2006
Writer's
Market®
Deluxe Edition

Kathryn S. Brogan, Editor
Robert Lee Brewer & Joanna Masterson,
   Assistant Editors

WRITER'S DIGEST BOOKS
CINCINNATI, OH

Complaint Procedure

If you feel you have not been treated fairly by a listing in *Writer's Market* or *Writer's Market Deluxe Edition*, we advise you to take the following steps:

- First try to contact the listing. Sometimes one phone call or a letter can quickly clear up the matter.

- Document all your correspondence with the listing. When you write to us with a complaint, provide the details of your submission, the date of your first contact with the listing and the nature of your subsequent correspondence.

- We will enter your letter into our files and attempt to contact the listing.

- The number and severity of complaints will be considered in our decision whether to delete the listing from the next edition.

Managing Editor, Writer's Digest Market Books: Alice Pope
Supervisory Editor, Writer's Digest Market Books: Donna Poehner

Writer's Market Website: www.writersmarket.com

Writer's Digest Website: www.writersdigest.com

Library of Congress Catalog Number 31-20772
International Standard Serial Number 0084-2729
International Standard Book Number 1-58297-394-6
International Standard Book Number 1-58297-401-2 (*Writer's Market Deluxe Edition*)

Cover design by Kelly Kofron

Interior design by Clare Finney

Production coordinated by Robin Richie

Attention Booksellers: This is an annual directory of F+W Publications. Return deadline for this edition is December 31, 2005.

Contents

THE BUSINESS OF WRITING

LITERARY AGENTS

BOOK PUBLISHERS

CANADIAN & INTERNATIONAL BOOK PUBLISHERS

SMALL PRESSES

CONSUMER MAGAZINES

TRADE JOURNALS

CONTESTS & AWARDS

RESOURCES

INDEXES

From the Editor

I don't have time to write—I'll do it tomorrow. I can't find the right words. I have the beginning and the end of my story, but I just can't seem to get everything in between. I have the worst case of writer's block. I just received my fifth rejection; I'm obviously not cut out to be a writer.

Do any of these excuses sound familiar? If you write—it doesn't matter whether it's fiction or nonfiction—you're kidding yourself if you think you don't relate to at least one. I'll share a secret with you: I've used each of these excuses more than once in my writing career. In fact, I used almost all of them as I attempted to write (or not write!) this letter.

So, how did I make myself sit down, put fingers to keyboard, and write? I read two of the articles featured in this edition. The first was **Writing on the Run: Finding Time to Write** by Allen and Linda Anderson. I chose to read this because so often I say, "I can't write today—I just don't have the time." And, if I actually do sit down to write, I'm usually overcome by feelings of guilt, that instead of writing, I should be focusing my attention on more "important" things—family, work, etc.

Next, I read Anthony Tedesco's **Overcoming Writer's Block** because once I actually get over my guilt, I find myself staring at a blank screen—I have writer's block!

While I found many gems in both articles (as I hope you'll find in *all* the articles in this edition), there was one thread appearing in both: Finding time to write and experiencing writer's block are inherent to writing; however, it's up to the writer to figure out what's causing these things to happen and, more importantly, how to conquer them.

"Writer's block isn't to be feared; it's to be expected and overcome. The trick is to figure out what's causing you to falter," says Tedesco. While he's specifically speaking about writer's block, I think the same can be said about finding time to write. I encourage you to read these articles, and figure out how best to apply their principles to your own writing—or, in many cases, your lack of writing.

Kathryn Struckel Brogan

Kathryn Struckel Brogan
Editor, *Writer's Market*
writersmarket@fwpubs.com

Getting Started

How to Use Writer's Market

Writer's Market is here to help you decide where and how to submit your writing to appropriate markets. Each listing contains information about the editorial focus of the market, how it prefers material to be submitted, payment information, and other helpful tips.

WHAT'S INSIDE?

Since 1921, *Writer's Market* has been giving you the information you need to knowledgeably approach a market. We've continued to develop improvements to help you access that information more efficiently.

Navigational tools. We've designed the pages of *Writer's Market* with you, the user, in mind. Within the pages you will find **readable market listings** and **accessible charts and graphs**. One such chart can be found in the ever-popular **How Much Should I Charge?** on page 68. We've taken all of the updated information in this feature and put it into an easy-to-read and navigate chart, making it more convenient than ever for you to find the rates that accompany the freelance jobs for which you are looking.

Tabs. You will also find user-friendly tabs for each section of *Writer's Market* so you can quickly find the section you need most. Once inside the Consumer Magazine, Trade Journals and Contests & Awards sections, you'll have subject headings at the top of the page to help guide and speed up your search.

Symbols. There are a variety of symbols that appear before each listing. A key to all of the symbols appears on the back inside cover and on a removable bookmark. However, there are a few symbols we'd like to point out. In book publishers, the ⚬⚬ quickly sums up a publisher's interests. In Consumer Magazines the ⚬⚬ zeroes in on what areas of that market are particularly open to freelancers—helping you break in. Other symbols let you know whether a listing is new to the book (**Ⓝ**), a book publisher accepts only agented writers (**Ⓐ**), comparative pay rates for a magazine (**$-$$$$**), and more.

Acquisition names, royalty rates, and advances. In the Book Publishers section we identify acquisition editors with the boldface word **Acquisitions** to help you get your manuscript to the right person. Royalty rates and advances are also highlighted in boldface, as is other important information on the percentage of first-time writers and unagented writers the company publishes, the number of books published, and the number of manuscripts received each year.

Editors, pay rates, and percentage of material written by freelance writers. In the Consumer Magazines and Trade Journal sections, we identify to whom you should send your query or article by the boldface word **Contact**. The amount (percentage) of material accepted from freelance writers, and the pay rates for features, columns and departments, and fillers are also highlighted in boldface to help you quickly identify the information you need to know when considering whether to submit your work.

Query formats. We asked editors how they prefer to receive queries and have indicated in the listings whether they prefer them by mail, e-mail, fax, or phone. Be sure to check an editor's individual preference before sending your query.

Articles. All of the articles, with the exception of a few standard pieces, are new to this edition. Newer, unpublished writers should be sure to read the articles in the **For Beginning Writers** section, while more experienced writers should focus on those in **The Business of Writing** section. In addition, there is a section devoted to **Interviews** with industry professionals and other career-oriented professionals, as well as best-selling authors.

IF *WRITER'S MARKET* IS NEW TO YOU . . .

A quick look at the **Contents** pages will familiarize you with the arrangement of *Writer's Market*. The three largest sections of the book are the market listings of Book Publishers;

Important Listing Information

Important

1. Listings are based on editorial questionnaires and interviews. They are not advertisements; publishers do not pay for their listings. The markets are not endorsed by *Writer's Market* editors. F + W Publications, Inc., Writer's Digest Books, and its employees go to great effort to ascertain the validity of information in this book. However, transactions between users of the information and individuals and/ or companies are strictly between those parties.

2. All listings have been verified before publication of this book. If a listing has not changed from last year, then the editor said the market's needs have not changed and the previous listing continues to accurately reflect its policies.

3. *Writer's Market* reserves the right to exclude any listing.

4. When looking for a specific market, check the index. A market may not be listed for one of these reasons:

   - It doesn't solicit freelance material.
   - It doesn't pay for material.
   - It has gone out of business.
   - It has failed to verify or update its listing for this edition.
   - It hasn't answered *Writer's Market* inquiries satisfactorily. (To the best of our ability, and with our readers' help, we try to screen fraudulent listings.)

5. Individual markets that appeared in last year's edition but are not listed in this edition are included in the General Index, with a notation giving the reason for their exclusion.

2006 WRITER'S MARKET KEY TO SYMBOLS

N market new to this edition

A market accepts agented submissions only

Ø market does not accept unsolicited manuscripts

✦ Canadian market

⊕ market located outside of the U.S. and Canada

▣ online opportunity

$ market pays 0-9¢/word or $0-$150/article

$ $ market pays 10-49¢/word or $151-$750/article

$ $ $ market pays 50-99¢/word or $751-$1,500/article

$ $ $ $ market pays $1/word or over $1,500/article

• comment from the editor of *Writer's Market*

⊙— tips to break into a specific market

ms, mss manuscript(s)

b&w black & white (photo)

SASE self-addressed, stamped envelope

SAE self-addressed envelope

IRC International Reply Coupon, for use in countries other than your own

(For words and expressions relating specifically to writing and publishing, see the Glossary in the back of this book.)

Find a handy pull-out bookmark, a quick reference to the icons used in this book, right inside the front cover.

Consumer Magazines; and Trade Journals. You will also find other sections of market listings for Literary Agents and Contests & Awards.

Narrowing your search

After you've identified the market categories in which you're interested, you can begin researching specific markets within each section.

Book Publishers are categorized, in the **Book Publishers Subject Index**, according to types of books they are interested in. If, for example, you plan to write a book on a religious topic, simply turn to the Book Publishers Subject Index on page 1054 and look under the Religion subhead in Nonfiction for the names and page numbers of companies that publish such books.

Consumer Magazines and Trade Journals are categorized by subject within their respective sections to make it easier for you to identify markets for your work. If you want to publish an article dealing with retirement, you could look under the Retirement category of Consumer Magazines to find an appropriate market. You would want to keep in mind, however, that magazines in other categories might also be interested in your article. (For example, women's magazines publish such material as well.)

Interpreting the markets

Once you've identified companies or publications that cover the subjects in which you're interested, you can begin evaluating specific listings to pinpoint the markets most receptive to your work and most beneficial to you.

In evaluating an individual listing, first check the location of the company, the types of material it is interested in seeing, submission requirements, and rights and payment policies. Depending upon your personal concerns, any of these items could be a deciding factor as you determine which markets you plan to approach. Many listings also include a reporting time, which lets you know how long it will typically take for the publisher to respond to your initial query or submission. (We suggest that you allow an additional two months for a response, just in case your submission is under further review or the publisher is backlogged.)

Check the Glossary on page 1051 in the back of the book for unfamiliar words. Specific symbols and abbreviations are explained in the key appearing on the back inside cover, as well as on a removable bookmark. The most important abbreviation is SASE—self-addressed, stamped envelope. Always enclose a SASE when you send unsolicited queries, proposals, or manuscripts.

A careful reading of the listings will reveal that many editors are very specific about their needs. Your chances of success increase if you follow directions to the letter. Often companies do not accept unsolicited manuscripts and return them unread. If a company does not accept unsolicited manuscripts, it is indicated in the listing with a (⊘) symbol.

Whenever possible, obtain writer's guidelines before submitting material. You can usually obtain guidelines by sending a SASE to the address in the listing. Magazines often post their guidelines on their website as well. Most of the listings indicate how writer's guidelines are made available. You should also familiarize yourself with the company's publications. Many of the listings contain instructions on how to obtain sample copies, catalogs, or market lists. The more research you do upfront, the better your chances of acceptance, publication, and payment.

Guide to listing features

Below is an example of the market listings you'll find in each section of *Writer's Market*. Note the callouts that identify various format features of the listing.

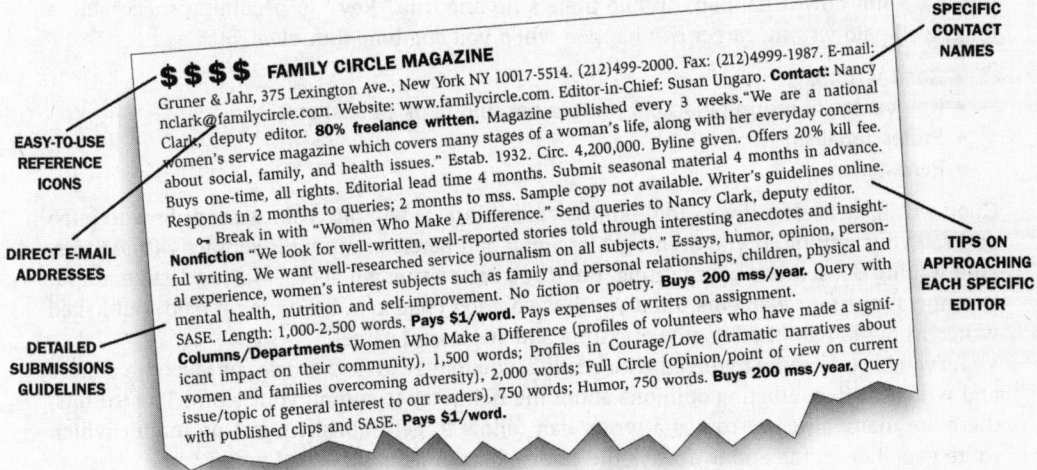

SPECIFIC CONTACT NAMES

EASY-TO-USE REFERENCE ICONS

DIRECT E-MAIL ADDRESSES

DETAILED SUBMISSIONS GUIDELINES

TIPS ON APPROACHING EACH SPECIFIC EDITOR

$ $ $ $ FAMILY CIRCLE MAGAZINE Gruner & Jahr, 375 Lexington Ave., New York NY 10017-5514. (212)499-2000. Fax: (212)4999-1987. E-mail: nclark@familycircle.com. Website: www.familycircle.com. Editor-in-Chief: Susan Ungaro. **Contact:** Nancy Clark, deputy editor. **80% freelance written.** Magazine published every 3 weeks. "We are a national women's service magazine which covers many stages of a woman's life, along with her everyday concerns about social, family, and health issues." Estab. 1932. Circ. 4,200,000. Byline given. Offers 20% kill fee. Buys one-time, all rights. Editorial lead time 4 months. Submit seasonal material 4 months in advance. Responds in 2 months to queries; 2 months to mss. Sample copy not available. Writer's guidelines online.
⚬ Break in with "Women Who Make A Difference." Send queries to Nancy Clark, deputy editor.
Nonfiction "We look for well-written, well-reported stories told through interesting anecdotes and insightful writing. We want well-researched service journalism on all subjects." Essays, humor, opinion, personal experience, women's interest subjects such as family and personal relationships, children, physical and mental health, nutrition and self-improvement. No fiction or poetry. **Buys 200 mss/year.** Query with SASE. Length: 1,000-2,500 words. **Pays $1/word.** Pays expenses of writers on assignment.
Columns/Departments Women Who Make a Difference (profiles of volunteers who have made a significant impact on their community), 1,500 words; Profiles in Courage/Love (dramatic narratives about women and families overcoming adversity), 2,000 words; Full Circle (opinion/point of view on current issue/topic of general interest to our readers), 750 words; Humor, 750 words. **Buys 200 mss/year.** Query with published clips and SASE. **Pays $1/word.**

Before Your First Sale

Everything in life has to start somewhere and that somewhere is always at the beginning. The same is true for writers. Stephen King, J.K. Rowling, John Grisham, Nora Roberts—they all had to start at the beginning. It would be great to say becoming a writer is as easy as waving a magic wand over your manuscript and "Poof!" you're published, but that's not how it happens. While there's no one true "key" to becoming successful, a long, well-paid writing career *can* happen when you combine four elements:

- Good writing
- Knowledge of writing markets (magazines and book publishers)
- Professionalism
- Persistence

Good writing is useless if you don't know which markets will buy your work or how to pitch and sell your writing. If you aren't professional and persistent in your contact with editors, your writing is just that—your writing. But if you are a writer who possesses, and can manipulate, the above four elements, then you have a good chance at becoming a paid, published writer who will reap the benefits of a long and successful career.

As you become more involved with writing, you may read new articles or talk with editors and writers with conflicting opinions about the right way to submit your work. The truth is, there are many different routes a writer can follow to get published, but no matter which route you choose, the end is always the same—becoming a published writer.

The following information on submissions has worked for many writers, but it is by no means the be-all-end-all of proper submission guidelines. It's very easy to get wrapped up in the specifics of submitting (Should I put my last name on every page of my manuscript?) and ignore the more important issues (Will this idea on ice fishing in Alaska be appropriate for a regional magazine in Seattle?). Don't allow yourself to become so blinded by submission procedures that you forget one of life's basic principles—common sense. If you use your common sense and develop professional, courteous relations with editors, you will eventually find your own submission style.

DEVELOP YOUR IDEAS, THEN TARGET THE MARKETS

Writers often think of an interesting story, complete the manuscript, and then begin the search for a suitable publisher or magazine. While this approach is common for fiction, poetry, and screenwriting, it reduces your chances of success in many nonfiction writing areas. Instead, try choosing categories that interest you and study those sections in *Writer's Market*. Select several listings you consider good prospects for your type of writing. Sometimes the individual listings will even help you generate ideas.

For Beginning Writers

Next, make a list of the potential markets for each idea. Make the initial contact with markets using the method stated in the market listings. If you exhaust your list of possibilities, don't give up. Instead, reevaluate the idea or try another angle. Continue developing ideas and approaching markets with the ideas. Identify and rank potential markets for an idea and continue the process.

As you submit to the various publications listed in *Writer's Market*, it's important to remember that every magazine is published with a particular audience and slant in mind. Probably the number one complaint we receive from editors is the submissions they receive are completely wrong for their magazines. The first mark of professionalism is to know your market well. That knowledge starts in *Writer's Market*, but you should also do your own detective work. Search out back issues of the magazines you wish to write for, pick up recent issues at your local newsstand, or visit magazines' websites—anything that will help you figure out what subjects specific magazines publish. This research is also helpful in learning what topics have been covered ad nauseum—the topics you should stay away from or approach in a fresh way. Magazines' websites are invaluable as most post the current issue of the magazine, as well as back issues, and most offer writer's guidelines.

Prepare for rejection and the sometimes lengthy wait. When a submission is returned, check your file folder of potential markets for that idea. Cross off the market that rejected the idea. If the editor has given you suggestions or reasons why the manuscript was not accepted, you might want to incorporate these suggestions when revising your manuscript. After revising your manuscript mail it to the next market on your list.

Take rejection with a grain of salt

Rejection is a way of life in the publishing world. It's inevitable in a business that deals with such an overwhelming number of applicants for such a limited number of positions. Anyone who has published has lived through many rejections, and writers with thin skin are at a distinct disadvantage. A rejection letter is not a personal attack. It simply indicates your submission is not appropriate for that market. Writers who let rejection dissuade them from pursuing their dream or who react to an editor's "No" with indignation or fury do themselves a disservice. Writers who let rejection stop them do not get published. Resign yourself to facing rejection now. You will live through it, and you'll eventually overcome it.

Reminder

QUERY AND COVER LETTERS

A query letter is a brief, one-page letter used as a tool to hook an editor and get him interested in your idea. When you send a query letter to a magazine, you are trying to get an editor to buy your idea or article. When you query a book publisher, you are attempting to get an editor interested enough in your idea to request your book proposal or your entire manuscript. (*Note:* Some book editors prefer to receive book proposals on first contact. Check individual listings for which method editors prefer.)

While there are no set rules for writing query letters, there are some basic guidelines to help you create one that's polished and well-organized:

- **Limit it to one page, single-spaced,** and address the editor by name (Mr. or Ms. and the surname). *Note:* Do not assume that a person is a Mr. or Ms. unless it is obvious from the name listed. For example, if you are contacting a D.J. Smith, do not assume that D.J. should be preceded by Mr. or Ms. Instead, address the letter to D.J. Smith.
- **Grab the editor's attention with a strong opening.** Some magazine queries begin with a paragraph meant to approximate the lead of the intended article.
- **Indicate how you intend to develop the article or book.** Give the editor some idea of the work's structure and content.

- **Let the editor know if you have photos** or illustrations available to accompany your magazine article.
- **Mention any expertise or training that qualifies** you to write the article or book. If you've been published before, mention it; if not, don't.
- **End with a direct request to write the article.** Or, if you're pitching a book, ask for the go-ahead to send in a full proposal or the entire manuscript. Give the editor an idea of the expected length and delivery date of your manuscript.

Another question that arises is: If I don't hear from an editor in the reported response time, how do I know when I can safely send the query to another market? Many writers find it helpful to indicate in their query that if they don't receive a response from the editor (slightly after the listed reporting time), they will assume the editor is not interested. It's best to take this approach, particularly if your topic is timely.

A brief, single-spaced cover letter is helpful when sending a manuscript as it helps personalize the submission. However, if you have previously queried the editor, use the cover letter to politely and briefly remind the editor of that query—when it was sent, what it contained, etc. "Here is the piece on low-fat cooking that I queried you about on December 12. I look forward to hearing from you at your earliest convenience." Do not use the cover letter as a sales pitch.

If you are submitting to a market that accepts unsolicited manuscripts, a cover letter is useful because it personalizes your submission. You can, and should, include information about the manuscript, yourself, your publishing history, and your qualifications.

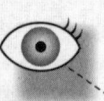

See Also

The Query Letter Clinic on page 16 offers eight different query letters, some that work and some that don't, as well as editors' comments on why the letters were either successful or failed to garner an assignment.

Querying for fiction

Fiction is sometimes queried, but more often not. Many fiction editors won't decide on a submission until they have seen the complete manuscript. When submitting a fiction book idea, most editors prefer to see at least a synopsis and sample chapters (usually the first three). For fiction published in magazines, most editors want to see the complete short story

Query Letter Resources

For More Info

The following list of books provide you with more detailed information on writing query letters, cover letters, and book proposals. All titles are published by Writer's Digest Books.

- *Formatting & Submitting Your Manuscript, Edition 2*, by Cynthia Laufenberg and the Editors of Writer's Digest Books.
- *How to Write Attention-Grabbing Query & Cover Letters*, by John Wood.
- *How to Write a Book Proposal, 3rd Edition*, by Michael Larsen.
- *The Marshall Plan for Getting Your Novel Published*, by Evan Marshall.
- *The Writer's Digest Writing Clinic*, edited by Kelly Nickell.
- *Writer's Market Companion, 2nd Edition*, by Joe Feiertag and Mary Cupito.

manuscript. If an editor does request a query for fiction, it should include a description of the main theme and story line, including the conflict and resolution. Take a look at individual listings to see what editors prefer to receive.

NONFICTION BOOK PROPOSALS

Most nonfiction books are sold by a book proposal—a package of materials that details what your book is about, who its intended audience is, and how you intend to write the book. It includes some combination of a cover or query letter, an overview, an outline, author's information sheet, and sample chapters. Editors also want to see information about the audience for your book and about titles that compete with your proposed book.

Submitting a nonfiction book proposal

A proposal package should include the following items:

- **A cover or query letter.** This letter should be a short introduction to the material you include in the proposal.
- **An overview.** This is a brief summary of your book. For nonfiction, it should detail your book's subject and give an idea of how that subject will be developed. If you're sending a synopsis of a novel, cover the basic plot.
- **An outline.** The outline covers your book chapter by chapter and should include all major points covered in each chapter. Some outlines are done in traditional outline form, but most are written in paragraph form.
- **An author's information sheet.** This information should acquaint the editor with your writing background and convince him of your qualifications regarding the subject of your book.
- **Sample chapters.** Many editors like to see sample chapters, especially for a first book. Sample chapters show the editor how you write and develop ideas from your outline.
- **Marketing information.** Facts about how and to whom your book can be successfully marketed are now expected to accompany every book proposal. If you can provide information about the audience for your book and suggest ways the book publisher can reach those people, you will increase your chances of acceptance.
- **Competitive title analysis.** Check the *Subject Guide* to *Books in Print* for other titles on your topic. Write a one- or two-sentence synopsis of each. Point out how your book differs and improves upon existing topics.

A WORD ABOUT AGENTS

An agent represents a writer's work to publishers, negotiates contracts, follows up to see that contracts are fulfilled, and generally handles a writer's business affairs, leaving the writer free to write. Effective agents are valued for their contacts in the publishing industry, their knowledge about who to approach with certain ideas, their ability to guide an author's career, and their business sense.

While most book publishers listed in *Writer's Market* publish books by unagented writers, some of the larger houses are reluctant to consider submissions that have not reached them through a literary agent. Companies with such a policy are noted by an ([A]) icon at the beginning of the listing, as well as in the submission information within the listing.

Writer's Market includes a list of 50 literary agents who are all members of the Association of Authors' Representatives and who are also actively seeking new and established writers. For a more comprehensive resource on finding and working with an agent, see *2006 Guide to Literary Agents*.

For Beginning Writers

MANUSCRIPT FORMAT

You can increase your chances of publication by following a few standard guidelines regarding the physical format of your manuscript. It should be your goal to make your manuscript readable. Follow these suggestions as you would any other suggestions: Use what works for you and discard what doesn't.

In general, when submitting a manuscript, you should use white, $8^{1}/_{2} \times 11$, 20 lb. paper, and you should also choose a legible, professional looking font (i.e., Times New Roman)—no all-italic or artsy fonts. Your entire manuscript should be double-spaced with a $1^{1}/_{2}$-inch margin on all sides of the page. Once you are ready to print your manuscript, you should print either on a laser printer or an ink-jet printer.

ESTIMATING WORD COUNT

Many computers will provide you with a word count of your manuscript. Your editor will count again after editing the manuscript. Although your computer is counting characters, an editor or production editor is more concerned about the amount of space the text will occupy on a page. Several small headlines or subheads, for instance, will be counted the same by your computer as any other word of text. However, headlines and subheads usually employ a different font size than the body text, so an editor may count them differently to be sure enough space has been estimated for larger type.

For short manuscripts, it's often quickest to count each word on a representative page and multiply by the number of pages. You can get a very rough count by multiplying the number of pages in your manuscript by 250 (the average number of words on a double-spaced typewritten page).

PHOTOGRAPHS AND SLIDES

In some cases, the availability of photographs and slides can be the deciding factor as to whether an editor will accept your submission. This is especially true when querying a publication that relies heavily on photographs, illustrations, or artwork to enhance the article (i.e., craft magazines, hobby magazines, etc.). In some instances, the publication may offer additional payment for photographs or illustrations.

Check the individual listings to find out which magazines review photographs and what their submission guidelines are. Most publications prefer that you do not send photographs with your submission. However, if photographs or illustrations are available, you should indicate as such in your query. As with manuscripts, never send the originals of your photographs or illustrations. Instead, send prints or duplicates of slides and transparencies.

SEND PHOTOCOPIES

If there is one hard-and-fast rule in publishing, it's this: *Never* send the original (or only) copy of your manuscript. Most editors cringe when they find out a writer has sent the only copy of their manuscript. You should always send photocopies of your manuscript.

Some writers choose to send a self-addressed, stamped postcard with a photocopied submission. In their cover letter they suggest if the editor is not interested in their manuscript, it may be tossed out and a reply sent on the postcard. This method is particularly helpful when sending your submissions to international markets.

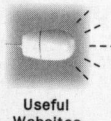

**Useful
Websites**

MAILING SUBMISSIONS

No matter what size manuscript you're mailing, always include a self-addressed, stamped envelope (SASE) with sufficient return postage. The website for the U.S. Postal Service (www.usps.com) and the website for the Canadian Post (www.canadapost.ca) both have postage calculators if you are unsure of how much postage you'll need to affix.

Manuscript Formatting Checklist

1 Type your real name (even if you use a pseudonym) and contact information.

2 Double-space twice.

3 Estimated word count and the rights you are offering.

4 Type your title in capital letters, double-space and type "by," double-space again, and type your name (or pseudonym if you're using one).

5 Double-space twice, then indent first paragraph and start text of your manuscript.

6 On subsequent pages, type your name, a dash, and the page number in the upper left or right corner.

Your name
Your street address
City, State ZIP code
Day and evening phone numbers
E-mail address

50,000 words
World rights

TITLE

by

Your Name

You can increase your chances of publication by following a few standard guidelines regarding the physical format of your article or manuscript. It should be your goal to make your manuscript readable. Use these suggestions as you would any other suggestions: Use what works for you and discard what doesn't.

In general, when submitting a manuscript, you should use white, $8^{1}/_{2} \times 11$, 20-lb. bond paper, and you should also choose a legible, professional-looking font (i.e., Times New Roman)—no all-italic or artsy fonts. Your entire manuscript should be double-spaced with a $1^{1}/_{2}$-inch margin

Your Name - 2

on all sides of the page. Once you are ready to print your article or manuscript, you should print either on a laser printer or an ink-jet printer.

Remember, though, articles should either be written after you send a one-page query letter to an editor, and the editor then asks you to write the article. If, however, you are sending an article "on spec" to an editor, you should send both a query letter and the complete article.

Fiction is a little different from nonfiction articles, in that it is only sometimes queried, but more often not. Many fiction editors won't decide on a submission until they have seen the complete manuscript. When submitting a fiction book idea, most editors prefer to see at least a synopsis and sample chapters (usually the first three). For fiction that is published

For Beginning Writers

Mailing Manuscripts

For More Info

- Fold manuscripts under five pages into thirds, and send in a #10 SASE.
- Mail manuscripts five pages or more unfolded in a 9×12 or 10×13 SASE.
- For return envelope, fold the envelope in half, address it to yourself, and add a stamp or, if going to Canada or another international destination, International Reply Coupons (available at most main branches of your local post office).
- Don't send by Certified mail—this is a sign of an amateur.

A book manuscript should be mailed in a sturdy, well-wrapped box. Enclose a self-addressed mailing label and paper clip your return postage to the label. However, be aware that some book publishers do not return unsolicited manuscripts, so make sure you know the practice of the publisher before sending any unsolicited material.

Types of mail service

There are many different mailing service options available to you whether you are sending a query letter or a complete manuscript. You can work with the U.S. Postal Service, United Parcel Service, Federal Express, or any number of private mailing companies. The following are the five most common types of mailing services offered by the U.S. Postal Service.

- **First Class** is an expensive way to mail a manuscript, but many writers prefer it. First-Class mail generally receives better handling and is delivered more quickly than Standard mail.
- **Priority mail** reaches its destination within two or three days.
- **Standard mail** rates are available for packages, but be sure to pack your materials carefully because they will be handled roughly. To make sure your package will be returned to you if it is undeliverable, print "Return Postage Guaranteed" under your address.
- **Certified mail** must be signed for when it reaches its destination.
- **Registered mail** is a high-security method of mailing where the contents are insured. The package is signed in and out of every office it passes through, and a receipt is returned to the sender when the package reaches its destination.

Is There a Secret to Getting Published?

by Paula Eykelhof

I t's human nature—we all want to know the secret: the inside knowledge, the formula, the password, the hidden piece of the puzzle, the shortcut that will lead us quickly and painlessly to our goals.

This is as true of writers as anyone else. Writers are constantly asking: "What do I have to do to get published? Who do I have to know? What kind of pitch do I have to make to an editor? What's the secret?"

Well, I'm here to give you an editor's answer. And the secret is—there *is* no secret.

GOOD WRITING

You may or may not be pleased by this answer, but what I can tell you is what will get you published—good writing. If it's fiction you're interested in, then write a great story with characters that are as real to you as the people in your life. If you write nonfiction, give the reader something *new*—whether it's a better way of doing something, a provocative idea, or an innovative and inspirational approach to life.

Good writing is far more than correct grammar and an accessible style—but knowledge of grammar, punctuation, and proper word use are the tools of your trade. Make sure those tools are in good condition. There are plenty of resources available to help you hone the basics and develop the fundamental skills you need in order to write well. These resources include *Eats, Shoots & Leaves* (Gotham) by Lynne Truss, *The Transitive Vampire* (Pantheon), and Bill Bryson's recently reissued *Troublesome Words* (Penguin UK). Above all, good writing is about clarity and precision. The resources I've mentioned will help you say *exactly* what you mean to say. Remember: The rules of grammar are essentially rules of logic.

Whatever kind of writer you are (and I'm making very broad distinctions here between fiction, including the various genres, and nonfiction), you'll need to know *what* you want to say before you figure out *how* to say it.

If you write fiction . . .

If you write fiction, good writing is a process of *showing* your characters and their lives. This doesn't mean loading the opening of your story with every background detail you've created for those characters—that kind of information needs to be seamlessly integrated, woven in

PAULA EYKELHOF is an executive editor at Harlequin Books. She currently works primarily on single-title women's fiction but has been involved with series romance for many years. She's also written for magazines, worked as a television researcher and writer, and was—briefly—a puppeteer.

at the right times and in appropriate amounts. A "secret" (or let's say an "important technique") of the fiction writer is knowing what facts or developments to reveal and when to reveal them. That means you're constantly making decisions, weighing the importance of each detail to the needs of your plot and the portrayal of your characters. Shaping your material is not simply a matter of arranging facts and details, but of deciding which to include and (equally important) which to leave out.

Any kind of storytelling requires you to create a narrative momentum that will drive readers to keep turning the pages and learn what happens next. Readers will only care about what happens next if they can care about your characters, connect with them in some way, and feel interested in their personalities and their fates.

If you write nonfiction . . .

The same "rules" that define good fiction writing can also be applied to nonfiction. Think of a piece of nonfiction in terms of a story. You need the same momentum and the same urgency to keep a reader reading, and—wherever possible—you need to get across a strong sense of the people you're writing about. Good examples of this type of approach to nonfiction can be found in true crime, in some travel books, in business books, and in works of popular history. For instance, Jon Krakauer's *Under the Banner of Heaven* (Doubleday) is as engrossing (and chilling) as any crime novel, yet it incorporates significant amounts of American history. Bill Bryson's wonderfully funny travel books, such as *In a Sunburned Country* (Broadway) and *A Walk in the Woods* (Broadway) tell the stories of one man's travels and, in the process, introduce the reader to an extremely likable narrator. It's Bryson's voice—his character (or the character he's created of himself)—that makes his books so entertaining and memorable.

THE BASIC ELEMENTS OF GOOD WRITING
Characters

If you're going to get your reader involved with your characters, you need a clear sense of those characters, of their personalities and the histories that formed them. Then, as I mentioned before, you need to plot out what to reveal when, and this means events taking place in the story's present, as well as things that happened in the past. Part of that is using the right point of view.

Something for fiction writers to consider: One interesting and often worthwhile exercise—especially if your story is stalled—is to rewrite a chapter or scene from another character's point of view. A new point of view can give you a different perspective on that character and on others, as well as your plot. You may even find the revised chapter or scene is actually more effective in moving your story forward.

In both fiction and nonfiction, you're leading your reader to a conclusion. In nonfiction, whether the point of your work is informative, inspirational, or provocative, you're building a structure that logically and inevitably draws your reader from the opening sentence, through your facts and arguments, to the conclusion.

Outlines

The idea of building a structure for your story leads me to outlines—a valuable and necessary tool for any kind of writing. However, the style of your outline should be whatever works for you, and it may take several attempts to discover what method suits you best. Maybe it's index cards you arrange on a bulletin board, or maybe it's a fairly rigid, numbered outline.

The amount of detail you include in an outline will vary, as will the amount of time invested in it. Some people work better from very precise and itemized outlines—like a road map with all the side roads, villages, and landmarks included—while others prefer a much simpler outline, more like a hand-drawn directional map taking you from point A to point B.

One thing to keep in mind with an outline, though, is not to become so attached to it that you're unable to take an occasional detour. In the process of writing, you will probably come across many interesting facts or connections that may mean diverging from, or revising, your original outline. You should never feel so committed to an outline, a conclusion, or an idea, that you're unable to change it if the story (and the reader) will benefit.

Openings

Your opening should entice and intrigue the reader (and, of course, the editor), but this doesn't mean devising an opening that shocks the reader solely for the purpose of grabbing his attention—unless the rest of your story, book, or article supports it.

Your opening should be consistent with the rest of the piece. For example, if you're writing a romance novel, starting the book with an extremely sexy scene probably isn't appropriate if the rest of the story is a quiet exploration of a relationship. Your opening sets up expectations, and you owe it to the reader to meet those expectations.

I use the word "probably" since there are always exceptions. For example, it can be effective and realistic—if jarring—to begin a mystery novel (or, for that matter, a true-crime piece) with a horrific and disturbing description of a murder and then spend the rest of the book detailing the police procedures that solve the crime. The expectation is the police protagonists will be as outraged by the crime as the reader is, and will devote all their resources to solving it.

If, on the other hand, you're writing a health-related article on diet for a women's magazine, you may be cheating the reader if you start with a flamboyant promise of quick weight-loss results and then just offer the usual sensible-eating-and-exercise plan.

Whatever you're writing, you have to keep your promise to the reader—meet the expectations you've raised and convey your story with integrity.

Professionalism

Professionalism is all about how you present yourself and your work to an editor. When you're submitting a manuscript or proposal, query letters and/or cover letters create the first impression the editor's going to have of you.

Your letter should be well written, succinct, and to the point. Strive to convey what's unique about your story or proposed article, but don't try too hard. Don't be cute and don't send gifts. I've received strange T-shirts, flowers, a package of coffee with the exhortation that I should drink it while reading the accompanying manuscript, and more. Editors don't want or need any of this from prospective authors!

Think of a letter to a publisher the same way you'd think about the letter you'd send with your résumé when applying for a job. You want to impress the editor with your writing skill, your qualifications, and with the fact there's something special about your work. You want him to ask for your manuscript or, in the case of a cover letter, to look forward to reading your manuscript.

If you hone your basic skills, know your characters, do your research, and learn how to shape your writing, you will reach your goal of being published—all without any secrets.

FOR BEGINNING WRITERS

Query Letter Clinic

by Kathryn S. Brogan and Cynthia Laufenberg

The query letter is the catalyst in the chemical reaction of publishing. Overall, writing a query letter is a fairly simple process that serves one purpose—selling an article.

There are two types of queries: a query for a finished manuscript, and a query for an idea that has yet to be developed into an article. Either way, a query letter is the tool that sells an idea using brief, attention-getting prose.

WHAT SHOULD I INCLUDE IN A QUERY LETTER?

A query should tell an editor how you plan to handle and develop the proposed article. Many writers even include the lead of the article as the first sentence of their query as a sales pitch to the editor. A query letter should also show that you are familiar with the publication and tell the editor why you are the most qualified person to write the article.

Beyond the information mentioned above, a query letter is also the appropriate place to state the availability of photographs or artwork. Do not send photographs with your query. You can include a working title and a projected word count as well. Some writers indicate whether a sidebar or other accompanying short would be appropriate, and the type of research they plan to conduct. It is also appropriate to include a tentative deadline and to indicate if the query is being simultaneously submitted.

WHAT SHOULD I *NOT* INCLUDE IN A QUERY LETTER?

The query letter is not the place to discuss pay rates. By mentioning what you would like to be paid, you are prematurely assuming the editor is going to buy your article. Plus, if you are really just looking to get published and get paid some amount of money, you could be doing yourself a disservice. If you offer a rate that is higher than what the editor is willing to pay, you could lose the assignment. And, if you offer a figure that's too low, you are short-changing yourself on what could possibly be a lucrative assignment.

Another thing you should avoid is requesting writer's guidelines or a sample copy of the publication. This is a red flag to the editor because it indicates you are not familiar with the magazine or its content. Don't use the query letter to list pages of qualifications. Only list those qualifications you feel would best help you land the gig. If you have too many qualifica-

---

KATHRYN S. BROGAN is the editor of *Writer's Market*, *Writer's Market Deluxe Edition*, and *Guide to Literary Agents*.

CYNTHIA LAUFENBERG is former managing editor of Writer's Digest Books and the author of *Formatting & Submitting Your Manuscript, Edition 2* (Writer's Digest Books). She lives in Narberth, Pennsylvania.

Things to Avoid in Queries

1. **Don't try any cute attention-getting devices,** like marking the envelope "Personal." This also includes fancy stationery that lists every publication you've ever sold to, or "clever" slogans.

2. **Don't talk about fees.**

3. **Keep your opinions to yourself.**

4. **Don't tell the editors what others think of your idea.** ("Several of my friends have read this and think it's marvelous . . ." is a certain sign of the amateur writer.) The same goes for comments from other editors.

5. **Don't name drop.** However, if you do know somebody who works for that magazine, or writes for it, or if you know an editor on another magazine who has bought your work and likes it, say so.

6. **Don't try to soft soap the editor** by telling him how great the magazine is, but definitely make it clear that you read it.

7. **Don't send any unnecessary enclosures,** such as a picture of yourself (or your prize-winning Labrador Retriever).

8. **Don't offer irrelevant information about yourself.** Simply tell the editor what there might be in your background that qualifies you to write this story.

9. **Know the magazine,** and send only those ideas that fit the format. Don't offer comments like, "I never read your magazine, but this seems to be a natural . . ." or "I know you don't usually publish articles about mountain climbing, but . . ."

10. **Don't ask for a meeting** to discuss your idea further. If the editor feels this is necessary, he will suggest it.

11. **Don't ask for advice,** like, "If you don't think you can use this, could you suggest another magazine that could?"

12. **Don't offer to rewrite,** as this implies you know the article's not good enough as you've submitted it. Editors will ask for rewrites if necessary—and they usually are.

13. **Don't make threats** like, "If I don't hear from you within four weeks I'll submit it elsewhere."

14. **Don't include a multiple-choice reply card** letting the editor check a box to indicate whether he likes the idea.

From *Magazine Writing That Sells*, by Don McKinney (Writer's Digest Books).

tions that you still feel would convince the editor to give you the assignment, include them as a separate page. Finally, never admit if five other editors rejected the query. This is your chance to shine.

HOW DO I FORMAT A QUERY LETTER?

There are no hard-and-fast rules when it comes to formatting your query letter, but there are some general, widely accepted guidelines like those listed below from *Formatting & Submitting Your Manuscript, Edition 2*, by Cynthia Laufenberg and the Editors of Writer's Digest Books (Writer's Digest Books).

- Use a standard font or typeface (avoid bold, script, or italics, except for publication titles).

Clips and E-mail Queries

When you send an e-mail query, you can provide clips five ways. Generally, there are no accepted standards for which is best, but the pros and cons of each method are described below.

1. **Include a line telling the editor that clips are available** on request. Then, mail, fax, or e-mail clips according to the editor's preference. This is a convenient solution for the writer, but not necessarily for the editor. The clips aren't available immediately, so you potentially slow the decision process by adding an additional step, and you lose any speed you've gained by e-mailing the query in the first place.

2. **Include electronic versions of the clips in the body** of the e-mail message. This can make for an awfully long e-mail, and it doesn't look as presentable as other alternatives, but it may be better than making the editor wait to download attachments or log on to a website.

3. **Include electronic versions of the articles as attachments.** The disadvantage here is the editor has to download the clips, which can take several minutes. Also, if there's a format disparity, the editor may not be able to read the attachment. The safest bet is to attach the documents as ".rtf" or ".txt" files, which should be readable with any word processing software, although you will lose formatting.

4. **Send the clips as a separate e-mail message.** This cuts the download time and eliminates software-related glitches, but it clutters the editor's e-mail queue.

5. **Set up a personal web page** and include your clips as hypertext links in or at the end of the e-mail (i.e., www.aolmembers.com/jackneff/smallbusinessclips). Setting up and maintaining the page takes a considerable amount of effort, but it may be the most convenient and reliable way for editors to access your clips electronically.

From *Formatting & Submitting Your Manuscript, Edition 2*, by Cynthia Laufenberg and the Editors of Writer's Digest Books (Writer's Digest Books).

- Your name, address, and phone number (plus e-mail and fax, if possible) should appear in the top right corner or on your letterhead.
- Use a 1-inch margin on all sides.
- Address the query to a specific editor, preferably the editor assigned to handle freelance submissions or the editor who handles the section for which you're writing. Note: The listings in *Writer's Market* provide a contact name for most submissions.
- Keep it to one page. If necessary, separately attach a résumé or list of credits to provide additional information.
- Include a SASE or postcard for reply; state you have done so, either in the body of the letter or in a listing of enclosures.
- Use block format (no indentations).
- Single-space the body of the letter and double-space between paragraphs.
- When possible, mention that you can send the manuscript on disk or via e-mail.
- Thank the editor for considering your proposal.

WHEN SHOULD I FOLLOW UP?

Sometimes things happen, and your query never reaches the editor's hands. Problems can arise with the mail delivery, the query may have been sent to a different department, or the editor may have inadvertently thrown the query away. Whatever the reason, there are a few simple guidelines you should use when you send a follow-up letter.

You should wait to follow up on your query at least until after the response time reported in the *Writer's Market* listing for that publication. If, after two months, you have not received a response to your query, you should compose a brief follow-up letter. The letter should describe the original query sent, the date the query was sent, and a reply postcard or a SASE. Some writers find it helpful to include a photocopy of the original query to help jog the editor's memory.

Above all, though, be polite and businesslike when following up. Don't take the lack of response personal. Editors are only human—situations can arise that are beyond their control.

WHAT THE CLINIC SHOWS YOU

Unpublished writers wonder how published writers break into print. It's not a matter of luck. Published writers know how to craft a well-written, hard-hitting query. What follows are eight actual queries submitted to editors (names and addresses have been altered). Four queries are strong; four are not. Detailed comments from the editors show what the writer did and did not do to secure a sale. As you'll see, there is not a cut-and-dry "good" query format; every strong query works because of its own merit.

For Beginning Writers

Good Nonfiction Magazine Query

Concrete information about the reporter's authority on the subject and experience as a writer. ——————

Hints of local color, indicating local impact of subject and writer's understanding of the need to set the stage for his reporting. ——————

Specific, anecdotal details about the central topic, in addition to specific cultural details about the broader significance of the story idea. ——————

Specific suggestion for word length and information about who the sources for the story would be. ——————

Bruce Steele, Editor-in-Chief
The Advocate
6922 Hollywood Blvd., 10th Floor
Los Angeles, CA 90028

Dear Mr. Steele,

I am *The Global Newspaper*'s lifestyle correspondent in Asian Nation. Our publication recently passed on a great story I think would be perfect for *The Advocate*.

Asian Nation Gay TV: Asian Nation's hottest new television series, "Crime Stories," has people gathering on sidewalks to watch communal TV sets and chattering over their tea the next day. It's not just the murder mystery generating buzz, but the controversial topic: It's Asian Nation's first open portrayal of gay characters on the screen.

To find out who is murdering young men in Capital City, a straight police officer must go undercover in the city's gay community. It's a world this officer especially hates and fears, because his estranged brother is gay and has been rejected by his family. That the TV series made it past Asian Nation's censors is a landmark for Asian Nation, where homosexuality is rarely discussed openly. The Asian Nation government routinely shuts down gay bars and refers to homosexuality as a "social evil" on par with drug addiction.

The author of the original novel has become an unlikely hero to Asian Nation's gay community. The author works for a state-run newspaper and he's straight. He wanted to write the book because it's a subject untouched in mainstream culture and he wants to encourage tolerance and understanding in a society traditionally hostile to gays. He hopes the TV adaptation makes people think, but he's upset at some of the changes made to the script to fit the government's official line.

I am suggesting a 2,000-word feature on this show with a look at the state of gay life in Asian Nation. I already have interviews with *Crime and the City*'s author and reactions from gay citizens.

If you are interested in this story, please contact me with details of what you want as well as rate information.

Yours,

George Good
123 Faraway Lane
Exotic Town 4323
Asian Nation
georgegood@email.an

This is a compelling, professional query. Good advice for writing queries: Have the best, most surprising, most dramatic, most revealing, most intimately reported, most human and engaging story that editor is going to see that day or even that week.

Bad Nonfiction Magazine Query

The entire pitch is angled to convince an editor of the moral imperative of doing the story. No consumer magazine makes editorial decisions on the basis of a reporter's assertion of moral imperative, nor because a reporter thinks the magazine's readers need to be spoon-fed certain content.

There's no real timeliness to the story. Magazines expect a writer to answer the question "Why now?"

Limited reference to 9/11 is several years old and a weak parallel to the advance of women's rights in Afghanistan.

Editors want details, names, dates, places. Editors want to know the writer can serve as an authority on the subject being pitched. Generalities are insufficient.

Susan Subpar
Box 789
Foreign City
Far East 9393

June 2, 2005

Bruce Steele
Editor-in-Chief
The Advocate
6922 Hollywood Blvd.
Los Angeles, CA 90028

Dear Mr. Steele,

I think in general there is a lack of knowledge about gay rights movements taking place, particularly in the Third World, and especially in the Muslim-dominated country where I live.

In Foreign City, Far East, many of the activists have taken the American gay rights movement as a model and are trying to learn from the struggle there.

On a more general level, however, as we live in a global world, it can only benefit Americans to be aware of a civil rights/human rights struggle in a society where the consequences for such actions are grave.

I thought it particularly telling that after September 11, the country became interested in the cause of women's rights in a place like Afghanistan. But no mention was made, to my knowledge, in any journal or magazine of public opinion, mainstream or otherwise, of the treatment of homosexuals in Afghanistan: a treatment so barbaric that it earned the condemnation of Kofi Annan himself but not Oprah Winfrey.

In short, these people in Far East, like those in Afghanistan, are very brave and are risking a great deal in doing what they are doing. They need solidarity and support from abroad, and their story needs to be told, for it has been untold for far too long. The struggle for human rights is not a local affair, for if it were, then we wouldn't call these rights "human."

If you're interested, I'll write something up and send it to you along with some clips of previously published material.

Warm regards,

Susan Subpar

Good Fiction Magazine Query

Frank Fabulous
20 Success Lane
Baltimore, MD 21202

January 24, 2005

Meagan Church, Editor
Peeks and Valleys
Brink Publications
202 Twyckenham Drive
South Bend, IN 46615

The writer in-
cludes pertinent
contact informa-
tion and begins
the letter
professionally. ——

Dear Ms. Church:

I'm a retired psychologist, and for the last seven years, I've been coordinating a program
of short story discussions at the Centennial Institute here in Baltimore—the country's
most highly rated institute of learning for seniors. In planning my courses, I've had the
pleasure of reading and evaluating over 2,500 short stories published in major anthologies, and that exposure to good writing has been a wonderful learning experience for me.

Though it's not
a requirement
for our maga-
zine, it is nice
to know he has
had some suc-
cess with being
published. ——

I wrote my first short story two years ago, at the age of 72, and it will shortly be published
by *Maryland Magazine*. A second story, "Farewell," appears in the current edition (Fall
2004) of *Oregon Literary Magazine*.

Shows he has
researched our ——
writer's guide-
lines and isn't
just blindly
submitting.

I'm submitting the enclosed 1,157 word story, "Outside the Kitchen Door," to you because of your willingness to consider new writers, and because of your interest in short
shorts.

I've taken the liberty of submitting the story to several other literary journals, and of
course I'll let you know immediately if it's been accepted for publication elsewhere.
Please consider the enclosed copy disposable.

Ends the letter
politely and men-
tions materials
he enclosed
along with the
cover letter. ——

Thanks in advance for considering "Outside the Kitchen Door." I look forward to hearing
from you, and I hope you enjoy the story, whatever its fate.

Cordially,

Frank Fabulous
Phone: 410-555-3838

Though it is
longer than
most, the writer
gives only perti-
nent information
that is intriguing
enough to make
us want to read
his submission.

Encl: Manuscript and SASE

Bad Fiction Magazine Query

This is to the former editor. It shows she did not fully research the publication. She also sent it to other e-mail addresses at the same time, which is unprofessional. She needs to take the time to individually send each submission.

Greeting is over the top and unprofessional.

Huh? This writer sounds cold and pretentious. Simple English in a cover letter is preferred. The submission, not the cover letter, is the time to show creativity.

She lists websites without saying what they are or why we should visit them.

Simplicity is key. This writer tries to make a big impression. She succeeds at doing it, but it's not the impression she intended to make. I have no interest in reading her submission.

To: cdavis@peekandvalleys.com; editor@otherpublication.com; editor@newpublication.com
Subject: Please allow me to share MY FORTUNE. GOD BLESS.

Hi and poignant greetings all.

I am aware that sharing of poems might not be in synergy with the most consummate temperament of both the Social and Business Lists, but please allow me just this one opportunity to share with all magnanimous patrons of art there, this poem which I have evolved just recently on the mantra to GOOD FORTUNE, the mantra which we all in some form or the other want to achieve in the chapter of our penuriously destined life.

Thank you for allowing me to share. My profound apologies if I trespass sentiments here.

God bless,

Donna

http://www.mywebsite.com/donnadismal
http://www.herwebsite.com/donnadismal
http://www.donnadismal.com

For Beginning Writers

Good Nonfiction Book Query

Perfect subject line: It defines it as a query and briefly sums up her book idea.

She reminds me of her previous contact without going into lengthy detail.

Wow! She gets some last-minute news relevant to a project she's wanted to work on and instantly uses the opportunity to enhance its worth and try to get me on board.

This is a bold statement, inappropriate for most proposals, but not this one. It's clear in a few paragraphs that she's probably right and that she's savvy about the publishing business.

It's hard to overlook the 200,000 figure.

Before she pushes us to act soon, she lets us know they're prepared to act very quickly as well.

To: Sharon@lakeclaremont.com
Subject: Query: Guide to Gay Chicago?

Dear Sharon,

I don't know if you recall, but I sent you an e-mail some time back introducing myself. My name is Emily Expert. I am a freelance writer, including contributing regularly as a food writer to the *Chicago Tribune* and functioning as the on-going editor of the *Anti-Tourist Guide to Chicago*.

Did you hear the news that Chicago was selected as the host city of the International Gay Games for 2006? The announcement came down last night. Thousands of gays and lesbians will be descending on Chicago for this event.

Gay guidebooks exist for San Francisco, Los Angeles, New York, even Seattle, but no guidebook to Gay Chicago currently exists. The need for one has never been greater. This is not a formal proposal (as I have just heard the news), just an antenna, feeling out whether you think this is a project you would like to take on. The fact is, somebody is going to put out this book.

Besides the games, thousands of gays and lesbians visit Chicago every year, including organized events like the Gay and Lesbian Pride Parade, which attracts 200,000 participants. Take it from someone with 10 years experience working in gay-affiliated bookstores, these people want guidance in where to go and what to do.

Here's what I propose. I would like to write this book with my friend Craig Creative (he'll take on the boy scene, I'll take on the girl scene). Craig, like myself, has many years experience being a gay and lesbian cultural ambassador to Chicago via his job at Rainbow Bookshop. Other credentials are listed on my attached resume and publishing history.

So, Sharon, what do you say? If you think you may be interested, let me know, and Craig and I can present you with a formal proposal within the next two weeks. Otherwise, we will work quickly to bring our proposal elsewhere.

Cordially yours,

Emily Expert

Bad Nonfiction Book Query

Larry Lacking
456 Off the Mark Ave.
Chicago, IL 60608
(312) 555-7777

May 31, 2005

Lake Claremont Press
4650 N. Rockwell St.
Chicago, IL 60625-2941
Attn: Susan (?)

Dear Susan (?):

I called Lake Claremont roughly a month ago about the bar guide I've been working on. I don't quite remember the name of the woman I spoke to, but I think it was Susan or Sarah, and I know she was about to leave on vacation. She also said there were already too many bar guides out there. I understand that, but I'm enclosing a copy of what I've produced anyway. I call it *Drinking Single*.

The idea I have is to produce bar guides for each neighborhood of Chicago, all with a bent toward the interests of a single guy out on his own. The focus is thus, of course, on what kind of women can be found. But *Drinking Single* is broader than that, as you'll see if you take a look.

So far, Wicker Park is the only neighborhood I've completed. The guide covers every drinking establishment therein. It treats each establishment on a list of criteria that make it easy for comparison. It also includes a map!

I'm hoping to get this published and distributed to hotel bookshops and stores in Wicker Park. Both the publication and the distribution would be, necessarily then, on a small scale. As I complete my reviews of other neighborhoods, the distribution area would naturally grow, until a city-wide guidebook could be produced.

Does this have any merit? Do you like it? Would you be interested in publishing something like this? Please respond, either to the address above or by calling me at (312) 555-7777.

Thank you for your attention.

Sincerely,

Larry Lacking

Despite calling to get my name, he still couldn't get it right and calls attention to his uncertainty.

He's forgotten from his call I wasn't just any person at the company, but the publisher and decision-maker.

The sample chapters reveal a book that would be offensive to most women, yet this author feels comfortable asking a woman publisher to personally finance his project.

These questions are plain silly as I answered them over the phone. If you make initial queries by phone or e-mail, listen to what an editor tells you.

It's unrealistic to expect a phone response to a query. And, there's no reason why any writer working today does not have an e-mail address.

Good Fiction Book Query

This is taken from our website, not from an outside source. That's very good: It means the author perused our site and read our guidelines.

Contact info is not necessary in an e-mail query, but it always looks professional and responsible.

Clearly the author has read our materials online and understands he has what we're looking for.

The premise of this social satire is an example of what ENC Press is looking for. It's also well written. It definitely deserves a look at least.

This tells me more about the author's irascible attitude, and I like it. While the tone of this query might antagonize some editors, it shows the author has understood our own attitude from our website.

To: olga@encpress.com
Subject: Death Entertainment, a satire

Joseph R. Brusque
P.O. Box 123, Anytown, RI 02345
(888) 555-1212

Dear Olga:

In the tradition of Edward Abbey's *The Monkey Wrench Gang, Death Entertainment* is a scathing commentary on the over-the-top sensationalism that is "news as entertainment," the insipid proliferation of "reality TV," and the super-sized corporate manifest destiny that is spreading its infectious mediocrity across our voyeuristic and rubbernecking society.

Death Entertainment is the story of one man's subversive plan to exploit the banal norm, and his hypocritical scheme by which to do so. Dean Barrett, fueled by a steady diet of caffeine, cigarettes, and anxiety, and with the patience of a hand grenade, wants to change society's downward trend, or at least what it looks like on TV.

Sitting listlessly on his threadbare couch, Barrett conveniently finds his scapegoat on CNN. Conrad Rangefork Thistle III basks in his precious 15 minutes at an impromptu press conference, claiming his client, a death-row inmate named Randall Cletus Hogg, deserves his choice of method by which to be executed to illustrate the cruel and unusual nature of capital punishment. Assembling an unlikely cult of personalities, Barrett sets the wheels of exploitation in motion. His goal: to broadcast the execution of Randall Cletus Hogg live, on pay-per-view television.

Death Entertainment is a completed 80,500 words. It is a satirical commentary that might be called "outrageous" and "irresponsible" by unimaginative and timidly politically correct critics. But beneath the layers of cynicism and disillusioned venom, one more-thoughtful might find a novel that foreshadows our culture's bleak future—or at least what it might look like on TV—lest we curb our appetites for the sensational and prevent the spread of infectious mediocrity.

My publishing credits include articles in a diverse collection of newspapers, magazines, alternative newsweeklies, trade journals, and reference sources. I hold degrees from both the Peabody Conservatory of Music at the Johns Hopkins University and the Juilliard School in New York, both of which hang above my toilet.

Quite sincerely,

Joseph R. Brusque

Bad Fiction Book Query

She's e-mailing her query to the right person at the wrong e-mail address. Our guidelines are very clear on whom to submit queries to.

I don't know what Clarion West is, nor have I heard of these publications—she erroneously assumes I would be impressed.

Who?

While these are positive reviews, including them in a query suggests the author thinks I don't have a mind of my own and need other people's opinions to guide me.

Urging a person who reviews queries to do their own legwork is always a bad idea.

Had this author looked at our website before sending in her query, and read our guidelines closer, she would have seen that a fantasy novel would not be a good fit for us.

To: pr@encpress.com
Subject: Query: The Fall of the Tarantula Emperor

Dear Ms. Galvin:

I am a graduate of Clarion West. My short stories have appeared in *Pulphouse*, *Marsdust*, *Paradox*, and *The Pedestal Magazine* among others. My first novel, *Macbeth Awakens*, was released in 2001 by Pinkwolf Press. Here's a sampling of the reviews:

"A fine opening turn upon the stage."
—*Asimov's Science Fiction*
"No reader will want to miss this unusual and compelling novel."
—*Midwest Book Review*
"Mimi Misguided's debut novel marks the emergence of a genuine talent."
—Paul DiMaggio
"Fine prose, likable characters, . . . and an interesting twist."
—*Science Fiction Chronicle*
"An unusually strong ending."
—*Booklist*

If you would like to read more from these reviews (and others), you can visit the publisher's website at www.pinkwolfpress.com.

I would like to submit for your consideration my fantasy novel, *The Fall of the Tarantula Emperor*. The premise is as follows:

The Emperor is dead. The Crown Prince and his five-year-old heir have been assassinated. The throne of Paleland lies vacant, and three people claim the right to sit on it.

For Michael Burke, who arranged the assassinations, the throne means a chance to save his kingdom from a war it cannot possibly win. For Peter Jones, whose father was wrongfully executed for the assassinations, the throne means a chance to win back his family's honor. For Beena Ditchie, the late Emperor's estranged daughter, the throne may be the only hope of escaping the assassin's knife or the headman's axe.

The completed manuscript is approximately 110,000 words. I look forward to hearing from you.

Sincerely,

Mimi Misguided

Writing Groups

Making the Most of Your Experience

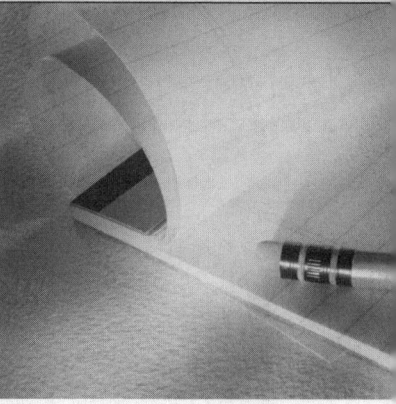

by John Moir

At a recent writing conference, a psychologist spoke about different personality types. He tried to divide the room into people who were lone wolves and those who liked to work in groups. A ripple of laughter rolled through the audience. We were writers, for goodness' sake—*everyone* was a lone wolf. And yet, sometimes even lone wolves run in packs.

That's why so many writers join writing groups. We need other writers to shine a light on blind spots in our work and to provide us with support, camaraderie, and a chance to talk about craft. Using other writers as a sounding board is far better than depending on family and friends, who may not know how to analyze writing or who may feel obliged to say nice things. Our writing skill improves with constructive criticism, but embracing such criticism isn't always easy, even for experienced writers.

Whether you're a beginning writer looking to join your first group or a veteran writing-group member, here are six questions to help you understand writing groups and make the most of your writing group experience.

1. How can a writing group help me?

Woody Allen said, "Ninety percent of success is showing up." A writing group provides an external motivator to help us keep writing. In addition, critiquing others can deepen our understanding of the writing craft.

As my own group discovered, it's wise to look for ways to expand a group beyond critiques. I'd finished a novel, and although the group's help had been invaluable, I knew I would have nothing else for them to read for months. When I suggested I should probably drop out, one member said, "What if you talked about getting an agent? Isn't that part of writing, too?" The light went on, and I turned my "reading time" into strategy sessions for finding an agent and then sharing the tribulations of watching the novel make the rounds of publishing houses.

A group can expand support for its members by allowing time for the discussion of various writing issues including brainstorming sessions, discussing a novel's narrative structure, or exchanging ideas on marketing and submissions.

JOHN MOIR lives in Santa Cruz, California, and is a writer for the National Science Teacher's Association. He's the author of a nonfiction book as well as numerous articles and stories, and he has won a dozen writing awards.

2. How can I find a writing group that's a good match for me?

First, ask yourself what you want from a writing group. Assess how your skill level, genre interests, and writing goals compare with those of the members of a prospective group. Stretch yourself by seeking a group working a little beyond your current ability. While no group offers a perfect match, look for one whose members are enthusiastic and committed writers.

Writing groups often evolve out of a writing class or from posting a sign-up sheet at a writing conference. Other groups start up through an ad in the local newspaper or a literary organization's newsletter. Writer friends, bookstore employees, or librarians may also know of groups. Online groups present another option, especially for writers in remote areas, although such groups may lack the personal connection of a face-to-face meeting.

For a list of active writing groups in the U.S. and other English-speaking countries, go to www.writepage.com/groups.htm.

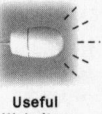

Useful Websites

3. What's the best way to conduct critiques?

Here's where the No. 2 pencil meets the 20 lb. bond paper. Effective critiques highlight both the strengths and weaknesses of the work, leaving a writer feeling supported, not slammed. When evaluating a piece, consider everything from language mechanics to narrative flow. Strive for specificity, and aim for description, not evaluation. It's better to say, "The question posed in the story's first sentence hooks the reader" rather than, "Great opening."

There are two commonly used methods for sharing a writer's work. In the first, a writer gives copies of the piece to be critiqued to other group members one meeting ahead of time. Members read the piece on their own and come to the next meeting ready to provide constructive comments and feedback. Advocates of this method say it allows time for a thorough reading and speeds up the meeting, since the focus remains entirely on critiquing. However, it also means an additional commitment for members to review the writing at home. It's worth considering if busy members will give the work a careful reading, and if they will remember the nuances behind their comments several days later.

A second method involves using part of the meeting time to read the work. A writer brings multiple copies of a piece and either reads it aloud or lets the group read it silently. In-group reading takes more time. However, it allows everyone to read the same thing together. I've been in writing groups using both methods, and while each works, I prefer the read-it-in-the-group method for providing a more cohesive critique. No matter which reading method a group uses, it's important to establish a page or time limit on how much material a writer may present.

Groups must also decide how to provide feedback to the writer. Methods vary from informal discussions to evaluating the piece page by page. The technique I favor gives each member a set amount of time to talk about the piece that was read aloud—no one else may speak. The next member repeats this process and so on. When everyone has finished providing feedback, the writer may ask clarifying questions. At the end, members hand the writer their copy of the piece with any written comments for further review. This method typically yields a clean, solid critique.

4. What should I do after a not-so-positive critique session?

Okay, so no one seemed to like your piece. Take a deep breath. Take another. Don't do anything for a while—give yourself the gift of time and perspective. Realize that criticism of your work is not personal. When you're calm, review the suggestions again—you might be surprised at what you find. Cherry-pick the best ideas, and work them into your writing.

5. How can I avoid common writing group pitfalls?

You've probably heard many a writer say: "My writing group said my story lacked a solid point of view and all the characters were undeveloped and flat. If I can't nail point of view or write believable characters, then why am I writing at all?" If you find yourself in such a group, consider modifying the group's structure to change the unhealthy dynamic. If that doesn't work, you'll need to find another group. In the end, measure your group's effectiveness by your comfort level and writing growth. You're looking for a synergy that encourages you. You still might have a twinge of nervousness before reading an important piece, but if you feel as if most of the time you get fair and thoughtful responses to your writing, consider your group a success.

Sometimes long-standing groups grow stale. Try something new to break the mold: Start the meeting with a 15-minute writing exercise, schedule a guest speaker, or invite a new member to join.

6. How do I start my own writing group?

Details left unattended can impair a writing group's effectiveness. When writing groups are started, it's in the best interest of the group to understand the members' general needs and to choose a leader to keep the group on track.

When starting a writing group, consider the following:

- **Attendance.** Regular attendance forms the foundation for everything a writing group does. Some groups meet as often as once a week, while others only get together once a month. A group must strike a balance between meeting too frequently (which can create burnout) and sporadic meetings (which can erode a group's cohesiveness).
- **Size.** Size matters in a writing group. The larger the group, the less individual attention your writing receives. Many groups settle on a limit of five or six writers so each person can reap the full benefits offered by membership in a writing group.
- **Location.** If you're starting a writing group that meets in person (versus one that meets online), you'll want to decide on a fixed or rotating meeting location. Many writing groups find it most convenient to meet at the local library or closest bookstore.
- **New members.** Sooner or later, every group has to replace a member, but choosing a new member in haste can leave the group regretting its decision. In order to find a suitable match, have potential members write a letter describing their background and writing goals, and have them include a sample of their work. This allows the group to gauge new prospects' abilities and interests before they meet them. A writer who passes this "try-out" can then be invited to sit in on a session to observe how the group operates. Some groups offer immediate membership, while others incorporate a probationary period to see how things work out.

E-mail Communication

The Art of Sending Effective E-mails

by Rob Spiegel

For the past five years, most of my communication with editors and agents has taken place through e-mail. Occasionally an editor will pick up the phone and call me, but that's an exception. Most of the communication, from the initial query and assignment to the delivery of the finished manuscript, is done by e-mail. In the past five years, I've not used postal mail for any communication other than returning a signed contract. I use e-mail to introduce myself to editors and agents, to send queries and articles, to send approved or rejected tracking changes on manuscripts, and to send invoices.

For many years, communicating by e-mail was a questionable practice, but today e-mail communication is accepted in all areas of publishing, from newspapers and magazines to book publishing companies, agents and, of course, websites and e-mail newsletters.

E-mail is the preferred form of communication for most editors because it's instant, yet unobtrusive, and it can cut the time from submission to acceptance (or rejection) from three weeks to three hours. However, if you use e-mail carelessly, you can instantly destroy a relationship with an editor.

E-mail introductions: Getting the right address

When you send an e-mail to an editor for the first time, use the same greeting format you would in a paper letter, "Dear Ms. Willis." In e-mail, there's a great temptation to simply say, "Hi Jill," since the more formal greeting can seem stilted. But go with the formal. It won't hurt and it may help. When you get a response signed, "Best, Jill," you can then move to the more natural use of the first name.

Like any other correspondence, make sure you're contacting the appropriate person. If you're not sure who that person is, send a quick e-mail note—or make a quick call—to an assistant at the publication.

Not all e-mail addresses are available on a publication's website. When I call a publication and ask whom the right contact person is and also request that person's e-mail address, I'm usually given the correct information. The least efficient way to request this information is through a site's general feedback form. If you do decide to fill out that form, understand that you may never receive a response or, if you do, it may not be as soon as you'd like or need.

ROB SPIEGEL writes for *Automation World, Electronic News,* and *Supply Chain Management Review.* He was senior editor at *Electronic News and Ecommerce Business.* Spiegel is author of five business books published by major publishers, and he writes a business column that appears in dozens of publications including *The Albuquerque Tribune.*

E-mail queries: Same content, different submission rules

E-mail queries follow the same basic rules as paper queries. The e-mail query should be roughly the same length as a paper query, and it should also include the same elements. As with a paper query, an e-mail query should open with a strong lead and follow up with information on your proposed book or magazine article that shows the editor you know the publication and have come up with a viable idea.

Where the queries differ is in the approach. For one, since editors typically respond to e-mail queries quickly, you can avoid the temptation of sending simultaneous queries. If the editor likes the idea, you'll likely get a response in two or three days—often, a positive response comes within hours. However, since e-mail is less formal than paper correspondence, you may not receive a formal rejection. So, instead of sending simultaneous queries, send your queries one at a time and simply wait two or three days before sending the next one. In rare instances, an editor may respond positively after two or three weeks, but it's not likely.

Quick notes: Sometimes assignments come through e-mail conversations

E-mail is a convenient form of communication to introduce yourself to an editor even before you send a query. There's no paper mail equivalent to a note that simply asks an editor, "Are you looking for new freelance writers?" I find this is a very effective question prior to sending a query if I'm not sure the publication is actively seeking queries. Consumer magazine editors generally always accept queries, but things are fuzzier with websites, newspapers, and trade publications. So it's handy to send along an e-mail note asking if the publication works with freelancers and whether they'd like to see a query. If you're a published writer, it helps to include one or two sentences explaining your experience.

Editors often respond to these quick questions by asking what type of subjects you've covered in the past. I've received more assignments through conversations prompted by a quick e-mail note than assignments prompted by a traditional query.

Working through problems with editors: Be careful with emotions

The most difficult aspect of any e-mail communication is effectively managing your emotions. Humor is always welcome, if not overdone. The most difficult emotion to manage in e-mail conversations is anger. Writing articles and books is difficult work—not all writers and editors hold the same view of what's expected in an article or book. Frustration is common and natural, but if you manage your frustration with humor, it's relatively easy to work through. However, if you resort to expressing anger in an e-mail, you can quickly destroy a potential relationship with an editor or agent.

What is it about e-mail that gives writers the courage to say what they really think? I've seen otherwise reasonable people tell someone off in an e-mail using horrid and distorted accusations. These are people who would never in a million years utter such flaming words in a phone call, in person, or even in a paper letter, yet they seem to feel perfectly comfortable blasting someone's character in an e-mail. I can think of at least a dozen professional relationships I've seen destroyed by poorly chosen words used in e-mail.

Don't succumb to the temptation to tell your editor off in an e-mail—count to ten, send it to a friend for editing, whatever it takes. If you're not sure whether you have the right tone in a difficult e-mail, pretend you're standing in front of the person you intend to e-mail. Would you use those same words and tone? If not, change your e-mail.

When things get difficult, the first thing you should do is to try to identify where and how the difficulties occurred. When communicating by e-mail, your strongest assets are humor and the ability to own up to your shortcomings—a little humble pie can win the day and preserve a relationship during a difficult moment. Humility or a self-effacing manner is the most effective stance in e-mail communication and, oddly, it's also the rarest.

Good E-mail Query

Even though it's common in e-mail correspondence, don't use the familiar "Hi, Jeff." If the editor or agent responds to the query and signs off, "Best, Jeff," then you can go to the first name in your next e-mail.

This paragraph quickly establishes the author is experienced in the subject matter and experienced in writing. It also establishes the potential market for the book is large.

This paragraph establishes there are few writers who cover this growing market and there is presently little competition.

This comment acknowledges there are general books on the topic but no specific books. In most cases, books succeed when they pinpoint an emerging subset of an established subject.

This paragraph shows the author has a "platform," which is agent and editor speak for the ability to promote books directly to a pre-existing audience.

Dear Mr. Herman,

For the past year, I've been editor of a biweekly print newsletter, "Marketing Smarter With Search Engines," which covers pay-per-click (PPC) advertising via search engines. This form of marketing has grown to a billion-dollar industry in two quick years. Google now has 275,000 PPC advertisers.

I'm the only seasoned business journalist covering search marketing on a daily basis. I think there's a great need for a book on the subject. Currently there are only two books on search marketing, and both are short e-books with price tags of $60 and $70. There are a number of books on search marketing, but none that cover pay-per-click advertising.

I write a syndicated column on business marketing, and I've published five books on Internet business and marketing. The column will provide a platform to help get the word out about this book when it comes out. We can also sell copies through the newsletter.

Want to try to sell this?

Thank you,
Rob Spiegel

This sign off may seem smirky—and it is—but it's also a very direct question.

Bad E-mail Query

Don't use the editor or agent's first name in an introductory letter.

Opening with a comment like this is amateur and prompts the skeptic in the reader.

The early communists came before Bob Dylan. Small detail, but it probably signals other inaccuracies in the book.

Frank McCourt wrote *Angela's Ashes*; not his brother Malachy. Also, *Angela's Ashes* is more than a decade old and is not sufficient evidence of a trend.

No agent or editor wants to hear the query is going out to a crowd of other agents and editors.

Hi Julie,

I have a great book idea. My mother came to America from Germany during World War II. She was just a child and was sent to the U.S. with an aunt and uncle. Her parents stayed behind and were killed during the War.

My mother suffered many hardships in New York during her early years. But later she married my father, Joe, and opened a butcher shop in Greenwich Village. That's where I grew up. I remember all of the colorful characters that came into the shop, from Bob Dylan to the early communists.

This memoir follows in the path of the bestselling *Angela's Ashes* by Malachy McCourt, so it's clear there is a market for memoirs that involve European emigrants that settle in New York. I'm certain my book will also succeed with this audience.

I've finished the book and it's 376 pages. Would you like to see sample chapters, or should I send along the whole manuscript? This is a simultaneous submission.

Let me know,
Rob Spiegel

Shelter Magazines

Finding a Home for Your Writing

by Will Allison

Once upon a time, the shelter magazine category was defined by titles such as *Architectural Digest*, *Elle Décor*, *Home*, *House & Garden*, *House Beautiful*, *Metropolitan Home*, and *Traditional Home*—home-decorating magazines that primarily targeted older, wealthy homeowners. But in the past few years, the category has seen an explosion of more lifestyle-oriented home magazines aimed at younger consumers—*Budget Living*, *Cottage Living*, *Dwell*, *InStyle Home*, *Martha Stewart Living*, *O at Home*, *Real Simple*, and *Readymade*.

These new titles focus less on the "ideal" home (picture a tastefully appointed Tuscan villa) in favor of a more individualized, more eclectic, do-it-yourself aesthetic. As Julie Lasky, editor of *I.D.* magazine, said in an interview with *Folio*, "Shelter magazines will always be dream books, but it is encouraging to see the attempts of many to come down to earth."

Industry analysts credit much of the category's growth to a "nesting" trend following 9/11. In the wake of the terrorist attacks, Americans traveled less, instead focusing on their homes. The stock market decline convinced many investors they were better off putting their money into their homes. Low mortgage rates fueled the trend, as did the popularity of TV shows such as *Trading Spaces* and *Extreme Makeover: Home Edition*.

In the following interview, editors from both new and old-school shelter magazines discuss how the category is changing and how freelancers can take advantage of the category's recent explosion.

Allison Arieff is the editor-in-chief of *Dwell* and was the magazine's founding senior editor. She is the author of the books *Prefab* (Gibbs Smith Publishers), *Trailer Travel: A Visual History of Mobile America* (Gibbs Smith Publishers), and *Spa* (Taschen). Prior to *Dwell*, Arieff spent most of her editorial career in book publishing, including stints at Random House, Oxford University Press, and Chronicle Books, where she edited titles on art, design, and popular culture, including *Airstream: The History of the Land Yacht* (Chronicle Books).

Charlotte Barnard is the deputy editor of *Country Living*, where she oversees content for the 26-year-old shelter and lifestyle magazine. Barnard has spent more than 20 years in publishing and media, most recently at Martha Stewart Omnimedia (MSO), where she was the copy director for retail merchandising, overseeing content for Martha Stewart Everyday and Martha Stewart Signature, the company's new line of home furnishings. Prior to her

WILL ALLISON (www.willallison.com) is a staff member at the Squaw Valley Community of Writers and teaches creative writing at Indiana University-Purdue University at Indianapolis. His short stories have appeared in *Zoetrope: All-Story*, *Kenyon Review*, *One Story*, *Shenandoah*, *American Short Fiction*, *Atlanta*, *Florida Review*, and *Kansas Quarterly/Arkansas Review*.

tenure at MSO, Barnard was an editor at numerous consumer and shelter publications, including *Glamour* and *Vogue*, as well as editor-in-chief of The Hearst Special Publications, a series of special-interest magazines focusing on home improvement and decorating.

Julie Saetre has more than 15 years professional experience in journalism and communications, and is the founding editor of *Indianapolis at Home*, which received a silver award for general excellence from the City and Regional Magazine Association in 2002. The publication relaunched in Spring 2005 as *Indianapolis Monthly Home*.

Alexa Yablonski is discovering what Target and Ikea have to offer while highlighting the inspiring homes of the not-so-rich and not-yet-famous for *Budget Living*. During her stints as associate editor at *Town and Country* and market editor at *Interior Design*, Yablonski, senior editor at *Budget Living*, wrote about Parisian haute couture and crystal chandeliers, among other price-is-no-object items.

What sets your magazine apart from others in the shelter category?

Arieff: *Dwell* has pushed the boundaries of the shelter category, and I'd really characterize the publication more as a lifestyle/design title. Our tagline, "At Home in the Modern World," is emblematic of our content. You'll find stories about home but also all the things one might be interested in relating to the design of that home—art, travel, culture, home entertaining, etc.

Allison Arieff

Photo by Emily Nathan

Barnard: *Country Living* supports, inspires, and, in many ways, defines the country lifestyle. Every issue features in-depth editorial on decorating and remodeling, cooking and entertaining, antiques and collecting, gardening and travel. With its inception 26 years ago, *Country Living* was the first magazine to identify country style, now a lifestyle that begins in the home and extends to all facets of everyday life. *Country Living* is the biggest shelter magazine, with a circulation of 1.7 million. It's also a large franchise that includes special interest publications like *Country Living Gardener* and *Country Living Holidays*, as well as a website, books, and a branded line of furniture with Lane. For over a quarter century, the magazine has maintained its success by consistently identifying and reporting on Americans' love for this way of living and decorating. The magazine celebrates the reader and her community. This reader is looking not for perfection, but for ways to realize her own personal style, and *Country Living* consistently provides attainable and actionable ideas.

Saetre: *Indianapolis Monthly Home* is a tightly targeted publication with an emphasis on "local." The information is personalized for affluent readers in the Indianapolis area, and all sources, products, shops, etc., are either based in Indianapolis or have a local tie or angle. We tell and show our readers how to adapt national trends in their own homes and gardens, using the resources we have here in the city.

Yablonski: Unlike many shelter magazines (which tend to highlight homes done up by professional designers), *Budget Living* primarily showcases places whose owners have put their own blood, sweat, and tears into the decorating. We've featured a range of residences— from a knick-knack filled Louisiana fish camp to an apartment that's so spare and mod it resembles a '60s sitcom set. The homes we publish may differ dramatically in style, but what they share is personality—and lots of it. And none of these nests cost a fortune to feather. We search out spots that have a deft mix of high and low—say a pair of $25 Ikea chairs cozied up next to a vintage Knoll table. We hope to inspire our readers and aim to give them the tools they'll need to keep from busting their decorating budget by including thrifty store listings in the back of the book, decorating tips, or pertinent do-it-yourself sidebars.

What departments and/or subject areas are most open to freelancers?

Arieff: Freelancers contribute to all departments—the shorter, front-of-the-book pieces—and the longer pieces in the feature well. We prefer to start people out with shorter articles, perhaps something in the Archive or Elsewhere departments.

Barnard: Personal projects, personal essays, and local or community-focused events. We read every letter that comes into the office, and some stories have been developed from these pitches or queries.

Saetre: We use freelance work extensively in our publication, from home features to our department roster. Topics include interior design (both big-picture room decor and details such as hardware, window coverings, lighting, etc.), major home renovations, gardening and landscaping, entertaining, and one-on-one interviews with local home and garden experts.

Yablonski: Our front-of-the-book Goods and Finance pages are primarily written in-house or by bimonthly columnists. Loose Change, our mixed bag news section, frequently publishes freelancers, as does Making It, which focuses on do-it-yourself projects. Most of our features are written by freelancers as well. For our home stories, we're always looking for projects big on personality and ideas (cheap wall treatments, small space solutions, easy home improvement projects, untapped resources, innovative and cheap materials, etc.). Typically, the owners know when to splurge and when to skimp. Their homes usually have a blend of big-ticket items and amazing steals. We're especially interested in pitches for homes outside of New York and Los Angeles.

What qualities do you look for in your writers?

Arieff: First and foremost, the writer should have a deep understanding of *Dwell*'s content. All too often, someone will pitch a story on a Tuscan villa, for example, despite *Dwell*'s explicit commitment to modern design. It becomes clear the freelancer has never seen the magazine or hasn't really spent any time with it. Writers for *Dwell* should be curious, intelligent, and have a sense of humor. We're interested in what they can bring to the table—different backgrounds, experiences, interests, writing styles—as that makes for a diverse and more interesting mix of content in the magazine.

Barnard: Clear, concise, direct, and accurate writing; professionalism, timeliness of ideas, and of delivery of piece.

Saetre: Writers should be familiar with the publication and its approach, and be able and willing to adapt to our editorial style. They should be willing to seek appropriate local sources, going beyond the easy public relations or sales contact to find individuals who adeptly speak to the subject at hand. They also need to be professional, not just in their dealings with me, but also in their contacts with our sources. Many times, the writers conduct interviews in the sources' homes, so they must represent our publication well. And, of course, the ability to meet deadlines is crucial.

Charlotte Barnard

Yablonski: Most of the writers we contract have been published before, but we're open to fresh voices, as long as they're attached to new and unusual ideas. Our favorite writers meet their deadlines, write cleverly and with clarity, have energy and enthusiasm that translates to the page, and can turn around an on-point revision (if it's needed).

Where do you see the shelter category moving in the coming years?

Arieff: I see two directions. On the one hand, I see the category moving more into the realm of catalogs, following the lead of magazines like *Lucky*. This results in a magazine almost entirely devoted to product. On the other hand, I also believe there's a big audience out there in search of real content, not catalogs. These readers want information, an interesting narrative, and a community of like-minded individuals. *Dwell* aims to reach the latter group with smart, thoughtful content.

Barnard: The home—and I think, in particular, country style and the way it embraces so many backgrounds and opportunities for personal expression—will continue to be a focus, providing inspiration, a creative outlet, and comfort to readers.

Saetre: I believe this category can only get stronger. As more and more shelter publications enter the marketplace, a title will need to find its proper niche and then completely fill that role to survive and thrive. People have strong emotional ties to their homes; shelter publications should continue to recognize those attachments. With the world an unsettled place, shelter pubs—like homes themselves—should offer a welcome respite and help readers celebrate the little joys present in day-to-day living.

Photo by Rob Whiteside

Alexa Yablonski

Yablonski: I think it's just going to get bigger and more interesting. Thanks to Ikea and Pottery Barn first—and later Target, Wal-Mart, etc.—design taste has been elevated, and now, more than ever, people can afford to make their homes stylish. Since almost anyone is able to tear out a page from a catalog and replicate it, magazines will be showing more and more unusual projects, ones that push boundaries.

Margaret Atwood

Unlocking the Door to Creativity
by Multitasking

by Kristin D. Godsey

Like many artists, Canadian writer Margaret Atwood seems uncomfortable with the notion of explaining her craft. She follows no formulas, has no set writing patterns and brushes off any attempts to dig into how the creative mind works.

But that's not to say this world-renowned author of such novels as *Cat's Eye* (Doubleday), *The Handmaid's Tale* (Cape), *Alias Grace* (Nan A. Talese) and her latest, *Oryx and Crake* (Doubleday), doesn't have any wisdom to offer her fellow writers. Her nonfiction book *Negotiating With the Dead: A Writer on Writing* (Anchor Books) is proof of that, and my interview with her revealed some interesting insights all writers can take to heart.

You're a poet, novelist, short-story writer, and essayist, and always have been, ever since you announced to your friends back in high school you were going to be a writer. Do you have a soft spot for one genre over the others?

I do when I'm writing it. When I'm in a poetry phase, I think this is the greatest thing and how could I write anything else? When I'm writing a novel, I'm very focused on that, and I can barely read poetry. There's no secret. I've always been a multitasker in all areas of life.

You have a distinct voice that shows through in all your published work. There's an intensity, a sense of menace beneath the surface, along with a wry, dark humor. Did you always write this way?

I think everybody goes through an apprenticeship period in which they try different forms. And I certainly did. When we were in high school in the '50s, in our high school anyway, we didn't read much modern poetry at all. So "The fog comes on little cat feet," and that was about it. Most of the other things we read, if it was prose, were most likely written before 1900. They taught rhyme, they taught scansion. I knew what the various kinds of sonnets were long before I hit university.

So presumably that's what you started trying to write?

[Laughing:] I started out sounding sort of like a combination of Lord Byron and Edgar Allen Poe. I wouldn't say what I was doing back in college was very much like what I sound like now. I'd say that didn't hit until I was 24 or 25.

KRISTIN D. GODSEY is editor of *Writer's Digest*. This interview originally appeared in *Writer's Digest* magazine, April 2004.

So what changed?

I was writing more formally before. I can't tell you what happened except it was a very noticeable shift, and it happened all at once. You can't account for anything that happens in the creative mind. It's the "eureka experience." The experience comes unbidden.

Is there a particular poem or novel you think introduces that change?

Yes, it's my first book of poetry, which you can't get in the States, called the *Circle Game* (House of Anansi). As for novels, it was the second one I wrote, *The Edible Woman* (Atlantic Little, Brown). My first novel was happily unpublished. I can look at *The Edible Woman*, and I can see where I was going. I can see things in it I later went on and developed.

So did you see the shift and decide, "Yes, this is the direction I want to go"?

I felt the shift. This is not an intellectual matter.

Was there any conscious effort then to develop it further?

It's not something you develop. It's something you have access to. It's not like scratching away at the architectural drawing board—maybe we need a doorknob here, or we can put this window over here. That may come in the editing process. But the experience you're talking about is more like opening a door, not developing something.

Then you say, "I didn't even know that door was there. Shall I go further down this corridor"?

Do you ever hesitate in that idea of whether you should go further?

Yes.

But do you generally plod through?

Eventually. But the hesitation can take years. So that's more like, "Okay, I know the door is there, but I'm not going in there now. I need to get my little vial of magic light or whatever it is we need for these expeditions." Or maybe you say, "I'm just not ready to go there yet."

And eventually you're ready.

Eventually, I go through the door. Or so far, that's been true. Let me give you an example: I wrote the first notes and chapters for *Cat's Eye* when I was 25. I didn't write the book itself for another 23 years. That's a long hesitation.

Again, is that just an instinctual thing—you know when you're ready to go back?

You know when you're not ready; you may be wrong about being ready, but you're rarely wrong about being not ready. You keep trying, but you may wait a while between the tries.

And in your case, you try something else.

I try something else. That's one of the virtues of being a multitasker. If something's not working, you can go dig up a flower or fix a drape. Or write a different book.

What are your thoughts on the "chick lit" phenomenon?

Well, I wrote the first one: *The Edible Woman*. It was published in 1969.

Do you think that compares with what's being done today?

Have a look! Have a look. It's very *Bridget Jones's Diary* when you come to think of it. She works in an office; it's a shit job—

But your voice doesn't match up with the tone of most of today's chick lit.
Well, some chick-lit books are better than others. I thought *Bridget Jones* was quite a howl. There's good, bad, and mediocre in everything. If you really wanted to, you could say the original chick-lit book is *Pride and Prejudice*. So what is it, if it's about young women we're not supposed to take it seriously? It should be judged on its merits like everything else. A lot of the books we regard as classics today were thought of as cheap junk when they came out. *Dracula* by Bram Stoker is one; so is Mary Shelley's *Frankenstein*. There's a long list.

Let's talk about your writing process. Do you write every day? Can you walk me through a typical writing day for you?
Not every day. I'd like to, but I never did. I've always had either a job or a very busy life. I can't describe my process. It's chaos around here all the time.

So you don't have any sort of weird rituals or anything before you get started?
Oh, I wish. I used to have the pencil-sharpening, pacing-the-floor, anxiety-attack ritual, but things got so I just couldn't afford the time. So I've got that narrowed down to about five minutes of screaming time. [Laughs.]
Sometimes you just come to a stop, and you go do something else. And you do get to a certain age where you realize the world will actually not stop turning if you don't write anymore.

I guess you don't really suffer from writer's block, then.
I never have, although I've had books that didn't work out. I had to stop writing them. I just abandoned them. It was depressing, but it wasn't the end of the world. When it really isn't working, and you've been bashing yourself against the wall, it's kind of a relief. I mean, sometimes you bash yourself against the wall and you get through it. But sometimes the wall is just a wall. There's nothing to be done but go somewhere else.

That sounds pretty practical.
I'm a very practical person. I grew up in a practical way; I grew up in the North. Make too many mistakes, and you're dead. You usually don't get a whole lot of second chances at certain kinds of mistakes. So let us say I'm cautious but practical.

So how does a Margaret Atwood novel come to be?
I usually start with some voices, an image, or a place. *The Handmaid's Tale* started with the scene of the bodies hanging from the wall. In the writing, that scene migrated quite far back into the book. But that was the first arresting image that made me feel I really had to go forward with this book.

Do you outline?
No. I did that once. It was a terrible mistake.

So you start with an image—
Yes. It's like overhearing someone talking in the next room. It's like seeing a village a long way off and thinking you have to go there. It's like seeing an object fraught with significance. You wonder why that's there. What is that blood-stained cleaver doing in the middle of the living room floor? I think we'd better look into this!
I'm compelled by something to go and find out more about it. And I've been wrong.

And do you just know when you're wrong?

You know eventually. It may take you 200 pages. That's unpleasant. But you know when you lose interest.

We all have those "this-is-drivel" moments. But it would be a "this-is-drivel" moment that lasts for quite a long time. It's not only drivel on Monday but on Tuesday, Wednesday, Thursday, Friday, and Saturday, too. What am I to make of this? Why did I write that?

You've won the Booker Prize, as well as numerous other prestigious awards for your body of work. Does such recognition change anything in how you approach your work?

I think if I hadn't won them, I'd be a more anxious and ulcer-ridden person.

Really? That's surprising, considering how practical you are.

I know it is. But having had the experience so many times . . . I'm probably the most short-listed person in the world. To be that short-listed, if I'd never won anything, think how weird it would be.

Can you tell me a little about your writing space?

I don't really have a writing space. I do a lot of writing on airplanes, in airports, in hotel rooms. I do write in my study here, where I have two desks. But I don't use my two desks, because I write on the floor. I lie on the floor—actually, I sort of crouch. I'm more comfortable.

So what are you working on now?

I'm not telling. Never, ever tell. I know if I told my editors at publishing companies what I was working on, they'd turn green and think I was crazy.

Because of the subject matter?

Yes. That's always been true.

Did you used to tell and then stopped?

I once told the title of a book, and then I changed it and everyone thought I'd written two books. So I never tell anyone anything.

You have to understand, my Western horoscope sign is the scorpion, and we're happiest in the toes of shoes where it's very dark. Nobody knows we're there. And on the Oriental calendar, I'm the rabbit, and we're very happy at the bottoms of burrows. We're very secretive.

Successful Freelancers

Four (More) Writers Share Their Secrets

by Kelly Kyrik

Success is a relative term, and each writer defines it differently. For some it's calculated in acceptance letters and publication credits; others use personal satisfaction as an index. Many writers, however, believe in an even more definitive gauge: income.

In 1995 the National Writers Union (www.nwu.org) attached a dollar figure to freelance success—which translates today to a little over $37,000 a year—and writers everywhere have embraced that as a goal.

So, what does it take to achieve that level of financial success? What are the secrets of those freelancers who've "made it"? Surprisingly enough, many will tell you there are no real secrets, no shortcuts when it comes to achieving success. A little bit of luck and a whole lot of work seem to be the main elements, although the four writers profiled (and the four featured in the last edition) admit perseverance, professionalism, and a dedication to the craft are all prerequisites. (For updates on the four writers profiled in *2005 Writer's Market*, see Still Successful on page 47.)

In addition, although they all took different paths on their journey toward success, each writer agrees success has been, and continues to be, a process. One that began with a single step: writing.

Karen Asp, columnist, www.karenasp.com

"I've been a fitness nut forever," says 35-year-old Karen Asp. "I started teaching fitness classes after college. I also very much wanted to be a writer and decided to combine my two passions. To that end, I started querying; first trade publications, then websites, then consumer magazines."

Photo by Karen Asp

Karen Asp

Her perseverance, along with her familiarity with the subject matter, led to numerous assignments both online and in print. It also landed Asp the gig as writer of Fitness News, *Allure* magazine's fitness column, a position she's held for three years. "It includes the latest, cutting-edge research readers can utilize in their own fitness pursuits," Asp explains. "The word count runs between 600-800 words, and I usually feature about three or four studies per column and offer practical take-home advice from the researchers."

KELLY KYRIK writes from her home in Colorado and her credits include *Writer's Digest*, *LowCarb Energy*, *Playgirl*, *Incredible Photography*, the *Denver Post*, and more. She can be reached at kyrik@comcast.net.

While she often writes for other publications, including *Family Circle*, *Prevention*, *Cooking Light*, and *Self*, Asp enjoys having steady work and has found the column has opened doors for her professionally. The only downside, she says, is finding studies and tracking down researchers is sometimes difficult. "The writing is actually sometimes the easiest part."

Asp attributes her freelance success to the fact she's always in motion, if not physically, then mentally. It doesn't hurt, she adds, that she's a bit of a Type A personality. "I do have a bit of a competitive spirit, and along with being motivated, I'm disciplined and organized beyond belief. I've always been a goal setter, and setting small goals along the way has pushed me along. It also helps I specialized in health, fitness, and nutrition, rather than starting as a generalist."

Asp has found her calling to be quite rewarding. "My first big break came when I wrote an article for *Shape* about a little-known eating disorder, and a reader wrote to me and thanked me for helping her diagnose her problem. My mantra in life is to make a difference in this world, no matter how big or small, and that's a prime example of how words can do that."

Words of Wisdom

"Your query is your sales pitch. It's the first impression you make on editors. Craft a good query, and even if the idea doesn't fly, the editor may ask for more. In addition, be passionate about your writing and about life. Writers are generally interested in learning about life, and they question what happens around them. Engage in that same curiosity." **—Karen Asp**

Peter Bowerman, commercial writer, www.wellfedwriter.com

"Writing is my fourth or fifth career. Even though I'd wanted to be a writer since college, I wasn't willing to starve doing it. Then I came across Robert Bly's *Secrets of a Freelance Writer* (Owl Books), and it was an epiphany; I never even knew the commercial field existed."

Photo by Jerry Mucklow, Atlanta (Rocket Photography)

Peter Bowerman

Eleven years later, Peter Bowerman, 46, is considered an expert in commercial writing where his work includes brochures, newsletters, and ad copy for clients such as Coca-Cola, IBM and American Express. In addition, he's also the author of *The Well-Fed Writer* and *The Well-Fed Writer: Back for Seconds* (both Fanove Publishing), and he believes most writers can achieve success in the commercial writing field, no matter what their level of experience.

"I had a sales background, and wasn't afraid of cold-calling, which is an important part of business writing. So, since I was entering a high-stakes field, I made use of what I did have, but what I didn't have was a writing background. I didn't have any experience, and I didn't have any credits. Everybody comes at it from a different angle."

Bowerman's found many writers are reluctant to try commercial writing because they believe it's boring or somehow less creative than writing for magazines. He stresses, however, crafting good commercial copy is every bit as challenging as in other genres. "The people who make the most money in this field are the ones who are the most creative. The more interesting you are as a writer, the more money you'll make. There are some really fun, creative challenges in this business, and, although you often don't get to choose your topic, you certainly choose how you're going to render that topic."

Interviews

In addition, Bowerman points out commercial writing usually pays very well, and, unlike other genres, where remuneration is often based on word count, business writers charge by the hour. A good business writer can bill between $50-$150 per hour. (That fee encompasses everything, including travel, meetings, phone conversations and what Bowerman calls "concepting" time.)

The financial reward, and the flexibility it affords him, is one of the main reasons Bowerman enjoys commercial writing. "Every day I get to create my life. I can wake up in the morning and decide what new directions I want to take my business."

Words of Wisdom

"Get convinced of your value. Then, find the people who recognize that value and are willing to pay for it. Don't put these big companies on a pedestal. It's easy to look at a company and assume you don't have what it takes to help them. You're probably wrong; good writers are in short supply. On the other hand, don't waste time looking for secrets. Instead, write." **—Peter Bowerman**

Pat Curry, trade writer

"Many people have the mistaken impression that writing for trade magazines isn't real journalism or that people only write for them because they aren't good enough to write for consumer publications," says 44-year-old Pat Curry.

Photo by John Curry

Pat Curry

Curry, who's been published in many of the top trade magazines, including *Builder*, *Industry Week*, and *Replacement Contractor*, knows better. "The staff at these magazines has strong journalistic backgrounds. They cover important topics, and they expect—and deserve—professional quality reporting and writing."

Curry is also quick to point out trade magazines pay as much or more than their consumer counterparts; the top trades pay $1 and up per word. In addition, it often takes less effort to break in at these magazines and their editorial make-up is sometimes more stable.

"It's easier to make and build long-term relationships with the editors at trade magazines because at consumer publications the editors seem to come and go rather quickly. Trade magazine editors aren't barraged with hundreds of queries a week, so they're easier to reach, plus they tend to have very small staffs so they appreciate and value their writers."

Curry believes much of her success in the trade market is her ability to take long, complex topics and translate them into clear, readable features. In addition, she has a strong newspaper background and has editing experience; she's a contributing editor at *Big Builder* and *ProSales*, and senior editor at *Builder Magazine*, which she calls the "*Cosmopolitan* of construction publications because it's fat with ads and everybody reads it."

It was a long-time goal of Curry's to write for *Builder Magazine*, and to be asked to be senior editor was a "dream come true." But there are other moments that have made her career worthwhile. "I was able to keep working when my daughter had a chronic illness and missed seven weeks of school," she says. "I was also able to take my family on a vacation to Europe. In addition, I went to South Africa with Habitat for Humanity to cover the Jimmy Carter Work Project as a volunteer. Freelancing is a fabulous way to achieve a balance between work and family."

Interviews

Words of Wisdom

"You're a business owner in a service industry—act like one. Your goal is to be the first person editors think of when they have an assignment. To accomplish that goal, do thorough research and reporting, write clear, readable copy turned in on time and in the desired format, and represent your clients with the highest level of professionalism and ethical behavior." **—Pat Curry**

Rick Walton, children's book writer, www.rickwalton.com

"I get a lot of writing done in the nooks and crannies of my life," explains Rick Walton, 47, a stay-at-home-dad to five children. "I brainstorm as I'm falling asleep at night, and while walking, driving, and showering. Any time my brain is free, I put it to work on my writing. And, fortunately, I write short things, which can survive constant interruptions."

Photo by Ann Walton

Rick Walton

Walton's niche is children's books, and he's written over 50 titles—including *Bunny Christmas* (HarperCollins) and *Suddenly, Alligator!* (Gibbs Smith)—in his 20 years as a professional writer. Although he didn't set out to write for kids, his career seemed to naturally follow that path.

"Once I started writing, I gravitated toward writing for children," he says. "When you write for kids, you can be sillier, weirder, more innovative. And I've always liked the idea of saying a lot in a few words. I also love the creative thrill, the giving birth to something brand new, something that never existed before."

Walton got his first break as a joke-book writer for Lerner Publishing, and, after that, he broke into the picture book market with the help of an agent. Once he'd made it that far, Walton quit "career-hopping" and began to focus on being a full-time writer.

Since then, Walton's found one of the many perks of his job is that children often tell him how much they enjoy his books. In addition, he finds satisfaction in the creation itself. "The best moments are when you put the period on the last sentence of a manuscript you know is really working," he explains. "The flower has bloomed. The apple is ripe. The baby is born."

Walton believes success is relative; he says he's always busy reaching toward the next level and re-defining his goals. "It's important to balance your life. Some writers are fortunate and can write full time. Other writers are fortunate and have families to care for, along with other worthwhile careers and interests. You define what success means."

Words of Wisdom

"It helps to be obsessed if you want to succeed as a writer. Also, productivity counts. Work on the diamond-mining theory of writing: The more earth you dig up, the more diamonds you find. The more you write, the more likely you are to write something publishable." **—Rick Walton**

Still Successful

It's been a very busy year for the crop of successful freelancers featured in *2005 Writer's Market*. Here's what they've been up to . . .

- **Jenna Glatzer** is currently writing Celine Dion's authorized biography, as well as *The Street-Smart Writer* for Nomad Press, and has just agreed to co-write a fertility book for Simon & Schuster. In the Spring, she released *Fear is No Longer My Reality* (McGraw-Hill), co-written with Jamie Blyth of the TV show *The Bachelorette*, and her children's picture book, *Hattie, Get a Haircut!* (Moo Press).

- **Jeremiah Healy's** third legal thriller—*A Stain Upon the Robe* (Putnam Adult), under the pseudonym Terry Devane—has been optioned for a feature film, and he's currently working on a police procedural series for television. In 2004, he concluded a four-year term as the president of the International Association of Crime Writers in Amsterdam and was also the American Guest of Honor at the 35th World Mystery Convention in Toronto.

- **Don Vaughan** reports he's never been busier. *Nursing Spectrum*, which has several regional editions across the country, has become a major market for him, and now assigns articles on a regular basis. He's also been writing for *Military Officer Magazine*, *Today's Officer Online*, *Cat Fancy*, *Your Money Report*, and the *Weekly World News*, among many others.

- **Christina Wood's** work took her from Arizona to Aruba and from St. Louis to St. Kitts last year—all without leaving her desk. In addition to contributing to a series of destination features for a nursing magazine and providing copy for resort brochures, Wood has explored new avenues on the Web by developing content for various sites.

Interviews

Alexander McCall Smith

Channeling Your Imagination

Photo by Chris Watt

by Christine Mersch

Alexander McCall Smith's books in The No. 1 Ladies' Detective Agency series typically hit best-seller lists around the world. But there's nothing typical about this writer.

The Zimbabwe-born author writes from a woman's point of view with such confidence his readers have no problem falling into a world revolving around a Botswana woman, Precious Ramotswe, and her detective agency. Smith, however, sees nothing strange about his unique voice.

"Writers always have to empathize with others, whomever the others may be," he says. "I suppose people find it a little bit odd a man should write in a woman's voice, but women writers do the equivalent very well."

While the books primarily focus on solving cases, Smith hesitates to categorize the series as "mystery." The stories are more about the relationships between people, he says, especially Precious Ramotswe and her friends.

Smith has finished writing the sixth book in the Agency series and plans to write two more. Also a medical law professor, he's written more than 50 books altogether, with topics ranging from children's stories to more scientific endeavors. He's also written a serial novel, published in a Scottish newspaper.

Lately, though, this busy author has found another woman to capture his interest— Isabel Dalhousie, the heroine of his new mystery series, launched with *The Sunday Philosophy Club* (Pantheon). Below, Smith discusses his writing process, favorite authors, and varied résumé.

What inspired you to create Precious Ramotswe?

The initial idea for an enterprising and impressive Botswana lady came years ago when I was staying with friends in Botswana. We went to see a woman who was preparing to give my friends a chicken for lunch. This woman chased this chicken through the yard— through feathers and dust—and then, rather coolly and with a great smile, rung the poor chicken's neck. And I thought, "What a remarkable woman. I might write about somebody like that."

CHRISTINE MERSCH is a freelance writer living in Cincinnati. This interview originally appeared in *Writer's Digest* magazine, January 2005.

When you first started writing The No. 1 Ladies' Detective Agency series, did you ever expect such a positive reaction?

I didn't imagine it would get as big as it did. In the very beginning, it was a short-short story. I expanded it because I rather liked Precious Ramotswe; I thought she was such an agreeable person. I was very much enjoying my conversation with her. It seemed to me that the whole situation she was in really asked for further treatment. So, I continued writing.

Have you found there's a difference in writing your first Agency book and your most recent?

A writer becomes more adept with each book. You learn something new about the world you're writing about, and you become a bit better at it. And, of course, it's practice. Every time one writes something, it's practice. One should try to get a little bit better with each book. So in some respects, it's easier to start a new book, but in other respects, each book should set higher standards.

What's different about your new heroine, Isabel Dalhousie of *The Sunday Philosophy Club*, and Precious Ramotswe?

Isabel is more sophisticated, in a sense, than Precious Ramotswe. Isabel's a nice woman, but she's less of a kitchen philosopher; she's the real thing. She's a very acute, moral philosopher. She's got a good sense of humor, as Precious Ramotswe has, so there may be similarities. But in other respects, they're pretty different.

How do you begin writing a new book?

First, I spend time thinking. And then I'll do an outline—just a vague set of notes. Then, I'll start writing and, of course, it'll transform and change as I go. As I near the end of my first draft, the book tends to almost be in final form. There will only be a tiny bit of fiddling about at the end.

What's the difference between writing novels and some of your other projects?

I get more pleasure out of novels. I wrote many children's books, but the Precious Ramotswe novels are particularly pleasurable for me. It's because I know the characters so well I can put humor in the story, and I like putting humor in books. With my novels, I just have good fun.

You're also writing a serialized novel for *The Scotsman* newspaper, which appears in 850-word installments five days a week over six months. How's that different from writing novels?

Since it's not a serialization of an existing novel, I'm writing it as I go. It's quite an interesting difference. I've discovered something has to happen in each installment; whereas, if you just wrote a novel and chopped it up into pieces and published it in a serial form, I think it would have a different feel. So it's quite a different technique, but it's a very enjoyable matter, and I'm getting great pleasure from it.

How are newspaper readers reacting to it?

I've had very nice feedback from readers, and also some suggestions for what I should put in. Some of the suggestions I've taken; others, no. There's one character who's a rather narcissistic young man, very good looking, and the female readers really like him. But they also want something unpleasant to happen to him—they want him to lose his job and be humiliated somehow. It's quite funny.

With all these writing projects going on, do you have a regular writing schedule?

When I've got the time to write, I like to start very early, at about 7:00 or 7:30 a.m., and then finish at 11 a.m. If I can get three or four hours done in a day that's great, but I have so many other things to do, it's rare I'll get a day like that. Therefore, I have to write in between my other duties. Sometimes I might get to write just an hour a day, if that.

Do you have any writing tips to offer aspiring writers?

Have the courage of your convictions, and persist and practice. It's really important when you finish a work to take a little break and then go straight into the next one. I think that's worth doing because then the next one will be better.

Minding the Details

Writers who've been successful in getting their work published know that publishing requires two different mind-sets. The first is the actual act of writing the manuscript. The second is the business of writing—the marketing and selling of the manuscript. This shift in perspective is necessary if you want to become a successful career writer. You must keep the business side of the industry in mind as you develop your writing.

Each of the following sections and accompanying sidebars discusses a writing business topic that affects anyone selling a manuscript. Our treatment of the business topics that follow is necessarily limited, so look for short blocks of information and resources throughout this section to help you further research the content.

CONTRACTS AND AGREEMENTS

If you've ever been a freelance writer, you know that contracts and agreements vary from publisher to publisher. Very rarely will you find two contracts that are exactly the same. Some magazine editors work only by verbal agreement, as do many agents; others have elaborate documents you must sign in duplicate and return to the editor before you even begin the assignment. It is essential that you consider all of the elements involved in a contract, whether verbal or written, and know what you stand to gain and lose by agreeing to the contract. Maybe you want to repurpose the article and resell it to a market that is different from the first publication to which you sold it. If that's the case, then you need to know what rights you want to sell.

In contract negotiations, the writer is usually interested in licensing the work for a particular use, but limiting the publisher's ability to make other uses of the work in the future. It's

Contracts and Contract Negotiation

For More Info

- **The Authors Guild** (www.authorsguild.org), 31 E. 28th St., 10th Floor, New York NY 10016-7923. (212)563-5904. Fax: (212)564-5363. E-mail: staff@authorsguild.org.

- **National Writers Union** (www.nwu.org), 113 University Place, 6th Floor, New York NY 10003. (212)254-0279. Fax: (212)254-0673. E-mail: nwu@nwu.org.

in the publisher's best interest, however, to secure as many rights as possible, both now and later on. Those are the basic positions of both parties. The contract negotiation involves compromising on questions relating to those basic points—and the amount of compensation to be given the writer for his work. If at any time you are unsure about any part of the contract, it is best to consult a lawyer who specializes in media law and contract negotiation.

A contract is rarely a take-it-or-leave-it proposition. If an editor tells you his company will allow no changes to the contract, you will then have to decide how important the assignment is to you. However, most editors are open to negotiations, so you need to learn how to compromise on points that don't matter to you, and stand your ground on those that do matter.

RIGHTS AND THE WRITER

A creative work can be used in many different ways. As the author of the work, you hold all rights to the work in question. When you agree to have your work published, you are granting a publisher the right to use your work in any number of ways. Whether that right is to publish the manuscript for the first time in a publication, or to publish it as many times and in many different ways as a publisher wishes, is up to you—it all depends on the agreed-upon terms. As a general rule, the more rights you license away, the less control you have over your work and the money you're paid. You should strive to keep as many rights to your work as you can.

Writers and editors sometimes define rights in a number of different ways. Below you will find a classification of terms as they relate to rights.

- **First Serial Rights**—Rights that the writer offers a newspaper or magazine to publish the manuscript for the first time in any periodical. All other rights remain with the writer. Sometimes the qualifier "North American" is added to these rights to specify a geographical limitation to the license.

  When content is excerpted from a book scheduled to be published, and it appears in a magazine or newspaper prior to book publication, this is also called first serial rights.
- **One-Time Rights**—Nonexclusive rights (rights that can be licensed to more than one market) purchased by a periodical to publish the work once (also known as simultaneous rights). That is, there is nothing to stop the author from selling the work to other publications at the same time.
- **Second Serial (Reprint) Rights**—Nonexclusive rights given to a newspaper or magazine to publish a manuscript after it has already appeared in another newspaper or magazine.
- **All Rights**—This is exactly what it sounds like. "All rights" means an author is selling every right he has to a work. If you license all rights to your work, you forfeit the right to ever use the work again. If you think you may want to use the article again, you should avoid submitting to such markets or refuse payment and withdraw your material.
- **Electronic Rights**—Rights that cover a broad range of electronic media, from online magazines and databases to CD-ROM magazine anthologies and interactive games. The contract should specify if—and which—electronic rights are included. The presumption is unspecified rights remain with the writer.
- **Subsidiary Rights**—Rights, other than book publication rights, that should be covered in a book contract. These may include various serial rights; movie, TV, audiotape, and other electronic rights; translation rights, etc. The book contract should specify who controls the rights (author or publisher) and what percentage of sales from the licensing of these rights goes to the author.
- **Dramatic, TV, and Motion Picture Rights**—Rights for use of material on the stage, on TV, or in the movies. Often a one-year option to buy such rights is offered (generally for 10 percent of the total price). The party interested in the rights then tries to sell the

idea to other people—actors, directors, studios, or TV networks. Some properties are optioned numerous times, but most fail to become full productions. In those cases, the writer can sell the rights again and again.

Sometimes editors don't take the time to specify the rights they are buying. If you sense that an editor is interested in getting stories, but doesn't seem to know what his and the writer's responsibilities are, be wary. In such a case, you'll want to explain what rights you're offering (preferably one-time or first serial rights only) and that you expect additional payment for subsequent use of your work.

The Copyright Law that went into effect January 1, 1978, states writers are primarily selling one-time rights to their work unless they—and the publisher—agree otherwise in writing. Book rights are covered fully by contract between the writer and the book publisher.

SELLING SUBSIDIARY RIGHTS

The primary right in book publishing is the right to publish the book itself. All other rights (movie rights, audio rights, book club rights, etc.) are considered secondary, or subsidiary, to the right to print publication. In contract negotiations, authors and their agents traditionally try to avoid granting the publisher subsidiary rights they feel comfortable marketing themselves. Publishers, on the other hand, want to obtain as many of the subsidiary rights as they can.

Larger agencies have experience selling subsidiary rights, and many authors represented by such agents prefer to retain those rights and let their agents do the selling. On the other

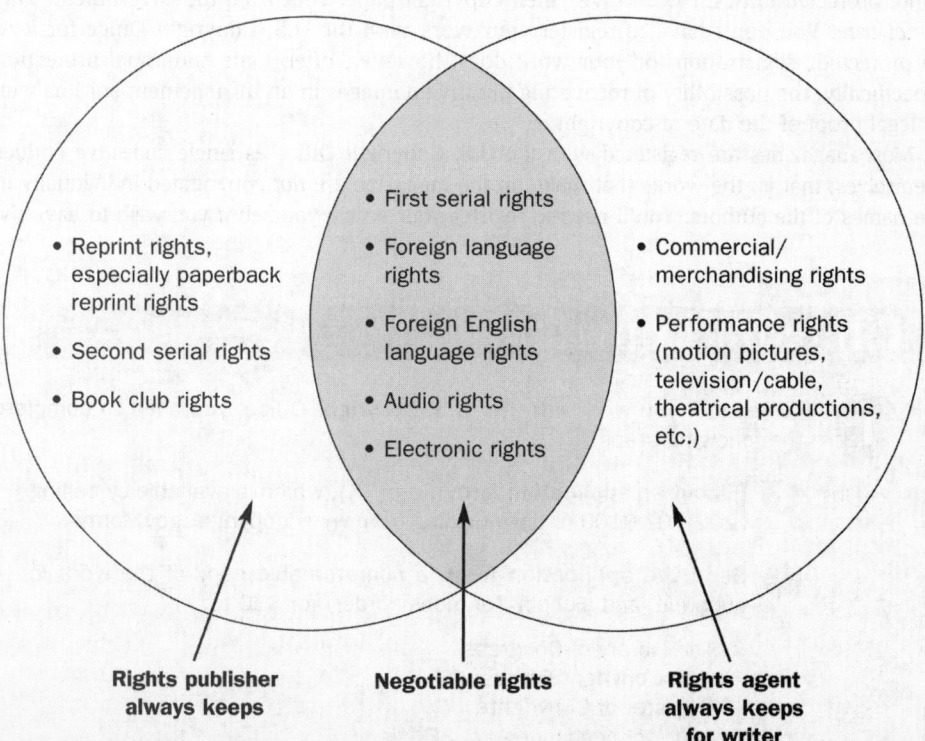

- Reprint rights, especially paperback reprint rights
- Second serial rights
- Book club rights

- First serial rights
- Foreign language rights
- Foreign English language rights
- Audio rights
- Electronic rights

- Commercial/ merchandising rights
- Performance rights (motion pictures, television/cable, theatrical productions, etc.)

Rights publisher always keeps **Negotiable rights** **Rights agent always keeps for writer**

Some subsidiary rights are always granted to the publisher. Some should always be retained by the author. The remainder are negotiable, and require knowledgeable advice from a literary agent or attorney in deciding whether it is more advantageous to grant the rights to the publisher or to reserve them.

The Business of Writing

hand, book publishers have subsidiary rights departments whose sole job is to exploit the subsidiary rights the publisher was able to retain during the contract negotiation.

The marketing of electronic rights can be tricky. With the proliferation of electronic and multimedia formats, publishers, agents, and authors are going to great lengths to make sure contracts specify exactly which electronic rights are being conveyed (or retained). Compensation for these rights is a major source of conflict because many book publishers seek control of them, and many magazines routinely include electronic rights in the purchase of all rights, often with no additional payment.

COPYRIGHT

Copyright law exists to protect creators of original works. It is also designed to encourage the production of creative works by ensuring that artists and writers hold the rights by which they can profit from their hard work.

The moment you finish a piece of writing—or in fact, the second you begin to pen the manuscript—the law recognizes only you can decide how the work is used. Copyright protects your writing, recognizes you (its sole creator) as its owner, and grants you all the rights and benefits that accompany ownership. With very few exceptions, anything you write today will enjoy copyright protection for your lifetime, plus 70 years. Copyright protects "original works of authorship" that are fixed in a tangible form of expression. *Copyright law cannot protect titles, ideas, and facts.*

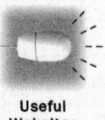

**Useful
Websites**

Some writers are under the mistaken impression that a registered copyright with the U.S. Copyright Office (www.copyright.gov) is necessary to protect their work, and that their work is not protected until they "receive" their copyright paperwork from the government. *This is not true.* You don't have to register your work with the U.S. Copyright Office for it to be protected. Registration for your work does, however, offer some additional protection (specifically, the possibility of recovering punitive damages in an infringement suit) as well as legal proof of the date of copyright.

Most magazines are registered with the U.S. Copyright Office as single collective entities themselves; that is, the works that make up the magazine are *not* copyrighted individually in the names of the authors. You'll need to register your article yourself if you wish to have the

Filing for Copyright

For More Info

To register you work with the U.S. Copyright Office, you need to complete the following steps.

1 **Fill out an application form** (Form TX), which is available by calling (202)707-9100 or downloading from www.copyright.gov/forms.

2 **Send the application form,** a nonreturnable copy of the work in question, and a check (or money order) for $30 to:

The Library of Congress
U.S. Copyright Office
Register of Copyrights
101 Independence Ave. SE
Washington DC 20559-6000

additional protection of copyright (your name, the year of first publication, and the copyright symbol ©) appended to any published version of your work. You may use the copyright symbol regardless of whether your work has been registered with the U.S. Copyright Office.

One thing you need to pay particular attention to is work-for-hire arrangements. If you sign a work-for-hire agreement, you are agreeing that your writing will be done as a work for hire, and you will not control the copyright of the completed work—the person or organization who hired you will be the copyright owner. These agreements and transfers of exclusive rights must appear in writing to be legal. In fact, it's a good idea to get every publishing agreement you negotiate in writing before the sale.

FINANCES AND TAXES

You will find that as your writing business expands, so will your need to keep track of writing-related expenses and incomes. Keeping a close eye on these details will prove very helpful when it comes time to report your income to the IRS. It will also help you pay as little tax as possible and keep you aware of the state of your freelance writing as a business. This means you need to set up a detailed tracking and organizing system to log all expenses and income. Without such a system, your writing as a business will eventually fold. If you dislike handling finance-related tasks, you can always hire a professional to oversee these duties for you. However, even if you do hire a professional, you still need to keep all original records.

The following tips will help you keep track of the finance-related tasks associated with your freelance business.

Tip

- Keep accurate records.
- Separate your writing income and expenses from your personal income and expenses.
- Maintain a separate bank account and credit card for business-related expenses.
- Record every transaction (expenses and earnings) related to your writing.
- Begin keeping records when you make your first writing-related purchase.
- Establish a working, detailed system of tracking expenses and income. Include the date; the source of income (or the vendor of your purchase); a description of what was sold or bought; how the payment was rendered (cash, check, credit card); and the amount of the transaction.
- Keep all check stubs and receipts (cash purchases and credit cards).
- Set up a record-keeping system, such as a file folder system, to store all receipts.

Tax Information

Important

While we cannot offer you tax advice or interpretations, we can suggest several sources for the most current information.

- Check the IRS website (www.irs.gov).

- Call your local IRS office.

- Obtain basic IRS publications by phone or by mail; most are available at libraries and some post offices.

The Business of Writing

Overcoming Writer's Block

by Anthony Tedesco

I hate to break the bad news, but if you're a writer and haven't yet experienced writer's block, you will eventually. That's not some literary hex on you, that's the truth, and an attempt to exorcise any unwarranted fear out of you. Writer's block isn't to be feared; it's to be expected and overcome.

The trick is to figure out what's causing you to falter—the seed beneath the symptom—so you can then accordingly choose and customize your elixir. With help from professional writers, I've diagnosed five causes of writer's block and put together a generic prescription of 12 cures to help you find the best antidote.

FIVE POTENTIAL CAUSES

Writer's block is an idiosyncratic malady with a myriad of personal sources. I'll spare you my amateur psychoanalysis and let you take a little alone time to consider whether any of these potential causes ring true.

1. Self-doubt

Self-doubt can insidiously creep into your subconscious at an early age. Then again, it can also explode into you with one fell swoop of a crass, insensitive critic or an abruptly orphaned book. Regardless of how you acquired the self-doubt that sparked a fear of failure, those little looped voices of negative criticism and naysaying will eventually translate into a knotted-up muse.

2. Perfectionism

Make sure your perfectionism isn't just a pretty name for "fear-of-failure-ism." If you truly are a perfectionist—the superhero arch nemesis of Mediocrity and all his writing minions—you'll be able to point to writing you've done you consider good. It's less a confidence issue and more a quality issue with your current effort. Perfectionists tend to get hung up on leads or even just opening lines. Their incessant inner critic will need to keep going back to craft a better (and better) sentence.

ANTHONY TEDESCO is co-founder of The Student Publishing Program (wwww.225pm.org) and co-author of free e-books for writers, including *Top 250 Free Resources For Writers: Working Writers Share the Free Resources that Have Helped Them Most in Their Careers* and *Words of the Wise: Working Writers Share the Celebrity Writing Advice that has Helped Them Most in Their Careers* (both available for free downloading only at MarketsForWriters.com/wm.html).

3. Ill-suited subject or genre

"Any writer who has difficulty in writing is probably not onto his true subject, but wasting time with false, petty goals," says Joyce Carol Oates. Until you find your true subject, style, voice, or genre, writing will often feel like insurmountable work.

4. Fatalistic career outlook

Kristi Holl, author of *Writer's First Aid* (The Writer's Bookstore, 2003), refers to this cause as "marketplace blues." She writes: "After a few months or years of nothing but rejection slips, it can become harder and harder to keep pouring your heart into your work. . . . After being rejected enough, the writer may feel unable to face another editorial comment, bad review, 'lost' manuscript, payment that never arrives, and stories that don't get published. In other words, he's blocked."

5. Poor time management

Writing takes time—for research, multiple drafts, recuperative breaks, etc.—and if you don't leave yourself enough time to go merrily through the process, you're going to crumble under the deadline pressure and deem it "writer's block."

12 PROVEN CURES

Ideally, you've thoroughly deduced the cause of your writer's block and are ready to choose your perfect prescription. Even if you're on deadline and desperately looking for a quick fix, one of these proven cures just might do the trick. Experiment voraciously. What might seem gimmicky to you now will seem 100 percent godsend if it works for you right at the buzzer.

1. Fight negative with positive

"The first thing you want to do is identify the inner voice who talks to you all the time—the voice that fills you with criticism, self-doubt, and negativity," says Rachel Ballon, Ph.D., the founder/director of the Writer's Center in Los Angeles and a psychotherapist who's coached hundreds of writers on their personal and professional issues. "Realize the voice isn't telling the truth, and take away its power to block you when you start writing."

Ballon suggests creating a written list of positive statements about yourself as a writer and reading them over and over until you memorize them. "Use these positive statements to silence the inner critic as soon as it starts criticizing you. These techniques really work if you read your positive affirmations for 21 days—every morning when you wake up and every evening before going to sleep."

2. Relax

Clear your mind in six calming breaths, each consisting of five slow seconds in through your nose, and five slow seconds out from your mouth. During each exhalation, gently place the tip of your tongue onto the roof of your mouth, right behind your front teeth.

Are you doing it right? Yes, because any way you do it that feels comfortable is right. The main thing is to focus on nothing but your breathing. If your mind wanders, don't worry. Just notice it, and bring yourself back to focusing on your breaths. It's one minute of meditation to help silence those nattering inner critics.

3. Get gratified

Instead of reaching for the pint of Vanilla Swiss Almond Hagen Daas, seek gratification from a market that publishes short, swift pieces to write—fillers, jokes, postcards, short-short stories, letters to the editor, etc. Online markets are particularly quick in their turnarounds, usually moving to "press" far faster than print publications, and they often run short pieces to spare readers from having to continuously scroll down the page.

To make your task less daunting still, you could even consider writing something for a publication that doesn't pay. "Real writers don't write for free" is a limiting myth, according to Jenna Glatzer, author of *Outwitting Writer's Block and Other Problems of the Pen* (The Lyons Press, 2003) and *Make a Real Living as a Freelance Writer* (Nomad Press, 2004). Glatzer understands the logic of not devaluing the industry, but knows it's not so black and white. "I've written for national magazines, books, and major anthologies, and I still write for free sometimes. . . . I do it when I particularly want to support a publication that can't afford to pay, or when I'll get valuable publicity from my efforts."

Writing for free could just be the trick you need to break into the industry and to break through any block you may be experiencing from those marketplace blues.

4. Freewrite

Whether it's a grocery list or your favorite writing prompt, anything that gets you writing is a good thing. If you haven't yet acquired a favorite writing prompt, fear not. The editors of *Writer's Digest* magazine have prepared 365 "idea joggers and brain starters to get your writing going." Visit www.writersdigest.com/writingprompts.asp for a new prompt every day, as well as access to all the previous prompts you may have missed.

Useful Websites

5. Start in the middle

Perfectionists, hear this: *The New York Post*'s Phil Mushnick points out "writer's block occurs most frequently at the very top of one's work." Mushnick goes on to say, "Lose that tortured lead you were laboring over—it probably wasn't any good, anyway—and write it straight. Halfway through the piece it'll come to you—and it'll better rhyme with what you were after when you began."

6. Write badly

I'm serious about this cure. Write badly, really badly—a first draft with run-on sentences, incoherent dialogue, typos, and ludicrous plot twists. Let it be the worst first draft you've ever written because it doesn't matter. According to Anne Lamott, author of *Bird by Bird: Some Instructions on Writing and Life* (Anchor, 1995), the only thing that matters about a first draft is that you finish it. She says, "All bad writing leads to good writing."

I know this advice sounds traumatic to perfectionists like me, but Lamott's rationale is sound. No one ever sees this first draft, and it enables you to get your raw ideas down on paper where they can be tweaked. Plus, let's be honest, it lets you actually finish something. It's a small victory, but a victory nonetheless, hopefully providing the vital confidence needed for your next victory.

7. Allow more time

I know, easier said than done, but your schedule will even out. Time allowed for pressure-free prewriting, brainstorming, bad drafts, and small goals will save you time previously spent staring at the screen or otherwise fearfully procrastinating.

8. Read

"One thing I do to get my creative juices flowing is to read," says Barbra Annino, a professional writer in McHenry, Illinois. "I read a favorite book or something about the topic I plan to write about."

You can also read some of the many self-help books dedicated to overcoming writer's block. In addition to the aforementioned resources, consider Heather Sellers' *Page After Page*

The Business of Writing

(Writer's Digest Books, 2004), which helps writers push through writer's block for both the sake of the stymied composition at hand, and for the potentially successful career at risk. "Ninety percent of beginning writers stop practicing their craft before they have a chance to discover their talents," says Sellers.

9. Change subjects and/or genres

"I don't necessarily believe in writer's block. However, subject block is another matter," says Thomas Nixon, a writer, academic counselor, and author of *Bears' Guide to Earning High School Diplomas Nontraditionally* (Ten Speed Press, 2003). "If I find I can't write about what I'm writing about, I work on my next book for a while. Still writing, still making progress, but using different information from my brain. Often, giving the other writing time to germinate will result in progress on both my book and the article." Working with multiple subjects and genres can help you find the writing that flows naturally from you.

10. Exercise

Ernest Hemingway was an advocate of exercise. He's quoted as saying, "It is better to produce half as much, get plenty of exercise, and not go crazy than to speed up so that your head is hardly normal." A 10-minute walk can get your blood flowing and, often, your ideas. Following Hemingway's advice, professional writer Amanda Castleman suggests taking a two-minute workout. "When fidgeting with a phrase, I sometimes crank out a few pushups to get the blood flowing. Yoga postures also help, if I'm feeling less Hemingway-esque."

11. Break from forcing it

Castleman also says to give yourself as many guilt-free breaks as you need until it's absolutely necessary to work. "I once was pottering about, procrastinating on deadline, when I bumped into two architect friends. One ordered me to 'stick my butt in a chair and produce.' The other (more successful) architect said, 'You're a professional. You know you'll get the work done, brilliantly, under last-minute pressure. So you might as well relax and enjoy yourself guilt-free, until the adrenaline kicks in. That's what I do.' The advice has proved invaluable."

Taking breaks is also a good way to treat yourself to nonwriting activities you enjoy, and to help you recognize yourself as a person as opposed to just a writer. This distinction is vital to staving off those "marketplace blues" mentioned earlier. Holl says, "Remember to keep your professional distance and separate yourself from your script, so when your writing is rejected, you just keep on writing no matter what happens."

12. Set a deadline

Set a deadline, or have a stern friend set one, and stick to it. Finish. Put a period somewhere, and call it the ending. Julia Cameron, author of *The Artist's Way* (Jeremy P. Tarcher, 2002) says, "All too often, it is audacity and not talent that moves an artist to center stage." Instead of being envious, be audacious. Be brave and be done with whatever piece is stressing you— and then move on to your next piece. The more you write, the faster you'll be at recognizing— and remedying—writer's block.

Writing on the Run

Finding Time to Write

by Allen and Linda Anderson

Guilt slithers onto the scene and masquerades as a writer's envious companion, and it reminds writers every minute they spend writing could be used in another way. Guilt is why writers transform themselves into brazen thieves of time.

No one is completely successful at eliminating every twinge of guilt when the "shoulds" start raining down, but there are simple and innovative ways to decrease the intensity of push-pull thoughts and feelings.

As a husband and wife writing team, we shared a strong desire to be published authors with a series of books about the spiritual connection between people and animals. Yet we were already busy people with complex lives and tons of responsibilities. We often felt guilty for taking time away from our children, our jobs, and each other, but we knew for us to be truly happy, we wanted and needed to write. Our passion for the subject, our willingness to work hard to achieve our goals, and our ability to find the in-between moments in life helped us learn what we call "writing on the run." We became proficient at writing any time, anywhere.

Allen's most recent day job, as a computer software trainer, required him to travel 80 to 90 percent of the time all over the United States, so his writing took place at airports and hotel rooms. Linda wrote at home where she had to keep up with the responsibilities of an active family of growing children and pets, a day job in public relations, an aging house, and tasks such as shoveling Minnesota snow in the winter. In order to write and find publishers for our books, articles, and columns, as well as to publicize and promote them, we had to devise systems for building writing time into almost every aspect of daily life as seamlessly as possible.

Following are some of the suggestions we and other writers have discovered for finding guilt-free time to enjoy the gift of writing.

Writing at home

People who write at home tend to rise earlier than others in their household, stay up later, and write when family members are otherwise occupied. They cook, clean, care for children,

ALLEN and **LINDA ANDERSON** are a husband and wife writing team and founders of the Angel Animals Network (www.angelanimals.net). Their new book, *Angel Cats: Divine Messengers of Comfort*, is the third book in an ongoing series with the theme of spiritual connection between people and animals. Their newest venture is a website (www.writingontherun.com) and newsletter designed to help professional and aspiring writers to find time and space for writing in their busy lives.

and perform chauffeur duties while writing, at least in their imaginations. Most often, they keep notebooks and pens easily accessible in every room.

Home writers devote drawers or shelves to holding writing materials. In various rooms, they place handheld tape recorders and laptop computers ready to capture their brilliant ideas for later transcription. They shield themselves away from interruptions by writing in bathrooms, in corners of bedrooms, in their laundry rooms, and at kitchen tables while kids and spouses are elsewhere. They write while meals cook, children do homework, and spouses watch television. They post "Do Not Disturb" and "Mom Will be Available Again at _____ O'Clock" signs on bedrooms they've converted into office spaces. They lose themselves in fantasy worlds and create white noise to eliminate distractions by running the vacuum cleaner or garbage disposal.

Parents of young children face challenges to their aspirations that would seem to defy solution. Yet writers can be terrific at creating ways to appease the guilt monster. Jennifer Scheel Bushman laments that, because she stays at home with her children, even though she is the author of *Hard Sleeper* (Cypress House), people don't understand she works at writing. She's found ways to be both a good parent and a published novelist. "I hire a babysitter, exchange babysitting with a friend, or write while my daughter takes a nap. I carry a notebook and pen and my work with me wherever I go. Most importantly, I've learned to push aside my guilt and steal away on the weekends to my home office with my husband tending to the children. I block out people's remarks about our grass being too long or that they can't believe I don't iron. I've stopped feeling guilty for doing something I love, pursuing a dream, and trying to do it all."

Writing on the job

Writers and best-selling authors weren't blessed with any more time to write than most of us. They usually started out their careers, and often continued them, while holding day jobs. In *I'd Rather Be Writing* (Writer's Digest Books), Marcia Golub writes, "Anton Chekhov was a doctor, William Carlos Williams was too. Franz Kafka worked in insurance, T.S. Eliot in banking. Henry Miller was a telegram messenger." In *Women Who Write* (Simon & Schuster), Lucinda Irwin reports Agatha Christie's job in a pharmacy gave her free time each day to study bottles of poison. Armed with this knowledge, she went on to write her mysteries, having researched how victims could meet their deaths.

Many writers think they shouldn't use time at work to write, but the guilt of writing at work, when an employer is paying for the time, doesn't have to be an obstacle. Every job requires taking breaks, and many people write during a portion of their lunchtime and through coffee breaks. On-the-job writers don't buy into the fallacy they can't write without having large blocks of time to devote to a project. Because they aren't gifted with hours or days for writing, on-the-job writers value minutes and transform them into opportunities for incrementally achieving goals—they quickly research a fact or statistic, or they write one more paragraph, sentence, snatch of dialogue, or detail about a character. For quick and easy access, at-work writers keep in a desk drawer, on a bookshelf, or in their briefcase an array of writing materials: notebooks, pens, a disk for saving and taking home, etc.

On-the-job writers learn to make better use of time spent driving to and from work. While making their daily commutes, they speak into tape recorders or lapel microphones when inspiration strikes. They keep a notebook handy and, while stalled in traffic or waiting at stop signs, quickly jot down notes. Those who ride buses, trains, subways, and taxis to work or to and from appointments, write paragraphs, poems, screenplays, and novels.

Writing at work provides rich resources for characters, plots, and experiences. We've found it's fun to notice the best in the people we meet on the job. We mentally record characteristics of co-workers and clients, listening for unique phrases and expressions and observing physical habits and appearance. These details provide fascinating quirks that can be mixed, matched, and adapted into fictional characters. We also allow for synchronicity to occur. Often the very example or anecdote we need to illustrate a point in an article or story will come when co-workers exchange news bulletins about their lives.

Writing while traveling

Writers often travel for business or pleasure, which enables them to write in airports and hotels during times that might otherwise be wasted or frittered away. These precious moments, when the weary traveler is relieved of other responsibilities, frees the imagination. While Allen traveled extensively for his work, many airline passengers became models for characters in his novel and screenplay.

Writing while traveling can yield other unexpected rewards. On the plane, Allen often edited one of our book manuscripts or wrote passages for them. Whenever he read a galley with its attractive cover, featuring adorable animals, flight attendants and seatmates asked about the book. He started taking along promotional postcards that contained ordering information and release dates for the books. There's no telling how many pre-orders online sellers and bookstores received for our books because Allen wrote during his travels.

Allen also figured out the best places to write at airports during layovers. His preference for all-time best writing space is the oversized rocking chairs at the Charlotte/Douglas, Boston, and Philadelphia airports. Chapels are also great spots for spending quiet moments writing or praying your writing gets published.

Writing on vacation

Vacations take a writer away from the ordinary and stimulate creativity. In addition to rest and relaxation, vacations and holidays offer opportunities for mixing it up with new people, hearing different dialects, experiencing exotic settings, and eavesdropping on conversations.

Joan Airey, a freelance magazine writer from Manitoba, takes a holiday every year and pays for the vacation by writing about the stories and people she meets along the way. "I enjoy having informal interviews with people, from artists to CEOs. One afternoon I visited a couple that had worked together for 50 years building their business. I took a walking tour with them of their orchards, market garden building, and gift store. I ended up with one main story and numerous mini-articles to sell. While on vacation, I always take my cameras and keep a diary."

Writing while you sleep

Most people dream four to six times each night. So why not put dreams to work by turning them into time for writing?

Linda uses a technique that's worked well to help her transform dream time into writing time. Prior to going to sleep, she writes a question about a project on which she's working on an index card. The question may relate to a character, plot point, article theme, or other aspect of her work. Then she places the written question under her pillow. This cues the subconscious mind to find answers and ideas in the dream-state. Upon awakening, she quickly jots down her dreams and ideas for interpreting them. These dream ideas have led to improvements in her individual and our joint writing projects. In one case, a dream teacher instructed Linda to write a title on a chalkboard ten times so she wouldn't risk forgetting it. Upon awakening, she did remember the dream, and the title turned out to be great!

In Naomi Epel's *Writers Dreaming* (Carol Southern Books), award-winning novelist, Reynolds Price says when he's writing intensely on a book, he'll often dream the dreams of a character that fascinates him. "I really feel as though, not only am I creating that person's life in the daytime while I'm writing the book, but I almost seem to be dreaming that character's dreams. I have literally transcribed some of those dreams and attributed them to the character."

Writing while sleeping and dreaming can become one of the most intriguing and useful times for devising fresh angles and resolving problem projects.

Daily life is the best resource for a constant supply of writing material. Using minutes in between tasks and activities yields hours of extra writing time. By seizing overlooked opportunities to think, plan, research, and imagine, writing becomes a guilt-free, enjoyable pleasure that enriches and serves rather than takes time away from family, jobs, vacations, and sleep.

Busy Lives, Productive Writers

Try these ideas to squeeze minutes of writing time into your busy daily life.

- **Schedule writing time.** As you plan your day or week, make appointments with yourself and put them in your appointment book or calendar. Be as diligent about keeping writing commitments as you are about other obligations.

- **Co-author with your children.** Rather than always reading books to your children at bedtime, try making up stories with and for them. Later, write the stories that elicited the most positive responses.

- **Give yourself a deadline.** Plan to enter your writing in a contest that has a deadline, or create an artificial deadline. For example: "I will write three pages by Wednesday." Make the deadline stick by putting it in your day planner and telling a friend what you intend to accomplish and by when. Reward yourself when you meet your deadline.

- **Give a twist to road rage.** While you're driving, observe the drivers in other cars. Are they friends or foes? Create lives for them. Turn them into characters. Give them dialogue to say.

- **Bust the telephone time-wasters.** Keep a notebook and pen by the phone. While you're waiting for service or if you're caught on the receiving end of a long-winded caller, jot down phrases and words that catch your attention. Compose a jingle or limerick to express how much you dislike being put on hold.

The Business of Writing

The Freelance Battlefield

14 Steps to Thrive and Survive

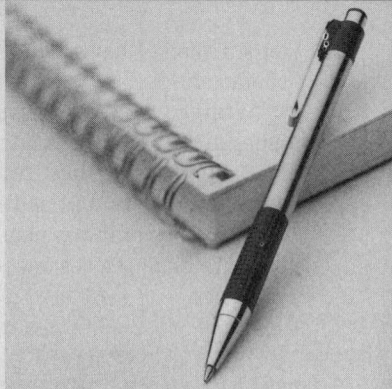

by I.J. Schecter

What's the easy part of becoming a successful writer? Learning how to write. What's the hard part? Making that ability work for you. Whether you write in the basement or on the terrace, about high finance or low golf scores, for national glossies or local circulars, success comes ultimately from developing—and embedding—positive, productive habits. Yes, the freelance battleground is formidable, but it's also continually expanding. Start ingraining these 14 principles, and you'll be well on your way to staking your own territory in a field alive with possibility.

1. Don't let frustration take root.

When you get a rejection letter, nobody expects you to cast it aside without a reaction. Let yourself feel angry, embarrassed, indignant, or despondent, but limit these feelings to five or 10 minutes—enough time for you to acknowledge your feelings but not long enough for them to get the better of you. Use the intensity of your response as fuel to plunge back in. It may just serve as the fire that produces your next acceptance.

"I wrote a query letter to a boys' magazine with a 1-million-plus circulation and a very specific voice," says freelancer Jeff Dewsbury. "The editor said, while the story I pitched was a bit off the mark, its style showed I understood the tone of the magazine, and he encouraged me to send others. Swallowing my pride—and suppressing the urge to tell him to take a long walk off a short pier—I promptly put together five story ideas. He bought one immediately and has since assigned two others. The lesson? Indignation will get you nowhere; responding positively and swiftly to an encouraging critique will get you everywhere."

2. Get organized.

Many writers feel having a messy workspace is merely a stamp of creativity. Let's face it: Such thinking is, in truth, nothing but counterproductive. The few steps required for a highly functional personal office—file folders, properly labeled disks or CDs, logical configuration of equipment—can make an enormous difference to your efficiency.

"It's worth your time to assess your workspace, and do what you can to optimize it," says writer Lisa Bendall. "I organize my active assignments, leads, publication samples, material to be read, and incoming mail into different areas and constantly refer to them. I also apply organization skills to planning my work schedule, and it serves as a major reason

---

I.J. SCHECTER (www.ijschecter.com) writes for top magazines including *Condé Nast Bride's*, *Golf Monthly*, *Maxim*, *Men's Exercise*, and *Parents*.

why I never miss a deadline. When juggling multiple projects, staying organized helps you stay in control, and staying in control helps you pull it all off."

3. Keep careful submission records.

In this business, you get exactly one chance to make a good first impression. Part of being organized is knowing exactly which manuscripts, queries, letters, or e-mails you've sent, when, and to whom. There's no greater poison to freelance success than inadvertently sending a query to an editor you'd already contacted about the same idea two months earlier. If you're going to be rigorous about anything in your career, be rigorous about this.

4. Keep raising your personal bar.

"I had a book I wanted to do for a number of years, but no success finding a publisher," says author Julie Watson. "I decided to really analyze why it wasn't taking and realized I'd been slotted into specific topic areas by publishers I'd worked with before. Some envisioned me purely as a regional writer because I do a lot of stuff about the Maritimes. Others had me pigeonholed in food and travel.

"Wanting to do a book on successful women in business, I chose a publisher I'd enjoyed working with in the past, started a dialogue, and worked hard to sell myself as someone qualified to write about female entrepreneurship. I got the contract, completed the manuscript on time, and the book is now selling nicely—plus I'm giving workshops to women in business groups. I've been a freelancer for 20 years and in the beginning found that creating a niche for myself was the way to generate sales. Now I feel like my career is starting all over again, and it's wonderful."

5. Do your homework.

Research doesn't just mean finding the proper editorial name or getting a publisher's address right. *Shape* contributor Amanda Vogel, for example, takes the process a step further. "One thing I always do is compare the manuscript I submitted with the published version of the article. I look to see what the editor kept and what she changed. This helps me ace my next assignment for that magazine because I get a better feel for its style and preferences." The point? Don't apply the same attention to detail as the next writer. Apply more.

6. Spell-check your e-mails—and don't stop there.

As a writer, you're justifiably held to higher standards even in casual correspondence. While others can get away with e-mails devoid of punctuation, endless emoticons, and stomach-turning grammar, you can't.

Before you send that three-line e-mail to the editor with whom you're just touching base, do a spell check. Ninety-nine times out of a hundred, you won't find anything, but the one mistake you catch might make or break a pivotal relationship. And if you're truly serious about ensuring a professional image, don't stop at the spell-check. Go word-by-word, even letter-by-letter, through your messages to make sure no homonyms have slipped by that might irredeemably alter things.

Your first instinct may tell you it isn't worth the time to do this, but keep in mind the next writer, or the one after that, is going to take the time, and bypassing that extra step means giving him an unnecessary edge. Worse, your error might be immortalized, like the unfortunate writer whose story describing a man who had "lapsed into a comma" found its way to the desk of *Washington Post* copy chief Bill Walsh—who used the gaffe as part of the title of his editors' and writers' guide, *Lapsing Into a Comma: A Curmudgeon's Guide to the Many Things That Can Go Wrong in Print—and How to Avoid Them* (McGraw-Hill).

The Business of Writing

7. Practice equilibrium.

Every writer needs to learn to resist, with equal vigilance, the exhilarating highs and desperate lows that are occupational hazards of the publishing trade. Mostly this requires time and experience, but diligent, bullheaded practice helps, too. "I tend to oscillate between thinking I'm a towering genius and the worst writer in the history of the world, all in the space of about three hours," says *Paradise Alley* (Perennial) author Kevin Baker. "The only thing that defeats this vicious cycle is to write. Eventually, I overcome the dread and artistic self-loathing and just get into the flow."

Landed a sweet assignment? Tell someone important to you, congratulate yourself in the mirror, then get back to work. Query rejected? Curse up a storm, have a piece of chocolate, give yourself a pep talk, then get back to work.

8. Don't write every day.

No, that isn't a typo. You've probably read dozens of times that, if you're a writer, you've got to write every single day, including Christmas and your birthday. Lawyers don't practice law every day, musicians don't compose every day, and painters don't paint every day. Even Stephen King takes time off on occasion. Sometimes the best thing you can do for yourself is to remove yourself from the writing realm to recharge. Being a writer means treating writing as your first priority, but not using guilt as your primary motivating tool.

9. Don't work in a vacuum.

Even if you don't think it's for you, force yourself to network with others, whether a local writing group or national association. (For more information on writing groups, see Writing Groups: Making the Most of Your Experience on page 28.) "The group back-and-forth has given me unparalleled new leads," says freelancer Veronica Leonard of her membership in the Periodical Writers Association of Canada (PWAC). "Recently, a fellow member posted a notice regarding *First For Women on the Go*, which prints 250-word articles about changes that made a difference in your life. I submitted one of these pieces and had it accepted, which paid three times my membership dues. I would never have gotten this lead without PWAC. It took me 10 years of freelance writing before I got around to joining, and I made back the outlay threefold within a month on a single market. This kind of return on investment has repeated itself every year for the past 14."

10. Respect your inner critic.

A writer's relationship with his inner voice is often tense, usually because he knows the voice is right. When it whispers the manuscript could still be improved before you send it off, listen. When it pesters you to get back to your current manuscript instead of watching the *Seinfeld* episode you've seen 47 times, listen. When it tells you to go for a jog and come back to the story an hour later, listen. You'll thank it—grudgingly—later.

11. Ignore your inner critic.

Sometimes—OK, often—that same voice talks simply because it likes the sound of itself. Like a friend who likes to bug you for sport, it will play head games, murmuring distracting, even paralyzing, words of self-doubt just to see if it can get a rise out of you. There isn't a thing you can do about this other than block it out, believe in yourself, and, in the words of Bob Dylan, "Keep on keepin' on."

12. Take the time to back up.

Maybe you have a super-powerful laptop with a dozen firewalls and state-of-the-art anti-virus software. Maybe you've never had a crash at an inopportune time. Maybe you're tired at the end of the day, and you just don't feel like taking those extra few minutes to save an extra copy of your work on floppy, CD, memory card or even by e-mailing it to yourself. But there will be some moment, somewhere down the line, when an editor asks you to re-send that story she loved so much on the same day an electrical storm takes down your entire operating system—and you'll want to kiss yourself for having taken those extra few minutes.

13. Never stop when you think it's great.

"Easy reading is damn hard writing," said Nathaniel Hawthorne—and he was damn right. Whenever you read through a manuscript and pronounce it ready for the mail, place it aside, and come back to it a few days later, committing to making it just a little better, even if that improvement amounts to tightening a single paragraph or replacing one "almost" word with the precise one. Since you possess a talent most others don't—the ability to make words sparkle—you owe it to yourself to set your own standards high.

Once a manuscript is done—that familiar feeling of quiet elation will let you know—get it out there, and don't worry if another edit occurs to you three days later. There is scarcely a writer in existence who looks back on a manuscript and believes it's perfect. Or, to place it in the more cynical words of Anthony Burgess, "You don't say, 'I've done it!' You come, with a horrible desperation, to realize that this will do."

14. Embrace the writing experience.

Says lauded British novelist Julian Barnes, "It's easy, after all, not to be a writer. Most people aren't writers, and very little harm comes to them." In other words, since your choice to write is probably less a choice than a fundamental, surging need, take it in your arms, squeeze it, cuddle it, and love it for all its worth. Don't buy into the stereotype that writers are lonely, unkempt figures forever despairing over what they haven't had published; instead, celebrate every word you write—even the ones that never see the light of day—as part of a lifelong process. This difference in attitude will translate into better consistency, higher productivity, and, in the end, greater success.

How Much Should I Charge?

by Lynn Wasnak

If you're a beginning freelancer, or don't know many other freelancers, you may wonder how anyone manages to earn enough to eat and pay the rent by writing or performing a mix of writing-related tasks. Yet, smart full-time freelance writers and editors annually gross $35,000 and up—sometimes up into the $150,000-200,000 category. These top-earning freelancers rarely have names known to the general public. (Celebrity writers earn fees far beyond the rates cited in this survey.) But, year after year, they sustain themselves and their families on a freelance income, while maintaining control of their hours and their lives.

Such freelancers take writing and editing seriously—it's their business.

Periodically, they sit down and think about the earning potential of their work, and how they can make freelancing more profitable and fun. They know their numbers: what it costs to run their business; what hourly rate they require; how long a job will take. Unless there's a real bonus (a special clip, or a chance to try something new) these writers turn down work that doesn't meet the mark and replace it with a better-paying project.

If you don't know your numbers, take a few minutes to figure them out. Begin by choosing your target annual income—whether it's $25,000 or $100,000. Add in fixed expenses: social security, taxes, and office supplies. Don't forget health insurance and something for your retirement. Once you've determined your yearly gross target, divide it by 1,000 billable hours—about 21 hours per week—to determine your target hourly rate.

Remember—this rate is flexible. You can continue doing low-paying work you love as long as you make up for the loss with more lucrative jobs. But you must monitor your rate of earning if you want to reach your goal. If you slip, remind yourself you're in charge. As a freelancer, you can raise prices, chase better-paying jobs, work extra hours, or adjust your spending.

"Sounds great," you may say. "But how do I come up with 1,000 billable hours each year? I'm lucky to find a writing-related job every month or two, and these pay a pittance."

That's where business attitude comes in: network, track your time, join professional organizations, and study the markets. Learn how to query, then query like mad. Take chances by reaching for the next level. Learn to negotiate for a fee you can live on—your plumber does! Then get it in writing!

You'll be surprised how far you can go, and how much you can earn, if you believe in your skills and act on your belief. The rates that follow are a guide to steer you in the right direction.

LYNN WASNAK (www.lynnwasnak.com) has freelanced full time for nearly three decades as a writer, editor, and small publisher. Her international newsletter for childhood trauma survivors, *Many Voices* (www.manyvoicespress.com), is now in its 17th year.

This report is based on input from sales finalized in 2004 and 2005 only. The data is generated from voluntary surveys completed by freelance members of numerous professional writers' and editors' organizations and specialty groups. We thank these responding groups, listed below, and their members for generously sharing information. Also, we welcome any writers who would like to contribute their rate experience to request a survey anytime. Your figures will be included in the next edition. To request a survey, send an e-mail to lwasnak@fuse.net.

Organizations

For More Info

For more information on determining freelance pay rates, negotiating contracts, etc., you can visit the following organizations' websites. (*Editor's note: A special thank you to the members of the organizations listed below for their thoughtful responses to our survey.*)

- **Association of Independents in Radio (AIR):** www.airmedia.org
- **American Literary Translators Association (ALTA):** www.literarytranslators.org
- **Association of Personal Historians (APH):** www.personalhistorians.org
- **American Society of Journalists & Authors (ASJA):** www.asja.org
- **American Society of Media Photographers (ASMP):** www.asmp.org
- **American Society of Picture Professionals (ASPP):** www.aspp.com
- **American Translators Association (ATA):** www.atanet.org
- **Editorial Freelancers Association (EFA):** www.the-efa.org
- **Freelance Success (FLX):** www.freelancesuccess.com
- **Independent Writers of Chicago (IWOC):** www.iwoc.org
- **International Association of Business Communicators (IABC):** www.iabc.com
- **Investigative Reporters & Editors (IRE):** www.ire.org
- **Media Communications Association International (MCA-I):** www.mca-i.org
- **National Writers Union (NWU):** www.nwu.org
- **Society of Professional Journalists (SPJ):** www.spj.org
- **Society for Technical Communication (STC):** www.stc.org
- **The Cartoon Bank:** www.cartoonbank.com
- **Washington Independent Writers (WIW):** www.washwriter.org
- **Women in Film (WIF):** www.wif.org
- **Writer's Guild of America East (WGAE):** www.wgae.org
- **Writer's Guild of America West (WGA):** www.wga.org

The Business of Writing

Advertising, Copywriting & Public Relations

	PER HOUR			PER PROJECT			OTHER		
	HIGH	LOW	AVG	HIGH	LOW	AVG	HIGH	LOW	AVG
Advertising copywriting	$125	$25	$84	$6,400	$300	$2,400	$3/word	$1/word	$1.50/word
Advertorials	$180	$75	$125	n/a	n/a	n/a	$2/word $1,875/page	67¢/word $300/page	$1/word $450/page
Book jacket copywriting	$100	$25	$67	$600	$100	$317	n/a	n/a	50¢/word
Campaign development or product launch	$125	$35	$77	$8,750	$1,500	$4,250	n/a	n/a	n/a
Catalog copywriting	$100	$25	$83	n/a	n/a	n/a	$150/item	$25/item	$60/item
Copyediting for advertising	$110	$20	$37	n/a	n/a	n/a	n/a	n/a	n/a
Direct-mail copywriting	$125	$25	$78	$6,000	$1,000	$2,725	$4/word $1,200/page	$1/word $200/page	$1.50/word $400/page
E-mail ad copywriting	$100	$20	$58	n/a	n/a	n/a	n/a	n/a	n/a
Event promotions/publicity	$100	$25	$54	n/a	n/a	n/a	n/a	n/a	$500/day
Fundraising campaign brochure	$100	$43	$81	$2,200	$1,000	$1,350	n/a	n/a	n/a
Political campaigns, public relations	$150	$43	$82	n/a	n/a	n/a	n/a	n/a	n/a
Press kits	$100	$43	$65	$5,000	$1,000	$2,334	n/a	n/a	n/a
Press/news release	$175	$20	$65	$1,000	$100	$425	n/a	n/a	n/a
Public relations for businesses	$100	$20	$70	n/a	n/a	n/a	n/a	n/a	n/a
Public relations for government	$60	$40	$50	n/a	n/a	n/a	n/a	n/a	n/a
Public relations for organizations or nonprofits	$100	$30	$52	n/a	n/a	n/a	n/a	n/a	n/a
Public relations for schools or libraries	$100	$30	$50	n/a	n/a	n/a	n/a	n/a	n/a
Speech writing/editing (general)[1]	$167	$43	$81	$10,000	$2,700	$5,480	n/a	n/a	n/a

1 Per project figures based on 30-minute speech.

	PER HOUR			PER PROJECT			OTHER		
	HIGH	LOW	AVG	HIGH	LOW	AVG	HIGH	LOW	AVG
Speech writing for government officials	$125	$30	$76	n/a	n/a	n/a	n/a	n/a	$4,500/20 min
Speech writing for political candidates	$150	$60	$92	n/a	n/a	n/a	n/a	n/a	$650/15 min
Audiovisuals & Electronic Communications									
Book summaries (narrative synopsis) for film producers[1]	n/a	n/a	n/a	n/a	n/a	n/a	$1,232/15 min $34/page	$2,052/30 min $15/page	$3,889/60 min $20/page
Business film scripts[2] (training and info)	$100	$40	$76	n/a	$600	n/a	$500/run min	$100/run min	$300/run min
Copyediting audiovisuals	$85	$22	$48	n/a	n/a	n/a	n/a	n/a	$50/page
Corporate product film	$100	$30	$70	n/a	n/a	n/a	$500/run min	$100/run min	$300/run min
Educational/training film scripts	$100	$35	$60	n/a	n/a	n/a	$500/run min	$100/run min	$300/run min
Movie novelization	$100	$35	n/a	$15,000	$3,000	$5,625	n/a	n/a	n/a
Radio commercials/PSAs	$85	$30	$56	n/a	n/a	n/a	$600/run min	$120/run min	$300/run min
Radio editorials & essays (no production)	$70	$50	$60	n/a	n/a	n/a	$200/run min	$65/run min	$125/run min
Radio interviews (3 minute interview)	n/a	n/a	n/a	$1,500	$150	$400	n/a	n/a	n/a
Radio stories (over 2 minutes with sound production)	n/a	n/a	n/a	$500	$100	$400	n/a	n/a	n/a
Screenwriting (original screenplay)	n/a	n/a	$50	$102,980	$54,854	$78,917	n/a	n/a	n/a
Script synopsis for agent or film producer	n/a	n/a	n/a	$120	$60	$65	n/a	n/a	n/a
Script synopsis for business	n/a	n/a	$70	$100	$60	$75	n/a	n/a	n/a

1 Other figures based on length of speech (min=minute).
2 Run min=run minute.

The Business of Writing

The Business of Writing

	PER HOUR			PER PROJECT			OTHER		
	HIGH	LOW	AVG	HIGH	LOW	AVG	HIGH	LOW	AVG
Scripts for nontheatrical films for education, business, industry	$100	$55	$75	$5,000	$3,000	$4,083	$500/run min	$100/run min	$300/run min
TV commercials/PSAs[1]	$85	$60	$73	n/a	n/a	n/a	n/a	n/a	$150/30 sec spot
TV news story/feature[2]	$100	$70	$90	n/a	n/a	n/a	n/a	n/a	n/a
TV scripts (nontheatrical)	$150	$70	$100	$20,000	$10,000	$15,000	$1,000/day	$550/day	$800/day
TV scripts (teleplay/MOW)[3]	n/a	n/a	n/a	n/a	n/a	n/a	$500/run min	$100/run min	$300/run min
Book Publishing									
Abstracting and abridging	$100	$25	$38	n/a	n/a	n/a			n/a
Anthology editing	$80	$23	$52	$3,000	$1,200	$2,050	n/a	n/a	n/a
Book proposal consultation	$100	$25	$53	$500	$350	$425	n/a	n/a	n/a
Book proposal writing	$100	$40	$78	$22,000	$2,500	$6,500	n/a	n/a	n/a
Book query critique	$100	$30	$40	n/a	n/a	$300	n/a	n/a	n/a
Book query writing	n/a	n/a	n/a	$500	$120	$200	n/a	n/a	n/a
Children's book writing (advance against royalties)	n/a	n/a	n/a	n/a	n/a	n/a	$4,500	$1,500	$2,720
Children's book writing (work for hire)	$75	$50	$63	n/a	n/a	n/a	$5/word	$1/word	$3/word
Content editing (scholarly)	$80	$20	$42	n/a	n/a	n/a	$20/page	$4/page	$6/page
Content editing (textbook)	$80	$16	$38	n/a	n/a	n/a	$9/page	$3/page	$4/page
Content editing (trade)	$100	$23	$52	n/a	n/a	n/a	$6/page	$3.75/page	$4.75/page
Copyediting	$50	$15	$29	n/a	n/a	n/a	$6/page	$1/page	$4.10/page
Fiction book writing (own)	n/a	n/a	n/a	$40,000	$500	$40,000	$40,000	$500	$14,193

1 30 sec spot=30-second spot

2 $1,201 Writers Guild of America minimum/story.

3 TV scripts 30 minutes or less average $6,535/story, $19,603 with teleplay; TV scripts 60 minutes or less average $11,504/story, $28,833 with teleplay.

	PER HOUR			PER PROJECT			OTHER		
	HIGH	LOW	AVG	HIGH	LOW	AVG	HIGH	LOW	AVG
Ghostwriting, as told to[1]	$100	$40	$60	$70,000	$5,000	$25,000	n/a	n/a	n/a
Ghostwriting, no credit	$100	$50	$69	$85,000	$5,000	$29,778	$2.20/word	50¢/word	$1/word
Indexing	$80	$25	$44	n/a	n/a	n/a	$5/page	$3/page	$4/page
Manuscript evaluation and critique	$100	$25	$46	$2,000	$200	$840	n/a	n/a	n/a
Nonfiction book writing (collaborative) (advance against royalties)	$100	$50	$70	n/a	n/a	n/a	$51,000	$5,000	$25,350
Nonfiction book writing (own) (advance against royalties)	n/a	n/a	n/a	n/a	n/a	n/a	$75,000	$2,000	$14,475
Novel synopsis (general)	$60	$45	$51	n/a	n/a	n/a	$30/page	$10/page	$15/page
Proofreading	$35	$12	$25	n/a	n/a	n/a	$3/page	$1/page	$2.25/page
Research for writers or book publishers	$50	$15	$33	n/a	n/a	n/a	n/a	n/a	$500/day
Rewriting	$100	$23	$50	$70,000	$3,000	$8,500	n/a	n/a	n/a
Translation (fiction)[2]	n/a	n/a	n/a	$10,000	$7,000	$8,500	12¢	6¢	9¢
Translation (nonfiction)	n/a	n/a	n/a	n/a	n/a	n/a	15¢	8¢	10¢
Translation (poetry)	n/a	n/a	n/a	n/a	n/a	n/a	$15/page	$0/page	$7.50/page
Business									
Annual reports	$125	$45	$85	$12,500	$3,000	$7,143	n/a	n/a	n/a
Associations and organizations (writing for)	$125	$43	$66	n/a	n/a	n/a	$400/day $800/page	$300/day $75/page	$350/day $434/page
Brochures, fliers, booklets for business	$120	$40	$72	$6,000	$500	$1,956	$31/word	30¢/word	$1.48/word
Business & sales letters	$100	$45	$74	$2,000	$100	$600	n/a	n/a	n/a
Business & government research	$100	$40	$59	n/a	n/a	n/a	n/a	n/a	n/a
Business editing (general)	$100	$28	$48	n/a	n/a	n/a	n/a	n/a	n/a

1 Per project figures do not include royalty arrangements, which vary from publisher to publisher.
2 Other figures in cents are per target word.

The Business of Writing

The Business of Writing

	PER HOUR			PER PROJECT			OTHER		
	HIGH	LOW	AVG	HIGH	LOW	AVG	HIGH	LOW	AVG
Business plan	$120	$30	$74	$5,000	$200	$1,995	n/a	n/a	n/a
Business-writing seminars	$200	$65	$83	$3,500	$1,000	$2,250	n/a	n/a	n/a
Catalogs for businesses	$90	$50	$76	$10,000	$2,000	$5,000	$980/page	$200/page	$516/page
Consultation on communications	$120	$40	$84	n/a	n/a	n/a	$1,200/day	$500/day	$850/day
Copyediting for businesses	$100	$28	$48	n/a	n/a	n/a	$4/page	$2/page	$3/page
Corporate histories	$100	$63	$84	$35,000	$1,000	$13,000	$2/word	$1/word	$1.50/word
Corporate periodicals, editing	$100	$25	$55	n/a	n/a	n/a	n/a	n/a	n/a
Corporate periodicals, writing	$100	$30	$74	$5,000	$1,000	$2,625	$2/word	$1/word	$1.50/word
Corporate profile	$100	$75	$85	n/a	n/a	n/a	$2/word	$1/word	$1.50/word
Ghostwriting for business (usually trade magazine articles for business columns)	$125	$50	$100	n/a	n/a	$750	$2/word	70¢/word	$1/word
Government writing	$75	$20	$50	n/a	n/a	n/a	n/a	n/a	n/a
Grant proposal writing for nonprofits	$100	$43	$65	$3,000	$1,800	$2,400	n/a	n/a	n/a
Newsletters, desktop publishing/production	$200	$35	$78	n/a	n/a	n/a	$750/page	$150/page	$391/page
Newsletters, editing	$100	$25	$46	n/a	n/a	n/a	$230/page	$150/page	$185/page
Newsletters, writing[1]	$125	$30	$64	$5,000	$800	$2,000	$5/word	$1/word	$2/word
Translation (commercial for government agencies, technical)	n/a	n/a	n/a	n/a	n/a	n/a	$1.40/ target line	$1/ target line	$1.20/ target line

Computer, Scientific & Technical

	PER HOUR			PER PROJECT			OTHER		
	HIGH	LOW	AVG	HIGH	LOW	AVG	HIGH	LOW	AVG
Computer-related manual writing	$75	$35	$62	n/a	n/a	n/a	n/a	n/a	n/a
E-mail copywriting	$125	$60	$89	n/a	n/a	n/a	$1/word	30¢/word	76¢/word

1 Per project figures based on four-page newsletters.

	PER HOUR			PER PROJECT			OTHER		
	HIGH	LOW	AVG	HIGH	LOW	AVG	HIGH	LOW	AVG
Engineering training manual (3 chapters)	n/a	n/a	n/a	n/a	n/a	n/a	n/a	n/a	$23,500
Medical and science editing	$110	$21	$54	n/a	n/a	n/a	$4/page	$3/page	$3.50/page
Medical and science proofreading	$33	$18	$27	n/a	n/a	n/a	n/a	n/a	n/a
Medical and science writing	$125	$30	$78	$4,800	$800	$2,520	$2/word	50¢/word	$1.03/word
Online editing	$80	$25	$45	n/a	n/a	n/a	$4/page	$3/page	$3.50/page
Technical editing	$75	$25	$53	n/a	n/a	n/a	n/a	n/a	n/a
Technical writing	$153	$45	$97	n/a	n/a	n/a	n/a	n/a	n/a
Web page design	$75	$35	$56	$4,000	$500	$2,000	n/a	n/a	n/a
Web page editing	$75	$25	$44	n/a	n/a	n/a	n/a	n/a	n/a
Web page writing	$150	$30	$83	$7,000	$100	$1,251	$1.50/word	20¢/word	63¢/word
White Papers	$125	$75	$100	n/a	n/a	n/a	n/a	n/a	n/a

Editorial/Design Packages[1]

	PER HOUR			PER PROJECT			OTHER		
	HIGH	LOW	AVG	HIGH	LOW	AVG	HIGH	LOW	AVG
Desktop publishing	$125	$30	$56	n/a	n/a	n/a	n/a	n/a	n/a
Greeting card ideas	n/a	n/a	n/a	n/a	n/a	n/a	$300/card	$25/card	$125/card
Photo brochures[2]	$75	$65	$70	$15,000	$400	n/a	n/a	n/a	n/a
Photo research	$70	$25	$40	n/a	n/a	n/a	n/a	n/a	n/a
Photography (corporate-commercial)	n/a	n/a	n/a	n/a	n/a	n/a	$2,500/day	$1,000/day	$2,000/day
Picture editing	$100	$40	$70	n/a	n/a	n/a	$65/picture	$35/picture	$45/picture
Slides/Overhead	n/a	n/a	$50	$2,500	$500	$1,000	n/a	n/a	n/a

Educational & Literary Services

	PER HOUR			PER PROJECT			OTHER		
	HIGH	LOW	AVG	HIGH	LOW	AVG	HIGH	LOW	AVG
Educational consulting and designing business/adult education courses	$100	$50	$81	n/a	n/a	n/a	n/a	n/a	n/a

1 For more information about photography rates, see *2006 Photographer's Market*.
2 Per project figures based on 4 pages/8 photos

The Business of Writing

The Business of Writing

	PER HOUR			PER PROJECT			OTHER		
	HIGH	LOW	AVG	HIGH	LOW	AVG	HIGH	LOW	AVG
Educational grant and proposal writing	$100	$75	$89	n/a	n/a	n/a	n/a	n/a	n/a
Manuscript evaluation for theses/dissertations	$90	$25	$60	$1,550	$250	$700	n/a	n/a	n/a
Poetry manuscript critique	$90	$30	$85	n/a	n/a	n/a	n/a	n/a	n/a
Presentations at national conventions (by well-known authors)	n/a	n/a	n/a	n/a	n/a	n/a	$30,000/event	$1,000/event	$5,000/event
Presentations at regional writers' conferences	n/a	n/a	n/a	n/a	n/a	n/a	$10,000/event	$50/event	$720/event
Presentations to local groups, librarians or teachers	n/a	n/a	n/a	n/a	n/a	n/a	$250/event	$35/event	$112/event
Presentations to school classes (5-day visiting artists program)	n/a	n/a	n/a	n/a	n/a	n/a	$3,400	$2,500	$2,750
Readings by poets, fiction writers (highest fees for celebrity writers)	n/a	n/a	n/a	n/a	n/a	n/a	$3,000/event	$50/event	$200/event
Short story manuscript critique	$100	$30	$55	n/a	n/a	n/a	n/a	n/a	n/a
Teaching college course/seminar (includes adult education)	$335	$35	$70	$35,000	$250	$2,260	$550/day	$150/day	$367/day
Writers' workshops	$220	$30	$75	n/a	n/a	n/a	$900/event	$220/event	$324/event
Writing for scholarly journals	n/a	n/a	n/a	n/a	n/a	n/a	$450/article	$100/article	$252/article
Magazines & Trade Journals[1]									
Article manuscript critique	$100	$30	$49	n/a	n/a	n/a	n/a	n/a	n/a
Arts reviewing	n/a	n/a	n/a	$300	$20	$140	$1.25/word	25¢/word	75¢/word
Book reviews	n/a	n/a	n/a	$500	$25	$133	$1/word	5¢/word	44¢/word
City magazine, calendar of events column	n/a	n/a	n/a	n/a	n/a	n/a	$150/column	$25/column	$75/column
Consultation on magazine editorial	$150	$30	$75	n/a	n/a	n/a	n/a	n/a	n/a

1 For specific pay rate information for feature articles, columns/departments, fillers, etc., see individual market listings.

	PER HOUR			PER PROJECT			OTHER		
	HIGH	LOW	AVG	HIGH	LOW	AVG	HIGH	LOW	AVG
Consumer magazine column	n/a	n/a	n/a	n/a	n/a	n/a	$3.50/word $625/column	30¢/word $75/column	$1.35/word $403/column
Consumer magazine feature articles	n/a	n/a	n/a	$7,500	$150	$1,842	$4/word	8¢/word	$1.24/word
Content editing	$75	$18	$39	n/a	n/a	n/a	$6,500/issue	$2,000/issue	$4.250/issue
Copyediting magazines	$50	$18	$32	n/a	n/a	n/a	n/a	n/a	n/a
Fact checking	$40	$20	$34	n/a	n/a	n/a	n/a	n/a	n/a
Ghostwriting articles (general)	$175	$40	$100	$3,500	$1,000	$2,880	$1.50/word	80¢/word	$1.08/word
Magazine research	$100	$15	$54	n/a	n/a	n/a	$150/item	$100/item	$125/item
Proofreading	$50	$15	$32	n/a	n/a	n/a	n/a	n/a	n/a
Reprint fees	n/a	n/a	n/a	$566	$5	$203	n/a	n/a	n/a
Rewriting	$95	$25	$65	n/a	n/a	n/a	n/a	n/a	n/a
Trade journal column	$70	$35	$56	n/a	n/a	n/a	$1.50/word $500/column	20¢/word $175/column	90¢/word $290/column
Trade journal feature article	$150	$43	$122	$4,950	$300	$1,412	$1.60/word	20¢/word	$1.23/word

Miscellaneous

	PER HOUR			PER PROJECT			OTHER		
	HIGH	LOW	AVG	HIGH	LOW	AVG	HIGH	LOW	AVG
Cartoons (gag, plus illustration)	n/a	n/a	n/a	n/a	n/a	n/a	$575	$15	$100
Comedy writing for nightclub entertainers	n/a	n/a	n/a	n/a	n/a	n/a	$50/joke $500/group	$5/joke $100/group	$38/joke $250/group
Craft projects with instructions	n/a	n/a	n/a	$600	$100	$250	n/a	n/a	n/a
Encyclopedia articles	n/a	n/a	n/a	n/a	n/a	n/a	$3,000/article 50¢/word	$50/article 30¢/word	$200/article 40¢/word
Family histories	$80	$30	$65	$25,000	$750	$9,188	n/a	n/a	n/a
Gagwriting for cartoonists	n/a	n/a	n/a	n/a	n/a	n/a	n/a	n/a	$30/gag
Institutional history (church school)	n/a	n/a	n/a	n/a	n/a	n/a	$125/page	$75/page	$100/page
Manuscript typing	n/a	n/a	n/a	n/a	n/a	n/a	$2.50/page	95¢/page	$1.27/page

The Business of Writing

The Business of Writing

	PER HOUR			PER PROJECT			OTHER		
	HIGH	LOW	AVG	HIGH	LOW	AVG	HIGH	LOW	AVG
Educational grant and proposal writing	$100	$75	$89	n/a	n/a	n/a	n/a	n/a	n/a
Manuscript evaluation for theses/dissertations	$90	$25	$60	$1,550	$250	$700	n/a	n/a	n/a
Poetry manuscript critique	$90	$30	$85	n/a	n/a	n/a	n/a	n/a	n/a
Presentations at national conventions (by well-known authors)	n/a	n/a	n/a	n/a	n/a	n/a	$30,000/event	$1,000/event	$5,000/event
Presentations at regional writers' conferences	n/a	n/a	n/a	n/a	n/a	n/a	$10,000/event	$50/event	$720/event
Presentations to local groups, librarians or teachers	n/a	n/a	n/a	n/a	n/a	n/a	$250/event	$35/event	$112/event
Presentations to school classes (5-day visiting artists program)	n/a	n/a	n/a	n/a	n/a	n/a	$3,400	$2,500	$2,750
Readings by poets, fiction writers (highest fees for celebrity writers)	n/a	n/a	n/a	n/a	n/a	n/a	$3,000/event	$50/event	$200/event
Short story manuscript critique	$100	$30	$55	n/a	n/a	n/a	n/a	n/a	n/a
Teaching college course/seminar (includes adult education)	$335	$35	$70	$35,000	$250	$2,260	$550/day	$150/day	$367/day
Writers' workshops	$220	$30	$75	n/a	n/a	n/a	$900/event	$220/event	$324/event
Writing for scholarly journals	n/a	n/a	n/a	n/a	n/a	n/a	$450/article	$100/article	$252/article
Magazines & Trade Journals[1]									
Article manuscript critique	$100	$30	$49	n/a	n/a	n/a	n/a	n/a	n/a
Arts reviewing	n/a	n/a	n/a	$300	$20	$140	$1.25/word	25¢/word	75¢/word
Book reviews	n/a	n/a	n/a	$500	$25	$133	$1/word	5¢/word	44¢/word
City magazine, calendar of events column	n/a	n/a	n/a	n/a	n/a	n/a	$150/column	$25/column	$75/column
Consultation on magazine editorial	$150	$30	$75	n/a	n/a	n/a	n/a	n/a	n/a

1 For specific pay rate information for feature articles, columns/departments, fillers, etc., see individual market listings.

Online PR

Creating a Buzz Without a Budget

by Kelly Milner Halls

It's a fact. Even the most promising new writers have a silent but formidable foe lurking just beyond paid publication—anonymity. Without public recognition, even award-worthy books slip, unnoticed, into bookstore remainder bins. However, there is something you can do to save your book from those bins. Dan Poynter (www.parapublishing.com) and John Kremer (www.bookmarket.com), mavericks of inventive public relations, insist the key to creating buzz about you and your book is mastering an Internet arsenal. The following seven steps will show you how to create a buzz—without a large budget.

Step 1: The website

If you build it, they will come. So say the lion's share of publicity gurus hired to jumpstart the media visibility of various authors. A website is no longer a writer's luxury, it's an essential. "I can't imagine anyone in any type of business not having a website," says Poynter. "But it's especially true if you're a writer. Writing is a creative act, but selling your work is all business."

Poynter, the author of *The Self-Publishing Manual* (Para Publishing), calls a writer's website an electronic storefront that saves time, space, and money. "Rather than having a number of brochures, documents, and other materials around your office," he says, "you simply keep [those things] on your website. Then, when someone wants a document, you direct him to that page. It saves a lot on printing and postage."

HarperCollins author Chris Crutcher (www.chriscrutcher.com), author of *Whale Talk* and *Staying Fat for Sarah Byrnes*, agrees. "My Web person has posted all the essentials—from an electronic press kit with photos and biographical details, to censorship news and briefs to my ongoing calendar of speaking engagements. If anyone has any reason to explore who I am, professionally, they can find an accurate overview, as well as publicity photos and book cover art, online."

Useful
Websites

Creating and hosting a website, however, can get pricey if you're not careful, but there are many companies offering inexpensive, yet professional, options. Roxyanne Young, co-owner of 2-Tiers Software/SmartWriters website hosting service (www.2-tiersoftware.com), where Crutcher's website has been parked for the past three years, says, "For $120 a year, just $10.00 a month, any author can create a beautiful, user-friendly website with up to 60

KELLY MILNER HALLS is a full-time freelance writer and single mom based in Spokane, Washington. Her work has appeared in *The Washington Post*, the *Chicago Tribune*, *The Atlanta Journal-Constitution*, the *Detroit Free Press*, the *Denver Post*, and dozens of children's publications.

unique pages, extensive visual files, a guest book, professional portfolio, traffic counters and much more.''

Step 2: The electronic press kit

Crutcher isn't the only author to make use of electronic availability. R.J. Garis, whose family publicity agency R.J. Garis Publicity Agency, has served the celebrity needs of luminaries like Theodore Geisel (Dr. Seuss), Bob Hope, Chuck Norris, and dozens of others, considers online press kits a virtual must.

''When I first started in publicity,'' Garis says, ''We'd have to mail out press kits by the thousands [which is] very expensive. But stories today move at lightening speed. E-mail has given us the ability to instantaneously flash information to media decision makers. So, we recommend all our clients have websites with their bio and basic information standing by in case a producer or editor wants to see it *now*.''

What elements are found in a good online press kit? A brief, but up-to-date author bio tops the list, including basic personal details—date and place of birth, current residence, educational background, etc.—book titles, significant awards, and recreational interests.

A close second, if not equal for first priority, is a group of professional, high-resolution, digital author photographs (scanned at 300 dots-per-inch). ''Include an unusual or dramatic photograph,'' Garis says. ''It should relate to you, as the author, and to the topic of your book, if possible. But anything you can add that will make your package stand out will liven up a press contact's day and increase your chance at being remembered and featured on TV or in print.''

Have you enjoyed good press coverage in the past? If so, feature excerpts in your online press kit. ''One thing that happens with all publicity is the bandwagon effect,'' says Kremer, author of *1,001 Ways to Market Your Books* (Open Horizons). ''If one person says, 'This is good,' everybody wants to join the parade. You see it all the time—*The New York Times* prints a review and suddenly every other newspaper in the country wants to do the same.''

Finally, your press kit should include contact information—mail, e-mail, and telephone— because, even if the background information's easy for a press contact to get, it's no substitute for a one-on-one interview. If you aren't available to frequently check your e-mail and phone messages, arrange for a family member or trusted assistant to handle the overflow so you don't miss a potential interview opportunity.

Step 3: The online newsletter

Once the electronic storefront has been created, Poynter says, ''The challenge is attracting people to the site. That's where your newsletter or e-zine comes into play.''

Established authors like Crutcher might balk at offering a free newsletter or other give- aways through subscriptions, but Poynter and Kremer insist a valuable newsletter is of recip- rocal value. ''It's a continuity device,'' Kremer says. ''In other words, a way for people to have regular and continuing contact with you. For example, I have a book marketing 'Tip of the Week' newsletter that goes out every week to my subscribers. It's free, and it's of value. A regular newsletter that offers something of value creates an army of potential book buyers who get to know you and become your champions.''

If you decide to offer a newsletter, however, you need to be aware of the time commitment. Marilyn Ross, director of the Small Publisher's Association of North America (www.spannet. org) says, ''I'm well past the 75th issue of the SPAN Connection newsletter, and it seems like I no more finish one issue, then it's time to start the next. So be willing to commit to a long-term situation if you want to create a newsletter.''

Ross also says drawing subscribers to your newsletter can be a challenge. ''You must get word out and drive traffic to your website, and that's not always easy to do.''

Step 4: Give it away—free advertising

Not easy, says Rick Frishman, president of Planned Television Arts and one of the authors of *Guerilla Marketing for Writers* (Writer's Digest Books), but also not impossible. Giving your time and expertise away for free can be a great place to start.

"We have an Internet campaign for just about every book client we represent," Frishman says. In an electronic blitz, Frishman clients do Internet chats, seek Internet book reviews, and even offer free interviews and expert article submissions just to guarantee cyber exposure.

"Even if only 20 people show up to participate in an Internet chat," Frishman says, "thousands more end up reading the transcripts." The author's Web address is regularly nestled within the chat, offering a live link from one active website to another.

Trading your writing for links rather than fiscal remuneration is bound to generate a flurry of negative reactions, but like Frishman, Ross believes free articles can be an investment in eventual sales. "I'm very willing to donate an article as long as it carries a nice bio at the end that includes full ordering information for my book. This applies to print publications as well as those on the Internet."

Step 5: Make use of search engines

Imagine typing your genre or subject of expertise into a search engine and finding your name at the top of the list? It can happen, according to Young, if you take the time to register your site. "There are lots of services that will submit your site for a fee," she says, "but you can do it yourself. Just go to the search engine's home page and look for their 'Add your URL' instructions, and follow them."

Beyond simple search engine registration, Young's best tip for search engine success is reciprocal links. According to Young, most popular search engines (like Google and Yahoo) send out automated "spiders" to search established websites for Internet links. Those with a large number of clickable resources move up on search engine registries much faster than those without them.

For websites already on the top of the search engine heap, Ross says she has an effective way to use these websites: "When I have a new book coming out, I enter the topic of the book and begin the merry chase for new links." Then, using a spreadsheet, Ross makes note of topic-related websites that answer the following questions: Do they offer book reviews? Do they sell books? Do they have expert articles featured on her book's topic? Do they have host chats? Do they offer a monthly newsletter? After careful analysis of the answers, Ross contacts the site webmasters and makes them an offer they aren't likely to refuse.

"The Internet is going to be even more important to marketing in years to come," Ross says. "By learning to use it well now, you put yourself in a more competitive position in the future."

Step 6: E-mail, e-mail, e-mail!

Spam—unwanted, unsolicited blanket-form e-mails—is a term that strikes fear in the hearts of all Internet citizens, so avoid sending it. Poynter, however, believes targeted e-mail notices are *not* spam. So, what is targeted e-mail? "It's mail that goes out to your address-book recipients based on identified interests," Poynter says. Using e-mail to contact those individuals "is faster than the postal service and less expensive than a brochure, it provides for instant response, and it requires a lot less work than traditional mail."

Frishman takes the e-mail approach a step further—the signature line on all outgoing e-mails. "You should always have information about your book in your e-mail signature line because you never know who's going to be forwarded your e-mail."

Step 7: Contact print media—online

Did you get a good review? Did one regional or national editor declare your book project an exceptional effort? Spread the word—online.

It's your responsibility to prepare a short press release with the review excerpt and your contact information. Hundreds of print publications are now Internet friendly, so make use of them—deliver your press release to newspaper and magazine editors whose e-mail addresses are listed online.

"Don't always depend on the book review sections, however" says Ross. "Get off the book pages, and look to sections like lifestyle, sports, religion, business, and family. Depending on the topic of your book, that's where your readers will be. In fact, many of them never even look at the book section."

Book Signings

Tricks and Tips for Successful Signings

by Paul Raymond Martin

On a crisp December evening in Cleveland, a disheveled man made a beeline for my table at the entrance to B. Dalton's. He appeared nervous, or perhaps harried. Rumpled hair, shirt bunched at the waist. He didn't fit with the holiday shoppers and movie-goers. He made me uneasy.

Nevertheless I sang out as usual, "Hi! I'm signing copies of my book tonight." He didn't smile or acknowledge my greeting; he just picked up a copy of my book and began reading. He turned a page, then another, and I saw a glimmer of a smile. He flipped ahead a few pages, read some more, and then surveyed the table as if to see what else I might have to offer. He set the book down, not unkindly, nodded and walked away. "Thank you for looking, sir," I called out with genuine goodwill.

Forty minutes later, the disheveled man made a beeline for my table, and my apprehension returned. He pulled a piece of paper from his pocket and handed it to me—it contained a list of names. "I'd like 17 of your books, signed and dated for the people on this list. Do I pay you?"

"No, sir," I answered, "They'll be happy to take care of you inside. And thank you!"

After more than 150 booksignings, the harried man with the rumpled hair and shirt bunched at the waist remains one of my favorite customers. But I love 'em all: writers and would-be writers and the friends who buy books for them.

When the original version of *The Writer's Little Instruction Book* (since reissued as three books published by Writer's Digest Books) was published in 1998, I drove back and forth across the country twice, from one bookstore to another holding book signings. I split the costs with my publisher who made most of the arrangements. Typically, I would drive three to eight hours, check into a motel, get a bite to eat, and head for the bookstore. I usually stayed longer than scheduled, often until the book sold out, and then I'd do it again the next day. Hardly a glamorous book tour, but it worked. The original edition sold more than 17,000 copies before it went out of print in 2003.

BEFORE YOUR SIGNING

As more publishers cut their budgets, more authors are required to take the reins and set up their own publicity campaigns and promotion efforts, including book signings. While

PAUL RAYMOND MARTIN has published more than 300 stories, poems, and nonfiction pieces. Martin's most recent titles, all published by Writer's Digest Books, include *Writer's Little Instruction Book: Inspiration & Motivation*; *Writer's Little Instruction Book: Craft & Technique*; and *Writer's Little Instruction Book: Getting Published*.

sometimes considered a daunting task, there are a few simple things you can do to set up and prepare for your signing.

- If you arrange a signing in a bookstore that publishes a newsletter at the beginning of the month, request a signing in the middle of the month for maximum draw.
- Telephone or e-mail the bookstore a week in advance to confirm your books are available at the bookstore and the date on which the store is expecting you.
- Provide names and addresses of friends and relatives in the city where you'll be signing; some bookstores will mail postcards announcing your signing.
- Ask your publisher to send a press release to local media, and arrange radio and television interviews on the day of the signing, especially in smaller markets.
- Ask your publisher to provide bag stuffers, as well as a copy of the book cover and an author photo in advance. Some bookstores will use the book cover and photo to create posters.
- Prepare a few standard inscriptions to accompany your autograph (i.e., "Best of luck with your writing," etc.), but make sure you ask each buyer if he would like a personalized inscription.
- Make a point of eating well, exercising, and resting properly. If you're rundown, you'll do a lousy job of presenting yourself.

DURING YOUR SIGNING
Setting up for the signing

Your reception at a bookstore can vary from a wine-and-cheese reception complete with balloons, fresh flowers, linen tablecloths, and scented candles to a sales associate asking, "What's the title of your book? Let me see if we have it somewhere." While it's hard to anticipate what kind of reception you'll receive, there are some things you can do in advance of the signing to make sure it at least looks like a concerted effort was put forth.

- **Bring two generic posters** with your photo and book cover—one for the entrance to the bookstore and one for the food court, and two fold-up easels.
- **Bring a smaller sign** ("Have you met our visiting author?") for display at the cash register or information desk.
- **Bring two tissue boxes** to place under your tablecloth—this will create platforms to display your books. Display your books casually, along with copies of your "praise sheet" (see below) and order forms.
- **Offer free bookmarks,** samples of your work, or other giveaways.
- **Offer fliers announcing upcoming appearances** and for other books from your publisher.
- **Affix a "Signed Copy" and/or "Local Author" sticker** to your books.
- **Wear a professional-looking nametag,** with "Visiting Author" printed under your name.

Attracting and interacting with customers

Once you've set up your physical location, it's time to take a seat and wait. However, there are some things you can do to attract customers and, once they arrive at your table, interact with them.

- **Invite friends or relatives to linger** at your table; this will attract passers-by.
- **Greet passers-by and engage them in conversation.** Make eye contact, and invite passers-by to look at some specific feature of your book.
- **Invite buyers and browsers to sign your mailing list.** If a customer buys your book as a gift, ask the customer to list the name and address of the person who will receive

the book. Check the customer's address on the mailing list for legibility before the customer leaves. Start the mailing list with a dummy entry or two, so your first customer doesn't appear to be the only one who bought your book. This list will become an invaluable marketing tool after the bookstore event.

Signing books and using each signature to your benefit

When it comes time to actually sign copies of your book—congratulations! You've hit the easiest part of the night, and you can now use each signature as an opportunity to track sales and garner valuable information about your reader and even more valuable feedback on your book.

- **Check the spelling of each customer's or gift recipient's name** before inscribing the book.
- **When bookstore personnel and customers praise your book,** ask them to fill out a permission-to-quote form. Your publisher may wish to use these endorsements in subsequent editions or future books.
- **Keep a tally of the number of books you sign** and of your customer mix (i.e., male/female, teacher/student/gift-buyer).
- **Plan to stay later than scheduled** but, near the end of your allotted time, ask the store manager for permission to do so.

AFTER YOUR SIGNING

Once your signing is over, there are a few housekeeping items you should take care of both before and also after you leave the store.

- **Take a photo with the bookstore staff** and mail a copy back to the store.
- **Ask the store manager how many books he'd like you to sign** before you leave the store. Most bookstores ask authors to sign additional copies of their book so they can sell them as "Autographed Copies."

Book Signings: What Doesn't Work

There are many things you should avoid when setting up and conducting book signings. Below are six "don'ts" you should always remember:

- **DON'T** stand, sit. You'll be more approachable.
- **DON'T** loan books from your own stock if the bookstore doesn't have any copies or sells out; it will be difficult to reclaim replacements for the borrowed books.
- **DON'T** read, write, or eat during your signing, even if no one is coming up to you.
- **DON'T** over-schedule yourself or schedule too tightly.
- **DON'T** provide your home address or telephone number to customers. If you're comfortable corresponding with customers, give them your e-mail address instead.
- **DON'T** expect the bookstore staff to fawn over you or even to promote your signing; though this often happens, you should consider it a bonus.

The Business of Writing

- **Carry copies of your book with you for "parking lot sales"** in case you sell out the store's stock.
- **Mail a handwritten thank-you note** to the store manager and staff (you're more likely to be invited back).

You'll have to give up something to make time for book signings. What's usually given up is writing time. Be wary of giving up time with family and friends, or all your leisure time. Book promotion can become an insatiable beast, but take joy in the process—remind yourself you're doing what you dreamed of doing as you wrote the book.

There's no way of predicting success, but weekends are better than weekdays. There's no optimal time for a signing, other than *not* at the dinner hour. There are always competing events, but a local football game or crafts show is a killer. Offering a presentation helps, as does rainy weather. Make no assumptions about who will buy your book. Make yourself approachable to everyone—even a harried guy with rumpled hair whose shirt's bunched at the waist.

Publishers and Their Imprints

The publishing world is constantly in transition. With all of the buying, selling, reorganizing, consolidating, and dissolving, it's hard to keep publishers and their imprints straight. To help you make sense of these changes, we offer this breakdown of major publishers (and their divisions)—who owns whom and which imprints are under each company umbrella. Keep in mind this information changes frequently. We have provided the websites of each of the publishers so you can continue to keep an eye on this ever-evolving business.

HARPERCOLLINS

www.harpercollins.com

HarperCollins Australia/New Zealand
Angus & Robertson
Flamingo
Fourth Estate
HarperBusiness
HarperCollins
HarperPerennial
HarperReligious
HarperSports
Voyager

HarperCollins Canada
HarperFlamingoCanada
PerennialCanada

HarperCollins Children's Books Group
Amistad
Julie Andrews Collection
Avon
Joanna Cotler books
Eos
Laura Geringer Books
Greenwillow Books
HarperCollins Children's Books
HarperFestival
HarperKidsEntertainment
HarperTempest
HarperTrophy
Rayo
Katherine Tegen Books

HarperCollins General Books Group
Access
Amistad
Avon
Caedmon
Dark Alley
Ecco
Eos
Fourth Estate
Harper Design
HarperAudio
HarperBusiness
HarperCollins
HarperEntertainment
HarperLargePrint
HarperResource
HarperSanFrancisco

HarperTorch
Harper Design International
William Morrow
William Morrow Cookbooks
Perennial
Perennial Currents
PerfectBound
Quill
Rayo
ReganBooks

HarperCollins UK
Bartholomew Maps

Collins
HarperCollins Children's Books
HarperCollins Crime & Thrillers
HarperCollins Freedom to Teach
Thorsons/Element
Voyager Books

Zondervan
Inspirio
Vida
Zonderkidz
Zondervan

HOLTZBRINCK PUBLISHERS

www.holtzbrinck.com

Farrar, Straus & Giroux
Books for Young Readers
Faber & Faber
Hill & Wang (division)
North Point Press

Henry Holt and Co. LLC
Books for Young Readers
Metropolitan Books
Owl Books
Times Books

The MacMillan Group
MacMillan Education
Nature Publishing Group
Palgrave MacMillan
Pan MacMillan
    Boxtree
    Campbell Books
    MacMillan
    MacMillan Children's
    Pan
    Picador
    Sidgwick & Jackson
    Young Picador

PENGUIN GROUP (USA), INC.

www.penguingroup.com

Penguin Adult Division
Ace Books
Alpha Books
Avery
Berkley Books
Chamberlain Bros.
Dutton
Gotham Books
Grosset & Dunlop
HPBooks
Hudson Street Press
Jove
New American Library
Penguin
Perigree
Plume

Portfolio
G.P. Putnam's Sons
Riverhead Books
Sentinel
Jeremy P. Tarcher
Viking
Frederick Warne

Penguin Children's Division
Dial Books for Young Readers
Dutton Children's Books
Firebird
Grosset & Dunlap
Philomel
Price Stern Sloan

Puffin Books
G.P. Putnam's Sons
Speak

Viking Children's Books
Frederick Warne

RANDOM HOUSE, INC.

www.randomhouse.com

Ballantine Publishing Group
Ballantine Books
Ballantine Reader's Circle
Del Rey
Del Rey/Lucas Books
Fawcett
Ivy
One World
Wellspring

Bantam Dell Publishing Group
Bantam Hardcover
Bantam Mass Market
Bantam Trade Paperback
Crimeline
Delacorte Press
Dell
Delta
The Dial Press
Domain
DTP
Fanfare
Island
Spectra

Crown Publishing Group
Shaye Arehart Books
Bell Tower
Clarkson Potter
Crown Business
Crown Forum
Crown Publishers, Inc.
Harmony Books
Three Rivers Press

Doubleday Broadway Publishing Group
Broadway Books
Currency
Doubleday
Doubleday Image
Doubleday Religious Publishing
  Three Leaves Press

Main Street Books
Nan A. Talese

Knopf Publishing Group
Anchor Books
Everyman's Library
Alfred A. Knopf
Pantheon Books
Schocken Books
Vintage Books

Random House Audio Publishing Group
Listening Library
Random House Audible
Random House Audio
Random House Audio Assets
Random House Audio Dimensions
Random House Audio Roads
Random House Audio Voices
Random House Price-less

Random House Children's Books
BooksReportsNow.com
GoldenBooks.com
Junie B. Jones
Kids@Random
Knopf/Delacorte/Dell Young
Readers Group
  Bantam
  Crown
  David Fickling Books
  Delacorte Press
  Dell Dragonfly
  Dell Laurel-Leaf
  Dell Yearling Books
  Doubleday
  Alfred A. Knopf
  Wendy Lamb Books
Random House Young Readers Group
  Akiko
  Arthur
  Barbie

Beginner Books
The Berenstain Bears
Bob the Builder
Disney
Dragon Tales
First Time Books
Golden Books
Landmark Books
Little Golden Books
Lucas Books
Mercer Mayer
Nickelodeon
Nick, Jr.
pat the bunny
Picturebacks
Precious Moments
Richard Scarry
Sesame Street Books
Step Into Reading
Stepping Stones
Star Wars
Thomas the Tank Engine and Friends
Seussville
Teachers@Random
Teens@Random

Random House Direct, Inc.
Bon Apetit
Gourmet Books
Pillsbury

Random House Information Group
Fodor's Travel Publications
House of Collectibles

Living Language
Prima Games
The Princeton Review
Random House Español
Random House Puzzles & Games
Random House Reference Publishing

Random House International
Arete
McClelland & Stewart Ltd.
Plaza & Janes
Random House Australia
Random House of Canada Ltd.
Random House of Mondadori
Random House South Africa
Random House South America
Random House United Kingdom
Transworld UK
Verlagsgruppe Random House

Random House Value Publishing
Children's Classics
Crescent
Derrydale
Gramercy
Testament
Wings

Waterbrook Press
Fisherman Bible Study Guides
Shaw Books
Waterbrook Press

SIMON & SCHUSTER

www.simonsays.com

Simon & Schuster Adult Publishing
Atria Books
    Washington Square Press
The Free Press
    Simon & Schuster Source
    Wall Street Journal Books
Kaplan
Pocket Books
    Downtown Press
    MTV Books
    Paraview Pocket
    Pocket Star
    Star Trek

VH-1 Books
World Wrestling Entertainment
Scribner
    Lisa Drew Books
    Scribner Classics
    Scribner Paperback Fiction
Simon & Schuster
    Simon & Schuster Classic Editions
The Touchstone & Fireside Group

Simon & Schuster Children's Publishing
Aladdin Paperbacks
Atheneum Books for Young Readers

Richard Jackson Books
Anne Schwartz Books
Little Simon
Margaret K. McElderry Books
Simon & Schuster Books for Young Readers
Paula Wiseman Books
Simon Pulse
Simon Spotlight

Simon & Schuster Audio
Pimsleur
Simon & Schuster Audioworks
Simon & Schuster Sound Ideas

Simon & Schuster International
Simon & Schuster Australia
Simon & Schuster Canada
Simon & Schuster UK

TIME WARNER BOOK GROUP

www.twbookmark.com

Warner Books
Aspect
Bulfinch Press
Little, Brown, and Co. Adult Trade Division
Back Bay Books
Little, Brown, and Co. Books for Young
Readers

Mysterious Press
Time Warner Audio Books
Warner Business Books
Warner Faith
Warner Forever
Warner Vision

The Business of Writing

Literary Agents

The 50 literary agencies listed in this section are either actively seeking new clients () or seeking both new and established writers ( ), and they all generate 98 to 100 percent of their income from commission on sales.

All 50 agencies are members of the Association of Authors' Representatives (AAR), which means they do not charge for reading, critiquing, or editing. Some agents in this section may charge clients for office expenses such as photocopying, foreign postage, long-distance phone calls, or express mail services. Make sure you have a clear understanding of what these expenses are before signing any agency agreement.

FOR MORE ON THE SUBJECT . . .

The *2006 Guide to Literary Agents* (Writer's Digest Books) offers more than 500 listings for both literary and script agents, as well as information on production companies, independent publicists, script contests, and writers' conferences. It also offers a wealth of information on the author/agent relationship and other related topics.

SUBHEADS

Each listing is broken down into subheads to make locating specific information easier. In the first section, you'll find contact information for each agency. Further information is provided which indicates an agency's size, its willingness to work with a new or previously unpublished writer, and its general areas of interest.

Member Agents Agencies comprised of more than one agent list member agents and their individual specialties to help you determine the most appropriate person for your query letter.

Represents Here agencies specify what nonfiction and fiction subjects they consider.

⚷ Look for the key icon to quickly learn an agent's areas of specialization or specific strengths.

How to Contact In this section agents specify the type of material they want to receive, how they want to receive it, and how long you should wait for their response.

Recent Sales To give a sense of the types of material they represent, agents provide specific titles they've sold as well as a sampling of clients' names.

Terms Provided here are details of an agent's commission, whether a contract is offered, and what additional office expenses you might have to pay if the agent agrees to represent you. Standard commissions range from 10-15 percent for domestic sales, and 15-20 percent for foreign or dramatic sales.

Writers' Conferences Here agents list the conferences they attend.

Tips Agents offer advice and additional instructions for writers looking for representation.

ALTAIR LITERARY AGENCY, LLC

P.O. Box 11656, Washington DC 20008. (202)237-8282. Website: www.altairliteraryagency.com. Estab. 1996. Member of AAR. Represents 50 clients. 20% of clients are new/unpublished writers. Currently handles: 95% nonfiction books; 5% novels.

Member Agents Andrea Pedolsky, partner; Nicholas Smith, partner.

Represents Nonfiction books. **Considers these nonfiction areas:** History; popular culture; sports; science (history of); illustrated; current events/contemporary issues; museum; organization; and corporate-brand books. **Considers these fiction areas:** Historical (pre-20th century mysteries only).

> This agency specializes in nonfiction with an emphasis on authors who have credentials and professional recognition for their topic, and a high level of public exposure. Actively seeking solid, well-informed authors who have a public platform for the subject specialty.

How to Contact Query with SASE; or see website for more specific query information and to send an online query. Considers simultaneous queries. Responds in 2-4 weeks to queries; 1 month to mss. Obtains most new clients through recommendations from others, solicitations, author queries.

Recent Sales *Performance Nutrition for Runners,* by Matt Fitzgerald (Rodale); *Online Roots,* by Pamela Porter, CGRS, CGL and Amy Johnson Crow (Rutledge Hill Press); *How Herbs Work,* by Suzette Holly Phaneuf (Marlowe/ Avalon Publshing).

Terms Agent receives 15% commission on domestic sales; 20% commission on foreign sales. Offers written contract, binding for 1 year; 2-month notice must be given to terminate contract. Charges clients for postage, copying, messengers and FedEx and UPS.

MIRIAM ALTSHULER LITERARY AGENCY

53 Old Post Rd. N., Red Hook NY 12571. (845)758-9408. **Contact:** Miriam Altshuler. Estab. 1994. Member of AAR. Represents 40 clients. Currently handles: 45% nonfiction books; 45% novels; 5% story collections; 5% juvenile books.

> • Ms. Altshuler has been an agent since 1982.

Represents Nonfiction books, novels, short story collections, juvenile books. **Considers these nonfiction areas:** Biography/autobiography; ethnic/cultural interests; history; language/literature/criticism; memoirs; multicultural; music/dance; nature/environment; popular culture; psychology; sociology; theater/film; women's issues/ studies. **Considers these fiction areas:** Literary; mainstream/contemporary; multicultural.

> Does not want self-help, mystery, how-to, romance, horror, spiritual, fantasy, poetry, screenplays, science fiction, techno-thriller.

How to Contact Query with SASE. Prefers to read materials exclusively. If no SASE is included, no response will be sent. *No unsolicited mss.* No e-mail or fax queries. Considers simultaneous queries. Responds in 2 weeks to queries; 3 weeks to mss. Returns materials only with SASE. Obtains most new clients through recommendations from others.

Terms Agent receives 15% commission on domestic sales; 20% commission on foreign sales. Charges clients for overseas mailing, photocopies, overnight mail when requested by author.

Writers' Conferences Bread Loaf Writers' Conference (Middlebury VT, August); Washington Independent Writers Conference (Washington DC, June), North Carolina Writers Network Conference (Carrboro NC, October).

ARCADIA

31 Lake Pl. N., Danbury CT 06810. E-mail: arcadialit@att.net. **Contact:** Victoria Gould Pryor. Member of AAR. **Represents** Nonfiction books (readable, serious), literary and commercial fiction. **Considers these nonfiction areas:** Biography/autobiography; business/economics; current affairs; history; memoirs; psychology; science/ technology; true crime/investigative; women's issues/studies; medicine; investigative journalism; culture; classical music; life transforming self-help.

> "I'm a very hands-on agent, necessary in this competitive marketplace. I work with authors on revisions until whatever we present to publishers is as perfect as it can be. I represent talented, dedicated, intelligent, and ambitious writers who are looking for a long-term relationship based on professional success and mutual respect." No science fiction/fantasy, or children's/YA. "We are only able to read fiction submissions from previously published authors."

How to Contact Query with SASE. E-mail queries accepted without attachments.

Recent Sales This agency prefers not to share information on specific sales.

BALKIN AGENCY, INC.

P.O. Box 222, Amherst MA 01004. (413)548-9835. Fax: (413)548-9836. **Contact:** Rick Balkin, president. Estab. 1972. Member of AAR. Represents 50 clients. 10% of clients are new/unpublished writers. Currently handles: 85% nonfiction books; 5% scholarly books; 5% textbooks; 5% reference books.

• Prior to opening his agency, Mr. Balkin served as executive editor with Bobbs-Merrill Company.

Represents Nonfiction books, scholarly books, textbooks. **Considers these nonfiction areas:** Animals; anthropology/archaeology; biography/autobiography; current affairs; health/medicine; history; how-to; language/literature/criticism; music/dance; nature/environment; popular culture; science/technology; sociology; translation; travel; true crime/investigative.

O⚓ This agency specializes in adult nonfiction. Does not want to receive fiction, poetry, screenplays, computer books.

How to Contact Query with SASE, proposal package, outline. No e-mail or fax queries. Responds in 1 week to queries; 2 weeks to mss. Returns materials only with SASE. Obtains most new clients through recommendations from others.

Recent Sales Sold 30 titles in the last year. *The Liar's Tale* (W.W. Norton Co.); *Adolescent Depression* (Henry Holt); *Eliz. Van Lew: A Union Spy in the Heart of the Confederacy* (Oxford U.P.).

Terms Agent receives 15% commission on domestic sales; 20% commission on foreign sales. Offers written contract, binding for 1 year. Charges clients for photocopying and express or foreign mail.

Tips "I do not take on books described as bestsellers or potential bestsellers. Any nonfiction work that is either unique, paradigmatic, a contribution, truly witty, or a labor of love is grist for my mill."

⬛ LORETTA BARRETT BOOKS, INC.

101 Fifth Ave., New York NY 10003. (212)242-3420. Fax: (212)807-9579. E-mail: mail@lorettabarrettbooks.com. **Contact:** Loretta A. Barrett or Nick Mullendore. Estab. 1990. Member of AAR. Currently handles: 60% nonfiction books; 40% novels.

• Prior to opening her agency, Ms. Barrett was vice president and executive editor at Doubleday and editor-in-chief of Anchor Books.

Represents Nonfiction books, novels. **Considers these nonfiction areas:** Biography/autobiography; business/economics; child guidance/parenting; creative nonfiction; current affairs; ethnic/cultural interests; gay/lesbian issues; government/politics/law; health/medicine; history; language/literature/criticism; memoirs; money/finance; multicultural; nature/environment; philosophy; popular culture; psychology; religious/inspirational; science/technology; self-help/personal improvement; sociology; spirituality; sports; women's issues/studies; nutrition. **Considers these fiction areas:** Action/adventure; contemporary issues; detective/police/crime; ethnic; family saga; historical; literary; mainstream/contemporary; mystery/suspense; psychic/supernatural; thriller.

O⚓ This agency specializes in general interest books. No children's, juvenile, science fiction or fantasy.

How to Contact Query with SASE. No e-mail or fax queries. Considers simultaneous queries. Responds in 6 weeks to queries. Returns materials only with SASE.

Recent Sales *Fantastic Voyage*, by Ray Kurzweil and Terry Grossman (Rodale); *The Singularity Is Near*, by Ray Kurzweil (Viking); *Invisible Heroes*, by Belleruth Naparstek (Bantam).

Terms Agent receives 15% commission on domestic sales; 20% commission on foreign sales. Offers written contract. Charges clients for shipping and photocopying.

Writers' Conferences San Diego State University Writer's Conference; Pacific Northwest Writer's Association; SEAK Medical Writer's Conference.

⬛ MEREDITH BERNSTEIN LITERARY AGENCY

2112 Broadway, Suite 503A, New York NY 10023. (212)799-1007. Fax: (212)799-1145. Estab. 1981. Member of AAR. Represents 85 clients. 20% of clients are new/unpublished writers. Currently handles: 50% nonfiction books; 50% fiction.

• Prior to opening her agency, Ms. Bernstein served in another agency for 5 years.

Member Agents Meredith Bernstein, Elizabeth Cavanaugh.

Represents Nonfiction books, fiction of all kinds. **Considers these nonfiction areas:** Any area of nonfiction in which the author has an established platform. **Considers these fiction areas:** Literary; mystery/suspense; romance; thriller; women's.

O⚓ This agency does not specialize. It is "very eclectic."

How to Contact Query with SASE. No e-mail or fax queries. Considers simultaneous queries. Obtains most new clients through recommendations from others, conferences, also develops and packages own ideas.

Recent Sales *Tripping the Prom Queen: Envy, Competition & Jealousy Among Women*, by Susan Shepiro Barash (St. Martin's Press); *Sleep on It*, by Carol Gordon (Hyperion); 3-book deal of contemporary romances by Sandra Hill to Warner Books.

Terms Agent receives 15% commission on domestic sales; 20% commission on foreign sales. Charges clients $75 disbursement fee/year.

Writers' Conferences SouthWest Writers Conference (Albuquereque NM); Rocky Moutnain Writers' Conference (Denver CO); Golden Triangle (Beaumont TX); Pacific Northwest Writers Conference; Austin League

Writers Conference; Willamette Writers Conference (Portland OR); Lafayette Writers Conference (Lafayette LA); Surrey Writers Conference (Surrey BC); San Diego State University Writers Conference (San Diego CA).

Ⓝ ⬤ BOOK DEALS, INC.

244 Fifth Ave., Suite 2164, New York NY 10001-7604. (212)252-2701. Fax: (212)591-6211. **Contact:** Caroline Francis Carney. Estab. 1996. Member of AAR. Represents 40 clients. 15% of clients are new/unpublished writers. Currently handles: 85% nonfiction books; 15% novels.

• Prior to opening her agency, Ms. Carney was editorial director for a consumer book imprint within Times Mirror and held senior editorial positions in McGraw-Hill and NYIF/Simon & Schuster.

Represents Nonfiction books, novels (commercial and literary). **Considers these nonfiction areas:** Business/economics; child guidance/parenting; ethnic/cultural interests; health/medicine (nutrition); history; how-to; money/finance; multicultural; popular culture; psychology (popular); religious/inspirational; science/technology; self-help/personal improvement; spirituality. **Considers these fiction areas:** Ethnic; literary; mainstream/contemporary; women's (contemporary); urban literature.

○ᛜ This agency specializes in highly commercial nonfiction and books for African-American readers and women. Actively seeking well-crafted fiction and nonfiction from authors with engaging voices and impeccable credentials.

How to Contact Query with SASE. Considers simultaneous queries.

Recent Sales *Eat Right for Your Personality Type*, by Dr. Robert Kushner and Nancy Kushner (St. Martin's Press); *Self-Proclaimed*, by Rochelle Shapiro (Simon & Schuster); *Par for the Course*, by Alice Dye and Mark Shaw (HarperCollins).

Terms Agent receives 15% commission on domestic sales; 20% commission on foreign sales. Offers written contract. Charges clients for photocopying and postage.

⬤ BRANDT & HOCHMAN LITERARY AGENTS, INC.

1501 Broadway, Suite 2310, New York NY 10036. (212)840-5760. Fax: (212)840-5776. **Contact:** Carl Brandt; Gail Hochman; Marianne Merola; Charles Schlessiger. Estab. 1913. Member of AAR. Represents 200 clients.

Represents Nonfiction books, novels, short story collections, juvenile books, journalism. **Considers these nonfiction areas:** Biography/autobiography; current affairs; ethnic/cultural interests; government/politics/law; history; women's issues/studies. **Considers these fiction areas:** Contemporary issues; ethnic; historical; literary; mainstream/contemporary; mystery/suspense; romance; thriller; young adult.

How to Contact Query with SASE. No e-mail or fax queries. Considers simultaneous queries. Responds in 1 month to queries. Returns materials only with SASE. Obtains most new clients through recommendations from others.

Recent Sales This agency prefers not to share information on specific sales. Clients include Scott Turow, Carlos Fuentes, Ursula Hegi, Michael Cunningham, Mary Pope Osborne, Julia Glass.

Terms Agent receives 15% commission on domestic sales; 20% commission on foreign sales. Charges clients for "manuscript duplication or other special expenses agreed to in advance."

Tips "Write a letter which will give the agent a sense of you as a professional writer, your long-term interests as well as a short description of the work at hand."

⬤ CURTIS BROWN, LTD.

10 Astor Place, New York NY 10003-6935. (212)473-5400. Also Peter Ginsberg, President at CBEF: 1750 Montgomery St., San Francisco CA 94111. (415)954-8566. Member of AAR; signatory of WGA.

Member Agents Laura Blake Peterson; Ellen Geiger; Emilie Jacobson, senior vice president; Maureen Walters, senior vice president; Ginger Knowlton, vice president (adult, children's); Timothy Knowlton, CEO (film, screenplays); Ed Wintle; Mitchell Waters; Elizabeth Harding; Kirsten Manges; Dave Barbor (translation rights).

Represents Nonfiction books, novels, short story collections, novellas, juvenile books, poetry books, movie scripts, feature film, TV movie of the week. **Considers these nonfiction areas:** Agriculture/horticulture; americana; animals; anthropology/archaeology; art/architecture/design; biography/autobiography; business/economics; child guidance/parenting; computers/electronic; cooking/foods/nutrition; crafts/hobbies; creative nonfiction; current affairs; education; ethnic/cultural interests; gardening; gay/lesbian issues; government/politics/law; health/medicine; history; how-to; humor/satire; interior design/decorating; juvenile nonfiction; language/literature/criticism; memoirs; military/war; money/finance; multicultural; music/dance; nature/environment; New Age/metaphysics; philosophy; photography; popular culture; psychology; recreation; regional; religious/inspirational; science/technology; self-help/personal improvement; sex; sociology; software; spirituality; sports; theater/film; translation; travel; true crime/investigative; women's issues/studies; young adult. **Considers these fiction areas:** Action/adventure; comic books/cartoon; confession; contemporary issues; detective/police/crime; erotica; ethnic; experimental; family saga; fantasy; feminist; gay/lesbian; glitz; gothic; hi-lo; historical; horror; humor/satire; juvenile; literary; mainstream/contemporary; military/war; multicultural;

multimedia; mystery/suspense; New Age; occult; picture books; plays; poetry; poetry in translation; psychic/supernatural; regional; religious/inspirational; romance; science fiction; short story collections; spiritual; sports; thriller; translation; westerns/frontier; young adult; women's.

How to Contact Query individual agent with SASE. Prefers to read materials exclusively. *No unsolicited mss.* No e-mail or fax queries. Responds in 3 weeks to queries; 5 weeks to mss. Obtains most new clients through recommendations from others, solicitations, conferences.

Recent Sales This agency prefers not to share information on specific sales.

Terms Offers written contract. Charges for photocopying, some postage.

⊠ ☑ ANDREA BROWN LITERARY AGENCY, INC.

1076 Eagle Dr., Salinas CA 93905. (831)422-5925. Fax: (831)422-5915. E-mail: andrea@andreabrownlit.com. Website: www.andreabrownlit.com. **Contact:** Andrea Brown, president. Estab. 1981. 10% of clients are new/unpublished writers. Currently handles: 95% juvenile nonfiction nonfiction books; 5% adult nonfiction and fiction.

- Prior to opening her agency, Ms. Brown served as an editorial assistant at Random House and Dell Publishing and as an editor with Alfred A. Knopf.

Member Agents Andrea Brown, Laura Rennert, Caryn Wiseman, Jennifer Jaeger, Robert Welsh.

Represents Nonfiction books (juvenile). **Considers these nonfiction areas:** Animals; anthropology/archaeology; art/architecture/design; biography/autobiography; current affairs; ethnic/cultural interests; history; how-to; juvenile nonfiction; nature/environment; photography; popular culture; science/technology; sociology; sports; All nonfiction subjects for juveniles and adults. **Considers these fiction areas:** Juvenile; young adult; All fiction genres for juveniles; some adult fiction but not genre fiction.

- ☛ This agency specializes in "all kinds of children's books—illustrators and authors." Considers all juvenile fiction areas; all genres of nonfiction.

How to Contact Query with SASE. Accepts e-mail queries. No fax queries. Considers simultaneous queries. Obtains most new clients through recommendations from others, referrals from editors, clients, and agents.

Recent Sales *Chloe*, by Catherine Ryan Hyde (Knopf); *Sasha Cohen Autobiography* (HarperCollins); *The Five Ancestors*, by Jeff Stone (Random House).

Terms Agent receives 15% commission on domestic sales; 20% commission on foreign sales. Offers written contract. Charges clients for shipping costs.

Writers' Conferences Austin Writers League; SCBWI, Orange County Conferences; Mills College Childrens Literature Conference (Oakland CA); Asilomar (Pacific Grove CA); Maui Writers Conference; Southwest Writers Conference; San Diego State University Writer's Conference; Big Sur Children's Writing Workshop (Director); William Saroyan Conference; Columbus Writers Conference; Willamette Writers Conference.

Tips "Query first—so many submissions come in it takes 3-4 months to get a response. Taking on very few picture books. Must be unique—no rhyme, no anthropomorphism. Handling some adult historical fiction."

☑ CASTIGLIA LITERARY AGENCY

1155 Camino Del Mar, Suite 510, Del Mar CA 92014. (858)755-8761. Fax: (858)755-7063. Estab. 1993. Member of AAR, PEN. Represents 50 clients. Currently handles: 55% nonfiction books; 45% novels.

Member Agents Julie Castiglia, Winifred Golden, Sally Van Haitsma.

Represents Nonfiction books, novels. **Considers these nonfiction areas:** Animals; anthropology/archaeology; biography/autobiography; business/economics; child guidance/parenting; cooking/foods/nutrition; current affairs; ethnic/cultural interests; health/medicine; history; language/literature/criticism; money/finance; nature/environment; New Age/metaphysics; psychology; religious/inspirational; science/technology; self-help/personal improvement; sociology; women's issues/studies. **Considers these fiction areas:** Contemporary issues; ethnic; literary; mainstream/contemporary; mystery/suspense; women's (especially).

- ☛ Does not want to receive horror, screenplays, or academic nonfiction.

How to Contact Query with SASE. No fax queries. Responds in 2 months to mss. Returns materials only with SASE. Obtains most new clients through recommendations from others, solicitations, conferences.

Recent Sales Sold 25 titles in the last year. *Courtyards*, by Douglas Keister (Gibbs Smith); *The New Vegan: Fresh, Fabulous and Fun*, by Janet Hudson (Thorsons/HarperCollins); *Will He Really Leave Her for Me*, by Rona Subotnik (Adams Media).

Terms Agent receives 15% commission on domestic sales; 25% commission on foreign sales. Offers written contract; 6-week notice must be given to terminate contract. Charges clients for Fed Ex or Messenger.

Writers' Conferences Southwestern Writers Conference (NM); National Writers Conference; Willamette Writers Conference (OR); San Diego State University (CA); Writers at Work (UT); Austin Conference (TX).

Tips "Be professional with submissions. Attend workshops and conferences before you approach an agent."

Literary Agents

❍ CORNERSTONE LITERARY, INC.

4500 Wilshire Blvd., 3rd Floor, Los Angeles CA 90010. (323)930-6037. Fax: (323)930-0407. Website: www.corne rstoneliterary.com. **Contact:** Helen Breitwieser. Estab. 1998. Member of AAR; Author's Guild; MWA; RWA. Represents 40 clients. 30% of clients are new/unpublished writers.

- Prior to founding her own boutique agency, Ms. Breitwieser was a literary agent at The William Morris Agency.

Represents Nonfiction books, novels. **Considers these fiction areas:** Detective/police/crime; erotica; ethnic; family saga; glitz; historical; literary; mainstream/contemporary; multicultural; mystery/suspense; romance; thriller; women's.

- ☛ Actively seeking first fiction, literary. Does not want to receive science fiction, westerns, children's books, poetry, screenplays, fantasy, gay/lesbian, horror, self-help, psychology, business or diet.

How to Contact Query with SASE. Responds in 6-8 weeks to queries; 2 months to mss. Returns materials only with SASE. Obtains most new clients through recommendations from others.

Recent Sales Sold 38 titles in the last year. *How Was It For You*, by Carmen Reid (Pocket); *Sisters in Pink*, by Kayla Perrin (St. Martin's Press); *What Angels Fear*, by Candice Proctor (NAL). Other clients include Stan Diehl, Elaine Coffman, Danielle Girard, Rachel Lee, Marilyn Jaye Lewis, Carole Matthews.

Terms Agent receives 15% commission on domestic sales; 20% commission on foreign sales. Offers written contract, binding for 1 year; 2-month notice must be given to terminate contract.

Tips "Don't query about more than 1 manuscript. Do not e-mail queries/submissions."

❍ JAMES R. CYPHER, THE CYPHER AGENCY

816 Wolcott Ave., Beacon NY 12508-4261. Phone/Fax: (845)831-5677. E-mail: jimcypher@prodigy.net. Website: pages.prodigy.net/jimcypher/. **Contact:** James R. Cypher. Estab. 1993. Member of AAR, Authors Guild. Represents 30 clients. 35% of clients are new/unpublished writers. Currently handles: 100% nonfiction books.

- Prior to opening his agency, Mr. Cypher worked as a corporate public relations manager for a Fortune 500 multi-national computer company for 28 years.

Represents Nonfiction books. **Considers these nonfiction areas:** Biography/autobiography; current affairs; government/politics/law; health/medicine; popular culture; science/technology; self-help/personal improvement; sports; true crime/investigative.

- ☛ Actively seeking a wide variety of topical nonfiction. Does not want to receive humor, pets, gardening, cookbooks, crafts, spiritual, religious, or New Age topics.

How to Contact Query with SASE, proposal package, outline, 2 sample chapters. Accepts e-mail and fax queries. Considers simultaneous queries. Responds in 2 weeks to queries; 6 weeks to mss. Obtains most new clients through recommendations from others, conferences, networking on online computer service.

Recent Sales Sold 9 titles in the last year. *The Man Who Predicts Earthquakes*, by Cal Orey (Sentient Publications); *No Cleansing Fire: A True Story of Jealousy, Deceit, Rage and Fiery Murder*, by Tom Basinski (Berkley Books); *True to the Roots: Excursions Off Country Music's Beaten Path*, by Monte Dutton (University of Nebraska Press). Other clients include Walter Harvey, Mark Horner, Charles Hustmyre, Glenn Puit, Robert L. Snow.

Terms Agent receives 15% commission on domestic sales; 20% commission on foreign sales. Offers written contract; 1-month notice must be given to terminate contract. 100% of business is derived from commissions on ms sales. Charges clients for postage, photocopying, overseas phone calls and faxes.

❍ DARHANSOFF, VERRILL, FELDMAN LITERARY AGENTS

236 W. 26th St., Suite 802, New York NY 10001. (917)305-1300. Fax: (917)305-1400. Estab. 1975. Member of AAR. Represents 120 clients. 10% of clients are new/unpublished writers. Currently handles: 25% nonfiction books; 60% novels; 15% story collections.

Member Agents Liz Darhansoff, Charles Verrill, Leigh Feldman.

Represents Nonfiction books, novels, short story collections.

How to Contact Obtains most new clients through recommendations from others.

❍ LIZA DAWSON ASSOCIATES

240 W. 35th St., Suite 500, New York NY 10001. (212)465-9071. **Contact:** Liza Dawson, Caitlin Blasdell. Member of AAR, MWA, Women's Media Group. Represents 50 clients. 15% of clients are new/unpublished writers. Currently handles: 60% nonfiction books; 40% novels.

- Prior to becoming an agent, Ms. Dawson was an editor for 20 years, spending 11 years at William Morrow as vice president and 2 at Putnam as executive editor. Ms. Blasdell was a senior editor at HarperCollins and Avon.

Member Agents Liza Dawson, Caitlin Blasdell.

Represents Nonfiction books, novels. **Considers these nonfiction areas:** Biography/autobiography; health/ medicine; history; memoirs; psychology; sociology; women's issues/studies; politics; business; parenting. **Con-**

siders these fiction areas: Ethnic; family saga; historical; literary; mystery/suspense; regional; science fiction (Blasdell only); thriller.

   ⚬⇥ This agency specializes in readable literary fiction, thrillers, mainstream historicals, women's fiction, academics, historians, business, journalists and psychology. Does not want to receive westerns, sports, computers, juvenile.

How to Contact Query with SASE. Responds in 3 weeks to queries; 6 weeks to mss. Obtains most new clients through recommendations from others, conferences.

Recent Sales Sold 40 titles in the last year. *Going for It*, by Karen E. Quinones Miller (Warner); *Mayada: Daughter of Iraq*, by Jean Sasson (Dutton); *It's So Much Work to Be Your Friend: Social Skill Problems at Home and at School*, by Richard Lavoie (Touchstone).

Terms Agent receives 15% commission on domestic sales; 20% commission on foreign sales. Offers written contract. Charges clients for photocopying and overseas postage.

🅐 DUNHAM LITERARY, INC.

156 Fifth Ave., Suite 625, New York NY 10010-7002. (212)929-0994. Website: www.dunhamlit.com. **Contact:** Jennie Dunham. Estab. 2000. Member of AAR. Represents 50 clients. 15% of clients are new/unpublished writers. Currently handles: 25% nonfiction books; 25% novels; 50% juvenile books.

   ● Prior to opening her agency, Ms. Dunham worked as a literary agent for Russell & Volkening. The Rhoda Weyr Agency is now a division of Dunham Literary, Inc.

Represents Nonfiction books, novels, short story collections, juvenile books. **Considers these nonfiction areas:** Anthropology/archaeology; biography/autobiography; ethnic/cultural interests; government/politics/law; health/medicine; history; language/literature/criticism; nature/environment; popular culture; psychology; science/technology; women's issues/studies. **Considers these fiction areas:** Ethnic; juvenile; literary; mainstream/contemporary; picture books; young adult.

How to Contact Query with SASE. No e-mail or fax queries. Responds in 1 week to queries; 2 months to mss. Obtains most new clients through recommendations from others, solicitations.

Recent Sales *America the Beautiful*, by Robert Sabuda; *Dahlia*, by Barbara McClintock; *Living Dead Girl*, by Tod Goldberg.

Terms Agent receives 15% commission on domestic sales; 20% commission on foreign sales.

🅐 DYSTEL & GODERICH LITERARY MANAGEMENT

1 Union Square W., Suite 904, New York NY 10003. (212)627-9100. Fax: (212)627-9313. E-mail: miriam@dystel.com. Website: www.dystel.com. **Contact:** Miriam Goderich. Estab. 1994. Member of AAR. Represents 300 clients. 50% of clients are new/unpublished writers. Currently handles: 65% nonfiction books; 25% novels; 10% cookbooks.

   ● Dystel & Goderich Literary Management recently acquired the client list of Bedford Book Works.

Member Agents Stacey Glick; Jane Dystel; Miriam Goderich; Michael Bourret; Leslie Josephs; Jim McCarthy.

Represents Nonfiction books, novels, cookbooks. **Considers these nonfiction areas:** Animals; anthropology/archaeology; biography/autobiography; business/economics; child guidance/parenting; cooking/foods/nutrition; current affairs; education; ethnic/cultural interests; gay/lesbian issues; government/politics/law; health/medicine; history; humor/satire; military/war; money/finance; New Age/metaphysics; popular culture; psychology; religious/inspirational; science/technology; true crime/investigative; women's issues/studies. **Considers these fiction areas:** Action/adventure; contemporary issues; detective/police/crime; ethnic; family saga; gay/lesbian; literary; mainstream/contemporary; mystery/suspense; thriller (especially).

   ⚬⇥ This agency specializes in commercial and literary fiction and nonfiction, plus cookbooks.

How to Contact Query with SASE. Considers simultaneous queries. Responds in 1 month to queries; 6 weeks to mss. Obtains most new clients through recommendations from others, solicitations, conferences.

Terms Agent receives 15% commission on domestic sales; 19% commission on foreign sales. Offers written contract, binding for book-to-book basis. Charges for photocopying. Galley charges and book charges from the publisher are passed on to the author.

Writers' Conferences West Coast Writers Conference (Whidbey Island WA, Columbus Day weekend); University of Iowa Writer's Conference; Pacific Northwest Writer's Conference; Pike's Peak Writer's Conference; Santa Barbara Writer's Conference; Harriette Austin's Writer's Conference; Sandhills Writers Conference; ASU Writers Conference.

Tips "Work on sending professional, well-written queries that are concise and addressed to the specific agent the author is contacting. No dear Sirs/Madam."

Ⓝ 🅐 ANN ELMO AGENCY, INC.

60 E. 42nd St., New York NY 10165. (212)661-2880, 2881. Fax: (212)661-2883. **Contact:** Lettie Lee. Estab. 1959. Member of AAR, MWA, Authors Guild.

Member Agents Lettie Lee; Mari Cronin (plays); A.L. Abecassis (nonfiction).

Represents Nonfiction books, novels. **Considers these nonfiction areas:** Biography/autobiography; current affairs; health/medicine; history; how-to; money/finance; music/dance; popular culture; psychology; science/technology; self-help/personal improvement; theater/film. **Considers these fiction areas:** Contemporary issues; ethnic; family saga; mainstream/contemporary; romance (contemporary, gothic, historical, regency); thriller; women's.

How to Contact Letter queries only with SASE. No fax queries. Responds in 3 months to queries. Obtains most new clients through recommendations from others.

Recent Sales This agency prefers not to share information on specific sales.

Terms Agent receives 15% commission on domestic sales; 20% commission on foreign sales. Offers written contract. Charges clients for "special mailings or shipping considerations or multiple international calls. No charge for usual cost of doing business."

Tips "Query first, and only when asked, please send properly prepared manuscript. A double-spaced, readable manuscript is the best recommendation. Include SASE, of course."

◖ ELAINE P. ENGLISH

Graybill & English, LLC, 1875 Connecticut Ave. NW, Suite 712, Washington DC 20009. (202)588-9798, ext. 143. Fax: (202)457-0662. E-mail: elaineengl@aol.com. Website: www.graybillandenglish.com. **Contact:** Elaine English. Member of AAR. Represents 18 clients. 50% of clients are new/unpublished writers. Currently handles: 100% novels.

• Ms. English is also an attorney specializing in media and publishing law.

Member Agents Elaine English (fiction, including women's fiction, romance, thrillers and mysteries).

Represents Novels. **Considers these fiction areas:** Historical; mainstream/contemporary; multicultural; mystery/suspense; romance (including single titles, historical, contemporary, romantic, suspense, chick lit, erotic); thriller; women's.

O┳ "While not as an agent per se, I have been working in publishing for over 15 years. Also, I'm affiliated with other agents who represent a broad spectrum of projects." Actively seeking women's fiction, including single-title romances. Does not want to receive any science fiction or time travel.

How to Contact Submit synopsis and first 3 chapters, SASE. Responds in 6-12 weeks to queries; 6 months to requested ms. Returns materials only with SASE. Obtains most new clients through recommendations from others, solicitations, conferences.

Terms Agent receives 15% commission on domestic sales; 20% commission on foreign sales. Offers written contract; 30-day notice must be given to terminate contract. Charges only for expenses directly related to sales of ms (long distance, postage, copying).

Writers' Conferences RWA Nationals (July); SEAK Medical Fiction Writing for Physcians (Cape Cod, September); Emerald City (Seattle WA, October); Novelists, Inc. (New York, April).

◖ FELICIA ETH LITERARY REPRESENTATION

555 Bryant St., Suite 350, Palo Alto CA 94301-1700. (650)375-1276. Fax: (650)401-8892. E-mail: feliciaeth@aol.com. **Contact:** Felicia Eth. Estab. 1988. Member of AAR. Represents 25-35 clients. Currently handles: 85% nonfiction books; 15% adult novels.

Represents Nonfiction books, novels. **Considers these nonfiction areas:** Animals; anthropology/archaeology; biography/autobiography; business/economics; child guidance/parenting; current affairs; ethnic/cultural interests; gay/lesbian issues; government/politics/law; health/medicine; history; nature/environment; popular culture; psychology; science/technology; sociology; true crime/investigative; women's issues/studies. **Considers these fiction areas:** Ethnic; feminist; gay/lesbian; literary; mainstream/contemporary; thriller.

O┳ This agency specializes in "provocative, intelligent, thoughtful nonfiction on a wide array of subjects which are commercial, and high-quality fiction—preferably mainstream and contemporary."

How to Contact Query with SASE, outline. Considers simultaneous queries. Responds in 3 weeks to queries; 4-6 weeks to mss.

Recent Sales Sold 7-10 titles in the last year. *Jane Austen in Boca*, by Paula Marantz Cohen (St. Martin's Press); *Beyond Pink and Blue*, by Dr. Leonard Sax (Doubleday/Random House); *Lavendar Road to Success*, by Kirk Snyder (Ten Speed Press).

Terms Agent receives 15% commission on domestic sales; 20% commission on foreign sales; 20% commission on dramatic rights sales. Charges clients for photocopying, express mail service—extraordinary expenses.

Writers' Conferences Independent Writers of LA (Los Angeles); Conference of National Coalition of Independent Scholars (Berkley CA); Writers Guild.

Tips "For nonfiction, established expertise is certainly a plus, as is magazine publication—though not a prerequisite. I am highly dedicated to those projects I represent, but highly selective in what I choose."

◙ GELFMAN, SCHNEIDER, LITERARY AGENTS, INC.

250 W. 57th St., Suite 2515, New York NY 10107. (212)245-1993. Fax: (212)245-8678. **Contact:** Jane Gelfman, Deborah Schneider. Estab. 1981. Member of AAR. Represents 300+ clients. 10% of clients are new/unpublished writers.

Represents Nonfiction books, novels, **Considers these fiction areas:** Literary; mainstream/contemporary; mystery/suspense.

O Does not want to receive romances, science fiction, westerns, or children's books.

How to Contact Query with SASE. No e-mail queries accepted. Responds in 1 month to queries; 2 months to mss. Obtains most new clients through recommendations from others.

Terms Agent receives 15% commission on domestic sales; 20% commission on foreign sales. Offers written contract. Charges clients for photocopying, messengers and couriers.

◙ SANFORD J. GREENBURGER ASSOCIATES, INC.

55 Fifth Ave., New York NY 10003. (212)206-5600. Fax: (212)463-8718. Website: www.greenburger.com. **Contact:** Heide Lange. Estab. 1945. Member of AAR. Represents 500 clients.

Member Agents Heide Lange, Faith Hamlin, Dan Mandel, Peter McGuigan, Matthew Bialer.

Represents Nonfiction books, novels. **Considers these nonfiction areas:** Agriculture/horticulture; americana; animals; anthropology/archaeology; art/architecture/design; biography/autobiography; business/economics; child guidance/parenting; computers/electronic; cooking/foods/nutrition; crafts/hobbies; current affairs; education; ethnic/cultural interests; gardening; gay/lesbian issues; government/politics/law; health/medicine; history; how-to; humor/satire; interior design/decorating; juvenile nonfiction; language/literature/criticism; memoirs; military/war; money/finance; multicultural; music/dance; nature/environment; New Age/metaphysics; philosophy; photography; popular culture; psychology; recreation; regional; religious/inspirational; science/technology; self-help/personal improvement; sex; sociology; software; sports; theater/film; translation; travel; true crime/investigative; women's issues/studies; young adult. **Considers these fiction areas:** Action/adventure; contemporary issues; detective/police/crime; ethnic; family saga; feminist; gay/lesbian; glitz; historical; humor/satire; literary; mainstream/contemporary; mystery/suspense; psychic/supernatural; regional; sports; thriller.

O Does not want to receive romances or westerns.

How to Contact Submit query, first 3 chapters, synopsis, brief bio, SASE. Considers simultaneous queries. Responds in 2 months.

Recent Sales Sold 200 titles in the last year. This agency prefers not to share information on specific sales. Clients include Andrew Ross, Margaret Cuthbert, Nicholas Sparks, Mary Kurcinka, Linda Nichols, Edy Clarke, Brad Thor, Dan Brown, Sallie Bissell.

Terms Agent receives 15% commission on domestic sales; 20% commission on foreign sales. Charges for photocopying, books for foreign and subsidiary rights submissions.

Ⓝ ◙ THE JOY HARRIS LITERARY AGENCY, INC.

156 Fifth Ave., Suite 617, New York NY 10010. (212)924-6269. Fax: (212)924-6609. E-mail: gen.office@jhlitagent.com. **Contact:** Joy Harris. Member of AAR. Represents over 100 clients. Currently handles: 50% nonfiction books; 50% novels.

Member Agents Leslie Daniels; Stéphanie Abou; Sara Lustg.

Represents Nonfiction books, novels. **Considers these fiction areas:** Contemporary issues; ethnic; experimental; family saga; feminist; gay/lesbian; glitz; hi-lo; historical; humor/satire; literary; mainstream/contemporary; multicultural; multimedia; mystery/suspense; picture books; regional; short story collections; spiritual; translation; women's.

O Does not want to receive screenplays.

How to Contact Query with sample chapter, outline/proposal, SASE. Considers simultaneous queries. Responds in 2 months to queries. Obtains most new clients through recommendations from clients and editors.

Recent Sales This agency prefers not to share information on specific sales.

Terms Agent receives 15% commission on domestic sales; 20% commission on foreign sales. Charges clients for some office expenses.

◙ HOPKINS LITERARY ASSOCIATES

2117 Buffalo Rd., Suite 327, Rochester NY 14624-1507. (585)352-6268. **Contact:** Pam Hopkins. Estab. 1996. Member of AAR, RWA. Represents 30 clients. 5% of clients are new/unpublished writers. Currently handles: 100% novels.

Represents Novels. **Considers these fiction areas:** Historical; mainstream/contemporary; romance; women's.

O This agency specializes in women's fiction, particularly historical, contemporary, and category romance, as well as mainstream work.

How to Contact Submit outline, 3 sample chapters. No e-mail or fax queries. Considers simultaneous queries. Responds in 2 weeks to queries; 1 month to mss. Returns materials only with SASE. Obtains most new clients through recommendations from others, solicitations, conferences.

Recent Sales Sold 50 titles in the last year. *The First Mistake*, by Merline Lovelace (Mira); *The Romantic*, by Madeline Hunter (Bantam); *The Damsel in This Dress*, by Marianne Stillings (Avon).

Terms Agent receives 15% commission on domestic sales; 20% commission on foreign sales. No written contract.

Writers' Conferences Romance Writers of America.

KIRCHOFF/WOHLBERG, INC., AUTHORS' REPRESENTATION DIVISION

866 United Nations Plaza, #525, New York NY 10017. (212)644-2020. Fax: (212)223-4387. **Contact:** Liza Pulitzer Voges. Director of Operations: John R. Whitman. Estab. 1930s. Member of AAR, AAP, Society of Illustrators, SPAR, Bookbuilders of Boston, New York Bookbinders' Guild, AIGA. Represents 50 clients. 10% of clients are new/unpublished writers. Currently handles: 5% nonfiction books; 25% novels; 5% young adult; 65% picture books.

• Kirchoff/Wohlberg has been in business for over 60 years.

Member Agents Liza Pulitzer Voges (juvenile and young adult authors).

○━ This agency specializes in only juvenile through young adult trade books.

How to Contact For novels, query with SASE, outline, a few sample chapters. For picture book submissions, please send entire ms. SASE required. No e-mail or fax queries. Considers simultaneous queries. Responds in 1 month to queries; 2 months to mss. Returns materials only with SASE. Obtains most new clients through recommendations from authors, illustrators, and editors.

Recent Sales Sold over 50 titles in the last year. *Three Nasty Gnarlies*, by Keith Graves (Scholastic); *Chu Ju's House*, by Gloria Whelan (HarperCollins); My Weird School Series, by Dan Gutman (HarperCollins).

Terms Offers written contract, binding for not less than 1 year. Agent receives standard commission, "depending upon whether it is an author only, illustrator only, or an author/illustrator book."

LINDA KONNER LITERARY AGENCY

10 W. 15th St., Suite 1918, New York NY 10011-6829. (212)691-3419. E-mail: ldkonner@cs.com. **Contact:** Linda Konner. Estab. 1996. Member of AAR, ASJA; signatory of WGA. Represents 85 clients. 30-35% of clients are new/unpublished writers. Currently handles: 100% nonfiction books.

Represents Nonfiction books (adult only). **Considers these nonfiction areas:** Gay/lesbian issues; health/medicine (diet/nutrition/fitness); how-to; money/finance (personal finance); popular culture; psychology; self-help/personal improvement; women's issues; African American and Latino issues; business; parenting; relationships.

○━ This agency specializes in health, self-help and how-to books.

How to Contact Query with SASE, synopsis, author bio, sufficient return postage. Prefers to read materials exclusively for 2 weeks. Considers simultaneous queries. Obtains most new clients through recommendations from others, occasional solicitation among established authors/journalists.

Recent Sales Sold 26 titles in the last year. *The Ultimate Body*, by Liz Neporent (Ballantine); *Strength for Their Journey: The Five Disciplines Every African-American Parent Must Teach Her Child*, by Robert Johnson, MD, and Paulette Stanford, MD (Doubleday).

Terms Agent receives 15% commission on domestic sales; 25% commission on foreign sales. Offers written contract. Charges $85 one-time fee for domestic expenses; additional expenses possible for foreign sales.

Writers' Conferences American Society of Journalists and Authors (New York City, Spring).

STUART KRICHEVSKY LITERARY AGENCY, INC.

381 Park Ave. S., Suite 914, New York NY 10016. Fax: (212)725-5275. E-mail: query@skagency.com. Member of AAR.

Represents Nonfiction books, novels.

How to Contact Prefers queries by e-mail (no attachments).

NANCY LOVE LITERARY AGENCY

250 E. 65th St., New York NY 10021-6614. (212)980-3499. Fax: (212)308-6405. E-mail: nloveag@aol.com. **Contact:** Nancy Love. Estab. 1984. Member of AAR. Represents 60-80 clients. 25% of clients are new/unpublished writers. Currently handles: 90% nonfiction books; 10% novels.

Member Agents Nancy Love; Miriam Tager.

Represents Nonfiction books, fiction. **Considers these nonfiction areas:** Biography/autobiography; child guidance/parenting; cooking/foods/nutrition; current affairs; ethnic/cultural interests; government/politics/law; health/medicine; history; how-to; nature/environment; New Age/metaphysics; popular culture; psychology;

religious/inspirational; science/technology; self-help/personal improvement; sociology; spirituality; travel (armchair only, no how-to travel); true crime/investigative; women's issues/studies. **Considers these fiction areas:** Mystery/suspense; thriller.

○┅ This agency specializes in adult nonfiction and mysteries. Actively seeking narrative nonfiction. Does not want to receive novels other than mysteries and thrillers.

How to Contact For nonfiction, send a proposal, chapter summary, and sample chapter. For fiction, query first. No e-mail or fax queries. Considers simultaneous queries. Responds in 3 weeks to queries; 6 weeks to mss. Returns materials only with SASE. Obtains most new clients through recommendations from others, solicitations.

Recent Sales Sold 18 titles in the last year. *Cutter Vaccine Incident*, by Paul Offit, MD (Yale U. Press); *Don't Panic*, by Stanton Peele, PhD (Crown); *Regime Change*, by Steven Kinzer (Henry Holt).

Terms Agent receives 15% commission on domestic sales; 20% commission on foreign sales. Offers written contract. Charges clients for photocopying "if it runs over $20."

Tips "Nonfiction author and/or collaborator must be an authority in subject area and have a platform. Send a SASE if you want a response."

◖ DONALD MAASS LITERARY AGENCY

160 W. 95th St., Suite 1B, New York NY 10025. (212)866-8200. Website: www.maassagency.com. **Contact:** Donald Maass, Jennifer Jackson, Rachel Vater, Cameron McClure. Estab. 1980. Member of AAR, SFWA, MWA, RWA. Represents over 100 clients. 5% of clients are new/unpublished writers. Currently handles: 100% novels.

● Prior to opening his agency, Mr. Maass served as an editor at Dell Publishing (New York) and as a reader at Gollancz (London). He also served as the president of AAR.

Member Agents Donald Maass (mainstream, literary, mystery/suspense, science fiction); Jennifer Jackson (commercial fiction, especially romance, science fiction, fantasy, mystery/suspense); Rachel Vater (chick lit, mystery, thriller, fantasy, commercial, literary); Cameron McClure (literary, historical, mystery/suspense, fantasy, women's fiction, narrative nonfiction and projects with multicultural, international and environmental themes).

Represents Novels. **Considers these fiction areas:** Detective/police/crime; fantasy; historical; horror; literary; mainstream/contemporary; mystery/suspense; psychic/supernatural; romance (historical, paranormal, time travel); science fiction; thriller; women's.

○┅ This agency specializes in commercial fiction, especially science fiction, fantasy, romance and suspense. Actively seeking "to expand the literary portion of our list and expand in women's fiction." Does not want to receive nonfiction, children's, or poetry.

How to Contact Query with SASE, synopsis, or first 5 pages. Returns material only with SASE. Considers simultaneous queries. Responds in 2 weeks to queries; 3 months to mss.

Recent Sales Sold over 100 titles in the last year. *The Shifting Tide*, by Anne Perry (Ballantine); *The Longest Night*, by Gregg Keizer (G.P. Putnam's Sons).

Terms Agent receives 15% commission on domestic sales; 20% commission on foreign sales.

Writers' Conferences *Donald Maass*: World Science Fiction Convention; Frankfurt Book Fair; Pacific Northwest Writers Conference; Bouchercon and others; *Jennifer Jackson*: World Science Fiction and Fantasy Convention; RWA National, and others; *Rachel Vater*: Pacific Northwest Writer's Conference, Pennwriters, and others.

Tips "We are fiction specialists, also noted for our innovative approach to career planning. Few new clients are accepted, but interested authors should query with SASE. Subagents in all principle foreign countries and Hollywood. No nonfiction or juvenile works considered."

◖ CAROL MANN AGENCY

55 Fifth Ave., New York NY 10003. (212)206-5635. Fax: (212)675-4809. E-mail: emily@carolmannagency.com. **Contact:** Emily Nurkin. Estab. 1977. Member of AAR. Represents 200 clients. 25% of clients are new/unpublished writers. Currently handles: 70% nonfiction books; 30% novels.

Member Agents Carol Mann (literary fiction, nonfiction); Emily Nurkin (fiction and nonfiction); Gareth Esersky.

Represents Nonfiction books, novels. **Considers these nonfiction areas:** Anthropology/archaeology; art/architecture/design; biography/autobiography; business/economics; child guidance/parenting; current affairs; ethnic/cultural interests; government/politics/law; health/medicine; history; money/finance; psychology; self-help/personal improvement; sociology; women's issues/studies. **Considers these fiction areas:** Literary; commercial.

○┅ This agency specializes in current affairs; self-help; popular culture; psychology; parenting; history. Does not want to receive "genre fiction (romance, mystery, etc.)."

How to Contact Query with outline/proposal and SASE. Responds in 3 weeks to queries.

Recent Sales Clients include Paul Auster, Marita Golden, Tim Egan, Hannah Storm, Willow Bay, Fox Butterfield,

Shelby Steele, Dr. William Julius Wilson, Thomas Sowell, Mary Dan, Michael Eades, Nadine Strossen, Mona Charen, Lauren Winner, Rick Smolan, David Cohen, Kevin Liles.
Terms Agent receives 15% commission on domestic sales; 20% commission on foreign sales. Offers written contract.

◙ MENZA-BARRON AGENCY

(formerly Claudia Menza Literary Agency), 1170 Broadway, Suite 807, New York NY 10001. (212)889-6850.
Contact: Claudia Menza, Manie Barron. Estab. 1983. Member of AAR. Represents 100 clients. 50% of clients are new/unpublished writers.
Represents Nonfiction books, novels. **Considers these nonfiction areas:** Current affairs; education; ethnic/cultural interests (especially African-American); health/medicine; history; multicultural; music/dance; photography; psychology; theater/film.

  ○┐ This agency specializes in African-American fiction and nonfiction, and editorial assistance.
How to Contact Query with SASE. Responds in 2-4 weeks to queries; 2-4 months to mss. Returns materials only with SASE.
Recent Sales This agency prefers not to share information on specific sales.
Terms Agent receives 15% commission on domestic sales; 20% (if co-agent is used) commission on foreign sales; 20% commission on dramatic rights sales. Offers written contract.

◙ WILLIAM MORRIS AGENCY, INC.

1325 Avenue of the Americas, New York NY 10019. (212)586-5100. Fax: (212)246-3583. Website: www.wma.com. California office: One William Morris Place, Beverly Hills CA 90212. (310)859-4000. Fax: (310)859-4462. Member of AAR.
Member Agents Owen Laster, Jennifer Rudolph Walsh, Suzanne Gluck, Joni Evans, Tracy Fisher, Mel Berger, Jay Mandel, Manie Barron.
Represents Nonfiction books, novels.
How to Contact Query with SASE. Considers simultaneous queries.
Recent Sales This agency prefers not to share information on specific sales.
Terms Agent receives 15% commission on domestic sales; 20% commission on foreign sales.

L. PERKINS ASSOCIATES

16 W. 36 St., New York NY 10018. (212)279-6418. Fax: (718)543-5354. E-mail: lperkinsagency@yahoo.com.
Contact: Lori Perkins or Amy Stout (astoutlperkinsagency@yahoo.com). Estab. 1990. Member of AAR. Represents 50 clients. 10% of clients are new/unpublished writers.
  ● Ms. Perkins has been an agent for 18 years. Her agency has an affiliate agency, Southern Literary Group. She is also the author of *The Insider's Guide to Getting an Agent* (Writer's Digest Books).
Represents Nonfiction books, novels. **Considers these nonfiction areas:** Popular culture. **Considers these fiction areas:** Fantasy; horror; literary (dark); science fiction.
  ○┐ Most of Ms. Perkins' clients write both fiction and nonfiction. "This combination keeps my clients publishing for years. I am also a published author, so I know what it takes to write a good book." Actively seeking a Latino *Gone With the Wind* and *Waiting to Exhale*, and urban ethnic horror. Does not want to receive "anything outside of the above categories, i.e., westerns, romance."
How to Contact Query with SASE. Considers simultaneous queries. Responds in 6 weeks to queries; 3 months to mss. Returns materials only with SASE. Obtains most new clients through recommendations from others, solicitations, conferences.
Recent Sales Sold 100 titles in the last year. *How to Make Love Like a Porn Star: A Cautionary Tale*, by Jenna Jameson (Reagan Books); *Dear Mom, I Always Wanted You to Know*, by Lisa Delman (Perigee Books); *The Illustrated Ray Bradbury*, by Jerry Weist (Avon).
Terms Agent receives 15% commission on domestic sales; 20% commission on foreign sales. No written contract. Charges clients for photocopying.
Writers' Conferences San Diego Writer's Conference; NECON; BEA; World Fantasy.
Tips "Research your field and contact professional writers' organizations to see who is looking for what. Finish your novel before querying agents. Read my book, *An Insider's Guide to Getting an Agent*, to get a sense of how agents operate."

◙ PINDER LANE & GARON-BROOKE ASSOCIATES, LTD.

159 W. 53rd St., Suite 14C, New York NY 10019-6005. (212)489-0880. E-mail: pinderl@interport.net. **Contact:** Robert Thixton. Member of AAR; signatory of WGA. Represents 30 clients. 20% of clients are new/unpublished writers. Currently handles: 25% nonfiction books; 75% novels.
Member Agents Dick Duane, Robert Thixton.

Represents Nonfiction books, novels. **Considers these fiction areas:** Contemporary issues; detective/police/crime; family saga; fantasy; gay/lesbian; literary; mainstream/contemporary; mystery/suspense; romance; science fiction.

    O➤ This agency specializes in mainstream fiction and nonfiction. Does not want to receive screenplays, TV series teleplays, or dramatic plays.

How to Contact Query with SASE. *No unsolicited mss.* Responds in 3 weeks to queries; 2 months to mss. Obtains most new clients through referrals, queries.

Recent Sales Sold 20 titles in the last year. *Diana & Jackie—Maidens, Mothers & Myths*, by Jay Mulvaney (St. Martin's Press); The Sixth Fleet series, by David Meadows (Berkley); *Dark Fires*, by Rosemary Rogers (Mira Books).

Terms Agent receives 15% commission on domestic sales; 30% commission on foreign sales. Offers written contract, binding for 3-5 years.

Tips "With our literary and media experience, our agency is uniquely positioned for the current and future direction publishing is taking. Send query letter first giving the essence of the manuscript, and a personal or career bio with SASE."

☑ HELEN REES LITERARY AGENCY

376 North St., Boston MA 02113-2013. (617)227-9014. Fax: (617)227-8762. E-mail: reesagency@reesagency.com (no unsolicited e-mail submissions). **Contact:** Joan Mazmanian, Ann Collette, Helen Rees, or Lorin Rees. Estab. 1983. Member of AAR, PEN. Represents 80 clients. 50% of clients are new/unpublished writers. Currently handles: 60% nonfiction books; 40% novels.

Member Agents Ann Collette (literary fiction, women's studies, health, biography, history); Helen Rees (business, money/finance/economics, government/politics/law, contemporary issues, literary fiction); Lorin Rees (business, money/finance, management, history, narrative nonfiction, science, literary fiction, memoir).

Represents Nonfiction books, novels. **Considers these nonfiction areas:** Biography/autobiography; business/economics; current affairs; government/politics/law; health/medicine; history; money/finance; women's issues/studies. **Considers these fiction areas:** Contemporary issues; historical; literary; mainstream/contemporary; mystery/suspense; thriller.

How to Contact Query with SASE, outline, 2 sample chapters. No e-mail or fax queries. Responds in 2-3 weeks to queries. Obtains most new clients through recommendations from others, solicitations, conferences.

Recent Sales Sold 30 titles in the last year. *Get Your Shipt Together*, by Capt. D. Michael Abrashoff; *Overpromise and Overdeliver*, by Rick Berrara; *MBA in a Box*, by Joel Kurtzman.

Terms Agent receives 15% commission on domestic sales; 20% commission on foreign sales.

☑ BARBARA RIFKIND LITERARY AGENCY

132 Perry St., 6th Floor, New York NY 10014. (212)229-0453. Fax: (212)229-0454. E-mail: barbara@barbararifkind.net. **Contact:** Barbara Rifkind. Estab. 2002. Member of AAR. Represents 20 clients. 50% of clients are new/unpublished writers. Currently handles: 80% nonfiction books; 10% scholarly books; 10% textbooks.

    ● Prior to becoming an agent, Ms. Rifkind was an acquisitions editor, editorial manager, and a general manager in educational publishing (Addison Wesley).

Represents Nonfiction books, scholarly books, textbooks. **Considers these nonfiction areas:** Anthropology/archaeology; art/architecture/design; biography/autobiography; business/economics; child guidance/parenting; current affairs; ethnic/cultural interests; government/politics/law; health/medicine; history; language/literature/criticism; money/finance; popular culture; psychology; science/technology; sociology; women's issues/studies.

    O➤ "We represent writers of smart nonfiction—academics, journalists, scientists, thinkers, people who've done something real and have something to say—writing for general trade audiences and occassionally for trade scholarly or textbook markets. We like to work in the areas of history; science writing; business and economics; applications of social sciences to important issues; public affairs and current events; narrative nonfiction; women's issues and parenting from a discipline." Actively seeking smart nonfiction from credentialed thinkers or published writers in selected areas of interest. Does not want commercial or category fiction, juvenile, and other nonselected areas.

How to Contact Query with SASE, submit proposal package, outline. Accepts e-mail queries. No fax queries. Responds in 2 weeks to queries. Obtains most new clients through recommendations from others.

Recent Sales Clients include Zvi Bodie, Juan Enriquez, Nancy Folbre, Walter Friedman, James Hoopes, Herminia Ibarra, Milind Lele, Barry Nalebuff, Raghu Rajan, Steven Wall, Luigi Zingales, Ian Ayres, Greg Stone, Bill Hammack.

Terms Agent receives 15% commission on domestic sales; 10% commission on foreign sales. Offers written contract, binding for 6 months; immediate upon written notice to terminate contract.

B.J. ROBBINS LITERARY AGENCY

5130 Bellaire Ave., North Hollywood CA 91607-2908. (818)760-6602. Fax: (818)760-6616. E-mail: robbinsliterary@ aol.com. **Contact:** (Ms.) B.J. Robbins. Estab. 1992. Member of AAR. Represents 40 clients. 50% of clients are new/unpublished writers. Currently handles: 50% nonfiction books; 50% novels.

Member Agents Missy Pontious (YA).

Represents Nonfiction books, novels. **Considers these nonfiction areas:** Biography/autobiography; child guidance/parenting; current affairs; ethnic/cultural interests; health/medicine; how-to; humor/satire; memoirs; music/dance; popular culture; psychology; self-help/personal improvement; sociology; sports; theater/film; travel; true crime/investigative; women's issues/studies. **Considers these fiction areas:** Contemporary issues; detective/police/crime; ethnic; literary; mainstream/contemporary; mystery/suspense; sports; thriller; young adult.

How to Contact Submit 3 sample chapters, outline/proposal, SASE. E-mail queries OK; no attachments. No fax queries. Considers simultaneous queries. Responds in 2 weeks to queries; 6 weeks to mss. Returns materials only with SASE. Obtains most new clients through conferences, referrals.

Recent Sales Sold 15 titles in the last year. *Quickening,* by Laura Catherine Brown (Random House/Ballantine); *Snow Mountain Passage,* by James D. Houston (Knopf); *The Last Summer,* by John Hough, Jr. (Simon & Schuster).

Terms Agent receives 15% commission on domestic sales; 20% commission on foreign sales. Offers written contract; 3-month notice must be given to terminate contract. 100% of business is derived from commissions on ms sales. Charges clients for postage and photocopying only. Writers charged for fees after the sale of ms.

Writers' Conferences Squaw Valley Fiction Writers Workshop (Squaw Valley CA, August); SDSU Writers Conference (San Diego CA, January).

THE ROSENBERG GROUP

23 Lincoln Ave., Marblehead MA 01945. (781)990-1341. Fax: (781)990-1344. Website: www.rosenberggroup.com. **Contact:** Barbara Collins Rosenberg. Estab. 1998. Member of AAR, recognized agent of the RWA. Represents 32 clients. 25% of clients are new/unpublished writers. Currently handles: 30% nonfiction books; 30% novels; 10% scholarly books; 30% textbooks.

• Prior to becoming an agent, Ms. Rosenberg was a senior editor for Harcourt.

Member Agents Barbara Collins Rosenberg.

Represents Nonfiction books, novels, textbooks. **Considers these nonfiction areas:** Current affairs; popular culture; psychology; sports; women's issues/studies; women's health; food/wine/beverages. **Considers these fiction areas:** Literary; romance; women's.

• Ms. Rosenberg is well-versed in the romance market (both category and single title). She is a frequent speaker at romance conferences. Actively seeking romance category or single title in contemporary chick lit, romantic suspense, and the historical sub-genres. Does not want to receive time-travel, paranormal, or inspirational/spiritual romances.

How to Contact Query with SASE. No e-mail or fax queries. Responds in 2 weeks to queries; 4-6 weeks to mss. Returns materials only with SASE. Obtains most new clients through recommendations from others, solicitations, conferences.

Recent Sales Sold 27 titles in the last year.

Terms Agent receives 15% commission on domestic sales; 15% commission on foreign sales. Offers written contract; 1-month notice must be given to terminate contract. Postage and photocopying limit of $350/year.

Writers' Conferences RWA Annual Conference (Reno NV); RT Booklovers Convention (St. Louis MO); BEA (New York).

JANE ROTROSEN AGENCY LLC

318 E. 51st St., New York NY 10022. (212)593-4330. Fax: (212)935-6985. E-mail: firstinitiallastname@janerotros en.com. Estab. 1974. Member of AAR, Authors Guild. Represents over 100 clients. Currently handles: 30% nonfiction books; 70% novels.

Member Agents Jane R. Berkey, Andrea Cirillo, Annelise Robey, Margaret Ruley, Perry Gordijn (director of translation rights).

Represents Nonfiction books, novels. **Considers these nonfiction areas:** Biography/autobiography; business/ economics; child guidance/parenting; cooking/foods/nutrition; current affairs; health/medicine; how-to; humor/satire; money/finance; nature/environment; popular culture; psychology; self-help/personal improvement; sports; true crime/investigative; women's issues/studies. **Considers these fiction areas:** Action/adventure; detective/police/crime; family saga; historical; horror; mainstream/contemporary; mystery/suspense; romance; thriller; women's.

How to Contact Query with SASE. By referral only. No e-mail or fax queries. Responds in 2 months to mss. Responds in 2 weeks to writers who have been referred by a client or colleague. Returns materials only with SASE.

Recent Sales This agency prefers not to share information on specific sales.

Terms Agent receives 15% commission on domestic sales; 20% commission on foreign sales. Offers written contract, binding for 3-5 years; 2-month notice must be given to terminate contract. Charges clients for photocopying, express mail, overseas postage, book purchase.

N O RUSSELL & VOLKENING

50 W. 29th St., #7E, New York NY 10001. (212)684-6050. Fax: (212)889-3026. **Contact:** Timothy Seldes, Kirsten Ringer. Estab. 1940. Member of AAR. Represents 140 clients. 20% of clients are new/unpublished writers. Currently handles: 45% nonfiction books; 50% novels; 3% story collections; 2% novellas.
Member Agents Timothy Seldes (nonfiction, literary fiction).

Represents Nonfiction books, novels, short story collections. **Considers these nonfiction areas:** Anthropology/archaeology; art/architecture/design; biography/autobiography; business/economics; cooking/foods/nutrition; creative nonfiction; current affairs; education; ethnic/cultural interests; gay/lesbian issues; government/politics/law; health/medicine; history; language/literature/criticism; military/war; money/finance; music/dance; nature/environment; photography; popular culture; psychology; science/technology; sociology; sports; theater/film; true crime/investigative; women's issues/studies. **Considers these fiction areas:** Action/adventure; detective/police/crime; ethnic; literary; mainstream/contemporary; mystery/suspense; picture books; sports; thriller.

    Oᴿ This agency specializes in literary fiction and narrative nonfiction.

Recent Sales *The Amateur Marriage*, by Anne Tyler (Knopf); *Loot*, by Nadine Gardiner; *Flying Crows*, by Jim Lehrer (Random House).

Terms Agent receives 15% commission on domestic sales; 20% commission on foreign sales. Charges clients for "standard office expenses relating to the submission of materials of an author we represent, i.e., photocopying, postage."

Tips "If the query is cogent, well written, well presented, and is the type of book we'd represent, we'll ask to see the manuscript. From there, it depends purely on the quality of the work."

O THE SAGALYN AGENCY

7201 Bethesda Ave., Suite 675, Bethesda MD 20814. (301)718-6440. Fax: (301)718-6444. E-mail: info@sagalyn.com. Website: sagalyn.com. **Contact:** Rebeca Sagalyn. Estab. 1980. Member of AAR. Currently handles: 85% nonfiction books; 5% novels; 10% scholarly books.
Member Agents Raphael Sagalyn, Rebeca Sagalyn.
Represents Nonfiction books (history, science, business).

    Oᴿ Does not want to receive stage plays, screenplays, poetry, science fiction, romance, children's books, or young adult books.

How to Contact Please send e-mail queries only, no attachments. Include 1 of these words in subject line: Query, submission, inquiry. Response time depends on number of current queries, generally within 3 weeks.
Recent Sales See website for sales information.
Tips "We receive between 1,000-1,200 queries a year, which in turn lead to 2 or 3 new clients."

N O THE SEYMOUR AGENCY

475 Miner St., Canton NY 13617. (315)386-1831. Fax: (315)386-1037. E-mail: marysue@slic.com. Website: www.theseymouragency.com. **Contact:** Mary Sue Seymour. Estab. 1992. Member of AAR, CBA, RWA and The Author's Guild. Represents 75 clients. 5% of clients are new/unpublished writers. Currently handles: 50% nonfiction books; 50% fiction.

    • Ms. Seymour is a retired New York State certified teacher.

Represents Nonfiction books, novels (romance). **Considers these nonfiction areas:** Business/economics; health/medicine; how-to; self-help/personal improvement; Christian books; cookbooks; any well-written nonfiction that includes a proposal in standard format and 1 sample chapter. **Considers these fiction areas:** Literary; religious/inspirational (Christian books); romance (any type); westerns/frontier.

How to Contact Query with SASE, synopsis, first 50 pages for romance. Accepts e-mail queries. No fax queries. Considers simultaneous queries. Responds in 1 month to queries; 3 months to mss. Returns materials only with SASE.

Recent Sales Penny McCusker's 3 books to Harlequin/Silhouette; Emilee Hines' 2-book deal to Warner Books; Dr. Val Dmitriev's Vocabulary book to Adams Media Corp.

Terms Agent receives 12% (from authors' material whose books the agency sold) and 15% (on new clients) commission on domestic sales.

Writers' Conferences Desert Rose (Scottsdale AZ); Mountain Laurel (Knoxville TN); Romantic Times Convention (New York City); RWA National (Dallas); CBA (Atlanta); Put Your Heart in a Book (New Jersey).

◖ WENDY SHERMAN ASSOCIATES, INC.

450 Seventh Ave., Suite 3004, New York NY 10123. (212)279-9027. Fax: (212)279-8863. Website: www.wsherm an.com. **Contact:** Wendy Sherman. Estab. 1999. Member of AAR. Represents 50 clients. 30% of clients are new/unpublished writers. Currently handles: 50% nonfiction books; 50% novels.

• Prior to opening the agency, Ms. Sherman worked for The Aaron Priest agency and was vice president, executive director of Henry Holt, associate publisher, subsidary rights director, sales and marketing director.

Member Agents Tracy Brown, Wendy Sherman.

Represents Nonfiction books, novels. **Considers these nonfiction areas:** Psychology; narrative nonfiction, practical. **Considers these fiction areas:** Literary; women's (suspense).

O→ ''We specialize in developing new writers as well as working with more established writers. My experi- ence as a publisher has proven to be a great asset to my clients.''

How to Contact Query with SASE, or send outline/proposal, 1 sample chapter. No e-mail queries. Considers simultaneous queries. Responds in 1 month to queries. Returns materials only with SASE. Obtains most new clients through recommendations from others.

Recent Sales Clients include Fiction: William Lashner, Nani Power, DW Buffa, Howard Bahr, Suzanne Chazin, Sarah Stonich, Ad Hudler, Mary Sharratt, Libby Street, Heather Estay, Darri Stephens, Megan Desales; Nonfic- tion: Rabbi Mark Borovitz, Alan Eisenstock, Esther Perel, Clifton Leaf, Maggie Estep, Greg Baer, Martin Fried- man, Lundy Bancroft, Alvin Ailey Dance, Lise Friedman, Liz Landers, Vicky Mainzer.

Terms Agent receives 15% commission on domestic sales; 20% commission on foreign sales. Offers written contract.

◖ STEELE-PERKINS LITERARY AGENCY

26 Island Lane, Canandaigua NY 14424. (585)396-9290. Fax: (585)396-3579. E-mail: pattiesp@aol.com. **Con- tact:** Pattie Steele-Perkins. Member of AAR, RWA. Currently handles: 100% romance and mainstream women's fiction.

Represents Novels. **Considers these fiction areas:** Mainstream/contemporary; multicultural; romance (inspira- tional); women's.

O→ Actively seeking inspirational, romance, women's fiction, and multicultural works.

How to Contact Submit outline, 3 sample chapters, SASE. Considers simultaneous queries. Responds in 6 weeks to queries. Returns materials only with SASE. Obtains most new clients through recommendations from others, queries/solicitations.

Recent Sales This agency prefers not to share information on specific sales.

Terms Agent receives 15% commission on domestic sales. Offers written contract, binding for 1 year; 1-month notice must be given to terminate contract.

Writers' Conferences National Conference of Romance Writers of America; BookExpo America Writers' Confer- ences; CBA; Romance Slam Jam.

Tips ''Be patient. E-mail rather than call. Make sure what you are sending is the best it can be.''

Ⓝ ◻ MARY M. TAHAN LITERARY, LLC

P.O. Box 1060 Gracie Station, New York NY 10028. E-mail: query.mary.tahan@earthlink.net. **Contact:** Mary M. Tahan. Member of AAR, Authors Guild.

Member Agents Mary M. Tahan and Jena H. Anderson.

Represents Nonfiction books, novels. **Considers these nonfiction areas:** Biography/autobiography; cooking/ foods/nutrition; health/medicine; history; how-to; memoirs; money/finance; psychology; writing books; fash- ion/beauty/style; relationships; also rights for books optioned for TV movies and feature films.

How to Contact Send via regular mail or e-mail. For nonfiction, query or proposal package and outline with SASE. For fiction, brief (1-2 pages single-spaced) synopsis, first 3 chapters with SASE. Responds in 4 weeks to queries. Returns materials only with SASE.

Recent Sales *The Siren of Solace Glen*, by Susan S. James (Berkley); *Finding the Right Words for the Holidays*, by J. Beverly Daniels (Pocket); *The Stinking Rose Restaurant Cookbook*, by Andrea Froncillo with Jennifer Jeffrey (Ten Speed Press).

Tips ''For nonfiction, it's crucial to research how to write a proposal, especially how to analyze your book's competing titles. For both fiction and nonfiction, do not send a full manuscript. Please do not phone or fax queries.''

◖ WALES LITERARY AGENCY, INC.

P.O. Box 9428, Seattle WA 98109-0428. (206)284-7114. E-mail: waleslit@waleslit.com. Website: www.waleslit. com. **Contact:** Elizabeth Wales, Josie di Bernardo. Estab. 1988. Member of AAR, Book Publishers' Northwest, Pacific Northwest Booksellers Association, PEN. Represents 65 clients. 10% of clients are new/unpublished writers. Currently handles: 60% nonfiction books; 40% fiction.

• Prior to becoming an agent, Ms. Wales worked at Oxford University Press and Viking Penguin.

Member Agents Elizabeth Wales, Adrienne Reed.

☞ This agency specializes in narrative nonfiction and quality mainstream and literary fiction. Does not handle screenplays, children's literature, genre fiction or most category nonfiction.

How to Contact Query with cover letter, writing sample (approx. 30 pages), and SASE. No phone or fax queries. Prefers regular mail queries, but accepts 1-page e-mail queries with no attachments. Considers simultaneous queries. Responds in 3 weeks to queries; 6 weeks to mss. Returns materials only with SASE.

Recent Sales *Breaking Ranks*, by Norman H. Stamper (Nation Books); *Birds of Central Park*, photographs by Cal Vornberger (Abrams); *Against Gravity*, by Farnoosh Moshiri (Penguin).

Terms Agent receives 15% commission on domestic sales; 20% commission on foreign sales.

Writers' Conferences Pacific NW Writers Conference (Seattle); Writers at Work (Salt Lake City); Writing Rendezvous (Anchorage); Willamette Writers (Portland).

Tips "Especially interested in work that espouses a progressive cultural or political view, projects a new voice, or simply shares an important, compelling story. Encourages writers living in the Pacific Northwest, West Coast, Alaska, and Pacific Rim countries, and writers from historically underrepresented groups, such as gay and lesbian writers and writers of color, to submit work (but does not discourage writers outside these areas). Most importantly, whether in fiction or nonfiction, the agency is looking for talented storytellers."

⬛ ☑ TED WEINSTEIN LITERARY MANAGEMENT

35 Stillman St., Suite 203, San Francisco CA 94107. Website: www.twliterary.com. **Contact:** Ted Weinstein. Estab. 2001. Member of AAR. Represents 50 clients. 75% of clients are new/unpublished writers. Currently handles: 100% nonfiction books.

Represents Nonfiction books. **Considers these nonfiction areas:** Biography/autobiography; business/economics; current affairs; government/politics/law; health/medicine; history; popular culture; science/technology; self-help/personal improvement; travel; environment, lifestyle.

How to Contact Accepts e-mail or paper submissions with SASE. Please visit website for detailed submission guidelines before submitting. Considers simultaneous queries. Responds in 3 weeks to queries.

Terms Agent receives 15% commission on domestic sales; 20-30% commission on foreign sales. Offers written contract, binding for 1 year. Charges clients for photocopying and express shipping.

☑ LYNN WHITTAKER, LITERARY AGENT

Graybill & English, LLC, 1875 Connecticut Ave. NW, Suite 712, Washington DC 20009. (202)588-9798, ext. 127. Fax: (202)457-0662. E-mail: lynnwhittaker@aol.com. Website: www.graybillandenglish.com. **Contact:** Lynn Whittaker. Estab. 1998. Member of AAR. Represents 24 clients. 10% of clients are new/unpublished writers. Currently handles: 80% nonfiction books; 20% novels.

• Prior to becoming an agent, Ms. Whittaker was an editor, owner of a small press, and taught at the college level.

Represents Nonfiction books, novels. **Considers these nonfiction areas:** Animals; biography/autobiography; current affairs; ethnic/cultural interests; health/medicine; history; memoirs; money/finance; multicultural; nature/environment; popular culture; science/technology; sports; women's issues/studies. **Considers these fiction areas:** Detective/police/crime; ethnic; historical; literary; multicultural; mystery/suspense; sports.

☞ "As a former editor, I especially enjoy working closely with writers to polish their proposals and manuscripts." Actively seeking literary fiction, sports, history, mystery/suspense. Does not want to receive romance/women's commercial fiction, children's/young adult, religious, fantasy/horror.

How to Contact Query with SASE. Responds in 2 weeks to queries; 1 month to mss. Returns materials only with SASE. Obtains most new clients through recommendations from others.

Terms Agent receives 15% commission on domestic sales; 20% commission on foreign sales. Offers written contract; 1-month notice must be given to terminate contract. Direct expenses for photocopying of proposals and mss, UPS/FedEx.

☑ WRITERS HOUSE

21 W. 26th St., New York NY 10010. (212)685-2400. Fax: (212)685-1781. Estab. 1974. Member of AAR. Represents 440 clients. 50% of clients are new/unpublished writers. Currently handles: 25% nonfiction books; 40% novels; 35% juvenile books.

Member Agents Albert Zuckerman (major novels, thrillers, women's fiction, important nonfiction); Amy Berkower (major juvenile authors, women's fiction, art and decorating, psychology); Merrilee Heifetz (quality children's fiction, science fiction and fantasy, popular culture, literary fiction); Susan Cohen (juvenile and YA fiction and nonfiction, Judaism, women's issues); Susan Ginsburg (serious and popular fiction, true crime, narrative nonfiction, personality books, cookbooks); Michele Rubin (serious nonfiction); Robin Rue (commercial fiction and nonfiction, YA fiction); Jennifer Lyons (literary, commercial fiction, international fiction, nonfiction, illustrated); Jodi Reamer (juvenile and YA fiction and nonfiction, adult commercial fiction, popular culture); Simon Lipskar (literary and commercial fiction, narrative nonfiction); Nicole Pitesa (juvenile and YA fiction, literary fiction); Steven Malk (juvenile and YA fiction and nonfiction).

Represents Nonfiction books, novels, juvenile books. **Considers these nonfiction areas:** Animals; art/architecture/design; biography/autobiography; business/economics; child guidance/parenting; cooking/foods/nutrition; health/medicine; history; interior design/decorating; juvenile nonfiction; military/war; money/finance; music/dance; nature/environment; psychology; science/technology; self-help/personal improvement; theater/film; true crime/investigative; women's issues/studies. **Considers these fiction areas:** Action/adventure; contemporary issues; detective/police/crime; erotica; ethnic; family saga; fantasy; feminist; gay/lesbian; gothic; hi-lo; historical; horror; humor/satire; juvenile; literary; mainstream/contemporary; military/war; multicultural; mystery/suspense; New Age; occult; picture books; psychic/supernatural; regional; romance; science fiction; short story collections; spiritual; sports; thriller; translation; westerns/frontier; young adult; women's; cartoon.

    ○┐ This agency specializes in all types of popular fiction and nonfiction. Does not want to receive scholarly, professional, poetry, plays, or screenplays.

How to Contact Query with SASE. No e-mail or fax queries. Responds in 1 month to queries. Obtains most new clients through recommendations from others.

Recent Sales Sold 200-300 titles in the last year. *Moneyball*, by Michael Lewis (Norton); *Cut and Run*, by Ridley Pearson (Hyperion); *Report from Ground Zero*, by Dennis Smith (Viking). Other clients include Francine Pascal, Ken Follett, Stephen Hawking, Linda Howard, F. Paul Wilson, Neil Gaiman, Laurel Hamilton, V.C. Andrews, Lisa Jackson, Michael Fruber, Chris Paolini, Barbara Delinsky, Ann Martin.

Terms Agent receives 15% commission on domestic sales; 20% commission on foreign sales. Offers written contract, binding for 1 year. Agency charges fees for copying mss and proposals, and overseas airmail of books.

Tips "Do not send manuscripts. Write a compelling letter. If you do, we'll ask to see your work."

☑ SUSAN ZECKENDORF ASSOC., INC.

171 W. 57th St., New York NY 10019. (212)245-2928. **Contact:** Susan Zeckendorf. Estab. 1979. Member of AAR. Represents 15 clients. 25% of clients are new/unpublished writers. Currently handles: 50% nonfiction books; 50% novels.

    ● Prior to opening her agency, Ms. Zeckendorf was a counseling psychologist.

Represents Nonfiction books, novels. **Considers these nonfiction areas:** Biography/autobiography; child guidance/parenting; health/medicine; history; music/dance; psychology; science/technology; sociology; women's issues/studies. **Considers these fiction areas:** Detective/police/crime; ethnic; historical; literary; mainstream/contemporary; mystery/suspense; thriller.

    ○┐ Actively seeking mysteries, literary fiction, mainstream fiction, thrillers, social history, parenting, classical music, biography. Does not want to receive science fiction, romance. "No children's books."

How to Contact Query with SASE. No e-mail or fax queries. Considers simultaneous queries. Responds in 10 days to queries; 3 weeks to mss. Returns materials only with SASE.

Recent Sales *How to Write a Damn Good Mystery*, by James N. Frey (St. Martin's); *Moment of Madness*, by Una-Mary Parker (Headline); *The Handscrabble Chronicles* (Berkley).

Terms Agent receives 15% commission on domestic sales; 20% commission on foreign sales. Charges for photocopying, messenger services.

Writers' Conferences Central Valley Writers Conference; The Tucson Publishers Association Conference; Writer's Connection; Frontiers in Writing Conference (Amarillo TX); Golden Triangle Writers Conference (Beaumont TX); Oklahoma Festival of Books (Claremont OK); SMU Writers Conference (NYC).

Tips "We are a small agency giving lots of individual attention. We respond quickly to submissions."

Book Publishers

The markets in this year's Book Publishers section offer opportunities in nearly every area of publishing. Large, commercial houses are here, as are their smaller counterparts.

The **Book Publishers Subject Index** on page 1054 is the best place to start your search. You'll find it in the back of the book, before the General Index. Subject areas for both fiction and nonfiction are broken out for all of the book publisher listings, including Canadian and international publishers and small presses.

When you have compiled a list of publishers interested in books in your subject area, read the detailed listings. Pare down your list by cross-referencing two or three subject areas and eliminating the listings only marginally suited to your book. When you have a good list, send for those publishers' catalogs and manuscript guidelines, or check publishers' websites, which often contain catalog listings, manuscript preparation guidelines, current contact names, and other information helpful to prospective authors. You want to use this information to make sure your book idea is in line with a publisher's list, but is not a duplicate of something already published.

You should also visit bookstores and libraries to see if the publisher's books are well represented. When you find a couple of books the house has published that are similar to yours, write or call the company to find out who edited those books. This extra bit of research could be the key to sending your proposal to precisely the right editor.

Publishers prefer different methods of submission on first contact. Most like to see a one-page query with SASE, especially for nonfiction. Others will accept a brief proposal package that might include an outline and/or a sample chapter. Some publishers will accept submissions from agents only. Each listing in the Book Publishers section includes specific submission methods, if provided by the publisher. Make sure you read each listing carefully to find out exactly what the publisher wants to receive.

When you write your one-page query, give an overview of your book, mention the intended audience, the competition for your book (check local bookstore shelves), and what sets your book apart from the competition. You should also include any previous publishing experience or special training relevant to the subject of your book.

Personalize your query by addressing the editor individually and mentioning what you know about the company from its catalog or books. Never send a form letter as a query. Envelopes addressed to "Editor" or "Editorial Department" end up in the dreaded slush pile. Under the heading **Acquisitions**, we list the names of editors who acquire new books for each company, along with the editors' specific areas of expertise. Try your best to send your query to the appropriate editor. Editors move around all the time, so it's in your best interest to look online or call the publishing house to make sure the editor to which you are addressing your query is still employed by that publisher.

Author-subsidy publishers' not included

Writer's Market is a reference tool to help you sell your writing, and we encourage you to work with publishers that pay a royalty. Subsidy publishing involves paying money to a publishing house to publish a book. The source of the money could be a government, foundation, or university grant, or it could be the author of the book. If one of the publishers listed in this book offers you an author-subsidy arrangement (sometimes called "cooperative publishing," "co-publishing," or "joint venture"); asks you to pay for part or all of the cost of any aspect of publishing (editing services, manuscript critiques, printing, advertising, etc.); or asks you to guarantee the purchase of any number of the books yourself, we would like you to inform us of that company immediately.

INFORMATION AT-A-GLANCE

There are a number of icons at the beginning of each listing that quickly convey certain information. In the Book Publisher sections, these icons identify new listings (**N**), Canadian markets (**✿**), publishers located outside of the U.S. and Canada (**⊕**), publishers that accept agented submissions only (**A**), and publishers who do not accept unsolicited manuscripts (**⊘**). Different sections of *Writer's Market* include other symbols; check the inside back cover for an explanation of all the symbols used throughout the book.

How much money? What are my odds?

We've also highlighted important information in boldface—the "quick facts" you won't find in any other market guide but should know before you submit your work. These items include: how many manuscripts a publisher buys per year; how many manuscripts from first-time authors; how many manuscripts from unagented writers; the royalty rate a publisher pays; and how large an advance is offered. Standard royalty rates for paperbacks generally range from $7\frac{1}{2}$ to $12\frac{1}{2}$ percent, and from 10 to 15 percent for hardcovers. Royalty rates for children's books are often lower, generally ranging from 5 to 10 percent; 10 percent for picture books (split between the author and the illustrator).

Publishers, their imprints, and how they are related

In this era of big publishing—and big mergers—the world of publishing has grown even more intertwined. A "family tree" on page 87 lists the imprints and divisions of the largest conglomerate publishers.

Keep in mind that most of the major publishers listed in this family tree do not accept unagented submissions or unsolicited manuscripts. You will find many of these publishers and their imprints listed within the Book Publishers section, and many contain only basic contact information. If you are interested in pursuing any of these publishers, we advise you to see each publisher's website for more information.

For a list of publishers according to their subjects of interest, see the Nonfiction and Fiction sections of the Book Publishers Subject Index. Information on book publishers listed in the previous edition of *Writer's Market*, but not included in this edition, can be found in the General Index.

⊘ ABDO PUBLISHING CO.

4940 Viking Dr., Suite 622, Edina MN 55435. (800)800-1312. Fax: (952)831-1632. E-mail: info@abdopub.com. Website: www.abdopub.com. **Acquisitions:** Paul Abdo, editor-in-chief. Estab. 1985. Publishes hardcover originals. **Publishes 300 titles/year.**

Imprints ABDO & Daughters; Buddy Books; Checkerboard Library; SandCastle.

- *No unsolicited mss.*
- ⚬⟆ ABDO publishes nonfiction children's books (pre-kindergarten to 8th grade) for school and public libraries—mainly history, sports, biography, geography, science, and social studies.

Nonfiction Biography, children's/juvenile, how-to. Subjects include animals, history, science, sports, geography, social studies. Query with SASE. Submit résumé to pabdo@abdopub.com.

Recent Title(s) *Lewis and Clark*, by John Hamilton (children's nonfiction); *Tiger Woods*, by Paul Joseph (children's biography).

ABI PROFESSIONAL PUBLICATIONS

P.O. Box 149, St. Petersburg FL 33731. (727)556-0950. Fax: (727)556-2560. E-mail: abipropub@vandamere.com. Website: www.abipropub.com. **Acquisitions:** Art Brown, publisher/editor-in-chief (prosthetics, rehabilitation, dental/medical research). Publishes hardcover and trade paperback originals. **Publishes 10 titles/year. Receives 20-30 queries and 5-10 mss/year. 25% of books from first-time authors; 100% from unagented writers. Pays royalty on revenues generated. Offers small advance.** Publishes book 1+ years after acceptance of ms. Accepts simultaneous submissions. Responds in 6 months to queries.

- No registered, certified, return-receipt submissions accepted.

Nonfiction Reference, technical, textbook. Subjects include health/medicine. Submit proposal package including outline, representative sample chapter(s), author bio, or submit complete ms. Reviews artwork/photos as part of ms package. Send photocopies.

Recent Title(s) *Cleft Palate Dentistry*, by Robert McKinstry (dental text); *Managing Stroke*, by Paul R. Rao and John E. Toerge (rehabilitation).

Tips Audience is allied health professionals, dentists, researchers, patients undergoing physical rehabilitation. "We will not review electronic submissions."

ABINGDON PRESS

Imprint of The United Methodist Publishing House, 201 Eighth Ave. S., Nashville TN 37203. (615)749-6000. Fax: (615)749-6512. Website: www.abingdonpress.com. President/Publisher: Neil M. Alexander. Senior Vice President/Publishing: Harriett Jane Olson. **Acquisitions:** Robert Ratcliff, senior editor (professional clergy and academic); Marj Pon (children's); Ron Kidd, senior editor (general interest). Estab. 1789. Publishes hardcover and paperback originals; church supplies. **Publishes 120 titles/year. Receives 3,000 queries and 250 mss/year. Small% of books from first-time authors; 85% from unagented writers. Pays 7½% royalty on retail price.** Publishes book 2 years after acceptance of ms. Does not accept simultaneous submissions. Responds in 2 months to queries. Book catalog free; ms guidelines online.

Imprints Dimensions for Living; Cokesbury; Abingdon Press.

- ⚬⟆ Abingdon Press, America's oldest theological publisher, provides an ecumenical publishing program dedicated to serving the Christian community—clergy, scholars, church leaders, musicians, and general readers—with quality resources in the areas of Bible study, the practice of ministry, theology, devotion, spirituality, inspiration, prayer, music and worship, reference, Christian education, and church supplies.

Nonfiction Children's/juvenile, gift book, reference, textbook, religious-lay, and professional, scholarly. Subjects include education, religion, theology. Query with outline and samples only.

Recent Title(s) *Making Love Last a Lifetime*, by Hamilton; *Global Bible Commentary*, edited by Patte; *God and the World in the Old Testament*, by Fretheim.

HARRY N. ABRAMS, INC.

Subsidiary of La Martiniere Groupe, 100 Fifth Ave., New York NY 10011. (212)206-7715. Fax: (212)645-8437. E-mail: submissions@abramsbooks.com. Website: www.abramsbooks.com. **Acquisitions:** Managing Editor. Estab. 1949. Publishes hardcover and "a few" paperback originals. **Publishes 250 titles/year.** Does not accept simultaneous submissions. Responds in 6 months. Only responds if interested.

Imprints Stewart; Tabori & Chang; Abrams Books for Young Readers; Abrams Gifts & Stationery.

- ⚬⟆ "We publish *only* high-quality illustrated art books, i.e., art, art history, museum exhibition catalogs, written by specialists and scholars in the field."

Nonfiction Illustrated book. Subjects include art/architecture, nature/environment, recreation (outdoor). Requires illustrated material for art and art history, museums. Submit queries, proposals, and mss via mail with SASE. No e-mail submissions. Reviews artwork/photos as part of ms package.

Recent Title(s) *1001 Reasons to Love Horses*, by Sheri Seggerman and Mary Tiegreen; *About NYC*, by Joanne Dugan; *Mother Teresa: A Life of Dedication*, by Raghu Rai.

Tips "We are one of the few publishers who publish almost exclusively illustrated books. We consider ourselves the leading publishers of art books and high-quality artwork in the U.S. Once the author has signed a contract to write a book for our firm the author must finish the manuscript to agreed-upon high standards within the schedule agreed upon in the contract."

ABSEY & CO.

23011 Northcrest Dr., Spring TX 77389. (281)257-2340. Fax: (281)251-4676. E-mail: abseyandco@aol.com. Website: www.absey.com. **Acquisitions:** Edward Wilson, editor-in-chief. New York Offices: 45 W. 21st St., Suite 5A, New York NY 10010. Publishes hardcover, trade paperback, and mass market paperback originals. **Publishes 6-10 titles/year. 50% of books from first-time authors; 50% from unagented writers. Royalty and advance vary.** Publishes book 1 year after acceptance of ms. Does not accept simultaneous submissions. Responds in 3 months to queries; 9 months to mss. Ms guidelines online.

    ○⇥ "Our goal is to publish original, creative works of literary merit." Currently emphasizing educational, young adult literature. De-emphasizing self-help.

Nonfiction Subjects include education, language/literature (language arts), general nonfiction. "We will not open anything without a return address. All submissions sent without return or insufficient postage are discarded." Query with SASE.

Fiction Juvenile, mainstream/contemporary, short story collections. "Since we are a small, new press, we are looking for book-length manuscripts with a firm intended audience." Query with SASE.

Poetry Publishes the Writers and Young Writers Series. Interested in thematic poetry collections of literary merit. Query.

Recent Title(s) *Saving the Scrolls*, by Mary Kerry; *Where I'm From*, by George Ella Lyon (poetry); *Regular Lu*, by Robin Nelson.

Tips "We work closely and attentively with authors and their work." Does not download mss or accept e-mail submissions.

ACADEMY CHICAGO PUBLISHERS

363 W. Erie St., Suite 7E., Chicago IL 60610-3125. (312)751-7300. Fax: (312)751-7306. E-mail: info@academychicago.com. Website: www.academychicago.com. **Acquisitions:** Anita Miller, editorial director/senior editor. Estab. 1975. Publishes hardcover originals and trade paperback reprints. **Publishes 10 titles/year. Pays 7-10% royalty on wholesale price. Offers modest advance.** Publishes book 18 months after acceptance of ms. Responds in 3 months to queries. Book catalog and ms guidelines online.

    ○⇥ "We publish quality fiction and nonfiction. Our audience is literate and discriminating. No novelized biography, history, or science fiction."

Nonfiction Biography. Subjects include history, travel. No religion or self-help. Submit proposal package including outline, 3 sample chapters, author bio.

Fiction Historical, mainstream/contemporary, military/war, mystery. "We look for quality work, but we do not publish experimental, avant garde novels." Submit proposal package including 3 sample chapters, synopsis.

Recent Title(s) *Sadika's Way*, by Hina Haq; *Alex: The Fathering of a Preemie*, by Jeff Stimpson; *Vinnie Ream: An American Sculptor*, by Ed Cooper.

Tips "At the moment, we are looking for good nonfiction; we certainly want excellent original fiction, but we are swamped. No fax queries, no disks. No electronic submissions. We are always interested in reprinting good out-of-print books."

ACE SCIENCE FICTION AND FANTASY

Imprint of The Berkley Publishing Group, Penguin Group (USA), Inc., 375 Hudson St., New York NY 10014. (212)366-2000. Website: www.penguin.com. **Acquisitions:** Anne Sowards, editor; John Morgan, editor. Estab. 1953. Publishes hardcover, paperback, and trade paperback originals and reprints. **Publishes 75 titles/year. Pays royalty. Offers advance.** Publishes book 1-2 years after acceptance of ms. Does not accept simultaneous submissions. Responds in 2 months to queries; 6 months to mss. Ms guidelines for #10 SASE.

    ○⇥ Ace publishes science fiction and fantasy exclusively.

Fiction Fantasy, science fiction. No other genre accepted. No short stories. Query first with SASE.

Recent Title(s) *Alphabet of Thorn*, by Patricia A. McKillip; *Iron Sunrise*, by Charles Stross.

ACEN PRESS

DNA Press, P.O. Box 572, Eagleville PA 19408. Fax: (501)694-5495. E-mail: dnapress@yahoo.com. Website: www.dnapress.com. **Acquisitions:** Xela Schenk, operations manager. Estab. 1998. Publishes trade paperback originals. **Publishes 10 titles/year; imprint publishes 5 titles/year. Receives 500 queries and 400 mss/year.**

90% of books from first-time authors; 100% from unagented writers. Pays 10-15% royalty. Publishes book 4 months after acceptance of ms. Accepts simultaneous submissions. Responds in 6 weeks to mss. Book catalog and ms guidelines free.

    O→ Book publisher for young adults, children, and adults.

Nonfiction Children's/juvenile (explaining science), how-to. Subjects include education, health/medicine, science, sports, travel. "We publish books for children which teach scientific concepts as part of the general context; or how-to for adults which carry scientific knowledge and contribute to learning." Submit complete ms. Reviews artwork/photos as part of ms package. Send photocopies.

Fiction Juvenile, science fiction, young adult. "All books should be oriented to explaining science even if they do not fall 100% under the category of science fiction." Submit complete ms.

Recent Title(s) *College Knowledge*; *DNA Array Image Analysis*; *The Prometheus Project*.

Tips "Quick response, great relationships, high commission/royalty."

ACTA PUBLICATIONS

4848 N. Clark St., Chicago IL 60640-4711. Fax: (773)271-7399. E-mail: actapublications@aol.com. Website: www.actapublications.com. **Acquisitions:** Gregory F. Augustine Pierce. Estab. 1958. Publishes trade paperback originals. **Publishes 12 titles/year. Receives 100 queries and 25 mss/year. 50% of books from first-time authors; 90% from unagented writers. Pays 10-12% royalty on wholesale price.** Publishes book 1 year after acceptance of ms. Does not accept simultaneous submissions. Responds in 1 month to proposals. Book catalog and ms guidelines for #10 SASE.

    O→ ACTA publishes nonacademic, practical books aimed at the mainline religious market.

Nonfiction Self-help. Subjects include religion, spirituality. Submit outline, 1 sample chapter. Reviews artwork/photos as part of ms package. Send photocopies.

Recent Title(s) *Invitation to Catholicism*, by Alice Camille (religious education); *Protect Us From All Anxiety: Meditations for the Depressed*, by William Burke (self-help).

Tips "Don't send a submission unless you have read our catalog or 1 of our books."

ADAMS MEDIA CORP.

Division of F+W Publications, Inc., 57 Littlefield St., Avon MA 02322. (508)427-7100. Fax: (800)872-5628. E-mail: submissions@adamsmedia.com. Website: www.adamsmedia.com. **Acquisitions:** Gary M. Krebs, publishing director; Paula Munier, director of product development; Jill Alexander, senior editor; Danielle Chiotti, editor; Kate Epstein, project editor. Estab. 1980. Publishes hardcover originals, trade paperback originals and reprints. **Publishes 200 titles/year. Receives 5,000 queries and 1,500 mss/year. 40% of books from first-time authors; 40% from unagented writers. Pays standard royalty or makes outright purchase. Offers variable advance.** Publishes book 12-18 months after acceptance of ms. Accepts simultaneous submissions. Responds in 3 months to queries. Ms guidelines online.

    O→ Adams Media publishes commercial nonfiction, including self-help, inspiration, women's issues, pop psychology, relationships, business, parenting, New Age, gift books, cookbooks, how-to, reference. Does not return unsolicited materials. Does not accept electronic submissions.

Recent Title(s) *Tao of Poker*; *Wabi Sabi Simple*; *Pregnancy Sucks for Men*.

ADAMS-BLAKE PUBLISHING

8041 Sierra St., Fair Oaks CA 95628. (916)962-9296. Website: www.adams-blake.com. Vice President: Paul Raymond. **Acquisitions:** Monica Blane, senior editor. Estab. 1992. Publishes trade paperback originals and reprints. **Publishes 10-15 titles/year. Receives 150 queries and 90 mss/year. 90% of books from first-time authors; 90% from unagented writers. Pays 10% royalty on wholesale price.** Publishes book 6 months after acceptance of ms. Accepts simultaneous submissions. Responds in 3 months to mss. Ms guidelines online.

    O→ Adams-Blake Publishing is looking for business, technology, and finance titles, as well as data that can be bound/packaged and sold to specific industry groups at high margins. "We publish technical and training material we can sell to the corporate market. We are especially looking for 'high ticket' items that sell to the corporate market for prices between $100-300." Currently emphasizing technical, computers, technology. De-emphasizing business, management.

Nonfiction How-to, technical. Subjects include business/economics, computers/electronic, health/medicine, money/finance, software. Query with sample chapters or complete ms. Reviews artwork/photos as part of ms package. Send photocopies.

Recent Title(s) *Computer Money*, by Alan N. Canton; *Success From Home! The Word Processing Business*, by Diana Ennen.

Tips "We will take a chance on material the big houses reject. Since we sell the majority of our material directly, we can publish material for a very select market. This year we seek niche market material that we can Docutech and sell direct to the corporate sector. Author should include a marketing plan. Sell us on the project!"

ADIRONDACK MOUNTAIN CLUB, INC.

814 Goggins Rd., Lake George NY 12845-4117. (518)668-4447. Fax: (518)668-3746. E-mail: pubs@adk.org. Website: www.adk.org. **Acquisitions:** John Kettlewell, editor (all titles); Neal Burdick, editor (*Adirondac* magazine, published bimonthly). Publishes hardcover and trade paperback originals and reprints. **Publishes 34 titles/year. Receives 36 queries and 12 mss/year. 95% of books from first-time authors; 95% from unagented writers. Pays 6-10% royalty on retail price. Offers $250-1,000 advance.** Publishes book 1-3 years after acceptance of ms. Does not accept simultaneous submissions. Responds in 3 months to queries; 4 months to proposals and mss. Book catalog free and online; ms guidelines free.

> O┓ "Our main focus is recreational guides to the Adirondack and Catskill Parks; however, our titles continue to include natural, cultural, and literary histories of these regions. Our main interest is in protecting the resource through environmental education. This is the focus of our magazine, *Adirondac*, as well."

Nonfiction Reference. Subjects include nature/environment, recreation, regional, sports, travel, trail maps. Query with SASE, or submit proposal package including outline, 1-2 sample chapters, with proposed illustrations and visuals. Reviews artwork/photos as part of ms package. Send photocopies.

Recent Title(s) *Canoe and Kayak Guide: East-Central New York State*; *Catskill Day Hikes for All Seasons*.

Tips "Our audience consists of outdoors people interested in muscle-powered recreation, natural history, and 'armchair traveling' in the Adirondacks and Catskills. Bear in mind the educational mandate implicit in our organization's mission. Note range of current ADK titles."

AERONAUTICAL PUBLISHERS

1 Oakglade Circle, Hummelstown PA 17036-9525. (717)566-0468. Fax: (717)566-6423. E-mail: possibilitypress@ aol.com. Website: www.aeronauticalpublishers.com. **Acquisitions:** Mike Markowski, publisher; Marjie Markowski, editor-in-chief. Estab. 1981. Publishes trade paperback originals. **Pays variable royalty.** Responds in 2 months to queries. Ms guidelines online.

Imprints American Aeronautical Archives; Aviation Publishers.

> O┓ "Our mission is to help people learn more about aviation and model aviation through the written word."

Nonfiction How-to, technical, general. Subjects include history (aviation), hobbies, recreation, radio control, free flight, indoor models, micro radio control, homebuilt aircraft, ultralights, and hang gliders. Prefers submission by mail. Include SASE.

Recent Title(s) *Flying Models*, by Don Ross; *Those Magnificent Fast Flying Machines*, by C.B. Hayward.

Tips "Our focus is on books of short to medium length that will serve the emerging needs of the hobby. We also want to help youth get started, while enhancing everyone's enjoyment of the hobby. We are looking for authors that are passionate about the hobby, and will champion the messages of their books."

AKTRIN FURNITURE INFORMATION CENTER

164 S. Main St., P.O. Box 898, High Point NC 27261. (336)841-8535. Fax: (336)841-5435. E-mail: aktrin@aktrin.c om. Website: www.furniture-info.com. **Acquisitions:** Donna Fincher, director of operations. Estab. 1985. Publishes trade paperback originals. **Publishes 8 titles/year. Receives 5 queries/year. 20% of books from first-time authors; 20% from unagented writers. Makes outright purchase of $1,500 minimum. Offers $300-600 advance.** Publishes book 2 months after acceptance of ms. Accepts simultaneous submissions. Responds in 1 month to queries. Book catalog free.

Imprints AKTRIN Furniture Information Center-Canada (151 Randall St., Oakville ON L6J 1P5 Canada. (905)845-3474. Contact: Stefan Wille).

> O┓ AKTRIN is a full-service organization dedicated to the furniture industry. "Our focus is on determining trends, challenges, and opportunities, while also identifying problems and weak spots." Currently emphasizing the wood industry.

Nonfiction Reference. Subjects include business/economics. "We are writing only about the furniture industry. Have an understanding of business/economics." Query.

Recent Title(s) *The American Demand for Household Furniture and Trends*, by Thomas McCormick (in-depth analysis of American household furniture market).

Tips Audience is executives of furniture companies (manufacturers and retailers), and suppliers and consultants to the furniture industry.

ALASKA NORTHWEST BOOKS

Graphic Arts Center Publishing, P.O. Box 10306, Portland OR 97296-0306. (503)226-2402. Fax: (503)223-1410. Website: www.gacpc.com. **Acquisitions:** Tricia Brown. Estab. 1959. Publishes hardcover and trade paperback originals and reprints. **Publishes 12 titles/year. 10% of books from first-time authors; 90% from unagented writers. Pays 10-14% royalty on net revenues. Buys mss outright (rarely). Offers advance.** Publishes book an average of 2 years after acceptance of ms. Accepts simultaneous submissions. Responds in 6 months to queries. Book catalog for 9×12 SAE with 6 first-class stamps; ms guidelines online.

Nonfiction Children's/juvenile, cookbook. Subjects include nature/environment, recreation, sports, travel, Native American culture, adventure, the arts. "All written for a general readership, not for experts in the subject." Submit outline, sample chapter(s).

Recent Title(s) *The Winterlake Lodge Cookbook: Culinary Adventures in the Wilderness*; *Portrait of the Alaska Railroad*; *Big-Enough Anna: The Little Sled Dog Who Braved the Arctic* (children's book).

Tips "Book proposals that are professionally written and polished with a clear understanding of the market, receive our most careful consideration. We are looking for originality. We publish a wide range of books for a wide audience. Some of our books are clearly for travelers, others for those interested in outdoor recreation or various regional subjects. If I were a writer trying to market a book today, I would research the competition (existing books) for what I have in mind, and clearly (and concisely) express why my idea is different and better. I would describe the book buyers (and readers)—where they are, how many of them are there, how they can be reached (organizations, publications), why they would want or need my book."

ALEXANDER BOOKS

Imprint of Creativity, Inc., 65 Macedonia Rd., Alexander NC 28701. (828)252-9515. Fax: (828)255-8719. E-mail: pat@abooks.com. Website: www.abooks.com. **Acquisitions:** Editor. Publishes hardcover originals, and trade paperback originals and reprints. **Pays royalty on net receipts.** Book catalog and ms guidelines online.

Imprints Farthest Star (science fiction from established professionals only); Mountain Church (Christian books from a mainly Protestant viewpoint); Blue/Gray Books (American Civil War); Elephant Books (cookbooks, books about elephants); Worldcomm (genealogical reference, how-to of all types); Land of the Sky (books about Asheville, North Carolina and the surrounding Southern Mountains).

- No e-mail or phone submissions.
- ⚬ Alexander Books publishes mostly nonfiction national titles, both new and reprints.

Nonfiction Biography, how-to, reference, self-help. Subjects include computers/electronic, government/politics, history, regional, religion, travel, collectibles. "We are interested in large, niche markets." Query, or submit 3 sample chapters and proposal package, including marketing plans with SASE. Reviews artwork/photos as part of ms package. Send photocopies.

Fiction "Unless you are a big name, do not submit." Query with SASE, or submit 3 sample chapters, synopsis.

Recent Title(s) *Sanders Price Guide to Autographs, 5th Ed.*, by Sanders and Roberts; *Birthright*, by Mike Resnick.

Tips "Send well-proofed manuscripts in final form. We will not read first rough drafts. Know your market."

ALGONQUIN BOOKS OF CHAPEL HILL

Workman Publishing, P.O. Box 2225, Chapel Hill NC 27515-2225. (919)967-0108. Website: www.algonquin.com. **Acquisitions:** Editorial Department. Publishes hardcover originals. **Publishes 24 titles/year.** query by mail before submitting work. No phone, e-mail or fax queries or submissions. Visit our website for full submission policy to queries. Ms guidelines online.

- ⚬ Algonquin Books publishes quality literary fiction and literary nonfiction.

ALGORA PUBLISHING

222 Riverside Dr., 16th Floor, New York NY 10025-6809. (212)678-0232. Fax: (212)666-3682. E-mail: editors@algora.com. Website: www.algora.com. **Acquisitions:** Martin DeMers, editor (sociology/philosophy/economics); Claudiu A. Secara, publisher (philosophy/international affairs). Publishes hardcover and trade paperback originals and reprints. **Publishes 25 titles/year. Receives 1,500 queries and 800 mss/year. 20% of books from first-time authors; 85% from unagented writers. Pays 7-12% royalty on net receipts. Offers $0-1,000 advance.** Publishes book 10-18 months after acceptance of ms. Accepts simultaneous submissions. Responds in 1-2 months to queries and proposals; 2-3 months to mss. Book catalog and ms guidelines online.

- ⚬ Algora Publishing is an academic-type press, focusing on works by North and South American, European, Asian, and African authors for the educated general reader.

Nonfiction General nonfiction for the educated reader. Subjects include anthropology/archeology, creative nonfiction, education, government/politics, history, language/literature, military/war, money/finance, music/dance, nature/environment, philosophy, psychology, religion, science, sociology, translation, women's issues/studies, economics. Query by e-mail (preferred) or submit proposal package including outline, 3 sample chapters or complete ms.

Recent Title(s) *Washington Diplomacy*, by John Shaw (international politics); *The Case for the Living Wage*, by Jerold Waltman (political economy); *Electoral Laws and Their Political Consequences*, by Bernard Grofman and Arend Lijphart (political science).

Tips "We welcome first-time writers; we help craft an author's raw manuscript into a literary work."

ALLWORTH PRESS

10 E. 23rd St., Suite 510, New York NY 10010-4402. Fax: (212)777-8261. E-mail: pub@allworth.com. Website: www.allworth.com. Publisher: Tad Crawford. **Acquisitions:** Nicole Potter, senior editor. Estab. 1989. Publishes hardcover and trade paperback originals. **Publishes 36-40 titles/year. Offers advance.** Does not accept simultaneous submissions. Responds in 1 month to queries and proposals. Book catalog and ms guidelines free and online.

 ⚬⚬ Allworth Press publishes business and self-help information for artists, designers, photographers, authors and film and performing artists, as well as books about business, money and the law for the general public. The press also publishes the best of classic and contemporary writing in art and graphic design. Currently emphasizing photography, graphic & industrial design, performing arts, fine arts and crafts, et al.

Nonfiction How-to, reference. Subjects include art/architecture, business/economics, film/cinema/stage, music/dance, photography, film, television, graphic design, performing arts, writing, as well as business and legal guides for the public. Query.

Recent Title(s) *Business & Legal Forms for Authors and Self-Publishers, 3rd Ed.*, by Tad Crawford; *The Radio Producer's Handbook*, by Rick Kaempfer and John Swanson; *Power Speaking: The Art of the Exceptional Public Speaker*, by Achim Nowak.

Tips "We are trying to give ordinary people advice to better themselves in practical ways—as well as helping creative people in the fine and commercial arts."

ALPINE PUBLICATIONS

225 S. Madison Ave., Loveland CO 80537. (970)667-9317. Fax: (970)667-9157. E-mail: alpinepubl@aol.com. Website: alpinepub.com. **Acquisitions:** Ms. B.J. McKinney, publisher. Estab. 1975. Publishes hardcover and trade paperback originals and reprints. **Publishes 6-10 titles/year. 40% of books from first-time authors; 95% from unagented writers. Pays 8-15% royalty on wholesale price. Offers advance.** Publishes book 18 months after acceptance of ms. Accepts simultaneous submissions. Responds in 1-3 months to queries; 1 month to proposals and mss. Book catalog free; ms guidelines online.

Imprints Blue Ribbon Books.

Nonfiction How-to, illustrated book, reference. Subjects include animals. "Alpine specializes in books that promote the enjoyment of and responsibility for companion animals with emphasis on dogs and horses." Reviews artwork/photos as part of ms package. Send photocopies.

Recent Title(s) *New Secrets of Successful Show Dog Handling*, by Peter Green and Mario Migliorini (dog); *Training for Trail Horse Classes*, by Laurie Truskauskas (horse); *The Japanese Chin*, by Elisabeth Legl (dogs).

Tips "Our audience is pet owners, breeders, exhibitors, veterinarians, animal trainers, animal care specialists, and judges. Look up some of our titles before you submit. See what is unique about our books. Write your proposal to suit our guidelines."

Ⓝ ALTHOS PUBLISHING

404 Wake Chapel Rd., Fuquay-Varina NC 27526-1936. (919)557-2260. Fax: (919)557-2261. E-mail: info@althos.com. Website: www.althos.com. Publisher: Lawrence Harte. **Acquisitions:** Karen Bunn. Publishes hardcover and trade paperback originals. **Publishes 50 titles/year. Receives 200 queries/year. Pays 10% royalty on sales.** Publishes book 1-3 months after acceptance of ms. Responds in 3 months to proposals; 6 months to mss. Book catalog online; ms guidelines free.

 ⚬⚬ Althos publishes books that solve problems, reduce cost, or save time.

Nonfiction Textbook. Subjects include telecommunications. Query with SASE. Reviews artwork/photos as part of ms package. Send photocopies.

AMACOM BOOKS

American Management Association, 1601 Broadway, New York NY 10019-7406. (212)586-8100. Fax: (212)903-8168. Website: www.amanet.org. President and Publisher: Hank Kennedy. **Acquisitions:** Adrienne Hickey, editorial director (management, human resources, leadership, organizational development, strategic planning, public policy, current affairs); Ellen Kadin, senior acquisitions editor (marketing, customer service, careers, manufacturing, communication skills); Jacquie Flynn, executive editor (personal development training, emerging science and technology, self-help, finance); Christina Parisi, acquisitions editor (real estate, project management, sales, supply chain management). Estab. 1923. Publishes hardcover and trade paperback originals, professional books in various formats.

 ⚬⚬ Amacom is the publishing arm of the American Management Association, the world's largest training organization for managers and executives. Amacom publishes books on business issues, strategies, and tasks to enhance organizational and individual effectiveness, as well as self-help books for more personal and professional growth, and books on science, current events, history.

Nonfiction Publishes business books of all types, including management, business strategy, organizational effectiveness, sales, marketing, training, technology applications, finance, career, professional skills for retail, direct mail, college, and corporate markets. Publishes books on public policy, science, current events, history, self-help. Submit sample chapter(s), author bio, brief book description, audience, competition, TOC, SASE.
Recent Title(s) *No! How One Simple Word Can Transform Your Life*, by Jana Kemp; *Hope of Hype: The Obsession With Medical Advances and the High Cost of False Promises*, by Richard A. Deyo, MD and Donald L. Patrick, PhD.

AMADEUS PRESS/LIMELIGHT EDITIONS

(formerly Limelight Editions), 933 Metropolitan Ave., #2L, Brooklyn NY 11211. Phone/Fax: (781)381-0421. E-mail: info@limelighteditions.com. Website: www.limelighteditions.com. **Acquisitions:** John Cerullo, publisher; Carol Flannery, editorial director. Estab. 1983. Publishes hardcover and trade paperback originals, trade paperback reprints. **Publishes 14 titles/year. Receives 150 queries and 40 mss/year. 15% of books from first-time authors; 20% from unagented writers. Pays 7½-10% royalty on retail price. Offers $500-2,000 advance.** Publishes book 10 months after acceptance of ms. Does not accept simultaneous submissions. Responds in 1 month to queries and proposals; 3 months to mss. Book catalog and ms guidelines free.

   O⊷ Limelight Editions publishes books on film, theater, music, and dance history. "Our books make a strong contribution to their fields and deserve to remain in print for many years."

Nonfiction "All books are on the performing arts *exclusively*." Biography, how-to (instructional), humor, illustrated book. Subjects include film/cinema/stage, history, multicultural, music/dance. Query with SASE, or submit proposal package including outline, 2-3 sample chapters. Reviews artwork/photos as part of ms package. Send photocopies.
Recent Title(s) *Film Noir Reader 4*, by Alain Silver and James Ursini; *Lucille Lortel: The Queen of Off Broadway*, by Alexis Greene; *My Dinner of Herbs*, by Efrem Zimbalist, Jr.

AMBASSADOR BOOKS, INC.

91 Prescott St., Worcester MA 01605. (508)756-2893. Fax: (508)757-7055. Website: www.ambassadorbooks.com. **Acquisitions:** Kathryn Conlan, acquisitions editor. Publishes hardcover and trade paperback originals. **Publishes 9 titles/year. Receives 2,000 queries and 100 mss/year. 50% of books from first-time authors; 90% from unagented writers. Pays 8-10% royalty on retail price.** Publishes book 1 year after acceptance of ms. Accepts simultaneous submissions. Responds in 3-4 months to queries. Book catalog free or online.

   O⊷ "We are a Christian publishing company looking for books of intellectual and/or spiritual excellence."

Nonfiction Books with a spiritual theme. Biography, children's/juvenile, illustrated book, self-help. Subjects include creative nonfiction, regional, religion, spirituality, sports, Catholic and Christian books. Query with SASE, or submit complete ms. Reviews artwork/photos as part of ms package. Send photocopies.
Fiction Books with a spiritual/religious theme. Juvenile, literary, picture books, religious, spiritual, sports, young adult, women's. Query with SASE, or submit complete ms.
Recent Title(s) *Spinner McClock and the Christmas Visit*, by Rick Dacey, illustrated by Hallie Gillett; *Survival Notes for Teens: Inspiration for the Emotional Journey*, by Robert Stofel.

AMBER BOOKS PUBLISHING

Imprint of Amber Communications Group, Inc., 1334 E. Chandler Blvd., Suite 5-D67, Phoenix AZ 85048. (480)460-1660. E-mail: amberbk@aol.com. Website: www.amberbooks.com. **Acquisitions:** Tony Rose, publisher. Estab. 1998. Publishes trade paperback and mass market paperback originals. Book catalog free or online.
Imprints Burta Books (celebrity bio); Amber Wiley (personal finance, beauty); Colossus (personalities and history-making topics); Ambrosia (nonfiction, fiction, novels, docu-dramas).

   O⊷ "Amber Books is the nation's largest African-American publisher of self-help and Career Guide books."

Nonfiction Biography (celebrity), children's/juvenile, how-to, self-help, Career Guides. Subjects include fashion/beauty, multicultural, personal finance, relationship advice. Submit proposal or outline with author biography. Please do not e-mail or mail mss unless requested by publisher. Reviews artwork/photos as part of ms package. Send photocopies.
Fiction Historic docudramas. Wants African-American topics and interest. Submit proposal or outline with author biography. Please do not e-mail or mail mss unless requested by publisher. Reviews artwork/photos as part if ms package. Send photocopies.
Recent Title(s) *101 Real Money Questions*, by Jesse B. Brown; *The African-American Women's Guide to Successful Make-Up and Skin Care*, by Alfred Fornay (revised); *The Jennifer Lopez Story*, by Stacy-Deanne.
Tips "The goal of Amber Books is to expand our catalog comprised of self-help books, and celebrity bio books; and expand our fiction department in print and on software, which pertain to, about, and for the African-American population."

AMERICAN BAR ASSOCIATION PUBLISHING

321 N. Clark St., Chicago IL 60610. (312)988-5000. Fax: (312)988-6030. Website: www.ababooks.org. **Acquisitions:** Adrienne Cook, Esq., director of new product development. Estab. 1878. Publishes hardcover and trade paperback originals. **Publishes 100 titles/year. Receives 50 queries/year. 20% of books from first-time authors; 95% from unagented writers. Pays 5-15% royalty on net receipts.** Publishes book 6 months after acceptance of ms. Accepts simultaneous submissions. Responds in 1 month to queries and proposals; 3 months to mss. Book catalog and ms guidelines online.

○┯ "We are interested in books that help lawyers practice law more effectively, whether it's help in handling clients, structuring a real estate deal, or taking an antitrust case to court."

Nonfiction All areas of legal practice. How-to (in the legal market), reference, technical. Subjects include business/economics, computers/electronic, money/finance, software, legal practice. "Our market is not, generally, the public. Books need to be targeted to lawyers who are seeking solutions to their practice problems. We rarely publish scholarly treatises." Query with SASE.

Recent Title(s) *The Attorney-Client Privilege and the Work-Product Doctrine*; *A Practical Guide to Real Estate Transactions*; *The Spine at Trial*.

Tips "ABA books are written for busy, practicing lawyers. The most successful books have a practical, reader-friendly voice. If you can build in features like checklists, exhibits, sample contracts, flow charts, and tables of cases, please do so." The Association also publishes over 50 major national periodicals in a variety of legal areas. Contact Kathleen Welton, director of book publishing, at the above address for guidelines.

AMERICAN CHEMICAL SOCIETY

Publications/Books Division, 1155 16th St. NW, Washington DC 20036. (202)452-2120. Fax: (202)452-8913. E-mail: b_hauserman@acs.org. Website: pubs.acs.org/books/. **Acquisitions:** Bob Hauserman, acquisitions editor. Estab. 1876. Publishes hardcover originals. **Publishes 35 titles/year. Pays royalty.** Accepts simultaneous submissions. Responds in 2 months to proposals. Book catalog free; ms guidelines online.

○┯ American Chemical Society publishes symposium-based books for chemistry.

Nonfiction Technical, semi-technical. Subjects include science. "Emphasis is on meeting-based books."

Recent Title(s) *Infrared Analysis of Peptides and Proteins*, edited by Singh.

AMERICAN CORRECTIONAL ASSOCIATION

4380 Forbes Blvd., Lanham MD 20706. (301)918-1800. Fax: (301)918-1886. E-mail: aliceh@aca.org. Website: www.corrections.com/aca. **Acquisitions:** Alice Heiserman, manager of publications and research. Estab. 1870. Publishes trade paperback originals. **Publishes 18 titles/year. 90% of books from first-time authors; 100% from unagented writers. Pays 10% royalty on net receipts.** Publishes book 1 year after acceptance of ms. Responds in 4 months to queries. Book catalog free; ms guidelines online.

○┯ American Correctional Association provides practical information on jails, prisons, boot camps, probation, parole, community corrections, juvenile facilities and rehabilitation programs, substance abuse programs, and other areas of corrections.

Nonfiction "We are looking for practical, how-to texts or training materials written for the corrections profession." How-to, reference, technical, textbook, correspondence courses. Subjects include corrections and criminal justice. No autobiographies or true-life accounts by current or former inmates or correctional officers, theses, or dissertations. No fiction or poetry. Query with SASE. Reviews artwork/photos as part of ms package.

Recent Title(s) *Working With Women Offenders in Correctional Institutions*, by Dr. Joann Brown Morton; *The Full Spectrum: Essays on Staff Diversity in Corrections*, edited by Carla Smalls; *Recess Is Over: Managing Youthful Offenders in Adult Correctional Systems*, by Barry Glick, PhD, William Sturgeon.

Tips Authors are professionals in the field and corrections. "Our audience is made up of corrections professionals and criminal justice students. No books by inmates or former inmates." This publisher advises out-of-town freelance editors, indexers, and proofreaders to refrain from requesting work from them.

AMERICAN COUNSELING ASSOCIATION

5999 Stevenson Ave., Alexandria VA 22304. (703)823-9800, ext. 356. Fax: (703)823-4786. E-mail: cbaker@counseling.org. Website: www.counseling.org. **Acquisitions:** Carolyn C. Baker, director of publications. Estab. 1952. Publishes paperback originals. Accepts simultaneous submissions. Responds in 1 month. Ms guidelines free.

○┯ The American Counseling Association is dedicated to promoting public confidence and trust in the counseling profession. "We publish scholarly texts for graduate level students and mental health professionals. We do not publish books for the general public."

Nonfiction Reference, scholarly, textbook (for professional counselors). Subjects include education, gay/lesbian, health/medicine, multicultural, psychology, religion, sociology, spirituality, women's issues/studies. ACA does not publish self-help books or autobiographies. Query with SASE, or submit proposal package including outline, 2 sample chapters, vitae.

Recent Title(s) *Assessment in Counseling, 3rd Ed.*, by Albert Hood and Richard Johnson; *Documentation in Counseling Records, 2nd Ed.*, by Robert Mitchell.

Tips "Target your market. Your books will not be appropriate for everyone across all disciplines."

AMERICAN FEDERATION OF ASTROLOGERS

6535 S. Rural Rd., Tempe AZ 85283. (480)838-1751. Fax: (480)838-8293. E-mail: afa@msn.com. Website: www.astrologers.com. **Acquisitions:** Kris Brandt Riske, publications manager. Estab. 1938. Publishes trade paperback originals and reprints. **Publishes 10-15 titles/year. Receives 10 queries and 20 mss/year. 50% of books from first-time authors; 100% from unagented writers. Pays 10% royalty.** Publishes book 10 months after acceptance of ms. Accepts simultaneous submissions. Responds in 6 months to mss. Book catalog and ms guidelines free.

○┬ American Federation of Astrologers publishes astrology books, calendars, charts, and related aids.

Nonfiction Subjects include astrology. Submit complete ms.

Recent Title(s) *The Vertex*, by Donna Henson; *Financial Astrology*, by David Williams; *Forensic Astrology*, by Dave Cambell.

⊘ AMERICAN PRESS

28 State St., Suite 1100, Boston MA 02109. (617)247-0022. **Acquisitions:** Jana Kirk, editor. Estab. 1911. Publishes college textbooks. **Publishes 25 titles/year. Receives 350 queries and 100 mss/year. 50% of books from first-time authors; 90% from unagented writers. Pays 5-15% royalty on wholesale price.** Publishes book 9 months after acceptance of ms. Does not accept simultaneous submissions. Responds in 3 months to queries.

Nonfiction Technical, textbook. Subjects include agriculture/horticulture, anthropology/archeology, art/architecture, business/economics, education, government/politics, health/medicine, history, music/dance, psychology, science, sociology, sports. "We prefer that our authors actually teach courses for which the manuscripts are designed." Query, or submit outline with tentative TOC. *No complete mss.*

Recent Title(s) *Basketball*, by Donald Staffo; *Basic Communication Course Annual #17 (2005)*, edited by Scott Titsworth; *Racquetball 3e*, by Linus Dowell and Tony Grice.

AMERICAN QUILTER'S SOCIETY

Schroeder Publishing, P.O. Box 3290, Paducah KY 42002-3290. (270)898-7903. Fax: (270)898-1173. E-mail: editor@aqsquilt.com. Website: www.aqsquilt.com. **Acquisitions:** Barbara Smith, executive book editor (primarily how-to and patterns, but other quilting books sometimes published). Estab. 1984. Publishes hardcover and trade paperback originals. **Publishes 20 titles/year. Receives 300 queries/year. 60% of books from first-time authors; 100% from unagented writers. Pays 5% royalty on retail price.** Publishes book 11 months after acceptance of ms. Accepts simultaneous submissions. Responds in same day to queries; 2 months to proposals. Book catalog and ms guidelines free or online.

○┬ American Quilter's Society publishes how-to and pattern books for quilters (beginners through intermediate skill level).

Nonfiction Coffee table book, how-to, reference, technical (about quilting). Subjects include creative nonfiction, hobbies (about quilting). Query with SASE, or submit proposal package including outline, 2 sample chapters, photos and patterns (if available). Reviews artwork/photos as part of ms package. Send photocopies; slides and drawings are also acceptable for a proposal.

Recent Title(s) *Affairs of the Heart*, by Aie Rossman; *Fabric Café: The Thrill of Chenille*, by Fran Morgan.

AMERICAN SOCIETY FOR TRAINING AND DEVELOPMENT

1640 King St., Alexandria VA 22313. (800)628-2783. Fax: (703)683-9591. E-mail: mmorrow@astd.org. Website: www.astd.org. **Acquisitions:** Mark Morrow, manager ASTD Press (acquisitions and development). Estab. 1944. Publishes trade paperback originals. **Publishes 10-12 titles/year. Receives 50 queries and 25-50 mss/year. 25% of books from first-time authors; 99% from unagented writers. Pays 10% royalty on net receipts. Offers $500-1,000 advance.** Publishes book up to 1 year after acceptance of ms. Accepts simultaneous submissions. Responds in 1 month. Book catalog and ms guidelines free.

Nonfiction Trade books for training and performance improvement professionals. Subjects include training and development. Submit proposal package including outline, 1 sample chapter. Reviews artwork/photos as part of ms package.

Recent Title(s) *Innovation Training*, by Ruth Ann Hattori and Joyce Wycoff; *Performance Basics*, by Joe Willmore; *Training Ain't Performance*, by Harold Stolovitch and Erica Keeps.

Tips Audience includes training professionals including frontline trainers, training managers and executives; performance professionals, including performance consultants; organizational development and human resource development professionals. "Send a good proposal targeted to our audience providing how-to advice that readers can apply now!"

AMERICAN WATER WORKS ASSOCIATION

6666 W. Quincy Ave., Denver CO 80235. (303)794-7711. Fax: (303)794-7310. E-mail: cmurcray@awwa.org. Website: www.awwa.org/communications/books. **Acquisitions:** Colin Murcray, senior acquisitions editor. Estab. 1881. Publishes hardcover and trade paperback originals. Does not accept simultaneous submissions. Responds in 4 months to queries. Book catalog and ms guidelines free.

> ⊶ AWWA strives to advance and promote the safety and knowledge of drinking water- and related issues to all audiences—from kindergarten through post-doctorate.

Nonfiction Subjects include nature/environment, science, software, drinking water, and wastewater-related topics, operations, treatment, sustainability. Query with SASE, or submit outline, 3 sample chapters, author bio. Reviews artwork/photos as part of ms package. Send photocopies.

Recent Title(s) *The Evolving Water Utility*, by Gary Westerhoff, et. al.

Tips "See website to download submission instructions."

AMERICANA PUBLISHING, INC.

303 San Mateo N.E., Suite 104 A, Albuquerque NM 87108. (505)265-6121. Fax: (505)255-6189. E-mail: editor@a mericanabooks.com. Website: www.americanabooks.com. **Acquisitions:** Managing Editor. Publishes audiobooks, most previously published in print, and a few trade paperbacks. **Publishes 150+ titles/year. Receives 500+ queries and 300+ mss/year. 5% of books from first-time authors; 50% from unagented writers. Pays 10% royalty.** Publishes book 1-2 years after acceptance of ms. Accepts simultaneous submissions. Book catalog online; ms guidelines by e-mail.

Fiction Adventure, fantasy (space fantasy), historical, military/war, mystery (amateur, sleuth, police procedural, private eye/hardboiled), science fiction, western, frontier. Does not accept short stories. Prefer 30,000-60,000 words. Prefer series. Does not want nonfiction, children's, poetry, sexually explicit (soft or hard porn), autobiographies, juvenile, gratuitous violence. Query with SASE, or submit 2 sample chapters. E-mail queries preferred.

Tips "Publish samples online."

AMG PUBLISHERS

6815 Shallowford Rd., Chattanooga TN 37421-1755. (423)894-6060. Fax: (423)894-9511. E-mail: danp@amginte rnational.org. Website: www.amgpublishers.com. **Acquisitions:** Dan Penwell, manager of product development and acquisitions. Publishes hardcover and trade paperback originals, electronic originals, and audio Bible and book originals. **Publishes 35-40 titles/year; imprint publishes 25 titles/year. Receives 1,500 queries and 500 mss/year. 25% of books from first-time authors; 40% from unagented writers. Pays 10-16% royalty on wholesale price.** Publishes book 12-15 months after acceptance of ms. Accepts simultaneous submissions. Responds in 1 week to queries; 6 months to proposals and mss. Book catalog and ms guidelines online.

Imprints Living Ink.

Nonfiction Reference, Bible study workbook, Bibles, commentaries. Looking for books that facilitate interaction with Bible, encourage and facilitate spiritual growth. Subjects include Christian living, women's, men's, and family issues, single and divorce issues, devotionals, inspirationals, prayer, contemporary issues, Biblical reference, applied theology and apologetics, Christian ministry and Bible study in the Following God Series format. "Note our Following God Series (www.followinggod.com) covers a variety of Bible study topics. This Bible study is designed in an interactive format." Prefer queries by e-mail.

Fiction Young adult Christian fantasy fiction. Prefer queries by e-mail.

Recent Title(s) *Raising Dragons*, by Bryan Davis; *For Women Only*, by Dr. Shay Roop; *The Twenty-Third Psalm for Caregivers*, by Carmen Leal.

Tips "AMG is open to well-written, niche books that meet immediate needs in the lives of adults and young adults."

ANCHORAGE PRESS PLAYS, INC.

P.O. Box 2901, Louisville KY 40201. Phone/Fax: (502)583-2288. E-mail: applays@bellsouth.net. Website: www. applays.com. **Acquisitions:** Marilee Miller, publisher. Estab. 1935. Publishes hardcover and trade paperback originals. **Publishes up to 10 titles/year. 50% of books from first-time authors; 80% from unagented writers. Pays 10-15% royalty. Playwrights also receive 50-75% royalties.** Publishes book 1-2 years after acceptance of ms. Accepts simultaneous submissions. Responds in 6 months to mss. Book catalog and ms guidelines online.

> ⊶ "We are an international agency for plays for young people. First in the field since 1935. We are primarily a publisher of theatrical plays with limited textbooks."

Nonfiction Textbook, plays. Subjects include education, theater, child drama, plays. "We are looking for texts for teachers of drama/theater." Query. Reviews artwork/photos as part of ms package.
Recent Title(s) *Curtain Time is Magic Time*, by Michael H. Hibbard; *The Rose of Treason*, by James DeVita; *The Pied Piper of Hamelin*, by Tim Wright.

WILLIAM ANDREW, INC.

13 Eaton Ave., Norwich NY 13815. (607)337-5000. Fax: (607)337-5090. E-mail: mtreloar@williamandrew.com. Website: www.williamandrew.com. **Acquisitions:** Millicent Treloar, senior editor. Estab. 1989. Publishes hardcover originals. Accepts simultaneous submissions. Book catalog online.

O— "We are looking for authors who want to write a book or compile data that can be employed by readers in day-to-day activities."

Nonfiction Reference, scholarly, technical, databooks, handbooks, literature reviews, patent reviews, data compilations, comprehensive fundamentals overviews, consultant-style training and evaluative works. Subject areas include agricultural/food technology, coatings/paints formulations, cosmetics/toiletries, diffusion/thin films, health/safety, industrial chemicals, MEMS/nanotechnology, materials engineers, packaging, plastics, processing/manufacturing, surface engineering. Submit outline with book propsal, SASE. Reviews artwork/photos as part of ms package. Send photocopies.
Recent Title(s) *Nanostructured Materials*, by Koch; *Handbook of Molded Part Shrinkage and Warpage*, by Fischer; *Fluoroplastics, Volumes 1 and 2*, by Ebnesajjad.

Ⓐ ANDREWS McMEEL UNIVERSAL

4520 Main St., Kansas City MO 64111-7701. (816)932-6700. **Acquisitions:** Christine Schillig, vice president/ editorial director. Estab. 1973. Publishes hardcover and paperback originals. **Publishes 200 titles/year. Pays royalty on retail price, or net receipts. Offers advance.**

O— Andrews McMeel publishes general trade books, humor books, miniature gift books, calendars, and stationery products.

Nonfiction How-to, humor, inspirational. Subjects include contemporary culture, general trade, relationships. Also produces gift books. *Agented submissions only.*
Recent Title(s) *The Complete Far Side*, by Gary Larsen.

ANKER PUBLISHING CO., INC.

P.O. Box 249, Bolton MA 01740-0249. (978)779-6190. Fax: (978)779-6366. E-mail: info@ankerpub.com. Website: www.ankerpub.com. **Acquisitions:** James D. Anker, president and publisher. Publishes hardcover and paperback professional books. **Publishes 10 titles/year. Pays royalty. Offers advance.** Publishes book 4 months after acceptance of ms. Accepts simultaneous submissions.

O— Publishes professional development books for higher education faculty and administrators.

Nonfiction Professional development. Subjects include education. Query with SASE, or submit proposal package including outline, 3 sample chapters.

APA BOOKS

American Psychological Association, 750 First St., NE, Washington DC 20002-4242. (800)374-2721 or (202)336-5792. E-mail: books@apa.org. Website: www.apa.org/books. Publishes hardcover and trade paperback originals. Book catalog and ms guidelines online.
Imprints Magination Press (children's books).
Nonfiction Reference, scholarly, textbook, professional. Subjects include education, gay/lesbian, multicultural, psychology, science, social sciences, sociology, women's issues/studies. Submit cv and prospectus with TOC, intended audience, selling points, and outside competition.
Recent Title(s) *The Dependent Patient: A Practitioner's Guide*, by Robert F. Bornstein, PhD; *A Place to Call Home: After-School Programs for Urban Youth*, by Barton J. Hirsch, PhD; *Law & Mental Health Professionals: Ohio*, by Leon VandeCreek, PhD and Marshall Kapp, JD.
Tips "Our press features scholarly books on empirically supported topics for professionals and students in all areas of psychology."

APPALACHIAN MOUNTAIN CLUB BOOKS

5 Joy St., Boston MA 02108. (617)523-0655. Fax: (617)523-0722. E-mail: sjshangraw@outdoors.org. Website: www.outdoors.org. **Acquisitions:** Sarah Jane Shangraw, publisher/editor. Estab. 1897. Publishes hardcover and trade paperback originals. Accepts simultaneous submissions. Ms guidelines online.

O— Appalachian Mountain Club publishes hiking guides, paddling guides, nature, conservation, and mountain-subject guides for America's Northeast. "We connect recreation to conservation and education."

Nonfiction Subjects include nature/environment, recreation, regional (Northeast outdoor recreation), literary nonfiction, guidebooks. Query with proposal and SASE. Reviews artwork/photos as part of ms package. Send photocopies or transparencies.

Recent Title(s) *Women on High*; *Northeastern Wilds*; *Outdoor Leadership, White Mountain Guide, 27th Ed.*

Tips "Our audience is outdoor recreationists, conservation-minded hikers and canoeists, family outdoor lovers, armchair enthusiasts. Visit our website for proposal submission guidelines and more information."

A-R EDITIONS, INC.

8551 Research Way, Suite 180, Middleton WI 53562. (608)836-9000. Fax: (608)831-8200. Website: www.areditions.com. **Acquisitions:** Paul L. Ranzini, managing editor (Recent Researches music editions); James L. Zychowicz, managing editor (Computer Music and Digital Audio Series). Estab. 1962. **Publishes 30 titles/year. Receives 40 queries and 30 mss/year. 75% of books from first-time authors; 100% from unagented writers. Pays royalty or honoraria.** Does not accept simultaneous submissions. Responds in 1 month to queries; 3 months to proposals; 6 months to mss. Book catalog and ms guidelines online.

> O— A-R Editions publishes modern critical editions of music based on current musicological research. Each edition is devoted to works by a single composer or to a single genre of composition. The contents are chosen for their potential interest to scholars and performers, then prepared for publication according to the standards that govern the making of all reliable, historical editions.

Nonfiction Subjects include computers/electronic, music/dance, software, historical music editions. Computer Music and Digital Audio Series titles deal with issues tied to digital and electronic media, and include both textbooks and handbooks in this area. Query with SASE, or submit outline.

Recent Title(s) *Audio Recording Handbook*, by Alan P. Kefauver; *Charles Ives: 129 Songs*, edited by H. Wiley Hitchcock; *Hyperimprovisation*, by Roger Dean.

ARABESQUE

BET Books, 850 Third Ave., 16th Floor, New York NY 10022. (212)407-1500. Website: www.bet.com/books. **Acquisitions:** Karen Thomas, editorial director. Publishes mass market paperback originals. Accepts simultaneous submissions. Responds in 3 months to mss. Book catalog for #10 SASE; ms guidelines online.

> O— Arabesque publishes contemporary romances about African-American couples.

Fiction Multicultural (romance), romance. "Arabesque books must be 85,000-100,000 words in length, and are contemporary genre romances only." Submit proposal package including 3 sample chapters, synopsis.

Recent Title(s) *His 1-800 Wife*, by Shirley Hailstock.

Tips "Please do not phone to see if your manuscript was received or returned, or to find out what we thought of it. A self-addressed, stamped postcard can be enclosed with your submission if you want confirmation of its arrival. Specify whether you would like your manuscript returned or recycled if it is not right for us."

Ⓐ ARCADE PUBLISHING

141 Fifth Ave., New York NY 10010. (212)475-2633. Website: www.arcadepub.com. **Acquisitions:** Richard Seaver, president/editor-in-chief; Jeannette Seaver, publisher/executive editor; Cal Barksdale, senior editor; Casey Ebro, editor; Savannah Ashour, assistant editor. Estab. 1988. Publishes hardcover originals, trade paperback reprints. **Publishes 45 titles/year. 5% of books from first-time authors. Pays royalty on retail price. 10 author's copies. Offers advance.** Publishes book within 18 months after acceptance of ms. Responds in 1 month to queries. Book catalog and ms guidelines for #10 SASE.

> O— Arcade prides itself on publishing top-notch literary nonfiction and fiction, with a significant proportion of foreign writers.

Nonfiction Biography, general nonfiction, general nonfiction. Subjects include government/politics, history, nature/environment, travel, popular science, current events. *Agented submissions only.* Reviews artwork/photos as part of ms package. Send photocopies.

Fiction Ethnic, historical, literary, mainstream/contemporary, mystery, short story collections. No romance, science fiction. *Agented submissions only.*

Recent Title(s) *Bibliophilia*, by Michael Griffith; *Weighing the Souls*, by Len Fisher; *The Last Song of Dusk*, by Siddharth Dhanvant Shanghvi.

ARCADIA PUBLISHING

420 Wando Park Blvd., Mt. Pleasant SC 29464. (843)853-2070. Fax: (843)853-0044. E-mail: sales@arcadiapublishing.com. Website: www.arcadiapublishing.com. **Acquisitions:** Editorial Director. Estab. 1993. Publishes trade paperback originals. **Publishes 500+ titles/year. 80% of books from first-time authors; 95% from unagented writers.** Accepts simultaneous submissions. Responds in 1 month to queries. Book catalog and ms guidelines online.

> O— Arcadia publishes photographic vintage regional histories. "We have more than 3,000 in print in our Images of America series. We have expanded our California program."

Nonfiction Subjects include history (local, regional, military, sports, African-American, college, rail, corporate). Query with SASE. Reviews artwork/photos as part of ms package. Send photocopies.

Recent Title(s) *South San Francisco*, by The South San Francisco Historical Society.

Tips "Writers should know that we only publish history titles. The majority of our books are on a city or region, and contain vintage images with limited text."

N A ARCHEBOOKS PUBLISHING

ArcheBooks Publishing Inc., 9101 W. Sahara Ave., Suite 105-112, Las Vegas NV 89117. (800)358-8101. Fax: (561)868-2127. E-mail: info@archebooks.com. Submissions E-mail: publisher@archebooks.com. Website: www.archebooks.com. **Acquisitions:** Robert E. Gelinas, publisher. Estab. 2003. Publishes hardcover originals, electronic originals and hardcover reprints. **Publishes 30-40 titles/year; imprint publishes 30-40 titles/year. Receives 100+ queries and 50+ mss/year. 90% of books from first-time authors. Pays royalty on retail price. Minimum of $2,500, subject to negotiation and keeping prior history and corporate policy in mind.** Publishes book 3-6 months after acceptance of ms. Does not accept simultaneous submissions. All submissions must be online only. Responds in 1 month. Book catalog and ms guidelines online.

Nonfiction Subjects include history, true crime. True crime is an emphasis, focusing on well-researched and documented sensational cases, both historical and contemporary. *Agented submissions only.* Reviews artwork/ photos as part of ms package. Digital e-mail attachments.

Fiction Adventure, fantasy, historical, horror, humor, literary, mainstream/contemporary, military/war, mystery, romance, science fiction, suspense, western, young adult. "Writers should be prepared to participate in very aggressive and orchestrated marketing and promotion campaigns, using all the promotional tools and training that we provide, at no charge. We're expanding in all areas." *Agented submissions only.*

Recent Title(s) *The Don Juan Con*, by Sara Williams; *The Mustard Seed*, by Robert E. Gelinas; *The Planters*, by Bill Rogers.

Tips "Learn to write a good book proposal. An article on this topic can be found for free on our website in the Author's Corner section of Writer's Resources."

ARKANSAS RESEARCH, INC.

P.O. Box 303, Conway AR 72033. (501)470-1120. E-mail: desmond@ipa.net. **Acquisitions:** Desmond Walls Allen, owner. Estab. 1985. Publishes trade paperback originals and reprints. **Publishes 12 titles/year. 10% of books from first-time authors; 100% from unagented writers. Pays 5-10% royalty on retail price.** Publishes book 6 months after acceptance of ms. Does not accept simultaneous submissions. Responds in 1 month to queries. Book catalog for $1; ms guidelines free.

Imprints Research Associates.

↪ "Our company opens a world of information to researchers interested in the history of Arkansas."

Nonfiction All Arkansas-related subjects. How-to (genealogy), reference, self-help. Subjects include Americana, ethnic, history, hobbies (genealogy), military/war, regional. "We don't print autobiographies or genealogies about 1 family." Query with SASE. Reviews artwork/photos as part of ms package. Send photocopies.

Recent Title(s) *Life & Times From The Clay County Courier Newspaper Published at Corning, Arkansas, 1893-1900.*

N ARROW PUBLICATIONS, LLC

9112 Paylley Bridge Lane, Potomac MD 20854-4432. Fax: (301)299-9423. E-mail: pwhite@arrowpub.com. Submissions E-mail: arrow_info@arrowpub.com (Tom King) or mcgib@sympatico.ca (Maryan Gibson). Website: www.arrowpub.com. **Acquisitions:** Tom King, assistant editor (romance/adventure/mystery); Maryan Gibson, acquisition editor (romance/adventure/mystery). Estab. 1987. Publishes mass market paperback and electronic originals. **Publishes 50 titles/year. Receives 80 queries and 60 mss/year. 80% of books from first-time authors; 100% from unagented writers. Makes outright purchase of $400-500.** Publishes book 4 months after acceptance of ms. Does not accept simultaneous submissions. Responds in 1 month. Ms guidelines online.

Fiction Adventure, humor, mystery, romance. "We are looking for outlines of stories heavy on romance with elements of adventure/intrigue/mystery. Humorous love stories are always appreciated. We need true-to-life romances between consenting adults, with believable conflicts and well-defined characterizations. We publish illustrated romance stories, so we are looking for good dialogue writers. Each story is formatted into a script of 60-64 panels, comprising narrative, dialogue, and art direction." Query with SASE, or submit proposal package including synopsis.

Recent Title(s) *Champion of Her Heart*, by Gail Hamilton (romance/adventure); *The Perfect Partner*, by Maryan Gibson (romance/adventure).

Tips "Our audience is primarily young and old adult women. Look at the website and review publications. Send query first."

ARTE PUBLICO PRESS

University of Houston, 452 Cullen Performance Hall, Houston TX 77204-2004. Fax: (713)743-3080. Website: www.artepublicopress.com. **Acquisitions:** Nicolas Kanellos, editor. Estab. 1979. Publishes hardcover originals, trade paperback originals and reprints. **Publishes 36 titles/year. Receives 1,000 queries and 2,000 mss/year. 50% of books from first-time authors; 80% from unagented writers. Pays 10% royalty on wholesale price. Provides 20 author's copies; 40% discount on subsequent copies. Offers $1,000-3,000 advance.** Publishes book 2 years after acceptance of ms. Accepts simultaneous submissions. Responds in 1 month to queries and proposals; 4 months to mss. Book catalog free; ms guidelines online.

Imprints Piñata Books.

○➝ "We are a showcase for Hispanic literary creativity, arts and culture. Our endeavor is to provide a national forum for U.S.-Hispanic literature."

Nonfiction Children's/juvenile, reference. Subjects include ethnic, language/literature, regional, translation, women's issues/studies. Hispanic civil rights issues for new series: The Hispanic Civil Rights Series. Query with SASE, or submit outline, 2 sample chapters.

Fiction Ethnic, literary, mainstream/contemporary, written by U.S.-Hispanic authors. Query with SASE, or submit outline/proposal, 2 sample chapters, synopsis, or submit complete ms.

Poetry Submit 10 sample poems.

Recent Title(s) *Shadows and Supposes*, by Gloria Vando (poetry); *Home Killings*, by Marcos McPeek Villatoro (mystery); *Message to Aztlár*, by Rodolfo "Corky" Gonzales (Hispanic Civil Rights Series book).

ASA, AVIATION SUPPLIES & ACADEMICS

7005 132nd Pl. SE, Newcastle WA 98059. (425)235-1500. E-mail: feedback@asa2fly.com. Website: www.asa2fly .com. Does not accept simultaneous submissions. Book catalog free.

○➝ ASA is an industry leader in the development and sales of aviation supplies, publications, and software for pilots, flight instructors, flight engineers and aviation technicians. All ASA products are developed by a team of researchers, authors and editors.

Nonfiction All subjects must be related to aviation education and training. How-to, technical. Subjects include education. "We are primarily an aviation publisher. Educational books in this area are our specialty; other aviation books will be considered." Query with outline. Send photocopies.

Recent Title(s) *The Savvy Flight Instructor: Secrets of the Successful CFI*, by Greg Brown.

Tips "Two of our specialty series include ASA's *Focus Series*, and ASA *Aviator's Library*. Books in our *Focus Series* concentrate on single-subject areas of aviation knowledge, curriculum and practice. The *Aviator's Library* is comprised of titles of known and/or classic aviation authors or established instructor/authors in the industry, and other aviation specialty titles."

ASCE PRESS

1801 Alexander Bell Dr., Reston VA 20191-4400. (703)295-6275. Fax: (703)295-6278. E-mail: ascepress@asce.o rg. Website: www.pubs.asce.org. Estab. 1989. **Pays royalty on net receipts.** Accepts simultaneous submissions. Request ASCE Press book proposal submission guidelines; ms guidelines online.

○➝ ASCE Press publishes technical volumes that are useful to both practicing civil engineers and graduate level civil engineering students. "We publish books by individual authors and editors to advance the civil engineering profession." Currently emphasizing management, construction engineering, geotechnical, hydrology, structural engineering, and bridge engineering. De-emphasizing highly specialized areas with narrow scope.

Nonfiction "We are looking for topics that are useful and instructive to the engineering practitioner." Subjects include civil engineering. Query with proposal, sample chapters, cv, TOC and target audience.

Recent Title(s) *The Tensioned Fabric Roof*, by Craig Huntington; *Handbook of Concrete Bridge Management*, by Fernando A. Branco and Jorge de Brito.

Tips "ASCE Press is a book publishing imprint of ASCE and produces authored and edited applications-oriented books for practicing civil engineers and graduate level civil engineering students. All proposals and manuscripts undergo a vigorous review process."

ASM INTERNATIONAL

9639 Kinsman Rd., Materials Park OH 44073-0002. (440)338-5151, ext. 5706. Fax: (440)338-4634. E-mail: books @asminternational.org. Website: www.asminternational.org. **Acquisitions:** Scott D. Henry, senior manager, new product development, publications (metallurgy/materials). Publishes hardcover originals. **Publishes 15-20 titles/year. Receives 50 queries and 10 mss/year. 50% of books from first-time authors; 100% from unagented writers. Pays royalty on wholesale price or makes outright purchase.** Does not accept simultaneous submissions. Responds in 1 month to queries; 4 months to proposals; 2 months to mss. Book catalog free or online at website; ms guidelines free.

○━ "We focus on practical information related to materials selection and processing."

Nonfiction Reference, technical, textbook. Subjects include engineering reference. Submit proposal package including outline, sample chapter, author bio. Reviews artwork/photos as part of ms package. Send photocopies.

Recent Title(s) *Introduction to Aluminum Alloys and Tempers*, by J.G. Kaufman; *Titanium: A Technical Guide, 2nd Ed.*, by M.J. Donachie, Jr.

Tips "Our audience consists of technically trained people seeking practical information on metals and materials to help them solve problems on the job."

ASSOCIATION FOR SUPERVISION AND CURRICULUM DEVELOPMENT

1703 N. Beauregard St., Alexandria VA 22311. (703)575-5693. Fax: (703)575-5400. E-mail: swillis@ascd.org. Website: www.ascd.org. **Acquisitions:** Scott Willis, acquisitions director. Estab. 1943. Publishes trade paperback originals. **Publishes 24-30 titles/year. Receives 100 queries and 100 mss/year. 50% of books from first-time authors; 95% from unagented writers. Pays negotiable royalty on actual monies received.** Publishes book 1 year after acceptance of ms. Accepts simultaneous submissions. Responds in 3 months to proposals. Book catalog and ms guidelines free or online.

○━ ASCD publishes high-quality professional books for educators.

Nonfiction Subjects include education (for professional educators). Submit outline, 2 sample chapters. Reviews artwork/photos as part of ms package. Send photocopies.

Recent Title(s) *Leadership for the Learning: How to Help Students Succeed*, by Carl Glickman; *The Multiple Intelligences of Reading and Writing*, by Thomas Armstrong; *Educating Oppositional and Defiant Children*, by Philip S. Hall, Nancy D. Hall.

⊘ ATHENEUM BOOKS FOR YOUNG READERS

Imprint of Simon & Schuster, 1230 Avenue of the Americas, New York NY 10020. (212)698-2715. Fax: (212)698-2796. Website: www.simonsayskids.com. Estab. 1960. Publishes hardcover originals. Accepts simultaneous submissions. Ms guidelines for #10 SASE.

○━ Atheneum Books for Young Readers publishes books aimed at children, pre-school through high school.

Nonfiction Biography, children's/juvenile, humor, self-help. Subjects include Americana, animals, art/architecture, business/economics, government/politics, health/medicine, history, music/dance, nature/environment, photography, psychology, recreation, religion, science, sociology, sports, travel. "Do remember, most publishers plan their lists as much as two years in advance. So if a topic is 'hot' right now, it may be 'old hat' by the time we could bring it out. It's better to steer clear of fads. Some writers assume juvenile books are for 'practice' until you get good enough to write adult books. Not so. Books for young readers demand just as much professionalism in writing as adult books. So save those 'practice' manuscripts for class, or polish them before sending them. *Query only for all submissions. We don't accept unsolicited mss.* It is recommended that you find an agent to represent your work."

Fiction All in juvenile versions. Adventure, ethnic, experimental, fantasy, gothic, historical, horror, humor, mainstream/contemporary, mystery, science fiction, sports, suspense, western, Animal. "We have few specific needs except for books that are fresh, interesting and well written. Fad topics are dangerous, as are works you haven't polished to the best of your ability. We also don't need safety pamphlets, ABC books, coloring books and board books. In writing picture book texts, avoid the coy and 'cutesy,' such as stories about characters with alliterative names." *Query only. No unsolicited mss.* No "paperback romance type" fiction.

Recent Title(s) *Billy and the Rebel*, by Deborah Hopkinson, illustrated by Brian Floca; *Imagine a Day*, by Sarah L. Thomson, illustrated by Rob Gonsalves; *Seeds*, written and illustrated by Ken Robbins.

Ⓝ ATLAS VARIETY PUBLISHING

737 Pinellas Bayway, #109, Tierra Verde FL 33715. E-mail: publisher@atlasvariety.com. Website: www.atlasvariety.com. **Acquisitions:** Elaine Koritsas, co-publisher (nonfiction); Christopher Rigoli, co-publisher (fiction). Estab. 2004. Publishes hardcover and trade paperback originals. **Publishes 10 titles/year. 50% of books from first-time authors; 50% from unagented writers. Pays 7-15% royalty on wholesale price.** Publishes book 12-18 months after acceptance of ms. Does not accept simultaneous submissions. Responds in 2 months to queries; 4 months to proposals and mss. Book catalog and ms guidelines for #10 SASE.

Nonfiction Autobiography, biography, booklets, children's/juvenile, cookbook, general nonfiction, how-to, humor, reference, self-help. Subjects include child guidance/parenting, contemporary culture, cooking/foods/nutrition, creative nonfiction, health/medicine, sex, travel, women's issues/studies. "Our books are as funny as they are informative. Please use wit and style in your manuscripts. We look for original, unique, detailed, informative, and interesting books." Submit proposal package including outline, 3 sample chapters, SASE.

Fiction Adventure, fantasy, historical, horror, mainstream/contemporary, military/war, multicultural, mystery, science fiction, suspense. "We seek and publish enterataining stories driven by characters readers can relate to. Keep query letters to 1 page, proposal/synopsis to 5 pages, and manuscripts to 50 pages (first 3 chapters).'' Submit proposal package including outline, 3 sample chapters, synopsis, SASE.

Recent Title(s) *The Savvy Patient's Medical Binder* (reference); *National Treasure: America's Best Pizza* (food/travel); *The Adventures of Puddin Pickney*, by Cecil P. Cole (fantasy).

Tips "Our readers turn to us to find interesting books that encourage, enrich, and inspire. We're open to new writers who have both a natural talent and a new, interesting voice."

ATRIAD PRESS, LLC

13820 Methuen Green, Dallas TX 75240. (972)671-0002. E-mail: editor@atriadpress.com. Website: www.atriadpress.com; www.hauntedencounters.com. President: Ginnie Bivona. **Acquisitions:** Mitchel Whitington, senior editor. Estab. 2002. Publishes trade paperback originals. Accepts simultaneous submissions. Book catalog and ms guidelines online.

> ○→ "We are currently accepting submissions for three different series: The Haunted Encounters Series (submissions@atriadpress.com); Encuentros Encantados (hector@atriadpress.com); Ghostly Tales from America's Jails (jails@atriadpress.com).

Nonfiction Ghost stories, haunted experiences. Does not want UFO or angels. Submit proposal package including outline, 3 sample chapters, author bio, via mail or e-mail.

Recent Title(s) *Haunted Encounters: Real-Life Stories of Supernatural Experiences* (anthology).

Tips "The market for ghost stories is huge! It seems to be very broad—and ranges from young to old. Currently, our books are for adults, but we would consider the teen market. Please check your manuscript carefully for errors in spelling and structure."

Ⓝ Ⓞ AUDIO RENAISSANCE

Division of Holtzbrinck Publishers, 175 Fifth Ave., New York NY 10010. (212)674-5151. Fax: (917)534-0980. Website: www.audiorenaissance.com. Estab. 1988.

> ○→ "Audio Renaissance publishes audio editions of the best fiction and nonfiction among the Holtzbrinck trade publishers. It has a strong tradition in the self-help, personal growth, and business categories."

Recent Title(s) *The Red Hat Club Rides Again*, by Haywood Smith; *The Illuminator*, by Brenda Rickman Vantrease.

AUGSBURG BOOKS

Imprint of Augsburg Fortress Publishers, P.O. Box 1209, Minneapolis MN 55440-1209. (612)330-3300. E-mail: booksub@augsburgfortress.org; lutheranvoices@augsburgfortress.org. Website: www.augsburgbooks.com. Publishes trade and mass market paperback originals and reprints, hardcover picture books. **Pays royalty.** Book catalog for 9×12 SAE with 3 first-class stamps; ms guidelines online.

Imprints Lutheran Voices (books of interest to ELCA members and wider Christian community that teach, inspire, renew); Fortress Press (academic and professional resources that inform and reform Christian faith).

> ○→ Augsburg Books is the publishing house of the Evangelical Lutheran Church in America. Augsburg Books are meant to nurture faith in daily life, enhancing the lives of Christians in their homes, churches, and schools.

Nonfiction Subjects include religion, spirituality (adult), grief/healing/wholeness, parenting, interactive books for children and families, seasonal and picture books. Query with SASE, or submit proposal package.

Recent Title(s) *The Passion of the Lord: African American Reflections*, edited by Matthew V. Johnson, Sr. and James A. Noel; *Two Worlds Are Ours: An Introduction to Christian Mysticism*, by John Macquarrie.

AVALON BOOKS

Thomas Bouregy & Co., Inc., 160 Madison Ave., 5th Floor, New York NY 10016. (212)598-0222. Fax: (212)979-1862. E-mail: editorial@avalonbooks.com. Website: www.avalonbooks.com. **Acquisitions:** Erin Cartwright-Niumata, editorial director; Abby Holcomb, assistant editor. Estab. 1950. Publishes hardcover originals. **Publishes 60 titles/year. Pays 15% royalty. Offers $1,000+ advance.** Publishes book 10-12 months after acceptance of ms. Responds in 1 month to queries. Ms guidelines online.

Fiction "We publish wholesome contemporary romances, mysteries, historical romances and westerns. Our books are read by adults as well as teenagers, and the characters are all adults. All mysteries are contemporary. We publish contemporary romances (4 every 2 months), historical romances (2 every 2 months), mysteries (2 every 2 months) and westerns (2 every 2 months). Submit first 3 sample chapters, a 2-3 page synopsis and SASE. The manuscripts should be between 40,000 to 70,000 words. Manuscripts that are too long will not be considered. Time period and setting are the author's preference. The historical romances will maintain the high level of reading expected by our readers. The books shall be wholesome fiction, without graphic sex, violence or strong language. We are actively looking for romantic comedy, chick lit." Query with SASE.

Recent Title(s) *Poppy's Place*, by Sylvia Renfro (romance); *Choices*, by Carolyn Brown (historical romance); *The Bride Wore Blood*, by Vicky Hunnings (mystery).

AVALON TRAVEL PUBLISHING

Avalon Publishing Group, 1400 65th St., Suite 250, Emeryville CA 94608. (510)595-3664. Fax: (510)595-4228. E-mail: acquisitions@avalonpub.com. Website: www.travelmatters.com. Estab. 1973. Publishes trade paperback originals. **Publishes 100 titles/year. Receives 800-1,000 queries/year. 50% of books from first-time authors; 95% from unagented writers. Pays royalty on net receipts. Offers up to $10,000 advance.** Publishes book an average of 9 months after acceptance of ms. Accepts simultaneous submissions. Responds in 4 months. Ms guidelines online.

Imprints *Series*: Dog Lover's Companion; Foghorn Outdoors; Living Abroad; Moon Handbooks; Moon Metro; Rick Steves; Road Trip USA.

> **0—** "Avalon travel guides feature a combination of practicality and spirit, offering a traveler-to-traveler perspective perfect for planning an afternoon hike, around-the-world journey, or anything in between. ATP publishes 7 major series. Each one has a different emphasis and a different geographic coverage. Our main areas of interest are North America, Central America, South America, the Caribbean, and the Pacific. At any given moment, we are seeking to acquire only a handful of specific titles in each of our major series. Check online guidelines for updated needs. Follow guidelines closely."

Nonfiction Subjects include regional, travel.

Recent Title(s) *Moon Handbooks Hudson River Valley*, by Nikki Goth Hoi; *California Golf*, by George Fuller.

Tips "Please note that ATP is only looking for books that fit into current series and is not interested in the following genres: fiction, children's books, and travelogues/travel diaries."

AVANT-GUIDE

Empire Press Media, 444 Madison Ave., 35th Floor, New York NY 10022. E-mail: info@avantguide.com. Website: www.avantguide.com. **Acquisitions:** Dan Levine, editor-in-chief (travel). Estab. 1997. Publishes trade paperback and electronic originals. **Publishes 20 titles/year. Receives 200 queries and 10 mss/year. 20% of books from first-time authors; 100% from unagented writers. Makes outright purchase of $10,000-30,000.** Publishes book 10 months after acceptance of ms. Accepts simultaneous submissions. Responds in 1 month. Book catalog free; ms guidelines online.

Nonfiction Subjects include travel (guide books). "Avant-Guide books live at the intersection of travel and style. They co-opt the best aspects of the guidebook genre—namely, being thorough and trustworthy. Then they add dynamic prose, innovative design and a brutally honest cosmopolitan perspective. Each new title in this boutique travel guidebook series is comprehensive in scope and includes authoritative reports on essential sights, hip new restaurants, nightclubs, hotels, and shops—all while making a fashion statement all its own. Avant-Guide is the first and only travel guidebook series for globally aware travelistas." Query by e-mail.

Tips "Avant-Guide readers are style-conscious, well-dressed, well-traveled city dwelling 25-49 year old men and women. They are sophisticated, brand-savvy, well-heeled, 21st century consumers searching for under-stated, cutting edge experiences. While they like to travel stylishly, our readers are busy people who don't have time to wade through exhaustive lists. When they travel they want to know only about the best hotels, restaurants, shops and nightlife. Our core audience resides in affluent city areas and gentrified multi-ethnic areas. They are predominantly single or unmarried-couples, highly qualified executives and creative professionals."

AVISSON PRESS, INC.

3007 Taliaferro Rd., Greensboro NC 27408. Fax: (336)288-6989. **Acquisitions:** M.L. Hester, editor. Estab. 1994. Publishes hardcover originals and trade paperback originals and reprints. **Publishes 8-10 titles/year. Receives 600 queries and 400 mss/year. 5% of books from first-time authors; 90% from unagented writers. Pays 8-10% royalty on wholesale price. Offers occasional small advance.** Publishes book 15 months after acceptance of ms. Accepts simultaneous submissions. Responds in 1 week to queries and proposals; 2 months to mss. Book catalog for #10 SASE.

> **0—** Currently emphasizing young-adult biography only. No fiction or poetry.

Nonfiction Biography. Subjects include ethnic, sports, women's issues/studies. Query with SASE, or submit outline, 1-3 sample chapters.

Recent Title(s) *Go, Girl!: Young Women Superstars of Pop Music*, by Jacqueline Robb; *The Experimenters: Eleven Great Chemists*, by Margery Everden.

Tips Audience is primarily public and school libraries.

Ⓐ AVON BOOKS

HarperCollins, 10 E. 53rd St., New York NY 10022. Website: www.avonbooks.com. **Acquisitions:** Editorial Submissions. Estab. 1941. Publishes hardcover trade and mass market paperback originals and reprints. **Royalty negotiable. Offers advance.** Accepts simultaneous submissions. Ms guidelines for #10 SASE.

Fiction Romance (contemporary, historical). *Agented submissions only.*

Recent Title(s) *Night Train to Lisbon*, by Emily Grayson; *Dirty South*, by Ace Atkins; *Sandstorm*, by James Rollins.

BACKCOUNTRY GUIDES

Imprint of The Countryman Press, P. O. Box 748, Woodstock VT 05091-0748. (802)457-4826. Fax: (802)457-1678. E-mail: countrymanpress@wwnorton.com. Website: www.countrymanpress.com. **Acquisitions:** Kermit Hummel, editorial director. Estab. 1973. Publishes trade paperback originals. **Publishes 50 titles/year.** Accepts simultaneous submissions. Responds in 3 months to proposals. Book catalog free; ms guidelines online.

Nonfiction Subjects include nature/environment, recreation (bicycling, hiking, canoeing, kayaking, fly fishing, walking, guidebooks, and series), sports, travel, food, gardening, country living, New England history. Query with SASE, or submit proposal package including outline, 2-3 sample chapters, market analysis. Reviews artwork/photos as part of ms package. Send transparencies.

Recent Title(s) *The King Arthur Flour Cookie Companion*; *Grand Canyon Wild*, by John Annerino; *50 Hikes in Arizona*, by Martin Tessmer.

Tips ''Look at our existing series of guidebooks to see how your proposal fits in.''

BAEN PUBLISHING ENTERPRISES

P.O. Box 1403, Riverdale NY 10471-0671. (718)548-3100. E-mail: slush@baen.com. Website: www.baen.com. **Acquisitions:** Jim Baen, editor-in-chief. Estab. 1983. Publishes hardcover, trade paperback and mass market paperback originals and reprints. Does not accept simultaneous submissions. Responds in 9-12 months to mss. Book catalog free; ms guidelines online.

- Electronic submissions are strongly preferred.
- ''We publish books at the heart of science fiction and fantasy.''

Fiction Fantasy, science fiction. Interested in science fiction novels (based on real science) and fantasy novels ''that at least strive for originality.'' Submit synopsis and complete ms.

Recent Title(s) *The Prometheus Project*, by Steve Shite; *The Course of Empire*, by Eric Flint and K.D. Wentworth; *E. Godz*, by Robert Asprin and Esther Friesner.

Tips ''See our books before submitting. Send for our writers' guidelines.''

⊘ BAKER ACADEMIC

Imprint of Baker Publishing Group, P.O. Box 6287, Grand Rapids MI 49516-6287. (616)676-9185. Fax: (616)676-2315. Website: www.bakeracademic.com. Editorial Director: Jim Kinney. Estab. 1939. Publishes hardcover and trade paperback originals. **Publishes 50 titles/year. 10% of books from first-time authors; 85% from unagented writers. Offers advance.** Publishes book 1 year after acceptance of ms. Book catalog for $9^{1}/_{2} \times 12^{1}/_{2}$ SAE with 3 first-class stamps; ms guidelines for #10 SASE.

- ''Baker Academic publishes religious academic and professional books for students and church leaders. Most of our authors and readers are Christians with academic interests, and our books are purchased from all standard retailers.'' Does not accept unsolicited queries.

Nonfiction Illustrated book, multimedia, reference, scholarly, textbook, dictionary, encyclopedia, reprint, professional book, CD-ROM. Subjects include anthropology/archeology, education, psychology, religion, women's issues/studies, Biblical studies, Christian doctrine, books for pastors and church leaders, contemporary issues.

Recent Title(s) *360-Degree Preaching*, by Michael J. Quicke (professional); *New Testament History*, by Ben Witherington III; *Deconstructing Evangelism*, by D.G. Hart.

⊘ BAKER BOOKS

Imprint of Baker Publishing Group, P.O. Box 6287, Grand Rapids MI 49516-6287. (616)676-9185. Fax: (616)676-9573. Website: www.bakerbooks.com. Estab. 1939. Publishes hardcover and trade paperback originals, and trade paperback reprints. Does not accept unsolicited proposals. Book catalog for $9^{1}/_{2} \times 12^{1}/_{2}$ SAE with 3 first-class stamps; ms guidelines for #10 SASE.

- ''Baker Books publishes popular religious nonfiction reference books and professional books for church leaders. Most of our authors and readers are evangelical Christians, and our books are purchased from Christian bookstores, mail-order retailers, and school bookstores.'' Does not accept unsolicited queries.

Nonfiction Biography, multimedia, reference, self-help, textbook, CD-ROM. Subjects include child guidance/parenting, psychology, religion, women's issues/studies, Christian doctrine, books for pastors and church leaders, seniors' concerns, singleness, contemporary issues.

Recent Title(s) *Being Sick Well: Joyful Living Despite Chronic Illness*, by Jeffrey H. Boyd, MD; *Leading Leaders: Empowering Church Boards for Ministry Excellence*, by Aubrey Malphurs; *Never Blink in a Hailstorm and Other Lessons on Leadership*, by David L. McKenna.

⊘ BAKER PUBLISHING GROUP

P.O. Box 6287, Grand Rapids MI 49516-6287. (616)676-9185. Fax: (616)676-2315. Website: www.bakerbooks.com. **Imprints** Baker Academic; Baker Books; Bethany House; Brazos Press; Chosen; Fleming H. Revell.

• *Does not accept unsolicited queries.*

BALCONY PRESS

512 E. Wilson, Suite 213, Glendale CA 91206. (818)956-5313. E-mail: ann@balconypress.com. **Acquisitions:** Ann Gray, publisher. Publishes hardcover and trade paperback originals. **Publishes 6-8 titles/year. Pays 10% royalty on wholesale price.** Accepts simultaneous submissions. Responds in 1 month to queries and proposals; 3 months to mss. Book catalog free.

• "We also now publish *LA Architect* magazine focusing on contemporary architecture and design in Southern California. Editor: Jesse Brink."

Nonfiction Subjects include art/architecture, ethnic, gardening, history (relative to design, art, and architecture), regional. "We are interested in the human side of design as opposed to technical or how-to. We like to think our books will be interesting to the general public who might not otherwise select an architecture or design book." Query by e-mail or letter. Submit outline and 2 sample chapters with introduction, if applicable.

Recent Title(s) *Iron: Erecting the Walt Disney Concert Hall,* by Gil Garcetti.

Tips Audience consists of architects, designers, and the general public who enjoy those fields. "Our books typically cover California subjects, but that is not a restriction. It's always nice when an author has strong ideas about how the book can be effectively marketed. We are not afraid of small niches if a good sales plan can be devised."

BALE BOOKS

Bale Publications, 5121 St. Charles Ave., Suite #13, New Orleans LA 70115. **Acquisitions:** Don Bale, Jr, editor-in-chief. Estab. 1963. Publishes hardcover and paperback originals and reprints. **Publishes 10 titles/year. 50% of books from first-time authors; 90% from unagented writers. Offers standard 10-12 1/2 % royalty contract on wholesale or retail price; sometimes makes outright purchases of $500.** Publishes book 3 years after acceptance of ms. Does not accept simultaneous submissions. Responds in 3 months to queries. Book catalog for #10 SAE with 2 first-class stamps.

○━ "Our mission is to educate numismatists about coins, coin collecting, and investing opportunities."

Nonfiction Numismatics. Subjects include hobbies, money/finance. "Our specialties are coin and stock market investment books; especially coin investment books and coin price guides." Submit outline, 3 sample chapters.

Recent Title(s) *How to Find Valuable Old & Scarce Coins,* by Jules Penn.

Tips "Most of our books are sold through publicity and ads in the coin newspapers. We are open to any new ideas in the area of numismatics. Write for a teenage through adult level. Lead the reader by the hand like a teacher, building chapter by chapter. Our books sometimes have a light, humorous treatment, but not necessarily. We look for good English, construction and content, and sales potential."

Ⓐ BALLANTINE PUBLISHING GROUP

Imprint of Random House, Inc., 1745 Broadway, 18th Floor, New York NY 10019. (212)782-9000. Website: www.randomhouse.com. Estab. 1952. Ms guidelines online.

Imprints Ballantine Books; Ballantine Reader's Circle; Del Rey; Del Rey/Lucas Books; Fawcett; Ivy; One World; Wellspring.

○━ Ballantine Books publishes a wide variety of nonfiction and fiction.

Nonfiction Biography, general nonfiction, gift book, how-to, humor, self-help. Subjects include animals, child guidance/parenting, community, cooking/foods/nutrition, creative nonfiction, education, gay/lesbian, health/medicine, history, language/literature, memoirs, military/war, recreation, religion, sex, spirituality, travel, true crime, women's issues/studies. *Agented submissions only.* Reviews artwork/photos as part of ms package. Send photocopies.

Fiction Confession, ethnic, fantasy, feminist, gay/lesbian, historical, humor, literary, mainstream/contemporary (women's), military/war, multicultural, mystery, romance, short story collections, spiritual, suspense, general fiction. *Agented submissions only.*

Ⓐ ⊘ BANTAM BOOKS FOR YOUNG READERS

Imprint of Random House Children's Books/Random House, Inc., 1745 Broadway, New York NY 10019. (212)782-9000. Website: www.randomhouse.com/kids.

• *Not seeking mss at this time.*

Ⓐ ⊘ BANTAM DELL PUBLISHING GROUP

Random House, Inc., 1745 Broadway, New York NY 10019. (212)782-9000. Website: www.bantamdell.com. Estab. 1945. Publishes hardcover, trade paperback and mass market paperback originals; mass market paperback reprints. Accepts simultaneous submissions.

Imprints Bantam Hardcover; Bantam Mass Market; Bantam Trade Paperback; Crimeline; Delacorte Press; Dell; Delta; The Dial Press; Domain; DTP; Fanfare; Island; Spectra.

   ⊶ Bantam Dell is a division of Random House, publishing both fiction and nonfiction. *No unsolicited mss*; send one-page queries.

Nonfiction Biography, how-to, humor, self-help. Subjects include Americana, child guidance/parenting, cooking/foods/nutrition, government/politics, health/medicine, history, military/war, New Age, philosophy, psychology, religion, science, sociology, spirituality, sports, true crime, women's issues/studies, fitness, mysticism/astrology.

Fiction Adventure, fantasy, historical, horror, literary, military/war, mystery, science fiction, suspense, women's fiction, general commercial fiction.

Recent Title(s) *The Glass Lake*, by Maeve Binchy; *Diabesity*, by Francine R. Kaufman, MD; *Charming Billy*, by Alice McDermott.

⊘ BANTAM DOUBLEDAY DELL BOOKS FOR YOUNG READERS

Random House Children's Publishing, Random House, Inc., 1745 Broadway, New York NY 10019. (212)782-9000. Fax: (212)782-8234. Website: www.randomhouse.com/kids. Vice President/Publisher: Beverly Horowitz. **Acquisitions:** Michelle Poploff, editorial director. Publishes hardcover, trade paperback and mass market paperback series originals, trade paperback reprints. **Publishes 300 titles/year. Receives thousands queries/year. 10% of books from first-time authors; small% from unagented writers. Pays royalty. Offers varied advance.** Publishes book 2 years after acceptance of ms. Does not accept simultaneous submissions. Responds in 2 months to queries. Book catalog for 9×12 SASE.

Imprints Delacorte Press Books for Young Readers; Doubleday Books for Young Readers; Dell Laurel Leaf (YA); Dell Yearling (middle grade).

   ⊶ "Bantam Doubleday Dell Books for Young Readers publishes award-winning books by distinguished authors and the most promising new writers." The best way to break in to this market is through its 2 contests, the Delacrote/Yearling Contest and the Delacorte Press Contest for a First Young Adult Novel.

Nonfiction Children's/juvenile. "Bantam Doubleday Dell Books for Young Readers publishes a very limited number of nonfiction titles." *No unsolicited mss.*

Fiction Adventure, fantasy, historical, humor, juvenile, mainstream/contemporary, mystery, picture books, suspense, chapter books, middle-grade. *No unsolicited mss.* Accepts unsolicited queries only.

Recent Title(s) *Sisterhood of the Traveling Pants*, by Ann Brashares; *Cuba 15*, by Nancy Osa.

BARBOUR PUBLISHING, INC.

P.O. Box 719, Uhrichsville OH 44683. (740)922-6045. Fax: (740)922-5948. Website: www.barbourpublishing.com. **Acquisitions:** Paul Muckley, editorial director (nonfiction); Rebecca Germany, senior editor (women's fiction). Estab. 1981. Publishes hardcover, trade paperback and mass market paperback originals and reprints. **Publishes 200 titles/year. Receives 500 queries and 1000 mss/year. 40% of books from first-time authors; 90% from unagented writers. Pays 0-12% royalty on net price or makes outright purchase of $500-5,000. Offers $500-5,000 advance.** Publishes book 2 years after acceptance of ms. Accepts simultaneous submissions. Responds in 1 month to queries. Book catalog online or for 9×12 SAE with 2 first-class stamps; ms guidelines for #10 SASE or online.

Imprints Heartsong Presents (contact Rebecca Germany, managing editor).

   ⊶ Barbour Books publishes inspirational/devotional material that is nondenominational and evangelical in nature; Heartsong Presents publishes Christian romance. "We're a Christian evangelical publisher."

Nonfiction Reference, devotional. Subjects include child guidance/parenting, cooking/foods/nutrition, money/finance, religion (evangelical Christian), women's issues/studies, inspirational/Christian living. "We look for book ideas with mass appeal—nothing in narrowly-defined niches. If you can appeal to a wide audience with an important message, creatively presented, we'd be interested to see your proposal." Submit outline, 3 sample chapters, SASE. Reviews artwork/photos as part of ms package. Send photocopies.

Fiction Romance (historical and contemporary), suspense, women's issues. "Heartsong romance is 'sweet'—no sex, no bad language. Other genres may be 'grittier'—real-life stories. All must have Christian faith as an underlying basis. Common writer's mistakes are a sketchy proposal, an unbelieveable story, and a story that doesn't fit our guidelines for inspirational romances." Submit 3 sample chapters, synopsis, SASE.

Recent Title(s) *Daily Wisdom for Working Women*, by Michelle Medlock Adams and Gena Maselli (devotional); *Dead as a Scone*, by Ron and Janet Benrey (fiction); *Mommy's Locked in the Bathroom*, by Cynthia Sumner (women's issues).

Tips "Audience is evangelical/Christian conservative, nondenominational, young and old. We're looking for great concepts, not necessarily a big name author or agent. We want to publish books that will sell millions, not just 'flash in the pan' releases. Send us your ideas!"

Book Publishers

BAREFOOT BOOKS

2067 Massachusettes Ave., Cambridge MA 02140. (617)576-0660. Fax: (617)576-0049. Website: www.barefootb ooks.com. **Acquisitions:** Submissions Editor. Publishes hardcover and trade paperback originals. **Publishes 30 titles/year. Receives 2,000 queries and 3,000 mss/year. 35% of books from first-time authors; 60% from unagented writers. Pays 2½-5% royalty on retail price, or makes outright purchase of $5.99-19.99. Offers advance.** Publishes book 2 years after acceptance of ms. Accepts simultaneous submissions. Responds in 4 months. Book catalog for 9×12 SAE stamped with $1.80 postage; ms guidelines online.

> ⚷ "We are a small, independent publishing company that publishes high-quality picture books for children of all ages and specializes in the work of artists and writers from many cultures. We focus on themes that support independence of spirit, encourage openness to others, and foster a life-long love of learning. Prefers full manuscript."

Fiction Juvenile. Barefoot Books only publishes children's picture books and anthologies of folktales. "We do not publish novels. We encourage authors to send their full manuscript. Always include SASE."

Recent Title(s) *We All Went on Safari: A Counting Journey Through Tanzania*, by Laurie Krebs (early learning picture book); *The Fairie's Gift*, by Tanya Robyn Batt (picture book); *The Lady of Ten Thousand Names: Goddess Stories From Many Cultures*, by Burleigh Mutén (illustrated anthology).

Tips "Our audience is made up of children and parents, teachers and students, of many different ages and cultures. Since we are a small publisher, and we definitely publish for a 'niche' market, it is helpful to look at our books and our website before submitting, to see if your book would fit into the type of book we publish."

BARRICADE BOOKS, INC.

185 Bridge Plaza N., Suite 308A, Fort Lee NJ 07024-5900. (201)944-7600. Fax: (201)944-6363. **Acquisitions:** Carole Stuart, publisher. Estab. 1991. Publishes hardcover and trade paperback originals, trade paperback reprints. **Publishes 30 titles/year. Receives 200 queries and 100 mss/year. 80% of books from first-time authors; 50% from unagented writers. Pays 10-12% royalty on retail price for hardcover. Offers advance.** Publishes book 18 months after acceptance of ms. Responds in 1 month to queries. Book catalog for $3.

> ⚷ Barricade Books publishes nonfiction, "mostly of the controversial type, and books we can promote with authors who can talk about their topics on radio and television and to the press."

Nonfiction Biography, how-to, reference, self-help. Subjects include business/economics, ethnic, gay/lesbian, government/politics, health/medicine, history, nature/environment, psychology, sociology, women's issues/ studies. Query with SASE, or submit outline, 1-2 sample chapters. Material will not be returned or responded to without SASE. Reviews artwork/photos as part of ms package. Send photocopies.

Recent Title(s) *Il Dottore*, by Ron Felber; *Palm Springs Confidential*, by Howard Johns.

Tips "Do your homework. Visit bookshops to find publishers who are doing the kinds of books you want to write. Always submit to a person—not just 'Editor.' Always enclose a SASE or you may not get a response."

BARRON'S EDUCATIONAL SERIES, INC.

250 Wireless Blvd., Hauppauge NY 11788. (800)645-3476. Fax: (631)434-3723. E-mail: waynebarr@barronsedu c.com. Website: barronseduc.com. **Acquisitions:** Wayne Barr, acquisitions editor. Estab. 1941. Publishes hardcover, paperback and mass market originals and software. **Publishes 400 titles/year. Receives 2,000 queries/ year. 25% of books from first-time authors; 75% from unagented writers. Pays 12-14% royalty on net receipts. Offers $3-4,000 advance.** Publishes book 18 months after acceptance of ms. Accepts simultaneous submissions. Responds in 3 months to queries; 8 months to mss. Book catalog free; ms guidelines online.

> ⚷ Barron's tends to publish series of books, both for adults and children. "We are always on the lookout for creative nonfiction ideas for children and adults."

Nonfiction Children's/juvenile, student test prep guides. Subjects include business/economics, child guidance/ parenting, education, health/medicine, hobbies, language/literature, New Age, sports, translation, travel, adult education, foreign language, review books, guidance, pets, literary guides, food/nutrition. Query with SASE, or submit outline, 2-3 sample chapters. Reviews artwork/photos as part of ms package.

Fiction Juvenile. Submit sample chapters, synopsis.

Recent Title(s) *Hex Appeal*, by Lucy Summers; *Rockwell: A Boy and His Dog*, by Loren Spiotta DiMare.

Tips "Audience is mostly educated self-learners and hobbyists. The writer has the best chance of selling us a book that will fit into one of our series. Children's books have less chance for acceptance because of the glut of submissions. SASE must be included for the return of all materials. Please be patient for replies."

BASIC BOOKS

Perseus Books, 387 Park Ave. S., 12th Floor, New York NY 10016. (212)340-8100. Website: www.basicbooks.c om. **Acquisitions:** Editor. Estab. 1952. Publishes hardcover and trade paperback originals and reprints. Accepts simultaneous submissions. Responds in at least 3 months to queries. Book catalog and ms guidelines free.

○━ "We want serious nonfiction by leading scholars, intellectuals, and journalists. No poetry, romance, children's books, conventional thrillers, or conventional horror."

Nonfiction Subjects include history, psychology, sociology, politics, current affairs. Submit proposal package including outline, sample chapters, TOC, cv, SASE. No e-mail or disk submissions.

Recent Title(s) *The Mystery of Capital*, by Hernando de Soto (economics); *The Hidden Hitler*, by Lothar Machton (history/biography); *The Truth Will Set You Free*, by Alice Miller (psychology).

BASIC HEALTH PUBLICATIONS, INC.

8200 Boulevard E., 25G, North Bergen NJ 07047. (201)868-8336. Fax: (201)868-2842. Website: www.letsliveonline.com. **Acquisitions:** Norman Goldfind, publisher. Estab. 2001. Publishes trade paperback and mass market paperback originals and reprints. Accepts simultaneous submissions. Book catalog online; ms guidelines for #10 SASE.

Nonfiction Booklets, trade paperback, mass market paperback. Subjects include health/medicine. "We are very highly focused on health, alternative medicine, nutrition, and fitness. Must be well researched and documented with appropriate references. Writing should be aimed at lay audience but also be able to cross over to professional market." Submit proposal package including outline, 2-3 sample chapters, introduction.

Recent Title(s) *Grow Younger With HGF*, by Ronald Klatz, MD, DO; *Breathe for Life*, by Sophie Gabriel.

Tips "Our audience is over 30, well educated, middle to upper income. We prefer writers with professional credentials (MDs, PhDs, NDs, etc.), or writers with backgrounds in health and medicine."

BATTELLE PRESS

505 King Ave., Columbus OH 43201. (614)424-6393. Fax: (614)424-3819. E-mail: press@battelle.org. Website: www.battelle.org/bookstore. **Acquisitions:** Joe Sheldrick. Estab. 1980. Publishes hardcover and paperback originals and markets primarily by direct mail. **Publishes 15 titles/year. Pays 10% royalty on wholesale price.** Publishes book 6 months after acceptance of ms. Accepts simultaneous submissions. Responds in 1 month to queries. Book catalog free; ms guidelines online.

○━ Battelle Press strives to be a primary source of books and software on science and technology management.

Nonfiction Subjects include science. "We are looking for management, leadership, project management and communication books specifically targeted to engineers and scientists." Query with SASE. Returns submissions with SASE only by writer's request. Reviews artwork/photos as part of ms package. Send photocopies.

Recent Title(s) *Communications Guide*; *Technically Speaking*.

Tips Audience consists of engineers, researchers, scientists and corporate researchers and developers.

BAY/SOMA PUBLISHING, INC.

444 DeHaro St., Suite 130, San Francisco CA 94107. (415)252-4350. Fax: (415)252-4352. E-mail: info@baybooks.com. Website: www.baybooks.com. President/Publisher: James Connolly. **Acquisitions:** Floyd Yearout, editorial director (floyd.yearout@baybooks.com). Publishes hardcover originals, trade paperback originals and reprints. Accepts simultaneous submissions. Book catalog for 9×12 SAE with 3 first-class stamps or see website.

Nonfiction Coffee table book, cookbook, gift book, how-to, humor, illustrated book, companion books for TV. Subjects include cooking/foods/nutrition, gardening, health/medicine, nature/environment, interior design. Query with SASE.

Recent Title(s) *The American Boulangerie*, by Pascal Rigo; *Compact Living*, by Jane Graining; *Dangerous Desserts*, edited by Orlando Murrin.

BAYLOR UNIVERSITY PRESS

P.O. Box 97363, Waco TX 76798. (254)710-3164. Fax: (254)710-3440. Website: www.baylorpress.com. **Acquisitions:** Carey C. Newman, editor. Publishes hardcover and trade paperback originals. **Publishes 14 titles/year. Pays 10% royalty on wholesale price.** Publishes book 9 months after acceptance of ms. Does not accept simultaneous submissions. Responds in 2 months to proposals. Ms guidelines online.

○━ "We publish contemporary and historical scholarly works on religion, ethics, church-state studies, and oral history, particularly as these relate to Texas and the Southwest." Currently emphasizing religious studies, history. De-emphasizing art, archaeology.

Nonfiction Subjects include politics/society, rhetoric/religion, sociology/religion, Judaism/Christianity, religion/higher education, Christianity/literature. Submit outline, 1-3 sample chapters.

Recent Title(s) *Building Jewish in the Roman East*, by Peter Richardson; *Encyclopedia of Evangelicalism*, by Randall Balmer; *Not Quite American? The Shaping of Muslim Identity in the United States*, by Yvonne Yazbeck Haddad.

Tips "Baylor University Press publishes academic books that explore the religious dimensions of selected academic disciplines. Through its publishing program, the press seeks to be a steward of public discourse about the role of religion in a global culture."

BAYWOOD PUBLISHING CO., INC.

26 Austin Ave., P.O. Box 337, Amityville NY 11701. (631)691-1270. Fax: (631)691-1770. E-mail: baywood@baywood.com. Website: www.baywood.com. **Acquisitions:** Stuart Cohen, managing editor. Estab. 1964. **Publishes 25 titles/year. Pays 7-15% royalty on retail price. Offers advance.** Publishes book within 1 year after acceptance of ms. Does not accept simultaneous submissions. Book catalog and ms guidelines free or online.

○╼ Baywood Publishing publishes original and innovative books in the humanities and social sciences, including areas such as health sciences, gerontology, death and bereavement, psychology, technical communications and archeology.

Nonfiction Scholarly, technical, scholarly. Subjects include anthropology/archeology, computers/electronic, education, health/medicine, nature/environment, psychology, sociology, women's issues/studies, gerontology, imagery, labor relations, death/dying, drugs. Submit proposal package.

Recent Title(s) *Common Threads: Nine Widows' Journeys Through Love, Loss and Healing*, by Diane S. Kaimann; *Invitation to the Life Course: Toward New Understandings of Later Life*, edited by Richard A. Settersten, Jr.; *Exploding Steamboats, Senate Debates and Technical Reports: The Convergence of Technology, Politics and Rhetoric in the Steamboat Bill of 1838*, by R. John Brockmann.

BEACON HILL PRESS OF KANSAS CITY

Nazarene Publishing House, P.O. Box 419527, Kansas City MO 64141. (816)931-1900. Fax: (816)753-4071. **Acquisitions:** Judi Perry, consumer editor. Publishes hardcover and paperback originals. **Publishes 30 titles/year. Pays royalty.** Publishes book 1 year after acceptance of ms. Responds in 3 months to queries.

○╼ "Beacon Hill Press is a Christ-centered publisher that provides authentically Christian resources faithful to God's word and relevant to life."

Nonfiction Accent on holy living; encouragement in daily Christian life. Subjects include applied Christianity, spiritual formation, leadership resources, contemporary issues, and Christian care. No fiction, autobiography, poetry, short stories, or children's picture books. Query with SASE, or submit proposal package. Average ms length: 30,000-60,000.

Recent Title(s) *My Faith Still Holds*, by Joyce Williams.

BEACON PRESS

25 Beacon St., Boston MA 02108-2892. (617)742-2110. Fax: (617)723-3097. E-mail: cvyce@beacon.org. Website: www.beacon.org. Director: Helene Atwan. **Acquisitions:** Gayatri Patnaik, senior editor (African-American, Asian-American, Latino, Native American, Jewish, and gay and lesbian studies, anthropology); Joanne Wyckoff, executive editor (child and family issues, environmental concerns); Amy Caldwell, senior editor (poetry, gender studies, gay/lesbian studies, and Cuban studies); Christopher Vyce, assistant editor; Brian Halley, assistant editor. Estab. 1854. Publishes hardcover originals and paperback reprints. **Publishes 60 titles/year. 10% of books from first-time authors. Pays royalty. Offers advance.** Accepts simultaneous submissions. Responds in 3 months to queries.

Imprints Bluestreak Series (innovative literary writing by women of color).

○╼ Beacon Press publishes general interest books that promote the following values: the inherent worth and dignity of every person; justice, equity, and compassion in human relations; acceptance of one another; a free and responsible search for truth and meaning; the goal of world community with peace, liberty, and justice for all; respect for the interdependent web of all existence. Currently emphasizing innovative nonfiction writing by people of all colors. De-emphasizing poetry, children's stories, art books, self-help.

Nonfiction Scholarly. Subjects include anthropology/archeology, child guidance/parenting, education, ethnic, gay/lesbian, nature/environment, philosophy, religion, women's issues/studies, world affairs. General nonfiction including works of original scholarship, religion, women's studies, philosophy, current affairs, anthropology, environmental concerns, African-American, Asian-American, Native American, Latino, and Jewish studies, gay and lesbian studies, education, legal studies, child and family issues, Irish studies. *Strongly prefers agented submissions.* Query with SASE, or submit outline, sample chapters, résumé, CV. *Strongly prefers referred submissions, on exclusive.*

Recent Title(s) *Radical Equation*, by Robert Moses and Charles Cobb; *All Souls*, by Michael Patrick McDonald; *Speak to Me*, by Marcie Hershman.

Tips "We probably accept only 1 or 2 manuscripts from an unpublished pool of 4,000 submissions/year. No fiction, children's book, or poetry submissions invited. An academic affiliation is helpful."

Ⓝ ∅ BEDFORD/ST. MARTIN'S

Division of Holtzbrinck Publishers, Boston Office: 75 Arlington St., Boston MA 02116. (617)399-4000. Fax: (617)426-8582. New York Office: 33 Irving Place, New York NY 10003. (212)375-7000. Fax: (212)614-1885. Website: www.bedfordstmartins.com. Estab. 1981. **Publishes 200 titles/year.** Book catalog online.

○→ College publisher specializing in English (composition, development, literature, and linguistics); history; communications; literature; philosophy; religion; business and technical writing; and music.

BEHRMAN HOUSE, INC.

11 Edison Place, Springfield NJ 07081. (973)379-7200. Fax: (973)379-7280. Website: www.behrmanhouse.com. **Acquisitions:** Editorial Committee. Estab. 1921. Accepts simultaneous submissions. Responds in 3 months to queries. Book catalog free; ms guidelines online.

○→ "Behrman House publishes quality books and supplementary materials of Jewish content—history, Bible, philosophy, holidays, ethics, Israel, Hebrew—for the classroom and the reading public."

Nonfiction Children's/juvenile (ages 1-18), reference, textbook. Subjects include ethnic, philosophy, religion. "We want Jewish textbooks for the el-hi market." Query with SASE, or submit 2 sample chapters, résumé, TOC, target audience. No electronic submissions.

Recent Title(s) *Great Israel Scavenger Hunt*, by Scott Blumenthal (Israel); *Rediscovering the Jewish Holidays*, by Nina Beth Cardin and Gila Gevirtz (Jewish Holidays).

FREDERIC C. BEIL, PUBLISHER, INC.

609 Whitaker St., Savannah GA 31401. (912)233-2446. Fax: (912)233-6456. E-mail: beilbook@beil.com. Website: www.beil.com. **Acquisitions:** Mary Ann Bowman, editor. Estab. 1982. Publishes hardcover originals and reprints. **Publishes 13 titles/year. Receives 3,500 queries and 13 mss/year. 80% of books from first-time authors; 100% from unagented writers. Pays 7½% royalty on retail price.** Publishes book 20 months after acceptance of ms. Accepts simultaneous submissions. Responds in 1 week to queries. Book catalog free.

Imprints The Sandstone Press; Hypermedia, Inc.

○→ Frederic C. Beil publishes in the fields of history, literature, and biography.

Nonfiction Biography, children's/juvenile, general nonfiction, illustrated book, reference, general trade. Subjects include art/architecture, history, language/literature, book arts. Query with SASE. Reviews artwork/photos as part of ms package. Send photocopies.

Fiction Historical, literary, regional, short story collections, biography. Query with SASE.

Recent Title(s) *Joseph Jefferson: Dean of the American Theatre*, by Arthur Bloom; *Goya, Are You With Me Now?*, by H.E. Francis.

Tips "Our objectives are (1) to offer to the reading public carefully selected texts of lasting value; (2) to adhere to high standards in the choice of materials and in bookmaking craftsmanship; (3) to produce books that exemplify good taste in format and design; and (4) to maintain the lowest cost consistent with quality."

Ⓝ BELLWETHER-CROSS PUBLISHING

Imprint of Star Publishing Co., Inc., P.O. Box 68, Belmont CA 94002. (650)591-3505. Fax: (650)591-3898. Website: www.starpublishing.com.

Nonfiction Submit cover letter and complete ms with SASE. Reviews artwork/photos as part of ms package. Send photocopies.

Recent Title(s) *Transitional Science*, by H. Sue Way and Gaines B. Jackson; *Daring to Be Different: A Manager's Ascent to Leadership*, by James A. Hatherley.

BENTLEY PUBLISHERS

1734 Massachusetts Ave., Cambridge MA 02138-1804. (617)423-4595. Fax: (617)876-9235. Website: www.bentleypublishers.com. Estab. 1950. Publishes hardcover and trade paperback originals and reprints. Does not accept simultaneous submissions. Book catalog and ms guidelines for 9×12 SAE with 4 first-class stamps. Proposal guidelines online.

○→ Bentley Publishers publishes books for automotive enthusiasts. "We are interested in books that showcase good research, strong illustrations, and valuable technical information."

Nonfiction Automotive subjects only. How-to, technical, theory of operation. Subjects include sports (motor sports). Query with SASE, or submit sample chapters, author bio, synopsis, target market. Reviews artwork/photos as part of ms package.

Recent Title(s) *Alex Zanardi: My Sweetest Victory*, by Alex Zanardi and Gianluca Gasparini; *Bosch Automotive Handbook*, by Robert Bosch (6th edition); *The British and Their Works*, by Markus Lupa.

Tips "Our audience is composed of serious, intelligent automobile, sports car, and racing enthusiasts, automotive technicians and high-performance tuners."

Ⓐ Ⓞ THE BERKLEY PUBLISHING GROUP

Penguin Putnam, Inc., 375 Hudson St., New York NY 10014. (212)366-2000. E-mail: online@penguinputnam.c om. Website: www.penguinputnam.com. President/Publishers: Leslie Gelbman. Estab. 1955. Publishes paperback and mass market originals and reprints. **Publishes more than 500 titles/year.** Does not accept simultaneous submissions.

Imprints Ace; Berkley; Jove.

- *Currently not accepting unsolicited submissions.*
- ⚷ The Berkley Publishing Group publishes a variety of general nonfiction and fiction including the traditional categories of romance, mystery and science fiction.

Nonfiction Biography, general nonfiction, how-to, reference, self-help. Subjects include business/economics, child guidance/parenting, creative nonfiction, gay/lesbian, health/medicine, history, New Age, psychology, true crime, women's issues/studies, job-seeking communication, positive thinking, general commercial publishing. No memoirs or personal stories. *Prefers agented submissions.*

Fiction Adventure, historical, literary, mystery, romance, spiritual, suspense, western, young adult. No occult fiction. *Prefers agented submissions.*

Recent Title(s) *Visions in Death*, by Norah Roberts; *Dark Secret*, by Christine Feehan.

Ⓝ BERRETT-KOEHLER PUBLISHERS, INC.

235 Montgomery St., #650, San Francisco CA 94104 USA. (415)288-0260. Fax: (415)362-2512. E-mail: bkpub@b kpub.com. Website: www.bkconnection.com. **Acquisitions:** Jeevan Sivasubramaniam. Publishes hardcover originals, trade paperback originals, mass market paperback originals, hardcover reprints, trade paperback reprints. **Publishes 40 titles/year. Receives 1,300 queries and 800 mss/year. 20-30% of books from first-time authors; 70% from unagented writers. Pays 10-20% royalty.** Publishes book 10 months after acceptance of ms. Accepts simultaneous submissions. Responds in 1 month. Book catalog and ms guidelines online.

Nonfiction General nonfiction, gift book, how-to, humor, scholarly, self-help, textbook. Subjects include business/economics, community, government/politics, New Age, spirituality, world affairs. Submit proposal package including outline, 1-2 sample chapters, author bio. Hard-copy proposals only. Do not e-mail, fax, or phone please. Reviews artwork/photos as part of ms package. Send photocopies or originals with SASE.

Recent Title(s) *Alternatives to Globalization*, by Jerry Mander & IFG (current affairs); *Leadership and the New Science*, by Margaret Wheatley (business); *Confessions of an Economic Hit Man*, by John Perkins (*New York Times* bestseller).

Tips "Our audience is business leaders, OD consultants, academics, economists, political leaders, and people with a popular platform. Use common sense, do your research, know what kind of books we publish, address the query properly, try not to have coffee-mug stains on your cover letter."

BET BOOKS

850 3rd Ave., New York NY 10022. Website: www.bet.com/books. **Acquisitions:** Glenda Howard, senior editor (Sepia and New Spirit); Karen Thomas, editorial director (Arabesque). Estab. 1998. Responds in 2-4 months to queries.

Imprints Arabesque (romance with predominantly African-American characters); Sepia (contemporary novels—thrillers, mystery, adventure, urban life); New Spirit (inspirational novels and motivational nonfiction in which characters overcome challenges through faith).

Tips "Please do not phone to see if your manuscript was received or returned, or to find out what we thought of it. A self-addressed, stamped postcard can be enclosed with your submission if you want confirmation of its arrival. Specify whether you would like your manuscript returned or recycled if it is not right for us."

Ⓞ BETHANY HOUSE PUBLISHERS

11400 Hampshire Ave. S., Minneapolis MN 55438. (952)829-2500. Fax: (952)996-1304. Website: www.bethanyh ouse.com. Estab. 1956. Publishes hardcover and trade paperback originals, mass market paperback reprints. **Publishes 90-100 titles/year. 2% of books from first-time authors; 50% from unagented writers. Pays royalty on net price. Offers advance.** Publishes book 1 year after acceptance of ms. Accepts simultaneous submissions. Responds in 3 months to queries. Book catalog for 9×12 SAE with 5 first-class stamps; ms guidelines online.

- *All unsolicited mss returned unopened.*
- ⚷ Bethany House Publishers specializes in books that communicate Biblical truth and assist people in both spiritual and practical areas of life. "While we do not accept unsolicited queries or proposals via telephone or e-mail, we will consider 1-page queries sent by fax and directed to Adult Nonfiction, Adult Fiction, or Young Adult/Children."

Nonfiction Children's/juvenile, gift book, how-to, reference, self-help, spiritual growth. Subjects include child guidance/parenting, Biblical disciplines, personal and corporate renewal, emerging generations, devotional, marriage and family, applied theology, inspirational.

Fiction Historical, young adult, contemporary.

Recent Title(s) *Under God*, by Toby Mae and Michael Tait (nonfiction); *Candle in the Darkness*, by Lynn Austin (fiction); *God Called a Girl*, by Shannon Kubiak Primicerio (YA nonfiction).

Tips ''Bethany House Publishers' publishing program relates Biblical truth to all areas of life—whether in the framework of a well-told story, of a challenging book for spiritual growth, or of a Bible reference work. We are seeking high quality fiction and nonfiction that will inspire and challenge our audience.''

BEYOND WORDS PUBLISHING, INC.

20827 NW Cornell Rd., Suite 500, Hillsboro OR 97124-9808. (503)531-8700. Fax: (503)531-8773. Website: www.beyondword.com. **Acquisitions:** Cynthia Black, editor-in-chief; Sarabeth Blakey, managing editor; Summer Steele, children's editor. Estab. 1984. Publishes hardcover and trade paperback originals and paperback reprints. **Publishes 10-15 titles/year. Receives 3,000 queries/year.** Accepts simultaneous submissions. Responds in 6 months to queries. Book catalog and ms guidelines for #10 SASE or online.

   • No electronic submissions or queries.

Nonfiction Children's/juvenile, coffee table book, gift book, how-to, self-help. Subjects include animals, child guidance/parenting, health/medicine, photography (selectively), psychology, spirituality, women's issues/studies. Query with SASE, or submit proposal package including outline, 3 sample chapters, author bio, publicity plans. Reviews artwork/photos as part of ms package. Send photocopies.

Fiction Ethnic (picture book), religious (children's). Does not accept adult fiction. Only wants children's/young adult fiction. Submit complete ms.

Tips ''*Beyond Words* markets to cultural, creative people, mostly women ages 30-60. Study our list before you submit and check out our website to make sure your book is a good fit for our list.''

⊘ BLACKBIRCH PRESS, INC.

Thomson Gale, 15822 Bernardo Center Dr., Suite C, San Diego CA 92127. Website: www.galegroup.com/blackbirch/. **Acquisitions:** Publisher. Estab. 1992. Publishes hardcover and trade paperback originals. Accepts simultaneous submissions. Replies only if interested to queries. Ms guidelines free.

   ⊶ Blackbirch Press publishes educational nonfiction books for elementary and middle school students.

Nonfiction Biography, children's/juvenile, illustrated book, reference. Subjects include animals, anthropology/archeology, art/architecture, education, health/medicine, history, nature/environment, science, sports, travel, women's issues/studies. Publishes in series—6-8 books at a time. ''No proposals for adult readers, please.'' *No unsolicited mss or proposals. No phone calls.* Query with SASE. Cover letters and résumés are useful for identifying new authors. Reviews artwork/photos as part of ms package. Send photocopies.

Recent Title(s) *A Whale on Her Own: The True Story of Wilma the Whale*, by Brian Skerry; *Flies*, by Elaine Pascoe.

Tips ''We cannot return submissions or send guidelines/replies without an enclosed SASE.''

Ⓝ BLEAK HOUSE BOOKS

953 E. Johnson St., Madison WI 53703. (608)259-8370. Website: www.bleakhousebooks.com. **Acquisitions:** Julie Kuczynski, mystery editor; Alison Embley, literary editor. Estab. 1995. **Publishes 6-10 titles/year. Receives 250+ queries and 50 mss/year. 50% of books from first-time authors; 90% from unagented writers. Pays 7¹/₂-15% royalty on wholesale price. Offers $500-4,000 advance.** Publishes book 12-18 months after acceptance of ms. Accepts simultaneous submissions. Responds in 1-2 months to queries; 2-3 months to mss. Book catalog online.

Fiction Literary, mystery. ''We are looking for gritty mystery/crime/suspense. Characters should be psychologically complex, flawed and human. We are rarely interested in cozies and are never interested in animals or inanimate objects that solve mysteries. We want books that are part of a planned series and we want authors that understand the business of publishing. We are also looking for dark and quirky literary fiction. Tell us a story that hasn't been told before. The most important thing is the quality of writing. Just because your best friends and family loved the book doesn't mean it's going to go over big with everybody else.'' Query with SASE. *All unsolicited mss returned unopened.*

Recent Title(s) *Blood of the Lamb*, by Michael Lister; *A Prayer for Dawn*, by Nathan Singer; *The Nail Knot*, by John Galligan.

Tips ''Our audience is made up of two groups. The first is mystery readers—a group dedicated to quality books that have a satisfaying conclusion to the age old questions of 'Whoodunit?' The second group reads books to get a different perspective on the human condition, to live through characters they haven't seen or heard from before. These readers aren't afraid of a book that is quirky or disturbed. Do not call us about submission guidelines, your query letter or anything else that can be answered in this book or others like it. Make sure your book is finished before contacting us. Our job is to clean up small stuff, not help rewrite a book. We are very loyal to our authors ... and work closely with our authors. We expect an author to be ready to work hard. It's a two way street.''

BLOOMBERG PRESS

Imprint of Bloomberg L.P., 100 Business Park Dr., P.O. Box 888, Princeton NJ 08542-0888. Website: www.bloomberg.com/books. **Acquisitions:** Jared Kieling. Estab. 1995. Publishes hardcover and trade paperback originals. **Publishes 18-22 titles/year. Receives 200 queries and 20 mss/year. 45% from unagented writers. Pays negotiable, competitive royalty. Offers negotiable advance.** Publishes book 9 months after acceptance of ms. Accepts simultaneous submissions. Responds in 1 month to queries with SASE. Book catalog for 10×13 SAE with 5 first-class stamps.

Imprints Bloomberg Professional Library.

> ⚷ Bloomberg Press publishes professional books for practitioners in the financial markets. ''We publish commercially successful, very high-quality books that stand out clearly from the competition by their brevity, ease of use, sophistication, and abundance of practical tips and strategies; books readers need, will use, and appreciate.''

Nonfiction How-to, reference, technical. Subjects include business/economics, money/finance, professional books on finance, investment and financial services, and books for financial advisors. ''We are looking for authorities and for experienced service journalists. Do not send us unfocused books containing general information already covered by books in the marketplace. We do not publish business, management, leadership, or career books.'' Submit outline, sample chapters, SAE with sufficient postage, or submit complete ms.

Tips ''*Bloomberg Professional Library*: Audience is upscale, financial professionals—traders, dealers, brokers, planners and advisors, financial managers, money managers, company executives, sophisticated investors. Authors are experienced financial journalists and/or financial professionals nationally prominent in their specialty for some time who have proven an ability to write a successful book. Research Bloomberg and look at our books in a library or bookstore, and peruse our website.''

Ⓝ BLOOMSBURY CHILDREN'S BOOKS

Imprint of Bloomsbury USA, 175 Fifth Ave., Suite 315, New York NY 10010. (646)307-5858. Fax: (212)982-2837. E-mail: bloomsburykids@bloomsburyusa.com. Website: www.bloomsburyusa.com. **Publishes 60 titles/year. 25% of books from first-time authors. Pays royalty. Offers advance.** Accepts simultaneous submissions. Responds in 6 months. Book catalog and ms guidelines online.

> ● No phone calls or e-mails.

Fiction Adventure, fantasy, historical, humor, juvenile, multicultural, mystery, picture books, poetry, science fiction, sports, suspense, young adult, animal, anthology, concept, contemporary, folktales, problem novels. ''We publish picture books, chapter books, middle grade, and YA novels, and some nonfiction.'' Query with SASE, or submit synopsis, first 3 chapters with SASE.

Recent Title(s) *Where Is Coco Going?*, by Sloane Tanen (picture books); *Once Upon a Curse*, by E.D. Baker (middle grade); *Enna Burning*, by Shannon Hale (young adult fantasy).

Tips ''Do not send originals or only copy. Be sure your work is appropriate for us. Familiarize yourself with our list by going to bookstores or libraries.''

Ⓩ BLUE MOON BOOKS, INC.

Imprint of Avalon Publishing Group, 245 W. 17th St., 11th Floor, New York NY 10011. (212)981-9919. Fax: (646)375-2571. Website: www.avalonpub.com. Estab. 1987. Publishes trade paperback and mass market paperback originals. Book catalog free.

> ⚷ ''Blue Moon Books is strictly an erotic press; largely fetish-oriented material, B&D, S&M, etc.''

Fiction Erotica. *No unsolicited mss.*

Recent Title(s) *Amateurs*, by Michael Hemmingson; *Venus in Lace*, by Marcus van Heller; *Confessions of a Left Bank Dominatrix*, by Gala Fur.

BLUEWOOD BOOKS

Imprint of The Siyeh Group, Inc., P.O. Box 689, San Mateo CA 94401. (650)548-0754. **Acquisitions:** Richard Michaels, director. Publishes trade paperback originals. **Publishes 8 titles/year. 20% of books from first-time authors; 100% from unagented writers. Makes work-for-hire assignments—fee depends upon book and writer's expertise. Offers ⅓ fee advance.** Does not accept simultaneous submissions.

> ⚷ ''We are looking for qualified writers for nonfiction series—history and biography oriented.''

Nonfiction Biography, illustrated book. Subjects include Americana, anthropology/archeology, art/architecture, business/economics, government/politics, health/medicine, history, military/war, multicultural, science, sports, women's issues/studies. Query with SASE.

Recent Title(s) *True Stories of Baseball's Hall of Famers,* by Russell Roberts (baseball history/biography); *100 Native Americans Who Shaped American History*, by Bonnie Juetner (American history/biography).

Tips "Our audience consists of adults and young adults. Our books are written on a newspaper level—clear, concise, well organized, and easy to understand. We encourage potential writers to send us a résumé, providing background qualifications and references."

BNA BOOKS

Imprint of The Bureau of National Affairs, Inc., 1231 25th St. NW, Washington DC 20037. (202)452-4343. Fax: (202)452-4997. E-mail: books@bna.com. Website: www.bnabooks.com. **Acquisitions:** Jim Fattibene, acquisitions manager. Estab. 1929. Publishes hardcover and softcover originals. Accepts simultaneous submissions. Book catalog and ms guidelines online.

O→ BNA Books publishes professional reference books written by lawyers, for lawyers.

Nonfiction Reference, scholarly. Subjects include labor and employment law, health law, legal practice, labor relations, intellectual property law, arbitration/ADR, occupational safety/health law, employee benefits law. No fiction, biographies, bibliographies, cookbooks, religion books, humor, or trade books. Submit detailed TOC or outline, cv, intended market, estimated word length.

Recent Title(s) *Computer and Intellectual Property Crime: Federal & State Law, 2004 Cumulative Supplement*; *Patent Litigation Strategies Handbooks, 2004 Cumulative Supplement.*

Tips "Our audience is made up of practicing lawyers and law librarians. We look for authoritative and comprehensive treatises that can be supplemented or revised every year or 2 on legal subjects of interest to those audiences."

BOA EDITIONS, LTD.

260 East Ave., Rochester NY 14604. (585)546-3410. Fax: (585)546-3913. E-mail: boaedit@frontiernet.net. Website: www.boaeditions.org. Estab. 1976. Publishes hardcover and trade paperback originals. **Publishes 11-13 titles/year. Receives 1,000 queries and 700 mss/year. 15% of books from first-time authors; 90% from unagented writers. Negotiates royalties. Offers variable advance.** Publishes book 18 months after acceptance of ms. Accepts simultaneous submissions. Responds in 1 week to queries; 5 months to mss. Ms guidelines online.

O→ BOA Editions publishes distinguished collections of poetry and poetry in translation. "Our goal is to publish the finest American contemporary poetry and poetry in translation."

Poetry BOA offers a first book poetry prize of $1,500 and book publication for the winner. For guidelines, see the home page of our website.

Recent Title(s) *Owner of the House*, by Louis Simpson; *Book of My Nights*, by Li-Young Lee.

Tips "Readers who, like Whitman, expect of the poet to 'indicate more than the beauty and dignity which always attach to dumb real objects. They expect him to indicate the path between reality and their souls,' are the audience of BOA's books."

Ⓝ BONUS BOOKS, INC.

1223 Wilshire Blvd. #597, Santa Monica CA 90403. E-mail: submissions@bonusbooks.com. Website: www.bonusbooks.com. **Acquisitions:** Editor. Estab. 1985. Publishes hardcover and trade paperback originals and reprints. Accepts simultaneous submissions. Responds in 6-8 weeks to queries. Book catalog for 9×11 SAE; ms guidelines for #10 SASE.

O→ Bonus Books publishes quality nonfiction in a variety of categories, including entertainment/pop culture, games/gambling, sports/sports biography, regional (Chicago), broadcasting, fundraising.

Nonfiction Biography, self-help. Subjects include business/economics, cooking/foods/nutrition, education, health/medicine, hobbies, money/finance, regional, sports (gambling), women's issues/studies, pop culture, automotive/self-help, current affairs, broadcasting, business/self-help, Chicago people and places, collectibles, education/self-help, fundraising, handicapping winners, home and health, entertainment. Query with SASE, or submit outline, 2-3 sample chapters, author bio, TOC, SASE. All submissions and queries must include SASE. Reviews artwork/photos as part of ms package.

Recent Title(s) *America's Right Turn*, by David Franke and Richard A. Viguerie; *The On Position*, by Katie Moran; *In the Midst of Wolves*, by Keith Remer.

BOOKWORLD, INC./BLUE STAR PRODUCTIONS

9666 E. Riggs Rd., #194, Sun Lakes AZ 85248. (480)390-4317. E-mail: bookworldinc@earthlink.net. Website: bluestarproductions.net. **Acquisitions:** Barbara DeBolt, editor. Publishes trade paperback originals. **Publishes 10-12 titles/year. 75% of books from first-time authors; 90% from unagented writers. Pays royalty.** Does not accept simultaneous submissions. Responds in 8 months to queries; 16 or more months to mss. Book catalog online.

○━ "We focus on UFOs, the paranormal, metaphysical, angels, psychic phenomena, visionary fiction, spiritual—both fiction and nonfiction. We're currently only taking referrals."

Nonfiction "To save time and reduce the amount of paper submissions, we are encouraging e-mail queries and submissions (no downloads or attachments without permission), or disk submissions formatted for Windows using WordPerfect or Microsoft Word. Our response will be via e-mail so no SASE will be needed in these instances, unless the disk needs to be returned. For those without computer access, a SASE is a must, and we prefer seeing the actual manuscript, a query letter. No phone queries."

Tips "Authors selected for publication must be prepared to promote their books via public appearances and/ or work with a publicist."

Ⓝ BOWTIE PRESS

BowTie, Inc., 3 Burroughs, Irvine CA 92618. E-mail: bowtiepress@fancypubs.com. Website: www.bowtiepress. com. **Acquisitions:** Karla Austin, business operations manager (adult nonfiction); Emily Little, acquisitions editor (adult nonfiction). Estab. 1995. Publishes hardcover and trade paperback originals. **Publishes 30 titles/ year. Receives 250 queries and 50 mss/year. 20% of books from first-time authors; 90% from unagented writers. Payment varies from author to author.** Publishes book 1 year after acceptance of ms. Accepts simultaneous submissions. Responds in 1 month to queries; 2 months to proposals; 3 months to mss. Book catalog and ms guidelines online.

Imprints Kennel Club Books (Andrew DePrisco); Doral Publishing (Emily Little).

Nonfiction Coffee table book, general nonfiction, gift book, how-to, illustrated book, reference. Subjects include agriculture/horticulture, animals, education, gardening, nature/environment, science, marine subjects, crafts, education. Submit proposal package including outline, sample chapters. Reviews artwork/photos as part of ms package. Send photocopies.

BOYDS MILLS PRESS

Highlights for Children, 815 Church St., Honesdale PA 18431-1895. (570)253-1164. Website: www.boydsmillspre ss.com. Publisher: Kent L. Brown. **Acquisitions:** Larry Rosler, editorial director. Estab. 1990. Publishes hardcover originals and trade paperback reprints. **Publishes 50 titles/year. Receives 10,000 queries and 7,500 mss/year. 40% of books from first-time authors; 60% from unagented writers. Pays royalty on retail price. Offers variable advance.** Accepts simultaneous submissions. Responds in 1 month to mss. Book catalog online.

Imprints Wordsong (poetry); Calkins Creek Books (American history).

○━ Boyds Mills Press, the book-publishing arm of *Highlights for Children*, publishes a wide range of children's books of literary merit, from preschool to young adult. Currently emphasizing picture books and novels (but no fantasy, romance, or horror). Time between acceptance and publication depends on acceptance of ms.

Nonfiction Children's/juvenile. Subjects include agriculture/horticulture, animals, ethnic, history, nature/environment, sports, travel. "Nonfiction should be accurate, tailored to young audience. Prefer simple, narrative style, but in compelling, evocative language. Too many authors overwrite for the young audience and get bogged down in minutiae. Boyds Mills Press is not interested in manuscripts depicting violence, explicit sexuality, racism of any kind, or which promote hatred. We also are not the right market for self-help books." Query with SASE, or submit proposal package including outline. Reviews artwork/photos as part of ms package.

Fiction Adventure, ethnic, historical, humor, juvenile, mystery, picture books, young adult (adventure, animal, contemporary, ethnic, historical, humor, mystery, sports). "We look for imaginative stories or concepts with simple, lively language that employs a variety of literary devices, including rhythm, repitition, and when composed properly, rhyme. The stories may entertain or challenge, but the content must be age appropriate for children. For middle and young adult fiction we look for stories told in strong, considered prose driven by well-imagined characters." No fantasy, romance, horror. Query with SASE. Submit outline/synopsis and 3 sample chapters for novel or complete ms for picture book.

Poetry "Poetry should be appropriate for young audiences, clever, fun language, with easily understood meaning. Too much poetry is either too simple and static in meaning, or too obscure." Collections should have a unifying theme.

Recent Title(s) *Rat*, by Jan Cheripko (novel); *The Alligator in the Closet*, by David Harrison (poetry); *The President Is Shot* (nonfiction).

Tips "Our audience is pre-school to young adult. Concentrate first on your writing. Polish it. Then—and only then—select a market. We need primarily picture books with fresh ideas and characters—avoid worn themes of 'coming-of-age,' 'new sibling,' and self-help ideas. We are always interested in multicultural settings. Please— no anthropomorphic characters."

Ⓩ BRANDEN PUBLISHING CO., INC.

P.O. Box 812094, Wellesley MA 02482. (781)235-3634. Fax: (781)790-1056. Website: www.branden.com. **Acquisitions:** Adolph Caso, editor. Estab. 1909. Publishes hardcover and trade paperback originals, reprints, and software. **Publishes 15 titles/year. 80% of books from first-time authors; 90% from unagented writers. Pays 5-10% royalty on net receipts. 10 author's copies. Offers $1,000 maximum advance.** Publishes book 10 months after acceptance of ms. Responds in 1 month to queries.

Imprints International Pocket Library and Popular Technology; Four Seas and Brashear; Branden Books.

    0-¬ Branden publishes books by or about women, children, military, Italian-American, or African-American themes.

Nonfiction Biography, children's/juvenile, general nonfiction, illustrated book, reference, technical, textbook. Subjects include Americana, art/architecture, computers/electronic, contemporary culture, education, ethnic, government/politics, health/medicine, history, military/war, music/dance, photography, sociology, software, classics. Especially looking for "about 10 manuscripts on national and international subjects, including biographies of well-known individuals. Currently specializing in Americana, Italian-American, African-American." No religion or philosophy. *No unsolicited mss.* Paragraph query only with author's vita and SASE. No telephone, e-mail, or fax inquiries. Reviews artwork/photos as part of ms package.

Fiction Ethnic (histories, integration), historical, literary, military/war, religious (historical-reconstructive), short story collections. Looking for "contemporary, fast pace, modern society." No science, mystery, experimental, horor, or pornography. *No unsolicited mss.* Query with SASE. Paragraph query only with author's vita and SASE. No telephone, e-mail, or fax inquiries.

Recent Title(s) *Quilt of America*, by Carole Gariepy; *The Wisdom of Angels*, by Martha Cummings; *Kaso English to Italian Dictionary*, by Adolph Caso.

BREAKAWAY BOOKS

P.O. Box 24, Halcottsville NY 12438. (212)898-0408. E-mail: information@breakawaybooks.com. Website: www.breakawaybooks.com. **Acquisitions:** Garth Battista, publisher. Estab. 1994. Publishes hardcover and trade paperback originals. **Publishes 8-10 titles/year. Receives 400 queries and 100 mss/year. 35% of books from first-time authors; 75% from unagented writers. Pays 6-15% royalty on retail price. Offers $2,000-3,000 advance.** Publishes book 9 months after acceptance of ms. Accepts simultaneous submissions. Responds in 1 month to queries and proposals; 2 months to mss. Book catalog and ms guidelines free and online.

    0-¬ "Breakaway Books is a sports literature specialty publisher—only fiction and narrative nonfiction. No how-tos."

Nonfiction Subjects include sports (narrative only, not how-to). Query with SASE or by e-mail.

Fiction Short story collections (sports stories). Query with SASE, or submit complete ms.

Recent Title(s) *The Runner and the Path*, by Dean Ottati; *Becoming an Ironman*, by Kara Douglass Thom; *Running Through the Wall*, by Neal Jamison.

Tips Audience is intelligent, passionately committed to athletes. "We're starting a new children's book line—only children's books dealing with running, cycling, swimming, triathlon, plus boating (canoes, kayaks and sailboats)."

BRENNER MICROCOMPUTING, INC.

Imprint of Brenner Information Group, P.O. Box 721000, San Diego CA 92172. (858)538-0093. Fax: (858)538-0380. E-mail: brenner@brennerbooks.com. Website: www.brennerbooks.com. **Acquisitions:** Jenny Hanson, acquisitions manager (pricing & ranges). Estab. 1982. Publishes trade paperback and electronic originals. **Publishes 15 titles/year. Receives 10 queries and 1 ms/year. 5% of books from first-time authors; 95% from unagented writers. Pays 5-15% royalty on wholesale price, or retail price, or net receipts. Offers $0-1,000 advance.** Publishes book 1 year after acceptance of ms. Accepts simultaneous submissions. Responds in 1 month. Book catalog free; ms guidelines for #10 SASE.

Nonfiction How-to, reference, self-help, technical. Subjects include business/economics, computers/electronic, marketing and pricing for small businesses.

BREVET PRESS, INC.

P.O. Box 1404, Sioux Falls SD 57101. **Acquisitions:** Donald P. Mackintosh, publisher (business); Peter E. Reid, managing editor (technical); A. Melton, editor (Americana); B. Mackintosh, editor (history). Estab. 1972. Publishes hardcover and paperback originals and reprints. **Publishes 15 titles/year. 50% of books from first-time authors; 100% from unagented writers. Pays 5% royalty. Offers $1,000 average advance.** Publishes book 1 year after acceptance of ms. Accepts simultaneous submissions. Responds in 2 months to queries. Book catalog free.

    0-¬ Brevet Books seeks nonfiction with "market potential and literary excellence."

Nonfiction Technical. Subjects include Americana, business/economics, history. Query with SASE. Reviews artwork/photos as part of ms package. Send photocopies.

Tips "Keep sexism out of the manuscripts."

BRIDGE WORKS PUBLISHING CO.

Box 1798, 221 Bridge Lane, Bridgehampton NY 11932. (631)537-3418. Fax: (631)537-5092. E-mail: bap@hampto
ns.com. **Acquisitions:** Barbara Phillips, editor/publisher. Estab. 1992. Publishes hardcover originals and reprints. **Publishes 6-9 titles/year. Receives 1,000 queries and 1,000 mss/year. 50% of books from first-time
authors; 40% from unagented writers. Offers $1,000 advance.** Publishes book 1 year after acceptance of ms.
Responds in 1 month to queries and proposals; 2 months to mss. Book catalog and ms guidelines for #10 SASE.

    O⟶ "Bridge Works is a small press dedicated to mainstream quality fiction and nonfiction."

Nonfiction Query with SASE, or submit proposal package including outline.

Fiction Literary (novels), mystery, short story collections. "Query with SASE before submitting manuscript.
First-time authors should have manuscripts vetted by freelance editors before submitting. We do not accept or
read multiple submissions."

Recent Title(s) *Find Courtney*, by Melissa Clark; *The Good Man*, by Ed Jae-Suk Lee.

Tips "Query letters should be 1 page, giving general subject or plot of the book and stating who the writer feels
is the audience for the work. In the case of novels, a portion of the work could be enclosed. We do not publish
self-help."

BRISTOL PUBLISHING ENTERPRISES

2714 McCone Ave., Hayward CA 94545. (800)346-4889. Fax: (800)346-7064. E-mail: orders@bristolpublishing.c
om. Website: bristolcookbooks.com. Estab. 1988. Publishes trade paperback originals. Accepts simultaneous
submissions. Book catalog online.

Imprints Nitty Gritty cookbooks; The Best 50 Recipe Series; Pet Care Series.

Nonfiction Cookbook, craft books, pet care books. Subjects include cooking/foods/nutrition. Send a proposal,
or query with possible outline, brief note about author's background, sample of writing, or chapter from ms.

Recent Title(s) *The Best 50 Chocolate Recipes*, by Christie Katona; *No Salt, No Sugar, No Fat*, by Jacqueline
Williams and Goldie Silverman (revised edition); *Wraps and Roll-Ups*, by Dona Z. Meilach (revised edition).

Tips Readers of cookbooks are novice cooks. "Our books educate without intimidating. We require our authors
to have some form of background in the food industry."

BROADMAN & HOLMAN PUBLISHERS

Lifeway Christian Resources, 127 Ninth Ave. N., Nashville TN 37234. (615)251-2438. Fax: (615)251-3752.
Website: www.broadmanholman.com. Publisher: David Shepherd. **Acquisitions:** Leonard G. Goss, editorial
director. Estab. 1934. Publishes hardcover and paperback originals. **Publishes 90-100 titles/year. Pays negotiable royalty.** Accepts simultaneous submissions. Responds in 6-9 months. Book catalog free; ms guidelines for
#10 SASE.

    O⟶ Broadman & Holman Publishers publishes books that provide biblical solutions that spiritually trans-
        form individuals and cultures. Currently emphasizing inspirational/gift books, general Christian living
        and books on Christianity and society.

Nonfiction Children's/juvenile, gift book, illustrated book, reference, textbook, devotional journals. Subjects
include religion, spirituality. Christian living, devotionals, prayer, women, youth, spiritual growth, Christian
history, parenting, home school, biblical studies, science and faith, current events, marriage and family concerns, church life, pastoral helps, preaching, evangelism. "We are open to submissions in all areas. Materials
in these areas must be suited for an evangelical Christian readership." No poetry, biography, or sermons. Query
with SASE.

Fiction Adventure, mystery, religious (general religious, inspirational, religious fantasy, religious mystery/
suspense, religious thriller, religious romance), western. "We publish fiction in all the main genres. We want
not only a very good story, but also one that sets forth Christian values. Nothing that lacks a positive Christian
emphasis (but do not preach, however); nothing that fails to sustain reader interest." Query with SASE.

Recent Title(s) *A Greater Freedom*, by Oliver North; *The Beloved Disciple*, by Beth Moore; *Against All Odds*,
by Chuck Norris.

Ⓐ BROADWAY BOOKS

Imprint of Doubleday Broadway Publishing Group, Random House, Inc., 1745 Broadway, New York NY 10019.
(212)782-9000. Fax: (212)782-9411. Website: www.broadwaybooks.com. Estab. 1995. Publishes hardcover and
trade paperback books.

    O⟶ Broadway publishes general interest nonfiction and fiction for adults.

Nonfiction Biography, cookbook, general nonfiction, illustrated book, reference, General interest adult books.
Subjects include business/economics, child guidance/parenting, contemporary culture, cooking/foods/nutri-
tion, gay/lesbian, government/politics, health/medicine, history, memoirs, money/finance, multicultural, New
Age, psychology, sex, spirituality, sports, travel (narrative), women's issues/studies, current affairs, motiva-
tional/inspirational, popular culture, consumer reference. *Agented submissions only.*

Fiction Publishes a limited list of commercial fiction, mainly chick lit. *Agented submissions only.*

Recent Title(s) *A Short History of Nearly Everything*, by Bill Bryson; *The Automatic Millionaire*, by David Bach; *Babyville*, by Jane Green.

BUCKNELL UNIVERSITY PRESS

Taylor Hall, Bucknell University, Lewisburg PA 17837. (570)577-1552. E-mail: clingham@bucknell.edu. Website: www.departments.bucknell.edu/univ_press. **Acquisitions:** Greg Clingham, director. Estab. 1969. Publishes hardcover originals. **Publishes 35-40 titles/year.** Does not accept simultaneous submissions. Book catalog free; ms guidelines online.

> Oᴙ "In all fields, our criteria are scholarly excellence, critical originality, and interdisciplinary and theoretical expertise and sensitivity."

Nonfiction Scholarly. Subjects include art/architecture, history, language/literature, philosophy, psychology, religion, sociology, English and American literary criticism, literary theory and cultural studies, historiography, art history, modern languages, classics, anthropology, ethnology, cultural and political geography, Hispanic and Latin American studies. Series: Bucknell Studies in Eighteenth-Century Literature and Culture, Bucknell Series in Latin American Literature and Theory, Eighteenth-Century Scotland. Submit proposal package including cv, SASE.

Recent Title(s) *The Selected Essays of Donald Greene*, edited by John Lawrence Abbott; *Brazilian Science Fiction: Cultural Myths and Nationhood in the Land of the Future*, by M. Elizabeth Ginway; *Borges and Translation: The Irreverence of Periphery*, by Sergio Waisman.

BUILDERBOOKS.COM™

National Association of Home Builders, 1201 15th St. NW, Washington DC 20005-2800. (800)368-5242. Fax: (202)266-8559. E-mail: publishing@nahb.com. Website: www.builderbooks.com. Managing Director: Larry Fox, ext. 8201. Senior Editor: Doris M. Thennyson, ext. 8368. Managing Editor: Aaron White, ext. 8476 (safety; multifamily; seniors housing; business and construction management for remodelers, builders, developers and others; land development; customer relations; computerization; construction how-to; economics; legal issues; marketing and selling for builders, remodelers, developers, suppliers, manufacturers and their sales and marketing directors). Publishes "books and electronic products for builders, remodelers, developers, sales and marketing professionals, manufacturers, suppliers, and consumers in the residential construction industry. Writers must be experts." **Publishes 20 titles/year. 33% of books from first-time authors; 99% from unagented writers. Pays royalty.** Publishes book 6-12 months after acceptance of ms. Does not accept simultaneous submissions. Responds in 1-2 months to queries. Book catalog free or on website; ms guidelines by e-mail.

Nonfiction "We prefer a detailed outline on a strong residential construction industry topic. Our readers like step-by-step how-to books and electronic products, no history or philosophy of the industry." How-to, reference, technical. Subjects include safety, multifamily, seniors housing, remodeling, land development, business and construction management, customer service, computerization, financial management, and sales and marketing. Query first. E-mail queries accepted. Include electronic and hard copy artwork/photos as part of ms package. Send photocopies.

Recent Title(s) *Building Community: Live, Gather, Play*, by Tom Kopf; *Customer Service for Home Builders*, by Carol Smith; *Jobsite Phrasebook, English/Spanish*, by Kent Shepard.

Tips Audience is primarily home builders, remodelers, developers, sales and marketing professionals, manufactuers, suppliers, and consumers in the residential construction industry. Ask for a sample outline.

Ⓩ BULFINCH PRESS

Imprint of Time Warner Book Group, Time Life Bldg., 1271 Avenue of the Americas, New York NY 10020. (212)522-8700. Website: www.bulfinchpress.com. Publishes hardcover and trade paperback originals. Accepts simultaneous submissions.

> ● *No unsolicited mss.* It is suggested that you enlist the help of an agent.
>
> Oᴙ Bulfinch Press publishes large format art books. "We are the home of Ansel Adams and Irving Penn."

Nonfiction Coffee table book, cookbook, gift book, illustrated book. Subjects include art/architecture, cooking/foods/nutrition, gardening, photography, interior design, lifestyle. Query with SASE.

Recent Title(s) *Brunscwig & Fils Up Close: From Grand Rooms to Your Rooms*, by Murray Douglas and Chippy Irvine; *The Party Planner*, by David Tutera; *Gardens to Go: Creating & Designing a Container Garden*, by Sydney Eddison.

BURFORD BOOKS

32 Morris Ave., Springfield NJ 07081. (973)258-0960. Fax: (973)258-0113. **Acquisitions:** Peter Burford, publisher. Estab. 1997. Publishes hardcover originals, trade paperback originals and reprints. **Publishes 25 titles/year. Receives 300 queries and 200 mss/year. 30% of books from first-time authors; 60% from unagented**

writers. **Pays royalty on wholesale price.** Publishes book 18 months after acceptance of ms. Accepts simultaneous submissions. Responds in 1 month to queries and proposals; 2 months to mss. Book catalog and ms guidelines free.

  O→ Burford Books publishes books on all aspects of the outdoors, from backpacking to sports, practical and literary.

Nonfiction How-to, illustrated book. Subjects include animals, cooking/foods/nutrition, hobbies, military/war, nature/environment, recreation, sports, travel. Query with SASE, or submit outline. Reviews artwork/photos as part of ms package. Send photocopies.

Recent Title(s) *Saltwater Fishing*, by Jim Freda; *One Hundred Stretches*, by Jim Brown.

BUTTE PUBLICATIONS, INC.

P.O. Box 1328, Hillsboro OR 97123-1328. (503)648-9791. Fax: (503)693-9526. E-mail: service@buttepublications .com. Website: www.buttepublications.com. Estab. 1992. **Publishes several titles/year.** Accepts simultaneous submissions. Responds in 6 or more months to mss. Book catalog and ms guidelines for #10 SASE or online; ms guidelines online.

  O→ Butte Publications, Inc., publishes classroom books related to deafness and language.

Nonfiction Children's/juvenile, textbook. Subjects include education (all related to field of deafness and education). Submit proposal package, including author bio, synopsis, market survey, 2-3 sample chapters, SASE and ms (if completed). Reviews artwork/photos as part of ms package. Send photocopies.

Fiction Submit complete ms.

Recent Title(s) *Cajun's Song*, by Darlene Toole; *Diccionario Visual Plus*, by Virginia McKinney; *Slangman Guides*, by Davie Burke.

Tips "Audience is students, teachers, parents, and professionals in the arena dealing with deafness and hearing loss. We are not seeking autobiographies or novels."

C&T PUBLISHING

1651 Challenge Dr., Concord CA 94520-5206. (925)677-0377. Fax: (925)677-0373. E-mail: ctinfo@ctpub.com. Website: www.ctpub.com. Estab. 1983. Publishes hardcover and trade paperback originals. **Publishes 40 titles/ year.** Accepts simultaneous submissions. Responds in 3 months to queries. Book catalog free; proposal guidelines online.

  O→ "C&T publishes well-written, beautifully designed books on quilting, embroidery, dollmaking, and other fiber crafts."

Nonfiction How-to (quilting), illustrated book. Subjects include art/architecture, hobbies, quilting books, occasional quilt picture books, quilt-related crafts, wearable art, needlework, fiber and surface embellishments, other books relating to fabric crafting. Extensive proposal guidelines are available on the company's website.

Recent Title(s) *Classic Four-Block Appliqué Quilts: A Back-to-Basics Approach*, by Gwen Marston; *Fast Knits Fat Needles*, by Sally Harding.

Tips "In our industry, we find that how-to books have the longest selling life. Quiltmakers, sewing enthusiasts, needle artists, and fiber artists are our audience. We like to see new concepts or techniques. Include some great samples, and you'll get our attention quickly. Dynamic design is hard to resist, and if that's your forte, show us what you've done."

CAMINO BOOKS, INC.

P.O. Box 59026, Philadelphia PA 19102. (215)413-1917. Fax: (215)413-3255. Website: www.caminobooks.com. **Acquisitions:** E. Jutkowitz, publisher. Estab. 1987. Publishes hardcover and trade paperback originals. **Publishes 8 titles/year. 20% of books from first-time authors. Pays 6-12% royalty on net receipts. Offers $1,000 average advance.** Publishes book 1 year after acceptance of ms. Responds in 2 weeks to queries. Ms guidelines online.

  O→ Camino Books, Inc., publishes nonfiction of regional interest to the Mid-Atlantic states.

Nonfiction Biography, children's/juvenile, cookbook, how-to. Subjects include agriculture/horticulture, Americana, art/architecture, child guidance/parenting, cooking/foods/nutrition, ethnic, gardening, government/politics, history, regional, travel. Query with SASE, or submit outline, sample chapters.

Tips "The books must be of interest to readers in the Middle Atlantic states, or they should have a clearly defined niche, such as cookbooks."

✪ CANDLEWICK PRESS

2067 Massachusetts Ave., Cambridge MA 02140. (617)661-3330. Fax: (617)661-0565. Website: www.candlewic k.com. President/Publisher: Karen Lotz. **Acquisitions:** Deb Wayshak (fiction); Monica Perez, editor (nonfiction, picture books); Joan Powers, editor-at-large (picture books); Liz Bicknell, editorial director/associate publisher (poetry, picture books, fiction); Mary Lee Donovan, executive editor (picture books, nonfiction/fiction); Kara

LaReau, senior editor; Sarah Ketchersid, editor (board, toddler). Estab. 1991. Publishes hardcover originals, trade paperback originals and reprints. **Publishes 200 titles/year. 5% of books from first-time authors; 40% from unagented writers.**

> **O⚓** Candlewick Press publishes high-quality, illustrated children's books for ages infant through young adult. "We are a truly child-centered publisher."

Nonfiction Children's/juvenile. "Good writing is essential; specific topics are less important than strong, clear writing." *No unsolicited mss.*

Fiction Juvenile, picture books, young adult. *No unsolicited mss.*

Recent Title(s) *Fairieality*, by Ellwand, Downton, and Bird; *Feed*, by M.T. Anderson (National Book Award finalist); *The Tale of Despereaux*, by Kate DiCamillo (Newberry Award winner).

Tips "*We no longer accept unsolicited mss.* See our website for further information about us."

CANON PRESS

P.O. Box 9025, Moscow ID 83843. (208)892-8074. Fax: (208)892-8143. E-mail: submissions@canonpress.org. Website: www.canonpress.org. **Acquisitions:** J. C. Evans. Estab. 1988. Publishes hardcover and trade paperback originals. **Publishes 10 titles/year. Receives 500 queries and 250 mss/year. 10% of books from first-time authors; 100% from unagented writers. Pays 5-10% royalty on wholesale price, or retail price.** Publishes book 18 months after acceptance of ms. Accepts simultaneous submissions. Responds in 1 month. Book catalog and ms guidelines online.

Nonfiction Subjects include creative nonfiction, education, humanities, language/literature, religion. "As we are generally dissatisfied with contemporary, evangelical Christian nonfiction, we recommend visiting our website and perusing our recent titles before submitting." Submit proposal package including outline, 3 sample chapters.

Fiction Adventure, historical, humor, juvenile, literary, poetry, poetry in translation, religious, short story collections. Submit proposal package including 3 sample chapters, synopsis.

Poetry "As we are generally dissatisfied with contemporary, evangelical Christian poetry (or lack thereof), we recommend perusing our website and new titles before submitting." Submit 15 sample poems.

Recent Title(s) *My Life for Yours* (family living); *Trinity & Reality* (apologetics); *Miniature & Morals* (literary criticism).

Tips "We seek to encourage Christians with God-honoring, Biblical books. Writers should possess a Trinitarian understanding of the good, true, and beautiful, and their submissions should reflect their understanding."

CAPITAL BOOKS

22841 Quicksilver Dr., Dulles VA 20166. (703)661-1571. Fax: (703)661-1547. E-mail: jennifer@booksintl.com. Website: www.capital-books.com. **Acquisitions:** Kathleen Hughes, publisher (reference, how-to, gardening, lifestyle, regional travel, business, women's studies). Estab. 1998. Publishes hardcover and trade paperback originals, and trade paperback reprints. **Publishes 20 titles/year. Receives 200 queries and 400 mss/year. 30% of books from first-time authors; 90% from unagented writers. Pays 1-10% royalty on net receipts. Offers up to $7,000 advance.** Publishes book 9 months after acceptance of ms. Accepts simultaneous submissions. Responds in 3 months. Book catalog free; ms guidelines online.

Nonfiction Cookbook, general nonfiction, how-to, reference, self-help. Subjects include animals, business/economics, child guidance/parenting, contemporary culture, cooking/foods/nutrition, gardening, health/medicine, money/finance, multicultural, nature/environment, psychology, regional, social sciences, travel, women's issues/studies. "We are looking for lifestyle and business books by experts with their own marketing and sales outlets." No religious titles, fiction, or children's books. Submit proposal package including outline, 3 sample chapters, query letter. Reviews artwork/photos as part of ms package. Send photocopies.

Recent Title(s) *Hannah's Art of Home*, by Hannah Keeley; *Now What Do I Do?*, by Jan Cannon; *Million Dollar Networking*, by Andrea Nierenberg.

Tips "Our audience is comprised of enthusiastic readers who look to books for answers and information. Do not send fiction, children's books, or religious titles. Please tell us how you, the author, can help market and sell the book."

⊘ CAPSTONE PRESS

151 Good Counsel Dr., P.O. Box 669, Mankato MN 56002. (507)345-8100. Fax: (507)625-4662. Website: www.capstone-press.com. Publishes hardcover originals. Book catalog and ms guidelines online.

Imprints Capstone High Interest; Blue Earth Books; Bridgestone Books; Pebble Books; LifeMatters; A+ Books; Pebble Plus; Yellow Umbrella Books; First Facts; Fact Finders; Spanish/Bilingual; Social Studies Grades 3-9; Let Freedom Ring.

> **O⚓** Capstone Press publishes nonfiction children's books for schools and libraries.

Nonfiction Children's/juvenile. Subjects include Americana, animals, child guidance/parenting, cooking/foods/

nutrition, health/medicine, history, military/war, multicultural, nature/environment, recreation, science, sports. "We do not accept proposals or manuscripts. Authors interested in writing for Capstone Press can request an author's brochure." Query via website.

Recent Title(s) *Achilles*, by Jason Glaser; *Can You Guess?*, by Jennifer VanVoorst; *Grasshoppers*, by Margaret Hall.

Tips Audience is made up of elementary, middle school, and high school students who are just learning how to read, who are experiencing reading difficulties, or who are learning English. Capstone Press does not publish unsolicited mss submitted by authors, and it rarely entertains proposals. Instead, Capstone hires freelance authors to write on nonfiction topics selected by the company. Authors may request a brochure via website.

CARDOZA PUBLISHING

857 Broadway, 3rd Floor, New York NY 10003. E-mail: submissions@cardozapub.com. Website: www.cardozapub.com. **Acquisitions:** Acquisitions Editor (gaming, gambling, card and casino games, and board games). Estab. 1981. Publishes trade paperback originals and reprints. **Publishes 35-40 titles/year. Receives 20-30 queries and 20-30 mss/year. 50% of books from first-time authors; 90% from unagented writers. Pays 5-6% royalty on retail price. Offers $1,000-10,000 advance.** Publishes book 7 months after acceptance of ms. Accepts simultaneous submissions. Responds in 1-2 months to queries and proposals; 2-3 months to mss. Book catalog online; ms guidelines by e-mail.

Nonfiction How-to. Subjects include hobbies, gaming, gambling, backgammon chess, card games. "Cardoza Publishing publishes exclusively gaming and gambling titles. In the past, we have specialized in poker and chess titles. While we always need more of those, we are currently seeking more books on various noncasino card games, such as bridge, hearts, spades, gin rummy, or canasta." Query with SASE, or submit complete ms. Reviews artwork/photos as part of ms package. Send photocopies.

Recent Title(s) *Super System*, by Doyle Brunson (poker); *Championship Hold 'Em*, by Tom McEvoy and T.J. Cloutier (poker); *Ken Warren Teaches Texas Hold 'Em*, by Ken Warren (poker).

Tips Audience is professional and recreational gamblers, chess players, card players. "We prefer not to deal with agents whenever possible. We publish only titles in a very specific niche market; please do not send us material that will not be relevant to our business."

THE CAREER PRESS, INC.

P.O. Box 687, 3 Tice Rd., Franklin Lakes NJ 07417. (201)848-0310 or (800)227-3371. E-mail: mlewis@careerpress.com. Website: www.careerpress.com; www.newpagebooks.com. **Acquisitions:** Michael Lewis, acquisitions editor. Estab. 1985. Publishes hardcover and paperback originals. Does not accept simultaneous submissions. Ms guidelines online.

Imprints New Page Books.

Oー Career Press publishes books for adult readers seeking practical information to improve themselves in careers, college, finance, parenting, retirement, spirituality and other related topics, as well as management philosophy titles for a small business and management audience. New Page Books publishes in the areas of New Age, self-help, health, parenting, general nonfiction and weddings/entertaining. Currently de-emphasizing Judaica.

Nonfiction How-to, reference, self-help. Subjects include business/economics, money/finance, recreation, nutrition. "Look through our catalog; become familiar with our publications. We like to select authors who are specialists on their topic." Submit outline, 1-2 sample chapters, author bio, marketing plan, SASE. Or, send complete ms (preferred).

Recent Title(s) *The Wisdom of Ginsu®*, by Barry Beecher and Edward Valenti; *Supernetworking for Sales Pros*, by Michael Salmon; *How to Win Any Argument*, by Robert Mayer.

CAROLRHODA BOOKS, INC.

Imprint of Lerner Publishing Group, 241 First Ave. N., Minneapolis MN 55401-1607. (612)332-3344. *No phone calls.* Fax: (612)332-7615. Website: www.lernerbooks.com. **Acquisitions:** Zelda Wagner, fiction submissions editor; Jennifer Zimian, nonfiction submissions editor. Estab. 1959. Publishes hardcover originals. Accepts simultaneous submissions. Book catalog for 9 × 12 SAE with $3.85 postage; ms guidelines online.

● Accepts submissions from November 1-30 only. Submissions received at other times of the year will be returned to sender.

Oー Carolrhoda Books is a children's publisher focused on producing high-quality, socially conscious nonfiction and fiction books with unique and well-developed ideas and angles for young readers that help them learn about and explore the world around them.

Nonfiction Carolrhoda Books seeks creative children's nonfiction. Biography. Subjects include ethnic, nature/environment, science. "We are always interested in adding to our biography series. Books on the natural and hard sciences are also of interest.'' Query with SASE. Prefers to receive complete ms, outline, résumé. Reviews artwork/photos as part of ms package. Send photocopies.

Fiction Historical, juvenile, multicultural, picture books, young reader, middle grade and young adult fiction. ''We continue to add fiction for middle grades and 8-10 picture books per year. Not looking for folktales or anthropomorphic animal stories.'' Carolrhoda does not publish alphabet books, puzzle books, song books, textbooks, workbooks, religious subject matter, or plays. Query with SASE. Prefers to receive complete ms, outline, and a few sample chapters.

Recent Title(s) *Blackberry Stew*, by Isabell Monk, illustrated by Janice Lee Porter; *A Style All Her Own*, by Laurie Friedman, illustrated by Sharon Watts; *Tooth Fairy's First Night*, by Anne Bowen, illustrated by Jon Berkeley.

▣ CARROLL & GRAF PUBLISHERS, INC.

Avalon Publishing Group, 245 W. 17th St., 11th Floor, New York NY 10011-5300. (212)981-9919. Fax: (646)375-2571. Website: www.avalonpub.com; www.carolandgraf.com. Publisher: Will Balliett. Estab. 1982. Publishes hardcover and trade paperback originals. Responds in a timely fashion to queries. Book catalog free.

    ○┓ Carroll and Graf Publishers offers quality fiction and nonfiction for a general readership.

Nonfiction Publish general trade books; interested in developing long term relations with authors. Biography, reference, self-help. Subjects include business/economics, contemporary culture, health/medicine, history, memoirs, military/war, psychology, sports, true crime, current affairs, adventure/exploration. *Agented submissions only.*

Fiction Literary, mainstream/contemporary, mystery, science fiction, suspense, thriller. No romance. *Agented submissions only.* Query with SASE.

Recent Title(s) *The Politics of Truth*, by Joseph Wilson; *Hiding the Elephant*, by Jim Steinmeyer.

CARSON-DELLOSA PUBLISHING CO., INC.

P.O. Box 35665, Greensboro NC 27425-5665. (336)632-0084. Fax: (336)856-9414. Website: www.carson-dellosa. com. **Acquisitions:** Pamela Hill, product acquistions. **Publishes 80-90 titles/year. 15-20% of books from first-time authors; 95% from unagented writers. Makes outright purchase.** Accepts simultaneous submissions. Responds in 3 months to proposals. Book catalog online; ms guidelines free.

Nonfiction We publish supplementary educational materials, such as teacher resource books, workbooks, and activity books. Subjects include education (including Christian education). No textbooks or trade children's books, please. Submit proposal package including sample chapters or pages, SASE. Reviews artwork/photos as part of ms package. Send photocopies.

Tips ''Our audience consists of pre-K through grade 8 educators, parents, and students. Ask for our submission guidelines and a catalog before you send us your materials. We do not publish fiction or nonfiction storybooks.''

CARSTENS PUBLICATIONS, INC.

Hobby Book Division, P.O. Box 700, Newton NJ 07860-0700. (973)383-3355. Fax: (973)383-4064. E-mail: hal@c arstens-publications.com. Website: www.carstens-publications.com. **Acquisitions:** Harold H. Carstens, publisher. Estab. 1933. Publishes paperback originals. **Publishes 8 titles/year. 100% from unagented writers. Pays 10% royalty on retail price. Offers advance.** Publishes book 1 year after acceptance of ms. Responds in 2 months to queries. Book catalog for #10 SASE.

    ○┓ Carstens specializes in books about railroads, model railroads, and airplanes for hobbyists.

Nonfiction Subjects include model railroading, toy trains, model aviation, railroads, and model hobbies. ''Authors must know their field intimately because our readers are active modelers. Writers cannot write about somebody else's hobby with authority. If they do, we can't use them. Our railroad books presently are primarily photographic essays on specific railroads.'' Query with SASE. Reviews artwork/photos as part of ms package.

Recent Title(s) *Pennsylvania Railroad Lines East*, by Steve Stewart and Dave Augsburger; *Track Design*, by Bill Schopp.

Tips ''We need lots of good photos. Material must be in model, hobby, railroad, and transportation field only.''

▣ ⊘ CARTWHEEL BOOKS

Imprint of Scholastic Trade Division, 557 Broadway, New York NY 10012. (212)343-6100. Website: www.schola stic.com. Vice President/Editorial Director: Ken Geist. Estab. 1991. Publishes novelty books, easy readers, board books, hardcover and trade paperback originals. Accepts simultaneous submissions. Book catalog for 9×12 SASE; ms guidelines free.

    ○┓ Cartwheel Books publishes innovative books for children, up to age 8. ''We are looking for 'novelties' that are books first, play objects second. Even without its gimmick, a Cartwheel Book should stand alone as a valid piece of children's literature.''

Nonfiction Children's/juvenile. Subjects include animals, history, music/dance, nature/environment, recreation, science, sports. ''Cartwheel Books publishes for the very young, therefore nonfiction should be written in a manner that is accessible to preschoolers through 2nd grade. Often writers choose topics that are too narrow or 'special' and do not appeal to the mass market. Also, the text and vocabulary are frequently too difficult for our young audience.'' Accepts mss from agents, previously published authors only. Reviews artwork/photos as part of ms package. Please do not send original artwork.

Fiction Humor, juvenile, mystery, picture books. ''Again, the subject should have mass market appeal for very young children. Humor can be helpful, but not necessary. Mistakes writers make are a reading level that is too difficult, a topic of no interest or too narrow, or manuscripts that are too long.'' Accepts mss from agents, previously published authors only.

Tips Audience is young children, ages 0-8. ''Know what types of books the publisher does. Some manuscripts that don't work for one house may be perfect for another. Check out bookstores or catalogs to see where your writing would 'fit' best.''

CATHOLIC UNIVERSITY OF AMERICA PRESS

620 Michigan Ave. NE, Washington DC 20064. (202)319-5052. Fax: (202)319-4985. E-mail: cua-press@cua.edu. Website: cuapress.cua.edu. **Acquisitions:** Dr. Gregory F. Lanave, acquisitions editor (philosophy, theology); Dr. David J. McGonagle, director (all other fields). Estab. 1939. **Publishes 30-35 titles/year. 50% of books from first-time authors; 100% from unagented writers. Pays variable royalty on net receipts.** Publishes book 2 years after acceptance of ms. Responds in 6 months to queries. Book catalog for #10 SASE; ms guidelines online.

   O— The Catholic University of America Press publishes in the fields of history (ecclesiastical and secular), literature and languages, philosophy, political theory, social studies, and theology. ''We have interdisciplinary emphasis on patristics, medieval studies, and Irish studies. Our principal interest is in works of original scholarship intended for scholars and other professionals, and for academic libraries, but we will also consider manuscripts whose chief contribution is to offer a synthesis of knowledge of the subject which may be of interest to a wider audience or suitable for use as supplementary reading material in courses.''

Nonfiction Scholarly. Subjects include government/politics, history, language/literature, philosophy, religion, Church-state relations. No unrevised doctoral dissertations. Length: 80,000-200,000 words. Query with outline, sample chapter, cv, and list of previous publications.

Recent Title(s) *Mediapolitik: How the Mass Media Have Transformed World Politics*, by Lee Edwards.

Tips ''Scholarly monographs and works suitable for adoption as supplementary reading material in courses have the best chance.''

CATO INSTITUTE

1000 Massachusetts Ave. NW, Washington DC 20001. (202)842-0200. Website: www.cato.org. **Acquisitions:** Gene Healy, senior editor. Estab. 1977. Publishes hardcover originals, trade paperback originals and reprints. **Publishes 12 titles/year. 25% of books from first-time authors; 90% from unagented writers. Makes outright purchase of $1,000-10,000. Offers advance.** Publishes book 9 months after acceptance of ms. Accepts simultaneous submissions. Responds in 3 months to queries. Book catalog online.

   O— Cato Institute publishes books on public policy issues from a free-market or libertarian perspective.

Nonfiction Scholarly. Subjects include business/economics, education, government/politics, health/medicine, money/finance, sociology, public policy, foreign policy, monetary policy. Query with SASE.

Recent Title(s) *Toward Liberty*, edited by David Boaz; *Voucher Wars*, by Clint Bolick.

CAXTON PRESS

312 Main St., Caldwell ID 83605-3299. (208)459-7421. Fax: (208)459-7450. Website: caxtonpress.com. Publisher: Scott Gipson. **Acquisitions:** Wayne Cornell, editor (Western Americana, regional nonfiction). Estab. 1907. Publishes hardcover and trade paperback originals. **Publishes 6-10 titles/year. 50% of books from first-time authors; 60% from unagented writers. Pays royalty. Offers advance.** Publishes book 18 months after acceptance of ms. Accepts simultaneous submissions. Responds in 3 months to queries. Book catalog for 9×12 SAE; ms guidelines online.

   O— ''Western Americana nonfiction remains our focus. We define Western Americana as almost any topic that deals with the people or culture of the west, past and present.'' Currently emphasizing regional issues—primarily Pacific Northwest. De-emphasizing ''coffee table'' or photograph-intensive books.

Nonfiction Biography, children's/juvenile, cookbook, scholarly. Subjects include Americana, history, regional. ''We need good Western Americana, especially the Northwest, emphasis on serious, narrative nonfiction.'' Query. Reviews artwork/photos as part of ms package.

Recent Title(s) *Salmon River Country*, by Mark Lisk and Stephen Stuebner; *Great Meals Dutch Oven Style*, by Dale Smith; *Ex America*, by Garet Garrett.

Tips "Books to us never can or will be primarily articles of merchandise to be produced as cheaply as possible and to be sold like slabs of bacon or packages of cereal over the counter. If there is anything that is really worthwhile in this mad jumble we call the 21st century, it should be books."

CELESTIAL ARTS

Ten Speed Press, P.O. Box 7123-S, Berkeley CA 94707. (510)559-1600. Fax: (510)524-1629. Website: www.tensp eed.com. Estab. 1966. Publishes trade paperback originals and reprints. Accepts simultaneous submissions. Responds in 6-8 weeks to queries. Book catalog and ms guidelines online.

O→ Celestial Arts publishes nonfiction for a forward-thinking, open-minded audience interested in psychology, self-help, spirituality, health and parenting.

Nonfiction Cookbook, how-to, reference, self-help. Subjects include child guidance/parenting, cooking/foods/nutrition, education, health/medicine, New Age, psychology, women's issues/studies. "We specialize in parenting, alternative health, how-to and spirituality. And please, no poetry!" Submit proposal package including outline, 1-2 sample chapters, author bio, SASE. Reviews artwork/photos as part of ms package. Send photocopies.

Recent Title(s) *Addiction to Love*, by Susan Peabody; *Your Right to Know*, by Andrew Kimbrell; *Girls Speak Out*, by Andrea Johnston.

Tips Audience is fairly well-informed, interested in psychology and sociology-related topics, open-minded, innovative, forward-thinking. "The most completely thought-out (developed) proposals earn the most consideration."

CENTERSTREAM PUBLICATIONS

P.O. Box 17878, Anaheim Hills CA 92807. (714)779-9390. Fax: (714)779-9390. E-mail: centerstrm@aol.com. Website: www.centerstream-usa.com. **Acquisitions:** Ron Middlebrook, Cindy Middlebrook, owners. Estab. 1980. Publishes hardcover and mass market paperback originals, trade paperback and mass market paperback reprints. **Publishes 12 titles/year. Receives 15 queries and 15 mss/year. 80% of books from first-time authors; 100% from unagented writers. Pays 10-15% royalty on wholesale price. Offers $300-3,000 advance.** Publishes book 8 months after acceptance of ms. Accepts simultaneous submissions. Responds in 3 months to queries. Book catalog and ms guidelines for #10 SASE.

O→ Centerstream publishes music history and instructional books.

Nonfiction How-to. Subjects include history, music/dance. Query with SASE.

Recent Title(s) *History of Dobro Guitars.*

CHALICE PRESS

P.O. Box 179, St. Louis MO 63166. (314)231-8500 or (615)452-3311. Fax: (314)231-8524 or (615)452-7781. E-mail: chalice@cbp21.com. Website: www.chalicepress.com. **Acquisitions:** Dr. Trent C. Butler, editorial director. Publishes hardcover and trade paperback originals. **Publishes 35 titles/year. Receives 300 queries and 250 mss/year. 10% of books from first-time authors; 100% from unagented writers. Pays 14% royalty on net receipts.** Publishes book 1 year after acceptance of ms. Accepts simultaneous submissions. Responds in 1 month to queries; 2 months to proposals; 3 months to mss. Book catalog and ms guidelines online.

Nonfiction Textbook. Subjects include religion, Christian spirituality. Submit proposal package including outline, 1-2 sample chapters.

Recent Title(s) *Solving the Da Vinci Code Mystery*, by Brandon Gilvin; *Chalice Introduction to the New Testament*, edited by Dennis E. Smith; *Martin Luther King on Creative Living*, by Michael G. Long.

Tips "We publish for professors, church ministers, and lay Christian readers."

CHARISMA HOUSE

Strang Communications, 600 Rinehart Rd., Lake Mary FL 32746. (407)333-0600. Fax: (407)333-7100. E-mail: charismahouse@strang.com. Website: www.charismahouse.com. **Acquisitions:** Acquisitions Assistant. Publishes hardcover and trade paperback originals. **Publishes 40-50 titles/year. Receives 600 mss/year. 2% of books from first-time authors; 95% from unagented writers. Pays 4-18% royalty on retail price. Offers $1,500-5,000 advance.** Publishes book 18 months after acceptance of ms. Accepts simultaneous submissions. Allow 3 months to review proposals. Ms guidelines online.

Imprints Creation House (customized publications of Christian fiction and nonfiction); Siloam (emphasizing health and fitness from the Christian perspective—topics include fitness, diet and nutrition, conventional and alternative medicine, and emotional and relationship health).

O→ Charisma House publishes nonfiction books about Christian living, the work of the Holy Spirit, prayer, scripture, adventures in evangelism and missions, and popular theology. "We now accept fiction submissions for speculative and historical fiction that focuses on the supernatural interventions of God."

Recent Title(s) *The Thorn in the Flesh*, by R.T. Kendall (nonfiction); *My Spiritual Inheritance*, by Juanita Bynum (nonfiction).

Tips "Request book proposal guidelines or go to our website before sending submissions."

THE CHARLES PRESS, PUBLISHERS

117 S. 17th St., Suite 310, Philadelphia PA 19103. (215)496-9616. Fax: (215)496-9637. E-mail: mailbox@charlesp resspub.com. Website: www.charlespresspub.com. **Acquisitions:** Lauren Meltzer, publisher. Estab. 1982. Publishes hardcover and trade paperback originals. Accepts simultaneous submissions. Responds in 2 months to proposals; 3 months to mss. Book catalog and ms guidelines online.

   Currently emphasizing how-to books, true crime, criminology, psychology (including suicide, anger and violence).

Nonfiction Subjects include child guidance/parenting, health/medicine (allied), psychology, counseling, criminology, true crime. No fiction, children's books, or poetry. Query or submit proposal package that includes a description of the book, a few representative sample chapters, intended audience, author's qualifications/ background and SASE. No e-mailed submissions. Reviews artwork/photos as part of ms package. Send photocopies or transparencies.

Recent Title(s) *The Golden Age of Medical Science and the Dark Age of Healthcare Delivery*, by Sylvan Weinberg, MD.

CHARLES RIVER MEDIA

10 Downer Ave., Hingham MA 02043-1132. (781)740-0400. Fax: (781)740-8816. E-mail: info@charlesriver.com. Website: www.charlesriver.com. **Acquisitions:** David Pallai, president (networking, Internet related); Jenifer Niles, publisher (computer graphics, animation, game programming). Publishes hardcover and trade paperback originals. **Publishes 60 titles/year. Receives 1,000 queries and 250 mss/year. 20% of books from first-time authors; 90% from unagented writers. Pays 5-20% royalty on wholesale price. Offers $3,000-20,000 advance.** Publishes book 4 months after acceptance of ms. Accepts simultaneous submissions. Responds in 2 weeks to queries. Book catalog for #10 SASE; ms guidelines online.

   "Our publishing program concentrates on 6 major areas: Internet, networking, game development, programming, engineering, and graphics. The majority of our titles are considered intermediate, not high-level research monographs, and not for lowest-level general users."

Nonfiction Multimedia (Win/Mac format), reference, technical. Subjects include computers/electronic. Query with SASE, or submit proposal package including outline, 2 sample chapters, résumé. Reviews artwork/photos as part of ms package. Send photocopies or GIF, TIFF, or PDF files.

Recent Title(s) *Game Programming Gems*; *Professional Web Design 2/E.*

Tips "We are very receptive to detailed proposals by first-time or nonagented authors. Consult our website for proposal outlines. Manuscripts must be completed within 6 months of contract signing."

CHARLESBRIDGE PUBLISHING, SCHOOL DIVISION

85 Main St., Watertown MA 02472. (800)225-3214. Fax: (800)926-5775. E-mail: schooleditorial@charlesbridge.c om. Website: www.charlesbridge.com/school. **Acquisitions:** Elena Dworkin Wright, vice president school division. Estab. 1980. Publishes educational curricula and hardcover and paperback nonfiction and fiction children's picture books. **Publishes 20 titles/year. 10-20% of books from first-time authors; 80% from unagented writers. Royalty and advance vary.** Publishes book 2 years after acceptance of ms. Ms guidelines online.

   "We're looking for compelling story lines, humor and strong educational content."

Nonfiction Children's/juvenile, textbook. Subjects include education, multicultural, nature/environment, science, math, astronomy, physical science, problem solving. Submit complete ms.

Fiction Multicultural, nature, science, social studies, bedtime, etc. Non-rhyming stories. Submit complete ms.

Recent Title(s) *A Place for Zero*, by Angeline Sparagna LoPresti; *Sir Cumference and the Sword in the Cone*, by Cindy Neuschwander.

CHARLESBRIDGE PUBLISHING, TRADE DIVISION

85 Main St., Watertown MA 02472. (617)926-0329. Fax: (617)926-5720. Website: www.charlesbridge.com. **Acquisitions:** Submission Editor. Estab. 1980. Publishes hardcover and trade paperback nonfiction, children's picture books (80%) and fiction picture books for the trade and library markets. **Publishes 30 titles/year. 10-20% of books from first-time authors; 80% from unagented writers. Pays royalty. Offers advance.** Publishes book 2-4 years after acceptance of ms. Ms guidelines online.

Imprints Charlesbridge.

   "We're always interested in innovative approaches to a difficult genre, the nonfiction picture book." Currently emphasizing nature, science, multiculturalism.

Nonfiction Children's/juvenile. Subjects include animals, creative nonfiction, history, multicultural, nature/

environment, science, social science. Strong interest in nature, environment, social studies, and other topics for trade and library markets. *Exclusive submissions only.*

Fiction "Strong stories with enduring themes." *Exclusive submissions only.*

Recent Title(s) *The Beetle Alphabet Book*, by Jerry Pallotta; *Mung-Mung*, by Linda Sue Park; *The Bumblebee Queen*, by April Pulley Sayre.

CHATHAM PRESS

Box 601, Greenwich CT 06870. **Acquisitions:** Jane Andrassi. Estab. 1971. Publishes hardcover and paperback originals, reprints, and anthologies. **Publishes 10 titles/year. 25% of books from first-time authors; 75% from unagented writers.** Publishes book 6 months after acceptance of ms. Responds in 2 months to queries. Book catalog and ms guidelines for 6×9 SAE with 6 first-class stamps.

• Chatham Press publishes "books that relate to the U.S. coastline from Maine to the Carolinas and which bring a new insight, visual or verbal, to the nonfiction topic."

Nonfiction Illustrated book. Subjects include history, nature/environment, regional (Northeast seaboard), translation (from French and German), natural history. Query with SASE. Reviews artwork/photos as part of ms package.

Recent Title(s) *Exploring Old Martha's Vineyard.*

Tips "Illustrated New England-relevant titles have the best chance of being sold to our firm. We have a slightly greater (15%) skew toward cooking and travel titles."

CHELSEA GREEN PUBLISHING CO.

P.O. Box 428, 85 N. Main St., White River Junction VT 05001-0428. (802)295-6300. Fax: (802)295-6444. Website: www.chelseagreen.com. **Acquisitions:** John Barstow, editor-in-chief. Estab. 1984. Publishes hardcover and trade paperback originals and reprints. **Publishes 12-15 titles/year. Receives 300-400 queries and 200-300 mss/year. 30% of books from first-time authors; 80% from unagented writers. Pays royalty on publisher's net. Offers $2,500-10,000 advance.** Publishes book 18 months after acceptance of ms. Responds in 2 weeks to queries; 1 month to proposals and mss. Book catalog free or online; ms guidelines online.

• Chelsea Green publishes and distributes books relating to issues of sustainability with a special concentration on books about nature, the environment, independent living and enterprise, organic gardening, renewable energy, alternative or natural building techniques, and the politics of sustainability. The books reflect positive options in a world of environmental turmoil. Emphasizing food/agriculture/gardening, innovative shelter and natural building, renewable energy, sustainable business, and enterprise. De-emphasizing nature/natural history.

Nonfiction Cookbook, how-to, reference, technical. Subjects include agriculture/horticulture, art/architecture, cooking/foods/nutrition, gardening, health/medicine, money/finance, nature/environment, forestry, current affairs/politics. Query with SASE, or submit proposal package including outline, 1-2 sample chapters. Reviews artwork/photos as part of ms package.

Recent Title(s) *The Slow Food Guide to New York City*, by Slow Food USA; *The Straw Bale House*, by Steen, Steen, Bainbridge; *Gaia's Garden*, by Toby Hemenway.

Tips "Our readers are passionately enthusiastic about ecological solutions for contemporary challenges in construction, energy harvesting, agriculture, and forestry. Our books are also carefully and handsomely produced to give pleasure to bibliophiles of a practical bent. It would be very helpful for prospective authors to have a look at several of our current books, as well as our catalog and website. For certain types of book, we are the perfect publisher, but we are exceedingly focused on particular areas."

CHELSEA HOUSE PUBLISHERS

Haights Cross Communications, 2080 Cabot Blvd. W., Suite 201, Langhorne PA 19047-1813. (800)848-BOOK. Fax: (800)780-7300. E-mail: editorial@chelseahouse.com. Website: www.chelseahouse.com. **Acquisitions:** Editorial Assistant. Publishes hardcover originals and reprints. Accepts simultaneous submissions. Book catalog online; ms guidelines for #10 SASE.

• "We publish curriculum-based nonfiction books for middle school and high school students."

Nonfiction Biography (must be common format, fitting under a series umbrealla), children's/juvenile. Subjects include Americana, animals, anthropology/archeology, ethnic, gay/lesbian, government/politics, health/medicine, history, hobbies, language/literature, military/war, multicultural, music/dance, nature/environment, recreation, regional, religion, science, sociology, sports, travel, women's issues/studies. "We are interested in expanding our topics to include more on the physical, life and environmental sciences." Query with SASE, or submit proposal package including outline, 2-3 sample chapters, résumé. Reviews artwork/photos as part of ms package. Send photocopies.

Recent Title(s) *Futuristics: Looking Ahead, Vol. 1* (Tackling Tomorrow Today series); *Hepatitis* (Deadly Disease & Epidemics series); *South Africa: A State of Apartheid* (Arbitrary Borders series).

Tips "Know our product. Do not waste your time or ours by sending something that does not fit our market. Be professional. Send clean, clear submissions that show you read the preferred submission format. Always include SASE."

CHEMICAL PUBLISHING CO., INC.

527 Third Ave., #427, New York NY 10016-4168. (212)779-0090. Fax: (212)889-1537. E-mail: chempub@aol.com. Website: www.chemicalpublishing.com. **Acquisitions:** Ms. S. Soto-Galicia, publisher. Estab. 1934. **Publishes hardcover originals. Publishes 8 titles/year. Receives 20 queries/year. 50% of books from first-time authors; 100% from unagented writers. Pays 10% royalty on retail price or makes negotiable outright purchase. Offers negotiable advance.** Publishes book 8 months after acceptance of ms. Does not accept simultaneous submissions. Responds in 3 weeks to queries; 5 weeks to proposals; 2 months to mss. Book catalog free; ms guidelines online.

> O-π Chemical Publishing Co., Inc., publishes professional chemistry-technical titles aimed at people employed in the chemical industry, libraries and graduate courses.

Nonfiction How-to, reference, applied chemical technology (cosmetics, cement, textiles). Subjects include agriculture/horticulture, cooking/foods/nutrition, health/medicine, nature/environment, science, analytical methods, chemical technology, cosmetics, dictionaries, engineering, environmental science, food technology, formularies, industrial technology, medical, metallurgy, textiles. Submit outline, few pages of 3 sample chapters, SASE. Reviews artwork/photos as part of ms package.

Recent Title(s) *Cooling Water Treatment, Principles and Practice*; *Harry's Cosmeticology, 8th Ed.*; *Library Handbook for Organic Chemists*.

Tips Audience is professionals in various fields of chemistry, corporate and public libraries, college libraries. "We request a fax letter with an introduction of the author and the kind of book written. Afterwards, we will reply. If the title is of interest, then we will request samples of the manuscript."

CHICAGO REVIEW PRESS

814 N. Franklin, Chicago IL 60610-3109. (312)337-0747. Fax: (312)337-5110. E-mail: csherry@chicagoreviewpress.com. Submissions E-mail: ytaylor@chicagoreviewpress.com. Website: www.chicagoreviewpress.com. **Acquisitions:** Cynthia Sherry, associate publisher (general nonfiction, children's); Yuval Taylor, senior editor (African-American and performing arts); Jerome Pohlen, senior editor (educational resources). Estab. 1973. Publishes hardcover and trade paperback originals, and trade paperback reprints. **Publishes 40-50 titles/year. Receives 400 queries and 800 mss/year. 50% of books from first-time authors; 50% from unagented writers. Pays 7-12½% royalty. Offers $3,000-10,000 average advance.** Publishes book 18 months after acceptance of ms. Accepts simultaneous submissions. Responds in 3 months to queries. Book catalog for $3.50; ms guidelines for #10 SASE or online at website.

Imprints Lawrence Hill Books; A Cappella Books (contact Yuval Taylor); Zephyr Press (contact Jerome Pohlen).

> O-π Chicago Review Press publishes intelligent nonfiction on timely subjects for educated readers with special interests.

Nonfiction Children's/juvenile (activity books only), how-to. Subjects include art/architecture, child guidance/parenting, creative nonfiction, education, gardening (regional), health/medicine, history, hobbies, memoirs, multicultural, nature/environment, recreation, regional, music. Query with outline, TOC, and 1-2 sample chapters. Reviews artwork/photos as part of ms package.

Recent Title(s) *In Plain Sight: The Startling Truth Behind the Elizabeth Smart Investigation*, by Tom Smart and Lee Benson.

Tips "Along with a table of contents and 1-2 sample chapters, also send a cover letter and a list of credentials with your proposal. Also, provide the following information in your cover letter: audience, market, and competition—who is the book written for and what sets it apart from what's already out there."

CHILD WELFARE LEAGUE OF AMERICA

440 First St. NW, 3rd Floor, Washington DC 20001. (202)638-2952. Fax: (202)638-4004. E-mail: books@cwla.org. Website: www.cwla.org/pubs. **Acquisitions:** Acquisitions Editor. Publishes hardcover and trade paperback originals. Book catalog and ms guidelines online.

Imprints CWLA Press (child welfare professional publications); Child & Family Press (children's books and parenting books for the general public).

> O-π CWLA is a privately supported, nonprofit, membership-based organization committed to preserving, protecting, and promoting the well-being of all children and their families.

Nonfiction Children's/juvenile. Subjects include child guidance/parenting, sociology. Submit complete ms and proposal with outline, TOC, sample chapter, intended audience, and SASE.

Recent Title(s) *Can You Hear Me Smiling*, by Aariane R. Jackson; *A Look in the Mirror: Freeing Yourself from the Body Image Blues*, by Valerie Rainon McManus; *A Pocket Full of Kisses*, by Audrey Penn.

Tips "We are looking for positive, kid-friendly books for ages 3-9. We are looking for books that have a positive message—a feel-good book."

CHILDREN'S PRESS/FRANKLIN WATTS
Imprint of Scholastic, Inc., 90 Old Sherman Turnpike, Danbury CT 06816. Website: publishing.grolier.com. Estab. 1946. Publishes nonfiction hardcover originals. Book catalog for #10 SASE.

- Children's Press publishes 90% nonfiction for the school and library market, and 10% early reader fiction and nonfiction. "Our books support textbooks and closely relate to the elementary and middle-school curriculum." Franklin Watts publishes nonfiction for middle and high school curriculum.

Nonfiction Biography, children's/juvenile, reference. Subjects include animals, anthropology/archeology, art/architecture, ethnic, health/medicine, history, hobbies, multicultural, music/dance, nature/environment, science, sports, general children's nonfiction. "We publish nonfiction books that supplement the school curriculum." No fiction, poetry, folktales, cookbooks or novelty books. Query with SASE.

Recent Title(s) *Arctic Tundra*, by Salvatore Tocci; *My Birthday Cake*, by Olivia George, illustrated by Martha Avilés; *You Have Healthy Bones!*, by Susan DerKazarian.

Tips Most of this publisher's books are developed inhouse; less than 5% come from unsolicited submissions. However, they publish several series for which they always need new books. Study catalogs to discover possible needs.

CHIPPEWA PUBLISHING LLC
678 Dutchman Dr. #3, Chippewa Falls WI 54729. E-mail: submissions@chippewapublishing.com. Website: www.chippewapublishing.com. **Acquisitions:** Kimberly Burton, executive managing editor. Estab. 2004. Publishes trade paperback and electronic originals. **Publishes 45 titles/year; imprint publishes 12 titles/year. 45% of books from first-time authors; 90% from unagented writers. Pays 40% royalty on wholesale or retail price.** Does not accept simultaneous submissions. Book catalog and writer's guidelines online.

Fiction Adventure, erotica, ethnic, experimental, fantasy, gay/lesbian, gothic, historical, horror, humor, juvenile, mainstream/contemporary, military/war, mystery, occult, romance (dark), science fiction, short story collections, suspense, young adult. "We specialize in dark romance, horror, science fiction, fantasy, and erotica, but we accept other titles too." Submit complete ms.

Recent Title(s) *Alexandru*, by Rebecca K. Rhodes; *Release Me*, by Melissa Swaim.

Tips "Our audience loves to be shocked by what they read. Our romance books take it beyond a simple kiss; our horror takes it beyond just blood and guts. We enjoy an exciting story. Edit your work before sending it to us and do not use passive voice. We will return manuscripts with excessive passive voice and general mistakes. If it is a good story, we'll let you know and ask you to try again. Please be professional. We are very busy and so are you."

CHIVALRY BOOKSHELF
3305 Mayfair Ln., Highland Village TX 75077. (978)418-4774. Fax: (978)418-4774. E-mail: chronique_editor@yahoo.com. Submissions E-mail: csr@chivalrybookshelf.com. Website: www.chivalrybookshelf.com. **Acquisitions:** Brian R. Price, publisher (history, art, philosophy, political science, military, martial arts, fencing); Gregory Mele, martial arts editor (martial arts, fencing, history). Estab. 1996. Publishes hardcover and trade paperback originals and reprints. **Publishes 12 titles/year. Receives 75 queries and 25 mss/year. 50% of books from first-time authors; 90% from unagented writers. Pays 5-12% royalty.** Publishes book 6 months after acceptance of ms. Does not accept simultaneous submissions. Responds in 1 month to queries and proposals; 2 months to mss. Book catalog free; ms guidelines online.

Nonfiction Biography, booklets, children's/juvenile, coffee table book, general nonfiction, gift book, how-to, humor, illustrated book, scholarly, technical. Subjects include art/architecture, creative nonfiction, education, government/politics, history, military/war, recreation, sports (martial arts/fencing especially), translation. "Chivalry Bookshelf began focusing on new works and important reprints relating to arms and armour, medieval knighthood, and related topics. Since then, we have become the largest publisher of books relating to 'Western' or 'historical' martial arts, including translations, interpretations, and fascimile reproductions done in partnership with major museums such as the J. Paul Getty Museum and the British Royal Armouries. During 2004, we are expanding our history and military line dramatically and will be seeking manuscripts, especially translations and biographies, relating to classical, medieval, Renaissance, or pre-21st century history. During 2005 we plan to launch a new imprint dealing with modern politics and military issues. Manuscripts that deal with military memoirs, arms and armour, martial arts, and medieval history will receive particular consideration." Query with SASE, or submit proposal package including outline, 1 sample chapter, sample illustrations, or submit complete ms. Reviews artwork/photos as part of ms package.

Recent Title(s) *The Medieval Art of Swordsmanship*, translated and interpreted by Dr. Jeffrey L. Forgeng, co-published with the British Royal Armouries (art history); *Jousts & Tournaments*, by Dr. Stephen Muhlberger (scholarly/popular translation); *Arte of Defence*, by William E. Wilson (historical fencing).

Tips "The bulk of our books are intended for serious amateur scholars and students of history and martial arts. The authors we select tend to have a strong voice, are well read in their chosen field, and submit relatively clean manuscripts."

CHOSEN BOOKS PUBLISHING CO., LTD.

3985 Bradwater St., Fairfax VA 22031-3702. (703)764-8250. Fax: (703)764-3995. E-mail: jecampbell@aol.com. Website: www.bakerbooks.com. **Acquisitions:** Jane Campbell, editorial director. Estab. 1971. Publishes hardcover and trade paperback originals. **Publishes 20-25 titles/year. 15% of books from first-time authors; 90% from unagented writers. Offers small advance.** Publishes book 12-18 months after acceptance of ms. Accepts simultaneous submissions. Responds in 3 months to queries. Ms guidelines for #10 SASE.

➚ "We publish well-crafted books that recognize the gifts and ministry of the Holy Spirit, and help the reader live a more empowered and effective life for Jesus Christ."

Nonfiction Subjects include religion (Christianity). "We publish books reflecting the current acts of the Holy Spirit in the world, books with a charismatic Christian orientation." No New Age, poetry, fiction, autobiographies, biographies, compilations, Bible studies, booklets, academic, or children's books. Submit synopsis, chapter outline, résumé, 2 chapters and SASE or e-mail address. No computer disks or e-mail attachments; brief query only by e-mail.

Recent Title(s) *Praying for Israel's Destiny*, by James W. Goll.

Tips "We look for solid, practical advice for the growing and maturing Christian from authors with professional or personal experience platforms. No conversion accounts or chronicling of life events, please. State the topic or theme of your book clearly in your cover letter."

CHRISTIAN ED. PUBLISHERS

P.O. Box 26639, San Diego CA 92196. (858)578-4700. Fax: (858)578-2431. Website: www.christianedwarehouse .com. **Acquisitions:** Janet Ackelson, assistant editor. **Publishes 80 titles/year. Makes outright purchase of 3¢/word.** Responds in 3 months on assigned material to mss. Book catalog for 9×12 SAE with 4 first-class stamps; ms guidelines for #10 SASE.

➚ Christian Ed. Publishers is an independent, nondenominational, evangelical company founded nearly 50 years ago to produce Christ-centered curriculum materials based on the Word of God for thousands of churches of different denominations throughout the world. "Our mission is to introduce children, teens, and adults to a personal faith in Jesus Christ, and to help them grow in their faith and service to the Lord. We publish materials that teach moral and spiritual values while training individuals for a lifetime of Christian service." Currently emphasizing Bible curriculum for preschool-preteen ages.

Nonfiction Children's/juvenile. Subjects include education (Christian), religion. "All subjects are on assignment." Query with SASE.

Fiction "All writing is done on assignment." Query with SASE.

Recent Title(s) *All-Stars for Jesus: Bible Curriculum for Preteens.*

Tips "Read our guidelines carefully before sending us a manuscript. All writing is done on assignment only and must be age appropriate (preschool-6th grade)."

Ⓜ CHRISTIAN PUBLICATIONS, INC.

3825 Hartzdale Dr., Camp Hill PA 17011. (717)761-7044. Fax: (717)761-7273. E-mail: dfessenden@christianpubl ications.com. Website: www.christianpublications.com. **Acquisitions:** Pamela Brossman, editor. Estab. 1883. Publishes hardcover and trade paperback originals. **Publishes 12 titles/year. Receives 200 queries and 100 mss/year. 50% of books from first-time authors; 99% from unagented writers. Pays 5-10% royalty on retail price or makes outright purchase. Offers varying advance.** Publishes book 14-18 months after acceptance of ms. Accepts simultaneous submissions. Responds in 1 month to queries; 3 months to proposals. Ms guidelines online.

Imprints Christian History Institute.

➚ "Our purpose is to exalt God and impact lives by producing and distributing biblically faithful resources."

Nonfiction Biblical studies, Christian living, homeschooling, deeper life/classics, missions, church resources/ pastoral helps. Subjects include Americana, religion (Evangelical Christian perspective), spirituality, devotionals, Bible studies (with practical application), family/marriage, children's books. Full proposal must accompany ms. Does not want fiction, poetry. Query with SASE, or submit proposal package, including chapter synopsis, 2 sample chapters (including chapter 1), audience and market ideas, author bio. Reviews artwork/photos as part of ms package. Send photocopies.

Recent Title(s) *The Radical Cross*; *Great Women in Christian History*; *You're Going to Be My Mom!*

Tips "We are owned by The Christian and Missionary Alliance denomination; while we welcome and publish authors from various denominations, their theological perspective must be compatible with The Christian and Missionary Alliance. We are especially interested in fresh, practical approaches to deeper life—sanctification with running shoes on. Readers are evangelical, regular church-goers, mostly female, usually leaders in their church. Your book should grow out of a thorough and faithful study of Scripture. You need not be a 'Bible scholar,' but you should be a devoted student of the Bible."

CHRONICLE BOOKS

85 Second St., 6th Floor, San Francisco CA 94105. (415)537-4200. Fax: (415)537-4460. E-mail: frontdesk@chroniclebooks.com. Website: www.chroniclebooks.com. **Acquisitions:** Jay Schaefer (fiction); Bill LeBlond (cookbooks); Alan Rapp (art and design); Sarah Malarkey (licensing and popular culture); Jodi Davis (sex, fitness and pop culture); Steve Mockus (popular culture); Debra Lande (gift books); Victoria Rock (children's). Estab. 1966. Publishes hardcover and trade paperback originals. **Publishes 175 titles/year.** Publishes book 18 months after acceptance of ms. Accepts simultaneous submissions. Responds in 3 months to queries. Book catalog for 11×14 SAE with 5 first-class stamps; ms guidelines online.

Imprints Chronicle Books for Children; GiftWorks (ancillary products, such as stationery, gift books).

- "Inspired by the enduring magic and importance of books, our objective is to create and distribute exceptional publishing that is instantly recognizable for its spirit, creativity and value. This objective informs our business relationships and endeavors, be they with customers, authors, suppliers or colleagues."

Nonfiction Coffee table book, cookbook, gift book. Subjects include art/architecture, cooking/foods/nutrition, gardening, nature/environment, photography, recreation, regional, design, pop culture, interior design. Query or submit outline/synopsis with artwork and sample chapters.

Fiction Submit complete ms.

Recent Title(s) *The Beatles Anthology*, by The Beatles; *Worst-Case Scenario Survival Handbook*, by David Borgenicht and Joshua Piven.

CHRONICLE BOOKS FOR CHILDREN

85 Second St., 6th Floor, San Francisco CA 94105. (415)537-4200. Fax: (415)537-4460. E-mail: frontdesk@chroniclebooks.com. Website: www.chroniclekids.com. **Acquisitions:** Victoria Rock, associate publisher; Beth Weber, managing editor; Monique Stephens, editor; Susan Pearson, editor-at-large. Publishes hardcover and trade paperback originals. **Publishes 50-60 titles/year. Receives 30,000 queries/year. 6% of books from first-time authors; 25% from unagented writers. Pays 8% royalty. Offers variable advance.** Publishes book 18-24 months after acceptance of ms. Accepts simultaneous submissions. Responds in 2-4 weeks to queries; 6 months to mss. Book catalog for 9×12 SAE with 3 first-class stamps; ms guidelines online.

- Chronicle Books for Children publishes an eclectic mixture of traditional and innovative children's books. "Our aim is to publish books that inspire young readers to learn and grow creatively while helping them discover the joy of reading. We're looking for quirky, bold artwork and subject matter." Currently emphasizing picture books. De-emphasizing young adult.

Nonfiction Biography, children's/juvenile (for ages 8-12), illustrated book, picture books (for ages up to 8 years). Subjects include animals, art/architecture, multicultural, nature/environment, science. Query with synopsis and SASE. Reviews artwork/photos as part of ms package.

Fiction Mainstream/contemporary, multicultural, young adult, picture books; middle grade fiction; young adult projects. "We do not accept proposals by fax, via e-mail, or on disk. When submitting artwork, either as a part of a project or as samples for review, do not send original art. Please be sure to include an SASE large enough to hold your materials. Projects submitted without an appropriate SASE will be recycled." Query with SASE. Send complete ms with SASE for picture books.

Recent Title(s) *The Man Who Went to the Far Side of the Moon*; *Just a Minute*; *Ruby's Wish*.

Tips "We are interested in projects that have a unique bent to them—be it in subject matter, writing style, or illustrative technique. As a small list, we are looking for books that will lend our list a distinctive flavor. Primarily we are interested in fiction and nonfiction picture books for children ages up to eight years, and nonfiction books for children ages up to twelve years. We publish board, pop-up, and other novelty formats as well as picture books. We are also interested in early chapter books, middle grade fiction, and young adult projects."

CLARION BOOKS

Houghton Mifflin Co., 215 Park Ave. S., New York NY 10003. Website: www.houghtonmifflinbooks.com. **Acquisitions:** Dinah Stevenson, vice president and associate publisher; Jennifer B. Greene, senior editor (contemporary fiction, picture books for all ages, nonfiction); Jennifer Wingertzahn, editor (fiction, picture books); Lynne Polvino, associate editor (fiction, nonfiction, picture books). Estab. 1965. Publishes hardcover originals for children. **Publishes 50 titles/year. Pays 5-10% royalty on retail price. Offers minimum of $4,000 advance.** Publishes book 2 years after acceptance of ms. Responds in 2 months to queries. Prefers no multiple submissions. Ms guidelines for #10 SASE or online.

> O–π Clarion Books publishes picture books, nonfiction, and fiction for infants through grade 12. Avoid telling your stories in verse unless you are a professional poet.

Nonfiction Biography, children's/juvenile, photo essay. Subjects include Americana, history, language/literature, nature/environment, photography, holiday. No unsolicited mss. Query with SASE, or submit proposal package including sample chapters, SASE. Reviews artwork/photos as part of ms package. Send photocopies.

Fiction Adventure, historical, humor, mystery, suspense, strong character studies. Clarion is highly selective in the areas of historical fiction, fantasy, and science fiction. A novel must be superlatively written in order to find a place on the list. Mss that arrive without an SASE of adequate size will *not* be responded to or returned. Accepts fiction translations. Submit complete ms. No queries, please. Send to only *one* Clarion editor.

Recent Title(s) *Lizzie Bright and the Buckminster Boy*, by Gary D. Schmidt (fiction); *The Firekeeper's Son*, by Linda Sue Park (picture book); *An American Plague*, by Jim Murphy (nonfiction).

Tips Looks for "freshness, enthusiasm—in short, life."

Ⓐ CLARKSON POTTER

The Crown Publishing Group, Random House, Inc., 1745 Broadway, 13th Floor, New York NY 10019. (212)782-9000. Website: www.clarksonpotter.com. Estab. 1959. Publishes hardcover and trade paperback originals. Accepts agented submissions only. Does not accept simultaneous submissions.

> O–π Clarkson Potter specializes in publishing cooking books, decorating and other around-the-house how-to subjects.

Nonfiction Biography, how-to, humor, self-help, crafts, cooking and foods, decorating, design gardening. Subjects include art/architecture, child guidance/parenting, cooking/foods/nutrition, language/literature, memoirs, nature/environment, photography, psychology, translation. *Agented submissions only.* Query or submit outline and sample chapter with tearsheets from magazines and artwork copies (e.g.—color photocopies or duplicate transparencies).

Recent Title(s) *Ranch House Style*, by Katherine Samon; *Half-Scratch Magic*, by Linda West Eckhardt and Katherine West Defoyd; *Wildflowers*, by David Stark and Avi Adler.

CLEAR LIGHT PUBLISHERS

823 Don Diego, Santa Fe NM 87505-4224. (505)989-9590. E-mail: publish@clearlightbooks.com. **Acquisitions:** Harmon Houghton, publisher. Estab. 1981. Publishes hardcover and trade paperback originals. **Publishes 20-24 titles/year. Receives 100 queries/year. 10% of books from first-time authors; 50% from unagented writers. Pays 10% royalty on wholesale price. Offers advance, a percent of gross potential.** Publishes book 1 year after acceptance of ms. Accepts simultaneous submissions. Responds in 3 months to queries. Book catalog free; ms guidelines online.

> O–π Clear Light publishes books that "accurately depict the positive side of human experience and inspire the spirit."

Nonfiction Biography, coffee table book, cookbook. Subjects include Americana, anthropology/archeology, art/architecture, cooking/foods/nutrition, ethnic, history, nature/environment, philosophy, photography, regional (Southwest). Query with SASE. Reviews artwork/photos as part of ms package. Send photocopies.

Recent Title(s) *American Indian History*, by Robert Venables; *Celebrations Cookbook*, by Myra Baucom; *American Indian Love Stories*, by Herman Grey.

CLEIS PRESS

P.O. Box 14697, San Francisco CA 94114. (415)575-4700. Fax: (415)575-4705. Website: www.cleispress.com. **Acquisitions:** Frederique Delacoste. Estab. 1980. Publishes trade paperback originals and reprints. **Publishes 20 titles/year. 10% of books from first-time authors; 90% from unagented writers. Pays variable royalty on retail price.** Publishes book 2 years after acceptance of ms. Responds in 1 month to queries.

> O–π Cleis Press specializes in feminist and gay/lesbian fiction and nonfiction.

Nonfiction Subjects include gay/lesbian, women's issues/studies, sexual politics, erotica, human rights, African-American studies. "We are interested in books on topics of sexuality, human rights and women's and gay and lesbian literature. Please consult our website first to be certain that your book fits our list." Query or submit outline and sample chapters.

Fiction Feminist, gay/lesbian, literary. "We are looking for high quality fiction by women and men." No romances. Submit complete ms. *Writer's Market* recommends sending a query with SASE first.

Recent Title(s) *Arts and Letters* (nonfiction); *Melymbrosia* (fiction); *Whole Lesbian Sex Book* (nonfiction).

Tips "Be familiar with publishers' catalogs; be absolutely aware of your audience; research potential markets;

present fresh new ways of looking at your topic; avoid 'PR' language and include publishing history in query letter.''

CLOVER PARK PRESS

P.O. Box 5067, Santa Monica CA 90409-5067. (310)452-7657. E-mail: cloverparkpr@earthlink.net. Website: www.cloverparkpress.com. **Acquisitions:** Martha Grant, acquisitions editor. Estab. 1991. Publishes hardcover and trade paperback originals. **Publishes 6-10 titles/year. Receives 800 queries and 500 mss/year. 80% from unagented writers. Pays royalty, or makes outright purchase. Offers modest advance.** Publishes book less than 1 year after acceptance of ms. Accepts simultaneous submissions. Responds in 2 months to queries and proposals; 4 months to mss. Book catalog online; ms guidelines for #10 SASE.

Nonfiction Biography, general nonfiction. Subjects include creative nonfiction, memoirs, multicultural, nature/environment, regional, science, travel, women's issues/studies, world affairs. ''We are accepting queries in the above subjects in order to expand our list.'' Query with SASE, or submit proposal package including outline, author bio, 30-50 pages (including the first chapter), SASE.

Recent Title(s) *Last Moon Dancing: A Memoir of Love and Real Life in Africa*, by Monique Maria Schmidt.

Tips ''Our audience is women, high school, and college students, readers with curiosity about the world. Initial contact by e-mail or query letter. We welcome good writing. Have patience, we will respond.''

COACHES CHOICE

P.O. Box 1828, Monterey CA 93942. (888)229-5745. E-mail: info@coacheschoice.com. Website: www.coacheschoice.com. Publishes trade paperback originals and reprints. Accepts simultaneous submissions. Book catalog free.

⊶ ''We publish books for anyone who coaches a sport or has an interest in coaching a sport—all levels of competition. Detailed descriptions, step-by-step instructions, and easy-to-follow diagrams set our books apart.''

Nonfiction How-to, reference. Subjects include sports, sports specific training, general physical conditioning. Submit proposal package including outline, 2 sample chapters, résumé. Reviews artwork/photos as part of ms package. Send photocopies or diagrams.

Recent Title(s) *Coaching the Multiple West Coast Offense*, by Ron Jenkins.

Ⓝ COASTAL PUBLISHING INTERNATIONAL

P.O. Box 910, Queen Creek AZ 85242. E-mail: acquisitions@coastalpublishingintl.com. Website: www.coastalpublishingintl.com. Estab. 2003. Publishes trade paperback, mass market paperback, and electronic originals. **Publishes 10 titles/year. Receives 300 queries and 50 mss/year. 90% of books from first-time authors; 90% from unagented writers. Pays 10-40% royalty on retail price.** Publishes book 6-12 months after acceptance of ms. Accepts simultaneous submissions. Responds in 1 month to queries and proposals; 2 months to mss. Ms guidelines online.

Nonfiction Audiocassettes, biography, children's/juvenile, coffee table book, cookbook, general nonfiction, how-to, humor, multimedia, reference, scholarly, self-help, technical, textbook. Subjects include agriculture/horticulture, alternative lifestyles, animals, anthropology/archeology, art/architecture, business/economics, child guidance/parenting, community, computers/electronic, cooking/foods/nutrition, creative nonfiction, education, gardening, health/medicine, hobbies, humanities, language/literature, money/finance, music/dance, nature/environment, New Age, philosophy, photography, psychology, recreation, regional, religion, science, sex, social sciences, sociology, software, spirituality, sports, travel, women's issues/studies, astrology/psychic, automotive, communications, counseling/career guidance, crafts, history, house/home, law, marine subjects, real estate, young adult. ''We do not publish military/war topics at all. We also do not accept manuscripts that have been previously published in any capacity.'' Query with SASE. Reviews artwork/photos as part of ms package. Send photocopies.

Tips ''We have a wide range or interests and audiences to match those interests. Let us know specifically how you are going to make this book a success. Just telling us you are available for interviews and promotions is not enough. Tell us your intended audience, and why that audience will feel compelled to buy the book.''

COFFEE HOUSE PRESS

27 N. Fourth St., Suite 400, Minneapolis MN 55401. (612)338-0125. Fax: (612)338-4004. Website: www.coffeehousepress.org. Publisher: Allan Kornblum. **Acquisitions:** Chris Fischbach, senior editor. Estab. 1984. Publishes hardcover and trade paperback originals. **Publishes 14 titles/year.** Responds in 4-6 weeks to queries; up to 6 months to mss. Book catalog and ms guidelines online.

Fiction Seeks essays, literary novels, and short story collections. No genre fiction or antholgies. Query first with outline, samples (20-30 pages) and SASE.

Poetry Full-length collections.

Recent Title(s) *The Impossibly*, by Laird Hunt; *That Kind of Sleep*, by Susan Atefat-Peckham; *Circle K Cycles*, by Karen Tei Yamashita.

Tips "Look for our books at stores and libraries to get a feel for what we like to publish. No phone calls, e-mails, or faxes."

COLLECTORS PRESS, INC.

P.O. Box 230986, Portland OR 97281-0986. (503)684-3030. Fax: (503)684-3777. Website: www.collectorspress.com. **Acquisitions:** Lisa Perry, publisher. Estab. 1992. Publishes hardcover and trade paperback originals. **Publishes 20 titles/year. Receives 500 queries and 200 mss/year. 75% of books from first-time authors; 75% from unagented writers. Pays royalty.** Publishes book 1 year after acceptance of ms. Responds in 1 month to queries. Book catalog and ms guidelines free.

   O─┐ Collectors Press, Inc., publishes award-winning popular-culture coffee table and gift books on 20th century, and modern collections and interests.

Nonfiction Illustrated book, reference. Subjects include art/architecture, photography, nostalgic pop culture, science-fiction art, fantasy art, graphic design, comic art, magazine art, historical art, poster art, genre-specific art. Submit proposal package, including market research, outline, 2 sample chapters, and SASE. Reviews artwork/photos as part of ms package. Send transparencies or very clear photos.

Recent Title(s) *Worlds of Tomorrow*; *Burlesque*; *Retro Kids Cooking*.

Tips "Your professional package must be typed. No computer disks accepted."

COLLEGE PRESS PUBLISHING CO.

P.O. Box 1132/223, 223 W. 3rd St., Joplin MO 64801. (800)289-3300. Fax: (417)623-8250. E-mail: jmcclarnon@collegepress.com. Website: www.collegepress.com. **Acquisitions:** Acquisitions Editor. Estab. 1959. Publishes hardcover and trade paperback originals and reprints. Accepts simultaneous submissions. Responds in 3 months to proposals; 2 months to mss. Book catalog for 9×12 SAE with 5 first-class stamps; ms guidelines online.

Imprints HeartSpring Publishing (nonacademic Christian, inspirational, devotional and Christian fiction).

   O─┐ "College Press is an evangelical Christian publishing house primarily associated with the Christian churches/Church of Christ."

Nonfiction Seeks Bible studies, topical studies, apologetic studies, historical biographies of Christians, and Sunday/Bible school curriculum. No poetry, games/puzzles, or any book without a Christian message. Query with SASE, or submit proposal package including outline, author bio, synopsis, TOC, target audience.

Recent Title(s) *Encounters With Christ*, by Mark E. Moore.

Tips "Our core market is Christian Churches/Churches of Christ and conservative evangelical Christians. Have your material critically reviewed prior to sending it. Make sure that it is non-Calvinistic and that it leans more amillennial (if it is apocalyptic writing)."

⊘ COMMON COURAGE PRESS

One Red Barn Rd. Box 702, Monroe ME 04951. (207)525-0900. Fax: (207)525-3068. Website: www.commoncouragepress.com. Publisher: Greg Bates. Estab. 1991. Publishes hardcover and trade paperback originals and trade paperback reprints. Accepts simultaneous submissions. Book catalog and ms guidelines online.

   O─┐ "Nonfiction leftist, activist, political, history, feminist, media issues are our niche. *We are not taking unsolicited mss at this time.*"

Nonfiction Reference, textbook. Subjects include anthropology/archeology, creative nonfiction, ethnic, gay/lesbian, government/politics, health/medicine, history, military/war, multicultural, nature/environment, science. Query with SASE or submit proposal package, including outline. Reviews artwork/photos as part of ms package.

Recent Title(s) *New Military Humanism*, by Noam Chomsky (leftist political); *Rogue State*, by William Blum (leftist political).

Tips Audience consists of left-wing activists, college audiences.

CONCORDIA PUBLISHING HOUSE

3558 S. Jefferson Ave., St. Louis MO 63118-3968. (314)268-1187. Fax: (314)268-1329. Website: www.cph.org. **Acquisitions:** Peggy Kuethe, acquisitions & production editor (children's product, adult devotional, teaching resources); Mark Sell, senior editor (adult nonfiction on Christian spirituality and culture, academic works of interest in Lutheran markets). Estab. 1869. Publishes hardcover and trade paperback originals. **Publishes 50 titles/year.** Ms guidelines online.

   O─┐ Concordia publishes Protestant, inspirational, theological, family, and juvenile material. All mss must conform to the doctrinal tenets of The Lutheran Church—Missouri Synod. No longer publishes fiction.

Nonfiction Children's/juvenile, adult. Subjects include child guidance/parenting (in Christian context), religion, inspirational.

Recent Title(s) *Faithfully Parenting Tweens: A Proactive Approach*, by John Bucka (parenting); *A Tree for Christmas*, by Dandi Daley Mackall (children's picture).

Tips "Call for information about what we are currently accepting."

Ⓝ CONSORTIUM PUBLISHING

640 Weaver Hill Rd., West Greenwich RI 02817-2261. (401)397-9838. Fax: (401)392-1926. John M. Carlevale, chief of publications. Estab. 1990. Publishes trade paperback originals and reprints. **Publishes 12 titles/year. Receives 150 queries and 50 mss/year. 50% of books from first-time authors; 95% from unagented writers. Pays 10-15% royalty.** Publishes book 3 months after acceptance of ms. Responds in 2 months to queries. Book catalog and ms guidelines for #10 SASE.

    ○➝ Consortium publishes books for all levels of the education market.

Nonfiction Autobiography, how-to, humor, illustrated book, reference, self-help, technical, textbook. Subjects include business/economics, child guidance/parenting, education, government/politics, health/medicine, history, music/dance, nature/environment, psychology, science, sociology, women's issues/studies. Query, or submit proposal package, including TOC, outline, 1 sample chapter, and SASE. Reviews artwork/photos as part of ms package. Send photocopies.

Recent Title(s) *Teaching the Child Under Six, 4th Ed.*, by James L. Hymes, Jr. (education).

Tips Audience is college and high school students and instructors, elementary school teachers and other trainers.

CONTEMPORARY BOOKS

Imprint of McGraw-Hill Co., 130 E. Randolph St., Suite 400, Chicago IL 60601. (800)621-1918. E-mail: mhceditorial@mcgraw-hill.com. Website: www.books.mcgraw-hill.com. Vice President: Philip Ruppel. Also: 2 Penn Plaza, New York NY 10121-2298. (212)904-2000. Estab. 1947. Publishes hardcover originals and trade paperback originals and reprints. Accepts simultaneous submissions. Ms guidelines for #10 SASE.

    ○➝ "We are a midsize, niche-oriented, backlist-oriented publisher. We publish adult basic education, GED, and ESL products."

Nonfiction How-to, reference, self-help. Query with SASE, or submit outline, sample chapters, cv. Reviews artwork/photos as part of ms package.

Recent Title(s) *American History 1 (Before 1865)*; *Achieving TABE Success in Reading/Mathematics/Language*.

CONTINUUM INTERNATIONAL PUBLISHING GROUP, LTD.

15 E. 26th St., Suite 1703, New York NY 10010. (212)953-5858. Fax: (212)953-5944. E-mail: info@continuumbooks.com. Website: www.continuumbooks.com. **Acquisitions:** Frank Oveis, VP/senior editor (religious, current affairs); Evander Lomke, VP/senior editor (literary criticism, performing arts, social thought, women's studies); David Barker, acquisitions editor (film, music, pop culture); Gabriella Page-Fort, assitant editor. Publishes hardcover originals and paperback textbooks. Does not accept simultaneous submissions. Book catalog and ms guidelines free.

    ○➝ Continuum publishes textbooks, monographs, and reference works in the humanities, arts, and social sciences for students, teachers, and professionals worldwide.

Nonfiction Reference, technical, textbook. Subjects include anthropology/archeology, business/economics, education, film/cinema/stage (performance), government/politics, history, language/literature, music/dance (popular), philosophy, religion, sociology, travel (tourism), therapy culture studies, linguistics. Submit outline.

Recent Title(s) *Jazz Writings*, by Philip Larkin; *Holocaust & Memory*, by Gunnar Paulsson and Barbara Engelking; *Children at War*, by Kate Agnew and Geoff Fox.

Ⓔ COOPER SQUARE PRESS

Taylor Trade Publishing, 5360 Manhattan Circle, #101, Boulder CO 80303. (303)543-7835. E-mail: tradeeditorial@rowman.com. Website: www.coopersquarepress.com. **Acquisitions:** Ross Plotkin, acquisitions editor. Estab. 1984. Publishes hardcover originals, trade paperback originals and reprints. **Publishes 40 titles/year. 15% of books from first-time authors; 65% from unagented writers. Pays 10-15% royalty on net receipts.** Publishes book 1 year after acceptance of ms. Responds in 2 months to queries. Book catalog and ms guidelines for 9×12 SAE with 4 first-class stamps.

Nonfiction Biography, reference (trade). Subjects include contemporary culture, history, contemporary affairs, music, film, theater, art, nature writing, exploration, women's studies, African-American studies, literary studies. All proposals may be sent via e-mail. *No unsolicited mss.* Query with SASE, or submit outline, sample chapters.

Ⓔ COPPER CANYON PRESS

P.O. Box 271, Port Townsend WA 98368. (360)385-4925. Fax: (360)385-4985. E-mail: poetry@coppercanyonpress.org. Website: www.coppercanyonpress.org. **Acquisitions:** Michael Wiegers, editor. Estab. 1972. Publishes trade paperback originals and occasional cloth-bound editions. **Publishes 18 titles/year. Receives 2,000 queries and 1,500 mss/year. 10% of books from first-time authors; 95% from unagented writers. Pays royalty.** Publishes book 2 years after acceptance of ms. Responds in 4 months to queries. Book catalog free; ms guidelines online.

O— Copper Canyon Press is dedicated to publishing poetry in a wide range of styles and from a full range of the world's cultures.

Poetry "First, second, and third book manuscripts are considered only for our Hayden Carruth Award, presented annually." Send SASE for entry form in September of each year. *No unsolicited mss.*

Recent Title(s) *Steal Away*, by C.D. Wright; *Nightworks*, by Marvin Bell; *The Complete Poems of Kenneth Rexroth*.

CORNELL MARITIME PRESS, INC.

P.O. Box 456, Centreville MD 21617-0456. (410)758-1075. Fax: (410)758-6849. E-mail: mslavin@cmptp.com. Website: www.cmptp.com. **Acquisitions:** Michelle Slavin, managing editor. Estab. 1938. Publishes hardcover originals and quality paperbacks. **Publishes 7-9 titles/year. 80% of books from first-time authors; 99% from unagented writers.** Publishes book 1 year after acceptance of ms. Responds in 2 months to queries. Book catalog for 10×13 SAE with 5 first-class stamps.

Imprints Tidewater (regional history, folklore, and wildlife of the Chesapeake Bay and the Delmarva Peninsula).

O— Cornell Maritime Press publishes books for the merchant marine and a few recreational boating books for professional mariners and yachtsmen.

Nonfiction How-to (on maritime subjects), technical, manuals. Subjects include marine subjects (highly technical). Query first, with writing samples and outlines of book ideas.

Recent Title(s) *Sequoia, Presidential Yacht*, by Giles M. Kelly; *The Mystery of Mary Surratt*, by Rebecca C. Jones; *Chesapeake Rainbow*, by Priscilla Cummings.

CORNELL UNIVERSITY PRESS

Sage House, 512 E. State St., Ithaca NY 14850. (607)277-2338. Fax: (607)277-2374. Website: www.cornellpress.cornell.edu. Estab. 1869. Publishes hardcover and paperback originals. **Publishes 150 titles/year. Pays royalty. Offers $0-5,000 advance.** Publishes book 1 year after acceptance of ms. Accepts simultaneous submissions. Book catalog and ms guidelines online.

Imprints Comstock (contact science editor); ILR Press (contact Frances Benson).

O— Cornell Press is an academic publisher of nonfiction with particular strengths in anthropology, Asian studies, biological sciences, classics, history, labor and business, literary criticism, politics and international relations, psychology, women's studies, Slavic studies, philosophy. Currently emphasizing sound scholarship that appeals beyond the academic community.

Nonfiction Biography, reference, scholarly, textbook. Subjects include agriculture/horticulture, anthropology/archeology, art/architecture, business/economics, education, ethnic, gay/lesbian, government/politics, history, language/literature, military/war, music/dance, philosophy, psychology, regional, religion, science, sociology, translation, women's issues/studies, classics. Submit résumé, cover letter, and prospectus.

Recent Title(s) *Corporate Warriors*, by Peter W. Singer; *The Venomous Reptiles of the Western Hemisphere*, by Jonathan A. Campbell and William W. Lamar; *Natural Life*, by David W. Robinson.

CORWIN PRESS, INC.

2455 Teller Rd., Thousand Oaks CA 91320. (805)499-9734. Fax: (805)499-2692. E-mail: robb.clouse@corwinpress.com. **Acquisitions:** Robb Clouse, editorial director; Lizzie Brenkus, acquisitions editor (administration); Kylee Liegl, acquisitions editor (content, curriculum and exceptional education); Rachel Livsey, acquisitions editor (staff development, diversity and research methods); Kathleen McLane, consulting acquisitions editor (exceptional education); Stacy Wagner, associate acquisitions editor (early childhood education and school counseling); Jean Ward, consulting senior acquisitions editor (teaching); Faye Zucker, executive editor (teaching). Estab. 1990. Publishes hardcover and paperback originals. **Publishes 140 titles/year.** Publishes book 7 months after acceptance of ms. Responds in 1 month to queries. Ms guidelines for #10 SASE.

O— Corwin Press, Inc., publishes leading-edge, user-friendly publications for education professionals.

Nonfiction Professional-level publications for administrators, teachers, school specialists, policymakers, researchers and others involved with K-12 education. Subjects include education. Seeking fresh insights, conclusions, and recommendations for action. Prefers theory or research-based books that provide real-world examples and practical, hands-on strategies to help busy educators be successful. No textbooks that simply summarize existing knowledge or mass-market books. Query with SASE.

COUNCIL OAK BOOKS

2105 E. 15th St., Suite B, Tulsa OK 74104. (918)743-BOOK. Fax: (918)743-4288. E-mail: publicity@counciloakbooks.com. **Acquisitions:** Acquisitions Editor. Estab. 1984. Publishes hardcover originals, trade paperback originals, and reprints. Accepts simultaneous submissions. Book catalog and ms guidelines for #10 SASE.

Imprints Wildcat Canyon Press (friendship, spirituality, women's issues, home, family, lifestyle, personal growth).

Nonfiction Autobiography, gift book, illustrated book, self-help. Subjects include Americana, memoirs, Native American history, alternative spiritual teachings, hidden wisdom & esoterica, alternative health for animals, relationship between humans and animals/nature. Query with SASE, or submit proposal package including outline, sample chapters, author bio. Reviews artwork/photos as part of ms package. Send photocopies.

Recent Title(s) *Water Crystal Oracle*, by Masaru Emoto; *Sworn to Fun!*, by Scout Cloud Lee; *Let It Be Easy*, by Tolly Burkan.

THE COUNTRYMAN PRESS

P.O. Box 748, Woodstock VT 05091-0748. (802)457-4826. Fax: (802)457-1678. E-mail: countrymanpress@wwn orton.com. Website: www.countrymanpress.com. Editorial Director: Kermit Hummel. Estab. 1973. Publishes hardcover originals, trade paperback originals and reprints. **Publishes 35 titles/year. Receives 1,000 queries/ year. 30% of books from first-time authors; 70% from unagented writers. Pays 5-15% royalty on retail price. Offers $1,000-5,000 advance.** Publishes book 18 months after acceptance of ms. Accepts simultaneous submissions. Responds in 2 months to proposals. Book catalog free; ms guidelines online.

Imprints Backcountry Guides, Berkshire House.

☌ Countryman Press publishes books that encourage physical fitness and appreciation for and understanding of the natural world, self-sufficiency, and adventure.

Nonfiction "We publish several series of regional recreation guidebooks—hiking, bicycling, walking, fly-fishing, canoeing, kayaking—and are looking to expand them. We're also looking for books of national interest on travel, gardening, rural living, nature, and fly-fishing." General nonfiction, how-to, guidebooks; general nonfiction. Subjects include cooking/foods/nutrition, gardening, history, nature/environment, recreation, regional, travel, country living. Submit proposal package including outline, 3 sample chapters, author bio, market information, SASE. Reviews artwork/photos as part of ms package. Send photocopies.

Recent Title(s) *The King Arthur Flour Cookie Companion*; *The Green Mountain Spinnery Knitting Book*; *Dog Friendly Washington DC and the Mid-Atlantic States.*

COVENANT COMMUNICATIONS, INC.

Box 416, American Fork UT 84003-0416. (801)756-1041. Website: www.covenant-lds.com. **Publishes 60+ titles/year. 35% of books from first-time authors; 100% from unagented writers. Pays 6½-15% royalty on retail price.** Publishes book 6-12 months after acceptance of ms. Responds in 4 months to mss. Ms guidelines online.

☌ Currently emphasizing inspirational, devotional, historical, biography. Our fiction is also expanding, and we are looking for new approaches to LDS literature and storytelling.

Nonfiction Biography, children's/juvenile, coffee table book, gift book, humor, illustrated book, multimedia (CD-ROM), reference, scholarly. Subjects include child guidance/parenting, creative nonfiction, history, memoirs, religion (LDS or Mormon), spirituality. Submit complete ms with synopsis and 1-page cover letter.

Fiction "We publish exclusively to the 'Mormon' (The Church of Jesus Christ of Latter-Day Saints) market. All work must appeal to that audience." Adventure, historical, humor, juvenile, literary, mainstream/contemporary, mystery, picture books, regional, religious, romance, spiritual, suspense, young adult. Submit complete ms with synopsis and 1-page cover letter.

Recent Title(s) *Between Husband and Wife*, by Brinley and Lamb (marriage/self-help); *Land of Promise*, by S. Michael Wilcox; *Saints at War II, Korea and Vietnam*, by Robert Freeman and Dennis Wright.

Tips "Our audience is exclusively LDS (Latter-Day Saints, 'Mormon')."

N COWLEY PUBLICATIONS

4 Brattle St., Cambridge MA 02138. (800)225-1534. Fax: (617)441-0120. E-mail: cowley@cowley.org. Website: www.cowley.org. Estab. 1979. Publishes trade paperback originals. **Publishes 16-20 titles/year. Receives 500 queries and 300 mss/year. 50% of books from first-time authors; 90% from unagented writers. Pays 10-15% royalty on wholesale price. Offers $0-5,000 advance.** Publishes book 12-18 months after acceptance of ms. Accepts simultaneous submissions. Responds in 2 months to queries; 3 months to proposals; 4 months to mss. Book catalog and ms guidelines online.

Nonfiction General nonfiction. Subjects include religion, spirituality. "We publish books and resources for those seeking spiritual and theological formation. We are committed to developing a new generation of writers and teachers who will encourage people to think and pray in new ways about spirituality, reconciliation, and the future. We are interested in the many ways that faith and spirituality intersect with the world, in arts, social concerns, ethics, and so on." Query with SASE, or submit proposal package including outline, 1 sample chapter, other materials as specified online.

Poetry "We consider poetry by invitation only."

Recent Title(s) *Spirited Men*, by Brian Doyle; *Light Theology and Heavy Cream*, by Robert Farrar Copon; *Mary: The Imagination of Her Heart*, by Penelope Duckworth (spirituality/Bible/Mary).

Tips "We envision an audience of committed Christians and spiritual seekers of various denominations and faiths. Familiarize yourself with our catalog and our outlook on spiritual and theological formation. Prepare proposals/manuscripts that are of professional caliber and demonstrate an understanding of and commitment to your book's reader."

CQ PRESS

Division of Congressional Quarterly, Inc., 1255 22nd St. NW, Suite 400, Washington DC 20037. (202)729-1800. E-mail: ckiino@cqpress.com. Website: www.cqpress.com. **Acquisitions:** Doug Goldenberg-Hart, Shana Wagger (library/reference); Clarisse Kiino (college), Barbara Rogers (staff directories). Estab. 1945. Publishes hardcover and online paperback titles. Accepts simultaneous submissions. Book catalog free.

Imprints College, Library/Reference, Staff Directories; CQ Electronic Library/CQ Researcher.

    ○┅ CQ Press seeks "to educate the public by publishing authoritative works on American and international politics, policy, and people."

Nonfiction "We are interested in American government, public administration, comparative government, and international relations." Reference, textbook (all levels of college political science texts), information directories (on federal and state governments, national elections, international/state politics and governmental issues). Subjects include government/politics, history. Submit proposal package including outline.

Tips "Our books present important information on American government and politics, and related issues, with careful attention to accuracy, thoroughness, and readability."

CRAFTSMAN BOOK CO.

6058 Corte Del Cedro, Carlsbad CA 92009-9974. (760)438-7828 or (800)829-8123. Fax: (760)438-0398. E-mail: jacobs@costbook.com. Website: www.craftsman-book.com. **Acquisitions:** Laurence D. Jacobs, editorial manager. Estab. 1957. Publishes paperback originals. **Publishes 12 titles/year. 85% of books from first-time authors; 98% from unagented writers. Pays 7½-12½% royalty on wholesale price or retail price.** Publishes book 2 years after acceptance of ms. Accepts simultaneous submissions. Responds in 2 months to queries. Book catalog and ms guidelines free.

    ○┅ Publishes how-to manuals for professional builders. Currently emphasizing construction software.

Nonfiction All titles are related to construction for professional builders. How-to, technical. Subjects include building, construction. Query with SASE. Reviews artwork/photos as part of ms package.

Recent Title(s) *Steel-Frame House Construction*, by Tim Waite.

Tips "The book should be loaded with step-by-step instructions, illustrations, charts, reference data, forms, samples, cost estimates, rules of thumb, and examples that solve actual problems in the builder's office and in the field. The book must cover the subject completely, become the owner's primary reference on the subject, have a high utility-to-cost ratio, and help the owner make a better living in his chosen field."

CREATIVE HOMEOWNER

24 Park Way, Upper Saddle River NJ 07458. (201)934-7100. Fax: (201)934-8971. E-mail: info@creativehomeowner.com. Website: www.creativehomeowner.com. Estab. 1978. Publishes trade paperback originals. Book catalog free.

    ○┅ Creative Homeowner is the one source for the largest selection of quality home-related how-to books, idea books, booklets, and project plans.

Nonfiction How-to, illustrated book. Subjects include gardening, crafts/hobbies, home remodeling/building, home repairs, home decorating/design, ideas, inspiration. Query, or submit proposal package, including competitive books (short analysis), outline, and SASE. Reviews artwork/photos as part of ms package.

Recent Title(s) *The Painted Home*, by Kerry Skinner; *So Simple Window Style*, by Gail Abbott and Cate Burren; *The Smart Approach to Baby Rooms*, by Joanne Still.

⊘ CRICKET BOOKS

Imprint of Carus Publishing, 30 Grove St., Suite C, Peterborough NH 03458. (603)924-7209. Fax: (603)924-7380. Website: www.cricketbooks.net. **Acquisitions:** Submissions Editor. Estab. 1999. Publishes hardcover originals. **Publishes 10 titles/year. Receives 1,500 queries and 5,000 mss/year. Pays 10% royalty on net receipts. Open to first-time authors. Pays up to 10% royalty on retail price. Offers $1,500 and up advance.** Publishes book 18 months after acceptance of ms. Accepts simultaneous submissions. Responds in 4 months to queries and proposals; 6 months to mss. Ms guidelines online.

    • *Currently not accepting queries or ms.* Check website for submissions details and updates.

    ○┅ Cricket Books publishes picture books, chapter books, and middle-grade novels.

Nonfiction Children's/juvenile. Send proposal, including sample chapters, TOC, and description of competition.

Fiction Juvenile (adventure, easy-to-read, fantasy/science fiction, historical, horror, mystery/suspense, problem novels, sports, western), early chapter books and middle-grade fiction. Submit complete ms.

Recent Title(s) *Breakout*, by Paul Fleischman; *Dare to be Scared*, by Robert San Souci; *Freedom Roads*, by Joyce Hansen and Gary McGowan.

Tips "Take a look at the recent titles to see what sort of materials we're interested in, especially for nonfiction. Please note that we aren't doing the sort of strictly educational nonfiction that other publishers specialize in."

Ⓐ CROWN BUSINESS

Random House, Inc., 1745 Broadway, New York NY 10019. (212)572-2275. Fax: (212)572-6192. E-mail: crownbiz@randomhouse.com. Website: www.randomhouse.com/crown. Estab. 1995. Publishes hardcover and trade paperback originals. Accepts simultaneous submissions. Book catalog online.

• *Agented submissions only.*

Nonfiction Subjects include business/economics, money/finance, management, technology. Query with proposal package including outline, 1-2 sample chapters, market analysis and SASE.

Recent Title(s) *Life 2.0*, by Rich Karlgaard; *Confronting Reality*, by Larry Bossidy and Ram Charan; *You're In Charge—Now What?*, by Thomas J. Neff and James M. Citrin.

Ⓐ Ⓩ CROWN PUBLISHING GROUP

Imprint of Random House, Inc., 1745 Broadway, New York NY 10019. (212)782-9000. Website: www.randomhouse.com/crown. Estab. 1933. Publishes popular fiction and nonfiction hardcover originals.

Imprints Bell Tower; Clarkson Potter; Crown Business; Crown Forum; Harmony Books; Shaye Arehart Books; Three Rivers Press.

• *Agented submissions only.* See website for more details.

Recent Title(s) *Electric Universe*, by David Bodanis; *Interior Desecrations*, by James Lileks; *Rammer Jammer Yellow Hammer*, by Warren St. John.

Ⓩ CRYSTAL DREAMS PUBLISHING

P.O. Box 698, Dover TN 37058. Phone/Fax: (931)232-4669. E-mail: dmawagner@bellsouth.net. Website: www.crystaldreamspub.com. **Acquisitions:** Dallas Wagner, head editor. Submission Address: 10826 N. Orva Dr., Citrus Springs FL 34434. Estab. 2001. Publishes trade paperback originals and reprints. Accepts simultaneous submissions. Responds in 1 month to queries; 2 months to proposals and mss. Book catalog and ms guidelines online.

• "Crystal Dreams is currently closed to new submissions so we may concentrate our energy on our current submissions."

Nonfiction Children's/juvenile, general nonfiction, humor. Subjects include alternative lifestyles, animals, creative nonfiction, gay/lesbian, history, hobbies, memoirs, military/war, New Age, regional, religion, science, spirituality, world affairs. Submit proposal package including outline, 3 sample chapters, preliminary marketing plan.

Fiction Adventure, experimental, fantasy, feminist, gay/lesbian, gothic, historical, horror, humor, juvenile, literary, mainstream/contemporary, military/war, mystery, occult, plays, poetry, regional, religious, romance, science fiction, short story collections, spiritual, sports, suspense, western, young adult. Submit proposal package including 3 sample chapters, synopsis, preliminary business plan.

Poetry "We are looking for poets who can get out and sell themselves to the public. All forms of poetry are accepted." Submit complete ms.

Recent Title(s) *Reflections of Soaring*, by Ed "Hawk" Marko.

Tips "Our audience varies a lot. We have readers who range from school children to retired persons. Wow us! Show us that you are an author who is willing to work and be known."

Ⓩ CSLI PUBLICATIONS

Ventura Hall, Stanford University, Stanford CA 94305-4115. (650)723-1839. Fax: (650)725-2166. E-mail: pubs@csli.stanford.edu. Website: cslipublications.stanford.edu. Publishes hardcover and scholarly paperback originals. Does not accept simultaneous submissions. Book catalog free; ms guidelines online.

• *No unsolicited mss.*

○┓ "CSLI Publications, part of the Center for the Study of Language and Information, specializes in books in the study of language, information, logic, and computation."

Nonfiction Reference, technical, textbook, scholarly. Subjects include anthropology/archeology, computers/electronic, language/literature (linguistics), science, logic, cognitive science. Query with SASE or by email.

Recent Title(s) *Handbook of French Semantics*, edited by Francis Corblin and Henriëtte de Swart; *Geometry & Meaning*, by Dominic Widdows.

CUMBERLAND HOUSE PUBLISHING

431 Harding Industrial Dr., Nashville TN 37211. (615)832-1171. Fax: (615)832-0633. E-mail: information@cumb
erlandhouse.com. Website: www.cumberlandhouse.com. Estab. 1996. Publishes hardcover, trade paperback
and mass market originals and reprints. Accepts simultaneous submissions. Responds in 4-6 months to mss.
Book catalog for 8×10 SAE with 4 first-class stamps; ms guidelines online.

Imprints Cumberland House Hearthside; Highland Books; WND Books.

● Accepts mss by US mail only. No electronic or telephone queries will be accepted.

○ᴚ Cumberland House publishes "market specific books. We evaluate in terms of how sure we are that
we can publish the book successfully and then the quality or uniqueness of a project." No longer
seeking to acquire fiction titles.

Nonfiction Cookbook, gift book, how-to, humor, reference. Subjects include Americana, cooking/foods/nutri-
tion, government/politics, history, military/war, recreation, regional, sports, travel, current affairs, popular
culture, civil war. Query with SASE, or submit proposal package including outline, 1 sample chapter, synopsis,
résumé, SASE. Reviews artwork/photos as part of ms package. Send photocopies only; not original copies.

Recent Title(s) *A Place to Stand*, by Gene Veith; *Buckeye Madness*, by Wilton Sharpe; *The Worst Baby Name
Book Ever*, by David Narter.

Tips Audience is "adventuresome people who like a fresh approach to things. Writers should tell what their
idea is, why it's unique and why somebody would want to buy it—but don't pester us."

Ⓐ CURRENCY

1745 Broadway, New York NY 10019. (212)782-9000. Website: www.randomhouse.com/doubleday/currency.
Estab. 1989.

○ᴚ Currency publishes "business books for people who want to make a difference, not just a living."

Nonfiction Subjects include marketing, investment. *Agented submissions only.*

Recent Title(s) *It's Not What You Say . . . It's What You Do*; *Shift: Inside Nissan's Historic Revival*; *The Fred
Factor.*

DA CAPO PRESS

Perseus Books Group, 11 Cambridge Center, Cambridge MA 02142. Website: www.dacapopress.com. Estab.
1975. Publishes hardcover originals and trade paperback originals and reprints. **Publishes 115 titles/year;
imprint publishes 115 titles/year. Receives 500 queries and 300 mss/year. 25% of books from first-time
authors; 1% from unagented writers. Pays 7-15% royalty. Offers $1,000-225,000 advance.** Publishes book
1 year after acceptance of ms. Accepts simultaneous submissions. Responds in 2-3 months. Book catalog and
ms guidelines online.

Nonfiction Autobiography, biography, coffee table book, general nonfiction, gift book. Subjects include art/
architecture, contemporary culture, creative nonfiction, government/politics, history, language/literature,
memoirs, military/war, social sciences, sports, translation, travel, world affairs. Does not accept electronic
submissions or take phone calls regarding submissions. Query with SASE, or submit proposal package including
outline, 3 sample chapters, cv. Reviews artwork/photos as part of ms package. Send photocopies.

Recent Title(s) *Arthur Miller*, by Martin Gottfried; *Da Capo Best Music Writing 2003*, edited by Matt Groening;
The Bedford Boys, by Alex Kershaw.

DAN RIVER PRESS

Conservatory of American Letters, P.O. Box 298, Thomaston ME 04861-0298. (207)354-0998. E-mail: cal@ameri
canletters.org. Website: www.americanletters.org. **Acquisitions:** Richard S. Danbury, fiction editor. Estab.
1977. Publishes hardcover and paperback originals. **Publishes 8-10 titles/year. Pays 10-15% royalty, 10
author's copies. Offers occassional advance.** Publishes book 3-4 months after acceptance of ms. Accepts
simultaneous submissions. Responds in 2-3 days to queries. Book catalog for 6×9 SAE with 60¢ postage affixed;
ms guidelines online.

○ᴚ "Small press publisher of fiction and biographies owned by a nonprofit foundation."

Fiction Accepts anything but porn, sedition, evangelical, and children's literature. Submit publishing history,
synopsis, author bio. Cover letter or query should include estimated word count, brief bio, and brief publishing
history. Query should also deal with marketing ideas. Be specific ("'All Women' is not a marketing idea we
can work with") and social security number, #10 SASE. "We do not read electronic submissions or queries."

Poetry Publishes poetry and fiction anthology (submission guidelines to *Dan River Anthology* online or send
#10 SASE).

Recent Title(s) *The Lutheran*, by Jack Britton Sullivan; *Blackbeard's Gift*, by James R. Clifford; *The Rat Catcher*,
by Andrew Laszlo.

Tips "Spend some time developing a following. Forget the advice that says, 'Your first job is to find a publisher!'
That's nonsense. Your first job as a writer is to develop an audience. Do that and a publisher will find you."

[N] DARBY CREEK PUBLISHING

7858 Industrial Pkwy., Plain City OH 43064. Website: www.darbycreekpublishing.com. Estab. 2002. Publishes hardcover, trade paperback, and mass market paperback originals and reprints. **Publishes 10-12 titles/year. Receives 500 queries and 750 mss/year. 25% of books from first-time authors; 75% from unagented writers. Pays royalty on retail price.** Publishes book 12-18 months after acceptance of ms. Accepts simultaneous submissions. Responds in 1 month to queries; 2 months to proposals and mss. Book catalog for #10 SASE; ms guidelines online.

Nonfiction Children's/juvenile, general nonfiction, illustrated book, hi-lo. Subjects include animals, anthropology/archeology, creative nonfiction, history, hobbies, nature/environment, science, social sciences, sports. "We are not a school library publisher. We do not do nonfiction series." Query with SASE, or submit complete ms. Reviews artwork/photos as part of ms package. Send photocopies.

Fiction Adventure, hi-lo, historical, humor, juvenile, mainstream/contemporary, multicultural, mystery, short story collections, sports, suspense, young adult. "We only want the highest-quality fiction for middle grade, hi-lo and young adults. We are not focused on picture books." Submit proposal package including 2 sample chapters, synopsis, or submit complete ms.

Recent Title(s) *Albino Animals*, by Kelly Milner Halls (photo/science); *Miracle: The True Story of the Wreck of the Sea Venture*, by Gail Karwoski (history); *Dog Days*, by David Lubar (realistic fiction).

Tips "We are looking for the 'Aha!' nonfiction title—the one no one else has done yet. All submissions should be comparable to or better than well-reviewed titles."

JONATHAN DAVID PUBLISHERS, INC.

68-22 Eliot Ave., Middle Village NY 11379-1194. (718)456-8611. Fax: (718)894-2818. E-mail: info@jdbooks.com. Website: www.jdbooks.com. **Acquisitions:** Alfred J. Kolatch, editor-in-chief. Estab. 1948. Publishes hardcover and trade paperback originals and reprints. **Publishes 20-25 titles/year. 50% of books from first-time authors; 90% from unagented writers. Pays royalty, or makes outright purchase.** Publishes book 18 months after acceptance of ms. Responds in 1 month to queries and proposals; 2 months to mss. Book catalog and ms guidelines online.

O— Jonathan David publishes "popular Judaica." Currently emphasizing projects geared toward children.

Nonfiction Biography, children's/juvenile, coffee table book, cookbook, gift book, how-to, humor, illustrated book, reference, self-help. Subjects include cooking/foods/nutrition, creative nonfiction, ethnic, humor, multicultural, religion, sex, sports. Query with SASE, or submit proposal package including outline, 3 sample chapters, résumé. Reviews artwork/photos as part of ms package. Send photocopies.

Recent Title(s) *Drawing a Crowd*, by Bill Gallo (sports cartoons/memoir).

DAW BOOKS, INC.

Distributed by Penguin Group (USA), 375 Hudson St., 3rd Floor, New York NY 10014-3658. (212)366-2096. Fax: (212)366-2090. E-mail: daw@us.penguingroup.com. Website: www.dawbooks.com. Publishers: Elizabeth Wollheim and Sheila Gilbert. **Acquisitions:** Peter Stampfel, submissions editor. Estab. 1971. Publishes hardcover and paperback originals and reprints. **Publishes 60-80 titles/year. Pays in royalties with an advance negotiable on a book-by-book basis.** Responds in 3 months to mss. Book catalog free; ms guidelines online.

● Simultaneous submissions "returned unread at once, unless prior arrangements are made by agent."

O— DAW Books publishes science fiction and fantasy.

Fiction Fantasy, science fiction. "We are interested in science fiction and fantasy novels. We need science fiction more than fantasy right now, but we're still looking for both. We like character-driven books with appealing characters. We accept both agented and unagented manuscripts. Long books are absolutely not a problem. We are not seeking collections of short stories or ideas for anthologies. We do not want any nonfiction manuscripts." Send complete ms and SASE.

Recent Title(s) *Phoenix and Ashes*, by Mercedes Lacky (fantasy); *Shadowmarch*, by Tad Williams (fantasy); *Destroyer*, by C.J. Cherryh (science fiction).

DEAD END STREET, LLC

813 Third St., Hoquiam WA 98550. Website: deadendstreet.com. Estab. 1997. Publishes all genres and seeks "cutting edge authors who represent the world's dead end streets." Accepts simultaneous submissions. Responds in 1 month to queries. Book catalog and ms guidelines online.

O— "Accepts fiction, nonfiction, and screenplay submissions. Submit 500-word synopsis through the online form. If interested, we will request the full manuscript within 30 days. If you are not contacted within 30 days, it's because we cannot pursue your project. At this time, we're particularly interested in screenplays for features and shorts."

[N] DEARBORN TRADE PUBLISHING

30 S. Wacker Dr., Suite 2500, Chicago IL 60606-1719. (312)836-4400. Fax: (312)836-1021. E-mail: kvillanosa@dearborn.com. Website: www.dearborntrade.com. **Acquisitions:** Cynthia Zigmund, VP/publisher/editorial director; Jonathan Malysiak, acquisitions editor (general business/management); Mary Good, acquisitions editor (consumer real estate, personal finance); Michael Cunningham, acquisitions editor (sales & marketing). Estab. 1959. Publishes hardcover and paperback originals. **Publishes 60 titles/year. 30% of books from first-time authors; 50% from unagented writers. Pays 10-15% royalty on wholesale price. Offers advance.** Publishes book 6 months after acceptance of ms. Accepts simultaneous submissions. Responds in 1 month to queries. Book catalog and ms guidelines free.

○━ The trade division of Dearborn publishes practical, solutions-oriented books for individuals and corporations on the subjects of finance, consumer real estate, business, and entrepreneurship. Currently emphasizing finance, general business/management, consumer real estate, small business.

Nonfiction How-to, reference, textbook. Subjects include business/economics, money/finance. Query with SASE.

Recent Title(s) *The Radical Leap*, by Steve Farber; *Why People Buy Things They Don't Need*, by Pamela Danziger; *Just Give Me the Answers*, by Sheryl Garrett.

IVAN R. DEE, PUBLISHER

Imprint of The Rowman & Littlefield Publishing Group, 1332 N. Halsted St., Chicago IL 60622-2694. (312)787-6262. Fax: (312)787-6269. E-mail: elephant@ivanrdee.com. Submissions E-mail: editorial@ivanrdee.com. Website: www.ivanrdee.com. **Acquisitions:** Ivan R. Dee, president; Hilary Meyer, managing editor. Estab. 1988. Publishes hardcover originals and trade paperback originals and reprints. **Publishes 50 titles/year. 10% of books from first-time authors; 70% from unagented writers. Pays royalty. Offers advance.** Publishes book 8 months after acceptance of ms. Accepts simultaneous submissions. Responds in 1 month. Book catalog free.

Imprints Elephant Paperbacks; New Amsterdam Books; J.S. Sanders Books.

○━ Ivan R. Dee publishes serious nonfiction for general-informed readers.

Nonfiction Biography. Subjects include art/architecture, government/politics, history, language/literature, world affairs, contemporary culture, baseball. "We publish history, biography, literature and letters, theater and drama, politics and current affairs, and literary baseball." Submit outline, sample chapters. Reviews artwork/photos as part of ms package.

Recent Title(s) *Fewer*, by Ben J. Wattenberg; *Vanishing Point*, by Richard J. Tofel; *Veritas*, by Andrew Schlesinger.

Tips "We publish for an intelligent lay audience and college course adoptions."

[A] DEL REY BOOKS

Imprint of Random House Publishing Group, 1745 Broadway, 18th Floor, New York NY 10019. (212)782-9000. E-mail: delrey@randomhouse.com. Website: www.randomhouse.com. Estab. 1977. Publishes hardcover, trade paperback, and mass market originals and mass market paperback reprints. **Pays royalty on retail price. Offers competitive advance.** Does not accept simultaneous submissions.

○━ Del Rey publishes top level fantasy, alternate history, and science fiction.

Fiction Fantasy (should have the practice of magic as an essential element of the plot), science fiction (well-plotted novels with good characterizations, exotic locales and detailed alien creatures), alternate history. *Agented submissions only.*

Recent Title(s) *The Salmon of Doubt*, by Douglas Adams; *Weapons of Choice*, by John Birmingham; *The Zenith Angle*, by Bruce Sterling.

Tips "Del Rey is a reader's house. Pay particular attention to plotting, strong characters, and dramatic, satisfactory conclusions. It must be/feel believable. That's what the readers like. In terms of mass market, we basically created the field of fantasy bestsellers. Not that it didn't exist before, but we put the mass into mass market."

[A] [Ø] DELACORTE BOOKS FOR YOUNG READERS

Imprint of Random House Children's Books/Random House, Inc., 1745 Broadway, New York NY 10019. (212)782-9000. Website: www.randomhouse.com.

● Although not currently seeking unsolicited mss, mss are being sought for 2 contests: Delacorte Dell Yearling Contest for a First Middle-Grade Novel and Delacorte Press Contest for a First Young Adult Novel. Submission guidelines can be found online.

[A] [Ø] DELL DRAGONFLY BOOKS FOR YOUNG READERS

Imprint of Random House Children's Books/Random House, Inc., 1745 Broadway, New York NY 10019. (212)782-9000. Website: www.randomhouse.com.

● Quality reprint paperback imprint for paperback books. *Does not accept mss.*

[A] [Ø] DELL LAUREL LEAF BOOKS FOR YOUNG READERS

Imprint of Random House Children's Books/Random House, Inc., 1745 Broadway, New York NY 10019. (212)782-9000. Website: www.randomhouse.com.

- Quality reprint paperback imprint for young adult paperback books. *Does not accept mss.*

Ⓐ Ⓩ DELL YEARLING BOOKS FOR YOUNG READERS
Imprint of Random House Children's Books/Random House, Inc., 1745 Broadway, New York NY 10019. (212)782-9000. Website: www.randomhouse.com.

- Quality reprint paperback imprint for middle grade paperback books. *Does not accept unsolicited mss.*

DEVORSS & CO.
DeVorss Publications, P.O. Box 1389, Camarillo CA 93011-1389. E-mail: editorial@devorss.com. Website: www. devorss.com. Publishes hardcover and trade paperback originals and reprints. **Receives 700 queries and 300 mss/year. 95% of books from first-time authors; 100% from unagented writers. 10% maximum royalty on retail price.** Publishes book 6 months after acceptance of ms. Accepts simultaneous submissions. Responds in 1 month to mss. Book catalog for #10 SASE; ms guidelines for #10 SASE.
Nonfiction Children's/juvenile, gift book, self-help, body, mind, and spirit. Subjects include creative nonfiction, philosophy, psychology, spirituality, Body, Mind, and Spirit. Query with SASE. Reviews artwork/photos as part of ms package. Send photocopies.
Recent Title(s) *Little Green Apples*, by O.C. Smith and James Shaw.
Tips "Our audience is people using their mind to improve health, finances, relationships, life changes, etc. Ask for guidelines first. Don't submit outlines, proposals, or manuscripts. Don't call. Please send submissions and inquiries by mail only."

Ⓐ DIAL BOOKS FOR YOUNG READERS
Imprint of Penguin Group USA, 345 Hudson St., 14th Floor, New York NY 10014. (212)366-2000. Website: www.penguinputnam.com. President/Publisher: Nancy Paulsen. Associate Publisher/Editorial Director: Lauri Hornik. **Acquisitions:** Submissions Editor. Estab. 1961. Publishes hardcover originals. **Publishes 50 titles/ year. Receives 5,000 queries/year. 20% of books from first-time authors. Pays royalty. Offers varies advance.** Does not accept simultaneous submissions. Responds in 4 months to queries. Book catalog for 9×12 SAE with 4 first-class stamps.
- ⌐ Dial Books for Young Readers publishes quality picture books for ages 18 months-8 years; lively, believable novels for middle readers and young adults; and occasional nonfiction for middle readers and young adults.
Nonfiction Children's/juvenile, illustrated book. Accepts unsolicited queries.
Fiction Adventure, fantasy, juvenile, picture books, young adult. Especially looking for "lively and well-written novels for middle grade and young adult children involving a convincing plot and believable characters. The subject matter or theme should not already be overworked in previously published books. The approach must not be demeaning to any minority group, nor should the roles of female characters (or others) be stereotyped, though we don't think books should be didactic, or in any way message-y. No topics inappropriate for the juvenile, young adult, and middle grade audiences. No plays." Query with SASE. Accepts unsolicited queries and up to 10 pages for longer works and unsolicited mss for picture books.
Recent Title(s) *A Cool Moonlight*, by Angela Johnson; *A Year Down Yonder*, by Richard Peck; *A Penguin Pup for Pinkerton*, by Steven Kellogg.
Tips "Our readers are anywhere from preschool age to teenage. Picture books must have strong plots, lots of action, unusual premises, or universal themes treated with freshness and originality. Humor works well in these books. A very well-thought-out and intelligently presented book has the best chance of being taken on. Genre isn't as much of a factor as presentation."

DISCOVERY ENTERPRISES, LTD.
31 Laurelwood Dr., Carlisle MA 01741. (978)287-5401. Fax: (978)287-5402. E-mail: ushistorydocs@aol.com. **Acquisitions:** JoAnne W. Deitch, president (plays for Readers Theatre, on American history). Publishes trade paperback originals. **Publishes 10 titles/year. Receives 50 queries and 20 mss/year. 5% of books from first-time authors; 90% from unagented writers. Pays 10-20% royalty.** Publishes book 3 months after acceptance of ms. Accepts simultaneous submissions. Responds in 1 month to queries. Book catalog for 6×9 SAE with 3 first-class stamps.
Fiction "We're interested in 40-minute plays (reading time) for students in grades 4-10 on topics in U.S. history." Historical, plays. Query with SASE, or submit complete ms.
Recent Title(s) *Life on the Road to Freedom: Sojourner Truth*, by Sharon Fennessey; *Salem Witch Hunt*, by Hilary Weisman; *Lewis and Clark: Across a Vast Land*, by Harold Torrance.
Tips "Call or send query letter on topic prior to sending ms for plays. We currently need a play on early colonists in Jamestown or Plymouth; a play on post-Civil War South; a play on the Revolutionary War, focusing on George Washington."

Ⓐ Ⓞ DK PUBLISHING, INC.

(formerly Dorling Kindersley), Pearson Plc, 375 Hudson St., New York NY 10014. (212)213-4800. Website: www.dk.com. **Pays royalty or flat fee.**
- Publishes picture books for middle-grade and older readers. Also, illustrated reference books for adults and children.

Fiction *Agented submissions only.*

TOM DOHERTY ASSOCIATES LLC

Subsidiary of Holtzbrinck Publishers, 175 Fifth Ave., 14th Floor, New York NY 10010. Fax: (212)388-0191. E-mail: inquiries@tor.com. Website: www.tor.com. **Acquisitions:** Patrick Nielsen Hayden (science fiction and fantasy); Melissa Singer (mainstream fiction). Estab. 1980. Publishes hardcover trade, paperback, and mass market originals. Does not accept simultaneous submissions. Book catalog and ms guidelines online.

Imprints Forge Books; Orb Books; Tor.

Nonfiction Biography.

Fiction Fantasy, horror, mystery, romance (paranormal), science fiction, suspense, western, techno thrillers, American historicals, true crime. Submit synopsis, first 3 chapters, cover letter stating genre and previous book sales or publications (if relevant).

Recent Title(s) *Gardens of the Moon*, by Steven Erikson (fantasy); *Ringworld's Children*, by Larry Nevin (science fiction).

DOLLAR$MART BOOKS

4320-C Ridgecrest, #150, Rio Rancho NM 87124. (505)681-2880. **Acquisitions:** Cheryl Gorder, publisher (financial education and business); Robin, editor (spirituality and New Age). Estab. 1985. Publishes trade paperback and electronic originals. **Publishes 12 titles/year. Receives 100 queries and 75 mss/year. 90% of books from first-time authors; 90% from unagented writers. Pays 10-15% royalty on retail price, or makes outright purchase of $500-3,000.** Publishes book 3 months after acceptance of ms. Accepts simultaneous submissions. Responds in 1 month. Book catalog free; ms guidelines for #10 SASE.

Nonfiction How-to, reference, self-help. Subjects include business/economics, education, money/finance, New Age, spirituality, real estate. Submit complete ms. Reviews artwork/photos as part of ms package. Send photocopies.

Fiction "The only fiction we publish is 'spiritual warrior' type." Submit complete ms.

Recent Title(s) *Dollar$mart Resource Guide for Kids*; *Dollar$mart Kid's Education at Home*.

Tips "We would prefer to see complete manuscripts, and we will return manuscripts if they are accompanied by an envelope with sufficient postage."

DORCHESTER PUBLISHING CO., INC.

200 Madison Ave., Suite 2000, New York NY 10016. (212)725-8811. Fax: (212)532-1054. Website: www.dorchesterpub.com. **Offers advance.** Does not accept simultaneous submissions. Ms guidelines online.

Imprints Love Spell (romance); Leisure Books (romance, westerns, horror, thrillers); Smooch (young adult); Making It (chick lit/trade).
- No submissions via e-mail or fax.

Ⓐ DOUBLEDAY BROADWAY PUBLISHING GROUP

Imprint of Random House, Inc., 1745 Broadway, New York NY 10019. (212)782-9000. Fax: (212)782-9700. Website: www.randomhouse.com. Estab. 1897. Publishes hardcover originals. **Receives thousands of queries and thousands of mss/year. Pays royalty on retail price. Offers advance.** Does not accept simultaneous submissions.

Imprints Broadway Books; Currency; Doubleday; Doubleday Image; Doubleday Religious Publishing; Main Street Books; Nan A. Talese.
- *Does not accept any unagented submissions.* No exceptions.
- Doubleday publishes high-quality fiction and nonfiction.

Nonfiction Biography. Subjects include Americana, anthropology/archeology, business/economics, computers/electronic, education, ethnic, government/politics, health/medicine, history, language/literature, money/finance, nature/environment, philosophy, religion, science, sociology, software, sports, translation, women's issues/studies. *Agented submissions only.*

Fiction Adventure, confession, ethnic, experimental, feminist, gay/lesbian, historical, humor, literary, mainstream/contemporary, religious, short story collections. *Agented submissions only.*

Ⓐ DOUBLEDAY RELIGIOUS PUBLISHING

Imprint of Doubleday Broadway Publishing Group, Division of Random House, Inc., 1745 Broadway, New York NY 10019. (212)782-9000. Website: www.randomhouse.com. Estab. 1897. Publishes hardcover and trade

paperback originals and reprints. Accepts simultaneous submissions. Book catalog for SAE with 3 first-class stamps.
Imprints Image Books; Anchor Bible Commentary; Anchor Bible Reference; Galilee; New Jerusalem Bible; Three Leaves Press.
Nonfiction Historical, philosophical, religious. *Agented submissions only.*
Fiction Religious. *Agented submissions only.*

DOUBLEDAY/IMAGE

Doubleday Broadway Publishing Group, Random House, Inc., 1745 Broadway, New York NY 10019. (212)782-9000. Fax: (212)302-7985. Website: www.randomhouse.com. **Acquisitions:** Trace Murphy, executive editor. Estab. 1956. Publishes hardcover, trade and mass market paperback originals and reprints. **Publishes 12 titles/year. Receives 500 queries and 300 mss/year. 10% of books from first-time authors. Pays royalty on retail price. Offers varied advance.** Publishes book 18 months after acceptance of ms. Accepts simultaneous submissions. Responds in 3 months to proposals.

   0–¬ Image Books has grown from a classic Catholic list to include a variety of current and future classics, maintaining a high standard of quality as the finest in religious paperbacks. Also publishes Doubleday paperbacks/hardcovers for general religion, spirituality, including works based in Buddhism, Islam, Judaism.
Nonfiction Biography, how-to, reference. Subjects include philosophy, religion, women's issues/studies. Query with SASE. Will review photocopies of artwork/photos.
Recent Title(s) *Papal Sin*, by Garry Wills; *Soul Survivor*, by Philip Yancey; *The Lamb's Supper*, by Scott Hahn.

DOWN EAST BOOKS

Imprint of Down East Enterprise, Inc., P.O. Box 679, Camden ME 04843-0679. Fax: (207)594-7215. **Acquisitions:** Chris Cornell, editor (Countrysport); Michael Steere, associate editor (general). Estab. 1967. Publishes hardcover and trade paperback originals, trade paperback reprints. **Publishes 24-30 titles/year. 50% of books from first-time authors; 90% from unagented writers. Pays 10-15% royalty on net receipts. Offers $500 average advance.** Publishes book 1 year after acceptance of ms. Accepts simultaneous submissions. Responds in 3 months to queries. Send SASE for ms guidlines. Send 9×12 SASE for guidelines, plus recent catalog.
Imprints Countrysport Press (fly fishing and wing-shooting market; Chris Cornell, editor, e-mail: ccornell@down east.com).

   0–¬ Down East Books publishes books that capture and illuminate the unique beauty and character of New England's history, culture, and wild places.
Nonfiction Children's/juvenile. Subjects include Americana, history, nature/environment, recreation, regional, sports. Books about the New England region, Maine in particular. "All of our regional books must have a Maine or New England emphasis." Query with SASE. Reviews artwork/photos as part of ms package.
Fiction Juvenile, mainstream/contemporary, regional. "We publish 2-4 juvenile titles/year (fiction and nonfiction), and 0-1 adult fiction titles/year." Query with SASE.
Recent Title(s) *The Maine Poets*, by Wesley McNair; *Visiting Aunt Sylvia's*, by Heather Austin; *Maine Sail*, by Margaret McCrea.

🄰 ⊘ LISA DREW BOOKS

Imprint of Scribner, Simon & Schuster Adult Publishing Group, 1230 Avenue of the Americas, New York NY 10020. (212)698-7000. Website: www.simonsays.com. **Acquisitions:** Lisa Drew, publisher. Publishes hardcover originals. **Publishes 10-14 titles/year. Receives 600 queries/year. 10% of books from first-time authors. Pays royalty on retail price. Offers variable advance.** Publishes book 1 year after acceptance of ms.

   • Accepts simultaneous agented submissions. Responds in 1 month.
   0–¬ "We publish narrative nonfiction. We do not want how-to books, fiction or self-help."
Nonfiction Subjects include government/politics, history, women's issues/studies. *No unsolicited material. Agented submissions only.*

🄰 THOMAS DUNNE BOOKS

Imprint of St. Martin's Press, 175 Fifth Ave., New York NY 10010. (212)674-5151. Website: www.stmartins.com. Publishes hardcover originals and trade paperback originals and reprints. Accepts simultaneous submissions. Book catalog and ms guidelines free.

   0–¬ Thomas Dunne publishes a wide range of fiction and nonfiction. Accepts submissions from agents only.
Nonfiction Biography. Subjects include government/politics, history, sports, political commentary. "Author's attention to detail is important. We get a lot of manuscripts that are poorly proofread and just can't be considered." Agents submit query, or an outline and 100 sample pages. Reviews artwork/photos as part of ms package. Send photocopies.

Fiction Mainstream/contemporary, mystery, suspense, thrillers, women's. Agents submit query, or submit synopsis and 100 sample pages.

Recent Title(s) *Snobs*, by Julian Fellowes; *Can't Stop Won't Stop*, by Jeff Chang; *Travels With My Donkey*, by Tim Moore.

Ⓐ Ⓞ DUTTON ADULT TRADE

Imprint of Penguin Group (USA), Inc., 375 Hudson St., New York NY 10014. (212)366-2000. Website: www.peng uinputnam.com. Estab. 1852. Publishers hardcover originals. **Pays royalty. Offers negotiable advance.** Accepts simultaneous submissions. Book catalog for #10 SASE.

  ○➔ Dutton publishes hardcover, original, mainstream, and contemporary fiction and nonfiction in the areas of memoir, self-help, politics, psychology, and science for a general readership.

Nonfiction General nonfiction, humor, reference, self-help, Memoir. *Agented submissions only. No unsolicited mss.*

Fiction Adventure, historical, literary, mainstream/contemporary, mystery, short story collections, suspense. *Agented submissions only. No unsolicited mss.*

Tips "Write the complete manuscript and submit it to an agent or agents. They will know exactly which editor will be interested in a project."

DUTTON CHILDREN'S BOOKS

Imprint of Penguin Group (USA), Inc., 345 Hudson St., New York NY 10014. (212)414-3700. Fax: (212)414-3397. Website: www.penguin.com. **Acquisitions:** Stephanie Owens Lurie, president and publisher (picture books and fiction); Maureen Sullivan, executive editor (books for all ages with distinctive narrative style); Lucia Monfried, senior editor (picture books, easy-to-read books, fiction). Estab. 1852. Publishes hardcover originals as well as novelty formats. **Publishes 100 titles/year. 15% of books from first-time authors. Pays royalty on retail price. Offers advance.**

  ○➔ Dutton Children's Books publishes high-quality fiction and nonfiction for readers ranging from pre-schoolers to young adults on a variety of subjects. Currently emphasizing middle-grade and young adult novels that offer a fresh perspective. De-emphasizing photographic nonfiction and picture books that teach a lesson.

Nonfiction Children's/juvenile, for preschoolers to young adults. Subjects include animals, history (US), nature/environment, science. Query with SASE.

Fiction Dutton Children's Books has a diverse, general interest list that includes picture books; easy-to-read books; and fiction for all ages, from "first chapter" books to young adult readers. Query with SASE.

Recent Title(s) *The Best Pet of All*, by David LaRochelle (picture book); *The Schwa Was Here*, by Neal Shusterman (novel); *Looking for Alaska*, by John Green (young adult novel).

E-DIGITAL BOOKS, LLC

1155 S. Havana St. #11-364, Aurora CO 80012. E-mail: submissions@edigitalbooks.com. Website: www.edigital bookstore.com. **Acquisitions:** T.R. Allen, manager and editor-in-chief (photography, art, travel, history, literary and short story collections, poetry, how-to, utility products, and Christian religious). Estab. 1999. **Publishes 10-15 titles/year. Receives 5 queries and 5 mss/year. 50% of books from first-time authors; 100% from unagented writers. Pays 30-60% royalty on retail price.** Publishes book 6 months after acceptance of ms. Accepts simultaneous submissions. Responds in 6 months via e-mail only to queries. Book catalog and ms guidlines by e-mail.

Nonfiction Children's/juvenile, general nonfiction, illustrated book. Subjects include animals, art/architecture, creative nonfiction, ethnic, history, language/literature, photography, religion, spirituality, travel. Query via e-mail with "Nonfiction Query" in the subject line. Reviews artwork/photos as part of ms package. Send JPEG initially.

Fiction Adventure, ethnic, fantasy, historical, humor, juvenile, literary, mainstream/contemporary, military/war, multicultural, multimedia, mystery, picture books, poetry, religious (Christian), romance (no bodice rippers), short story collections, spiritual, suspense, western, young adult. "General guidelines: family audience with respect to language and subject matter." Query via e-mail with "Fiction Query" in subject line.

Poetry "We are interested in Christian religious or secular poetry that embraces uplifting, positive, and inspirational themes." Query.

Recent Title(s) *E-Digital E-Calendars: Artistic Impressions of Italy 2005*, by Cathy Lynn; *E-Digital E-Stickers: Holiday Edition*, by E-Digital Books staff (utility).

Tips "Audience is family, Christian, travel oriented, interested in the efficacy and convenience of our published utility e-books. Overall, we are specifically interested in subject matter that involves bringing a positive light into the world. We will consider material that is of a more complicated and dark nature if it provides informed and intelligent solutions to whatever area of difficulty is examined or problem that is presented."

EAKIN PRESS

P.O. Drawer 90159, Austin TX 78709-0159. (512)288-1771. Fax: (512)288-1813. Website: www.eakinpress.com. **Acquisitions:** Virginia Messer, publisher. Estab. 1978. Publishes hardcover and paperback originals and reprints. Accepts simultaneous submissions. Responds in up to 1 year to queries. Book catalog for $1.25; ms guidelines online.

- No electronic submissions.
- O— Eakin specializes in Texana and Western Americana for adults and juveniles. Currently emphasizing women's studies.

Nonfiction Biography, cookbook (regional). Subjects include Americana (Western), business/economics, cooking/foods/nutrition, ethnic, history, military/war, regional, sports, African American studies, Civil War, Texas history. Juvenile nonfiction: includes biographies of historic personalities, prefer with Texas or regional interest, or nature studies; and easy-read illustrated books for grades 1-3. Submit sample chapters, author bio, synopsis, publishing credits, SASE.

Fiction Historical, juvenile. Juvenile fiction for grades K-12, preferably relating to Texas and the Southwest or contemporary. No adult fiction. Query or submit outline/synopsis, author bio, publishing credits, and sample chapters. For children's books or books under 100 pgs, send complete ms.

Recent Title(s) *Sam Houston Slept Here*, by Bill O'Neal; *Grape Man of Texas*, by Sherrie S. McLeRoy and Roy E. Renfro, Jr., PhD; *Playbills and Popcorn*, by Michael A. Jenkins.

EASTERN WASHINGTON UNIVERSITY PRESS

705 W. 1st Ave., Spokane WA 99201. (509)623-4284. Fax: (509)623-4283. E-mail: ewupress@ewu.edu. Website: ewupress.ewu.edu. **Acquisitions:** Chris Howell, senior editor (poetry, fiction); Ivar Nelson, interim publisher; Joelean Copeland, managing editor. Estab. 1994. Publishes hardcover and trade paperback originals and reprints. **Publishes 12 titles/year. Receives 150 queries/year. 25% of books from first-time authors. Pays 10% royalty.** Publishes book 2-4 years after acceptance of ms. Accepts simultaneous submissions. Responds in 1-2 months to queries; 3 months to proposals; 6-9 months to mss. Book catalog and ms guidelines free.

Nonfiction Subjects include anthropology/archeology, history, language/literature, philosophy, regional, translation.

Fiction Accepts novels and entries for the short fiction contest. Query before sending complete ms.

Poetry Accepts any poetry.

Tips "Submit complete ms in hard copy—no digital ms submissions. May query by e-mail."

ECLIPSE PRESS

The Blood-Horse, Inc., 3101 Beaumont Centre Circle, Lexington KY 40513. Website: www.eclipsepress.com. **Acquisitions:** Jacqueline Duke, editor (equine). Estab. 1916. Publishes hardcover and trade paperback originals. **Publishes 12-15 titles/year. Receives 100 queries and 50 mss/year. 20% of books from first-time authors; 40% from unagented writers. Pays 10-15% royalty on net receipts, or makes outright purchase. Offers $3,000-12,000 advance.** Publishes book 18 months after acceptance of ms. Accepts simultaneous submissions. Responds in 2-3 months. Book catalog free.

Nonfiction Subjects include sports (equine, equestrian). "We only accept nonfiction works on equine and equestrian topics." Query with SASE, or submit outline, sample chapters. Reviews artwork/photos as part of ms package.

Tips "Our audience is sports, horse, and racing enthusiasts."

EDUCATOR'S INTERNATIONAL PRESS, INC.

18 Colleen Rd., Troy NY 12180. (518)271-9886. Fax: (518)266-9422. E-mail: bill@edint.com. Website: www.edint.com. **Acquisitions:** William Clockel, publisher. Estab. 1996. Publishes hardcover and trade paperback originals and reprints. Accepts simultaneous submissions. Book catalog and ms guidelines free.

- O— Educator's International publishes books in all aspects of education, broadly conceived, from prekindergarten to postgraduate. "We specialize in texts, professional books, videos and other materials for students, faculty, practitioners and researchers. We also publish a full list of books in the areas of women's studies, and social and behavioral sciences."

Nonfiction Textbook, supplemental texts; conference proceedings. Subjects include education, gay/lesbian, language/literature, philosophy, psychology, software, women's issues/studies. Submit TOC, outline, 2-3 chapters, résumé with SASE. Reviews artwork/photos as part of ms package.

Recent Title(s) *Journal of Curriculum and Pedagogy*; *Democratic Responses in an Era of Standardization* (Relationship and the Arts in Teacher Education).

Tips Audience is professors, students, researchers, individuals, libraries.

EDUCATORS PUBLISHING SERVICE

P.O. Box 9031, Cambridge MA 02139-9031. (617)547-6706. Fax: (617)547-3805. Website: www.epsbooks.com. **Acquisitions:** Charles H. Heinle, vice president, Publishing Group. Estab. 1952. **Publishes 26 titles/year. Receives 200 queries and 200 mss/year. 50% of books from first-time authors; 90% from unagented writers. Pays 5-10% royalty on retail price.** Publishes book 8 months (minimum) after acceptance of ms. Accepts simultaneous submissions. Responds in 1 month to queries; 3 months to proposals and mss. Book catalog and ms guidelines free or online.

    O⊷ EPS accepts queries from educators writing for a school market, authoring materials (primarily K-8) in the reading and language areas. "We are interested in materials following pedagogical restraints (such as decodable texts and leveled readers) that we can incorporate into ongoing or future projects, or that form a complete program in themselves."

Nonfiction Workbooks (language arts) and some professional books. Subjects include education (reading comprehension, phonics vocabulary development and writing), supplementary texts and workbooks (reading and language arts). Query with SASE.

Recent Title(s) *Words Are Wonderful, Book 3*, by Dorothy Grant Hennings; *Ten Essential Vocabulary Strategies*, by Lee Mountain; *Write About Me*, by Elsie Wilmerding.

Tips Student (K-8) audiences.

EDUPRESS, INC.

W5527 State Road 106, P.O. Box 800, Fort Atkinson WI 53538-0800. (920)563-9571. E-mail: edupress@highsmith.com. Website: www.edupressinc.com. Estab. 1979. Publishes trade paperback originals. Book catalog and ms guidelines free.

    O⊷ Edupress, Inc., publishes supplemental resources for classroom curriculum. Currently emphasizing more science, math, language arts emphasis than in the past.

Nonfiction Subjects include education (resources for pre-school through middle school).

Tips Audience is classroom teachers and homeschool parents.

EERDMANS BOOKS FOR YOUNG READERS

William B. Eerdmans Publishing Co., 255 Jefferson Ave. SE, Grand Rapids MI 49503. (616)459-4591. Fax: (616)776-7638. Website: www.eerdmans.com/youngreaders. **Acquisitions:** Judy Zylstra, editor. Publishes picture books and middle reader and young adult fiction and nonfiction. **Publishes 12-15 titles/year. Receives 4,000 queries/year. Pays 5-7½% royalty on retail price.** Publishes book Publishes middle reader and YA books in 1 year; publishes picture books in 2-3 years after acceptance of ms. Accepts simultaneous submissions. Responds in 6 weeks to queries. Book catalog for #10 SASE; ms guidelines online.

    • No queries or submissions via e-mail or fax.

    O⊷ "We publish books for children and young adults that deal with spiritual themes—but never in a preachy or heavy-handed way. Some of our books are clearly religious, while others (especially our novels) look at spiritual issues in very subtle ways. We look for books that are honest, wise and hopeful." Currently emphasizing general picture books (also picture book biographies), novels (middle reader and YA). De-emphasizing retellings of Bible stories. "We also have been expanding to publish books for library, school and general trade markets."

Nonfiction Children's/juvenile, picture books, middle reader, young adult nonfiction. "Do not send illustrations unless you are a professional illustrator." Submit complete mss for picture books and novels or biographies under 200 pages with SASE. For longer books, send query letter and 3 or 4 sample chapters with SASE. Reviews artwork/photos as part of ms package. Send color photocopies rather than original art.

Fiction Juvenile, picture books, young adult, middle reader. "Do not send illustrations unless you are a professional illustrator." Submit complete mss for picture books and novels or biographies under 200 pages with SASE. For longer books, send query letter and 3 or 4 sample chapters with SASE.

Recent Title(s) *Mississippi Morning*, by Ruth Vanderzee, illustrated by Floyd Cooper; *Something to Tell Grandcows*, by Eileen Spinelli, illustrated by Bill Slarin; *Going for the Record*, by Julie A. Swanson.

WILLIAM B. EERDMANS PUBLISHING CO.

255 Jefferson Ave. SE, Grand Rapids MI 49503. (616)459-4591. Fax: (616)459-6540. E-mail: info@eerdmans.com. Website: www.eerdmans.com. **Acquisitions:** Jon Pott, editor-in-chief. Estab. 1911. Publishes hardcover and paperback originals and reprints. Accepts simultaneous submissions. Responds in 4 weeks to queries; several months to mss. Book catalog and ms guidelines free.

Imprints Eerdmans Books for Young Readers (Judy Zylstra, editor).

- Will not respond to or accept mss, proposals, or queries sent by e-mail or fax.
- ⚷ "The majority of our adult publications are religious and most of these are academic or semi-academic in character (as opposed to inspirational or celebrity books), though we also publish general trade books on the Christian life. Our nonreligious titles, most of them in regional history or on social issues, aim, similarly, at an educated audience."

Nonfiction Children's/juvenile, reference, textbook, monographs. Subjects include history (religious), language/literature, philosophy (of religion), psychology, regional (history), religion, sociology, translation, Biblical studies, theology, ethics. "We prefer that writers take the time to notice if we have published anything at all in the same category as their manuscript before sending it to us." Query with TOC, 2-3 sample chapters, and SASE for return of ms. Reviews artwork/photos as part of ms package.

Fiction Religious (children's, general, fantasy). Query with SASE.

Recent Title(s) *Christ Plays in Ten Thousand Places*, by Eugene H. Peterson; *Did God Have a Wife?*, by William G. Dever; *Cruel Paradise*, by Hylke Speerstra.

ELEPHANT BOOKS

65 Macedonia Rd., Alexander NC 28701. (828)252-9515. Fax: (828)255-8719. E-mail: pat@abooks.com. Website: abooks.com. **Acquisitions:** Editor. Publishes trade paperback originals and reprints. Book catalog and ms guidelines online.

- No e-mail or phone submissions.

Nonfiction Cookbook, books about elephants. Subjects include cooking/foods/nutrition, history, military/war (Civil War). Query, or submit outline with 3 sample chapters and proposal package, including potential marketing plans with SASE. Reviews artwork/photos as part of ms package. Send photocopies.

ELLORA'S CAVE PUBLISHING, INC.

1337 Commerce Dr. #13, Stow OH 44224. E-mail: service@ellorascave.com. Submissions E-mail: submissions@ellorascave.com. Website: www.ellorascave.com. **Acquisitions:** Raelene Gorlinsky, managing editor. Estab. 2000. Publishes electronic originals and reprints. **Pays 37.5% royalty on gross (cover price).** Accepts simultaneous submissions. Responds in 2 months. Book catalog and ms guidelines online.

Fiction Erotica, fantasy, gay/lesbian, gothic, historical, horror, mainstream/contemporary, multicultural, mystery, romance, science fiction, suspense, western. All must be under genre romance. All must have erotic content or author be willing to add sex during editing. Submit proposal package including 3 sample chapters, synopsis. Send via e-mail in doc or rtf format.

Recent Title(s) *Caught!*, by Lorie O'Clare; *Eden's Curse*, by Elisa Adams; *Immaculate*, by Kate Hill.

Tips "Our audience is romance readers who want to read more sex, more detailed sex. They come to us, because we offer not erotica, but Romantica™. Sex with romance, plot, emotion. Remember Ellora's Cave is a Romantica™ site. We publish romance books with an erotic nature. More sex is the motto, but there has to be a storyline—a logical plot and a happy ending."

Ⓝ ELSEVIER, INC.

Reed-Elsevier (USA) Inc., 30 Corporate Dr., Suite 400, Burlington MA 01803. (800)470-1199. Fax: (781)904-2640. Website: www.bh.com. **Acquisitions:** Jim DeWolf, vice president of technical publishing (engineering, electronics, computing, media and visual, security); Joanne Tracy, publisher (Focal Press); Theron Shreve, publisher (Digital Press); Susan Pioli, publishing director (medical); Mark Listewnik, associate acquisitions editor (security). Estab. 1975. Publishes hardcover and trade paperback originals. **Publishes 250 titles/year; imprint publishes 40-50 titles/year. 25% of books from first-time authors; 95% from unagented writers. Pays 10-12% royalty on wholesale price. Offers modest advance.** Publishes book 9 months after acceptance of ms. Responds in 1 month to proposals. Book catalog free; ms guidelines online.

Imprints Butterworth-Heinemann/Academic Press (engineering, business); Morgan Kauffman/Digital Press (computing); Focal Press (media and visual technology); Newnes (electronics); Butterworth Heinemann Security; Acadmic Press (life sciences, physical science).

- ⚷ Elsevier publishes technical professional and academic books in technology, medicine and business; no fiction.

Nonfiction How-to (in our selected areas), reference, technical, textbook. Subjects include business/economics, computers/electronic, health/medicine, photography, science, security/criminal justice, audio-video broadcast, communication technology. Query with SASE, or submit outline, 1-2 sample chapters, competing books and how yours is different/better. Reviews artwork/photos as part of ms package. Send photocopies.

Tips Elsevier has been serving professionals and students for over 5 decades. "We remain committed to publishing materials that forge ahead of rapidly changing technology and reinforce the highest professional standards. Our goal is to give you the competitive advantage in this rapidly changing digital age."

EMMIS BOOKS

(formerly Guild Press), The Old Firehouse, 3rd Floor, 1700 Madison Rd., Cincinnati OH 45206. (513)861-4045. Fax: (513)861-4430. E-mail: info@emmis.com. Website: www.emmisbooks.com. Editorial Director: Jack Heffron. **Acquisitions:** Acquisitions Editor. Estab. 2003. Publishes hardcover and trade paperback originals and reprints. **Pays royalty on wholesale price, or retail price.** Does not accept simultaneous submissions. Responds in 1 month to queries; 3 weeks to proposals; 2 months to mss. Book catalog for #10 SASE.

Nonfiction Biography, children's/juvenile (regional), coffee table book, humor. Subjects include Americana, psychology, religion, sports, travel, women's issues/studies, current events, pets, food, pop culture, social studies, music, comedy/performing arts, humor, reference. Query with SASE, or submit proposal package including outline, sample chapters, credentials, marketing plan.

Fiction Adventure, juvenile, mystery, young adult. "We do not normally accept fiction submissions."

Recent Title(s) *Best Food in Town*, by Dawn Simonds; *Ain't It Funny?*, by the editors of *Texas Monthly*; *The Fine Art of Fundraising*, by Carolyn Farb.

EMPIRE PUBLISHING SERVICE

P.O. Box 1344, Studio City CA 91614-0344. **Acquisitions:** Joseph Witt. Estab. 1960. Publishes hardcover reprints and trade paperback originals and reprints. **Publishes 40 titles/year; imprint publishes 15 titles/year. Receives 500 queries and 85 mss/year. 50% of books from first-time authors; 95% from unagented writers. Pays 6-10% royalty on retail price. Offers variable advance.** Publishes book up to 2 years after acceptance of ms. Does not accept simultaneous submissions. Responds in 1 month to queries; 2 months to proposals; up to 1 year to mss. Book catalog for #10 SASE; ms guidelines for $1 or #10 SASE.

Imprints Gaslight Publications; Gaslight Books; Empire Publications; Empire Books; Empire Music.

○╍ "Submit only Sherlock Holmes, performing arts and health."

Nonfiction How-to, humor, reference, technical, textbook. Subjects include health/medicine, humor, music/dance, Sherlock Holmes. Query with SASE. Reviews artwork/photos as part of ms package. Send photocopies.

Fiction Historical (pre-18th century), mystery (Sherlock Holmes). Query with SASE.

Recent Title(s) *On the Scent With Sherlock Holmes*, by Jacy Tracy; *Elementary My Dear Watson*, by William Alan Landes; *The Magic of Food*, by James Cohen.

Ⓐ Ⓔ ENCOUNTER BOOKS

665 Third St., Suite 330, San Francisco CA 94107-1951. (415)538-1460. Fax: (415)538-1461. E-mail: read@encounterbooks.com. Website: www.encounterbooks.com. Publisher: Peter Collier. **Acquisitions:** Leota A. Higgins. Hardcover originals and trade paperback reprints. Accepts simultaneous submissions. Book catalog free or online; ms guidelines online.

● *Accepts agented material only. No unsolicited mss/queries.* Reading period is March 1-November 1.

○╍ Encounter Books publishes serious nonfiction—books that can alter our society, challenge our morality, stimulate our imaginations—in the areas of history, politics, religion, biography, education, public policy, current affairs, and social sciences.

Nonfiction Biography, reference. Subjects include child guidance/parenting, education, ethnic, government/politics, health/medicine, history, language/literature, memoirs, military/war, multicultural, philosophy, psychology, religion, science, sociology, women's issues/studies, gender studies. Submit proposal package, including outline and 1 sample chapter, SASE. Do not send via e-mail.

Recent Title(s) *Black Rednecks and White Liberals*, by Thomas Sowell; *Dawn Over Baghdad*, by Karl Zinsmeister; *The Future of Marriage*, by David Blankenhorn.

ENSLOW PUBLISHERS, INC.

40 Industrial Rd., Box 398, Berkeley Heights NJ 07922. (973)771-9400. Website: www.enslow.com. **Acquisitions:** Brian D. Enslow, editor. Estab. 1977. Publishes hardcover originals. 10% require freelance illustration. **Publishes 250 titles/year. Pays royalty on net price with advance or flat fee. Offers advance.** Publishes book 1 year after acceptance of ms. Responds in 1 month to queries. Ms guidelines for #10 SASE.

○╍ Enslow publishes hardcover nonfiction series books for young adults and school-age children.

Nonfiction Biography, children's/juvenile, reference. Subjects include health/medicine, history, recreation (Sports), science, sociology. Interested in new ideas for series of books for young people. No fiction, fictionalized history, or dialogue.

Recent Title(s) *TV News: Can It Be Trusted?*, by Ray Spangenburg and Kit Moser; *Resisters and Rescuers—Standing Up Against the Holocaust*, by Linda Jacobs Attman.

Tips "We love to receive résumés from experienced writers with good research skills who can think like young people."

Book Publishers

ENTREPRENEUR PRESS

2445 McCabe Way, Irvine CA 92614. (949)261-2325. Fax: (949)261-7729. Website: www.entrepreneurpress.c om. **Acquisitions:** Jere Calmes, editorial director; Leanne Harvey, marketing director. Publishes quality hardcover and trade paperbacks. **Publishes 50+ titles/year. Receives 1,200 queries and 600 mss/year. 40% of books from first-time authors; 60% from unagented writers. Pays competitive net royalty.** Accepts simultaneous submissions. Ms guidelines online.

Nonfiction Subjects include business/economics, start-up, marketing, finance, personal finance, accounting, motivation, leadership, and management. Query with SASE, or submit proposal package including outline, 2 sample chapters, author bio, preface or executive summary, competition. Reviews artwork/photos as part of ms package. Send transparencies.

Recent Title(s) *Masters of Success*, by Ivan R. Misner and Don Morgan; *No B.S. Series*, by Dan Kennedy; *Start Your Own Business*, by Rieva Lesonsky.

Tips Audience is "people who are thinking about starting or growing their own business, and people who want to become successful and effective in business and management. Also general business skills, including finance, marketing, presentation, leadership, etc."

Ⓐ Ⓞ EOS

Imprint of HarperCollins General Books Group, 10 E. 53rd St., New York NY 10022. (212)207-7000. E-mail: eossubs@harpercollins.com. Website: www.eosbooks.com. Estab. 1998. Publishes hardcover originals, trade and mass market paperback originals, and reprints. **Pays royalty on retail price. Offers variable advance.** Ms guidelines for #10 SASE.

 ○┐ Eos publishes "quality science fiction/fantasy with broad appeal."

Fiction Fantasy, science fiction. No horror or juvenile. *Agented submissions only. All unsolicited mss returned unopened.*

Recent Title(s) *Black Juice*, by Margo Lanagan; *Exile's Return*, by Raymond E. Feist; *The Hidden Queen*, by Alma Alexander.

Tips "The official HarperCollins submissions policy has changed, and we can no longer accept unsolicited submissions. To submit your science fiction or fantasy novel to Eos, please query first. We strongly urge you to query via e-mail. Your query should be brief—no more than a 2-page description of your book. Do not send chapters or full synopsis at this time. You will receive a response—either a decline or a request for more material—in approximately 1-2 months."

EPICENTER PRESS, INC.

P.O. Box 82368, Kenmore WA 98028. (425)485-6822. Fax: (425)481-8253. E-mail: info@epicenterpress.com. Website: www.epicenterpress.com. **Acquisitions:** Lael Morgan. Estab. 1987. Publishes hardcover and trade paperback originals. **Publishes 10 titles/year. Receives 200 queries and 100 mss/year. 75% of books from first-time authors; 90% from unagented writers.** Publishes book 1-2 years after acceptance of ms. Responds in 2 months to queries. Book catalog and ms guidelines on website.

 ○┐ "We are a regional press founded in Alaska whose interests include but are not limited to the arts, history, environment, and diverse cultures and lifestyles of the North Pacific and high latitudes.

Nonfiction "Our focus is Alaska and the Pacific Northwest. We do not encourage nonfiction titles from outside this region." Biography, humor. Subjects include animals, ethnic, history, nature/environment, recreation, regional, women's issues/studies. Submit outline and 3 sample chapters. Reviews artwork/photos as part of ms package. Send photocopies.

Recent Title(s) *Echoes of Fury*, by Frank Parchman.

ETC PUBLICATIONS

700 E. Vereda Sur, Palm Springs CA 92262-4816. (760)325-5352. Fax: (760)325-8841. **Acquisitions:** Dr. Richard W. Hostrop, publisher (education and social sciences); Lee Ona S. Hostrop, editorial director (history and works suitable below the college level). Estab. 1972. Publishes hardcover and paperback originals. **Publishes 6-12 titles/year. 75% of books from first-time authors; 90% from unagented writers. Offers 5-15% royalty, based on wholesale and retail price.** Publishes book 9 months after acceptance of ms.

 ○┐ ETC publishes works that "further learning as opposed to entertainment."

Nonfiction Textbook, educational management, gifted education, futuristics. Subjects include education, translation (in above areas). Submit complete ms with SASE. Reviews artwork/photos as part of ms package.

Recent Title(s) *The Artilect War; The Cosmists vs. The Terrans.*

Tips "Special consideration is given to those authors who are capable and willing to submit their completed work in camera-ready, typeset form. We are particularly interested in works suitable for both the Christian school market and homeschoolers; e.g., state history texts below the high school level with a Christian-oriented slant."

EVAN-MOOR EDUCATIONAL PUBLISHERS

18 Lower Ragsdale Dr., Monterey CA 93940-5746. (800)976-1915. Fax: (800)777-4332. E-mail: editorial@evan-moor.com. Website: www.evan-moor.com. **Acquisitions:** Acquisitions Editor. Estab. 1979. Publishes teaching materials. **Publishes 40-60 titles/year.** Accepts simultaneous submissions. Responds in 3 months to queries. Book catalog and ms guidelines free or on website.

- ○→ "Our books are teaching ideas, lesson plans, and blackline reproducibles for grades pre-K through 6th in all curriculum areas except music and bilingual." Currently emphasizing writing/language arts, practice materials for home use. De-emphasizing thematic materials. "We do not publish children's literary fiction or literary nonfiction."

Nonfiction Subjects include education, teaching materials, grades pre-K through 6th. No children's fiction or nonfiction literature. Submit proposal package, including outline and 3 sample chapters, résumé, SASE.

Recent Title(s) *Basic Phonics Skills*; *Read and Understand Poetry*; *U.S. Facts & Fun*.

Tips "Writers should know how classroom/educational materials differ from trade publications. They should request catalogs and submission guidelines before sending queries or manuscripts. Visiting our website will give writers a clear picture of the type of materials we publish."

⊘ Ⓐ M. EVANS AND CO., INC.

216 E. 49th St., New York NY 10017-1502. (212)688-2810. Fax: (212)486-4544. E-mail: editorial@mevans.com. Website: www.mevans.com. **Acquisitions:** Editor. Estab. 1960. Publishes hardcover and trade paperback originals. **Publishes 30-40 titles/year. 5% from unagented writers. Pays negotiable royalty. Offers advance.** Publishes book 8 months after acceptance of ms. Responds in 2 months to queries. Book catalog for 9 × 12 SAE with 3 first-class stamps; ms guidelines online.

- ○→ Evans has a strong line of health and self-help books but is interested in publishing quality titles on a wide variety of subject matters. "We publish a general trade list of adult nonfiction, cookbooks and semi-reference works. The emphasis is on selectivity, publishing commercial works with quality." Currently emphasizing health, relationships, nutrition.

Nonfiction Cookbook, general nonfiction, self-help. Subjects include cooking/foods/nutrition, health/medicine, relationships. "Our most successful nonfiction titles have been related to health and the behavioral sciences. No limitation on subject." No memoirs. Query with SASE. *No unsolicited mss.*

Fiction "Our very small general fiction list represents an attempt to combine quality with commercial potential. We publish no more than one novel per season. Small, general trade publisher specializing in nonfiction titles on health, nutrition, diet, cookbooks, parenting, popular psychology." Query with SASE. *No unsolicited mss.*

Recent Title(s) *Dr. Atkins' Diet Revolution* (health); *This Is How Love Works*, by Steven Carter.

Tips "A writer should clearly indicate what his book is all about, frequently the task the writer performs least well. His credentials, although important, mean less than his ability to convince this company that he understands his subject and that he has the ability to communicate a message worth hearing. Writers should review our book catalog before making submissions."

EXCELSIOR CEE PUBLISHING

P.O. Box 5861, Norman OK 73070. (405)329-3909. Fax: (405)329-6886. **Acquisitions:** J.C. Marshall. Estab. 1989. Publishes hardcover and trade paperback originals. **Publishes 15 titles/year. Receives 400 queries/year. Pays royalty, or makes outright purchase (both negotiable); will consider co-op publishing some titles.** Publishes book 1 year after acceptance of ms. Accepts simultaneous submissions. Responds in 1 month to queries. Book catalog for #10 SASE.

- ○→ "All of our books speak to the reader through words of feeling—whether they are how-to, educational, humor, or memoir, the reader comes away with feeling, truth, and inspiration." Currently emphasizing how-to, family history, memoirs, inspiration. De-emphasizing childrens.

Nonfiction Biography, gift book, how-to, humor, self-help, inspiration. Subjects include Americana, education, history, language/literature, memoirs, women's issues/studies, general nonfiction, writing. Query with SASE.

Recent Title(s) *Goodbye Kite*, by Lois Redpath; *About Face . . . Forward March*, by Robert Seikel; *Oklahoma Jim*, by James Shears.

Tips "We have a general audience, bookstore browsers interested in nonfiction reading. We publish titles that have a mass appeal and can be enjoyed by a large reading public."

F+W PUBLICATIONS, INC. (BOOK DIVISION)

4700 E. Galbraith Rd., Cincinnati OH 45236. (513)531-2690. Website: www.fwpublications.com. President: William Budge Wallis. Executive Vice President/Product Development: David Lewis. **Acquisitions:** See individual listings for the names of specific acquisitions editors. Estab. 1913. Publishes trade paperback originals and reprints. **Publishes 200+ titles/year.** Ms guidelines online.

Imprints Adams Media (general interest series); Betterway Books (consumer reference, genealogy); David &

Charles (crafts, equestrian, railroads, soft crafts); HOW Design Books (graphic design); IMPACT Books (drawing and creative comics); KP Books (antiques and collectibles, automotive, coins and paper money, comics, crafts, games, firearms, militaria, outdoors and hunting, records and CDs, sports, toys); Memory Makers (scrapbooking); North Light Books (crafts, decorative painting, fine art); Popular Woodworking Books (shop skills, woodworking); Warman's (antiques and collectibles, field guides); Writer's Digest Books (photography, writing).

- Please see individual listings for specific submission information about the company's imprints.
- O→ "With more than 3,000 titles in print and nearly a century of publishing history, F+W is proud to be one of the largest enthusiast book publishers in the world. Across subjects, age, gender, or geographic and economic demographics, readers share one common characteristic: passion. Whether it's a passion for novel writing, painting, collecting, or crafts, F+W book titles encourage readers to express their creativity, gain expertise, and achieve self-fulfillment."

FACTS ON FILE, INC.

132 W. 31st St., 17th Floor, New York NY 10001. (212)967-8800. Fax: (212)967-9196. E-mail: llikoff@factsonfile.com. Website: www.factsonfile.com. **Acquisitions:** Laurie Likoff, editorial director (science, fashion, natural history); Frank Darmstadt (science & technology, nature, reference); Nicole Bowen, senior editor (American history, women's studies, young adult reference); James Chambers, trade editor (health, pop culture, true crime, sports); Jeff Soloway, acquisitions editor (language/literature). Estab. 1941. Publishes hardcover originals and reprints. **Publishes 135-150 titles/year. 25% from unagented writers. Pays 10% royalty on retail price. Offers $5,000-10,000 advance.** Accepts simultaneous submissions. Responds in 2 months to queries. Book catalog free; ms guidelines online.
Imprints Checkmark Books.

- O→ Facts on File produces high-quality reference materials on a broad range of subjects for the school library market and the general nonfiction trade.

Nonfiction "We publish serious, informational books for a targeted audience. All our books must have strong library interest, but we also distribute books effectively to the trade. Our library books fit the junior and senior high school curriculum." Reference. Subjects include contemporary culture, education, health/medicine, history, language/literature, multicultural, recreation, religion, sports, careers, entertainment, natural history, popular culture. No computer books, technical books, cookbooks, biographies (except YA), pop psychology, humor, fiction or poetry. Query or submit outline and sample chapter with SASE. No submissions returned without SASE.
Tips "Our audience is school and public libraries for our more reference-oriented books and libraries, schools and bookstores for our less reference-oriented informational titles."

FAIRLEIGH DICKINSON UNIVERSITY PRESS

285 Madison Ave., Madison NJ 07940. (973)443-8564. Fax: (973)443-8364. E-mail: fdupress@fdu.edu. **Acquisitions:** Harry Keyishian, director. Estab. 1967. Publishes hardcover originals and occasional paperbacks. **Publishes 45 titles/year. 33% of books from first-time authors; 95% from unagented writers.** Publishes book approximately 1 year after acceptance of ms. Responds in 2 weeks to queries.

- "Contract is arranged through Associated University Presses of Cranbury, New Jersey. We are a selection committee only." Nonauthor subsidy publishes 2% of books.
- O→ Fairleigh Dickinson publishes scholarly books for the academic market, mainly—but not exclusively—in the humanities.

Nonfiction Biography, reference, scholarly, scholarly books. Subjects include art/architecture, business/economics, ethnic, film/cinema/stage, gay/lesbian, government/politics, history, music/dance, philosophy, psychology, sociology, women's issues/studies, Civil War, film, Jewish studies, literary criticism, scholarly editions. Looking for scholarly books in all fields; no nonscholarly books. Query with outline, detailed abstract, and sample chapters (if possible). Reviews artwork/photos as part of ms package. Send only copies of illustrations during the evaluation process.
Recent Title(s) *The Carlyle Encyclopedia*, edited by Mark Cummings; *Sleuthing Ethnicity: The Detective in Multiethnic Crime Fiction*, edited by D. Fischer-Hornung and Monika Mueller; *Whig's Progress: Tom Wharton Between Revolutions*, by J. Kent Clark.
Tips "Research must be up to date. Poor reviews result when bibliographies and notes don't reflect current research. We follow *Chicago Manual of Style* (15th edition) in scholarly citations. We welcome collections of unpublished conference papers or essay collections, if they relate to a strong central theme and have scholarly merit. For further details, consult our online catalogue."

FAIRVIEW PRESS

2450 Riverside Ave., Minneapolis MN 55454. (800)544-8207. Fax: (612)672-4980. E-mail: press@fairview.org. Website: www.fairviewpress.org. **Acquisitions:** Lane Stiles, director; Stephanie Billecke, senior editor. Estab.

1988. Publishes hardcover and trade paperback originals and reprints. **Publishes 8-12 titles/year. Receives 3,000 queries and 1,500 mss/year. 40% of books from first-time authors; 65% from unagented writers. Advance and royalties negotiable.** Publishes book 1 year after acceptance of ms. Accepts simultaneous submissions. Responds in 6 months to proposals. Book catalog free; ms guidelines online.

- **O—** Fairview Press publishes books and related materials that educate individuals and families about their physical, emotional, and spiritual health and motivate them to make positive changes in themselves and their communities.

Nonfiction Submit proposal package including outline, 2 sample chapters, author bio, marketing ideas, SASE. Reviews artwork/photos as part of ms package. Send photocopies.

Tips Audience is general reader.

FAITH KIDZ BOOKS

Cook Communications Ministries, 4050 Lee Vance View, Colorado Springs CO 80918. (800)708-5550. Website: www.cookministries.com. **Acquisitions:** Heather Gemmen, acquisitions editor. Publishes hardcover and paperback originals. Accepts simultaneous submissions. Responds in 6 months to queries.

- • Not currently accepting unsolicited book proposals.
- **O—** Faith Kids Books publishes inspirational works for children, ages 0-12, with a strong underlying Christian theme or clearly stated Biblical value, designed to foster spiritual growth in children and positive interaction between parent and child. Currently emphasizing Bible storybooks, Christian living books, life issue books, early readers, and picture books.

Nonfiction Biography, children's/juvenile. Subjects include religion (Bible stories, devotionals), picture books on nonfiction subjects.

Fiction Historical, juvenile, picture books, religious, toddler books. "Picture books, devotionals, Bible storybooks, for an age range of 1-12. We're particularly interested in materials for beginning readers." No teen fiction. Previously published or agented authors preferred.

Recent Title(s) *God Is There*, by Dan Foote; *Baby Bible 123*.

FANTAGRAPHICS BOOKS

7563 Lake City Way NE, Seattle WA 98115. (206)524-1967. Fax: (206)524-2104. E-mail: fbicomx@fantagraphics.com. Website: www.fantagraphics.com. Co-owners: Gary Groth, Kim Thompson. **Acquisitions:** Submissions Editor. Estab. 1976. Publishes original trade paperbacks. Responds in 2-3 months to queries. Book catalog and ms guidelines online.

- **O—** Publishes comics for thinking readers. Does not want mainstream genres of superhero, vigilante, horror, fantasy, or science fiction.

Fiction Comic books. "Fantagraphics is an independent company with a modus operandi different from larger, factory-like corporate comics publishers. If your talents are limited to a specific area of expertise (i.e. inking, writing, etc.), then you will need to develop your own team before submitting a project to us. We want to see an idea that is fully fleshed-out in your mind, at least, if not on paper. Submit a minimum of 5 fully-inked pages of art, a synopsis, SASE, and a brief note stating approximately how many issues you have in mind."

Recent Title(s) *In My Darkest Hour*, by Wilfred Santiago; *When We Were Very Maakies*, by Tony Millionaire.

Tips "Take note of the originality and diversity of the themes and approaches to drawing in such Fantagraphics titles as *Love & Rockets* (stories of life in Latin America and Chicano L.A.), *Palestine* (journalistic autobiography in the Middle East), *Eightball* (surrealism mixed with kitsch culture in stories alternately humorous and painfully personal), and *Naughty Bits* (feminist humor and short stories which both attack and commiserate). Try to develop your own, equally individual voice; originality, aesthetic maturity, and graphic storytelling skill are the signs by which Fantagraphics judges whether or not your submission is ripe for publication."

FARRAR, STRAUS & GIROUX BOOKS FOR YOUNG READERS

Farrar Straus Giroux, Inc., 19 Union Square W., New York NY 10003. (212)741-6900. Fax: (212)633-2427. Website: www.fsgkidsbooks.com. **Acquisitions:** Margaret Ferguson, editorial director. Estab. 1946. Publishes hardcover originals and trade paperback reprints. **Publishes 75 titles/year. Receives 6,000 queries and mss/year. 5% of books from first-time authors; 50% from unagented writers. Pays royalty. Pays 2-6% royalty on retail price for paperbacks, 3-10% for hardcovers. Offers $3,000-25,000 advance.** Publishes book 18 months after acceptance of ms. Accepts simultaneous submissions. Responds in 2 months to queries; 4 months to mss. Book catalog for 9 × 12 SAE with $1.95 postage; ms guidelines online.

Imprints Frances Foster Books; Melanie Kroupa Books.

- **O—** "We publish original and well-written material for all ages."

Fiction Juvenile, picture books, young adult, nonfiction. "Do not query picture books; just send manuscript. Do not fax queries or manuscripts." Query with SASE.

Recent Title(s) *Jack Adrift*, by Jack Gantos (ages 10 up); *The Canning Season*, by Polly Horvath (National Book Award); *Tree of Life*, by Peter Sis (all ages).

Tips Audience is full age range, preschool to young adult. Specializes in literary fiction.

N FATCAT PRESS

P.O. Box 130281, Ann Arbor MI 48113. E-mail: editorial@fatcatpress.com. Submissions E-mail: inbox@fatcatpress.com. Website: www.fatcatpress.com. **Acquisitions:** Ellen Bauerle, publisher/acquiring editor (technology, mysteries, Buddhist studies, travel, science fiction). Estab. 2003. Publishes electronic originals and occasional reprints. **Publishes 20 titles/year. Receives 360 queries and 120 mss/year. 60% of books from first-time authors; 95% from unagented writers. Pays 50% royalty on net receipts.** Publishes book 3 months after acceptance of ms. Does not accept simultaneous submissions. Responds in 1 month. Book catalog and ms guidelines online.

Nonfiction General nonfiction. Subjects include travel, eastern religion and spirituality, technology and society. ''Follow submission information on our website. We only publish in specific areas, as noted there.'' Query with SASE, or submit proposal package including outline, 4 sample chapters, current e-mail address.

Fiction Fantasy, mystery, science fiction. ''We want top-flight writing, unusual points of view, unusual characters.'' Query with e-mail address via e-mail, or submit complete ms.

Tips ''Our readers are educated, well read, and technologically competent. Many travel extensively.''

A ⊘ FAWCETT

The Ballantine Publishing Group, A Division of Random House, Inc., 1745 Broadway, New York NY 10019. E-mail: bfi@randomhouse.com. Website: www.randomhouse.com. Estab. 1955. Publishes paperback originals and reprints.

　O⇥ Major publisher of mystery mass market and trade paperbacks.

Fiction Mystery. *Agented submissions only. All unsolicited mss returned unopened.*

FC2

Dept. of English, Florida State University, Tallahassee FL 32306-1580. (850)644-2260. E-mail: fc2@english.fsu.edu. Website: fc2.org. **Acquisitions:** Production Manager. Submissions: Publications Unit, Campus Box 4241, Illinois State University, Normal IL 61790-4241 Estab. 1974. Publishes hardcover and paperback originals. **Publishes 6-10 titles/year. Receives 200-300 queries and 35-50 mss/year. Pays royalty.** Publishes book 18 months after acceptance of ms. Accepts simultaneous submissions. Responds in 3-9 months to mss. Ms guidelines online.

　● Accepts mss September 1-February 1 only.

　O⇥ Publisher of innovative fiction. No nonfiction, poetry, children's, or plays.

Fiction Experimental, feminist, gay/lesbian, innovative; modernist/postmodern; avant-garde; anarchist; minority; cyberpunk. Submit cover letter, 50 pages of ms, SASE.

Recent Title(s) *The Body Parts Shop*, by Lynda Schor; *Disability*, by Cris Mazza; *Last Fall*, by Ronald Sukenick.

Tips ''Be familiar with our list.''

FREDERICK FELL PUBLISHERS, INC.

2131 Hollywood Blvd., Suite 305, Hollywood FL 33020. (954)925-5242. Fax: (954)925-5244. E-mail: info@fellpub.com. Website: www.fellpub.com. **Acquisitions:** Barbara Newman, senior editor. Publishes hardcover and trade paperback originals. **Publishes 40 titles/year. Receives 4,000 queries and 1,000 mss/year. 95% of books from first-time authors; 95% from unagented writers. Pays negotiable royalty on retail price. Offers up to $10,000 advance.** Publishes book 1 year after acceptance of ms. Accepts simultaneous submissions. Responds in 1 month to queries; 3 months to proposals. Ms guidelines online.

　O⇥ ''Fell has just launched 25 titles in the *Know-It-All* series. We will be publishing over 125 titles in all genres. Prove to us that your title is the best in this new exciting nonfiction format.''

Nonfiction ''We are reviewing in all categories. Advise us of the top three competitive titles for your work and the reasons why the public would benefit by having your book published.'' How-to, reference, self-help. Subjects include business/economics, child guidance/parenting, education, ethnic, film/cinema/stage, health/medicine, hobbies, money/finance, spirituality. Submit proposal package, including outline, 3 sample chapters, author bio, publicity ideas, market analysis. Reviews artwork/photos as part of ms package. Send photocopies.

Recent Title(s) *Venus & Serena: My Seven Years as Hitting Coach for the Williams Sisters*; *Greatest Salesman in the World*, by Og Mandino (gift edition).

Tips ''We are most interested in well-written, timely nonfiction with strong sales potential. We will not consider topics that appeal to a small, select audience. Learn markets and be prepared to help with sales and promotion. Show us how your book is unique or better than the competition.''

THE FEMINIST PRESS AT THE CITY UNIVERSITY OF NEW YORK

365 Fifth Ave., Suite 5406, New York NY 10016. (212)817-7920. Fax: (212)817-1593. E-mail: ltenzer@gc.cuny.edu. Website: www.feministpress.org. **Acquisitions:** Livia Tenzer, publisher/director. Estab. 1970. Publishes hardcover and trade paperback originals and reprints. Publishes no original fiction; exceptions are anthologies and international works. Accepts simultaneous submissions. Book catalog and ms guidelines online.

O⌐ Our primary mission is to publish works of fiction by women which preserve and extend women's literary traditions. We emphasize work by multicultural/international women writers.

Nonfiction Subjects include ethnic, gay/lesbian, government/politics, health/medicine, history, language/literature, memoirs, multicultural, music/dance, sociology, translation, women's issues/studies. "We look for nonfiction work which challenges gender-role stereotypes and documents women's historical and cultural contributions. Note that we generally publish for the college classroom as well as the trade." Send e-mail queries only, limited to 200 words with Submission as the subject line. "We regret that submissions are no longer accepted through the mail and unsolicited packages will be discarded."

Fiction Ethnic, feminist, gay/lesbian, literary, short story collections, women's. "The Feminist Press publishes only fiction reprints by classic American women authors and imports and translations of distinguished international women writers. Absolutely no original fiction is considered." Needs fiction by "U.S. women of color writers from 1920-1970 who have fallen out of print." Query by e-mail only; limit 200 words with Submission as the subject line.

Recent Title(s) *The Stories of Fannie Hurst*, by Fannie Hurst; edited by Susan Koppelman; *Developing Power*, by Arvonne S. Fraser and Irene Tinker; *Bunny Lake Is Missing*, by Evelyn Piper.

Tips We cannot accept telephone inquiries regarding proposed submissions.

FERGUSON PUBLISHING CO.

Imprint of Facts on File, 132 W. 31st St., 17th Floor, New York NY 10001. (800)322-8755. E-mail: editorial@factsonfile.com. Website: www.fergpubco.com. **Acquisitions:** Editorial Director. Estab. 1940. Publishes hardcover and trade paperback originals. **Publishes 50 titles/year. Pays by project.** Responds in 6 months to queries. Ms guidelines online.

O⌐ "We are primarily a career education publisher that publishes for schools and libraries. We need writers who have expertise in a particular career or career field (for possible full-length books on a specific career or field)."

Nonfiction "We publish work specifically for the elementary/junior high/high school/college library reference market. Works are generally encyclopedic in nature. Our current focus is career encyclopedias. We consider manuscripts that cross over into the trade market." Reference. Subjects include careers. "No mass market, poetry, scholarly, or juvenile books, please." Query or submit an outline and 1 sample chapter.

Recent Title(s) *Ferguson Career Biographies: Colin Powell, Bill Gates, etc.* (20 total books in series); *Careers in Focus: Geriatric Care, Design, etc.*

Tips "We like writers who know the market—former or current librarians or teachers or guidance counselors."

FIRE ENGINEERING BOOKS & VIDEOS

Imprint of PennWell Corp., 1421 S. Sheridan Rd., Tulsa OK 74112. (918)831-9420. Fax: (918)831-9555. E-mail: bookproposals@pennwell.com. Website: www.pennwellbooks.com. **Acquisitions:** Jared Wicklund, supervising editor. Publishes hardcover and softcover originals. Does not accept simultaneous submissions. Responds in 1 month to proposals. Book catalog free.

O⌐ Fire Engineering publishes textbooks relevant to firefighting and training. Currently emphasizing strategy and tactics, reserve training, preparedness for terrorist threats, natural disasters, first response to fires and emergencies.

Nonfiction Reference, technical, textbook. Subjects include firefighter training, public safety. Submit proposal via e-mail.

Recent Title(s) *Vehicle Extrication*, by Brian G. Anderson; *Crew Resource Management for the Fire Service*, by Randy Okray and Thomas Lubnau II.

Tips "No human-interest stories; technical training only."

FLORIDA ACADEMIC PRESS

P.O. Box 540, Gainesville FL 32602. (352)332-5104. Fax: (352)331-6003. E-mail: fapress@worldnet.att.net. **Acquisitions:** Max Vargas, CEO; Sam Decalo, acquisitions editor (scholarly, nonfiction); Florence Dusek, assistant editor (fiction). **Publishes 10 titles/year. Receives 500 queries and 300 mss/year. 65% of books from first-time authors; 100% from unagented writers.**

● "We were twice the publisher of *Choice*'s 'Best Book of the Year.'"

O⌐ "We are primarily interested in: scholarly works in the social sciences and history; world literature and literary criticism; and serious U.S. fiction. No polemics, poetry, science fiction, religion, autobiography, self-improvement, collections of stories, or children's books."

Recent Title(s) *Antinomy*, by Lucian Whyte; *Love & Delusion*, by Daniel Martinez; *Sweet Prince: The Passion of Hamlet*, by Doug Brode.

Tips Only completed mss are considered, accompanied by SASE. "Books we accept for publication must be submitted in camera-ready format."

FOCAL PRESS

Imprint of Elsevier (USA), Inc., 200 Wheeler Rd., Burlington MA 01803. Fax: (781)221-1615. Website: www.foca lpress.com. **Acquisitions:** Joanne Tracy, publisher; for further editorial contacts, visit the contacts page on the company's website. Estab. US, 1981; UK, 1938. Publishes hardcover and paperback originals and reprints. **Publishes 80-120 UK-US titles/year; entire firm publishes over 1,000 titles/year. 25% of books from first-time authors; 90% from unagented writers. Pays 10-12% royalty on net receipts. Offers modest advance.** Publishes book 9-12 months after acceptance of ms. Accepts simultaneous submissions. Responds in 2 months to queries. Book catalog for #10 SASE; ms guidelines online.

   ○┐ Focal Press provides excellent books for students, advanced amateurs, and working professionals involved in all areas of media technology. Topics of interest include photography (digital and traditional techniques), film/video, audio, broadcasting, and cinematography, through to journalism, radio, television, video, and writing. Currently emphasizing graphics, gaming, animation, and multimedia.

Nonfiction How-to, reference, scholarly, technical, textbook, media arts. Subjects include film/cinema/stage, photography, film, cinematography, broadcasting, theater and performing arts, audio, sound and media technology. "We do not publish collections of photographs or books composed primarily of photographs." Query preferred, or submit outline and sample chapters. Reviews artwork/photos as part of ms package.

Recent Title(s) *Adobe Photoshop 7.0 for Photographers*, by Martin Evening (nonfiction).

Ⓐ FODOR'S TRAVEL PUBLICATIONS, INC.

Imprint of Random House, Inc., 1745 Broadway, New York NY 10019. Website: www.fodors.com. **Acquisitions:** Editorial Director. Estab. 1936. Publishes trade paperback originals. **Most titles are collective works, with contributions as works for hire. Most contributions are updates of previously published volumes.** Accepts simultaneous submissions. Responds in 2 months to queries. Book catalog free.

   ○┐ Fodor's publishes travel books on many regions and countries.

Nonfiction How-to (travel), illustrated book (travel), travel guide. Subjects include travel. "We are interested in unique approaches to favorite destinations. Writers seldom review our catalog or our list and often query about books on topics that we're already covering. Beyond that, it's important to review competition and to say what the proposed book will add. Do not send originals without first querying as to our interest in the project. We're not interested in travel literature or in proposals for general travel guidebooks." *Agented submissions only.* Submit proposal and résumé via mail.

Recent Title(s) *Fodor's Cape Code 2005*; *Fodor's German for Travelers, 3rd Ed.* (phrase book); *Solo Traveler: Tales & Tips for Great Trips*, by Lea Lane.

Tips "In preparing your query or proposal, remember that it's the only argument Fodor's will hear about why your book will be a good one, and why you think it will sell; and it's also best evidence of your ability to create the book you propose. Craft your proposal well and carefully so that it puts your best foot forward."

FOGHORN OUTDOORS

Avalon Travel Publishing, Avalon Publishing Group, 1400 65th St., Suite 250, Emeryville CA 94608. (510)595-3664. Fax: (510)595-4228. E-mail: acquisitions@avalonpub.com. Website: www.travelmatters.com/acquisitions; www.foghorn.com. **Acquisitions:** Acquisitions Manager. Estab. 1985. Publishes trade paperback originals and reprints. **Publishes 20 titles/year. Receives 500 queries and 200 mss/year. 40% of books from first-time authors; 98% from unagented writers. Pays 12% royalty on wholesale price; occasional work-for-hire.** Publishes book 18 months after acceptance of ms. Accepts simultaneous submissions. Responds in 4 months to queries. Book catalog free; ms guidelines online.

   ○┐ Foghorn publishes outdoor recreation guidebooks. Editorial mission is "to produce current, informative and complete travel information for specific types of travelers."

Nonfiction Outdoor recreation guidebooks. Subjects include nature/environment, recreation (camping, biking, fishing), sports, outdoors, leisure. Query first via e-mail, Attn: acquisitions manager.

Recent Title(s) *Foghorn Outdoors: California Camping*, by Tom Stienstra.

Tips "We are expanding our list nationally in the formats we already publish (camping, hiking, fishing, dogs) as well as developing new formats to test California."

FORDHAM UNIVERSITY PRESS

University Box L, Bronx NY 10458. (718)817-4795. Fax: (718)817-4785. Website: www.fordhampress.com. Editorial Director: Helen Tartar. **Acquisitions:** Mary-Lou Elias-Peña. Publishes hardcover and trade paperback originals and reprints. Book catalog and ms guidelines free.

⚬⚬ "We are a publisher in humanities, accepting scholarly monographs, collections, occasional reprints and general interest titles for consideration. No fiction."

Nonfiction Biography, textbook, scholarly. Subjects include anthropology/archeology, art/architecture, education, film/cinema/stage, government/politics, history, language/literature, military/war (World War II), philosophy, regional (New York), religion, science, sociology, translation, business, Jewish studies, media, music. Submit query letter, CV, SASE.

Recent Title(s) *The Search for Major Plagge*, by Michael Good; *Red Tail Captured, Red Tail Free*, by Alexander Jefferson, with Lewis Carlson.

Tips "We have an academic and general audience."

N FORT ROSS INC. RUSSIAN-AMERICAN PUBLISHING PROJECTS

26 Arthur Place, Yonkers NY 10701. (914)375-6448. Fax: (914)375-6439. E-mail: fort.ross@verizon.net. Submissions E-mail: vkartsev2000@yahoo.com. Website: www.fortross.net. **Acquisitions:** Dr. Vladimir P. Kartsev, executive director. Estab. 1992. Publishes paperback originals. **Publishes 10 titles/year. Receives 100 queries and 100 mss/year. Pays 4-7% royalty on wholesale price or makes outright purchase of $500-1,500. Offers $500-$1,000; negotiable advance.** Publishes book 1 year after acceptance of ms. Accepts simultaneous submissions. Responds in 1 month to queries and proposals; 3 months to mss.

⚬⚬ "Generally, we publish Russia-related books in English or Russian. Sometimes we publish various fiction and nonfiction books in collaboration with the East European publishers in translation. We are looking mainly for well-established authors."

Nonfiction Biography, illustrated book (for adults and children), reference.

Fiction Adventure, fantasy (space fantasy, sword and sorcery), horror, mainstream/contemporary, mystery (amateur sleuth, police procedural, private eye/hardboiled), romance (contemporary, futuristic/time travel), science fiction (hard science/technological, soft/sociological), suspense. Query with SASE.

Recent Title(s) *Cosack Galloped Far Away*, by Nikolas Feodoroff; *Verses*, by Filip Novikov; *Bay of Cross*, by Yury Egorov (in Russian).

FORTRESS PRESS

P.O. Box 1209, Minneapolis MN 55440-1209. (612)330-3300. E-ail: booksub@augsburgfortress.org. Website: www.fortresspress.com. Publishes hardcover and trade paperback originals. **Pays royalty on retail price.** Accepts simultaneous submissions. Book catalog free (call 1-800-328-4648); ms guidelines online.

⚬⚬ Fortress Press publishes academic books in Biblical studies, theology, Christian ethics, church history, and professional books in pastoral care and counseling.

Nonfiction Subjects include religion, women's issues/studies, church history, African-American studies. Query with annotated TOC, brief cv, sample pages, SASE. Please study guidelines before submitting.

Recent Title(s) *God & Power: Counter-Apocalyptic Journeys*, by Catherine Keller; *New Testament Theology: Communion and Community*, by Philip F. Esler; *Radical Wisdom: A Feminist Mystical Theology*, by Beverly J. Lanzetta.

FORUM PUBLISHING CO.

383 E. Main St., Centerport NY 11721. (631)754-5000. Fax: (631)754-0630. Website: www.forum123.com. **Acquisitions:** Martin Stevens. Estab. 1981. Publishes trade paperback originals. **Publishes 12 titles/year. Receives 200 queries and 25 mss/year. 75% of books from first-time authors; 75% from unagented writers. Makes outright purchase of $250-750.** Publishes book 4 months after acceptance of ms. Accepts simultaneous submissions. Responds in 1 month to mss. Book catalog free.

⚬⚬ "Forum publishes only business titles."

Nonfiction Subjects include business/economics, money/finance. Submit outline. Reviews artwork/photos as part of ms package. Send photocopies.

Recent Title(s) *Selling Information By Mail*, by Glen Gilcrest.

WALTER FOSTER PUBLISHING, INC.

23062 La Cadena Dr., Laguna Hills CA 92653. (800)426-0099. Fax: (949)380-7575. E-mail: info@walterfoster.com. Website: www.walterfoster.com. Publishes trade paperback originals. Accepts simultaneous submissions. Book catalog free.

⚬⚬ Walter Foster publishes instructional how-to/craft instruction as well as licensed products.

Nonfiction How-to. Subjects include arts and crafts. Submit proposal package, including query letter, color photos/examples of artwork. Reviews artwork/photos as part of ms package. Submit color photocopies or color photos. Samples cannot be returned.

Recent Title(s) *Glass Painting; Ceramic Painting; Paper Crafts* (art instruction).

FOX CHAPEL PUBLISHING

1970 Broad St., East Petersburg PA 17520. (717)560-4703. Fax: (717)560-4702. E-mail: editors@carvingworld.com. Website: www.foxchapelpublishing.com. **Acquisitions:** Alan Giagnocavo, publisher; Peg Couch, acquisitions editor; Gretchen Bacon, editor. Publishes hardcover and trade paperback originals and trade paperback reprints. **Publishes 25-40 titles/year. 50% of books from first-time authors; 100% from unagented writers. Pays royalty or makes outright purchase. Offers variable advance.** Publishes book 6-18 months after acceptance of ms. Accepts simultaneous submissions. Responds in 2 months to queries.

○→ Fox Chapel publishes woodworking and woodcarving titles for professionals and hobbyists.

Nonfiction Subjects include woodworking, wood carving, scroll saw and woodturning. Write for query submission guidelines. Reviews artwork/photos as part of ms package. Send photocopies.

Recent Title(s) *Woodworking Projects for Women*; *Whittling Twigs & Branches*; *Great Book of Fairy Patterns*.

Tips "We're looking for knowledgeable artists, woodworkers first, writers second to write for us. Our market is for avid woodworking hobbyists and professionals."

Ⓐ FREE PRESS

Simon & Schuster, 1230 Avenue of the Americas, New York NY 10020. (212)698-7000. Fax: (212)632-4989. Website: www.simonsays.com. Publisher: Martha Levin. **Acquisitions:** Bruce Nichols, vice president/senior editor (history/serious nonfiction); Leslie Meredith, vice president/senior editor (psychology/sprituality/self-help); Fred Hills (business/serious nonfiction); Amy Scheibe, senior editor (literary fiction); Elizabeth Stein, senior editor (history, current events, biography, memoir); Dominick Anfuso, vice president/editorial director (self-help/serious nonfiction). Estab. 1947. **Publishes 85 titles/year. 15% of books from first-time authors; 10% from unagented writers. Pays variable royalty. Offers advance.** Publishes book 1 year after acceptance of ms. Responds in 2 months to queries.

○→ The Free Press publishes nonfiction.

Nonfiction *Does not accept unagented submissions.* Query with 1-3 sample chapters, outline before submitting mss.

Recent Title(s) *Against All Enemies*, by Richard Clarke; *The 8th Habit*, by Stephen R. Covey.

FREE SPIRIT PUBLISHING, INC.

217 Fifth Ave. N., Suite 200, Minneapolis MN 55401-1299. (612)338-2068. Fax: (612)337-5050. E-mail: acquisitions@freespirit.com. Website: www.freespirit.com. Publisher: Judy Galbraith. **Acquisitions:** Acquisitions Editor. Estab. 1983. Publishes trade paperback originals and reprints. **Publishes 18-24 titles/year. 25% of books from first-time authors; 50% from unagented writers. Offers advance.** Book catalog and ms guidelines free or online.

Imprints Self-Help for Kids®; Learning to Get Along® Series; Self-Help for Teens®; Laugh & Learn™ Series; How Rude!™ Handbooks for Teens; Adding Assets Series for Kids.

○→ "We believe passionately in empowering kids to learn to think for themselves and make their own good choices."

Nonfiction Children's/juvenile (young adult), self-help (parenting). Subjects include child guidance/parenting, education (pre-K-12, study and social skills, special needs, differentiation but not textbooks or basic skills books like reading, counting, etc.), health/medicine (mental/emotional health for/about children), psychology (for/about children), sociology (for/about children). "Many of our authors are educators, mental health professionals, and youth workers involved in helping kids and teens." No fiction or picture storybooks, poetry, single biographies or autobiographies, books with mythical or animal characters, or books with religious or New Age content. Query with cover letter stating qualifications, intent, and intended audience and how your book stands out from the field, along with outline, 2 sample chapters, résumé, SASE. Do not send original copies of work.

Recent Title(s) *100 Things Guys Need to Know*; *Too Stressed to Think?*; *26 Big Things Small Hands Do*.

Tips "Our books are issue-oriented, jargon-free, and solution-focused. Our audience is children, teens, teachers, parents and youth counselors. We are especially concerned with kids' social and emotional well-being and look for books with ready-to-use strategies for coping with today's issues at home or in school—written in everyday language. We are not looking for academic or religious materials, or books that analyze problem's with the nation's school systems. Instead, we want books that offer practical, positive advice so kids can help themselves and parents and teachers can help kids succeed."

FRONT STREET

862 Haywood Rd., Asheville NC 28806. (828)236-3097. Fax: (828)221-2112. E-mail: contactus@frontstreetbooks.com. Website: www.frontstreetbooks.com. **Acquisitions:** Joy Neaves, editor. Estab. 1994. Publishes hardcover originals. **Publishes 10-15 titles/year; imprint publishes 6-12 titles/year. Receives 2,000 queries and 5,000 mss/year. 50% of books from first-time authors; 80% from unagented writers. Pays royalty on retail price. Offers advance.** Publishes book 1 year after acceptance of ms. Accepts simultaneous submissions. Responds

in 1 month to queries; 2 months to proposals; 4 months to mss. Book catalog and ms guidelines online.

○┓ "We are an independent publisher of books for children and young adults."

Nonfiction Children's/juvenile, humor, illustrated book.

Fiction Adventure, historical, humor, juvenile, literary, picture books, young adult (adventure, fantasy/science fiction, historical, mystery/suspense, problem novels, sports). Query with SASE. Submit complete ms, if under 100 pages, with SASE. Keeps illustration samples on file. Reviews artwork/photos with ms. Send photocopies.

Poetry Submit 25 sample poems.

Recent Title(s) *Honeysuckle House*, by Andrea Cheng; *The Big House*, by Carolyn Coman; *Fortune's Bones*, by Marilyn Nelson.

FUTURE HORIZONS

721 W. Abram St., Arlington TX 76013. (817)277-0727. Fax: (817)277-2270. E-mail: victoria@futurehorizons-autism.com. Website: www.futurehorizons-autism.com. **Acquisitions:** Victoria Ulmer. Publishes hardcover originals, trade paperback originals and reprints. **Publishes 10 titles/year. Receives 250 queries and 125 mss/ year. 75% of books from first-time authors; 95% from unagented writers. Pays 10% royalty, or makes outright purchase.** Publishes book 2 months after acceptance of ms. Accepts simultaneous submissions. Responds in 1 month to queries; 2 months to proposals. Book catalog free; ms guidelines online.

Nonfiction Children's/juvenile (pertaining to autism), cookbook (for autistic individuals), humor (about autism), self-help (detailing with autism/Asperger's syndrome). Subjects include education (about autism/Asperger's syndrome), autism. Submit proposal package including outline. Reviews artwork/photos as part of ms package. Send photocopies.

Recent Title(s) *Diagnosing Jefferson*, by Norm Ledgin (nonfiction); *Tobin Learns to Make Friends*, by Diane Murrell (childrens fiction).

Tips Audience is parents, teachers, professionals dealing with individuals with autism or Asperger's syndrome. "Books that sell well, have practical and useful information on how to help individuals and/or care givers of individuals with autism. Personal stories, even success stories, are usually not helpful to others in a practical way."

GATFPRESS

Graphic Arts Technical Foundation, 200 Deer Run Rd., Sewickley PA 15143-2600. (412)741-6860. Fax: (412)741-2311. E-mail: tdestree@piagatf.org. Submissions E-mail: awoodall@piagatf.org. Website: www.gain.net. **Acquisitions:** Tom Destree, editor in chief; Amy Woodall, managing editor (graphic arts, communication, book publishing, printing). Estab. 1924. Publishes trade paperback originals and hardcover reference texts. **Publishes 20 titles/year. 50% of books from first-time authors; 100% from unagented writers. Pays 5-15% royalty on wholesale price.** Publishes book 18 months after acceptance of ms. Responds in 1 month to queries. Book catalog for 9×12 SAE with 2 first-class stamps; ms guidelines for #10 SASE.

○┓ "GATF's mission is to serve the graphic communications community as the major resource for technical information and services through research and education." Currrently emphasizing career guides for graphic communications and turnkey training curriculums."

Nonfiction How-to, reference, technical, textbook. Subjects include printing/graphic communications, electronic publishing. "We primarily want textbook/reference books about printing and related technologies. However, we are expanding our reach into electronic communications." Query with SASE, or submit outline, sample chapters, and SASE. Reviews artwork/photos as part of ms package.

Recent Title(s) *Color and Its Reproduction, 3rd Ed.*, by Gary G. Field; *To Be a Profitable Printer*, by Michael Moffit.

Tips "We are publishing titles that are updated more frequently, such as *On-Demand Publishing*. Our scope now includes reference titles geared toward general audiences interested in computers, imaging, and Internet, as well as print publishing."

GEM GUIDES BOOK CO.

315 Cloverleaf Dr., Suite F, Baldwin Park CA 91706-6510. (626)855-1611. Fax: (626)855-1610. E-mail: gembooks @aol.com. Website: www.gemguidesbooks.com. **Acquisitions:** Kathy Mayerski, editor. Estab. 1965. **Publishes 6-8 titles/year. 60% of books from first-time authors; 100% from unagented writers. Pays 6-10% royalty on retail price.** Publishes book 1 year after acceptance of ms. Accepts simultaneous submissions. Responds in 5 months to queries.

Imprints Gembooks.

○┓ "Gem Guides prefers nonfiction books for the hobbyist in rocks and minerals; lapidary and jewelry-making; travel and recreation guide books for the West and Southwest; and other regional local interest." Currently emphasizing how-to, field guides, West/Southwest regional interest. De-emphasizing stories, history, poetry.

Nonfiction Subjects include history (Western), hobbies (lapidary and jewelry-making), nature/environment, recreation, regional (Western US), science (earth), travel. Query with outline/synopsis and sample chapters with SASE. Reviews artwork/photos as part of ms package.

Recent Title(s) *Fee Mining and Mineral Adventures in the Eastern U.S.*, by James Martin Monaco and Jeannette Hathaway Monaco; *Geology Trails of Northern California*, by Robin C. Johnson and Dot Loftsrom; *Baby's Day Out in Southern California: Fun Places to Go With Babies and Toddlers*, by JoBea Holt.

Tips "We have a general audience of people interested in recreational activities. Publishers plan and have specific book lines in which they specialize. Learn about the publisher and submit materials compatible with that publisher's product line."

GENESIS PRESS, INC.

1213 Hwy. 45 N., Columbus MS 39705. (888)463-4461. Fax: (662)329-9399. E-mail: books@genesis-press.com. Website: www.genesis-press.com. Estab. 1993. Publishes hardcover and trade paperback originals and reprints. Responds in 2 months to queries; 4 months to mss. Ms guidelines online.

Imprints Indigo (romance); Black Coral (fiction); Indigo Love Spectrum (interracial romance); Indigo After Dark (erotica); Obsidian (thriller/myster); Indigo Glitz (love stories for young adults); Indigo Vibe (for stylish audience under 35 years old); Mount Blue (Christian); Inca Books (teens); Sage (self-help/inspirational).

    O➠ Genesis Press is the largest privately owned African-American publisher in the country, focusing on African American, Hispanic, Asian, and interracial fiction.

Nonfiction Autobiography, biography, self-help. Submit outline, 3 sample chapters, SASE.

Fiction Adventure, erotica, ethnic, multicultural, mystery, romance, science fiction, women's. Submit 3 sample chapters, synopsis, SASE.

Recent Title(s) *Falling*, by Natalie Dunbar; *Hearts Awakening*, by Veronica Parker.

Tips "Be professional. Always include a cover letter and SASE. Follow the submission guidelines posted on our website or send SASE for a copy."

GLENBRIDGE PUBLISHING, LTD.

19923 E. Long Ave., Centennial CO 80016. (720)870-8381. Fax: (720)870-5598. E-mail: glenbr@eazy.net. **Acquisitions:** James A. Keene, editor. Estab. 1986. Publishes hardcover originals and reprints, trade paperback originals. **Publishes 6-8 titles/year. Pays 10% royalty.** Publishes book 1 year after acceptance of ms. Accepts simultaneous submissions. Responds in 2 months to queries. Book catalog online; ms guidelines for #10 SASE.

    O➠ "Glenbridge has an eclectic approach to publishing. We look for titles that have long-term capabilities."

Nonfiction Subjects include Americana, business/economics, cooking/foods/nutrition, health/medicine, history, philosophy, psychology, sociology, music. Query with outline/synopsis, sample chapters, and SASE.

Recent Title(s) *E-Motion Picture Magic*, by Birgit Wolz; *Keep Your WITS About You*, by Michelle Gall; *Would Somebody Please Send Me to My Room!*, by Bob Schwartz.

THE GLOBE PEQUOT PRESS, INC.

P.O. Box 480, Guilford CT 06437. (203)458-4500. Fax: (203)458-4604. Website: www.globepequot.com. President/Publisher: Linda Kennedy. **Acquisitions:** Shelley Wolf, submissions editor. Estab. 1947. Publishes paperback originals, hardcover originals and reprints. **Publishes 600 titles/year. 30% of books from first-time authors; 70% from unagented writers. Average print order for a first book is 4,000-7,500. Makes an outright purchase, or pays 10% royalty on net price. Offers advance.** Publishes book 1 year after acceptance of ms. Accepts simultaneous submissions. Responds in 3 months to queries. Ms guidelines online.

    O➠ Globe Pequot is the largest publisher of regional travel books and outdoor recreation in the United States and offers the broadest selection of travel titles of any vendor in this market.

Nonfiction Regional travel guidebooks, outdoor recreation guides, natural history field guides, topics of local interest and state pride, popular western and women's history. Subjects include cooking/foods/nutrition (regional), history (popular, regional), nature/environment, recreation (outdoor), regional travel. No doctoral theses, fiction, genealogies, travel memoirs, poetry, or textbooks. Submit brief synopsis of work, TOC or outline, sample chapter, résumé/vita, definition of target audience, and an analysis of competing titles. Reviews artwork/photos as part of ms package. Do not send originals.

Recent Title(s) *Iowa Curiosities*; *Hiking the Columbia River Gorge*; *Myths and Mysteries of the Old West*.

Ⓐ ⊘ DAVID R. GODINE, PUBLISHER, INC.

9 Hamilton Place, Boston MA 02108. (617)451-9600. Fax: (617)350-0250. E-mail: info@godine.com. Website: www.godine.com. Estab. 1970. Publishes hardcover and trade paperback originals and reprints. **Publishes 35 titles/year. Pays royalty on retail price.** Publishes book 3 years after acceptance of ms. Book catalog for 5 × 8 SAE with 3 first-class stamps.

O– "Our particular strengths are books about the history and design of the written word, literary essays, and the best of world fiction in translation. We also have an unusually strong list of children's books, all of them printed in their entirety with no cuts, deletions, or side-stepping to keep the political watchdogs happy."

Nonfiction Biography, children's/juvenile, coffee table book, cookbook, illustrated book. Subjects include Americana, art/architecture, gardening, nature/environment, photography, literary criticism, book arts, typography. *No unsolicited mss.* Query with SASE.

Fiction Historical, literary. *No unsolicited mss.* Query with SASE.

Recent Title(s) *A Rage for Rock Gardening*, by Nicola Schulman; *Sustenance and Desire*, edited with paintings by Bascove; *As We Were*, by Rosamond Vaule.

Tips "Please visit our website for more information about our books and detailed submission policy. No phone calls, please."

ⓃⓏ GOLLEHON PRESS, INC.

6157 28th St., SE, Grand Rapids MI 49546. (616)949-3515. Fax: (616)949-8674. E-mail: john@gollehonbooks.com. Website: www.gollehonbooks.com. Editor: John Gollehon. **Acquisitions:** Lori Adams, editor. Publishes hardcover, trade paperback and mass market paperback originals. **Publishes 6-8 titles/year. Receives 100 queries and 30 mss/year. 85% of books from first-time authors; 90% from unagented writers. Pays 7% royalty on retail price. Offers $500-1,000 advance.** Publishes book usually 6 months after acceptance of ms. Accepts simultaneous submissions. Responds in 1 month to queries and proposals if interested; 2 months to mss. Book catalog and ms guidelines online.

O– Currently emphasizing theology (life of Christ), political, current events, pets (dogs only, rescue/heroic), self-help, poker (Texas hold 'em only), and gardening. *No unsolicited mss*; brief proposals only with first 5 pages of Chapter 1. "Writer must have strong credentials to author work."

Nonfiction See information listed above for current needs. Submit brief proposal package only with bio and first 5 pages of Chapter 1. "We do not return materials unless we specifically request the full manuscript." Reviews artwork/photos as part of ms package. Writer must be sure he/she owns all rights to photos, artwork, illustrations, etc., submitted for consideration (all submissions must be free of any third-party claims). Never send original photos or art.

Tips "Mail brief book proposal, bio, and and a few sample pages only. We will request full manuscript if interested. We cannot respond to all queries. Full manuscript will be returned if we requested it, and if writer provides SASE. We do not return proposals. Simultaneous submissions are encouraged."

THE GRADUATE GROUP

P.O. Box 370351, West Hartford CT 06137-0351. (860)233-2330. Fax: (860)233-2330. E-mail: graduategroup@hotmail.com. Website: www.graduategroup.com. **Acquisitions:** Mara Whitman, partner; Amy Gibson, partner; Robert Whitman, vice president. Estab. 1964. Publishes trade paperback originals. **Publishes 50 titles/year. Receives 100 queries and 70 mss/year. 60% of books from first-time authors; 85% from unagented writers. Pays 20% royalty on retail price.** Publishes book 3 months after acceptance of ms. Accepts simultaneous submissions. Responds in 1 month to queries. Book catalog free; ms guidelines online.

O– "The Graduate Group helps college and graduate students better prepare themselves for rewarding careers and helps people advance in the workplace." Currently emphasizing test preparation, career advancement, and materials for prisoners, law enforcement, books on unique careers.

Nonfiction Reference. Subjects include business/economics, education, government/politics, health/medicine, money/finance, law enforcement. Submit complete ms and SASE with sufficient postage.

Recent Title(s) *Real Life 101: Winning Secrets You Won't Find in Class*, by Debra Yergen; *Getting In: Applicant's Guide to Graduate School Admissions*, by David Burrell.

Tips Audience is career planning offices; colleges, graduate schools, and public libraries. "We are open to all submissions, especially those involving career planning, internships, and other nonfiction titles. Looking for books on law enforcement, books for prisoners, and reference books on subjects/fields students would be interested in. We want books on helping students and others to interview, pass tests, gain opportunity, understand the world of work, network, build experience, prepare for advancement, prepare to enter business, improve personality, and build relationships."

GRAYWOLF PRESS

2402 University Ave., Suite 203, St. Paul MN 55114. Website: www.graywolfpress.org. Editor/Publisher: Fiona McCrae. Executive Editor: Anne Czarniecki. Poetry Editor: Jeffrey Shotts. **Acquisitions:** Katie Dublinski, editor (nonfiction, fiction). Estab. 1974. Publishes trade cloth and paperback originals. **Publishes 20 titles/year. Receives 2,500 queries/year. 20% of books from first-time authors; 50% from unagented writers. Pays**

royalty on retail price. Offers $1,000-15,000 advance. Publishes book 18 months after acceptance of ms. Responds in 3 months to queries. Book catalog free; ms guidelines online.

    O— Graywolf Press is an independent, nonprofit publisher dedicated to the creation and promotion of thoughtful and imaginative contemporary literature essential to a vital and diverse culture.

Nonfiction Subjects include contemporary culture, language/literature, culture. Submit cover letter and proposal with sample chapter.

Fiction Short story collections, literary novels. "Familiarize yourself with our list first." No genre books (romance, western, science fiction, suspense). Query with SASE and 30-page sample. "Please do not fax or e-mail queries or submissions."

Poetry "We are interested in linguistically challenging work." Query with SASE and 10-poem sample.

Recent Title(s) *Cocktails*, by D.A. Powell; *The Weatherman*, by Clint McCown; *Coin of the Realm*, by Carl Phillips.

GREENHAVEN PRESS, INC.

15822 Bernardo Center Dr., Suite C, San Diego CA 92127. Website: www.gale.com/greenhaven. **Acquisitions:** Chandra Howard, senior aquisitions editor. Estab. 1970. Publishes approximately 200 anthologies/year; all anthologies are works for hire. **Makes outright purchase of $1,000-3,000.**

    O— Greenhaven Press publishes hard and softcover educational supplementary materials and (nontrade) nonfiction anthologies on contemporary issues, scientific discoveries, and history for high school and college readers. These anthologies serve as supplementary educational material for high school and college libraries and classrooms. Currently emphasizing social-issue anthologies.

Nonfiction Subjects include history, social issues. "We produce tightly formatted anthologies on contemporary issues and history for high school and college-level readers. We are looking for freelance book editors to research and compile these anthologies; we are not interested in submissions of single-author manuscripts. Each series has specific requirements. Potential book editors should familiarize themselves with our catalog and anthologies." Send query letter and résumé. *No unsolicited ms.*

Recent Title(s) *Opposing Viewpoints: Israel; At Issue: Does the World Hate the U.S.?; The Bill of Rights: Freedom of Speech.*

GREENLINE PUBLICATIONS

P.O. Box 590780, San Francisco CA 94159-0780. (415)386-8646, ext. 35. Fax: (415)386-8049. E-mail: samia@greelinepub.com. Website: www.greenlinepub.com. **Acquisitions:** Christina Henry, senior editor. Estab. 1998. Publishes trade paperback originals. **Publishes 8 titles/year; imprint publishes 6 (Fun); 2 (Historic) titles/ year. Makes outright purchase of $15,000-20,000. Offers $5,000 advance.** Does not accept simultaneous submissions. Responds in 2 months. Book catalog free.

Imprints Fun Seeker's Guides; Greenline Historical Travel Guides.

Nonfiction Subjects include history, travel. Submit proposal package including outline. Reviews artwork/photos as part of ms package.

Recent Title(s) *The 25 Best World War II Sites: European Theater*, by Chuck Thompson (travel); *The Fun Seeker's Athens*, by Coral Davenport and Jane Foster (travel); *The Fun Seeker's Miami*, by Gretchen Schmidt (travel).

Tips Audience is adult travelers.

GREENWILLOW BOOKS

HarperCollins Publishers, 1350 Avenue of the Americas, New York NY 10019. (212)261-6500. Website: www.harperchildrens.com/hch. Estab. 1974. Publishes hardcover originals and reprints.

    O— Greenwillow Books publishes quality picture books and fiction for young readers of all ages, and nonfiction primarily for children under seven years of age.

Fiction Juvenile. Fantasy, humor, literary, mystery, picture books.

Recent Title(s) *The Train of States*, by Peter Sis; *If Not for the Cat*, by Jack Prelutsky, illustrated by Ted Rand; *Happy Haunting, Amelia Bedelia*, by Herman Parish, illustrated by Lynn Sweat.

Tips "Currently not accepting unsolicited mail, mss or queries."

GREENWOOD PRESS

Greenwood Publishing Group, 88 Post Rd. W., Box 5007, Westport CT 06881. (203)226-3571. Fax: (203)222-1502. E-mail: editorial@greenwood.com. Website: www.greenwood.com. **Acquisitions:** Gary Kuris, editorial director; Emily Birch, managing editor. Publishes hardcover originals. **Publishes 200 titles/year. Receives 1,000 queries/year. 25% of books from first-time authors. Pays variable royalty on net price. Offers rare advance.** Publishes book 1 year after acceptance of ms. Accepts simultaneous submissions. Responds in 6 months to queries. Book catalog and ms guidelines online.

O– Greenwood Press publishes reference materials for high school, public and academic libraries in the humanities and the social and hard sciences.

Nonfiction Reference, scholarly. Subjects include humanities, social sciences, humanities and the social and hard sciences. Query with proposal package, including scope, organization, length of project, whether complete ms is available or when it will be, cv or résumé and SASE. *No unsolicited mss.*

Recent Title(s) *All Things Shakespeare*, by Kirstin Olsen.

GREENWOOD PUBLISHING GROUP

Reed-Elsevier (USA) Inc., 88 Post Rd. W., Box 5007, Westport CT 06881-5007. (203)226-3571. Fax: (203)222-1502. E-mail: editorial@greenwood.com. Website: www.greenwood.com. **Acquisitions:** See website for list of contact editors by subject area. **Pays variable royalty on net price.** Accepts simultaneous submissions. Book catalog and ms guidelines online.

Imprints Praeger (general nonfiction in the social sciences, business, and humanities); Greenwood Press (reference titles for middle, high school, public, and academic libraries).

O– The Greenwood Publishing Group consists of two distinguished imprints with one unifying purpose: to provide the best possible reference and general interest resources in the humanities and the social and hard sciences.

Nonfiction Reference, scholarly. Subjects include business/economics, child guidance/parenting, education, government/politics, history, humanities, language/literature, music/dance, psychology, religion, social sciences, sociology, sports, women's issues/studies. Query with proposal package, including scope, organization, length of project, whether a complete ms is available or when it will be, cv or résumé and SASE. *No unsolicited mss.*

Recent Title(s) *Listener Supported*, by Jack W. Mitchell; *Empires at War*, by Richard A. Gabriel; *The Case for Shakespeare*, by Scott McCrea.

Tips "No interest in fiction, drama, poetry—looking for reference materials and materials for educated general readers. Most of our authors are college professors who have distinguished credentialsa and who have published research widely in their fields." Greenwood Publishing maintains an excellent website, providing complete catalog, ms guidelines and editorial contacts.

ⒶⓄ GROSSET & DUNLAP PUBLISHERS

Penguin Putnam Inc., 345 Hudson St., New York NY 10014. Website: www.penguingroup.com. President/Publisher: Debra Dorfman. Estab. 1898. Publishes hardcover (few) and mass market paperback originals. **Publishes 100-125 titles/year. Pays royalty. Offers advance.** Does not accept simultaneous submissions.

● *Not currently accepting submissions.*

O– Grosset & Dunlap publishes children's books that show children that reading is fun, with books that speak to their interests, and that are affordable so that children can build a home library of their own. Focus on licensed properties, series and readers.

Nonfiction Children's/juvenile. Subjects include nature/environment, science. *Agented submissions only.*

Fiction Juvenile. *Agented submissions only.*

Recent Title(s) *Winner Takes All!*, by Maria Gallagher; *A Light From Within: Zenda*, by Ken Petti, John Amodeo, and Cassandra Westwood.

Tips "Nonfiction that is particularly topical or of wide interest in the mass market; new concepts for novelty format for preschoolers; and very well-written easy readers on topics that appeal to primary graders have the best chance of selling to our firm."

GROUP PUBLISHING, INC.

1515 Cascade Ave., Loveland CO 80538. (970)669-3836. Fax: (970)679-4370. E-mail: kloesche@grouppublishing.com. Website: www.group.com. **Acquisitions:** Kerri Loesche, editorial assistant/copyright coordinator. Estab. 1974. Publishes trade paperback originals. **Publishes 40 titles/year. Receives 500 queries and 500 mss/year. 40% of books from first-time authors; 95% from unagented writers. Pays up to 10% royalty on wholesale price or makes outright purchase or work for hire. Offers up to $1,000 advance.** Publishes book 18 months after acceptance of ms. Accepts simultaneous submissions. Responds in 1 month to queries; 6 months to proposals and mss. Book catalog for 9×12 SAE with 2 first-class stamps; ms guidelines online.

O– "Our mission is to equip churches to help children, youth, and adults grow in their relationship with Jesus."

Nonfiction How-to, multimedia, textbook (pastor/Sunday school teacher/youth leader). Subjects include education, religion. "We're an interdenominational publisher of resource materials for people who work with adults, youth or children in a Christian church setting. We also publish materials for use directly by youth or children (such as devotional books, workbooks or Bibles stories). Everything we do is based on concepts of active and interactive learning as described in *Why Nobody Learns Much of Anything at Church: And How to Fix It*, by

Thom and Joani Schultz. We need new, practical, hands-on, innovative, out-of-the-box ideas—things that no one's doing . . . yet.'' Query with SASE, or submit proposal package including outline, 3 sample chapters, cover letter, introduction to book, and sample activities if appropriate.

Recent Title(s) *An Unstoppable Force*, by Erwin McManus; *The 1 Thing*™, by Thom and Joani Schultz (effective teaching and learning).

Tips ''Our audience consists of pastors, Christian education directors, youth leaders, and Sunday school teachers.''

Ⓐ ⊘ GROVE/ATLANTIC, INC.

841 Broadway, 4th Floor, New York NY 10003. (212)614-7850. Fax: (212)614-7886. Estab. 1952. Publishes hardcover and trade paperback originals, and reprints. **Publishes 60-70 titles/year. 10-15% of books from first-time authors. Pays 7½-15% royalty on retail price. Offers considerably varies advance.** Book catalog free.

Imprints Grove Press (estab. 1952); Atlantic Monthly Press (estab. 1917); Black Cat (estab. 2004).

   o┐ Grove/Atlantic publishes serious nonfiction and literary fiction. Accepts simultaneous submissions from agents only.

Nonfiction Biography. Subjects include government/politics, history. *No unsolicited mss.*

Fiction Literary. *Agented submissions only. No unsolicited mss.*

Poetry ''We publish 3 titles/year.'' *No unsolicited mss.*

Recent Title(s) *The Divine Husband*, by Francisco Goldman; *The Lost German Slave Girl*, by John Bailey.

ALDINE DE GRUYTER

Imprint of Walter de Gruyter, Inc., Division of Transaction Publishers, Rutgers—The State University of New Jersey, 35 Berrue Circle, Piscataway NJ 08854. E-mail: trans@transactionpub.com. Website: www.degruyter.com. **Acquisitions:** Irving Louis Horowitz, editorial director. Publishes hardcover and academic paperback originals. Accepts simultaneous submissions. Book catalog free; ms guidelines only after contract.

   o┐ Aldine de Gruyter is an academic nonfiction publisher.

Nonfiction Scholarly, textbook (rare), course-related monographs; edited volumes. Subjects include anthropology/archeology, humanities, psychology (evolutionary), sociology, criminology, social psychology (not clinical), human services. ''Aldine's authors are academics with PhD's and strong publication records. No poetry or fiction.'' Submit proposal package including 1-2 sample chapters, cv, market, competing texts, reviews of early work.

Recent Title(s) *A Handbook of Varieties of English*, edited by B. Kortmann and E.W. Schneider; *Rhetoric & Renaissance Culture*, by Heinrich F. Plett; *Trauma & Guilt*, by Susanne Vees-Galani.

Tips Audience is professors and upper level and graduate students. ''Never send unsolicited manuscripts; always query before sending anything.''

GRYPHON HOUSE, INC.

P.O. Box 207, Beltsville MD 20704. (301)595-9500. Fax: (301)595-0051. Website: www.gryphonhouse.com. **Acquisitions:** Kathy Charner, editor-in-chief. Estab. 1971. Publishes trade paperback originals. **Publishes 12-15 titles/year. Pays royalty on wholesale price.** Does not accept simultaneous submissions. Responds in 3-6 months to queries. Ms guidelines online.

   o┐ Gryphon House publishes books that teachers and parents of young children (birth-age 8) consider essential to their daily lives.

Nonfiction Children's/juvenile, how-to. Subjects include child guidance/parenting, education (early childhood). Currently emphasizing reading; de-emphasizing after-school activities. Submit outline, 2-3 sample chapters, SASE.

Recent Title(s) *The Busy Family's Guide to Volunteering*, by Jenny Friedman; *Science Is Simple*, by Peggy Ashbrook; *Zen Parenting*, by Judith Costello and Jurgen Haver.

GRYPHON PUBLICATIONS

P.O. Box 209, Brooklyn NY 11228. **Acquisitions:** Gary Lovisi, owner/publisher. Publishes trade paperback originals and reprints. **Publishes 10 titles/year. Receives 500 queries and 1,000 mss/year. 20% of books from first-time authors; 90% from unagented writers. Makes outright purchase by contract, price varies. Offers no advance.** Publishes book 1-2 years after acceptance of ms. Responds in 1 month to queries. Book catalog and ms guidelines for #10 SASE.

Imprints Paperback Parade Magazine; Hardboiled Magazine; Gryphon Books; Gryphon Doubles.

   o┐ ''I publish very genre-oriented work (science fiction, crime, pulps) and nonfiction on these topics, authors and artists. It's best to query with an idea first.''

Nonfiction Reference, scholarly, bibliography. Subjects include hobbies, language/literature, book collecting.

"We need well-written, well-researched articles, but query first on topic and length. Writers should not submit material that is not fully developed/researched." Query with SASE. Reviews artwork/photos as part of ms package. Send photocopies; slides, transparencies may be necessary later.

Fiction Crime, hard-boiled fiction. "We want cutting-edge fiction, under 3,000 words with impact." For short stories, query or submit complete ms. For novels, send 1-page query letter with SASE.

Recent Title(s) *Barsom: Edgar Rice Burroughs & the Martian Myth*, by Richard A. Lysoff; *Sherlock Holmes & the Terror Out of Time*, by Ralph Vaughan; *A Trunk Full of Murder*, by Julius Fast.

Tips "We are very particular about novels and book-length work. A first-timer has a better chance with a short story or article. On anything over 4,000 words do not send manuscript, send only query letter with SASE."

HALF HALT PRESS, INC.

P.O. Box 67, Boonsboro MD 21713. (301)733-7119. Fax: (301)733-7408. E-mail: mail@halfhaltpress.com. Website: www.halfhaltpress.com. **Acquisitions:** Elizabeth Carnes, publisher. Estab. 1986. Publishes 90% hardcover and trade paperback originals and 10% reprints. **Publishes 15 titles/year. 25% of books from first-time authors; 50% from unagented writers. Pays 10-12½% royalty on retail price.** Publishes book 1 year after acceptance of ms. Does not accept simultaneous submissions. Responds in 1 month to queries. Book catalog for 6×9 SAE 2 first-class stamps.

  O— "We publish high-quality nonfiction on equestrian topics, books that help riders and trainers do something better."

Nonfiction How-to. Subjects include animals (horses), sports. "We need serious instructional works by authorities in the field on horse-related topics, broadly defined." Query with SASE. Reviews artwork/photos as part of ms package.

Recent Title(s) *Dressage in Harmony*, by Walter Zettl.

Tips "Writers have the best chance selling us well-written, unique works that teach serious horse people how to do something better. If I were a writer trying to market a book today, I would offer a straightforward presentation, letting the work speak for itself, without hype or hard sell. Allow the publisher to contact the writer, without frequent calling to check status. They haven't forgotten the writer but may have many different proposals at hand; frequent calls to 'touch base,' multiplied by the number of submissions, become an annoyance. As the publisher/author relationship becomes close and is based on working well together, early impressions may be important, even to the point of being a consideration in acceptance for publication."

HANSER GARDNER PUBLICATIONS

6915 Valley Ave., Cincinnati OH 45244. (513)527-8894. Fax: (513)527-8801. Website: www.hansergardner.com. **Acquisitions:** Woody Chapman (metalworking—wchapman@gardnerweb.com); Christine Strohm (plastics—cstrohm@gardnerweb.com). Estab. 1993. Publishes hardcover and paperback originals, and digital educational and training programs. **Publishes 10-15 titles/year. Receives 100 queries and 10-20 mss/year. 50% of books from first-time authors; 100% from unagented writers. Pays 10-15% royalty on net receipts.** Publishes book 10 months after acceptance of ms. Accepts simultaneous submissions. Responds in 2 weeks to queries; 1 month to proposals and mss. Book catalog free; ms guidelines online.

  O— Hanser Gardner publishes books and electronic media for the manufacturing (both metalworking and plastics) industries. Publications range from basic training materials to advanced reference books.

Nonfiction "We publish how-to texts, references, and technical books, and computer-based learning materials for the manufacturing industries. Titles include award-winning management books, encyclopedic references, and leading references." Submit outline, sample chapters, résumé, preface, and comparison to competing or similar titles.

Recent Title(s) *Modern Machine Shop's Handbook for the Metalworking Industries*, by W. Chapman; *Polymer Extrusion, 4th Ed.*, by Chris Rauwendaal.

Tips "E-mail submissions speed up response time."

Ⓓ HARCOURT, INC., CHILDREN'S BOOKS DIVISION

525 B St., Suite 1900, San Diego CA 92101. (619)281-6616. Fax: (619)699-6777. Website: www.harcourtbooks. com/htm/childrens_index.asp. Estab. 1919. Publishes hardcover originals and trade paperback reprints.

Imprints Harcourt Children's Books; Gulliver Books; Red Wagon Books; Harcourt Young Classics; Green Light Readers; Voyager Books/Libros Viajeros; Harcourt Paperbacks; Odyssey Classics; Magic Carpet Books; Silver Whistle.

  O— Harcourt, Inc., owns some of the world's most prestigious publishing imprints—imprints which distinguish quality products for the juvenile, educational, scientific, technical, medical, professional and trade markets worldwide.

Nonfiction *No unsolicited mss or queries.* No phone calls.

Fiction Young adult. *No unsolicited mss or queries.* No phone calls.

Recent Title(s) *Harvesting Hope*, by Kathleen Krull, illustrated by Yuyi Morales; *Tails*, by Matthew Van Fleet; *Pinduli*, by Janell Cannon.

Ⓐ ⊘ HARCOURT, INC., TRADE DIVISION

525 B St., Suite 1900, San Diego CA 92101. (619)699-6560. Fax: (619)699-5555. Website: www.harcourtbooks.com. **Acquisitions:** Rebecca Saletan, editor-in-chief; David Hough, managing editor; Drenka Willen, senior editor (poetry, fiction in translation, history); Andrea Schulz (nonfiction, American fiction, history, science); Ann Patty (American fiction); Tim Bent (nonfiction). Also: 15 E. 26th St., New York NY 10010. Publishes hardcover and trade paperback originals and trade paperback reprints. **Publishes 120 titles/year. 5% of books from first-time authors; 5% from unagented writers. Pays 6-15% royalty on retail price. Offers $2,000 minimum advance.** Accepts simultaneous submissions. Book catalog for 9×12 SAE; ms guidelines online.

Imprints Harvest Books (contact Andre Bernard).

O→ Harcourt, Inc., owns some of the world's most prestigious publishing imprints—imprints which distinguish quality products for the juvenile, educational, scientific, technical, medical, professional, and trade markets worldwide. Currently emphasizing science and math.

Nonfiction Biography, children's/juvenile, coffee table book, general nonfiction, gift book, illustrated book, multimedia, reference, technical. Subjects include anthropology/archeology, art/architecture, child guidance/parenting, creative nonfiction, education, ethnic, gay/lesbian, government/politics, health/medicine, history, language/literature, memoirs, military/war, multicultural, philosophy, psychology, religion, science, sociology, spirituality, sports, translation, travel, women's issues/studies. Published all categories except business/finance (university texts), cookbooks, self-help, sex. *No unsolicited mss. Agented submissions only.*

Fiction Historical, mystery, picture books. *Agented submissions only.*

Recent Title(s) *Life of Pi*, by Yann Martel (fiction); *The Time Traveler's Wife*, by Audrey Niffenegger (fiction); *Odd Girl Out*, by Rachel Simmons (nonfiction).

Ⓐ HARPERBUSINESS

Imprint of HarperCollins General Books Group, 10 E. 53rd St., New York NY 10022. (212)207-7000. Website: www.harpercollins.com. Estab. 1991. Publishes hardcover, trade paperback originals and reprints. **Pays royalty on retail price. Offers advance.** Accepts simultaneous submissions.

O→ HarperBusiness publishes "the inside story on ideas that will shape business practices with cutting-edge information and visionary concepts."

Nonfiction Biography (economics). Subjects include business/economics, Marketing subjects. "We don't publish how-to, textbooks or things for academic market; no reference (tax or mortgage guides), our reference department does that. Proposals need to be top notch. We tend not to publish people who have no business standing. Must have business credentials." *Agented submissions only.*

Recent Title(s) *The Flight of the Creative Class*, by Richard Florida; *Fortune Favors the Bold*, by Lester C. Thurow; *Reinventing the Wheel*, by Steve Kemper.

Ⓐ ⊘ HARPERCOLLINS

10 E. 53rd St., New York NY 10022. (212)207-7000. Website: www.harpercollins.com. Publishes hardcover and paperback originals and paperback reprints. **Pays royalty. Offers negotiable advance.**

Imprints **HarperCollins Australia/New Zealand:** Angus & Robertson, Fourth Estate, HarperBusiness, HarperCollins, HarperPerenniel, HarperReligious, HarperSports, Voyager; **HarperCollins Canada:** HarperFlamingoCanada, PerennialCanada; **HarperCollins Children's Books Group:** Amistad, Julie Andrews Collection, Avon, Joanna Cotler Books, Eos, Laura Geringer Books, Greenwillow Books, HarperAudio, HarperCollins Children's Books, HarperFestival, HarperTempest, HarperTrophy, Rayo, Katherine Tegen Books; **HarperCollins General Books Group:** Access, Amistad, Avon, Caedmon, Ecco, Eos, Fourth Estate, HarperAudio, HarperBusiness, HarperCollins, HarperEntertainment, HarperLargePrint, HarperResource, HarperSanFrancisco, HarperTorch, Harper Design International, Perennial, PerfectBound, Quill, Rayo, ReganBooks, William Morrow, William Morrow Cookbooks; **HarperCollins UK:** Collins Bartholomew, Collins, HarperCollins Crime & Thrillers, Collins Freedom to Teach, HarperCollins Children's Books, Thorsons/Element, Voyager Books; **Zondervan:** Inspirio, Vida, Zonderkidz, Zondervan.

O→ "HarperCollins, one of the largest English language publishers in the world, is a broad-based publisher with strengths in academic, business and professional, children's, educational, general interest, and religious and spiritual books, as well as multimedia titles."

Nonfiction *Agented submissions only.*

Fiction Adventure, fantasy, gothic, historical, literary, mystery, science fiction, suspense, western. "We look for a strong story line and exceptional literary talent." *Agented submissions only. All unsolicited mss returned unopened.*

Recent Title(s) *Don't Know Much About Mummies*, by Kenneth C. Davis; *Looking for Jaguar*, by Susan Katz; *Runny Babbit*, by Shel Silverstein.

Tips "We do not accept any unsolicited material."

Ⓐ ⊘ HARPERCOLLINS CHILDREN'S BOOKS GROUP

Imprint of HarperCollins Children's Books Group, 1350 Avenue of the Americas, New York NY 10019. (212)261-6500. Website: www.harperchildrens.com. Publishes hardcover and paperback originals.

Imprints Amistad; Julie Andrews Collection; Avon; Joanna Cotler Books; Eos; Laura Geringer Books; Greenwillow Books; HarperAudio; HarperCollins Children's Books; HarperFestival; HarperTempest; HarperTrophy; Rayo; Katherine Tegen Books.

> �⇥ *No unsolicited mss and/or unagented mss or queries.* "The volume of these submissions is so large that we cannot give them the attention they deserve. Such submissions will not be reviewed or returned."

Nonfiction Picture books, middle grade, young adult, board books, novelty books, TV/Movie tie-ins. *No unsolicited mss or queries. Agented submissions only.*

Fiction Picture books, young adult, chapter books, middle grade, early readers. *Agented submissions only. No unsolicited mss or queries.*

Recent Title(s) *A Dance of Sisters*, by Tracey Porter; *Down the Rabbit Hole*, by Peter Abrahams; *California Holiday*, by Kate Cann.

Ⓐ ⊘ HARPERCOLLINS GENERAL BOOKS GROUP

Division of HarperCollins Publishers, 10 E. 53 St., New York NY 10022. (212)207-7000. Fax: (212)207-7633. Website: www.harpercollins.com.

Imprints Access; Amistad; Avon; Caedmon; Dark Alley; Ecco; Eos; Fourth Estate; HarperAudio; HarperBusiness; HarperCollins; HarperEntertainment; HarperLargePrint; HarperResource; HarperSanFranciso; HarperTorch; Harper Design International; Perennial; PerfectBound; Quill; Rayo; ReganBooks; William Morrow; William Morrow Cookbooks.

> • See website for further details.

Ⓝ HARPERENTERTAINMENT

HarperCollins Publishers, 10 E. 53rd St., New York NY 10022. (212)207-7000. Website: www.harpercollins.com. Estab. 1997.

> o⇥ "HarperEntertainment is dedicated to publishing sports, movie and TV tie-ins, celebrity bios and books reflecting trends in popular culture."

Nonfiction Biography, children's/juvenile, humor, Movie and TV tie-ins. Subjects include film/cinema/stage, humor. "The bulk of our work is done by experienced writers for hire, but we are open to original ideas." Query with SASE.

Fiction Humor, juvenile, Movie and TV tie-ins. Query with SASE.

Recent Title(s) *Chore Whore*, by Heather H. Howard; *Dizzy*, by Donald L. Maggin; *Thoroughbred #71: Calamity Jinx*, by Joanna Campbell.

Tips "We are demanding about the quality of proposals; in addition to strong writing skills and thorough knowledge of the subject matter, we require a detailed analysis of the competition."

⊘ HARPERSANFRANCISCO

Imprint of HarperCollins General Books Group, 353 Sacramento St., Suite 500, San Francisco CA 94111-3653. (415)477-4400. Fax: (415)477-4444. E-mail: hcsanfrancisco@harpercollins.com. **Acquisitions:** Michael Maudlin, editorial director (Christian spirituality, religious history and biography, Biblical studies); Eric Brandt, senior editor (world religions, politics/current events and religion, biblical studies, sciene/psychology and religion); Gideon Weil, senior editor (gift/inspiration, self-help, history, biography and current events which include prominent religious themes, inspirational or transformational fiction, Buddhism, Judaica); Renee Sedliar, editor (fiction and narrative nonfiction with religious/spiritual or inspirational focus, self-help, gift/inspiration, religion and culture—especially women's interest). Estab. 1977. Publishes hardcover originals, trade paperback originals and reprints. **Publishes 75 titles/year. 5% of books from first-time authors. Pays royalty. Offers advance.** Publishes book within 18 months after acceptance of ms.

> o⇥ HarperSanFrancisco "strives to be the preeminent publisher of the most important books across the full spectrum of religion and spiritual literature, adding to the wealth of the world's wisdom by respecting all traditions."

Nonfiction Biography, how-to, reference, self-help. Subjects include psychology (inspiration), religion, spirituality. *No unsolicited mss.*

Recent Title(s) *The Gift of Change*, by Marianne Williamson; *In Search of Paul*, by Dominic Crossan and Jonathan Reed; *The Heart of Christianity*, by Marcus Borg.

HARVARD BUSINESS SCHOOL PRESS

Imprint of Harvard Business School Publishing Corp., 60 Harvard Way, Boston MA 02163. (617)783-7400. Fax: (617)783-7489. E-mail: bookpublisher@hbsp.harvard.edu. Website: www.hbsp.harvard.edu. Director: David Goehring. **Acquisitions:** Hollis Heimbouch, editorial director; Kirsten Sandberg, executive editor; Melinda Adams Merino, executive editor; Jeff Kehoe, senior editor; Jacque Murphy, senior editor; Astrid Sandoval, associate editor. Estab. 1984. Publishes hardcover originals and several paperback series. **Publishes 40-50 titles/year. Pays escalating royalty on retail price. Advances vary widely depending on author and market for the book.** Accepts simultaneous submissions. Responds in 1 month. Book catalog and ms guidelines online.

> ⚓ The Harvard Business School Press publishes books for senior and general managers and business scholars. HBS Press is the source of the most influential ideas and conversations that shape business worldwide.

Nonfiction Trade and professional. Subjects include business, general management, strategy, leadership, marketing, technology management and innovation, human resources. Submit proposal package including outline, sample chapters.

Recent Title(s) *The Innovator's Solution*, by Clayton Christense and Michael Raynor; *Why Not?*, by Barry Nalebuff and Ian Ayres; *Changing Minds*, by Howard Gardner.

Tips "Take care to look into the type of business books we publish. They are generally not policy-oriented, dissertations, or edited collections."

THE HARVARD COMMON PRESS

535 Albany St., Boston MA 02118-2500. (617)423-5803. Fax: (617)695-9794. Website: www.harvardcommonpress.com. Publisher/President: Bruce P. Shaw. **Acquisitions:** Valerie Cimino, executive editor. Estab. 1976. Publishes hardcover and trade paperback originals and reprints. **Publishes 16 titles/year. 20% of books from first-time authors; 40% from unagented writers. Pays royalty. Offers average $4,000 advance.** Publishes book 1 year after acceptance of ms. Accepts simultaneous submissions. Responds in 2 months to queries. Book catalog for 9×12 SAE with 3 first-class stamps; ms guidelines for #10 SASE or online.

Imprints Gambit Books.

> ⚓ "We want strong, practical books that help people gain control over a particular area of their lives." Currently emphasizing cooking, child care/parenting, health. De-emphasizing general instructional books, travel.

Nonfiction Subjects include child guidance/parenting, cooking/foods/nutrition, health/medicine. "A large percentage of our list is made up of books about cooking, child care, and parenting; in these areas we are looking for authors who are knowledgeable, if not experts, and who can offer a different approach to the subject. We are open to good nonfiction proposals that show evidence of strong organization and writing, and clearly demonstrate a need in the marketplace. First-time authors are welcome." Submit outline, 1-3 sample chapters. Reviews artwork/photos as part of ms package.

Recent Title(s) *Icebox Desserts*, by Lauren Chattman; *Pie*, by Ken Haedrich; *Not Your Mother's Slow Cooker Cookbook*, by Beth Hensperger and Julie Kaufmann.

Tips "We are demanding about the quality of proposals; in addition to strong writing skills and thorough knowledge of the subject matter, we require a detailed analysis of the competition."

🄰 ⊘ HARVEST HOUSE PUBLISHERS

990 Owen Loop N., Eugene OR 97402. (541)343-0123. Fax: (541)302-0731. Website: www.harvesthousepublishers.com. Estab. 1974. Publishes hardcover, trade paperback, and mass market paperback originals and reprints. **Publishes 160 titles/year. Receives 1,500 queries and 1,000 mss/year. 1% of books from first-time authors; 5% from unagented writers. Pays royalty.** Book catalog free.

Nonfiction Reference, self-help. Subjects include anthropology/archeology, business/economics, child guidance/parenting, health/medicine, money/finance, religion, women's issues/studies, Bible studies. *No unsolicited mss. Agented submissions only.*

Fiction *No unsolicited mss, proposals, or artwork. Agented submissions only.*

Recent Title(s) *Power of a Praying Husband*, by Stormie Omartial (Christian living); *Life Management for Busy Women*, by Elizabeth George (Christian living); *After Anne*, by Roxanne Henke (relationship).

Tips "For first time/nonpublished authors we suggest building their literary résumé by submitting to magazines, or perhaps accruing book contributions."

HASTINGS HOUSE/DAYTRIPS PUBLISHERS

(formerly Hastings House), LINI LLC, 2601 Wells Ave., Suite 161, Fern Park FL 32730-2000. (407)339-3600. Fax: (407)339-5900. E-mail: hastings_daytrips@earthlink.net. Website: www.hastingshousebooks.com. Publisher: Peter Leers. **Acquisitions:** Earl Steinbicker, senior travel editor (edits Daytrips Series). Publishes trade paperback originals and reprints. **Publishes 20 titles/year. Receives 600 queries and 900 mss/year. 10% of books** from first-time authors; 40% from unagented writers. Pays 8-10% royalty on net receipts.** Publishes book 6-10 months after acceptance of ms. Responds in 2 months to queries.

    O→ "We are primarily focused on expanding our Daytrips Travel Series (facts/guide) nationally and internationally." Currently de-emphasizing all other subjects.

Nonfiction Subjects include travel. Submit outline. Query.

Recent Title(s) *Daytrips Eastern Australia*, by James Postell; *Daytrips Italy*, by Earl Steinbicker (5th edition); *Daytrips Scotland & Wales*, by Judith Frances Duddle.

HAWK PUBLISHING GROUP

7107 S. Yale Ave., #345, Tulsa OK 74136. (918)492-3677. Fax: (918)492-2120. Website: www.hawkpub.com. Estab. 1999. Publishes hardcover and trade paperback originals. **Publishes 6-8 titles/year. 25% of books from first-time authors; 50% from unagented writers. Pays royalty.** Publishes book 1-2 years after acceptance of ms. Accepts simultaneous submissions. Ms guidelines online.

    O→ "Please visit our website and read the submission guidelines before sending anything to us. The best way to learn what might interest us is to visit the website, read the information there, look at the books, and perhaps even read a few of them."

Nonfiction Looking for subjects of broad appeal and interest.

Fiction Looking for good books of all kinds. Not interested in juvenile, poetry, or short story collections. Does not want childrens or young adult books. Submissions will not be returned, so send only copies. No SASE. No submissions by e-mail or by "certified mail or any other service that requires a signature." Replies "only if interested. If you have not heard from us within 3 months after the receipt of your submission, you may safely assume that we were not able to find a place for it in our list."

Recent Title(s) *The Darkest Night*, by Jodie Larsen; *Mama Used to Say*, by Hannibal B. Johnson; *Bury My Heart at Redtree*, by Patrick Chalfant.

▲ HAY HOUSE, INC.

P.O. Box 5100, Carlsbad CA 92018-5100. (760)431-7695. Fax: (760)431-6948. E-mail: slittrell@hayhouse.com. Website: www.hayhouse.com. Editorial Director: Jill Kramer. **Acquisitions:** Shannon Littrell, acquisitions editor. Estab. 1985. Publishes hardcover and trade paperback originals. **Publishes 50 titles/year. Pays standard royalty.** Publishes book 14-16 months after acceptance of ms. Accepts simultaneous submissions. Responds in 2 months to mss. No e-mail submissions; ms guidelines online.

Imprints Astro Room; Hay House Lifestyles; New Beginnings Press; Smiley Books.

    O→ "We publish books, audios, and videos that help heal the planet."

Nonfiction Biography, self-help. Subjects include cooking/foods/nutrition, education, health/medicine, money/finance, nature/environment, New Age, philosophy, psychology, sociology, women's issues/studies. "Hay House is interested in a variety of subjects as long as they have a positive self-help slant to them. No poetry, children's books, or negative concepts that are not conducive to helping/healing ourselves or our planet." *Agented submissions only.*

Recent Title(s) *The Mommy Chronicles*, by Sara Ellington and Stephanie Triplett.

Tips "Our audience is concerned with our planet, the healing properties of love, and general self-help principles. If I were a writer trying to market a book today, I would research the market thoroughly to make sure there weren't already too many books on the subject I was interested in writing about. Then I would make sure I had a unique slant on my idea. SASE a must! Simultaneous submissions from agents must include SASEs. No e-mail submissions."

HAZELDEN PUBLISHING AND EDUCATIONAL SERVICES

P.O. Box 176, Center City MN 55012. (651)257-4010. Website: www.hazelden.org. Editorial Director: Rebecca Post. Estab. 1954. Publishes trade paperback originals and educational materials (videos, workbooks, pamphlets, etc.) for treatment centers, schools, hospitals, and correctional institutions. **Publishes 100 titles/year. Receives 2,500 queries and 2,000 mss/year. 30% of books from first-time authors; 50% from unagented writers. Pays 8% royalty on retail price. Offers variable advance.** Publishes book 1 year after acceptance of ms. Accepts simultaneous submissions. Responds in 6 months to queries. Book catalog and ms guidelines online.

    O→ Hazelden is a trade, educational and professional publisher specializing is psychology, self-help, and spiritual books that help enhance the quality of people's lives. Products include gift books, curriculum, workbooks, audio and video, computer-based products, and wellness products. "We specialize in books on addiction/recovery, spirituality/personal growth, and prevention topics related to chemical and mental health."

Nonfiction How-to, multimedia, self-help. Subjects include child guidance/parenting, memoirs, psychology, sex (sexual addiction), spirituality, addiction/recovery, eating disorders, codependency/family issues. Query with SASE.

Recent Title(s) *When Painkillers Become Dangerous*, by Drew Pinsky, MD, et al; *Get Me Out of Here: My Recovery From Borderline Personality Disorder*, by Rachel Reiland; *Little Book of Big Emotions*, by Erika M. Hunter.

Tips Audience includes ''consumers and professionals interested in the range of topics related to chemical and emotional health, including spirituality, self-help, and addiction recovery.''

HEALTH COMMUNICATIONS, INC.

3201 SW 15th St., Deerfield Beach FL 33442. (954)360-0909. Fax: (954)360-0034. Website: www.hcibooks.com. **Acquisitions:** Bret Witter, editorial director; Allison Janse, executive editor; Amy Hughes, religion editor; Elisabeth Rinaldi, editor. Estab. 1976. Publishes hardcover and trade paperback nonfiction only. **Publishes 50 titles/ year.** Responds in 3 months. Ms guidelines online.

> O⃞ ''We are the Life Issues Publisher. Health Communications, Inc., strives to help people grow and improve their lives, from physical and emotional health to finances and interpersonal relationships.''

Nonfiction Self-help. Subjects include child guidance/parenting, health/medicine, psychology, women's issues/ studies.

Recent Title(s) *How to Be Like Women of Influence*, by Pat Williams; *A Teen's Guide to Christian Living*, by Bettie Youngs; *How Not to Be My Patient*, by Edward T. Creagan, MD.

HEALTH PRESS

P.O. Box 37470, Albuquerque NM 87176. (505)888-1394. Fax: (505)888-1521. E-mail: goodbooks@healthpress.com. Website: www.healthpress.com. **Acquisitions:** K. Frazer, editor. Estab. 1988. Publishes hardcover and trade paperback originals. **Publishes 8 titles/year. 90% of books from first-time authors; 90% from unagented writers. Pays standard royalty on wholesale price.** Publishes book 1 year after acceptance of ms. Accepts simultaneous submissions. Responds in 3 months to proposals. Book catalog free; ms guidelines online.

> O⃞ Health Press publishes books by healthcare professionals on cutting-edge patient education topics.

Nonfiction How-to, reference, self-help, textbook. Subjects include education, health/medicine. Submit proposal package including outline, 3 complete sample chapters, résumé. Reviews artwork/photos as part of ms package. Send photocopies.

Recent Title(s) *Keeping a Secret: A Story About Juvenile Rheumatoid Arthritis*; *Peanut Butter Jam: A Story About Peanut Allergy*; *Health and Nutrition Secrets*.

HEALTH PROFESSIONS PRESS

P.O. Box 10624, Baltimore MD 21285-0624. (410)337-9585. Fax: (410)337-8539. E-mail: acquis@healthpropress. com. Website: www.healthpropress.com. **Acquisitions:** Mary Magnus, director of publications (aging, long-term care, health administration). Publishes hardcover and trade paperback originals. **Publishes 6-8 titles/ year. Receives 70 queries and 12 mss/year. 50% of books from first-time authors; 100% from unagented writers. Pays 8-18% royalty on wholesale price.** Publishes book 10 months after acceptance of ms. Accepts simultaneous submissions. Responds in 1 month to queries; 3 months to proposals; 4 months to mss. Book catalog free or online; ms guidelines online.

> O⃞ ''We are a specialty publisher. Our primary audiences are professionals, students, and educated consumers interested in topics related to aging and eldercare.''

Nonfiction How-to, reference, self-help, textbook. Subjects include health/medicine, psychology. Query with SASE, or submit proposal package including outline, 1-2 sample chapters, résumé, cover letter.

Recent Title(s) *The Best Friends Book of Alzheimer's Activities*; *The Caring Spirit Approach to Eldercare: A Training Guide for Professionals and Families*; *Ethics in Health Services Management, 4th Ed.*

WILLIAM S. HEIN & CO., INC.

1285 Main St., Buffalo NY 14209-1987. (716)882-2600. Fax: (716)883-8100. E-mail: mail@wshein.com. Website: www.wshein.com. **Acquisitions:** Sheila Jarrett, publications manager. Estab. 1961. **Publishes 50 titles/year. Receives 80 queries and 40 mss/year. 20% of books from first-time authors; 100% from unagented writers. Pays 10-20% royalty on net price.** Publishes book 9 months after acceptance of ms. Accepts simultaneous submissions. Responds in 2 months to queries. Book catalog online; ms guidelines for #10 SASE.

> O⃞ William S. Hein & Co. publishes reference books for law librarians, legal researchers, and those interested in legal writing. Currently emphasizing legal research, legal writing, and legal education.

Nonfiction Law, reference, scholarly. Subjects include education, government/politics, women's issues/studies, world affairs, legislative histories.

Recent Title(s) *1000 Days to the Bar*, by Dennis J. Tonsing; *Librarian's Copyright Companion*, by James S. Heller.

HEINEMANN

Reed Elsevier (USA) Inc., 361 Hanover St., Portsmouth NH 03801-3912. (603)431-7894. Fax: (603)431-7840. E-mail: proposals@heinemann.com. Website: www.heinemann.com. Estab. 1977. Publishes hardcover and trade paperback originals. **Publishes 80-100 titles/year. 50% of books from first-time authors; 75% from unagented writers. Pays royalty on wholesale price. Offers variable advance.** Does not accept simultaneous submissions. Responds in 6-8 weeks to proposals. Book catalog free; ms guidelines online.

Imprints Boynton/Cook Publishers.

O→ Heinemann specializes in professional resources for educators and theater professionals. "Our goal is to offer a wide selecton of books that satisfy the needs and interests of educators from kindergarten to college." Currently emphasizing literacy education, social studies, mathematics, science, K-12 education through technology, drama and drama education.

Nonfiction "Our goal is to provide books that represent leading ideas within our niche markets. We publish very strictly within our categories. We do not publish classroom textbooks." Query with SASE, or submit proposal package including outline, 1-2 sample chapters, TOC.

Recent Title(s) *Word Matters*, by Irene Fountas and Gay-Su Pinnell.

Tips "Keep your queries (and manuscripts!) short, study the market, be realistic and prepared to promote your book."

⊘ HELLGATE PRESS

P.O. Box 3531, Ashland OR 97520. (541)855-5566. E-mail: harley@hellgatepress.com. Website: www.hellgatepress.com. **Acquisitions:** Harley B. Patrick, editor. Estab. 1996. **Publishes 15-20 titles/year. Pays royalty.** Publishes book 6-8 months after acceptance of ms. Responds in 2 months to queries.

O→ Hellgate Press specializes in military history, other military topics, and travel adventure.

Nonfiction Subjects include history, memoirs, military/war, travel adventure. Query/proposal only with SASE or by e-mail. *Do not send mss.* Reviews artwork/photos as part of ms package. Send photocopies.

Recent Title(s) *XVIII Airborne Corps in Desert Storm*, by Charles Lane Toomey; *Charlie Battery*, by Andrew Lubin; *My Life in Capitals*, by Bobbie Bergesen.

HENDRICKSON PUBLISHERS, INC.

140 Summit St., P.O. Box 3473, Peabody MA 01961-3473. Fax: (978)531-8146. E-mail: editorial@hendrickson.com. **Acquisitions:** Shirley Decker-Lucke, editorial director. Estab. 1983. Publishes trade reprints and scholarly material in the areas of New Testament; Hebrew Bible; religion and culture; patristics; Judaism; and practical, historical, and Biblical theology. **Publishes 35 titles/year. Receives 600 queries/year. 10% of books from first-time authors; 90% from unagented writers.** Publishes book an average of 1 year after acceptance of ms. Does not accept simultaneous submissions. Responds in 2 months to queries. Book catalog and ms guidelines for #10 SASE.

O→ Hendrickson is an academic publisher of books that "give insight into Bible understanding (academically) and encourage spiritual growth (popular trade)." Currently emphasizing Biblical helps and reference, ministerial helps, Biblical studies and de-emphasizing fiction and biography.

Nonfiction Reference. Subjects include religion. "We will consider any quality manuscript specifically related to Biblical studies and related fields." Submit outline, sample chapters, and CV.

Recent Title(s) *Getting the Gospels*, by Steven L. Bridge.

JOSEPH HENRY PRESS

National Academy Press, 500 5th St., NW, Lockbox 285, Washington DC 20001. (202)334-3336. Fax: (202)334-2793. E-mail: jrobbins@nas.edu. Website: www.jhpress.org. **Acquisitions:** Jeffrey Robbins, senior editor. Publishes hardcover and trade paperback originals. **Publishes 15-20 titles/year. Receives 200 queries and 60 mss/year. 30% of books from first-time authors; 50% from unagented writers. Pays standard trade book list-price royalties. Offers occasional, varying royalty advance.** Publishes book 1 year after acceptance of ms. Accepts simultaneous submissions. Responds in 1 month to queries.

● Submit to: Jeffrey Robbins, senior editor, The Joseph Henry Press, 4701 Willard Ave. #1731, Chevy Chase MD 02148. (301)654-5188. Fax: (301)654-8931.

O→ "The Joseph Henry Press seeks manuscripts in general science and technology that will appeal to young scientists and established professionals or to interested lay readers within the overall categories of science, technology and health. We'll be looking at everything from astrophysics to the environment to nutrition."

Nonfiction Technical. Subjects include health/medicine, nature/environment, psychology, technology, nutrition, physical sciences. Submit proposal package including author bio, TOC, prospectus (via mail or e-mail), SASE.

Recent Title(s) *Prime Obsession: Berhard Riemann and the Greatest Unsolved Problem in Mathematics*, by John

Derbyshire; *Einstein Defiant: Genius Versus Genius in the Quantum Revolution*, by Edmund Blair Bolles; *Mendel in the Kitchen: A Scientist's View of Genetically Modified Foods*, by Nina V. Fedoroff and Nancy Marie Brown.

HERITAGE BOOKS, INC.

65 E. Main St., Westminster MD 21157. (410)876-0371. E-mail: submissions@heritagebooks.com. **Acquisitions:** Editorial Director. Estab. 1978. Publishes hardcover and paperback originals and reprints. **Publishes 200 titles/ year. 25% of books from first-time authors; 100% from unagented writers. Pays 10% royalty on list price.** Accepts simultaneous submissions. Responds in 3 months to queries. Book catalog and ms guidelines free.

    O—¬ "Our goal is to celebrate life by exploring all aspects of American life: settlement, development, wars, and other significant events, including family histories, memoirs, etc." Currently emphasizing early American life, early wars and conflicts, ethnic studies.

Nonfiction Biography, how-to (genealogical, historical), reference, scholarly. Subjects include Americana, ethnic (origins and research guides), history, memoirs, military/war, regional (history). Query with SASE. Submit outline via e-mail. Reviews artwork/photos as part of ms package.

Fiction Historical (relating to early American life, 1600-1900). Query with SASE. Submit outline via e-mail.

Tips "The quality of the book is of prime importance; next is its relevance to our fields of interest."

HIDDENSPRING

997 Macarthur Blvd., Mahwah NJ 07430. (201)825-7300. Fax: (201)825-8345. Website: www.hiddenspringbook s.com. **Acquisitions:** Paul McMahon, managing editor (nonfiction/spirituality). Publishes hardcover and trade paperback originals and reprints. **Publishes 10-12 titles/year. 5% of books from first-time authors; 10% from unagented writers. Royalty varies. Offers variable advance.** Accepts simultaneous submissions. Responds in 2 months to queries.

    O—¬ "Books should always have a spiritual angle—nonfiction with a spiritual twist."

Nonfiction Biography, self-help. Subjects include Americana, anthropology/archeology, art/architecture, creative nonfiction, ethnic, history, multicultural, psychology, religion, travel. Submit proposal package including outline, 1 sample chapter, SASE.

Recent Title(s) *The Spiritual Traveler: Boston and New England*, by Jana Riess; *Christian Mystics*, by Ursula King; *Tolkien and C.S. Lewis*, by Colin Duriez.

HILL AND WANG

Farrar Straus & Giroux, Inc., 19 Union Square W., New York NY 10003. (212)741-6900. Fax: (212)633-9385. Website: www.fsgbooks.com. **Acquisitions:** Thomas LeBien, publisher; Elisabeth Sifton, editor. Estab. 1956. Publishes hardcover and trade paperbacks. **Publishes 12 titles/year. Receives 1,500 queries/year. 50% of books from first-time authors; 50% from unagented writers. Pays 10% royalty on retail price to 5,000 copies sold, 12½% to 10,000 copies, 15% thereafter on hardcover; 7½% on retail price for paperback.** Publishes book 1 year after acceptance of ms. Accepts simultaneous submissions. Book catalog free.

    O—¬ Hill and Wang publishes serious nonfiction books, primarily in history and the social sciences. "We are not considering new fiction, drama, or poetry."

Nonfiction Subjects include government/politics, history (American). Submit outline, sample chapters. SASE and a letter explaining rationale for book.

HILL STREET PRESS

191 E. Broad St., Suite 209, Athens GA 30601-2848. (706)613-7200. Fax: (706)613-7204. E-mail: editorial@hillstr eetpress.com. Website: www.hillstreetpress.com. **Acquisitions:** Judy Long, editor-in-chief. Estab. 1998. Publishes hardcover originals, trade paperback originals and reprints. **Publishes 20 titles/year. Receives 300 queries/year. 5% of books from first-time authors; 2% from unagented writers. Pays 9-12½% royalty on wholesale price.** Publishes book 1 year after acceptance of ms. Accepts simultaneous submissions. Responds in 1 month to queries; 3 months to proposals; 6 months to mss. Book catalog and ms guidelines online.

    O—¬ "HSP is a Southern regional press. While we are not a scholarly or academic press, our nonfiction titles must meet the standards of research for an exacting general audience."

Nonfiction Biography, coffee table book, cookbook, gift book, humor, illustrated book. Subjects include Americana, cooking/foods/nutrition, creative nonfiction, gardening, gay/lesbian, history, memoirs, nature/environment, recreation, regional (Southern), sports, travel. Submit proposal package including outline, 3 sample chapters, résumé.

Fiction Must have a strong connection with the American South. Gay/lesbian, historical, humor, literary, mainstream/contemporary, military/war, regional (southern US), religious, sports, African-American. "Reasonable length projects (50,000-85,000 words) stand a far better chance of review. Do not submit proposals for works in excess of 125,000 words in length." No short stories. "No cornball moonlight-and-magnolia stuff."

Query with SASE, or submit proposal package including 3 sample chapters, résumé, synopsis, press clips. "Let us know at the point of submission if you are represented by an agent."

Recent Title(s) *Strange Birds in the Tree of Heaven*, by Karen Salyer McElmurray (literary fiction); *The Worst Day of My Life, So Far*, by M.A. Harper (literary fiction); *How I Learned to Snap* (memoir).

Tips "Audience is discerning with an interest in the fiction, history, current issues, and food of the American South"

HIPPOCRENE BOOKS, INC.

171 Madison Ave., New York NY 10016. (212)685-4371. Fax: (212)779-9338. E-mail: hippocrene.books@verizon.net. Website: www.hippocrenebooks.com. President/Publisher: George Blagowidow. **Acquisitions:** Rebecca Cole, editor (food and wine); Robert Martin, editor (foreign language, dictionaries, language guides); Sophie Fels, editor (history, nonfiction). Estab. 1971. Publishes hardcover and trade paperback originals. **Publishes 60-80 titles/year. 10% of books from first-time authors; 95% from unagented writers. Pays 6-10% royalty on retail price. Offers $1,500 advance.** Publishes book 16 months after acceptance of ms. Accepts simultaneous submissions. Responds in 2 months to queries. Book catalog for 9×12 SAE with 5 first-class stamps; ms guidelines for #10 SASE.

> ⚬┯ "We focus on ethnic-interest and language-related titles, particularly on less frequently published languages and often overlooked cultures." Currently emphasizing concise foreign language dictionaries.

Nonfiction Biography, cookbook, reference. Subjects include cooking/foods/nutrition, ethnic, history, language/literature, military/war, multicultural, travel. No contemporary fiction or memoir. Submit proposal package including outline, 2 sample chapters, TOC.

Recent Title(s) *Yoruba Practical Dictionary*; *A History of the Islamic World*; *Secrets of Colombian Cooking*.

Tips "Our recent successes in publishing general books considered midlist by larger publishers are making us more of a general trade publisher. We continue to do well with reference books like dictionaries and other language related titles. We ask for proposal, sample chapter, and TOC. If we are interested, we will reply with a request for more material."

HOHM PRESS

P.O. Box 31, Prescott AZ 86302. (800)381-2700. Fax: (928)717-1779. Website: www.hohmpress.com. **Acquisitions:** Regina Sara Ryan, managing editor. Estab. 1975. Publishes hardcover and trade paperback originals. **Publishes 6-8 titles/year. 50% of books from first-time authors. Pays 10% royalty on net sales.** Publishes book 18 months after acceptance of ms. Accepts simultaneous submissions. Responds in 3 months to queries.

> ⚬┯ Hohm Press publishes a range of titles in the areas of transpersonal psychology and spirituality, herbistry, alternative health methods, and nutrition. Currently emphasizing health alternatives. Not interested in personal health survival stories.

Nonfiction Subjects include health/medicine (natural/alternative health), philosophy, religion (Hindu, Buddhist, Sufi, or translations of classic texts in major religious traditions), yoga. "We look for writers who have an established record in their field of expertise. The best buy of recent years came from 2 women who fully substantiated how they could market their book. We believed they could do it. We were right." Query with SASE. No e-mail inquiries, please.

Poetry "We are not accepting poetry at this time except for translations of recognized religious/spiritual classics."

HOLIDAY HOUSE, INC.

425 Madison Ave., New York NY 10017. (212)688-0085. Fax: (212)421-6134. Editor-in-Chief: Regina Griffin. Estab. 1935. Publishes hardcover originals and paperback reprints. **Publishes 60 titles/year. 2-5% of books from first-time authors; 50% from unagented writers. Pays royalty on list price, range varies. Offers Flexible, depending on whether the book is illustrated. advance.** Publishes book 1-2 years after acceptance of ms. Does not accept simultaneous submissions. Ms guidelines for #10 SASE.

> ⚬┯ Holiday House publishes children's and young adult books for the school and library markets. "We have a commitment to publishing first-time authors and illustrators. We specialize in quality hardcovers from picture books to young adult, both fiction and nonfiction, primarily for the school and library market." Currently emphasizing literary middle-grade novels.

Nonfiction Subjects include Americana, history, science, Judaica. Query with SASE. Reviews artwork/photos as part of ms package. Send photocopies—no originals—to Jacquline Byrne, editorial assistant.

Fiction Adventure, historical, humor, literary, mainstream/contemporary, Judaica and holiday, animal stories for young readers. Children's books only. Query with SASE. "No phone calls, please."

Recent Title(s) *In Defense of Liberty: The Story of America's Bill of Rights*, by Russell Freedman; *Blues Journey*, by Walter Dean Myers, illustrated by Christopher Myers.

Tips "We need novels with strong stories and writing. We do not publish board books or novelties."

HENRY HOLT & CO. BOOKS FOR YOUNG READERS

Imprint of Henry Holt & Co., LLC, 115 W. 18th St., New York NY 10011. (212)886-9200. Website: www.henryhol t.com. Vice President, Publisher and Editorial Director: Laura Godwin. Executive Editor: Christy Ottaviano. Editor-at-Large: Nina Ignatowicz. Editor: Reka Simonsen. Editor: Kate Farrell. **Acquisitions:** Submissions Editor. Estab. 1866 (Holt). Publishes hardcover originals of picture books, chapter books, middle grade and young adult novels. **Publishes 70-80 titles/year. 10% of books from first-time authors; 50% from unagented writers. Pays royalty on retail price. Offers $3,000 and up advance.** Publishes book 18-36 months after acceptance of ms. Does not accept simultaneous submissions. Responds in 4-5 months to queries. Book catalog for 8½ × 11 SAE with $1.75 postage; ms guidelines online.

    O→ ''Henry Holt Books for Young Readers publishes highly original and cutting-edge fiction and nonfiction for all ages, from the very young to the young adult.''

Nonfiction Children's/juvenile, illustrated book. Submit complete ms.

Fiction Adventure, fantasy, historical, mainstream/contemporary, multicultural, picture books, young adult. Juvenile: adventure, animal, contemporary, fantasy, history, multicultural. Picture books: animal, concept, history, mulitcultural, sports. Young adult: contemporary, fantasy, history, multicultural, nature/environment, problem novels, sports. Submit complete ms.

Recent Title(s) *Hondo and Fabian*, by Peter McCarty; *Keeper of the Night*, by Kimberly Willis Holt.

⊘ HENRY HOLT & CO. LLC

Holtzbrinck Publishers, 115 W. 18th St., New York NY 10011. (212)886-9200. Fax: (212)633-0748. Website: www.henryholt.com. Estab. 1866. Does not accept simultaneous submissions.

Imprints Books for Young Readers; John Macrae Books; Metropolitan Books; Owl Books; Times Books.

    • *Does not accept unsolicited queries or mss.*

    O→ Holt is a general-interest publisher of quality fiction and nonfiction.

Recent Title(s) *The Many Lives of Marilyn Monroe*, by Sarah Churchwell; *Science Fiction: Where the Known Meets the Unknown*, by Michael Shermer; *American Mafia: A History of Its Rise to Power*, by Thomas Reppetto.

HOMA & SEKEY BOOKS

P.O. Box 103, Dumont NJ 07628. (201)384-6692. Fax: (201)384-6055. E-mail: info@homabooks.com. Submissions E-mail: submission@homabooks.com. Website: www.homabooks.com. **Acquisitions:** Shawn Ye, editor (fiction and nonfiction). Estab. 1997. Publishes hardcover originals and trade paperback originals and reprints. **Publishes 10 titles/year. Receives 300-500 queries and 100-200 mss/year. 50% of books from first-time authors; 90% from unagented writers. Pays 5-10% royalty on retail price.** Publishes book 1 year after acceptance of ms. Accepts simultaneous submissions. Responds in 2 months to queries; 3 months to proposals; 4 months to mss. Book catalog and ms guidelines online.

Nonfiction Autobiography, biography, coffee table book, general nonfiction, illustrated book, reference, scholarly, textbook. Subjects include alternative lifestyles, art/architecture, business/economics, contemporary culture, creative nonfiction, ethnic, health/medicine, history, language/literature, memoirs, multicultural, New Age, photography, social sciences, translation, travel, world affairs. ''We publish books on Asian topics. Books should have something to do with Asia.'' Submit proposal package including outline, 2 sample chapters, or submit complete ms. Reviews artwork/photos as part of ms package. Send photocopies.

Fiction Adventure, ethnic, feminist, historical, literary, multicultural, mystery, plays, poetry, poetry in translation, romance, short story collections, young adult. ''We publish books on Asian topics. Books should be Asia-related.'' Submit proposal package including 2 sample chapters, synopsis, or submit complete ms.

Poetry ''We publish books on Asian topics. Poetry should have things to do with Asia.'' Submit complete ms.

Recent Title(s) *The Haier Way: The Making of a Chinese Business Leader and a Global Brand*, by Dr. Jeannie Yi; *Father and Son*, by Han Sung-won (novel); *Selected Short Stories*, by Korean women writers (Korean translation).

Tips General readership with a leaning on Asian cultures. ''Authors should be willing to participate in publicity and promotion activities.''

Ⓐ ⊘ HONOR BOOKS

Cook Communications Ministries, 4050 Lee Vance View, Colorado Springs CO 80918. (719)536-0100. E-mail: info@honorbooks.com. Website: www.honorbooks.com. Publishes hardcover and trade paperback originals. **Pays royalty on wholesale price, makes outright purchase or assigns work for hire. Offers negotiable advance.**

    • Currently closed to book proposals.

    O→ ''We are a Christian publishing house with a mission to inspire and encourage people to draw near to God and to enjoy His love and grace. We are no longer accepting unsolicited mss from writers.'' Currently emphasizing humor, personal and spiritual growth, children's books, devotions, personal stories.

Nonfiction Subjects include religion, motivation, devotionals. Subjects are geared toward the "felt needs" of people. No autobiographies or teaching books.

Recent Title(s) *Welcome Home*, by Liz Cowen Furman; *Breakfast for the Soul*, by Judy Couchman.

Tips "Our books are for busy, achievement-oriented people who are looking for a balance between reaching their goals and knowing that God loves them unconditionally. Our books encourage spiritual growth, joyful living and intimacy with God. Write about what you are for and not what you are against. We look for scripts that are biblically based and which inspire readers."

HOUGHTON MIFFLIN BOOKS FOR CHILDREN

Imprint of Houghton Mifflin Trade & Reference Division, 222 Berkeley St., Boston MA 02116. (617)351-5959. Fax: (617)351-1111. E-mail: children's_books@hmco.com. Website: www.houghtonmifflinbooks.com. **Acquisitions:** Hannah Rodgers, editorial associate; Ann Rider, Margaret Raymo, Eden Edwards, senior editors; Kate O'Sullivan, editor. Publishes hardcover originals and trade paperback originals and reprints. **Publishes 100 titles/year. Receives 5,000 queries and 14,000 mss/year. 10% of books from first-time authors; 60% from unagented writers. Pays 5-10% royalty on retail price. Offers variable advance.** Publishes book 18-24 months after acceptance of ms. Accepts simultaneous submissions. Responds in 4 months to queries. Book catalog for 9×12 SASE with 3 first-class stamps; ms guidelines online.

Imprints Sandpiper Paperback Books; Graphia (Eden Edwards, senior editor).

- Does not respond to or return mss unless interested.
- "Houghton Mifflin gives shape to ideas that educate, inform, and above all, delight."

Nonfiction Biography, children's/juvenile, humor, illustrated book. Subjects include animals, anthropology/archeology, art/architecture, ethnic, history, language/literature, music/dance, nature/environment, science, sports. Interested in innovative books and subjects about which the author is passionate. Query with SASE, or submit sample chapters, synopsis. Reviews artwork/photos as part of ms package. Send photocopies.

Fiction Adventure, ethnic, historical, humor, juvenile (early readers), literary, mystery, picture books, suspense, young adult, board books. Submit complete ms with appropriate-sized SASE.

Recent Title(s) *The Red Book*, by Barbara Lehman; *Actual Size*, by Steve Jenkins; *Remember*, by Toni Morrison.

Tips "Faxed or e-mailed manuscripts and proposals are not considered. Complete submission guidelines available on website."

Ⓐ HOUGHTON MIFFLIN CO.

222 Berkeley St., Boston MA 02116. (617)351-5000. Website: www.hmco.com. **Acquisitions:** Submissions Editor. Estab. 1832. Publishes hardcover originals and trade paperback originals and reprints. Accepts simultaneous submissions. Book catalog online.

Imprints American Heritage Dictionaries; Clarion Books; Great Source Education Group; Houghton Mifflin; Houghton Mifflin Books for Children; Houghton Mifflin Paperbacks; Mariner Books; McDougal Littell; Peterson Field Guides; Riverside Publishing; Sunburst Technology; Taylor's Gardening Guides; Edusoft; Promissor; Walter Lorraine Books; Kingfisher.

- "Houghton Mifflin gives shape to ideas that educate, inform and delight. In a new era of publishing, our legacy of quality thrives as we combine imagination with technology, bringing you new ways to know."

Nonfiction Audiocassettes, autobiography, biography, children's/juvenile, cookbook, general nonfiction, gift book, how-to, illustrated book, reference, self-help. Subjects include agriculture/horticulture, animals, anthropology/archeology, cooking/foods/nutrition, ethnic, gardening, gay/lesbian, health/medicine, history, memoirs, military/war, social sciences. "We are not a mass market publisher. Our main focus is serious nonfiction. We do practical self-help but not pop psychology self-help." *Agented submissions only.*

Fiction Literary. "We are not a mass market publisher. Study the current list." *Agented submissions only.*

Recent Title(s) *The Namesake*, by Jhumpa Lahiri; *The Plot Against America*, by Philip Roth.

Tips "Our audience is high end literary."

HOUSE OF COLLECTIBLES

Imprint of Random House, Inc., 1745 Broadway, 15th Floor, New York NY 10019. E-mail: houseofcollectibles@randomhouse.com. Website: www.houseofcollectibles.com. Publishes trade and mass market paperback originals. **Royalty on retail price varies. Offers varied advance.** Does not accept simultaneous submissions. Book catalog free.

Imprints Official Price Guide series.

- "One of the premier publishing companies devoted to books on a wide range of antiques and collectibles, House of Collectibles publishes books for the seasoned expert and the beginning collector alike."

Nonfiction How-to (related to collecting antiques and coins), reference. Subjects include art/architecture (fine art), sports, comic books, American patriotic memorabilia, clocks, character toys, coins, stamps, costume jewelry, knives, books, military, glassware, records, arts and crafts, Native American collectibles, pottery, fleamarkets. Accepts unsolicited proposals.

Recent Title(s) *The Official Price Guide to Records*, by Jerry Osborne; *The One-Minute Coin Expert*, by John Travers.

Tips "We have been publishing price guides and other books on antiques and collectibles for over 35 years and plan to meet the needs of collectors, dealers, and appraisers well into the 21st century."

HOWELL PRESS, INC.

1125 Stoney Ridge Rd., Suite A, Charlottesville VA 22902. (434)977-4006. Fax: (434)971-7204. E-mail: rhowell@howellpress.com. Website: www.howellpress.com. **Acquisitions:** Ross A. Howell, president. Estab. 1985. **Publishes 6-8 titles/year. Receives 500 queries/year. 30% of books from first-time authors; 80% from unagented writers. Pays 5-10% royalty. Offers advance.** Publishes book 18 months after acceptance of ms. Book catalog for 9×12 SAE with 4 first-class stamps; ms guidelines online.

    O—ᖇ "While our aviation, history, and transportation titles are produced for the enthusiast market, writing must be accessible to the general adult reader." Currently emphasizing regional (Mid-Atlantic and Southeast), aviation history, motorsport, and gift books.

Nonfiction Illustrated book. Subjects include history, regional, aviation, transportation, gourmet, quilts. "Generally open to most ideas, as long as writing is accessible to average adult reader. Our line is targeted, so it would be advisable to look over our catalog before querying to better understand what Howell Press does." Query with SASE, or submit outline, sample chapter(s). Does not return mss without SASE. Reviews artwork/photos as part of ms package.

Recent Title(s) *The Nation's Hangar: The Aircraft Collection of the Steven F. Udvar-Hazy Center, Smithsonian National Air and Space Museum*, by Robert Van Der Linden; *Vietnam Graffiti: Messages From a Forgotten Troopship*, by Art and Lee Beltrone; *Godfather's Pasta: Italian Cooking You Can't Refuse*, by Olindo Chiocca.

Tips "Focus of our program has been illustrated books, but we will also consider nonfiction manuscripts that would not be illustrated."

HQN BOOKS

Imprint of Harlequin, 233 Broadway, Suite 1001, New York NY 10279. **Acquisitions:** Tracy Farrell, executive editor. Publishes hardcover, trade paperback, and mass market paperback originals. **Pays royalty. Offers advance.**

Fiction Romance (contemporary and historical). Accepts unagented material. Does not accept e-mail queries.

HUDSON HILLS PRESS, INC.

74-2 Union St., Box 205, Manchester VT 05254. (802)362-6450. Fax: (802)362-6459. E-mail: sbutterfield@hudsonhills.com. Website: www.hudsonhills.com. **Acquisitions:** Sarah Butterfield, assistant to publisher. Estab. 1978. Publishes hardcover and paperback originals. **Publishes 15+ titles/year. 15% of books from first-time authors; 90% from unagented writers. Pays 4-6% royalty on retail price. Offers $3,500 average advance.** Publishes book 1 year after acceptance of ms. Accepts simultaneous submissions. Responds in 2 months to queries. Book catalog for 6×9 SAE with 2 first-class stamps.

    O—ᖇ Hudson Hills Press publishes books about art and photography, including monographs.

Nonfiction Subjects include art/architecture, photography. Query first, then submit outline and sample chapters. Reviews artwork/photos as part of ms package.

Recent Title(s) *Systems of Color*, by Ida Kohlmeyer.

HUNTER HOUSE

P.O. Box 2914, Alameda CA 94501. (510)865-5282. Fax: (510)865-4295. E-mail: acquisitions@hunterhouse.com. Website: www.hunterhouse.com. **Acquisitions:** Jeanne Brondino, acquisitions editor; Kiran S. Rana, publisher. Estab. 1978. Publishes trade paperback originals and reprints. **Publishes 24 titles/year. Receives 200-300 queries and 100 mss/year. 50% of books from first-time authors; 80% from unagented writers. Pays 12% royalty on net receipts, defined as selling price. Offers $500-3,000 advance.** Publishes book 1-2 years after acceptance of ms. Accepts simultaneous submissions. Responds in 2 months to queries; 3 months to proposals; 6 months to mss. Book catalog for 8½×11 SAE with 3 first-class stamps; ms guidelines online.

    O—ᖇ Hunter House publishes health books (especially women's health), self-help health, sexuality and couple relationships, violence prevention and intervention. De-emphasizing reference, self-help psychology.

Nonfiction Subjects include health/medicine, self-help, women's health, fitness, relationships, sexuality, personal growth, and violence prevention. "Health books (especially women's health) should focus on emerging health issues or current issues that are inadequately covered and be written for the general population. Family books: Our current focus is sexuality and couple relationships, and alternative lifestyles to high stress. Community topics include violence prevention/violence intervention. We also publish specialized curricula for counselors and educators in the areas of violence prevention and trauma in children.'' Query with proposal package, including synopsis, TOC, and chapter outline, sample chapter, target audience information, competition, and what distinguishes the book. Reviews artwork/photos as part of ms package. Send photocopies, proposals generally not returned, requested mss returned with SASE. Reviews artwork/photos as part of ms package.

Recent Title(s) *The Cortisol Connection*, by Shawn Talbott; *Tantric Sex for Women*, by Christa Schulte; *How to Spot a Dangerous Man*, by Sandra Brown.

Tips Audience is concerned people who are looking to educate themselves and their community about real-life issues that affect them. ''Please send as much information as possible about who your audience is, how your book addresses their needs, and how you reach that audience in your ongoing work.''

HUNTER PUBLISHING, INC.

130 Campus Dr., Edison NJ 08818. Fax: (772)546-8040. E-mail: hunterp@bellsouth.net. Website: www.hunterp ublishing.com. President: Michael Hunter. **Acquisitions:** Kim Andre, editor; Lissa Dailey. Estab. 1985. **Publishes 100 titles/year. 10% of books from first-time authors; 75% from unagented writers. Pays royalty. Offers negotiable advance.** Publishes book 5 months after acceptance of ms. Accepts simultaneous submissions. Responds in 3 weeks to queries; 1 month to mss. Book catalog for #10 SAE with 4 first-class stamps.
Imprints Adventure Guides; Romantic Weekends Guides; Alive Guides.

   O→ Hunter Publishing publishes practical guides for travelers going to the Caribbean, US, Europe, South America, and the far reaches of the globe.

Nonfiction Reference. Subjects include regional, travel (travel guides). ''We need travel guides to areas covered by few competitors: Caribbean Islands, South and Central America, Europe, Asia from an active 'adventure' perspective.'' No personal travel stories or books not directed to travelers. Query, or submit outline/synopsis and sample chapters. Reviews artwork/photos as part of ms package.

Recent Title(s) *Adventure Guide to Canada's Atlantic Provinces*, by Barbara Radcliffe-Rogers.

Tips ''Guides should be destination-specific, rather than theme-based alone. Thus, 'Travel with Kids' is too broad; 'Italy with Kids' is OK. Make sure the guide doesn't duplicate what other guide publishers do.''

IBEX PUBLISHERS

P.O. Box 30087, Bethesda MD 20824. (301)718-8188. Fax: (301)907-8707. E-mail: info@ibexpub.com. Website: www.ibexpub.com. Publishes hardcover and trade paperback originals and reprints. **Publishes 10-12 titles/year. Payment varies.** Accepts simultaneous submissions. Book catalog free.
Imprints Iranbooks Press.

   O→ IBEX publishes books about Iran and the Middle East.

Nonfiction Biography, cookbook, reference, textbook. Subjects include cooking/foods/nutrition, language/literature. Query with SASE, or submit propsal package, including outline and 2 sample chapters.

Poetry Translations of Persian poets will be considered.

ICONOGRAFIX, INC.

1830A Hanley Rd., P.O. Box 446, Hudson WI 54016. (715)381-9755. Fax: (715)381-9756. E-mail: dcfrautschi@ic onografixinc.com. **Acquisitions:** Dylan Frautschi, acquisitions manager (transportation). Estab. 1992. Publishes trade paperback originals. **Publishes 24 titles/year. Receives 100 queries and 20 mss/year. 50% of books from first-time authors; 100% from unagented writers. Pays 8-12% royalty on wholesale price or makes outright purchase of $1,000-3,000. Offers $1,000-3,500 advance.** Publishes book 1 year after acceptance of ms. Accepts simultaneous submissions. Responds in 1 month to queries; 3 months to proposals and mss. Book catalog and ms guidelines free.

   O→ Iconografix publishes special, historical-interest photographic books for transportation equipment enthusiasts. Currently emphasizing emergency vehicles, buses, trucks, railroads, automobiles, auto racing, construction equipment, snowmobiles.

Nonfiction Interested in photo archives. Coffee table book, illustrated book (photographic), photo albums. Subjects include Americana (photos from archives of historic places, objects, people), history, hobbies, military/war, transportation (older photos of specific vehicles). Query with SASE, or submit proposal package, including outline. Reviews artwork/photos as part of ms package. Send photocopies.

Recent Title(s) *Greyhound Buses 1914-2000 Photo Archive*, by William A. Luke; *Indianapolis Racing Cars of Frank Kurtis, 1941-1963 Photo Archive*, by Gordon Eliot White; *The American Ambulance 1900-2002: An Illustrated History*, by Walter M.P. McCall.

IDEALS CHILDREN'S BOOKS

Ideals Publications, Inc., 535 Metroplex Dr., Nashville TN 37211. (615)333-0478. Estab. 1944. **Offers varied advance.** Publishes hardbound books and children's titles. **Offers varied advance.** Accepts simultaneous submissions. Ms guidelines for #10 SASE.

○━ Ideals Childrens Books publishes picture books for children ages 5-8.

Nonfiction Biography, religious, holiday. Subjects include history, travel, inspirational, nostalgic, patriotic.

Recent Title(s) *Discover George Washington*; *Let's Be Thankful*; *You're My Little Love Bug*.

Ⓝ IMPACT BOOKS

Imprint of F+W Publications, Inc., 4700 E. Galbraith Rd., Cincinnati OH 45236. Fax: (513)531-2686. E-mail: pam.wissman@fwpubs.com. Website: www.fwpublications.com. **Acquisitions:** Pamela Wissman, acquisitions editor (art instruction for comics, manga, anime, fantasy). Estab. 2004. Publishes trade paperback originals and reprints. **Publishes 8 titles/year. Receives 40 queries and 10 mss/year. 80% of books from first-time authors; 100% from unagented writers. Pays 10-15% royalty on net receipts.** Publishes book 11 months after acceptance of ms. Accepts simultaneous submissions. Responds in 2 months. Book catalog free; ms guidelines online.

Nonfiction Children's/juvenile, how-to, illustrated book, reference. Subjects include art/architecture, contemporary culture, creative nonfiction, hobbies. "We are looking for authors who can teach beginners how to create comics and fantasy in traditional and Japanese manga styles step-by-step, including working from photo references, drawing monsters, anatomy, and creating characters." Submit proposal package including outline, 1 sample chapter, at least 7 examples of sample art. Reviews artwork/photos as part of ms package. Send transparencies or anything that represents the art well, preferably in the form the author plans to submit art if contracted.

Recent Title(s) *Manga Madness*, by David Okum (art instruction); *Comics Crash Course*, by Vincent Garrano (art instruction).

Tips "Audience comprised of 13- to 18-year-old beginners along the lines of comic buyers, in general—mostly teenage boys—but also appealing to a broader audience of young adults 19-30 who need basic techniques. Art must appeal to teenage boys and be submitted in a form that will reproduce well. Authors need to know how to teach beginners step-by-step. A sample step-by-step is important."

IMPACT PUBLISHERS, INC.

P.O. Box 6016, Atascadero CA 93423-6016. (805)466-5917. Fax: (805)466-5919. E-mail: info@impactpublishers. com. Website: www.impactpublishers.com. **Acquisitions:** Freeman Porter, acquisitions editor. Estab. 1970. Publishes trade paperback originals. **Publishes 6-10 titles/year. Receives 250 queries and 250 mss/year. 20% of books from first-time authors; 60% from unagented writers. Pays 10% royalty on net receipts. Offers advance.** Publishes book 12-18 months after acceptance of ms. Accepts simultaneous submissions. Responds in 5 months to proposals. Book catalog free; ms guidelines online.

Imprints American Source Books; Little Imp Books; Rebuilding Books; Practical Therapist series.

○━ "Our purpose is to make the best human services expertise available to the widest possible audience: children, teens, parents, couples, individuals seeking self-help and personal growth, and human service professionals." Currently emphasizing books on divorce recovery for The Rebuilding Books Series. Deemphasizing children's books.

Nonfiction "All our books are written by qualified human service professionals and are in the fields of mental health, personal growth, relationships, aging, families, children, and professional psychology." Children's/juvenile, self-help. Subjects include child guidance/parenting, health/medicine, psychology (professional), caregiving/eldercare. "We do not publish general fiction for children, poetry, or New Age/spiritual works." Submit proposal package, including short résumé or vita, book description, audience description, outline, 1-3 sample chapters, and SASE.

Recent Title(s) *Calming the Family Storm: Anger Management for Moms, Dads, and All Their Kids*, by Gary McKay, PhD, and Steve Maybell, PhD.

Tips "Don't call to see if we have received your submission. Include a self-addressed, stamped postcard if you want to know if your manuscript arrived safely. We prefer a nonacademic, readable style. We publish only popular and professional psychology and self-help materials written in 'everyday language' by professionals with advanced degrees and significant experience in the human services. Our theme is 'psychology you can use, from professionals you can trust.'"

INDIANA HISTORICAL SOCIETY PRESS

450 W. Ohio St., Indianapolis IN 46202-3269. (317)233-6073. Fax: (317)233-0857. **Acquisitions:** Submissions Editor. Estab. 1830. Publishes hardcover originals. **Publishes 10 titles/year. Pays 6% royalty on net revenue received.** Responds in 1 month to queries.

Nonfiction Biography. Subjects include agriculture/horticulture, art/architecture, business/economics, ethnic, government/politics, history, military/war, sports, children's books. All topics must relate to Indiana. "We seek book-length manuscripts that are solidly researched and engagingly written on topics related to Indiana:

biography, history, literature, music, politics, transportation, sports, agriculture, architecture, and children's books." Query with SASE.

Recent Title(s) *Gus Grissom: The Lost Astronaut*, by Ray E. Boomhower; *Skirting the Issue: Stories of Indiana's Historical Women Artists*, by Judith Vale Newton and Carol Ann Weiss; *Affectionately Yours: The Civil War Home-Front Letters of the Ovid Butler Family*, edited by Barbara Butler Davis.

INFORMATION TODAY, INC.

143 Old Marlton Pike, Medford NJ 08055. (609)654-6266. Fax: (609)654-4309. E-mail: jbryans@infotoday.com. Website: www.infotoday.com. **Acquisitions:** John B. Bryans, editor-in-chief. Publishes hardcover and trade paperback originals. **Publishes 15-20 titles/year. Receives 100 queries and 30 mss/year. 30% of books from first-time authors; 90% from unagented writers. Pays 10-15% royalty on wholesale price. Offers $500-2,500 advance.** Publishes book 9 months after acceptance of ms. Accepts simultaneous submissions. Responds in 1 month to queries; 2 months to proposals; 3 months to mss. Book catalog free or on website; ms guidelines free or via e-mail as attachment.

Imprints ITI (academic, scholarly, library science); CyberAge Books (high-end consumer and business technology books—emphasis on Internet/WWW topics including online research).

> **O—** "We look for highly-focused coverage of cutting-edge technology topics, written by established experts and targeted to a tech-savvy readership. Virtually all our titles focus on how information is accessed, used, shared, and transformed into knowledge that can benefit people, business, and society." Currently emphasizing Internet/online technologies, including their social significance; biography, how-to, technical, reference. De-emphasizing fiction.

Nonfiction Biography, how-to, multimedia, reference, self-help, technical, scholarly. Subjects include business/economics, computers/electronic, education, science, Internet and cyberculture, library and information science. Query with SASE. Reviews artwork/photos as part of ms package. Send photocopies.

Recent Title(s) *Knowledge Management Lessons Learned*, edited by M. Koenig and T. Srikantaiah; *Building & Running a Successful Research Business*, by Mary Ellen Bates; *The Extreme Searcher's Internet Handbook: A Guide for the Serious Searcher*, by Randolph Hock.

Tips "Our readers include scholars, academics, indexers, librarians, information professionals (ITI imprint), as well as high-end consumer and business users of Internet/WWW/online technologies, and people interested in the marriage of technology with issues of social significance (i.e., cyberculture)."

⊘ INNER OCEAN PUBLISHING, INC.

P.O. Box 1239, Makawao HI 96768. (808)573-8000. Fax: (808)573-0700. E-mail: info@innerocean.com. Website: www.innerocean.com. **Acquisitions:** Karen Bouris, publisher; John Elder, executive publisher. Estab. 1999. Publishes hardcover originals and trade paperback originals and reprints. **Publishes 20+ titles/year. Pays 10-15% roaylty on net sales. Offers modest advance.** Accepts simultaneous submissions. Responds in 2-3 months to queries. Book catalog free; ms guidelines online.

Nonfiction General trade. Subjects include spirituality, women's issues/studies, personal growth, sexuality, environmental, and political call to action. Query with SASE. *Do not send ms.*

Recent Title(s) *Roar Softly & Carry a Great Lipstick*; *MoveOn's 50 Ways to Love Your Country*; *Sexy Mamas: Keeping Your Sex Life Alive While Raising Kids*.

Tips Audience is a wide range of readers interested in improving their lives through self-awareness, personal empowerment, and community involvement.

INNER TRADITIONS

Bear & Co., P.O. Box 388, Rochester VT 05767. (802)767-3174. Fax: (802)767-3726. E-mail: submissions@gotoit.com. Website: www.innertraditions.com. Managing Editor: Jeanie Levitan. **Acquisitions:** Jon Graham, editor. Estab. 1975. Publishes hardcover and trade paperback originals and reprints. **Publishes 60 titles/year. Receives 5,000 queries/year. 10% of books from first-time authors; 20% from unagented writers. Pays 8-10% royalty on net receipts. Offers $1,000 average advance.** Publishes book 1 year after acceptance of ms. Responds in 3 months to queries; 6 months to mss. Book catalog and ms guidelines free or online.

Imprints Destiny Audio Editions; Destiny Books; Destiny Recordings; Healing Arts Press; Inner Traditions; Inner Traditions En Espanol; Inner Traditions India; Park Street Press; Bear & Company; Bear Cub; Bindu Books.

> **O—** Inner Traditions publishes works representing the spiritual, cultural and mythic traditions of the world and works on alternative medicine and holistic health that combine contemporary thought with the knowledge of the world's great healing traditions. Currently emphasizing sacred sexuality, indigenous spirituality, ancient history.

Nonfiction "We are interested in the relationship of the spiritual and transformative aspects of world cultures." Children's/juvenile, self-help. Subjects include animals, art/architecture, child guidance/parenting, contemporary culture, ethnic, fashion/beauty, health/medicine (alternative medicine), history (ancient history and mythology), music/dance, nature/environment, New Age, philosophy (esoteric), psychology, religion (world religions), sex, spirituality, women's issues/studies, indigenous cultures, ethnobotany business. No fiction. Query, or submit outline and sample chapters with SASE. Does not return mss without SASE. Reviews artwork/photos as part of ms package.

Recent Title(s) *Science and the Akashie Field*, by Ervin Laszlo; *The Knights Templar in the New World*, by William F. Mann; *The Secret Teachings of Plants*, by Stephen Harrod Buhner.

Tips "We are not interested in autobiographical stories of self-transformation. We do accept electronic submissions (via e-mail). We are not currently looking at fiction."

INSTITUTE OF POLICE TECHNOLOGY AND MANAGEMENT

University of North Florida, 12000 Alumni Dr., Jacksonville FL 32224-2678. (904)620-4786. Fax: (904)620-2453. E-mail: rhodge@unf.edu. Website: www.iptm.org. **Acquisitions:** Richard C. Hodge, editor. Estab. 1980. Usually publishes trade paperback originals. **Publishes 8 titles/year. Receives 30 queries and 12 mss/year. 50% of books from first-time authors; 100% from unagented writers. Pays 25% royalty on actual sale price, or makes outright purchase of $300-2,000.** Publishes book 6 months after acceptance of ms. Does not accept simultaneous submissions. Responds in 3 weeks to queries.

O→ "Our publications are principally for law enforcement. Will consider works in nearly every area of law enforcement."

Nonfiction Illustrated book, reference, technical, textbook. Subjects include traffic crash investigation and reconstruction, management and supervision, criminal investigations, security. "Our authors are mostly active or retired law enforcement officers with excellent, up-to-date knowledge of their particular areas. However, some authors are highly regarded professionals in other specialized fields that in some way intersect with law enforcement." Reviews artwork/photos as part of ms package.

Tips "Manuscripts should not be submitted before the author has contacted IPTM's editor by e-mail or telephone. It is best to make this contact before completing a lengthy work such as a manual."

[N] INTEL PRESS

2111 NE 25 Ave., JF3-330, Hillsboro OR 97124. E-mail: intelpress@intel.com. Website: www.intel.com/intelpress. **Acquisitions:** David B. Spencer, managing editor (computer technology). Estab. 1999. Publishes hardcover and trade paperback originals. **Publishes 10 titles/year. Receives 200 queries and 6 mss/year. 80% of books from first-time authors; 100% from unagented writers. Pays 7-10% royalty on retail price.** Publishes book 1 year after acceptance of ms. Accepts simultaneous submissions. Responds in 2 months to queries; 1 month to proposals and mss. Ms guidelines online.

Nonfiction Reference, technical. Subjects include computers/electronic, software. "We publish books about technologies, initiatives, or products in which Intel Corp. has an interest." Submit proposal package including outline, form from website. Reviews artwork/photos as part of ms package. Send photocopies.

Recent Title(s) *Programming With Hyper-Threading Technology*, by Richard Gerber and Andrew Binstock (software engineering); *PCI Express Electrical Interface Design*, by Dave Coleman, et al (computer architecture).

Tips "Our books are written by engineers for engineers. They should solve a commonly recognized problem faced by computer developers. Review the information on our website. Submit a clear, 25-word summary of the book concept via e-mail."

INTERCULTURAL PRESS, INC.

P.O. Box 700, Yarmouth ME 04096. (866)372-2665 or (207)846-5168. Fax: (207)846-5181. E-mail: books@interculturalpress.com. Website: www.interculturalpress.com. **Acquisitions:** Judy Carl-Hendrick, managing editor. Estab. 1980. Publishes hardcover and paperback originals. **Publishes 8-12 titles/year. 50% of books from first-time authors; 95% from unagented writers. Pays royalty. Offers small advance occasionally.** Publishes book within 18 months after acceptance of ms. Accepts simultaneous submissions. Responds in 1 month to queries. Book catalog free; ms guidelines online.

O→ Intercultural Press publishes materials related to intercultural relations, including the practical concerns of living and working in foreign countries, the impact of cultural differences on personal and professional relationships, and the challenges of interacting with people from unfamiliar cultures, whether at home or abroad. Currently emphasizing international business.

Nonfiction "We want books with an international or domestic intercultural or multicultural focus, including those on business operations (how to be effective in intercultural business activities), education (textbooks for teaching intercultural subjects, for instance), and training (for Americans abroad or foreign nationals coming to the United States)." Reference, textbooks, theory. Subjects include world affairs, business, education, diversity and multicultural, relocation and cultural adaptation, culture learning, training materials, country-specific guides. "Our books are published for educators in the intercultural field, business people engaged in international business, managers concerned with cultural diversity in the workplace, and anyone who works in an occupation where cross-cultural communication and adaptation are important skills. No manuscripts that don't have an intercultural focus.'' Accepts nonfiction translations. Submit proposals, outline, résumé, cv, and potential market information.

Recent Title(s) *The Cultural Imperative: Global Trends in the 21st Century*, by Richard D. Lewis; *Exploring Culture: Excercises, Stories and Synthetic Cultures*, by Gert Jan Hofstede, Paul B. Pedersen and Geert Hofstede.

INTERLINK PUBLISHING GROUP, INC.

46 Crosby St., Northampton MA 01060. (413)582-7054. Fax: (413)582-7057. E-mail: info@interlinkbooks.com. Website: www.interlinkbooks.com. **Acquisitions:** Michel Moushabeck, publisher. Estab. 1987. Publishes hardcover and trade paperback originals. **Publishes 50 titles/year. 30% of books from first-time authors; 50% from unagented writers. Pays 6-8% royalty on retail price. Offers small advance.** Publishes book 18 months after acceptance of ms. Accepts simultaneous submissions. Responds in 3-6 months to queries. Book catalog free; ms guidelines online.

Imprints Crocodile Books, USA; Interlink Books; Olive Branch Press.

   O─┐ Interlink publishes a general trade list of adult fiction and nonfiction with an emphasis on books that have a wide appeal while also meeting high intellectual and literary standards.

Nonfiction Subjects include world travel, world history and politics, ethnic cooking, world music. Submit outline and sample chapters.

Fiction Ethnic, international. ''Adult—We are looking for translated works relating to the Middle East, Africa or Latin America.'' No science fiction, romance, plays, erotica, fantasy, horror. Query with SASE, or submit outline, sample chapters.

Recent Title(s) *House of the Winds*, by Mia Yun.

Tips ''Any submissions that fit well in our publishing program will receive careful attention. A visit to our website, your local bookstore, or library to look at some of our books before you send in your submission is recommended.''

INTERNATIONAL CITY/COUNTY MANAGEMENT ASSOCIATION

777 N. Capitol St., NE, Suite 500, Washington DC 20002. (202)962-4262. Fax: (202)962-3500. Website: www.icma.org. **Acquisitions:** Christine Ulrich, editorial director. Estab. 1914. Publishes hardcover and paperback originals. **Publishes 10-15 titles/year. Receives 50 queries and 20 mss/year. 20% of books from first-time authors; 100% from unagented writers. Makes negotiable outright purchase. Offers occasional advance.** Publishes book 18 months after acceptance of ms. Responds in 2 months to queries. Book catalog and ms guidelines online.

   O─┐ ''Our mission is to create excellence in local government by developing and fostering professional local government management worldwide.''

Nonfiction Reference, textbook, training manuals. Subjects include government/politics. Query with outline and 1 sample chapter. Reviews artwork/photos as part of ms package. Send photocopies.

Recent Title(s) *Capital Budgeting and Finance: A Guide for Local Governments*; *The Effective Local Government Manager*.

Tips ''Our mission is to enhance the quality of local government and to support and assist professional local administrators in the United States and other countries.''

INTERNATIONAL FOUNDATION OF EMPLOYEE BENEFIT PLANS

P.O. Box 69, Brookfield WI 53008-0069. (262)786-6700. Fax: (262)786-8780. E-mail: books@ifebp.org. Website: www.ifebp.org. **Acquisitions:** Dee Birschel, senior director of publications. Estab. 1954. Publishes trade paperback originals. **Publishes 10 titles/year. 15% of books from first-time authors; 80% from unagented writers. Pays 5-15% royalty on wholesale and retail price.** Publishes book 1 year after acceptance of ms. Responds in 3 months to queries. Book catalog free; ms guidelines for #10 SASE.

   O─┐ IFEBP publishes general and technical monographs on all aspects of employee benefits—pension plans, health insurance, etc.

Nonfiction Subjects limited to health care, pensions, retirement planning and employee benefits and compensation. Reference, technical, textbook. Subjects include consumer information. Query with outline.

Recent Title(s) *Integrated Disability Management: An Employers Guide*, by Janet R. Douglas.

Tips ''Be aware of interests of employers and the marketplace in benefits topics, for example, how AIDS affects employers, healthcare cost containment.''

INTERNATIONAL MEDICAL PUBLISHING

1313 Dolley Madison Blvd., Suite 302, McLean VA 22101. (703)356-2037. Fax: (703)734-8987. E-mail: contact@ medicalpublishing.com. Website: www.medicalpublishing.com. **Acquisitions:** Thomas Masterson, MD, editor. Estab. 1991. Publishes mass market paperback originals. **Publishes 30 titles/year. Receives 100 queries and**

20 mss/year. **5% of books from first-time authors; 100% from unagented writers. Pays royalty on gross receipts.** Publishes book 8 months after acceptance of ms. Responds in 2 months to queries.

O→ IMP publishes books to make life easier for doctors in training. "We're branching out to also make life easier for people with chronic medical problems."

Nonfiction Reference, textbook. Subjects include health/medicine. "We distribute only through medical and scientific bookstores. Think about practical material for doctors-in-training. We are interested in handbooks. Online projects are of interest." Query with outline.

Recent Title(s) *Healthy People 2010*, by the US Department of Health and Human Services; *Day-by-Day Diabetes*, by Resa Levetan.

INTERNATIONAL SOCIETY FOR TECHNOLOGY IN EDUCATION (ISTE)

480 Charnelton St., Eugene OR 97401. (541)434-8928. E-mail: sharter@iste.org. Website: www.iste.org. **Acquisitions:** Scott Harter, acquisitions editor. Publishes trade paperback originals. **Publishes 15 titles/year. Receives 150 queries and 50 mss/year. 75% of books from first-time authors; 95% from unagented writers. Pays 10% royalty on retail price.** Publishes book 6 months after acceptance of ms. Accepts simultaneous submissions. Responds in 1 month. Book catalog and ms guidelines free.

O→ Currently emphasizing books on educational technology standards, curriculum integration, professional development, and assessment. De-emphasizing software how-to books.

Nonfiction Reference, technical, curriculum. Subjects include educational technology, educational software, educational administration. Submit proposal package including outline, sample chapters, TOC, vita. Reviews artwork/photos as part of ms package. Send photocopies.

Recent Title(s) *Palm OS Handhelds in the Elementary Classroom*, by Michael Curtis, et al; *Videoconferencing for K-12 Classrooms*, by Camille Cole, et al; *The Technology Coordinator's Handbook*.

Tips "Our audience is K-12 teachers, teacher educators, technology coordinators, and school and district administrators."

INTERNATIONAL WEALTH SUCCESS

P.O. Box 186, Merrick NY 11570-0186. (516)766-5850. Fax: (516)766-5919. **Acquisitions:** Tyler G. Hicks, editor. Estab. 1967. **Publishes 10 titles/year. 100% of books from first-time authors; 100% from unagented writers. Pays 10% royalty on wholesale or retail price. Offers usual advance of $1,000, but this varies depending on author's reputation and nature of book. Buys all rights.** Publishes book 4 months after acceptance of ms. Responds in 1 month to queries. Book catalog and ms guidelines for 9×12 SAE with 3 first-class stamps.

O→ "Our mission is to publish books, newsletters, and self-study courses aimed at helping beginners and experienced business people start, and succeed in, their own small business in the fields of real estate, import-export, mail order, licensing, venture capital, financial brokerage, etc. The large number of layoffs and downsizings have made our publications of greater importance to people seeking financial independence in their own business, free of layoff threats and snarling bosses."

Nonfiction How-to, self-help. Subjects include business/economics, financing, business success, venture capital, etc. "Techniques, methods, sources for building wealth. Highly personal, how-to-do-it with plenty of case histories. Books are aimed at wealth builders and are highly sympathetic to their problems. These publications present a wide range of business opportunities while providing practical, hands-on, step-by-step instructions aimed at helping readers achieve their personal goals in as short a time as possible while adhering to ethical and professional business standards." Length: 60,000-70,000 words. Query. Reviews artwork/photos as part of ms package.

Recent Title(s) *How to Buy and Flip Real Estate for a Profit*, by Rod L. Griffin.

Tips "With the mass layoffs in large and medium-size companies there is an increasing interest in owning your own business. So we focus on more how-to, hands-on material on owning—and becoming successful in—one's own business of any kind. Our market is the BWB—Beginning Wealth Builder. This person has so little money that financial planning is something they never think of. Instead, they want to know what kind of a business they can get into to make some money without a large investment. Write for this market and you have millions of potential readers. Remember—there are a lot more people without money than with money."

⊘ INTERVARSITY PRESS

P.O. Box 1400, Downers Grove IL 60515. (630)734-4000. Fax: (630)734-4200. E-mail: mail@ivpress.com. Website: www.ivpress.com. **Acquisitions:** David Zimmerman, associate editor; Andy Le Peau, editorial director; Jim Hoover, associate editorial director (academic, reference); Cindy Bunch, editor (Bible study, Christian living); Gary Deddo, associate editor (academic); Dan Reid, editor (reference, academic); Al Hsu, associate editor (general). Estab. 1947. Publishes hardcover originals, trade paperback and mass market paperback originals. **Publishes 80-90 titles/year. Receives 1,500 queries and 1,000 mss/year. 15% of books from first-time authors; 85% from unagented writers. Pays negotiable flat fee or royalty on retail price. Offers negotiable**

advance. Publishes book 1 year after acceptance of ms. Accepts simultaneous submissions. Responds in 3 months to proposals. Book catalog for 9 × 12 SAE and 5 first-class stamps; ms guidelines online.
Imprints Academic (contact Gary Deddo); Bible Study (contact Cindy Bunch); General (contact Al Hsu); Reference (contact Dan Reid).

> **O→** InterVarsity Press publishes a full line of books from an evangelical Christian perspective targeted to an open-minded audience. "We serve those in the university, the church, and the world, by publishing books from an evangelical Christian perspective."

Nonfiction Subjects include religion. Query with SASE. *No unsolicited mss.*
Recent Title(s) *Finding God in the Questions*, by Timothy Johnson; *The Gospel Code*, by Ben Witherington III.

THE INVISIBLE COLLEGE PRESS

P.O. Box 209, Woodbridge VA 22194-0209. (703)590-4005. E-mail: submissions@invispress.com. Website: www.invispress.com. **Acquisitions:** Dr. Phillip Reynolds, editor (nonfiction); Paul Mossinger, submissions editor (fiction). Publishes trade paperback originals and reprints. **Publishes 12 titles/year. Receives 120 queries and 30 mss/year. 75% of books from first-time authors; 75% from unagented writers. Pays 10-25% royalty on wholesale price. Offers $100 advance.** Publishes book 4 months after acceptance of ms. Accepts simultaneous submissions. Responds in 1 month to queries and proposals; 3 months to mss. Book catalog and ms guidelines online.
Nonfiction Reference. Subjects include creative nonfiction, government/politics, religion, spirituality, conspiracy. "We only publish nonfiction related to conspiracies, UFOs, government cover-ups, and the paranormal." Query with SASE, or submit proposal package including outline, 1 sample chapter.
Fiction Experimental, fantasy, gothic, horror, literary, mainstream/contemporary, occult, religious, science fiction, spiritual, suspense, conspiracy. "We only publish fiction related to conspiracies, UFOs, government cover-ups, and the paranormal." Query with SASE, or submit proposal package including 1 sample chapter, synopsis.
Recent Title(s) *UFO Politics at the White House*, by Larry Bryant (nonfiction); *City of Pillars*, by Dominic Peloso (fiction); *The Third Day*, by Mark Graham (fiction).
Tips "Our audience tends to be fans of conspiracies and UFO mythology. They go to UFO conventions, they research who shot JFK, they believe that they are being followed by Men in Black, they wear aluminum-foil hats to stop the CIA from beaming them thought-control rays. We are only interested in work dealing with established conspiracy/UFO mythology. Rosicrucians, Illuminatti, Men in Black, Area 51, Atlantis, etc. If your book doesn't sound like an episode of the *X-Files*, we probably won't consider it."

IRON GATE PUBLISHING

P.O. Box 999, Niwot CO 80544-0999. (303)530-2551. Fax: (303)530-5273. E-mail: editor@irongate.com. Website: www.irongate.com; www.reunionsolutions.com. **Acquisitions:** Dina C. Carson, publisher (how-to, genealogy). Publishes hardcover and trade paperback originals. **Publishes 6-10 titles/year; imprint publishes 2-6 titles/year. Receives 100 queries and 20 mss/year. 30% of books from first-time authors; 10% from unagented writers. Pays royalty on a case-by-case basis.** Publishes book 1 year after acceptance of ms. Accepts simultaneous submissions. Responds in 2 months to proposals. Book catalog and ms guidelines free or online.
Imprints Reunion Solutions Press; KinderMed Press.

> **O→** "Our readers are people who are looking for solid, how-to advice on planning reunions or self-publishing a genealogy."

Nonfiction Subjects include child guidance/parenting, health/medicine, hobbies. Query with SASE, or submit proposal package, including outline, 2 sample chapters, and marketing summary. Reviews artwork/photos as part of ms package. Send photocopies.
Recent Title(s) *The Genealogy and Local History Researcher's Self-Publishing Guide*; *Reunion Solutions: Everything You Need to Know to Plan a Family, Class, Military, Association or Corporate Reunion.*
Tips "Please look at the other books we publish and tell us in your query letter why your book would fit into our line of books."

JAYJO BOOKS, LLC

Imprint of The Guidance Channel, P.O. Box 760, 135 Dupont St., Plainview NY 11803-0769. (516)349-5520. Fax: (516)349-5521. **Acquisitions:** Rosie Dellorso, merchandising manager (for elementary school age youth). Publishes trade paperback originals. **Publishes 8-12 titles/year. Receives 100 queries/year. 25% of books from first-time authors; 100% from unagented writers. Makes outright purchase of $500-1,000.** Publishes book 9 months after acceptance of ms. Accepts simultaneous submissions. Responds in 2 months. Book catalog and writer's guidelines for #10 SASE.
Imprints Each book published is for a specific series. Series include: Special Family and Friends, Health Habits for Kids, Substance Free Kids, Special Kids in School. Series publish 1-5 titles/year.

Nonfiction Children's/juvenile, illustrated book. Subjects include health/medicine (issues for children). "JayJo Books is a publisher of nonfiction books to help teachers, parents, and children cope with chronic illnesses, special needs, and health education in classroom, family, and social settings. Each JayJo series has a particular style and format it must follow. Writers should send query letter with areas of expertise or interest and suggested focus of book." No animal character books or illustrated books. Query with SASE.

Tips "Send a query letter—since we only publish books adapted to our special formats—we contact appropriate potential authors and work with them to customize manuscript."

JEWISH LIGHTS PUBLISHING

LongHill Partners, Inc., P.O. Box 237, Sunset Farm Offices, Rt. 4, Woodstock VT 05091. (802)457-4000. Fax: (802)457-4004. Website: www.jewishlights.com. Editor: Stuart Matlins. **Acquisitions:** Acquisitions Editor. Estab. 1990. Publishes hardcover and trade paperback originals, trade paperback reprints. **Publishes 30 titles/year. 30% of books from first-time authors; 99% from unagented writers. Pays royalty on net sales, 10% on first printing, then increases.** Publishes book 1 year after acceptance of ms. Accepts simultaneous submissions. Responds in 3 months to queries. Book catalog and ms guidelines free.

> Oᴚ "People of all faiths and backgrounds yearn for books that attract, engage, educate and spiritually inspire. Our principal goal is to stimulate thought and help all people learn about who the Jewish people are, where they come from, and what the future can be made to hold."

Nonfiction Children's/juvenile, illustrated book, reference, self-help. Subjects include business/economics (with spiritual slant, finding spiritual meaning in one's work), health/medicine (healing/recovery, wellness, aging, life cycle), history, nature/environment, philosophy, religion (theology), spirituality (and inspiration), women's issues/studies. "We do *not* publish haggadot, biography, poetry, or cookbooks." Submit proposal package, including cover letter, TOC, 2 sample chapters and SASE (postage must cover weight of ms). Reviews artwork/photos as part of ms package. Send photocopies.

Recent Title(s) *The Rituals and Practices of a Jewish Life: A Handbook for Personal Spiritual Renewal*, by Kerry M. Oliteky and Daniel Judson; *The Jewish Prophet: Visionary Words From Moses and Miriam to Henrietta Szold and A.J. Heschel*, by Michael J. Shire; *Noah's Wife: The Story of Naamah*, by Sandy Eisenberg Sasso.

Tips "We publish books for all faiths and backgrounds that also reflect the Jewish wisdom tradition."

THE JOHNS HOPKINS UNIVERSITY PRESS

2715 N. Charles St., Baltimore MD 21218. (410)516-6900. Fax: (410)516-6968. E-mail: tcl@mail.press.jhu.edu. Website: www.press.jhu.edu. **Acquisitions:** Trevor Lipscombe, editor-in-chief (physics, astronomy, mathematics; tcl@mail.press.jhu.edu); Jacqueline C. Wehmueller, executive editor (consumer health, history of medicine, education; jwehmueller@mail.press.jhu.edu); Henry Y.K. Tom, executive editor (social sciences; htom@mail.press.jhu.edu); Wendy Harris, senior acquisitions editor (clinical medicine, public health, health policy; wharris@mail.press.jhu.edu); Robert J. Brugger, senior acquisitions editor (American history, history of science and technology, regional books; rbrugger@mail.press.jhu.edu); Vincent J. Burke, acquisitions editor (biology; vjb@mail.press.jhu.edu); Michael B. Lonegro, acquisitions editor (humanities, classics, and ancient studies; mlonegro@mail.press.jhu.edu). Estab. 1878. Publishes hardcover originals and reprints, and trade paperback reprints. **Publishes 125 titles/year. Pays royalty.** Publishes book 1 year after acceptance of ms.

Nonfiction Biography, general nonfiction, reference, scholarly, textbook. Subjects include government/politics, health/medicine, history, humanities, regional, religion, science, social sciences. Submit proposal package including outline, 1 sample chapter, curriculum vita. Reviews artwork/photos as part of ms package. Send photocopies.

Recent Title(s) *In Albert's Shadow*, by Milan Popovic (collection of letters); *An Alliance at Risk*, by Laurent Cohen-Tanugi, translated by George A. Holoch, Jr. (international relations); *Living With Rheumatoid Arthritis*, by Tammi L. Shlotzhauer, MD, and James L. McGuire, MD (health).

JOHNSON BOOKS

Johnson Publishing Co., 1880 S. 57th Court, Boulder CO 80301. (303)443-9766. Fax: (303)998-7594. E-mail: books@jpcolorado.com. **Acquisitions:** Mira Perrizo, publisher. Estab. 1979. Publishes hardcover and paperback originals and reprints. **Publishes 10-12 titles/year. 30% of books from first-time authors; 90% from unagented writers. Royalties vary.** Publishes book 1 year after acceptance of ms. Responds in 3 months to queries. Book catalog for 9×12 SAE with 5 first-class stamps.

Imprints Spring Creek Press.

> Oᴚ Johnson Books specializes in books on the American West, primarily outdoor, "useful" titles that will have strong national appeal.

Nonfiction Subjects include anthropology/archeology, history, nature/environment (environmental subjects), recreation (outdoor), regional, science, travel (regional), general nonfiction, books on the West, natural history, paleontology, geology. "We are primarily interested in books for the informed popular market, though we will consider vividly written scholarly works.'' Looks for ''good writing, thorough research, professional presentation, and appropriate style. Marketing suggestions from writers are helpful.'' Submit outline/synopsis and 3 sample chapters.

Recent Title(s) *Montana Surround*, by Phil Condon (nature); *The Thin Green Line*, by Terry Grosz (environment); *Butterflies of the Lower Rio Grande Valley*, by Ro Wauer (field guide).

JOSSEY-BASS/PFEIFFER

John Wiley & Sons, Inc., 989 Market St., San Francisco CA 94103. (415)433-1740. Fax: (415)433-0499. Website: www.josseybass.com; www.pfeiffer.com. **Acquisitions:** Paul Foster, publisher (public health and health administration, education K-12, higher and adult education, trade psychology, parenting, relationships, religion and spirituality); Cedric Crocker, publisher (business, nonprofit and public management, training and human resources developement). **Publishes 250 titles/year. Pays variable royalties. Offers occasional advance.** Publishes book 1 year after acceptance of ms. Accepts simultaneous submissions. Responds in 2-3 months to queries. Ms guidelines online.

Nonfiction Subjects include business/economics, education, health/medicine, money/finance, psychology, religion. Jossey-Bass publishes first-time and unagented authors. Publishes books on topics of interest to a wide range of readers: business & management, conflict resolution, mediation and negotiation, K-12 education, higher and adult education, healthcare management, psychology/behavioral healthcare, nonprofit & public management, religion, human resources & training. Also publishes 25 periodicals.

Recent Title(s) *No More Misbehavin'*, by Michele Borba; *Hidden Wholeness*, by Parker Palmer; *Teaching With Fire*, by Sam Intrator.

Ⓝ JOURNEY STONE CREATIONS, LLC

A.W.A. Gang (Angels with Attitudes), 3533 Danbury Rd., Fairfield OH 45014. (513)860-5616. Fax: (513)860-0176. E-mail: pat@journeystonecreations.com. Submissions E-mail: info@journeystonecreations.com. Website: www.journeystonecreations.com; www.awagang.com. **Acquisitions:** Patricia Stirnkorb, president (women's publications, business, children's books). Estab. 2004. Publishes hardcover, trade paperback, and mass market paperback originals. **Publishes 15-20 titles/year. Receives 100+ queries and 100+ mss/year. Pays 5-12% royalty on wholesale price, or makes outright purchase.** Publishes book 1 year after acceptance of ms. Accepts simultaneous submissions. Responds in 1 month to queries and proposals; 1-3 months to mss. Book catalog online; ms guidelines by e-mail.

    ○┐ ''We are a new and growing publisher with great plans for the future. All our products must be moral and conservative material to be considered.''

Nonfiction Children's/juvenile, coffee table book, gift book, illustrated book. Query with SASE, or submit proposal package including 3-5 sample chapters, or submit complete ms. Reviews artwork/photos as part of ms package. Send photocopies.

Fiction Juvenile, picture books, religious (juvenile or adult light reading—no theology), young adult, women's and men's inspirational. Query with SASE, or submit proposal package including 3-5 sample chapters, synopsis, or submit complete ms.

Recent Title(s) *Meet the Angels*, by Patricia Stirnkurs (children's board book); *A Place for the King*, by Patricia Stirnkurs (Christian story book); *In the Beginning*, by Patricia Stirnkurs (children's picture book).

Tips Audience is kids ages 2-12; adults of all ages. ''Be thorough and concise when explaining your work. Don't waste words. Be sure it is letter perfect, and punctuation and grammar are correct. We won't weed through poor grammar and spelling to get to the heart of the story.''

JOURNEYFORTH

Imprint of BJU Press, 1700 Wade Hampton Blvd., Greenville SC 29614. (864)242-5100, ext. 4350. Fax: (800)525-8398. E-mail: jb@bjup.com. Website: www.bjup.com. **Acquisitions:** Nancy Lohr, acquisitions editor. Estab. 1974. Publishes paperback original and reprints. **Pays royalty.** Accepts simultaneous submissions. Responds in 1 month to queries; 3 months to mss. Book catalog free; ms guidelines online.

    ○┐ ''Small independent publisher of excellent, trustworthy novels, information books, audio tapes and ancillary materials for readers pre-school through high school. We desire to develop in our children a love for and understanding of the written word, ultimately helping them love and understand God's word.''

Fiction Adventure (children's/juvenile, young adult), historical (children's/juvenile, young adult), juvenile (animal, easy-to-read, series), mystery (children's/juvenile, young adult), sports (children's/juvenile, young adult), suspense (young adult), western (young adult), young adult (series). ''Our fiction is all based on a moral and Christian worldview.'' Submit 5 sample chapters, synopsis, SASE.

Tips ''Study the publisher's guidelines. Make sure your work is suitable or you waste time for you and the publisher.''

JUDAICA PRESS

123 Ditmas Ave., Brooklyn NY 11218. (718)972-6200. Fax: (718)972-6204. E-mail: info@judaicapress.com. Website: www.judaicapress.com. **Acquisitions:** Nachum Shapiro, managing editor. Estab. 1963. Publishes hardcover and trade paperback originals and reprints. **Publishes 12 titles/year.** Responds in 3 months to queries. Book catalog in print and online.

    O— ''We cater to the Orthodox Jewish market.''

Nonfiction ''Looking for Orthodox Judaica in all genres.'' Children's/juvenile, cookbook, textbook, outreach books. Subjects include religion (Bible commentary), prayer, holidays, life cycle. Submit ms with SASE.

Fiction Novels.

Recent Title(s) *Scattered Pieces*, by Allison Cohen; *The Practical Guide to Kashrus*, by Rabbi Shaul Wagschal; *How Mitzvah Giraffe Got His Long, Long Neck*, by David Sokoloff.

[N] JUDSON PRESS

P.O. Box 851, Valley Forge PA 19482-0851. (610)768-2118. Fax: (610)768-2441. E-mail: judson.press@abc-usa.org. Website: www.judsonpress.com. Associate Publisher: Linda Peavy. **Acquisitions:** Randy Frame. Estab. 1824. Publishes hardcover and paperback originals. **Publishes 12-15 titles/year. Receives 750 queries/year. Pays royalty or makes outright purchase.** Publishes book 10 months after acceptance of ms. Accepts simultaneous submissions. Responds in 3 months to queries. Book catalog for 9 × 12 SAE with 4 first-class stamps; ms guidelines for #10 SASE.

    O— ''Our audience is mostly church members and leaders who seek to have a more fulfilling personal spiritual life and want to serve Christ in their churches and other relationships. We have a large African-American readership.'' Currently emphasizing worship resources/small group resources. De-emphasizing biography, poetry.

Nonfiction Adult religious nonfiction of 30,000-80,000 words. Subjects include multicultural, religion. Query with SASE, or submit outline, sample chapters.

Recent Title(s) *The Gospel According to Dr. Seuss*, by James W. Kemp; *The Real Deal*, by Billie Montgomery Cook; *40 Days to a Life of G.O.L.D.*, by Ed Gray.

Tips ''Writers have the best chance selling us practical books assisting clergy or laypersons in their ministry and personal lives. Our audience consists of Protestant church leaders and members. Be sensitive to our workload and adapt to the market's needs. Books on multicultural issues are very welcome. Also seeking books that heighten awareness and sensitivity to issues related to the poor and to social justice.''

KAEDEN BOOKS

P.O. Box 16190, Rocky River OH 44116. (800)890-7323. Fax: (440)617-1403. E-mail: jhoyer@kaeden.com. Website: www.kaeden.com. Estab. 1986. Publishes paperback originals. **Publishes 8-16 titles/year. Pays flat fee or royalty by individual arrangement with author depending on book.** Ms guidelines online.

    O— Children's book publisher for education K-3 market: reading stories, fiction/nonfiction, chapter books, science, math, and social studies materials, also poetry.

Nonfiction Grades K-3 only. Needs all subjects, especially biography, science, nature, and history. Send complete ms and SASE. Only responds ''if interested.''

Fiction Grades K-3 only. Adventure, ethnic, fantasy, historical, humor, mystery, science fiction (soft/sociological), short story collections, sports, suspense (amateur sleuth). Send a disposable copy of ms and SASE. Responds only ''if interested.''

Tips ''Our line is expanding with particular interest in nonfiction for grades K-3 only. Material must be suitable for use in the public school classroom, be multicultural, and be high interest with appropriate word usage and a positive tone for the respective grade.''

KALMBACH PUBLISHING CO.

21027 Crossroads Circle, P.O. Box 1612, Waukesha WI 53187-1612. (262)796-8776. Fax: (262)798-6468. E-mail: books@kalmbach.com. Website: corporate.kalmbach.com. **Acquisitions:** Candice St. Jacques, editor-in-chief; Lawrence Hansen, senior editor (hobbies); Julia Gerlach, associate editor (jewelry-making); Kristin Schneidler, crafts editor. Estab. 1934. Publishes hardcover and paperback originals, paperback reprints. **Publishes 20-30 titles/year. 50% of books from first-time authors; 99% from unagented writers. Pays 7% royalty on net receipts. Offers $2,500 advance.** Publishes book 18 months after acceptance of ms. Responds in 2 months to queries.

Nonfiction Kalmbach publishes reference materials and how-to publications for hobbyists, jewelry-makers, and crafters. Concentration in the railfan, model railroading, plastic modeling, and toy train collecting/operating hobbies. Focus on beading, wirework, and one-of-a-kind artisan creations for jewelry-making and crafts. ''Kalmbach Publications enhance our readers' enjoyment of their hobby and leisure-time interests.'' Query with 2-3 page detailed outline, sample chapter with photos, drawings, and how-to text. Reviews artwork/photos as part of ms package.

Recent Title(s) *Legendary Lionel Trains*, by John A. Grams and Terry D. Thompson; *The Model Railroader's Guide to Industries Along the Tracks*, by Jeff Wilson; *Easy Beading: The Best Projects From the First Year of Beadstyle Magazine*.

Tips "Our how-to books are highly visual in their presentation. Any author who wants to publish with us must be able to furnish good photographs and rough drawings before we'll consider his or her book."

KAR-BEN PUBLISHING

11430 Strand Dr. #2, Rockville MD 20852. (301)984-8826. Fax: (301)881-9195. E-mail: karben@aol.com. Website: www.karben.com. **Acquisitions:** Madeline Wikler and Judye Groner, editors (juvenile Judaica). Estab. 1976. Publishes hardcover and trade paperback originals. **Publishes 10-15 titles/year. Receives 50-100 queries and 300-400 mss/year. 5% of books from first-time authors; 100% from unagented writers. Pays 5-8% royalty on net receipts. Offers $500-2,500 advance.** Accepts simultaneous submissions. Responds in 1 month to queries. Book catalog free or on website; ms guidelines online.

　○→ Kar-Ben Publishing publishes high-quality materials on Jewish themes for young children and families.

Nonfiction "Jewish themes only!" Children's/juvenile (Judaica only). Subjects include religion. Submit complete ms.

Fiction "Jewish themes and young kids only!" Juvenile, religious.

Recent Title(s) *Six Million Paper Clips*; *It's Hanukkah Time*.

Tips "Do a literature search to make sure similar title doesn't already exist."

Ⓐ ⊘ KENSINGTON PUBLISHING CORP.

850 Third Ave., 16th Floor, New York NY 10022. (212)407-1500. Fax: (212)935-0699. Website: www.kensingtonbooks.com. **Acquisitions:** Michaela Hamilton, editor-in-chief (thrillers, mysteries, mainstream fiction, true crime, current events); Kate Duffy, editorial director, romance and women's fiction (historical romance, Regency romance, Brava erotic romance, women's contemporary fiction); John Scognamiglio, editorial director, fiction (historical romance, Regency romance, women's contemporary fiction, gay and lesbian fiction and nonfiction, mysteries, suspense, mainstream fiction); Karen Thomas, editorial director, Dafina Books (African-American fiction and nonfiction); Audrey LaFehr, editorial director (women's fiction, thrillers); Gene Brissie, editor-in-chief, Citadel Press (narrative nonfiction, business, pop culture, how-to, biography, cooking, history and military history); Bob Shuman, senior editor, Citadel Press (politics, military, wicca, business, Judaica, sports); Jeremie Ruby-Strauss, senior editor (nonfiction, pop culture, pop reference, true crime); Gary Goldstein, senior editor (westerns, true crime, military, sports, how-to, narrative nonfiction); Richard Ember, editor, Citadel Press (biography, film, sports, New Age, spirituality); Miles Lott, assistant editor (mainstream fiction, thrillers, horror, women's fiction, general nonfiction, popular culture, entertainment); Hilary Sares, consulting editor (historical romance, Regency romance, women's fiction). Estab. 1975. Publishes hardcover and trade paperback originals, mass market paperback originals and reprints. **Publishes over 500 titles/year. Receives 5,000 queries and 2,000 mss/year. 10% of books from first-time authors. Pays 6-15% royalty on retail price, or makes outright purchase. Offers $2,000 and up advance.** Publishes book 9-12 months after acceptance of ms. Accepts simultaneous submissions. Responds in 1 month to queries and proposals; 4 months to mss. Book catalog online.

Imprints Kensington Books; Brava Books; Citadel Press; Dafina Books; Pinnacle Books; Zebra Books.

　● Kensington recently purchased the assets of Carol Publishing Group.

　○→ Kensington focuses on profitable niches and uses aggressive marketing techniques to support its books.

Nonfiction Biography, cookbook, gift book, how-to, humor, illustrated book, reference, self-help. Subjects include Americana, animals, business/economics, child guidance/parenting, contemporary culture, cooking/foods/nutrition, gay/lesbian, health/medicine (alternative), history, hobbies, memoirs, military/war, money/finance, multicultural, nature/environment, philosophy, psychology, recreation, regional, sex, sports, travel, true crime, women's issues/studies, pop culture, true crime, current events. *Agented submissions only. No unsolicited mss.* Reviews artwork/photos as part of ms package. Send photocopies.

Fiction Ethnic, gay/lesbian, historical, horror, mainstream/contemporary, multicultural, mystery, occult, romance (contemporary, historical, regency), suspense, western (epic), thrillers, women's. No science fiction/fantasy, experimental fiction, business texts or children's titles. *Agented submissions only. No unsolicited mss.*

Recent Title(s) *Sullivan's Law*, by Nancy Taylor Rosenberg (fiction); *Sex, Lies, and Politics*, by Larry Flynt (nonfiction).

Tips Agented submissions only, except for submissions to romance lines. For those lines, query with SASE or submit proposal package including 3 sample chapters, synopsis.

KENT STATE UNIVERSITY PRESS

P.O. Box 5190, Kent OH 44242-0001. (330)672-7913. Fax: (330)672-3104. Website: www.kentstateuniversitypress.com. **Acquisitions:** Joanna H. Craig, editor-in-chief. Estab. 1965. Publishes hardcover and paperback originals and some reprints. **Publishes 30-35 titles/year. Nonauthor subsidy publishes 20% of books. Standard minimum book contract on net sales.** Responds in 3 months to queries. Book catalog free.

　O⟶ Kent State publishes primarily scholarly works and titles of regional interest. Currently emphasizing US history, literary criticism.

Nonfiction Biography, general nonfiction, scholarly. Subjects include anthropology/archeology, art/architecture, history, language/literature, regional, true crime, literary criticism, material culture, textile/fashion studies, US foreign relations. Especially interested in scholarly works in history and literary studies of high quality, any titles of regional interest for Ohio, scholarly biographies, the arts, and general nonfiction. Send a letter of inquiry before submitting mss. Decisions based on in-house readings and 2 by outside scholars in the field of study. Enclose return postage.

N ⊘ KIDHAVEN PRESS

Imprint of Gale, 15822 Bernardo Center Dr., Suite C, San Diego CA 92127. E-mail: chandra.howard@thomson.com. Website: www.gale.com/kidhaven. **Acquisitions:** Chandra Howard. Estab. 2001. Publishes hardcover originals. **Publishes 400 titles/year; imprint publishes 100 titles/year. Receives 300 queries/year. 10% of books from first-time authors; 99% from unagented writers. Makes outright purchase of $1,000-3,000.** Does not accept simultaneous submissions. Responds in 3 months to queries. Book catalog online; ms guidelines free.
Nonfiction Children's/juvenile. Subjects include animals, art/architecture, history, humanities, multicultural, nature/environment, religion, science, social sciences, world affairs. Query with SASE. *All unsolicited mss returned unopened.*
Recent Title(s) *What Makes Me a Buddhist?*, by Charles George; *Great Structures in History: The Roman Colosseum*, by Lynn Kuntz; *Cockroach*, by Toney Allman.
Tips "KidHaven Press books are written for upper elementary grade readers. All manuscripts must be contracted and adhere to our guidelines. As a series publisher, we do not accept unsolicited manuscripts. After your query is answered, you can discuss the titles available for assignment with the acquisitions editor. When submitting your query, include a list of pertinent publications and the subject areas in which you are interested."

KNOPF PUBLISHING GROUP

Imprint of Random House, Inc., 1745 Broadway, New York NY 10019. Website: www.aaknopf.com. **Acquisitions:** Senior Editor. Estab. 1915. Publishes hardcover and paperback originals. **Royalty and advance vary.** Accepts simultaneous submissions. Responds in 2-6 months to queries. Book catalog for $7\frac{1}{2} \times 10\frac{1}{2}$ SAE with 5 first-class stamps; ms guidelines online.
Imprints Alfred A. Knopf; Everyman's Library; Pantheon Books; Schocken Books; Vintage Anchor Publishing (Vintage Books, Anchor Books).

　• "We usually only accept work through an agent, but you may still send a query to our slush pile."

　O⟶ Knopf is a general publisher of quality nonfiction and fiction.

Nonfiction General nonfiction, scholarly, book-length nonfiction, including books of scholarly merit. Subjects include general scholarly nonfiction. "A good nonfiction writer should be able to follow the latest scholarship in any field of human knowledge, and fill in the abstractions of scholarship for the benefit of the general reader by means of good, concrete, sensory reporting." Preferred length: 50,000-150,000 words. Submit query, 25-50 page sample, SASE. Reviews artwork/photos as part of ms package.
Fiction Publishes book-length fiction of literary merit by known or unknown writers. Length: 40,000-150,000 words. Submit query, 25-50 page sample, SASE.
Recent Title(s) *Soldiers and Slaves*, by Roger Cohen; *The Power of the Dog*, by Don Winslow; *Falling Water Rising*, by Franklin Toker.

KOENISHA PUBLICATIONS

3196 53rd St., Hamilton MI 49419-9626. Phone/Fax: (269)751-4100. E-mail: koenisha@macatawa.org. Website: www.koenisha.com. **Acquisitions:** Sharolett Koenig, publisher; Flavia Crowner, proof editor; Earl Leon, acquisition editor. Publishes trade paperback originals. **Publishes 10-12 titles/year. Receives 500 queries and 500 mss/year. 95% of books from first-time authors; 100% from unagented writers. Pays 15-25% royalty on net receipts.** Publishes book 1 year after acceptance of ms. Accepts simultaneous submissions. Responds in 2 months to queries; 3 months to proposals and mss. Book catalog and ms guidelines online.
Nonfiction Autobiography, children's/juvenile, cookbook, how-to. Subjects include gardening, hobbies, memoirs, nature/environment. Query with SASE, or submit complete ms. Reviews artwork/photos as part of ms package. Send photocopies.
Fiction Humor, mainstream/contemporary, mystery, romance, suspense, young adult. "We do not accept manuscripts that contain unnecessary foul language, explicit sex or gratuitous violence." Query with SASE, or submit proposal package including 3 sample chapters, synopsis.
Poetry Submit 3 sample poems.

Recent Title(s) *Beaver Village Adventures*, by Linda Petty and Sharon Parrett (children's read-along); *Crucial Judgment*, by Al Blanchard (mystery); *A Writer's Concordance: Every Thing the Bible Says About Writing*, by Sharolett Koenig (inspirational).

Tips "We're not interested in books written to suit a particular line or house or because it's trendy. Instead write a book from your heart—the inspiration or idea that kept you going through the writing process."

KP BOOKS

Imprint of F+W Publications, Inc., 700 E. State St., Iola WI 54990. (715)445-2214. Fax: (715)445-4087. E-mail: info@krause.com. Website: www.krause.com. **Acquisitions:** Acquisitions Editor. Publishes hardcover and trade paperback originals. **Publishes 170 titles/year. Receives 400 queries and 40 mss/year. 10% of books from first-time authors; 90% from unagented writers. Pays 9-12% royalty on net or makes outright purchase of $2,000-10,000. Offers $1,500-4,000 advance.** Publishes book 18 months after acceptance of ms. Does not accept simultaneous submissions. Responds in 3 months to proposals; 2 months to mss. Book catalog for free or on website; ms guidelines free.

O→ "We are the world's largest hobby and collectibles publisher."

Nonfiction How-to, illustrated book, reference, technical, price guides. Subjects include hobbies (antiques, collectibles, toys), sports (outdoors, hunting, fishing), coins, firearms, knives, records, sewing, quilting, ceramics. Submit proposal package, including outline, 1-3 sample chapters, and letter explaining your project's unique contributions. Reviews artwork/photos as part of ms package. Send sample photos.

Recent Title(s) *Antique Trader® Antiques & Collectibles Price Guide 2005*, by Kyle Husfloen (reference/price guide); *The ABC's of Reloading*, by Bill Chevalier (how-to/reference); *Easy-to-Sew Playful Toys*, by Debra Quartermain (how-to).

Tips Audience consists of serious hobbyists. "Your work should provide a unique contribution to the special interest."

KREGEL PUBLICATIONS

Kregel, Inc., P.O. Box 2607, Grand Rapids MI 49501. (616)451-4775. Fax: (616)451-9330. Website: www.kregelpublications.com. **Acquisitions:** Dennis R. Hillman, publisher. Estab. 1949. Publishes hardcover and trade paperback originals and reprints. **Publishes 90 titles/year. Receives 1,000 queries and 300 mss/year. 10% of books from first-time authors; 70% from unagented writers. Pays 8-16% royalty on wholesale price. Offers $200-2,000 advance.** Publishes book 16 months after acceptance of ms. Accepts simultaneous submissions. Responds in 4 months to queries. Book catalog for 9×12 SASE; ms guidelines online.

Imprints Editorial Portavoz (Spanish-language works); Kregel Academic & Professional; Kregel Kidzone.

O→ "Our mission as an evangelical Christian publisher is to provide—with integrity and excellence—trusted, Biblically-based resources that challenge and encourage individuals in their Christian lives. Works in theology and Biblical studies should reflect the historic, orthodox Protestant tradition."

Nonfiction "We serve evangelical Christian readers and those in career Christian service."

Fiction Religious (children's, general, inspirational, mystery/suspense, relationships), young adult. Fiction should be geared toward the evangelical Christian market. Wants "books with fast-paced, contemporary storylines presenting a strong Christian message in an engaging, entertaining style."

Recent Title(s) *Clopper, The Christmas Donkey*, by Emily King; *The Case for the Resurrection of Jesus*, by Gary Habermas and Michael Licona; *Firestorm*, by Jeanette Windle (mystery).

Tips "Our audience consists of conservative, evangelical Christians, including pastors and ministry students. Think through very clearly the intended audience for the work."

KRIEGER PUBLISHING CO.

P.O. Box 9542, Melbourne FL 32902-9542. (321)724-9542. Fax: (321)951-3671. E-mail: info@krieger-publishing.com. Website: www.krieger-publishing.com. **Acquisitions:** Sharan B. Merriam and Ronald M. Cervero, series editor (adult education); David E. Kyvig, series director (local history); James B. Gardner, series editor (public history). Also publishes in the fields of history and space sciences. Estab. 1969. Publishes hardcover and paperback originals and reprints. **Publishes 30 titles/year. 30% of books from first-time authors; 100% from unagented writers. Pays royalty on net price.** Publishes book 9-18 months after acceptance of ms. Responds in 3 months to queries. Book catalog free.

Imprints Anvil Series; Orbit Series; Public History; Professional Practices in Adult Education and Lifelong Learning Series.

O→ "We are a short-run niche publisher providing accurate and well-documented scientific and technical titles for text and reference use, college level and higher."

Nonfiction Reference, technical, textbook, scholarly. Subjects include agriculture/horticulture, animals, education (adult), history, nature/environment, science (space), herpetology, chemistry, physics, engineering, veterinary medicine, natural history, math. Query with SASE. Reviews artwork/photos as part of ms package.

Recent Title(s) *Amphibian Medicine & Captive Husbandry*, edited by Kevin R. Wright and Brent R. Whitaker; *A History of Christian Education: Protestant, Catholic, and Orthodox Perspectives*, by John L. Elias.

WENDY LAMB BOOKS

Imprint of Random House Children's Books/Random House, Inc., 1745 Broadway, New York NY 10019. (212)782-9000. Website: www.randomhouse.com. Estab. 2001. Publishes hardcover originals. **Pays royalty.** Accepts simultaneous submissions. Ms guidelines for #10 SASE.

• Literary fiction and nonfiction for readers 8-15. Query with SASE.

Nonfiction Children's/juvenile.

Fiction Juvenile (ages 2-18).

Poetry Submit 4 sample poems.

Tips "A query letter should briefly describe the book you want to write, the intended age group, and your publishing credentials, if any. If you like, you may send no more than 5 pages of the manuscript of shorter works (picture books) and a maximum of 10 pages of longer works (novels). Please do not send more than the specified amount. Also, do not send cassette tapes, videos, or other materials along with your query or excerpt. Manuscript pages will not be returned. Do not send original art."

LANGENSCHEIDT PUBLISHING GROUP

46-35 54th Rd., Maspeth NY 11378. (888)774-7979. Fax: (718)784-0640. E-mail: spohja@langenscheidt.com. **Acquisitions:** Sue Pohja, vice president of trade. Estab. 1983. Publishes hardcover and trade paperback originals. **Publishes 100 titles/year. Receives 100 queries and 50 mss/year. 90% from unagented writers. Pays royalty, or makes outright purchase.** Publishes book 6 months after acceptance of ms. Accepts simultaneous submissions. Responds in 2 months to proposals. Book catalog free.

Imprints ADC Map; American Map; Hagstrom Map; Insight Guides; Hammond World Atlas Corp.; Langenscheidt Trade; Berlitz Publishing.

O── Langenscheidt Publishing Group publishes maps, travel guides, language reference, and dictionary titles, world atlases, educational materials, and language learning audio products.

Nonfiction Reference. Subjects include education, travel, foreign language. "Any title that fills a gap in our line is welcome for review." Submit outline and 2 sample chapters (complete ms preferred). For return of unsolicited queries, include a SASE.

Recent Title(s) *Hammond World Almanac*; *Insight Guide Utah*.

Tips "Any item related to our map, foreign language dictionary, audio, atlas, and travel lines could have potential for us. Of particular interest are titles that have a sizeable potential customer base and have little in the way of good competition."

LARK BOOKS

67 Broadway, Asheville NC 28801. (828)253-0467. Fax: (828)253-7952. Website: www.larkbooks.com. President/Publisher: Carol Taylor. **Acquisitions:** Nicole Tuggle, submissions coordinator. Estab. 1976. Publishes hardcover and trade paperback originals and reprints. **Publishes 60 titles/year. Receives 300 queries and 100 mss/year. 80% of books from first-time authors; 90% from unagented writers. Offers up to $4,000 advance.** Publishes book 1 year after acceptance of ms. Accepts simultaneous submissions. Responds in 3 months to queries. Ms guidelines online.

O── Lark Books publishes high quality, highly illustrated books, primarily in the crafts/leisure markets celebrating the creative spirit. We work closely with bookclubs. Our books are either how-to, 'gallery' or combination books."

Nonfiction Children's/juvenile, coffee table book, how-to, illustrated book. Subjects include gardening, hobbies, nature/environment, crafts, books for enthusiasts. Query first. If asked, submit outline and 1 sample chapter, sample projects, TOC, visuals. Reviews artwork/photos as part of ms package. Send transparencies.

Recent Title(s) *Exquisite Little Knits, Design!*.

Tips "We publish both first-time and seasoned authors. In either case, we need to know that you have substantial expertise on the topic of the proposed book—that we can trust you to know what you're talking about. If you're great at your craft but not so great as a writer, you might want to work with us as a coauthor or as a creative consultant."

LEE & LOW BOOKS

95 Madison Ave., New York NY 10016. (212)779-4400. Fax: (212)532-6035. Website: www.leeandlow.com. **Acquisitions:** Louise May, editor-in-chief. Estab. 1991. Publishes hardcover originals—picture books, middle-grade works only. **Publishes 12-16 titles/year. Pays royalty. Offers advance.** Accepts simultaneous submissions. Responds in 2-4 months. Book catalog for SASE with $1.98 postage; ms guidelines online.

○⇥ "Our goals are to meet a growing need for books that address children of color, and to present literature that all children can identify with. We only consider multicultural children's books." Currently emphasizing material for 5-12 year olds. Sponsors a yearly New Voices Award for first-time picture book authors of color. Contest rules online at website or for SASE.

Nonfiction Children's/juvenile, illustrated book. Subjects include ethnic, multicultural.

Fiction Ethnic, juvenile, multicultural, illustrated. "We do not consider folktales, fairy tales, or animal stories." Send complete ms with cover letter or through an agent.

Recent Title(s) *The Pot That Juan Built*, by Nancy Andrews-Goebel; *Mama's Window*, by Lynn Rubright.

Tips "Of special interest are stories set in contemporary America. We are interested in fiction as well as nonfiction."

LEGACY PRESS

Imprint of Rainbow Publishers, P.O. Box 261129, San Diego CA 92196. (858)668-3260. **Acquisitions:** Christy Scannell, editor,. Estab. 1997. **Publishes 20 titles/year. Receives 250 queries and 100 mss/year. 50% of books from first-time authors. Pays royalty based on wholesale price. Offers negotiable advance.** Publishes book 1-3 years after acceptance of ms. Accepts simultaneous submissions. Book catalog for 9×12 SAE with 2 first-class stamps; ms guidelines for #10 SASE.

○⇥ "Legacy Press strives to publish Bible-based materials that inspire Christian spiritual growth and development in children." Currently emphasizing nonfiction for kids, particularly pre-teens and more specifically girls, although we are publishing boys and girls 2-12. No picture books, fiction without additional activities, poetry or plays.

Nonfiction Subjects include creative nonfiction, education, hobbies, religion. Submit outline, 3-5 sample chapters, market analysis, SASE.

Recent Title(s) *God and Me!* (series for girls); *Gotta Have God* (series for boys); *The Christian Girl's Guide To . . .* (series for girls).

Tips "We are looking for Christian versions of general market nonfiction for kids, as well as original ideas."

LEGEND BOOKS

69 Lansing St., Auburn NY 13021. (315)258-8012. **Acquisitions:** Joseph P. Berry, editor. Publishes paperback monographs, scholarly books, and college textbooks. **Publishes 15 titles/year. Receives 100 queries and 60 mss/year. 50% of books from first-time authors; 100% from unagented writers. Pays 20% royalty on net sales.** Publishes book 9 months after acceptance of ms. Accepts simultaneous submissions. Responds in 2 months.

○⇥ Legend Books publishes a variety of books used in the college classroom, including workbooks. However, it does not publish any books on mathematics or hard sciences.

Nonfiction Biography, scholarly, textbook, community/public affairs, speech/mass communication. Subjects include business/economics, child guidance/parenting, community, education, government/politics, health/medicine, history, humanities, philosophy, psychology, recreation, social sciences, sociology, sports, journalism, public relations, television. Query with SASE, or submit complete ms (include SASE if ms is to be returned). Reviews artwork/photos as part of ms package. Send photocopies.

Recent Title(s) *The Conversion of the King of Bissau*, by Timothy Coates, PhD (world history); *Values, Society & Evolution*, by H. James Birx, PhD (anthropology and sociology).

Tips "We seek college professors who actually teach courses for which their books are designed."

LEHIGH UNIVERSITY PRESS

Linderman Library, 30 Library Dr., Lehigh University, Bethlehem PA 18015-3067. (610)758-3933. Fax: (610)758-6331. E-mail: inlup@lehigh.edu. Website: fpl.cc.lehigh.edu/inlup. **Acquisitions:** Philip A. Metzger, director. Estab. 1985. Publishes hardcover originals. **Publishes 10 titles/year. Receives 90-100 queries and 50-60 mss/year. 70% of books from first-time authors; 100% from unagented writers. Pays royalty.** Publishes book 18 months after acceptance of ms. Accepts simultaneous submissions. Responds in 3 months to queries. Book catalog and ms guidelines free.

○⇥ "Currently emphasizing works on 18th-century studies, history of technology, East-Asian studies, and literary criticism. Accepts all subjects of academic merit."

Nonfiction Lehigh University Press is a conduit for nonfiction works of scholarly interest to the academic community. Biography, reference, scholarly. Subjects include Americana, art/architecture, history, language/literature, science. Submit proposal package including 1 sample chapter.

Recent Title(s) *An American Musical Dynasty: A Biography of the Wolle Family of Bethlehem, Pennsylvania*, by Paul S. Larson; *The Widow's Quest: The Byers Extraterritorial Case in Hairas, China, 1924-1925*, by Kathleen L. Loawica; *A Wonderful World of God: Puritanism and the Great Awakening*, by Robert W. Brockway.

LEISURE BOOKS

Imprint of Dorchester Publishing Co., 200 Madison Ave., Suite 2000, New York NY 10016. (212)725-8811. Fax: (212)532-1054. Website: www.dorchesterpub.com. **Acquisitions:** Kate Seaver, editor; Alicia Condon, editorial director; Don D'Auria, executive editor (westerns, thrillers, horror); Christopher Keeslar, senior editor. Estab. 1970. Publishes mass market paperback originals and reprints. Publishes romances, westerns, horrors, young adult, chick lit, and thrillers only. **Publishes 240 titles/year. 20% of books from first-time authors; 20% from unagented writers. Pays royalty on retail price. Offers negotiable advance.** Publishes book 18 months after acceptance of ms. Does not accept simultaneous submissions. Responds in 6 months to queries. Book catalog for free by calling (800)481-9191; ms guidelines online.

Imprints Love Spell (romance); Leisure (romance, western, thriller, horror).

O— Leisure Books/Love Spell is seeking historical, contemporary, time travel, and paranormal romances.

Fiction Historical (romance), horror, romance, western, chick lit. "All historical romance should be set pre-1900. Horrors and westerns are growing as well. No sweet romance, science fiction, erotica, mainstream, or action/adventure. New YA line, contemporary, and paranormal, 45,000 words." Query with SASE, or submit outline, first 3 sample chapters, synopsis. "All manuscripts must be typed, double-spaced on one side, and left unbound."

Recent Title(s) *The Pirate Prince*, by Connie Mason (romance); *The Lake*, by Richard Laymon (horror); *Calendar Girl*, by Naomi Neale (chick lit).

LERNER PUBLISHING CO.

241 First Ave. N., Minneapolis MN 55401. (612)332-3344. Fax: (612)332-7615. Website: www.lernerbooks.com. **Acquisitions:** Jennifer Zimian, nonfiction submissions editor; Zelda Wagner, fiction submissions editor. Estab. 1959. Publishes hardcover originals, trade paperback originals and reprints. Accepts simultaneous submissions. Book catalog for 9×12 SAE with $3.85 postage; ms guidelines online.

Imprints Carolrhoda Books; First Avenue Editions (paperback reprints for hard/soft deals only); Lerner Publications; LernerSports; LernerClassroom; Kar-Ben Publishing.

• Only accepts submissions in November. Anything sent another month will be returned unopened.

O— "Our goal is to publish children's books that educate, stimulate and stretch the imagination, foster global awareness, encourage critical thinking and inform, inspire and entertain."

Nonfiction Biography, children's/juvenile. Subjects include art/architecture, ethnic, history, nature/environment, science, sports. Query with SASE, or submit outline, 1-2 sample chapters.

Fiction Young adult (problem novels, sports, adventure, mystery). Looking for "well-written middle grade and young adult. *No adult fiction or single short stories.*" Query with SASE, or submit outline, 2 sample chapters, synopsis.

Recent Title(s) *Discovering Nature's Laws*, by Laura Purdie Salas; *Mallory vs. Max*, by Laurie Friedman.

Tips "No alphabet, puzzle, song or text books, religious subject matter or plays. Submissions are accepted in the months of November only. Work received in any other month will be returned unopened. SASE required for authors who wish to have their material returned or business-sized SASE for response only. Submissions without an SASE will receive no reply. Please allow 4-6 months for a response. No phone calls."

⊘ ARTHUR A. LEVINE BOOKS

Imprint of Scholastic Inc., 557 Broadway, New York NY 10012. (212)343-4436. Website: www.arthuralevinebooks.com. **Acquisitions:** Arthur Levine, editorial director. **Publishes 10-14 titles/year. Pays variable royalty on retail price. Offers variable advance.** Book catalog for 9×12 SASE.

Fiction Juvenile, picture books, young adult, middle grade novels. Query with SASE. *All unsolicited mss returned unopened.* "We are willing to work with first-time authors, with or without an agent. However, we only accept query letters."

Recent Title(s) *The Guild of Geniuses*, by Dan Santat; *Millicent Min, Girl Genius*, by Lisa Yee; *The Story of a Seagull and the Cat Who Taught Her How to Fly*, by Luis Sepulveda.

LIBRARIES UNLIMITED, INC.

88 Post Rd. W., Westport CT 06881. (800)225-5800. Fax: (203)222-1502. Website: www.lu.com. **Acquisitions:** Barbara Ittner, acquisitions editor (public library titles); Sharon Coatney (school library titles); Sue Easun (academic library titles). Estab. 1964. Publishes hardcover and paperback originals. **Publishes 100 titles/year. Receives 400 queries and 100 mss/year. 50% of books from first-time authors; 100% from unagented writers.** Publishes book 9 months after acceptance of ms. Accepts simultaneous submissions. Responds in 1 month to queries; 2 months to proposals and mss. Book catalog and ms guidelines online.

O— Libraries Unlimited publishes resources for libraries, librarians, and educators. "We are currently emphasizing readers' advisory guides, academic reference works, readers' theatre, literary and technology resources."

Nonfiction Biography (collections), reference, textbook. Subjects include agriculture/horticulture, anthropology/archeology, art/architecture, business/economics, education, ethnic, health/medicine, history, language/literature, music/dance, philosophy, psychology, religion, science, sociology, women's issues/studies, technology. "We are interested in library applications and tools for all subject areas." Submit proposal package including outline, 1 sample chapter, résumé. Reviews artwork/photos as part of ms package. Send photocopies.
Recent Title(s) *Information Literacy: Essential Skills for the Information Age*, by Michael B. Eisenberg, Carrie A. Lowe, and Kathleen L. Spitzer; *Picture This! Using Picture Books for Character Education in the Classroom*, by Claire Gatrell Stephens.
Tips "We welcome any ideas that combine professional expertise, writing ability, and innovative thinking. Audience is librarians (school, public, academic, and special) and teachers (K-12)."

LIGUORI PUBLICATIONS

One Liguori Dr., Liguori MO 63057. (636)464-2500. Fax: (636)464-8449. Website: www.liguori.org. Publisher: Harry Grile. **Acquisitions:** Daniel Michaels, acquisitions editor. Estab. 1947. Publishes paperback originals and reprints under the Ligouri and Libros Ligouri imprints. **Publishes 20-25 titles/year. Pays royalty, or makes outright purchase. Offers varied advance.** Publishes book 2 years after acceptance of ms. Does not accept simultaneous submissions. Responds in 2 months to queries and proposals; 3 months to mss. Ms guidelines online.
Imprints Libros Liguori; Liguori Books; Liguori/Triumph; Liguori Lifespan.
- Liguori Publications, faithful to the charism of St. Alphonsus, is an apostolate within the mission of the Denver Province. Its mission, a collaborative effort of Redemptorists and laity, is to spread the gospel of Jesus Christ primarily through the print and electronic media. It shares in the Redemptorist priority of giving special attention to the poor and the most abandoned. Currently emphasizing practical spirituality, prayers and devotions, "how-to" spirituality.

Nonfiction Mss with Catholic sensibility. Self-help. Subjects include religion, spirituality. Mostly adult audience; limited children/juvenile. Query with SASE, or submit outline, 1 sample chapter.

LILLENAS PUBLISHING CO.

Imprint of Lillenas Drama Resources, 2923 Troost Ave., Kansas City MO 64109. (816)931-1900. Fax: (816)412-8390. E-mail: drama@lillenas.com. Website: www.lillenasdrama.com. **Acquisitions:** Kim Messer, product manager (Christian drama). Publishes mass market paperback and electronic originals. **Publishes 50+ titles/year; imprint publishes 12+ titles/year. Pays royalty on wholesale price, or makes outright purchase.**
Nonfiction Plays, collections of scripts. Subjects include religion, life issues. Query with SASE, or submit complete ms.

[N] LION BOOKS

210 Nelson Rd., Suite B, Scarsdale NY 10583. (914)725-2280. Fax: (914)725-3572. **Acquisitions:** Harriet Ross, editor. Estab. 1966. Publishes hardcover originals and reprints, trade paperback reprints. **Publishes 8 titles/year. Receives 60-150 queries and 100 mss/year. Pays 7-15% royalty on wholesale price. Offers advance.** Does not accept simultaneous submissions. Responds in 1 week to queries; 1 month to mss.
Nonfiction Biography, how-to. Subjects include Americana, ethnic, government/politics, history, recreation, sports. No fiction. Submit complete ms with SASE.

[A] LISTEN & LIVE AUDIO, INC.

P.O. Box 817, Roseland NJ 07068. (973)781-1444. Fax: (973)781-0333. E-mail: alfred@listenandlive.com. Website: www.listenandlive.com. **Acquisitions:** Alisa Weberman, publisher (mss/books for audiobook consideration). **Publishes 20 titles/year. Receives 200 mss/year. Offers advance.** Publishes book 3-6 months after acceptance of ms. Accepts simultaneous submissions. Responds in 1 month to mss. Audiobook catalog online.
- Listen & Live publishes fiction and nonfiction books on audio cassette/CD.

Nonfiction Multimedia (audio format), self-help, true life. Subjects include business/economics, relationships. *Agented submissions only.*
Fiction Mystery, young adult, contemporary, women's fiction, children's. *Agented submissions only.*
Recent Title(s) *The Darwin Awards I & II*; *Jump the Shark*; *The Jane Austen Book Club*.
Tips Agents/publishers only may submit mss/books.

[A] [∅] LITTLE, BROWN AND CO., INC.

Subsidiary of Time Warner Book Group, 1271 Avenue of the Americas, New York NY 10017. Website: www.twbookgroup.com. **Acquisitions:** Editorial Department, Trade Division. Estab. 1837. Publishes adult and juvenile hardcover and paperback originals, and reprints. **Pays royalty. Offers varying advance.** Does not accept simultaneous submissions. Ms guidelines online.

Imprints Little, Brown and Co. Adult Trade; Bulfinch Press; Back Bay; Little, Brown Books for Young Readers.
- *No unsolicited submissions. Agented submissions only.*
- ⊶ "The general editorial philosophy for all divisions continues to be broad and flexible, with high quality and the promise of commercial success as always the first considerations."

Nonfiction Autobiography, biography, cookbook. Subjects include contemporary culture, cooking/foods/nutrition, history, memoirs, nature/environment, science, sports.

Fiction Experimental, literary, mainstream/contemporary, mystery, short story collections, suspense, thrillers/espionage, translations.

Ⓐ ⊘ LITTLE, BROWN AND CO. ADULT TRADE BOOKS

Division of Time Warner Book Group, 1271 Avenue of the Americas, New York NY 10020. (212)522-8700. Fax: (212)522-2067. Website: www.twbookmark.com. Estab. 1837. Publishes hardcover originals and paperback originals and reprints.
- *Does not accept unsolicited mss.*

Recent Title(s) *The Way Out*, by Craig Childs; *The True and Outstanding Adventures of the Hunt Sisters*, by Elisabeth Robinson; *Searching for the Sound*, by Phil Lesh.

Ⓐ LITTLE, BROWN AND CO. BOOKS FOR YOUNG READERS

Subsidiary of Time Warner Book Group, Time Life Bldg., 1271 Avenue of the Americas, 11th Floor, New York NY 10020. (212)522-8700. Website: www.twbookmark.com. Editor-in-Chief/VP/Associate Publisher: Megan Tingley. Marketing Director VP/Associate Publisher: Bill Boedeker. Executive Editors: Cindy Eagan and Andrea Spooner. Executive Editor/Director of Special Projects (novelty & merchandise): Liza Baker. Senior Editor; Jennifer Hunt. Estab. 1837. Publishes hardcover originals, trade paperback reprints. **Publishes 70-100 titles/year. Pays royalty on retail price. Offers negotiable advance.** Publishes book 1-2 years after acceptance of ms. Accepts simultaneous submissions. Responds in 1 month to queries; 2 months to proposals and mss.

Imprints Megan Tingley Books (Megan Tingley, editorial director).
- ⊶ Little, Brown and Co. Children's Publishing publishes all formats including board books, picture books, middle grade fiction, and nonfiction YA titles. "We are looking for strong writing and presentation, but no predetermined topics."

Nonfiction Children's/juvenile. Subjects include animals, art/architecture, ethnic, gay/lesbian, history, hobbies, nature/environment, recreation, science, sports. Writers should avoid "looking for the 'issue' they think publishers want to see, choosing instead topics they know best and are most enthusiastic about/inspired by." *Agented submissions only.*

Fiction Picture books, middle grade and young adult. Adventure, fantasy, feminist, gay/lesbian, historical, humor, mystery, science fiction, suspense, chick lit, multicultural. "We are looking for strong fiction for children of all ages in any area. We always prefer full manuscripts for fiction." *Agented submissions only.*

Recent Title(s) *Gossip Girl*, by Cecily von Ziegesar; *Toot & Puddle: The New Friend*, by Holly Hobbie; *The Feel Good Book*, by Todd Parr.

Tips "Our audience is children of all ages, from preschool through young adult. We are looking for quality material that will work in hardcover—send us your best."

Ⓐ ⊘ LITTLE SIMON

Imprint of Simon & Schuster Children's Publishing Division, Simon & Schuster, 1230 Avenue of the Americas, New York NY 10020. (212)698-1295. Fax: (212)698-2794. Website: www.simonsayskids.com. Publishes novelty and branded books only. **Offers advance and royalties.**
- *Currently not accepting unsolicited mss.*
- ⊶ "Our goal is to provide fresh material in an innovative format for preschool to age 8. Our books are often, if not exclusively, format driven."

Nonfiction "We publish very few nonfiction titles." Children's/juvenile. No picture books. Query with SASE.

Fiction "Novelty books include many things that do not fit in the traditional hardcover or paperback format, such as pop-up, board book, scratch and sniff, glow in the dark, lift the flap, etc." Children's/juvenile. No picture books. Large part of the list is holiday-themed.

Recent Title(s) *Mother's Day Ribbons*, by Michelle Knudsen, illustrated by John Wallace; *Dear Zoo*, by Rod Campbell; *My Blankie*, by Patricia Ryan Lampl, illustrated by Valeria Petrone.

⊘ LIVINGSTON PRESS

University of West Alabama, Station 22, Livingston AL 35470. E-mail: jwt@uwa.edu. Website: www.livingstonpress.uwa.edu. **Acquisitions:** Joe Taylor, director. Estab. 1974. Publishes hardcover and trade paperback originals. **Publishes 10-12 titles/year. 50% of books from first-time authors; 100% from unagented writers. Pays**

150 contributor's copies, after sales of 1,500, standard royalty. Publishes book 18 months after acceptance of ms. Accepts simultaneous submissions. Responds in 1 month to queries; 1 year to mss. Book catalog for SASE; ms guidelines online.

Imprints Swallow's Tale Press.

- Reads mss in March only. *Not accepting unsolicited material until 2006.*
- Livingston Press publishes topics such as Southern literature and quirky fiction. Currently emphasizing novels. "We typically only publish short story collections through our Tartt Frist Fiction Award."

Fiction Experimental, literary, short story collections, off-beat or Southern. "We are interested in form and, of course, style." Query with SASE. Accepts unsolicited mss only during March, except for Tartt Frist Fiction Award, which closes in December.

Recent Title(s) *The Soft Room*, by Karen Heuler; *B. Horror and Other Stories*, by Wendell Mayo.

Tips "Our readers are interested in literature, often quirky literature that emphasizes form and style. Please visit our website for current needs."

LLEWELLYN ESPAÑOL

P.O. Box 64383, St. Paul MN 55164-0383. (651)291-1970. Fax: (651)291-1908. E-mail: lwlpc@llewellyn.com. Website: www.llewellyn.com. Estab. 1993. Publishes mass market and trade paperback originals and reprints. Accepts simultaneous submissions. Book catalog and ms guidelines online.

- Publishes Spanish-language books for people of any age interested in material discussing "mind, body and spirit."

Nonfiction General nonfiction, gift book, how-to, self-help, teen/young adult. Subjects include health/medicine, New Age, psychology, sex, spirituality, foods/nutrition; angels; magic. "Have it edited, including all ortographic punctuation and accents." Submit proposal package including outline, sample chapters, SASE, or submit complete ms. Reviews artwork/photos as part of ms package. Send photocopies.

Recent Title(s) *Miguel: Comunicÿndose con el Arcÿngel para la orientación y protección*; *Las llaves del reino: Jesús y la cábala cristiana*, by Migene Gonzalez-Wippler.

LLEWELLYN PUBLICATIONS

Imprint of Llewellyn Worldwide, Ltd., P.O. Box 64383, St. Paul MN 55164-0383. (800)THE-MOON. Fax: (651)291-1908. E-mail: lwlpc@llewellyn.com. Website: www.llewellyn.com. **Acquisitions:** Nancy J. Mostad (New Age, metaphysical, occult, astrology, tarot, pagan, magick, alternative health, self-help, how-to books). Estab. 1901. Publishes trade and mass market paperback originals. **Publishes 100 titles/year. 30% of books from first-time authors; 90% from unagented writers. Pays 10% royalty on wholesale price, or retail price.** Accepts simultaneous submissions. Responds in 3 months to queries. Book catalog for 9×12 SAE with 4 first-class stamps.

- Llewellyn publishes New Age fiction and nonfiction exploring "new worlds of mind and spirit." Currently emphasizing astrology, alternative health and healing, tarot. De-emphasizing fiction, channeling.

Nonfiction How-to, self-help. Subjects include cooking/foods/nutrition, health/medicine, nature/environment, New Age, psychology, women's issues/studies. Submit outline, sample chapters. Reviews artwork/photos as part of ms package.

Fiction "Authentic and educational, yet entertaining." Occult, spiritual (metaphysical).

Recent Title(s) *Authentic Spirituality*, by Richard N. Potter; *You Are Psychic*, by Debra Katz.

LONELY PLANET PUBLICATIONS

150 Linden St., Oakland CA 94607-2538. (510)893-8555. Fax: (510)893-8563. E-mail: info@lonelyplanet.com. Website: www.lonelyplanet.com. Australia Office: Locked Bag 1, Footscray, Victoria 3011, Australia. Estab. 1973. Publishes trade paperback originals. **Work-for-hire: 1/3 on contract, 1/3 on submission, 1/3 on approval. Offers advance.** Accepts simultaneous submissions. Responds in 3 months to queries. Book catalog and ms guidelines online.

- Lonely Planet publishes travel guides, atlases, travel literature, phrasebooks, condensed pocket guides, diving and snorkeling guides.

Nonfiction "We only work with contract writers on book ideas that we originate. We do not accept original proposals. Request our writer's guidelines. Send résumé and clips of travel writing." Subjects include travel. "Request our catalog first to make sure we don't already have a similar book or call and see if a similar book is on our production schedule." Query with SASE.

Recent Title(s) *Europe on a Shoestring, 4th Ed.*, by China Williams; *Morocco, 7th Ed.*, by Mara Vorhees; *Vietnam, 8th Ed.*, by Wendy Yanagihara.

LOOMPANICS UNLIMITED

P.O. Box 1197, Port Townsend WA 98368-0997. Fax: (360)385-7785. E-mail: editorial@loompanics.com. Website: www.loompanics.com. **Acquisitions:** Michael Hoy, president. Estab. 1975. Publishes trade paperback originals. **Publishes 12 titles/year. 40% of books from first-time authors; 100% from unagented writers. Pays 10-12% royalty on wholesale and/or retail sales, or makes outright purchase of $100-1,200. Offers $500 average advance.** Publishes book 6 months after acceptance of ms. Accepts simultaneous submissions. Responds in 3 months to queries. Book catalog for $5, postage paid; ms guidelines online.

　　O⟶ "Our motto 'No more secrets-no more excuses-no more limits' says it all, whatever the subject. Our books are somewhat 'edgy.' From computer hacking to gardening to tax avoision, we are the name in beat-the-system books." Always emphasizing unusual takes on subjects that are controversial and how-to books. "We do not want anything that's already been done or New Age."

Nonfiction "In general, we like works on edgy topics or obscure-but-useful technology written with confidence in a matter-of-fact way. We are looking for how-to books in the fields of espionage, investigation, the underground economy, police methods, how to beat the system, crime and criminal techniques." How-to, reference, self-help, technical. Subjects include agriculture/horticulture, Americana, anthropology/archeology, computers/electronic, government/politics, health/medicine, money/finance, psychology, science, film/cinema/stage. "We are also looking for articles on similar subjects for our catalog and its supplements." Query with SASE, or submit outline, sample chapters. Electronic submissions will not be considered. Reviews artwork/photos as part of ms package.

Recent Title(s) *Rancho Costa Nada: The Dirt Cheap Desert Homestead*, by Phil Garlington; *Speak Up, Speak Out and Be Heard: How to Protest and Make It Count*, by Jeremy Holcomb; *Uberhacker II! More Ways to Break Into a Computer*, by Carolyn Meinel.

Tips "Our audience is primarily people who think outside the box and believers in the first amendment and our constitutional rights looking for hard-to-find information on alternatives to 'The System.' Your chances for success are greatly improved if you can show us how your proposal fits in with our catalog."

LOUISIANA STATE UNIVERSITY PRESS

P.O. Box 25053, Baton Rouge LA 70894-5053. (225)578-6434. Fax: (225)578-6461. Website: www.lsu.edu/lsupress. Director: MaryKatherine Callaway. Estab. 1935. Publishes hardcover and paperback originals, and reprints. Publishes 12 poetry titles per year and 1 work of original fiction as part of the Yellow Shoe Fiction series. **Publishes 80-90 titles/year. 33% of books from first-time authors; 95% from unagented writers. Pays royalty.** Publishes book 1 year after acceptance of ms. Does not accept simultaneous submissions. Responds in 1 month to queries. Book catalog and ms guidelines free.

Nonfiction Biography. Subjects include art/architecture, ethnic, government/politics, history, language/literature, music/dance, photography, regional, women's issues/studies, geography and environmental studies. Query with SASE, or submit outline, sample chapters.

Recent Title(s) *Habitat: New and Selected Poems, 1965-2005*, by Brendan Galvin (poetry); *Sixty-Cent Coffee and a Quarter Dance*, by Judy Jordan (poetry); *The Great Southern Babylon: Sex, Race, and Respectability in New Orleans, 1865-1920*, by Alecia P. Long (history).

Tips "Our audience includes scholars, intelligent laymen, general audience."

[N] LOVE INSPIRED

Imprint of Steeple Hill, 233 Broadway, Suite 1001, New York NY 10279. (212)553-4200. Fax: (212)227-8969. Website: www.steeplehill.com. **Acquisitions:** Joan Marlow Golan, executive editor (inspirational fiction); Mavis Allen, associate senior editor (inspirational fiction); Krista Stroever, editor (inspirational fiction); Diane Dietz, assistant editor (inspirational fiction). Estab. 1997. Publishes mass market paperback originals. **Publishes 78-90 titles/year. Pays royalty on retail price. Offers advance.** Does not accept simultaneous submissions. Responds in 3 months. Ms guidelines online.

Fiction Religious, romance. "The Love Inspired line is a series of contemporary, inspirational romances that feature Christian characters facing the many challenges of life and love in today's world. We only publish inspirational romance between 70,000 and 75,000 words." Query with SASE.

Recent Title(s) *Holiday Homecoming*, by Jillian Hart; *A Dry Creek Christmas*, by Janet Tronstad.

Tips "Please read our guidelines."

[N] LOVE INSPIRED SUSPENSE

Imprint of Steeple Hill, 233 Broadway, Suite 1001, New York NY 10279. (212)553-4200. Fax: (212)227-8969. Website: www.steeplehill.com. **Acquisitions:** Joan Marlow Golan, executive editor (inspirational fiction); Mavis Allen, associate senior editor (inspirational fiction); Krista Stroever, editor (inspirational fiction); Diane Dietz, assistant editor (inspirational fiction). Estab. 1997. Publishes mass market paperback originals. **Publishes 78-90 titles/year. Pays royalty on retail price. Offers advance.** Does not accept simultaneous submissions. Responds in 3 months. Ms guidelines online.

　　● This program launches in July 2005, so you will not find any recent titles listed. Please read the imprint's guidelines before submitting.

Fiction Religious, romance, suspense. "This new brand is a series of edge-of-the-seat, comtemporary romantic suspense tales or intrigue and romance featuring Christian characters facing challenges to their faith and to their lives. We only publish novels between 70,000 and 75,000 words.'' Query with SASE.

Tips ''Please read our guidelines.''

LOVE SPELL

Imprint of Dorchester Publishing Co., Inc., 200 Madison Ave., Suite 2000, New York NY 10016. (212)725-8811. Fax: (212)532-1054. Website: www.dorchesterpub.com. **Acquisitions:** Kate Seaver, editor; Christopher Keeslar, senior editor; Alicia Condon, editorial director. Publishes mass market paperback originals. **Publishes 48 titles/ year. Receives 1,500-2,000 queries and 150-500 mss/year. 30% of books from first-time authors; 25-30% from unagented writers. Pays 4% royalty on retail price. Offers variable advance.** Publishes book 1 year after acceptance of ms. Does not accept simultaneous submissions. Responds in 8 months to mss. Book catalog for free or by calling (800)481-9191; ms guidelines online.

> ⊶ Love Spell publishes the quirky sub-genres of romance: time-travel, paranormal, futuristic. ''Despite the exotic settings, we are still interested in character-driven plots.''

Fiction Romance (futuristic, time travel, paranormal, historical), whimsical contemporaries. ''Books industry-wide are getting shorter; we're interested in 90,000 words.'' Query with SASE, or submit 3 sample chapters, synopsis. No material will be returned without SASE. No queries by fax. ''All manuscripts must be typed, double-spaced on one side, and left unbound.''

Recent Title(s) *Night Bites*, by Nina Bangs; *The Scarlet Empress*, by Susan Grant.

LOYOLA PRESS

3441 N. Ashland Ave., Chicago IL 60657-1397. (773)281-1818. Fax: (773)281-0152. E-mail: editorial@loyolapress.com. Website: www.loyolapress.org. **Acquisitions:** Joseph Durepos, acquisitions editor. Publishes hardcover and trade paperback. **Publishes 20-30 titles/year. Receives 500 queries/year. Pays standard royalties. Offers reasonable advance.** Accepts simultaneous submissions. Book catalog and ms guidelines online.

Imprints Jesuit Way (focus on Jesuit life and history as well as on Ignatian spirituality and ministry).

Nonfiction Subjects include religion, spirituality, inspirational, prayer, Catholic life, grief and loss, marriage and family. Query with SASE.

Recent Title(s) *Notre Dame Vs. the Klan*, by Todd Tucker; *In the Arms of Angels*, by Joan Webster Anderson; *Lessons for Living*, by Pope John Paul II.

Tips ''We're looking for authors who have a fresh approach to religion and spirituality, especially for readers looking for a way to respond to God in their daily lives.''

Ⓝ LRP PUBLICATIONS, INC.

P.O. Box 980, Horsham PA 19044. (215)784-0860. Fax: (215)784-9639. E-mail: custserve@lrp.com. Website: www.lrp.com. **Acquisitions:** See website for contacts by product group. Estab. 1977. Publishes hardcover and trade paperback originals. **Pays royalty.** Does not accept simultaneous submissions. Book catalog and ms guidelines free.

Nonfiction Reference. Subjects include business/economics, education. Submit proposal package including outline.

Ⓞ LUCENT BOOKS

15822 Bernardo Center Dr., Suite C, San Diego CA 92127. E-mail: chandra.howard@thomson.com. Website: www.gale.com/lucent. **Acquisitions:** Chandra Howard, senior acquisitions editor. Estab. 1988. **Publishes 200 titles/year. 10% of books from first-time authors; 99% from unagented writers. Makes outright purchase of $2,500-3,000.**

> ⊶ Lucent Books is a nontrade publisher of nonfiction for the middle school audience providing students with resource material for academic studies and for independent learning.

Nonfiction Children's/juvenile. Subjects include history, world affairs, cultural and social issues. Tightly formatted books for middle grade readers. Each series has specific requirements. Potential writers should familiarize themselves with the material. All are works for hire, by assignment only. *No unsolicited mss.* E-mail query with cover letter, résumé, list of publications to Chandra Howard.

Recent Title(s) *J.K. Rowling*, by Bradley Steffens; *Life in the Trenches*, by Stephen Currie; *Women of the American Revolution*, by Louise Chipley Slavicek.

Tips ''We expect writers to do thorough research using books, magazines, and newspapers. Biased writing, whether liberal or conservative, has no place in our books. We prefer to work with writers who have experience writing nonfiction for middle grade students. We are looking for experienced writers, especially those who have written nonfiction books at young adult level.''

THE LYONS PRESS

Imprint of The Globe Pequot Press, Inc., Box 480, 246 Goose Lane, Guilford CT 06437. (203)458-4500. Fax: (203)458-4668. Website: www.lyonspress.com. **Acquisitions:** Jay Cassell, editorial director (fishing, hunting, survival, military, history); Tom McCarthy, senior editor (sports & fitness, history, outdoor adventure, current events); George Donahue, senior editor (military history, martial arts, narrative nonfiction, sports, current affairs); Ann Treistman, senior editor (narrative nonfiction, adventure, sports, animals, cooking); Jay McCullough, editor (narrative nonfiction, adventure, military, espionage, international current events, history); Holly Rubino, associate editor (narrative nonfiction, home); Lilly Golden, editor-at-large (nature, narrative nonfiction); Lisa Purcell, editor-at-large (history, adventure, narrative nonfiction); Steve Price, editor-at-large (equestrian). Estab. 1984 (Lyons & Burford), 1997 (The Lyons Press). Publishes hardcover and trade paperback originals and reprints. **Publishes 300 titles/year. 50% of books from first-time authors; 30% from unagented writers. Pays 5-10% royalty on wholesale price. Offers $2,000-7,000 advance.** Publishes book 1 year after acceptance of ms. Accepts simultaneous submissions. Responds in 2 months to queries and proposals; 3 months to mss. Book catalog and ms guidelines online.

- The Lyons Press has teamed up to develop books with The Explorers Club, Orvis, L.L. Bean, *Field & Stream*, Outward Bound, Buckmasters, and *Golf Magazine*.
- O— The Lyons Press publishes practical and literary books, chiefly centered on outdoor subjects—natural history, all sports, gardening, horses, fishing, hunting, survival, self-reliant living.

Nonfiction Biography, how-to, reference. Subjects include agriculture/horticulture, Americana, animals, cooking/foods/nutrition, history, military/war, nature/environment, recreation, sports, adventure, fitness. "Visit our website and note the featured categories." Query with SASE, or submit proposal package including outline, 3 sample chapters, marketing description. Reviews artwork/photos as part of ms package. Send photocopies or nonoriginal prints.

Recent Title(s) *Believe*, by Buck Brannaman (horses); *The Orvis Ultimate Book of Fly Fishing*, by Tom Rosenbauer (fishing); *Lost in Tibet*, by Richard Starks and Miriam Murcutt (adventure/military history).

Ⓝ MACADAM/CAGE PUBLISHING, INC.

155 Sansome St., Suite 550, San Francisco CA 94104. (415)986-7502. Fax: (415)986-7414. E-mail: jason@macad amcage.com. Website: www.macadamcage.com. Publisher: David Poindexter. **Acquisitions:** Patrick Walsh, editor; Anika Streitfeld, editor; Kate Nitze, assistant editor; Jason Wood, assistant editor. Estab. 1999. Publishes hardcover and trade paperback originals. **Publishes 25-30 titles/year. Receives 5,000 queries and 1,500 mss/year. 75% of books from first-time authors; 50% from unagented writers. Pays negotiable royalties. Offers negotiable advance.** Publishes book up to 1 year after acceptance of ms. Accepts simultaneous submissions. Responds in 4 months. Ms guidelines for SASE or check the website.

- O— MacAdam/Cage publishes quality works of literary fiction that are carefully crafted and tell a bold story. De-emphasizing romance, poetry, Christian or New Age mss.

Nonfiction Biography. Subjects include history, memoirs, science, social sciences. "Narrative nonfiction that reads like fiction." No self-help or New Age. Submit proposal package including outline, up to 3 sample chapters, SASE.

Fiction Historical, literary, mainstream/contemporary. No electronic or faxed submissions. No romance, science fiction, Christian, New Age. Submit proposal package including up to 3 sample chapters, synopsis, SASE.

Recent Title(s) *How to be Lost*, by Amanda Eyre Ward (fiction); *The Time Traveler's Wife*, by Audrey Niffenegger (fiction); *Pinkerton's Sister*, by Peter Rushforth (fiction).

Tips "We like to keep in close contact with writers. We publish for readers of quality fiction and nonfiction."

Ⓝ Ⓩ JOHN MACRAE BOOKS

Henry Holt & Co., Inc., 115 W. 18th St., New York NY 10011. (212)886-9200. Estab. 1991. Publishes hardcover originals. **Publishes 20-25 titles/year. Pays royalty. Offers varies advance.** Publishes book 9-12 months after acceptance of ms.

Fiction Literary, mainstream/contemporary.

Ⓝ MANDALEY PRESS

Subsidiary of Solution Resources, 720 Rio Grande Dr., Suite 100, Alpharetta GA 30022. E-mail: msatt@mindspring.com. **Acquisitions:** Mark Satterfield, president (business books with a particular interest in sales training). Estab. 2001. Publishes hardcover, trade paperback, and mass market paperback originals. **Publishes 10 titles/year; imprint publishes 10 titles/year. Receives 50 queries and 50 mss/year. 80% of books from first-time authors; 100% from unagented writers. Pays 10-20% royalty on wholesale price.** Publishes book 6 months after acceptance of ms. Accepts simultaneous submissions. Responds in 1 month to queries; 2 months to proposals and mss.

Nonfiction Audiocassettes, booklets, how-to, self-help. Subjects include business/economics. "We are looking for authors in the sales marketing arena with a value-added message. There are many books currently available that focus on 'what' successful sales professionals do. We are interested in 'how' specifically to achieve success.'' No books on a ''winning attitude.'' Query with SASE. Reviews artwork/photos as part of ms package.

Ⓐ Ⓩ MARINER BOOKS

Houghton Mifflin Trade Division, 222 Berkeley St., Boston MA 02116. (617)351-5000. Fax: (617)351-1202. Website: www.hmco.com. Estab. 1997. Publishes trade paperback originals and reprints. **Pays royalty on retail price, or makes outright purchase. Offers variable advance.** Book catalog free.

   ○━ Houghton Mifflin books give shape to ideas that educate, inform and delight. Mariner has an eclectic list that notably embraces fiction.

Nonfiction Biography. Subjects include education, government/politics, history, nature/environment, philosophy, sociology, women's issues/studies, political thought. *Agented submissions only.*

Fiction Literary, mainstream/contemporary. *Agented submissions only.*

Recent Title(s) *Self-Portrait With Turtles*, by David M. Carroll (memoir); *Two Souls Indivisible*, by James S. Hirsch (history); *Empress Orchid*, by Anchee Min (historical fiction).

Ⓩ MARLOWE & CO.

Imprint of Avalon Publishing Group, 245 W. 17th St., 11th Floor, New York NY 10011. (212)981-9919. Fax: (212)375-2571. Website: www.avalonpub.com. Publisher: Matthew Lore. Estab. 1994.

   ○━ Marlowe & Co. publishes widely in the areas of health and fitness, food and cooking, psychology and personal growth, religion and spirituality, current affairs, pregnancy and parenting, and folklore and mythology.

Nonfiction Self-help. Subjects include health and fitness, food and cooking, psychology and personal growth, religion and spirituality, current affairs, pregnancy and parenting, and folklore and mythology. *No unsolicited mss.*

Recent Title(s) *Anti-Aging Plan*, by Roy L. Walford, MD and Lisa Walford; *Away With Wrinkles*, by Nick Lowe; *Bike for Life*, by Roy M. Wallack and Bill Katovsky.

Ⓝ MARVEL COMICS

10 E. 40th St., New York NY 10016. Website: www.marvel.com. Publishes hardcover originals and reprints, trade paperback reprints, mass market comic book originals, electronic reprints. **Pays on a per page work for hire basis or creator-owned which is then contracted. Pays negotiable advance.** Does not accept simultaneous submissions. Responds in 3-5 weeks to queries. Ms guidelines online.

Fiction Adventure, comic books, fantasy, horror, humor, science fiction, young adult. ''Our shared universe needs new heroes and villains; books for younger readers and teens needed.'' Submit inquiry letter, idea submission form (download from website), SASE.

Tips Marvel currently appeals to 12-30 year-old males. ''We'd like to expand that both up and down the age range. We're looking for strong voices and people who have read things beyond the last 40 years of comics publishing. Life experience helps a lot.''

Ⓩ MCBOOKS PRESS

ID Booth Building, 520 N. Meadow St., Ithaca NY 14850. (607)272-2114. Fax: (607)273-6068. E-mail: jackie@mcbooks.com. Website: www.mcbooks.com. Publisher: Alexander G. Skutt. **Acquisitions:** Jackie Swift, editorial director. Estab. 1979. Publishes trade paperback and hardcover originals and reprints. **Publishes 20 titles/year. Pays 5-10% royalty on retail price. Offers $1,000-5,000 advance.** Accepts simultaneous submissions. Responds in 2 months. Ms guidelines online.

   • ''We can only consider the highest quality projects in our narrow interest areas.''

   ○━ Currently emphasizing nautical and military historical fiction, preferably with at least 1 strong female character.

Nonfiction Subjects include regional (New York state), vegetarianism, and veganism. ''Authors' ability to promote a plus.'' *No unsolicited mss.* Query with SASE.

Fiction Historical, nautical, naval and military historical. Query with SASE.

Recent Title(s) *The Only Life That Mattered*, by James L. Nelson; *Storm Force to Narvik*, by Alexander Fullerton; *Wine Tour of the Finger Lakes*, by Grady Wells.

MCDONALD & WOODWARD PUBLISHING CO.

431-B E. Broadway, Granville OH 43023-1310. (740)321-1140. Fax: (740)321-1141. Website: www.mwpubco.com. **Acquisitions:** Jerry N. McDonald, managing partner/publisher. Estab. 1986. Publishes hardcover and trade paperback originals. **Publishes 8 titles/year. Receives 100 queries and 20 mss/year. 50% of books from first-time authors; 100% from unagented writers. Pays 10% royalty on net receipts.** Publishes book 1 year after acceptance of ms. Accepts simultaneous submissions. Responds in 2 weeks to queries. Book catalog free.

⚬— "McDonald & Woodward publishes books in natural and cultural history." Currently emphasizing travel, natural and cultural history.

Nonfiction Biography, coffee table book, illustrated book. Subjects include Americana, anthropology/archeology, ethnic, history, nature/environment, science, travel. Query with SASE, or submit outline, sample chapter(s). Reviews artwork/photos as part of ms package. Send photocopies.

Recent Title(s) *The Carousel Keepers: An Oral History of American Carousels*, by Carrie Papa; *A Guide to Common Freshwater Invertebrates of North America*, by J. Reese Voshell; *Vernal Pools: Natural History and Conservation*, by Elizabeth A. Colburn.

Tips "We are especially interested in additional titles in our Guides to the American Landscape Series. Should consult titles in print for guidance. We want well-organized, clearly written, substantive material."

✇ MARGARET K. MCELDERRY BOOKS

Imprint of Simon & Schuster Children's Publishing Division, Simon & Schuster, 1230 Sixth Ave., New York NY 10020. (212)698-2761. Fax: (212)698-2797. Website: www.simonsayskids.com. **Acquisitions:** Emma D. Dryden, vice president/editorial director; Karen Wojtyla, senior editor; Sarah Sevier, associate editor. Estab. 1971. Publishes quality material for preschoolers to 18-year-olds. Publishes hardcover originals. **Publishes 30 titles/year. Receives 4,000 queries/year. 15% of books from first-time authors; 50% from unagented writers. Average print order is 5,000-10,000 for a first middle grade or young adult book; 7,500-20,000 for a first picture book. Pays royalty on hardcover retail price: 10% fiction; picture book, 5% author and 5% illustrator. Offers $5,000-8,000 advance for new authors.** Publishes book up to 3 years after acceptance of ms. Ms guidelines for #10 SASE.

⚬— "We are more interested in superior writing and illustration than in a particular 'type' of book." Currently emphasizing young picture books and funny middle grade fiction.

Nonfiction Biography, children's/juvenile. Subjects include history, adventure. "Read. The field is competitive. See what's been done and what's out there before submitting. Looks for originality of ideas, clarity and felicity of expression, well-organized plot and strong characterization (fiction) or clear exposition (nonfiction); quality. Accept query letters with SASE only." *No unsolicited mss.*

Fiction Adventure, fantasy, historical, mainstream/contemporary, mystery, picture books, young adult (or middle grade), All categories (fiction and nonfiction) for juvenile and young adult. "We will consider any category. Results depend on the quality of the imagination, the artwork, and the writing." *No unsolicited mss.* Send query letter with SASE only for picture books; query letter with first 3 chapters, SASE for middle grade and young adult novels.

Poetry *No unsolicited mss.* Query, or submit 3 sample poems.

Recent Title(s) *Bear Stays Up for Christmas*, by Karma Wilson, illustrated by Jane Chapman (picture book); *Indigo's Star*, by Hilary McKay (middle-grade fiction); *The Legend of Buddy Bush*, by Shelia P. Moses (teen fiction).

Tips "Read! The children's book field is competitive. See what's been done and what's out there before submitting. We look for high quality: an originality of ideas, clarity and felicity of expression, a well-organized plot, and strong character-driven stories."

Ⓜ MCFARLAND & CO., INC., PUBLISHERS

Box 611, Jefferson NC 28640. (336)246-4460. Fax: (336)246-5018. E-mail: info@mcfarlandpub.com. Website: www.mcfarlandpub.com. **Acquisitions:** Steve Wilson, executive editor (automotive, general); Virginia Tobiassen, editorial development chief (general, medieval history, bilingual works); Gary Mitchem, acquisitions editor (general, baseball). Estab. 1979. Publishes hardcover and "quality" paperback originals; a "nontrade" publisher. **Publishes 250 titles/year. 70% of books from first-time authors; 95% from unagented writers. Pays 10-12½% royalty on net receipts.** Publishes book 10 months after acceptance of ms. Responds in 1 month to queries. Ms guidelines online.

⚬— McFarland publishes serious nonfiction in a variety of fields, including general reference, performing arts, sports (particularly baseball); women's studies, librarianship, literature, Civil War, history and international studies. Currently emphasizing medieval history, automotive history, Spanish-English bilingual works. De-emphasizing memoirs.

Nonfiction Reference (and scholarly), scholarly, technical, professional monographs. Subjects include art/architecture, business/economics, contemporary culture, ethnic, film/cinema/stage, health/medicine, history, music/dance, recreation, sociology, sports (very strong), women's issues/studies (very strong), world affairs, African-American studies (very strong), chess, Civil War, drama/theater, cinema/radio/TV (very strong), librarianship (very strong), pop culture, world affairs (very strong). Reference books are particularly wanted—fresh material (i.e., not in head-to-head competition with an established title). "We prefer manuscripts of 250 or more double-spaced pages." No fiction, New Age, exposés, poetry, children's books, devotional/inspirational works, Bible studies, or personal essays. Query with SASE, or submit outline, sample chapters. Reviews artwork/photos as part of ms package.

Recent Title(s) *Encyclopedia of Abortion in the United States*, by Louis J. Palmer; *The Women of Afghanistan Under the Taliban*, by Rosemarie Skaine.

Tips ''We want well-organized knowledge of an area in which there is not information coverage at present, plus reliability so we don't feel we have to check absolutely everything. Our market is worldwide and libraries are an important part.'' McFarland also publishes the *Journal of Information Ethics* and *North Korean Review*.

MCGRAW-HILL TRADE

Imprint of The McGraw-Hill Companies, 2 Penn Plaza, New York NY 10121-2298. Website: www.books.mcg raw-hill.com. Publisher: Philip Ruppel. Editor-in-Chief: Jeffrey Krames. **Acquisitions:** Jonathan Eaton, editorial director (International Marine/Ragged Mountain Press); Barbara Gilson, editorial director (Schaum's Outlines). Accepts simultaneous submissions. Ms guidelines online.

- ● Publisher not responsible for returning mss or proposals.
- ○┅ McGraw Hill Trade is a publishing leader in business/investing, management, careers, self-help, consumer health, language reference, test preparation, sports/recreation, and general interest titles.

Nonfiction How-to, reference, self-help, technical. Subjects include business/economics, child guidance/parenting, education (study guides), health/medicine, money/finance, sports (fitness), management, consumer reference, English and foreign language reference. ''Current, up-to-date, original ideas are needed. Good self-promotion is key.'' Submit proposal package including outline, concept of book, competition and market info, cv.

Recent Title(s) *World Out of Balance*, by Paul A. Laudicina; *You Play to Win the Game*, by Herman Edwards and Shelly Smith; *SAT Vocabulary Express*, by Jacqueline Byrne and Michael Ashley.

Ⓝ MCGRAW-HILL/OSBORNE MEDIA

The McGraw-Hill Companies, 2100 Powell St., 10th Floor, Emeryville CA 94608. (800)227-0900. Website: www. osborne.com. Estab. 1979. Publishes computer trade paperback originals. Book catalog and ms guidelines online.

- ○┅ Publishes self-paced computer training materials.

Nonfiction Reference, technical. Subjects include computers/electronic, software (and hardware). Submit proposal package including outline, sample chapters, résumé, competition analysis, SASE. Reviews artwork/photos as part of ms package.

Tips ''A leader in self-paced training and skills development tools on information technology and computers.''

MEADOWBROOK PRESS

5451 Smetana Dr., Minnetonka MN 55343. (952)930-1100. Fax: (952)930-1940. Website: www.meadowbrookpr ess.com. **Acquisitions:** Submissions Editor. Estab. 1975. Publishes trade paperback originals and reprints. **Publishes 12 titles/year. Receives 1,500 queries/year. 10% of books from first-time authors. Pays 10% royalty. Offers small advance.** Publishes book 1 year after acceptance of ms. Accepts simultaneous submissions. Responds in 6 months to queries. Book catalog for #10 SASE; ms guidelines online.

- ○┅ Meadowbrook is a family-oriented press which specializes in parenting and pregnancy books, party planning books.

Nonfiction How-to, reference. Subjects include child guidance/parenting, cooking/foods/nutrition, pregnancy, childbirth, party planning, children's activities, relationships. ''We prefer a query first; then we will request an outline and/or sample material.'' Send for guidelines. No children's fiction, poetry, academic, or biography. Query with SASE, or submit outline, sample chapters.

Recent Title(s) *Wiggle & Giggle Busy Book*, by Trish Kuffner (children's activities); *Pregnancy Q&A*, by Trish Booth (pregnancy).

Tips ''Always send for guidelines before submitting material. We do not accept unsolicited picture book submissions.''

MEDALLION PRESS, INC.

27825 N. Forest Garden Rd., Wauconda IL 60084. Website: www.medallionpress.com. **Acquisitions:** Wendy Burbank, acquisitions (all fiction for adults and young adults; no erotica, inspirational, children's books, graphic novels, poetry, anthologies, or short stories). Estab. 2003. Publishes trade paperback originals, mass market paperback originals and hardcover books. **Publishes 30-40 titles/year. 80% of books from first-time authors; 80% from unagented writers. Pays 6-8% royalty. Offers advance.** Publishes book up to 2 years after acceptance of ms. Accepts simultaneous submissions. Responds in 6 months to queries; 1 year to mss.

Imprints Platinum (hardcover); Gold (mass market paperback); Silver (trade paperback); Bronze (young adult fiction); Jewel (romance mass market paperback).

- Always view the guidelines and FAQs on the website for the most updated information prior to sending your submission. If the guidelines aren't followed completely, your package will be returned. No e-mail queries, previously published works or packages requiring a signature. Do not send e-mails inquiring as to the status of your submission.

Fiction Adventure, historical, mainstream/contemporary, mystery, science fiction, suspense, young adult (no YA fantasy), political action thriller, espionage. No Celtic/Medieval romances. Query with SASE. Include genre and word count, chapter-by-chapter synopsis and first 3 sequential chapters only.

Recent Title(s) *Charmed*, by Beth Ciotta (contemporary romance mass market paperback); *The Secret of Shabaz*, by Jennifer Macaire (young adult fantasy trade paperback); *More Than Magick*, by Rick Taubold (science fiction mass market paperback).

Tips "Our audience is general mainstream adults and young adults. Lead a trend rather than follow here. We are seeking original ideas, not those that have been done over and over again. We do not offer large advances. Our funds are reserved for marketing our books. Please consider another publisher if you are seeking large financial compensation."

MEMORY MAKERS BOOKS

Imprint of F+W Publications, Inc., 12365 Huron, Suite 500, Denver CO 80234. Website: www.memorymakersm agazine.com. Book proposal submissons: MaryJo Regier, senior editor. Estab. 1998. Publishes trade paperback originals. **Publishes 18 titles/year. 30% of books from first-time authors; 95% from unagented writers. Pays royalty or flat fee. Offers advance.** Publishes book 12-15 months after acceptance of ms. Accepts simultaneous submissions. Responds in 2 months to queries.

- "Memory Makers Books exclusively publishes titles for the consumer scrapbooking industry in the form of fresh and innovative scrapbooking and paper-craft books. Authors who submit proposal packages must conduct their own up-to-the-minute-and-beyond research and have a good working knowledge of the industry's current and future specialty-niche voids. Authors must be outstanding scrapbook artists, as well as apt photographers and writers familiar with AP style. Authors must possess a well-rounded knowledge of the industry in order to present their special book idea in a concise and complete proposal package to ensure proper evaluation and timely feedback."

Nonfiction Submit a proposal package that includes 5 working titles and 5 subtitles; 40-word promotional blurb or synopsis of the book; detailed outline (front and back matter, chapters, sidebars) for a 96-, 112- or 128-page book; thumbnail sketches that follow the outline page-for-page; no less than 10 pieces of sample art (color photocopies or transparencies) that illustrate the subject/techniques to be covered in the book; a brief biography and published clips. Theme, how-to technique and/or general-interest. Subjects include craft/scrapbooking.

Recent Title(s) *How to Take Perfect Scrapbook Pictures*, by Joann Zocchi; *Creative Stamping for Scrapbookers*, by Memory Makers Books editors; *A Passion for Patterned Paper*, by Brandi Ginn and Pam Klassen.

Tips "Our readers are savvy scrapbook and paper artists—from beginning to advanced—who are on the lookout for cutting-edge scrapbooking styles, themes, approaches and techniques with photo illustration that they can recreate in their own albums with their own photos and journaling. Study our books to see how we present material, then ptich us something fresh, innovative and unlike anything other consumer scrapbooking publishers are producing."

☒ MENASHA RIDGE PRESS

P.O. Box 43059, Birmingham AL 35243. (205)322-0439. E-mail: rhelms@menasharidge.com. Website: www.me nasharidge.com. **Acquisitions:** Molly Merkle, associate publisher (travel, reference); Russell Helms, senior acquisitions editor. Publishes hardcover and trade paperback originals. **Publishes 20 titles/year. 30% of books from first-time authors; 85% from unagented writers. Pays varying royalty. Offers varying advance.** Publishes book 1 year after acceptance of ms. Accepts simultaneous submissions. Responds in 2 months to queries. Book catalog for 9×12 SAE with 4 first-class stamps.

- Menasha Ridge Press publishes "distinctive books in the areas of outdoor sports, travel, and diving. Our authors are among the best in their fields."

Nonfiction How-to, humor, travel guides. Subjects include recreation (outdoor), sports (adventure), travel, outdoors. "Most concepts are generated in-house, but a few come from outside submissions." Submit proposal package including résumé, synopsis. Reviews artwork/photos as part of ms package.

Recent Title(s) *Sex in the Outdoors*, by Buck Tilton.

Tips Audience is 25-60, 14-18 years' education, white collar and professional, $30,000 median income, 75% male, 55% east of the Mississippi River.

MERIWETHER PUBLISHING, LTD.

885 Elkton Dr., Colorado Springs CO 80907-3557. (719)594-4422. Fax: (719)594-9916. E-mail: merpeds@aol.c om. Website: www.meriwetherpublishing.com; www.contemporarydrama.com. **Acquisitions:** Arthur Zapel,

Theodore Zapel, Rhonda Wray, editors. Estab. 1969. Publishes paperback originals and reprints. **50% of books from first-time authors; 90% from unagented writers. Pays 10% royalty, or makes outright purchase.** Publishes book 6-12 months after acceptance of ms. Accepts simultaneous submissions. Responds in 3 weeks to queries; 2 months to mss. Book catalog and ms guidelines for $2 postage.

O→ Meriwether publishes theater/arts books, games and videos; speech resources; plays, skits, and musicals; and drama resources for gifted students. "We specialize in books on the theatre arts and religious plays for Christmas, Easter, and youth activities. We also publish musicals for high school performers and churches." Currently emphasizing how-to books for theatrical arts and church youth activities.

Nonfiction "We publish unusual textbooks or trade books related to the communication of performing arts and how-to books on staging, costuming, lighting, etc." How-to, reference, textbook. Subjects include performing arts, theater/drama. "We prefer mainstream religion theatre titles." Query, or submit outline/synopsis and sample chapters.

Fiction Plays and musical comedies for middle grades through college only. Mainstream/contemporary, plays (and musicals), religious (children's plays and religious Christmas and Easter plays), suspense, all in playscript format, comedy. Query with SASE.

Recent Title(s) *100 Great Monologs*, by Rebecca Young; *Group Improvisation*, by Peter Gwinn; *112 Acting Games*, by Gavin Levy.

Tips "Our educational books are sold to teachers and students at college, high school, and middle school levels. Our religious books are sold to youth activity directors, pastors, and choir directors. Our trade books are directed at the public with a tie to the performing arts. Another group of buyers is the professional theater, radio, and TV category. We focus more on books of plays and short scenes and textbooks on directing, staging, make-up, lighting, etc."

MERRIAM PRESS

218 Beech St., Bennington VT 05201-2611. (802)447-0313. Fax: (802)217-1051. E-mail: ray@merriam-press.com. Website: www.merriam-press.com. Publishes hardcover and softcover originals and reprints. **Publishes 12 + titles/year. 70-90% of books from first-time authors; 95% from unagented writers. Pays 10% royalty on actual selling price.** Publishes book 1 year or less after acceptance of ms. Does not accept simultaneous submissions. Responds quickly to queries; e-mail preferred. Book catalog for $1 or visit website to view all available titles and access writer's guidelines and info.

O→ Merriam Press publishes only World War II military history.

Nonfiction Biography, illustrated book, reference, technical. Subjects include military/war (World War II). Query with SASE or by e-mail first. Reviews artwork/photos as part of ms package. Send photocopies or on floppy disk/CD.

Recent Title(s) *The Cow Spoke French: The Story of Sgt. William True, An American Paratrooper in World War II*, By William True, Company F, 2nd Battalion, 506th Parachute Infantry Regiment, 101st Airborne Division, ETO, and Deryck Tufts True; *Dogface Soldiers: The Story of B Company, 15th Regiment, 3rd Infantry Division, From Fedala to Salzburg: Audie Murphy and His Brothers in Arms*, by Daniel R. Champagne; *Not All Were Heroes: A Private in the Corps of Engineers in the Pacific During World War II*, by Herbert L. Martin.

Tips "Our books are geared for WWII historians, collectors, model kit builders, wargamers, veterans, general enthusiasts. We do not publish any fiction or poetry, only WWII military history."

N MESSIANIC JEWISH PUBLISHERS

6204 Park Heights Ave., Baltimore MD 21215. (410)358-6471. E-mail: website@messianicjewish.net. Website: www.messianicjewish.net. **Acquisitions:** Janet Chaier, managing editor. Publishes hardcover and trade paperback originals and reprints. **Publishes 6-12 titles/year. Pays 7-15% royalty on wholesale price.** Ms guidelines by e-mail.

Nonfiction Jewish themes only. Gift book, reference. Subjects include religion (Messianic Judaism, Jewish roots of the Christian faith). Text must demonstrate keen awareness of Jewish culture and thought, and Biblical literacy. Query with SASE. Unsolicited mss are not returned. "We rarely review artwork/photos, but will consider them."

Fiction "We publish very little fiction. Jewish or Biblical themes are a must." Religious. Text must demonstrate keen awareness of Jewish culture and thought. Query with SASE. Unsolicited mss are not returned.

Recent Title(s) *Blessing the King of the Universe: Transforming Your Life Through the Practice of Biblical Praise*, by Irene Lipson (religious reference/devotional); *The Distortion: 2,000 Years of Misrepresenting the Relationship Between Jesus the Messiah and the Jewish People*, by Dr. John Fischer and Dr. Patrice Fischer (nonfiction); *Celebrations of the Bible: A Messianic Children's Curriculum*.

Tips "Our audience is Christians, Messianic Jews, and Jewish people of all backgrounds. Be familiar with titles we have already published and the kind of books we consider."

Ⓝ METAL POWDER INDUSTRIES FEDERATION

105 College Rd. E., Princeton NJ 08540. (609)452-7700. Fax: (609)987-8523. E-mail: info@mpif.org. Website: www.mpif.org. **Acquisitions:** Jim Adams, director of technical services; Peggy Lebedz, assistant publications manager. Estab. 1946. Publishes hardcover originals. **Publishes 10 titles/year. Pays 3-12½% royalty on wholesale or retail price. Offers $3,000-5,000 advance.** Responds in 1 month to queries.

> ⓞ Metal Powder Industries publishes monographs, textbooks, handbooks, design guides, conference proceedings, standards, and general titles in the field of powder metallurgy or particulate materials.

Nonfiction Work must relate to powder metallurgy or particulate materials. Technical, textbook.

Recent Title(s) *Advances in Powder Metallurgy and Particulate Materials* (conference proceeding).

MICHIGAN STATE UNIVERSITY PRESS

1405 S. Harrison Rd., Manly Miles Bldg., Suite 25, East Lansing MI 48823-5202. (517)355-9543. Fax: (517)432-2611. E-mail: msupress@msu.edu. Website: www.msupress.msu.edu. **Acquisitions:** Acquisitions Editor. Estab. 1947. Publishes hardcover and softcover originals. **Pays variable royalty.** Does not accept simultaneous submissions. Book catalog and ms guidelines for 9×12 SASE or online.

> • Distributes books for: University of Calgary Press, Penumbra Press, National Museum of Science (UK), African Books Collective, University of Alberta Press, University of Manitoba Press.
>
> ⓞ Michigan State University publishes scholarly books that further scholarship in their particular field. In addition, they publish nonfiction that addresses, in a more contemporary way, social concerns, such as diversity, civil rights, and the environment.

Nonfiction Scholarly. Subjects include Americana (American studies), business/economics, creative nonfiction, ethnic (Afro-American studies), government/politics, history (contemporary civil rights), language/literature, regional (Great Lakes regional, Canadian studies), women's issues/studies. Submit letter of inquiry and proposal/outline. Reviews artwork/photos as part of ms package.

Recent Title(s) *Arab Americans in Michigan*, by Rosina J. Hassoun; *Intimate Strangers*, by Margaret Lawrence and Gabrielle Roy, edited by Paul Socken; *Wise Leadership*, by Linda A. McLyman.

MILKWEED EDITIONS

1011 Washington Ave. S., Suite 300, Minneapolis MN 55415. (612)332-3192. Fax: (612)215-2550. Website: www.milkweed.org. **Acquisitions:** H. Emerson Blake, editor-in-chief; Elisabeth Fitz, first reader (fiction, nonfiction, children's fiction, poetry). Estab. 1980. Publishes hardcover originals and paperback originals and reprints. **Publishes 15 titles/year. 30% of books from first-time authors; 70% from unagented writers. Pays 6% royalty on retail price. Offers varied advance.** Publishes book 1-2 years after acceptance of ms. Accepts simultaneous submissions. Responds in 2 months to queries; 6 months to mss. Book catalog for $1.50 postage; ms guidelines online.

Imprints Milkweeds for Young Readers.

> • Reads poetry in January and June only.
>
> ⓞ Milkweed Editions publishes literary fiction for adults and middle grade readers, nonfiction, and poetry. "Our vision is focused on giving voice to writers whose work is of the highest literary quality and whose ideas engender personal reflection and cultural action."

Nonfiction Literary. Subjects include nature/environment, human community. Submit complete ms with SASE.

Fiction Literary. Novels for adults and for readers 8-13. High literary quality. For adult readers: literary fiction, nonfiction, poetry, essays. For children (ages 8-13): literary novels. Translations welcome for both audiences. No romance, mysteries, science fiction. Send for guidelines first, then submit complete ms.

Recent Title(s) *Ordinary Wolves*, by Seth Kantner (fiction); *Cross-Pollinations*, by Gary Paul Nabhan (nonfiction); *Atlas*, by Katrina Vandenberg (poetry).

Tips "We are looking for excellent writing with the intent of making a humane impact on society. Send for guidelines. Acquaint yourself with our books in terms of style and quality before submitting. Many factors influence our selection process, so don't get discouraged. Nonfiction is focused on literary writing about the natural world, including living well in urban environments."

MINNESOTA HISTORICAL SOCIETY PRESS

Minnesota Historical Society, 345 Kellogg Blvd. W., St. Paul MN 55102-1906. (651)296-2264. Fax: (651)297-1345. Website: www.mnhs.org/mhspress. **Acquisitions:** Gregory M. Britton, director; Ann Regan, managing editor. Estab. 1849. Publishes hardcover and trade paperback originals, trade paperback reprints. **Publishes 25 titles/year; imprint publishes 1-4 titles/year. Receives 200 queries and 75 mss/year. 50% of books from first-time authors; 85% from unagented writers. Royalties are negotiated. Offers advance.** Publishes book 14 months after acceptance of ms. Accepts simultaneous submissions. Responds in 1 month to queries. Book catalog free.

Imprints Borealis Books.

O⌐ Minnesota Historical Society Press publishes both scholarly and general interest books that contribute to the understanding of the Midwest.

Nonfiction Regional works only. Biography, coffee table book, cookbook, illustrated book, reference, scholarly. Subjects include anthropology/archeology, art/architecture, cooking/foods/nutrition, ethnic, history, memoirs, photography, regional, women's issues/studies. Query with SASE, or submit proposal package including outline, 1 sample chapter. Reviews artwork/photos as part of ms package. Send photocopies.

Recent Title(s) *Potato City: Nature, History, and Community in the Age of Sprawl*, by Sue Leaf; *A Northern Front: New and Selected Essays*, by John Hildebrand.

Tips A regional connection is required.

⊘ MITCHELL LANE PUBLISHERS, INC.

P.O. Box 196, Hockessin DE 19707. (302)234-9426. Fax: (302)234-4742. **Acquisitions:** Barbara Mitchell, publisher. Estab. 1993. Publishes hardcover and library bound originals. **Publishes 65 titles/year. Receives 100 queries and 5 mss/year. 0% of books from first-time authors; 90% from unagented writers. Makes outright purchase on work-for-hire basis.** Publishes book 1 year after acceptance of ms. Does not accept simultaneous submissions. Responds only if interested to queries. Book catalog free.

O⌐ "Mitchell Lane publishes quality nonfiction for children and young adults."

Nonfiction Biography, children's/juvenile. Subjects include ethnic, multicultural. Query with SASE. *All unsolicited mss returned unopened.*

Recent Title(s) *The Life and Times of Johann Sebastian Bach* (Masters of Music); *Alfred Nobel and the Story Behind the Nobel Prize* (Great Achievement Awards); *Eminem* (Blue Banner Biographies).

Tips "We hire writers on a 'work-for-hire' basis to complete book projects we assign. Send résumé and writing samples that do not need to be returned."

MODERN LANGUAGE ASSOCIATION OF AMERICA

26 Broadway, 3rd Floor, New York NY 10004-1789. (646)576-5000. Fax: (646)458-0030. Director of MLA Book Publications: David G. Nicholls. **Acquisitions:** Joseph Gibaldi, director of book acquisitions and development; Sonia Kane, acquisitions editor. Estab. 1883. Publishes hardcover and paperback originals. **Publishes 15 titles/year. 100% from unagented writers. Pays 4-8% royalty on net receipts.** Publishes book 1 year after acceptance of ms. Does not accept simultaneous submissions. Responds in 2 months to mss. Book catalog free.

O⌐ The MLA publishes on current issues in literary and linguistic research and teaching of language and literature at postsecondary level.

Nonfiction Reference, scholarly, professional. Subjects include education, language/literature, translation (with companion volume in foreign language, for classroom use). No critical monographs. Query with SASE, or submit outline.

Recent Title(s) *Teaching the Representation of the Holocaust*, edited by Marianne Hirsch and Irene Kacandes; *Brazilian Narrative in a Comparative Context*, by Earl E. Fritz.

Ⓝ Ⓐ ⊘ MOODY PUBLISHERS

Moody Bible Institute, 820 N. LaSalle Blvd., Chicago IL 60610. (312)329-8047. Fax: (312)329-2019. Website: www.moodypublishers.org. Vice President/Executive Editor: Greg Thornton. **Acquisitions:** Acquisitions Coordinator. Estab. 1894. Publishes hardcover, trade, and mass market paperback originals. **Publishes 60 titles/year; imprint publishes 5-10 titles/year. Receives 1,500 queries and 2,000 mss/year. 1% of books from first-time authors; 80% from unagented writers. Royalty varies. Offers $1,000-10,000 advance.** Publishes book 9-12 months after acceptance of ms. Does not accept simultaneous submissions. Responds in 2-3 months to queries. Book catalog for 9×12 SAE with 4 first-class stamps; ms guidelines for SASE and on website.

Imprints Northfield Publishing; Lift Every Voice (African American-interest).

O⌐ "The mission of Moody Publishers is to educate and edify the Christian and to evangelize the non-Christian by ethically publishing conservative, evangelical Christian literature and other media for all ages around the world; and to help provide resources for Moody Bible Institute in its training of future Christian leaders."

Nonfiction Children's/juvenile, gift book, general Christian living. Subjects include child guidance/parenting, money/finance, religion, spirituality, women's issues/studies. "We are no longer reviewing queries or unsolicited manuscripts unless they come to us through an agent. Unsolicited proposals will be returned only if proper postage is included. We are not able to acknowledge the receipt of your unsolicited proposal." *Agented submissions only.*

Fiction Fantasy, historical, mystery, religious (children's religious, inspirational, religious mystery/suspense), science fiction, young adult (adventure, fantasy/science fiction, historical, mystery/suspense, series). Query with 1 chapter and SASE.

Recent Title(s) *Letters for Lizzie*, by James O'Donnell; *Nightsong*, by Tricia Goyer; *Gun Lake*, by Travis Thrasher.

Tips "In our fiction list, we're looking for Christian storytellers rather than teachers trying to present a message. Your motivation should be to delight the reader. Using your skills to create beautiful works is glorifying to God."

Ⓝ MOREHOUSE PUBLISHING CO.

4475 Linglestown Rd., Harrisburg PA 17112. (717)541-8130. Fax: (717)541-8136. E-mail: morehouse@morehou segroup.com. Website: www.morehousepublishing.com. **Acquisitions:** Nancy Fitzgerald, senior editor. Estab. 1884. Publishes hardcover and paperback originals. **Publishes 35 titles/year. 50% of books from first-time authors. Pays 10% royalty on net receipts. Offers small advance.** Publishes book 18 months after acceptance of ms. Accepts simultaneous submissions. Responds in 2 months to queries. Ms guidelines online.

    O— Morehouse Publishing publishes mainline Christian books, primarily Episcopal/Anglican works. Currently emphasizing Christian spiritual direction.

Nonfiction Subjects include religion (Christian), women's issues/studies, Christian spirituality, Liturgies, congregational resources, issues around Christian life. Submit outline, 1-2 sample chapters, résumé, market analysis.

Recent Title(s) *Welcome to Sunday*, by Christopher Webber; *101 Reasons to Be Episcopalian*, by Louie Crew.

MORNINGSIDE HOUSE, INC.

Morningside Bookshop, 260 Oak St., Dayton OH 45410. (937)461-6736. Fax: (937)461-4260. E-mail: msbooks@e rinet.com. Website: www.morningsidebooks.com. **Acquisitions:** Robert J. Younger, publisher. Publishes hardcover and trade paperback originals. **Publishes 10 titles/year; imprint publishes 5 titles/year. Receives 30 queries and 10 mss/year. 20% of books from first-time authors; 80% from unagented writers. Pays 10% royalty on retail price. Offers $1,000-2,000 advance.** Publishes book 15 months after acceptance of ms. Accepts simultaneous submissions. Book catalog for $5 or on website.

Imprints Morningside Press; Press of Morningside Bookshop.

    O— Morningside publishes books for readers interested in the history of the American Civil War.

Nonfiction Subjects include history, military/war. Query with SASE, or submit complete ms. Reviews artwork/photos as part of ms package. Send photocopies.

Recent Title(s) *The Mississippi Brigade of Brig. Gen. Joseph R. Davis*, by T.P. Williams; *The 16th Michigan Infantry*, by Kim Crawford.

Tips "We are only interested in previously unpublished material."

MOTORCYCLING

Imprint of Bristol Fashion Publications, Inc., P.O. Box 4676, Harrisburg PA 17111-4676. (800)478-7147. E-mail: jpk@bfpbooks.com. Website: www.bfpbooks.com. **Acquisitions:** John Kaufman, publisher. Publishes trade paperback originals and limited hardback. **Publishes 15-25 titles/year. Receives 100 queries and 50 mss/ year. 50% of books from first-time authors; 99% from unagented writers. Pays 7-11% royalty on retail price.** Publishes book 3 months after acceptance of ms. Responds in 1 month to queries. Ms guidelines online.

    ● Motorcycling (BFP, Inc.) publishes books on motorcycling and motorcycling history.

Nonfiction General interest relating to touring, guide books, how-to subjects, and motorcycling history. "We are interested in any title related to these fields. Query with a list of ideas. Include phone number. Our title plans rarely extend past 6 months, although we know the type and quantity of books we will publish over the next 2 years. We prefer good knowledge with simple-to-understand writing style containing a well-rounded vocabulary." Query with SASE. Reviews artwork/photos as part of ms package. Send photocopies or JPEG files on CD.

Tips "All of our staff and editors are riders. As such, we publish what we would want to read relating to the subject. Our audience in general are active riders at the beginner and intermediate level of repair knowledge and riding skills, and history buffs wanting to learn more about the history of motorcycles in this country. Many are people new to motorcycles, attempting to learn all they can before starting out on that first long ride or even buying their first bike. Keep it easy and simple to follow. Use motorcycle jargon sparingly. Do not use complicated technical jargon, terms, or formulas without a detailed explanation of the same. Use experienced riders and mechanics as a resource for knowledge. Please read our guidelines before submitting your manuscript."

MOUNTAIN PRESS PUBLISHING CO.

P.O. Box 2399, Missoula MT 59806-2399. (406)728-1900 or (800)234-5308. Fax: (406)728-1635. E-mail: info@mt npress.com. Website: www.mountain-press.com. **Acquisitions:** Gwen McKenna, editor (history); Jennifer Carey, editor (Roadside Geology, Field Guides, and Tumblweed Series, natural history, science). Estab. 1948. Publishes hardcover and trade paperback originals. **Publishes 15 titles/year. 50% of books from first-time**

authors; 90% from unagented writers. Pays 7-12% royalty on wholesale price. Publishes book 2 years after acceptance of ms. Responds in 3 months to queries. Book catalog online.

- Expanding children's/juvenile nonfiction titles.
- **O─** "We are expanding our Roadside Geology, Geology Underfoot, and Roadside History series (done on a state-by-state basis). We are interested in well-written regional field guides—plants and flowers—and readable history and natural history."

Nonfiction How-to. Subjects include animals, history (Western), nature/environment, regional, science (Earth science). "No personal histories or journals." Query with SASE, or submit outline, sample chapters. Reviews artwork/photos as part of ms package.

Recent Title(s) *Plants of the Lewis and Clark Expedition*, by H. Wayne Phillips; *Loons: Diving Birds of the North*, by Donna Love; *Encyclopedia of Indian Wars*, by Gregory F. Michno.

Tips "Find out what kind of books a publisher is interested in and tailor your writing to them; research markets and target your audience. Research other books on the same subjects. Make yours different. Don't present your manuscript to a publisher—sell it. Give the information needed to make a decision on a title. Please learn what we publish before sending your proposal. We are a 'niche' publisher."

N MOYER BELL, LTD.

549 Old North Rd., Kingston RI 02881-1220. (401)783-5480. Fax: (401)284-0959. E-mail: contact@moyerbellboo ks.com. Website: www.moyerbellbooks.com. Publisher: Britt Bell. Estab. 1984. Book catalog online.

- **O─** Moyer Bell publishes literature, reference, and art books.

A Ø MULTNOMAH PUBLISHERS, INC.

P.O. Box 1720, Sisters OR 97759. (541)549-1144. Fax: (541)549-8048. Website: www.multnomahbooks.com. Estab. 1987. Publishes hardcover and trade paperback originals. **Publishes 75 titles/year. 2% of books from first-time authors; 50% from unagented writers. Pays royalty on wholesale price. Provides 100 author's copies. Offers advance.** Publishes book 1-2 years after acceptance of ms. Accepts simultaneous submissions. Ms guidelines online.

Imprints Multnomah Books; Multnomah Gifts; Multnomah Fiction.

- Multnomah is currently not accepting unsolicited queries, proposals, or mss. Queries will be accepted through agents and at writers' conferences at which a Multnomah representative is present.
- **O─** Multnomah publishes books on Christian living, family enrichment, devotional and gift books, and fiction.

Nonfiction Subjects include child guidance/parenting, religion, Christian living. *Agented submissions only.*

Fiction Adventure, historical, humor, literary, mystery, religious, romance, suspense, western. *Agented submissions only.*

Recent Title(s) *The Prayer of Jabez*, by Bruce Wilkinson (nonfiction); *Turn*, by Max Lucado (nonfiction); *Marriage Under Fire*, by James Dobson (nonfiction).

Tips "We are not interested in first-person travel accounts or memoirs."

A THE MYSTERIOUS PRESS

Imprint of Warner Books, 1271 Avenue of the Americas, New York NY 10020. (212)522-7200. Fax: (212)522-7990. Website: www.mysteriouspress.com. **Acquisitions:** Kristen Weber, editor. Estab. 1976. Publishes hardcover, trade paperback and mass market editions. **Publishes 20 titles/year. Pays standard, but negotiable, royalty on retail price. Offers negotiable advance.** Publishes book an average of 1 year after acceptance of ms. Ms guidelines online.

- **O─** The Mysterious Press publishes well-written crime/mystery/suspense fiction.

Fiction Mystery, suspense, Crime/detective novels. No short stories. *Agented submissions only.*

Recent Title(s) *Bury the Lead*, by David Rosenfelt; *High Country Fall*, by Margaret Maron.

MYSTIC SEAPORT

75 Greenmanville Ave., Mystic CT 06355-0990. (860)572-0711. Fax: (860)572-5321. **Acquisitions:** Andy German, publications director. Estab. 1970. Publishes hardcover and trade paperback originals and reprints. **Publishes 8-10 titles/year. Pays royalty on wholesale price.** Does not accept simultaneous submissions. Responds in 3 months to proposals.

Imprints American Maritime Library.

- **O─** "We strive to publish significant new work in the areas of American maritime, yachting and small-craft history and biography." Mystic Seaport has enlarged its focus from New England to North America.

Nonfiction Biography, how-to, reference, studies of economic, social, artistic, or musical elements of American maritime (not naval) history; books on traditional boat and ship types and construction (how to). Subjects include Americana, art/architecture, history. "We need serious, well-documented biographies, studies of economic, social, artistic, or musical elements of American maritime history; books on traditional boat and ship types and construction (how-to). We are now interested in all North American maritime history—not, as in the past, principally New England. We like to see anything and everything, from queries to finished work." Query with SASE, or submit outline, 3 sample chapters.

Recent Title(s) *America and the Sea: A Maritime History*, Benjamin W. Labaree, et. al; *Sailing at Fishers*, by John Rousmaniere; *Eugene O'Neill & "Dat Ole Davil Sea,"* by Robert Richter.

NAVAL INSTITUTE PRESS

US Naval Institute, 291 Wood Ave., Annapolis MD 21402-5034. (410)268-6110. Fax: (410)295-1084. E-mail: esecunda@usni.org. Website: www.usni.org. Press Director: Mark Gatlin. **Acquisitions:** Paul Wilderson, executive editor; Tom Cutler, senior acquisitions editor; Eric Mills, acquisitions editor. Estab. 1873. **Publishes 80-90 titles/year. 50% of books from first-time authors; 90% from unagented writers.** Ms guidelines online.

   O→ The Naval Institute Press publishes trade and scholarly nonfiction and some fiction. "We are interested in national and international security, naval, military, military jointness, intelligence, and special warfare, both current and historical."

Nonfiction Submit proposal package with outline, author bio, TOC, description/synopsis, sample chapters, page/word count, number of illustrations, ms completion date, intended market; or submit complete ms. Send SASE with sufficient postage for return of ms.

Fiction Submit complete ms. Send SASE with sufficient postage for return of ms.

NAVPRESS PUBLISHING GROUP

P.O. Box 35001, Colorado Springs CO 80935. Fax: (719)260-7223. E-mail: bookeditorial@navpress.com. Website: www.navpress.com. Estab. 1975. Publishes hardcover, trade paperback and mass market paperback originals and reprints. **Publishes 50 titles/year. Pays royalty.** Book catalog free.

Imprints Piñon Press.

Nonfiction Reference, self-help, inspirational, Christian living, Bible studies. Subjects include business/economics, child guidance/parenting, religion, sociology, spirituality, marriage. Submit outline, 2-3 sample chapters, author bio, competition summary, audience profile, SASE.

Fiction Submit outline, 2-5 sample chapters, author bio, reader profile, word count.

Recent Title(s) *Ask Me Anything: Provocative Answers for College Students*, by J. Budziszewski; *5 Minute Theologian: Maximum Truth in Minimum Time*, by Rick Cornish.

NEAL-SCHUMAN PUBLISHERS, INC.

100 William St., Suite 2004, New York NY 10038-4512. (212)925-8650. Fax: (212)219-8916. E-mail: miguel@n eal-schuman.com. Website: www.neal-schuman.com. **Acquisitions:** Miguel A. Figueroa, assistant director of publishing. Estab. 1976. Publishes trade paperback originals. **Publishes 30 titles/year. 75% of books from first-time authors; 90% from unagented writers. Pays 10% royalty on net receipts. Offers infrequent advance.** Publishes book 4 months after acceptance of ms. Does not accept simultaneous submissions. Responds in 1 month to proposals. Book catalog and ms guidelines free.

   O→ "Neal-Schuman publishes books about libraries, information science, and the use of information technology, especially in education and libraries." Especially soliciting proposals for undergraduate information studies, knowledge management textbooks.

Nonfiction Reference, technical, textbook, professional. Subjects include computers/electronic, education, software, Internet guides, library and information science. "We are looking for many books about the Internet." Submit proposal package including outline, sample chapters, résumé, preface.

Recent Title(s) *Foundations of Library and Information Science, 2nd Ed.*, by Richard E. Rubin; *Copyright for Teachers and Librarians*, by Rebecca P. Butler; *The Medical Library Association Encyclopedic Guide to Searching and Finding Health Information on the Web*, by P.F. Anderson and Nancy J. Allee.

Ⓝ Ⓩ THOMAS NELSON, INC.

Box 141000, Nashville TN 37214-1000. (615)889-9000. Website: www.thomasnelson.com. **Acquisitions:** Acquisitions Editor. Publishes hardcover and paperback orginals. **Publishes 100-150 titles/year. Rates negotiated for each project. Offers advance.** Publishes book 1-2 years after acceptance of ms. Accepts simultaneous submissions. Responds in 3 months to queries. Ms guidelines online.

Imprints Nelson Books; W Publishing; Rutledge Hill Press; J. Countryman; Cool Springs Press; Reference & Electronic Publishing; Editorial Caribe; Nelson Curriculum; Tommy Nelson; Nelson Current; WestBow Press.

   • *Corporate address does not accept unsolicited mss*; no phone queries.

   O→ Thomas Nelson publishes Christian lifestyle nonfiction and fiction, and general nonfiction.

Nonfiction Cookbook, reference, self-help. Subjects include business/economics (business development), cooking/foods/nutrition, gardening, health/medicine (and fitness), religion, spirituality, adult inspirational, motiva-

Book Publishers

tional, devotional, Christian living, prayer and evangelism, Bible study, personal development, political, biography/autobiography.

Fiction Publishes commercial fiction authors who write for adults from a Christian perspective.

Recent Title(s) *Live Like You Were Dying*, with Tim McGraw; *Epic*, by John Eldredge; *When the Enemy Strikes*, by Charles Stanley.

ⓝ ⊘ TOMMY NELSON

Imprint of Thomas Nelson, Inc., P.O. Box 141000, Nashville TN 37214-1000. (615)889-9000. Fax: (615)902-2219. Website: www.tommynelson.com. Publishes hardcover and trade paperback originals. **Publishes 50-75 titles/year.** Does not accept simultaneous submissions. Ms guidelines online.

- *Does not accept unsolicited mss.*
- ⚬┑ Tommy Nelson publishes children's Christian nonfiction and fiction for boys and girls up to age 14. "We honor God and serve people through books, videos, software and Bibles for children that improve the lives of our customers."

Nonfiction Children's/juvenile. Subjects include religion (Christian evangelical).

Fiction Adventure, juvenile, mystery, picture books, religious. "No stereotypical characters."

Recent Title(s) *Hermie the Common Caterpillar*, by Max Lucado; *Bible for Me Series*, by Andy Holmes; *Shaoey and Dot*, by Mary Beth and Steven Curtis Chapman.

Tips "Know the Christian Booksellers Association market. Check out the Christian bookstores to see what sells and what is needed."

Ⓐ ⊘ NEW AMERICAN LIBRARY

Penguin Putnam, Inc., 375 Hudson St., New York NY 10014. (212)366-2000. Fax: (212)366-2889. Website: www.penguinputnam.com. Estab. 1948. Publishes mass market and trade paperback originals and reprints. **Pays negotiable royalty. Offers negotiable advance.** Does not accept simultaneous submissions. Book catalog for SASE.

Imprints Onyx; ROC; Signet; Signet Classic; NAL trade paperback; Accent.

- ⚬┑ NAL publishes commercial fiction and nonfiction for the popular audience.

Nonfiction How-to, reference, self-help. Subjects include animals, child guidance/parenting, ethnic, health/medicine, military/war, psychology, sports, movie tie-in. *Agented submissions only.*

Fiction Erotica, ethnic, fantasy, historical, horror, mainstream/contemporary, mystery, romance, science fiction, suspense, western, chicklit. "All kinds of commercial fiction." *Agented submissions only.* Query with SASE. "State type of book and past publishing projects."

Recent Title(s) *How to Be Famous*, by Alison Bond; *Secret Commandos*, by John Plaster; *Notes From the Underbelly*, by Risa Green.

NEW HARBINGER PUBLICATIONS

5674 Shattuck Ave., Oakland CA 94609. (510)652-0215. Fax: (510)652-5472. E-mail: proposals@newharbinger.com. Website: www.newharbinger.com. **Acquisitions:** Catharine Sutker, acquisitions manager; Melissa Kirk, senior acquisitions editor. Estab. 1973. **Publishes 50 titles/year. Receives 1,000 queries and 300 mss/year. 60% of books from first-time authors; 75% from unagented writers. Pays 10% royalty on net receipts.** Publishes book 1 year after acceptance of ms. Accepts simultaneous submissions. Responds in 1 month to queries and proposals; 2 months to mss. Book catalog free; ms guidelines online.

- ⚬┑ "We look for step-by-step self-help titles on psychology, health, and balanced living that teach the average reader how to master essential skills. Our books are also read by mental health professionals who want simple, clear explanations of important psychological techniques and health issues."

Nonfiction Self-help (psychology/health). Subjects include health/medicine, psychology, women's issues/studies, balanced living, anger management, anxiety, coping. "Authors need to be qualified psychotherapists or health practitioners to publish with us." Submit proposal package including outline, 2 sample chapters, competing titles, and a compelling, supported reason why the book is unique.

Recent Title(s) *The Anxiety & Phobia Workbook, 3rd Ed.*, by Edmund J. Bourne; *Rosacea: A Self-Help Guide*, by Arlen Brownstein; *Brave New You*, by Mary and John Valentis.

Tips Audience includes psychotherapists and lay readers wanting step-by-step strategies to solve specific problems. "Our definition of a self-help psychology or health book is one that teaches essential life skills. The primary goal is to train the reader so that, after reading the book, he or she can deal more effectively with health and/or psychological challenges."

NEW HOPE PUBLISHERS

Woman's Missionary Union, P.O. Box 12065, Birmingham AL 35202-2065. (205)991-8100. Fax: (205)991-4015. E-mail: new_hope@wmu.org. Website: www.newhopepublishers.com. **Acquisitions:** Acquisitions Editor. **Pub-**

lishes 20-28 titles/year. **Receives several hundred queries/year. 25% of books from first-time authors; small% from unagented writers. Pays royalty on net receipts.** Publishes book 2 years after acceptance of ms. Book catalog for 9×12 SAE with 3 first-class stamps.

○→ "Our goal is to create unique books that help women and families to grow in Christ and share His hope."
Nonfiction "We publish books dealing with all facets of Christian life for women and families, including health, discipleship, missions, ministry, Bible studies, spiritual development, parenting, and marriage. We currently do not accept adult fiction or children's picture books. We are particularly interested in niche categories and books on lifestyle development and change." Children's/juvenile (religion). Subjects include child guidance/ parenting (from Christian perspective), education (Christian church), health/medicine (Christian), multicultural, religion (spiritual development, Bible study, life situations from Christian perspective, ministry), women's issues/studies (Christian), church leadership, evangelism. Prefers a query and prospectus.
Recent Title(s) *Running on Ice*, by Vonetta Flowers; *Love Notes in Lunchboxes*, by Linda Gilden; *5 Leadership Essentials for Women*, compiled by Linda Clark.

NEW HORIZON PRESS

P.O. Box 669, Far Hills NJ 07931. (908)604-6311. Fax: (908)604-6330. E-mail: nhp@newhorizonpressbooks.c om. Website: www.newhorizonpressbooks.com. **Acquisitions:** Dr. Joan S. Dunphy, publisher (nonfiction, social issues, true crime). Estab. 1983. Publishes hardcover and trade paperback originals. **Publishes 12 titles/ year. 90% of books from first-time authors; 50% from unagented writers. Pays standard royalty on net receipts. Offers advance.** Publishes book within 2 years after acceptance of ms. Accepts simultaneous submissions. Book catalog free; ms guidelines online.
Imprints Small Horizons.

○→ New Horizon publishes adult nonfiction featuring true stories of uncommon heroes, true crime, social issues, and self help.
Nonfiction Biography, children's/juvenile, how-to, self-help. Subjects include child guidance/parenting, creative nonfiction, government/politics, health/medicine, nature/environment, psychology, women's issues/ studies, true crime. Submit proposal package including outline, 3 sample chapters, résumé, author bio, photo, marketing information.
Recent Title(s) *Dead Center*, by Frank J. Daniels; *Mending Wounded Minds*, by Beth Friday Henry; *Race Against Evil*, by David Race Bannon.
Tips "We are a small publisher, thus it is important that the author/publisher have a good working relationship. The author must be willing to promote his book."

NEW SPIRIT

Imprint of BET Books, 850 Third Ave., 16th Floor, New York NY 10022. Website: www.bet.com/books. **Acquisitions:** Glenda Howard, senior editor. Responds in 4 months to proposals.
Nonfiction "Our nonfiction books objective is to encourage and motivate readers by offering messages advocating personal growth, empowerment, and strong personal relationships." Submit proposal package including outline, 3 sample chapters.
Fiction "We are looking to acquire fiction novels that are well crafted, and will feature strong characters who overcome challenges and obstacles through the power of prayer and faith. The New Spirit fiction titles will appeal to a broad audience because they will address contemporary issues such as love, betrayal, tragedy, and triumph over adversity, while keeping a spiritual message throughout." Submit proposal package including 3 sample chapters, synopsis.
Tips "Please do not phone to see if your manuscript was received or returned, or to find out what we thought of it. A self-addressed, stamped postcard can be enclosed with your submission if you want confirmation of its arrival. Specify whether you would like your manuscript returned or recycled if it is not right for us."

NEW WORLD LIBRARY

14 Pamaron Way, Novato CA 94949. (415)884-2100. Fax: (415)884-2199. Website: www.newworldlibrary.com. Publisher: Marc Allen. **Acquisitions:** Submissions Editor. Estab. 1979. Publishes hardcover and trade paperback originals and reprints. **Publishes 35-40 titles/year.** Accepts simultaneous submissions. Responds in 3 months to queries. Book catalog free; ms guidelines online.
Imprints Nataraj; H.J. Kramer; Amber-Allen Publishing.

● Does not accept e-mail submissions. No longer accepting unsolicited children's mss.

○→ "NWL is dedicated to publishing books and audio projects that inspire and challenge us to improve the quality of our lives and our world."
Nonfiction Gift book, self-help. Subjects include alternative lifestyles (health), business/economics (prosperity), ethnic (African/American, Native American), health/medicine (natural), money/finance, nature/environment, psychology, religion, spirituality, women's issues/studies, personal growth, parenting. Submit outline, 2-3 sam-

ple chapters, author bio, SASE. Reviews artwork/photos as part of ms package. Send photocopies.
Recent Title(s) *Coaching the Artist Within*, by Eric Maisel; *Forever Ours*, by Janis Amatuzio.

NEW YORK UNIVERSITY PRESS

838 Broadway, New York NY 10003. (212)998-2575. Fax: (212)995-3833. Website: www.nyupress.org. **Acquisitions:** Eric Zinner (cultural studies, literature, media, history); Jennifer Hammer (Jewish studies, psychology, religion, women's studies); Ilene Kalish (social sciences); Deborah Gershenowitz (law, American history). Estab. 1916. Hardcover and trade paperback originals. **Publishes 100 titles/year. Receives 800-1,000 queries/year. 30% of books from first-time authors; 90% from unagented writers. Pays royalty on net receipts.** Publishes book 9-11 months after acceptance of ms. Accepts simultaneous submissions. Responds in 1-4 months (peer reviewed) to proposals. Ms guidelines online.

> O— New York University Press embraces ideological diversity. "We often publish books on the same issue from different poles to generate dialogue, engender and resist pat categorizations."

Nonfiction Subjects include anthropology/archeology, business/economics, ethnic, gay/lesbian, government/politics, history, language/literature, military/war, psychology, regional, religion, sociology, sports, women's issues/studies. Query with SASE, or submit proposal package including outline, 1 sample chapter. Reviews artwork/photos as part of ms package. Send photocopies.

NEWMARKET PRESS

18 E. 48th St., New York NY 10017. (212)832-3575. Fax: (212)832-3629. E-mail: mailbox@newmarketpress.com. Website: www.newmarketpress.com. President/Publisher: Esther Margolis. **Acquisitions:** Editorial Department. Publishes hardcover and trade paperback originals and reprints. **Publishes 15-20 titles/year. Pays royalty. Offers varied advance.** Accepts simultaneous submissions. Ms guidelines for #10 SASE or online.

> O— Currently emphasizing movie tie-in/companion books, health, psychology, parenting. De-emphasizing fiction.

Nonfiction Biography, coffee table book, general nonfiction, reference, self-help. Subjects include child guidance/parenting, cooking/foods/nutrition, health/medicine, history, psychology, business/personal finance, film/performing arts. Submit proposal package including complete ms, or 1-3 sample chapters, TOC, marketing info, author credentials, SASE.

Recent Title(s) *Condi*, by Antonia Felix; *Hotel Rwanda: Bringing the True Story of an African Hero to Film*, edited by Terry George; *In Good Company*, by Paul Weitz.

NO STARCH PRESS, INC.

555 De Haro St., Suite 250, San Francisco CA 94107. (415)863-9900. Fax: (415)863-9950. E-mail: info@nostarch.com. Website: www.nostarch.com. **Acquisitions:** William Pollock, publisher. Estab. 1994. Publishes trade paperback originals. **Publishes 20-25 titles/year. Receives 100 queries and 5 mss/year. 80% of books from first-time authors; 90% from unagented writers. Pays 10-15% royalty on wholesale price. Offers advance.** Publishes book 4 months after acceptance of ms. Accepts simultaneous submissions. Book catalog free.
Imprints Linux Journal Press.

> O— No Starch Press, Inc., is an independent publishing company committed to producing easy-to-read and information-packed computer books. Currently emphasizing open source, Web development, computer security issues, programming tools, and robotics. "More stuff, less fluff."

Nonfiction How-to, reference, technical. Subjects include computers/electronic, hobbies, software (Open Source). Submit outline, 1 sample chapter, author bio, market rationale. Reviews artwork/photos as part of ms package. Send photocopies.

Recent Title(s) *Hacking: The Art of Exploitation*, by Jon Erickson; *Art of Assembly Language*, by Randall Hyde; *Hacking the XBox*, by Andrew "bunnie" Huang.

Tips "No fluff—content, content, content or just plain fun. Understand how your book fits into the market. Tell us why someone, anyone, will buy your book. Be enthusiastic."

N: NOLO

950 Parker St., Berkeley CA 94710. (510)549-1976. Fax: (510)859-0025. E-mail: acquisitions@nolo.com. Website: www.nolo.com. **Acquisitions:** Editorial Department. Estab. 1971. Publishes trade paperback originals. **Publishes 75 new editions and 15 new titles/year. 20% of books from first-time authors. Pays 10-12% royalty on net receipts. Offers advance.** Accepts simultaneous submissions. Responds in 3 weeks to queries; 5 weeks to proposals. Ms guidelines online.

> O— "We publish practical, do-it-yourself books, software and various electronic products on financial and legal issues that affect individuals, small business, and nonprofit organizations. We specialize in helping people handle their own legal tasks; i.e., write a will, file a small claims lawsuit, start a small business or nonprofit, or apply for a patent."

Nonfiction General nonfiction, how-to, reference, self-help, child guidance/parenting. Subjects include business/economics, money/finance, legal guides in various topics including employment, small business, intellectual property, parenting and education, finance and investment, landlord/tenant, real estate, and estate planning. Query with SASE, or submit outline, 1 sample chapter.

Recent Title(s) *Credit Repair*, by Robin Leonard; *The Small Business Start-Up Kit*, by Pevi Pakroo; *Effective Fundraising for Nonprofits*, by Ilona Bray.

NOMAD PRESS

2456 Christian St., White River Junction VT 05001. (802)649-1995. Fax: (802)649-2667. E-mail: info@nomadpress.net. Website: www.nomadpress.net. Publisher: Alex Kahan. **Acquisitions:** Acquisitions Editor. Publishes trade paperback originals. **Publishes 8+ titles/year. 10% of books from first-time authors; 90% from unagented writers. Pays royalty on retail price, or makes outright purchase. Offers negotiable advance.** Publishes book 1 year after acceptance of ms. Does not accept simultaneous submissions. Responds in 1-2 months to mss. Book catalog and ms guidelines online.

Nonfiction Parenting, how-to, teaching/education, children's activity/science titles. Subjects include child guidance/parenting, sports, teacher training/education, writing/journalism. Actively seeking well-written nonfiction. No disorder-specific parenting mss, cookbooks, poetry, fiction, memoir, or technical manuals. Submit complete ms. Reviews artwork/photos as part of ms package. Send photocopies.

Recent Title(s) *Make a Real Living as a Freelance Writer*, by Jenna Glatzer (journalism/career); *Playing the Game: Inside Athletic Recruiting in the Ivy League*, by Chris Lincoln (sports); *How to Handle School Snafus: A Go Parents! Guide*, by Carmella Van Vleet (parenting).

Ⓝ NORTH LIGHT BOOKS

Imprint of F+W Publications, Inc., 4700 E. Galbraith Rd., Cincinnati OH 45236. **Acquisitions:** Jamie Markle, executive editor of fine art books (books on painting); Pam Wissman, acquisitions editor of fine art books (books on drawing); Tricia Waddell, editorial director of craft books (books on craft instruction); Graphic Design Books (books on graphic design instruction and inspiration). Publishes hardcover and trade paperback how-to books. **Publishes 70-75 titles/year. Pays 10% royalty on net receipts. Offers $5,000 advance.** Accepts simultaneous submissions. Responds in 1 month to queries. Book catalog for 9×12 SAE with 6 first-class stamps.

    ○→ North Light Books publishes art, craft and design books, including watercolor, drawing, colored pencil and decorative painting titles that emphasize illustrated how-to art instruction. Currently emphasizing table-top crafts using materials found in craft stores like Michael's, Hobby Lobby, and comic drawing including traditional American-style comics and Japanese-style comics.

Nonfiction Art how-to. Subjects include hobbies, watercolor, realistic drawing, colored pencil, creativity, decorative painting, comics drawing, craft and graphic design instruction books. Interested in books on watercolor painting, basic drawing, pen and ink, colored pencil, decorative painting, table-top crafts, basic design, computer graphics, layout and typography. Do not submit coffee table art books without how-to art instruction. Query with SASE, or submit outline. Send photocopies or duplicate transparencies.

Recent Title(s) *Manga Secrets*, by Lea Hernandez; *Beautiful Botanicals*, by Bente Starke King; *Collage Discovery Workshop*, by Claudine Hellmuth.

NORTH POINT PRESS

Imprint of Farrar Straus & Giroux, Inc., 19 Union Square W., New York NY 10003. (212)741-6900. E-mail: fsg.editorial@fsgbooks.com. Website: www.fsgbooks.com. Estab. 1980. Publishes hardcover and paperback originals. **Pays standard royalty. Offers varied advance.** Accepts simultaneous submissions. Ms guidelines for #10 SASE.

    ○→ "We are a broad-based literary trade publisher—high quality writing only."

Nonfiction Subjects include history, nature/environment, religion (no New Age), travel, cultural criticism, music, cooking/food. "Be familiar with our list. No genres." Query with SASE, or submit outline, 1-2 sample chapters.

Recent Title(s) *Chocolate: A Bittersweet Saga of Dark and Light*, by Mort Rosenblum; *In Fond Remembrance of Me*, by Howard Norman.

NORTHERN ILLINOIS UNIVERSITY PRESS

310 N. Fifth St., DeKalb IL 60115-2854. (815)753-1826. Fax: (815)753-1845. Director/Editor-in-Chief: Mary L. Lincoln. **Acquisitions:** Melody Herr, acquisitions editor (history, politics). Estab. 1965. **Publishes 20-22 titles/year. Pays 10-15% royalty on wholesale price. Offers advance.** Does not accept simultaneous submissions. Book catalog free.

○━ NIU Press publishes scholarly work and books of general interest to the informed public. "We publish mainly history, politics, anthropology, and other social sciences. We are interested also in studies on the Chicago area and Midwest, and in literature in translation." Currently emphasizing history, the social sciences, and cultural studies.

Nonfiction "Publishes mainly history, political science, social sciences, philosophy, literary and cultural studies, and regional studies." Subjects include anthropology/archeology, government/politics, history, language/literature, philosophy, regional, social sciences, translation, cultural studies. No collections of previously published essays or unsolicited poetry. Query with SASE, or submit outline, 1-3 sample chapters.

Recent Title(s) *Possessed: Women, Witches and Demons in Imperial Russia.*

NORTHLAND PUBLISHING, INC.

P.O. Box 1389, Flagstaff AZ 86002-1389. (928)774-5251. Fax: (928)774-0592. Website: www.northlandbooks.com. **Acquisitions:** Tammy Gales-Biber, managing editor; Theresa Howell, managing children's editor (picture books, especially with Southwest appeal). Estab. 1958. Publishes hardcover and trade paperback originals. **Publishes 8-10 titles/year; imprint publishes 8-10 titles/year. 20% of books from first-time authors; 20% from unagented writers. Pays royalty. Offers advance.** Publishes book 1-2 years after acceptance of ms. Accepts simultaneous submissions. Responds in 3 months to queries. Call for book catalog; ms guidelines online.

Imprints Rising Moon (books for children); Luna Rising (bilingual Spanish/English books for children).

○━ "Northland Publishing acquires nonfiction books intended for general trade audiences on the American West and Southwest, including Native American arts, crafts, and culture; Mexican culture; regional cookery; Western lifestyle; and interior design and architecture. Northland is not accepting poetry or fiction at this time."

Nonfiction Query with SASE, or submit outline, 2-3 sample chapters. No fax or e-mail submissions.

Fiction Picture books. Submit complete ms.

Recent Title(s) *Outdoor Style,* by Suzanne Pickett Martinson; *Southwest Lite,* by Bob Wiseman; *Sedona: Treasure of the Southwest,* by Kathleen Bryant.

Tips "Our audience is composed of general-interest readers."

NORTHWORD BOOKS FOR YOUNG READERS

(formerly NorthWord Press), Imprint of T&N Children's Publishing, 11571 K-Tel Dr., Minnetonka MN 55343. (952)933-7537. Fax: (952)933-3630. Website: www.tnkidsbooks.com. **Acquisitions:** Kristin McCurry (children's books). Estab. 1984. Publishes children's nonfiction trade hardcovers and paperback originals. **Publishes 20 titles/year. 25% of books from first-time authors; 50% from unagented writers. Pays 5% royalty on list price. Offers $2,000-10,000 advance.** Publishes book 1-2 years after acceptance of ms. Accepts simultaneous submissions. Responds in 3 months to queries. Ms guidelines for #10 SASE.

○━ NorthWord Books for Young Readers exclusively publishes nonfiction nature, wildlife, natural history, and outdoor titles for children.

Nonfiction Formats include board books, picture books and series. Query with SASE.

Recent Title(s) *John Muir and Stickeen: An Icy Adventure with a No-Good Dog,* by Marybeth Lorbiecki and Julie Dunlap, illustrated by Bill Farnsworth (nonfiction picture book, ages 5-8); *Everything Reptile,* by Cherie Winner (kids' FAQs series, ages 8-11); *Yoga Bear: Yoga for Youngsters,* by Karen Pierce, illustrated by Paula Brinkman (nonfiction picture book, ages 2-6).

W.W. NORTON CO., INC.

500 Fifth Ave., New York NY 10110. Fax: (212)869-0856. E-mail: manuscripts@wwnorton.com. Website: www.wwnorton.com. **Acquisitions:** Starling Lawrence, editor-in-chief; Robert Weil, executive editor; Edwin Barber; Jill Bialosky (literary fiction, biography, memoirs); Amy Cherry (history, biography, women's issues, African-American, health); Carol Houck-Smith (literary fiction, creative nonfictions, memoir/biography); Angela von der Lippe (trade nonfiction, behavioral sciences, earth sciences, astronomy, neuro-science, education); Jim Mairs (history, biography, illustrated books); Alane Mason (serious nonfiction cultural and intellectual history, illustrated books, literary fiction and memoir); W. Drake McFeely, president (nonfiction, particularly science and social science); Maria Guarnaschelli (cookbooks, food & travel writing, literary fiction, memoir, serious nonfiction—esepcially language, psychology, physics, history, math, nature). Estab. 1923. Publishes hardcover and paperback originals and reprints. **Publishes 300 titles/year. Pays royalty. Offers advance.** Does not accept simultaneous submissions. Responds in 2 months to queries. Ms guidelines online.

Imprints Backcountry Publication; Countryman Press; W.W. Norton.

○━ General trade publisher of fiction, poetry and nonfiction, educational and professional books. "W. W. Norton Co. strives to carry out the imperative of its founder to 'publish books not for a single season, but for the years' in the areas of fiction, nonfiction and poetry."

Nonfiction Autobiography, biography, reference, self-help. Subjects include agriculture/horticulture, art/architecture, business/economics, child guidance/parenting, community, computers/electronic, cooking/foods/nutrition, government/politics, health/medicine, history, hobbies, language/literature, memoirs, music/dance, nature/environment, photography, psychology, religion, science, sports, travel, antiques and collectibles, current affairs, family, games, law, mystery, nautical subjects, poetry, political science, sailing, transportation. College Department: Subjects include biological sciences, economics, psychology, political science and computer science. Professional Books specializes in psychotherapy. "We are not interested in considering books from the following categories: juvenile or young adult, religious, occult or paranormal, and arts and crafts." Query with SASE, or submit 2-3 sample chapters, one of which should be the first chapter. Please give a brief description of your submission, your writing credentials, and any experience, professional or otherwise, which is relevant to your submission. No phone calls. Address envelope and letter to The Editors.
Fiction Literary, poetry, poetry in translation, religious. High-qulity literary fiction. "We are not interested in considering books from the following categories: juvenile or young adult, religious, occult or paranormal, genre fiction (formula romances, sci-fi or westerns)." Accepts e-mail submissions. No phone calls.
Recent Title(s) *Guns, Germs and Steel*, by Jared Diamond; *Island*, by Alistir MacLeod.

NURSESBOOKS.ORG
American Nurses Association, 8515 Georgia Ave., Suite 400, Silver Spring MD 20901-3492. (301)628-5212. Fax: (301)628-5003. E-mail: cwurzbac@ana.org. Website: www.nursesbooks.org. **Acquisitions:** Rosanne O'Connor, publisher; Eric Wurzbacher, editor/project manager. Publishes professional paperback originals and reprints. **Publishes 10 titles/year. Receives 300 queries and 8-10 mss/year. 75% of books from first-time authors; 100% from unagented writers. Pays 12% royalty on net receipts. Offers negotiable advance.** Publishes book 4 months after acceptance of ms. Does not accept simultaneous submissions. Responds in 3 months. Book catalog online; ms guidelines free.

> O—¬ Nursebooks.org publishes books designed to help professional nurses in their work and careers. Through the publishing program, Nursebooks.org provides nurses in all practice settings with publications that address cutting-edge issues and form a basis for debate and exploration of this century's most critical health care trends.

Nonfiction Reference, technical, textbook, handbooks; resource guides. Subjects include health/medicine. Subjects include advanced practice, computers, continuing education, ethics, health care policy, nursing administration, psychiatric and mental health, quality, nursing history, workplace issues, key clinical topics. Submit outline, 1 sample chapter, cv. Reviews artwork/photos as part of ms package. Send photocopies.
Recent Title(s) *Florence Nightingale Today: Healing, Leadership, and Global Action*; *Genetics Nursing Portfolios: A New Model for Credentialing*; *Person Centered Care: A New Model for Nursing Homes*.

OAK KNOLL PRESS
310 Delaware St., New Castle DE 19720. (302)328-7232. Fax: (302)328-7274. E-mail: oakknoll@oakknoll.com. Website: www.oakknoll.com. **Acquisitions:** John Von Hoelle, director of publishing. Estab. 1976. Publishes hardcover and trade paperback originals and reprints. **Publishes 40 titles/year. Receives 250 queries and 100 mss/year. 50% of books from first-time authors; 100% from unagented writers.** Publishes book 12 months after acceptance of ms. Accepts simultaneous submissions. Ms guidelines online.

> O—¬ Oak Knoll specializes in books about books and manuals on the book arts—preserving the art and lore of the printed word.

Nonfiction How-to. Subjects include book arts, printing, papermaking, bookbinding, book collecting, etc. Reviews artwork/photos as part of ms package. Send photocopies.
Recent Title(s) *ABC for Book Collectors, 8th Ed.*, by John Carter and Nicolas Barker; *Early Type Specimens*, by John Lane; *The Great Libraries*, by Konstantinos Staikos.

THE OAKLEA PRESS
6912-B Three Chopt Rd., Richmond VA 23226. (804)281-5872. Fax: (804)281-5686. E-mail: info@oakleapress.com. **Acquisitions:** S.H. Martin, publisher. Publishes hardcover and trade paperback originals. **Receives 300 queries and 50 mss/year. 50% of books from first-time authors; 90% from unagented writers. Pays 10-20% royalty on wholesale price.** Publishes book 6 months after acceptance of ms. Accepts simultaneous submissions. Responds in 1 month to queries and proposals; 3 months to mss. Book catalog online.
Nonfiction How-to, self-help. Subjects include business management, lean enterprise. "We like how-to books and currently are actively looking for those that can help businesses and organizations increase the productivity of workers and staff." Submit proposal package including outline, 1 sample chapter.
Recent Title(s) *Buried Alive! Digging Out of a Management Dumpster*, by Anna Versteeg et al; *Secrets of Success: Key Insights for Life's Journey From the Great Western Myths*, by Gerald W. Morton, PhD; *Product Development for the Lean Enterprise*, by Michael Kennedy.

OHIO STATE UNIVERSITY PRESS

1070 Carmack Rd., Columbus OH 43210-1002. (614)292-6930. Fax: (614)292-2065. E-mail: ohiostatepress@osu. edu. Website: www.ohiostatepress.org. **Acquisitions:** Malcolm Litchfield, director; Heather Miller, acquisitions editor. Estab. 1957. **Publishes 30 titles/year. Pays royalty. Offers advance.** Responds in 3 months to queries. Ms guidelines online.

> Ohio State University Press publishes scholarly nonfiction, and offers short fiction and short poetry prizes. Currently emphasizing history, literary studies, political science, women's health, classics, Victoria studies.

Nonfiction General nonfiction, scholarly. Subjects include business/economics, education, government/politics, history (American), language/literature, multicultural, regional, sociology, women's issues/studies, criminology, literary criticism, women's health. Query with SASE.

Recent Title(s) *Saving Lives*, by Albert Goldbarth (poetry); *Ohio: History of People*, by Andrew Cayton (nonfiction).

OHIO UNIVERSITY PRESS

Scott Quadrangle, Athens OH 45701. (740)593-1155. Fax: (740)593-4536. Website: www.ohio.edu/oupress/. **Acquisitions:** Gillian Berchowitz, senior editor (American history and popular culture, legal history, African studies, Appalachian studies); David Sanders, director (literature, literary criticism, midwest and frontier studies, Ohioana). Estab. 1964. Publishes hardcover and trade paperback originals and reprints. **Publishes 45-50 titles/year. Receives 500 queries and 50 mss/year. 20% of books from first-time authors; 95% from unagented writers. Pays 7-10% royalty on net receipts.** Publishes book 1 year after acceptance of ms. Responds in 1 month to queries and proposals; 2 months to mss. Book catalog free; ms guidelines online.

Imprints Ohio University Research in International Studies (Gillian Berchowitz); Swallow Press (David Sanders).

> Ohio University Press publishes and disseminates the fruits of research and creative endeavor, specifically in the areas of literary studies, regional works, philosophy, contemporary history, African studies, and frontier Americana. Its charge to produce books of value in service to the academic community and for the enrichment of the broader culture is in keeping with the university's mission of teaching, research and service to its constituents.

Nonfiction Reference, scholarly. Subjects include Americana, anthropology/archeology, art/architecture, ethnic, gardening, government/politics, history, language/literature, military/war, nature/environment, philosophy, regional, sociology, travel, women's issues/studies, African studies. "We prefer queries or detailed proposals, rather than manuscripts, pertaining to scholarly projects that might have a general interest. Proposals should explain the thesis and details of the subject matter, not just sell a title." Query with SASE. Reviews artwork/photos as part of ms package. Send photocopies.

Recent Title(s) *Body Story*, by Julia K. De Pree; *Mencken's America*, edited by S.T. Soshi; *A Poet's Prose: Selected Writings of Louise Bogan*, edited by Mary Kinzie.

Tips "Rather than trying to hook the editor on your work, let the material be compelling enough and well-presented enough to do it for you."

Ø ONE ON ONE COMPUTER TRAINING

Mosaic Media, 751 Roosevelt Rd., Suite 108, Glen Ellyn IL 60137-5905. Website: www.ooo training.com. Estab. 1976. Does not accept simultaneous submissions. Book catalog free.

Imprints OneOnOne Computer Training; Working Smarter; Professional Training Associates.

> One On One Computer Training publishes ongoing computer training and soft skills training for computer users and office professionals.

Nonfiction How-to, self-help, technical. Subjects include computers/electronic, software, soft skills for businesses and creative use of digital media, Internet. *All unsolicited mss returned unopened.* Query.

Ⓐ ONE WORLD BOOKS

Ballantine Publishing Group, Inc., 1745 Broadway, 18th Floor, New York NY 10019. (212)782-9000. Fax: (212)572-4949. Website: www.randomhouse.com. Estab. 1991. Publishes hardcover, trade and mass market paperback originals and trade paperback reprints. Accepts simultaneous submissions.

> "All One World Books must be specifically written for either an African-American, Asian, Native American, or Hispanic audience. No exceptions."

Nonfiction Biography, cookbook, how-to, humor, self-help. Subjects include Americana, cooking/foods/nutrition, creative nonfiction, ethnic, government/politics, history, memoirs, multicultural, philosophy, psychology, recreation, travel, women's issues/studies, African-American studies. *Agented submissions only.*

Fiction Adventure, comic books, confession, erotica, ethnic, historical, humor, literary, mainstream/contemporary, multicultural, mystery, regional, romance, suspense, strong need for commercial women's fiction. No poetry. *Agented submissions only.*

Recent Title(s) *A One Woman Man*, by Travis Hunter; *Space Between the Stars*, by Deborah Santana; *Black Titan*, by Carol Jenkins and Elizabeth Gardner Hines.

Tips All books must be written in English.

[N] OPEN COURT PUBLISHING CO.

315 Fifth St., Peru IL 61354. Estab. 1887. Publishes hardcover and trade paperback originals. **Publishes 20 titles/year. Pays 5-15% royalty on wholesale price.** Publishes book 8 months after acceptance of ms. Does not accept simultaneous submissions. Book catalog online; ms guidelines free.

Nonfiction General nonfiction, scholarly. Subjects include contemporary culture (popular culture), philosophy, Asian thought, religious studies. Query with SASE, or submit proposal package including outline, 1 sample chapter, TOC, author's VITA, cover letter, intended audience.

Recent Title(s) *The Matrix and Philosophy*, edited by William Irwin (philosophy); *Tool-Being*, by Graham Harman (philosophy).

Tips Audience consists of philosophers and intelligent general readers.

OPEN ROAD PUBLISHING

P.O. Box 284, Cold Spring Harbor NY 11724. (631)692-7172. Fax: (631)692-7193. E-mail: jopenroad@aol.com. Website: openroadpub.com. Publisher: Jonathan Stein. Publishes trade paperback originals. **Publishes 22-27 titles/year. Receives 200 queries and 75 mss/year. 30% of books from first-time authors; 98% from un-agented writers. Pays 5-6% royalty on retail price. Offers $1,000-5,000 advance.** Publishes book 3 months after acceptance of ms. Accepts simultaneous submissions. Responds in 1 month to queries; 2 months to proposals. Book catalog and ms guidelines free.

   O→ Open Road publishes travel guides and has expanded into other areas with its new imprint, Cold Spring Press, particularly sports/fitness, topical, biographies, history, fantasy.

Nonfiction How-to. Subjects include travel. Query with SASE.

Recent Title(s) *Tahiti & French Polynesia Guide*, by Jon Prince; *Book of the Three Dragons*, by Kennedy Morris; *The Sillymarillion*, by D.R. Lloyd.

⊘ ORCHARD BOOKS

Imprint of Scholastic Trade Division, 557 Broadway, New York NY 10012. (212)343-6100. Website: www.schola stic.com. Estab. 1987. Publishes hardcover and trade paperback originals.

   O→ Orchard specializes in children's picture books. Currently emphasizing picture books and middle grade novels (ages 8-12). De-emphasizing young adult.

Nonfiction Children's/juvenile, illustrated book. Subjects include animals, history, nature/environment. *"No unsolicited mss.* Be as specific and enlightening as possible about your book." Query with SASE. Reviews artwork/photos as part of ms package. Send photocopies.

Fiction Picture books, young adult, middle reader; novelty. *No unsolicited mss.* Query with SASE.

Recent Title(s) *Katie's Sunday Afternoon*, by James Mayhew; *The Wheels on the Race Car*, by Alexander Zane, illustrated by James Warhola; *What's Going on in There?*, by Geoffrey Grahn.

Tips "Go to a bookstore and read several Orchard Books to get an idea of what we publish. Write what you feel and query us if you think it's 'right.' It's worth finding the right publishing match."

[N] OUR SUNDAY VISITOR PUBLISHING

200 Noll Plaza, Huntington IN 46750-4303. (260)356-8400. Fax: (260)359-9117. E-mail: booksed@osv.com. Website: www.osv.com. President/Publisher: Greg Erlandson. Editorial Director: Beth McNamara. Editorial Development Manager: Jacquelyn Lindsey. **Acquisitions:** Michael Dubruiel, Kelley Renz, acquisitions editors. Estab. 1912. Publishes paperback and hardbound originals. **Publishes 30-40 titles/year. 10% of books from first-time authors; 90% from unagented writers. Pays variable royalty on net receipts. Offers $1,500 average advance.** Publishes book 1-2 years after acceptance of ms. Does not accept simultaneous submissions. Responds in 3 months to queries. Book catalog for 9×12 SAE; ms guidelines for #10 SASE or online.

   O→ "We are a Catholic publishing company seeking to educate and deepen our readers in their faith." Currently emphasizing reference, apologetics, and catechetics. De-emphasizing inspirational.

Nonfiction Catholic viewpoints on family, prayer, and devotional books, and Catholic heritage books. Reference. Prefers to see well-developed proposals as first submission with annotated outline and definition of intended market. Reviews artwork/photos as part of ms package.

Recent Title(s) *De-Coding DaVinci*, by Amy Welborn.

Tips "Solid devotional books that are not first person, or lives of the saints and catechetical books have the best chance of selling to our firm. Make it solidly Catholic, unique, without pious platitudes."

THE OVERLOOK PRESS

141 Wooster St., New York NY 10012. (212)673-2210. Fax: (212)673-2296. Website: www.overlookpress.com. Publisher: Peter Mayer. Estab. 1971. Publishes hardcover and trade paperback originals and hardcover reprints. **Publishes 100 titles/year.** Does not accept simultaneous submissions. Book catalog free.

Oₙ Overlook Press publishes fiction, children's books, and nonfiction.

Nonfiction Biography. Subjects include art/architecture, film/cinema/stage, history, regional (New York State), current events, design, health/fitness, how-to, lifestyle, martial arts. No pornography. *Agented submissions only.*

Fiction Literary, some commercial, foreign literature in translation. *Agented submissions only.*

Recent Title(s) *Dragon's Eye*, by Andy Oakes; *The Brontes*, by Juliet Barker; *Triomf*, translated from the Afrikaans by Leon de Kock.

THE OVERMOUNTAIN PRESS

P.O. Box 1261, Johnson City TN 37605. (423)926-2691. Fax: (423)232-1252. E-mail: submissions@overmtn.com. Website: www.overmountainpress.com. Publisher: Beth Wright; Managing Editor: Daniel Lewis. Estab. 1970. Publishes hardcover and trade paperback originals and reprints. Accepts simultaneous submissions. Responds in 1-4 months to mss. Book catalog free; ms guidelines online.

Imprints Silver Dagger Mysteries.

Oₙ The Overmountain Press publishes primarily Appalachian history. Audience is people interested in history of Tennessee, Virginia, North Carolina, Kentucky, and all aspects of this region—Revolutionary War, Civil War, county histories, historical biographies, etc.

Nonfiction Regional works only. Coffee table book, cookbook. Subjects include Americana, cooking/foods/nutrition, ethnic, history, military/war, nature/environment, photography, regional, women's issues/studies, Native American, ghostlore, guidebooks, folklore. Submit proposal package including outline, 3 sample chapters, marketing suggestions. Reviews artwork/photos as part of ms package. Send photocopies.

Fiction Picture books (must have regional flavor). Submit complete ms.

Tips "Please, no phone calls."

RICHARD C. OWEN PUBLISHERS, INC.

P.O. Box 585, Katonah NY 10536. (914)232-3903. Website: www.rcowen.com. **Acquisitions:** Janice Boland, director, children's books; Amy Finney, project editor (professional development, teacher-oriented books). Estab. 1982. Publishes hardcover and paperback originals. **Publishes 23 titles/year. Receives 50 queries and 1,000 mss/year. 99% of books from first-time authors; 100% from unagented writers. Pays 5% royalty on wholesale price. Books for Young Learners Anthologies: flat fee for all rights.** Publishes book 2-5 years after acceptance of ms. Accepts simultaneous submissions. Responds in 1 month to queries and proposals; 5 months to mss. Ms guidelines online.

Oₙ "In addition to publishing good literature, stories for 8-9-year-old children, we are also seeking manuscripts for 8-9-year-old children. Subjects include humor, careers, mysteries, science fiction, folktales, women, fashion trends, sports, music, myths, journalism, history, inventions, planets, architecture, plays, adventure, technology, vehicles."

Nonfiction Children's/juvenile. Subjects include animals, art/architecture, fashion/beauty, gardening, history, music/dance, nature/environment, recreation, science, sports, women's issues/studies, contemporary culture. "Our books are for kindergarten, first- and second-grade children to read on their own. The stories are very brief—under 1,000 words—yet well structured and crafted with memorable characters, language, and plots." Send for ms guidelines, then submit complete ms with SASE via mail only or visit website.

Fiction Picture books. "Brief, strong story line, believable characters, natural language, exciting—child-appealing stories with a twist. No lists books, alphabet, or counting books." Seeking short, snappy stories and articles for 7-8-year-old children (2nd grade). Subjects include humor, careers, mysteries, science fiction, folktales, women, fashion trends, sports, music, mysteries, myths, journalism, history, inventions, planets, architecture, plays, adventure, technology, vehicles. Send for ms guidelines, then submit full ms with SASE via mail only. No e-mail submissions, please.

Poetry "Poems that excite children are fun, humorous, fresh, and interesting. If rhyming, must be without force or contrivance. Poems should tell a story or evoke a mood or atmostphere and have rhythmic language." No jingles. Submit complete ms.

Recent Title(s) *Powwow*, by Rhonda Cox (nonfiction); *Concrete*, by Ellen Javernich (fiction); *Bunny Magic*, by Suzanne Hardin (humor).

Tips "We don't respond to queries or e-mails. Please do *not* fax or e-mail us. Because our books are so brief it is better to send entire manuscript. We publish story books with inherent educational value for young readers—books they can read with enjoyment and success. We believe students become enthusiastic, independent, lifelong learners when supported and guided by skillful teachers using good books. The professional development work we do and the books we publish support these beliefs.''

△ OWL BOOKS

Henry Holt & Co., Inc., 115 W. 18th St., New York NY 10011. (212)886-9200. Fax: (212)633-0748. Website: www.henryholt.com. Estab. 1996. Publishes paperback originals and reprints. Accepts simultaneous submissions. Ms guidelines online.

    O━ ''We are looking for original, great ideas that have commercial appeal, but that you can respect.''

Nonfiction Biography, self-help. Subjects include health/medicine, history (American, military), regional, science, women's issues/studies, current affairs, parenting, business/finance. *Agented submissions only.*

Recent Title(s) *The G Spot*, by Alice Kahn Ladas, Beverly Whipple, and John D. Perry; *The Gluten-Free Gourmet Cooks Comfort Foods*, by Bette Hagman; *I'm OK, You're My Parents*, by Dale Atkins, PhD.

P & R PUBLISHING CO.

P.O. Box 817, Phillipsburg NJ 08865. Fax: (908)454-0859. Website: www.prpbooks.com. **Acquisitions:** Allan Fisher, director of publications. Estab. 1930. Publishes hardcover originals and trade paperback originals and reprints. **Publishes 40 titles/year. Receives 300 queries and 100 mss/year. 5% of books from first-time authors; 95% from unagented writers. Pays 10-14% royalty on wholesale price.** Accepts simultaneous submissions. Responds in 1 month to queries; 2 months to proposals; 4 months to mss. Book catalog free; ms guidelines online.

Nonfiction Biography, booklets, children's/juvenile, gift book, scholarly. Subjects include history, religion, spirituality, translation. Query with SASE.

Recent Title(s) *Justification and the New Perspectives on Paul*, by Guy Waters (Biblical studies); *The Afternoon of Life*, by Elyse Fitzpatrick (women); *Rebel's Keep*, by Douglas Bond (children's historical fiction).

Tips ''Our audience is evangelical Christians, other Christians, and seekers. All of our publications are consistent with Biblical teaching, as summarized in the Westminster Standards.''

PACIFIC PRESS PUBLISHING ASSOCIATION

Trade Book Division, P.O. Box 5353, Nampa ID 83653-5353. (208)465-2500. Fax: (208)465-2531. E-mail: booksubmissions@pacificpress.com. Website: www.pacificpress.com. **Acquisitions:** Tim Lale, acquisitions editor (children's stories, biography, Christian living, spiritual growth); David Jarnes, book editor (theology, doctrine, inspiration). Estab. 1874. Publishes hardcover and trade paperback originals and reprints. **Publishes 35 titles/year. 35% of books from first-time authors; 100% from unagented writers. Pays 8-16% royalty on wholesale price.** Publishes book up to 2 years after acceptance of ms. Does not accept simultaneous submissions. Responds in 3 months to queries. Ms guidelines online.

    O━ ''We publish books that fit Seventh-day Adventist beliefs only. All titles are Christian and religious. For guidance, see www.adventist.org/beliefs/index.html. Our books fit into the categories of this retail site: www.adventistbookcenter.com.''

Nonfiction Biography, booklets, children's/juvenile, cookbook (vegetarian), how-to, humor. Subjects include child guidance/parenting, cooking/foods/nutrition (vegetarian only), health/medicine, history, nature/environment, philosophy, religion, spirituality, women's issues/studies, family living, Christian lifestyle, Bible study, Christian doctrine, eschatology. Query with SASE or e-mail, or submit 3 sample chapters, cover letter with overview of book. Electronic submissions accepted. Reviews artwork/photos as part of ms package.

Fiction Religious. ''Pacific Press rarely publishes fiction, but we're interested in developing a line of Seventh-day Adventist fiction in the future. Only proposals accepted; no full manuscripts.''

Recent Title(s) *Graffiti in the Holy of Holies*, by Clifford Goldstein (doctrine); *Parenting by the Spirit*, by Sally Hohnberger (practical Christianity); *I Miss Grandpa*, by Karen Holford (children's).

Tips ''Our primary audience is members of the Seventh-day Adventist denomination. Almost all are written by Seventh-day Adventists. Books that do well for us relate the Biblical message to practical human concerns and focus more on the experiential rather than theoretical aspects of Christianity. We are assigning more titles, using less unsolicited material—although we still publish manuscripts from freelance submissions and proposals.''

PALADIN PRESS

7077 Winchester Circle, Boulder CO 80301. (303)443-7250. Fax: (303)442-8741. E-mail: editorial@paladin-press.com. Website: www.paladin-press.com. President/Publisher: Peder C. Lund. **Acquisitions:** Jon Ford, editorial director. Estab. 1970. Publishes hardcover originals and paperback originals and reprints. **Publishes 50 titles/year. 50% of books from first-time authors; 100% from unagented writers. Pays 10-15% royalty on net receipts. Offers advance.** Publishes book 1 year after acceptance of ms. Accepts simultaneous submissions. Responds in 2 months to proposals. Book catalog free.

Imprints Sycamore Island Books; Flying Machines Press; Outer Limits Press.

O—¬ Paladin Press publishes the "action library" of nonfiction in military science, police science, weapons, combat, personal freedom, self-defense, survival.

Nonfiction "Paladin Press primarily publishes original manuscripts on military science, weaponry, self-defense, personal privacy, financial freedom, espionage, police science, action careers, guerrilla warfare, and fieldcraft." How-to, reference. Subjects include government/politics, military/war. "If applicable, send sample photographs and line drawings with complete outline and sample chapters." Query with SASE.

Recent Title(s) *Surviving Workplace Violence: What to Do Before a Violent Incident; What to Do When the Violence Explodes*, by Loren W. Christensen.

Tips "We need lucid, instructive material aimed at our market and accompanied by sharp, relevant illustrations and photos. As we are primarily a publisher of 'how-to' books, a manuscript that has step-by-step instructions, written in a clear and concise manner (but not strictly outline form) is desirable. No fiction, first-person accounts, children's, religious, or joke books. We are also interested in serious, professional videos and video ideas (contact Michael Rigg)."

N PALGRAVE MACMILLAN

St. Martin's Press, 175 Fifth Ave., New York NY 10010. (212)982-3900. Fax: (212)777-6359. Website: www.palgrave-usa.com. **Acquisitions:** Airié Stuart (history, business, economics, current events, psychology, biography); Anthony Wahl (political economy, political theory, Asian studies, international relations theory, Western European studies); David Pervin (political science, Middle East & Central Asia, American politics, international relations, Russia & Eastern Europe); Farideh Koohi-Kamali (literature, anthropology, cultural studies, performing arts, Islamic World & Middle East); Amanda Johnson (education, religion, women's studies/history); Ella Pearce (African studies, Latin American studies); Alessandra Bastagli (American history, American studies, world history). Publishes hardcover and trade paperback originals. Accepts simultaneous submissions. Book catalog and ms guidelines online.

O—¬ Palgrave wishes to "expand on our already successful academic, trade, and reference programs so that we will remain at the forefront of publishing in the global information economy of the 21st century. We publish high-quality academic works and a distinguished range of reference titles, and we expect to see many of our works available in electronic form. We do not accept fiction or poetry."

Nonfiction Biography, reference, scholarly. Subjects include business/economics, creative nonfiction, education, ethnic, gay/lesbian, government/politics, history, language/literature, military/war, money/finance, multicultural, music/dance, philosophy, regional, religion, sociology, spirituality, translation, women's issues/studies, humanities, social studies, film/cinema/stage, contemporary culture, general nonfiction, world affairs. "We are looking for good solid scholarship." Query with proposal package including outline, 3-4 sample chapters, prospectus, cv and SASE. Reviews artwork/photos as part of ms package.

Recent Title(s) *John Jay*, by Walter Stahr; *America on the Brink*, by Richard Buel; *The Timeline History of Baseball*, by Don Jensen.

A PANTHEON BOOKS

Imprint of Knopf Publishing Group, Division of Random House, Inc., 1745 Broadway 21-2, New York NY 10019. (212)782-9000. Fax: (212)572-6030. Website: www.pantheonbooks.com. **Acquisitions:** Adult Editorial Department. Estab. 1942. Publishes hardcover and trade paperback originals and trade paperback reprints. **Pays royalty. Offers advance.** Does not accept simultaneous submissions.

● "We only accept mss submitted by an agent. You may still send a 20-50 page sample and a SASE to our slushpile. Allow 2-6 months for a response."

O—¬ Pantheon Books publishes both Western and non-Western authors of literary fiction and important nonfiction.

Nonfiction Autobiography, biography, general nonfiction, literary; international. Subjects include government/politics, history, memoirs, science, travel.

Fiction Quality fiction, including graphic novels and fairytales/folklore.

Recent Title(s) *In the Company of Cheerful Ladies*, by Alexander McCall Smith; *The Way Home*, by Ernestine Bradley; *Reef Madness*, by David Dobbs.

PARACLETE PRESS

P.O. Box 1568, Orleans MA 02653. (508)255-4685. Fax: (508)255-5705. Website: www.paracletepress.com. **Acquisitions:** Editorial Review Committee. Estab. 1981. Publishes hardcover and trade paperback originals. **Publishes 20 titles/year. Receives 250 mss/year.** Publishes book up to 2 years after acceptance of ms. Accepts simultaneous submissions. Responds in 2 months. Book catalog for 8½×11 SASE; ms guidelines for #10 SASE.

O—¬ Publisher of devotionals, new editions of classics, books on prayer, Christian living, spirituality, compact discs, and videos.

Nonfiction Subjects include religion. No poetry or children's books. Query with SASE, or submit 2-3 sample chapters, TOC, chapter summaries.

Recent Title(s) *The Jesus Creed*, by Scot McKnight; *Engaging the World With Merton*, by M. Basil Pennington, O.C.S.O; *The Illuminated Heart*, by Frederica Mathewes-Green.

PARAGON HOUSE PUBLISHERS

1925 Oakcrest Ave., Suite 7, St. Paul MN 55113-2619. (651)644-3087. Fax: (651)644-0997. E-mail: paragon@paragonhouse.com. Website: www.paragonhouse.com. **Acquisitions:** Rosemary Yokoi, acquisitions editor. Estab. 1962. Publishes hardcover and trade paperback originals and trade paperback reprints. **Publishes 12-15 titles/year; imprint publishes 2-5 titles/year. Receives 1,500 queries and 150 mss/year. 7% of books from first-time authors; 90% from unagented writers. Offers $500-1,500 advance.** Publishes book 1 year after acceptance of ms. Accepts simultaneous submissions. Ms guidelines online.

Imprints *Series*: Paragon Issues in Philosophy, Genocide and Holocaust Studies; Omega Books.

> ⦿ "We publish general-interest titles and textbooks that provide the readers greater understanding of society and the world." Currently emphasizing religion, philosophy, economics, and society."

Nonfiction Biography, reference, textbook. Subjects include child guidance/parenting, government/politics, memoirs, multicultural, nature/environment, philosophy, religion, sex, sociology, women's issues/studies, world affairs. Submit proposal package including outline, 2 sample chapters, market breakdown, SASE.

Recent Title(s) *One Cosmos Under God*, by Robert W. Godwin; *Corporate Scandals*, by Kenneth R. Gray et. al; *Philosophy of the United States*, by Gordon L. Anderson.

PARALLAX PRESS

P.O. Box 7355, Berkeley CA 94707. (510)525-0101, ext. 113. Fax: (510)525-7129. E-mail: rachel@parallax.org. Website: www.parallax.org. **Acquisitions:** Rachel Neumann, senior editor. Estab. 1985. Publishes hardcover and trade paperback originals. **Publishes 5-8 titles/year.** Does not accept simultaneous submissions. Responds in 6-8 weeks to queries. Book catalog for 1 SAE with 3 first-class stamps; Ms guidelines for #10 SASE or online.

> ⦿ "We focus primarily on engaged Buddhism."

Nonfiction Children's/juvenile, coffee table book, self-help. Subjects include multicultural, religion (Buddhism), spirituality. Query with SASE, or submit 1 sample chapter, 1-page proposal. Reviews artwork/photos as part of ms package. Send photocopies.

Recent Title(s) *Journeying East*, by Victoria Jean Dimidjian; *Touching the Earth*, by Thich Nhat Hanh; *Wild Grace*, by Eric Alan.

PARKWAY PUBLISHERS, INC.

Box 3678, Boone NC 28607. (828)265-3993. Fax: (828)265-3993. E-mail: parkwaypub@hotmail.com. Website: www.parkwaypublishers.com. **Acquisitions:** Rao Aluri, president. Publishes hardcover and trade paperback originals. **Publishes 10-12 titles/year. Receives 15-20 queries and 20 mss/year. 75% of books from first-time authors; 100% from unagented writers.** Publishes book 8 months after acceptance of ms. Does not accept simultaneous submissions.

> ⦿ Parkway publishes books on the local history and culture of western North Carolina. "We are located on Blue Ridge Parkway and our primary industry is tourism. We are interested in nonfiction books which present the history and culture of western North Carolina to the tourist market." Will consider fiction if it highlights the region.

Nonfiction Technical. Subjects include history, biography, tourism, and natural history. Query with SASE, or submit complete ms.

Recent Title(s) *Shuffletown USA and One Woman's Century: The Remarkable Story of Angela Marsh Peterson.*

PASSEGGIATA PRESS

420 W. 14th St., Pueblo CO 81003-3404. (719)544-1038. Fax: (719)544-7911. E-mail: passeggiata@compuserve.com. **Acquisitions:** Donald E. Herdeck, publisher/editor-in-chief. Estab. 1973. Publishes hardcover and paperback originals. **Publishes 10-20 titles/year. 15% of books from first-time authors; 99% from unagented writers. Pays 5-10% royalty. Foundation or institution receives 20-30 copies of book and at times royalty on first printing. Pays royalties once yearly (against advance) as a percentage of net paid receipts. Offers $300 average advance.** Accepts simultaneous submissions. Responds in 1 week to queries; 1 month to mss.

> ⦿ "We search for literary works that will make clear the complexity and value of non-Western literature and culture. Mostly we do fiction in translation. We also publish literary criticism and memoirs."

Fiction Specializes in African, Caribbean, Middle Eastern (Arabic and Persian), and Asian-Pacific literature, criticism and translation, Third World literature and history, fiction, poetry, criticism, history and translations of creative work. Ethnic, historical, literary, multicultural, regional, scholarly. "We publish original fiction only by writers from Africa, the Caribbean, the Middle East, Asia, and the Pacific." Query with SASE, or submit outline, TOC. State origins (non-Western), education and previous publications. "Send inquiry letter first and ms only if so requested by us. We are not a subsidy publisher, but do a few specialized titles a year with grants. In those cases we accept institutional subventions. We review artwork/photos as part of ms package. State availability of photos/illustrations."

Poetry Submit 5-10 sample poems.

Recent Title(s) *History of Syriac Literature and Sciences*; *Ghost Songs: A Palestinian Love Story*.

Tips "We are always interested in genuine contributions to understanding non-Western culture. We need a polished translation, or original prose or poetry by non-Western authors only. Critical and cross-cultural studies are accepted from any scholar from anywhere."

PAULINE BOOKS AND MEDIA

Daughters of St. Paul, 50 St. Paul's Ave., Boston MA 02130. (617)522-8911. Fax: (617)541-9805. E-mail: editorial @pauline.org. Website: www.pauline.org. **Acquisitions:** Sr. Donna William Giaimo, FSP; Sr. Madonna therese, acquisitions editor. Estab. 1948. Publishes trade paperback originals and reprints. Does not accept simultaneous submissions. Responds in 2-3 months to queries. Book catalog for 9×12 SAE with 4 first-class stamps; ms guidelines online.

　　○┅ Submissions are evaluated on adherence to Gospel values, harmony with the Catholic tradition, relevance of topic, and quality of writing.

Nonfiction Subjects include spirituality, scripture, catechetics, family life, teacher resources, lives of the saints, mariology, prayer, peer pressure, substance abuse, self-esteem, "coping" books. No biography/autobiography, poetry, or strictly nonreligious works considered. Submit 2-3 sample chapters, query, synopsis, SASE.

Fiction Bible stories, prayerbooks, coloring/activity books. Children only. No strictly nonreligious works considered. Submit 2-3 sample chapters, synopsis, query, SASE.

Recent Title(s) *Lent: An Uncommon Love Story*, by Antoinette Bosco; *Experiencing Bereavement*, by Helen Alexander; *Saint Jude*, by Michael Aquilina III.

PAULIST PRESS

997 Macarthur Blvd., Mahwah NJ 07430. (201)825-7300. Fax: (201)825-8345. E-mail: info@paulistpress.com. Website: www.paulistpress.com. **Acquisitions:** Rev. Lawrence Boadt, CSP, editorial director for general submissions; Susan O'Keefe, children's editor. Estab. 1865. Publishes hardcover and paperback originals and paperback reprints. **Usually pays royalty on net, but occasionally on retail price. Offers advance.** Does not accept simultaneous submissions. Responds in 6-8 weeks to queries. Book catalog and ms guidelines online.

　　○┅ "Paulist Press publishes ecumenical theology, Roman Catholic studies, and books on scripture, liturgy, spirituality, church history, and philosophy, as well as works on faith and culture. Our publishing is oriented toward adult-level nonfiction, although we offer a growing selection of children's stories (about 12/year). We do not publish poetry."

Nonfiction Biography (young adult), gift book, self-help, textbook (religious). Subjects include philosophy, religion. Submit 1-2 page summary with rationale for ms, content description, audience info, projected length. Reviews artwork/photos as part of ms package. Picture books (ages 2-5), chapter books (ages 8-12). Must have Christian and Catholic themes. Submit résumé, ms, SASE. Accepts unsolicited mss, but most titles are commissioned.

Recent Title(s) *101 Questions & Answers on the Bible*, by Raymond E. Brown; *Saint Brendan and the Voyage Before Columbus*, by Mike McGrew; *Abiding in the Indwelling Trinity*, by Goerge A. Maloney.

PEACHTREE CHILDREN'S BOOKS

Peachtree Publishers, Ltd., 1700 Chattahoochee Ave., Atlanta GA 30318-2112. (404)876-8761. Fax: (404)875-2578. E-mail: hello@peachtree-online.com. Website: www.peachtree-online.com. **Acquisitions:** Helen Harriss, submissions editor. Publishes hardcover and trade paperback originals. **Publishes 30 titles/year. 25% of books from first-time authors; 25% from unagented writers. Pays royalty on retail price; Advance varies.** Publishes book 1 year or more after acceptance of ms. Accepts simultaneous submissions. Responds in 6 months. Book catalog for 6 first-class stamps; ms guidelines online.

Imprints Freestone; Peachtree Jr.

　　○┅ "We publish a broad range of subjects and perspectives, with emphasis on innovative plots and strong writing."

Nonfiction Children's/juvenile. Subjects include animals, child guidance/parenting, creative nonfiction, education, ethnic, gardening, health/medicine, history, language/literature, multicultural, music/dance, nature/environment, recreation, regional, science, social sciences, sports, travel. No e-mail or fax queries of mss. Submit complete ms with SASE, or summary and 3 sample chapters with SASE.

Fiction Juvenile, picture books, young adult. Looking for very well-written middle grade and young adult novels. No collections of poetry or short stories; no romance or science fiction. Submit complete ms with SASE.

Book Publishers

Recent Title(s) *About Amphibians*, Cathryn Sill (children's picture book); *Yellow Star*, by Carmen Agra Deedy; *My Life and Death by Alexandra Canarsie*, by Susan Heyboer O'Keefe.

Ⓝ PEACHTREE PUBLISHERS

1700 Chattahoochee Ave., Atlanta GA 30318-2112. (404)876-8761. Fax: (404)875-2578. E-mail: hello@peachtree-online.com. Website: www.peachtree-online.com. **Acquisitions:** Helen Harriss, submissions editor. Estab. 1978. Publishes hardcover and trade paperback originals. **Publishes 30 titles/year. 25% of books from first-time authors; 75% from unagented writers. Pays royalty. Royalty varies. Offers advance.** Publishes book 1 year or more after acceptance of ms. Accepts simultaneous submissions. Responds in 6 months. Book catalog for 9×12 SAE with 6 first-class stamps; ms guidelines online.

Imprints Peachtree Children's Books (Peachtree Jr., FreeStone).

○┐ Peachtree Publishers specializes in children's books, middle reader and books, young adult, regional guidebooks, parenting and self-help.

Nonfiction Children's/juvenile, general nonfiction, self-help, regional guides. Subjects include health/medicine, recreation. No technical or reference. No e-mail or fax submissions or queries. Submit outline, 3 sample chapters, or submit complete ms. Include SASE for response.

Fiction Juvenile, young adult. "Absolutely no adult fiction! We are seeking young adult and juvenile works, including mystery and historical fiction, of high literary merit." No adult fiction, fantasy, science fiction, or romance. No collections of poetry or short stories. Query with SASE. Query, submit outline/synopsis, and 3 sample chapters, or submit complete ms with SASE. Inquires/submissions by US Mail only. E-mail and fax will not be answered.

Recent Title(s) *Around Atlanta With Children*, by Denise Black and Janet Schwartz; *Yellow Star*, by Carmen Agra Deedy; *Surviving Jamestown: The Adventures of Young Sam Collier*, by Gail Langer Karwoski.

PELICAN PUBLISHING CO.

1000 Burmaster St., Gretna LA 70053. (504)368-1175. Website: www.pelicanpub.com. **Acquisitions:** Nina Kooij, editor-in-chief. Estab. 1926. Publishes hardcover, trade paperback and mass market paperback originals and reprints. **Publishes 65 titles/year. 30% of books from first-time authors; 90% from unagented writers. Pays royalty on actual receipts. Advance considered.** Publishes book 9-18 months after acceptance of ms. Does not accept simultaneous submissions. Responds in 1 month to queries; 3 months to mss. Book catalog and ms guidelines for SASE or online.

○┐ "We believe ideas have consequences. One of the consequences is that they lead to a best-selling book. We publish books to improve and uplift the reader." Currently emphasizing business and history titles.

Nonfiction Biography, children's/juvenile, coffee table book (limited), cookbook, gift book, illustrated book, self-help. Subjects include Americana (especially Southern regional, Ozarks, Texas, Florida, and Southwest), art/architecture, contemporary culture, ethnic, government/politics, history (popular), multicultural, regional, religion (for popular audience mostly, but will consider others), sports, travel (regional and international), motivational (with business slant), inspirational (author must be someone with potential for large audience), Scottish, Irish, editorial cartoon. "We look for authors who can promote successfully. We require that a query be made first. This greatly expedites the review process and can save the writer additional postage expenses." No multiple queries or submissions. Query with SASE. Reviews artwork/photos as part of ms package.

Fiction Historical, juvenile (regional or historical focus). "We publish maybe 1 novel a year, usually by an author we already have. Almost all proposals are returned. We are most interested in historical Southern novels." No young adult, romance, science fiction, fantasy, gothic, mystery, erotica, confession, horror, sex, or violence. Also no "psychological" novels. Query with SASE, or submit outline, 2 sample chapters, synopsis, SASE. "Not responsible if writer's only copy is sent."

Recent Title(s) *Douglas Southall Freeman*, by David E. Johnson (biography).

Tips "We do extremely well with cookbooks, popular histories, and business. We will continue to build in these areas. The writer must have a clear sense of the market and knowledge of the competition. A query letter should describe the project briefly, give the author's writing and professional credentials, and promotional ideas."

Ⓩ PENDRAGON PUBLISHING, INC.

P.O. Box 31665, Chicago IL 60631. (847)720-0600. Fax: (847)720-0601. E-mail: info@pendragonpublishinginc.com. Website: www.pendragonpublishinginc.com. **Acquisitions:** Kate Palandech, managing director (all areas). Estab. 2002. Publishes hardcover, trade paperback, and mass market originals. **Publishes 10 titles/year. 75% of books from first-time authors; 75% from unagented writers. Pays 10% royalty on retail price. Offers $250 advance.** Publishes book 1 year after acceptance of ms. Accepts simultaneous submissions. Responds in 6 months. Book catalog and ms guidelines online.

Nonfiction General nonfiction, gift book, self-help. Subjects include creative nonfiction, health/medicine, mind/

body/spirit, Eastern philosophy, yoga. "Review our titles online. We are looking for writers who can inspire their readers by bringing a fresh perspective or new knowledge to their subject matter. We are happy to consider first-time authors." Submit proposal package including outline, 2 sample chapters. *All unsolicited mss returned unopened.* Reviews artwork/photos as part of ms package. Send photocopies.

Recent Title(s) *Guiding Yoga's Light*, by Nancy Gerstein; *Afterimages*, by Carrie Karegeannes; *The Spiritual Philosophy of the Tao Te Ching*, by Dr. Joseph Magno.

Tips "We are a small publishing house that works very closely with our authors in the entire process from manuscript drafts to marketing and sales. Authors must be flexible and open to the creative process that is publishing and must be willing to promote and sell their books beyond Pendragon's broad marketing and PR."

PENGUIN GROUP (USA), Inc.

375 Hudson St., New York NY 10014. (212)366-2000. Website: www.penguin.com. General interest publisher of both fiction and nonfiction.

Imprints Penguin Adult Division: Ace Books, Alpha Books, Avery, Berkley Books, Chamberlain Bros., Dutton, Gotham Books, Grosset & Dunlap, HPBooks, Hudson Street Press, Jove, New American Library, Penguin, Perigee, Plume, Portfolio, G.P. Putnam's Sons, Riverhead, Sentinel, Jeremy P. Tarcher, Viking, Frederick Warne; **Penguin Children's Division:** Dial Books for Young Readers, Dutton Children's Books, Firebird, Grosset & Dunlap, Philomel, Price Stern Sloan, Puffin Books, G.P. Putnam's Sons, Speak, Viking Children's Books, Frederick Warne.

- *No unsolicited mss.* Submit work through a literary agent. Exceptions are DAW Books and G.P. Putnam's Sons Books for Young Readers, which are accepting submissions. See individual listings for more information.

Recent Title(s) *Two-Dollar Bill*, by Stone Barrington; *In the Company of Liars*, by David Ellis; *Gossip Times Three*, by Amy Goldman Koss.

PERENNIAL

HarperCollins Publishers, 10 E. 53rd St., New York NY 10022. (212)207-7000. Website: www.harpercollins.com. **Acquisitions:** Acquisitions Editor. Estab. 1963. Publishes trade paperback originals and reprints. Book catalog free.

- "Perennial publishes a broad range of adult literary fiction and nonfiction paperbacks that create a record of our culture."

Nonfiction Subjects include Americana, animals, business/economics, child guidance/parenting, cooking/foods/nutrition, education, ethnic, gay/lesbian, history, language/literature, military/war, money/finance, music/dance, nature/environment (and environment), philosophy, psychology (self-help psychotherapy), recreation, regional, religion (spirituality), science, sociology, sports, translation, travel, women's issues/studies, mental health, health, classic literature. "Our focus is ever-changing, adjusting to the marketplace. Mistakes writers often make are not giving their background and credentials - why they are qualified to write the book. A proposal should explain why the author wants to write this book; why it will sell; and why it is better or different from others of its kind." *Agented submissions only.*

Fiction Ethnic, feminist, literary. *Agented submissions only.*

Poetry Don't send poetry unless you have been published in several established literary magazines already. *Agented submissions only.*

Recent Title(s) *Bradbury Stories*, by Ray Bradbury; *Ugly Americans*, by Ben Mezrich; *Goodnight Steve McQueen*, by Louise Wener.

Tips "See our website for a list of titles or write to us for a free catalog."

PERIGEE BOOKS

Imprint of Penguin Group (USA), Inc., 375 Hudson St., New York NY 10014. (212)366-2000. Publisher: John Duff. **Acquisitions:** Marian Lizzi, senior editor (health, reference); Michelle Howry, editor (personal growth, personal finance, women's issues). Editors also acquire for Putnam for hard/soft joint ventures in all areas of prescriptive nonfiction. Publishes hardcover and trade paperback originals and reprints. **Publishes 55-60 titles/ year. Receives hundreds queries/year. 30% of books from first-time authors; 10% from unagented writers. Pays 6-7½% royalty. Offers $5,000-150,000 advance.** Publishes book within 18 months after acceptance of ms. Accepts simultaneous submissions. Responds in 2 months to queries. Book catalog free; ms guidelines given on contract.

- Publishes in all areas of self-help and how-to. Currently emphasizing popular psychology, women's issues in health, fitness, and careers and lifestyles.

Nonfiction How-to, reference (popular), self-help, prescriptive books. Subjects include child guidance/parenting, cooking/foods/nutrition, health/medicine, hobbies, money/finance (personal finance), psychology, sex, sports, women's issues/studies, career, fashion/beauty. Prefers agented mss, but accepts unsolicited queries. Query with SASE, or submit outline.

THE PERMANENT PRESS/SECOND CHANCE PRESS

4170 Noyac Rd., Sag Harbor NY 11963. (631)725-1101. Fax: (631)725-8215. Website: www.thepermanentpress. com. **Acquisitions:** Judith Shepard, editor. Estab. 1978. Publishes hardcover originals. **Publishes 12 titles/ year. 60% of books from first-time authors; 60% from unagented writers. Pays 10-15% royalty on wholesale price. Offers $1,000 advance for Permanent Press books; royalty only on Second Chance Press titles.** Publishes book 18 months after acceptance of ms. Accepts simultaneous submissions. Responds in 3 weeks to queries; 6 months to mss. Book catalog for 8×10 SAE with 7 first-class stamps; ms guidelines for #10 SASE.

- O➤ Permanent Press publishes literary fiction. Second Chance Press devotes itself exclusively to re-publishing fine books that are out of print and deserve continued recognition. "We endeavor to publish quality writing—primarily fiction—without regard to authors' reputations or track records." Currently emphasizing literary fiction. No poetry, short story collections.

Nonfiction Autobiography, biography. Subjects include history, memoirs. No scientific and technical material, academic studies. Query with SASE.

Fiction Literary, mainstream/contemporary, mystery. Especially looking for high-line literary fiction, "artful, original and arresting." Accepts any fiction category as long as it is a "well-written, original full-length novel." Query with SASE and first 20 pages. No queries by fax.

Recent Title(s) *Mutual Life and Casualty*, by Elizabeth Polinar; *The Widow's Husband*, by Shelia Evans; *Ideal Marriage*, by Peter Friedman.

Tips "Audience is the silent minority—people with good taste. We are interested in the writing more than anything and dislike long outlines. The SASE is vital to keep track of things, as we are receiving ever more submissions. No fax queries will be answered. We aren't looking for genre fiction but a compelling, well-written story." Permanent Press does not employ readers and the number of submissions it receives has grown. If the writer sends a query or manuscript that the press is not interested in, a reply may take 6 weeks. If there is interest, it may take 3-6 months.

PETER PAUPER PRESS, INC.

202 Mamaroneck Ave., White Plains NY 10601-5376. E-mail: bpaulding@peterpauper.com. **Acquisitions:** Barbara Paulding, editorial director. Estab. 1928. Publishes hardcover originals. **Publishes 40-50 titles/year. Receives 100 queries and 150 mss/year. 5% from unagented writers. Makes outright purchase only. Offers advance.** Publishes book 1 year after acceptance of ms. Does not accept simultaneous submissions. Responds in 1 month to queries. Ms guidelines for #10 SASE or may request via e-mail for a faxed copy.

- O➤ PPP publishes small and medium format, illustrated gift books for occasions and in celebration of specific relationships such as mom, sister, friend, teacher, grandmother, granddaughter. PPP has expanded into the following areas: books for teens and tweens, books on popular topics of nonfiction for adults and licensed books by best-selling authors.

Nonfiction Gift book. Subjects include specific relationships or special occasions (graduation, Mother's Day, Christmas, etc.). "We do publish interactive journals and workbooks but not narrative manuscripts or fiction. We publish brief, original quotes, aphorisms, and wise sayings. Please do not send us other people's quotes." Query with SASE.

Recent Title(s) *The Essential Writer's Notebook*, by Natalie Goldberg; *The Feng Shui Journal*, by Teresa Polanco; *My Life as a Baby*.

Tips "Our readers are primarily female, age 10 and over, who are likely to buy a 'gift' book or gift book set in a stationery, gift, book, or boutique store or national book chain. Writers should become familiar with our previously published work. We publish only small- and medium-format, illustrated, hardcover gift books and sets of between 1,000-4,000 words. We have much less interest in work aimed at men."

N PETERSON'S

2000 Lenox Dr., Princeton Pike Corporate Center, 3rd Floor, Lawrenceville NJ 08648. (609)896-1800. Website: www.petersons.com. Estab. 1966. Publishes trade and reference books. **Pays royalty. Offers advance.** Does not accept simultaneous submissions. Book catalog free.

- O➤ "Peterson's publishes guides to graduate and professional programs, colleges and universities, financial aid, distance learning, private schools, summer programs, international study, executive education, job hunting and career opportunities, educational and career test prep, as well as online products and services offering educational and career guidance and information for adult learners and workplace solutions for education professionals."

Nonfiction Authored titles; education directories; career directories. Subjects include business/economics, education, careers. Looks for "appropriateness of contents to our markets, author's credentials, and writing style suitable for audience."

Recent Title(s) *Best College Admissions Essays, 3rd Ed.*; *Study Abroad 2005, 12th Ed.*; *Summer Opportunities for Kids & Teenagers 2005, 22nd Ed.*

Tips Many of Peterson's reference works are updated annually. Peterson's markets strongly to libraries and institutions, as well as to the corporate sector.

PFLAUM PUBLISHING GROUP

N90 W16890 Roosevelt Dr., Menomonee Falls WI 53051-7933. (262)502-4222. Fax: (262)502-4224. E-mail: kcannizzo@pflaum.com. Vice President: Annie Galvin Teich (Catechetical products and services). **Acquisitions:** Karen A. Cannizzo, editorial director. Other Address: 2621 Dryden Rd., Suite 300, Dayton OH 45439. Fax: (937)293-1310. E-mail: ateich@pflaum.com. **Publishes 20 titles/year. Payment may be outright purchase, royalty, or down payment plus royalty.** Book catalog and ms guidelines free.

> O→ "Pflaum Publishing Group, a division of Peter Li, Inc., serves the specialized market of religious education, primarily Roman Catholic. We provide high quality, theologically sound, practical, and affordable resources that assist religious educators of and ministers to children from preschool through senior high school."

Nonfiction Religious education programs and catechetical resources. Query with SASE.

Recent Title(s) *Totally Lent! A Teen's Journey to Easter 2004*; *Changing Lives*; *Welcome Children! A Beginner's Mass Book.*

PHAIDON PRESS

180 Varick St., Suite 1420, New York NY 10014. (212)652-5400. Fax: (212)652-5410. Website: www.phaidon.com. **Acquisitions:** Editorial Submissions. Publishes hardcover and trade paperback originals and reprints. **Publishes 100 titles/year. Receives 500 mss/year. 40% of books from first-time authors; 90% from unagented writers. Pays royalty on wholesale price, if appropriate. Offers advance, if appropriate.** Publishes book 1 year after acceptance of ms. Accepts simultaneous submissions. Responds in 3 months to proposals. Book catalog free; ms guidelines online.

Imprints Phaidon.

Nonfiction Subjects include art/architecture, photography, design. Submit proposal package and outline, or submit complete ms. Reviews artwork/photos as part of ms package. Send photocopies.

PHI DELTA KAPPA EDUCATIONAL FOUNDATION

P.O. Box 789, Bloomington IN 47402. (812)339-1156. Fax: (812)339-0018. E-mail: special.pubs@pdkintl.org. Website: www.pdkintl.org. **Acquisitions:** Donovan R. Walling, director of publications and research. Estab. 1906. Publishes hardcover and trade paperback originals. **Publishes 24-30 titles/year. Receives 100 queries and 50-60 mss/year. 50% of books from first-time authors; 100% from unagented writers. Pays honorarium of $500-5,000.** Publishes book 9 months after acceptance of ms. Does not accept simultaneous submissions. Responds in 3 months to proposals. Book catalog and ms guidelines free.

> O→ "We publish books for educators—K-12 and higher education. Our professional books are often used in college courses but are never specifically designed as textbooks."

Nonfiction How-to, reference, scholarly, essay collections. Subjects include child guidance/parenting, education, legal issues. Query with SASE, or submit outline, 1 sample chapter. Reviews artwork/photos as part of ms package.

Recent Title(s) *The Nation's Report Card*, edited by Lyle V. Jones and Ingram Olkin; *Evaluating Principals*, by James E. Green.

⊘ PHILOMEL BOOKS

Imprint of Penguin Group (USA), Inc., 345 Hudson St., New York NY 10014. (212)414-3610. **Acquisitions:** Patricia Lee Gauch, editor-at-large; Michael Green, editorial director. Estab. 1980. Publishes hardcover originals. **Pays royalty. Offers negotiable advance.** Accepts simultaneous submissions. Book catalog for 9 × 12 SAE with 4 first-class stamps; ms guidelines for #10 SASE.

> O→ "We look for beautifully written, engaging manuscripts for children and young adults."

Fiction Adventure, ethnic, fantasy, historical, juvenile (5-9 years), literary, picture books, regional, short story collections, western (young adult), young adult (10-18 years). Children's picture books (ages 3-8); middle-grade fiction and illustrated chapter books (ages 7-10); young adult novels (ages 10-15). Looking for "story-driven novels with a strong cultural voice but which speak universally." No series or activity books. No "generic, mass-market oriented fiction." *No unsolicited mss.*

Recent Title(s) *Scorpia*, by Alex Rider; *Nikolai, the Only Bear*, by Barbara Joosee and Renata Liwska.

Ⓐ Ⓞ PICADOR USA

Subsidiary of Holtzbrinck Publishers Holdings LLC, 175 Fifth Ave., New York NY 10010. (212)674-5151. Fax: (212)253-9627. Website: www.picadorusa.com. Estab. 1994. Publishes hardcover and trade paperback originals and reprints.

• *No unsolicited mss or queries. Agented submissions only.*

O Picador publishes high-quality literary fiction and nonfiction.

Recent Title(s) *Housekeeping*, by Marilynne Robinson; *Life on the Outside*, by Jennifer Gonnerman; *Dry*, by Augusten Burroughs.

PICTON PRESS

Picton Corp., P.O. Box 250, Rockport ME 04856-0250. (207)236-6565. Fax: (207)236-6713. E-mail: sales@picton press.com. Website: www.pictonpress.com. Publishes hardcover and mass market paperback originals and reprints, and CDs. **Publishes 30 titles/year. Receives 30 queries and 15 mss/year. 50% of books from first-time authors; 100% from unagented writers. Pays 0-10% royalty on wholesale price, or makes outright purchase.** Publishes book 6 months after acceptance of ms. Does not accept simultaneous submissions. Responds in 2 months to queries and proposals; 3 months to mss. Book catalog free.

Imprints Cricketfield Press; New England History Press; Penobscot Press; Picton Press.

O "Picton Press is one of America's oldest, largest, and most respected publishers of genealogical and historical books specializing in research tools for the 17th, 18th, and 19th centuries."

Nonfiction Reference, textbook. Subjects include Americana, history, hobbies, genealogy, vital records. Query with SASE, or submit outline.

Recent Title(s) *Norden: A Guide to Scandinavian Genealogical Research in a Digital World*, by Art Jura.

THE PILGRIM PRESS

700 Prospect Ave. E., Cleveland OH 44115-1100. (216)736-3755. Fax: (216)736-2207. E-mail: tstaveteig@thepilg rimpress.com. Website: www.thepilgrimpress.com. **Acquisitions:** Timothy G. Staveteig, publisher. Publishes hardcover and trade paperback originals. **Publishes 55 titles/year. 60% of books from first-time authors; 80% from unagented writers. Pays standard royalties. Offers advance.** Publishes book an average of 18 months after acceptance of ms. Does not accept simultaneous submissions. Responds in 3 months to queries. Book catalog and ms guidelines online.

Nonfiction Scholarly. Subjects include business/economics, gay/lesbian, government/politics, nature/environment, religion, ethics, social issues with a strong commitment to justice—addressing such topics as public policy, sexuality and gender, human rights and minority liberation—primarily in a Christian context, but not exclusively.

Tips "We are concentrating more on academic and trade submissions. Writers should send books about contemporary social issues. Our audience is liberal, open-minded, socially aware, feminist, church members and clergy, teachers, and seminary professors."

PIÑATA BOOKS

Imprint of Arte Publico Press, University of Houston, Houston TX 77204-2004. (713)743-2841. Fax: (713)743-3080. Website: www.artepublicopress.com. **Acquisitions:** Nicolas Kanellos, director. Estab. 1994. Publishes hardcover and trade paperback originals. **Publishes 10-15 titles/year. 40% of books from first-time authors. Pays 10% royalty on wholesale price. Offers $1,000-3,000 advance.** Publishes book 2 years after acceptance of ms. Accepts simultaneous submissions. Responds in 1 month to queries; 6 months to mss. Book catalog and ms guidelines available via website or with #10 SASE.

O Piñata Books is dedicated to the publication of children's and young adult literature focusing on US Hispanic culture by US Hispanic authors.

Nonfiction "Piñata Books specializes in publication of children's and young adult literature that authentically portrays themes, characters and customs unique to U.S. Hispanic culture." Children's/juvenile. Subjects include ethnic. Query with SASE, or submit outline, 2 sample chapters, synopsis.

Fiction Adventure, juvenile, picture books, young adult. Query with SASE, or submit 2 sample chapters, synopsis, SASE.

Poetry Appropriate to Hispanic theme. Submit 10 sample poems.

Recent Title(s) *Walking Stars*, by Victor Villasenor; *The Bakery Lady*, by Pat Mora.

Tips "Include cover letter with submission explaining why your manuscript is unique and important, why we should publish it, who will buy it, etc."

PINEAPPLE PRESS, INC.

P.O. Box 3889, Sarasota FL 34230. (941)739-2219. Fax: (941)739-2296. Website: www.pineapplepress.com. **Acquisitions:** June Cussen, editor. Estab. 1982. Publishes hardcover and trade paperback originals. **Publishes**

25 titles/year. 20% of books from first-time authors; 80% from unagented writers. Pays 6½-15% royalty on net receipts. Offers rare advance. Publishes book 18 months after acceptance of ms. Accepts simultaneous submissions. Responds in 3 months to queries. Book catalog for 9×12 SAE with $1.25 postage.

○┅ "We are seeking quality nonfiction on diverse topics for the library and book trade markets."

Nonfiction Biography, how-to, reference. Subjects include animals, gardening, history, nature/environment, regional (Florida). "We will consider most nonfiction topics. Most, though not all, of our fiction and nonfiction deals with Florida." No pop psychology or autobiographies. Query, or submit outline/brief synopsis, sample chapters, and SASE.

Fiction Historical, literary, mainstream/contemporary, regional (Florida). No romance or science fiction. Query with SASE, or submit outline, sample chapters, synopsis. Submit outline/brief synopsis and sample chapters.

Recent Title(s) *Those Funny Flamingos*, by Jan Lee Wicker.

Tips "Learn everything you can about book publishing and publicity, and agree to actively participate in promoting your book. A query on a novel without a brief sample seems useless."

PLAYERS PRESS, INC.

P.O. Box 1132, Studio City CA 91614-0132. (818)789-4980. **Acquisitions:** Robert W. Gordon, vice president, editorial. Estab. 1965. Publishes hardcover originals and trade paperback originals and reprints. **Publishes 35-70 titles/year. 15% of books from first-time authors; 80% from unagented writers. Pays royalty on wholesale price. Offers advance.** Publishes book 3 months-2 years after acceptance of ms. Does not accept simultaneous submissions. Book catalog for 9×12 SAE with 6 first-class stamps; ms guidelines for #10 SASE.

○┅ Players Press publishes support books for the entertainment industries: theater, film, television, dance and technical. Currently emphasizing plays for all ages, theatre crafts, monologues and short scenes for ages 5-9, 11-15, and musicals.

Nonfiction Children's/juvenile, theatrical drama/entertainment industry. Subjects include film/cinema/stage, performing arts, costume, theater crafts, film crafts, dance. Needs quality plays and musicals, adult or juvenile. Query with SASE. Reviews music as part of ms package.

Fiction Plays: Subject matter includes adventure, confession, ethnic, experimental, fantasy, historical, horror, humor, mainstream, mystery, religious romance, science fiction, suspense, western. Submit complete ms for theatrical plays only. Plays must be previously produced. "No novels or story books are accepted."

Recent Title(s) *Women's Wear of the 1930's*, by Hopper/Countryman; *Rhyme Tyme*, by William-Alan Landes; *Borrowed Plumage*, by David Crawford.

Tips "Plays, entertainment industry texts, theater, film and TV books have the only chances of selling to our firm."

⊘ PLAYHOUSE PUBLISHING

1566 Akron-Peninsula Rd., Akron OH 44313. (330)926-1313. Fax: (330)926-1315. E-mail: webmaster@playhousepublishing.com. Website: www.playhousepublishing.com. **Acquisitions:** Children's Acquisitions Editor. Publishes novelty board books. **Publishes 10-15 titles/year. Work-for-hire. Makes outright purchase.** Publishes book 18-24 months after acceptance of ms. Accepts simultaneous submissions. Responds in 2 months to proposals. Book catalog and ms guidelines online.

Imprints Picture Me Books (board books with photos); Nibble Me Books (board books with edibles).

● Playhouse Publishing will no longer accept unsolicited mss sent for review in the mail. Any items sent in the mail will be destroyed. The company encourages writers to submit query letters/book proposals electronically to webmaster@playhousepublishing.com. All copy must be contained in the body of an e-mail. Attachments will not be opened.

○┅ "We publish novelty board books and juvenile fiction appropriate for children from birth to first grade. All Picture Me Books titles incorporate the 'picture me' photo concept. All Nibble Me Books titles incorporate an edible that completes the illustrations."

Fiction Juvenile.

Recent Title(s) *Squeaky Clean*, by Merry North; *All Gone*, by Merry North; *Pretend & Play Superhero*, by Cathy Hapka.

Ⓐ ⊘ PLUME

Division of Penguin Group (USA), Inc., 375 Hudson St., New York NY 10014. (212)366-2000. Website: www.penguinputnam.com. Estab. 1970. Publishes paperback originals and reprints. **Pays in royalties and author's copies. Offers advance.** Accepts simultaneous submissions. Book catalog for SASE.

Nonfiction Serious and historical nonfiction, including pop culture, current events, politics. *Agented submissions only.*

Fiction "All kinds of commercial and litearary fiction, including mainstream, historical, New Age, western, erotica, gay. Full-length novels and collections." *Agented submissions only.*

Recent Title(s) *Leonard Maltin's Classic Movie Guide*, by Leonard Maltin; *Summer in the City*, by Robyn Sisman; *Swimming Naked*, by Stacy Sims.

Ⓐ Ⓞ POCKET BOOKS

Simon & Schuster, 1230 Avenue of the Americas, New York NY 10020. (212)698-7000. Website: www.simonsays .com. Estab. 1939. Publishes paperback originals and reprints, mass market and trade paperbacks. Does not accept simultaneous submissions. Book catalog free; ms guidelines online.

    O–π Pocket Books publishes commercial fiction and genre fiction (WWE, Downtown Press, Star Trek).

Nonfiction Reference. Subjects include cooking/foods/nutrition. *Agented submissions only.*

Fiction Mystery, romance, suspense (psychological suspense, thriller), western, *Star Trek* novels. *Agented submissions only.*

Recent Title(s) *My Wicked Highlander*, by Jen Holling; *The Givenchy Code*, by Julie Kenner; *Awaken Me Darkly*, by Gena Showalter.

Ⓝ POISONED PEN PRESS

6962 E. 1st Ave., #103, Scottsdale AZ 85251. (480)945-3375. Fax: (480)949-1707. E-mail: editor@poisonedpenpr ess.com. Submissions E-mail: editor@poisonedpenpress.com. Website: www.poisonedpress.com. Estab. 1996. Publishes hardcover originals, and hardcover and trade paperback reprints. **Publishes 36 titles/year. Receives 1,000 queries and 300 mss/year. 35% of books from first-time authors; 65% from unagented writers. Pays 9-15% royalty on retail price.** Publishes book 6-8 months after acceptance of ms. Does not accept simultaneous submissions. Responds in 2-3 months to queries and proposals; 6 months to mss. Book catalog and ms guidelines online.

    O–π "Our publishing goal is to offer well-written mystery novels of crime and/or detection where the puzzle and its resolution are the main forces that move the story forward."

Fiction Mystery. Mss should generally be longer than 65,000 words and shorter than 100,000 words. Does not want novels "centered on serial killers, spousal or child abuse, drugs, or extremist groups, although we do not entirely rule such works out." Query with SASE, or submit synopsis, first 30 pages. "We must receive both the synopsis and manuscript pages electronically as separate attachments to an e-mail message or as a disk or CD which we will not return."

Tips Audience is adult readers of mystery fiction.

POPULAR WOODWORKING BOOKS

Imprint of F+W Publications, Inc., 4700 Galbraith Rd., Cincinnati OH 45236. (513)531-2690. Website: www.pop ularwoodworking.com. **Acquisitions:** Jim Stack, acquisitions editor. Publishes trade paperback originals and reprints. **Publishes 10-12 titles/year. Receives 30 queries and 10 mss/year. 50% of books from first-time authors; 95% from unagented writers. Offers $5,000 advance.** Publishes book 1 year after acceptance of ms. Accepts simultaneous submissions. Responds in 1 month to queries. Book catalog and ms guidelines for 9×12 SAE with 6 first-class stamps.

    O–π Popular Woodworking publishes how-to woodworking books that use photos with captions to show and tell the reader how to build projects. Technical illustrations and materials lists supply all the rest of the information needed. Currently emphasizing woodworking jigs and fixtures, furniture and cabinet projects, smaller finely crafted boxes, all styles of furniture. De-emphasizing woodturning, woodcarving, scroll saw projects.

Nonfiction "We publish heavily illustrated how-to woodworking books that show, rather than tell, our readers how to accomplish their woodworking goals." How-to, illustrated book. Subjects include hobbies, woodworking/wood crafts. Query with SASE, or submit proposal package including outline, transparencies. Reviews artwork/photos as part of ms package.

Recent Title(s) *Design & Build Your Own Entertainment Center*, by the editors of Popular Woodworking; *Woodworking Wit & Wisdom*, by Jim Tolpin; *Build Your Own Kitchen Cabinets*, by Danny Proulx.

Tips "Our books are for beginning to advanced woodworking enthusiasts."

POTOMAC BOOKS, INC.

(formerly Brassey's, Inc.), 22841 Quicksilver Dr., Dulles VA 20166. (703)661-1548. Fax: (703)661-1547. E-mail: djacobs@booksintl.com. Website: www.potomacbooksinc.com. **Acquisitions:** Don McKeon, vice president/ publisher; Don Jacobs, acquisitions editor (general inquiries). Estab. 1984. Publishes hardcover and trade paperback originals and reprints. **Publishes 60 titles/year. Receives 900 queries/year. 20% of books from first-time authors; 70% from unagented writers. Pays royalty on wholesale price. Offers five figure maximum advance.** Publishes book 1 year after acceptance of ms. Accepts simultaneous submissions. Responds in 2 months to queries. Book catalog free; send 9×12 SAE with 4 first-class stamps for ms guidelines.

Imprints Potomac Sports.

O— Potomac Books specializes in national and international affairs, history (especially military and diplomatic), intelligence, biography, reference, and sports. "We are particularly interested in authors who can communicate a sophisticated understanding of their topic to general readers, as well as specialists."

Nonfiction Biography, coffee table book, reference, textbook. Subjects include government/politics, history, military/war, sports, world affairs, national and international affairs, intelligence studies. When submitting nonfiction, be sure to include sufficient biographical information (e.g., track records of previous publications), and "make clear in the query letter how your work might differ from other such works already published and with which yours might compete." Query letter should provide a summary of the project, a description of the author's credentials and an analysis of the work's competition. SASE must be included to receive a response. No e-mail submissions, please.

Recent Title(s) *Imperial Hubris: Why the West Is Losing the War on Terror*; *Brassey's D-Day Encyclopedia: The Normandy Invasion From A to Z*, by Barrett Tillman; *Pro Football Prospectus*, by Sean Lahman and Todd Greanier.

Tips "Our audience consists of general nonfiction readers, as well as students, scholars, policymakers and the military."

PRACTICE MANAGEMENT INFORMATION CORP. (PMIC)

4727 Wilshire Blvd., #300, Los Angeles CA 90010. (323)954-0224. Fax: (323)954-0253. E-mail: arthur.gordon@pmicmail.com. Website: www.medicalbookstore.com. **Acquisitions:** Arthur Gordon, managing editor. Estab. 1986. Publishes hardcover originals. **Publishes 21 titles/year. Receives 100 queries and 50 mss/year. 10% of books from first-time authors; 90% from unagented writers. Pays 12½% royalty on net receipts. Offers $1,000-5,000 advance.** Publishes book 18 months after acceptance of ms. Does not accept simultaneous submissions. Responds in 6 months to queries.

Imprints PMIC; Health Information Press (HIP).

O— PMIC helps healthcare workers understand the business of medicine by publishing books for doctors, medical office and hospital staff, medical managers, insurance coding/billing personnel. HIP seeks to simplify health care for consumers.

Nonfiction Reference, technical, textbook, medical practice management, clinical. Subjects include business/economics, health/medicine, science. Submit proposal package including outline, 3-5 sample chapters, résumé, letter stating who is the intended audience and the need/market for such a book.

Recent Title(s) *ICD-9-CM Coding Made Easy*, by James Davis; *Medicare Rules & Regulations*, by Maxine Lewis; *Medical Practice Forms*, by Keith Borglum.

PRAEGER PUBLISHERS

The Greenwood Publishing Group, Inc., 88 Post Road W., Westport CT 06881. (203)226-3571. Fax: (203)226-6009. Managing Editor: Anthony Chiffolo. **Acquisitions:** Heather Stainer (history, military); Debbie Carvalko (psychology); Suzanne Staszak-Silva (sociology); Nicholas Philipson (business); Eric Levy (cultural studies, media); Hilary Claggett (politics/journalism); Elizabeth Polenza (psychology). Estab. 1949. Publishes hardcover originals. **Publishes 250 titles/year. 5% of books from first-time authors; 90% from unagented writers. Pays 6½-12% royalty on net receipts. Offers rare advance.** Publishes book an average of 1 year after acceptance of ms. Accepts simultaneous submissions. Responds in 1 month to queries. Book catalog and ms guidelines online.

O— Praeger publishes scholarly trade and advanced texts in the the social and behavioral sciences and communications, international relations, and military studies.

Nonfiction Scholarly. Subjects include business/economics, government/politics, history, psychology, sociology, women's issues/studies. "We are looking for scholarly works in women's studies, sociology, psychology, contemporary history, military studies, political science, economics, international relations. No language and literature." Query with proposal package, including: scope; organization; length of project; whether a complete ms is available, or when it will be; cv or résumé with SASE. *No unsolicited mss.*

Recent Title(s) *An American Paradox: Censorship in a Nation of Free Speech*, Patrick Garry; *Pharmacracy: Medicine and Politics in America*, edited by Thomas Szasz.

PREP PUBLISHING

Prep, Inc., 111012 Hay St., Fayetteville NC 28305. E-mail: preppub@aol.com. Website: www.prep-pub.com. **Acquisitions:** Anne McKinney, editor (nonfiction, careers). Estab. 1995. Publishes hardcover and trade paperback originals. **Publishes 10-12 titles/year; imprint publishes 2 each titles/year. Receives 1,000 queries and 40 mss/year. 90% of books from first-time authors; 70% from unagented writers. Pays 6-10% royalty on retail price.** Publishes book 3 months after acceptance of ms. Accepts simultaneous submissions. Response time varies to queries; 1 month to mss. Book catalog and ms guidelines online.

Imprints Judeo-Christian Ethics; Real-Résumés; Government Jobs; Business Success.

Nonfiction Biography, how-to, self-help. Subjects include business/economics, computers/electronic, creative

nonfiction, education, health/medicine, money/finance, religion, spirituality. Query with SASE.
Fiction Literary, mainstream/contemporary, military/war, mystery, spiritual. Query with SASE.

PRESTWICK HOUSE, INC.
P.O. Box 246, Cheswold DE 19936. (800)932-4593. Fax: (302)734-0549 or (888)718-9333. E-mail: info@prestwic
khouse.com. Website: www.prestwickhouse.com. Estab. 1980.
Nonfiction Reference, textbook, teaching supplements. Subjects include grammar, writing, test taking. Submit
proposal package including outline, 1 sample chapter, résumé, TOC.
Tips "We market our books primarily for middle and high school English teachers. Submissions should address
a direct need of grades 7-12 language arts teachers. Current and former English teachers are encouraged to
submit materials developed and used by them successfully in the classroom."

✪ PRICE STERN SLOAN, INC.
Penguin Group (USA), 345 Hudson, New York NY 10014. (212)414-3590. Fax: (212)414-3396. Website: www.pe
nguinputnam.com. Estab. 1963. **Publishes 75 titles/year. Makes outright purchase. Offers advance.** Does
not accept simultaneous submissions. Book catalog for 9×12 SAE with 5 first-class stamps; ms guidelines for
#10 SASE.
Imprints Mad Libs; Mad Libs Jr.; Mr. Men & Little Miss; Serendipity; Wee Sing.
- ○┓ Price Stern Sloan publishes quirky mass market novelty series for children as well as licensed tie-in
  books.
Nonfiction Children's/juvenile, humor. "Most of our titles are unique in concept as well as execution." Do not
send *original* artwork or ms. *No unsolicited mss.*
Fiction "Quirky, funny picture books, novelty books and quirky full color series."
Recent Title(s) *123 Look at Me!*, by Roberta Intrater.
Tips "Price Stern Sloan has a unique, humorous, off-the-wall feel."

PROFESSIONAL PUBLICATIONS, INC.
1250 Fifth Ave., Belmont CA 94002-3863. (650)593-9119. Fax: (650)592-4519. E-mail: acquisitions@ppi2pass.c
om. Website: www.ppi2pass.com. Estab. 1975. Publishes hardcover, electronic and paperback originals, video
and audio cassettes, CD-ROMs. **Publishes 10 titles/year.** Publishes book 4-18 months after acceptance of ms.
Accepts simultaneous submissions. Responds in 1 month to queries. Book catalog and ms guidelines free.
- ○┓ PPI publishes professional career, reference, and licensing preparation materials. Professional Publications wants only professionals practicing in the field to submit material. Currently emphasizing engineering, interior design, architecture, and landscape architecture exam review.
Nonfiction Multimedia, reference, technical, textbook. Subjects include science, architecture, landscape architecture, engineering mathematics, engineering, land surveying, interior design, and other professional licensure
and development subjects. Especially needs "review and reference books for all professional licensing examinations." Please submit ms and proposal outlining market potential, etc. Proposal template available upon request.
Reviews artwork/photos as part of ms package.
Recent Title(s) *Six-Minute Solutions for the Civil PE Exam*, various authors; *The Fantastical Engineer*, by Celeste
Baine.
Tips "We specialize in books for working professionals and those who want to enter the profession: engineers,
architects, land surveyors, interior designers, etc. The more technically complex the manuscript, the happier
we are. We love equations, tables of data, complex illustrations, mathematics, etc. Demonstrating your understanding of the market, competition, and marketing ideas will help sell us on your proposal."

PROMETHEUS BOOKS
59 John Glenn Dr., Amherst NY 14228-2197. (800)421-0351. Fax: (716)564-2711. E-mail: slmitchell@prometheu
sbooks.com. Website: www.prometheusbooks.com. **Acquisitions:** Steven L. Mitchell, editor-in-chief. Estab.
1969. Publishes hardcover originals, trade paperback originals and reprints. Accepts simultaneous submissions.
Responds in 1 month to queries; 2 months to proposals; 3 months to mss. Book catalog free or online; ms
guidelines for #10 SASE.
Imprints Humanity Books (scholarly and professional monographs in philosophy, social science, sociology,
archaeology, black stuides, womens studies, Marxist studies, etc.).
- ○┓ "Prometheus Books is a leading independent publisher in philosophy, popular science, and critical
  thinking. We publish authoritative and thoughtful books by distinguished authors in many categories.
  We are a niche, or specialized, publisher that features critiques of the paranormal and pseudoscience,
  critiques of religious extremism and right wing fundamentalism and creationism; Biblical and Koranic
  criticism: human sexuality, etc. Currently emphasizing popular science, health, psychology, social science."

Nonfiction Biography, children's/juvenile, reference, self-help, general, historical, popular. Subjects include education, government/politics, health/medicine, history, language/literature, New Age (critiquing of), philosophy, psychology, religion (not religious, but critiquing), contemporary issues, current events, Islamic studies, law, popular science, critiques of the paranormal and UFO sightings, sexuality. "Ask for a catalog, go to the library or our website, look at our books and others like them to get an idea of what our focus is." Submit proposal package including outline, synopsis, potential market, tentative ms length, résumé, and a well-developed query letter with SASE. Reviews artwork/photos as part of ms package. Send photocopies.

Recent Title(s) *Affirmations*, by Paul Kurtz; *Should Parents Be Licensed?*, edited by Peg Tittle; *Of Molecules and Men*, by Francis Crick.

Tips "Audience is highly literate with multiple degrees; an audience that is intellectually mature and knows what it wants. They are aware, and we try to provide them with new information on topics of interest to them in mainstream and related areas."

N PROSTAR PUBLICATIONS, INC.

3 Church Circle, #109, Annapolis MD 21401. (800)481-6277. Fax: (800)487-6277. Website: www.prostarpublications.com. **Acquisitions:** Peter Griffes, president (marine-related/how-to/business/technical); Susan Willson, editor (history/memoirs). Estab. 1965. Publishes trade paperback originals. **Publishes 150 titles/year; imprint publishes 10-15 titles/year. Receives 120 queries and 25 mss/year. 50% of books from first-time authors; 100% from unagented writers. Pays 15% royalty on wholesale price. Rarely offers advance.** Publishes book 1 year after acceptance of ms. Accepts simultaneous submissions. Responds in 3 months. Book catalog online.

Imprints Lighthouse Press (Peter Griffes).

➤ "Originally, ProStar published only nautical books. Any quality nonfiction book would be of interest."

Nonfiction How-to, illustrated book, technical. Subjects include history, memoirs, nature/environment, travel, nautical. Query with SASE. Reviews artwork/photos as part of ms package. Send photocopies.

Recent Title(s) *Age of Cunard*, by Daniel Butler; *They Call Me Kendra*, by Julie Posey; *No More Mondays*, by LaVonne Misner.

Tips "We prefer to work directly with the author and seldom work with agents. Please send in a well-written query letter, and we will give your book serious consideration."

PRUETT PUBLISHING

P.O. Box 2140, Boulder CO 80306. (303)449-4919. Fax: (303)443-9019. **Acquisitions:** Jim Pruett, publisher. Estab. 1959. Publishes hardcover and trade paperback originals and reprints. **Publishes 10-15 titles/year. 60% of books from first-time authors; 95% from unagented writers. Pays 10-12% royalty on net receipts. Offers advance.** Publishes book 18 months after acceptance of ms. Accepts simultaneous submissions. Responds in 2 months to queries. Book catalog and ms guidelines free.

➤ "Pruett Publishing strives to convey to our customers and readers a respect of the American West, in particular the spirit, traditions, and attitude of the region. We publish books in the following subject areas: outdoor recreation, regional history, environment and nature, travel and culture. We especially need books on outdoor recreation."

Nonfiction "We are looking for nonfiction manuscripts and guides that focus on the Rocky Mountain West." Guidebooks. Subjects include Americana (Western), anthropology/archeology (Native American), cooking/foods/nutrition (Native American, Mexican, Spanish), ethnic, history (Western), nature/environment, recreation (outdoor), regional, sports (cycling, hiking, fly fishing), travel. Submit proposal package. Reviews artwork/photos as part of ms package.

Recent Title(s) *Flyfishing the Texas Coast: Back Country Flats to Bluewater*, by Chuck Scales and Phil Shook, photography by David J. Sams; *Trout Country: Reflections on Rivers, Flyfishing & Related Addictions*, by Bob Saile; *Rocky Mountain Christmas*, by John H. Monnett.

Tips "There has been a movement away from large publisher's mass market books toward small publisher's regional-interest books, and in turn distributors and retail outlets are more interested in small publishers. Authors don't need to have a big name to have a good publisher. Look for similar books that you feel are well produced—consider design, editing, overall quality, and contact those publishers. Get to know several publishers, and find the one that feels right—trust your instincts."

PRUFROCK PRESS, INC.

5926 Balcones Dr., Ste. 220, Austin TX 78731. (512)300-2220. Fax: (513)300-2221. E-mail: info@prufrock.com. Website: www.prufrock.com. Publisher: Joel McIntosh. **Acquisitions:** Jennifer Jolly, Jennifer Robins. Publishes trade paperback originals and reprints. Does not accept simultaneous submissions. Book catalog and ms guidelines free.

➤ "Prufrock Press publishes exciting, innovative and current resources supporting the education of gifted and talented learners."

Nonfiction How-to, textbook, scholarly. Subjects include child guidance/parenting, education. "We publish for the education market. Our readers are typically teachers or parents of gifted and talented children. Our product line is built around professional development books for teachers and activity books for gifted children. Our products support innovative ways of making learning more fun and exciting for gifted and talented children." Submit book prospectus (download form on website).

Recent Title(s) *Mathability*, by Michael Cain; *Analogy Roundup*, by Bonnie Risby; *The Periodic Table*, by Cindy Blobaum.

Tips "We are looking for practical, classroom-ready materials that encourage children to creatively learn and think."

⊘ PUFFIN BOOKS

Imprint of Penguin Putnam, Inc., 375 Hudson St., New York NY 10014. (212)366-2000. Website: www.penguinputn am.com. Publishes trade paperback originals and reprints. **Publishes 225 titles/year. Royalty varies. Offers varies advance.** Does not accept simultaneous submissions. Book catalog for 9×12 SAE with 7 first-class stamps.

> ○⊓ Puffin Books publishes high-end trade paperbacks and paperback reprints for preschool children, beginning and middle readers, and young adults.

Nonfiction Biography, children's/juvenile, illustrated book, Young children's concept books (counting, shapes, colors). Subjects include education (for teaching concepts and colors, not academic), history, women's issues/studies. *No unsolicited mss.*

Fiction Picture books, young adult, middle grade, easy-to-read grades 1-3. "We publish mostly paperback reprints. We do very few original titles. We do not publish original picture books." *No unsolicited mss.*

Recent Title(s) *Dear World*, by Takayo Noda; *The Night Journey*, by Kathryn Lasky; *Prep*, by Jake Coburn.

Tips "Our audience ranges from little children 'first books' to young adult (ages 14-16). An original idea has the best luck."

PURDUE UNIVERSITY PRESS

South Campus Courts, Bldg. E, 509 Harrison St., West Lafayette IN 47907-2025. (765)494-2038. E-mail: pupress@pur due.edu. Website: www.thepress.purdue.edu. Director: Thomas Bacher. **Acquisitions:** Margaret Hunt, managing editor. Estab. 1960. Publishes hardcover and trade paperback originals and trade paperback reprints. **Publishes 35-40 titles/year.** Does not accept simultaneous submissions. Book catalog and ms guidelines for 9×12 SASE.

Imprints PUP Books (juvenile reprint series that brings back to publication out-of-print stories illuminating other times in American history).

> ○⊓ "We look for books that look at the world as a whole and offer new thoughts and insights into the standard debate." Currently emphasizing technology, human-animal issues, business. De-emphasizing literary studies.

Nonfiction "We publish work of quality scholarship and titles with regional (Midwest) flair. Especially interested in innovative contributions to the social sciences and humanities that break new barriers and provide unique views on current topics. Expanding into veterinary medicine, technology, and business topics." Biography, scholarly. Subjects include agriculture/horticulture, Americana, business/economics, government/politics, health/medicine, history, language/literature, philosophy, regional, science, social sciences, sociology. "Always looking for new authors who show creativity and thoroughness of research." Print and electronic projects accepted. Query before submitting.

Recent Title(s) *Lay Your Cards on the Table*, by Rosanne D'Ausilio; *St. Benedict's Rule for Business Success*, by Quentin R. Skrabec, Jr; *Feeding the Media Beast*, by Mark E. Mathis.

Ⓝ G.P. PUTNAM'S SONS BOOKS FOR YOUNG READERS

Penguin Young Readers Group, Penguin Group USA, 345 Hudson St., 14th Floor, New York NY 10014. (212)414-3610. Website: www.penguin.com. Publishes hardcover originals. **Pays standard royalty. Offers negotiable advance.** Accepts simultaneous submissions. Ms guidelines for SASE.

Nonfiction Submit 1-2 sample chapters, query letter, synopsis, TOC, SASE.

Fiction Children's picture books (ages 0-8); middle-grade fiction and illustrated chapter books (ages 7-10); older middle-grade fiction (ages 10-14); some young adult (14-18). Particularly interested in middle-grade fiction with strong voice, literary quality, high interest for audience, poignancy, humor, unusual settings or plots. Historical fiction OK. No series or activity books, no board books. Submit proposal package including 1-3 sample chapters, synopsis, query letter, SASE. Send complete ms for picture books. No response without SASE.

Ⓐ ⊘ G.P. PUTNAM'S SONS HARDCOVER

Imprint of Penguin Group (USA), Inc., 375 Hudson, New York NY 10014. (212)366-2000. Fax: (212)366-2664. Website: www.penguinputnam.com. Publishes hardcover originals. **Pays variable royalties on retail price. Offers varies advance.** Accepts simultaneous submissions. Request book catalog through mail order department.

Nonfiction Biography, cookbook, self-help. Subjects include animals, business/economics, child guidance/parenting, contemporary culture, cooking/foods/nutrition, health/medicine, military/war, nature/environment, religion, science, sports, travel, women's issues/studies, celebrity-related topics. *Agented submissions only. No unsolicited mss.*

Fiction Adventure, literary, mainstream/contemporary, mystery, suspense, women's. *Agented submissions only. No unsolicited mss.*

Recent Title(s) *A Voice for the Dead*, by James Starrs and Katherine Ramsland; *Prince of Fire*, by Daniel Silva.

QUE

Pearson Education, 800 E. 96th St., Indianapolis IN 46240. (317)581-3500. E-mail: proposals@quepublishing.com. Website: www.quepublishing.com. Publisher: Paul Boger. Estab. 1981. Publishes hardcover, trade paperback and mass market paperback originals and reprints. **Publishes 100 titles/year. 80% from unagented writers. Pays variable royalty on wholesale price or makes work-for-hire arrangements. Offers varying advance.** Accepts simultaneous submissions. Book catalog and ms guidelines online.

Nonfiction Subjects include computers/electronic. Submit proposal package including résumé, TOC, writing sample, competing titles.

Recent Title(s) *MySQL, 3rd Ed.*, by Paul Dubois; *Absolute Beginner's Guide to Project Management*, by Greg Horine; *Teach Yourself to Create Web Pages*, by Preston Gralla and Matt Brown.

QUEST BOOKS

Imprint of Theosophical Publishing House, 306 W. Geneva Rd., Wheaton IL 60187. (630)665-0130. Fax: (630)665-8791. E-mail: permissions@questbooks.net. Website: www.questbooks.net. **Acquisitions:** Karen Schweizer. Publishes hardcover originals and trade paperback originals and reprints. **Publishes 8-10 titles/year. Receives 600 queries/year. 50% of books from first-time authors; 90% from unagented writers. Pays royalty. Offers varying advance.** Publishes book 20 months after acceptance of ms. Accepts simultaneous submissions. Responds in 2 months to queries. Book catalog free; ms guidelines online.

    O→ "Quest Books is the imprint of the Theosophical Publishing House, the publishing arm of the Theosophical Society in America. Since 1965, Quest books has sold millions of books by leading cultural thinkers on such increasingly popular subjects as transpersonal psychology, comparative religion, deep ecology, spiritual growth, the development of creativity, and alternative health practices."

Nonfiction Subjects include anthropology/archeology, art/architecture, health/medicine, music/dance, nature/environment, philosophy (holistic), psychology (transpersonal), religion (Eastern and Western), science, spirituality (Native American, etc.), travel, women's issues/studies, biography, self-help, theosophy, comparative religion, men's and women's spirituality, holistic implications in science, health and healing, yoga, meditation, astrology. "Our speciality is high-quality spiritual nonfiction with a self-help aspect. Great writing is a must. We seldom publish 'personal spiritual awakening' stories. No submissions accepted that do not fit the needs outlined above." Accepts nonfiction translations. No fiction, poetry, children's books, or any literature based on channeling or personal psychic impressions. Query with SASE, or submit proposal package including sample chapters, author bio, TOC. Prefers online submissions; no attachments please. Reviews artwork/photos as part of ms package. Send photocopies.

Recent Title(s) *The Yoga of Time Travel*; *In Search of P.D. Ouspensley*; *The Zen of Listening*.

Tips "Our audience includes cultural creatives, seekers in all religions, students of religion, general public, professors, and health professionals. Read a few recent Quest titles. Know our books and our company goals. Explain how your book or proposal relates to other Quest titles. Quest gives preference to writers with established reputations/successful publications."

QUILL DRIVER BOOKS/WORD DANCER PRESS

1831 Industrial Way #101, Sanger CA 93657. (559)876-2170. Fax: (559)876-2180. Website: www.quilldriverbooks.com. **Acquisitions:** Stephen Blake Mettee, publisher. Publishes hardcover and trade paperback originals and reprints. **Publishes 10-12 (Quill Driver Books: 6-8/year, Word Dancer Press: 4/year) titles/year. 50% of books from first-time authors; 95% from unagented writers. Pays 4-10% royalty on retail price. Offers $500-5,000 advance.** Publishes book 9 months after acceptance of ms. Accepts simultaneous submissions. Responds in 1 month to queries and proposals; 3 months to mss. Book catalog and ms guidelines for #10 SASE.

    O→ "We publish a modest number of books per year, each of which, we hope, makes a worthwhile contribution to the human community, and we have a little fun along the way. We are strongly emphasizing our book series: The Best Half of Life series—on subjects which will serve to enhance the lifestyles, life skills, and pleasures of living for those over 50."

Nonfiction Biography, general nonfiction, how-to, reference, general. Subjects include regional (California), writing, aging. Query with SASE, or submit proposal package. Reviews artwork/photos as part of ms package. Send photocopies.

Recent Title(s) *Live Longer, Live Better*, by Peter H. Gott, MD; *Help Your Kids Get It Done Right at Home and School*, by Donna M. Genett, PhD; *Dr. Ruth's Sex After 50*, by Dr. Ruth K. Westheimer.

✪ QUITE SPECIFIC MEDIA GROUP, LTD.

7373 Pyramid Place, Hollywood CA 90046. (323)851-5797. Fax: (323)851-5798. E-mail: info@quitespecificmedia .com. Website: www.quitespecificmedia.com. **Acquisitions:** Ralph Pine, editor-in-chief. Estab. 1967. Publishes hardcover originals, trade paperback originals and reprints. **Publishes 12 titles/year. Receives 300 queries and 100 mss/year. 75% of books from first-time authors; 85% from unagented writers. Pays royalty on wholesale price. Offers varies advance.** Publishes book 18 months after acceptance of ms. Accepts simultaneous submissions. Responds to queries. Book catalog online; ms guidelines free.

Imprints Costume & Fashion Press; Drama Publishers; By Design Press; Entertainment Pro; Jade Rabbit.

O— Quite Specific Media Group is an umbrella company of 5 imprints specializing in costume and fashion, theater and design.

Nonfiction For and about performing arts theory and practice: acting, directing; voice, speech, movement; makeup, masks, wits; costumes, sets, lighting, sound; design and execution; technical theater, stagecraft, equipment; stage management; producing; arts management, all varieties; business and legal aspects; film, radio, television, cable, video; theory, criticism, reference; theater and performance history; costume and fashion. How-to, multimedia, reference, textbook, guides; manuals; directories. Subjects include fashion/beauty, film/ cinema/stage, history, translation. Accepts nonfiction and technical works in translations also. Query with SASE, or submit 1-3 sample chapters. *No complete ms.* Reviews artwork/photos as part of ms package.

RAGGED MOUNTAIN PRESS

The McGraw Hill Companies, P.O. Box 220, Camden ME 04843-0220. (207)236-4837. Fax: (207)236-6314. Website: www.raggedmountainpress.com. Editorial Director: Jonathan Eaton. **Acquisitions:** Bob Holtzman, acquisitions/ms submissions. Estab. 1993. Publishes hardcover and trade paperback originals and reprints. Accepts simultaneous submissions. Ms guidelines online.

Imprints International Marine (books about boats and the sea).

O— Ragged Mountain Press publishes books that take you off the beaten path.

Nonfiction "Ragged Mountain publishes nonconsumptive outdoor and environmental issues books of literary merit or unique appeal." How-to (outdoor-related), humor, guidebooks, essays. Subjects include cooking/ foods/nutrition, nature/environment, recreation, sports, team sports, adventure, camping, fly fishing, snowshoeing, backpacking, canoeing, outdoor cookery, skiing, snowboarding, survival skills, wilderness know-how, birdwatching, natural history, climbing, kayaking. "Be familiar with the existing literature. Find a subject that hasn't been done or has been done poorly, then explore it in detail and from all angles." Submit outline, rationale, cv, suggested reviewers, competition and market information. Reviews artwork/photos as part of ms package. Send photocopies.

Recent Title(s) *Stitch-and-Glue Boatbuilding*, by Chris Kulczycki; *In the Wake of the Jomon*, by Jon Turk; *The Complete RV Handbook*, by Jayne Freeman.

RAILROADING

Imprint of Bristol Fashion Publications, Inc., P.O. Box 4676, Harrisburg PA 17111-4676. (800)478-7147. E-mail: jpk@bfpbooks.com. Website: www.bfpbooks.com. **Acquisitions:** John Kaufman, publisher. Publishes trade paperback originals and limited hardback. **Publishes 15-25 titles/year. Receives 100 queries and 50 mss/ year. 50% of books from first-time authors; 99% from unagented writers. Pays 7-11% royalty on retail price.** Publishes book 3-4 months after acceptance of ms. Responds in 1 month to queries. Ms guidelines online.

• Railroading (BFP, Inc.) publishes books on model railroading and railroad history.

Nonfiction General nonfiction (relating to model railroading and railroad history), how-to, reference. "We are interested in any title related to these fields. Query with a list of ideas. Include phone number. This is a fast-changing market. Our title plans rarely extend past 6 months, although we know the type and quantity of books we will publish over the next 2 years. We prefer good knowledge with simple-to-understand writing style containing a well-rounded vocabulary." Query with SASE. Reviews artwork/photos as part of ms package. Send photocopies or JPEG files on CD.

Recent Title(s) *Track Plans for Beginners in N-Scale*; *Track Plans for Beginners in HO-Scale*; *Track Plans for Beginners in O-Scale*.

Tips "All of our staff and editors are model railroaders. As such, we publish what we would want to read relating to the subject. Our audience in general are active model railroaders at the beginner and intermediate level, and history buffs wanting to learn more about the history of railroads in this country. Many are people new to the hobby, attempting to learn all they can before starting their first layout. Keep it easy and simple to follow. Use railroad terms and jargon sparingly. Do not use complicated technical jargon, terms, or formulas without detailed explanation of the same. Use experienced craftsmen as a resource for knowledge. Please read our guidelines before submitting your manuscript.''

Ⓝ Ⓐ ⊘ RANDOM HOUSE AUDIO PUBLISHING GROUP

Subsidiary of Random House, Inc., 1745 Broadway, New York NY 10019. (212)782-9720. Fax: (212)782-9600. Website: www.randomhouse.com.

Imprints Listening Library; Random House Audible; Random House Audio; Random House Audio Assets; Random House Audio Dimensions; Random House Audio Roads; Random House Audio Voices; Random House Price-less.

    O⚊ Audio publishing for adults and children, offering titles in both abridged and unabridged formats on cassettes, compact discs, and by digital delivery.

Recent Title(s) *Confronting Reality*, by Larry Bossidy and Ram Charan; *To the Last Man*, by Jeff Shaara; *Dragon Rider*, by Cornelia Funke.

Ⓐ ⊘ RANDOM HOUSE CHILDREN'S BOOKS

Imprint of Random House, Inc., 1745 Broadway, New York NY 10019. (212)782-9000. Website: www.randomhouse.com. Estab. 1925.

Imprints BooksReportsNow.com, GoldenBooks.com, Junie B. Jones, Kids@Random, Seusville, Teachers@Random, Teens@Random; **Knopf/Delacorte/ Dell Young Readers Group:** Bantam, Crown, David Fickling Books, Delacorte Press, Dell Dragonfly, Dell Laurel-Leaf, Dell Yearling, Doubleday, Alfred A. Knopf, Wendy Lamb Books; **Random House Young Readers Group:** Akiko, Arthur, Barbie, Beginner Books, The Berenstain Bears, Bob the Builder, Disney, Dragon Tales, First Time Books, Golden Books, Landmark Books, Little Golden Books, Lucas Books, Mercer Mayer, Nickelodeon, Nick, Jr., pat the bunny, Picturebacks, Precious Moments, Richard Scarry, Sesame Street Books, Step Into Reading, Stepping Stones, Star Wars, Thomas the Tank Engine and Friends.

    ● Only accepts unsolicited mss through Delacorte Dell Yearling Contest for a First Middle Grade Novel and Delacorte Press Contest for a First Young Adult Novel. Otherwise, submit through a literary agent.

Recent Title(s) *Toad Heaven*, by Morris Gleitzman; *The Haunting*, by Joan Lowery Nixon; *Melanie in Manhattan*, by Carol Weston.

Ⓝ Ⓐ ⊘ RANDOM HOUSE DIRECT, INC.

Affiliate of Random House, Inc., 1745 Broadway, New York NY 10019. Website: www.randomhouse.com.

Imprints Bon Apetit; Gourmet Books; Pillsbury.

Ⓐ ⊘ RANDOM HOUSE, INC.

Division of Bertelsmann Book Group, 1745 Broadway, New York NY 10019. (212)782-9000. Website: www.randomhouse.com. Estab. 1925. **Pays royalty. Offers advance.**

Imprints Ballantine Publishing Group: Ballantine Books, Ballantine Reader's Circle, Del Rey, Del Rey/Lucas Books, Fawcett, Ivy, One World, Wellspring; **Bantam Dell Publishing Group:** Bantam Hardcover, Bantam Mass Market, Bantam Trade Paperback, Crimeline, Delacorte Press, Dell, Delta, The Dial Press, Domain, DTP, Fanfare, Island, Spectra; **Crown Publishing Group:** Bell Tower, Clarkson Potter, Crown Business, Crown Forum, Crown Publishers, Inc., Harmony Books, Shaye Arehart Books, Three Rivers Press; **Doubleday Broadway Publishing Group:** Broadway Books, Currency, Doubleday, Doubleday Image, Doubleday Religious Publishing, Main Street Books, Nan A. Talese; **Knopf Publishing Group:** Alfred A. Knopf, Everyman's Library, Pantheon Books, Schocken Books, Vintage Anchor Publishing (Vintage Books, Anchor Books); **Random House Audio Publishing Group:** Listening Library, Random House Audible, Random House Audio, Random House Audio Assets, Random House Audio Dimensions, Random House Audio Roads, Random House Audio Voices, Random House Price-less; **Random House Children's Books:** BooksReportsNow.com, GoldenBooks.com, Junie B. Jones, Kids@Random, Seusville, Teachers@Random, Teens@Random, Knopf/Delacorte/Dell Young Readers Group (Alfred A. Knopf, Bantam, Crown, David Fickling Books, Delacorte Press, Dell Dragonfly, Dell Laurel-Leaf, Dell Yearling Books, Doubleday, Wendy Lamb Books), Random House Young Readers Group (Akiko, Arthur, Barbie, Beginner Books, The Berenstain Bears, Bob the Builder, Disney, Dragon Tales, First Time Books, Golden Books, Landmark Books, Little Golden Books, Lucas Books, Mercer Mayer, Nickelodeon, Nick, Jr., pat the bunny, Picturebacks, Precious Moments, Richard Scarry, Sesame Street Books, Step Into Reading, Stepping Stones, Star Wars, Thomas the Tank Engine and Friends), **Random House Direct, Inc.:** Bon Appetit, Gourmet Books, Pillsbury; **Random House Information Group:** Fodor's Travel Publications, House of Collectibles, Living Language, Prima Games, The Princeton Review, Random House Espanol, Random House Puzzles & Games, Random House Reference; **Random House International:** Arete, McClelland & Stewart Ltd., Plaza & Janes, Random House Australia, Random House of Canada Ltd., Random House Mondadori, Random House South Africa, Random House South America, Random House United Kingdom, Transworld UK, Verlagsgruppe Ran-

dom House; **Random House Value Publishing:** Children's Classics, Crescent, Derrydale, Gramercy, Testament, Wings; **Waterbrook Press:** Fisherman Bible Study Guides, Shaw Books, Waterbrook Press.
- *Agented submissions only. No unsolicited mss.*
- "Random House has long been committed to publishing the best literature by writers both in the United States and abroad."

ℕ Ⓐ ∅ RANDOM HOUSE INFORMATION GROUP

Division of Random House, Inc., 1745 Broadway, New York NY 10019. (212)782-9000. Website: www.randomhouse.com.
Imprints Fodor's Travel Publications; Living Language; House of Collectibles; Prima Games; The Princeton Review; Random House Español; Random House Puzzles & Games; Random House Reference Publishing.

ℕ Ⓐ ∅ RANDOM HOUSE INTERNATIONAL

Division of Random House, Inc., 1745 Broadway, New York NY 10019. (212)572-6106. Fax: (212)572-6045. Website: www.randomhouse.com.
Imprints Arete; McClelland & Stewart Ltd.; Plaza & Janes; Random House Australia; Random House of Canada Ltd.; Random House Mondadori; Random House South Africa; Random House South America; Random House United Kingdom; Transworld UK; Verlagsgruppe Random House.
Recent Title(s) *Saturday*, by Ian McEwan (Random House Australia); *The Family Tree*, by Carole Cadwalladr (Transworld UK); *The Bird Factory*, by David Layton (McClelland & Stewart).

ℕ Ⓐ ∅ RANDOM HOUSE LARGE PRINT

Division of Random House, Inc., 1745 Broadway, New York NY 10019. (212)782-9720. Fax: (212)782-9600. Website: www.randomhouse.com. Estab. 1990. **Publishes 60 titles/year.**
- Acquires and publishes general interest fiction and nonfiction in large print editions.

Ⓐ ∅ RANDOM HOUSE PUBLISHING GROUP

Division of Random House, Inc., 1745 Broadway, New York NY 10019. (212)782-9000. Website: www.randomhouse.com. Estab. 1925. Publishes hardcover and paperback trade books. **Publishes 120 titles/year.**
Imprints Ballantine Books; Del Rey; Modern Library; One World; Presidio Press; Random House; Random House Trade Paperbacks; Villard.
- See website for details.
- "Random House is the world's largest English-language general trade book publisher. It includes an array of prestigious imprints that publish some of the foremost writers of our time—in hardcover, trade paperback, mass market paperback, electronic, multimedia and other formats."

Nonfiction *Agented submissions only.*
Fiction *Agented submissions only.*

ℕ Ⓐ ∅ RANDOM HOUSE VALUE PUBLISHING

Affiliate of Random House, Inc., 1745 Broadway, New York NY 10019. (212)940-7422. Fax: (212)572-2114. Website: www.randomhouse.com. Estab. 1933. Publishes hardcover and illustrated/nonillustrated nonfiction, adult fiction, and gifts.
Imprints Children's Classics; Crescent; Derrydale; Gramercy; Testament; Wings.
Recent Title(s) *The Celebrate-Your-Life Quote Book*, by Allen Klein; *The Complete Mom's Little Instruction Book*, by Annie Pigeon; *Paris Boulangerie-Patisserie*, by Linda Dannenberg.

Ⓐ ∅ RANDOM HOUSE/GOLDEN BOOKS FOR YOUNG READERS GROUP

Imprint of Random House Children's Books/Random House, Inc., 1745 Broadway, New York NY 10019. (212)782-9000. Website: www.randomhouse.com/kids. Vice President/Publisher: Kate Klimo. Vice President/Publisher (Random House): Mallory Loehr. Estab. 1935. Publishes hardcover, trade paperback, and mass market paperback originals and reprints. **Publishes 375 titles/year. Receives 1,000 queries/year. Pays 1-6% royalty, or makes outright purchase. Offers variable advance.** Accepts simultaneous submissions. Book catalog free.
Imprints Beginner Books; Disney; First Time Books; Landmark Books; Picturebacks; Sesame Workshop; Step into Reading; Stepping Stones; Little Golden Books.
- Color & activity; board & novelty; fiction and nonfiction for beginning readers; hardcover and paperback fiction for kids ages 7-YA.
- "Our aim is to create books that nurture the hearts and minds of children, providing and promoting quality books and a rich variety of media that entertain and educate readers from birth to 16 years."

Nonfiction Children's/juvenile. Subjects include animals, history, nature/environment, science, sports, popular culture. *No unsolicited mss. Agented submissions only.*

Fiction Horror, juvenile, mystery, picture books, young adult. "Familiarize yourself with our list. We look for original, unique stories. Do something that hasn't been done." *Agented submissions only. No unsolicited mss.*

Recent Title(s) *The Best Place to Read*, by Debbie Bertram & Susan Bloom; *Top-Secret, Personal Beeswax: A Journal by Junie B. (and Me)*, by Barbara Park; *The Pup Speaks Up*, by Anna Jane Hays.

RAVEN TREE PRESS, LLC

200 S. Washington St., Suite 306, Green Bay WI 54301. (920)438-1605. Fax: (920)438-1607. E-mail: amy@ravent reepress.com. Website: www.raventreepress.com. **Acquisitions:** Amy Crane Johnson, editor (children's picture books). Estab. 2000. Publishes hardcover and trade paperback originals. **Publishes 10 titles/year. Receives 1,500 mss/year. 75% of books from first-time authors; 100% from unagented writers. Pays royalty. Offers variable advance.** Publishes book 2 years after acceptance of ms. Accepts simultaneous submissions. Responds in 4 months to mss. Book catalog and ms guidelines online.

  • Currently, Raven Tree press is not accepting any unsolicited manuscripts or illustrations.

Nonfiction Children's/juvenile. Stories will be translated upon acceptance. Submit complete ms. Reviews artwork/photos as part of ms package. Send photocopies.

Fiction Juvenile, picture books. Looking for lower reading levels (K-3)—math, science, social studies. Bilingual—no wordplay, no rhyming, 500 words or less. Submit complete ms.

Recent Title(s) *On the Banks of the Amazon*, by Nancy Kelly Allen; *Oh, Crumps!*, by Lee Bock (bilingual children's picture book).

Tips "Follow submission guidelines on website."

Ⓝ RAVENHAWK™ BOOKS

The 6DOF Group, 7739 Broadway Blvd., #95, Tucson AZ 85710. E-mail: ravenhawk6dof@yahoo.com. Website: www.ravenhawk.biz. Estab. 1998. Publishes hardcover and paperback originals. **Pays 45-60% royalty.** Publishes book 18 months after acceptance of ms. Does not accept simultaneous submissions. Book catalog online.

Fiction Fantasy (space fantasy, sword and sorcery), horror (dark fantasy, futuristic, psychological, supernatural), humor, literary, mainstream/contemporary, mystery (amateur sleuth, cozy, police procedural, private eye/hardboiled), religious (religious mystery/suspense, religious thriller), romance (contemporary, romantic suspense), science fiction (hard science/technological, soft/sociological), short story collections, young adult (adventure, easy-to-read, fantasy/science fiction, horror, mystery/suspense, problem novels, series). Query by invitation only.

Ⓝ RED DRESS INK

Harlequin Enterprises, Ltd., 233 Broadway, New York NY 10279. Website: www.eharlequin.com; www.reddres sink.com. **Acquisitions:** Margaret O'Neill Marbury, senior editor; Farrin Jacobs, associate editor. Also: P.O. Box 5190, Buffalo NY 14240-5190. Publishes hardcover and trade paperback originals. Accepts simultaneous submissions. Book catalog and ms guidelines online.

Fiction Adventure, confession, humor, literary, mainstream/contemporary, multicultural, regional, romance, short story collections, contemporary women's fiction. Red Dress Ink publishes "stories that reflect the lifestyles of today's urban, single women. They show life as it is, with a strong touch of humor, hipness and energy." Word length: 80,000-110,000 words. Point of view: no restriction but must have a strong female protagonist. Tone: vibrant. Query with SASE.

Recent Title(s) *Sleeping Over*, by Stacey Ballis; *Lisa Maria Takes Off*, by Susan Hubbard; *Love Like That*, by Amanda Hill.

Tips Audience is women 18-55. "These books are *Ally McBeal* meets *Sex and the City*, *Bridget Jones's Diary* meets *The Girls' Guide to Hunting and Fishing*. The style of writing is light, highly accessible, clever, funny and full of witty observations. The dialogue is sharp and true-to-life. These are characters you can immediately identify with in a story you just can't put down!"

Ⓞ RED HEN PRESS

P.O. Box 3537, Granada Hills CA 91394. (818)831-0649. Fax: (818)831-6659. E-mail: editor@redhen.org. Website: www.redhen.org. **Acquisitions:** Mark E. Cull, publisher/editor (fiction); Katherine Gale, poetry editor (poetry, literary fiction). Estab. 1993. Publishes trade paperback originals. **Publishes 10 titles/year. Receives 2,000 queries and 500 mss/year. 10% of books from first-time authors; 90% from unagented writers.** Publishes book 1 year after acceptance of ms. Accepts simultaneous submissions. Responds in 1 month to queries; 2 months to proposals; 3 months to mss. Book catalog free; ms guidelines online.

  ☛ Red Hen Press is a nonprofit organization specializing in literary fiction and nonfiction. "We currently have a backlog and are not accepting unsolicited manuscripts." Currently de-emphasizing poetry.

Nonfiction Biography, children's/juvenile. Subjects include ethnic, gay/lesbian, language/literature, memoirs, women's issues/studies, political/social interest. Query with SASE. Reviews artwork/photos as part of ms package. Send photocopies.

Fiction "We prefer high-quality literary fiction." Ethnic, experimental, feminist, gay/lesbian, historical, literary, mainstream/contemporary, poetry, poetry in translation, short story collections. "We prefer high-quality literary fiction." Query with SASE.

Poetry Query, or submit 5 sample poems.

Recent Title(s) *The Misread City: New Literary Los Angeles*, edited by Dana Gioia and Scott Timberg; *Rebel*, by Tom Hayden.

Tips "Audience reads poetry, literary fiction, intelligent nonfiction. If you have an agent, we may be too small since we don't pay advances. Write well. Send queries first. Be willing to help promote your own book."

RED WHEEL/WEISER AND CONARI PRESS

368 Congress St., Boston MA 02210. (617)542-1324. Fax: (617)482-9676. Website: www.redwheelweiser.com. **Acquisitions:** Pat Bryce, acquisitions editor. Estab. 1956. Publishes hardcover and trade paperback originals and reprints. **Publishes 60-75 titles/year; imprint publishes 20-25 titles/year. Receives 2,000 queries and 2,000 mss/year. 20% of books from first-time authors; 50% from unagented writers. Pays royalty.** Publishes book 1 year after acceptance of ms. Accepts simultaneous submissions. Responds in 3 months to queries; 3-6 months to proposals and mss. Book catalog free; ms guidelines online.

Imprints Red Wheel; Conari Press; Weiser.

Nonfiction Gift book, self-help, inspirational, esoteric subjects including magic, Wicca, astrology, tarot. Subjects include New Age, spirituality, women's issues/studies, parenting. Query with SASE, or submit proposal package including outline, 2 sample chapters, TOC. Reviews artwork/photos as part of ms package. Send photocopies.

Recent Title(s) *The Blackberry Tea Club*, by Barbara Herrick; *What Is Goth?*, by Voltaire; *Shining Through*, by Hugh Prather.

REFERENCE SERVICE PRESS

5000 Windplay Dr., Suite 4, El Dorado Hills CA 95762. (916)939-9620. Fax: (916)939-9626. E-mail: findaid@aol.com. Website: www.rspfunding.com. **Acquisitions:** Stuart Hauser, acquisitions editor. Estab. 1977. Publishes hardcover originals. **Publishes 10-20 titles/year. 100% from unagented writers. Pays 10% royalty. Offers advance.** Publishes book 6 months after acceptance of ms. Accepts simultaneous submissions. Responds in 2 months to queries. Book catalog for #10 SASE.

> O—★ "Reference Service Press focuses on the development and publication of financial aid resources in any format (print, electronic, e-book, etc.). We are interested in financial aid publications aimed at specific groups (e.g., minorities, women, veterans, the disabled, undergraduates majoring in specific subject areas, specific types of financial aid, etc.)."

Nonfiction Specializes in financial aid opportunities for students in or having these characteristics: women, minorities, veterans, the disabled, etc. Subjects include agriculture/horticulture, art/architecture, business/economics, education, ethnic, health/medicine, history, religion, science, sociology, women's issues/studies, disabled. Submit outline, sample chapters.

Recent Title(s) *Financial Aids for Women, 2005-2007.*

Tips "Our audience consists of librarians, counselors, researchers, students, re-entry women, scholars, and other fundseekers."

Ⓐ Ø REGAN BOOKS

HarperCollins, 10 E. 53rd St., New York NY 10022. (212)207-7400. Fax: (212)207-6951. Website: www.reganbooks.com. Estab. 1994. Publishes hardcover and trade paperback originals. **Pays royalty on retail price. Offers variable advance.** Accepts simultaneous submissions.

> O—★ Regan Books publishes general fiction and nonfiction: biography, self-help, style and gardening books, and is known for contemporary topics and controversial authors and titles.

Nonfiction Subjects include agriculture/horticulture, alternative lifestyles, Americana, animals, anthropology/archeology, art/architecture, business/economics, child guidance/parenting, community, computers/electronic, contemporary culture, cooking/foods/nutrition, creative nonfiction, education, ethnic, fashion/beauty, film/cinema/stage, gardening, gay/lesbian, government/politics, health/medicine, history, hobbies, humanities, language/literature, memoirs, military/war, money/finance, multicultural, music/dance, nature/environment, New Age, philosophy, photography, psychology, recreation, regional, religion, science, sex, social sciences, sociology, software, spirituality, sports, translation, travel, true crime, women's issues/studies, world affairs. *No unsolicited mss. Agented submissions only.* Reviews artwork/photos as part of ms package. Send photocopies.

Fiction Adventure, comic books, confession, erotica, ethnic, experimental, fantasy, feminist, gay/lesbian, gothic, hi-lo, historical, horror, humor, juvenile, literary, mainstream/contemporary, military/war, multicultural, multimedia, mystery, occult, picture books, plays, poetry, poetry in translation, regional, religious, romance, science fiction, short story collections, spiritual, sports, suspense, western, young adult. *No unsolicited mss. Agented submissions only.*

Recent Title(s) *Handmade Modern*, by Todd Oldham; *A Deadly Game*, by Catherine Crier; *The Private Passion of Jackie Kennedy Onassis*, by Vicky Moon.

[N] [A] [⊘] REGENERY PUBLISHING, INC.

Subsidiary of Eagle Publishing, One Massachusetts Ave., NW, Washington DC 20001. (202)216-0600. Website: www.regnery.com. Publisher: Marji Ross. **Acquisitions:** Harry Crocker, executive editor. Estab. 1947. Publishes hardcover and paperback originals and reprints. **Publishes 30 titles/year. Pays 8-15% royalty on retail price. Offers $0-50,000 advance.** Publishes book 1 year after acceptance of ms. Does not accept simultaneous submissions. Responds in 3 months.

Imprints Gateway Editions; Capital Press.

  ०⌐ Regnery publishes conservative, well-written, well-produced, sometimes controversial books.

Nonfiction Biography, current affairs. Subjects include business/economics, history, money/finance, politics, national security. *Agented submissions only. No unsolicited mss.*

Recent Title(s) *Unfit for Command: Swift Boat Veterans Speak Out Against John Kerry*; *Dereliction of Duty: The Eyewitness Account of How Bill Clinton Compromised America's National Security*; *The Final Days: The Last, Desparate Abuses of Power by the Clinton White House*, by Barbara Olson.

Tips "We seek high-impact, headline-making, best-seller treatments of pressing current issues by established experts in the field."

REPUBLIC OF TEXAS PRESS

Imprint of Taylor Trade Publishing, 3164 Harbinger Lane, Dallas TX 75287. Phone/Fax: (972)307-1186. E-mail: dundeeh@aol.com. **Acquisitions:** Janet Harris, acquisitions editor. Publishes trade and paperback originals. **Publishes 10-15 titles/year. 95% from unagented writers. Pays industry-standard royalty on net receipts. Offers small advance.** Publishes book 9 months to 1 year after acceptance of ms. Accepts simultaneous submissions. Responds in 1 month to queries.

  ०⌐ Republic of Texas Press specializes in Texas history and general Texana nonfiction, including ethnic, history, nature/environment, regional, sports, travel, women's issues/studies, Old West, Texas military, and ghost accounts.

Nonfiction Submit TOC, 2 sample chapters, target audience, author bio, and SASE.

Recent Title(s) *Texas Bandits: From Real to Reel*, by Mona Sizer; *Texas Women in World War II*, by Cindy Wiegand; *Alamo Traces: New Evidence and New Conclusions*, by Thomas Ricks Lindley.

Tips "Our market is adult. We are interested in anything relating to Texas. Nonfiction, from the whimsical to the most informative, will be considered."

[A] [⊘] FLEMING H. REVELL PUBLISHING

Imprint of Baker Book House, P.O. Box 6287, Grand Rapids MI 49516. (800)877-2665. Fax: (800)398-3111. Website: www.bakerbooks.com. Estab. 1870. Publishes hardcover, trade paperback and mass market paperback originals. Book catalog and ms guidelines online.

  • *No longer accepts unsolicited mss.*

  ०⌐ Revell publishes to the heart (rather than to the head). For 125 years, Revell has been publishing evangelical books for the personal enrichment and spiritual growth of general Christian readers.

Nonfiction How-to, self-help. Subjects include child guidance/parenting, religion, Christian living, marriage.

Fiction Historical, religious, suspense, contemporary.

Recent Title(s) *Suddenly Unemployed*, by Helen Kooiman Hosier; *The Bride's Handbook*, by Amy J. Tol; *Just Give Me a Little Peace and Quiet*, by Lorilee Craker.

MORGAN REYNOLDS PUBLISHING

620 S. Elm St., Suite 223, Greensboro NC 27406. (336)275-1311. Fax: (336)275-1152. E-mail: editorial@morganr eynolds.com. Website: www.morganreynolds.com. Founder/Publisher: John Riley. **Acquisitions:** Casey Cornelius, editor-in-chief. Estab. 1994. Publishes hardcover originals. **Publishes 35 titles/year. Receives 250-300 queries and 100-150 mss/year. 50% of books from first-time authors; 100% from unagented writers. Pays advance and 10% royalty.** Publishes book 12-18 months after acceptance of ms. Accepts simultaneous submissions. Responds in 3 months to queries. Book catalog and ms guidelines online.

  ०⌐ Morgan Reynolds publishes nonfiction books for young-adult readers. "We prefer lively, well-written biographies of interesting, contemporary and historical figures for our biography series. Books for our Great Events Series should be insightful and exciting looks at critical periods." Currently emphasizing great scientists and scientific subjects, world history, and world writers. De-emphasizing sports figures.

Nonfiction "We do not always publish the obvious subjects. Don't shy away from less-popular subjects." Biography. Subjects include Americana (young-adult oriented), business/economics, government/politics, history, language/literature, military/war, money/finance, women's issues/studies. No picture books or fiction. Query with SASE.

Recent Title(s) *Catherine dé Medici and the Protestant Reformation*, by Nancy Whitelaw; *Restless Genius: The Story of Virginia Woolf*, by Virginia Brackett; *Louis Pasteur and the Founding of Microbiology*, by Jane Ackerman and Richmond Wagner.

Tips "Read our writer's guidelines, look at our books, and visit our website."

RFF PRESS

Resources for the Future, 1616 P St., NW, Washington DC 20036. (202)328-5086. Fax: (202)328-5002. E-mail: rffpress@rff.org. Website: www.rffpress.org. **Acquisitions:** Don Reisman, publisher. Publishes hardcover, trade paperback and electronic originals. **Publishes 20 titles/year. Pays royalty on wholesale price.** Publishes book 6 months after acceptance of ms. Accepts simultaneous submissions. Responds in 1 month to queries and proposals; 2 months to mss. Book catalog online; ms guidelines free.

Nonfiction "We focus on social science approaches to environmental and natural resource issues." Reference, technical, textbook, trade. Subjects include agriculture/horticulture, business/economics, government/politics, history, nature/environment, science. "We do not publish works that are purely opinion driven. Inquire via e-mail or letter; no phone calls." Submit proposal package including outline. Reviews artwork/photos as part of ms package. Send photocopies.

Recent Title(s) *Northern Landscapes: The Struggle for Wilderness Alaska*, by Daniel Nelson; *Private Rights and Public Resources: Equity and Property Allocation in Market-Based Environmental Policy*, by Leigh Raymond; *Determining the Economic Value of Water: Concepts and Methods*, by Robert A. Young.

Tips Audience is scholars, policy makers, activists, businesses, government, the general public. Distributed by Johns Hopkins University Press.

RIO NUEVO PUBLISHERS

Imprint of Treasure Chest Books, P.O. Box 5250, Tucson AZ 85703. Fax: (520)624-5888. E-mail: info@rionuevo. com. Submissions E-mail: theresak@rionuevo.com. Website: www.rionuevo.com. **Acquisitions:** Theresa Kennedy, acquiring editor (adult nonfiction titles about the Southwest). Estab. 1975. Publishes hardcover and trade paperback originals and reprints. **Publishes 12-20 titles/year. Receives 20 queries and 10 mss/year. 30% of books from first-time authors; 100% from unagented writers. Pays 7-10% royalty on net receipts, or makes outright purchase. Offers $1,000-4,000 advance.** Publishes book 1 year after acceptance of ms. Accepts simultaneous submissions. Responds in 6 months. Book catalog online; ms guidelines by e-mail.

Nonfiction Cookbook, general nonfiction, gift book, illustrated book. Subjects include animals, cooking/foods/nutrition, gardening, history, nature/environment, regional, religion, spirituality, travel. "We cover the Southwest but prefer titles that are not too narrow in their focus. We want our books to be of broad enough interest that people from other places will also want to read them." Query with SASE, or submit proposal package including outline, 2 sample chapters. Reviews artwork/photos as part of ms package. Send photocopies.

Recent Title(s) *Yard Full of Sun: The Story of a Gardener's Obsession That Got a Little Out of Hand*; *The Prickley Pear Cookbook*; *Clouds for Dessert: Sweet Treats From the Wild West*.

Tips "We have a general audience of intelligent people interested in the Southwest—nature, history, culture. Many of our books are sold in gift shops throughout the region; we are also distributed nationally by W.W. Norton."

RISING MOON

Imprint of Northland Publishing, Inc., P.O. Box 1389, Flagstaff AZ 86002-1389. (928)774-5251. Fax: (928)774-0592. E-mail: editorial@northlandpub.com. Website: www.risingmoonbooks.com. **Acquisitions:** Theresa Howell, kids editor. Estab. 1988. Publishes hardcover and trade paperback originals. **Publishes 8-10 titles/year. 20% of books from first-time authors; 20% from unagented writers. Pays royalty. Sometimes pays flat fee. Offers advance.** Publishes book 1-2 years after acceptance of ms. Accepts simultaneous submissions. Responds in 3 months to queries. Call for book catalog; ms guidelines online.

O— Rising Moon's objective is to provide children with entertaining and informative books that follow the heart and tickle the funny bone. Rising Moon is no longer publishing middle-grade children's fiction.

Fiction Picture books (with Southwest or Latino themes). "We are looking for exceptional bilingual stories (Spanish/English), fractured fairy tales, and original stories with a Southwest themes." Submit complete ms with SASE of adequate size and postage. No e-mail submissions.

Recent Title(s) *Bedtime in the Southwest*, by Mona Hodgson, illustrated by Renee Graef.

Tips "Our audience is composed of regional Southwest-interest readers."

RIVER CITY PUBLISHING

River City Publishing, LLC, 1719 Mulberry St., Montgomery AL 36106. (334)265-6753. Fax: (334)265-8880. E-mail: jgilbert@rivercitypublishing.com. Website: www.rivercitypublishing.com. **Acquisitions:** Jim Gilbert, editor. Estab. 1989. Publishes hardcover and trade paperback originals and reprints. **Publishes 12 titles/year. Receives 1,250 queries and 200 mss/year. 20% of books from first-time authors; 75% from unagented writers. Pays 10% royalty on net revenue. Offers $500-5,000 advance.** Publishes book 1 year after acceptance of ms. Accepts simultaneous submissions. Responds in 3 months to queries; 4 months to proposals; 1 year to mss. Ms guidelines free.

Imprints Starrhill Press; Elliott & Clark; River City Kids.

Nonfiction Biography, coffee table book, illustrated book. Subjects include art/architecture, creative nonfiction, government/politics, history, memoirs, regional, sports, travel. Submit proposal package including outline, 2 sample chapters, author's bio/résumé. Reviews artwork/photos as part of ms package. Send photocopies.

Fiction Ethnic, historical, literary, multicultural, poetry, regional (southern), short story collections. Submit proposal package including 3 sample chapters, résumé, synopsis, author bio.

Poetry Query.

Recent Title(s) *Speaks the Nightbird*, by Robert McCammon (historical fiction); *My Mother's Witness*, by Carolyn Haines (creative nonfiction); *Love to the Spirits*, by Stephen March (short story).

◩ ROC BOOKS

Imprint of New American Library, A Division of Penguin Putnam, Inc., 375 Hudson St., New York NY 10014. (212)366-2000. Website: www.penguinputnam.com. Publishes mass market, trade, and hardcover originals. **Pays royalty. Offers negotiable advance.** Accepts simultaneous submissions.

    ○┑ "We're looking for books that are a good read, that people will want to pick up time and time again."

Fiction Fantasy, horror, science fiction. "Roc tries to strike a balance between fantasy and science fiction. We strongly discourage unsolicited submissions."

Recent Title(s) *The Soul Weaver*, by Carol Berg; *Deathstalker Return*, by Simon R. Green.

JAMES A. ROCK & CO., PUBLISHERS

9710 Traville Gateway Dr., #305, Rockville MD 20850. Fax: (301)294-1683. Website: www.rockpublishing.com. **Acquisitions:** James A. or Lynne A. Rock, editors. Estab. 1977. Publishes hardcover, trade paperback, and electronic originals and reprints. **Publishes 10-15 titles/year; imprint publishes 3-7 titles/year. 10% of books from first-time authors; 25% from unagented writers. Pays 5-15% royalty. Offers $0-2,000 advance.** Publishes book 9 months after acceptance of ms. Does not accept simultaneous submissions. Responds in 1 month. Book catalog online.

Imprints Sense of Wonder Press; Yellow Back Mysteries; Castle Keep Press.

Nonfiction Audiocassettes, autobiography, biography, booklets, children's/juvenile, coffee table book, cookbook, general nonfiction, gift book, how-to, humor, illustrated book, multimedia, reference, scholarly, self-help, technical, textbook, bibliography. Subjects include Americana, animals, anthropology/archeology, art/architecture, business/economics, child guidance/parenting, community, computers/electronic, contemporary culture, cooking/foods/nutrition, creative nonfiction, education, gardening, government/politics, health/medicine, history, hobbies, humanities, language/literature, memoirs, military/war, money/finance, multicultural, music/dance, nature/environment, New Age, philosophy, science, software, travel, women's issues/studies, world affairs. "Grammar, language, punctuation, and spelling count heavily. We edit all manuscripts for style and content, and we do not want to read sloppy, unschooled, or badly written manuscripts. If you are composing in English, we expect you to be in control of your instrument. We are rather conservative when it comes to punctuation." Query with SASE. Reviews artwork/photos as part of ms package. Send photocopies.

Fiction Adventure, comic books, experimental, fantasy, gothic, horror, humor, juvenile, literary, mainstream/contemporary, multicultural, multimedia, mystery, picture books, plays, poetry, poetry in translation, regional, religious, romance, science fiction, short story collections, suspense, young adult, ghost. Query with SASE.

Poetry "Good poetry sometimes develops its own conventions. Feel free to do so if you feel up to it." Submit 5 sample poems.

Recent Title(s) *Rex Stout: A Majesty's Life*, by John McAleer (biography); *Sci-Fi Womanthology*, edited by Forrest J. Ackerman and Pam Keesey (short story anthology).

Tips "Exhibit a love of language, of Western Culture, and of writing. A 'gift of laughter and sense that the world is mad' won't hurt."

◩ THE ROSEN PUBLISHING GROUP

29 E. 21st St., New York NY 10010. Estab. 1950. Publishes nonfiction hardcover originals. **50% of books from first-time authors; 95% from unagented writers. Makes outright purchase of $200-3,000 for sale to school**

and public libraries. Publishes book approximately 9 months after acceptance of ms. Does not accept simultaneous submissions. Responds in 2 months to proposals. Book catalog and ms guidelines free.

Imprints PowerKids Press (nonfiction books for grades K-4 that are supplementary to the curriculum), including conflict resolution, character building, history, science, social studies, and multicultural titles. Contact: Joanne Randolph, editorial director; Rosen Central (nonfiction for grades 5-8 on a wide range of topics); Rosen Young Adult (social issues, health, sports, self-esteem, history and science. Contact: Iris Rosoff, editorial director).

Nonfiction Children's/juvenile, reference, self-help, textbook, young adult. Subjects include ethnic, health/medicine, history, multicultural (ethnographic studies), religion, science. Areas of particular interest include American history, science, health, sports, careers, coping with social, medical, and personal problems, social studies, high interest subjects. Submit outline, 1 sample chapter.

Recent Title(s) *Primary Sources of E American History*; *When Disaster Strikes!*; *Terrorist Attacks*.

Tips "The writer has the best chance of selling our firm a book on vocational guidance, personal social adjustment, a topic corellated directly to the 5-12 grade social studies or science curriculum, or high-interest, low reading-level material for teens."

ℕ ROWMAN & LITTLEFIELD PUBLISHING GROUP

4501 Forbes Blvd., Suite 200, Lanham MD 20706. (301)459-3366. Fax: (301)429-5748. Website: www.rowmanlittlefield.com. Editorial Director: Jeremy Langford. **Acquisitions:** See website for a detailed list of editors and addresses by subject area. Estab. 1949. Publishes hardcover and trade paperback originals and reprints. **Offers advance.** Does not accept simultaneous submissions. Ms guidelines online.

Imprints Lexington Books; Rowman & Littlefield Publishers; Madison Books; Scarecrow Press; Cooper Square.

Recent Title(s) *Crime, Punishment, and Policing in China*, by Børge Bakken; *The Making of Arab News*, by Noha Mellor; *African Americans in the U.S. Economy*, edited by Cecilia A. Conrad, John Whitehead, Patrick Mason, and James Stewart.

ROXBURY PUBLISHING CO.

P.O. Box 491044, Los Angeles CA 90049. (310)473-3312. **Acquisitions:** Claude Teweles, publisher. Estab. 1981. Publishes hardcover and paperback originals and reprints. **Publishes 15-20 titles/year. Pays royalty.** Accepts simultaneous submissions. Responds in 2 months to queries.

○━ Roxbury publishes college textbooks in the humanities and social sciences only.

Nonfiction Textbook (college-level textbooks and supplements only). Subjects include humanities, social sciences, sociology, political science, family studies, criminology, criminal justice. Query with SASE, or submit outline, sample chapters, synopsis, or submit complete ms.

RUTGERS UNIVERSITY PRESS

100 Joyce Kilmer Ave., Piscataway NJ 08854-8099. (732)445-7762. Fax: (732)445-7039. Website: rutgerspress.rutgers.edu. **Acquisitions:** Leslie Mitchner, editor-in-chief/associate director (humanities); Kristi Long, senior editor (social sciences); Audra Wolfe, editor (science, health & medicine); Melanie Halkias, editor (history, American studies, Asian-American studies). Estab. 1936. Publishes hardcover and trade paperback originals, and reprints. **Publishes 90 titles/year. Receives 1,500 queries and 300 mss/year. 30% of books from first-time authors; 70% from unagented writers. Pays 7$\frac{1}{2}$-15% royalty. Offers $1,000-10,000 advance.** Publishes book 1 year after acceptance of ms. Responds in 1 month to proposals. Book catalog online or with SASE; ms guidelines online.

○━ "Our Press aims to reach audiences beyond the academic community with accessible scholarly and regional books."

Nonfiction Reference. Subjects include art/architecture (art history), ethnic, film/cinema/stage, gay/lesbian, government/politics, health/medicine, history, multicultural, nature/environment, regional, religion, sociology, women's issues/studies, African-American studies, Asian-American studies, history of science and technology, literature, literary criticism, human evolution, ecology, media studies. Books for use in undergraduate courses. Submit outline, 2-3 sample chapters. Reviews artwork/photos as part of ms package. Send photocopies.

Recent Title(s) *Einstein on Race and Racism*, by Fred Jerome and Rodger Taylor; *Beasts of the Earth: Animals, Humans, and Disease*, by E. Fuller Torrey, MD and Robert H. Yolken, MD; *The Brooklyn Bridge: A Cultural History*, by Richard Haw.

Tips Both academic and general audiences. "Many of our books have potential for undergraduate course use. We are more trade-oriented than most university presses. We are looking for intelligent, well-written, and accessible books. Avoid overly narrow topics."

SABLE PUBLISHING

P.O. Box 4496, Palm Springs CA 92263. (760)408-1881. E-mail: sablepublishing@aol.com. Website: www.sablepublishing.com. CEO: Ed Baron. **Acquisitions:** Glory Harley, submissions editor. Estab. 2000. Publishes hardcover and trade paperback originals and reprints. **Publishes 24 titles/year. Receives 300+ queries/year. 40% of books from first-time authors; 90% from unagented writers. Pays 7-12% royalty on retail price.** Publishes book 18 months after acceptance of ms. Accepts simultaneous submissions. Responds in 3 months. Book catalog online; ms guidelines by e-mail.

Nonfiction Autobiography, biography, how-to, humor, illustrated book, self-help. Subjects include alternative lifestyles, contemporary culture, cooking/foods/nutrition, creative nonfiction, ethnic, hobbies, humanities, language/literature, memoirs, money/finance, multicultural, New Age, philosophy, photography, psychology, regional, religion, sex, social sciences, sociology, spirituality, women's issues/studies. Query with SASE, or submit proposal package including outline, 3 sample chapters, author bio. Reviews artwork/photos as part of ms package. Send photocopies.

Fiction Adventure, confession, erotica, ethnic, experimental, fantasy, feminist, gothic, horror, humor, literary, mainstream/contemporary, multicultural, multimedia, mystery, occult, poetry, regional, religious, romance, science fiction, short story collections, spiritual, suspense, western. ''We look for originality, and we are interested in screenplays for motion pictures, scripts for half-hour TV shows, and scripts for TV series.'' Query with SASE, or submit proposal package including 3 sample chapters, synopsis, author bio.

Poetry ''We love epic poems, rhyming poetry that isn't forced, and expressions of complete ideas expressed in a poetic form. We especially love illustrated poetry.'' Query, or submit 10 sample poems, or submit complete ms.

Recent Title(s) *The Jewish Maven Cookbook*, by Shoshana Barer (cooking, advice, humor, wisdom); *Creativity, Making Your Mark*, by Hyacinthe Baron (how-to, self-help-art, self-improvement); *Pure Gold, An Economic Goldmine*, by Jack Bentley (economics, business, finance, self-help).

SAE INTERNATIONAL

Society of Automotive Engineers, 400 Commonwealth Dr., Warrendale PA 15096. (724)776-4841. E-mail: writea book@sae.org. Website: www.sae.org. **Acquisitions:** Jeff Worsinger, product developer; Martha Swiss, product developer; Kris Hattman, product developer; Erin Moore, associate product developer; Matt Miller, product manager; Theresa Wertz, product manager; Emily Kroll, associate product developer. Estab. 1905. Publishes hardcover and trade paperback originals, Web and CD-ROM based electronic product. **Publishes 30-40 titles/year. Receives 250 queries and 75 mss/year. 30-40% of books from first-time authors; 100% from unagented writers. Pays royalty. Offers possible advance.** Publishes book 9-10 months after acceptance of ms. Accepts simultaneous submissions. Responds in 2 months to queries. Book catalog free; ms guidelines online.

    O→ ''Automotive means anything self-propelled. We are a professional society serving this area, which includes aircraft, spacecraft, marine, rail, automobiles, trucks, and off-highway vehicles.'' Currently emphasizing engineering.

Nonfiction Biography, multimedia (CD-ROM, Web-based), reference, technical, textbook. Query with SASE. Reviews artwork/photos as part of ms package. Send photocopies.

Recent Title(s) *Hands-On Race Car Engineer*; *Ferrari Formula 1*.

Tips ''Audience is automotive engineers, technicians, car buffs, aerospace engineers, technicians, and historians.''

SAFARI PRESS, INC.

15621 Chemical Lane, Bldg. B, Huntington Beach CA 92649-1506. (714)894-9080. Fax: (714)894-4949. E-mail: info@safaripress.com. Website: www.safaripress.com. **Acquisitions:** Jacqueline Neufeld, editor. Estab. 1985. Publishes hardcover originals and reprints, and trade paperback reprints. **Publishes 25-30 titles/year. 50% of books from first-time authors; 65% from unagented writers. Pays 8-15% royalty on wholesale price.** Does not accept simultaneous submissions. Book catalog for $1; ms guidelines online.

    ● The editor notes that she receives many mss outside the areas of big-game hunting, wingshooting, and sporting firearms, and these are always rejected.

    O→ Safari Press publishes books only on big-game hunting, sporting, firearms, and wingshooting; this includes African, North American, European, Asian, and South American hunting and wingshooting. Does not want books on 'outdoors' topics (hiking, camping, canoeing, etc.).

Nonfiction Biography (of hunters), how-to (hunting and wingshooting stories), hunting adventure stories. Subjects include hunting, firearms, wingshooting, ''We discourage autobiographies, unless the life of the hunter or firearms maker has been exceptional. We routinely reject manuscripts along the lines of 'Me and my buddies went hunting for . . . and a good time was had by all!'' No outdoors topics (hiking, camping, canoeing, fishing, etc.). Query with SASE, or submit outline.

Recent Title(s) *Royal Quest: The Hunting Saga of H.I.H. Prince Abdorreza of Iran*; *The Best of Holland & Holland: England's Premier Gunmaker*; *African Hunter II*.

ST. ANTHONY MESSENGER PRESS

28 W. Liberty St., Cincinnati OH 45202-6498. (513)241-5615. Fax: (513)241-0399. E-mail: books@americancath olic.org. Website: www.americancatholic.org. Publisher: The Rev. Jeremy Harrington, O.F.M. **Acquisitions:** Lisa Biedenbach, editorial director. Estab. 1970. Publishes trade paperback originals. **Publishes 20-25 titles/ year; imprint publishes 12-15 titles/year. Receives 300 queries and 50 mss/year. 5% of books from first-time authors; 99% from unagented writers. Pays 10-12% royalty on net receipts. Offers $1,000 average advance.** Publishes book 18 months after acceptance of ms. Responds in 2 months. Book catalog for 9×12 SAE with 4 first-class stamps; ms guidelines online.

Imprints Servant Books.

O— "St. Anthony Messenger Press/Franciscan Communications seeks to communicate the word that is Jesus Christ in the styles of Saints Francis and Anthony. Through print and electronic media marketed in North America and worldwide, we endeavor to evangelize, inspire, and inform those who search for God and seek a richer Catholic, Christian, human life. Our efforts help support the life, ministry, and charities of the Franciscan Friars of St. John the Baptist Province, who sponsor our work." Currently emphasizing prayer/spirituality.

Nonfiction Family-based religious education programs. Subjects include church history and practices, Catholic identity and teaching, prayer and spirituality resources, Scripture study. Query with SASE, or submit outline, Attn: Lisa Biedenbach. Reviews artwork/photos as part of ms package.

Recent Title(s) *Life With Mother Teresa*, by Sebastian Vazhakala, M.C; *Franciscan Prayer*, by Ilia Delio, OSF; *Spirituality of Sport*, by Susan Saint Sing.

Tips "Our readers are ordinary 'folks in the pews' and those who minister to and educate these folks. Writers need to know the audience and the kind of books we publish. Manuscripts should reflect best and current Catholic theology and doctrine." St. Anthony Messenger Press especially seeks books which will sell in bulk quantities to parishes, teachers, pastoral ministers, etc. They expect to sell at least 5,000 to 7,000 copies of a book.

N ST. AUGUSTINE'S PRESS

P.O. Box 2285, South Bend IN 46680-2285. (219)-291-3500. Fax: (219)291-3700. E-mail: bruce@staugustine.net. Website: www.staugustine.net. **Acquisitions:** Bruce Fingerhut, president (philosophy). Publishes hardcover originals and trade paperback originals and reprints. **Publishes 30 titles/year. Receives 200 queries and 100 mss/year. 5% of books from first-time authors; 95% from unagented writers. Pays 6-20% royalty. Offers $500-5,000 advance.** Publishes book 8 months after acceptance of ms. Accepts simultaneous submissions. Responds in 2-6 months to queries; 3-8 months to proposals; 4-8 months to mss. Book catalog free.

Imprints Carthage Reprints.

O— "Our market is scholarly in the humanities. We publish in philosophy, religion, cultural history, and history of ideas only."

Nonfiction Biography, textbook. Subjects include history (of ideas), philosophy, religion. Query with SASE. Reviews artwork/photos as part of ms package. Send photocopies.

Recent Title(s) *Introduction to the Summa Theologiae of Thomas Aquinas*, by John of St. Thomas (medieval philosophy); *The American Catholic Voter: 200 Years of Political Impact*, by George J. Marlin (cultural history); *A Theater of Envy: William Shakespeare*, by René Girard (philosophy of literature).

Tips Scholarly and student audience.

A Ø ST. MARTIN'S PRESS, LLC

Holtzbrinck Publishers, 175 Fifth Ave., New York NY 10010. (212)674-5151. Fax: (212)420-9314. Website: www.stmartins.com. Estab. 1952. Publishes hardcover, trade paperback and mass market originals. **Publishes 1,500 titles/year. Pays royalty. Offers advance.** Ms guidelines online.

Imprints Minotaur; Thomas Dunne Books; Griffin; Palgrave MacMillan (division); Priddy Books; St. Martin's Press Paperback & Reference Group; St. Martin's Press Trade Division; Truman Talley Books.

O— General interest publisher of both fiction and nonfiction.

Nonfiction Biography, cookbook, reference, scholarly, self-help, textbook. Subjects include business/economics, cooking/foods/nutrition, sports, general nonfiction, contemporary culture, true crime. *Agented submissions only. No unsolicited mss.*

Fiction Fantasy, historical, horror, literary, mainstream/contemporary, mystery, science fiction, suspense, western (contemporary), general fiction; thriller. *Agented submissions only. No unsolicited mss.*

SAINT MARY'S PRESS

702 Terrace Heights, Winona MN 55987-1318. (800)533-8095. Fax: (800)344-9225. E-mail: submissions@smp.o rg. Website: www.smp.org. Ms guidelines online or by e-mail.

Nonfiction Subjects include religion (prayers), spirituality. Titles for Catholic youth and their parents, teachers, and youth ministers. Query with SASE, or submit proposal package including outline, 1 sample chapter, SASE. Brief author biography.

Recent Title(s) *The Catholic Faith Handbook for Youth*; *The Total Faith Initiative*; *Take Ten: Daily Bible Reflections for Teens*.

Tips "Request product catalog and/or do research online of Saint Mary Press book lists before submitting proposal."

ST PAULS/ALBA HOUSE

Society of St Paul, 2187 Victory Blvd., Staten Island NY 10314-6603. (718)761-0047. Fax: (718)761-0057. E-mail: edmund_lane@juno.com. Website: www.alba-house.com. **Acquisitions:** Victor L. Viberti, SSP, acquisitions editor. Estab. 1957. Publishes trade paperback and mass market paperback originals and reprints. **Publishes 22 titles/year. Receives 250 queries and 150 mss/year. 10% of books from first-time authors; 100% from unagented writers. Pays 5-10% royalty.** Publishes book 10 months after acceptance of ms. Does not accept simultaneous submissions. Responds in 1 month to queries and proposals; 2 months to mss. Book catalog and ms guidelines free.

Nonfiction Reference, scholarly, textbook, religious biographies. Subjects include philosophy, religion, spirituality. "Alba House is the North American publishing division of St. Paul, an International Roman Catholic Missionary Religious Congregation dedicated to spreading the Gospel message via the media of communications." Does not want fiction, children's books, poetry, personal testimonies, or autobiographies. Submit complete ms. Reviews artwork/photos as part of ms package. Send photocopies.

Recent Title(s) *Ethics: The Drama of the Moral Life*, by Piotr Jaroszynski and Matthew Anderson (textbook); *Have You Heard the Good News?*, by Edward T. Dowling, S.J. (homiletics).

Tips "Our audience is educated Roman Catholic readers interested in matters related to the Church, spirituality, Biblical and theological topics, moral concerns, lives of the saints, etc."

SALEM PRESS, INC.

Magill's Choice, 131 N. El Molino, Suite 350, Pasadena CA 91101. (626)584-0106. Fax: (626)584-1525. Website: www.salempress.com. **Acquisitions:** Dawn P. Dawson. **Publishes 20-22 titles/year. Receives 15 queries/year. Work-for-hire pays 5-15¢/word.** Responds in 1 month. Book catalog online.

Nonfiction Reference. Subjects include business/economics, ethnic, government/politics, health/medicine, history, language/literature, military/war, music/dance, nature/environment, philosophy, psychology, science, sociology, women's issues/studies. "We accept vitas for writers interested in supplying articles/entries for encyclopedia-type entries in library reference books. Will also accept multi-volume book ideas from people interested in being a general editor." Query with SASE.

⊘ SANTA MONICA PRESS LLC

P.O. Box 1076, Santa Monica CA 90406. Website: www.santamonicapress.com. **Acquisitions:** Acquistions Editor. Estab. 1991. Publishes trade paperback originals. **Publishes 15 titles/year. 25% of books from first-time authors; 75% from unagented writers. Pays 4-10% royalty on wholesale price. Offers $500-2,500 advance.** Publishes book 6-18 months after acceptance of ms. Accepts simultaneous submissions. Responds in 1-2 months to proposals. Book catalog for 9×12 SASE with 83¢ postage; ms guidelines online.

    Oⁿ "At Santa Monica Press, we're not afraid to cast a wide editorial net. Our vision extends from lively and modern how-to books to offbeat looks at popular culture, from film history to literature."

Nonfiction Biography, gift book, how-to, humor, illustrated book, reference. Subjects include Americana, creative nonfiction, film/cinema/stage, health/medicine, language/literature, memoirs, music/dance, spirituality, sports, travel, contemporary culture, film/cinema/stage, general nonfiction. *All unsolicited mss returned unopened.* Submit proposal package, including outline, 2-3 sample chapters, biography, marketing and publicity plans, analysis of competitive titles, SASE with appropriate postage. Reviews artwork/photos as part of ms package. Send photocopies.

Recent Title(s) *James Dean Died Here: The Locations of America's Pop Culture Landmarks*, by Chris Epting; *Footsteps in the Fog: Alfred Hitchcock's San Francisco*, by Jeff Kraft and Aaron Leventhal; *Atomic Wedgies, Wet Willies, & Other Acts of Roguery*, by Greg Tanabaum and Dan Martin.

Tips "Visit our website before submitting to get a clear idea of the types of books we publish. Carefully analyze your book's competition and tell us what makes your book different—and what makes it better. Also let us know what promotional and marketing opportunities you, as the author, bring to the project."

SARABANDE BOOKS, INC.

2234 Dundee Rd., Suite 200, Louisville KY 40205. (502)458-4028. Fax: (502)458-4065. E-mail: info@sarabandebooks.org. Website: www.sarabandebooks.org. **Acquisitions:** Sarah Gorham, editor-in-chief. Estab. 1994. Publishes hardcover and trade paperback originals. **Publishes 10 titles/year. Receives 500 queries and 3,000** mss/year. **35% of books from first-time authors; 75% from unagented writers. Pays royalty. 10% on actual income received. Also pays in author's copies. Offers $500-1,000 advance.** Publishes book 18 months after acceptance of ms. Accepts simultaneous submissions. Responds in 3 months to queries; 6 months to mss. Book catalog free; ms and contest guidelines for #10 SASE or on website.

○┅ "Sarabande Books was founded to publish poetry, short fiction, and creative nonfiction. We look for works of lasting literary value. We are actively seeking creative nonfiction."

Fiction Literary, short story collections, novellas, short novels (300 pages maximum, 150 pages minimum).

Poetry "Poetry of superior artistic quality; otherwise no restraints or specifications."

Recent Title(s) *Portrait of My Mother Who Posed Nude in Wartime*, by Marjorie Sandor; *October*, by Louise Glück.

Tips Sarabande publishes for a general literary audience. "Know your market. Read—and buy—books of literature." Sponsors contests.

SAS PUBLISHING

SAS Campus Dr., Cary NC 27513-2414. (919)531-0585. Fax: (919)677-4444. E-mail: sasbbu@sas.com. Website: support.sas.com/bbu. **Acquisitions:** Julie M. Platt, editor-in-chief. Estab. 1976. Publishes hardcover and trade paperback originals. **Publishes 40 titles/year. 50% of books from first-time authors; 100% from unagented writers. Payment negotiable. Offers negotiable advance.** Does not accept simultaneous submissions. Responds in 2 weeks to queries. Book catalog and ms guidelines via website or with SASE; ms guidelines online.

○┅ SAS publishes books for SAS and JMP software users, "both new and experienced."

Nonfiction Technical, textbook. Subjects include software, statistics. "SAS Publishing develops and writes books inhouse. Through Books by Users Press, we also publish books by SAS users on a variety of topics relating to SAS software. Books by Users Press titles enhance users' abilities to use SAS effectively. We're interested in publishing manuscripts that describe or illustrate using any of SAS products, including JMP software. Books must be aimed at SAS or JMP users, either new or experienced. Tutorials are particularly attractive, as are descriptions of user-written applications for solving real-life business, industry or academic problems. Books on programming techniques using SAS are also desirable. Manuscripts must reflect current or upcoming software releases, and the author's writing should indicate an understanding of SAS and the technical aspects covered in the manuscript." Query with SASE, or submit outline, sample chapters. Reviews artwork/photos as part of ms package.

Recent Title(s) *The Little SAS Book: A Primer, Third Ed.*, by Lora D. Delwiche and Susan J. Slaughter.

Tips "If I were a writer trying to market a book today, I would concentrate on developing a manuscript that teaches or illustrates a specific concept or application that SAS users will find beneficial in their own environments or can adapt to their own needs."

SASQUATCH BOOKS

119 S. Main, Suite 400, Seattle WA 98104. (206)467-4300. Fax: (206)467-4301. E-mail: custserve@sasquatchboo ks.com. Website: www.sasquatchbooks.com. President: Chad Haight. **Acquisitions:** Gary Luke, editorial director; Terence Maikels, acquisitions editor; Heidi Lenze, acquisitions editor. Estab. 1986. Publishes regional hardcover and trade paperback originals. **Publishes 30 titles/year. 20% of books from first-time authors; 75% from unagented writers. Pays royalty on cover price. Offers wide range advance.** Publishes book 6 months after acceptance of ms. Does not accept simultaneous submissions. Responds in 3 months to queries. Book catalog for 9×12 SAE with 2 first-class stamps; ms guidelines online.

○┅ Sasquatch Books publishes books for a West Coast regional audience—Alaska to California. Currently emphasizing outdoor recreation, cookbooks, and history.

Nonfiction "We are seeking quality nonfiction works about the Pacific Northwest and West Coast regions (including Alaska to California). The literature of place includes how-to and where-to as well as history and narrative nonfiction." Reference. Subjects include animals, art/architecture, business/economics, cooking/foods/nutrition, gardening, history, nature/environment, recreation, regional, sports, travel, women's issues/studies, outdoors. Query first, then submit outline and sample chapters with SASE.

Recent Title(s) *Out of Left Field*, by Art Thiel; *Book Lust*, by Nancy Pearl; *The Traveling Curmudgeon*, by Jon Winokur.

Tips "We sell books through a range of channels in addition to the book trade. Our primary audience consists of active, literate residents of the West Coast."

Ⓝ SCARECROW PRESS, INC.

Imprint of Rowman & Littlefield Publishing Group, 4501 Forbes Blvd., Suite 200, Lanham MD 20706. (301)459-3366. Fax: (301)429-5748. Website: www.scarecrowpress.com. Vice President/Publisher: Edward Kurdyla. **Acquisitions:** Martin Dillon, acquisitions editor (information studies, interdisciplinary studies, general reference); Bruce Phillips, acquisitions editor (music); Stephen Ryan (film and theater); Kim Tabor (young adult literature).

Estab. 1955. Publishes hardcover originals. **Publishes 165 titles/year. 70% of books from first-time authors; 99% from unagented writers. Pays 8% royalty on net of first 1,000 copies; 10% of net price thereafter.** Publishes book 18 months after acceptance of ms. Does not accept simultaneous submissions. Responds in 2 months to queries. Catalog and ms guidelines online.

O— Scarecrow Press publishes several series: Historical Dictionaries (includes countries, religions, international organizations, and area studies); Studies and Documentaries on the History of Popular Entertainment (forthcoming); Society, Culture and Libraries. "Emphasis is on any title likely to appeal to libraries." Currently emphasizing jazz, Africana, and educational issues of contemporary interest.

Nonfiction Reference (criminology, guides, military history, bibliographies), scholarly. Subjects include film/cinema/stage, language/literature, religion, sports, annotated bibliographies, handbooks and biographical dictionaries in the areas of women's studies and ethnic studies, parapsychology, fine arts and handicrafts, genealogy, sports history, music, movies, stage, library and information science. Query with SASE.

Ⓐ SCHOCKEN BOOKS

Imprint of Random House, Inc., a Division of Bertlesmann AG, 1745 Broadway, New York NY 10019. (212)572-2838. Fax: (212)572-6030. Website: www.schocken.com. Estab. 1945. Publishes hardcover and trade paperback originals and reprints. **Publishes 9-12 titles/year. Small% of books from first-time authors; small% from unagented writers. Offers varied advance.** Accepts simultaneous submissions.

O— "Schocken publishes quality Judaica in all areas—fiction, history, biography, current affairs, spirituality and religious practices, popular culture, and cultural studies."

Recent Title(s) *One People Two Worlds*, by Ammiel Hirsch and Yosef Reinman; *The Rebbe's Army*, by Sue Fishkoff; *Reading the Women of the Bible*, by Tikva Frymer-Kensky.

Ⓐ SCHOLASTIC LIBRARY PUBLISHING

A division of Scholastic, Inc., 90 Old Sherman Turnpike, Danbury CT 06816. (203)797-3500. Fax: (203)797-3197. Website: www.scholastic.com/librarypublishing. Estab. 1895. Publishes hardcover and trade paperback originals. Does not accept simultaneous submissions.

Imprints Grolier; Children's Press; Franklin Watts; Grolier Online.

● *This publisher accepts agented submissions only.*

O— "Scholastic Library is a leading publisher of reference, educational, and children's books. We provide parents, teachers, and librarians with the tools they need to enlighten children to the pleasure of learning and prepare them for the road ahead."

Ⓐ SCHOLASTIC PRESS

Imprint of Scholastic, Inc., 557 Broadway, New York NY 10012. (212)343-6100. Fax: (212)343-4713. Website: www.scholastic.com. **Acquisitions:** Elizabeth Szabla, editorial director; Dianne Hess and Tracy Mack, executive editors; Laruen Thompson, senior editor; Leslie Budnick and Jennifer Rees, associate editors. Publishes hardcover originals. **Publishes 30 titles/year. Receives 2,500 queries/year. 5% of books from first-time authors. Pays royalty on retail price. Offers variable advance.** Publishes book 18-24 months after acceptance of ms. Does not accept simultaneous submissions. Responds in 2 months to queries; 6-8 months to mss.

O— Scholastic Press publishes "fresh, literary picture book fiction and nonfiction; fresh, literary nonseries or nongenre-oriented middle grade and young adult fiction." Currently emphasizing "subtly handled treatments of key relationships in children's lives; unusual approaches to commonly dry subjects, such as biography, math, history, or science." De-emphasizing fairy tales (or retellings), board books, genre, or series fiction (mystery, fantasy, etc.).

Nonfiction Children's/juvenile, general interest. *Agented submissions and previously published authors only.*

Fiction Juvenile, picture books, novels. Wants "fresh, exciting picture books and novels—inspiring, new talent." *Agented submissions and previously published authors only.*

Recent Title(s) *Here Today*, by Ann M. Martin; *Chasing Vermeer*, by Blue Balliett, illustrated by Brett Helquist; *Detective LaRue: Letters From the Investigation*, by Mark Teague.

SCHREIBER PUBLISHING, INC.

51 Monroe St., Suite 101, Rockville MD 20850. (301)424-7737 ext. 28. Fax: (301)424-2336. E-mail: spbooks@aol.com. Website: www.schreiberpublishing.com. President: Morry Schreiber. **Acquisitions:** Linguistics Editor; Judaica Editor. Publishes hardcover and trade paperback originals and reprints. **Publishes 8 titles/year. Receives 40 queries and 12 mss/year. 80% of books from first-time authors; 95% from unagented writers. Pays negotiable royalty on retail price.** Publishes book 6 months after acceptance of ms. Accepts simultaneous submissions. Responds in 1 month. Book catalog free or on website; ms guidelines free.

O— Schreiber publishes reference books and dictionaries for better language and translation work, as well as Judaica books emphasizing Jewish culture and religion. Currently emphasizing multicultural dictionaries and parochial books.

Nonfiction Biography, children's/juvenile, coffee table book, gift book, humor, multimedia (CD-ROM), reference, textbook. Subjects include history, language/literature, memoirs, money/finance, multicultural, religion, science, translation. Query with SASE, or submit proposal package including outline, 1 sample chapter, and TOC. Reviews artwork/photos as part of ms package. Send photocopies.
Recent Title(s) *Questioning the Bible*, by Morry Soffer; *Spanish Business Dictionary*.

Ⓐ SCRIBNER

Imprint of Simon & Schuster Adult Publishing Group, 1230 Avenue of the Americas, New York NY 10020. (212)698-7000. Website: www.simonsays.com. **Acquisitions:** Nan Graham (literary fiction, nonfiction); Sarah McGrath (fiction, nonfiction); Susanne Kirk (fiction); Lisa Drew (nonfiction); Alexis Gargagliano (fiction, nonfiction); Brant Rumble (fiction, nonfiction); Colin Harrison (fiction, nonfiction). Publishes hardcover originals. **Publishes 70-75 titles/year. Receives thousands queries/year. 20% of books from first-time authors; 0% from unagented writers. Pays 7½-15% royalty. Offers variable advance.** Publishes book 9 months after acceptance of ms. Accepts simultaneous submissions. Responds in 3 months to queries.
Imprints Lisa Drew Books; Scribner Classics (reprints only); Scribner Poetry (by invitation only).
Nonfiction Biography. Subjects include education, ethnic, gay/lesbian, health/medicine, history, language/literature, nature/environment, philosophy, psychology, religion, science, criticism. *Agented submissions only.*
Fiction Literary, mystery, suspense. *Agented submissions only.*
Recent Title(s) *That Old Ace in the Hole*, by Annie Proulx; *Cosmopolis*, by Don DeLillo; *Random Family*, by Adrian Nicole LeBlanc.

Ⓝ SEAL PRESS

1400 65th St., Suite 250, Emeryville CA 94608. (510)595-3664. Fax: (510)595-4228. Website: www.sealpress.com. **Acquisitions:** Attn: Seal Press. Estab. 1976. Publishes trade paperback originals. **Publishes 25 titles/year. Receives 1,000 queries and 750 mss/year. 25% of books from first-time authors; 50% from unagented writers. Pays 7-10% royalty on retail price. Offers $3,000-10,000 advance.** Publishes book 6-12 months after acceptance of ms. Accepts simultaneous submissions. Responds in 2 months to queries. Book catalog and ms guidelines for SASE or online.

> ⊶ "Seal Press is an imprint of Avalon Publishing Group, feminist book publisher interested in original, lively, radical, empowering and culturally diverse nonfiction by women addressing contemporary issues from a feminist perspective or speaking positively to the experience of being female." Currently emphasizing women outdoor adventurists, young feminists, political issues for women, health issues, and suriving abuse. De-emphasizing fiction.

Nonfiction Biography (women only), literary nonfiction essays. Subjects include Americana, child guidance/parenting, contemporary culture, creative nonfiction, ethnic, gay/lesbian, memoirs, multicultural, nature/environment, sex, travel, women's issues/studies, popular culture, politics, domestic violence, sexual abuse. Query with SASE. Reviews artwork/photos as part of ms package. Send photocopies. No original art or photos accepted.
Fiction Ethnic, feminist, gay/lesbian, literary, multicultural. "We are interested in alternative voices." Query with SASE, or submit outline, 2 sample chapters, synopsis. Does not accept queries by e-mail or phone.
Recent Title(s) *No Touch Monkey*, by Ayun Halliday; *The F-word*, by Kristin Rowe-Finkbeiner.
Tips "Our audience is generally composed of women interested in reading about women's issues addressed from a feminist perspective."

SEAWORTHY PUBLICATIONS, INC.

207 S. Park St., Port Washington WI 53074. (262)268-9250. Fax: (262)268-9208. E-mail: publisher@seaworthy.com. Website: www.seaworthy.com. **Acquisitions:** Joseph F. Janson, publisher. Publishes trade paperback originals, hardcover originals, and reprints. **Publishes 8 titles/year. Receives 150 queries and 40 mss/year. 60% of books from first-time authors; 100% from unagented writers. Pays 15% royalty on wholesale price. Offers $1,000 advance.** Publishes book 6 months after acceptance of ms. Does not accept simultaneous submissions. Responds in 1 month to queries. Book catalog on website or for #10 SASE; ms guidelines online.

> ⊶ Seaworthy Publications is a nautical book publisher that primarily publishes books of interest to recreational boaters and bluewater cruisers, including cruising guides, how-to books about boating. Currently emphasizing how-to.

Nonfiction Illustrated book, reference, technical. Subjects include hobbies (sailing, boating), regional (boating guide books). Regional guide books, first-person adventure, reference, technical—all dealing with boating. Query with SASE, or submit 3 sample chapters, TOC. Prefers electronic query via e-mail. Reviews artwork/photos as part of ms package. Send photocopies or color prints.

Recent Title(s) *The Solitude of the Open Sea*, by Gregory Newell Smith.
Tips "Our audience consists of sailors, boaters, and those interested in the sea, sailing, or long-distance cruising."

SEEDLING PUBLICATIONS, INC.

20 W. Kanawha Ave., Columbus OH 43214-1432. Phone/Fax: (614)888-4140. E-mail: lsalem@jinl.com. Website: www.seedlingpub.com. **Acquisitions:** Josie Stewart, vice president. Estab. 1992. Publishes in an 8-, 12-, or 16-page format for beginning readers. **Publishes 10-20 titles/year. Receives 450 mss/year. 50% of books from first-time authors; 100% from unagented writers. Makes outright purchase.** Publishes book 1 year after acceptance of ms. Accepts simultaneous submissions. Responds in 9-12 months to queries. Ms guidelines for #10 SASE.

O→ "We are an education niche publisher, producing books for beginning readers. Stories must include language that is natural to young children and story lines that are interesting to 5-7-year-olds and written at their beginning reading level."

Nonfiction Children's/juvenile. Science, math, or social studies concepts are considered. Does not accept mss or queries via fax. Reviews artwork/photos as part of ms package. Send photocopies.
Fiction Juvenile. Submit complete ms.
Recent Title(s) *Sherman in the Talent Show*, by Betty Erickson; *Moth or Butterfly?*, by Ryan Durney; *The Miller, His Son, and the Donkey*, by Lynn Salem and Josie Stewart.
Tips "Follow our guidelines. Do not submit full-length picture books or chapter books. We are an education niche publisher. Our books are for children, ages 5-7, who are just beginning to read independently. We do not accept stories that rhyme or poetry at this time. Try your manuscript with young readers. Listen for text that doesn't flow when the child reads the story. Rewrite until the text sounds natural to beginning readers. Visit our website to be sure your manuscript fits our market." Does not accept mss via fax. Does not accept queries at all.

[N] SELF-COUNSEL PRESS

1704 N. State St., Bellingham WA 92225. (360)676-4530. Website: www.self-counsel.com. **Acquisitions:** Richard Day, managing editor. Estab. 1971. Publishes trade paperback originals. **Publishes 30 titles/year. Receives 1,500 queries/year. 30% of books from first-time authors; 90% from unagented writers. Pays 10% royalty on net receipts. Offers rare advance.** Publishes book 8 months after acceptance of ms. Accepts simultaneous submissions. Responds in 2 months to queries. Book catalog via website or upon request; ms guidelines online.

O→ Self-Counsel Press publishes a range of quality self-help books written in practical, nontechnical style by recognized experts in the fields of business, financial, or legal guidance for people who want to help themselves.

Nonfiction How-to, reference, self-help. Subjects include business/economics, computers/electronic, money/finance, legal issues for lay people. Submit proposal package including outline, 2 sample chapters, résumé.
Recent Title(s) *Write Your Legal Will in 3 Easy Steps*, by Craig Waters; *Start & Run an Event Planning Business*, by Cindy Lemaise and M. Foster Walker; *Family Medical History Kit*, by Self-Counsel Press.

SEPIA

Imprint of BET Books, 850 Third Ave., 16th Floor, New York NY 10022. Website: www.bet.com/books. **Acquisitions:** Glenda Howard, senior editor. Responds in 4 months to proposals.
Fiction Historical, mainstream/contemporary. "Manuscripts submitted in consideration for Sepia should be 90,000-100,000 words in length. We will review both contemporary and historical novels that display strong characters with intriguing plots." Submit proposal package including 3 sample chapters, synopsis.
Tips "Please do not phone to see if your manuscript was received or returned, or to find out what we thought of it. A self-addressed, stamped postcard can be enclosed with your submission if you want confirmation of its arrival. Specify whether you would like your manuscript returned or recycled if it is not right for us."

[N] [⊘] SEVEN STORIES PRESS

140 Watts St., New York NY 10013. (212)226-8760. Fax: (212)226-1411. E-mail: info@sevenstories.com. Website: www.sevenstories.com. **Acquisitions:** Daniel Simon; Greg Ruggiero. Estab. 1995. Publishes hardcover and trade paperback originals. **Publishes 40-50 titles/year. 15% of books from first-time authors; 5% from unagented writers. Pays 7-15% royalty on retail price. Offers advance.** Publishes book 1-3 years after acceptance of ms. Accepts simultaneous submissions. Book catalog and ms guidelines free.

O→ Seven Stories Press publishes literary/activist fiction and nonfiction "on the premise that both are works of the imagination and that there is no contradiction in publishing the 2 side by side." Currently emphasizing politics, social justice, biographies, foreign writings.

Nonfiction Biography. Subjects include general nonfiction. Responds only if interested. Query with SASE. *All unsolicited mss returned unopened.*

Fiction Literary. Query with SASE. *All unsolicited mss returned unopened.*

Recent Title(s) *Power and Terror*, by Noam Chomsky; *First Loves*, by Ted Solotaroff; *A History of Color*, by Stanley Moss.

SHAMBHALA PUBLICATIONS, INC.

300 Massachusetts Ave., Boston MA 02115. (617)424-0030. Fax: (617)236-1563. E-mail: editors@shambhala.c om. Website: www.shambhala.com. President: Peter Turner. **Acquisitions:** Eden Steinberg, editor; Emily Bower, editor; David O'Neal, senior editor; Beth Frankl, editor. Estab. 1969. Publishes hardcover and trade paperback originals and reprints. **Publishes 90-100 titles/year. Receives 2,000 queries and 500-700 mss/ year. 30% of books from first-time authors; 80% from unagented writers. Pays 8% royalty on retail price.** Publishes book 1 year after acceptance of ms. Accepts simultaneous submissions. Responds in 1 month to queries; 2 months to proposals and mss. Book catalog and ms guidelines free.

Nonfiction Biography, general nonfiction, reference, self-help. Subjects include alternative lifestyles, art/architecture, creative nonfiction. Query with SASE, or submit proposal package including outline, 2 sample chapters, résumé, synopsis, TOC, or submit complete ms. Reviews artwork/photos as part of ms package.

Fiction Health/medicine, humanities, language/literature, memoirs, philosphy, religion, spirituality, women's issues/studies. Query with SASE, or submit proposal package including outline, 2 sample chapters, résumé, synopsis, TOC, or submit complete ms.

N ⊘ SHAW BOOKS

Imprint of WaterBrook Press, 2375 Telstar Dr. #160, Colorado Springs CO 80920-1029. (719)590-4999. Fax: (719)590-8977. **Acquisitions:** Elisa Fryling Stanford, editor. Estab. 1967. Publishes mostly trade paperback originals. **Publishes 25 titles/year. Receives 350 queries/year. 10-20% of books from first-time authors. Offers advance.** Publishes book 18 months after acceptance of ms. Responds in 6 months to queries.

- ⊶ "We are looking for unique manuscripts from a Christian perspective on the topics below. Queries accepted but not unsolicited manuscripts."

Nonfiction General nonfiction, books that blend faith, life, and the arts. Subjects include creative nonfiction, education, language/literature, spiritual growth, parenting, health and wellness, literary topics all from a Christian perspective. "We are looking for adult nonfiction with different twists—self-help manuscripts with fresh insight and colorful, vibrant writing style." *No fiction, poetry or unsolicited mss.* Query with SASE.

Recent Title(s) *God in the Alley*, by Greg Paul; *Mom, I Hate My Life!*, by Sharon Hersh; *Falling for God*, by Gary Moon.

SHEED & WARD BOOK PUBLISHING

Imprint of Rowman & Littlefield Publishing Group, 4501 Forbes Blvd., Suite 200, Lanham MD 20706. (301)459-3366. Fax: (301)429-5747. Website: www.sheedandward.com. Publisher: Jon Sisk. Editorial Director: Jeremy Langford (1427 Brummel St., Evanston IL 60202). **Acquisitions:** Katie Lane. Publishes hardcover and paperback originals. Does not accept simultaneous submissions. Book catalog free or on website; ms guidelines online.

- ⊶ "We are looking for books that help our readers, most of whom are college educated, gain access to the riches of the Catholic/Christian tradition. We publish in the areas of history, biography, spirituality, prayer, ethics, ministry, justice, liturgy."

Nonfiction Biography. Subjects include religion, spirituality, family life, theology, ethics. Submit proposal package including outline, 2 sample chapters, strong cover letter indicating why the project is unique and compelling. Reviews artwork/photos as part of ms package. Send photocopies.

Recent Title(s) *Becoming Fully Human*, by Joan Chittister, OSB; *Exploring Catholic Literature*, by Mary R. Reichardt.

Tips "We prefer that writers get our author guidelines either from our website or via mail before submitting proposals."

⊘ SIERRA CLUB BOOKS

85 Second St., San Francisco CA 94105. (415)977-5500. Fax: (415)977-5792. E-mail: books.publishing@sierraclu b.org. Website: www.sierraclub.org/books. **Acquisitions:** Danny Moses, editor-in-chief. Estab. 1962. Publishes hardcover and paperback originals and reprints. **Publishes approximately 15 titles/year. 50% from unagented writers. Pays royalty. Offers $5,000-15,000 average advance.** Publishes book 1 year after acceptance of ms. Accepts simultaneous submissions. Responds in 1 month to queries; 2 months to proposals; 3 months to mss. Book catalog and ms guidelines online.

Imprints Sierra Club Books for Children.

- *Currently not accepting unsolicited mss* or proposals for children's books.
- ⊶ The Sierra Club was founded to help people to explore, enjoy, and preserve the nation's forests, waters, wildlife, and wilderness. The books program publishes quality trade books about the outdoors and the protection of the natural world.

Nonfiction General nonfiction. Subjects include nature/environment. A broad range of environmental subjects: outdoor adventure, women in the outdoors; literature, including travel and works on the spiritual aspects of the natural world; natural history and current environmental issues. Does not want "proposals for large, color-photographic books without substantial text; how-to books on building things outdoors; books on motorized travel; or any but the most professional studies of animals." No fiction or poetry. Query with SASE. Reviews artwork/photos as part of ms package. Send photocopies.

Recent Title(s) *Caribou Rising: Defending the Porcupine Herd*, by Rick Bass; *Nature's Operating Instructions: The True Biotechnologies*, edited by Kenny Ausubel with J.P. Harpignies; *Paper or Plastic: Searching for Solutions to an Overpackaged World*, by Daniel Imhoff.

⊘ SILHOUETTE BOOKS

233 Broadway, New York NY 10279. (212)553-4200. Fax: (212)227-8960. Website: www.eharlequin.com. Director, Global Series Editorial: Randall Toye. Executive Editor, Silhouette Books: Mary-Theresa Hussey. **Acquisitions:** Ann Leslie Tuttle, associate senior editor (Silhouette Romance); Gail Chasan, senior editor (Silhouette Special Edition); Melissa Jeglinski, senior editor (Silhouette Desire); Patience Smith, associate senior editor (Silhouettee Intimate Moments); Natashya Wilson, associate senior editor (Silhouette Bombshell). Estab. 1979. Publishes mass market paperback originals. **Publishes over 350 titles/year. Pays royalty. Offers advance.** Publishes book 1-3 years after acceptance of ms. Does not accept simultaneous submissions. Ms guidelines online.

Imprints Silhouette Romance (contemporary adult romances, 53,000-58,000 words); Silhouette Desire (contemporary adult romances, 55,000-60,000 words); Silhouette Intimate Moments (contemporary adult romances, 80,000 words); Silhouette Bombshell (contemporary adult suspense/adventure fiction, 80,000-85,000 words); Silhouette Special Edition (contemporary adult romances, 75,000-80,000 words).

○⇥ Silhouette publishes contemporary adult romances.

Fiction Romance (contemporary romance for adults). "We are interested in seeing submissions for all our lines. No manuscripts other than the types outlined. Manuscript should follow our general format, yet have an individuality and life of its own that will make them stand out in the readers' minds." *No unsolicited mss.* Send query letter, 2 page synopsis, and SASE to head of line.

Recent Title(s) *Marrying Molly*, by Christine Rimmer; *AKA Goddess*, by Evelyn Vaughn.

Tips "The romance market is constantly changing, so when you read for research, read the latest books and those that have been recommended to you by people knowledgeable in the genre. We are actively seeking new authors for all our lines, contemporary and historical."

SILMAN-JAMES PRESS

3624 Shannon Rd., Los Angeles CA 90027. (323)661-9922. Fax: (323)661-9933. E-mail: silmanjamespress@earth link.net. Website: www.silmanjamespress.com. Publishes trade paperback originals and reprints. **Pays variable royalty on retail price.** Book catalog free.

Imprints Siles Press (publishes chess books and other nonfiction subjects).

Nonfiction Pertaining to film, theatre, music, peforming arts. Biography, how-to, reference, technical, textbook. Submit proposal package including outline, 1+ sample chapter(s), or submit complete ms. Reviews artwork/photos as part of ms package. Send photocopies.

Recent Title(s) *John Carpenter: The Prince of Darkness*, by Gilles Boulenger; *Screenplay: Writing the Picture*, by Robin U. Russin and William Missouri Downs; *Total Directing*, by Tom Kingdon.

Tips "Our audience ranges from people with a general interest in film (fans, etc.) to students of film and performing arts to industry professionals. We will accept 'query' phone calls."

⊘ SILVER DAGGER MYSTERIES

The Overmountain Press, 325 Walnut St., Johnson City TN 37605. E-mail: contactsd@silverdaggermysteries.com. Website: www.silverdaggermysteries.com. Estab. 1999. Publishes hardcover and trade paperback originals and reprints. Accepts simultaneous submissions. Book catalog and ms guidelines online.

● *Currently closed to submissions.*

○⇥ Silver Dagger publishes mysteries that take place in the American South. Emphasizing cozies, police procedurals, hard-boiled detectives.

Fiction Mystery (amateur sleuth, cozy, police procedural, private eye/hardboiled), young adult (mystery). "We look for average-length books of 60-80,000 words." No horror or science fiction. *All unsolicited mss returned unopened.*

Recent Title(s) *Death by Dissertation*, by Dean James; *Execute the Office*, by Daniel Bailey; *Criminal Appetite*, presented by Jeffrey Marks.

SILVER LAKE PUBLISHING

111 E. Wishkah St., Aberdeen WA 98520. (360)532-5758. Fax: (360)532-5728. E-mail: publisher@silverlakepub. com. Website: www.silverlakepub.com. Estab. 1998. Publishes hardcover and trade paperback originals and reprints. **Pays royalty.** Accepts simultaneous submissions. Responds in 6-8 weeks to proposals. Book catalog and ms guidelines free.

Nonfiction How-to, reference. Subjects include business/economics, money/finance. No fiction or poetry. Submit outline, 2 sample chapters, résumé, cover letter, synopsis. Submit via mail only.

Recent Title(s) *The Elements of Small Business*, by John Thaler; *Liberty in Troubled Times*, by James Walsh; *Use History Like a Tool*, by Steven Levi.

SIMON & SCHUSTER BOOKS FOR YOUNG READERS

Imprint of Simon & Schuster Children's Publishing, 1230 Avenue of the Americas, New York NY 10020. (212)698-7000. Fax: (212)698-2796. Website: www.simonsayskids.com. **Acquisitions:** Elizabeth Law, vice president/associate publisher; Kevin Lewis, executive editor; Paula Wiseman, editorial director. Publishes hardcover originals. **Publishes 75 titles/year. Pays variable royalty on retail price.** Publishes book 2-4 years after acceptance of ms. Accepts simultaneous submissions. Responds in 2 months. Ms guidelines for #10 SASE.

Imprints Paula Wiseman Books.

- *No unsolicited mss.* Queries are accepted via mail.
- ⚬┓ "We publish high-quality fiction and nonfiction for a variety of age groups and a variety of markets. Above all, we strive to publish books that we are passionate about."

Nonfiction Children's/juvenile. Subjects include history, nature/environment, biography. *All unsolicited mss returned unopened.* Query with SASE only.

Fiction Fantasy, historical, humor, juvenile, mystery, picture books, science fiction, young adult (adventure, historical, mystery, contemporary fiction). *All unsolicited mss returned unopened.* Query with SASE only.

Recent Title(s) *Duck for President*, by Doreen Cronin; *Spiderwick*, by Holly Black, illustrated by Tony Di Terlizzi; *Shrimp*, by Rachel Cohn.

SIMON & SCHUSTER CHILDREN'S PUBLISHING

Division of Simon & Schuster, Inc., 1230 Avenue of the Americas, New York NY 10020. (212)698-7000. Website: www.simonsays.com. Publishes hardcover and paperback fiction, nonfiction, trade, library, mass market titles, and novelty books for preschool through young adult readers. **Publishes 650 titles/year.**

Imprints Aladdin Paperbacks; Atheneum Books for Young Readers (Richard Jackson Books, Anne Schwartz Books); Libros Para Ninos; Little Simon; Margaret K. McElderry Books; Simon & Schuster Books for Young Readers (Paula Wiseman Books); Simon Pulse; Simon Spotlight; Simon Spotlight Entertainment.

SIMON & SCHUSTER, INC.

1230 Avenue of the Americas, New York NY 10020. (212)698-7000. Website: www.simonsays.com. **Pays royalty. Offers advance.** Ms guidelines online.

Imprints Simon & Schuster Adult Publishing Group: Atria Books (Washington Square Press), The Free Press (Simon & Schuster Source, Wall Street Journal Books), Kaplan, Pocket Books (Downtown Press, MTV Books, Paraview Pocket, Pocket Star, Star Trek, VH-1 Books, World Wrestling Entertainment), Scribner (Lisa Drew Books, Scribner Classics, Scribner Paperback Fiction), Simon & Schuster (Simon & Schuster Classic Editions), Simon & Schuster Trade Paperbacks (Fireside, Libros en Espanol, Touchstone) **Simon & Schuster Australia:** Audio, Fireside, Kangaroo Press, Martin Books, Pocket Books, Scribner, Simon & Schuster, Touchstone; **Simon & Schuster Children's Publishing:** Aladdin Paperbacks; Atheneum Books for Young Readers (Richard Jackson Books, Anne Schwartz Books), Libros Para Ninos, Little Simon, Margaret K. McElderry Books, Simon & Schuster Books for Young Readers (Paula Weisman Books), Simon Pulse, Simon Spotlight and Simon Spotlight Entertainment; **Simon & Schuster Audio** (Encore, Nightingale-Conant, Pimsleur Language Programs, Simon & Schuster Audioworks, Simon & Schuster Sound Ideas); **Simon & Schuster Online**; **Simon & Schuster UK:** Fireside, The Free Press, Martin Books, Pocket Books, Scribner, Simon & Schuster, Simon & Schuster Audio, Touchstone, Town House.

- See website for more details.

SKINNER HOUSE BOOKS

The Unitarian Universalist Association, 25 Beacon St., Boston MA 02108. (617)742-2100 ext. 601. Fax: (617)742-7025. Website: www.uua.org/skinner. **Acquisitions:** Mary Benard, project editor. Estab. 1975. Publishes trade paperback originals and reprints. **Publishes 10-20 titles/year. 50% of books from first-time authors; 100% from unagented writers. Pays 5-10% royalty on net receipts.** Publishes book 1 year after acceptance of ms. Does not accept simultaneous submissions. Responds in 3 months to queries. Book catalog for 6×9 SAE with 3 first-class stamps; ms guidelines online.

○━ "We publish titles in Unitarian Universalist faith, liberal religion, history, biography, worship, and issues of social justice. We also publish inspirational titles of poetic prose and meditations. Writers should know that Unitarian Universalism is a liberal religious denomination committed to progressive ideals." Currently emphasizing social justice concerns.

Nonfiction Biography, self-help. Subjects include gay/lesbian, memoirs, religion, women's issues/studies, inspirational, church leadership. Query with SASE. Reviews artwork/photos as part of ms package. Send photocopies.

Recent Title(s) *In Nature's Honor*, by Patricia Montley; *Simply Pray*, by Erik Wikstrom; *Faith Without Certainty*, by Paul Rasor.

Tips "From outside our denomination, we are interested in manuscripts that will be of help or interest to liberal churches, Sunday School classes, parents, ministers, and volunteers. Inspirational/spiritual and children's titles must reflect liberal Unitarian Universalist values. Fiction for youth is being considered."

N SMITH AND KRAUS PUBLISHERS, INC.

P.O. Box 127, Lyme NH 03768. (603)643-6431. Fax: (603) 643-1831. **Acquisitions:** Marisa Smith, president/publisher. Estab. 1990. Publishes hardcover and trade paperback originals. **Publishes 35-40 titles/year. 10% of books from first-time authors; 10-20% from unagented writers. Pays 7% royalty on retail price. Offers $500-2,000 advance.** Publishes book 1 year after acceptance of ms. Does not accept simultaneous submissions. Responds in 1 month to queries; 2 months to proposals; 4 months to mss. Book catalog free.

Nonfiction Subjects include film/cinema/stage, drama, theater. Does not return submissions. Query with SASE.

Fiction Drama, theater. Does not return submissions. Query with SASE.

Recent Title(s) *On Broadway Men Still Wear Hats: Fascinating Lives Led on the Borders of Broadway*, by Robert Simonson; *Ingenue in White: Reflections of a Costume Designer*, by Marcia Dixcy Jory; *Provoking Theater: Koma Ginkas Directs*, by Koma Ginkas and John Freedman.

GIBBS SMITH, PUBLISHER

P.O. Box 667, Layton UT 84041. (801)544-9800. Fax: (801)546-8853. E-mail: info@gibbs-smith.com. Website: www.gibbs-smith.com. **Acquisitions:** Suzanne Taylor, editorial director, humor. Estab. 1969. Publishes hardcover and trade paperback originals. **Publishes 80 titles/year. Receives 3,000-4,000 queries/year. 50% of books from first-time authors; 75% from unagented writers. Pays 8-14% royalty on gross receipts. Offers advance based on first year saleability projections.** Publishes book 1-2 years after acceptance of ms. Accepts simultaneous submissions. Responds in 1 month to queries; 10 weeks to proposals and mss. Book catalog for 9×12 SAE and $2.13 in postage; ms guidelines online.

○━ "We publish books that enrich and inspire humankind." Currently emphasizing interior decorating and design, home reference. De-emphasizing novels and short stories.

Nonfiction Humor, illustrated book, textbook, children's. Subjects include art/architecture, nature/environment, regional, interior design, cooking, business, western, outdoor/sports/recreation. Query with SASE, or submit outline, several completed sample chapters, author's cv. Reviews artwork/photos as part of ms package. Send sample illustrations, if applicable.

Fiction Only short works oriented to gift market. No novels or short stories. Submit synopsis with sample illustration, if applicable. Send query letter or short gift book ms directly to the editorial director.

Recent Title(s) *Secrets of French Design*, by Betty Lou Phillips (nonfiction); *101 More Things to Do with a Slow Cooker*, by Stephanie Ashcraft and Janet Eyring (cookbook).

N SOCRATES MEDIA, LLC

227 W. Monroe, Suite 500, Chicago IL 60606. (312)762-5600. Fax: (312)762-5601. Website: www.socrates.com. **Acquisitions:** Paul Barrett, senior VP/general manager for sales, marketing, editorial, operations, and customer service. Publishes trade paperback and electronic originals. Accepts simultaneous submissions. Book catalog free.

○━ Publishes self-help business forms, legal forms, software, books, kits, and certificates.

Nonfiction How-to. Subjects include business/economics, money/finance, real estate, law. Submit complete ms.

Tips "Our audience is interested in business, legal, and financial matters."

SOHO PRESS, INC.

853 Broadway, New York NY 10003. (212)260-1900. Fax: (212)260-1902. E-mail: soho@sohopress.com. Website: www.sohopress.com. **Acquisitions:** Juris Jurjevics, editor-in-chief. Estab. 1986. Publishes hardcover and trade paperback originals. Accepts simultaneous submissions. Book catalog for 6×9 SAE with 2 first-class stamps; ms guidelines online.

o-т Soho Press publishes primarily fiction, with the occasional autobiogrpahy or historical account. No electronic submissions.

Nonfiction Autobiography, biography, autobiography; literary. Subjects include contemporary culture, history, memoirs, military/war, translation, travel. No self-help, how-to, or cookbooks. Submit outline, sample chapter(s), publishing history, SASE.

Fiction Adventure, ethnic, feminist, historical, literary, mainstream/contemporary, mystery (police procedural), suspense. Submit outline, 3 sample chapters, publishing history, synopsis, SASE.

Recent Title(s) *The Midnight Band of Mercy*, by Michael Blaine; *Political Animal*, by David Mizner; *truecrime*, by Jake Arnott.

Tips "Soho Press publishes discerning authors for discriminating readers, finding the strongest possible writers and publishing them."

[N] SOUNDPRINTS

Division of Trudy Corp., 353 Main Ave., Norwalk CT 06851. Website: www.soundprints.com. Publishes hardcover and trade paperback originals. **Publishes 30 titles/year; imprint publishes 10 titles/year. Receives 500 queries and 500 mss/year. 10% of books from first-time authors; 100% from unagented writers. Makes outright purchase of $500-1,000.** Book catalog for #10 SASE.

o-т "Whether your children are fascinated by life in the blue ocean or the green grass of their own backyards, Soundprints storybooks, read-along audiobooks, and adorable stuffed toys offer something to delight every child."

Nonfiction Children's/juvenile. Subjects include animals, nature/environment. Query with SASE.

Fiction Query with SASE.

Recent Title(s) *Pepper: A Snowy Search*; *Pteranodon Soars*; *Red Bat at Sleepy Hollow Lane*.

Tips "Before submitting, you should have a knowledge of what we publish."

[S] SOURCEBOOKS, INC.

P.O. Box 4410, Naperville IL 60567. (630)961-3900. Fax: (630)961-2168. Website: www.sourcebooks.com. Publisher: Dominique Raccah. **Acquisitions:** Todd Stocke, VP/editorial director (nonfiction trade); Deborah Werksman (Sourcebooks Hysteria, Sourcebooks Casablanca); Dianne Wheeler (Sphinx Publishing). Estab. 1987. Publishes hardcover and trade paperback originals. **Publishes 150 titles/year. 30% of books from first-time authors; 25% from unagented writers. Pays royalty on wholesale price. Offers advance.** Publishes book 1 year after acceptance of ms. Accepts simultaneous submissions. Responds in 3 months to queries. Book catalog and ms guidelines online.

Imprints Sourcebooks Casablanca (love/relationships); Sourcebooks Hysteria (women's humor/gift book); Sourcebooks Landmark; Sourcebooks MediaFusion (multimedia); Sphinx Publishing (self-help legal).

o-т Sourcebooks publishes many forms of nonfiction titles, generally in the how-to and reference areas, including books on parenting, self-help/psychology, business, and health. Focus is on practical, useful information and skills. It also continues to publish in the reference, New Age, history, current affairs, and travel categories. Currently emphasizing gift, women's interest, history, reference.

Nonfiction "We seek unique books on traditional subjects and authors who are smart and aggressive." Biography, gift book, how-to, illustrated book, multimedia, reference, self-help, technical, textbook. Subjects include art/architecture, business/economics, child guidance/parenting, history, military/war, money/finance, psychology, science, sports, women's issues/studies, contemporary culture. Books for small business owners, entrepreneurs, and students. "A key to submitting books to us is to explain how your book helps the reader, why it is different from the books already out there (please do your homework), and the author's credentials for writing this book. Books likely to succeed with us are self-help, parenting and childcare, psychology, women's issues, how-to, history, reference, biography, humor, gift books, or books with strong artwork." Query with SASE, 2-3 sample chapters (not the first). *No complete mss.* Reviews artwork/photos as part of ms package.

Recent Title(s) *1,000 Best Wedding Bargains*, by Sharon Naylor; *E.E. Cummings: A Biography*, by Christopher Sawyer-Laucanno.

Tips "Our market is a decidedly trade-oriented bookstore audience. We also have very strong penetration into the gift-store market. Books which cross over between these 2 very different markets do extremely well with us. Our list is a solid mix of unique and general audience titles and series-oriented projects. In other words, we are looking for products that break new ground either in their own areas or within the framework of our series of imprints. We love to develop books in new areas or develop strong titles in areas that are already well developed."

SOUTHERN ILLINOIS UNIVERSITY PRESS

P.O. Box 3697, Carbondale IL 62902-3697. (618)453-2281. Fax: (618)453-1221. Website: www.siu.edu/~siupress. **Acquisitions:** Karl Kageff, editor-in-chief (film/theater, history, baseball, poetry, regional and US history, rhetoric); Kristine Priddy, editor (civil rights, women's studies, true crime); Sylvia Rodrigue (Civil War, Reconstruction). Estab. 1956. Publishes hardcover and trade paperback originals and reprints. **Publishes 50-60 titles/ year. Receives 700 queries and 300 mss/year. 40% of books from first-time authors; 99% from unagented writers. Pays 5-10% royalty on wholesale price. Rarely offers advance.** Publishes book 1-1½ years after acceptance of ms. Does not accept simultaneous submissions. Responds in 4 months to queries. Book catalog and ms guidelines free.

Imprints Shawnee Books; Shawnee Classics (regional reprint); Writing Baseball; Crab Orchard Series in Poetry; Theater in the Americas; Studies in Rhetorics and Feminisms; Studies in Writing and Rhetoric.

> O⊸ "Scholarly press specializes in film and theater studies, civil rights, rhetoric and composition studies, American history, Civil War, regional and nonfiction trade, women's studies, baseball, poetry. No fiction." Currently emphasizing film, theater and American history, especially Civil War.

Recent Title(s) *Breaking Into Baseball: Women and the National Pastime*, by Jean Hastings Ardell (trade baseball); *Framing Monsters: Fantasy Film and Social Alienation*, by Joshua David Bellin (film); *Labor, Loyalty, and Rebellion: Southwestern Illinois Coal Miners and World War I*, by Carl R. Weinberg (American history).

SOUTHERN METHODIST UNIVERSITY PRESS

P.O. Box 750415, Dallas TX 75275-0415. (214)768-1433. Fax: (214)768-1428. Website: www.tamu.edu/upress. **Acquisitions:** Kathryn Lang, senior editor. Estab. 1937. Publishes hardcover and trade paperback originals and reprints. **Publishes 10-12 titles/year. Receives 500 queries and 500 mss/year. 75% of books from first-time authors; 95% from unagented writers. Pays up to 10% royalty on wholesale price, 10 author's copies. Offers $500 advance.** Publishes book 1 year after acceptance of ms. Does not accept simultaneous submissions. Responds in 1 week to queries; 1 month to proposals; up to 1 year to mss. Book catalog free; ms guidelines online.

> O⊸ Southern Methodist University publishes for the general, educated audience in the fields of literary fiction, sports, ethics and human values, film and theater, regional studies. Currently emphasizing literary fiction. De-emphasizing scholarly, narrowly focused academic studies.

Nonfiction Subjects include creative nonfiction, medical ethics/human values, film/theater, regional history. Query with SASE, or submit outline, 3 sample chapters, author bio, TOC. Reviews artwork/photos as part of ms package. Send photocopies.

Fiction Literary, short story collections, novels. "We are willing to look at 'serious' or 'literary' fiction." No "mass market, science fiction, formula, thriller, romance." Query with SASE.

Recent Title(s) *In the River Province: A Novella and Stories*, by Lisa Sandlin; *Shambles: A Novel*, by Debra Monroe.

Ⓐ ⊘ SPECTRA BOOKS

Subsidiary of Random House, Inc., 1745 Broadway, New York NY 10019. (212)782-8632. Fax: (212)782-9174. Website: www.bantamdell.com. Estab. 1985. Publishes hardcover originals, paperback originals, and trade paperbacks. **Pays royalty. Offers negotiable advance.** Accepts simultaneous submissions. Ms guidelines for #10 SASE.

Fiction Fantasy, literary, science fiction. Needs include novels that attempt to broaden the traditional range of science fiction and fantasy. Strong emphasis on characterization. Especially well-written, traditional science fiction and fantasy will be considered. No fiction without at least some element of speculation or the fantastic.

Recent Title(s) *The Mysteries*, by Lisa Tuttle; *Pashazade*, by Jon Courtenay Grimwood; *A Secret Atlas*, by Michael A. Stackpole.

THE SPEECH BIN, INC.

1965 25th Ave., Vero Beach FL 32960-3062. (561)770-0007. **Acquisitions:** Jan J. Binney, senior editor. Estab. 1984. Publishes trade paperback originals. **Publishes 10-20 titles/year. Receives 500 mss/year. 50% of books from first-time authors; 90% from unagented writers. Pays negotiable royalty on wholesale price. Offers advance.** Publishes book 1 year after acceptance of ms. Does not accept simultaneous submissions. Responds in 3 months to queries. Book catalog for 9×12 SASE.

> O⊸ Publishes professional materials for specialists in rehabilitation, particularly speech-language pathologists and audiologists, special educators, occupational and physical therapists, and parents and caregivers of children and adults with developmental and post-trauma disabilities."

Nonfiction Booklets, children's/juvenile (preschool-teen), how-to, illustrated book, reference, textbook, games for children and adults. Subjects include education, health/medicine, communication disorders, education for handicapped persons. Query with SASE, or submit outline, sample chapters. Reviews artwork/photos as part of ms package. Send photocopies.

Fiction "Booklets or books for children and adults about handicapped persons, especially with communication disorders. This is a potentially new market for The Speech Bin.'' Query with SASE, or submit outline, sample chapters, synopsis.

Recent Title(s) *I Can Say S*; *I Can Say R*.

Tips ''Books and materials must be clearly presented, well written, and competently illustrated. We have added books and materials for use by other allied health professionals. We are also looking for more materials for use in treating adults and very young children with communication disorders. Please do not fax or e-mail manuscripts to us.'' The Speech Bin is increasing their number of books published per year and is especially interested in reviewing treatment materials for adults and adolescents.

⊘ SPENCE PUBLISHING CO.

111 Cole St., Dallas TX 75207. (214)939-1700. Fax: (214)939-1800. E-mail: muncy@spencepublishing.com. Website: www.spencepublishing.com. **Acquisitions:** Mitchell Muncy, editor-in-chief. Estab. 1995. Publishes hardcover and trade paperback originals.

• *No longer accepting unsolicited proposals.*

Ⓝ SPHINXBOOKS.COM

140 South Blvd., San Mateo CA 94402. E-mail: submissions@sphinxbooks.com. Website: www.sphinxbooks.com. Estab. 2004. Publishes original eBooks. Responds in 1 month to queries. Ms guidelines online.

Fiction Fantasy, horror, mystery, science fiction. Needs novel-length mysteries, science fiction, fantasy, and horror. Query via e-mail with a 2-3 page synopsis and the first 30 pages of the ms. No paper submissions, please.

Ⓝ SPI BOOKS

99 Spring St., 3rd Floor, New York NY 10012. (212)431-5011. Fax: (212)431-8646. E-mail: publicity@spibooks.com. Website: www.spibooks.com. **Acquisitions:** Ian Shapolsky, acquisitions editor (pop culture, how-to, exposé, entertainment, Judaica, business, conspiracy, children's); Jill Olofsson, acquisitions editor (how-to, self-help, health). Estab. 1991. Publishes hardcover and trade paperback originals and reprints. **Publishes 20-30 titles/year. 5% of books from first-time authors; 50% from unagented writers. Pays 6-15% royalty on retail price. Offers $1,000-10,000 advance.** Publishes book 3-6 months after acceptance of ms. Accepts simultaneous submissions. Responds in 2 months. Book catalog online; ms guidelines free.

Nonfiction Autobiography, biography, children's/juvenile, coffee table book, cookbook, general nonfiction, gift book, how-to, humor, illustrated book, reference, scholarly, self-help, textbook. Subjects include Americana, animals, business/economics, child guidance/parenting, community, contemporary culture, cooking/foods/nutrition, creative nonfiction, education, ethnic, government/politics, health/medicine, history, hobbies, humanities, language/literature, memoirs, military/war, money/finance, multicultural, music/dance, nature/environment, New Age, philosophy, psychology, regional, religion, sex, social sciences, sociology, spirituality, sports, translation, travel, women's issues/studies, world affairs, exposé, conspiracy. ''Aside from a quality editorial product, we request a marketing plan, suggested by the author, to supplement our own ideas for successfully marketing/promoting their book.'' Query with SASE, or submit proposal package including outline, sample chapters. Reviews artwork/photos as part of ms package. Send photocopies.

Recent Title(s) *Don't Be a Slave to What You Crave*, by Dr. Daisy Merey (health); *Princess Diana: The Hidden Evidence*, by King & Beveridge (conspiracy); *Steve Martin: The Magic Years*, by Morris Walker (biography).

Tips ''Advise us how to reach the market for the legions of interested buyers of your book. Be specific if you can help us target marketing opportunities and promotional possibilities, particularly those that are not obvious. Also, let us know if there are any friends/contacts/connections you can draw upon to assist us in getting the message out about the significance of your book.''

SQUARE ONE PUBLISHERS, INC.

115 Herricks Rd., Garden City Park NY 11040. (516)535-2010. Fax: (516)535-2014. Website: www.squareonepublishers.com. Publisher: Rudy Shur. **Acquisitions:** Acquisitions Editor. Publishes trade paperback originals. **Publishes 20 titles/year. Receives 500 queries and 100 mss/year. 95% of books from first-time authors; 95% from unagented writers. Pays 10-15% royalty on wholesale price. Offers variable advance.** Publishes book 10 months after acceptance of ms. Accepts simultaneous submissions. Responds in 1 month. Book catalog and ms guidelines free or online.

Nonfiction Cookbook, how-to, reference, self-help. Subjects include business/economics, child guidance/parenting, health/medicine, hobbies, money/finance, nature/environment, psychology, religion, spirituality, sports, travel, writers' guides, cooking/foods, gaming/gambling. Query with SASE, or submit proposal package including outline, author bio, introduction, synopsis, SASE. Reviews artwork/photos as part of ms package. Send photocopies.

Recent Title(s) *Talking With Your Hands, Listening With Your Eyes*, by Gabriel Grayson (reference/sign language); *Retiring Right, 3rd Ed.*, by Lawrence Kaplan (personal finance); *How to Publish Your Articles*, by Shirley Kawa-Jump (reference/writing).

Tips "We focus on making our books accessible, accurate, and interesting. They are written for people who are looking for the best place to start, and who don't appreciate the terms 'dummy,' 'idiot,' or 'fool,' on the cover of their books. We look for smartly written, informative books that have a strong point of view, and that are authored by people who know their subjects well."

STACKPOLE BOOKS

5067 Ritter Rd., Mechanicsburg PA 17055. Fax: (717)796-0412. E-mail: jschnell@stackpolebooks.com. Website: www.stackpolebooks.com. **Acquisitions:** Judith Schnell, editorial director (fly fishing, sports); Chris Evans, editor (history); Mark Allison, editor (nature); Ed Skender, editor (military guides); Kyle Weaver, editor (Pennsylvania/regional). Estab. 1935. Publishes hardcover and paperback originals and reprints. **Publishes 90 titles/ year. Offers industry standard advance.** Publishes book 1 year after acceptance of ms. Does not accept simultaneous submissions. Responds in 1 month to queries.

    ○┯ "Stackpole maintains a growing and vital publishing program by featuring authors who are experts in their fields."

Nonfiction Subjects include history, military/war, nature/environment, recreation, sports, wildlife, outdoor skills, fly fishing, paddling, climbing. Query with SASE. Does not return unsolicited mss. Reviews artwork/ photos as part of ms package.

Recent Title(s) *Mayflies*; *Careers With Animals*; *In the Company of Moose*.

Tips "Stackpole seeks well-written, authoritative manuscripts for specialized and general trade markets. Proposals should include chapter outline, sample chapter, illustrations, and author's credentials."

STANFORD UNIVERSITY PRESS

1450 Page Mill Rd., Palo Alto CA 94304-1124. (650)723-9434. Fax: (650)725-3457. E-mail: info@www.sup.org. Website: www.sup.org. **Acquisitions:** Muriel Bell (Asian studies, US foreign policy, Asian-American studies); Amanda M. Moran (law, political science, public policy); Martha Cooley (economics, finance, business); Kate Wahl (sociology, anthropology, education, Middle Eastern studies). Estab. 1925. **Pays variable royalty (sometimes none). Offers occasional advance.** Does not accept simultaneous submissions. Ms guidelines online.

    ○┯ Stanford University Press publishes scholarly books in the humanities and social sciences, along with professional books in business, economics and management science; also high-level textbooks and some books for a more general audience.

Nonfiction Scholarly, textbook, professional books. Subjects include anthropology/archeology, business/economics, ethnic (studies), gay/lesbian, government/politics, history, humanities, language/literature, nature/ environment, philosophy, psychology, religion, science, social sciences, sociology, political science, law, education, history and culture of China, Japan and Latin America, European history, linguistics, geology, medieval and classical studies. Query with prospectus and an outline. Reviews artwork/photos as part of ms package.

Recent Title(s) *Culture and Public Action*; *The Sovereignty Revolution*; *Maps, Myths, and Men*.

Tips "The writer's best chance is a work of original scholarship with an argument of some importance."

STEEPLE HILL

Imprint of Harlequin Enterprises, 233 Broadway, New York NY 10279. Website: www.steeplehill.com. **Acquisitions:** Krista Stroever, editor. Also: P.O. Box 5190, Buffalo NY 14240-5190. Estab. 1997. Publishes mass market and trade paperback originals. **Pays royalty. Offers advance.** Does not accept simultaneous submissions. Ms guidelines online.

Imprints Love Inspired.

    ○┯ "This series of contemporary, inspirational love stories portrays Christian characters facing the many challenges of life, faith, and love in today's world."

Fiction Romance (Christian, inspirational). Query with SASE.

Recent Title(s) *Hero Dad*, by Marta Perrty; *Love the Sinner*, by Lynn Bulock; *Last Resort*, by Hannah Alexander.

Tips "Drama, humor, and even a touch of mystery all have a place in Steeple Hill. Subplots are welcome and should further the story's main focus or intertwine in a meaningful way. Secondary characters (children, family, friends, neighbors, fellow church members, etc.) may all contribute to a substantial and satisfying story. These wholesome tales include strong family values and high moral standards. While there is no premarital sex between characters, in the case of romance, a vivid, exciting tone presented with a mature perspective is essential. Although the element of faith must clearly be present, it should be well integrated into the characterizations and plot. The conflict between the main characters should be an emotional one, arising naturally from the well-developed personalities you've created. Suitable stories should also impart an important lesson about the powers of trust and faith."

[N] STEEPLE HILL WOMEN'S FICTION

Imprint of Steeple Hill, 233 Broadway, Suite 1001, New York NY 10279. (212)553-4200. Fax: (212)227-8969. Website: www.steeplehill.com. **Acquisitions:** Joan Marlow Golan, executive editor (inspirational fiction); Mavis Allen, associate senior editor (inspirational fiction); Krista Stroever, editor (inspirational fiction); Diane Dietz, assistant editor (inspirational fiction). Estab. 1997. Publishes hardcover, trade paperback, and mass market paperback originals. **Publishes 78-90 titles/year. Pays royalty on retail price. Offers advance.** Does not accept simultaneous submissions. Responds in 3 months. Ms guidelines online.

Imprints Steeple Hill Café.

Fiction Literary, mystery, religious, romance, chick lit. "This program is dedicated to publishing inspirational Christian women's fiction that depicts the struggles characters encounter as they learn important lessons about trust and the power of faith. See listing for subgenres. The Steeple Hill Café line is a new subbrand within the Steeple Hill Women's Fiction Program, and it is dedicated to publishing inspirational fiction for the hip, modern women of faith. These distinctively smart and spirited books will depict the unique and varied situations women encounter as they learn important lessons about life, love, and the power of faith." Query with SASE.

Recent Title(s) *Hideaway*, by Hannah Alexander; *The Whitney Chronicles*, by Judy Baer.

Tips "Please read our guidelines."

STENHOUSE PUBLISHERS

477 Congress St., Suite 4B, Portland ME 04101-3451. (207)253-1600. Fax: (207)253-5121. E-mail: wvarner@stenhouse.com. Website: www.stenhouse.com. **Acquisitions:** William Varner, senior editor. Estab. 1993. Publishes paperback originals. **Publishes 15 titles/year. Receives 300 queries/year. 30% of books from first-time authors; 99% from unagented writers. Pays royalty on wholesale price. Offers very modest advance.** Accepts simultaneous submissions. Responds in 2 weeks to queries; 1 month to mss. Book catalog free or online; ms guidelines online.

O— Stenhouse publishes exclusively professional books for teachers, K-12.

Nonfiction Subjects include education (specializing in literacy). "All our books are a combination of theory and practice." No children's books or student texts. Query with SASE, or submit outline. Reviews artwork/photos as part of ms package. Send photocopies.

Recent Title(s) *Reconsidering Read-Aloud*, by Mary Lee Hahn; *Writing for Real*, by Ross M. Burkhardt; *Knowing How*, by Mary C. McMackin and Barbara Seigel.

STERLING PUBLISHING

387 Park Ave. S., New York NY 10016. (212)532-7160. Fax: (212)213-2495. Website: www.sterlingpub.com. **Acquisitions:** Category Editor (i.e., Craft Editor or Children's Editor). Estab. 1949. Publishes hardcover and paperback originals and reprints. **Pays royalty. Offers advance.** Does not accept simultaneous submissions. Ms guidelines online.

Imprints Sterling/Chapelle; Lark; Sterling/Tamos; Sterling/Prolific Impressions.

O— Sterling publishes highly illustrated, accessible, hands-on, practical books for adults and children.

Nonfiction Publishes nonfiction only. Children's/juvenile, how-to, humor, reference, adult. Subjects include alternative lifestyles, animals, art/architecture, ethnic, gardening, health/medicine, hobbies, New Age, recreation, science, sports, fiber arts, games and puzzles, children's humor, children's science, nature and activities, pets, wine, home decorating, dolls and puppets, ghosts, UFOs, woodworking, crafts, medieval, Celtic subjects, alternative health and healing, new consciousness. Submit outline, 1 sample chapter, publishing history, SASE. Reviews artwork/photos as part of ms package. Send photocopies.

Recent Title(s) *AARP Crash Course in Estate Planning*, by Michael Palermo and Ric Edelman.

STIPES PUBLISHING LLC

P.O. Box 526, Champaign IL 61824-9933. (217)356-8391. Fax: (217)356-5753. E-mail: stipes@soltec.net. Website: www.stipes.com. **Acquisitions:** Benjamin H. Watts, (engineering, science, business); Robert Watts (agriculture, music, and physical education). Estab. 1925. Publishes hardcover and paperback originals. **Publishes 15-30 titles/year. 50% of books from first-time authors; 95% from unagented writers. Pays 15% maximum royalty on retail price.** Publishes book 4 months after acceptance of ms. Does not accept simultaneous submissions. Responds in 2 months to queries. Ms guidelines online.

O— Stipes Publishing is "oriented towards the education market and educational books with some emphasis in the trade market."

Nonfiction Technical (some areas), textbook (on business/economics, music, chemistry, CADD, agriculture/horticulture, environmental education, recreation, physical education). Subjects include agriculture/horticulture, business/economics, music/dance, nature/environment, recreation, science. "All of our books in the trade area are books that also have a college text market. No books unrelated to educational fields taught at the college level." Submit outline, 1 sample chapter.

Recent Title(s) *The AutoCAD 2004 Workbook*, by Philip Age and Ronald Sutliff.

STOEGER PUBLISHING CO.

17603 Indian Head Hwy., Suite 200, Accokeek MD 20607. (301)283-6300. Fax: (301)283-4783. Website: www.st oegerindustries.com. **Acquisitions:** Jay Langston, publisher. Estab. 1925. Publishes hardback and trade paperback originals. **Publishes 12-15 titles/year. Royalty varies, depending on ms. Offers advance.** Accepts simultaneous submissions. Responds in 2 months to queries. Book catalog online.

○→ Stoeger publishes books on hunting, shooting sports, fishing, cooking, nature, and wildlife.

Nonfiction Specializes in reference and how-to books that pertain to hunting, fishing, and appeal to gun enthusiasts. How-to, reference. Subjects include cooking/foods/nutrition, sports. Submit outline, sample chapters.

Fiction Specializes in outdoor-related fiction.

Recent Title(s) *Escape in Iraq: The Thomas Hamill Story*; *Gun Trader's Guide, 26th Ed.*; *Hunting Whitetails East & West.*

SUN BOOKS/SUN PUBLISHING

P.O. Box 5588, Santa Fe NM 87502-5588. (505)471-5177. E-mail: info@sunbooks.com. Website: www.sunbooks .com. **Acquisitions:** Skip Whitson, director. Publishes trade paperback originals and reprints. **Publishes 10-15 titles/year. 5% of books from first-time authors; 90% from unagented writers. Pays 5% royalty on retail price, or makes outright purchase.** Publishes book 16 months after acceptance of ms. Responds in 2 months to queries and proposals; 6 months to mss. Book catalog online.

Nonfiction Biography, cookbook, how-to, humor, illustrated book, reference, self-help, technical. Subjects include Americana, anthropology/archeology, business/economics, cooking/foods/nutrition, creative nonfiction, education, government/politics, health/medicine, history, language/literature, memoirs, money/finance, multicultural, nature/environment, philosophy, psychology, regional, religion, sociology, travel, women's issues/ studies, metaphysics, motivational, inspirational, Oriental studies. Query with SASE, preferably via e-mail. Reviews artwork/photos as part of ms package. Send photocopies.

Recent Title(s) *Eight Pillars of Prosperity*, by James Allen; *Ambition and Success*, by Orson Swett Marden; *Cheerfulness as a Life Power*, by Orson Swett Marden.

SUNBELT PUBLICATIONS

1250 Fayette St., El Cajon CA 92020. (619)258-4911. Fax: (619)258-4916. E-mail: mail@sunbeltpub.com. Website: www.sunbeltbooks.com. **Acquisitions:** Jennifer Redmond, publications coordinator; Lowell Lindsay, publisher. Publishes hardcover and trade paperback originals and reprints. **Publishes 6-10 titles/year. Receives 30 queries and 20 mss/year. 80% of books from first-time authors; 100% from unagented writers. Pays 10-14% royalty.** Accepts simultaneous submissions. Responds in 1 month to queries and proposals; 3 months to mss. Book catalog free or online; ms guidelines online.

○→ "We are interested in the cultural and natural history of the 'The Californias' in the U.S. and Mexico."

Nonfiction "We publish multi-language pictorials, natural science and outdoor guidebooks, regional references, and stories that celebrate the land and its people." Coffee table book, how-to, reference, guidebooks. Subjects include anthropology/archeology, history (regional), nature/environment (natural history), recreation, regional, travel. Query with SASE, or submit proposal package including outline, 1-2 sample chapters. Reviews artwork/photos as part of ms package. Send photocopies.

Recent Title(s) *Mexican Slang*, by Linton Robinson (language/reference); *Weekend Driver San Diego*, by Jack Brandais (regional guidebook).

Tips "Our audience is interested in natural science or the cultural history of California and Baja California, Mexico. They want specific information that is accurate and up-to-date. Our books are written for an adult audience that is primarily interested in adventure and the outdoors. Our guidebooks lead to both personal and armchair adventure and travel. Authors must be willing to actively promote their book through book signings, the media, and lectures/slide shows for intended audiences."

SYRACUSE UNIVERSITY PRESS

621 Skytop Road, Suite 110, Syracuse NY 13244-5290. (315)443-5534. Fax: (315)443-5545. Website: syracuseuni versitypress.syr.edu. **Acquisitions:** Peter B. Webber, director. Estab. 1943. **Publishes 50 titles/year. 25% of books from first-time authors; 75% from unagented writers. Pays royalty on net receipts. Offers advance.** Publishes book an average of 15 months after acceptance of ms. Does not accept simultaneous submissions. Book catalog for 9×12 SAE with 3 first-class stamps; ms guidelines online.

○→ Currently emphasizing television, Jewish studies, Middle East topics. De-emphasizing peace studies.

Nonfiction Subjects include regional. "Special opportunity in our nonfiction program for freelance writers of books on New York state, sports history, Jewish studies, the Middle East, religious studies, television, and popular culture. Provide precise descriptions of subjects, along with background description of project. The author must make a case for the importance of his or her subject.'' Query with SASE, or submit outline, 2 sample chapters. Reviews artwork/photos as part of ms package.

Recent Title(s) *A Time Between Ashes and Roses*, by Adonis, translated from Arabic by Shawkat M. Toorawa; *In the Path of Hizbullah*, by A. Nizar Hamzeh; *Anything for a T-Shirt: Fred Lebow and the New York City Marathon, the World's Greatest Footrace*, by Ron Rubin.

Tips ''We're seeking well-written and well-researched books that will make a significant contribution to the subject areas listed above and will be well-received in the marketplace.''

NAN A. TALESE

Imprint of Doubleday, 1745 Broadway, New York NY 10019. (212)782-8918. Fax: (212)782-8448. Website: www.nanatalese.com. **Acquisitions:** Nan A. Talese, publisher and editorial director; Coates Bateman, editor; Lorna Owen, associate editor. Publishes hardcover originals. **Publishes 15 titles/year. Receives 400 queries and 400 mss/year. Pays variable royalty on retail price. Offers varying advance.** Publishes book 1 year after acceptance of ms. Accepts simultaneous submissions. Responds in 1 week to queries; 2 weeks to proposals and mss. *Agented submissions only.*

    ○━ Nan A. Talese publishes nonfiction with a powerful guiding narrative and relevance to larger cultural interests, and literary fiction of the highest quality.

Nonfiction Biography. Subjects include contemporary culture, history, philosophy, sociology.

Fiction Literary. Well-written narratives with a compelling story line, good characterization and use of language. ''We like stories with an edge.''

Recent Title(s) *Saturday*, by Ian McEwan; *Albion: The Origins of the English Imagination*, by Peter Ackroyd; *Oryx and Crake*, by Margaret Atwood.

Tips ''Audience is highly literate people interested in story, information and insight. We want well-written material submitted by agents only. See our website.''

JEREMY P. TARCHER, INC.

Imprint of Penguin Group (USA), Inc., 375 Hudson St., New York NY 10014. (212)366-2000. Website: www.peng uinputnam.com. Publisher: Joel Fotinos. **Acquisitions:** Mitch Horowitz, executive editor; Terri Hennessy, associate editor; Sara Carder, senior editor. Estab. 1972. Publishes hardcover and trade paperback originals and reprints. **Publishes 40-50 titles/year. Receives 750 queries and 750 mss/year. 10% of books from first-time authors; 15% from unagented writers. Pays royalty. Offers advance.** Accepts simultaneous submissions. Book catalog free.

    ○━ Tarcher's vision is to publish ideas and works about human consciousness that are large enough to include all aspects of human experience.

Nonfiction Self-help, spirituality, social issues. Subjects include gay/lesbian, health/medicine, nature/environment, philosophy, psychology, religion, women's issues/studies, Eastern and Western religions, metaphysics, politics. Query with SASE.

Recent Title(s) *The Faith of George W. Bush*, by Stephen Mansfield; *The European Dream*, by Jeremy Rifkin; *The Secret Teachings of All Ages*, by Manly P. Hall.

Tips ''Our audience seeks personal growth through books. Understand the imprint's focus and categories.''

TCU PRESS

P.O. Box 298300, TCU, Fort Worth TX 76129. (817)257-7822. Fax: (817)257-5075. **Acquisitions:** Judy Alter, director; James Ward Lee, acquisitions editor; Susan Petty, editor. Estab. 1966. Publishes hardcover originals, some reprints. **Publishes 9-12 titles/year. 10% of books from first-time authors; 75% from unagented writers. Pays 10% royalty on net receipts.** Publishes book 16 months after acceptance of ms. Does not accept simultaneous submissions. Responds in 3 months to queries.

    ○━ TCU publishes ''scholarly works and regional titles of significance focusing on the history and literature of the American West.''

Nonfiction Biography, coffee table book, scholarly. Subjects include Americana, art/architecture, contemporary culture, ethnic, history, language/literature, multicultural, regional, women's issues/studies, American studies, criticism. Query with SASE. Reviews artwork/photos as part of ms package.

Fiction Historical, young adult, contemporary. No mysteries or science fiction.

Recent Title(s) *Adventures With a Texas Humanist*, by James Ward Lee; *Jim Coartright of Fort Worth: His Life and Legend*, by Robert K. Dearment; *Texas Literary Outlaws*, by Steven L. Davis.

Tips ''Regional and/or Texana nonfiction has best chance of breaking into our firm. Our list focuses on the history of literature of the American West, although recently we have branched out into literary criticism, women's studies, and Mexican-American studies.''

⦿ TEACHER CURRICULUM LLC

1710 E. Trent, Suite B, Spokane WA 99202. Fax: (509)533-1915. E-mail: dennisr@goteachit.com. Submissions E-mail: steved@goteachit.com. Website: www.goteachit.com. Estab. 2004. Publishes electronic originals. **Publishes 1,000 titles/year. Receives 500 queries and 500 mss/year. 90% of books from first-time authors; 100% from unagented writers. Pays 10-20% royalty on retail price.** Publishes book 3 months after acceptance of ms. Accepts simultaneous submissions. Responds in 1 month. Book catalog online.

Nonfiction Booklets, children's/juvenile, reference, textbook, traditional or non-traditional curriculum. Subjects include animals, education, history, social sciences, world affairs, curriculum. "We generally write using established templates or formats. We accept ideas for development into our formats." Submit proposal package including outline, and clearly state object of curriculum. Reviews artwork/photos as part of ms package. Send photocopies.

Fiction Adventure, comic books, confession, erotica, ethnic, experimental, fantasy, feminist, gay/lesbian, gothic, hi-lo, historical, horror, humor, juvenile, literary, mainstream/contemporary, military/war, multicultural, multimedia, mystery, occult, picture books, plays, poetry, poetry in translation, regional, religious, romance, science fiction, short story collections, spiritual, sports, suspense, western, young adult. "We publish curriculum in any of the above areas. We publish original fiction, but it must be developed into a usable curriculum for use in a classroom." Submit synopsis, curriculum outline.

Poetry "We publish original poetry with a usable curriculum for use in primary and secondary classrooms." Submit any sample poems.

Recent Title(s) *Rollercoaster*, by Marcia Davis (elementary curriculum, nonfiction); *Statehood*, by Steven Denny (secondary curriculum, nonfiction); *Frindle Curriculum*, by Steven Denny (primary curriculum, fiction).

Tips "Go to our website and order a product in the specific area of interest."

⦿ TEACHERS COLLEGE PRESS

1234 Amsterdam Ave., New York NY 10027. (212)678-3929. Fax: (212)678-4149. Website: www.teacherscollegepress.com. Director: Carole P. Saltz. **Acquisitions:** Brian Ellerbeck, executive acquisitions editor. Estab. 1904. Publishes hardcover and paperback originals and reprints. **Publishes 60 titles/year. Pays industry standard royalty. Offers advance.** Publishes book 1 year after acceptance of ms. Does not accept simultaneous submissions. Responds in 2 months to queries. Book catalog free; ms guidelines online.

 ○➔ Teachers College Press publishes a wide range of educational titles for all levels of students: early childhood to higher education. "Publishing books that respond to, examine, and confront issues pertaining to education, teacher training, and school reform."

Nonfiction Subjects include computers/electronic, education, film/cinema/stage, government/politics, history, philosophy, sociology, women's issues/studies. "This university press concentrates on books in the field of education in the broadest sense, from early childhood to higher education: good classroom practices, teacher training, special education, innovative trends and issues, administration and supervision, film, continuing and adult education, all areas of the curriculum, computers, guidance and counseling, and the politics, economics, philosophy, sociology, and history of education. We have recently added women's studies to our list. The Press also issues classroom materials for students at all levels, with a strong emphasis on reading and writing and social studies." Submit outline, sample chapters.

Recent Title(s) *Cultural Miseducation: In Search of a Democratic Solution*, by Jane Roland Martin.

TEN SPEED PRESS

P.O. Box 7123, Berkeley CA 94707. (510)559-1600. Fax: (510)524-1052. E-mail: info@tenspeed.com. Website: www.tenspeed.com. **Acquisitions:** Phil Wood, president; Lorena Jones, Ten Speed Press publisher; Aaron Wehmer, Ten Speed Press editorial director; Jo Ann Deck, Celestial Arts/Crossing Press publisher. Estab. 1971. Publishes trade paperback originals and reprints. **Publishes 120 titles/year; imprint publishes 70 titles/year. 40% of books from first-time authors; 40% from unagented writers. Pays 15-20% royalty on net receipts. Offers $2,500 average advance.** Publishes book 1 year after acceptance of ms. Accepts simultaneous submissions. Responds in 3 months to queries. Book catalog for 9×12 SAE with 6 first-class stamps; ms guidelines online.

Imprints Celestial Arts; Crossing Press; Tricycle Press.

 ○➔ Ten Speed Press publishes authoritative books for an audience interested in innovative ideas. Currently emphasizing cookbooks, career, business, alternative education, and offbeat general nonfiction gift books.

Nonfiction Subjects include business/economics, child guidance/parenting, cooking/foods/nutrition, gardening, health/medicine, money/finance, nature/environment, New Age (mind/body/spirit), recreation, science. "No fiction." Query with SASE, or submit proposal package including sample chapters.

Recent Title(s) *How to Be Happy, Dammit*, by Karen Salmansohn; *The Bread Baker's Apprentice*, by Peter Reinhart.

Tips "We like books from people who really know their subject, rather than people who think they've spotted a trend to capitalize on. We like books that will sell for a long time, rather than nine-day wonders. Our audience consists of a well-educated, slightly weird group of people who like food, the outdoors, and take a light, but serious, approach to business and careers. Study the backlist of each publisher you're submitting to and tailor your proposal to what you perceive as their needs. Nothing gets a publisher's attention like someone who knows what he or she is talking about, and nothing falls flat like someone who obviously has no idea who he or she is submitting to."

N TEXAS A&M UNIVERSITY PRESS

College Station TX 77843-4354. (979)845-1436. Fax: (979)847-8752. E-mail: fdl@tampress.tamu.edu. Website: www.tamu.edu/upress. **Acquisitions:** Mary Lenn Dixon, editor-in-chief (presidential studies, anthropology, borderlands, western history); Shannon Davies, senior editor (natural history, agriculture). Estab. 1974. **Publishes 60 titles/year. Pays royalty.** Publishes book 1 year after acceptance of ms. Does not accept simultaneous submissions. Responds in 1 month to queries. Book catalog free; ms guidelines online.

> O— Texas A&M University Press publishes a wide range of nonfiction, scholarly trade, and crossover books of regional and national interest, "reflecting the interests of the university, the broader scholarly community, and the people of our state and region."

Nonfiction Subjects include agriculture/horticulture, anthropology/archeology, art/architecture, business/economics, government/politics, history (American and Western), language/literature (Texas and western), military/war, nature/environment, regional (Texas and the Southwest), Mexican-US borderlands studies, nautical archaeology, ethnic studies, presidential studies, business history. Query with SASE.

Recent Title(s) *The White House World*, edited by Martha Joynt Kuma and Terry Sullivan.

Tips Proposal requirements are posted on the website.

N TEXAS STATE HISTORICAL ASSOCIATION

2.306 Richardson Hall, University Station, Austin TX 78712. (512)471-1525. Fax: (512)471-1551. Website: www.tsha.utexas.edu. **Acquisitions:** J. Kent Calder, director of publications. Estab. 1897. Publishes hardcover and trade paperback originals and reprints. **Publishes 8 titles/year. Receives 50 queries and 50 mss/year. 10% of books from first-time authors; 95% from unagented writers. Pays 10% royalty on net cash proceeds.** Publishes book 1 year after acceptance of ms. Does not accept simultaneous submissions. Responds in 2-3 months to mss. Book catalog and ms guidelines free.

> O— "We are interested in scholarly historical articles and books on any aspect of Texas history and culture."

Nonfiction Biography, coffee table book, illustrated book, reference, scholarly. Subjects include history. Query with SASE. Reviews artwork/photos as part of ms package. Send photocopies.

Recent Title(s) *Sea of Mud: The Retreat of the Mexican Army after San Jacinto*, by Gregg J. Dimmick; *Civil War and Revolution on the Rio Grande Frontier: A Narrative and Photographic History*, by Jerry Thompson and Lawrence T. Jones III.

THIRD WORLD PRESS

P.O. Box 19730, Chicago IL 60619. (773)651-0700. Fax: (773)651-7286. E-mail: twpress3@aol.com. Publisher: Haki R. Madhubuti. **Acquisitions:** Bennett Johnson. Estab. 1967. Publishes hardcover and trade paperback originals and reprints. **Publishes 20 titles/year. Receives 200-300 queries and 200 mss/year. 20% of books from first-time authors; 80% from unagented writers. Compensation based upon royalties. Individual arrangement with author depending on the book, etc.** Publishes book 18 months after acceptance of ms. Accepts simultaneous submissions. Responds in 6 months to queries; 5 months to mss. Book catalog free; ms guidelines for #10 SASE.

> • Third World Press is open to submissions in July only.

Nonfiction Children's/juvenile, illustrated book, reference, self-help, textbook, ethnic/African-centered; African-American materials. Subjects include anthropology/archeology, education, ethnic, government/politics, health/medicine, history, language/literature, philosophy, psychology, regional, religion, sociology, women's issues/studies, Black studies, literary criticism. Query with SASE, or submit outline, 5 sample chapters. Reviews artwork/photos as part of ms package. Send photocopies.

Fiction Ethnic, feminist, historical, juvenile (animal, easy-to-read, fantasy, historical, contemporary), literary, mainstream/contemporary, picture books, plays, short story collections, young adult (easy-to-read/teen, folktales, historical), African-centered, African-American materials, preschool/picture book. "We primarily publish nonfiction, but will consider fiction by and about Blacks." Query with SASE, or submit outline, 5 sample chapters, synopsis.

Poetry Ethnic/African-centered and African-American materials. Submit complete ms.

Recent Title(s) *Asunder*, by Eric Lee Bauers (novel); *Run Toward Fear*, by Haki R. Madhubuti; *My Thoughts, Your Journal, Our Book*, by Abe Thompson.

N ⊘ THUNDER'S MOUTH PRESS

Imprint of Avalon Publishing Group, 245 W. 17th St., New York NY 10011. (646)375-2570. Fax: (646)375-2571. Website: www.thundersmouth.com. Publisher: John Oakes. **Acquisitions:** Acquisitions Editor. Estab. 1982. Publishes hardcover and trade paperback originals and reprints, almost exclusively nonfiction. **Publishes 70-80 titles/year. Receives 4,000 queries/year. 15% from unagented writers. Pays 7-10% royalty on retail price. Offers $2,500 average advance.** Publishes book 8 months after acceptance of ms. Does not accept simultaneous submissions. Responds in 2 months to queries.

Nonfiction Biography. Subjects include government/politics, popular culture. *No unsolicited mss.*

Recent Title(s) *Chance*, by Amir Aczel.

TIDEWATER PUBLISHERS

Cornell Maritime Press, Inc., P.O. Box 456, Centreville MD 21617-0456. (410)758-1075. Fax: (410)758-6849. Website: www.cmptp.com. **Acquisitions:** Michelle M. Slavin, managing editor. Estab. 1938. Publishes hardcover and paperback originals. **Publishes 7-9 titles/year. 41% of books from first-time authors; 99% from unagented writers. Pays 7½-15% royalty on retail price.** Publishes book 1 year after acceptance of ms. Does not accept simultaneous submissions. Responds in 2 months to queries.

    O⟶ Tidewater Publishers issues adult nonfiction works related to the Chesapeake Bay area, Delmarva, or Maryland in general.

Nonfiction Regional subjects only. Children's/juvenile, cookbook, illustrated book, reference. Subjects include art/architecture, history, regional, natural history, folklore, Chesapeake watercraft. Query with SASE, prospectus, list of publications, outline, and 1 sample chapter.

Fiction Regional juvenile fiction only. Query with SASE, prospectus, list of publications, outline, and 1 sample chapter.

Recent Title(s) *Sequoia: Presidential Yacht*, by Giles Kelly; *The Mystery of Mary Surratt*, by Rebecca C. Jones.

Tips "Our audience is made up of readers interested in works that are specific to the Chesapeake Bay and Delmarva Peninsula area. We do not publish personal narratives, adult fiction, or poetry."

TILBURY HOUSE, PUBLISHERS

Imprint of Harpswell Press, Inc., 2 Mechanic St., Gardiner ME 04345. (207)582-1899. Fax: (207)582-8227. E-mail: tilbury@tilburyhouse.com. Website: www.tilburyhouse.com. Publisher: Jennifer Bunting (New England, maritime, children's). **Acquisitions:** Audrey Maynard, children's book editor. Estab. 1990. Publishes hardcover originals, trade paperback originals. **Publishes 10 titles/year. Pays royalty.** Book catalog free; ms guidelines online.

Nonfiction Regional adult biography/history/maritime/nature, and children's picture books. Submit complete ms. Reviews artwork/photos as part of ms package. Send photocopies.

Recent Title(s) *Sea Struck*; *Say Something*, by Peggy Moss; *The Goat Lady*, by Jane Bregoli.

TIMBERWOLF PRESS, INC.

Website: www.timberwolfpress.com. Ms guidelines online.

    • "We accept electronic queries only."

A MEGAN TINGLEY BOOKS

Imprint of Little, Brown & Co., 1271 Avenue of the Americas, New York NY 10020. (212)522-8700. Fax: (212)522-7997. Website: www.lb-kids.com. **Acquisitions:** Megan Tingley, editor-in-chief; Nancy Consescu, assistant editor. Publishes hardcover and trade paperback originals and reprints. **Publishes 80-100 titles/year; imprint publishes 10-20 titles/year. Receives 500-1,000 queries and 500-1,000 mss/year. 2% of books from first-time authors; 5% from unagented writers. Pays 0-15% royalty on retail price, or makes outright purchase.** Publishes book 1-2 years after acceptance of ms. Accepts simultaneous submissions. Responds in 1 month to queries; 6-8 weeks to proposals and mss.

    O⟶ Megan Tingley Books is an imprint of the children's book department of Little, Brown and Company. Currently looking for all formats with special interest in humor, music, multicultural, supernatural, narrative nonfiction, poetry, and unusual art styles. No fairy tales.

Nonfiction Children's/juvenile. Subjects include animals, art/architecture, cooking/foods/nutrition, creative nonfiction, ethnic, gay/lesbian, history, language/literature, memoirs, multicultural, music/dance, photography. *Agented submissions and queries only.* Ideally, books should be about a subject that hasn't been dealt with for children before. Reviews artwork/photos as part of ms package. Send photocopies. No original pieces.

Fiction Picture books, middle grade, young adult. Adventure, fantasy, gay/lesbian, historical, humor, multicultural, suspense, political, chick lit. *Agented submissions only.* No genre novels (romance, mystery, science fiction, etc.).

Recent Title(s) *Luna*, by Julie Ann Peters; *Harlem Stomp!*, by Laban Carrick Hill; *You Read to Me, I'll Read to You*, by Mary Ann Hoberman; illustrated by Michael Emberley.

Tips "Do your research. Know our submission policy. Do not fax or call."

THE TOBY PRESS, LTD.

P.O. Box 8531, New Milford CT 06776-8531. Fax: (203)830-8512. Website: www.tobypress.com. **Acquisitions:** Editorial Director (fiction, biography). Publishes hardcover originals and paperbacks. **Publishes 20-25 titles/ year. Receives over 2,000 queries/year. 20% of books from first-time authors; 10% from unagented writers. Offers advance.** Publishes book up to 2 year after acceptance of ms. Accepts simultaneous submissions.

O➝ The Toby Press publishes literary fiction.

Nonfiction Biography.

Fiction Literary.

Recent Title(s) *Foiglman*, by Aharon Megged; *With*, by Donald Harington.

N TORAH AURA PRODUCTIONS

4423 Fruitland Ave., Los Angeles CA 90058. (800)238-6724. Fax: (323)585-0327. E-mail: misrad@torahaura.com. Website: www.torahaura.com. **Acquisitions:** Jane Golub. Estab. 1982. Publishes hardcover and trade paperback originals. **Publishes 25 titles/year; imprint publishes 10 titles/year. Receives 5 queries and 10 mss/year. 2% of books from first-time authors; 100% from unagented writers. Pays 10% royalty on whole- sale price.** Publishes book 2-3 years after acceptance of ms. Accepts simultaneous submissions. Responds in 6 months to mss. Book catalog free.

O➝ Torah Aura only publishes educational materials for Jewish classrooms.

Nonfiction Children's/juvenile, textbook. Subjects include language/literature (Hebrew), religion (Jewish). No picture books. Query with SASE. Reviews artwork/photos as part of ms package. Send photocopies.

Fiction Juvenile, religious, young adult. All fiction must have Jewish interest. No picture books. Query with SASE. Reviews artwork/photos as part of ms package. Send photocopies.

Recent Title(s) *I Have Some Questions About God*, by Rabbis Bradley Shavit Artson, Ed Feinstein, Elyse Frish- man, Joshua Hammerman, Jeffrey K. Salkin, and Sybil Sheridan; *Let's Talk About God*, by Dorothy K. Kripke.

N TOWER PUBLISHING

588 Saco Rd., Standish ME 04084. (207)642-5400. Fax: (207)642-5463. E-mail: info@towerpub.com. Website: www.towerpub.com. **Acquisitions:** Michael Lyons, president. Estab. 1772. Publishes hardcover originals and reprints, trade paperback originals. **Publishes 22 titles/year. Receives 60 queries and 30 mss/year. 10% of books from first-time authors; 90% from unagented writers. Pays royalty on net receipts.** Publishes book 6 months after acceptance of ms. Accepts simultaneous submissions. Responds in 1 month to queries; 2 months to proposals and mss. Book catalog and ms guidelines online.

O➝ Tower Publishing specializes in business and professional directories and legal books.

Nonfiction Reference. Subjects include business/economics. Looking for legal books of a national stature. Query with SASE, or submit outline.

N TOWLEHOUSE PUBLISHING CO.

394 W. Main St., Suite B-9, Hendersonville TN 37075. (615)338-0283. E-mail: vermonte@aol.com. Website: www.towlehouse.com. **Acquisitions:** Mike Towle, president/publisher (nonfiction, sports). Publishes hard- cover, trade paperback, and mass market paperback originals, and hardcover and trade paperback reprints. **Publishes 8-10 titles/year. Receives 100-250 mss/year. 75% of books from first-time authors; 80% from unagented writers. Pays 8-20% royalty on wholesale price. Offers $500-2,000 advance.** Publishes book 9 months after acceptance of ms. Accepts simultaneous submissions. Responds in 4-6 months to queries.

O➝ "We publish nonfiction books about America that are informative and entertaining." Currently empha- sizing Potent Quotables and Good Golf! series of books.

Nonfiction "I don't solicit children's books, poetry, or non-Christian religious titles. Authors using profanity, obscenities, or other vulgar or immoral language in their books need not contact me." Query with SASE, or submit proposal package including outline, 2 sample chapters, author bio, letter containing marketing plan. Reviews artwork/photos as part of ms package. Send photocopies.

Recent Title(s) *Quotable Dean Smith*, by David Scott (Potent Quotables); *Golf in the Year 2100*, by Bob Labbance (Good Golf!).

Tips "Send 1 proposal for 1 book at a time. If you send me a query listing 3, 4 or more 'ideas' for books, I will immediately know that you lack the commitment needed to author a book. Send a SASE for anything you send me. I don't accept fiction unless you're a bestselling fiction author."

TRAFALGAR SQUARE PUBLISHING

P.O. Box 257, N. Pomfret VT 05053-0257. (802)457-1911. Fax: (802)457-1913. E-mail: tsquare@sover.net. Website: www.horseandriderbooks.com. Publisher: Caroline Robbins. **Acquisitions:** Martha Cook, managing editor. Estab. 1985. Publishes hardcover and trade paperback originals and reprints. **Publishes 10 titles/year. Pays royalty. Offers advance.** Responds in 2 months to queries.

- ''We publish high quality instructional books for horsemen and horsewomen, always with the horse's welfare in mind.''

Nonfiction ''We publish books for intermediate to advanced riders and horsemen.'' Subjects include animals (horses). ''No stories, children's books, or horse biographies.'' Query with SASE, or submit proposal package including 1-2 sample chapters, outline or TOC, letter of writer's qualifications, and audience for book's subject.

Recent Title(s) *Bombproof Your Horse*, by Rick Relicano; *Clinton Anderson's Down Under Horsemanship*, by Clinton Anderson.

TRAILS MEDIA GROUP, INC.

P.O. Box 317, Black Earth WI 53515. (608)767-8100. Fax: (608)767-5444. E-mail: books@wistrails.com. Website: www.trailsbooks.com. Director: Eva Solcova. **Acquisitions:** Stan Stoga, acquisitions editor. Publishes hardcover originals, trade paperback originals, and reprints. **Publishes 12 titles/year. Pays royalty. Offers advance.** Does not accept simultaneous submissions. Responds in 2 months to proposals. Ms guidelines online.

Imprints Trails Books; Prairie Oak Press.

- Follow online submission guidelines.
- Trails Media Group publishes exclusively Midwest regional nonfiction. Currently emphasizing travel, sports, recreation, home and garden.

Nonfiction ''Any work considered must have a strong tie to Wisconsin and/or the Midwest region.'' General nonfiction. Subjects include art/architecture, gardening, history, regional, sports, travel, folklore, general trade subjects. No poetry or fiction. Query with SASE, or submit outline, 1 sample chapter.

Recent Title(s) *Before They Were the Packers*, by Dennis J. Gullickson and Carl Hanson; *Great Wisconsin Romantic Weekends*, by Christine des Garennes; *Horsing Around in Wisconsin*, by Anne M. Connor.

Tips ''We publish works about Wisconsin, Minnesota, Illinois, Iowa, and Indiana.''

TRANS NATION

2715 Buford Hwy. NE, Atlanta GA 30324. Fax: (404)634-3739. E-mail: info@transnation.us. Website: www.transnation.us. **Acquisitions:** Ronald Ashley, editor (general submissions); and Juan Maldonado, editor (Spanish submissions). Estab. 2001. Publishes hardcover, trade paperback, mass market paperback originals, and electronic originals and reprints. **Publishes 10-15 titles/year. Receives 45 queries and 20 mss/year. 80% of books from first-time authors; 100% from unagented writers. Pays 15-20% royalty on wholesale price.** Publishes book 9 months after acceptance of ms. Accepts simultaneous submissions. Responds in 1 month to queries; 3 months to proposals and mss. Book catalog online; ms guidelines by e-mail.

Nonfiction Audiocassettes, booklets, children's/juvenile, multimedia, reference, bilingual safety training materials (especially English-Spanish and Spanish-English). Subjects include contemporary culture, education, language/literature, multicultural, translation, training materials. ''We specialize in Spanish/English publications, translation, and education materials.'' Submit complete ms with cover letter and outline. Reviews artwork/photos as part of ms package. Send photocopies.

Fiction Erotica, ethnic, multicultural, will consider quality work in other categories. Does not want poetry or science fiction. ''We will begin publishing fiction in 2004, and are interested in manuscripts geared toward a multicultural audience.'' Submit proposal package including 1 sample chapter, synopsis.

Recent Title(s) *1,000 Spanish Commands: Public Safety*, by Irene Walsh (translation); *Ingles Rapido 1,000: Construccion*, by Irene Welsh (translation).

Tips ''Audience is multicultural, English and Spanish speakers. Please be sure to include appropriate contact information. If we are interested, we will contact you normally within 30 days of receipt of manuscript.''

TRANSNATIONAL PUBLISHERS, INC.

410 Saw Mill River Rd., Ardsley NY 10502. (914)693-5100. Fax: (914)693-4430. E-mail: info@transnationalpubs.com. Website: www.transnationalpubs.com. Publisher: Heike Fenton. Estab. 1980. **Publishes 45-50 titles/year. Receives 40-50 queries and 30 mss/year. 60% of books from first-time authors; 95% from unagented writers. Pays royalty.** Publishes book 6-9 months after acceptance of ms. Accepts simultaneous submissions. Responds in 1 month to queries. Book catalog and ms guidelines free.

- ''We provide specialized international law publications for the teaching of law and law-related subjects in law school classroom, clinic, and continuing legal education settings.'' Currently emphasizing any area of international law that is considered a current issue/event.

Nonfiction Reference, technical, textbook. Subjects include business/economics, government/politics, women's issues/studies, international law. Query with SASE, or submit proposal package including sample chapters, TOC, and introduction.

Recent Title(s) *Defending the Environment: Civil Society Strategies to Enforce International Environmental Law*, by Linda A. Malone and Scott Pasternack; *Forum Non Conveniens in the Modern Age*, by Michael Karayanni; *The First Decade of Nafta: The Future of Free Trade in North America*, by Kevin C. Kennedy.

TRAVELERS' TALES

853 Alma St., Palo Alto CA 94301. (650)462-2110. Fax: (650)462-2114. E-mail: ttales@travelerstales.com. Website: www.travelerstales.com. **Acquisitions:** James O'Reilly and Larry Habegger, series editors; Sean O'Reilley, editor-at-large (sales/publicity). Publishes inspirational travel books, mostly anthologies and travel advice books. **Publishes 8-10 titles/year. Pays $100 honorarium for anthology pieces.** Accepts simultaneous submissions. Ms guidelines online.

Imprints Travelers' Tales Guides; Footsteps; Travelers' Tales Classics.

• "Due to the volume of submissions, we do not respond unless the material submitted meets our immediate editorial needs. All stories are read and filed for future use contingent upon meeting editorial guidelines."

Nonfiction Subjects include all aspects of travel.

Recent Title(s) *The Best Travelers' Tales 2004*; *Hyenas Laughed at Me and Now I Know Why*; *Who's Panties Are Those?* (women & travel humor book).

Tips "We publish personal nonfiction stories and anecdotes—funny, illuminating, adventurous, frightening, or grim. Stories should reflect that unique alchemy that occurs when you enter unfamiliar territory and begin to see the world differently as a result. Stories that have already been published, including book excerpts, are welcome as long as the authors retain the copyright or can obtain permission from the copyright holder to reprint the material. We do not publish fiction."

☑ TREBLE HEART BOOKS

1284 Overlook Dr., Sierra Vista AZ 85635. (520)458-5602. Fax: (520)458-5618. E-mail: submissions@trebleheart books.com. Website: www.trebleheartbooks.com. **Acquisitions:** Lee Emory, owner/publisher (fiction, nonfiction, romance, mystery, suspense, paranormal, metaphysical, historical, Westerns, thrillers—no children's books, poetry, autobiography). Estab. 2001. Publishes trade paperback originals and reprints (limited), and electronic originals. **Publishes approximately 48 titles/year. Receives 500 queries and 1,000 mss/year. 30% of books from first-time authors; 90% from unagented writers. Pays 15-35% royalty on wholesale price, or retail price.** Publishes book 8-12 months after acceptance of ms. Does not accept simultaneous submissions. Responds in 3 weeks to queries; 2 months to proposals; 3-4 months to mss. Ms guidelines online.

Imprints MountainView (inspirational fiction and nonfiction, most faiths); Sundowners (Westerns); Whooodoo Mysteries (from cozy to hardboiled).

○⌐ New submissions closed until late Spring 2005.

Nonfiction General nonfiction, how-to, humor, self-help. Subjects include creative nonfiction, health/medicine, New Age, psychology, religion, spirituality, women's issues/studies. "Writing skills must be top notch to make it here. We have 10 editors to serve. Study the guidelines and write in the lively, active voice with a fresh slant." Submit complete ms. Query by e-mail. Reviews artwork/photos as part of ms package. Send TIFF or PDF files on CD or via e-mail.

Fiction Adventure, fantasy, historical, horror, humor, mainstream/contemporary, mystery, occult, religious, romance, science fiction, short story collections, spiritual, suspense, western. "Follow our guidelines. Authors are encouraged to write outside of the box here, but traditional stories and plots are also accepted if handled with a fresh twist or approach." Submit complete ms. Query by e-mail. Hardcopy submissions are not accepted.

Recent Title(s) *Fortress America*, by Alan Wayne Burch; *The Ways of the Sorcerer*, by William Henry; *Troubled Sea*, by Jinx Schwartz.

Tips "We love book lovers who want to be entertained or are interested in religion, spirituality (metaphysical) fiction, and nonfiction. Ages from 13-100. We accept unagented submissions, but do not accept hard copy manuscripts even from agents. All submissions must come to us via e-mail or attachment. We require a 90-day exclusive to have time to move the manuscript through our reading staff before you submit elsewhere. Study and follow our guidelines and style sheets."

TRICYCLE PRESS

P.O. Box 7123, Berkeley CA 94707. (510)559-1600. Website: www.tenspeed.com. **Acquisitions:** Nicole Geiger, publisher; Abigail Samoun, project editor. Estab. 1993. Publishes hardcover and trade paperback originals. **Publishes 18-20 titles/year. 20% of books from first-time authors; 60% from unagented writers. Pays 15-20% royalty on net receipts. Offers $0-9,000 advance.** Publishes book 1-2 years after acceptance of ms. Accepts simultaneous submissions. Responds in 4-6 months to mss. Book catalog for 9×12 SASE with 3 first-class stamps or visit the website; ms guidelines online.

O→ "Tricycle Press looks for something outside the mainstream; books that encourage children to look at the world from a possibly alternative angle. We have been trying to publish educational books with strong trade appeal and high quality middle grade fiction."

Nonfiction Biography, children's/juvenile, gift book, humor, illustrated book, picture books. Subjects include animals, art/architecture, creative nonfiction, film/cinema/stage, gardening, health/medicine, multicultural, music/dance, nature/environment, photography, science, travel, health, geography, math. Submit 2-3 chapters, or 20 pages and TOC. Reviews artwork/photos as part of ms package. Send photocopies.

Fiction Preteen. "One-off middle grade novels—quality fiction, 'tween fiction." Board books and picture books: Submit complete ms. Middle grade books and other longer projects: Send complete outline and 2-3 sample chapters (ages 9-14).

Recent Title(s) *Yesterday I Had the Blues*, by Jeron Frame, illustrated by Gregory Christie; *The Young Adventurer's Guide to Everest: From Avalanche to Zopkio*, by Jonathan Chester; *The Bossqueen, Little Big Bark, and the Sentinel Pup*, by Sarah Jordan.

TRINITY PRESS INTERNATIONAL

Division of Continuum International Publishing Group, 15 E. 26th St., Suite 1703, New York NY 10010. (212)953-5858. Fax: (212)953-5944. E-mail: hcarriga@morehousegroup.com. Website: www.tandtclarkinternational.com. **Acquisitions:** Henry Carrigan, publisher. Estab. 1989. Publishes trade paperback originals and reprints. Accepts simultaneous submissions. Responds in 4-6 weeks to query. Book catalog free.

O→ Trinity Press International is an ecumenical publisher of serious books on theology and the Bible for the religious academic community, religious professionals, and serious book readers. Currently emphasizing religion and science, ethics, Biblical studies, film and religion, and religion and culture books.

Nonfiction Textbook. Subjects include history (as relates to the Bible), religion, Christian/theological studies. Submit proposal form (download from website).

Recent Title(s) *To Our Bodies Turn We Then*, by Felecia Wright McDuffie; *Priests in Love*, by Jane Anderson; *Jesus, a Jewish Galilean*, by Sean Freyne.

TRIUMPH BOOKS

601 S. LaSalle St., Suite 500, Chicago IL 60605. (312)939-3330. Fax: (312)663-3557. Website: www.triumphbooks.com. Editorial Director: Thomas Bast. **Acquisitions:** Mike Emmerich. Estab. 1989. Publishes hardcover originals and trade paperback originals and reprints. Accepts simultaneous submissions. Book catalog free.

Nonfiction Biography, coffee table book, gift book, humor, illustrated book. Subjects include recreation, sports, health, sports business/motivation. Query with SASE. Reviews artwork/photos as part of ms package. Send photocopies.

Recent Title(s) *It's Only Me: The Ted Williams We Hardly Knew*, by John Underwood; *For the Love of NASCAR*, by Michael Fresina; *Bobby Jones and the Quest for the Grand Slam*, by Catherine Lewis.

TRUMAN STATE UNIVERSITY PRESS

100 E. Normal St., Kirksville MO 63501-4221. (660)785-7336. Fax: (660)785-4480. E-mail: tsup@truman.edu. Website: tsup.truman.edu. **Acquisitions:** Barbara Smith-Mandell (regional, poetry); Raymond Mentzer (early modern studies). **Publishes 10 titles/year. Pays 7% royalty on net receipts.** Ms guidelines online.

Nonfiction Early modern, regional, poetry.

Recent Title(s) *When the Railroad Leaves Town*; *The Empty Boat*; *Renaissance in Siena*.

TURTLE BOOKS

866 United Nations Plaza, Suite #525, New York NY 10017. (212)644-2020. Fax: (212)223-4387. Website: www.turtlebooks.com. **Acquisitions:** John Whitman, publisher (children's picture books). Publishes hardcover and trade paperback originals. **Publishes 6-8 titles/year. Receives 1,000 mss/year. 25% of books from first-time authors; 50% from unagented writers. Pays royalty on retail price. Offers advance.** Publishes book 12 months after acceptance of ms. Accepts simultaneous submissions.

O→ Turtle Books publishes children's picture books.

Nonfiction Children's/juvenile, illustrated book. Subjects include animals, education, history, language/literature, multicultural, nature/environment, regional, any subject suitable for a children's picture book. Submit complete ms. Reviews artwork/photos as part of ms package. Send photocopies, no original art.

Fiction Adventure, ethnic, fantasy, historical, multicultural, regional, sports, western. Subjects suitable for children's picture books. "We are looking for good stories which can be illustrated as children's picture books." Submit complete ms.

Poetry Must be suitable for an illustrated children's book format. Submit complete ms.

Recent Title(s) *Finding Daddy: A Story of the Great Depression*, by Jo Harper; *The Crab Man*, by Patricia Van West; *Alphabet Fiesta*, by Anne Miranda (children's picture books).

Tips "Our preference is for stories rather than concept books. We will consider only children's picture book manuscripts."

TUTTLE PUBLISHING

153 Milk St., 4th Floor, Boston MA 02109. Publishing Director: Ed Walters. **Acquisitions:** Editorial Acquisitions. Estab. 1832. Publishes hardcover and trade paperback originals and reprints. **Publishes 125 titles/year. Receives 1,000 queries/year. 20% of books from first-time authors; 40% from unagented writers. Pays 5-10% royalty on net or retail price, depending on format and kind of book. Offers advance.** Publishes book 18 months after acceptance of ms. Accepts simultaneous submissions. Responds in 4 months to proposals.

○→ "Tuttle is America's leading publisher of books on Japan and Asia."

Nonfiction Subjects include martial arts, arts/crafts, antiques/collectibles, architecture/interior design, cooking, language, and children's. Query with SASE, or submit outline. Cannot guarantee return of ms.

Recent Title(s) *The Complete Book of Sushi*, by Hideo Dekura, Brigid Treloar, and Ryuichi Yoshii; *Aikido Basics*, by Phong Thong Dany and Lynn Seiser; *Contemporary Asian Kitchens and Dining Rooms*, by Chami Jotisalikorn and Karina Zabihi.

Ⓝ Ⓐ ⊘ TWENTY-FIRST CENTURY BOOKS

Imprint of Lerner Publishing Group, 241 First Ave. N., Minneapolis MN 55401-1607. (612)332-3344. Fax: (612)332-7615. Website: www.lernerbooks.com. **Acquisitions:** Editorial Department. Publishes hardcover originals. Does not accept simultaneous submissions.

● Accepts submissions during the month of November only.

○→ Twenty-First Century Books publishes nonfiction science, technology and social issues titles for children and young adults. "We no longer accept unsolicited manuscripts. Agented submissions only, please."

Nonfiction Children's/juvenile, young adult. Subjects include government/politics, health/medicine, history, military/war, nature/environment, science, current events, social issues. "We publish primarily in series of four or more titles, for ages 12 and up, and single titles for grades 7 and up. No picture books, fiction or adult books." *Agented submissions only.*

Recent Title(s) *Fabulous Fish* (What a Pet! series); *Mercury and Pluto* (Worlds Beyond series).

Ⓝ TWO DOT

Imprint of The Globe Pequot Press., 825 Great Northern Blvd., Suites 327 & 328, Helena MT 59601. (406)442-6597. Fax: (406)457-5461. Website: www.globepequot.com. **Acquisitions:** Erin Turner, executive editor. Publishes hardcover and trade paperback originals. **Publishes 20 titles/year. 30% of books from first-time authors; 80% from unagented writers. Pays royalty on net price.** Accepts simultaneous submissions. Responds in 3 months to queries. Book catalog and ms guidelines online.

○→ "Two Dot looks for lively writing for a popular audience, well-researched, on regional themes." Currently emphasizing popular history, western history, regional history, biography collections, western Americana. De-emphasizing scholarly writings, children's books, memoirs fiction, poetry.

Nonfiction Subjects include Americana (western), history, regional. Three state-by-state series of interest: More than Petticoats (notable women); It Happened In . . . (state histories); and Outlaw Tales (by state). Submit outline, 1-2 sample chapters, SASE. Reviews artwork/photos as part of ms package. Send photocopies.

Recent Title(s) *Love Untamed: Romances of the Old West*, by Chris Enss and Jo Ann Chartier; *Sacagawea Speaks*, by Joyce Badgley Hunsaker; *It Happened in the Civil War*, by Michael R. Bradley.

Ⓐ ⊘ TYNDALE HOUSE PUBLISHERS, INC.

351 Executive Dr., Carol Stream IL 60188. (800)323-9400. Fax: (800)684-0247. Website: www.tyndale.com. **Acquisitions:** Manuscript Review Committee. Estab. 1962. Publishes hardcover and trade paperback originals and mass paperback reprints. **Pays negotiable royalty. Offers negotiable advance.** Accepts simultaneous submissions. Ms guidelines for 9×12 SAE and $2.40 for postage or visit website.

○→ Tyndale House publishes "practical, user-friendly Christian books for the home and family."

Nonfiction Children's/juvenile, self-help (Christian growth). Subjects include child guidance/parenting, religion, devotional/inspirational, theology/Bible doctrine, contemporary/critical issues. Prefers agented submissions. *No unsolicited mss.*

Fiction Romance, Christian (children's, general, inspirational, mystery/suspense, thriller, romance). Christian truths must be woven into the story organically. No short story collections. Youth books: character building stories with Christian perspective. Especially interested in ages 10-14. "We primarily publish Christian historical romances, with occasional contemporary, suspense, or standalones." *Agented submissions only. No unsolicited mss.*

Recent Title(s) *Danzig Passage*, by Bodie & Brock Thoene; *Croutons for Breakfast*, by Lissa Halls Johnson and Kathy Wierenga; *Stolen Secrets*, by Jerry B. Jenkins and Chris Fabry.

N: THE UNDERGROUND WHO CHAPBOOK PRESS

A company under Rembrandt and Company Publishers International, P.O. Box 13486, St. Petersburg FL 33733. E-mail: submissions@undergroundwho.com. Website: www.rembrandtandcompany.com. **Acquisitions:** Benjamin M. Scarlato, chief editor. Estab. 2004. Publishes trade paperback and mass market paperback originals. **Publishes 24 titles/year. Receives 100 queries and 400 mss/year. 50% of books from first-time authors; 100% from unagented writers. Pays 10-20% royalty on retail price.** Publishes book 6 months after acceptance of ms. Accepts simultaneous submissions. Responds in 1 month to queries and proposals; 6 months to mss. Book catalog online; ms guidelines by e-mail.

Nonfiction Autobiography, biography, general nonfiction, humor. Subjects include art/architecture, business/economics, education, ethnic, history, memoirs, music/dance, science, sports, world affairs. "At the moment, I am seeking nonfiction with subjects that talk about current affairs in world politics." 10,000 words is the maximum length for mss. Query with SASE and proposal package, including outline, or submit complete ms. Reviews artwork/photos as part of ms package. Send photocopies.

Fiction Adventure, confession, erotica, ethnic, experimental, fantasy, feminist, gay/lesbian, gothic, horror, literary, mainstream/contemporary, mystery, poetry, religious, romance, science fiction, short story collections, spiritual, sports, suspense, young adult. 10,000 words is the maximum length for mss. Query with SASE and proposal package including synopsis, or submit complete ms.

Poetry "Send as much poetry as you wish. The world needs more poetry." Submit 20 sample poems, or submit complete ms.

Recent Title(s) *Love Orbits Venus*, by John Ramos (fantasy); *Resolution 258*, by Peter Ebsworth (science fiction); *LAM*, by M.J. Hewitt (horror).

Tips "No need for an agent, just be creative in your work."

UNITY HOUSE

Unity, 1901 NW Blue Pkwy., Unity Village MO 64065-0001. (816)524-3550, ext. 3190. Fax: (816)251-3557. Website: www.unityonline.org. **Acquisitions:** Adrienne Ford, product manager. Estab. 1903. Publishes hardcover and trade paperback originals and reprints. **Publishes 16 titles/year. 30% of books from first-time authors; 95% from unagented writers. Pays 10-15% royalty on net receipts. Offers advance.** Publishes book 13 months after acceptance of ms. Does not accept simultaneous submissions. Responds in 2 weeks to queries and proposals; 1 month to mss. Ms guidelines online.

> O-n "Unity House publishes metaphysical Christian books based on Unity principles, as well as inspirational books on metaphysics and practical spirituality. All manuscripts must reflect a spiritual foundation and express the Unity philosophy, practical Christianity, universal principles, and/or metaphysics."

Nonfiction "Writers should be familiar with principles of metaphysical Christianity but not feel bound by them. We are interested in works in the related fields of holistic health, spiritual psychology, and the philosophy of other world religions." Reference (spiritual/metaphysical), self-help, inspirational. Subjects include health/medicine (holistic), philosophy (perennial/New Thought), psychology (transpersonal), religion (spiritual/metaphysical Bible interpretation/modern Biblical studies). Query with book proposal, including cover letter summarizing unique features, suggested sales and marketing strategies, TOC or project outline, and 1-3 sample chapters with SASE. Reviews artwork/photos as part of ms package. Send photocopies.

Fiction Spiritual, visionary fiction, inspirational, metaphysical. Query with SASE.

Recent Title(s) *Looking in for Number One*, by Alan Cohen; *That's Just How My Spirit Travels*, by Rosemary Fillmore Rhea.

THE UNIVERSITY OF AKRON PRESS

374B Bierce Library, Akron OH 44325-1703. (330)972-5342. Fax: (330)972-8364. E-mail: uapress@uakron.edu. Website: www.uakron.edu/uapress. **Acquisitions:** Michael Carley, director. Estab. 1988. Publishes hardcover and trade paperback originals. **Publishes 8-12 titles/year. Receives 400-500 queries and 100 mss/year. 40% of books from first-time authors; 100% from unagented writers. Pays 5-10% royalty. Offers (possible) advance.** Publishes book 10-12 months after acceptance of ms. Responds in 2 months to queries and proposals; 3 months to mss. Book catalog free; ms guidelines online.

> O-n "The University of Akron Press strives to be the University's ambassador for scholarship and creative writing at the national and international levels." Currently emphasizing technology and the environment, Ohio history and culture, poetry, history of law, political science, and international, political, and economic history. De-emphasizing fiction.

Nonfiction Scholarly. Subjects include history, regional, science, environment, technology, law, political science. "We publish mostly in our 4 nonfiction series: Technology and the Environment; Ohio History and Culture; Law, Politics and Society, and International, Political, and Economic History." Query with SASE. Reviews artwork/photos as part of ms package. Send photocopies.

Poetry Follow the guidelines and submit mss only for the contest: www.uakron.edu/uapress/poetry.html.

Recent Title(s) *Transport of Delight*, by Jonathan Richmond; *The Ohio Hopewell Episode*, by A. Martin Byers.
Tips "We have mostly an audience of general educated readers, with a more specialized audience of public historians, sociologists and political scientists for the scholarly series."

UNIVERSITY OF ALABAMA PRESS

Box 870380, Tuscaloosa AL 35487. (205)348-5180. Fax: (205)348-9201. Website: www.uapress.ua.edu. **Acquisitions:** Daniel J.J. Ross, director (American history, Southern history and culture, American military history, American religious history, Latin American history, Jewish studies); Daniel Waterman, acquisitions editor for humanities (American literature and criticism, rhetoric and communication, literary journalism, African-American studies, women's studies, public administration, theater, natural history and environmental studies, regional studies, including regional trade titles); Judith Knight, senior acquisitions editor (American archaeology, Caribbean archaeology, historical archaeology, ethnohistory, anthropology). Estab. 1945. Publishes nonfiction hardcover and paperbound originals, and fiction paperback reprints. **Publishes 55-60 titles/year. 70% of books from first-time authors; 95% from unagented writers. Offers advance.** Responds in 2 weeks to queries. Book catalog free.
Nonfiction Biography, scholarly. Subjects include anthropology/archeology, community, government/politics, history, language/literature, religion, translation. Considers upon merit almost any subject of scholarly interest, but specializes in communications, military history, public administration, literary criticism and biography, history, Jewish studies, and American archeology. Accepts nonfiction translations. Query with SASE. Reviews artwork/photos as part of ms package.
Fiction Reprints of works by contemporary, Southern writers. Query with SASE.
Tips Please direct inquiry to appropriate acquisitions editor. University of Alabama Press responds to an author within 2 weeks upon receiving the ms. If they think it is unsuitable for Alabama's program, they tell the author at once. If the ms warrants it, they begin the peer-review process, which may take 2-4 months to complete. During that process, they keep the author fully informed.

☒ UNIVERSITY OF ALASKA PRESS

P.O. Box 756240, Fairbanks AK 99775-6240. (907)474-5831 or (888)252-6657. Fax: (907)474-5502. E-mail: fypress@uaf.edu. Website: www.uaf.edu/uapress. Estab. 1967. Publishes hardcover originals, trade paperback originals and reprints. **Publishes 10 titles/year. Pays 7½% royalty on net receipts.** Publishes book within 2 years after acceptance of ms. Responds in 2 months to queries. Book catalog free; ms guidelines online.
Imprints Classic Reprints; Oral Biographies; Rasmuson Library Historical Translation Series.
  • "The mission of the University of Alaska Press is to encourage, publish, and disseminate works of scholarship that will enhance the store of knowledge about Alaska and the North Pacific Rim, with a special emphasis on the circumpolar regions."
Nonfiction Biography, reference, scholarly nonfiction relating to Alaska-circumpolar regions. Subjects include Americana (Alaskana), animals, anthropology/archeology, art/architecture, education, ethnic, government/politics, health/medicine, history, language/literature, military/war, nature/environment, regional, science, translation, women's issues/studies. Northern or circumpolar only. Query with SASE and proposal. Reviews artwork/photos as part of ms package.
Recent Title(s) *Russians in Alaska*, by Lydia T. Black; *Eastern Arctic Kayaks*, by John D. Heath and E. Arima; *Into Brown Bear Country*, by Will Troyer.
Tips "Writers have the best chance with scholarly nonfiction relating to Alaska, the circumpolar regions and North Pacific Rim. Our audience is made up of scholars, historians, students, libraries, universities, individuals, and the general Alaskan public."

UNIVERSITY OF ARIZONA PRESS

355 S. Euclid Ave., Suite 103, Tucson AZ 85719. (520)621-1441. Fax: (520)621-8899. E-mail: uap@uapress.arizona.edu. Website: www.uapress.arizona.edu. Director: Christin Szuter. **Acquisitions:** Patti Hartmann, acquiring editor (humanities); Allyson Carter, acquiring editor (social sciences and science). Estab. 1959. Publishes hardcover and paperback originals and reprints. **Royalty terms vary; usual starting point for scholarly monography is after sale of first 1,000 copies. Offers advance.** Does not accept simultaneous submissions. Responds in 3 months to queries. Book catalog available via website or upon request; ms guidelines online.
  • "University of Arizona is a publisher of scholarly books and books of the Southwest."
Nonfiction Subjects include Americana, anthropology/archeology, ethnic, nature/environment, regional, environmental studies, western, and environmental history. Scholarly books about anthropology, Arizona, American West, archeology, Native American studies, Latino studies, environmental science, global change, Latin America, Native Americans, natural history, space sciences, and women's studies. Submit sample chapters, résumé, TOC, ms length, audience, comparable books. Reviews artwork/photos as part of ms package.

Recent Title(s) *Elegy for Desire*, by Luis Omar Salinas; *In-Between Places*, by Diane Glancy; *Beyond Desert Walls: Essays from Prison*, by Ken Lamberton.

Tips "Perhaps the most common mistake a writer might make is to offer a book manuscript or proposal to a house whose list he or she has not studied carefully. Editors rejoice in receiving material that is clearly targeted to the house's list ('I have approached your firm because my books complement your past publications in . . .') and presented in a straightforward, businesslike manner."

THE UNIVERSITY OF ARKANSAS PRESS

201 Ozark Ave., Fayetteville AR 72701-1201. (479)575-3246. Fax: (479)575-6044. E-mail: uapress@uark.edu. Website: www.uapress.com. **Acquisitions:** Lawrence J. Malley, director and editor-in-chief. Estab. 1980. Publishes hardcover and trade paperback originals and reprints. **Publishes 30 titles/year. 30% of books from first-time authors; 95% from unagented writers. Pays royalty on net receipts.** Publishes book 1 year after acceptance of ms. Responds in 3 months to proposals. Book catalog and ms guidelines on website or on request.

O➔ The University of Arkansas Press publishes series on Ozark studies, the Civil War in the West, poetry and poetics, and sport and society.

Nonfiction Subjects include government/politics, history (Southern), humanities, nature/environment, regional, Arkansas, African-American studies, Middle Eastern studies, poetry/poetics. Accepted mss must be submitted on disk. Query with SASE, or submit outline, sample chapters, résumé.

Recent Title(s) *Reading With Oprah*, by Kathleen Rooney; *Looking Back to See*, by Maxine Brown; *Chattahoochee*, by Patrick Phillips.

UNIVERSITY OF CALIFORNIA PRESS

2120 Berkeley Way, Berkeley CA 94720-1012. (510)642-4247. Fax: (510)643-7127. E-mail: askucp@ucpress.edu. Website: www.ucpress.edu. **Acquisitions:** Lynne Withey (public health); Reed Malcolm (religion, politics, Asian studies); Niels Hooper (history); Deborah Kirshman (museum copublications); Sheila Levine (food, regional); Jenny Wapner (natural history, organismal biology); Naomi Schneider (sociology, politics, anthropology, Latin American studies); Blake Edgar (biology, archaeology, viticulture & enology); Stephanie Fay (art); Stan Holwitz (anthropology, public health, Jewish studies); Laura Cerruti (literature, poetry, classics); Mary Francis (music, film); Chuck Crumly (evolution, environment, ecology, biology). Estab. 1893. Publishes hardcover and paperback originals and reprints. **Offers advance.** Response time varies, depending on the subject. Enclose return postage to queries. Ms guidelines online.

O➔ University of California Press publishes mostly nonfiction written by scholars.

Nonfiction Scholarly. Subjects include history, nature/environment, translation, art, literature, natural sciences, some high-level popularizations. No length preference. Submit sample chapters, letter of introduction, cv, TOC.

Fiction Publishes fiction only in translation.

Recent Title(s) *William Dean Howells: A Writer's Life*, by Susan Goodman and Carl Dawson; *A History of Wine in America: From Prohibition to the Present*, by Thomas Pinney; *Biology of Gila Monsters and Beaded Lizards*, by Daniel Beck.

UNIVERSITY OF GEORGIA PRESS

330 Research Dr., Athens GA 30602-4901. (706)369-6130. Fax: (706)369-6131. E-mail: books@ugapress.uga.edu. Website: www.ugapress.org. Estab. 1938. Publishes hardcover originals, trade paperback originals, and reprints. **Publishes 85 titles/year. Offers rare, varying advance.** Publishes book 1 year after acceptance of ms. Does not accept simultaneous submissions. Responds in 2 months to queries. Book catalog and ms guidelines for #10 SASE or online.

Nonfiction Biography. Subjects include government/politics, history (American), nature/environment, regional, environmental studies, literary nonfiction. Query with SASE, or submit 1 sample chapter, author bio. Reviews artwork/photos as part of ms package. Send if essential to book.

Fiction Short story collections published in Flannery O'Connor Award Competition. Query #10 SASE for guidelines and submission periods. Charges $20 submission fee. "No phone calls accepted."

Poetry Published only through contemporary poetry series competition. Query first for guidelines and submission periods. Charges $20 submission fee. #10 SASE for guidelines.

Recent Title(s) *Deep in Our Hearts: Nine White Women in the Freedom Movement*, by Connie Curry et al; *As Eve Said to the Serpent: On Landscape, Gender and Art*, by Rebecca Solnit; *Big Bend*, by Bill Roorbach.

UNIVERSITY OF IDAHO PRESS

312 Main St., Caldwell ID 83605. (800)657-6465. E-mail: publish@caxtonpress.com.

● University of Idaho Press is not currently accepting queries or mss for New York.

O➔ Major subjects published by the Press include the history of Idaho, the northern Rocky Mountains and the region; the natural history of the same area; Native American culture and history; mining history;

Hemingway studies; Idaho human rights series; ecological literary criticism, resource, and policy studies; and literature of the region and the West.

Nonfiction Biography, reference, technical, textbook. Subjects include Americana, anthropology/archeology, ethnic, history, language/literature, nature/environment, recreation, regional, women's issues/studies, folklore. "Writers should contact us to discuss projects in advance. Be aware of the constraints of scholarly publishing, and avoid submitting queries and manuscripts in areas in which the press doesn't publish." Query with SASE, or submit proposal package including sample chapters, contents, and vita. Reviews artwork/photos as part of ms package. Send photocopies.

Recent Title(s) *Bold Spirit*, by Linda L. Hunt; *Common Courage*, by Andrea Vogt.

[N] UNIVERSITY OF ILLINOIS PRESS

1325 S. Oak St., Champaign IL 61820-6903. (217)333-0950. Fax: (217)244-8082. E-mail: sears@uillinois.edu. Website: www.press.uillinois.edu. **Acquisitions:** Willis Regier, director (literature, classics, music, military history); Joan Catapano, associate director and editor-in-chief (women's studies, film, African-American studies); Elizabeth Dulany (American religion, anthropology, western history, Native American studies); Laurie Matheson (American history, labor history, American studies); Judy McCulloh (American music, folklore); Kerry Callahan (sociology, criminology, communications, philosophy); Richard Wentworth (sport history). Estab. 1918. Publishes hardcover and trade paperback originals and reprints. **Publishes 150 titles/year. 50% of books from first-time authors; 95% from unagented writers. Pays 0-10% royalty on net receipts. Offers $1,000-1,500 (rarely) advance.** Publishes book 1 year after acceptance of ms. Responds in 1 month to queries. Book catalog for 9×12 SAE with 2 first-class stamps; ms guidelines online.

O→ University of Illinois Press publishes "scholarly books and serious nonfiction" with a wide range of study interests. Currently emphasizing American history, especially immigration, labor, African-American, and military; American religion, music, women's studies, and film.

Nonfiction Biography, reference, scholarly, scholarly. Subjects include Americana, animals, cooking/foods/nutrition, government/politics, history (especially American history), language/literature, military/war, music/dance (especially American music), philosophy, regional, sociology, sports, translation, film/cinema/stage. Always looking for "solid, scholarly books in American history, especially social history; books on American popular music, and books in the broad area of American studies." Query with SASE, or submit outline.

Recent Title(s) *Philosophical Writings*, by Simone de Beauvoir (philosophy); *March of the Machines: The Breakthrough in Artificial Intelligence*, by Kevin Warwick (nonfiction); *Myths American Lives By*, by Richard T. Hughes (nonfiction).

Tips "As a university press, we are required to submit all manuscripts to rigorous scholarly review. Manuscripts need to be clearly original, well written, and based on solid and thorough research. We cannot encourage memoirs or autobiographies."

UNIVERSITY OF IOWA PRESS

100 Kuhl House, Iowa City IA 52242-1000. (319)335-2000. Fax: (319)335-2055. Website: www.uiowapress.org. **Acquisitions:** Holly Carver, director; Prasenjit Gupta, acquisitions editor. Estab. 1969. Publishes hardcover and paperback originals. **Publishes 35 titles/year. 30% of books from first-time authors; 95% from unagented writers. Pays 7-10% royalty on net receipts.** Publishes book 1 year after acceptance of ms. Responds in 6 months to queries. Book catalog free; ms guidelines online.

O→ "We publish authoritative, original nonfiction that we market mostly by direct mail to groups with special interests in our titles, and by advertising in trade and scholarly publications."

Nonfiction Subjects include anthropology/archeology, creative nonfiction, history (regional), language/literature, nature/environment, American literary studies. Looks for evidence of original research, reliable sources, clarity of organization, complete development of theme with documentation, supportive footnotes and/or bibliography, and a substantive contribution to knowledge in the field treated. Use *Chicago Manual of Style*. Query with SASE, or submit outline. Reviews artwork/photos as part of ms package.

Fiction Currently publishes the Iowa Short Fiction Award selections. Competition guidelines available on website. See Competition and Awards section for further information.

Poetry Currently publishes winners of the Iowa Poetry Prize Competition, Kuhl House Poets, poetry anthologies. Competition guidelines available on website.

Recent Title(s) *The Menu in My Country*, by Marilyn Abildskov.

UNIVERSITY OF MISSOURI PRESS

2910 LeMone Blvd., Columbia MO 65201. (573)882-7641. Fax: (573)884-4498. Website: www.umsystem.edu/upress. **Acquisitions:** (Mr.) Clair Willcox and Gary Kass, acquisitions editors; Beverly Jarrett, editor-in-chief (history, literature, political philosophy, intellectual history, women's studies, African-American studies). Estab. 1958. Publishes hardcover and paperback originals and paperback reprints. **Publishes 65 titles/year. 40-50%**

of books from first-time authors; 90% from unagented writers. Pays up to 10% royalty on net receipts. Publishes book within 1 year after acceptance of ms. Responds immediately to queries; 3 months to mss. Book catalog free; ms guidelines online.

    O→ University of Missouri Press publishes primarily scholarly nonfiction in the humanities and social sciences. Currently emphasizing American history, political philosophy, literary criticism, African-American studies, women's studies.

Nonfiction Scholarly. Subjects include history (American), regional (studies of Missouri and the Midwest), social sciences, women's issues/studies, political philosophy, African-American studies. Consult *Chicago Manual of Style*. No mathematics or hard sciences. Query with SASE, or submit outline, sample chapters.

Recent Title(s) *Don't Let the Fire Go Out!*, by Jean Carnahan; *Wilderness Journey: The Life of William Clark*, by William E. Foley.

UNIVERSITY OF NEBRASKA PRESS

233 N. 8th St., Lincoln NE 68588-0225. (402)472-3581. Fax: (402)472-0308. E-mail: pressmail@unl.edu. Submissions E-mail: edemers2@unl.edu. Website: nebraskapress.unl.edu. **Acquisitions:** Elizabeth Demers. Publishes hardcover and trade paperback originals and trade paperback reprints. Book catalog free; ms guidelines online.

Imprints Bison Books.

Nonfiction Biography, cookbook, reference, textbook. Subjects include agriculture/horticulture, animals, anthropology/archeology, creative nonfiction, history, memoirs, military/war, multicultural, nature/environment, religion, sports, translation, women's issues/studies, Native American studies, American Lives series, experimental fiction by American-Indian writers. Submit book proposal.

Fiction Series and translation only. Occasionaly reprint fiction of established reputation.

Poetry Contemporary, regional.

Recent Title(s) *Mending Skins*, by Eric Gansworth; *Baseball Before We Knew It*, by David Block; *Wells Fargo*, by Ralph Moody.

UNIVERSITY OF NEVADA PRESS

MS 166, Reno NV 89557. (775)784-6573. Fax: (775)784-6200. Website: www.nvbooks.nevada.edu. **Acquisitions:** Joanne O'Hare, director and editor-in-chief. Estab. 1961. Publishes hardcover and paperback originals and reprints. **Publishes 25 titles/year.** Does not accept simultaneous submissions. Ms guidelines online.

Nonfiction Subjects include anthropology/archeology, ethnic (studies), history (regional and natural), nature/environment, regional (history and geography), western literature, current affairs, gambling and gaming, Basque studies. No juvenile books. Submit proposal. No online submissions. Reviews artwork/photos as part of ms package. Send photocopies.

Fiction Query with SASE, or submit outline, 2-4 sample chapters, synopsis.

UNIVERSITY OF NEW MEXICO PRESS

1601 Randolph Rd. SW, Suite 2005, Albuquerque NM 87106. (505)277-2346 or (800)249-7737. E-mail: unmpress @unm.edu. Website: www.unmpress.com. **Acquisitions:** Maya Allen-Gallegos, managing editor; David Holtby, editor-in-chief; Elizabeth Hadas, editor. Also: Editorial Dept., University of New Mexico Press, M5C11 6290, Albuquerque NM 87131-0001. Estab. 1929. Publishes hardcover originals and trade paperback originals and reprints. **Pays variable royalty. Offers advance.** Does not accept simultaneous submissions. Book catalog free; ms guidelines online.

    O→ "The Press is well known as a publisher in the fields of anthropology, archeology, Latin American studies, photography, architecture and the history and culture of the American West, fiction, some poetry, Chicano/a studies and works by and about American Indians. We focus on American West, Southwest and Latin American regions."

Nonfiction Biography, children's/juvenile, illustrated book, multimedia, scholarly. Subjects include Americana, anthropology/archeology, art/architecture, creative nonfiction, ethnic, gardening, gay/lesbian, government/politics, history, language/literature, memoirs, military/war, multicultural, music/dance, nature/environment, photography, regional, religion, science, translation, travel, women's issues/studies, contemporary culture, cinema/stage, true crime, general nonfiction. "No how-to, humor, juvenile, self-help, software, technical or textbooks." Query with SASE. Reviews artwork/photos as part of ms package. Send photocopies.

Recent Title(s) *Jemez Spring*, by Rudolfo Anaya; *The Cherokee Nation*, by Robert J. Conley; *Blood of Our Earth*, by Dan C. Jones.

THE UNIVERSITY OF NORTH CAROLINA PRESS

P.O. Box 2288, Chapel Hill NC 27515-2288. (919)966-3561. Fax: (919)966-3829. E-mail: uncpress@unc.edu. Website: www.uncpress.unc.edu. **Acquisitions:** David Perry, editor-in-chief (regional trade, Civil War); Charles Grench, senior editor (American history, European history, law and legal studies, business and economic history, classics, political or social science); Elaine Maisner, editor (Latin American studies, religious studies, anthropology, regional trade, folklore); Sian Hunter, editor (literary studies, gender studies, American studies, African American studies, social medicine, Appalachian studies, media studies); Mark Simpson-Vos, associate editor (electronic publishing and special projects, American-Indian studies). Publishes hardcover originals, trade paperback originals and reprints. **Publishes 90 titles/year. Receives 500 queries and 200 mss/year. 50% of books from first-time authors; 90% from unagented writers. Pays variable royalty on wholesale price. Offers variable advance.** Publishes book 1 year after acceptance of ms. Responds in 3-4 weeks to queries and proposals; 2 weeks to mss. Book catalog free or on website; ms guidelines online.

O→ "UNC Press publishes nonfiction books for academic and general audiences. We have a special interest in trade and scholarly titles about our region. We do not, however, publish original fiction, drama, or poetry, memoirs of living persons, or festshriften."

Nonfiction Biography, cookbook, multimedia (CD-ROM). Subjects include Americana, anthropology/archeology, art/architecture, cooking/foods/nutrition, gardening, government/politics, health/medicine, history, language/literature, military/war, multicultural, music/dance, nature/environment, philosophy, photography, regional, religion, translation, women's issues/studies, African-American studies, American studies, cultural studies, Latin-American studies, American-Indian studies, media studies, gender studies, social medicine, Appalachian studies. Submit proposal package including outline, cv, cover letter, abstract, and TOC. Reviews artwork/photos as part of ms package. Send photocopies.

UNIVERSITY OF NORTH TEXAS PRESS

P.O. Box 311336, Denton TX 76203-1336. Fax: (940)565-4590. E-mail: rchrisman@unt.edu; kdevinney@unt.edu. Website: www.unt.edu/untpress. Director: Ronald Chrisman. **Acquisitions:** Karen DeVinney, managing editor. Estab. 1987. Publishes hardcover and trade paperback originals and reprints. **Publishes 14-16 titles/ year. Receives 500 queries/year. 95% from unagented writers. Pays 7-10% royalty on net receipts.** Publishes book 1-2 years after acceptance of ms. Does not accept simultaneous submissions. Responds in 1 month to queries. Book catalog for 8½×11 SASE; ms guidelines online.

O→ "We are dedicated to producing the highest quality scholarly, academic, and general interest books. We are committed to serving all peoples by publishing stories of their cultures and experiences that have been overlooked. Currently emphasizing military history, Texas history and Texas literature, Mexican-American studies."

Nonfiction Subjects include agriculture/horticulture, Americana, ethnic, government/politics, history, language/literature, military/war, nature/environment, regional, women's issues/studies. Query with SASE. Reviews artwork/photos as part of ms package. Send photocopies.

Fiction "The only fiction we publish is the winner of the Katherine Anne Porter Prize in Short Fiction, an annual, national competition with a $1,000 prize, and publication of the winning manuscript each Fall."

Poetry "The only poetry we publish is the winner of the Vassar Miller Prize in Poetry, an annual, national competition with a $1,000 prize and publication of the winning manuscript each Spring." Query.

Recent Title(s) *Interpreters With Lewis and Clark*; *The Royal Air Force in Texas*.

Tips "We publish series called War and the Southwest; Texas Folklore Society Publications; the Western Life Series; practical guide series; Al-Filo: Mexican-American studies; North Texas crime and criminal justice; Katherine Anne Porter Prize in Short Fiction."

UNIVERSITY OF OKLAHOMA PRESS

2800 Venture Dr., Norman OK 73069. E-mail: cerankin@ou.edu. Website: www.oupress.com. **Acquisitions:** Charles E. Rankin, editor-in-chief. Estab. 1928. Publishes hardcover and paperback originals and reprints. **Publishes 90 titles/year. Pays standard royalty.** Does not accept simultaneous submissions. Responds promptly to queries. Book catalog for 9×12 SAE with 6 first-class stamps.

Imprints Plains Reprints.

O→ University of Oklahoma Press publishes books for both scholarly and nonspecialist readers.

Nonfiction Subjects include political science (Congressional, area and security studies), history (regional, military, natural), language/literature (American Indian, US West), American Indian studies, classical studies. Query with SASE, or submit outline, 1-2 sample chapters, résumé. Use *Chicago Manual of Style* for ms guidelines. Reviews artwork/photos as part of ms package.

Recent Title(s) *The Uncivil War: Irregular Warfare in the Upper South, 1861-1865*, by Robert R. Mackey (history); *Ojibwa Warrior*, by Dennis Banks and Richard Erdoes (American Indian studies); *Oklahoma Breeding Bird Atlas*, by Dan L. Reinking (natural history).

⊘ UNIVERSITY OF PENNSYLVANIA PRESS

3905 Spruce St., Philadelphia PA 19104. (215)898-6261. Fax: (215)898-0404. Website: www.upenn.edu/pennpress. Director: Eric Halpern. **Acquisitions:** Jerome Singerman, humanities editor; Peter Agree, social sciences editor; Jo Joslyn, art and architecture editor; Robert Lockhart, history editor. Estab. 1890. Publishes hardcover and paperback originals, and reprints. **Publishes 85 titles/year. 20-30% of books from first-time authors; 95% from unagented writers. Royalty determined on book-by-book basis. Offers advance.** Publishes book 10 months after delivery of ms after acceptance of ms. Does not accept simultaneous submissions. Responds in 3 months to queries. Book catalog and ms guidelines online.

Nonfiction "Serious books that serve the scholar and the professional, student and general reader." Scholarly. Subjects include Americana, art/architecture, history (American, art), sociology, anthropology, literary criticism, cultural studies, ancient studies, medieval studies, urban studies, human rights. Follow the *Chicago Manual of Style. No unsolicited mss.* Query with SASE, or submit outline, résumé. Reviews artwork/photos as part of ms package. Send photocopies.

UNIVERSITY OF SCRANTON PRESS

University of Scranton, Smufit Hall, 445 Madison Ave., Scranton PA 18510. Website: www.scrantonpress.com. **Acquisitions:** Richard W. Rousseau, director. Estab. 1981. Publishes paperback originals. Does not accept simultaneous submissions. Book catalog and ms guidelines free.

Imprints Ridge Row Press.

    ➤ The University of Scranton Press, a member of the Association of Jesuit University Presses, publishes primarily scholarly monographs in theology, philosophy, and the culture and history of Northeast Pennsylvania.

Nonfiction Looking for clear editorial focus: theology/religious studies; philosophy/philosophy of religion; scholarly treatments; the culture of Northeast Pennsylvania. Scholarly monographs. Subjects include art/architecture, language/literature, philosophy, regional, religion, sociology. Query with SASE, or submit outline, 2 sample chapters.

Poetry Only poetry related to Northeast Pennsylvania.

Recent Title(s) *Not My Kid 2*, by Mary Muscari, PhD; *Jesuit Generals*, by Thomas E. Zeyen, S.J; *Becoming a Bar Mitzvah*, by Arnine Cumsky Weiss.

UNIVERSITY OF SOUTH CAROLINA PRESS

1600 Hampton St., 5th Floor, Columbia SC 29208. (803)777-5243. Fax: (803)777-0160. Website: www.sc.edu/uscpress. **Acquisitions:** Linda Fogle, assistant director (trade books); Barry Blose, acquisitions editor (literature, religious studies, rhetoric, communication, social work); Alexander Moore, acquisitions editor (history, regional studies). Estab. 1944. Publishes hardcover originals, trade paperback originals and reprints. **Publishes 50-55 titles/year. Receives 1,000 queries and 250 mss/year. 30% of books from first-time authors; 95% from unagented writers.** Publishes book 1 year after acceptance of ms. Accepts simultaneous submissions. Responds in 3 months to mss. Book catalog free; ms guidelines online.

    ➤ "We focus on scholarly monographs and regional trade books of lasting merit."

Nonfiction Biography, illustrated book, monograph. Subjects include art/architecture, history (American, Civil War, culinary, maritime, women's), language/literature, regional, religion, rhetoric, communication. "Do not submit entire unsolicited manuscripts or projects with limited scholarly value." Query with SASE, or submit proposal package and outline, and 1 sample chapter and résumé with SASE. Reviews artwork/photos as part of ms package. Send photocopies.

Recent Title(s) *Journey of a Hope Merchant: From Apartheid to the Elite World of Solo Yacht Racing*, by Neal Petersen with William P. Baldwin and Patty Fulcher; *Wild Orchids of South Carolina: A Popular Natural History*, by James Alexander Fowlder; *The Art of Brevity: Excursions in Short Fiction Theory and Analysis*, edited by Per Winther, Jakob Lothe, and Hans H. Skei.

Ⓝ THE UNIVERSITY OF TENNESSEE PRESS

600 Henley St., UT Conference Center, Suite 110, Knoxville TN 37902. (865)974-3321. Fax: (865)974-3724. E-mail: custserv@utpress.org. Website: www.utpress.org. **Acquisitions:** Scot Danforth, acquisitions editor (scholarly books); Jennifer Siler, director (regional trades, fiction). Estab. 1940. **Publishes 35 titles/year. 35% of books from first-time authors; 99% from unagented writers. Pays negotiable royalty on net receipts.** Does not accept simultaneous submissions. Book catalog for 12×16 SAE with 2 first-class stamps; ms guidelines online.

    ➤ "Our mission is to stimulate scientific and scholarly research in all fields; to channel such studies, either in scholarly or popular form, to a larger number of people; and to extend the regional leadership of the University of Tennessee by stimulating research projects within the South and by nonuniversity authors."

Nonfiction Scholarly, American studies only. Subjects include Americana, anthropology/archeology (historical), art/architecture (vernacular), history, language/literature, regional, religion (history sociology, anthropology, biography only), women's issues/studies, African-American studies, Appalachian studies, folklore/folklife, material culture. Prefers "scholarly treatment and a readable style. Authors usually have PhDs." Submissions in other fields, and submissions of poetry, textbooks, plays and translations are not invited. Submit outline, 2 sample chapters, author bio. Reviews artwork/photos as part of ms package.

Fiction Query with SASE, or submit synopsis, author bio.

Recent Title(s) *Dictionary of Smoky Mountain English*, by Michael B. Montgomery and Joseph S. Hall.

Tips "Our market is in several groups: scholars; educated readers with special interests in given scholarly subjects; and the general educated public interested in Tennessee, Appalachia, and the South. Not all our books appeal to all these groups, of course, but any given book must appeal to at least one of them."

UNIVERSITY OF TEXAS PRESS

P.O. Box 7819, Austin TX 78713-7819. (512)471-7233. Fax: (512)232-7178. E-mail: utpress@uts.cc.utexas.edu. Website: www.utexaspress.com. **Acquisitions:** Theresa May, assistant director/editor-in-chief (social sciences, Latin American studies); James Burr, sponsoring editor (humanities, classics); William Bishel, sponsoring editor (natural sciences, Texas history). Estab. 1952. **Publishes 90 titles/year. 50% of books from first-time authors; 99% from unagented writers. Pays royalty on net receipts. Offers occasional advance.** Publishes book 18-24 months after acceptance of ms. Does not accept simultaneous submissions. Responds in 3 months to queries. Book catalog free; ms guidelines online.

> ⊶ "In addition to publishing the results of advanced research for scholars worldwide, UT Press has a special obligation to the people of its state to publish authoritative books on Texas. We do not publish fiction or poetry, except for some Latin American and Middle Eastern literature in translation."

Nonfiction Biography, scholarly. Subjects include anthropology/archeology, art/architecture, ethnic, film/cinema/stage, history, language/literature, nature/environment, regional, science, translation, women's issues/studies, natural history, American, Latin American, Native American, Latino, and Middle Eastern studies; classics and the ancient world, film, contemporary regional architecture, geography, ornithology, biology. Also uses specialty titles related to Texas and the Southwest, national trade titles and regional trade titles. Query with SASE, or submit outline, 2 sample chapters. Reviews artwork/photos as part of ms package.

Fiction No poetry. Query with SASE, or submit outline, 2 sample chapters.

Recent Title(s) *Citizen's Primer for Conservation Activism*, by Perlman; *Understanding the Chiapas Rebellion*, by Higgins; *Coming Attractions: Reading American Moive Trailers*, by Kernan.

Tips "It's difficult to make a manuscript over 400 double-spaced pages into a feasible book. Authors should take special care to edit out extraneous material. We look for sharply focused, in-depth treatments of important topics."

UNIVERSITY PRESS OF COLORADO

5589 Arapahoe, Suite 206C, Boulder CO 80303. (720)406-8849. Fax: (720)406-3443. Director: Darrin Pratt. **Acquisitions:** Sandy Crooms, editor. Estab. 1965. Publishes hardcover and paperback originals. **Publishes 30-40 titles/year. 50% of books from first-time authors; 95% from unagented writers. Pays 5-15% royalty on net receipts. Offers advance.** Publishes book within 2 years after acceptance of ms. Accepts simultaneous submissions. Responds in 6 months to queries. Book catalog free.

> ⊶ "We are a university press that publishes scholarly nonfiction in the disciplines of the American West, Native-American studies, archeology, environmental studies, and regional-interest titles." Currently de-emphasizing fiction, poetry, biography.

Nonfiction Scholarly. Subjects include nature/environment, regional. Length: 250-500 pages. Query with SASE. Reviews artwork/photos as part of ms package.

Recent Title(s) *Reversing the Lens: Ethnicity Race, Gender, and Sexuality Through Film*, by Jun Xing and Lane Ryo Hirabayashi; *International Environmental Cooperation: Politics and Diplomacy in Pacific Asia*, by Paul G. Harris.

Tips "We have series on mining history and on Mesoamerican worlds."

UNIVERSITY PRESS OF KANSAS

2501 Bob Billings Pkwy., Lawrence KS 66049-3905. (785)864-4154. Fax: (785)864-4586. E-mail: upress@ku.edu. Website: www.kansaspress.ku.edu. **Acquisitions:** Michael J. Briggs, editor-in-chief (military history, political science, law); Nancy Scott Jackson, acquisitions editor (western history, American studies, environmental studies, women's studies); Fred M. Woodward, director, (political science, presidency, regional). Estab. 1946. Publishes hardcover originals, trade paperback originals and reprints. **Publishes 55 titles/year. Receives 600 queries/year. 20% of books from first-time authors; 98% from unagented writers. Pays 5-15% royalty on net receipts. Offers selective advance.** Publishes book 10 months after acceptance of ms. Does not accept simultaneous submissions. Responds in 1 month to proposals. Book catalog and ms guidelines free.

> ⊶ The University Press of Kansas publishes scholarly books that advance knowledge and regional books that contribute to the understanding of Kansas, the Great Plains, and the Midwest.

Nonfiction Biography, scholarly. Subjects include Americana, anthropology/archeology, government/politics, history, military/war, nature/environment, regional, sociology, women's issues/studies. "We are looking for books on topics of wide interest based on solid scholarship and written for both specialists and informed general readers. Do not send unsolicited, complete manuscripts." Submit outline, sample chapter(s), cover letter, cv, prospectus. Reviews artwork/photos as part of ms package. Send photocopies.

Recent Title(s) *The FBI and American Democracy: A Brief Critical History*, by Athan Theoharis; *The Legend of John Wilkes Booth: Myth, Memory, and a Mummy*, by C. Wyatt Evans; *Colossus Reborn: The Red Army at War, 1941-1943*, by David M. Glantz.

UNIVERSITY PRESS OF KENTUCKY

663 S. Limestone, Lexington KY 40508-4008. (859)257-2951. Fax: (859)323-1873. Website: www.kentuckypress. com. **Acquisitions:** Joyce Harrison, editor-in-chief. Estab. 1943. Publishes hardcover and paperback originals and reprints. **Publishes 60 titles/year. Royalty varies.** Publishes book 1 year after acceptance of ms. Responds in 2 months to queries. Book catalog free; ms guidelines online.

○┬ "We are a scholarly publisher, publishing chiefly for an academic and professional audience, as well as books about Kentucky, the upper South, Appalachia, and the Ohio Valley."

Nonfiction Biography, reference, scholarly (monographs). Subjects include history, military/war (history), regional, women's issues/studies, political science, film studies, American and African-American studies, folklore, Kentuckiana and regional books, Appalachian studies. "No textbooks, genealogical material, lightweight popular treatments, how-to books, or books unrelated to our major areas of interest. The Press does not consider original works of fiction or poetry." Query with SASE.

UNIVERSITY PRESS OF MISSISSIPPI

3825 Ridgewood Rd., Jackson MS 39211-6492. (601)432-6205. Fax: (601)432-6217. E-mail: press@ihl.state.ms.us. Website: www.upress.state.ms.us. **Acquisitions:** Craig Gill, editor-in-chief (regional studies, art, folklore, fiction, memoirs); Seetha Srinivasan, director (African-American studies, popular culture, literature). Estab. 1970. Publishes hardcover and paperback originals and reprints. **Publishes 60 titles/year. 20% of books from first-time authors; 90% from unagented writers. Competitive royalties and terms. Offers advance.** Publishes book 1 year after acceptance of ms. Does not accept simultaneous submissions. Responds in 3 months to queries.

Imprints Muscadine Books (regional trade); Banner Books (literary reprints).

○┬ "University Press of Mississippi publishes scholarly and trade titles, as well as special series, including: American Made Music; Conversations with Comic Artists; Conversations with Filmmakers; Faulkner and Yoknapatawpha; Literary Conversations; Studies in Popular Culture; Hollywood Legends; Understanding Health and Sickness."

Nonfiction Biography, scholarly. Subjects include Americana, art/architecture, ethnic (minority studies), government/politics, health/medicine, history, language/literature, music/dance, photography, regional (Southern), folklife, literary criticism, popular culture with scholarly emphasis, literary studies. "We prefer a proposal that describes the significance of the work and a chapter outline." Submit outline, sample chapters, cv.

Fiction Commissioned trade editions by prominent writers.

Recent Title(s) *Voodoo Queen: The Spiritual Lives of Marie Laveau*, by Martha Ward; *Shebang*, by Valerie Vogrin.

UNIVERSITY PRESS OF NEW ENGLAND

1 Court St., Suite 250, Lebanon NH 03766. (603)448-1533. Fax: (603)448-7006. E-mail: university.press@dartmouth.edu. Website: www.upne.com. Director: Richard Abel. **Acquisitions:** Phyllis Deutsch, senior editor; Ellen Wicklum, editor; John Landrigan, editor. Estab. 1970. Publishes hardcover and paperback originals. **Publishes 90 titles/year. Pays standard royalty. Offers occasional advance.** Responds in 2 months to queries. Book catalog and ms guidelines for 9×12 SASE and 5 first-class stamps; ms guidelines online.

Imprints Brandies University Press; Dartmouth College Press; University of New Hampshire Press; Northeastern University Press; Tufts University Press; University of Vermont Press; University Press of New England; Hardscrabble Books (publishing fiction of New England).

Nonfiction Biography. Subjects include Americana (New England material culture), art/architecture, nature/environment, regional (New England), music, American studies, Jewish studies, criminal justice. Submit outline, 1-2 sample chapters. No electronic submissions.

Fiction Literary. Only New England novels, literary fiction, and reprints. Query with SASE, or submit sample chapters.

Recent Title(s) *The Fate of Family Farming*, by Ronald Jager (nonfiction); *New England covered Bridges: A Complete Guide*, by Benjamin and June Evans (nonfiction/regional); *From Madness to Mutiny: Why Mothers Are Running from the Family Courts and What Can Be Done About It*, by Amy Neustein and Michael Lesher (nonfiction).

THE URBAN LAND INSTITUTE

1025 Thomas Jefferson St. NW, Washington DC 20007-5201. (202)624-7000. Fax: (202)624-7140. Website: www.uli.org. **Acquisitions:** Rachelle Levitt, executive vice president/publisher. Estab. 1936. Publishes hardcover and trade paperback originals. **Publishes 15-20 titles/year. 2% of books from first-time authors; 100% from unagented writers. Pays 10% royalty on gross sales. Offers $1,500-2,000 advance.** Publishes book 6 months after acceptance of ms. Does not accept simultaneous submissions. Book catalog and ms guidelines via website or 9×12 SAE.

○₩ The Urban Land Institute publishes technical books on real estate development and land planning.

Nonfiction Technical. Subjects include money/finance, design and development. "The majority of manuscripts are created in-house by research staff. We acquire 2 or 3 outside authors to fill schedule and subject areas where our list has gaps. We are not interested in real estate sales, brokerages, appraisal, making money in real estate, opinion, personal point of view, or manuscripts negative toward growth and development." Query with SASE. Reviews artwork/photos as part of ms package.

Recent Title(s) *Better Places, Better Lives: A Biography of James Fowse*; *Creating a Vibrant City Center*.

N URJ PRESS

633 Third Ave., New York NY 10017-6778. (212)650-4120. Fax: (212)650-4119. E-mail: press@urj.org. Website: www.urjpress.com. **Acquisitions:** Rabbi Hara Person, editor (subjects related to Judaism). Publishes hardcover and trade paperback originals. **Publishes 22 titles/year. Receives 500 queries and 400 mss/year. 70% of books from first-time authors; 90% from unagented writers. Pays 3-5% royalty on retail price, or makes outright purchase of $500-2,000. Offers $500-2,000 advance.** Publishes book 9 months after acceptance of ms. Does not accept simultaneous submissions. Responds in 2 months to queries; 6 months to proposals and mss. Book catalog and ms guidelines free or on website.

○₩ URJ Press publishes books related to Judaism.

Nonfiction Biography, children's/juvenile, coffee table book, cookbook, gift book, how-to, illustrated book, multimedia (CD), reference, textbook. Subjects include art/architecture (synagogue), child guidance/parenting (Jewish), cooking/foods/nutrition (Jewish), education (Jewish), ethnic (Judaism), government/politics, history (Jewish), language/literature (Hebrew), military/war (as relates to Judaism), music/dance, nature/environment, philosophy (Jewish), religion (Judaism only), sex (as it relates to Judaism), spirituality (Jewish). Submit proposal package including outline, 1-2 sample chapters, author bio.

Fiction Jewish, liberal content. Picture book length only. Juvenile, children's picture books. Submit complete ms with author bio.

Recent Title(s) *Talmud for Everyday Living: Employer-Employee Relations*, by Hillel Gamoran (nonfiction); *The Gift of Wisdom*, by Steven E. Steinbock (textbook for grades 5-7); *Solomon and the Trees*, by Matt Biers-Ariel (picture book).

Tips "Look at some of our books. Have an understanding of the Reform Judaism community. In addition to bookstores, we sell to Jewish congregations and Hebrew day schools."

UTAH STATE UNIVERSITY PRESS

7800 Old Main Hill, Logan UT 84322-7800. (435)797-1362. Fax: (435)797-0313. Website: www.usu.edu/usupress. **Acquisitions:** Michael Spooner, director (composition, poetry); John Alley, editor (history, folklore, fiction). Estab. 1972. Publishes hardcover and trade paperback originals and reprints. **Publishes 18 titles/year. 8% of books from first-time authors. Pays royalty on net receipts.** Publishes book 18 months after acceptance of ms. Does not accept simultaneous submissions. Responds in 1 month to queries. Book catalog free; ms guidelines online.

○₩ Utah State University Press publishes scholarly works in the academic areas noted below. Currently interested in book-length scholarly mss dealing with folklore studies, composition studies, Native American studies, and history.

Nonfiction Biography, reference, scholarly, textbook. Subjects include history (of the West), regional, folklore, the West, Native-American studies, studies in composition and rhetoric. Query with SASE. Reviews artwork/photos as part of ms package. Send photocopies.

Recent Title(s) *Alaska's Daughter: An Eskimo Memoir of the Early Twentieth Century*, by Elizabeth Bernhardt Pinson; *Building the Goodly Fellowship of Faith: A History of the Episcopal Church in Utah, 1867-1996*, by Frederick Quinn; *Once Upon a Virus: AIDS Legends and Vernacular Risk Perception*, by Diane E. Goldstein.

Tips Utah State University Press also sponsors the annual May Swenson Poetry Award.

VANDAMERE PRESS

P.O. Box 149, St. Petersburg FL 33731. **Acquisitions:** Jerry Frank, senior acquistions editor. Estab. 1984. Publishes hardcover and trade paperback originals and reprints. **Publishes 8-15 titles/year. Receives 750 queries and 2,000 mss/year. 25% of books from first-time authors; 90% from unagented writers. Pays royalty on** revenues generated. **Offers advance.** Publishes book 1-3 years after acceptance of ms. Accepts simultaneous submissions. Responds in 6 months to queries.

O➡ Vandamere publishes high-quality work with solid, well-documented research and minimum author/political bias.

Nonfiction Biography, illustrated book, reference. Subjects include Americana, education, health/medicine, history, military/war, photography, regional (Washington D.C./Mid-Atlantic), women's issues/studies, disability/healthcare issues. No New Age. Submit outline, 2-3 sample chapters. Send photocopies.

Fiction Adventure, humor, mystery, suspense. Submit 5-10 sample chapters, synopsis.

Recent Title(s) *Ask What You Can Do for Your Country*, by Dan Fleming (nonfiction); *Cry Me a River*, by Patricia Hagan (fiction).

Tips "Authors who can provide endorsements from significant published writers, celebrities, etc., will always be given serious consideration. Clean, easy-to-read, dark copy is essential. Patience in waiting for replies is essential. All unsolicited work is looked at, but at certain times of the year our review schedule will stop. No response without SASE. No electronic submissions or queries."

VANDERBILT UNIVERSITY PRESS

VU Station B 351813, Nashville TN 37235. (615)322-3585. Fax: (615)343-8823. E-mail: vupress@vanderbilt.edu. Website: www.vanderbilt.edu/vupress. **Acquisitions:** Michael Ames, director. Publishes hardcover originals and trade paperback originals and reprints. **Publishes 20-25 titles/year. Receives 500 queries/year. 25% of books from first-time authors; 90% from unagented writers. Pays 8% royalty on net receipts. Offers rare advance.** Publishes book 10 months after acceptance of ms. Accepts simultaneous submissions. Responds in 2 weeks to proposals. Book catalog free; ms guidelines online.

● Also distributes for and co-publishes with Country Music Foundation.

O➡ "Vanderbilt University Press publishes books on healthcare, social sciences, education, and regional studies, for both academic and general audiences that are intellectually significant, socially relevant, and of practical importance."

Nonfiction Biography, scholarly, textbook. Subjects include Americana, anthropology/archeology, education, ethnic, government/politics, health/medicine, history, language/literature, multicultural, music/dance, nature/environment, philosophy, women's issues/studies. Submit prospectus, sample chapter, cv. Reviews artwork/photos as part of ms package. Send photocopies.

Recent Title(s) *A Good-Natured Riot: The Birth of the Grand Ole Opry*, by Charles K. Wolfe; *Invisible Work: Borges and Translation*, by Efrain Kristal; *Smoke in Their Eyes: Lessons Learned in Movement Leadership from the Tobacco Wars*, by Michael Pertschuk.

Tips "Our audience consists of scholars and educated, general readers."

VENTURE PUBLISHING, INC.

1999 Cato Ave., State College PA 16801. (814)234-4561. Fax: (814)234-1651. E-mail: vpublish@venturepublish.com. Website: www.venturepublish.com. Estab. 1978. Publishes hardcover and paperback originals and reprints. **Pays royalty on wholesale price. Offers advance.** Does not accept simultaneous submissions. Book catalog and ms guidelines for SASE or online.

O➡ Venture Publishing produces quality educational publications, also workbooks for professionals, educators, and students in the fields of recreation, parks, leisure studies, therapeutic recreation and long term care.

Nonfiction Scholarly (college academic), textbook, professional. Subjects include nature/environment (outdoor recreation management and leadership texts), recreation, sociology (leisure studies), long-term care nursing homes, therapeutic recreation. "Textbooks and books for recreation activity leaders high priority." Submit 1 sample chapter, book proposal, competing titles.

Recent Title(s) *Bordeom Busters: Themed Special Events to Dazzle and Delight Your Group*, by Annette C. Moore; *Constraints to Leisure*, edited by Edgar L. Jackson; *Introduction to Therapeutic Recreation: U.S. & Canadian Perspectives*, by Kenneth E. Mobily and Lisa J. Ostiguy.

Ⓝ VERSO

180 Varick St., 10th Floor, New York NY 10014-4606. (212)807-9680. Fax: (212)807-9152. E-mail: versony@versobooks.com. Website: www.versobooks.com. **Acquisitions:** Editorial Department. Estab. 1970. Publishes hardcover and trade paperback originals. **Pays royalty. Offers advance.** Accepts simultaneous submissions. Book catalog free; ms guidelines online.

O➡ "Our books cover economics, politics, cinema studies, and history (among other topics), but all come from a critical, Leftist viewpoint, on the border between trade and academic."

Nonfiction Illustrated book. Subjects include business/economics, government/politics, history, philosophy, sociology, women's issues/studies. Submit proposal package.

Recent Title(s) *A Sultan in Palermo*, by Tariq Ali; *Planet of Slums*, by Mike Davis; *Water, Inc.*, by Varda Burstyn.

Ⓐ VIKING

Imprint of Penguin Group (USA), Inc., 375 Hudson St., New York NY 10014. (212)366-2000. Estab. 1925. Publishes hardcover and originals. **Publishes 100 titles/year.** Accepts simultaneous submissions.

   O━ Viking publishes a mix of academic and popular fiction and nonfiction.

Nonfiction Biography. Subjects include business/economics, child guidance/parenting, cooking/foods/nutrition, health/medicine, history, language/literature, music/dance, philosophy, women's issues/studies. *Agented submissions only.*

Fiction Literary, mainstream/contemporary, mystery, suspense. *Agented submissions only.*

Recent Title(s) *The Mermaid Chair*, by Sue Monk Kidd; *Mountain Peril*, by Tom Eslick; *House*, by Michael Ruhlman.

Ⓒ VIKING CHILDREN'S BOOKS

Imprint of Penguin Group (USA), Inc., 345 Hudson St., New York NY 10014-3657. (212)414-3600. Fax: (212)414-3399. Website: www.penguin.com. **Acquisitions:** Catherine Frank, editor; Tracy Gates, executive editor; Joy Peskin, senior editor; Jill Davis, senior editor; Anne Gunton, associate editor; Rachel Nugen, assistant editor; Janet Pascal, editor. Publishes hardcover originals. **Publishes 70 titles/year. Pays 2-10% royalty on retail price or flat fee. Offers negotiable advance.** Publishes book 1-2 years after acceptance of ms. Responds in 6 months. *Does not accept unsolicited submissions.*

   O━ Viking Children's Books publishes high-quality trade books for children including fiction, nonfiction, picture books and novelty books for pre-schoolers through young adults.

Nonfiction Children's/juvenile. Query with SASE, or submit outline, 3 sample chapters, SASE.

Fiction Juvenile, picture books, young adult. For picture books, submit complete ms and SASE. For novels, submit outline with 3 sample chapters and SASE.

Recent Title(s) *Prom*, by Laurie Halse Anderson; *Science Verse*, by Jon Scieszka, et al.

Ⓐ VILLARD BOOKS

Imprint of Random House Publishing Group, 1745 Broadway, New York NY 10019. (212)572-2600. Website: www.atrandom.com. Estab. 1983. Publishes hardcover and trade paperback originals. **Pays negotiable royalty. Offers negotiable advance.** Accepts simultaneous submissions.

   O━ "Villard Books is the publisher of savvy and sometimes quirky, best-selling hardcovers and trade paperbacks."

Nonfiction General nonfiction. Subjects include commercial nonfiction. *Agented submissions only.*

Fiction Commercial fiction. *Agented submissions only.*

Recent Title(s) *Serpent Girl*, by Matthew Carnahan; *Mr. Lucky*, by James Swain; *Swing*, by Rupert Holmes.

Ⓐ VINTAGE BOOKS & ANCHOR BOOKS

Division of Random House, Inc., 1745 Broadway Ave., New York NY 10019. Website: www.vintagebooks.com; www.anchorbooks.com. Publishes trade paperback originals and reprints. Accepts simultaneous submissions.

Nonfiction Subjects include history, science, sociology, women's issues/studies.

Fiction Literary, mainstream/contemporary, short story collections. *Agented submissions only.*

Recent Title(s) *The Dew Breaker*, by Edwidge Danticat; *A Distant Shore*, by Caryl Phillips; *Operating Instructions*, by Anne Lammott.

VITAL HEALTH PUBLISHING

34 Mill Plain Rd., Danbury CT 06811. (203)794-1009. Fax: (203)794-1085. E-mail: info@vitalhealthbooks.com. Website: www.vitalhealthbooks.com. **Acquisitions:** David Richard, publishing director (health, nutrition, ecology, creativity). Estab. 1997. Publishes trade paperback originals and reprints. **Publishes 10 titles/year; imprint publishes 5-6 titles/year. Receives 150 queries and 25 mss/year. 25% of books from first-time authors; 90% from unagented writers. Pays 15-20% royalty on wholesale price for top authors; pays in copies 30-40% of the time. Offers $1,000-5,000 advance.** Publishes book 6-8 months after acceptance of ms. Does not accept simultaneous submissions. Responds in 2 months to queries; 1-3 months to proposals; 2-4 months to mss. Book catalog online.

Imprints Vital Health Publishing; Enhancement Books.

   O━ Nonfiction books for a health-conscious, well-educated, creative audience.

Nonfiction Audiocassettes, children's/juvenile, cookbook, self-help. Subjects include health/medicine, music/dance, New Age, philosophy, spirituality. "All titles must be related to health. Because we have a holistic philosophy, this includes nutrition, ecology, creativity, and spirituality. Submit proposal package including outline, 1 sample chapter, cover letter describing the project. Reviews artwork/photos as part of ms package. Send photocopies or color prints.

Recent Title(s) *Cultivate Health from Within: Dr. Shahani's Guide to Probiotics*, by Khem Shahani, Ph.D.

(nonfiction); *Our Children's Health*, by Bonnie Minsky, L.C.N. (nonfiction); *The Color Pathway to the Soul: The Diamond Color Meditation*, by John Diamond, MD.

Tips "View our website to compare our titles to your manuscript."

N VIVISPHERE PUBLISHING

675 Dutchess Turnpike, Poughkeepsie NY 12603. (845)463-1100. Fax: (845)463-0018. Website: www.vivisphere .com. Estab. 1995. Publishes paperback originals and paperback reprints. **Pays 10-15% royalty and 25 author's copies.** Publishes book 3-12 months after acceptance of ms. Accepts simultaneous submissions. Responds in 3 months to queries. Book catalog free; ms guidelines free or online.

Fiction Adventure, ethnic, fantasy, feminist, gay/lesbian, historical, horror, literary, mainstream/contemporary, military/war, mystery, religious, romance, science fiction, suspense, western, the game of Bridge. Query with SASE.

N VOYAGEUR PRESS

123 N. Second St., Stillwater MN 55082. (651)430-2210. Fax: (651)430-2211. E-mail: mdregni@voyageurpress. com; jleventhal@voyageurpress.com. **Acquisitions:** Michael Dregni, editorial director; Josh Leventhal, acquisitions editor. Estab. 1972. Publishes hardcover and trade paperback originals. **Publishes 50 titles/year. Receives 1,200 queries and 500 mss/year. 10% of books from first-time authors; 90% from unagented writers. Pays royalty. Offers advance.** Publishes book 1 year after acceptance of ms. Accepts simultaneous submissions. Responds in 3 months to queries.

> O→ "Voyageur Press is internationally known as a leading publisher of quality natural history, wildlife, and regional books. No children's or poetry books."

Nonfiction Coffee table book (smaller format photographic essay books), cookbook. Subjects include Americana, cooking/foods/nutrition, history (natural), hobbies, nature/environment, regional, collectibles, outdoor recreation. Query with SASE, or submit outline. Reviews artwork/photos as part of ms package. Send transparencies (duplicates and tearsheets only).

Recent Title(s) *This Old Tractor* (stories and photos about farm tractors); *The Snowflake* (pop science and microphotography look at snow crystals); *For the Love of Knitting* (anthology of essays and art).

Tips "We publish books for a sophisticated audience interested in natural history and cultural history of a variety of subjects. Please present as focused an idea as possible in a brief submission (1-page cover letter; 2-page outline or proposal). Note your credentials for writing the book. Tell all you know about the market niche and marketing possibilities for proposed book."

N WADSWORTH PUBLISHING CO.

10 Davis Dr., Belmont CA 94002. (650)595-2350. Fax: (650)637-7544. Website: www.thomson.com. **Acquisitions:** Sean Wakely, president; Steve Wainwright, editor (philosophy/religion); Holly Allen, publisher (communications, radio/TV/film/theater); David Tatum, editor (political science); Clark Baxter, publisher (history/music); Annie Mitchell, editor (communications and speech); Lin Marshall, editor (sociology/anthropology [upper level]); Lisa Gebo, senior editor (psychology and helping professions); Dan Alpert, editor (education/special education); Vicki Knight, publisher (psychology); Peter Marshall, publisher (health/nutrition); Michele Sordi, editor (psychology); Marianne Tafliner, senior editor (psychology). Estab. 1956. Publishes hardcover and paperback originals and software. **Publishes 300 titles/year. 35% of books from first-time authors; 99% from unagented writers. Pays 5-15% royalty on net receipts.** Publishes book 1 year after acceptance of ms. Accepts simultaneous submissions. Book catalog and ms guidelines via website or with SASE.

> O→ Wadsworth publishes college-level textbooks in social sciences, humanities, education, and college success.

Nonfiction Multimedia, textbook, multimedia products: higher education only. Subjects include anthropology/archeology, education, health/medicine, language/literature, music/dance, nature/environment, philosophy, psychology, religion (studies), science, sociology, software, nutrition, counseling, criminal justice, speech and mass communications, broadcasting, TV and film productions, college success. Query with SASE, or submit outline, sample chapters, synopsis.

WALKER AND CO.

Walker Publishing Co., 104 Fifth Ave., 7th Floor, New York NY 10011. (212)727-8300. Fax: (212)727-0984. Website: www.walkeryoungreaders.com. **Acquisitions:** Submissions to Adult Nonfiction Editor limited to agents, published authors, and writers wtih professional credentials in their field of expertise. Children's books to "Submissions Editor-Juvenile." Estab. 1959. Publishes hardcover trade originals. Does not accept simultaneous submissions. Book catalog for 9×12 SAE with 3 first-class stamps.

> O→ Walker publishes general nonfiction on a variety of subjects, as well as children's books.

Nonfiction Autobiography, biography, Adult. Subjects include business/economics, health/medicine, history (science and technology), nature/environment, science, sports. *Adult: agented submissions only*; Juvenile: send synopsis.

Fiction Juvenile, mystery (adult), picture books. Query with SASE. Send complete ms for picture books.

Recent Title(s) *Blood Red Horse*, by K.M. Grant; *The Driving Book*, by Karen Gravelle; *Shelf Life*, by Robert Corbet.

WALTSAN PUBLISHING, LLC

5000 Barnett St., Fort Worth TX 76103-2006. (817)492-0188. E-mail: sandra@waltsan.com. Website: www.walts an.com. **Publishes 40-60 titles/year. Receives 1,500 queries and 1,000 mss/year. 95% of books from first-time authors; 95% from unagented writers. Pays 20% royalty on wholesale price.** Publishes book 1-2 years after acceptance of ms. Accepts simultaneous submissions. Responds in 2 months to queries and proposals; 4-6 months to mss. Book catalog and ms guidelines online.

• Not accepting new queries until January 2006.

Nonfiction Subjects include general nonfiction. "We look at any nonfiction subject." Query with SASE or via website, or submit proposal package, including outline and 3 sample chapters, or submit complete ms. Reviews artwork/photos as part of ms package. Send photocopies.

Fiction "We look at all fiction." Full-length or collections equal to full-length only. 50,000 word minimum. Query with SASE, or submit proposal package including 3 sample chapters, synopsis, or submit complete ms.

Recent Title(s) *The Last Knight of Camelot*, by Guy Ward; *Diana the Dragon Spirit of Briarsglen*, by M.R. Crutchfield; *The Pennant Man*, by Daniel Wyatt.

Tips Audience is computer literate, generally higher income and intelligent. "When possible, authors record their manuscript to include audio on the CD. Check our website for guidelines and sample contract." Initial queries and proposals may be submitted on paper. Mss accepted for publication must be submitted electronically—no exceptions. Only publishes on CDs and other removable media.

Ⓐ WARNER ASPECT

Imprint of Warner Books, 1271 Avenue of the Americas, New York NY 10020. (212)522-7200. Website: twbookm ark.com. Editorial Director: Jaime Levine. Publishes hardcover, trade paperback, mass market paperback originals and mass market paperback reprints. **Publishes 30 titles/year. Receives 500 queries and 350 mss/year. 5-10% of books from first-time authors; 1% from unagented writers. Pays royalty on retail price. Offers $5,000-up advance.** Publishes book 14 months after acceptance of ms. Responds in 3 months to mss.

○┑ "We're looking for 'epic' stories in both fantasy and science fiction. Also seeking writers of color to add to what we've already published by Octavia E. Butler, Nalo Hopkinson, Walter Mosley, etc."

Fiction Fantasy, science fiction. Mistake writers often make is "hoping against hope that being unagented won't make a difference. We simply don't have the staff to look at unagented projects." *Agented submissions only.*

Recent Title(s) *Hidden Empire*, by Kevin J. Anderson; *The Elder Gods*, by David & Leigh Eddings.

Ⓐ Ⓞ WARNER BOOKS

Imprint of Time Warner Book Group, Time & Life Building, 1271 Avenue of the Americas, New York NY 10020. (212)522-7200. Fax: (212)522-7993. Website: www.twbookmark.com. President/Time Warner Book Group: Maureen Egen. **Acquisitions:** (Ms.) Jamie Raab, senior vice president/publisher (general nonfiction and fiction); Les Pockell, associate publisher (general nonfiction); Amy Einhorn, vice president/editorial director, trade paperback (popular culture, business, fitness, self-help); Beth de Guzman, editorial director, mass market (fiction, romance, nonfiction); Rick Wolff, vice president/executive editor (business, humor, sports); Kristen Weber, editor-in-chief, Mysterious Press (mysteries, suspense); Caryn Karmatz Rudy, senior editor (fiction, general nonfiction, popular culture); Diana Baroni, vice president/executive editor (health, fitness, general nonfiction and fiction); Ms. Jaime Levine, editor/Aspect (science fiction); Karen Kosztolnyik, senior editor (women's fiction). Estab. 1960. Publishes hardcover, trade paperback and mass market paperback originals and reprints and e-books. **Publishes 250 titles/year. Pays variable royalty. Offers variable advance.** Publishes book 2 years after acceptance of ms. *Accepts no unsolicited mss.*

Imprints Aspect; Mysterious Press; Walk Worthy Press; Warner Business; Warner Faith; Warner Forever; Warner Vision; Warner Wellness.

○┑ Warner publishes general interest fiction and nonfiction.

Nonfiction Biography, humor, reference, self-help. Subjects include business/economics, contemporary culture, cooking/foods/nutrition, health/medicine, history, psychology, spirituality, sports, current affairs, human potential. *No unsolicited mss.*

Fiction Fantasy, horror, mainstream/contemporary, mystery, romance, science fiction, suspense, thrillers. *Agented submissions only. No unsolicited mss.*

Recent Title(s) *Hour Game*, by David Baldacci; *Nice Girls Don't Get the Corner Office*, by Lois Frankel; *The Perricone Promise*, by Nicholas Perricone.

WASHINGTON STATE UNIVERSITY PRESS

P.O. Box 645910, Pullman WA 99164-5910. (800)354-7360. Fax: (509)335-8568. E-mail: wsupress@wsu.edu. Website: www.wsupress.wsu.edu. **Acquisitions:** Glen Lindeman, editor. Estab. 1928. Publishes hardcover originals, trade paperback originals and reprints. **Publishes 8-10 titles/year. 40% of books from first-time authors. Most books from unagented writers. Pays 5% royalty graduated according to sales.** Publishes book 18 months after acceptance of ms. Responds in 2 months to queries. Ms guidelines online.

> ⊶ WSU Press publishes books on the history, pre-history, culture, and politics of the West, particularly the Pacific Northwest.

Nonfiction Biography. Subjects include cooking/foods/nutrition (history), government/politics, history, nature/environment, regional, essays. "We seek manuscripts that focus on the Pacific Northwest as a region. No poetry, novels, literary criticism, how-to books. We welcome innovative and thought-provoking titles in a wide diversity of genres, from essays and memoirs to history, archaeology, and political science." Submit outline, sample chapters. Reviews artwork/photos as part of ms package.

Recent Title(s) *Lewis and Clark Lexicon of Discovery*; *Color: Latino Voices in the Pacific Northwest*; *Washington State Government and Politics*.

Tips "We have developed our marketing in the direction of regional and local history and have attempted to use this as the base upon which to expand our publishing program. In regional history, the secret is to write a good narrative—a good story—that is substantiated factually. It should be told in an imaginative, clever way. Have visuals (photos, maps, etc.) available to help the reader envision what has happened. Tell the regional history story in a way that ties it to larger, national, and even international events. Weave it into the large pattern of history."

ⒶWATERBROOK PRESS

Subsidiary of Random House, 2375 Telstar Dr., Suite 160, Colorado Springs CO 80920. (719)590-4999. Fax: (719)590-8977. Website: www.waterbrookpress.com. **Acquisitions:** Ron Lee (nonfiction); Dudley Delffs, editor (fiction). Estab. 1996. Publishes hardcover and trade paperback originals. **Publishes 70 titles/year; imprint publishes 18 titles/year. Receives 2,000 queries/year. 15% of books from first-time authors. Pays royalty.** Publishes book 11 months after acceptance of ms. Accepts simultaneous submissions. Responds in 2-3 months. Book catalog online.

Imprints Fisherman Bible Study Guides; Shaw Books (Elisa Stanford, editor); Waterbrook Press.

Nonfiction General nonfiction, self-help, juvenile. Subjects include child guidance/parenting, health/medicine, money/finance, religion, spirituality. "We publish books on unique topics with a Christian perspective." *Agented submissions only.*

Fiction Adventure, historical, literary, mainstream/contemporary, mystery, religious (inspirational, religious mystery/suspense, religious thriller, religious romance), romance (contemporary, historical), science fiction, spiritual, suspense. *Agented submissions only.*

Recent Title(s) *Every Woman's Battle*, by Shannon Ethridge; *Hold Tight the Thread*, by Jane Kirkpatrick; *How Children Raise Parents*, by Dan Allender.

WATSON-GUPTILL PUBLICATIONS

Imprint of Billboard Publications, Inc., 770 Broadway, New York NY 10003. (646)654-5000. Fax: (646)654-5486. Website: www.watsonguptill.com. **Acquisitions:** Candace Raney, executive editor (fine art, art technique, pop culture, graphic design); Bob Nirkind, executive editor (Billboard-music, popular culture); Joy Acquilino, senior editor (crafts); Victoria Craven, senior editor (Amphoto-photography, lifestyle, architecture); Julie Mazur (children's books). Publishes hardcover and trade paperback originals and reprints. **Receives 150 queries and 50 mss/year. 50% of books from first-time authors; 75% from unagented writers. Pays royalty on wholesale price.** Publishes book 9 months after acceptance of ms. Responds in 2 months to queries; 3 months to proposals. Book catalog free; ms guidelines online.

Imprints Watson-Guptill; Amphoto; Whitney Library of Design; Billboard Books; Back Stage Books.

> ⊶ Watson-Guptill is an arts book publisher.

Nonfiction How-to (instructionals). Subjects include art/architecture, music/dance, photography, lifestyle, pop culture, theater. "Writers should be aware of the kinds of books (arts, crafts, graphic designs, instructional) Watson-Guptill publishes before submitting. Although we are growing and will consider new ideas and approaches, we will not consider a book if it is clearly outside of our publishing program." Query with SASE, or submit proposal package including outline, 1-2 sample chapters. Reviews artwork/photos as part of ms package. Send photocopies or transparencies.

Recent Title(s) *Manga Mania Shoujo*, by Christopher Hart; *Scared! How to Draw Horror Comic Characters*, by Steve Miller and Bryan Baugh; *Days of Hope and Dreams: An Intimate Portrait of Bruce Springsteen*, by Frank Stefanko.

Tips "We are an art book publisher."

WEATHERHILL, INC.

Imprint of Shambhala Publications, P.O. Box 308, Boston MA 02117. (617)424-0030. Fax: (617)236-1563. E-mail: editors@shambhala.com. Website: www.shambhala.com. Estab. 1962. Publishes hardcover and trade paperback originals and reprints. Accepts simultaneous submissions. Book catalog and ms guidelines free.

⊶ Weatherhill publishes exclusively Asia-related nonfiction and Asian fiction and poetry in translation.

Nonfiction Asia related topics only. Biography, coffee table book, cookbook, gift book, how-to, humor, illustrated book, reference, self-help. Subjects include anthropology/archeology, art/architecture, cooking/foods/nutrition, gardening, history, language/literature, music/dance, nature/environment, photography, regional, religion, sociology, translation, travel, martial arts. Submit outline, 2-3 sample chapters, résumé, TOC, SASE. Reviews artwork/photos as part of ms package. Send photocopies.

Fiction "We publish only important Asian writers in translation. Asian fiction is a hard sell. Authors should check funding possibilities from appropriate sources: Japan Foundation, Korea Foundation, etc."

Poetry Accepts very few poetry books. Send ms, SASE.

WESLEYAN UNIVERSITY PRESS

215 Long Lane, Middletown CT 06459. (860)685-7711. Fax: (860)685-7712. E-mail: stamminen@wesleyan.edu. Website: www.wesleyan.edu/wespress. Director: Tom Radko. **Acquisitions:** Suzanna Tamminen, editor-in-chief. Estab. 1959. Publishes hardcover originals and paperbacks. Accepts simultaneous submissions. Book catalog free; ms guidelines online or with #10 SASE.

⊶ Wesleyan University Press is a scholarly press with a focus on poetry, music, dance and cultural studies.

Nonfiction Biography, scholarly, textbook. Subjects include music/dance, film/TV & media studies, science fiction studies. Submit proposal package including outline, 2-3 sample chapters, cover letter, curriculum vitae, TOC, anticipated length of ms and date of completion. Reviews artwork/photos as part of ms package. Send photocopies.

Poetry "We will accept unsolicited poetry mss starting June 2005. See website for details."

Recent Title(s) *The Coming Race*, edited by Edward Bulwer-Lytton and David Seed; *Staging Whiteness*, by Mary F. Brewer; *Watching Daytime Soap Operas*, by Louise Spence.

WESTCLIFFE PUBLISHERS

P.O. Box 1261, Englewood CO 80150. (303)935-0900. Fax: (303)935-0903. E-mail: editor@westcliffepublishers.com. Website: www.westcliffepublishers.com. Linda Doyle, associate publisher. **Acquisitions:** Jenna Samelson, managing editor. Estab. 1981. Publishes hardcover originals, trade paperback originals, and reprints. **Publishes 18 titles/year. Receives 100 queries and 60 mss/year. 50% of books from first-time authors; 100% from unagented writers. Pays royalty on retail price. Offers advance.** Publishes book 18 months after acceptance of ms. Accepts simultaneous submissions. Responds in 1 month to queries. Book catalog free; ms guidelines online.

⊶ "Westcliffe Publishers produces the highest quality in regional photography and essays for our outdoor guidebooks, coffee table-style books, and calendars. As an eco-publisher our mission is to foster environmental awareness by showing the beauty of the natural world." Strong concentration on color guide books, outdoor sports, history.

Nonfiction Coffee table book, gift book, illustrated book, reference. Subjects include Americana, animals, gardening, history, nature/environment, photography, regional, sports (outdoor), travel. "Writers need to do their market research to justify a need in the marketplace." Submit proposal package including outline. Westcliffe will contact you for photos, writing samples.

Recent Title(s) *Colorado: 1870-2000*, by John Fielder; *Haunted Texas Vacations*, by Lisa Farwell.

Tips Audience are nature and outdoors enthusiasts and photographers. "Just call us!"

ℕ WESTERNLORE PRESS

P.O. Box 35305, Tucson AZ 85740. (520)297-5491. Fax: (520)297-1722. **Acquisitions:** Lynn R. Bailey, editor. Estab. 1941. **Publishes 6-12 titles/year. Pays standard royalty on retail price.** Does not accept simultaneous submissions. Responds in 2 months to queries.

⊶ Westernlore publishes Western Americana of a scholarly and semischolarly nature.

Nonfiction Biography, scholarly. Subjects include Americana, anthropology/archeology, history, regional, historic sights, restoration, ethnohistory pertaining to the American West. Re-publication of rare and out-of-print books. Length: 25,000-100,000 words. Query with SASE.

Recent Title(s) *Too Tough to Die*, by Bailey; *Men & Women of American Mining*, by Bailey & Chaput (2 volumes); *Cochise County Stalwarts, Vol. I & II*, by Bailey & Chaput.

WESTMINSTER JOHN KNOX PRESS

Division of Presbyterian Publishing Corp., 100 Witherspoon St., Louisville KY 40202-1396. (502)569-5613. Fax: (502)569-5113. Website: www.wjkbooks.com. **Acquisitions:** Lori Dowell. Publishes hardcover and trade paperback originals and reprints. **Publishes 100 titles/year. Receives 2,500 queries and 750 mss/year. 10% of books from first-time authors. Pays royalty on retail price. Offers advance.** Publishes book up to 18 months after acceptance of ms. Accepts simultaneous submissions. Book catalog for #10 SASE; ms guidelines online.

> ○━ "All WJK books have a religious/spiritual angle, but are written for various markets—scholarly, professional, and the general reader." Westminster John Knox is affiliated with the Presbyterian Church USA.

Nonfiction Biography, reference, self-help, textbook. Subjects include child guidance/parenting, education, ethnic, gay/lesbian, history, multicultural, philosophy, psychology, religion, sociology, spirituality, women's issues/studies. Submit proposal package according to WJK book proposal guidelines.

Ⓝ WHITEHORSE PRESS

107 E. Conway Rd., Center Conway NH 03813-4012. (603)356-6556. Fax: (603)356-6590. **Acquisitions:** Dan Kennedy, publisher. Estab. 1988. Publishes trade paperback originals. **Publishes 10-20 titles/year. Pays 10% royalty on wholesale price.** Does not accept simultaneous submissions. Responds in 1 month to queries.

Nonfiction "We are actively seeking nonfiction books to aid motorcyclists in topics such as motorcycle safety, restoration, repair, and touring. We are especially interested in technical subjects related to motorcycling." How-to, reference. Subjects include travel. Query with SASE.

Recent Title(s) *How to Set Up Your Motorcycle Workshop*, by Charlie Masi (trade paperback).

Tips "We like to discuss project ideas at an early stage and work with authors to develop those ideas to fit our market."

Ⓝ ALBERT WHITMAN AND CO.

6340 Oakton St., Morton Grove IL 60053-2723. (847)581-0033. Website: www.albertwhitman.com. **Acquisitions:** Kathleen Tucker, editor-in-chief. Estab. 1919. Publishes hardcover originals and paperback reprints. **Publishes 30 titles/year. 20% of books from first-time authors; 70% from unagented writers. Pays 10% royalty for novels; 5% for picture books. Offers advance.** Publishes book an average of 18 months after acceptance of ms. Accepts simultaneous submissions. Responds in 6 weeks to queries; 3-4 months to mss. Book catalog for 8×10 SAE with 3 first-class stamps; ms guidelines for #10 SASE.

> ○━ Albert Whitman publishes good books for children on a variety of topics: holidays (i.e., Halloween), special needs (such as diabetes), and problems like divorce. The majority of our titles are picture books with less than 1,500 words." De-emphasizing bedtime stories.

Nonfiction All books are for ages 2-12. Children's/juvenile, illustrated book. Subjects include animals, anthropology/archeology, art/architecture, computers/electronic, cooking/foods/nutrition, ethnic, gardening, health/medicine, history, hobbies, language/literature, music/dance, nature/environment, photography, recreation, religion, science, sports, travel, social studies, math. Submit complete ms if ms is picture book length; otherwise query with SASE.

Fiction All books are for ages 2-12. Adventure, ethnic, fantasy, historical, humor, mystery, holiday, concept books (to help children deal with problems), family. Currently emphasizing picture books; de-emphasizine folf tales and bedtime stories. No young adult and adult books. Submit complete ms for picture books; for longer works submit query with outline and sample chapters.

Recent Title(s) *Pumpkin Jack*, by Will Hubbell.

Tips "We sell mostly to libraries, but our bookstore sales are growing. We recommend you study our catalog, or visit our website before submitting your work."

WHITSTON PUBLISHING CO., INC.

1717 Central Ave., Suite 201, Albany NY 12205. (518)452-1900. Fax: (518)452-1777. E-mail: whitston@capital.n et. Website: www.whitston.com. **Acquisitions:** Michael Laddin, publisher. Estab. 1969. Publishes hardcover and trade paperback originals. **Publishes 15-25 titles/year. Receives 500 queries/year. 20% of books from first-time authors; 100% from unagented writers. Pays royalities after sale of 500 copies.** Publishes book 1-2 years after acceptance of ms. Does not accept simultaneous submissions. Responds in 6 months to queries.

> ○━ Whitston focuses on literature, politics, history, business, and the sciences.

Nonfiction "We publish nonfiction books in the humanities. We also publish reference bibliographies and indexes." Subjects include art/architecture, business/economics, government/politics, health/medicine, history, language/literature, social sciences. Query with SASE. Reviews artwork/photos as part of ms package.

Recent Title(s) *Mark Twain Among the Scholars*; *Autobiographies by Americans of Color*; *Into the Dragon's Teeth: Warriors' Tales of the Battle of the Bulge.*

Ⓝ MARKUS WIENER PUBLISHERS, INC.

231 Nassau St., Princeton NJ 08542. (609)921-1141. **Acquisitions:** Shelley Frisch, editor-in-chief. Estab. 1981. Publishes hardcover and trade paperback originals and reprints. **Publishes 15 titles/year; imprint publishes**

5 titles/year. Receives 50-150 queries and 50 mss/year. Pays 10% royalty on net receipts. Publishes book 1 year after acceptance of ms. Does not accept simultaneous submissions. Responds in 2 months. Book catalog free.

Imprints Princeton Series on the Middle East; Topics in World History.

○┐ Markus Wiener publishes textbooks on history subjects and regional world history.

Nonfiction Textbook. Subjects include history, world affairs, Caribbean studies, Middle East, Africa.

Recent Title(s) *The US & Mexico: The Bear and the Porcupine*, by Jeffrey Davidow; *The Chinese in the Caribbean*, by Dex Wilson; *Puerto Rico 1896, The War after the War*, by Fernando Pico.

⋈ MICHAEL WIESE PRODUCTIONS

11288 Ventura Blvd., Suite 621, Studio City CA 91604. (818)379-8799 or (206)283-2948. Fax: (818)986-3408. E-mail: kenlee@mwp.com. Website: www.mwp.com. **Acquisitions:** Ken Lee, vice president. Estab. 1981. Publishes trade paperback originals. Accepts simultaneous submissions. Book catalog online.

○┐ Michael Wiese publishes how-to books for professional film or video makers, film schools and bookstores.

Nonfiction How-to. Subjects include professional film and videomaking. Call before submitting.

Recent Title(s) *Filmmaking for Teens*, by Troy Lanier and Clay Nichols; *The Hollywood Standard*, by Christopher Riley; *The Working Director*, by Charles Wilkinson.

Tips Audience is professional filmmakers, writers, producers, directors, actors and university film students.

⋈ WILDCAT CANYON PRESS

Council Oak Books, 2105 E. 15th St., Suite B, Tulsa OK 74105. (918)743-2665. Fax: (918)743-4288. Website: www.counciloakbooks.com. **Acquisitions:** Acquisitions Editor. Accepts simultaneous submissions. Responds in 6 months to queries. Book catalog and ms guidelines free or online.

○┐ Wildcat Canyon Press publishes quality books on relationships, women's issues, home and family, and personal growth.

Nonfiction Gift book, self-help, lifestyle. Query with SASE, or submit proposal package including outline, sample chapters, author bio, SASE. Reviews artwork/photos as part of ms package. Send photocopies.

Recent Title(s) *Brenda's Bible*, by Brenda Kinsel; *Growing Season: A Healing Journey Into the Heart of Nature*, by Arlene Bernstein.

Tips "We are looking for fun and practical book projects that work well in both the traditional bookstore and gift markets."

WILDERNESS PRESS

1200 Fifth St., Berkeley CA 94710. (510)558-1666. Fax: (510)558-1696. E-mail: editor@wildernesspress.com. Website: www.wildernesspress.com. **Acquisitions:** Managing Editor. Estab. 1967. Publishes paperback originals. **Publishes 12 titles/year.** Publishes book 8-12 months after acceptance of ms. Responds in 2 months to queries. Book catalog and ms guidelines online.

○┐ "Wilderness Press has a 35-year tradition of publishing the highest quality, most accurate hiking and other outdoor activity guidebooks."

Nonfiction How-to (outdoors). Subjects include nature/environment, recreation, trail guides for hikers and backpackers. "We publish books about the outdoors. Most are trail guides for hikers and backpackers, but we also publish climbing, kayaking, and other outdoor activity guides, how-to books about the outdoors. The manuscript must be accurate. The author must research an area in person. If writing a trail guide, you must walk all the trails in the area your book is about. Outlook must be strongly conservationist. Style must be appropriate for a highly literate audience." Download proposal guidelines from website.

Recent Title(s) *Afoot & Afield San Francisco Bay Area*; *Hiking & Backpacking Big Sur*; *Fixing Your Feet*.

⋈ JOHN WILEY & SONS, INC.

111 River St., Hoboken NJ 07030. (201)748-6000. Fax: (201)748-6088. Website: www.wiley.com. **Acquisitions:** Editorial Department. Estab. 1807. Publishes hardcover originals, trade paperback originals and reprints. **Pays competitive rates. Offers advance.** Accepts simultaneous submissions. Book catalog and ms guidelines online.

Imprints Jossey-Bass (business/management, leadership, human resource development, education, health, psychology, religion, and public and nonprofit sectors).

○┐ The General Interest group publishes nonfiction books for the consumer market.

Nonfiction Biography, children's/juvenile, reference, narrative nonfiction. Subjects include history, memoirs, psychology, science (popular), African American interest, health/self-improvement, technical, medical. Submit proposal package, or submit complete ms. See website for more details.

Recent Title(s) *Bordeaux and Its Wines, 17th Ed.*, by Charles Cocks; *Penthouse Living*, by Jonathan Bell; *Prevention of Type 2 Diabetes*, edited by Manfred Ganz.

Ⓝ Ⓐ Ⓞ WILLIAM MORROW

HarperCollins, 10 E. 53rd St., New York NY 10022. (212)207-7000. Fax: (212)207-7145. Website: www.harpercol lins.com. **Acquisitions:** Acquisitions Editor. Estab. 1926. **Pays standard royalty on retail price. Offers varying advance.** Book catalog free.

    ○➔ William Morrow publishes a wide range of titles that receive much recognition and prestige. A most selective house.

Nonfiction Biography, cookbook, general nonfiction, how-to. Subjects include art/architecture, cooking/foods/ nutrition, history. Length 50,000-100,000 words. *No unsolicited mss or proposals. Agented submissions only.*

Fiction Publishes adult ficiton. Morrow accepts only the highest quality submissions in adult fiction. *No unsolic ited mss or proposals. Agented submissions only.*

Recent Title(s) *Serpent on the Crown*, by Elizabeth Peters; *The Baker's Apprentice*, by Judith R. Hendricks; *Freakonomics*, by Steven D. Levitt and Stephen J. Dubner.

Ⓝ WILLIAMSON PUBLISHING CO.

P.O. Box 185, Charlotte VT 05445. E-mail: susan@kidsbks.net. Website: www.williamsonbooks.com. **Acquisi tions:** Susan Williamson, editorial director. Estab. 1983. Publishes trade paperback originals. **Publishes 8-10 titles/year. Receives 1,000 queries/year. 75% of books from first-time authors; 90% from unagented writ ers. Pays royalty on net receipts, or makes outright purchase. Offers standard advance.** Publishes book 18-24 months after acceptance of ms. Does not accept simultaneous submissions. Responds in 3 months to queries. Book catalog for $8^{1}/_{2} \times 11$ SAE with 6 first-class stamps; ms guidelines online.

    ○➔ "Much of Williamson's success is based on our strong philosophy of how children learn best and on our reputation for excellence. Our books win top awards year in and year out, including Parents Choice (4 in Fall 2004), Teacher's Choice, and Children's Book Council. Our mission is to help every child fulfull his/her potential and experience personal growth through active learning. We want 'our kids' to be able to work toward a culturally rich, ethnically diverse, peaceful nation and global community." Currently emphasizing creative approaches to specific areas of science, history, cultural experiences, diversity.

Nonfiction All for children ages 3-14. Subjects include animals, anthropology/archeology, art/architecture, business/economics, cooking/foods/nutrition, ethnic, government/politics, health/medicine, history, hobbies, language/literature, memoirs, money/finance, multicultural, music/dance, nature/environment, photography, psychology, science, women's issues/studies, world affairs, geography, early learning skills, careers, arts, crafts. "Williamson has five very successful children's book series: Little Hands® (ages 3-6), Kids Can® (ages 7-14), Quick Starts for Kids® (64 pages, ages 8 and up), Tales Alive® (folktales plus activities, ages 4-10) and Kaleido scope Kids® (96 pages, single subject, ages 8-14). They must incorporate learning through doing. No picture books, story books, or fiction please! Please don't call concerning your submission. It never helps your review, and it takes too much of our time. With an SASE, you'll hear from us." Query with SASE, or submit 1-2 sample chapters, TOC, SASE.

Recent Title(s) *Kids Easy-to-Make Wildlife Habitats*, by Emily Stetson; *Using Color in Your Art*, by Sandi Henry; *Wordplay Café*, by Michael Kline.

Tips "Our children's books are used by kids, their parents, and educators. They encourage self-discovery, creativity, and personal growth. Our books are based on the philosophy that children learn best by doing, by being involved, and by asking questions—that's how memorable learning takes place, setting the stage for future learning. Our authors need to be excited about their subject area and equally important, excited about kids. Please, no storybooks of any kind."

WILLOW CREEK PRESS

P.O. Box 147, 9931 Highway 70 W., Minocqua WI 54548. (715)358-7010. Fax: (715)358-2807. E-mail: andread@ willowcreekpress.com. Website: www.willowcreekpress.com. **Acquisitions:** Andrea Donner, managing editor. Estab. 1986. Publishes hardcover and trade paperback originals and reprints. **Publishes 25 titles/year. Receives 400 queries and 150 mss/year. 15% of books from first-time authors; 50% from unagented writers. Pays 6-15% royalty on wholesale price. Offers $2,000-5,000 advance.** Publishes book within 18 months after acceptance of ms. Accepts simultaneous submissions. Responds in 2 months to queries. Ms guidelines online.

    ○➔ "We specialize in nature, outdoor, and sporting topics, including gardening, wildlife, and animal books. Pets, cookbooks, and a few humor books and essays round out our titles." Currently emphasizing pets (mainly dogs and cats), wildlife, outdoor sports (hunting, fishing). De-emphasizing essays, fiction.

Nonfiction Coffee table book, cookbook, how-to, humor, illustrated book, reference. Subjects include animals, cooking/foods/nutrition, gardening, humor, nature/environment, recreation, sports, travel, wildlife, pets. Sub mit outline, 1 sample chapter, SASE. Reviews artwork/photos as part of ms package.

Recent Title(s) *Ocean Friendly Cuisine*; *Horse Rules*; *What Labs Teach Us*.

WILSHIRE BOOK CO.

12015 Sherman Rd., North Hollywood CA 91605-3781. (818)765-8579. Fax: (818)765-2922. E-mail: mpowers@ mpowers.com. Website: www.mpowers.com. Publisher: Melvin Powers. **Acquisitions:** Rights Department. Estab. 1947. Publishes trade paperback originals and reprints. **Publishes 25 titles/year. Receives 1,200 queries/year. 70% of books from first-time authors; 90% from unagented writers. Pays standard royalty. Offers advance.** Publishes book 6-9 months after acceptance of ms. Accepts simultaneous submissions. Responds in 2 months.

Nonfiction How-to, self-help, motivational/inspiration, recovery. Subjects include psychology, personal success, entrepreneurship, Internet marketing, mail order, horsmanship. Minimum 30,000 words. Submit 3 sample chapters, or submit complete ms. Include outline, author bio, analysis of book's competition and SASE. No e-mail or fax submissions. Reviews artwork/photos as part of ms package. Send photocopies.

Fiction Adult allegories that teach principles of psychological growth or offer guidance in living. Minimum 30,000 words. No standard fiction. Submit 3 sample chapters, or submit complete ms. Include outline, author bio, analysis of book's competition and SASE. No e-mail or fax queries.

Recent Title(s) *The Dragon Slayer With a Heavy Heart*, by Marcia Powers; *The Secret of Overcoming Verbal Abuse*, by Albert Ellis, PhD, and Marcia Grad Powers; *The Princess Who Believed in Fairy Tales*, by Marcia Grad.

Tips "We are vitally interested in all new material we receive. Just as you are hopeful when submitting your manuscript for publication, we are hopeful as we read each one submitted, searching for those we believe could be successful in the marketplace. Writing and publishing must be a team effort. We need you to write what we can sell. We suggest you read the successful books similar to the one you want to write. Analyze them to discover what elements make them winners. Duplicate those elements in your own style, using a creative new approach and fresh material, and you will have written a book we can catapult onto the bestseller list. You are welcome to telephone or e-mail us for immediate feedback on any book concept you may have. To learn more about us and what we publish—and for complete manuscript guidelines—visit our website."

⊘ WINDRIVER PUBLISHING, INC.

72 N. WindRiver Ln., Silverton ID 83867-0446. (208)752-1836. Fax: (208)752-1876. E-mail: info@windriverpubli shing.com. Website: www.windriverpublishing.com. **Acquisitions:** E. Keith Howick, Jr., president; Gail Howick, vice president/editor-in-chief. Estab. 2003. Publishes hardcover originals and reprints, trade paperback originals, mass market originals. **Publishes 24 titles/year. Receives 1,000 queries and 300 mss/year. 95% of books from first-time authors; 90% from unagented writers. Pays 5-10% royalty on retail price.** Publishes book 1 year after acceptance of ms. Accepts simultaneous submissions. Responds in 1 month to queries; 4 months to proposals and mss. Book catalog and ms guidelines online.

Nonfiction Autobiography, biography, children's/juvenile, general nonfiction, humor, self-help. Subjects include gardening, government/politics, history, hobbies, New Age, religion, science, spirituality. Follow online instructions for submitting proposal, including synopsis and 3 sample chapters. *Ms submissions by invitation only.* Reviews artwork/photos as part of ms package.

Fiction Adventure, fantasy, historical, humor, juvenile, literary, military/war, mystery, religious, science fiction, spiritual, suspense, young adult. Follow online instructions for submitting proposal, including synopsis and 3 sample chapters. *Ms submissions by invitation only.*

Recent Title(s) *Don't Put Lipstick on the Cat!*; *The American St. Nick*; *Waldo Chicken Wakes the Dead*.

Tips "We do not accept manuscripts containing graphic or gratuitous profanity, sex, or violence. See online instructions for details."

Ⓝ WINDSTORM CREATIVE, LTD

P.O. Box 28, Port Orchard WA 98366. E-mail: wsc@windstormcreative.com. Submissions E-mail: submissions @windstormcreative.com. Website: www.windstormcreative.com. **Acquisitions:** (Ms.) Cris DiMarco, senior editor; Joy Garcia, managing editor (children's picture books); David Lambert, managing editor (nonfiction); Sarah Gee, managing editor; Talis Pelucir, managing editor (Internet and episode guides). Estab. 1989. Publishes trade and mass market paperback and electronic originals. **Publishes 100-200 titles/year. Receives 25,000 queries and 20,000 mss/year. 90% of books from first-time authors; 100% from unagented writers. Pays 15% royalty on gross monies received.** Publishes book 18 months after acceptance of ms. Accepts simultaneous submissions. Responds in 3 months to queries and proposals; 6 months to mss. Book catalog and ms guidelines online.

Imprints Blue Works; Digital Leaf ePress; Faith's Compass Press; Fandom Press; House with Bee; Immortal Day Publishing; Lightning Rod Publishers; Little Blue Works; Orchard Academy Press; Paper Frog Productions.

○┯ Publisher of fiction, poetry, Internet guides, episode guides, nonfiction.

Nonfiction Autobiography, biography, children's/juvenile, coffee table book, cookbook, general nonfiction, how-to, reference, self-help. Subjects include anthropology/archeology, child guidance/parenting, contemporary culture, creative nonfiction, gay/lesbian, history, military/war, photography, software. "Be familiar with all of our divisions and our philosophy." Query with SASE. Reviews artwork/photos as part of ms package. Send photocopies.

Fiction Adventure, comic books, erotica, fantasy, gay/lesbian, historical, literary, multicultural, mystery, picture books, plays, poetry, poetry in translation, regional, science fiction, short story collections, spiritual, young adult. "Read the comparison books for your genre which are listed at the website." No horror, explicit sexual violence, violence against children, "bestseller" fiction, spy or espionage novels, thrillers, any work which describes childhood sexual abuse or in which this theme prominently figures. Submit proposal package including synopsis.

Poetry "Read what we've already published and the comparison books listed at the website." Submit 10 sample poems, or submit complete ms.

Recent Title(s) *The American Space Program: Apollo Missions*, by Beverly Durfee; *This New Breed: Gents, Bad Boys & Barbarians 2*, edited by Rudy Kikel; *A Manual for Normal*, by Rebecca McEldowney.

Tips "Each division has its own audience. We are a gay-friendly press. If you are not comfortable with that, please look elsewhere. I cannot stress enough how important it is for writers to read and follow the guidelines for the division and genre to which they are submitting. We will discard any submissions that don't come in with a submission label and form. We are author/artist friendly and give authors and artists a higher royalty and more control over their books than any other press. Because of this, we are deluged with submissions and have to be very strict about enforcing the guidelines."

WINDWARD PUBLISHING, INC.

Imprint of Finney Company, 3943 Meadowbrook Road, Minneapolis MN 55426. (952)938-9330. Fax: (952)938-7353. E-mail: feedback@finney-hobar.com. Website: www.finney-hobar.com. **Acquisitions:** Alan E. Krysan, president. Estab. 1973. Publishes trade paperback originals. **Publishes 6-10 titles/year. Receives 120 queries and 50 mss/year. 50% of books from first-time authors; 100% from unagented writers. Pays 10% royalty on wholesale price. Offers advance.** Publishes book 6-12 months after acceptance of ms. Accepts simultaneous submissions. Responds in 8-10 weeks to queries.

○➔ Windward publishes illustrated natural history and recreation books.

Nonfiction Illustrated book, handbooks, field guides. Subjects include agriculture/horticulture, animals, gardening, nature/environment, recreation, science, sports, natural history. Query with SASE. Reviews artwork/photos as part of ms package.

Recent Title(s) *Nighlight*, by Jeannine Anderson; *Space Station Science*, by Marianne Dyson; *Daddy Played Music for the Cows*, by Maryann Weidt.

N WISDOM PUBLICATIONS

199 Elm St., Somerville MA 02144. (617)776-7416, ext. 28. Fax: (617)776-7841. E-mail: editorial@wisdompubs.org. Website: www.widsompubs.org. Publisher: Timothy McNeill. **Acquisitions:** David Kittlestrom, senior editor. Estab. 1976. Publishes hardcover originals and trade paperback originals and reprints. **Publishes 20-25 titles/year. Receives 300 queries/year. 50% of books from first-time authors; 95% from unagented writers. Pays 4-8% royalty on wholesale price. Offers advance.** Publishes book within 2 years after acceptance of ms. Does not accept simultaneous submissions. Book catalog and ms guidelines online.

○➔ Wisdom Publications is dedicated to making available authentic Buddhist works for the benefit of all. "We publish translations, commentaries, and teachings of past and contemporary Buddhist masters and original works by leading Buddhist scholars." Currently emphasizing popular applied Buddhism, scholarly titles.

Nonfiction Reference, self-help, textbook (Buddhist). Subjects include philosophy (Buddhist or comparative Buddhist/Western), psychology, religion, Buddhism, Tibet. Query with SASE. Reviews artwork/photos as part of ms package. Send photocopies.

Poetry Buddhist. Query.

Recent Title(s) *Essence of the Heart Sutra*, by The Dalai Lama.

Tips "We are basically a publisher of Buddhist books—all schools and traditions of Buddhism. Please see our catalog or our website before you send anything to us to get a sense of what we publish."

WIZARDS OF THE COAST

Subsidiary of Hasbro, Inc., P.O. Box 707, Renton WA 98057-0707. (425)226-6500. Website: www.wizards.com. **Acquisitions:** Peter Archer, director. Publishes hardcover and trade paperback originals and trade paperback reprints. Wizard of the Coast publishes games as well, including Dungeons & Dragons role-playing game. **Pays based on royalty, flat fee, or work-for hire assignment.** Accepts simultaneous submissions. Responds in 4 months to queries. Ms guidelines online.

Imprints Dragonlance; Forgotten Realms; Magic: The Gathering; Eberron.

○ Wizards of the Coast publishes only science fiction and fantasy shared-world titles. Currently emphasizing solid fantasy writers. De-emphasizing gothic fiction.

Fiction Fantasy, short story collections. "We currently publish only work-for-hire novels set in our trademarked worlds. No violent or gory fantasy or science fiction." Query with author credentials, synopsis, 10-page writing sample, and SASE.

Recent Title(s) *Crown of Fire*, by Ed Greenwood; *The Crystal Shard*, by R.A. Salvatore; *Lore of the Rose*, by Douglas Niles.

Tips "Our audience is largely comprised of highly imaginative 12-30 year-old males."

WOODBINE HOUSE

6510 Bells Mill Rd., Bethesda MD 20817. (301)897-3570. Fax: (301)897-5838. E-mail: ngpaul@woodbinehouse.com. Website: www.woodbinehouse.com. **Acquisitions:** Nancy Gray Paul, acquisitions editor. Estab. 1985. Publishes hardcover and trade paperback originals. **Publishes 8 titles/year. 90% from unagented writers. Pays 10-12% royalty.** Publishes book 18 months after acceptance of ms. Accepts simultaneous submissions. Responds in 8 months to queries. Book catalog for 6×9 SAE with 3 first-class stamps; ms guidelines online.

○ Woodbine House publishes books for or about individuals with disabilities to help those individuals and their families live fulfilling and satisfying lives in their homes, schools, and communities.

Nonfiction Publishes books for and about children with disabilities. Reference. Subjects include health/medicine. No personal accounts or general parenting guides. Submit outline, 3 sample chapters. Reviews artwork/photos as part of ms package.

Fiction Picture books (children's). Submit complete ms with SASE.

Recent Title(s) *Activity Schedules for Children With Autism: Teaching Independent Behavior*, by Lynn McClannahan and Patricia Krantz; *Children With Fragile X Syndrome: A Parents' Guide*, by Jayne Dixon Weber, Ed.

Tips "Do not send us a proposal on the basis of this description. Examine our catalog or website and a couple of our books to make sure you are on the right track. Put some thought into how your book could be marketed (aside from in bookstores). Keep cover letters concise and to the point; if it's a subject that interests us, we'll ask to see more."

Ⓝ WOODLAND PUBLISHING, INC.

448 E. 800 North, Orem UT 84097. (801)434-8113. Fax: (801)334-1913. Website: www.woodlandpublishing.com. Estab. 1974. Publishes perfect bound and trade paperback originals. **Offers advance.** Accepts simultaneous submissions. Book catalog and ms guidelines for #10 SASE or via e-mail.

○ "Our readers are interested in herbs and other natural health topics. Most of our books are sold through health food stores."

Nonfiction Subjects include health/medicine (alternative). Query with SASE and author credentials.

Recent Title(s) *Soy Smart Health, 2nd Ed.*, by Rita Elkins, MH; *100 and Healthy*, by W. Shaffer Fox.

Tips "Our readers are interested in herbs and other natural health topics. Most of our books are sold through health food stores."

Ⓝ WORDWARE PUBLISHING, INC.

2320 Los Rios Blvd., Suite 200, Plano TX 75074. (972)423-0090. Fax: (972)881-9147. E-mail: tmcevoy@wordware.com. Website: www.wordware.com. President: Russell A. Stultz. **Acquisitions:** Wes Beckwith, acquisitions editor. Estab. 1983. Publishes trade paperback and mass market paperback originals. **Publishes 20-25 titles/year. Receives 75-100 queries and 30-50 mss/year. 40% of books from first-time authors; 95% from unagented writers. Royalties/advances negotiated per project.** Publishes book 6 months after acceptance of ms. Accepts simultaneous submissions. Responds in 2 weeks to queries. Book catalog free; ms guidelines online.

○ Wordware publishes computer/electronics books covering a broad range of technologies for professional programmers and developers with special emphasis in game development, animation, and modeling.

Nonfiction Reference, technical, textbook. Subjects include computers/electronic. "Wordware publishes advanced titles for developers and professional programmers." Submit proposal package including 2 sample chapters, TOC, target audience summation, competing books.

Recent Title(s) *3DS Max Lighting; Modeling a Character in 3DS Max, 2nd Ed.*; *LightWave 3D 8 Character Animation; Essential LightWave 3D 8*; *OpenGL Game Development.*

WORKMAN PUBLISHING CO.

708 Broadway, New York NY 10003. (212)254-5900. Fax: (212)254-8098. Website: www.workman.com. Editor-in-Chief: Susan Bolotin. **Acquisitions:** Suzanne Rafer, executive editor (cookbook, child care, parenting, teen interest); Ruth Sullivan, Jennifer Griffin, Margot Herrera, Richard Rosen, senior editors. David Allender, senior editor (juvenile). Estab. 1967. Publishes hardcover and trade paperback originals. **Publishes 40 titles/year.**

Receives thousands of queries/year. Open to first-time authors. Pays variable royalty on retail price. Offers variable advance. Publishes book approximately 1 year after acceptance of ms. Accepts simultaneous submissions. Responds in 5 months to queries. Ms guidelines online.

Imprints Algonquin, Artisan, Greenwich Workshop Press, Storey.

○╌ ''We are a trade paperback house specializing in a wide range of popular nonfiction. We publish no adult fiction and very little children's fiction. We also publish a full range of full-color wall and Page-A-Day calendars.''

Nonfiction Cookbook, gift book, how-to, humor. Subjects include business/economics, child guidance/parenting, cooking/foods/nutrition, gardening, health/medicine, sports, travel. Query with SASE first for guidelines. Reviews artwork/photos as part of ms package.

Recent Title(s) *Stich 'n Bitch*, by Debbie Stoller; *Bad Cat*, by Jim Edgar; *Younger Next Year*, by Chris Crowley and Henry S. Lodge, MD.

Tips ''No phone calls, please. We do not accept submissions via fax or e-mail.''

WRITER'S DIGEST BOOKS

Imprint of F+W Publications, Inc., 4700 E. Galbraith Rd., Cincinnati OH 45236. (513)531-2690, ext. 1408. Website: www.writersdigest.com. **Acquisitions:** Jane Friedman, executive editor. Estab. 1920. Publishes hardcover originals and trade paperbacks. **Publishes 20-25 titles/year. Receives 300 queries and 50 mss/year. 30% from unagented writers. Pays 10-20% royalty on net receipts. Offers average $5,000 and up advance.** Publishes book 18 months after acceptance of ms. Accepts simultaneous submissions. Responds in 3 months to queries. Book catalog for 9×12 SAE with 6 first-class stamps.

○╌ Writer's Digest Books is the premiere source for books about writing, publishing instructional and reference books for writers. Typical mss are 80,000 words.

Nonfiction How-to, reference, instructional books for writers. ''Our instruction books stress results and how specifically to achieve them. Should be well-researched, yet lively and readable. We do not want to see books telling readers how to crack specific nonfiction markets: *Writing for the Computer Market* or *Writing for Trade Publications*, for instance. We are most in need of fiction-technique books written by published authors. Be prepared to explain how the proposed book differs from existing books on the subject.'' No fiction or poetry. Query with SASE, or submit outline, sample chapters, SASE.

Recent Title(s) *The Little Red Writing Book*, by Brandon Royal; *Page After Page*, by Heather Sellers; *First Draft in 30 Days*, by Karen Wiesner.

Tips ''Most queries we receive are either too broad (how to write fiction) or too niche (how to write erotic horror), and don't reflect a knowledge of our large backlist of 150 titles. We rarely publish books on niche topics such as songwriting, scriptwriting, or poetry, unless the author has outstanding credentials or an outstanding manuscript. We are actively seeking: briefer books (20,000-40,000 words) that distill vast amounts of writing advice into skimmable rules and principles; light or humorous reads about the writing life, superbly written; interactive and visual writing instruction books, similar to *Pocket Muse*, by Monica Wood; and general reference works that appeal to an audience beyond writers, such as specialized word finders, eccentric dictionaries, or pocket guides.''

Ⓝ WRITINGCAREER.COM

P.O. Box 14061, Surfside Beach SC 29575. Website: www.writingcareer.com. **Acquisitions:** Brian Konradt, publisher (how-to). Estab. 2003. Publishes electronic originals and reprints. **Publishes 12 titles/year. 100% from unagented writers. Pays 50% royalty on retail price.** Publishes book 1 month after acceptance of ms. Accepts simultaneous submissions. Responds in 1 month to queries. Book catalog and ms guidelines online.

Nonfiction Subjects include writing, freelancing, screenwriting, editing, marketing, copywriting, style guides, etc. ''We are a niche market with specific needs. We only publish nonfiction how-to books on the creative and business aspects of writing.'' Query at www.writingcareer.com/epublishing.shtml.

Recent Title(s) *Writing Industry Reports*, by Jennie S. Bev; *Freelance Writing for Vet Hospitals*, by Stanley Burkhardt.

Tips WritingCareer.com targets writers—freelancers, staff writers, hobbyists—who want to master their writing, marketing, and business skills. ''Browse our book titles at WritingCareer.com to better understand what we publish and sell.''

Ⓢ YALE UNIVERSITY PRESS

302 Temple St., New Haven CT 06511. (203)432-0960. Fax: (203)432-0948. Website: www.yale.edu/yup. **Acquisitions:** Jonathan Brent, editorial director (literature, literary studies, theater); Jean E. Thomson Black (science, medicine); Lauren Shapiro (reference books); Keith Condon (education, behavioral/social sciences); Michelle Komie (art, architecture); Patricia Fidler, publisher (art, architecture); Mary Jane Peluso, publisher (languages, ESL); John Kulka (literature, literary studies, philosophy, political science); Michael O'Malley (busi-

ness, economics, law); Molly Egland (history). Also: P.O. Box 209040, New Haven CT 06520-9040. Estab. 1908. Publishes hardcover and trade paperback originals. Accepts simultaneous submissions. Book catalog and ms guidelines online.

O→ Yale University Press publishes scholarly and general interest books.

Nonfiction Biography, illustrated book, reference, scholarly, textbook. Subjects include Americana, anthropology/archeology, art/architecture, business/economics, education, health/medicine, history, language/literature, military/war, music/dance, philosophy, psychology, religion, science, sociology, women's issues/studies. "Our nonfiction has to be at a very high level. Most of our books are written by professors or journalists, with a high level of expertise. Submit proposals only. We'll ask if we want to see more. *No unsolicited mss.* We won't return them." Submit sample chapters, cover letter, prospectus, cv, TOC, SASE. Reviews artwork/photos as part of ms package. Send photocopies.

Poetry Publishes 1 book each year. Submit to Yale Series of Younger Poets Competition. Open to poets under 40 who have not had a book previously published. Submit ms of 48-64 pages by November 15. Rules and guidelines available online or with SASE. Submit complete ms.

Recent Title(s) *Methodism: Empire of the Spirit*, by David Hempton; *A Drawing Manual*, by Thomas Eakins; *The Eighties: America in the Age of Reagan*, by John Ehrman.

Tips "Audience is scholars, students and general readers."

N A ZEBRA BOOKS

Kensington, 850 Third Ave., 16th Floor, New York NY 10022. (212)407-1500. Website: www.kensingtonbooks.com. Publishes hardcover originals, trade paperback and mass market paperback originals and reprints. Accepts simultaneous submissions. Book catalog online.

O→ Zebra Books is dedicated to women's fiction, which includes, but is not limited to romance.

Fiction Mostly historical romance. Some contemporary romance, westerns, horror, and humor. *Agented submissions only.*

Recent Title(s) *Calder Promise*, by Janet Dailey; *Come Up and See Me Sometime*, by Lucy Monroe; *A Perfect Wedding*, by Anne Robins.

MARKETS

Canadian & International Book Publishers

anadian and international book publishers share the same mission as their U.S. counterparts—publishing timely books on subjects of concern and interest to a targetable audience. Most of the publishers listed in this section, however, differ from U.S. publishers in that their needs tend toward subjects specific to their country or are intended for a Canadian or international audience. Some are interested in submissions from writers outside the U.S. only. There are many regional publishers that concentrate on region-specific subjects.

U.S. writers hoping to do business with Canadian or international publishers should follow specific paths of research to find out as much about their intended markets as possible. The listings will inform you about what kinds of books the Canadian and international companies publish and tell you whether they are open to receiving submissions from writers in the U.S. To further target your markets and see specific examples of the books these houses are publishing, send for catalogs from publishers, or check their websites.

Once you have determined which publishers will accept your work, it is important to understand the differences that exist between U.S. mail and international mail. U.S. postage stamps are useless on mailings originating outside of the U.S. When enclosing a SASE for return of your query or manuscript from a publisher outside the U.S. (including Canada), you must include International Reply Coupons (IRCs) or postage stamps from that country.

Canadian publishers are indicated by the ✛ icon, and markets located outside of the U.S. and Canada are indicated by the 🌐 icon.

For a list of publishers according to their subjects of interest, see the Nonfiction and Fiction sections of the Book Publishers' Subject Index. Information on book publishers listed in the previous edition of *Writer's Market*, but not included in this edition, can be found in the General Index.

Book Publishers

A&C BLACK PUBLISHERS, LTD.

Bloomsbury Plc, 37 Soho Square, London W1D 3QZ United Kingdom. (020)7758-0200. Fax: (020)7758-0222. **Acquisitions:** Sarah Fecher, editor (children's nonfiction); Susila Baglars, editor (children's fiction); Janet Murphy, editor (nautical); Charlotte Jenkins (sport); Linda Lambert, editor (arts and crafts); Jenny Ridout, editor (theater, writing, reference); Nigel Redman, editor (ornithology). Publishes hardcover and trade paperback originals, trade paperback reprints. **Publishes 170 titles/year; imprint publishes 10-20 titles/year. Receives 3,000 queries and 650 mss/year. 5% of books from first-time authors; 70% from unagented writers. Pays royalty on retail price or net receipts; makes outright purchase very occasionally on short children's books. Offers £1,500-6,000 advance.** Publishes book 9 months after acceptance of ms. Accepts simultaneous submissions. Responds in 1 month to queries; 2 months to proposals and mss. Book catalog free.

Imprints Adlard Coles Nautical (Janet Murphy, editor); Christopher Helm/Pica Press (Nigel Redman, editor); Herbert Press (Linda Lambert, editor).

Nonfiction Children's/juvenile, how-to, illustrated book, reference. Subjects include art/architecture, creative nonfiction, education, multicultural, music/dance, nature/environment, recreation, sports, travel, nutrition. Query with SASE, or submit proposal package including outline, 2 sample chapters, or submit complete ms. Reviews artwork/photos as part of ms package. Send transparencies.

Fiction Juvenile. Submit 2 sample chapters, synopsis, or submit complete ms.

Recent Title(s) *Marathon From Start to Finish*, by Sam Murphy; *The Last Great Adventure of Sir Peter Blake*, by Sir Peter Blake.

IAN ALLAN PUBLISHING, LTD.

Riverdene Business Park, Molesey Rd., Hersham Surrey KT12 4RG United Kingdom. (+44)1932 266600. Fax: (+44)1932 266601. E-mail: info@ianallanpub.co.uk. Website: www.ianallanpub.co.uk. **Acquisitions:** Peter Waller, publishing manager. Publishes hardcover, trade paperback and mass market paperback originals and reprints. **Publishes 120 titles/year. Receives 300 queries and 50 mss/year. 5% of books from first-time authors; 95% from unagented writers. Payment is subject to contract and type of publication.** Publishes book 6 months after acceptance of ms. Accepts simultaneous submissions. Book catalog free.

Imprints OPC; Dial House; Midland Publishing; Ian Allan Publishing.

Nonfiction Illustrated book. Subjects include history, hobbies, military/war, sports, travel. Query with SASE. Reviews artwork/photos as part of ms package.

Recent Title(s) *War Without Garlands*, by Kershaw (military history); *Enigma U-Boats*, by Showell (naval history); *Without Enigma*, by Macksey (military history).

Tips Audience is enthusiasts and historians. "We don't publish books with a strong autobiographical bias—e.g., military reminiscences—and no fiction/children's/poetry."

AMBER LANE PRESS, LTD.

Church St., Charlbury OX7 3PR United Kingdom. 01608 810024. Fax: 01608 810024. E-mail: info@amberlanepress.co.uk. Website: www.amberlanepress.co.uk. **Acquisitions:** Judith Scott, managing editor (drama/theater/music). Publishes hardcover and trade paperback originals, trade paperback reprints. **Publishes 5 titles/year. Receives 10 queries and 6 mss/year. 20% of books from first-time authors; 10% from unagented writers. Pays 7¹/₂-12% royalty. Offers £250-1,000 (sterling pounds) advance.** Publishes book 18 months after acceptance of ms. Accepts simultaneous submissions. Responds in 1 month to queries. Book catalog free.

Amber Lane Press aims "to help promote British theater and modern drama in general."

Nonfiction Biography, how-to, reference. Subjects include music/dance. Submit proposal package including outline, 2 sample chapters.

Fiction Plays. "All plays need to be staged professionally by a major theater/theater company." Submit complete ms.

Recent Title(s) *Theatre in a Cool Climate*, Vera Gottlieb and Colin Chambers, eds; *Oroonoko*, Aphra Behn, adapted by Biyi Bandele (play); *Strindberg and Love*, by Eivor Martinus (biography).

Tips "Explain why the book would be different from anything else already published on the subject."

ANNICK PRESS, LTD.

15 Patricia Ave., Toronto ON M2M 1H9 Canada. (416)221-4802. Fax: (416)221-8400. E-mail: annickpress@annickpress.com. Website: www.annickpress.com. **Acquisitions:** Rick Wilks, director; Colleen MacMillan, associate publisher. Publishes picture books, juvenile and YA fiction and nonfiction; specializes in trade books. **Publishes 25 titles/year. Receives 5,000 queries and 3,000 mss/year. 20% of books from first-time authors; 80-85% from unagented writers.** Publishes book 2 years after acceptance of ms. Book catalog and ms guidelines online.

- *Does not accept unsolicited mss.*
- Annick Press maintains "a commitment to high quality books that entertain and challenge. Our publications share fantasy and stimulate imagination, while encouraging children to trust their judgment and abilities."

Recent Title(s) *Chanda's Secrets*, by Allen Stratton; *Hoodwinked: Deception and Resistance*, by Stephen Shapiro and Lena Forrester; illustrated by David Craig; *The Sidewalk Rescue*, by Hazel Hutchins.

ANVIL PRESS

3008 MPO, Vancouver BC V6B 3X5 Canada. (604)876-8710. Fax: (604)879-2667. E-mail: info@anvilpress.com. Website: www.anvilpress.com. **Acquisitions:** Brian Kaufman. Estab. 1988. Publishes trade paperback originals. **Publishes 8-10 titles/year. Receives 300 queries/year. 80% of books from first-time authors; 70% from unagented writers. Pays 15% royalty on net receipts. Offers $500 advance.** Publishes book 8 months after acceptance of ms. Accepts simultaneous submissions. Responds in 2 months to queries; 6 months to mss. Book catalog for 9 × 12 SAE with 2 first-class stamps; ms guidelines online.

- Canadian authors only.
- "Anvil Press publishes contemporary adult fiction, poetry, and drama, giving voice to up-and-coming Canadian writers, exploring all literary genres, discovering, nurturing, and promoting new Canadian literary talent." Currently emphasizing urban/suburban themed fiction and poetry; de-emphasizing historical novels.

Fiction Experimental, literary, short story collections. Contemporary, modern literature—no formulaic or genre. Query with SASE.

Poetry "Get our catalog, look at our poetry. We do very little poetry—maybe 1-2 titles per year." Query, or submit 12 sample poems.

Recent Title(s) *Tight Like That*, by Jim Christy (fiction); *Rattlesnake Plantain*, by Heidi Greco (poetry).

Tips Audience is young, informed, educated, aware, with an opinion, culturally active (films, books, the performing arts). "No US authors. Research the appropriate publisher for your work."

ARSENAL PULP PRESS

Suite 103, 1014 Homer St., Vancouver BC V6B 2W9 Canada. (604)687-4233. Fax: (604)687-4283. E-mail: contact @arsenalpulp.com. Website: www.arsenalpulp.com. **Acquisitions:** Brian Lam, publisher. Estab. 1980. Publishes trade paperback originals, and trade paperback reprints. Rarely publishes non-Canadian authors. **Publishes 20 titles/year. Receives 400 queries and 200 mss/year. 40% of books from first-time authors; 100% from unagented writers.** Publishes book 1 year after acceptance of ms. Accepts simultaneous submissions. Responds in 2 months to queries; 4 months to proposals and mss. Book catalog for 9 × 12 SAE with 2 first-class stamps or online; ms guidelines online.

Nonfiction Cookbook, illustrated book, literary, cultural studies. Subjects include art/architecture, cooking/foods/nutrition, creative nonfiction, ethnic (Canadian, aboriginal issues), gay/lesbian, history (cultural), language/literature, multicultural, regional (British Columbia), sex, sociology, travel, women's issues/studies, film. Submit proposal package including outline, 2-3 sample chapters. Reviews artwork/photos as part of ms package.

Fiction Erotica, ethnic (general), feminist, gay/lesbian, literary, multicultural, short story collections. No children's books or genre fiction, i.e., westerns, romance, horror, mystery, etc. Submit proposal package including outline, 2-3 sample chapters, synopsis.

Recent Title(s) *The Greenpeace to Amchitka*, by Robert Hunter (nonfiction); *Vive le Vegan*, by Dreena Burton (nonfiction cookbook); *When Fox Is a Thousand*, by Larissa Lai (fiction).

BEACH HOLME PUBLISHERS, LTD.

1010-409 Granville St., Vancouver BC V6C 1T2 Canada. (604)733-4868. Fax: (604)733-4860. E-mail: bhp@beach holme.bc.ca. Website: www.beachholme.bc.ca. **Acquisitions:** Michael Carroll, publisher (adult and young adult fiction, poetry, creative nonfiction); Jen Hamilton, production manager; Sarah Warren, publicity and marketing coordinator. Estab. 1971. Publishes trade paperback originals. **Publishes 10-14 titles/year. 40% of books from first-time authors; 75% from unagented writers. Pays 10% royalty on retail price. Offers $500 average advance.** Publishes book 1 year after acceptance of ms. Does not accept simultaneous submissions. Responds in 4-6 months to queries. Ms guidelines online.

Imprints Porcepic Books (literary); Sandcastle Books (children's/YA); Prospect Books (nonfiction).

- Beach Holme seeks "to publish excellent, emerging Canadian fiction, nonfiction, and poetry and to contribute to Canadian materials for children with quality young adult historical novels."

Nonfiction Subjects include creative nonfiction. Query with SASE, or submit outline, 2 sample chapters.

Fiction Experimental, literary, poetry, young adult (Canada historical/regional), quality imaginative adult literary fiction from authors published in Canadian literary magazines. Query with SASE, or submit outline, 2 sample chapters.

Recent Title(s) *Kameleon Man*, by Kim Barry Brunhuber; *Last Days in Africville*, by Dorothy Perkyns.

Tips "Make sure the manuscript is well written. We see so many that only the unique and excellent can't be put down. Prior publication is a must. This doesn't necessarily mean book-length manuscripts, but a writer should try to publish his or her short fiction or poetry."

Ⓝ ⓦ BERG PUBLISHERS

Oxford International Publishers, 1st Floor, Angel Court, 81 St. Clements St., Oxford Oxfordshire OX4 1AW United Kingdom. (44)1865-245104. Fax: (44)1865-791165. E-mail: hshakespeare@bergpublishers.com. Website: www.bergpublishers.com. **Acquisitions:** Hannah Shakespeare, editorial assistant. Publishes hardcover and trade paperback originals. **Publishes 50 titles/year. Receives 700 queries and 100 mss/year. 98% from unagented writers. Pays royalty on wholesale price.** Publishes book 9 months after acceptance of ms. Does not accept simultaneous submissions. Responds in 2 months to queries and proposals; 4 months to mss. Book catalog free; ms guidelines online.

> ⚷ Berg Publishers publishes "academic books aimed at an undergraduate and postgraduate readership only." Currently emphasizing fashion, sport, material culture, leisure studies, consumption, cultural history. De-emphasizing literary studies.

Nonfiction Textbook. Subjects include anthropology/archeology, history, sociology, sports, fashion. Submit proposal package including outline.

Recent Title(s) *'Don We Now Our Gay Apparel': Gay Men's Dress in the 20th Century*, by Shaun Cole; *The Internet: An Ethnographic Approach*, by Daniel Miller and Don Slater; *Filming Women in the Third Reich*, by Jo Fox.

ⓦ BETWEEN THE LINES

720 Bathurst St., Suite #404, Toronto ON M5S 2R4 Canada. (416)535-9914. Fax: (416)535-1484. E-mail: btlbooks @web.ca. Website: www.btlbooks.com. **Acquisitions:** Paul Eprile, editorial coordinator. Publishes trade paperback originals. **Publishes 8 titles/year. Receives 350 queries and 50 mss/year. 80% of books from first-time authors; 95% from unagented writers. Pays 8% royalty.** Publishes book 1 year after acceptance of ms. Accepts simultaneous submissions. Responds in 2 months to queries and proposals; 4 months to mss. Book catalog and ms guidelines for 8½×11 SAE and IRCs; ms guidelines online.

> ⚷ "We are a small independent house concentrating on politics and public policy issues, social issues, gender issues, international development, education, and the environment. We publish mainly Canadian authors."

Nonfiction Subjects include education, gay/lesbian, government/politics, health/medicine, history, memoirs, social sciences, sociology, women's issues/studies. Submit proposal package including outline, 2-3 sample chapters. Reviews artwork/photos as part of ms package.

Recent Title(s) *Booze: A Distilled History*; *User Error: Resisting Computer Culture*.

Ⓝ ⓦ BIRLINN, LTD.

West Newington House, 10 Newington Rd., Edinburgh Scotland EH9 1QS United Kingdom. +44(0)131 668 4371. Fax: +44(0)131 668 4466. E-mail: info@birlinn.co.uk. Website: www.birlinn.co.uk. **Acquisitions:** Hugh Andrew, managing director. Publishes hardcover, trade and mass market originals; trade and mass market reprints. **Publishes 80 titles/year; imprint publishes 5 titles/year. Receives 50 queries and 25 mss/year. 10% of books from first-time authors; 90% from unagented writers. Pays 8% royalty on net receipts. Offers £0-2,000 advance.** Publishes book 1 year after acceptance of ms. Accepts simultaneous submissions. Responds in 1 month. Book catalog free.

Imprints John Donald, Ltd. (Hugh Andrew, managing director).

Nonfiction Biography, gift book, humor, reference, textbook, academic. Subjects include anthropology/archeology, creative nonfiction, education, history, language/literature, memoirs, military/war, nature/environment, religion, sports, travel. Query with SASE, or submit proposal package including outline. Reviews artwork/photos as part of ms package. Send photocopies.

Fiction Historical, military/war, regional, sports. Query with SASE, or submit proposal package including 2 sample chapters, synopsis.

Recent Title(s) *Mull*, Jo Currie; *Shackleton's Boat Journey*, Frank Worsley; *Queen's Country*, Robert Smith.

Tips A wide and varied national and international audience.

ⓞ ⓦ BOREALIS PRESS, LTD.

110 Bloomingdale St., Ottawa ON K2C 4A4 Canada. (613)829-0150. Fax: (613)829-7783. E-mail: drt@borealispress.com. Website: www.borealispress.com. **Acquisitions:** Glenn Clever, senior editor. Estab. 1972. Publishes

hardcover and paperback originals and reprints. **Publishes 20 titles/year. 80% of books from first-time authors; 95% from unagented writers. Pays 10% royalty on net receipts; plus 3 free author's copies.** Publishes book 18 months after acceptance of ms. Does not accept simultaneous submissions. Responds in 2 months to queries; 4 months to mss. Book catalog and ms guidelines online.

Imprints Tecumseh Press.

    O⟳ "Our mission is to publish work which will be of lasting interest in the Canadian book market." Currently emphasizing Canadian fiction, nonfiction, drama, poetry. De-emphasizing children's books.

Nonfiction Biography, children's/juvenile, reference. Subjects include government/politics, history, language/literature, regional. "Only material Canadian in content." Looks for "style in tone and language, reader interest, and maturity of outlook." Query with SASE, or submit outline, 2 sample chapters. *No unsolicited mss.* Reviews artwork/photos as part of ms package.

Fiction Adventure, ethnic, historical, juvenile, literary, mainstream/contemporary, romance, short story collections, young adult. "Only material Canadian in content and dealing with significant aspects of the human situation." Query with SASE, or submit 1-2 sample chapters, synopsis. *No unsolicited mss.*

Recent Title(s) *Canada's Governors General At Play*, by James Noonan; *James McGill of Montreal*, by John Cooper; *Musk Oxen of Gango*, by Mary Burpee.

⬔ THE BOSTON MILLS PRESS

132 Main St., Erin ON N0B 1T0 Canada. (519)833-2407. Fax: (519)833-2195. E-mail: books@bostonmillspress.com. Website: www.bostonmillspress.com. President: John Denison. **Acquisitions:** Noel Hudson, managing editor. Estab. 1974. Publishes hardcover and trade paperback originals. **Publishes 20 titles/year. 40% of books from first-time authors; 95% from unagented writers. Pays 8% royalty on retail price. Offers advance.** Publishes book 6 months-2 years after acceptance of ms. Accepts simultaneous submissions. Responds in 2 months to queries. Book catalog free.

    O⟳ Boston Mills Press publishes specific market titles of Canadian and American interest including history, transportation, and regional guidebooks. "We like very focused books aimed at the North American market."

Nonfiction Coffee table book, gift book, illustrated book. Subjects include Americana, art/architecture, cooking/foods/nutrition, creative nonfiction, gardening, history, military/war, nature/environment, photography, recreation, regional, sports, travel, Canadiana. "We're interested in anything to do with Canadian or American history—especially transportation." No autobiographies. Query with SASE. Reviews artwork/photos as part of ms package. Send photocopies.

⬡ BRADT TRAVEL GUIDES, LTD.

19 High St., Chalfont St. Peter Bucks SL9 9QE United Kingdom. 01753 893444. Fax: 01753 892333. E-mail: info@bradt-travelguides.com. Website: www.bradtguides.com. **Acquisitions:** Tricia Hayne, editorial director; Adrian Phillips, senior editor. Estab. 1974. Publishes mass market paperback originals. **Publishes 25 titles/year. Receives 150 queries and 60 mss/year. 30% of books from first-time authors; 95% from unagented writers. Pays 11½% royalty on wholesale price. Offers advance.** Publishes book 6 months after acceptance of ms. Does not accept simultaneous submissions. Responds in 1 month. Book catalog online; ms guidelines by e-mail.

Nonfiction Subjects include focus on travel, including a series of mini guides to more unusual European and other cities. "We specialize in unusual destinations or unusual ways of looking at more popular destinations. Wildlife, history, culture and responsible travel important." Submit outline, details of competition and author's suitability for the title. Query with SAE.

Recent Title(s) *Faroe Islands: The Bradt Travel Guide*, by James Proctor; *Cameroon: The Bradt Travel Guide*, by Ben West; *Budapest: The Bradt City Guide*, by Adrian Phillips.

Tips "Audience includes thinking, responsible travelers who are interested in destinations off the beaten tourist track. Be enthusiastic about the country you want to cover—we often commission energetic first-time authors in preference to seasoned hacks. Include an e-mail address for replies if possible."

⬚ ⬔ BROADVIEW PRESS, INC.

P.O. Box 1243, Peterborough ON K9J 7H5 Canada. (705)743-8990. Fax: (705)743-8353. E-mail: customerservice@broadviewpress.com. Website: www.broadviewpress.com. **Acquisitions:** Julia Gaunce, humanities editor (English, philosophy); Mical Moser, history editor; Michael Harrison, president/politics editor; Anne Brackenbury, anthropology & sociology editor. Estab. 1985. **Publishes over 60 titles/year. Receives 500 queries and 200 mss/year. 10% of books from first-time authors; 99% from unagented writers. Pays royalty.** Publishes book 1 year after acceptance of ms. Accepts simultaneous submissions. Responds in 1 month to queries; 2 months to proposals; 4 months to mss. Book catalog free; ms guidelines online.

○━ "We publish in a broad variety of subject areas in the arts and social sciences. We are open to a broad range of political and philosophical viewpoints, from liberal and conservative to libertarian and Marxist, and including a wide range of feminist viewpoints."

Nonfiction Biography, reference, textbook. Subjects include anthropology/archeology, gay/lesbian, history, language/literature, philosophy, religion, sociology, women's issues/studies, politics. "All titles must have some potential for university or college-level course use. Crossover titles are acceptable." Query with SASE, or submit proposal package. Reviews artwork/photos as part of ms package. Send photocopies.

Recent Title(s) *A Short History of the Middle Ages, 2nd Ed.*, by Barbara Rosenwein; *Seeing Medieval Art*, by Herbert L. Kessler.

Tips "Our titles often appeal to a broad readership; we have many books that are as much of interest to the general reader as they are to academics and students."

■ BROKEN JAW PRESS

Box 596, Station A, Fredericton NB E3B 5A6 Canada. (506)454-5127. Fax: (506)454-5127. E-mail: jblades@broke njaw.com. Website: www.brokenjaw.com. Publisher: Joe Blades. **Acquisitions:** Editorial Board. Publishes mostly Canadian-authored literary trade paperback originals and reprints. **Publishes 8-12 titles/year. 50% of books from first-time authors; 100% from unagented writers. Pays 10% royalty on retail price. Offers $0-500 advance.** Publishes book 18 months after acceptance of ms. Does not accept simultaneous submissions. Responds in 1 year to mss. Book catalog for 6×9 SAE with 2 first-class Canadian stamps in Canada or download PDF from website; ms guidelines online.

Imprints Book Rat; Broken Jaw Press; SpareTime Editions; Dead Sea Physh Products; Maritimes Arts Projects Productions.

○━ "We publish poetry, fiction, drama and literary nonfiction, including translations and multilingual books."

Nonfiction Illustrated book, essays, artist books, literary nonfiction. Subjects include gay/lesbian, history, language/literature, regional, women's issues/studies, contemporary culture. Reviews artwork/photos as part of ms package.

Fiction Literary (novels and short stories).

Recent Title(s) *The Space of Light/El Espacio de la Luz*, by Nela Rio; edited and translated by Elizabeth Gamble Miller (fiction/poetry); *Sculpture: A Journey to the Circumference of the Earth*, by Robin Peck (essays/art).

Tips "Unsolicited manuscripts are welcome only in the context of the Poets' Corner Award. Please see the award guidelines on our website."

● BROWN SKIN BOOKS

Pentimento, Ltd., P.O. Box 46504, London N1 3NT United Kingdom. E-mail: info@brownskinbooks.co.uk. Website: www.brownskinbooks.co.uk. **Acquisitions:** Vastiana Belfon, managing director (erotic fiction by women of color). Estab. 2002. Publishes trade paperback originals. **Publishes 7 titles/year. 75% of books from first-time authors; 80% from unagented writers. Pays 5-50% royalty, or makes outright purchase.** Publishes book 9-12 months after acceptance of ms. Accepts simultaneous submissions. Responds in 1 month to queries; 2 months to proposals and mss. Book catalog and ms guidelines online.

Fiction Erotica. "We are looking for erotic short stories or novels written by women of color." Submit proposal package including 2 sample chapters, synopsis.

Recent Title(s) *Personal Business*, by Isabel Baptiste; *Body and Soul*, by Jade Williams.

Tips "Audience is women of color aged 18 to 50, living in the US, Canada, Europe, Africa, and the Caribbean. Please make sure there is a strong story with believable characters. This is just as important as the sex in our erotic fiction."

■ CANADIAN LIBRARY ASSOCIATION

328 Frank St., Ottawa ON K2P 0X8 Canada. (613)232-9625. Fax: (613)563-9895. E-mail: publishing@cla.ca. Website: www.cla.ca. Publishes trade paperback originals. **Publishes 4 titles/year. Receives 10 queries and 5 mss/year. 50% of books from first-time authors; 100% from unagented writers. Pays 10% royalty on wholesale price.** Publishes book 6 months after acceptance of ms. Does not accept simultaneous submissions. Responds in 1 month to queries; 3 months to proposals and mss. Book catalog and ms guidelines free.

○━ "CLA publishes practical/professional/academic materials with a Canadian focus or direct Canadian application as a service to CLA members and to contribute to the professional development of library staff."

Nonfiction Reference, textbook. Subjects include history, language/literature, library science. Query with SASE, or submit outline. Reviews artwork/photos as part of ms package. Send photocopies.

Recent Title(s) *The Canadian Genealogical Sourcebook*; *Access to Information in a Digital World*.

Tips Audience is library and information scientists.

◨ CANADIAN PLAINS RESEARCH CENTER

University of Regina, Regina SK S4S 0A2 Canada. (306)585-4795. Fax: (306)585-4699. E-mail: brian.mlazgar@ur egina.ca. Website: www.cprc.uregina.ca. **Acquisitions:** Brian Mlazgar, coordinator. Estab. 1973. Publishes scholarly paperback originals and some casebound originals. **Publishes 8-10 titles/year. 35% of books from first-time authors.** Publishes book 2 years after acceptance of ms. Does not accept simultaneous submissions. Responds in 6 months to queries. Book catalog and ms guidelines free.

　　O₋₇ Canadian Plains Research Center publishes scholarly research on the Canadian plains.

Nonfiction Biography, illustrated book, technical, textbook. Subjects include business/economics, government/ politics, history, nature/environment, regional, sociology. "The Canadian Plains Research Center publishes the results of research on topics relating to the Canadian Plains region, although manuscripts relating to the Great Plains region will be considered. Material *must* be scholarly. Do not submit health, self-help, hobbies, music, sports, psychology, recreation, or cookbooks unless they have a scholarly approach." Query with SASE, or submit complete ms. Reviews artwork/photos as part of ms package.

Recent Title(s) *I Could Not Speak My Heart: Education and Social Justice for Gay and Lesbian Youth*, edited by James McNinch and Mary Cronin (19 articles intended for education about the problems faced by gay and lesbian youth).

Tips "Pay attention to manuscript preparation and accurate footnoting, according to *Chicago Manual of Style.*"

◨ ◉ CAPALL BANN PUBLISHING

Auton Farm, Milverton, Somerset TA4 1NE United Kingdom. (0044)1823 401528. Fax: (0044)1823 401529. E-mail: enquiries@capallbann.co.uk. Website: www.capallbann.co.uk. **Acquisitions:** Julia Day (MBS, healing, animals); Jon Day (MBS, religion). Publishes trade and mass market paperback originals and trade paperback and mass market paperback reprints. **Publishes 46 titles/year. Receives 800 queries and 450 mss/year. 50% of books from first-time authors; 100% from unagented writers. Pays 10% royalty on net sales.** Publishes book 8 months after acceptance of ms. Accepts simultaneous submissions. Responds in 2-6 weeks to queries; 2 months to proposals and mss. Book catalog free; ms guidelines online.

　　O₋₇ "Our mission is to publish books of real value to enhance and improve readers' lives."

Nonfiction Illustrated book, reference, self-help. Subjects include animals, anthropology/archeology, gardening, health/medicine, music/dance, nature/environment, philosophy, religion, spirituality, women's issues/studies, new age. Submit outline. Reviews artwork/photos as part of ms package. Send photocopies.

Recent Title(s) *Everything You Wanted to Know About Your Body, But So Far Nobody's Been Able to Tell You*; *Real Fairies*, by David Tame.

◨ ◨ CARSWELL THOMSON

One Corporate Plaza 2075 Kennedy Rd., Scarborough ON M1T 3V4 Canada. (416)298-5024. Fax: (416)298-5094. E-mail: robert.freeman@thomson.com. Website: www.carswell.com. **Acquisitions:** Robert Freeman, vice president, legal, accounting and finance, and corporate groups. Publishes hardcover originals. **Publishes 150-200 titles/year. 30-50% of books from first-time authors. Pays 5-15% royalty on wholesale price.** Publishes book 6 months after acceptance of ms. Accepts simultaneous submissions. Responds in 3 months to queries. Book catalog and ms guidelines free.

　　O₋₇ Carswell Thomson is Canada's national resource of information and legal interpretations for law, accounting, tax and business professionals.

Nonfiction Reference (legal, tax). "Canadian information of a regulatory nature is our mandate." Submit proposal package including outline, résumé.

Tips Audience is Canada and persons interested in Canadian information; professionals in law, tax, accounting fields; business people interested in regulatory material.

◨ CHA PRESS

17 York St., Ottawa ON K1N 9J6 Canada. (613)241-8005, ext. 264. Fax: (613)241-5055. E-mail: chapress@cha. ca. Website: www.cha.ca. **Acquisitions:** Eleanor Sawyer, director of publishing. **Publishes 4-5 titles/year. Receives 5 queries and 3 mss/year. 40% of books from first-time authors; 90% from unagented writers. Pays 10-17% royalty on retail price, or makes outright purchase of $250-1,000. Offers $500-1,500 advance.** Responds in 3 months to queries. Book catalog and ms guidelines free.

　　O₋₇ CHA Press strives to be Canada's health administration textbook publisher. "We serve readers in our broad continuum of care in regional health authorities, hospitals, and health care facilities and agencies, which are governed by trustees." Currently emphasizing history of regionalization; accountability of boards/executives; executives and leadership. De-emphasizing hospital-based issues of any type.

Nonfiction How-to, textbook, guides. Subjects include health/medicine, history. Query with SASE, or submit outline.

Recent Title(s) *Governance for Health System Trustees*, by Jannice E. Moore; *The Road to Eden North: How Five*

Canadian Long-Term Care Facilities Became Eden Alternatives, edited by Eleanor Sawyer, with Cynthia Rurak.

Tips Audience is healthcare facility managers (senior/middle); policy analysts/researchers; nurse practitioners and other healthcare professionals; trustees. "CHA Press is looking to expand its frontlist in 2005 to include accountability, risk management, security and safety, fundraising, and quality assessment. Don't underestimate amount of time it will take to write or mistake generic 'how-to health for mass media' as appropriate for CHA's specialty press."

CHEMTEC PUBLISHING

38 Earswick Dr., Toronto-Scarborough ON M1E 1C6 Canada. (416)265-2603. Fax: (416)265-1399. E-mail: info@ chemtec.org. Website: www.chemtec.org. **Acquisitions:** Anna Wypych, president. Publishes hardcover originals. **Publishes 5 titles/year. Receives 10 queries and 7 mss/year. 20% of books from first-time authors. Pays 5-15% royalty on retail price.** Publishes book 6 months after acceptance of ms. Accepts simultaneous submissions. Responds in 2 months to queries; 4 months to mss. Book catalog and ms guidelines free.

⊶ Chemtec publishes books on polymer chemistry, physics, and technology. "Special emphasis is given to process additives and books which treat subject in comprehensive manner."

Nonfiction Technical, textbook. Subjects include science, environment, chemistry, polymers. Submit outline, sample chapters.

Recent Title(s) *Handbook of Plastisizers*, by George Wypych; *Handbook of Antibloekiny, Release, and Slip Additives*, by George Wypych.

Tips Audience is industrial research and universities.

COACH HOUSE BOOKS

401 Huron St. on bpNichol Lane, Toronto ON M5S 2G5 Canada. (416)979-2217. Fax: (416)977-1158. Website: www.chbooks.com. **Acquisitions:** Alana Wilcox, editor. Publishes trade paperback originals. **Publishes 16 titles/year. 80% of books from first-time authors; 100% from unagented writers. Pays 10% royalty on retail price.** Publishes book 1 year after acceptance of ms. Does not accept simultaneous submissions. Responds in 6 months to queries. Ms guidelines online.

Nonfiction Artists' books. Query with SASE. *All unsolicited mss returned unopened.*

Fiction Experimental, literary, plays. "Consult website for submissions policy." *All unsolicited mss returned unopened.*

Poetry Consult website for guidelines. Query.

Recent Title(s) *Eunoia*, by Christian Bök (poetry); *Lenny Bruce Is Dead*, by Jonathan Goldstein (fiction); *All My Friends Are Superheroes*, by Andrew Kaufman (fiction).

Tips "We are not a general publisher, and publish only Canadian poetry, fiction, artist books and drama. We are interested primarily in innovative or experimental writing."

CONSTABLE & ROBINSON, LTD.

Constable & Robinson, 3 The Lanchesters, 162 Fulham Palace Rd., London WB 9ER United Kingdom. 0208-741-3663. Fax: 0208-748-7562. **Acquisitions:** (Ms.) Carol O'Brien (biography: historical and literary, Celtic interest, pre-WWII military history, travel literature); Krystyna Green (crime fiction); Dan Hind (politics, current affairs, nonfiction); Pete Duncan (popular science, photographic, true crime, nonfiction); Sandra Rigby (health, psychology); Becky Hardie (literary fiction, history). Publishes hardcover and trade paperback originals. **Publishes 160 titles/year. Receives 3,000 queries and 1,000 mss/year. Pays royalty. Offers advance.** Publishes book 1 year after acceptance of ms. Accepts simultaneous submissions. Responds in 1 month to queries and proposals; 3 months to mss. Book catalog free.

Imprints Constable Hardback; Robinson Paperback.

Nonfiction Biography. Subjects include health/medicine, history, military/war, psychology, science (popular), travel, politics, current affairs. Query with SASE, or submit 3 sample chapters, list of chapter titles. Reviews artwork/photos as part of ms package. Send photocopies.

Fiction Crime/whodunnit and some literary fiction. Length 80,000 words minimum; 130,000 words maximum. *Agented submissions only.* Submit 3 sample chapters, synopsis, SASE.

Recent Title(s) *The Best Democracy Money Can Buy* (current affairs); *Love All the People: Complete Works of Bill Hicks* (biography/humor); *Hunting Midnight*, by Richard Zimler (literary fiction).

CORMORANT BOOKS, INC.

215 Spadina Ave., Studio 230, Toronto ON M5T 2C7 Canada. (416)929-4957. Fax: (416)929-3596. Website: www.cormorantbooks.com. **Acquisitions:** Marc Côté, publisher. Publishes hardcover, trade paperback originals and reprints. **Publishes 16-20 titles/year. Receives 500 queries and 300 mss/year. 50% of books from first-time authors; 50% from unagented writers. Pays 8-15% royalty on retail price. Offers $500-15,000**

advance. Publishes book 1-2 years after acceptance of ms. Accepts simultaneous submissions. Responds in 1 months to queries and proposals; 3 months to mss. Book catalog and ms guidelines free or online.

⚷ Cormorant publishes Canadian fiction and essay collections, occasional nonfiction titles, usually on literary themes. Currently emphasizing novels. De-emphasizing short stories.

Nonfiction Biography. Subjects include creative nonfiction, history, memoirs, philosophy. Query with SASE.

Fiction Cormorant is a highly literary company with hundreds of awards for literary excellence. Adventure, confession, ethnic, experimental, feminist, gay/lesbian, historical, humor, literary, mainstream/contemporary, multicultural, mystery, plays, poetry, regional, short story collections. Query with SASE, or submit 3 sample chapters, synopsis, or submit complete ms.

Recent Title(s) *Beyond Measure*, by Pauline Holdstock (novel); *Still Life With June*, by Darren Greer (novel).

Tips "Writers should determine, from a study of our list, whether their fiction or essay collection would be appropriate. *Canadian authors only.*"

⚌ COTEAU BOOKS

Thunder Creek Publishing Co-operative Ltd., 401-2206 Dewdney Ave., Regina SK S4R 1H3 Canada. (306)777-0170. Fax: (306)522-5152. E-mail: coteau@coteaubooks.com. Website: www.coteaubooks.com. **Acquisitions:** Geoffrey Ursell, publisher. Estab. 1975. Publishes trade paperback originals and reprints. **Publishes 16 titles/ year. Receives 200 queries and 200 mss/year. 25% of books from first-time authors; 90% from unagented writers. Pays 10% royalty on retail price.** Publishes book 1 year after acceptance of ms. Does not accept simultaneous submissions. Responds in 3 months to queries and mss. Book catalog free; ms guidelines online.

⚷ "Our mission is to publish the finest in Canadian fiction, nonfiction, poetry, drama, and children's literature, with an emphasis on Saskatchewan and prairie writers." De-emphasizing science fiction, picture books.

Nonfiction Coffee table book, reference. Subjects include creative nonfiction, ethnic, history, language/literature, memoirs, regional, sports, travel. Canadian authors only. Submit 3-4 sample chapters, author bio, SASE.

Fiction Ethnic, fantasy, feminist, gay/lesbian, historical, humor, juvenile, literary, mainstream/contemporary, multicultural, multimedia, mystery, plays, poetry, regional, short story collections, spiritual, sports, young adult, novels, short fiction, middle years. *Canadian authors only*. No science fiction. No children's picture books. Submit 3-4 sample chapters, author bio, SASE.

Poetry Submit 20-25 sample poems, or submit complete ms.

Recent Title(s) *The Kalifax Trilogy*, juvenile fiction series for ages 9 and up; *Penelope's Way*, by Blanche Howard (novel); *A Song for Nettie Johnson*, by Gloria Swaii (novel).

Tips "Look at past publications to get an idea of our editorial program. We do not publish romance, horror, or picture books but are interested in juvenile and teen fiction from Canadian authors. Submissions may be made by e-mail (maximum 20 pages) with attachments."

🌐 CRESSRELLES PUBLISHING CO., LTD.

10 Station Rd., Industrial Estate, Colwall Malvern Worcestershire WR13 6RN United Kingdom. Phone/Fax: 01684 540154. E-mail: simonsmith@cressrelles4drama.fsbusiness.co.uk. Publishes hardcover and trade paperback originals. **Publishes 10-20 titles/year. Pays royalty on retail price.** Book catalog free.

Imprints Kenyon-Deane; J. Garnet Miller; New Playwright's Network; Actinic Press.

Nonfiction Subjects include drama (plays), theater. Submit complete ms.

🌐 DAY BOOKS

Orchard Piece, Crawborough, Charlbury Oxfordshire OX7 3TX United Kingdom. E-mail: lives@day-books.com. Website: www.day-books.com. Estab. 1997. Publishes hardcover originals and trade paperback reprints. **Publishes 4 titles/year. Receives 30 queries and 30 mss/year. 10% of books from first-time authors; 80% from unagented writers. Pays 10% royalty on wholesale price. Offers $1,000-2,500 advance.** Publishes book 1 year after acceptance of ms. Accepts simultaneous submissions. Responds in 1 month. Book catalog online; ms guidelines free.

Nonfiction Autobiography, biography, general nonfiction, scholarly. Subjects include history, memoirs, regional. Query with SASE, submit proposal package, or submit complete ms. Reviews artwork/photos as part of ms package. Send photocopies.

Recent Title(s) *Inside Stalin's Russia: The Diaries of Reader Bullard, 1930-1934*, by Julian and Margaret Bullard (history/biography); *Lifting the Latch: A Life on the Land*, by Sheila Stewart (social history/biography).

⚌ DUNDURN PRESS, LTD.

8 Market St., Suite 200, Toronto ON M5E 1M6 Canada. (416)214-5544. Website: www.dundurn.com. **Acquisitions:** Acquisitions Editor. Estab. 1972. Publishes hardcover and trade paperback originals and reprints. **Receives 600 queries/year. 25% of books from first-time authors; 50% from unagented writers. Pays 10%**

royalty on net receipts. Publishes book an average of 1 year after acceptance of ms. Accepts simultaneous submissions. Responds in 3 months to queries. Ms guidelines online.

   Oπ Dundurn publishes books by Canadian authors.

Nonfiction Subjects include art/architecture, history (Canadian and military), music/dance (drama), regional, art history, theater, serious and popular nonfiction.

Fiction Literary, mystery, young adult. ''No romance, science fiction, or experimental.'' Query with SASE, and submit sample chapters, synopsis, author bio.

Recent Title(s) *A Man in a Distant*, by Theresa Kishkan (novel); *D-Day: Juno Beach, Canada's 24 Hours of Destiny*, by Lance Goddard (military history); *Now You Know More: The Book of Answers, Vol. 2*, by Doug Lennox (popular nonfiction).

ECCENOVA EDITIONS

P.O. Box 50001, 15-1594 Fairfield Rd., Victoria BC V8S 5L8 Canada. Fax: (250)595-8401. E-mail: editor2@ecceno va.com. Website: www.eccenova.com. Estab. 2003. Publishes trade paperback originals. **Publishes 4 titles/year. Receives 40-50 queries and 15 mss/year. 30% of books from first-time authors; 90% from unagented writers. Pays 15% royalty on wholesale price.** Publishes book 9 months after acceptance of ms. Does not accept simultaneous submissions. Responds in 1 week to e-mail queries; 1 month to proposals and mss. Book catalog and ms guidelines online.

   Oπ ''Our purpose is to offer an opportunity for exposure of valid but unorthodox approaches to controversial subjects.''

Nonfiction Subjects include religious and scientific nonfiction only. ''We are actively seeking out unique and well-written research-based nonfiction works in the fields of religion and science. We have no denominational or political bias and seek titles that reflect open-minded and well-reasoned investigation. Interdisciplinary works are welcomed. Research-based implies historical, analytical or theoretical dissertation, and implies a certain degree of author credentials. We will publish ufology alongside biblical interpretation, ancient mythology along-side quantum mechanics. Other areas we will consider include paranormal investigations, physical sciences (for the lay reader), philosophy of science or religion, biographies (of famous scientists or religious figures), university-level study aids (in religion/science). If in doubt, ask. We are not accepting submissions of fiction, children's books, textbooks, spiritual workbooks/guides, or books with color images. We are not currently in the market to purchase rights to foreign-language books.'' Query via e-mail or with SASE. Please use Canadian stamps or IRC, or supply e-mail address. Reviews artwork/photos as part of ms package. Send photocopies.

Recent Title(s) *The Book of Ancient Revelations*, by Hugh Fox, PhD; *Is Et Here*, by Robert Trundle, PhD.

Tips ''Our books are aimed at the intelligent layperson and will employ a language suitable for a broad, but well-read audience. Include your CV. Explain a little about the book in the body of your letter/e-mail. (What is it about? How many words is it? Who is your intended audience?) Provide some idea of how you intend to promote your own work (e.g. public talks/lectures, journal articles, advertising, radio interviews). We rely on our authors to help in the promotional aspect of the enterprise. Obtain some pre-submission endorsements of your work from those in the public eye or in the field. These can be invaluable when attempting to solicit reviews later.''

ECRITS DES FORGES

C.P. 335, 1497 Laviolette, Trois-Rivieres QC G9A 5G4 Canada. (819)379-9813. Fax: (819)376-0774. E-mail: ecrits.desforges@tr.cgocable.ca. **Acquisitions:** Gaston Bellemare, president. Publishes hardcover originals. **Publishes 40 titles/year. Receives 30 queries and 1,000 mss/year. 10% of books from first-time authors; 90% from unagented writers. Pays 10-30% royalty. Offers 50% advance.** Publishes book 9 months after acceptance of ms. Accepts simultaneous submissions. Responds in 9 months to queries. Book catalog free.

   Oπ Ecrits des Forges publishes only poetry written in French.

Poetry Submit 20 sample poems.

Recent Title(s) *Ode au St-Laurent*, by Gatien Lapointe (poetry).

ECW PRESS

2120 Queen St. E., Suite 200, Toronto ON M4E 1E2 Canada. (416)694-3348. Fax: (416)698-9906. E-mail: info@ec wpress.com. Website: www.ecwpress.com. **Acquisitions:** Jack David, president (nonfiction); Michael Holmes, literary editor (fiction, poetry); Jennifer Hale, associate editor (pop culture, entertainment); Joy Gugeler, literary and arts editor. Estab. 1979. Publishes hardcover and trade paperback originals. **Publishes 40 titles/year; imprint publishes 6 titles/year. Receives 500 queries and 300 mss/year. 30% of books from first-time authors. Pays 8-12% royalty on net receipts. Offers $300-5,000 advance.** Publishes book 18 months after acceptance of ms. Accepts simultaneous submissions. Book catalog free; ms guidelines online.

   Oπ ECW publishes nonfiction about people or subjects that have a substantial fan base. Currently emphasizing books about music, gambling, TV and movie stars.

Nonfiction Biography (popular), general nonfiction, humor. Subjects include business/economics, creative nonfiction, gay/lesbian, government/politics, health/medicine, history, memoirs, money/finance, regional, sex, sports, women's issues/studies, contemporary culture, Wicca, gambling, TV and movie stars. Submit proposal package including outline, 4-5 sample chapters, IRC, SASE. Reviews artwork/photos as part of ms package. Send photocopies.

Fiction "We publish literary fiction and poetry from Canadian authors exclusively. Literary, mystery, poetry, short story collections, suspense. Visit company website to view submission guidelines."

Poetry "We publish Canadian poetry exclusively." Query, or submit 4-5 sample poems.

Recent Title(s) *Too Close to the Falls*, by Catherine Gildiner; *Ghost Rider*, by Neil Peart; *Ashland*, by Gil Anderson (poetry).

Tips "Visit our website and read a selection of our books."

N ✉ ÉDITIONS LA LIBERTE, INC.

3020 Chemin Ste-Foy, Ste-Foy QC G1X 3V6 Canada. (418)658-3763. Fax: (418)658-3763. **Acquisitions:** Hugues Doré, director of operations. Publishes trade paperback originals. **Publishes 4-5 titles/year. Receives 125 queries and 100 mss/year. 75% of books from first-time authors; 90% from unagented writers. Pays 10% royalty on retail price.** Publishes book 4 months after acceptance of ms. Accepts simultaneous submissions. Book catalog free.

- Distributor for Canada: OECD, UNESCO, United Nations, World Bank, WTO, ILO, Council of Europe, Eurostat, IMF, WHO, EUR-OP.
- ⚬⚞ Accepts only mss written in French. Specializes in history. De-emphasizing fiction and poetry.

Nonfiction Biography, children's/juvenile. Subjects include Americana, animals, anthropology/archeology, child guidance/parenting, cooking/foods/nutrition, education, government/politics, history, hobbies, language/literature, music/dance, nature/environment, psychology, science, sociology. Submit proposal package including complete ms.

Fiction Historical, juvenile, literary, mainstream/contemporary, short story collections, young adult. Query with SASE.

Recent Title(s) *Au coeur de la Litterature D'enfance et de Jeunesse*, by Charlotte Guerette (nonfiction); *Le Cahier des dix (collectif)* (history); *Le domaine aquatique*, by Pierre L. Landry (scientific).

⊘ 🌐 FERNHURST BOOKS

Duke's Path, High St., Arundel BN18 9AG United Kingdom. 01903-882277. Fax: 01903-882715. Website: www.fernhurstbooks.co.uk. **Acquisitions:** Tim Davison, publisher. Publishes mass market paperback originals. **Publishes 12 titles/year. Receives 2-4 queries/year. 50% of books from first-time authors; 90% from unagented writers. Pays 10% royalty. Offers advance.** Publishes book up to 1 year after acceptance of ms. Does not accept simultaneous submissions. Book catalog free.

- ⚬⚞ Fernhurst publishes books on watersports, producing practical, highly-illustrated handbooks on sailing and watersports. Currently emphasizing sailing and maintenance.

Nonfiction Gift book, how-to, humor. Subjects include sports. Submit proposal package including outline. *No unsolicited mss.* Reviews artwork/photos as part of ms package.

N ✉ FERNWOOD PUBLISHING, LTD.

32 Ocenavista Lane, Site 2A, Box 5, Black Pointe NS B0J 1B0 Canada. (902)857-1388. E-mail: info@fernwoodbooks.ca. Website: www.fernwoodbooks.ca. **Acquisitions:** Errol Sharpe, publisher (social science); Wayne Antony, editor (social science). Publishes trade paperback originals. **Publishes 15-20 titles/year. Receives 80 queries and 30 mss/year. 40% of books from first-time authors; 100% from unagented writers. Pays 7-10% royalty on wholesale price. Offers advance.** Publishes book 1 year after acceptance of ms. Accepts simultaneous submissions. Responds in 6 weeks to proposals. Ms guidelines online.

- ⚬⚞ "Fernwood's objective is to publish critical works which challenge existing scholarship."

Nonfiction Reference, textbook, scholarly. Subjects include agriculture/horticulture, anthropology/archeology, business/economics, education, ethnic, gay/lesbian, government/politics, health/medicine, history, language/literature, multicultural, nature/environment, philosophy, regional, sex, sociology, sports, translation, women's issues/studies, contemporary culture, world affairs. "Our main focus is in the social sciences and humanities, emphasizing labor studies, women's studies, gender studies, critical theory and research, political economy, cultural studies, and social work—for use in college and university courses." Submit proposal package including outline, sample chapters. Reviews artwork/photos as part of ms package. Send photocopies.

Recent Title(s) *My Union, My Life: Jean-Claude Parrot*, by Jean-Claude Parrot; *Beyond Token Change: Breaking the Cycle of Oppression in Institutions*, by Anne Bishop; *Inference and Persuasion: An Introduction to Logic and Critical Thinking*, by Leslie Armour and Richard Feist.

Ⓐ Ⓞ Ⓖ DAVID FICKLING BOOKS

61-63 Uxbridge Rd., Ealing, London W5 5SA United Kingdom. Website: www.davidficklingbooks.co.uk.
• High-quality fiction and picture books for ages 0-18. Submit synopsis, first few chapters, and SASE.

Ⓖ FINDHORN PRESS

305A The Park, Findhorn, Forres Scotland IV36 3TE United Kingdom. 01309-690582. Fax: 01309-690036. E-mail: info@findhornpress.com. Website: www.findhornpress.com. **Acquisitions:** Thierry Bogliolo, publisher. Publishes trade paperback originals. **Publishes 12 titles/year. Receives 1,000 queries/year. 50% of books from first-time authors. Pays 10-15% royalty on wholesale price.** Publishes book 1 year after acceptance of ms. Book catalog and ms guidelines online.
Nonfiction Self-help. Subjects include health/medicine, nature/environment, spirituality. Submit proposal package including outline, 1 sample chapter, author bio, marketing plan. Please submit as e-mail attachments.

Ⓝ ☒ FORMAC PUBLISHING CO. LTD.

5502 Atlantic St., Halifax NS B3H 1G4 Canada. (902)421-7022. Website: www.formac.ca. **Acquisitions:** Elizabeth Eve, senior editor (Canadian history and geography). Estab. 1977. Publishes hardcover and trade paperback originals. **Publishes 15-20 titles/year. Receives 200 queries and 150 mss/year. 20% of books from first-time authors; 75% from unagented writers. Pays 5-10% royalty on wholesale price.** Publishes book 1 year after acceptance of ms. Accepts simultaneous submissions. Responds in 2 months to queries and proposals; 4 months to mss. Book catalog free; ms guidelines online.
Nonfiction Autobiography, biography, children's/juvenile, cookbook, general nonfiction, illustrated book, reference. Subjects include animals, art/architecture, cooking/foods/nutrition, creative nonfiction, government/politics, history, military/war, multicultural, nature/environment, regional, travel, marine subjects, transportation. Submit proposal package including outline, 2 sample chapters, cv or résumé of author(s).
Recent Title(s) *Fastest in the World: The Saga of Canada's Revolutionary Hydrofoils*, by John Boileau (military, transportation, history, illustrated).
Tips "For our illustrated books, our audience includes adults interested in regional topics. For our travel titles, the audience is Canadians and visitors looking for cultural and outdoor experiences. Check out our website and see if you think your book fits anywhere in our list before submitting it. We are primarily interested in the work of Canadian authors only."

Ⓝ Ⓖ FOUR COURTS PRESS

7 Malpas St., Dublin 8 Ireland. (03531)4534668. Fax: (03531)4534672. E-mail: info@four-courts-press.ie. Website: www.four-courts-press.ie. **Acquisitions:** Martin Fanning. Publishes hardcover and trade paperback originals. **Publishes 60 titles/year. Receives 200 queries and 100 mss/year. 30% of books from first-time authors; 90% from unagented writers. Pays 10% royalty on wholesale price.** Publishes book 6 months after acceptance of ms. Does not accept simultaneous submissions. Responds in 2 months to mss. Book catalog free online; ms guidelines free.
Nonfiction Subjects include art/architecture, health/medicine, history, military/war, philosophy, religion, spirituality, scholarly. Submit proposal package.
Recent Title(s) *Dublin Through Space and Time* (modern history); *The Irish Storyteller* (arts and literature); *The Navarre Bible: New Testament* (theology & spirituality).

Ⓝ ☒ GOOSE LANE EDITIONS

469 King St., Fredericton NB E3B 1E5 Canada. (506)450-4251. Fax: (506)459-4991. Website: www.gooselane.com. **Acquisitions:** Laurel Boone, editorial director. Estab. 1954. Publishes hardcover and paperback originals and occasional reprints. **Publishes 16-20 titles/year. 20% of books from first-time authors; 60% from unagented writers. Pays 8-10% royalty on retail price. Offers $500-3,000, negotiable advance.** Does not accept simultaneous submissions. Responds in 6 months to queries.
☞ Goose Lane publishes literary fiction and nonfiction from well-read and highly skilled Canadian authors.
Nonfiction Biography, illustrated book. Subjects include art/architecture, history, language/literature, nature/environment, regional, women's issues/studies. Query with SASE.
Fiction Literary (novels), short story collections, contemporary. "Our needs in fiction never change: Substantial, character-centered literary fiction." No children's, YA, mainstream, mass market, genre, mystery, thriller, confessional or science fiction. Query with SAE with Canadian stamps or IRCs. No US stamps.
Recent Title(s) *Tattycoram*, by Audrey Thomas (fiction); *The Right Fight: Bernard Lord and the Conservative Dilemma*, by Jacques Poitras (nonfiction).
Tips "Writers should send us outlines and samples of books that show a very well-read author who, in either fiction or nonfiction, has highly developed literary skills. Our books are almost all by Canadians living in Canada; we seldom consider submissions from outside Canada. If I were a writer trying to market a book today,

I would contact the targeted publisher with a query letter and synopsis, and request manuscript guidelines. Purchase a recent book from the publisher in a relevant area, if possible. Always send an SASE with IRCs or suffient return postage in Canadian stamps for reply to your query and for any material you'd like returned should it not suit our needs."

⊘ ⚄ GUERNICA EDITIONS

Box 117, Station P, Toronto ON M5S 2S6 Canada. (416)658-9888. Fax: (416)657-8885. E-mail: guernicaeditions@cs. com. Website: www.guernicaeditions.com. **Acquisitions:** Antonio D'Alfonso, editor/publisher (poetry, nonfiction, novels); Ken Scambray, editor (US reprints). Estab. 1978. Publishes trade paperback originals, reprints, and software. **Publishes 25 titles/year. Receives 750 mss/year. 20% of books from first-time authors; 99% from unagented writers. Pays 8-10% royalty on retail price, or makes outright purchase of $200-5,000. Offers $200-2,000 advance.** Publishes book 15 months after acceptance of ms. Does not accept simultaneous submissions. Responds in 1 month to queries; 6 months to proposals; 1 year to mss. Book catalog online.

   O–π Guernica Editions is an independent press dedicated to the bridging of cultures. "We do original and translations of fine works. We are seeking essays on authors and translations with less emphasis on poetry."

Nonfiction Biography. Subjects include art/architecture, creative nonfiction, ethnic, film/cinema/stage, gay/lesbian, government/politics, history, language/literature, memoirs, multicultural, music/dance, philosophy, psychology, regional, religion, sex, translation, women's issues/studies. Query with SASE. *All unsolicited mss returned unopened.* Reviews artwork/photos as part of ms package. Send photocopies.

Fiction Erotica, feminist, gay/lesbian, literary, multicultural, plays, poetry, poetry in translation. "We wish to open up into the fiction world and focus less on poetry. We specialize in European, especially Italian, translations." Query with SASE. *All unsolicited mss returned unopened.*

Poetry Feminist, gay/lesbian, literary, multicultural, poetry in translation. "We wish to have writers in translation. Any writer who has translated Italian poetry is welcomed. Full books only. No single poems by different authors, unless modern, and used as an anthology. First books will have no place in the next couple of years." Query.

Recent Title(s) *Surface Roots*, by Kenneth Scambray; *Naked in the Sanctuary*, by Julie Roorda; *Prague Memories*, by Tecia Werbowski.

⚄ GYNERGY BOOKS

Ragweed Press, P.O. Box 2023, Charlottetown PE C1A 7N7 Canada. (902)566-5750. Fax: (902)566-4473. E-mail: editor@gynergy.com. **Acquisitions:** Sibyl Frei, managing editor. Publishes trade paperback originals. **Publishes 3-5 titles/year; imprint publishes 3-5 titles/year. Receives 200 queries and 1,500-2,000 mss/year. 50% of books from first-time authors; 95% from unagented writers. Pays 8-10% royalty on wholesale price, or retail price. Offers confidential advance.** Publishes book 1-2 years after acceptance of ms. Does not accept simultaneous submissions. Responds in 6 months to mss. Book catalog free; ms guidelines for #10 SASE.

   O–π Gynergy publishes lesbian fiction and nonfiction.

Nonfiction Gift book, illustrated book. Subjects include child guidance/parenting, creative nonfiction, gay/lesbian, women's issues/studies. "For nonfiction, we prefer to review proposals and, if accepted, work with the author or editor on developing the book from concept through to final manuscript." Submit proposal package including outline, synopsis.

Fiction Fantasy, gay/lesbian, mystery. "We are interested in series, looking to add line of feminist/lesbian fantasy or science fiction." Query with SASE, or submit complete ms.

Recent Title(s) *Fragment by Fragment: Feminist Perspectives in Memory and Child Sexual Abuse*, Margo Rivera (feminist nonfiction anthology); *The Mennonite Madonna*, Diane Drieger (poetry).

⊕ HAMBLEDON AND LONDON

102 Gloucester Ave., London NW1 8HX United Kingdom. 0044 207 586 0817. Fax: 0044 207 586 9970. E-mail: office@hambledon.co.uk. Submissions E-mail: ajm@hambledon.co.uk. Website: www.hambledon.co.uk. **Acquisitions:** Tony Morris, commissioning director (all history); Martin Sheppard, director (commissioning, editorial marketing). Publishes hardcover and trade paperback originals. **Publishes 20-30 titles/year; imprint publishes 20-30 titles/year. Receives 750 queries and 150 mss/year. 10% of books from first-time authors; 90% from unagented writers. Pays 0-10% royalty on retail price.** Publishes book 6 months after acceptance of ms. Accepts simultaneous submissions. Responds in 1 week to queries; 2 weeks to proposals; 1 month to mss. Book catalog online; ms guidelines free.

   O–π "We publish high quality history at an affordable price for the general reader as well as the specialist."

Nonfiction Biography (historical). Subjects include history, language/literature. Submit outline. Reviews artwork/photos as part of ms package. Send photocopies.

Recent Title(s) *Churchill: A Study in Greatness*, by Geoffrey Best; *Pilgrimage in Medieval England*, by Diana Webb.

HARLEQUIN ENTERPRISES, LTD.

225 Duncan Mill Rd., Don Mills ON M3B 3K9 Canada. (416)445-5860. **Acquisitions:** Tara Gavin, editorial director New York (Silhouette, Harlequin, Steeple Hill, Luna); Dianne Moggy, editorial director Toronto (MIRA, Red Dress Ink, HQN Books); Randall Toye, editorial director Toronto (Gold Eagle, Worldwide Library); Karin Stoecker, editorial director UK. US Address: 233 Broadway, Suite 1001, New York NY 10279. (212)553-4200. UK: Eton House, 18-24 Paradise Lane, Richmond, Surrey TW9 1SR United Kingdom. Estab. 1949. Publishes mass market paperback, trade paperback, and hardcover originals and reprints. **Publishes 1,500 titles/year. Pays royalty. Offers advance.** Publishes book 1-2 years after acceptance of ms. Responds in 6 weeks to queries; 3 months to mss. Ms guidelines online.

Imprints Harlequin Books; Silhouette; MIRA; Gold Eagle; Luna; HQN Books; World Wide Library; Mills & Boon; Steeple Hill; Red Dress Ink.

- Websites: www.eharlequin.com; www.mirabooks.com; www.reddressink.com; www.steeplehill.com; www.luna-books.com.

Fiction Considers all types of serious romance and strong, mainstream, women's fiction. For series, query with SASE. For MIRA, *agented submissions only*.

Tips "The quickest route to success is to check www.eharlequin.com, other websites listed above, or write or call for submission guidlines. We acquire first novelists. Before submitting, read as many current titles in the imprint or line of your choice as you can. It's very important to know the genre, what readers are looking for, and the series or imprint most appropriate for your submission."

HARLEQUIN MILLS & BOON, LTD.

Harlequin Enterprises, Ltd., Eton House, 18-24 Paradise Rd., Richmond Surrey TW9 1SR United Kingdom. (44)0208-288-2800. Website: www.millsandboon.co.uk. **Acquisitions:** Bryon Green, associate senior editor (Harlequin Romance); Tessa Shapcott, senior editor (Harlequin Presents); Linda Fildew, senior editor (historical/romance); and Sheila Hodgson, senior editor (medical/romance). Estab. 1908-1909. Publishes mass market paperback originals. **Pays advance against royalty.** Does not accept simultaneous submissions. Responds in 3 months to mss. Ms guidelines online.

Imprints Harlequin; Silhouette; Mills & Boon; MIRA.

- "World's largest publisher of brand name category romance and general women's fiction; books are available for translation into more than 20 languages and distributed in more than 100 international markets. We are accepting submissions in any women fiction genre."

Fiction Romance (contemporary, historical, regency period, medical). Query with SASE, 3 sample chapters, synopsis.

Recent Title(s) *The Salvatore Marriage*, by Michelle Reid; *The Last Year of Being Single*, by Sarah Tucker; *Consultant in Crisis*, by Alison Roberts.

Tips "Study a wide selection of our current paperbacks to gain an understanding of our requirements, then write from the heart."

HARPERCOLLINS AUSTRALIA

Imprint of HarperCollins, 25 Ryde Rd., P.O. Box 321, Pymble NSW 2073 Australia. (612)9952 5000. Fax: (612)9952 5555. Website: www.harpercollins.com.au. Estab. 1989.

Imprints Angus & Robertson; Collins; Fourth Estate; Harper Perenniel; HarperCollins; HarperSports; Voyager.

HARPERCOLLINS CANADA, LTD.

2 Bloor St. E., 20th Floor, Toronto ON M4W 1A8 Canada. (416)975-9334. Fax: (416)975-5223. Website: www.harpercollins.ca.

- *HarperCollins is not accepting unsolicited material at this time.*

HARPERCOLLINS UK

Imprint of HarperCollins, 77-85 Fulham Palace Rd., Hammersmith London W6 8JB United Kingdom. (0208)307 4000. Website: www.harpercollins.co.uk.

Imprints Bartholomew Maps; Collins; Collins Crime; Collins Education; HarperCollins Children's Books; Thorsons/Element; Voyager Books.

HELTER SKELTER PUBLISHING

South Bank House, Black Prince Rd., London SE1 7SJ United Kingdom. (44)20 7463 2204. Fax: (44)20 7463 2295. E-mail: sean@helterskelterbooks.com. **Acquisitions:** Sean Body, editor (music, film). Publishes hardcover and trade paperback originals and trade paperback reprints. **Publishes 10 titles/year. Receives 50 queries and 30 mss/year. 50% of books from first-time authors; 60% from unagented writers. Pays 8-12½% royalty on** retail price. **Offers $1,000-6,000 advance.** Publishes book 6 months after acceptance of ms. Accepts simultaneous submissions. Responds in 1 month to queries. Book catalog free.

Imprints Firefly.

O— "Our mission is to publish high quality books about music and cinema subjects of enduring appeal."

Nonfiction Biography. Subjects include music/dance. Submit outline, 2 sample chapters. Reviews artwork/photos as part of ms package. Send photocopies.

Recent Title(s) *Waiting for the Man*, Harry Shapiro.

Tips "The subject artist should have a career spanning at least five years."

HERITAGE HOUSE PUBLISHING CO., LTD.

301-3555 Outrigger Rd., Nanoose Bay BC V9P 9K1 Canada. (250)468-5328. Fax: (250)468-5318. E-mail: publisher@heritagehouse.ca. Website: www.heritagehouse.ca. **Acquisitions:** Rodger Touchie, publisher/president. Publishes trade paperback originals. **Publishes 10-12 titles/year. Receives 200 queries and 60 mss/year. 50% of books from first-time authors; 100% from unagented writers. Pays 9% royalty. Offers advance.** Publishes book 1 year after acceptance of ms. Does not accept simultaneous submissions. Responds in 2 months to queries. Book catalog for #10 SASE; ms guidelines online.

O— Heritage House is primarily a regional publisher of Western Canadiana and the Pacific Northwest. "We aim to publish and distribute good books that entertain and educate our readership regarding both historic and contemporary Western Canada and Pacific Northwest."

Nonfiction Biography, how-to, illustrated book. Subjects include animals, anthropology/archeology, cooking/foods/nutrition, history, nature/environment, recreation, regional, sports. "Writers should include a sample of their writing, an overview sample of photos or illustrations to support the text, and a brief letter describing who they are writing for." Query with SASE, or submit outline, 2-3 sample chapters. Reviews artwork/photos as part of ms package. Send photocopies.

Fiction Children's books. Very limited. Only author/illustrator collaboration.

Recent Title(s) *Simply the Best: Insights and Strategies From Great Hockey Coaches*, by Mike Johnson and Ryan Walters; *Fortress of the Grizzlies: The Khutzeymateen Grizzly Bear Sanctuary*, by Dan Wakeman and Wendy Shymanski; *Mountie Makers: Putting the Canadian in RCMP*, by Bob Teather.

Tips "Our books appeal to residents and visitors to the northwest quadrant of the continent. Present your material only after you have done your best."

HIPPOPOTAMUS PRESS

22 Whitewell Rd., Frome, Somerset BA11 4EL United Kingdom. 0173-466653. Fax: 01373-466653. E-mail: rjhippopress@aol.com. **Acquisitions:** R. John, editor; M. Pargitter (poetry); Anna Martin (translation). Publishes hardcover and trade paperback originals. **Publishes 6-12 titles/year. 90% of books from first-time authors; 90% from unagented writers. Pays 7½-10% royalty on retail price. Offers advance.** Publishes book 10 months after acceptance of ms. Accepts simultaneous submissions. Responds in 1 month to queries. Book catalog free.

Imprints Hippopotamus Press; *Outposts* Poetry Quarterly, distributor for University of Salzburg Press.

O— Hippopotamus Press publishes first, full collections of verse by those well represented in the mainstream poetry magazines of the English-speaking world.

Nonfiction Subjects include language/literature, translation. Query with SASE, or submit complete ms.

Poetry "Read one of our authors! Poets often make the mistake of submitting poetry not knowing the type of verse we publish." Query, or submit complete ms.

Recent Title(s) *Mystic Bridge*, Edward Lowbury.

Tips "We publish books for a literate audience. We have a strong link to the Modernist tradition. Read what we publish."

HOUSE OF ANANSI PRESS

110 Spadina Ave., Suite 801, Toronto ON M5V 2K4 Canada. Fax: (416)363-1017. Website: www.anansi.ca. **Acquisitions:** Martha Sharpe, publisher. Estab. 1967. Publishes hardcover and trade paperback originals and paperback reprints. **Publishes 10-15 titles/year. Receives 750 queries/year. 5% of books from first-time authors; 99% from unagented writers. Pays 8-15% royalty on retail price. Offers $500-2,000 advance.** Publishes book 9 months after acceptance of ms. Accepts simultaneous submissions. Responds in 2 months to queries; 3 months to proposals; 4 months to mss. Book catalog free; ms guidelines online.

O— "Our mission is to publish the best new literary writers in Canada and to continue to grow and adapt along with the Canadian literary community, while maintaining Anansi's rich history."

Nonfiction Biography. Subjects include anthropology/archeology, gay/lesbian, government/politics, history, language/literature, philosophy, science, sociology, women's issues/studies. "Our nonfiction list is literary, but not overly academic. Some writers submit academic work better suited for university presses or pop-psychology books, which we do not publish." Query with SASE, or submit outline, 2 sample chapters. Reviews artwork/photos as part of ms package. Send photocopies.

Fiction Ethnic (general), experimental, feminist, gay/lesbian, literary, short story collections. "We publish literary fiction by Canadian authors. Authors must have been published in established literary magazines and/or journals. We only want to consider sample chapters." Query with SASE, or submit outline, 2 sample chapters, synopsis.

Poetry "We only publish book-length works by Canadian authors. Poets must have a substantial résumé of published poems in literary magazines or journals. We only want samples from a manuscript." Submit 10-15 sample poems.

Recent Title(s) *The Big Why*, by Michael Winter; *Moving Targets*, by Margaret Atwood; *Paradise*, by A.L. Kennedy.

Tips "Submit often to magazines and journals. Read and buy other writers' work. Know and be a part of your writing community."

🌐 HOW TO BOOKS, LTD.

3 Newtec Place, Magdalen Rd., Oxford OX4 1RE United Kingdom. (00144)1865 793806. Fax: (00144)1865 248780. E-mail: read@howtobooks.co.uk. Website: www.howtobooks.co.uk. **Acquisitions:** Nikki Read, commissioning editor (self-help, business, careers, home & family, living & working abroad). Publishes trade paperback originals and reprints. **Publishes 100 titles/year. Receives 200 queries and 100 mss/year. 80% of books from first-time authors; 90% from unagented writers.** Accepts simultaneous submissions. Responds in 1 month to queries and proposals; 2 months to mss. Book catalog free or on website; ms guidelines free.

Nonfiction How-to, reference, self-help. Subjects include child guidance/parenting, creative nonfiction, money/finance, small business. "Submit a proposal you feel strongly about and can write knowledgably. Have a look at our catalog/website to see what we publish. We ask authors to send a synopsis for initial consideration." Submit proposal package including outline, 1 sample chapter.

Recent Title(s) *Voices of Experience*, by Jacqui Harper; *Presenting With Power 2*, by Shay McConnon; *Getting a Job in America 8*, by Roger Jones.

Tips "Our books are aimed at people who want to improve their lives, their careers, their general skills. Our authors have to have a passion and extensive knowledge about their subject area."

🅽 🌐 JOHN HUNT PUBLISHING, LTD./O BOOKS

Deershot Lodge, Park Lane, Ropley, Hampshire SO24 0BE United Kingdom. Website: www.o-books.net. Publishes hardcover, trade paperback and mass market paperback originals. **Publishes 50 titles/year. Receives 300 queries and 200 mss/year. 1% of books from first-time authors; 50% from unagented writers. Pays 5-15% royalty on wholesale price. Offers $100-10,000 advance.** Publishes book 1 year after acceptance of ms. Does not accept simultaneous submissions. Responds in 1 month. Book catalog for #10 SASE; ms guidelines online.

Nonfiction Children's/juvenile (religious), gift book, illustrated book, reference. Subjects include philosophy, religion, spirituality. Submit proposal package including outline, 1 sample chapter. Reviews artwork/photos as part of ms package. Send photocopies.

🅽 💭 INSOMNIAC PRESS

192 Spadina Ave., Suite 403, Toronto ON M5T 2C2 Canada. (416)504-6270. Fax: (416)504-9313. E-mail: mike@insomniacpress.com. Website: www.insomniacpress.com. **Acquisitions:** Mike O'Connor, publisher. Estab. 1992. Publishes trade paperback originals and reprints, mass market paperback originals, and electronic originals and reprints. **Publishes 20 titles/year. Receives 250 queries and 1,000 mss/year. 50% of books from first-time authors; 80% from unagented writers. Pays 10-15% royalty on retail price. Offers $500-1,000 advance.** Publishes book 6 months after acceptance of ms. Accepts simultaneous submissions. Responds in 1 week to queries; 2 months to proposals and mss. Ms guidelines online.

Nonfiction Gift book, humor, self-help. Subjects include business/economics, creative nonfiction, gay/lesbian, government/politics, health/medicine, language/literature, money/finance, multicultural, religion, true crime. Very interested in areas such as true crime and well-written and well-researched nonfiction on topics of wide interest. Query via e-mail, submit proposal package including outline, 2 sample chapters, or submit complete ms. Reviews artwork/photos as part of ms package. Send photocopies.

Fiction Comic books, ethnic, experimental, gay/lesbian, humor, literary, mainstream/contemporary, multicultural, mystery, poetry, suspense. We publish a mix of commercial (mysteries) and literary fiction. Query via e-mail, submit proposal package including synopsis or submit complete ms.

Poetry "Our poetry publishing is limited to 2-4 books per year and we are often booked up a year or two in advance." Submit complete ms.

Recent Title(s) *Belong*, by Jennifer Morton; *Certifiable*, by David McGimpsey; *Creating Love*, by Samantha Stevens.

Tips "We envision a mixed readership that appreciates up-and-coming literary fiction and poetry as well as solidly researched and provocative nonfiction. Peruse our website and familiarize yourself with what we've published in the past."

◪ INSTITUTE OF PSYCHOLOGICAL RESEARCH, INC.

34 Fleury St. W., Montréal QC H3L 1S9 Canada. (514)382-3000. Fax: (514)382-3007. **Acquisitions:** Robert Chevrier, advisor. Estab. 1958. Publishes hardcover and trade paperback originals and reprints. **Publishes 12 titles/year. 10% of books from first-time authors; 100% from unagented writers. Pays 10-12% royalty.** Publishes book 6 months after acceptance of ms. Responds in 2 months to queries.

  ⊶ Institute of Psychological Research publishes psychological tests and science textbooks for a varied professional audience.

Nonfiction Textbook. Subjects include philosophy, psychology, science, translation. "We are looking for psychological tests in French or English." Query with SASE, or submit complete ms.

Recent Title(s) *Épreuve individuelle d'habileté mentale*, by Jean-Marc Chevrier (intelligence test).

Tips "Psychologists, guidance counselors, professionals, schools, school boards, hospitals, teachers, government agencies and industries comprise our audience."

Ⓝ ◪ KEY PORTER BOOKS

6 Adelaide St. E, 10th Floor, Toronto ON M5C 1H6 Canada. (416)862-7777. Fax: (416)862-2304. E-mail: info@keyporter.com. Website: www.keyporter.com. **Acquisitions:** Anna Porter, publisher; Jordan Fenn, associate publisher. Estab. 1979. Publishes hardcover and trade paperback originals and reprints. **Publishes 100 titles/year. Receives 1,000 queries and 500 mss/year. Pays royalty.** Accepts simultaneous submissions. Responds in 4 months to queries; 6 months to proposals and mss.

Imprints Key Porter Kids; Sarasota; L&OD.

  ⊶ Key Porter specializes in autobiography, biography, children's, cookbook, gift book, how-to, humor, illustrated book, self-help, young adult. Subjects include art, architecture, business, economics, parenting, food, creative nonfiction, gardening, general nonfiction, politics, health, history, humanities, memoirs, military, personal finance, nature, environment, photography, psychology, science, social sciences, sociology, sports, translation, travel, women's issues, world affairs, and literary fiction. Query with SASE. Reviews artwork/photos as part of ms package. Send photocopies.

Ⓝ ⊕ JESSICA KINGSLEY PUBLISHERS, LTD.

116 Pentonville Rd., London N1 9JB United Kingdom. (44)171-833-2307. Fax: (44)171-837-2917. E-mail: post@jkp.com. Website: www.jkp.com. **Acquisitions:** Jessica Kingsley, managing director (autism, pastoral thealogy, arts therapy/psychiatry). Publishes hardcover and trade paperback originals and trade paperback reprints. **Publishes 100 titles/year. Receives 500 queries and 30 mss/year. 20% of books from first-time authors; 99% from unagented writers. Pays royalty on wholesale price. Offers advance.** Publishes book 5 months after acceptance of ms. Does not accept simultaneous submissions. Responds in 1 month to queries and proposals; 3 months to mss. Book catalog for free or on website; ms guidelines free.

  ⊶ "We publish titles that present a combination of theory and practice." Currently emphasizing autism spectrum.

Nonfiction Reference, self-help, technical, textbook, scholarly. Subjects include child guidance/parenting, health/medicine, psychology, religion, sex, spirituality. Submit proposal package including outline, 1 sample chapter, résumé. Reviews artwork/photos as part of ms package. Send photocopies.

Recent Title(s) *Adam's Alternative Sports Day*, by Jude Welton; *Brain Injury and Returning to Employment*, by James Japp; *How to Understand Autism—The Easy Way*, by Alex Durig.

Tips "Do not go through an agent. Proposals must be for books within the subject areas we publish. No fiction or poetry."

◪ LES ÉDITIONS DU VERMILLON

305 St. Patrick St., Ottawa ON K1N 5K4 Canada. (613)241-4032. Fax: (613)241-3109. E-mail: leseditionsduvermillon@rogers.com. **Acquisitions:** Jacques Flamand, editorial director. Publishes trade paperback originals. **Publishes 15-20 titles/year. Pays 10% royalty.** Publishes book 18 months after acceptance of ms. Responds in 6 months to mss. Book catalog free.

Fiction Juvenile, literary, religious, short story collections, young adult. Query with SASE.

Recent Title(s) *Ce pays qui est le mien*, by Didier Leclair (novel); *Une twiga â Ottawa*, by Mireille Messier (children, 8-10 years); *Ombres et lueurs*, by Gabrielle Poulin (poetry).

Ⓝ ◪ LEXISNEXIS CANADA, INC.

123 Commerce Valley Dr. E., Suite 700, Markham ON L3T 7W8 Canada. (905)479-2665. Fax: (905)479-2826. E-mail: info@lexisnexis.ca. Website: www.lexisnexis.ca. **Acquisitions:** Product Development Director. **Publishes**

100 titles/year. 50% of books from first-time authors; 100% from unagented writers. Pays 5-15% royalty on wholesale price. Publishes book 4 months after acceptance of ms. Accepts simultaneous submissions. Responds in 1 month to queries. Book catalog free; ms guidelines online.

 O─⫶ LexisNexis Canada, Inc., publishes professional reference material for the legal, business, and accounting markets under the Butterworths imprint and operates the Quicklaw and LexisNexis online services.

Nonfiction Multimedia (CD-ROM, Quicklaw, and LexisNexis online services), reference (legal and law for business), legal and accounting newspapers.

Recent Title(s) *The Canada-U.S. Tax Treaty Text and Commentary*, by Vern Krishna; *The Public Purchasing Law Handbook*, by Robert C. Worthington; *Corporate Law in Quebec*, by Stephan Rousseau.

Tips Audience is legal community, business, medical, accounting professions.

LOBSTER PRESS

1620 Sherbrooke St. W, Suites C & D, Montreal QC H3H 1C9 Canada. (514)904-1100. Fax: (514)904-1101. Website: www.lobsterpress.com. **Acquisitions:** Stephanie Normandin, publishing assistant. Publishes hardcover, trade paperback, and mass market paperback originals. **Publishes 12-20 titles/year. Receives 200 queries and 1,500 mss/year. 90% of books from first-time authors; 75% from unagented writers. Pays 5-10% royalty on retail price. Offers $1,000-6,000 (Canadian) advance.** Publishes book 1-2 years after acceptance of ms. Does not accept simultaneous submissions. Responds in 3 months to queries; 10 months to proposals; 1 year to mss.

 • Lobster Press is once again accepting new mss, primarily in YA fiction, ages 15 and up.

Nonfiction Children's/juvenile, illustrated book, self-help. Subjects include child guidance/parenting, creative nonfiction, history, sex, travel. Query with SASE (IRC or Canadian postage only), or submit complete ms. Reviews artwork/photos as part of ms package. Send photocopies.

Fiction Adventure for children, historical for children, juvenile, picture books, young adult. Submit complete ms.

Recent Title(s) *Penelope and the Monsters*, by Sheri Radford, illustrated by Christine Tripp (picture book); *The Baseball Card*, by Jack Siemiatycki and Avi Slodovick, illustrated by Laura Watson (picture book); *The Gaggle Sisters River Tour*, written and illustrated by Chris Jackson (picture book).

LONE PINE PUBLISHING

10145 81st Ave., Edmonton AB T6E 1W9 Canada. (403)433-9333. Fax: (403)433-9646. Website: www.lonepinepublishing.com. **Acquisitions:** Nancy Foulds, editorial director. Estab. 1980. Publishes trade paperback originals and reprints. **Publishes 30-40 titles/year. 75% of books from first-time authors; 95% from unagented writers. Pays royalty.** Does not accept simultaneous submissions. Responds in 3 months to queries. Book catalog free.

Imprints Lone Pine; Home World; Pine Candle; Pine Cone; Ghost House Books.

 O─⫶ Lone Pine publishes natural history and outdoor recreation—including gardening—titles and some popular history and ghost story collections by region. "'The World Outside Your Door' is our motto— helping people appreciate nature and their own special place." Currently emphasizing ghost stories by region and gardening by region.

Nonfiction Subjects include animals, gardening, nature/environment, recreation, regional. The list is set for the next year and a half, but we are interested in seeing new material. Query with SASE, or submit outline, sample chapters. Reviews artwork/photos as part of ms package.

Recent Title(s) *Essential Christmas Cookbook*, by Lovoni Walker; *Birds of Minnesota and Wisconsin*, by Robert Janssen, Daryl Tessen and Gregory Kennedy; *Tree & Shrub Gardening for Ohio*, by Fred Hower and Allison Beck.

Tips "Writers have their best chance with recreational or nature guidebooks. Most of our books are strongly regional in nature."

LTDBOOKS

200 N. Service Rd. W., Unit 1, Suite 301, Oakville ON L6M 2Y1 Canada. (905)847-6060. Fax: (905)847-6060. E-mail: editor@ltdbooks.com. Website: www.ltdbooks.com. **Acquisitions:** Dee Lloyd, editor; Terry Shiels, editor. Estab. 1999. Publishes electronic originals by download, as well as selected trade paperback titles. **Publishes 15 titles/year. Pays 30% royalty on electronic titles and flat rate on trade paperbacks.** Publishes book 6 months after acceptance of ms. Accepts simultaneous submissions. Responds in 1-2 months to queries. Ms guidelines online.

 • Only accepts electronic submissions. Paper submissions are automatically rejected.

 O─⫶ "LTDBooks, an energetic presence in the rapidly expanding e-book market, is a multi-genre, royalty-paying fiction publisher specializing in high quality stories with strong characters and great ideas."

Fiction Adventure, fantasy (space fantasy, sword and sorcery), historical (general), horror (dark fantasy, futuristic, psychological, supernatural), literary, mainstream/contemporary, mystery (amateur sleuth, cozy, police procedural, private eye/hardboiled), romance (contemporary, futuristic/time travel, gothic, historical, regency period, romantic suspense), science fiction (hard science/technological, soft/sociological), suspense (amateur sleuth, cozy, police procedural, private eye/hardboiled), western, young adult (adventure, fantasy/science fiction, historical, horror, mystery/suspense, problem novels, romance, series, sports, thriller/espionage, western). Follow guidelines on website. Queries via e-mail only.

Recent Title(s) *The Marriage Committee*, by Catherine Snodgrass; *Seven Words for Sand*, by Allan Serafino.

Tips "We publish only fiction. All of our books are electronic (as download) with ongoing additions to our new trade paperback program. All submitting authors must have a working e-mail address for correspondence."

N ⬚ LYNX IMAGES, INC.

P.O. Box 5961, Station A, Toronto ON M5W 1P4 Canada. Phone/Fax: (416)925-8422. E-mail: submissions@lynx images.com. Website: www.lynximages.com. **Acquisitions:** Russell Floren, president; Andrea Gutsche, director; Barbara Chisholm, producer. Publishes hardcover and trade paperback originals. **Publishes 6 titles/year. Receives 100 queries and 50 mss/year. 80% of books from first-time authors; 80% from unagented writers. Offers 40% advance.** Publishes book 1 year after acceptance of ms. Accepts simultaneous submissions. Ms guidelines online.

　　O﹁ Lynx publishes historical tourism, travel, Canadian history, Great Lakes history. Currently emphasizing travel, history, nature. De-emphasizing boating, guides.

Nonfiction Coffee table book, gift book, multimedia. Subjects include history, nature/environment, travel. Reviews artwork/photos as part of ms package.

Recent Title(s) *General Stores of Canada*, by R.B. Fleming; *Ghosts of the Great Lakes*, by Megan Long; *Places Lost*, by Scott Walden.

⬚ MANOR HOUSE PUBLISHING, INC.

452 Cottingham Crescent, Ancaster ON L9G 3V6 Canada. (905)648-2193. Fax: (905)648-8369. E-mail: mdavie@t hestar.ca. Website: www.manor-house.biz. **Acquisitions:** Mike Davie, president (novels, poetry, and nonfiction). Estab. 1998. Publishes hardcover, trade paperback, and mass market paperback originals, and mass market paperback reprints. **Publishes 5-6 titles/year. Receives 30 queries and 20 mss/year. 90% of books from first-time authors; 90% from unagented writers. Pays 10-15% royalty on retail price.** Publishes book 12-14 months after acceptance of ms. Accepts simultaneous submissions. Responds in 1 month. Book catalog online; ms guidelines by e-mail.

Nonfiction Biography, coffee table book, general nonfiction, how-to, humor, illustrated book, self-help. Subjects include alternative lifestyles, anthropology/archeology, business/economics, community, history, sex, social sciences, sociology, spirituality. "We are a Canadian publisher, so manuscripts should be Canadian in content and aimed as much as possible at a wide, general audience." Query with SASE, or submit proposal package including outline, 3 sample chapters, author bio, or submit complete ms. Reviews artwork/photos as part of ms package. Send photocopies.

Fiction Adventure, experimental, gothic, historical, horror, humor, juvenile, literary, mainstream/contemporary, mystery, occult, poetry, regional, romance, short story collections, young adult. "Stories should have Canadian settings and characters should be Canadian, but content should have universal appeal to wide audience." Query with SASE, or submit proposal package including 3 sample chapters, synopsis, author bio, or submit complete ms.

Poetry "Poetry should engage, provoke, involve the reader. (I don't like yawning when I read.)" Query, or submit 12-20 sample poems, or submit complete ms.

Recent Title(s) *Political Losers*, by Michael B. Davie (politics/science); *Broken Dreams*, by Amanda Hyde (young adult novel); *Mystical Poetry*, by Deborah Morrison (poetry).

Tips "Our audience includes everyone—the general public/mass audience. Self-edit your work first, make sure it is well written with strong Canadian content."

N ⬚ MARQLAR INTERNATIONAL TRADERS

Life Untangled Publishing, 31 St. Dennis Dr., Suite 509, Toronto ON M3C 1G7 Canada. Website: www.lifeuntang led.com. Estab. 2005. Publishes hardcover, trade paperback, mass market, and electronic originals. **Publishes up to 30 titles/year. Receives up to 100 queries and around 50 mss/year. 90% of books from first-time authors; 90% from unagented writers. Pays 10-50% royalty on wholesale price, or makes outright purchase of $100-1,000.** Publishes book 6 months after acceptance of ms. Accepts simultaneous submissions. Responds in 1 month. Book catalog and ms guidelines online.

　　O﹁ "We specialize in Canadian topics and world events. We are looking for submissions from opinionated writers that explore progressive issues and non-traditional views."

Nonfiction Autobiography, biography, booklets, coffee table book, general nonfiction, how-to, humor, multimedia, self-help. Subjects include alternative lifestyles, animals, art/architecture, business/economics, community, contemporary culture, creative nonfiction, education, ethnic, gay/lesbian, government/politics, history, memoirs, money/finance, multicultural, nature/environment, New Age, philosophy, photography, psychology, religion, science, sex, social sciences, sociology, spirituality, translation, travel, women's issues/studies, world affairs. Query with SASE, or submit proposal package including outline, 1 sample chapter. Reviews artwork/photos as part of ms package. Send photocopies.

Recent Title(s) *How to Come to Canada*, by Kiran Mehdee and Polina Skibinskaya (softcover/e-book).

Tips "Our audience includes progressive readers interested in unorthodox views on world events and cultural and sociological studies, as well as readers looking for uniquely Canadian content."

⊘ 🔁 McCLELLAND & STEWART, LTD.

The Canadian Publishers, 481 University Ave., Suite 900, Toronto ON M5G 2E9 Canada. (416)598-1114. Fax: (416)598-7764. E-mail: editorial@mcclelland.com. Website: www.mcclelland.com. Publishes hardcover, trade paperback, and mass market paperback originals and reprints. **Publishes 80 titles/year. Receives 1,500 queries/year. 10% of books from first-time authors; 30% from unagented writers. Pays 10-15% royalty on retail price (hardcover rates). Offers advance.** Publishes book 1 year after acceptance of ms. Responds in 3 months to proposals.

Imprints McClelland & Stewart; New Canadian Library; Douglas Gibson Books; Emblem Editions (Ellen Seligman, editor).

Nonfiction "We publish books primarily by Canadian authors." Subjects include art/architecture, business/economics, gay/lesbian, government/politics, health/medicine, history, language/literature, military/war, music/dance, nature/environment, philosophy, photography, psychology, recreation, religion, science, sociology, sports, translation, travel, women's issues/studies, Canadiana. Submit outline. *All unsolicited mss returned unopened.*

Fiction Literary novels (some short story collections, including novels with a historical setting) and some crime writing. "We publish work by established authors, as well as the work of new and developing authors." *All unsolicited mss returned unopened.* Query.

Poetry "Only Canadian poets should apply. We publish only 4 titles each year." Query. *No unsolicited mss.*

Recent Title(s) *Runaway*, by Alice Munro; *Norman Bray in the Performance of His Life*, by Trevor Cole; *The Mysteries*, by Robert McGill.

🌐 MERCAT PRESS

10 Coates Crescent, Edinburgh EH3 7AL Scotland. E-mail: enquiries@mercatpress.com. Website: www.mercatpress.com. **Acquisitions:** Sean Costello, managing editor; Tom Johnstone, managing editor. Publishes hardcover and trade paperback originals and reprints. **Publishes 30 titles/year. Receives 200 queries and 100 mss/year. 10% of books from first-time authors; 70% from unagented writers. Pays 7½-10% royalty on retail price.** Publishes book 6 months after acceptance of ms. Accepts simultaneous submissions. Responds in 1 month to queries. Book catalog free or online.

Nonfiction Biography, children's/juvenile, cookbook, reference, textbook, fiction. Subjects include agriculture/horticulture, art/architecture, cooking/foods/nutrition, gardening, government/politics, history, language/literature, memoirs, music/dance, nature/environment, photography, regional, sociology. Scottish interest only. Query with IRCs, or submit proposal package, including outline and 2 sample chapters.

Recent Title(s) *A Sense of Belonging to Scotland*, by Andy Hall; *Jessie's Journey*, by Jess Smith; *The One*, by Paul Reed.

Tips "Consult our website for an idea of the type of books we publish."

🅐 🔁 MIRA BOOKS

Imprint of Harlequin, 225 Duncan Mill Rd., Don Mills ON M3B 3K9 Canada. Website: www.mirabooks.com. **Acquisitions:** Margaret Marbury, executive editor. Publishes hardcover, trade paperback, and mass market originals. **Pays royalty. Offers advance.**

Fiction Relationship novels; political, psychological and legal thrillers; family sagas; commercial literary fiction. *Agented submissions only.* No e-mail queries.

🌐 MONARCH BOOKS

Imprint of Lion Hudson Plc, Mayfield House, 256 Banbury Rd., Oxford OX2 7DH United Kingdom. (44)1865 302750. Fax: (44)1865 302757. E-mail: tonyc@lionhudson.com. **Acquisitions:** Tony Collins, editorial director (whole list). Estab. 1988. Publishes hardcover, trade paperback, and mass market paperback originals and reprints. **Publishes 35 titles/year. Receives 2,000 queries and 1,500 mss/year. 25% of books from first-time authors; 90% from unagented writers. Pays 10-15% royalty on wholesale price. Offers negotiable advance.** Publishes book 9 months after acceptance of ms. Accepts simultaneous submissions. Responds in 2 months to proposals; 1 month to queries and mss. Book catalog and ms guidelines free.

Imprints Monarch.

- O→ "We publish primarily for the evangelical Christian market, providing tools and resources for Christian leaders." Monarch Books publishes and distributes in the US and Canada through an arrangement with Kregel Books (Grand Rapids MI).

Nonfiction Biography, humor, reference, self-help. Subjects include child guidance/parenting, philosophy, psychology, religion, science, sex, sociology, Christian fiction. All subjects must have a Christian treatment. Submit proposal package including outline, 2 sample chapters. Query by e-mail.

Recent Title(s) *The Heavenly Man*, by Brother Yun (biography).

Tips "Think about who you are writing for. What will a reader get as benefit from reading your book?"

N ⊠ MUSSIO VENTURES PUBLISHING LTD.

5811 Beresford St., Burnaby BC V5J1K1 Canada. (604)438-3474. Fax: (604)438-3470. Website: www.backroadmapbooks.com. Estab. 1993. **Publishes 5 titles/year. Receives 5 queries and 2 mss/year. 25% of books from first-time authors; 0% from unagented writers. Makes outright purchase of $2,000-4,800. Offers $1,000 advance.** Publishes book 12 months after acceptance of ms. Accepts simultaneous submissions. Responds in 1 month. Book catalog free.

Nonfiction Map and Guide books. Subjects include nature/environment, maps and guides. Submit proposal package including outline/proposal, 1 sample chapter. Reviews artwork/photos as part of ms package. Send photocopies or Digital files.

Recent Title(s) *Le Sud-Quest de Quebec*, by Christine Butt and Jason Marleau; *Southpeace Alberta*, by Trent Ernst.

Tips "Audience includes outdoor recreation enthusiasts and travellers. Provide a proposal including an outline and samples."

N ⊠ NAPOLEON PUBLISHING/RENDEZVOUS PRESS

178 Willowdale Ave., Suite 201, Toronto ON M2N 4Y8 Canada. (416)730-9052. Fax: (416)730-8096. Website: www.rendezvouspress.com. **Acquisitions:** A. Thompson, editor. Estab. 1990. Publishes hardcover and trade paperback originals and reprints. **Publishes 8 titles/year; imprint publishes 4 titles/year. Receives 200 queries and 100 mss/year. 50% of books from first-time authors; 80% from unagented writers.** Publishes book 18 months after acceptance of ms. Accepts simultaneous submissions. Responds in 1 month to queries; 3 months to proposals; 6 months to mss. Book catalog and ms guidelines online.

- Napoleon is not accepting children's novels, biographies or picture book mss at this time. Rendezvous is not accepting mysteries. Check website for updates.
- O→ Rendezvous publishes adult fiction. Napoleon publishes children's books.

Nonfiction Query with SASE, or submit outline, 1 sample chapter.

Recent Title(s) *Little Boy Blues*, by Mary Jane Maffini; *Dead Cow in Aisle Three*, by H. Mel Malton; *Death Goes Shopping*, by Jessica Burton.

Tips "Canadian resident authors only."

⊠ NATURAL HERITAGE/NATURAL HISTORY, INC.

P.O. Box 95, Station O, Toronto ON M4A 2M8 Canada. (416)694-7907. Fax: (416)690-0819. E-mail: info@natural heritagebooks.com. Submissions E-mail: submissions@naturalheritagebooks.com. Website: www.naturalherit agebooks.com. **Acquisitions:** Barry Penhale, publisher. Publishes trade paperback originals. **Publishes 10-12 titles/year. 50% of books from first-time authors; 85% from unagented writers. Pays 8-10% royalty on retail price.** Publishes book 2-3 years after acceptance of ms. Accepts simultaneous submissions. Responds in 4 months to queries; 6 months to proposals and mss. Book catalog free; ms guidelines online.

Imprints Natural Heritage Books.

- O→ Currently emphasizing heritage, history, nature.

Nonfiction Subjects include ethnic, history, nature/environment, recreation, regional. Submit outline.

Fiction Children's (age 8-12), biography/memoir. Query with SASE.

Recent Title(s) *Canoeing a Continent: On the Trail of Alexander Mackenzie*, by Max Finkelstein (nonfiction); *Algonquin Wildlife: Lessons in Survival*, by Norm Quinn (nonfiction); *The Underground Railroad: Next Stop, Toronto!*, by Adrienne Shadd, Afua Cooper, and Karolyn Smardz Frost (young adult nonfiction).

Tips "We are a Canadian publisher in the natural heritage and history fields. We publish only Canadian authors or books with significant Canadian content."

⊠ NEW SOCIETY PUBLISHERS

P.O. Box 189, Gabriola Island BC V0R 1X0 Canada. (250)247-9737. Fax: (250)247-7471. E-mail: info@newsociety.com. Website: www.newsociety.com. **Acquisitions:** Chris Plant, editor. Publishes trade paperback originals and reprints and electronic originals. **Publishes 20 titles/year. Receives 300 queries and 200 mss/year. 50% of books from first-time authors; 80% from unagented writers. Pays 10-12% royalty on wholesale price.**

Offers $0-5,000 advance. Publishes book 9 months after acceptance of ms. Accepts simultaneous submissions. Responds in 1 month to queries; 2 months to proposals. Book catalog free or online; ms guidelines online.

Nonfiction Biography, how-to, illustrated book, self-help. Subjects include business/economics, child guidance/parenting, creative nonfiction, education, government/politics, memoirs, nature/environment, philosophy, regional. Query with SASE, or submit proposal package including outline, 2 sample chapters. Reviews artwork/photos as part of ms package. Send photocopies.

Recent Title(s) *The Party's Over: Oil, War & the Fate of Industrial Societies*, by Richard Heinberg (current affairs).

Tips Audience is activists, academics, progressive business people, managers. "Don't get an agent!"

NEWEST PUBLISHERS LTD.

201, 8540-109 St., Edmonton AB T6G 1E6 Canada. (780)432-9427. Fax: (780)433-3179. E-mail: info@newestpress.com. Website: www.newestpress.com. **Acquisitions:** Ruth Linka, general manager. Estab. 1977. Publishes trade paperback originals. **Publishes 13-16 titles/year. 40% of books from first-time authors; 85% from unagented writers. Pays 10% royalty.** Publishes book 2-3 years after acceptance of ms. Accepts simultaneous submissions. Responds in 6-8 months to queries. Book catalog for 9×12 SASE; ms guidelines online.

NeWest publishes Western Canadian fiction, nonfiction, poetry, and drama.

Nonfiction Literary/essays (Western Canadian authors, Western Canadian and Northern themes). Subjects include ethnic, government/politics, history (Western Canada), nature/environment (northern), Canadiana. Query.

Fiction Literary. "Our press is interested in Western Canadian writing." Submit complete ms.

Recent Title(s) *Big Rig 2*, by Don McTavish (nonfiction); *Better Than Life*, by Margaret Gunning (fiction); *Playing Dead*, by Rudy Wiebe (nonfiction).

NOVALIS

Bayard Presse Canada, 49 Front St. E, Toronto ON M5E 1B3 Canada. (416)363-3303. Fax: (416)363-9409. E-mail: cservice@novalis.ca. Website: www.novalis.ca. **Acquisitions:** Kevin Burns, commissioning editor; Michael O'Hearn, publisher; Anne Louise Mahoney, managing editor. Editorial offices: Novalis, St. Paul University, 223 Main St., Ottawa ON K1S 1C4 Canada. Phone: (613)782-3039. Fax: (613)751-4020. E-mail: kburns@ustpaul.ca. Publishes hardcover and trade paperback originals and trade paperback reprints. **Publishes 40 titles/year. 20% of books from first-time authors; 80% from unagented writers. Pays 10-15% royalty on wholesale price. Offers $300-2,000 advance.** Publishes book 12-18 months after acceptance of ms. Responds in 2 months to queries; 1 month to proposals; 3 months to mss. Book catalog for free or online; ms guidelines free.

"Novalis publishes books about faith, religion, and spirituality in their broadest sense. Based in the Catholic tradition, our interest is strongly ecumenical. Regardless of their denominational perspective, our books speak to the heart, mind, and spirit of people seeking to deepen their faith and understanding."

Nonfiction Biography, children's/juvenile, gift book, humor, illustrated book, reference, self-help. Subjects include child guidance/parenting, education (Christian or Catholic), memoirs, multicultural, nature/environment, philosophy, religion, spirituality. Query with SASE.

Recent Title(s) *Restless Churches*, by Reginald W. Bibby; *Drawn to the Mystery of Jesus Through the Gospel of John*, by Jean Vanier; *At the Edge of Our Longing*, by James Conlon.

N ⊕ ONEWORLD PUBLICATIONS

185 Banbury Rd., Oxford OX2 7AR United Kingdom. (44)(0)1865-310597. Fax: (44)(0)1865-310598. E-mail: info@oneworld-publications.com. Submissions E-mail: submissions@oneworld-publications.com. Website: www.oneworld-publications.com. **Acquisitions:** Novin Doostdar, commissioning editor (religion, Middle East); Victoria Roddam, commissioning editor (popular science, philosophy, current events). Publishes hardcover and trade paperback originals and trade paperback reprints. **Publishes 35 titles/year. Receives 200 queries and 50 mss/year. 20% of books from first-time authors; 100% from unagented writers. Pays 10% royalty on wholesale price. Offers $500-4,000 advance.** Publishes book 15 months after acceptance of ms. Does not accept simultaneous submissions. Responds in 1 month to queries and proposals; 3 months to mss. Book catalog and ms guidelines online.

"We publish authoritative books by academics for a general readership and cross-over student market. Authors must be well qualified." Currently emphasizing religion, history, philosophy. De-emphasizing self-help.

Nonfiction Gift book, reference, self-help, textbook. Subjects include government/politics, history, multicultural, philosophy, psychology, religion, science, sociology, women's issues/studies. Query with SASE, or submit proposal package including outline, 1-3 sample chapters.

Recent Title(s) *Islam: Faith and History*, by Mahmoud M. Ayoub; *Our Sacred Land*, by Kenizé Mourad; *Global Outrage*, by Peter Stearns.

Tips "We don't require agents—just good proposals with enough hard information."

N ☑ ORCA BOOK PUBLISHERS

P.O. Box 5626, Stn. B, Victoria BC V8R 6S4 Canada. Fax: (877)408-1551. E-mail: orca@orcabook.com. Website: www.orcabook.com. **Acquisitions:** Maggie DeVries, editor (picture books, young readers); Andrew Wooldridge, editor (juvenile fiction, teen fiction); Bob Tyrrell, publisher (YA, teen). Estab. 1984. Publishes hardcover and trade paperback originals, and mass market paperback originals and reprints. **Publishes 30 titles/year. Receives 2,500 queries and 1,000 mss/year. 20% of books from first-time authors; 75% from unagented writers. Pays 10% royalty.** Publishes book 12-18 months after acceptance of ms. Does not accept simultaneous submissions. Responds in 1 month to queries and proposals; 1-2 months to mss. Book catalog for 8½×11 SASE; ms guidelines online.

- Only publishes Canadian authors.

Nonfiction Subjects include multicultural, picture books. Query with SASE.

Fiction Hi-lo, juvenile (5-9 years), literary, mainstream/contemporary, young adult (10-18 years). "Ask for guidelines, find out what we publish." Looking for childrens fiction. No romance, science fiction. Query with SASE, or submit proposal package including outline, 2-5 sample chapters, synopsis, SASE.

Recent Title(s) *Before Wings*, by Beth Goobie (teen fiction); *No Two Snowflakes*, by Sheree Fitch (picture book).

Tips "Our audience is for students in grades K-12. Know our books, and know the market."

N 🌐 PETER OWEN PUBLISHERS

73 Kenway Rd., London SW5 0RE United Kingdom. 020-7373 5628. Fax: 020-7373 6760. E-mail: antonia@peterowen.com. Website: www.peterowen.com. **Acquisitions:** Antonia Owen. Publishes hardcover originals and trade paperback originals and reprints. **Publishes 20-30 titles/year. Receives 3,000 queries and 800 mss/year. 70% from unagented writers. Pays 7½-10% royalty. Offers negotiable advance.** Publishes book 1 year after acceptance of ms. Accepts simultaneous submissions. Responds in 2 months to queries; 3 months to proposals and mss. Book catalog for SASE, SAE with IRC or on website.

- "We are far more interested in proposals for nonfiction than fiction at the moment." No poetry or short stories.

Nonfiction Biography. Subjects include art/architecture, history, language/literature, memoirs, translation, travel, women's issues/studies. Query with SASE, or submit outline, 1-3 sample chapters. Submit complete ms with return postage.

Fiction Literary. "No first novels—Authors should be aware that we publish very little new fiction these days." Does not accept short stories, only excerpts from novels of normal length. Submit sample chapters, synopsis. Query with SASE or by e-mail. Submissions by agent preferred.

Recent Title(s) *Almodóvar: Labrynths of Passion*, by Gwynne Edwards (nonfiction); *Doubting Thomas*, by Atle Naess (translation, novel).

N ☑ PEMMICAN PUBLICATIONS, INC.

150 Henry Ave., Winnipeg MB R3B 0J7 Canada. (204)589-6346. Fax: (204)589-2063. E-mail: dramsay@pemmican.mb.ca. Submissions E-mail: dramsay@pemmican.mb.ca. Website: www.pemmican.mb.ca. **Acquisitions:** Diane Ramsay, managing editor (First Nations, Metis, and Inuit culture and heritage. Estab. 1980. Publishes trade paperback originals and reprints, and electronic reprints. **Publishes 7-10 titles/year. Receives 120 queries and 120 mss/year. 50% of books from first-time authors; 100% from unagented writers. Pays 10% royalty on retail price.** Publishes book 1-2 years after acceptance of ms. Accepts simultaneous submissions. Responds in 1 month to queries and proposals; 1 year to mss. Book catalog and ms guidelines free.

Nonfiction Autobiography, biography, children's/juvenile, coffee table book, general nonfiction, illustrated book, reference, scholarly. Subjects include alternative lifestyles, creative nonfiction, education, ethnic, government/politics, history, language/literature, military/war, nature/environment, spirituality. "All of our books are culture and heritage related (Aboriginal), Metis, First Nations, or Inuit. Submit proposal package including outline and 3 sample chapters, or submit complete ms. Reviews artwork/photos as part of ms package. Send photocopies.

Fiction Adventure, ethnic, fantasy, historical, juvenile, literary, military/war, multicultural, mystery, picture books, short story collections, spiritual, sports, suspense, western, young adult. "All manuscripts must be culture and heritage related." Submit proposal package including 3 sample chapters, or submit complete ms.

Poetry "Must be a Metis, First Nations, or Inuit author." Submit 10 sample poems, or submit complete ms.

Recent Title(s) *My Children Are My Reward*, by Alex Harpelle (biography); *The Tobanz*, by Edgar Desjarlais (young adult sports); *The Dream Catcher Pool*, by Jane Chartrand (children's fiction).

Tips Audience is anyone who has an interest in Metis, First Nations, and Inuit culture. No agent is necessary.

🌐 PIPERS' ASH, LTD.

Pipers' Ash, Church Rd., Christian Malford, Chippenham, Wiltshire SN15 4BW United Kingdom. +44(01249)720-563. Fax: 0870 0568917. E-mail: pipersash@supamasu.com. Website: www.supamasu.com. **Acquisitions:** Manuscript Evaluation Desk. Estab. 1976. Publishes hardcover and paperback editions. **Publishes**

12 titles/year. Receives 1,000 queries and 400 mss/year. **90% of books from first-time authors; 99% from unagented writers. Pays 10% royalty on wholesale price. and 5 author's copies.** Publishes book 6 months after acceptance of ms. Does not accept simultaneous submissions. Responds in 1 month to queries and proposals; 3 months to mss. Book catalog for A5 SASE and on website; ms guidelines online.

Imprints Salisbury; Canterbury; Lincoln; Gloucester; Durham; Ely.

Nonfiction Autobiography, biography, how-to, self-help, children's/juvenile/teenagers. Subjects include creative nonfiction, ethnic, history, humanities, language/literature, military/war, philosophy, recreation, religion, translation. "Visit our website." Query with SASE.

Fiction Adventure, confession, feminist, historical, juvenile, literary, mainstream/contemporary, military/war, plays, poetry, poetry in translation, regional, religious, romance (contemporary, romantic suspense), science fiction (hard science/technological, soft/sociological), short story collections, sports, suspense. "We publish 30,000-word novels and short story collections. Visit our website." Query with SASE, or submit sample chapter(s), 25-word synopsis (that sorts out the writers from the wafflers).

Poetry Submit 60 sample poems.

Recent Title(s) *Cross to Bear*, by Chris Spiller; *Science Quicktion*, by Steve Fitzsimmons; *Henry's Navy Blue Hair*, by Gwyneth Hughes.

PLAYWRIGHTS CANADA PRESS

215 Spadina Ave., Suite 230, Toronto ON M5T 2C7 Canada. (416)703-0013. Fax: (416)408-3402. Website: www.playwrightscanada.com. **Acquisitions:** Betony Main, editorial coordinator. Estab. 1984. Publishes paperback originals and reprints of plays. **50% of books from first-time authors; 50% from unagented writers. Pays 10% royalty on retail price.** Publishes book 6 months-1 year after acceptance of ms. Responds in 2-3 months to queries. Ms guidelines online.

> O─ Playwrights Canada Press publishes only drama by Canadian citizens or landed immigrants, which has received professional production.

Recent Title(s) *Butler's Marsh* and *Tempting Providence*, by Robert Chafe; *Rune Alridge*, by Michael Healey; *The Red Priest*, by Mieko Ouchi.

DAVID PORTEOUS EDITIONS

P.O. Box 5, Chudleigh, Newton Abbot, Devon TQ13 0YZ United Kingdom. E-mail: editorial@davidporteous.com. Website: www.davidporteous.com. **Acquisitions:** David Porteous, publisher (arts, crafts, hobbies). Estab. 1992. Publishes hardcover originals and trade paperback originals and reprints. **Publishes 3-5 titles/year. 90% of books from first-time authors; 99% from unagented writers.** Does not accept simultaneous submissions. Responds in 1 month to queries; 2 months to proposals and mss. Book catalog online.

Nonfiction How-to, illustrated book. Subjects include hobbies, arts, crafts. "We publish practical, illustrated books showing step-by-step instructions." Query with SASE. Reviews artwork/photos as part of ms package. Send photocopies or digital images.

Recent Title(s) *Create Greeting Cards With Glass Painting Techniques*, by Joan Dale (craft); *Paul Riley's Watercolour Workshop*, by Paul Riley (art instruction); *Painting With Stitches*, by Sue Dove (craft).

Tips "We publish for an international market, so the content must be suitable for the USA, UK, South Africa, Australia, and New Zealand."

PRESSES DE L'UNIVERSITÉ DE MONTREAL

Case postale 6128, Succursale Centre-ville, Montreal QC H3C 3J7 Canada. (514)343-6933. Fax: (514)343-2232. E-mail: pum@umontreal.ca. Website: www.pum.umontreal.ca. **Acquisitions:** Rene Bonenfant, editor-in-chief. Street Address: 3535 Queen-Mary, Suite 410, Montreal QC H3V 1H8 Canada. Publishes hardcover and trade paperback originals. **Publishes 40 titles/year. Pays 8-12% royalty on net receipts.** Publishes book 6 months after acceptance of ms. Responds in 1 month to queries and proposals; 3 months to mss. Book catalog and ms guidelines free.

Nonfiction Reference, textbook. Subjects include education, health/medicine, history, language/literature, philosophy, psychology, sociology, translation. Submit outline, 2 sample chapters.

PRODUCTIVE PUBLICATIONS

P.O. Box 7200 Station A, Toronto ON M5W 1X8 Canada. (416)483-0634. Fax: (416)322-7434. **Acquisitions:** Iain Williamson, owner. Estab. 1985. Publishes trade paperback originals. **Publishes 24 titles/year. Receives 160 queries and 40 mss/year. 80% of books from first-time authors; 100% from unagented writers. Pays 10-15% royalty on wholesale price.** Publishes book 6 months after acceptance of ms. Accepts simultaneous submissions. Responds in 1 month to queries and proposals; 3 months to mss. Book catalog free.

> O─ "Productive Publications publishes books to help readers succeed and to help them meet the challenges of the new information age and global marketplace." Interested in books on business, computer soft-

ware, the Internet for business purposes, investment, stock market and mutual funds, etc. Currently emphasizing computers, software, small business, business management, entrepreneurship. De-emphasizing jobs, how to get employment.

Nonfiction How-to, reference, self-help, technical. Subjects include business/economics (small business and management), computers/electronic, money/finance, software (business). "We are interested in small business/entrepreneurship/self-help (business)—100-300 pages." Submit outline. Reviews artwork/photos as part of ms package. Send photocopies.

Recent Title(s) *How to Deliver Excellent Customer Service: A Step-by-Step Guide for Every Business*, by Julie Olley; *Market Your Professional Service*, by Jerome Shure.

Tips "We are looking for books written by knowledgable, experienced experts who can express their ideas clearly and simply."

🖳 PURICH PUBLISHING

Box 23032, Market Mall Post Office, Saskatoon SK S7J 5H3 Canada. (306)373-5311. Fax: (306)373-5315. E-mail: purich@sasktel.net. Website: www.purichpublishing.com. **Acquisitions:** Donald Purich, publisher (law, Aboriginal issues); Karen Bolstad, publisher (law, history, education). Publishes trade paperback originals. **Publishes 3-5 titles/year. 20% of books from first-time authors. Pays 8-12% royalty on retail price.** Publishes book within 4 months of completion of editorial work, after acceptance of ms. Accepts simultaneous submissions. Responds in 1 month to queries; 3 months to mss. Book catalog free.

    0➥ Purich publishes books on law, Aboriginal/Native American issues, and Western Canadian history and education for the academic and professional trade reference market.

Nonfiction Reference, technical, textbook. Subjects include education, government/politics, history, Aboriginal issues. "We are a specialized publisher and only consider work in our subject areas." Query with SASE.

Recent Title(s) *Tough on Kids: Rethinking Approaches to Youth Justice*, by Ross Green and Kearney Healy; *Reclaiming Aboriginal Justice, Identity, and Community*, by Craig Proulx; *Who Are Canada's Aboriginal Peoples?*, edited by Paul Chartrand.

🖳 🖉 🖳 RAINCOAST BOOK DISTRIBUTION, LTD.

9050 Shaughnessy St., Vancouver BC V6P 6E5 Canada. (604)323-7128. Fax: (604)323-2600. E-mail: info@raincoast.com. Website: raincoast.com. Publisher: Michelle Benjamin. **Acquisitions:** Lynn Henry, associate publisher. Publishes hardcover and trade paperback originals and reprints. **Publishes 60 titles/year. Receives 3,000 queries/year. 10% of books from first-time authors; 40% from unagented writers. Pays 8-12% royalty on retail price. Offers $1,000-6,000 advance.** Publishes book within 2 years after acceptance of ms. Book catalog for #10 SASE.

Imprints Raincoast Books; Polestar Books (fiction, poetry, literary nonfiction); Press Gang (lesbian and feminist nonfiction).

Nonfiction Children's/juvenile, coffee table book, cookbook, gift book, illustrated book. Subjects include animals, art/architecture, business/economics, cooking/foods/nutrition, ethnic, history, nature/environment, photography, recreation, regional, sports, travel. *No unsolicited mss.* Query with SASE.

Fiction Literary, short story collections, young adult. *No unsolicited mss.*

Recent Title(s) *The Man Who Mapped the Arctic*, by Peter Steele (literary nonfiction); *Beyond the Outer Shores*, by Eric Enno Tamm (biography); *The Five Books of Moses Lapinsky*, by Karen X.

🖳 ROCKY MOUNTAIN BOOKS

406-13th Ave. NE, Calgary AB T2E 1C2 Canada. (403)249-9490. Fax: (403)249-2968. E-mail: rmb@heritagehouse.ca. Website: www.rmbooks.com. **Acquisitions:** David Finch, associate publisher. Publishes trade paperback originals. **Publishes 10 titles/year. Receives 30 queries/year. 75% of books from first-time authors; 100% from unagented writers. Pays 12% royalty on net receipts. Rarely offers advance.** Publishes book 1 year after acceptance of ms. Does not accept simultaneous submissions. Responds in 1 month to queries. Book catalog and ms guidelines free.

    0➥ Rocky Mountain Books publishes books on outdoor recreation, mountains, and mountaineering in Western Canada.

Nonfiction Biography, how-to. Subjects include nature/environment, recreation, regional, travel. "Our main area of publishing is outdoor recreation guides to Western and Northern Canada." Query with SASE.

Recent Title(s) *Caves of the Canadian Rockies and Columbia Mountains*, by Jon Rollins; *Exploring Prince George*, by Mike Nash.

🖳 RONSDALE PRESS

3350 W. 21st Ave., Vancouver BC V6S 1G7 Canada. (604)738-4688. Fax: (604)731-4548. Website: www.ronsdalepress.com. **Acquisitions:** Ronald B. Hatch, director (fiction, poetry, social commentary); Veronica Hatch, managing director (children's literature). Estab. 1988. Publishes trade paperback originals. **Publishes 10 titles/ year. Receives 300 queries and 800 mss/year. 60% of books from first-time authors; 95% from unagented writers. Pays 10% royalty on retail price.** Publishes book 6 months after acceptance of ms. Accepts simultaneous submissions. Responds in 2 weeks to queries; 1 month to proposals; 3 months to mss. Book catalog for #10 SASE; ms guidelines online.

    O┐ Canadian authors only. Ronsdale publishes fiction, poetry, regional history, biography and autobiography, books of ideas about Canada, as well as young adult historical fiction.

Nonfiction Biography, children's/juvenile. Subjects include history (Canadian), language/literature, nature/ environment, regional.

Fiction Literary, short story collections, novels. *Canadian authors only.* Query with at least the first 80 pages. Short story collections must have some previous magazine publication.

Poetry ''Poets should have published some poems in magazines/journals and should be well-read in contemporary masters.'' Submit complete ms.

Recent Title(s) *Adrift in Time*, by John Wilson (YA historical fiction); *When Eagles Call*, by Susan Dobbie (novel).

Tips ''Ronsdale Press is a literary publishing house, based in Vancouver, and dedicated to publishing books from across Canada, books that give Canadians new insights into themselves and their country. We aim to publish the best Canadian writers.''

🌐 ROTOVISION

Sheridan House, 112-116A Western Rd., Hove East Sussex BN3 IDD England. +44 (0) 1273 716010. Fax: +44 (0) 1273 727269. Website: www.rotovision.com. **Acquisitions:** Lindy Dunlop and Chris Middleton, acquisitions editors. Publishes hardcover and trade paperback originals, and trade paperback reprints. Accepts simultaneous submissions. Book catalog and ms guidelines free.

Nonfiction Coffee table book, general nonfiction, how-to, illustrated book. Subjects include art/architecture, creative nonfiction, photography, travel, design, graphic design, stage and screen, advertising. ''Our books are aimed at keen amateurs and professionals who want to improve their skills.'' Query with SASE. Reviews artwork/photos as part of ms package. Send transparencies or PDFs.

Recent Title(s) *Art Directors Annual 83*; *Motion Design*, by Matt Woolman; *Underwater Photography*, by Larry and Denise Tackett.

Tips ''Our audience includes professionals, keen amateurs, and students of visual arts including graphic design, general design, advertising, and photography. Make your approach international in scope. Content not to be less than 35% U.S.''

📧 SAXON HOUSE CANADA

P.O. Box 6947, Station A, Toronto ON M5W 1X6 Canada. (416)488-7171. Fax: (416)488-2989. **Acquisitions:** Dietrich Hummell, editor-in-chief; W.H. Wallace, general manager (history, philosophy); Carla Saxon, CEO (printed music). Publishes hardcover originals. **Publishes 4 titles/year. Receives approximately 60 queries and 20 mss/year. 20% of books from first-time authors; 80% from unagented writers. Pays royalty on wholesale price, or makes outright purchase.** Publishes book 15 months after acceptance of ms. Accepts simultaneous submissions. Responds in 4 months to mss.

Nonfiction Illustrated book. Subjects include history, philosophy, religion, music (printed music). Submit proposal package including 3 sample chapters, résumé. Reviews artwork/photos as part of ms package. Send photocopies.

Fiction Historical, literary. Submit proposal package including 3 sample chapters, résumé.

Recent Title(s) *The Journey to Canada*, by David Mills (history); *Voices From the Lake*, by E.M. Watts (illustrated ancient American Indian legend); *The Wine of Babylon*, by David Mills (epic poem).

Tips ''We want books with literary integrity, historical accuracy, and fresh narrative skills.''

Ⓐ ⊘ 📧 SCHOLASTIC CANADA, LTD.

175 Hillmount Rd., Markham ON L6C 1Z7 Canada. (905)887-7323. Fax: (905)887-3643. Website: www.scholasti c.ca. Publishes hardcover and trade paperback originals. **Publishes 40 titles/year; imprint publishes 4 titles/ year. 3% of books from first-time authors; 50% from unagented writers. Pays 5-10% royalty on retail price. Offers $1,000-5,000 (Canadian) advance.** Publishes book 1 year after acceptance of ms. Does not accept simultaneous submissions. Responds in 3 months to queries; 6 months to proposals. Book catalog for 8½ × 11 SAE with 2 first-class stamps (IRC or Canadian stamps only).

Imprints North Winds Press; Les Editions Scholastic.

    O┐ Scholastic publishes books by Canadians and/or about Canada. Currently emphasizing Canadian interest, middle-grade fiction.

Nonfiction Biography, children's/juvenile. Subjects include history, hobbies, nature/environment, recreation, science, sports. *Agented submissions only. No unsolicited mss.*

Fiction Juvenile (middle grade), young adult. *No unsolicited mss. Agented submissions only.* Canadian authors only.

Recent Title(s) *A Very Unusual Dog*, by Dorothy Joan Harris; *A Poppy Is to Remember*, by Heather Patterson; *Dead and Gone*, by Norah McClintock.

N A ⊕ SEVERN HOUSE PUBLISHERS

9-15 High St., Sutton Surrey SM1 1DF United Kingdom. (0208)770-3930. Fax: (0208)770-3850. **Acquisitions:** Amanda Stewart, editorial director. Publishes hardcover and trade paperback originals and reprints. **Publishes 150 titles/year. Receives 400-500 queries and 50 mss/year. Pays 7½-15% royalty on retail price. Offers $750-5,000 advance.** Accepts simultaneous submissions. Responds in 3 months to proposals. Book catalog free.

○━ Severn House is currently emphasizing suspense, romance, mystery. Large print imprint from existing authors.

Fiction Adventure, fantasy, historical, horror, mainstream/contemporary, mystery, romance, short story collections, suspense. *Agented submissions only.*

Recent Title(s) *The Streets of Town*, by John Gardner; *The Networks*, by Ted Albeury; *Weekend Warriors*, by Fern Michaels.

N ♣ J. GORDON SHILLINGFORD PUBLISHING INC.

P.O. Box 86, RPO Corydon Ave., Winnipeg MB R3M 3S3 Canada. Phone/Fax: (204)779-6967. Website: www.jgs hillingford.com. **Acquisitions:** Catherine Hunter, poetry editor; Glenda MacFarlone, drama editor. Estab. 1993. Publishes trade paperback originals. **Publishes 15 titles/year. Receives 100 queries and 50 mss/year. 15% of books from first-time authors; 60% from unagented writers. Pays 10% royalty on retail price.** Accepts simultaneous submissions. Responds in 1 month to queries and proposals; 3 months to mss. Book catalog and ms guidelines online.

Nonfiction Biography, general nonfiction, humor. Subjects include creative nonfiction, history. Query with SASE.

Fiction Plays, poetry. Query with SASE.

Recent Title(s) *The Golden Woman*, by Kay Stone (body/mind/spirit); *Orchi Delirium*, by Dave Carley (drama).

N ♣ SHORELINE

23 Ste-Anne, Ste-Anne-de-Bellevue, Quebec H9X 1L1 Canada. Phone/Fax: (514)457-5733. E-mail: shoreline@sy mpatico.ca. Website: www.shorelinepress.ca. **Acquisitions:** Judy Isherwood, editor. Estab. 1991. Publishes trade book and paperback originals. **Publishes 3-4 titles/year. Pays 10% royalty on retail price.** Publishes book 1 year after acceptance of ms. Does not accept simultaneous submissions. Responds in 1 month to queries. Book catalog for 75¢; ms guidelines online.

○━ "Our mission is to support new authors by publishing works of considerable merit." Currently emphasizing biographies, memoirs and local history. Do not send mss.

Fiction Ethnic, historical, literary, regional (Canada), religious, short story collections, education, memoir, local history, poetry. Query with SASE, or submit 1-5 sample chapters.

Recent Title(s) *Chasing Grandma*, by Barbara Young (family history); *Walk Up the Creek*, by Marjorie Ludgate (memoir/education); *This Business of Family*, by Dennis Dwyer (conflict resolution in family businesses).

Tips "See our website for submission guide, then query by e-mail or mail query with bio and sample chapters."

N A ⊘ ⊕ SIMON & SCHUSTER AUSTRALIA

Division of Simon & Schuster, Inc., Suite 2, Lower Ground Floor, 14-16 Suakin St. (P.O. Box 33), Pymble NSW 2073 Australia. (61) 2 9983 6600. Fax: (61) 2 9983 6600. Website: www.simonsays.com. Publishes fiction and nonfiction by local authors.

Imprints Audio; Fireside; Kangaroo Press; Martin Books; Pocket Books; Scribner; Simon & Schuster; Touchstone.

N A ⊘ ⊕ SIMON & SCHUSTER UK LTD.

Division of Simon & Schuster, Inc., Africa House, 64-78 Kingsway, London WC2B 6AH United Kingdom. (+44)(0)20 7316 1900. Fax: (+44)(0)20 7316 0332. E-mail: editorial.enquiries@simonandschuster.co.uk. Website: www.simonsays.co.uk. Estab. 1987.

Imprints Earthlight; Fireside; Free Press; International; Martin Books; Pocket Books; Scribner; Simon & Schuster; Simon & Schuster Audio; Simon & Schuster Children's; Touchstone; Town House.

○━ Publisher committed to ongoing literary and commercial success across a wide range of imprints.

⊕ SUMAIYAH DISTRIBUTORS PVT. LTD.

42281 Ansari Rd., Daryaganj, 2nd Floor, New Delhi Delhi 110002 India. (011)23244148. Fax: (011)23244133. E-mail: sumaiyah@vsnl.net. **Acquisitions:** Mohd. Aslam Khan, managing director (medical and allied health sciences); Mrs. Feroza Khanam, acquisitions editor (marketing sales, customer service and development). Estab.

2000. **Publishes 10 titles/year. Receives 8 queries and 5 mss/year. 90% of books from first-time authors. Pays 10-12% royalty. Offers $400-800 advance.** Publishes book 3 months after acceptance of ms. Accepts simultaneous submissions. Responds in 1 month to mss. Book catalog and ms guidelines free.

Nonfiction Illustrated book, technical, textbook, medical and allied health sciences management, quick reference manual, and self-guide book. Subjects include health/medicine. Submit complete ms. Reviews artwork/photos as part of ms package.

Recent Title(s) *Understanding Human Histology*, by Dr. Abrar Khan (textbook for undergraduate medical and allied health); *Topics in Colorectal Surgery*, by P. Sivalingam; *Otolaryngology at 11th Hour*, by Anupam Mishra.

Tips "We place strong emphasis on materials that teach quick grasp of the subject for the busy student, practitioners, and researchers. And the writers should clearly indicate what the book is about and who the audience is."

THOMPSON EDUCATIONAL PUBLISHING, INC.

6 Ripley Ave., Suite 200, Toronto ON M6S 3N9 Canada. (416)766-2763. Fax: (416)766-0398. E-mail: publisher@thompsonbooks.com. Website: www.thompsonbooks.com. **Acquisitions:** Keith Thompson, president. **Publishes 10 titles/year. Receives 15 queries and 10 mss/year. 80% of books from first-time authors; 100% from unagented writers. Pays 10% royalty on net receipts.** Publishes book 1 year after acceptance of ms. Does not accept simultaneous submissions. Responds in 1 month to queries. Book catalog free; ms guidelines online.

O➔ Thompson Educational specializes in high-quality educational texts in the social sciences and humanities.

Nonfiction Textbook. Subjects include business/economics, education, ethnic, government/politics, multicultural, sociology, sports, women's issues/studies. Submit outline, 1 sample chapter, résumé.

Recent Title(s) *Social Work: A Critical Turn*, edited by Steven Hick, Jan Foot and Richard Pozzuto.

TITAN BOOKS, LTD.

144 Southwark St., London SE1 0UP United Kingdom. (0207)620 0200. Fax: (0207)620 0032. E-mail: editorial@titanemail.com. Website: www.titanbooks.com. **Acquisitions:** D. Barraclough, editorial manager. Publishes trade and mass market paperback originals and reprints. **Publishes about 200 titles/year. Receives 500 queries and 200 mss/year. 1% of books from first-time authors; 50% from unagented writers. Pays 6-8% royalty on retail price. Offers variable advance.** Accepts simultaneous submissions. Responds in 1 month to queries; 3 months to proposals; 6 months to mss. Ms guidelines for #10 SASE.

O➔ Titan Books publishes film and TV titles.

Nonfiction Biography, how-to, illustrated books. Subjects include film/cinema/stage, film and TV. Submit outline, sample chapters, SASE.

Recent Title(s) *Batman: War Drums; Simpsons Comics Barn Burner; Superman: Unconventional Warfare; The Battlestar Galactica Companion; Smallville Season 2 Companion; Stargate SG-1 Companion Seasons 7 & 8; CSI: Dominos; Scooby-Doo & the Monster Menace; Star Wars: Clone Wars Adventures 3.*

TRADEWIND BOOKS

1809 Maritime Mews, Granville Island, Vancouver BC V6H 3W7 Canada. (604)662-4405. Fax: (604)730-0454. E-mail: tradewindbooks@eudoramail.com. Website: www.tradewindbooks.com. **Acquisitions:** Michael Katz, publisher (picturebooks, young adult); Carol Frank, art director (picturebooks); Tiffany Stone (acquisitions editor). Publishes hardcover and trade paperback originals. **Publishes 5 titles/year. 10% of books from first-time authors; 50% from unagented writers. Pays 7% royalty on retail price. Offers variable advance.** Publishes book 3 years after acceptance of ms. Accepts simultaneous submissions. Responds in 2 months to mss. Book catalog and ms guidelines online.

O➔ Tradewind Books publishes juvenile picture books and young adult novels. Requires that submissions include evidence that author has read at least 3 titles published by Tradewind Books.

Fiction Juvenile. Query with SASE, or submit proposal package including 2 sample chapters, synopsis.

Recent Title(s) *The Bone Collector's Son; The Sorcerer's Letterbox; For Sure for Sure.*

TRENTHAM BOOKS, LTD.

Westview House, 734 London Rd., Stoke on Trent ST4 5NP United Kingdom. (0044)1782 745567. Fax: (0044)745553. E-mail: tb@trentham-books.co.uk. Website: www.trentham-books.co.uk. **Acquisitions:** Gillian Klein, commissioning editor (education, race). Publishes hardcover and trade paperback originals. **Publishes 32 titles/year. Receives 1,000 queries and 600 mss/year. 60% of books from first-time authors; 70% from unagented writers. Pays 7½% royalty on wholesale price.** Publishes book 4 months after acceptance of ms. Does not accept simultaneous submissions. Responds in 1 month to queries. Book catalog for #10 SASE; ms guidelines online.

O➔ "Our mission is to enhance the work of professionals in education, law, and social work." Currently emphasizing curriculum, professional behavior. De-emphasizing theoretical issues.

Nonfiction Technical, textbook. Subjects include education, ethnic, multicultural, psychology, women's issues/studies, language/literacy. Query with SASE.

Recent Title(s) *Children's Literature and National Identity*, by Margaret Meek, ed; *Lifelong Learning and the New Educational Order*, by John Field.

TURNSTONE PRESS

607-100 Arthur St., Winnipeg MB R3B 1H3 Canada. (204)947-1555. Fax: (204)942-1555. E-mail: info@ravenstonebooks.com. Website: www.ravenstonebooks.com. **Acquisitions:** Todd Besant, managing editor; Sharon Caseburg, acquisitions editor. Estab. 1976. Publishes trade paperback originals, mass market for literary mystery imprint. **Publishes 10-12 titles/year. Receives 800 mss/year. 25% of books from first-time authors; 75% from unagented writers. Pays 10% royalty on retail price, and 10 author's copies. Offers advance.** Publishes book 18 months-2 years after acceptance of ms. Does not accept simultaneous submissions. Responds in 4 months to queries. Book catalog for #10 SASE; ms guidelines online.

Imprints Ravenstone (literary mystery fiction).

> Turnstone Press is a literary press that publishes Canadian writers with an emphasis on writers from, and writing on, the Canadian West. Currently emphasizing novels, nonfiction travel, adventure travel, poetry. Does not consider formula or mainstream work.

Nonfiction Subjects include travel, adventure travel, cultural/social issues, Canadian literary criticism. Query with SASE, literary cv, and 50-page sample.

Fiction Literary, regional (Western Canada), short story collections, contemporary, novels. *Canadian authors only*. Query with SASE, literary cv, and 50-page sample.

Poetry Submit complete ms.

Recent Title(s) *Kornukopia*, by David Annandale (action/thriller); *Leaving Wyoming*, by Brent Robillard (novel); *Loving Gertrude Stein*, by Deborah Schnitzer (poetry).

Tips "Writers are encouraged to view our list and check if submissions are appropriate. Although we publish new authors, we prefer first-time authors to have publishing credits in literary magazines. We would like to see more adventure travel, as well as eclectic novels. We would like to see 'nonformula' writing for the Ravenstone imprint, especially literary thrillers, urban mystery, and noir."

THE UNIVERSITY OF ALBERTA PRESS

Ring House 2, Edmonton AB T6G 2E1 Canada. (780)492-3662. Fax: (780)492-0719. E-mail: uap@ualberta.ca. Website: www.uap.ualberta.ca. Estab. 1969. Publishes orginals and reprints. **Publishes 18-25 titles/year. Royalties are negotiated.** Publishes book within 2 years (usually) after acceptance of ms. Does not accept simultaneous submissions. Responds in 3 months to queries. Ms guidelines online.

> "Award-winning publisher The University of Alberta Press has published excellent scholarly works and fine books for general audiences. Our program is particularly strong in the areas of biography, history, literature, natural history, and books of regional interest. Within each of those broad subject areas, we have published in a variety of specific fields. We are pursuing academic manuscripts in our areas of strength and expertise, as listed above, and inviting submissions in several new areas, including travel/adventure writing, business, health, and social policy. We do not accept unsolicited novels, short story collections, or poetry. Please see our website for details."

Tips Query with SASE.

UNIVERSITY OF CALGARY PRESS

2500 University Dr. NW, Calgary AB T2N 1N4 Canada. (403)220-7578. Fax: (403)282-0085. Website: www.uofcpress.com. **Acquisitions:** Walter Hildebrandt, director. Publishes hardcover and trade paperback originals and reprints. **Publishes 30-40 titles/year.** Publishes book 20 months after acceptance of ms. Does not accept simultaneous submissions. Responds in 1 month to queries; 2 months to proposals and mss. Book catalog free; ms guidelines online.

> "University of Calgary Press is committed to the advancement of scholarship through the publication of first-rate monographs, and academic and scientific journals."

Nonfiction Scholarly. Subjects include art/architecture, philosophy, travel, women's issues/studies, world affairs. Canadian studies, post-modern studies, native studies, history, international relations, artic studies, Africa, Latin American and Caribbean studies, and heritage of the Canadian and American heartland. "The UC Press has recently launched a new Open Spaces series presenting some of the region's finest literary works that resonate with prarie themes, voices, and experiences." Submit outline, 2 sample chapters. SASE. Reviews artwork/photos as part of ms package. Send photocopies.

Recent Title(s) *Animals of the Rolling Hills: An Alberta Bestiary*, by Zahava Hanen; *Passages: Explorations in the Contemporary City*, by Graham Livesey; *New Owners in Their Own Land*, by Robert McPherson.

〔N〕 ⬚ UNIVERSITY OF MANITOBA PRESS

301 St. John's College, University of Manitoba, Winnipeg MB R3T 2M5 Canada. (204)474-9495. Fax: (204)474-7566. E-mail: carr@cc.umanitoba.ca. Website: www.umanitoba.ca/uofmpress. **Acquisitions:** David Carr, director. Estab. 1967. Publishes nonfiction hardcover and trade paperback originals. **Publishes 4-6 titles/year. Pays 5-15% royalty on wholesale price. Offers advance.** Does not accept simultaneous submissions. Responds in 3 months to queries.

Nonfiction Scholarly. Subjects include ethnic, history, regional, women's issues/studies, Western Canadian history. Query with SASE.

Recent Title(s) *Rural Life*, by P.J. Giffen; *Fresh Water Fishes of Manitoba*, by Kenneth Stewart and Douglas Watkinson; *Formidible Heritage*, by Jim Mochoruk.

Tips "Western Canadian focus or content is important."

〔N〕 ⊕ UNIVERSITY OF NEW SOUTH WALES PRESS

University of New South Wales, Sydney NSW 2052 Australia. +612 9664 0900. Fax: +612 9664 5420. E-mail: info.press@unsw.edu.au. Website: www.unswpress.com.au. Estab. 1962. Publishes hardcover and trade paperback originals. **Publishes 40 titles/year. Pays royalty on wholesale price.** Ms guidelines online.

Nonfiction Biography, general nonfiction, reference, scholarly, textbook. Subjects include community, contemporary culture, gardening, government/politics, health/medicine, history, humanities, nature/environment, science, social sciences. Submit proposal package including outline.

Recent Title(s) *Refuge Australia*, by Klaus Neumann; *A Spirit of True Learning*, by Matthew Jordan; *Personality and Performance*, by Robert Spillane and John Martin.

Tips "We have readers of serious nonfiction in Australia and beyond, including books of ideas, trade reference, and tertiary text books."

⬚ UNIVERSITY OF OTTAWA PRESS

542 King Edward, Ottawa ON K1N 6N5 Canada. (613)562-5246. Fax: (613)562-5247. E-mail: press@uottawa.ca. Website: www.uopress.uottawa.ca. **Acquisitions:** Ruth Bradley-St-Cyr, director. Estab. 1936. **Publishes 25 titles/year. 20% of books from first-time authors; 95% from unagented writers. Pays 5-10% royalty on net receipts.** Publishes book 6-12 months after acceptance of ms. Does not accept simultaneous submissions. Responds in 1 month to queries; 6 months to mss. Book catalog and ms guidelines free.

○─┬ The University of Ottawa Press publishes books for scholarly and serious nonfiction audiences. They were "the first *officially* bilingual university publishing house in Canada. Our goal is to help the publication of cutting-edge research—books written to be useful to active researchers but accessible to an interested public." Currently emphasizing French in North America, language rights, translation, Canadian studies, criminology, international development, governance. De-emphasizing medieval studies.

Nonfiction Reference, scholarly, textbook. Subjects include education, government/politics, history, philosophy, religion, sociology, translation, women's studies, Canadian literature. Submit outline, sample chapters, cv.

Recent Title(s) *Ashore and Afloat: The British Navy and the Halifax Naval Yard Before 1820*, by Julian Gwyn; *Canada's Religions*, by Robert Choquette (Choice Outstanding Academic title).

Tips "No unrevised theses! Envision audience of academic specialists and readers of serious nonfiction."

⬚ VÉHICULE PRESS

Box 125, Place du Parc Station, Montreal QC H2X 4A3 Canada. (514)844-6073. Fax: (514)844-7543. Website: www.vehiculepress.com. **Acquisitions:** Simon Dardick, president/publisher. Estab. 1973. Publishes trade paperback originals by Canadian authors only. **Publishes 15 titles/year. 20% of books from first-time authors; 95% from unagented writers. Pays 10-15% royalty on retail price. Offers $200-500 advance.** Publishes book 1 year after acceptance of ms. Responds in 4 months to queries. Book catalog for 9×12 SAE with IRCs.

Imprints Signal Editions (poetry); Dossier Quebec (history, memoirs); Esplanade Editions (fiction).

● Canadian authors only.

○─┬ "Montreal's Véhicule Press has published the best of Canadian and Quebec literature—fiction, poetry, essays, translations, and social history."

Nonfiction Autobiography, biography. Subjects include government/politics, history, language/literature, memoirs, regional, sociology. Especially looking for Canadian social history. Query with SASE. Reviews artwork/photos as part of ms package.

Fiction Contact Andrew Steinmet. Feminist, literary, regional, short story collections. No romance or formula writing. Query with SASE.

Poetry Contact Carmine Starnino.

Recent Title(s) *Mirabel*, by Pierre Nepreu, translated by Judith Cowan (winner of Governor General's Award); *Seventeen Tomatoes*, by Jasprect Singh (winner of QWF First Book Prize); *The Man Who Killed Houdini*, by Don Bell.

[N] [globe] WHICH?, LTD.

2 Marylebone Rd., London NW1 4DF United Kingdom. 020 7770 7000. Fax: 020 7770 7600. E-mail: which@which.co.uk. Website: www.which.net. **Publishes 25-30 titles/year. Receives 30 queries/year. 95% from unagented writers. Pays royalty on retail price.** Publishes book 6 months after acceptance of ms. Responds in 1 month to queries. Book catalog free or online at website.

Nonfiction How-to, reference, self-help. Subjects include business/economics, computers/electronic, gardening, health/medicine, hobbies, money/finance, software, travel. Query with SASE.

Recent Title(s) *The Which? Book of Wiring and Lighting*, by Mike Lawrence (manual for amateur electricians).

Tips "We rarely take on proposals from authors, and when we do we expect to have a lot of influence on the content, tone, etc., of the text. But occasionally a relevant submission comes in that fulfills our requirements of independence, reliability, where a successful commission and publication, has resulted."

[globe] WHITECAP BOOKS, LTD.

351 Lynn Ave., North Vancouver BC V7J 2C4 Canada. (604)980-9852. Fax: (604)980-8197. Website: www.whitecap.ca. Publishes hardcover and trade paperback originals. **Publishes 20 titles/year. Receives 500 queries and 1,000 mss/year. 20% of books from first-time authors; 90% from unagented writers. Pays royalty. Offers negotiated advance.** Publishes book 18 months after acceptance of ms. Accepts simultaneous submissions. Responds in 3 months to proposals.

  O– Whitecap Books publishes a wide range of nonfiction with a Canadian and international focus. Currently emphasizing children's nonfiction, natural history. De-emphasizing children's illustrated fiction.

Nonfiction Children's/juvenile, coffee table book, cookbook. Subjects include animals, cooking/foods/nutrition, gardening, history, nature/environment, recreation, regional, travel. "We require an annotated outline. Writers should take the time to research our list and read the submission guidelines on our website. This is especially important for children's writers." Submit outline, 1 sample chapter, SASE. Reviews artwork/photos as part of ms package. Send photocopies.

Recent Title(s) *Vancouver's Glory Years*, by Heather Conn and Henry Ewert (nonfiction); *Accidental Alphabet*, by Dianne Bonder (children's illustrated fiction); *Mustang Mountain Series*, by Sharon Siamon (children's/YA fiction).

Tips "We want well-written, well-researched material that presents a fresh approach to a particular topic."

[globe] WOODHEAD PUBLISHING, LTD.

Abington Hall, Abington Cambridge CB1 6AH United Kingdom. (+44)1223-891358. Fax: (+44)1223-893694. E-mail: wp@woodheadpublishing.com. Website: www.woodheadpublishing.com. **Acquisitions:** Francis Dodds (food science, technology, and nutrition); Gwen Jones (materials engineering, textile technology, welding and joining). Publishes hardcover originals. **Publishes 40 titles/year. 75% of books from first-time authors; 99% from unagented writers. Pays 10% royalty on wholesale price.** Publishes book 6 months after acceptance of ms. Does not accept simultaneous submissions. Book catalog for free or on website; ms guidelines online.

Nonfiction Technical. Subjects include food science, materials engineering, textile technology, welding and joining. Submit proposal package including outline. Reviews artwork/photos as part of ms package. Send photocopies.

Recent Title(s) *Yoghurt: Science and Technology*; *Food Preservation Techniques*; *Fatigue in Composites*.

[globe] ZED BOOKS

7 Cynthia St., London N1 9JF United Kingdom. 44-71-837-4014. Fax: 44-71-833-3960. Website: www.zedbooks.co.uk. **Acquisitions:** Robert Molten (international affairs, politics, development, environment, Third World, gender studies, cultural studies, social sciences). Publishes hardcover and trade paperback originals. **Publishes 40-45 titles/year. Receives 300 queries and 150 mss/year. 25% of books from first-time authors; 95-100% from unagented writers. Pays 7½-10% royalty on retail price, or net receipts. Offers $1,000 advance.** Publishes book 9 months after acceptance of ms. Accepts simultaneous submissions. Responds in 1 week to queries; 1 month to proposals; 3 months to mss. Book catalog free; ms guidelines online.

Nonfiction Textbook. Subjects include agriculture/horticulture, anthropology/archeology, business/economics, education, government/politics, health/medicine, history, money/finance, multicultural, nature/environment, sociology, women's issues/studies. Submit proposal package including outline, 2 sample chapters, or submit complete ms.

Recent Title(s) *Iran in Crisis?*, by Roger Howard; *North Korea*, by Paul French; *State Terrorism and the United States*, by Frederick H. Gareau.

Small Presses

Small press is a relative term. Compared to the dozen or so conglomerates, the rest of the book publishing world may seem to be comprised of small presses. A number of the publishers listed in the Book Publishers section consider themselves small presses and cultivate the image. For our classification, small presses are those that publish, on average, no more than six books per year.

The publishing opportunities are slightly more limited with the companies listed here than with those in the Book Publishers section. Not only are they publishing fewer books, but small presses are usually not able to market their books as effectively as larger publishers, and their print runs and royalty arrangements are usually smaller.

However, realistic small press publishers don't try to compete with Penguin Group (USA), Inc., or Random House. Most small press publishers get into book publishing for the love of it, not solely for the profit. Of course, every publisher, small or large, wants successful books, but small press publishers often measure success in different ways.

Many writers actually prefer to work with small presses. Since small publishing houses are usually based on the publisher's commitment to the subject matter, and since they work with far fewer authors than the conglomerates, small press authors and their books usually receive more personal attention than the larger publishers can afford to give them. Promotional dollars at the big houses tend to be siphoned toward a few books each season that they have decided are likely to succeed, leaving hundreds of "midlist" books underpromoted. Since small presses only commit to a very small number of books every year, they are quite interested in the promotion and distribution of each book.

Just because they publish fewer titles than large publishing houses does not mean small press editors have the time to look at complete manuscripts. In fact, the editors with smaller staffs often have even less time for submissions. The procedure for contacting a small press with your book idea is exactly the same as it is for a larger publisher. Send a one-page query with SASE first. If the press is interested in your proposal, be ready to send an outline or synopsis, and/or a couple sample chapters.

For more information on small presses, see *Novel & Short Story Writer's Market* and *Poet's Market* (Writer's Digest Books).

For a list of publishers according to their subjects of interest, see the Nonfiction and Fiction sections of the Book Publishers Subject Index. Information on book publishers listed in the previous edition of *Writer's Market*, but not included in this edition, can be found in the General Index.

⚠ ACTIVE BLADDER

P.O. Box 24607, Philadelphia PA 19111. Website: www.activebladder.com. **Acquisitions:** John Osborn. Estab. 2004. **30% of profits.** Accepts simultaneous submissions. Responds in 1 month. Ms guidelines online.

Nonfiction Biography, general nonfiction. Subjects include music/dance. All materials must deal with punk rock. "Queries and submissions are discouraged, since we approach punk-rock celebrities that we would like to work with." Query with SASE.

Fiction Horror, mainstream/contemporary, mystery, romance, science fiction, suspense. Looking for genre fiction (horror, sci-fi, mystery, romance) with a suspenseful edge. Length should be 20,000-100,000 words. Novel should stress story-telling; author shouldn't be obsessed with theme, metaphors and symbolism. Novelists who would fit in with the Active Bladder roster would be ones whose literary heroes include Stephen King, Michael Crichton, Robert Parker and/or Jayne Ann Krentz. Submit 1 sample chapter, SASE.

Recent Title(s) *The Olfactory Empath*, Johnny Ostenatious (mystery/sci-fi/horror fiction).

AD LIB BOOKS, LLC

217 E. Foxwood Dr., Raymore MO 64083. Phone/Fax: (816)331-6160. E-mail: info@adlibbooks.com. Website: www.adlibbooks.com. **Acquisitions:** Julie Henry, publication director (general fiction). Estab. 2004. Publishes trade paperback originals. **Publishes 4 titles/year. 95% of books from first-time authors; 75% from unagented writers. Pays 7% royalty on wholesale price.** Publishes book 4 months after acceptance of ms. Accepts simultaneous submissions. Responds in 1 month to queries; 3 months to mss. Ms guidelines for #10 SASE or online.

Fiction Adventure, experimental, horror, humor, literary, mainstream/contemporary, mystery, romance, sports, suspense. Query with SASE. No e-mail queries.

Recent Title(s) *Reign of the Rat*, by Gil Smolin (medical thriller); *A Matter of Time*, by Julie Mears Henry (romance).

ADAMS-HALL PUBLISHING

P.O. Box 491002, Los Angeles CA 90049. (800)888-4452. E-mail: adamshallpublish@aol.com. Website: www.adams-hall.com. **Acquisitions:** Sue Ann Bacon, editorial director. Publishes hardcover and trade paperback originals and reprints. **Publishes 3-4 titles/year. Pays 10% royalty on net receipts. Offers negotiable advance.** Does not accept simultaneous submissions. Responds in 1 month to queries.

Nonfiction Subjects include money/finance, business. Small successful house that aggressively promotes select titles. Only interested in business or personal finance titles with broad appeal. Submit query, title, synopsis, your qualifications, a list of 3 competitive books and how it's widely different from other books. Do not send ms or sample chapters.

Recent Title(s) *Fail Proof Your Business*.

ADDICUS BOOKS, INC.

P.O. Box 45327, Omaha NE 68145. (402)330-7493. Website: www.addicusbooks.com. **Acquisitions:** Acquisitions Editor. Estab. 1994. **Publishes 5-10 nonfiction titles/year. 70% of books from first-time authors; 60% from unagented writers. Pays royalty on retail price. Offers advance.** Publishes book 9 months after acceptance of ms. Accepts simultaneous submissions. Responds in 1 month to proposals. Ms guidelines online.

    ⚬⚯ Addicus Books, Inc. seeks mss with strong national or regional appeal.

Nonfiction How-to, self-help. Subjects include Americana, business/economics, health/medicine, psychology, regional, true crime. "We are expanding our line of consumer health titles." Query with SASE. Do not send entire ms unless requested. When querying electronically, send only 1-page e-mail, giving an overview of your book and its market. Please do not send attachments unless invited to do so. Additional submission guidelines online.

Recent Title(s) *A Simple Guide to Thyroid Disorders*, by Paul Ruggieri, MD; *Understanding Lumpectomy—A Guide to Breast Cancer Treatment*, by Rosalind Benedet, RN and Mark Rounsaville, MD.

Tips "We are looking for quick-reference books on health topics. Do some market research to make sure the market is not already flooded with similar books. We're also looking for good true-crime manuscripts, with an interesting story, with twists and turns, behind the crime."

AMERICAN CATHOLIC PRESS

16565 S. State St., South Holland IL 60473. (312)331-5845. Fax: (708)331-5484. E-mail: acp@acpress.org. Website: www.acpress.org. **Acquisitions:** Rev. Michael Gilligan, PhD, editorial director. Estab. 1967. Publishes hardcover originals and hardcover and paperback reprints. **Publishes 4 titles/year. Makes outright purchase of $25-100.** Does not accept simultaneous submissions. Ms guidelines online.

Nonfiction Subjects include education, music/dance, religion, spirituality. "We publish books on the Roman

Catholic liturgy—for the most part, books on religious music and educational books and pamphlets. We also publish religious songs for church use, including Psalms, as well as choral and instrumental arrangements. We are interested in new music, meant for use in church services. Books, or even pamphlets, on the Roman Catholic Mass are especially welcome. We have no interest in secular topics and are not interested in religious poetry of any kind.''

Tips "Most of our sales are by direct mail, although we do work through retail outlets.''

ANACUS PRESS

Imprint of Finney Co., 3943 Meadowbrook Rd., Minneapolis MN 55426. (952)938-9330. Fax: (952)938-7353. E-mail: feedback@finney-hobar.com. Website: www.anacus.com. **Acquisitions:** Alan Krysan, president (bicycling guides, travel). Publishes trade paperback originals. **Publishes variable number of titles/year. Pays 10% royalty on wholesale price. Offers $500 advance.** Book catalog online.

Nonfiction Subjects include recreation, regional, travel (travel guides, travelogue). Query with SASE.

Recent Title(s) *Bed, Breakfast & Bike Mississippi Valley*, by Dale Lally (travel guide); *The Adventure of Two Lifetimes*, by Peggy and Brian Goetz (travelogue); *Bed, Breakfast & Bike Midwest*, by Robert and Theresa Russell (travel guide).

Tips Audience is cyclists and armchair adventurers.

ANHINGA PRESS

P.O. Box 10595, Tallahassee FL 32302. (850)422-1408. Fax: (850)442-6323. E-mail: info@anhinga.org. Website: www.anhinga.org. **Acquisitions:** Rick Campbell or Joann Gardner, editors. Publishes hardcover and trade paperback originals. **Publishes 3-4 titles/year. Pays 10% royalty on retail price. Offers Anhinga Prize of $2,000.** Accepts simultaneous submissions. Responds in 3 months to queries; 3 months to proposals; 3 months to mss. Book catalog for #10 SASE or online; ms guidelines online.

   O— Publishes only full-length collections of poetry (60-80 pages). No individual poems or chapbooks.

Poetry Query with SASE and 10-page sample (not full ms) by mail. No e-mail queries.

Recent Title(s) *Ornithologies*, by Joshua Poteat (2004 Anhinga Prize for Poetry winner); *The Pyramids of Malpighi*, by Steven Gehrke (2003 Levine Prize in Poetry winner); *Musical Chair*, by Rhonda J. Nelson (2004 Florida Poetry Series).

ANVIL PUBLISHERS, INC.

3852 Allsborough Dr., Tucker GA 30084. (770)938-0289. Fax: (770)493-7232. E-mail: info@anvilpub.com. **Acquisitions:** Lee Xavier, editor-in-chief. Publishes hardcover and paperback originals, CD-ROMs. **Publishes 3-5 titles/year. Pays royalty.** Responds in 3 months to mss.

Nonfiction Biography, Christian. Subjects include health/medicine, history (American), military/war. No autobiography or memoir. Query with SASE.

Recent Title(s) *New Hope: Avoiding Lung Cancer*; *How to Work With Angry People and Outraged Publics*; *How to Manage Organizational Communication During Crisis*.

ARCHIMEDES PRESS, INC.

6 Berkley Rd., Glenville NY 12302. (518)265-3269. Fax: (518)384-1313. E-mail: archimedespress@verizon.net. Website: www.archimedespress.com. President: Kim Gorham. **Acquisitions:** Richard DiMaggio, chief editor. Estab. 2002. Publishes broad-based hardcover, trade paperback, and mass market paperback originals. **Publishes 3-6 titles/year. Pays 5-15% royalty.** Publishes book 6 months after acceptance of ms. Does not accept simultaneous submissions. Responds in 2 months to queries.

Nonfiction General nonfiction, how-to, illustrated book, multimedia, self-help. Subjects include alternative lifestyles, business/economics, child guidance/parenting, community, cooking/foods/nutrition, creative nonfiction, education, government/politics, history, humanities, language/literature, money/finance, photography, sex, social sciences, travel. "E-mail submissions acceptable. Please snail mail complete manuscripts. If a consumer wants it, so do we." Query with SASE, or submit sample chapter(s), marketing plan, SASE, or submit complete ms. Reviews artwork/photos as part of ms package. Send photocopies.

Recent Title(s) *Real Estate Professionals Liability Review*; *Financial Empowerment Infomercials*.

Tips "Our audience is the consumer, plain and simple. That means everyone. We are a small press and try hard to avoid the limitations of the industry. While agented submissions are preferred, they are not necessary with professional submissions. We want fresh, creative ideas and will accept unsolicited manuscripts. These, however, will not be returned without a SASE. E-mails are OK. No phone calls, please."

ARDEN PRESS, INC.

P.O. Box 418, Denver CO 80201-0418. (303)697-6766. Fax: (303)697-3443. **Acquisitions:** Susan Conley, publisher. Estab. 1980. Publishes hardcover and trade paperback originals and reprints. **Publishes 4-6 titles/year.**

20% of books from first-time authors; 80% from unagented writers. Pays 8-15% royalty on wholesale price. Offers $2,000 average advance. Publishes book 6 months after acceptance of ms. Accepts simultaneous submissions. Responds in 2 months to queries. Ms guidelines free.

O⇥ Arden Press publishes nonfiction on women's history and women's issues. ''We sell to general and women's bookstores as well as public and academic libraries. Many of our titles are adopted as texts for use in college courses.''

Nonfiction Subjects include women's issues/studies. No personal memoirs or autobiographies. Query with outline/synopsis and sample chapters.

Recent Title(s) *Whatever Happened to the Year of the Woman?*, by Amy Handlin.

Tips ''Writers have the best chance selling us nonfiction on women's subjects. If I were a writer trying to market a book today, I would learn as much as I could about publishers' profiles *then* contact those who publish similar works.''

ⓝ ARTEMIS CREATIONS PUBLISHING

100 Chatham E., West Palm Beach FL 33417-1817. **Acquisitions:** President: Shirley Oliveira. Publishes trade paperback and mass market paperback originals. **Publishes 4 titles/year. Pays 50% royalty on retail price for eBooks only.**

Imprints FemSuprem Books.

O⇥ ''Our publications explore femme supremacy, matriarchy, sex, gender, relationships, etc., masochism (male only).''

Nonfiction Subjects include language/literature, religion (pagan), science, sex, women's issues/studies. ''Strong feminine archetypes, subjects only.'' Query with SASE, or submit outline, 3 sample chapters, author bio, marketing plan.

Fiction Erotica, experimental, fantasy, feminist, gothic, horror, mystery, occult, religious, science fiction. Submit synopsis, SASE.

Recent Title(s) *Lady Killer: Tale of Horror and the Erotic*, by Tony Malo; *Gospel of Goddess*, by Bond and Suffield (metaphysical).

Tips ''Our readers are looking for strong, powerful feminine archetypes in fiction and nonfiction. Graphic sex and language are OK.''

ASIAN HUMANITIES PRESS

Jain Publishing Co., P.O. Box 3523, Fremont CA 94539. (510)659-8272. Fax: (510)659-0501. E-mail: mail@jainpub.com. Website: www.jainpub.com. **Acquisitions:** M.K. Jain, editor-in-chief. Estab. 1989. Publishes hardcover and trade paperback originals and reprints. **Publishes 6 titles/year. 100% from unagented writers. Pays 5-15% royalty on net receipts.** Publishes book 1-2 years after acceptance of ms. Does not return proposal material. Responds in 3 months to mss. Book catalog and ms guidelines online.

O⇥ Asian Humanities Press publishes in the areas of humanities and social sciences pertaining to Asia, commonly categorized as ''Asian Studies.'' Currently emphasizing undergraduate-level textbooks.

Nonfiction Reference, textbook, general trade books. Subjects include language/literature, philosophy, psychology, religion, spirituality, Asian classics, social sciences, art/culture. Submit proposal package including vita, list of prior publications. Reviews artwork/photos as part of ms package. Send photocopies.

Recent Title(s) *Adhidharmasamuccaya*, by Walpola Rahula.

ASTRAGAL PRESS

P.O. Box 239, Mendham NJ 07945. (866)543-3045 or (973)543-3045. Fax: (973)543-3044. E-mail: info@astragalpress.com. Website: www.astragalpress.com. Estab. 1983. Publishes trade paperback originals and reprints. Does not accept simultaneous submissions. Book catalog and ms guidelines free.

O⇥ ''Our primary audience includes those interested in antique tool collecting, metalworking, carriage building,e arly sciences and early trades, and railroading.''

Nonfiction Books on early tools, trades & technology, and railroads. Query with SASE, or submit sample chapter(s), TOC, book overview, illustration descriptions, or submit complete ms. Send photocopies.

Recent Title(s) *Vintage Woodworking Machinery*, by Dana M. Batory (Vol. 2); *Tales From the Blue Ox*, by Dan Brett; *A Source Book for Rule Collectors*, by Philip Stanley.

Tips ''We sell to niche markets. We are happy to work with knowledgeable amateur authors in developing titles.''

AVANYU PUBLISHING, INC.

P.O. Box 27134, Albuquerque NM 87125. (505)341-1280. Fax: (505)341-1281. Website: www.avanyu-publishing.com. **Acquisitions:** J. Brent Ricks, president. Estab. 1984. Publishes hardcover and trade paperback originals and reprints. **Publishes 4 titles/year. 30% of books from first-time authors; 90% from unagented writers.**

Pays 8% maximum royalty on wholesale price. Offers advance. Publishes book 1 year after acceptance of ms. Does not accept simultaneous submissions. Responds in 2 months to queries. Book catalog for #10 SASE.

> ○ₐ Avanyu publishes highly-illustrated, history-oriented books on American Indians and adventures in the Southwest.

Nonfiction Biography, children's/juvenile, coffee table book, illustrated book, reference, scholarly. Subjects include Americana (Southwest), anthropology/archeology, art/architecture, ethnic, history, multicultural, photography, regional, sociology, spirituality. Query with SASE. Reviews artwork/photos as part of ms package.

Recent Title(s) *Kachinas Spirit Beings of the Hopi*; *Mesa Verde Ancient Architecture*; *Hopi Snake Ceremonies*.

Tips "Our audience consists of libraries, art collectors, and history students. We publish subjects dealing with modern and historic American Indian matters of all kinds."

⊘ AVOCET PRESS, INC.

19 Paul Court, Pearl River NY 10965-1539. (845)620-0986. Fax: (845)735-6807. Website: www.avocetpress.com. Estab. 1997. Publishes hardcover and trade paperback originals. Does not accept simultaneous submissions. Book catalog and ms guidelines online.

> • *Currently not accepting any mss.* Check online for updates.

Fiction Feminist, literary, mainstream/contemporary, multicultural, mystery, poetry. "Read our books! Plot and characters are very important." Query with SASE.

Poetry "Read our books! Must have already published in literary journals." Submit 4 sample poems.

Tips "Avocet Press is a small, independent publisher of a wide variety of quality literature. Our offerings range from important contemporary poetry to mysteries to beautifully written historical fiction. We are particularly interested in work that is different, exciting, and awakens us to angles of the world we haven't noticed before."

BALL PUBLISHING

335 N. River St., Batavia IL 60510-0009. (630)208-9080. Fax: (630)208-9350. E-mail: info@ballpublishing.com; rblanchette@ballpublishing.com. Website: www.ballpublishing.com. **Acquisitions:** Rick Blanchette, managing editor. Publishes hardcover and trade paperback originals. **Publishes 4-6 titles/year.** Accepts simultaneous submissions. Book catalog for 8½×11 SAE with 3 first-class stamps.

> ○ₐ "We publish for the book trade and the horticulture trade. Books on both home gardening/landscaping and commercial production are considered."

Nonfiction How-to, reference, technical, textbook. Subjects include agriculture/horticulture, gardening, floriculture. Query with SASE, or submit proposal package including outline, 2 sample chapters. Reviews artwork/photos as part of ms package. Send photocopies.

Recent Title(s) *Great Flowering Landscape Shrubs*, by Vincent A. Simeone; *Flower Seeds: Biology and Technology*, edited by M.B. McDonald and F.Y. Kwong; *Lighting Up Profits: Understanding Greenhouse Lighting*, by Paul Fisher and Erik Runkle.

Tips "We are expanding our book line to home gardeners, while still publishing for green industry professionals. Gardening books should be well thought out and unique in the market. Actively looking for photo books on specific genera and families of flowers and trees."

BANCROFT PRESS

P.O. Box 65360, Baltimore MD 21209-9945. (410)358-0658. Fax: (410)764-1967. E-mail: bruceb@bancroftpress. com. Website: www.bancroftpress.com. **Acquisitions:** Bruce Bortz, editor and publisher (health, investments, politics, history, humor, literary novels, mystery/thrillers, young adult). Publishes hardcover and trade paperback originals. **Publishes 6 titles/year. Pays 6-8% royalty. Pays various royalties on retail price. Offers $750 advance.** Publishes book up to 3 years after acceptance of ms. Accepts simultaneous submissions. Responds in 6-12 months. Ms guidelines online.

> ○ₐ Bancroft Press is a general trade publisher. "We are currently moving into soley publishing young adult fiction and nonfiction as well as adult fiction for young adults (single titles and series). Please, nothing that would be too graphic for anyone under 17 years old."

Nonfiction "Our No. 1 priority is publishing books appropriate for young adults, ages 10-18. All quality books on any subject that fit that category will be considered." Biography, how-to, humor, self-help. Subjects include business/economics, government/politics, health/medicine, money/finance, regional, sports, women's issues/studies, popular culture, essays. "We advise writers to visit the website." Submit proposal package including outline, 2 sample chapters, competition/market survey.

Fiction "Our No. 1 priority is publishing books appropriate for young adults, ages 10-18. All quality books on any subject that fit that category will be considered." Ethnic (general), feminist, gay/lesbian, historical, humor, literary, mainstream/contemporary, military/war, mystery (amateur sleuth, cozy, police procedural, private eye/hardboiled), regional, science fiction (hard science/technological, soft/sociological), young adult (historical, problem novels, series), thrillers. Query with SASE, or submit outline, 2 sample chapters, synopsis, by mail or e-mail, or submit complete ms.

Recent Title(s) *Like We Care*, by Tom Matthews; *Finding the Forger*, by Libby Sternberg; *Gradebusters*, by Stephen Schmidtz, PhD.

Ⓝ BARBICAN BOOKS

P.O. Box 763, Berkeley CA 94701. E-mail: grace@barbicanbooks.com. Website: www.barbicanbooks.com. **Acquisitions:** Grace Ebron, publisher (ethnic literature, feminist literature, social consciousness). Estab. 2004. Publishes hardcover and trade paperback originals. **Publishes 3-5 titles/year. Receives 100 queries and 50 mss/year. 100% from unagented writers. Pays 5-10% royalty on retail price.** Publishes book 10 months after acceptance of ms. Accepts simultaneous submissions. Responds in 1 month to queries; 2 months to proposals; 3 months to mss. Book catalog and ms guidelines online.

Nonfiction Biography, children's/juvenile, general nonfiction. Subjects include creative nonfiction, ethnic, gay/lesbian, humanities, multicultural, women's issues/studies. Query with SASE, or submit proposal package including outline, 1 sample chapter. Reviews artwork/photos as part of ms package. Send photocopies.

Fiction Ethnic, feminist, gay/lesbian, juvenile, literary, poetry, poetry in translation, short story collections, young adult. Query with SASE, or submit proposal package including 1 sample chapter, synopsis.

Poetry Query, or submit 10 sample poems.

Recent Title(s) *The Star Café and Other Stories*, by Brian A. Belton (short story collection); *The Remembered Art of Seagull Training, 2nd Ed.*, by Sean Jackson.

BEARMANOR MEDIA

P.O. Box 750, Boalsburg PA 16827. (814)466-7555. Fax: (814)690-1559. E-mail: ben@ritzbros.com. Website: www.bearmanormedia.com. Estab. 2001. Publishes trade paperback originals and reprints. **Publishes 6 titles/year.** Accepts simultaneous submissions. Book catalog for #10 SASE; ms guidelines by e-mail.

Nonfiction Autobiography, biography, general nonfiction. Subjects include old-time radio, voice actors, old movies. Query with SASE, or submit proposal package including outline, list of credits on the subject.

Recent Title(s) *Jingle of the Silver Spurs: The Hopalong Cassidy Radio Program*, by Bernard A. Drew; *Comic Strips and Comic Books of Radio's Golden Age*, by Ron Lackmann.

Tips "My readers love the past. Radio, old movies, old television. My own tastes include voice actors and scripts, especially of radio and television no longer available. I prefer books on subjects that haven't previously been covered as full books. Doesn't matter to me if you're a first-time author or have a track record. Just know your subject!"

BEARPAW PUBLISHING

9120 Thorton Rd., #343, Stockton CA 95209. (888)266-5704. Fax: (209)951-7284. E-mail: stories@bearpawpublishing.com. Website: www.bearpawpublishing.com. **Acquisitions:** Jiana Behr, owner (gay fiction). Estab. 2002. Publishes trade paperback originals. Does not accept simultaneous submissions. Responds in 2-4 months to mss. Book catalog and ms guidelines online.

Imprints Bearpaw will soon be expanding with She Bear (lesbian fiction) and Honey Bear (transgender fiction).

Fiction Adventure, confession, erotica, ethnic, fantasy, gay/lesbian, gothic, historical, horror, humor, mainstream/contemporary, military/war, multicultural, mystery, occult, romance, science fiction, short story collections, spiritual, sports, suspense, western. All submissions should include gay characters as the main characters. Sex in the book is requested but not required. Submit complete ms and SASE.

Recent Title(s) *Cost of Love*, by Alexis Rogers (contemporary).

Tips "Audience is gay men. I prefer submissions via e-mail in text format. I will accept attachments and large loads."

BEEMAN JORGENSEN, INC.

7510 Allisonville Rd., Indianapolis IN 46250. (317)841-7677. Fax: (317)849-2001. **Acquisitions:** Brett Johnson, president (automotive/auto racing). Publishes hardcover and trade paperback originals and hardcover reprints. **Publishes 4 titles/year. Receives 10 queries/year. 50% of books from first-time authors; 100% from unagented writers. Pays 15-30% royalty on wholesale price. Offers up to $1,000 advance.** Publishes book 8 months after acceptance of ms. Responds in 1 month to queries; 2 months to proposals. Book catalog free.

Nonfiction Publishes books on automobiles and auto racing. Coffee table book, illustrated book, reference. Subjects include sports (auto racing). Query with SASE, or submit proposal package including outline, 1 sample chapter.

Recent Title(s) *Drag Racing Basics*, by Cindy Crawford (illustrated book); *Road America*, by Tom Schultz (illustrated book); *Porshe 356, Guide to D-I-Y Restoration*, by Jim Kellogg (illustrated book).

Tips Audience is automotive enthusiasts, specific marque owners/enthusiasts, auto racing fans, and participants.

BICK PUBLISHING HOUSE

307 Neck Rd., Madison CT 06443. (203)245-0073. Fax: (203)245-5990. E-mail: bickpubhse@aol.com. Website: www.bickpubhouse.com. **Acquisitions:** Dale Carlson, president (psychology); Hannah Carlson (special needs, disabilities); Irene Ruth (wildlife). Estab. 1994. Publishes trade paperback originals. **Publishes 4 titles/year. Receives 100 queries and 100 mss/year. 55% of books from first-time authors; 55% from unagented writers. Pays 10% royalty on net receipts. Offers $500-1,000 advance.** Publishes book 1 year after acceptance of ms. Responds in 1 month to queries; 2 months to proposals; 3 months to mss. Book catalog free; ms guidelines for #10 SASE.

○ᆓ Bick Publishing House publishes step-by-step, easy-to-read professional information for the general adult public about physical, psychological, and emotional disabilities or special needs. Currently emphasizing science, psychology for teens.

Nonfiction Subjects include health/medicine (disability/special needs), psychology, young adult or teen science, psychology, wildlife rehabilitation. Query with SASE, or submit proposal package including outline, 3 sample chapters, résumé.

Recent Title(s) *The Courage to Lead Support Groups: Mental Illnesses and Addictions*, by Hannah Carlson; *In and Out of Your Mind Teen Science*, by Dale Carlson; *Who Said What, Philosophy Quotes for Teens: What Are You Doing With Your Life?*, by J. Krishnamurti.

BKMK PRESS

University of Missouri-Kansas City, 5101 Rockhill Rd., Kansas City MO 64110-2499. (816)235-2558. Fax: (816)235-2611. E-mail: bkmk@umkc.edu. Website: www.umkc.edu/bkmk. **Acquisitions:** Ben Furnish, managing editor. Estab. 1971. Publishes trade paperback originals. Accepts simultaneous submissions. Responds in 4-6 months to queries. Ms guidelines online.

○ᆓ BkMk Press publishes fine literature. Reading period January-June.

Nonfiction Creative nonfiction essays. Query with SASE.

Fiction Literary, short story collections. Query with SASE.

Poetry Submit 10 sample poems.

Recent Title(s) *I'll Never Leave You*, by H.E. Francis; *Circe, After Hours*, by Marilyn Kallet; *A Bed of Nails*, by Ron Tanner.

Tips "We skew toward readers of literature, particularly contemporary writing. Because of our limited number of titles published per year, we discourage apprentice writers or 'scattershot' submissions."

BLACK DOME PRESS CORP.

1011 Route 296, Hensonville NY 12439. (518)734-6357. Fax: (518)734-5802. E-mail: blackdome@aol.com. Website: www.blackdomepress.com. Estab. 1990. Publishes cloth and trade paperback originals and reprints. Accepts simultaneous submissions. Book catalog online.

Nonfiction Subjects include history, nature/environment, photography, regional (New York state), Native Americans, grand hotels, geneology, colonial life, quilting, architecture, railroads. New York state regional material only. Submit proposal package including outline, 1 sample chapter, author bio.

Recent Title(s) *Katerskill Clove: Where Nature Met Art*, by Raymond Beecher; *The Catskill Park: Inside the Blue Line*, by Norman J. Van Valkenburgh and Christopher W. Olney.

Tips "Our audience is comprised of New York state residents, tourists, and visitors."

BLACK HERON PRESS

P.O. Box 95676, Seattle WA 98145. Website: www.blackheronpress.com. **Acquisitions:** Jerry Gold, publisher. Estab. 1984. Publishes hardcover and trade paperback originals. **Publishes 4-6 titles/year.** Accepts simultaneous submissions.

○ᆓ "Black Heron Press publishes primarily literary fiction."

Fiction Literary. "We don't want to see fiction written for the mass market. If it sells to the mass market, fine, but we don't see ourselves as a commercial press." Submit first 30-40 pages of the book, SASE. No e-mail queries.

Recent Title(s) *How I Learned That I Could Push the Button*, by Jerome Gold; *Mehkti*, by Amy Bassan; *The Crazy Dervish & the Pomegranite*, by Farnoosh Moshiri.

Tips "Readers should look at some of our books before submitting—they are easily available. Most submissions we see are done competently but have been sent to the wrong place. We do not publish self-help books or romances."

BLUE POPPY PRESS

Imprint of Blue Poppy Enterprises, Inc., 5441 Western Ave., #2, Boulder CO 80301-2733. (303)447-8372. Fax: (303)245-8362. E-mail: info@bluepoppy.com. Website: www.bluepoppy.com. **Acquisitions:** Bob Flaws, editor-in-chief. Estab. 1981. Publishes hardcover and trade paperback originals. **Publishes 3-4 titles/year. Receives 50-100 queries and 20 mss/year. 30-40% of books from first-time authors; 100% from unagented writers. Pays 8-12% royalty.** Publishes book 1 year after acceptance of ms. Does not accept simultaneous submissions. Responds in 1 month to queries. Book catalog free; ms guidelines online.

○━ Blue Poppy Press is dedicated to expanding and improving the English language literature on acupuncture and Asian medicine for both professional practitioners and lay readers.

Nonfiction Self-help, technical, textbook (related to acupuncture and Oriental medicine). Subjects include ethnic, health/medicine. "We only publish books on acupuncture and Oriental medicine by authors who can read Chinese and have a minimum of 5 years clinical experience. We also require all our authors to use Wiseman's *Glossary of Chinese Medical Terminology* as their standard for technical terms." Query with SASE, or submit outline, 1 sample chapter.

Recent Title(s) *Chinese Medical Psychiatry*, by Bob Flaws and James Lake, MD.

Tips Audience is "practicing acupuncturists, interested in alternatives in healthcare, preventive medicine, Chinese philosophy, and medicine."

BLUE/GRAY BOOKS

Imprint of Creativity, Inc., 65 Macedonia Rd., Alexander NC 28701. (828)252-9515. Fax: (828)255-8719. Website: abooks.com. **Acquisitions:** Pat Roberts, acquisitions editor. Publishes trade paperback originals and reprints. **Publishes 4 titles/year. Pays negotiable royalty on wholesale price. Offers advance.** Publishes book 18 months after acceptance of ms.

○━ Blue/Gray Books specializes in Civil War history.

Nonfiction Biography. Subjects include military/war (Civil War). Query with SASE, or submit proposal package including 3 sample chapters, original book if wanting reprint. Reviews artwork/photos as part of ms package. Send photocopies.

Recent Title(s) *Deo Vindice: Heroes in Gray Forever*, by Lee Jacobs.

Ⓝ BLUEWATERPRESS

2220 CR 210 W., Suite 108, #132, Jacksonville FL 32259-4060. E-mail: jfclark@bluewaterpress.com. Submissions E-mail: editors@bluewaterpress.com. Website: www.bluewaterpress.com. Estab. 2002. Publishes trade paperback and mass market paperback originals. **Publishes 5-10 titles/year. 75-90% of books from first-time authors; 100% from unagented writers. Pays 10-20% royalty.** Publishes book 3-6 months after acceptance of ms. Accepts simultaneous submissions. Responds in 1 month to queries; 2 months to proposals; 4 months to mss. Book catalog and ms guidelines online.

Nonfiction Autobiography, biography, children's/juvenile, coffee table book, cookbook, general nonfiction, gift book, how-to, humor, illustrated book, scholarly, self-help, technical, textbook. Subjects include Americana, animals, anthropology/archeology, art/architecture, business/economics, child guidance/parenting, community, computers/electronic, contemporary culture, cooking/foods/nutrition, creative nonfiction, education, history, hobbies, memoirs, military/war, money/finance, New Age, philosophy, photography, recreation, regional, religion, science, social sciences, sociology, spirituality, travel, women's issues/studies, world affairs, automotive, astrology/psychic, aviation, communications, counseling/career guidance, crafts, house/home, real estate, transportation, young adult. Query with SASE, or submit proposal package including 3 sample chapters, synopsis, or submit complete ms. Reviews artwork/photos as part of ms package. Send photocopies.

Fiction Adventure, historical, humor, juvenile, literary, mainstream/contemporary, military/war, mystery, picture books, poetry, regional, religious, romance, science fiction, short story collections, spiritual, suspense, western, young adult. Query with SASE, or submit proposal package including synopsis, 3 sample chapters, or submit complete ms.

Poetry Query.

Recent Title(s) *Yo, Boatman! A Boatman Shares the Secrets of the Journey* (fiction).

BOOKHOME PUBLISHING

P.O. Box 5900, Navarre FL 32566. (850)936-4184. Fax: (850)939-4953. E-mail: info@bookhome.com. Website: www.bookhome.com. **Acquisitions:** Shirley Siluk Gregory, publisher; Scott Gregory, managing editor. Estab. 1996. Publishes hardcover and trade paperback originals. Accepts simultaneous submissions. Book catalog for #10 SAE with 2 first-class stamps; ms guidelines online.

○━ "Our goal is to help people live better lives by crafting lifestyles and businesses that are ideal for them."

Nonfiction How-to, self-help. Subjects include business/economics, creative nonfiction, lifestyles, career. Query with SASE, or submit proposal package including 2 sample chapters. Marketing plan.

Recent Title(s) *Get Published Get Paid*, by Janet Groene.

Tips "Ask for our guidelines (include SASE) or review our guidelines at our website. Do your homework, then make your proposal irresistible!Make sure a publicity plan is part of your proposal. We work hard to tell the world about our wonderful books, and we expect our authors to do the same.''

BRIGHT MOUNTAIN BOOKS, INC.

206 Riva Ridge Dr., Fairview NC 28730. (828)628-1768. Fax: (828)628-1755. E-mail: booksbmb@charter.net. **Acquisitions:** Cynthia F. Bright, editor. Publishes hardcover originals and trade paperback originals and reprints. **Publishes 6 titles/year. Pays 5-10% royalty on retail price.** Responds in 1 month to queries; 3 months to mss.

Imprints Historical Images.

Nonfiction Biography. Subjects include history, regional. ''Our current emphasis is on regional titles set in the Southern Appalachians and Carolinas, which can include nonfiction by local writers.'' Query with SASE.

Recent Title(s) *My Journey to Appalachia: A Year at the Folk School*, by Eleanor L. Wilson.

BROOKS BOOKS

3720 N. Woodridge Dr., Decatur IL 62526. (217)877-2966. E-mail: brooksbooks@sbcglobal.net. Website: www. brooksbookshaiku.com. **Acquisitions:** Randy Brooks, editor (haiku poetry, tanka poetry). Publishes trade paperback originals. **Publishes 3-5 titles/year. Receives 100 queries and 25 mss/year. 10% of books from first-time authors; 100% from unagented writers. Pays 10-15% royalty on retail price or makes outright purchase of $100-500.** Publishes book 16 months after acceptance of ms. Responds in 1 month to queries; 3 months to proposals; 6 months to mss. Book catalog for #10 SASE or online at website; ms guidelines for #10 SASE.

- ○→ Brooks Books, formerly High/Coo Press, publishes English-language haiku books, chapbooks, magazines, and bibliographies.

Poetry Submit 10 sample poems.

Recent Title(s) *Almost Unseen: Selected Haiku of George Swede*, by George Swede; *To Hear the Rain: Selected Haiku*, by Peggy Lyles.

Tips ''Our readers enjoy contemporary haiku based on the literary tradition of Japanese aesthetics (not 5-7-5 Internet jokes).''

N MARTIN BROWN PUBLISHERS, LLC

1138 S. Webster St., Kokomo IN 46902. (765)459-8258. E-mail: submissions@mbpubs.com. Website: www.mbp ubs.com. Estab. 2004. Publishes trade paperback originals and mass market paperback originals. **Publishes 4-6 titles/year. Receives 400 queries and 24 mss/year. 50% of books from first-time authors; 90% from unagented writers. Pays 10-15% royalty on wholesale price.** Publishes book 1 year after acceptance of ms. Accepts simultaneous submissions. Responds in 1 month. Book catalog by e-mail; ms guidelines online.

Fiction Juvenile, literary, mainstream/contemporary, mystery, picture books, romance, science fiction, young adult. ''We are still growing, so writers should always check our website before submitting to get updated descriptions of what we seek.'' Query via e-mail only according to guidelines on the website.

Recent Title(s) *Digging Up Otis*, by T. Dawn Richard (cozy mystery); *Poetic License*, by Joyce Yarrow (detective).

Tips ''People of all ages who enjoy a great reading experience are in our target audience. A book's appeal begins at its cover. A book is a product, nothing more and nothing less. Word-of-mouth sells books; if yours is great, word will get around. A great book begins at word one, page. Great books live in the minds of readers forever.''

CAROLINA WREN PRESS

120 Morris St., Durham NC 27701. (919)560-2738. E-mail: carolina@carolinawrenpress.org. Website: www.car olinawrenpress.org. Estab. 1976. ''We publish poetry, fiction, nonfiction, biography, autobiography, literary nonfiction work by, and/or about people of color, women, gay/lesbian issues, health and mental health topics in children's literature.'' Publishes book 1 year after acceptance of ms. Responds in 3 months to queries; 6 months to mss. Ms guidelines online.

- ● Reads unsolicited mss of fiction and nonfiction from September 1 to December 1 and poetry and children's lit from February 1 to June 1, but prefers writers to wait and enter their contests—poetry contest in Fall 2006 and 2008; fiction and nonfiction contest in Fall 2005 and 2007.

Fiction Ethnic, experimental (poetry), feminist, gay/lesbian, literary, short story collections. ''We are especially interested in children's literature on the subjects of health, illness, mental illness, healing, etc.'' Query by mail only with SASE and short (10-page) sample. Do not send a query letter without an actual (10-page) writing sample.

Tips ''Manuscripts are read year-round, but reply time is long unless submitting for a contest.''

N CCC PUBLICATIONS, LLC

9725 Lurline Ave., Chatsworth CA 91311. (818)718-0507. **Acquisitions:** Mark Chutick, publisher. Estab. 1983. Publishes trade paperback originals. **Publishes 4 titles/year. Receives 1,000 mss/year. 30% of books from** first-time authors; 50% from unagented writers. Pays 8-12% royalty on wholesale price. Offers variable advance. Publishes book 8 months after acceptance of ms. Accepts simultaneous submissions. Responds in 3 months to queries. Book catalog for 10×13 SAE with 2 first-class stamps.

> O— CCC publishes humor that is "today" and will appeal to a wide demographic. Currently emphasizing "short, punchy pieces with *lots* of cartoon illustrations."

Nonfiction How-to, humor. "We are looking for *original, clever* and *current* humor that is not too limited in audience appeal or that will have a limited shelf life. All of our titles are as marketable five years from now as they are today. No rip-offs of previously published books, or too special interest manuscripts." Query with SASE, or submit complete ms. Reviews artwork/photos as part of ms package.

Recent Title(s) *Humorous Mini Dictionary of Sex*, by Joel Rotham.

Tips "Humor—we specialize in the subject and have a good reputation with retailers and wholesalers for publishing super-impulse titles. SASE is a must!"

N CELLAR DOOR PUBLISHING, LLC

3439 NE Sandy Blvd., Suite 309, Portland OR 97232-1959. E-mail: info@cellardoorpublishing.com. Website: www.cellardoorpublishing.com. Publisher: Jade Dodge. Estab. 2004. Publishes hardcover originals, trade paperback originals and electronic originals. **Publishes 3-4 titles/year. Pays 30-50% royalty on wholesale price.** Accepts simultaneous submissions. Ms guidelines by e-mail.

> O— Interested in illustrated literature and graphic novels.

Nonfiction Children's/juvenile, coffee table book, gift book, illustrated book, multimedia, reference. "We specialize in the publication of illustrated literature and graphic novels. While it is not required that you have an artist before submitting, it is encouraged. We do accept a limited number of submissions for books without illustrations. This is generally reserved for books that are either unique in content or controversial in nature. Nonfiction submissions will also be considered if they fall into one of the previously mentioned categories." Query with SASE, or submit proposal package including outline, 3 sample chapters, artwork, if available, or submit complete ms. Reviews artwork/photos as part of ms package. Send photocopies.

Fiction Adventure, comic books, erotica, experimental, fantasy, gothic, historical, horror, humor, juvenile, literary, mainstream/contemporary, multimedia, mystery, occult, picture books, romance, science fiction, suspense, western, young adult, translation. Query with SASE, or submit proposal package including 3 sample chapters, synopsis, artwork, if available, or submit complete ms.

CHAPULTEPEC PRESS

4222 Chambers, Cincinnati OH 45223. (513)681-1976. E-mail: chapultepecpress@hotmail.com. Website: www.tokyoroserecords.com. **Acquisitions:** David Garza. Estab. 2001. Publishes trade paperback originals. **Publishes 5 titles/year. Receives 50 queries and 10 mss/year. 75% of books from first-time authors; 100% from unagented writers. Pays 10-50% royalty on wholesale price.** Publishes book 6 months after acceptance of ms. Accepts simultaneous submissions. Responds in 2 months. Book catalog online; ms guidelines by e-mail.

Nonfiction Autobiography, biography, booklets, general nonfiction, humor, illustrated book, multimedia. Subjects include alternative lifestyles, art/architecture, contemporary culture, creative nonfiction, ethnic, government/politics, history, humanities, language/literature, memoirs, multicultural, music/dance, nature/environment, philosophy, photography, recreation, regional, translation, world affairs. Submit proposal package including outline, 2-3 sample chapters, artwork samples. Reviews artwork/photos as part of ms package. Send photocopies.

Fiction Comic books, erotica, ethnic, experimental, humor, literary, multicultural, multimedia, occult, picture books, plays, poetry, poetry in translation, regional, short story collections. Submit proposal package including 2-3 sample chapters, synopsis, artwork samples.

Poetry Submit 5-15 sample poems.

Recent Title(s) *The Compact Duchamp*, by Guy R. Beining; *A Beautiful Woman*, by Roesing Ape.

Tips Chapultepec Press specializes in shorter-length publications (100 pages or less).

CHITRA PUBLICATIONS

2 Public Ave., Montrose PA 18801. (570)278-1984. E-mail: chitraed@epix.net. Website: www.quilttownusa.com. **Acquisitions:** Acquisitions Editors. Publishes trade paperback originals. Does not accept simultaneous submissions. Book catalog and ms guidelines for #10 SASE; ms guidelines online.

> O— "We publish quality quilting magazines and pattern books that recognize, promote, and inspire self expression."

Nonfiction How-to. Subjects include quilting. Query with SASE, or submit proposal package including sample chapters, TOC, photos/illustrations, intended audience. Reviews artwork/photos as part of ms package. Send photocopies or transparencies.

CHURCH GROWTH INSTITUTE

P.O. Box 7, Elkton MD 21922-0007. (434)525-0022. Fax: (434)525-0608. E-mail: cgimail@churchgrowth.org. Website: www.churchgrowth.org. **Acquisitions:** Cindy Spear, administrator/resource development director. Estab. 1978. Publishes trade paperback originals, 3-ring-bound manuals, mixed media resource packets. **Publishes 4 titles/year. Pays 6% royalty on retail price.** Publishes book 1 year after acceptance of ms. Accepts simultaneous submissions. Responds in 3 months to queries. Book catalog for 9×12 SAE with 4 first-class stamps; ms guidelines given after query and outline is received.

    O→ "Our mission is to provide practical resources to help pastors, churches, and individuals reach their potential for Christ; to promote spiritual and numerical growth in churches, thereby leading Christians to maturity and lost people to Christ; and to equip pastors so they can equip their church members to do the work of the ministry."

Nonfiction "Material should originate from a conservative Christian view and cover topics that will help churches grow, through leadership training, self-evaluation, and new or unique ministries, or enhancing existing ministries. Self-discovery inventories regarding spiritual growth, relationship improvement, etc., are hot items." How-to. Subjects include education, religion (church-growth related), ministry, how-to manuals, spiritual growth, relationship-building, evangelism. "Accepted manuscripts will be adapted to our resource packet, manual, or inventory format. All material must be practical and easy for the average Christian to understand." Query, or submit outline and brief explanation of what the packet will accomplish in the local church and whether it is leadership or lay oriented. Queries accepted by mail or e-mail. No phone queries. Reviews artwork/photos as part of ms package. Send photos or images on CD (in TIFF, EPS, or PDF format).

Recent Title(s) *Ministry Descriptions*; *Ask Me to Pray for You*; *Evaluating Your Friendship Skills*.

Tips "We are not publishing many textbooks. Concentrate on how-to manuals and ministry evaluation and diagnostic tools and spiritual or relationship-oriented 'inventories' for individual Christians."

CLARITY PRESS, INC.

3277 Roswell Rd. NE, #469, Atlanta GA 30305. (877)613-1495. Fax: (404)231-3899 and (877)613-7868. E-mail: claritypress@usa.net. Website: www.claritypress.com. **Acquisitions:** Diana G. Collier, editorial director (contemporary social justice issues). Estab. 1984. Publishes hardcover and trade paperback originals. **Publishes 4 titles/year.** Accepts simultaneous submissions. Submit by e-mail, no SASE. Responds in 1 month to queries.

Nonfiction Publishes books on contemporary issues in US, Middle East and Africa. Subjects include ethnic, world affairs, human rights/socio-economic and minority issues. No fiction. Query with synopsis, TOC, résumé, publishing history.

Recent Title(s) *State Terrorism and the United States*, by Frederick H. Gareau; *Destroying World Order*, by Francis A. Boyle.

Tips "Check our titles on website."

CLEAR VIEW PRESS

P.O. Box 11574, Marina del Rey CA 90295. E-mail: publisher@clearviewpress.com. Website: www.clearviewpress.com. Estab. 2003. Publishes hardcover, trade paperback, and electronic originals.

Nonfiction Audiocassettes, how-to, self-help, technical. Subjects include computers/electronic, education, hobbies, memoirs, New Age, spirituality, literary criticism. Query with SASE, or submit proposal package including outline, 1 sample chapter.

Fiction Adventure, comic books, literary, mainstream/contemporary, spiritual.

Recent Title(s) *Advanced Nanotechnology*, by Steiner (technology/science); *The River Beneath the River*, by Susan Tabin (fiction).

COUNTRYSPORT PRESS

Down East Enterprises, P.O. Box 679, Camden ME 04843. (207)594-9544. Fax: (207)594-0147. E-mail: msteere@countrysportpress.com. Website: www.countrysportpress.com. **Acquisitions:** Michael Steere, managing editor. Estab. 1988. Publishes hardcover originals and reprints. **Publishes 4 titles/year. 20% of books from first-time authors; 90% from unagented writers. Pays royalty on wholesale or retail price. Offers variable advance.** Publishes book 1 year after acceptance of ms. Accepts simultaneous submissions. Responds in 1 month to queries; 3 months to proposals and mss. Book catalog free via website or with SASE.

    ● E-mail queries only. Submissions of mss or proposals via e-mail will not be considered.

    O→ "Our audience is upscale sportsmen with interests in wingshooting, fly fishing, fine guns and other outdoor activities."

Nonfiction Coffee table book, how-to, illustrated book. Subjects include sports, wingshooting, fly fishing, fine guns, other outdoor-related subjects. "We are looking for high-quality writing that is often reflective, anecdotal, and that offers a complete picture of an outdoor experience." Query with SASE, or submit outline, 3 sample chapters.

Recent Title(s) *Arctic Aurora*, by John Holt; *A Fisherman's Guide to Maine*, by Kevin Tracewski; *Grouse and Lesser Gods*, by Ted Lundrigan.

⊘ CROSSQUARTER PUBLISHING GROUP

P.O. Box 8756, Santa Fe NM 87504. (505)438-9846. E-mail: info@crossquarter.com. Website: www.crossquarter .com. **Acquisitions:** Anthony Ravenscroft. Publishes case and trade paperback originals and reprints. **Publishes 5-10 titles/year. Receives 250 queries/year. 90% of books from first-time authors. Pays 8-10% royalty on wholesale or retail price.** Publishes book 1 year after acceptance of ms. Accepts simultaneous submissions. Responds in 3 months to queries. Book catalog for $1.75; ms guidelines online.

- Query letters are required. *No unsolicited mss.*
- ⚷ "We emphasize personal sovereignty, self responsibility and growth with pagan or pagan-friendly emphasis for young adults and adults."

Nonfiction Biography, how-to, self-help. Subjects include health/medicine, nature/environment, New Age, philosophy, psychology, religion (pagan only), spirituality, autobiography. Query with SASE. Reviews artwork/ photos as part of ms package. Send photocopies.

Fiction Science fiction, visionary fiction. Query with SASE.

Recent Title(s) *Dead as I'll Ever Be: Psychic Adventures That Changed My Life*, by Pamela Evans; *Beyond One's Own*, by Gabriel Constans; *The Shamrock and The Feather*, by Dori Dalton.

Tips "Audience is earth-conscious people looking to grow into balance of body, mind, heart and spirit."

CYCLE PUBLISHING

Van der Plas Publications, 1282 Seventh Ave., San Francisco CA 94122. (415)665-8214. Fax: (415)753-8572. E-mail: pubrel@vanderplas.net. Website: www.cyclepublishing.com. **Acquisitions:** Rob van der Plas, publisher/ editor. Estab. 1997. Publishes hardcover and trade paperback originals. **Publishes 4 titles/year.** Accepts simultaneous submissions. Book catalog and ms guidelines for #10 SASE.

Nonfiction How-to, technical. Subjects include recreation, sports, manufactured homes. Submit complete ms. Reviews artwork/photos as part of ms package.

Recent Title(s) *Mountain Bike Maintenance*; *Buying a Manufactured Home*.

Tips "Writers have a good chance selling us books with better and more illustrations and a systematic treatment of the subject. First check what is on the market and ask yourself whether you are writing something that is not yet available and wanted."

DANA PRESS

900 15th St. NW, Washington DC 20005. (202)408-8800. Fax: (202)408-5599. Website: www.dana.org/books/ press. **Acquisitions:** Jane Nevins, editor-in-chief; Dan Gordon, editor. Publishes hardcover and trade paperback originals. **Publishes 4 titles/year. 50% of books from first-time authors; 90% from unagented writers. Pays 7-10% royalty on list price. Offers $10,000-35,000 advance.** Publishes book 1 year after acceptance of ms. Accepts simultaneous submissions. Responds in 2 weeks to queries; 1 month to proposals; 2 months to mss. Book catalog and ms guidelines online.

Nonfiction Subjects include health/medicine, memoirs, psychology, science. "We are interested in the brain, arts and cognition, and immunology." Reviews artwork/photos as part of ms package. Send photocopies.

Recent Title(s) *A Well-Tempered Mind: Using Music to Help Children Listen and Learn*, by Peter Perret and Janet Fox; *Neuroscience and the Law: Brain, Mind and the Scales of Justice*, edited by Brent Garland; *Back From the Brink: How Crises Spur Doctors to New Discoveries About the Brain*, by Edward J. Sylvester.

Tips "The science must be solid, the perspective interesting. Coherent proposals are key. What is new or different about the book? Who is the reader?"

JOHN DANIEL AND CO.

Daniel & Daniel, Publishers, Inc., P.O. Box 2790, McKinleyville CA 95519. (707)839-3495. Fax: (707)839-3242. E-mail: dandd@danielpublishing.com. Website: www.danielpublishing.com. **Acquisitions:** John Daniel, publisher. Estab. 1980. Publishes hardcover originals and trade paperback originals. Publishes poetry, fiction and nonfiction. **Publishes 4 or fewer titles/year. Pays 10% royalty on wholesale price. Offers $0-500 advance.** Publishes book 1 year after acceptance of ms. Accepts simultaneous submissions. Responds in 1 month to queries and proposals; 2 months to mss. Book catalog and ms guidelines online.

Nonfiction Biography, essay. Subjects include creative nonfiction, memoirs. "We seldom publish books over 70,000 words. Other than that, we're looking for books that are important and well-written." Query with SASE, or submit proposal package including outline, 50 pages.

Fiction Literary, short story collections. Publishes poetry, fiction and nonfiction; specializes in belles lettres, literary memoir. Query with SASE, or submit proposal package including synopsis, 50 pages.

Poetry "We publish very little poetry, I'm sorry to say." Query, or submit complete ms.

Recent Title(s) *Out of the Kitchen: Adventures of a Food Writer*, by Jeannette Ferrary (memoir); *Yellow Swing*, by Rosalind Brackenbury (poetry).

Tips "Audience includes literate, intelligent general readers. We are very small and very cautious, and we publish fewer books each year, so any submission to us is a long shot. But we welcome your submissions, by mail only, please. We don't want submissions by phone, fax, disk, or e-mail."

DANTE UNIVERSITY OF AMERICA PRESS, INC.

P.O. Box 812158, Wellesley MA 02482. Fax: (781)790-1056. E-mail: danteu@danteuniversity.org. Website: www.danteuniversity.org/dpress.html. **Acquisitions:** Adolph Caso, president. Estab. 1975. Publishes hardcover and trade paperback originals and reprints. **Publishes 5 titles/year. 50% of books from first-time authors; 50% from unagented writers. Pays royalty. Offers negotiable advance.** Publishes book 10 months after acceptance of ms. Responds in 2 months to queries.

⚬━ "The Dante University Press exists to bring quality, educational books pertaining to our Italian heritage as well as the historical and political studies of America. Profits from the sale of these publications benefit the Foundation, bringing Dante University closer to a reality."

Nonfiction Biography, reference, scholarly, reprints. Subjects include history (Italian-American), humanities, translation (from Italian and Latin), general scholarly nonfiction, Renaissance thought and letter, Italian language and linguistics, Italian-American culture, bilingual education. Query with SASE. Reviews artwork/photos as part of ms package.

Fiction Translations from Italian and Latin. Query with SASE.

Poetry "There is a chance that we would use Renaissance poetry translations."

Recent Title(s) *The Prince*, by Machiavelli (social sciences); *The Kaso Dictionary—English-Italian* (reference).

MAY DAVENPORT, PUBLISHERS

26313 Purissima Rd., Los Altos Hills CA 94022. (650)947-1275. Fax: (650)947-1373. E-mail: mdbooks@earthlink .net. Website: www.maydavenportpublishers.com. **Acquisitions:** May Davenport, editor/publisher. Estab. 1976. Publishes hardcover and paperback originals. **Publishes 4 titles/year. 95% of books from first-time authors; 100% from unagented writers. Pays 15% royalty on retail price. Offers no advance.** Publishes book 1 year after acceptance of ms. Responds in 1 month to queries. Book catalog and ms guidelines for #10 SASE.

Imprints md Books (nonfiction and fiction).

⚬━ May Davenport publishes "literature for teenagers (before they graduate from high schools) as supplementary literary material in English courses nationwide." Looking particularly for authors able to write for the "teen Internet" generation who don't like to read in-depth. Currently emphasizing more upper-level subjects for teens.

Nonfiction Subjects include Americana, language/literature, humorous memoirs for chldren/young adults. "For children ages 6-8: stories to read with pictures to color in 500 words. For preteens and young adults: Exhibit your writing skills and entertain them with your literary tools." Query with SASE.

Fiction Humor, literary. "We want to focus on novels junior and senior high school teachers can share with their reluctant readers in their classrooms." Query with SASE.

Recent Title(s) *Senioritis*, by Tate Thompson; *Significant Footsteps*, by Ashleigh E. Grange (fiction); *A Warm Familiar Feeling*, by Colby King Farley (fiction).

Tips "If you have to write only about the ills of today's society of incest, murders, homelessness, divorce, 1-parent families, just write your fictional novel humorously. If you can't write that way, create youthful characters so teachers, as well as 15-18-year-old high school readers, will laugh at your descriptive passages and contemporary dialogue. Avoid 1-sentence paragraphs. The audience we want to reach is past Nancy Drew and Hardy Boy readers."

DAWN PUBLICATIONS

12402 Bitney Springs Rd., Nevada City CA 95959. (530)274-7775. Fax: (530)274-7778. Website: www.dawnpub. com. **Acquisitions:** Glenn Hovemann, editor. Estab. 1979. Publishes hardcover and trade paperback originals. **Publishes 6 titles/year. Receives 550 queries and 2,500 mss/year. 15% of books from first-time authors; 90% from unagented writers. Pays royalty on net receipts. Offers advance.** Publishes book 1 to 2 years after acceptance of ms. Accepts simultaneous submissions. Responds in 2 months to queries. Book catalog and ms guidelines online.

⚬━ Dawn Publications is dedicated to inspiring in children a sense of appreciation for all life on earth. Dawn looks for nature awareness and appreciation titles that promote a relationship with the natural world and specific habitats, usually through inspiring treatment and nonfiction.

Nonfiction Children's/juvenile. Subjects include animals, nature/environment. Query with SASE.

Recent Title(s) *Salmon Stream*, by Carol Reed-Jones; *In One Tidepool*, by Anthony Fredericks; *The Okomi Series*, with Jane Goodall.

Tips Publishes mostly nonfiction with lightness and inspiration.

DBS PRODUCTIONS

P.O. Box 1894, Charlottesville VA 22903. (800)745-1581. Fax: (434)293-5502. E-mail: robert@dbs-sar.com. Website: www.dbs-sar.com. **Acquisitions:** Bob Adams, publisher. Estab. 1989. Publishes hardcover and trade paperback originals. **Publishes 6 titles/year. Receives 5 queries/year. 5% of books from first-time authors; 100% from unagented writers. Pays 5-20% royalty on retail price.** Publishes book 1 year after acceptance of ms. Does not accept simultaneous submissions. Responds in 2 months to queries. Book catalog on request or on website; ms guidelines for #10 SASE.

    ○→ dbS Productions produces search and rescue and outdoor first-aid related materials and courses. It offers a selection of publications, videotapes, management kits and tools, and instructional modules.

Nonfiction Technical, textbook. Subjects include health/medicine. Submit proposal package including outline, 2 sample chapters. Reviews artwork/photos as part of ms package. Send photocopies.

Recent Title(s) *Field Operations Guide for Search and Rescue, 2nd Ed.*, by R. Koester.

◎ THE DENALI PRESS

P.O. Box 021535, Juneau AK 99802-1535. (907)586-6014. Fax: (907)463-6780. E-mail: denalipress@alaska.com. Website: www.denalipress.com. **Acquisitions:** Alan Schorr, editorial director; Sally Silvas-Ottumwa, editorial associate. Estab. 1986. Publishes trade paperback originals. **Publishes 5 titles/year. 50% of books from first-time authors; 80% from unagented writers. Pays 10% royalty on wholesale price, or makes outright purchase. Offers advance.** Publishes book 1 year after acceptance of ms. Accepts simultaneous submissions. Responds in 1 month to queries.

    ○→ The Denali Press looks for reference works suitable for the educational, professional, and library market. "Though we publish books on a variety of topics, our focus is most broadly centered on multiculturalism, public policy, Alaskana, and general reference works."

Nonfiction Reference. Subjects include Americana, anthropology/archeology, ethnic, government/politics, history, multicultural, recreation, regional. "We need reference books—ethnic, refugee, and minority concerns." Query with SASE, or submit outline, sample chapters. *All unsolicited mss returned unopened.*

Recent Title(s) *Winning Political Campaigns: A Comprehensive Guide to Electoral Success*, by William S. Bike.

DIAMOND EYES PUBLISHING

P.O. Box 681, Ocoee FL 34761. (407)654-6652. E-mail: info@depublishing.com. Submissions E-mail: wordsarelife@yahoo.com. Website: www.depublishing.com. **Acquisitions:** Jessica Adriel, senior editor (fiction). Estab. 1999. Publishes trade paperback originals. **Publishes 6 titles/year. Receives 1,000 queries and 50 mss/year. 80% of books from first-time authors; 100% from unagented writers. Pays 8-10% royalty on net receipts.** Publishes book 1 year after acceptance of ms. Accepts simultaneous submissions. Responds in 2 months to queries; 4 months to mss. Book catalog and ms guidelines online.

Nonfiction General nonfiction, self-help. Subjects include money/finance, religion, true crime, motivational books, workbooks, church dramas, plays. "Diamond Eyes is looking for 'How-to Manuals' that can be marketed to churches. We are especially interested in leadership ideas for teens, and ideas for how to grow/develop a drama department. We are looking for short plays to comprise for churches or youth organizations. Biblical finance or controversial biblical topics welcome. Authors should note that we have a charismatic viewpoint on most issues." Query via e-mail.

Fiction Mainstream/contemporary, plays, young adult. "Trident Books is seeking fresh ideas for mainstream fiction, or any story that teaches a moral or lesson. Books are marketed toward a secular audience but teach a moral or ethical virtue. We are also interested in books that possess supernatural perspectives or characters. Lauren's Box is a women's fiction imprint of Diamond Eyes and is looking for authors who write about everyday characters who embrace grief, trauma, divorce, or any other issue except medical that women face today. We are looking for romance novels as well. Submit your ideas on all subjects if you are looking for a publisher who is interested in the purpose of your book and not just publishing another title." Query via e-mail.

Poetry "We only publish the winners of our contest. The winners will be published in a gift book along with inspirational photos. The fee to enter the contest is $7/poem. There is no deadline. Our goal is to enhance the meaning and purpose of poetry by sharing the beauty of the writer through their own expression. We welcome poems on various topics. Entrants can view the topics on our website."

Recent Title(s) *Writing His Way*, by Jessica Adriel (Christian writing manual); *Dance for the Piper*; *Christian Plays for Pre-K*.

Tips "We are a Christian publisher looking for fiction that has a message and provides the reader with more than just entertainment. Read a few articles on query letters, and know how the industry works. Understand that writing talent is secondary to how an author conducts him/herself. Your query is your first impression. Do not rush; be more than prepared when you send out your query and pray.''

EASTLAND PRESS

P.O. Box 99749, Seattle WA 98139. (206)217-0204. Fax: (206)217-0205. E-mail: info@eastlandpress.com. Website: www.eastlandpress.com. **Acquisitions:** John O'Connor, managing editor. Estab. 1981. Publishes hardcover and trade paperback originals. **Publishes 3-4 titles/year. Receives 25 queries/year. 30% of books from first-time authors; 90% from unagented writers. Pays 12-15% royalty on receipts.** Publishes book 2 years after acceptance of ms. Accepts simultaneous submissions. Responds in 1 month to queries. Book catalog free.

○━ Eastland Press is interested in textbooks for practitioners of alternative medical therapies primarily Chinese and physical therapies, and related bodywork.

Nonfiction Reference, textbook, alternative medicine (Chinese and physical therapies, and related bodywork). Subjects include health/medicine. ''We prefer that a manuscript be completed or close to completion before we will consider publication. Proposals are rarely considered, unless submitted by a published author or teaching institution.'' Submit outline and 2-3 sample chapters. Reviews artwork/photos as part of ms package. Send photocopies.

Recent Title(s) *Cranial Sutures*, by Marc Pick; *Acupuncture in the Treatment of Children*, by Julian Scott.

EIH PUBLISHING

AHU Press, P.O. Box 249, Goshen VA 24439. (540)997-0325. E-mail: allenchips@holistictree.com. Website: www.holistictree.com. **Acquisitions:** Dr. Allen Chips, acquisitions/publishing director (holistic texts and how-to/self-help). Estab. 1999. Publishes hardcover originals and reprints, trade paperback originals and reprints, electronic originals and reprints, and mass market paperback reprints. **Publishes 3-7 titles/year. Receives 35 queries/year. 50% of books from first-time authors; 95% from unagented writers. Pays 10% royalty.** Publishes book 9-12 months after acceptance of ms. Accepts simultaneous submissions. Responds in 1 month to queries; 2 months to proposals; 3 months to mss. Book catalog and ms guidelines online.

Nonfiction Audiocassettes, how-to, self-help, textbook. Subjects include education, health/medicine, psychology, spirituality. ''We are looking for textbooks, and self-help, how-to books with a holistic health or transpersonal therapy orientation.'' Query, then submit TOC with 2 sample chapters. Reviews artwork/photos as part of ms package. Send photocopies.

Recent Title(s) *Script Magic: A Hypnotherapist's Desk Reference*, by Dr. Allen Chips, Henry Bolduc, Dr. Masud Ansari, and others; *Life Patterns: Soul Lessons & Forgiveness*, by Henry Bolduc; *Inspirational Poetry*, by Dee Chips.

Tips Audience is people desiring to learn about mind-body-spirit oriented therapies/practices that lead to healing and/or enlightenment. ''The best authors are engaged in regular travel and seminars/workshops, demonstrating dedication, self-motivation, and a people orientation.''

ENC PRESS

(formerly Emperor's New Clothes Press). E-mail: info@encpress.com. Submissions E-mail: publisher@encpress.com. Website: www.encpress.com. **Acquisitions:** Olga Gardner Galvin, publisher; Justin Bryant, editorial advisor. Estab. 2003. Publishes trade paperback originals. **Publishes 4-6 titles/year. 90% of books from first-time authors; 100% from unagented writers. Pays 50% royalty on retail price.** Publishes book 18 months after acceptance of ms. Does not accept simultaneous submissions. Responds in 2-3 weeks to queries; 3-4 months to mss. Book catalog and ms guidelines online.

Fiction Adventure, humor, literary, mainstream/contemporary, science fiction, suspense, political satire, utopias/dystopias, social satire, picaresque novel. Query through e-mail.

Recent Title(s) *Exit Only*, by Liam Bracken (suspense/current affairs/Saudi Arabia/terrorism); *Devil Jazz*, by Craig Forgrave (satire/religion/parable); *Cherry Whip*, by Michael Antman (literary/Japanese culture/jazz).

Tips Audience is well-informed, socially liberal, fiscally conservative, decidedly not politically correct readers. ''Don't be afraid to offend. We're not publishing for the 'broadest possible audience.' We're publishing for the politically incorrect audience with a good sense of humor. If it's not at all funny, we don't want to read it.''

EXCALIBUR PUBLICATIONS

P.O. Box 89667, Tucson AZ 85752-9667. (520)575-9057. E-mail: excalibureditor@earthlink.net. **Acquisitions:** Alan M. Petrillo, editor. Publishes trade paperback originals. **Publishes 4-6 titles/year. Pays royalty or makes outright purchase.** Responds in 1 month.

○━ Excalibur publishes historical and military works from all time periods.

Nonfiction Subjects include history (military), military/war (strategy and tactics, as well as the history of battles, firearms, arms, and armour), historical personalities. ''We are seeking well-researched and documented works.

Unpublished writers are welcome.'' Query with outline, first 3 chapters, SASE. Include notes on photos, illustrations, and maps.

Recent Title(s) *Famous Faces of World War II*, by Robert Van Osdol; *Present Sabers: A History of the U.S. Horse Cavalry*, by Allan Heninger.

Tips ''Know your subject matter, and present it in a clear and precise manner. Please give us a brief description of your background or experience as it relates to your submission, as well as any marketing insight you might have on your subject.''

FILBERT PUBLISHING

140 3rd St., Box 326, Kandiyohi MN 56251. E-mail: filbertpublishing@filbertpublishing.com. Website: www.filbertpublishing.com. **Acquisitions:** Maurice Erickson, director of acquistions. Estab. 1995. Publishes trade paperback originals and reprints, and electronic originals. **Publishes 6 titles/year. Receives 200+ queries and 20 mss/year. 70% of books from first-time authors; 100% from unagented writers. Pays 10-15% royalty on retail price.** Publishes book 6-9 months after acceptance of ms. Accepts simultaneous submissions. Responds in 2 months to queries; 3 months to proposals; 3-4 months to mss. Book catalog for 6×9 SAE with 4 first-class stamps; ms guidelines online.

Nonfiction General nonfiction, how-to, reference. Subjects include creative nonfiction, hobbies, regional, reference books for writers, subjects small business owners would find helpful, and a very small amount of fiction. ''Writers who keep their eye on *Writing Etc.* (our free e-mag for writers) will get a feel for the style we're looking for.'' Query with SASE, or submit proposal package including outline, 2 sample chapters, strong query. Reviews artwork/photos as part of ms package. Send photocopies.

Fiction Adventure, historical, mainstream/contemporary, mystery, regional, romance, suspense. ''If your manuscript follows a formula of any kind, please submit it elsewhere. We enjoy unpredictable plots and strong characters supported by great writing.'' Query with SASE, or submit proposal package including 2 sample chapters, synopsis, strong query.

Recent Title(s) *Bob Bly's Guide to Freelance Writing Success*, by Robert W. Bly; *Secrets of a Writing Hustler*, by Roscoe Barnes III; *Pump Up Your Prose*, by Shaunna Privratsky.

Tips ''The people who purchase our books tend to be very educated, discriminating readers. Many are writers who are interested in finding information that will make their jobs easier and more profitable. I'd suggest that authors subscribe to our e-magazine, *Writing Etc.* It's free and will give them a feel for what we're looking for. We also use *Writing Etc.* as a way to promote our author's books as well as keep in touch with our readership. When you know *Writing Etc.*, you know a lot about Filbert Publishing.''

FILTER PRESS, LLC

P.O. Box 95, Palmer Lake CO 80133-0095. (719)481-2420. Fax: (719)481-2420. E-mail: info@filterpressbooks.com. Website: www.filterpressbooks.com. **Acquisitions:** Doris Baker, president. Estab. 1957. Publishes trade paperback originals and reprints. **Publishes 4-6 titles/year. Pays 10-12% royalty on wholesale price.** Publishes book 1 year after acceptance of ms.

    O↝ Filter Press specializes in nonfiction of the West.

Nonfiction Subjects include Americana, anthropology/archeology, ethnic, history, regional, crafts and crafts people of the Southwest. Query with outline and SASE. Reviews artwork/photos as part of ms package.

Recent Title(s) *Kokopelli Drum in Belly*, by Gail E. Haley (children's picture book); *Meadow Lark*, by Mary Peace Finley (YA fiction).

FLORICANTO PRESS

Inter American Development, 650 Castro St., Suite 120-331, Mountain View CA 94041-2055. (415)552-1879. Fax: (702)995-1410. E-mail: editor@floricantopress.com. Website: www.floricantopress.com. Estab. 1982. Publishes hardcover and trade paperback originals and reprints. Book catalog for #10 SASE; ms guidelines online.

    O↝ Floricanto Press is ''dedicated to promoting Latino thought and culture.''

Nonfiction Biography, cookbook, reference, academic, educational, professional, literary. Subjects include anthropology/archeology, cooking/foods/nutrition, ethnic (Hispanic), health/medicine, history, language/literature, psychology, women's issues/studies. ''We are looking primarily for nonfiction popular (but serious) titles that appeal to the general public on Hispanic subjects.'' Submit ms with word count, author bio, SASE.

Recent Title(s) *Bring Me More Stories: Tales of the Sephardim*, by Sally Benforado; *The Salvation of La Purísima*, by T.M. Spooner.

Tips Audience is general public interested in Hispanic culture. ''We need authors that are willing to promote their work heavily.''

FOCUS PUBLISHING, INC.

P.O. Box 665, Bemidji MN 56619-0665. (800)913-6287. Fax: (218)751-7210. E-mail: info@focuspubilshing.com. Website: www.focuspublishing.com. Estab. 1993. Publishes hardcover and trade paperback originals and reprints. Book catalog free.

  O→ "Focus Publishing is a small press primarily devoted to adult Christian books with a Bible study emphasis."

Nonfiction Subjects include religion, Christian living, Bible studies for men and women. Submit proposal package, including marketing ideas with SASE. Reviews artwork/photos as part of ms package. Send photocopies.

Recent Title(s) *Morning Will Come*, by Sandy Day; *Communication and Conflict Resolution*, by Dr. Stuart Scott.

FORWARD MOVEMENT PUBLICATIONS

300 W. 4th St., Cincinnati OH 45202-2666. (513)721-6659. Fax: (513)721-0729. E-mail: esgleason@forwarddaybyday.com. Website: www.forwardmovement.org. Estab. 1934. Publishes trade and mass market paperback originals, trade paperback reprints and tracts. Book catalog and ms guidelines free.

  O→ "Forward Movement was established 'to help reinvigorate the life of the church.' Many titles focus on the life of prayer, where our relationship with God is centered, death, marriage, baptism, recovery, joy, the Episcopal Church and more." Currently emphasizing prayer/spirituality.

Nonfiction "We publish a variety of types of books, but they all relate to the lives of Christians. We are an agency of the Episcopal Church." Biography, children's/juvenile, reference, self-help (about religion and prayer). Subjects include religion. Query with SASE or submit complete ms.

Fiction Episcopal for middle school (ages 8-12) readers. Juvenile. Query with SASE.

Recent Title(s) *Body Language*, by Lundy Pentz; *De-Cluttering as a Spiritual Activity*, by Donna Schaper; *A Letter Never Sent*, by Alanson B. Houghton.

Tips Audience is primarily Episcopalians and other Christians.

Ø GAY SUNSHINE PRESS and LEYLAND PUBLICATIONS

P.O. Box 410690, San Francisco CA 94141-0690. Fax: (415)626-1802. Website: www.gaysunshine.com. **Acquisitions:** Winston Leyland, editor. Estab. 1970. Publishes hardcover originals, trade paperback originals and reprints. **Publishes 3-4 titles/year. Pays royalty, or makes outright purchase.** Responds in 6 weeks to queries; 2 months to mss. Book catalog for $1.

  O→ Gay history, sex, politics, and culture are the focus of the quality books published by Gay Sunshine Press. Leyland Publications publishes books on popular aspects of gay sexuality and culture.

Nonfiction "We're interested in innovative literary nonfiction which deals with gay lifestyles." How-to. Subjects include gay/lesbian. No long personal accounts, academic or overly formal titles. Query with SASE. *All unsolicited mss returned unopened.*

Fiction Interested in innovative well-written novels on gay themes; also short story collections. Erotica, experimental, historical, literary, mystery, science fiction, All gay male material only. "We have a high literary standard for fiction. We desire fiction on gay themes of high literary quality and prefer writers who have already had work published in literary magazines. We also publish erotica—short stories and novels." Query with SASE. *All unsolicited mss returned unopened.*

Recent Title(s) *Out of the Closet Into Our Hearts: Celebration of Our Gay/Lesbian Family Members*.

N Ø GIFTED EDUCATION PRESS

10201 Yuma Court, Manassas VA 20109. (703)369-5017. E-mail: mfisher345@comcast.net. Website: www.giftedpress.com. **Acquisitions:** Maurice Fisher, publisher. Estab. 1981. Publishes trade paperback originals. **Publishes 5 titles/year. Receives 20 queries and 10 mss/year. 90% of books from first-time authors; 100% from unagented writers. Pays 10% royalty on retail price.** Publishes book 4 months after acceptance of ms. Accepts simultaneous submissions. Responds in 1 month. Book catalog and ms guidelines online.

  O→ Searching for rigorous texts on teaching science, math and humanities to gifted students.

Nonfiction Textbook, Subject matter guides in different fields of education. Subjects include child guidance/parenting, computers/electronic, education, history, humanities, philosophy, science, math, biology. Query with SASE. *All unsolicited mss returned unopened.* Reviews artwork/photos as part of ms package.

Recent Title(s) *Introducing Gifted Students to the Wonders of Mathematics*, by Francis Seanga; *Beyond Classroom Enrichment*, by Mark Wood.

Tips Audience includes teachers, parents, gifted program supervisors. "Be knowledgeable about your subject. Write clearly and don't use educational jargon."

GOLDEN WEST BOOKS

P.O. Box 80250, San Marino CA 91118. (626)458-8148. Fax: (626)458-8148. E-mail: trainbook@earthlink.net. Website: www.goldenwestbooks.com. **Acquisitions:** Donald Duke, publisher. Publishes hardcover originals.

Publishes 3-4 titles/year. Receives 8-10 queries and 5 mss/year. 75% of books from first-time authors; 100% from unagented writers. Pays 8-10% royalty on wholesale price. Offers no advance. Publishes book 3 months after acceptance of ms. Does not accept simultaneous submissions. Responds in 3 months to queries. Book catalog and ms guidelines free.

    O– Golden West Books specializes in railroad history.

Nonfiction Illustrated book (railroad history). Subjects include Americana, history. Query with SASE. Reviews artwork/photos as part of ms package.

Recent Title(s) *The Ulster & Delaware Railroad Through the Catskills*, by Gerald M. Best; *The Streamline Era*, by Robert C. Reed; *Electric Railways Around San Francisco Bay*, by Donald Duke.

GRAND CANYON ASSOCIATION

P.O. Box 399, 1 Tonto St., Grand Canyon AZ 86023. (928)638-7021. Fax: (928)638-2484. E-mail: tberger@grandc anyon.org. Website: www.grandcanyon.org. **Acquisitions:** Todd R. Berger, managing editor (Grand Canyon-related geology, natural history, outdoor activities, human history, photography, ecology, etc., posters, post-cards and other nonbook products). Estab. 1932. Publishes hardcover originals and reprints, and trade paper-back originals and reprints. **Publishes 6 titles/year. Receives 100 queries/year. 70% of books from first-time authors; 99% from unagented writers. Pays royalty on wholesale price, or makes outright purchase.** Publishes book 1 month-1 year after acceptance of ms. Accepts simultaneous submissions. Responds in 2 months. Book catalog online; ms guidelines by e-mail.

Nonfiction Autobiography, biography, booklets, children's/juvenile, coffee table book, general nonfiction, gift book, how-to, illustrated book, scholarly. Subjects include animals, anthropology/archeology, art/architecture, creative nonfiction, history, nature/environment, photography, recreation, regional, science, sports, travel, geology. Grand Canyon Association (GCA) is a nonprofit organization established in 1932 to support education, research, and other programs for the benefit of Grand Canyon National Park and its visitors. GCA operates bookstores throughout the park, publishes books and other materials related to the Grand Canyon region, supports wildlife surveys and other research, funds acquisitions for the park's research library, and produces a wide variety of free publications and exhibits for park visitors. Since 1932, GCA has provided Grand Canyon National Park with over $20 million in financial support. All publications and other products are related to Grand Canyon National Park and the surrounding region. Query with SASE, or submit proposal package includ-ing outline, 3-4 sample chapters, list of publication credits, and samples of previous work, or submit complete ms. Reviews artwork/photos as part of ms package. Send transparencies, color or b&w prints, or digital samples of images.

Recent Title(s) *Phantom Ranch*, by Scott Thybony (illustrated history); *Grand Canyon: The Vault of Heaven*, by Susan Lamb (photographic scenic book); *An Introduction to Grand Canyon Geology*, by L. Greer Price (illustrated geology).

Tips "All books, articles, and other products must be about the Grand Canyon. We also publish some things, to a much lesser extent, on the surrounding region, particularly geology-related titles with a connection to the Grand Canyon."

GRANITE PUBLISHING, LLC

P.O. Box 1429, Columbus NC 28722. (828)894-8444. Fax: (828)894-8454. E-mail: granitepub@5thworld.com. Website: www.5thworld.com. President: Pam Meyer. **Acquisitions:** Brian Crissey. Publishes trade paperback originals and reprints. **Publishes 4 titles/year. Receives 50 queries and 150 mss/year. 70% of books from first-time authors; 90% from unagented writers. Pays 7½-10% royalty.** Publishes book 16 months after acceptance of ms. Accepts simultaneous submissions. Responds in 6 months to mss.

Imprints Wild Flower Press; Swan-Raven & Co.; Agents of Change.

    O– "Granite Publishing strives to preserve the Earth by publishing books that develop new wisdom about our emerging planetary citizenship, bringing information from the outerworlds to our world." Currently emphasizing indigenous ideas, planetary healing.

Nonfiction Multimedia. Subjects include New Age, planetary paradigm shift. Submit proposal. Reviews artwork/photos as part of ms package. Send photocopies.

Recent Title(s) *Reconciliation*, by Ida Kannenberg; *Raechel's Eyes Volume I & II*, by Helen Littrell and Jean Bilodeaux.

GREAT POTENTIAL PRESS

P.O. Box 5057, Scottsdale AZ 85261. (602)954-4200. Fax: (602)954-0185. E-mail: info@giftedbooks.com. Web-site: www.giftedbooks.com. **Acquisitions:** Janet Gore, editor (gifted curriculum in schools); James Webb, president (parenting and social and emotional needs). Estab. 1986. Publishes trade paperback originals. **Pub-lishes 4-5 titles/year. Receives 10 queries and 10-15 mss/year. 25% of books from first-time authors; 100% from unagented writers. Pays 10% royalty on retail price.** Publishes book 6-12 months after acceptance of ms. Accepts simultaneous submissions. Responds in 2 months to queries; 3 months to proposals; 4 months to mss. Book catalog free or on website; ms guidelines online.

- O— Great Potential Press publishes books on the social/emotional/interpersonal/creative needs of gifted and talented children and adults for parents and teachers of gifted and talented youngsters. Currently emphasizing books regarding gifted and talented children, their parents and teachers. De-emphasizing research-based books.

Nonfiction Biography, children's/juvenile, humor, reference, self-help, textbook, assessment scales, advocacy, parenting tips. Subjects include child guidance/parenting, education, multicultural, psychology, translation, travel, women's issues/studies, gifted/talented children and adults. No research-based books, dissertations. Submit proposal package, including preface or introduction, TOC, outline, 3 sample chapters and an explanation of how work differs from similar published books.

Recent Title(s) *Misdiagnosis and Dual Diagnoses of Gifted Children and Adults*, by James T. Webb, PhD; *Being Smart about Gifted Children*, by Dona J. Matthews, PhD and Joanne F. Foster, EdD; *Grandparents' Guide to Gifted Children*, by James T. Webb, PhD.

Tips "Manuscripts should be clear, cogent, and well-written and should pertain to gifted, talented, and creative persons and/or issues."

GREENE BARK PRESS

P.O. Box 1108, Bridgeport CT 06601. (203)372-4861. Fax: (203)371-5856. Website: www.greenebarkpress.com. **Acquisitions:** Thomas J. Greene, publisher; Tara Maroney, associate publisher. Estab. 1991. Publishes hardcover originals. **Publishes 5 titles/year. Receives 100 queries and 6,000 mss/year. 60% of books from first-time authors; 100% from unagented writers. Pays 10-15% royalty on wholesale price.** Publishes book 1 year after acceptance of ms. Accepts simultaneous submissions. Responds in 1 month to queries; 6 months to mss. Book catalog for $2; ms guidelines for SASE.

- O— Greene Bark Press only publishes books for children and young adults, mainly picture and read-to books. "All of our titles appeal to the imagination and encourage children to read and explore the world through books. We only publish children's fiction—all subjects—but in reading picture book format appealing to ages 3-9 or all ages."

Fiction Juvenile. Submit complete ms. No queries or ms by e-mail.

Recent Title(s) *The Magical Trunk*, by Gigi Tegge; *Hey! There's a Goblin Under My Throne!*, by Rhett Ransom Pennell; *Edith Ellen Eddy*, by Julee Ann Granger.

Tips Audience is "children who read to themselves and others. Mothers, fathers, grandparents, godparents who read to their respective children, grandchildren. Include SASE, be prepared to wait, do not inquire by telephone."

HACHAI PUBLISHING

156 Chester Ave., Brooklyn NY 11218. (718)633-0100. Website: www.hachai.com. **Acquisitions:** Devorah Leah Rosenfeld, editor. Estab. 1988. Publishes hardcover originals. **Publishes 4 titles/year. Makes outright purchase of $600 and up.** Accepts simultaneous submissions. Responds in 2 months to mss. Book catalog free; ms guidelines online.

- O— "Hachai is dedicated to producing high quality Jewish children's literature, ages 2-10. Story should promote universal values such as sharing, kindness, etc."

Nonfiction Children's/juvenile. Subjects include ethnic, religion. Submit complete ms, SASE. Reviews artwork/photos as part of ms package. Send photocopies.

Recent Title(s) *The Key Under the Pillow*, by Leah Shollar; *The Secret Tunnel*, by Joy Nelkin Wieder; *I Go to the Doctor*, by Rikki Benenfeld.

Tips "We are looking for books that convey the traditional Jewish experience in modern times or long ago; traditional Jewish observance such as Sabbath and holidays and mitzvos such as mezuzah, blessings etc; positive character traits (middos) such as honesty, charity, respect, sharing, etc. We are also interested in historical fiction for young readers (7-10) written with a traditional Jewish perspective and highlighting the relevance of Torah in making important choices. Please, no animal stories, romance, violence, preachy sermonizing."

ALEXANDER HAMILTON INSTITUTE

70 Hilltop Rd., Ramsey NJ 07446-1119. (201)825-3377. Fax: (201)825-8696. Website: www.ahipubs.com. **Acquisitions:** Brian L.P. Zevnik, editor-in-chief; Gloria Ju, editor. Estab. 1909. Publishes 3-ring binder and paperback originals. **Publishes 5-10 titles/year. Receives 50 queries and 10 mss/year. 25% of books from first-time authors; 95% from unagented writers. Pays 5-8% royalty on retail price, or makes outright purchase of $3,500-7,000. Offers $3,500-7,000 advance.** Publishes book 10 months after acceptance of ms. Accepts simultaneous submissions. Responds in 1 month to queries; 2 months to mss.

O→ Alexander Hamilton Institute publishes management books for upper-level managers and executives. Currently emphasizing legal issues for HR/personnel.

Nonfiction The main audience is US personnel executives and high-level management. Subjects include legal personnel matters. "These books combine court case research and practical application of defensible programs."

Recent Title(s) *Employer's Guide to Record-Keeping Requirements.*

Tips "We sell exclusively by direct mail or through electronic means to managers and executives. A writer must know his/her field and be able to communicate legal and practical systems and programs."

HARTMAN PUBLISHING, INC.

8529 Indian School NE, Albuquerque NM 87112. (505)291-1274. Fax: (505)291-1284. E-mail: susan@hartmanonline.com. Website: www.hartmanonline.com. **Acquisitions:** Susan Alvare, managing editor (healthcare education). Publishes trade paperback originals. **Publishes 5-10 titles/year. Receives 50 queries and 25 mss/year. 50% of books from first-time authors; 100% from unagented writers. Pays 6-12% royalty on wholesale or retail price, or makes outright purchase of $200-600.** Publishes book 4-12 months after acceptance of ms. Accepts simultaneous submissions. Responds in 2 months to proposals; 3 months to mss. Book catalog free; ms guidelines online.

Imprints Care Spring (Mark Hartman, publisher).

O→ We publish educational and inspirational books for employees of nursing homes, home health agencies, hospitals, and providers of eldercare.

Nonfiction Textbook. Subjects include health/medicine. "Writers should request our books-wanted list, as well as view samples of our published material." Submit proposals via e-mail.

HEMINGWAY WESTERN STUDIES SERIES

Imprint of Boise State University, 1910 University Dr., Boise ID 83725. (208)426-1999. Fax: (208)426-4373. E-mail: ttrusky@boisestate.edu. Website: www.boisestate.edu/hemingway. **Acquisitions:** Tom Trusky, editor. Publishes multiple edition artists' books which deal with Rocky Mountain political, social, and environmental issues. **Offers advance.** Does not accept simultaneous submissions. Ms guidelines free.

HENDRICK-LONG PUBLISHING CO., INC.

10635 Toweroaks D., Houston TX 77070. (832)912-7323. Fax: (832)912-7353. E-mail: hendrick-long@worldnet. att.net. Website: hendricklongpublishing.com. **Acquisitions:** Vilma Long. Estab. 1969. Publishes hardcover and trade paperback originals and hardcover reprints. **Publishes 4 titles/year. 90% from unagented writers. Pays royalty. Pays royalty on selling price. Offers advance.** Publishes book 18 months after acceptance of ms. Does not accept simultaneous submissions. Responds in 3 months to queries. Book catalog for 8½×11 or 9×12 SASE with 4 first-class stamps; ms guidelines online.

O→ Hendrick-Long publishes historical fiction and nonfiction about Texas and the Southwest for children and young adults.

Nonfiction Biography, children's/juvenile. Subjects include history, regional. Query, or submit outline and 2 sample chapters. Reviews artwork/photos as part of ms package. Send photocopies.

Fiction Juvenile, young adult. Query with SASE, or submit outline, 2 sample chapters, synopsis.

Recent Title(s) *Catholic Texans, HB & Teachers Guide; My Texas.*

HENSLEY PUBLISHING

6116 E. 32nd St., Tulsa OK 74135-5494. (918)664-8520. E-mail: editorial@hensleypublishing.com. Website: www.hensleypublishing.com. **Acquisitions:** Acquisitions Department. Publishes trade paperback originals. **Publishes 5 titles/year. Receives 200 queries/year. 50% of books from first-time authors; 50% from unagented writers.** Publishes book 18 months after acceptance of ms. Responds in 2 months to queries. Ms guidelines online.

O→ Hensley Publishing publishes Bible studies that offer the reader a wide range of topics. Currently emphasizing 192-page workbook studies.

Nonfiction Subjects include child guidance/parenting, money/finance, religion, women's issues/studies, marriage/family. "We publish only Bible studies. We do not want to see anything non-Christian." No New Age, poetry, plays, sermon collections. Query with synopsis and sample chapters.

Recent Title(s) *Balance at the Speed of Life,* by Barb Folkerts (women's edition); *Balance at the Speed of Life,* by Dave Folkerts (men's edition); *Journey to Jesus,* by Florence & Marita Littauer.

Tips "Submit something that crosses denominational lines directed toward the large Christian market, not small specialized groups. We serve an interdenominational market—all Christian persuasions. Our goal is to get readers back into studying the Bible instead of studying about the Bible."

HIGH PLAINS PRESS

P.O. Box 123, 539 Cassa Rd., Glendo WY 82213. (307)735-4370. Fax: (307)735-4590. E-mail: editor@highplainspress .com. Website: www.highplainspress.com. **Acquisitions:** Nancy Curtis, publisher. Estab. 1986. Publishes hardcover and trade paperback originals. **Publishes 4 titles/year. Receives 300 queries and 200 mss/year. 80% of books from first-time authors; 95% from unagented writers. Pays 10% royalty on wholesale price. Offers $200-800 advance.** Publishes book 2 years after acceptance of ms. Accepts simultaneous submissions. Responds in 1 month to queries; 3 months to proposals and mss. Book catalog for 9×12 SASE; ms guidelines online.

> O— "What we sell best is history of the Old West, particularly things relating to Wyoming. We also publish 1 book of poetry a year in our Poetry of the American West series."

Nonfiction "We focus on books of the American West, mainly history. We like books on the history and culture of Wyoming and the West." Biography. Subjects include Americana, art/architecture, history, nature/ environment, regional. Submit outline, 3 sample chapters. Reviews artwork/photos as part of ms package. Send photocopies.

Poetry "We only seek poetry closely tied to the Rockies. Do not submit single poems." Query, or submit complete ms.

Recent Title(s) *Slade: The True Story of the Notorious Badman*, by Bob Scott; *Cloud Seeding: Poetry of the American West*, by Stacy Gillett Coyle; *A Triceratops Hunt in Pioneer Wyoming: The Journals of Barnum Brown & J.P. Sams*, edited by Michael F. Kohl, Larry D. Martin, and Paul Brinkman.

LAWRENCE HILL BOOKS

Chicago Review Press, 814 N. Franklin St., 2nd Floor, Chicago IL 60610. (312)337-0747. Fax: (312)337-5985. **Acquisitions:** Yuval Taylor, senior editor. Publishes hardcover originals and trade paperback originals and reprints. **Publishes 3-10 titles/year. Receives 20 queries and 10 mss/year. 40% of books from first-time authors; 50% from unagented writers. Pays 7¹/₂-12¹/₂% royalty on retail price. Offers $1,500-7,500 advance.** Publishes book 1 year after acceptance of ms. Accepts simultaneous submissions. Responds in 1 month. Book catalog free.

Nonfiction Biography, reference, general nonfiction. Subjects include ethnic, government/politics, history, multicultural. Submit proposal package including outline, 2 sample chapters.

Recent Title(s) *When Race Becomes Real*, edited by Bernestine Singley.

Ⓝ HOBAR PUBLICATIONS

A division of Finney Co., 3943 Meadowbrook Rd., Minneapolis MN 55426. (952)938-9330. Fax: (952)938-7353. E-mail: feedback@finney-hobar.com. Website: www.finney-hobar.com. **Acquisitions:** Alan E. Krysan, president. Publishes trade paperback originals. **Publishes 4-6 titles/year. Receives 30 queries and 10 mss/ year. 35% of books from first-time authors; 100% from unagented writers. Pays 10% royalty on wholesale price. Offers advance.** Publishes book 6-12 months after acceptance of ms. Accepts simultaneous submissions. Responds in 8-10 weeks to queries.

> O— Hobar publishes career and technical educational materials.

Nonfiction How-to, illustrated book, reference, technical, textbook, handbooks, field guides. Subjects include agriculture/horticulture, animals, business/economics, education, gardening, nature/environment, science, building trades. Query with SASE. Reviews artwork/photos as part of ms package.

Recent Title(s) *Horsemanship Handbook*, by Susan J. Stuska; *Forest Management Digest*, edited by Allen Wickman; *Concrete & Concrete Masonry*, by Donald L. Ahrens.

Ⓝ HOLLIS PUBLISHING CO.

Division of Puritan Press, Inc., 95 Runnells Bridge Rd., Hollis NH 03049. (603)889-4500. Fax: (603)889-6551. E-mail: books@hollispublishing.com. Website: www.hollispublishing.com. **Acquisitions:** Frederick Lyford, editor. Publishes hardcover and trade paperback originals. **Publishes 5 titles/year. Receives 25 queries and 15 mss/year. 50% of books from first-time authors; 100% from unagented writers. Pays 5-10% royalty on retail price.** Publishes book 6 months after acceptance of ms. Does not accept simultaneous submissions. Responds in 1 month to queries; 2 months to mss. Book catalog free; ms guidelines for #10 SASE.

> O— Hollis publishes books on social policy, government, politics, and current and recent events intended for use by professors and their students, college and university libraries, and the general reader. Currently emphasizing works about education, the Internet, government, history-in-the-making, social values and politics.

Nonfiction Biography. Subjects include Americana, anthropology/archeology, education, ethnic, government/ politics, health/medicine, history, memoirs, nature/environment, regional, sociology, travel. Query with SASE, or submit outline, 2 sample chapters.

Recent Title(s) *Basic Lymphoedema Management: Treatment and Prevention of Problems Associated With Lymphatic Filariasis*, by Gerusa Dreyer, MD, et. al.

IDYLL ARBOR, INC.

P.O. Box 720, Ravensdale WA 98051. (425)432-3231. Fax: (425)432-3726. E-mail: editors@idyllarbor.com. Website: www.idyllarbor.com. **Acquisitions:** Tom Blaschko. Publishes hardcover and trade paperback originals, and trade paperback reprints. **Publishes 6 titles/year. 50% of books from first-time authors; 100% from unagented writers. Pays 8-15% royalty on wholesale price or retail price.** Publishes book 1 year after acceptance of ms. Accepts simultaneous submissions. Responds in 1 month to queries; 2 months to proposals; 6 months to mss. Book catalog and ms guidelines free.

Imprints Issues Press; Pine Winds Press.

○➤ Idyll Arbor publishes practical information on the current state and art of healthcare practice. Currently emphasizing therapies (recreational, aquatic, occupational, music, horticultural), activity directors in long-term care facilities, and social service professionals.

Nonfiction Reference, technical, textbook. Subjects include health/medicine (for therapists, social service providers and activity directors), psychology, recreation (as therapy), horticulture (used in long-term care activities or health care therapy). "Idyll Arbor is currently developing a line of books under the imprint Issues Press, which treats emotional issues in a clear-headed manner. The latest books are *Female Sex Offenders: What Therapists, Law Enforcement and Child Protective Services Need to Know* and *Situational Mediation: Sensible Conflict Resolution.* Another series of *Personal Health* books explains a condition or a closely related set of medical or psychological conditions. The target audience is the person or the family of the person with the condition. We want to publish a book that explains a condition at the level of detail expected of the average primary care physician so that our readers can address the situation intelligently with specialists. We look for manuscripts from authors with recent clinical experience. Good grounding in theory is required, but practical experience is more important." Query preferred with outline and 1 sample chapter. Reviews artwork/photos as part of ms package. Send photocopies.

Recent Title(s) *The Enduring Human Spirit: Thought-Provoking Stories on Caring for Our Elders*, by Charles Tindell; *Aquatic Therapy: Techniques and Interventions*, by Luis G. Vargas.

Tips "The books must be useful for the health practitioner who meets face to face with patients or the books must be useful for teaching undergraduate and graduate level classes. We are especially looking for therapists with a solid clinical background to write on their area of expertise."

ILLUMINATION ARTS

P.O. Box 1865, Bellevue WA 98009. (425)644-7185. Fax: (425)644-9274. E-mail: liteinfo@illumin.com. Website: www.illumin.com. **Acquisitions:** Ruth Thompson, editorial director (ms submissions); Terri Cohlene, creative director (artwork submissions); Carol Morris, publisher's assistant (artwork submissions). Publishes hardcover originals. **Publishes 4-5 titles/year. Pays royalty on wholesale price. Offers advance for artists.** Book catalog and ms guidelines online.

○➤ Illumination Arts publishes inspirational/spiritual (not religious) children's picture books.

Nonfiction Children's/juvenile. "Our books are all high quality and exquisitely illustrated. Stories need to be exciting and inspirational for children." Submit complete ms with SASE. Reviews artwork/photos as part of ms package. Send photocopies.

Fiction Picture books (children's). Prefer under 1,000 words; 1,500 words max. No electronic submissions.

Recent Title(s) *The Errant Knight*; *A Mother's Promise*; *We Share One World*.

Tips "A smart writer researches publishing companies thoroughly before submitting and then follows submission guidelines closely."

IMAGES SI, INC.

Imprint of Images Publishing, 109 Woods of Arden Rd., Staten Island NY 10312. (718)966-3694. Fax: (718)966-3695. Website: www.imagesco.com. **Acquisitions:** Ronald Chironna. Estab. 1990. Publishes hardcover originals, trade paperback originals and audio. **Publishes 5 titles/year. 10% of books from first-time authors; 75% from unagented writers. Pays 10-20% royalty on wholesale price. Offers advance.** Publishes book 6 months after acceptance of ms. Accepts simultaneous submissions. Responds in 2 months. Book catalog online.

○➤ "We are currently looking for science fiction and fantasy stories and books more than anything else."

Nonfiction Audiocassettes, booklets, how-to, technical, CDs. Subjects include computers/electronic, photography, science, software. Query with SASE.

Fiction Fantasy, science fiction, audiocassetes, CDs, and printed books. "We are looking for short stories as well as full-length novels." Query with SASE.

Recent Title(s) *Centauri III*, by George L. Griggs (science fiction print book); *Nova-Audio, Issues 1-3*, by Hoyt, Franklin, Schoen, Wild, Silverberg, and Catelli (science fiction audio); *Kirlian Photography*, by John Iovine (photo/how-to).

INFO NET PUBLISHING

21142 Canada Rd., Unit 1-C, Lake Forest CA 92630. (949)458-9292. Fax: (949)462-9595. E-mail: herb@infonetpublishing.com. Website: www.infonetpublishing.com. **Acquisitions:** Herb Wetenkamp, president. Estab. 1987. Publishes hardcover and trade paperback originals. **Publishes 6 titles/year. Receives 50 queries and 20 mss/year. 80% of books from first-time authors; 85% from unagented writers. Pays 7-10% royalty on wholesale price, or makes outright purchase of $1,000-5,000. Offers $1,000-2,000 advance in some cases.** Publishes book 10 months after acceptance of ms. Accepts simultaneous submissions. Responds in 2 months to queries. Book catalog for 10×12 SAE with 2 first-class stamps; ms guidelines for #10 SASE.

    O➤ Info Net publishes for easily identified niche markets; specific markets with some sort of special interest, hobby, avocation, profession, sport, or lifestyle. New emphasis on collectibles and a series of books on retailing with CD-Roms.

Nonfiction Biography, children's/juvenile, gift book, how-to, reference, self-help, technical. Subjects include Americana (and collectibles), business/economics (retailing), history, hobbies, military/war, nature/environment (and environment), recreation, regional, sports, travel, women's issues/studies, aviation/aircraft archaeology. "We are looking for specific niche market books, not general titles, other than self-help. Do not repeat same formula as other books. In other words, offer something new." Submit outline, 3 sample chapters, proposal package, including demographics, marketing plans/data with SASE. Reviews artwork/photos as part of ms package. Send photocopies.

Recent Title(s) *Aircraft Wrecks in the Mountains and Deserts of California, 3rd Ed.*

Tips "Please check to be sure similar titles are not already published covering the exact same subject matter. Research the book you are proposing."

INTERCONTINENTAL PUBLISHING

P.O. Box 7242, Fairfax Station VA 22039. E-mail: icpub@worldnet.att.net. Website: home.att.net/~icpub/. **Acquisitions:** H.G. Smittenaar, publisher. Publishes hardcover and trade paperback originals. **Publishes 3-4 titles/year. Pays 5% minimum royalty.** Accepts simultaneous submissions. Responds ASAP to proposals.

    O➤ Intercontinental publishes mystery and suspense novels.

Fiction Mystery, suspense. Submit proposal package, including 1-3 sample chapters, estimated word count and SASE.

Recent Title(s) *The Dog That Belonged to No One*, by Gerald Schiller (children's); *The Cop Was White as Snow*, by Joyce Spizer; *Twisted*, by Cahroul Cramer.

Tips "Be original, write proper English, be entertaining."

Ⓝ INTERMEDIA PUBLISHING, LLC

P.O. Box 14932, Silver Spring MD 20911. (301)920-1186. E-mail: editor@intermediapublishing.com. Website: www.intermediapublishing.com. **Acquisitions:** Angel Robles, editorial director (Spanish-language legal, how-to guides). Estab. 2004. Publishes trade paperback originals. **Publishes 5-20 titles/year. Pays royalty or makes outright purchase.** Book catalog online; ms guidelines for SASE.

Imprints Libros Simples Para Su Exito.

Nonfiction How-to, illustrated book, reference, self-help. Subjects include child guidance/parenting, education, ethnic, money/finance, multicultural. Query with SASE, or submit proposal package including outline, 3 sample chapters. Reviews artwork/photos as part of ms package. Send photocopies.

Recent Title(s) *Guía y Formularios de Inmigración*, by Angel Robles-Pena.

Tips "Our audience is Spanish-speaking Latinos in the US."

ITALICA PRESS

595 Main St., Suite 605, New York NY 10044-0047. (212)935-4230. Fax: (212)838-7812. E-mail: inquiries@italicapress.com. Website: www.italicapress.com. **Acquisitions:** Ronald G. Musto and Eileen Gardiner, publishers. Estab. 1985. Publishes trade paperback originals. **Publishes 6 titles/year. Receives 600 queries and 60 mss/year. 5% of books from first-time authors; 100% from unagented writers. Pays 7-15% royalty on wholesale price. author's copies.** Publishes book 1 year after acceptance of ms. Accepts simultaneous submissions. Responds in 1 month to queries; 4 months to mss. Book catalog and ms guidelines online.

    O➤ Italica Press publishes English translations of modern Italian fiction and medieval and Renaissance nonfiction.

Nonfiction Subjects include translation. "We publish English translations of medieval and Renaissance source materials and English translations of modern Italian fiction." Query with SASE. Reviews artwork/photos as part of ms package. Send photocopies.

Fiction Translations of 20th century Italian fiction. Query with SASE.

Poetry Poetry titles are always translations and generally dual language.

Tips "We are interested in considering a wide variety of medieval and Renaissance topics (not historical fiction), and for modern works we are only interested in translations from Italian fiction by well-known Italian authors.''

JAIN PUBLISHING CO.

P.O. Box 3523, Fremont CA 94539. (510)659-8272. Fax: (510)659-0501. E-mail: mail@jainpub.com. Website: www.jainpub.com. **Acquisitions:** M. Jain, editor-in-chief. Estab. 1989. Publishes hardcover and paperback originals and reprints. **Publishes 6 titles/year. Receives 300 queries/year. 100% from unagented writers. Pays 5-15% royalty on net sales.** Publishes book 1-2 years after acceptance of ms. Responds in 3 months to mss. Book catalog and ms guidelines online.

Imprints Asian Humanities Press.

O┐ Jain Publishing Co. publishes college textbooks and supplements, as well as professional and scholarly references and AV materials.

Nonfiction Reference, textbook. Subjects include humanities, social sciences, Asian studies, medical, business, scientific/technical. Submit proposal package including publishing history. Reviews artwork/photos as part of ms package. Send photocopies.

Recent Title(s) *A Student Guide to College Composition*, by William Murdiek.

ALICE JAMES BOOKS

238 Main St., Farmington ME 04938. (207)778-7071. Fax: (207)778-7071. E-mail: ajb@umf.maine.edu. Website: www.alicejamesbooks.org. **Acquisitions:** April Ossmann, director (poetry). Publishes trade paperback originals. **Publishes 6 titles/year. Receives 1,000 mss/year. 50% of books from first-time authors; 99% from unagented writers. Pays through competition awards.** Publishes book 1 year after acceptance of ms. Accepts simultaneous submissions. Responds in 1 month to queries; 4 months to mss. Book catalog for free or on website; ms guidelines for #10 SASE or on website.

O┐ Alice James Books is a nonprofit poetry press.

Poetry Query.

Recent Title(s) *The Art of the Lathe*, by B.H. Fairchild; *The River at Wolf*, by Jean Valentine; *Pity the Bathtub Its Forced Embrace of the Human Form*, by Matthea Harvey.

Tips ''Send SASE for contest guidelines or check website. Do not send work without consulting current guidelines.''

Ⓝ JAMESON BOOKS, INC.

722 Columbus St., P.O. Box 738, Ottawa IL 61350. (815)434-7905. Fax: (815)434-7907. **Acquisitions:** Jameson G. Campaigne, publisher/editor. Estab. 1986. Publishes hardcover originals. **Publishes 6 titles/year. Receives 500 queries and 300 mss/year. 33% of books from first-time authors; 33% from unagented writers. Pays 6-15% royalty on retail price. Offers $1,000-25,000 advance.** Publishes book 1 year after acceptance of ms. Accepts simultaneous submissions. Responds in 6 months to queries.

O┐ Jameson Books publishes conservative politics and economics, Chicago area history, and biographies.

Nonfiction Biography. Subjects include business/economics, government/politics, history, regional (Chicago area). Query with SASE, or submit 1 sample chapter. Submissions not returned without SASE.

Fiction Very well-researched western (frontier pre-1850). Interested in pre-cowboy ''mountain men'' in American west, before 1820 in east frontier fiction. No cowboys, no science fiction, mystery, poetry, et al. Query with SASE, or submit outline, 1 sample chapter, synopsis.

Recent Title(s) *Politics as a Noble Calling*, by F. Clifton White (memoirs); *Capitalism*, by George Reisman; *The Citizen's Guide to Fighting Government*, by Steve Symms and Larry Grupp.

KAMEHAMEHA SCHOOLS PRESS

Kamehameha Schools, 1887 Makuakane St., Honolulu HI 96817-1887. (808)842-8719. Fax: (808)842-8895. E-mail: kspress@ksbe.edu. Website: kspress.ksbe.edu. **Acquisitions:** Acquisitions Editor. Publishes hardcover and trade paperback originals and reprints. **Publishes 3-5 titles/year. 10-25% of books from first-time authors; 100% from unagented writers. Makes outright purchase.** Publishes book up to 2 years after acceptance of ms. Responds in 3 months to queries. Book catalog online or request print copy.

Imprints Kamehameha Schools Press; Kamehameha Schools; Kamehameha Schools Bishop Estate.

O┐ ''Only writers with substantial and documented expertise in Hawaiian history, Hawaiian culture, Hawaiian language, and/or Hawaiian studies should consider submitting to Kamehameha Schools Press. We prefer to work with writers available to physically meet at our Honolulu offices.''

Nonfiction Biography, children's/juvenile, reference, textbook. Subjects include education (Hawaiian), history (Hawaiian), regional (Hawaii), translation (Hawaiian). Query with SASE. Reviews artwork/photos as part of ms package. Send photocopies.

DENIS KITCHEN PUBLISHING CO., LLC

P.O. Box 2250, Amherst MA 01004-2250. (413)259-1627. Fax: (413)259-1812. E-mail: publishing@deniskitchen.com. Website: www.deniskitchen.com. **Acquisitions:** Denis Kitchen, publisher (graphic novels, classic comic strips, postcard books, boxed trading cards, graphics, pop culture, alternative culture). Publishes hardcover and trade paperback originals and reprints. **Publishes 4 titles/year. 15% of books from first-time authors; 50% from unagented writers. Pays 6-10% royalty on retail price. Occasionally makes deals based on percentage of wholesale if idea and/or bulk of work is done in-house. Offers $1-5,000 advance.** Publishes book 9-12 months after acceptance of ms. Does not accept simultaneous submissions. Responds in 4-6 weeks.

● This publisher strongly discourages e-mail submissions.

Nonfiction Coffee table book, illustrated book, graphic novels. Subjects include art, comic art, pop culture, alternative culture. Query with SASE, or submit proposal package including outline, illustrative matter, or submit complete ms. Reviews artwork/photos as part of ms package. Send photocopies or transparencies.

Fiction Adventure, erotica, historical, horror, humor, literary, mystery, occult, science fiction (only if in graphic novel form). "We do not want pure fiction. We seek cartoonists or writer/illustrator teams who can tell compelling stories with a combination of words and pictures." No pure fiction (meaning text only). Query with SASE, or submit sample illustrations/comic pages, or submit complete ms.

Recent Title(s) *Mr. Natural Postcard Book*, by R. Crumb; *The Grasshopper and the Ant*, by Harvey Kurtzman; *Jazz Greats*, by R. Crumb.

Tips "Our audience is readers who embrace the graphic novel revolution, who appreciate historical comic strips and books, and those who follow popular and alternative culture. Readers who supported Kitchen Sink Press for 3 decades will find that Denis Kitchen Publishing continues the tradition and precedents established by KSP. We like to discover new talent. The artist who has a day job but a great idea is encouraged to contact us. The pop culture historian who has a new take on an important figure is likewise encouraged. We have few preconceived notions about manuscripts or ideas, though we are decidedly selective. Historically, we have published many first-time authors and artists, some of whom developed into award-winning creators with substantial followings. Artists or illustrators who do not have confidence in their writing should send us self-promotional postcards (our favorite way of spotting new talent)."

Ⓝ B. KLEIN PUBLICATIONS

P.O. Box 6578, Delray Beach FL 33482. (561)496-3316. Fax: (561)496-5546. **Acquisitions:** Bernard Klein, editor-in-chief. Estab. 1946. Publishes hardcover and paperback originals. **Publishes 5 titles/year. Pays 10% royalty on wholesale price.** Accepts simultaneous submissions. Responds in 2 months to queries. Book catalog for #10 SASE.

○━ B. Klein Publications specializes in directories, annuals, who's who books, bibliography, business opportunity, reference books. Markets books by direct mail and mail order.

Nonfiction How-to, reference, self-help, directories; bibliographies. Subjects include business/economics, hobbies. Query with SASE, or submit outline, sample chapters.

Recent Title(s) *Guide to American Directories*, by Bernard Klein.

H.J. KRAMER, INC.

Imprint of New World Library, P.O. Box 1082, Tiburon CA 94920. (415)435-5367. Fax: (415)435-5364. E-mail: hjkramer@jps.net. **Acquisitions:** Jan Phillips, managing editor. Estab. 1984. Publishes hardcover and trade paperback originals. **Publishes 5-7 titles/year. Receives 1,000 queries and 500 mss/year. 20% of books from first-time authors. Advance varies.** Publishes book 18 months after acceptance of ms. Book catalog free.

Imprints Starseed Press Children's Illustrated Books.

Nonfiction Subjects include health/medicine (holistic), spirituality, metaphysical.

Fiction Juvenile, picture books with themes of self-esteem, nonviolence, and spirituality. Prospective authors please note: Kramer's list is selective and is normally fully slated several seasons in advance.

Recent Title(s) *Saying What's Real*, by Dr. Susan Campbell (nonfiction); *A Goose Named Gilligan*, by Jerry M. Hay (nonfiction for children); *Just for Today*, by Jan Phillips (fiction).

Tips "Our books are for people who are interested in personal growth and consciousness-raising. We are not interested in personal stories unless they have universal appeal. We do not accept e-mail submissions of mss although queries will be answered."

LAKE CLAREMONT PRESS

4650 N. Rockwell St., Chicago IL 60625. (773)583-7800. Fax: (773)583-7877. E-mail: sharon@lakeclaremont.com. Website: www.lakeclaremont.com. **Acquisitions:** Sharon Woodhouse, publisher. Publishes trade paperback originals. **Publishes 5-7 titles/year. Receives 300 queries and 50 mss/year. 50% of books from first-time authors; 100% from unagented writers. Pays 10-15% royalty on wholesale price. Offers $500-1,000**

Small Presses

advance. Publishes book 4-12 months after acceptance of ms. Accepts simultaneous submissions. Responds in 1 month to queries; 2 months to proposals; 2-6 months to mss. Book catalog online.

☞ "We specialize in books on the Chicago area and its history, and may consider regional titles for the Midwest. We also like nonfiction books on ghosts and cemeteries."

Nonfiction Subjects include Americana, ethnic, history, nature/environment (regional), regional, travel, women's issues/studies, film/cinema/stage (regional), urban studies. Query with SASE, or submit proposal package, including outline and 2 sample chapters, or submit complete ms (e-mail queries and proposals preferred).

Recent Title(s) *The Chicago River: A Natural and Unnatural History*, by Libby Hill; *Chicago's Midway Airport: The First Seventy-Five Years*, by Christopher Lynch.

Tips "Please include a market analysis in proposals (who would buy this book and where) and an analysis of similar books available for different regions. Please know what else is out there."

LANGMARC PUBLISHING

P.O. Box 90488, Austin TX 78709-0488. (512)394-0989. Fax: (512)394-0829. E-mail: langmarc@booksails.com. Website: www.langmarc.com. **Acquisitions:** Lois Qualben, president (inspirational). Publishes trade paperback originals. **Publishes 3-5 titles/year; imprint publishes 1 title/year. Receives 150 queries and 80 mss/year. 60% of books from first-time authors; 100% from unagented writers. Pays 10-13% royalty on wholesale price.** Publishes book 18 months after acceptance of ms. Accepts simultaneous submissions. Responds in 3 months to queries. Book catalog free; ms guidelines online.

Imprints North Sea Press; Harbor Lights Series.

Nonfiction Self-help, inspirational. Subjects include child guidance/parenting, education, health/medicine. Query with SASE. Reviews artwork/photos as part of ms package. Send photocopies.

Recent Title(s) *Cut Me Some Slack, Lord*; *Little Things Remembered*; *The Leapin' Deacon*.

LARSON PUBLICATIONS/PBPF

4936 Rt. 414, Burdett NY 14818-9729. (607)546-9342. Fax: (607)546-9344. E-mail: larson@lightlink.com. Website: www.larsonpublications.org. **Acquisitions:** Paul Cash, director. Estab. 1982. Publishes hardcover and trade paperback originals. **Publishes 4-5 titles/year. 5% of books from first-time authors. Pays variable royalty. Seldom offers advance.** Publishes book 1-2 years after acceptance of ms. Accepts simultaneous submissions. Responds in 4-6 months to queries. Visit website for book catalog.

Nonfiction Subjects include philosophy, psychology, religion, spirituality. Query with SASE and outline.

Recent Title(s) *Astronoesis*, by Anthony Damiani.

Tips "We look for original studies of comparative spiritual philosophy or personal fruits of independent (transsectarian viewpoint) spiritual research/practice."

Ⓜ J & L LEE CO.

P.O. Box 5575, Lincoln NE 68505. **Acquisitions:** Jim McKee, acquisitions editor. Publishes trade paperback originals and reprints. **Publishes 5 titles/year. Receives 25 queries and 5-10 mss/year. 20% of books from first-time authors; 60% from unagented writers. Pays 10% royalty on retail price, or makes outright purchase. Offers advance.** Publishes book 18 months after acceptance of ms. Accepts simultaneous submissions. Responds in 1 month to proposals; 6 months to queries and mss. Book catalog free.

Imprints Salt Creek Press; Young Hearts.

☞ "Virtually everything we publish is of a Great Plains nature."

Nonfiction Biography, reference. Subjects include Americana, history, regional. Query with SASE.

Recent Title(s) *The Good Old Days*, by Van Duling; *Bipartisan Efforts and Other Mutations*, by Paul Fell.

Tips "We do not publish poetry or fiction."

LIBRARY OF VIRGINIA

800 E. Broad St., Richmond VA 23219-8000. (804)692-3500. Fax: (804)692-3594. E-mail: gkimball@lva.lib.va.us. Website: www.lva.lib.va.us. **Acquisitions:** Gregg D. Kimball, assistant director (Virginia history and culture). Publishes hardcover originals and reprints. **Publishes 3-4 titles/year. Pays royalty on retail price, or makes outright purchase.** Does not accept simultaneous submissions. Responds in 1 month to queries and proposals; 3 months to mss. Book catalog online.

Nonfiction The Library of Virginia publishes works that draw from the library's collections. Biography, coffee table book, illustrated book. Subjects include history, regional. Submit proposal package including outline, 1 sample chapter.

Recent Title(s) *A Little Parliament: The Virginia Assembly in the 17th Century*, by Warren M. Billings; *The Unboxing of Henry Brown*, by Jeffrey Ruggles; *The Capital of Virginia: A Landmark of American Architecture*, by Fiske Kimball.

Ⓝ LIFE CYCLE BOOKS

P.O. Box 1008, Niagara Falls NY 14304. (416)690-5860. Fax: (416)690-8532. Website: www.lifecyclebooks.com. **Acquisitions:** Paul Broughton, general manager. Estab. 1973. Publishes trade paperback originals and reprints, and mass market reprints. **Publishes 6 titles/year. Receives 100+ queries/year. 50% of books from first-time authors; 100% from unagented writers. Pays 8-10% royalty on wholesale price. Offers $250-1,000 advance.** Publishes book 1 year after acceptance of ms. Does not accept simultaneous submissions. Responds in 1 month. Book catalog online.

Nonfiction Booklets, children's/juvenile, reference, scholarly. Subjects include health/medicine, religion, social sciences, women's issues/studies. ''We specialize in human life issues.'' Query with SASE, or submit complete ms. Reviews artwork/photos as part of ms package.

Recent Title(s) *Don't Panic: How to Tell Your Parents You're Pregnant*, by Elaine Depaw; *Men and Abortion: A Path to Healing*, by Catherine T. Coyle, PhD.

LOST HORSE PRESS

105 Lost Horse Lane, Sandpoint ID 83864. (208)255-4410. Fax: (208)255-1560. E-mail: losthorsepress@mindspring.com. Website: www.losthorsepress.org. **Acquisitions:** Christine Holbert, editor (novels, novellas). Estab. 1998. Publishes hardcover and paperback originals. **Publishes 4 titles/year.** Publishes book 1-2 years after acceptance of ms.

Fiction Literary, poetry, regional (Pacific Northwest), short story collections.

Recent Title(s) *Woman on the Cross*, by Pierre Delattre (novel); *Iron Fever*, by Stephan Torre (poetry); *Hiding From Salesmen*, by Scott Poole (poetry).

MAGE PUBLISHERS, INC.

1032 29th St. NW, Washington DC 20007. (202)342-1642. Fax: (202)342-9269. E-mail: info@mage.com. Submissions E-mail: as@mage.com. Website: www.mage.com. **Acquisitions:** Amin Sepehri, assistant to publisher. Estab. 1985. Publishes hardcover originals and reprints, trade paperback originals. **Pays royalty.** Accepts simultaneous submissions. Responds in 1 month to queries. Book catalog free; ms guidelines online.

○→ Mage publishes books relating to Persian/Iranian culture.

Nonfiction Autobiography, biography, children's/juvenile, coffee table book, cookbook, gift book, illustrated book. Subjects include anthropology/archeology, art/architecture, cooking/foods/nutrition, ethnic, history, language/literature, music/dance, sociology, translation. Submit outline, author bio, SASE. Query via mail or e-mail. Reviews artwork/photos as part of ms package. Send photocopies.

Fiction Ethnic, feminist, historical, literary, mainstream/contemporary, short story collections. Must relate to Persian/Iranian culture. Submit outline, SASE. Query via mail or e-mail.

Poetry Must relate to Persian/Iranian culture. Query.

Recent Title(s) *The Films of Makhmalbaf*, by Eric Egan; *Masters and Masterpieces of Iranian Cinema*, by Hamid Dabashi; *Land of the Lion and Sun*, by C.J. Wills.

Tips Audience is the Iranian-American community in America and Americans interested in Persian culture.

THE MAGNI GROUP, INC.

7106 Wellington Point Rd., McKinney TX 75070. (972)540-2050. Fax: (972)540-1057. E-mail: info@magnico.com. Website: www.magnico.com. **Acquisitions:** Evan Reynolds, president. Publishes hardcover originals and trade paperback reprints. **Publishes 5-10 titles/year. Receives 20 queries and 10-20 mss/year. 50% of books from first-time authors; 80% from unagented writers. Pays royalty on wholesale price, or makes outright purchase. Offers advance.** Publishes book 6 months after acceptance of ms. Does not accept simultaneous submissions. Responds in 2 months to queries. Book catalog and ms guidelines online.

Imprints Magni Publishing.

Nonfiction Cookbook, how-to, self-help. Subjects include child guidance/parenting, cooking/foods/nutrition, health/medicine, money/finance, sex. Submit complete ms. Reviews artwork/photos as part of ms package. Send photocopies.

Recent Title(s) *Home Owner's Diary*; *Foods That Cause You to Lose Weight*; *Live Your Life Pain Free.*

MAISONNEUVE PRESS

P.O. Box 2980, Washington DC 20013-2980. (301)277-7505. Fax: (301)277-2467. E-mail: editors@maisonneuvepress.com. Website: www.maisonneuvepress.com. **Acquisitions:** Robert Merrill, editor (politics, literature, philosophy, intellectual history); Dennis Crow, editor (architecture, urban studies, sociology). Publishes hardcover and trade paperback originals. **Publishes 6 titles/year. 5% of books from first-time authors; 100% from unagented writers. Pays 5% royalty on cover price.** Publishes book 1 year after acceptance of ms. Accepts simultaneous submissions. Responds in 1 month. Book catalog free; send letter for guidelines, individual response.

☨ "Maisonneuve provides solid, first-hand information for serious adult readers: academics and political activists. We do not publish poetry, fiction, or autobiography."

Nonfiction Subjects include education, government/politics, history, language/literature, military/war, philosophy, psychology, sociology, translation, women's issues/studies, intellectual history, literary criticism, social theory, economics, essay collections. "We make decisions on completed manuscripts only. Will correspond on work in progress. Some books submitted are too narrowly focused; not marketable enough. We are eager to read manuscripts on the current crisis, war, and the rise of fundamentalists and neo-conservatism in America. The commercial media—TV and newspapers—are not doing a very good job of cutting through the government propaganda." Query with SASE, or submit complete ms. Reviews artwork/photos as part of ms package.

Recent Title(s) *Man's Rage for Chaos: Biology, Behavior and the Arts*, by Morse Peckham; *The Perpetual Consequences of Fear and Violence: Rethinking the Future*, by Chris Maser; *Iraq and the International Oil System: Why America Went to War in the Gulf*, by Stephen Pelletiere.

MARINE TECHNIQUES PUBLISHING, INC.

126 Western Ave., Suite 266, Augusta ME 04330-7252. (207)622-7984. Fax: (207)621-0821. E-mail: marinetechniques@midmaine.com. **Acquisitions:** James L. Pelletier, president/CEO (commercial marine or maritime international); Christopher S. Pelletier, vice president operations (national and international maritime related properties). **Publishes 3-5 titles/year. Receives 5-20 queries and 1-4 mss/year. 15% of books from first-time authors. Pays 25-43% royalty on wholesale or retail price.** Publishes book 6-12 months after acceptance of ms. Accepts simultaneous submissions. Responds in 2 months to queries; 4 months to proposals; 6 months to mss. Book catalog free.

☨ Publishes only books related to the commercial marine industry.

Nonfiction Reference, self-help, technical, maritime company directories. Subjects include the commerical maritime industry only. Submit proposal package, including ms, with all photos (photocopies OK).

Fiction Must be commercial maritime/marine related. Submit complete ms.

Poetry Must be related to maritime/marine subject matter. Submit complete ms.

Tips Audience consists of commercial marine/maritime firms, persons employed in all aspects of the marine/maritime commercial and recreational fields, persons interested in seeking employment in the commercial marine industry; firms seeking to sell their products and services to vessel owners, operators, and managers in the commercial marine industry worldwide, etc.

Ⓢ MARLOR PRESS, INC.

4304 Brigadoon Dr., St. Paul MN 55126. (651)484-4600. E-mail: marlin.marlor@minn.net. **Acquisitions:** Marlin Bree, publisher. Estab. 1981. Publishes trade paperback originals. **Publishes 6 titles/year. Receives 100 queries and 25 mss/year. Pays 8-10% royalty on wholesale price.** Publishes book 1 year after acceptance of ms. Does not accept simultaneous submissions. Responds in 3-6 weeks to queries. Ms guidelines for #10 SASE.

☨ Currently emphasizing general interest nonfiction children's books and nonfiction boating books. De-emphasizing travel.

Nonfiction Children's/juvenile, how-to. Subjects include travel, boating. "Primarily how-to stuff." *No unsolicited mss.* No anecdotal reminiscences or biographical materials. No fiction or poetry. Query first; submit outline with sample chapters only when requested. Do not send full ms. Reviews artwork/photos as part of ms package.

Recent Title(s) *Going Abroad: The Bathroom Survival Guide*, by Eva Newman; *Wake of the Green Storm: A Survivor's Tale*, by Marlin Bree.

Ⓛ MEDICAL PHYSICS PUBLISHING

4513 Vernon Blvd., Madison WI 53705. (608)262-4021. Fax: (608)265-2121. E-mail: mpp@medicalphysics.org. Website: www.medicalphysics.org. **Acquisitions:** John Cameron, president; Betsey Phelps, managing editor. Estab. 1985. Publishes hardcover and paperback originals and reprints. **Publishes 5-6 titles/year. Receives 10-20 queries/year. 100% from unagented writers. Pays 10% royalty on wholesale price.** Publishes book 1 year after acceptance of ms. Accepts simultaneous submissions. Responds in 6 months to mss. Book catalog available via website or upon request.

☨ "We are a nonprofit, membership organization publishing affordable books in medical physics and related fields." Currently emphasizing biomedical engineering. De-emphasizing books for the general public.

Nonfiction Reference, technical, textbook. Subjects include health/medicine, symposium proceedings in the fields of medical physics and radiology. Submit complete ms. Reviews artwork/photos as part of ms package. Send disposable copies.

Recent Title(s) *A Practical Guide to Intensity-Modulated Radiation Therapy*, by members of the staff of Memorial Sloan-Kettering Cancer Center; *Physics of the Body*, by John R. Cameron, James G. Skofronick and Roderick M. Grant.

MEYERBOOKS, PUBLISHER

P.O. Box 427, Glenwood IL 60425-0427. (708)757-4950. **Acquisitions:** David Meyer, publisher. Estab. 1976. Publishes hardcover and trade paperback originals and reprints. **Publishes 5 titles/year. Pays 10-15% royalty on wholesale or retail price.** Responds in 3 months to queries.

Imprints David Meyer Magic Books; Waltham Street Press.

    O→ "We are currently publishing books on stage magic history. We only consider subjects which have never been presented in book form before. We are not currently considering books on health, herbs, cookery, or general Americana."

Nonfiction Reference. Subjects include history of stage magic. Query with SASE.

Recent Title(s) *Inclined Toward Magic: Encounters With Books, Collectors and Conjurors' Lives*, by David Meyer; *Houdini and the Indescribable Phenomenon*, by Robert Lund.

MID-LIST PRESS

4324 12th Ave S., Minneapolis MN 55407-3218. (612)822-3733. Fax: (612)823-8387. Website: www.midlist.org. Publisher: Lane Stiles. Estab. 1989. Publishes hardcover and trade paperback originals. **Publishes 6 titles/year. Pays 40-50% royalty on net receipts. Offers $1,000 advance.** Publishes book 12-18 months after acceptance of ms. Accepts simultaneous submissions. Responds in 3 weeks to queries; 3 months to mss. Ms guidelines online.

    O→ Mid-List Press publishes books of high literary merit and fresh artistic vision by new and emerging writers.

Fiction General fiction. No children's, juvenile, romance, young adult. See guidelines.

Recent Title(s) *The Trouble With You Is*, by Susan Jackson Rodgers (short fiction); *Ask*, by Lou Suarez (poetry); *Odd Men In*, by Michael Milburn (creative nonfiction).

Tips Mid-List Press is an independent press. In addition to publishing the annual winners of the Mid-List Press First Series Awards, Mid-List Press publishes fiction, poetry, and creative nonfiction by established writers.

N MINE FALLS PRESS

1 Clocktower Place, Unit 315-1, Nashua NH 03060. E-mail: janice@minefallspress.com. Submissions E-mail: submissions@minefallspress.com. Website: www.minefallspress.com. **Acquisitions:** Ruth Barton, editor (mainstream fiction); Janice Schad, publisher (fantasy, mystery, science fiction). Estab. 2004. Publishes trade paperback originals. **Publishes 4 titles/year. Receives 200 queries and 20 mss/year. 50% of books from first-time authors; 50% from unagented writers. Pays 15-25% royalty on wholesale price.** Publishes book 4 months after acceptance of ms. Accepts simultaneous submissions. Responds in 1 month. Book catalog and ms guidelines online.

Nonfiction Biography, general nonfiction, how-to, self-help. Subjects include alternative lifestyles, Americana, community, contemporary culture, crafts, government/politics, history, humanities, memoirs, New Age, philosophy, spirituality, world affairs. Submit proposal package including outline, 1 sample chapter.

Fiction Adventure, fantasy, gothic, historical, horror, humor, literary, mainstream/contemporary, military/war, multicultural, mystery, occult, regional, religious, romance, science fiction, suspense, western. Submit proposal package including 1 sample chapter, synopsis.

Recent Title(s) *The Wheelwright's Son*, by Michael Alan (historical fiction); *The Taos Monster*, by J. Delphine Cheney (mystery).

Tips "Our target readers are deep and insightful. They are after stories of substance and emotional nuance, stories that excite the mind and fill the soul. Our entire operation is based on a web infrastructure. We prefer all initial communication through our website."

MOMENTUM BOOKS, LLC

117 W. Third St., Royal Oak MI 48067. (800)758-1870. Fax: (248)691-4531. E-mail: momentumbooks@glis.net. Website: www.momentumbooks.com. **Acquisitions:** Franklin Foxx, editor. Estab. 1987. **Publishes 6 titles/ year. Receives 100 queries and 30 mss/year. 95% of books from first-time authors; 100% from unagented writers. Pays 10-15% royalty.** Does not accept simultaneous submissions. Ms guidelines online.

    O→ Momentum Books publishes regional books and general interest nonfiction.

Nonfiction Biography, cookbook, guides. Subjects include cooking/foods/nutrition, history, memoirs, sports, travel, automotive, current events. Submit proposal package including outline, 3 sample chapters, marketing outline.

Recent Title(s) *Rockin' Down the Dial*, by David Carson (regional history); *Offbeat Cruises & Excursions*, by Len Barnes (travel); *The Way It Was* (regional history).

N MONTANA HISTORICAL SOCIETY PRESS

225 N. Roberts St., Helene MT 59620-1201. (406)444-4741. E-mail: cwhitehorn@state.mt.us. Website: www.montanahistoricalsociety.org. **Acquisitions:** Clark Whitehorn. Estab. 1956. Publishes hardcover originals, trade

paperback originals and trade paperback reprints. **Publishes 4 titles/year. Receives 24 queries and 16 mss/year. 50% of books from first-time authors; 100% from unagented writers. Pays 5-10% royalty on wholesale price.** Publishes book 1 year after acceptance of ms. Does not accept simultaneous submissions. Responds in 1 month to queries; 2 months to proposals; 4 months to mss. Book catalog and ms guidelines online.

Nonfiction Biography, cookbook, general nonfiction. Subjects include anthropology/archeology, history, military/war, nature/environment, regional, travel. "We publish history and environmental studies books focusing on the northern plains and Rocky Mountains." Query with SASE. Send photocopies.

Recent Title(s) *Hope in Hard Times*, by Mary Murphy (photo and interpretive essays about Depression-era photographers); *Tenderfoot in Montana*, by Francis Thomson (historical account of the Vigilante era in Montana).

Tips Audience includes history buffs; people with an interest in Yellowstone National Park.

[N] MOUNTAIN N'AIR BOOKS

P.O. Box 12540, La Crescenta CA 91224. (818)248-9345. Website: www.mountain-n-air.com. **Acquisitions:** Gilberto d'Urso, owner. Publishes trade paperback originals. **Publishes 6 titles/year. Receives 50 queries and 35 mss/year. 75% of books from first-time authors; 100% from unagented writers. Pays 5-10% royalty on retail price, or makes outright purchase.** Publishes book 6 months after acceptance of ms. Does not accept simultaneous submissions. Responds in 2 weeks to queries; 2 months to mss. Ms guidelines online.

Imprints Bearly Cooking.

○→ Mountain N'Air publishes books for those generally interested in the outdoors and travel.

Nonfiction Biography, cookbook, how-to. Subjects include cooking/foods/nutrition, nature/environment, recreation, travel. Submit outline, 2 sample chapters. Reviews artwork/photos as part of ms package. Send photocopies.

Recent Title(s) *We Aspired*; *Bible Drama*; *Eighty Years of Adventures*.

THE NAUTICAL & AVIATION PUBLISHING CO.

2055 Middleburg Lane, Mt. Pleasant SC 29464. (843)856-0561. Fax: (843)856-3164. **Acquisitions:** Melissa A. Pluta, acquisitions editor. Estab. 1979. Publishes hardcover originals and reprints. **Publishes 5-10 titles/year. Receives 200 queries/year. Pays 10-12% royalty on net receipts. Offers rare advance.** Accepts simultaneous submissions. Responds in 3 weeks to queries. Book catalog free.

○→ The Nautical & Aviation Publishing Co. publishes naval and military history, fiction, and reference.

Nonfiction Reference. Subjects include military/war (American), naval history. Query with SASE, or submit 3 sample chapters, synopsis. Reviews artwork/photos as part of ms package.

Fiction Historical, military/war (Revolutionary War, War of 1812, Civil War, WW I and II, Persian Gulf, and Marine Corps history). Looks for "novels with a strong military history orientation." Submit complete ms with cover letter and brief synopsis.

Recent Title(s) *The Civil War in the Carolinas*, by Dan L. Morrill; *Christopher and the Quasi War With France*, by William P. Mack; *A Guide to Airborne Weapons*, by David Crosby.

Tips "We are primarily a nonfiction publisher, but we will review historical fiction of military interest with strong literary merit."

[N] NEW CANAAN PUBLISHING CO., INC.

P.O. Box 752, New Canaan CT 06840. (203)548-3408. Fax: (203)358-9072. E-mail: info@newcanaanpublishing.com. Website: www.newcanaanpublishing.com. Publishes hardcover trade and paperback originals and reprints. Does not accept simultaneous submissions. Responds in 3 months to queries; 3 months to proposals; 4 months to mss. Book catalog and ms guidelines available via website or #10 SASE.

○→ New Canaan publishes children's, young adult, and Christian titles. Only wants submissions in the following categories: joke books addressing contemporary religious, political, or other societal themes; Christian books for any age group; books for children of military families; historical fiction; middle readers and young adult books addressing Christian themes. Submit proposal package including ms, synopsis, query letter, competition, marketing plans, résumé. Does not guarantee a response or return of materials.

[N] NEW ENGLAND LEAGUE OF MIDDLE SCHOOLS (NELMS)

460 Boston St., Suite 4, Topsfield MA 01983-1223. (978)887-6263. Fax: (978)887-6504. E-mail: nelms@nelms.org. Submissions E-mail: lwhealy@nelms.org. Website: www.nelms.org. **Acquisitions:** Lyn Ward Healy, associate executive editor. Estab. 1974. Publishes trade paperback originals and reprints. Does not accept simultaneous submissions. Book catalog and ms guidelines online.

Nonfiction Scholarly. Subjects include education. "We have a juried review and offer an educational journal. Our focus is on middle level education." Submit complete ms.

Recent Title(s) *Combinations: Opening the Door to Student Leadership*, by Ed Gerety.

NEW VICTORIA PUBLISHERS

P.O. Box 27, Norwich VT 05055-0027. (802)649-5297. Fax: (802)649-5297. E-mail: newvic@aol.com. Website: www.newvictoria.com. Editor: ReBecca Beguin. **Acquisitions:** Claudia Lamperti, editor. Estab. 1976. Publishes trade paperback originals. **Publishes 4-6 titles/year. 50% of books from first-time authors; large% from unagented writers. Pays 10% royalty.** Publishes book 1 year after acceptance of ms. Does not accept simultaneous submissions. Book catalog free; ms guidelines for SASE.

    ⊙⌐ "New Victoria is a nonprofit literary and cultural organization producing the finest in lesbian fiction and nonfiction." Emphasizing mystery. De-emphasizing coming-of-age stories.

Nonfiction Biography. Subjects include gay/lesbian, history (feminist), women's issues/studies. "We are interested in feminist history or biography and interviews with or topics relating to lesbians." No poetry. Submit outline, sample chapters.

Fiction Adventure, erotica, fantasy, feminist, historical, humor, mystery (amateur sleuth), romance, science fiction, western. "Looking for strong feminist characters, also strong plot and action. We will consider most anything if it is well written and appeals to a lesbian/feminist audience. Hard copy only—no disks." Submit outline, sample chapters, synopsis.

Recent Title(s) *Theoretically Dead*, by Tinker Marks (mystery); *Circles of Power*, by Barbara Summerhawk.

Tips "Try to appeal to a specific audience and not write for the general market. We're still looking for well-written, hopefully humorous, lesbian fiction and well-researched biography or nonfiction."

NEW VOICES PUBLISHING

Imprint of KidsTerrain, Inc., P.O. Box 560, Wilmington MA 01887. (978)658-2131. Fax: (978)988-8833. E-mail: rschiano@kidsterrain.com. Website: www.kidsterrain.com. **Acquisitions:** Rita Schiano, executive editor (children's books). Estab. 2000. Publishes hardcover and trade paperback originals. **Publishes 5 titles/year. Receives 30 queries and 20 mss/year. 95% of books from first-time authors; 95% from unagented writers. Pays 10-15% royalty on wholesale price.** Publishes book 1 year after acceptance of ms. Does not accept simultaneous submissions. Responds in 1 month to queries; 3 months to proposals and mss. Book catalog and ms guidelines online.

    ⊙⌐ The audience for this company is children ages 4-9.

Nonfiction Children's/juvenile, illustrated book. Subjects include child guidance/parenting. Query with SASE. Reviews artwork/photos as part of ms package. Send photocopies.

Fiction Juvenile. Query with SASE.

Recent Title(s) *The Magic in Me*, by Maggie Moran (children's fiction); *Aunt Rosa's House*, by Maggie Moran (children's fiction); *Last Night I Left Earth for Awhile*, by Natalie Brown-Douglas (children's fiction).

Tips "Know, specifically, what your story/book is about."

NEWSAGE PRESS

P.O. Box 607, Troutdale OR 97060-0607. (503)695-2211. Fax: (503)695-5406. E-mail: info@newsagepress.com. Website: www.newsagepress.com. **Acquisitions:** Maureen R. Michelson, publisher; Sherry Wachter, marketing and communications. Estab. 1985. Publishes trade paperback originals. Ms guidelines online.

    ⊙⌐ "We focus on nonfiction books. No 'how to' books or cynical, despairing books." Currently emphasizing books that explore the animal/human bond and death and grieving, and are written intelligently. Photo-essay books in large format are no longer published by Newsage Press. No novels or other forms of fiction.

Nonfiction Subjects include animals, multicultural, nature/environment, women's issues/studies, death/dying. Submit 2 sample chapters, proposal (no more than 10 pgs), SASE.

Recent Title(s) *Looking Like the Enemy: My Story of Imprisonment in a Japanese-American Internment Camp*, by Mary Matsuda Gruenewald; *Whales: Touching the Mystery*, by Doug Thompson.

NODIN PRESS

530 N. Third St., Suite 120, Minneapolis MN 55401. (612)333-6300. Fax: (612)333-6303. E-mail: nstill4402@aol.com. **Acquisitions:** Norton Stillman, publisher. Publishes hardcover and trade paperback originals. **Publishes 5 titles/year. Receives 20 queries and 20 mss/year. 75% of books from first-time authors; 100% from unagented writers. Pays 7½% royalty.** Publishes book 6 months after acceptance of ms. Accepts simultaneous submissions. Responds in 6 months to queries. Book catalog and ms guidelines free.

    ⊙⌐ Nodin Press publishes Minnesota regional titles: nonfiction, memoir, sports, poetry.

Nonfiction Biography, regional guide book. Subjects include history (ethnic), regional, sports, travel. Query with SASE.

Poetry Regional (Minnesota poets). Submit 10 sample poems.

Recent Title(s) *Stories Teachers Tell*, by Gretchen and Jon Hassler; *Let's Fondue*, by Susan Lukens; *Why Still Dance*, by Phoebe Hanson.

⊘ NONETHELESS PRESS

20332 W. 98th St., Lenexa KS 66220. (913)254-7266. Fax: (913)393-3245. E-mail: info@nonethelesspress.com. Website: www.nonethelesspress.com. **Acquisitions:** Marie-Christine Ebershoff. Estab. 2002. Publishes hardcover, trade paperback and electronic originals and reprints. **Publishes 3-10 titles/year. Receives 900 queries and 100 mss/year. 50% of books from first-time authors; 60% from unagented writers. Pays 20% royalty on wholesale price.** Publishes book 8 months after acceptance of ms. Accepts simultaneous submissions. Responds in 6 months. Book catalog and ms guidelines online.

Nonfiction Biography, general nonfiction, reference, scholarly, textbook. Subjects include art/architecture, contemporary culture, creative nonfiction, history, humanities, language/literature, multicultural, philosophy, religion, world affairs, women's studies. Nonetheless Press is a new publisher that is following the best traditions of the small press movement, with an ambitious initial list. At a time when most independent publishers are crowding their titles into ever smaller niches, Nonetheless defies that convention and chooses mss for the best of all possible reasons—because they are good. Query with SASE. *All unsolicited mss returned unopened.* Reviews artwork/photos as part of ms package. Send photocopies.

Fiction Historical, literary, short story collections, spiritual. Query with SASE. *All unsolicited mss returned unopened.*

Recent Title(s) *Strange Birds From Zoroaster's Nest*, by Laina Farhat-Holzman (religion/world affairs); *The Ecumenical Cruise*, by Walter Benesch (philosophy/short story collection); *Secrets of Successful Query Letters*, by Pam Brodowsky (reference/writing).

Tips "Provide a detailed, specific proposal. Don't waste your time or ours with half-formed ideas vaguely expressed."

NORTH CAROLINA OFFICE OF ARCHIVES AND HISTORY

Historical Publications Section, 4622 Mail Service Center, Raleigh NC 27699-4622. (919)733-7442. Fax: (919)733-1439. E-mail: donna.kelly@ncmail.net. Website: www.ncpublications.com. **Acquisitions:** Donna E. Kelly, administrator (North Carolina and southern history). Publishes hardcover and trade paperback originals. **Publishes 4 titles/year. Receives 20 queries and 25 mss/year. 5% of books from first-time authors; 100% from unagented writers. Makes one-time payment upon delivery of completed ms.** Publishes book 2 years after acceptance of ms. Accepts simultaneous submissions. Responds in 1 week to queries and proposals; 2 months to mss. Ms guidelines for $3.

    ○┰ "We publish *only* titles that relate to North Carolina. The North Carolina Office of Archives and History also publishes the *North Carolina Historical Review*, a scholarly journal of history."

Nonfiction Hardcover and trade paperback books relating to North Carolina. Subjects include history (related to North Carolina), military/war (related to North Carolina), regional (North Carolina and Southern history). Query with SASE. Reviews artwork/photos as part of ms package. Send photocopies.

Recent Title(s) *The North Carolina State Fair: The First 150 Years*, by Melton A. McLaurin; *Phantom Pain: North Carolina's Artificial Limbs Program for Confederate Veterans*, by Ansley Herring Wegner; *Photographers in North Carolina: The First Century, 1842-1941*, by Stephen E. Massengill.

Tips Audience is public school and college teachers and students, librarians, historians, genealogists, North Carolina citizens, tourists.

Ⓝ Ⓐ NORTHFIELD PUBLISHING

Imprint of Moody Publishers, 215 W. Locust St., Chicago IL 60610. (800)678-8001. Fax: (312)329-2019. E-mail: acquisitions@moody.edu. Website: www.moodypublishers.org. **Acquisitions:** Acquisitions Coordinator. **Publishes 5-10 titles/year. 1% of books from first-time authors. Pays royalty on net receipts. Offers $500-50,000 advance.** Publishes book 1 year after acceptance of ms. Accepts simultaneous submissions. Book catalog for 9 × 12 SAE with 2 first-class stamps.

    ○┰ "Northfield publishes a line of books for non-Christians or those exploring the Christian faith. While staying true to Biblical principles, we eliminate some of the Christian wording and scriptual references to avoid confusion."

Nonfiction Biography (classic). Subjects include business/economics, child guidance/parenting, money/finance, religion. *Agented submissions only.*

Recent Title(s) *The Five Love Languages, Men's Edition*, by Gary Chapman; *Beautiful Spiritual Places*, by Sharon Hanby-Robie and Deb Strubel.

NOVA PRESS

11659 Mayfield Ave., Suite 1, Los Angeles CA 90049. (310)207-4078. Fax: (310)571-0908. E-mail: novapress@aol.com. Website: www.novapress.net. **Acquisitions:** Jeff Kolby, president. Estab. 1993. Publishes trade paperback originals. **Publishes 4 titles/year. Pays 10-22½% royalty on net receipts. Offers advance.** Publishes book 6 months after acceptance of ms. Does not accept simultaneous submissions. Book catalog free.

　　O→ Nova Press publishes only test prep books for college entrance exams (SAT, GRE, GMAT, LSAT, etc.), and closely related reference books, such as college guides and vocabulary books.

Nonfiction How-to, self-help, technical, test prep books for college entrance exams. Subjects include education, software.

Recent Title(s) *The MCAT Chemistry Book*, by Ajikumar Aryangat.

N ◯ ORCHISES PRESS

P.O. Box 20602, Alexandria VA 22320-1602. (703)683-1243. Fax: (703)993-1161. E-mail: lathbury@gmu.edu. Website: mason.gmu.edu/~rlathbur. **Acquisitions:** Roger Lathbury, editor-in-chief. Estab. 1983. Publishes hardcover and trade paperback originals and reprints. **Publishes 4-5 titles/year. 1% of books from first-time authors; 95% from unagented writers. Pays 36% of receipts after Orchises has recouped its costs.** Publishes book 1 year after acceptance of ms. Accepts simultaneous submissions. Responds in 3 months to queries. Book catalog for #10 SASE; ms guidelines online.

　　• *Orchises Press no longer reads unsolicited mss.*

　　O→ Orchises Press is a general literary publisher specializing in poetry with selected reprints and textbooks. No new fiction or children's books.

Nonfiction Biography, how-to, humor, reference, technical, textbook. Subjects include literary. No real restrictions on subject matter. Query with SASE. Reviews artwork/photos as part of ms package. Send photocopies.

Poetry Poetry must have been published in respected literary journals. Publishes free verse, but has strong formalist preferences. Query, or submit 5 sample poems.

Recent Title(s) *Library*, by Stephen Akey (nonfiction); *I Think I Am Going to Call My Wife Paraguay*, by David Kirby (poetry).

OZARK MOUNTAIN PUBLISHING, INC.

P.O. Box 754, Huntsville AR 72740. (479)738-2348. Fax: (479)738-2348. Website: www.ozarkmt.com. **Acquisitions:** Nancy Garrison. Publishes hardcover and trade paperback originals and mass market paperback reprints. **Publishes 3-4 titles/year. Pays 10% royalty on retail price. Offers $500 advance.** Accepts simultaneous submissions. Responds in 6 months to queries. Book catalog free or online; ms guidelines online.

Nonfiction Subjects include New Age, spirituality (New Age/metaphysical). "No phone calls please." Query with SASE, or submit proposal package including outline, 2 sample chapters.

Recent Title(s) *Holiday in Heaven*, by Aron Abrahamsen; *Is Jehovah an E.T.?*, by Dorothy Leon; *The Ultimate Dictionary of Dream Language*, by Briceida Ryan.

PALARI PUBLISHING

P.O. Box 9288, Richmond VA 23227-0288. (866)570-6724. Fax: (804)883-5234. E-mail: palaripub@aol.com. Website: www.palaribooks.com. **Acquisitions:** David Smitherman, fiction publisher. Estab. 1998. Publishes hardcover and trade paperback originals. **Pays royalty.** Publishes book 1 year after acceptance of ms. Does not accept simultaneous submissions. Responds in 1 month to queries; 2-3 months to mss. Ms guidelines online.

　　• Member of Publishers Marketing Association.

　　O→ Small publisher specializing in southern mysteries and nonfiction. Distributes titles through Baker & Taylor, Ingram, Amazon, mail order and website. Promotes titles through book signings, direct mail and the Internet. Published 2 debut authors in the last year.

Fiction Adventure, ethnic, gay/lesbian, historical, literary, mainstream/contemporary, multicultural, mystery, suspense. "Tell why your idea is unique or interesting. Make sure we are interested in your genre before submitting." Query with SASE, or submit author bio, estimated word count, list of publishing credits. Accepts queries via e-mail, fax. Often comments on rejected mss.

Recent Title(s) *Poor Man's Philanthropist: The Thomas Cannon Story* (inspirational); *The 7 Most Powerful Selling Secrets* (business); *The Guessing Game* (mystery).

Tips "Send a good bio. I'm interested in a writer's experience and unique outlook on life."

PARADISE CAY PUBLICATIONS

P.O. Box 29, Arcata CA 95518-0029. (707)822-7038. Fax: (707)822-9163. E-mail: paracay@humboldt1.com. Website: www.paracay.com. **Acquisitions:** Matt Morehouse, publisher. Publishes hardcover and trade paperback originals and reprints. **Publishes 5 titles/year; imprint publishes 2 titles/year. Receives 360-480 queries and 240-360 mss/year. 10% of books from first-time authors; 100% from unagented writers. Pays 10-15% royalty on wholesale price, or makes outright purchase of $1,000-10,000. Offers $0-2,000 advance.** Publishes book 4 months after acceptance of ms. Responds in 1 month to queries and proposals; 2 months to mss. Book catalog and ms guidelines free on request or online.

Imprints Pardey Books.

Nonfiction Must have strong nautical theme. Cookbook, how-to, illustrated book, reference, technical, textbook. Subjects include cooking/foods/nutrition, recreation, sports, travel. Query with SASE, or submit proposal package including 2-3 sample chapters, call first. Reviews artwork/photos as part of ms package. Send photocopies.

Fiction Adventure (nautical, sailing). All fiction must have a nautical theme. Query with SASE, or submit proposal package including 2-3 sample chapters, synopsis.

Recent Title(s) *American Practical Navigator*, by Nathaniel Bowditch; *Voyage Toward Vengeance* (fiction); *Rescue at the Top of the World*.

Tips Audience is recreational sailors and powerboaters. Call Matt Morehouse (publisher).

ℕ PASSPORT PRESS

P.O. Box 1346, Champlain NY 12919-1346. **Acquisitions:** Jack Levesque, publisher. Estab. 1975. Publishes trade paperback originals. **Publishes 4 titles/year. 25% of books from first-time authors; 100% from unagented writers. Pays 6% royalty on retail price. Offers advance.** Publishes book 9 months after acceptance of ms. Does not accept simultaneous submissions.

Imprints Travel Line Press.

○━ Passport Press publishes practical travel guides on specific countries. Currently emphasizing offbeat countries.

Nonfiction Subjects include travel. Especially looking for mss on practical travel subjects and travel guides on specific countries. No travelogues. Send 1-page query only. Reviews artwork/photos as part of ms package.

Recent Title(s) *Costa Rica Guide: New Authorized Edition*, by Paul Glassman.

ℕ PATHFINDER PUBLISHING, INC.

3600 Harbor Blvd., #82, Oxnard CA 93035. (805)984-7756. Fax: (805)985-3267. E-mail: bmosbrook@adelphia.net. Website: www.pathfinderpublishing.com. Publishes hardcover and trade paperback originals. **Publishes 4 titles/year. Receives 100 queries and 75 mss/year. 80% of books from first-time authors; 70% from unagented writers. Pays 9-15% royalty on net receipts. Offers $200-1,000 advance.** Publishes book 4 months after acceptance of ms. Does not accept simultaneous submissions. Responds in 1 month to queries. Book catalog online.

○━ Pathfinder Publishing, Inc. was founded to seek new ways to help people cope with psychological and health problems resulting from illness, accidents, losses or crime.

Nonfiction Self-help. Subjects include creative nonfiction, health/medicine, hobbies, psychology, sociology. Submit complete ms. "We do not open envelopes from people we do not know. We require e-mail proposals or manuscripts now." Reviews artwork/photos as part of ms package. Send photocopies.

Recent Title(s) *When Our Parents Need Us*; *Coffee in the Cereal*.

ℕ PENCIL POINT PRESS, INC.

P.O. Box 634, New Hope PA 18938-0634. (800)356-1299. E-mail: penpoint@ix.netcom.com. Website: www.pencilpointpress.com/index.html. **Acquisitions:** Gene Garone, publisher (all areas). **Publishes 4-12 titles/year. Receives 4-12 queries and 12 mss/year. 100% of books from first-time authors. Pays 5-16% royalty. Pays 5-16% royalty or makes outright purchase by contract.** Publishes book 1 year after acceptance of ms. Accepts simultaneous submissions. Responds in 2 months to proposals. Book catalog free.

○━ Pencil Point publishes educational supplemental materials for teachers of all levels. Currently emphasizing mathematics and science. De-emphasizing language arts.

Nonfiction Prefers supplemental resource materials for teachers grades K-12 and college (especially mathematics). Reference, technical, textbook. Subjects include education, language/literature, music/dance, science. Education subjects, including professional reference, music, science, mathematics, language arts, ESL and special needs. Submit proposal package including outline, 2 sample chapters, memo stating rationale and markets.

Recent Title(s) *Investigations in Geometry Using CABRI Jr. and the Graphing Calculator,* by Aki Margaritas; *Skill and Practice Masters in Algebra Using the TI-84 Graphing Calculator,* by David P. Lawrence; *TI-84 Easy Warm Ups in Pre-Algebra*, by David P. Lawrence.

Tips Audience is K-8 teachers, 9-12 teachers, and college-level supplements. No children's trade books or poetry.

PENMARIN BOOKS, INC.

1044 Magnolia Way, Roseville CA 95661. (916)771-5869. Fax: (916)771-5879. E-mail: penmarin@penmarin.com. Website: www.penmarin.com. **Acquisitions:** Virginia Ray, editorial director. Estab. 1987. Publishes hardcover and trade paperback originals. **Publishes 4 titles/year. Receives 200 queries and 100 mss/year. 40% of books from first-time authors; 60% from unagented writers. Pays 7-15% royalty on retail price. Offers**

$3,000-10,000 advance. Publishes book 1 year after acceptance of ms. Accepts simultaneous submissions. Responds in 2 days to queries; 1 month to proposals. Book catalog and ms guidelines online.

Nonfiction Autobiography, biography, general nonfiction, illustrated book, self-help. Subjects include child guidance/parenting, contemporary culture, health/medicine, history, memoirs, psychology, world affairs. Submit proposal package including outline, 1-3 sample chapters, and all material listed in proposal/submission guidelines on website. Query by e-mail first. Reviews artwork/photos as part of ms package. Send photocopies.

Recent Title(s) *Stepping Into Greatness: Success Is Up to You!*, by Gutierrez (self-help/success); *Every Third House*, by Freed (novel); *Carl Rogers: The Quiet Revolutionary*, by Rogers/Russell (oral history/biography).

PHILOSOPHY DOCUMENTATION CENTER

P.O. Box 7147, Charlottesville VA 22906-7147. (434)220-3300. Fax: (434)220-3301. E-mail: order@pdcnet.org. Website: www.pdcnet.org. **Acquisitions:** Dr. George Leaman, director. Estab. 1966. **Publishes 4 titles/year. Receives 4-6 queries and 4-6 mss/year. 50% of books from first-time authors. Pays 2½-10% royalty. Offers advance.** Publishes book 1 year after acceptance of ms. Does not accept simultaneous submissions. Responds in 2 months to queries. Book catalog free.

- ○→ The Philosophy Documentation Center works in cooperation with publishers, database producers, software developers, journal editors, authors, librarians, and philosophers to create an electronic clearinghouse for philosophical publishing.

Nonfiction Reference, textbook, guidebooks; directories in the field of philosophy. Subjects include philosophy, software. "We want to increase our range of philosophical titles and are especially interested in electronic publishing." Query with SASE, or submit outline.

Recent Title(s) *Proceedings of the World Congress of Philosophy*; *2002-2003 Directory of American Philosophers*.

PICCADILLY BOOKS, LTD.

P.O. Box 25203, Colorado Springs CO 80936-5203. (719)550-9887. Website: www.piccadillybooks.com. **Acquisitions:** Submissions Department. Estab. 1985. Publishes hardcover originals and trade paperback originals and reprints. **Publishes 5-8 titles/year. 70% of books from first-time authors; 95% from unagented writers. Pays 6-10% royalty on retail price.** Publishes book 1 year after acceptance of ms. Accepts simultaneous submissions. Responds only if interested, unless accompanied by a SASE to queries.

- ○→ Picadilly publishes nonfiction, diet, nutrition, and health-related books with a focus on alternative and natural medicine.

Nonfiction How-to, reference, self-help. Subjects include cooking/foods/nutrition, health/medicine, performing arts, writing, small business. "Do your research. Let us know why there is a need for your book, how it differs from other books on the market, and how you will promote the book." No phone calls. Submit outline and sample chapters.

Recent Title(s) *Heart Frauds*, by Charles T. McGee, MD.

Tips "We publish nonfiction, general interest, self-help books currently emphasizing alternative health."

N THE PINE LAKE MEDIA GROUP

P.O. Box 211054, Columbus OH 43221-1054. Website: www.pinelakemedia.com. **Acquisitions:** Keith W. Kimmel, owner. Estab. 2004. Publishes trade paperback originals and mass market paperback originals. **Publishes 5 titles/year. Receives 500 queries and 100 mss/year. 90% of books from first-time authors; 80% from unagented writers. Pays 1-20% royalty on retail price. Royalties are handled on a case-by-case basis depending on many factors. Also work on a set amount per copy sold (i.e. $1.10/copy).** Publishes book 1 year after acceptance of ms. Accepts simultaneous submissions. Responds in 6 months to queries and proposals; 1 year to mss. Book catalog and ms guidelines online.

Nonfiction General nonfiction, humor, reference, scholarly, technical. Subjects include alternative lifestyles, business/economics, community, computers/electronic, government/politics, history, hobbies, money/finance, science, world affairs. "We are looking for titles that go against the grain, that teach people to think independently of the establishment." Query with SASE, or submit proposal package including 3 sample chapters. Indicate whether electronic version of the ms is available. Reviews artwork/photos as part of ms package. Send photocopies.

Fiction Adventure, historical, mystery, regional, political. "We are especially interested in political titles, satire, parody, spoof. No short stories or collections." Query with SASE, or submit proposal package including 3 sample chapters. Indicate whether electronic version of ms is available.

Recent Title(s) *Deception*, by Charles R. Smith (political); *The Gibbs' Place Mystery*, by Richard D. Baldwin (political fiction).

Tips "Our buyers are independent thinkers. They want titles off the beaten path. We hate telephone calls, faxes and emails. Please do not send/make them."

⊘ PIPPIN PRESS

229 E. 85th St., P.O. Box 1347, Gracie Station, New York NY 10028. (212)288-4920. Fax: (908)237-2407. **Acquisitions:** Barbara Francis, publisher and editor-in-chief; Joyce Segal, senior editor. Estab. 1987. Publishes juvenile hardcover originals. **Publishes 4 titles/year. Receives 1,500 queries/year. 80% from unagented writers. Pays royalty. Offers advance.** Publishes book 2 years after acceptance of ms. Does not accept simultaneous submissions. Responds in 3 weeks to queries. Book catalog for 6×9 SASE; ms guidelines for #10 SASE.

○⊓ Pippin publishes general nonfiction and fiction for children ages 4-12.

Nonfiction Biography, children's/juvenile, humor, autobiography. Subjects include animals, memoirs, literature, general nonfiction for children ages 4-12. *No unsolicited mss.* Query with SASE only. Reviews artwork/photos as part of ms package. Send photocopies.

Fiction Historical, humor, mystery. "We're especially looking for small chapter books for 7- to 11-year olds, including those by people of many cultures." Also interested in humorous fiction for ages 7-11. "At this time, we are especially interested in historical novels, 'autobiographical' novels, historical, and literary biographies, and humor." Query with SASE only.

Recent Title(s) *A Visit From the Leopard: Memories of a Ugandan Childhood*, by Catherine Mudibo-Piwang and Edward Frascino; *Abigail's Drum*, by John A. Minahan, illustrated by Robert Quackenbush (historical fiction).

Tips "Read as many of the best children's books published in the last 5 years as you can. We are looking for multi-ethnic fiction and nonfiction for ages 7-10, as well as general fiction for this age group. I would pay particular attention to children's books favorably reviewed in *School Library Journal, The Booklist, The New York Times Book Review*, and *Publishers Weekly.*"

PLANNERS PRESS

Imprint of the American Planning Association, 122 S. Michigan Ave., Chicago IL 60603. Fax: (312)431-9985. E-mail: slewis@planning.org. Website: www.planning.org. **Acquisitions:** Sylvia Lewis, director of publications. Estab. 1978. Publishes hardcover and trade paperback originals. **Publishes 4-6 titles/year. Receives 20 queries and 6-8 mss/year. 50% of books from first-time authors; 100% from unagented writers. Pays 10-12% royalty on retail price. Offers advance.** Publishes book 1 year after acceptance of ms. Does not accept simultaneous submissions. Responds in 1 month to queries; 2 months to proposals and mss. Book catalog and ms guidelines free.

○⊓ "Our books have a narrow audience of city planners and often focus on the tools of city planning."

Nonfiction Technical (public policy and city planning). Subjects include government/politics. Submit 2 sample chapters and TOC. Reviews artwork/photos as part of ms package. Send photocopies.

Recent Title(s) *Redesigning Cities: Principles, Practice, Implementation; Making Places Special: Stories of Real Places Made Better by Planning; Above and Beyond: Visualizing Change in Small Towns and Rural Areas.*

PLANNING/COMMUNICATIONS

7215 Oak Ave., River Forest IL 60305-1935. (708)366-5200. Fax: (708)366-5280. E-mail: dl@planningcommunic ations.com. Website: jobfindersonline.com; dreamitdoit.net. **Acquisitions:** Daniel Lauber, president. Estab. 1979. Publishes hardcover, trade, and mass market paperback originals, trade paperback reprints. **Publishes 3-6 titles/year. Receives 30 queries and 20 mss/year. 50% of books from first-time authors; 100% from unagented writers. Pays 10-16% royalty on net receipts.** Publishes book 1 year after acceptance of ms. Accepts simultaneous submissions. Responds in 3 months to queries. Book catalog for $2 or free on website; ms guidelines online.

○⊓ Planning/Communications publishes books on careers, improving your life, dream fulfillment, ending discrimination, sociology, urban planning, and politics.

Nonfiction Self-help. Subjects include business/economics (careers), education, government/politics, money/finance, sociology, ending discrimination, careers, résumés, cover letters, interviewing. Submit outline, 3 sample chapters, SASE. Reviews artwork/photos as part of ms package. Send photocopies.

Recent Title(s) *Dream It Do It: Inspiring Stories of Dreams Come True*, by Sharon Cook and Graciela Sholander; *How to Get a Job in Europe*, by Cheryl Matherly and Robert Sanborn; *International Job Finder*, by Daniel Lauber and Kraig Rice.

Tips "Our editorial mission is to publish books that can make a difference in people's lives—books of substance, not glitz."

Ⓝ PLASTIC SUGAR PRESS

P.O. Box 55, New York NY 10276. E-mail: info@plasticsugar.com. Website: www.plasticsugar.com. **Acquisitions:** Nicole Hughes, publisher (fiction, nonfiction, cultural studies, politics, media). Estab. 2004. Publishes trade paperback originals. **Publishes 5 titles/year. Receives 650 queries and 900 mss/year. 70% of books from first-time authors; 85% from unagented writers. Pays 7-12% royalty on retail price.** Publishes book

9 months after acceptance of ms. Accepts simultaneous submissions. Responds in 2 months. Book catalog and ms guidelines online.

Nonfiction Submit proposal package including 3 sample chapters, synopsis, chapter outline. Reviews artwork/photos as part of ms package. Send photocopies.

Fiction Submit proposal package including 3 sample chapters, synopsis, chapter outline.

Ⓝ Ⓞ PLATYPUS MEDIA, LLC

627 A St. NE, Washington DC 20002. (202)546-1674. Fax: (202)546-2356. E-mail: info@platypusmedia.com. Website: www.platypusmedia.com. **Acquisitions:** Wendy Catbagan, editorial assistant (children's—early childhood and science, birth, lactation). Estab. 2000. Publishes hardcover and trade paperback originals. **Publishes 3-4 titles/year. Receives 100 queries and 250 mss/year. 5% of books from first-time authors; 100% from unagented writers. Pays royalty on wholesale price, or makes outright purchase.** Publishes book 9 months after acceptance of ms. Accepts simultaneous submissions. Responds in 2-4 months. Book catalog free; ms guidelines online.

Oⲛ "All content should focus on family closeness and child development."

Nonfiction Booklets, children's/juvenile. Subjects include child guidance/parenting, education, health/medicine, women's issues/studies, breastfeeding, childbirth, children's science books. Query with SASE. *All unsolicited mss returned unopened.* Reviews artwork/photos as part of ms package. Send photocopies.

Fiction Juvenile. Query with SASE. *All unsolicited mss returned unopened.*

Recent Title(s) *If My Mom Were a Platypus*, by Dia L. Michels; *Look What I See! Where Can I Be? Visiting China*, by Dia L. Michels; *I Was Born to Be a Brother*, by Zaydek G. Michels-Gualtieri.

Tips "Audience includes parents, children, teachers, and parenting professionals. We publish just a handful of books each year and most are generated in-house."

PLEXUS PUBLISHING, INC.

143 Old Marlton Pike, Medford NJ 08055-8750. (609)654-6500. Fax: (609)654-4309. E-mail: jbryans@infotoday.com. **Acquisitions:** John B. Bryans, editor-in-chief. Estab. 1977. Publishes hardcover and paperback originals. **Publishes 4-5 titles/year. 70% of books from first-time authors; 90% from unagented writers. Pays 10-15% royalty on net receipts. Offers $500-1,000 advance.** Accepts simultaneous submissions. Responds in 3 months to proposals. Book catalog and ms guidelines for 10×13 SAE with 4 first-class stamps.

Oⲛ Plexus publishes mainly regional-interest (southern New Jersey) fiction and nonfiction including mysteries, field guides, history. Also health/medicine, biology, ecology, botany, astronomy.

Nonfiction How-to, illustrated book, reference, textbook, natural, historical references, and scholarly. Subjects include agriculture/horticulture, education, gardening, health/medicine, history (southern New Jersey), nature/environment, recreation, regional (southern New Jersey), science, botany, medicine, biology, ecology, astronomy. "We will consider any book on a nature/biology subject, particularly those of a reference (permanent) nature that would be of lasting value to high school and college audiences, and/or the general reading public (ages 14 and up). Authors should have authentic qualifications in their subject area, but qualifications may be by experience as well as academic training." Also interested in mss of about 20-40 pages in length for feature articles in *Biology Digest* (guidelines available for SASE). No gardening, philosophy, or psychology; generally not interested in travel but will consider travel that gives sound ecological information. Query with SASE. Reviews artwork/photos as part of ms package. Send photocopies.

Fiction Mysteries and literary novels with a strong regional (southern New Jersey) angle. Query with SASE.

Recent Title(s) *Boardwalk Empire: The Birth, High Times, and Corruption of Atlantic City*, by Nelson Johnson; *Wildflowers of the Pine Barrens of New Jersey*, by Howard P. Boyd.

POSSIBILITY PRESS

One Oakglade Circle, Hummelstown PA 17036-9525. (717)566-0468. Fax: (717)566-6423. E-mail: possibilitypress@aol.com. Website: www.possibilitypress.com. **Acquisitions:** Mike Markowski, publisher; Marjie Markowski, editor-in-chief. Estab. 1981. Publishes trade paperback originals. **Publishes 4-6 titles/year. 90% of books from first-time authors; 95% from unagented writers. Royalties vary.** Responds in 2 months to queries. Ms guidelines online.

Imprints Aeronautical Publishers; Possibility Press.

Oⲛ "Our mission is to help the people of the world grow and become the best they can be, through the written and spoken word."

Nonfiction How-to, self-help, inspirational. Subjects include psychology (pop psychology), business, success/motivation, inspiration, entrepreneurship, sales marketing, network, MLM and home-based business topics, and human interest success stories. Prefers submissions to be mailed. Include SASE.

Fiction Parables that teach lessons about life and success.

Recent Title(s) *The Power of Talking Out Loud to Yourself*, by Bill Wayne; *The Power of Positive Productivity*, by William E. Hensley; *The Power to Make It Happen*, by William I. McGrane.

Tips "Our focus is on creating and publishing short- to medium-length bestsellers written by authors who speak and consult. We're looking for kind and compassionate authors who are passionate about making a difference in the world, and will champion their mission to do so."

✷ THE POST-APOLLO PRESS

35 Marie St., Sausalito CA 94965. (415)332-1458. Fax: (415)332-8045. E-mail: postapollo@earthlink.net. Website: www.postapollopress.com. **Acquisitions:** Simone Fattal, publisher. Estab. 1982. Publishes trade paperback originals and reprints. **Publishes 4 titles/year. Pays 5-7% royalty on wholesale price.** Publishes book 1½ years after acceptance of ms. Responds in 3 months to queries. Book catalog and ms guidelines for #10 SASE.
• *Not accepting new mss.*

Nonfiction Essay; letters. Subjects include art/architecture, language/literature, translation, women's issues/studies. Query.

Fiction Experimental, literary (plays), spiritual. "Many of our books are first translations into English." No juvenile, horror, sports, or romance. Submit 1 sample chapter, SASE. "The Post-Apollo Press is not accepting manuscripts or queries currently due to a full publishing schedule."

Poetry Experimental/translations.

Recent Title(s) *Memnoir*, by Jack Retallack; *Self-Destruction*, by Laura Moriarty; *Mind-God and the Properties of Nitrogen*, by Fouad Gabriel Naffah, translated from the French by Norma Cole.

Tips "We are interested in writers with a fresh and original vision. We often publish foreign literature that is already well known in its original country, but new to the American reader."

PRINCETON BOOK CO.

614 Route 130, Hightstown NJ 08520. (609)426-0602. Fax: (609)426-1344. E-mail: pbc@dancehorizons.com. Website: www.dancehorizons.com. **Acquisitions:** Charles Woodford, president (dance and adult nonfiction). Publishes hardcover and trade paperback originals and reprints. **Publishes 5-6 titles/year. Receives 50 queries and 100 mss/year. 80% of books from first-time authors; 100% from unagented writers. Pays negotiable royalty on net receipts.** Publishes book 9-12 months after acceptance of ms. Accepts simultaneous submissions. Responds in 1 week to queries and proposals. Book catalog free on request or online; ms guidelines online.

Imprints Dance Horizons; Elysian Editions.

Nonfiction "We publish all sorts of dance-related books including ones on fitness and health." Biography, children's/juvenile, gift book, how-to, illustrated book, reference. Subjects include music/dance. Submit proposal package including outline, 3 sample chapters. Reviews artwork/photos as part of ms package. Send photocopies.

Recent Title(s) *The Nutcracker Backstage*, by Angela Whitehill and William Noble; *The Pointe Book, 2nd Ed.*, by Janice Barringer and Sarah Schlesinger; *Pelvic Power*, by Eric Franklin.

PUCKERBRUSH PRESS

76 Main St., Orono ME 04473-1430. (207)581-3832. **Acquisitions:** Constance Hunting, publisher/editor. Estab. 1971. Publishes trade paperback originals and reprints of literary fiction and poetry. **Publishes 3-4 titles/year. Pays 10-15% royalty on wholesale price.** Does not accept simultaneous submissions. Responds in 1 month to queries; 2 months to proposals; 3 months to mss. Book catalog for large SASE and 34¢; ms guidelines for SASE.

Nonfiction Subjects include language/literature, translation, belles lettres. Query with SASE.

Fiction Literary, short story collections. Submit complete ms, and include cover letter.

Poetry Highest literary quality. Submit complete ms.

Recent Title(s) *At Water's Edge*, by Margaret Shipley (poetry).

Tips "No religious subjects, crime per se, tired prose. For sophisticated readers who retain love of literature. Maine writers continue to be featured."

PULPLIT PUBLISHING

411A Highland Ave., #376, Somerville MA 02144-2516. E-mail: editor@pulplit.com. Submissions E-mail: submissions@pulplit.com. Website: www.pulplit.com. **Acquisitions:** John O'Brien, editor-in-chief (fiction, nonfiction, and criticism); Ben Henry, poetry editor. Estab. 2002. Publishes hardcover, trade paperback, and electronic originals. **Publishes 4 titles/year. 100% of books from first-time authors; 100% from unagented writers. Pays 5-10% royalty on wholesale price.** Publishes book 3 months after acceptance of ms. Accepts simultaneous submissions. Responds in 1 month to queries and proposals; 3 months to mss. Book catalog and ms guidelines online.

Nonfiction Booklets, humor, scholarly. Subjects include humanities. Submit complete ms online. Reviews artwork/photos as part of ms package.

Fiction Adventure, comic books, erotica, experimental, fantasy, gothic, hi-lo, historical, humor, juvenile, literary, mainstream/contemporary, plays, poetry, science fiction, short story collections, western, young adult. Want edgy, smart, hip, and sassy. Submit complete ms online.

Poetry "To give you some idea, we enjoy Simic, Russell Edson, Nash, Kerouac, and Ferlinghetti to name but a few. We look for humor, topic, but always resonance and never for meter. Flow is more important than anything." Submit complete ms.

Recent Title(s) *The Kabbalah Killings*, by Arthur Asa Berger.

Tips "We're tiny. We sell primarily through the website. We're risky but full of heart."

RED SAGE PUBLISHING, INC.

P.O. Box 4844, Seminole FL 33775. (727)391-3847. Website: www.redsagepub.com. **Acquisitions:** Alexandria Kendall, publisher; Judith Pich, executive editor. Estab. 1995. **Publishes 4 titles/year. 50% of books from first-time authors.** Does not accept simultaneous submissions. Ms guidelines online.

○┐ Publishes books of romance fiction, written for the adventurous woman.

Recent Title(s) *Secrets, Volume 10* (an anthology of 4 novellas); *Forever Kissed* (sexy paranormal featuring vampires).

Tips "We define romantic erotica. Sensuous, bold, spicy, untamed, hot, and sometimes politically incorrect, *Secrets* stories concentrate on the sophisticated, highly intense adult relationship. We look for character-driven stories that concentrate on the love and sexual relationship between a hero and the heroine. Red Sage expanded into single-title books in 2004. Author voice, excellent writing, and strong emotions are all important ingredients to the fiction we publish."

REFERENCE PRESS INTERNATIONAL

P.O. Box 4126, Greenwich CT 06831. (203)622-6860. **Acquisitions:** Cheryl Lacoff, senior editor. Publishes hardcover and trade paperback originals. **Publishes 6 titles/year. Receives 50 queries and 20 mss/year. 75% of books from first-time authors; 90% from unagented writers. Pays royalty, or makes outright purchase. Offers determined by project advance.** Publishes book 6 months after acceptance of ms. Accepts simultaneous submissions. Responds in 3 months to queries.

○┐ Reference Press specializes in gift books, instructional, reference, and how-to titles.

Nonfiction Gift book, how-to, illustrated book, multimedia (audio, video, CD-ROM), reference, technical, instructional. Subjects include anything related to the fine arts or crafts field. "Follow the guidelines as stated concerning subjects and types of books we're looking for." Query with SASE, or submit outline, 1-3 sample chapters. Reviews artwork/photos as part of ms package. photocopies, not originals.

Recent Title(s) *Who's Who in the Peace Corps* (alumni directory).

Ⓝ RICHBORO PRESS

P.O. Box 6, Southampton PA 18966. (215)355-6084. Fax: (215)364-2212. **Acquisitions:** George Moore, editor. Estab. 1979. Publishes hardcover and trade paperback originals, and software. **Publishes 4 titles/year. 90% from unagented writers. Pays 15% royalty on retail price. Offers advance.** Publishes book 1 year after acceptance of ms. Does not accept simultaneous submissions. Responds in 2 months to queries. Book catalog free; ms guidelines for $1 and #10 SASE.

Nonfiction Cookbook, how-to. Subjects include cooking/foods/nutrition, gardening, software. Query with SASE. Prefers complete ms via electronic media.

RISING STAR PRESS

2532 NW Shields, Bend OR 97701. (541)330-9119. Fax: (541)389-5768. E-mail: editor@risingstarpress.com. Website: www.risingstarpress.com. **Acquisitions:** Acquisitions Editor. Publishes hardcover and trade paperback originals. **Publishes 3-4 titles/year. Pays 10-15% royalty on wholesale price. Offers advance.** Publishes book 9 months after acceptance of ms. Accepts simultaneous submissions. Responds in 2 months to proposals. Ms guidelines online.

Nonfiction Biography, reference, self-help. Subjects include education, health/medicine, language/literature, philosophy, regional, religion, sociology. "Rising Star Press publishes books that cause people to think and be inspired to act in some positive and proactive way to improve their own life as well as the lives of those around them. Authors are treated as partners in the production and marketing process. Books are selected based on the combination of fit with the company mission, consistency between the author's words and life, and marketability." Currently emphasizing social and religious issues. De-emphasizing metaphysical, personal finance. "Authors need to be able to answer these questions: Who will benefit from reading this? Why? Mistakes writers often make are not identifying their target market early and shaping the work to address it." Query with SASE, or submit outline, 2 sample chapters. Must include e-mail address with query/proposal.

Fiction "Must illuminate topics, as listed for nonfiction submissions, for the reader who is more drawn to fiction writing."

Recent Title(s) *Dancing With Diagnosis—Steps for Taking the Lead When Facing Cancer*, by Michelle Waters; *The Dishonest Church*, by Jack Good; *Warrior Mothers—Stories to Awaken the Flames of the Heart*, by Thais Mazur.

[N] RIVER'S BEND PRESS

P.O. Box 606, Stillwater MN 55082. E-mail: editor@riversbendpress.com. Website: www.riversbendpress.com. **Acquisitions:** Jane Esbensen. Estab. 2001. Publishes hardcover, trade paperback, and mass market paperback originals. **Publishes 4 titles/year. Receives 250 queries and 200 mss/year. 90% of books from first-time authors; 100% from unagented writers. Pays 15-20% royalty on net receipts. Offers $500 advance.** Publishes book 9-12 months after acceptance of ms. Accepts simultaneous submissions. Responds in 3-6 weeks to queries and proposals; 3-6 months to mss. Book catalog and ms guidelines online.

Nonfiction Autobiography, biography, general nonfiction, humor, illustrated book, reference, scholarly. Subjects include Americana, anthropology/archeology, art/architecture, creative nonfiction, ethnic, history, hobbies, humanities, language/literature, memoirs, military/war, translation, objectivism. No children's stories, religious stories, or self-help/abuse/recovery stories. Query with SASE, or submit first 3 sample chapters. Reviews artwork/photos as part of ms package. Send photocopies.

Fiction Adventure, comic books, historical, humor, literary, mainstream/contemporary, military/war, mystery, short story collections, suspense, western, young adult, gen-X. No children's stories, religious stories or epic battles between heaven and hell.

Recent Title(s) *Irma: Memoirs of a Vampire Gone Dry*, by Laine Jacob (fiction); *Pick Up Stick City*, by Steve Semken (fiction); *Motor Oil for the Car Guy's Soul*, by Kevin Clemens (essay).

Tips "We are willing to consider anything that's well written, except heaven/hell stories and demons."

[N] ROLENTA PRESS

P.O. Box 1365, Springfield NJ 07081-5365. Phone/Fax: (973)564-7252. E-mail: info@rolentapress.com. Website: www.rolentapress.com. Publisher: Leonard Herman. Estab. 1994. Publishes trade paperback originals and reprints. **Publishes 5 titles/year. Pays 12-15% royalty on wholesale price.** Publishes book 6 months after acceptance of ms. Accepts simultaneous submissions. Responds in 1 month to queries and proposals; 2-3 months to mss. Book catalog online.

    Oⁿ "Submissions must be video or computer-game related. No stragey guides or how to break into the business."

Nonfiction Autobiography, biography, coffee table book, general nonfiction, how-to, reference, scholarly, technical, textbook. Subjects include computers/electronic, software. Query with SASE, or submit proposal package including outline. Reviews artwork/photos as part of ms package. Send photocopies.

Recent Title(s) *Videogames: In the Beginning*, by Ralph H. Baer; *Phoenix: The Fall & Rise of Videogames*, by Leonard Herman.

Tips "Audience includes gamers, collectors, and students. Know your subject. It helps to be an authority in the field. We are publishing books by the inventor of videogames and the co-founder of the first videogame magazine."

ROSE PUBLISHING

4455 Torrance Blvd., #259, Torrance CA 90503. (310)370-7152. Fax: (310)370-7492. E-mail: rosepubl@aol.com. Website: www.rose-publishing.com. **Acquisitions:** Carol R. Witte, editor. **Publishes 25-30 titles/year. 2% of books from first-time authors; 100% from unagented writers. Makes outright purchase.** Publishes book 18 months after acceptance of ms. Accepts simultaneous submissions. Responds in 3 months to proposals; 2 months to mss. Book catalog for $1.29 in postage.

    Oⁿ "We publish Bible reference materials in wall chart, pamphlet, and Powerpoint form, easy-to-understand and appealing to children, teens or adults on Bible study, prayer, basic beliefs, Scripture memory, salvation, sharing the gospel, worship, abstinence, creation, apologetics, marriage, family, grief, and comfort."

Nonfiction Reference, pamphlets, group study books. Subjects include religion, science, sex, spirituality, Bible studies, Christian history, counseling aids, cults/occult, curriculum, Christian discipleship, evangelism/witnessing, Christian living, marriage, prayer, creation, singles issues. No fiction or poetry. Submit proposal package including outline, photocopies of chart contents or poster artwork. Reviews artwork/photos as part of ms package. Send photocopies.

Recent Title(s) *Islam and Christianity*; *Answers to Evolution*; *How to Study the Bible*.

Tips Audience includes both church (Bible study leaders, Sunday school teachers [all ages], pastors, youth leaders), and home (parents, home schoolers, children, youth, high school, and college). Open to topics that supplement Sunday School curriculum or Bible study, junior high creation materials, Bible study, reasons to believe, books of the Bible.

SAFER SOCIETY PRESS

P.O. Box 340, Brandon VT 05733. (802)247-3132. Fax: (802)247-4233. Website: www.safersociety.org. **Acquisitions:** Steve Zeoli, director of public relations. Estab. 1985. Publishes trade paperback originals. **Publishes 3-4 titles/year. Receives 15-20 queries and 15-20 mss/year. 90% of books from first-time authors; 100% from unagented writers. Pays 5% royalty on retail price.** Publishes book 1 year after acceptance of ms. Accepts simultaneous submissions. Book catalog free; ms guidelines online.

O⤳ "Our mission is the prevention and treatment of sexual abuse."

Nonfiction Self-help (sex abuse prevention and treatment). Subjects include psychology (sexual abuse). "We are a small, nonprofit, niche press. We want well-researched books dealing with any aspect of sexual abuse: treatment, prevention, understanding; works on subject in Spanish." Query with SASE, submit proposal package, or complete ms. Reviews artwork/photos as part of ms package. Send photocopies.

Recent Title(s) *Supervision of the Sex Offender: Community Management, Risk Assessment & Treatment*, by Georgia F. Cumming and Robert J. McGrath.

Tips Audience is persons working in mental health/persons needing self-help books. Pays small fees or low royalties.

ST. BEDE'S PUBLICATIONS

St. Scholastica Priory, P.O. Box 545, Petersham MA 01366-0545. (978)724-3213. Fax: (978)724-3216. President: Sister Mary Clare Vincent. **Acquisitions:** Acquisitions Editor. Estab. 1977. Publishes hardcover originals, trade paperback originals and reprints. **Publishes 3-4 titles/year. 30-40% of books from first-time authors; 98% from unagented writers. Pays 5-10% royalty on wholesale price, or retail price.** Publishes book 2 years after acceptance of ms. Accepts simultaneous submissions. Responds in 2 months to queries. Book catalog and ms guidelines for 9×12 SAE with 2 first-class stamps.

O⤳ St. Bede's Publications is owned and operated by the Roman Catholic nuns of St. Scholastica Priory. The publications are seen as an apostolic outreach. Their mission is to make available to everyone quality books on spiritual subjects such as prayer, scripture, theology, and the lives of holy people.

Nonfiction Textbook (theology). Subjects include history, philosophy, religion, sex, spirituality, translation, prayer, hagiography, theology, church history, related lives of saints. No submissions unrelated to religion, theology, spirituality, etc., and no poetry, fiction, or children's books. Does not return submissions without adequate postage. Query, or submit outline and sample chapters with SASE.

Recent Title(s) *Reading the Gospels with Gregory the Great*, translated by Santha Bhattacharji; *Why Catholic?*, by Father John Pasquini.

Tips "There seems to be a growing interest in monasticism among lay people, and we will be publishing more books in this area. For our theology/philosophy titles our audience is scholars, colleges and universities, seminaries, etc. For our other titles (i.e. prayer, spirituality, lives of saints, etc.) the audience is above-average readers interested in furthering their knowledge in these areas."

SALINA BOOKSHELF

1254 W. University Ave., Suite 130, Flagstaff AZ 86001. (928)527-0070. Fax: (928)526-0386. E-mail: jessier@salinabookshelf.com. Website: www.salinabookshelf.com. **Acquisitions:** Jessie Ruffenach, editor. Publishes trade paperback originals and reprints. **Publishes 4-5 titles/year. 50% of books from first-time authors; 100% from unagented writers. Pays varying royalty. Offers advance.** Publishes book 1 year after acceptance of ms. Accepts simultaneous submissions. Responds in 3 months to queries.

Nonfiction Children's/juvenile, textbook (Navajo language). Subjects include education, ethnic, science. "We publish childrens' bilingual readers. Nonfiction should be appropriate to science and social studies curriculum grades 3-8." Query with SASE. Reviews artwork/photos as part of ms package. Send photocopies.

Fiction Juvenile. "Submissions should be in English or Navajo. All our books relate to the Navajo language and culture." Query with SASE.

Poetry "We accept poetry in English/Southwest language for children." Submit 3 sample poems.

Recent Title(s) *Dine Bizaad: Speak, Read, Write Navajo*, by Irvy W. Goossen.

SALVO PRESS

P.O. Box 7396, Beaverton OR 97007. E-mail: info@salvopress.com. Website: www.salvopress.com. **Acquisitions:** Scott Schmidt, publisher. Estab. 1998. Publishes paperback originals and e-books in most formats. **Publishes 3 titles/year. Receives 500 queries/year. 50% of books from first-time authors; 80% from unagented writers. Pays 10% royalty.** Publishes book 9 months after acceptance of ms. Does not accept simultaneous submissions. Responds in 1 month to queries; 2 months to mss. Book catalog and ms guidelines online.

Fiction Adventure, literary, mystery (amateur sleuth, police procedural, private/hard boiled), science fiction (hard science/technological), suspense, espionage, thriller. "Our needs change. Check our website." Query with SASE.

Recent Title(s) *Silver Thaw & Selected Stories*, by Ron Johnson; *House of the Rising Sun*, by Chuck Hustmyre; *Poised to Kill*, by Brian Lutterman.

[N] SANTA ANA RIVER PRESS

P.O. Box 5473, Norco CA 92860-8016. E-mail: admin@santaanariverpress.com. Submissions E-mail: editorial@santaanariverpress.com. Website: www.santaanariverpress.com. Estab. 2003. Publishes trade paperback originals and reprints. **Publishes 6 titles/year. Pays 10-25% royalty on wholesale price. Advance varies.** Accepts simultaneous submissions. Responds in 1 month. Ms guidelines online.

○━ "Our focus, at least for the present, is California history. This includes traditional nonfiction, fiction, and biography set in California."

Nonfiction Biography, general nonfiction. Subjects include history, regional. Submit proposal package and cover letter describing the book and first 50 pages, or submit complete ms. Prefers electronic submissions. Reviews artwork/photos as part of ms package.

Fiction Historical, regional. Historical fiction set in California only. Submit proposal package with cover letter describing the book and the first 50 pages, or submit complete ms. Prefers electronic submissions.

Recent Title(s) *Life by Land and Sea*, by Prentice Mulford (humorous memoir); *Sleeping Fires*, by Gertrude Atherton (melodramatic Victorian novel).

Tips "We prefer to receive completed manuscripts or the first 50 pages by e-mail in a Microsoft Word attachment or plain text, accompanied by a cover letter describing the book. Material submitted by mail will not be returned. We set a high standard for literary quality, but we welcome first-time authors and experimental approaches."

[N] SOCIETY OF MANUFACTURING ENGINEERS

One SME Dr., P.O. Box 930, Dearborn MI 48121. (313)425-3280. Fax: (313)425-3417. E-mail: sbollinger@sme.org. Website: www.sme.org. **Acquisitions:** Manager. Publishes hardcover and trade paperback originals. **Publishes 6 titles/year. Receives 20 queries and 10 mss/year. 90% of books from first-time authors; 100% from unagented writers. Pays 5-10% royalty on wholesale or retail price.** Publishes book 8 months after acceptance of ms. Responds in 1 month. Book catalog and ms guidelines free or online.

Nonfiction "Seeking manuscripts that would assist manufacturing practitioners in increasing their productivity, quality, and/or efficiency." Technical, textbook. Subjects include engineering, industry. Query with SASE. Reviews artwork/photos as part of ms package. Send photocopies.

Recent Title(s) *Lean Manufacturing for the Small Shop*; *Quick Die Change*.

Tips Audience is "manufacturing practitioners and management, individuals wishing to advance their careers in the industry or to enhance productivity, quality, and efficiency within a manufacturing operation."

⊘ STAND! PUBLISHING

2744 S. Seneca, Suite T-12, Wichita KS 67207. E-mail: standbooks@yahoo.com. **Acquisitions:** Jheri Aubrey, editor. Estab. 2000. Publishes hardcover and trade paperback originals. **Publishes 5-10 titles/year. 99% of books from first-time authors; 100% from unagented writers. Pays 5-10% royalty on retail price. Offers $250-500 advance.** Publishes book 1 year after acceptance of ms. Accepts simultaneous submissions. Responds in 1 month to queries; 2 months to proposals. Book catalog for #10 SASE; ms guidelines online.

Nonfiction Biography, children's/juvenile, general nonfiction, self-help. Subjects include alternative lifestyles, anthropology/archeology, community, contemporary culture, creative nonfiction, ethnic, gay/lesbian, government/politics, history, humanities, multicultural, religion, sex, social sciences, women's issues/studies, world affairs. The current publishing program emphasizes multicultural interests, anthropology, current events, gay/lesbian/gender issues, religious interests and societal concerns, and women's studies/interests. Query with SASE. *All unsolicited mss returned unopened.* Reviews artwork/photos as part of ms package. Send photocopies or If color, send color photocopies.

Recent Title(s) *Natural Blues*, by Jheri Shayler; *The World I Know*, by Melanie Price; *Southern Ritual*, by Nella Banks.

Tips "Query with a short overview of the book's main theme(s), also include some background on the author or contributors. If we like the sound of a proposal, we will contact you to request sample sections or a completed manuscript."

STONE BRIDGE PRESS

P.O. Box 8208, Berkeley CA 94707. (510)524-8732. Fax: (510)524-8711. E-mail: sbpedit@stonebridge.com. Website: www.stonebridge.com. **Acquisitions:** Peter Goodman, publisher. Estab. 1989. Publishes hardcover and trade paperback originals. **Publishes 6 titles/year. Receives 100 queries and 75 mss/year. 15-20% of books from first-time authors; 90% from unagented writers. Pays royalty on wholesale price. Offers variable advance.** Publishes book 2 years after acceptance of ms. Accepts simultaneous submissions. Responds in 4 months to queries; 6 months to proposals; 8 months to mss. Book catalog for 2 first-class stamps and SASE; ms guidelines online.

Imprints The Rock Spring Collection of Japanese Literature.

O─ Stone Bridge Press strives "to publish and distribute high-quality informational tools about Japan." Currently emphasizing art/design, spirituality. De-emphasizing business, current affairs, fiction.

Nonfiction How-to, reference, popular culture. Subjects include art/architecture, business/economics, ethnic, language/literature, philosophy, travel, popular culture. "We publish Japan- (and some Asia-) related books only." Query with SASE. Reviews artwork/photos as part of ms package. Send photocopies.

Fiction "Primarily looking at material relating to Japan. Translations only." Query with SASE.

Recent Title(s) *The Yakuza Movie Book*; *Cruising the Anime City*.

Tips Audience is "intelligent, worldly readers with an interest in Japan based on personal need or experience. No children's books or commercial fiction. Realize that interest in Japan is a moving target. Please don't submit yesterday's trends or rely on a view of Japan that is outmoded. Stay current!"

STONEYDALE PRESS

523 Main St., Stevensville MT 59870. (406)777-2729. Fax: (406)777-2521. E-mail: daleburk@montana.com. Website: www.stoneydale.com. **Acquisitions:** Dale A. Burk, publisher. Estab. 1976. Publishes hardcover and trade paperback originals. **Publishes 4-6 titles/year. Receives 40-50 queries and 6-8 mss/year. 90% from unagented writers. Pays 12-15% royalty. Offers advance.** Publishes book 18 months after acceptance of ms. Does not accept simultaneous submissions. Responds in 2 months to queries. Book catalog available.

O─ "We seek to publish the best available source books on big game hunting, historical reminiscence, and outdoor recreation in the Northern Rocky Mountain region."

Nonfiction How-to (hunting books). Subjects include regional, sports, historical reminiscences. Query with SASE.

Recent Title(s) *We Called This Creek Traveller's Rest*, by The Discovery Writers; *Mule Tracks: The Last of the Story*, by Howard Copenhaver; *Hunting Chukar*, by Richard O'Toole.

STRIDER NOLAN PUBLISHING, INC.

68 S. Main St., Doylestown PA 18901. (215)887-3821. Fax: (215)340-3926. E-mail: stridernolanmedia@yahoo.c om. Website: www.stridernolanmedia.com. VP Marketing & Development: Jill S. Katz. President: Michael S. Katz. Publishes hardcover, trade paperback, and electronic originals. **Publishes 5-10 titles/year. Receives 50-100 queries and 25-75 mss/year. 50% of books from first-time authors; 50% from unagented writers. Pays royalty on retail price.** Accepts simultaneous submissions. Responds in 2 months. Book catalog and ms guidelines online.

Nonfiction Children's/juvenile, coffee table book, cookbook, general nonfiction, how-to, illustrated book, reference, scholarly, self-help. Subjects include Americana, animals, art/architecture, child guidance/parenting, cooking/foods/nutrition, creative nonfiction, health/medicine, history, hobbies, nature/environment, New Age, philosophy, recreation, sports, women's issues/studies, martial arts. Query with SASE. Reviews artwork/photos as part of ms package. Send photocopies.

Fiction Adventure, experimental, fantasy, gothic, historical, horror, humor, juvenile, mainstream/contemporary, military/war, mystery, occult, picture books, science fiction, short story collections, spiritual, sports, suspense, western, young adult, martial arts. Query with SASE.

SUCCESS PUBLISHING

3419 Dunham Rd., Warsaw NY 14569-9735. **Acquisitions:** Allan H. Smith, president (home-based business); Ginger Smith (business); Dana Herbison (home/craft); Robin Garretson (fiction). Estab. 1982. Publishes mass market paperback originals. **Publishes 6 titles/year. Receives 10 mss/year. 90% of books from first-time authors; 100% from unagented writers. Pays 7-12% royalty. Offers $500-1,000 advance.** Publishes book 10 months after acceptance of ms. Accepts simultaneous submissions. Responds in 2 months to queries. Book catalog and ms guidelines for #10 SAE with 2 first-class stamps.

O─ Success publishes guides that focus on the needs of the home entrepreneur to succeed as a viable business. Currently emphasizing starting a new business. De-emphasizing self-help/motivation books. Success Publishing notes that it is looking for ghostwriters.

Nonfiction Children's/juvenile, how-to, self-help. Subjects include business/economics, child guidance/parenting, hobbies, money/finance, craft/home-based business. "We are looking for books on how-to subjects such as home business and sewing." Query with SASE.

Recent Title(s) *How to Find a Date/Mate*, by Dana Herbison.

Tips ''Our audience is made up of housewives, hobbyists, and owners of home-based businesses.''

SWEDENBORG FOUNDATION PUBLISHERS
320 North Church St., West Chester PA 19380. (610)430-3222. Fax: (610)430-7982. E-mail: editor@swedenborg. com. Website: www.swedenborg.com. **Acquisitions:** Mary Lou Bertucci, senior editor. Estab. 1849. Publishes trade paperback originals and reprints. **Publishes 5 titles/year.** Does not accept simultaneous submissions. Responds in 1 month to queries; 3 months to proposals and mss. Book catalog free; ms guidelines online.
Imprints Chrysalis Books; Swedenborg Foundation Press.

> ○━ ''The Swedenborg Foundation publishes books by and about Emanuel Swedenborg (1688-1772), his ideas, how his ideas have influenced others, and related topics. A Chrysalis book is a spiritually focused book presented with a nonsectarian perspective that appeals to open-minded, well-educated seekers of all traditions. Appropriate topics include—but are not limited to—science, mysticism, spiritual growth and development, wisdom traditions, healing and spirituality, as well as subjects that explore Swedenborgian concepts, such as: near-death experience, angels, Biblical interpretation, mysteries of good and evil, etc. Although Chrysalis Books explore topics of general spirituality, a work must actively engage the thought of Emanuel Swedenborg and show an understanding of his philosophy in order to be accepted for publication.''

Nonfiction Self-help, spiritual growth and development. Subjects include philosophy, psychology, religion, science. Query with SASE, or submit proposal package including outline, sample chapters, synopsis. ''I personally prefer e-mail.'' Reviews artwork/photos as part of ms package. Send photocopies.
Recent Title(s) *Healing as a Sacred Path: A Story of Personal, Medical, and Spiritual Transformation*, by L. Robert Keck; *Emanuel Swedenborg: Visionary Savant in the Age of Reason*, by Ernst Benz; *Kant on Swedenborg*, edited and translated by Gregory Johnson.

Ⓝ THE SYSTEMSWARE CORPORATION
973 Russell Ave., Suite D, Gaithersburg MD 20879. (301)948-4890. Fax: (301)926-4243. **Acquisitions:** Pat White, editor. Estab. 1987. Does not accept simultaneous submissions.
Nonfiction Technical, textbook. Subjects include computers/electronic, software. ''We specialize in innovative books and periodicals on Knowledge Engineering or Applied Artificial Intelligence and Knowledge Based Systems. We also develop intelligent procurement-related software packages for large procurement systems.'' Query with SASE.

Ⓝ TAMARACK BOOKS, INC.
P.O. Box 190313, Boise ID 83719. (208)922-2229. Fax: (208)922-5880. President/Owner: Kathy Gaudry. Publishes trade paperback originals and reprints. **Publishes 3-5 titles/year. Pays 5-15% royalty. Offers advance.** Does not accept simultaneous submissions. Responds in 4 months to queries; 6 months to mss.

> ○━ ''We publish nonfiction history of the American West and are avidly seeking women's books. Time period preference is for pre-1900s.'' Currently emphasizing ''pioneer women who have made a difference, whether they have name recognition or not.''

Nonfiction Illustrated book. Subjects include history, regional. ''We are looking for manuscripts for a popular audience, but based on solid research. We specialize in mountain man, women's issues, and outlaw history prior to 1940 in the West, but will look at any good manuscript on Western history prior to 1940.'' Query with SASE, or submit outline.
Recent Title(s) *Competitive Struggle, America's Western Fur Trading Posts, 1764-1865*, R.G. Robertson.
Tips ''We look for authors who want to actively participate in the marketing of their books.''

Ⓝ THREE FORKS BOOKS
Imprint of The Globe Pequot Press, 825 Great Northern Blvd., Suites 327 & 328, Helena MT 59601. (406)442-6597. Fax: (406)457-5461. Website: www.globepequot.com. **Acquisitions:** Erin Turner, executive editor. Publishes hardcover and trade paperback originals. **Publishes 4 titles/year. 80% of books from first-time authors; 80% from unagented writers. Pays variable royalty.** Does not accept simultaneous submissions. Responds in 2 months to queries. Book catalog and ms guidelines free.

> ○━ Three Forks specializes in regional cookbooks *or* cookbooks with a unique, nonfood theme. ''We do not publish single-food themed cookbooks.''

Nonfiction Cookbook. Subjects include regional. Query with SASE, or submit proposal package. Reviews artwork/photos as part of ms package. Send photocopies, no originals.
Recent Title(s) *Whistleberries, Stirabout, & Depression Cake* (food history); *Chocolate Snowball* (cookbook).

Ⓝ TOP PUBLICATIONS, LTD.
3100 Independence Parkway, Suite 311-349, Plano TX 75075. (972)490-9686. Fax: (972)233-0713. E-mail: info@ toppub.com. Submissions E-mail: submissions@toppub.com. Website: www.toppub.com. **Acquisitions:** Bill

Manchee, editor. Estab. 1999. Publishes harcover originals. **Publishes 4 titles/year. Receives 100 queries and 20 mss/year. 90% of books from first-time authors; 95% from unagented writers. Pays 15-20% royalty on wholesale price. Offers $500-2,500 advance.** Publishes book 8 months after acceptance of ms. Accepts simultaneous submissions. Responds in 3 months to queries; 6 months to mss. Book catalog free; ms guidelines online.

Fiction Adventure, historical, horror, juvenile, mainstream/contemporary, military/war, mystery, poetry, regional, romance, science fiction, short story collections, suspense, young adult. "It is imperative that our authors realize they will be required to promote their book extensively for it to be a success. Unless they are willing to make this commitment, they shouldn't submit to TOP." Query with SASE, or submit 3 sample chapters.

Recent Title(s) *Green Streak*, by Matthew LaBrot and Daniel Hale; *Keeper of the Empire*, by H.J. Ralles; *Yes, We're Open: Defending the Small Business Under Siege*, by William Manchee.

Tips "Because of the intense competition in this industry, we recommend that our authors write books that appeal to a large mainstream audience to make marketing easier and increase the chances of success. Be patient and don't get your hopes up. We only publish a few titles a year so the odds at getting published at TOP are slim. If we reject your work, don't give it a second thought. It probably doesn't have any reflection on your work. We have to pass on a lot of good material each year simply by the limitations of our time and budget."

ℕ ⊘ TOY BOX PRODUCTIONS

7532 Hickory Hills Court, Whites Creek TN 37189. (615)299-0822. Fax: (615)876-3931. E-mail: toybox@crttoybox.com. Website: www.crttoybox.com. Estab. 1995. Publishes mass market paperback originals. **Publishes 4 titles/year. 100% of books from first-time authors; 100% from unagented writers. Pays 10-15% royalty on wholesale price.** Does not accept simultaneous submissions. Book catalog online.

• "We are not accepting new submissions at this time."

Nonfiction Audiocassettes, biography, children's/juvenile. Subjects include Americana, education, religion. *All unsolicited mss returned unopened.*

Recent Title(s) *The Tuskegee Airmen & Lions, Lions Everywhere*, by Joe Loesch.

⊘ TRANSPERSONAL PUBLISHING/AHU PRESS

P.O. Box 249, Goshen VA 24439. E-mail: allenchips@holistictree.com. Website: www.transpersonalpublishing.com. **Acquisitions:** Dr. Allen Chips, managing director (holistic health texts and metaphysics). Estab. 1999. Publishes hardcover, trade paperback, and electronic originals and reprints; and mass market paperback reprints. **Publishes 3-7 titles/year. Receives 100 queries/year. 50% of books from first-time authors; 99% from unagented writers. Pays 10% royalty.** Publishes book 9-12 months after acceptance of ms. Accepts simultaneous submissions. Responds in 1 month to queries; 2 months to proposals; 3 months to mss. Book catalog and ms guidelines online.

• *Unsolicited mss are discarded.* If asked for a submission, will not return materials.

Nonfiction Subjects include alternative health/medicine, transpersonal pyschology, paranormal/metaphysics. "We are looking for textbooks and how-to in the fields of naturopathy, hypnotherapy, energy therapies, natural health, and controversial health recovery programs. Also books that focus on paranormal experiences, but none should be primarily autobiographical in nature (unless the author is already well known)." Query by e-mail with "Query" in the subject line. Have good proposal ready if asked for, with speaking/workshop bio, marketing plan, endorsements (if any), market niche. Reviews artwork/photos as part of ms package. Send photocopies.

Recent Title(s) *Life Patterns: Soul Lessons & Forgiveness*, by Henry Bolduc; *Alive and Well: Into the New Millennium With Edgar Cayce's Health Care Wisdom*, by Bette S. Margolis; *Clinical Hypnotherapy: A Transpersonal Approach*, by George Schwimmer, PhD (educational guidebook, 2nd edition).

Tips "The best authors are already engaged in regular travel and seminars/workshops so that book signings are self-initiated. They also demonstrate integrity, honesty, a track record of success, dedication, self-motivation, and a people orientation."

THE TRINITY FOUNDATION

PO Box 68, Unicoi TN 37692. (423)743-0199. Fax: (423)743-2005. E-mail: jrob1517@aol.com. Website: www.trinityfoundation.org. **Acquisitions:** John Robbins. Publishes hardcover and paperback originals and reprints. **Publishes 5 titles/year. Makes outright purchase of $1-1,500.** Publishes book 9 months after acceptance of ms. Responds in 1 month to queries and proposals; 3 months to mss. Book catalog online.

Nonfiction "Only books that conform to the philosophy and theology of the Westminster Confession of Faith." Textbooks subjects include business/economics, education, government/politics, history, philosophy, religion, science. Query with SASE.

TURTLE PRESS

S.K. Productions, P.O. Box 290206, Wethersfield CT 06129-0206. (860)721-1198. Fax: (860)436-2360. E-mail: editorial@turtlepress.com. Website: www.turtlepress.com. **Acquisitions:** Cynthia Kim, editor. Publishes hardcover originals, trade paperback originals and reprints. **Publishes 4-8 titles/year. Pays 8-10% royalty. Offers $500-1,500 advance.** Accepts simultaneous submissions. Responds in 1 month to queries. Ms guidelines online.

O— Turtle Press publishes sports and martial arts nonfiction for a specialty niche audience. Currently emphasizing martial arts, eastern philosophy. De-emphasizing self-help.

Nonfiction How-to, self-help. Subjects include philosophy, sports, martial arts. "We prefer tightly targeted topics on which there is little or no information available in the market, particularly for our sports and martial arts titles." Query with SASE.

Recent Title(s) *Warrior Speed*, by Ted Weimann; *The Art of Harmony*, by Sang H. Kim; *Fighting Science*, by Martina Sprague.

UNION SQUARE PUBLISHING

Cardoza Publishing, 857 Broadway, 3rd Floor, New York NY 10003. E-mail: submissions@cardozapub.com. **Acquisitions:** Acquisition Editor (biographies, word books, cultural studies, sports, general nonfiction and fiction). Estab. 2002. Publishes hardcover originals, trade paperback originals and reprints, mass market paperback originals. **Publishes 5-10 titles/year. Receives 10 queries and 5 mss/year. 80% of books from first-time authors; 95% from unagented writers. Pays 5-6% royalty on retail price. Offers $1,000-10,000 advance.** Publishes book 7 months after acceptance of ms. Accepts simultaneous submissions. Responds in 1-2 months to queries and proposals; 2-3 months to mss. Ms guidelines by e-mail.

Nonfiction Autobiography, biography, cookbook, general nonfiction, how-to, self-help. Subjects include anthropology/archeology, community, contemporary culture, cooking/foods/nutrition, education, ethnic, government/politics, history, hobbies, humanities, language/literature, memoirs, multicultural, music/dance, nature/environment, philosophy, recreation, religion, social sciences, sociology, spirituality, sports, translation. "Union Square Publishing is a new imprint of a long-established company, and we have yet to determine the exact role it will fill in the publishing world. We began by publishing books on writing, words, and language." Query with SASE, or submit complete ms. Reviews artwork/photos as part of ms package. Send photocopies.

Recent Title(s) *The Complete Guide to Successful Publishing*, by Avery Cardoza (how-to); *Drinking Companion*, by Kelly Boler; *Write in Style*, by Bobbie Christmas.

Tips "We will never reject a book based solely on genre. Our audience is the general market interested in original concepts."

VISIONS COMMUNICATIONS

200 E. 10th St., #714, New York NY 10003. (212)529-4029. Fax: (212)529-4029. E-mail: info@visionsbooks.com. **Acquisitions:** Beth Bay. Estab. 1994. Visions specializes in trade and reference books. Publishes hardcover originals and paperback originals and reprints. **Publishes 5 titles/year. Pays 5-20% royalty on retail price.** Publishes book 8 months after acceptance of ms. Responds in 2 months to queries; 4 months to mss. Ms guidelines free.

Nonfiction How-to, reference, self-help, technical, textbook. Subjects include art/architecture, business/economics, health/medicine, psychology, religion, science, women's issues/studies, scholarly, engineering. Submit proposal package including outline, 3 sample chapters.

Recent Title(s) *Illuminating Engineering*, by Joseph Murdoch; *Restructuring Electricity Markets*, by Charles Cichetti.

Ⓝ VOLCANO PRESS, INC.

P.O. Box 270, Volcano CA 95689-0270. (209)296-4991. Fax: (209)296-4995. E-mail: ruth@volcanopress.com. Website: www.volcanopress.com. **Acquisitions:** Ruth Gottstein, publisher; Adam Gottstein, associate publisher. Estab. 1969. Publishes trade paperback originals. **Publishes 4-6 titles/year. Pays royalty on net receipts. Offers $500-1,000 advance.** Does not accept simultaneous submissions. Responds in 1 month to queries. Book catalog free.

O— "We believe that the books we are producing today are of even greater value than the gold of yesteryear and that the sybolism of the term 'Mother Lode' is still relevant to our work."

Nonfiction Self-help. Subjects include health/medicine, multicultural, women's issues/studies. "We publish women's health and social issues, particularly in the field of domestic violence." Query with SASE. No e-mail or fax submissions.

Recent Title(s) *Family & Friends Guide to Domestic Violence: How to Listen, Talk & Take Action When Someone You Care About Is Being Abused*, by Elaine Weiss, EdD; *Surviving Domestic Violence: Voices of Women Who Broke Free*, by Elaine Weiss, EdD.

Tips "Look at our titles on the Web or in our catalog, and submit materials consistent with what we already publish."

WESCOTT COVE PUBLISHING CO.

Subsidiary of NetPV, P.O. Box 560989, Rockledge FL 32956. (321)690-2224. Fax: (321)690-0853. E-mail: publish er@wescottcovepublishing.com. Website: www.wescottcovepublishing.com. **Acquisitions:** Will Standley, publisher. Also: 1227 S. Florida Ave., Rockledge FL 32955. Estab. 1968. Publishes trade paperback originals and reprints. **Publishes 4 titles/year.** Accepts simultaneous submissions. Responds in 1 week to queries. Book catalog free.

○→ *"We publish the most complete cruising guides, each one an authentic reference for the area covered."*
Nonfiction "All titles are nautical books; half of them are cruising guides. Mostly we seek out authors knowledgeable in sailing, navigation, cartography and the area we want covered. Then we commission them to write the book." How-to, humor, illustrated book, reference. Subjects include history, hobbies, regional, sports, travel, nautical. Query publisher via e-mail.

WESTWINDS PRESS

Imprint of Graphic Arts Center Publishing, P.O. Box 10306, Portland OR 97296-0306. (503)226-2402. Fax: (503)223-1410. Website: www.gacpc.com. **Acquisitions:** Tricia Brown, acquisitions editor. Estab. 1999. Publishes hardcover and trade paperback originals and reprints. **Publishes 5-7 titles/year. 10% of books from first-time authors; 90% from unagented writers. Pays 10-14% royalty on net receipts, or makes outright purchase. Offers advance.** Publishes book an average of 2 years after acceptance of ms. Accepts simultaneous submissions. Responds in 6 months to queries. Book catalog for 9×12 SAE with 6 first-class stamps; ms guidelines online.

Nonfiction Children's/juvenile, cookbook. Subjects include history, memoirs, regional (Western regional states—nature, travel, cookbooks, Native American culture, adventure, outdoor recreation, sports, the arts, and children's books), guidebooks.

Recent Title(s) *Stone Fruit* (Northwest Homegrown cookbook series); *The Exploding Whale* (memoir); *Portland Confidential* (true crime).

Tips "Book proposals that are professionally written and polished with a clear understanding of the market receive our most careful consideration. We are looking for originality. We publish a wide range of books for a wide audience. Some of our books are clearly for travelers, others for those interested in outdoor recreation or various regional subjects. If I were a writer trying to market a book today, I would research the competition (existing books) for what I have in mind, and clearly (and concisely) express why my idea is different and better. I would describe the book buyers (and readers)—where they are, how many of them are there, how they can be reached (organizations, publications), why they would want or need my book."

WHITE CLIFFS MEDIA, INC.

Editorial Dept., P.O. Box 6083, Incline Village NV 89450. E-mail: wcm@wcmedia.com. Website: www.wcmedia. com. **Acquisitions:** Larry Aynesmith. Estab. 1985. Publishes hardcover and trade paperback originals. Does not accept simultaneous submissions. Book catalog online.

○→ Publishes music titles for an academic and general audience.
Nonfiction Biography, textbook. Subjects include anthropology/archeology, ethnic, music/dance. Query. Reviews artwork/photos as part of ms package. Send photocopies.

Recent Title(s) *Mother Mountain and Father Sea*, by Dr. Phong Nguyen and Dr. Terry Miller; *A Garden of Music*, by Joyce E. Depow; *Rhythm, Musical Time and Society*, by Dr. Michael W. Morse.

Tips "Distribution is more difficult due to the large number of publishers. Writers should send proposals that have potential for mass markets as well as college texts, and that will be submitted and completed on schedule. Our audience reads college texts, general interest trade publications. If I were a writer trying to market a book today, I would send a book on music comparable in quality and mass appeal to a book like Stephen Hawking's *A Brief History of Time*."

WILDER PUBLISHING CENTER

919 Lafond Ave., St. Paul MN 55104. (651)659-6013. Fax: (651)642-2061. E-mail: vlh@wilder.org. Website: www.wilderpubs.org. **Acquisitions:** Vincent Hyman, director. Publishes professional trade paperback originals. **Publishes 6 titles/year. Receives 30 queries and 15 mss/year. 75% of books from first-time authors; 100% from unagented writers. Pays 10% royalty on net receipts. Books are sold through direct mail; average discount is 20%. Offers $1,000-3,000 advance.** Publishes book 18 months after acceptance of ms. Accepts simultaneous submissions. Responds in 6 weeks to queries and proposals; 3 months to mss. Book catalog and ms guidelines free or online.

○→ Wilder Publishing Center emphasizes community development and nonprofit organization management. Actively seeking authors of color.
Nonfiction Subjects include nonprofit management, funder's guides, board guides, organizational development, community building. "We are seeking manuscripts that report 'best practice' methods using handbook or

workbook formats for nonprofit and community development managers." Submit 3 sample chapters, complete topical outline, and full proposal based on online guidelines. Phone query OK before submitting proposal with detailed chapter outline, SASE, statement of the goals of the book, statement of unique selling points, identification of audience, author qualification, competing publications, marketing potential.

Recent Title(s) *The Lobbying and Advocacy Handbook for Nonprofit Organizations*; *The Wilder Nonprofit Guide to Crafting Effective Mission and Vision Statements*; *The Five Life Stages of Nonprofit Organizations*.

Tips "Writers must be practitioners with a passion for their work in nonprofit management or community building and experience presenting their techniques at conferences. We seek practical, not academic books. Our books identify professional challenges faced by our audiences and offer practical, step-by-step solutions. Do not send us a manuscript without first checking our online guidelines."

N WISH PUBLISHING

P.O. Box 10337, Terre Haute IN 47801. (812)299-5700. Fax: (928)447-1836. E-mail: holly@wishpublishing.com. Website: www.wishpublishing.com. **Acquisitions:** Holly Kondras, president. Publishes hardcover and trade paperback originals. **Publishes 5-10 titles/year. Pays 10-18% royalty on wholesale price.** Accepts simultaneous submissions. Responds in 2 months. Book catalog and ms guidelines free or online.

Nonfiction Biography, children's/juvenile, reference. Subjects include health/medicine, sports, women's issues/studies. Query with SASE, or submit proposal package including outline, 2 sample chapters, author bio. Reviews artwork/photos as part of ms package. Send photocopies.

Recent Title(s) *Hard Fought Victories: Women Coaches Making a Difference* (sports); *Total Fitness for Women* (fitness); *Girls' Basketball: Building a Winning Team* (sports).

Tips Audience is women and girls who play sports, and their coaches, parents, and supporters.

N ⊘ WOMEN IN PRINT

Datamaster Publishing, LLC, P.O. Box 1527, Williston VT 05495. E-mail: womeninprint@surfglobal.net. Website: www.womeninprint.com. Brette McWhorter Sember, senior editor. **Acquisitions:** Arlene Cardoza, editor of all genres; Heather Long, fiction editor; Jennifer Sadler, fiction editor; Melissa Sheffels, nonfiction editor; Stephanie Maull, nonfiction editor; Olga Cossi, children's editor. Estab. 1995. Publishes hardcover originals, trade paperback originals and mass market paperback originals. **Publishes 6 titles/year; imprint publishes 3 titles/year. Receives 5,000 queries and 500 mss/year. 90% from unagented writers. Pays royalty on wholesale price.** Publishes book 1 year after acceptance of ms. Accepts simultaneous submissions. Responds in 1 month to queries; 1-2 months to proposals and mss. Book catalog and ms guidelines online.

• *Closed to submissions for 2005-2006.*

Nonfiction Biography, children's/juvenile, general nonfiction, gift book, how-to, humor, illustrated book, reference, self-help. Subjects include business/economics, community, contemporary culture, creative nonfiction, education, health/medicine, hobbies, multicultural, nature/environment, philosophy, psychology, women's issues/studies. The writer should be an expert in the field chosen to write about and have a solid platform for marketing. Query with SASE. Reviews artwork/photos as part of ms package. Send photocopies.

Fiction Adventure, historical, humor, juvenile, literary, mainstream/contemporary, mystery, science fiction, short story collections, suspense, young adult. "We are looking for original ideas, creative writing and strong character development." Query with SASE.

Tips "Our audience is male and female, mid to upper income, 25-45 years of age. We prefer e-mail queries and ask that writers follow our submission guidelines."

WORLD LEISURE

P.O. Box 160, Hampstead NH 03841. (617)569-1966. Fax: (603)947-0838. E-mail: leocha@worldleisure.com. Website: www.worldleisure.com. **Acquisitions:** Charles Leocha, president. Estab. 1977. Publishes trade paperback originals. **Publishes 3-5 titles/year. Pays royalty, or makes outright purchase.** Accepts simultaneous submissions. Responds in 2 months to queries. Book catalog and ms guidelines online.

⊶ World Leisure specializes in travel books, activity guidebooks, and self-help titles.

Nonfiction Self-help. Subjects include recreation, sports (skiing/snowboarding), travel. "We will be publishing annual updates to *Ski Snowboard Europe* and *Ski Snowboard America & Canada*. Writers planning any winter resort stories should contact us for possible add-on assignments at areas not covered by our staff." Submit outline, intro sample chapters, annotated TOC, SASE.

Recent Title(s) *Ski Snowboard America and Canada*, by Charles Leocha; *Ski Snowboard Europe*, by Charles Leocha.

YMAA PUBLICATION CENTER

4354 Washington St., Roslindale MA 02131. (617)323-7215. Fax: (617)323-7417. E-mail: ymaa@aol.com. **Acquisitions:** David Ripianzi, director. Estab. 1982. Publishes trade paperback originals and reprints. **Publishes 6**

titles/year. Receives 50 queries and 20 mss/year. 25% of books from first-time authors; 100% from un-agented writers. Pays 10% royalty on net receipts. Publishes book 18 months after acceptance of ms. Accepts simultaneous submissions. Responds in 3 months to proposals. Book catalog online; ms guidelines free.

O━ "YMAA publishes books on Chinese Chi Kung (Qigong), Taijiquan, (Tai Chi) and Asian martial arts. We are expanding our focus to include books on healing, wellness, meditation and subjects related to Asian culture and Asian medicine." De-emphasizing fitness books.

Nonfiction "We are most interested in Asian martial arts, Chinese medicine, and Chinese Qigong. We publish Eastern thought, health, meditation, massage, and East/West synthesis." How-to, multimedia, self-help. Subjects include ethnic, health/medicine (Chinese), history, philosophy, spirituality, sports, Asian martial arts, Chinese Qigong. "We no longer publish or solicit books for children. We also produce instructional DVDs and videos to accompany our books on traditional Chinese martial arts, meditation, massage, and Chi Kung." Submit proposal package including outline, 1 sample chapter, author bio, SASE. Reviews artwork/photos as part of ms package. Send photocopies and 1-2 originals to determine quality of photo/line art.

Recent Title(s) *Qigong Meditation-Embryonic Breathing*, by Dr. Yang Jwing-Ming; *The Martial Way and Its Virtues*, by F.J. Chu.

Tips "If you are submitting health-related material, please refer to an Asian tradition. Learn about author publicity options as your participation is mandatory."

Consumer Magazines

Selling your writing to consumer magazines is as much an exercise of your marketing skills as it is of your writing abilities. Editors of consumer magazines are looking not only for good writing, but for good writing that communicates pertinent information to a specific audience—their readers.

Approaching the consumer magazine market

Marketing skills will help you successfully discern a magazine's editorial slant, and write queries and articles that prove your knowledge of the magazine's readership. You can gather clues about a magazine's readership—and establish your credibility with the magazine's editor—in a number of ways:

- **Read** the magazine's listing in *Writer's Market*.
- **Study** a magazine's writer's guidelines.
- **Check** a magazine's website.
- **Read** several current issues of the target magazine.
- **Talk** to an editor by phone.

Writers who can correctly and consistently discern a publication's audience and deliver stories that speak to that target readership will win out every time over writers who submit haphazardly.

What editors want

In nonfiction, editors continue to look for short feature articles covering specialized topics. Editors want crisp writing and expertise. If you are not an expert in the area about which you are writing, make yourself one through research. Always query before sending your manuscript. Don't e-mail or fax a query to an editor unless the listing mentions it is acceptable to do so.

Fiction editors prefer to receive complete manuscripts. Writers must keep in mind that marketing fiction is competitive, and editors receive far more material than they can publish. For this reason, they often do not respond to submissions unless they are interested in using the story. More comprehensive information on fiction markets can be found in *Novel & Short Story Writer's Market* (Writer's Digest Books).

Payment

Most magazines listed here have indicated pay rates; some give very specific payment-per-word rates, while others state a range. **(Note: All of the magazines listed in the Consumer**

Magazines section are paying markets. However, some of the magazines are not identified by payment icons (**$ – $ $ $ $**) because the magazines preferred not to disclose specific payment information.) Any agreement you come to with a magazine, whether verbal or written, should specify the payment you are to receive and when you are to receive it. Some magazines pay writers only after the piece in question has been published (on publication). Others pay as soon as they have accepted a piece and are sure they are going to use it (on acceptance). In *Writer's Market*, those magazines that pay on acceptance have been highlighted with the phrase **pays on acceptance** set in bold type.

So what is a good pay rate? There are no standards; the principle of supply and demand operates at full throttle in the business of writing and publishing. As long as there are more writers than opportunities for publication, wages for freelancers will never skyrocket. Rates vary widely from one market to the next. Smaller circulation magazines and some departments of the larger magazines will pay a lower rate.

Editors know the listings in *Writer's Market* are read and used by writers with a wide range of experience, from those unpublished writers just starting out, to those with a successful, profitable freelance career. As a result, many magazines publicly report pay rates in the lower end of their actual pay ranges. Experienced writers will be able to successfully negotiate higher pay rates for their material. Newer writers should be encouraged that as their reputation grows (along with their clip file), they will be able to command higher rates. The article "How Much Should I Charge?" on page 68, gives you an idea of pay ranges for different freelance jobs, including those directly associated with magazines.

INFORMATION AT-A-GLANCE

In the Consumer Magazine section, icons identify comparative payment rates (**$ – $ $ $ $**); new listings (N); and magazines that do not accept unsolicited manuscripts (⊘). Different sections of *Writer's Market* include other symbols; check the inside back cover for an explanation of all the symbols used throughout the book.

Important information is highlighted in boldface—the "quick facts" you won't find in any other market book, but should know before you submit your work. The word **Contact** identifies the appropriate person to query at each magazine. We also highlight what percentage of the magazine is freelance written; how many manuscripts a magazine buys per year of nonfiction, fiction, poetry, and fillers; and respective pay rates in each category.

Information on publications listed in the previous edition of *Writer's Market*, but not included in this edition, can be found in the General Index.

ANIMAL

$ $ AKC GAZETTE

American Kennel Club, 260 Madison Ave., New York NY 10016. E-mail: gazette@akc.org. Website: www.akc. org/pubs/index.cfm. **85% freelance written.** Monthly magazine. "Geared to interests of fanciers of purebred dogs as opposed to commercial interests or pet owners. We require solid expertise from our contributors—we are *not* a pet magazine." Estab. 1889. Circ. 60,000. Pays on publication. Publishes ms an average of 6 months after acceptance. Byline given. Offers 10% kill fee. Buys first North American serial, electronic, international rights. Submit seasonal material 6 months in advance. Accepts queries by mail. Responds in 2 months to queries. Writer's guidelines for #10 SASE.

Nonfiction General interest, how-to, humor, interview/profile, photo feature, travel, dog art, training and canine performance sports. No poetry, tributes to individual dogs, or fiction. **Buys 30-40 mss/year.** Length: 1,000-3,000 words. **Pays $300-500.** Pays expenses of writers on assignment.

Photos Photo contest guidelines for #10 SASE. State availability with submission. Reviews color transparencies, prints. Buys one-time rights. Pays $50-200/photo. Captions, identification of subjects, model releases required.

Fiction Annual short fiction contest only. Guidelines for #10 SASE.

Tips "Contributors should be involved in the dog fancy or be an expert in the area they write about (veterinary, showing, field trialing, obedience training, dogs in legislation, dog art or history or literature). All submissions are welcome but author must be a credible expert or be able to interview and quote the experts. Veterinary articles must be written by or with veterinarians. Humorous features or personal experiences relative to purebred dogs should have broader applications. For features, know the subject thoroughly and be conversant with jargon peculiar to the sport of dogs."

$ $ APPALOOSA JOURNAL

Appaloosa Horse Club, 2720 West Pullman Rd., Moscow ID 83843-0903. (208)882-5578. Fax: (208)882-8150. E-mail: journal@appaloosa.com. Website: www.appaloosajournal.com. **Contact:** Diane Rice, editor. **40% freelance written.** Monthly magazine covering Appaloosa horses. Estab. 1946. Circ. 25,000. Pays on publication. Publishes ms an average of 3 months after acceptance. Byline given. Buys first North American serial, electronic rights. Responds in 1 month to queries; 2 months to mss. Sample copy for free. Writer's guidelines online.

• *Appaloosa Journal* no longer accepts material for columns.

Nonfiction Historical/nostalgic, interview/profile, photo feature. **Buys 15-20 mss/year.** Query with or without published clips or send complete ms. Length: 800-1,800 words. **Pays $200-400.**

Photos Send photos with submission. Payment varies. Captions, identification of subjects required.

🖳 The online magazine carries original content not found in the print edition. Contact: Jennie Archer, online editor.

Tips "Articles by writers with horse knowledge, news sense, and photography skills are in great demand. If it's a strong article about an Appaloosa, the writer has a pretty good chance of publication. A good understanding of the breed and the industry, breeders, and owners is helpful. Make sure there's some substance and a unique twist."

$ $ AQUARIUM FISH MAGAZINE

Fishkeeping—the Art and the Science, Bowtie, Inc., P.O. Box 6050, Mission Viejo CA 92690. Fax: (949)855-3045. E-mail: aquariumfish@fancypubs.com. Website: www.aquariumfish.com. Editor: Russ Case. Managing Editor: Patricia Knight. **Contact:** Dave Cravotta, associate editor. **90% freelance written.** Monthly magazine covering fish and other aquatic pets. "Our focus is on beginning and intermediate fish keeping. Most of our articles concentrate on general fish and aquarium care, but we will also consider other types of articles that may be helpful to those in the fishkeeping hobby. Freshwater and saltwater tanks, and ponds are covered." Estab. 1988. Pays on publication. Byline given. Buys first North American serial, electronic rights. Accepts queries by mail, e-mail, fax. Responds in 1 month to queries; 6 months to mss. Writer's guidelines for #10 SASE.

Nonfiction General interest (species profiles, natural history with home care info), interview/profile (of well-known people in fish keeping), new product (press releases only for Product Showcase section), photo feature, caring for fish in aquariums. Special issues: "We do have 2 annuals; freelancers should query." No fiction, anthropomorphism, articles on sport fishing, or animals that cannot be kept as pets (i.e., whales, dolphins, manatees, etc.). **Buys 60 mss/year.** Query with or without published clips or send complete ms. Length: 1,500-2,000 words. **Pays 10¢/word.**

Photos State availability with submission. Reviews 35mm transparencies, 4×5 prints. Buys first North American serial rights. Offers $15-200/photo. Identification of subjects required.

Fillers Facts, gags to be illustrated by cartoonist, newsbreaks. **Buys variable number/year.** Length: 50-200 words.

Tips "Take a look at our guidelines before submitting. Writers are not required to provide photos for submitted articles, but we do encourage it, if possible. It helps if writers are involved in fish keeping themselves. Our writers tend to be experienced fish keepers, detailed researchers, and some scientists."

$ $ CAT FANCY

For the Love of Cats, Fancy Publications, a division of BowTie Inc., P.O. Box 6050, Mission Viejo CA 92690. (949)855-8822. E-mail: query@catfancy.com. Website: www.catfancy.com. **Contact:** Susan Logan, editor. **90% freelance written.** Monthly magazine covering all aspects of responsible cat ownership. Estab. 1965. Pays on publication. Buys first North American serial rights. Editorial lead time 6 months. Responds in 3 months to queries. Writer's guidelines online.

- *Cat Fancy* does not accept unsolicited mss and only accepts queries from January-May. Queries sent after May will be returned or discarded.

Nonfiction Engaging presentation of expert, up-to-date information. Must be cat oriented. Writing should not be gender specific. How-to, humor, photo feature, travel, behavior, health, lifestyle, cat culture, entertainment. **Buys 70 mss/year.** Query with published clips. Length: 600-1,200 words. **Pays $50-450.**

Photos Seeking photos of happy, healthy, well-groomed cats and kittens in studio or indoor settings. Buys one-time rights. Negotiates payment individually. Captions, identification of subjects, model releases required.

Tips "No fiction or poetry. Please read recent issues to become acquainted with our style and content. Show us in your query how you can contribute something new and unique. No phone queries."

$ $ THE CHRONICLE OF THE HORSE

P.O. Box 46, Middleburg VA 20118-0046. (540)687-6341. Fax: (540)687-3937. E-mail: bethr@chronofhorse.com. Website: www.chronofhorse.com. Editor: John Strassburger. Managing Editor: Tricia Booker. **Contact:** Beth Rasin, assistant editor. **80% freelance written.** Weekly magazine covering horses. "We cover English riding sports, including horse showing, grand prix jumping competitions, steeplechase racing, foxhunting, dressage, endurance riding, handicapped riding, and combined training. We are the official publication for the national governing bodies of many of the above sports. We feature news, how-to articles on equitation and horse care, and interviews with leaders in the various fields." Estab. 1937. Circ. 22,000. Pays for features on acceptance; news and other items on publication. Publishes ms an average of 4 months after acceptance. Byline given. Buys first North American serial rights, makes work-for-hire assignments. Submit seasonal material 3 months in advance. Accepts queries by mail, e-mail. Responds in 5-6 weeks to queries. Sample copy for $2 and 9×12 SAE. Writer's guidelines online.

- Break in by "clearing a small news assignment in your area ahead of time."

Nonfiction General interest, historical/nostalgic (history of breeds, use of horses in other countries and times, art, etc.), how-to (trailer, train, design a course, save money, etc.), humor (centered on living with horses or horse people), interview/profile (of nationally known horsemen or the very unusual), technical (horse care, articles on feeding, injuries, care of foals, shoeing, etc.). Special issues: Steeplechase Racing (January); American Horse in Sport and Grand Prix Jumping (February); Horse Show (March); Intercollegiate (April); Kentucky 4-Star Preview (April); Junior and Pony (April); Dressage (June); Horse Care (July); Combined Training (August); Hunt Roster (September); Amateur (November); Stallion (December). No Q&A interviews, clinic reports, Western riding articles, personal experience or wild horses. **Buys 300 mss/year.** Query with or without published clips or send complete ms. Length: 6-7 pages. **Pays $150-250.**

Photos State availability with submission. Reviews prints or color slides; accepts color for b&w reproduction. Buys one-time rights. Pays $25-30. Identification of subjects required.

Columns/Departments Dressage, Combined Training, Horse Show, Horse Care, Racing over Fences, Young Entry (about young riders, geared for youth), Horses and Humanities, Hunting, Vaulting, Handicapped Riding, Trail Riding, 1,000-1,225 words; News of major competitions ("clear assignment with us first"), 1,500 words. Query with or without published clips or send complete ms. **Pays $25-200.**

Tips "Get our guidelines. Our readers are sophisticated, competitive horsemen. Articles need to go beyond common knowledge. Freelancers often attempt too broad or too basic a subject. We welcome well-written news stories on major events, but clear the assignment with us."

$ COONHOUND BLOODLINES

The Complete Magazine for the Houndsman and Coon Hunter, United Kennel Club, Inc., 100 E. Kilgore Rd., Kalamazoo MI 49002-5584. (269)343-9020. Fax: (269)343-7037. E-mail: vrand@ukcdogs.com. Website: www.ukcdogs.com. **Contact:** Vicki Rand, editor. **40% freelance written.** Monthly magazine covering all aspects of the 6 Coonhound dog breeds. "Writers must retain the 'slang' particular to dog people and to our readers—many of whom are from the South." Estab. 1925. Circ. 16,000. Pays on publication. Publishes ms an average of 6 months after acceptance. Byline given. Buys first North American serial rights, makes work-for-hire assignments. Editorial lead time 6 months. Submit seasonal material 6 months in advance. Accepts queries by mail,

e-mail, fax, phone. Accepts simultaneous submissions. Responds in 6 weeks to queries. Sample copy for $4.50.
Nonfiction General interest, historical/nostalgic, humor, interview/profile, new product, personal experience, photo feature, breed-specific. Special issues: Six of our 12 issues are each devoted to a specific breed of Coonhound. Treeing Walker (February); English (March); Black & Tan (April); Bluetick (May); Redbone (June); Plott Hound (July), 1,000-3,000 words and photos. **Buys 12-36 mss/year.** Query. Length: 1,000-5,000 words. **Pays $100.** Sometimes pays expenses of writers on assignment.
Photos State availability with submission. Reviews contact sheets. Buys one-time rights. Negotiates payment individually. Captions, identification of subjects required.
Columns/Departments Buys 6-12 mss/year. Pays $100.
Fiction Must be about the Coonhound breeds or hunting with hounds. Adventure, historical, humorous, mystery. **Buys 3-6 mss/year.** Query. Length: 1,000-3,000 words. **Pays $100.**
Tips "Hunting with hounds is a two-century old American tradition and an important part of the American heritage, especially east of the Mississippi. It covers a lifestyle as well as a wonderful segment of the American population, many of whom still live by honest, friendly values."

$ $ DOG FANCY

P.O. Box 6050, Mission Viejo CA 92690-6050. Fax: (949)855-3045. E-mail: barkback@dogfancy.com. Website: www.dogfancy.com. **95% freelance written.** Monthly magazine for men and women of all ages interested in all phases of dog ownership. Estab. 1970. Circ. 250,000. Pays on publication. Publishes ms an average of 6 months after acceptance. Byline given. Offers negotiable kill fee. Buys first North American serial, nonexclusive electronic and other rights. Submit seasonal material 6 months in advance. Accepts queries by mail. Responds in 2 months to queries. Sample copy for $5.50. Writer's guidelines online.
Nonfiction Book excerpts, general interest, how-to, humor, inspirational, interview/profile, personal experience, photo feature, travel. "No stories written from a dog's point of view." **Buys 100 mss/year.** Query. Length: 850-1,500 words. **Pays $200-500.**
Photos State availability with submission. Reviews contact sheets, transparencies, prints. Buys electronic rights. Offers no additional payment for photos accepted with ms.
Columns/Departments Health and Medicine, 600-700 words; Training and Behavior, 800 words. **Buys 24 mss/year.** Query by mail only. **Pays $300-400.**
Tips "We're looking for the unique experience that enhances the dog/owner relationship—with the dog as the focus of the story, not the owner. Medical articles are assigned to veterinarians. Note that we write for a lay audience (nontechnical), but we do assume a certain level of intelligence. Read the magazine before making a pitch. Make sure your query is clear, concise, and relevant."

N $ DOG SPORTS MAGAZINE

4215 S. Lowell Rd., St. Johns MI 48879. (989)224-7225. Fax: (989)224-6033. E-mail: chercar@acd.net. Website: www.dogsports.com. Editor: Cheryl Carlson. **5% freelance written.** Monthly tabloid covering working dogs. Estab. 1979. Circ. 2,000. Pays on publication. Publishes ms an average of 1 month after acceptance. Byline given. Buys first North American serial, second serial (reprint) rights. Editorial lead time 1 month. Submit seasonal material 1 month in advance. Accepts queries by mail, e-mail. Accepts previously published material. Accepts simultaneous submissions. Sample copy free or online.
Nonfiction Essays, general interest, how-to (working dogs), humor, interview/profile, technical. **Buys 5 mss/year.** Send complete ms. **Pays $50.**
Photos State availability with submission. Reviews prints. Buys all rights. Offers no additional payment for photos accepted with ms. Captions, identification of subjects required.

DOG WORLD

BowTie, Inc., P.O. Box 6050, Mission Viejo CA 92690. E-mail: letters@dogworld.com. Website: www.dogworld mag.com. **95% freelance written.** Monthly magazine covering dogs. "We write for the serious dog enthusiast and participant, including breeders, veterinarians, exhibitors, groomers, agility competitors, etc., as well as a general audience interested in in-depth information about dogs." Estab. 1915. Circ. 58,000. Pays on publication. Byline given. Buys exclusive worldwide print rights for 6 months and nonexclusive electronic rights. Editorial lead time 6 months. Submit seasonal material 6 months in advance. Accepts queries by mail. Responds in 3 months to queries. Writer's guidelines for #10 SASE.
Nonfiction General interest (on dogs including health care, veterinary medicine, grooming, legislation, responsible ownership, obedience training, kennel operations, dog sports, breed spotlights and histories), new product. No fluffy poems or pieces about dogs. **Buys approximately 50 mss/year.** Query by mail only with SASE. Query should include a list of points the story will cover and a list of experts the writer plans to interview. Length: 2,000-2,500 words. **Pays negotiable rate.** Sometimes pays expenses of writers on assignment.
Photos State availability with submission. Buys one-time rights. Offers no additional payment for photos ac-

cepted with ms; negotiates payment individually for professional photos. Current rate for cover photo is $500; inside color photo $50-175; b&w $25-50, depending on size used. Payment on publication.

Tips "Get a copy of the magazine and our writer's guidelines. Stories should cover a very narrowly focused topic in great depth. Be able to translate technical and medical articles into language the average reader can understand. Be ready to quote experts through live interviews."

$ EQUINE JOURNAL

103 Roxbury St., Keene NH 03431-8801. (603)357-4271. Fax: (603)357-7851. E-mail: editorial@equinejournal.com. Website: www.equinejournal.com. **Contact:** Kathleen Labonville, managing editor. **90% freelance written.** Monthly tabloid covering horses—all breeds, all disciplines. "To educate, entertain, and enable amateurs and professionals alike to stay on top of new developments in the field. Covers horse-related activities from all corners of New England, New York, New Jersey, Pennsylvania, and the Midwest." Estab. 1988. Circ. 26,000. Pays on publication. Byline given. Buys first North American serial, electronic rights. Editorial lead time 3 months. Submit seasonal material 4 months in advance. Accepts queries by mail, e-mail, fax, phone. Responds in 2 months to queries. Writer's guidelines online.

Nonfiction General interest, how-to, interview/profile. **Buys 100 mss/year.** Query with published clips or send complete ms. Length: 1,500-3,000 words.

Photos Send photos with submission. Reviews prints. Pays $10.

Columns/Departments Horse Health (health-related topics), 1,200-1,500 words. **Buys 12 mss/year.** Query.

Fillers Short humor. Length: 500-1,000 words. **Pays $40-75.**

EQUUS

Primedia Enthusiast Group, 656 Quince Orchard Rd., Suite 600, Gaithersburg MD 20878-1409. (301)977-3900. Fax: (301)990-9015. E-mail: equuslts@aol.com. Website: www.equisearch.com. Editor: Laurie Prinz. Monthly magazine covering equine behavior. Provides the latest information from the world's top veternarians, equine researchers, riders, and trainers. Circ. 149,482. Sample copy not available.

$ $ FIELD TRIAL MAGAZINE

Androscoggin Publishing, Inc., P.O. Box 98, Milan NH 03588. (603)449-6767. Fax: (603)449-2462. E-mail: birddog@ncia.net. Website: www.fielddog.com/ftm. **Contact:** Craig Doherty, editor. **75% freelance written.** Quarterly magazine covering field trials for pointing dogs. "Our readers are knowledgeable sports men and women who want interesting and informative articles about their sport." Estab. 1997. Circ. 6,000. Pays on publication. Publishes ms an average of 6 months after acceptance. Byline given. Buys first North American serial rights. Editorial lead time 3 months. Submit seasonal material 6 months in advance. Accepts queries by mail, e-mail, fax. Accepts simultaneous submissions. Responds in 2 weeks to queries; 2 months to mss. Sample copy for free. Writer's guidelines online.

Nonfiction Book excerpts, essays, general interest, historical/nostalgic, how-to, interview/profile, opinion, personal experience. No hunting articles. **Buys 12-16 mss/year.** Query. Length: 1,000-3,000 words. **Pays $100-300.**

Photos Send photos with submission. Buys one-time rights. Offers no additional payment for photos accepted with ms. Captions, identification of subjects required.

Fiction Fiction that deals with bird dogs and field trials. **Buys 4 mss/year.** Send complete ms. Length: 1,000-2,500 words. **Pays $100-250.**

Tips "Make sure you have correct and accurate information—we'll work with a writer who has good solid info even if the writing needs work."

$ $ THE GAITED HORSE

The One Magazine for All Gaited Horses, P.O. Box 3070, Deer Park WA 99006-3070. Phone/Fax: (509)276-4930. E-mail: tgheditor@thegaitedhorse.com. Website: www.thegaitedhorse.com. **Contact:** Rhonda Hart Poe, editor. Quarterly magazine. "Subject matter must relate in some way to gaited horses." Estab. 1998. Circ. 15,000. Pays on publication. Publishes ms an average of 2 months after acceptance. Byline given. Buys first North American serial rights, makes work-for-hire assignments. Editorial lead time 4 months. Submit seasonal material 4 months in advance. Accepts queries by mail, e-mail. Accepts simultaneous submissions. Responds in 6 weeks to queries; 1 month to mss. Sample copy for $3. Writer's guidelines online.

Nonfiction Wants anything related to gaited horses, lifestyles, art, etc. Book excerpts, essays, exposé, general interest (gaited horses), historical/nostalgic, how-to, humor, interview/profile, new product, personal experience, photo feature, travel. **Buys 25 mss/year.** Query or send complete ms. Length: 1,000-2,500 words. **Pays $50-300.**

Photos State availability of or send photos with submission. Reviews prints (3×5 or larger). Buys one-time rights. Negotiates payment individually. Captions, identification of subjects, model releases required.

Columns/Departments Legal Paces (equine owners rights & responsibilities); Horse Cents (financial advice for horse owners); Health Check (vet advice); Smoother Trails (trail riding), all 500-1,000 words. **Buys 24 mss/year.** Query. **Pays $100.**

Fillers Anecdotes, short humor, NewsBits. **Buys 20/year.** Length: 5-300 words. **Pays $10-50.**

Tips "We are actively seeking to develop writers from within the various gaited breeds and equine disciplines. If you have a unique perspective on these horses, we would love to hear from you. Submit a query that targets any aspect of gaited horses and you'll have my attention."

$THE GREYHOUND REVIEW

P.O. Box 543, Abilene KS 67410-0543. (785)263-4660. Fax: (785)263-4689. E-mail: nga@ngagreyhounds.com. Website: www.ngagreyhounds.com. Editor: Gary Guccione. **Contact:** Tim Horan, managing editor. **20% freelance written.** Monthly magazine covering greyhound breeding, training, and racing. Estab. 1911. Circ. 4,000. **Pays on acceptance.** Byline given. Buys first rights. Submit seasonal material 2 months in advance. Responds in 2 weeks to queries; 1 month to mss. Sample copy for $3. Writer's guidelines free.

Nonfiction "Articles must be targeted at the greyhound industry: from hard news, to special events at racetracks, to the latest medical discoveries." How-to, interview/profile, personal experience. Do not submit gambling systems. **Buys 24 mss/year.** Query. Length: 1,000-10,000 words. **Pays $85-150.**

Reprints Send photocopy. Pays 100% of amount paid for original article.

Photos State availability with submission. Reviews 35mm transparencies, 8×10 prints. Buys one-time rights. Pays $10-50 photo. Identification of subjects required.

$ ▣ HORSE & COUNTRY CANADA

Equine Publications, Inc., 422 Kitley Line 3, Toledo ON K0E 1Y0 Canada. (613)275-1684. Fax: (613)275-1807. **Contact:** Editor. **40% freelance written.** Bimonthly magazine covering equestrian issues. "A celebration of equestrian sport and the country way of life." Estab. 1994. Circ. 14,000. Pays on publication. Publishes ms an average of 3 months after acceptance. Byline sometimes given. Buys one-time rights. Accepts queries by mail.

Nonfiction Book excerpts, historical/nostalgic, how-to, inspirational, new product, travel. Query with published clips. Length: 1,200-1,700 words. **Pays $25-150.** Sometimes pays expenses of writers on assignment.

Photos Send photos with submission. Reviews prints. Buys one-time rights. Pays $15-125/photo or negotiates payment individually. Captions required.

Columns/Departments Back to Basics (care for horses); Ask the Experts (how-to with horses); Nutrition (for horses), all 800 words. Query with published clips. **Pays $25-150.**

$ $ $HORSE & RIDER

The Magazine of Western Riding, Primedia, 4101 International Parkway, Carrollton TX 75007. (972)309-5700. Fax: (972)309-5670. E-mail: horse&rider@primediamags.com. Website: www.horseandrider.com. **Contact:** Darrell Dodds, editor/associate publisher. **10% freelance written.** Monthly magazine covering Western horse industry, competition, recreation. "*Horse & Rider*'s mission is to educate, inform, and entertain both competitive and recreational riders with tightly focused training articles, practical stable management techniques, hands-on healthcare tips, safe trail-riding practices, well-researched consumer advice, and a behind-the-scenes, you-are-there approach to major equine events." Estab. 1961. Circ. 164,000. **Pays on acceptance.** Publishes ms an average of 1 year after acceptance. Byline given. Offers $75 kill fee. Buys first North American serial rights. Editorial lead time 2 months. Submit seasonal material 6 months in advance. Accepts queries by mail. Responds in 3 months. Sample copy and writer's guidelines online.

• Does *not accept* e-mail submissions.

Nonfiction Book excerpts, general interest, how-to (horse training, horsemanship), humor, interview/profile, new product, personal experience, photo feature, travel, horse health care, trail riding. **Buys 5-10 mss/year.** Send complete ms. Length: 1,000-3,000 words. **Pays $150-1,000.**

Photos State availability of or send photos with submission. Buys rights on assignment or stock. Negotiates payment individually. Captions, identification of subjects, model releases required.

▣ The online magazine carries original content not found in the print edition. Contact: Darrell Dodds.

Tips Writers should have "patience, ability to accept critical editing, and extensive knowledge of the Western horse industry and our publication."

$ $HORSE ILLUSTRATED

The Magazine for Responsible Horse Owners, BowTie, Inc., P.O. Box 6050, Mission Viejo CA 92690-6050. (949)855-8822. Fax: (949)855-3045. Website: www.horseillustrated.com. **Contact:** Moira Harris, editor. **90% freelance written.** Prefers to work with published/established writers but will work with new/unpublished writers. Monthly magazine covering all aspects of horse ownership. "Our readers are adults, mostly women, between the ages of 18 and 40; stories should be geared to that age group and reflect responsible horse care."

Estab. 1976. Circ. 216,930. Pays on publication. Publishes ms an average of 8 months after acceptance. Byline given. Buys one-time rights, requires first North American rights among equine publications. Submit seasonal material 6 months in advance. Accepts queries by mail. Responds in 3 months to queries. Writer's guidelines for #10 SASE.

Nonfiction "We are looking for authoritative, in-depth features on trends and issues in the horse industry. Such articles must be queried first with a detailed outline of the article and clips. We rarely have a need for fiction." General interest, historical/nostalgic, how-to (horse care, training, veterinary care), inspirational, photo feature. No "little girl" horse stories, "cowboy and Indian" stories or anything not *directly* relating to horses. **Buys 20 mss/year.** Query or send complete ms. Length: 1,000-2,000 words. **Pays $200-400.**

Photos Send photos with submission. Reviews 35mm and medium format transparencies, 4×6 prints.

Tips "Freelancers can break in at this publication with feature articles on Western and English training methods; veterinary and general care how-to articles; and horse sports articles. We rarely use personal experience articles. Submit photos with training and how-to articles whenever possible. We have a very good record of developing new freelancers into regular contributors/columnists. We are always looking for fresh talent, but certainly enjoy working with established writers who 'know the ropes' as well. We are accepting less unsolicited freelance work—much is now assigned and contracted."

$ $THE HORSE

Your Guide to Equine Health Care, P.O. Box 4680, Lexington KY 40544-4680. (859)276-6771. Fax: (859)276-4450. E-mail: kherbert@thehorse.com. Website: www.thehorse.com. Managing Editor: Christy West. **Contact:** Kimberly S. Herbert, editor. **85% freelance written.** Monthly magazine covering equine health and care. *The Horse* is an educational/news magazine geared toward the hands-on horse owner. Estab. 1983. Circ. 55,000. **Pays on acceptance.** Publishes ms an average of 6 months after acceptance. Byline given. Buys first world and electronic rights Accepts queries by mail, e-mail. Responds in 3 months to queries. Sample copy for $2.95 or online. Writer's guidelines online.

○⇥ Break in with short horse health news items.

Nonfiction How-to, technical, topical interviews. "No first-person experiences not from professionals; this is a technical magazine to inform horse owners." **Buys 90 mss/year.** Query with published clips. Length: 250-4,000 words. **Pays $50-750 for assigned articles.**

Photos Send photos with submission. Reviews transparencies. $35-350. Captions, identification of subjects required.

Columns/Departments News Front (news on horse health), 100-500 words; Equinomics (economics of horse ownership); Step by Step (feet and leg care); Nutrition; Reproduction; Back to Basics, all 1,500-2,200 words. **Buys 50 mss/year.** Query with published clips. **Pays $50-400.**

▣ The online magazine carries original content not found in the print edition—mostly news items.

Tips "We publish reliable horse health care and management information from top industry professionals and researchers around the world. Manuscript must be submitted electronically or on disk."

$▧ HORSEPOWER

Magazine for Young Horse Lovers, Horse Publications Group, P.O. Box 670, Aurora ON L4G 4J9 Canada. Fax: (905)841-1530. E-mail: editor@horse-canada.com. Website: www.horse-canada.com. **50% freelance written.** Bimonthly magazine covering horse care and training for teens and preteens (ages 8-16). "Safety when dealing with horses is our first priority. Also, explaining techniques, etc., in terms kids can understand without over-simplifying." Estab. 1988. Circ. 10,000. Pays on publication. Publishes ms an average of 6 months after acceptance. Byline given. Buys one-time rights. Editorial lead time 2 months. Submit seasonal material 4 months in advance. Accepts queries by mail, e-mail, fax. Accepts simultaneous submissions. Responds in 3 weeks to queries; 6 months to mss. Sample copy for $2.95. Writer's guidelines for #10 SASE.

Nonfiction How-to (horse care, grooming, training, etc.), humor, interview/profile (famouse riders). **Buys 6 mss/year.** Query or send complete ms. Length: 500-1,200 words. **Pays $50-75.** Pays in contributor copies upon request.

Photos Send photos with submission. Reviews 4×6 prints, GIF/JPEG files. Buys one-time rights. Offers $10-15/photo. Captions required.

Columns/Departments How To . . . (step-by-step), 1,000 words. **Buys 3 mss/year.** Query or send complete ms. **Pays $50-75.**

Fiction Adventure, humorous, slice-of-life vignettes. Nothing too young for the readership or stories about "How I Won the Big Race," etc. **Buys 2 mss/year.** Length: 500-1,200 words. **Pays $50-75.**

Tips "Writers must have a firm grasp on all aspects of horse ownership, training, health care, etc. Most of our readers are quite intelligent and do not want to be talked down to. Articles must not be too simplistic."

$I LOVE CATS

I Love Cats Publishing, 16 Meadow Hill Lane, Armonk NY 10504. (908)222-0990. Fax: (908)222-8228. E-mail: ilovecatseditor@sbcglobal.net. Website: www.iluvcats.com. **Contact:** Lisa Allmendinger, editor. **100% free-lance written.** Bimonthly magazine. "*I Love Cats* is a general interest cat magazine for the entire family. It caters to cat lovers of all ages. The stories in the magazine include fiction, nonfiction, how-to, humorous, and columns for the cat lover." Estab. 1989. Circ. 25,000. Pays on publication. Publishes ms an average of 2 years after acceptance. Byline given. Must sign copyright consent form. Buys all rights. Editorial lead time 6 months. Submit seasonal material 9 months in advance. Accepts queries by mail, e-mail. Responds in 3 months to queries. Sample copy for $5. Writer's guidelines online.

Nonfiction Essays, general interest, how-to, humor, inspirational, interview/profile, new product, opinion, personal experience, photo feature. No poetry. **Buys 50 mss/year.** Send complete ms. Length: 500-1,000 words. **Pays $50-100, or contributor copies or other premiums if requested.** Sometimes pays expenses of writers on assignment.

Photos Please send copies; art will no longer be returned. Send photos with submission. Buys all rights. Offers no additional payment for photos accepted with ms. Identification of subjects required.

Fiction Adventure, fantasy, historical, humorous, mainstream, mystery, novel excerpts, slice-of-life vignettes, suspense. "This is a family magazine. No graphic violence, pornography, or other inappropriate material. *I Love Cats* is strictly 'G-rated.'" **Buys 50 mss/year.** Send complete ms. Length: 500-1,000 words. **Pays $25-100.**

Fillers Anecdotes, facts, short humor. **Buys 25/year. Pays $25.**

Tips "Please keep stories short and concise. Send complete manuscript with photos, if possible. I buy lots of first-time authors. Nonfiction pieces with color photos are always in short supply. With the exception of the standing columns, the rest of the magazine is open to freelancers. Be witty, humorous, or offer a different approach to writing."

$ $KITTENS USA

Adopting and Caring for Your Kitten, Fancy Publications, Inc., P.O. Box 6050, Mission Viejo CA 92690. (949)855-8822. **Contact:** Editor. **90% freelance written.** Annual publication for kitten buyers. Estab. 1997. Pays on publication. Buys first North American serial rights. Editorial lead time 6 months. Responds in 3 months to queries. Sample copy not available. Writer's guidelines for #10 SASE.

Nonfiction Healthcare, training, adoption. **Buys 20 mss/year.** Query with published clips. Length: 1,000-2,000 words. **Pays $50-450.**

Photos Looking for happy, healthy, well-groomed kittens in studio or indoor settings. Guidelines for #10 SASE. Buys one-time rights. Negotiates payment individually. Captions, identification of subjects, model releases required.

Tips "No fiction or poetry. Please read recent issues to become acquainted with our style and content. Show us in your query how you can contribute something new and unique. No phone queries."

$MINIATURE DONKEY TALK

Miniature Donkey Talk, Inc., 1338 Hughes Shop Rd., Westminster MD 21158-2911. (410)875-0118. Fax: (410)857-9145. E-mail: minidonk@qis.net. Website: www.qis.net/~minidonk/mdt.htm. Bonnie Gross, editor. **65% freelance written.** Bimonthly magazine covering donkeys, with articles on healthcare, promotion, and management of donkeys for owners, breeders, or donkey lovers. Estab. 1987. Circ. 4,925. **Pays on acceptance.** Publishes ms an average of 4 months after acceptance. Byline given. Buys first, second serial (reprint) rights. Editorial lead time 2 months. Submit seasonal material 3 months in advance. Accepts queries by mail, e-mail, fax. Accepts previously published material. Responds in 2 weeks to queries; 1 month to mss. Sample copy for $5. Writer's guidelines free.

Nonfiction "We accept breeder profiles—either of yourself or another breeder. (The full address and/or telephone number of the breeder will not appear in the article as this would constitute advertising.) We cover nonshow events such as fairs, donkey gatherings, holiday events, etc. (We do not pay for coverage of an event that you were involved in organizing.) We want relevant, informative equine health pieces. We much prefer they deal specifically with donkeys, but will consider articles geared toward horses. If at all possible, substitute the word 'horse' for 'donkey.' We reserve the right to edit, change, delete, or add to health articles. Please be careful in the accuracy of advice or treatment and review the material with a veterinarian. We are also interested in detailed instructional or training material, as well as farm management articles and fictional stories on donkeys." Book excerpts, humor, interview/profile, personal experience. **Buys 6 mss/year.** Query with published clips. Length: 700-7,000 words. **Pays $25-150.**

Tips "Simply send your manuscript. If on topic and appropriate, there is a good possibility it will be published."

$ $MUSHING

Stellar Communications, Inc., P.O. Box 149, Ester AK 99725-0149. (907)479-0454. Fax: (907)479-3137. E-mail: editor@mushing.com. Website: www.mushing.com. Publisher: Todd Hoener. **Contact:** Mary Haley, managing editor. Bimonthly magazine covering all aspects of the growing sports of dogsledding, skijoring, carting, dog packing, and weight pulling. "*Mushing* promotes responsible dog care through feature articles and updates on working animal health care, safety, nutrition, and training." Estab. 1987. Circ. 6,000. Pays within 3 months of publication. Publishes ms an average of 4 months after acceptance. Byline given. Buys first, second serial (reprint) rights. Submit seasonal material 4 months in advance. Accepts queries by mail, e-mail, fax, phone. Responds in 8 months to queries. Sample copy for $5 ($6 US to Canada). Writer's guidelines online.

Nonfiction "We consider articles on canine health and nutrition, sled dog behavior and training, musher profiles and interviews, equipment how-to's, trail tips, expedition and race accounts, innovations, sled dog history, current issues, personal experiences, and humor." Historical/nostalgic, how-to. Special issues: Iditarod and Long-Distance Racing (January/February); Ski or Sprint Racing (March/April); Health and Nutrition (May/June); Musher and Dog Profiles, Summer Activities (July/August); Equipment, Fall Training (September/October); Races and Places (November/December). Query with or without published clips. Considers complete ms with SASE. Length: 1,000-2,500 words. **Pays $50-250.** Sometimes pays expenses of writers on assignment.

Photos "We look for good b&w and quality color for covers and specials." Send photos with submission. Reviews contact sheets, negatives, transparencies, prints. Buys one-time and second reprint rights. Pays $20-165/photo. Captions, identification of subjects, model releases required.

Columns/Departments Query with or without published clips or send complete ms.

Fillers Anecdotes, facts, newsbreaks, short humor, cartoons, puzzles. Length: 100-250 words. **Pays $20-35.**

Tips "Read our magazine. Know something about dog-driven, dog-powered sports."

$$ PAINT HORSE JOURNAL

American Paint Horse Association, P.O. Box 961023, Fort Worth TX 76161-0023. (817)834-2742. Fax: (817)222-8466. E-mail: jnice@apha.com. Website: www.painthorsejournal.com. **Contact:** Jennifer Nice, editor. **10% freelance written.** Works with a small number of new/unpublished writers each year. Monthly magazine for people who raise, breed and show Paint Horses. Estab. 1966. Circ. 30,000. **Pays on acceptance.** Byline given. Offers negotiable kill fee. Buys first North American serial rights. Submit seasonal material 3 months in advance. Accepts queries by mail, e-mail, fax. Sample copy for $4.50. Writer's guidelines online.

Nonfiction General interest (personality pieces on well-known owners of Paints), historical/nostalgic (Paint Horses in the past—particular horses and the breed in general), how-to (train and show horses), photo feature (Paint Horses). **Buys 4-5 mss/year.** Query. Length: 1,000-2,000 words. **Pays $100-650.**

Photos Photos must illustrate article and must include registered Paint Horses. Send photos with submission. Reviews 35mm or larger transparencies, 3×5 or larger color glossy prints, digital images on CD or DVD. Offers no additional payment for photos accepted with accompanying ms. Captions required.

Tips "Well-written first person articles are welcomed. Submit items that show a definite understanding of the horse business. Be sure you understand precisely what a Paint Horse is as defined by the American Paint Horse Association. Use proper equine terminology. Photos with copy are almost always essential."

$ ROCKY MOUNTAIN RIDER MAGAZINE

Regional All-Breed Horse Monthly, P.O. Box 1011, Hamilton MT 59840. (406)363-4085. Fax: (406)363-1056. Website: www.rockymountainrider.com. **Contact:** Natalie Riehl, editor. **90% freelance written.** Monthly magazine for horse owners and enthusiasts. Estab. 1993. Circ. 14,500. Pays on publication. Publishes ms an average of 6 months after acceptance. Byline given. Buys one-time rights. Submit seasonal material 6 months in advance. Accepts simultaneous submissions. Responds in 1 month to queries; 2 months to mss. Sample copy for free. Writer's guidelines for #10 SASE.

Nonfiction Book excerpts, essays, general interest, historical/nostalgic, humor, interview/profile, new product, personal experience, photo feature, equine medical. **Buys 100 mss/year.** Send complete ms. Length: 500-2,000 words. **Pays $15-90.**

Photos Send photos with submission. Reviews 3×5 prints, e-mail digital photos. Buys one-time rights. Pays $5/photo. Captions, identification of subjects required.

Poetry Light verse, traditional. **Buys 25 poems/year.** Submit maximum 10 poems. Length: 6-36 lines. **Pays $10.**

Fillers Anecdotes, facts, gags to be illustrated by cartoonist, short humor. Length: 200-750 words. **Pays $15.**

Tips "*RMR* is looking for positive, human interest stories that appeal to an audience of horsepeople. We accept profiles of unusual people or animals, history, humor, anecdotes, cowboy poetry, coverage of regional events, and new products. We aren't looking for many 'how-to' or training articles, and are not currently looking at any fiction."

N $$ ZOO VIEW

Greater Los Angeles Zoo Association, 5333 Zoo Dr., Los Angeles CA 90027. E-mail: bposada@lazoo.org. Website: www.lazoo.org. Managing Editor: Sandy Masuo. **Contact:** Brenda Posada, director of publications. **20% freelance written.** Quarterly magazine covering animals, wildlife and conservation. "The zoo's mission is 'nurturing wildlife and enriching the human experience.' Our readers are knowledgeable and passionate about animals and respectful of nature and the environment. We seek to educate about animals in the zoo and the wild, as well as the people who care for them." Estab. 1965. Circ. 66,000. **Pays on acceptance.** Publishes ms an average of 2 months after acceptance. Byline given. Offers 25% kill fee. Buys first, electronic rights. Editorial lead time 2 months. Accepts queries by mail. Responds in 4-6 weeks to queries. Sample copy for 9 × 12 SAE with 3 first class stamps or $2. Writer's guidelines free.

Nonfiction General interest, interview/profile. Does not want "my trip to the zoo" or articles that anthropomorphize animals (give them human characteristics). **Buys 4-10 mss/year.** Query with published clips. Length: 750-2,500 words. **Pays $75-300.**

Photos State availability with submission. Buys one-time rights. Offers no additional payment for photos accepted with ms. Identification of subjects required.

Tips "Demonstrate in your query or samples a lively, engaging writing style and a knowledge of your proposed subject."

ART & ARCHITECTURE

$ $ AMERICAN ARTIST

VNU Business Media, 770 Broadway, New York NY 10003-9595. (646)654-5506. E-mail: mail@myamericanartist.com. Website: www.myamericanartist.com. Monthly magazine covering art. Written to provide information on outstanding representational artists living in the US. Estab. 1937. Circ. 116,526. Editorial lead time 18 weeks. Accepts queries by mail. Responds in 6-8 weeks to queries. Sample copy for $3.95. Writer's guidelines by e-mail.

Nonfiction Essays, exposé, interview/profile, personal experience, technical. Query with published clips and résumé. Length: 1,500-2,000 words. **Pays $500.**

$ $ AMERICAN INDIAN ART MAGAZINE

American Indian Art, Inc., 7314 E. Osborn Dr., Scottsdale AZ 85251. (480)994-5445. Fax: (480)945-9533. E-mail: info@aiamagazine.com. Website: www.aiamagazine.com. **97% freelance written.** Works with many new/unpublished writers/year. Quarterly magazine covering Native American art, historic and contemporary, including new research on any aspect of Native American art north of the US-Mexico border. Estab. 1975. Circ. 30,000. Pays on publication. Publishes ms an average of 3 months after acceptance. Byline given. Buys first, one-time rights. Responds in 6 weeks to queries; 3 months to mss. Sample copy not available. Writer's guidelines for #10 SASE or online.

Nonfiction New research on any aspect of Native American art. No previously published work or personal interviews with artists. **Buys 12-18 mss/year.** Query. Length: 6,000-7,000 words. **Pays $75-300.**

Photos An article usually requires 8-15 photographs. Buys one-time rights. Fee schedules and reimbursable expenses are decided upon by the magazine and the author.

Tips "The magazine is devoted to all aspects of Native American art. Some of our readers are knowledgeable about the field and some know very little. We seek articles that offer something to both groups. Articles reflecting original research are preferred to those summarizing previously published information."

$ $ $ AMERICANSTYLE MAGAZINE

The Rosen Group, 3000 Chestnut Ave., Suite 304, Baltimore MD 21211. (410)889-3093. Fax: (410)243-7089. E-mail: hoped@rosengrp.com. Website: www.americanstyle.com. **Contact:** Hope Daniels, editor-in-chief. **80% freelance written.** Bimonthly magazine covering arts, crafts, travel, and interior design. "*AmericanStyle* is a full-color lifestyle publication for people who love art. Our mandate is to nurture collectors with information that will increase their passion for contemporary art and craft and the artists who create it. *AmericanStyle*'s primary audience is contemporary craft collectors and enthusiasts. Readers are college-educated, age 35+, high-income earners with the financial means to collect art and craft, and to travel to national art and craft events in pursuit of their passions." Estab. 1994. Circ. 60,000. Pays on publication. Publishes ms an average of 9 months after acceptance. Buys first North American serial rights. Editorial lead time 9 months. Submit seasonal material at least 1 year in advance. Accepts queries by mail, e-mail, fax. Sample copy for $3. Writer's guidelines online. Editorial calendar online.

○→ *AmericanStyle* is especially interested in freelance ideas about arts travel, profiles of contemporary craft collectors, and established studio craft artists.

Nonfiction Specialized arts/crafts interests. Length: 600-1,500 words. **Pays $500-800.** Sometimes pays expenses of writers on assignment.

Photos Send photos with submission. Reviews oversized transparencies, 35mm slides, high resolution e-images. Negotiates payment individually. Captions required.

Columns/Departments Portfolio (profiles of emerging and established artists); Arts Walk; Origins; One on One, all 600-900 words. Query with published clips. **Pays $500-700.**

Tips ''This is not a hobby-crafter magazine. Country crafts or home crafting is not our market. We focus on contemporary American craft art, such as ceramics, wood, fiber, glass, metal.''

$ $ $ART & ANTIQUES

TransWorld Publishing, Inc., 2100 Powers Ferry Rd., Suite 300, Atlanta GA 30339. (770)955-5656. Fax: (770)952-0669. E-mail: pverbanas@billian.com. Editor: Barbara S. Tapp. **Contact:** Patti Verbanas, managing editor. **90% freelance written.** Monthly magazine covering fine art and antique collectibles and the people who collect them and/or create them. ''*Art & Antiques* is the authoritative source for elegant, sophisticated coverage of the treasures collectors love, the places to discover them, and the unique ways collectors use them to enrich their environments.'' Circ. 125,800. **Pays on acceptance.** Byline given. Offers 25% kill fee or $250. Buys all rights. Editorial lead time 8 months. Submit seasonal material 8 months in advance. Accepts queries by mail, e-mail. Responds in 6 weeks to queries; 2 months to mss. Sample copy and writer's guidelines free.

Nonfiction ''We publish 1 'interior design with art and antiques' focus feature a month.'' Essays. Special issues: Designing with art & antiques (April); contemporary art (September). **Buys 200 mss/year.** Query with or without published clips. Length: 150-1,200 words. **Pays $150-1,200 for assigned articles.** Pays $50 toward expenses of writers on assignment.

Photos Scouting shots. Send photos with submission. Reviews contact sheets, transparencies, prints. Captions, identification of subjects required.

Columns/Departments Art & Antiques News (trend coverage and timely news of issues and personalities), 100-350 words; Preview/Review (thoughts and criticisms on a variety of worldwide art exhibitions throughout the year), 600-800 words; Market Value (experts highlight popular to undiscovered areas of collecting), 600-800 words; Emerging Artist (an artist on the cusp of discovery), 600-800 words; Discoveries (collections in lesser-known museums and homes open to the public), 800-900 words; Today's Masters (peek into the studio of an artist who is currently hot or is a revered veteran allowing the reader to watch the artist in action), 800-900 words; Then & Now (the best reproductions being created today and the craftspeople behind the work), 800-900 words; World View (major art and antiques news worldwide; visuals preferred but not necessary), 600-800 words; Traveling Collector (hottest art and antiques destinations, dictated by those on editorial calendar; visuals preferred but not necessary), 800-900 words; Essay (first-person piece tackling a topic in a nonacademic way; visuals preferred but not necessary); A&A Insider (a how-to column on collecting topics); Art and Design (highlights 1 genre of decorative arts and shows revolutionary and innovative designs of that genre over the decades). **Buys 200 mss/year.** Query by mail only with or without published clips. **Pays $150-900.**

Fillers Facts, newsbreaks. **Buys 22/year.** Length: 150-300 words. **Pays $150-300.**

🖥 The online magazine carries original content not found in the print edition, though there is no payment at this time.

Tips ''Send scouting shots with your queries. We are a visual magazine and no idea will be considered without visuals. We are good about responding to writers in a timely fashion—excessive phone calls are not appreciated, but do check in if you haven't heard from us in 2 months. We like colorful, lively, and creative writing.''

$ $ART PAPERS

Atlanta Art Papers, Inc., P.O. Box 5748, Atlanta GA 31107-0748. (404)588-1837. Fax: (404)588-1836. E-mail: editor@artpapers.org. Website: www.artpapers.org. **Contact:** Sylvie Fortin, editor-in-chief. **95% freelance written.** Bimonthly magazine covering contemporary art and artists. ''*Art Papers*, about regional and national contemporary art and artists, features a variety of perspectives on current art concerns. Each issue presents topical articles, interviews, reviews from across the US, and an extensive and informative artists' classified listings section. Our writers and the artists they cover represent the scope and diversity of the country's art scene.'' Estab. 1977. Circ. 12,000. Pays on publication. Publishes ms an average of 3 months after acceptance. Byline given. Not copyrighted. Buys all rights. Editorial lead time 2 months. Submit seasonal material 2 months in advance. Sample copy not available.

Nonfiction Feature articles and reviews. **Buys 240 mss/year. Pays $60-325; unsolicited articles are on spec.**

Photos Send photos with submission. Reviews color slides, b&w prints. Offers no additional payment for photos accepted with ms. Identification of subjects required.

Columns/Departments Buys 8-10 mss/year. Query. **Pays $100-175.**

$ART TIMES

Commentary and Reasons for the Fine and Performing Arts, P.O. Box 730, Mount Marion NY 12456-0730. (845)246-6944. Fax: (845)246-6944. E-mail: info@arttimesjournal.com. Website: www.arttimesjournal.com. **Contact:** Raymond J. Steiner, editor. **10% freelance written.** Monthly tabloid covering the arts (visual, theater, dance, music, literary, etc.). ''*Art Times* covers the art fields and is distributed in locations most frequented by those enjoying the arts. Our copies are distributed throughout the Northeast as well as in most of the galleries of Soho, 57th Street and Madison Avenue in the metropolitan area; locations include theaters, galleries, museums, cultural centers and the like. Our readers are mostly over 40, affluent, art-conscious and sophisticated. Subscribers are located across US and abroad (Italy, France, Germany, Greece, Russia, etc.)." Estab. 1984. Circ. 27,000. Pays on publication. Publishes ms an average of 3 years after acceptance. Byline given. Buys first North American serial, first rights. Submit seasonal material 8 months in advance. Accepts simultaneous submissions. Responds in 6 months. Sample copy for 9×12 SAE and 6 first-class stamps. Writer's guidelines for #10 SASE or on website.

Fiction Raymond J. Steiner, fiction editor. "We're looking for short fiction that aspires to be literary." Adventure, ethnic, fantasy, historical, humorous, mainstream, science fiction, contemporary. "We seek quality literary pieces. Nothing violent, sexist, erotic, juvenile, racist, romantic, political, off-beat, or related to sports or juvenile fiction." **Buys 8-10 mss/year.** Send complete ms. Length: 1,500 words maximum. **Pays $25 maximum (honorarium) and 1 year's free subscription.**

Poetry "We prefer well-crafted 'literary' poems. No excessively sentimental poetry." Raymond J. Steiner, poetry editor. Avant-garde, free verse, haiku, light verse, traditional, poet's niche. **Buys 30-35 poems/year.** Submit maximum 6 poems. Length: 20 lines maximum. **Offers contributor copies and 1 year's free subscription.**

Tips "Be advised that we are presently on an approximate 3-year lead for short stories, 2-year lead for poetry. We are now receiving 300-400 poems and 40-50 short stories per month. We only publish 2-3 poems and 1 story each issue. Be familiar with *Art Times* and its special audience. *Art Times* has literary leanings with articles written by a staff of scholars knowledgeable in their respective fields. Although an 'arts' publication, we observe no restrictions (other than noted) in accepting fiction/poetry other than a concern for quality writing—subjects can cover anything and not specifically arts."

$🖂 ARTICHOKE

Writings About the Visual Arts, Artichoke Publishing, 208-901 Jervis St., Vancouver BC V6E 2B6 Canada. Fax: (604)683-1941. E-mail: editor@artichoke.ca. Website: www.artichoke.ca. **Contact:** Paula Gustafson, editor. **90% freelance written.** Triannual magazine. "*Artichoke* is Western Canada's visual arts magazine. Writers must be familiar with Canadian art and artists." Estab. 1989. Circ. 1,500. **Pays on acceptance.** Publishes ms an average of 6 months after acceptance. Byline given. Offers 50% kill fee. Buys one-time rights. Editorial lead time 6 months. Accepts queries by mail, e-mail, fax. Accepts simultaneous submissions. Responds in 1 week to queries; 2 weeks to mss. Sample copy for free. Writer's guidelines online.

Nonfiction Essays, interview/profile, opinion, critical reviews about Canadian visual art. "*Artichoke* does not publish fiction, poetry, or academic jargon." **Buys 100 mss/year.** Query with or without published clips or send complete ms. Length: 1,000-2,500 words. **Pays $125.**

Photos State availability of or send photos with submission. Reviews transparencies, prints. Buys one-time rights. Offers no additional payment for photos accepted with ms. Captions, identification of subjects required.

Ⓝ $ $ ARTISAN NORTHWEST

The Magazine of Northwest Art and Artists, 48906 284th Ave. SE, Enumclaw WA 98022. E-mail: editorial@artisannorthwest.com. Website: www.artisannorthwest.com. **Contact:** Diane Mettler, managing editor. **90% freelance written.** Quarterly magazine covering fine art and craft in the Northwest. "Our goal is to promote the artists and galleries of the great Northwest. We are trying to inform people about Northwest fine art and craft through the voices of artists, gallery owners, and collectors." Estab. 2004. Circ. 6,000. **Pays on acceptance.** Publishes ms an average of 2 months after acceptance. Byline given. Offers 50% kill fee. Buys first rights, makes work-for-hire assignments. Editorial lead time 4 months. Submit seasonal material 3 months in advance. Accepts queries by mail, e-mail, fax. Responds in 2 weeks to queries; 1 month to mss. Sample copy for $2.50. Writer's guidelines for #10 SASE.

Nonfiction Interview/profile, photo feature. No how-to pieces. **Buys 16-18 mss/year.** Query with published clips. Length: 900-1,200 words. **Pays $250 for assigned articles.** Pays expenses of writers on assignment.

Photos Send photos with submission. Reviews transparencies, prints, GIF/JPEG files. Buys one-time rights. Offers no additional payment for photos accepted with ms. Captions required.

Columns/Departments Gallery Openings (brief description of new galleries), 300-350 words; Events (review of previous art event in the last 3 months), 250-300 words; Art at Work (interesting work an organization is doing), 350 words; Outside Artist (short profile of self-taught artist), 450 words. Query with published clips. **Pays $75-150.**

Tips "Please write articles so that the subject matter is accessible to everyone—not just those with an art major. Profiles should focus on artists who create exceptionally unique and expressive work and whose work is of gallery quality. The pictures will let the readers see the art, the article should tell the story of the artists behind it."

[N] $ $ THE ARTIST'S MAGAZINE

F+W Publications, Inc., 4700 E. Galbraith Rd., Cincinnati OH 45236. (513)531-2690, ext. 1421. Fax: (513)891-7153. E-mail: tamedit@fwpubs.com. Website: www.artistsmagazine.com. **Contact:** Steve Smith, senior editor. **50% freelance written.** Works with a large number of new/unpublished writers each year. Monthly magazine covering primarily two-dimensional art instruction for working artists. "Ours is a highly visual approach to teaching the serious amateur and professional artists techniques that will help them improve their skills and market their work. The style should be crisp and immediately engaging, written in a voice that speaks directly to artists." Circ. 175,000. Pays on publication. Publishes ms an average of 6 months-1 year after acceptance. Bionote given for feature material. Offers 25% kill fee. Buys first North American serial, second serial (reprint) rights. Responds in 3 months to queries. Sample copy for $4.99. Writer's guidelines online.

> O—w Writers must have working knowledge of art techniques. This magazine's most consistent need is for instructional feature articles written in the artist's voice.

Nonfiction "The emphasis must be on how the reader can learn some method of improving his artwork; or the marketing of it." Mostly instructional—how an artist uses a particular technique, how he handles a particular subject or medium, or how he markets his work. Will also consider informational and human interest pieces related to the world of representational fine art. No unillustrated articles; no pieces aimed solely at collectors or art appreciators. "We do not cover sculpture or digital art." **Buys 60 mss/year.** Length: 500-1,200 words. **Pays $200-350 and up.** Sometimes pays expenses of writers on assignment.

Photos "Images of artwork must be in the form of 35mm slides or larger transparencies. High-quality digital files can be used for other images. Full captions must accompany these." Buys one-time rights.

Tips "Look at several current issues and read the author's guidelines carefully. Submissions must include artwork. Remember that our readers are fine artists."

ARTNEWS

ABC, 48 W. 38th St., New York NY 10018. (212)398-1690. Fax: (212)819-0394. E-mail: info@artnews.com. Website: www.artnews.com. Monthly magazine. "*ARTnews* reports on art, personalities, issues, trends and events that shape the international art world. Investigative features focus on art ranging from old masters to contemporary, including painting, sculpture, prints, and photography. Regular columns offer exhibition and book reviews, travel destinations, investment and appreciation advice, design insights, and updates on major art world figures." Estab. 1902. Circ. 83,017. Accepts queries by mail, e-mail, fax, phone. Sample copy not available.

[A] AZURE DESIGN, ARCHITECTURE AND ART

460 Richmond St. W., Suite 601, Toronto ON M5V 1Y1 Canada. (416)203-9674. Fax: (416)203-9842. E-mail: azure@azureonline.com. Website: www.azuremagazine.com. **Contact:** Nelda Rodger, editor. **50% freelance written.** Magazine covering design and architecture. Estab. 1985. Circ. 20,000. Pays on publication. Publishes ms an average of 1 month after acceptance. Offers variable kill fee. Buys first rights. Editorial lead time up to 45 days. Responds in 6 weeks to queries. Sample copy not available.

Nonfiction Buys 25-30 mss/year. Length: 350-2,000 words. **Payment varies.**

Columns/Departments Trailer (essay/photo on something from the built environment); and Forms & Functions (coming exhibitions, happenings in world of design), both 300-350 words. **Buys 30 mss/year.** Query. **Payment varies.**

Tips "Try to understand what the magazine is about. Writers must be well versed in the field of architecture and design. It's very unusual to get something from someone I haven't worked quite closely with and gotten a sense of who the writer is. The best way to introduce yourself is by sending clips or writing samples and describing what your background is in the field."

$ BOMB MAGAZINE

New Arts Publications, 80 Hanson Place, Suite 703, Brooklyn NY 11217. (718)636-9100. Fax: (718)636-9200. E-mail: info@bombsite.com. Website: www.bombsite.com. Editor: Betsy Sussler. Managing Editor: Lucy Raven. Quarterly magazine providing interviews between artists, writers, musicians, directors and actors. Written, edited and produced by industry professionals and funded by those interested in the arts. Publishes "work which is unconventional and contains an edge, whether it be in style or subject matter." Estab. 1981. Circ. 36,000. Pays on publication. Publishes ms an average of 3-6 months after acceptance. Buys first, one-time rights. Editorial lead time 3-4 months. Accepts queries by mail. Responds in 3-5 months to mss. Sample copy for $7, plus $1.42 postage and handling. Writer's guidelines by e-mail.

Fiction Send completed ms with SASE. Experimental, novel excerpts, contemporary. No genre: romance, science fiction, horror, western. Length: 10-12 pages average. **Pays $100, and contributor's copies.**

Poetry Send completed ms with SASE. Submit no more than 25 pages. Length: No more than 25 pages in length.

Tips Mss should be typed, double-spaced, proofread and should be final drafts.

$ $ ☑ C

international contemporary art, C The Visual Arts Foundation, P.O. Box 5, Station B, Toronto ON M5T 2T2 Canada. (416)539-9495. Fax: (416)539-9903. E-mail: editor@cmagazine.com. Website: www.cmagazine.com. **Contact:** Rosemary Heather, editor. **80% freelance written.** Quarterly magazine covering international contemporary art. "*C* provides a vital and vibrant forum for the presentation of contemporary art and the discussion of issues surrounding art in our culture, including feature articles, reviews and reports, as well as original artists' projects." Estab. 1983. Circ. 7,000. Pays on publication. Publishes ms an average of 4 months after acceptance. Byline given. Offers kill fee. Editorial lead time 3 months. Accepts queries by mail, e-mail, fax. Accepts simultaneous submissions. Responds in 6 weeks to queries; 4 months to mss. Sample copy for $10 (US). Writer's guidelines for #10 SASE.

Nonfiction Essays, general interest, opinion, personal experience. **Buys 50 mss/year.** Length: 1,000-3,000 words. **Pays $150-500 (Canadian), $105-350 (US).**

Photos State availability of or send photos with submission. Reviews 35mm transparencies or 8×10 prints. Buys one-time rights; shared copyright on reprints. Offers no additional payment for photos accepted with ms. Captions required.

Columns/Departments Reviews (review of art exhibitions), 500 words. **Buys 30 mss/year.** Query. **Pays $125 (Canadian).**

ℕ $ $ DIRECT ART MAGAZINE

Slow Art Productions, P.O. Box 503, Phoenicia NY 12464. E-mail: directartmag@aol.com. Website: www.slowart.com. **75% freelance written.** Semiannual fine art magazine covering alternative, anti-establishment, left-leaning fine art. Estab. 1998. Circ. 10,000. **Pays on acceptance.** Byline sometimes given. Buys one-time, electronic rights. Editorial lead time 2 months. Submit seasonal material 3 months in advance. Accepts queries by mail, e-mail. Accepts simultaneous submissions. Responds in 2 weeks to queries; 1 month to mss. Sample copy for 9×12 SAE and 10 first-class stamps. Writer's guidelines for #10 SASE.

Nonfiction Essays, exposé, historical/nostalgic, how-to, humor, inspirational, interview/profile, opinion, personal experience, photo feature, technical. **Buys 4-6 mss/year.** Query with published clips. Length: 1,000-3,000 words. **Pays $100-500.**

Reprints Accepts previously published submissions.

Photos State availability of or send photos with submission. Reviews 35mm slide transparencies, digital files on CD (TIF format). Buys one-time rights. Negotiates payment individually.

Columns/Departments Query with published clips. **Pays $100-500.**

ℕ $ ☑ ESPACE

Sculpture, Centre de Diffusion 3D, 4888 St. Denis, Montreal QC H2J 2L6 Canada. (514)844-9858. Fax: (514)844-3661. E-mail: espace@espace-sculpture.com. Website: www.espace-sculpture.com. **Contact:** S. Fisette, editor. **95% freelance written.** Quarterly magazine covering sculpture events. "Canada's only sculpture publication, *Espace* represents a critical tool for the understanding of contemporary sculpture. Published 4 times a year, in English and French, *Espace* features interviews, in-depth articles, and special issues related to various aspects of three dimensionality. Foreign contributors guarantee an international perspective and diffusion." Estab. 1987. Circ. 1,400. Pays on publication. Publishes ms an average of 3 months after acceptance. Byline given. Buys all rights. Editorial lead time 5 months. Submit seasonal material 3 months in advance. Accepts queries by mail. Accepts simultaneous submissions. Sample copy for free.

Nonfiction Essays, exposé. **Buys 60 mss/year.** Query. Length: 1,000-1,400 words. **Pays $60/page.**

Reprints Accepts previously published submissions.

Photos Send photos with submission. Reviews transparencies, prints. Offers no additional payment for photos accepted with ms.

L.A. ARCHITECT

The Magazine of Design in Southern California, Balcony Press, 512 E. Wilson, Suite 213, Glendale CA 91206. (818)956-5313. Fax: (818)956-5904. E-mail: jesse@balconypress.com. Website: www.laarch.com. **Contact:** Jesse Brink, editor. **80% freelance written.** Bimonthly magazine covering architecture, interiors, landscape, and other design disciplines. "*L.A. Architect* is interested in architecture, interiors, product, graphics, and landscape design as well as news about the arts. We encourage designers to keep us informed on projects, techniques, and products that are innovative, new, or nationally newsworthy. We are especially interested in new and renovated projects that illustrate a high degree of design integrity and unique answers to typical problems in the urban cultural and physical environment." Estab. 1999. Circ. 20,000. Pays on publication. Publishes ms an average of 3 months after acceptance. Byline given. Makes work-for-hire assignments. Editorial lead time 4 months. Submit seasonal material 4 months in advance. Accepts queries by mail, e-mail, fax. Responds in 1 month. Sample copy for $3. Writer's guidelines online.

Nonfiction Book excerpts, essays, historical/nostalgic, interview/profile, new product. "No technical, foo-foo interiors, or non-Southern California subjects." **Buys 20 mss/year.** Length: 500-2,000 words. **Payment negotiable.**

Photos State availability with submission. Buys one-time rights. Offers no additional payment for photos accepted with ms. Captions, identification of subjects, model releases required.

Tips "Our magazine focuses on contemporary and cutting-edge work either happening in Southern California or designed by a Southern California designer. We like to find little-known talent which has not been widely published. We are not like *Architectural Digest* in flavor so avoid highly decorative subjects. Each project, product, or event should be accompanied by a story proposal or brief description and select images. Do not send original art without our written request; we make every effort to return materials we are unable to use, but this is sometimes difficult and we must make advance arrangements for original art."

$ $ $ $ METROPOLIS

The Magazine of Architecture and Design, Bellerophon Publications, 61 W. 23rd St., 4th Floor, New York NY 10010. (212)627-9977. Fax: (212)627-9988. E-mail: edit@metropolismag.com. Website: www.metropolismag.com. Executive Editor: Martin Pedersen. **Contact:** Ariana Donalds, managing editor. **80% freelance written.** Monthly magazine (combined issues February/March and August/September) for consumers interested in architecture and design. Estab. 1981. Circ. 45,000. Pays 60-90 days after acceptance. Publishes ms an average of 3 months after acceptance. Byline given. Makes work-for-hire assignments. Submit seasonal material 3 months in advance. Accepts queries by mail, e-mail, fax. Responds in 8 months to queries. Sample copy for $7. Writer's guidelines online.

Nonfiction Martin Pedersen, executive editor. Essays (design, architecture, urban planning issues and ideas), interview/profile (of multi-disciplinary designers/architects). No profiles on individual architectural practices, information from public relations firms, or fine arts. **Buys 30 mss/year.** Length: 1,500-4,000 words. **Pays $1,500-4,000.**

Photos Reviews contact sheets, 35mm or 4×5 transparencies, 8×10 b&w prints. Buys one-time rights. Payment offered for certain photos. Captions required.

Columns/Departments The Metropolis Observed (architecture, design, and city planning news features), 100-1,200 words, **pays $100-1,200**; Perspective (opinion or personal observation of architecture and design), 1,200 words, **pays $1,200**; Enterprise (the business/development of architecture and design), 1,500 words, **pays $1,500**; In Review (architecture and book review essays), 1,500 words, **pays $1,500**. Direct queries to Julien Devereux, managing editor. **Buys 40 mss/year.** Query with published clips.

    The online magazine carries original content not found in the print edition. Contact: Julie Taraska (jtaraska@metropolismag.com).

Tips "*Metropolis* strives to tell the story of design to a lay person with an interest in the built environment, while keeping the professional designer engaged. The magazine examines the various design disciplines (architecture, interior design, product design, graphic design, planning, and preservation) and their social/cultural context. We're looking for the new, the obscure, or the wonderful. Also, be patient and don't expect an immediate answer after submission of query."

$ $ MIX

Independent Art and Culture Magazine, Parallelogramme Artist-Run Culture and Publishing, Inc., 401 Richmond St., Suite 446, Toronto ON M5V 3A8 Canada. (416)506-1012. Fax: (416)506-0141. E-mail: info@mixmagazine.com. Website: www.mixmagazine.com. **95% freelance written.** Quarterly magazine covering Artist-Run gallery activities. "*Mix* represents and investigates contemporary artistic practices and issues, especially in the progressive Canadian artist-run scene." Estab. 1975. Circ. 3,500. Pays on publication. Publishes ms an average of 6 months after acceptance. Byline given. Offers 40% kill fee. Buys first North American serial rights. Editorial lead time 6 months. Submit seasonal material 4 months in advance. Accepts queries by mail, e-mail, fax. Responds in 2 months to queries; 3 months to mss. Sample copy for $6.95, 8½×10¼ SAE and 6 first-class stamps. Writer's guidelines online.

Nonfiction Essays, interview/profile. **Buys 12-20 mss/year.** Query with published clips. Length: 750-3,500 words. **Pays $100-450.**

Reprints Send photocopy of article and information about when and where the article previously appeared.

Photos State availability with submission. Buys one-time rights. Captions, identification of subjects required.

Columns/Departments Features, 1,000-3,000 words; Art Reviews, 500 words. Query with published clips. **Pays $100-450.**

Tips "Read the magazine and other contemporary art magazines. Understand the idea 'artist-run.' We're not interested in 'artsy-phartsy' editorial, but rather pieces that are critical, dynamic, and would be of interest to nonartists too."

$ $MODERNISM MAGAZINE

333 N. Main St., Lambertville NJ 08530. (609)397-4104. Fax: (609)397-4409. E-mail: andrea@modernismmagazi ne.com. Website: www.modernismmagazine.com. Publisher: David Rago. **Contact:** Andrea Truppin, editor-in-chief. **70% freelance written.** Quarterly magazine covering 20th century art and design. ''We are interested in objects and the people who created them. Our coverage begins in the 1920s with Art Deco and related movements, and ends with 1980s Post-Modernism, leaving contemporary design to other magazines. Our emphasis is on the decorative arts—furniture, pottery, glass, textiles, metalwork, and so on—but we're moving toward more coverage of interiors.'' Estab. 1998. Circ. 20,000. Pays on publication. Publishes ms an average of 4 months after acceptance. Byline given. Offers 25% kill fee. Buys all rights. Editorial lead time 6 months. Submit seasonal material 6 months in advance. Accepts queries by mail, e-mail, fax. Accepts previously published material. Accepts simultaneous submissions. Responds in 1 month to queries. Sample copy for $6.95. Writer's guidelines free.

Nonfiction Book excerpts, essays, historical/nostalgic, interview/profile, new product, photo feature. ''No first-person.'' **Buys 20 mss/year.** Query with published clips. Length: 2,000-2,500 words. **Pays $400 for assigned articles.**

Reprints Accepts previously published submissions.

Photos State availability of or send photos with submission. Reviews contact sheets, transparencies, prints. Buys one-time rights. Negotiates payment individually. Captions, identification of subjects required.

Tips ''Articles should be well researched, carefully reported, and directed at a popular audience with a special interest in the Modernist movement. Please don't assume readers have prior familiarity with your subject; be sure to tell us the who, what, why, when, and how of whatever you're discussing.''

$ $WATERCOLOR

VNU Business Media, 770 Broadway, New York NY 10003. (646)654-5506. Fax: (646)654-5514. E-mail: mail@m yamericanartist.com. Website: www.myamericanartist.com. **Contact:** M. Stephen Doherty, editor-in-chief. Quarterly magazine devoted to watermedia artists. Circ. 80,000. Editorial lead time 4 months.

Nonfiction Essays, exposé, interview/profile, personal experience, technical. Query with published clips. Length: 1,500-2,000 words. **Pays $500.**

$ $WILDLIFE ART

The Art Journal of the Natural World, Pothole Publications, Inc., 1428 E. Cliff Rd., Burnsville MN 55337. Fax: (952)736-1030. E-mail: mnelson@wildlifeartmag.com. Website: www.wildlifeartmag.com. Publisher: Robert Koenke. **Contact:** Mary Nelson, editor. **60% freelance written.** Bimonthly magazine. ''*Wildlife Art* is the world's foremost magazine of the natural world, featuring wildlife, landscape, and western art. Features living artists as well as wildlife art masters, illustrators, and conservation organizations. Special emphasis on landscape and plein-air paintings. Audience is collectors, galleries, museums, show promoters worldwide.'' Estab. 1982. Circ. 30,000. Pays on publication. Publishes ms an average of 6 months after acceptance. Byline given. Offers negotiable kill fee. Buys second serial (reprint) rights. Accepts queries by mail, e-mail. Responds in 6 months to queries. Sample copy for 9×12 SAE and 10 first-class stamps. Writer's guidelines online.

Nonfiction General interest, historical/nostalgic, interview/profile. **Buys 40 mss/year.** Query with published clips, include artwork samples. Length: 800-1,500 words. **Pays $150-500.**

Tips ''Best way to break in is to offer concrete story ideas, new talent, and a new unique twist of artistic excellence.''

ASSOCIATIONS

$ $ $ $AMERICAN EDUCATOR

American Federation of Teachers, 555 New Jersey Ave., Washington DC 20001. (202)879-4420. Fax: (202)879-4534. E-mail: amered@aft.org. Website: www.aft.org/american_educator/index.html. **Contact:** Ruth Wattenberg, editor. **50% freelance written.** Quarterly magazine covering education, condition of children, and labor issues. ''*American Educator*, the quaterly magazine of the American Federation of Teachers, reaches over 800,000 public school teachers, higher education faculty, and education researchers and policymakers. The magazine concentrates on significant ideas and practices in education, civics, and the condition of children in America and around the world.'' Estab. 1977. Circ. 850,000. Pays on publication. Publishes ms an average of 2-6 months after acceptance. Byline given. Offers 50% kill fee. Buys one-time, electronic rights. Editorial lead time 1 year. Submit seasonal material 6 months in advance. Accepts queries by mail, e-mail, fax. Accepts previously published material. Accepts simultaneous submissions. Responds in 2 months to queries; 6 months to mss. Sample copy and writer's guidelines online.

Nonfiction Book excerpts, essays, historical/nostalgic, interview/profile, discussions of educational research.

No pieces that are not supportive of the public schools. **Buys 8 mss/year.** Query with published clips. Length: 1,000-7,000 words. **Pays $750-3,000 for assigned articles; $300-1,000 for unsolicited articles.** Pays expenses of writers on assignment.

Photos State availability with submission. Reviews contact sheets, negatives, transparencies, 8×10 prints, GIF/JPEG files. Buys one-time rights. Negotiates payment individually. Captions, identification of subjects, model releases required.

$ $ DAC NEWS

Official Publication of the Detroit Athletic Club, Detroit Athletic Club, 241 Madison Ave., Detroit MI 48226. (313)442-1034. Fax: (313)442-1047. E-mail: kenv@thedac.com. **Contact:** Kenneth Voyles, editor/publisher. **20% freelance written.** Magazine published 10 times/year. "*DAC News* is the magazine for Detroit Athletic Club members. It covers club news and events, plus general interest features." Estab. 1916. Circ. 5,000. Pays on publication. Publishes ms an average of 3 months after acceptance. Byline given. Buys one-time rights, makes work-for-hire assignments. Editorial lead time 3 months. Submit seasonal material 3 months in advance. Accepts queries by mail, phone. Responds in 1 month to queries. Sample copy for free.

Nonfiction General interest, historical/nostalgic, photo feature. "No politics or social issues—this is an entertainment magazine. We do not acccept unsolicited manuscripts or queries for travel articles." **Buys 2-3 mss/year.** Length: 1,000-2,000 words. **Pays $100-500.** Sometimes pays expenses of writers on assignment.

Photos Illustrations only. State availability with submission. Reviews transparencies, 4×6 prints. Buys one-time rights. Negotiates payment individually. Captions, identification of subjects, model releases required.

Tips "Review our editorial calendar. It tends to repeat from year to year, so a freelancer with a fresh approach to one of these topics will get our attention quickly. It helps if articles have some connection with the DAC, but this is not absolutely necessary. We also welcome articles on Detroit history, Michigan history, or automotive history."

$ $ $ DCM

Data Center Management: Bringing Insight and Ideas to the Data Center Community, AFCOM, 742 E. Chapman Ave., Orange CA 92866. Fax: (714)997-9743. E-mail: cdrysdale@afcom.com. Website: www.afcom.com. Executive Editor: Jill Eckhaus. **Contact:** Chelsey Drysdale, managing editor. **50% freelance written.** Bimonthly magazine covering data center management. "*DCM* is the slick, 4-color, bimonthly publication for members of AFCOM, the leading association for data center management." Estab. 1988. Circ. 4,000 worldwide. Pays on acceptance for assigned articles and on publication for unsolicited articles. Publishes ms an average of 3 months after acceptance. Byline given. Offers 0-10% kill fee. Buys all rights. Editorial lead time 6-12 months. Submit seasonal material 6 months in advance. Responds in 1-3 weeks to queries; 1-3 months to mss. Writer's guidelines online.

● Prefers queries by e-mail.

Nonfiction How-to, technical, management as it relates to and includes examples of data centers and data center managers. Special issues: "The January/February issue is the annual 'Emerging Technologies' issue. Articles for this issue are visionary and product neutral." No product reviews or general tech articles. **Buys 15 + mss/year.** Query with published clips. Length: 2,000 word maximum. **Pays 50¢/word and up, based on writer's expertise.**

Photos "We rarely consider freelance photos." State availability with submission. Reviews GIF/JPEG files. Buys one-time rights. Offers no additional payment for photos accepted with ms. Identification of subjects, model releases required.

Tips "See 'Top 10 Reasons for Rejection' and editorial guidelines online."

$ $ THE ELKS MAGAZINE

425 W. Diversey P, Chicago IL 60614-6196. (773)755-4740. E-mail: elksmag@elks.org. Website: www.elks.org/elksmag. Editor: Cheryl T. Stachura. **Contact:** Anna L. Idol, managing editor. **25% freelance written.** Magazine published 10 times/year with basic mission of being the "voice of the Elks." All material concerning the news of the Elks is written in-house. Estab. 1922. Circ. 1,037,000. **Pays on acceptance.** Buys first North American serial rights. Responds in 1 month with a yes/no on ms purchase. Responds in 2 weeks to queries. Sample copy for 9×12 SAE with 5 first-class stamps or online. Writer's guidelines online.

● Accepts queries by mail, but purchase decision is based on final mss only.

Nonfiction "We're really interested in seeing manuscripts on business, technology, sports, health, Americana, science, history, or just intriguing topics." No fiction, religion, controversial issues, first-person, fillers, or verse. **Buys 20-30 mss/year.** Send complete ms. Length: 1,500-2,500 words. **Pays 25¢/word.**

Photos If possible, please advise where photographs may be found. Photographs taken and submitted by the writer are paid for separately at $25 each. Send transparencies, slides. Pays $475 for one-time cover rights.

Tips "Please try us first. We'll get back to you soon."

$ $⊠ FRANCHISE CANADA MAGAZINE

August Communications, 225-530 Century St., Winnipeg MB R3H 0Y4 Canada. Fax: (866)957-0217. E-mail: k.hodgson@august.ca. Website: www.august.ca. **Contact:** Kathleen Hodgson, editor. **70% freelance written.** Bimonthly magazine covering the franchising industry in Canada. "*Franchise Canada Magazine* is the Canadian Franchise Association publication for all franchise industry stakeholders, including current and future franchisees and franchisors." Estab. 1999. Circ. 6,500. Pays 30 days after publication. Publishes ms an average of 2 months after acceptance. Byline given. Buys all rights. Accepts queries by e-mail, fax.

Nonfiction How-to (investigate a franchise system—research methods), interview/profile (CFA franchise members/businesses), technical (aspects of franchising). **Buys 12 mss/year.** Query with published clips. Length: 1,000-1,800 words. **Pays 15-30¢/word.**

Photos State availability with submission. Reviews GIF/JPEG files. Buys all rights. Negotiates payment individually. Captions required.

Columns/Departments Franchisor Profiles (profiles of CFA members), 1,500-1,800 words. **Buys 10 mss/year.** Query with published clips. **Pays 15-30¢/word.**

Tips "Research the Canadian Franchise Association website, www.cfa.ca."

$ $ THE KEEPER'S LOG

U.S. Lighthouse Society, 244 Kearny St., San Francisco CA 94108. (415)362-7255. **Contact:** Wayne Wheeler, editor. **10% freelance written.** Quarterly magazine covering lighthouses, lightships, and human interest relating to them. "Our audience is national (some foreign members). The magazine carries historical and contemporary information (articles) relating to technical, human interest, history, etc." Estab. 1984. Circ. 11,000. Pays on publication. Publishes ms an average of 6 months after acceptance. Byline given. Buys first rights. Editorial lead time 6 months. Accepts queries by mail. Responds in 1 week to queries. Sample copy for $7. Writer's guidelines for #10 SASE.

Nonfiction Historical/nostalgic, personal experience, photo feature, technical. Ghost stories need not apply. Buys 1 ms/year. Query. Length: 2,500-5,000 words. **Pays $200-400.**

Photos State availability with submission. Reviews 5×7 prints. Offers no additional payment for photos accepted with ms. Identification of subjects required.

$ $⊘ KIWANIS

3636 Woodview Trace, Indianapolis IN 46268. (317)875-8755. Fax: (317)879-0204. E-mail: magazine@kiwanis.org. Website: www.kiwanis.org. **10% freelance written.** Magazine published 6 times/year for business and professional persons and their families. Estab. 1917. Circ. 240,000. **Pays on acceptance.** Publishes ms an average of 6 months after acceptance. Byline given. Offers 40% kill fee. Buys first rights. Accepts queries by mail, e-mail, fax. Responds in 1 month to queries. Sample copy and writer's guidelines for 9×12 SAE with 5 first class stamps. Writer's guidelines online.

• No unsolicited mss.

Nonfiction Articles about social and civic betterment, small-business concerns, children, science, education, religion, family, health, recreation, etc. Emphasis on objectivity, intelligent analysis, and thorough research of contemporary issues. Positive tone preferred. Concise, lively writing, absence of clichés, and impartial presentation of controversy required. Articles must include information and quotations from international sources. "We have a continuing need for articles that concern helping youth, particularly prenatal through age 5: day care, developmentally appropriate education, early intervention for at-risk children, parent education, safety and health. No fiction, personal essays, profiles, travel pieces, fillers, or verse of any kind. A light or humorous approach is welcomed where the subject is appropriate and all other requirements are observed." **Buys 20 mss/year.** Length: 500-1,200 words. **Pays $300-600.** Sometimes pays expenses of writers on assignment.

Photos "We accept photos submitted with manuscripts. Our rate for a manuscript with good photos is higher than for one without." Buys one-time rights. Identification of subjects, model releases required.

Tips "We will work with any writer who presents a strong feature article idea applicable to our magazine's audience and who will prove he or she knows the craft of writing. First, obtain writer's guidelines and a sample copy. Study for general style and content. When querying, present detailed outline of proposed manuscript's focus and editorial intent. Indicate expert sources to be used, as well as possible Kiwanis sources for quotations and anecdotes. Present a well-researched, smoothly written manuscript that contains a 'human quality' with the use of anecdotes, practical examples, quotations, etc."

$ $ LEGACY MAGAZINE

National Association for Interpretation, P.O. Box 2246, Fort Collins CO 80522. (970)484-8283. Fax: (970)484-8179. Website: www.interpnet.com/interpnet/miscpages/publication.htm. **80% freelance written.** Bimonthly magazine covering heritage interpretation (national parks, museums, nature centers, aquaria, etc.). "The National Association for Interpretation's premier publication, *Legacy Magazine*, offers a thought-provoking look at the field of heritage interpretation through articles about individuals who interpret natural and cultural history, biographies of important figures in or related to the field, discussions of interpretive sites, and trends in interpretation. The magazine, published 6 times a year, appeals to those interested in learning about natural or cultural heritage and interpretive sites around the world.'' Estab. 1989. Circ. 5,000. Pays on publication. Publishes ms an average of 4 months after acceptance. Byline given. Offers 80% kill fee. Buys first North American serial rights. Editorial lead time 6 months. Submit seasonal material 4 months in advance. Accepts queries by mail, e-mail, fax, phone. Accepts simultaneous submissions. Responds in 1 month to queries; 4 months to mss. Sample copy online. Writer's guidelines by e-mail.

Nonfiction Essays, historical/nostalgic, opinion, personal experience, photo feature, travel, heritage interpretation. **Buys 12-20 mss/year.** Query. Length: 500-2,500 words. **Pays $75-350.** Sometimes pays expenses of writers on assignment.

Photos State availability with submission. Reviews contact sheets, 4×6 prints, GIF/JPEG files. Buys one-time rights. Offers $75-100/photo. Captions required.

Columns/Departments Visitor's View (review of personal experience at a heritage interpretation site), 500 words. **Buys 6 mss/year.** Query. **Pays $75-150.**

Tips ''Please review the article descriptions in our writer's guidelines before submitting a query.''

$ $ THE LION

300 W. 22nd St., Oak Brook IL 60523-8815. (630)571-5466. Fax: (630)571-8890. E-mail: rkleinfe@lionsclubs.org. Website: www.lionsclubs.org. **Contact:** Robert Kleinfelder, senior editor. **35% freelance written.** Works with a small number of new/unpublished writers each year. Monthly magazine covering service club organization for Lions Club members and their families. Estab. 1918. Circ. 490,000. **Pays on acceptance.** Publishes ms an average of 5 months after acceptance. Byline given. Buys all rights. Accepts queries by mail, e-mail, fax, phone. Responds in 1 month to queries. Sample copy and writer's guidelines free.

Nonfiction Welcomes humor, if sophisticated but clean; no sensationalism. Prefers anecdotes in articles. Photo feature (must be of a Lions Club service project), informational (issues of interest to civic-minded individuals). No travel, biography, or personal experiences. **Buys 40 mss/year.** Length: 500-1,500 words. **Pays $100-750.** Sometimes pays expenses of writers on assignment.

Photos Purchased with accompanying ms. ''Photos should be at least 5×7 glossies; color prints or slides are preferred. We also accept digital photos by e-mail. Be sure photos are clear and as candid as possible.'' Total purchase price for ms includes payment for photos accepted with ms. Captions required.

Tips ''Send detailed description of proposed article. Query first and request writer's guidelines and sample copy. Incomplete details on how the Lions involved actually carried out a project and poor quality photos are the most frequent mistakes made by writers in completing an article assignment for us. No gags, fillers, quizzes, or poems are accepted. We are geared increasingly to an international audience. Writers who travel internationally could query for possible assignments, although only locally related expenses could be paid.''

$ $ $ THE MEETING PROFESSIONAL

Meeting Professionals International, 3030 LBJ Freeway, Suite 1700, Dallas TX 75234. Fax: (972)702-3096. E-mail: publications@mpiweb.org. Website: www.themeetingprofessional.org. Associate Publisher: Bruce Mac-Millan. Editor-in-Chief: John Delavan. **Contact:** Kirsten Rockwood, publications coordinator. **60% freelance written.** Monthly magazine covering the global meeting idustry. ''*The Meeting Professional* delivers strategic editorial content on meeting industry trends, opportunities and items of importance in the hope of fostering professional development and career enhancement. The magazine is mailed monthly to 19,000 MPI members and 11,500 qualified nonmember subscribers and meeting industry planners. It is also distributed at major industry shows, such as IT&ME and EIBTM, at MPI conferences, and upon individual request.'' Circ. 32,000. **Pays on acceptance.** Publishes ms an average of 2-3 months after acceptance. Byline given. Offers a negotiable kill fee. Buys all rights. Editorial lead time 2 months. Submit seasonal material 3 months in advance. Accepts queries by mail, e-mail, fax. Sample copy for free. Writer's guidelines by e-mail.

Nonfiction General interest, how-to, interview/profile, travel, industry-related. No duplications from other industry publications. **Buys 60 mss/year.** Query with published clips. Length: 1,000-2,500 words. **Pays 50-75¢/ word for assigned articles.**

Tips ''Understand and have experience within the industry. Writers who are familiar with our magazine and our competitors are better able to get our attention, send better queries, and get assignments.''

ℕ $ $ PENN LINES

Pennsylvania Rural Electric Association, 212 Locust St., P.O. Box 1266, Harrisburg PA 17108. E-mail: pas@prea. com. Website: www.prea.com/pennlines/plonline.htm. **Contact:** Perry Stambaugh, editor. Monthly magazine covering rural life in Pennsylvania. News magazine of Pennsylvania electric cooperatives. Features should be balanced, and they should have a rural focus. Electric cooperative sources (such as consumers) should be used.

Estab. 1966. Circ. 140,000. Pays on publication. Publishes ms an average of 3 months after acceptance. Byline given. Buys first rights. Editorial lead time 4 months. Submit seasonal material 4 months in advance. Accepts queries by mail, e-mail. Sample copy and writer's guidelines online.

Nonfiction General interest, historical/nostalgic, how-to, interview/profile, travel (rural PA only). **Buys 6 mss/year.** Query or send complete ms. Length: 500-2,000 words. **Pays $300-650.**

Photos Reviews transparencies, prints, GIF/JPEG files. Buys one-time rights and right to publish online. Negotiates payment individually. Captions required.

Tips "Find topics of statewide interest to rural residents. Detailed information on *Penn Lines'* readers, gleaned from a reader survey, is available online."

$ $ PERSPECTIVES IN HEALTH

Pan American Health Organization, 525 23rd St. NW, Washington DC 20037-2895. (202)974-3122. Fax: (202)974-3143. E-mail: eberwind@paho.org. Website: www.paho.org. **Contact:** Donna Eberwine, editor. **80% freelance written.** Magazine published 3 times/year covering international public health with a focus on the Americas. "*Perspectives in Health,* the popular magazine of the Pan American Health Organization (PAHO), was created in 1996 to serve as a forum on current issues in the area of international public health and human development. PAHO works with the international community, government institutions, nongovernmental organizations, universities, community groups, and others to strengthen national and local public health systems and to improve the health and well-being of the peoples of the Americas." Estab. 1996. Circ. 10,000. **Pays on acceptance.** Publishes ms an average of 6 months after acceptance. Byline given. Buys first North American serial rights and electronic rights to post articles on the PAHO website. Editorial lead time 2 months. Accepts queries by mail, e-mail, fax, phone. Responds in 2 months to faxed/mailed queries; 1 week to e-mail queries. Sample copy and writer's guidelines free.

• Each issue of *Perspectives in Health* is published in English and Spanish.

Nonfiction Subject matter: Culturally insightful and scientifically sound articles related to international public health and human development issues and programs affecting North America, Latin America, and the Caribbean. The story angle should have wide relevancy—i.e., capturing national and particularly international concerns, even if the setting is local—and should be high in human interest content: "international public health with a human face." General topics may include (but are not limited to) AIDS and other sexually transmitted diseases, maternal and child health, the environment, food and nutrition, cardiovascular diseases, cancer, mental health, oral health, violence, veterinary health, disaster preparedness, health education and promotion, substance abuse, water and sanitation, and issues related to the health and well-being of women, adolescents, workers, the elderly, and minority groups in the countries of the Americas. Historical pieces on the region's public health "trail blazers" and innovators are also welcome. General interest, historical/nostalgic, interview/profile, opinion, personal experience, photo feature. No highly technical, highly bureaucratic articles. **Buys 12 mss/year.** Query with or without published clips or send complete ms. Length: 1,500-3,000 words. **Pays $250.** Sometimes pays expenses of writers on assignment.

Photos State availability with submission. Reviews contact sheets, negatives, transparencies, prints. Buys one-time rights. Negotiates payment individually. Captions, identification of subjects, model releases required.

Columns/Departments Last Word, 750 words. **Buys 2 mss/year.** Query with or without published clips or send complete ms. **Pays $100.**

Tips "*Perspectives* puts the human face on international public health issues and programs. All facts must be documented. Quote people involved with the programs described. Get on-site information—not simply an Internet-researched story."

$ $ RECREATION NEWS

Official Publication of the ESM Association of the Capital Region, 7339 Hanover Pkwy., Suite D, Greenbelt MD 20770. (301)474-4600. Fax: (301)474-6283. Website: www.recreationnews.com. **85% freelance written.** Monthly guide to leisure-time activities for federal and private industry workers covering outdoor recreation, travel, fitness and indoor pasttimes. Estab. 1979. Circ. 110,000. Pays on publication. Publishes ms an average of 8 months after acceptance. Byline given. Buys first, second serial (reprint) rights. Submit seasonal material 10 months in advance. Accepts queries by mail, e-mail, fax, phone. Accepts previously published material. Accepts simultaneous submissions. Responds in 2 months to queries. Sample copy and writer's guidelines for 9×12 SAE with $1.05 in postage.

Nonfiction Historical/nostalgic (Washington-related), personal experience (with recreation, life in Washington), travel (mid-Atlantic travel only), sports; hobbies. Special issues: skiing (December). **Buys 45 mss/year.** Query with published clips. Length: 800-2,000 words. **Pays $50-300.**

Reprints Send tearsheet or typed ms with rights for sale noted and information about when and where the material previously appeared. Pays $50.

Photos Call for details.

Tips "Our writers generally have a few years of professional writing experience and their work runs to the lively and conversational. We like more manuscripts in a wide range of recreational topics, including the off-beat. The areas of our publication most open to freelancers are general articles on travel and sports, both participational and spectator, also historic in the DC area. In general, stories on sites visited need to include info on nearby places of interest and places to stop for lunch, to shop, etc."

N $ $ $ THE ROTARIAN

Rotary International, 1560 Sherman Ave., Evanston IL 60201-4818. (847)866-3000. Fax: (847)866-9732. E-mail: chamberj@rotaryintl.org. Website: www.rotary.org. **Contact:** Janice Chambers, managing editor. **40% freelance written.** Monthly magazine for Rotarian business and professional men and women and their families, schools, libraries, hospitals, etc. "Articles should appeal to an international audience and in some way help Rotarians help other people. The organization's rationale is one of hope, encouragement, and belief in the power of individuals talking and working together." Estab. 1911. Circ. 510,000. **Pays on acceptance.** Byline sometimes given. Kill fee negotiable. Buys one-time, all rights. Accepts queries by mail, e-mail. Accepts previously published material. Sample copy for 9×12 SAE with 6 first-class stamps. Writer's guidelines for #10 SASE.

Nonfiction General interest, humor, inspirational, photo feature, travel, sports, business, environmental. No fiction, religious, or political articles. Query with published clips. Length: about 1,500 words. **Pays negotiable rate.**

Reprints Send tearsheet, photocopy or typed ms with rights for sale noted and information about when and where the material previously appeared. Negotiates payment.

Photos State availability with submission. Reviews contact sheets, transparencies. Buys one-time rights.

Columns/Departments Manager's Memo (business); Database; Health Watch; Earth Diary; Travel Tips, all 650 words. Query.

Tips "The chief aim of *The Rotarian* is to report Rotary International news. Most of this information comes through Rotary channels and is staff written or edited. The best field for freelance articles is in the general interest category. We prefer queries with a Rotary angle. These stories run the gamut from humor pieces and 'how-to' stories to articles about such significant concerns as business management, technology, world health, and the environment."

$ $ $ SCOUTING

Boy Scouts of America, 1325 W. Walnut Hill Lane, P.O. Box 152079, Irving TX 75015-2079. (972)580-2367. Fax: (972)580-2079. Website: www.scoutingmagazine.org. Executive Editor: Scott Daniels. **Contact:** Jon C. Halter, editor. **80% freelance written.** Magazine published 6 times/year covering Scouting activities for adult leaders of the Boy Scouts, Cub Scouts, and Venturing. Estab. 1913. Circ. 1,000,000. Pays on acceptance for major features and some shorter features. Publishes ms an average of 18 months after acceptance. Byline given. Buys first North American serial rights. Editorial lead time 1 year. Submit seasonal material 1 year in advance. Accepts queries by mail, fax. Accepts previously published material. Accepts simultaneous submissions. Responds in 1 month to queries; 2 months to mss. Sample copy for $2.50 and 9×12 SAE with 4 first-class stamps or online. Writer's guidelines online.

- **O—** Break in with "a profile of an outstanding Scout leader who has useful advice for new volunteer leaders (especially good if the situation involves urban Scouting or Scouts with disabilities or other extraordinary roles)."

Nonfiction Program activities, leadership techniques and styles, profiles, inspirational, occasional general interest for adults (humor, historical, nature, social issues, trends). Inspirational, interview/profile. **Buys 20-30 mss/year.** Query with published clips and SASE. Length: 600-1,200 words. **Pays $750-1,000 for major articles, $300-500 for shorter features.** Pays expenses of writers on assignment.

Reprints Send photocopy of article and information about when and where the article previously appeared. "First-person accounts of meaningful Scouting experiences (previously published in local newspapers, etc.) are a popular subject."

Photos State availability with submission. Reviews transparencies, prints. Buys one-time rights. Identification of subjects required.

Columns/Departments Way It Was (Scouting history), 600-750 words; Family Talk (family—raising kids, etc.), 600-750 words. **Buys 8-12 mss/year.** Query. **Pays $300-500.**

Fillers "Limited to personal accounts of humorous or inspirational Scouting experiences." Anecdotes, short humor. **Buys 15-25/year.** Length: 50-150 words. **Pays $25 on publication.**

Tips "*Scouting* magazine articles are mainly about successful program activities conducted by or for Cub Scout packs, Boy Scout troops, and Venturing crews. We also include features on winning leadership techniques and styles, profiles of outstanding individual leaders, and inspirational accounts (usually first person) or *Scouting*'s impact on an individual, either as a youth or while serving as a volunteer adult leader. Because most volunteer

Scout leaders are also parents of children of Scout age, *Scouting* is also considered a family magazine. We publish material we feel will help parents in strengthening their families (because they often deal with communicating and interacting with young people, many of these features are useful to a reader in both roles as parent and Scout leader)."

ℕ $ $ THE TOASTMASTER

Toastmasters International, P.O. Box 9052, Mission Viejo CA 92690. (949)858-8255. E-mail: kmurphy@toastmasters.org. Website: www.toastmasters.org. **Contact:** Kelly Murphy. **50% freelance written.** Monthly magazine on public speaking, leadership, and club concerns. "This magazine is sent to members of Toastmasters International, a nonprofit educational association of men and women throughout the world who are interested in developing their communication and leadership skills. Members range from novice to professional speakers and from a wide variety of ethnic and cultural backgrounds, as Toastmasters is an international organization." Estab. 1933. Circ. 185,000. **Pays on acceptance.** Publishes ms an average of 1 year after acceptance. Byline given. Buys first, second serial (reprint), all rights. Submit seasonal material 3-4 months in advance. Accepts previously published material. Accepts simultaneous submissions. Responds in 2-3 months. Sample copy for 9×12 SASE with 4 first-class stamps. Writer's guidelines for #10 SASE, online or by e-mail.

Nonfiction "Toastmasters members are requested to view their submissions as contributions to the organization. Sometimes asks for book excerpts and reprints without payment, but original contribution from individuals outside Toastmasters will be paid for at stated rates." How-to, humor, interview/profile (well-known speakers and leaders), communications, leadership, language use. **Buys 50 mss/year.** Query by mail or e-mail (e-mail preferred). Length: 1,000-2,500 words. **Pays $250-350.** Sometimes pays expenses of writers on assignment.

Reprints Send ms with rights for sale noted and information about when and where the material previously appeared. Pays 50-70% of amount paid for an original article.

Tips "We are looking primarily for 'how-to' articles on subjects from the broad fields of communications and leadership which can be directly applied by our readers in their self-improvement and club programming efforts. Concrete examples are useful. *Avoid sexist or nationalist language and 'Americanisms' such as football examples, etc.*"

ℕ $ $ U MAG

A Magazine for Young USAA Members, USAA, 9800 Fredericksburg Rd., San Antonio TX 78288. Fax: (210)498-0030. E-mail: shari.biediger@usaa.com. **Contact:** Shari Biediger, senior editor. **75% freelance written.** Quarterly magazine covering money, safety, history, human interest, military related. Estab. 1995. Circ. 439,000. **Pays on acceptance.** Publishes ms an average of 6 months after acceptance. Buys all rights. Editorial lead time 6 months. Submit seasonal material 9 months in advance. Accepts queries by mail, e-mail, fax. Accepts simultaneous submissions. Sample copy and writer's guidelines free.

Nonfiction General interest, historical/nostalgic, how-to, humor, interview/profile, personal experience. Nothing religious. **Buys 4-6 mss/year.** Query with published clips. Length: 250-500 words.

Fiction Adventure, historical, humorous. Buys 1 ms/year.

Fillers Anecdotes, facts, gags to be illustrated by cartoonist, short humor. **Buys 2/year.**

Tips "Write for a tween audience (ages 9-12). Shouldn't sound like textbook material."

ℕ $ $ U-TURN

For Teen USAA Members, USAA, 9800 Fredericksburg Rd., San Antonio TX 78288. Fax: (210)498-0030. E-mail: shari.biediger@usaa.com. **Contact:** Shari Biediger, senior editor. **85% freelance written.** Quarterly magazine covering driving, college prep, lifestyle, and money. Estab. 1998. Circ. 545,000. **Pays on acceptance.** Publishes ms an average of 6 months after acceptance. Offers 30% kill fee. Buys all rights. Editorial lead time 6 months. Submit seasonal material 9 months in advance. Accepts queries by mail, e-mail, fax. Responds in 6 weeks to queries; 6 months to mss. Sample copy and writer's guidelines free.

Nonfiction How-to, humor, interview/profile. **Buys 6 mss/year.** Query with published clips. Length: 250-500 words. Sometimes pays expenses of writers on assignment.

Tips "Read other magazines targeted at this age group (13-17)."

$ $ $ UPDATE

New York Academy of Sciences, 2 E. 63rd St., New York NY 10021. E-mail: dvanatta@nyas.org. Website: www.nyas.org. **Contact:** Dan Van Atta, editor. **40% freelance written.** Magazine published 7 times/year covering science, health issues. Scientific newsletter for members of the New York Academy of Sciences. Estab. 2001. Circ. 25,000. Pays on publication. Publishes ms an average of 1 month after acceptance. Byline sometimes given. Not copyrighted. Buys first, electronic rights, makes work-for-hire assignments. Editorial lead time 2 months. Submit seasonal material 2 months in advance. Accepts queries by mail, e-mail. Sample copy online.

Nonfiction All articles "must be science or medical related in every case." Book excerpts, essays, general interest, historical/nostalgic, interview/profile, technical. No science fiction, any pieces exceeding 1,000 words, or subjects that aren't current. **Buys 6-7 mss/year.** Query. Length: 300-1,000 words. **Pays $200-1,200.** Sometimes pays expenses of writers on assignment.

Photos State availability with submission. Reviews GIF/JPEG files. Buys one-time rights. Negotiates payment individually. Captions, identification of subjects, model releases required.

Tips "Submit detailed summary or outline of the proposed article's content. Subject matter must be current and topical, as well as scientific, technical, or medical in nature. We prefer interviews with noted scientific and medical researchers whose work is cutting edge and credible. Articles should be relatively brief and contain some 'news' element, i.e., important recent development or unusual, attention-getting element. All sources must be identified and credible."

$ $ VFW MAGAZINE

Veterans of Foreign Wars of the United States, 406 W. 34th St., Kansas City MO 64111. (816)756-3390. Fax: (816)968-1169. E-mail: jcarter@vfw.org. Website: www.vfw.org. **Contact:** Rich Kolb, editor-in-chief. **40% freelance written.** Monthly magazine on veterans' affairs, military history, patriotism, defense, and current events. "*VFW Magazine* goes to its members worldwide, all having served honorably in the armed forces overseas from World War II through the war on terrorism." Circ. 1,800,000. **Pays on acceptance.** Byline given. Offers 50% kill fee. Buys first rights. Submit seasonal material 6 months in advance. Accepts queries by mail, e-mail, fax. Responds in 2 months to queries. Sample copy for 9×12 SAE with 5 first-class stamps.

> O— Break in with "fresh and innovative angles on veterans' rights; stories on little-known exploits in US military history. Will be particularly in the market for Vietnam War battle accounts during 2005. Upbeat articles about severely disabled veterans who have overcome their disabilities; feel-good patriotism pieces; current events as they relate to defense policy; and health and retirement pieces are always welcome."

Nonfiction Veterans' and defense affairs, recognition of veterans and military service, current foreign policy, American armed forces abroad, and international events affecting US national security are in demand. **Buys 25-30 mss/year.** Query with 1-page outline, résumé, and published clips. Length: 1,000 words. **Pays up to $500 maximum unless otherwise negotiated.**

Photos Send photos with submission. Reviews contact sheets, negatives, color (2¼×2¼) preferred transparencies, 5×7 or 8×10 b&w prints. Buys first North American rights. Captions, identification of subjects required.

Tips "Absolute accuracy and quotes from relevant individuals are a must. Bibliographies useful if subject required extensive research and/or is open to dispute. Counsult *The Associated Press Stylebook* for correct grammar and punctuation. Please enclose a 3-sentence biography describing your military service and your military experience in the field in which you are writing. No phone queries."

VINTAGE SNOWMOBILE MAGAZINE

Vintage Snowmobile Club of America, P.O. Box 508, Luverne MN 56156. (507)283-1860. E-mail: info@vsca.com. Website: www.vsca.com. **Contact:** Terry Hoffman, editor. **75% freelance written.** Quarterly magazine covering vintage snowmobiles and collectors. *Vintage Snowmobile Magazine* deals with vintage snowmobiles and is sent to members of the Vintage Snowmobile Club of America. Estab. 1987. Circ. 2,400. **Pays on acceptance.** Publishes ms an average of 3 months after acceptance. Byline sometimes given. Buys first North American serial rights. Editorial lead time 2 months. Submit seasonal material 3 months in advance. Accepts queries by mail, e-mail, fax, phone.

Nonfiction General interest, historical/nostalgic, humor, photo feature, coverage of shows. Query with published clips. Length: 200-2,000 words.

Photos Send photos with submission. Reviews 3×5 prints, GIF/JPEG files. Buys all rights. Negotiates payment individually.

Columns/Departments Featured Sleds Stories, 500 words. Query with published clips.

ASTROLOGY, METAPHYSICAL & NEW AGE

$ $ FATE MAGAZINE

P.O. Box 460, Lakeville MN 55044. (952)431-2050. E-mail: fate@fatemag.com. Website: www.fatemag.com. **Contact:** Editor. **70% freelance written.** Estab. 1948. Circ. 20,000. Pays on publication. Byline given. Buys all rights. Responds in 3 months.

Nonfiction Personal psychic and mystical experiences, 350-500 words. **Pays $25.** Articles on parapsychology, Fortean phenomena, cryptozoology, spiritual healing, flying saucers, new frontiers of science, and mystical aspects of ancient civilizations, 500-3,000 words. Must include complete authenticating details. Prefers interesting accounts of single events rather than roundups. "We very frequently accept manuscripts from new writers;

the majority are people's first-person accounts of their own psychic/mystical/spiritual experiences. We do need to have all details, where, when, why, who and what, included for complete documentation. We ask for a notarized statement attesting to truth of the article." Query. **Pays 10¢/word.**

Photos Buys slides, prints, or digital photos/illustrations with ms. Pays $10.

Fillers Fillers are especially welcomed and must be be fully authenticated also, and on similar topics. Length: 50-300 words.

Tips "We would like more stories about current paranormal or unusual events."

$ MAGICAL BLEND MAGAZINE

A Primer for the 21st Century, P.O. Box 600, Chico CA 95927. (530)893-9037. Fax: (530)893-9076. E-mail: editor@magicalblend.com. Website: www.magicalblend.com. **Contact:** Michael Peter Langevin, editor. **50% freelance written.** Bimonthly magazine covering social and mystical transformation. "*Magical Blend* endorses no one pathway to spiritual growth, but attempts to explore many alternative possibilities to help transform the planet." Estab. 1980. Circ. 100,000. Pays on publication. Publishes ms an average of 2 months after acceptance. Byline given. Responds in 2-6 months to mss. Sample copy for free. Writer's guidelines for #10 SASE.

> **O━** Break in by "writing a great article that gives our readers something they can use in their daily lives or obtain 'name' interviews."

Nonfiction "Articles must reflect our standards; see our magazine." Book excerpts, essays, general interest, inspirational, interview/profile, religious, travel. No poetry or fiction. **Buys 24 mss/year.** Send complete ms. Length: 1,000-2,000 words. **Pays $35-100.**

Photos State availability with submission. Reviews transparencies. Buys all rights. Negotiates payment individually. Identification of subjects, model releases required.

Fillers Newsbreaks. **Buys 12-20/year.** Length: 300-450 words. **Pays variable rate.**

$ NEW YORK SPIRIT MAGAZINE

107 Sterling Place, Brooklyn NY 11217. (800)634-0989. Fax: (718)230-3459. E-mail: office@nyspirit.com. Website: www.nyspirit.com. Bimonthly tabloid covering spirituality and personal growth and transformation. "We are a magazine that caters to the holistic health community in New York City." Circ. 50,000. **Pays on acceptance.** Publishes ms an average of 3 months after acceptance. Byline given. Buys first rights. Editorial lead time 1 month. Accepts previously published material. Accepts simultaneous submissions. Responds in 1 month to queries. Sample copy for 8×10 SAE and 10 first-class stamps. Writer's guidelines online.

Nonfiction Essays, how-to, humor, inspirational, interview/profile, photo feature. **Buys 30 mss/year.** Query with or without published clips. Length: 1,000-3,500 words. **Pays $150 maximum.**

Photos State availability with submission. Model releases required.

Columns/Departments Fitness (new ideas in staying fit), 1,500 words. **Pays $150.**

Fiction Humorous, mainstream, inspirational. **Buys 5 mss/year.** Query with published clips. Length: 1,000-3,500 words. **Pays $150.**

Tips "Be vivid and descriptive. We are very interested in hearing from new writers."

$ PANGAIA

Earthwise Spirituality, Blessed Bee, Inc., P.O. Box 641, Point Arena CA 95468. Fax: (707)882-2793. E-mail: info@pangaia.com. Website: www.pangaia.com. Editor: Anne Newkirk Niven. Managing Editor: Elizabeth Barrette. **50% freelance written.** Quarterly magazine of Earth spirituality covering Earth-based religions. "We publish articles pertinent to an Earth-loving readership. Mysticism, science, humor, tools all are described." Estab. 1994. Circ. 10,000. Pays on publication. Publishes ms an average of 6 months after acceptance. Byline given. Offers $10 kill fee. Buys first North American serial, electronic rights. Editorial lead time 6 months. Submit seasonal material 6 months in advance. Accepts queries by mail, e-mail. Responds in 2-8 weeks to queries. Sample copy for $5. Writer's guidelines online.

Nonfiction Book excerpts, essays, how-to, humor, inspirational, interview/profile, photo feature, religious, Reviews. Special issues: Contact editor for upcoming themes. No material on unrelated topics. **Buys 30 mss/ year.** Query. Length: 500-5,000 words. **Pays 1-3¢/word.** Sometimes pays with contributor copies or other premiums rather than a cash payment if negotiated/requested by writer. Sometimes pays expenses of writers on assignment.

Photos State availability with submission. Reviews 5×7 prints, GIF/JPEG files. Buys one-time rights. Negotiates payment individually. Model releases required.

Fiction Ethnic, fantasy, religious, science fiction, Pagan/Gaian. No grim or abstract stories. **Buys 5 mss/year.** Send complete ms. Length: 500-5,000 words. **Pays 1-3¢/word.**

Poetry Will consider most forms. Free verse, traditional. "Avoid clichés like the burning times. Do not send forms with rhyme/meter unless those features are executed perfectly." **Buys 12 poems/year.** Submit maximum 5 poems. Length: 3-100 lines. **Pays $10.**

Tips "Share a spiritual insight that can enlighten others. Back up your facts with citations where relevant, and make those facts sound like the neatest thing since self-lighting charcoal. Explain how to solve a problem; offer a new way to make the world a better place. We would also like to see serious scholarship on nature religion topics, material of interest to intermediate or advanced practicioners, which is both accurate and engaging."

$ SHAMAN'S DRUM

A Journal of Experiential Shamanism, Cross-Cultural Shamanism Network, P.O. Box 270, Williams OR 97544. (541)846-1313. Fax: (541)846-1204. **Contact:** Timothy White, editor. **75% freelance written.** Quarterly educational magazine of cross-cultural shamanism. "*Shaman's Drum* seeks contributions directed toward a general but well-informed audience. Our intent is to expand, challenge, and refine our readers' and our understanding of shamanism in practice. Topics include indigenous medicineway practices, contemporary shamanic healing practices, ecstatic spiritual practices, and contemporary shamanic psychotherapies. Our overall focus is cross-cultural, but our editorial approach is culture-specific—we prefer that authors focus on specific ethnic traditions or personal practices about which they have significant firsthand experience. We are looking for examples of not only how shamanism has transformed individual lives but also practical ways it can help ensure survival of life on the planet. We want material that captures the heart and feeling of shamanism and that can inspire people to direct action and participation, and to explore shamanism in greater depth." Estab. 1985. Circ. 14,000. Publishes ms an average of 6 months after acceptance. Byline given. Buys first North American serial, first rights. Editorial lead time 1 year. Accepts previously published material. Responds in 3 months to queries. Sample copy for $7. Writer's guidelines for #10 SASE.

Nonfiction Book excerpts, essays, interview/profile (please query), opinion, personal experience, photo feature. No fiction, poetry, or fillers. **Buys 16 mss/year.** Send complete ms. Length: 5,000-8,000 words. **Pays 5-8¢/word, "depending on how much we have to edit."**

Reprints Send ms with rights for sale noted and information about when and where the material previously appeared. Pays 50% of amount paid for an original article.

Photos Send photos with submission. Reviews contact sheets, transparencies, All size prints. Buys one-time rights. Offers $40-50/photo. Identification of subjects required.

Columns/Departments Judy Wells, Earth Circles. Timothy White, Reviews. Earth Circles (news format, concerned with issues, events, organizations related to shamanism, indigenous peoples, and caretaking Earth); Reviews (in-depth reviews of books about shamanism or closely related subjects such as indigenous lifestyles, ethnobotany, transpersonal healing, and ecstatic spirituality), 500-1,500 words. **Buys 8 mss/year.** Query. **Pays 5¢/word.**

Tips "All articles must have a clear relationship to shamanism, but may be on topics which have not traditionally been defined as shamanic. We prefer original material that is based on, or illustrated with, first-hand knowledge and personal experience. Articles should be well documented with descriptive examples and pertinent background information. Photographs and illustrations of high quality are always welcome and can help sell articles."

N $ WHOLE LIFE TIMES

21225 Pacific Coast Highway, Malibu CA 90265. (310)317-4200. E-mail: editor@wholelifetimes.com. Website: www.wholelifetimes.com. **Contact:** Eliza Thomas, associate editor. Monthly tabloid for cultural creatives. Estab. 1979. Circ. 58,000. Pays within 1-2 months after publication. Byline given. Buys first North American serial rights. Accepts queries by mail, e-mail. Sample copy for $3. Writer's guidelines for #10 SASE.

Nonfiction Social justice, food health, alternative healing, eco-travel, political issues, spiritual, conscious business, leading-edge information, relevant celebrity profiles. Special issues: Healing Arts, Food and Nutrition, Spirituality, New Beginnings, Relationships, Longevity, Arts/Cultures Travel, Vitamins and Supplements, Women's Issues, Sexuality, Science and Metaphysics, Environment/Simple Living. **Buys 60 mss/year.** Query with published clips or send complete ms. **Payment varies.**

Reprints Send ms with rights for sale noted and information about when and where the material previously appeared. Pays 50% of amount paid for an original article.

Columns/Departments Healing; Parenting; Finance; Food; Personal Growth; Relationships; Humor; Travel; Politics; Sexuality; Spirituality; and Psychology. Length: 750-1,200 words.

Tips "Queries should be professionally written and show an awareness of current topics of interest in our subject area. We welcome investigative reporting and are happy to see queries that address topics in a political context. We are especially looking for articles on health and nutrition. No monthly columns sought."

AUTOMOTIVE & MOTORCYCLE

$ AMERICAN MOTORCYCLIST

American Motorcyclist Association, 13515 Yarmouth Dr., Pickerington OH 43147. (614)856-1900. Fax: (614)856-1920. E-mail: bwood@ama-cycle.org. Website: www.ama-cycle.org. **Contact:** Bill Wood, managing editor. **10%**

freelance written. Monthly magazine for "enthusiastic motorcyclists investing considerable time and money in the sport. We emphasize the motorcyclist, not the vehicle." Estab. 1947. Circ. 260,000. Pays on publication. Byline given. Buys first North American serial rights. Editorial lead time 3 months. Submit seasonal material 4 months in advance. Accepts queries by mail, e-mail. Responds in 5 weeks to queries; 6 weeks to mss. Sample copy for $1.25. Writer's guidelines free.

Nonfiction Interview/profile (with interesting personalities in the world of motorcycling), personal experience, travel. **Buys 8 mss/year.** Query with or without published clips or send complete ms. Length: 1,000-2,500 words. **Pays minimum $8/published column inch.**

Photos Send photos with submission. Reviews transparencies, prints. Buys one-time rights. Pays $50/photo minimum. Captions, identification of subjects required.

Tips "Our major category of freelance stories concerns motorcycling trips to interesting North American destinations. Prefers stories of a timeless nature."

$ $ AUTO RESTORER

BowTie, Inc., 3 Burroughs, Irvine CA 92618. (949)855-8822. Fax: (949)855-3045. E-mail: tkade@fancypubs.com. Website: www.autorestorermagazine.com. **Contact:** Ted Kade, editor. **85% freelance written.** Monthly magazine covering auto restoration. "Our readers own old cars and they work on them. We help our readers by providing as much practical, how-to information as we can about restoration and old cars." Estab. 1989. Pays on publication. Publishes ms an average of 3 months after acceptance. Buys first North American serial, one-time rights. Submit seasonal material 4 months in advance. Accepts queries by mail, e-mail, fax. Responds in 2 months to queries. Sample copy for $7. Writer's guidelines free.

Nonfiction How-to (auto restoration), new product, photo feature, technical, product evaluation. **Buys 60 mss/year.** Query with or without published clips. Length: 200-2,500 words. **Pays $150/published page, including photos and illustrations.**

Photos Technical drawings that illustrate articles in black ink are welcome. Send photos with submission. Reviews contact sheets, transparencies, 5×7 prints. Offers no additional payment for photos accepted with ms.

Tips "Query first. Interview the owner of a restored car. Present advice to others on how to do a similar restoration. Seek advice from experts. Go light on history and nonspecific details. Make it something that the magazine regularly uses. Do automotive how-tos."

$ $ AUTOMOBILE QUARTERLY

The Connoisseur's Magazine of Motoring Today, Yesterday, and Tomorrow, Automobile Heritage Publishing & Communications LLC, 800 E. 8th St., New Albany IN 47150. (812)948-2886. Fax: (812)948-2816. Website: www.autoquarterly.com. Publisher: Gerald Durnell. **Contact:** Mr. Tracy L. Powell, managing editor. **85% freelance written.** Quarterly magazine covering "automotive history, with excellent photography." Estab. 1962. Circ. 8,000. **Pays on acceptance.** Publishes ms an average of 1 year after acceptance. Byline given. Buys first international serial rights. Editorial lead time 9 months. Responds in 1 month to queries; 2 months to mss. Sample copy for $19.95.

Nonfiction Historical/nostalgic, photo feature, technical, biographies. **Buys 25 mss/year.** Query. Length: 2,500-5,000 words. **Pays approximately 35¢/word or more.** Sometimes pays expenses of writers on assignment.

Photos State availability with submission. Reviews 4×5; 35mm; 120 transparencies; historical prints. Buys perpetual rights of published photography per work-for-hire freelance agreement.

Tips "Please query, with clips, via snail mail. No phone calls, please. Study *Automobile Quarterly*'s unique treatment of automotive history first."

$ $ $ $ AUTOWEEK

Crain Communications, Inc., 1155 Gratiot Ave., Detroit MI 48207. (313)446-6000. Fax: (313)446-1027. E-mail: bgritzinger@crain.com. Website: www.autoweek.com. Editor: Dutch Mandel. Managing Editor: Roger Hart. **Contact:** Bob Gritzinger, news editor. **3% freelance written,** all by regular contributors. Weekly magazine. "*AutoWeek* is the country's only weekly magazine for the auto enthusiast." Estab. 1958. Circ. 350,000. Pays on publication. Publishes ms an average of 1 month after acceptance. Byline given. Buys all rights. Accepts queries by mail, e-mail, fax.

Nonfiction Historical/nostalgic, interview/profile. **Buys 5 mss/year.** Query. Length: 100-400 words. **Pays $1/word.**

$ $ BACKROADS

Motorcycles, Travel & Adventure, Backroads, Inc., P.O. Box 317, Branchville NJ 07826. (973)948-4176. Fax: (973)948-0823. E-mail: editor@backroadsusa.com. Website: www.backroadsusa.com. Managing Editor: Shira Kamil. **Contact:** Brian Rathjen, editor/publisher. **80% freelance written.** Monthly tabloid covering motorcycle touring. "*Backroads* is a motorcycle tour magazine geared toward getting motorcyclists on the road and traveling. We provide interesting destinations, unique roadside attractions and eateries, plus Rip & Ride Route Sheets. We cater to all brands. If you really ride, you need *Backroads*.'' Estab. 1995. Circ. 40,000. Pays on publication. Publishes ms an average of 3 months after acceptance. Byline given. Buys one-time rights. Editorial lead time 1 month. Submit seasonal material 3 months in advance. Accepts queries by mail, e-mail, fax. Accepts previously published material. Responds in 3 weeks to queries. Sample copy for $2. Writer's guidelines free.

Nonfiction Shira Kamil, editor/publisher. Essays (motorcycle/touring), how-to, humor, new product, opinion, personal experience, technical, travel. ''No long diatribes on 'How I got into motorcycles.''' **Buys 2-4 mss/ year.** Query. Length: 500-2,500 words. **Pays 10¢/word minimum for assigned articles; 5¢/word minimum for unsolicited articles.** Pays writers contributor copies or other premiums for short pieces.

Photos Send photos with submission. Reviews contact sheets. Offers no additional payment for photos accepted with ms.

Columns/Departments We're Outta Here (weekend destinations), 500-750 words; Great All-American Diner Run (good eateries with great location), 300-800 words; Thoughts from the Road (personal opinion/insights), 250-500 words; Mysterious America (unique and obscure sights), 300-800 words; Big City Getaway (day trips), 500-750 words. **Buys 20-24 mss/year.** Query. **Pays 2¢/word-$50/article.**

Fiction Adventure, humorous. **Buys 2-4 mss/year.** Query. Length: 500-1,500 words. **Pays 2-4¢/word.**

Fillers Facts, newsbreaks. Length: 100-250 words.

Tips ''We prefer destination-oriented articles in a light, layman's format, with photos (negatives or transparencies preferred). Stay away from any name-dropping and first-person references.''

$ $ $ ☑ CANADIAN BIKER MAGAZINE

735 Market St., Victoria BC V8T 2E2 Canada. (250)384-0333. Fax: (250)384-1832. E-mail: edit@canadianbiker.c om. Website: canadianbiker.com. **Contact:** John Campbell, editor. **65% freelance written.** Magazine covering motorcycling. ''A family-oriented motorcycle magazine whose purpose is to unite Canadian motorcyclists from coast to coast through the dissemination of information in a non-biased, open forum. The magazine reports on new product, events, touring, racing, vintage and custom motorcycling as well as new industry information.'' Estab. 1980. Circ. 20,000. Publishes ms an average of 1 year after acceptance. Byline given. Buys first rights. Editorial lead time 3 months. Accepts queries by mail, e-mail, fax, phone. Responds in 6 weeks to queries; 6 months to mss. Sample copy for $5 or online. Writer's guidelines free.

Nonfiction All nonfiction must include photos and/or illustrations. General interest, historical/nostalgic, how-to, interview/profile (Canadian personalities preferred), new product, technical, travel. **Buys 12 mss/year.** Query with or without published clips or send complete ms. Length: 500-1,500 words. **Pays $100-200 for assigned articles; $80-150 for unsolicited articles.**

Photos State availability of or send photos with submission. Reviews 4×4 transparencies, 3×5 prints. Buys one-time rights. Negotiates payment individually. Captions, identification of subjects, model releases required.

Tips ''We're looking for more racing features, rider profiles, custom sport bikes, quality touring stories, 'extreme' riding articles. Contact editor first before writing anything. Have original ideas, an ability to write from an authoritative point of view, and an ability to supply quality photos to accompany text. Writers should be involved in the motorcycle industry and be intimately familiar with some aspect of the industry which would be of interest to readers. Observations of the industry should be current, timely, and informative.''

☑ $ $ $ $ CAR AND DRIVER

Hachette Filipacchi Magazines, Inc., 2002 Hogback Rd., Ann Arbor MI 48105-9795. (734)971-3600. Fax: (734)971-9188. E-mail: editors@caranddriver.com. Website: www.caranddriver.com. Monthly magazine for auto enthusiasts; college-educated, professional, median 24-35 years of age. Estab. 1956. Circ. 1,300,000. **Pays on acceptance.** Byline given. Offers 25% kill fee. Buys first North American serial rights. Accepts queries by mail, e-mail, fax. Responds in 2 months to queries.

Nonfiction Seek stories about people and trends, including racing. Two recent freelance purchases include news-feature on cities across America banning ''cruising'' and feature on how car companies create ''new car smells.'' All road tests are staff-written. ''Unsolicited manuscripts are not accepted. Query letters must be addressed to the Managing Editor. Rates are generous, but few manuscripts are purchased from outside.'' **Buys 1 mss/year. Pays max $3,000/feature; $750-1,500/short piece.** Pays expenses of writers on assignment.

Photos Color slides and b&w photos sometimes purchased with accompanying ms.

■ The online magazine carries original content not found in the print edition. Contact: Sue Conroy, online editor.

Tips ''It is best to start off with an interesting query and to stay away from nuts-and-bolts ideas because that will be handled in-house or by an acknowledged expert. Our goal is to be absolutely without flaw in our presentation of automotive facts, but we strive to be every bit as entertaining as we are informative. We do not print this sort of story: 'My Dad's Wacky, Lovable Beetle.' ''

N $ $ CLASSIC TRUCKS

Primedia/McMullen Argus Publishing, 2400 E. Katella Ave., Suite 1100, Anaheim CA 92806. (714)939-2589. Fax: (714)978-6390. E-mail: rob.fortier@primedia.com. Website: www.classictrucks.com. **Contact:** Rob Fortier, editor. Monthly magazine covering classic trucks from the 1930s to 1973. Estab. 1994. Circ. 60,000. Pays on publication. Byline given. Buys first North American serial rights. Editorial lead time 4 months. Submit seasonal material 4 months in advance. Writer's guidelines free.

Nonfiction How-to, interview/profile, new product, technical, travel. Query. Length: 1,500-5,000 words. **Pays $75-200/page; $100/page maximum for unsolicited articles.**

Photos Send photos with submission. Reviews transparencies, 5×7 prints. Buys one-time rights. Negotiates payment individually. Captions, identification of subjects, model releases required.

Columns/Departments Buys 24 mss/year. Query.

N $ $ $ FOUR WHEELER MAGAZINE

6420 Wilshire Blvd., Los Angeles CA 90048. E-mail: fourwheeleditor@primedia.com. Website: www.fourwheeler.com. **Contact:** Douglas McColloch, editorial director. **20% freelance written.** Works with a small number of new/unpublished writers each year. Monthly magazine covering four-wheel-drive vehicles, back-country driving, competition, and travel adventure. Estab. 1963. Circ. 355,466. Pays on publication. Publishes ms an average of 4 months after acceptance. Buys all rights. Submit seasonal material 4 months in advance. Accepts queries by mail. Sample copy not available.

Nonfiction 4WD competition and travel/adventure articles, technical, how-tos, and vehicle features about unique four-wheel drives. "We like the adventure stories that bring four wheeling to life in word and photo: mud-running deserted logging roads, exploring remote, isolated trails or hunting/fishing where the 4x4 is a necessity for success." Query with photos. Length: 1,200-2,000 words; average 4-5 pages when published. **Pays $200-300/feature vehicles; $350-600/travel and adventure; $100-800/technical articles.**

Photos Requires professional quality color slides and b&w prints for every article. Prefers Kodachrome 64 or Fujichrome 50 in 35mm or 2¼ formats. "Action shots a must for all vehicle features and travel articles." Captions required.

Tips "Show us you know how to use a camera as well as the written word. The easiest way for a new writer/photographer to break into our magazine is to read several issues of the magazine, then query with a short vehicle feature that will show his or her potential as a creative writer/photographer."

$ $ ⊘ FRICTION ZONE

Motorcycle Travel and Information, 60166 Hop Patch Spring Rd., Mountain Center CA 92561. (909)659-9500. E-mail: editor@friction-zone.com. Website: www.friction-zone.com. **60% freelance written.** Monthly magazine covering motorcycles. Estab. 1999. Circ. 26,000. Pays on publication. Publishes ms an average of 1 month after acceptance. Byline given. Buys first North American serial rights. Editorial lead time 6 weeks. Submit seasonal material 2 months in advance. Sample copy for $4.50 or on website.

Nonfiction General interest, historical/nostalgic, how-to, humor, inspirational, interview/profile, new product, opinion, photo feature, technical, travel, medical (relating to motorcyclists), book reviews (relating to motorcyclists). Does not accept first-person writing. **Buys 1 mss/year.** Query. Length: 1,000-3,000 words. **Pays 20¢/word.** Sometimes pays expenses of writers on assignment.

Photos Send photos with submission. Reviews negatives, slides. Buys one-time rights. Offers $15/published photo. Captions, identification of subjects, model releases required.

Columns/Departments Health Zone (health issues relating to motorcyclists); Motorcycle Engines 101 (basic motorcycle mechanics); Road Trip (California destination review including hotel, road, restaurant), all 2,000 words. **Buys 60 mss/year.** Query. **Pays 20¢/word.**

Fiction "We want stories concerning motorcycling or motorcyclists. No 'first-person' fiction." Query. Length: 1,000-2,000 words. **Pays 20¢/word.**

Fillers Anecdotes, facts, gags to be illustrated by cartoonist, newsbreaks, short humor. Length: 2,000-3,000 words. **Pays 20¢/word.**

Tips "Query via e-mail with sample writing. Visit our website for more detailed guidelines."

N $ HOT ROD MAGAZINE

Primedia Enthusiast Group, 6420 Wilshire Bvld., 10th Floor, Los Angeles CA 90048-5502. (323)782-2000. Fax: (323)782-2223. E-mail: hotrod@primedia.com. Website: www.hotrod.com. Editor: David Freiburger. Monthly magazine covering hot rods. Focuses on 50s and 60s cars outfitted with current drive trains and the nostalgia associated with them. Circ. 700,000. Editorial lead time 3 months. Sample copy not available.

⊘ LATINOS ON WHEELS

On Wheels, Inc., 585 E. Larned St., Suite 100, Detroit MI 48226-4369. (313)963-2209. Fax: (313)963-7778. E-mail: editor@onwheelsinc.com. Website: www.onwheelsinc.com/lowmagazine. Editor: Lyndon Conrad Bell.

Quarterly magazine. Supplement to leading Latino newspapers in the US. Provides Latino car buyers and car enthusiasts with the most relevant automotive trends. Circ. 500,000.

- Query before submitting.

◎ LOWRIDER MAGAZINE

Primedia Enthusiast Group, 2100 E. Howell Ave., Suite 209, Anaheim CA 92806. E-mail: ralph.fuentes@primedia.com. Website: www.lowridermagazine.com. Editor: Ralph Fuentes. Monthly magazine covering the national and international lowriding scene with high impact, full-color vehicle and event features. Circ. 212,500. Editorial lead time 3 months.

- Query before submitting.

MOMENTUM

Hachette Filipacchi Media U.S., Inc., 1633 Broadway, 40th Floor, New York NY 10019. (212)767-6000. Fax: (212)767-4757. Magazine published 3 times/year. Published exclusively for the Mercedes-Benz owner who appreciates quality, elegance, adventure and style. Circ. 750,000. Sample copy not available.

$ $ $ MOTOR TREND

Primedia, 6420 Wilshire Blvd., Los Angeles CA 90048. (323)782-2220. E-mail: motortrend@primedia.com. Website: www.motortrend.com. **Contact:** Matt Stone, executive editor. **5-10% freelance written.** Only works with published/established writers. Monthly magazine for automotive enthusiasts and general interest consumers. Circ. 1,250,000. Publishes ms an average of 3 months after acceptance. Buys all rights. Accepts queries by mail. Responds in 1 month to queries. Sample copy not available.

Nonfiction "Automotive and related subjects that have national appeal. Emphasis on domestic and imported cars, road tests, driving impressions, auto classics, auto, travel, racing, and high-performance features for the enthusiast. Packed with facts. Freelancers should confine queries to photo-illustrated exotic drives and other feature material; road tests and related activity are handled inhouse. Fact-filled query suggested for all freelancers."

Photos Buys photos of prototype cars and assorted automotive matter. Pays $25-500 for transparencies.

Columns/Departments Car care.

OUTLAW BIKER

Outlaw Biker Enterprises, Inc., 5 Marine View Plaza, Suite 207, Hoboken NJ 07030. (201)653-2700. Fax: (201)653-7892. Website: www.outlawbiker.com. **50% freelance written.** Magazine published 6 times/year covering bikers and their lifestyle. "All writers must be insiders of biker lifestyle. Features include coverage of biker events, profiles, and humor." Estab. 1983. Circ. 150,000. Pays on publication. Publishes ms an average of 3 months after acceptance. Byline given. Buys first rights. Editorial lead time 3 months. Submit seasonal material 5 months in advance. Accepts queries by mail, e-mail, fax. Accepts previously published material. Accepts simultaneous submissions. Responds in 2 weeks to queries; 2 months to mss. Sample copy for $5.98. Writer's guidelines for #10 SASE.

Nonfiction Historical/nostalgic, humor, new product, personal experience, photo feature, travel. Special issues: Daytona Special, Sturgis Special (annual bike runs). "No first time experiences—our readers already know." **Buys 10-12 mss/year.** Send complete ms. Length: 100-1,000 words.

Photos Send photos with submission. Reviews transparencies, prints. Buys one-time rights. Offers $0-10/photo. Captions, identification of subjects, model releases required.

Columns/Departments Buys 10-12 mss/year. Send complete ms.

Fiction Adventure, erotica, fantasy, historical, humorous, romance, science fiction, slice-of-life vignettes, suspense. No racism. **Buys 10-12 mss/year.** Send complete ms. Length: 500-2,500 words.

Poetry Avant-garde, free verse, haiku, light verse, traditional. **Buys 10-12 poems/year.** Submit maximum 12 poems. Length: 2-1,000 lines.

Fillers Anecdotes, facts, gags to be illustrated by cartoonist, newsbreaks, short humor. **Buys 10-12/year.** Length: 500-2,000 words.

Tips "Writers must be insiders of the biker lifestyle. Manuscripts with accompanying photographs as art are given higher priority."

◎ POPULAR HOT RODDING

Primedia Enthusiast Group, 2400 E. Katella Ave., Suite 1100, Anaheim CA 92806. (714)939-2400. E-mail: john.hunkins@primedia.com. Website: www.popularhotrodding.com. Editor: John Hunkins. Monthly magazine for the automotive enthusiast; highlights features that emphasize performance, bolt-on accessories, replacement parts, safety, and the sport of drag racing. Circ. 182,000.

- Query before submitting.

$ $RIDER MAGAZINE

Ehlert Publishing Group, 2575 Vista Del Mar Dr., Ventura CA 93001. E-mail: editor@ridermagazine.com. Website: www.ridermagazine.com. **Contact:** Mark Tuttle, editor. **60% freelance written.** Monthly magazine covering motorcycling. "*Rider* serves the all-brand motorcycle lifestyle/enthusiast with a slant toward travel and touring." Estab. 1974. Circ. 107,000. Pays on publication. Publishes ms an average of 6-12 months after acceptance. Byline given. Offers 25% kill fee. Buys first North American serial, electronic rights. Editorial lead time 4 months. Submit seasonal material 6 months in advance. Accepts queries by mail. Responds in 2 months to queries. Sample copy for $2.95. Writer's guidelines for #10 SASE.

- ⚷ "The articles we do buy often share the following characteristics: 1) The writer queried us in advance by regular mail (not by telephone or e-mail) to see if we needed or wanted the story; 2) The story was well written and of proper length; 3) The story had sharp, uncluttered photos taken with the proper film—*Rider* does not buy stories without photos."

Nonfiction General interest, historical/nostalgic, how-to, humor, interview/profile, personal experience, travel. Does not want to see "fiction or articles on 'How I Began Motorcycling.'" **Buys 40-50 mss/year.** Query. Length: 750-2,000 words. **Pays $150-750.**

Photos Send photos with submission. Reviews contact sheets, transparencies, 5×7 (b&w only) prints. Buys one-time and electronic rights. Offers no additional payment for photos accepted with ms. Captions required.

Columns/Departments Favorite Rides (short trip), 850-1,100 words. **Buys 12 mss/year.** Query. **Pays $150-750.**

Tips "We rarely accept manuscripts without photos (slides or b&w prints). Query first. Follow guidelines available on request. We are most open to feature stories (must include excellent photography) and material for 'Rides, Rallies and Clubs.' Include information on routes, local attractions, restaurants, and scenery in favorite ride submissions."

$ $ROAD KING

Parthenon Publishing, 28 White Bridge Rd., Suite 209, Nashville TN 37205. Fax: (615)627-2197. Website: www.roadking.com. **Contact:** Lisa Waddle, editor. **25% freelance written.** Bimonthly magazine covering the trucking industry. Pays 3 weeks from acceptance. Publishes ms an average of 3 months after acceptance. Byline given. Offers 30% kill fee. Buys first North American serial, all electronic rights. Editorial lead time 3-4 months. Submit seasonal material 4 months in advance. Accepts queries by mail, fax. Accepts previously published material. Accepts simultaneous submissions. Responds in 3-4 weeks to queries. Sample copy for #10 SASE. Writer's guidelines free.

Nonfiction Book excerpts, general interest, how-to, humor, new product, health. **Buys 12 mss/year.** Query with published clips. Length: 100-1,000 words. **Pays $50-500.** Pays expenses of writers on assignment.

Photos Michael Nott, art director. Send photos with submission. Negotiates payment individually.

$ $ROADBIKE

TAM Communications, 1010 Summer St., Stamford CT 06905. (203)425-8777. Fax: (203)425-8775. E-mail: jessicap@roadbikemag.com. **Contact:** Jessica Prokup, editor. **40% freelance written.** Monthly magazine covering motorcycling tours, project and custom bikes, products, news, and tech. Estab. 1993. Circ. 50,000. Pays on publication. Publishes ms an average of 6 months after acceptance. Byline given. Editorial lead time 4 months. Submit seasonal material 6 months in advance. Accepts queries by mail, e-mail, fax. Writer's guidelines free.

Nonfiction How-to (motorcycle tech, travel, camping), interview/profile (motorcycle related), new product, photo feature (motorcycle events or gathering places with maximum of 1,000 words text), travel. No fiction. **Buys 100 mss/year.** Query with or without published clips or send complete ms. Length: 1,000-2,500 words. **Pays $15-400.**

Photos Send photos with submission (slides preferred, prints and high resolution digital images accepted). Buys one-time rights. Offers no additional payment for photos accepted with ms. Captions required.

Fillers Facts.

Ⓝ $ $SPEED, STYLE & SOUND

RPM Communications LLC, 1093 Badder Dr., Troy MI 48083. E-mail: info@speedstylesound.com. Website: www.speedstylesound.com. Editor: Marco Trejo. **Contact:** Todd Lamb, managing editor. **60% freelance written.** Monthly magazine covering custom and performance vehicles. "*Speed, Style & Sound* caters to educated automobile enthusiasts between the ages of 18 and 35." Estab. 2002. Circ. 35,000. Pays on publication. Publishes ms an average of 1-2 months after acceptance. Byline sometimes given. Buys all rights. Editorial lead time 1-2 months. Submit seasonal material 3 months in advance. Accepts queries by e-mail. Responds in 1 week to queries; 1 month to mss. Sample copy online.

Nonfiction How-to, humor, interview/profile, new product, photo feature, technical. Query with published clips. Length: 200-2,000 words. **Pays $250-500 for assigned articles; $100-400 for unsolicited articles.** Sometimes pays expenses of writers on assignment.

Photos Send photos with submission. Reviews GIF/JPEG files. Rights purchased depends on subject. Negotiates payment individually. Captions, identification of subjects required.

Tips "Submissions should be related to the automotive aftermarket."

⊘ SPORT COMPACT CAR

Primedia Enthusiast Group, 774 S. Placentia Ave., Placentia CA 92870. (714)939-2584. E-mail: scott.oldham@primedia.com. Website: www.sportcompactcarweb.com. Editor: Scott Oldham. Monthly magazine for owners and potential buyers of new compacts who seek inside information regarding performance, personalization, and cosmetic enhancement of the vehicles. Circ. 117,000. Editorial lead time 4 months.

- Query before submitting.

Ⓝ ⊘ SPORT RIDER

Primedia Enthusiast Group, 6420 Wilshire Blvd., Los Angeles CA 90048. (323)782-2584. Fax: (323)782-2372. E-mail: srmail@primedia.com. Website: www.sportrider.com. Bimonthly magazine for enthusiast of sport/street motorcycles and emphasizes performance, both in the motorcycle and the rider. Circ. 108,365.

- Query before submitting.

⊘ SUPER CHEVY

Primedia Enthusiast Group, 2400 Katella Ave., 11th Floor, Anaheim CA 92806. (714)939-2540. E-mail: terry.cole @primedia.com. Website: www.superchevy-web.com. Editor: Terry Cole. Monthly magazine covering various forms of motorsports where Cheverolet cars and engines are in competition. Circ. 198,995.

- Query before submitting.

TRAINS

Kalmbach Publishing Co., P.O. Box 1612, Waukesha WI 53187-1612. (262)796-8776. Fax: (262)796-1142. E-mail: editor@trainsmag.com. Website: www.trainsmag.com. Editor: Jim Wrinn. Monthly magazine that appeals to consumers interested in learning about the function and history of the train industry. Circ. 110,000. Editorial lead time 2 months. Sample copy not available.

TRUCK TREND

The SUV & Pickup Authority, Primedia, 260 Madison Ave., 8th Floor, New York NY 10016. (212)726-4300. Website: www.trucktrend.com. **Contact:** Mark Willliams, editor. **60% freelance written.** Bimonthly magazine covering light trucks, SUVs, minivans, vans, and travel. *"Truck Trend* readers want to know about what's new in the world of sport-utilities, pickups, and vans. What to buy, how to fix up, and where to go." Estab. 1998. Circ. 125,000. Pays on publication. Publishes ms an average of 3 months after acceptance. Byline given. Buys all rights. Editorial lead time 5 months. Submit seasonal material 6 months in advance. Accepts queries by mail. Sample copy for #10 SASE. Writer's guidelines not available.

Nonfiction How-to, travel. **Buys 12 mss/year.** Query. Length: 500-1,800 words.

Photos Send photos with submission. Reviews transparencies. Buys all rights. Offers no additional payment for photos accepted with ms. Captions, identification of subjects, model releases required.

▮ The online magazine carries original content not found in the print edition.

Tips "Know the subject/audience. Start by using a previous story as a template. Call editor for advice after flushing story out. Understand the editor is looking to freelancers to make life easier."

$ $ $ $ VIPER MAGAZINE

The Magazine for Dodge Viper Enthusiasts, J.R. Thompson Co., 26970 Haggerty Rd., Farmington Hills MI 48331. (800)998-1110. E-mail: ed@vipermagazine.com. Website: www.vipermagazine.com. **20% freelance written.** Quarterly magazine covering all Vipers—all the time. Also the official magazine of the Viper Club of America. "Speak to *VM* readers from a basis of Viper knowledge and enthusiasm. We take an honest, journalistic approach to all stories, but we're demonstrably and understandably proud of the Dodge Viper sports car, its manufacturer and employees." Estab. 1995. Circ. 15,000. **Pays on acceptance.** Publishes ms an average of 4 months after acceptance. Byline given. Buys first, second serial (reprint) rights. Editorial lead time 5 months. Submit seasonal material 6 months in advance. Accepts queries by mail, e-mail, fax, phone. Accepts previously published material. Responds in 1 week to queries. Writer's guidelines for #10 SASE or by e-mail.

Nonfiction Query. Length: 400-1,500 words. **Pays $1/word.** Sometimes pays expenses of writers on assignment.

Photos State availability of or send photos with submission. Buys all rights. Negotiates payment individually. Captions, identification of subjects, model releases required.

Columns/Departments SnakeBites (coverage of Viper Club of America events such as local chapter activities, fundraising, track days, etc.), under 200 words; Competition (competitive Viper events such as road-racing, drag-racing, etc.), under 200 words. **Pays $1/word.**

Fillers Anecdotes, facts, gags to be illustrated by cartoonist, newsbreaks, short humor. Length: 25-100 words. **Pays $1/word.**

Tips "Being a Viper owner is a good start, since you have been exposéd to our 'culture' and probably receive the magazine. This is an even more specialized magazine than traditional auto-buff books, so knowing Vipers is essential."

AVIATION

$ $ $ $ AIR & SPACE MAGAZINE

Smithsonian Institution, P.O. Box 37012, Victor Bldg. 7100, MRC 951, Washington DC 20013-7012. (202)275-1230. Fax: (202)275-1886. E-mail: editors@airspacemag.si.edu. Website: www.airspacemag.com. Editor: George Larson. **Contact:** Linda Shiner, executive editor (features); Patricia Trenner, senior editor (departments). **80% freelance written.** Bimonthly magazine covering aviation and aerospace for a nontechnical audience. "The emphasis is on the human rather than the technological, on the ideas behind the events. Features are slanted to a technically curious, but not necessarily technically knowledgeable, audience. We are looking for unique angles to aviation/aerospace stories, history, events, personalities, current and future technologies, that emphasize the human-interest aspect." Estab. 1985. Circ. 225,000. **Pays on acceptance.** Byline given. Offers kill fee. Buys first North American serial rights. Accepts queries by mail, e-mail, fax. Responds in 3 months to queries. Sample copy for $5. Writer's guidelines online.

> ○→ "We're looking for 'reader service' articles—a collection of helpful hints and interviews with experts that would help our readers enjoy their interest in aviation. An example: An article telling readers how they could learn more about the space shuttle, where to visit, how to invite an astronaut to speak to their schools, what books are most informative, etc. A good place to break in is our 'Soundings' department."

Nonfiction The editors are actively seeking stories covering space and general or business aviation. Book excerpts, essays, general interest (on aviation/aerospace), historical/nostalgic, humor, photo feature, technical. **Buys 50 mss/year.** Query with published clips. Length: 1,500-3,000 words. **Pays $1,500-3,000.** Pays expenses of writers on assignment.

Photos Refuses unsolicited material. State availability with submission. Reviews 35 mm transparencies, digital files.

Columns/Departments Above and Beyond (first person), 1,500-2,000 words; Flights and Fancy (whimsy), approximately 800 words. Soundings (brief items, timely but not breaking news), 500-700 words. **Buys 25 mss/year.** Query with published clips. **Pays $150-300.**

> ▣ The online version carries original content not found in the print edition. Contact: Linda Shiner, Patricia Trenner.

Tips "We continue to be interested in stories about space exploration. Also, writing should be clear, accurate, and engaging. It should be free of technical and insider jargon, and generous with explanation and background. The first step every aspiring contributor should take is to study recent issues of the magazine."

$ $ AIR LINE PILOT

The Magazine of Professional Flight Deck Crews, Air Line Pilots Association, 535 Herndon Pkwy., P.O. Box 1169, Herndon VA 20172. (703)481-4460. Fax: (703)464-2114. E-mail: magazine@alpa.org. Website: www.alpa.org. **Contact:** Gary DiNunno, editor. **2% freelance written.** Prefers to work with published/established writers; works with a small number of new/unpublished writers each year. Magazine published 10 times/year for airline pilots covering commercial aviation industry information—economics, avionics, equipment, systems, safety—that affects a pilot's life in a professional sense. Also includes information about management/labor relations trends, contract negotiations, etc. Estab. 1931. Circ. 90,000. **Pays on acceptance.** Publishes ms an average of 6 months after acceptance. Offers 50% kill fee. Buys all rights except book rights. Submit seasonal material 6 months in advance. Responds in 2 months to queries. Sample copy for $2. Writer's guidelines online.

Nonfiction Humor, inspirational, photo feature, technical. **Buys 5 mss/year.** Query with or without published clips or send complete ms and SASE. Length: 700-3,000 words. **Pays $100-600 for assigned articles; $50-600 for unsolicited articles.**

Reprints Send photocopy of article or typed ms with rights for sale noted and information about when and where the material previously appeared. Payment varies.

Photos "Our greatest need is for strikingly original cover photographs featuring ALPA flight deck crew members and their airlines in their operating environment. See list of airlines with ALPA Pilots online." Send photos with submission. Reviews contact sheets, 35mm transparencies, 8×10 prints, digital (must be 300 dpi at 8×11). Will review low res thumbnail images. Buys all rights for cover photos, one-time rights for inside color. Offers $10-35/b&w photo, $30-50 for color used inside and $450 for color used as cover. For cover photography, shoot vertical rather than horizontal. Identification of subjects required.

Tips "For our feature section, we seek aviation industry information that affects the life of a professional pilot's career. We also seek material that affects a pilot's life from a job security and work environment standpoint. Any airline pilot featured in an article must be an Air Line Pilot Association member in good standing. Our readers are very experienced and require a high level of technical accuracy in both written material and photographs."

$ $AVIATION HISTORY

Primedia History Group, 741 Miller Dr., SE, Suite D-2, Leesburg VA 20175-8920. (703)771-9400. Fax: (703)779-8345. E-mail: aviationhistory@thehistorynet.com. Website: www.thehistorynet.com. Managing Editor: Carl von Wodtke. **Contact:** Arthur Sanfelici, editor. **95% freelance written.** Bimonthly magazine covering military and civilian aviation from first flight to the jet age. It aims to make aeronautical history not only factually accurate and complete, but also enjoyable to a varied subscriber and newsstand audience. Estab. 1990. Circ. 60,000. Pays on publication. Publishes ms an average of 2 years after acceptance. Byline given. Buys all rights. Editorial lead time 6 months. Submit seasonal material 1 year in advance. Accepts queries by mail, e-mail, fax. Accepts simultaneous submissions. Responds in 3 months to queries; 6 months to mss. Sample copy for $5. Writer's guidelines for #10 SASE or online.

Nonfiction Historical/nostalgic, interview/profile, personal experience. **Buys 24 mss/year.** Query. Length: Feature articles should be 3,500-4,000 words, each with a 500-word sidebar, author's biography, and book suggestions for further reading. **Pays $300.**

Photos State availability of art and photos with submissions, cite sources. "We'll order." Reviews contact sheets, negatives, transparencies. Buys one-time rights. Identification of subjects required.

Columns/Departments People and Planes; Enduring Heritage; Aerial Oddities; Art of Flight, all 2,000 words. **Pays $150.** Book reviews, 300-750 words, **pays minimum $40.**

■ The online magazine carries original content not found in the print edition and includes writer's guidelines. Contact: Roger Vance.

Tips "Choose stories with strong art possibilities. Include a hard copy as well as an IBM- or Macintosh-compatible floppy disk. Write an entertaining, informative, and unusual story that grabs the reader's attention and holds it. All stories must be true. We do not publish fiction or poetry."

$BALLOON LIFE

P.O. Box 7, Lichtfield CT 06759. (203)629-1241. E-mail: editorballoon@aol.com. Website: www.balloonlife.com. **Contact:** William G. Armstrong. **75% freelance written.** Monthly magazine covering sport of hot air ballooning. Readers participate as pilots, crew, and official observers at events and spectators." Estab. 1986. Circ. 7,000. Pays on publication. Publishes ms an average of 3-4 months after acceptance. Byline given. Offers 50-100% kill fee. Buys first North American serial, one-time rights. Buys nonexclusive, all rights. Submit seasonal material 4 months in advance. Accepts queries by e-mail, fax. Accepts previously published material. Accepts simultaneous submissions. Responds in 3 weeks to queries; 1 month to mss. Sample copy for 9×12 SAE with $2 postage. Writer's guidelines for #10 SASE.

Nonfiction Book excerpts, general interest, how-to (flying hot air balloons, equipment techniques), interview/profile, new product, technical, events/rallies, safety seminars, balloon clubs/organizations, letters to the editor. **Buys 150 mss/year.** Query with or without published clips or send complete ms. Length: 1,000-1,500 words. **Pays $50-75 for assigned articles; $25-50 for unsolicited articles.** Pays expenses of writers on assignment.

Reprints Send tearsheet, photocopy, or typed ms with rights for sale noted and information about when and where the material previously appeared. Pays 100% of amount paid for an original article or story.

Photos Send photos with submission. Reviews transparencies, prints. Buys nonexclusive, all rights. Offers $15/inside photos, $50/cover. Identification of subjects required.

Columns/Departments Hangar Flying (real-life flying experience that others can learn from), 800-1,500 words; Crew Quarters (devoted to some aspect of crewing), 900 words; Preflight (a news and information column), 100-500 words; **pays $50.** Logbook (balloon events that have taken place in last 3-4 months), 300-500 words; **pays $20.** Buys 60 mss/year. Send complete ms. **Pays $20-50.**

Fiction Humorous, related to hot air ballooning. **Buys 3-5 mss/year.** Send complete ms. Length: 800-1,500 words. **Pays $25-75 and contributor's copies.**

Tips "This magazine slants toward the technical side of ballooning. We are interested in articles that help to educate and provide safety information. Also stories with manufacturers, important individuals, and/or historic events and technological advances important to ballooning. The magazine attempts to present articles that show 'how-to' (fly, business opportunities, weather, equipment). Both our Feature Stories section and Logbook section are where most manuscripts are purchased."

N $ $ CESSNA OWNER MAGAZINE

Jones Publishing, Inc., N7450 Aanstad Rd., P.O. Box 5000, Iola WI 54945. (715)445-5000. Fax: (715)445-4053. E-mail: markm@cessnaowner.org. Website: www.cessnaowner.org. **Contact:** Mark Mitchell, editor. **50% freelance written.** Monthly magazine covering Cessna single and twin-engine aircraft. "*Cessna Owner Magazine* is the official publication of the Cessna Owner Organization (C.O.O.). Therefore, our readers are Cessna aircraft owners, renters, pilots, and enthusiasts. Articles should deal with buying/selling, flying, maintaining, or modifying Cessnas. The purpose of our magazine is to promote safe, fun, and affordable flying." Estab. 1975. Circ. 6,000. Pays on publication. Publishes ms an average of 3 months after acceptance. Byline given. Buys first, one-time, second serial (reprint) rights, makes work-for-hire assignments. Editorial lead time 1 month. Submit seasonal material 3 months in advance. Accepts queries by mail, e-mail, fax, phone. Accepts previously published material. Responds in 2 weeks to queries; 1 month to mss. Sample copy and writer's guidelines free or on website.

Nonfiction "We are always looking for articles about Cessna aircraft modifications. We also need articles on Cessna twin-engine aircraft. April, July, and October are always big issues for us because we attend various airshows during these months and distribute free magazines. Feature articles on unusual, highly modified, or vintage Cessnas are especially welcome during these months. Good photos are also a must." Historical/nostalgic (of specific Cessna models), how-to (aircraft repairs and maintenance), new product, personal experience, photo feature, technical (aircraft engines and airframes). Special issues: Engines (maintenance, upgrades); Avionics (purchasing, new products). **Buys 48 mss/year.** Query. Length: 1,500-3,500 words. **Pays 10-14¢/word.**

Reprints Send mss via e-mail with rights for sale noted and information about when and where the material previously appeared.

Photos Send photos with submission. Reviews 3×5 and larger prints. Captions, identification of subjects required.

FLYING MAGAZINE

Hachette Filipacchi Media U.S., Inc., 1633 Broadway, 45th Floor, New York NY 10019. (212)767-6000. Fax: (212)767-4932. E-mail: flyedit@hfmus.com. Website: www.flyingmag.com. Monthly magazine covering aviation. Edited for active pilots through coverage of new product development and application in the general aviation market. Estab. 1927. Circ. 303,000. Editorial lead time 3 months. Accepts queries by mail, e-mail, fax. Sample copy for $3.99.

● *Flying* is almost entirely staff written; use of freelance material is limited.

Nonfiction "We are looking for the most unusual and best-written material that suits *Flying*. Most subjects in aviation have already been done so fresher ideas and approaches to stories are particularly valued. We buy 'I Learned About Flying From That' articles, as well as an occasional feature with and without photographs supplied." Send complete ms.

◯ $ $ GENERAL AVIATION NEWS

Flyer Media, Inc., P.O. Box 39099, Lakewood WA 98439-0099. (888)333-5937. Fax: (253)471-9911. E-mail: janice@generalaviationnews.com. Website: www.generalaviationnews.com. **Contact:** Janice Wood, editor. **30% freelance written.** Prefers to work with published/established writers. Biweekly tabloid covering general, regional, national, and international aviation stories of interest to pilots, aircraft owners, and aviation enthusiasts. Estab. 1949. Circ. 35,000. Pays 1 month after publication. Publishes ms an average of 3 months after acceptance. Byline given. Buys first North American serial, second serial (reprint) rights. Submit seasonal material 6 months in advance. Accepts queries by mail, e-mail, fax, phone. Responds in 2 months to queries. Sample copy for $3.50. Writer's guidelines online.

● Always query first. Unsolicited mss will not be considered.

o— Break in by having "an aviation background, including a pilot's license, being up to date on current events, and being able to write. A 1,000-word story with good photos is the best way to see your name in print.

Nonfiction "News is covered by our staff. What we're looking for from freelancers is personality features, including stories of people who use their aircraft in an unusual way, builder and pilot reports, and historical features." **Buys 100 mss/year.** Query with published clips. Length: 500-2,000 words. **Pays $75-500.** Sometimes pays expenses of writers on assignment.

Photos Shoot clear, up-close photos, preferably color prints or slides. Send photos with submission. Payment negotiable. Captions, identification of subjects required.

Tips "The longer the story, the less likely it is to be accepted. If you are covering controversy, send us both sides of the story. Most of our features and news stories are assigned in response to a query."

N $ $ PIPERS MAGAZINE

Jones Publishing, Inc., N7450 Aanstad Rd., P.O. Box 5000, Iola WI 54945. (715)445-5000. Fax: (715)445-4053. E-mail: markm@piperowner.org. Website: www.piperowner.org. **Contact:** Mark Mitchell, editor. **50% freelance written.** Monthly magazine covering Piper single and twin engine aircraft. *"Pipers Magazine* is the official publication of the Piper Owner Society (P.O.S). Therefore, our readers are Piper aircraft owners, renters, pilots, mechanics, and enthusiasts. Articles should deal with buying/selling, flying, maintaining, or modifying Pipers. The purpose of our magazine is to promote safe, fun and affordable flying." Estab. 1988. Circ. 5,000. Pays on publication. Publishes ms an average of 3 months after acceptance. Buys first, one-time, second serial (reprint) rights, makes work-for-hire assignments. Editorial lead time 1 month. Submit seasonal material 3 months in advance. Accepts queries by mail, e-mail, fax, phone. Accepts previously published material. Responds in 2 weeks to queries; 1 month to mss. Sample copy and writer's guidelines free.

Nonfiction "We are always looking for articles about Piper aircraft modifications. We also are in need of articles on Piper twin engine aircraft, and late-model Pipers. April, July, and October are always big issues for us, because we attend airshows during these months and distribute free magazines." Feature articles on unusual, highly-modified, vintage, late-model, or ski/float equipped Pipers are especially welcome. Good photos are a must. Historical/nostalgic (of specific models of Pipers), how-to (aircraft repairs and maintenance), new product, personal experience, photo feature, technical (aircraft engines and airframes). **Buys 48 mss/year.** Query. Length: 1,500-3,500 words. **Pays 10-14¢/word.**

Reprints Send mss by e-mail with rights for sale noted and information about when and where the material previously appeared.

Photos Send photos with submission. Reviews transparencies, 3×5 and larger prints. Offers no additional payment for photos accepted. Captions, identification of subjects required.

$ $ PLANE AND PILOT

Werner Publishing Corp., 12121 Wilshire Blvd., Suite 1200, Los Angeles CA 90025. (310)820-1500. Fax: (310)826-5008. E-mail: editors@planeandpilotmag.com. Website: www.planeandpilotmag.com. **80% freelance written.** Monthly magazine covering general aviation. "We think a spirited, conversational writing style is most entertaining for our readers. We are read by private and corporate pilots, instructors, students, mechanics and technicians—everyone involved or interested in general aviation." Estab. 1964. Circ. 150,000. Pays on publication. Publishes ms an average of 4 months after acceptance. Byline given. Offers kill fee. Buys all rights. Submit seasonal material 4 months in advance. Accepts previously published material. Responds in 4 months to queries. Sample copy for $5.50. Writer's guidelines online.

Nonfiction How-to, new product, personal experience, technical, travel, pilot efficiency, pilot reports on aircraft. **Buys 75 mss/year.** Query. Length: 1,200 words. **Pays $200-500.** Pays expenses of writers on assignment.

Reprints Send tearsheet, photocopy, or typed ms with rights for sale noted and information about when and where the material previously appeared. Pays 50% of amount paid for original article.

Photos Submit suggested heads, decks and captions for all photos with each story. Submit b&w photos, 8×10 prints with glossy finish. Submit color photos in the form of 2¼×2¼, 4×5 or 35mm transparencies in plastic sleeves. Buys all rights. Offers $50-300/photo.

Columns/Departments Readback (any newsworthy items on aircraft and/or people in aviation), 1,200 words; Jobs & Schools (a feature or an interesting school or program in aviation), 900-1,000 words. **Buys 30 mss/ year.** Send complete ms. **Pays $200-500.**

Tips "Pilot proficiency articles are our bread and butter. Manuscripts should be kept under 1,800 words—1,200 words is ideal."

$ $ PRIVATE PILOT

Y-Visionary, Inc., 265 S. Anita Dr., Suite 120, Orange CA 92868. (714)939-9991. Fax: (714)939-9909. E-mail: nogoyer@aol.com. Website: www.privatepilotmag.com. **Contact:** Norm Goyer, editor. **40% freelance written.** Monthly magazine covering general aviation. "*Private Pilot* is edited for owners and pilots of single and multi-engine aircraft." Estab. 1965. Circ. 85,000. Pays on publication. Publishes ms an average of 4 months after acceptance. Byline given. Offers 15% or $75 kill fee. Buys first North American serial rights. Editorial lead time 3 months. Submit seasonal material 6 months in advance. Accepts queries by mail, fax. Responds in 2 months to queries. Writer's guidelines for #10 SASE.

Nonfiction General interest, historical/nostalgic, how-to, humor, inspirational, interview/profile, new product, opinion, personal experience, technical, travel, aircraft types. **Buys 12-15 mss/year.** Query. Length: 800-3,000 words. **Pays $250-650.** Sometimes pays expenses of writers on assignment.

Photos State availability with submission. Reviews 35mm transparencies. Buys one-time rights. Negotiates payment individually. Captions, identification of subjects, model releases required.

Tips "Send good queries. Readers are pilots who want to read about aircraft, places to go, and ways to save money."

BUSINESS & FINANCE

NATIONAL

$ $ THE BUSINESS JOURNAL

Serving San Jose and Silicon Valley, American City Business Journals, Inc., 96 N. Third St., Suite 100, San Jose CA 95112. (408)295-3800. Fax: (408)295-5028. E-mail: sanjose@bizjournals.com. Website: sanjose.bizjournals. com. Editor: Norman Bell. **Contact:** Susan Futterman, managing editor. **2-5% freelance written.** Weekly tabloid covering a wide cross-section of industries. "Our stories are written for business people. Our audience is primarily upper-level management." Estab. 1983. Circ. 13,200. Pays on publication. Byline given. Offers $75 kill fee. Buys all rights. Editorial lead time 1 month. Accepts queries by e-mail. Responds in 2 weeks to queries. Sample copy and writer's guidelines free.

Nonfiction News/feature articles specifically assigned. **Buys 300 mss/year.** Query. Length: 700-2,500 words. **Pays $175-400.**

Photos State availability with submission. Reviews 5×7 prints. Offers $25/photo used.

Tips "Just call or e-mail (preferable) and say you are interested. We give almost everyone a chance."

$ $ $ $ BUSINESS 2.0 MAGAZINE

Time, Inc., One California St., 29th Floor, San Francisco CA 94111. E-mail: freelancers@business2.com. Website: www.business2.com. **Contact:** Josh Quittner, editor. Monthly magazine covering business in the Internet economy. Estab. 1998. Circ. 600,000. Pays on publication. Publishes ms an average of 3 months after acceptance. Byline given. Offers 20% kill fee. Buys all rights. Editorial lead time 2 months. Submit seasonal material 4 months in advance. Accepts queries by e-mail. Accepts simultaneous submissions. Writer's guidelines online.

    ○➝ Break in with fresh ideas on business transformation—from the way companies are conceived and financed to how they develop markets and retain customers.

Nonfiction Essays, exposé, new product, opinion, travel, new business ideas. **Buys 40-50 mss/year.** Query with published clips. Length: 150-3,000 words. **Pays $1/word.** Pays expenses of writers on assignment.

⊘ BUSINESSWEEK

McGraw-Hill, Inc., 1221 Avenue of the Americas, 43rd Floor, New York NY 10020-1001. (212)512-2511. Fax: (212)512-4938. Website: www.businessweek.com. Editor-in-Chief: Stephen J. Adler. Weekly magazine. Circ. 991,000.

    • *BusinessWeek* does not accept freelance submissions.

$ $ DOLLARS AND SENSE: THE MAGAZINE OF ECONOMIC JUSTICE

Economic Affairs Bureau, 740 Cambridge St., Cambridge MA 02141. (617)876-2434. Fax: (617)876-0008. E-mail: dollars@dollarsandsense.org. Website: www.dollarsandsense.org. **Contact:** Amy Gluckman or Adria Scharf, co-editors. **10% freelance written.** Bimonthly magazine covering economic, environmental, and social justice. "We explain the workings of the US and international economics, and provide left perspectives on current economic affairs. Our audience is a mix of activists, organizers, academics, unionists, and other socially concerned people." Estab. 1974. Circ. 8,000. Pays on publication. Publishes ms an average of 4 months after acceptance. Byline given. Editorial lead time 3 months. Submit seasonal material 2 months in advance. Accepts queries by mail, e-mail, fax, phone. Sample copy for $5 or on website. Writer's guidelines online.

Nonfiction Exposé, political economics. **Buys 6 mss/year.** Query with published clips. Length: 700-2,500 words. **Pays $0-200.** Sometimes pays expenses of writers on assignment.

Photos State availability with submission. Buys one-time rights. Negotiates payment individually. Captions, identification of subjects required.

Tips "Be familiar with our magazine and the types of communities interested in reading us. *Dollars and Sense* is a progressive economics magazine that explains in a popular way both the workings of the economy and struggles to change it. Articles may be on the environment, the World Bank, community organizing, urban conflict, inflation, unemployment, union reform, welfare, changes in government regulation—a broad range of topics that have an economic theme. Find samples of our latest issue on our homepage."

$ $ ENTREPRENEUR MAGAZINE

Entrepreneur Media, 2445 McCabe Way, Irvine CA 92614. E-mail: pbennett@entrepreneur.com. Website: www. entrepreneur.com. **Contact:** Peggy Reeves Bennett, articles editor. **60% freelance written.** *Entrepreneur* readers already run their own businesses. They have been in business for several years and are seeking innovative methods and strategies to improve their business operations. They are also interested in new business ideas and opportunities, as well as current issues that affect their companies. Circ. 540,000. **Pays on acceptance.** Publishes ms an average of 5 months after acceptance. Byline given. Buys first worldwide rights. Submit seasonal material 6 months in advance. Accepts queries by mail, e-mail. Responds in 3 months to queries. Sample copy for $7.20. Writer's guidelines online.

Nonfiction How-to (information on running a business, dealing with the psychological aspects of running a business, profiles of unique entrpreneurs), current news/trends (and their effect on small business). **Buys 10-20 mss/year.** Query with published clips. Length: 1,800 words. **Payment varies.**

Photos "Ask for photos or transparencies when interviewing entrepreneurs; send them with the article." Buys one-time rights.

Columns/Departments Snapshots (profiles of interesting entrepreneurs); Money Smarts (financial management); Marketing Smarts; Web Smarts (Internet news); Tech Smarts; Management Smarts; Viewpoint (first-person essay on entrepreneurship), all 300 words. **Pays $1/word.**

Tips "Read several issues of the magazine! Study the feature articles versus the columns. Probably 75% of our freelance rejections are for article ideas covered in one of our regular columns. Go beyond the typical, flat 'business magazine query'—how to write a press release, how to negotiate with vendors, etc.—and instead investigate a current trend and develop a story on how that trend affects small business. In your query, mention companies you'd like to use to illustrate examples and sources who will provide expertise on the topic."

⊘ FORBES

Forbes, Inc., 60 5th Ave., New York NY 10011. (212)660-2200. Fax: (212)620-1873. Website: www.forbes.com. Biweekly magazine. Edited for top business management professionals and for those aspiring to positions of corporate leadership. Circ. 1,000,000. Editorial lead time 2 months.

• Query before submitting.

ℕ ⊘ FORBES FYI

Forbes, Inc., 60 5th Ave., New York NY 10011. (212)620-2200. Fax: (212)620-2426. Website: www.forbes.com/fyi. Editor: Christopher Buckley. Quarterly magazine. "*Forbes FYI* provides business professionals with insider tips to turn their dreams into reality." Circ. 860,000.

• Does not buy freelance material or use freelance writers.

⊘ FORTUNE

Time, Inc., 1271 Avenue of the Americas, New York NY 10020. (212)522-1212. Fax: (212)522-0810. E-mail: fortunemail_letters@fortunemail.com. Website: www.fortune.com. Editor: Peter Petre. Biweekly magazine. Edited primarily for high-demographic business people. Specializes in big stories about companies, business personalities, technology, managing, Wall Street, media, marketing, personal finance, politics and policy. Circ. 1,066,000. Editorial lead time 6 weeks. Sample copy not available.

• Does not accept freelance submissions.

$ $ $ $ HISPANIC BUSINESS

Hispanic Business, Inc., 425 Pine Ave., Santa Barbara CA 93117. Fax: (805)964-5539. E-mail: judi.erickson@hbinc.com. Website: www.hispanicbusiness.com. Editor: Jesus Chavarria. **Contact:** Judi Erickson, managing editor. **40-50% freelance written.** Monthly magazine covering Hispanic business. "For more than 2 decades, *Hispanic Business* magazine has documented the growing affluence and power of the Hispanic community. Our magazine reaches the most educated, affluent Hispanic business and community leaders. Stories should have relevance for the Hispanic business community." Estab. 1979. Circ. 220,000 (rate base); 990,000 (readership base). Pays on publication. Publishes ms an average of 1 month after acceptance. Byline given. Offers 50% kill fee. Buys all rights. Editorial lead time 1-3 months. Submit seasonal material 2 months in advance. Accepts queries by mail, e-mail. Accepts simultaneous submissions. Responds in 3 weeks to queries; 1 month to mss. Sample copy for free.

Nonfiction Interview/profile, travel. **Buys 120 mss/year.** Query résumé and published clips. Length: 650-2,000 words. **Pays $50-1,500.** Sometimes pays expenses of writers on assignment.

Photos State availability with submission. Reviews GIF/JPEG files. Buys all rights. Negotiates payment individually. Captions required.

Columns/Departments Tech Pulse (technology); Money Matters (financial), both 800 words. **Buys 40 mss/year.** Query with résumé and published clips. **Pays $50-450.**

Tips "E-mail or snail mail queries with résumé and published clips are the most effective."

$ $ $ $ INDUSTRYWEEK

Leadership in Manufacturing, Penton Media, Inc., Penton Media Bldg., 1300 E. 9th St., Cleveland OH 44114. (216)696-7000. Fax: (216)696-7670. E-mail: tvinas@industryweek.com. Website: www.industryweek.com. **Contact:** Tonya Vinas, managing editor. **30% freelance written.** Magazine published 12 times/year. "*Industry-Week* provides information that helps manufacturers drive continuous improvement throughout the enterprise.

Every issue of *IndustryWeek* is edited for the management teams of today's most competitive manufacturing companies, as well as decision-makers in the service industries that support manufacturing growth and productivity.'' Estab. 1970. Circ. 200,000. **Pays on acceptance.** Publishes ms an average of 2 months after acceptance. Byline given. Buys all rights. Accepts queries by e-mail. Responds in 1 month to queries. Sample copy and writer's guidelines online.

Nonfiction Book excerpts, exposé, interview/profile. ''No first-person articles.'' **Buys 25 mss/year.** Query with published clips. Length: 1,800-3,000 words. **Pays average of $1/word for all articles; reserves right to negotiate.** Sometimes pays expenses of writers on assignment.

Photos Reviews contact sheets, negatives, transparencies, prints. Buys one-time rights. Negotiates payment individually. Captions, identification of subjects required.

Tips ''Pitch wonderful ideas targeted precisely at our audience. Read, re-read, and understand the writer's guidelines and stories published. *IndustryWeek* readers are primarily senior executives—people with the title of vice president, executive vice president, senior vice president, chief executive officer, chief financial officer, chief information officer, chairman, managing director, and president. *IW*'s executive readers oversee global corporations. While *IW*'s primary target audience is a senior executive in a US firm, your story should provide information that any executive anywhere in the world can use. *IW*'s audience is primarily in companies in manufacturing and manufacturing-related industries.''

⊘ MONEY

Time, Inc., 1271 Avenue of the Americas, 17th Floor, New York NY 10020. (212)522-1212. Fax: (212)522-0189. E-mail: money_letters@moneymail.com. Website: money.cnn.com. Editor: Norman Pearlstine. Managing Editor: Eric Schurenberg. Monthly magazine covering finance. ''*Money* magazine offers sophisticated coverage in all aspects of personal finance for individuals, business executives, and personal investors.'' Estab. 1972. Circ. 1,967,420. Editorial lead time 2 months. Sample copy for $3.99.

• ''*Money* magazine does not accept unsolicited manuscripts and almost never uses freelance writers.''

$ $ $ MYBUSINESS MAGAZINE

Hammock Publishing, 3322 W. End Ave., Suite 700, Nashville TN 37203. Fax: (615)690-3401. E-mail: sscully@hammock.com. Website: www.mybusinessmag.com. **Contact:** Shannon Scully, managing editor. **75% freelance written.** Bimonthly magazine for small businesses. ''We are a guide to small business success, however that is defined in the new small business economy. We explore the methods and minds behind the trends and celebrate the men and women leading the creation of the new small business economy.'' Estab. 1999. Circ. 600,000. **Pays on acceptance.** Publishes ms an average of 4 months after acceptance. Byline given. Offers 30% kill fee. Buys first North American serial, electronic rights. Editorial lead time 4 months. Submit seasonal material 5 months in advance. Accepts queries by mail, fax. Accepts simultaneous submissions. Responds in 3 weeks to queries. Sample copy free. Writer's guidelines online.

Nonfiction Book excerpts, how-to (small business topics), new product. **Buys 8 mss/year.** Query with published clips. Length: 200-1,800 words. **Pays $75-1,000.** Pays expenses of writers on assignment.

Tips *MyBusiness* is sent bimonthly to the 600,000 members of the National Federation of Independent Business. ''We're here to help small business owners by giving them a range of how-to pieces that evaluate, analyze, and lead to solutions.''

$ $ THE NETWORK JOURNAL

Black Professional and Small Business News, The Network Journal Communication, 39 Broadway, Suite 2120, New York, NY 10006. (212)962-3791. Fax: (212)962-3537. E-mail: editors@tnj.com. Website: www.tnj.com. **25% freelance written.** Monthly magazine covering business and career articles. *The Network Journal* caters to Black professionals and small-business owners, providing quality coverage on business, financial, technology and career news germane to the black community. Estab. 1993. Circ. 15,000. Pays on publication. Byline given. Buys all rights. Editorial lead time 2 months. Submit seasonal material 3 months in advance. Accepts queries by mail, e-mail, fax, phone. Accepts previously published material. Accepts simultaneous submissions. Sample copy for $1 or online. Writer's guidelines for SASE or online.

Nonfiction How-to, interview/profile. Send complete ms. Length: 1,200-1,500 words. **Pays $150-200.** Sometimes pays expenses of writers on assignment.

Photos Send photos with submission. Buys one-time rights. Offers $25/photo. Identification of subjects required.

Columns/Departments Book reviews, 700-800 words; career management and small business development, 800 words. **Pays $100.**

Tips ''We are looking for vigorous writing and reporting for our cover stories and feature articles. Pieces should have gripping leads, quotes that actually say something and that come from several sources. Unless it is a column, please do not submit a 1-source story. Always remember that your article must contain a nutgraph—that's usually the third paragraph telling the reader what the story is about and why you are telling it now. Editorializing should be kept to a minimum. If you're writing a column, make sure your opinions are well-supported.''

PERDIDO

Leadership with a Conscience, High Tide Press, 3650 W. 183rd St., Homewood IL 60430-2603. (708)206-2054. Fax: (708)206-2044. E-mail: editor1@hightidepress.com. Website: www.perdidomagazine.com. **Contact:** Mary Rundell-Holmes, editor. **60% freelance written.** Quarterly magazine covering leadership and management as they relate to mission-oriented organizations. ''We are concerned with what's happening in organizations that are mission-oriented—as opposed to merely profit-oriented. *Perdido* is focused on helping conscientious leaders put innovative ideas into practice. We seek pragmatic articles on management techniques as well as esoteric essays on social issues. The readership of *Perdido* is comprised mainly of CEOs, executive directors, vice presidents, and program directors of nonprofit and for-profit organizations. We try to make the content of *Perdido* accessible to all decision-makers, whether in the nonprofit or for-profit world, government, or academia. *Perdido* actively pursues diverse opinions and authors from many different fields.'' Estab. 1994. Circ. 3,000. Pays on publication. Publishes ms an average of 3 months after acceptance. Byline given. Buys first North American serial, second serial (reprint) rights. Editorial lead time 4 months. Submit seasonal material 6 months in advance. Accepts queries by mail, e-mail, fax, phone. Accepts previously published material. Accepts simultaneous submissions. Responds in 2 months to queries. Sample copy for 6×9 SASE with 2 first-class stamps or online. Writer's guidelines for #10 SASE or by e-mail.

Nonfiction Book excerpts, humor, inspirational, interview/profile, informative articles. **Buys 6-10 mss/year.** Query with published clips. Length: 1,000-3,000 words.

Photos State availability with submission. Reviews 5×7 prints. Buys one-time rights. Negotiates payment individually. Captions, identification of subjects, model releases required.

Columns/Departments Book Review (new books on management/leadership), 800 words.

Tips ''Potential writers for *Perdido* should rely on the magazine's motto—Leadership with a Conscience—as a starting point. We're looking for thoughtful reflections on management that help people succeed. While instructive articles are good, we avoid step-by-step recipes. Data and real life examples are very important.''

$ $ $ $☑ PROFIT

Your Guide to Business Success, 1 Mt. Pleasant Rd., 11th Floor, Toronto ON M4Y 2Y5 Canada. (416)764-1402. Fax: (416)764-1404. E-mail: profit@profit.rogers.com. Website: www.profitguide.com. Publisher: Deborah Rosser. **Contact:** Ian Portsmouth, editor. **80% freelance written.** Magazine published 6 times/year covering small and medium businesses. ''We specialize in specific, useful information that helps our readers manage their businesses better. We want Canadian stories only.'' Estab. 1982. Circ. 110,000. **Pays on acceptance.** Publishes ms an average of 2 months after acceptance. Byline given. Offers variable kill fee. Buys first North American serial, electronic rights. Submit seasonal material 6 months in advance. Accepts queries by mail, e-mail, fax, phone. Responds in 1 month to queries; 6 weeks to mss. Sample copy for 9×12 SAE with 84¢ postage. Writer's guidelines free.

Nonfiction How-to (business management tips), strategies and Canadian business profiles. **Buys 50 mss/year.** Query with published clips. Length: 800-2,000 words. **Pays $500-2,000.** Pays expenses of writers on assignment.

Columns/Departments Finance (info on raising capital in Canada), 700 words; Marketing (marketing strategies for independent business), 700 words. **Buys 80 mss/year.** Query with published clips. **Pays $150-600.**

   📖 The online magazine carries original content not found in the print edition. Contact: Ian Portsmouth, editor.

Tips ''We're wide open to freelancers with good ideas and some knowledge of business. Read the magazine and understand it before submitting your ideas—which should have a Canadian focus.''

Ⓝ ⊘ SMARTMONEY MAGAZINE

250 W. 55th St., 10th Floor, New York NY 10019. E-mail: editors@smartmoney.com. Website: www.smartmoney.com. Editor: Robert Hunter. **Contact:** Igor Greenwald, senior editor; Stephanie AuWerter, senior editor; Stacey L. Bradford, associate editor.

   • Query before submitting.

$ $TECHNICAL ANALYSIS OF STOCKS & COMMODITIES

The Traders' Magazine, Technical Analysis, Inc., 4757 California Ave. SW, Seattle WA 98116-4499. (206)938-0570. Fax: (206)938-1307. E-mail: editor@traders.com. Website: www.traders.com. Publisher: Jack K. Hutson. **Contact:** Jayanthi Gopalakrishnan, editor. **85% freelance written.** Magazine covers methods of investing and trading stocks, bonds and commodities (futures), options, mutual funds, and precious metals using technical analysis. Estab. 1982. Circ. 65,000. Pays on publication. Publishes ms an average of 6 months after acceptance. Byline given. Buys all rights. Responds in 2 months to queries. Sample copy for $8. Writer's guidelines online.

● Eager to work with new/unpublished writers.

Nonfiction How-to (trade), humor (cartoons), technical (trading and software aids to trading), reviews, utilities, real world trading (actual case studies of trades and their results). "No newsletter-type, buy-sell recommendations. The article subject must relate to technical analysis, charting or a numerical technique used to trade securities or futures. Almost universally requires graphics with every article." **Buys 150 mss/year.** Query with published clips or send complete ms. Length: 1,000-4,000 words. **Pays $100-500.**

Reprints Send tearsheet with rights for sale noted and information about when and where the material previously appeared.

Photos Christine M. Morrison, art director. State availability with submission. Buys one time and reprint rights. Pays $60-350 for b&w or color negatives with prints or positive slides. Captions, identification of subjects, model releases required.

Columns/Departments Length: 800-1,600 words. **Buys 100 mss/year.** Query. **Pays $50-300.**

Fillers Karen Wasserman, fillers editor. Must relate to trading stocks, bonds, options, mutual funds, commodities, or precious metals. Cartoons on investment humor. **Buys 20/year.** Length: 500 words. **Pays $20-50.**

Tips "Describe how to use technical analysis, charting, or computer work in day-to-day trading of stocks, bonds, commodities, options, mutual funds, or precious metals. A blow-by-blow account of how a trade was made, including the trader's thought processes, is the very best-received story by our subscribers. One of our primary considerations is to instruct in a manner that the layperson can comprehend. We are not hypercritical of writing style."

REGIONAL

$ $ ALASKA BUSINESS MONTHLY

Alaska Business Publishing, 501 W. Northern Lights Blvd., Suite 100, Anchorage AK 99503-2577. (907)276-4373. Fax: (907)279-2900. E-mail: editor@akbizmag.com. Website: www.akbizmag.com. **Contact:** Debbie Cutler, editor. **80% freelance written.** Magazine covering Alaska-oriented business and industry. "Our audience is Alaska businessmen and women who rely on us for timely features and up-to-date information about doing business in Alaska." Estab. 1985. Circ. 10,000. Pays on publication. Publishes ms an average of 4 months after acceptance. Byline given. Offers $50 kill fee. Buys all rights. Editorial lead time 5 months. Submit seasonal material 5 months in advance. Accepts queries by mail, e-mail, fax. Accepts previously published material. Responds in 1 month to queries. Sample copy for 9×12 SAE and 4 first-class stamps. Writer's guidelines free.

Nonfiction General interest, how-to, interview/profile, new product (Alaska), opinion. No fiction, poetry, or anything not pertinent to Alaska. **Buys approximately 130 mss/year.** Send complete ms. Length: 500-2,000 words. **Pays $150-300.** Sometimes pays expenses of writers on assignment.

Photos State availability with submission.

Columns/Departments Required Reading (business book reviews); Right Moves; Alaska this Month; Monthly Calendars (all Alaska related), all 500-1,200 words. **Buys 12 mss/year.** Send complete ms. **Pays $50-75.**

Tips "Send a well-written manuscript on a subject of importance to Alaska businesses. We seek informative, entertaining articles on everything from entrepreneurs to heavy industry. We cover all Alaska industry to include mining, tourism, timber, transportation, oil and gas, fisheries, finance, insurance, real estate, communications, medical services, technology, and construction. We also cover Native and environmental issues, and occasionally feature Seattle and other communities in the Pacific Northwest."

$ $ ▣ ATLANTIC BUSINESS MAGAZINE

Communications Ten, Ltd., 197 Water St., St. John's NL A1C 6E7 Canada. (709)726-9300. Fax: (709)726-3013. E-mail: dchafe@atlanticbusinessmagazine.com. Website: www.atlanticbusinessmagazine.com. Managing Editor: Edwina Hutton. **Contact:** Dawn Chafe, editor. **80% freelance written.** Bimonthly magazine covering business in Atlantic Canada. "We discuss positive business developments, emphasizing that the 4 Atlantic provinces are a great place to do business." Estab. 1989. Circ. 30,000. Pays within 30 days of publication. Publishes ms an average of 2 months after acceptance. Byline given. Buys one-time rights. Editorial lead time 6 months. Accepts queries by mail, e-mail, fax. Sample copy and writer's guidelines free.

Nonfiction Exposé, general interest, interview/profile, new product. "We don't want religious, technical, or scholarly material. We are not an academic magazine. We are interested only in stories concerning business topics specific to the 4 Canadian provinces of Nova Scotia, New Brunswick, Prince Edward Island, and Newfoundland and Labrador." **Buys 36 mss/year.** Query with published clips. Length: 1,200-2,500 words. **Pays $300-750.** Sometimes pays expenses of writers on assignment.

Photos Send photos with submission. Reviews contact sheets, transparencies, prints. Buys one-time rights. Negotiates payment individually. Captions, identification of subjects required.

Columns/Departments Query with published clips.

Tips "Writers should submit their areas of interest as well as samples of their work and, if possible, suggested story ideas."

$ $☒ BUSINESS LONDON

Bowes Publishers, 1147 Gainsburough Rd., London ON N5Y 4X3 Canada. (519)472-7601. Fax: (519)473-7859. **Contact:** Gord Delamont, editor. **70% freelance written.** Monthly magazine covering London business. "Our audience is primarily small and medium businesses and entrepreneurs. Focus is on success stories and how to better operate your business." Estab. 1987. Circ. 14,000. Pays on publication. Publishes ms an average of 3 months after acceptance. Byline given. Offers 50% kill fee. Buys first rights. Editorial lead time 3 months. Responds in 3 months to mss. Sample copy for #10 SASE. Writer's guidelines free.

Nonfiction How-to (business topics), humor, interview/profile, new product (local only), personal experience (must have a London connection). **Buys 30 mss/year.** Query with published clips. Length: 250-1,500 words. **Pays $125-500.**

Photos Send photos with submission. Reviews contact sheets, transparencies. Buys one-time rights. Negotiates payment individually. Identification of subjects required.

Tips "Phone with a great idea. The most valuable things a writer owns are ideas. We'll take a chance on an unknown if the idea is good enough."

☒ CANADIAN MONEYSAVER

Canadian MoneySaver, Inc., Box 370, Bath ON K0H 1G0 Canada. (613)352-7448. Fax: (613)352-7700. E-mail: moneyinfo@canadianmoneysaver.ca. Website: www.canadianmoneysaver.ca. **Contact:** Dale Ennis, editor. **10% freelance written.** Monthly magazine covering personal finance. "*Canadian MoneySaver* contains practical money articles on tax, investment, retirement, and financial planning for everyday use." Estab. 1981. Circ. 76,300. Pays on publication. Publishes ms an average of 1 month after acceptance. Byline given. Buys first rights. Editorial lead time 1 month. Accepts queries by mail, e-mail, fax, phone. Responds in 2 weeks to queries; 1 month to mss. Sample copy online. Writer's guidelines free.

Nonfiction How-to (personal finance), personal experience. Query with published clips. Length: 800-2,000 words. **Pays negotiable rates for assigned articles.**

$ CRAIN'S DETROIT BUSINESS

Crain Communications, Inc., 1155 Gratiot, Detroit MI 48207-2997. (313)446-1654. Fax: (313)446-1687. E-mail: sselby@crain.com. Website: www.crainsdetroit.com. Editor: Mary Kramer. Executive Editor: Cindy Goodaker. **Contact:** Shawn Selby, special sections editor. **15% freelance written.** Weekly tabloid covering business in the Detroit metropolitan area—specifically Wayne, Oakland, Macomb, Washtenaw, and Livingston counties. Estab. 1985. Circ. 150,000. Pays on publication. Publishes ms an average of 1 month after acceptance. Byline given. Buys all rights. Accepts queries by mail, e-mail. Sample copy for $1.50. Writer's guidelines online.

• *Crain's Detroit Business* uses only area writers and local topics.

Nonfiction New product, technical, business. **Buys 50 mss/year.** Query with published clips. Length: 30-40 words/column inch. **Pays $10-15/column inch.** Pays expenses of writers on assignment.

Photos State availability with submission.

Tips "Contact special sections editor in writing with background and, if possible, specific story ideas relating to our type of coverage and coverage area."

№ $ $☒ HOME BUSINESS REPORT

Working for People Working from Home, The Dream Launchers Project, 439A Marmont St., Coquitlam BC V3K 4S4 Canada. (604)936-5815. Fax: (604)936-5805. E-mail: info@homesbusinessreport.com. Website: www.homebusinessreport.com. **Contact:** Susan Ward, editor-in-chief. **95% freelance written.** Quarterly magazine covering home-based business/small business. "Our focus is on practical strategies that small and home-based business owners can use to increase their business success. We prefer articles about real people having real experiences, as opposed to lists of how-tos. We run 2 types of articles: features and Regional Reports, which profile successful Canadian home-based businesses." Estab. 1989. Circ. 125,000. **Pays on acceptance.** Publishes ms an average of 2 months after acceptance. Byline given. Buys first North American serial, first rights. Editorial lead time 1-3 months. Submit seasonal material 3-6 months in advance. Accepts queries by mail, e-mail. Responds in 1-6 weeks to queries; 1-6 months to mss. Sample copy and writer's guidelines online.

Nonfiction "We have an ongoing need for freelance writers comfortable with researching and writing about products, services, and technology related to starting and running a successful home-based business, and for Regional Report writers to cover specific areas of Canada—the Yukon, Nunavut, NWT, and Saskatchewan."

Interview/profile, business articles. Special issues: Creating Cash Flow (October). Does not want "articles solely on theory or 'puff' pieces that do little more than promote your own business or product." **Buys 35-40 mss/year.** Query with or without published clips. Length: 1,000-3,000 words. **Pays $200-350.**

Photos State availability with submission. Buys one-time rights. Offers no additional payment for photos accepted with ms. Captions required.

Tips "The best way to break into our magazine is to be responsive to our specific needs. We are often looking for articles that are specific to the theme of a particular issue."

$ ☐ IN BUSINESS WINDSOR

Cornerstone Publications, Inc., 1775 Sprucewood Ave., Unit 1, LaSalle ON N9J 1X7 Canada. (519)250-2880. Fax: (519)250-2881. E-mail: gbaxter@inbusinesswindsor.com. Website: www.inbusinesswindsor.com. **Contact:** Gary Baxter, general manager/publisher. **70% freelance written.** Monthly magazine covering business. "We focus on issues/ideas which are of interest to businesses in and around Windsor and Essex County (Ontario). Most stories deal with business and finance; occasionally we will cover health and sports issues that affect our readers." Estab. 1988. Circ. 10,000. **Pays on acceptance.** Byline given. Buys first rights. Editorial lead time 3 months. Submit seasonal material 3 months in advance. Accepts queries by mail, e-mail, fax. Responds in 2 weeks to queries; 1 month to mss. Sample copy for $3.50.

Nonfiction General interest, how-to, interview/profile. **Buys 25 mss/year.** Query with published clips. Length: 800-1,500 words. **Pays $70-150.** Sometimes pays expenses of writers on assignment.

ℕ $ $ THE LANE REPORT

Lane Communications Group, 201 E. Main St., 14th Floor, Lexington KY 40507. (859)244-3500. Fax: (859)244-3555. E-mail: editorial@lanereport.com. Website: www.kybiz.com. Editor: Andy Olsen. **Contact:** Karen Baird, associate editor. **70% freelance written.** Monthly magazine covering statewide business. Estab. 1986. Circ. 15,000. Pays on publication. Byline given. Buys one-time rights. Editorial lead time 6 weeks. Submit seasonal material 3 months in advance. Accepts queries by mail, e-mail, fax. Accepts previously published material. Accepts simultaneous submissions. Responds in 1 month to queries. Sample copy and writer's guidelines free.

Nonfiction Essays, interview/profile, new product, photo feature. No fiction. **Buys 30-40 mss/year.** Query with published clips. Length: 500-2,000 words. **Pays $150-375.** Sometimes pays expenses of writers on assignment.

Photos State availability with submission. Reviews contact sheets, negatives, transparencies, prints, digital images. Buys one-time rights. Negotiates payment individually. Identification of subjects required.

Columns/Departments Technology and Business in Kentucky; Advertising; Exploring Kentucky; Perspective; Spotlight on the Arts, all less than 1,000 words.

▣ The online magazine carries original content not included in the print edition. Contact: Karen Baird, online editor.

Tips "As Kentucky's only statewide business and economics publication, we look for stories that incorporate perspectives from the Commonwealth's various regions and prominent industries—tying it into the national picture when appropriate. We also look for insightful profiles and interviews of Kentucky's entrepreneurs and business leaders."

$ $ $ $ ☑ OREGON BUSINESS

MEDIAmerica, Inc., 610 SW Broadway, Suite 200, Portalnd OR 97205. (503)223-0304. Fax: (503)221-6544. E-mail: queries@oregonbusiness.com. Website: www.oregonbusiness.com. **Contact:** Mitchell Hartman, editor. **15-25% freelance written.** Monthly magazine covering business in Oregon. "Our subscribers inlcude owners of small and medium-sized businesses, government agencies, professional staffs of banks, insurance companies, ad agencies, attorneys and other service providers. We accept *only* stories about Oregon businesses, issues and trends." Estab. 1981. Circ. 50,000. Pays on publication. Byline given. Buys first North American serial, electronic rights. Editorial lead time 2 months. Accepts queries by mail, e-mail. Sample copy for $4. Writer's guidelines online.

Nonfiction Features should focus on "major trends shaping the state; noteworthy businesses, practices, and leaders; stories with sweeping implications across industry sectors." Query with résumé and 2-3 published clips. Length: 1,200-3,000 words.

Columns/Departments First Person (opinion piece on an issue related to business), 750 words; Around the State (recent news and trends, and how they might shape the future), 100-600 words; Business Tools (practical, how-to suggestions for business managers and owners), 400-600 words; In Character (profile of interesting or "quirky" member of the business community), 850 words. Query with résumé and 2-3 published clips.

Tips "An *Oregon Business* story must meet at least 2 of the following criteria: **Size and location**: The topic must be relevant to Northwest businesses. Featured companies (including franchises) must be based in Oregon or Southwest Washington. **Service**: Our sections (1,200 words) are reserved largely for service pieces focusing on finance, marketing, management or other general business topics. These stories are meant to be instructional, emphasizing problem-solving by example. **Trends**: These are sometimes covered in a section piece, or perhaps a feature story. We aim to be the state's leading business publication so we want to be the first to spot trends that affect Oregon companies. **Exclusivity or strategy**: of an event, whether it's a corporate merger, a dramatic turnaround, a marketing triumph or a PR disaster."

$ROCHESTER BUSINESS JOURNAL

Rochester Business Journal, Inc., 45 E. Ave., Suite 500, Rochester NY 14604. (585)546-8303. Fax: (585)546-3398. E-mail: sjacob@rbj.net. Website: www.rbjdaily.com. Editor: Paul Ericson. Managing Editor: Mike Dickinson. **Contact:** Smriti Jacob, associate editor. **10% freelance written.** Weekly tabloid covering local business. "The *Rochester Business Journal* is geared toward corporate executives and owners of small businesses, bringing them leading-edge business coverage and analysis first in the market." Estab. 1984. Circ. 10,000. Pays on publication. Publishes ms an average of 1 month after acceptance. Byline given. Buys first, second serial (reprint), electronic rights. Editorial lead time 6 weeks. Accepts queries by mail, e-mail, fax. Responds in 1 week to queries. Sample copy for free or by e-mail. Writer's guidelines online.

Nonfiction How-to (business topics), news features, trend stories with local examples. Do not query about any topics that do not include several local examples—local companies, organizations, universities, etc. **Buys 110 mss/year.** Query with published clips. Length: 1,000-2,000 words. **Pays $150.**

Tips "The *Rochester Business Journal* prefers queries from local published writers who can demonstrate the ability to write for a sophisticated audience of business readers. Story ideas should be about business trends illustrated with numerous examples of local companies participating in the change or movement."

$ $VERMONT BUSINESS MAGAZINE

2 Church St., Burlington VT 05401-4445. (802)863-8038. Fax: (802)863-8069. E-mail: mcq@vermontbiz.com. Website: www.vermontbiz.com. **Contact:** Timothy McQuiston, editor. **80% freelance written.** Monthly tabloid covering business in Vermont. Circ. 8,000. Pays on publication. Publishes ms an average of 1 month after acceptance. Byline given. Buys one-time rights. Responds in 2 months to queries. Sample copy for 11 × 14 SAE and 7 first-class stamps.

Nonfiction Business trends and issues. **Buys 200 mss/year.** Query with published clips. Length: 800-1,800 words. **Pays $100-200.**

Reprints Send tearsheet and information about when and where the material previously appeared.

Photos Send photos with submission. Reviews contact sheets. Offers $10-35/photo. Identification of subjects required.

Tips "Read daily papers and look for business angles for a follow-up article. We look for issue and trend articles rather than company or businessman profiles. Note: Magazine accepts Vermont-specific material only. The articles must be about Vermont."

CAREER, COLLEGE & ALUMNI

$ $AMERICAN CAREERS

Career Communications, Inc., 6701 W. 64th St., Overland Park KS 66202. (800)669-7795. Fax: (913)362-7788. Website: www.carcom.com. **Contact:** Mary Pitchford, editor. **50% freelance written.** Student publication covering careers, career statistics, skills needed to get jobs. "*American Careers* provides career, salary, and education information to middle school and high school students. Self-tests help them relate their interests and abilities to future careers. Articles on résumés, interviews, etc., help them develop employability skills." Estab. 1989. Circ. 500,000. Pays 1 month after acceptance. Byline given. Buys all rights, makes work-for-hire assignments. Accepts queries by mail. Accepts simultaneous submissions. Sample copy for $3. Writer's guidelines for #10 SASE.

  ⊶ Break in by "sending us query letters with samples and résumés. We want to 'meet' the writer before making an assignment."

Nonfiction Career and education features related to career paths, including arts and communication, business, law, government, finance, construction, technology, health services, human services, manufacturing, engineering, and natural resources and agriculture. "No preachy advice to teens or articles that talk down to students." **Buys 20 mss/year.** Query by mail only with published clips. Length: 300-1,000 words. **Pays $100-450.** Pays expenses of writers on assignment.

Photos State availability with submission. Buys all rights. Negotiates payment individually. Captions, identification of subjects, model releases required.

Tips "Letters of introduction or query letters with samples and résumés are ways we get to know writers. Samples should include how-to articles and career-related articles. Articles written for teenagers also would make good samples. Short feature articles on careers, career-related how-to articles, and self-assessment tools (10-20 point quizzes with scoring information) are primarily what we publish.''

BROWN ALUMNI MAGAZINE

Brown University, 71 George St., Providence RI 02912. E-mail: alumni_magazine@brown.edu. Website: www.brownalumnimagazine.com. Editor: Norman Boucher. **Contact:** Elizabeth Smith, office manager. Bimonthly magazine covering the world of Brown University and its alumni. ''We are an editorially independent, general interest magazine covering the on-campus world of Brown University and the off-campus world of its alumni.'' Estab. 1900. Circ. 80,000. **Pays on acceptance.** Publishes ms an average of 3 months after acceptance. Byline given. Buys North American serial and Web rights. Editorial lead time 3 months. Submit seasonal material 4 months in advance. Accepts queries by mail, e-mail, fax. Sample copy for free. Writer's guidelines not available.

Nonfiction Book excerpts, essays, exposé, general interest, historical/nostalgic, humor, interview/profile, opinion, personal experience, photo feature, travel, profiles. No articles unconnected to Brown or its alumni. **Buys 50 mss/year.** Query with published clips. Length: 150-4,000 words.

Photos State availability with submission. Reviews contact sheets, transparencies, prints. Buys one-time rights. Negotiates payment individually. Captions, identification of subjects required.

Columns/Departments Under the Elms (news items about campus), 100-400 words; Arts & Culture (reviews of Brown-authored works), 200-500 words; Alumni P.O.V. (essays by Brown alumni), 750 words; Sports (reports on Brown sports teams and athletes), 200-500 words. **Buys 10-20 mss/year.** Query with published clips.

Tips ''Be imaginative and be specific. A Brown connection is required for all stories in the magazine, but a Brown connection alone does not guarantee our interest. Ask yourself: Why should readers care about your proposed story? Also, we look for depth and objective reporting, not boosterism.''

$ $ CIRCLE K MAGAZINE

3636 Woodview Trace, Indianapolis IN 46268-3196. (317)875-8755. Fax: (317)879-0204. E-mail: ckimagazine@kiwanis.org. Website: www.circlek.org. **Contact:** Christopher Martz, executive editor. **60% freelance written.** Magazine published 5 times/year. ''Our readership consists almost entirely of above-average college students interested in voluntary community service and leadership development. They are politically and socially aware and have a wide range of interests.'' Circ. 12,000. **Pays on acceptance.** Byline given. Buys first North American serial rights. Accepts queries by mail, e-mail, fax. Responds in 2 weeks to queries. Sample copy for large SAE with 3 first-class stamps or on website. Writer's guidelines online.

   O— Break in by offering ''fresh ideas for stories dealing with college students who are not only concerned with themselves. Our readers are concerned with making their communities better.''

Nonfiction Articles published in *Circle K* are of 2 types—serious and light nonfiction. ''We are interested in general interest articles on topics concerning college students and their lifestyles, as well as articles dealing with careers, community concerns, and leadership development. No first-person confessions, family histories, or travel pieces.'' Query. Length: 1,500-2,000 words. **Pays $150-400.**

Photos Purchased with accompanying ms; total price includes both photos and ms. Captions required.

Tips ''Query should indicate author's familiarity with the field and sources. Subject treatment must be objective and in-depth, and articles should include illustrative examples and quotes from persons involved in the subject or qualified to speak on it. We are open to working with new writers who present a good article idea and demonstrate that they've done their homework concerning the article subject itself, as well as concerning our magazine's style. We're interested in college-oriented trends, for example: entrepreneur schooling, high-tech classrooms, music, leisure, and health issues.''

$ $ CONCORDIA UNIVERSITY MAGAZINE

Concordia University, 1455 de Maisonneuve Blvd. W., FB520, Montreal QC H3G 1M8 Canada. (514)848-2424, ext. 3826. Fax: (514)848-2826. E-mail: howard.bokser@concordia.ca. Website: www.magazine.concordia.ca. **Contact:** Howard Bokser, editor. **60% freelance written.** Quarterly magazine covering matters relating to Concordia University and its alumni. ''We only cover topics related to research and teaching at Concordia, and student or administrator news, and we profile university alumni.'' Estab. 1977. Circ. 70,000. **Pays on acceptance.** Publishes ms an average of 1 month after acceptance. Byline given. Offers 50% kill fee. Not copyrighted. Buys first rights. Editorial lead time 2 months. Submit seasonal material 2 months in advance. Accepts queries by mail, e-mail. Accepts previously published material. Accepts simultaneous submissions. Responds in 1 month. Sample copy online. Writer's guidelines free.

Nonfiction Book excerpts, general interest, historical/nostalgic, humor, interview/profile, opinion, personal experience, photo feature. **Buys 10 mss/year.** Query with published clips. Length: 1,500-2,000 words. **Pays $300-350.** Sometimes pays expenses of writers on assignment.

Photos State availability with submission. Reviews contact sheets, 2×2 transparencies, 4×6 prints, GIF/JPEG files. Buys one-time rights. Negotiates payment individually. Identification of subjects required.

Columns/Departments End Piece (opinion or essay), 650 words. **Buys 4 mss/year.** Query with published clips. **Pays $200.**

$ $ EQUAL OPPORTUNITY

The Nation's Only Multi-Ethnic Recruitment Magazine for African-American, Hispanic, Native-American & Asian-American College Grads, Equal Opportunity Publications, Inc., 445 Broad Hollow Rd., Suite 425, Melville NY 11747. (631)421-9421. Fax: (631)421-0359. E-mail: jschneider@eop.com. Website: www.eop.com. **Contact:** James Schneider, editor. **70% freelance written.** Prefers to work with published/established writers. Triannual magazine covering career guidance for minorities. "Our audience is 90% college juniors and seniors; 10% working graduates. An understanding of educational and career problems of minorities is essential." Estab. 1967. Circ. 11,000. Pays on publication. Publishes ms an average of 6 months after acceptance. Byline given. Buys first rights. Editorial lead time 6 months. Submit seasonal material 6 months in advance. Accepts queries by mail, e-mail, fax, phone. Accepts previously published material. Responds in 2 weeks to queries; 1 month to mss. Sample copy and writer's guidelines for 9 × 12 SAE with 5 first-class stamps.

● Distributed through college guidance and placement offices.

Nonfiction General interest (specific minority concerns), how-to (job hunting skills, personal finance, better living, coping with discrimination), interview/profile (minority role models), opinion (problems of minorities), personal experience (professional and student study experiences), technical (on career fields offering opportunities for minorites), coverage of minority interests. **Buys 10 mss/year.** Query with or without published clips or send complete ms. Length: 1,000-2,000 words. **Pays 10¢/word.** Sometimes pays expenses of writers on assignment.

Reprints Send information about when and where the material previously appeared. Pays 10¢/word.

Photos Reviews 35mm color slides and b&w. Buys all rights. Pays $15/photo use. Captions, identification of subjects required.

Tips "Articles must be geared toward questions and answers faced by minority and women students. We would like to see role-model profiles of professions."

$ FLORIDA LEADER

P.O. Box 14081, Gainesville FL 32604-2081. (352)373-6907. Fax: (352)373-8120. E-mail: stephanie@studentleader.com. Website: www.floridaleader.com. Publisher: W.H. Oxendine, Jr. **Contact:** Stephanie Reck, editor. **10% freelance written.** Triannual magazine. College magazine, feature-oriented, especially activities, events, interests and issues pertaining to college students. Estab. 1983. Circ. 50,000. Pays on publication. Publishes ms an average of 2 months after acceptance. Byline given. Submit seasonal material 6 months in advance. Accepts queries by mail, e-mail, fax. Responds in 2 months to queries. Sample copy for $3.50, 9 × 12 SAE with 5 first-class stamps. Writer's guidelines online.

Nonfiction Practical tips for going to college, student life and leadership development. How-to, humor, interview/profile, Feature (All multi-sourced and Florida college related). "No lengthy individual profiles or articles without primary and secondary sources of attribution." Length: 900 words. **Pays $35-75.** Sometimes pays expenses of writers on assignment.

Photos State availability with submission. Reviews negatives, transparencies. Captions, identification of subjects, model releases required.

Columns/Departments College Life, The Lead Role, In Every Issue (quizzes, tips), Florida Forum (features Florida high school students), 250-1,000 words. **Buys 2 mss/year.** Query.

Tips "Read other high school and college publications for current issues, interests. Send manuscripts or outlines for review. All sections open to freelance work. Always looking for lighter, humorous articles, as well as features on Florida colleges and universities, careers, jobs. Multi-sourced (5-10) articles are best."

$ $ $ $ HARVARD MAGAZINE

Harvard Magazine, Inc., 7 Ware St., Cambridge MA 02138. (617)495-5746. Fax: (617)495-0324. Website: www.harvardmagazine.com. **Contact:** John S. Rosenberg, editor. **35-50% freelance written.** Bimonthly magazine for Harvard University faculty, alumni, and students. Estab. 1898. Circ. 225,000. Pays on publication. Publishes ms an average of 4 months after acceptance. Byline given. Buys one-time print and website rights. Editorial lead time 1 year. Accepts queries by mail, fax. Responds in 1 month. Sample copy online. Writer's guidelines not available.

Nonfiction Book excerpts, essays, interview/profile, journalism on Harvard-related intellectual subjects. **Buys 20-30 mss/year.** Query with published clips. Length: 800-10,000 words. **Pays $250-2,000.** Pays expenses of writers on assignment.

$ $ $ $ NOTRE DAME MAGAZINE

University of Notre Dame, 538 Grace Hall, Notre Dame IN 46556-5612. (574)631-5335. Fax: (574)631-6767. E-mail: ndmag@nd.edu. Website: www.nd.edu/ ~ ndmag. Managing Editor: Carol Schaal. **Contact:** Kerry Temple, editor. **75% freelance written.** Quarterly magazine covering news of Notre Dame and education and issues affecting contemporary society. ''We are a university magazine with a scope as broad as that found at a university, but we place our discussion in a moral, ethical, and spiritual context reflecting our Catholic heritage.'' Estab. 1972. Circ. 150,000. **Pays on acceptance.** Publishes ms an average of 1 year after acceptance. Byline given. Buys first, electronic rights. Accepts queries by mail, e-mail, fax. Responds in 2 months to queries. Sample copy and writer's guidelines online.

Nonfiction Opinion, personal experience, religious. **Buys 35 mss/year.** Query with published clips. Length: 600-3,000 words. **Pays $250-3,000.** Sometimes pays expenses of writers on assignment.

Photos State availability with submission. Reviews transparencies, 8×10 prints, b&w contact sheets. Buys one-time and electronic rights. Identification of subjects, model releases required.

Columns/Departments Perspectives (essays, often written in first person, deal with a wide array of issues—some topical, some personal, some serious, some light). Query with or without published clips or send complete ms.

The online version carries original content not found in the print edition and includes writer's guidelines. Contact: Carol Schaal.

Tips ''The editors are always looking for new writers and fresh ideas. However, the caliber of the magazine and frequency of its publication dictate that the writing meet very high standards. The editors value articles strong in storytelling quality, journalistic technique, and substance. They do not encourage promotional or nostalgia pieces, stories on sports, or essays which are sentimentally religious.''

$ $ OREGON QUARTERLY

The Northwest Perspective from the University of Oregon, 130 Chapman Hall, 5228 University of Oregon, Eugene OR 97403-5228. (541)346-5048. Fax: (541)346-5571. E-mail: gmaynard@uoregon.edu. Website: www.uoregon.edu/ ~ oq. Managing Editor: Ross West. **Contact:** Guy Maynard, editor. **50% freelance written.** Quarterly magazine covering people and ideas at the University of Oregon and the Northwest. Estab. 1919. Circ. 100,000. **Pays on acceptance.** Publishes ms an average of 3 months after acceptance. Byline given. Offers 20% kill fee. Buys first North American serial rights. Accepts queries by mail, e-mail. Accepts previously published material. Responds in 2 months to queries. Sample copy for 9×12 SAE with 4 first-class stamps or on website. Writer's guidelines online.

Break in to the magazine with a profile (400 or 800 words) of a University of Oregon alumnus. Best to query first.

Nonfiction Northwest issues and culture from the perspective of UO alumni and faculty. **Buys 30 mss/year.** Query with published clips. Length: 500-3,000 words. **Pays 20¢/word.** Sometimes pays expenses of writers on assignment.

Reprints Send photocopy and information about when and where the material previously appeared. Pays 50% of amount paid for an original article.

Photos State availability with submission. Reviews 8×10 prints. Buys one-time rights. Offers $10-25/photo. Identification of subjects required.

Fiction Publishes novel excerpts.

Tips ''Query with strong, colorful lead; clips.''

THE PENN STATER

Penn State Alumni Association, Hintz Family Alumni Center, University Park PA 16802. (814)865-2709. Fax: (814)863-5690. E-mail: pennstater@psu.edu. Website: www.alumni.psu.edu. **Contact:** Tina Hay, editor. **75% freelance written.** Bimonthly magazine covering Penn State and Penn Staters. Estab. 1910. Circ. 123,000. **Pays on acceptance.** Publishes ms an average of 4 months after acceptance. Byline given. Offers 50% kill fee. Buys first North American serial, second serial (reprint) rights. Editorial lead time 3 months. Submit seasonal material 8 months in advance. Accepts queries by mail, e-mail, fax. Accepts previously published material. Accepts simultaneous submissions. Responds in 3 months to queries. Sample copy and writer's guidelines free.

Nonfiction Stories must have Penn State connection. Book excerpts (by Penn Staters), general interest, historical/nostalgic, interview/profile, personal experience, photo feature, book reviews, science/research. No unsolicited mss. **Buys 20 mss/year.** Query with published clips. Length: 200-3,000 words. **Pays competitive rates.** Pays expenses of writers on assignment.

Reprints Send photocopy and information about when and where the material previously appeared. Payment varies.

Photos Send photos with submission. Reviews transparencies, prints. Buys one-time rights. Negotiates payment individually. Captions required.

Tips "We are especially interested in attracting writers who are savvy in creative nonfiction/literary journalism. Most stories must have a Penn State tie-in. No phone calls."

$ $ THE PURDUE ALUMNUS

Purdue Alumni Association, Dick and Sandy Dauch Alumni Center, 403 W. Wood St., West Lafayette IN 47907-2007. (765)494-5182. Fax: (765)494-9179. E-mail: slmartin@purdue.edu. Website: www.purdue.edu/PAA. **Contact:** Sharon Martin, editor. **50% freelance written.** Prefers to work with published/established writers; works with small number of new/unpublished writers each year. Bimonthly magazine covering subjects of interest to Purdue University alumni. Estab. 1912. Circ. 65,000. Pays on publication. Publishes ms an average of 2 months after acceptance. Byline given. Buys first rights, makes work-for-hire assignments. Submit seasonal material 6 months in advance. Accepts queries by mail. Accepts previously published material. Accepts simultaneous submissions. Responds in 6 weeks to queries. Sample copy for 9×12 SAE with 2 first-class stamps. Writer's guidelines online.

Nonfiction Focus is on alumni, campus news, issues, and opinions of interest to 65,000 members of the Alumni Association. Feature style, primarily university-oriented. Issues relevant to education. General interest, historical/nostalgic, humor, interview/profile, personal experience. **Buys 12-20 mss/year.** Length: 1,500-2,500 words. **Pays $250-500 for assigned articles.** Pays expenses of writers on assignment.

Photos State availability with submission. Reviews 5×7 prints, b&w contact sheets.

Tips "We have more than 350,000 living, breathing Purdue alumni. If you can find a good story about one of them, we're interested. We use local freelancers to do campus pieces."

Ⓝ $ $ ⊠ QUEEN'S ALUMNI REVIEW

Queen's University, 99 University Ave., Kingston ON K7L 3N6 Canada. Fax: (613)533-6828. E-mail: cuthberk@post.queensu.ca. Website: www.alumni.queensu.ca/alumniprograms. **Contact:** Ken Cuthbertson, editor. **25% freelance written.** Quarterly magazine. Estab. 1927. Circ. 99,000. **Pays on acceptance.** Publishes ms an average of 3 months after acceptance. Byline given. Buys first North American serial, electronic rights. Editorial lead time 3 months. Submit seasonal material 9 months in advance. Accepts queries by mail, e-mail. Responds in 2 weeks. Sample copy and writer's guidelines online.

Nonfiction "We publish feature articles, columns, and articles about alumni, faculty, and staff who are doing unusual or worthwile things." Does not want religious or political rants, travel articles, how-to, or general interest pieces that do not refer to or make some reference to our core audience." **Buys 40 mss/year.** Query with or without published clips or send complete ms. Length: 200-2,500 words. **Pays 40¢/word for assigned articles.** Sometimes pays expenses of writers on assignment.

Photos Send photos with submission. Reviews transparencies, prints, GIF/JPEG files. Offers $25 minimum or negotiates payment individually. Identification of subjects required.

Columns/Departments "Potential freelancers should study our magazine before submitting a query for a column." **Buys 40 mss/year.** Query with published clips or send complete ms. **Pays 40¢/word.**

Tips "We buy freelance material, but our budget is limited, and so we choose carefully. All articles should have a Queen's angle—one that shows how Queen's alumni, faculty, staff, or friends of the university are involved and engaged in the world. We also look for topical articles that start Queen's specific and go from there to look at issues of a wide topical interest. The writing should be professional, snappy, informative, and engaging. We always have far more editorial material in hand than we can ever publish. Study our magazine before you submit a query. Our circulation is primarily in Canada, but we also have readers in the US, the United Kingdom, Hong Kong, Australia, and elsewhere. Our readers are young and old, male and female, well educated, well traveled, and sophisticated. We look for material that will appeal to a broad constituency."

Ⓝ $ $ RIPON COLLEGE MAGAZINE

P.O. Box 248, Ripon WI 54971-0248. (920)748-8364. Fax: (920)748-9262. E-mail: booneL@ripon.edu. Website: www.ripon.edu. **Contact:** Loren J. Boone, editor. **15% freelance written.** Quarterly magazine that "contains information relating to Ripon College and is mailed to alumni and friends of the college." Estab. 1851. Circ. 14,000. Pays on publication. Publishes ms an average of 3 months after acceptance. Byline given. Makes work-for-hire assignments. Accepts queries by mail, e-mail, fax, phone. Responds in 2 weeks to queries.

Nonfiction Historical/nostalgic, interview/profile. **Buys 4 mss/year.** Query with or without published clips or send complete ms. Length: 250-1,000 words. **Pays $25-350.**

Photos State availability with submission. Reviews contact sheets. Buys one-time rights. Offers additional payment for photos accepted with ms. Captions, model releases required.

Tips "Story ideas must have a direct connection to Ripon College."

RUTGERS MAGAZINE

Rutgers University, 96 Davidson Rd., Piscataway NJ 08854-8062. (732)445-3710. Fax: (732)445-5925. E-mail: rutgersmagazine@ur.rutgers.edu. **Contact:** Renee Olson, editor. **30% freelance written.** Published 3 times/

year. University magazine of general interest, but articles must have a Rutgers University or alumni tie-in. Circ. 70,000. **Pays on acceptance.** Publishes ms an average of 4 months after acceptance. Byline given. Offers kill fee. Buys first North American serial rights. Submit seasonal material 8 months in advance. Accepts queries by mail, e-mail, fax.

Nonfiction Essays, general interest, historical/nostalgic, interview/profile, photo feature, science/research; art/humanities. No fillers/shorts, how-to articles, or articles without a Rutgers connection. **Buys 10-15 mss/year.** Query with published clips. Length: 1,000-4,000 words. **Payment varies.**

Photos State availability with submission. Buys one-time rights. Payment varies. Identification of subjects required.

Columns/Departments Sports; Alumni Profiles (related to Rutgers), all 1,200-1,800 words. **Buys 4-6 mss/year.** Query with published clips. **Pays competitively.**

Tips "Send an intriguing query backed by solid clips. We'll evaluate clips and topic for most appropriate use."

SCHOLASTIC ADMINISTR@TOR MAGAZINE

Scholastic, Inc., 557 Broadway, 5th Floor, New York NY 10012. (212)965-7429. Fax: (212)965-7497. E-mail: lrenwick@scholastic.com. Website: www.scholastic.com/administrator. **Contact:** Lucile Renwick, senior managing editor. Magazine published 8 times/year. Focuses on helping today's school administrators and education technology leaders in their efforts to improve the management of schools. Circ. 100,000. Editorial lead time 1 month. Sample copy for free.

TRANSFORMATIONS

A Journal of People and Change, Worcester Polytechnic Institute, 100 Institute Rd., Worcester MA 01609-2280. Fax: (508)831-5820. E-mail: transformations@wpi.edu. Website: www.wpi.edu/+transformations. **Contact:** Amy Dean, editor. **70% freelance written.** Quarterly alumni magazine covering science and engineering/education/business personalities and related technologies and issues for 25,000 alumni, primarily engineers, scientists, managers, media. Estab. 1897. Circ. 34,000. Pays on publication. Publishes ms an average of 6 months after acceptance. Byline given. Buys one-time rights. Accepts queries by mail, e-mail. Accepts previously published material. Accepts simultaneous submissions. Responds in 1 month to queries. Sample copy online.

Nonfiction Interview/profile (alumni in engineering, science, etc.), photo feature, features on people and programs at WPI. Query with published clips. Length: 300-3,000 words. **Pays negotiable rate.** Sometimes pays expenses of writers on assignment.

Photos State availability with submission. Reviews contact sheets. Pays negotiable rate. Captions required.

The online magazine carries original content not found in the print edition.

Tips "Submit outline of story, story idea, or published work. Features are most open to freelancers with excellent narrative skills, and an ability to understand and convey complex technologies in an engaging way. Keep in mind that this is an alumni magazine, so most articles focus on the college and its graduates."

$ $U.S. BLACK ENGINEER/HISPANIC ENGINEER

And Information Technology, Career Communications Group, Inc., 729 E. Pratt St., Suite 504, Baltimore MD 21202-3101. (410)244-7101. Fax: (410)752-1837. E-mail: editors@ccgmag.com. Website: www.blackengineer.com. **Contact:** Eric Addison, managing editor. **80% freelance written.** Quarterly magazine. "Both of our magazines are designed to bring technology issues home to people of color. We look at careers in technology and what affects career possibilities, including education. But we also look at how technology affects Black Americans and Latinos." Estab. 1976. Circ. 40,000. Pays on publication. Publishes ms an average of 1 month after acceptance. Byline given. Offers 50% kill fee. Makes work-for-hire assignments. Editorial lead time 2 months. Accepts queries by mail, e-mail, fax, phone. Responds in 2 months to queries. Sample copy and writer's guidelines for #10 SASE.

Nonfiction How-to (plan a career, get a first job, get a good job), interview/profile, new product, technical (new technologies and people of color involved with them), Capitol Hill/federal reportage on technology and EEO issues. No opinion pieces, first-person articles, routine profiles with no news peg or grounding in science/technology issues. Length: 650-1,800 words. **Pays $250-600 for assigned articles.** Sometimes pays expenses of writers on assignment.

Photos State availability with submission. Buys all rights. Negotiates payment individually. Captions, identification of subjects, model releases required.

Columns/Departments Buys 30 mss/year. **Pays $250-300.**

Tips "Call or come see me. Also contact us about covering our conferences, Black Engineer of the Year Awards and Women of Color Technology Awards."

CHILD CARE & PARENTAL GUIDANCE

$ $ ALL ABOUT KIDS MAGAZINE

Midwest Parenting Publications, 1901 Broad Ripple Ave., Indianapolis IN 46220. E-mail: jasonjones@aak.com. Website: www.aak.com. **Contact:** Tom Wynne, editor. Cincinnati Address: 1077 Celestial, Suite 101, Cincinnati OH 45202. (513)684-0501. Fax: (513)684-0507. **Contact:** Jason Jones, managing editor. **100% freelance written.** Monthly magazine covering a myriad of parenting topics and pieces of information relative to families and children in greater Cincinnati. Estab. 1985. Circ. 60,000. Pays on publication. Publishes ms an average of 6 months after acceptance. Byline given. Buys first, electronic rights. Editorial lead time 3 months. Submit seasonal material 6 months in advance. Accepts queries by mail. Writer's guidelines online.

Nonfiction Exposé, general interest, historical/nostalgic, how-to (family projects, crafts), humor, inspirational, interview/profile, opinion, photo feature, travel. Special issues: Maternity (January); Special Needs Children (May). No product or book reviews. **Buys 50 mss/year.** Send complete ms. Length: 750-3,000 words. **Pays $50-250 for assigned articles; $50-100 for unsolicited articles.**

Photos State availability with submission.

Fillers Anecdotes, facts, gags to be illustrated by cartoonist, short humor. **Buys 20/year.** Length: 350-800 words. **Pays $50-100.**

Tips "Submit full-text articles with query letter. Keep in mind the location of the magazine and try to include relevant sidebars, sources, etc. Include 'Editorial Submission' on the outside of the envelope."

$ ATLANTA PARENT/ATLANTA BABY

2346 Perimeter Park Dr., Suite 100, Atlanta GA 30341. (770)454-7599. Fax: (770)454-7699. E-mail: atlantaparent @atlantaparent.com. Website: www.atlantaparent.com. Publisher: Liz White. **50% freelance written.** Pays on publication. Publishes ms an average of 3 months after acceptance. Byline given. Buys one-time rights. Submit seasonal material 6 months in advance. Accepts queries by mail, e-mail. Accepts previously published material. Responds in 4 months to queries. Sample copy for $3.

Nonfiction General interest, how-to, humor, interview/profile, travel. Special issues: Private School (January); Camp (February); Birthday Parties (March and September); Maternity and Mothering (May and October); Childcare (July); Back-to-School (August); Teens (September); Holidays (November/December). No religious or philosophical discussions. **Buys 60 mss/year.** Query with or without published clips or send complete ms. Length: 800-1,500 words. **Pays $5-50.** Sometimes pays expenses of writers on assignment.

Reprints Send tearsheet or photocopy with rights for sale noted and information about when and where the material previously appeared. **Pays $30-50.**

Photos State availability of or send photos with submission. Reviews 3 × 5 photos. Buys one-time rights. Offers $10/photo.

Tips "Articles should be geared to problems or situations of families and parents. Should include down-to-earth tips and be clearly written. No philosophical discussions. We're also looking for well-written humor."

N $ $ ⊡ BEST WISHES

Family Communications Inc., 65 The East Mall, Toronto ON M8Z 5W3 Canada. (416)537-2604. Fax: (416)538-1794. E-mail: admin@parentscanada.com. Website: www.parentscanada.com. **Contact:** Tracy Cooper. **80% freelance written.** Semiannual magazine. Practical information for parents of babies from birth to 6 months of age. Written by Canadian healthcare professionals. Estab. 1948. Circ. 120,000. **Pays on acceptance.** Publishes ms an average of 3-6 months after acceptance. Byline given. Buys all rights. Editorial lead time 3-6 months. Accepts queries by mail. Responds in 1 month to queries. Writer's guidelines free.

Nonfiction Query. Length: 500-1,500 words.

Photos State availability of or send photos with submission. Reviews 4 × 6 or larger prints, GIF/JPEG files (300 dpi or scanned from 4 × 6 or larger). Reprint rights. Offers no additional payment for photos accepted with ms.

$ BIG APPLE PARENT/QUEENS PARENT/WESTCHESTER PARENT/BROOKLYN PARENT

Family Communications, LLC, 9 E. 38th St., 4th Floor, New York NY 10016. (212)889-6400. Fax: (212)689-4958. E-mail: hellonwheels@parentsknow.com. Website: www.parentsknow.com. **Contact:** Helen Freedman, executive editor. **90% freelance written.** Monthly tabloid covering New York City family life. "*BAP* readers live in high-rise Manhattan apartments; it is an educated, upscale audience. Often both parents are working full time in professional occupations. Child-care help tends to be one on one, in the home. Kids attend private schools for the most part. While not quite a suburban approach, some of our *QP* and *BK* readers do have backyards (though most live in high-rise apartments). It is a more middle-class audience in Queens and Brooklyn. More kids are in day care centers; majority of kids are in public schools. Our Westchester county edition is for suburban parents." Estab. 1985. Circ. 80,000, *Big Apple*; 70,000, *Queens Parent*; 70,000, *Westchester Parent*; 45,000, *Brooklyn Parent*. Pays 2 months after publication. Byline given. Offers 50% kill fee. Buys first

New York area rights. Submit seasonal material 3 months in advance. Accepts queries by mail, e-mail, fax. Accepts simultaneous submissions. Responds immediately to queries. Sample copy and writer's guidelines free.

> **O—** Break in with "any kind of piece, but remember that everything should be targeted to parents. We love journalistic pieces (as opposed to essays, which is what we mostly get)."

Nonfiction Book excerpts, exposé, general interest, how-to, inspirational, interview/profile, opinion, personal experience, family health, education. "We're always looking for news and coverage of controversial issues." **Buys 150 mss/year.** Query with or without published clips or send complete ms. Length: 600-1,000 words. **Pays $35-50.** Sometimes pays expenses of writers on assignment.

Reprints Send tearsheet or typed ms with rights for sale noted and information about when and where the material previously appeared. Pays same as article rate.

Columns/Departments Dads; Education; Family Finance. **Buys 50-60 mss/year.** Send complete ms.

Tips "We have a very local focus; our aim is to present articles our readers cannot find in national publications. To that end, news stories and human interest pieces must focus on New York and New Yorkers. We are always looking for news and newsy pieces; we keep on top of current events, frequently giving issues that may relate to parenting a local focus so that the idea will work for us as well. We are not currently looking for essays, humor, general child raising, or travel."

$CATHOLIC PARENT

Our Sunday Visitor, 200 Noll Plaza, Huntington IN 46750-4310. (260)356-8400. Fax: (260)356-8472. E-mail: cparent@osv.com. Website: www.osv.com. **95% freelance written.** Bimonthly magazine. "We look for practical, realistic parenting articles written for a primarily Roman Catholic audience. The key is practical, not pious." Estab. 1993. Circ. 36,000. **Pays on acceptance.** Publishes ms an average of 6 months after acceptance. Byline given. Offers variable kill fee. Buys first North American serial rights. Editorial lead time 6 months. Submit seasonal material 6 months in advance. Accepts simultaneous submissions. Responds in 2 months to queries. Sample copy for $3.

> • *Catholic Parent* is extremely receptive to first-person accounts of personal experiences dealing with parenting issues that are moving, emotionally engaging, and uplifting for the reader. Bear in mind the magazine's mission to provide practical information for parents.

Nonfiction Essays, how-to, humor, inspirational, personal experience, religious. **Buys 50 mss/year.** Send complete ms. Length: 800-1,000 words. **Payment varies.** Sometimes pays expenses of writers on assignment.

Photos State availability with submission.

Columns/Departments This Works (parenting tips), 200 words. **Buys 50 mss/year.** Send complete ms. **Pays $15-25.**

Tips No poetry or fiction.

$CHESAPEAKE FAMILY

Jefferson Communications, 929 West St., Suite 307, Annapolis MD 21401. (410)263-1641. Fax: (410)280-0255. E-mail: editor@chesapeakefamily.com. Website: www.chesapeakefamily.com. **Contact:** Suzette Guiffré, editor. **80% freelance written.** Monthly magazine covering parenting. "*Chesapeake Family* is a free, regional parenting publication serving readers in the Anne Arundel, Calvert, Prince George's, and Queen Anne's counties of Maryland. Our goal is to identify tips, resources, and products that will make our readers' lives easier. We answer the questions they don't have time to ask, doing the research for them so they have the information they need to make better decisions for their families' health, education, and well-being." Estab. 1990. Circ. 40,000. Publishes ms an average of 2 months after acceptance. Byline given. Buys first, one-time, second serial (reprint), electronic rights, makes work-for-hire assignments. Editorial lead time 3-6 months. Submit seasonal material 4 months in advance. Accepts queries by mail, e-mail, fax. Accepts previously published material. Accepts simultaneous submissions. Sample copy for SASE with 3 First-Class stamps. Writer's guidelines online.

Nonfiction How-to (parenting topics: sign your kids up for sports, find out if your child needs braces, etc.), interview/profile (local personalities), travel (family-fun destinations). No general, personal essays (however, personal anecdotes leading into a story with general applicability is fine). **Buys 25 mss/year.** Send complete ms. Length: 800-1,200 words. **Pays $75-125; $35-50 for unsolicited articles.**

Photos State availability with submission. Reviews prints, GIF/JPEG files. Offers no additional payment for photos accepted with ms, unless original, assigned photo is selected for the cover. Model releases required.

Columns/Departments Buys 25 mss/year. **Pays $35-50.**

Tips "A writer's best chance is to know the issues specific to our local readers. Know how to research the issues well, answer the questions our readers need to know, and give them information they can act on—and present it in a friendly, conversational tone."

$ $CHICAGO PARENT

Wednesday Journal, Inc., 141 S. Oak Park Ave., Oak Park IL 60302-2972. (708)386-5555. Fax: (708)524-8360. E-mail: sschultz@chicagoparent.com. Website: www.chicagoparent.com. **Contact:** Susy Schultz, editor. **60%**

freelance written. Monthly tabloid. "*Chicago Parent* has a distinctly local approach. We offer information, inspiration, perspective and empathy to Chicago-area parents. Our lively editorial mix has a 'we're all in this together' spirit, and articles are thoroughly researched and well written." Estab. 1988. Circ. 125,000 in 3 zones covering the 6-county Chicago metropolitan area. Pays on publication. Publishes ms an average of 2 months after acceptance. Byline given. Offers 10-50% kill fee. Buys first, electronic rights. Editorial lead time 4 months. Submit seasonal material 4 months in advance. Accepts queries by mail. Responds in 6 weeks to queries. Sample copy for $3.95 and 11×17 SAE with $1.65 postage. Writer's guidelines for #10 SASE.

   Oᴙ Break in by "writing 'short stuff' items (front-of-the-book short items on local people, places and things of interest to families)." Local writers only.

Nonfiction Essays, exposé, how-to (parent-related), humor, interview/profile, travel, local interest; investigative features. Special issues: include Chicago Baby and Healthy Child. "No pot-boiler parenting pieces, simultaneous submissions, previously published pieces or non-local writers (from outside the 6-county Chicago metropolitan area)." **Buys 40-50 mss/year.** Query with published clips. Length: 200-2,500 words. **Pays $25-300 for assigned articles; $25-100 for unsolicited articles.** Pays expenses of writers on assignment.

Photos State availability with submission. Reviews contact sheets, negatives, prints. Buys one-time rights. Offers $0-40/photo; negotiates payment individually. Captions, identification of subjects required.

Columns/Departments Healthy Child (kids' health issues), 850 words; Getaway (travel pieces), up to 1,200 words; other columns not open to freelancers. **Buys 30 mss/year.** Query with published clips or send complete ms. **Pays $100.**

Tips "We don't like pot-boiler parenting topics and don't accept many personal essays unless they are truly compelling."

$ $ $ $ CHILD

Gruner + Jahr, 375 Lexington Ave., New York NY 10017-5514. (212)499-2000. Fax: (212)499-2038. Website: www.child.com. Editor-in-Chief: Miriam Arond. Managing Editor: Dawn Roode. **Contact:** Submissions. **95% freelance written.** Monthly magazine covering parenting. Estab. 1986. Circ. 1,020,000. **Pays on acceptance.** Byline given. Offers 25% kill fee. Buys all rights. Editorial lead time 8 months. Submit seasonal material 6 months in advance. Accepts queries by mail. Responds in 2 months to queries. Sample copy for $3.95. Writer's guidelines for #10 SASE.

Nonfiction Book excerpts, essays, interview/profile, personal experience, travel, health, timely trend stories on topics that affect today's parents. No poetry or fiction. **Buys 50 feature, 20-30 short mss/year.** Query with published clips. Length: 650-2,500 words. **Pays $1/word and up for assigned articles.** Sometimes pays expenses of writers on assignment.

Photos State availability with submission. Reviews transparencies. Buys one-time rights. Negotiates payment individually.

Columns/Departments What I Wish Every Parent Knew (personal essay); How They Do It (highlighting the experience of real parents in unique situations, explaining how they keep their lives in balance). **Buys 10 mss/year.** Query with published clips. **Pays $1/word and up.**

   ▣ **The online magazine carries original content not found in the print edition. Contact: Kathleen Tripp, online editor.**

Tips "Stories should include opinions from experts as well as anecdotes from parents to illustrate the points being made. Lifestyle is key. Send a well-written query that meets our editorial needs. *Child* receives too many inappropriate submissions. Please consider your work carefully before submitting."

Ⓝ $ $ CHRISTIAN PARENTING TODAY

Christianity Today International, 465 Gundersen Dr., Carol Stream IL 60188-2489. (630)260-6200. Fax: (630)260-0114. E-mail: cpt@christianparenting.net. Website: www.christianparenting.net. Managing Editor: Caryn Riva-doneira. Assistant Editor: Dawn Zemker. **Contact:** Raelynn Eickhoff, editorial coordintor. **90% freelance written.** Quarterly magazine. "Strives to be a positive, practical magazine that targets real needs of today's family with authoritative articles based on real experience, fresh research, and the timeless truths of the Bible. *CPT* provides parents information that spans birth to 14 years of age in the following areas of growth: spiritual, social, emotional, physical, academic." Estab. 1988. Circ. 90,000. **Pays on acceptance.** Byline given. Buys first North American serial, second serial (reprint) rights. Submit seasonal material 8 months in advance. Accepts previously published material. Responds in 2 months to mss. Sample copy for 9×12 SAE with $3 postage. Writer's guidelines for #10 SASE.

Nonfiction Feature topics of greatest interest: practical guidance in spiritual/moral development and values transfer; practical solutions to everyday parenting issues; tips on how to enrich readers' marriages; ideas for nurturing healthy family ties; family activities that focus on parent/child interaction; humorous pieces about everyday family life. Book excerpts, how-to, humor, inspirational, religious. **Buys 50 mss/year.** Length: 750-2,000 words. **Pays 12-20¢/word.**

Reprints Send tearsheet, photocopy or typed ms with rights for sale noted and information about when and where the material previously appeared.

Photos Do not submit photos without permission. State availability with submission. Reviews transparencies. Buys one-time rights. Model releases required.

Tips "Tell it like it is. Readers have a 'get real' attitude that demands a down-to-earth, pragmatic take on topics. Don't sugar-coat things. Give direction without waffling. If you've 'been there,' tell us. The first-person, used appropriately, is OK. Don't distance yourself from readers. They trust people who have walked in their shoes. Get reader friendly. Fill your article with nuts and bolts: developmental information, age-specific angles, multiple resources, sound-bite sidebars, real-life people and anecdotes and realistic, vividly explained suggestions."

$CONNECTICUT'S COUNTY KIDS

Journal Register Co., 877 Post Rd. E., Westport CT 06880-5224. (203)226-8877, ext. 125. Fax: (203)221-7540. E-mail: countykids@ctcentral.com. Website: www.countykids.com. **Contact:** Linda Greco, editor. **80-90% freelance written.** Monthly tabloid covering parenting. "We publish positive articles (nonfiction) that help parents of today raise children." Estab. 1987. Circ. 35,000. Pays on publication. Publishes ms an average of 2 months after acceptance. Byline given. Buys first North American serial, first, one-time, second serial (reprint) rights. Editorial lead time 6 weeks. Submit seasonal material 2-3 months in advance. Accepts queries by e-mail. Accepts previously published material. Sample copy not available. Writer's guidelines by e-mail.

Nonfiction Essays, general interest, humor, inspirational, new product, opinion, personal experience. Special issues: Birthday; Maternity; Birthing Services. No fiction. **Buys 24-35 mss/year.** Send complete ms. Length: 600-1,500 words. **Pays $40-100 for assigned articles; $25-40 for unsolicited articles.**

Columns/Departments Mom's View (humorous experiences), 800-1,000 words; Pediatric Health (medical situations), 800 words; Active Family (events shared as a family), 800 words. **Buys 15-20 mss/year.** Send complete ms. **Pays $25-40.**

Tips "We like to use Connecticut writers when we can, but we do use writers from all over the US. We like all kinds of writing styles."

N ∅ EPREGNANCY

Majestic Publishing, 5742 W. Harold Getty Dr., Suite 113, Salt Lake City UT 84116. (888)894-4232. Fax: (801)517-7002. E-mail: editorial@mjstc.com. Website: www.epregnancy.com. Managing Editor: Misty Bott. Monthly magazine. "*EPregnancy* offers information, support, and research to couples planning pregnancy, those currently expecting, and new parents." Circ. 435,000.

● Does not buy freelance material or use freelance writers.

$ $ EXPECTING

Family Communications, 65 The East Mall, Toronto ON M8Z 5W3 Canada. (416)537-2604. Fax: (416)538-1794. **Contact:** Tracy Cooper, editor. **100% freelance written.** Semiannual digest-sized magazine. Writers must be Canadian health professionals. Articles address all topics relevant to expectant parents. Estab. 1995. Circ. 100,000. **Pays on acceptance.** Publishes ms an average of 6 months after acceptance. Byline given. Buys all rights. Editorial lead time 6 months. Accepts queries by mail, fax. Responds in 2 months to queries.

Nonfiction Medical. **Buys 6 mss/year.** Query with published clips. Length: 1,000-2,000 words. **Pays $300 (more for some articles).** Sometimes pays expenses of writers on assignment.

Photos State availability with submission. Buys all rights. Negotiates payment individually. Identification of subjects required.

$ $ FAMILY DIGEST

The Black Mom's Best Friend!, Family Digest Association, P.O. Box 342373, Austin TX 78734. Fax: (512)795-2078. E-mail: editor@familydigest.com. **Contact:** John Starch, associate editor. **90% freelance written.** Quarterly magazine. "Our mission: Help black moms/female heads-of-household get more out of their roles as wife, mother, homemaker. Editorial coverage includes parenting, health, love and marriage, travel, family finances, and beauty and style. All designed to appeal to black moms." Estab. 1997. Circ. 400,000. Pays on publication. Publishes ms an average of 6 months after acceptance. Buys first North American serial, all rights. Editorial lead time 2 months. Submit seasonal material 3 months in advance. Accepts queries by e-mail. Accepts previously published material. Accepts simultaneous submissions. Responds in 1 month to queries. Writer's guidelines by e-mail.

Nonfiction "We are not political. We do not want articles that blame others. We do want articles that improve the lives of our readers." Book excerpts, general interest (dealing with relationships), historical/nostalgic, how-to, humor, inspirational, interview/profile, personal experience. Query with published clips. Length: up to 3,000 words. **Pays $100-500.** Sometimes pays expenses of writers on assignment.

Photos Reviews negatives, transparencies, prints. Offers no additional payment for photos accepted with ms. Captions, identification of subjects, model releases required.

Columns/Departments Food; Travel; Family; Parenting; Love and Marriage; Health; Family Finances; Beauty and Style. **Buys 100 mss/year.** Query with published clips. **Pays $100-500.**

Fiction Erotica, ethnic, historical, humorous, novel excerpts, romance. Query with published clips.

Fillers Anecdotes, facts, gags to be illustrated by cartoonist, short humor. **Buys 100 mss/year.** Length: 50-250 words.

$THE FAMILY DIGEST

P.O. Box 40137, Fort Wayne IN 46804. **Contact:** Corine B. Erlandson, manuscript editor. **95% freelance written.** Bimonthly magazine. *"The Family Digest* is dedicated to the joy and fulfillment of the Catholic family and its relationship to the Catholic parish." Estab. 1945. Circ. 150,000. Pays within 1-2 months of acceptance. Byline given. Buys first North American serial rights. Submit seasonal material 7 months in advance. Accepts previously published material. Responds in 1-2 months to queries. Sample copy and writer's guidelines for 6×9 SAE with 2 first-class stamps.

Nonfiction Family life, parish life, prayer life, Catholic traditions. How-to, inspirational, religious. **Buys 60 unsolicited mss/year.** Send complete ms. Length: 750-1,200 words. **Pays $40-60 for accepted articles.**

Reprints Send ms with rights for sale noted and information about when and where the material previously appeared.

Fillers Anecdotes, tasteful humor based on personal experience. **Buys 18/year.** Length: 25-100 words. **Pays $25.**

Tips "Prospective freelance contributors should be familiar with the publication and the types of articles we accept and publish. We are especially looking for upbeat articles which affirm the simple ways in which the Catholic faith is expressed in daily life. Articles on family and parish life, including seasonal articles, how-to pieces, inspirational, prayer, spiritual life, and Church traditions, will be gladly reviewed for possible acceptance and publication."

$ $ $ $FAMILYFUN

Disney Publishing, Inc., 244 Main St., Northampton MA 01060-3107. (413)585-0444. Fax: (413)586-5724. Website: www.familyfun.com. **Contact:** Features Editor. Magazine covering activities for families with kids ages 3-12. *"FamilyFun* is about all the great things families can do together. Our writers are either parents or authorities in a covered field." Estab. 1991. Circ. 1,850,000. **Pays on acceptance.** Byline sometimes given. Offers 25% kill fee. Makes work-for-hire assignments. Editorial lead time 6 months. Submit seasonal material 6 months in advance. Accepts simultaneous submissions. Responds in 3 months to queries. Sample copy for $5. Writer's guidelines online.

Nonfiction Book excerpts, essays, general interest, how-to (crafts, cooking, educational activities), humor, interview/profile, personal experience, photo feature, travel. **Buys dozens of mss/year.** Query with published clips. Length: 850-3,000 words. **Pays $1.25/word.** Pays expenses of writers on assignment.

Photos State availability with submission. Reviews contact sheets, negatives, transparencies. Buys all rights. Offers $75-500/photo. Identification of subjects, model releases required.

Columns/Departments Family Almanac, Nicole Blasenak, associate editor (simple, quick, practical, inexpensive ideas and projects—outings, crafts, games, nature activities, learning projects, and cooking with children), 200-400 words; query or send ms; **pays per word or $200 for ideas.** Family Traveler, Adrienne Stolarz, assistant editor (brief, newsy items about family travel, what's new, what's great, and especially, what's a good deal), 100-125 words; send ms; **pays per word or $50 for ideas.** Family Ties, Kathy Whittemore, senior editor (first-person column that spotlights some aspect of family life that is humorous, inspirational, or interesting), 1,300 words; send ms; **pays $1,625.** My Great Idea, Mary Giles, senior editor (explains fun and inventive ideas that have worked for writer's own family), 1,000 words; query or send ms; **pays $1,250 on acceptance.** Also publishes best letters from writers and readers following column, send to My Great Idea: From Our Readers Editor, 100-150 words, **pays $75 on publication. Buys 60-80 letters/year; 10-12 mss/year.**

Tips "Many of our writers break into *FF* by writing for Family Almanac or Family Traveler (front-of-the-book departments)."

$GRAND RAPIDS FAMILY

Gemini Publications, 549 Ottawa Ave., NW, Suite 201, Grand Rapids MI 49503. (616)459-4545. Fax: (616)459-4800. E-mail: cvalde@geminipub.com. Website: www.grfamily.com. **Contact:** Carole Valade, editor. Monthly magazine covering local parenting issues. *"Grand Rapids Family* seeks to inform, instruct, amuse, and entertain its readers and their families." Circ. 30,000. Pays on publication. Byline given. Offers $25 kill fee. Buys first North American serial, simultaneous, all rights, makes work-for-hire assignments. Editorial lead time 3 months.

Submit seasonal material 4 months in advance. Accepts simultaneous submissions. Responds in 2 months to queries; 6 months to mss. Writer's guidelines for #10 SASE.

Nonfiction "The publication recognizes that parenting is a process that begins before conception/adoption and continues for a lifetime. The issues are diverse and ever changing. *Grand Rapids Family* seeks to identify these issues and give them a local perspective, using local sources and resources." Query. **Pays $25-50.**

Photos State availability with submission. Reviews contact sheets. Buys one-time or all rights. Offers $25/ photo. Captions, identification of subjects, model releases required.

Columns/Departments Pays $25.

HEALTHY BEGINNINGS, HEALTHY GROWING, HEALTHY CHOICES

Bridge Communications, Inc., 1450 Pilgrim Rd., Birmingham MI 48009-1006. (248)646-1020. E-mail: bridgecom m@aol.com. Website: www.bridge-comm.com. Editor: Alice R. McCarthy, PhD. Semiannual (March and October publication dates) 4-page, 4-color newsletters written for parents of children in grades preK-3, 4-5, and 6-8. Mental and physical health topics, plus strong support for school health programs including student health education. No advertising except books related to children's health. Circ. 100,000 yearly. Editorial lead time 4 months. Sample copies available.

 • Rarely use unsolicited mss.

$HOME EDUCATION MAGAZINE

P.O. Box 1083, Tonasket WA 98855. (509)486-1351. E-mail: editor@homeedmag.com. Website: www.homeed mag.com. **Contact:** Carol Narigon, articles editor. **80% freelance written.** Bimonthly magazine covering home-based education. We feature articles which address the concerns of parents who want to take a direct involvement in the education of their children—concerns such as socialization, how to find curriculums and materials, testing and evaluation, how to tell when your child is ready to begin reading, what to do when homeschooling is difficult, teaching advanced subjects, etc. Estab. 1983. Circ. 32,000. **Pays on acceptance.** Publishes ms an average of 4 months after acceptance. Byline given. Buys first North American serial, first, one-time, electronic rights. Submit seasonal material 6 months in advance. Accepts queries by mail, e-mail. Responds in 2 months to queries. Sample copy for $6.50. Writer's guidelines for #10 SASE or via e-mail.

 ○┓ Break in by "reading our magazine, understanding how we communicate with our readers, having an understanding of homeschooling, and being able to communicate that understanding clearly."

Nonfiction Essays, how-to (related to homeschooling), humor, interview/profile, personal experience, photo feature, technical. **Buys 40-50 mss/year.** Query with or without published clips or send complete ms. Length: 750-2,500 words. **Pays $50-100.** Sometimes pays expenses of writers on assignment.

Photos Send photos with submission. Reviews enlargements, 35mm prints, b&w, CD-ROMs. Buys one-time rights. Pays $100/cover; $12/inside b&w photos. Identification of subjects required.

Tips "We would like to see how-to articles (that don't preach, just present options); articles on testing, account-ability, working with the public schools, socialization, learning disabilities, resources, support groups, legislation, and humor. We need answers to the questions that homeschoolers ask. Please, no teachers telling parents how to teach. Personal experience with homeschooling is the preferred approach."

$HOMESCHOOLING TODAY

P.O. Box 468, Barker TX 77413. Fax: (832)201-7620. E-mail: publisher@homeschooltoday.com. Website: www. homeschooltoday.com. **Contact:** Stacy McDonald, editor. **75% freelance written.** Bimonthly magazine covering homeschooling. "We are a practical magazine for homeschoolers with a broadly Christian perspective." Estab. 1992. Circ. 25,000. Pays on publication. Publishes ms an average of 1 year after acceptance. Byline given. Offers 25% kill fee. Buys first rights. Editorial lead time 6 months. Submit seasonal material 1 year in advance. Accepts queries by mail, e-mail, fax. Accepts simultaneous submissions. Responds in 1 month to queries; 2 months to mss. Sample copy and writer's guidelines free.

Nonfiction Book excerpts, how-to, inspirational, interview/profile, new product. No fiction or poetry. **Buys 30 mss/year.** Query. Length: 500-2,500 words. **Pays 8¢/word.**

Photos State availability with submission. Buys one-time rights. Offers no additional payment for photos accepted with ms. Captions, identification of subjects required.

INSTRUCTOR MAGAZINE

For Teachers of Grades K-8, Scholastic, Inc., 557 Broadway, New York NY 10012. (212)343-6100. Fax: (212)343-4799. E-mail: instructor@scholastic.com. Website: www.scholastic.com/instructor. Editor: Bernadette Grey. Managing Editor: Jennifer Prescott. Published 8 times/year. Geared toward teachers, curriculum coordinators, principals, and supervisors of kindergarten through 8th grade classes. Circ. 200,391. Editorial lead time 4 months. Submit seasonal material 6 months in advance. Accepts queries by mail. Responds in 6 months. Sample copy available by calling (866)436-2455. Writer's guidelines online.

Nonfiction Classroom management and practice; education trends and issues; professional development; lesson plans. Query with or without published clips or send complete ms. Length: 800-1,200 words.

Columns/Departments Activities and Tips (for teachers), 250 words; Lesson Units (lesson-planning units on a specific curriculum area or theme), 400-800 words; Cyber Hunt Activities (tech-based activities in the classroom), 250 words; End of the Day (personal essays about a teacher's experience with kids), 400-500 words. Query with or without published clips or send complete ms.

Tips "As you write, think: How can I make this article most useful for teachers? Write in your natural voice. We shy away from wordy, academic prose. Let us know what grade/subject you teach and name and location of your school."

N $LIVING

Encouragement for the Whole Family, Shalom Foundation, 1251 Virginia Ave., Harrisonburg VA 22802. E-mail: tgether@aol.com. Website: www.churchoutreach.com. Managing Editor: Dorothy Hartman. **Contact:** Melodie Davis, editor. **90% freelance written.** Quarterly tabloid covering family living. Articles focus on giving general encouragement for families of all ages and stages. Estab. 1985. Circ. 250,000. Pays on publication. Publishes ms an average of 6-12 months after acceptance. Byline given. Buys one-time, electronic rights. Editorial lead time 4-6 months. Submit seasonal material 6 months in advance. Accepts queries by mail, e-mail. Accepts previously published material. Accepts simultaneous submissions. Responds in 2 months to queries; 2-4 months to mss. Sample copy for 9×12 SAE and 4 first-class stamps. Writer's guidelines free.

  • "Our bias is to use articles 'showing' rather than telling readers how to raise families (stories rather than how-to). We aim for articles that are well written, understandable, challenging (not the same old thing you've read elsewhere); they should stimulate readers to dig a little deeper, but not too deep with academic or technical language; that are interesting and fit our theological perspective (Christian), but are not preachy or overly patriotic. No favorable mentions of smoking, drinking, cursing, etc."

Nonfiction General interest, how-to, humor, inspirational, personal experience. "We do not use devotional materials intended for Christian audiences. We seldom use pet stories and receive way too many grief/death/dealing with serious illness stories to use. We encourage stories from non-white writers (excuse the phrase). We publish in March, June, September, and December so holidays that occur in other months are not usually the subject of articles." **Buys 48-52 mss/year.** Query. Length: 500-1,200 words. **Pays $35-60.**

Photos Dorothy Hartman. State availability with submission. Reviews 4×6 prints, GIF/JPEG files. Buys one-time rights. Offers $15-25/photo. Captions, identification of subjects, model releases required.

Tips "We prefer 'good news' stories that are uplifting and non-controversial in nature. We want articles that tell stories of people solving problems and dealing with personal issues rather than essays or 'preaching.' If you submit electronically, it is very helpful if you put the specific title of the submission in the subject line and please include your e-mail address in the body of the e-mail or on your manuscript. Also, always please include your address and phone number."

N $$LONG ISLAND MOTHERS JOURNAL

Richner Communications, P.O. Box 220, Lawrence NY 11559. E-mail: limjedit@optonline.net. Managing Editor: Andrew Elias. **Contact:** Pat Simms-Elias, editorial director. **90% freelance written.** Bimonthly magazine covering women and children. Estab. 2004. Circ. 35,000. Pays 30 days after publication. Publishes ms an average of 2-6 months after acceptance. Byline given. Offers 50% kill fee. Buys one-time rights. Editorial lead time 1-2 months. Submit seasonal material 2-6 months in advance. Accepts queries by e-mail. Accepts previously published material. Accepts simultaneous submissions. Responds in 1-2 months to queries; 1-3 months to mss. Sample copy for $3. Writer's guidelines by e-mail.

Nonfiction Book excerpts, essays, general interest, how-to, humor, interview/profile, opinion, personal experience, travel. **Buys 25-35 mss/year.** Send complete ms. Length: 500-2,000 words. **Pays $50-200; may barter for advertising space.** Sometimes pays expenses of writers on assignment.

Photos State availability of or send photos with submission. Reviews GIF/JPEG files. Buys one-time rights. Offers $10-100/photo. Captions, identification of subjects, model releases required.

Columns/Departments Arts & Letters; Health & Fitness; House & Garden; Travel + Leisure; Cooking & Dining; Reflections; Education & Learning; Pregnancy & Newborns; Challenged Children; Books & Enlightenment, all 500-1,500 words. **Buys 25-35 mss/year.** Send complete ms. **Pays $50-150.**

Fiction Humorous, slice-of-life vignettes.

$$METRO PARENT MAGAZINE

Metro Parent Publishing Group, 24567 Northwestern Hwy., Suite 150, Southfield MI 48075. (248)352-0990. Fax: (248)352-5066. E-mail: sdemaggio@metroparent.com. Website: www.metroparent.com. **Contact:** Susan DeMaggio, editor. **75% freelance written.** Monthly magazine covering parenting, women's health, education. "We are a local magazine on parenting topics and issues of interest to Detroit-area parents. Related issues: *Ann*

Arbor Parent; African/American Parent; Metro Baby Magazine.'' Circ. 85,000. Pays on publication. Publishes ms an average of 3 months after acceptance. Byline given. Buys first rights. Editorial lead time 3 months. Submit seasonal material 3 months in advance. Accepts queries by mail, e-mail. Accepts previously published material. Accepts simultaneous submissions. Responds in 2 weeks to queries; 3 months to mss. Sample copy for $2.50.
Nonfiction Essays, humor, inspirational, personal experience. **Buys 100 mss/year.** Send complete ms. Length: 1,500-2,500 words. **Pays $50-300 for assigned articles.**
Photos State availability with submission. Buys one-time rights. Offers $100-200/photo or negotiates payment individually. Captions required.
Columns/Departments Women's Health (latest issues of 20-40 year olds), 750-900 words; Solo Parenting (advice for single parents); Family Finance (making sense of money and legal issues); Tweens 'N Teens (handling teen issues), 750-800 words. **Buys 50 mss/year.** Send complete ms. **Pays $75-150.**

$ METROFAMILY MAGAZINE

Inprint Publishing, 1015 Waterford Pkwy., Suite G, Box H-1, Edmond OK 73034. (405)340-1404. E-mail: editor@ metrofamilymagazine.com. Website: www.metrofamilymagazine.com. Publisher: Sarah Taylor. **Contact:** Denise Springer, editor. **60% freelance written.** Monthly tabloid covering parenting. *''MetroFamily Magazine* provides local parenting and family fun information for our Central Oklahoma readers. Send us (by e-mail, please) information parents can use and relate to. Keep it light and bring on the humor.''* Circ. 20,000. Pays on publication. Publishes ms an average of 1-2 months after acceptance. Byline given. Offers 100% kill fee. Buys first North American serial, second serial (reprint), simultaneous, electronic rights. Editorial lead time 2-3 months. Submit seasonal material 3 months in advance. Accepts queries by e-mail. Accepts previously published material. Accepts simultaneous submissions. Responds in 3 weeks to queries; 1 month to mss. Sample copy for 10×13 SAE and 3 first-class stamps. Writer's guidelines for #10 SASE.
Nonfiction How-to (parenting issues, education), humor, inspirational, travel. No poetry, fiction (except for humor column), or anything that doesn't support good, solid family values. Send complete ms. Length: 300-600 words. **Pays $25-50, plus 1 contributor copy.**
Photos State availability with submission. Reviews GIF/JPEG files. Buys one-time rights. Negotiates payment individually. Captions, identification of subjects, model releases required.
Columns/Departments You've Just Gotta Laugh, humor (600 words). **Buys 12 mss/year.** Send complete ms. **Pays $25-35.**
Fillers Facts, short humor. **Buys 12/year.** Length: 300-600 words. **Pays $25-35.**

$ METROKIDS MAGAZINE

The Resource for Delaware Valley Families, Kidstuff Publications, Inc., 4623 S. Broad St., Philadelphia PA 19122. (215)291-5560. Fax: (215)291-5563. Website: www.metrokids.com. **25% freelance written.** Monthly tabloid providing information for parents and kids in Philadelphia, South Jersey, and surrounding counties. Estab. 1990. Circ. 125,000. Pays on publication. Byline given. Buys one-time rights. Submit seasonal material 4 months in advance. Accepts queries by e-mail. Accepts previously published material. Writer's guidelines by e-mail.
  • Responds only if interested.
Nonfiction General interest, how-to, new product, travel, parenting, health. Special issues: Educator's Edition— (March & September) field trips, school enrichment, teacher, professional development; Camps—(December & June); Special Kids—(August) children with special needs; Vacations and Theme Parks—(May & June); What's Happening—(January) guide to events and activities; Kids 'N Care—(July) guide to childcare. **Buys 40 mss/ year.** Query with published clips. Length: 800-1,500 words. **Pays $1-50.** Sometimes pays expenses of writers on assignment.
Reprints Send photocopy and information about when and where the material previously appeared. Pays $20-40.
Photos State availability with submission. Buys one-time rights. Captions required.
Columns/Departments Techno Family (CD-ROM and website reviews); Body Wise (health); Style File (fashion and trends); Woman First (motherhood); Practical Parenting (financial parenting advice); all 800-1,000 words. **Buys 25 mss/year.** Query. **Pays $1-50.**
Tips ''We prefer e-mail queries or submissions. Because they're so numerous, we don't reply unless interested. We are interested in feature articles (on specified topics) or material for our regular departments (with a regional/seasonal base). Articles should cite expert sources and the most up-to-date theories and facts. We are looking for a journalistic style of writing. Editorial calendar available on request. We are also interested in finding local writers for assignments.''

PARENTS

Gruner + Jahr, 375 Lexington Ave., New York NY 10017. (212)499-2000. Fax: (212)499-2083. Website: www.pa rents.com. Monthly magazine. Estab. 1,700,000. Responds in 6 weeks to queries. Writer's guidelines online.

Nonfiction ''Before you query us, please take a close look at our magazine at the library or newsstand. This will give you a good idea of the different kinds of stories we publish, as well as their tempo and tone. In addition, please take the time to look at the masthead to make sure you are directing your query to the correct department.'' Query.

Tips ''We're a national publication, so we're mainly interested in stories that will appeal to a wide variety of parents. We're always looking for compelling human-interest stories, so you may want to check your local newspaper for ideas. Keep in mind that we can't pursue stories that have appeared in competing national publications.''

$PEDIATRICS FOR PARENTS

Pediatrics for Parents, Inc., P.O. Box 63716, Philadelphia PA 19147-3321. Fax: (419)858-7221. E-mail: rich.sagall @pobox.com. **Contact:** Richard J. Sagall, editor. **50% freelance written.** Monthly newsletter covering children's health. ''*Pediatrics For Parents* emphasizes an informed, common-sense approach to childhood health care. We stress preventative action, accident prevention, when to call the doctor and when and how to handle a situation at home. We are also looking for articles that describe general, medical and pediatric problems, advances, new treatments, etc. All articles must be medically accurate and useful to parents with children—prenatal to adolescence.'' Estab. 1981. Circ. 500. Pays on publication. Publishes ms an average of 4 months after acceptance. Byline given. Buys first North American serial, electronic rights. Accepts queries by mail, e-mail, fax. Accepts previously published material. Accepts simultaneous submissions. Responds in 1 month to queries. Sample copy and writer's guidelines online.

Nonfiction Medical. No first person or experience. **Buys 25 mss/year.** Query with or without published clips or send complete ms. Length: 500-1,000 words. **Pays $10-50.**

Reprints Accepts previously published submissions.

$SAN DIEGO FAMILY MAGAZINE

San Diego County's Leading Resource for Parents & Educators Who Care!, P.O. Box 23960, San Diego CA 92193-3960. (619)685-6970. Fax: (619)685-6978. Website: www.sandiegofamily.com. **Contact:** Claire Yezbak Fadden, editor. **75% freelance written.** Monthly magazine for parenting and family issues. ''*SDFM* strives to provide informative, educational articles emphasizing positive parenting for our typical readership of educated mothers, ages 25-45, with an upper-level income. Most articles are factual and practical, a few are humor and personal experience. Editorial emphasis is uplifting and positive.'' Estab. 1982. Circ. 120,000. Pays on publication. Byline given. Buys first, one-time, second serial (reprint) rights. Editorial lead time 2 months. Submit seasonal material 3 months in advance. Accepts previously published material. Responds in 1 month to queries. Sample copy for $4.50 with 9×12 SAE. Writer's guidelines online.

• No e-mail or fax queries accepted.

Nonfiction How-to, interview/profile (influential or noted persons or experts included in parenting or the welfare of children), parenting, new baby help, enhancing education, family activities, articles of specific interest to San Diego. ''No rambling, personal experience pieces.'' **Buys 75 mss/year.** Send complete ms. Length: 800-1,200 words. **Pays $1.25/column inch.**

Reprints Send ms with rights for sale noted and information about when and where the material previously appeared. Will respond only if SASE is included.

Photos State availability with submission. Identification of subjects required.

Fillers Facts, newsbreaks (specific to family market). **Buys 10/year.** Length: 50-200 words. **Pays $1.25/column inch minimum.**

$ $SOUTH FLORIDA PARENTING

6501 Nob Hill Rd., Sunrise FL 33321. (954)747-3050. Fax: (954)747-3055. E-mail: vmccash@sfparenting.com. Website: www.sfparenting.com. **Contact:** Vicki McCash Brennan, managing editor. **90% freelance written.** Monthly magazine covering parenting, family. ''*South Florida Parenting* provides news, information, and a calendar of events for readers in Southeast Florida. The focus is on positive parenting and things to do or information about raising children in South Florida.'' Estab. 1990. Circ. 110,000. Pays on publication. Byline given. Buys one-time, second serial (reprint) rights, makes work-for-hire assignments. Editorial lead time 4 months. Submit seasonal material 5 months in advance. Accepts queries by mail, e-mail, fax. Accepts previously published material. Responds in 3 months to queries; 6 months to mss. Sample copy for 9×12 SAE with $2.95 postage. Writer's guidelines for #10 SASE.

• Preference given to writers based in South Florida.

o— Best bet to break in: ''Be a local South Florida resident (particular need for writers from the Miami-Dade area) and address contemporary parenting topics and concerns.''

Nonfiction How-to (parenting issues), interview/profile, family and children's issues. Special issues: Education/ Women's Health (January); Birthday Party (October); Summer Camp (February); Maternity (April); Florida/

Vacation Guide (April); Back to School (July); Education (September); Holiday (December). **Buys 60+ mss/ year.** Send complete ms. Length: 500-2,000 words. **Pays $40-300.**

Reprints Send photocopy or e-mail on spec. **Pays $25-50.**

Photos State availability with submission. Reviews negatives, transparencies, prints. Buys one-time rights. Sometimes offers additional payment for photos accepted with ms.

Columns/Departments Baby Basics (for parents of infants); Preteen Power (for parents of preteens); Family Money (family finances), all 500-750 words.

Tips "We want information targeted to the South Florida market. Multicultural and well-sourced is preferred. A unique approach to a universal parenting concern will be considered for publication. Profiles or interviews of courageous parents. Opinion pieces on child rearing should be supported by experts and research should be listed. First-person stories should be fresh and insightful. All writing should be clear and concise. Submissions can be typewritten, double-spaced, but the preferred format is by e-mail attachment."

$ $ $ $ TODAY'S PARENT

Today's Parent Group, One Mt. Pleasant Rd., 8th Floor, Toronto ON M4Y 2Y5 Canada. (416)764-2883. Fax: (416)764-2801. Website: www.todaysparent.com. Monthly magazine for parents with children up to the age of 12. Circ. 175,000. Editorial lead time 5 months.

Nonfiction Runs features with a balance between the practical and the philosophical, the light-hearted and the investigative. All articles should be grounded in the reality of Canadian family life. Length: 1,800-2,500 words. **Pays $1,500-2,200.**

Columns/Departments Profile (Canadian who has accomplished something remarkable for the benefit of children), 250 words. **Pays $250.** Your Turn (parents share their experiences), 800 words; **pays $200.** Beyond Motherhood (deals with topics not directly related to parenting), 700 words; **pays $800.** Education (tackles straightforward topics and controversial or complex topics), 1,200 words; **pays $1,200-1,500.** Health Behavior (child development and discipline), 1,200 words; **pays $1,200-1,500.** Slice of Life (explores lighter side of parenting), 750 words; **pays $650.**

Tips "Because we promote ourselves as a Canadian magazine, we use only Canadian writers."

$ $ $ $ TODAY'S PARENT PREGNANCY & BIRTH

One Mt. Pleasant Rd., 8th Floor, Toronto ON M4Y 2Y5 Canada. (416)764-2883. Fax: (416)764-2801. Website: www.todaysparent.com. **Contact:** Editor. **100% freelance written.** Magazine published 3 times/year. "*P&B* helps, supports and encourages expectant and new parents with news and features related to pregnancy, birth, human sexuality and parenting." Estab. 1973. Circ. 200,000. **Pays on acceptance.** Publishes ms an average of 8 months after acceptance. Buys first North American serial rights. Editorial lead time 6 months. Responds in 6 weeks to queries. Sample copy and writer's guidelines for #10 SASE.

Nonfiction Features about pregnancy, labor and delivery, post-partum issues. **Buys 12 mss/year.** Query with published clips. Length: 1,000-2,500 words. **Pays up to $1/word.** Sometimes pays expenses of writers on assignment.

Photos State availability with submission. Rights negotiated individually. Pay negotiated individually.

Tips "Our writers are professional freelance writers with specific knowledge in the childbirth field. *P&B* is written for a Canadian audience using Canadian research and sources."

$ $ TOLEDO AREA PARENT NEWS

Adams Street Publishing, 1120 Adams St., Toledo OH 43624-1509. (419)244-9859. Fax: (419)244-9871. E-mail: editor@toldeoparent.com. Website: www.toledoparent.com. **Contact:** Collette Jacobs, publisher. Monthly tabloid for Northwest Ohio/Southeast Michigan parents. Estab. 1992. Circ. 40,000. Pays on publication. Publishes ms an average of 1 month after acceptance. Byline given. Editorial lead time 3 months. Accepts queries by mail, e-mail, fax. Responds in 1 month to queries. Sample copy for $1.50.

○┰ Break in with "local interest articles—Ohio/Michigan regional topics and examples preferred."

Nonfiction "We use only local writers by assignment. We accept queries and opinion pieces only. Send cover letter to be considered for assignments." General interest, interview/profile, opinion. **Buys 10 mss/year.** Length: 1,000-2,500 words. **Pays $75-125.**

Photos State availability with submission. Buys all rights. Negotiates payment individually. Identification of subjects required.

Tips "We love humorous stories that deal with common parenting issues or features on cutting-edge issues."

TREASURE VALLEY FAMILY MAGAZINE

(formerly *Boise Family Magazine*), Family Magazine & Media, Inc., 13191 W. Scotfield St., Boise ID 83713-0899. (208)938-2119. Fax: (208)938-2117. E-mail: magazine@tresurevalleyfamily.com. Website: www.treasure valleyfamily.com. **Contact:** Liz Buckingham, editor. **90% freelance written.** Monthly magazine covering parenting, education, child development. "Geared to parents with children 12 years and younger. Focus on education, interest, activities for children. Positive parenting and healthy families." Estab. 1993. Circ. 20,000. Pays on publication. Publishes ms an average of 3 months after acceptance. Byline given. Offers 50% kill fee. Buys first North American serial rights. Editorial lead time 3 months. Submit seasonal material 3 months in advance. Accepts queries by mail, e-mail. Accepts simultaneous submissions. Responds in 2 months to queries. Sample copy for $2. Writer's guidelines online.

Nonfiction Special issues: Family Health and Wellness (January); Early Childhood Education (February); Secondary and Higher Education (March); Summer Camps (April); Youth Sports Guide (May); Family Recreation and Fairs & Festivals (June/July); Back-to-School and extra-curricular Activities (August/September); Teens and College Planning (October); Birthday Party Fun (November); Youth in the Arts and Holiday Traditions (December). Query with published clips. Length: 1,000-1,300 words.

Photos State availability with submission. Buys one-time rights. Negotiates payment individually. Captions required.

Columns/Departments Crafts, travel, finance, parenting. Length: 700-1,000 words. Query with published clips.

$ $ TWINS

The Magazine for Parents of Multiples, The Business Word, Inc., 11211 E. Arapahoe Rd., Suite 101, Centennial CO 80112-3851. (303)967-0111. Fax: (303)290-9025. E-mail: sharon.withers@businessword.com. Website: www.twinsmagazine.com. **Contact:** Sharon Withers, managing editor. **80% freelance written.** Bimonthly magazine covering parenting multiples. "*TWINS* is an international publication that provides informational and educational articles regarding the parenting of twins, triplets, and more. All articles must be multiple specific and have an upbeat, hopeful, and/or positive ending." Estab. 1984. Circ. 55,000. Pays on publication. Byline given. Buys first North American serial rights. Editorial lead time 6 months. Submit seasonal material 8 months in advance. Accepts queries by mail, e-mail, fax. Response time varies to queries. Sample copy for $5 or on website. Writer's guidelines online.

Nonfiction Interested in seeing twin-specific discipline articles. Personal experience (first-person parenting experience), professional experience as it relates to multiples. Nothing on cloning, pregnancy reduction, or fertility issues. **Buys 12 mss/year.** Query with or without published clips or send complete ms. Length: 650-1,300 words. **Pays $25-250 for assigned articles; $25-100 for unsolicited articles.**

Photos State availability with submission. Offers no additional payment for photos accepted with ms. Identification of subjects required.

Columns/Departments Special Miracles (miraculous stories about multiples with a happy ending), 800-850 words. **Buys 12-20 mss/year.** Query with or without published clips or send complete ms. **Pays $40-75.**

Tips "All department articles must have a happy ending, as well as teach a lesson helpful to parents of multiples."

$ WESTERN NEW YORK FAMILY

Western New York Family, Inc., 3147 Delaware Ave., Suite B, Buffalo NY 14217. (716)836-3486. Fax: (716)836-3680. E-mail: feedback@wnyfamilymagazine.com. Website: www.wnyfamilymagazine.com. **Contact:** Michele Miller, editor/publisher. **90% freelance written.** Monthly magazine covering parenting in Western New York State. "Readership is largely composed of families with children ages newborn to 14 years. Although most subscriptions are in the name of the mother, 91% of fathers also read the publication. Strong emphasis is placed on how and where to find family-oriented events, as well as goods and services for children, in the Buffalo/Niagara Falls area." Estab. 1984. Circ. 22,500. Pays on publication. Publishes ms an average of 3 months after acceptance. Byline given. Buys one-time, second serial (reprint), simultaneous rights. Editorial lead time 2 months. Submit seasonal material 3 months in advance. Accepts previously published material. Accepts simultaneous submissions. Responds only if interested to queries. Sample copy for $2.50 and 9×12 SAE with $1.06 postage. Writer's guidelines online.

    ○▸ Break in with either a "cutting edge" topic that is new and different in its relevance to current parenting challenges and trends or a "timeless" topic which is "evergreen" and can be kept on file to fill last minute holes.

Nonfiction How-to (craft projects for kids, holiday, costume, etc.), humor (as related to parenting), personal experience (parenting related), travel (family destinations). Special issues: Birthday Celebrations (January); Cabin Fever (February); Seeking Spring/Eldercare Guide (March); Having a Baby/Home Buying, Building & Beautifying; (April); Mother's Day (May); Father's Day (June); Summer Fun (July and August); Back to School (September); Halloween Happenings (October); Family Issues (November); and Holiday Happenings/Exploring Education (December). **Buys 125 mss/year.** Send complete ms by mail or e-mail. Unsolicited e-mail attachments are not accepted; paste text of article into body of e-mail. Length: 750-3,000 words. **Pays $50-150 for assigned articles; $35-50 for unsolicited articles.** Sometimes pays expenses of writers on assignment.

Reprints Accepts previously published submissions.

Photos State availability with submission. Reviews 3×5 prints, JPEG files via e-mail. Buys one-time rights. Offers no additional payment for photos accepted with ms. Captions, identification of subjects, model releases required.

Tips "We are interested in well-researched, nonfiction articles on surviving the newborn, preschool, school age, and adolescent years. Our readers want practical information on places to go and things to do in the Buffalo area and nearby Canada. They enjoy humorous articles about the trials and tribulations of parenthood as well as 'how-to' articles (i.e., choosing a musical instrument for your child, keeping your sanity while shopping with preschoolers, ideas for holidays and birthdays, etc.). Articles on making a working parent's life easier are of great interest as are articles written by fathers. We also need more material on preteen and young teen (13-15) issues. More material on multicultural families and their related experiences, traditions, etc., would be of interest in 2005. Our annual 'Eldercare Guide: Caring for Our Aging Parents' has become very popular, and more material is needed on that subject."

$ ⊡ WHAT'S UP KIDS? FAMILY MAGAZINE

496 Metler Rd., Ridgeville ON L0S 1M0 Canada. E-mail: susan@whatsupkids.com. Website: www.whatsupkids.com. **Contact:** Susan Pennell-Sebekos, editor-in-chief. **95% freelance written.** Bimonthly magazine covering topics of interest to young families. "Editorial is aimed at parents of kids birth-age 14. Kids Fun Section offers a section just for kids. We're committed to providing top-notch content." Estab. 1995. Circ. 200,000. Pays 30 days after publication. Publishes ms an average of 4 months after acceptance. Byline given. Buys all rights. Editorial lead time 6 months. Submit seasonal material 6 months in advance. Accepts queries by mail, e-mail. Responds in 2 weeks if interested to queries. Writer's guidelines online.

Nonfiction Service articles for families. No religious (one sided) or personal experience. **Buys 50 mss/year.** Query with published clips. Length: 500-900 words. **Pays variable amount for assigned articles.** Sometimes pays expenses of writers on assignment.

Columns/Departments Understanding Families; Learning Curves; Family Finances, all 400-600 words. **Buys variable number of mss/year.** Query with published clips. **Pays $150.**

Tips "We only accept submissions from Canadian writers. Writers should send résumé, clips, and query. Please do not call, and include e-mail address on all queries."

WORKING MOTHER MAGAZINE

60 E. 42nd St., Suite 2700, New York NY 10165. Website: www.workingmother.com. Editor-in-Chief: Susan Lapinski. **Contact:** Editorial Department. **90% freelance written.** Prefers to work with published/established writers; works with a small number of new/unpublished writers each year. Monthly magazine for women who balance a career, home, and family. Circ. 925,000. Publishes ms an average of 4 months after acceptance. Byline given. Offers kill fee. Buys all rights. Submit seasonal material 6 months in advance. Accepts queries by mail. Sample copy for $5; available by calling (800)925-0788. Writer's guidelines online.

Nonfiction Service, humor, child development, material pertinent to the working mother's predicament. Humor, service, child development, material perinent to the working mother's predicament. **Buys 9-10 mss/year.** Query with published clips. Length: 700-1,500 words.

Tips "We are looking for pieces that help the reader. In other words, we don't simply report on a trend without discussing how it specifically affects our readers' lives and how they can handle the effects. Where can they look for help if necessary?"

COMIC BOOKS

$ THE COMICS JOURNAL

Fantagraphics Books, 7563 Lake City Way NE, Seattle WA 98115. (206)524-1967. Fax: (206)524-2104. E-mail: dirk@tcj.com. Website: www.tcj.com. Editor: Gary Groth. **Contact:** Dirk Deppey. Monthly magazine covering the comics medium from an arts-first perspective. *The Comics Journal* is one of the nation's most respected single-arts magazines, providing its readers with an eclectic mix of industry news, professional interviews, and reviews of current work. Due to its reputation as the American magazine with an interest in comics as an art form, the *Journal* has subscribers worldwide, and in this country serves as an important window into the world of comics for several general arts and news magazines. Byline given. Buys exclusive rights to articles that run in print or online versions for 6 months after initial publication. Rights then revert back to the writer. Accepts queries by mail, e-mail. Writer's guidelines online.

Nonfiction "We're not the magazine for the discussion of comic 'universes,' character re-boots, and Spider-Man's new costume—beyond, perhaps, the business or cultural implications of such events." Essays, general interest, how-to, humor, interview/profile, opinion. Send complete ms. Length: 2,000-3,000 words. **Pays 4¢/word, and 1 contributor's copy.**

Columns/Departments On Theory, Art and Craft (2,000-3,000 words); Firing Line (600-1,000 words); Bullets (100 words); Comics Library (up to 5,000 words). Send complete ms. **Pays 4¢/word, and 1 contributor's copy.**

Tips "Like most magazines, the best writers guideline is to look at the material within the magazine and give something that approximates that material in terms of approach and sophistication. Anything else is a waste of time."

CONSUMER SERVICE & BUSINESS OPPORTUNITY

CONSUMER REPORTS

Consumers Union of U.S., Inc., 101 Truman Ave., Yonkers NY 10703-1057. (914)378-2000. Fax: (914)378-2904. Website: www.consumerreports.org. Managing Editor: Kimberly Kleman. **Contact:** Margot Slade, editor. **5% freelance written.** Monthly magazine. "*Consumer Reports* is the leading product-testing and consumer-service magazine in the US. We buy very little freelance material, mostly from proven writers we have used before for finance and health stories." Estab. 1936. Circ. 14,000,000. **Pays on acceptance.** Publishes ms an average of 2 months after acceptance. Offers negotiable kill fee. Buys all rights. Editorial lead time 4 months. Submit seasonal material 6 months in advance. Accepts queries by mail.

Nonfiction Technical, personal finance, personal health. **Buys 12 mss/year.** Query. Length: 1,000 words. **Pays variable rate.**

$ $ HOME BUSINESS MAGAZINE

United Marketing & Research Co., Inc., 9582 Hamilton Ave., PMB 368, Huntington Beach CA 92646. Fax: (714)962-7722. Website: www.homebusinessmag.com. **Contact:** Stacy Henderson, online editor. **75% freelance written.** "*Home Business Magazine* covers every angle of the home-based business market including: cutting edge editorial by well-known authorities on sales and marketing, business operations, the home office, franchising, business opportunities, network marketing, mail order and other subjects to help readers choose, manage and prosper in a home-based business; display advertising, classified ads and a directory of home-based businesses; technology, the Internet, computers and the future of home-based business; home-office editorial including management advice, office set-up, and product descriptions; business opportunities, franchising and work-from-home success stories." Estab. 1993. Circ. 100,000. Pays on publication. Publishes ms an average of 6 months after acceptance. Byline given. Makes work-for-hire assignments. Editorial lead time 4 months. Submit seasonal material 6 months in advance. Accepts queries by mail, e-mail, fax. Accepts previously published material. Accepts simultaneous submissions. Sample copy for 9 × 12 SAE and 8 first-class stamps. Writer's guidelines for #10 SASE.

Nonfiction Book excerpts, general interest, how-to (home business), inspirational, interview/profile, new product, personal experience, photo feature, technical, mail order, franchise, business management, internet, finance network marketing. No non-home business related topics. **Buys 40 mss/year.** Send complete ms. Length: 200-1,000 words. **Pays 20¢/word for assigned articles; 50-word byline for unsolicited articles.**

Photos Send photos with submission. Buys one-time rights. Offers no additional payment for photos accepted with ms. Identification of subjects required.

Columns/Departments Marketing & Sales; Money Corner; Home Office; Management; Technology; Working Smarter; Franchising; Network Marketing, all 650 words. Send complete ms.

▣ The online magazine carries original content not found in the print edition. Contact: Herb Wetenkamp, online editor.

Tips "Send complete information by mail as per our writer's guidelines and e-mail if possible. We encourage writers to submit Feature Articles (2-3 pages) and Departmental Articles (1 page). Please submit polished, well-written, organized material. It helps to provide subheadings within the article. Boxes, lists, and bullets are encouraged because they make your article easier to read, use, and reference by the reader. A primary problem in the past is that articles do not stick to the subject of the title. Please pay attention to the focus of your article and to your title. Please don't call to get the status of your submission. We will call if we're interested in publishing the submission."

KIPLINGER'S PERSONAL FINANCE

1729 H St. NW, Washington DC 20006. (202)887-6400. Fax: (202)331-1206. Website: www.kiplinger.com. Editor: Fred W. Frailey. **Contact:** Dayl Sanders, office manager. **10% freelance written.** Prefers to work with published/established writers. Monthly magazine for general, adult audience intersted in personal finance and consumer information. "*Kiplinger's* is a highly trustworthy source of information on saving and investing, taxes, credit, home ownership, paying for college, retirement planning, automobile buying, and many other personal finance topics." Estab. 1947. Circ. 1,300,000. **Pays on acceptance.** Publishes ms an average of 2 months after acceptance. Buys all rights. Responds in 1 month to queries.

Nonfiction "Most material is staff-written, but we accept some freelance. Thorough documentation is required for fact-checking." Query with published clips. Pays expenses of writers on assignment.

Tips "We are looking for a heavy emphasis on personal finance topics. Currently all work is provided by in-house writers."

CONTEMPORARY CULTURE

$ $ $ $ A&U

America's AIDS Magazine, Art & Understanding, Inc., 25 Monroe St., Suite 205, Albany NY 12210-2729. (888)245-4333. Fax: (888)790-1790. E-mail: editor@aumag.org. Website: www.aumag.org. **Contact:** David Waggoner, editor-in-chief. **50% freelance written.** Monthly magazine covering cultural, political, and medical responses to AIDS/HIV. Estab. 1991. Circ. 205,000. Pays 2 months after publication. Publishes ms an average of 3 months after acceptance. Byline given. Offers 20% kill fee. Buys first North American serial rights. Editorial lead time 6 months. Accepts queries by mail, fax, phone. Accepts simultaneous submissions. Responds in 1 month to queries; 2 months to mss. Sample copy for $5. Writer's guidelines online.

Nonfiction Book excerpts, essays, general interest, how-to, humor, interview/profile, new product, opinion, personal experience, photo feature, travel, reviews (film, theater, art exhibits, video, music, other media), medical news. **Buys 120 mss/year.** Query with published clips. Length: 800-4,800 words. **Pays $250-2,500 for assigned articles.** Sometimes pays expenses of writers on assignment.

Photos State availability with submission. Reviews contact sheets, up to 4×5 transparencies, 5×7 to 8×10 prints. Buys one-time rights. Offers $50-500/photo. Captions, identification of subjects, model releases required.

Columns/Departments The Culture of AIDS (reviews of books, music, film), 800 words; Viewpoint (personal opinion), 900-1,500 words. **Buys 100 mss/year.** Send complete ms. **Pays $100-250.**

Fiction Unpublished work only; accepts prose, poetry, and drama. Send complete ms. Length: less than 3,500 words. **Pays $50-200.**

Poetry Any length/style (shorter works preferred). **Pays $50.**

Tips "We're looking for more articles on youth and HIV/AIDS; more international coverage; more small-town America coverage."

$ $ $ ☒ ADBUSTERS

Journal of the Mental Environment, The Media Foundation, 1243 W. 7th Ave., Vancouver BC V6H 1B7 Canada. (604)736-9401. Fax: (604)737-6021. Website: www.adbusters.org. Managing Editor: Tim Querengesser. **Contact:** Kalle Lasn, editor. **50% freelance written.** Bimonthly magazine. "We are an activist journal of the mental environment." Estab. 1989. Circ. 90,000. Pays 1 month after publication. Byline given. Buys first rights. Accepts queries by mail, e-mail, fax. Accepts simultaneous submissions. Writer's guidelines online.

Nonfiction Essays, exposé, interview/profile, opinion. **Buys variable mss/year.** Query. Length: 250-3,000 words. **Pays $100/page for unsolicited articles; 50¢/word for solicited articles.**

Fiction Inquire about themes.

Poetry Inquire about themes.

$ $ THE AMERICAN SCHOLAR

Phi Beta Kappa, 1606 New Hampshire Ave. NW, Washington DC 20009. (202)265-3808. Fax: (202)265-0083. E-mail: scholar@pbk.org. Editor: Robert Wilson. **Contact:** Jean Stipicevic, managing editor. **100% freelance written.** Quarterly journal. "Our intent is to have articles written by scholars and experts but written in nontechnical language for an intelligent audience. Material covers a wide range in the arts, sciences, current affairs, history, and literature." Estab. 1932. Circ. 25,000. Pays on publication. Publishes ms an average of 1 year after acceptance. Byline given. Offers 50% kill fee. Buys first rights. Editorial lead time 6 months. Submit seasonal material 6 months in advance. Accepts queries by mail, e-mail, fax. Responds in 2 weeks to queries; 2 months to mss. Sample copy for $9. Writer's guidelines for #10 SASE.

Nonfiction Essays, historical/nostalgic, humor. **Buys 40 mss/year.** Query. Length: 3,000-5,000 words. **Pays $500 maximum.**

Poetry "We have no special requirements of length, form, or content for original poetry." Sandra Costich, poetry editor. **Buys 25 poems/year.** Submit maximum 3-4 poems. **Pays $50.**

$ BOSTON REVIEW

E53-407, M.I.T., Cambridge MA 02139. (617)258-0805. Fax: (617)252-1549. E-mail: review@mit.edu. Website: www.bostonreview.net. Editors: Deb Chasman and Josh Cohen. **Contact:** Joshua J. Friedman, managing editor. **90% freelance written.** Bimonthly magazine of cultural and political analysis, reviews, fiction, and poetry. "The editors are committed to a society and culture that foster human diversity and a democracy in which we seek common grounds of principle amidst our many differences. In the hope of advancing these ideals, the *Review* acts as a forum that seeks to enrich the language of public debate.'' Estab. 1975. Circ. 20,000. Publishes ms an average of 4 months after acceptance. Byline given. Buys first North American serial, first rights. Accepts simultaneous submissions. Responds in 4 months to queries. Sample copy for $5 or online. Writer's guidelines online.

Nonfiction Critical essays and reviews. ''We do not accept unsolicited book reviews. If you would like to be considered for review assignments, please send your résumé along with several published clips.'' **Buys 50 mss/ year.** Query with published clips.

Fiction Junot Diaz, fiction editor. ''I'm looking for stories that are emotionally and intellectually substantive and also interesting on the level of language. Things that are shocking, dark, lewd, comic, or even insane are fine so long as the fiction is *controlled* and purposeful in a masterly way. Subtlety, delicacy, and lyricism are attractive too.'' Ethnic, experimental, contemporary, prose poem. ''No romance, erotica, genre fiction.'' **Buys 5 mss/year.** Send complete ms. Length: 1,200-5,000 words. **Pays $50-100, and 5 contributor's copies.**

Poetry Reads poetry between September 15 and May 15 each year. Mary Jo Bang and Timothy Donnelly, poetry editors.

$ $BRUTARIAN

The Magazine of Brutiful Art, 9405 Ulysses Ct., Burke VA 22015. E-mail: brutarian@msn.com. **Contact:** Dominick J. Salemi, publisher/editor. **100% freelance written.** Quarterly magazine covering trash, carnival culture, the ridiculous and the sublime. ''A healthy knowledge of the great works of antiquity and an equally healthy contempt for most of what passes today as culture.'' Estab. 1991. Circ. 5,000. Pays on publication. Publishes ms an average of 3 months after acceptance. Byline given. Buys first, electronic rights. Editorial lead time 2 months. Submit seasonal material 3 months in advance. Accepts queries by mail. Accepts simultaneous submissions. Responds in 1 week to queries; 2 months to mss. Sample copy for $6. Writer's guidelines online.

  O→ Break in with an interview with an interesting musical group, film actor/actress or director, or unusual writer.

Nonfiction Book excerpts, essays, exposé, general interest, historical/nostalgic, humor, interview/profile, opinion, photo feature, travel, reviews of books, film, and music. **Buys 30 mss/year.** Send complete ms. Length: No length limits. **Pays up to 10¢/word.** Sometimes pays expenses of writers on assignment.

Reprints Send ms with rights for sale noted and information about when and where the material previously appeared. Pays 50% of amount paid for an original article.

Photos State availability with submission. Reviews contact sheets. Buys one-time rights. Offers no additional payment for photos accepted with ms. Captions, identification of subjects, model releases required.

Columns/Departments Celluloid Void (critiques of cult and obscure films), 500-1,000 words; Brut Library (critiques of books), 500-1,000 words. **Buys 20-30 mss/year.** Send complete ms. **Pays $50 average for book reviews; 5-10¢/word for feature articles.**

Fiction Adventure, confessions, erotica, experimental, fantasy, horror, humorous, mystery, novel excerpts, suspense. **Buys 8-10 mss/year.** Send complete ms. Length: No length limit. **Pays up to 10¢/word.**

Poetry Avant-garde, free verse, traditional. **Buys 10-15 poems/year.** Submit maximum 3 poems. Length: 25-1,000 lines. **Pays $20-200.**

Tips ''Send résumé with completed manuscript. Avoid dry tone and excessive scholasticism. Do not cover topics or issues which have been done to death unless you have a fresh approach or new insights on the subject. Pays $25/illustration; $100 for cover art.''

$ CANADIAN DIMENSION

Dimension Publications, Inc., 91 Albert St., Room 2-B, Winnipeg MB R3B 1G5 Canada. (204)957-1519. Fax: (204)943-4617. E-mail: info@canadiandimension.mb.ca. Website: www.canadiandimension.mb.ca. **80% freelance written.** Bimonthly magazine covering socialist perspective. ''We bring a socialist perspective to bear on events across Canada and around the world. Our contributors provide in-depth coverage on popular movements, peace, labour, women, aboriginal justice, environment, third world and eastern Europe.'' Estab. 1963. Circ. 2,000. Pays on publication. Publishes ms an average of 6 months after acceptance. Accepts previously published material. Accepts simultaneous submissions. Responds in 6 weeks to queries. Sample copy for $2. Writer's guidelines online.

Nonfiction Interview/profile, opinion, reviews; political commentary and analysis; journalistic style. **Buys 8 mss/year.** Length: 500-2,000 words. **Pays $25-100.**

Reprints Send ms with rights for sale noted and information about when and where the material previously appeared.

$ $ $COMMENTARY

American Jewish Committee, 165 E. 56th St., New York NY 10022. (212)891-1400. Fax: (212)891-6700. E-mail: editorial@commentarymagazine.com. Website: www.commentarymagazine.com. Editor: Neal Kozodoy.

Managing Editor: Gary Rosen. Monthly magazine. Estab. 1945. Pays on publication. Publishes ms an average of 2 months after acceptance. Byline given. Buys all rights. Accepts queries by mail, e-mail. Writer's guidelines not available.

Nonfiction Essays, opinion. **Buys 4 mss/year.** Query. Length: 2,000-8,000 words. **Pays $400-1,200.**

Tips "Unsolicited manuscripts must be accompanied by a self-addressed, stamped envelope."

$ $⬚ COMMON GROUND

Common Ground Publishing, 201-3091 W. Broadway, Vancouver BC V6K 2G9 Canada. (604)733-2215. Fax: (604)733-4415. E-mail: editor@commonground.ca. Website: www.commonground.ca. Senior Editor: Joseph Roberts. **90% freelance written.** Monthly tabloid covering health, environment, spirit, creativity, and wellness. "We serve the cultural creative community." Estab. 1982. Circ. 65,900. Pays on publication. Publishes ms an average of 1 month after acceptance. Byline given. Buys one-time, second serial (reprint) rights. Editorial lead time 2 months. Submit seasonal material 3 months in advance. Accepts queries by e-mail. Accepts simultaneous submissions. Responds in 6 weeks to queries; 3 months to mss. Sample copy for $5. Writer's guidelines online.

Nonfiction Topics include health, personal growth, creativity, spirituality, ecology, or short inspiring stories on environment themes. Book excerpts, how-to, inspirational, interview/profile, opinion, personal experience, travel, call to action. **Buys 12 mss/year.** Send complete ms. Length: 500-2,500 words. **Pays 10¢/word (Canadian).**

Reprints Accepts previously published submissions.

Photos State availability with submission. Buys one-time rights. Captions, photo credits required.

$ $ $ FIRST THINGS

Institute on Religion & Public Life, 156 Fifth Ave., Suite 400, New York NY 10010. (212)627-1985. Fax: (212)627-2184. E-mail: ft@firstthings.com. Website: www.firstthings.com. Editor-in-Chief: Richard John Neuhaus. Managing Editor: Matthew Boudway. **Contact:** Damon Linker, editor. **70% freelance written.** "Intellectual journal published 10 times/year containing social and ethical commentary in broad sense, religious and ethical perspectives on society, culture, law, medicine, church and state, morality and more." Estab. 1990. Circ. 32,000. Pays on publication. Publishes ms an average of 4 months after acceptance. Byline given. Buys all rights. Editorial lead time 2 months. Submit seasonal material 5 months in advance. Responds in 3 weeks to mss. Sample copy and writer's guidelines for #10 SASE.

Nonfiction Essays, opinion. **Buys 60 mss/year.** Send complete ms. Length: 1,500-6,000 words. **Pays $400-1,000.** Sometimes pays expenses of writers on assignment.

Poetry Joseph Bettum, poetry editor. Traditional. **Buys 25-30 poems/year.** Length: 4-40 lines. **Pays $50.**

Tips "We prefer complete manuscripts (hard copy, double-spaced) to queries, but will reply if unsure."

Ⓝ $ $ FRANCE TODAY

The Journal of French Travel & Culture, 944 Market St., Suite 200, San Francisco CA 94102. (415)981-9088. Fax: (415)981-9177. E-mail: info@francetoday.com. Website: www.francetoday.com. **Contact:** Anne Sengès, managing editor. **70% freelance written.** Tabloid published 10 times/year covering contemporary France. "*France Today* is a feature publication on contemporary France including sociocultural analysis, business, trends, current events, food, wine, and travel." Estab. 1989. Circ. 12,000. Pays on publication. Byline given. Buys first North American serial, second serial (reprint) rights. Submit seasonal material 4 months in advance. Accepts queries by mail, e-mail, fax. Accepts previously published material. Responds in 3 months to queries. Sample copy for 10×13 SAE with 5 first-class stamps.

Nonfiction Essays, exposé, general interest, humor, interview/profile, personal experience, travel, historical. Special issues: Paris, France on the Move, France On a Budget, Summer Travel, France Adventure. "No travel pieces about well-known tourist attractions." Query with published clips, or articles sent on spec. Length: 500-1,500 words. **Pays 10¢/word.**

Reprints Send ms with rights for sale noted and information about when and where the material previously appeared. Payment varies.

Photos Buys one-time rights. Offers $25/photo. Identification of subjects required.

$ $ $⬚ FW MAGAZINE

FW Omni Media Corp., 460 Richmond St. W., Suite 500, Toronto ON M5V 1Y1 Canada. (416)591-6537. Fax: (416)591-2390. E-mail: editors@myfw.com. Website: www.myfw.com. **80% freelance written.** Bimonthly magazine. "We are a lifestyle magazine that is geared to both males and females. Our readership is 18-34 years old. We focus on the hottest new trends for our readers. We profile people in their 20s doing exciting ventures." Estab. 1993. Circ. 500,000. Pays on publication. Byline given. Offers 50% kill fee. Buys first, electronic rights. Editorial lead time 2 months. Submit seasonal material 3 months in advance. Accepts queries by fax, phone.

Accepts simultaneous submissions. Responds to queries in 1 month if interested to queries; 2 months to mss. Sample copy for free. Writer's guidelines online.

Nonfiction Exposé, general interest, how-to, interview/profile, new product, personal experience, photo feature, travel. **Buys 83 mss/year.** Query with published clips. Length: 500-3,000 words. **Pays $300-1,000.** Sometimes pays expenses of writers on assignment.

Photos State availability with submission. Reviews contact sheets, negatives. Buys one-time rights. Negotiates payment individually. Captions, identification of subjects, model releases required.

Columns/Departments Body (the newest trends in fitness); Travel (the new "hotspots" on a budget); Work (interesting jobs for people in their 20s); Fashion (profile new designers and trends); all 1,000 words. **Buys 50 mss/year.** Query. **Pays $300-1,000.**

$ GENERATION X NATIONAL JOURNAL

Speaking for Our Generation, 411 W. Front, Wayland IA 52654. (319)256-4221. E-mail: genxjournal2004@yahoo .com. Website: www.genxnatljournal.com. Editor: Les Stoops. **Contact:** Kathy Stoops, managing editor. **95% freelance written.** Quarterly creative journal covering the generation who came of age in the late 80s and early 90s. Estab. 2003. Pays on publication. Publishes ms an average of 3 months after acceptance. Buys one-time rights. Editorial lead time 4 months. Submit seasonal material 6 months in advance. Accepts queries by mail, e-mail. Accepts simultaneous submissions. Responds in 2 months to queries; 3 months to mss. Sample copy for $3. Writer's guidelines for #10 SASE.

Nonfiction Book excerpts, essays, general interest, historical/nostalgic, how-to, humor, inspirational, interview/ profile, opinion, personal experience, religious (but practical), travel. No sexually explicit material; religious pieces are fine, but cannot be preachy. Send complete ms. Length: 500-2,500 words. **Pays $5-10.**

Columns/Departments Politicrat Corner (any political views), 500-2,000 words; Ethnic View (views life from a minority's perspective), 500-2,000 words; Gen-X Poetry (realistic, humorous poetry), 5-15 lines; Success Stories (a Gen-xer who is successful, how they did it, etc.), 500-2,000 words. **Pays $5-10.**

Fiction Adventure, confessions, ethnic, experimental, fantasy, historical, humorous, mainstream, religious, romance, slice-of-life vignettes, political pieces, success stories. No erotica or horror. Length: 500-2,500 words. **Pays $5-10.**

Poetry "Share your heritage. Discuss the challenges of gaining understanding of one another's differences." Avant-garde, free verse, haiku, light verse, traditional. Submit maximum 5 poems. Length: 5-25 lines.

Fillers Anecdotes, short humor. Length: 10-100 words. **Pays $5-10.**

Tips "Be thought provoking in your ideas. Gen-X can spot half-baked thinking and are ruthlessly realistic. We are seeking classy material. Seeking to escape the gutter, meaning: No reality TV crass, date arranging stuff. Let's stay away from trash talk and curse words. Good writers don't need shock and awe. We are looking for optimism. Keep in touch with Kathy and learn more about monthly contests coming in the near future."

$ $ ⊡ HEADS MAGAZINE

Worldwide Heads, P.O. Box 1319, Hudson QC J0P 1H0 Canada. E-mail: editor@headsmagazine.com. Website: www.headsmagazine.com. **Contact:** Editor. **100% freelance written.** Magazine published every 6 weeks covering the marijuana lifestyle. "*Heads Magazine* is a counter-culture publication concerning the lifestyle surrounding marijuana use and propogation." Estab. 2000. Circ. 75,000. Pays 3 months after publication. Publishes ms an average of 3 months after acceptance. Byline given. Buys all rights. Editorial lead time 3 months. Submit seasonal material 4 months in advance. Accepts queries by mail, e-mail, fax. Accepts simultaneous submissions. Sample copy for $5 (US) or online at website. Writer's guidelines for $5 (US) or by e-mail.

• The editor will contact the writer only if query/ms is usable.

Nonfiction Book excerpts, exposé, general interest, how-to (grow info), humor, interview/profile, new product, opinion, personal experience, photo feature, travel. **Buys 150 mss/year.** Query with published clips or send complete ms. Length: 600-1,500 words. **Pays $50-200.**

Photos Send photos with submission. Reviews contact sheets, prints, GIF/JPEG files. Buys all rights. Negotiates payment individually. Captions, model releases required.

Columns/Departments Marijuana Notes & News (news items about marijuana), 80-150 words; Heads Destination (travel stories), 1,000-2,000 words; Heads Musician (feature story about a musician—pot oriented), 1,000-2,000 words; Ahead of Their Times (groundbreaking member of the counter-culture), 600-1,000 words. **Buys 64 mss/year.** Send complete ms. **Pays $50-200.**

Fillers Facts, newsbreaks. Length: 50-150 words. **Pays $5-15.**

$ ⊕ THE LIST

The List, Ltd., 14 High St., Edinburgh EH1 1TE Scotland. (0131) 550 3050. Fax: (0131) 557 8500. E-mail: editor@list.co.uk. Website: www.list.co.uk. Publisher/General Editor: Robin Hodge. **Contact:** Nick Barley, editor. **25% freelance written.** Biweekly magazine covering Glasgow and Edinburgh arts, events, listings, and lifestyle. *"The List* is pitched at educated 18-35 year olds." Estab. 1985. Circ. 15,000. Pays on publication. Publishes ms an average of 2 weeks after acceptance. Byline given. Offers 100% kill fee. Buys first, second serial (reprint) rights. Editorial lead time 1 month. Submit seasonal material 1 month in advance. Accepts queries by mail, e-mail. Accepts simultaneous submissions.

Nonfiction Interview/profile, opinion, travel. Query with published clips. Length: 300 words. **Pays £60-80.** Sometimes pays expenses of writers on assignment.

Columns/Departments Reviews, 50-650 words; **pays £16-35**; Book Reviews, 150 words; **pays £14**; Comic Reviews, 100 words; **pays £10**; TV/Video Reviews, 100 words; **pays £10**; Record Reviews, 100 words; **pays £10**. Query with published clips.

$ $ $ $ MOTHER JONES

Foundation for National Progress, 222 Shutter St., Suite 600, San Francisco CA 94108. (415)321-1700. Fax: (415)321-1701. E-mail: query@motherjones.com. Website: www.motherjones.com. **Contact:** Clara Jeffery, deputy editor; Alastair Paulin, managing editor; Monika Bauerlein, senior editor; Tim Dickinson, articles editor. **80% freelance written.** Bimonthly magazine covering politics, investigative reporting, social issues, and pop culture. *"Mother Jones* is a 'progressive' magazine—but the core of its editorial well is reporting (i.e., fact-based). No slant required. MotherJones.com is an online sister publication." Estab. 1976. Circ. 235,000. Pays on publication. Publishes ms an average of 4 months after acceptance. Byline given. Offers 33% kill fee. Buys first North American serial, first, one-time, electronic rights. Editorial lead time 4 months. Submit seasonal material 6 months in advance. Responds in 2 months to queries. Sample copy for $6 and 9×12 SAE. Writer's guidelines online.

Nonfiction Exposé, interview/profile, photo feature, current issues, policy, investigative reporting. **Buys 70-100 mss/year.** Query with published clips. Length: 2,000-5,000 words. **Pays $1/word.** Sometimes pays expenses of writers on assignment.

Columns/Departments Outfront (short, newsy and/or outrageous and/or humorous items), 200-800 words; Profiles of "Hellraisers," 500 words. **Pays $1/word.**

Tips "We're looking for hard-hitting, investigative reports exposing government cover-ups, corporate malfeasance, scientific myopia, institutional fraud or hypocrisy; thoughtful, provocative articles which challenge the conventional wisdom (on the right or the left) concerning issues of national importance; and timely, people-oriented stories on issues such as the environment, labor, the media, healthcare, consumer protection, and cultural trends. Send a great, short query and establish your credibility as a reporter. Explain what you plan to cover and how you will proceed with the reporting. The query should convey your approach, tone and style, and should answer the following: What are your specific qualifications to write on this topic? What 'ins' do you have with your sources? Can you provide full documentation so that your story can be fact-checked?"

N $ $ $ THE NEW CANADIAN MAGAZINE

Canadian Culture, Business and Politics, The NewCanadian Publishing Inc., 151 Jean-Leman, Suite 2001, Candiac QC J5R 4V5 Canada. (450)444-0341. Fax: (514)221-2427. E-mail: editorial@newcanadian.com. Website: www.newcanadian.com. **Contact:** Amy Luft, editorial manager. **80% freelance written.** Quarterly magazine covering Canadian culture, business, and politics. This magazine is a modern and thought-provoking take on social issues of concern to an intelligent and affluent Canadian reader. Estab. 2002. Circ. 30,000. Pays on publication. Publishes ms an average of 3 months after acceptance. Byline given. Buys all rights, with the exception of personal stories rights. Editorial lead time 4-5 months. Submit seasonal material 5 months in advance. Accepts queries by e-mail. Accepts simultaneous submissions. Responds in 2-3 weeks to queries. Sample copy online. Writer's guidelines not available; editor will answer any questions via e-mail if requested.

Nonfiction Essays, general interest, historical/nostalgic, interview/profile, personal experience, travel. **Buys 50-60 mss/year.** Query with published clips. Length: 800-2,500 words. **Pays $240-1,250.** Sometimes pays expenses of writers on assignment.

Photos State availability with submission. Reviews prints, GIF/JPEG files. Buys all rights. Mainly offers no additional payment for photos accepted with ms; occasionally will negotiate payment individually. Captions, identification of subjects, model releases required.

Columns/Departments Routes (historical and cultural overview of various Canadian cultural communities), 1,800-2,000 words; Features (thought-provoking modern social issue), 1,800-2,500 words; Business, 1,800-2,000 words; Lifestyle, 1,200-1,800 words; Destination (travel stories in Canada and worldwide), 1,500-2,000 words. **Buys 50-60 mss/year.** Query with published clips. **Pays $240-1,250.**

Tips "Articles should discuss timeless social issues with a modern hook. Let us know why you're the best person to write it, and what insight you have into this issue. Also, submissions are all well-received for our Routes section."

$NEW HAVEN ADVOCATE

News & Arts Weekly, New Mass Media, Inc., 900 Chapel St., Suite 1100, New Haven CT 06510. (203)789-0010. Fax: (203)787-1418. E-mail: pbass@newhavenadvocate.com. Website: www.newhavenadvocate.com. **Contact:** Tom Gogola, managing editor. **10% freelance written.** Weekly tabloid. "Alternative, investigative, cultural reporting with a strong voice. We like to shake things up." Estab. 1975. Circ. 55,000. Pays on publication. Byline given. Buys one-time rights. Buys on speculation. Editorial lead time 1 month. Submit seasonal material 2 months in advance. Accepts simultaneous submissions. Responds in 1 month to queries. Sample copy not available.

Nonfiction Book excerpts, essays, exposé, general interest, humor, interview/profile. **Buys 15-20 mss/year.** Query with published clips. Length: 750-2,000 words. **Pays $50-150.** Sometimes pays expenses of writers on assignment.

Photos State availability with submission. Buys one-time rights. Captions, identification of subjects, model releases required.

Tips "Strong local focus; strong literary voice, controversial, easy-reading, contemporary, etc."

$ $ $THE SUN

The Sun Publishing Co., 107 N. Roberson St., Chapel Hill NC 27516. (919)942-5282. Fax: (919)932-3101. Website: www.thesunmagazine.org. **Contact:** Sy Safransky, editor. **90% freelance written.** Monthly magazine. "We are open to all kinds of writing, though we favor work of a personal nature." Estab. 1974. Circ. 70,000. Pays on publication. Publishes ms an average of 6-12 months after acceptance. Byline given. Buys first, one-time rights. Accepts previously published material. Responds in 3-6 months. Sample copy for $5. Writer's guidelines online.

Nonfiction Book excerpts, essays, general interest, interview/profile, opinion, personal experience, spiritual. **Buys 50 mss/year.** Send complete ms. Length: 7,000 words maximum. **Pays $300-1,250.** Complimentary subscription is given in addition to payment (applies to payment for *all* works, not just nonfiction).

Reprints Send photocopy and information about when and where the material previously appeared. Pays 50% of amount paid for original article or story.

Photos Send photos with submission. Reviews b&w prints. Buys one-time rights. Offers $50-200/photo. Model releases required.

Fiction "We avoid stereotypical genre pieces like science fiction, romance, western, and horror. Read an issue before submitting." Literary. **Buys 20 mss/year.** Send complete ms. Length: 7,000 words maximum. **Pays $300-750.**

Poetry Free verse, prose poems, short and long poems. **Buys 24 poems/year.** Submit maximum 6 poems. **Pays $50-250.**

UTNE READER

1624 Harmon Place, Suite 330, Minneapolis MN 55403. (612)338-5040. Fax: (612)338-6043. E-mail: editor@utne .com. Website: www.utne.com. Accepts queries by mail, e-mail. Writer's guidelines online.

Reprints Send tearsheet or photocopy with rights for sale noted and information about when and where the material previously appeared.

Tips "State the theme(s) clearly, let the narrative flow, and build the story around strong characters and a vivid sense of place. Give us rounded episodes, logically arranged. We do not publish fiction or poetry."

$THE WORLD & I

The Magazine for Lifelong Learners, News World Communications, Inc., 3600 New York Ave. NE, Washington DC 20002. (202)635-4000. Fax: (202)269-9353. E-mail: editor@worldandimag.com. Website: www.worldandi.c om. Editor: Morton A. Kaplan. Associate Executive Editor: Eric P. Olsen. **Contact:** Gary Rowe, editorial office manager. **90% freelance written.** Monthly magazine. "A broad interest magazine for the thinking, educated person." Estab. 1986. Circ. 30,000. Pays on publication. Publishes ms an average of 6 months after acceptance. Byline given. Offers 20% kill fee. Submit seasonal material 5 months in advance. Accepts queries by mail. Accepts previously published material. Responds in 6 weeks to queries; 10 weeks to mss. Sample copy for $5 and 9 × 12 SASE. Writer's guidelines online.

Nonfiction *Current Issues:* Politics, economics and strategic trends covered in a variety of approaches, including special report, analysis, commentary and photo essay. *The Arts:* International coverage of music, dance, theater, film, television, craft, design, architecture, photography, poetry, painting and sculpture—through reviews, features, essays, opinion pieces and a 6-page gallery of full-color reproductions. *Life:* Surveys all aspects of life in 22 rotating subsections which include: Travel and Adventure (first person reflections, preference given to authors who provide photographic images), Profile (people or organizations that are 'making a difference'), Food and Garden (must be accompanied by photos), Education, Humor, Hobby, Family, Consumer, Trends, and Health. Send SASE for complete list of subsections. *Natural Science:* Covers the latest in science and technology, relating it to the social and historical context, under these headings: At the Edge, Impacts, Nature Walk, Science and Spirit, Science and Values, Scientists: Past and Present, Crucibles of Science and Science Essay. *Book World*: Excerpts from important, timely books (followed by commentaries) and 10-12 scholarly reviews of significant new books each month, including untranslated works from abroad. Covers current affairs, intellectual issues, contemporary fiction, history, moral/religious issues and the social sciences. *Currents in Modern Thought*: Examines scholarly research and theoretical debate across the wide range of disciplines in the humanities and social sciences. Featured themes are explored by several contributors. Investigates theoretical issues raised by certain current events, and offers contemporary reflection on issues drawn from the whole history of human thought. *Culture*: Surveys the world's people in these subsections: Peoples (their unique characteristics and cultural symbols), Crossroads (changes brought by the meeting of cultures), Patterns (photo essay depicting the daily life of a distinct culture), Folk Wisdom (folklore and practical wisdom and their present forms), and Heritage (multicultural backgrounds of the American people and how they are bound to the world). *Photo Essay*: Patterns, a 6- or 8-page photo essay, appears monthly in the Culture section. Emphasis is placed on comprehensive photographic coverage of a people or group, their private or public lifestyle, in a given situation or context. Accompanying word count: 300-500 words. Photos must be from existing stock, no travel subsidy. Life & Ideals, a 6- or 8-page photo essay, occasionally appears in the Life section. First priority is given to those focused on individuals or organizations that are 'making a difference.' Accompanying word count: 700-1,000 words." No *National Enquirer*-type articles. **Buys 1,200 mss/year.** Query with published clips. Length: 1,000-5,000 words. **Pays on a per article basis.** Seldom pays expenses of writers on assignment.

Reprints Send ms with rights for sale noted and information about when and where the material previously appeared.

Photos State availability with submission. Reviews contact sheets, transparencies, prints. Buys one-time rights. Payment negotiable. Identification of subjects, model releases required.

Fiction Novel excerpts.

Poetry Arts Editor. Avant-garde, free verse, haiku, light verse, traditional. **Buys 4-6 poems/year.** Submit maximum 5 poems. **Pays $30-75.**

Tips "We accept articles from journalists, but also place special emphasis on scholarly contributions. It is our hope that the magazine will enable the best of contemporary thought, presented in accessible language, to reach a wider audience than would normally be possible through the academic journals appropriate to any given discipline."

$ YES!

A Journal of Positive Futures, Positive Futures Network, P.O. Box 10818, Bainbridge Island WA 98110. (206)842-0216. Fax: (206)842-5208. E-mail: editors@yesmagazine.org. Website: www.futurenet.org. Executive Editor: Sarah Ruth van Gelder. Quarterly magazine covering sustainability and community. "Interested in stories on building a positive future: sustainability, overcoming divisiveness, ethical business practices, etc." Estab. 1996. Circ. 23,000. Pays on publication. Byline given. Editorial lead time 4 months. Accepts queries by mail. Accepts previously published material. Accepts simultaneous submissions. Responds in 1 month to queries; 3 months to mss. Sample copy and writer's guidelines online.

Nonfiction "Please check website for a detailed call for submission before each issue." Book excerpts, essays, humor, interview/profile, personal experience, photo feature, technical, environmental. Query with published clips. Length: 1,500-2,500 words. **Pays up to $100/page for original, researched material.** Pays writers with 1-year subscition and 2 contributor copies.

Reprints Send photocopy or typed ms with rights for sale noted and information about when and where the material previously appeared. Pays 100% of amount paid for an original article.

Photos State availability with submission. Reviews contact sheets, negatives, transparencies, prints. Buys one-time rights. Offers $20-75/photo. Identification of subjects required.

Tips "Read and become familiar with the publication's purpose, tone and quality. We are about facilitating the creation of a better world. We are looking for writers who want to participate in that process. *Yes!* is less interested in bemoaning the state of our problems than in highlighting promising solutions. We are highly unlikely to accept submissions that simply state the author's opinion on what needs to be fixed and why. Our readers know *why* we need to move towards sustainability; they are interested in *how* to do so."

DISABILITIES

$ $ ABILITIES

Canada's Lifestyle Magazine for People with Disabilities, Canadian Abilities Foundation, 650-340 College St., Toronto ON M5T 3A9 Canada. (416)923-1885. Fax: (416)923-9829. E-mail: able@abilities.ca. Website: www.abilities.ca. Editor: Raymond Cohen. **Contact:** Lisa Bendall, managing editor. **50% freelance written.** Quarterly magazine covering disability issues. "*Abilities* provides information, inspiration, and opportunity to its readers with articles and resources covering health, travel, sports, products, technology, profiles, employment, recreation, and more." Estab. 1987. Circ. 45,000. Pays on publication. Publishes ms an average of 3 months after acceptance. Byline given. Offers 50% kill fee. Buys first rights. Editorial lead time 3 months. Submit seasonal material 4 months in advance. Accepts queries by mail, e-mail, fax. Responds in 3 months to queries. Sample copy for free. Writer's guidelines for #10 SASE, online, or by e-mail.

Nonfiction Book excerpts, general interest, how-to, humor, inspirational, interview/profile, new product, opinion, personal experience, photo feature, travel. Does not want "articles that 'preach to the converted'—contain info that people with disabilities likely already know, such as what it's like to have a disability." **Buys 30-40 mss/year.** Query or send complete ms. Length: 500-2,500 words. **Pays $50-400 (Canadian) for assigned articles; $50-300 (Canadian) for unsolicited articles.**

Reprints Sometimes accepts previously published submissions (if stated as such).

Photos State availability with submission.

Columns/Departments The Lighter Side (humor), 700 words; Profile, 1,200 words.

Tips "Do not contact by phone—send something in writing. Send a great idea that we haven't done before, and make a case for why you'd be able to do a good job with it. Must be Canadian-focused. Be sure to include a relevant writing sample."

$ $ $ $ ARTHRITIS TODAY

Arthritis Foundation, 1330 W. Peachtree St. NW, Suite 100, Atlanta GA 30309. (404)872-7100. Fax: (404)872-9559. E-mail: contactus@arthritis.org. Website: www.arthritis.org. Editor: Marcy O'Koon Moss. Managing Editor: Lissa Poirot. Medical Editor: Donna Siegfried. **50% freelance written.** Bimonthly magazine covering living with arthritis and the latest in research/treatment. "*Arthritis Today* is a consumer health magazine and is written for the more than 70 million Americans who have arthritis and for the millions of others whose lives are touched by an arthritis-related disease. The editorial content is designed to help the person with arthritis live a more productive, independent, and pain-free life. The articles are upbeat and provide practical advice, information and inspiration." Estab. 1987. Circ. 650,000. **Pays on acceptance.** Byline given. Offers kill fee. Buys first North American serial, second serial (reprint), electronic rights. Editorial lead time 6 months. Submit seasonal material 6 months in advance. Accepts queries by mail, e-mail, fax. Accepts simultaneous submissions. Responds in 2 months to queries. Sample copy for 9×11 SAE with 4 first-class stamps. Writer's guidelines online.

Nonfiction General interest, how-to (tips on any aspect of living with arthiritis), inspirational, new product (arthritis related), opinion, personal experience, photo feature, technical, travel (tips, news), service, nutrition, general health, lifestyle. **Buys 12 unsolicited mss/year.** Query with published clips. Length: 150-2,500 words. **Pays $100-2,500.** Pays expenses of writers on assignment.

Photos Send photos with submission. Reviews prints. Buys one-time rights. Negotiates payment individually. Identification of subjects required.

Columns/Departments Nutrition, 100-600 words; Fitness, 100-600 words; Balance (emotional coping), 100-600 words; MedWatch, 100-800 words; Solutions, 100-600 words; Life Makeover, 400-600 words.

Fillers Facts, gags to be illustrated by cartoonist, short humor. **Buys 2/year.** Length: 40-100 words. **Pays $80-150.**

Tips "Our readers are already well informed. We need ideas and writers that give in-depth, fresh, interesting information that truly adds to their understanding of their condition and their quality of life. Quality writers are more important than good ideas. The staff generates many of our ideas but needs experienced, talented writers who are good reporters to execute them. Please provide published clips. In addition to articles specifically about living with arthritis, we look for articles to appeal to an older audience on subjects such as hobbies, general health, lifestyle, etc."

$ $ CAREERS & THE DISABLED

Equal Opportunity Publications, 445 Broad Hollow Rd., Suite 425, Melville NY 11747. (631)421-9421. Fax: (631)421-0359. E-mail: jschneider@eop.com. Website: www.eop.com. **Contact:** James Schneider, editor. **60% freelance written.** Quarterly magazine offering "role-model profiles and career guidance articles geared toward disabled college students and professionals, and promotes personal and professional growth." Estab. 1967. Circ. 10,000. Pays on publication. Publishes ms an average of 6 months after acceptance. Byline given. Buys first North American serial rights. Editorial lead time 6 months. Submit seasonal material 6 months in advance. Accepts queries by mail, e-mail, fax, phone. Accepts previously published material. Accepts simultaneous submissions. Responds in 3 weeks to queries. Sample copy for 9×12 SAE with 5 first-class stamps.

Nonfiction Essays, general interest, how-to, interview/profile, new product, opinion, personal experience. **Buys 30 mss/year.** Query. Length: 1,000-2,500 words. **Pays 10¢/word.** Sometimes pays expenses of writers on assignment.

Reprints Accepts previously published submissions and information about when and where the material previously appeared.

Photos Reviews transparencies, prints. Buys one-time rights. Offers $15-50/photo. Captions, identification of subjects, model releases required.

Tips "Be as targeted as possible. Role-model profiles and specific career guidance strategies that offer advice to disabled college students are most needed."

$ $DIABETES HEALTH

6 School St., Suite 160, Fairfax CA 94930. (415)258-2828. Fax: (415)387-3604. Website: www.diabetesinterview. com. Editor-in-Chief: Scott King. **Contact:** Daniel Trecroci, managing editor. **40% freelance written.** Monthly tabloid covering diabetes care. "*Diabetes Interview* covers the latest in diabetes care, medications, and patient advocacy. Personal accounts are welcome as well as medical-oriented articles by MDs, RNs, and CDEs (certified diabetes educators)." Estab. 1991. Circ. 40,000. Pays on publication. Publishes ms an average of 2 months after acceptance. Byline given. Buys all rights. Editorial lead time 2 months. Submit seasonal material 2 months in advance. Accepts queries by mail, e-mail, fax, phone. Sample copy online. Writer's guidelines free.

Nonfiction Essays, how-to, humor, inspirational, interview/profile, new product, opinion, personal experience. **Buys 25 mss/year.** Send complete ms. Length: 500-1,500 words. **Pays 20¢/word.**

Reprints Accepts previously published submissions.

Photos State availability of or send photos with submission. Negotiates payment individually.

Tips "Be actively involved in the diabetes community or have diabetes. However, writers need not have diabetes to write an article, but it must be diabetes-related."

$ $DIABETES SELF-MANAGEMENT

R.A. Rapaport Publishing, Inc., 150 W. 22nd St., Suite 800, New York NY 10011-2421. (212)989-0200. Fax: (212)989-4786. E-mail: editor@diabetes-self-mgmt.com. Website: www.diabetesselfmanagement.com. **Contact:** Ingrid Strauch, managing editor. **20% freelance written.** Bimonthly magazine. "We publish how-to health care articles for motivated, intelligent readers who have diabetes and who are actively involved in their own health care management. All articles must have immediate application to their daily living." Estab. 1983. Circ. 480,000. Pays on publication. Byline given. Offers 20% kill fee. Buys all rights. Submit seasonal material 6 months in advance. Accepts queries by mail, e-mail, fax. Responds in 6 weeks to queries. Sample copy for $4 and 9×12 SAE with 6 first-class stamps or online. Writer's guidelines for #10 SASE.

⚬━ Break in by having extensive knowledge of diabetes. "We are extremely generous regarding permission to republish."

Nonfiction How-to (exercise, nutrition, diabetes self-care, product surveys), technical (reviews of products available, foods sold by brand name, pharmacology), travel (considerations and prep for people with diabetes). No personal experiences, personality profiles, exposés, or research breakthroughs. **Buys 10-12 mss/year.** Query with published clips. Length: 2,000-2,500 words. **Pays $400-700 for assigned articles; $200-700 for unsolicited articles.**

Tips "The rule of thumb for any article we publish is that it must be clear, concise, useful, and instructive, and it must have immediate application to the lives of our readers. If your query is accepted, expect heavy editorial supervision."

$DIALOGUE

Blindskills, Inc., P.O. Box 5181, Salem OR 97304-0181. (800)860-4224; (503)581-4224. Fax: (503)581-0178. E-mail: blindskl@teleport.com. Website: www.blindskills.com. **Contact:** Carol M. McCarl, publisher. **60% freelance written.** Bimonthly journal covering visually impaired people. Estab. 1962. Circ. 1,100. Pays on publication. Publishes ms an average of 6 months after acceptance. Byline given. Buys first rights. Editorial lead time 3 months. Accepts queries by e-mail. One free sample on request. Available in large print, Braille, 4-track audio cassette, and disk (for compatible IBM computer). Writer's guidelines online.

⚬━ Break in by "using accurate punctuation, grammar, and structure, and writing about pertinent subject matter."

Nonfiction Mostly features material written by visually impaired writers. Essays, general interest, historical/nostalgic, how-to (life skills methods used by visually impaired people), humor, interview/profile, personal experience, sports, recreation, hobbies. No controversial, explicit sex, religious, or political topics. **Buys 80 mss/year.** Send complete ms. Length: 200-1,000. **Pays $15-35 for assigned articles; $15-25 for unsolicited articles.**

Columns/Departments All material should be relative to blind and visually impaired readers. Living with Low Vision, 1,000 words; Hear's How (dealing with sight loss), 1,000 words. Technology Answer Book, 800 words. **Buys 80 mss/year.** Send complete ms. **Pays $10-25.**

$KALEIDOSCOPE

Exploring the Experience of Disability Through Literature and the Fine Arts, Kaleidoscope Press, 701 S. Main St., Akron OH 44311-1019. (330)762-9755. Fax: (330)762-0912. E-mail: mshiplett@udsakron.org. Website: www.udsakron.org. **Contact:** Gail Willmott, editor-in-chief. **75% freelance written.** Eager to work with new/unpublished writers. Semiannual magazine. Subscribers include individuals, agencies, and organizations that assist people with disabilities and many university and public libraries. Appreciates work by established writers as well. Especially interested in work by writers with a disability, but features writers both with and without disabilities. "Writers without a disability must limit themselves to our focus, while those with a disability may explore any topic (although we prefer original perspectives about experiences with disability)." Estab. 1979. Circ. 1,000. Pays on publication. Byline given. Buys first rights. Rights return to author upon publication. Accepts queries by mail, fax. Accepts previously published material. Accepts simultaneous submissions. Responds in 3 weeks to queries; 6 months to mss. Sample copy for $6 prepaid. Writer's guidelines online.

> Submit photocopies with SASE for return of work. Please type submissions (double spaced). Include SASE with sufficient postage for return of work. All submissions should be accompanied by an autobiographical sketch. May include art or photos that enhance works, prefer b&w with high contrast.

Nonfiction Articles related to disability. Book excerpts, essays, humor, interview/profile, personal experience, book reviews, articles related to disability. Special issues: A Thematic Collage (January 2006, deadline August 2005); Potrayals of Disability in the Media (July 2006, deadline March 2006); Disability & Humor (January 2007, deadline August 2006). **Buys 8-15 mss/year.** Length: 5,000 words maximum. **Pays $25-125, plus 2 copies.**

Reprints Send ms with rights for sale noted and information about when and where the material previously appeared. Reprints permitted with credit given to original publication.

Photos Send photos with submission.

Fiction Fiction Editor. Short stories, novel excerpts. Traditional and experimental styles. Works should explore experiences with disability. Use people-first language. "We look for well-developed plots, engaging characters, and realistic dialogue. We lean toward fiction that emphasizes character and emotions rather than action-oriented narratives. No fiction that is stereotypical, patronizing, sentimental, erotic, or maudlin. No romance, religious or dogmatic fiction; no children's literature." Length: 5,000 words maximum. **Pays $10-125, and 2 contributor's copies; additional copies $6.**

Poetry "Do not get caught up in rhyme scheme. High quality with strong imagery and evocative language." Reviews any style. **Buys 12-20 poems/year.** Submit maximum 5 poems.

Tips "Articles and personal experiences should be creative rather than journalistic and with some depth. Writers should use more than just the simple facts and chronology of an experience with disability. Inquire about future themes of upcoming issues. Sample copy very helpful. Works should not use stereotyping, patronizing, or offending language about disability. We seek fresh imagery and thought-provoking language."

N $$SPECIALIVING

P.O. Box 1000, Bloomington IL 61702. (309)820-9277. E-mail: gareeb@aol.com. Website: www.specialiving.com. **Contact:** Betty Garee, managing editor. **90% freelance written.** Quarterly magazine covering the physically disabled/mobility impaired. Estab. 2001. Circ. 12,000. Pays on publication. Byline given. Buys one-time rights. Editorial lead time 3 months. Submit seasonal material 6 months in advance. Accepts queries by mail, e-mail, fax, phone. Accepts simultaneous submissions. Responds in 3 weeks to queries. Sample copy for $3.

Nonfiction How-to, humor, inspirational, interview/profile, new product, personal experience, technical, travel. **Buys 40 mss/year.** Query. Length: 800 words. **Pays 10¢/word.** Pays in contributor copies, only if requested.

Photos State availability with submission. Reviews GIF/JPEG files. Buys one-time rights. Offers $10/photo. Captions, identification of subjects required.

Columns/Departments Shopping Guide; Items. **Buys 10 mss/year.** Query. **Pays $50.**

ENTERTAINMENT

$CINEASTE

America's Leading Magazine on the Art and Politics of the Cinema, Cineaste Publishers, Inc., 304 Hudson St., 6th Floor, New York NY 10013-1015. (212)366-5720. Fax: (212)366-5724. E-mail: cineaste@cineaste.com. **Contact:** Gary Crowdus, editor-in-chief. **30% freelance written.** Quarterly magazine covering motion pictures with an emphasis on social and political perspective on cinema. Estab. 1967. Circ. 11,000. Pays on publication. Publishes ms an average of 4 months after acceptance. Byline given. Offers 50% kill fee. Buys first North American serial rights. Editorial lead time 3 months. Submit seasonal material 4 months in advance. Accepts queries by mail, e-mail, fax. Responds in 1 month to queries. Sample copy for $5. Writer's guidelines for #10 SASE.

○┓ Break in by "being familiar with our unique editorial orientation—we are not just another film magazine."

Nonfiction Book excerpts, essays, exposé, historical/nostalgic, humor, interview/profile, opinion. **Buys 20-30 mss/year.** Query with published clips. Length: 2,000-5,000 words. **Pays $30-100.**

Photos State availability with submission. Reviews transparencies, 8×10 prints. Buys one-time rights. Offers no additional payment for photos accepted with ms. Identification of subjects required.

Columns/Departments Homevideo (topics of general interest or a related group of films); A Second Look (new interpretation of a film classic or a reevaluation of an unjustly neglected release of more recent vintage); Lost and Found (film that may or may not be released or otherwise seen in the US but which is important enough to be brought to the attention of our readers), all 1,000-1,500 words. Query with published clips. **Pays $50 minimum.**

Tips "We dislike academic jargon, obtuse Marxist terminology, film buff trivia, trendy 'buzz' phrases, and show biz references. We do not want our writers to speak of how they have 'read' or 'decoded' a film, but to view, analyze, and interpret. The author's processes and quirks should be secondary to the interests of the reader. Warning the reader of problems with specific films is more important to us than artificially 'puffing' a film because its producers or politics are agreeable. One article format we encourage is an omnibus review of several current films, preferably those not reviewed in a previous issue. Such an article would focus on films that perhaps share a certain political perspective, subject matter, or generic concerns (i.e., films on suburban life, or urban violence, or revisionist Westerns). Like individual film reviews, these articles should incorporate a very brief synopsis of plots for those who haven't seen the films. The main focus, however, should be on the social issues manifested in each film, and how it may reflect something about the current political/social/esthetic climate."

$ ⊠ DANCE INTERNATIONAL

Scotiabanti Dance Centre, 677 Davie St., Vancouver BC V6B 2G6 Canada. (604)681-1525. Fax: (604)681-7732. E-mail: danceint@direct.ca. Website: www.danceinternational.org. **Contact:** Maureen Riches, editor. **100% freelance written.** Quarterly magazine covering dance arts. "Articles and reviews on current activities in world dance, with occasional historical essays; reviews of dance films, video, and books." Estab. 1973. Circ. 4,500. Pays on publication. Publishes ms an average of 3 months after acceptance. Byline given. Offers 50% kill fee. Buys one-time rights. Editorial lead time 3 months. Submit seasonal material 6 weeks in advance. Accepts queries by mail, e-mail, fax, phone. Responds in 2 weeks to queries; 1 month to mss. Sample copy for $7. Writer's guidelines for #10 SASE.

Nonfiction Book excerpts, essays, historical/nostalgic, interview/profile, personal experience, photo feature. **Buys 100 mss/year.** Query. Length: 1,200-2,200 words. **Pays $40-150.**

Photos Send photos with submission. Reviews prints. Offers no additional payment for photos accepted with ms. Identification of subjects required.

Columns/Departments Dance Bookshelf (recent books reviewed), 700-800 words; Regional Reports (events in each region), 1,200 words. **Buys 100 mss/year.** Query. **Pays $80.**

Tips "Send résumé and samples of recent writings."

$ DANCE SPIRIT

Lifestyle Media, Inc., 110 William St., 23rd Floor, New York NY 10038. (646)459-4800. Fax: (646)459-4900. E-mail: sjarrett@lifestylemedia.com. Website: www.dancespirit.com. **Contact:** Sara Jarrett, editor-in-chief. **50% freelance written.** Monthly magazine covering all dance disciplines. "*Dance Spirit* is a special interest teen magazine for girls and guys who study and perform either through a studio or a school dance performance group." Estab. 1997. Circ. 100,000. Pays on publication. Publishes ms an average of 4 months after acceptance. Byline given. Offers 25% kill fee. Buys all rights. Editorial lead time 3 months. Submit seasonal material 8 months in advance. Accepts queries by e-mail. Responds in 3 months to queries; 4 months to mss. Sample copy for $4.95.

Nonfiction Personal experience, photo feature, dance-related articles only. **Buys 100 mss/year.** Query with published clips. Length: 500-1,200 words. **Pays $150.** Sometimes pays expenses of writers on assignment.

Photos Reviews transparencies. Buys all rights. Negotiates payment individually. Captions, identification of subjects, model releases required.

Columns/Departments Ballet; Jazz; Tap; Swing; Hip Hop; Lyrical; Dance Team; Health; Beauty; Los Angeles and New York City Focuses; Choreography; Celebrities; Nutrition.

■ The online magazine carries original content not found in the print edition. Contact: Sara Jarrett.

Tips "Reading the magazine can't be stressed enough. We look for writers with a dance background and experienced dancers/choreographers to contribute; succinct writing style, hip outlook."

$ $ DIRECTED BY

The Cinema Quarterly, Visionary Media, P.O. Box 1722, Glendora CA 91740-1722. Fax: (309)276-0309. E-mail: visionarycinema@yahoo.com. Website: www.directed-by.com. **Contact:** Carsten Dau, editor. **10% freelance**

written. Quarterly magazine covering the craft of directing a motion picture. "Our articles are for readers particularly knowledgeable about the art and history of movies from the director's point of view. Our purpose is to communicate our enthusiasm and interest in the craft of cinema." Estab. 1998. Circ. 42,000. Pays on publication. Publishes ms an average of 3 months after acceptance. Byline given. Offers 25% kill fee. Buys all rights. Editorial lead time 3 months. Submit seasonal material 3 months in advance. Accepts queries by mail, e-mail. Accepts simultaneous submissions. Responds in 6 weeks to queries. Sample copy for $5. Writer's guidelines free or by e-mail.

Nonfiction Interview/profile, photo feature, on-set reports. No gossip, celebrity-oriented material, or movie reviews. **Buys 5 mss/year.** Query. Length: 500-7,500 words. **Pays $50-750.** Sometimes pays expenses of writers on assignment.

Photos State availability with submission. Reviews contact sheets. Buys all rights. Offers no additional payment for photos accepted with ms. Captions, identification of subjects required.

Columns/Departments Trends (overview/analysis of specific moviemaking movements/genres/subjects), 1,500-2,000 words; Focus (innovative take on the vision of a contemporary director), 1,500-2,000 words; Appreciation (overview of deceased/foreign director), 1,000-1,500 words; Final Cut (spotlight interview with contemporary director), 3,000 words; Perspectives (interviews/articles about film craftspeople who work with a featured director), 1,500-2,000 words. **Buys 5 mss/year.** Query. **Pays $50-750.**

Tips "We have been inundated with 'shelf-life' article queries and cannot publish even a small fraction of them. As such, we have restricted our interest in freelancers to writers who have direct access to a notable director of a current film which has not been significantly covered in previous issues of magazines; said director must be willing to grant an exclusive peronal interview to *DIRECTED BY*. This is a tough task for a writer, but if you are a serious freelancer and have access to important filmmakers, we are interested in you."

ELECTRONIC GAMING MONTHLY

Ziff-Davis Media, Inc., 101 2nd St., 8th Floor, San Francisco CA 94105. (415)547-8000. Fax: (415)547-8777. Website: www.egmmag.com. Monthly magazine. Focuses on electronic games for console video game units. Circ. 600,000. Sample copy not available.

$ $FANGORIA

Horror in Entertainment, Starlog Communications, Inc., 475 Park Ave. S., 7th Floor, New York NY 10016. (212)689-2830. Fax: (212)889-7933. Website: www.fangoria.com. **Contact:** Anthony Timpone, editor. **95% freelance written.** Works with a small number of new/unpublished writers each year. Magazine published 10 times/year covering horror films, TV projects, comics, videos, and literature, and those who create them. "We provide an assignment sheet (deadlines, info) to writers, thus authorizing queried stories that we're buying." Estab. 1979. Pays on publication. Publishes ms an average of 3 months after acceptance. Byline given. Buys all rights. Submit seasonal material 4 months in advance. Accepts queries by mail. Responds in 6 weeks to queries. Sample copy for $8 and 10×13 SAE with 4 first-class stamps. Writer's guidelines for #10 SASE.

* Avoids most articles on science-fiction films—see listing for sister magazine *Starlog* in *Writer's Market* science fiction consumer magazine section.

○╍ Break in by "reading the magazine regularly and exhibiting a professional view of the genre."

Nonfiction Book excerpts, interview/profile of movie directors, makeup FX artists, screenwriters, producers, actors, noted horror/thriller novelists and others—with genre credits; special FX and special makeup FX how-it-was-dones (on filmmaking only). Occasional "think" pieces, opinion pieces, reviews, or sub-theme overviews by industry professionals. **Buys 120 mss/year.** Query with published clips. Length: 1,000-3,500 words. **Pays $100-250.** Sometimes pays expenses of writers on assignment.

Photos State availability with submission. Reviews transparencies, prints (b&w, color) electronically. Captions, identification of subjects required.

Columns/Departments Monster Invasion (exclusive, early information about new film productions; also mini-interviews with filmmakers and novelists). Query with published clips. **Pays $45-75.**

▣ The online magazine carries original content not found in the print edition.

Tips "Other than recommending that you study one or several copies of *Fangoria*, we can only describe it as a horror film magazine consisting primarily of interviews with technicians and filmmakers in the field. Be sure to stress the interview subjects' words—not your own opinions as much. We're very interested in small, independent filmmakers working outside of Hollywood. These people are usually more accessible to writers, and more cooperative. *Fangoria* is also sort of a *de facto* bible for youngsters interested in movie makeup careers and for young filmmakers. We are devoted only to *reel* horrors—the fakery of films, the imagery of the horror fiction of a Stephen King or a Clive Barker—we do not want nor would we ever publish articles on real-life horrors, murders, etc. A writer must like and enjoy horror films and horror fiction to work for us. If the photos in *Fangoria* disgust you, if the sight of (*stage*) blood repels you, if you feel 'superior' to horror (and its fans), you aren't a writer for us and we certainly aren't the market for you. We love giving new writers their first chance to break into print in a national magazine. We are currently looking for Arizona- and Las Vegas-based correspondents, as well as writers stationed in Spain (especially Barcelona)."

N FILM COMMENT

Film Society of Lincoln Center, 70 Lincoln Center Plaza, New York NY 10023. (212)875-5610. E-mail: editor@filmlinc.com; chang@filmlinc.com. Website: www.filmlinc.com. **Contact:** Chris Chang, senior editor. **100% freelance written.** Bimonthly magazine covering film criticism and film history. Estab. 1962. Circ. 30,000. Pays on publication. Byline given. Editorial lead time 6 weeks. Accepts queries by mail, e-mail, fax, phone. Accepts simultaneous submissions.

Nonfiction Essays, historical/nostalgic, interview/profile, opinion. **Buys 100 mss/year.** Send complete ms. We respond to queries, but rarely assign a writer we don't know. Length: 800-8,000 words.

Photos State availability with submission. Buys one-time rights. No additional payment for photos accepted with ms.

Tips "We are more or less impervious to 'hooks,' don't worry a whole lot about 'who's hot who's not,' or tying in with next fall's surefire big hit. (We think people should write about films they've seen, not films that haven't even been finished.) We appreciate good writing (writing, not journalism) on subjects in which the writer has some personal investment and about which he or she has something noteworthy to say. Demonstrate ability and inclination to write *FC*-worthy articles. We read and consider everything we get, and we do print unknowns and first-timers. Probably the writer with a shorter submission (1,000-2,000 words) has a better chance than with an epic article that would fill half the issue."

$ 5678 MAGAZINE

Champion Media, P.O. Box 8886, Gaithersburg MD 20898. (301)871-7160. Fax: (301)519-1019. E-mail: durand5678@aol.com. Website: www.5678magazine.com. **Contact:** Barry Durand, publisher. **50% freelance written.** Quarterly magazine covering dance: couples, line, country, swing. "All articles with a dance or dance music slant. Interviews, reviews, features—today's social dance." Estab. 1999. Circ. 10,000. Pays on publication. Publishes ms an average of 2 months after acceptance. Byline given. Buys first rights. Editorial lead time 2 months. Accepts queries by e-mail. Sample copy for free. Writer's guidelines by e-mail.

Nonfiction Historical/nostalgic, how-to, humor, interview/profile, photo feature. **Buys 60 mss/year.** Query. Length: 600-2,000 words. **Pays $35-100.** Sometimes pays expenses of writers on assignment.

Photos Send photos with submission. Buys one-time rights. Negotiates payment individually. Captions, identification of subjects required.

Fiction Humorous, slice-of-life vignettes. **Buys 10 mss/year.** Query. Length: 600-1,500 words. **Pays $35-100.**

N $ $ FLICK MAGAZINE

Your Movie Souvenir, Decipher, Inc., 253 Granby St., Norfolk VA 23510. (757)623-3600. Fax: (757)623-8368. E-mail: julie.matthews@decipher.com. Website: www.flickmagazine.com. Managing Editor: Julie Matthews. **Contact:** Peter Lobred, vice president, publishing. **30-40% freelance written.** Mini magazine that comes out in conjunction with selected movies; distributed in movie theaters. *Flick*'s mission is to match the passion and personality of fans, taking readers inside Hollywood and increasing their connection to the film they are about to view. Estab. 2005. Circ. 2.5 million. **Pays on acceptance.** Publishes ms an average of 4 months after acceptance. Makes work-for-hire assignments. Editorial lead time 4-5 months. Accepts queries by mail, e-mail.

Nonfiction Essays, humor, interview/profile, opinion, personal experience. Query. Length: 500-1,000 words. **Pays $200-500.** Sometimes pays expenses of writers on assignment.

Photos Art Director (jeff.hellerman@decipher.com).

Columns/Departments Pays $200-500. Gags to be illustrated by cartoonist, short humor. **Buys 5-10/year. Pays $200-500.**

Tips "Writing for *Flick* is about research, story angles, subject knowledge, and access to movie cast and crew."

N HOME THEATER

Primedia Enthusiast Group, 6420 Wilshire Blvd., Los Angeles CA 90048-5502. (323)782-2000. Fax: (323)782-2080. E-mail: htletters@primedia.com. Website: www.hometheatermag.com. Executive Editor: Adrienne Maxwell. **Contact:** Maureen Jenson, editor. Monthly magazine covering audio, video, high-end components, and movies and music. Covers the home theater lifestyle. Estab. 1995. Circ. 109,422. Accepts queries by e-mail. Sample copy for $4.95.

Nonfiction Send résumé.

Columns/Departments Query with published clips.

$ $ MOVIEMAKER MAGAZINE

MovieMaker Publishing Co., 121 Fulton St., Fifth Floor, New York NY 10038. (212)766-4100. Fax: (212)766-4102. E-mail: jwood@moviemaker.com. Website: www.moviemaker.com. Editor: Timothy Rhys. **Contact:** Jennifer Wood, managing editor. **95% freelance written.** Quarterly magazine covering film, independent cinema, and Hollywood. "*MovieMaker*'s editorial is a progressive mix of in-depth interviews and criticism, combined with practical techniques and advice on financing, distribution, and production strategies. Behind-the-scenes discussions with Hollywood's top moviemakers, as well as independents from around the globe, are routinely found in *MovieMaker*'s pages." Estab. 1993. Circ. 50,000. Pays within 1 month of publication. Publishes ms an average of 2 months after acceptance. Byline given. Offers variable kill fee. Buys all rights. Editorial lead time 3 months. Submit seasonal material 4 months in advance. Accepts queries by mail, e-mail, fax. Accepts simultaneous submissions. Responds in 2 months. Sample copy online. Writer's guidelines by e-mail.

Nonfiction Exposé, general interest, historical/nostalgic, how-to, interview/profile, new product, technical. **Buys 10 mss/year.** Query with published clips. Length: 800-3,000 words. **Pays $75-500 for assigned articles.**

Photos State availability with submission. Rights purchased negotiable. Payment varies for photos accepted with ms. Identification of subjects required.

Columns/Departments Documentary; Home Cinema (home video/DVD reviews); How They Did It (first-person filmmaking experiences); Festival Beat (film festival reviews); World Cinema (current state of cinema from a particular country). Query with published clips. **Pays $75-300.**

Tips "The best way to begin working with *MovieMaker* is to send a list of 'pitches' along with your résumé and clips. As we receive a number of résumés each week, we want to get an early sense of not just your style of writing, but the kinds of subjects that interest you most as they relate to film. E-mail is the preferred method of correspondence, and please allow 2 months before following up on a query or résumé. Queries should be submitted in writing, rather than phone calls."

⊘ PREMIERE MAGAZINE

Hachette Filipacchi Magazines, 1633 Broadway, 41st Floor, New York NY 10019. (212)767-5400. Fax: (212)767-5450. Website: www.premiere.com. Magazine published 10 times/year.

- Does not buy freelance material or use freelance writers.

$ $⊠ RUE MORGUE

Horror in Culture & Entertainment, Marrs Media, Inc., 700 Queen St. E., Toronto ON M4M 1G9 Canada. E-mail: info@rue-morgue.com. Website: www.rue-morgue.com. Editor: Rod Gudino. Associate Editor: Mary Beth Hollyer. **Contact:** Jen Vuckovic, managing editor. **50% freelance written.** Bimonthly magazine covering horror entertainment. Estab. 1997. Pays on publication. Publishes ms an average of 4 months after acceptance. Byline given. Buys all rights. Editorial lead time 2 months. Submit seasonal material 4 months in advance. Accepts queries by e-mail. Responds in 6 weeks to queries; 2 months to mss. Writer's guidelines by e-mail.

Nonfiction Essays, exposé, historical/nostalgic, interview/profile, new product, travel. No fiction. Reviews done by staff writers. **Buys 10 mss/year.** Query with published clips or send complete ms. Length: 500-2,000 words. **Pays $75-300.**

Columns/Departments Classic Cut (historical essays on classic horror films, books, games, comic books, music), 500-700 words. **Buys 1-2 mss/year.** Query with published clips. **Pays $60.**

Tips "The editors are most responsive to special interest articles and analytical essays on cultural/historical topics relating to the horror genre—published examples: Leon Theremin, Soren Kierkegaard, Horror in Fine Art, Murderbilia."

⊘ SOAP OPERA DIGEST

Primedia Broad Reach Magazines, 216 Madison Ave., 10th Floor, New York NY 10016. Website: www.soapdigest.com. Weekly magazine for the daytime and primetime soap opera viewer. Circ. 1,040,142.

- Does not buy freelance material or use freelance writers.

$ $ $ $SOUND & VISION

Hachette Filipacchi Media U.S., Inc., 1633 Broadway, New York NY 10019. (212)767-6000. Fax: (212)767-5615. E-mail: soundandvision@hfmus.com. Website: www.soundandvisionmag.com. Editor-in-Chief: Bob Ankosko. Entertainment Editor: Ken Richardson. **Contact:** Michael Gaughn, features editor. **50% freelance written.** Published 10 times/year. Provides readers with authoritative information on the entertainment technologies and products that will impact their lives. Estab. 1958. Circ. 400,000. **Pays on acceptance.** Publishes ms an average of 4 months after acceptance. Byline given. Buys first North American serial, electronic rights. Accepts queries by mail, e-mail, fax. Sample copy for 9×12 SAE and 11 first-class stamps.

Nonfiction Home theater, audio, video and multimedia equipment plus movie, music, and video game reviews, how-to-buy and how-to-use A/V gear, interview/profile. **Buys 25 mss/year.** Query with published clips. Length: 1,500-3,000 words. **Pays $1,000-1,500.**

Tips "Send proposals or outlines, rather than complete articles, along with published clips to establish writing ability. Publisher assumes no responsibility for return or safety of unsolicited art, photos, or manuscripts."

N ⊘ STAR MAGAZINE

American Media, Inc., 1000 American Media Way, Boca Raton FL 33464. E-mail: letters@starmagazine.com. Website: www.starmagazine.com..

- Query before submitting.

$ $ TAKE ONE

Film & Television in Canada, Canadian Independent Film & Television Publishing Association, 252-128 Danforth Ave., Toronto ON M4K 1N1 Canada. (416)944-1096. Fax: (416)465-4356. E-mail: editor@takeonemagazine.ca. Website: www.takeonemagazine.ca. **Contact:** Wyndham Wise, editor-in-chief. **100% freelance written.** Quarterly magazine covering Canadian film and television. *"Take One* is a special interest magazine that focuses exclusively on Canadian cinema, filmmakers, and Canadian television." Estab. 1992. Circ. 5,000/issue. Pays on publication. Publishes ms an average of 2 months after acceptance. Byline given. Offers 50% kill fee. Buys one-time, electronic rights. Editorial lead time 3 months. Submit seasonal material 3 months in advance. Accepts queries by mail, e-mail, fax, phone. Sample copy online.

Nonfiction Essays, historical/nostalgic, interview/profile, opinion. Query. Length: 2,000-4,000 words. **Pays 12¢/word.** Sometimes pays expenses of writers on assignment.

N $ TELE REVISTA

Su Mejor Amiga, Teve Latino Publishing, Inc., P.O. Box 142179, Coral Gables FL 33114-5170. (305)445-1755. Fax: (305)445-3907. E-mail: info@telerevista.com. Website: www.telerevista.com. **Contact:** Ana Pereiro, editor. **100% freelance written.** Monthly magazine covering Hispanic entertainment (US and Puerto Rico). "We feature interviews, gossip, breaking stories, behind-the-scenes happenings, etc." Estab. 1986. Pays on publication. Publishes ms an average of 3 months after acceptance. Byline sometimes given. Buys all rights. Editorial lead time 2 months. Submit seasonal material 3 months in advance. Accepts queries by mail, e-mail, fax. Sample copy for free.

Nonfiction Exposé, interview/profile, opinion, photo feature. **Buys 200 mss/year.** Query. **Pays $25-75.**

Photos State availability of or send photos with submission. Buys all rights. Negotiates payment individually. Captions required.

Columns/Departments Buys 60 mss/year. Query. **Pays $25-75.**

Fillers Anecdotes, facts, gags to be illustrated by cartoonist, newsbreaks, short humor.

⊘ TV GUIDE

Gemstar- TV Guide Ineternational, Inc., 1211 Avenue of The Americas, 4th Floor, New York NY 10036. (212)852-7500. Fax: (212)852-7470. Website: www.tv.guide.com. Editor: Steve Sonsky. Weekly magazine. Focuses on all aspects of network, cable, and pay television programming and how it affects and reflects audiences. Circ. 9,097,762. Editorial lead time 2 months. Sample copy not available.

- Does not buy freelance material or use freelance writers.

⊘ VARIETY

Reed Business Information, 5700 Wilshire Blvd., Suite 120, Los Angeles CA 90036. (323)965-4476. Fax: (323)857-0494. E-mail: news@reedbusiness.com. Website: www.variety.com. Editor-in-Chief: Peter Bart. Deputy Editor: Elizabeth Guider. Weekly magazine. Circ. 34,000.

- Does not buy freelance material or use freelance writers.

XXL MAGAZINE

Harris Publications, 1115 Broadway, 8th Floor, New York NY 10010. (212)807-7100. Fax: (212)620-7787. E-mail: xxl@harris-pub.com. Website: www.xxlmag.com. Publisher: Dennis S. Page. Editor-in-Chief: Elliott Wilson. **Contact:** Juleyka Lantigua, managing editor; Vanessa Satten, deputy editor; Dave Bry, features editor; Bonsu Thompson, music editor; Leah Rose, associate music editor; Jermaine Hall, contributing editor. **50% freelance written.** Monthly magazine. *"XXL* is hip-hop on a higher level, an upscale urban lifestyle magazine." Estab. 1997. Circ. 350,000. Pays on publication. Byline given. Buys all rights. Editorial lead time 2 months. Submit seasonal material 3 months in advance. Accepts queries by mail.

Nonfiction Interview/profile, music, entertainment, luxury materialism. Query with published clips. Length: 200-5,000 words.

Photos State availability with submission. Reviews contact sheets, transparencies, prints. Captions, model releases required.

Tips Please send clips, query, and cover letter by mail.

ETHNIC & MINORITY

$AIM MAGAZINE

Aim Publishing Co., P.O. Box 1174, Maywood IL 60153. (708)344-4414. Fax: (206)543-2746. E-mail: mapilado@ aol.com. Website: aimmagazine.org. **Contact:** Dr. Myron Apilado, editor. **75% freelance written.** Works with a small number of new/unpublished writers each year. Quarterly magazine on social betterment that promotes racial harmony and peace for high school, college, and general audience. Publishes material "to purge racism from the human bloodstream through the written word." Estab. 1975. Circ. 10,000. Pays on publication. Publishes ms an average of 3 months after acceptance. Byline given. Offers 60% kill fee. Buys first, one-time rights. Submit seasonal material 6 months in advance. Accepts queries by mail, e-mail. Accepts simultaneous submissions. Responds in 2 months to queries; 1 month to mss. Sample copy and writer's guidelines for $4 and 9×12 SAE with $1.70 postage or online.

Nonfiction Exposé (education), general interest (social significance), historical/nostalgic (Black or Indian), how-to (create a more equitable society), interview/profile (one who is making social contributions to community), book reviews, reviews of plays. No religious material. **Buys 16 mss/year.** Send complete ms. Length: 500-800 words. **Pays $25-35.**

Photos Reviews b&w prints. Captions, identification of subjects required.

Fiction Ruth Apilado, associate editor. "Fiction that teaches the brotherhood of man." Ethnic, historical, mainstream, suspense. Open. No religious mss. **Buys 20 mss/year.** Send complete ms. Length: 1,000-1,500 words. **Pays $25-35.**

Poetry Avant-garde, free verse, light verse. No "preachy" poetry. **Buys 20 poems/year.** Submit maximum 5 poems. Length: 15-30 lines. **Pays $3-5.**

Fillers Anecdotes, newsbreaks, short humor. **Buys 30/year.** Length: 50-100 words. **Pays $5.**

Tips "Interview anyone of any age who unselfishly is making an unusual contribution to the lives of less fortunate individuals. Include photo and background of person. We look at the nations of the world as part of one family. Short stories and historical pieces about Blacks and Indians are the areas most open to freelancers. Subject matter of submission is of paramount concern for us rather than writing style. Articles and stories showing the similarity in the lives of people with different racial backgrounds are desired."

$ $AMBASSADOR MAGAZINE

National Italian American Foundation, 186019 St. NW, Washington DC 20009. (202)387-0600. Fax: (202)387-0800. E-mail: kevin@niaf.org. Website: www.niaf.org. **Contact:** Kevin Heitz. **50% freelance written.** Magazine for Italian-Americans covering Italian-American history and culture. "We publish nonfiction articles on little-known events in Italian-American history and articles on Italian-American culture, traditions, and personalities living and dead." Estab. 1989. Circ. 25,000. Pays on approval of final draft. Byline given. Offers $50 kill fee. Buys second serial (reprint) rights. Editorial lead time 3 months. Accepts queries by mail, e-mail, fax. Accepts previously published material. Accepts simultaneous submissions. Responds in 2 months to queries. Sample copy and writer's guidelines free.

Nonfiction Historical/nostalgic, interview/profile, photo feature. **Buys 12 mss/year.** Send complete ms. Length: 1,500-2,000 words. **Pays $250.**

Photos Send photos with submission. Reviews contact sheets, prints. Buys one-time rights. Offers no additional payment for photos accepted with ms. Captions, identification of subjects required.

Tips "Good photos, clear prose, and a good storytelling ability are all prerequisites."

$ CELTIC HERITAGE

Clansman Publishing, Ltd., P.O. Box 8805, Station A, Halifax NS B3K 5M4 Canada. (902)835-6244. Fax: (902)835-0080. E-mail: celtic@hfx.eastlink.ca. Website: www.celticheritage.ns.ca. **Contact:** Alexa Thompson, managing editor. **95% freelance written.** Bimonthly magazine covering culture of North Americans of Celtic descent. "The magazine chronicles the stories of Celtish people who have settled in North America, with a focus on the stories of those who are not mentioned in history books. We also feature Gaelic language articles, history of Celtic people, traditions, music, and folklore. We profile Celtic musicians and include reviews of Celtic books, music, and videos." Estab. 1987. Circ. 8,000 (per issue). Pays 1 month after publication. Publishes ms an average of 2 months after acceptance. Byline given. Buys all rights. Editorial lead time 2 months. Submit seasonal material 3 months in advance. Accepts queries by mail, e-mail, fax, phone. Accepts previously published material. Responds in 1 week to queries; 1 month to mss. Sample copy for free. Writer's guidelines online.

Nonfiction Essays, general interest, historical/nostalgic, interview/profile, opinion, personal experience, travel, Gaelic language, Celtic music reviews, profiles of Celtic musicians, Celtic history, traditions, and folklore. No fiction, poetry, historical stories already well publicized. **Buys 100 mss/year.** Query or send complete ms.

Length: 800-2,500 words. **Pays $50-75 (Canadian). All writers receive a complimentary subscription.** ''We have, on rare occasion, run an advertisement for a writer in lieu of payment.''

Photos State availability with submission. Reviews 35mm transparencies, 5×7 prints, JPEG files (200 dpi). ''We do not pay for photographs.'' Captions, identification of subjects, model releases required.

Columns/Departments Query. **Pays $50-75 (Canadian).**

Fillers Anecdotes, facts. **Buys 2-3/year.** Length: 300-500 words. **Pays $30-50 (canadian).**

Tips ''The easiest way to get my attention is to submit a query by e-mail. We are so short staffed that we do not have much time to start a correspondence by regular post.''

N $ $ ESTYLO MAGAZINE

Mandalay Publishing, 3600 Wilshire Blvd., Suite 1903, Los Angeles CA 90010. (213)383-6300. Fax: (213)632-2666. E-mail: info@estylo.com. Editor: Linda Cauthen. **25% freelance written.** Magazine published 10 times/year covering fashion, beauty and entertainment for the affluent and mobile Latina. ''It contains a variety of features and departments devoted to cuisine, fitness, beauty, fashion and entertainment topics. Particularly interested in celebrity interviews.'' Estab. 1997. Circ. 160,000. Pays on publication. Publishes ms an average of 2 months after acceptance. Byline given. Buys first rights. Editorial lead time 3 months. Submit seasonal material 4 months in advance. Accepts queries by mail, e-mail. Accepts simultaneous submissions.

- E-mail queries preferred.

Photos State availability with submission. Reviews contact sheets. Buys all rights. Negotiates payment individually. Captions, identification of subjects, model releases required.

$ FILIPINAS

A Magazine for All Filipinos, Filipinas Publishing, Inc., 1486 Huntington Ave., Suite 300, South San Francisco CA 94080. (650)872-8650. Fax: (650)872-8651. E-mail: editorial@filipinasmag.com. Website: www.filipinasmag.com. **Contact:** Mona Lisa Yuchengco, editor/publisher. Monthly magazine focused on Filipino-American affairs. ''*Filipinas* answers the lack of mainstream media coverage of Filipinos in America. It targets both Filipino immigrants and American-born Filipinos, gives in-depth coverage of political, social, and cultural events in the Philippines and in the Filipino-American community. Features role models, history, travel, food and leisure, issues, and controversies.'' Estab. 1992. Circ. 40,000. Pays on publication. Publishes ms an average of 5 months after acceptance. Byline given. Offers $10 kill fee. Buys first, all rights. Editorial lead time 2 months. Submit seasonal material 4 months in advance. Accepts queries by mail, e-mail, fax. Responds in 3 weeks to queries; 5 months to mss. Writer's guidelines for 9½×4 SASE or on website.

- Unsolicited mss will not be paid.
- Break in with ''a good idea outlined well in the query letter. Also, tenacity is key. If one idea is shot down, come up with another.''

Nonfiction Interested in seeing ''more issue-oriented pieces, unusual topics regarding Filipino-Americans, and stories from the Midwest and other parts of the country other than the coasts.'' Exposé, general interest, historical/nostalgic, inspirational, interview/profile, opinion, personal experience, travel. No academic papers. **Buys 80-100 mss/year.** Query with published clips. Length: 800-1,500 words. **Pays $50-75.**

Photos State availability with submission. Reviews 2¼×2¼ and 4×5 transparencies. Offers $15-25/photo. Captions, identification of subjects required.

Columns/Departments Cultural Currents (Filipino traditions and beliefs), 1,000 words; New Voices (first-person essays by Filipino Americans ages 10-25), 800 words; First Person (open to all Filipinos), 800 words. Query with published clips. **Pays $50-75.**

$ $ GERMAN LIFE

Zeitgeist Publishing, Inc., 1068 National Hwy., LaVale MD 21502. (301)729-6190. Fax: (301)729-1720. E-mail: mslider@germanlife.com. Website: www.germanlife.com. **Contact:** Mark Slider, editor. **50% freelance written.** Bimonthly magazine covering German-speaking Europe. ''*German Life* is for all interested in the diversity of German-speaking culture—past and present—and in the various ways that the US (and North America in general) has been shaped by its German immigrants. The magazine is dedicated to solid reporting on cultural, historical, social, and political events.'' Estab. 1994. Circ. 40,000. Pays on publication. Byline given. Buys first North American serial rights. Editorial lead time 4 months. Submit seasonal material 6 months in advance. Accepts queries by mail, e-mail. Responds in 2 months to queries; 3 months to mss. Sample copy for $4.95 and SAE with 4 first-class stamps. Writer's guidelines online.

Nonfiction General interest, historical/nostalgic, interview/profile, photo feature, travel. Special issues: Oktoberfest-related (October); Seasonal Relative to Germany, Switzerland, or Austria (December); Travel to German-speaking Europe (April). **Buys 50 mss/year.** Query with published clips. Length: 800-1,500 words. **Pays $200-500 for assigned articles; $200-350 for unsolicited articles.**

Photos State availability with submission. Reviews color transparencies, 5×7 color or b&w prints. Buys one-time rights. Offers no additional payment for photos accepted with ms. Identification of subjects required.

Columns/Departments German-Americana (regards specific German-American communities, organizations, and/or events past or present), 1,200 words; Profile (portrays prominent Germans, Americans, or German-Americans), 1,000 words; At Home (cuisine, etc. relating to German-speaking Europe), 800 words; Library (reviews of books, videos, CDs, etc.), 300 words. **Buys 30 mss/year.** Query with published clips. **Pays $50-150.**

Fillers Facts, newsbreaks. Length: 100-300 words. **Pays $50-150.**

Tips "The best queries include several informative proposals. Writers should avoid overemphasizing autobiographical experiences/stories."

$ HERITAGE FLORIDA JEWISH NEWS

207 O'Brien Rd., Suite 101, Fern Park FL 32730. (407)834-8787. E-mail: heritagefl@aol.com. Website: www.heritagefl.com. **Contact:** Lyn Payne, associate editor. **20% freelance written.** Weekly tabloid on Jewish subjects of local, national and international scope, except for special issues. "Covers news of local, national and international scope of interest to Jewish readers and not likely to be found in other publications." Estab. 1976. Circ. 3,500. Pays on publication. Byline given. Buys first North American serial, first, one-time, second serial (reprint), simultaneous rights. Submit seasonal material 3 months in advance. Accepts queries by e-mail. Accepts previously published material. Responds in 1 month to queries. Sample copy for $1 and 9 × 12 SASE.

Nonfiction "Especially needs articles for these annual issues: Rosh Hashanah, Financial, Chanukah, Celebration (wedding and bar mitzvah), Passover, Health and Fitness, House and Home, Back to School, Travel and Savvy Seniors. No fiction, poems, first-person experiences." General interest, interview/profile, opinion, photo feature, religious, travel. **Buys 50 mss/year.** Send query only. Length: 500-1,000 words. **Pays 75¢/column inch.**

Reprints Send ms with rights for sale noted.

Photos State availability with submission. Reviews 8 × 10 prints. Buys one-time rights. Offers $5/photo. Captions, identification of subjects required.

$ HORIZONS

The Jewish Family Journal, Targum Press, 22700 W. Eleven Mile Rd., Southfield MI 48034. Fax: (888)298-9992. E-mail: horizons@netvision.net.il. Website: www.targum.com. Managing Editor: Moshe Dombey. **Contact:** Miriam Zakon, chief editor. **100% freelance written.** Quarterly magazine covering the Orthodox Jewish family. "We include fiction and nonfiction, memoirs, essays, historical, and informational articles—all of interest to the Orthodox Jew." Estab. 1994. Circ. 5,000. Pays 4-6 weeks after publication. Publishes ms an average of 6 months after acceptance. Byline given. Buys one-time rights. Editorial lead time 6 months. Submit seasonal material 8 months in advance. Accepts queries by mail, e-mail, fax. Accepts simultaneous submissions. Responds in 1 week to queries; 2 months to mss. Writer's guidelines available.

Nonfiction Essays, historical/nostalgic, humor, inspirational, interview/profile, opinion, personal experience, photo feature, travel. **Buys 150 mss/year.** Send complete ms. Length: 350-3,000 words. **Pays $5-150.**

Photos State availability with submission. Buys one-time rights. Offers no additional payment for photos accepted with ms.

Fiction Historical, humorous, mainstream, slice-of-life vignettes. Nothing not suitable to Orthodox Jewish values. **Buys 10-15 mss/year.** Send complete ms. Length: 300-3,000 words. **Pays $20-100.**

Poetry Free verse, haiku, light verse, traditional. **Buys 30-35 poems/year.** Submit maximum 4 poems. Length: 3-28 lines. **Pays $5-10.**

Fillers Anecdotes, short humor. **Buys 20/year.** Length: 50-120 words. **Pays $5.**

Tips "*Horizons* publishes for the Orthodox Jewish market and therefore only accepts articles that are of interest to this market. We do not accept submissions dealing with political issues or Jewish legal issues. The tone is light and friendly and we therefore do not accept submissions that are of a scholarly nature. Our writers must be very familiar with our market. Anything that is not suitable for our readership doesn't stand a chance, no matter how high its literary merit."

$ INTERNATIONAL EXAMINER

622 S. Washington, Seattle WA 98104. (206)624-3925. Fax: (206)624-3046. E-mail: editor@iexaminer.org. Website: www.iexaminer.org. **Contact:** Nhien Nguyen, managing editor. **75% freelance written.** Biweekly journal of Asian-American news, politics, and arts. "We write about Asian-American issues and things of interest to Asian-Americans. We do not want stuff about Asian things (stories on your trip to China, Japanese Tea Ceremony, etc. will be rejected). Yes, we are in English." Estab. 1974. Circ. 12,000. Pays on publication. Publishes ms an average of 1 month after acceptance. Buys one-time rights. Editorial lead time 1 month. Submit seasonal material 2 months in advance. Accepts simultaneous submissions. Writer's guidelines for #10 SASE.

Nonfiction Essays, exposé, general interest, historical/nostalgic, humor, interview/profile, opinion, personal experience, photo feature. **Buys 100 mss/year.** Query by mail, fax, or e-mail with published clips. Length: 750-

5,000 words depending on subject. **Pays $25-100.** Sometimes pays expenses of writers on assignment.

Reprints Accepts previously published submissions (as long as not published in same area). Send typed ms with rights for sale noted and information about when and where the material previously appeared. Payment negotiable.

Photos State availability with submission. Reviews contact sheets. Buys one-time rights. Negotiates payment individually. Captions, identification of subjects required.

Fiction Asian-American authored fiction by or about Asian-Americans. Novel excerpts. **Buys 1-2 mss/year.** Query.

Tips "Write decent, suitable material on a subject of interest to the Asian-American community. All submissions are reviewed; all good ones are contacted. It helps to call and run an idea by the editor before or after sending submissions."

$ $ ITALIAN AMERICA

Official Publication of the Order Sons of Italy in America, 219 E St. NE, Washington DC 20002. (202)547-2900. Fax: (202)546-8168. E-mail: ddesanctis@osia.org. Website: www.osia.org. **Contact:** Dr. Dona De Sanctis, editor/deputy executive director. **20% freelance written.** Quarterly magazine. "*Italian America* provides timely information about OSIA, while reporting on individuals, institutions, issues, and events of current or historical significance in the Italian-American community." Estab. 1996. Circ. 65,000. Pays on publication. Publishes ms an average of 3 months after acceptance. Byline given. Offers 50% kill fee. Buys worldwide nonexclusive rights. Editorial lead time 3 months. Accepts queries by mail, e-mail, fax. Accepts simultaneous submissions. Sample copy for free. Writer's guidelines online.

Nonfiction Historical/nostalgic (little known historical facts that must relate to Italian Americans), interview/profile, opinion, current events. **Buys 8 mss/year.** Query with published clips. Length: 750-1,000 words. **Pays $50-250.**

Tips "We pay particular attention to the quality of graphics that accompany the stories. We are interested in little known facts about historical/cultural Italian America."

$ $ JEWISH ACTION

Union of Orthodox Jewish Congregations of America, 11 Broadway, New York NY 10004. (212)613-8146. Fax: (212)613-0646. E-mail: ja@ou.org. Website: www.ou.org. Editor: Nechama Carmel. **Contact:** Dassi Zeidel, assistant editor. **80% freelance written.** Quarterly magazine covering a vibrant approach to Jewish issues, Orthodox lifestyle, and values. Circ. 40,000. Pays 2 months after publication. Byline given. Not copyrighted. Submit seasonal material 4 months in advance. Responds in 3 months to queries. Sample copy online. Writer's guidelines for #10 SASE or by e-mail.

- Prefers queries by e-mail. Mail and fax OK.
- O—n Break in with a query for "Just Between Us" column.

Nonfiction Current Jewish issues, history, biography, art, inspirational, humor, music, book reviews. "We are not looking for Holocaust accounts. We welcome essays about responses to personal or societal challenges." **Buys 30-40 mss/year.** Query with published clips. Length: 1,000-3,000 words. **Pays $100-400 for assigned articles; $75-150 for unsolicited articles.**

Photos Send photos with submission. Identification of subjects required.

Columns/Departments Just Between Us (personal opinion on current Jewish life and issues), 1,000 words. **Buys 4 mss/year.**

Fiction Must have relevance to Orthodox reader. Length: 1,000-2,000 words.

Poetry Buys limited number of poems/year. Pays $25-75.

Tips "Remember that your reader is well educated and has a strong commitment to Orthodox Judaism. Articles on the holidays, Israel, and other common topics should offer a fresh insight. Because the magazine is a quarterly, we do not generally publish articles which concern specific timely events."

$ KHABAR

The Community Magazine, Khabar, Inc., 3790 Holcomb Bridge Rd., Suite 101, Norcross GA 30092. (770)451-7666. Fax: (770)234-6115. E-mail: parthiv@khabar.com. Website: www.khabar.com. **Contact:** Parthiv N. Parekh, editor. **50% freelance written.** Monthly magazine covering the Asian and Indian community in Georgia. "Content relating to Indian-American and/or immigrant experience." Estab. 1992. Circ. 14,000. Pays on publication. Publishes ms an average of 2 months after acceptance. Offers 35% kill fee. Buys one-time, second serial (reprint), simultaneous, electronic rights. Editorial lead time 2 months. Submit seasonal material 2 months in advance. Accepts queries by mail, e-mail. Accepts previously published material. Accepts simultaneous submissions. Sample copy for free. Writer's guidelines by e-mail.

Nonfiction Essays, interview/profile, opinion, personal experience, travel. **Buys 5 mss/year.** Query with or without published clips or send complete ms. Length: 750-4,000 words. **Pays $50-125 for assigned articles; $25-100 for unsolicited articles.**

Reprints Accepts previously published submissions.

Photos State availability of or send photos with submission. Negotiates payment individually. Captions, identification of subjects required.

Columns/Departments Book Review, 1,200 words; Music Review, 800 words; Spotlight (profiles), 1,200-3,000 words. **Buys 5 mss/year.** Query with or without published clips or send complete ms. **Pays $25-100.**

Fiction Ethnic. **Buys 5 mss/year.** Query with or without published clips or send complete ms. **Pays $25-100.**

Tips "Ask for our 'content guidelines' document by e-mail or otherwise by writing to us."

$ $ $ $ LATINA MAGAZINE

Latina Media Ventures, 1500 Broadway, 7th Floor, New York NY 10036. (212)642-0200. E-mail: editor@latina.com. Website: www.latina.com. **40-50% freelance written.** Monthly magazine covering Latina lifestyle. "*Latina Magazine* is the leading bilingual lifestyle publication for Hispanic women in the US today. Covering the best of Latino fashion, beauty, culture, and food, the magazine also features celebrity profiles and interviews." Estab. 1996. Circ. 250,000. Pays on publication. Publishes ms an average of 2-3 months after acceptance. Byline given. Offers 25% kill fee. Buys first, second serial (reprint), electronic rights. Editorial lead time 3 months. Submit seasonal material 4-5 months in advance. Accepts queries by e-mail. Responds in 1 month to queries; 1-2 months to mss. Sample copy online.

- Editors are in charge of their individual sections and pitches should be made directly to them. Do not make pitches directly to the editor-in-chief or the editorial director as they will only be routed to the relevant section editor.

Nonfiction Essays, how-to, humor, inspirational, interview/profile, new product, personal experience. Special issues: The 10 Latinas Who Changed the World (December). "We do not feature an extensive amount of celebrity content or entertainment content, and freelancers should be sensitive to this. The magazine does not contain book or album reviews, and we do not write stories covering an artist's new project. We do not attend press junkets and do not cover press conferences. Please note that we are a lifestyle magazine, not an entertainment magazine." **Buys 15-20 mss/year.** Query with published clips. Length: 300-2,200 words. **Pays $1/word.** Pays expenses of writers on assignment.

Photos State availability with submission. Reviews contact sheets, transparencies, GIF/JPEG files. Buys one-time rights. Negotiates payment individually. Identification of subjects required.

Tips "*Latina*'s features cover a wide gamut of topics, including fashion, beauty, wellness, and personal essays. The magazine runs a wide variety of features on news and service topics (from the issues affecting Latina adolescents to stories dealing with anger). If you are going to make a pitch, please keep the following things in mind. All pitches should include statistics or some background reporting that demonstrates why a developing trend is important. Also, give examples of women who can provide a personal perspective. Profiles and essays need to have a strong personal journey angle. We will not cover someone just because they are Hispanic. When pitching stories about a particular person, please let us know the following: timeliness (Is this someone who is somehow tied to breaking news events? Has their story been heard?); the 'wow' factor (Why is this person remarkable? What elements make this story a standout? What sets your subject apart from other women?); target our audience (please note that the magazine targets acculturated, English-dominant Latina women between the ages of 18-39)."

$ $ $ MOMENT

The Magazine of Jewish Culture, Politics and Religion, 4115 Wisconsin Ave. NW, Suite 102, Washington DC 20016. (202)364-3300. Fax: (202)364-2636. E-mail: editor@momentmag.com. Website: www.momentmag.com. **90% freelance written.** Bimonthly magazine. "*Moment* is an independent Jewish bimonthly general interest magazine that specializes in cultural, political, historical, religious, and lifestyle articles relating chiefly to the North American Jewish community and Israel." Estab. 1975. Circ. 65,000. Pays on publication. Publishes ms an average of 6 months after acceptance. Byline given. Buys first North American serial rights. Editorial lead time 3 months. Submit seasonal material 6 months in advance. Accepts queries by mail, e-mail, fax. Accepts simultaneous submissions. Responds in 1 month to queries; 3 months to mss. Sample copy for $4.50 and SAE. Writer's guidelines online.

Nonfiction "We look for meaty, colorful, thought-provoking features and essays on Jewish trends and Israel. We occasionally publish book excerpts, memoirs, and profiles." **Buys 25-30 mss/year.** Query with published clips. Length: 2,500-7,000 words. **Pays $200-1,200 for assigned articles; $40-500 for unsolicited articles.**

Photos State availability with submission. Buys one-time rights. Negotiates payment individually. Identification of subjects required.

Columns/Departments 5765 (snappy pieces about quirky events in Jewish communities, news and ideas to improve Jewish living), 250 words maximum; Olam (first-person pieces, humor, and colorful reportage), 600-1,500 words; Book reviews (fiction and nonfiction) are accepted but generally assigned, 400-800 words. **Buys 30 mss/year.** Query with published clips. **Pays $50-250.**

Tips "Stories for *Moment* are usually assigned, but unsolicited manuscripts are often selected for publication. Successful features offer readers an in-depth journalistic treatment of an issue, phenomenon, institution, or individual. The more the writer can follow the principle of 'show, don't tell,' the better. The majority of the submissions we receive are about The Holocaust and Israel. A writer has a better chance of having an idea accepted if it is not on these subjects."

$ $ NA'AMAT WOMAN

Magazine of NA'AMAT USA, The Women's Labor Zionist Organization of America, 350 Fifth Ave., Suite 4700, New York NY 10118. (212)563-5222. Fax: (212)563-5710. **Contact:** Judith A. Sokoloff, editor. **80% freelance written.** Magazine published 4 times/year covering Jewish themes and issues, Israel, women's issues, and social and political issues. "Magazine covering a wide variety of subjects of interest to the Jewish community—including political and social issues, arts, profiles, and many articles about Israel and women's issues. Fiction must have a Jewish theme. Readers are the American Jewish community." Estab. 1926. Circ. 20,000. Pays on publication. Byline given. Buys first North American serial, first, one-time, second serial (reprint) rights, makes work-for-hire assignments. Accepts queries by mail, fax. Responds in 3 months. Sample copy for $9 \times 11\frac{1}{2}$ SAE and $1.20 postage. Writer's guidelines for #10 SASE.

Nonfiction "All articles must be of particular interest to the Jewish community." Exposé, general interest (Jewish), historical/nostalgic, interview/profile, opinion, personal experience, photo feature, travel, art, music, social, and political issues, Israel. **Buys 20 mss/year.** Query with or without published clips or send complete ms. **Pays 10-15¢/word.**

Photos State availability with submission. Buys one-time rights. Pays $25-55 for 4×5 or 5×7 prints. Captions, identification of subjects required.

Columns/Departments Buys 20 mss/year. Query with published clips or send complete ms. **Pays 10¢/word.**

Fiction "Intelligent fiction with Jewish slant. No maudlin nostalgia or trite humor." Ethnic, historical, humorous, novel excerpts, women-oriented. **Buys 3 mss/year.** Query with published clips or send complete ms. Length: 2,000-3,000 words. **Pays 10¢/word and 2 contributor's copies.**

$ $ NATIVE PEOPLES MAGAZINE

5333 N. 7th St., Suite C-224, Phoenix AZ 85014. (602)265-4855. Fax: (602)265-3113. E-mail: dgibson@nativepeoples.com. Website: www.nativepeoples.com. **Contact:** Daniel Gibson, editor. Bimonthly magazine covering Native Americans. "High-quality reproduction with full color throughout. The primary purpose of this magazine is to offer a sensitive portrayal of the arts and lifeways of Native peoples of the Americas." Estab. 1987. Circ. 50,000. Pays on publication. Byline given. Buys one-time rights. Accepts queries by mail, e-mail, fax. Responds in 2 months to queries. Writer's guidelines online.

Nonfiction Pathways (travel section) and Viewpoint (opinion) most open to freelancers. Looking for articles on educational, economic and political development; occasional historic pieces; Native events. Interview/profile (of interesting and leading Natives from all walks of life, with an emphasis on arts), personal experience. **Buys 35 mss/year.** Query with published clips. Length: 1,000-2,500 words. **Pays 25¢/word.**

Photos State availability with submission. Reviews transparencies, prefers 35mm slides. Also accepts high resolution electronic photo images. Inquire for details. Buys one-time rights. Offers $45-150/page rates, $250/ cover photos. Identification of subjects required.

Tips "We are focused upon authenticity and a positive portrayal of present-day Native American life and cultural practices. Our stories portray role models of Native people, young and old, with a sense of pride in their heritage and culture. Therefore, it is important that the Native American point of view be incorporated in each story."

$ $ RUSSIAN LIFE

RIS Publications, P.O. Box 567, Montpelier VT 05601. (802)223-4955. Fax: (802)223-6105. Website: www.rispubs.com. Editor: Lina Rozovskya. **Contact:** Paul Richardson, publisher. **75% freelance written.** Bimonthly magazine covering Russian culture, history, travel, and business. "Our readers are informed Russophiles with an avid interest in all things Russian. But we do not publish personal travel journals or the like." Estab. 1956. Circ. 15,000. Pays on publication. Publishes ms an average of 3-6 months after acceptance. Byline given. Offers $25 kill fee. Buys first rights. Editorial lead time 2 months. Submit seasonal material 3 months in advance. Accepts queries by mail. Accepts previously published material. Responds in 1 month to queries. Sample copy for 9×12 SAE and 6 first-class stamps. Writer's guidelines online.

O→ Break in with a "good travel essay piece covering remote regions of Russia."

Nonfiction General interest, photo feature, travel. No personal stories, i.e., "How I came to love Russia." **Buys 15-20 mss/year.** Query. Length: 1,000-6,000 words. **Pays $100-300.**

Reprints Accepts previously published submissions

Photos Send photos with submission. Reviews contact sheets. Buys one-time rights. Negotiates payment individually. Captions required.

▣ The online magazine carries original content not found in the print editions.
Tips "A straightforward query letter with writing sample or manuscript (not returnable) enclosed."

$ $ SCANDINAVIAN REVIEW

The American-Scandinavian Foundation, 58 Park Ave., New York NY 10016. (212)879-9779. E-mail: editor@am scan.org. Website: www.amscan.org. **75% freelance written.** Triannual magazine for contemporary Scandinavia. Audience: Members, embassies, consulates, libraries. Slant: Popular coverage of contemporary affairs in Scandinavia. Estab. 1913. Circ. 4,000. Pays on publication. Publishes ms an average of 2 months after acceptance. Byline given. Buys first North American serial, second serial (reprint) rights. Editorial lead time 3 months. Submit seasonal material 3 months in advance. Accepts previously published material. Responds in 6 weeks to queries. Sample copy online. Writer's guidelines free.
Nonfiction General interest, interview/profile, photo feature, travel (must have Scandinavia as topic focus). Special issues: Scandinavian travel. No pornography. **Buys 30 mss/year.** Query with published clips. Length: 1,500-2,000 words. **Pays $300 maximum.**
Photos Reviews 3×5 transparencies, prints. Buys one-time rights. Pays $25-50/photo; negotiates payment individually. Captions required.

$ TODAY'S LATINO MAGAZINE

217 N. Broad St., Middletown DE 19709. (302)376-1129. Fax: (302)376-1129. E-mail: info@todayslatino.com. Website: www.todayslatino.com. Managing Editor: Hector Correa. **Contact:** Milton Delgado, editor. **80% freelance written.** Quarterly magazine covering issues and stories affecting latinos. "We seek to inform, educate, and entertain the upwardly mobile Latino and English speaking people interested in our rich culture and language." Estab. 2003. Circ. 7,000. Pays on publication. Publishes ms an average of 2 months after acceptance. Byline given. Buys one-time rights. Editorial lead time 1 month. Submit seasonal material 2 months in advance. Accepts queries by mail, e-mail, phone. Accepts previously published material. Sample copy and writer's guidelines free.
Nonfiction Length: 500-1,500 words. **Pays $75-125.** Sometimes pays expenses of writers on assignment.
Photos Send photos with submission. Reviews TIFF/JPEG files. Buys one-time rights. Pays $25-100. Captions, identification of subjects, model releases required.
Columns/Departments Politics; Celebrities; Travel, all 1,000 words. **Buys 10 mss/year.** Query with or without published clips. **Pays $75-125.**
Fiction Ethnic. Does not want vulgar, street urban. Buys 1 ms/year. Send complete ms.
Poetry Avant-garde, free verse, traditional. Does not want vulgar writing. **Buys 4 poems/year.** Submit maximum 4 poems. Length: 5-20 lines.
Fillers Anecdotes, facts, newsbreaks, short humor. **Buys 4/year.** Length: 500-750 words. **Pays $75-100.**
Tips "I really appreciate a professional writer who can write in English and Spanish, and whose style would be attractive for the professional Latino."

UPSCALE MAGAZINE

Bronner Brothers, 600 Bronner Brothers Way SW, Atlanta GA 30310. (404)758-7467. E-mail: features@upscalem ag.com. Website: www.upscalemagazine.com. Monthly magazine covering topics for "upscale African-American/black interests. *Upscale* offers to take the reader to the 'next level' of life's experience. Written for the black reader and consumer, *Upscale* provides information in the realms of business, news, lifestyle, fashion and beauty, and arts and entertainment." Estab. 1989. Circ. 250,000. Pays on publication. Publishes ms an average of 4 months after acceptance. Byline given. Offers 25% kill fee. Buys first North American serial rights. Editorial lead time 3-4 months. Accepts queries by mail. Accepts simultaneous submissions. Responds in 1 month to queries; 2 months to mss. Sample copy and writer's guidelines online.
Photos State availability with submission. Negotiates payment individually. Captions, identification of subjects, model releases required.
Columns/Departments News & Business (factual, current); Lifestyle (travel, home, wellness, etc.); Beauty & Fashion (tips, trends, upscale fashion, hair); and Arts & Entertainment (artwork, black celebrities, entertainment). **Buys 6-10 mss/year.** Query with published clips. **Payment different for each department.**
Tips "Make queries informative and exciting. Include entertaining clips. Be familiar with issues affecting black readers. Be able to write about them with ease and intelligence."

$ ▣ WINDSPEAKER

Aboriginal Multi-Media Society of Alberta, 13245-146 St., Edmonton AB T5L 4S8 Canada. (800)661-5469. Fax: (780)455-7639. E-mail: edwind@ammsa.com. Website: www.ammsa.com. **Contact:** Debora Steel, editor-in-chief. **25% freelance written.** Monthly tabloid covering native issues. "Focus on events and issues that affect and interest native peoples, national or local." Estab. 1983. Circ. 27,000. Pays on publication. Publishes ms an average of 1 month after acceptance. Byline given. Offers kill fee. Buys first rights. Editorial lead time 1 month. Submit seasonal material 2 months in advance. Accepts queries by mail, e-mail, phone. Accepts simultaneous submissions. Sample copy for free. Writer's guidelines online.

Nonfiction Opinion, photo feature, travel, news interview/profile, reviews: books, music, movies. Special issues: Powwow (June); Travel supplement (May). **Buys 200 mss/year.** Query with published clips and SASE or by phone. Length: 500-800 words. **Pays $3-3.60/published inch.** Sometimes pays expenses of writers on assignment.

Photos Send photos with submission. Buys one-time rights. Offers $25-100/photo. Will pay for film and processing. Identification of subjects required.

Tips ''Knowledge of Aboriginal culture and political issues is a great asset.''

FOOD & DRINK

BON APPETIT

America's Food and Entertaining Magazine, Conde Nast Publications, Inc., 4 Times Square, 15th Floor, New York NY 10036. (212)286-2106. Fax: (212)286-2363. Website: www.bonappetit.com. Editor-in-Chief: Barbara Fairchild. **Contact:** Victoria von Biel, executive editor. **50% freelance written.** Monthly magazine covering fine food, restaurants, and home entertaining. *''Bon Appetit* readers are upscale food enthusiasts and sophisticated travelers. They eat out often and entertain 4-6 times a month.'' Estab. 1975. Circ. 1,300,000. **Pays on acceptance.** Byline given. Buys all rights. Submit seasonal material 1 year in advance. Accepts queries by mail. Responds in 6 weeks to queries. Writer's guidelines for #10 SASE.

Nonfiction Travel (food-related), food feature, personal essays. ''No cartoons, quizzes, poetry, historic food features, or obscure food subjects.'' **Buys 50 mss/year.** Query with published clips. No phone calls or e-mails. Length: 150-2,000 words. **Pays $100 and up.** Pays expenses of writers on assignment.

Photos Never send photos.

Tips ''We are not generally interested in receiving specific queries, but we do look for new good writers. They must have a good knowledge of *Bon Appetit* and the related topics of food, travel and entertaining (as shown in accompanying clips). A light, lively style is a plus.''

⊘ COOK'S ILLUSTRATED

Boston Common Press, 17 Station St., Brookline MA 02445-7995. (617)232-1000. Fax: (617)232-1572. E-mail: cooks@bcpress.com. Website: cooksillustrated.com. Bimonthly magazine. Circ. 500,000.
  • Does not buy freelance material or use freelance writers.

⊘ FOOD & WINE

American Express Publishing Corp., 1120 Avenue of the Americas, 9th Floor, New York NY 10036. (212)382-5600. Fax: (212)764-2177. Website: www.foodandwine.com. **Contact:** Dana Cowin, editor-in-chief. Monthly magazine for the reader who enjoys the finer things in life. Editorial focuses on upscale dining, covering resturants, entertaining at home, and travel destinations. Circ. 964,000. Editorial lead time 6 months.
  • Does not buy freelance material or use freelance writers.

$ $HOME COOKING

House of White Birches, 306 E. Parr Rd., Berne IN 46711. (260)589-4000 ext. 337. Fax: (260)589-8093. E-mail: editor@homecookingmagazine.com. Website: www.homecookingmagazine.com. Associate Editor: Barb Sprunger. **Contact:** Alice Robinson and Judy Shaw, editors. **35% freelance written.** Bimonthly magazine. Circ. 58,000. Pays within 45 days of acceptance. Publishes ms an average of 4 months after acceptance. Byline given. Buys all rights. Editorial lead time 6 months. Submit seasonal material 6 months in advance. Accepts queries by mail, e-mail. Responds in 1 month to queries. Sample copy for 6×9 SAE and 5 first-class stamps.

Nonfiction How-to, humor, personal experience, recipes, all in food/cooking area. No health/fitness or travel articles. **Buys 36 mss/year.** Query or send complete ms. Length: 200-350 words, plus 6-10 recipes. **Pays $75-200 for assigned articles; $25-200 for unsolicited articles.**

Columns/Departments Pinch of Sage (hints for the home cook), 200-500 words; Kitchen Know-How, 250-1,000 words. **Buys 12 mss/year.** Query or send complete ms.

Tips ''You must request our writer's guidelines and editorial calendar for issue themes. We will gladly e-mail or mail them to you. Please follow our guidelines and schedule for all submissions.''

Ⓝ $ $KASHRUS MAGAZINE

The Bimonthly for the Kosher Consumer and the Trade, The Kashrus Institute, P.O. Box 204, Parkville Station, Brooklyn NY 11204. (718)336-8544. **Contact:** Rabbi Yosef Wikler, editor. **25% freelance written.** Prefers to work with published/established writers, but will work with new/unpublished writers. Bimonthly magazine covering the kosher food industry and food production. Estab. 1980. Circ. 10,000. Pays on publication. Publishes ms an average of 2 months after acceptance. Byline given. Offers 50% kill fee. Buys first, second serial (reprint) rights. Submit seasonal material 2 months in advance. Accepts queries by mail, phone. Accepts previously published material. Accepts simultaneous submissions. Responds in 1 week to queries; 2 weeks to mss. Sample copy for $2.

Nonfiction General interest, interview/profile, new product, personal experience, photo feature, religious, technical, travel. Special issues: International Kosher Travel (October); Passover Shopping Guide (March); Domestic Kosher Travel Guide (June). **Buys 8-12 mss/year.** Query with published clips. Length: 1,000-1,500 words. **Pays $100-250 for assigned articles; up to $100 for unsolicited articles.** Sometimes pays expenses of writers on assignment.

Reprints Send tearsheet or photocopy and information about when and where the material previously appeared. Pays 25-50% of amount paid for an original article.

Photos No guidelines; send samples or call. State availability with submission. Buys one-time rights. Offers no additional payment for photos accepted with ms.

Columns/Departments Book Review (cookbooks, food technology, kosher food), 250-500 words; People In the News (interviews with kosher personalities), 1,000-1,500 words; Regional Kosher Supervision (report on kosher supervision in a city or community), 1,000-1,500 words; Food Technology (new technology or current technology with accompanying pictures), 1,000-1,500 words; Travel (international, national—must include Kosher information and Jewish communities), 1,000-1,500 words; Regional Kosher Cooking, 1,000-1,500 words. **Buys 8-12 mss/year.** Query with published clips. **Pays $50-250.**

Tips *"Kashrus Magazine* will do more writing on general food technology, production, and merchandising as well as human interest travelogs and regional writing in 2005 than we have done in the past. Areas most open to freelancers are interviews, food technology, cooking and food preparation, dining, regional reporting, and travel, but we also feature healthy eating and lifestyles, redecorating, catering, and hospitals and health care. We welcome stories on the availability and quality of kosher foods and services in communities across the US and throughout the world. Some of our best stories have been by non-Jewish writers about kosher observance in their region. We also enjoy humorous articles. Just send a query with clips and we'll try to find a storyline that's right for you, or better yet, call us to discuss a storyline."

[N] SAVEUR

World Publications, Inc., 304 Park Ave. S., 8th Floor, New York NY 10010. (212)219-7400. Website: www.saveur.com. Magazine published 8 times/year covering exotic foods. Written for sophisticated, upscale lovers of food, wine, travel, and adventure. Estab. 1994. Circ. 390,589. Accepts queries by mail. Sample copy for $5 at newsstands. Writer's guidelines by e-mail.

Nonfiction Query with published clips.

Columns/Departments Query with published clips.

Tips "Queries and stories should be detailed and specific, and personal ties to the subject matter are important—let us know why you should be the one to write the story. Familiarize yourself with our departments, and the magazine style as a whole, and pitch your stories accordingly. Also, we rarely assign restaurant-based pieces, and the selections 'Classis' and 'Source' are almost always staff-written."

[N] [Ø] TASTE OF HOME

Reader's Digest Association, Inc., 5400 S. 60th St., Greendale WI 53129. (414)423-0100. Fax: (414)423-8463. E-mail: editors@tasteofhome.com. Website: www.tasteofhome.com. Executive Editor: Kathy Pohl. Managing Editor: Ann Kaiser. Bimonthly magazine. *"Taste of Home* is dedicated to home cooks, from beginners to the very experienced. Editorial includes recipes and serving suggestions, interviews and ideas from the publication's readers and field editors based around the country, and reviews of new cooking tools and gadgets." Circ. 4.5 million.

● Does not buy freelance material or use freelance writers.

$ $ WINE PRESS NORTHWEST

P.O. Box 2608, Tri-Cities WA 99302. (509)582-1564. Fax: (509)585-7221. E-mail: editor@winepressnw.com. Website: www.winepressnw.com. Associate Editor: Eric Degerman. **Contact:** Andy Perdue, editor. **50% freelance written.** Quarterly magazine covering Pacific Northwest wine (Washington, Oregon, British Columbia, Idaho). "We focus narrowly on Pacific Northwest wine. If we write about travel, it's where to go to drink NW wine. If we write about food, it's what goes with NW wine. No beer, no spirits." Estab. 1998. Circ. 12,000. Pays on publication. Publishes ms an average of 3 months after acceptance. Byline given. Offers 20% kill fee. Buys first North American serial, electronic rights. Editorial lead time 3 months. Submit seasonal material 3 months in advance. Accepts queries by mail, e-mail, fax. Accepts simultaneous submissions. Responds in 1 month to queries. Sample copy free or online. Writer's guidelines free.

Nonfiction General interest, historical/nostalgic, interview/profile, new product, photo feature, travel. No "beer, spirits, non-NW (California wine, etc.)" **Buys 30 mss/year.** Query with published clips. Length: 1,500-2,500 words. **Pays $300.** Sometimes pays expenses of writers on assignment.

Photos State availability with submission. Reviews contact sheets. Buys one-time rights. Negotiates payment individually. Identification of subjects required.

■ The online magazine carries original content not found in the print edition. Contact: Andy Perdue, online editor.

Tips "Writers must be familiar with *Wine Press Northwest* and should have a passion for the region, its wines, and cuisine."

$ $ $ WINE SPECTATOR

M. Shanken Communications, Inc., 387 Park Ave. S., 8th Floor, New York NY 10016. (212)684-4224. Fax: (212)684-5424. E-mail: winespec@mshanken.com. Website: www.winespectator.com. **Contact:** Thomas Matthews, executive editor. **20% freelance written.** Prefers to work with published/established writers. Monthly news magazine. Estab. 1976. Circ. 350,000. Pays within 30 days of publication. Publishes ms an average of 2 months after acceptance. Byline given. Buys all rights, makes work-for-hire assignments. Submit seasonal material 4 months in advance. Accepts queries by mail, fax. Responds in 3 months to queries. Writer's guidelines for #10 SASE.

Nonfiction General interest (news about wine or wine events), interview/profile (of wine, vintners, wineries), opinion, photo feature, travel, dining and other lifestyle pieces. No "winery promotional pieces or articles by writers who lack sufficient knowledge to write below just surface data." Query. Length: 100-2,000 words. **Pays $100-1,000.**

Photos Send photos with submission. Buys all rights. Pays $75 minimum for color transparencies. Captions, identification of subjects, model releases required.

■ The online magazine carries original content not found in the print edition. Contact: Dana Nigro, news editor.

Tips "A solid knowledge of wine is a must. Query letters essential, detailing the story idea. New, refreshing ideas which have not been covered before stand a good chance of acceptance. *Wine Spectator* is a consumer-oriented news magazine, but we are interested in some trade stories; brevity is essential."

Ⓝ $ $ WINE X MAGAZINE

Wine, Food and an Intelligent Slice of Vice, X Publishing, Inc., 4184 Sonoma Mountain Rd., Santa Rosa CA 95404. (707)545-0992. E-mail: jenna@winexmagazine.com. Website: www.winexmagazine.com. **Contact:** Jenna Corwin, associate editor. **100% freelance written.** Bimonthly magazine covering wine and other beverages. "*Wine X* is a lifestyle magazine for young adults featuring wine, beer, spirits, music, movies, fashion, food, coffee, celebrity interviews, health/fitness." Estab. 1997. Circ. 35,000. Pays on publication. Publishes ms an average of 3 months after acceptance. Byline given. Not copyrighted. Buys first North American and international serial, electronic rights for 3 years. Editorial lead time 3 months. Submit seasonal material 4 months in advance. Accepts queries by e-mail. Responds in 3 weeks to queries. Sample copy for $7. Writer's guidelines online.

Nonfiction Essays, new product, personal experience, photo feature, travel. No restaurant reviews, wine collector profiles. **Buys 6 mss/year.** Query. Length: 1,000-1,200 words. **Pays $50-250 for assigned articles; $50-150 for unsolicited articles.** Sometimes pays expenses of writers on assignment.

Photos Reviews transparencies. Buys one-time rights. Offers no additional payment for photos accepted with ms. Identification of subjects, model releases required.

Columns/Departments Wine; Other Beverages; Lifestyle, all 1,000 words. **Buys 72 mss/year.** Query.

Fiction Buys 6 mss/year. Query. Length: 1,000-1,500 words. **No payment for fiction.**

Poetry Avant-garde, free verse, haiku, light verse, traditional. **Buys 2 poems/year.** Submit maximum 3 poems. Length: 10-1,500 lines.

Fillers Short humor. **Buys 6/year.** Length: 100-500 words. **Pays $0-50.**

GAMES & PUZZLES

$ THE BRIDGE BULLETIN

American Contract Bridge League, 2990 Airways Blvd., Memphis TN 38116-3847. (901)332-5586, ext. 1291. Fax: (901)398-7754. E-mail: editor@acbl.org. Website: www.acbl.org. Managing Editor: Paul Linxwiler. **Contact:** Brent Manley, editor. **20% freelance written.** Monthly magazine covering duplicate (tournament) bridge. Estab. 1938. Circ. 155,000. Pays on publication. Publishes ms an average of 3 months after acceptance. Byline given. Buys first, second serial (reprint) rights. Editorial lead time 2 months. Accepts queries by mail, e-mail. Accepts previously published material. Accepts simultaneous submissions.

O→ Break in with a ''humorous piece about bridge.''

Nonfiction Book excerpts, essays, how-to (play better bridge), humor, interview/profile, new product, personal experience, photo feature, technical, travel. **Buys 6 mss/year.** Query. Length: 500-2,000 words. **Pays $100/page.**

Photos Color required. State availability with submission. Buys all rights. Negotiates payment individually. Identification of subjects required.

Tips ''Articles must relate to contract bridge in some way. Cartoons on bridge welcome.''

$ $ CHESS LIFE

United States Chess Federation, 3068 US Route 9W, Suite 100, New Windsor NY 12553-7698. (845)562-8350, ext. 152. Fax: (845)236-4852. E-mail: editor@uschess.org. Website: www.uschess.org. **Contact:** Kalev Pehme, editor. **15% freelance written.** Works with a small number of new/unpublished writers/year. Monthly magazine. ''*Chess Life* is the official publication of the United States Chess Federation, covering news of most major chess events, both here and abroad, with special emphasis on the triumphs and exploits of American players.'' Estab. 1939. Circ. 85,000. Publishes ms an average of 8 months after acceptance. Byline given. Buys first rights. Submit seasonal material 8 months in advance. Accepts queries by mail, e-mail, fax, phone. Accepts simultaneous submissions. Responds in 3 months to mss. Sample copy and writer's guidelines for 9×11 SAE with 5 first-class stamps.

Nonfiction All must have some relation to chess. General interest, historical/nostalgic, humor, interview/profile (of a famous chess player or organizer), photo feature (chess centered), technical. No ''stories about personal experiences with chess.'' **Buys 30-40 mss/year.** Query with samples if new to publication. Length: 3,000 words maximum. **Pays $100/page (800-1,000 words).** Sometimes pays expenses of writers on assignment.

Reprints Send tearsheet, photocopy or typed ms with rights for sale noted and information about when and where the material previously appeared.

Photos Reviews b&w contact sheets and prints, and color prints and slides. Buys all or negotiable rights. Pays $25-35 inside; $100-300 for covers. Captions, identification of subjects, model releases required.

Columns/Departments Chess Review (brief articles on unknown chess personalities) and ''Chess in Everyday Life.''

Fillers Submit with samples and clips. Buys first or negotiable rights to cartoons and puzzles. **Pays $25 upon acceptance.**

Tips ''Articles must be written from an informed point of view—not from view of the curious amateur. Most of our writers are specialized in that they have sound credentials as chess players. Freelancers in major population areas (except New York and Los Angeles, which we already have covered) who are interested in short personality profiles and perhaps news reporting have the best opportunities. We're looking for more personality pieces on chess players around the country; not just the stars, but local masters, talented youths, and dedicated volunteers. Freelancers interested in such pieces might let us know of their interest and their range. Could be we know of an interesting story in their territory that needs covering. Examples of published articles include a locally produced chess television program, a meeting of chess set collectors from around the world, chess in our prisons, and chess in the works of several famous writers.''

[N] GAMEPRO

IDG Entertainment, 555 12th St., Oakland CA 94607. (510)768-2700. Fax: (510)768-2701. Website: www.gamepro.com. Monthly magazine. ''*GamePro* is the industry leader among independent multiplatform video gaming magazines.'' Circ. 517,000. Byline given.

● Contact specific editor. Mostly staff written.

Nonfiction New product. Query.

$ $ $ GAMES MAGAZINE

Games Publications, a division of Kappa Publishing Group, Inc., 6198 Butler Pike, Blue Bell PA 19422. (215)643-6385. Fax: (215)628-3571. E-mail: games@kappapublishing.com. **Contact:** R. Wayne Schmittberger, editor-in-chief. **50% freelance written.** Magazine published 10 times/year covering puzzles and games. ''*Games* is a magazine of puzzles, contests, and features pertaining to games and ingenuity. It is aimed primarily at adults and has an emphasis on pop culture.'' Estab. 1977. Circ. 75,000. Pays on publication. Publishes ms an average of 4 months after acceptance. Byline given. Offers 25% kill fee. Buys first North American serial, first, one-time, second serial (reprint), all rights, makes work-for-hire assignments. Editorial lead time 3 months. Submit seasonal material 6 months in advance. Accepts queries by mail, e-mail. Accepts previously published material. Accepts simultaneous submissions. Responds in 6 weeks to queries; 3 months to mss. Sample copy for $5. Writer's guidelines for #10 SASE.

Nonfiction Photo feature, puzzles; games. **Buys 100 puzzles/year and 3 mss/year.** Query. Length: 1,500-2,500 words. **Pays $300-1,000.** Sometimes pays expenses of writers on assignment.

Photos State availability with submission. Reviews contact sheets, negatives, transparencies, prints. Buys one-time rights. Negotiates payment individually. Captions, identification of subjects, model releases required.

Columns/Departments Gamebits (game/puzzle news), 250 words; Games & Books (product reviews), 350 words; Wild Cards (short text puzzles), 100 words. **Buys 50 mss/year.** Query. **Pays $25-250.**

Fiction Adventure, mystery. **Buys 1-2 mss/year.** Query. Length: 1,500-2,500 words. **Pays $500-1,200.**

Tips "Look for real-life people, places, or things that might in some way be the basis for a puzzle."

ℕ $ $ $ INQUEST GAMER

151 Wells Ave., Congers NY 10920-2036. (845)268-2000. Fax: (845)268-0053. E-mail: iqtom@hotmail.com. Website: www.wizarduniverse.com. **Contact:** Kyle Ackerman, editor. Monthly magazine covering all gaming, particularly video and computer gaming, collectible and miniature gaming, and role-playing and board games. Pays on publication. Publishes ms an average of 2 months after acceptance. Byline given. Buys one-time, all rights. Accepts queries by mail, e-mail, fax, phone. Responds in 6 weeks to mss. Sample copy for $5. Writer's guidelines for #10 SASE.

   ○─ Break in with short news pieces.

Nonfiction Interview/profile (Q&As with big-name personalities or properties in gaming). No advertorials or stories on older, non-current games. **Buys 60 mss/year.** Query with published clips. Length: 2,000-4,000 words. **Pays $350-1,000.**

Columns/Departments Technical columns on how to play currently popular games. **Buys 100 mss/year.** Query with published clips. **Pays $50-250.**

Tips "*InQuest* is always looking for good freelance news and feature writers who are interested in card, roleplaying, or electronic games. A love of fantasy or science fiction books, movies, or art is desirable. Experience is preferred; sense of humor a plus; a flair for writing mandatory. Above all you must be able to find interesting new angles to a story, work hard, and meet deadlines."

GAY & LESBIAN INTEREST

ℕ $ $ THE ADVOCATE

Liberation Publications, Inc., 6922 Hollywood Blvd., Suite 1000, Los Angeles CA Z90028-6148. (323)871-1225. Fax: (323)467-6805. E-mail: newsroom@advocate.com. Website: www.advocate.com. **Contact:** Bruce Steele, editor-in-chief. Biweekly magazine covering national news events with a gay and lesbian perspective on the issues. Estab. 1967. Circ. 120,000. Pays on publication. Byline given. Buys first North American serial rights. Responds in 1 month to queries. Sample copy for $3.95. Writer's guidelines by e-mail.

Nonfiction "Here are elements we look for in all articles: *Angling:* An angle is the one editorial tool we have to attract a reader's attention. An *Advocate* editor won't make an assignment unless he or she has worked out a very specific angle with you. Once you've worked out the angle with an editor, don't deviate from it without letting the editor know. Some of the elements we look for in angles are: a news hook; an open question or controversy; a 'why' or 'how' element or novel twist; national appeal; and tight focus. *Content:* Lesbian and gay news stories in all areas of life: arts, sciences, financial, medical, cyberspace, etc. *Tone:* Tone is the element that makes an emotional connection. Some characteristics we look for: toughness; edginess; fairness and even-handedness; multiple perspectives." Exposé, interview/profile, news reporting and investigating. Special issues: gays on campus, coming out interviews with celebrities, HIV and health. Query. Length: 1,200 words. **Pays $550.**

Columns/Departments Arts & Media (news and profiles of well-known gay or lesbians in entertainment) is most open to freelancers, 750 words. Query. **Pays $100-500.**

Tips "*The Advocate* is a unique newsmagazine. While we report on gay and lesbian issues and are published by one of the country's oldest and most established gay-owned companies, we also play by the rules of mainstream-not-gay-community-journalism."

ℕ $ $ CURVE MAGAZINE

Outspoken Enterprises, Inc., 1550 Bryant St., Suite 510, San Francisco CA 94103. Fax: (415)863-1609. E-mail: editor@curvemag.com. Website: www.curvemag.com. Editor-in-Chief: Frances Stevens. **Contact:** Diane Anderson-Minshall, executive editor. **60% freelance written.** Magazine published 8 times/year covering lesbian entertainment, culture, and general interest categories. "We want dynamic and provocative articles that deal with issues, ideas, or cultural moments that are of interest or relevance to gay women." Estab. 1990. Circ. 70,000. Pays on publication. Byline given. Offers 25% kill fee. Buys first North American serial rights. Editorial lead time 6 months. Submit seasonal material 6 months in advance. Accepts queries by mail, e-mail, fax. Sample copy for $3.95 with $2 postage. Writer's guidelines online.

Nonfiction General interest, photo feature, travel, celebrity interview/profile. Special issues: Sex (February); Travel (April); Pets (May); Pride (June); Music (August); School (September); Money/Careers (November); Gift Guide (December). No fiction or poetry. **Buys 25 mss/year.** Query. Length: 200-2,500 words. **Pays 15¢/word.**

Photos Send photos with submission. Buys one-time rights. Offers $50-100/photo; negotiates payment individually. Captions, identification of subjects, model releases required.

Tips "Feature articles generally fit into 1 of the following categories: Celebrity profiles (lesbian, bisexual, or straight women who are icons for the lesbian community or actively involved in coalition-building with the lesbian community); community segment profiles—i.e., lesbian firefighters, drag kings, sports teams (multiple interviews with a variety of women in different parts of the country representing a diversity of backgrounds); noncelebrity profiles (activities of unknown or low-profile lesbian and bisexual activists/political leaders, athletes, filmmakers, dancers, writers, musicians, etc.); controversial issues (spark a dialogue about issues that divide us as a community, and the ways in which lesbians of different backgrounds fail to understand and support one another). We are not interested in inflammatory articles that incite or enrage readers without offering a channel for action, but we do look for challenging, thought-provoking work."

$ECHO MAGAZINE

ACE Publishing, Inc., P.O. Box 16630, Phoenix AZ 85011-6630. (602)266-0550. Fax: (602)266-0773. E-mail: editor@echomag.com. Website: www.echomag.com. **Contact:** Buddy Early, managing editor. **30-40% freelance written.** Biweekly magazine covering gay and lesbian issues. *"Echo Magazine* is a newsmagazine for gay, lesbian, bisexual, and transgendered persons in the Phoenix metro area and throughout the state of Arizona. Editorial content needs to be pro-gay, that is, supportive of GLBT equality in all areas of American life." Estab. 1989. Circ. 15,000-18,000. Pays on publication. Publishes ms an average of less than 1 month after acceptance. Byline given. Buys all rights. Editorial lead time 1-2 months. Submit seasonal material 1-2 months in advance. Accepts queries by e-mail. Responds in 2 weeks to queries; 1 month to mss. Sample copy online. Writer's guidelines by e-mail.

Nonfiction Book excerpts, essays, historical/nostalgic, humor, interview/profile, opinion, personal experience, photo feature, travel. Special issues: Pride Festival (April); Arts issue (August); Holiday Gift/Decor (December). No "articles on topics unrelated to our GLBT readers, or anything that is not pro-gay." **Buys 10-20 mss/year.** Query. Length: 500-2,000 words. **Pays $30-40.**

Photos State availability with submission. Reviews contact sheets, GIF/JPEG files. Buys all rights. Negotiates payment individually. Captions, identification of subjects, model releases required.

Columns/Departments Guest Commentary (opinion on GLBT issues), 500-1,000 words; Arts/Entertainment (profiles of GLBT or relevant celebrities, or arts issues), 800-1,500 words. **Buys 5-10 mss/year.** Query. **Pays $30-40.**

Tips "Know Phoenix (or other areas of Arizona) and its GLBT community. Please don't send nongay-related or nonpro-gay material. Research your topics thoroughly and write professionally. Our print content and online contenty are very similar."

$THE GAY & LESBIAN REVIEW

Gay & Lesbian Review, Inc., P.O. Box 180300, Boston MA 02118. (617)421-0082. E-mail: editor@glreview.com. Website: www.glreview.com. **100% freelance written.** Bimonthly magazine covers gay & lesbian history, culture, and politics. "In-depth essays on GLBT history, biography, the arts, political issues, written in clear, lively prose targeted to the 'literate nonspecialist.'" Estab. 1994. Circ. 12,000. Pays on publication. Byline given. Buys first rights. Editorial lead time 2 months. Accepts queries by mail, e-mail, phone. Accepts simultaneous submissions. Sample copy for free. Writer's guidelines free.

Nonfiction Essays, historical/nostalgic, humor, interview/profile, opinion, book reviews. Does not want fiction, memoirs, personal reflections. Query. Length: 1,500-5,000 words. **Pays $100.** "Writer can waive payment for five gift subscriptions."

Poetry Avant-garde, free verse, traditional.

Tips "We prefer that a proposal be e-mailed before a completed draft is sent."

ℕ $ $ $ $GENRE

Genre Publishing, 213 W. 35th St., Suite 402, New York NY 10001. (212)594-8181. Fax: (212)594-8263. E-mail: genre@genremagazine.com. Website: www.genremagazine.com. Editor: Bill Henning. **60% freelance written.** Monthly magazine. "*Genre*, America's best-selling gay men's lifestyle magazine, covers entertainment, fashion, travel, and relationships in a hip, upbeat, upscale voice." Estab. 1991. Circ. 50,000. Pays on publication. Publishes ms an average of 3 months after acceptance. Byline given. Offers 25% kill fee. Buys first North

American serial, electronic rights. Editorial lead time 10 weeks. Submit seasonal material 10 weeks in advance. Accepts queries by mail, e-mail, fax. Sample copy for $6.95 ($5 plus $1.95 postage).
Nonfiction Essays, exposé, general interest, historical/nostalgic, how-to, humor, inspirational, interview/profile, new product, opinion, personal experience, photo feature, religious, travel, relationships, fashion. Not interested in articles on 2 males negotiating a sexual situation or coming out stories. **Buys variable number mss/year.** Query with published clips. Length: 500-1,500 words. **Pays $150-1,600.**
Photos State availability with submission. Reviews contact sheets, 3×5 or 5×7 prints. Buys one-time rights. Negotiates payment individually. Model releases required.
Columns/Departments Body (how to better the body); Mind (how to better the mind); Spirit (how to better the spirit), all 700 words; Reviews (books, movies, music, travel, etc.), 500 words. **Buys variable number of mss/year.** Query with published clips or send complete ms. **Pays $200 maximum.**
Fiction Adventure, experimental, horror, humorous, mainstream, mystery, novel excerpts, religious, romance, science fiction, slice-of-life vignettes, suspense. **Buys 10 mss/year.** Send complete ms. Length: 2,000-4,000 words.
Tips ''Like you, we take our journalistic responsibilities and ethics very seriously, and we subscribe to the highest standards of the profession. We expect our writers to represent original work that is not libelous and does not infringe upon the copyright or violate the right of privacy of any other person, firm or corporation.''

$ $ GIRLFRIENDS MAGAZINE

Lesbian Culture, Politics, and Entertainment, 3415 Cèsar Châvez, Suite 101, San Francisco CA 94110. (415)648-9464. Fax: (415)648-4705. E-mail: staff@girlfriendsmag.com. Website: www.girlfriendsmag.com. **Contact:** Editor. Monthly lesbian magazine. *''Girlfriends* provides its readers with intelligent, entertaining and visually pleasing coverage of culture, politics, and entertainment—all from an informed and critical lesbian perspective.'' Estab. 1994. Circ. 75,000. Pays on publication. Publishes ms an average of 6 months after acceptance. Byline given. Offers 50% kill fee. Buys first rights and use for advertising/promoting *girlfriends*. Editorial lead time 3 months. Submit seasonal material 6 months in advance. Accepts queries by mail, e-mail. Accepts simultaneous submissions. Responds in 3 weeks to queries; 2 months to mss. Sample copy for $4.95 plus $1.50 postage or online. Writer's guidelines online.
   • *Girlfriends* is not accepting fiction, poetry or fillers.
   O— Break in by sending a letter detailing interests and story ideas, plus résumé and published samples.
Nonfiction Book excerpts, essays, exposé, historical/nostalgic, humor, interview/profile, new product, opinion, personal experience, photo feature, religious, technical, travel, investigative features. Special issues: Sex, music, bridal, sports and Hollywood issues, breast cancer issue. Special features: Best lesbian restaurants in the US; best places to live. **Buys 20-25 mss/year.** Query with published clips. Length: 1,000-3,500 words. **Pays 15¢/word.**
Reprints Send photocopy or typed ms with rights for sale noted and information about when and where the material previously appeared. Negotiable payment.
Photos Send photos with submission. Reviews contact sheets, 4×5 or 2¼×2¼ transparencies, prints. Buys one-time rights. Offers $30-50/photo. Captions, identification of subjects, model releases required.
Columns/Departments Book reviews, 900 words; Music reviews, 600 words; Travel, 600 words; Opinion pieces, 1,000 words; Humor, 600 words. Query with published clips. **Pays 15¢/word.**
Tips ''Be unafraid of controversy—articles should focus on problems and debates raised in lesbian culture, politics, and sexuality. Avoid being 'politically correct.' We don't just want to know what's happening in the lesbian world, we want to know how what's happening in the world affects lesbians.''

$ $ THE GUIDE

To Gay Travel, Entertainment, Politics, and Sex, Fidelity Publishing, P.O. Box 990593, Boston MA 02115. (617)266-8557. Fax: (617)266-1125. E-mail: letters@guidemag.com. Website: www.guidemag.com. **25% freelance written.** Monthly magazine on the gay and lesbian community. Estab. 1981. Circ. 30,000. **Pays on acceptance.** Publishes ms an average of 2 months after acceptance. Offers negotiable kill fee. Buys first rights. Submit seasonal material 2 months in advance. Accepts queries by mail, e-mail. Accepts previously published material. Accepts simultaneous submissions. Responds in 3 months to queries. Sample copy for 9×12 SAE and 8 first-class stamps. Writer's guidelines for #10 SASE.
Nonfiction Book excerpts (if yet unpublished), essays, exposé, general interest, historical/nostalgic, humor, interview/profile, opinion, personal experience, photo feature, religious. **Buys 24 mss/year.** Query with or without published clips or send complete ms. Length: 500-5,000 words. **Pays $85-240.**
Reprints Occasionally buys previously published submissions. Pays 100% of amount paid for an original article.
Photos Send photos with submission. Reviews contact sheets. Buys one-time rights. Pays $15/image used. Captions, identification of subjects, model releases required.
Tips ''Brevity, humor, and militancy appreciated. Writing on sex, political analysis, and humor are particularly

appreciated. We purchase very few freelance travel pieces; those that we do buy are usually on less commercial destinations.''

$HX MAGAZINE

Two Queens, Inc., 230 W. 17th St., 8th Floor, New York NY 10011. (212)352-3535. E-mail: info@hx.com. Website: www.hx.com. **25% freelance written.** Weekly magazine covering gay New York City nightlife and entertainment. Estab. 1991. Circ. 39,000. Pays on publication. Publishes ms an average of 1 month after acceptance. Byline given. Buys first North American serial, second serial (reprint), electronic rights. Editorial lead time 2 months. Submit seasonal material 2 months in advance. Only responds if interested to queries. Sample copy not available.

Nonfiction General interest, arts and entertainment, celebrity profiles, reviews. **Buys 50 mss/year.** Query with published clips. Length: 500-2,000 words. **Pays $50-150; $25-100 for unsolicited articles.**

Reprints Send tearsheet or photocopy with rights for sale noted and information about when and where the material previously appeared. Pays 50% of amount paid for an original article.

Photos State availability with submission. Reviews contact sheets, negatives, 8×10 prints. Buys one-time, reprint and electronic reprint rights. Captions, identification of subjects, model releases required.

Columns/Departments Buys 200 mss/year. Query with published clips. **Pays $25-125.**

$ $INSTINCT MAGAZINE

Instinct Publishing, 15335 Morrison St., Suite 325, Sherman Oaks CA 91403. (818)205-9033. Fax: (818)205-9093. E-mail: editor@instinctmag.com. Website: www.instinctmag.com. Editor: Parker Ray. **60% freelance written.** Monthly magazine covering gay men's life and style issues. ''*Instinct* is a blend of *Cosmo* and *Maxim* for gay men. We're smart, sexy, irreverent, and more than a bit un-PC—a unique style that has made us the No. 1 gay men's magazine in the US.'' Estab. 1997. Circ. 60,000+. Pays on publication. Byline given. Offers 20% kill fee. Buys all rights. Editorial lead time 2 months. Accepts queries by mail, e-mail, phone. Accepts simultaneous submissions. Sample copy and writer's guidelines online.

Nonfiction ''Be inventive and specific—an article on 'dating' isn't saying much and will need a twist, for example.'' Exposé, general interest, humor, interview/profile, travel. Does not want first-person accounts or articles. Query with or without published clips. Length: 800-2,400 words. **Pays $150-300.** Sometimes pays expenses of writers on assignment.

Photos Buys all rights. Negotiates payment individually. Captions, identification of subjects, model releases required.

Columns/Departments Health (gay, off-kilter), 800 words; Fitness (irreverent), 500 words; Movies, Books (edgy, sardonic), 800 words; Music, Video Games (indie, underground), 800 words. **Pays $150-250.**

Tips ''While *Instinct* publishes a wide variety of features and columns having to do with gay men's issues, we maintain our signature irreverent, edgy, un-PC tone throughout. When pitching stories (e-mail is preferred), be as specific as possible, and try to think beyond the normal scope of 'gay relationship' features. An article on 'Dating Tips,' for example, will not be considered, while an article on 'Tips on Dating Two Guys At Once' is more our slant. We rarely accept finished articles. We keep a special eye out for pitches on investigational/exposé-type stories geared toward our audience.''

$ $ $METROSOURCE

MetroSource Publishing, Inc., 180 Varick St., 5th Floor, New York NY 10014. (212)691-5127. Fax: (212)741-2978. Website: www.metrosource.com. **70% freelance written.** Magazine published 6 times/year. ''*MetroSource* is an upscale, glossy, 4-color lifestyle magazine targeted to an urban, professional gay and lesbian readership.'' Estab. 1990. Circ. 120,000. Pays on publication. Publishes ms an average of 2 months after acceptance. Byline given. Editorial lead time 3 months. Submit seasonal material 4 months in advance. Accepts queries by mail, e-mail, fax, phone. Accepts simultaneous submissions. Sample copy for $5.

Nonfiction Exposé, interview/profile, opinion, photo feature, travel. **Buys 20 mss/year.** Query with published clips. Length: 1,000-2,500 words. **Pays $100-900.**

Photos State availability with submission. Negotiates payment individually. Captions, model releases required.

Columns/Departments Book, film, television, and stage reviews; health columns; and personal diary and opinion pieces. Word lengths vary. Query with published clips. **Pays $200.**

OUT

245 W. 17th St., Suite 1200, New York NY 10011. (212)242-8100. Fax: (212)242-8364. E-mail: editor@out.com. Website: www.out.com. **Contact:** Department Editor. **70% freelance written.** Monthly national magazine covering gay and lesbian general-interest topics. ''Our subjects range from current affairs to culture, from fitness to finance.'' Estab. 1992. Circ. 120,000. Pays on publication. Publishes ms an average of 3 months after acceptance. Byline given. Offers 25% kill fee. Buys first North American serial rights. second serial (reprint) rights

for anthologies (additional fee paid) and 30-day reprint rights (additional fee paid if applicable) Editorial lead time 3 months. Submit seasonal material 5 months in advance. Accepts queries by mail. Accepts simultaneous submissions. Responds in 6 weeks to queries; 2 months to mss.

Nonfiction Book excerpts, essays, exposé, general interest, historical/nostalgic, humor, interview/profile, new product, opinion, personal experience, photo feature, fashion/lifestyle. **Buys 200 mss/year.** Query with published clips and SASE. Length: 50-1,500 words. **Pays variable rate.** Sometimes pays expenses of writers on assignment.

Photos State availability with submission. Reviews contact sheets, transparencies, prints. Buys one-time rights. Negotiates payment individually. Captions, identification of subjects, model releases required.

Tips *"Out*'s contributors include editors and writers from the country's top consumer titles: skilled reporters, columnists, and writers with distinctive voices and specific expertise in the fields they cover. But while published clips and relevant experience are a must, the magazine also seeks out fresh, young voices. The best guide to the kind of stories we publish is to review our recent issues. Is there a place for the story you have in mind? Be aware of our long lead time. No phone queries, please."

OUTSMART

Up & Out Communications, 3406 Audubon Place, Houston TX 77006. (713)520-7237. Fax: (713)522-3275. Website: www.outsmartmagazine.com. **50% freelance written.** Monthly magazine concerned with gay, lesbian, bisexual, and transgender issues. *"OutSmart* offers vibrant and thoughtful coverage of the stories that appeal most to an educated gay audience." Estab. 1994. Circ. 60,000. Pays on publication. Byline given. Buys one-time, simultaneous rights. Permission to publish on website. Editorial lead time 3 months. Submit seasonal material 4 months in advance. Accepts queries by mail, e-mail, fax. Responds in 6 weeks to queries; 2 months to mss. Sample copy and writer's guidelines online.

Nonfiction Historical/nostalgic, interview/profile, opinion, personal experience, photo feature, travel, health/wellness; local/national news. **Buys 24 mss/year.** Send complete ms. Length: 450-2,000 words. **Negotiates payment individually.**

Reprints Send photocopy.

Photos State availability with submission. Reviews 4×6 prints. Buys one-time rights. Negotiates payment individually. Identification of subjects required.

    ◘ The online magazine carries original content not found in the print edition and includes writer's guidelines.

Tips *"OutSmart* is a mainstream publication that covers culture, politics, personalities, and entertainment as well as local and national news and events. We work to address the diversity of the lesbian, gay, bisexual, and transgender community, fostering understanding among all our readers."

Ⓝ $ $ ⊠ XTRA

Toronto's Lesbian & Gay Biweekly, Pink Triangle Press, 491 Church St., Suite 200, Toronto ON M4Y 2C6 Canada. (416)925-6665. Fax: (416)925-6503. E-mail: info@xtra.ca. Website: www.xtra.ca. Editor-in-Chief: David Walberg. **Contact:** Paul Gallant, managing editor. **80% freelance written.** Biweekly tabloid covering gay, lesbian, bisexual and transgender issues, news, arts and events of interest in Toronto. *"Xtra* is dedicated to lesbian and gay sexual liberation. We publish material that advocates this end, according to the mission statement of the not-for-profit organization Pink Triangle Press, which operates the paper." Estab. 1984. Circ. 45,000. Pays on publication. Byline given. Buys first North American serial, electronic rights. Editorial lead time 1 month. Accepts queries by e-mail. Accepts previously published material. Accepts simultaneous submissions. Responds in 2 weeks to queries. Sample copy online. Writer's guidelines by e-mail.

Nonfiction Book excerpts, essays, interview/profile, opinion, personal experience, travel. US-based stories or profiles of straight people who do not have a direct connection to the LGBT community. Query with published clips. Length: 200-1,600 words. Sometimes pays expenses of writers on assignment.

Photos Send photos with submission. Buys Internet rights. Offers $60 minimum. Captions, identification of subjects, model releases required.

Columns/Departments *Xtra* rarely publishes unsolicited columns. **Buys 6 mss/year.** Query with published clips.

GENERAL INTEREST

Ⓝ $ $ ALL AMERICAN FESTIVALS

Rangoon Moon Inc., P.O. Box 904, Dahlonega GA 30533 USA. E-mail: sesails@yahoo.com. **Contact:** Kevin Gralton, managing editor. **20% freelance written.** Bimonthly magazine. Covers US festivals and special events that are fun, well-attended, enthusiastic and provide pictures. Estab. 2000. Circ. 25,000. **Pays on acceptance.**

Not copyrighted. Buys first, all rights. Editorial lead time 3 months. Submit seasonal material 3 months in advance. Accepts queries by e-mail. Accepts previously published material. Accepts simultaneous submissions. Sample copy not available.

Nonfiction General interest, historical/nostalgic, humor, personal experience, travel. **Buys 15 mss/year.** Send complete ms. Length: 300-700 words.

Photos State availability with submission. Reviews JPEG/TIFF files, the bigger the better. Buys one-time rights. $10 maximum per photo.

$ $ THE AMERICAN LEGION MAGAZINE

P.O. Box 1055, Indianapolis IN 46206-1055. (317)630-1200. Fax: (317)630-1280. E-mail: magazine@legion.org. Website: www.legion.org. Editorial Administrator: Patricia Marschand. **Contact:** John Raughter, editor. **70% freelance written.** Prefers to work with published/established writers, but works with a small number of new/unpublished writers each year. Monthly magazine. "Working through 15,000 community-level posts, the honorably discharged wartime veterans of The American Legion dedicate themselves to God, country and traditional American values. They believe in a strong defense; adequate and compassionate care for veterans and their families; community service; and the wholesome development of our nation's youth. We publish articles that reflect these values. We inform our readers and their families of significant trends and issues affecting our nation, the world and the way we live. Our major features focus on the American flag, national security, foreign affairs, business trends, social issues, health, education, ethics and the arts. We also publish selected general feature articles, articles of special interest to veterans, and question-and-answer interviews with prominent national and world figures." Estab. 1919. Circ. 2,700,000. **Pays on acceptance.** Publishes ms an average of 6 months after acceptance. Byline given. Buys first North American serial rights. Accepts queries by mail, e-mail, fax. Responds in 2 months to queries. Sample copy for $3.50 and 9×12 SAE with 6 first-class stamps. Writer's guidelines for #10 SASE.

Nonfiction Well-reported articles or expert commentaries cover issues/trends in world/national affairs, contemporary problems, general interest, sharply-focused feature subjects. Monthly Q&A with national figures/experts. General interest, interview/profile. No regional topics or promotion of partisan political agendas. No personal experiences or war stories. **Buys 50-60 mss/year.** Query with SASE should explain the subject or issue, article's angle and organization, writer's qualifications, and experts to be interviewed. Length: 300-2,000 words. **Pays 40¢/word and up.**

Photos On assignment.

Tips "Queries by new writers should include clips/background/expertise; no longer than 1½ pages. Submit suitable material showing you have read several issues. *The American Legion Magazine* considers itself '*the* magazine for a strong America.' Reflect this theme (which includes economy, educational system, moral fiber, social issues, infrastructure, technology and national defense/security). We are a general interest, national magazine, not a strictly military magazine. We are widely read by members of the Washington establishment and other policy makers."

AMERICAN PROFILE

Publishing Group of America, 341 Cool Springs Blvd., Suite 400, Franklin TN 37067. (615)468-6000. Fax: (615)468-6100. E-mail: editorial@americanprofile.com. Website: www.americanprofile.com. **90% freelance written.** Weekly magazine with national and regional editorial celebrating the people, places, and experiences of hometowns across America. The 4-color magazine is distributed through small to medium-size community newspapers. Estab. 2000. Circ. 7,000,000. **Pays on acceptance.** Byline given. Buys first, electronic, 6-month exclusive rights rights. Editorial lead time 6 months. Submit seasonal material 1 year in advance. Accepts queries by mail. Responds in 1 month. Writer's guidelines online.

O→ In addition to a query, first-time writers should include 2-3 published clips.

Nonfiction General interest, how-to, interview/profile. No fiction, nostalgia, poetry, essays. **Buys 250 mss/ year.** Query with published clips. Length: 400-1,200 words. Pays expenses of writers on assignment.

Photos State availability with submission. Reviews transparencies. Buys one-time rights, nonexclusive after 6 months. Negotiates payment individually. Captions, identification of subjects, model releases required.

Columns/Departments Health; Family; Finances; Home; Gardening.

Tips "Please visit the website to see our content and writing style."

$ $ $ $ THE ATLANTIC MONTHLY

77 N. Washington St., Boston MA 02114. (617)854-7700. Fax: (617)854-7876. E-mail: letters@theatlantic.com. Website: www.theatlantic.com. Managing Editor: Cullen Murphy. **Contact:** C. Michael Curtis, senior editor (fiction). Monthly magazine of arts and public affairs. General magazine for an educated readership with broad cultural interests. Estab. 1857. Circ. 500,000. **Pays on acceptance.** Byline given. Buys first North American serial rights. Accepts queries by mail. Responds in 2 months to mss. Writer's guidelines online.

Nonfiction Reportage preferred. Book excerpts, essays, general interest, humor, personal experience, religious, travel. Query with or without published clips or send complete ms. All unsolicited mss must be accompanied by SASE. Length: 1,000-6,000 words. **Payment varies**. Sometimes pays expenses of writers on assignment.

Fiction "Seeks fiction that is clear, tightly written with strong sense of 'story' and well-defined characters. No longer publishes fiction in the regular magazine. Instead, it will appear in a special newsstand-only fiction issue." Literary and contemporary fiction. Send complete ms. Length: 2,000-6,000 words.

Poetry Peter Davison, poetry editor. **Buys 40-60 poems/year.**

Tips Writers should be aware that this is not a market for beginner's work (nonfiction and fiction), nor is it truly for intermediate work. Study this magazine before sending only your best, most professional work. When making first contact, "cover letters are sometimes helpful, particularly if they cite prior publications or involvement in writing programs. Common mistakes: melodrama, inconclusiveness, lack of development, unpersuasive characters and/or dialogue."

$⊘ BIBLIOPHILOS

A Journal of History, Literature, and the Liberal Arts, The Bibliophile Publishing Co., Inc., 200 Security Building, Fairmont WV 26554. (304)366-8107. **Contact:** Dr. Gerald J. Bobango, editor. **65-70% freelance written.** Quarterly literary magazine concentrating on 19th century American and European history and literature. "We see ourself as a forum for new and unpublished writers, historians, philosophers, literary critics and reviewers, and those who love animals. Audience is academic-oriented, college graduate, who believes in traditional Aristotelian-Thomistic thought and education, and has a fair streak of the Luddite in him/her. Our ideal reader owns no television, has never sent nor received e-mail, and avoids shopping malls at any cost. He loves books." Estab. 1981. Circ. 400. Pays on publication. Publishes ms an average of 1 year after acceptance. Byline given. Buys first North American serial rights. Editorial lead time 6 months. Submit seasonal material 6 months in advance. Accepts queries by mail. Responds in 2 weeks to queries; 1 month to mss. Sample copy for $5.25. Writer's guidelines for $9^{1}/_{2} \times 4$ SAE with 2 first-class stamps.

- Query first only, unaccompanied by any ms.
- O→ Break in with "either prose or poetry which is illustrative of man triumphing over and doing without technology, pure Ludditism, if need be. Send material critical of the socialist welfare state, constantly expanding federal government (or government at all levels), or exposing the inequities of affirmative action, political correctness, and the mass media packaging of political candidates. We want to see a pre-1960 worldview."

Nonfiction Book excerpts, essays, general interest, historical/nostalgic, humor, interview/profile, opinion, personal experience, photo feature, travel, book review-essay, literary criticism. Special issues: Upcoming theme issues include an annual all book-review issue, containing 10-15 reviews and review-essays, or poetry about books and reading. Does not want to see "anything that Oprah would recommend, or that Erma Bombeck or Ann Landers would think humorous or interesting. No 'I found Jesus and it changed my life' material." **Buys 25-30 mss/year.** Query by mail only first, not with any ms included. Length: 1,500-3,000 words. **Pays $5-35.**

Photos State availability with submission. Reviews b&w 4×6 prints. Buys one-time rights. Negotiates payment individually. Identification of subjects required.

Columns/Departments Features (fiction and nonfiction, short stories), 1,500-3,000 words; Poetry (batches of 5, preferably thematically related), 3-150 lines; Reviews (book reviews or review essays on new books or individual authors, current and past), 1,000-1,500 words; Opinion (man triumphing over technology and technocrats, the facade of modern education, computer fetishism), 1,000-1,500 words. **Buys 20 mss/year.** Query by mail only. **Pays $25-40.**

Fiction Gerald J. Bobango, editor. Adventure, ethnic, historical, horror, humorous, mainstream, mystery, novel excerpts, romance, slice-of-life vignettes, suspense, western, utopian, Orwellian. "No 'I remember Mama, who was a saint and I miss her terribly'; no gay or lesbian topics; no drug culture material; nothing harping on political correctness; nothing to do with healthy living, HMOs, medical programs, or the welfare state, unless it is against statism in these areas." **Buys 25-30 mss/year.** Length: 1,500-3,000 words. **Pays $25-40.**

Poetry "Formal and rhymed verse gets read first." Free verse, light verse, traditional, political satire, doggerel.

Tips "Query first. Do not send material unsolicited. We shall not respond if you do."

$ CAPPER'S

Ogden Publications, Inc., 1503 SW 42nd St., Topeka KS 66609-1265. (785)274-4300. Website: www.cappers.com. **25% freelance written.** Works with a small number of new/unpublished writers each year. Biweekly tabloid emphasizing home and family for readers who live mainly in the rural Midwest. "*Capper's* is upbeat, focusing on the homey feelings people like to share, as well as hopes and dreams." Estab. 1879. Circ. 240,000. Pays for poetry and fiction on acceptance; articles on publication. Publishes ms an average of 2-12 months after acceptance. Byline given. Buys first North American serial rights. Submit seasonal material 4 months in advance.

Accepts queries by mail. Responds in 2-3 months to queries; 6 months to mss. Sample copy and writer's guidelines online.

Nonfiction General interest, historical/nostalgic (local museums, etc.), inspirational, travel, nostalgic, human interest, family-oriented. **Buys 75 mss/year.** Send complete ms. Length: 900 words maximum. **Pays $2.50/ printed inch. Pays additional $5 if used on website.**

Reprints Accepts occasionally from noncompeting venues. Send typed ms with rights for sale noted and information about when and where the material previously appeared.

Photos Send photos with submission. Buys one-time rights. Pays $5-15 for b&w glossy prints; $20-40 for color prints (inside); $40 for cover. Captions required.

Columns/Departments Send complete ms. **Pays approximately $2/printed inch. Payment for recipes is $5. Hints used earn $2 gift certificate.**

Fiction ''We buy very few fiction pieces—longer than short stories, shorter than novels.'' Adventure, historical, humorous, mainstream, mystery, romance, serialized novels, western. No explicit sex, violence, profanity, or alcohol use. **Buys 4-5 mss/year.** Length: 7,500-50,000 words. **Pays $100-400.**

Poetry ''The poems that appear in *Capper's* are not too difficult to read. They're easy to grasp. We're looking for everyday events and down-to-earth themes.'' Free verse, light verse, traditional, nature, inspiration. **Buys 150 poems/year.** Submit maximum 5-6 poems. Length: 4-16 lines. **Pays $10-15.**

Tips ''Study a few issues of our publication. Most rejections are for material that is too long, unsuitable or out of character for our magazine (too sexy, too much profanity, wrong kind of topic, etc.). On occasion, we must cut material to fit column space. No electronic submissions.''

$ $ CIA—CITIZEN IN AMERICA

CIA—Citizen in America, Inc., 30 Ford St., Glen Cove, Long Island NY 11542. (516)671-4047. E-mail: jjm@citize ninamerica.com. Website: www.citizeninamerica.com. **Contact:** John J. Maddox, magazine coordinator. **100% freelance written.** Magazine published 9 times/year covering first amendment responsibilities. ''*CIA—Citizen in America* tries to strengthen democracy here and abroad by allowing the freedom of expression in all forms possible through the press. *CIA* does not shy away from controversy.'' Estab. 2002. Pays on publication. Publishes ms an average of 3 months after acceptance. Byline sometimes given. Buys one-time rights. Accepts queries by mail, e-mail. Accepts previously published material. Accepts simultaneous submissions. Responds in 3 weeks to queries; 1-2 months to mss. Sample copy for $6.95. Writer's guidelines for #10 SASE, e-mail or on website.

Nonfiction Essays, exposé, general interest, historical/nostalgic, humor, inspirational, opinion, personal experience, religious, travel. Does not want ''any manuscript that deliberately exploits or promotes racial, religious, or gender bigotry.'' **Buys 150+ mss/year.** Send complete ms. Length: 2,500 words maximum. **Pays $40-100, plus 1 contributor copy.**

Photos State availability with submission. Offers no additional payment for photos accepted with ms.

Columns/Departments There are numerous columns where paid articles are accepted. See writer's guidelines for details. Send complete ms.

Fiction Adventure, erotica, ethnic, experimental, historical, humorous, mainstream, religious, romance, science fiction, slice-of-life vignettes, western, war stories. No screen or plays. No works that deliberately promote racism, prejudice, or gender oriented violence. Send complete ms. Length: 250-2,500 words.

Poetry Avant-garde, free verse, light verse, traditional. Submit maximum 5 poems. Length: 25 lines maximum.

Fillers Anecdotes, facts, short humor.

Tips ''Writers should consciously shy away from getting an 'ego' or 'celebrity' boost in this publication. Therefore, writers should have a fervent desire to publish work for others to read. Rule of thumb is: If the writer feels good writing it, *CIA* will feel the same reading and, hopefully, publishing it. The purchase of sample copy is strongly recommended before submission.''

$ $ $ $ DIVERSION

888 Seventh Ave., New York NY 10019. (212)969-7500. Fax: (212)969-7557. E-mail: shartford@hearst.com. Website: www.diversion.com. **Contact:** Shari Hartford. Monthly magazine covering travel and lifestyle, edited for physicians. ''*Diversion* offers an eclectic mix of interests beyond medicine. Regular features include stories on domestic and foreign travel destinations, food and wine, cars, gardening, photography, books, electronic gear, and the arts. Although *Diversion* doesn't cover health subjects, it does feature profiles of doctors who excel at nonmedical pursuits or who engage in medical volunteer work.'' Estab. 1973. Circ. 176,000. Pays 3 months after acceptance. Byline given. Offers 25% kill fee. Editorial lead time 4 months. Responds in 1 month to queries. Sample copy for $4.50. Guidelines available.

   O— Break in by ''querying with a brief proposal describing the focus of the story. It should be on a topic in which you have demonstrated expertise.''

Nonfiction ''We get so many travel and food queries that we're hard pressed to even read them all. Far better to query us on culture, the arts, sports, technology, etc.'' **Buys 50 mss/year.** Query with proposal, published clips, and author's credentials. Length: 1,800-2,000 words. **Pays 50¢-$1/word.**

Columns/Departments Travel, food & wine, photography, gardening, cars, technology. Length: 1,200 words.

Ⓩ EBONY

Johnson Publishing Co., Inc., 820 S. Michigan Ave., Chicago IL 60605. Website: www.ebony.com. Monthly magazine covering topics ranging from education and history to entertainment, art, government, health, travel, sports and social events. African-American oriented consumer interest magazine. Circ. 1,728,986. Editorial lead time 3 months.

• Query before submitting.

$ EDUCATION IN FOCUS

Books for All Times, Inc., P.O. Box 202, Warrenton VA 20188. (540)428-3175. E-mail: staff@bfat.com. Website: www.bfat.com. **Contact:** Joe David, editor. **80% freelance written.** Semiannual newsletter for public interested in education issues at all levels. ''We are always looking for intelligent articles that provide educationally sound ideas that enhance the understanding of what is happening or what should be happening in our schools today. We are not looking for material that might be published by the Department of Education. Instead we want material from liberated and mature thinkers and writers, tamed by reason and humanitarianism.'' Estab. 1989. Circ. 1,000. **Pays on acceptance.** Publishes ms an average of 2 months after acceptance. Byline given. Buys first, one-time, second serial (reprint), book, newsletter and internet rights rights. Editorial lead time 2 months. Accepts queries by mail, e-mail. Accepts simultaneous submissions. Responds in 1 month to queries. Sample copy for #10 SASE.

Nonfiction ''We prefer documented, intelligent articles that deeply inform. The best way to be quickly rejected is to send articles that defend the public school system as it is today, or was!'' Book excerpts, exposé, general interest. **Buys 4-6 mss/year.** Query with published clips or send complete ms. Length: 1,000 words. Some longer articles can be broken into 2 articles—1 for each issue. **Pays $25-75.**

Tips ''Maintain an honest voice and a clear focus on the subject.''

$ $ GRIT

American Life and Traditions, Ogden Publications, 1503 SW 42nd St., Topeka KS 66609-1265. (785)274-4300. Fax: (785)274-4305. E-mail: grit@grit.com. Website: www.grit.com. **Contact:** Ann Crahan, editor-in-chief. **90% freelance written.** Open to new writers. Monthly magazine. ''*Grit* is good news. As a wholesome, family-oriented magazine published for more than a century and distributed nationally, *Grit* features articles about family lifestyles, traditions, values, and pastimes. *Grit* accents the best of American life and traditions—past and present. Our readers are ordinary people doing extraordinary things, with courage, heart, determination, and imagination. Many of them live in small towns and rural areas across the country; others live in cities but share many of the values typical of small-town America.'' Estab. 1882. Circ. 100,000. Pays on publication. Byline given. Buys first North American serial rights. Submit seasonal material 6 months in advance. Accepts queries by mail. Sample copy and writer's guidelines for $4 and 11 × 14 SASE with 4 first-class stamps. Sample articles on website.

➤ Break in through departments such as Best Friends, Looking Back, Poetry.

Nonfiction The best way to sell work is by reading each issue cover to cover. Features (timely, newsworthy, touching but with a *Grit* angle), readers' true stories, outdoor hobbies, collectibles, gardening, crafts, hobbies, leisure pastimes. Query by mail only. Prefers full ms with photos. Length: Main features run 1,200-1,500 words. Department features average 800-1,000 words. **Pays 15¢/word for features; plays flat rate for departments.**

Photos Professional quality photos (b&w prints or color slides/prints) increase acceptability of articles. Send photos with submission. Pays up to $25 each in features according to quality, placement, and color/b&w. Payment for department photos included in flat rate.

Fiction Short stories, 1,500-3,500 words; may also purchase accompanying art if of high quality and appropriate. Need serials (romance, westerns, mysteries), 3,500-10,000 words. Send ms with SASE to Fiction Dept. Adventure, condensed novels, mainstream, mystery, religious, romance, western, nostalgia. ''No sex, violence, drugs, obscene words, abuse, alcohol, or negative diatribes.''

Tips ''Articles should be directed to a national audience, mostly 40 years and older. Sources identified fully. Our readers are warm and loving. They want to read about others with heart. Tell us stories about someone unusual, an unsung hero, an artist of the backroads, an interesting trip with an emotional twist, a memory with a message, an ordinary person accomplishing extraordinary things. Tell us stories that will make us cry with joy.'' Send complete ms with photos for consideration.

$ $ $ $ HARPER'S MAGAZINE

666 Broadway, 11th Floor, New York NY 10012. (212)420-5720. Fax: (212)228-5889. Website: www.harpers.o rg. Editor: Lewis H. Lapham. **90% freelance written.** Monthly magazine for well-educated, socially concerned,

widely read men and women who value ideas and good writing. *"Harper's Magazine* encourages national discussion on current and significant issues in a format that offers arresting facts and intelligent opinions. By means of its several shorter journalistic forms—Harper's Index, Readings, Forum, and Annotation—as well as with its acclaimed essays, fiction, and reporting, *Harper's* continues the tradition begun with its first issue in 1850: to inform readers across the whole spectrum of political, literary, cultural, and scientific affairs." Estab. 1850. Circ. 230,000. **Pays on acceptance.** Publishes ms an average of 3 months after acceptance. Offers negotiable kill fee. Accepts previously published material. Responds in 6 weeks to queries. Sample copy for $5.95.

Nonfiction "For writers working with agents or who will query first only, our requirements are: public affairs, literary, international and local reporting, and humor." Publishes 1 major report/issue. Length: 4,000-6,000 words. Publishes 1 major essay/issue. Length: 4,000-6,000 words. "These should be construed as topical essays on all manner of subjects (politics, the arts, crime, business, etc.) to which the author can bring the force of passionate and informed statement." Humor. No interviews; no profiles. **Buys 2 mss/year.** Query. Length: 4,000-6,000 words.

Reprints Accepted for Readings section. Send typed ms with rights for sale noted and information about when and where the article previously appeared.

Photos Occasionally purchased with ms; others by assignment. Stacey Clarkson, art director. State availability with submission. Pays $50-500.

Fiction Lewis H. Lapham, editor. Will consider unsolicited fiction. Humorous. **Buys 12 mss/year.** Query. Length: 3,000-5,000 words. **Generally pays 50¢-$1/word.**

Tips "Some readers expect their magazines to clothe them with opinions in the way that Bloomingdale's dresses them for the opera. The readers of *Harper's Magazine* belong to a different crowd. They strike me as the kind of people who would rather think in their own voices and come to their own conclusions."

$ $ $ $ NATIONAL GEOGRAPHIC MAGAZINE

1145 17th St. NW, Washington DC 20036. (202)857-7000. Fax: (202)492-5767. Website: www.nationalgeograph ic.com. Editor-in-Chief: Chris Johns. **Contact:** Oliver Payne, senior editor. **60% freelance written.** Prefers to work with published/established writers. Monthly magazine for members of the National Geographic Society. "Timely articles written in a compelling, 'eyewitness' style. Arresting photographs that speak to us of the beauty, mystery, and harsh realities of life on earth. Maps of unprecedented detail and accuracy. These are the hallmarks of *National Geographic* magazine. Since 1888, the *Geographic* has been educating readers about the world." Estab. 1888. Circ. 6,800,000.

   O→ Before querying, study recent issues and check a *Geographic Index* at a library since the magazine seldom returns to regions or subjects covered within the past 10 years.

Nonfiction *National Geographic* publishes general interest, illustrated articles on science, natural history, exploration, cultures and geographical regions. Of the freelance writers assigned, a few are experts in their fields; the remainder are established professionals. Fewer than 1% of unsolicited queries result in assignments. Query (500 words with clips of published articles by mail to Senior Assitant Editor Oliver Payne. Do not send mss. Length: 2,000-8,000 words. Pays expenses of writers on assignment.

Photos Query in care of the Photographic Division.

   ▣ The online magazine carries original content not included in the print edition. Contact: Valerie May, online editor.

Tips "State the theme(s) clearly, let the narrative flow, and build the story around strong characters and a vivid sense of place. Give us rounded episodes, logically arranged."

Ⓝ $ $ NAVIGO MAGAZINE

Partridge Hill Press, P.O. Box 310, Charlton MA 01507. (508)248-1113. E-mail: nissa.gadbois@navigo-online.c om. Website: www.navigo-online.com. **Contact:** Nissa Gadbois, editor. **50-100% freelance written.** Magazine published 8 times/year. "We aim to speak to readers who appreciate well-written, in-depth articles with an educational focus (rather than a litany of how-to advice), beautiful photography, and quality resources." Estab. 2005. Circ. 40,000. Pays on publication. Publishes ms an average of 3 months after acceptance. Byline given. Offers 15% kill fee. Buys all rights. Editorial lead time 3 months. Submit seasonal material 3 months in advance. Accepts queries by mail, e-mail. Responds in 3 weeks to queries; 2 months to mss. Sample copy for $8. Writer's guidelines free.

Nonfiction Interview/profile, new product, photo feature, travel. Special issues: Elite Sports (summer and winter). Query. Length: 500-1,200 words. **Pays $40-500.** Sometimes pays expenses of writers on assignment.

Photos Send photos with submission. Reviews contact sheets, 5×7 prints, GIF/JPEG files. Buys all rights. Negotiates payment individually. Captions, identification of subjects, model releases required.

Columns/Departments Travel feature (road scholars); Product reviews and recommended books/products; Humor, Student/Family (highlighting work of a home-educated child/family); Focus on History; Focus on Science; Focus on Culture; Geography Sidebars (with factoids). **Buys 24 mss/year.** Query. **Pays $40-500.**

Tips "We're targeting home learners who are more adventurous types—who travel frequently for educational and recreational purposes, who go out of their way to avail themselves of more in-depth educational opportunities, are focused on getting the most from their educational experience as a family, are goal driven, and don't mind spending more for better resources. *Navigo* magazine's voice is one of educated sophistication and intelligence, but which can be enjoyed by parents and children (ages 10 and up) alike. Our audience is made up of mainly home learners who educate for excellence and achievement (by a variety of methods), but will also appeal to 'traditional schoolers' who want to augment what their children are learning at school."

⊘ NEW YORK TIMES UPFRONT

Scholastic, Inc., 557 Broadway, New York NY 10012-3999. Website: www.upfrontmagazine.com. Biweekly magazine collaboration between *The New York Times* and Scholastic, Inc. designed as a news magazine specifically for teenagers. Circ. 200,000. Editorial lead time 1-2 months.
- Query before submitting.

THE NEW YORKER

4 Times Square, New York NY 10036. (212) 286-5900. Website: www.newyorker.com. Weekly magazine. A quality magazine of distinct news stories, articles, essays and poems for a literate audience. Estab. 1925. Circ. 1,000,000. **Pays on acceptance.** Accepts queries by e-mail. Responds in 3 months to mss. Writer's guidelines online.
- *The New Yorker* receives approximately 4,000 submissions per month.
- ⊶ For e-mail submissions: fiction@newyorker.com (fiction); talkofthetown@newyorker.com (Talk of the Town); shouts@newyorker.com (Shouts & Murmurs); poetry@newyorker.com (poetry); newsbreaks@newyorker.com (newsbreaks).

Fiction Publishes 1 ms/issue. Send complete ms. **Payment varies.**

Poetry Send poetry to "Poetry Department."

Tips "Be lively, original, not overly literary. Write what you want to write, not what you think the editor would like."

$ $ $ NEWSWEEK

251 W. 57th St., 17th Floor, New York NY 10019. E-mail: letters@newsweek.com. Website: www.newsweek.com. "*Newsweek* is edited to report the week's developments on the newsfront of the world and the nation through news, commentary and analysis." Accepts unsolicited mss for *My Turn*, a column of personal opinion. The 850-900 word essays for the column must be original, not published elsewhere, and contain verifiable facts. **Payment is $1,000** on publication. Circ. 3,180,000. Acquires non-exclusive world-wide rights. Responds in 2 months (only on submissions with SASE) to mss.

$ $ $ THE OLD FARMER'S ALMANAC

Yankee Publishing, Inc., Main St., Dublin NH 03444. (603)563-8111. Fax: (603)563-8252. Website: www.almanac.com. **Contact:** Janice Stillman, editor. **95% freelance written.** Annual magazine covering weather, gardening, history, oddities, lore. "*The Old Farmer's Almanac* is the oldest continuously published periodical in North America. Since 1792, it has provided useful information for people in all walks of life: tide tables for those who live near the ocean; sunrise tables and planting charts for those who live on the farm or simply enjoy gardening; recipes for those who like to cook; and forecasts for those who don't like the question of weather left up in the air. The words of the *Almanac*'s founder, Robert B. Thomas, guide us still: 'Our main endeavor is to be useful, but with a pleasant degree of humour.'" Estab. 1792. Circ. 3,750,000. **Pays on acceptance.** Publishes ms an average of 9 months after acceptance. Byline given. Offers 25% kill fee. Buys first North American serial, electronic, all rights. Editorial lead time 6 months. Submit seasonal material 1 year in advance. Accepts queries by mail. Responds in 3 weeks to queries; 2 months to mss. Sample copy for $5 at bookstores or online. Writer's guidelines online.

Nonfiction General interest, historical/nostalgic, how-to (garden, cook, save money), humor, weather, natural remedies, obscure facts, history, popular culture. No personal weather recollections/accounts, personal/family histories. Query with published clips. Length: 800-2,500 words. **Pays 65¢/word.** Sometimes pays expenses of writers on assignment.

Fillers Anecdotes, short humor. **Buys 1-2/year.** Length: 100-200 words. **Pays $25.**

▣ The online magazine carries original content not found in the print edition.

Tips "*The Old Farmer's Almanac* is a reference book. Our readers appreciate obscure facts and stories. Read it. Think differently. Read writer's guidelines online."

OPEN SPACES

Open Spaces Publications, Inc., PMB 134, 6327-C SW Capitol Hwy., Portland OR 97239-1937. (503)227-5764. Fax: (503)227-3401. E-mail: info@open-spaces.com. Website: www.open-spaces.com. President: Penny Harrison. Managing Editor: James Bradley. **Contact:** Elizabeth Arthur, editor. **95% freelance written.** Quarterly general interest magazine. "*Open Spaces* is a forum for informed writing and intelligent thought. Articles are written by experts in various fields. Audience is varied (CEOs and rock climbers, politicos and university presidents, etc.) but is highly educated and loves to read good writing." Estab. 1997. Pays on publication. Publishes ms an average of 6 months after acceptance. Byline given. Offers 20% kill fee. Rights purchased vary with author and material. Editorial lead time 9 months. Accepts queries by mail, fax. Accepts simultaneous submissions. Sample copy for $10. Writer's guidelines online.

Nonfiction Essays, general interest, historical/nostalgic, how-to (if clever), humor, interview/profile, personal experience, travel. **Buys 35 mss/year.** Query with published clips. Length: 1,500-2,500 words; major articles: up to 6,000 words. **Pays variable amount.**

Photos State availability with submission. Buys one-time rights. Captions, identification of subjects required.

Columns/Departments David Williams, departments editor. Books (substantial topics such as the Booker Prize, The Newbery, etc.); Travel (must reveal insight); Sports (past subjects include rowing and swing dancing); Unintended Consequences, 1,500-2,500 words. **Buys 20-25 mss/year.** Query with published clips or send complete ms. **Payment varies.**

Fiction Ellen Teicher, fiction editor. "Quality is far more important than type. Read the magazine. Excellence is the issue—not subject matter." **Buys 8 mss/year.** Length: 2,000-6,000 words. **Payment varies.**

Poetry "Again, quality is far more important than type." Susan Juve-Hu Bucharest, poetry editor. Submit maximum 3 poems with SASE.

Fillers Anecdotes, short humor, cartoons; interesting or amusing Northwest facts; expressions, etc.

Tips "*Open Spaces* reviews all manuscripts submitted in hopes of finding writing of the highest quality. We present a Northwest perspective as well as a national and international one. Best advice is read the magazine."

$ $ $ $ PARADE

The Sunday Magazine, Parade Publications, Inc., 711 Third Ave., New York NY 10017. (212)450-7000. Fax: (212)450-7284. Website: www.parade.com. Editor: Lee Kravitz. **Contact:** Sharon Male, articles editor. **95% freelance written.** Weekly magazine for a general interest audience. Estab. 1941. Circ. 81,000,000. **Pays on acceptance.** Publishes ms an average of 5 months after acceptance. Kill fee varies in amount. Buys worldwide exclusive rights for 7 days, plus nonexclusive electronic and other rights in perpetuity. Editorial lead time 1 month. Accepts queries by mail, fax. Accepts simultaneous submissions. Sample copy and writer's guidelines online.

• Does not accept e-mail queries.

Nonfiction Publishes general interest (on health, trends, social issues or anything of interest to a broad general audience), interview/profile (of news figures, celebrities and people of national significance), and "provocative topical pieces of news value." Spot news events are not accepted, as *Parade* has a 2-month lead time. No fiction, fashion, travel, poetry, cartoons, nostalgia, regular columns, personal essays, quizzes, or fillers. Unsolicited queries concerning celebrities, politicians, sports figures, or technical are rarely assigned. **Buys 150 mss/year.** Query with published clips. Length: 1,200-1,500 words. **Pays $2,500 minimum.** Pays expenses of writers on assignment.

Tips "If the writer has a specific expertise in the proposed topic, it increases a writer's chances for breaking in. Send a well-researched, well-written 1-page proposal and enclose a SASE. Do not submit completed manuscripts."

Ⓝ $ THE POLISHING STONE

Refining the Life You Live Into the Life You Love, 3616 Colby Ave., #707, Everett WA 98201 USA. E-mail: submissions@polishingstone.com. Website: www.polishingstone.com. **Contact:** Lee Revere. **50% freelance written.** Magazine published 5 times/year. *The Polishing Stone* takes an optimistic and realistic look at the environment and quality of life: whole foods, alternative health, earth-friendly and handcrafted products, mindful parenting, relationships, and social and environmental issues. "We focus on healthy lifestyles that are close to the earth, sustainable, and in balance. The issues we cover are serious, but we seek a tone of ease because our personal beliefs lean toward hopefulness about possibilities and opportunities for healing. Facts are encouraged as an accurate assessment of a situation, but should not overshadow the offering of solutions and inspiration. In a world where reporting has become synonymous with shock tactics, speaking from the heart is an effective alternative." Estab. 2004. Pays on publication. Publishes ms an average of 4 months after acceptance. Byline given. Buys first North American serial rights. Editorial lead time 4 months. Submit seasonal material 4 months in advance. Accepts queries by mail. Accepts simultaneous submissions. Responds in 1 month to queries; 2 months to mss. Sample copy and writer's guidelines online.

o— "Our readers range from those relatively new to taking charge of their own health and that of our planet, to that tighter core of people who are dedicated environmentalists. Regardless, they want an accurate recap of the situation and straightforward solutions—dished out with as light a hand as possible."

Nonfiction Book excerpts, essays, general interest, how-to (accepted for the following columns: Whole Foods, From the Ground Up, Everything Herbal, With our Hands and Treading Lightly), humor, inspirational, interview/profile, new product, personal experience. Special issues: The Polishing Stone is published in February, April, July, September and December. Articles often relate to the season in which they appear. "We do not accept travel, religious or technical articles, or any article that focuses on problems without offering solutions. We do not publish reprints." **Buys 75 mss/year.** Query with published clips. Length: 200-1,600 words.

Columns/Departments Whole Foods (preparation of primarily vegetarian foods); From the Ground Up (earth-friendly gardening); Everything Herbal (information about the healing power of herbs); A Balance of Health (practical alternatives for returning to balanced health); Treading Lightly (sustainable products, processes and services); With our Hands (artisans share design for simple hand-made products); Life out Loud (an honest look at how children shape us); Looking Within (spiritual and psychological insights); In Community (the people responsible for healing/changing communities); This Spinning Earth (information and inspiration to heal the earth); In Print & On Screen (reviews of books and movies that explain and encourage). **Buys 75 mss/year.** Query with published clips or send complete ms. **Pays $25-100.**

Poetry Free verse, haiku, light verse. **Buys 5-10 poems/year.** Submit maximum 4 poems. Length: 5-25 lines.

Fillers Anecdotes, facts, short humor. **Buys 10-20/year.** Length: 50-175 words. **Pays $10.**

Tips If previously published, send query letter and clips. Otherwise, send a completed ms of no more than 1,600 words. Send both queries and completed mss by mail only. "We want to give new writers a chance, especially those who are willing to do the work. For queries, this means providing a clear description of your topic, angle, sources, lead, and reason why the article is a good fit for *The Polishing Stone.* Completed manuscripts should be carefully edited and fact-checked prior to submission. As always, read our magazine as a guide to our content and writing style. Draw on your own experiences and expertise and share from the heart."

PORTLAND MAGAZINE

Maine's City Magazine, 722 Congress St., Portland ME 041012. (207)775-4339. Fax: (207)775-2334. Website: www.portlandmagazine.com. **Contact:** Colin Sargent, editor. Monthly "city lifestyle magazine—fiction, style, business, real estate, controversy, fashion, cuisine, interviews and art relating to the Maine area." Estab. 1985. Circ. 100,000. Pays on publication. Buys first North American serial rights.

Fiction Colin Sargent, editor. Send complete ms. Length: 700 words or less.

$ $ READER'S DIGEST

The Reader's Digest Association, Inc., Box 100, Pleasantville NY 10572-0100. Website: www.rd.com. Monthly magazine.

Columns/Departments Life in These United States; All in a Day's Work; Humor in Uniform, **pays $300.** Laughter, the Best Medicine; Quotable Quotes, **pays $100.** Address your submission to the appropriate humor category.

Tips "Full-length, original articles are usually assigned to regular contributors to the magazine. We do not accept or return unpublished manuscripts. We do, however, accept 1-page queries that clearly detail the article idea—with special emphasis on the arc of the story, your interview access to the main characters, your access to special documents, etc. We look for dramatic narratives, articles about everyday heroes, crime dramas, adventure stories. Do include a separate page of your writing credits. We are not interested in poetry, fiction, or opinion pieces. Please submit article proposals on the website."

$ REUNIONS MAGAZINE

P.O. Box 11727, Milwaukee WI 53211-0727. (414)263-4567. Fax: (414)263-6331. E-mail: reunions@execpc.com. Website: www.reunionsmag.com. **Contact:** Edith Wagner, editor. **75% freelance written.** Bimonthly magazine covering reunions—all aspects and types. "*Reunions Magazine* is primarily for people actively planning family, class, military, and other reunions. We want easy, practical ideas about organizing, planning, researching/searching, attending, or promoting reunions." Estab. 1990. Circ. 20,000. Pays on publication. Publishes ms an average of 1 year after acceptance. Byline given. Buys one-time rights. Editorial lead time 6 months. Submit seasonal material 1 year in advance. Accepts queries by mail, e-mail, fax. Accepts previously published material. Responds in about 1 year to queries. Sample copy and writer's guidelines for #10 SASE or online.

Nonfiction "We can't get enough about reunion activities, particularly family reunions with multigenerational activities. We would also like more reunion food-related material." Needs reviewers for books, videos, software (include your requirements). Special features: Ethnic/African-American family reunions; food, kids stuff, theme parks, small venues (bed & breakfasts, dormitories, condos); golf, travel and gaming features; themes, cruises, ranch reunions and reunions in various US locations. Historical/nostalgic, how-to, humor, interview/profile, new product, personal experience, photo feature, travel. **Buys 50 mss/year.** Query with published clips. Length: 500-2,500 (prefers work on the short side). **Pays $25-50.** Often rewards with generous copies.

Reprints Send tearsheet, photocopy or typed ms with rights for sale noted and information about when and where the material previously appeared. Usually pays $10.

Photos Always looking for vertical cover photos screaming: "Reunion!" Prefers print or e-mail pictures. State availability with submission. Reviews contact sheets, negatives, 35mm transparencies, prints, TIFF/JPEG files (300 dpi or higher) as e-mail attachments. Offers no additional payment for photos accepted with ms. Captions, identification of subjects, model releases required.

Fillers Must be reunion-related. Anecdotes, facts, short humor. **Buys 20-40/year.** Length: 50-250 words. **Pays $5.**

■ The online magazine carries original content and includes writer's guidelines and articles. Contact: Edith Wagner, online editor.

Tips "All copy must be reunion-related with strong, real reunion examples and experiences. Write a lively account of an interesting or unusual reunion, either upcoming or soon after while it's hot. Tell readers why the reunion is special, what went into planning it, and how attendees reacted. Our 'Masterplan' section, about family reunion planning, is a great place for a freelancer to start by telling her/his own reunion story. Send us how-tos or tips about any of the many aspects of reunion organizing or activities. Open your minds to different types of reunions—they're all around!"

$ $ $ $ ROBB REPORT

The Magazine for the Luxury Lifestyle, Curtco Media Labs, 1 Acton Place, Acton MA 01720. (978)264-7500. Fax: (978)264-7505. E-mail: miken@robbreport.com. Website: www.robbreport.com. **Contact:** Mike Nolan, editor. **60% freelance written.** Monthly magazine. "We are a lifestyle magazine geared toward active, affluent readers. Addresses upscale autos, luxury travel, boating, technology, lifestyles, watches, fashion, sports, investments, collectibles." Estab. 1976. Circ. 111,000. Pays on publication. Byline given. Offers 25% kill fee. Buys first North American serial, all rights. Submit seasonal material 5 months in advance. Accepts queries by mail, fax. Responds in 2 months to queries; 1 month to mss. Sample copy for $10.95, plus shipping and handling. Writer's guidelines for #10 SASE.

Nonfiction General interest (autos, lifestyle, etc), interview/profile (prominent personalities/entrepreneurs), new product (autos, boats, consumer electronics), travel (international and domestic). Special issues: Home (October); Recreation (March). **Buys 60 mss/year.** Query with published clips. Length: 500-3,500 words. **Pays $150-2,000.** Sometimes pays expenses of writers on assignment.

Photos State availability with submission. Buys one-time rights. Payment depends on article.

■ The online magazine carries original content not found in the print edition. Contact: Mike Nolan.

Tips "Show zest in your writing, immaculate research, and strong thematic structure, and you can handle most any assignment. We want to put the reader there, whether the article is about test driving a car, fishing for marlin, touring a luxury home, or profiling a celebrity. The best articles will be those that tell compelling stories. Anecdotes should be used liberally, especially for leads, and the fun should show in your writing."

$ $ THE SATURDAY EVENING POST

The Saturday Evening Post Society, 1100 Waterway Blvd., Indianapolis IN 46202. (317)634-1100. Fax: (317)637-0126. Website: www.satevepost.org. Travel Editor: Holly Miller. Medical/Fitness Editor: Cory SerVaas, MD. **30% freelance written.** Bimonthly general interest, family-oriented magazine focusing on physical fitness, preventive medicine. "Ask almost any American if he or she has heard of *The Saturday Evening Post*, and you will find that many have fond recollections of the magazine from their childhood days. Many readers recall sitting with their families on Saturdays awaiting delivery of their *Post* subscription in the mail. *The Saturday Evening Post* has forged a tradition of 'forefront journalism.' *The Saturday Evening Post* continues to stand at the journalistic forefront with its coverage of health, nutrition, and preventive medicine." Estab. 1728. Circ. 350,000. Pays on publication. Publishes ms an average of 3 months after acceptance. Byline given. Buys all rights. Submit seasonal material 4 months in advance. Accepts queries by mail, fax. Accepts simultaneous submissions. Responds in 3 weeks to queries; 6 weeks to mss.

Nonfiction Book excerpts, how-to (gardening, home improvement), humor, interview/profile, travel, medical, health, fitness. "No political articles or articles containing sexual innuendo or hypersophistication." **Buys 25 mss/year.** Query with or without published clips or send complete ms. Length: 2,500-3,000 words. **Pays $25-400.** Sometimes pays expenses of writers on assignment.

Photos State availability with submission. Reviews negatives, transparencies. Buys one-time or all rights. Offers $50 minimum, negotiable maximum per photo. Identification of subjects, model releases required.

Columns/Departments Travel (destinations); Post Scripts (well-known humorists); Post People (activities of celebrities). Length 750-1,500. **Buys 16 mss/year.** Query with published clips or send complete ms. **Pays $150 minimum, negotiable maximum.**

Fiction Fiction Editor.

Poetry Light verse.

Fillers Post Scripts Editor: Steve Pettinga. Anecdotes, short humor. **Buys 200/year.** Length: 300 words. **Pays $15.**

Tips ''Areas most open to freelancers are Health, Fitness, Research Breakthroughs, Nutrition, Post Scripts, and Travel. For travel we like text-photo packages, pragmatic tips, side bars and safe rather than exotic destinations. Query by mail, not phone. Send clips.''

⚎ SHARED VISION

Raven Eagle Partners Co., 873 Beatty St., Suite 203, Vancouver BC V6B 2H6 Canada. (604)733-5062. Fax: (604)731-1050. E-mail: editor@shared-vision.com. Website: www.shared-vision.com. **Contact:** Beverley Sinclair, editor/associate publisher. **75% freelance written.** Monthly magazine covering health and wellness, environment, personal growth, spirituality, social justice, and issues related to food. Estab. 1988. Circ. 40,000 monthly. Byline given. Editorial lead time 3 months. Submit seasonal material 3 months in advance. Accepts queries by mail, e-mail, fax. Accepts previously published material. Sample copy for $3 Canadian, postage paid. Writer's guidelines by e-mail.

Nonfiction Book excerpts, general interest, inspirational, personal experience, travel, health, environment. Query with published clips.

Columns/Departments Footnotes (first-person inspirational). Query with published clips.

Tips ''Reading the magazine is the optimum method. E-mail the editor for writer's guidelines.''

$ $ $ $ SMITHSONIAN MAGAZINE

MRC 951, P.O. Box 37012, Washington DC 20013-7012. (202)275-2000. Website: www.smithsonianmag.com. **90% freelance written.** Monthly magazine for associate members of the Smithsonian Institution; 85% with college education. ''*Smithsonian Magazine's* mission is to inspire fascination with all the world has to offer by featuring unexpected and entertaining editorial that explores different lifestyles, cultures and peoples, the arts, the wonders of nature and technology, and much more. The highly educated, innovative readers of *Smithsonian* share a unique desire to celebrate life, seeking out the timely as well as timeless, the artistic as well as the academic, and the thought-provoking as well as the humorous.'' Circ. 2,300,000. **Pays on acceptance.** Publishes ms an average of 6 months after acceptance. Offers 33% kill fee. Buys first North American serial rights. Editorial lead time 2 months. Submit seasonal material 3 months in advance. Accepts queries by e-mail. Responds in 2 months to queries. Sample copy for $5. Writer's guidelines online.

    ⊶ ''We consider focused subjects that fall within the general range of Smithsonian Institution interests, such as: cultural history, physical science, art, and natural history. We are always looking for offbeat subjects and profiles. We do not consider fiction, poetry, political and news events, or previously published articles. We publish only 12 issues a year, so it is difficult to place an article in *Smithsonian*, but please be assured that all proposals are considered.''

Nonfiction ''Our mandate from the Smithsonian Institution says we are to be interested in the same things which now interest or should interest the institution: Cultural and fine arts, history, natural sciences, hard sciences, etc.'' **Buys 120-130 feature (up to 5,000 words) and 12 short (500-650 words) mss/year.** Use online submission form. **Pays various rates per feature, $1,500 per short piece.** Pays expenses of writers on assignment.

Photos Purchased with or without ms and on assignment. ''Illustrations are not the responsibility of authors, but if you do have photographs or illustration materials, please include a selection of them with your submission. In general, 35mm color transparencies or black-and-white prints are perfectly acceptable. Photographs published in the magazine are usually obtained through assignment, stock agencies, or specialized sources. No photo library is maintained and photographs should be submitted only to accompany a specific article proposal.'' Send photos with submission. Pays $400/full color page. Captions required.

Columns/Departments Last Page humor, 550-700 words. Use online submission form. **Pays $1,000-1,500.**

HEALTH & FITNESS

$ $ AMERICAN FITNESS

15250 Ventura Blvd., Suite 200, Sherman Oaks CA 91403. (818)905-0040. Fax: (818)990-5468. Website: www.afaa.com. Publisher: Roscoe Fawcett. **Contact:** Dr. Meg Jordan, editor. **75% freelance written.** Bimonthly magazine covering exercise and fitness, health, and nutrition. ''We need timely, in-depth, informative articles on health, fitness, aerobic exercise, sports nutrition, age-specific fitness, and outdoor activity.'' Absolutely no first-person accounts. Need well-reserched articles for professional readers. Circ. 42,000. Pays 30 days after publication. Publishes ms an average of 6 months after acceptance. Byline given. Submit seasonal material 4 months in advance. Accepts queries by mail, fax. Accepts previously published material. Accepts simultaneous submissions. Responds in 2 months to queries. Sample copy for $4.50 and SAE with 6 first-class stamps.

Nonfiction Needs include health and fitness, including women's issues (pregnancy, family, pre- and post-natal, menopause, and eating disorders); new research findings on exercise techniques and equipment; aerobic exercise; sports nutrition; sports medicine; innovations and trends in aerobic sports; tips on teaching exercise and humorous accounts of fitness motivation; physiology; youth and senior fitness. Historical/nostalgic (history of various athletic events), inspirational, interview/profile (fitness figures), new product (plus equipment review), personal experience (successful fitness story), photo feature (on exercise, fitness, new sport), travel (activity adventures). No articles on unsound nutritional practices, popular trends, or unsafe exercise gimmicks. **Buys 18-25 mss/year.** Query with published clips or send complete ms. Length: 800-1,200 words. **Pays $200 for features, $80 for news.** Sometimes pays expenses of writers on assignment.

Photos Sports, action, fitness, aquatic aerobics competitions, and exercise class. "We are especially interested in photos of high-adrenalin sports like rock climbing and mountain biking." Reviews transparencies, prints. Usually buys all rights; other rights purchased depend on use of photo. Pays $35 for transparencies. Captions, identification of subjects, model releases required.

Columns/Departments Research (latest exercise and fitness findings); Alternative paths (nonmainstream approaches to health, wellness, and fitness); Strength (latest breakthroughs in weight training); Clubscene (profiles and highlights of fitness club industry); Adventure (treks, trails, and global challenges); Food (low-fat/nonfat, high-flavor dishes); Homescene (home-workout alternatives); Clip 'n Post (concise exercise research to post in health clubs, offices or on refrigerators). Length: 800-1,000 words. Query with published clips or send complete ms. **Pays $100-200.**

Tips "Make sure to quote scientific literature or good research studies and several experts with good credentials to validate exercise trend, technique, or issue. Cover a unique aerobics or fitness angle, provide accurate and interesting findings, and write in a lively, intelligent manner. Please, no first-person accouts of 'how I lost weight or discovered running.' *AF* is a good place for first-time authors or regularly published authors who want to sell spin-offs or reprints."

$ $ ⬛ AMERICAN HEALTH & FITNESS

CANUSA Publishing, 5775 McLaughlin Rd., Mississauga ON L5R 3P9 Canada. Fax: (905)507-2372. E-mail: editorial@ahfmag.com. Website: www.ahfmag.com. Bimonthly magazine. "*American Health & Fitness* is designed to help male fitness enthusiasts (18-39) stay fit, strong, virile, and healthy through sensible diet and exercise." Estab. 2000. Circ. 310,000. **Pays on acceptance.** Publishes ms an average of 6 months after acceptance. Byline given. Buys all rights. Editorial lead time 4 months. Submit seasonal material 6 months in advance. Accepts queries by mail, e-mail, fax. Responds in 4 months. Sample copy for $5.

Nonfiction How-to, humor, inspirational, interview/profile, new product, personal experience, photo feature, bodybuilding and weight training, health & fitness tips, diet, medical advice, workouts, nutrition. **Buys 80-100 mss/year.** Send complete ms. Length: 800-1,500 words. **Pays 25-45¢/word.**

Photos Send photos with submission. Reviews 35mm transparencies, 8×10 prints. Buys all rights. Offers $35 and up/photo. Captions, identification of subjects required.

Columns/Departments Personal Training; Strength & Conditioning; Fitness; Longevity; Natural Health; Sex. **Buys 40 mss/year.** Send complete ms.

Fillers Anecdotes, facts, gags to be illustrated by cartoonist, newsbreaks (fitness, nutrition, health), short humor. **Buys 50-100/year.** Length: 100-200 words.

$ $ ⬛ ASCENT MAGAZINE

Yoga for an Inspired Life, Timeless Books, 837 Rue Gilford, Montreal QC H2J 1P1 Canada. (514)499-3999. Fax: (514)499-3904. E-mail: info@ascentmagazine.com. Website: www.ascentmagazine.com. Editor: Sarah E. Truman. **Contact:** Anurag Dhir, managing editor. **75% freelance written.** Quarterly magazine covering engaged spirituality, with a focus on yoga philosophy and practice. "*Ascent* publishes unique and personal perspectives on yoga and spirituality. Our goal is to explore what it means to be truly human, to think deeply, and live a meaningful life in today's world." Estab. 1999. Circ. 6,000. Pays on publication. Publishes ms an average of 3 months after acceptance. Byline given. Offers 20% kill fee. Buys first North American serial, with exclusive rights for 6 months after publication rights. Editorial lead time 4 months. Submit seasonal material 6 months in advance. Accepts queries by e-mail. Responds in 1 month. Sample copy for $5. Writer's guidelines online.

Nonfiction Essays, interview/profile, personal experience, photo feature, spiritual. Special issues: Liberation (Fall); Health & Healing (Winter); Family (Spring). No academic articles or promotional articles for specific yoga school or retreats. **Buys 30 mss/year.** Query with published clips. Length: 800-3,500 words. **Pays 20¢/word (Canadian).** Sometimes pays expenses of writers on assignment.

Photos Joe Ollmann, designer. Reviews GIF/JPEG files. Buys one-time rights. Negotiates payment individually.

Columns/Departments Reviews (books and CDs), 500 words. **Buys 10 mss/year.** Query based on online guidelines. **Pays $50-150 (Canadian).**

Tips "*Ascent* publishes mainly personal, reflective nonfiction. Make sure to tell us how you will bring a personal, intimate tone to your article. Send a detailed query with writing samples. Give us a good idea of your potential as a writer."

$ $ BETTER HEALTH

Hospital of Saint Raphael, 1450 Chapel St., New Haven CT 06511. (203)789-3972. Fax: (203)789-4053. E-mail: cboynton@srhs.org. Website: www.srhs.org/betterhealth. **Contact:** Cynthia Wolfe Boynton, editor/publishing director. **90% freelance written.** Prefers to work with published/established writers; will consider new/unpublished writers. Bimonthly magazine devoted to health, wellness, medicine, fitness, and nutrition. Estab. 1979. Circ. 500,000. **Pays on acceptance.** Byline given. Offers 20% kill fee. Buys first North American serial rights. Sample copy for $2.50. Writer's guidelines online.

Nonfiction Wellness/prevention issues are of primary interest. New medical techniques or nonmainstream practices are not considered. No fillers, poems, quizzes, seasonal, heavy humor, inspirational or personal experience. **Buys 30 mss/year.** Query with published clips. Length: 1,500-3,000 words. **Pays $250-700.**

$ $ $ BETTER NUTRITION

Active Interest Media, 301 Concourse Blvd., Suite 350, Glen Allen VA 23059. (804)346-0990. Fax: (804)346-1223. E-mail: editorial@betternutrition.com. Website: www.betternutrition.com. **Contact:** Jerry Shaver, managing editor. **57% freelance written.** Monthly magazine covering nutritional news and approaches to optimal health. "The new *Better Nutrition* helps people (men, women, families, old and young) integrate nutritious food, the latest and most effective dietary supplements, and exercise/personal care into healthy lifestyles." Estab. 1938. Circ. 460,000. Pays on publication. Publishes ms an average of 2 months after acceptance. Byline given. Buys varies according to article rights. Editorial lead time 3 months. Accepts queries by mail, e-mail. Sample copy for free.

Nonfiction Each issue has multiple features, clinical research crystallized into accessible articles on nutrition, health, alternative medicine, disease prevention. **Buys 120-180 mss/year.** Query. Length: 400-1,200 words. **Pays $400-1,000.**

Photos State availability with submission. Reviews 4×5 transparencies, 3×5 prints. Buys one-time rights or non-exclusive reprint rights. Negotiates payment individually. Captions, identification of subjects, model releases required.

Tips "Be on top of what's newsbreaking in nutrition and supplementation. Interview experts. Fact-check, fact-check, fact-check. Send in a résumé (including Social Security/IRS number), a couple of clips, and a list of article possibilities."

$ $ CLIMBING

Primedia Enthusiast Group, 0326 Highway 133, Suite 190, Carbondale CO 81623. (970)963-9449. Fax: (970)963-9442. Website: www.climbing.com. Editor: Jeff Achey. Magazine published 9 times/year covering climbing and mountaineering. Provides features on rock climbing and mountaneering worldwide. Estab. 1970. Circ. 51,000. Pays on publication. Editorial lead time 6 weeks. Accepts queries by e-mail. Sample copy for $4.99. Writer's guidelines online.

Nonfiction SASE returns. Interview/profile (interesting climbers), personal experience (climbing adventures), Surveys of different areas. Query. Length: 2,000-5,000 words. **Pays 35¢/word.**

Photos State availability with submission. Reviews negatives, 35mm transparencies, prints. Pays $75-700.

Columns/Departments Query. **Payment varies.**

Ⓝ $ $ DELICIOUS LIVING!

Feel Good/Live Well, New Hope Natural Media, 1401 Pearl St., Suite 200, Boulder CO 80302. (303)939-8440. Fax: (303)939-9886. E-mail: delicious@newhope.com. Website: www.healthwell.com. **85% freelance written.** Monthly magazine covering natural products, nutrition, alternative medicines, herbal medicines. "*Delicious Living!* magazine empowers natural foods store shoppers to make health-conscious choices in their lives. Our goal is to improve consumers' perception of the value of natural methods in achieving health. To do this, we educate consumers on nutrition, disease prevention, botanical medicines and natural personal care products." Estab. 1985. Circ. 420,000. **Pays on acceptance.** Publishes ms an average of 6 months after acceptance. Byline given. Offers 20% kill fee. Editorial lead time 6 months. Submit seasonal material 8 months in advance. Accepts simultaneous submissions. Responds in 3 months to queries. Sample copy and writer's guidelines free.

Nonfiction Book excerpts, how-to, interview/profile, personal experience (regarding natural or alternative health), health nutrition, herbal medicines, alternative medicine, environmental. **Buys 150 mss/year.** Query with published clips. Length: 500-2,000 words. **Pays $100-700 for assigned articles; $50-300 for unsolicited articles.**

Photos State availability with submission. Reviews 3×5 prints. Buys one-time rights. Offers no additional payment for photos accepted with ms. Identification of subjects required.

Columns/Departments Herbs (scientific evidence supporting herbal medicines), 1,500 words; Nutrition (new research on diet for good health), 1,200 words; Dietary Supplements (new research on vitamins/minerals, etc.), 1,200 words. Query with published clips. **Pays $100-500.**

Tips "Highlight any previous health/nutrition/medical writing experience. Demonstrate a knowledge of natural medicine, nutrition, or natural products. Health practitioners who demonstrate writing ability are ideal freelancers."

☑ FIT PREGNANCY

Weider Publications, Inc., 21100 Erwin St., Woodland Hills CA 91367-3712. Website: www.fitpregnancy.com. Bimonthly magazine. Circ. 505,000.
- Does not buy freelance material or use freelance writers.

$ $ HEALING LIFESTYLES & SPAS

P.O. Box 90110, Santa Barbara CA 93190. (202)441-9557. Fax: (805)684-4397. E-mail: editorial@healinglifestyles.com. Website: www.healinglifestyles.com. Editor: Melissa B. Williams. **90% freelance written.** *"Healing Lifestyles & Spas* is a bimonthly magazine committed to healing, health, and living a well-rounded, more natural life. In each issue we cover retreats, spas, organic living, natural food, herbs, beauty, yoga, alternative medicine, bodywork, spirituality, and features on living a healthy lifestyle." Estab. 1996. Circ. 45,000. Pays on publication. Publishes ms an average of 2-10 months after acceptance. Editorial lead time 6 months. Submit seasonal material 6-9 months in advance. Accepts queries by mail, e-mail. Responds in 6 weeks to queries.

Nonfiction "We will consider all in-depth features relating to spas, retreats, lifestyle issues, mind/body well being, yoga, enlightening profiles, and women's health issues." Travel (domestic and international). No fiction or poetry. Query. Length: 1,000-2,000 words. **Pays $150-500, depending on length, research, experience, and availability and quality of images.**

Photos "If you will be providing your own photography, you must use slide film or provide a Mac-formatted CD with image resolution of at least 300 dpi." Send photos with submission. Captions required.

Columns/Departments All Things New & Natural (short pieces outlining new health trends, alternative medicine updates, and other interesting tidbits of information), 50-200 words; Urban Retreats (focuses on a single city and explores its spas and organic living features), 1,200-1,600 words; Health (features on relevant topics ranging from nutrition to health news and updates), 900-1,200 words; Food (nutrition or spa-focused food articles and recipes), 1,000-1,200 words; Seasonal Spa (focuses on a seasonal ingredient on the spa menu), 500-700 words; Spa Origins (focuses on particular modalities and healing beliefs from around the world, 1,000-1,200 words; Yoga, 400-800 words; Spa a la carte (explores a new treatment or modality on the spa menu), 600-1,000 words; Insight (focuses on profiles, theme-related articles, and new therapies, healing practices, and newsworthy items), 1,000-2,000 words. Query.

$ $ $ $ HEALTH

Time, Inc., Southern Progress Corp., 2100 Lakeshore Dr., Birmingham AL 35209. (205)445-6000. Fax: (205)445-5123. E-mail: health@timeinc.com. Website: www.health.com. Vice President/Editor: Doug Crichton. Magazine published 10 times/year covering health, fitness, and nutrition. "Our readers are predominantly college-educated women in their 30s, 40s, and 50s. Edited to focus not on illness, but on wellness news, events, ideas, and people." Estab. 1987. Circ. 1,360,000. **Pays on acceptance.** Byline given. Offers 33% kill fee. Buys first publication and online rights. Accepts queries by mail, fax. Accepts simultaneous submissions. Responds in 2 months to queries to mss. Sample copy for $5 to Back Issues. Writer's guidelines for #10 SASE.

Nonfiction No unsolicited mss. **Buys 25 mss/year.** Query with published clips and SASE. Length: 1,200 words. **Pays $1-1.50/word.** Pays expenses of writers on assignment.

Columns/Departments Food, Mind, Healthy Looks, Fitness, Relationships.

Tips "We look for well-articulated ideas with a narrow focus and broad appeal. A query that starts with an unusual local event and hooks it legitimately to some national trend or concern is bound to get our attention. Use quotes, examples and statistics to show why the topic is important and why the approach is workable. We need to see clear evidence of credible research findings pointing to meaningful options for our readers. Stories should offer practical advice and give clear explanations."

$ $ HEPATITIS

Management and Treatment—A Practical Guide for Patients, Families, and Friends, Quality Publishing, Inc., 523 N. Sam Houston Tollway E., Suite 300, Houston TX 77060. (281)272-2744. Fax: (281)847-5440. E-mail: gdrushel@hepatitismag.com. Website: www.hepatitismag.com. **Contact:** Managing Editor. **70-80% freelance written.** Quarterly magazine covering Hepatitis health news. Estab. 1999. Circ. 25,000. Pays on publication. Publishes ms an average of 2 months after acceptance. Byline given. Buys first North American serial, electronic rights. Editorial lead time 6 months. Submit seasonal material 4 months in advance. Accepts queries by mail, e-mail. Accepts simultaneous submissions. Responds in 6 weeks to queries. Sample copy and writer's guidelines free.

Nonfiction Inspirational, interview/profile, new product, personal experience. "We do not want any one-source or no-source articles." **Buys 42-48 mss/year.** Query with or without published clips. Length: 1,500-2,500 words. Sometimes pays expenses of writers on assignment.

Photos Send photos with submission. Reviews transparencies, prints, GIF/JPEG files. Rights negotiated, usually purchases one-time rights. Offers no additional payment for photos accepted with ms. Identification of subjects required.

Columns/Departments General news or advice on Hepatitis written by a doctor or healthcare professional, 1,500-2,000 words. **Buys 12-18 mss/year.** Query. **Pays $375-500.**

Tips "Be specific in your query. Show me that you know the topic you want to write about, and show me that you can write a solid, well-rounded story."

N $ $ $ LET'S LIVE MAGAZINE

Basic Media Group, Inc., 11050 Santa Monica Blvd., 3rd Floor, Los Angeles CA 90025-3594. (310)445-7500. Fax: (310)445-7583. E-mail: info@letslivemag.com. Website: www.letsliveonline.com. Editor-in-Chief: Beth Salmon. **Contact:** Ayn Nix, senior editor. **95% freelance written.** Monthly magazine emphasizing health and preventive medicine. "We're especially looking for stories that profile a hot, new supplement with growing research to validate its benefits to health and wellness." Estab. 1933. Circ. 1,700,000. Pays within 1 month. Publishes ms an average of 4 months after acceptance. Byline given. Buys all rights. Submit seasonal material 6 months in advance. Accepts queries by mail, e-mail, fax. Responds in 2 months to queries; 3 months to mss. Sample copy for $5 and 10×13 SAE with 6 first-class stamps or on website. Writer's guidelines for #10 SASE.

    ○━ The editors are looking for more cutting-edge, well-researched natural health information that is substantiated by experts and well-respected scientific research literature. Works with a small number of new/unpublished writers each year; expertise in health field helpful.

Nonfiction Mss must be well-researched, reliably documented and written in a clear, readable style. General interest (effects of vitamins, minerals, herbs and nutrients in improvement of health or afflictions), historical/nostalgic (documentation of experiments or treatments establishing value of nutrients as boon to health), how-to (enhance natural beauty, exercise/bodybuilding, acquire strength and vitality, improve health of adults and/or children and prepare tasty, health meals), interview/profile (benefits of research in establishing prevention as key to good health, background and/or medical history of preventive medicine, MDs or PhDs, in advancement of nutrition), opinion (views of orthomolecular doctors or their patients on balue of health foods toward maintaining good health). "No pre-written articles or mainstream medicine pieces such as articles on drugs or surgery." **Buys 2-4 mss/year.** Query with published clips and SASE. Length: 800-1,400 words. **Pays $700-1,200 for features.**

Photos Send photos with submission. Reviews transparencies, prints. Pays $50 for 8×10 color prints, 35mm transparencies. Captions, model releases required.

Columns/Departments Natural Medicine Chest. Query with published clips and SASE. **Payment varies.**

Tips "We want writers with experience in researching nonsurgical medical subjects and interviewing experts with the ability to simplify technical and clinical information for the layman. A captivating lead and structural flow are essential. The most frequent mistakes made by writers are in writing articles that are too technical, in poor style, written for the wrong audience (publication not thoroughly studied), or have unreliable documentation or overzealous faith in the topic reflected by flimsy research and inappropriate tone."

$ $ $ $ MAMM MAGAZINE

Courage, Respect & Survival, MAMM, LLC, 54 W. 22nd St., 4th Floor, New York NY 10010. (646)365-1355. Fax: (646)365-1369. E-mail: editorial@mamm.com. Website: www.mamm.com. **80% freelance written.** Magazine published 10 times/year covering cancer prevention, treatment, and survival for women. "*MAMM* gives its readers the essential tools and emotional support they need before, during and after diagnosis of breast, ovarian and other gynecologic cancers. We offer a mix of survivor profiles, conventional and alternative treatment information, investigative features, essays, and cutting-edge news." Estab. 1997. Circ. 100,000. Pays within 30 days of publication. Publishes ms an average of 3 months after acceptance. Byline given. Offers 50% kill fee. Buys exclusive rights up to 3 months after publishing. Submit seasonal material 3-4 months in advance. Accepts simultaneous submissions. Sample copy and writer's guidelines free.

Nonfiction Book excerpts, essays, exposé, how-to, humor, inspirational, interview/profile, opinion, personal experience, photo feature, historic/nostalgic. **Buys 90 mss/year.** Query with published clips. Length: 200-3,000 words. **Pays $100-3,000.** Negotiates coverage of expenses of writers on assignment.

Photos Send photos with submission. Reviews contact sheets, negatives. Buys first rights. Negotiates payment individually. Identification of subjects required.

Columns/Departments Opinion (cultural/political); International Dispatch (experience); Q and A (interview format), all 600 words. **Buys 30 mss/year.** Query with published clips. **Pays $400-800.**

$ $ $ $ MEN'S HEALTH

Rodale, 33 E. Minor St., Emmaus PA 18098. (610)967-5171. Fax: (610)967-7725. E-mail: mhletters@rodale.com. Website: www.menshealth.com. Editor-in-Chief: David Zinczenko. Executive Editor: Peter Moore. **Contact:** Bill Stieg, senior editor. **50% freelance written.** Magazine published 10 times/year covering men's health and fitness. *"Men's Health* is a lifestyle magazine showing men the practical and positive actions that make their lives better, with articles covering fitness, nutrition, relationships, travel, careers, grooming, and health issues." Estab. 1986. Circ. 1,600,000. **Pays on acceptance.** Offers 25% kill fee. Buys all rights. Accepts queries by mail, fax. Responds in 3 weeks to queries. Writer's guidelines for #10 SASE.

○╌ Freelancers have the best chance with the front-of-the-book piece, Malegrams.

Nonfiction "Authoritative information on all aspects of men's physical and emotional health. We rely on writers to seek out the right experts and to either tell a story from a first-person vantage or get good anecdotes." **Buys 30 features/year; 360 short mss/year.** Query with published clips. Length: 1,200-4,000 words for features, 100-300 words for short pieces. **Pays $1,000-5,000 for features; $100-500 for short pieces.**

Columns/Departments Length: 750-1,500 words. **Buys 80 mss/year. Pays $750- 2,000.**

▣ The online magazine carries original content not included in the print edition. Contact: Rob Gerth, online editor.

Tips "We have a wide definition of health. We believe that being successful in every area of your life is being healthy. The magazine focuses on all aspects of health, from stress issues and nutrition, to exercise and sex. It is 50% staff written, 50% from freelancers. The best way to break in is not by covering a particular subject, but by covering it within the magazine's style. There is a very particular tone and voice to the magazine. A writer has to be a good humor writer as well as a good service writer. Prefers mail queries. No phone calls, please."

Ⓝ $ $ $ MUSCLE & FITNESS

Weider Health & Fitness, 21100 Erwin St., Woodland Hills, CA 91367. (818)884-6800. Fax: (818)595-0463. Website: www.muscle-fitness.com. **Contact:** Maureen Meyers Farrar, managing editor. **50% freelance written.** Monthly magazine covering bodybuilding and fitness for healthy, active men and women. It contains a wide range of features and monthly departments devoted to all areas of bodybuilding, health, fitness, sport, injury prevention and treatment, and nutrition. Editorial fulfills 2 functions: information and entertainment. Special attention is devoted to how-to advice and accuracy. Estab. 1950. Circ. 500,000. Pays on publication. Publishes ms an average of 2 months after acceptance. Editorial lead time 5 months. Submit seasonal material 6 months in advance. Accepts queries by mail. Accepts previously published material. Responds in 1 month to queries.

Nonfiction "All features and departments are written on assignment." Book excerpts, how-to (training), humor, interview/profile, photo feature. **Buys 120 mss/year.** Does not accept unsolicited mss. Length: 800-1,800 words. **Pays $400-1,000 for assigned articles.** Pays expenses of writers on assignment.

Reprints Send photocopy with rights for sale noted and information about when and where the material previously appeared. Payment varies.

Photos State availability with submission.

Tips "Know bodybuilders and bodybuilding. Read our magazine regularly (or at least several issues), come up with new information or a new angle on our subject matter (bodybuilding training, psychology, nutrition, diets, fitness, sports, etc.), then pitch us in terms of providing useful, unique, how-to information for our readers. Send a 1-page query letter (as described in *Writer's Market*) to sell us on your idea and on you as the best writer for that article. Send a sample of your published work."

$ NATURAL BEAUTY & HEALTH MAGAZINE

A Primer for Holistic Health and Natural Living, P.O. Box 600, Chico CA 95927. (530)893-9037. E-mail: editor@ magicalblend.com. Website: www.nbhonline.com. **50% freelance written.** Bimonthly magazine covering alternative healing practices, bodywork, self-help, and spiritual perspectives on wellness. *"Natural Beauty & Health Magazine* exists to aid individuals in achieving better lives, both physically and spiritually. We hold that health is as much a state of the mind as a condition of the body." Estab. 2001. Circ. 100,000. Pays on publication. Publishes ms an average of 2 months after acceptance. Byline given. Responds in 2-6 months to mss. Sample copy for free. Writer's guidelines for #10 SASE.

○╌ Break in by "writing an engaging article about some unique perspective on healthy or balanced living or some form of healing trasnformation with practical advice for readers on how to achieve it or interview a recognizable celebrity with a natural lifestyle."

Nonfiction "Articles must reflect our standards; see our magazine." Book excerpts, essays, general interest, inspirational, interview/profile, travel, spiritual. No poetry or fiction. **Buys 24 mss/year.** Send complete ms. Length: 500-2,000 words. **Pays $35-100.**

Photos State availability with submission. Reviews transparencies. Buys all rights. Negotiates payment individually. Identification of subjects, model releases required.

Fillers Alternative health news. **Buys 12-20/year.** Length: 200-500 words. **Pays variable rate.**

$ $ $ $ POZ

CDM Publishing, LLC, 500 Fifth Ave., Suite 320, New York NY 10110. (212)242-2163. Fax: (212)675-8505. E-mail: poz-editor@poz.com. Website: www.poz.com. Managing Editor: Jennifer Morton. **Contact:** Walter Armstrong, editor. **75% freelance written.** Monthly national magazine for people impacted by HIV and AIDS. "POZ is a trusted source of conventional and alternative treatment information, investigative features, survivor profiles, essays and cutting-edge news for people living with AIDS and their caregivers. POZ is a lifestyle magazine with both health and cultural content." Estab. 1994. Circ. 100,000. Pays 45 days after acceptance. Publishes ms an average of 3 months after acceptance. Byline given. Offers 25% kill fee. Buys first rights. Editorial lead time 4 months. Submit seasonal material 4 months in advance. Accepts simultaneous submissions. Sample copy and writer's guidelines free.

Nonfiction Book excerpts, essays, exposé, historical/nostalgic, how-to, humor, inspirational, interview/profile, opinion, personal experience, photo feature. **Buys 180 mss/year.** Query with published clips. "We take unsolicited mss on speculation only." Length: 200-3,000 words. **Pays $1/word.** Sometimes pays expenses of writers on assignment.

Photos Send photos with submission. Reviews contact sheets, negatives. Buys first rights. Negotiates payment individually. Identification of subjects required.

Columns/Departments Life (personal experience); Back Page (humor); Data Dish (opinion/experience/information), all 600 words. **Buys 120 mss/year.** Query with published clips. $1/word.

Fiction Buys 10 mss/year. Send complete ms. Length: 700-2,000 words. Payment negotiable.

Poetry Avant-garde, free verse, haiku, light verse, traditional. **Buys 12 poems/year.** Submit maximum 3 poems. Length: 10-40 lines. **Payment negotiable.**

Fillers Anecdotes, facts, gags to be illustrated by cartoonist, newsbreaks, short humor. **Buys 90/year.** Length: 50-150 words. **Pays $50-75.**

PREVENTION'S GUIDE: FIT AND FIRM AT 35 PLUS

Rodale, Inc., 33 E. Minor St., Emmaus PA 18098-7726. (610)967-5171. Fax: (610)967-7654. E-mail: preventionspecials@rodale.com. Website: www.prevention.com. Executive Editor: Cindi Caciolo. Semiannual magazine. Targeted to the 35+ women who want to look and feel their best. Circ. 650,000. Sample copy not available.

PREVENTION'S GUIDE: WALKING FIT

Rodale, Inc., 33 E. Minor St., Emmaus PA 18098-0001. (610)967-5171. Fax: (610)967-7654. E-mail: preventionspecials@rodale.com. Website: www.prevention.com. Executive Editor: Cindi Caciolo. Biannual magazine. Serves as a guide for those looking to experience the many benefits of fitness walking. Circ. 650,000. Sample copy not available.

$ $ $ $ SHAPE MAGAZINE

Weider Publications, Inc., 21100 Erwin St., Woodland Hills CA 91367. (818)595-0593. Fax: (818)704-7620. Website: www.shapemag.com. Editor-in-Chief: Anne Russell. **Contact:** Bethany Gumper, assistant editor. **70% freelance written.** Prefers to work with published/established writers. Monthly magazine covering women's health and fitness. "Shape reaches women who are committed to healthful, active lifestyles. Our readers are participating in a variety of fitness-related activities, in the gym, at home and outdoors, and they are also proactive about their health and are nutrition conscious." Estab. 1981. Circ. 1,600,000. **Pays on acceptance.** Offers 33% kill fee. Buys second serial (reprint), all rights. Submit seasonal material 8 months in advance. Responds in 2 months to queries. Sample copy for 9×12 SAE and 4 first-class stamps.

Nonfiction "We use some health and fitness articles written by professionals in their specific fields." Book excerpts, exposé (health, fitness, nutrition related), how-to (get fit), health/fitness, recipes. "No articles that haven't been queried first." **Buys 27 features/year and 36-54 short mss/year.** Query by mail only with published clips. Length: 2,500 words for features, 1,000 words for shorter pieces. **Pays $1.50/word, on average.**

Tips "Review a recent issue of the magazine. Not responsible for unsolicited material. We reserve the right to edit any article."

$ $ ⊘ VIBRANT LIFE

A Magazine for Healthful Living, Review and Herald Publishing Association, 55 W. Oak Ridge Dr., Hagerstown MD 21740-7390. (301)393-4019. Fax: (301)393-4055. E-mail: vibrantlife@rhpa.org. Website: www.vibrantlife.com. **Contact:** Charles Mills, editor. **80% freelance written.** Enjoys working with published/established writers; works with a small number of new/unpublished writers each year. Bimonthly magazine covering health articles (especially from a prevention angle and with a Christian slant). "The average length of time between acceptance of a freelance-written manuscript and publication of the material depends upon the topics: some immediately used; others up to 2 years." Estab. 1885. Circ. 30,000. **Pays on acceptance.** Byline given. Offers 50% kill fee. Buys first serial, first world serial, or sometimes second serial (reprint) rights. Submit seasonal material 9 months in advance. Accepts queries by mail, e-mail, fax. Accepts previously published material. Responds in 1 month to queries. Sample copy for $1. Writer's guidelines online.

- Currently closed to submissions.

Nonfiction ''We seek practical articles promoting better health and a more fulfilled life. We especially like features on breakthroughs in medicine, and most aspects of health. We need articles on how to integrate a person's spiritual life with their health. We'd like more in the areas of exercise, nutrition, water, avoiding addictions of all types, and rest—all done from a wellness perspective.'' Interview/profile (with personalities on health). **Buys 50-60 feature articles/year and 6-12 short mss/year.** Send complete ms. Length: 500-1,500 words for features, 25-250 words for short pieces. **Pays $75-300 for features, $50-75 for short pieces.**

Reprints Send tearsheet and information about when and where the material previously appeared. Pays 50% of amount paid for an original article.

Photos Not interested in b&w photos. Send photos with submission. Reviews 35mm transparencies.

Columns/Departments Pays $75-175.

Tips ''*Vibrant Life* is published for baby boomers, particularly young professionals, age 40-55. Articles must be written in an interesting, easy-to-read style. Information must be reliable; no faddism. We are more conservative than other magazines in our field. Request a sample copy, and study the magazine and writer's guidelines.''

$ $ $ $ VIM & VIGOR

America's Family Health Magazine, 1010 E. Missouri Ave., Phoenix AZ 85014-2601. (602)395-5850. Fax: (602)395-5853. E-mail: betht@mcmurry.com. **Contact:** Stephanie Conner, sernior editor. **90% freelance written.** Quarterly magazine covering health and healthcare. Estab. 1985. Circ. 650,000. **Pays on acceptance.** Publishes ms an average of 6 months after acceptance. Byline given. Buys all rights. Sample copy for 9×12 SAE with 8 first-class stamps. Writer's guidelines for #10 SASE.

Nonfiction ''Absolutely no complete manuscripts will be accepted/returned. All articles are assigned. Send published samples for assignment consideration. Any queries regarding story ideas will be placed on the following year's conference agenda and will be addressed on a topic-by-topic basis.'' Health, disease, medical breakthroughs, exercise/fitness trends, wellness, healthcare. Send published clips and résumé by mail or e-mail. Length: 500-1,200 words. **Pays 90¢-$1/word.** Pays expenses of writers on assignment.

Tips ''Writers must have consumer healthcare experience.''

$ $ $ $ YOGA JOURNAL

475 Sasome St., Suite 850, San Francisco CA 94111. (510)841-9200. Website: www.yogajournal.com. **Contact:** Matthew Solan, senior editor; Todd Jones, senior editor; Phil Catalfo, senior editor; Nora Isaacs, managing editor; Vasela Simic, copy editor. **75% freelance written.** Bimonthly magazine covering the practice and philosophy of yoga. Estab. 1975. Circ. 130,000. Pays within 90 days of acceptance. Publishes ms an average of 10 months after acceptance. Byline given. Offers kill fee on assigned articles. Buys first North American serial rights. Submit seasonal material 4 months in advance. Accepts queries by mail. Accepts previously published material. Responds in 3 months to queries. Sample copy for $4.99. Writer's guidelines online.

Nonfiction ''Yoga is a main concern, but we also highlight other conscious living/New Age personalities and endeavors (nothing too 'woo-woo'). In particular we welcome articles on the following themes: 1) Leaders, spokepersons, and visionaries in the yoga community; 2) The practice of hatha yoga; 3) Applications of yoga to everyday life; 4) Hatha yoga anatomy and kinesiology, and therapeutic yoga; 5) Nutrition and diet, cooking, and natural skin and body care.'' Book excerpts, how-to (yoga, exercise, etc.), inspirational, interview/profile, opinion, photo feature, travel (yoga-related). Does not want unsolicited poetry or cartoons. ''Please avoid New Age jargon and in-house buzz words as much as possible.'' **Buys 50-60 mss/year.** Query with SASE. Length: 3,000-5,000 words. **Pays $800-2,000.**

Reprints Send tearsheet or photocopy with rights for sale noted and information about when and where the material previously appeared.

Columns/Departments Health (self-care, well-being); Body-Mind (hatha Yoga, other body-mind modalities, meditation, yoga philosophy, Western mysticism); Community (service, profiles, organizations, events), all 1,500-2,000 words. **Pays $400-800.** Living (books, video, arts, music), 800 words. **Pays $200-250.** World of Yoga; Spectrum (brief yoga and healthy living news/events/fillers), 150-600 words. **Pays $50-150.** ''We encourage a well-written query letter outlining your subject and describing its appeal.''

Tips ''Please read our writer's guidelines before submission. Do not e-mail or fax unsolicited manuscripts.''

HISTORY

$ $ AMERICA'S CIVIL WAR

Primedia History Group, 741 Miller Dr., Suite D-2, Leesburg VA 20175-8994. (703)771-9400. Fax: (703)779-8345. Website: www.thehistorynet.com. **Contact:** Dana Shoaf, editor. **95% freelance written.** Bimonthly magazine covering "popular history and straight historical narrative for both the general reader and the Civil War buff covering strategy, tactics, personalities, arms and equipment." Estab. 1988. Circ. 78,000. Pays on publication. Byline given. Buys all rights. Accepts queries by mail, e-mail, fax. Sample copy for $5. Writer's guidelines for #10 SASE.

Nonfiction Historical/nostalgic, book notices, preservation news. **Buys 24 mss/year.** Query. Length: 3,500-4,000 words and a 500-word sidebar. **Pays $300 and up.**

Photos Send photos with submission or cite sources. Captions, identification of subjects required.

Columns/Departments Personality (profiles of Civil War personalities); Men & Material (about weapons used); Commands (about units); Eyewitness to War (historical letters and diary excerpts). Length: 2,000 words. **Buys 24 mss/year.** Query. **Pays $150 and up.**

▣ The online magazine carries original content not found in the print edition. Contact: Roger Vance.

Tips "All stories must be true. We do not publish fiction or poetry. Write an entertaining, well-researched, informative and unusual story that grabs the reader's attention and holds it. Include suggested readings in a standard format at the end of your piece. Manuscript must be typed, double-spaced on one side of standard white $8\frac{1}{2} \times 11$, 16-30 pound paper—no onion skin paper or dot matrix printouts. All submissions are on speculation. Prefer subjects to be on disk (IBM- or Macintosh-compatible floppy disk) as well as a hard copy. Choose stories with strong art possibilities."

AMERICAN HERITAGE

90 Fifth Ave., New York NY 10011. (212)367-3100. E-mail: mail@americanheritage.com. Website: www.americanheritage.com. **Contact:** Richard Snow, editor. **70% freelance written.** Magazine published 6 times/year. "*American Heritage* writes from a historical point of view on politics, business, art, current and international affairs, and our changing lifestyles. The articles are written with the intent to enrich the reader's appreciation of the sometimes nostalgic, sometimes funny, always stirring panorama of the American experience." Circ. 350,000. **Pays on acceptance.** Publishes ms an average of 6-12 months after acceptance. Byline given. Buys first North American serial, all rights. Submit seasonal material 1 year in advance. Responds in 2 months to queries. Writer's guidelines for #10 SASE.

⊶ Before submitting material, "check our index to see whether we have already treated the subject."

Nonfiction Wants "historical articles by scholars or journalists intended for intelligent lay readers rather than for professional historians." Emphasis is on authenticity, accuracy, and verve. "Interesting documents, photographs, and drawings are always welcome. Style should stress readability and accuracy." **Buys 30 unsolicited mss/year.** Query. Length: 1,500-6,000 words. **Payment varies.** Sometimes pays expenses of writers on assignment.

Tips "We have over the years published quite a few 'firsts' from young writers whose historical knowledge, research methods, and writing skills met our standards. The scope and ambition of a new writer tell us a lot about his or her future usefulness to us. A major article gives us a better idea of the writer's value. Everything depends on the quality of the material. We don't really care whether the author is 20 and unknown, or 80 and famous, or vice versa. No phone calls, please."

⊘ AMERICAN HISTORY

Primedia History Group, 741 Miller Dr., Suite D-2, Leesburg VA 20175-8994. (703)771-9400. Fax: (703)779-8345. Website: www.thehistorynet.com. **Contact:** Douglas Brinkley, editor. **60% freelance written.** Bimonthly magazine of cultural, social, military, and political history published for a general audience. Estab. 1966. Circ. 95,000. **Pays on acceptance.** Byline given. Buys first rights. Responds in 10 weeks to queries. Sample copy and guidelines for $5 (includes 3rd class postage) or $4 and 9×12 SAE with 4 first-class stamps. Writer's guidelines for #10 SASE.

Nonfiction Features events in the lives of noteworthy historical figures and accounts of important events in American history. Also includes pictorial features on artists, photographers, and graphic subjects. "Material is presented on a popular rather than a scholarly level." **Buys 20 mss/year.** Query by mail only with published clips and SASE. Length: 2,000-4,000 words depending on type of article.

Photos Welcomes suggestions for illustrations.

Tips "Key prerequisites for publication are thorough research and accurate presentation, precise English usage, and sound organization, a lively style, and a high level of human interest. Unsolicited manuscripts not considered. Inappropriate materials include: fiction, book reviews, travelogues, personal/family narratives not of national significance, articles about collectibles/antiques, living artists, local/individual historic buildings/landmarks, and articles of a current editorial nature. Currently seeking articles on significant Civil War subjects. No phone, fax, or e-mail queries, please."

🅽 ⊘ AMERICAN LEGACY

Forbes, Inc., 28 W. 23rd St., 10th Floor, New York NY 10010-5254. (212)367-3100. Fax: (212)367-3151. E-mail: apeterson@forbes.com. Website: www.americanlegacymagazine.net. Editor: Audrey Peterson. Quarterly magazine spotlighting the historical and cultural achievements of African American men and women throughout history. Editorial lead time 6 months.

- Query before submitting.

$ THE ARTILLERYMAN

Historical Publications, Inc., 234 Monarch Hill Rd., Tunbridge VT 05077. (802)889-3500. Fax: (802)889-5627. E-mail: mail@civilwarnews.com. **Contact:** Kathryn Jorgensen, editor. **60% freelance written.** Quarterly magazine covering antique artillery, fortifications, and crew-served weapons 1750-1900 for competition shooters, collectors, and living history reenactors using artillery. "Emphasis on Revolutionary War and Civil War but includes everyone interested in pre-1900 artillery and fortifications, preservation, construction of replicas, etc." Estab. 1979. Circ. 2,000. Pays on publication. Publishes ms an average of 6 months after acceptance. Byline given. Not copyrighted. Buys one-time rights. Accepts queries by mail, e-mail, fax. Accepts previously published material. Accepts simultaneous submissions. Responds in 3 weeks to queries. Sample copy and writer's guidelines for 9×12 SAE with 4 first-class stamps.

   O➔ Break in with a historical or travel piece featuring artillery—the types and history of guns and their use.

Nonfiction Interested in "artillery only, for sophisticated readers. Not interested in other weapons, battles in general." Historical/nostalgic, how-to (reproduce ordnance equipment/sights/implements/tools/accessories, etc.), interview/profile, new product, opinion (must be accompanied by detailed background of writer and include references), personal experience, photo feature, technical (must have footnotes), travel (where to find interesting antique cannon). **Buys 24-30 mss/year.** Send complete ms. Length: 300 words minimum. **Pays $20-60.** Sometimes pays expenses of writers on assignment.

Reprints Send tearsheet or photocopy and information about when and where the material previously appeared. Pays 100% of amount paid for an original article.

Photos Send photos with submission. Pays $5 for 5×7 and larger b&w prints. Captions, identification of subjects required.

Tips "We regularly use freelance contributions for Places-to-Visit, Cannon Safety, The Workshop, and Unit Profiles departments. Also need pieces on unusual cannon or cannon with a known and unique history. To judge whether writing style and/or expertise will suit our needs, writers should ask themselves if they could knowledgeably talk artillery with an expert. Subject matter is of more concern than writer's background."

BRITISH HERITAGE

Primedia History Group, 741 Miller Dr., Suite D-2, Leesburg VA 20175-8994. (703)771-9400. Fax: (703)779-8345. Website: www.thehistorynet.com. Editor: Dana Huntley. Bimonthly magazine covering British heritage. Presents comprehensive information and background of British culture for admirers and those interested in learning about life (past and present) in England, Scotland, and Wales. Circ. 77,485. **Pays on acceptance.** Buys all rights. Editorial lead time 6 months. Accepts queries by mail, e-mail. Sample copy not available.

Nonfiction Historical/nostalgic (British History), interview/profile, travel. **Buys 30 mss/year.** Send complete ms.

Columns/Departments In History's Court (2 writers take opposing sides in a historical debate), 1,500 words; Great Britons (biographical sketches of interesting British personalities), 2,000 words; Rendezvous with Destiny (highlight a specific historical personality focusing on a historic turning point) 1,500 words; It Happened Here (describe a historic home, castle, cathedral, etc.) 2,000 words; Wayfaring (travel oriented features) 2,000 words; Historymakers (interviews with eyewitnesses to historic events) 2,000 words. *British Heritage* does not accept unsolicited mss for In History's Court. The following departments are generally written by the editorial staff or by a regularly commissioned contributing editor: The Game's Afoot; Hindsight; Timeline; The Private Side; Keepsakes; and Reviews.

$ $ $ CIVIL WAR TIMES

741 Miller Dr. SE, Suite D-2, Leesburg VA 20175. (703)779-8371. Fax: (703)779-8345. E-mail: civilwartimes.mag azine@primedia.com. Website: www.thehistorynet.com. Editor: James P. Weeks. **90% freelance written.** Works with a small number of new/unpublished writers each year. Magazine published 6 times/year. "*Civil War Times* is the full-spectrum magazine of the Civil War. Specifically, we look for nonpartisan coverage of battles, prominent military and civilian figures, the home front, politics, military technology, common soldier life, prisoners and escapes, period art and photography, the naval war, blockade-running, specific regiments, and much more." Estab. 1962. Circ. 108,000. Pays on acceptance and on publication. Publishes ms an average of 18 months after acceptance. Buys unlimited usage rights. Submit seasonal material 1 year in advance. Responds in 3-6 months to queries. Sample copy for $6. Writer's guidelines for #10 SASE.

Nonfiction Interview/profile, photo feature, Civil War historical material. "Don't send us a comprehensive article on a well-known major battle. Instead, focus on some part or aspect of such a battle, or some group of soldiers in the battle. Similar advice applies to major historical figures like Lincoln and Lee. Positively no fiction or poetry." **Buys 20 freelance mss/year.** Query with clips and SASE. **Pays $75-800.**

Photos Michael Caplanis, art director.

Tips "We're very open to new submissions. Send query after examining writer's guidelines and several recent issues. Include photocopies of photos that could feasibly accompany the article. Confederate soldiers' diaries and letters are especially welcome."

$ $GATEWAY

(formerly *Gateway Heritage*), Missouri Historical Society, P.O. Box 11940, St. Louis MO 63112-0040. (314)746-4558. Fax: (314)746-4548. E-mail: vwmonks@mohistory.org. Website: www.mohistory.org. **Contact:** Victoria W. Monks, editor. **75% freelance written.** Quarterly magazine covering Missouri history and culture. "*Gateway* is a popular cultural history magazine that is primarily a member benefit of the Missouri Historical Society. Thus, we have a general audience with an interest in the history and culture of Missouri, and St. Louis in particular." Estab. 1980. Circ. 9,000. Pays on publication. Publishes ms an average of 6 months after acceptance. Byline given. Offers $100 kill fee. Buys first North American serial rights. Editorial lead time 6 months. Submit seasonal material 1 year in advance. Accepts queries by mail, e-mail, fax. Responds in 1 month to queries; 2 months to mss. Sample copy for $8. Writer's guidelines for #10 SASE.

Nonfiction Book excerpts, interview/profile, photo feature, historical, scholarly essays, Missouri biographies, viewpoints on events, first-hand historical accounts, regional architectural history, literary history. No genealogies. **Buys 12-15 mss/year.** Query with published clips. Length: 3,500-5,000 words. **Pays $300-400 (average).**

Photos State availability with submission.

Columns/Departments Origins (essays on the beginnings of organizations, movements, and immigrant communities in St. Louis and Missouri), 1,500-2,500 words; Missouri Biographies (biographical sketches of famous and interesting Missourians), 1,500-2,500 words; Gateway Conversations (interviews); Letters Home (excerpts from letters, diaries, and journals), 1,500-2,500 words. **Buys 6-8 mss/year. Pays $250-300.**

Tips "You'll get our attention with queries reflecting new perspectives on historical and cultural topics."

$GOOD OLD DAYS

America's Premier Nostalgia Magazine, House of White Birches, 306 E. Parr Rd., Berne IN 46711. Fax: (260)589-8093. E-mail: editor@goodolddaysonline.com. Website: www.goodolddaysonline.com. **Contact:** Ken Tate, editor. **75% freelance written.** Monthly magazine of first person nostalgia, 1935-1960. "We look for strong narratives showing life as it was in the first half of the 20th century. Our readership is comprised of nostalgia buffs, history enthusiasts, and the people who actually lived and grew up in this era." Pays on contract. Publishes ms an average of 8 months after acceptance. Byline given. Prefers all rights, but will negotiate for First North American serial and one-time rights. Submit seasonal material 10 months in advance. Responds in 2 months to queries. Sample copy for $2. Writer's guidelines online.

- Queries accepted, but are not necessary.

Nonfiction Regular features: Good Old Days on Wheels (auto, plane, horse-drawn, tram, bicycle, trolley, etc.); Good Old Days In the Kitchen (favorite foods, appliances, ways of cooking, recipes); Home Remedies (herbs and poultices, hometown doctors, harrowing kitchen table operations). Historical/nostalgic, humor, personal experience, photo feature, favorite food/recipes, year-round seasonal material, biography, memorable events, fads, fashion, sports, music, literature, entertainment. No fiction accepted. **Buys 350 mss/year.** Query or send complete ms. Length: 500-1,500 words. **Pays $20-100, depending on quality and photos.**

Photos "Send original or professionally copied photographs. Do not submit laser-copied prints." Send photos with submission. Identification of subjects required.

Tips "Most of our writers are not professionals. We prefer the author's individual voice, warmth, humor, and honesty over technical ability."

Ⓝ $ $KANSAS JOURNAL OF MILITARY HISTORY

P.O. Box 828, Topeka KS 66601. (785)357-0510. Fax: (785)357-0579. E-mail: karen@ksjournal.com. Website: www.ksjournal.com. Managing Editor: Deb Goodrich. **Contact:** Tom Goodrich, editor. **20% freelance written.** Quarterly magazine that celebrates and explores the military history of Kansas and its territories and the Kansans who have served here and abroad, and promotes tourism by showcasing historic sites and landmarks. Estab. 2004. Circ. 4,000. Pays on publication. Publishes ms an average of 6 months after acceptance. Byline given. Buys first North American serial rights. Editorial lead time 6 months. Submit seasonal material 1 year in advance. Accepts queries by mail, e-mail. Accepts previously published material. Accepts simultaneous submissions. Responds in 2 weeks to queries; 2 months to mss. Sample copy and writer's guidelines online.

Nonfiction Book excerpts, essays, historical/nostalgic, humor, interview/profile opinion, personal experience, photo feature. Special issues: Lights, Camera, Kansas: movie stills, posters, etc. relating to film in Kansas. Does not want to receive fiction or poetry. **Buys 10 mss/year.** Query with published clips. Length: 500-1,500 words. **Pays $50-200.**

Photos Send photos with submission. Reviews contact sheets, GIF/JPEG files. Buys one-time rights. Offers no additional payment for photos accepted with ms. Captions, identification of subjects, model releases required.

Columns/Departments Hand to Hand (opinion, pro/con, historic figures), 800-1,000 words. **Buys 5 mss/year. Pays $50-200.**

Fillers Anecdotes, facts, gags to be illustrated by cartoonist, short humor. **Buys 20/year.** Length: 200-300 words. **Pays $25-50.**

Tips "We are interested in history that is fun, compelling, and interesting—not academic. The audience is made up of military members, veterans, tourists, and history buffs (novice and knowledgeable)."

MHQ

The Quarterly Journal of Military History, Primedia History Group, 741 Miller Dr., Suite D-2, Leesburg VA 20175-8994. (703)771-9400. Fax: (703)779-8345. Website: www.thehistorynet.com. Editor: Rod Paschall. **100% freelance written.** Quarterly journal covering military history. "*MHQ* offers readers in-depth articles on the history of warfare from ancient times into the 20th century. Authoritative features and departments cover military strategies, philosophies, campaigns, battles, personalities, weaponry, espionage and perspectives, all written in a lively and readable style. Articles are accompanied by classic works of art, photographs and maps. Readers include serious students of military tactics, strategy, leaders and campaigns, as well as general world history enthusiasts. Many readers are currently in the military or retired officers." Estab. 1988. Circ. 40,000. Pays on publication. Byline given. Buys all rights. Editorial lead time 1 year. Submit seasonal material 1 year in advance. Accepts queries by mail, e-mail, fax. Accepts simultaneous submissions. Sample copy for $23 (hardcover), $13 (softcover); some articles on website. Writer's guidelines for #10 SASE.

Nonfiction Historical/nostalgic, personal experience, photo feature. No fiction or stories pertaining to collectibles or reenactments. **Buys 50 mss/year.** Query preferred; also accepts complete ms. Length: 1,500-6,000 words.

Photos Send photos/art with submission. Reviews transparencies, prints. Buys all rights. Negotiates payment individually. Identification of subjects required.

Columns/Departments Artists on War (description of artwork of a military nature); Experience of War (first-person accounts of military incidents); Strategic View (discussion of military theory, strategy); Arms & Men (description of military hardware or unit), all up to 2,500 words. **Buys 20 mss/year.** Send complete ms.

Tips "All stories must be true—we publish no fiction. Although we are always looking for variety, some subjects—World War II, the American Civil War, and military biography, for instance—are the focus of so many proposals that we are forced to judge them by relatively rigid criteria. We are always glad to consider articles on these subjects. However, less common ones—medieval, Asian, or South American military history, for example—are more likely to attract our attention. The likelihood that articles can be effectively illustrated often determines the ultimate fate of manuscripts. Many otherwise excellent articles have been rejected due to a lack of suitable art or photographs. Regular departments—columns on strategy, tactics, and weaponry—average 1,500 words. While the information we publish is scholarly and substantive, we prefer writing that is light, anecdotal, and above all, engaging, rather than didactic."

MILITARY HISTORY

Primedia History Group, 741 Miller Dr., Suite D-2, Leesburg VA 20175-8994. (703)771-9400. Fax: (703)779-8345. Website: www.thehistorynet.com. **Contact:** Jon Guttman, editor. **95% freelance written.** "We'll work with anyone, established or not, who can provide the goods and convince us of its accuracy." Bimonthly magazine covering all military history of the world. "We strive to give the general reader accurate, highly readable, often narrative popular history, richly accompanied by period art." Circ. 112,000. Pays 30 days after publication. Publishes ms an average of 2 years after acceptance. Byline given. Buys all rights. Submit seasonal material 1 year in advance. Accepts queries by mail, e-mail, fax. Sample copy for $5. Writer's guidelines for #10 SASE.

Nonfiction "The best way to break into our magazine is to write an entertaining, informative, and unusual story that grabs the reader's attention and holds it." Historical/nostalgic, interview/profile (military figures of commanding interest), personal experience (only occasionally). **Buys 30 mss/year.** Query with published clips. "Submit a short, self-explanatory query summarizing the story proposed, its highlights, and/or significance. State also your own expertise, access to sources, or proposed means of developing the pertinent information." Length: 4,000 words with a 500-word sidebar.

Columns/Departments Intrigue; Weaponry; Perspectives; Personality; Reviews (books, video, CD-ROMs, software—all relating to military history). Length: 2,000 words. **Buys 24 mss/year.** Query with published clips.

Tips "We would like journalistically 'pure' submissions that adhere to basics, such as full name at first reference, same with rank, and definition of prior or related events, issues cited as context or obscure military 'hardware.'

Read the magazine, discover our style, and avoid subjects already covered. Pick stories with strong art possibilities (real art and photos), send photocopies, tell us where to order the art. Avoid historical overview; focus upon an event with appropriate and accurate context. Provide bibliography. Tell the story in popular but elegant style. Include a hard copy as well as an IBM- or Macintosh-compatible floppy disk.''

NOSTALGIA MAGAZINE

Enriching Today with the Stories of Yesterday, King's Publishing Group, Inc., 1703 N. Normandie St., Spokane WA 99205. (509)323-2086. Fax: (509)323-2096. E-mail: editor@nostalgiamagazine.net. Website: www.nostalgiamagazine.net. **Contact:** Mark Carter, editor. **90% freelance written.** Monthly magazine covering stories and photos of personal, historical, nostalgic experiences: ''I remember when . . .'' *Nostalgia Magazine* is a journal that gathers photos, personal remembrance stories, diaries, and researched stories of well-known—and more often little-known—people, places, and events, and puts them into 1 monthly volume. ''We glean the best of the past to share and enrich life now.'' Pays on publication. Publishes ms an average of 4 months after acceptance. Byline given. ''Buys simultaneous rights and right to reprint in our regional editions and affiliated media.'' Editorial lead time 3 months. Submit seasonal material 4 months in advance. Accepts queries by mail, e-mail. Accepts previously published material. Accepts simultaneous submissions. Responds in 2 months to queries; 3 months to mss. Sample copy for $1. Writer's guidelines available via e-mail or mail.

Nonfiction Book excerpts, exposé, general interest, historical/nostalgic, how-to, humor, inspirational, interview/profile, personal experience, photo feature, religious, travel. Does not want genealogies, current events/news, divisive politics (in historical setting sometimes OK), or glorification of immorality. **Buys 120 mss/year.** Send complete ms. Length: 400-2,000 words.

Photos Send photos with submission. Reviews negatives, transparencies, prints, GIF/JPEG files. Buys use in all publications and affiliated media only. Offers no additional payment for photos accepted with ms. Captions, identification of subjects required.

Poetry Free verse, light verse, traditional, historical. Does not want avant-garde, contemporary/modern experiences, simple junk. **Buys 6 poems/year.** Submit maximum 1 poems. **Pays in copies.**

Fillers Anecdotes, facts, gags to be illustrated by cartoonist, short humor. **Buys 50/year.** Length: 50-200 words. **Pays with copies of the magazine.**

Tips ''Start with an interesting photograph from the past you know, or your own past. Good photos are the key to people reading an interesting story in our magazine. Write the who, what, when, where, why, and how. We need 1 interesting photo for every 400 words of text.''

$ $ PERSIMMON HILL

National Cowboy & Western Heritage Museum, 1700 NE 63rd St., Oklahoma City OK 73111. (405)478-6404. Fax: (405)478-4714. E-mail: editor@nationalcowboymuseum.org. Website: www.nationalcowboymuseum.org. **Contact:** M.J. Van Deventer, editor. **70% freelance written.** Prefers to work with published/established writers; works with a small number of new/unpublished writers each year. Quarterly magazine for an audience interested in Western art, Western history, ranching, and rodeo, including historians, artists, ranchers, art galleries, schools, and libraries. Estab. 1970. Circ. 15,000. Pays on publication. Publishes ms an average of 2 years after acceptance. Byline given. Buys first rights. Responds in 3 months to queries. Sample copy for $10.50, including postage. Writer's guidelines for #10 SASE or on website.

⊶ ''We need more material on rodeo, both contemporary and historical. And we need more profiles on contemporary working ranches in the West.''

Nonfiction Historical and contemporary articles on famous Western figures connected with pioneering the American West, Western art, rodeo, cowboys, etc. (or biographies of such people), stories of Western flora and animal life and environmental subjects. ''We want thoroughly researched and historically authentic material written in a popular style. May have a humorous approach to subject. No broad, sweeping, superficial pieces; i.e., the California Gold Rush or rehashed pieces on Billy the Kid, etc.'' **Buys 35-50 mss/year.** Query by mail only with clips. Length: 1,500 words. **Pays $150-250.**

Photos Purchased with ms or on assignment. Reviews color transparencies, glossy b&w prints. Pays according to quality and importance for b&w and color photos. Captions required.

Tips ''Send us a story that captures the spirit of adventure and indvidualism that typifies the Old West or reveals a facet of the Western lifestyle in comtemporary society. Excellent illustrations for articles are essential! We lean towards scholarly, historical, well-researched articles. We're less focused on Western celebrities than some of the other contemporary Western magazines.''

PRESERVATION MAGAZINE

National Trust for Historic Preservation, 1785 Massachusetts Ave. NW, Washington DC 20036. (202)588-6388. Fax: (202)588-6266. E-mail: preservation@nthp.org. Website: www.preservationonline.org. **Contact:** James Conaway, editor-in-chief. **75% freelance written.** Prefers to work with published/established writers. Bimonthly magazine covering preservation of historic buildings in the US. "We cover subjects related in some way to place. Most entries are features, department, or opinion pieces." Circ. 250,000. Pays on publication. Publishes ms an average of 1 month after acceptance. Byline given. Offers variable kill fee. Buys one-time rights. Accepts queries by mail, e-mail, fax. Responds in 2 months to queries. Writer's guidelines online.

Nonfiction Book excerpts, essays, historical/nostalgic, humor, interview/profile, new product, opinion, photo feature, travel, features, news. **Buys 30 mss/year.** Query with published clips. Length: 500-3,500 words. Sometimes pays expenses of writers on assignment, but not long-distance travel.

The online magazine carries original content not found in the print edition. Contact: Margaret Foster.

Tips "Do not send or propose histories of buildings, descriptive accounts of cities or towns, or long-winded treatises. Best bet for breaking in is via Preservation Online, Preservation News (news features, 500-1,000 words), House Rules (brief profile or article, 250-500 words)."

$ $ $ TIMELINE

Ohio Historical Society, 1982 Velma Ave., Columbus OH 43211-2497. (614)297-2360. Fax: (614)297-2367. E-mail: timeline@ohiohistory.org. **Contact:** David A. Simmons, editor. **90% freelance written.** Works with a small number of new/unpublished writers each year. Quarterly magazine covering history, prehistory, and the natural sciences, directed toward readers in the Midwest. Estab. 1984. Circ. 19,000. **Pays on acceptance.** Publishes ms an average of 1 year after acceptance. Byline given. Offers $75 minimum kill fee. Buys first North American serial, all rights. Submit seasonal material 6 months in advance. Accepts queries by mail, e-mail, fax. Responds in 3 weeks to queries; 6 weeks to mss. Sample copy for $8 and 9 × 12 SAE. Writer's guidelines for #10 SASE.

Nonfiction Topics include the traditional fields of political, economic, military, and social history; biography; the history of science and technology; archaeology and anthropology; architecture; the fine and decorative arts; and the natural sciences including botany, geology, zoology, ecology, and paleontology. Book excerpts, essays, historical/nostalgic, interview/profile (of individuals), photo feature. **Buys 22 mss/year.** Query. Length: 1,500-6,000 words. Also vignettes of 500-1,000 words. **Pays $100-900.**

Photos Submissions should include ideas for illustration. Send photos with submission. Reviews contact sheets, transparencies, 8 × 10 prints. Buys one-time rights. Captions, identification of subjects, model releases required.

Tips "We want crisply written, authoritative narratives for the intelligent lay reader. An Ohio slant may strengthen a submission, but it is not indispensable. Contributors must know enough about their subject to explain it clearly and in an interesting fashion. We use high-quality illustration with all features. If appropriate illustration is unavailable, we can't use the feature. The writer who sends illustration ideas with a manuscript has an advantage, but an often-published illustration won't attract us."

$ $ TRACES OF INDIANA AND MIDWESTERN HISTORY

Indiana Historical Society, 450 W. Ohio St., Indianapolis IN 46202-3269. (317)232-1877. Fax: (317)233-0857. E-mail: rboomhower@indianahistory.org. Website: www.indianahistory.org/traces.htm. **Contact:** Ray E. Boomhower, managing editor. **80% freelance written.** Quarterly magazine on Indiana history. "Conceived as a vehicle to bring to the public good narrative and analytical history about Indiana in its broader contexts of region and nation, *Traces* explores the lives of artists, writers, performers, soldiers, politicians, entrepreneurs, homemakers, reformers, and naturalists. It has traced the impact of Hoosiers on the nation and the world. In this vein, the editors seek nonfiction articles that are solidly researched, attractively written, and amenable to illustration, and they encourage scholars, journalists, and freelance writers to contribute to the magazine." Estab. 1989. Circ. 10,000. Publishes ms an average of 6 months after acceptance. Byline given. Buys one-time rights. Submit seasonal material 1 year in advance. Responds in 3 months to mss. Sample copy and writer's guidelines for $5.25 (make checks payable to Indiana Historical Society) and 9 × 12 SAE with 7 first-class stamps or on website.

Nonfiction Book excerpts, historical essays, historical photographic features on topics of biography, literature, folklore, music, visual arts, politics, economics, industry, transportation, and sports. **Buys 20 mss/year.** Send complete ms. Length: 2,000-4,000 words. **Pays $100-500.**

Photos Send photos with submission. Reviews contact sheets, transparencies, photocopies, prints. Buys one-time rights. Pays "reasonable photographic expenses." Captions, identification of subjects, permissions required.

Tips "Freelancers should be aware of prerequisites for writing history for a broad audience. Should have some awareness of this magazine and other magazines of this type published by Midwestern historical societies. Preference is given to subjects with an Indiana connection and authors who are familiar with *Traces*. Quality of potential illustration is also important."

$ $ $ ⊘ TRUE WEST

True West Publishing, Inc., P.O. Box 8008, Cave Creek AZ 85327. (888)687-1881. Fax: (480)575-1903. E-mail: editor@twmag.com. Website: www.twmag.com. Executive Editor: Bob Boze Bell. **Contact:** R.G. Robertson, editor. **70% freelance written.** Works with a small number of new/unpublished writers each year. Magazine published 10 times/year covering Western American history from prehistory 1800 to 1930. "We want reliable research on significant historical topics written in lively prose for an informed general audience. More recent topics may be used if they have a historical angle or retain the Old West flavor of trail dust and saddle leather." Estab. 1953. Pays on publication. Byline given. Buys first North American serial rights. Editorial lead time 3 months. Accepts queries by mail, e-mail. Sample copy for $3. Writer's guidelines online.

- No unsolicited mss.
- "We are looking for historically accurate stories on the Old West that make you wonder 'What happens next?'"

Nonfiction No fiction, poetry, or unsupported, undocumented tales. **Buys 30 mss/year.** Query. Length: 1,000-3,000 words. **Pays $50-800.**

Photos State availability with submission. Reviews contact sheets, negatives, 4×5 transparencies, 4×5 prints. Buys one-time rights. Offers $10-75/photo. Captions, identification of subjects, model releases required.

Columns/Departments Book Reviews, 50-60 words (no unsolicited reviews). **Pays $25.**

Fillers Anecdotes, facts, gags to be illustrated by cartoonist, newsbreaks, short humor. **Buys 30/year.** Length: 50-600 words.

Tips "Read our magazines and follow our guidelines. A freelancer is most likely to break in with us by submitting thoroughly researched, lively prose on relatively obscure topics or by being assigned to write for 1 of our departments. First-person accounts rarely fill our needs. Historical accuracy and strict adherence to the facts are essential. We much prefer material based on primary sources (archives, court records, documents) and should not be based mainly on secondary sources (published books, magazines, and journals)."

VIETNAM

Primedia History Group, 741 Miller Dr., Suite D-2, Leesburg VA 20175-8994. (703)771-9400. Fax: (703)779-8345. Website: www.thehistorynet.com. **Contact:** David T. Zabecki, editor. **90% freelance written.** Bimonthly magazine providing in-depth and authoritative accounts of the many complexities that made the war in Vietnam unique, including the people, battles, strategies, perspectives, analysis, and weaponry. Estab. 1988. Circ. 46,000. Pays on publication. Byline given. Buys all rights. Accepts queries by mail, e-mail, fax. Sample copy for $5. Writer's guidelines for #10 SASE.

Nonfiction Historical/nostalgic (military), interview/profile, personal experience. "Absolutely no fiction or poetry; we want straight history, as much personal narrative as possible, but not the gung-ho, shoot-'em-up variety, either." **Buys 24 mss/year.** Query. Length: 4,000 words maximum; sidebars 500 words.

Photos Send photos with submission or state availability and cite sources. Identification of subjects required.

Columns/Departments Arsenal (about weapons used, all sides); Personality (profiles of the players, all sides); Fighting Forces (various units or types of units: air, sea, rescue); Perspectives. Length: 2,000 words. Query.

Tips "Choose stories with strong art possibilities. Send hard copy plus an IBM- or Macintosh-compatible floppy disk. All stories must be true. We do not publish fiction or poetry. All stories should be carefully researched third-person articles or firsthand accounts that give the reader a sense of experiencing historical events."

$ $ WILD WEST

Primedia History Group, 741 Miller Dr., SE, Suite D-2, Leesburg VA 20175-8920. (703)771-9400. Fax: (703)779-8345. E-mail: wildwest@thehistorynet.com. Website: www.thehistorynet.com. Managing Editor: Carl von Wodtke. **Contact:** Gregory Lalire, editor. **95% freelance written.** Bimonthly magazine covering the history of the American frontier, from its eastern beginnings to its western terminus. "*Wild West* covers the popular (narrative) history of the American West—events, trends, personalities, anything of general interest." Estab. 1988. Circ. 83,500. Pays on publication. Publishes ms an average of 2 years after acceptance. Byline given. Not copyrighted. Buys all rights. Editorial lead time 10 months. Submit seasonal material 1 year in advance. Accepts queries by mail, e-mail. Accepts simultaneous submissions. Responds in 3 months to queries; 6 months to mss. Sample copy for $6. Writer's guidelines for #10 SASE or online.

Nonfiction Historical/nostalgic (Old West). No excerpts, travel, etc. Articles can be "adapted from" book. No fiction or poetry—nothing current. **Buys 36 mss/year.** Query. Length: 3,500 words with a 500-word sidebar. **Pays $300.**

Photos State availability with submission. Reviews negatives, transparencies. Buys one-time rights. Offers no additional payment for photos accepted with ms. Captions, identification of subjects required.

Columns/Departments Gunfighters & Lawmen, 2,000 words; Westerners, 2,000 words; Warriors & Chiefs, 2,000 words; Western Lore, 2,000 words; Guns of the West, 1,500 words; Artists West, 1,500 words; Books Reviews, 250 words. **Buys 36 mss/year.** Query. **Pays $150 for departments; book reviews paid by the word, minimum $40.**

The online magazine carries original content not found in the print edition. Contact: Roger Vance, online editor.

Tips "Always query the editor with your story idea. Successful queries include a description of sources of information and suggestions for color and b&w photography or artwork. The best way to break into our magazine is to write an entertaining, informative, and unusual story that grabs the reader's attention and holds it. We favor carefully researched, third-person articles that give the reader a sense of experiencing historical events. Include a hard copy as well as an IBM- or Macintosh-compatible floppy disk."

$ $WORLD WAR II

Primedia History Group, 741 Miller Dr., Suite D-2, Leesburg VA 20175-8994. (703)771-9400. Fax: (703)779-8345. Website: www.thehistorynet.com. **Contact:** Christopher Anderson, editor. **95% freelance written.** Prefers to work with published/established writers. Bimonthly magazine covering military operations in World War II—events, personalities, strategy, national policy, etc. Estab. 1986. Circ. 146,000. Pays on publication. Byline given. Buys all rights. Accepts queries by mail, e-mail, fax. Sample copy for $5. Writer's guidelines for #10 SASE.

Nonfiction World War II military history. Submit anniversary-related material 1 year in advance. No fiction. **Buys 24 mss/year.** Query. Length: Length: 4,000 words with a 500-word sidebar. **Pays $300 and up.**

Photos For photos and other art, send photocopies and cite sources. "We'll order." State availability with submission. Captions, identification of subjects required.

Columns/Departments Undercover (espionage, resistance, sabotage, intelligence gathering, behind the lines, etc.); Personality (WWII personalities of interest); Armament (weapons, their use and development); Commands (unit histories); One Man's War (personal profiles), all 2,000 words. Book reviews, 300-750 words. **Buys 30 (plus book reviews) mss/year.** Query. **Pays $150 and up.**

Tips "List your sources and suggest further readings in standard format at the end of your piece—as a bibliography for our files in case of factual challenge or dispute. All submissions are on speculation. Include a hard copy as well as an IBM- or Macintosh-compatible floppy disk. All stories must be true. We do not publish fiction or poetry. Stories should be carefully researched."

HOBBY & CRAFT

$ANTIQUE JOURNAL

Krause Publications, a Division of F+W Publications, Inc., 500 Fesler St., Suite 201, El Cajon CA 92020. (619)593-2925. Fax: (619)447-7187. E-mail: antiquejournal@krause.com. Website: www.collect.com. **Contact:** Jennifer Edwards, editor. **90% freelance written.** Monthly magazine covering antiques and collectibles. *Antique Journal* serves antique dealers and collectors in Northern California, Washington, Oregon, and Nevada. Estab. 1992. Circ. 25,000. Pays on publication. Publishes ms an average of 1 month after acceptance. Byline given. Buys first North American serial rights. Editorial lead time 1 month. Submit seasonal material 2 months in advance. Accepts queries by mail, e-mail, fax, phone. Accepts previously published material. Accepts simultaneous submissions. Responds in 2 weeks to queries. Sample copy for $3. Writer's guidelines free.

Nonfiction General interest, historical/nostalgic, how-to (start a collection display and sell antiques), interview/profile. Does not want religious articles, opinion pieces, exposés. Query. Length: 500-700 words. **Pays $25-60.**

Photos Send photos with submission. Reviews 5×7 transparencies, 5×7 prints, GIF/JPEG files. Buys all rights. Offers no additional payment for photos accepted with ms. Identification of subjects required.

Columns/Departments Cover Stories (on specific antique merchandise or trends), 1,000 words; Show Producer Profile (profiles antiques show promoters), 500-700 words; California Profile, Washington Profile, Nevada Profile, Oregon Profile (profiles antiques shops/malls in specific states), 500 words; Vintage Fashions (on vintage clothing, hats, shoes, etc.), 500-700 words. **Buys 108 mss/year.** Query. **Pays $25-60.**

Tips "Talk directly to the editor or publisher either by phone or e-mail."

$ $ANTIQUE REVIEW

Krause Publications, a Division of F+W Publications, Inc., P.O. Box 1050, Dubuque IA 52004-1050. (800)482-4150. E-mail: kunkell@krause.com. Website: www.collect.com. **Contact:** Linda Kunkel, editor. **60% freelance written.** Eager to work with new/unpublished writers. Monthly tabloid for an antique-oriented readership, "generally well-educated, interested in Early American furniture and decorative arts, as well as folk art." Estab. 1975. Circ. 6,000. Pays on publication. Publishes ms an average of 3 months after acceptance. Byline given. Buys first North American serial, second serial (reprint) rights. Accepts queries by mail, e-mail, phone. Accepts previously published material. Responds in 3 months to queries. Inquire for sample copy.

Nonfiction "The articles we desire concern history and production of furniture, pottery, china, and other quality Americana. In some cases, contemporary folk art items are acceptable. We are also interested in reporting on antiques shows and auctions with statements on conditions and prices." Query should show "author's familiarity with antiques, an interest in the historical development of artifacts relating to early America, and an awareness of antiques market.'' **Buys 10-15 mss/year.** Query with published clips. Length: 600-1,500 words. **Pays $100-200.** Sometimes pays expenses of writers on assignment.

Reprints Send tearsheet, photocopy or typed ms with rights for sale noted and information about when and where the material previously appeared.

Photos Articles with photographs receive preference. Accepts and prefers digital photos (200 dpi, JPEG format). Send photos with submission. Reviews 3 × 5 or larger glossy b&w or color prints. Payment included in ms price. Captions required.

Tips ''Give us a call and let us know of specific interests. We are most concerned with the background in antiques than in writing abilities. The writing can be edited, but the knowledge imparted is of primary interest. A frequent mistake is being too general, not becoming deeply involved in the topic and its research. We are interested in primary research into America's historic material culture.''

$ $ANTIQUE TRADER

Krause Publications, a Division of F+W Publications, Inc., 700 E. State St., Iola WI 54990-0001. (715)445-2214. Fax: (715)445-4087. E-mail: antiquetrader@krause.com. Website: www.antiquetrader.com. **Contact:** Patricia DuChene, associate editor. **60% freelance written.** Weekly tabloid covering antiques. ''We publish quote-heavy stories of timely interest in the antiques field. We cover antiques shows, auctions, and news events.'' Estab. 1957. Circ. 30,000. Pays on publication. Publishes ms an average of 1-3 months after acceptance. Byline given. Offers 50% kill fee. Buys exclusive rights. Editorial lead time 2 months. Accepts queries by mail, e-mail, fax. Responds in 1 week to queries; 2 months to mss. Sample copy for cover price, plus postage. Writer's guidelines online.

Nonfiction Book excerpts, general interest, interview/profile, personal experience, show and auction coverage. Does not want the same, dry textbook, historical stories on antiques that appear elsewhere. ''I want personality and timeliness.'' **Buys 1,000+ mss/year.** Query with or without published clips or send complete ms. Length: 750-1,200 words. **Pays $50-200, plus contributor copy.**

Photos State availability with submission. Reviews transparencies, prints, GIF/JPEG files. Buys one-time rights. Offers no additional payment for photos accepted with ms. Identification of subjects required.

Columns/Departments Dealer Profile (interviews with interesting antiques dealers), 750-1,200 words; Collector Profile (interviews with interesting collectors), 750-1,000 words. **Buys 30-60 mss/year.** Query with or without published clips or send complete ms.

$ANTIQUE & COLLECTABLES NEWSMAGAZINE

Krause Publications, a Division of F+W Publications, Inc., 500 Fesler St., Suite 201, El Cajon CA 92022. (619)593-2933. Fax: (619)447-7187. E-mail: ac@krause.com. Website: www.collect.com. **Contact:** Jennifer Edwards, managing editor. **90% freelance written.** Monthly magazine covering antiques and collectibles. *Antique & Collectables Newsmagazine* serves dealers, collectors, and the general public in Southern California, Arizona and Southern Nevada on the antiques and collectibles industry. Estab. 1979. Circ. 27,500. Pays on publication. Publishes ms an average of 1 month after acceptance. Byline given. Buys first North American serial rights. Editorial lead time 1 month. Submit seasonal material 2 months in advance. Accepts queries by mail, e-mail, fax, phone. Accepts previously published material. Accepts simultaneous submissions. Responds in 2 weeks to queries. Sample copy for $2.50. Writer's guidelines free.

Nonfiction General interest, historical/nostalgic, how-to (start a collection, display and sell antiques), interview/ profile, photo feature. Does not want religious articles, opinion pieces, and exposés. Query. Length: 500-700 words. **Pays $25-70.**

Photos Send photos with submission. Reviews 5 × 7 transparencies, 5 × 7 prints, GIF/JPEG files. Buys all rights. Offers no additional payment for photos accepted with ms.

Columns/Departments Focus on San Diego (antique shops, malls and dealers), 500-600 words; Focus on Old Towne Orange (antique shops, malls and dealers), 500-600 words; Focus on Arizona (antique shops, malls and dealers), 500-600 words; Collector's Spotlight (collectors of antiques), 700-900 words; On with the Show (profiles on show producers), 700-900 words; Cover Stories (on specific antique merchandise or trends), 1,000 words. **Buys 96 mss/year.** Query. **Pays $25-70.**

Tips ''Talk directly to the editor or publisher either by phone or e-mail.''

N $AUTOGRAPH COLLECTOR

Odyssey Publications, 510-A South Corona Mall, Corona CA 92879. (951)734-9636. Fax: (951)371-7139. E-mail: editorev@telus.net. Website: www.autographcollector.com. **Contact:** Ev Phillips, editor. **80% freelance written.** Monthly magazine covering the autograph collecting hobby. ''The focus of *Autograph Collector* is on documents, photographs, or any collectible item that has been signed by a famous person, whether a current celebrity or historical figure. Articles stress how and where to locate celebrities and autograph material, authenticity of signatures and what they are worth.'' Byline given. Offers negotiable kill fee. Buys all rights. Editorial lead time 2 months. Submit seasonal material 3 months in advance. Accepts queries by mail, e-mail, fax, phone. Responds in 2 weeks to queries. Sample copy and writer's guidelines free.

Nonfiction "Articles must address subjects that appeal to autograph collectors and should answer 6 basic questions: Who is this celebrity/famous person? How do I go about collecting this person's autograph? Where can I find it? How scarce or available is it? How can I tell if it's real? What is it worth?" Historical/nostalgic, how-to, interview/profile, personal experience. **Buys 25-35 mss/year.** Query. Length: 1,600-2,000 words. **Pays 5¢/word.** Sometimes pays expenses of writers on assignment.

Photos State availability with submission. Reviews transparencies, prints. Buys one-time rights. Offers $3/ photo. Captions, identification of subjects required.

Columns/Departments Buys 90-100 mss/year. Query. **Pays $50 or as determined on a per case basis.**

Fillers Anecdotes, facts. **Buys 20-25/year.** Length: 200-300 words. **Pays $15.**

Tips "Ideally writers should be autograph collectors themselves and know their topics thoroughly. Articles must be well-researched and clearly written. Writers should remember that *Autograph Collector* is a celebrity-driven magazine and name recognition of the subject is important."

$ $ BEAD & BUTTON

Kalmbach Publishing, P.O. Box 1612, Waukesha WI 53187. E-mail: web@beadandbutton.com. Website: www.beadandbutton.com. **50% freelance written.** "*Bead & Button* is a bimonthly magazine devoted to techniques, projects, designs and materials relating to beads, buttons, and accessories. Our readership includes both professional and amateur bead and button makers, hobbyists, and enthusiasts who find satisfaction in making beautiful things." Estab. 1994. Circ. 80,000. **Pays on acceptance.** Publishes ms an average of 4 months after acceptance. Byline given. Offers $75 kill fee. Buys all rights. Accepts queries by mail, e-mail, fax. Writer's guidelines online.

Nonfiction Historical/nostalgic (on beaded jewelry history), how-to (make beaded jewelry and accessories), humor (or inspirational), interview/profile. **Buys 24-30 mss/year.** Send complete ms. Length: 750-3,000 words. **Pays $75-300.**

Photos Send photos with submission. Offers no additional payment for photos accepted with ms. Identification of subjects required.

Columns/Departments Chic & Easy (fashionable jewelry how-to); Beginner (easy-to-make jewelry how-to); Simply Earrings (fashionable earring how-to); Fun Fashion (trendy jewelry how-to), all 1,000 words. **Buys 12 mss/year.** Send complete ms. **Pays $75-150.**

Tips "*Bead & Button* magazine primarily publishes how-to articles by the artists who have designed the piece. We publish 2 profiles and 1 historical piece per issue. These would be the only applicable articles for non-artisan writers. Also our humorous and inspirational endpiece might apply."

$ $ BIG REEL

Movie, Video & Hollywood Collectibles, Krause Publications, a Division of F+W Publications, Inc., P.O. Box 1050, Dubuque IA 52004. (800)482-4143. Fax: (800)531-0880. E-mail: fliessc@krause.com. Website: www.bigreel.com. **Contact:** Claire R. Fliess, editor. **95% freelance written.** Monthly tabloid covering movie, video and Hollywood collectibles. "The audience is 50+ years old, deals with film (most advertisers) and old movies, serials." Circ. 5,870. Pays on publication. Publishes ms an average of 9 months after acceptance. Byline given. Offers $25 kill fee. Buys all rights. Editorial lead time 2 months. Submit seasonal material 2 months in advance. Accepts queries by mail, e-mail, fax, phone. Accepts simultaneous submissions. Responds in 1 month to mss. Sample copy and writer's guidelines free.

Nonfiction Essays, historical/nostalgic, interview/profile, personal experience, photo feature. Special issues: Western (April); Horror (October); Poster (June). Does not want opinion pieces. **Buys 120 mss/year.** Query. Length: 1,500-3,000 words. **Pays $100-300.**

Photos Send photos with submission. Reviews 8×10 prints, JPEG files. Buys all rights. Offers no additional payment for photos accepted with ms. Captions, identification of subjects, model releases required.

Tips "Ask if we would be interested in the topic, or send manuscript."

$ $ BLADE MAGAZINE

The World's #1 Knife Publication, Krause Publications, a Division of F+W Publications, Inc., 700 E. State St., Iola WI 54990-0001. (715)445-2214. Fax: (715)445-4087. E-mail: blademagazine@krause.com. Website: www.blademag.com. Editor: Steve Shackleford. **Contact:** Joe Kertzman, managing editor. **5% freelance written.** Monthly magazine covering working and using, collectible, popular knives. "*Blade* prefers in-depth articles focusing on groups of knives, whether military, collectible, high-tech, pocket knives or hunting knives, and how they perform." Estab. 1973. Circ. 39,000. Pays on publication. Publishes ms an average of 9 months after acceptance. Byline given. Buys all rights. Editorial lead time 9 months. Submit seasonal material 9 months in advance. Accepts queries by mail, e-mail, fax. Responds in 3 months to queries; 6 months to mss. Sample copy for $4.99. Writer's guidelines for 8×11 SAE with 3 first-class stamps.

Nonfiction General interest, historical/nostalgic, how-to, interview/profile, new product, photo feature, technical. Query with or without published clips or send complete ms. Length: 700-1,400 words. **Pays $200-350.**

Photos Send photos with submission. Reviews transparencies, prints. Buys all rights. Offers no additional payment for photos accepted with ms. Captions, identification of subjects required.

Fillers Anecdotes, facts, newsbreaks. **Buys 1-2/year.** Length: 50-200 words. **Pays $25-50.**

Tips "We are always willing to read submissions from anyone who has read a few copies and studied the market. The ideal article for us is a piece bringing out the romance, legend, and love of man's oldest tool—the knife. We like articles that place knives in peoples' hands—in life saving situations, adventure modes, etc. (Nothing gory or with the knife as the villain.) People and knives are good copy. We are getting more well-written articles from writers who are reading the publication beforehand. That makes for a harder sell for the quickie writer not willing to do his homework. Go to knife shows and talk to the makers and collectors. Visit knifemakers' shops and knife factories. Read anything and everything you can find on knives and knifemaking."

$ BREW YOUR OWN

The How-to Homebrew Beer Magazine, Battenkill Communications, 5053 Main St., Suite A, Manchester Center VT 05255. (802)362-3981. Fax: (802)362-2377. E-mail: edit@byo.com. Website: www.byo.com. **Contact:** Chris Colby, editor. **85% freelance written.** Monthly magazine covering home brewing. "Our mission is to provide practical information in an entertaining format. We try to capture the spirit and challenge of brewing while helping our readers brew the best beer they can." Estab. 1995. Circ. 40,000. **Pays on acceptance.** Publishes ms an average of 4 months after acceptance. Byline given. Offers 25% kill fee. Buys all rights. Editorial lead time 3 months. Submit seasonal material 3 months in advance. Accepts queries by mail, e-mail, fax. Responds in 2 months to queries. Writer's guidelines online.

    ○→ Break in by "sending a detailed query in 1 of 2 key areas: how to brew a specific, interesting style of beer (with step-by-step recipes), or how to build your own specific piece of brewing equipment."

Nonfiction Informational pieces on equipment, ingredients, and brewing methods. Historical/nostalgic, how-to (home brewing), humor (related to home brewing), interview/profile (of professional brewers who can offer useful tips to home hobbyists), personal experience, trends. **Buys 75 mss/year.** Query with published clips or description of brewing expertise. Length: 800-3,000 words. **Pays $50-150, depending on length, complexity of article, and experience of writer.** Sometimes pays expenses of writers on assignment.

Photos State availability with submission. Reviews contact sheets, transparencies, 5×7 prints, slides, and electronic images. Buys all rights. Negotiates payment individually. Captions required.

Columns/Departments News (humorous, unusual news about homebrewing), 50-250 words; Last Call (humorous stories about homebrewing), 700 words. **Buys 12 mss/year.** Query with or without published clips. **Pays $50.**

Tips *"Brew Your Own* is for anyone who is interested in brewing beer, from beginners to advanced all-grain brewers. We seek articles that are straightforward and factual, not full of esoteric theories or complex calculations. Our readers tend to be intelligent, upscale, and literate."

$ $ CERAMICS MONTHLY

735 Ceramic Place, Westerville OH 43081. (614)895-4213. Fax: (614)891-8960. E-mail: editorial@ceramicsmonthly.org. Website: www.ceramicsmonthly.org. **Contact:** Renée Fairchild, assistant editor. **70% freelance written.** Monthly magazine (except July and August) covering the ceramic art and craft field. "Each issue includes articles on potters and ceramics artists from throughout the world, exhibitions, and production processes, as well as critical commentary, book and video reviews, clay and glaze recipes, kiln designs and firing techniques, advice from experts in the field, and ads for available materials and equipment. While principally covering contemporary work, the magazine also looks back at influential artists and events from the past." Estab. 1953. Circ. 39,000. Pays on publication. Byline given. Editorial lead time 3 months. Submit seasonal material 6 months in advance. Accepts queries by mail, e-mail, fax, phone. Responds in 2 months to mss. Writer's guidelines online.

Nonfiction Essays, how-to, interview/profile, opinion, personal experience, technical. **Buys 100 mss/year.** Send complete ms. Length: 500-3,000 words. **Pays 10¢/word.**

Photos Send photos with submission. Reviews original slides or $2\frac{1}{4}$ or 4×5 transparencies. Offers $25 for photos. Captions required.

Columns/Departments Upfront (workshop/exhibition review), 500-1,000 words. **Buys 20 mss/year.** Send complete ms.

$ $ CLASSIC TOY TRAINS

Kalmbach Publishing Co., 21027 Crossroads Circle, Waukesha WI 53187. (262)796-8776. Fax: (262)796-1142. E-mail: editor@classictoytrains.com. Website: www.classictoytrains.com. **Contact:** Neil Besougloff, editor. **80%**

freelance written. Magazine published 9 times/year covering collectible toy trains (O, S, Standard, G scale, etc.) like Lionel, American Flyer, Marx, Dorfan, etc. "For the collector and operator of toy trains, *CTT* offers full-color photos of layouts and collections of toy trains, restoration tips, operating information, new product reviews and information, and insights into the history of toy trains." Estab. 1987. Circ. 65,000. **Pays on acceptance.** Publishes ms an average of 1 year after acceptance. Byline given. Buys all rights. Editorial lead time 3 months. Submit seasonal material 6 months in advance. Accepts queries by mail, e-mail. Responds in 3 weeks to queries; 1 month to mss. Sample copy for $5.50, plus postage. Writer's guidelines online.

Nonfiction General interest, historical/nostalgic, how-to (restore toy trains; design a layout; build accessories; fix broken toy trains), interview/profile, personal experience, photo feature, technical. **Buys 90 mss/year.** Query. Length: 500-5,000 words. **Pays $75-500.** Sometimes pays expenses of writers on assignment.

Photos Send photos with submission. Reviews 4×5 transparencies, 5×7 prints or 35mm slides preferred. Also accepts hi-res digital photos. Buys all rights. Offers no additional payment for photos accepted with ms or $15-75/photo. Captions required.

Tips "It's important to have a thorough understanding of the toy train hobby; most of our freelancers are hobbyists themselves. One-half to two-thirds of *CTT*'s editorial space is devoted to photographs; superior photography is critical."

$ $COLLECTOR MAGAZINE & PRICE GUIDE

Krause Publications, a Division of F+W Publications, Inc., P.O. Box 1050, Dubuque IA 52004. (800)482-4143. Fax: (800)531-0880. E-mail: fliessc@krause.com. Website: www.collect.com. **Contact:** Claire R. Fliess, editor. **20% freelance written.** Monthly magazine covering collectibles—all kinds. "Our readers like all collectibles. Antiques, furniture, glass, and ceramics are most often written about." Estab. 1994. Circ. approximately 30,000. Byline given. Offers $25 kill fee. Buys all rights. Editorial lead time 3 months. Submit seasonal material 3 months in advance. Accepts queries by mail, e-mail, fax, phone. Accepts simultaneous submissions. Responds in 1 month to mss. Sample copy for free. Writer's guidelines free.

Nonfiction Essays, historical/nostalgic, interview/profile, show reports, price guide information. Does not want opinion pieces. **Buys 40 mss/year.** Query. Length: 1,000-2,000 words. **Pays $100-200.**

Photos Send photos with submission. Reviews 8×10 prints, JPEG files. Buys all rights. Offers no additional payment for photos accepted with ms. Captions, identification of subjects, model releases required.

Columns/Departments Oh, You Beautiful Doll! (history and prices on 1 doll/month), 500 words and pictures. **Buys 20 mss/year.** Query. **Pays $100-150.**

Tips "This magazine stresses prices of collectible items. We are open to all subjects."

$COLLECTORS NEWS

P.O. Box 306, Grundy Center IA 50638. (319)824-6981. Fax: (319)824-3414. E-mail: collectors@collectors-news.com. Website: collectors-news.com. **Contact:** Linda Kruger, managing editor. **20% freelance written.** Works with a small number of new/unpublished writers each year. Monthly magazine-size publication on offset, glossy cover, covering antiques, collectibles, and nostalgic memorabilia. Estab. 1959. Circ. 9,000. Pays on publication. Publishes ms an average of 1 year after acceptance. Byline given. Buys first rights, makes work-for-hire assignments. Submit seasonal material 3 months in advance. Accepts queries by mail, e-mail, fax, phone. Responds in 2 weeks to queries; 6 weeks to mss. Sample copy for $4 and 9×12 SAE. Writer's guidelines free.

○┰ Break in with articles on collecting online; history and values of collectibles and antiques; collectors with unique and/or extensive collections; using collectibles in the home decor; and any 20th century and timely subjects.

Nonfiction General interest (collectibles, antique to modern), historical/nostalgic (relating to collections or collectors), how-to (display your collection, care for, restore, appraise, locate, add to, etc.), interview/profile (covering individual collectors and their hobbies, unique or extensive; celebrity collectors, and limited edition artists), technical (in-depth analysis of a particular antique, collectible, or collecting field), travel ("hot" antiquing places in the US). Special issues: 12-month listing of antique and collectible shows, flea markets, and conventions (January includes events January-December; June includes events June-May); Care & Display of Collectibles (September); holidays (October-December). **Buys 36 mss/year.** Query with sample of writing. Length: 800-1,000 words. **Pays $1.10/column inch.**

Photos "Articles must be accompanied by photographs for illustration." A selection of 2-8 images is suggested. "Articles are eligible for full-color front page consideration when accompanied by quality color prints, high resolution electronic images and/or color transparencies. Only 1 article is highlighted on the cover/month. Any article providing a color photo selected for front page use receives an additional $25." Reviews color or b&w images. Buys first rights. Payment for photos included in payment for ms. Captions required.

Tips "Present a professionally written article with quality illustrations—well-researched and documented information."

COUNTRY ALMANAC

Harris Publications, Inc., 1115 Broadway, New York NY 10010. (212)807-7100. Fax: (212)463-9958. E-mail: countryletters@yahoo.com. Website: www.countryalmanacmag.com. Editor: Jodi Zucker. Quarterly magazine. Home service magazine containing articles ranging from country living, crafts, home-spun decorating, food, and outdoor hobbies. Circ. 300,000. Editorial lead time 4-5 months.

COUNTRY MARKETPLACE

707 Kautz Rd., Saint Charles IL 60174-5330. (630)377-8000. Fax: (630)377-8194. Website: www.sampler.com. Editor: Amy Wiegman. Bimonthly magazine. Edited for active crafters who are interested in current crafting trends, ideas and products. Circ. 300,000. Editorial lead time 3 months. Sample copy not available.

$ CQ AMATEUR RADIO

The Radio Amateur's Journal, CQ Communications, Inc., 25 Newbridge Rd., Hicksville NY 11801. (516)681-2922. Fax: (516)681-2926. E-mail: cq@cq-amateur-radio.com. Website: www.cq-amateur-radio.com. Managing Editor: Gail Schieber. **Contact:** Richard Moseson, editor. **40% freelance written.** Monthly magazine covering amateur (ham) radio. "*CQ* is published for active ham radio operators and is read by radio amateurs in over 100 countries. All articles must deal with amateur radio. Our focus is on operating and on practical projects. A thorough knowledge of amateur radio is required." Estab. 1945. Circ. 60,000. Pays on publication. Publishes ms an average of 6 months after acceptance. Byline given. Buys first North American serial rights. Editorial lead time 4 months. Submit seasonal material 4 months in advance. Accepts queries by mail, e-mail, fax. Responds in 3 weeks to queries; 3 months to mss. Sample copy for free. Writer's guidelines online.

Nonfiction Historical/nostalgic, how-to, interview/profile, personal experience, technical, all related to amateur radio. **Buys 50-60 mss/year.** Query. Length: 2,000-4,000 words. **Pays $40/published page.**

Photos State availability with submission. Reviews contact sheets, 4×6 prints, TIFF or JPEG files with 300 dpi resolution. Buys one-time rights. Offers no additional payment for photos accepted with ms. Captions, identification of subjects, model releases required.

Tips "You must know and understand ham radio and ham radio operators. Most of our writers (95%) are licensed hams. Because our readers span a wide area of interests within amateur radio, don't assume they are already familiar with your topic. At the same time, don't write down to the readers. They are intelligent, well-educated people who will understand what you're saying when written and explained in plain English."

$ $ DECORATIVE ARTIST'S WORKBOOK

F+W Publications, Inc., 4700 E. Galbraith Rd., Cincinnati OH 45236. (513)531-2690, ext. 1461. E-mail: dawedit @fwpubs.com. Website: www.decorativeartist.com. **Contact:** Anne Hevener, editor. **75% freelance written.** Bimonthly magazine covering decorative painting step-by-step projects. Offers "straightforward, personal instruction in the techniques of decorative painting." Estab. 1987. Circ. 85,000. **Pays on acceptance.** Byline given. Offers 25% kill fee. Buys first North American serial rights. Submit seasonal material 8 months in advance. Accepts queries by mail, e-mail. Responds in 3 weeks to queries. Sample copy for $8 and 9×12 SAE with 5 first-class stamps. Writer's guidelines online.

Nonfiction How-to (related to decorative painting projects), new product, technique. **Buys 30 mss/year.** Query with slides or photos. Length: 1,200-1,800 words. **Pays 15-25¢/word.**

The online magazine carries original content not found in the print edition. Contact: Anne Hevener, online editor.

Tips "Create a design, surface, or technique that is fresh and new to decorative painting. I'm looking for experts in the field who, through their own experience, can accurately describe the techniques involved. How-to articles are most open to freelancers skilled in decorative painting. Be sure to query with photo/slides, and show that you understand the extensive graphic requirements for these pieces and can provide painted progressives—painted illustrations that show painting in progress."

N DISCOVERIES

For Record & CD Collectors, Krause Publications, a Division of F+W Publications, Inc., 700 E. State St., Iola WI 54990. (715)445-2214. Fax: (715)445-4087. E-mail: youngbloodw@krause.com. Website: www.collect.com. **Contact:** Wayne Youngblood, editor. **90% freelance written.** Monthly magazine covering recorded music collecting, music collectibles, popular music history, market trends, pricing, all topics related to collecting music and memorabilia. "We are all about collecting. Whether that be vinyl, compact discs, memorabilia, *Discoveries* is about information for collectors. Pricing, market values and trends, what is hot, what isn't, history, some discographies." Estab. 1982. Circ. 9,000. Pays on publication. Publishes ms an average of 4 months after acceptance. Byline given. Offers 50% kill fee. Buys all rights, makes work-for-hire assignments. Editorial lead time 2-4 months. Accepts queries by e-mail. Responds in 2-4 weeks no answer to queries. Sample copy for free. Writer's guidelines by e-mail.

$ $DOLLHOUSE MINIATURES

Madavor Media, P.O. Box 595, Boston MA 02117. (800)437-5828. E-mail: dollreader.edit@verizon.net. Website: www.dhminiatures.com. Editor: Marianne Clay. **80% freelance written.** Monthly magazine covering dollhouse scale miniatures. *"Dollhouse Miniatures* is America's best-selling miniatures magazine and the definitive resource for artisans, collectors, and hobbyists. It promotes and supports the large national and international community of miniaturists through club columns, short reports, and by featuring reader projects and ideas." Estab. 1971. Circ. 25,000. **Pays on acceptance.** Byline given. Buys all rights. Editorial lead time 6 months. Submit seasonal material 6 months in advance. Accepts queries by mail, e-mail. Responds in 1 month to queries; 2 months to mss. Sample copy for $4.95. Writer's guidelines online.

Nonfiction How-to (miniature projects of various scales in variety of media), interview/profile (artisans, collectors), photo feature (dollhouses, collections, museums). No articles on miniature shops or essays. **Buys 50-60 mss/year.** Query with or without published clips or send complete ms. Length: 500-1,500 words. **Pays $50-350 for assigned articles; $0-200 for unsolicited articles.**

Photos Send photos with submission. Reviews 35mm slides and larger, 3×5 prints. Buys all rights. Photos are paid for with ms. Seldom buys individual photos. Captions, identification of subjects required.

Tips "Familiarity with the miniatures hobby is very helpful. Accuracy to scale is extremely important to our readers. A complete package (manuscripts/photos) has a better chance of publication."

$ $DOLLS

Jones Publishing, Inc., 217 Passaic Ave., Hasbrouck Heights NJ 07684. (715)445-5000. Fax: (715)445-4053. E-mail: nrdollsmagazine@earthlink.net. Website: www.jonespublishing.com. Assistant Editor: Trina Laube. **Contact:** Nayda Rondon, editor. **75% freelance written.** Magazine published 10 times/year covering dolls, doll artists, and related topics of interest to doll collectors and enthusiasts. *"Dolls* enhances the joy of collecting by introducing readers to the best new dolls from around the world, along with the artists and designers who create them. It keeps readers up-to-date on shows, sales and special events in the doll world. With beautiful color photography, *Dolls* offers an array of easy-to-read, informative articles that help our collectors select the best buys." Estab. 1982. Circ. 100,000. Pays on publication. Byline given. Buys first North American serial rights. Accepts queries by mail, e-mail. Responds in 1 month to queries.

Nonfiction Historical/nostalgic, how-to, interview/profile, new product, photo feature. **Buys 55 mss/year.** Query with published clips or send complete ms. Length: 750-1,200 words. **Pays $75-300.**

Photos Send photos with submission. Reviews transparencies. Buys one-time rights. Offers no additional payment for photos accepted with ms. Captions, identification of subjects, model releases required.

Tips "Know the subject matter and artists. Having quality artwork and access to doll artists for interviews are big pluses. We need original ideas of interest to doll lovers."

ℕ F+W PUBLICATIONS, INC. (MAGAZINE DIVISION)

4700 E. Galbraith Rd., Cincinnati OH 45236. (513)531-2690. Website: www.fwpublications.com. **Iola Magazine Group:** Jim Gleim, executive vice president. **Cincinnati and Satellite Magazines:** Colleen Cannon, senior vice president/group publisher. "Each month, more than 3.7 million readers turn to the magazines from F+W for inspiration, instruction, and encouragement. Readers are as varied as the range of titles. F+W titles assure readers they're getting the best possible coverage of their favorite hobby." Publishes magazines in the following categories: **antiques and collectibles** (*Antique & Collectables Monthly,* Antique Journal, *Antique Review, Big Reel, Collector Magazine & Price Guide, Collector's Mart, Cotton & Quail Antique Gazette, Postcard Collector*); **automotive** (*Military Vehicles, Old Cars Price Guide, Old Cars Weekly*); **coins and paper money** (*Bank Note Reporter, Coins Magazine, Coin Prices, Numismatic News, World Coin News*); **comics** (*Comic Buyers Guide, Comics & Games Retailer*); **construction** (*Country's Best Log Homes, Frame Building News, Metal Roofing, Rural Builder*); **crafts** (*CNA Magazine*); **decorative painting** (*Decorative Artist's Workbook*); **fine art** (*Pastel Journal, The Artist's Magazine, Watercolor Magic, Artist's Sketchbook*); **firearms and knives** (*Blade, Blade Trade, Gun List*); **games** (*Comics & Games Retailer, SCRYE*); **gardening** (*Horticulture Magazine*); **genealogy** (*Family Tree Magazine*); **graphic design** (*HOW Magazine, I.D., PRINT*); **militaria** (*Military Trader*); **outdoors and hunting** (*Deer & Deer Hunting, Trapper & Predator Caller, Turkey & Turkey Hunting, Wisconsin Outdoor Journal*); **records and CDs** (*Discoveries, Goldmine*); **scrapbooking** (*Memory Makers Magazine*); **sports** (*Card Trade, Fantasy Sports, Sports Collectors Digest, Tuff Stuff*); **toys** (*Toy Cars & Models, Toy Shop*); **water sports** (*Scuba Diving*); **woodworking** (*Popular Woodworking*); **writing** (*Writer's Digest*).

● Please see individual listings in the Consumer Magazines and Trade Journals sections for specific submission information about each magazine.

$ $ $FAMILY TREE MAGAZINE

F+W Publications, 4700 E. Galbraith Rd., Cincinnati OH 45236. (513)531-2690. Fax: (513)891-7153. E-mail: ftmedit@fwpubs.com. Website: www.familytreemagazine.com. **Contact:** Allison Stacy, editor. **75% freelance**

written. Bimonthly magazine covering family history, heritage, and genealogy research. *"Family Tree Magazine* is a general-interest consumer magazine that helps readers discover, preserve, and celebrate their family's history. We cover genealogy, ethnic heritage, genealogy websites and software, scrapbooking, photography and photo preservation, and other ways that families connect with their past." Estab. 1999. Circ. 80,000. **Pays on acceptance.** Publishes ms an average of 6 months after acceptance. Byline given. Offers 25% kill fee. Buys first, electronic rights. Editorial lead time 8 months. Submit seasonal material 8 months in advance. Accepts queries by mail, e-mail. Responds in 1 month to queries. Sample copy for $7 from website. Writer's guidelines online.

O⟶ Break in by suggesting a "useful, timely idea for our Toolkit section on a resource that our readers would love to discover."

Nonfiction "Articles are geared to beginners but never talk down to the audience. We emphasize sidebars, tips, and other reader-friendly 'packaging,' and each article aims to give the reader the resources necessary to take the next step in his or her quest for the past." Book excerpts, historical/nostalgic, how-to (genealogy), new product (photography, computer), technical (genealogy software, photography equipment). **Buys 60 mss/year.** Query with published clips. Length: 250-4,500 words. **Pays $25-800.**

Photos State availability with submission. Reviews color transparencies. Buys one-time rights. Negotiates payment individually. Captions required.

Tips "Always query with a specific story idea. Look at sample issues before querying to get a feel for appropriate topics and angles. We see too many broad, general stories on genealogy or records, and personal accounts of 'How I found great-aunt Sally' without how-to value."

$ $ FIBERARTS

Contemporary Textile Art and Craft, Interweave Press, 201 E. Fourth St., Loveland CO 80537. (970)613-4679. Fax: (970)669-6117. E-mail: lizg@fiberarts.com. Website: www.fiberarts.com. **Contact:** Liz Good, assistant editor. **85% freelance written.** Magazine published 5 times/year covering textiles as art and craft (contemporary trends in fiber sculpture, weaving, quilting, surface design, stitchery, papermaking, basketry, felting, wearable art, knitting, fashion, crochet, mixed textile techniques, ethnic dying, eccentric tidbits, etc.) for textile artists, craftspeople, collectors, teachers, museum and gallery staffs, and enthusiasts. Estab. 1975. Circ. 22,500. Pays on publication. Publishes ms an average of 4 months after acceptance. Byline given. Buys first rights. Accepts queries by mail. Sample copy for $6. Writer's guidelines online.

Nonfiction "Please be very specific about your proposal. Also, an important consideration in accepting an article is the kind of photos that you can provide as illustration. We like to see photos in advance." Essays, interview/profile (artist), opinion, personal experience, photo feature, technical, education, trends, exhibition reviews, textile news, book reviews, ethnic. Query with brief synopsis, SASE, and visuals. No phone queries. Length: 250-2,000 words. **Pays $70-550.**

Photos Color slides, large-format transparencies, or 300 dpi 5-inch-high TIFF images must accompany every query. The more photos to choose from, the better. Please include caption information. The names and addresses of those mentioned in the article or to whom the visuals are to be returned are necessary.

Columns/Departments Commentary (thoughtful opinion on a topic of interest to our readers), 400 words; Notable Events; Worldwide Connections; Profiles; The Creative Process; Fiber Hot Spots; Collections; Practical Matters, 450 words and 2-4 photos; Reviews (exhibits and shows; summarize quality, significance, focus and atmosphere, then evaluate selected pieces for aesthetic quality, content and technique—because we have an international readership, brief biographical notes or quotes might be pertinent for locally or regionally known artists), 500 words and 3-5 photos. (Do not cite works for which visuals are unavailable; you are not eligible to review a show in which you have participated as an artist, organizer, curator or juror.) **Pays $150.**

Tips "Our writers are usually familiar with textile techniques and textile-art history, but expertise in historical textiles, art, or design can also qualify a new writer. The writer should also be familiar with *Fiberarts* magazine. The professional is essential to the editorial depth of *Fiberarts* and must find timely information in the pages of the magazine, but our editorial philosophy is that the magazine must provide the non-professional textile enthusiast with the inspiration, support, useful information, and direction to keep him or her excited, interested, and committed. Although we address serious issues relating to the fiber arts as well as light, we're looking for an accessible rather than overly scholarly tone."

$ FIBRE FOCUS

Magazine of the Ontario Handweavers and Spinners, 10 Teanaustaye Dr., Hillsdale ON L0L 1V0 Canada. E-mail: jettevdm@sympatico.ca. Website: www.ohs.on.ca. **Contact:** Jette Vandermeiden, editor. **90% freelance written.** Quarterly magazine covering handweaving, spinning, basketry, beading, and other fibre arts. "Our readers are weavers and spinners who also do dyeing, knitting, basketry, feltmaking, papermaking, sheep raising, and craft supply. All articles deal with some aspect of these crafts." Estab. 1957. Circ. 1,000. Pays within 30 days after publication. Byline given. Buys one-time rights. Editorial lead time 6 months. Submit seasonal material 6 months in advance. Accepts previously published material. Responds in 1 month to queries. Sample copy for $5 Canadian. Writer's guidelines online.

Nonfiction How-to, interview/profile, new product, opinion, personal experience, technical, travel, book reviews. **Buys 40-60 mss/year.** Length: Varies. **Pays $30 Canadian/published page.**

Photos Send photos with submission. Reviews 4×6 color prints. Buys one-time rights. Offers additional payment for photos accepted with ms. Captions, identification of subjects required.

Fiction Humorous, slice-of-life vignettes. **Pays $30 Canadian/published page.**

Tips "Visit the OHS website for current information."

$ $ FINE BOOKS & COLLECTIONS

(formerly *OP*), OP Media, LLC, P.O. Box 106, Eureka CA 95502. E-mail: scott@finebooksmagazine.com. Website: www.finebooksmagazine.com. **Contact:** P. Scott Brown, managing editor. **90% freelance written.** Bimonthly magazine covering used and antiquarian bookselling and book collecting. "We cover all aspects of selling and collecting out-of-print books. We emphasize good writing, interesting people, and unexpected viewpoints." Estab. 2002. Circ. 3,000. Pays on publication. Publishes ms an average of 4 months after acceptance. Byline given. Offers negotiable kill fee. Buys first North American serial, second serial (reprint), electronic rights, makes work-for-hire assignments. Editorial lead time 4 months. Submit seasonal material 4 months in advance. Accepts queries by mail, e-mail. Accepts previously published material. Accepts simultaneous submissions. Responds in 1 month to queries; 2 months to mss. Sample copy for $6.50. Writer's guidelines online.

Nonfiction Book excerpts, essays, exposé, general interest, historical/nostalgic, how-to, humor, interview/profile, opinion, personal experience, photo feature, travel. Does not want tales of the "gold in my attic" vein; stories emphasizing books as an investment. **Buys 40 mss/year.** Query with published clips. Length: 1,000-5,000 words. **Pays $100-400.** Sometimes pays expenses of writers on assignment.

Photos State availability with submission. Reviews GIF/JPEG files. Buys one-time, plus nonexclusive electronic rights. Negotiates payment individually. Captions, identification of subjects required.

Columns/Departments Digest (news about collectors, booksellers, and bookselling), 350 words; Book Reviews (reviews of books about books, writers, publishers, collecting), 400-800 words.

Tips "Tell compelling stories about people and the passion for book collecting. We aim to make academic writing on books accessible to a broad audience and to enliven the writing of aficionados with solid editing and story development."

$ $ FINE TOOL JOURNAL

Antique & Collectible Tools, Inc., 27 Fickett Rd., Pownal ME 04069. (207)688-4962. Fax: (207)688-4831. E-mail: ceb@finetoolj.com. Website: www.finetoolj.com. **Contact:** Clarence Blanchard, president. **90% freelance written.** Quarterly magazine specializing in older or antique hand tools from all traditional trades. Readers are primarily interested in woodworking tools, but some subscribers have interests in such areas as leatherworking, wrenches, kitchen, and machinist tools. Readers range from beginners just getting into the hobby to advanced collectors and organizations. Estab. 1970. Circ. 2,500. Pays on publication. Publishes ms an average of 6 months after acceptance. Byline given. Offers $50 kill fee. Buys first, second serial (reprint) rights. Editorial lead time 9 months. Submit seasonal material 6 months in advance. Accepts queries by mail. Accepts previously published material. Responds in 2 months to queries; 3 months to mss. Sample copy for $5. Writer's guidelines for #10 SASE.

Nonfiction "We're looking for articles about tools from all trades. Interests include collecting, preservation, history, values and price trends, traditional methods and uses, interviews with collectors/users/makers, etc. Most articles published will deal with vintage, pre-1950, hand tools. Also seeking articles on how to use specific tools or how a specific trade was carried out. However, how-to articles must be detailed and not just of general interest. We do on occasion run articles on modern toolmakers who produce traditional hand tools." General interest, historical/nostalgic, how-to (make, use, fix and tune tools), interview/profile, personal experience, photo feature, technical. **Buys 24 mss/year.** Send complete ms. Length: 400-2,000 words. **Pays $50-200.** Pays expenses of writers on assignment.

Photos Send photos with submission. Reviews 4×5 prints. Buys all rights. Negotiates payment individually. Identification of subjects, model releases required.

Columns/Departments Stanley Tools (new finds and odd types), 300-400 words; Tips of the Trade (how to use tools), 100-200 words. **Buys 12 mss/year.** Send complete ms. **Pays $30-60.**

Tips "The easiest way to get published in the *Journal* is to have personal experience or know someone who can supply the detailed information. We are seeking articles that go deeper than general interest and that knowledge requires experience and/or research. Short of personal experience, find a subject that fits our needs and that interests you. Spend some time learning the ins and outs of the subject and with hard work and a little luck you will earn the right to write about it."

$ $ FINE WOODWORKING

The Taunton Press, P.O. Box 5506, Newtown CT 06470-5506. (800)926-8776. Fax: (203)270-6753. E-mail: achristiana@taunton.com. Website: www.taunton.com. Publisher: Tim Schreiner. **Contact:** Asa Christiana. Bimonthly magazine on woodworking in the small shop. "All writers are also skilled woodworkers. It's more important that a contributor be a woodworker than a writer. Our editors (also woodworkers) will provide assistance." Estab. 1975. Circ. 270,000. **Pays on acceptance.** Byline given. Offers variable kill fee. Buys first rights and rights to republish in anthologies and use in promo pieces. Submit seasonal material 6 months in advance. Accepts simultaneous submissions. Responds in 2 months to queries. Writer's guidelines free and online.

> O→ "We're looking for good articles on almost all aspects of woodworking from the basics of tool use, stock preparation and joinery, to specialized techniques and finishing. We're especially keen on articles about shop-built tools, jigs and fixtures, or any stage of design, construction, finishing and installation of cabinetry and furniture. Whether the subject involves fundamental methods or advanced techniques, we look for high-quality workmanship, thoughtful designs, and safe and proper procedures."

Nonfiction How-to (woodworking). "No specs—our editors would rather see more than less." **Buys 120 mss/year.** Query with proposal letter. **Pays $150/magazine page for assigned articles.** Sometimes pays expenses of writers on assignment.

Photos Send photos with submission. Reviews contact sheets, negatives, transparencies, prints. Buys one-time rights. Captions, identification of subjects, model releases required.

Columns/Departments Notes & Comment (topics of interest to woodworkers); Question & Answer (woodworking Q&A); Methods of Work (shop tips); Tools & Materials (short reviews of new tools). **Buys 400 mss/year. Pays $10-150/published page.**

Tips "Look for authors guidelines and follow them. Stories about woodworking reported by non-woodworkers are *not* used. Our magazine is essentially reader-written by woodworkers."

$ FINESCALE MODELER

Kalmbach Publishing Co., P.O. Box 1612, Waukesha WI 53187. Website: www.finescale.com. **Contact:** Jim Haught, associate editor. **80% freelance written.** Eager to work with new/unpublished writers. Magazine published 10 times/year "devoted to how-to-do-it modeling information for scale model builders who build non-operating aircraft, tanks, boats, automobiles, figures, dioramas, and science fiction and fantasy models." Circ. 60,000. **Pays on acceptance.** Publishes ms an average of 14 months after acceptance. Byline given. Buys all rights. Responds in 6 weeks to queries; 3 months to mss. Sample copy for 9 × 12 SAE and 3 first-class stamps.

> O→ *Finescale Modeler* is especially looking for how-to articles for car modelers.

Nonfiction How-to (build scale models), technical (research information for building models). Query or send complete ms. Length: 750-3,000 words. **Pays $55 published page minimum.**

Photos Send photos with submission. Reviews transparencies, color prints. Buys one-time rights. Pays $7.50 minimum for transparencies and $5 minimum for color prints. Captions, identification of subjects required.

Columns/Departments *FSM* Showcase (photos plus description of model); *FSM* Tips and Techniques (model building hints and tips). **Buys 25-50 mss/year.** Send complete ms. **Pays $25-50.**

Tips "A freelancer can best break in first through hints and tips, then through feature articles. Most people who write for *FSM* are modelers first, writers second. This is a specialty magazine for a special, quite expert audience. Essentially, 99% of our writers will come from that audience."

$ $ THE HOME SHOP MACHINIST

2779 Aero Park Dr., Traverse City MI 49686. (616)946-3712. Fax: (616)946-3289. E-mail: nknopf@villagepress.com. Website: www.homeshopmachinist.net. **Contact:** Neil Knopf, editor. **95% freelance written.** Bimonthly magazine covering machining and metalworking for the hobbyist. Circ. 34,000. Pays on publication. Publishes ms an average of 2 years after acceptance. Byline given. Buys first North American serial rights. Responds in 2 months to queries. Sample copy for free. Writer's guidelines for 9 × 12 SASE.

Nonfiction How-to (projects designed to upgrade present shop equipment or hobby model projects that require machining), technical (should pertain to metalworking, machining, drafting, layout, welding or foundry work for the hobbyist). No fiction or "people" features. **Buys 40 mss/year.** Query with or without published clips or send complete ms. Length: open—"whatever it takes to do a thorough job." **Pays $40/published page, plus $9/published photo.**

Photos Send photos with submission. Pays $9-40 for 5 × 7 b&w prints; $70/page for camera-ready art; $40 for b&w cover photo. Captions, identification of subjects required.

Columns/Departments Book Reviews; New Product Reviews; Micro-Machining; Foundry. Length: 600-1,500 words. **Buys 25-30 mss/year.** Query. **Pays $40-70.**

Fillers Machining tips/shortcuts. **Buys 12-15/year.** Length: 100-300 words. **Pays $30-48.**

Tips "The writer should be experienced in the area of metalworking and machining; should be extremely thorough in explanations of methods, processes—always with an eye to safety; and should provide good quality b&w photos and/or clear dimensioned drawings to aid in description. Visuals are of increasing importance to our readers. Carefully planned photos, drawings and charts will carry a submission to our magazine much farther along the path to publication."

$ $ KITPLANES

For Designers, Builders, and Pilots of Experimental Aircraft, A Primedia Publication, 239 New Rd., Suite B-201, Parsippany NJ 07054. (973)227-7660. Fax: (973)227-7630. E-mail: editorial@kitplanes.com. Website: www.kitplanes.com. **Contact:** Brian Clark, editor. **80% freelance written.** Eager to work with new/unpublished writers. Monthly magazine covering self-construction of private aircraft for pilots and builders. Estab. 1984. Circ. 72,000. Pays on publication. Publishes ms an average of 3 months after acceptance. Byline given. Buys complete rights, except book rights. Submit seasonal material 6 months in advance. Accepts queries by mail, e-mail. Responds in 2 weeks to queries; 6 weeks to mss. Sample copy for $6. Writer's guidelines online.

Nonfiction "We are looking for articles on specific construction techniques, the use of tools—both hand and power—in aircraft building, the relative merits of various materials, conversions of engines from automobiles for aviation use, and installation of instruments and electronics." General interest, how-to, interview/profile, new product, personal experience, photo feature, technical. No general-interest aviation articles, or "My First Solo" type of articles. **Buys 80 mss/year.** Query. Length: 500-3,000 words. **Pays $70-600 including story photos for assigned articles.**

Photos State availability of or send photos with submission. Buys one-time rights. Pays $300 for cover photos. Captions, identification of subjects required.

Tips "*Kitplanes* contains very specific information—a writer must be extremely knowledgeable in the field. Major features are entrusted only to known writers. I cannot emphasize enough that articles must be directed at the individual aircraft builder. We need more 'how-to' photo features in all areas of homebuilt aircraft."

$ $ KNIVES ILLUSTRATED

The Premier Cutlery Magazine, 265 S. Anita Dr., Suite 120, Orange CA 92868. (714)939-9991. Fax: (714)939-9909. E-mail: editorial@knivesillustrated.com. Website: www.knivesillustrated.com. **Contact:** J. Bruce Voyles, editor. **40-50% freelance written.** Bimonthly magazine covering high-quality factory and custom knives. "We publish articles on different types of factory and custom knives, how-to make knives, technical articles, shop tours, articles on knife makers and artists. Must have knowledge about knives and the people who use and make them. We feature the full range of custom and high tech production knives, from miniatures to swords, leaving nothing untouched. We're also known for our outstanding how-to articles and technical features on equipment, materials and knife making supplies. We do not feature knife maker profiles as such, although we do spotlight some makers by featuring a variety of their knives and insight into their background and philosophy." Estab. 1987. Circ. 35,000. Pays on publication. Byline given. Editorial lead time 3 months. Accepts queries by mail, e-mail, fax. Responds in 2 weeks to queries. Sample copy available. Writer's guidelines for #10 SASE.

Nonfiction General interest, historical/nostalgic, how-to, interview/profile, new product, photo feature, technical. **Buys 35-40 mss/year.** Query. Length: 400-2,000 words. **Pays $100-500.**

Photos Send photos with submission. Reviews 35mm, $2\frac{1}{4} \times 2\frac{1}{4}$, 4×5 transparencies, 5×7 prints, electronic images in TIFF, GIF or JPEG Mac format. Negotiates payment individually. Captions, identification of subjects, model releases required.

Tips "Most of our contributors are involved with knives, either as collectors, makers, engravers, etc. To write about this subject requires knowledge. Writers can do OK if they study some recent issues. If you are interested in submitting work to *Knives Illustrated* magazine, it is suggested you analyze at least 2 or 3 different editions to get a feel for the magazine. It is also recommended that you call or mail in your query to determine if we are interested in the topic you have in mind. While verbal or written approval may be given, all articles are still received on a speculation basis. We cannot approve any article until we have it in hand, whereupon we will make a final decision as to its suitability for our use. Bear in mind we do not suggest you go to the trouble to write an article if there is doubt we can use it promptly."

LAPIDARY JOURNAL

300 Chesterfield Parkway, Suite 100, Malvern PA 19355. (610)232-5700. Fax: (610)232-5756. E-mail: lj.editorial @primedia.com. Website: www.lapidaryjournal.com. **70% freelance written.** Monthly magazine covering gem, bead and jewelry arts. "Our audience is hobbyists who usually have some knowledge of and proficiency in the subject before they start reading. Our style is conversational and informative. There are how-to projects and profiles of artists and materials." Estab. 1947. Circ. 53,000. **Pays on acceptance.** Publishes ms an average

of 4 months after acceptance. Byline given. Acquires one-time and worldwide rights. Editorial lead time 3 months. Accepts queries by mail, e-mail. Sample copy online.

Nonfiction Looks for conversational and lively narratives with quotes and anecdotes; Q&As; interviews. How-to (jewelry/craft), interview/profile, new product, personal experience, technical, travel. Special issues: Bead Annual, Jewelry Design issue, Jewelry Arts Awards, Bead Arts Awards, Gemmy's, Annual Buyers' Directory. **Buys 100 mss/year.** Query. Length: 1,500-2,500 words preferred; 1,000-3,500 words acceptable; longer works occasionally published serially.

Reprints Send photocopy.

Tips "Some knowledge of jewelry, gemstones and/or minerals is a definite asset. Step-by-Step is a section within *Lapidary Journal* that offers illustrated, step-by-step instruction in gem cutting, jewelry making, and beading. Please request a copy of the Step-by-Step guidelines for greater detail."

$ $ THE LEATHER CRAFTERS & SADDLERS JOURNAL

331 Annette Court, Rhinelander WI 54501-2902. (715)362-5393. Fax: (715)362-5391. E-mail: tworjournal@new north.net. Co-Publisher: Dorothea Reis. **Contact:** William R. Reis, editor/co-publisher. **100% freelance written.** Bimonthly magazine. "A leather-working publication with how-to, step-by-step instructional articles using full-size patterns for leathercraft, leather art, custom saddle, boot and harness making, etc. A complete resource for leather, tools, machinery, and allied materials, plus leather industry news." Estab. 1990. Circ. 9,000. Pays on publication. Publishes ms an average of 2 months after acceptance. Byline given. Buys first North American serial, second serial (reprint) rights. Submit seasonal material 6 months in advance. Accepts queries by mail, e-mail, fax, phone. Accepts previously published material. Accepts simultaneous submissions. Responds in 1 month to mss. Sample copy for $5. Writer's guidelines for #10 SASE.

    ○→ Break in with a how-to, step-by-step leather item article from beginner through masters and saddlemaking.

Nonfiction "I want only articles that include hands-on, step-by-step, how-to information." How-to (crafts and arts, and any other projects using leather). **Buys 75 mss/year.** Send complete ms. Length: 500-2,500 words. **Pays $20-250 for assigned articles; $20-150 for unsolicited articles.**

Reprints Send tearsheet or photocopy. Pays 50% of amount paid for an original article.

Photos Send good contrast color print photos and full-size patterns and/or full-size photo-carve patterns with submission. Lack of these reduces payment amount. Captions required.

Columns/Departments Beginners; Intermediate; Artists; Western Design; Saddlemakers; International Design; and Letters (the open exchange of information between all peoples). Length: 500-2,500 words on all. **Buys 75 mss/year.** Send complete ms. **Pays 5¢/word.**

Fillers Anecdotes, facts, gags to be illustrated by cartoonist, newsbreaks. Length: 25-200 words. **Pays $5-20.**

Tips "We want to work with people who understand and know leathercraft and are interested in passing on their knowledge to others. We would prefer to interview people who have achieved a high level in leathercraft skill."

N $ LINN'S STAMP NEWS

Amos Press, P.O. Box 29, Sidney OH 45365. (937)498-0801. Fax: (937)498-0886. Website: www.linns.com. **50% freelance written.** Weekly tabloid on the stamp collecting hobby. All articles must be about philatelic collectibles. Our goal at *Linn's* is to create a weekly publication that is indispensable to stamp collectors. Estab. 1928. Circ. 46,000. Pays within one month of publication. Publishes ms an average of 3 months after acceptance. Byline given. Buys first print and electronic rights. Submit seasonal material 2 months in advance. Responds in 6 weeks to queries. Sample copy for free. Writer's guidelines online.

Nonfiction General interest, historical/nostalgic, how-to, interview/profile, technical, club and show news, current issues, auction realization and recent discoveries. "No articles merely giving information on background of stamp subject. Must have philatelic information included." **Buys 50 mss/year.** Send complete ms. Length: 500 words maximum. **Pays $50.** Sometimes pays expenses of writers on assignment.

Photos Good illustrations a must. Provide captions on a separate sheet of paper. Send scans with submission. Reviews digital color at twice actual size (300 dpi). Buys all rights. Offers no additional payment for photos accepted with ms. Captions required.

Tips "Check and double check all facts. Footnotes and bibliographies are not appropriate to newspaper style. Work citation into the text. Even though your subject might be specialized, write understandably. Explain terms. *Linn's* features are aimed at a broad audience of relatively novice collectors. Keep this audience in mind. Provide information in such a way to make stamp collecting more interesting to more people."

$ LOST TREASURE, INC.

P.O. Box 451589, Grove OK 74345. (918)786-2182. Fax: (918)786-2192. E-mail: managingeditor@losttreasure.c om. Website: www.losttreasure.com. **Contact:** Jann Clark, managing editor. **75% freelance written.** Monthly and annual magazines covering lost treasure. Estab. 1966. Circ. 55,000. Pays on publication. Byline given. Buys all rights. Accepts queries by mail, e-mail, fax. Responds in 1 month to queries; 2 months to mss. Sample copy for #10 SASE. Writer's guidelines for 10×13 SAE with $1.47 postage or online.

Nonfiction *Lost Treasure* is composed of lost treasure stories, legends, how-to articles, treasure hunting club news, who's who in treasure hunting, tips. Length: 500-1,200 words. *Treasure Cache*, an annual, contains stories about documented treasure caches with a sidebar from the author telling the reader how to search for the cache highlighted in the story. **Buys 225 mss/year.** Query on *Treasure Cache* only. Length: 1,000-2,000 words. **Pays 4¢/word.**

Photos Black & white or color prints, hand-drawn or copied maps, art with source credit with mss will help sell your story. We are always looking for cover photos with or without accompanying ms. Pays $100/published cover photo. Must be vertical 35mm color slides or negatives. Pays $5/published photo. Captions required.

Tips "We are only interested in treasures that can be found with metal detectors. Queries welcome but not required. If you write about famous treasures and lost mines, be sure we haven't used your selected topic recently—the story must have a new slant or new information. Source documentation required. How-tos should cover some aspect of treasure hunting and how-to steps should be clearly defined. If you have a *Treasure Cache* story we will, if necessary, help the author with the sidebar telling how to search for the cache in the story. *Lost Treasure* articles should coordinate with theme issues when possible."

MCCALL'S QUILTING

Primedia Enthusiast Group, 741 Corporate Circle, Suite A, Golden CO 80401. (303)278-1010. Fax: (303)277-0370. Website: www.mccallsquilting.com. Publisher: Tina Battock. **Contact:** Beth Hayes, editor. Bimonthly magazine covering quiltmaking. Attracts quilters of all skill levels with a variety of complete, how-to quilting projects, including bed size quilts, wall hangings, wearables, and small projects. Estab. 1993. Circ. 162,000. Buys limited exclusive copyright license. Editorial lead time 6-9 months. Submit seasonal material 6-9 months in advance. Accepts queries by mail. Sample copy for $5.95. Writer's guidelines by e-mail.

Tips "For any design or article, include a detailed description of the project to help us make an informed decision."

ℕ $ $ MEMORY MAKERS

The First Source for Scrapbooking Ideas, F+W Publications, Inc., 12365 Huron St., Suite 500, Denver CO 80234. (303)452-1968. Fax: (303)452-2164. E-mail: editorial@memorymakersmagazine.com. Website: www.memory makersmagazine.com. **Contact:** Deborah Mock, executive editor. **50% freelance written.** Magazine published 9 times/year covering creative scrapbook ideas and craft techniques. "*Memory Makers* is an international magazine that showcases ideas and stories of scrapbookers. It includes articles with information, instructions, and products that apply to men and women who make creative scrapbooks." Estab. 1996. Circ. 285,000. Pays on project completion. Publishes ms an average of 6 months after acceptance. Byline given. Buys first rights. Editorial lead time 6 months. Submit seasonal material 6 months in advance. Accepts queries by mail, e-mail. Accepts simultaneous submissions. Writer's guidelines online.

⊶ Break in with articles on "unique craft techniques that can apply to scrapbooking, and personal stories of how scrapbooking has impacted someone's life."

Nonfiction Historical/nostalgic, how-to (scrapbooking), inspirational, interview/profile, new product, personal experience, photography. No "all-encompassing how-to scrapbook" articles. **Buys 6-10 mss/year.** Query with published clips. Length: 1,000-1,500 words. **Pays $500-750.**

Columns/Departments Keeping It Safe (issues surrounding the safe preservation of scrapbooks); Scrapbooking 101 (how-to scrapbooking techniques for beginners); Photojournaling (new and useful ideas for improving scrapbook journaling); Modern Memories (computer and modern technology scrapbooking issues), all 600-800 words. Query with published clips. **Pays $200-350.**

ℕ $ $ MILITARY TRADER

Krause Publications, a Division of F+W Publications, Inc., 700 E. State St., Iola WI 54990-0001. (715)445-4612. E-mail: militarytrader@krause.com. Website: www.militarytrader.com. **Contact:** John Adams-Graf, editor. **50% freelance written.** Magazine covering military collectibles. "Dedicated to serving people who collect, preserve, and display military relics." Estab. 1994. Circ. 6,500. Pays on publication. Publishes ms an average of 1 month after acceptance. Byline given. Buys first North American serial rights. Accepts queries by mail, e-mail. Accepts simultaneous submissions. Responds in 1 week to queries; 1 month to mss. Sample copy for $5. Writer's guidelines not available.

Nonfiction Historical/nostalgic, collection comparisons, artifact identification, reproduction alert. **Buys 40 mss/year.** Send complete ms. Length: 1,300-2,600 words. **Pays $0-200.**

Photos Send photos with submission. Reviews contact sheets. Buys all rights. Negotiates payment individually. 25-50 word captions (not repeating ms text) required.

Columns/Departments Pays $0-50.

Tips "Be knowledgeable on military collectibles and/or military history. Plenty of good photos will make it easier to be published in our publication. Write for the collector: Assume that they already know the basics of historical context. Provide tips on where and how to collect specific items. Articles that teach the reader how to recognize fakes or forgeries are given the highest priority."

Ⓝ $ $ MILITARY VEHICLES

Krause Publications, a Division of F+W Publications, Inc., 700 E. State St., Iola WI 54990-0001. (715)445-4612. E-mail: militaryvehicles@krause.com. Website: www.militaryvehiclesmagazine.com. **Contact:** John Adams-Graf, editor. **50% freelance written.** Bimonthly magazine covering historic military vehicles. "Dedicated to serving people who collect, restore, and drive historic military vehicles." Circ. 19,000. Pays on publication. Publishes ms an average of 1 month after acceptance. Byline given. Buys first North American serial rights. Accepts queries by mail, e-mail. Accepts simultaneous submissions. Responds in 1 week to queries; 1 month to mss. Sample copy for $5.

Nonfiction Historical/nostalgic, how-to, technical. **Buys 20 mss/year.** Send complete ms. Length: 1,300-2,600 words. **Pays $0-200.**

Photos Buys all rights. 25-50 word captions (not repeating ms text) required.

Columns/Departments Pays $0-75.

Tips "Be knowledgeable about military vehicles. This magazine is for a very specialized audience. General automotive journalists will probably not be able to write for this group. The bulk of our content addresses US-manufactured and used vehicles. Plenty of good photos will make it easier to be published in our publication. Write for the collector/restorer: Assume that they already know the basics of historical context. Articles that show how to restore or repair military vehicles are given the highest priority."

$ MINIATURE QUILTS

Chitra Publications, 2 Public Ave., Montrose PA 18801. (570)278-1984. Fax: (570)278-2223. E-mail: chitraed@epix.net. Website: www.quilttownusa.com. **Contact:** Phyllis Montange, production coordinator. **40% freelance written.** Bimonthly magazine on miniature quilts. "We seek articles of an instructional nature (all techniques), profiles of talented quiltmakers, and informational articles on all aspects of miniature quilts. Miniature is defined as quilts made up of blocks smaller than 5 inches." Estab. 1990. Circ. 70,000. Pays on publication. Publishes ms an average of 6 months after acceptance. Byline given. Buys second serial (reprint) rights. Submit seasonal material 8 months in advance. Accepts queries by mail, fax. Responds in 2 months to queries. Writer's guidelines online.

   ○┐ "Best bet—a quilter writing about a new or unusual quilting technique."

Nonfiction How-to, interview/profile (quilters who make small quilts), photo feature (about noteworthy miniature quilts or exhibits). Query. Length: 1,500 words maximum. **Pays $75/published page of text.**

Photos Send photos with submission. Reviews 35mm slides and larger transparencies. Offers $20/photo. Captions, identification of subjects, model releases required.

$ MODEL RAILROADER

P.O. Box 1612, Waukesha WI 53187. Fax: (262)796-1142. E-mail: mrmag@mrmag.com. Website: www.trains.com. **Contact:** Jim Slocum, publisher; Terry Thompson, editor. Monthly magazine for hobbyists interested in scale model railroading. "We publish articles on all aspects of model-railroading and on prototype (real) railroading as a subject for modeling." Byline given. Buys exclusive rights. Accepts queries by mail, e-mail, fax. Responds in 2 months to queries.

   ○┐ "Study publication before submitting material." First-hand knowledge of subject almost always necessary for acceptable slant.

Nonfiction Wants construction articles on specific model railroad projects (structures, cars, locomotives, scenery, benchwork, etc.). Also photo stories showing model railroads. Query. **Pays base rate of $90/page.**

Photos Buys photos with detailed descriptive captions only. Pays $15 and up, depending on size and use. Full color cover earns $200.

Tips "Before you prepare and submit any article, you should write us a short letter of inquiry describing what you want to do. We can then tell you if it fits our needs and save you from working on something we don't want."

$ MONITORING TIMES

Grove Enterprises, Inc., 7540 Hwy. 64 W., Brasstown NC 28902-0098. (828)837-9200. Fax: (828)837-2216. E-mail: editor@monitoringtimes.com. Website: www.monitoringtimes.com. Publisher: Robert Grove. **Contact:** Rachel Baughn, editor. **15% freelance written.** Monthly magazine for radio hobbyists. Estab. 1982. Circ. 20,000. Pays on publication. Publishes ms an average of 4 months after acceptance. Byline given. Buys first North

American serial, second serial (reprint) rights. Submit seasonal material 4 months in advance. Accepts queries by mail, e-mail. Accepts previously published material. Responds in 1 month to queries. Sample copy for 9 × 12 SAE and 9 first-class stamps. Writer's guidelines online.

☞ Break in with a shortwave station profile or topic, or scanning topics of broad interest.

Nonfiction General interest, how-to, humor, interview/profile, personal experience, photo feature, technical. **Buys 50 mss/year.** Query. Length: 1,500-3,000 words. **Pays average of $50/published page.**

Reprints Send photocopy and information about when and where the material previously appeared. Pays 25% of amount paid for an original article.

Photos Send photos with submission. Buys one-time rights. Captions required.

Tips "Need articles on radio communications systems and shortwave broadcasters. We are accepting more technical projects."

$NUMISMATIST MAGAZINE

American Numismatic Association, 818 N. Cascade Ave., Colorado Springs CO 80903-3279. (719)632-2646. Fax: (719)634-4085. E-mail: magazine@money.org. **Contact:** Barbara Gregory, editor. Monthly magazine covering numismatics (study of coins, tokens, medals, and paper money). Estab. 1888. Circ. 30,000. Pays on publication. Publishes ms an average of 1 year after acceptance. Byline given. Buys perpetual, but nonexclusive rights. Editorial lead time 2 months. Sample copy for free.

Nonfiction "Submitted material should present new information and/or constitute a contribution to numismatic education for the experienced collector and beginner alike." Book excerpts, essays, historical/nostalgic, opinion, technical. **Buys 60 mss/year.** Query or send complete ms. Length: 2,500 words maximum. **Pays 7¢/word.** Sometimes pays expenses of writers on assignment.

Photos Send photos with submission. Negotiates payment individually. Captions, identification of subjects required.

Columns/Departments Send complete ms. **Pays $25-100.**

Ⓝ ⊘ OLD CARS PRICE GUIDE

Krause Publications, a Division of F+W Publications, Inc., 700 E. State St., Iola WI 54990-0001. (715)445-2214. Fax: (715)445-4087. E-mail: oldcarspg@krause.com. Website: www.oldcarspriceguide.net. Editor: Ron Kowalke. Bimonthly magazine covering collector vehicle values. Estab. 1978. Circ. 60,000. Sample copy for free.

• This publication is testing a new format and is not accepting freelance submissions at this time.

PACK-O-FUN

Projects For Kids & Families, Clapper Communications, 2400 Devon Ave., Des Plaines IL 60018-4618. (847)635-5800. Website: www.craftideas.com. **85% freelance written.** Bimonthly magazine covering crafts and activities for kids and those working with kids. Estab. 1951. Circ. 102,000. Pays 45 days after signed contract. Byline given. Buys all rights. Editorial lead time 6 months. Submit seasonal material 6 months in advance. Accepts queries by mail, fax. Accepts previously published material. Accepts simultaneous submissions. Responds in 2 months to queries. Sample copy for $3.50 or online.

Nonfiction "We request quick and easy, inexpensive crafts and activities. Projects must be original, and complete instructions are required upon acceptance." **Payment negotiable.**

Reprints Send tearsheet and information about when and where the material previously appeared.

Photos Photos of project may be submitted in place of project at query stage.

Tips "*Pack-O-Fun* is looking for original how-to projects for kids and those working with kids. Write simple instructions for crafts to be done by children ages 5-13 years. We're looking for recyclable ideas for throwaways. We accept fiction if accompanied by a craft or in skit form (appropriate for classrooms, scouts, or Bible school groups). It would be helpful to check out our magazine before submitting."

$ $PAPERCRAFTS MAGAZINE

Primedia Magazines, 14850 Pony Express Rd., Bluffdale UT 84065. (801)984-2070. Fax: (801)984-2080. E-mail: editor@papercraftsmag.com. Website: www.papercraftsmag.com. Magazine published 10 times/year designed to help readers make creative and rewarding handmade crafts. The main focus is fresh, craft-related projects our reader can make and display in her home or give as gifts. Estab. 1978. Circ. 300,000. **Pays on acceptance.** Byline given. Buys all rights. Editorial lead time 6 months. Accepts queries by mail, e-mail. Responds in 1 month to queries. Writer's guidelines for #10 SASE.

Nonfiction How-to. **Buys 300 mss/year.** Query with photo or sketch of how-to project. Do not send the actual project until request. **Pays $100-500 for assigned articles.**

Tips "We are looking for projects that are fresh, innovative, and in sync with today's trends. We accept projects made with a variety of techniques and media. Projects can fall in several categories, ranging from home decor to gifts, garden accessories to jewelry, and other seasonal craft projects. Submitted projects must be original, never-before-published, copyright-free work that use readily available materials.''

$PIECEWORK MAGAZINE

Interweave Press, Inc., 201 E. 4th St., Loveland CO 80537-5655. (970)669-7672. Fax: (970)667-8317. E-mail: piecework@interweave.com. Website: www.interweave.com. **90% freelance written.** Bimonthly magazine covering needlework history. ''*PieceWork* celebrates the rich tradition of needlework and the history of the people behind it. Stories and projects on embroidery, cross-stitch, knitting, crocheting, and quilting, along with other textile arts, are featured in each issue.'' Estab. 1993. Circ. 60,000. Pays on publication. Byline given. Offers 30% kill fee. Buys first North American serial rights. Editorial lead time 6 months. Submit seasonal material 6 months in advance. Accepts queries by mail, e-mail, fax, phone. Responds in 6 months to queries. Sample copy and writer's guidelines free.

Nonfiction Book excerpts, historical/nostalgic, how-to, interview/profile, new product. No contemporary needlework articles. **Buys 25-30 mss/year.** Send complete ms. Length: 1,000-5,000 words. **Pays $100/printed page.**

Photos State availability of or send photos with submission. Reviews transparencies, prints. Buys one-time rights. Captions, identification of subjects, model releases required.

Tips ''Submit a well-researched article on a historical aspect of needlework complete with information on visuals and suggestion for accompanying project.''

$POPULAR COMMUNICATIONS

CQ Communications, Inc., 25 Newbridge Rd., Hicksville NY 11801. (516)681-2922. Fax: (516)681-2926. E-mail: popularcom@aol.com. Website: www.popular-communications.com. **Contact:** Harold Ort, editor. **25% freelance written.** Monthly magazine covering the radio communications hobby. Estab. 1982. Circ. 40,000. Pays on publication. Publishes ms an average of 6 months after acceptance. Byline given. Buys first North American serial rights. Editorial lead time 3 months. Submit seasonal material 6 months in advance. Accepts queries by mail, e-mail. Responds in 1 month to queries; 2 months to mss. Sample copy for free. Writer's guidelines for #10 SASE.

Nonfiction General interest, how-to (antenna construction), humor, new product, photo feature, technical. **Buys 6-10 mss/year.** Query. Length: 1,800-3,000 words. **Pays $35/printed page.**

Photos State availability with submission. Negotiates payment individually. Captions, identification of subjects, model releases required.

Tips ''Either be a radio enthusiast or know one who can help you before sending us an article.''

$ $ $ $POPULAR MECHANICS

Hearst Corp., 810 Seventh Ave., 6th Floor, New York NY 10019. (212)649-2000. E-mail: popularmechanics@hearst.com. Website: www.popularmechanics.com. **Contact:** Don Chaikin (auto); Tobey Grumet (technology, electronics, computers); Jerry Beilinson (outdoors); Steve Willson (home); David Dunbar (science). **Up to 50% freelance written.** Monthly magazine on technology, science, automotive, home, outdoors. ''We are a men's service magazine that addresses the diverse interests of today's male, providing him with information to improve the way he lives. We cover stories from do-it-yourself projects to technological advances in aerospace, military, automotive and so on.'' Estab. 1902. Circ. 1,200,000. Publishes ms an average of 6 months after acceptance. Offers 25% kill fee. Submit seasonal material 6 months in advance.

- **Pays $1/word and up.**

    The online magazine contains material not found in the print edition. Contact: Ken Juran, online editor.

$ $POPULAR WOODWORKING

F+W Publications, Inc., 4700 E. Galbraith Rd., Cincinnati OH 45236. (513)531-2690, ext. 1348. E-mail: kara.gebhart@fwpubs.com. Website: www.popularwoodworking.com. Editor/Publisher: Steve Shanesy. Executive Editor: Christopher Schwarz. **Contact:** Kara Gebhart, associate editor. **45% freelance written.** Magazine published 7 times/year. ''*Popular Woodworking* invites woodworkers of all levels into a community of professionals who share their hard-won shop experience through in-depth projects and technique articles, which help the readers hone their existing skills and develop new ones. Related stories increase the readers' understanding and enjoyment of their craft. Any project submitted must be aesthetically pleasing, of sound construction, and offer a challenge to readers. On the average, we use 4 freelance features per issue. Our primary needs are 'how-to' articles on woodworking. Our secondary need is for articles that will inspire discussion concerning woodworking. Tone of articles should be conversational and informal, as if the writer is speaking directly to the reader. Our readers are the woodworking hobbyist and small woodshop owner. Writers should have an extensive knowledge of woodworking, or be able to communicate information gained from woodworkers.'' Estab. 1981. Circ. 200,000. **Pays on acceptance.** Publishes ms an average of 10 months after acceptance. Byline given. Buys first world rights rights. Submit seasonal material 6 months in advance. Accepts queries by mail, e-mail, fax, phone. Accepts previously published material. Responds in 2 months to queries. Sample copy for $4.50 and 9×12 SAE with 6 first-class stamps or online. Writer's guidelines online.

O→ ''The project must be well-designed, well-constructed, well-built, and well-finished. Technique pieces must have practical application.''

Nonfiction How-to (on woodworking projects, with plans), humor (woodworking anecdotes), technical (woodworking techniques). Special issues: Workshop issue; Tool buying guide. No tool reviews. **Buys 40 mss/year.** Query with or without published clips or send complete ms. **Pay starts at $150/published page.**

Reprints Send photocopy with rights for sale noted and information about when and where the material previously appeared. Pays 25% of amount paid for an original article.

Photos Photographic quality affects acceptance. Need sharp close-up color photos of step-by-step construction process. Send photos with submission. Reviews (color only), slides and transparencies, 3×5 glossies acceptable. Captions, identification of subjects required.

Columns/Departments Tricks of the Trade (helpful techniques), Out of the Woodwork (thoughts on woodworking as a profession or hobby, can be humorous or serious), 500-1,500 words. **Buys 20 mss/year.** Query.

Tips ''Write an 'Out of the Woodwork' column for us and then follow up with photos of your projects. Submissions should include materials list, complete diagrams (blueprints not necessary), and discussion of the step-by-step process. We have become more selective on accepting only practical, attractive projects with quality construction. We are also looking for more original topics for our other articles.''

$ $ POSTCARD COLLECTOR

Krause Publications, a Division of F+W Publications, Inc., P.O. Box 1050, Dubuque IA 52004. (800)482-4143. Fax: (800)531-0880. E-mail: fliessc@krause.com. Website: www.postcardcollector.com. **Contact:** Claire R. Fliess, editor. **98% freelance written.** Monthly magazine covering postcard collecting. ''The publication prints columns and articles about postcard collections. Sometimes they are historical—some are modern. Dealers and collectors subscribe.'' Estab. 1983. Circ. 6,165. Pays on publication. Publishes ms an average of 9 months after acceptance. Byline given. Offers $25 kill fee. Buys all rights. Editorial lead time 3 months. Submit seasonal material 3 months in advance. Accepts queries by mail, e-mail, fax, phone. Accepts simultaneous submissions. Responds in 1 month to mss. Sample copy and writer's guidelines free.

Nonfiction Essays, historical/nostalgic, interview/profile, personal experience, photo feature. Does not want poorly researched articles. **Buys 120 mss/year.** Query. Length: 800-1,500 words. **Pays $75-200.**

Photos Send photos with submission. Reviews 4×6 prints, JPEG files. Buys negotiable rights. Offers no additional payment for photos accepted with ms. Captions, identification of subjects required.

Columns/Departments Book Reviews (review of content including images), 500-800 words. **Buys 120 mss/year.** Query. **Pays $75-200.**

Tips ''Need good images of postcards, well-researched article—unusual topic.''

$ THE PYSANKA

Starwind Press, P.O. Box 98, Ripley OH 45167. (937)392-4549. E-mail: susannah@techgallery.com. **Contact:** Susannah West, editor. **90% freelance written.** Quarterly newsletter covering wax-resist egg decoration. ''*The Pysanka* examines the art of wax-resist egg decoration (pysanky). Its audience is artists and hobbyists who create this style egg.'' Estab. 2000. Circ. 100. **Pays on acceptance.** Publishes ms an average of 3 months after acceptance. Byline given. Offers 100% kill fee. Buys first North American serial rights. Editorial lead time 3 months. Submit seasonal material 3 months in advance. Accepts queries by mail, e-mail. Accepts previously published material. Responds in 2 months. Sample copy for $3.50. Writer's guidelines for #10 SASE.

Nonfiction Historical/nostalgic, how-to, interview/profile, new product, opinion, personal experience, photo feature, travel. **Buys 16-20 mss/year.** Query or send complete ms. Length: 500-900 words. **Pays $10.**

Reprints Accepts previously published submissions.

Photos State availability with submission. Negotiates payment individually. Identification of subjects required.

Columns/Departments Around and About (reviews of interesting places to visit related to the craft), 300-500 words; Passing the Torch (workshop experiences), 200-500 words; On the Pysanky Bookshelf (book reviews), 100-200 words; Issues and Answers (issues of interest), 500-900 words. **Buys 8-12 mss/year.** Query. **Pays $5-10.**

Fiction Ethnic. **Buys 4 mss/year.** Send complete ms. Length: 2,000-5,000 words. **Pays 1¢/word.**

Tips ''The writer should be familiar with the wax-resist style of egg decoration, ideally an artist or hobbyist who makes this style of egg.''

QUILTER'S NEWSLETTER MAGAZINE

Primedia Enthusiast Group, 741 Corporate Circle, Suite A, Golden CO 80401. (303)278-1010. Fax: (303)277-0370. Website: www.quiltersnewsletter.com. Publisher: Tina Battock. **Contact:** Mary Leman Austin, editor. Magazine published 10 times/year covering quilt making. Written for quilt enthusiasts. Estab. 1969. Circ. 185,000. Pays on publication. Accepts queries by mail. Sample copy and writer's guidelines online.

Nonfiction SASE Returns. Historical/nostalgic, how-to (design techniques, presentation of a single technique or concept with step-by-step approach), interview/profile, new product, reviews (quilt books and videos). Send complete ms.

Photos Color only, no b&w. Reviews 2×2, 4×5 or larger transparencies, 35mm slides. Negotiates payment individually. Captions required.

Tips ''Our decision will be based on the freshness of the material, the interest of the material to our readers, whether we have recently published similar material or already have something similar in our inventory, how well it fits into the balance of the material we have on hand, how much rewriting or editing we think it will require, and the quality of the slides, photos or illustrations you include.''

$ $THE QUILTER

All American Crafts, Inc., 7 Waterloo Rd., Stanhope NJ 07874. (973)347-6900. E-mail: editors@thequiltermag.com. Website: www.thequiltermag.com. **Contact:** Laurette Koserowski, editor. **45% freelance written.** Bimonthly magazine on quilting. Estab. 1988. Pays on publication. Publishes ms an average of 6 months after acceptance. Byline given. Submit seasonal material 6 months in advance. Accepts queries by mail, phone. Responds in 2 months to queries. Sample copy for 9×12 SAE and 4 first-class stamps. Writer's guidelines online.

Nonfiction Quilts and quilt patterns with instructions, quilt-related projects, interview/profile, photo feature—all quilt related. Query with published clips. Length: 350-1,000 words. **Pays 10-12¢/word.**

Photos Send photos with submission. Reviews transparencies, prints. Buys one-time or all rights. Offers $10-15/photo. Captions, identification of subjects required.

Columns/Departments Feature Teacher (qualified quilt teachers with teaching involved—with slides); Profile (award-winning and interesting quilters). Length: 1,000 words maximum. **Pays 10¢/word, $15/photo.**

$RENAISSANCE MAGAZINE

One Controls Dr., Shelton CT 06484. (800)232-2224. Fax: (800)775-2729. E-mail: editor@renaissancemagazine.com. Website: www.renaissancemagazine.com. **Contact:** Kim Guarnaccia, managing editor. **90% freelance written.** Bimonthly magazine covering the history of the Middle Ages and the Renaissance. ''Our readers include historians, reenactors, roleplayers, medievalists, and Renaissance Faire enthusiasts.'' Estab. 1996. Circ. 33,000. Pays on publication. Publishes ms an average of 1 year after acceptance. Byline given. Buys first North American serial rights. Editorial lead time 6 months. Submit seasonal material 4 months in advance. Accepts queries by mail, e-mail, fax, phone. Accepts previously published material. Responds in 3 weeks to queries; 2 months to mss. Sample copy for $9. Writer's guidelines online.

● The editor reports an interest in seeing costuming ''how-to'' articles; and Renaissance Festival ''insider'' articles.

○⇥ Break in by submitting short (500-1,000 word) articles as fillers or querying on upcoming theme issues.

Nonfiction Essays, exposé, historical/nostalgic, how-to, interview/profile, new product, opinion, photo feature, religious, travel. **Buys 25 mss/year.** Query or send ms. Length: 1,000-5,000 words. **Pays 8¢/word.**

Photos State availability with submission. Reviews contact sheets, negatives, transparencies, prints. Buys all rights. Pays $7.50/photo. Captions, identification of subjects, model releases required.

Tips ''Send in all articles in the standard manuscript format with photos/slides or illustrations for suggested use. Writers *must* be open to critique, and all historical articles should also include a recommended reading list. A SASE must be included to receive a response to any submission.''

$ $ROCK & GEM

The Earth's Treasures, Minerals and Jewelry, Miller Magazines, Inc., 290 Maple Court, Suite 232, Ventura CA 93003-7783. (805)644-3824, ext. 29. Fax: (805)644-3875. E-mail: editor@rockngem.com. Website: www.rockngem.com. **Contact:** Lynn Varon, managing editor. **99% freelance written.** Monthly magazine covering rockhounding field trips, how-to lapidary projects, minerals, fossils, gold prospecting, mining, etc. ''This is not a scientific journal. Its articles appeal to amateurs, beginners, and experts, but its tone is conversational and casual, not stuffy. It's for hobbyists.'' Estab. 1971. Circ. 55,000. Pays on publication. Byline given. Buys first North American serial, electronic rights. Editorial lead time 4 months. Submit seasonal material 6 months in advance. Accepts queries by mail. Writer's guidelines online.

Nonfiction General interest, how-to, personal experience, photo feature, travel. Does not want to see ''The 25th Anniversary of the Pet Rock,'' or anything so scientific that it could be a thesis. **Buys 156-200 mss/year.** Send complete ms. Length: 2,000-4,000 words. **Pays $100-250.**

Photos Accepts prints, slides or digital art on disk or CD only (provide thumbnails). Send photos with submission. Offers no additional payment for photos accepted with ms. Captions required.

Tips ''We're looking for more how-to articles and field trips with maps. Read writers guidelines very carefully and follow all instructions in them. Then be patient. Your manuscript may be published within a month or even a year from date of submission.''

$SCALE AUTO

Kalmbach Publishing Co., 21027 Crossroads Circle, P.O. Box 1612, Waukesha WI 53187-1612. (262)796-8776. Fax: (262)796-1383. E-mail: jhaught@kalmbach.com. Website: www.scaleautomag.com. **Contact:** Jim Haught, editor. **70% freelance written.** Bimonthly magazine covering model car building. ''We are looking for model builders, collectors, and enthusiasts who feel their models and/or modeling techniques and experiences would be of interest and benefit to our readership.'' Estab. 1979. Circ. 35,000. Pays on publication. Publishes ms an average of 1 year after acceptance. Byline given. Buys all rights. Editorial lead time 4 months. Submit seasonal material 4 months in advance. Accepts queries by mail, e-mail, fax, phone. Responds in 3 months. Sample copy and writer's guidelines online.

Nonfiction Book excerpts, historical/nostalgic, how-to (build models, do different techniques), interview/profile, personal experience, photo feature, technical. Query or send complete ms. Length: 750-3,000 words. **Pays $60/published page.**

Photos When writing how-to articles be sure to take photos during the project. Send photos with submission. Reviews negatives, 35mm color transparencies, color glossy. Buys all rights. Negotiates payment individually. Captions, identification of subjects, model releases required.

Columns/Departments Buys 50 mss/year. Query. **Pays $60/page.**

Tips ''First and foremost, our readers like how-to material: how-to paint, how-to scratchbuild, how-to chop a roof, etc. Basically, our readers want to know how to make their own models better. Therefore, any help or advice you can offer is what modelers want to read. Also, the more photos you send, taken from a variety of views, the better choice we have in putting together an outstanding article layout. Send us more photos than you would ever possibly imagine we could use. This permits us to pick and choose the best of the bunch.''

$ $SEW NEWS

The Magazine for People Who Sew, Primedia Enthusiast Group, 741 Corporate Circle, Suite A, Golden CO 80401. (303)278-1010. Fax: (303)277-0370. E-mail: sewnews@sewnews.com. Website: www.sewnews.com. **Contact:** Marla Stefanelli, editor. **70% freelance written.** Works with a small number of new/unpublished writers each year. Monthly magazine covering fashion, gift, and home-dec sewing. ''Our magazine is for the beginning home sewer to the professional dressmaker. It expresses the fun, creativity, and excitement of sewing.'' Estab. 1980. Circ. 150,000. **Pays on acceptance.** Publishes ms an average of 6 months after acceptance. Byline given. Buys all rights. Submit seasonal material 6 months in advance. Accepts queries by mail, e-mail, fax. Responds in 2 months to mss. Sample copy for $5.99. Writer's guidelines for #10 SAE with 2 first-class stamps or online.

● All stories submitted to *Sew News* must be on disk or by e-mail.

Nonfiction How-to (sewing techniques), interview/profile (interesting personalities in home-sewing field). **Buys 200-240 mss/year.** Query with published clips if available. Length: 500-2,000 words. **Pays $25-500 for assigned articles.**

Photos Prefers digital images, color photos, or slides. Send photos with submission. Buys all rights. Payment included in ms price. Identification of subjects required.

The online magazine carries some original content not found in the print edition and includes writer's guidelines. *Sew News* has a free online newsletter.

Tips ''Query first with writing sample and outline of proposed story. Areas most open to freelancers are how-to and sewing techniques; give explicit, step-by-step instructions, plus rough art. We're using more home decorating and soft craft content.''

$SHUTTLE SPINDLE & DYEPOT

Handweavers Guild of America, Inc., 1255 Buford Hwy., Suite 211, Suwanee GA 30024. (678)730-0010. Fax: (678)730-0836. E-mail: hga@weavespindye.org. Website: www.weavespindye.org. Assistant Editor: Trish Fowler. Advertising Manager: Dorothy Holt. **Contact:** Sandra Bowles, editor-in-chief. **60% freelance written.** Quarterly magazine. ''Quarterly membership publication of the Handweavers Guild of America, Inc., *Shuttle Spindle & Dyepot* magazine seeks to encourage excellence in contemporary fiber arts and to support the preservation of techniques and traditions in fiber arts. It also provides inspiration for fiber artists of all levels and develops public awareness and appreciation of the fiber arts. *Shuttle Spindle & Dyepot* appeals to a highly educated, creative, and very knowledgeable audience of fiber artists and craftsmen—weavers, spinners, dyers, and basket makers.'' Estab. 1969. Circ. 30,000. Pays on publication. Publishes ms an average of 6 months after acceptance. Byline given. Buys first North American serial, second serial (reprint), electronic rights. Editorial lead time 8 months. Submit seasonal material 8 months in advance. Accepts queries by mail, e-mail, fax, phone. Sample copy for $7.50 plus shipping. Writer's guidelines online.

0⤙ Articles featuring up-and-coming artists, new techniques, cutting-edge ideas and designs, fascinating children's activities, and comprehensive fiber collections are a few examples of "best bet" topics.

Nonfiction Inspirational, interview/profile, new product, personal experience, photo feature, technical, travel. "No self-promotional and no articles from those without knowledge of area/art/artists." **Buys 40 mss/year.** Query with published clips. Length: 1,000-2,000 words. **Pays $75-150.**

Photos State availability with submission. Offers no additional payment for photos accepted with ms. Captions, identification of subjects, model releases required.

Columns/Departments Books and Videos, News and Information, Calendar and Conference, Travel and Workshop, Guildview (all fiber/art related).

Tips "Become knowledgeable about the fiber arts and artists. The writer should provide an article of importance to the weaving, spinning, dyeing and basket making community. Query by telephone (once familiar with publication) by appointment helps editor and writer.

$ $ SPORTS COLLECTORS DIGEST

Voice for the Hobby, Krause Publications, a Division of F+W Publications, Inc., 700 E. State St., Iola WI 54990. (715)445-2214. Fax: (715)445-4087. E-mail: scd@krause.com. Website: www.sportscollectorsdigest.com; www .krause.com. **Contact:** T.S. O'Connell, editor. **10% freelance written.** Weekly tabloid covering sports collectibles. Estab. 1973. Circ. 30,000. Pays on publication. Publishes ms an average of 2 months after acceptance. Byline given. Makes work-for-hire assignments. Editorial lead time 2 months. Submit seasonal material 1 month in advance. Accepts queries by e-mail. Sample copy for free. Writer's guidelines not available.

Nonfiction General interest (new card issues, research older sets), historical/nostalgic (old stadiums, old collectibles, etc.), how-to (buy cards, sell cards and other collectibles, display collectibles, ways to get autographs, jerseys and other memorabilia), interview/profile (well-known collectors, ball players—but must focus on collectibles), new product (new card sets), personal experience (what I collect and why-type stories). No non-collecting sports stories. "We are not competing with *The Sporting News*, *Sports Illustrated*, or your daily paper. Sports collectibles only." **Buys 50-75 mss/year.** Query. Length: 300-3,000 words. **Pays $100-200.**

Reprints Send tearsheet. Pays 100% of amount paid for an original article.

Photos Unusual collectibles. Send photos with submission. Buys all rights. Pays $25-150 for b&w prints. Identification of subjects required.

Columns/Departments Length: 500-1,500 words. **Buys 100-150 mss/year.** Query. **Pays $90-150.**

Tips "Sports collectibles submissions only, e-mailed or mailed to T.S. O'Connell (oconnellt@krause.com)."

N $ SUNSHINE ARTIST

America's Premier Show & Festival Publication, Palm House Publishing Inc., 3210 Dade Ave., Orlando FL 32804. (407)228-9772. Fax: (407)228-9862. E-mail: editor@sunshineartist.com. Website: www.sunshineartist.c om. Monthly magazine covering art shows in the US. "We are the premiere marketing/reference magazine for artists and crafts professionals who earn their living through art shows nationwide. We list more than 2,000 shows monthly, critique many of them, and publish articles on marketing, selling and other issues of concern to professional show circuit artists." Estab. 1972. Circ. 12,000. Pays on publication. Publishes ms an average of 3 months after acceptance. Byline given. Buys first North American serial rights. Responds in 2 months to queries. Sample copy for $5.

Nonfiction "We publish articles of interest to artists and crafts professionals who travel the art show circuit. Current topics include marketing, computers, and RV living." No how-to. **Buys 5-10 freelance mss/year.** Query with or without published clips or send complete ms. Length: 1,000-2,000 words. **Pays $50-150.**

Reprints Send photocopy and information about when and where the material previously appeared.

Photos Send photos with submission. Offers no additional payment for photos accepted with ms. Captions, identification of subjects, model releases required.

N $ $ TOY CARS & MODELS

Krause Publications, a Division of F+W Publications, Inc., 700 E. State St., Iola WI 54990-0001. Fax: (715)445-4087. E-mail: contacttoycars@krause.com. Website: www.toycarsmag.com. **Contact:** Merry Dudley, editor. **90% freelance written.** Monthly magazine covering die-cast metal, plastic, resin and white-metal model cars. "*Toy Cars & Models* provides comprehensive coverage of the model car hobby without bias toward scale, subject, manufacturer or material. Each month, *TC&M* offers columns and news stories featuring models made of die-cast, white metal, plastic, resin and more while getting readers in touch with the manufacturers, distributors and retailers who sell these model cars." Estab. 1998. Circ. 20,000. Pays on publication. Publishes ms an average of 1 year after acceptance. Byline given. Offers kill fee. Editorial lead time 3 months. Submit seasonal material 3 months in advance. Accepts queries by mail, e-mail, fax. Accepts simultaneous submissions. Responds in 1 month to queries; 2 months to mss. Writer's guidelines free.

Nonfiction Essays, general interest, historical/nostalgic, how-to (build models, assemble collections, protect/

display collection), interview/profile, new product, photo feature, technical. Query. Length: 300-1,500 words. **Pays $50-200 for assigned articles; $50-100 for unsolicited articles.**

Photos Send photos with submission. Reviews transparencies, 3×5 prints, GIF/JPEG files (300 resolution, 4 inches wide). Buys negotiable rights. No additional payment for photos accepted with ms. Captions, identification of subjects, model releases required.

📭 The online magazine carries original content not found in the print version. Contact: Merry Dudley, online editor.

Tips ''Our magazine is for serious hobbyists looking for info about kit building, model quality, new products, and collectible value.''

$ $ TOY FARMER

Toy Farmer Publications, 7496 106 Ave. SE, LaMoure ND 58458-9404. (701)883-5206. Fax: (701)883-5209. E-mail: info@toyfarmer.com. Website: www.toyfarmer.com. President/Publisher: Cathy Scheibe. **Contact:** Cheryl Hegvik, editorial assistant. **70% freelance written.** Monthly magazine covering farm toys. Estab. 1978. Circ. 27,000. Pays on publication. Byline given. Buys first North American serial rights. Editorial lead time 3 months. Submit seasonal material 3 months in advance. Accepts queries by mail, e-mail, fax, phone. Accepts previously published material. Responds in 1 month to queries; 2 months to mss. Sample copy for $4. Writer's guidelines available upon request.

• Youth involvement is strongly encouraged.

Nonfiction General interest, historical/nostalgic, humor, interview/profile, new product, personal experience, technical, book introductions. **Buys 100 mss/year.** Query with published clips. Length: 800-1,500 words. **Pays 10¢/word.** Sometimes pays expenses of writers on assignment.

Photos Must be 35mm originals or very high resolution digital images. State availability with submission. Buys one-time rights. Offers no additional payment for photos accepted with ms.

$ $ TOY SHOP

Krause Publications, a Division of F+W Publications, Inc., 700 E. State St., Iola WI 54990-0001. (715)445-4612. Fax: (715)445-4087. E-mail: toyshop@krause.com. Website: www.toyshopmag.com; www.collect.com. **Contact:** Tom Bartsch, editor. **20% freelance written.** Biweekly tabloid covering toys. ''Our publication features writing that's easy to understand and lively.'' Estab. 1988. Circ. 15,000. Pays on publication. Publishes ms an average of 3 months after acceptance. Byline given. Offers kill fee. Editorial lead time 2 months. Submit seasonal material 2 months in advance. Accepts queries by mail, e-mail, phone. Accepts previously published material. Accepts simultaneous submissions. Responds in 1 week to queries; 1 month to mss. Sample copy and writer's guidelines free.

Nonfiction General interest, historical/nostalgic, humor, interview/profile, personal experience. **Buys 60 mss/ year.** Query. Length: 600-800 words. **Pays $125-175.** Sometimes pays expenses of writers on assignment.

Reprints Send photocopy and information about when and where the material previously appeared.

Photos Send photos with submission. Reviews 5×7 prints, GIF/JPEG files. Offers no additional payment for photos accepted with ms. Captions, identification of subjects required.

Columns/Departments Buys 20 mss/year. Query. **Pays $125-175.**

Tips ''Submit well-worded queries. Know our magazine and style before submitting.''

$ $ TOY TRUCKER & CONTRACTOR

Toy Farmer Publications, 7496 106th Ave. SE, LaMoure ND 58458-9404. (701)883-5206. Fax: (701)883-5209. E-mail: info@toyfarmer.com. Website: www.toyfarmer.com. President/Publisher: Cathy Scheibe. **Contact:** Cheryl Hegvik, editorial assistant. **40% freelance written.** Monthly magazine covering collectible toys. ''We are a magazine on hobby and collectible toy trucks and construction pieces.'' Estab. 1990. Circ. 6,500. Pays on publication. Byline given. Buys first North American serial rights. Editorial lead time 3 months. Submit seasonal material 3 months in advance. Accepts queries by mail, e-mail, fax, phone. Accepts previously published material. Responds in 1 month to queries; 2 months to mss. Sample copy for $4. Writer's guidelines available on request.

Nonfiction Historical/nostalgic, interview/profile, new product, personal experience, technical. **Buys 35 mss/ year.** Query. Length: 800-1,400 words. **Pays 10¢/word.** Sometimes pays expenses of writers on assignment.

Photos Must be 35mm originals or very high resolution digital images. Send photos with submission. Offers no additional payment for photos accepted with ms. Captions, identification of subjects, model releases required.

Tips ''Send sample work that would apply to our magazine. Also, we need more articles on collectors, builders, model kit enthusiasts and small company information. We have regular columns, so a feature should not repeat what our columns do.''

TUFF STUFF

Krause Publications, a Division of F+W Publications, Inc., 700 E. State St., Iola WI 54990-0001. (715)445-2214. Fax: (715)445-4087. E-mail: tuffstuff@krause.com. Website: www.tuffstuff.com. Editor: Rocky Landsverk. **Contact:** Tom Hultman, managing editor (hultmant@krause.com). Monthly magazine covering sports collectibles. "Collectibles expertise is necessary." Estab. 1984. Circ. 190,000. Pays on publication. Publishes ms an average of 2 months after acceptance. Byline given. Offers negotiable kill fee. Makes work-for-hire assignments. Editorial lead time 3 months. Submit seasonal material 3 months in advance. Accepts queries by e-mail. Sample copy for free. Writer's guidelines not available.

Photos State availability with submission. Reviews GIF/JPEG files. Buys one-time rights. Negotiates payment individually.

Tips "No general interest sports submissions. Collectibles writers only."

✪ VOGUE KNITTING

Soho Publishing Co., Inc., 233 Spring St., 8th Floor, New York NY 10013. (212)937-2555. Fax: (646)336-3960. E-mail: miriam@sohopublishingco.com. Website: www.vogueknitting.com. Quarterly magazine created for participants in and enthusiasts of high fashion knitting. Circ. 175,000.

• Query before submitting.

$WESTERN & EASTERN TREASURES

People's Publishing Co., Inc., P.O. Box 219, San Anselmo CA 94979. E-mail: treasurenet@prodigy.net. Website: www.treasurenet.com. **Contact:** Rosemary Anderson, managing editor. **100% freelance written.** Monthly magazine covering hobby/sport of metal detecting/treasure hunting. *"Western & Eastern Treasures provides concise, yet comprehensive coverage of every aspect of the sport/hobby of metal detecting and treasure hunting with a strong emphasis on current, accurate information; innovative, field-proven advice and instruction; and entertaining, effective presentation."* Estab. 1966. Circ. 50,000. Pays on publication. Publishes ms an average of 3 months after acceptance. Byline given. Buys all rights. Editorial lead time 4 months. Submit seasonal material 3-4 months in advance. Responds in 3 months to mss. Sample copy for 9×12 SAE and 5 first-class stamps. Writer's guidelines for #10 SASE.

Nonfiction How-to (tips and finds for metal detectorists), interview/profile (only people in metal detecting), personal experience (positive metal detector experiences), technical (only metal detecting hobby-related), helping in local community with metal detecting skills (i.e., helping local police locate evidence at crime scenes—all volunteer basis). Special issues: Silver & Gold Annual (editorial deadline February each year)—looking for articles 1,500 words maximum, plus photos on the subject of locating silver and/or gold using a metal detector. No fiction, poetry, or puzzles. **Buys 150+ mss/year.** Send complete ms. Length: 600-1,500 words. **Pays 2¢/word for assigned articles.** Sometimes pays in contributor copies as trade for advertising space.

Photos Steve Anderson, vice president. Send photos with submission. Reviews 35mm transparencies, prints, digital scans (minimum 300 dpi). Buys all rights. Offers $5 minimum/photo. Captions, identification of subjects required.

$ $WOODSHOP NEWS

Soundings Publications, Inc., 10 Bokum Rd., Essex CT 06426-1185. (860)767-8227. Fax: (860)767-0645. E-mail: editorial@woodshopnews.com. Website: www.woodshopnews.com. **Contact:** Tod Riggio, editor. **20% freelance written.** Monthly tabloid "covering woodworking for professionals. Solid business news and features about woodworking companies. Feature stories about interesting professional woodworkers. Some how-to articles." Estab. 1986. Circ. 85,000. Pays on publication. Publishes ms an average of 3 months after acceptance. Byline given. Offers 25% kill fee. Buys first North American serial rights. Submit seasonal material 4 months in advance. Accepts queries by mail, e-mail, fax. Responds in 1 month to queries. Sample copy online. Writer's guidelines free.

• *Woodshop News* needs writers in major cities in all regions except the Northeast. Also looking for more editorial opinion pieces.

Nonfiction How-to (query first), interview/profile, new product, opinion, personal experience, photo feature. Key word is "newsworthy." No general interest profiles of "folksy" woodworkers. **Buys 15-25 mss/year.** Query with published clips or send complete ms. Length: 100-1,200 words. **Pays $50-500 for assigned articles; $40-250 for unsolicited articles.** Pays expenses of writers on assignment.

Photos Send photos with submission. Reviews contact sheets, prints. Buys one-time rights. Offers $20-35/color photo; $250/color cover, usually with story. Captions, identification of subjects required.

Columns/Departments Pro Shop (business advice, marketing, employee relations, taxes, etc., for the professional written by an established professional in the field); Finishing (how-to and techniques, materials, spraybooths, staining; written by experienced finishers), both 1,200-1,500 words. **Buys 18 mss/year.** Query. **Pays $200-300.**

Fillers Small filler items, briefs, or news tips that are followed up by staff reporters. **Pays $10.**

Tips "The best way to start is a profile of a professional woodworker in your area. Find a unique angle about the person or business and stress this as the theme of your article. Avoid a broad, general-interest theme that would be more appropriate to a daily newspaper. Our readers are professional woodworkers who want more depth and more specifics than would a general readership. If you are profiling a business, we need standard business information such as gross annual earnings/sales, customer base, product line and prices, marketing strategy, etc. Color 35mm or high-res digital photos are a must. We need more freelance writers from the Mid-Atlantic, Midwest, and West Coast."

$ $WOODWORK

A Magazine For All Woodworkers, Ross Periodicals, 42 Digital Dr., #5, Novato CA 94949. (415)382-0580. Fax: (415)382-0587. E-mail: woodwork@rossperiodicals.com. Website: www.woodwork-mag.com. Publisher: Tom Toldrian. **Contact:** John Lavine, editor. **90% freelance written.** Bimonthly magazine covering woodworking. "We are aiming at a broad audience of woodworkers, from the enthusiast to professional. Articles range from intermediate to complex. We cover such subjects as carving, turning, furniture, tools old and new, design, techniques, projects, and more. We also feature profiles of woodworkers, with the emphasis being always on communicating woodworking methods, practices, theories, and techniques. Suggestions for articles are always welcome." Estab. 1986. Circ. 50,000. Pays on publication. Byline given. Buys first North American serial, second serial (reprint) rights. Accepts queries by mail, e-mail, fax. Sample copy for $5 and 9×12 SAE with 6 first-class stamps. Writer's guidelines for #10 SASE.

Nonfiction How-to (simple or complex, making attractive furniture), interview/profile (of established woodworkers that make attractive furniture), photo feature (of interest to woodworkers), technical (tools, techniques). "Do not send a how-to unless you are a woodworker." Query. Length: 1,500-2,000 words. **Pays $150/ published page.**

Photos Send photos with submission. Reviews 35mm slides. Buys one-time rights. Pays higher page rate for photos accepted with ms. Captions, identification of subjects required.

Columns/Departments Tips and Techniques column, **pays $35-75.** Interview/profiles of established woodworkers (bring out woodworker's philosophy about the craft, opinions about what is happening currently). Good photos of attractive furniture a must. Section on how-to desirable. Query with published clips.

Tips "Our main requirement is that each article must directly concern woodworking. If you are not a woodworker, the interview/profile is your best chance. Good writing is essential, as are good photos. The interview must be entertaining, but informative and pertinent to woodworkers' interests. Include sidebar written by the profile subject."

HOME & GARDEN

$THE ALMANAC FOR FARMERS & CITY FOLK

Greentree Publishing, Inc., 840 S. Rancho Dr., Suite 4-319, Las Vegas NV 89106. (702)387-6777. Website: www.thealmanac.com. **Contact:** Lucas McFadden, editor. **30-40% freelance written.** Annual almanac of "down-home, folksy material pertaining to farming, gardening, homemaking, animals, etc." Deadline: March 31. Estab. 1983. Circ. 400,000. Pays on publication. Publishes ms an average of 6 months after acceptance. Byline given. Buys first North American serial rights. Sample copy for $4.99. Writer's guidelines not available.

    O➞ Break in with short, humorous solutions to everyday problems; gardening; or how-to pieces.

Nonfiction Essays, general interest, historical/nostalgic, how-to (any home or garden project), humor. No fiction or controversial topics. "Please, no first-person pieces!" **Buys 30-40 mss/year.** No queries please. Editorial decisions made from ms only. Send complete ms by mail. Length: 350-1,400 words. **Pays $45/page.**

Poetry Buys 1-6 poems/year. **Pays $45 for full pages or $15 for short poems.**

Fillers Uses 60/year. Anecdotes, facts, short humor, gardening hints. Length: 125 words maximum. **Pays $15 for short fillers or page rate for longer fillers.**

Tips "Typed submissions essential as we scan manuscript. Short, succinct material is preferred. Material should appeal to a wide range of people and should be on the 'folksy' side, preferably with a thread of humor woven in. No first-person pieces (using 'I' or 'my')."

$ $THE AMERICAN GARDENER

A Publication of the American Horticultural Society, 7931 E. Boulevard Dr., Alexandria VA 22308-1300. (703)768-5700. Fax: (703)768-7533. E-mail: editor@ahs.org. Website: www.ahs.org. Managing Editor: Mary Yee. **Contact:** David J. Ellis, editor. **70% freelance written.** Bimonthly magazine covering gardening and horticulture. "*The American Gardener* is the official publication of the American Horticultural Society (AHS), a national, nonprofit, membership organization for gardeners, founded in 1922. The AHS mission is to open the eyes of all Americans to the vital connection between people and plants, and to inspire all Americans to become responsible caretakers of the earth, to celebrate America's diversity through the art and science of horticulture, and to lead this effort by sharing the society's unique national resources with all Americans." All articles in *The American Gardener* are also published on members-only website. Estab. 1922. Circ. 36,000. Pays on publication. Publishes ms an average of 6 months after acceptance. Byline given. Offers 25% kill fee. Buys first North American serial rights. Editorial lead time 4 months. Submit seasonal material at least 1 year in advance. Accepts queries by mail. Responds in 3 months to queries. Sample copy for $5. Writer's guidelines by e-mail.

Nonfiction "Feature-length articles include in-depth profiles of individual plant groups; profiles of prominent American horticulturists and gardeners (living and dead); profiles of unusual public or private gardens; descriptions of historical developments in American gardening; descriptions of innovative landscape design projects (especially relating to use of regionally native plants or naturalistic gardening); and descriptions of important plant breeding and research programs tailored to a lay audience. We run a few how-to articles; these should address relatively complex or unusual topics that most other gardening magazines won't tackle—photography must be provided." **Buys 30 mss/year.** Query with published clips. Length: 1,500-2,500 words. **Pays $300-500, depending on complexity and author's experience.**

Reprints Rarely purchases second rights. Send photocopy of article with information about when and where the material previously appeared. Payment varies.

Photos E-mail for guidelines before submitting. Must be accompanied by postage-paid return mailer. Buys one-time print rights, plus limited rights to run article on members-only website. Offers $60-300/photo. Identification of subjects required.

Columns/Departments Conservationist's Notebook (addresses issues in plant conservation that are relevant or of interest to gardeners); Natural Connections (explains a natural phenomenon—plant and pollinator relationships, plant and fungus relationships, parasites—that may be observed in nature or in the garden), 750-1,200 words. **Buys 10 mss/year.** Query with published clips. **Pays $100-250.**

Tips "The majority of our readers are advanced, passionate amateur gardeners; about 20 percent are horticultural professionals. Most prefer not to use synthetic chemical pesticides. Our articles are intended to bring this knowledgeable group new information, ranging from the latest scientific findings that affect plants, to in-depth profiles of specific plant groups, and the history of gardening and gardens in America."

$ $ ATLANTA HOMES AND LIFESTYLES

Weisner Publishing, LLC, 1100 Johnson Ferry Rd., Suite 595, Atlanta GA 30342. (404)252-6670. Fax: (404)252-6673. Website: www.atlantahomesmag.com. **Contact:** Oma Blaise, editor-in-chief. **65% freelance written.** Magazine published 8 times/year. "*Atlanta Homes and Lifestyles* is designed for the action-oriented, well-educated reader who enjoys his/her shelter, its design and construction, its environment, and living and entertaining in it." Estab. 1983. Circ. 33,091. Pays on publication. Publishes ms an average of 6 months after acceptance. Byline given. Buys all rights. Accepts queries by mail, fax. Responds in 3 months to queries. Sample copy for $3.95. Writer's guidelines online.

Nonfiction Interview/profile, new product, photo feature, well-designed homes, gardens, local art, remodeling, food, preservation, entertaining. "We do not want articles outside respective market area, not written for magazine format, or that are excessively controversial, investigative or that cannot be appropriately illustrated with attractive photography." **Buys 35 mss/year.** Query with published clips. Length: 500-1,200 words. **Pays $100-500.** Sometimes pays expenses of writer on assignment.

Photos Most photography is assigned. State availability with submission. Reviews transparencies. Buys one-time rights. Pays $40-50/photo. Captions, identification of subjects, model releases required.

Columns/Departments Short Takes (newsy items on home and garden topics); Quick Fix (simple remodeling ideas); Cheap Chic (stylish decorating that is easy on the wallet); Digging In (outdoor solutions from Atlanta's gardeners); Big Fix (more extensive remodeling projects); Real Estate News. Length: 350-500 words. Query with published clips. **Pays $50-200.**

Tips "Query with specific new story ideas rather than previously published material."

$ $ AUSTIN HOME & LIVING

Publications & Communications, Inc., 11675 Jollyville Rd., Suite 150, Austin TX 78759. (512)381-0576. Fax: (512)331-3950. E-mail: bronas@pcinews.com. Website: www.austinhomeandliving.com. Editor: Taylor Bowles. **Contact:** Brona Stockton, associate publisher. **75% freelance written.** Bimonthly magazine. "*Austin Home & Living* showcases the homes found in Austin and provides tips on food, gardening, and decorating." Estab. 1994. Circ. 20,000. Pays on publication. Publishes ms an average of 4 months after acceptance. Byline given. Offers 100% kill fee. Buys all rights. Editorial lead time 4 months. Submit seasonal material 6 months in advance. Accepts queries by mail, e-mail, fax. Responds in 1 month to queries; 2 months to mss. Sample copy for free. Writer's guidelines online.

Nonfiction How-to, interview/profile, new product, travel. **Buys 18 mss/year.** Query with published clips. Length: 500-2,000 words. **Pays $200 for assigned articles.** Pays expenses of writers on assignment.

Photos State availability of or send photos with submission. Reviews negatives, transparencies, prints. Buys all rights. Offers no additional payment for photos accepted with ms. Captions required.

$BACKHOME

Your Hands-On Guide to Sustainable Living, Wordsworth Communications, Inc., P.O. Box 70, Hendersonville NC 28793. (828)696-3838. Fax: (828)696-0700. E-mail: backhome@ioa.com. Website: www.backhomemagazin e.com. **Contact:** Lorna K. Loveless, editor. **80% freelance written.** Bimonthly magazine. *BackHome* encourages readers to take more control over their lives by doing more for themselves: productive organic gardening; building and repairing their homes; utilizing alternative energy systems; raising crops and livestock; building furniture; toys and games and other projects; creative cooking. *BackHome* promotes respect for family activities, community programs, and the environment. Estab. 1990. Circ. 26,000. Pays on publication. Publishes ms an average of 1 year after acceptance. Byline given. Offers $25 kill fee at publisher's discretion. Buys first North American serial rights. Editorial lead time 3 months. Submit seasonal material 6 months in advance. Accepts queries by mail, e-mail, fax, phone. Accepts previously published material. Responds in 6 weeks to queries; 2 months to mss. Sample copy $5 or online. Writer's guidelines online.

- The editor reports an interest in seeing "more alternative energy experiences, *good* small houses, workshop projects (for handy persons, not experts), and community action others can copy."
- Break in by writing about personal experience (especially in overcoming challenges) in fields in which *BackHome* focuses.

Nonfiction How-to (gardening, construction, energy, homebusiness), interview/profile, personal experience, technical, self-sufficiency. No essays or old-timey reminiscences. **Buys 80 mss/year.** Query. Length: 750-5,000 words. **Pays $35 (approximately)/printed page.**

Reprints Send photocopy and information about when and where the material previously appeared. Pays $35/ printed page.

Photos Send photos with submission. Reviews color prints, 35mm slides, JPEG photo attachments of 300 dpi. Buys one-time rights. Offers additional payment for photos published. Identification of subjects required.

Tips "Very specific in relating personal experiences in the areas of gardening, energy, and homebuilding how-to. Third-person approaches to others' experiences are also acceptable but somewhat less desirable. Clear color photo prints, especially those in which people are prominent, help immensely when deciding upon what is accepted."

$$$$BETTER HOMES AND GARDENS

1716 Locust St., Des Moines IA 50309-3023. (515)284-3044. Fax: (515)284-3763. Website: www.bhg.com. Editor-in-Chief: Karol DeWulf Nickell; Editor (Building): Laura O' Neil; Editor (Food & Nutrition): Nancy Hopkins; Editor (Garden/Outdoor Living): Elvin McDonald; Editor (Health): Christian Millman; Editor (Education & Parenting): Stephen George; Editor (Automotive): Lamont Olson; Editor (Home Design): Oma Ford; Editor (Features and Family Matters): Stephen George. **10-15% freelance written.** Magazine "providing home service information for people who have a serious interest in their homes." "We read all freelance articles, but much prefer to see a letter of query rather than a finished manuscript." Estab. 1922. Circ. 7,605,000. **Pays on acceptance.** Buys all rights. Sample copy and writer's guidelines not available.

Nonfiction Travel, education, gardening, health, cars, home, entertainment. "We do not deal with political subjects or with areas not connected with the home, community, and family." No poetry or fiction. **Pay rates vary.**

Tips Most stories published by this magazine go through a lengthy process of development involving both editor and writer. Some editors will consider only query letters, not unsolicited manuscripts. Direct queries to the department that best suits your storyline.

$$BIRDS & BLOOMS

Reiman Publications, 5925 Country Lane, Greendale WI 53129. (414)423-0100. E-mail: editors@birdsandblooms .com. Website: www.birdsandblooms.com. **15% freelance written.** Bimonthly magazine focusing on the "beauty in your own backyard. *Birds & Blooms* is a sharing magazine that lets backyard enthusiasts chat with each other by exchanging personal experiences. This makes *Birds & Blooms* more like a conversation than a magazine, as readers share tips and tricks on producing beautiful blooms and attracting feathered friends to their backyards." Estab. 1995. Circ. 1,900,000. Pays on publication. Publishes ms an average of 7 months after acceptance. Byline given. Buys all rights. Editorial lead time 2 months. Submit seasonal material 4 months in advance. Accepts queries by mail, e-mail. Accepts simultaneous submissions. Responds in 2 months. Sample copy for $2, 9×12 SAE and $1.95 postage. Writer's guidelines for #10 SASE.

Nonfiction Essays, how-to, humor, inspirational, personal experience, photo feature, natural crafting and plan items for building backyard accents. No bird rescue or captive bird pieces. **Buys 12-20 mss/year.** Send complete ms. Length: 250-1,000 words. **Pays $100-400.**

Photos Trudi Bellin, photo coordinator. Send photos with submission. Reviews transparencies, prints. Buys one-time rights. Identification of subjects required.

Columns/Departments Backyard Banter (odds, ends and unique things); Bird Tales (backyard bird stories); Local Lookouts (community backyard happenings), all 200 words. **Buys 12-20 mss/year.** Send complete ms. **Pays $50-75.**

Fillers Anecdotes, facts, gags to be illustrated by cartoonist. **Buys 25/year.** Length: 10-250 words. **Pays $10-75.**

Tips "Focus on conversational writing—like you're chatting with a neighbor over your fence. Manuscripts full of tips and ideas that people can use in backyards across the country have the best chance of being used. Photos that illustrate these points also increase chances of being used."

$ $CALIFORNIA HOMES

The Magazine of Architecture, the Arts and Distinctive Design, McFadden-Bray Publishing Corp., P.O. Box 8655, Newport Beach CA 92658. (949)640-1484. Fax: (949)640-1665. E-mail: edit@calhomesmagazine.com. **Contact:** Susan McFadden, editor. **80% freelance written.** Bimonthly magazine covering California interiors, architecture, some food, travel, history, and current events in the field. Estab. 1997. Circ. 80,000. Pays on publication. Publishes ms an average of 3 months after acceptance. Byline given. Offers 50% kill fee. Buys first North American serial rights. Editorial lead time 3 months. Submit seasonal material 6 months in advance. Accepts queries by mail, e-mail, fax. Responds in 1 month to queries; 2 months to mss. Sample copy for $7.50. Writer's guidelines for #10 SASE.

Nonfiction Query. Length: 500-1,000 words. **Pays $250-750.** Sometimes pays expenses of writers on assignment.

Photos State availability with submission. Buys one-time rights. Negotiates payment individually. Captions required.

CANADIAN GARDENING MAGAZINE

Transcontinental Media G.P., 25 Sheppard Ave. W., Suite 100, Toronto ON M2N 6S7 Canada. E-mail: satterthwaite@canadiangardening.com. Website: www.canadiangardening.com. Managing Editor: Christina Selby. **Contact:** Aldona Satterthwaite, editor. Mostly freelance written. Magazine published 8 times/year covering Canadian gardening. "*Canadian Gardening* is a national magazine aimed at the avid home gardener. Our readers are city gardeners with tiny lots, country gardeners with rolling acreage, indoor gardeners, rooftop gardeners, and enthusiastic beginners and experienced veterans. Estab. 1990. Circ. 152,000. **Pays on acceptance.** Byline given. Offers 25-50% kill fee. Buys electronic rights. Editorial lead time 3 months. Submit seasonal material 3 months in advance. Accepts queries by mail, e-mail, fax. Accepts simultaneous submissions. Responds in 4 months to queries. Writer's guidelines online.

Nonfiction How-to (planting and gardening projects), humor, personal experience, technical, plant and garden profiles, practical advice. **Buys 100 mss/year.** Query. Length: 200-2,000 words. **Pays variable amount.** Sometimes pays expenses of writers on assignment.

Photos Send photos with submission. Reviews color transparencies, and high resolution digital images. Negotiates payment individually.

$ $ CANADIAN HOMES & COTTAGES

The In-Home Show, Ltd., 2650 Meadowvale Blvd., Unit 4, Mississauga ON L5N 6M5 Canada. (905)567-1440. Fax: (905)567-1442. E-mail: jnaisby@homesandcottages.com. Website: www.homesandcottages.com. Managing Editor: Steven Chester. **Contact:** Janice Naisby, editor-in-chief. **75% freelance written.** Magazine published 6 times/year covering building and renovating; "technically comprehensive articles." Estab. 1987. Circ. 79,000. Pays on publication. Publishes ms an average of 2 months after acceptance. Byline given. Offers 10% kill fee. Buys first North American serial rights. Editorial lead time 3 months. Submit seasonal material 3 months in advance. Accepts queries by mail. Sample copy for SAE. Writer's guidelines for #10 SASE.

Nonfiction Looking for how-to projects and simple home improvement ideas. Humor (building and renovation related), new product, technical. **Buys 32 mss/year.** Query. Length: 1,000-2,000 words. **Pays $300-750.** Sometimes pays expenses of writers on assignment.

Photos Send photos with submission. Reviews transparencies, prints. Buys one-time rights. Negotiates payment individually. Captions, identification of subjects required.

Tips "Read our magazine before sending in a query. Remember that you are writing to a Canadian audience."

$CAROLINA HOMES & INTERIORS

MediaServices, Inc., P.O. Box 22617, Charleston SC 29413. (843)881-1481. Fax: (843)849-6717. E-mail: editorial@carolinahomes.net. Website: www.carolinahomes.net. **Contact:** Andrew Mosier, managing editor. **80% freelance written.** Quarterly magazine covering coastal Carolina homes and lifestyles. "We feature the finest in coastal living. Highlighting builders, designers, communities, vendors and the many recreational alternatives in the Carolinas, coastal Georgia and Florida, *CH&I* is the region's premiere home and lifestyle guide." Estab. 1983. Circ.

65,000. Pays 30 days after publication. Publishes ms an average of 2 months after acceptance. Byline given. Offers 50% kill fee. Buys one-time rights. Editorial lead time 2 months. Submit seasonal material 4 months in advance. Accepts queries by mail, e-mail. Accepts previously published material. Accepts simultaneous submissions. Responds in 2 weeks to queries; 1-2 months to mss. Sample copy for free. Writer's guidelines by e-mail.

Nonfiction Exposé, general interest, historical/nostalgic, how-to, inspirational, interview/profile, new product, personal experience, technical, travel. **Buys 50 mss/year.** Query with published clips. Length: 300-2,000 words. **Pays $30.** Sometimes pays expenses of writers on assignment.

Columns/Departments Inner Beauty, 300 words; Outer Beauty, 300 words; Coastal Custom Builders, 600 words; Hot Retirement Towns, 400 words; Things to Do, 500 words; Four!, 500 words; Day Trips, 750 words; Smiling Faces, 600 words; Important People, 600 words; Top, maximum 300 words; Night Out, 750 words. **Buys 50 mss/year.** Query with published clips. **Pays $30.**

Tips "Be creative. Story ideas should reflect the beauty of the region. All writers are welcome, but local writers are preferred. New writers are encouraged to query."

$ $ $ $ COASTAL LIVING

Southern Progress Corp., 2100 Lakeshore Dr., Birmingham AL 35209. (205)445-6053. Website: www.coastalliving.com. **Contact:** Cathy Still Johnson, home & garden; Susan Haynes, West Coast travel; Steve Millburg, non-West Coast travel; Jennifer Chappell, lifestyle; Julia Rutland, food & entertainment. Bimonthly magazine for those who live or vacation along our nation's coasts. The magazine emphasizes home design and travel, but also covers a wide variety of other lifestyle topics and coastal concerns. Estab. 1997. Circ. 660,000. **Pays on acceptance.** Offers 25% kill fee. Responds in 2 months to queries. Sample copy and writer's guidelines online.

Nonfiction The magazine is roughly divided into 5 areas, with regular features, columns and departments for each area. **Currents** offers short, newsy features of 25-200 words written mostly by staff members on new products, seaside events, beach fashions, etc. **Travel** includes outdoor activities, nature experiences, and lodging and dining stories. **Homes** places the accent on casual living, with warm, welcoming houses and rooms designed for living. **Food & Entertainment** is divided into *In the Coastal Kitchen* (recipes and tips) and *Seafood Primer* (basics of buying and preparing seafood). The **Lifestyle** section is a catch all of subjects to help readers live better and more comfortably: *The Good Life* (profiles of people who have moved to the coast), *Coastal Character* (profile of someone connected to a coastal environment), *Collectibles* (treasured items/accessories with a marine connection), *So You Want to Live In . . .* (profiles of coastal communities), etc. Query with clips and SASE. **Pays $1/word.**

Photos State availability with submission.

Tips "Query us with ideas that are very specifically targeted to the columns that are currently in the magazine."

$ $ COLORADO HOMES & LIFESTYLES

Wiesner Publishing, LLC, 7009 S. Potomac St., Centennial CO 80112-4029. (303)397-7600. Fax: (303)397-7619. E-mail: mdakotah@coloradohomesmag.com. Website: www.coloradohomesmag.com. **75% freelance written.** Upscale shelter magazine published 9 times/year containing beautiful homes, landscapes, architecture, calendar, antiques, etc. All of Colorado is included. Geared toward home-related and lifestyle areas, personality profiles, etc. Estab. 1981. Circ. 36,000. **Pays on acceptance.** Publishes ms an average of 3 months after acceptance. Byline given. Offers 15% kill fee. Buys first North American serial rights. Editorial lead time 3 months. Submit seasonal material 1 year in advance. Accepts queries by mail, e-mail. Accepts simultaneous submissions. Responds in 2 months to queries. Sample copy for #10 SASE.

Nonfiction Fine homes and furnishings, regional interior design trends, shopping information, interesting personalities and lifestyles—all with a Colorado slant. No personal essays, religious, humor, technical. **Buys 50-75 mss/year.** Query with published clips. Length: 900-1,500 words. **Pays $200-400.** Sometimes pays expenses of writers on assignment.

Photos Send photos with submission. Reviews transparencies, b&w glossy prints, CDs, digital images, slides. Identification of subjects, title and caption suggestions appreciated. Photographic credits required.

Tips "Send query, lead paragraph, clips. Send ideas for story or stories. Include some photos, if applicable. The more interesting and unique the subject the better. A frequent mistake made by writers is failure to provide material with a style and slant appropriate for the magazine, due to poor understanding of the focus of the magazine."

$ $ CONCRETE HOMES

Publications and Communications, Inc. (PCI), 11675 Jollyville Rd., Suite 150, Austin TX 78759. Fax: (512)331-3950. E-mail: homes@pcinews.com. Website: concretehomesmagazine.com. Editor: Taylor Bowles. **Contact:** Brona Stockton, associate publisher. **85% freelance written.** Bimonthly magazine covering homes built with concrete. "*Concrete Homes* is a publication designed to be informative to consumers, builders, contractors, architects, etc., who are interested in concrete homes. The magazine profiles concrete home projects (they must be complete) and offers how-to and industry news articles." Estab. 1999. Circ. 25,000. Pays on publication. Publishes ms an average of 2 months after acceptance. Byline given. Offers 100% kill fee. Buys all rights. Editorial lead time 2 months. Submit seasonal material 3-4 months in advance. Accepts queries by mail, e-mail. Accepts simultaneous submissions. Responds in 1 month. Sample copy and writer's guidelines online.

Nonfiction How-to, interview/profile, new product, technical. **Buys 30-40 mss/year.** Query or query with published clips. Length: 800-2,000 words. **Pays $200-250.** Sometimes pays expenses of writers on assignment.

Photos State availability with submission. Reviews 8×10 transparencies, prints, GIF/JPEG files. Buys all rights. Offers no additional payment for photos accepted with ms. Captions required.

Tips "Demonstrate awareness of concrete homes and some knowledge of the construction/building industry."

$ $ $ $ ⊠ COTTAGE LIFE

Quarto Communications, 54 St. Patrick St., Toronto ON M5T 1V1 Canada. (416)599-2000. Fax: (416)599-4070. E-mail: editorial@cottagelife.com. Website: www.cottagelife.com. Editor: Penny Caldwell. **Contact:** Michelle Kelly, associate editor. **80% freelance written.** Bimonthly magazine. "*Cottage Life* is written and designed for the people who own and spend time at waterfront cottages throughout Canada and bordering US states, with a strong focus on Ontario. The magazine has a strong service slant, combining useful 'how-to' journalism with coverage of the people, trends, and issues in cottage country. Regular columns are devoted to boating, fishing, watersports, projects, real estate, cooking, design and decor, nature, personal cottage experience, and environmental, political, and financial issues of concern to cottagers." Estab. 1988. Circ. 70,000. **Pays on acceptance.** Publishes ms an average of 2 months after acceptance. Byline given. Offers 50-100% kill fee. Buys first North American serial rights. Sample copy not available. Writer's guidelines free.

Nonfiction Book excerpts, exposé, historical/nostalgic, how-to, humor, interview/profile, personal experience, photo feature, technical. **Buys 90 mss/year.** Query with published clips and SAE with Canadian postage or IRCs. Length: 150-3,500 words. **Pays $100-3,000.** Pays expenses of writers on assignment.

Columns/Departments On the Waterfront (front department featuring short news, humor, human interest, and service items), 400 words maximum. **Pays $50-400.** Cooking, Real Estate, Fishing, Nature, Watersports, Decor, Personal Experience, and Issues, all 150-1,200 words. **Pays $100-1,200.** Query with published clips and SAE with Canadian postage or IRCs.

Tips "If you have not previously written for the magazine, the 'On the Waterfront' section is an excellent place to break in."

⊘ COUNTRY DECORATING IDEAS

Harris Publications, Inc., 1115 Broadway, New York NY 10010. (212)807-7100. E-mail: countryletters@yahoo.com. Website: www.countrydecoratingideas.com. Quarterly magazine features do-it-yourself ideas and affordable advice on country decorating for the home. Circ. 360,183. Editorial lead time 2 months.

• Query before submitting.

COUNTRY LIVING

The Hearst Corp., 224 W. 57th St., New York NY 10019. (212)649-3500. E-mail: clmail@hearst.com. Editor-in-Chief: Nancy Mernit Soriano. Monthly magazine covering home design and interior decorating with an emphasis on country style. "A lifestyle magazine for readers who appreciate the warmth and traditions associated with American home and family life. Each monthly issue embraces American country decorating and includes features on furniture, antiques, gardening, home building, real estate, cooking, entertaining and travel." Estab. 1978. Circ. 1,600,000. Sample copy not available. Writer's guidelines not available.

Nonfiction Subjects covered include decorating, collecting, cooking, entertaining, gardening/landscaping, home building/remodeling/restoring, travel, and leisure activities. **Buys 20-30 mss/year.** Send complete ms and SASE. **Payment varies.**

Columns/Departments Query first.

Tips "Know the magazine, know the market, and know how to write a good story that will interest *our* readers."

COUNTRY SAMPLER

707 Kautz Rd., St. Charles IL 60174. (630)377-8000. Fax: (630)377-8194. Website: www.sampler.com. Bimonthly magazine. "*Country Sampler* is a country decorating, antiques, and collectibles magazine and a country product catalog." Estab. 1984. Circ. 426,771. Accepts queries by mail, fax.

Nonfiction "Furniture, accessories, and decorative accents created by artisans throughout the country are displayed and offered for purchase directly from the maker. Fully decorated room settings show the readers how to use the items in their homes to achieve the warmth and charm of the country look."

Tips "Send photos and story idea for a country-style house tour. Story should be regarding decorating tips and techniques."

$ $ COUNTRY SAMPLER DECORATING IDEAS

707 Kautz Rd., St. Charles IL 60174. Fax: (630)377-8194. Website: www.decoratingideas.com. **Contact:** Ann Wilson, editor. **60% freelance written.** Bimonthly magazine on home decor and home improvement. "This magazine is devoted to providing do-it-yourself decorating solutions for the average homeowner, through step-by-step projects, topical articles, and real-life feature stories that inspire readers to create the country home of their dreams." **Pays on acceptance.** Publishes ms an average of 6 months after acceptance. Byline given. Makes work-for-hire assignments. Editorial lead time 4 months. Submit seasonal material 6 months in advance. Accepts queries by mail, e-mail, fax. Responds in 1 month to queries; 3 months to mss. Sample copy not available. Writer's guidelines free.

Nonfiction Book excerpts, how-to (decorating projects), interview/profile, photo feature, house tours. Special issues: Decorate With Paint (March, May, July, September, and November). No opinion or fiction. **Buys 50 mss/year.** Query with published clips. Length: 500-1,500 words. **Pays $250-375.**

Photos State availability with submission. Reviews transparencies, 3×5 prints. Buys negotiable rights. Negotiates payment individually. Captions, identification of subjects, model releases required.

Tips "Query letters accompanied by published clips are your best bet. We do not accept unsolicited articles, but pay on acceptance for assigned articles. So it is best to sell us on an article concept and support that concept with similar published articles."

$ $ ⊘ COUNTRY'S BEST LOG HOMES

F+W Publications, Inc., 441 Carlisle Dr., Herndon VA 20170-4884. E-mail: laura.cleveland@fwpubs.com. Website: www.countrysbestloghomesmag.com. Editor: Brooke C. Stoddard. **Contact:** Laura Cleveland, managing editor. **90% freelance written.** Bimonthly magazine covering milled log homes. "*Country's Best Log Homes* focuses solely on milled log homes and related subject matter. It is designed for people who are interested in building a log home and giving them the information they need to finance, design, buy, build, decorate, landscape, and maintain a log home. The feature articles describe individual home owners' experiences in building a log home. Departments discuss the nuts and bolts of log home construction." Estab. 1996. Circ. 220,000. Pays on publication. Publishes ms an average of 2 months after acceptance. Byline given. Offers 50% kill fee. Buys first North American serial, electronic rights. Editorial lead time 2 months. Accepts queries by mail, e-mail. Accepts simultaneous submissions. Responds in 1 month to queries. Sample copy for free.

● Magazine looking for new freelance writers that would work by assignment only. No unsolicited mss.

Nonfiction Historical/nostalgic (deals with historical buildings made of log, such as lodges, Adirondack camps, famous homes, railway stations, etc.), how-to (covers anything dealing with building a log home; i.e., how to select a log home producer, builder contractor, etc.), interview/profile (with homeowners, builders, architects, craftspeople of log homes). No unsolicited mss; articles by assignment only. **Buys 60 mss/year.** Query with published clips. Length: 1,200-1,800 words. **Pays $300-400 for assigned articles.** Sometimes pays expenses of writers on assignment.

Photos State availability with submission. Reviews 4×5 transparencies, GIF/JPEG files. Buys one-time rights. Negotiates payment individually. Captions, identification of subjects, model releases required.

Columns/Departments Design (how to design the log home you want); Money (how to find financing for construction; getting the best mortgage rates); Traditions (focus on historic log buildings); Step-by-Step (log home building); all 1,600 words. **Buys 30 mss/year.** Query with published clips. **Pays $300-400.**

Tips "Send clips that reflect the content of the magazine (architecture, design, decorating, landscaping, building); the clips do not have to be specific to the log home industry."

$ $ EARLY AMERICAN LIFE

Firelands Media Group LLC, P.O. Box 221228, Shaker Heights OH 44122-0996. E-mail: queries@firelandsmedia.com. Website: www.ealonline.com. **Contact:** Jeanmarie Andrews, executive editor. **60% freelance written.** Bimonthly magazine for "people who are interested in capturing the warmth and beauty of the 1600-1840 period and using it in their homes and lives today. They are interested in antiques, traditional crafts, architecture, restoration, and collecting." Estab. 1970. Circ. 90,000. **Pays on acceptance.** Publishes ms an average of 1 year after acceptance. Byline given. Buys worldwide rights. Accepts queries by mail, e-mail. Responds in 3 months to queries. Sample copy and writer's guidelines for 9×12 SAE with 4 first-class stamps.

○→ Break in "by offering highly descriptive, entertaining, yet informational articles on social culture, decorative arts, antiques, or well-restored and appropriately furnished homes that reflect middle-class American life prior to 1850."

Nonfiction "Social history (the story of the people, not epic heroes and battles), travel to historic sites, antiques and reproductions, restoration, architecture, and decorating. We try to entertain as we inform. We're always on the lookout for good pieces on any of our subjects. Would like to see more on how real people did something great to their homes." **Buys 40 mss/year.** Query with or without published clips or send complete ms. Length: 750-3,000 words. **Pays $350-700, additionally for photos.**

Tips "Our readers are eager for ideas on how to bring early America into their lives. Conceive a new approach to satisfy their related interests in arts, crafts, travel to historic sites, and especially in houses decorated in the Early American style. Write to entertain and inform at the same time. We are visually oriented to having photos available or helping us with sources for illustrations."

$ $ $ FINE GARDENING

Taunton Press, 63 S. Main St., P.O. Box 5506, Newtown CT 06470-5506. (203)426-8171. Fax: (203)426-3434. E-mail: fg@taunton.com. Website: www.finegardening.com. **Contact:** Todd Meier, editor-in-chief. Bimonthly magazine. "High-value magazine on landscape and ornamental gardening. Articles written by avid gardeners—first person, hands-on gardening experiences." Estab. 1988. Circ. 200,000. **Pays on acceptance.** Publishes ms an average of 6 months after acceptance. Byline given. Buys all rights. Editorial lead time 1 year. Submit seasonal material 1 year in advance. Accepts queries by mail, e-mail, fax. Sample copy not available. Writer's guidelines free.

Nonfiction How-to, personal experience, photo feature, book review. **Buys 60 mss/year.** Query. Length: 1,000-3,000 words. **Pays $300-1,200.**

Photos Send photos with submission. Reviews digital images. Acquires serial rights.

Columns/Departments Book, video and software reviews (on gardening); Last Word (essays/serious, humorous, fact or fiction). Length: 250-500 words. **Buys 30 mss/year.** Query. **Pays $50- 200.**

Tips "It's most important to have solid first-hand experience as a gardener. Tell us what you've done with your own landscape and plants."

N $ GARDEN COMPASS

Streamopolis, 1450 Front St., San Diego CA 92101. (619)239-2202. Fax: (619)239-4621. E-mail: editor@gardencompass.com. Website: www.gardencompass.com. **Contact:** Siri Jostad, editor. **70% freelance written.** Bimonthly magazine covering gardening. *Garden Compass* is "entertaining and offers sound practical advice for West Coast gardeners." Estab. 1992. Circ. 112,000. Pays on publication. Publishes ms an average of 10 weeks after acceptance. Byline given. Offers $50 kill fee. Not copyrighted. Buys first North American serial rights. Editorial lead time 6 months. Submit seasonal material 6 months in advance. Accepts queries by mail, e-mail. Accepts simultaneous submissions. Responds in 1 month to queries. Sample copy for free.

Photos State availability of or send photos with submission. Reviews contact sheets, transparencies, GIF/JPEG files. Buys one-time rights. Negotiates payment individually. Identification of subjects required.

Columns/Departments Pest Patrol (plant posts/diseases), 400-800 words; e-Gardening (garden info on the Web), 400-800 words; Book Review (gardening books), 400-600 words; Fruit Trees, 800-1,200 words. Query with published clips. **Payment varies.**

Fillers Anecdotes, facts, newsbreaks. Length: 30-150 words. **Pays $25.**

THE HERB COMPANION

Ogden Publications, Inc., 1503 SW 42nd St., Topeka KS 66609. (785)274-4300. Fax: (785)274-4305. E-mail: editor@herbcompanion.com. Website: www.herbcompanion.com. **Contact:** Dawna Edwards, editor. **80% freelance written.** Bimonthly magazine about herbs: culture, history, culinary, crafts and some medicinal use for both experienced and novice herb enthusiasts. Pays on publication. Byline given. Buys all rights. Editorial lead time 4 months. Accepts queries by mail, e-mail, fax. Responds in 2 months to queries. Sample copy for $6. Writer's guidelines online.

Nonfiction Practical horticultural, original recipes, historical, herbal crafts, helpful hints, and book reviews. How-to, interview/profile. Submit by mail only detailed query or ms. Length: 4 pages or 1,000 words. **Pays according to length, story type, and experience.**

Photos Returns photos and artwork. Send photos with submission. Reviews transparencies.

Tips "New approaches to familiar topics are especially welcome. Technical accuracy is essential. Please use scientific as well as popular names for plants and cover the subject in depth while avoiding overly academic presentation. Information should be made accessible to the reader, and we find this is best accomplished by writing from direct personal experience where possible and always in an informal style."

$ $ THE HERB QUARTERLY

EGW Publishing Co., 1041 Shary Circle, Concord CA 94518. (925)671-9852. E-mail: jenniferbarrett@earthlink.net. Website: www.herbquarterly.com. **Contact:** Jennifer Barrett, editor. **95% freelance written.** Quarterly magazine covering herbs and their uses. "Now in its 27th year, *The Herb Quarterly* brings readers the joy of herbs and the herb garden each season, with recipes, remedies, and growing advice." Estab. 1978. Circ. 45,000. Pays on publication. Publishes ms an average of 3 months after acceptance. Byline given. Offers 25% kill fee. Buys first North American serial rights. Editorial lead time 6 months. Submit seasonal material 6-12 months in advance. Accepts queries by mail, e-mail. Responds in 1 month to queries; 2 months to mss. Sample copy for free. Writer's guidelines free.

Nonfiction Book excerpts, historical/nostalgic, how-to (cooking, crafts, gardening), interview/profile (herbalist), new product, opinion, personal experience, photo feature, technical (gardening), travel (gardeners around the world). **Buys 21+ mss/year.** Query with or without published clips or send complete ms. Length: 250-2,500 words. **Pays $50-350.** Provides contributor copies in addition to payment. Sometimes pays expenses of writers on assignment.

Tips "Please read the magazine before submitting. We prefer specific information (whether natural health approaches or gardening advice) rather than general."

$ ⊠ HOME DIGEST

Your Guide to Home and Life Improvement, Home Digest International, Inc., 268 Lakeshore Rd. E., Unit 604, Oakville ON L6J 7S4 Canada. (905)844-3361. Fax: (905)849-4618. E-mail: homedigesteditor@sympatico.ca. Website: www.home-digest.com. **Contact:** William Roebuck, editor. **25% freelance written.** Quarterly magazine covering home and life management for families in the greater Toronto region. "*Home Digest* has a strong service slant, combining useful how-to journalism with coverage of the trends and issues of home ownership and family life. In essence, our focus is on the concerns of families living in their own homes." Estab. 1995. Circ. 710,000. Pays on publication. Publishes ms an average of 3 months after acceptance. Byline given. Buys first North American serial rights and the rights to archive articles on the magazine's website. Editorial lead time 3 months. Submit seasonal material 5 months in advance. Accepts queries by mail, e-mail. Accepts previously published material. Accepts simultaneous submissions. Responds in 1 month to queries. Sample copy for 9×6 SAE and 2 Canadian first-class stamps. Writer's guidelines online.

Nonfiction General interest, how-to (household hints, home renovation tip, decorating tips), humor (living in Toronto). No opinion, fashion, or beauty. **Buys 8 mss/year.** Query. Length: 350-700 words. **Pays $35-100 (Canadian).**

Photos Send photos with submission. Reviews prints, JPEGs. Buys one-time rights. Pays $10-20/photo. Captions, identification of subjects, model releases required.

Columns/Departments Household Hints (tested tips that work); Home Renovation Tips; all 300-350 words. **Buys 4-6 mss/year.** Query. **Pays $40-50 (Canadian).**

Tips "Base your ideas on practical experiences. We're looking for 'uncommon' advice that works."

Ⓝ ⊘ HOME MAGAZINE

Hachette Filipacchi Media U.S., Inc., 1633 Broadway, New York NY 10019. E-mail: homemag@hfnm.com. Website: www.homemag.com. Monthly magazine written for the American home owner and home enthusiast. Circ. 1,020,938.

• Query before submitting.

$ $ $ $ HORTICULTURE

Gardening at Its Best, F+W Publications, Inc., 98 N. Washington St., Boston MA 02114. (617)742-5600. Fax: (617)367-6364. E-mail: sara.begg@hortmag.com. Website: www.hortmag.com. **Contact:** Sara Begg, senior editor. Bimonthly magazine. "*Horticulture*, the country's oldest gardening magazine, is designed for active amateur gardeners. Our goal is to offer a blend of text, photographs and illustrations that will both instruct and inspire readers." Circ. 240,000. Byline given. Offers kill fee. Buys first North American serial, one-time rights. Submit seasonal material 10 months in advance. Accepts queries by mail, e-mail, fax. Responds in 3 months to queries. Sample copy not available. Writer's guidelines for SASE or by e-mail.

Nonfiction "We look for an encouraging personal experience, anecdote and opinion. At the same time, a thorough article should to some degree place its subject in the broader context of horticulture." **Buys 15 mss/year.** Query with published clips, subject background material and SASE. Length: 1,000-2,000 words. **Pays $600-1,500.** Pays expenses of writers on assignment if previously arranged with editor.

Columns/Departments Query with published clips, subject background material and SASE. Include disk where possible. **Pays $50-750.**

Tips "We believe every article must offer ideas or illustrate principles that our readers might apply on their own gardens. No matter what the subject, we want our readers to become better, more creative gardeners."

$ $ $ $ HOUSE BEAUTIFUL

The Hearst Corp., 1700 Broadway, New York NY 10019. (212)903-5084. Website: www.housebeautiful.com. Editor: Mark Mayfield. Monthly magazine. Targeted toward affluent, educated readers ages 30-40. Covers home design and decoration, gardening and entertaining, interior design, architecture and travel. Circ. 865,352. Editorial lead time 3 months. Sample copy not available.

$ $ $ LAKESTYLE

Celebrating Life on the Water, Bayside Publications, Inc., P.O. Box 170, Excelsior MN 55331. (952)470-1380. Fax: (952)470-1389. E-mail: editor@lakestyle.com. Website: www.lakestyle.com. **50% freelance written.** Quarterly magazine. "*Lakestyle* is committed to celebrating the lifestyle chosen by lake home and cabin owners." Estab. 2000. Circ. 40,000. Pays on publication. Publishes ms an average of 3 months after acceptance. Byline given. Offers 10% kill fee. Buys all rights. Editorial lead time 2 months. Submit seasonal material 3 months in advance. Accepts queries by mail, e-mail, fax, phone. Accepts previously published material. Responds in 3 weeks to queries; 1 month to mss. Sample copy for $5. Writer's guidelines online.

Nonfiction Essays, historical/nostalgic, how-to, humor, inspirational, interview/profile, new product, photo feature. No direct promotion of product. **Buys 15 mss/year.** Query with or without published clips or send complete ms. Length: 500-2,500 words. **Pays 25-50¢/word for assigned articles; 10-25¢/word for unsolicited articles.** Sometimes pays expenses of writers on assignment.

Photos State availability of or send photos with submission. Rights purchased vary. Offers no additional payment for photos accepted with ms. Captions, identification of subjects, model releases required.

Columns/Departments Lakestyle Entertaining (entertaining ideas); Lakestyle Gardening (gardening ideas); On the Water (boating/playing on the lake); Hidden Treasures (little known events); At the Cabin (cabin owner's information); all approximately 1,000 words. **Buys 10 mss/year.** Query with or without published clips or send complete ms. **Pays 10-25¢/word.**

Tips "*Lakestyle* is interested in enhancing the lifestyle chosen by our readers, a thorough knowledge of cabin/lake home issues helps writers fulfill this goal."

N $ $ ⊘ LUXURY LOG HOMES & TIMBER FRAMES

F+W Publications, Inc., 441 Carlisle Dr., Herndon VA 20170-4884. E-mail: laura.cleveland@fwpubs.com. Website: www.countrysbestloghomesmag.com. **Contact:** Laura Cleveland, editor. **90% freelance written.** Bimonthly magazine covering high-end timber frame, handcrafted log, and milled log homes. "*Luxury Log Homes & Timber Frame* showcases luxury log and timber frame homes through interviews with architects, builders, interior designers, decorators, and homeowners. The articles cover selecting a building site, choosing a builder/architect, log home company, or timber framer. The magazine sells the log/timber frame lifestyle and generally puts a positive spin on the log/timber frame industry." Estab. 2002. Circ. 140,000. Pays on publication. Publishes ms an average of 2 months after acceptance. Byline given. Offers 50% kill fee. Buys first North American serial, electronic rights. Editorial lead time 2 months. Accepts simultaneous submissions. Responds in 1 month to queries. Sample copy for free.

● Magazine looking for new freelance writers that would work by assignment only. No unsolicited mss.

Nonfiction How-to (work with builders, architects, designers, landscapers; select flooring, windows, wall treatments, appliances, etc.), interview/profile (homeowners, architects, designers, etc.), photo feature (specific rooms, decorating style, building location, decks and porches, landscaping, etc.). No unsolicited mss; queries only. **Buys 48 mss/year.** Query with published clips. Length: 1,200-1,800 words. **Pays $300-400 for assigned articles.** Sometimes pays expenses of writers on assignment.

Photos State availability with submission. Reviews negatives, 4×5 transparencies, GIF/JPEG files. Buys one-time rights. Negotiates payment individually. Captions, identification of subjects, model releases required.

Columns/Departments Design (building site/architecture); Decor (style/accessories/materials); Exteriors (materials/landscaping/windows/doors); House Tour (designing specific rooms); Timber Frame Construction (building issues specific to timber-frame homes); Log Homes Construction (building issues specific to log homes); all 1,600 words. **Buys 24 mss/year.** Query with published clips.

Tips "Send in clips that reflect the content of the magazine (architecture, design, decorating, landscaping, building). The clips do not have to be specific to the log and timber frame industry."

METROPOLITAN HOME

Hachette Filipacchi Media U.S., Inc., 1633 Broadway, New York NY 10019. (212)767-6000. Editor: Donna Warner. Magazine published 10 times/year. Written for style-conscious individuals interested in keeping up on the latest offerings from the design and architecture worlds. Estab. 1981. Circ. 615,230. Editorial lead time 5 months. Sample copy not available.

MIDWEST HOME AND GARDEN

U.S. Trust Bldg., 730 S. Second Ave., Suite 600, Minneapolis MN 55402. Fax: (612)371-5801. E-mail: kmeewes@mnmo.com. Website: www.midwesthomemag.com. **Contact:** Kori Meewes. **50% freelance written.** "*Midwest Home and Garden* is an upscale shelter magazine showcasing innovative architecture, interesting interior design, and beautiful gardens of the Midwest." Estab. 1997. Circ. 80,000. **Pays on acceptance.** Byline given. Accepts queries by mail, e-mail, fax. Writer's guidelines online.

Nonfiction Profiles of regional designers, architects, craftspeople related to home and garden. Photo-driven articles on home decor and design, and gardens. Book excerpts, essays, how-to (garden and design), interview/profile (brief), new product, photo feature. Query with résumé, published clips, and SASE. Length: 300-1,000 words. **Payment negotiable.**

Columns/Departments Back Home (essay on home/garden topics), 800 words; Design Directions (people and trends in home and garden), 300 words.

Tips "We are always looking for great new interior design, architecture, and gardens—in Minnesota and in the Midwest."

$ $ MOUNTAIN LIVING

Wiesner Publishing, 7009 S. Potomac St., Centennial CO 80112. (303)397-7600. Fax: (303)397-7619. E-mail: irawlings@mountainliving.com. Website: www.mountainliving.com. **Contact:** Irene Rawlings, editor-in-chief. **50% freelance written.** Bimonthly magazine covering "shelter and lifestyle issues for people who live in, visit, or hope to live in the mountains." Estab. 1994. Circ. 35,000. **Pays on acceptance.** Publishes ms an average of 4 months after acceptance. Byline given. Buys one-time magazine rights, plus right to run piece online. Editorial lead time 6 months. Submit seasonal material 8 months in advance. Accepts queries by mail, e-mail, phone. Responds in 6 weeks to queries; 2 months to mss. Sample copy for $5 or on website.

Nonfiction Photo feature, travel, home features. **Buys 30 mss/year.** Query with published clips. Length: 1,200-2,000 words. **Pays $250-500.** Sometimes pays expenses of writers on assignment.

Photos Provide photos (slides, transparencies, or on disk, saved as TIFF and at least 300 dpi). State availability with submission. Buys one-time rights. Negotiates payment individually.

Columns/Departments Art; Insider's Guide; Entertaining. Length: 300-1,500 words. **Buys 35 mss/year.** Query with published clips. **Pays $50-500.**

Tips "A deep understanding of and respect for the mountain environment is essential. Think out of the box. We love to be surprised. Write a brilliant, short query, and always send clips. Before you query, read the magazine to get a sense of who we are and what we like."

Ⓝ $ $ $ NATURAL HOME

201 E. 4th St., Loveland CO 80537. (970)669-7672. Fax: (970)613-4678. Website: www.naturalhomemag.com. Editor: Robyn Griggs Lawrence. Managing Editor: Joyanna Laughlin. **Contact:** Karen Brock, editorial assistant. **85% freelance written.** Bimonthly magazine covering sustainable, green lifestyle. Estab. 1999. Circ. 87,000. **Pays on acceptance.** Publishes ms an average of 6-8 months after acceptance. Byline given. Offers 30% kill fee. Buys first North American serial rights. Editorial lead time 6 month. Submit seasonal material 6 months in advance. Accepts queries by mail. Responds in 1 month to queries. Writer's guidelines online.

Nonfiction How-to (use natural building techniques), travel, natural building; sustainable homes and gardens. Does not want personal experience articles that do not relate to green building or sustainable lifestyle. No self-help. **Buys 100 mss/year.** Query. **Pays 30-50¢/word.** Sometimes pays expenses of writers on assignment.

Photos State availability with submission. Reviews contact sheets. Buys one-time rights. Negotiates payment individually. Captions, identification of subjects required.

Columns/Departments Nuts and Bolts (natural products), 1,200 words; Can This Home Be Greened? (green remodel), 1,500 words. **Buys 6 mss/year.** Query. **Pays $500.**

$ $ PEOPLE, PLACES & PLANTS

512 Memorial Hwy., N. Yarmouth ME 04097. (207)827-4783. Fax: (207)829-6814. E-mail: paul@ppplants.com. Website: www.ppplants.com. Paul Tukey, editor-in-chief. **50% freelance written.** Gardening magazine published 6 times/year focused on the Northeast. Circ. 52,000. **Pays on acceptance.** Publishes ms an average of 3 months after acceptance. Buys first rights. Responds in 1 month to queries. Sample copy by e-mail. Writer's guidelines by e-mail.

Nonfiction Know the subject at hand; anecdotes help get readers interested in stories. Query. **Pays $50-500.**

Photos Reviews slides. $50-500.

$ $ ROMANTIC HOMES

Y-Visionary Publishing, 265 Anita Dr., Suite 120, Orange CA 92868. E-mail: editorial@romantichomes.com. Website: www.romantichomesmag.com. **70% freelance written.** Monthly magazine covering home decor. "*Romantic Homes* is the magazine for women who want to create a warm, intimate, and casually elegant home—a haven that is both a gathering place for family and friends and a private refuge from the pressures of the outside world. The *Romantic Homes* reader is personally involved in the decor of her home. Features offer unique ideas and how-to advice on decorating, home furnishings, and gardening. Departments focus on floor and wall coverings, paint, textiles, refinishing, architectural elements, artwork, travel, and entertaining. Every article responds to the reader's need to create a beautiful, attainable environment, providing her with the style ideas and resources to achieve her own romantic home.'' Estab. 1994. Circ. 200,000. Pays 30-60 days upon receipt of invoice. Publishes ms an average of 4 months after acceptance. Byline given. Buys all rights. Editorial lead time 5 months. Submit seasonal material 6 months in advance. Accepts queries by mail, fax. Accepts simultaneous submissions. Responds in 2 weeks to queries; 2 months to mss. Writer's guidelines for #10 SASE.

Nonfiction ''Not just for dreaming, *Romantic Homes* combines unique ideas and inspirations with practical how-to advice on decorating, home furnishings, remodeling, and gardening for readers who are actively involved in improving their homes. Every article responds to the reader's need to know how to do it and where to find it.'' Essays, how-to, new product, personal experience, travel. **Buys 150 mss/year.** Query with published clips. Length: 1,000-1,200 words. **Pays $500.**

Photos State availability of or send photos with submission. Reviews transparencies. Buys all rights. Captions, identification of subjects, model releases required.

Columns/Departments Departments cover antiques, collectibles, artwork, shopping, travel, refinishing, architectural elements, flower arranging, entertaining, and decorating. Length: 400-600 words. **Pays $250.**

Tips ''Submit great ideas with photos.''

$ $SAN DIEGO HOME/GARDEN LIFESTYLES

McKinnon Enterprises, Box 719001, San Diego CA 92171-9001. (858)571-1818. Fax: (858)571-6379. E-mail: carlson@sdhg.net; ditler@sdhg.net. **Contact:** Wayne Carlson, editor; Eva Ditler, managing editor. **50% freelance written.** Monthly magazine covering homes, gardens, food, intriguing people, real estate, art, culture, and local travel for residents of San Diego city and county. Estab. 1979. Circ. 50,000. Pays on publication. Publishes ms an average of 3 months after acceptance. Byline given. Buys first North American serial rights. Submit seasonal material 3 months in advance. Accepts queries by mail, e-mail, fax, phone. Responds in 3 months to queries. Sample copy for $4.

Nonfiction Residential architecture and interior design (San Diego-area homes only), remodeling (must be well-designed—little do-it-yourself), residential landscape design, furniture, other features oriented toward upscale readers interested in living the cultured good life in San Diego. Articles must have a local angle. Query with published clips. Length: 700-2,000 words. **Pays $50-350 for assigned articles.**

Tips ''No out-of-town, out-of-state subject material. Most freelance work is accepted from local writers. Gear stories to the unique quality of San Diego. We try to offer only information unique to San Diego—people, places, shops, resources, etc.''

$ $SEATTLE HOMES & LIFESTYLES

Wiesner Publishing, LLC, 1221 E. Pike St., Suite 305, Seattle WA 98122-3930. (206)322-6699. Fax: (206)322-2799. E-mail: falbert@seattlehomesmag.com. Website: www.seattlehomesmag.com. **Contact:** Fred Albert, editor-in-chief. **60% freelance written.** Magazine published 8 times/year covering home design and lifestyles. ''*Seattle Homes and Lifestyles* showcases the finest homes and gardens in the Northwest, and the personalities and lifestyles that make this region special. We try to help our readers take full advantage of the resources the region has to offer with in-depth coverage of events, entertaining, shopping, food, and wine. And we write about it with a warm, personal approach that underscores our local perspective.'' Estab. 1996. Circ. 30,000. **Pays on acceptance.** Publishes ms an average of 2 months after acceptance. Byline given. Offers 25% kill fee. Buys first, electronic rights. Editorial lead time 3 months. Submit seasonal material 4 months in advance. Accepts previously published material. Accepts simultaneous submissions. Responds in 4 months to queries.

Nonfiction General interest, how-to (decorating, cooking), interview/profile, photo feature. ''No essays, travel stories, sports coverage.'' **Buys 95 mss/year.** Query with published clips via mail. Length: 300-1,500 words. **Pays $150-400.**

Photos State availability with submission. Reviews contact sheets, transparencies, prints. Buys one-time rights. Negotiates payment individually. Captions, identification of subjects, model releases required.

Tips ''We're always looking for experienced journalists with clips that demonstrate a knack for writing engaging, informative features. We're also looking for writers knowledgeable about architecture and decorating who can communicate a home's flavor and spirit through the written word. Since all stories are assigned by the editor, please do not submit manuscripts. Send a résumé and 3 published samples of your work. Story pitches are not encouraged. Please mail all submissions—do not e-mail or fax. Please don't call—we'll call you if we have an assignment. Writers from the Seattle area only.''

SOUTHERN ACCENTS

Southern Progress Corp., 2100 Lakeshore Dr., Birmingham AL 35209. (205)445-6000. Fax: (205)445-6990. Website: www.southernaccents.com. **Contact:** Frances MacDougall, executive editor. ''*Southern Accents* celebrates the finest of the South.'' Estab. 1977. Circ. 370,000. Accepts queries by mail. Responds in 2 months to queries.

Nonfiction ''Each issue features the finest homes and gardens along with a balance of features that reflect the affluent lifestyles of its readers, including architecture, antiques, entertaining, collecting, and travel.'' Query by mail with SASE, bio, clips, and photos.

    ◪ The online magazine carries original content not found in the print edition. Contact: Garrett Lane, online editor.

Tips ''Query us only with specific ideas targeted to our current columns.''

◪ MARTHA STEWART LIVING

Time Publishing, Inc., 11 W. 42nd St., 25th Floor, New York NY 10036. E-mail: mstewart@marthastewart.com. Website: www.marthastewart.com. **Contact:** Editorial. Monthly magazine offering readers a unique combination of inspiration and how-to information focusing on our 8 core areas: Home, Cooking & Entertaining, Gardening, Crafts, Holidays, Keeping, Weddings, and Baby.

    • Query before submitting.

$ $ $◪ STYLE AT HOME

Transcontinental Media, G.P., 25 Sheppard Ave. W., Suite 100, Toronto ON M2N 6S7 Canada. (416)733-7600. Fax: (416)218-3632. E-mail: letters@styleathome.com. Associate Editor: Laurie Grassi. **Contact:** Gail Johnston Habs, editor-in-chief. **85% freelance written.** Magazine published 11 times/year. ''The No. 1 magazine choice of Canadian women aged 25 to 54 who have a serious interest in decorating. Provides an authoritative, stylish collection of inspiring and accessible Canadian interiors, decor projects; reports on style design trends.'' Estab. 1997. Circ. 230,000. **Pays on acceptance.** Byline given. Offers 50% kill fee. Buys first, electronic rights. Editorial lead time 4 months. Submit seasonal material 6 months in advance. Accepts queries by e-mail. Responds in 1 month to queries; 2 weeks to mss. Writer's guidelines by e-mail.

    o┐ Break in by ''familiarizing yourself with the type of interiors we show. Be very up to date with the design and home decor market in Canada. Provide a lead to a fabulous home or garden.''

Nonfiction Interview/profile, new product. ''No how-to; these are planned in-house.'' **Buys 80 mss/year.** Query with published clips; include scouting shots with interior story queries. Length: 300-700 words. **Pays $300-1,000.** Sometimes pays expenses of writers on assignment.

Columns/Departments Humor (fun home decor/renovating experiences), 500 words. Query with published clips. **Pays $250-500.**

$ $ TEXAS GARDENER

The Magazine for Texas Gardeners, by Texas Gardeners, Suntex Communications, Inc., P.O. Box 9005, Waco TX 76714-9005. (254)848-9393. Fax: (254)848-9779. E-mail: suntex@aenbb.net. **Contact:** Chris Corby, editor. **80% freelance written.** Works with a small number of new/unpublished writers each year. Bimonthly magazine covering vegetable and fruit production, ornamentals, and home landscape information for home gardeners in Texas. Estab. 1981. Circ. 30,000. Pays on publication. Publishes ms an average of 4 months after acceptance. Byline given. Buys first North American serial, all rights. Submit seasonal material 6 months in advance. Accepts queries by mail, e-mail, fax. Responds in 2 months to queries. Sample copy for $2.95 and SAE with 5 first-class stamps. Writer's guidelines for #10 SASE.

Nonfiction ''We use articles that relate to Texas gardeners. We also like personality profiles on hobby gardeners and professional horticulturists who are doing somehting unique.'' How-to, humor, interview/profile, photo feature. **Buys 50-60 mss/year.** Query with published clips. Length: 800-2,400 words. **Pays $50-200.**

Photos ''We prefer superb color and b&w photos; 90% of photos used are color.'' Send photos with submission. Reviews contact sheets, 2¼×2¼ or 35mm color transparencies, 8×10 b&w prints. Pays negotiable rates. Identification of subjects, model releases required.

Columns/Departments Between Neighbors. **Pays $25.**

Tips ''First, be a Texan. Then come up with a good idea of interest to home gardeners in this state. Be specific. Stick to feature topics like 'How Alley Gardening Became a Texas Tradition.' Leave topics like 'How to Control Fire Blight' to the experts. High quality photos could make the difference. We would like to add several writers to our group of regular contributors and would make assignments on a regular basis. Fillers are easy to come up with in-house. We want good writers who can produce accurate and interesting copy. Frequent mistakes made by writers in completing an article assignment for us are that articles are not slanted toward Texas gardening, show inaccurate or too little gardening information, or lack good writing style.''

TRADITIONAL HOME

Meredith Corp., 1716 Locust St., Des Moines 50309-3023. (515)284-3762. Fax: (515)284-2083. E-mail: traditional home@meredith.com. Website: www.traditionalhome.com. Executive Editor: Marsha Raisch. Senior Decorating Editor: Candace Ord Manroe. Senior Architecture and Art Editor: Eliot Nusbaum. Entertaining and Travel Editor: Carroll Stoner. Senior Features and Antiques Editor: Doris Athineos. Garden Editor: Ethne Clarke. Magazine published 8 times/year. Features articles on building and decorating homes in the traditional style. Circ. 925,000. Editorial lead time 6 months. Sample copy not available.

$ $ UNIQUE HOMES

Network Communications, Inc., 327 Wall St., Princeton NJ 08540. (609)688-1110. Fax: (609)688-0201. E-mail: lkim@uniquehomes.com. Website: www.uniquehomes.com. Editor: Kathleen Carlin-Russell. **Contact:** Lauren Baier Kim, managing editor. **30% freelance written.** Bimonthly magazine covering luxury real estate for consumers and the high-end real estate industry. "Our focus is the luxury real estate market, i.e., the business of buying and selling luxury homes, as well as regional real estate market trends." Pays on publication. Publishes ms an average of 3 months after acceptance. Byline given. Buys all rights. Editorial lead time 4 months. Submit seasonal material 4 months in advance. Accepts queries by mail, e-mail, fax. Responds in 1 month to queries; 4 months to mss. Sample copy online. Writer's guidelines not available.

Nonfiction Looking for high-end luxury real estate profiles on cities and geographical regions. Luxury real estate, interior design, landscaping, home features. Special issues: Golf Course Living; Resort Living; Ski Real Estate; Farms, Ranches and Country Estates; Waterfront Homes; International Homes. **Buys 36 mss/year.** Query with published clips and résumé. Length: 500-1,500 words. **Pays $150-500.**

Photos State availability with submission. Reviews transparencies, prints. Buys all rights. Offers no additional payment for photos accepted with ms. Captions required.

Tips "For profiles on specific geographical areas, seeking writers with an in-depth personal knowledge of the luxury real estate trends in those locations. Writers with in-depth knowledge of the high-end residential market (both domestic and abroad) are especially needed."

Ø VERANDA

The Hearst Corp., 455 E. Paces Ferry Road NE, Suite 216, Atlanta GA 30305-3319. (404)261-3603. Fax: (404)364-9772. Website: www.veranda.com. Bimonthly magazine. Written as an interior design magazine featuring creative design across the country and around the world. Circ. 380,890. Editorial lead time 5 months. Sample copy not available.

● Does not buy freelance materials or use freelance writers.

$ $ VICTORIAN HOMES

Y-Visionary Publishing, LP, 265 S. Anita Dr., Suite 120, Orange CA 92868-3310. E-mail: editorial@victorianhome s.com. Website: www.victorianhomesmag.com. **90% freelance written.** Bimonthly magazine covering Victorian home restoration and decoration. "*Victorian Homes* is read by Victorian home owners, restorers, house museum management and others interested in the Victorian revival. Feature articles cover home architecture, interior design, furnishings, and the home's history. Photography is very important to the feature." Estab. 1981. Circ. 100,000. **Pays on acceptance.** Publishes ms an average of 1 year after acceptance. Byline given. Offers $50 kill fee. Buys first North American serial, one-time rights. Editorial lead time 4 months. Submit seasonal material 1 year in advance. Accepts queries by mail, e-mail, fax. Accepts simultaneous submissions. Responds in 6 weeks to queries; 2 months to mss. Sample copy and writer's guidelines for SAE.

O→ Break in with "access to good photography and reasonable knowledge of the Victorian era."

Nonfiction "Article must deal with structures—no historical articles on Victorian people or lifestyles." How-to (create period style curtains, wall treatments, bathrooms, kitchens, etc.), photo feature. **Buys 30-35 mss/year.** Query. Length: 800-1,800 words. **Pays $300-500.** Sometimes pays expenses of writers on assignment.

Photos State availability with submission. Reviews $2\frac{1}{4} \times 2\frac{1}{4}$ transparencies. Buys one-time rights. Negotiates payment individually. Captions required.

$ $ WATER GARDENING

The Magazine for Pondkeepers, The Water Gardeners, Inc., P.O. Box 607, St. John IN 46373. (219)374-9419. Fax: (219)374-9052. E-mail: wgmag@watergardening.com. Website: www.watergardening.com. **50% freelance written.** Bimonthly magazine. *Water Gardening* is for hobby water gardeners. "We prefer articles from a first-person perspective." Estab. 1996. Circ. 25,000. Pays on publication. Publishes ms an average of 6 months after acceptance. Byline given. Offers 50% kill fee. Buys first North American serial rights. Editorial lead time 6 months. Submit seasonal material 6-12 months in advance. Accepts queries by mail, e-mail, fax. Responds in 1 month to queries; 3 months to mss. Sample copy for $3. Writer's guidelines for #10 SASE.

Nonfiction How-to (construct, maintain, improve ponds, water features), interview/profile, new product, personal experience, photo feature. **Buys 18-20 mss/year.** Query. Length: 600-1,500 words.

Photos State availability with submission. Reviews contact sheets, 3×5 transparencies, 3×5 prints. Buys one-time rights. Negotiates payment individually. Captions, identification of subjects, model releases required.

HUMOR

$FUNNY TIMES

A Monthly Humor Review, Funny Times, Inc., P.O. Box 18530, Cleveland Heights OH 44118. (216)371-8600. Fax: (216)371-8696. E-mail: ft@funnytimes.com. Website: www.funnytimes.com. **Contact:** Raymond Lesser, Susan Wolpert, editors. **10% freelance written.** Monthly tabloid for humor. "*Funny Times* is a monthly review of America's funniest cartoonists and writers. We are the *Reader's Digest* of modern American humor with a progressive/peace-oriented/environmental/politically activist slant." Estab. 1985. Circ. 74,000. Pays on publication. Publishes ms an average of 3 months after acceptance. Byline given. Buys one-time, second serial (reprint) rights. Editorial lead time 2 months. Accepts previously published material. Accepts simultaneous submissions. Responds in 3 months to mss. Sample copy for $3 or 9×12 SAE with 3 first-class stamps (83¢ postage). Writer's guidelines online.

Nonfiction "We only publish humor or interviews with funny people (comedians, comic actors, cartoonists, etc.). Everything we publish is very funny. If your piece isn't extremely funny then don't bother to send it. Don't send us anything that's not outrageously funny. Don't send anything that other people haven't already read and told you they laughed so hard they peed their pants." Essays (funny), humor, interview/profile, opinion (humorous), personal experience (absolutely funny). **Buys 36 mss/year.** Send complete ms. Length: 500-700 words. **Pays $60 minimum.**

Reprints Accepts previously published submissions.

Columns/Departments Query with published clips.

Fiction Ray Lesser and Susan Wolpert, editors. Humorous. "Anything funny." **Buys 6 mss/year.** Query with published clips. Length: 500-700 words. **Pays $50-150.**

Fillers Short humor. **Buys 6/year. Pays $20.**

Tips "Send us a small packet (1-3 items) of only your very funniest stuff. If this makes us laugh we'll be glad to ask for more. We particularly welcome previously published material that has been well-received elsewhere."

$ $MAD MAGAZINE

1700 Broadway, New York NY 10019. (212)506-4850. E-mail: submissions@madmagazine.com. Website: www .madmag.com. **Contact:** *MAD* Submissions Editor. **100% freelance written.** Monthly magazine "always on the lookout for new ways to spoof and to poke fun at hot trends." Estab. 1952. **Pays on acceptance.** Publishes ms an average of 6 months after acceptance. Byline given. Buys all rights. Submit seasonal material 6 months in advance. Responds in 10 weeks to queries. Sample copy and writer's guidelines online.

Nonfiction "Submit a premise with 3 or 4 examples of how you intend to carry it through, describing the action and visual content. Rough sketches desired but not necessary. One-page gags: 2- to 8-panel cartoon continuities as minimum very funny, maximum hilarious!" Satire; parody. "We're not interested in formats we're already doing or have done to death like 'what they say and what they really mean.' Don't send previously published submissions, riddles, advice columns, TV or movie satires, book manuscripts, top ten lists, articles about Alfred E. Neuman, poetry, essays, short stories or other text pieces." **Buys 400 mss/year. Pays minimum of $500/** *MAD* page.

Tips "Have fun! Remember to think visually! Surprise us! Freelancers can best break in with satirical nontopical material. Include SASE with each submission. Originality is prized. We like outrageous, silly and/or satirical humor."

INFLIGHT

$ $ $ $ATTACHÉ MAGAZINE

Pace Communications, 1301 Carolina St., Greensboro NC 27401. E-mail: attacheedit@attachemag.com. Website: www.attachemag.com. Editor: Lance Elko. **Contact:** Submissions Editor. **60% freelance written.** Monthly magazine for travelers on US Airways. "We focus on 'the best of the world' and use a humorous view." Estab. 1997. Circ. 441,000. **Pays on acceptance.** Publishes ms an average of 4 months after acceptance. Byline given. Offers kill fee. Buys first global serial rights. Editorial lead time 3 months. Accepts queries by mail, e-mail. Responds in 6 weeks to queries; 1 month to mss. Sample copy for $7.50 or online. Writer's guidelines online.

Nonfiction Features are highly visual, focusing on some unusual or unique angle of travel, food, business, or other topic approved by an *Attaché* editor. Book excerpts, essays, general interest, personal experience, travel, food, lifestyle, sports. **Buys 50-75 mss/year.** Query with published clips. Length: 350-2,500 words. **Pays $350-2,500.** Sometimes pays expenses of writers on assignment.

Photos State availability with submission. Reviews contact sheets, negatives, transparencies. Buys one-time rights. Negotiates payment individually. Identification of subjects, model releases required.

Columns/Departments Passions includes several topics such as Vices, Food, Golf, Sporting, Shelf Life, and

Things That Go; Paragons features short lists of the best in a particular field or category, as well as 400-word pieces describing the best of something—for example, the best home tool, the best ice cream in Paris, and the best reading library. Each piece should lend itself to highly visual art. Informed Sources are departments of expertise and first-person accounts; they include How It Works, Home Front, Improvement, and Genius at Work. **Buys 50-75 mss/year.** Query. **Pays $500-2,000.**

Tips "We look for cleverly written, entertaining articles with a unique angle, particularly pieces that focus on 'the best of' something. Study the magazine for content, style and tone. Queries for story ideas should be to the point and presented clearly. Any correspondence should include SASE."

$ $ $ HEMISPHERES

Pace Communications for United Airlines, Pace Communications, 1301 Carolina St., Greensboro NC 27401. (336)383-5690. E-mail: hemiedit@aol.com. Website: www.hemispheresmagazine.com. **95% freelance written.** Monthly magazine for the educated, sophisticated business and recreational frequent traveler on an airline that spans the globe. "*Hemispheres* is an inflight magazine that interprets 'inflight' to be a mode of delivery rather than an editorial genre. As such, Hemispheres' task is to engage, intrigue and entertain its primary readers—an international, culturally diverse group of affluent, educated professionals and executives who frequently travel for business and pleasure on United Airlines. The magazine offers a global perspective and a focus on topics that cross borders as often as the people reading the magazine. That places our emphasis on ideas, concepts, and culture rather than products. We present that perspective in a fresh, artful and sophisticated graphic enviroment." Estab. 1992. Circ. 500,000. **Pays on acceptance.** Publishes ms an average of 4-6 months after acceptance. Byline given. Offers 20% kill fee. Buys first worldwide rights. Editorial lead time 8 months. Submit seasonal material 8 months in advance. Accepts queries by mail. Responds in 2 months to queries; 4 months to mss. Sample copy for $7.50. Writer's guidelines for #10 SASE.

Nonfiction "Keeping 'global' in mind, we look for topics that reflect a modern appreciation of the world's cultures and environment. No 'What I did (or am going to do) on a trip.'" General interest, humor, personal experience. Query with published clips. Length: 500-3,000 words. **Pays 50¢/word and up.**

Photos Reviews photos "only when we request them." State availability with submission. Buys one-time rights. Negotiates payment individually. Captions, identification of subjects, model releases required.

Columns/Departments Making a Difference (Q&A format interview with world leaders, movers, and shakers. A 500-600 word introduction anchors the interview. "We want to profile an international mix of men and women representing a variety of topics or issues, but all must truly be making a difference. No puffy celebrity profiles."); 15 Fascinating Facts (a snappy selection of 1- or 2-sentence obscure, intriguing, or travel-service-oriented items that the reader never knew about a city, state, country, or destination.); Executive Secrets (things that top executives know); Case Study (Business strategies of international companies or organizations. No lionizations of CEOs. Strategies should be the emphasis. "We want international candidates."); Weekend Breakway (Takes us just outside a major city after a week of business for several activities for a physically active, action-packed weekend. This isn't a sedentary "getaway" at a "property."); Roving Gourmet (Insider's guide to interesting eating in major city, resort area, or region. The slant can be anything from ethnic to expensive; not just "best." The 4 featured eateries span a spectrum from "hole in the wall," to "expense account lunch," and on to "big deal dining."); Collecting (occasional 800-word story on collections and collecting that can emphasize travel); Eye on Sports (global look at anything of interest in sports); Vintage Traveler (options for mature, experienced travelers); Savvy Shopper (Insider's tour of best places in the world to shop. Savvy Shopper steps beyond all those stories that just mention the great shopping at a particular destination. A shop-by-shop, gallery-by-gallery tour of the best places in the world.); Science and Technology (Substantive, insightful stories on how technology is changing our lives and the business world. Not just another column on audio components or software. No gift guides!); Aviation Journal (For those fascinated with aviation. Topics range widely.); Terminal Bliss (a great airports guide series); Grape And Grain (wine and spirits with emphasis on education, not one-upmanship); Show Business (films, music, and entertainment); Musings (humor or just curious musings); Quick Quiz (tests to amuse and educate); Travel Trends (brief, practical, invaluable, global, trend-oriented); Book Beat (Tackles topics like the Wodehouse Society, the birth of a book, the competition between local bookshops and national chains. Please, no review proposals.); What the World's Reading (residents explore how current bestsellers tell us what their country is thinking). Length: 1,400 words. Query with published clips. **Pays 50¢/word and up.**

Fiction Adventure, ethnic, historical, humorous, mainstream, mystery, explorations of those issues common to all people but within the context of a particular culture. **Buys 14 mss/year.** Send complete ms. Length: 1,000-4,000 words. **Pays 50¢/word and up.**

Tips "We increasingly require writers of 'destination' pieces or departments to 'live whereof they write.' Increasingly want to hear from US, UK, or other English-speaking/writing journalists (business & travel) who reside outside the US in Europe, South America, Central America, and the Pacific Rim—all areas that United flies. We're not looking for writers who aim at the inflight market. *Hemispheres* broke the fluffy mold of that tired domestic genre. Our monthly readers are a global mix on the cutting edge of the global economy and culture. They don't need to have the world filtered by US writers. We want a Hong Kong restaurant writer to speak for that city's eateries, so we need English-speaking writers around the globe. That's the 'insider' story our readers respect. We use resident writers for departments such as Roving Gourmet, Savvy Shopper, On Location, 3 Perfect Days, and Weekend Breakaway, but authoritative writers can roam in features. Sure we cover the US, but with a global view: No 'in this country' phraseology. 'Too American' is a frequent complaint for queries. We use UK English spellings in articles that speak from that tradition and we specify costs in local currency first before US dollars. Basically, all of above serves the realization that today, 'global' begins with respect for 'local.' That approach permits a wealth of ways to present culture, travel, and business for a wide readership. We anchor that with a reader-service mission that grounds everything in 'how to do it.'''

N $ $ HORIZON AIR MAGAZINE

Paradigm Communications Group, 2701 First Ave., Suite 250, Seattle WA 98121. Fax: (206)448-6939. **Contact:** Michele Andrus Dill, editor. **90% freelance written.** Monthly inflight magazine covering travel, business, and leisure in the Pacific Northwest. "*Horizon Air Magazine* serves a sophisticated audience of business and leisure travelers. Stories must have a Northwest slant." Estab. 1990. Circ. 425,000/month. Pays on publication. Publishes ms an average of 1 year after acceptance. Byline given. Offers 33% kill fee. Buys first North American serial, electronic rights. Editorial lead time 6 months. Submit seasonal material 5 months in advance. Accepts queries by mail, fax. Sample copy for 10×12 SASE. Writer's guidelines for #10 SASE.

Nonfiction Essays (personal), general interest, historical/nostalgic, how-to, humor, interview/profile, personal experience, photo feature, travel, business. Special issues: Meeting planners' guide, golf, gift guide. No material unrelated to the Pacific Northwest. **Buys approximately 36 mss/year.** Query with published clips or send complete ms. Length: 1,500-3,000 words. **Pays $300-700.** Sometimes pays expenses of writers on assignment.

Photos State availability with submission. Reviews transparencies, prints. Buys one-time rights. Negotiates payment individually. Captions, identification of subjects, model releases required.

Columns/Departments Region (Northwest news/profiles), 200-400 words; Air Time (personal essays), 700 words. **Buys 15 mss/year.** Query with published clips. **Pays $100 (Region), $250 (Air Time).**

$ MIDWEST AIRLINES MAGAZINE

Paradigm Communications Group, 2701 First Ave., Suite 250, Seattle WA 98121. **Contact:** Eric Lucas, managing editor. **90% freelance written.** Semimonthly magazine for Midwest Airlines. "Positive depiction of the changing economy and culture of the US, plus travel and leisure features." Estab. 1993. Circ. 35,000. Pays on publication. Byline given. Buys first North American serial rights. Editorial lead time 9 months. Accepts queries by mail. Responds in 6 weeks to queries. Sample copy for 9×12 SASE. Writer's guidelines free.

O— *Midwest Airlines Magazine* continues to look for sophisticated travel and golf writing.

Nonfiction Travel, business, sports and leisure. Special issues: "Need good ideas for golf articles in spring." No humor, how-to, or fiction. **Buys 20-25 mss/year.** Query by mail only with published clips and résumé. Length: 250-3,000 words. **Pays $100 minimum.** Sometimes pays expenses of writers on assignment.

Columns/Departments Preview (arts and events), 200-400 words; Portfolio (business), 200-500 words. **Buys 12-15 mss/year.** Query with published clips. **Pays $100-150.**

Tips "Article ideas must encompass areas within the airline's route system. We buy quality writing from reliable writers. Editorial philosophy emphasizes innovation and positive outlook. Do not send manuscripts unless you have no clips."

N $ $ SKYLIGHTS

The Inflight Magazine of Spirit Airlines, Worth International Media Group, Inc., 5979 NW 151 St., Suite 120, Miami Lakes FL 33014. (305)828-0123. Fax: (305)828-0799. Website: www.worthit.com. Executive Editor: Gretchen Schmidt; Managing Editor: Millie Acebal Rousseau. **Contact:** Skylights Editorial Department. Bimonthly magazine. Like Spirit Airlines, *Skylights* will be known for its practical and friendly sensibility. This publication is a clean, stylish, user-friendly product. This is not an old-school airline, and *Skylights* is not an old-school inflight. Circ. 5.5 million. Pays on publication. Byline sometimes given. Buys first North American serial rights. Editorial lead time 3-6 months. Submit seasonal material 4 months in advance. Accepts queries by mail. Responds in 4-6 weeks to queries. Sample copy not available. Writer's guidelines via e-mail at millie@worthit.com.

O— "We're not going to bore readers with ponderous dissertations on weighty or esoteric topics, ho-hum something-for-everyone destination pieces, the stuffy de rigueur which-mutual-funds-to-watch business article. Instead, we're going to give readers the quick and practical lowdown on where they're going, what's going on once they get there, where they can sleep, eat, play, buy, relax. We'll present who and what they're talking about—names, faces, music, movies, books, gadgets, fashion—in chatty culture-current language. Our voice reflects a youthful sassy edge that—while never speaking down to our readers— amuses and delights our wide-ranging readership. Our readers are both leisure and business travelers."

Nonfiction General interest, humor, interview/profile, new product, travel. No first-person accounts or weighty topics. Stories should be practical and useful, but not something-for-everyone-type articles. **Buys 18 mss/year.** Query with published clips. Length: 350-1,200 words. **Pays 25-40¢/word.**

Photos State availability with submission. Reviews GIF/JPEG files. Buys one-time rights. Negotiaties payment individually. Captions, identification of subjects, model releases required.

Columns/Departments Events calendar (based on Spirit destinations), 1,200 words; Gizmos (latest and greatest gadgets), between 4 and 5 250-word descriptions; Biz (bizz buzz), 650-800 words; Fast Reads (Quick finds, books, movies, music, food, wine); Skybuys (hot buys and smart shopping options), between 4 and 6 150-word descriptions; Beauty and Health Story (specific aspects of staying well), 800 words. **Buys 36 mss/year.** Query with published clips. **25-40¢/word.**

Fillers Crossword puzzles, think and do ideas for kids (entertainment for children, such as new DVDs). Length: 250-400 words. **Pays 25-40¢/word.**

$ $ $ $ SOUTHWEST AIRLINES SPIRIT

4333 Amon Carter Blvd., Fort Worth TX 76155. (817)967-1803. Fax: (817)931-3015. E-mail: editors@spiritmag.com. Website: www.spiritmag.com. **Contact:** Ross McCammon, editor. Monthly magazine for passengers on Southwest Airlines. Estab. 1992. Circ. 380,000. **Pays on acceptance.** Byline given. Buys first North American serial, electronic rights. Responds in 1 month to queries.

Nonfiction "Seeking lively, accessible, entertaining, relevant, and trendy travel, business, lifestyle, sports, celebrity, food, tech-product stories on newsworthy/noteworthy topics in destinations served by Southwest Airlines; well-researched and reported; multiple source only. Experienced magazine professionals only." **Buys about 40 mss/year.** Query by mail only with published clips. Length: 1,500 words (features). **Pays $1/word.** Pays expenses of writers on assignment.

Columns/Departments Length: 800-900 words. **Buys about 21 mss/year.** Query by mail only with published clips.

Fillers Buys 12/year. Length: 250 words. **Pays variable amount.**

Tips "*Southwest Airlines Spirit* magazine reaches more than 2.8 million readers every month aboard Southwest Airlines. Our median reader is a college-educated, 32- to 40-year-old traveler with a household income around $90,000. Writers must have proven magazine capabilities, a sense of fun, excellent reporting skills, a smart, hip style, and the ability to provide take-away value to the reader in sidebars, charts, and/or lists."

$ $ SPIRIT OF ALOHA

The Inflight Magazine of Aloha Airlines, Honolulu Publishing Co., Ltd., 707 Richards St., Suite 525, Honolulu HI 96813. (808)524-7400. Fax: (808)531-2306. E-mail: tchapman@honpub.com. Website: www.spiritofaloha.com. **Contact:** Tom Chapman, editor. **80% freelance written.** Bimonthly magazine covering Hawaii and other Aloha Airlines destinations. Estab. 1978. Circ. 100,000. **Pays on acceptance.** Publishes ms an average of 2 months after acceptance. Byline given. Buys first rights. Editorial lead time 2 months. Submit seasonal material 4 months in advance. Accepts queries by mail, e-mail. Responds in up to 1 month to queries. Writer's guidelines by e-mail.

Nonfiction Should be related to Hawaii and other mainland destinations of airline. **Buys 40 mss/year.** Query with published clips. Length: 1,500-2,500 words. **Pays $500 and up.**

Photos State availability with submission. Reviews transparencies. Buys one-time rights. Negotiates payment individually. Captions, identification of subjects, model releases required.

$ $ $ WASHINGTON FLYER MAGAZINE

1707 L St., NW, Suite 800, Washington DC 20036. (202)331-9393. Fax: (202)331-2043. E-mail: lauren@themagazinegroup.com. Website: www.fly2dc.com. **Contact:** Lauren Paige Kennedy, editor-in-chief. **60% freelance written.** Bimonthly magazine for business and pleasure travelers at Washington National and Washington Dulles International airports INSI. "Primarily affluent, well-educated audience that flies frequently in and out of Washington, DC." Estab. 1989. Circ. 182,000. **Pays on acceptance.** Byline given. Offers 25% kill fee. Buys first North American serial rights. Submit seasonal material 4 months in advance. Accepts queries by mail, e-mail, fax. Responds in 10 weeks to queries. Sample copy for 9×12 SAE with $2 postage. Writer's guidelines and editorial calendar online.

⊙π "First understand the magazine—from the nuances of its content to its tone. Best departments to get your foot in the door are 'Washington Insider' and 'Mini Escapes.' The former deals with new business, the arts, sports, etc. in Washington. The latter: getaways that are within 4 hours of Washington by car. Regarding travel, we're less apt to run stories on sedentary pursuits (i.e., inns, B&Bs, spas). Our readers want to get out and discover an area, whether it's DC or Barcelona. Action-oriented activities work best. Also, the best way to pitch is via e-mail. Our mail is sorted by interns, and sometimes I never get queries. E-mail is so immediate, and I can give a more personal response."

Nonfiction One international destination feature per issue, determined 6 months in advance. One feature per issue on aspect of life in Washington. General interest, interview/profile, travel, business. No personal experiences, poetry, opinion or inspirational. **Buys 20-30 mss/year.** Query with published clips. Length: 800-1,200 words. **Pays $500-900.**

Photos State availability with submission. Reviews negatives, almost always color transparencies. Buys one-time rights. Considers additional payment for top-quality photos accepted with ms. Identification of subjects required.

Columns/Departments Washington Insider, Travel, Hospitality, Airports and Airlines, Restaurants, Shopping, all 800-1,200 words. Query. **Pays $500-900.**

Tips ''Know the Washington market and issues relating to frequent business/pleasure travelers as we move toward a global economy. With a bimonthly publication schedule it's important that stories remain viable as possible during the magazine's 2-month 'shelf life.' No telephone calls, please and understand that most assignments are made several months in advance. Queries are best sent via e-mail.''

JUVENILE

$ $ AMERICAN GIRL

8400 Fairway Place, Middleton WI 53562. Website: www.americangirl.com. **Contact:** Magazine Department Assistant. **5% freelance written.** Bimonthly 4-color magazine covering hobbies, crafts, profiles, and history of interest to girls ages 8-12. ''We want thoughtfully developed children's literature with good characters and plots.'' Estab. 1992. Circ. 700,000. **Pays on acceptance.** Byline given for larger features, not departments. Offers 50% kill fee. Buys first North American serial, all rights. Editorial lead time 6 months. Submit seasonal material 6 months in advance. Accepts queries by mail. Accepts previously published material. Accepts simultaneous submissions. Responds in 3 months to queries. Sample copy for $3.95 (check made out to *American Girl*) and 9 × 12 SAE with $1.98 postage. Writer's guidelines online.

   O—π Best opportunity for freelancers is the Girls Express section. ''We're looking for short profiles of girls who are into sports, the arts, interesting hobbies, cultural activities, and other areas. A key: The girl must be the 'star' and the story must be from her point of view. Be sure to include the age of the girls you're pitching to us. If you have any photo leads, please send those, too. We also welcome how-to stories—how to send away for free things, hot ideas for a cool day, how to write the President and get a response. In addition, we're looking for easy crafts that can be explained in a few simple steps. Stories in Girls Express have to be told in no more than 175 words. We prefer to receive ideas in query form rather than finished manuscripts.''

Nonfiction Pays $300 minimum for feature articles. Pays expenses of writers on assignment.

Photos ''We prefer to shoot.'' State availability with submission. Buys all rights.

Columns/Departments Girls Express (short profiles of girls with unusual and interesting hobbies that other girls want to read about), 175 words; Giggle Gang (puzzles, games, etc.—especially looking for seasonal). Query.

Fiction Adventure, condensed novels, ethnic, historical, humorous, slice-of-life vignettes. No romance, science fiction, fantasy. **Buys 6 mss/year.** Query with published clips. Length: 2,300 words maximum. **Pays $500 minimum.**

$ $ ARCHAEOLOGY'S DIG MAGAZINE

Cobblestone Publishing, 30 Grove St., Suite C, Peterborough NH 03458-1454. (603)924-7209. Fax: (603)924-7380. E-mail: cfbakeriii@meganet.net. Website: www.digonsite.com. **Contact:** Rosalie Baker, editor. **75% freelance written.** Magazine published 9 times/year covering archaeology for kids ages 9-14. Estab. 1999. Circ. 20,000. Pays on publication. Publishes ms an average of 1 year after acceptance. Byline given. Buys all rights. Editorial lead time 1 year. Accepts queries by mail. Responds in several months to queries. Sample copy for $4.95 with 8 × 11 SASE or $9 without SASE. Writer's guidelines online.

Nonfiction Personal experience, photo feature, travel, archaeological excavation reports. No fiction. Occasional paleontology stories accepted. **Buys 30-40 mss/year.** Query with published clips. Length: 100-1,000 words. **Pays 20-25¢/word.**

Photos State availability with submission. Buys one-time rights. Negotiates payment individually. Identification of subjects required.

Tips ''Please remember that this is a children's magazine for kids ages 9-14 so the tone is as kid-friendly as possible given the scholarship involved in researching and describing a site or a find.''

$ BABYBUG

Carus Publishing Co., P.O. Box 300, Peru IL 61354. (815)224-5803, ext. 656. Website: www.cricketmag.com. Editor-in-Chief: Marianne Carus. **Contact:** Paula Morrow, executive editor. **50% freelance written.** Board-book magazine published monthly except for combined May/June and July/August issues. "*Babybug* is 'the listening and looking magazine for infants and toddlers,' intended to be read aloud by a loving adult to foster a love of books and reading in young children ages 6 months-2 years." Estab. 1994. Circ. 45,000. Pays on publication. Byline given. Buys variable rights. Editorial lead time 10 months. Accepts simultaneous submissions. Sample copy for $5. Writer's guidelines online.

Nonfiction General interest. **Buys 10-20 mss/year.** Send complete ms. Length: up to 4 short sentences. **Pays $25.**

Fiction Anything for infants and toddlers. Adventure, humorous. **Buys 10-20 mss/year.** Send complete ms. Length: 2-8 short sentences. **Pays $25 and up.**

Poetry Buys 30 poems/year. Submit maximum 5 poems. Length: 2-8 lines. **Pays $25.**

Tips "Imagine having to read your story or poem—out loud—50 times or more! That's what parents will have to do. Babies and toddlers demand, 'Read it again'—your material must hold up under repetition."

N $BEYOND CENTAURI

Sam's Dot Publishing, P.O. Box 782, Cedar Rapids IA 52406-0782. E-mail: beyondcentauri@samsdotpublishing. com. Website: www.samsdotpublishing.com. **Contact:** Tyree Campbell, editor. **100% freelance written.** Quarterly magazine. *Beyond Centauri* is a magazine for younger readers (ages 10 and up) that publishes science fiction, fantasy, very mild horror, sword & sorcery, and slipstream short stories that are well-plotted and have memorable characters. It also publishes poetry in these genres that addresses the human condition in space or in magic. Estab. 2003. Circ. 60. Pays on publication. Publishes ms an average of 3-6 months after acceptance. Byline given. Offers 100% kill fee. Buys first North American serial, one-time, second serial (reprint) rights. Editorial lead time 6 months. Submit seasonal material 6 months in advance. Accepts queries by e-mail. Accepts previously published material. Responds in 2 weeks to queries; 2-3 months to mss. Sample copy for $6. Writer's guidelines online.

Nonfiction "*Beyond Centauri* buys/publishes science fiction, fantasy, and horror movie and book reviews, and interviews with noted individuals in those genres. We are also interested in short science articles about space exploration, astronomy, opinions, and so forth. If in doubt, submit it." **Buys 5 mss/year.** Send complete ms. Length: 500 words. **Pays $1 for unsolicited articles.** Pays in contributor copies at the author's request.

Fiction Fantasy, horror, science fiction, sword & sorcery, slipstream. Do not send blood and gore horror, bad language, or "adult" themes. **Buys 30-40 mss/year.** Send complete ms. Length: 2,000 words. **Pays $3-5.**

Poetry Avant-garde, free verse, light verse, traditional. **Buys 24-30 poems/year.** Submit maximum 5 poems. Length: 100 lines.

Tips "*Beyond Centauri* loves to publish younger writers, as well as beginning writers and seasoned veterans. Be sure to read and follow the guidelines before you submit your work. The best advice for beginning writers is to send your best effort, not your first draft."

$ $ $ $BOYS' LIFE

Boy Scouts of America, P.O. Box 152079, Irving TX 75015-2079. (972)580-2366. Fax: (972)580-2079. Website: www.boyslife.org. **Contact:** Michael Goldman, senior editor. **75% freelance written.** Prefers to work with published/established writers; works with small number of new/unpublished writers each year. Monthly magazine covering activities of interest to all boys ages 6-18. Most readers are Boy Scouts or Cub Scouts. "*Boys' Life* covers Boy Scout activities and general interest subjects for ages 8-18, Boy Scouts, Cub Scouts and others of that age group." Estab. 1911. Circ. 1,300,000. **Pays on acceptance.** Publishes ms an average of 1 year after acceptance. Buys one-time rights. Accepts queries by mail, fax. Responds in 2 months to queries. Sample copy for $3.60 and 9×12 SAE. Writer's guidelines for #10 SASE or online.

Nonfiction Subject matter is broad, everything from professional sports to American history to how to pack a canoe. Look at a current list of the BSA's more than 100 merit badge pamphlets for an idea of the wide range of subjects possible. Uses strong photo features with about 500 words of text. Separate payment or assignment for photos. How-to, photo feature, hobby and craft ideas. **Buys 60 mss/year.** Query with SASE. No phone queries. Length: Major articles run 500-1,500 words; preferred length is about 1,000 words, including sidebars and boxes. **Pays $400-1,500.** Pays expenses of writers on assignment.

Columns/Departments Darrin Scheid, associate editor. "Science, nature, earth, health, sports, space and aviation, cars, computers, entertainment, pets, history, and music are some of the columns for which we use 300-750 words of text. This is a good place to show us what you can do." **Buys 75-80 mss/year.** Query. **Pays $250-300.**

Fiction Rich Haddaway, associate editor. Adventure, humorous, mystery, science fiction, western, sports. **Buys 12-15 mss/year.** Send complete ms with SASE. Length: 1,000-1,500 words. **Pays $750 minimum.**

Fillers Freelance comics pages and scripts.

Tips "We strongly recommend reading at least 12 issues of the magazine before you submit queries. We are a good market for any writer willing to do the necessary homework."

$BREAD FOR GOD'S CHILDREN

Bread Ministries, Inc., P.O. Box 1017, Arcadia FL 34265. (863)494-6214. Fax: (863)993-0154. E-mail: bread@sun line.net. Editor: Judith M. Gibbs. **Contact:** Donna Wade, editorial secretary. **10% freelance written.** Published 6-8 times/year. ''An interdenominational Christian teaching publication written to aid children and youth in leading a Christian life.'' Estab. 1972. Circ. 10,000. Pays on publication. Publishes ms an average of 6 months after acceptance. Byline given. Buys first rights. Accepts queries by mail. Accepts simultaneous submissions. Responds in 6 months to mss. Three sample copies for 9×12 SAE and 5 first-class stamps. Writer's guidelines for #10 SASE.

    O→ Break in with a good story about a 6-10 year old gaining insight into a spiritual principle—without an adult preaching the message to him.

Reprints Send tearsheet and information about when and where the material previously appeared.

Columns/Departments Let's Chat (children's Christian values), 500-700 words; Teen Page (youth Christian values), 600-800 words; Idea Page (games, crafts, Bible drills). **Buys 5-8 mss/year.** Send complete ms. **Pays $30.**

Fiction ''We are looking for writers who have a solid knowledge of Biblical principles and are concerned for the youth of today living by those principles. Our stories must be well written, with the story itself getting the message across—no preaching, moralizing, or tag endings.'' No fantasy, science fiction, or nonChristian themes. **Buys 15-20 mss/year.** Send complete ms. Length: 600-800 words (young children), 900-1,500 words (older children). **Pays $40-50.**

Tips ''We're looking for more submissions on healing miracles and reconciliation/restoration. Follow usual guidelines for careful writing, editing, and proofreading. We get many manuscripts with misspellings, poor grammar, careless typing. Know your subject—writer should know the Lord to write about the Christian life. Study the publication and our guidelines.''

$CADET QUEST MAGAZINE

P.O. Box 7259, Grand Rapids MI 49510-7259. (616)241-5616. Fax: (616)241-5558. E-mail: submissions@calvinis tcadets.org. Website: www.calvinistcadets.org. **Contact:** G. Richard Broene, editor. **40% freelance written.** Works with a small number of new/unpublished writers each year. Magazine published 7 times/year. ''*Cadet Quest Magazine* shows boys 9-14 how God is at work in their lives and in the world around them.'' Estab. 1958. Circ. 10,000. **Pays on acceptance.** Publishes ms an average of 4-11 months after acceptance. Byline given. Buys first North American serial, one-time, second serial (reprint), simultaneous rights. Rights purchased vary with author and material. Accepts previously published material. Accepts simultaneous submissions. Responds in 2 months to submissions to queries. Sample copy for 9×12 SASE. Writer's guidelines for #10 SASE.

    ● Accepts submissions by mail, or by e-mail (must include ms in text of e-mail). Will not open attachments.

Nonfiction Articles about young boys' interests: sports (articles about athletes and developing Christian character through sports; photos appreciated), outdoor activities (camping skills, nature study, survival exercises; practical 'how to do it' approach works best. 'God in nature' themes appreciated), science, crafts, and problems. Emphasis is on a Christian perspective, but no simplistic moralisms. How-to, humor, inspirational, interview/profile, personal experience, informational. Special issues: Write for new themes list in February. **Buys 20-25 mss/year.** Send complete ms. Length: 500-1,500 words. **Pays 2-5¢/word.**

Reprints Send ms with rights for sale noted. Payment varies.

Photos Pays $4-25 for photos purchased with ms.

Columns/Departments Project Page (uses simple projects boys 9-14 can do on their own made with easily accessible materials; must provide clear, accurate instructions).

Fiction ''Considerable fiction is used. Fast-moving stories that appeal to a boy's sense of adventure or sense of humor are welcome.'' Adventure, religious, spiritual, sports, comics. ''Avoid preachiness. Avoid simplistic answers to complicated problems. Avoid long dialogue and little action.'' No fantasy, science fiction, fashion, horror or erotica. Send complete ms. Length: 900-1,500 words. **Pays 4-6¢/word, and 1 contributor's copy.**

Fillers Short humor, any type of puzzles.

Tips ''Best time to submit stories/articles is early in calendar year (February-April). Also remember readers are boys ages 9-14. Stories must reflect or add to the theme of the issue and be from a Christian perspective.''

$ $CALLIOPE

Exploring World History, Cobblestone Publishing Co., 30 Grove St., Suite C, Peterborough NH 03458-1454. (603)924-7209. Fax: (603)924-7380. Website: www.cobblestonepub.com. Editors: Rosalie and Charles Baker. **Contact:** Rosalie F. Baker, editor. **More than 50% freelance written.** Magazine published 9 times/year covering world history (East and West) through 1800 AD for 8-14 year olds. Articles must relate to the issue's theme. ''*Calliope* covers world history (east/west) and lively, original approaches to the subject are the primary concerns of the editors in choosing material.'' Estab. 1990. Circ. 11,000. Pays on publication. Byline given. Buys all rights. Responds in several months (if interested, responds 5 months before publication date) to mss. Sample copy for $4.50 and 7½ × 10½ SASE with 4 first-class stamps or online. Writer's guidelines for #10 SAE and 1 first-class stamp or online.

O⟶ Break in with a "well-written query on a topic that relates directly to an upcoming issue's theme, a writing sample that is well-researched and concise, and a bibliography that includes new research."

Nonfiction Articles must relate to the theme. Essays, general interest, historical/nostalgic, how-to (activities), humor, interview/profile, personal experience, photo feature, technical, travel, recipes. No religious, pornographic, biased, or sophisticated submissions. **Buys 30-40 mss/year.** Query by mail only with published clips. Length: 700-800 words for feature articles; 300-600 words for supplemental nonfiction. **Pays 20-25¢/printed word.**

Photos State availability with submission. Reviews contact sheets, color slides and b&w prints. Buys one-time rights. Pays $15-100 (color cover negotiated).

Columns/Departments Activities (crafts, recipes, projects), up to 700 words. Query by mail only with published clips. **Pays on individual basis.**

Fiction Rosalie Baker, editor. All fiction must be theme-related. **Buys 10 mss/year.** Query with or without published clips. Length: 1,000 words maximum. **Pays 20-25¢/word.**

Fillers Puzzles and games (no word finds); crossword and other word puzzles using the vocabulary of the issue's theme; mazes and picture puzzles that relate to the theme. **Pays on individual basis.**

Tips "A query must consist of all of the following to be considered (please use nonerasable paper): a brief cover letter stating the subject and word length of the proposed article; a detailed 1-page outline explaining the information to be presented in the article; an extensive bibliography of materials the author intends to use in preparing the article; a self-addressed stamped envelope. (Authors are urged to use primary resources and up-to-date scholarly resources in their bibliography.) Writers new to *Calliope* should send a writing sample with the query. In all correspondence, please include your complete address and a telephone number where you can be reached."

$ CHARACTERS

Kids Short Story & Poetry Outlet, Davis Publications, P.O. Box 708, Newport NH 03773-0708. (603)863-5896. Fax: (603)863-8198. E-mail: hotdog@nhvt.net. **Contact:** Cindy Davis, editor. **100% freelance written.** Quarterly magazine for kids. "We accept submissions by all, but when space is limited, give preference to ones written by kids." Estab. 2003. Pays on publication. Publishes ms an average of 6 months after acceptance. Byline given. Not copyrighted. Buys one-time, second serial (reprint) rights. Editorial lead time 4 months. Submit seasonal material 6 months in advance. Accepts queries by mail, e-mail. Accepts previously published material. Accepts simultaneous submissions. Responds in 2 weeks to queries; 1 month to mss. Sample copy for $5. Writer's guidelines by e-mail or snail mail.

Fiction All genres accepted. **Buys 40 mss/year.** Send complete ms. Length: 1,500 words maximum. **Pays $5, plus contributor copy.**

Poetry Light verse, traditional. **Buys 8 poems/year.** Submit maximum 2 poems. Length: up to 16 lines.

$ $ CHILDREN'S PLAYMATE MAGAZINE

Children's Better Health Institute, P.O. Box 567, Indianapolis IN 46206-0567. Website: www.childrensplaymate mag.org. **40% freelance written.** Eager to work with new/unpublished writers. Magazine published 8 times/year for children ages 6-8. "We are looking for articles, poems, and activities with a health, fitness, or nutrition theme. We try to present our material in a positive light, and we try to incorporate humor and a light approach wherever possible without minimizing the seriousness of what we are saying." Estab. 1929. Circ. 114,907. Pays on publication. Byline given. Buys all rights. Submit seasonal material 8 months in advance. Responds in 3 months to queries. Sample copy for $1.75. Writer's guidelines for SASE or on website.

• May hold mss for up to 1 year before acceptance/publication.

O⟶ Include word count. Material will not be returned unless accompanied by a SASE.

Nonfiction "We are especially interested in material concerning sports and fitness, including profiles of famous amateur and professional athletes; 'average' atheletes (especially children) who have overcome obstacles to excel in their areas; and new or unusual sports, particularly those in which children can participate. Nonfiction articles dealing with health subjects should be fresh and creative. Avoid encyclopedic or 'preachy' approach. We try to present our health material in a positive manner, incorporate humor and a light approach wherever possible without minimizing the seriousness of the message." Interview/profile (famous amateurs and professional athletes), photo feature, recipes (ingredients should be healthful). **Buys 25 mss/year.** Send complete ms. Length: 300-700 words. **Pays up to 17¢/word.**

Photos State availability with submission. Buys one-time rights. $15 minimum. Captions, model releases required.

Fiction Terry Harshman, editor. Not buying much fiction right now except for rebus stories of 100-300 words and occasional poems. Vocabulary suitable for ages 6-8. Include word count. No adult or adolescent fiction.

Send complete ms. Length: 300-700 words. **Pays minimum of 17¢/word and 10 contributor's copies.**

Fillers Recipes, puzzles, dot-to-dots, color-ins, hidden pictures, mazes. Prefers camara-ready activities. Activity guidelines for #10 SASE. **Buys 25/year. Pays variable amount.**

Tips "We would especially like to see more holiday stories, articles, and activities. Please send seasonal material at least 8 months in advance."

$ $CICADA MAGAZINE

Cricket Magazine Group, P.O. Box 300, Peru IL 61354. (815)224-5803 ext. 656. Fax: (815)224-6615. Website: www.cricketmag.com. Editor-in-Chief: Marianne Carus. Executive Editor: Deborah Vetter. Senior Editor: Tracy C. Schoenle. Senior Art Director: Ron McCutchan. **Contact:** Submissions Editor. **80% freelance written.** Bi-monthly magazine for teenagers and young adults. "*Cicada*, for ages 14 and up, publishes original short stories, poems, and first-person essays written for teens and young adults." Estab. 1998. Circ. 17,000. Pays on publication. Publishes ms an average of 1 year after acceptance. Byline given. Rights vary. Accepts previously published material. Accepts simultaneous submissions. Responds in 3 months to mss. Sample copy for $8.50. Writer's guidelines for SASE and on website.

Nonfiction Looking for first-person experiences that are relevant and interesting to teenagers. Essays, personal experience. Send complete ms. Length: up to 5,000 words. **Pays 25¢/word.**

Reprints Send ms. Payment varies.

Fiction Looking for realistic, contemporary, historical fiction, adventure, humor, fantasy, science fiction. Main protagonist should be age 14 or older. Stories should have a genuine teen sensibility and be aimed at readers in high school or college. Adventure, fantasy, historical, humorous, mainstream, mystery, romance, science fiction, western, sports. Send complete ms. Length: 3,000-15,000 words. **Pays 25¢/word, plus 6 contributor's copies.**

Poetry Looking for serious or humorous; rhymed or free verse. Free verse, light verse, traditional. Length: up to 25 lines. **Pays up to $3/line.**

Tips "An exact word count should be noted on each manuscript submitted. For poetry, indicate number of lines instead. Word count includes every word, but does not include the title of the manuscript or the author's name."

$CLUB CONNECTION

A Missionettes Magazine for Girls, The General Council of the Assemblies of God, 1445 N. Boonville Ave., Springfield MO 65802. (417)862-2781. Fax: (417)862-0503. E-mail: clubconnection@ag.org. Website: missionettes.ag.org/clubconnection. Editor: Debby Seler. Managing Editor: Lori VanVeen. **Contact:** Kelly Kirksey, assistant editor. **25% freelance written.** Quarterly magazine covering Christian discipleship. "*Club Connection* is a Christian-based magazine for girls ages 6-12." Estab. 1997. Circ. 12,000. Pays on publication. Publishes ms an average of 6-12 months after acceptance. Buys first, one-time rights. Editorial lead time 6 months. Submit seasonal material 9-12 months in advance. Accepts queries by mail, e-mail, fax. Responds in 1-2 months. Sample copy for free. Writer's guidelines online.

Nonfiction Historical/nostalgic, how-to (fun activities for girls), humor, inspirational, interview/profile, personal experience, religious. Special issues: A Look At Nature: trees, flowers, insects, butterflies, etc. (Spring 2005); A View of the World: geography, mountains, oceans and seas, summer vacation (Summer 2005); The Bigger Picture: science, the universe, astronauts, back to school (Fall 2005); The Perfect Plan: God's unique design in all creation, Jesus, salvation, Christmas (Winter 2005). No songs or poetry. **Buys 8 mss/year.** Send complete ms. Length: 250-800 words. **Pays $35-50 for assigned articles; $25-40 for unsolicited articles.**

Photos Send photos with submission. Reviews 3½×5 prints. Buys one-time rights with online options. Offers $10/photo. Captions, identification of subjects required.

Fiction Adventure, confessions, ethnic, historical, humorous, mainstream, mystery, religious. No songs or poetry. **Buys 8 mss/year.** Send complete ms. Length: 250-800 words. **Pays $25-50.**

Tips "Our goal is to offer a Christ-centered, fun magazine for girls. We look for word count, age appropriateness, and relevancy to today's girls when selecting articles. Writing to theme's is also helpful. They can be found on our website."

$ $COBBLESTONE

Discover American History, Cobblestone Publishing, 30 Grove St., Suite C, Peterborough NH 03458. Fax: (603)924-7380. Website: www.cobblestonepub.com. **Contact:** Meg Chorlian, editor. Monthly magazine (September-May) covering American history for children ages 8-14. Prefers to work with published/established writers. "Each issue presents a particular theme, making it exciting as well as informative. Half of all subscriptions are for schools." All material must relate to monthly theme. Estab. 1979. Circ. 30,000. Pays on publication. Publishes ms an average of 4 months after acceptance. Byline given. Offers 50% kill fee. Buys all rights. Editorial lead time 8 months. Accepts queries by mail, fax. Responds in 4 months to queries. Sample copy for $4.95 and

$7^1/_2 \times 10^1/_2$ SAE with 4 first-class stamps. Writer's guidelines for #10 SASE and 1 first-class stamp or on website.

Nonfiction "Request a copy of the writer's guidelines to find out specific issue themes in upcoming months." Historical/nostalgic, interview/profile, personal experience, plays, biography, recipes, activities. No material that editorializes rather than reports. **Buys 80 mss/year.** Query by mail with published clips, outline, and bibliography. Length: Feature articles 600-800 words; supplemental nonfiction 300-500 words. **Pays 20-25¢/printed word.**

Photos Photos must relate to theme. State availability with submission. Reviews contact sheets, transparencies, prints. Buys one-time rights. Offers $15-50 for nonprofessional quality, up to $100 for professional quality. Captions, identification of subjects required.

Columns/Departments Puzzles and Games (no word finds); crosswords and other word puzzles using the vocabulary of the issue's theme.

Fiction Adventure, ethnic, historical, biographical fiction relating to theme. Has to be very strong and accurate. **Buys 5 mss/year.** Query with published clips. Length: 500-800 words. **Pays 20-25¢/word.**

Poetry Must relate to theme. Free verse, light verse, traditional. **Buys 3 poems/year.** Length: Up to 50 lines.

Tips "Review theme lists and past issues of magazine to see what we look for."

$ $CRICKET

Carus Publishing Co., P.O. Box 300, Peru IL 61354-0300. (815)224-5803, ext. 656. Website: www.cricketmag.com. Editor-in-Chief: Marianne Carus. Executive Editor: Deborah Vetter. Senior Editor: Tracy C. Schoenle. Assistant Editor: Ron McCutchan. **Contact:** Submissions Editor. Monthly magazine for children ages 9-14. Estab. 1973. Circ. 73,000. Pays on publication. Publishes ms an average of 6-24 months after acceptance. Byline given. Rights vary. Submit seasonal material 1 year in advance. Accepts previously published material. Responds in 3 months to mss. Sample copy for $5 and 9×12 SAE. Writer's guidelines for SASE and on website.

- *Cricket* is looking for more fiction and nonfiction for the older end of its 9-14 age range, as well as contemporary stories set in other countries. It also seeks humorous stories and mysteries (not detective spoofs), fantasy and original fairy tales, stand-alone excerpts from unpublished novels, and well-written/researched science articles.

Nonfiction A bibliography is required for all nonfiction articles. Travel, adventure, biography, foreign culture, geography, history, natural science, science, social science, sports, technology. Send complete ms. Length: 200-1,500 words. **Pays 25¢/word maximum.**

Reprints Send ms with rights for sale noted and information about when and where the material previously appeared. Pays 50% of amount paid for an original article.

Fiction Marianne Carus, editor-in-chief. Adventure, ethnic, fantasy, historical, humorous, mystery, novel excerpts, science fiction, suspense, western, folk and fairy tales. No didactic, sex, religious, or horror stories. **Buys 75-100 mss/year.** Send complete ms. Length: 200-2,000 words. **Pays 25¢/word maximum, and 6 contributor's copies; $2.50 charge for extras.**

Poetry Buys 20-30 poems/year. Length: 25 lines maximum. **Pays $3/line maximum.**

$DISCOVERIES

Word Action Publishing Co., 6401 The Paseo, Kansas City MO 64131. (816)333-7000, ext. 2728. Fax: (816)333-4439. E-mail: sweatherwax@nazarene.org. Editor: Virginia Folsom. **Contact:** Sarah Weatherwax, editorial assistant. **80% freelance written.** Weekly Sunday school take-home paper. "Our audience is third and fourth graders. We require that the stories relate to the Sunday school lesson for that week." Circ. 18,000. **Pays on acceptance.** Publishes ms an average of 1-2 year after acceptance. Byline given. Buys multi-use rights. Accepts queries by mail, e-mail, fax. Accepts previously published material. Accepts simultaneous submissions. Responds in 6 weeks to queries. Sample copy for SASE. Writer's guidelines for SASE.

- "Query before sending submissions. Make sure content is Biblically correct and relevant where necessary."

Fiction Submit contemporary, true-to-life portrayals of 8-10 year olds, written for a third- to fourth-grade reading level. Religious themes. Must relate to our theme list. No fantasy, science fiction, abnormally mature or precocious children, personification of animals. Nothing preachy. No unrealistic dialogue. **Buys 50 mss/year.** Send complete ms. **Pays $25.**

Fillers Spot cartoons, puzzles (related to the theme), trivia (any miscellaneous area of interest to 8-10 year olds). Length: 50-100 words. **Pays $15 for trivia, puzzles, and cartoons.**

Tips "Follow our theme list and read the Bible verses that relate to the theme."

$ $FACES

People, Places and Cultures, Cobblestone Publishing, 30 Grove St., Suite C, Peterborough NH 03458. (603)924-7209. Fax: (603)924-7380. E-mail: facesmag@yahoo.com. Website: www.cobblestonepub.com. **Contact:** Elizabeth Carpentiere, editor. **90-100% freelance written.** Monthly magazine published during school year. "*Faces* covers world culture for ages 9-14. It stands apart from other children's magazines by offering a solid look at one subject and stressing strong editorial content, color photographs throughout, and original illustrations. *Faces* offers an equal balance of feature articles and activities, as well as folktales and legends." Estab. 1984. Circ. 15,000. Pays on publication. Publishes ms an average of 4 months after acceptance. Byline given. Offers 50% kill fee. Buys all rights. Editorial lead time 1 year. Accepts queries by mail, e-mail. Accepts simultaneous submissions. Sample copy for $4.95 and 7½×10½ (or larger) SAE with $2 postage or online. Writer's guidelines for SASE or on website.

    O→ All material must relate to the theme of a specific upcoming issue in order to be considered. Writers new to *Faces* should send a writing sample with the query.

Nonfiction Historical/nostalgic, humor, interview/profile, personal experience, photo feature, travel, recipes, activities, puzzles, mazes. All must relate to theme. **Buys 45-50 mss/year.** Query with published clips. Length: 800 words for feature articles; 300-600 for supplemental nonfiction; up to 700 words for activities. **Pays 20-25¢/word.**

Photos State availability of photos with submission or send copies of related images for photo researcher. Reviews contact sheets, transparencies, prints. Buys one-time rights. Captions, identification of subjects, model releases required.

Fiction Ethnic, historical, retold legends or folktales. Depends on theme. Query with published clips. Length: Up to 800 words. **Pays 20-25¢/word.**

Tips "Freelancers should send for a sample copy of magazine and a list of upcoming themes and writer's guidelines. The magazine is based on a monthly theme (upcoming themes include Bolivia, Japan, Nelson Mandela, Afghanistan, Child Labor, and Extreme Places). We appreciate professional queries that follow our detailed writer's guidelines."

$ $THE FRIEND

50 E. North Temple, Salt Lake City UT 84150-3226. Fax: (801)240-2270. **Contact:** Vivian Paulsen, managing editor. **50% freelance written.** Eager to work with new/unpublished writers as well as established writers. Monthly publication of The Church of Jesus Christ of Latter-Day Saints for children ages 3-11. Circ. 275,000. **Pays on acceptance.** Buys all rights. Submit seasonal material 1 year in advance. Responds in 2 months to mss. Sample copy and writer's guidelines for $1.50 and 9×12 SAE with 4 first-class stamps.

Nonfiction "*The Friend* is interested in only stories based on true experiences." Special issues: Christmas, Easter. Submit complete ms with SASE. No queries, please. Length: 1,000 words maximum. **Pays $100 (200-300 words); $250 (400 words and up) minimum.**

Poetry Serious, humorous, holiday. Any form with child appeal. **Pays $50 minimum.**

Tips "Do you remember how it feels to be a child? Can you write stories that appeal to children ages 3-11 in today's world? We're interested in stories with an international flavor and those that focus on present-day problems. Send material of high literary quality slanted to our editorial requirements. Let the child solve the problem—not some helpful, all-wise adult. No overt moralizing. Nonfiction should be creatively presented—not an array of facts strung together. Beware of being cutesy."

$ $GIRLS' LIFE

Monarch Publishing, 4517 Harford Rd., Baltimore MD 21214. E-mail: karen@girlslife.com. Website: www.girlslife.com. **Contact:** Karen Bokram, editor. Bimonthly magazine covering girls ages 9-15. Estab. 1994. Circ. 2,000,000. Pays on publication. Publishes ms an average of 3 months after acceptance. Byline given. Buys all rights. Editorial lead time 4 months. Submit seasonal material 5 months in advance. Accepts queries by mail. Responds in 1 month to queries. Sample copy for $5 or online. Writer's guidelines online.

Nonfiction Book excerpts, essays, general interest, how-to, humor, inspirational, interview/profile, new product, travel, beauty, relationship, sports. Special issues: Back to School (August/September); Fall, Halloween (October/November); Holidays, Winter (December/January); Valentine's Day, Crushes (February/March); Spring, Mother's Day (April/May); and Summer, Father's Day (June/July). **Buys 40 mss/year.** Query by mail with published clips. Submit complete mss on spec only. Length: 700-2,000 words. **Pays $350/regular column; $500/feature.**

Photos State availability with submission. Reviews contact sheets, negatives, transparencies. Negotiates payment individually. Captions, identification of subjects, model releases required.

Columns/Departments Buys 20 mss/year. Query with published clips. **Pays $150-450.**

Tips Send queries with published writing samples and detailed résumé. "Have new ideas, a voice that speaks to our audience—not *down* to our audience—and supply artwork source."

$GUIDE

True Stories Pointing to Jesus, Review and Herald Publishing Association, 55 W. Oak Ridge Dr., Hagerstown MD 21740. (301)393-4037. Fax: (301)393-4055. E-mail: guide@rhpa.org. Website: www.guidemagazine.org.

Contact: Randy Fishell, editor, or Rachel Whitaker, assistant editor. **90% freelance written.** Weekly magazine featuring all-true stories showing God's involvement in 10- to 14-year-olds' lives. Estab. 1953. Circ. 32,000. **Pays on acceptance.** Publishes ms an average of 8 months after acceptance. Byline given. Buys first North American serial, second serial (reprint) rights. Editorial lead time 8 months. Submit seasonal material 8 months in advance. Accepts queries by mail, e-mail, fax. Responds in 1 month to queries. Sample copy for 6×9 SAE and 2 first-class stamps. Writer's guidelines online.

- Prefers electronic ms submissions.
- Break in with "a true story that shows in a clear way that God is involved in a 10- to 14-year-old's life."

Nonfiction Religious. "No fiction. Nonfiction should set forth a clearly evident spiritual application." **Buys 300 mss/year.** Send complete ms. Length: 750-1,500 words. **Pays $25-125.**

Reprints Send photocopy. Pays 50% of usual rates.

Fillers Games, puzzles, religious. **Buys 75/year. Pays $25-40.**

Tips "The majority of 'misses' are due to the lack of a clearly evident (not 'preachy') spiritual application."

$HIGH ADVENTURE

General Council of the Assemblies of God/Royal Rangers, 1445 N. Boonville Ave., Springfield MO 65802-1894. (417)862-2781, ext. 4177. Fax: (417)831-8230. E-mail: royalrangers@ag.org. Website: www.royalrangers.ag.org. **Contact:** Rev. Jerry Parks, editor. **60-70% freelance written.** Quarterly magazine. "*High Adventure* is a quarterly Royal Rangers magazine for boys. This 16-page, 4-color periodical is designed to provide boys with worthwhile leisure reading to challenge them to higher ideals and greater spiritual dedication; and to perpetuate the spirit of Royal Rangers ministry through stories, crafts, ideas, and illustrations." Estab. 1971. Circ. 87,000. Pays on publication. Publishes ms an average of 6-12 months after acceptance. Buys one-time, electronic rights. Buys first or all rights. Editorial lead time 3 months. Submit seasonal material 3 months in advance. Accepts queries by mail, e-mail, fax. Accepts previously published material. Accepts simultaneous submissions. Responds in 4-6 weeks to queries; 3-6 months to mss. Sample copy and writer's guidelines for 9×12 SAE and 2 first-class stamps. Writer's guidelines for SASE, by e-mail or fax. Editorial calendar for #10 SASE.

Nonfiction General interest, historical/nostalgic, humor, inspirational, personal experience, religious. No objectionable language, innuendo, immoral, or non-Christian materials. **Buys 10-12 mss/year.** Send complete ms. Length: 200-1,000 words. **Pays 6¢/word for assigned articles.**

Fiction Rev. Jerry Parks, editor. Adventure, historical, humorous, religious, camping. No objectionable language, innuendo, immoral, or non-Christian materials. **Buys 30 mss/year.** Send complete ms. Length: 200-1,000 words. **Pays 6¢/word, plus 3 contributor's copies.**

Fillers Anecdotes, facts, short humor. **Buys 25-30/year.** Length: 25-100 words. **Pays 6¢/word.**

Tips "Consider the (middle/upper elementary) average age of readership when making a submission."

$HIGHLIGHTS FOR CHILDREN

803 Church St., Honesdale PA 18431-1824. (570)253-1080. Fax: (570)251-7847. Website: www.highlights.com. Editor: Christine French Clark. **Contact:** Manuscript Submissions. **80% freelance written.** Monthly magazine for children ages 2-12. "This book of wholesome fun is dedicated to helping children grow in basic skills and knowledge, in creativeness, in ability to think and reason, in sensitivity to others, in high ideals, and worthy ways of living—for children are the world's most important people. We publish stories for beginning and advanced readers. Up to 500 words for beginners (ages 3-7), up to 800 words for advanced (ages 8-12)." Estab. 1946. Circ. 2,000,000+. **Pays on acceptance.** Buys all rights. Accepts queries by mail. Responds in 2 months to queries. Sample copy for free. Writer's guidelines for SASE or on website.

Nonfiction "We need articles on science, technology, and nature written by persons with strong backgrounds in those fields. Contributions always welcomed from new writers, especially engineers, scientists, historians, teachers, etc., who can make useful, interesting facts accessible to children. Also writers who have lived abroad and can interpret the ways of life, especially of children, in other countries in ways that will foster world brotherhood. Sports material, arts features, biographies, and articles of general interest to children. Direct, original approach, simple style, interesting content, not rewritten from encyclopedias. State background and qualifications for writing factual articles submitted. Include references or sources of information. Articles geared toward our younger readers (3-7) especially welcome, up to 500 words. Also buys original party plans for children ages 4-12, clearly described in 300-600 words, including drawings or samples of items to be illustrated. Also, novel but tested ideas in crafts, with clear directions. Include samples. Projects must require only free or inexpensive, easy-to-obtain materials. Especially desirable if easy enough for early primary grades. Also, finger-plays with lots of action, easy for very young children to grasp and to dramatize. Avoid wordiness. We need creative-thinking puzzles that can be illustrated, optical illusions, brain teasers, games of physical agility, and other 'fun' activities." Query. Length: 800 words maximum. **Pays $50 for party plans; $25 for craft ideas; $25 for fingerplays.**

Photos Reviews color 35mm slides, photos, or electronic files.

Fiction Unusual, meaningful stories appealing to both girls and boys, ages 2-12. "Vivid, full of action. Engaging plot, strong characterization, lively language." Prefers stories in which a child protagonist solves a dilemma through his or her own resources. Seeks stories that the child ages 8-12 will eagerly read, and the child ages 2-7 will like to hear when read aloud (500-800 words). "Stories require interesting plots and a number of illustration possiblities. Also need rebuses (picture stories 125 words or under), stories with urban settings, stories for beginning readers (100-500 words), sports and humorous stories and mysteries. We also would like to see more material of 1-page length (300-400 words), both fiction and factual. War, crime, and violence are taboo." Adventure, fantasy, historical, humorous, animal, contemporary, folktales, multi-cultural, problem-solving, sports. "No war, crime or violence." Send complete ms. **Pays $100 minimum.**

▢ The online magazine carries original content not found in the print edition.

Tips "We are pleased that many authors of children's literature report that their first published work was in the pages of *Highlights*. It is not our policy to consider fiction on the strength of the reputation of the author. We judge each submission on its own merits. With factual material, however, we do prefer that writers be authorities in their field or people with first-hand experience. In this manner we can avoid the encyclopedic article that merely restates information readily available elsewhere. We don't make assignments. Query with simple letter to establish whether the nonfiction subject is likely to be of interest. A beginning writer should first become familiar with the type of material that *Highlights* publishes. Include special qualifications, if any, of author. Write for the child, not the editor. Write in a voice that children understand and relate to. Speak to today's kids, avoiding didactic, overt messages. Even though our general principles haven't changed over the years, we are contemporary in our approach to issues. Avoid worn themes."

$ $▢ HUMPTY DUMPTY'S MAGAZINE

Children's Better Health Institute, P.O. Box 567, Indianapolis IN 46206-0567. (317)636-8881. Fax: (317)684-8094. E-mail: plybarger@cbhi.org. Website: www.humptydumptymag.org. **Contact:** Phyllis Lybarger, editor. **25% freelance written.** Magazine published 8 times/year covering health, nutrition, hygiene, fitness, and safety for children ages 4-6. "Our publication is designed to entertain and to educate young readers in healthy lifestyle habits. Fiction, poetry, pencil activities should have an element of good nutrition or fitness." Estab. 1948. Circ. 350,000. Pays on publication. Publishes ms an average of 8 months after acceptance. Byline given. Buys all rights. Editorial lead time 8 months. Submit seasonal material 10 months in advance. Accepts simultaneous submissions. Sample copy for $2.95. Writer's guidelines for SASE or on website.

• All work is on speculation only; queries are not accepted nor are stories assigned.

Nonfiction "Material must have a health theme—nutrition, safety, exercise, hygiene. We're looking for articles that encourage readers to develop better health habits without preaching. Very simple factual articles that creatively teach readers about their bodies. We use several puzzles and activities in each issue—dot-to-dot, hidden pictures, and other activities that promote following instructions, developing finger dexterity, and working with numbers and letters." Include word count. **Buys 3-4 mss/year.** Send complete ms. Length: 300 words maximum. **Pays 22¢/word.**

Photos Send photos with submission. Buys all rights. Offers no additonal payment for photos accepted with ms.

Columns/Departments Mix & Fix (no-cook recipes), 100 words. All ingredients must be nutritious—low fat, no sugar, etc.—and tasty. **Buys 8 mss/year.** Send complete ms. **Payment varies.**

Fiction Phyllis Lybarger, editor. "We use some stories in rhyme and a few easy-to-read stories for the beginning reader. All stories should work well as read-alouds. Currently we need health/sports/fitness stories. We try to present our health material in a positive light, incorporating humor and a light approach wherever possible. Avoid stereotyping. Characters in contemporary stories should be realistic and reflect good, wholesome values." Include word count. Juvenile health-related material. "No inanimate talking objects, animal stories, or science fiction." **Buys 4-6 mss/year.** Send complete ms. Length: 350 words maximum. **Pays 22¢/word for stories, plus 10 contributor's copies.**

Tips "We would like to see more holiday stories, articles, and activities. Please send seasonal material at least 8 months in advance."

$ $ JACK AND JILL

Children's Better Health Institute, P.O. Box 567, Indianapolis IN 46206-0567. (317)636-8881. Fax: (317)684-8094. E-mail: cbhiseif@tcon.net. Website: www.jackandjillmag.org. **Contact:** Daniel Lee, editor. **50% freelance written.** Bimonthly Magazine published 8 times/year for children ages 7-10. "Material will not be returned unless accompanied by SASE with sufficient postage." No queries. May hold material being seriously considered for up to 1 year. Estab. 1938. Circ. 200,000. Pays on publication. Publishes ms an average of 8 months after acceptance. Byline given. Buys all rights. Submit seasonal material 8 months in advance. Responds in 10 weeks to mss. Sample copy for $2.95. Writer's guidelines online.

➤ Break in with nonfiction about ordinary kids with a news hook—something that ties in with current events, matters the kids are seeing on television and in mainstream news—i.e., space exploration, scientific advances, sports, etc.

Nonfiction "Because we want to encourage youngsters to read for pleasure and for information, we are interested in material that will challenge a young child's intelligence and be enjoyable reading. Our emphasis is on good health, and we are in particular need of articles, stories, and activities with health, safety, exercise, and nutrition themes. We try to present our health material in a positive light—incorporating humor and a light approach wherever possible without minimizing the seriousness of what we are saying. Straight factual articles are OK if they are short and interestingly written. We would rather see, however, more creative alternatives to the straight factual article. Items with a news hook will get extra attention. We'd like to see articles about interesting kids involved in out-of-the-ordinary activities. We're also interested in articles about people with unusual hobbies for our Hobby Shop department." **Buys 10-15 mss/year.** Send complete ms. Length: 500-800 words. **Pays 17¢/word minimum.**

Photos When appropriate, photos should accompany ms. Reviews sharp, contrasting b&w glossy prints. Sometimes uses color slides, transparencies, or good color prints. Buys one-time rights. Pays $15/photo.

Fiction May include, but is not limited to, realistic stories, fantasy, adventure—set in past, present, or future. "All stories need a well-developed plot, action, and incident. Humor is highly desirable. Stories that deal with a health theme need not have health as the primary subject." Adventure, historical, humorous, mystery, science fiction, sports. Wants health-related stories with a subtle lesson. **Buys 20-25 mss/year.** Send complete ms. Length: 500-800 words. **Pays 15¢/word minimum.**

Fillers Puzzles (including various kinds of word and crossword puzzles), poems, games, science projects, and creative craft projects. "We get a lot of these. To be selected, an item needs a little extra spark and originality. Instructions for activities should be clearly and simply written and accompanied by models or diagram sketches. We also have a need for recipes. Ingredients should be healthful; avoid sugar, salt, chocolate, red meat, and fats as much as possible. In all material, avoid references to eating sugary foods, such as candy, cakes, cookies, and soft drinks."

Tips "We are constantly looking for new writers who can tell good stories with interesting slants—stories that are not full of out-dated and time-worn expressions. We like to see stories about kids who are smart and capable, but not sarcastic or smug. Problem-solving skills, personal responsibility, and integrity are good topics for us. Obtain current issues of the magazine and study them to determine our present needs and editorial style."

$ $ LADYBUG

The Magazine for Young Children, Carus Publishing Co., P.O. Box 300, Peru IL 61354-0300. (815)224-5803 ext. 656. Website: www.cricketmag.com. Editor-in-Chief: Marianne Carus. **Contact:** Paula Morrow, executive editor. Monthly magazine for children ages 2-6. "We look for quality writing—quality literature, no matter the subject. For young children, ages 2-6." Estab. 1990. Circ. 134,000. Pays on publication. Byline given. For recurring features, pays flat fee and copyright becomes property of Cricket Magazine Group. Rights purchased vary. Accepts previously published material. Responds in 3 months to mss. Sample copy for $5 and 9×12 SAE. Guidelines only for #10 SASE or online. Writer's guidelines online.

➤ *Ladybug* needs imaginative activities based on concepts and interesting, appropriate nonfiction. See sample issues. Also needs articles and parent-child activities for its online parent's companion.

Nonfiction Can You Do This?, 1-2 pages; The World Around You, 2-4 pages; activities based on concepts (size, color, sequence, comparison, etc.), 1-2 pages. "Most *Ladybug* nonfiction is in the form of illustration. We'd like more simple science, how things work, and behind the scenes on a preschool level." **Buys 35 mss/year.** Send complete ms; no queries. Length: 250-300 words. **Pays 25¢/word.**

Fiction "Looking for age-appropriate read-aloud stories for preschoolers." **Buys 30 mss/year.** Send complete ms. Length: 800 words maximum. **Pays 25¢/word (less for reprints).**

Poetry Light verse, traditional, humorous. **Buys 40 poems/year.** Submit maximum 5 poems. Length: 20 lines maximum. **Pays $3/line, with $25 minimum.**

Fillers "We welcome interactive activities: rebuses, up to 100 words; original fingerplays and action rhymes (up to 8 lines)." **Buys 10/year.** Length: 100 words maximum. **Pays 25¢/word.**

Tips "Reread manuscript before sending in. Keep within specified word limits. Study back issues before submitting to learn about the types of material we're looking for. Writing style is paramount. We look for rich, evocative language and a sense of joy or wonder. Remember that you're writing for preschoolers—be age-appropriate but not condescending. A story must hold enjoyment for both parent and child through repeated read-aloud sessions. Remember that people come in all colors, sizes, physical conditions, and have special needs. Be inclusive!"

$MY FRIEND

The Catholic Magazine for Kids, Pauline Books & Media/Daughters of St. Paul, 50 Saint Pauls Ave., Jamaica Plain, Boston MA 02130-3491. (617)522-8911. Fax: (617)541-9805. E-mail: myfriend@paulinemedia.org. Website: www.myfriendmagazine.org. Editor-in-Chief: Sister Donna William Giaimo. **Contact:** Sister Maria Grace Dateno, editor. **25% freelance written.** Magazine published 10 times/year for children ages 7-12. "*My Friend* is a 32-page monthly Catholic magazine for boys and girls. Its goal is to communicate religious truths and positive values in an enjoyable and attractive way." Theme list available. Send a SASE to the above address, or see website (click on "For Contributors"). Estab. 1979. Circ. 8,000. **Pays on acceptance.** Publishes ms an average of 6 months after acceptance. Buys worldwide publication rights. Responds in 2 months to mss. Sample copy for $2 and 9×12 SASE ($1.29). Writer's guidelines and theme list for #10 SASE.

Fiction "We are looking for stories that immediately grab the imagination of the reader. Good dialogue, realistic character development, and current lingo are necessary. A child protagonist must resolve a dilemma through his or her own resources. Not all the stories of each issue have to be directly related to the theme. We continue to need stories that are simply fun and humorous." Religious, sports. Send complete ms. Length: 600-1,200 words. **Pays $75-150.**

Tips "For fiction, please send manuscripts. Do not query. If you are not sure whether a story would be appropriate for *My Friend*, please request our complete guidelines, theme list, and a sample issue (see above). For nonfiction articles, you may query by e-mail, but most are written by staff and contributing authors."

N $ $ $ $NATIONAL GEOGRAPHIC KIDS

Dare to Explore, National Geographic Society, 1145 17th St. NW, Washington DC 20036. Website: www.national geographic.com/ngkids. Editor: Melina Gerosa Bellows. **Contact:** Julie Vasburgh Agnone, executive editor. **70% freelance written.** Magazine published 10 times/year. "It's our mission to excite kids about their world. We are the children's magazine that makes learning fun." Estab. 1975. **Pays on acceptance.** Publishes ms an average of 6 months after acceptance. Byline given. $100. Buys all rights, makes work-for-hire assignments. Editorial lead time 6+ months. Submit seasonal material 6+ months in advance. Accepts queries by mail. Accepts simultaneous submissions. Sample copy for #10 SAE. Writer's guidelines free.

Nonfiction General interest, how-to, humor, interview/profile, photo feature, technical, travel, animals, human interest, science, technology, entertainment, archaeology, pets. Special issues: "We do not release our editorial calendar. We do not want poetry, sports, fiction, or story ideas that are too young—our audience is between ages 8-14." Query with published clips. Length: 100-1,000 words. **Pays $1/word for assigned articles.** Pays expenses of writers on assignment.

Photos Jay Sumner, photo director. State availability with submission. Reviews contact sheets, negatives, transparencies, prints. Negotiates payment individually. Captions, identification of subjects, model releases required.

Columns/Departments Amazing Animals (animal heroes, stories about animal survivors, interesting/funny animal tales), 100 words; Kids Did It! (stories about kids who have survived or overcome obstacles), 100 words; World News (fun, kid-friendly news items), 50-70 words. Query with published clips. **Pays $1/word.**

Tips Submit relevant clips. Writers must have demonstrated experience writing for kids. Read the magazine before submitting. Send query and clips via snail mail—materials will not be returned. No SASE required unless sample copy is requested.

$ $NEW MOON

The Magazine for Girls & Their Dreams, New Moon Publishing, Inc., 34 E. Superior St., #200, Duluth MN 55802. (218)728-5507. Fax: (218)728-0314. E-mail: girl@newmoon.org. Website: www.newmoon.org. **Contact:** Editorial Department. **25% freelance written.** Bimonthly magazine covering girls ages 8-14, edited by girls aged 8-14. "In general, all material should be pro-girl and feature girls and women as the primary focus. *New Moon* is for every girl who wants her voice heard and her dreams taken seriously. *New Moon* celebrates girls, explores the passage from girl to woman, and builds healthy resistance to gender inequities. The *New Moon* girl is true to herself and *New Moon* helps her as she pursues her unique path in life, moving confidently into the world." Estab. 1992. Circ. 30,000. Pays on publication. Publishes ms an average of 6 months after acceptance. Byline given. Buys all rights. Editorial lead time 6 months. Submit seasonal material 8 months in advance. Accepts queries by mail, e-mail, fax. Accepts simultaneous submissions. Responds in 2 months to mss. Sample copy for $6.75 or online. Writer's guidelines for SASE or online.

⊶ Adult writers can break in with "Herstory articles about less well-known women from all over the world, especially if it relates to one of our themes. Same with Women's Work articles. Girls can break in with essays and articles (nonfiction) that relate to a theme."

Nonfiction Essays, general interest, humor, inspirational, interview/profile, opinion, personal experience (written by girls), photo feature, religious, travel, multicultural/girls from other countries. No fashion, beauty, or dating. **Buys 20 mss/year.** Query with or without published clips or send complete ms. Length: 600 words. **Pays 6-12¢/word.**

Photos State availability with submission. Buys one-time rights. Negotiates payment individually. Captions, identification of subjects required.

Columns/Departments Women's Work (profile of a woman and her job relating the the theme), 600 words; Herstory (historical woman relating to theme), 600 words. **Buys 10 mss/year.** Query. **Pays 6-12¢/word.**

Fiction Prefers girl-written material. All girl-centered. Adventure, fantasy, historical, humorous, slice-of-life vignettes. **Buys 6 mss/year.** Send complete ms. Length: 900-1,200 words. **Pays 6-12¢/word.**

Poetry No poetry by adults.

Tips "We'd like to see more girl-written feature articles that relate to a theme. These can be about anything the girl has done personally, or she can write about something she's studied. Please read *New Moon* before submitting to get a sense of our style. Writers and artists who comprehend our goals have the best chance of publication. We love creative articles—both nonfiction and fiction—that are not condescending to our readers. Keep articles to suggested word lengths; avoid stereotypes. Refer to our guidelines and upcoming themes."

$ ON THE LINE

Mennonite Publishing House, 616 Walnut Ave., Scottdale PA 15683-1999. (724)887-8500. Fax: (724)887-3111. E-mail: ofl@mph.org. Website: www.mph.org. **Contact:** Mary Clemens Meyer, editor. **90% freelance written.** Works with a small number of new/unpublished writers each year. Monthly Christian magazine for children ages 9-14. "*On the Line* helps upper elementary and junior high children understand and appreciate God, the created world, themselves, and others." Estab. 1908. Circ. 5,500. **Pays on acceptance.** Publishes ms an average of 1 year after acceptance. Byline given. Buys one-time rights. Submit seasonal material 6 months in advance. Accepts queries by e-mail. Accepts previously published material. Accepts simultaneous submissions. Responds in 1 month to mss. Sample copy for 9×12 SAE, 2 first-class stamps and $2. Writer's guidelines for 9×12 SAE and 2 first-class stamps.

Nonfiction How-to (things to make with easy-to-get materials including food recipes), informational (300-500 word articles on wonders of nature, people who have made outstanding contributions). **Buys 95 mss/year.** Send complete ms. **Pays $15-35.**

Reprints Send ms with rights for sale noted and information about when and where the material previously appeared. Pays 75% of amount paid for an original article.

Fiction Mary Clemens Meyer. Adventure, humorous, religious, everyday problems. No fantasy or fictionalized Bible stories. Wants more mystery and humorous. **Buys 50 mss/year.** Send complete ms. Length: 1,000-1,800 words. **Pays 3-5¢/word.**

Poetry Light verse, religious. Length: 3-12 lines. **Pays $10-25.**

Fillers Appropriate puzzles, cartoons, and quizzes.

Tips "Study the publication first. We need short, well-written how-to and craft articles; also more puzzles. Don't send query; we prefer to see the complete manuscript."

$ $ POCKETS

The Upper Room, 1908 Grand Ave., P.O. Box 340004, Nashville TN 37203-0004. (615)340-7333. Fax: (615)340-7267. E-mail: pockets@upperroom.org. Website: www.pockets.org; www.upperroom.org/pockets. **Contact:** Cary Graham, editorial assistant. **60% freelance written.** Monthly (except February) magazine covering children's and families' spiritual formation. "We are a Christian, inter-denominational publication for children 6-11 years of age. Each issue reflects a specific theme available online." Estab. 1981. Circ. 96,000. **Pays on acceptance.** Publishes ms an average of 1 year to 18 months after acceptance. Byline given. Buys first North American serial rights. Submit seasonal material 1 year in advance. Accepts previously published material. Responds in 6 weeks to mss. Each issue reflects a specific theme. Sample copy, writers' guidelines, and themes available with a 9×12 SASE.

● *Pockets* publishes fiction and poetry, as well as short-short stories (no more than 600 words) for children 5-7. Eager to work with new/unpublished writers.

Nonfiction Each issue reflects a specific theme. Articles should be related to the theme for a particular issue. Seek biographical sketches of persons, famous or unknown, whose lives reflect their Christian commitment. Write in a way that appeals to children. We welcome retold scripture stories that remain true to the Bible and are related to the theme. Interview/profile, personal experience, religious (retold scripture stories). No violence, science fiction, romance, fantasy, or talking animal stories. **Buys 10 mss/year.** Length: 400-1,000 words. **Pays 14¢/word.**

Reprints Accepts one-time previously published submissions. Send typed ms with rights for sale noted and information about when and where the material previously appeared.

Photos Photos accepted when accompanied with ms. Send photos with submission. Reviews contact sheets, transparencies, prints. Buys one-time rights. Pays $25/photo.

Columns/Departments Poetry and Prayer (related to themes), maximum 24 lines; Pocketsful of Love (family communications activities), 300 words; Peacemakers at Work (profiles of children working for peace, justice, and ecological concerns), 300-800 words. **Pays 14¢/word.** Activities/Games (related to themes). **Pays $25 and up**. Kids Cook (simple recipes children can make alone or with minimal help from an adult). **Pays $25. Buys 20 mss/year.**

Fiction "Submissions do not need to be overtly religious. They should reflect daily living, lifestyle, and problem-solving based on living as faithful disciples. They should help children experience the Christian life that is not always a neatly wrapped moral package but is open to the continuing revelation of God's will for their lives." Adventure, ethnic, historical, religious, slice-of-life vignettes. No violence, science fiction, romance, fantasy, or talking animal stories. **Buys 25-30 mss/year.** Send complete ms. Length: 600-1,400 words. **Pays 14¢/word, plus 2-5 contributor's copies.**

Poetry Buys 22 poems/year. Length: 4-24 lines. **Pays $2/line, $25 minimum.**

▢ The online magazine carries original content not found in the print edition and includes writers' guidelines, themes, and annual fiction-writing contest guidelines. Contact: Cary Graham, editorial assistant.

Tips "Theme stories, role models, and retold scripture stories are most open to freelancers. Poetry is also open. It is very helpful if writers read our writers' guidelines and themes on our website."

$ SHINE BRIGHTLY

GEMS Girls' Clubs, P.O. Box 7259, Grand Rapids MI 49510. (616)241-5616. Fax: (616)241-5558. E-mail: sara@gemsgc.org. Website: www.gospelcom.net/gems. Editor: Jan Boone. **Contact:** Sara Lynne Hilton, managing editor. **80% freelance written.** Works with new and published/established writers. Monthly magazine. "Our purpose is to lead girls into a living relationship with Jesus Christ and to help them see how God is at work in their lives and the world around them. Puzzles, crafts, stories, and articles for girls ages 9-14." Estab. 1971. Circ. 13,000. Pays on publication. Publishes ms an average of 1 year after acceptance. Byline given. Buys first North American serial, second serial (reprint), simultaneous rights. Submit seasonal material 1 year in advance. Accepts previously published material. Accepts simultaneous submissions. Responds in 2 months to queries. Sample copy for 9×12 SAE with 3 first class stamps and $1. Writer's guidelines online.

Nonfiction "We do not want easy solutions or quick character changes from good to bad. No pietistic characters. No 'new girl at school starting over after parents' divorce' stories. Constant mention of God is not necessary if the moral tone of the story is positive. We do not want stories that always have a happy ending." Needs include: biographies and autobiographies of "heroes of the faith," informational (write for issues themes), multicultural materials. Humor (need much more), inspirational, interview/profile, personal experience (avoid the testimony approach), photo feature (query first), religious, travel. **Buys 35 unsolicited mss/year.** Send complete ms. Length: 100-400 words. **Pays 3¢/word, plus 2 copies.**

Reprints Send ms with rights for sale noted and information about when and where the material previously appeared.

Photos Purchased with or without ms. Appreciate multicultural subjects. Reviews 5×7 or 8×10 clear color glossy prints. Pays $25-50 on publication.

Columns/Departments How-to (crafts); puzzles and jokes; quizzes. Length: 200-400 words. Send complete ms. **Pay varies.**

Fiction Adventure, ethnic, historical, humorous, mystery, religious, romance, slice-of-life vignettes, suspense. **Buys 20 mss/year.** Send complete ms. Length: 400-900 words. **Pays up to $35.**

Poetry Free verse, haiku, light verse, traditional. **Pays $5-15.**

Tips "Prefers not to see anything on the adult level, secular material, or violence. Writers frequently oversimplify the articles and often write with a Pollyanna attitude. An author should be able to see his/her writing style as exciting and appealing to girls ages 9-14. The style can be fun, but also teach a truth. Subjects should be current and important to *SHINE brightly* readers. Use our theme update as a guide. We would like to receive material with a multicultural slant."

$ $ SPIDER

The Magazine for Children, Cricket Magazine Group, P.O. Box 300, Peru IL 61354. (815)224-5803. Fax: (815)224-6615. Website: www.cricketmag.com. Editor: Heather Delabre. **Contact:** Submissions Editor. **85% freelance written.** Monthly magazine covering literary, general interest. "*Spider* introduces 6- to 9-year-old children to the highest quality stories, poems, illustrations, articles, and activities. It was created to foster in beginning readers a love of reading and discovery that will last a lifetime. We're looking for writers who respect children's intelligence." Estab. 1994. Circ. 70,000. Pays on publication. Publishes ms an average of 2-3 years after acceptance. Byline given. Rights vary. Editorial lead time 9 months. Accepts previously published material. Accepts simultaneous submissions. Responds in 4 months to mss. Sample copy for $5. Writer's guidelines for #10 SASE or on website.

Nonfiction A bibliography is required with all nonfiction submissions. Nature, animals, science & technology, environment, foreign culture, history. Send complete ms. Length: 300-800 words. **Pays 25¢/word.**

Reprints Send photocopy with rights for sale noted and information about when and where the material previously appeared.

Photos Send photos with submission. Reviews contact sheets, 35mm to 4×4 transparencies, 8×10 prints. Buys one-time rights. Offers $35-50/photo. Captions, identification of subjects, model releases required.

Fiction Adventure, ethnic, fantasy, historical, humorous, mystery, science fiction, suspense, realistic fiction, folk tales, fairy tales. No romance, horror, religious. Send complete ms. Length: 300-1,000 words. **Pays 25¢/word and 2 contributor's copies; additional copies $2.**

Poetry Free verse, traditional, nonsense, humorous, serious. No forced rhymes, didactic. Submit maximum 5 poems. Length: 20 lines maximum. **Pays $3/line maximum.**

Fillers Puzzles, crafts, recipes, mazes, games, brainteasers, engaging math and word activities. **Pays various amounts depending on type of filler.**

Tips "We'd like to see more of the following: engaging nonfiction, fillers, and 'takeout page' activities; folktales, fairy tales, science fiction, and humorous stories. Most importantly, do not write down to children."

$ STONE SOUP

The Magazine by Young Writers and Artists, Children's Art Foundation, P.O. Box 83, Santa Cruz CA 95063-0083. (831)426-5557. Fax: (831)426-1161. E-mail: editor@stonesoup.com. Website: www.stonesoup.com. **Contact:** Ms. Gerry Mandel, editor. **100% freelance written.** Bimonthly magazine of writing and art by children, including fiction, poetry, book reviews, and art by children through age 13. Audience is children, teachers, parents, writers, artists. "We have a preference for writing and art based on real-life experiences; no formula stories or poems." Estab. 1973. Circ. 20,000. Pays on publication. Publishes ms an average of 4 months after acceptance. Buys all rights. Submit seasonal material 6 months in advance. Sample copy for $5 or online. Writer's guidelines online.

> ○╼ Don't send queries, just submissions. No e-mail submissions. "Please do not enclose a SASE. We only respond to work we want to publish. If you do not hear from us within 6 weeks, it means we could not use your work."

Nonfiction Historical/nostalgic, personal experience, book reviews. **Buys 12 mss/year. Pays $40.**

Fiction Adventure, ethnic, experimental, fantasy, historical, humorous, mystery, science fiction, slice-of-life vignettes, suspense. "We do not like assignments or formula stories of any kind." **Buys 60 mss/year.** Send complete ms. Length: 150-2,500 words. **Pays $40 for stories. Authors also receive 2 copies, a certificate, and discounts on additional copies and on subscriptions.**

Poetry Avant-garde, free verse. **Buys 12 poems/year. Pays $40/poem.**

> ▣ The online magazine carries original content not found in the print edition and includes writer's guidelines. Contact: Ms. Gerry Mandel, online editor.

Tips "All writing we publish is by people ages 13 and under. We do not publish any writing by adults. We can't emphasize enough how important it is to read a couple of issues of the magazine. We have a strong preference for writing on subjects that mean a lot to the author. If you feel strongly about something that happened to you or something you observed, use that feeling as the basis for your story or poem. Stories should have good descriptions, realistic dialogue, and a point to make. In a poem, each word must be chosen carefully. Your poem should present a view of your subject, and a way of using words that are special and all your own."

Ⓝ $ STORY FRIENDS

Mennonite Publishing Network, 616 Walnut Ave., Scottdale PA 15683. (724)887-8500. Fax: (724)887-3111. E-mail: storyfriends@mph.org. Website: www.mph.org. **Contact:** Susan R. Swan, editor. **80% freelance written.** Monthly magazine. "*Story Friends* is planned to nurture faith development in 4-9 year olds." Estab. 1905. Circ. 7,000. **Pays on acceptance.** Publishes ms an average of 1 year after acceptance. Byline given. Buys one-time, second serial (reprint) rights. Submit seasonal material 6 months in advance. Accepts simultaneous submissions. Responds in 2 months to queries. Sample copy for $2 plus 9×12 SAE and 2 first-class stamps. Writer's guidelines for #10 SASE.

Nonfiction How-to (craft ideas for young children), photo feature. **Buys 20 mss/year.** Length: 300-500 words. **Pays 3-5¢/word.**

Reprints Send photocopy with rights for sale noted and information about when and where the material previously appeared. Pays 100% of amount paid for an original article.

Fiction Susan Reith, editor. Stories of everyday experiences at home, in church, in school or at a play, which provide models of Christian values. "Wants to see more fiction set in African-American, Latino, or Hispanic settings. No stories about children and their grandparents or children and their elderly neighbors. I have more than enough." **Buys 50 mss/year.** Send complete ms. Length: 300-800 words. **Pays 3-5¢/word.**

Poetry Traditional. **Buys 20 poems/year.** Length: 4-16 lines. **Pays $10/poem.**

Tips "Send stories that children from a variety of ethnic backgrounds can relate to; stories that deal with experiences similar to all children. Send stories with a humorous twist. We're also looking for well-planned puzzles that challenge and promote reading readiness."

$ $ TURTLE MAGAZINE FOR PRESCHOOL KIDS

Children's Better Health Institute, P.O. Box 567, Indianapolis IN 46206-0567. Website: www.turtlemag.org. Bimonthly magazine. General interest, interactive magazine with the purpose of helping preschoolers develop healthy minds and bodies. Magazine of picture stories and articles for preschool children 2-5 years old. Estab. 1978. Circ. 300,000. Pays on publication. Byline given. Buys all rights. Submit seasonal material 8 months in advance. Responds in 3 months to queries. Sample copy for $1.75. Writer's guidelines for #10 SASE.

• May hold mss for up to 1 year before acceptance/publication.

Nonfiction "We use very simple science experiments. These should be pretested. We also publish simple, healthful recipes." Length: 100-300 words. **Pays up to 22¢/word.**

Fiction "Not buying much fiction right now except for rebus stories. All material should have a health or fitness slant. We no longer buy stories about 'generic' turtles because we now have PokeyToes, our own trade-marked turtle character. All should 'move along' and lend themselves well to illustration. Writing should be energetic, enthusiastic, and creative—like preschoolers themselves." No queries. Send complete ms. Length: 150-300 words. **Pays up to 22¢/word, plus 10 contributor's copies.**

Poetry "We use short verse on our inside front cover and back cover."

Tips "We are looking for more short rebus stories, easy science experiments, and simple, nonfiction health articles. We are trying to include more material for our youngest readers. Material must be entertaining and written from a healthy lifestyle perspective."

N $ $ U.S. KIDS

A Weekly Reader Magazine, Children's Better Health Institute, P.O. Box 567, Indianapolis IN 46206-0567. (317)636-8881. Fax: (317)684-8094. E-mail: cbhiseif@tcon.net. Website: www.cbhi.org/magazines/uskids/index.shtml. **Contact:** Daniel Lee, editor. **50% freelance written.** Magazine published 8 times/year featuring "kids doing extraordinary things, especially activities related to health, sports, the arts, interesting hobbies, the environment, computers, etc." Estab. 1987. Circ. 230,000. Pays on publication. Publishes ms an average of 4 months after acceptance. Byline given. Buys all rights. Editorial lead time 6 months. Submit seasonal material 6 months in advance. Responds in 4 months to mss. Sample copy for $2.95 or online. Writer's guidelines for #10 SASE.

• U.S. Kids is being retargeted to a younger audience.

Nonfiction Especially interested in articles with a health/fitness angle. General interest, how-to, interview/profile, science, kids using computers, multicultural. **Buys 16-24 mss/year.** Send complete ms. Length: 400 words maximum. **Pays up to 25¢/word.**

Photos State availability with submission. Reviews contact sheets, negatives, transparencies, color photocopies, or prints. Buys one-time rights. Negotiates payment individually. Captions, identification of subjects, model releases required.

Columns/Departments Real Kids (kids doing interesting things); Fit Kids (sports, healthy activities); Computer Zone. Length: 300-400 words. Send complete ms. **Pays up to 25¢/word.**

Fiction Buys very little fictional material. **Buys 1-2 mss/year.** Send complete ms. Length: 400 words. **Pays up to 25¢/word.**

Poetry Light verse, traditional, kid's humorous, health/fitness angle. **Buys 6-8 poems/year.** Submit maximum 6 poems. Length: 8-24 lines. **Pays $25-50.**

Fillers Facts, newsbreaks, short humor, puzzles, games, activities. Length: 200-500 words. **Pays 25¢/word.**

Tips "We are retargeting the magazine for first-, second-, and third-graders, and looking for fun and informative articles on activities and hobbies of interest to younger kids. Special emphasis on fitness, sports, and health. Availability of good photos a plus."

LITERARY & "LITTLE"

$ THE ABSINTHE LITERARY REVIEW

P.O. Box 328, Spring Green WI 53588. Website: www.absinthe-literary-review.com. **Contact:** Charles Allen Wyman, editor. "ALR publishes short stories, novel excerpts, poems and literary essays. Our target audience is the literate individual who enjoys creative language use, character-driven fiction and the clashing of worlds—real and surreal, poetic and prosaic, sacred and transgressive." Accepts queries by mail, e-mail. Sample copy not available.

Fiction "Transgressive works dealing with sex, death, disease, madness, and the like; the clash of archaic with modern-day; archetype, symbolism; surrealism, philosophy, physics; existential and post-modern flavoring;

experimental or flagrantly textured (but not sloppy or casual) fiction; intense crafting of language from the writer's writer. See website for information on the Absinthe Editors' Prize. Anathemas: mainstream storytellers, 'Oprah' fiction, high school or beginner fiction, poetry or fiction that contains no capital letters or punctuation, 'hot' trends, genre prose or poetry, first, second or third drafts, pieces that exceed our stated word count (5,000 max.) by thousands of words, writers who do not read and follow our onsite guidelines." **Pays $2-10. Poetry Pays $1-10.**

$ AFRICAN AMERICAN REVIEW

Saint Louis University, Humanities 317, 3800 Lindell Blvd., St. Louis MO 63108. (314)977-3703. Fax: (314)977-1514. E-mail: keenanam@slu.edu. Website: aar.slu.edu. Editor: Jocelyn Moody. **Contact:** Aileen Keenan, managing editor. **65% freelance written.** Quarterly magazine covering African-American literature and culture. "Essays on African-American literature, theater, film, art and culture generally; interviews; poetry and fiction by African-American authors; book reviews." Estab. 1967. Circ. 2,067. Pays on publication. Publishes ms an average of 1-2 years after acceptance. Byline given. Buys first North American serial rights. Editorial lead time 1 year. Responds in 1 month to queries; 6 months to mss. Sample copy for $12. Writer's guidelines online.

Nonfiction Essays, interview/profile. **Buys 30 mss/year.** Query. Length: 3,500-6,000 words. **Pays $50-150.** Pays in contributors copies upon request.

Photos State availability with submission. Pays $100 for covers. Captions required.

Fiction Joe Weixlmann, editor. Ethnic, experimental, mainstream. "No children's/juvenile/young adult/teen." **Buys 5 mss/year.** Length: 2,500-5,000 words. **Pays $25-100, 3 contributor's copies and 10 offprints.**

$ AGNI

Creative Writing Program, Boston University, 236 Bay State Rd., Boston MA 02215. (617)353-7135. Fax: (617)353-7134. E-mail: agni@bu.edu. Website: www.agnimagazine.org. **Contact:** Sven Birkerts, editor. Biannual magazine. "Eclectic literary magazine publishing first-rate poems, essays, translations, and stories." Estab. 1972. Circ. 4,000. Pays on publication. Publishes ms an average of 6 months after acceptance. Byline given. Buys first North American serial rights. Rights to reprint in *AGNI* anthology (with author's consent). Editorial lead time 1 year. Accepts queries by mail. Accepts simultaneous submissions. Responds in 2 weeks to queries; 4 months to mss. Sample copy for $10 or online. Writer's guidelines online.

● Reading period September 1-May 31 only.

Fiction Stories, prose poems. "No science fiction or romance." **Buys 6-12 mss/year. Pays $10/page up to $150, 2 contributor's copies, 1-year subscription, and 4 gift copies.**

Poetry Buys more than 60 poems/year. Submit maximum 5 poems. **Pays $20-150.**

🖥 The online magazine carries original content not found in the print edition. Contact: Sven Birkerts, editor.

Tips "We're looking for extraordinary translations from little-translated languages. It is important to look at a copy of *AGNI* before submitting, to see if your work might be compatible. Please write for guidelines or a sample."

N $ 🖵 THE AMBASSADOR

Canada Cuba Literary Journal, Canada Cuba Literary Alliance, 109 Bayshore Rd., RR #4, Brighton ON K0K 1H0 Canada. E-mail: info@canadacubaliteraryalliance.org. Website: www.canadacubaliteraryalliance.org. **Contact:** Manuel Leon, editor-in-chief (written submissions); Richard Grove, managing editor (visual submissions). **80% freelance written.** Quarterly magazine covering poetry, prose, art, photography, reviews, articles. "The goal of the Canada Cuba Literary Alliance is to advance literary solidarity between Canada and Cuba through the creative expression of poetry, prose, and photography." Estab. 2004. Circ. 500. Pays on publication. Byline given. Buys one-time rights. Editorial lead time 6-9 months. Submit seasonal material 6 months in advance. Accepts queries by e-mail. Accepts previously published material. Accepts simultaneous submissions. Sample copy and writer's guidelines online.

Nonfiction Anything Cuba, Canada, literary, or art related. **Buys 10 mss/year.** Query. **Pays $5-100, plus 1 contributor copy.**

Fiction Anything nonpolitical that's related to Canada or Cuba. Does not want political fiction **Buys 2-6 mss/ year.** Query. **Pays $5-100, plus 1 contributor copy.**

Poetry All types of poetry accepted, except political. No line limit. **Buys 25-100 poems/year.** Submit maximum 5 poems.

N $ AMERICAN BOOK REVIEW

The Writer's Review, Inc., Campus Box 4241, Illinois State University, Normal IL 61790-4241. (309)438-2127. Fax: (309)438-3523. E-mail: lasavag@ilstu.edu. Website: www.litline.org/abr. Editor/Publisher: Charles B. Harris. **Contact:** Lisa Savage, managing editor. Bimonthly magazine covering book reviews. "We specialize in reviewing books published by independent presses." Estab. 1977. Circ. 15,000. Pays on publication. Publishes ms an average of 2-4 months after acceptance. Byline given. Offers $50 kill fee. Buys one-time rights. Editorial lead time 1 month. Accepts queries by mail, e-mail, fax, phone. Responds in 2 weeks to queries; 1-2 months to mss. Sample copy for $4. Writer's guidelines online.

Nonfiction Book reviews. Does not want fiction, poetry, or interviews. Query with published clips. Length: 750-1,250 words. **Pays $50.**

Tips "Most of our reviews are assigned, but we occasionally accept unsolicited reviews. Send query and samples of published reviews."

$THE AMERICAN DISSIDENT

ContraOstrich Press, 1837 Main St., Concord MA 01742. E-mail: enmarge@aol.com. Website: www.geocities. com/enmarge. **Contact:** G. Tod Slone, editor. **100% freelance written.** Semiannual magazine "offering hardcore criticism of all American icons and institutions in English, French, or Spanish. Writers must be free of dogma, clear in mind, critical in outlook, and courageous in behavior." Estab. 1998. Circ. 200. Pays on publication. Publishes ms an average of 9 months after acceptance. Byline given. Buys first North American serial, one-time rights. Editorial lead time 6 months. Accepts queries by mail. Responds in 3 weeks to queries; 2 months to mss. Sample copy for $8. Writer's guidelines online.

Nonfiction Essays, interview/profile, opinion, personal experience. **Buys 2-4 mss/year.** Query. Length: 250-750 words. **Pays $5 for assigned articles.** Pays in contributor's copies for poetry submissions and book reviews.

Photos State availability with submission. Reviews prints. Buys one-time rights. Negotiates payment individually. Identification of subjects required.

Poetry Free verse. Poetry with a message, not poetry for the sake of poetry. Submit maximum 3-5 poems.

Tips "*The American Dissident* is subversive and samizdat in nature, providing a forum for the examining the dark side of the academic/literary industrial complex, questioning, challenging, and angering (if need be) of entrenched professors, poets, writers, editors, actors, workshop leaders, MFA program directors, town mothers and fathers, and whoever else has sold out to the machine. It fights, satirizes, and exposes, wielding logic and reason against celebrity, diversion, groupthink, herd mentality, and conformity. Writing should be on the edge with a dash of personal risk and stemming from personal experience, conflict with power and/or involvement. Submissions should be iconoclastic and parrhesiastic in nature."

$ANCIENT PATHS

Christian Literary Magazine, P.O. Box 7505, Fairfax Station VA 22039. E-mail: ssburris@msn.com. Website: www.editorskylar.com. **Contact:** Skylar Hamilton Burris, editor. **99% freelance written.** Annual magazine with subtle Christian and universal religious themes. "*Ancient Paths* publishes quality fiction and creative nonfiction for a literate Christian audience. Religious themes are usually subtle, and the magazine has non-Christian readers as well as some content by non-Christian authors. However, writers should be comfortable appearing in a Christian magazine." Estab. 1998. Circ. 175-200. Pays on publication. Publishes ms an average of 2 months after acceptance. Byline given. Not copyrighted. Buys one-time rights. Submit seasonal material 3 months in advance. Accepts queries by mail, e-mail. Accepts previously published material. Accepts simultaneous submissions. Responds in 1 week to queries; 4-5 weeks to mss. Sample copy for $5; make checks payable to Skylar Burris. Writer's guidelines online. Editorial calendar online.

Nonfiction Book excerpts, historical/nostalgic, religious, Book reviews of poetry chapbooks. No devotions, sermons, or lessons. **Buys 1-10 mss/year.** Send complete ms. Length: 250-2,500 words. **Pays $2, 1 copy, and discount on additional copies.**

Fiction Fantasy, historical, humorous, mainstream, mystery, novel excerpts, religious, science fiction, slice-of-life vignettes, western. No retelling of Bible stories. Literary fiction favored over genre fiction. **Buys 4-10 mss/year.** Send complete ms. Length: 250-2,500 words. **Pays $2, 1 copy, and discount on additional copies.**

Poetry Free verse, traditional. No avant-garde, prose poetry, or poor meter. **Buys 25-60 poems/year.** Submit maximum 5 poems. Length: 4-60 lines. **Pays $1/poem, 1 copy, and discount on additional copies.**

Tips "Make the reader think as well as feel. Do not simply state a moral message; no preaching, nothing didactic. You should have something meaningful to say, but be subtle. Show, don't tell."

$ANTIETAM REVIEW

Washington County Arts Council, 41 S. Potomac St., Hagerstown MD 21740-5512. (301)791-3132. Fax: (240)420-1754. E-mail: antietamreview@washingtoncountyarts.com (queries only). Website: www.washingtoncountyarts.com. **Contact:** Mary Jo Vincent, managing editor. **90% freelance written.** Annual magazine covering fiction, poetry, and b&w photography. Estab. 1982. Circ. 1,000. Buys first North American serial rights. Sample copy for $6.30 (back issue); $8.40 (current issue).

Photos Seeks b&w photos. All subject matter is considered. Contact via mail or e-mail for photo guidelines.

Fiction Condensed novels, ethnic, experimental, novel excerpts, short stories of a literary quality. No religious, romance, erotica, confession, or horror. Length: Maximum 5,000 words. **Pays $50-100 and 2 contributor's copies.**

Poetry Avant-garde, free verse, traditional. No haiku, religious or rhyme. Submit maximum 3 poems. Length: 30 lines maximum. **Pays $25/poem and 2 contributor copies.**

Tips "We seek high-quality, well-crafted work with significant character development and shift. We look for work that is interesting, involves the reader, and teaches us a new way to view the world. A manuscript stands out because of its energy and flow. Most of our submissions reflect the times (news/current events) more than industry trends. Works should have a compelling voice, originality, and magic. Contributors are encouraged to review past issues."

$ ⬚ THE ANTIGONISH REVIEW

St. Francis Xavier University, P.O. Box 5000, Antigonish NS B2G 2W5 Canada. (902)867-3962. Fax: (902)867-5563. E-mail: tar@stfx.ca. Website: www.antigonishreview.com. Managing Editor: Josephine Mensch. **Contact:** Jeanette Lynes, co-editor. **100% freelance written.** Quarterly magazine. Literary magazine for educated and creative readers. Estab. 1970. Circ. 850. Pays on publication. Publishes ms an average of 8 months after acceptance. Byline given. Offers variable kill fee. Rights retained by author. Editorial lead time 4 months. Submit seasonal material 4 months in advance. Accepts queries by mail, fax. Responds in 1 month to queries; 6 months to mss. Sample copy for $7 or online. Writer's guidelines for #10 SASE or online.

Nonfiction Essays, interview/profile, book reviews/articles. No academic pieces. **Buys 15-20 mss/year.** Query. Length: 1,500-5,000 words. **Pays $50-150.**

Fiction Literary. Contemporary, prose poem. No erotica. **Buys 35-40 mss/year.** Send complete ms. Length: 500-5,000 words. **Pays $50 for stories.**

Poetry Buys 100-125 poems/year. Submit maximum 5 poems. **Pays in copies.**

Tips "Send for guidelines and/or sample copy. Send ms with cover letter and SASE with submission."

$ ANTIOCH REVIEW

P.O. Box 148, Yellow Springs OH 45387-0148. Website: www.review.antioch.edu. **Contact:** Robert S. Fogarty, editor. Quarterly magazine for general, literary, and academic audience. "Literary and cultural review of contemporary issues, and literature for general readership." Estab. 1941. Circ. 5,100. Pays on publication. Publishes ms an average of 10 months after acceptance. Byline given. Buys first, one-time rights. Accepts queries by mail. Responds in 3 months to mss. Sample copy for $7. Writer's guidelines online.

Nonfiction "Contemporary articles in the humanities and social sciences, politics, economics, literature, and all areas of broad intellectual concern. Somewhat scholarly, but never pedantic in style, eschewing all professional jargon. Lively, distinctive prose insisted upon. We do not read simultaneous submissions." Length: 2,000-8,000 words. **Pays $10/printed page.**

Fiction Fiction editor. "Quality fiction only, distinctive in style with fresh insights into the human condition." Experimental, contemporary. No science fiction, fantasy, or confessions. Length: generally under 8,000. **Pays $10/printed page.**

Poetry "No light or inspirational verse."

$ ⬚ ARC

Canada's National Poetry Magazine, Arc Poetry Society, P.O. Box 81060, Ottawa ON K1P 1A0 Canada. E-mail: reviews@arcpoetry.ca. Website: www.arcpoetry.ca. **Contact:** Anita Lahey, managing editor. Semiannual magazine featuring poetry, poetry-related articles, and criticism. "Our focus is poetry, and Canadian poetry in general, although we do publish writers from elsewhere. We are looking for the best poetry from new and established writers. We often have special issues. Send a SASE for upcoming special issues and contests." Estab. 1978. Circ. 1,500. Pays on publication. Publishes ms an average of 6 months after acceptance. Byline given. Buys one-time rights. Responds in 4 months to queries. Writer's guidelines for #10 SASE.

Nonfiction Essays, interview/profile, book reviews. Query first. Length: 500-4,000 words. **Pays $40/printed page (Canadian), and 2 copies.**

Photos Query first. Buys one-time rights. Pays $300 for 10 photos.

Poetry Avant-garde, free verse. **Buys 60 poems/year.** Submit maximum 6 poems. **Pays $40/printed page (Canadian).**

Tips "Please include brief biographical note with submission."

$ ARTFUL DODGE

Dept. of English, College of Wooster, Wooster OH 44691. (330)263-2577. Website: www.wooster.edu/artfuldodge. **Contact:** Philip Brady, poetry editor. Annual magazine that "takes a strong interest in poets who are continually testing what they can get away with successfully in regard to subject, perspective, language, etc., but who also show mastery of the current American poetic techniques—its varied textures and its achievement in the illumination of the particular. There is no theme in this magazine, except literary power. We also have an ongoing interest in translations from Central/Eastern Europe and elsewhere." Estab. 1979. Circ. 1,000. Buys first North American serial rights. Accepts queries by mail. Accepts simultaneous submissions. Responds in 1 year to mss. Sample copy for $7. Writer's guidelines for #10 SASE.

Fiction Experimental, prose poem. "We judge by literary quality, not by genre. We are especially interested in fine English translations of significant prose writers. Translations should be submitted with original texts." **Pays 2 contributor's copies and honorarium of $5/page, "thanks to funding from the Ohio Arts Council."**

Poetry "We are interested in poems that utilize stylistic persuasions both old and new to good effect. We are not afraid of poems which try to deal with large social, political, historical, and even philosophical questions—especially if the poem emerges from one's own life experience and is not the result of armchair pontificating. We don't want cute, rococo surrealism, someone's warmed-up, left-over notion of an avant-garde that existed 10-100 years ago, or any last bastions of rhymed verse in the civilized world." **Buys 20 poems/year.** Submit maximum 6 poems.

Tips "Poets may send books for review consideration; however, there is no guarantee we can review them."

$ARTS & LETTERS

Journal of Contemporary Culture, Georgia College & State University, Campus Box 89, Milledgeville GA 31061. E-mail: al@gcsu.edu. Website: al.gcsu.edu. **Contact:** Martin Lammon, editor. Semiannual magazine covering poetry, fiction, creative nonfiction, and commentary on contemporary culture. "The journal features the mentors interview series and the world poetry translation series. Also, it is the only journal nationwide to feature authors and artists that represent such an eclectic range of creative work." Estab. 1999. Circ. 1,500. Pays on publication. Publishes ms an average of 6-12 months after acceptance. Rights revert to author after publication. Responds in 2 months to mss. Sample copy for $5, plus $1 for postage. Writer's guidelines online.

Nonfiction Karen Salyer McElmurray, creative nonfiction editor. Looking for creative nonfiction.

Fiction Allen Gee, fiction editor. No genre fiction. **Buys 6 mss/year.** Length: 3,000-7,500 words. **Pays $50 minimum or $10/published page.**

Poetry Alice Friman, poetry editor.

Tips "An obvious, but not gimmicky, attention to fresh usage of language. A solid grasp of the craft of story writing. Fully realized work."

$BLACK WARRIOR REVIEW

P.O. Box 862936, Tuscaloosa AL 35486-0027. (205)348-4518. Website: www.webdelsol.com/bwr. **90% freelance written.** Semiannual magazine of fiction, poetry, essays, art, and reviews. "We publish contemporary fiction, poetry, reviews, essays, and art for a literary audience. We publish the freshest work we can find." Estab. 1974. Circ. 2,000. Pays on publication. Publishes ms an average of 6 months after acceptance. Byline given. Buys first rights. Accepts simultaneous submissions. Responds in 4 months to mss. Sample copy for $8. Writer's guidelines online.

Nonfiction Laura Hendrix, editor. Interview/profile, literary/personal essays. **Buys 5 mss/year.** No queries; send complete ms. **Pays up to $100, copies, and a 1-year subscription.**

Fiction Sarah Blackman, fiction editor. Publishes novel excerpts if under contract to be published. One story/chapter per envelope, please. Contemporary, short and short-short fiction. Want "work that is conscious of form and well-crafted. We are open to good experimental writing and short-short fiction. No genre fiction please." **Buys 10 mss/year.** Length: 7,500 words. **Pays up to $150, copies, and a 1-year subscription.**

Poetry Amir Kenan, poetry editor. **Buys 35 poems/year.** Submit maximum 3-6 poems. **Pays up to $75, copies, and a 1-year subscription.**

Tips "Read *BWR* before submitting. Send us only your best work. Address all submissions to the appropriate genre editor."

Ⓝ ∅ BOOKLIST

American Library Association, 50 E. Huron St., Chicago IL 60611. (312)280-5715. Fax: (312)337-6787. E-mail: booklist@ala.org. Website: www.ala.org/booklist. **Contact:** Bill Ott, editor. **30% freelance written.** Biweekly magazine covering library selection, book publishing. Estab. 1905. Circ. 26,000. Pays on publication. Publishes ms an average of 6 weeks after acceptance. Byline given. Buys all rights. Editorial lead time 3 months. Submit seasonal material 6 months in advance. Accepts queries by mail, fax. Sample copy for free. Writer's guidelines online.

● *Booklist* does not accept unsolicited mss.

Nonfiction No unsolicited mss. Reviews must be assigned by editors. Query with published clips. Length: 140-200 words. **Payment varies for assigned articles.**

Columns/Departments Writers & Readers (established writers talk about writing for the library audience), 1,000 words. **Buys 4 mss/year.** Query with published clips. **Payment varies.**

Tips "Already-published reviewers are the best prospects. Must demonstrate an understanding of the subject matter and of the public and/or school library markets. Unsolicited reviews or articles are not welcome."

$ $ BOULEVARD

Opojaz, Inc., 6614 Clayton Rd., PMB 325, Richmond Heights MO 63117. (314)862-2643. Fax: (314)862-2982. Website: www.richardburgin.com. **Contact:** Richard Burgin, editor. **100% freelance written.** Triannual magazine covering fiction, poetry, and essays. "*Boulevard* is a diverse literary magazine presenting original creative work by well-known authors, as well as by writers of exciting promise." Estab. 1985. Circ. 11,000. Pays on publication. Publishes ms an average of 9 months after acceptance. Byline given. Offers no kill fee. Buys first North American serial rights. Accepts queries by mail, phone. Accepts simultaneous submissions. Responds in 2 weeks to queries; 3 months to mss. Sample copy for $8. Writer's guidelines online.

    O─ Break in with "a touching, intelligent, and original story, poem or essay."

Nonfiction Book excerpts, essays, interview/profile, opinion, photo feature. "No pornography, science fiction, children's stories, or westerns." **Buys 10 mss/year.** Send complete ms. Length: 10,000 words maximum. **Pays $20/page, minimum $150.**

Fiction Confessions, experimental, mainstream, novel excerpts. "We do not want erotica, science fiction, romance, western, or children's stories." **Buys 20 mss/year.** Send complete ms. Length: 8,000 words maximum. **$20/page; minimum $150.**

Poetry Avant-garde, free verse, haiku, traditional. "Do not send us light verse." **Buys 80 poems/year.** Submit maximum 5 poems. Length: 200 lines. **$25-250 (sometimes higher).**

Tips "Read the magazine first. The work *Boulevard* publishes is generally recognized as among the finest in the country. We continue to seek more good literary or cultural essays. Send only your best work."

BRAIN, CHILD

The Magazine for Thinking Mothers, March Press, P.O. Box 5566, Charlottesville VA 22905. (434)977-4151. E-mail: editor@brainchildmag.com. Website: www.brainchildmag.com. Co-Editors: Jennifer Niesslein and Stephanie Wilkinson. **90% freelance written.** Quarterly magazine covering the experience of motherhood. "*Brain, Child* reflects modern motherhood—the way it really is. We like to think of *Brain, Child* as a community, for and by mothers who like to think about what raising kids does for (and to) the mind and soul. *Brain, Child* isn't your typical parenting magazine. We couldn't cupcake-decorate our way out of a paper bag. We are more 'literary' than 'how-to,' more *New Yorker* than *Parents*. We shy away from expert advice on childrearing in favor of first-hand reflections by great writers (Jane Smiley, Barbara Ehrenreich, Anne Tyler) on life as a mother. Each quarterly issue is full of essays, features, humor, reviews, fiction, art, cartoons, and our readers' own stories. Our philosophy is pretty simple: Motherhood is worthy of literature. And there are a lot of ways to mother, all of them interesting. We're proud to be publishing articles and essays that are smart, down to earth, sometimes funny, and sometimes poignant." Estab. 2000. Circ. 30,000. Pays on publication. Publishes ms an average of 6 months after acceptance. Byline given. Buys first North American serial, electronic, and *Brain, Child* anthology rights. Editorial lead time 3 months. Submit seasonal material 6 months in advance. Accepts queries by mail, e-mail. Accepts simultaneous submissions. Responds in 1-3 months. Sample copy and writer's guidelines online.

Nonfiction Essays (including debate), humor, in-depth features. No how-to articles, advice, or tips. **Buys 40-50 mss/year.** Query with published clips for features and debate essays; send complete ms for essays. Length: 800-5,000 words. **Payment varies.** Sometimes pays expenses of writers on assignment.

Photos State availability with submission. Reviews contact sheets, prints, GIF/JPEG files. Model releases required.

Fiction "We publish fiction that has a strong motherhood theme." Mainstream, literary. No genre fiction. **Buys 4 mss/year.** Send complete ms. Length: 800-5,000 words. **Payment varies.**

Ⓝ $ BRAVE HEARTS

Ogden Publications, 1503 SW 42nd St., Topeka KS 66609-1265. Website: www.braveheartsmagazine.com. Executive Editor: Ann Crahan; Managing Editors: Jean Teller and Traci Smith. **Contact:** Darrah Buren, assistant editor. **100% freelance written.** Quarterly magazine covering inspirational topics. "*Brave Hearts* is written by and for ordinary people who have an inspirational message to share on an issue's topic." Estab. 2001. Circ. 1,000. Pays on publication. Publishes ms an average of 6 months after acceptance. Byline given. Buys all rights. Editorial lead time 3 months. Submit seasonal material 6 months in advance. Responds in 1 month to queries. Sample copy for $4.95. Writer's guidelines online.

Nonfiction Essays (short), general interest, humor, inspirational, personal experience, photo feature. Does not want overly religious, opinion, negative situations (sex/drugs/violence). Send complete ms. Length: 300-900 words. **Pays $5-12.**

Photos Send photos with submission. Reviews prints. Buys all rights. Pays maximum $5/photo. Captions, identification of subjects required.

Poetry Free verse, light verse, traditional. Does not want negative situations (sex/drugs/violence). **Buys 30 + poems/year.** Submit maximum 5 poems. **Pays $10.**

Tips "Be succinct and on topic. Indicate in your cover letter which topic/issue that submission is on. Be inspirational, yet not overtly religious. Topics for upcoming issues are printed on the inside cover of each issue."

$ $ 💻 BRICK

A Literary Journal, Brick, Box 537, Station Q, Toronto ON M4T 2M5 Canada. E-mail: info@brickmag.com. Website: www.brickmag.com. Publisher: Michael Redhill. **Contact:** Rebecca Silver Slayter, managing editor. **90% freelance written.** Semiannual magazine covering literature and the arts. "We publish literary nonfiction of a very high quality on a range of arts and culture subjects." Estab. 1978. Circ. 4,000. Pays on publication. Publishes ms an average of 3 months after acceptance. Byline given. Buys first world, first serial, one-time English language rights. Editorial lead time 5 months. Responds in 6 months to mss. Sample copy for $12, plus $3 shipping. Writer's guidelines online.

Nonfiction Essays, historical/nostalgic, interview/profile, opinion, travel. No fiction, poetry, personal real-life experience, or book reviews. **Buys 30-40 mss/year.** Send complete ms. Length: 250-2,500 words. **Pays $75-500 (Canadian).**

Photos State availability with submission. Reviews transparencies, prints, TIFF/JPEG files. Buys one-time rights. Offers $25-50/photo.

Tips "*Brick* is interested in polished work by writers who are widely read and in touch with contemporary culture. The magazine is serious, but not fusty. We like to feel the writer's personality in the piece, too."

Ⓝ $ BUTTON

New England's Tiniest Magazine of Poetry, Fiction and Gracious Living, Box 26, Lunenburg MA 01462. E-mail: sally@moonsigns.net. Website: www.moonsigns.net. **Contact:** Sally Cragin, editor. **10% freelance written.** Annual literary magazine. "*Button* is New England's tiniest magazine of poetry, fiction, and gracious living, published once a year. As 'gracious living' is on the cover, we like wit, brevity, cleverly-conceived essay/recipe, poetry that isn't sentimental or song lyrics. I started *Button* so that a century from now, when people read it in landfils or, preferably, libraries, they'll say, 'Gee, what a great time to have lived. I wish I lived back then.'" Estab. 1993. Circ. 1,500. Pays on publication. Publishes ms an average of 3-9 months after acceptance. Byline given. Buys first North American serial rights. Editorial lead time 6 months. Responds in 1 month to queries; 2 months to mss. Sample copy for $2 and 1 37¢ stamp. Writer's guidelines for #10 SASE.

Nonfiction Personal experience, cooking stories. Does not want "the tired, the trite, the sexist, the multiply-folded, the single-spaced, the sentimental, the self-pitying, the swaggering, the infantile (i.e., coruscated whimsy and self-conscious quaint), poems about Why You Can't Be together and stories about How Complicated Am I. Before you send us anything, sit down and read a poem by Stanley Kunitz or a story by Evelyn Waugh, Louisa May Alcott, or anyone who's visited the poles, and if you still think you've written a damn fine thing, have at it. A word-count on the top of the page is fine—a copyright or 'all rights reserved' reminder makes you look like a beginner." **Buys 1-2 mss/year.** Length: 300-2,000 words. **Pays $10 and up, depending on length of piece.**

Fiction W.M. Davies, fiction editor. Seeking quality fiction. "No genre fiction, science fiction, techno-thriller." Wants more of "anything Herman Melville, Henry James, or Betty MacDonald would like to read." **Buys 1-2 mss/year.** Send complete ms. Length: 300-2,000 words. **Pays $25.**

Poetry Seeking quality poetry. Free verse, traditional. **Buys 2-4 poems/year.** Submit maximum 3 poems. **Pays $10-25.**

Tips "*Button* writers have been widely published elsewhere, in virtually all the major national magazines. They include, Ralph Lombreglia, Lawrence Millman, They Might Be Giants, Combustible Edison, Sven Birkerts, Stephen McCauley, Amanda Powell, Wayne Wilson, David Barber, Romayne Dawnay, Brendan Galvin, and Diana DerHovanessian. It's $2 for a sample, which seems reasonable. Follow the guidelines, make sure you read your work aloud, and don't inflate or deflate your publications and experience. We've published plenty of new folks, but on the merits of the work."

Ⓝ $ $ 💻 THE CAPILANO REVIEW

2055 Purcell Way, North Vancouver BC V7J 3H5 Canada. E-mail: tcr@capcollege.bc.ca. Website: www.capcollege.bc.ca/thecapilanoreview. **Contact:** Sharon Thesen, editor. **100% freelance written.** "Triannual visual and literary arts magazine that publishes only what the editors consider to be the very best fiction, poetry, drama, or visual art being produced. *TCR* editors are interested in fresh, original work that stimulates and challenges readers. Over the years, the magazine has developed a reputation for pushing beyond the boundaries of traditional art and writing. We are interested in work that is new in concept and in execution." Estab. 1972. Circ. 900. Pays on publication. Publishes ms an average of 2-4 months after acceptance. Byline given. Buys first North American serial rights. Accepts queries by mail. Responds in 1 month to queries; 4 months to mss. Sample copy for $9. Writer's guidelines for #10 SASE with IRC or Canadian stamps or online.

Fiction Query by mail or send complete ms with SASE and Canadian postage or IRCs. Experimental, novel excerpts, literary. "No traditional, conventional fiction. Want to see more innovative, genre-blurring work." **Buys 10-15 mss/year.** Length: 8,000 words. **Pays $50-200.**

Poetry Submit maximum 6-8 poems (with SASE and Canadian postage or IRCs). Avant-garde, free verse. **Buys 40 poems/year. Pays $50-200.**

$THE CHARITON REVIEW

English Dept., Brigham Young University, Provo UT 84602. (660)785-4499. **Contact:** Jim Barnes, editor. **100% freelance written.** Semiannual (fall and spring) magazine covering contemporary fiction, poetry, translation, and book reviews. "We demand only excellence in fiction and fiction translation for a general and college readership." Estab. 1975. Circ. 600. Pays on publication. Publishes ms an average of 6 months after acceptance. Byline given. Buys first North American serial rights. Accepts queries by mail. Responds in 1 week to queries; 1 month to mss. Sample copy for $5 and 7×10 SAE with 4 first-class stamps.

Nonfiction Essays (reviews of books). **Buys 2-5 mss/year.** Send complete ms. Length: 1,000-5,000 words. **Pays $15.**

Fiction Fiction editor. Ethnic, experimental, mainstream, novel excerpts, traditional. "We are not interested in slick or sick material." **Buys 6-10 mss/year.** Send complete ms. Length: 1,000-6,000 words. **Pays $5/page (up to $50).**

Poetry Avant-garde, traditional. **Buys 50-55 poems/year.** Submit maximum 5 poems. Length: Open. **Pays $5/page.**

Tips "Read *Chariton*. Know the difference between good and bad literature. Know what magazine might be interested in your work. We are not a trendy magazine. We publish only the best. All sections are open to freelancers. Know your market or you are wasting your time—and mine. Do not write for guidelines; the only guideline is excellence."

$THE CHATTAHOOCHEE REVIEW

Georgia Perimeter College, 2101 Womack Rd., Dunwoody GA 30338-4497. (770)551-3019. Website: www.chattahoochee-review.org. **Contact:** Lawrence Hetrick, editor. Quarterly magazine. "We publish a number of Southern writers, but *Chattahoochee Review* is not by design a regional magazine. All themes, forms, and styles are considered as long as they impact the whole person: heart, mind, intuition, and imagination." Estab. 1980. Circ. 1,350. Pays on publication. Publishes ms an average of 3 months after acceptance. Byline given. Buys first rights. Accepts queries by mail. Responds in 2 weeks to queries; 4 months to mss. Sample copy for $6. Writer's guidelines online.

Nonfiction "We look for distinctive, honest personal essays and creative nonfiction of any kind, including the currently popular memoiristic narrative. We publish interviews with writers of all kinds: literary, academic, journalistic, and popular. We also review selected current offerings in fiction, poetry, and nonfiction, including works on photography and the visual arts, with an emphasis on important southern writers and artisits. We do not often, if ever, publish technical, critical, theoretical, or scholarly work about literature, although we are interested in essays written for general readers about writers, their careers, and their work." Essays (interviews with authors, reviews). **Buys 10 mss/year.** Send complete ms. Length: 5,000 words maximum.

Photos State availability with submission. Buys one-time rights. Negotiates payment individually. Identification of subjects required.

Fiction Accepts all subject matter except juvenile, science fiction, and romance. **Buys 12 mss/year.** Send complete ms. Length: 6,000 words maximum. **Pays $20/page, $250 max and 2 contributor's copies.**

Poetry Avant-garde, free verse, haiku, light verse, traditional. **Buys 60 poems/year.** Submit maximum 5 poems. **Pays $30/poem.**

Tips "Become familiar with our journal and the type of work we regularly publish."

$CHELSEA

Chelsea Associates, P.O. Box 773 Cooper Station, New York NY 10276-0773. **Contact:** Alfredo de Palchi, editor. **70% freelance written.** Semiannual magazine. "We stress style, variety, originality. No special biases or requirements. Flexible attitudes, eclectic material. We take an active interest, as always, in cross-cultural exchanges, superior translations, and are leaning toward cosmopolitan, interdisciplinary techniques, but maintain no strictures against traditional modes." Estab. 1958. Circ. 2,200. Pays on publication. Publishes ms an average of 6 months after acceptance. Byline given. Buys first North American serial rights. Accepts queries by mail. Responds in 3-5 months to mss. Sample copy for $6. Writer's guidelines and contest guidelines available for #10 SASE.

● *Chelsea* also sponsors fiction and poetry contests. Poetry Deadline: December 15; Fiction Deadline: June 15. Send SASE for guidelines.

Nonfiction Essays, book reviews (query first with sample). **Buys 6 mss/year.** Send complete ms with SASE. Length: 6,000 words. **Pays $15/page.**

Fiction Mainstream, novel excerpts, literary. **Buys 12 mss/year.** Send complete ms. Length: 5,000-6,000 words. **Pays $15/page.**

Poetry Avant-garde, free verse, traditional. **Buys 60-75 poems/year. Pays $15/page.**

Tips "We only accept written correspondence. We are looking for more super translations, first-rate fiction, and work by writers of color. No need to query; submit complete manuscript. We suggest writers look at a recent issue of *Chelsea*."

Ⓝ $ $ CHICKEN SOUP FOR THE SOUL

101 Stories to Open the Heart and Rekindle the Spirit, Chicken Soup for the Soul Enterprises, Inc., P.O, Box 30880, Santa Barbara CA 93130. (805)563-2935. Fax: (805)563-2945. E-mail: nautio@chickensoup.com. Website: www.chickensoup.com. **95% freelance written.** Paperback with 8-12 publications/year featuring inspirational, heartwarming, uplifting short stories. Estab. 1993. Circ. Over 40 titles; 60 million books in print. Pays on publication. Publishes ms an average of 8 months after acceptance. Byline given. Buys all rights. Accepts queries by mail, e-mail, fax. Accepts previously published material. Accepts simultaneous submissions. Responds upon consideration to queries. Sample copy not available. Writer's guidelines online.

Nonfiction Humor, inspirational, personal experience, religious. Special issues: Traveling sisterhood, Mother-Daughter stories, Christian teen, Christmas stories, stories by and/or about men on love, kindness, parenting, family, Nascar racing, athletes, teachers, fishing, adoption, volunteers. No sermon, essay, eulogy, term paper, journal entry, political, or controversial issues. **Buys 1,000 mss/year.** Send complete ms. Length: 300-1,200 words. **Pays $300.**

Poetry Traditional. No controversial poetry. **Buys 50 poems/year.** Submit maximum 5 poems. **Pays $300.**

Fillers Anecdotes, facts, gags to be illustrated by cartoonist, short humor. **Buys 50/year. Pays $300.**

Tips "We prefer submissions to be sent via our website. Print submissions should be on 8½×11 paper in 12 point Times New Roman font. Type author's contact information on the first page of story. Stories are to be nonfiction. No anonymous or author unknown submissions are accepted. We do not return submissions."

$ THE CINCINNATI REVIEW

P.O. Box 210069, Cincinnati OH 45221-0069. (513)556-3954. E-mail: editors@cincinnatireview.com. Website: www.cincinnatireview.com. Managing Editor: Nicola Mason. **Contact:** Don Bogen, poetry editor; Brock Clarke, fiction editor. **100% freelance written.** Semiannual magazine. "A journal devoted to publishing the best new literary fiction and poetry as well as book reviews, essays, and interviews." Estab. 2003. Pays on publication. Publishes ms an average of 6 months after acceptance. Byline given. Buys first North American serial, electronic rights. Accepts queries by mail. Responds in 2 weeks to queries; 1 month to mss. Sample copy for $7, subscription for $12. Writer's guidelines online.

● Reads submissions September 1-May 31.

Nonfiction Book excerpts, essays, interview/profile, new book fiction and poetry reviews. Query. Length: 1,000-5,000 words. **Pays $25/page.**

Columns/Departments Book Reviews; Literary Fiction; Poetry, 1,500 words. **Buys 20 mss/year.** Query. **Pays $25/page.**

Fiction Brock Clarke, fiction editor. Literary. Does not want genre fiction. **Buys 13 mss/year.** Query. Length: 125-10,000 words. **Pays $25/page.**

Poetry Don Bogen, poetry editor. Avant-garde, free verse, traditional. **Buys 120 poems/year.** Submit maximum 10 poems. **Pays $30/page.**

$ $ CITY SLAB

Urban Tales of the Grotesque, City Slab Publications, 1705 Summit Ave., #314, Seattle WA 98122. (206)226-7430. E-mail: dave@cityslab.com. Website: www.cityslab.com. **Contact:** Dave Lindschmidt, editor. **90% freelance written.** Quarterly magazine covering horror and horror/crime mix. "*City Slab* magazine is hard-edged, adult fiction." Estab. 2002. Pays on publication. Publishes ms an average of 3 months after acceptance. Byline given. Buys first North American serial rights. Accepts queries by mail, e-mail. Responds in 3 weeks to queries; 2 months to mss. Sample copy for $6. Writer's guidelines online.

Nonfiction Essays, interview/profile, photo feature. **Buys 4 mss/year.** Send complete ms. Length: 2,000-3,000 words. **Pays $50-100, plus contributor copies.**

Photos State availability of or send photos with submission. Reviews JPEG files. Buys one-time rights. Offers no additional payment for photos accepted with ms. Model releases required.

Fiction "*City Slab* wants to publish well thought out, literary-quality horror." Erotica, experimental, horror.

Does not want to see children/youth in sexually oriented stories. **Buys 24 mss/year.** Send complete ms. Length: 5,000 words maximum. **Pays 1-10¢/word.**

Tips "Read not only the horror greats—Barker, King, Campbell, Lovecraft, etc.—but also the classics—Dickens, Hemingway, Oates, Steinbeck—to see how a great tale is woven. Recently published fiction by Gerard Hoaurner, Christa Faust, and P.D. Cacek."

$COLORADO REVIEW

Center for Literary Publishing, Department of English, Colorado State University, Fort Collins CO 80523. (970)491-5449. E-mail: creview@colostate.edu. Website: coloradoreview.colostate.edu. **Contact:** Stephanie G'Schwind, editor. Literary magazine published 3 times/year. Estab. 1956. Circ. 1,300. Pays on publication. Publishes ms an average of 1 year after acceptance. Byline given. Buys first North American serial rights. Rights revert to author upon publication. Editorial lead time 1 year. Responds in 2 months to mss. Sample copy for $10. Writer's guidelines online.

● Mss are read from September 1 to April 30. Mss recieved between May 1 and August 30 will be returned unread.

Nonfiction Personal essays, creative nonfiction. **Buys 6-9 mss/year.** Send complete ms. **Pays $5/page.**

Fiction Short fiction. No genre fiction. Ethnic, experimental, mainstream, contemporary. **Buys 15-20 mss/year.** Send complete ms. Length: under 30 ms pages. **Pays $5/page.**

Poetry Considers poetry of any style. Send no more than 5 poems at one time. Don Revell or Jorie Graham, poetry editors. **Buys 60-100 poems/year. Pays $5/page.**

$ $CONFRONTATION

A Literary Journal, Long Island University, Brookville NY 11548. (516)299-2720. Fax: (516)299-2735. E-mail: mtucker@liu.edu. Assistant to Editor: Jonna Semeik. **Contact:** Martin Tucker, editor-in-chief. **75% freelance written.** Semiannual magazine. "We are eclectic in our taste. Excellence of style is our dominant concern." Estab. 1968. Circ. 2,000. Pays on publication. Publishes ms an average of 1 year after acceptance. Byline given. Offers kill fee. Buys first North American serial, first, one-time, all rights. Accepts queries by mail, e-mail, phone. Accepts simultaneous submissions. Responds in 3 weeks to queries; 2 months to mss. Sample copy for $3. Writer's guidelines not available.

● *Confrontation* does not read mss during June, July, or August.

Nonfiction Essays, personal experience. **Buys 15 mss/year.** Send complete ms. Length: 1,500-5,000 words. **Pays $100-300 for assigned articles; $15-300 for unsolicited articles.**

Photos State availability with submission. Buys one-time rights. Offers no additional payment for photos accepted with ms.

Fiction "We judge on quality, so genre is open." Experimental, mainstream, novel excerpts, slice-of-life vignettes, contemporary, prose poem. "No 'proselytizing' literature or genre fiction." **Buys 60-75 mss/year.** Send complete ms. Length: 6,000 words. **Pays $25-250.**

Poetry Avant-garde, free verse, haiku, light verse, traditional. **Buys 60-75 poems/year.** Submit maximum 6 poems. Length: Open. **Pays $10-100.**

Tips "Most open to fiction and poetry. Study our magazine."

$THE CONNECTICUT POETRY REVIEW

The Connecticut Poetry Review Press, P.O. Box 818, Stonington CT 06378. Managing Editor: Harley More. **Contact:** J. Claire White. **60% freelance written.** Annual magazine covering poetry/literature. Estab. 1981. Circ. 500. **Pays on acceptance.** Byline sometimes given. Buys first rights. Editorial lead time 4 months. Submit seasonal material 4 months in advance. Accepts queries by mail. Responds in 1 month to queries; 3 months to mss. Sample copy for $3.50 and #10 SASE. Writer's guidelines for #10 SASE.

Nonfiction Book excerpts, essays. **Buys 18 mss/year.**

Fiction Experimental.

Poetry Avant-garde, free verse, haiku, traditional. No light verse. **Buys 20-30 poems/year.** Submit maximum 4 poems. Length: 3-25 lines. **Pays $5-10.**

$⬛ CONTEMPORARY VERSE 2

The Canadian Journal of Poetry and Critical Writing, Contemporary Verse 2, Inc., 207-100 Arthur St., Winnipeg MB R3B 1H3 Canada. (204)949-1365. Fax: (204)942-5754. E-mail: cv2@mb.sympatico.ca. Website: www.contemporaryverse2.ca. **Contact:** Clarise Foster, managing editor. **75% freelance written.** Quarterly magazine covering poetry and critical writing about poetry. "*CV2* publishes poetry of demonstrable quality as well as critical writing in the form of interviews, essays, articles, and reviews. With the critical writing we tend to create a discussion of poetry which will interest a broad range of readers, including those who might be skeptical about the value of poetry." Estab. 1975. Circ. 600. Pays on publication. Byline given. Offers 50% kill fee. Not copyrighted. Buys first North American serial, second serial (reprint) rights. Editorial lead time 3-6 months. Submit seasonal material 3-6 months in advance. Accepts queries by mail, e-mail, phone. Responds in 2-3 weeks to queries; 3-8 months to mss. Sample copy for $8. Writer's guidelines online.

Nonfiction Essays, interview/profile, book reviews. No content that is not about poetry. **Buys 10-30 mss/year.** Query. Length: 800-3,000 words. **Pays $40-130 for assigned articles.** Pays in contributor copies only if requested by the author.

Poetry Avant-garde, free verse. No rhyming verse, traditionally inspirational. **Buys 110-120 poems/year.** Submit maximum 6 poems. **Pays $20/poem.**

$CRAB ORCHARD REVIEW

A Journal of Creative Works, Southern Illinois University at Carbondale, English Department, Faner Hall, Carbondale IL 62901-4503. (618)453-6833. Fax: (618)453-8224. Website: www.siu.edu/~crborchd. "We are a general interest literary journal published twice/year. We strive to be a journal that writers admire and readers enjoy. We publish fiction, poetry, creative nonfiction, fiction translations, interviews and reviews." Estab. 1995. Circ. 2,200. Publishes ms an average of 9-12 months after acceptance. Buys first North American serial rights. Accepts simultaneous submissions. Responds in 3 weeks to queries; 9 months to mss. Sample copy for $8. Writer's guidelines for #10 SASE.

Fiction Jon Tribble, managing editor. Ethnic, excerpted novel. No science fiction, romance, western, horror, gothic or children's. Wants more nove excerpts that also stand alone as pieces. Length: 1,000-6,500 words. **Pays $100 minimum; $20/page maximum, 2 contributor's copies and a year subscription.**

Tips "We publish two issues per volume—one has a theme (we read from May to November for the theme issue), the other doesn't (we read from January through April for the nonthematic issue). Consult our website for information about our upcoming themes."

$CREATIVE NONFICTION

Creative Nonfiction Foundation, 5501 Walnut St., Suite 202, Pittsburgh PA 15232. (412)688-0304. Fax: (412)683-9173. E-mail: information@creativenonfiction.org. Website: www.creativenonfiction.org. **Contact:** Lee Gutkind, editor. **100% freelance written.** Magazine published 3 times/year covering nonfiction—personal essay, memoir, literary journalism. "*Creative Nonfiction* is the first journal to focus exclusively upon the genre of creative nonfiction. It publishes personal essay, memoir, and literary journalism on a broad range of subjects. Interviews with prominent writers and commentary about the genre also appear on its pages." Estab. 1993. Circ. 4,000. Pays on publication. Publishes ms an average of 1 year after acceptance. Byline given. Buys all rights. Editorial lead time 6 months. Accepts simultaneous submissions. Responds in 6 months to mss. Sample copy for $10. Writer's guidelines online.

Nonfiction Essays, interview/profile, personal experience, narrative journalism. No poetry, fiction. **Buys 30 mss/year.** Send complete ms. Length: 5,000 words maximum. **Pays $10/page—more if grant money available for assigned articles.**

Tips "Points to remember when submitting to *Creative Nonfiction:* strong reportage; well-written prose, attentive to language, rich with detail and distinctive voice; an informational quality or 'teaching element'; a compelling, focused, sustained narrative that's well-structured and conveys meaning. Manuscripts will not be accepted via fax or e-mail."

$ DESCANT

Descant Arts & Letters Foundation, P.O. Box 314, Station P, Toronto ON M5S 2S8 Canada. (416)593-2557. Fax: (416)593-9362. E-mail: descant@web.net. Website: www.descant.on.ca. Editor: Karen Mulhallen. **Contact:** Mary Newberry, managing editor. Quarterly journal. Estab. 1970. Circ. 1,200. Pays on publication. Publishes ms an average of 16 months after acceptance. Editorial lead time 1 year. Accepts queries by mail, e-mail, phone. Sample copy for $8.50 plus postage. Writer's guidelines online.

• Pays $100 honorarium, plus 1-year's subscription for accepted submissions of any kind.

Nonfiction Book excerpts, essays, interview/profile, personal experience, historical.

Photos State availability with submission. Reviews contact sheets, prints. Buys one-time rights. Offers no additional payment for photos accepted with ms.

Fiction Karen Mulhallen, editor. Short stories or book excerpts. Maximum length 6,000 words; 3,000 words or less preferred. Ethnic, experimental, historical, humorous. No gothic, religious, beat. Send complete ms. **Pays $100 (Canadian); additional copies $8.**

Poetry Free verse, light verse, traditional. Submit maximum 6 poems.

Tips "Familiarize yourself with our magazine before submitting."

$ DOWNSTATE STORY

1825 Maple Ridge, Peoria IL 61614. (309)688-1409. E-mail: ehopkins@prairienet.org. Website: www.wiu.edu/users/mfgeh/dss. **Contact:** Elaine Hopkins, editor. Annual magazine covering short fiction with some connection with Illinois or the Midwest. Estab. 1992. Circ. 500. **Pays on acceptance.** Publishes ms an average of 1 year after acceptance. Buys first rights. Accepts simultaneous submissions. Responds "ASAP" to mss. Sample copy for $8. Writer's guidelines online.

Fiction Adventure, ethnic, experimental, historical, horror, humorous, mainstream, mystery, romance, science fiction, suspense, western. No porn. **Buys 10 mss/year.** Length: 300-2,000 words. **Pays $50.**

Tips Wants more political fiction. Publishes short shorts and literary essays.

$ ☑ DREAMS & VISIONS

Spiritual Fiction, Skysong Press, 35 Peter St. S., Orillia ON L3V 5A8 Canada. (705)329-1770. Fax: (705)329-1770. E-mail: skysong@bconnex.net. Website: www.bconnex.net/~skysong. **Contact:** Steve Stanton, editor. **100% freelance written.** Semiannual magazine. "Innovative literary fiction for adult Christian readers." Estab. 1988. Circ. 300. Pays on publication. Publishes ms an average of 4 months after acceptance. Byline given. Buys first North American serial, one-time, second serial (reprint) rights. Editorial lead time 6 months. Accepts queries by mail, e-mail. Accepts simultaneous submissions. Responds in 3 weeks to queries; 3 months to mss. Sample copy for $4.95. Writer's guidelines online.

Fiction Experimental, fantasy, humorous, mainstream, mystery, novel excerpts, religious, science fiction, slice-of-life vignettes. "We do not publish stories that glorify violence or perversity. All stories should portray a Christian world view or expand upon Biblical themes or ethics in an entertaining or enlightening manner." **Buys 12 mss/year.** Send complete ms. Length: 2,000-6,000 words. **Pays 1¢/word.**

$ ELLIPSIS MAGAZINE

Westminster College of Salt Lake City, 1840 S. 1300 E., Salt Lake City UT 84105. (801)832-2321. E-mail: ellipsis@westminstercollege.edu. Website: www.westminstercollege.edu/ellipsis. **Contact:** *Ellipsis* Editor. Annual magazine. *Ellipsis Magazine* needs good literary poetry, fiction, essays, plays and visual art. Estab. 1967. Circ. 2,500. Pays on publication. Publishes ms an average of 3 months after acceptance. Byline given. Not copyrighted. Buys first North American serial rights. Accepts queries by mail. Accepts simultaneous submissions. Responds in 6 months to mss. Sample copy for $7.50. Writer's guidelines online.

• Reads submissions August 1 to November 1.

Nonfiction Essays. Send ms with SASE and brief bio.

Fiction Martin Murphy (revolving editor; changes every year). Needs good literary fiction and plays. Send complete ms. Length: 6,000 words. **Pays $50 per story and 1 contributor's copy; additional copies $3.50.**

Poetry All accepted poems are eligible for the *Ellipsis* Award which includes a $100 prize. Past judges have included Jorie Graham, Sandra Cisneros, and Stanley Plumly. Submit maximum 3-5 poems. Include SASE and brief bio.

$ EPOCH

Cornell University, 251 Goldwin Smith Hall, Cornell University, Ithaca NY 14853. (607)255-3385. Fax: (607)255-6661. Editor: Michael Koch. **Contact:** Joseph Martin, senior editor. **100% freelance written.** Magazine published 3 times/year. "Well-written literary fiction, poetry, personal essays. Newcomers always welcome. Open to mainstream and avant-garde writing." Estab. 1947. Circ. 1,000. Pays on publication. Publishes ms an average of 6 months after acceptance. Byline given. Offers 100% kill fee. Buys first North American serial rights. Editorial lead time 6 months. Submit seasonal material 8 months in advance. Accepts queries by mail. Responds in 2 weeks to queries; 6 weeks to mss. Sample copy for $5. Writer's guidelines for #10 SASE.

Nonfiction Send complete ms. Essays, interview. No inspirational. **Buys 6-8 mss/year.** Send complete ms. Length: Open. **Pays $5-10/printed page.**

Photos Send photos with submission. Reviews contact sheets, transparencies, any size prints. Buys one-time rights. Negotiates payment individually.

Fiction Ethnic, experimental, mainstream, novel excerpts, literary short stories. "No genre fiction. Would like to see more Southern fiction (Southern US)." **Buys 25-30 mss/year.** Send complete ms. Length: Open. **Pays $5 and up/printed page.**

Poetry Nancy Vieira Couto. Avant-garde, free verse, haiku, light verse, traditional, all types. **Buys 30-75 poems/year.** Submit maximum 7 poems.

Tips "Tell your story, speak your poem, straight from the heart. We are attracted to language and to good writing, but we are most interested in what the good writing leads us to, or where."

$ $ ☑ EVENT

Douglas College, P.O. Box 2503, New Westminster BC V3L 5B2 Canada. (604)527-5293. Fax: (604)527-5095. Website: event.douglas.bc.ca. **Contact:** Ian Cockfield, assistant editor. **100% freelance written.** Magazine published 3 times/year containing fiction, poetry, creative nonfiction, notes on writing, and reviews. "We are eclectic and always open to content that invites involvement. Generally, we like strong narrative." Estab. 1971. Circ. 1,250. Pays on publication. Publishes ms an average of 8 months after acceptance. Byline given. Buys first North American serial rights. Accepts queries by mail, fax. Accepts simultaneous submissions. Responds in 1 month to queries; 6 months to mss. Sample copy for $5. Writer's guidelines online.

• *Event* does not read mss in July, August, December, and January. No e-mail submissions. All submissions must include SASE (Canadian postage or IRCs only).

Fiction "We look for readability, style, and writing that invites involvement." Submit maximum 2 stories. Humorous, contemporary. "No technically poor or unoriginal pieces." **Buys 12-15 mss/year.** Send complete ms. Length: 5,000 words maximum. **Pays $22/page, up to $500.**

Poetry "We tend to appreciate the narrative and sometimes the confessional modes." Free verse, prose. No light verse. **Buys 30-40 poems/year.** Submit maximum 10 poems. **Pays $25-500.**

Tips "Write well and read some past issues of *Event*."

Ⓝ $ FICTION

℅ Department of English, City College, 138th St. & Covenant Ave., New York NY 10031. (212)650-6319. E-mail: fiction@fictioninc.com. Website: www.fictioninc.com. **Contact:** Mark J. Mirsky, editor. Semiannual magazine. "As the name implies, we publish only fiction; we are looking for the best new writing available, leaning toward the unconventional. *Fiction* has traditionally attempted to make accessible the unaccessible, to bring the experimental to a broader audience." Estab. 1972. Circ. 4,000. Publishes ms an average of 1 year after acceptance. Buys first rights. Accepts simultaneous submissions. Responds in 3 months to mss. Sample copy for $5. Writer's guidelines online.

• Reading period for unsolicited mss is September 15-April 15.

Fiction Experimental, humorous, contemporary, literary. translations. No romance, science fiction, etc. **Buys 24-40 mss/year.** Length: 5,000 words. **Pays $114.**

Tips "The guiding principle of *Fiction* has always been to go to terra incognita in the writing of the imagination and to ask that modern fiction set itself serious questions, if often in absurd and comedic voices, interrogating the nature of the real and the fantastic. It represents no particular school of fiction, except the innovative. Its pages have often been a harbor for writers at odds with each other. As a result of its willingness to publish the difficult, experimental, and unusual, while not excluding the well known, *Fiction* has a unique reputation in the US and abroad as a journal of future directions."

$ FIELD: CONTEMPORARY POETRY & POETICS

Oberlin College Press, 50 N. Professor St., Oberlin OH 44074-1091. (440)775-8408. Fax: (440)775-8124. E-mail: oc.press@oberlin.edu. Website: www.oberlin.edu/ocpress. **Contact:** Linda Slocum, managing editor. **60% freelance written.** Biannual magazine of poetry, poetry in translation, and essays on contemporary poetry by poets. No electronic submissions. Estab. 1969. Circ. 1,500. Pays on publication. Byline given. Buys first rights. Editorial lead time 4 months. Accepts queries by mail, e-mail, fax, phone. Responds in 6 weeks to mss. Sample copy for $7. Writer's guidelines online.

Poetry Buys 100 poems/year. Submit maximum 5 with SASE poems. **Pays $15/page.**

Tips "Submit 3-5 of your best poems with a cover letter and SASE. No simultaneous submissions. Keep trying! Submissions are read year-round."

$ THE FIRST LINE

Blue Cubicle Press, LLC, P.O. Box 250382, Plano TX 75025-0382. E-mail: info@thefirstline.com. Website: www.thefirstline.com. Co-editors: David LaBounty and Jeff Adams. **Contact:** Robin LaBounty, ms coordinator. **95% freelance written.** Quarterly magazine. *The First Line* is a magazine that explores the different directions writers can take when they start from the same place. All stories must be written with the first line provided by the magazine. Estab. 1999. Circ. 800. Pays on publication. Publishes ms an average of 1 month after acceptance. Byline given. Buys first North American serial, electronic rights. Editorial lead time 2 months. Accepts queries by mail, e-mail. Responds in 1 week to queries; 2 months to mss. Sample copy for $3. Writer's guidelines online.

Nonfiction Essays, interview/profile, book reviews. **Buys 4-8 mss/year.** Query. Length: 300-1,000 words. **Pays $10.**

Fiction Adventure, ethnic, experimental, fantasy, historical, horror, humorous, mainstream, mystery, romance, science fiction, suspense, western. No stories that do not start with the issue's first sentence. **Buys 40-60 mss/year.** Send complete ms. Length: 300-3,000 words. **Pays $10.**

$ FIVE POINTS

A Journal of Literature and Art, Georgia State University, P.O. Box 3999, Atlanta GA 30302-3999. Fax: (404)651-3167. E-mail: info@langate.gsu.edu. Website: www.webdelsol.com/five_points. Triannual *Five Points* is "committed to publishing work that compels the imagination through the use of fresh and convincing language.'' Estab. 1996. Circ. 2,000. Publishes ms an average of 6 months after acceptance. Buys first North American serial rights. Sample copy for $7. Editorial calendar online.

Fiction Megan Sexton, executive editor. **Pays $15/page minimum; $250 maximum, free subscription to magazine and 2 contributor's copies; additional copies $4.**

$ 🌐 FRANK

An International Journal of Contemporary Writing & Art, Association Frank, 32 rue Edouard Vaillant, Montreuil France. (33)(1)48596658. Fax: (33)(1)48596668. E-mail: submissions@readfrank.com. Website: www.readfran k.com; www.frank.ly. **80% freelance written.** Magazine published twice/year covering contemporary writing of all genres. Bilingual. ''Writing that takes risks and isn't ethnocentric is looked upon favorably.'' Estab. 1983. Circ. 4,000. Pays on publication. Publishes ms an average of 1 year after acceptance. Byline given. Buys one-time rights. Editorial lead time 6 months. Responds in 1 month to queries; 2 months to mss. Sample copy for $10. Writer's guidelines online.

Nonfiction Interview/profile, travel. **Buys 2 mss/year.** Query. **Pays $100 for assigned articles.**

Photos State availability with submission. Buys one-time rights. Negotiates payment individually.

Fiction Experimental, novel excerpts, international. ''At *Frank,* we publish fiction, poetry, literary and art interviews, and translations. We like work that falls between existing genres and has social or political consciousness.'' **Buys 8 mss/year.** Send complete ms. Length: 1,000-3,000 words. **Pays $10/printed page.**

Poetry Avant-garde, translations. **Buys 20 poems/year.** Submit maximum 10 poems. **Pays $20.**

Tips ''Suggest what you do or know best. Avoid query form letters—we won't read the manuscript. Looking for excellent literary/cultural interviews with leading American writers or cultural figures. Very receptive to new Foreign Dossiers of writing from a particular country.''

$ THE GEORGIA REVIEW

The University of Georgia, 012 Gilbert Hall, University of Georgia, Athens GA 30602-9009. (706)542-3481. Fax: (706)542-0047. E-mail: garev@uga.edu. Website: www.uga.edu/garev. Managing Editor: Annette Hatton. **Contact:** T.R. Hummer, editor. **99% freelance written.** Quarterly journal. ''Our readers are educated, inquisitive people who read a lot of work in the areas we feature, so they expect only the best in our pages. All work submitted should show evidence that the writer is at least as well-educated and well-read as our readers. Essays should be authoritative but accessible to a range of readers.'' Estab. 1947. Circ. 5,000. Pays on publication. Publishes ms an average of 6 months after acceptance. Byline given. Buys first North American serial rights. Accepts queries by mail. Responds in 2 weeks to queries; 3 months to mss. Sample copy for $7. Writer's guidelines online.

• No simultaneous or electronic submissions.

Nonfiction Essays. ''For the most part we are not interested in scholarly articles that are narrow in focus and/ or overly burdened with footnotes. The ideal essay for *The Georgia Review* is a provocative, thesis-oriented work that can engage both the intelligent general reader and the specialist.'' **Buys 12-20 mss/year.** Send complete ms. **Pays $40/published page.**

Photos Send photos with submission. Reviews 5×7 prints or larger. Buys one-time rights. Offers no additional payment for photos accepted with ms.

Fiction ''We seek original, excellent writing not bound by type. ''Ordinarily we do not publish novel excerpts or works translated into English, and we strongly discourage authors from submitting these.'' **Buys 12-20 mss/ year.** Send complete ms. Length: Open. **Pays $40/published page.**

Poetry ''We seek original, excellent poetry.'' **Buys 60-75 poems/year.** Submit maximum 5 poems. **Pays $3/line.**

Tips ''Unsolicited manuscripts will not be considered from May 15-August 15 (annually); all such submissions received during that period will be returned unread.''

$ THE GETTYSBURG REVIEW

Gettysburg College, Gettysburg PA 17325. (717)337-6770. Fax: (717)337-6775. Website: www.gettysburgreview .com. **Contact:** Peter Stitt, editor. Quarterly magazine. ''Our concern is quality. Manuscripts submitted here should be extremely well written.'' Reading period September-May. Estab. 1988. Circ. 3,000. Pays on publication. Publishes ms an average of 1 year after acceptance. Byline given. Buys first North American serial rights. Editorial lead time 1 year. Submit seasonal material 9 months in advance. Accepts queries by mail, fax. Accepts simultaneous submissions. Responds in 1 month to queries; 3-6 months to mss. Sample copy for $7. Writer's guidelines online.

Nonfiction Essays. **Buys 20 mss/year.** Send complete ms. Length: 3,000-7,000 words. **Pays $30/page.**

Fiction Mark Drew, assisant editor. High quality, literary. Experimental, historical, humorous, mainstream, novel excerpts, serialized novels, contemporary. ''We require that fiction be intelligent, and esthetically written.'' **Buys 20 mss/year.** Send complete ms. Length: 2,000-7,000 words. **Pays $30/page.**

Poetry Buys 50 poems/year. Submit maximum 3 poems. **Pays $2.50/line.**

$ $ GLIMMER TRAIN STORIES

Glimmer Train Press, Inc., 1211 NW Glisan St., Suite 207, Portland OR 97209. (503)221-0836. Fax: (503)221-0837. E-mail: linda@glimmertrain.com. Website: www.glimmertrain.com. **Contact:** Linda Swanson-Davies, co-editor. **90% freelance written.** Quarterly magazine of literary short fiction. "We are interested in well-written, emotionally-moving short stories published by unknown, as well as known, writers." Estab. 1991. Circ. 16,000. **Pays on acceptance.** Publishes ms an average of 18 months after acceptance. Byline given. Buys first rights. Responds in 3 months to mss. Sample copy for $11 on website. Writer's guidelines online.

Fiction "Open to stories of all themes, all subjects." **Buys 32 mss/year.** Length: up to 12,000. **Pays $500.**

Tips To submit a story, use the form on the website. All stories should be submitted via this electronic format. See *Glimmer Train*'s contest listings in Contest and Awards section.

$ $ ◩ GRAIN LITERARY MAGAZINE

Saskatchewan Writers Guild, P.O. Box 67, Saskatoon SK S7K 3K1 Canada. (306)244-2828. Fax: (306)244-0255. E-mail: grainmag@sasktel.net. Website: www.grainmagazine.ca. Buisiness Administrator: Bobbi Clackson-Walker. **Contact:** Kent Bruyneel, editor. **100% freelance written.** Quarterly magazine covering poetry, fiction, creative nonfiction, drama. "*Grain* publishes writing of the highest quality, both traditional and innovative in nature. The *Grain* editors' aim: To publish work that challenges readers; to encourage promising new writers; and to produce a well-designed, visually interesting magazine." Estab. 1973. Circ. 1,600. Pays on publication. Byline given. Buys first, canadian serial rights. Editorial lead time 6 months. Accepts queries by mail. Responds in 1 month to queries; 4 months to mss. Sample copy for $13 or online. Writer's guidelines for #10 SASE or online.

Nonfiction Interested in creative nonfiction.

Photos Submit 12-20 slides and b&w prints, short statement (200 words), and brief résumé. Reviews transparencies, prints. Pays $100 for front cover art, $30/photo.

Fiction David Carpenter, fiction editor. Literary fiction of all types. Experimental, mainstream, contemporary, prose poem. "No romance, confession, science fiction, vignettes, mystery." **Buys 40 mss/year.** Length: "No more than 30 pages." **Pays $40-175.**

Poetry "High quality, imaginative, well-crafted poetry. Submit maximum 8 poems and SASE with postage or IRC's. Avant-garde, free verse, haiku, traditional. No sentimental, end-line rhyme, mundane." **Buys 78 poems/year. Pays $40-175.**

Tips "Sweat the small stuff. Pay attention to detail, credibility. Make sure you have researched your piece and that the literal and metaphorical support one another."

⊕ GRANTA

The Magazine of New Writing, Granta Publications, 2-3 Hanover Yard, Noel Rd., London N1 8BE United Kingdom. (44)(0)20 7704 9776. E-mail: hgordon@granta.com. Website: www.granta.com. Editor: Ian Jack. **Contact:** Helen Gordon, editorial assistant. **100% freelance written.** Quarterly 256-page paperback book. "*Granta* magazine publishes fiction, reportage, biography and autobiography, history, travel and documentary photography. It does not publish 'writing about writing.' The realistic narrative—the story—is its primary form." Estab. 1979. Circ. 80,000. Pays on publication. Byline given. Offers kill fee, amount determined by arrangement. Buys world English language rights, first serial rights (minimum). "We hold more rights in pieces we commission." Editorial lead time 3 months. Accepts simultaneous submissions. Responds in 3 months to mss. Sample copy for $14.95. Writer's guidelines online.

  • Queries not necessary.

Nonfiction No articles or reporting whose relevancy will not last the life span of the magazine. The pieces we publish should last for several years (as the issues themselves do).

Fiction Buys no more than 2 short stories or synopsis and first chapter of a novel. "Please do not send more than 2 stories at a time." Novel excerpts, literary. No genre fiction. Length: No limits on length. **Payment varies.**

Tips "You must be familiar with the magazine and ask yourself honestly if you feel your piece meets our criteria. We receive many submissions every day, many of which are completely unsuitable for *Granta* (however well written)."

$ HAPPY

240 E. 35th St., Suite 11A, New York NY 10016. E-mail: bayardx@aol.com. **Contact:** Bayard, editor. Quarterly Estab. 1995. Circ. 500. Pays on publication. Publishes ms an average of 6-12 months after acceptance. Byline given. Buys one-time rights. Accepts queries by mail. Accepts simultaneous submissions. Responds in 1 month to queries. Sample copy for $20. Writer's guidelines for #10 SASE.

Fiction "We accept anything that's beautifully written. Genre isn't important. It just has to be incredible writing." Erotica, ethnic, experimental, fantasy, horror, humorous, novel excerpts, science fiction, short stories. No "televi-

sion rehash or religious nonsense." Want more work that is "strong, angry, empowering, intelligent, God-like, expressive." **Buys 100-130 mss/year.** Send complete ms. Length: 6,000 words maximum. **Pays 1-5¢/word.**
Tips "Don't bore us with the mundane—blast us out of the water with the extreme!"

$HAYDEN'S FERRY REVIEW

Arizona State University, Box 871502, Arizona State University, Tempe AZ 85287-1502. (480)965-1243. Fax: (480)965-2191. E-mail: hfr@asu.edu. Website: www.asu.edu/clas/pipercwcenter/publications/haydensferryre view. **Contact:** Fiction, Poetry, or Art Editor. **85% freelance written.** Semiannual magazine. "*Hayden's Ferry Review* publishes the best quality fiction, poetry, and creative nonfiction from new, emerging, and established writers." Estab. 1986. Circ. 1,300. Pays on publication. Publishes ms an average of 6 months after acceptance. Byline given. Buys first North American serial rights. Editorial lead time 3 months. Accepts queries by mail. Accepts simultaneous submissions. Responds in 2 weeks to queries; 3 months to mss. Sample copy for $7.50. Writer's guidelines online.

● No electronic submissions.

Nonfiction Essays, interview/profile, personal experience. **Buys 2 mss/year.** Send complete ms. Length: Open. **Pays $25-100.**

Photos Send photos with submission. Reviews slides. Buys one-time rights. Offers $25/photo.

Fiction Editors change every 1-2 years. Ethnic, experimental, humorous, slice-of-life vignettes, contemporary, prose poem. **Buys 10 mss/year.** Send complete ms. Length: Open. **Pays $25-100.**

Poetry Avant-garde, free verse, haiku, light verse, traditional. **Buys 60 poems/year.** Submit maximum 6 poems. Length: Open. **Pays $25-100.**

$THE HOLLINS CRITIC

P.O. Box 9538, Hollins University, Roanoke VA 24020-1538. E-mail: acockrell@hollins.edu. Website: www.holli ns.edu/academics/critic. Editor: R.H.W. Dillard. Managing Editor: Amanda Cockrell. **Contact:** Cathryn Hankla, poetry editor. **100% freelance written.** Magazine published 5 times/year. Estab. 1964. Circ. 400. Pays on publication. Publishes ms an average of 2 years after acceptance. Byline given. Buys first North American serial rights. Accepts queries by mail. Accepts simultaneous submissions. Responds in 2 months to mss. Sample copy for $1.50. Writer's guidelines for #10 SASE.

● No e-mail submissions. Send complete ms.

Poetry "We read poetry only from September 1-December 15." Avant-garde, free verse, traditional. **Buys 16-20 poems/year.** Submit maximum 5 poems. **Pays $25.**

Tips "We accept unsolicited poetry submissions; all other content is by prearrangement."

$THE HUDSON REVIEW

A magazine of literature and the arts, The Hudson Review, Inc., 684 Park Ave., New York NY 10021. (212)650-0020. Fax: (212)774-1911. E-mail: info@hudsonreview.com. Website: www.hudsonreview.com. Managing Editor: Ronald Koury. **Contact:** Paula Deitz, editor. **100% freelance written.** Quarterly magazine publishing fiction, poetry, essays, book reviews; criticism of literature, art, theatre, dance, film and music; and articles on contemporary cultural developments. Estab. 1948. Circ. 5,000. Pays on publication. Publishes ms an average of 6 months after acceptance. Byline given. Only assigned reviews are copyrighted. Editorial lead time 3 months. Accepts queries by mail. Responds in 2 months to queries; 3 months to mss. Sample copy for $9. Writer's guidelines for #10 SASE.

Nonfiction Paula Deitz. Essays, general interest, historical/nostalgic, opinion, personal experience, travel. **Buys 4-6 mss/year.** Send complete ms between January 1 and March 31 only. Length: 3,500 words maximum. **Pays 2¹/₂¢/word.**

Fiction Ronald Koury. Read between September 1 and November 30 only. **Buys 4 mss/year. Pays 2¹/₂¢/word.**

Poetry Read poems only between April 1 and June 30. Shannon Bond, associate editor. **Buys 12-20 poems/year.** Submit maximum 7 poems. **Pays 50¢/line.**

Tips "We do not specialize in publishing any particular 'type' of writing; our sole criterion for accepting unsolicited work is literary quality. The best way for you to get an idea of the range of work we publish is to read a current issue. We do not consider simultaneous submissions. Unsolicted manuscripts submitted outside of specified reading times will be returned unread. Do not send submissions via e-mail."

$HUNGER MOUNTAIN

The Vermont College Journal of Arts & Letters, Vermont College/Union Institute & University, 36 College St., Montpelier VT 05602. Fax: (802)828-8649. E-mail: hungermtn@tui.edu. Website: www.hungermtn.org. **Contact:** Caroline Mercurio, managing editor. **30% freelance written.** Semiannual perfect-bound journal covering high quality fiction, poetry, creative nonfiction, interviews, photography, and artwork reproductions. Accepts high quality work from unknown, emerging, or successful writers and artists. No genre fiction, drama, children's writing, or academic articles, please. Estab. 2002. Pays on publication. Publishes ms an average of 1 year after acceptance. Byline given. Buys first North American serial rights. Submit seasonal material 6 months in advance. Accepts queries by mail. Responds in 1 month to queries; 3 months to mss. Sample copy for $10. Writer's guidelines online or by e-mail.

Nonfiction Creative nonfiction only. All book reviews and interviews will be solicited. Book excerpts, essays, opinion, personal experience, photo feature, religious, travel. Special issues: "We will publish special issues, hopefully yearly, but we do not know yet the themes of these issues." No informative or instructive articles, please. Query with published clips. **Pays $5/page (minimum $30).** Sometimes pays expenses of writers on assignment.

Photos Send photos with submission. Reviews contact sheets, transparencies, prints, GIF/JPEG files. Slides preferred. Buys one-time rights. Negotiates payment individually. Query with published clips. **Pays $25-100.**

Poetry Avant-garde, free verse, haiku, traditional, nature, narrative, experimental, etc. No light verse, humor/quirky/catchy verse, greeting card verse. **Buys 10 poems/year.**

Tips "We want high quality work! Submit in duplicate. Manuscripts must be typed, prose double-spaced. Poets submit at least 3 poems. No multiple genre submissions. We need more b&w photography and short shorts. Fresh viewpoints and human interest are very important, as is originality. We are committed to publishing an outstanding journal of arts & letters. Do not send entire novels, manuscripts, or short story collections. Do not send previously published work."

$ THE ICONOCLAST

1675 Amazon Rd., Mohegan Lake NY 10547-1804. **Contact:** Phil Wagner, editor. **90% freelance written.** Bi-monthly literary magazine. "Aimed for a literate general audience with interests in fine (but accessible) fiction and poetry." Estab. 1992. Circ. 600. Pays on publication. Publishes ms an average of 9-12 months after acceptance. Byline given. Buys first North American serial rights. Editorial lead time 1-2 months. Accepts queries by mail. Responds in 2 weeks to queries; 1 month to mss. Sample copy for $2.50. Writer's guidelines for #10 SASE.

Nonfiction Essays, humor, reviews, literary/cultural matters. Does not want "anything that would be found in the magazines on the racks of supermarkets or convenience stores." **Buys 6-10 mss/year.** Query. Length: 250-2,500 words. **Pays 1¢/word.** Pays in contributor copies for previously published articles.

Photos Line drawings preferred. State availability with submission. Reviews 4×6, b&w prints. Buys one-time rights. Negotiates payment individually.

Columns/Departments Book reviews (fiction/poetry), 250-500 words. **Buys 6 mss/year.** Query. **Pays 1¢/word.**

Fiction Buys more fiction and poetry than anything else. Adventure, ethnic, experimental, fantasy, humorous, mainstream, novel excerpts, science fiction, literary. No character studies, slice-of-life, pieces strong on attitude/weak on plot. **Buys 25 mss/year.** Send complete ms. Length: 250-3,000 words. **Pays 1¢/word.**

Poetry Avant-garde, free verse, haiku, light verse, traditional. No religious, greeting card, beginner rhyming. **Buys 75 poems/year.** Submit maximum 4 poems. Length: 2-50 lines. **Pays $2-5.**

Tips "Professional conduct and sincerity help. Know it's the best you can do on a work before sending it out. Skill is the luck of the prepared. Everything counts. We love what we do, and are serious about it—and expect you to share that attitude. Remember: You're writing for paying subscribers. Ask Yourself: Would I pay money to read what I'm sending? We don't reply to submissions without a SASE, nor do we e-mail replies."

N $ ILLUMEN

Sam's Dot Publishing, P.O. Box 782, Cedar Rapids IA 52406-0782. E-mail: illumensdp@yahoo.com. Website: www.samsdotpublishing.com/aoife/cover.htm. **Contact:** Tyree Campbell. **100% freelance written.** Semiannual magazine. *Illumen* publishes speculative poetry and articles about speculative poetry, and reviews of poetry and collections. Estab. 2004. Circ. 40. Publishes ms an average of 1-3 months after acceptance. Byline given. Offers 100% kill fee. Buys first North American serial, one-time, second serial (reprint) rights. Editorial lead time 2 months. Submit seasonal material 6 months in advance. Accepts queries by e-mail. Responds in 2 weeks to queries; 3-4 months to mss. Sample copy for $8. Writer's guidelines online.

Nonfiction *Illumen* buys/publishes reviews of poetry and poetry collections, and interviews with poets, writers, and teachers, so long as the interviews are related to the magazine's specialty. **Buys 5-8 mss/year.** Send complete ms. Length: 2,000 words. **Pays $10 for unsolicited articles.** Pays in contributor copies at the author's request.

Poetry Avant-garde, free verse, haiku, light verse, traditional. "Scifaiku is a difficult sell with us because we also publish a specialty magazine—*Scifaikuest*—for scifaiku and related forms." **Buys 40-50 poems/year.** Submit maximum 5 poems. Length: 200 lines.

Tips "*Illumen* publishes beginning writers, as well as seasoned veterans. Be sure to read and follow the guidelines before submitting your work. The best advice for beginning writers is to send your best effort, not your first draft."

Ⓝ $ $ IMAGE

3307 Third Ave. W., Seattle WA 98119. (206)281-2988. E-mail: image@imagejournal.org. Website: www.imagej ournal.org. **Editor:** Gregory Wolfe. **Managing Editor:** Mary Kenagy. **50% freelance written.** Quarterly magazine covering the intersection between art and faith. *Image* is a unique forum for the best writing and artwork that is informed by—or grapples with—religious faith. "We have never been interested in art that merely regurgitates dogma or falls back on easy answers or didacticism. Instead, our focus has been on writing and visual artwork that embody a spiritual struggle, that seek to strike a balance between tradition and a profound openness to the world. Each issue explores this relationship through outstanding fiction, poetry, painting, sculpture, architecture, film, music, interviews, and dance. *Image* also features 4-color reproductions of visual art." Estab. 1989. Circ. 5,200. Pays on publication. Publishes ms an average of 8 months after acceptance. Byline given. Buys first North American serial rights. Accepts queries by mail, e-mail, phone. Responds in 1 month to queries; 2 months to mss. Sample copy for $12 or online. Writer's guidelines for #10 SASE or online.

    Oⁿ "We seek well-crafted essays, stories and poetry that use language in new and surprising ways and engage with timeless themes, like grace, redemption, and incarnation."

Nonfiction Essays. No sentimental, preachy, moralistic, or obvious essays. **Buys 10 mss/year.** Send complete ms. Length: 4,000-6,000 words. **Pays $10/page; $200 maximum for all prose articles.**

Fiction No sentimental, preachy, moralistic, obvious stories, or genre stories (unless they manage to transcend their genre). **Buys 8 mss/year.** Send complete ms. Length: 4,000-6,000 words. **Pays $10/page; $200 maximum.**

Poetry Buys 24 poems/year. Submit maximum 5 poems. **Pays $2/line; $150 maximum.**

Tips "Read the publication."

$ INDIANA REVIEW

Indiana University, Ballantine Hall 465, 1020 E. Kirkwood, Bloomington IN 47405-7103. (812)855-3439. E-mail: inreview@indiana.edu. Website: www.indiana.edu/~inreview. **Contact:** Esther Lee, editor. **100% freelance written.** Biannual magazine. "*Indiana Review*, a nonprofit organization run by IU graduate students, is a journal of previously unpublished poetry and fiction. Literary interviews and essays are also considered. We publish innovative fiction and poetry. We're interested in energy, originality, and careful attention to craft. While we publish many well-known writers, we also welcome new and emerging poets and fiction writers." Estab. 1976. Circ. 2,000. Pays on publication. Publishes ms an average of 3-6 months after acceptance. Byline given. Buys first North American serial rights. Accepts queries by mail. Accepts simultaneous submissions. Responds in 2 or more weeks to queries; 4 or more months to mss. Sample copy for $9. Writer's guidelines online.

    Oⁿ Break in with 500-1,000 word book reviews of fiction, poetry, nonfiction, and literary criticism published within the last 2 years, "since this is the area in which there's the least amount of competition."

Nonfiction Essays, interview/profile, creative nonfiction, reviews. No "coming of age/slice of life pieces." **Buys 5-7 mss/year.** Send complete ms. Length: 9,000 words maximum. **Pays $5/page ($10 minimum), plus 2 contributor's copies.**

Fiction Will Boast, fiction editor. "We look for daring stories which integrate theme, language, character, and form. We like polished writing, humor, and fiction which has consequence beyond the world of its narrator." Ethnic, experimental, mainstream, novel excerpts, literary, short fictions, translations. No genre fiction. **Buys 14-18 mss/year.** Send complete ms. Length: 250-10,000 words. **Pays $5/page ($10 minimum), plus 2 contributor's copies.**

Poetry "We look for poems that are skillfull and bold, exhibiting an inventiveness of language with attention to voice and sonics." Experimental, free verse, prose poem, traditional form, lyrical, narrative. Kyle Dorgan, poetry editor. **Buys 80 poems/year.** Submit maximum 6 poems. Length: 5 lines minimum. **Pays $5/page ($10 minimum), plus 2 contributor's copies.**

Tips "We're always looking for nonfiction essays that go beyond merely autobiographical revelation and utilize sophisticated organization and slightly radical narrative strategies. We want essays that are both lyrical and analytical where confession does not mean nostalgia. Read us before you submit. Often reading is slower in summer and holiday months. Only submit work to journals you would proudly subscribe to, then subscribe to a few. Take care to read the latest 2 issues and specifically mention work you identify with and why. Submit work that 'stacks up' with the work we've published." Offers annual poetry, fiction, short-short/prose-poem prizes. See website for details.

Ⓝ INK POT

Lit Pot Press, Inc., 3909 Reche Rd., Suite 96, Fallbrook CA 92028. Phone/fax: (760)731-3111. E-mail: inkpot@ver yfast.biz. Website: www.inkpots.net. **Contact:** Beverly Jackson, editor-in-chief/publisher. **100% freelance written.** Semiannual perfect-bound book/journal. "*Ink Pot* publishes fresh, edgy work of the highest literary quality from both the unheralded as well as the known professionals." Estab. 2003. Circ. 100. Publishes ms an average of 6-8 months after acceptance. Byline given. Buys first, electronic rights. Editorial lead time 8 months.

Submit seasonal material 8 months in advance. Accepts queries by e-mail. Accepts simultaneous submissions. Responds in 1 week to mss. Sample copy for $12. Writer's guidelines online.

- E-mail submissions only. Do not submit to this publication more than once a month to the same category/ editor.

Nonfiction "We want creative nonfiction in the literary genre only." Essays, general interest, humor, interview/ profile, opinion, personal experience, photo feature, criticism/diary. "We do not publish religious, political, medical, improvement, or mainstream work." **Buys 12 mss/year.** Send complete ms. Length: 500-5,000 words. **Pays writers with choice of cash or copies.**

Photos Reviews GIF/JPEG files (400×600). Buys one-time rights. Offers $20 (or copies) minimum/photo. Model releases required.

Fiction Experimental, humorous, suspense, literary. No science fiction, romance, religious, mainstream, mystery, or erotica (unless it is literary). **Buys 25 mss/year.** Send complete ms. Length: 100-5,000 words. **Pays writers with choice of cash or copies.**

Poetry Free verse, haiku. "We're not interested in rhymed poetry unless it's exceptional; no confessional/ romance." **Buys 25 poems/year.** Submit maximum 5 poems. Length: 3-100 lines.

Tips "We aren't looking for traditional work. We are interested in writers trying to create universal themes in new and exciting ways. We appreciate professionalism but support newcomers with serious writing work ethics. Send only your best. Don't batter us with everything in your inventory."

Ⓝ $ $ INKWELL

Manhattanville College, 2900 Purchase St., Purchase NY 10577. (914)323-7239. Fax: (914)323-3122. E-mail: inkwell@mville.edu. Website: www.inkwelljournal.org. Editor: Christine Adler. **Contact:** Fiction editor; Poetry editor. **100% freelance written.** Semiannual magazine covering poetry, fiction, essays, artwork, and photography. Estab. 1995. Pays on publication. Publishes ms an average of 4 months after acceptance. Byline given. Buys first North American serial rights. Editorial lead time 4 months. Accepts simultaneous submissions. Responds in 1 month to queries; 4-6 months to mss. Sample copy for $6. Writer's guidelines free.

Nonfiction Book excerpts, essays, literary essays, memoirs. Does not want children's literature, erotica, pulp adventure, or science fiction. **Buys 3-4 mss/year.** Query with or without published clips or send complete ms. Length: Length: 5,000 words maximum. **Pays $150-350.**

Photos Send photos with submission. Reviews 5×7 prints, GIF/JPEG files on diskette/cd. Buys one-time rights. Negotiates payment individually.

Fiction Mainstream, novel excerpts, literary. Does not want children's literature, erotica, pulp adventure, or science fiction. **Buys 20 mss/year.** Send complete ms. Length: 5,000 words maximum. **Pays $75-150.**

Poetry Avant-garde, free verse, traditional. Does not want doggerel, funny poetry, etc. **Buys 40 poems/year.** Submit maximum 6 poems. **Pays $5-10/page.**

Tips "We cannot accept electronic submissions."

$ THE IOWA REVIEW

308 EPB, The University of Iowa, Iowa City IA 52242. Website: iowareview.org. **Contact:** David Hamilton, editor. Triannual magazine "Stories, essays, and poems for a general readership interested in contemporary literature." Estab. 1970. Circ. 2,500. Pays on publication. Publishes ms an average of 8-12 months after acceptance. Buys first North American serial, nonexclusive anthology, classroom, and online serial rights. Responds in 3 months. Sample copy for $7 and online. Writer's guidelines online.

- This magazine uses the help of colleagues and graduate assistants. Its reading period for unsolicited work is September 1-December 1. "From January through April, we read entries to our annual Iowa Awards competition. Check our website for further information."

Fiction "We are open to a range of styles and voices and always hope to be surprised by work we then feel we need." **Pays $25 for the first page and $15 for each additional page, plus 2 contributor's copies; additional copies 30% off cover price.**

Tips "We publish essays, reviews, novel excerpts, stories, and poems, and would like for our essays not always to be works of academic criticism. We have no set guidelines as to content or length, but strongly recommend that writers read a sample issue before submitting." **Buys 65-80 unsolicited ms/year.** Submit complete ms with SASE. **Pays $25 for the first page and $15 for each subsequent page of poetry or prose.**

$ IRREANTUM

A Review of Mormon Literature and Film, The Association for Mormon Letters, P.O. Box 51364, Provo UT 84605. (801)355-3756. E-mail: editor@irreantum.org. Website: www.irreantum.org. **Contact:** Laraine Wilkins. Literary journal published 3 times/year. "While focused on Mormonism, *Irreantum* is a cultural, humanities-oriented magazine, not a religious magazine. Our guiding principle is that Mormonism is grounded in a sufficiently unusual, cohesive, and extended historical and cultural experience that it has become like a nation, an ethnic culture. We can speak of Mormon literature at least as surely as we can of a Jewish or Southern literature. *Irreantum* publishes stories, one-act dramas, stand-alone novel and drama excerpts, and poetry by, for, or about Mormons (as well as author interviews, essays, and reviews). The journal's audience includes readers of any or no religious faith who are interested in literary exploration of the Mormon culture, mindset, and worldview through Mormon themes and characters either directly or by implication. *Irreantum* is currently the only magazine devoted to Mormon literature." Estab. 1999. Circ. 500. Pays on publication. Publishes ms an average of 3-12 months after acceptance. Buys one-time, electronic rights. Accepts queries by e-mail. Accepts previously published material. Accepts simultaneous submissions. Responds in 2 weeks to queries; 2 months to mss. Sample copy for $6. Writer's guidelines by e-mail.

● Also publishes short shorts, literary essays, literary criticism, and poetry.

Fiction Adventure, ethnic, experimental, fantasy, historical, horror, humorous, mainstream, mystery, religious, romance, science fiction, suspense. **Buys 12 mss/year.** Length: 1,000-5,000 words. **Pays $0-100.**

Tips "*Irreantum* is not interested in didactic or polemical fiction that primarily attempts to prove or disprove Mormon doctrine, history, or corporate policy. We encourage beginning writers to focus on human elements first, with Mormon elements introduced only as natural and organic to the story. Readers can tell if you are honestly trying to explore human experience or if you are writing with a propagandistic agenda either for or against Mormonism. For conservative, orthodox Mormon writers, beware of sentimentalism, simplistic resolutions, and foregone conclusions."

Ⓝ $⊡ ISLAND

P.O. Box 210, Sandy Bay Tasmania 7006 Australia. 03 6226 2325. Fax: 03 6226 2172. E-mail: island@tassie.net. au. Website: www.islandmag.com. **Contact:** David Owen, editor. Quarterly magazine. "*Island* seeks quality fiction, poetry, essays, and articles. Our philosophy is general, with some emphasis on environment." Circ. 1,000. Buys one-time rights. Accepts queries by mail, e-mail, fax. Sample copy for $8.95 (Australian). Writer's guidelines online.

Nonfiction Articles and reviews. **Pays $100 (Australian)/1,000 words.**

Fiction Length: 4,000 words. **Pays $100 (Australian).**

Poetry Pays $60.

$ THE KENYON REVIEW

Walton House, 104 College Dr., Gambier OH 43022. (740)427-5208. Fax: (740)427-5417. E-mail: kenyonreview @kenyon.edu. Website: www.kenyonreview.org. **Contact:** David H. Lynn, editor. **100% freelance written.** Quarterly magazine covering contemporary literature and criticism. An international journal of literature, culture, and the arts dedicated to an inclusive representation of the best in new writing (fiction, poetry, essays, interviews, criticism) from established and emerging writers. Length: 3-15 typeset pages preferred. **Pays $30-40/page.** Estab. 1939. Circ. 6,000. Pays on publication. Publishes ms an average of 1 year after acceptance. Byline given. Buys first rights. Editorial lead time 1 year. Submit seasonal material 1 year in advance. Accepts queries by mail. Responds in 3-4 months. Sample copy $12, includes postage and handling. Please call or e-mail to order. Writer's guidelines online.

Tips "Work may be submitted through our website, but not through e-mail. See our website for instructions."

$ THE KIT-CAT REVIEW

244 Halstead Ave., Harrison NY 10528. (914)835-4833. **Contact:** Claudia Fletcher, editor. **100% freelance written.** Quarterly magazine. *The Kit-Cat Review* is named after the 18th Century Kit-Cat Club, whose members included Addison, Steele, Congreve, Vanbrugh, and Garth. Its purpose is to promote/discover excellence and originality. Estab. 1998. Circ. 500. Pays on publication. Publishes ms an average of 6-12 months after acceptance. Byline given. Buys first rights. Accepts queries by mail, phone. Accepts simultaneous submissions. Responds in 1 week to queries; 2 months to mss. Sample copy for $7 (payable to Claudia Fletcher). Writer's guidelines for SASE.

Nonfiction "Shorter pieces stand a better chance of publication." Book excerpts, essays, general interest, historical/nostalgic, humor, interview/profile, personal experience, travel. **Buys 6 mss/year.** Send complete ms with brief bio and SASE. Length: 5,000 words maximum. **Pays $25-100.**

Fiction Ethnic, experimental, novel excerpts, slice-of-life vignettes. No stories with "O. Henry-type formula endings. Shorter pieces stand a better chance of publication." No science fiction, fantasy, romance, horror, or new age. **Buys 20 mss/year.** Send complete ms. Length: 5,000 words maximum. **Pays $25-100 and 2 contributor's copies; additional copies $5.**

Poetry Free verse, traditional. No excessively obscure poetry. **Buys 100 poems/year. Pays $10-100.**

Tips "Obtaining a sample copy is strongly suggested. Include a short bio, SASE, and word count for fiction and nonfiction submissions."

$ ⊕ THE LONDON MAGAZINE

Review of Literature and the Arts, The London Magazine, 32 Addison Grove, London W4 1ER United Kingdom. (00)44 0208 400 5882. Fax: (00)44 0208 994 1713. E-mail: editorial@thelondonmagazine.net. Website: www.the londonmagazine.net. **Contact:** Sebastian Barker, editor. **100% freelance written.** Bimonthly magazine covering literature and the arts. Estab. 1732. Circ. 5,000. Pays on publication. Publishes ms an average of 4 months after acceptance. Byline given. Kill fee negotiable. Buys first rights. Editorial lead time 3 months. Submit seasonal material 6 months in advance. Accepts queries by mail. Responds in 1 month to queries; 3 months to mss. Sample copy for £7.50. Writer's guidelines online.

Nonfiction Book excerpts, essays, interview/profile, memoirs. No journalism, reportage, or quasi-marketing. **Buys 16 mss/year.** Send complete ms. Length: 6,000 words maximum. **Pays minimum £20; average £30-50; maximum £150 for a major contribution.**

Fiction Adventure, confessions, erotica, ethnic, experimental, fantasy, historical, horror, humorous, mainstream, mystery, novel excerpts, religious, romance, science fiction, slice-of-life vignettes, suspense. **Buys 32 mss/year.** Send complete ms. Length: 6,000 words maximum. **Pays minimum £20; average £30-50; maximum £150 for a major contribution.**

Poetry Avant-garde, free verse, haiku, light verse, traditional. **Buys 60 poems/year.** Submit maximum 6 poems. Length: 1,000 words maximum (negotiable).

$ LULLABY HEARSE

26 Fifth St., Bangor ME 04401-6022. E-mail: editor@lullabyhearse.com. Website: www.lullabyhearse.com. Editor: Sarah Ruth Jacobs. **95% freelance written.** Quarterly magazine. "*Lullaby Hearse* seeks dark, literary fiction in which the protagonist never gets a free ride. Stories that are event-driven rather than character-driven or that utilize traditional horror themes will generally get the back door treatment. Stark imagery and powerful characterization are desirable." Estab. 2002. Circ. 200. **Pays on acceptance.** Publishes ms an average of 3 months after acceptance. Buys first rights. Submit seasonal material 5 months in advance. Accepts queries by mail, e-mail. Accepts simultaneous submissions. Responds in 2 weeks to queries; 2 months to mss. Sample copy for $6. Writer's guidelines online.

Nonfiction Book excerpts, interview/profile, reviews of lost cult movie directors and films, reviews of other literary magazines. No essays on the craft of writing. **Buys 20 mss/year.** Send complete ms. Length: 500-2,500 words. **Pays $10-20 for assigned articles; $10-15 for unsolicited articles.**

Photos State availability of or send photos with submission. Reviews contact sheets, 4×6 and larger prints, GIF/JPEG files. Offers $10-20/photo. Negotiates payment individually.

Columns/Departments Film Criticism (write-ups of old or obscure movies), 750 words. **Buys 7 mss/year.** Send complete ms. **Pays $10-15.**

Fiction "We look for uniquely structured stories that ultimately cohere in a strong, decisive ending. Black humor is sometimes accepted, but humor alone isn't enough to take a story where it needs to go. Keenness of imagery and overall literary quality are important deciding factors. Crudity crosses the line when it insults the intelligence of the reader." Experimental, horror, science fiction. "Please don't send stories about writers, formulaic horror stories, or crime/mystery narratives that drag themselves down the beaten path. Fantasy and science fiction works are considered, but imagery must always be grounded in reality; miracles will be shot down." **Buys 30 mss/year.** Send complete ms. Length: 1,000-6,000 words. **Pays $10-20.**

Poetry Avant-garde, free verse. No first-person narrated poems that are often lacking in description. Generalized images or statements are undesirable—the shorter the poem, the more overwhelming the imagery should be. **Buys 25 poems/year.** Length: 10 lines minimum.

Tips "Often, subs are rejected because they go overboard on the horror component. Horror is a subtle craft, and its readers have indeed seen almost everything. *Lullaby Hearse* looks for characters and situations that invite the reader to linger after the story is put down. Each story and poem is chosen for its lasting quality, and shorts with predictable punchline endings are the anathema."

N $ LYNX EYE

ScribbleFest Literary Group, 581 Woodlawn Dr., Los Osos CA 93402. (805)528-8146. E-mail: pamccully@aol.c om. Co-Editor: Kathryn Morrison. **Contact:** Pam McCully, co-editor. **100% freelance written.** Quarterly journal. "Each issue of *Lynx Eye* offers thoughtful and thought-provoking reading." Estab. 1994. Circ. 500. **Pays on acceptance.** Publishes ms an average of 6 months after acceptance. Byline given. Offers 100% kill fee. Buys first North American serial rights. Editorial lead time 6 months. Submit seasonal material 6 months in advance. Accepts queries by mail. Accepts simultaneous submissions. Responds in 3 weeks to queries; 4 months to mss. Sample copy for $7.95. Writer's guidelines for #10 SASE.

Nonfiction Essays. No memoirs. **Buys 6 mss/year.** Send complete ms. Length: 500-5,000 words. **Pays $10.**

Fiction Pam McCully. Adventure, condensed novels, erotica, ethnic, experimental, fantasy, historical, horror, humorous, mainstream, mystery, novel excerpts, romance, science fiction, serialized novels, western. "No horror with gratuitous violence or YA stories." **Buys 50 mss/year.** Send complete ms. Length: 500-5,000 words. **Pays $10.**

Poetry Pam McCully. Avant-garde, free verse, haiku, light verse, traditional. **Buys 50 poems/year.** Submit maximum 6 poems. Length: 30 lines. **Pays $10.**

Tips "Know your craft, including grammar, usage, active verbs, well-constructed sentences and paragraphs, and fully developed characters. We accept never-before-published work only"

$⬚ THE MALAHAT REVIEW

The University of Victoria, P.O. Box 1700, STN CSC, Victoria BC V8W 2Y2 Canada. (250)721-8524. E-mail: malahat@uvic.ca (for queries only). Website: www.malahatreview.com. **Contact:** John Barton, editor. **100% freelance written.** Eager to work with new/unpublished writers. Quarterly magazine covering poetry, fiction, and reviews. "We try to achieve a balance of views and styles in each issue. We strive for a mix of the best writing by both established and new writers." Estab. 1967. Circ. 1,000. **Pays on acceptance.** Publishes ms an average of 6 months after acceptance. Byline given. Offers 100% kill fee. Buys second serial (reprint) rights and first world rights. Accepts queries by mail. Responds in 2 weeks to queries; 3 months to mss. Sample copy for $12 (US). Writer's guidelines online.

Nonfiction "Query first about review articles, critical essays, interviews, and visual art, which we generally solicit." Include SASE with Canadian postage or IRCs. **Pays $30/magazine page.**

Fiction "General ficton and poetry." **Buys 20 mss/year.** Send complete ms. Length: 20 pages maximum. **Pays $30/magazine page.**

Poetry Avant-garde, free verse, traditional. **Buys 100 poems/year.** Length: 5-10 pages. **Pays $30/magazine page.**

Tips "Please do not send more than 1 manuscript (the one you consider your best) at a time. See *The Malahat Review's* long poem and novella contests in Contest & Awards section."

$MAN'S STORY 2 MAGAZINE

Man's Story 2 Publishing Co., P.O. Box 1082, Roswell GA 30077. E-mail: mansstory2@aol.com. Website: www.mansstory2.com. Editor: Glenn Dunn. **80% freelance written.** Quarterly magazine and monthly online zine. "*Man's Story 2 Magazine* strives to recreate the pulp fiction that was published in the magazines of the 1960s. As the title implies, they are stories slanted toward the heterosexual male. Story subjects tend to slant toward the damsel in distress." Estab. 2001. Circ. 300. Pays on publication. Publishes ms an average of 3-6 months after acceptance. Buys one-time, second serial (reprint) rights. Accepts queries by e-mail. Accepts previously published material. Accepts simultaneous submissions. Writer's guidelines online.

Fiction Adventure, erotica, fantasy, horror, suspense, pulp fiction. **Buys 30-50 mss/year.** Send complete ms. Length: 1,500-5,000 words. **Pays $25.**

Tips "Since pulp fiction is pretty much a dead art form and not everyone can write a good action packed pulp fiction story, we suggest interested writers visit our website and read our writer's guidelines. Then, read the 1960s style pulp fiction stories posted in our online mini-magazine and/or read one of our magazines, or find an old pulp fiction magazine that was published in the 1960s. If all else fails, e-mail us."

$ $MANOA

A Pacific Journal of International Writing, English Dept., University of Hawaii, Honolulu HI 96822. (808)956-3070. Fax: (808)956-3083. E-mail: fstewart@hawaii.edu. Website: manoajournal.hawaii.edu. **Contact:** Frank Stewart, editor. Semiannual magazine. "High quality literary fiction, poetry, essays, personal narrative. Most of each issue is devoted to new work from Pacific and Asian nations. Our audience is primarily in the US, although expanding in Pacific countries. US writing need not be confined to Pacific settings or subjects." Estab. 1989. Circ. 2,500. Pays on publication. Byline given. Buys first North American serial rights and non-exclusive, one-time print rights. Editorial lead time 9 months. Accepts simultaneous submissions. Responds in 3 weeks to queries; 1 month to poetry mss; 6 months to fiction to mss. Sample copy for $10 (US). Writer's guidelines online.

Nonfiction Book excerpts, essays, interview/profile, creative nonfiction or personal narrative related to literature or nature. No Pacific exotica. **Buys 1-2 mss/year.** Send complete ms. Length: 1,000-5,000 words. **Pays $25/printed page.**

Fiction "We're potentially open to anything of literary quality, though usually not genre fiction as such." Mainstream, contemporary, excerpted novel. No Pacific exotica. **Buys 1-2 in the US (excluding translation) mss/year.** Send complete ms. Length: 1,000-7,500 words. **Pays $100-500 normally ($25/printed page).**

Poetry No light verse. **Buys 10-20 poems/year.** Submit maximum 5-6 poems. **Pays $25/poem.**

Tips "Although we are a Pacific journal, we are a general interest US literary journal, not limited to Pacific settings or subjects."

$THE MASSACHUSETTS REVIEW

South College, University of Massachusetts, Amherst MA 01003-9934. (413)545-2689. Fax: (413)577-0740. E-mail: massrev@external.umass.edu. Website: www.massreview.org. **Contact:** Corwin Ericson, managing editor; Ellen Watson, David Lenson, editors. Quarterly magazine. Estab. 1959. Circ. 1,200. Pays on publication. Publishes ms an average of 18 months after acceptance. Buys first North American serial rights. Accepts queries by mail. Accepts simultaneous submissions. Responds in 3 months to mss. Sample copy for $8. Writer's guidelines online.

● Does not respond to mss without SASE.

Nonfiction Articles on all subjects. No reviews of single books. Send complete ms or query with SASE. Length: 6,500 words maximum. **Pays $50.**

Fiction Short stories. Wants more prose less than 30 pages. **Buys 10 mss/year.** Send complete ms. Length: 25-30 pages maximum. **Pays $50.**

Poetry Submit maximum 6 poems. **Pays 35¢/line to $10 maximum.**

Tips "No manuscripts are considered June-October. No fax or e-mail submissions. No simultaneous submissions."

$MICHIGAN QUARTERLY REVIEW

3574 Rackham Bldg., 915 E. Washington, University of Michigan, Ann Arbor MI 48109-1070. (734)764-9265. E-mail: mqr@umich.edu. Website: www.umich.edu/~mqr. **Contact:** Laurence Goldstein, editor. **75% freelance written.** Quarterly magazine. "An interdisciplinary journal which publishes mainly essays and reviews, with some high-quality fiction and poetry, for an intellectual, widely read audience." Estab. 1962. Circ. 1,500. Pays on publication. Publishes ms an average of 1 year after acceptance. Byline given. Buys first serial rights. Accepts queries by mail. Responds in 2 months. Sample copy for $4. Writer's guidelines online.

● The Laurence Goldstein Award is a $1,000 annual award to the best poem published in the *Michigan Quarterly Review* during the previous year. The Lawrence Foundation Award is a $1,000 annual award to the best short story published in the *Michigan Quarterly Review* during the previous year.

Nonfiction "*MQR* is open to general articles directed at an intellectual audience. Essays ought to have a personal voice and engage a significant subject. Scholarship must be present as a foundation, but we are not interested in specialized essays directed only at professionals in the field. We prefer ruminative essays, written in a fresh style and which reach interesting conclusions. We also like memoirs and interviews with significant historical or cultural resonance." **Buys 35 mss/year.** Query. Length: 2,000-5,000 words. **Pays up to $75.**

Fiction Fiction Editor. No restrictions on subject matter or language. "We are very selective. We like stories which are unusual in tone and structure, and innovative in language. No genre fiction written for a market. Would like to see more fiction about social, political, cultural matters, not just centered on a love relationship or dysfunctional family." **Buys 10 mss/year.** Send complete ms. Length: 1,500-7,000 words. **Pays $10/published page.**

Poetry Buys 8 poems/issue **Pays $10/published page.**

Tips "Read the journal and assess the range of contents and the level of writing. We have no guidelines to offer or set expectations; every manuscript is judged on its unique qualities. On essays—query with a very thorough description of the argument and a copy of the first page. Watch for announcements of special issues which are usually expanded issues and draw upon a lot of freelance writing. Be aware that this is a university quarterly that publishes a limited amount of fiction and poetry that it is directed at an educated audience, one that has done a great deal of reading in all types of literature."

$MID-AMERICAN REVIEW

Department of English, Box W, Bowling Green State University, Bowling Green OH 43403. (419)372-2725. Website: www.bgsu.edu/midamericanreview. **Contact:** Michael Czyzniejewski, editor-in-chief. Willing to work with new/unpublished writers. Biannual magazine of "the highest quality fiction, poetry, and translations of contemporary poetry and fiction." Also publishes critical articles and book reviews of contemporary literature. "We try to put the best possible work in front of the biggest possible audience. We publish serious fiction and poetry, as well as critical studies in contemporary literature, translations and book reviews." Estab. 1981. Pays on publication when funding is available. Publishes ms an average of 6 months after acceptance. Byline given. Buys first North American serial, one-time rights. Accepts queries by mail, phone. Responds in 5 months to mss. Sample copy for $7 (current issue); $5 (back issue); $10 (rare back issues). Writer's guidelines online.

○Ɽ "Grab our attention with something original—even experimental—but most of all, well-written."

Nonfiction Essays (articles focusing on contemporary authors and topics of current literary interest), short book reviews (500-1,000 words). **Pays $10/page up to $50, pending funding.**

Fiction Michael Czyzniejewski, fiction editor. Character-oriented, literary, experimental, short short. Experimental, Memoir, prose poem, traditional. "No genre fiction. Would like to see more short shorts." **Buys 12 mss/year.** Length: 6,000 words. **Pays $10/page up to $50, pending funding.**

Poetry Karen Craigo, poetry editor. Strong imagery and sense of visio. **Buys 60 poems/year. Pays $10/page up to $50, pending funding.**

Tips "We are seeking translations of contemporary authors from all languages into English; submissions must include the original and proof of permission to translate. We would also like to see more creative nonfiction."

$ MILLER'S POND

H&H Press, RR 2, Box 239, Middlebury Center PA 16935. (570)376-3361. Website: www.millerspondpoetry.com. **Contact:** David Cazden, editor. **100% freelance written.** Annual magazine featuring poetry with poetry book/chapbook reviews and interviews of poets. E-mail submissions must be on the form from the website. Estab. 1998. Circ. 200. Pays on publication. Publishes ms an average of 1 year after acceptance. Byline given. Buys one-time rights. Editorial lead time 1 year. Accepts queries by mail, e-mail. Accepts simultaneous submissions. Responds in 10 months. Sample copy for $7, plus $3 postage. Writer's guidelines online.

Nonfiction Interview/profile (2,000 words), poetry chapbook reviews (500 words). **Buys 1-2 mss/year.** Query or send complete ms. **Pays $5.**

Poetry Free verse. No religious, horror, vulgar, rhymed, preachy, lofty, trite, overly sentimental. **Buys 30-35 poems/year.** Submit maximum 3-5 poems. Length: 40 lines maximum. **Pays $2.**

▣ The online magazine carries original content not found in the print edition and includes writer's guidelines. No payment for material appearing online. Contact: Julie Damerell, online editor.

Tips "View our website to see what we like. Study the contemporary masters: Billy Collins, Maxine Kumin, Colette Inez, Vivian Shipley. Always enclose SASE."

$ $ THE MISSOURI REVIEW

1507 Hillcrest Hall, University of Missouri, Columbia MO 65211. (573)882-4474. Fax: (573)884-4671. E-mail: tmr@missourireview.com. Website: www.missourireview.com. Associate Editor: Evelyn Somers. Poetry Editor: Steve Gehrke. Managing Editor: Richard Sowienski. **Contact:** Speer Morgan, editor. **90% freelance written.** Triannual magazine. "We publish contemporary fiction, poetry, interviews, personal essays, cartoons, special features—such as History as Literature series and Found Text series—for the literary and the general reader interested in a wide range of subjects." Estab. 1978. Circ. 5,500. Offers signed contract. Byline given. Editorial lead time 6 months. Accepts queries by mail. Responds in 2 weeks to queries; 10 weeks to mss. Sample copy for $8 or online. Writer's guidelines online.

Nonfiction Evelyn Somers, associate editor. Book excerpts, essays. No literary criticism. **Buys 10 mss/year.** Send complete ms. **Pays $30/printed page up to $750.**

Fiction Ethnic, humorous, mainstream, novel excerpts, literary. No genre or flash fiction. **Buys 25 mss/year.** Send complete ms. Length: no preference. **Pays $30/printed page up to $750.**

Poetry Publishes 3-5 poetry features of 6-12 pages per issue. "Please familiarize yourself with the magazine before submitting poetry." Steve Gehrke, poetry editor. **Buys 50 poems/year. Pays $30/printed page.**

▣ The online magazine carries original content not found in the print edition and includes writer's guidelines. Contact: Richard Sowienski, managing editor.

Tips "Send your best work."

$ MODERN HAIKU

An Independent Journal of Haiku and Haiku Studies, P.O. Box 68, Lincoln IL 62656. Website: www.modernhaik u.org. **Contact:** Lee Gurga, editor. **85% freelance written.** Magazine published 3 times/year. "*Modern Haiku* publishes high quality material only. Haiku and related genres, articles on haiku, haiku book reviews, and translations compose its contents. It has an international circulation and is widely subscribed to by university, school, and public libraries. Estab. 1969. Circ. 625. Pays on acceptance for poetry; on publication for prose. Publishes ms an average of 3 months after acceptance. Byline given. Buys first North American serial rights. Editorial lead time 4 months. Accepts queries by mail. Responds in 1 week to queries; 2 weeks to mss. Sample copy for $8 in North America, $12 elsewhere. Writer's guidelines online.

Nonfiction Essays (anything related to haiku). **Buys 40 mss/year.** Send complete ms. **Pays $5/page.**

Columns/Departments Haiku & Senryu; Haibun; Articles (on haiku and related genres); book reviews (books of haiku or related genres), 4 pages maximum. **Buys 15 mss/year.** Send complete ms. **Pays $5/page.**

Poetry Haiku, senryu. Does not want "general poetry, sentimental, and pretty-pretty haiku or overtly pornographic." **Buys 500 poems/year.** Submit maximum 24 poems. **Pays $1.**

Tips "Study the history of haiku, read books about haiku, learn the aesthetics of haiku and methods of composition. Write about your sense perceptions of the suchness of entities, avoid ego-centered interpretations."

$ NEW ENGLAND REVIEW

Middlebury College, Middlebury VT 05753. (802)443-5075. E-mail: nereview@middlebury.edu. Website: www. middlebury.edu/~nereview/. **Contact:** On envelope: Poetry, Fiction, or Nonfiction Editor; on letter: Stephen

Donadio, editor. Quarterly magazine. Serious literary only. Reads September 1-May 31 (postmarked dates). Estab. 1978. Circ. 2,000. Pays on publication. Publishes ms an average of 6 months after acceptance. Byline given. Buys first North American serial, first, second serial (reprint) rights. Accepts simultaneous submissions. Responds in 2 weeks to queries; 3 months to mss. Sample copy for $8. Writer's guidelines online.

● No e-mail submissions.

Nonfiction Serious literary only. Rarely accepts previously published submissions (out of print or previously published abroad only.) **Buys 20-25 mss/year.** Send complete ms. Length: 7,500 words maximum, though exceptions may be made. **Pays $10/page ($20 minimum), and 2 copies.**

Fiction Send 1 story at a time. Serious literary only, novel excerpts. **Buys 25 mss/year.** Send complete ms. Length: Prose length: 10,000 words maximum, double spaced. Novellas: 30,000 words maximum. **Pays $10/page ($20 minimum), and 2 copies.**

Poetry Buys 75-90 poems/year. Submit maximum 6 poems. **Pays $10/page ($20 minimum), and 2 copies.**

Tips "We consider short fiction, including shorts, short-shorts, novellas, and self-contained extracts from novels. We consider a variety of general and literary, but not narrowly scholarly nonfiction; long and short poems; speculative, interpretive, and personal essays; book reviews; screenplays; graphics; translations; critical reassessments; statements by artists working in various media; interviews; testimonies; and letters from abroad. We are committed to exploration of all forms of contemporary cultural expression in the US and abroad. With few exceptions, we print only work not published previously elsewhere."

$NEW LETTERS

University of Missouri-Kansas City, University House, 5101 Rockhill Rd., Kansas City MO 64110-2499. (816)235-1168. Fax: (816)235-2611. E-mail: newletters@umkc.edu. Website: www.newletters.org. Editor: Robert Stewart. **100% freelance written.** Quarterly magazine. "*New Letters* is intended for the general literate reader. We publish literary fiction, nonfiction, essays, poetry. We also publish art." Estab. 1934. Circ. 5,000. Pays on publication. Publishes ms an average of 6 months after acceptance. Byline given. Buys first North American serial rights. Editorial lead time 6 months. Submit seasonal material 6 months in advance. Accepts queries by mail. Responds in 1 month to queries; 3 months to mss. Sample copy for $7 or sample articles on website. Writer's guidelines online.

● Submissions are not read between May 1 and October 1.

Nonfiction Essays. No self-help, how-to, or nonliterary work. **Buys 8-10 mss/year.** Send complete ms. Length: 5,000 words maximum. **Pays $40-100.**

Photos Send photos with submission. Reviews contact sheets, 2 × 4 transparencies, prints. Buys one-time rights. Pays $10-40/photo.

Fiction Robert Stewart, editor. Ethnic, experimental, humorous, mainstream, contemporary. No genre fiction. **Buys 15-20 mss/year.** Send complete ms. Length: 5,000 words maximum. **Pays $30-75.**

Poetry Avant-garde, free verse, haiku, traditional. No light verse. **Buys 40-50 poems/year.** Submit maximum 6 poems. Length: Open. **Pays $10-25.**

Tips "We aren't interested in essays that are footnoted, or essays usually described as scholarly or critical. Our preference is for creative nonfiction or personal essays. We prefer shorter stories and essays to longer ones (an average length is 3,500-4,000 words). We have no rigid preferences as to subject, style, or genre, although commercial efforts tend to put us off. Even so, our only fixed requirement is on good writing."

$NEW ORLEANS REVIEW

Box 195, Loyola University, New Orleans LA 70118. (504)865-2295. Website: www.loyno.edu/~noreview/. Biannual magazine "publishing poetry, fiction, translations, photographs, and nonfiction on literature, art and film. Readership: those interested in contemporary literature and culture." Estab. 1968. Circ. 1,500. Pays on publication. Buys first North American serial rights. Accepts simultaneous submissions. Responds in 4 months to mss. Sample copy for $7.

Nonfiction Book reviews around 1,000 words.

Fiction Christopher Chambers, editor. "Good writing, from conventional to experimental." Length: up to 6,500 words. **Pays $25-50 and 2 copies.**

Poetry Submit maximum 3-5 poems.

Tips "Submissions should be complete, legible, with a brief cover letter and SASE."

$ THE NEW QUARTERLY

Canadian Writers & Writing, St. Jerome's University, 290 University Ave. N., Waterloo ON N2L 3G3 Canada. (519)884-8111, ext. 290. E-mail: newquart@watarts.uwaterloo.ca. Website: newquarterly.uwaterloo.ca. Editor: Kim Jernigan. **95% freelance written.** Quarterly book covering Canadian fiction and poetry. "Emphasis on emerging writers and genres, but we publish more traditional work as well if the language and narrative structure are fresh." Estab. 1981. Circ. 1,000. Pays on publication. Publishes ms an average of 4 months after acceptance. Byline given. Buys first Canadian rights. Editorial lead time 6 months. Accepts queries by mail, e-mail. Accepts simultaneous submissions. Responds in 2 weeks to queries; 4 months to mss. Sample copy for $15 (cover price, plus mailing). Writer's guidelines for #10 SASE or online.

- Open to Canadian writers only.

Fiction Kim Jernigan, Rae Crossman, Mark Spielmacher, Rosalynn Worth, fiction editors. *Canadian work only.* "We are not interested in genre fiction. We are looking for innovative, beautifully crafted, deeply felt literary fiction." **Buys 20-25 mss/year.** Send complete ms. Length: 20 pages maximum. **Pays $150/story.**

Poetry *Canadian work only.* Lesley Elliott, Randi Patterson, John Vardon, Erin Noteboom, poetry editors. Avant-garde, free verse, traditional. **Buys 40 poems/year.** Submit maximum 5 poems. Length: 4½ inches typeset.

Tips "Reading us is the best way to get our measure. We don't have preconceived ideas about what we're looking for other than that it must be Canadian work (Canadian writers, not necessarily Canadian content). We want something that's fresh, something that will repay a second reading, something in which the language soars and the feeling is complexly rendered."

⊘ $⊞ THE NEW WRITER

P.O. Box 60, Cranbrook Kent TN17 2ZR United Kingdom. 01580 212626. Fax: 01580 212041. E-mail: editor@thenewwriter.com. Website: www.thenewwriter.com. Publishes 6 issues per annum. Contemporary writing magazine which publishes "the best in fact, fiction and poetry." Estab. 1996. Circ. 1,500. Pays on publication. Publishes ms an average of 1 year after acceptance. Buys one-time rights. Accepts queries by e-mail, fax. Accepts simultaneous submissions. Responds in 2 months to queries; 4 months to mss. Sample copy for SASE and A4 SAE with IRCs only. Writer's guidelines for SASE.

Nonfiction Content should relate to writing. Query. Length: 1,000-2,000 words. **Pays £20-40.**

Fiction No unsolicited mss. Accepts fiction from subscribers only. "We will consider most categories apart from stories written for children. No horror, erotic, or cosy fiction." Query with published clips. Length: 2,000-5,000 words. **Pays £10 per story by credit voucher; additional copies for £1.50.**

Poetry Buys 50 poems/year. Submit maximum 3 poems. Length: 40 lines maximum. **Pays £3/poem.**

Ⓝ $ $ NEW YORK STORIES

LaGuardia/CUNY, 31-10 Thomson Ave., Long Island City NY 11101. (718)482-5673. E-mail: nystories@lagcc.cuny.edu. Website: www.newyorkstories.org. **Contact:** Daniel Caplice Lynch, editor-in-chief. **100% freelance written.** Magazine published 3 times/year. "Our purpose is to publish quality short fiction and New York-centered nonfiction. We look for fresh approaches, artistic daring, and story telling talent. We are especially interested in work that explores NYC's diversity—ethnic, social, sexual, psychological, economic, and geographical." Estab. 1998. Circ. 1,500. Pays on publication. Publishes ms an average of 6 months after acceptance. Byline given. Buys first North American serial rights. Editorial lead time 6 months. Submit seasonal material 6 months in advance. Accepts queries by mail. Accepts simultaneous submissions. Responds in 2 weeks to queries; 6 months to mss. Sample copy for $4. Writer's guidelines online.

Nonfiction Essays, personal experience, all must be related to New York City. **Buys 25-30 mss/year.** Send complete ms. Length: 300-6,000 words. **Pays $100-750.**

Photos Send photos with submission. Buys one-time rights. Negotiates payment individually. Model releases required.

Fiction Daniel Caplice Lynch, editor. Seeks quality above all; also minority writers, New York City themes. Ethnic, experimental, humorous, mainstream. **Buys 25 mss/year.** Send complete ms. Length: 300-6,000 words. **Pays $100-750.**

Tips "Send your best work. Try briefer pieces, cultivate a fresh approach. For the NYC nonfiction pieces, look on your doorstep. Fresh angles of vision and psychological complexity are the hallmarks of our short stories."

$ ☑ NFG MAGAZINE

Writing with Attitude, NFG Media, Sheppard Centre, P.O. Box 43112, Toronto ON M2N 6N1 Canada. Fax: (416)226-0994. E-mail: mrspeabody@nfg.ca. Website: www.nfg.ca. Publisher/Editor-in-Chief: Shar O'Brien. Managing Editor: J. Dale Hand-Humphries. **Contact:** Debbie Moorhouse, senior submissions manager. **100% freelance written.** Triannual magazine covering fiction. "We offer fiction without boundaries; content based on merit, not classification. From poetry to short stories, comics to art—if it titillates the mind, twists the subconscious, or delivers an unexpected slap, we want to see it. Artists who submit to *NFG* log in as a member and may check the status of their work as it moves through the editorial process. Work accepted for review is read by a minimum of 5 editors, who leave constructive comments for the author." Estab. October 2001; first issue January 2003. Circ. 5,000. **Pays on acceptance.** Publishes ms an average of 6 months after acceptance. Byline given. Offers 100% kill fee. Buys first, second serial (reprint) rights. Editorial lead time 2 months. Accepts queries by e-mail. Sample copy for $11. Writer's guidelines online.

Nonfiction Kelly A. Harmon, senior articles editor. Book excerpts (unpublished novels), essays, exposé, general interest, historical/nostalgic, humor, inspirational, interview/profile, new product, personal experience, photo feature, technical, travel. **Buys 6 mss/year.** Send complete ms. Length: 7,500 words maximum. **Pays $50 for unsolicited articles.**

Photos Sue Miller, senior art editor. Send photos with submission. Reviews JPEG files (600×800 at 100 dpi or smaller for initial view). Buys one-time rights. Offers no additional payment for photos accepted with ms. Identification of subjects, permission for rights required.

Fiction Adventure, condensed novels, confessions, erotica, ethnic, experimental, fantasy, historical, horror, humorous, mainstream, mystery, novel excerpts, religious, romance, science fiction, serialized novels, slice-of-life vignettes, suspense, western. **Buys 25-30 mss/year.** Send complete ms. Length: 7,500 words maximum. **Pays 3¢/word, minimum $50.**

Poetry Sue Miller, senior poetry editor. Avant-garde, free verse, haiku, light verse, traditional. Submit maximum 1 poem. **Buys 30-40 poems/year. Pays $35/poem.**

Fillers Anecdotes, facts, newsbreaks, short humor. **Buys 10-20/year.** Length: 1,000 words maximum. **Pays 5¢/word; $15 minimum.**

$THE NORTH AMERICAN REVIEW

University of Northern Iowa, 1222 W. 27th St., Cedar Falls IA 50614-0516. (319)273-6455. Fax: (319)273-4326. E-mail: nar@uni.edu. Website: www.webdelsol.com/northamreview/nar/. **Contact:** Grant Tracey, editor. **90% freelance written.** Bimonthly magazine. "The *NAR* is the oldest literary magazine in America and one of the most respected; though we have no prejudices about the subject matter of material sent to us, our first concern is quality." Estab. 1815. Circ. under 5,000. Pays on publication. Publishes ms an average of 9 months after acceptance. Byline given. Buys first North American serial, first rights. Accepts queries by mail, e-mail, phone. Responds in 4 months to mss. Sample copy for $5. Writer's guidelines online.

- This is the oldest literary magazine in the country and one of the most prestigious. Also one of the most entertaining—and a tough market for the young writer.
- ⦿ Break in with the "highest quality poetry, fiction, and nonfiction on any topic, but particularly interested in the environment, gender, race, ethnicity, and class."

Nonfiction Ron Sandvik, nonfiction editor. No restrictions; highest quality only. Length: Open. **Pays $5/350 words; $20 minimum, $100 maximum.**

Fiction Grant Tracey, fiction editor. No restrictions; highest quality only. "No flat narrative stories where the inferiority of the character is the paramount concern." Wants to see more "well-crafted literary stories that emphasize family concerns." Length: Open. **Pays $5/350 words; $20 minimum, $100 maximum.**

Poetry No restrictions; highest quality only. Length: Open. **Pays $1/line; $20 minimum, $100 maximum.**

Tips "We like stories that start quickly and have a strong narrative arc. Poems that are passionate about subject, language, and image are welcome, whether they are traditional or experimental, whether in formal or free verse (closed or open form). Nonfiction should combine art and fact with the finest writing. We do not accept simultaneous submissions; these will be returned unread. We read poetry, fiction, and nonfiction year-round."

$NORTH CAROLINA LITERARY REVIEW

A Magazine of North Carolina Literature, Culture, and History, English Dept., East Carolina University, Greenville NC 27858-4353. (252)328-1537. Fax: (252)328-4889. E-mail: bauerm@mail.ecu.edu. Website: www.ecu.edu/nclr. **Contact:** Margaret Bauer, editor. Annual magazine published in fall covering North Carolina writers, literature, culture, history. "Articles should have a North Carolina slant. First consideration is always for quality of work. Although we treat academic and scholarly subjects, we do not wish to see jargon-laden prose; our readers, we hope, are found as often in bookstores and libraries as in academia. We seek to combine the best elements of magazine for serious readers with best of scholarly journal." Estab. 1992. Circ. 750. Pays on publication. Publishes ms an average of 1 year after acceptance. Byline given. Buys first North American serial rights. Rights returned to writer on request. Editorial lead time 6 months. Accepts queries by mail, e-mail. Responds in 1 month to queries; 6 months to mss. Sample copy for $10-25. Writer's guidelines online.

- ⦿ Break in with an article related to the special feature topic. Check the website for upcoming topics and deadlines.

Nonfiction North Carolina-related material only. Book excerpts, essays, exposé, general interest, historical/nostalgic, humor, interview/profile, opinion, personal experience, photo feature, travel, reviews, short narratives, surveys of archives. "No jargon-laden academic articles." **Buys 25-35 mss/year.** Query with published clips. Length: 500-5,000 words. **Pays $50-100 honorarium, extra copies, back issues or subscription, negotiable.**

Photos State availability with submission. Reviews 5×7 or 8×10 prints; snapshot size or photocopy OK. Buys one-time rights. Pays $25-250. Captions and identification of subjects required; releases (when appropriate) required.

Columns/Departments NC Writers (interviews, biographical/bibliographic essays); Reviews (essay reviews of North Carolina-related or fiction, creative nonfiction, poetry). Query with published clips. **Pays $50-100 honorarium, extra copies, back issues or subscription (negotiable).**

Fiction Must be either by a North Carolina-connected writer or set in North Carolina. **Buys 3-4 mss/year.** Query. Length: 5,000 words maximum. **$50-100 honorarium, extra copies, back issues or subscription (negotiable).**

Poetry *North Carolina poets only.* **Buys 8-10 poems/year.** Length: 30-150 lines. **$50-100 honorarium, extra copies, back issues or subscription (negotiable).**

Fillers Buys 2-5/year. Length: 50-500 words. **Pays $50-100 honorarium, extra copies, back issues or subscription (negotiable).**

Tips "By far the easiest way to break in is with special issue sections. We are especially interested in reports on conferences, readings, meetings that involve North Carolina writers, and personal essays or short narratives with a strong sense of place. See back issues for other departments. Interviews are probably the other easiest place to break in; no discussions of poetics/theory, etc., except in reader-friendly (accessible) language; interviews should be personal, more like conversations, that explore connections between a writer's life and his/her work."

$ NOTRE DAME REVIEW

University of Notre Dame, 840 Flanner Hall, Notre Dame IN 46556. (574)631-6952. Fax: (574)631-4795. E-mail: english.ndreview.1@nd.edu. Website: www.nd.edu/~ndr/review.htm. Executive Editor: Kathleen J. Canavan. Poetry Editor: John Matthias. **Contact:** William O'Rourke, fiction editor. Semiannual magazine. "The *Notre Dame Review* is an indepenent, noncommercial magazine of contemporary American and international fiction, poetry, criticism, and art. We are especially interested in work that takes on big issues by making the invisible seen, that gives voice to the voiceless. In addition to showcasing celebrated authors like Seamus Heaney and Czelaw Milosz, the *Notre Dame Review* introduces readers to authors they may have never encountered before, but who are doing innovative and important work. In conjunction with the *Notre Dame Review*, the online companion to the printed magazine, the *Notre Dame Review* engages readers as a community centered in literary rather than commercial concerns, a community we reach out to through critique and commentary as well as aesthetic experience." **Buys 10 mss/year.** Length: 3,000 words. **Pays $5-25.** Estab. 1995. Circ. 2,000. Pays on publication. Publishes ms an average of 6 months after acceptance. Buys first North American serial rights. Accepts simultaneous submissions. Responds in 4 months to mss. Sample copy for $6. Writer's guidelines online.

Tips "We're looking for high quality work that takes on big issues in a literary way. Please read our back issues before submitting."

$ $ ⬚ ON SPEC MAGAZINE

Copper Pig Writers Society, Box 4727, Edmonton AB T6E 5G6 Canada. E-mail: editor@onspec.ca. Website: www.onspec.ca. **Contact:** Diane L. Walton, editor. **100% freelance written.** Quarterly magazine. "*On Spec Magazine* was launched in 1989 by the nonprofit Copper Pig Writers' Society to provide a voice and a paying market for Canadian writers working in the speculative genre. Aside from the then-biannual *Tesseracts* anthology, there were almost no speculative fiction markets in Canada for Canadian writers. *On Spec* was created to provide this market. *On Spec* is published quarterly by the Copper Pig Writers Society, a collective whose members (all writers themselves) donate their professional services and their time. Our readers have told us what they want is fiction, fiction and more fiction, and that's what we give them: each 112-page issue of the digest-size magazine typically contains 1 or 2 poems and nonfiction pieces, some illustrations, and at least 10 short stories, all in the speculative genre." Estab. 1989. **Pays on acceptance.** Byline given. Buys first rights. Accepts queries by mail. Sample copy not available. Writer's guidelines free.

Fiction Fantasy, horror, science fiction. **Buys 40-50 mss/year.** Send complete ms. Length: 1,000-6,000 words. **Pays $50-180 (Canadian).**

Tips "The *On Spec* editors are looking for original, unpublished science fiction—fantasy, horror, ghost stories, fairy stories, magic realism, or any other speculative material. Since our mandate is to provide a market for the Canadian viewpoint, strong preference is given to submissions by Canadians."

$ ONE-STORY

One-Story, LLC, P.O. Box 1326, New York NY 10156. Website: www.one-story.com. **Contact:** Maribeth Batcha, publisher and Hannah Tinti, editor. **100% freelance written.** Literary magazine covering 1 short story. "*One-Story* is a literary magazine that contains, simply, **1 story**. It is a subscription-only magazine. Every 3 weeks subscribers are sent *One-Story* in the mail. *One-Story* is artfully designed, lightweight, easy to carry, and ready to entertain on buses, in bed, in subways, in cars, in the park, in the bath, in the waiting rooms of doctor's offices, on the couch, or in line at the supermarket. Subscribers also have access to a website, where they can learn more about *One-Story* authors, and hear about *One-Story* readings and events. There is always time to read *One-Story*." Estab. 2002. Circ. 3,500. Pays on publication. Publishes ms an average of 3-6 months after acceptance. Byline given. Buys first North American serial rights. Buys the rights to publish excerpts on website and in promotional materials. Editorial lead time 3-4 months. Accepts simultaneous submissions. Responds in 2-6 months to mss. Sample copy for $5. Writer's guidelines online.

- Accepts submissions via website only.

Fiction Literary short stories. *One-Story* only accepts short stories. Do not send excerpts. Do not send more than 1 story at a time. **Buys 18 mss/year.** Send complete ms. Length: 3,000-8,000 words. **Pays $100.**

Tips "*One-Story* is looking for stories that are strong enough to stand alone. Therefore they must be very good. We want the best you can give. We want our socks knocked off."

N $ ORCHID: A LITERARY REVIEW

Celebrating Stories and the Art of Storytelling, Critical Connection Fiction Workshops, Inc., P.O. Box 131457, Ann Arbor MI 48113-1457. E-mail: editors@orchidlit.org. Website: www.orchidlit.org. **Contact:** Keith Hood and Amy Sumerton, executive editors. **100% freelance written.** Semiannual magazine. "We want great fiction. It's that simple. We publish the best fiction by new and emerging writers while showcasing new work by established writers. Our audience is anyone who loves great fiction." Estab. 2001. Circ. 800. Pays on publication. Publishes ms an average of 6 months after acceptance. Byline given. Buys first North American serial, first, second serial (reprint) rights. Editorial lead time 3-6 months. Accepts simultaneous submissions. Responds in 1 week to queries; 3 months to mss. Sample copy for $8. Writer's guidelines online.

Nonfiction Interview/profile. **Buys 2 mss/year.** Send complete ms. Length: 3,000-4,000 words. **Pays $75.**

Photos Send photos with submission. Reviews prints, GIF/JPEG files. Buys one-time rights. Offers $20-75/photo.

Columns/Departments Interview (interviews with fiction writers that focus on the craft of fiction writing), 3,000-4,000 words. **Buys 2-4 mss/year.** Send complete ms. **Pays $75.**

Fiction Novel excerpts, slice-of-life vignettes, literary. Does not want genre fiction. **Buys 30-40 mss/year.** Send complete ms. Length: 30,000 words maximum. **Pays $75-150.**

Tips "Send us your best work, stories that are well written and show an understanding of craft. Cover letters should be brief. Don't describe your story in the cover letter. Visit our website for more specifics."

OTHER VOICES

University of Illinois at Chicago, 601 S. Morgan St., Chicago IL 60607. (312)413-2209. E-mail: othervoices@listserv.uic.edu. Website: www.othervoicesmagazine.org. **Contact:** Gina Frangello and JoAnne Ruvoli, editors. Semiannual magazine "publishing original, fresh, diverse stories and novel excerpts" for literate adults. Estab. 1985. Circ. 1,500. Buys one-time rights. Accepts simultaneous submissions. Responds in 10-12 weeks to mss. Sample copy for $7 (includes postage). Writer's guidelines for #10 SASE.

Fiction Humorous, contemporary, excerpted novel and one act-plays. Fiction only. "No taboos, except ineptitude and murkiness. No science fiction, romance, horror, chick lit or futuristic." Length: 5,000 words. **Pays in contributor's copies and modest cash gratuity.**

$ $ $ THE PARIS REVIEW

541 E. 72nd St., New York NY 10021. (212)861-0016. Fax: (212)861-4504. E-mail: queries@theparisreview.org. Website: www.theparisreview.com. Editor: Philip Gourevitch. **Contact:** Fiction Editor, Poetry Editor. Quarterly magazine. "Fiction and poetry of superlative quality, whatever the genre, style or mode. Our contributors include prominent, as well as less well-known and previously unpublished writers. Writers at Work interview series includes important contemporary writers discussing their own work and the craft of writing." Pays on publication. Buys all, first english-language rights. Accepts simultaneous submissions. Responds in 4 months to mss. Sample copy for $15 (includes postage). Writer's guidelines online.

- Address submissions to proper department. Do not make submissions via e-mail.

Fiction Study the publication. Annual Aga Khan Fiction Contest award of $1,000. Send complete ms. Length: no limit. **Pays $500-1,000.**

Poetry Richard Howard, poetry editor.

$ $ PARNASSUS

Poetry in Review Foundation, 205 W. 89th St., #8-F, New York NY 10024. (212)362-3492. Fax: (212)875-0148. E-mail: parnew@aol.com. Website: www.parnassuspoetry.com. Co-Editor: Ben Downing. **Contact:** Herbert Leibowitz, editor. Semiannual magazine covering poetry and criticism. Estab. 1972. Circ. 1,500. Pays on publication. Publishes ms an average of 5 months after acceptance. Byline given. Buys one-time rights. Accepts queries by mail. Responds in 2 months to mss. Sample copy for $15. Writer's guidelines not available.

Nonfiction Essays. **Buys 30 mss/year.** Query with published clips. Length: 1,500-7,500 words. **Pays $500.**

Poetry Accepts most types of poetry. Avant-garde, free verse, traditional. **Buys 3-4 unsolicited poems/year.**

Tips "Be certain you have read the magazine and are aware of the editor's taste. Blind submissions are a waste of everybody's time. We'd like to see more poems that display intellectual acumen and curiosity about history, science, music, etc., and fewer trivial lyrical poems about the self, or critical prose that's academic and dull. Prose should sing."

$ PEEKS & VALLEYS

Fiction Journal, South Bend IN. E-mail: peeksandvalleys@earthlink.net. Website: www.peeksandvalleys.com. **Contact:** Meagan Church, editor. **100% freelance written.** Quarterly magazine covering short stories. "*Peeks & Valleys* is a fiction journal that seeks quality writing and storytelling of various genres. We look for writing that leaves an impression and has a purpose—however tangible that may be. Our goal is to encourage and offer an outlet for both accomplished and new writers, and to cause contemplation on the part of the reader." Estab. 1999. Pays on publication. Publishes ms an average of 8 months after acceptance. Byline given. Buys one-time, second serial (reprint) rights. Editorial lead time 4 months. Submit seasonal material 6 months in advance. Accepts queries by e-mail. Accepts previously published material. Accepts simultaneous submissions. Responds in 2 months to mss. Sample copy for $5.75. Writer's guidelines online.

Fiction "Genres aren't as important as quality writing. We seek depth and development." No sci-fi, fantasy, sex, or obscenity. **Buys 30 mss/year.** Send complete ms. Length: 2,600 words. **Pays $5.**

Poetry "We seek quality poetry that offers insight." **Buys 5 poems/year.** Submit maximum 2 poems. Length: 30 lines.

Tips "Follow the submission guidelines, and don't exceed the recommended length. Study the journal to get a clear idea of what is needed. Be sure to check the website for information on the Annual Flash Fiction Contest."

$ ⊕ PLANET-THE WELSH INTERNATIONALIST

P.O. Box 44, Aberystwyth Ceredigion SY23 3ZZ United Kingdom. 01970-611255. Fax: 01970-611197. E-mail: planet.enquiries@planetmagazine.org.uk. Website: www.planetmagazine.org.uk. **Contact:** John Barnie, editor. Bimonthly journal. "A literary/cultural/political journal centered on Welsh affairs but with a strong interest in minority cultures in Europe and elsewhere." Circ. 1,400. Sample copy for £4. Writer's guidelines online.

Fiction Would like to see more "inventive, imaginative fiction that pays attention to language and experiments with form." No magical realism, horror, science fiction. Length: 1,500-4,000 words. **Pays £50/1,000 words.**

Tips "We do not look for fiction which necessarily has a 'Welsh' connection, which some writers assume from our title. We try to publish a broad range of fiction and our main criterion is quality. Try to read copies of any magazine you submit to. Don't write out of the blue to a magazine which might be completely inappropriate for your work. Recognize that you are likely to have a high rejection rate, as magazines tend to favor writers from their own countries."

$ PLEIADES

Pleiades Press, Department of English & Philosophy, Central Missouri State University, Martin 336, Warrensburg MO 64093. (660)543-4425. Fax: (660)543-8544. E-mail: kdp8106@cmsu2.cmsu.edu. Website: www.cmsu.edu/englphil/pleiades. **Contact:** Kevin Prufer, editor. **100% freelance written.** Semiannual journal ($5\frac{1}{2} \times 8\frac{1}{2}$ perfect bound). "We publish contemporary fiction, poetry, interviews, literary essays, special-interest personal essays, and reviews for a general and literary audience." Estab. 1991. Circ. 3,000. Pays on publication. Publishes ms an average of 9 months after acceptance. Byline given. Buys first North American serial, second serial (reprint) rights. Occasionally requests rights for TV, radio reading, website. Editorial lead time 9 months. Accepts queries by mail. Accepts simultaneous submissions. Responds in 2 months. Sample copy for $5 (back issue); $6 (current issue). Writer's guidelines for #10 SASE.

> • Also sponsors the Lena-Miles Wever Todd Poetry Series competition, a contest for the best book ms by an American poet. The winner receives $1,000, publication by Pleiades Press, and distribution by Louisiana State University Press. Deadline September 30. Send SASE for guidelines.

Nonfiction Book excerpts, essays, interview/profile, reviews. "Nothing pedantic, slick, or shallow." **Buys 4-6 mss/year.** Send complete ms. Length: 2,000-4,000 words. **Pays $10.**

Fiction Susan Steinberg, fiction editor. Ethnic, experimental, humorous, mainstream, novel excerpts, magic realism. No science fiction, fantasy, confession, erotica. **Buys 16-20 mss/year.** Send complete ms. Length: 2,000-6,000 words. **Pays $10.**

Poetry Avant-garde, free verse, haiku, light verse, traditional. "Nothing didactic, pretentious, or overly sentimental." **Buys 40-50 poems/year.** Submit maximum 6 poems. **Pays $3/poem, and contributor copies.**

Tips "Show care for your material and your readers—submit quality work in a professional format. Include cover letter with brief bio and list of publications. Include SASE."

$ $ PLOUGHSHARES

Emerson College, Department M, 120 Boylston St., Boston MA 02116. Website: www.pshares.org. **Contact:** Don Lee, editor. Triquarterly magazine for "readers of serious contemporary literature. Our mission is to present dynamic, contrasting views on what is valid and important in contemporary literature, and to discover and advance significant literary talent. Each issue is guest-edited by a different writer. We no longer structure issues around preconceived themes." Estab. 1971. Circ. 6,000. Pays on publication. Publishes ms an average of 6 months after acceptance. Offers 50% kill fee for assigned ms not published. Buys first North American serial rights. Accepts simultaneous submissions. Responds in 5 months to mss. Sample copy for $9 (back issue). Writer's guidelines online.

● A competitive and highly prestigious market. Rotating and guest editors make cracking the line-up even tougher, since it's difficult to know what is appropriate to send. The reading period is August 1-March 31.

Nonfiction Essays (personal and literary; accepted only occasionally). Length: 6,000 words maximum. **Pays $25/printed page, $50-250.**

Fiction Mainstream. "No genre (science fiction, detective, gothic, adventure, etc.), popular formula, or commerical fiction whose purpose is to entertain rather than to illuminate." **Buys 25-35 mss/year.** Length: 300-6,000 words. **Pays $25/printed page, $50-250.**

Poetry Avant-garde, free verse, traditional, blank verse. Length: Open. **Pays $25/printed page, $50-250.**

Tips "We no longer structure issues around preconceived themes. If you believe your work is in keeping with our general standards of literary quality and value, submit at any time during our reading period."

$ POETRY

The Poetry Foundation, 1030 N. Clark St., Chicago IL 60610. (312)787-7070. Fax: (312)787-6650. E-mail: poetry @poetrymagazine.org. Website: www.poetrymagazine.org. Editor: Christian Wiman. Business Manager: Helen Klaviter. Assistant Editor: Fred Sasaki. Reader: Christina Pugh. **Contact:** Editors. **100% freelance written.** Monthly magazine. Estab. 1912. Circ. 16,000. Pays on publication. Publishes ms an average of 9 months after acceptance. Byline given. Buys all rights. Copyright returned to author on request. Accepts queries by mail. Responds in 1 month to queries; 4 months to mss. Sample copy for $5.50 or online at website. Writer's guidelines online.

Nonfiction Reviews (most are solicited). **Buys 14 mss/year.** Query. Length: 1,000-2,000 words. **Pays $150/page.**

Poetry All styles and subject matter. **Buys 180-250 poems/year.** Submit maximum 4 poems. Length: Open. **Pays $6/line.**

⊕ POETRY IRELAND REVIEW

Poetry Ireland, 120 St. Stephen's Green, Dublin. 01-4789974. Fax: 01-4780205. E-mail: publications@poetryirela nd.ie. Website: www.poetryireland.ie. Editor: Peter Sirr. Managing Editor: Joseph Woods. Quarterly literary magazine in book form. Estab. 1978. Circ. 5,000. Pays on publication. Not copyrighted. Accepts queries by mail, e-mail, fax, phone. Responds in 1 week to queries; 2 months to mss.

Poetry Avant-garde, free verse, haiku, light verse, traditional. **Buys 200 poems/year.** Submit maximum 6 poems.

$ ⊡ THE PRAIRIE JOURNAL

Journal of Canadian Literature, Prairie Journal Trust, P.O. Box 61203, Brentwood P.O., Calgary AB T2L 2K6 Canada. E-mail: prairiejournal@yahoo.com. Website: www.geocities.com/prairiejournal. **Contact:** A. Burke, editor. **100% freelance written.** Semiannual magazine publishing quality poetry, short fiction, drama, literary criticism, reviews, bibliography, interviews, profiles, and artwork. "The audience is literary, university, library, scholarly, and creative readers/writers." Estab. 1983. Circ. 600. Pays on publication. Publishes ms an average of 4-6 months after acceptance. Byline given. Buys first North American serial, electronic rights. In Canada, author retains copyright with acknowledgment appreciated. Editorial lead time 4-6 months. Accepts queries by mail, e-mail. Responds in 2 weeks to queries; 6 months to mss. Sample copy for $5. Writer's guidelines online.

Nonfiction Essays, humor, interview/profile, literary. No inspirational, news, religious, or travel. **Buys 25-40 mss/year.** Query with published clips. Length: 100-3,000 words. **Pays $100, plus contributor's copy.**

Photos State availability with submission. Rights purchased is negotiable. Offers additional payment for photos accepted with ms.

Columns/Departments Reviews (books from small presses publishing poetry, short fiction, essays, and criticism), 200-1,000 words. **Buys 5 mss/year.** Query with published clips. **Pays $10-50.**

Fiction Literary. No genre (romance, horror, western—sagebrush or cowboys), erotic, science fiction, or mystery. **Buys 6 mss/year.** Send complete ms. Length: 100-3,000 words. **Pays $10-75.**

Poetry Avant-garde, free verse, haiku. No heroic couplets or greeting card verse. **Buys 25-35 poems/year.** Submit maximum 6-8 poems. Length: 3-50 lines. **Pays $5-50.**

Tips "We publish many, many new writers and are always open to unsolicited submissions because we are 100% freelance." Do not send US stamps, always use IRCs.

$⬚ PRISM INTERNATIONAL

Department of Creative Writing, Buch E462 Main Mall, University of British Columbia, Vancouver BC V6T 1Z1 Canada. (604)822-2514. Fax: (604)822-3616. E-mail: prism@interchange.ubc.ca. Website: prism.arts.ubc.ca. Executive Editor: Brenda Leifso. **Contact:** Catherine Chen, editor. **100% freelance written.** Works with new/unpublished writers. "A quarterly international journal of contemporary writing—fiction, poetry, drama, creative nonfiction and translation." Readership: "public and university libraries, individual subscriptions, bookstores—a world-wide audience concerned with the contemporary in literature." Estab. 1959. Circ. 1,200. Pays on publication. Publishes ms an average of 4 months after acceptance. Buys first North American serial rights. Selected authors are paid an additional $10/page for digital rights. Accepts queries by mail, fax, phone. Responds in 4 months. Sample copy for $7 or on website. Writer's guidelines online.

⊶ Break in by "sending unusual or experimental work (we get mostly traditional submissions) and playing with forms (i.e., nonfiction, prose poetry, etc.)."

Nonfiction "Creative nonfiction that reads like fiction. Nonfiction pieces should be creative, exploratory, or experimental in tone rather than rhetorical, academic, or journalistic." No reviews, tracts, or scholarly essays. **Pays $20/printed page.**

Fiction Billeh Nickerson, editor. For Drama: one-acts preferred. Also interested in seeing dramatic monologues. **Buys 3-5 mss/year.** Send complete ms. Length: 25 pages maximum. **Pays $20/printed page.** Experimental, novel excerpts, traditional. New writing that is contemporary and literary. Short stories and self-contained novel excerpts. Works of translation are eagerly sought and should be accompanied by a copy of the original. Would like to see more translations. "No gothic, confession, religious, romance, pornography, or sci-fi." **Buys 12-16 mss/year.** Send complete ms. Length: 25 pages maximum. **Pays $20/printed page, and 1-year subscription.**

Poetry Buys 10 poems/issue. Avant-garde, traditional. Submit maximum 6 poems. **Pays $40/printed page, and 1-year subscription.**

Tips "We are looking for new and exciting fiction. Excellence is still our No. 1 criterion. As well as poetry, imaginative nonfiction and fiction, we are especially open to translations of all kinds, very short fiction pieces, and drama which work well on the page. Translations must come with a copy of the original language work. We pay an additional $10/printed page to selected authors whose work we place on our online version of *Prism*."

$ QUARTERLY WEST

University of Utah, 200 S. Central Campus Dr., Room 317, Salt Lake City UT 84112-9109. (801)581-3938. E-mail: dhawk@earthlink.net. Website: www.utah.edu/quarterlywest. **Contact:** David Hawkins, editor-in-chief. Semiannual magazine. "We publish fiction, poetry, and nonfiction in long and short formats, and will consider experimental as well as traditional works." Estab. 1976. Circ. 1,900. Pays on publication. Publishes ms an average of 6 months after acceptance. Buys first North American serial, all rights. Accepts queries by mail. Accepts simultaneous submissions. Responds in 6 months to mss. Sample copy for $7.50 or online. Writer's guidelines online.

Nonfiction Essays, interview/profile, personal experience, travel, book reviews. **Buys 6-8 mss/year.** Send complete ms. Length: 10,000 words maximum. **Pays $20-100.**

Fiction No preferred lengths; interested in longer, fuller short stories and short shorts. Ethnic, experimental, humorous, mainstream, novel excerpts, slice-of-life vignettes, short shorts, translations. No detective, science fiction or romance. **Buys 6-10 mss/year.** Send complete ms. **Pays $15-100, and 2 contributor's copies.**

Poetry Avant-garde, free verse, traditional. **Buys 40-50 poems/year.** Submit maximum 5 poems. **Pays $15-100.**

Tips "We publish a special section of short shorts every issue, and we also sponsor a biennial novella contest. We are open to experimental work—potential contributors should read the magazine! Don't send more than 1 story/submission. Biennial novella competition guidelines available upon request with SASE. We prefer work with interesting language and detail—plot or narrative are less important. We don't do Western themes or religious work."

$ $⬚ QUEEN'S QUARTERLY

A Canadian Review, Queen's University, Kingston ON K7L 3N6 Canada. (613)533-2667. Fax: (613)533-6822. E-mail: qquarter@post.queensu.ca. Website: info.queensu.ca/quarterly. **Contact:** Joan Harcourt, literary editor. **95% freelance written.** Quarterly magazine covering a wide variety of subjects, including science, humanities, arts and letters, politics, and history for the educated reader. "A general interest intellectual review, featuring articles, book reviews, poetry, and fiction." Estab. 1893. Circ. 3,000. Pays on publication. Publishes ms an average of 6-12 months after acceptance. Byline given. Buys first North American serial rights. Responds in 2-3 months to queries. Sample copy and writer's guidelines online.

⊶ Submissions can be sent as e-mail attachment or on hard copy with a SASE (Canadian postage).

Fiction Boris Castel, editor. Historical, mainstream, novel excerpts, short stories, women's. Length: 2,500-3,000

words. **Pays $100-300, 2 contributor's copies and 1-year subscription; additional copies $5.**
Poetry Buys 25 poems/year. Submit maximum 6 poems.

$ 🌐 QWF (QUALITY WOMEN'S FICTION)

Breaking the Boundaries of Women's Fiction, 18 Warwick Crescent, Harrogate N. Yorks HG2 8JA United Kingdom. 01788 334302. Fax: 01788 334702. E-mail: sally_zigmond@yahoo.co.uk. Website: www.qwfmagazine.co.uk. Editor: Jo Good. **Contact:** Sally Zigmond, assistant editor. Bimonthly magazine. "*QWF* gets under the skin of the female experience and exposes emotional truth." Estab. 1994. Circ. 2,000. Pays on publication. Publishes ms an average of 18 months after acceptance. Buys first British serial rights. Accepts queries by mail, e-mail. Accepts previously published material. Responds in 2 weeks to queries; 3 months to mss. Writer's guidelines by e-mail.

Fiction Does not read mss June-August. Erotica, ethnic, experimental, fantasy, horror, humorous, science fiction, feminist, gay, lesbian, literary, New Age, psychic/supernatural/occult, translations. **Buys 72 mss/year.** Length: 1,000-4,500 words. **Pays £10 sterling maximum, or 3 voucher copies to US contributors.**

Tips "Take risks with subject matter. Study at least 1 copy of *QWF*. Ensure story is technically sound."

Ⓝ $ RATTAPALLAX

Rattapallax Press, 532 LaGuardia Place, #353, New York NY 10012. (212)560-7459. E-mail: info@rattapallax.com. Website: www.rattapallax.com. Editor: Alan Cheuse. Managing Editor: Ram Devineni. **10% freelance written.** Magazine published 2 times/year covering fiction, poetry, and international issues. "*Rattapallax* is a literary magazine that focuses on issues dealing with globalization." Estab. 1999. Circ. 3,000. Pays on publication. Publishes ms an average of 6 months after acceptance. Byline given. Buys first North American serial rights. Editorial lead time 6 months. Submit seasonal material 6 months in advance. Accepts queries by e-mail. Responds in 2 weeks to queries; 6 months to mss. Sample copy and writer's guidelines online.

Nonfiction Alan Cheuse, fiction editor. Essays, interview/profile. Does not want interviews. **Buys 4 mss/year.** Query. Length: 500-2,000 words. **Pays $100 for assigned articles.**

Photos Ram Devineni, publisher. State availability of or send photos with submission. Reviews GIF/JPEG files. Buys one-time rights. Offers no additional payment for photos accepted with ms. Captions required.

Fiction Alan Cheuse, fiction editor. Mainstream. Does not want children's fiction. **Buys 6 mss/year.** Query. Length: 500-2,000 words. **Pays $100.**

Poetry Martin Mitchell, poetry editor. Avant-garde, free verse, traditional. **Buys 100 poems/year.** Submit maximum 5 poems. Length: 5-200 lines.

$ 🔲 ROOM OF ONE'S OWN

A Canadian Quarterly of Women's Literature and Criticism, West Coast Feminist Literary Magazine Society, P.O. Box 46160, Station D, Vancouver BC V6J 5G5 Canada. Website: www.roommagazine.com. **Contact:** Growing Room Collective. **100% freelance written.** Quarterly journal of feminist literature. "*Room of One's Own* is Canada's oldest feminist literary journal. Since 1975, *Room* has been a forum in which women can share their unique perspectives on the world, each other, and themselves." Estab. 1975. Circ. 1,000. Pays on publication. Publishes ms an average of 1 year after acceptance. Byline given. Buys first North American serial rights. Editorial lead time 9 months. Responds in 3 months to queries; 6 months to mss. Sample copy for $7 or online. Writer's guidelines online.

Nonfiction Reviews. **Buys 1-2 mss/year.** Send complete ms. Length: 500-1,500 words. **Pays $35 (Canadian), and a 1-year subscription.**

Fiction Feminist literature—short stories, creative nonfiction, essays by, for, and about women. "No humor, science fiction, romance." **Buys 40 mss/year.** Length: 2,000-5,000 words. **Pays $35 (Canadian), and a 1-year subscription.**

Poetry Avant-garde, free verse. "Nothing light, undeveloped." **Buys 40 poems/year.** Submit maximum 6 poems. Length: 3-80 lines. **Pays $35 (Canadian), and a 1-year subscription.**

$ $ THE SAINT ANN'S REVIEW

A Journal of Contemporary Arts and Letters, Saint Ann's School, 129 Pierrepont St., Brooklyn NY 11201. (718)522-1660. Fax: (718)522-2599. E-mail: sareview@saintanns.k12.ny.us. Website: www.saintannsreview.com. **Contact:** Beth Bosworth, editor. **100% freelance written.** Semiannual literary magazine. "We seek fully realized work, distinguished by power and craft." Estab. 2000. Circ. 2,000. Pays on publication. Publishes ms an average of 4 months after acceptance. Byline given. Buys first North American serial rights. Submit seasonal material 4 months in advance. Accepts queries by mail. Responds in 1 month to queries; 4 months to mss. Sample copy for $8. Writer's guidelines online.

Nonfiction Book excerpts (occasionally), essays, humor, interview/profile, personal experience, photo feature.

Buys 10 mss/year. Query with or without published clips or send complete ms. Length: 7,500 words maximum. **Pays $40/published page, $250/maximum.**

Photos Send photos with submission. Reviews transparencies, prints, GIF/JPEG files, b&w art. Buys one-time rights. Offers $50/photo page or art page, $250 maximum.

Columns/Departments Book reviews, 1,500 words. **Buys 10 mss/year.** Send complete ms by mail only. **Pays $40/published page, $250 maximum.**

Fiction Ethnic, experimental, fantasy, historical, humorous, mainstream, slice-of-life vignettes, translations. **Buys 15 mss/year.** Length: 7,500 words maximum. **Pays $40/published page, $250 maximum.**

Poetry Avant-garde, free verse, haiku, light verse, traditional, translations. **Buys 30 poems/year.** Submit maximum 5 poems. **Pays $50/page, $250 maximum.**

[N] $ THE SEATTLE REVIEW

Box 354330, University of Washington, Seattle WA 98195. (206)543-2302. E-mail: seaview@u.washington.edu. Website: depts.washington.edu/engl/seaview1.html. Semiannual magazine. "Includes general fiction, poetry, craft essays on writing, and one interview per issue with a Northwest writer." Estab. 1978. Circ. 1,000. Pays on publication. Buys first North American serial rights. Responds in 8 months to mss. Sample copy for $6. Writer's guidelines online.

● Editors accept submissions only from October 1 through May 31.

Fiction Colleen J. McElroy, editor. Wants more creative nonfiction. "We also publish a series called Writers and their Craft, which deals with aspects of writing fiction (also poetry)—point of view, characterization, etc, rather than literary criticism, each issue." Ethnic, experimental, fantasy, historical, horror, humorous, mainstream, mystery, novel excerpts, science fiction, suspense, western, contemporary, feminist, gay, lesbian, literary, psychic/supernatural/occult, regional, translations. Nothing in "bad taste (porn, racist, etc.)." **Buys 4-10 mss/year.** Send complete ms. Length: 500-10,000 words. **Pays $0-100.**

Poetry Colleen J. McElroy, editor. Pros.

Tips "Beginners do well in our magazine if they send clean, well-written manuscripts. We've published a lot of 'first stories' from all over the country and take pleasure in discovery."

THE SEWANEE REVIEW

University of the South, 735 University Ave., Sewanee TN 37383-1000. (931)598-1246. Website: www.sewanee. edu/sreview/home.html. **Contact:** Fiction Editor. Quarterly magazine. "A literary quarterly, publishing original fiction, poetry, essays on literary and related subjects, and book reviews for well-educated readers who appreciate good American and English literature." Estab. 1892. Circ. 3,000. Pays on publication. Buys first North American serial, second serial (reprint) rights. Responds in 4-6 weeks to mss. Sample copy for $8.50 ($9.50 outside US). Writer's guidelines online.

● Does not read mss June 1-August 31.

Fiction Send query letter for essays and reviews. Send complete ms for fiction. Literary, contemporary. No erotica, science fiction, fantasy or excessively violent or profane material. **Buys 10-15 mss/year.** Length: 3,500-7,500 words.

Poetry Send complete ms. Submit maximum 6 poems. Length: 40 lines or less.

$ SHENANDOAH

The Washington and Lee University Review, Washington and Lee University, Mattingly House, 2 Lee Ave., Lexington VA 24450-0303. (540)458-8765. Fax: (540)458-8461. Website: shenandoah.wlu.edu. Managing Editor: Lynn Leech. **Contact:** R.T. Smith, editor. Quarterly magazine. Estab. 1950. Circ. 2,000. Pays on publication. Publishes ms an average of 10 months after acceptance. Byline given. Buys first North American serial, one-time rights. Responds in 3 months to mss. Sample copy for $8. Writer's guidelines online.

Nonfiction Book excerpts, essays. **Buys 6 mss/year.** Send complete ms. **Pays $25/page.**

Fiction Mainstream, novel excerpts. No sloppy, hasty, slight fiction. **Buys 15 mss/year.** Send complete ms. **Pays $25/page.**

Poetry No inspirational, confessional poetry. **Buys 70 poems/year.** Submit maximum 6 poems. Length: Open. **Pays $2.50/line.**

[N] [Ø] SHORT STUFF MAGAZINE

Bowman Publications, 712 W. 10th St., Loveland CO 80537. (970)669-9139. E-mail: shortstf89@aol.com. Copy Editor: Greg Palmer. **Contact:** Donnalee Bowman, editor. **98% freelance written.** Bimonthly magazine. "We are perhaps an enigma in that we publish only clean stories in any genre. We'll tackle any subject, but don't allow obscene language or pornographic description. Our magazine is for grown-ups, not X-rated 'adult' fare." Estab. 1989. Circ. 10,400. Payment and contract upon publication. Byline given. Buys first North American serial rights. Editorial lead time 3 months. Submit seasonal material 3 months in advance. Responds in 6 months to mss. Sample copy for $1.50 and 9×12 SAE with 5 first-class stamps. Writer's guidelines for #10 SASE.

● Closed to submissions for the time being due to backlog.

🔾 Break in with "a good, tight story. Cover letters stating what a great story is enclosed really turn me off, just a personal bit about the author is sufficient. Please do not submit any essays. We're not considering any essays at this time. No exceptions."

Nonfiction Most nonfiction is staff written. Humor. Special issues: "We are holiday oriented and each issue reflects the appropriate holidays." **Buys 30 mss/year.** Send complete ms. Length: 500-1,500 words. **Payment varies.**

Photos Send photos with submission. Buys one-time rights. Offers no additional payment for photos accepted with ms. Identification of subjects required.

Fiction Adventure, historical, humorous, mainstream, mystery, romance, science fiction, suspense, western. "We want to see more humor—not essay format—real stories with humor; 1,000-word mysteries, modern lifestyles. The 1,000-word pieces have the best chance of publication." No erotica; nothing morbid or pornographic. **Buys 144 mss/year.** Send complete ms. Length: 500-1,500 words. **Payment varies.**

Fillers Anecdotes, short humor. **Buys 200/year.** Length: 20-500 words. **Pays variable amount.**

Tips "Don't send floppy disks or cartridges. Do include cover letter about the author, not a synopsis of the story. We are holiday oriented; mark on outside of envelope if story is for Easter, Mother's Day, etc. We receive 500 manuscripts each month. This is up about 200%. Because of this, I implore writers to send 1 manuscript at a time. I would not use stories from the same author more than once an issue and this means I might keep the others too long. Please don't e-mail your stories! If you have an e-mail address, please include that with cover letter so we can contact you. If no SASE, we destroy the manuscript."

Ⓝ $SOLEADO

Revista de Literatura y Cultura, Dept. of International Language and Culture Studies, IPFW, CM 267, 2101 E. Coliseum Blvd., Fort Wayne IN 46805. (260)481-6630. Fax: (260)481-6985. E-mail: summersj@ipfw.edu. Website: users.ipfw.edu/summersj/soleportada.htm. **Contact:** Jason Summers, editor. **100% freelance written.** Annual magazine covering Spanish-language literary, cultural, and creative writing. "Our readers are interested in literature and culture, from creative writing to personal essays and beyond. Spanish is of an ever-growing importance in the US and the world, and our readers and writers are people using that language. *Soleado* is a literary magazine, so academic treatises are not on the list of texts we would be excited to see. The focus of the magazine is on Spanish-language writing, although the national origin of the writer does not matter. The subject matter doesn't have to be Hispanic, either. The one exception to the Spanish-language requirement is that certain texts deal with the difficulties of being bilingual and/or bicultural are welcome to be written in 'Spanglish' when that usage is essential to the text." Estab. 2004. **Pays on acceptance.** Publishes ms an average of 8 months after acceptance. Byline given. Buys first North American serial, first, one-time, second serial (reprint), simultaneous, electronic rights. Editorial lead time 6 months. Submit seasonal material 1 year in advance. Accepts queries by mail, e-mail. Accepts previously published material. Responds in 1 week to queries; 3 months to mss. Sample copy and writer's guidelines online.

Nonfiction Book excerpts, essays, humor, interview/profile, opinion, personal experience, travel, translations, creative nonfiction. No how-to, general travel, inspirational, religious or anything written in English. All nonfiction must have a literary or cultural slant. **Buys up to 3 mss/year.** Query with or without published clips. **Pays maximum $50.**

Fiction "We are looking for good literary writing in Spanish, from Magical Realism a la García Márquez, to McOndo-esque writing similar to that of Edmundo Paz-Soldá and Alberto Fuguet, to Spanish pulp realism like that of Arturo Pérez-Reverte. Testimonials, experimental works like those of Diamela Eltit, and women's voices like Marcela Serrano and Zoé Valdés are also encouraged. We are not against any particular genre writing, but such stories do have to maintain their hold on the literary, as well as the genre, which is often a difficult task." Adventure, ethnic, experimental, fantasy, historical, humorous, mainstream, mystery, novel excerpts, science fiction, slice-of-life vignettes, suspense, translations, magical realism. **Buys 2-6 mss/year.** Query with or without published clips or send complete ms. Length: 8,000 words. **Pays $50.**

Poetry Avant-garde, free verse, light verse, traditional, translation. "Avoid poetry that takes us to places we have already seen. The best kind of poetry takes readers somewhere unexpected, departing from the familiar just when they thought they had things figured out." **Buys 10-15 poems/year.** Submit maximum 4 poems. Length: 400 words.

Fillers Short humor. **Buys up to 4/year.** Length: 1,000 words. **Pays $10.**

Tips "Whether you are or are not a native speaker of Spanish, have someone read over your manuscript for obvious grammatical errors, flow, and continuity of ideas. We are interested in literary translations into Spanish, as well as original writing. Query before sending submission as an e-mail attachment. We publish annually, and the reading period runs from September 1 to March 31 of the following year. Anything that comes between April and August won't get a reply until the new reading period begins."

$THE SOUTHERN REVIEW

43 Allen Hall, Louisiana State University, Baton Rouge LA 70803-5001. (225)578-5108. Fax: (225)578-5098. E-mail: southernreview@lsu.edu. Website: www.lsu.edu/thesouthernreview. **Contact:** Donna Perreault, associate editor. **100% freelance written.** Works with a moderate number of new/unpublished writers each year. Quarterly magazine "with emphasis on contemporary literature in the US and abroad, and with special interest in Southern culture and history." Reading period: September-May. Estab. 1935. Circ. 3,100. Pays on publication. Publishes ms an average of 6 months after acceptance. Byline given. Buys first North American serial rights. Accepts queries by mail. Responds in 2 months to mss. Sample copy for $8. Writer's guidelines online.

Nonfiction Essays with careful attention to craftsmanship, technique, and seriousness of subject matter. "Willing to publish experimental writing if it has a valid artistic purpose. Avoid extremism and sensationalism. Essays should exhibit thoughtful and sometimes severe awareness of the necessity of literary standards in our time." Emphasis on contemporary literature, especially southern culture and history. No footnotes. **Buys 25 mss/year.** Length: 4,000-10,000 words. **Pays $30/page.**

Fiction John Easterly, associate editor. Short stories of lasting literary merit, with emphasis on style and technique; novel excerpts. "We emphasize style and substantial content. No mystery, fantasy or religious mss." Length: 4,000-8,000 words. **Pays $30/page.**

Poetry Length: 1-4 pages. **Pays $20/page.**

Ⓝ $SPRING HILL REVIEW

A Journal of Northwest Culture, P.O. Box 621, Brush Prairie WA 98606. (360)892-1178. E-mail: springhillreview @aol.com. **Contact:** Lucy S. R. Austen, editor. **70% freelance written.** Monthly tabloid covering contemporary Pacific Northwest culture—fiction, nonfiction, essays, poetry, book and movie reviews, humor, history, politics, religion. "*Spring Hill Review* is a journal of contemporary Northwest US culture commenting on and challenging Northwest politics, arts, and current social and spiritual issues. Edited from a gently Christian worldview and with a target market of baby boomers, *Spring Hill Review* is nonetheless a general market publication and accepts submissions from writers of a variety of faiths and belief systems." Estab. 2000. Circ. 6,100. Pays on publication. Publishes ms an average of 3 months after acceptance. Byline given. Buys first, one-time, second serial (reprint), simultaneous rights. Editorial lead time 3 month. Submit seasonal material 3 months in advance. Accepts queries by mail, e-mail. Accepts previously published material. Accepts simultaneous submissions. Responds in 4-6 weeks to queries; 3 months to mss. Sample copy for $2. Writer's guidelines for #10 SASE.

Nonfiction Book excerpts, essays, general interest, historical/nostalgic, humor, interview/profile, opinion, personal experience, photo feature, travel, book and movie reviews, seasonal pieces, Pacific Northwest topics. Special issues: "In December we try to focus particularly on Christmas, so we need articles dealing with that theme. In July, we do a combined July/August issue in which we focus on a laid-back summer-time feeling with fewer 'hard' pieces and more fiction, poetry, and book and movie reviews." **Buys 80-90 mss/year.** Send complete ms. Length: 300-1,000 words. **Pays $10-15, plus 1 contributor copy.** Sometimes pays expenses of writers on assignment.

Photos Send photos with submission. Reviews 3×5-8½×11 prints. Buys one-time rights.

Columns/Departments Northwest Book Nook (books with a Pacific Northwest connection); The Reel Deal (movie reviews for films in the theater); Video Corner (video reviews of new and old releases); The Play's the Thing (Pacific Northwest theater reviews), all 600-800 words. **Buys 40 mss/year.** Query. **Pays $10-15.**

Fiction Adventure, ethnic, experimental, fantasy, historical, humorous, mainstream, mystery, science fiction, slice-of-life vignettes, suspense, western. "We don't want fiction about elderly men/women and the children/animals in their lives, unless it's handled in a very unusual manner. We see a lot of fiction dealing with parent/child relationships, especially parent/adult child relationships, and a lot of fiction dealing with people for whom career is everything, who suddenly see the light and realize that family is more important—both of those themes need to be treated in very fresh, new ways to be of interest." **Buys 12-15 mss/year.** Send complete ms. Length: 300-1,000 words. **Pays $10-15.**

Poetry Avant-garde, free verse, haiku, light verse, traditional. Does not want anything that is "intentionally obscure." **Buys 36 poems/year.** Submit maximum 6 poems. Length: 35 lines maximum. **Pays $10-15.**

Fillers Facts, short humor, puzzles, particularly crosswords (with Pacific Northwest themes) and cartoons, both single panel and strip. **Buys 8-10/year.** Length: 300 words maximum. **Pays $5-10.**

Tips Follow the writer's guidelines. "The best way to get into our publication is to send work that's of particular interest to residents of the Pacific Northwest. We're always looking for good book reviews, especially of Northwest authors, and movie reviews. We particularly look for essay-style reviews which not only review the book/movie, but discuss the larger life themes implicit in the work. We look for poetry that looks at the world in a new way and that plays on an important human theme through specific images and situations, rather than dealing directly with ideas."

$ STAND MAGAZINE

Dept. of English, VCU, Richmond VA 23284-2005. (804)828-1331. E-mail: dlatane@vcu.edu. Website: www.peo ple.vcu.edu/~dlatane/stand.htm. Managing Editor: Jon Glover. **Contact:** David Latané, US editor. **75% freelance written.** Quarterly magazine covering short fiction, poetry, criticism, and reviews. "*Stand Magazine* is concerned with what happens when cultures and literatures meet, with translation in its many guises, with the mechanics of language, with the processes by which the policy receives or disables its cultural makers. *Stand* promotes debate of issues that are of radical concern to the intellectual community worldwide." Estab. 1952. Circ. 3,000 worldwide. Pays on publication. Publishes ms an average of 10 months after acceptance. Byline given. Acquires first world rights. Editorial lead time 2 months. Accepts queries by mail. Responds in 6 weeks to queries; 3 months to mss. Sample copy for $12. Writer's guidelines for #10 SASE with sufficient number of IRCs or online.

Nonfiction "Reviews are commissioned from known freelancers." Reviews of poetry/fiction. **Buys 8 mss/year.** Query. Length: 200-5,000 words. **Pays $30/1,000 words.**

Fiction Adventure, ethnic, experimental, historical, mainstream. "No genre fiction." **Buys 12-14 mss/year.** Send complete ms. Length: 8,000 words maximum. **Payment varies.**

Poetry Avant-garde, free verse, traditional. **Buys 100-120 poems/year.** Submit maximum 6 poems. **Pays $37.50/poem.**

Tips "Poetry/fiction areas are most open to freelancers. *Stand* is published in England and reaches an international audience. North American writers should submit work to the US address. While the topic or nature of submissions does not have to be 'international,' writers may do well to keep in mind the range of *Stand*'s audience."

N $ ⊘ THE STRAND MAGAZINE

P.O. Box 1418, Birmingham MI 48012-1418. (248)788-5948. Fax: (248)874-1046. E-mail: strandmag@strandmag .com. Website: strandmag@strandmag.com. **Contact:** Andrew Gulli, editor. Quarterly magazine covering mysteries, short stories, essays, book reviews. "After an absence of nearly half a century, the magazine known to millions for bringing Sir Arthur Conan Doyle's ingenious detective, Sherlock Holmes, to the world has once again appeared on the literary scene. First launched in 1891, *The Strand* included in its pages the works of some of the greatest writers of the 20th century: Agatha Christie, Dorothy Sayers, Margery Allingham, W. Somerset Maugham, Graham Greene, P.G. Wodehouse, H.G. Wells, Aldous Huxley and many others. In 1950, economic difficulties in England caused a drop in circulation which forced the magazine to cease publication." Estab. 1998. Circ. 50,000. **Pays on acceptance.** Publishes ms an average of 4 months after acceptance. Byline given. Buys first North American serial rights. Responds in 1 month to queries. Sample copy not available. Writer's guidelines for #10 SASE.

• No longer accepts unsolicited mss.

Fiction A.F. Gulli, editor. Horror, humorous, mystery, suspense, tales of the unexpected, tales of terror and the supernatural "written in the classic tradition of this century's great authors. "We are not interested in submissions with any sexual content." Length: 2,000-6,000 words. **Pays $50-175.**

Tips "No gratuitous violence, sexual content, or explicit language, please."

N $ TALEBONES

5203 Quincy Ave. SE, Auburn WA 98092. E-mail: info@talebones.com. Website: www.talebones.com. Associate Editor: Kevin Kerr. **Contact:** Patrick and Honna Swenson, editors. **100% freelance written.** Magazine covering science fiction and dark fantasy. "*Talebones* publishes an eclectic mix of speculative fiction. We want literate stories that entertain readers." Estab. 1995. Circ. 1,000. Pays before publication. Publishes ms an average of 6 months after acceptance. Byline given. Offers 100% kill fee. Buys first North American serial, electronic rights. Accepts queries by mail, e-mail. Responds in 1 week to queries; 2 months to mss. Sample copy for $6. Writer's guidelines online.

Fiction Fantasy, horror, science fiction. Does not want vampire stories, writer stories, or stories about or narrated by young adults or children. **Buys 16 mss/year.** Send complete ms. Length: 6,000 words maximum. **Pays $10.**

Poetry Avant-garde, free verse, light verse, traditional. **Buys 5-8 poems/year.** Submit maximum 8 poems. **Pays $10.**

Tips "We publish a wide variety of speculative fiction. Reading a sample copy of *Talebones* will help the writer understand our eclectic tastes. Be professional and humble. We do publish a lot of new writers."

$ TAMPA REVIEW

University of Tampa Press, 401 W. Kennedy Blvd., Tampa FL 33606. (813)253-6266. Fax: (813)258-7593. Website: tampareview.ut.edu. **Contact:** Richard B. Mathews, editor. Semiannual magazine published in hardback format. An international literary journal publishing art and literature from Florida and Tampa Bay as well as new work and translations from throughout the world. Estab. 1988. Circ. 500. Pays on publication. Publishes ms an average of 10 months after acceptance. Byline given. Buys first North American serial rights. Editorial lead time 18 months. Accepts queries by mail. Responds in 5 months to mss. Sample copy for $7. Writer's guidelines online.

Nonfiction Elizabeth Winston, nonfiction editor. General interest, interview/profile, personal experience, creative nonfiction. No "how-to" articles, fads, journalise reprise, etc. **Buys 6 mss/year.** Send complete ms. Length: 250-7,500 words. **Pays $10/printed page.**

Photos State availability with submission. Reviews contact sheets, negatives, transparencies, prints, digital files. Buys one-time rights. Offers $10/photo. Captions, identification of subjects required.

Fiction Lisa Birnbaum and Kathleen Ochshorn, fiction editors. Ethnic, experimental, fantasy, historical, mainstream, literary. "We are far more interested in quality than in genre. Nothing sentimental as opposed to genuinely moving, nor self-conscious style at the expense of human truth." **Buys 6 mss/year.** Send complete ms. Length: 200-5,000 words. **Pays $10/printed page.**

Poetry Don Morrill and Martha Serpas, poetry editors. Avant-garde, free verse, haiku, light verse, traditional, visual/experimental. No greeting card verse, hackneyed, sing-song, rhyme-for-the-sake-of-rhyme. **Buys 45 poems/year.** Submit maximum 10 poems. Length: 2-225 lines.

Tips "Send a clear cover letter stating previous experience or background. Our editorial staff considers submissions between September and December for publication in the following year."

$ THEMA

Box 8747, Metairie LA 70011-8747. (504)887-1263. E-mail: thema@cox.net. Website: members.cox.net/thema. **Contact:** Virginia Howard, editor. **100% freelance written.** Triannual magazine covering a different theme for each issue. Upcoming themes for SASE. "*Thema* is designed to stimulate creative thinking by challenging writers with unusual themes, such as 'bookstore cowboy' and 'umbrellas in the snow.' Appeals to writers, teachers of creative writing, and general reading audience." Estab. 1988. Circ. 350. **Pays on acceptance.** Publishes ms an average of within 6 months after acceptance. Byline given. Buys one-time rights. Accepts queries by mail. Accepts previously published material. Accepts simultaneous submissions. Responds in 1 week to queries; 5 months to mss. Sample copy for $8. Writer's guidelines for #10 SASE.

Reprints Send ms with rights for sale noted and information about when and where the material previously appeared. Pays the same amount paid for original.

Fiction Special Issues Deadlines: Just Describe Them to Me (November 2005); Rage Over a Lost Penny (March 2006); The Perfect Cup of Coffee (July 2006). Adventure, ethnic, experimental, fantasy, historical, humorous, mainstream, mystery, novel excerpts, religious, science fiction, slice-of-life vignettes, suspense, western, contemporary, sports, prose poem. "No erotica." **Buys 30 mss/year.** Length: fewer than 6,000 words preferred. **Pays $10-25.**

Poetry Avant-garde, free verse, haiku, light verse, traditional. "No erotica." **Buys 27 poems/year.** Submit maximum 3 poems. Length: 4-50 lines. **Pays $10.**

Tips "Be familiar with the themes. Don't submit unless you have an upcoming theme in mind. Specify the target theme on the first page of your manuscript or in a cover letter. Put your name on first page of manuscript only. (All submissions are judged in blind review after the deadline for a specified issue.) Most open to fiction and poetry. Don't be hasty when you consider a theme—mull it over and let it ferment in your mind. We appreciate interpretations that are carefully constructed, clever, subtle, and well thought out."

$ $ THE THREEPENNY REVIEW

P.O. Box 9131, Berkeley CA 94709. (510)849-4545. Website: www.threepennyreview.com. **Contact:** Wendy Lesser, editor. **100% freelance written.** Works with small number of new/unpublished writers each year. Quarterly tabloid. "We are a general interest, national literary magazine with coverage of politics, the visual arts, and the performing arts as well." Estab. 1980. Circ. 9,000. **Pays on acceptance.** Publishes ms an average of 1 year after acceptance. Byline given. Buys first North American serial rights. Responds in 1 month to queries; 2 months to mss. Sample copy for $12 or online. Writer's guidelines online.

  • Does not read mss from September to December.

Nonfiction Essays, exposé, historical/nostalgic, personal experience, book, film, theater, dance, music, and art reviews. **Buys 40 mss/year.** Query with or without published clips or send complete ms. Length: 1,500-4,000 words. **Pays $200.**

Fiction No fragmentary, sentimental fiction. **Buys 10 mss/year.** Send complete ms. Length: 800-4,000 words. **Pays $100 per poem or Table Talk piece.**

Poetry Free verse, traditional. No poems "without capital letters or poems without a discernible subject." **Buys 30 poems/year.** Submit maximum 5 poems. **Pays $100.**

Tips "Nonfiction (political articles, memoirs, reviews) is most open to freelancers."

⑬ $ $ $ TIN HOUSE

McCormack Communications, Box 10500, Portland OR 97210. (503)274-4393. Fax: (503)222-1154. Website: www.tinhouse.com. Editor-in-Chief: Win McCormack. Managing Editor: Holly Macarthur. Editor: Rob Spillman. Senior Editor: Lee Montgomery. Poetry Editor: Brenda Shaunessy. **90% freelance written.** "We are a general interest literary quarterly. Our watchword is quality. Our audience includes people interested in literature in all its aspects, from the mundane to the exalted." Estab. 1998. Circ. 11,000. Pays on publication. Publishes ms an average of 6 months after acceptance. Byline given. Buys first North American serial rights and anthology rights. Editorial lead time 6 months. Submit seasonal material 6 months in advance. Accepts queries by mail. Accepts simultaneous submissions. Responds in 6 weeks to queries; 3 months to mss. Sample copy for $15. Writer's guidelines online.

Nonfiction Book excerpts, essays, interview/profile, personal experience. Send complete ms. Length: 5,000 words maximum. **Pays $50-800 for assigned articles; $50-500 for unsolicited articles.** Sometimes pays expenses of writers on assignment.

Columns/Departments Lost and Found (mini-reviews of forgotten or underappreciated books), up to 500 words; Readable Feasts (fiction or nonfiction literature with recipes), 2,000-3,000 words; Pilgrimage (journey to a personally significant place, especially literary), 2,000-3,000 words. **Buys 15-20 mss/year.** Send complete ms. **Pays $50-500.**

Fiction Rob Spillman, fiction editor. Experimental, mainstream, novel excerpts, literary. **Buys 15-20 mss/year.** Send complete ms. Length: 5,000 words maximum. **Pays $200-800.**

Poetry Brenda Shaunessy, poetry editor. Avant-garde, free verse, traditional. No prose masquerading as poetry. **Buys 40 poems/year.** Submit maximum 5 poems. **Pays $50-150.**

Tips "Remember to send a SASE with your submission."

⑬ $ TRACE OF THE HAND

The All-5-Senses Zine Experience, DSAME, 12400 Ventura Blvd., #134, Studio City CA 91604. Website: www.1d-same.com.; geocities.com/loveandunity2020. Semiannual magazine. "Two things will cause your submission to be immediately discarded faster than anything else: Numerous misspelled words (except in handwritten diary format poems), and any submission from nonmembers. Unlike print-on-demand publishers, publishers that charge reading fees, and vanity publishers, we do not charge you anything at any time to join our band, to join our writers group. We are strictly an independent, not-for-profit effort attempting to help circulate positive creations in an effort to make the world a better place." Estab. 2004. Pays on publication. Publishes ms an average of 6 months after acceptance. Byline given. Buys first rights. Accepts queries by e-mail. Writer's guidelines online.

● Must be a member of the writer's group to submit.

Nonfiction Essays, exposé, general interest, historical/nostalgic, how-to, humor, inspirational, interview/profile, opinion, personal experience, photo feature, travel, experimental diary format writing. "We do not accept translations of another author's work or anything that promotes, rationalizes and/or justifies violence (including violent activism), ageism, ableism (which includes the physically and mentally disabled/challenged), classism, racism, sexism, or any form of discrimination against any person's sexual orientation, religion, or lack of religion." **Buys 10 mss/year.** Query. Length: 500-5,000 words. **Pays $25.** Sometimes pays expenses of writers on assignment.

Photos Send photos with submission. Reviews GIF/JPEG files. Buys one-time rights. Negotiates payment individually.

Poetry "We desire to receive all topics and tones of poetry from members no matter how juvenile (such as poems and writing for children) or how serious. Also, authors who are fluent in Spanish have the option of submitting a Spanish version of their English material provided that the English material accompanies it." Avant-garde, free verse, haiku, light verse, traditional, experimental diary format. **Buys 20 poems/year.** Length: open.

Tips "Stay sincere. Allow your writing to be written in a fresh, alive and perhaps even an experimental and spontaneous manner from your sincere feelings rather than limited to the rehearsed and reconstructed confines of 'allegedly unbiased news reporting,' rhythm, meter, and the traditional styles of ancient celebrities who established so-called 'rules' of journalism, poetry, and standard writing."

⑬ ⬛ VALLUM

Contemporary Poetry, Vallum Society for Arts & Letters Education, P.O. Box 48003, Montreal QC H2V 4S8 Canada. Phone/Fax: (514)278-4999. E-mail: vallummag@sympatico.ca. Website: www.vallummag.com. Editors: Joshua Auerbach and Eleni Zisimatos. Managing Editor: Andrea Belcham. **Contact:** Editor. **100% freelance written.** Biannual magazine covering poetry. "*Vallum* publishes the best in new poetry by emerging and established writers from around the world. Poetry that is fresh, avant garde, and challenging will be considered. *Vallum* also publishes essays on poetics, interviews with noted poets, and reviews of recent books of poetry and translations. Occasional theme issues." Estab. 2001. Circ. 2,500. Pays on publication. Publishes ms an average of 6-12 months after acceptance. Byline given. Offers 100% kill fee. Buys first North American serial rights. Accepts queries by mail. Responds in 1-2 months to queries; 6-12 months to mss. Sample copy for $7 (US); $8.25 (Canadian); $8.75 (outside North America). Writer's guidelines online.

- Reads submissions from October-March only. Work received outside this time frame will be returned unread (exceptions are made for specified theme issues, where submissions should be clearly marked as such).

Nonfiction Reviews of books of poetry. Special issues: Theme issues and deadlines are regularly posted on the website. Does not want content not specific to poetry/poetics. **Buys 20 mss/year.** Query. Length: 700-2,000 words. **Negotiates payment individually.**

Photos Send photos with submission. Reviews contact sheets, prints. Buys first North American serial rights. Negotiates payment individually.

Columns/Departments Book Reviews (critiques of new releases of poetry), 700-1,000 words. **Buys 10 mss/ year.** Query. **Negotiates payment individually.**

Poetry Avant-garde, free verse, haiku, light verse, traditional, concrete. **Buys 100 poems/year.** Submit maximum 5-8 poems.

Tips "Be sure to follow our submission guidelines—submit only by mail and only within the reading period (October-March). Include sufficient postage for the return of submissions. Include a cover letter and a brief bio, including writing credits."

N $ $ VERBATIM

The Language Quarterly, Word, Inc., 4907 N. Washtenaw, Chicago IL 60625. (773)275-1516. E-mail: editor@verbatimmag.com. Website: www.verbatimmag.com. **Contact:** Erin McKean, editor. **75-80% freelance written.** Quarterly magazine covering language and linguistics. "*Verbatim* is the only magazine of language and linguistics for the lay person." Estab. 1974. Circ. 1,600. Pays on publication. Publishes ms an average of 6-9 months after acceptance. Byline given. Buys all rights. Editorial lead time 3 months. Submit seasonal material 6 months in advance. Accepts queries by mail, e-mail. Responds in 3 weeks to queries; 2 months to mss. Sample copy for 9×12 SAE and 6 first-class stamps. Writer's guidelines online.

Nonfiction Essays, humor, personal experience. Does not want puns or overly cranky prescriptivism. **Buys 24-28 mss/year.** Query. **Pays $25-400 for assigned articles; $25-300 for unsolicited articles.**

Poetry "We only publish poems explicitly about language. Poems written in language not enough." **Buys 4-6 poems/year.** Submit maximum 3 poems. Length: 3-75 lines. **Pays $25-50.**

Tips "Humorously write about an interesting language, language topic, or jargon. Also, when querying, include 3-4 lines of biographical information about yourself."

$ $ VESTAL REVIEW

A flash fiction magazine, 2609 Dartmouth Dr., Vestal NY 13850. E-mail: submissions@vestalreview.net. Website: www.vestalreview.net. **Contact:** Mark Budman, publisher/editor; Sue O'Neill, co-editor. Quarterly magazine specializing in flash fiction. "We accept only e-mail submissions." Circ. 1,500. Pays on publication. Publishes ms an average of 2-3 months after acceptance. Buys first North American serial, electronic rights. Accepts queries by e-mail. Accepts simultaneous submissions. Responds in 1 week to queries; 2 months to mss. Sample copy for $5. Writer's guidelines online.

Fiction Ethnic, horror, mainstream, speculative fiction. Does not read new submissions in March, June, September, and December. All submissions received during these months will be returned unopened. Length: 50-500 words. **Pays 3-10¢/word and 1 contributor's copy; additional copies $5.**

Tips "We like literary fiction, with a plot, that doesn't waste words. Don't send jokes masked as stories."

$ THE VILLAGE RAMBLER MAGAZINE

The Flying Typewriter, P.O. Box 5070, Chapel Hill NC 27514-5001. (919)545-9789. Fax: (919)545-0921. E-mail: editor@villagerambler.com. Website: www.villagerambler.com. **Contact:** Elizabeth Oliver, editor. **85% freelance written.** Bimonthly magazine. "*The Village Rambler Magazine* is distributed in North Carolina and features area and national talent. We are interested in fiction, poetry, and nonfiction." Estab. 2003. Circ. 3,000. Pays on publication. Publishes ms an average of 6-12 months after acceptance. Byline given. Buys first rights, makes work-for-hire assignments. Accepts queries by mail. Accepts previously published material. Responds in 1 month to queries; 4 months to mss. Sample copy for $8. Writer's guidelines for #10 SASE.

Nonfiction Book excerpts, essays, general interest, historical/nostalgic, humor, interview/profile, personal experience, photo feature. **Buys 24 mss/year.** Send complete ms. Length: 10,000 words maximum. **Pays $50, plus 1 contributor copy.**

Photos State availability with submission. Reviews 4×6 prints, GIF/JPEG files. Buys one-time rights. Negotiates payment individually. Captions, identification of subjects, model releases required.

Fiction Ethnic, experimental, historical, humorous, mainstream, novel excerpts, serialized novels, short shorts. No genre fiction (science fiction, horror, romance, or children's). **Buys 6-12 mss/year.** Send complete ms. Length: 10,000 words maximum. **Pays $50, plus 1 contributor copy.**

Poetry "We are open to all types of poetry." **Buys 12-18 poems/year.** Submit maximum 5 poems.

Tips "Send us your strongest work. We are interested in writing that knows its objective and achieves it with talent and technique."

$ VIRGINIA QUARTERLY REVIEW

University of Virginia, One West Range, P.O. Box 400223, Charlottesville VA 22904-4223. (434)924-3124. Fax: (434)924-1397. Website: www.virginia.edu/vqr. **Contact:** Ted Genoways, editor. Quarterly magazine. "A national journal of literature and thought. A lay, intellectual audience; people who are not out-and-out scholars but who are interested in ideas and literature." Estab. 1925. Circ. 4,000. Pays on publication. Publishes ms an average of 1 year after acceptance. Byline given. Buys first rights. Editorial lead time 6 months. Submit seasonal material 6 months in advance. Responds in 2 weeks to queries; 4 months to mss. Sample copy for $11. Writer's guidelines online.

Nonfiction Book excerpts, essays, general interest, historical/nostalgic, humor, inspirational, personal experience, travel. Send complete ms. Length: 2,000-4,000 words. **Pays $100/page maximum.**

Fiction Adventure, ethnic, historical, humorous, mainstream, mystery, novel excerpts, romance, serialized novels. "No pornography." Send complete ms. Length: 3,000-7,000 words. **Pays $100/page maximum.**

Poetry All type. Submit maximum 5 poems. **Pays $5/line.**

N $ VISIONS-INTERNATIONAL

Black Buzzard Press, 3503 Ferguson Rd., Austin TX 78754. (512)674-3977. **Contact:** B.R. Strahan, editor. **95% freelance written.** Magazine published 2 times/year featuring poetry, essays and reviews. Estab. 1979. Circ. 750. Pays on publication. Publishes ms an average of 6 months after acceptance. Byline given. Buys first North American serial rights. Editorial lead time 4 months. Accepts queries by mail. Responds in 3 weeks to queries; 2 months to mss. Sample copy for $4.95. Writer's guidelines for #10 SASE.

Nonfiction Essays (by assignment after query reviews). Query. Length: 1 page maximum. **Pays $10 and complimentary copies.** Pays with contributor copies when grant money is unavailable.

Poetry Avant-garde, free verse, traditional, translations into English. No sentimental, religious, scurrilous, sexist, racist, amaturish, or over 3 pages. **Buys 110 poems/year.** Submit 3-6 poems Length: 2-120 lines.

Tips "Know your craft. We are not a magazine for amateurs. We also are interested in translation from modern poets writing in any language into English. No e-mail submissions please."

N $ $ WEBER STUDIES

Voices and Viewpoints of the Contemporary World, Weber State University, 1214 University Circle, Ogden UT 84404-1214. (801)626-6616 or (801)626-6473. E-mail: weberstudies@weber.edu. Website: weberstudies.weber. edu. Editor: Brad L. Roghaar. **Contact:** Kay Anderson, editorial assistant. **20% freelance written.** Magazine and online text archive published 3 times/year covering preservation of and access to wilderness, environmental cooperation, insight derived from living in the West, cultural diversity, changing federal involvement in the region, women and the West, implications of population growth, the contributions of individuals (scholars, artists and community leaders), a sense of place. "We seek works that provide insight into the environment and culture (both broadly defined) of the contemporary western US. We look for good writing that reveals human nature, as well as natural environment." Estab. 1981. Circ. 800-1,000. Pays on publication. Publishes ms an average of 6-12 months after acceptance. Byline given. Buys one-time, electronic rights. (copyrights revert to authors after publication) Editorial lead time 6 months. Submit seasonal material 6 months in advance. Accepts queries by mail, e-mail, phone. Accepts simultaneous submissions. Responds in 1 month to queries; 6-9 months to mss. Sample copy for $8. Writer's guidelines for #10 SASE, on website or by e-mail.

Nonfiction Essays, historical/nostalgic, interview/profile, opinion, personal experience, photo feature. **Buys 20-30 mss/year.** Send complete ms. Length: 5,000 words. **Pays $150-300, plus 1 contributor copy and 1-year subscription.**

Photos State availability with submission. Reviews 4×6 prints, 4×6 GIF/JPEG files at 300 dpi. Buys one-time rights. Negotiates pay individually. Captions, identification of subjects, model releases required.

Columns/Departments Send complete ms. **Pays $100-200.**

Fiction Adventure, ethnic, historical, humorous, mainstream, novel excerpts, religious, slice-of-life vignettes, western. Send complete ms. Length: 5,000 words. **Pays $150-300.**

Poetry Buys 15-20 sets of poems/year. Submit maximum 6 poems. **Pays $70-150.**

$ WEST BRANCH

Bucknell Hall, Bucknell University, Lewisburg PA 17837-2029. (570)577-1853. Fax: (570)577-1885. E-mail: westbranch@bucknell.edu. Website: www.bucknell.edu/westbranch. Managing Editor: Andrew Ciotola. **Con-**

tact: Paula Closson Buck, editor. Semiannual literary magazine. *"West Branch* is an aesthetic conversation between the traditional and the innovative in poetry, fiction and nonfiction. It brings writers, new and established, to the rooms where they will be heard, and where they will, no doubt, rearrange the furniture." Pays on publication. Byline given. Buys first North American serial rights. Accepts queries by mail. Sample copy for $3. Writer's guidelines online.

Nonfiction Essays, general interest, literary. **Buys 4-5 mss/year.** Send complete ms. **Pays $20-100 ($10/page).**

Fiction Novel excerpts, short stories. No genre fiction. **Buys 10-12 mss/year.** Send complete ms. **Pays $20-100 ($10/page).**

Poetry Free verse, formal, experimental. **Buys 30-40 poems/year.** Submit maximum 6 poems. **Pays $20-100 ($10/page).**

Tips "Please send only 1 submission at a time and do not send another work until you have heard about the first. Send no more than 6 poems or 30 pages of prose at once. We accept simultaneous submissions if they are clearly marked as such, and if we are notified immediately upon acceptance elsewhere. Manuscripts must be accompanied by the customary return materials; we cannot respond by e-mail or postcard, except to foreign submissions. All manuscripts should be typed, with the author's name on each page; prose must be double-spaced. We recommend that you acquaint yourself with the magazine before submitting."

🅽 $🗗 WEST COAST LINE

A Journal of Contemporary Writing & Criticism, West Coast Review Publishing Society, 2027 E. Annex, 8888 University Dr., Simon Fraser University, Burnaby BC V5A 1S6 Canada. (604)291-4287. Fax: (604)291-4622. E-mail: wcl@sfu.ca. Website: www.sfu.ca/west-coast-line. **Contact:** Roger Farr, managing editor. Triannual magazine of contemporary literature and criticism. Estab. 1990. Circ. 500. Pays on publication. Buys one-time rights. Editorial lead time 4 months. Accepts queries by mail, e-mail. Responds in up to 6 months. Sample copy for $10. Writer's guidelines for SASE (US must include IRC).

Nonfiction Essays (literary/scholarly/critical), experimental prose. "No journalistic articles or articles dealing with nonliterary material." **Buys 8-10 mss/year.** Send complete ms. Length: 1,000-5,000 words. **Pays $8/page, 2 contributor's copies and a 1-year subscription.**

Fiction Experimental, novel excerpts. **Buys 3-6 mss/year.** Send complete ms. Length: 1,000-7,000 words. **Pays $8/page.**

Poetry Avant-garde. "No light verse, traditional." **Buys 10-15 poems/year.** Submit maximum maximum 5-6 poems.

Tips "Submissions must be either scholarly or formally innovative. Contributors should be familiar with current literary trends in Canada and the US Scholars should be aware of current schools of theory. All submissions should be accompanied by a brief cover letter; essays should be formatted according to the MLA guide. The publication is not divided into departments. We accept innovative poetry, fiction, experimental prose and scholarly essays."

$ WESTERN HUMANITIES REVIEW

University of Utah, English Department, 255 S. Central Campus Dr., Room 3500, Salt Lake City UT 84112-0494. (801)581-6070. Fax: (801)585-5167. E-mail: whr@mail.hum.utah.edu. Website: www.hum.utah.edu/whr. **Contact:** David McGlynn, managing editor. Semiannual magazine for educated readers. Estab. 1947. Circ. 1,000. Pays on publication. Publishes ms an average of 1 year after acceptance. Buys all rights. Accepts simultaneous submissions. Sample copy for $10. Writer's guidelines online.

• Reads mss September 1-May 1. Mss sent outside of these dates will be returned unread.

Nonfiction Barry Weller, editor-in-chief. Authoritative, readable articles on literature, art, philosophy, current events, history, religion, and anything in the humanities. Interdisciplinary articles encouraged. Departments on films and books. **Buys 4-5 unsolicited mss/year.** Send complete ms. **Pays $5/published page.**

Fiction Karen Brennan and Robin Hemley, fiction editors. Experimental. Does not want genre (romance, sci-fi, etc.). **Buys 8-12 mss/year.** Send complete ms. Length: 5,000 words. **Pays $5/published page (when funds available).**

Poetry Richard Howard, poetry editor.

Tips "Because of changes in our editorial staff, we urge familiarity with recent issues of the magazine. Inappropriate material will be returned without comment. We do not publish writer's guidelines because we think that the magazine itself conveys an accurate picture of our requirements. Please, no e-mail submissions."

🅽 $🗗 WINDSOR REVIEW

A Journal of the Arts, Dept. of English, University of Windsor, Windsor ON N9B 3P4 Canada. (519)253-3000. Fax: (519)971-3676. E-mail: uwrevu@uwindsor.ca. Website: zeus.uwindsor.ca/english/review.htm. **Contact:** Alistair MacLeod, fiction editor. Semiannual magazine. "We try to offer a balance of fiction and poetry distinguished by excellence." Estab. 1965. Circ. 250. Pays on publication. Publishes ms an average of 6 months after acceptance. Buys one-time rights. Accepts queries by e-mail. Responds in 1 month to queries; 6 weeks to mss. Sample copy for $7 (US). Writer's guidelines online.

Fiction Literary. No genre fiction (science fiction, romance), "but would consider if writing is good enough." Send complete ms. Length: 1,000-5,000 words. **Pays $30, 1 contributor's copy and a free subscription.**

Poetry Submit maximum 6 poems.

Tips "Good writing, strong characters, and experimental fiction is appreciated."

$WRITERS NOTES

Stories, Craft, Experience, Hopewell Publications, LLC, P.O. Box 11, Titusville NJ 08560-0011. E-mail: editor@h opepubs.com. Website: www.writersnotes.com. Managing Editor: Karin Seidel. **Contact:** Christopher Klim, editor. **90% freelance written.** Semiannual magazine covering fiction, nonfiction, poetry, photos, graphic arts, and writing craft. "*Writers Notes* is a community of working writers and curious readers seeking entertainment and information. Good writing is paramount. The editorial staff is open to compelling prose and experience, including photo essays and graphic arts." Estab. 2003. Circ. 1,500. Pays on publication. Publishes ms an average of 18 months after acceptance. Byline given. Buys first, electronic, one-time anthology rights. Editorial lead time 6 months. Submit seasonal material 6 months in advance. Accepts queries by mail, e-mail. Accepts simultaneous submissions. Responds in 3 weeks to queries; 3 months to mss. Sample copy and writer's guidelines online.

● E-mail queries are OK, but do not send mss electronically.

Nonfiction Book excerpts, essays, exposé, general interest, how-to (writing craft), humor, interview/profile, opinion, personal experience, photo feature. Does not want to see "the same tired party line." **Buys 10-20 mss/year.** Query with or without published clips or send complete ms. Length: 250-5,000 words. **Pays $10-150.** Author advertising/promotion offered in magazine.

Photos State availability with submission. Reviews GIF/JPEG files. Buys one-time anthology rights. Negotiates payment individually.

Fiction Adventure, condensed novels, confessions, erotica, experimental, fantasy, horror, humorous, mainstream, mystery, novel excerpts, suspense. Does not want genre-specific formula stories. **Buys 10-20 mss/year.** Send complete ms. Length: 250-5,000 words. **Pays $10-150.**

Poetry All types accepted. Does not want greeting card, saccharin prose. **Buys 4-8 poems/year.** Submit maximum 10 poems.

Tips "There is a form and craft to great stories and articles. You must engage the reader from the first sentence, while informing, entertaining, and lending insight into a facet of writing craft or life in general. A topic or story that jars common thought, without being obtuse or paranoid, expands the mind. If you think we've seen it before, then don't submit it. Finally, we all need more humor. Make sure the work is complete and professional."

$THE WRITERS POST JOURNAL

Let's Be 'Frank', P.O. Box 7989, Pittsburgh PA 15216. (412)207-9120. E-mail: submissions@lbfbooks.com. Website: www.lbfbooks.com. Editor: Jacqueline Druga-Marchetti. Managing Editor: Teresa Tunaley. **Contact:** Michael Evanitz, submissions editor. **90% freelance written.** Monthly magazine based on a literary organization established in 1996. *The Writers Post Journal* features and focuses on new and emerging literary voices. We also encourage articles on writing." Estab. 2003. Pays on publication. Publishes ms an average of 3 months after acceptance. Buys one-time rights. Editorial lead time 3 months. Submit seasonal material 4 months in advance. Accepts queries by mail, e-mail. Accepts previously published material. Accepts simultaneous submissions. Responds in 6 weeks to queries; 3 months to mss. Sample copy by e-mail. Writer's guidelines online.

Nonfiction Essays, exposé, general interest, how-to, humor, inspirational, opinion, personal experience. Does not want "vulgar material." **Buys 12-20 mss/year.** Query. Length: 1,700 maximum. **Pays $5-25.** Pays contributor copies for poetic pieces, some short fiction pieces, letters to the editor.

Photos Jacqueline Druga. State availability with submission. Reviews GIF/JPEG files. Buys one-time rights. Offers no additional payment for photos accepted with ms.

Fiction Confessions, ethnic, experimental, horror, humorous, mainstream, religious, romance, science fiction, slice-of-life vignettes, young adult. Does not want porn. **Buys 20-40 mss/year.** Query with or without published clips or send complete ms. Length: 2,000 words maximum. **Pays $5-25.**

Poetry Avant-garde, free verse, light verse. Does not want haiku. **Buys 60 poems/year.** Submit maximum 5 poems. Length: 25 lines maximum.

Tips "Be professional. Be patient. We are not as strict as others if you veer off normal queries. Impress us with freshness. We'd like to see more young writer submissions (ages 12-16)."

$ $THE YALE REVIEW

Yale University, P.O. Box 208243, New Haven CT 06520-8243. (203)432-0499. Fax: (203)432-0510. Website: www.yale.edu. Associate Editor: Susan Bianconi. **Contact:** J.D. McClatchy, editor. **20% freelance written.** Quarterly magazine. Estab. 1911. Circ. 7,000. Pays prior to publication. Publishes ms an average of 6 months after acceptance. Buys one-time rights. Responds in 2 months. Sample copy for $9, plus postage. Writer's guidelines online.

Nonfiction Authoritative discussions of politics, literature and the arts. No previously published submissions. Send complete ms with cover letter and SASE. Length: 3,000-5,000 words. **Pays $400-500.**

Fiction Buys quality fiction. Length: 3,000-5,000 words. **Pays $400-500.**

Poetry Pays $100-250.

N $THE YALOBUSHA REVIEW

The Literary Journal of the University of Mississippi, University of Mississippi Press, P.O. Box 1848, Dept. of English, University MS 38677. (662)915-3175. Website: www.olemiss.edu/yalobusha. Annual literary journal seeking quality submissions from around the globe. Reading period is July 15-November 15. Estab. 1995. Circ. 1,000. Buys first North American serial rights. Accepts queries by mail. Responds in 2-4 months to mss. Sample copy for $5. Writer's guidelines for #10 SASE.

Nonfiction Nonfiction Editor. Essays, general interest, humor, interview/profile, personal experience, travel. Buys 1-3 mss/year. Send complete ms. Length: 500-5,000 words. **Pays honorarium when funding available.**

Fiction Fiction Editor. Experimental, historical, humorous, mainstream, novel excerpts, short shorts. **Buys 4-6 mss/year.** Send complete ms. Length: 500-4,000 words. **Pays honorarium when funding available.**

Poetry Avant-garde, free verse, light verse, traditional. **Buys 10-20 poems/year.** Submit maximum 5 poems.

$ZAHIR

Unforgettable Tales, Zahir Publishing, 315 South Coast Hwy. 101, Suite U8, Encinitas CA 92024. E-mail: stempch in@zahirtales.com. Website: www.zahirtales.com. **Contact:** Sheryl Tempchin, editor. **100% freelance written.** Triannual magazine covering speculative fiction. "We publish quality speculative fiction for intelligent adult readers. Our goal is to bridge the gap between literary and genre fiction, and present a publication that is both entertaining and aesthetically pleasing." Estab. 2003. Pays on publication. Publishes ms an average of 2-12 months after acceptance. Byline given. Buys first, second serial (reprint) rights. Accepts queries by e-mail. Accepts previously published material. Responds in 1-2 weeks to queries; 1-3 months to mss. Sample copy for $5 (US), $6.50 elsewhere. Writer's guidelines for #10 SASE, by e-mail, or online.

Fiction Fantasy, science fiction, surrealism, magical realism. No children's stories or stories that deal with excessive violence or anything pornographic. **Buys 18-25 mss/year.** Send complete ms. Length: 6,000 words maximum. **Pays $10, and 2 contributor's copies.**

Tips "We look for great storytelling and fresh ideas. Let your imagination run wild and capture it in concise, evocative prose."

$ $ $ZOETROPE: ALL STORY

AZX Publications, The Sentinel Bldg., 916 Kearny St., San Francisco CA 94133. (415)788-7500. E-mail: info@all-story.com. Website: www.all-story.com. **Contact:** Francis Ford Coppola, publisher; Michael Ray, editor. Quarterly magazine specializing in the best of contemporary short fiction. "*Zoetrope: All Story* presents a new generation of classic stories." Estab. 1997. Circ. 20,000. Publishes ms an average of 5 months after acceptance. Byline given. Buys first serial rights rights. Accepts queries by mail. Accepts simultaneous submissions. Responds in 5 months (if SASE included) to mss. Sample copy for $6.95. Writer's guidelines online.

Fiction Literary short stories, one-act plays. **Buys 25-35 mss/year.** Send complete ms. **Pays $1,000.**

Current and select back issues can be found online. "The website features current news, events, contests, workshops, writer's guidelines, and more. In addition, the site links to Francis Ford Coppola's Virtual Studio, which is host to an online workshop for short story writers."

$ZYZZYVA

The Last Word: West Coast Writers & Artists, P.O. Box 590069, San Francisco CA 94159-0069. (415)752-4393. Fax: (415)752-4391. E-mail: editor@zyzzyva.org. Website: www.zyzzyva.org. **Contact:** Howard Junker, editor. **100% freelance written.** Works with a small number of new/unpublished writers each year. Magazine published in March, August, and November. "We feature work by writers currently living on the West Coast or in Alaska and Hawaii only. We are essentially a literary magazine, but of wide-ranging interests and a strong commitment to nonfiction." Estab. 1985. Circ. 3,500. **Pays on acceptance.** Publishes ms an average of 3 months after acceptance. Byline given. Acquires first North American serial and one-time anthology rights. Accepts queries by mail, e-mail. Responds in 1 week to queries; 1 month to mss. Sample copy for $7 or online. Writer's guidelines online.

Nonfiction Book excerpts, general interest, historical/nostalgic, humor, personal experience. **Buys 50 mss/year.** Query by mail or e-mail. Length: Open. **Pays $50.**

Photos Reviews copies or slides only—scans at 300 dpi, 5½" wide.

Fiction Ethnic, experimental, humorous, mainstream. **Buys 20 mss/year.** Send complete ms. Length: 100-7,500 words. **Pays $50.**

Poetry **Buys 20 poems/year.** Submit maximum 5 poems. Length: 3-200 lines. **Pays $50.**

Tips "West Coast writers means those currently living in California, Alaska, Washington, Oregon, or Hawaii."

MEN'S

$ $ $ $ESQUIRE

Hearst Corp., 1790 Broadway, New York NY 10019. (212)649-4020. E-mail: esquire@hearst.com. Website: www.esquire.com. Editor-in-Chief: David Granger. Monthly magazine covering the ever-changing trends in American culture. Geared toward smart, well-off men. General readership is college educated and sophisticated, between ages 30 and 45. Written mostly by contributing editors on contract. Rarely accepts unsolicited mss. Estab. 1933. Circ. 720,000. Publishes ms an average of 2-6 months after acceptance. Retains first worldwide periodical publication rights for 90 days from cover date. Editorial lead time at least 2 months. Accepts simultaneous submissions. Writer's guidelines for SASE.

Nonfiction Focus is the ever-changing trends in American culture. Topics include current events and politics, social criticism, sports, celebrity profiles, the media, art and music, men's fashion. Queries must be sent by letter. **Buys 4 features and 12 shorter mss/year.** Length: Columns average 1,500 words; features average 5,000 words; short front of book pieces average 200-400 words. **Payment varies.**

Photos Uses mostly commissioned photography. Payment depends on size and number of photos.

Fiction "Literary excellence is our only criterion." Novel excerpts, short stories, some poetry, memoirs, and plays. No "pornography, science fiction or 'true romance' stories." Send complete ms.

Tips "A writer has the best chance of breaking in at *Esquire* by querying with a specific idea that requires special contacts and expertise. Ideas must be timely and national in scope."

$GC MAGAZINE

Handel Publishing, P.O. Box 331775, Fort Worth TX 76163. (817)640-1306. Fax: (817)633-9045. E-mail: rosa.gc @sbcglobal.net. Managing Editor: Rosa Atwood-Flores. **80% freelance written.** Monthly magazine. "*GC Magazine* is a general entertainment magazine for men. We include entertainment celebrity interviews (movies, music, books) along with general interest articles for adult males." Estab. 1994. Circ. 53,000. Pays on publication. Publishes ms an average of 3 months after acceptance. Buys one-time rights. Editorial lead time 3 months. Submit seasonal material 6 months in advance. Accepts queries by mail, e-mail, fax. Accepts previously published material. Accepts simultaneous submissions. Responds in 3 months to queries. Sample copy for $1.50. Writer's guidelines for #10 SASE.

Nonfiction Book excerpts, essays, exposé, general interest, historical/nostalgic, how-to, humor, interview/profile, technical, travel, dating tips. **Buys 100 mss/year.** Query. Length: 1,000-2,000 words. **Pays 2¢/word.** Sometimes pays expenses of writers on assignment.

Reprints Accepts previously published submissions.

Photos State availability with submission. Reviews 3×5 prints, GIF/JPEG files. Buys one-time rights. Offers no additional payment for photos accepted with ms. Model releases required.

Columns/Departments Actress feature (film actress interviews), 2,500 words; Author feature (book author interviews), 1,500 words; Music feature (singer or band interviews), 1,500 words. **Buys 50 mss/year.** Query. **Pays 2¢/word.**

Tips "Submit material typed and free of errors. Writers should think of magazines like *Maxim* and *Details* when determining article ideas for our magazine. Our primary readership is adult males and we are seeking original and unique articles."

$ $ $INDY MEN'S MAGAZINE

The Guy's Guide to the Good Life, Table Moose Media, 8500 Keystone Crossing, Suite 100, Indianapolis IN 46240. (317)255-3850. Fax: (317)254-5944. E-mail: lou@indymensmagazine.com. Website: www.indymensma gazine.com. **Contact:** Lou Harry, editor-in-chief. **50% freelance written.** Monthly magazine. Estab. 2002. Circ. 50,000. Pays on publication. Byline given. Offers 10% kill fee. Buys first North American serial rights. Editorial lead time 3 months. Submit seasonal material 1 year in advance. Accepts queries by e-mail. Accepts simultaneous submissions. Responds in 3 weeks to queries; 2 months to mss. Sample copy for $5. Writer's guidelines by e-mail.

Nonfiction Essays, travel. No generic pieces that could run anywhere. No advocacy pieces. **Buys 50 mss/year.** Query. Length: 100-2,000 words. **Pays $75-500 for assigned articles; $50-400 for unsolicited articles.** Sometimes pays expenses of writers on assignment.

Photos State availability with submission. Reviews contact sheets, transparencies, prints, GIF/JPEG files. Buys one-time rights. Negotiates payment individually. Identification of subjects required.
Columns/Departments Balls (opinionated sports pieces), 1,400 words; Dad Files (introspective parenting essays), 1,400 words; Men At Work (Indianapolis men and their jobs), 100-600 words; Trippin' (experiential travel), 1,500 words. **Buys 30 mss/year.** Query with published clips. **Pays $75-400.**
Fiction "The piece needs to hold our attention from the first paragraph." Adventure, fantasy, historical, horror, humorous, mainstream, mystery, science fiction, suspense. **Buys 12 mss/year.** Send complete ms. Length: 1,000-4,000 words. **Pays $50-250.**
Tips "We don't believe in wasting our reader's time, whether it's in a 50-word item or a 6,000-word Q&A. Our readers are smart, and they appreciate our sense of humor. Write to entertain and engage."

N KING
Harris Publications, Inc., 1115 Broadway, 8th Floor, New York NY 10010. (212)807-7100. Fax: (212)807-0216. E-mail: kingmag@harris-pub.com. Website: www.king-mag.com. Editor: Datwon Thomas. Managing Editor: Siobhan O'Connor. Magazine published 8 times/year for today's urban male. Circ. 300,000. Editorial lead time 3 months. Sample copy not available.

MAXIM
Dennis Publishing, 1040 Avenue of the Americas, 16th Floor, New York NY 10018-3703. (212)302-2626. Fax: (212)302-2635. E-mail: editors@maximmag.com. Website: www.maximonline.com. Editor: Keith Blanchard. Monthly magazine covering relationships, sex, women, careers and sports. Written for young, professional men interested in fun and informative articles. Circ. 2,500,000. Editorial lead time 5 months. Sample copy for $3.99 at newstands.

MEN'S FITNESS
Weider Publications, 21100 Erwin St., Woodland Hills CA 91367. Website: www.mensfitness.com. Editor: Neal Boulton. Monthly magazine written for the sophisticated man who knows what he wants. *Men's Fitness* delivers the tools he needs to perform to his maximum potential and to live an active and healthy lifestyle. Circ. 635,145.

MEN'S JOURNAL
Wenner Media, Inc., 1290 Avenue of the Americas, 2nd Floor, New York NY 10104-0295. (212)484-1616. Fax: (212)484-3434. E-mail: letters@mensjournal.com. Website: www.mensjournal.com. Monthly magazine covering general lifestyle for men, ages 25-49. "*Men's Journal* is for active men with an interest in participatory sports, travel, fitness, and adventure. It provides practical, informative articles on how to spend quality leisure time." Estab. 1992. Circ. 650,000. Accepts queries by mail, fax.
Nonfiction Features and profiles 2,000-7,000 words; shorter features of 400-1,200 words; equipment and fitness stories, 400-1,800 words. Book excerpts, essays, exposé, general interest, historical/nostalgic, how-to, humor, new product, personal experience, photo feature, travel. Query with SASE. **Payment varies.**

$ $ $ $ SMOKE MAGAZINE
Life's Burning Desires, Lockwood Publications, 26 Broadway, Floor 9M, New York NY 10004. (212)391-2060. Fax: (212)827-0945. E-mail: editor@smokemag.com. Website: www.smokemag.com. Editor: Ted Hoyt. **50% freelance written.** Quarterly magazine covering cigars and men's lifestyle issues. "A large majority of *Smoke's* readers are affluent men, ages 28-50; active, educated and adventurous." Estab. 1995. Circ. 175,000. Pays 2 months after publication. Publishes ms an average of 3 months after acceptance. Byline given. Offers 25% kill fee. Buys first rights. Editorial lead time 2 months. Submit seasonal material 6 months in advance. Accepts queries by mail, e-mail. Accepts simultaneous submissions. Responds in 6 weeks to queries; 3 months to mss. Sample copy for $4.99.
    0→ Break in with "good nonfiction that interests guys—beer, cuisine, true-crime, sports, cigars. Be original."
Nonfiction Essays, exposé, general interest, historical/nostalgic, how-to, humor, interview/profile, opinion, personal experience, photo feature, technical, travel, true crime. **Buys 8 mss/year.** Query with published clips. Length: 1,500-3,000 words. **Pays $500-1,200.** Sometimes pays expenses of writers on assignment.
Photos State availability with submission. Reviews $2\frac{1}{4} \times 2\frac{1}{4}$ transparencies. Negotiates payment individually. Identification of subjects required.
Columns/Departments Smoke Undercover (investigative journalism, personal experience); Smoke Screen (TV/film/entertainment issues); Smoke City (cigar-related travel), all 1,500 words. **Buys 8 mss/year.** Query with published clips. **Pays $500-1,000.**
Tips "Send a short, clear query with clips. Go with your field of expertise: cigars, sports, music, true crime, etc."

$ $⌨ UMM (URBAN MALE MAGAZINE)

Canada's Only Lifestyle and Fashion Magazine for Men, UMM Publishing Inc., 70 George St., Suite 200, Ottawa ON K1N 5V9 Canada. (613)723-6216. Fax: (613)723-1702. E-mail: editor@umm.ca. Website: www.umm.ca. **100% freelance written.** Bimonthly magazine covering men's interests. "Our audience is young men, aged 18-24. We focus on Canadian activities, interests, and lifestyle issues. Our magazine is fresh and energetic and we look for original ideas carried out with a spark of intelligence and/or humour (and you'd better spell humour with a 'u')." Estab. 1998. Circ. 90,000. Pays 1 month after publication. Publishes ms an average of 3 months after acceptance. Byline given. Buys first North American serial rights. Editorial lead time 3 months. Submit seasonal material 4 months in advance. Accepts queries by e-mail. Accepts simultaneous submissions. Responds in 6 weeks.

Nonfiction Book excerpts, exposé, general interest, historical/nostalgic, how-to, humor, interview/profile, new product, personal experience, travel, adventure, cultural, sports, music. **Buys 80 mss/year.** Query with published clips. Length: 1,200-3,500 words. **Pays $100-400.** Sometimes pays expenses of writers on assignment.

Photos State availability with submission. Reviews contact sheets, prints. Buys one-time rights. Negotiates payment individually.

Fillers Anecdotes, facts, short humor. **Buys 35/year.** Length: 100-500 words. **Pays $50-150.**

Tips "Be familiar with our magazine before querying. We deal with all subjects of interest to young men, especially those with Canadian themes. We are very open-minded. Original ideas and catchy writing are key."

MILITARY

$ $ AIR FORCE TIMES

Army Times Publishing Co., 6883 Commercial Dr., Springfield VA 22159. (703)750-8646. Fax: (703)750-8601. E-mail: lbacon@airforcetimes.com. Website: www.airforcetimes.com. **Contact:** Lance Bacon, managing editor. Weeklies edited separately for Army, Navy, Marine Corps, and Air Force military personnel and their families. They contain career information such as pay raises, promotions, news of legislation affecting the military, housing, base activities and features of interest to military people. Estab. 1940. **Pays on acceptance.** Byline given. Offers kill fee. Buys first rights. Accepts queries by mail, e-mail, phone. Accepts simultaneous submissions. Responds in 1 month to queries. Sample copy for #10 SASE. Writer's guidelines for #10 SASE.

Nonfiction Features of interest to career military personnel and their families. No advice pieces. **Buys 150-175 mss/year.** Query. Length: 750-2,000 words. **Pays $100-500.**

Columns/Departments Length: 500-900. **Buys 75 mss/year. Pays $75-125.**

◻ The online magazines carry original content not found in the print editions. Websites: www.armytimes. com; www.navytimes.com; www.airforcetimes.com; www.marinecorpstimes.com. Contact: Kent Miller, online editor.

Tips Looking for "stories on active duty, reserve and retired military personnel; stories on military matters and localized military issues; stories on successful civilian careers after military service."

$ $ ARMY MAGAZINE

2425 Wilson Blvd., Arlington VA 22201-3385. (703)841-4300. Fax: (703)841-3505. E-mail: armymag@ausa.org. Website: www.ausa.org. **Contact:** Mary Blake French, editor-in-chief. **70% freelance written.** Prefers to work with published/established writers. Monthly magazine emphasizing military interests. Estab. 1904. Circ. 90,000. Pays on publication. Publishes ms an average of 5 months after acceptance. Byline given. Buys all rights. Submit seasonal material 3 months in advance. Accepts queries by mail. Sample copy for 9×12 SAE with $1 postage or online. Writer's guidelines for 9×12 SAE with $1 postage or online.

● *Army Magazine* looks for shorter articles.

Nonfiction "We would like to see more pieces about little-known episodes involving interesting military personalities. We especially want material lending itself to heavy, contributor-supplied photographic treatment. The first thing a contributor should recognize is that our readership is very savvy militarily. 'Gee-whiz' personal reminiscences get short shrift, unless they hold their own in a company in which long military service, heroism and unusual experiences are commonplace. At the same time, *Army* readers like a well-written story with a fresh slant, whether it is about an experience in a foxhole or the fortunes of a corps in battle." Historical/nostalgic (military and original), humor (military feature-length articles and anecdotes), interview/profile, photo feature. No rehashed history. No unsolicited book reviews. **Buys 40 mss/year.** Submit complete ms (hard copy and disk). Length: 1,000-1,500 words. **Pays 12-18¢/word.**

Photos Send photos with submission. Reviews prints, slides, high resolution digital photos. Buys all rights. Pays $50-100 for 8×10 b&w glossy prints; $50-350 for 8×10 color glossy prints and 35mm and high resolution digital photos. Captions required.

$ $ ARMY TIMES

Army Times Publishing Co., 6883 Commercial Dr., Springfield VA 22159. (703)750-9000. Fax: (703)750-8622. E-mail: aneill@armytimes.com. Website: www.armytimes.com. **Contact:** Alex Neill, managing editor. Weekly for Army military personnel and their families containing career information such as pay raises, promotions, news of legislation affecting the military, housing, base activities and features of interest to military people. Estab. 1940. Circ. 230,000. **Pays on acceptance.** Byline given. Offers kill fee. Makes work-for-hire assignments. Accepts queries by mail, e-mail. Accepts simultaneous submissions. Responds in 1 month to queries. Sample copy and writer's guidelines for #10 SASE.

> O—¬ Break in by "proposing specific feature stories that only you can write—things we wouldn't be able to get from 'generic' syndicated or wire material. The story must contain an element of mystery and/or surprise, and be entertaining as well as informative. Above all, your story must have a direct connection to military people's needs and interests."

Nonfiction Features of interest to career military personnel and their families: food, relationships, parenting, education, retirement, shelter, health, and fitness, sports, personal appearance, community, recreation, personal finance, entertainment. No advice please. **Buys 150-175 mss/year.** Query. Length: 750-2,000 words. **Pays $100-500.**

Columns/Departments Length: 500-900 words. **Buys 75 mss/year. Pays $75-125.**

Tips Looking for "stories on active duty, reserve and retired military personnel; stories on military matters and localized military issues; stories on successful civilian careers after military service."

$ $ MARINE CORPS TIMES

Army Times Publishing Co., 6883 Commercial Dr., Springfield VA 22159. (703)750-9000. Fax: (703)750-8767. E-mail: rcolenso@marinecorpstimes.com. Website: www.marinecorpstimes.com. **Contact:** Rob Colenso, managing editor, *Marine Corps Times*. Weeklies edited separately for Army, Navy, Marine Corps, and Air Force military personnel and their families. They contain career information such as pay raises, promotions, news of legislation affecting the military, housing, base activities and features of interest to military people. Estab. 1940. Circ. 230,000 (combined). Pays on publication. Byline given. Offers kill fee. Buys first rights. Accepts queries by mail, e-mail, phone. Accepts simultaneous submissions. Responds in 1 month to queries. Sample copy for #10 SASE. Writer's guidelines for #10 SASE.

Nonfiction Features of interest to career military personnel and their families, including stories on current military operations and exercises. No advice pieces. **Buys 150-175 mss/year.** Query. Length: 750-2,000 words. **Pays $100-500.**

Columns/Departments Length: 500-900 words. **Buys 75 mss/year. Pays $75-125.**

> ▣ The online magazines carry original content not found in the print editions. Websites: www.armytimes. com; www.navytimes.com; www.airforcetimes.com. Contact: Kent Miller, online editor.

Tips Looking for "stories on active duty, reserve and retired military personnel; stories on military matters and localized military issues; stories on successful civilian careers after military service."

$ $ $ MILITARY OFFICER

201 N. Washington St., Alexandria VA 22314-2539. (800)234-6622. Fax: (703)838-8179. E-mail: editor@moaa.org. Website: www.moaa.org. Editor: Col. Warren S. Lacy, USA-Ret. **Contact:** Managing Editor. **60% freelance written.** Prefers to work with published/established writers. Monthly magazine for officers of the 7 uniformed services and their families. "*Military Officer* covers topics such as current military/political affairs, military history, travel, finance, hobbies, health and fitness, and military family and retirement lifestyles." Estab. 1945. Circ. 389,000. **Pays on acceptance.** Publishes ms an average of 1 year after acceptance. Byline given. Buys first North American serial rights. Accepts queries by mail, e-mail, fax. Responds in 3 months to queries. Sample copy and writer's guidelines for 9 × 12 SAE with 6 first-class stamps or online.

Nonfiction Current military/political affairs, health and wellness, recent military history, travel, military family life-style. Emphasis now on current military and defense issues. "We rarely accept unsolicited manuscripts." **Buys 48 mss/year.** Query with résumé, sample clips and SASE. Length: 800-2,500 words. **Pays 80¢/word.**

Photos Query with list of stock photo subjects. Original slides and transparencies must be suitable for color separation. Reviews transparencies. Pays $20 for each 8 × 10 b&w photo (normal halftone) used. Pays $75-250 for inside color; $300 for cover.

> ▣ The online magazine carries original content not found in the print edition and includes writer's guidelines. Contact: Ronda Reid, online editor.

$ $ MILITARY TIMES

Times News Group, Inc. (subsidiary of Gannett Corp.), 6883 Commercial Dr., Springfield VA 22159. Fax: (703)750-8781. E-mail: features@atpco.com. **Contact:** Phillip Thompson, Lifeline editor. **25% freelance written.** Weekly tabloid covering lifestyle topics for active, retired, and reserve military members and their families.

"Features need to have real military people in them, and appeal to readers in all the armed services. Our target audience is 90% male, young, fit and adventurous, mostly married and often with young children. They move frequently. Writer queries should approach ideas with those demographics and facts firmly in mind." Circ. 300,000. Pays on publication. Publishes ms an average of 2 months after acceptance. Byline given. Buys first, electronic rights. Editorial lead time 2 months. Submit seasonal material 3 months in advance. Accepts queries by e-mail. Accepts simultaneous submissions. Responds in 6 weeks to queries. Sample copy for $2.75 or online. Writer's guidelines for SAE with 1 first-class stamp or by e-mail.

Nonfiction How-to, new product, technical, travel, sports, recreation, entertainment, health, personal fitness, self-image (fashion, trends), relationships, personal finance, food. "No poems, war memoirs or nostalgia, fiction, travel pieces that are too upscale (luxury cruises) or too focused on military monuments/museums." Query with published clips. Length: 300-500 words. **Pays $100-500.** Sometimes pays expenses of writers on assignment.

Photos State availability with submission. Reviews transparencies. Offers work-for-hire. Offers $75/photo. Captions, identification of subjects required.

Columns/Departments Running (how-to for experienced runners, tips, techniques, problem-solving), 500 words; Personal Fitness (how-to, tips, techniques for working out, improving fitness), 500 words. **Buys 25 mss/year.** Query. **Pays $100-200.**

Tips "Our Lifelines section appears every week with a variety of services, information, and entertainment articles on topics that relate to readers' off-duty lives; or to personal dimensions of their on-duty lives. Topics include food, relationships, parenting, education, retirement, shelter, health and fitness, sports, personal appearances, community, recreation, personal finance, and entertainment. We are looking for articles about military life, its problems and how to handle them, as well as interesting things people are doing, on the job and in their leisure. Keep in mind that our readers come from all of the military services. For instance, a story can focus on an Army family, but may need to include families or sources from other services as well. The editorial 'voice' of the section is familiar and conversational; good-humored without being flippant; sincere without being sentimental; savvy about military life but in a relevant and subtle way, never forgetting that our readers are individuals first, spouses or parents or children second, and service members third."

$ $ NAVAL HISTORY

U.S. Naval Institute, 291 Wood Rd., Annapolis MD 21402-5034. (410)295-1079. Fax: (410)295-1049. E-mail: fschultz@usni.org. Website: www.navalinstitute.org. Associate Editor: Colin Babb. **Contact:** Fred L. Schultz, editor-in-chief. **90% freelance written.** Bimonthly magazine covering naval and maritime history, worldwide. "We are committed, as a publication of the 130-year-old US Naval Institute, to presenting the best and most accurate short works in international naval and maritime history. We do find a place for academicians, but they should be advised that a good story generally wins against a dull topic, no matter how well researched." Estab. 1988. Circ. 40,000. **Pays on acceptance.** Publishes ms an average of 2 years after acceptance. Byline given. Buys all rights. Editorial lead time 6 months. Submit seasonal material 6 months in advance. Accepts queries by mail, e-mail, fax, phone. Responds in 1 month to queries; 2 months to mss. Sample copy for $4.99 and SASE, or on website. Writer's guidelines online.

Nonfiction Book excerpts, essays, historical/nostalgic, humor, inspirational, interview/profile, personal experience, photo feature, technical. **Buys 50 mss/year.** Query. Length: 1,000-3,000 words. **Pays $300-500 for assigned articles; $75-400 for unsolicited articles.**

Photos State availability with submission. Reviews contact sheets, transparencies, 4×6 or larger prints, and digital submissions or CD-ROM. Buys one-time rights. Offers $10 minimum. Captions, identification of subjects, model releases required.

Fillers Anecdotes, newsbreaks (naval-related), short humor. **Buys 40-50/year.** Length: 50-1,000 words. **Pays $10-50.**

Tips "A good way to break in is to write a good, concise, exciting story supported by primary sources and substantial illustrations. Naval history-related news items (ship decommissionings, underwater archaeology, etc.) are also welcome. Because our story bank is substantial, competition is severe. Tying a topic to an anniversary many times is an advantage. We still are in need of Korean and Vietnam War-era material."

$ PARAMETERS

U.S. Army War College Quarterly, U.S. Army War College, 122 Forbes Ave., Carlisle PA 17013-5238. (717)245-4943. E-mail: parameters@carlisle.army.mil. Website: www.carlisle.army.mil/usawc/parameters. **Contact:** Col. Robert H. Taylor, USA Ret., editor. **100% freelance written.** Prefers to work with published/established writers or experts in the field. Readership consists of senior leaders of US defense establishment, both uniformed and civilian, plus members of the media, government, industry and academia. Subjects include national and international security affairs, military strategy, military leadership and management, art and science of warfare, and military history with contemporary relevance. Estab. 1971. Circ. 13,500. Pays on publication. Publishes ms an average of 6 months after acceptance. Byline given. Buys first North American serial rights. Accepts queries by mail, e-mail, phone. Responds in 6 weeks to queries. Sample copy free or online. Writer's guidelines online.

Nonfiction Prefers articles that deal with current security issues, employ critical analysis, and provide solutions or recommendations. Liveliness and verve, consistent with scholarly integrity, appreciated. Theses, studies, and academic course papers should be adapted to article form prior to submission. Documentation in complete endnotes. Send complete ms. Length: 4,500 words average. **Pays $150 average.**

Tips "Make it short; keep it interesting; get criticism and revise accordingly. Write on a contemporary topic. Tackle a subject only if you are an authority. No fax submissions." Encourage e-mail submissions.

$ $ PROCEEDINGS

U.S. Naval Institute, 291 Wood Rd., Annapolis MD 21402-5034. (410)268-6110. Fax: (410)295-7940. E-mail: articlesubmissions@navalinstitute.org. Website: www.usni.org. Editor: Fred H. Rainbow. **Contact:** Gordon Keiser, senior editor. **80% freelance written.** Monthly magazine covering Navy, Marine Corps, Coast Guard issues. Estab. 1873. Circ. 100,000. **Pays on acceptance.** Publishes ms an average of 9 months after acceptance. Byline given. Buys all rights. Editorial lead time 3 months. Responds in 2 months to queries. Sample copy for $3.95. Writer's guidelines online.

Nonfiction Essays, historical/nostalgic, interview/profile, photo feature, technical. **Buys 100-125 mss/year.** Query with or without published clips or send complete ms. Length: 3,000 words. **Pays $60-150/printed page for unsolicited articles.**

Photos State availability of or send photos with submission. Reviews transparencies, prints. Buys one-time rights. Offers $25/photo maximum.

Columns/Departments Comment & Discussion (letters to editor), 750 words; Commentary (opinion), 900 words; Nobody Asked Me, But . . . (opinion), less than 1,000 words. **Buys 150-200 mss/year.** Query or send complete ms. **Pays $34-150.**

Fillers Anecdotes. **Buys 20/year.** Length: 100 words. **Pays $25.**

$ $ $ $ SOLDIER OF FORTUNE

The Journal of Professional Adventurers, 5735 Arapahoe Ave., Suite A-5, Boulder CO 80303-1340. (303)449-3750. E-mail: editorsof@aol.com. Website: www.sofmag.com. **50% freelance written.** Monthly magazine covering military, paramilitary, police, combat subjects, and action/adventure. "We are an action-oriented magazine; we cover combat hot spots around the world. We also provide timely features on state-of-the-art weapons and equipment; elite military and police units; and historical military operations. Readership is primarily active-duty military, veterans, and law enforcement." Estab. 1975. Circ. 60,000. Byline given. Offers 25% kill fee. Buys first rights. Responds in 3 weeks to queries; 1 month to mss. Sample copy for $5. Writer's guidelines for #10 SASE.

Nonfiction Exposé, general interest, historical/nostalgic, how-to (on weapons and their skilled use), humor, interview/profile, new product, personal experience, photo feature (No. 1 on our list), technical, travel, combat reports, military unit reports, and solid Vietnam and Operation Iraqi Freedom articles. "No 'How I won the war' pieces; no op-ed pieces unless they are fully and factually backgrounded; no knife articles (staff assignments only). All submitted articles should have good art; art will sell us on an article." **Buys 75 mss/year.** Query with or without published clips or send complete ms. Send mss to articles editor; queries to managing editor. Length: 2,000-3,000 words. **Pays $150-250/page.**

Reprints Send disk copy, photocopy of article and information about when and where the material previously appeared. Pays 25% of amount paid for an original article.

Photos Send photos with submission. Reviews contact sheets, transparencies. Buys one-time rights. Pays $500 for cover photo. Captions, identification of subjects required.

Fillers Bulletin Board editor. Newsbreaks (military/paramilitary related has to be documented). Length: 100-250 words. **Pays $50.**

Tips "Submit a professionally prepared, complete package. All artwork with cutlines, double-spaced typed manuscript with 5.25 or 3.5 IBM-compatible disk, if available, cover letter including synopsis of article, supporting documentation where applicable, etc. Manuscript must be factual; writers have to do their homework and get all their facts straight. One error means rejection. Vietnam features, if carefully researched and art heavy, will always get a careful look. Combat reports, again, with good art, are No. 1 in our book and stand the best chance of being accepted. Military unit reports from around the world are well received, as are law-enforcement articles (units, police in action). If you write for us, be complete and factual; pros read *Soldier of Fortune*, and are very quick to let us know if we (and the author) err."

MUSIC

ℕ $AMERICAN COUNTRY

Music Monthly, Publishing Services, Inc., 1336 Edna SE, Suite 6, Grand Rapids MI 49507. (616)458-1011. Fax: (616)458-2285. E-mail: brucep@gogrand.com. **Contact:** Bruce L. Parrott, editor. **50% freelance written.** Monthly tabloid covering country music. *"American Country* is a country music publication syndicated to radio stations around the country and featuring articles on country artists, album reviews, recipes, etc." Estab. 1992. Circ. 300,000. Pays on publication. Publishes ms an average of 2 months after acceptance. Byline given. Buys one-time rights, makes work-for-hire assignments. Editorial lead time 2 months. Accepts queries by e-mail, fax. Accepts simultaneous submissions. Responds in 1 week to queries.
Nonfiction Interview/profile, new product (all pertaining to country music). No country music news. **Buys 40-50 mss/year.** Query with published clips. Length: 1,000-2,000 words. **Pays $10-50.**
Columns/Departments Buys 35-50 mss/year. Query with published clips. **Pays $10.**
Tips "Call and tell me the kind of stuff you're doing and send some copies. Have existing contacts within the Nashville music scene."

$AMERICAN SONGWRITER MAGAZINE

50 Music Square W., Suite 604, Nashville TN 37203-3227. (615)321-6096. Fax: (615)321-6097. E-mail: info@americansongwriter.com. Website: www.americansongwriter.com. **Contact:** Douglas Waterman, editor. **90% freelance written.** Bimonthly magazine about songwriters and the craft of songwriting for many types of music, including pop, country, rock, metal, jazz, gospel, and r&b. Estab. 1984. Circ. 5,000. Pays on publication. Publishes ms an average of 2 months after acceptance. Offers 25% kill fee. Buys first North American serial rights. Accepts previously published material. Responds in 2 months to queries. Sample copy for $4. Writer's guidelines for #10 SASE or by e-mail.
Nonfiction General interest, interview/profile, new product, technical, home demo studios, movie and TV scores, performance rights organizations. **Buys 20 mss/year.** Query with published clips. Length: 300-1,200 words. **Pays $25-60.**
Reprints Send tearsheet or photocopy and information about when and where the material previously appeared. Pays same amount as paid for an original article.
Photos Send photos with submission. Reviews 3×5 prints. Buys one-time rights. Offers no additional payment for photos accepeted with ms. Identification of subjects required.
Tips *"American Songwriter* strives to present articles which can be read a year or 2 after they were written and still be pertinent to the songwriter reading them."

ℕ BLACK BEAT

Dorchester Media, 333 7th Ave., 11th Floor, New York NY 10001. (212)780-3500. Fax: (212)979-4825. Website: www.blackbeat.com. Editor: Danica Daniel. Monthly magazine covering the nouveau hip-hop culture and all the gloss that lifestyle promotes. Circ. 80,000.

ℕ BLENDER

The Ultimate Music Magazine, Dennis Publishing, 1040 Avenue of The Americas, New York NY 10018. (212)302-2626. Fax: (212)302-2635. E-mail: info@blender.com. Website: www.blender.com. Editor-in-Chief: Craig Marks. Managing Editor: Adam Bell. Bimonthly magazine covering music for ages 18-34. "Discusses cutting-edge trends across several musical genres." Circ. 410,000. Byline given. Editorial lead time 2 months. Accepts queries by e-mail. Sample copy for $2.99.
Nonfiction Book excerpts, interview/profile (bands, musical artists), new product, Reviews—CD, concert, film.
Photos Photography Editor: Tanya Martin.

$ $BLUEGRASS UNLIMITED

Bluegrass Unlimited, Inc., P.O. Box 771, Warrenton VA 20188-0771. (540)349-8181 or (800)BLU-GRAS. Fax: (540)341-0011. E-mail: editor@bluegrassmusic.com. Website: www.bluegrassmusic.com. Editor: Peter V. Kuykendall. **Contact:** Sharon McGraw, managing editor. **10% freelance written.** Prefers to work with published/established writers. Monthly magazine covering bluegrass, acoustic, and old-time country music. Estab. 1966. Circ. 27,000. Pays on publication. Publishes ms an average of 4 months after acceptance. Byline given. Offers negotiated kill fee. Buys first North American serial, one-time, second serial (reprint), all rights. Submit seasonal material 4 months in advance. Accepts queries by mail, e-mail, fax. Responds in 2 weeks to queries; 2 months to mss. Sample copy for free. Writer's guidelines for #10 SASE.
Nonfiction General interest, historical/nostalgic, how-to, interview/profile, personal experience, photo feature, travel. No "fan"-style articles. **Buys 30-40 mss/year.** Query with or without published clips. Length: Open. **Pays 10-13¢/word.**

Reprints Send photocopy with rights for sale noted and information about when and where the material previously appeared. Payment is negotiable.

Photos State availability of or send photos with submission. Reviews 35mm transparencies and 3×5, 5×7 and 8×10 b&w and color prints. Buys all rights. Pays $50-175 for transparencies; $25-60 for b&w prints; $50-250 for color prints. Identification of subjects required.

Fiction Ethnic, humorous. **Buys 3-5 mss/year.** Query. Length: Negotiable. **Pays 10-13¢/word.**

Tips "We would prefer that articles be informational, based on personal experience or an interview with lots of quotes from subject, profile, humor, etc."

$ $ CHAMBER MUSIC

Chamber Music America, 305 Seventh Ave., 5th Floor, New York NY 10001-6008. (212)242-2022. Fax: (212)242-7955. Website: www.chamber-music.org. **Contact:** Editor. Bimonthly magazine covering chamber music. Estab. 1977. Circ. 13,000. Pays on publication. Publishes ms an average of 5 months after acceptance. Byline given. Offers kill fee. Buys first rights. Editorial lead time 4 months. Accepts queries by mail, phone.

Nonfiction Book excerpts, essays, humor, opinion, personal experience, issue-oriented stories of relevance to the chamber music fields written by top music journalists and critics, or music practitioners. No artist profiles, no stories about opera or symphonic work. **Buys 35 mss/year.** Query with published clips. Length: 2,500-3,500 words. **Pays $500 minimum.** Sometimes pays expenses of writers on assignment.

Photos State availability with submission. Offers no payment for photos accepted with ms.

N $ CHART MAGAZINE

Canada's Music Magazine, Chart Communications, Inc., 41 Britain St., Suite 200, Toronto ON M5A 1R7 Canada. (416)363-3101. Fax: (416)363-3109. E-mail: chart@chartattack.com. Website: www.chartattack.com. Editor: Nada Laskovski. **Contact:** Aaron Brophy, managing editor. **90% freelance written.** Monthly magazine. *Chart Magazine* has a "cutting edge attitude toward music and pop culture to fit with youth readership." Estab. 1990. Circ. 40,000 (paid). Pays on publication. Publishes ms an average of 3-6 months after acceptance. Byline given. Buys first North American serial, electronic rights. Editorial lead time 2 months. Submit seasonal material 3 months in advance. Accepts queries by mail, e-mail, fax, phone. Responds in 4-6 weeks to queries; 2-3 months to mss. Sample copy for $6 US (via mail order). Writer's guidelines free.

Nonfiction All articles must relate to popular music and/or pop culture. Book excerpts, essays, exposé, humor, interview/profile, personal experience, photo feature. Nothing that isn't related to popular music and pop culture (i.e., film, books, video games, fashion, etc., that would appeal to a hip youth demographic). Query with published clips and send complete ms. Length: varies. **Payment varies.**

Photos Claman Chu, art director. Send photos with submission. Buys all rights. Negotiates payment individually.

$ $ $ GUITAR ONE

The Magazine You Can Play, 149 5th St., 9th Floor, New York NY 10010. (212)768-2966. Fax: (212)944-9279. E-mail: editors@guitaronemag.com. Website: www.guitaronemag.com. **75% freelance written.** Monthly magazine covering guitar news, artists, music, gear. Estab. 1996. Circ. 140,000. Pays on publication. Publishes ms an average of 1 month after acceptance. Byline given. Offers 50% kill fee. Buys one-time rights. Editorial lead time 3 months. Accepts queries by mail, e-mail, fax. Accepts simultaneous submissions. Sample copy online.

Nonfiction Interview/profile (with guitarists). **Buys 15 mss/year.** Query with published clips. Length: 2,000-5,000 words. **Pays $300-1,200 for assigned articles; $150-800 for unsolicited articles.** Sometimes pays expenses of writers on assignment.

Photos State availability with submission. Reviews negatives, transparencies, prints. Buys one-time rights. Negotiates payment individually.

Tips "Find an interesting feature with a nice angle that pertains to guitar enthusiasts. Submit a well-written draft or samples of work."

$ $ GUITAR PLAYER MAGAZINE

United Entertainment Media, Inc., 2800 Campus Dr., San Mateo CA 94403. (650)513-4300. Fax: (650)513-4616. E-mail: mmolenda@musicplayer.com. Website: www.guitarplayer.com. **Contact:** Michael Molenda, editor-in-chief. **50% freelance written.** Monthly magazine for persons "interested in guitars, guitarists, manufacturers, guitar builders, equipment, careers, etc." Circ. 150,000. **Pays on acceptance.** Publishes ms an average of 3 months after acceptance. Byline given. Buys first serial and all reprint rights. Accepts queries by e-mail. Responds in 6 weeks to queries. Writer's guidelines for #10 SASE.

Nonfiction Publishes "wide variety of articles pertaining to guitars and guitarists: interviews, guitar craftsmen profiles, how-to features—anything amateur and professional guitarists would find fascinating and/or helpful. In interviews with 'name' performers, be as technical as possible regarding strings, guitars, techniques, etc.

We're not a pop culture magazine, but a magazine for musicians. The essential question: What can the reader take away from a story to become a better player?'' **Buys 30-40 mss/year.** Query. Length: Open. **Pays $250-450.** Sometimes pays expenses of writers on assignment.
Photos Reviews 35 mm color transparencies, b&w glossy prints. Buys one-time rights. Payment varies.

$MUSIC FOR THE LOVE OF IT

67 Parkside Dr., Berkeley CA 94705. (510)654-9134. Fax: (510)654-4656. E-mail: tedrust@musicfortheloveofit.c om. Website: www.musicfortheloveofit.com. **Contact:** Ted Rust, editor. **20% freelance written.** Bimonthly newsletter covering amateur musicianship. ''A lively, intelligent source of ideas and enthusiasm for a musically literate audience of adult amateur musicians.'' Estab. 1988. Circ. 600. Pays on publication. Publishes ms an average of 2 months after acceptance. Byline given. Buys one-time rights. Editorial lead time 1 month. Submit seasonal material 1 month in advance. Accepts queries by mail, e-mail, fax, phone. Responds in 1 week to queries; 1 month to mss. Sample copy for $6. Writer's guidelines online.

O— Break in with ''a good article, written from a musician's point of view, with at least 1 photo.''

Nonfiction Essays, historical/nostalgic, how-to, personal experience, photo feature. No concert reviews, star interviews, CD reviews. **Buys 6 mss/year.** Query. Length: 500-1,500 words. **Pays $50, or gift subscriptions.**
Photos State availability with submission. Reviews 4×6 prints or larger. Buys one-time rights. Offers no additional payment for photos accepted with ms. Identification of subjects required.
Tips ''We're looking for more good how-to articles on musical styles. Love making music. Know something about it.''

RELIX MAGAZINE

Music for the Mind, 180 Varick St., 4th Floor, New York NY 10014. (646)230-0100. Website: www.relix.com. **Contact:** Aeve Baldwin, editor-in-chief. **40% freelance written.** Bimonthly magazine focusing on new and independent bands, classic rock, lifestyles, and music alternatives such as roots, improvisational music, psychedelia, and jambands. Estab. 1974. Circ. 100,000. Pays on publication. Publishes ms an average of 4 months after acceptance. Byline given. Buys one-time rights. Accepts queries by mail, e-mail. Responds in 6 months to queries. Sample copy for $5. Writer's guidelines online.
Nonfiction Feature topics include jambands, reggae, Grateful Dead, bluegrass, jazz, rock, experimental, electronic, and world music; also deals with environmental, cultural, and lifestyle issues. Historical/nostalgic, humor, interview/profile, photo feature, technical, live reviews, new artists, hippy lifestyles, food, mixed media, books. Query by e-mail with published clips if available or send complete ms. Length: 300-1,500 words. **Pays variable rates.**
Columns/Departments Query with published clips or send complete ms. **Pays variable rates.**
Tips ''The best part of working with freelance writers is discovering new music we might never have stumbled across.''

Ⓝ Ⓞ REVOLVER

Harris Publication, Inc., 1115 Broadway, New York NY 10010-2803. (212)807-7100. E-mail: letters@revolverma g.com. Website: www.revolvermag.com. Editor-in-Chief: Tom Beaujour. Quarterly magazine covering artists from indie pop, classic rock, acid jazz, hip-hop, punk and more. Targets young men ages 18-34. Circ. 150,000.
● Query before submitting.

Ⓞ ROLLING STONE

Wenner Media, 1290 Avenue of the Americas, New York NY 10104. (212)484-1616. Fax: (212)484-1664. E-mail: letters@rollingstone.com. Website: www.rollingstone.com. Editor: Jann S. Wenner. Biweekly magazine geared towards young adults interested in news of popular music, entertainment and the arts, current news events, politics and American culture. Circ. 1,254,200. Editorial lead time 1 month.
● Query before submitting.

SPIN

205 Lexington Ave., 3rd Floor, New York NY 10016. (212)231-7400. Fax: (212)231-7312. E-mail: feedback@spin .com. Website: www.spin.com. **Contact:** Sia Michel, editor-in-chief. Monthly magazine covering music and popular culture. ''*Spin* covers progressive rock as well as investigative reporting on issues from politics, to pop culture. Editorial includes reviews, essays, profiles and interviews on a wide range of music from rock to jazz. It also covers sports, movies, politics, humor, fashion and issues—from AIDS research to the environment. The editorial focuses on the progressive new music scene and young adult culture more from an 'alternative' perspective as opposed to mainstream pop music. The magazine discovers new bands as well as angles for the familiar stars.'' Estab. 1985. Circ. 540,000.
Nonfiction Features are not assigned to writers who have not established a prior relationship with *Spin*. Cultural,

political or social issues. New writers: submit complete ms with SASE. Established writers: query specific editor with published clips.

Columns/Departments Most open to freelancers: Exposure (short articles on popular culture, TV, movies, books), 200-500 words; Reviews (record reviews), 100 words; Noise (music and new artists). Query before submitting.

Tips "The best way to break into the magazine is the Exposure and Reviews sections. We primarily work with seasoned, professional writers who have extensive national magazine experience and very rarely make assignments based on unsolicited queries."

$ $ $ $ VIBE

215 Lexington Ave., 6th Floor, New York NY 10016. (212)448-7300. Fax: (212)448-7400. Website: www.vibe.com. **Contact:** Individual editors. Monthly magazine covering urban music and culture. "*Vibe* chronicles and celebrates urban music and the youth culture that inspires and consumes it." Estab. 1993. Circ. 800,000. Pays on publication. Buys first North American serial rights. Editorial lead time 4 months. Responds in 2 months to queries. Sample copy available on newsstands. Writer's guidelines for #10 SASE.

Nonfiction Cultural, political or social issues. Query with published clips, résumé and SASE. Length: 800-3,000 words. **Pays $1/word.**

Columns/Departments Start (introductory news-based section), 350-740 words; Revolutions (music reviews), 100-800 words; Book reviews. Query with published clips, résumé and SASE. **Pays $1/word.**

Tips "A writer's best chance to be published in *Vibe* is through the Start or Revolutions sections. Keep in mind that *Vibe* is a national magazine, so ideas should have a national scope. People in Cali should care as much about the story as people in NYC. Also, *Vibe* has a 4-month lead time. What we work on today will appear in the magazine 4 or more months later. Stories must be timely with respect to this fact."

MYSTERY

$ HARDBOILED

Gryphon Publications, P.O. Box 209, Brooklyn NY 11228. Website: www.gryphonbooks.com. **Contact:** Gary Lovisi, editor. **100% freelance written.** Semiannual book covering crime/mystery fiction and nonfiction. "Hard-hitting crime fiction and private-eye stories—the newest and most cutting-edge work and classic reprints." Estab. 1988. Circ. 1,000. Pays on publication. Publishes ms an average of 18 months after acceptance. Byline given. Offers 100% kill fee. Buys first North American serial, one-time rights. Editorial lead time 1 year. Submit seasonal material 9 months in advance. Accepts queries by mail, fax. Accepts previously published material. Accepts simultaneous submissions. Responds in 2 weeks to queries; 1 month to mss. Sample copy for $10 or double issue for $20 (add $1.50 book postage). Writer's guidelines for #10 SASE.

Nonfiction Book excerpts, essays, exposé. **Buys 4-6 mss/year.** Query. Length: 500-3,000 words. **Pays 1 copy.**

Reprints Query first.

Photos State availability with submission.

Columns/Departments **Buys 2-4 mss/year.** Query.

Fiction Mystery, hardboiled crime, and private-eye stories, all on the cutting edge. No "pastches, violence for the sake of violence." **Buys 40 mss/year.** Query with or without published clips or send complete ms. Length: 500-3,000 words. **Pays $5-50.**

Tips "Your best bet for breaking in is short hard crime fiction filled with authenticity and brevity. Try a subscription to *Hardboiled* to get the perfect idea of what we are after."

ALFRED HITCHCOCK'S MYSTERY MAGAZINE

Dell Magazines, 475 Park Ave. S., 11th Floor, New York NY 10016. (212)686-7188. Website: www.themysteryplace.com. Editor: Linda Landrigan. **100% freelance written.** Monthly magazine featuring new mystery short stories. Estab. 1956. Circ. 150,000 readers. Pays on publication. Byline given. Buys first, foreign rights. Submit seasonal material 7 months in advance. Responds in 3 months to mss. Sample copy for $5. Writer's guidelines for SASE or on website.

Fiction Linda Landrigan, editor. Original and well-written mystery and crime fiction. "Because this is a mystery magazine, the stories we buy must fall into that genre in some sense or another. We are interested in nearly every kind of mystery: stories of detection of the classic kind, police procedurals, private eye tales, suspense, courtroom dramas, stories of espionage, and so on. We ask only that the story be about crime (or the threat or fear of one). We sometimes accept ghost stories or supernatural tales, but those also should involve a crime." No sensationalism. Send complete ms. Length: Up to 12,000 words. **Payment varies.**

Tips "No simultaneous submissions, please. Submissions sent to *Alfred Hitchcock's Mystery Magazine* are not considered for or read by *Ellery Queen's Mystery Magazine*, and vice versa."

$ELLERY QUEEN'S MYSTERY MAGAZINE

Dell Magazines Fiction Group, 475 Park Ave. S., 11th Floor, New York NY 10016. (212)686-7188. Fax: (212)686-7414. E-mail: elleryqueen@dellmagazines.com. Website: www.themysteryplace.com. **Contact:** Janet Hutchings, editor. **100% freelance written.** Magazine published 10 times/year featuring mystery fiction. *''Ellery Queen's Mystery Magazine* welcomes submissions from both new and established writers. We publish every kind of mystery short story: the psychological suspense tale, the deductive puzzle, the private eye case—the gamut of crime and detection from the realistic (including the policeman's lot and stories of police procedure) to the more imaginative (including 'locked rooms' and 'impossible crimes'). *EQMM* has been in continuous publication since 1941. From the beginning, 3 general criteria have been employed in evaluating submissions: We look for strong writing, an original and exciting plot, and professional craftsmanship. We encourage writers whose work meets these general criteria to read an issue of *EQMM* before making a submission.'' Estab. 1941. Circ. 180,780. **Pays on acceptance.** Publishes ms an average of 6-12 months after acceptance. Byline given. Buys first North American serial rights. Accepts simultaneous submissions. Responds in 3 months to mss. Sample copy for $5. Writer's guidelines for SASE or online.

Fiction ''We always need detective stories. Special consideration given to anything timely and original.'' No explicit sex or violence, no gore or horror. Seldom publishes parodies or pastiches. **Buys up to 120 mss/year.** Send complete ms. Length: Most stories 2,500-8,000 words. Accepts longer and shorter submissions—including minute mysteries of 250 words, and novellas of up to 20,000 words from established authors. **Pays 5-8¢/word; occasionally higher for established authors.**

Poetry Short mystery verses, limericks. Length: 1 page, double spaced maximum.

Tips ''We have a Department of First Stories to encourage writers whose fiction has never before been in print. We publish an average of 10 first stories every year.''

NATURE, CONSERVATION & ECOLOGY

$⬛ ALTERNATIVES JOURNAL

Canadian Environmental Ideas and Action, Alternatives, Inc., Faculty of Environmental Studies, University of Waterloo, Waterloo ON N2L 3G1 Canada. (519)888-4442. Fax: (519)746-0292. E-mail: editor@alternativesjournal.ca. Website: www.alternativesjournal.ca. **Contact:** Tara Flynn, executive editor. **90% freelance written.** Quarterly magazine covering environmental issues with Canadian relevance. Estab. 1971. Circ. 4,800. Pays on publication. Publishes ms an average of 5 months after acceptance. Byline given. Offers 50% kill fee. Buys first rights. Editorial lead time 7 months. Submit seasonal material 5 months in advance. Accepts queries by mail, e-mail, fax. Accepts simultaneous submissions. Sample copy free for Canadian writers only. Writer's guidelines online.

Nonfiction Book excerpts, essays, exposé, humor, interview/profile, opinion. **Buys 50 mss/year.** Query with published clips. Length: 800-3,000 words. **Pays $50-150 (Canadian).** All contributors receive a free subscription in addition to payment. Sometimes pays expenses of writers on assignment.

Photos State availability with submission. Buys one-time rights. Offers $35-75/photo. Identification of subjects required.

$ $ $AMERICAN FORESTS

American Forests, P.O. Box 2000, Washington DC 20013. E-mail: mrobbins@amfor.org. Website: www.americanforests.org. **Contact:** Michelle Robbins, editor. **75% freelance written.** Quarterly magazine ''of trees and forests published by a nonprofit citizens' organization that strives to help people plant and care for trees for ecosystem restoration and healthier communities.'' Estab. 1895. Circ. 25,000. **Pays on acceptance.** Publishes ms an average of 8 months after acceptance. Byline given. Buys one-time rights. Submit seasonal material 5 months in advance. Accepts queries by mail, e-mail. Accepts previously published material. Responds in 2 months to queries. Sample copy for $2. Writer's guidelines online.

    O⌐ Break in with ''stories that resonate with city dwellers who love trees, or small, forestland owners (private). This magazine is looking for more urban and suburban-oriented pieces.

Nonfiction All articles should emphasize trees, forests, forestry, and related issues. General interest, historical/nostalgic, how-to, humor, inspirational. **Buys 8-12 mss/year.** Query. Length: 1,200-2,000 words. **Pays $250-1,000.**

Reprints Send tearsheet or typed ms with rights for sale noted and information about when and where the material previously appeared. Pays 50% of amount paid for original article.

Photos Originals only. Send photos with submission. Reviews 35mm or larger transparencies, glossy color prints. Buys one-time rights. Offers no additional payment for photos accompanying ms. Captions required.

Tips ''We're looking for more good urban forestry stories, and stories that show cooperation among disparate elements to protect/restore an ecosystem. Query should have honesty and information on photo support. We do not accept fiction or poetry at this time.''

ℕ $ $ APPALACHIAN TRAILWAY NEWS

Appalachian Trail Conservancy, P.O. Box 807, Harpers Ferry WV 25425-0807. (304)535-6331. Fax: (304)535-2667. E-mail: editor@appalachiantrail.org. Website: www.appalachiantrail.org. **40% freelance written.** Bi-monthly magazine. Estab. 1925. Circ. 32,000. Pays on publication. Byline given. Buys first North American serial, second serial (reprint), Web reprint rights. Responds in 2 months to queries. Sample copy and writer's guidelines online.

● Articles must relate to Appalachian Trail.

Nonfiction Publishes but does not pay for hiking ''reflections.'' Essays, general interest, historical/nostalgic, how-to, humor, inspirational, interview/profile, photo feature, technical, travel. **Buys 5-10 mss/year.** Query with or without published clips, or send complete ms. Prefers e-mail queries. Length: 250-3,000 words. **Pays $25-300.** Pays expenses of writers on assignment.

Reprints Send photocopy with rights for sale noted and information about when and where the material previously appeared.

Photos State availability with submission. Reviews contact sheets, 5×7 prints, slides, digital images. Offers $25-125/photo; $250/cover. Identification of subjects required.

Tips ''Contributors should display a knowledge of or interest in the Appalachian Trail. Those who live in the vicinity of the trail may opt for an assigned story and should present credentials and subject of interest to the editor.''

$ $ $ THE ATLANTIC SALMON JOURNAL

The Atlantic Salmon Federation, P.O. Box 5200, St. Andrews NB E5B 3S8 Canada. Fax: (506)529-4985. E-mail: martinsilverstone@sympatico.ca. Website: www.asf.ca. **Contact:** Martin Silverstone, editor. **50-68% freelance written.** Quarterly magazine covering conservation efforts for the Atlantic salmon, catering to the dedicated angler and conservationist. Circ. 11,000. Pays on publication. Publishes ms an average of 6 months after acceptance. Byline given. Buys first North American serial rights. Buys one-time rights to photos. Submit seasonal material 3 months in advance. Accepts simultaneous submissions. Responds in 2 months to queries. Sample copy for 9×12 SAE with $1 (Canadian), or IRC. Writer's guidelines free.

Nonfiction ''We are seeking articles that are pertinent to the focus and purpose of our magazine, which is to inform and entertain our membership on all aspects of the Atlantic salmon, its environment, and conservation.'' Exposé, historical/nostalgic, how-to, humor, interview/profile, new product, opinion, personal experience, photo feature, technical, travel, conservation, science, research, and management. **Buys 15-20 mss/year.** Query with published clips. Length: 2,000 words. **Pays $400-800 for articles with photos.** Sometimes pays expenses of writers on assignment.

Photos State availability with submission. Pays $50 minimum; $350-500 for covers; $300 for 2-page spread; $175 for full page photo; $100 for ½-page photo. Captions, identification of subjects required.

Columns/Departments Fit To Be Tied (conservation issues and salmon research; the design, construction and success of specific flies); interesting characters in the sport and opinion pieces by knowledgeable writers, 900 words; Casting Around (short, informative, entertaining reports, book reviews and quotes from the world of Atlantic salmon angling and conservation). Query. **Pays $50-300.**

Tips ''Articles must reflect informed and up-to-date knowledge of Atlantic salmon. Writers need not be authorities, but research must be impeccable. Clear, concise writing is essential, and submissions must be typed.''

$ $ THE BEAR DELUXE MAGAZINE

Orlo, P.O. Box 10342, Portland OR 97296. (503)242-1047. E-mail: bear@orlo.org. Website: www.orlo.org. **Contact:** Tom Webb, editor. **80% freelance written.** Quarterly magazine. ''*The Bear Deluxe Magazine* is a national independent environmental magazine publishing significant works of reporting, creative nonfiction, literature, visual art, and design. Based in the Pacific Northwest, *The Bear Deluxe* reaches across cultural and political divides to engage readers on vital issues effecting the environment.'' Estab. 1993. Circ. 19,000. Pays on publication. Publishes ms an average of 6 months after acceptance. Byline given. Offers 25% kill fee. Buys first, one-time rights. Editorial lead time 6 months. Submit seasonal material 9 months in advance. Accepts queries by mail, e-mail. Accepts previously published material. Accepts simultaneous submissions. Responds in 3 months to queries; 6 months to mss. Sample copy for $3. Writer's guidelines for #10 SASE or on website.

Nonfiction Book excerpts, essays, exposé, general interest, interview/profile, new product, opinion, personal experience, photo feature, travel, artist profiles. Special issues: Publishes 1 theme/2 years. **Buys 40 mss/year.** Query with published clips. Length: 250-4,500 words. **Pays $25-400, depending on piece.** Sometimes pays expenses of writers on assignment.

Photos State availability with submission. Reviews contact sheets, transparencies, 8×10 prints. Buys one-time rights. Offers $30/photo. Identification of subjects, model releases required.

Columns/Departments Reviews (almost anything), 300 words; Front of the Book (mix of short news bits, found writing, quirky tidbits), 300-500 words; Portrait of an Artist (artist profiles), 1,200 words; Back of the Book (creative opinion pieces), 650 words. **Buys 16 mss/year.** Query with published clips. **Pays $25-400, depending on piece.**

Fiction "Stories must have some environmental context, but we view that in a broad sense." Adventure, condensed novels, historical, horror, humorous, mystery, novel excerpts, western. "No detective, children's, or horror." **Buys 8 mss/year.** Query with or without published clips or send complete ms. Length: 750-4,500 words. **Pays free subscription to the magazine, contributor's copies and $25-400, depending on piece; additional copies for postage.**

Poetry Avant-garde, free verse, haiku, light verse, traditional. **Buys 16-20 poems/year.** Submit maximum 5 poems. Length: 50 lines maximum. **Pays $20, subscription, and copies.**

Fillers Facts, newsbreaks, short humor. **Buys 10/year.** Length: 100-750 words. **Pays $25, subscription, and copies.**

Tips "Offer to be a stringer for future ideas. Get a copy of the magazine and guidelines, and query us with specific nonfiction ideas and clips. We're looking for original, magazine-style stories, not fluff or PR. Fiction, essay, and poetry writers should know we have an open and blind review policy and should keep sending their best work even if rejected once. Be as specific as possible in queries."

$ BIRD WATCHER'S DIGEST

Pardson Corp., P.O. Box 110, Marietta OH 45750. (740)373-5285. Fax: (740)373-8443. E-mail: editor@birdwatchersdigest.com. Website: www.birdwatchersdigest.com. **60% freelance written.** Works with a small number of new/unpublished writers each year. Bimonthly magazine covering natural history—birds and bird watching. "*BWD* is a nontechnical magazine interpreting ornithological material for amateur observers, including the knowledgeable birder, the serious novice, and the backyard bird watcher. We strive to provide good reading and good ornithology." Estab. 1978. Circ. 90,000. Pays on publication. Publishes ms an average of 2 years after acceptance. Byline given. Buys one-time, second serial (reprint) rights. Submit seasonal material 6 months in advance. Accepts previously published material. Responds in 2 months to queries. Sample copy for $3.99 or online. Writer's guidelines online.

Nonfiction "We are especially interested in fresh, lively accounts of closely observed bird behavior and displays and of bird-watching experiences and expeditions. We often need material on backyard subjects such as bird feeding, housing, and gardenening on less common species or on unusual or previously unreported behavior of common species." Book excerpts, how-to (relating to birds, feeding and attracting, etc.), humor, personal experience, travel (limited, we get many). No articles on pet or caged birds; none on raising a baby bird. **Buys 45-60 mss/year.** Send complete ms. Length: 600-3,500 words. **Pays from $100.**

Photos Send photos with submission. Reviews transparencies, prints. Buys one-time rights. Pays $75 minimum for transparencies.

Tips "We are aimed at an audience ranging from the backyard bird watcher to the very knowledgeable birder; we include in each issue material that will appeal at various levels. We always strive for a good geographical spread, with material from every section of the country. We leave very technical matters to others, but we want facts and accuracy, depth and quality, directed at the veteran bird watcher and at the enthusiastic novice. We stress the joys and pleasures of bird watching, its environmental contribution, and its value for the individual and society."

$$ BIRDER'S WORLD

Enjoying Birds at Home and Beyond, Kalmbach Publishing Co., P.O. Box 1612, Waukesha WI 53187-1612. Fax: (262)798-6468. E-mail: mail@birdersworld.com. Website: www.birdersworld.com. Editor: Charles J. Hagner. Managing Editor: Melanie Buellesbach. Associate Editor: Matt Mendenhall. **Contact:** Rosemary Nowak, editorial assistant. Bimonthly magazine covering wild birds and birdwatching. "*Birder's World* is a magazine designed for people with a broad interest in wild birds and birdwatching. Our readers are curious and generally well-educated with varying degrees of experience in the world of birds. No poetry, fiction, or puzzles please." Estab. 1987. Circ. 70,000. **Pays on acceptance.** Byline given. Offers $100 kill fee. Buys one-time rights. Accepts queries by mail. Writer's guidelines for #10 SASE or by e-mail.

Nonfiction Essays, how-to (attracting birds), interview/profile, personal experience, photo feature (bird photography), travel (birding trips in North America), book reviews, product reviews/comparisons, bird biology, endangered or threatened birds. No poetry, fiction, or puzzles. **Buys 60 mss/year.** Query with published clips or send complete ms. Length: 500-2,400 words. **Pays $200-450.** Sometimes pays expenses of writers on assignment.

Photos State availability with submission. Buys one-time rights. Identification of subjects required.

$ $ $ CALIFORNIA WILD

Natural Science for Thinking Animals, California Academy of Sciences, 875 Howard St., San Francisco CA 94103. (415)321-8188. Fax: (415)321-8625. E-mail: kkhowell@calacademy.org. Website: www.calacademy.org/calwild. **Contact:** Keith Howell, editor. **75% freelance written.** Quarterly magazine covering natural sciences and the environment. "Our readers' interests range widely from ecology to geology, from endangered species to anthropology, from field identification of plants and birds to armchair understanding of complex scientific issues." Estab. 1948. Circ. 32,000. Pays prior to publication. Publishes ms an average of 3 months after acceptance. Byline given. Offers 50% kill fee; maximum $200. Buys first North American serial, one-time rights. Editorial lead time 3 months. Submit seasonal material 6 months in advance. Accepts queries by mail, fax. Responds in 6 weeks to queries; 6 months to mss. Sample copy for 9 × 12 SASE or online. Writer's guidelines online.

Nonfiction Personal experience, photo feature, biological, and earth sciences. Mostly California pieces, but also from Pacific Ocean countries. No travel pieces. **Buys 20 mss/year.** Query with published clips. Length: 1,000-3,000 words. **Pays $250-1,000 for assigned articles; $200-800 for unsolicited articles.** Sometimes pays expenses of writers on assignment.

Photos State availability with submission. Reviews transparencies. Buys one-time rights. Offers $75-150/photo. Identification of subjects, model releases required.

Columns/Departments A Closer Look (unusual places); Wild Lives (description of unusual plant or animal); In Pursuit of Science (innovative student, teacher, young scientist), all 1,000-1,500 words; Skywatcher (research in astronomy), 2,000-3,000 words. **Buys 12 mss/year.** Query with published clips. **Pays $200-400.**

Tips "We are looking for unusual and/or timely stories about California environment or biodiversity."

$ $ $ ⊡ CANADIAN WILDLIFE

350 Michael Cowpland Dr., Kanata ON K2M 2W1 Canada. (613)599-9594. Fax: (613)271-9591. E-mail: wild@cwf-fcf.org. Senior Editor: Andrea Fajrajsl. **Contact:** Asha Jhamandas, assistant editor. **90% freelance written.** Magazine published 5 times/year covering wildlife conservation. Includes topics pertaining to wildlife, endangered species, conservation, and natural history. When possible, it is beneficial if articles have a Canadian slant or the topic has global appeal. Estab. 1995. Circ. 15,000. **Pays on acceptance.** Publishes ms an average of 3 months after acceptance. Byline given. Offers 15% kill fee. Buys first North American serial rights. Editorial lead time 3 months. Submit seasonal material 4 months in advance. Accepts queries by mail, e-mail, fax. Responds in 6 weeks to queries; 2 months to mss. Sample copy for $5 (Canadian). Writer's guidelines free.

Nonfiction Book excerpts, interview/profile, photo feature, science/nature. No standard travel stories. **Buys 20 mss/year.** Query with published clips. Length: 800-2,500 words. **Pays $500-1,200 for assigned articles; $300-1,000 for unsolicited articles.**

Photos Send photos with submission. Reviews transparencies. Buys one-time rights. Negotiates payment individually. Captions, identification of subjects, model releases required.

Columns/Departments Vistas (science news), 200-500 words; Book Reviews, 100-150 words. **Buys 15 mss/year.** Query with published clips. **Pays $50-250.**

Tips "*Canadian Wildlife* is a benefit of membership in the Canadian Wildlife Federation. Nearly 15,000 people currently receive the magazine. The majority of these men and women are already well versed in topics concerning the environment and natural science; writers, however, should not make assumptions about the extent of a reader's knowledge of topics."

$ $ $ CONSCIOUS CHOICE

The Journal of Ecology & Natural Living, Dragonfly Chicago, LLC, 920 N. Franklin St., Suite 202, Chicago IL 60610-3179. Fax: (312)751-3973. E-mail: editor@consciouschoice.com. Website: www.consciouschoice.com. **Contact:** Marla Donato, editor. **95% freelance written.** Monthly tabloid covering the environment, natural health and medicine, and personal growth and spirituality. Estab. 1988. Circ. 55,000. Pays on publication. Publishes ms an average of 6 months after acceptance. Byline given. Offers 50% kill fee. Buys first North American serial, electronic rights. Editorial lead time 6 months. Submit seasonal material 6 months in advance. Accepts queries by mail. Accepts simultaneous submissions. Responds in 6 weeks to queries; 1 month to mss. Sample copy online. Writer's guidelines free or by e-mail.

Nonfiction General interest (to cultural creatives), interview/profile (emphasis on narrative, storytelling), personal experience, environment. **Buys 24 mss/year.** Query with 2-3 published clips. Length: 1,800 words. **Pays $150-1,000.** Sometimes pays expenses of writers on assignment.

$ $ E THE ENVIRONMENTAL MAGAZINE

Earth Action Network, P.O. Box 5098, Westport CT 06881-5098. (203)854-5559. Fax: (203)866-0602. E-mail: info@emagazine.com. Website: www.emagazine.com. **Contact:** Jim Motavalli, editor. **60% freelance written.** Bimonthly magazine. "*E Magazine* was formed for the purpose of acting as a clearinghouse of information, news, and commentary on environmental issues.'' Estab. 1990. Circ. 50,000. Pays on publication. Byline given. Buys first North American serial rights. Editorial lead time 3 months. Submit seasonal material 6 months in advance. Accepts queries by mail, e-mail, fax. Accepts simultaneous submissions. Sample copy for $5 or online. Writer's guidelines online.

• The editor reports an interest in seeing more investigative reporting. On spec or free contributions welcome.

Nonfiction On spec or free contributions welcome. Exposé (environmental), how-to, new product, book review, feature (in-depth articles on key natural environmental issues). **Buys 100 mss/year.** Query with published clips. Length: 100-4,000 words. **Pays 30¢/word.**

Photos State availability with submission. Reviews printed samples, i.e., magazine tearsheets, postcards, etc., to be kept on file. Buys one-time rights. Negotiates payment individually. Identification of subjects required.

Columns/Departments In Brief/Currents (environmental news stories/trends), 400-1,000 words; Conversations (Q&As with environmental ''movers and shakers''), 2,000 words; Tools for Green Living; Your Health; Eco-Travel; Eco-Home; Eating Right; Green Business; Consumer News, all 700-1,200 words. Query with published clips.

📧 Contact: Jim Motavalli, online editor.

Tips ''Contact us to obtain writer's guidelines and back issues of our magazine. Tailor your query according to the department/section you feel it would be best suited for. Articles must be lively, well researched, balanced, and relevant to a mainstream, national readership.''

$ $HIGH COUNTRY NEWS

High Country Foundation, P.O. Box 1090, Paonia CO 81428. (970)527-4898. E-mail: greg@hcn.org. Website: www.hcn.org. **Contact:** Greg Hanscom, editor. **80% freelance written.** Weekly tabloid covering Rocky Mountain West, the Great Basin, and Pacific Northwest environment, rural communities, and natural resource issues in 10 western states for environmentalists, politicians, companies, college classes, government agencies, grass roots activists, public land managers, etc. Estab. 1970. Circ. 23,000. Pays on publication. Publishes ms an average of 2 months after acceptance. Byline given. Buys one-time rights. Accepts queries by mail. Responds in 1 month to queries. Sample copy for SAE or online. Writer's guidelines online.

Nonfiction Exposé (government, corporate), interview/profile, personal experience, photo feature (center-spread), reporting (local issues with regional importance). **Buys 100 mss/year.** Query. Length: up to 3,000 words. **Pays 20¢/word minimum.** Sometimes pays expenses of writers on assignment.

Reprints Send tearsheet and information about when and where the material previously appeared. Pays 15¢/word.

Photos Send photos with submission. Reviews b&w prints. Captions, identification of subjects required.

Columns/Departments Roundups (topical stories), 800 words; opinion pieces, 1,000 words.

Tips ''We use a lot of freelance material, though very little from outside the Rockies. Familiarity with the newspaper is a must. Start by writing a query letter. We define 'resources' broadly to include people, culture, and aesthetic values, not just coal, oil, and timber.''

$ $ $MINNESOTA CONSERVATION VOLUNTEER

Minnesota Department of Natural Resources, 500 Lafayette Rd., St. Paul MN 55155-4046. Website: www.dnr.state.mn.us. **50% freelance written.** Bimonthly magazine covering Minnesota natural resources, wildlife, natural history, outdoor recreation, and land use. ''*Minnesota Conservation Volunteer* is a donor-supported magazine advocating conservation and wise use of Minnesota's natural resources. Material must reflect an appreciation of nature and an ethic of care for the environment. We rely on a variety of sources in our reporting. More than 128,000 Minnesota households, businesses, schools, and other groups subscribe to this conservation magazine.'' Estab. 1940. **Pays on acceptance.** Publishes ms an average of 1 month after acceptance. Byline given. Offers 30% kill fee. Buys first North American serial, rights to post to website, and archive rights. Editorial lead time 8 months. Submit seasonal material 8 months in advance. Accepts queries by mail, e-mail, fax. Accepts previously published material. Accepts simultaneous submissions. Responds in 1 month to queries; 2 months to mss. Sample copy free or on website. Writer's guidelines by e-mail.

Nonfiction Book excerpts, essays, exposé, general interest, historical/nostalgic, humor, interview/profile, opinion, personal experience, photo feature, travel, ''Young Naturalist'' for children. Does not publish poetry or uncritical advocacy. **Buys 10 mss/year.** Query with published clips. Length: up to 1,500 words. **Pays 50¢/word for full-length feature articles.** Pays expenses of writers on assignment.

Photos State availability with submission. Reviews 35mm or large format transparencies. Buys one-time rights, will negotiate for Web use separately. Offers $100/photo.

Columns/Departments Close Encounters (unusual, exciting, or humorous personal wildlife experience in Minnesota); Sense of Place (first- or third-person essay developing character of a Minnesota place); Viewpoint (well-researched and well-reasoned opinion piece), all up to 1,500 words; Minnesota Profile (concise description of emblematic state species or geographic feature), 400 words. **Buys 10 mss/year.** Query with published clips. **Pays 50¢/word.**

Tips "In submitting queries, look beyond topics to stories: What is someone doing and why? How does the story end? In submitting a query addressing a particular issue, think of the human impacts and the sources you might consult. Summarize your idea, the story line, and sources in 2 or 3 short paragraphs. While topics must have relevance to Minnesota and give a Minnesota character to the magazine, feel free to round out your research with out-of-state sources."

$ $ $ NATIONAL PARKS

1300 19th St. NW, Suite 300, Washington DC 20036. (202)223-6722. Fax: (202)659-0650. E-mail: npmag@npca. org. Website: www.npca.org/magazine/. Editor-in-chief: Linda Rancourt. **Contact:** Amy Leinbach, assistant editor. **60% freelance written.** Prefers to work with published/established writers. Quarterly magazine for a largely unscientific but highly educated audience interested in preservation of National Park System units, natural areas, and protection of wildlife habitat. Estab. 1919. Circ. 300,000. **Pays on acceptance.** Publishes ms an average of 2 months after acceptance. Offers 33% kill fee. Responds in 5 months to queries. Sample copy for $3 and 9×12 SASE or online. Writer's guidelines online.

Nonfiction All material must relate to US national parks. Exposé (on threats, wildlife problems in national parks), descriptive articles about new or proposed national parks and wilderness parks; natural history pieces describing park geology, wildlife or plants; new trends in park use; legislative issues. No poetry, philosophical essays, or first-person narratives. No unsolicited mss. Length: 1,500 words. **Pays $1,300 for full-length features; $1,000 for excursions articles.**

Photos No color prints or negatives. Send for guidelines. Not responsible for unsolicited photos. Send photos with submission. Reviews color slides. Pays $150-350 inside; $525 for covers. Captions required.

Tips "Articles should have an original slant or news hook and cover a limited subject rather than attempt to treat a broad subject superficially. Specific examples, descriptive details, and quotes are always preferable to generalized information. The writer must be able to document factual claims, and statements should be clearly substantiated with evidence within the article. *National Parks* does not publish fiction, poetry, personal essays, or 'My trip to . . .' stories."

N $ $ $ $ NATIONAL WILDLIFE

National Wildlife Federation, 11100 Wildlife Center Dr., Reston VA 20190. (703)438-6510. Fax: (703)438-6544. E-mail: pubs@nwf.org. Website: www.nwf.org/nationalwildlife. **Contact:** Mark Wexler, editor. **75% freelance written.** Assigns almost all material based on staff ideas. Assigns few unsolicited queries. Bimonthly magazine. "Our purpose is to promote wise use of the nation's natural resources and to conserve and protect wildlife and its habitat. We reach a broad audience that is largely interested in wildlife conservation and nature photography." Estab. 1963. Circ. 500,000. **Pays on acceptance.** Publishes ms an average of 1 year after acceptance. Offers 25% kill fee. Buys all rights. Submit seasonal material 8 months in advance. Accepts queries by mail, e-mail, fax. Responds in 6 weeks to queries. Writer's guidelines for #10 SASE.

Nonfiction General interest (2,500 word features on wildlife, new discoveries, behavior, or the environment), how-to (an outdoor or nature related activity), interview/profile (people who have gone beyond the call of duty to protect wildlife and its habitat, or to prevent environmental contamination and people who have been involved in the environment or conservation in interesting ways), personal experience (outdoor adventure), photo feature (wildlife), short 700-word features on an unusual individual or new scientific discovery relating to nature. "Avoid too much scientific detail. We prefer anecdotal, natural history material." **Buys 50 mss/ year.** Query with or without published clips. Length: 750-2,500 words. **Pays $800-3,000.** Sometimes pays expenses of writers on assignment.

Photos John Nuhn, photo editor. Send photos with submission. Reviews Kodachrome or Fujichrome transparencies. Buys one-time rights.

Tips "Writers can break in with us more readily by proposing subjects (initially) that will take only 1 or 2 pages in the magazine (short features)."

N $ $ $ $ NATURAL HISTORY

Natural History, Inc., 36 W. 25th St., 5th Floor, New York NY 10010. E-mail: nhmag@naturalhistorymag.com. Website: www.naturalhistorymag.com. **15% freelance written.** Magazine published 10 times/year for well-educated audience: professional people, scientists, and scholars. Circ. 225,000. **Pays on acceptance.** Publishes ms an average of 3 months after acceptance. Byline given. Buys first North American serial rights. Becomes an agent for second serial (reprint) rights. Submit seasonal material 6 months in advance.

Nonfiction "We are seeking new research on mammals, birds, invertebrates, reptiles, ocean life, anthropology, and astronomy, preferably written by principal investigators in these fields. Our slant is toward unraveling problems in behavior, ecology, and evolution." **Buys 60 mss/year.** Query by mail or send complete ms. Length: 1,500-3,000 words. **Pays $500-2,500.**

Photos Rarely uses 8×10 b&w glossy prints; pays $125/page maximum. Much color is used; pays $300 for inside, and up to $600 for cover. Buys one-time rights.

Columns/Departments Journal (reporting from the field); Findings (summary of new or ongoing research); Naturalist At Large; The Living Museum (relates to the American Museum of Natural History); Discovery (natural or cultural history of a specific place).

Tips "We expect high standards of writing and research. We do not lobby for causes, environmental, or other. The writer should have a deep knowledge of his subject, then submit original ideas either in query or by manuscript."

🌐 NATURE

Nature Publishing Group, The Macmillan Building, 4 Crinan St., London N1 9XW United Kingdom. (0044)20 7833 4000. Fax: (0044)20 7843 4596. E-mail: nature@nature.com. Website: www.nature.com/nature. Editor: Philip Campbell. **5% freelance written.** Weekly magazine covering multidisplinary science. "*Nature* is the top multidisciplinary journal of science, publishing news, views, commentary, reviews, and ground-breaking research." Estab. 1869. Circ. 60,000. Publishes ms an average of 2 months after acceptance. Byline given.

$ $ $🔲 NATURE CANADA

1 Nicholas St., Suite 606, Ottawa ON K1N 7B7 Canada. Fax: (613)562-3371. E-mail: magazine@naturecanada. ca. Website: www.naturecanada.ca. **Contact:** Pamela Feeny, editor. Quarterly magazine covering conservation, natural history and environmental/naturalist community. "Editorial content reflects the goals and priorities of Nature Canada as a conservation organization with a focus on our program areas: federally protected areas (national parks, national wildlife areas, etc.), endangered species, and bird conservation through Canada's important bird areas. Nature Canada is written for an audience interested in nature conservation. *Nature Canada* celebrates, preserves, and protects Canadian nature. We promote the awareness and understanding of the connection between humans and nature and how natural systems support life on Earth. We strive to instill a sense of ownership and belief that these natural systems should be protected." Estab. 1971. Circ. 27,000. Pays on publication. Publishes ms an average of 3 months after acceptance. Byline given. Offers $100 kill fee. Buys all *Nature Canada* rights (including electronic). Author retains resale rights elsewhere. Editorial lead time 4 months. Submit seasonal material 6 months in advance. Responds in 4 months to mss. Sample copy for $5. Writer's guidelines online.

Nonfiction Subjects include: Canadian conservation issues; nature education; reconnecting with nature; enviro-friendly lifestyles, products and consumer reports; federal protected areas; endangered species; birds; sustainable development; company and individual profiles; urban nature; how-to; natural history. **Buys 12 mss/year.** Query with published clips. Length: 650-2,000 words. **Pays up to 50¢/word (Canadian).**

Photos State availability with submission. Buys one-time rights. Offers $50-200/photo (Canadian). Identification of subjects required.

Tips "Our readers are well-educated and knowledgeable about nature and the environment so contributors should have a good understanding of the subject. We also deal exclusively with Canadian issues and species, except for those relating directly to our international program. E-mail queries preferred. Do not send unsolicited manuscripts. We receive many BC-related queries but need more for the rest of Canada, particularly SK, MB, QC and the Maritimes. Articles must focus on the positive and be supported by science when applicable. We are looking for strong, well-researched writing that is lively, entertaining, enlightening, provocative and, when appropriate, amusing."

$ $ NORTHERN WOODLANDS MAGAZINE

Center for Woodlands Education, Inc., 1776 Center Rd., P.O. Box 471, Corinth VT 05039-0471. (802)439-6292. Fax: (802)439-6296. E-mail: anne@northernwoodlands.org. Website: www.northernwoodlands.org. **Contact:** Anne Margolis. **40-60% freelance written.** Quarterly magazine covering natural history, conservation, and forest management in the Northeast. "*Northern Woodlands* strives to inspire landowners' sense of stewardship by increasing their awareness of the natural history and the principles of conservation and forestry that are directly related to their land. We also hope to increase the public's awareness of the social, economic, and environmental benefits of a working forest." Estab. 1994. Circ. 12,000. Pays 1 month prior to publication. Publishes ms an average of 6 months after acceptance. Byline given. Buys one-time rights. Editorial lead time 6 months. Submit seasonal material 6 months in advance. Accepts queries by mail, e-mail. Accepts previously published material. Accepts simultaneous submissions. Responds in 2 weeks to queries; 1½ months to mss. Sample copy and writer's guidelines online.

Nonfiction Stephen Long, editor. Book excerpts, essays, how-to (related to woodland management), interview/profile (related to the Northeastern US). No product reviews, first-person travelogues, cute animal stories, opinion, or advocacy pieces. **Buys 15-20 mss/year.** Query with published clips. Length: 500-3,000 words. **Pays 10¢/word.** Sometimes pays expenses of writers on assignment.

Photos State availability with submission. Reviews transparencies, prints, high resolution digital photos. Buys one-time rights. Offers $35-75/photo. Identification of subjects required.

Columns/Departments Stephen Long, editor. A Place in Mind (essays on places of personal significance), 600-800 words. **Pays $100.** Knots and Bolts (seasonal natural history items or forest-related news items), 300-600 words. **Pays 10¢/word.** Wood Lit (book reviews), 600 words. **Pays $25.** Field Work (profiles of people who work in the woods, the wood-product industry, or conservation field), 1,500 words. **Pays 10¢/word. Buys 30 mss/year.** Query with published clips.

Poetry Jim Schley, poetry editor. Free verse, light verse, traditional. **Buys 4 poems/year.** Submit maximum 5 poems. **Pays $25.**

Tips "We will work with subject-matter experts to make their work suitable for our audience."

N $ $ $ ONEARTH

The Natural Resources Defense Council, 40 W. 20th St., New York NY 10011. Website: www.nrdc.org. **Contact:** Douglas S. Barasch, editor-in-chief. **75% freelance written.** Quarterly magazine covering national and international environmental issues. "*OnEarth* is intended to provide the general public with a journal of thought and opinion on environmental affairs, particularly those relating to policies of national and international significance." Estab. 1979. Circ. 250,000. Pays on publication. Publishes ms an average of 6 months after acceptance. Byline given. Offers variable kill fee. Buys first North American serial, simultaneous, electronic rights. Submit seasonal material 6 months in advance. Accepts queries by mail. Responds in 3 months to queries. Sample copy for $5. Writer's guidelines for #10 SASE.

Nonfiction Environmental features. **Buys 12 mss/year.** Query with published clips. Length: 3,000. **Pays 50¢/word.** Sometimes pays expenses of writers on assignment.

Photos State availability with submission. Reviews contact sheets, color transparencies, 8×10 b&w prints. Buys one-time rights. Negotiates payment individually. Captions, identification of subjects, model releases required.

Columns/Departments News & Comment (summary reporting of environmental issues, tied to topical items), 700-2,000 words; International Notebook (new or unusual international environmental stories), 700-2,000 words; People, 2,000 words; Reviews (in-depth reporting on issues and personalities, well-informed essays on books of general interest to environmentalists interested in policy and history), 500-1,000 words. Query with published clips. **Payment negotiable.**

Poetry All poetry should be rooted in nature. Brian Swann, poetry editor. Avant-garde, free verse, haiku. **Buys 12 poems/year.** Length: 1 ms page. **Pays $75.**

Tips "Please stay up to date on environmental issues, and review *OnEarth* before submitting queries. Except for editorials all departments are open to freelance writers. Queries should precede manuscripts, and manuscripts should conform to the *Chicago Manual of Style*. *Amicus* needs interesting environmental stories—of local, regional or national import—from writers who can offer an on-the-ground perspective. Accuracy, high-quality writing, and thorough knowledge of the environmental subject are vital."

$ $ $ $ ORION

The Orion Society, 187 Main St., Great Barrington MA 01230. E-mail: orion@orionsociety.org. Website: www.ori ononline.org. Editor: Jennifer Sahn. **Contact:** Submissions, *Orion* magazine. **90% freelance written.** Bimonthly magazine covering nature and culture. "*Orion* is a magazine about the issues of our time: how we live, what we value, what sustains us. *Orion* explores an emerging alternative worldview through essays, literary journalism, short stories, interviews, and reviews, as well as photo essays and portfolios of art." Estab. 1982. Circ. 22,000. Pays on publication. Publishes ms an average of 3-12 months after acceptance. Byline given. Buys first North American serial rights. Editorial lead time 3-9 months. Submit seasonal material 9 months in advance. Accepts queries by mail, e-mail. Accepts simultaneous submissions. Responds in 1-2 months to queries; 4-6 months to mss. Sample copy and writer's guidelines online.

Nonfiction Essays, exposé, historical/nostalgic, humor, personal experience, photo feature, reported feature. No "What I learned during my walk in the woods"; personal hiking/adventure/travel anecdotes; unsolicited poetry; writing that deals with the natural world in only superficial ways. **Buys 40-50 mss/year.** Send complete ms. Length: 2,000-4,500 words. **Pays $300-2,000.** Pays expenses of writers on assignment.

Photos State availability with submission. Reviews contact sheets, prints. Buys one-time rights. Negotiates payment individually.

Columns/Departments Point of View (opinion essay by a noted authority), 625 words; Sacred & Mundane (funny, ironic or awe-inspiring ways nature exists within or is created by contemporary culture), 200-600 words; Blueprint for Change (groundbreaking, visionary, replicable projects that are working in areas related to *Orion*'s mission), 1,300 words; Health & the Environment (emphasizes and explores relationship between human health and a healthy natural world, or forces that threaten both simultaneously), 1,300 words; Reviews (new books, films and recordings related to *Orion's* mission), 250-600 words; Coda (an endpaper), 650 words. **Buys 85 mss/ year.** Send complete ms. **Pays $25-300.**

Fiction Ethnic, historical, humorous, mainstream, slice-of-life vignettes. No manuscripts that don't carry an environmental message or involve the landscape/nature as a major character. Buys up to 1 ms/year. Send complete ms. Length: 1,200-4,000 words. **Pays 10-20¢/word.**

Tips "We are most impressed by and most likely to work with writers whose submissions show they know our magazine. If you are proposing a story, your query must: 1) Be detailed in its approach and reflect the care you will give the story itself; 2) Define where in the magazine you believe the story would be appropriate; 3) Include 3 tear sheets of previously published work. If you are submitting a manuscript, it must be double-spaced and typed or printed in black ink. Please be sure your name and a page number appear on each page of your submission, and that we have your phone number.''

Ⓝ $ $ $ $SIERRA

85 Second St., 2nd Floor, San Francisco CA 94105. Website: www.sierraclub.org. **Contact:** Managing Editor. Works with a small number of new/unpublished writers each year. Bimonthly magazine emphasizing conservation and environmental politics for people who are well educated, activist, outdoor-oriented, and politically well informed with a dedication to conservation. Estab. 1893. Circ. 695,000. **Pays on acceptance.** Publishes ms an average of 4 months after acceptance. Byline given. Offers negotiable kill fee. Buys first North American serial rights. Accepts queries by mail, fax. Accepts previously published material. Responds in 2 months to queries. Sample copy for $3 and SASE, or online. Writer's guidelines online.

- The editor reports an interest in seeing pieces on environmental "heroes," thoughtful features on new developments in solving environmental problems, and outdoor adventure stories with a strong environmental element.

Nonfiction Exposé (well-documented articles on environmental issues of national importance such as energy, wilderness, forests, etc.), general interest (well-researched nontechnical pieces on areas of particular environmental concern), interview/profile, photo feature (photo essays on threatened or scenic areas), journalistic treatments of semitechnical topic (energy sources, wildlife management, land use, waste management, etc.). No "My trip to . . ." or "Why we must save wildlife/nature" articles; no poetry or general superficial essays on environmentalism; no reporting on purely local environmental issues. **Buys 30-36 mss/year.** Query with published clips. Length: 1,000-3,000 words. **Pays $800-3,000.**

Reprints Send photocopy with rights for sale noted and information about when and where the material previously appeared. Payment negotiable.

Photos Send photos with submission. Buys one-time rights. Pays maximum $300 for transparencies; more for cover photos.

Columns/Departments Food for Thought (food's connection to environment); Good Going (adventure journey); Hearth & Home (advice for environmentally sound living); Body Politics (health and the environment); Profiles (biographical look at environmentalists); Hidden Life (exposure of hidden environmental problems in everyday objects); Lay of the Land (national/international concerns), 500-700 words; Mixed Media (essays on environment in the media; book reviews), 200-300 words. **Pays $50-500.**

- The online magazine carries original content not found in the print edition and includes writer's guidelines.

Tips "Queries should include an outline of how the topic would be covered and a mention of the political appropriateness and timeliness of the article. Statements of the writer's qualifications should be included.''

$SNOWY EGRET

The Fair Press, P.O. Box 29, Terre Haute IN 47808. Editor: Philip C. Repp. Managing Editor: Ruth C. Acker. **Contact:** Editors. **95% freelance written.** Semiannual literary magazine featuring nature writing. "We publish works which celebrate the abundance and beauty of nature, and examine the variety of ways in which human beings interact with landscapes and living things. Nature writing from literary, artistic, psychological, philosophical, and historical perspectives.'' Estab. 1922. Circ. 400. Pays on publication. Publishes ms an average of 6 months after acceptance. Byline given. Buys first North American serial, second serial (reprint), one-time anthology rights, or reprints rights. Editorial lead time 2 months. Accepts queries by mail. Accepts simultaneous submissions. Responds in 1 month to queries; 2 months to mss. Sample copy for 9 × 12 SASE and $8. Writer's guidelines for #10 SASE.

- Break in with "an essay, story, or short description based on a closely observed first-hand encounter with some aspect of the natural world.''

Nonfiction Essays, general interest, interview/profile, personal experience, travel. **Buys 10 mss/year.** Send complete ms. Length: 500-10,000 words. **Pays $2/page.**

Columns/Departments Jane Robertson, Woodnotes editor. Woodnotes (short descriptions of personal encounters with wildlife or natural settings), 200-2,000 words. **Buys 12 mss/year. Pays $2/page.**

Fiction Fiction Editor. Nature-oriented works (in which natural settings, wildlife, or other organisms and/or characters who identify with the natural world are significant components. "No genre fiction, i.e., horror, western romance, etc." **Buys 4 mss/year.** Send complete ms. Length: 500-10,000 words. **Pays $2/page.**

Poetry Avant-garde, free verse, traditional. **Buys 30 poems/year.** Submit maximum 5 poems. **Pays $4/poem or page.**

Tips "The writers we publish invariably have a strong personal identification with the natural world, have examined their subjects thoroughly, and write about them sincerely. They know what they're talking about and show their subjects in detail, using, where appropriate, detailed description and dialogue."

Ⓝ $ $ $ $ WILDLIFE CONSERVATION

2300 Southern Blvd., Bronx NY 10460. E-mail: nsimmons@wcs.org. Website: www.wcs.org. **Contact:** Nancy Simmons, senior editor. Bimonthly magazine for environmentally aware readers. Offers 25% kill fee. Buys first North American serial rights. Accepts simultaneous submissions. Responds in 1 month to queries. Sample copy for $4.95 (includes postage). Writer's guidelines available for SASE or via e-mail.

Nonfiction "We want well-reported articles on conservation issues, conservation successes, and straight natural history based on author's research." **Buys 30 mss/year.** Query with published clips. Length: 300-2,000 words. **Pays $1/word for features and department articles, and $150 for short pieces.**

PERSONAL COMPUTERS

Ⓔ BASELINE

Ziff Davis Media, Inc., 28 E. 28th St., New York NY 10016. (212)503-5435. Fax: (212)503-5454. E-mail: baseline @ziffdavis.com. Website: www.baselinemag.com. Editor-in-Chief: Tom Steinert-Threlkeld. Managing Editor: Anna Maria Virzi. **Contact:** Elizabeth Bennett, associate editor. Monthly magazine covering "pricing, planning, and managing the implementation of next generation IT solutions. *Baseline* is edited for senior IT and coroporate management business leaders." Circ. 125,000. Editorial lead time 3 months.

● Managing Editor Maria Virzi says, "Most of the reporting and writing is done by staff writers and editors."

Ⓝ COMPUTER WORLD

The Voice of IT Management, IDG, Inc., One Speen St., Framingham MA 01701. (508)879-0700. Website: www.computerworld.com. **Contact:** Editor. Weekly magazine. "We provide readers with a lively variety of everything from the latest IT news, in-depth analysis and feature stories, to special reports, case studies, industry updates, product information, advice and opinion." Estab. 1967. Circ. 180,000.

● Contact specific editor.

Nonfiction How-to, opinion. Query.

$ COMPUTOREDGE

Computer and Internet Magazine, The Byte Buyer, Inc., P.O. Box 83086, San Diego CA 92138. E-mail: submission s@computoredge.com. Website: www.computoredge.com. Editor: Patricia Smith. **Contact:** Gretchen Grunburg, marketing/technical editor. **75% freelance written.** "We are the nation's largest regional computer weekly with editions in Southern California and Colorado." Estab. 1983. Circ. 100,000. Pays 1 month after publication. Publishes ms an average of 2-4 months after acceptance. Byline given. Buys first North American serial, electronic rights. Editorial lead time 2 months. Submit seasonal material 2 months in advance. Accepts queries by e-mail. Sample copy and writer's guidelines online.

● Accepts electronic submissions only. Put the issue number for which you wish to write in the subject line of your e-mail message. No attachments.

Nonfiction How-to (computer processes), humor (limited), interview/profile (limited), new product, personal experience, technical. **Buys 200 mss/year.** Query. Length: 1,000-1,200 words. **Pays $100-150.**

Columns/Departments Mac Madness (Macintosh-related), 900 words; I Don't Do Windows (alternative operating systems), 900 words. **Buys 85 mss/year.** Query. **Pays $75-110.**

Ⓝ $ $ EZ TECH: WINDOWS XP

Future Network USA, 150 N. Hill Dr., Suite 40, Brisbane CA 94005. (415)468-4684. Fax: (415)468-4686. E-mail: editor@eztechguides.com. Website: futurenetworkusa.com/publications/eztechguides.html. **Contact:** Robert Strohmeyer, editor. **80% freelance written.** Bimonthly magazine covering Microsoft Windows XP and related software and hardware. "*EZ Tech: Windows XP* is America's leading Windows XP resource, packed with in-depth tutorials, advice, and news about Microsoft's Windows XP operating system and its related hardware and software. Our international team of seasoned technology writers brings authority, humor, and expertise to readers whose technology experience levels range from beginner to itermediate. We are the smart person's alternative to technical manuals, and we satisfy our readers' desires for both information and enteratinment through lively, crisp copy that redefines what a technology magazine can be.'' Estab. 2003. **Pays on acceptance.** Publishes ms an average of 2 months after acceptance. Byline given. Offers 10% kill fee. Buys all rights. Editorial lead time 3 months. Submit seasonal material 3 months in advance. Accepts queries by e-mail. Responds in 2-3 weeks to queries. Sample copy online. Writer's guidelines by e-mail.

Nonfiction How-to, new product, technical. **Buys 60 mss/year.** Query with published clips. Length: 500-8,000 words. **Pays 25-50¢/word.** Sometimes pays expenses of writers on assignment.

Tips ''We're looking for writers who are absolute experts with Windows XP and can bring the world of technology to life with fun, exciting, and entertaining copy. Our magazine is the smart person's alternative to the technical manual, and we need writers who can speak to an audience of intelligent readers who are too busy for jargon. If you're a world-class Windows XP geek with a flair for the written word and an astoundingly nuanced sense of humor, we welcome your pitches. Your query should demonstrate both your technical expertise and your writing voice, and should be accompanied by clips from a major technology publication. Hint: We are a technology magazine, and you will be judged on your use of technology in communicating with us. Clips should be sent as PDF attachments of URLs. Please do not send queries via snail mail. First-time writers and hobbyists need not apply.''

N INFOWORLD

Lead with Knowledge, InfoWorld Media Group, 501 2nd St., Suite 500, San Francisco CA 94107. Website: www.infoworld.com. Editor-in-Chief: Steve Fox. Weekly magazine. ''*InfoWorld* provides in-depth technical analysis on key products, solutions, and technologies for sound buying decisions and business gain.'' Circ. 220,000. Editorial lead time 2 months. Accepts queries by e-mail.

• Contact specific editor.

Nonfiction Reviews, features, and news.

N $ $ $ LAPTOP

Bedford Communications, 1410 Broadway, 21st Floor, New York NY 10018. (212)807-8220. Fax: (212)807-1098. E-mail: ccummings@bedfordmags.com. Website: www.laptopmag.com. Editor-in-Chief: Mark Spoonauer. **Contact:** Corrine Cummings, assistant editor. **60% freelance written.** Monthly magazine covering mobile computing, such as laptop computers, PDAs, software and peripherals, and industry trends. ''Publication is geared toward the mobile technology laptop computer buyer, with an emphasis on the small office.'' Estab. 1991. Pays on publication. Publishes ms an average of 3 months after acceptance. Byline given. Offers 20% kill fee. Buys all rights. Editorial lead time 4 months. Accepts queries by e-mail. Responds in 4 months to queries. Sample copy online.

Nonfiction How-to (i.e., install a CD-ROM drive), technical, hands-on reviews, features. **Buys 80-100 mss/year.** Length: 300-3,500 words. **Pays $150-1,250.** Sometimes pays expenses of writers on assignment.

Tips ''Send résumé with feature-length clips (technology-related, if possible) to editorial offices. Unsolicited manuscripts are not accepted or returned.''

$ $ $ $ MACADDICT

Imagine Media, 150 North Hill Dr., Suite 40, Brisbane CA 94005. (415)468-4684. Fax: (415)468-4686. E-mail: editor@macaddict.com. Website: www.macaddict.com. **Contact:** Rik Myslewski, editor-in-chief. **35% freelance written.** Monthly magazine covering Macintosh computers. ''*MacAddict* is a magazine for Macintosh computer enthusiasts of all levels. Writers must know, love and own Macintosh computers.'' Estab. 1996. Circ. 160,000. Pays on publication. Publishes ms an average of 3 months after acceptance. Byline given. Buys all rights. Editorial lead time 3 months. Submit seasonal material 2 months in advance. Accepts queries by mail, e-mail. Responds in 1 month to queries.

Nonfiction How-to, new product, technical. No humor, case studies, personal experience, essays. **Buys 30 mss/year.** Query with or without published clips. Length: 250-7,500 words. **Pays $50-2,500.**

Columns/Departments Reviews (always assigned), 300-750 words; how-to's (detailed, step-by-step), 500-2,500 words; features, 1,000-3,500 words. **Buys 20 mss/year.** Query with or without published clips. **Pays $50-2,500.**

The online magazine carries original content not found in the print edition. Contact: Niko Coucouvanis, online editor.

Tips ''Send us an idea for a short 1-2 page how-to and/or send us a letter outlining your publishing experience and areas of Mac expertise so we can assign a review to you (reviews editor is Roman Loyola). Your submission should have great practical hands-on benefit to a reader, be fun to read in the author's natural voice, and include lots of screenshot graphics. We require electronic submissions. Impress our reviews editor with well-written reviews of Mac products and then move up to bigger articles from there.''

N ONLINE MAGAZINE

Information Today, Inc., P.O. Box 78225, Indianapolis IN 46278. (317)870-1994. Fax: (317)870-1996. E-mail: marydee@infotoday.com. Website: www.infotoday.com/online. **Contact:** Marydee Ojala, editor. Bimonthly magazine for librarians and other professionals who routinely use online services for information delivery, research, and knowledge management. *"Online* provides evaluation and informed opinion about selecting, using, and managing electronic information products, as well as industry and professional information about online database systems." Estab. 1977. Circ. 9,000. Byline given. Editorial lead time 3-4 months. Sample copy and writer's guidelines online.

 • Unaccepted mss will not be returned.

Nonfiction Query. **Pays variable amount.**

Tips Read online guidelines.

N PC GAMER

Future Network USA, 150 N. Hill Dr., Suite 40, Brisbane CA 94005. (415)468-4684. Fax: (415)468-4686. E-mail: editor@pcgamer.com. Website: www.pcgamer.com. Monthly magazine. Accepts queries by e-mail.

Nonfiction General interest, new product. Query.

Tips "Audience is serious Windows-based gamers."

⊘ PC MAGAZINE

Ziff-Davis Media, Inc., 28 E. 28th St., New York NY 10016. (212)503-3500. Fax: (212)503-5799. E-mail: pcmag@ziffdavis.com. Website: www.pcmag.com. Editor: Michael Miller. Managing Editor: Paul Ross. Magazine published 22 times/year. Circ. 1,228,658. Editorial lead time 4 months.

 • Query before submitting.

$ $ $⊘ PC UPGRADE

Bedford Communications, 1410 Broadway, 21st Floor, New York NY 10018. (212)807-8220. Website: www.techworthy.com. **70% freelance written.** Magazine published 8 times/year covering computer hardware, software and peripherals, and industry trends. "Publication is geared toward the computer owner interested in upgrading." Estab. 1991. Pays on publication. Publishes ms an average of 3 months after acceptance. Byline given. Offers 25% kill fee. Buys all rights. Editorial lead time 4 months. Accepts queries by mail, e-mail. Responds in 1 month to queries.

Nonfiction How-to (i.e., install a DVD-ROM drive), technical, hands-on reviews. **Buys 80-100 mss/year.** Query with published clips. "Will not accept unsolicited articles or manuscripts." Length: 600-3,500 words. Sometimes pays expenses of writers on assignment.

Tips "Send résumé with feature-length (technology-related, if possible) clips to editorial offices. Unsolicited manuscripts are not accepted or returned."

⊘ PC WORLD

PC World Communications, Inc., 501 2nd St., Suite 600, San Francisco CA 94107. (415)243-0500. Fax: (415)442-1891. E-mail: letters@pcworld.com. Website: www.pcworld.com. Editor: Harry McCracken. Managing Editor: Kimberly Brinson. Senior Associate Editor: Grace Aquino. Senior Editor: Anush Yegyazarian. **Contact:** Article Proposals. Monthly magazine covering personal computers. *"PC World* was created to give PC-proficient managers advice on which technology products to buy, tips on how to use those products most efficiently, news about the latest technological developments, and alerts regarding current problems with products and manufacturers." Circ. 1,100,000. Editorial lead time 3 months. Accepts queries by mail. Sample copy not available. Writer's guidelines by e-mail.

 ○┐ "We have very few opportunities for writers who are not already contributing to the magazine. One way we discover new talent is by assigning short tips and how-to pieces."

Nonfiction How-to, reviews, news items, features. Query. **Payment varies.**

Tips "Once you're familiar with *PC World,* you can write us a query letter. Your letter should answer the following questions as specifically and consisely as possible. What is the problem, technique, or product you want to discuss? Why will *PC World* readers be interested in it? Which section of the magazine do you think it best fits? What is the specific audience for the piece (i.e., database or LAN users, desktop publishers, and so on)?"

$ $ $SMART COMPUTING

Sandhills Publishing, 131 W. Grand Dr., Lincoln NE 68521. (800)544-1264. Fax: (402)479-2104. E-mail: editor@smartcomputing.com. Website: www.smartcomputing.com. Editor: Rod Scher. **Contact:** Ron Kobler, editor-in-chief. **45% freelance written.** Monthly magazine. "We focus on plain-English computing articles with an emphasis on tutorials that improve productivity without the purchase of new hardware." Estab. 1990. Circ.

200,000. **Pays on acceptance.** Publishes ms an average of 2 months after acceptance. Byline given. Offers 25% kill fee. Buys all rights. Editorial lead time 4 months. Submit seasonal material 4 months in advance. Accepts queries by mail, e-mail. Accepts simultaneous submissions. Responds in 1 month to queries. Sample copy for $7.99. Writer's guidelines for #10 SASE.

○━ Break in with "any article containing little-known tips for improving software and hardware performance and Web use. We're also seeking clear reporting on key trends changing personal technology."

Nonfiction How-to, new product, technical. No humor, opinion, personal experience. **Buys 250 mss/year.** Query with published clips. Length: 800-3,200 words. **Pays $240-960.** Pays expenses of writers on assignment up to $75.

Photos Send photos with submission. Buys all rights. Offers no additional payment for photos accepted with ms. Captions required.

Tips "Focus on practical, how-to computing articles. Our readers are intensely productivity-driven. Carefully review recent issues. We receive many ideas for stories printed in the last 6 months."

PHOTOGRAPHY

Ⓝ $ NATURE PHOTOGRAPHER

Nature Photographer Publishing Co., Inc., P.O. Box 220, Lubec ME 04652. (207)733-4201. Fax: (207)733-4202. E-mail: nature_photographer@yahoo.com. Website: www.naturephotographermag.com. **Contact:** Helen Longest-Saccone, editor-in-chief/photo editor. Quarterly magazine written by field contributors and editors; write to above address to become a "Field Contributor." *Nature Photographer* emphasizes nature photography that uses low-impact and local less-known locations, techniques and ethics. Articles include how-to, travel to worldwide wilderness locations, and how nature photography can be used to benefit the environment and environmental education of the public. Estab. 1990. Circ. 34,000. Pays on publication. Buys one-time rights. Submit seasonal material 8 months in advance. Accepts queries by mail, e-mail. Accepts simultaneous submissions. Responds in 2 months to queries. Sample copy for 9×12 SAE and 6 first-class stamps. Writer's guidelines online.

Nonfiction How-to (underwater, exposure, creative techniques, techniques to make photography easier, low-impact techniques, macro photography, large-format wildlife), photo feature, technical, travel. No articles about photographing in zoos or on game farms. **Buys 56-72 mss/year.** Query with published clips or writing samples. Length: 750-2,500 words. **Pays $75-150.**

Reprints Send photocopy and information about when and where the material previously appeared. Pays 75% of amount *Nature Photographer* pays for an original article.

Photos Send photos upon request. Do not send with submission. Reviews 35mm, 2¼×2¼ and 4×5 transparencies. Buys one-time rights. Offers no additional payment for photos accepted with ms. Identification of subjects required.

Tips "Query with original, well-thought-out ideas and good writing samples. Make sure you send a SASE. Areas most open are travel, how-to, and conservation articles with dramatic slides to illustrate the articles. Must have good, solid research and knowledge of subject. Be sure to obtain guidelines by sending a SASE with request before submitting query. If you have not requested guidelines within the last year, request an updated version because *Nature Photographer* is now written by editors and field contributors, and guidelines will outline how you can become a field contributor."

$ $ PC PHOTO

Werner Publishing Corp., 12121 Wilshire Blvd., 12th Floor, Los Angeles CA 90025. (310)820-1500. Fax: (310)826-5008. E-mail: pceditors@wernerpublishing.com. Website: www.pcphotomag.com. Managing Editor: Chris Robinson. **Contact:** Rob Sheppard, editor. **60% freelance written.** Bimonthly magazine covering digital photography. "Our magazine is designed to help photographers better use digital technologies to improve their photography." Estab. 1997. Circ. 175,000. Pays on publication. Publishes ms an average of 4 months after acceptance. Byline given. Buys one-time rights. Editorial lead time 6 months. Submit seasonal material 6 months in advance. Accepts queries by mail. Responds in 1 month to queries. Sample copy for #10 SASE or online. Writer's guidelines online.

Nonfiction How-to, personal experience, photo feature. **Buys 30 mss/year.** Query. Length: 1,200 words. **Pays $500 for assigned articles; approximately $400 for unsolicited articles.**

Photos Do not send original transparencies or negatives. Send photos with submission. Buys one-time rights. Offers $100-200/photo.

Tips "Since *PC Photo* is a photography magazine, we must see photos before any decision can be made on an article, so phone queries are not appropriate. Ultimately, whether we can use a particular piece or not will depend greatly on the photographs and how they fit in with material already in our files. We take a fresh look at the modern photographic world by encouraging photography and the use of new technologies. Editorial is intended to demystify the use of modern equipment by emphasizing practical use of the camera and the computer, highlighting the technique rather than the technical.''

$ $⊡ PHOTO LIFE

Canada's Photography Magazine, Apex Publications, Inc., One Dundas St. W., Suite 2500, P.O. Box 84, Toronto ON M5G 1Z3 Canada. (800)905-7468. Fax: (800)664-2739. E-mail: editor@photolife.com. Website: www.photolife.com. **Contact:** Anita Dammer, editor-in-chief. **15% freelance written.** Bimonthly magazine. ''*Photo Life* is geared to an audience of advanced amateur photographers. *Photo Life* is not a technical magazine per se, but techniques should be explained in enough depth to make them clear.'' Estab. 1976. Circ. 45,000. Pays on publication. Publishes ms an average of 1 year after acceptance. Byline given. Buys one-time rights. Editorial lead time 4 months. Submit seasonal material 6 months in advance. Accepts queries by mail, e-mail. Accepts simultaneous submissions. Responds in 3 months to queries. Sample copy for $5.50. Writer's guidelines online.
Nonfiction How-to (photo tips, technique), inspirational, photo feature, technical, travel. **Buys 10 mss/year.** Query with published clips or send complete ms. **Pays $100-600 (Canadian).**
Photos Reviews transparencies, prints. Buys one-time rights. Negotiates payment individually. Captions, model releases required.
Tips ''We will review any relevant submissions that include a full text or a detailed outline of an article proposal. Accompanying photographs are necessary, as the first decision of acceptance will be based upon images. Most of the space available in the magazine is devoted to our regular contributors. Therefore, we cannot guarantee publication of other articles within any particular period of time.''

$ $ PHOTO TECHNIQUES

Preston Publications, Inc., 6600 W. Touhy Ave., Niles IL 60714. (847)647-2900. Fax: (847)647-1155. E-mail: slewis@prestonpub.com. Website: www.phototechmag.com. **Contact:** Scott Lewis, editor. **50% freelance written.** Prefers to work with experienced photographer-writers; happy to work with excellent photographers whose writing skills are lacking. Bimonthly publication covering photochemistry, lighting, optics, processing, and printing, Zone System, digital imaging/scanning/printing, special effects, sensitometry, etc. Aimed at serious amateurs. Article conclusions should be able to be duplicated by readers. Estab. 1979. Circ. 30,000. Pays within 3 weeks of publication. Publishes ms an average of 8 months after acceptance. Byline given. Buys one-time rights. Sample copy for $5. Writer's guidelines by e-mail.
Nonfiction How-to, photo feature, technical (product review), special interest articles within the above listed topics. Query or send complete ms. Length: most features run approximately 2,500 words or 3-4 magazine pages. **Pays $100-450 for well-researched technical articles.**
Photos Photographers have a much better chance of having their photos published if the photos accompany a written article. Prefers JPEGs scanned at 300 dpi and sent via e-mail or CD-ROM; accepts prints, slides, and transparencies. Buys one-time rights. Ms payment includes payment for photos. Captions, technical information required.
Tips ''Study the magazine! Virtually all writers we publish are readers of the magazine. We are now more receptive than ever to articles about photographers, history, aesthetics, and informative backgrounders about specific areas of the photo industry or specific techniques. Successful writers for our magazine are doing what they write about.''

ℕ $ PICTURE MAGAZINE

41 Union Square W., Suite 504, New York NY 10003. (212)352-2700. Fax: (212)352-2155. E-mail: picmag@aol.com. Website: www.picturemagazine.com. **100% freelance written.** Bimonthly magazine covering professional photography topics. Estab. 1995. Circ. 16,000. Pays on publication. Publishes ms an average of 2 months after acceptance. Byline given. Buys one-time rights. Editorial lead time 3 months. Submit seasonal material 3 months in advance. Accepts queries by e-mail. Accepts previously published material. Accepts simultaneous submissions. Sample copy and writer's guidelines free.
Nonfiction General interest, how-to, interview/profile, new product, photo feature, technical. **Buys 5 mss/year.** Send complete ms. Length: 1,500-2,500 words. **Pays $150.** Pays expenses of writers on assignment.
Photos State availability with submission. Buys one-time rights. Offers no additional payment for photos accepted with ms. Captions required.

⊘ POPULAR PHOTOGRAPHY & IMAGING

Hachette Filipacchi Media U.S., Inc., 1633 Broadway, New York NY 10019. (212)767-6000. Fax: (212)767-5602. E-mail: popeditor@aol.com. Website: www.popphoto.com. **Contact:** Jason Schneider, editor-in-chief. Monthly magazine edited for amateur to professional photographers. Provides incisive instructional articles, authoritative tests of photographic equipment; covers still and digital imaging, travel, color, nature, and large-format columns; plus up-to-date industry information. Circ. 453,944. Editorial lead time 2 months.

- Query before submitting.

Ⓝ $ $ VIDEOMAKER

Videomaker, Inc., P.O. Box 4591, Chico CA 95927-4591. (530)891-8410. Fax: (530)891-8443. E-mail: editor@videomaker.com. Website: www.videomaker.com. Editor: Stephen Muratore. Managing Editor: Jennifer O'Rourke. **Contact:** Charles Fulton, associate editor. Monthly magazine covering audio and video production, camcorders, editing, computer video, DVDs. Estab. 1985. Circ. 89,182. Pays on publication. Publishes ms an average of 4 months after acceptance. Byline given. Buys electronic, all rights. Editorial lead time 5 months. Submit seasonal material 5 months in advance. Accepts queries by mail, e-mail. Responds in 3 weeks to queries. Sample copy and writer's guidelines online.

- The magazine's voice is friendly, encouraging; never condescending to the audience.

Nonfiction How-to, technical. Special issues: Annual Buyer's Guide in October (13th issue of the year). **Buys 34 mss/year.** Query. Length: 800-1,500 words. **Pays $100-300.** Sometimes pays expenses of writers on assignment.
Photos Brent Holland, art director. Negotiates payment individually. Model releases required.
Columns/Departments Basic Training (introduction to video production techniques), 1,400 words. **Buys 14 mss/year.** Query. **Pays $150-225.**
Fiction Storyboards for readers to reproduce. **Buys 3 mss/year.** Query. Length: 400-600 words. **Pays $150-200.**

POLITICS & WORLD AFFAIRS

THE AMERICAN SPECTATOR

1611 N. Kent St., Suite 901, Arlington VA 22209. (703)807-2011. Fax: (703)807-2013. E-mail: editor@spectator.org. Website: www.spectator.org. Managing Editor: George Neumayr. Monthly magazine. "For many years, one ideological viewpoint dominated American print and broadcast journalism. Today, that viewpoint still controls the entertainment and news divisions of the television networks, the mass-circulation news magazines, and the daily newspapers. *American Spectator* has attempted to balance the Left's domination of the media by debunking its perceived wisdom and advancing alternative ideas through spirited writing, insightful essays, humor and, most recently, through well-researched investigative articles that have themselves become news." Estab. 1967. Circ. 50,000. Accepts queries by mail.
Nonfiction "Topics include politics, the press, foreign relations, the economy, culture. Stories most suited for publication are timely articles on previously unreported topics with national appeal. Articles should be thoroughly researched with a heavy emphasis on interviewing and reporting, and the facts of the article should be verifiable. We prefer articles in which the facts speak for themselves and shy away from editorial and first person commentary. No unsolicited poetry, fiction, satire, or crossword puzzles. Query with résumé, clips and SASE.
Columns/Departments The Continuing Crisis and Current Wisdom (humor); On the Prowl ("Washington insider news"). Query with résumé, clips and SASE.

$ $ CHURCH & STATE

Americans United for Separation of Church and State, 518 C St. NE, Washington DC 20002. (202)466-3234. Fax: (202)466-3353. E-mail: americansunited@au.org. Website: www.au.org. **Contact:** Joseph Conn, editor. **10% freelance written.** Monthly magazine emphasizing religious liberty and church/state relations matters. Strongly advocates separation of church and state. Readership is well-educated. Estab. 1947. Circ. 40,000. **Pays on acceptance.** Publishes ms an average of 2 months after acceptance. Buys all rights. Accepts queries by mail. Accepts simultaneous submissions. Responds in 2 months to queries. Sample copy and writer's guidelines for 9×12 SAE with 3 first-class stamps.
Nonfiction Exposé, general interest, historical/nostalgic, interview/profile. **Buys 11 mss/year.** Query. Length: 800-1,600 words. **Pays $150-300 for assigned articles.** Sometimes pays expenses of writers on assignment.
Reprints Send tearsheet, photocopy or typed ms with rights for sale noted and information about when and where the material previously appeared.
Photos Send photos with submission. Buys one-time rights. Pays negotiable fee for b&w prints. Captions required.
Tips "We're looking for feature articles on underreported local church-state controversies. We also consider 'viewpoint' essays that offer a unique or personal take on church-state issues. We are not a religious magazine. You need to see our magazine before you try to write for it."

$COMMONWEAL

A Review of Public Affairs, Religion, Literature and the Arts, Commonweal Foundation, 475 Riverside Dr., Room 405, New York NY 10115. (212)662-4200. Fax: (212)662-4183. E-mail: editors@commonwealmagazine.org. Website: www.commonwealmagazine.org. Editor: Paul Baumann. **Contact:** Patrick Jordan, managing editor. Biweekly journal of opinion edited by Catholic lay people, dealing with topical issues of the day on public affairs, religion, literature, and the arts. Estab. 1924. Circ. 20,000. Pays on publication. Byline given. Buys all rights. Submit seasonal material 2 months in advance. Responds in 2 months to queries. Sample copy for free. Writer's guidelines online.

Nonfiction Essays, general interest, interview/profile, personal experience, religious. **Buys 30 mss/year.** Query with published clips. Length: 2,000-2,500 words. **Pays $75-100.**

Columns/Departments Upfronts (brief, newsy reportorials, giving facts, information and some interpretation behind the headlines of the day), 750-1,000 words; Last Word (usually of a personal nature, on some aspect of the human condition: spiritual, individual, political, or social), 800 words.

Poetry Rosemary Deen, editor. Free verse, traditional. **Buys 20 poems/year. Pays 75¢/line.**

Tips "Articles should be written for a general but well-educated audience. While religious articles are always topical, we are less interested in devotional and churchy pieces than in articles which examine the links between 'worldly' concerns and religious beliefs."

⊘ ⊕ THE ECONOMIST

Economist Group of London, 25 St. James St., London England SW1A 1HG United Kingdom. Fax: (44207)839-2968. Website: www.economist.com. Weekly magazine for senior management and policy makers in business, government, and finance throughout the world. Estab. 1843. Circ. 403,131.

• Query before submitting.

Ⓝ $ $THE FREEMAN: IDEAS ON LIBERTY

30 S. Broadway, Irvington-on-Hudson NY 10533. (914)591-7230. Fax: (914)591-8910. E-mail: freeman@fee.org. Website: www.fee.org. Publisher: Foundation for Economic Education. **85% freelance written.** Monthly publication for "the layman and fairly advanced students of liberty." Estab. 1946. Pays on publication. Publishes ms an average of 5 months after acceptance. Byline given. Acquires all rights, including reprint rights. Sample copy for $7\frac{1}{2} \times 10\frac{1}{2}$ SASE with 4 first-class stamps.

• Eager to work with new/unpublished writers.

Nonfiction "We want nonfiction clearly analyzing and explaining various aspects of the free market, private property, limited-government philosophy. Though a necessary part of the literature of freedom is the exposure of collectivistic cliches and fallacies, our aim is to emphasize and explain the positive case for individual responsibility and choice in a free-market economy. We avoid name-calling and personality clashes. Ours is an intelligent analysis of the principles underlying a free-market economy. No political strategies or tactics." **Buys 100 mss/year.** Query with SASE. Length: 3,500 words. **Pays 10¢/word.** Sometimes pays expenses of writers on assignment.

Tips "It's most rewarding to find freelancers with new insights, fresh points of view. Facts, figures and quotations cited should be fully documented, to their original source, if possible."

THE LABOR PAPER

Serving Southern Wisconsin, Union-Cooperative Publishing, 3030 39th Ave., Suite 110, Kenosha WI 53144. (262)657-6116. Fax: (262)657-6153. **Contact:** Mark T. Onosko, publisher. **30% freelance written.** Weekly tabloid covering union/labor news. Estab. 1935. Circ. 12,000. Pays on publication. Publishes ms an average of 2 months after acceptance. Byline given. Buys all rights. Editorial lead time 1 month. Submit seasonal material 1 month in advance. Accepts queries by mail, fax. Accepts simultaneous submissions. Sample copy and writer's guidelines free.

Nonfiction Exposé, general interest, historical/nostalgic, humor, inspirational. **Buys 4 mss/year.** Query with published clips. Length: 300-1,000 words. Sometimes pays expenses of writers on assignment.

Photos State availability with submission. Negotiates payment individually. Captions required.

Ⓝ $ $THE NATION

33 Irving Place, New York NY 10003. (212)209-5400. Fax: (212)982-9000. Website: www.thenation.com. **75% freelance written.** Works with a small number of new/unpublished writers each year. Weekly magazine "firmly committed to reporting on the issues of labor, national politics, business, consumer affairs, environmental politics, civil liberties, foreign affairs and the role and future of the Democratic Party." Estab. 1865. Buys first rights. Accepts queries by mail, e-mail, fax. Sample copy for free. Writer's guidelines online.

• See the Contests & Awards section for the Discovery-*The Nation* poetry contest.

Nonfiction "We welcome all articles dealing with the social scene from an independent perspective." Queries encouraged. **Buys 100 mss/year. Pays $350-500.** Sometimes pays expenses of writers on assignment.

Columns/Departments Editorial, 500-700 words. **Pays $150.**

Poetry *The Nation* publishes poetry of outstanding aesthetic quality. Send poems with SASE. **Payment negotiable.**

Tips "We are a journal of left/liberal political opinion covering national and international affairs. We are looking both for reporting and for fresh analysis. On the domestic front, we are particularly interested in civil liberties, civil rights, labor, economics, environmental and feminist issues, and the role and future of the Democratic Party. Because we have readers all over the country, it's important that stories with a local focus have real national significance. In our foreign affairs coverage we prefer pieces on international political, economic, and social developments. As the magazine which published Ralph Nader's first piece (and there is a long list of *Nation* 'firsts'), we are seeking new writers."

THE NATIONAL VOTER

League of Women Voters, 1730 M St. NW, Suite 1000, Washington DC 20036. (202)429-1965. Fax: (202)429-0854. E-mail: nationalvoter@lwv.org. Website: www.lwv.org. Magazine published 3 times/year. "*The National Voter* provides background, perspective and commentary on public policy issues confronting citizens and their leaders at all levels of government. And it empowers people to make a difference in their communities by offering guidance, maturation and models for action." Estab. 1951. Circ. 100,000. Pays on publication. Byline given. Makes work-for-hire assignments. Editorial lead time 2 months. Accepts queries by mail, e-mail. Sample copy for free.

Nonfiction Exposé, general interest, interview/profile. No essays, personal experience, religious, opinion. **Buys 2-3 mss/year.** Query with published clips. Length: 200-4,000 words. **Payment always negotiated.** Pays expenses of writers on assignment.

Photos State availability with submission. Reviews contact sheets. Buys one-time rights. Offers no additional payment for photos accepted with ms. Captions, identification of subjects required.

THE NEW REPUBLIC

1331 H St. NW, Suite 700, Washington DC 20005. (202)508-4444. Fax: (202)628-9383. E-mail: letters@tnr.com. Website: www.tnr.com. Editor-in-Chief: Martin Peretz. Editor: Peter Beinart. Weekly magazine covering issues before they hit the mainstream, from energy to the environment, from foreign to fiscal policy. By publishing the best writing from a variety of view points, *The New Republic* continues to be America's best and most influential journal of opinion." Responds in 6-8 weeks.

Tips "Poetry submissions should be sent by regular mail. No phone calls please."

THE ONION

Onion, Inc., 536 Broadway, 10th Floor, New York NY 10012. (212)627-1972. Fax: (212)627-1711. E-mail: infomat@theonion.com. Website: www.theonion.com. Editor-in-Chief: Carol Kolb. Weekly magazine. "*The Onion* offers satirical editorial which uses invented names in all its stories, except when public figures are being satirized." Circ. 153,000.

- Does not buy freelance material or use freelance writers.

$ PROGRESSIVE POPULIST

Journal from America's Heartland, P.O. Box 150517, Austin TX 78715-0517. (512)447-0455. E-mail: populist@usa.net. Website: www.populist.com. Managing Editor: Art Cullen. **Contact:** Jim Cullen, editor. **90% freelance written.** Biweekly tabloid covering politics and economics. "We cover issues of interest to workers, small businesses, and family farmers and ranchers." Estab. 1995. Circ. 10,000. Pays quarterly. Publishes ms an average of 1 month after acceptance. Byline given. Buys first North American serial, second serial (reprint) rights. Editorial lead time 3 weeks. Submit seasonal material 1 month in advance. Accepts queries by mail, e-mail, fax, phone. Accepts previously published material. Accepts simultaneous submissions. Sample copy and writer's guidelines free.

Nonfiction "We cover politics and economics. We are interested not so much in the dry reporting of campaigns and elections, or the stock markets and GNP, but in how big business is exerting more control over both the government and ordinary people's lives, and what people can do about it." Essays, exposé, general interest, historical/nostalgic, humor, interview/profile, opinion. "We are not much interested in 'sound-off' articles about state or national politics, although we accept letters to the editor. We prefer to see more 'journalistic' pieces in which the writer does enough footwork to advance a story beyond the easy realm of opinion." **Buys 400 mss/year.** Query. Length: 600-1,000 words. **Pays $15-50.** Pays writers with contributor copies or other premiums if preferred by writer.

Reprints Send photocopy with rights for sale noted and information about when and where the material previously appeared.

Photos State availability with submission. Buys one-time rights. Negotiates payment individually. Identification of subjects required.

Tips "We do prefer submissions by e-mail. I find it's easier to work with e-mail and for the writer it probably increases the chances of getting a response."

$ $ THE PROGRESSIVE

409 E. Main St., Madison WI 53703. (608)257-4626. Fax: (608)257-3373. E-mail: editorial@progressive.org. Website: www.progressive.org. **Contact:** Matthew Rothschild, editor. **75% freelance written.** Monthly magazine. Estab. 1909. Pays on publication. Publishes ms an average of 6 weeks after acceptance. Byline given. Accepts queries by mail. Responds in 1 month to queries. Sample copy for 9 × 12 SAE with 4 first-class stamps or sample articles online. Writer's guidelines online.

Nonfiction Investigative reporting (exposé of corporate malfeasance and governmental wrongdoing); electoral coverage (a current electoral development that has national implications); social movement pieces (important or interesting event or trend in the labor movement, or the GLBT movement, or in the area of racial justice, disability rights, the environment, women's liberation); foreign policy pieces (a development of huge moral importance where the US role may not be paramount); interviews (a long Q&A with a writer, activist, political figure, or musician who is widely known for doing especially worthwhile work); activism (highlights the work of activists and activist groups; increasingly, we are looking for good photographs of a dynamic or creative action, and we accompany the photos with a caption); book reviews (cover 2-3 current titles on a major issue of concern). Primarily interested in articles that interpret, from a progressive point of view, domestic and world affairs. Occasional lighter features. "*The Progressive* is a political publication. General interest is inappropriate. We do not want editorials, satire, historical pieces, philosophical peices or columns." Query. Length: 500-4,000 words. **Pays $500-1,300.**

Poetry Publishes 1 original poem a month. "We prefer poems that connect up—in one fashion or another, however obliquely—with political concerns." **Pays $150.**

Tips "Sought-after topics include electoral coverage, social movement, foreign policy, activism and book reviews."

$ $ $ $ REASON

Free Minds and Free Markets, Reason Foundation, 3415 S. Sepulveda Blvd., Suite 400, Los Angeles CA 90034. (310)391-2245. Fax: (310)390-8986. E-mail: jsanchez@reason.com. Website: www.reason.com. Editor-in-Chief: Nick Gillespie. **Contact:** Brian Doherty (by mail) or Julian Sanchez (by e-mail). **30% freelance written.** Monthly magazine covering politics, current events, culture, ideas. "*Reason* covers politics, culture, and ideas from a dynamic libertarian perspective. It features reported works, opinion pieces, and book reviews." Estab. 1968. Circ. 55,000. **Pays on acceptance.** Byline given. Offers kill fee. Buys first North American serial, first, all rights. Editorial lead time 2 months. Submit seasonal material 3 months in advance. Accepts queries by mail, e-mail. Responds in 6 weeks to queries; 2 months to mss. Sample copy for $4. Writer's guidelines online.

Nonfiction Book excerpts, essays, exposé, general interest, humor, interview/profile, opinion. No products, personal experience, how-to, travel. **Buys 50-60 mss/year.** Query with published clips. Length: 850-5,000 words. **Pays $300-2,000.** Sometimes pays expenses of writers on assignment.

  The online magazine carries original content not found in the print edition and includes writer's guidelines. Contact: Nick Gillespie.

Tips "We prefer queries of no more than 1-2 pages with specifically developed ideas about a given topic rather than more general areas of interest. Enclosing a few published clips also helps."

N ∅ U.S. NEWS & WORLD REPORT

U.S. News & World Report, Inc., 1050 Thomas Jefferson St. NW, Washington DC 20007. (202)955-2000. Website: www.usnews.com. Weekly magazine devoted largely to reporting and analyzing national and international affairs, politics, business, health, science, technology, and social trends. Circ. 2,018,621. Editorial lead time 10 days.

  • Query before submitting.

$ $ WASHINGTON MONTHLY

The Washington Monthly Co., 733 15th St. NW, Suite 520, Washington DC 20005. (202)393-5155. Fax: (202)393-2444. E-mail: editors@washingtonmonthly.com. Website: www.washingtonmonthly.com. Editor-in-Chief: Paul Glastris. **50% freelance written.** Monthly magazine covering politics, policy, media. "We are a neo-liberal publication with a long history and specific views—please read our magazine before submitting." Estab. 1969. Circ. 28,000. Pays on publication. Publishes ms an average of 2 months after acceptance. Byline given. Buys all rights. Editorial lead time 2 months. Submit seasonal material 4 months in advance. Accepts queries by mail, e-mail, fax, phone. Responds in 3 weeks to queries; 2 months to mss. Sample copy for 11×17 SAE with 5 first-class stamps or by e-mail. Writer's guidelines online.

Nonfiction Book excerpts, essays, exposé, general interest, historical/nostalgic, interview/profile, opinion, personal experience, technical, first-person political. "No humor, how-to, or generalized articles." **Buys 20 mss/year.** Query with or without published clips or send complete ms. Length: 1,500-5,000 words. **Pays 10¢/word.**

Photos State availability with submission. Reviews contact sheets, prints. Buys one-time rights. Negotiates payment individually.

Columns/Departments 10 Mile Square (about DC); On Political Books, Booknotes (both reviews of current political books), 1,500-3,000 words. **Buys 10 mss/year.** Query with published clips or send complete ms. **Pays 10¢/word.**

Tips "Call our editors to talk about ideas. Always pitch articles showing background research. We're particularly looking for first-hand accounts of working in government. We also like original work showing that the government is or is not doing something important. We have writer's guidelines, but do your research first."

Ⓝ Ⓢ THE WEEKLY STANDARD

News America, Inc., 1150 17th St., NW, Suite 505, Washington DC 20036. E-mail: editor@weeklystandard.com. Website: www.weeklystandard.com. Publisher: Terry Eastland. **Contact:** William Kristol, editor; Fred Barnes, executive editor. Weekly magazine.

- Query before submitting.

Ⓢ WHISTLE BLOWER

WorldNetDaily.com, Inc., P.O. Box 1087, Grants Pass OR 97528. (541)474-1776. Website: www.worldnetdaily.com. Monthly magazine. "*Whistle Blower* focuses on current events and controversies in the US and abroad."

- Does not buy freelance material or use freelance writers.

WORLD POLICY JOURNAL

World Policy Institute, 66 Fifth Ave., 9th Floor, New York NY 10011. (212)229-5808. Fax: (212)229-5579. Website: www.worldpolicy.org. **Contact:** Linda Wrigley, managing editor. **10% freelance written.** Quarterly journal covering international politics, economics, and security isssues, as well as historical and cultural essays, book reviews, profiles, and first-person reporting from regions not covered in the general media. "We hope to bring principle and proportion, as well as a sense of reality and direction to America's discussion of its role in the world." Circ. 8,000. Pays on publication. Publishes ms an average of 3 months after acceptance. Byline given. Buys all rights. Accepts queries by mail. Responds in 3 months to queries. Sample copy for $7.95 and 9×12 SASE with 10 first-class stamps. Writer's guidelines online.

Nonfiction Articles that "define policies that reflect the shared needs and interests of all nations of the world." Query. Length: 2,500-4,500 words. **Pays variable commission rate.**

PSYCHOLOGY & SELF-IMPROVEMENT

$PLUS ATTITUDE MAGAZINE

Success Through Positive Action + Positive Attitude, Plus Attitude, 209 W. Millcreek Way, Tooele UT 84074-2929. (435)882-4116. E-mail: joyehenrie@msn.com. Website: www.plusattitude.com. **Contact:** Joye L. Henrie, editor. **95% freelance written.** Monthly newsletter focused on enhancement in all areas of the lives of our readers. "It is our goal to motivate and inspire our readers to work toward their personal goals of success. Our audience is comprised of individuals who value achievement. Our primary focus isn't necessarily on monetary achievement, so our writers must think in broader terms, beyond the dollar sign. We are open to all styles of writing, as long as the piece speaks to, rather than 'at,' the reader. It has to draw a person in, help him or her visualize the goal, and motivate positive action." Estab. 2003. Pays on publication. Publishes ms an average of 6 months after acceptance. Byline sometimes given. Buys one-time, simultaneous rights. Editorial lead time 4 months. Submit seasonal material 6 months in advance. Accepts queries by mail, e-mail. Accepts previously published material. Accepts simultaneous submissions. Responds in 1 month to queries; 3 months to mss. Sample copy not available. Writer's guidelines for #10 SASE, online or by e-mail.

- This magazine only pays for printed material. It does not pay for material posted online.

Nonfiction Book excerpts, essays, general interest, historical/nostalgic, how-to, humor, inspirational, interview/profile, new product, opinion, personal experience, photo feature, technical, travel, anything that encompasses the theme of the publication. Does not want to see religious themes. "While religion is inspirational to many, our publication is not a forum for this. We don't want to see memoirs that disconnect the reader from the picture of success, but we don't discourage memoirs. If in doubt, please query with your idea." **Buys 50 mss/year.** Query with or without published clips or send complete ms. Length: 200-1,200 words. **Pays $10-30.**

Photos State availability with submission. Rights negotiable. Negotiates payment individually. Captions, model releases required.

Columns/Departments Principles of Success (application tools/goal setting), 1,200-1,500 words; Innovators of the Past (historical figures that modeled principles of success), 800-1,000 words; Rags to Riches (present figures that model principles of success), 1,000-1,200 words; Inspirational Retreats (places to visit for relaxation, fun and inspirational), 600-700 words; What Is Plus Attitude? (introduction: ongoing summary), 600-650 words; Dwellings (luxury and/or inspirational homes to own), 600-700 words; PA Forward Thinking Schedule Planner (how to use/benefits), 50-75 words; Fun to Own (the buzz on the latest products), 600-700 words. **Buys 96 mss/year.** Query with or without published clips or send complete ms. **Pays $25-75.**

Fiction "We accept a very limited amount of fiction. The only types of fiction we want to see are pieces that help our readers visualize components of success." Experimental, historical, humorous. **Buys 12 mss/year.** Query with or without published clips or send complete ms. Length: 600-1,000 words. **Pays $10-30.**

Fillers Anecdotes, facts, gags to be illustrated by cartoonist, newsbreaks, short humor. **Buys 24/year.** Length: 25-200 words. **Pays $2-10.**

Tips "We are still a young publication and able to give some level of personal attention to our writers. We still have the leverage to work with writers who have a good piece that needs to be altered some to fit our magazine. If you need further information on the type of content needed, pick up one of the top selling 'self-help' books, and it should give you some good ideas on the angle we're going for. If you send your query or manuscript in the mail, please include a SASE to receive a response and/or have your material returned."

$ $ $ $ PSYCHOLOGY TODAY

Sussex Publishers, Inc., 115 E. 23rd St., 9th Floor, New York NY 10010. (212)260-7210. Fax: (212)260-7445. E-mail: kat@psychologytoday.com. Website: www.psychologytoday.com. **Contact:** Kathleen McGowan, senior editor. Bimonthly magazine. "*Psychology Today* explores every aspect of human behavior, from the cultural trends that shape the way we think and feel to the intricacies of modern neuroscience. We're sort of a hybrid of a science magazine, a health magazine and a self-help magazine. While we're read by many psychologists, therapists, and social workers; most of our readers are simply intelligent and curious people interested in the psyche and the self." Estab. 1967. Circ. 331,400. Pays on publication. Publishes ms an average of 3 months after acceptance. Byline given. Buys first North American serial rights. Editorial lead time 5 months. Accepts queries by mail. Responds in 1 month to queries. Sample copy for $3.50. Writer's guidelines for #10 SASE.

Nonfiction "Nearly any subject related to psychology is fair game. We value originality, insight and good reporting; we're not interested in stories or topics that have already been covered ad nauseum by other magazines unless you can provide a fresh new twist and much more depth. We're not interested in simple-minded 'pop psychology.'" No fiction, poetry or first-person essays on "How I Conquered Mental Disorder X." **Buys 20-25 mss/year.** Query with published clips. Length: 1,500-4,000 words. **Pays $1,000-2,500.**

Columns/Departments News Editor. News & Trends, 150-300 words. Query with published clips. **Pays $150-300.**

$ ROSICRUCIAN DIGEST

Rosicrucian Order, AMORC, 1342 Naglee Ave., San Jose CA 95191-0001. (408)947-3600. Website: www.rosicrucian.org. **Contact:** Robin M. Thompson, editor-in-chief. Quarterly magazine (international) emphasizing mysticism, science, philosophy, and the arts for educated men and women of all ages seeking alternative answers to life's questions. **Pays on acceptance.** Publishes ms an average of 6 months after acceptance. Byline given. Buys first, second serial (reprint) rights. Accepts queries by mail, phone. Responds in 3 months to queries. Writer's guidelines for #10 SASE.

Nonfiction How to deal with life—and all it brings us—in a positive and constructive way. Informational articles—new ideas and developments in science, the arts, philosophy, and thought. Historical sketches, biographies, human interest, psychology, philosophical, and inspirational articles. "We are always looking for good articles on the contributions of ancient civilizations to today's civilizations, the environment, ecology, inspirational (nonreligious) subjects. Know your subject well and be able to capture the reader's interest in the first paragraph. Be willing to work with the editor to make changes in the manuscript." No religious, astrological or political material, or articles promoting a particular group or system of thought. Most articles are written by members or donated, but we're always open to freelance submissions. No book-length mss. Query. Length: 1,500-2,000 words. **Pays 6¢/word.**

Reprints Prefers typed ms with rights for sale noted and information about when and where the article previously appeared, but tearsheet or photcopy acceptable. Pays 50% of amount paid for an original article.

Tips "We're looking for more pieces on these subjects: our connection with the past—the important contributions of ancient civilizations to today's world and culture and the relevance of this wisdom to now; how to channel teenage energy/angst into positive, creative, constructive results (preferably written by teachers or others who work with young people—written for frustrated parents); and the vital necessity of raising our environmental consciousness if we are going to survive as a species on this planet."

REGIONAL

GENERAL

$ $ AAA CAROLINAS GO MAGAZINE

6600 AAA Dr., Charlotte NC 28212. Fax: (704)569-7815. Website: www.aaacarolinas.com. Managing Editor: Sarah B. Davis. **Contact:** Tom Crosby, editor. **20% freelance written.** Member publication for the Carolina affiliate of American Automobile Association covering travel and auto-related issues. "We prefer stories that focus on travel and auto safety in North and South Carolina and surrounding states." Estab. 1922. Circ. 800,000. Pays on publication. Byline given. Buys all rights. Editorial lead time 2 months. Accepts queries by mail. Sample copy and writer's guidelines for #10 SASE.

Nonfiction Travel, auto safety. Length: 750 words. **Pays $150.**

Photos Send photos with submission. Reviews slides. Buys all rights. Offers no additional payment for photos accepted with ms. Identification of subjects required.

The online magazine carries original content not found in the print edition. Contact: Sarah B. Davis.

Tips "Submit regional stories relating to Carolinas travel."

$ $ BLUE RIDGE COUNTRY

Leisure Publishing, 3424 Brambleton Ave., Roanoke VA 24018. (540)989-6138. Fax: (540)989-7603. E-mail: editorial@leisurepublishing.com. Website: www.blueridgecountry.com. **Contact:** Cora Ellen Modisett, editor. **75% freelance written.** Bimonthly magazine. "The magazine is designed to celebrate the history, heritage and beauty of the Blue Ridge region. It is aimed at adult, upscale readers who enjoy living or traveling in the mountain regions of Virginia, North Carolina, West Virginia, Maryland, Kentucky, Tennessee, South Carolina, Alabama, and Georgia." Estab. 1988. Circ. 100,000. Pays on publication. Publishes ms an average of 8 months after acceptance. Byline given. Offers $50 kill fee for commissioned pieces only. Buys first, second serial (reprint) rights. Submit seasonal material 6 months in advance. Accepts queries by mail, e-mail, fax. Responds in 2 months. Sample copy for 9×12 SAE with 6 first-class stamps or online. Writer's guidelines online.

Nonfiction "Looking for more backroads travel, first person outdoor recreation pieces, environmental news, baby boomer era, regional history and legend/lore pieces." General interest, historical/nostalgic, personal experience, photo feature, travel. **Buys 25-30 mss/year.** Query with or without published clips or send complete ms. Length: 200-1,500 words. **Pays $50-250 for assigned articles; $25-250 for unsolicited articles.**

Photos Send photos with submission. Reviews transparencies. Buys one-time rights. Pays $25-50/photo. Identification of subjects required.

Columns/Departments Country Roads (shorts on people, destinations, events, travel, ecology, history, antiques, books); Mountain Inns (reviews of inns); Mountain Delicacies (cookbooks and recipes); The Hike; Mountainside (outdoor recreation pieces). **Buys 30-42 mss/year.** Query. **Pays $10-40.**

Tips "Would like to see more pieces dealing with contemporary history (1940s-70s). Freelancers needed for regional departmental shorts and 'macro' issues affecting whole region. Need field reporters from all areas of Blue Ridge region. We are also looking for updates on the Blue Ridge Parkway, Appalachian Trail, national forests, ecological issues, preservation movements."

$ CHRONOGRAM

Luminary Publishing, P.O. Box 459, New Paltz NY 12561. Fax: (914)256-0349. E-mail: info@chronogram.com. Website: www.chronogram.com. **Contact:** Brian K. Mahoney, editor. **50% freelance written.** Monthly magazine covering regional arts and culture. "*Chronogram* features accomplished, literary writing on issues of cultural, spiritual, and idea-oriented interest." Estab. 1994. Circ. 20,000. Pays on publication. Publishes ms an average of 3 months after acceptance. Byline given. Buys one-time rights. Editorial lead time 2 months. Submit seasonal material 3 months in advance. Accepts queries by mail, e-mail. Accepts simultaneous submissions. Responds in 2 weeks to queries; 6-8 weeks to mss. Sample copy and writer's guidelines online.

Nonfiction Book excerpts, essays, exposé, general interest, historical/nostalgic, humor, interview/profile, opinion, personal experience, photo feature, religious, travel. "No health practitioners writing about their own healing modality." **Buys 24 mss/year.** Query with published clips. Length: 1,000-3,500 words. **Pays $75-150.**

Photos State availability with submission. Reviews contact sheets. Buys one-time rights. Negotiates payment individually. Captions required.

Poetry Phillip Levine, poetry editor. Avant-garde, free verse, haiku, traditional.

Tips "The editor's ears are always open for new voices and all story ideas are invited for pitching. *Chronogram* welcomes all voices and viewpoints as long as they are expressed well. We discriminate solely based on the quality of the writing, nothing else. Clear, thoughtful writing on any subject will be considered for publication in *Chronogram*. We publish a good deal of introspective first-person narratives and find that in the absence of objectivity, subjectivity at least is a quantifiable middle ground between ranting opinion and useless facts."

$\boxed{\text{N}}$ $ $ $ $ COWBOYS & INDIANS MAGAZINE

The Premier Magazine of the West, USFR Media Group, 6688 N. Central Expressway, Suite 650, Dallas TX 75206. E-mail: queries@cowboysindians.com. Website: www.cowboysindians.com. **Contact:** Queries. **60% freelance written.** Magazine published 8 times/year covering people and places of the American West. "The Premier Magazine of the West, *Cowboys & Indians* captures the romance, drama, and grandeur of the American frontier—both past and present—like no other publication. Undeniably exclusive, the magazine covers a broad range of lifestyle topics: art, home interiors, travel, fashion, Western film, and Southwestern cuisine." Estab. 1993. Circ. 101,000. Pays on publication. Publishes ms an average of 2 months after acceptance. Byline given. Offers 20% kill fee. Buys first North American serial, electronic rights. Editorial lead time 4 months. Submit seasonal material 6 months in advance. Accepts queries by mail, e-mail, fax. Sample copy for $5. Writer's guidelines by e-mail.

Nonfiction Book excerpts, exposé, general interest, historical/nostalgic, interview/profile, photo feature, travel, art. No essays, humor, poetry, or opinion. **Buys 40-50 mss/year.** Query. Length: 500-3,000 words. **Pays $250-5,000 for assigned articles; $250-1,000 for unsolicited articles.**

Photos State availability with submission. Reviews contact sheets, $2\frac{1}{4} \times 2\frac{1}{4}$ transparencies. Buys one-time rights. Negotiates payment individually. Captions, identification of subjects required.

Columns/Departments Art; Travel; Music; Home Interiors, all 200-1,000 words. **Buys 50 mss/year.** Query. **Pays $200-1,500.**

Tips "Our readers are educated, intelligent, and well-read Western enthusiasts, many of whom collect Western Americana, read other Western publications, attend shows, and have discerning tastes. Therefore, articles should assume a certain level of prior knowledge of Western subjects on the part of the reader. Articles should be readable and interesting to the novice and general interest reader as well. Please keep your style lively, above all things, and fast-moving, with snappy beginnings and endings. Wit and humor are always welcome."

$ $ GUESTLIFE

Monterey Bay/New Mexico/El Paso/St. Petersburg/Clearwater/Houston/Vancouver, Desert Publications, Inc., 303 N. Indian Canyon Dr., Palm Springs CA 92262. (760)325-2333. Fax: (760)325-7008. E-mail: steven@palmspringslife.com. Website: www.guestlife.com. **Contact:** Steven R. Biller, editorial director. **95% freelance written.** Annual prestige hotel room magazine covering history, highlights, and activities of the area named (i.e., *Monterey Bay GuestLife*). "*GuestLife* focuses on its respective area and is placed in hotel rooms in that area for the affluent vacationer." Estab. 1979. Pays on publication. Publishes ms an average of 9 months after acceptance. Byline given. Offers 25% kill fee. Buys electronic, all rights. Editorial lead time 4 months. Submit seasonal material 3 months in advance. Accepts queries by e-mail. Responds in 1 month. Sample copy for $10. Writer's guidelines not available.

Nonfiction General interest (regional), historical/nostalgic, photo feature, travel. **Buys 3 mss/year.** Query with published clips. Length: 300-1,500 words. **Pays $100-500.**

Photos State availability with submission. Reviews contact sheets. Buys all rights. Negotiates payment individually. Identification of subjects required.

Fillers Facts. **Buys 3/year.** Length: 50-100 words. **Pays $50-100.**

$ $ NOW AND THEN

The Appalachian Magazine, Center for Appalachian Studies and Services, P.O. Box 70556-ETSU, Johnson City TN 37614. (423)439-7865. Fax: (423)439-7870. E-mail: nowandthen@etsu.edu. Website: cass.etsu.edu/n&t/. Managing Editor: Nancy Fischman. **80% freelance written.** Triannual magazine covering Appalachian region from Southern New York to Northern Mississippi. "*Now & Then* accepts a variety of writing genres: fiction, poetry, nonfiction, essays, interviews, memoirs, and book reviews. All submissions must relate to Appalachia and to the issue's specific theme. Our readership is educated and interested in the region." Estab. 1984. Circ. 1,000. Pays on publication. Publishes ms an average of 4 months after acceptance. Byline given. Buys all, holds copyright rights. Editorial lead time 6 months. Accepts queries by mail, e-mail, fax. Accepts simultaneous submissions. Responds in 5 months. Sample copy for $5. Writer's guidelines online.

Nonfiction Book excerpts, essays, general interest, historical/nostalgic, humor, interview/profile, opinion, personal experience, photo feature, book reviews from and about Appalachia. "We don't consider articles which have nothing to do with Appalachia or articles which blindly accept and employ regional stereotypes (dumb hillbillies, poor and downtrodden hillfolk, and miners)." Query with published clips. Length: 1,000-2,500 words. **Pays $30-250 for assigned articles; $30-100 for unsolicited articles.** Sometimes pays expenses of writers on assignment.

Reprints Send ms with rights for sale noted and information about when and where the material previously appeared. Pays 100% of amount paid for original article (typically $15-60).

Photos State availability with submission. Buys one-time rights. Offers no additional payment for photos accepted with ms. Captions, identification of subjects required.

Fiction "Fiction has to relate to Appalachia and to the issue's theme in some way." Adventure, ethnic, experimental, fantasy, historical, humorous, mainstream, slice-of-life vignettes, excerpted novel, prose poem. "Absolutely has to relate to Appalachian theme. Can be about adjustment to new environment, themes of leaving and returning, for instance. Nothing unrelated to region." **Buys 3-4 mss/year.** Send complete ms. Length: 750-2,500 words. **Pays $30-100.**

Poetry Free verse, haiku, light verse, traditional. "No stereotypical work about the region. I want to be surprised and embraced by the language, the ideas, even the form." **Buys 25-30 poems/year.** Submit maximum 5 poems. **Pays $10.**

Tips "Get a copy of the magazine and read it. Then make sure your submission has a connection to Appalachia (check out http://cass.etsu.edu/cass/apregion.htm) and fits in with an upcoming theme."

SOUTHERN LIVING

Southern Progress Corp., 2100 Lakeshore Dr., Birmingham AL 35209. (205)445-6000. Fax: (205)445-6700. E-mail: sara_askew_jones@timeinc.com. Website: www.southernliving.com. Editor: John Floyd. Managing Editor: Clay Norden. **Contact:** Sara Askew Jones. Monthly magazine covering the southern lifestyle. Publication addressing the tastes and interest of contemporary southerners. Estab. 1966. Circ. 2,526,799. Buys all rights. Editorial lead time 3 months. Accepts queries by mail. Sample copy for $4.99 at newsstands. Writer's guidelines by e-mail.

N $ $ $ $ SUNSET MAGAZINE

Sunset Publishing Corp., 80 Willow Rd., Menlo Park CA 94025-3691. (650)321-3600. Fax: (650)327-7537. E-mail: travelquery@sunset.com. Website: www.sunset.com. Monthly magazine covering the lifestyle of the Western states. "*Sunset* is a Western lifestyle publication for educated, active consumers. Editorial provides localized information on gardening and travel, food and entertainment, home building, and remodeling." Freelance articles should be timely and only about the 13 Western states. Garden section accepts queries by mail. Travel section prefers queries by e-mail. **Pays on acceptance.** Byline given. Writer's guidelines online.

Nonfiction "Travel items account for the vast majority of *Sunset*'s freelance assignments, although we also contract out some short garden items. However *Sunset* is largely staff-written." Travel (in the West). **Buys 50-75 mss/year.** Query. Length: 550-750 words. **Pays $1/word.**

Columns/Departments Building & Crafts, Food, Garden, Travel (length: 300-350 words). Direct queries to specific editorial department.

Tips "Here are some subjects regularly treated in *Sunset*'s stories and Travel Guide items: Outdoor recreation (bike tours, bird-watching spots, walking or driving tours of historic districts); indoor adventures (new museums and displays, hands-on science programs at aquariums or planetariums, specialty shopping); special events (festivals that celebrate a region's unique social, cultural, or agricultural heritage). Also looking for great weekend getaways, backroad drives, urban adventures and culinary discoveries such as ethnic dining enclaves. Planning and assigning begins a year before publication date."

N $ $ Y'ALL

The Magazine of Southern People, GRM, LLC, P.O. Box 1217, Oxford MS 38655. (662)236-1928. E-mail: mail@yall.com. Website: yall.com. **Contact:** Molly Fergusson, Managing Editor. **20% freelance written.** Bimonthly magazine covering the south and its people. Y'All features celebrities from the south, and extraordinary southerners. Estab. 2003. Circ. 100,000. Pays on publication. Publishes ms an average of 2 months after acceptance. Byline given. Offers 25% kill fee. Editorial lead time 3 months. Submit seasonal material 4 months in advance. Accepts queries by mail, e-mail. Accepts simultaneous submissions. Responds in 3 weeks to queries; 1 month to mss. Sample copy not available. Writer's guidelines online.

Nonfiction General interest, historical/nostalgic, humor, interview/profile, photo feature, South. Does not want fiction or poetry. **Buys 15 mss/year.** Query with published clips. **Pays $50-400.** Sometimes pays expenses of writers on assignment.

Photos Carroll Moore, Art Director. Send photos with submission. Reviews GIF or JPEG files. Buys one-time rights. Captions, identification of subjects, model releases required.

N YANKEE

Yankee Publishing, Inc., P.O. Box 520, Dublin NH 03444-0520. (603)563-8111. Fax: (603)563-8252. E-mail: queries@yankeepub.com. Website: www.yankeemagazine.com. Editor: Michael Carlton. **Contact:** (Ms.) Sam Darley, editorial assistant. **60% freelance written.** Monthly magazine covering New England. "Our mission is to express and perhaps, indirectly, preserve the New England culture—and to do so in an entertaining way. Our audience is national and has 1 thing in common—it loves New England." Estab. 1935. Circ. 500,000. Pays within 1 month of acceptance. Publishes ms an average of 10 months after acceptance. Byline given. Offers kill fee. Buys all rights. Submit seasonal material 1 year in advance. Accepts queries by mail. Accepts simultaneous submissions. Responds in 2 months to queries. Writer's guidelines for #10 SASE.

- Include SASE for a response. Does not respond to e-mail queries unless interested.

Nonfiction Essays, general interest, interview/profile. "No 'good old days' pieces, no dialect, humor or anything outside New England!" **Buys 30 mss/year.** Query with published clips and SASE. Length: Not to exceed 2,500 words. **Pays per assignment.** Pays expenses of writers on assignment when appropriate.

Photos Leonard Loria, art director. Reviews contact sheets, transparencies. Buys one-time rights. Identification of subjects required.

Columns/Departments Food; Home; Travel.

Tips "Submit lots of ideas. Don't censor yourself—let us decide whether an idea is good or bad. We might surprise you. Remember we've been publishing for 65 years, so chances are we've already done every 'classic' New England subject. Try to surprise us—it isn't easy. Study the ones we publish—the format should be apparent. It is to your advantage to read several issues of the magazine before sending us a query or a manuscript. *Yankee* does not publish fiction, poetry, or cartoons as a routine format, nor do we solicit submissions."

ALABAMA

$ $ ALABAMA HERITAGE

University of Alabama, Box 870342, Tuscaloosa AL 35487-0342. (205)348-7467. Fax: (205)348-7473. Website: www.alabamaheritage.com. **Contact:** Donna L. Cox, editor. **90% freelance written.** "*Alabama Heritage* is a nonprofit historical quarterly published by the University of Alabama and the Alabama Department of Archives and History for the intelligent lay reader. We are interested in lively, well-written, and thoroughly researched articles on Alabama/Southern history and culture. Readability and accuracy are essential." Estab. 1986. Pays on publication. Byline given. Buys all rights. Accepts queries by mail, e-mail. Sample copy for $6, plus $2.50 for shipping. Writer's guidelines for #10 SASE or online.

Nonfiction Buys 12-16 feature mss/year and 10-14 short pieces. Historical. "We do not publish fiction, poetry, book reviews, articles on current events or living artists, and personal/family reminiscences." Query. Length: 750-4,000 words. **Pays $50-350.** Sends 10 copies to each author.

Photos Reviews contact sheets. Buys one-time rights. Identification of subjects required.

Tips "Authors need to remember that we regard history as a fascinating subject, not as a dry recounting of dates and facts. Articles that are lively and engaging, in addition to being well researched, will find interested readers among our editors. No term papers, please. All areas are open to freelance writers. Best approach is a written query."

$ $ ALABAMA LIVING

Alabama Rural Electric Assn., P.O. Box 244014, Montgomery AL 36124. (334)215-2732. Fax: (334)215-2733. E-mail: info@areapower.com. Website: www.alabamaliving.com. Editor: Darryl Gates. **Contact:** Editor. **80% freelance written.** Monthly magazine covering topics of interest to rural and suburban Alabamians. "Our magazine is an editorially balanced, informational and educational service to members of rural electric cooperatives. Our mix regularly includes Alabama history, Alabama features, gardening, outdoor, and consumer pieces." Estab. 1948. Circ. 380,000. **Pays on acceptance.** Byline given. Not copyrighted. Editorial lead time 4 months. Submit seasonal material 4 months in advance. Accepts queries by mail, e-mail. Accepts simultaneous submissions. Responds in 1 month to queries. Sample copy for free.

- Break in with a bit of history or nostalgia about Alabama or the Southeast and pieces about "little-known" events in Alabama history or "little-known" sites.

Nonfiction Historical/nostalgic (rural-oriented), inspirational, personal experience (Alabama). Special issues: Gardening (March); Travel (April); Home Improvement (May); Holiday Recipes (December). **Buys 20 mss/year.** Send complete ms. Length: 500-750 words. **Pays $250 minimum for assigned articles; $100 minimum for unsolicited articles.**

Reprints Send ms with rights for sale noted. Pays $75.

ALASKA

$ $ $ ALASKA

Exploring Life on the Last Frontier, 301 Arctic Slope Ave., Suite 300, Anchorage AK 99518. (907)272-6070. E-mail: luke.smith@alaskamagazine.com. Website: www.alaskamagazine.com. **Contact:** Luke Smith, editor. **70% freelance written.** Eager to work with new/unpublished writers. Magazine published 10 times/year covering topics "uniquely Alaskan." Estab. 1935. Circ. 180,000. Pays on publication. Publishes ms an average of 6 months after acceptance. Byline given. Buys first, one-time rights. Submit seasonal material 1 year in advance. Accepts queries by mail. Responds in 2 months. Sample copy for $3 and 9×12 SAE with 7 first-class stamps. Writer's guidelines online.

O→ Break in by "doing your homework. Make sure a similar story has not appeared in the magazine within the last 5 years. It must be about Alaska."

Nonfiction Historical/nostalgic, humor, interview/profile, personal experience, photo feature, travel, adventure, outdoor recreation (including hunting, fishing), Alaska destination stories. No fiction or poetry. **Buys 40 mss/year.** Query. Length: 100-2,500 words. **Pays $100-1,250.**

Photos Send photos with submission. Reviews 35mm or larger transparencies and slides labeled with your name. Captions, identification of subjects required.

Tips "We're looking for top-notch writing—original, well researched, lively. Subjects must be distinctly Alaskan. A story on a mall in Alaska, for example, won't work for us; every state has malls. If you've got a story about a Juneau mall run by someone who is also a bush pilot and part-time trapper, maybe we'd be interested. The point is *Alaska* stories need to be vivid, focused and unique. Alaska is like nowhere else—we need our stories to be the same way."

ARIZONA

$ $ $ ARIZONA HIGHWAYS

2039 W. Lewis Ave., Phoenix AZ 85009-9988. (602)712-2024. Fax: (602)254-4505. E-mail: queryeditor@azhighways.com. Website: www.arizonahighways.com. **Contact:** Beth Deveny, senior editor. **100% freelance written.** Magazine that is state-owned, designed to help attract tourists into and through Arizona. Estab. 1925. Circ. 425,000. **Pays on acceptance.** Buys first North American serial rights. Accepts queries by mail, e-mail, fax. Responds in 1 month. Sample copy not available. Writer's guidelines online.

O→ Break in with "a concise query written with flair, backed by impressive clips that reflect the kind of writing that appears in *Arizona Highways*. The easiest way to break into the magazine for writers new to us is to propose short items for the Off-Ramp section or submit 750-word pieces for the Along the Way column."

Nonfiction Feature subjects include narratives and exposition dealing with history, anthropology, nature, wildlife, armchair travel, out of the way places, small towns, Old West history, Indian arts and crafts, travel, etc. Travel articles are experience-based. All must be oriented toward Arizona. "We deal with professionals only, so include a list of current credits." **Buys 50 mss/year.** Query with a lead paragraph and brief outline of story. Length: 600-1,800 words. **Pays up to $1/word.** Pays expenses of writers on assignment.

Photos "We use transparencies of medium format, 4×5, and 35mm when appropriate to the subject matter, or they display exceptional quality or content. If submitting 35mm, we prefer 100 ISO or slower. Each transparency must be accompanied by information attached to each photograph: where, when, what. No photography will be reviewed by the editors unless the photographer's name appears on each and every transparency." Peter Ensenberger, director of photography. Buys one-time rights. Pays $125-600.

Columns/Departments Focus on Nature (short feature in first or third person dealing with the unique aspects of a single species of wildlife), 800 words; Along the Way (short essay dealing with life in Arizona, or a personal experience keyed to Arizona), 750 words; Back Road Adventure (personal back-road trips, preferably off the beaten path and outside major metro areas), 1,000 words; Hike of the Month (personal experiences on trails anywhere in Arizona), 500 words. **Pays $50-1,000, depending on department.**

▣ The online magazine carries original content not found in the print edition. Contact: Beth Deveny, senior editor.

Tips "Writing must be of professional quality, warm, sincere, in-depth, well peopled, and accurate. Avoid themes that describe first trips to Arizona, the Grand Canyon, the desert, Colorado River running, etc. Emphasis is to be on Arizona adventure and romance as well as flora and fauna, when appropriate, and themes that can be photographed. Double check your manuscript for accuracy. Our typical reader is a 50-something person with the time, the inclination, and the means to travel."

📖 $ $ $ ARIZONA MONTHLY

Metro Media Group, LLC, 2400 E. Arizona Biltmore Circle, Suite 1170, Phoenix AZ 85016. (602)522-8100. E-mail: info@arizonamonthly.net. Website: www.arizonamonthly.net. Editor: Leigh Flayton. **Contact:** Jeff Ficker, managing editor. **75% freelance written.** Monthly magazine. "Arizona Monthly celebrates the state that is our home." Estab. 2003. Pays on publication. Publishes ms an average of 5 months after acceptance. Byline given. Buys all rights. Editorial lead time 5 months. Submit seasonal material 6 months in advance. Accepts queries by mail, e-mail. Accepts simultaneous submissions. Sample copy online.

Nonfiction General interest. No columns. Query with published clips. Length: 1,000-3,000 words. **Pays 50¢/word.**

Photos Valerie Moreno. State availability with submission.

Tips "We're looking for smart stories with a strong Arizona angle."

$ $ DESERT LIVING

342 E. Thomas, Phoenix AZ 85012. (602)667-9798. Fax: (602)508-9454. E-mail: david@desertlivingmag.com. Website: www.desertlivingmag.com. **Contact:** David Tyda, editor. **75% freelance written.** Lifestyle and culture magazine published 8 times/year "with an emphasis on modern design, culinary trends, cultural trends, fashion, great thinkers of our time, and entertainment." Estab. 1997. Circ. 50,000. Pays 1 month after publication. Byline given. Offers 50% kill fee. Buys first, electronic rights. Editorial lead time 3 months. Submit seasonal material 3 months in advance. Accepts queries by mail, e-mail, fax. Responds in 3 weeks to queries; 2 months to mss. Sample copy for e-mail request. Writer's guidelines free.

Nonfiction General interest, interview/profile, new product, photo feature, travel, architecture. Query with published clips. Length: 300-1,500 words. **Pays $25-400.**

Photos State availability with submission. Reviews contact sheets, negatives, transparencies, prints. Buys one-time or electronic rights. Negotiates payment individually. Identification of subjects, model releases required.

Columns/Departments See website.

$ $ TUCSON LIFESTYLE

Conley Publishing Group, Ltd., Suite 12, 7000 E. Tanque Verde Rd., Tucson AZ 85715-5318. (520)721-2929. Fax: (520)721-8665. E-mail: tucsonlife@aol.com. **Contact:** Scott Barker, executive editor. **90% freelance written.** Prefers to work with published/established writers. Monthly magazine covering Tucson-related events and topics. Estab. 1982. Circ. 32,000. **Pays on acceptance.** Publishes ms an average of 6 months after acceptance. Byline given. Buys first North American serial rights. Submit seasonal material 1 year in advance. Accepts queries by mail, e-mail, fax. Responds in 2 months to queries; 3 months to mss. Sample copy for $2.95, plus $3 postage. Writer's guidelines free.

   O╌ Features are not open to freelancers.

Nonfiction All stories need a Tucson angle. "Avoid obvious tourist attractions and information that most residents of the Southwest are likely to know. No anecdotes masquerading as articles. Not interested in fish-out-of-water, Easterner-visiting-the-Old-West pieces." **Buys 20 mss/year. Pays $50-500.**

Photos Query about electronic formats. Reviews contact sheets, 2¼×2¼ transparencies, 5×7 prints. Buys one-time rights. Pays $25-100/photo. Identification of subjects required.

Columns/Departments Lifestylers (profiles of interesting Tucsonans). Query. **Pays $100-200.**

Tips "Style is not of paramount importance; good, clean copy with an interesting lead is a must."

CALIFORNIA

Ⓝ $ $ BRENTWOOD MAGAZINE

PTL Productions, 2118 Wilshire Blvd., #1060, Santa Monica CA 90403. (310)390-0251. Fax: (310)390-0261. E-mail: dawnya@brentwoodmagazine.com. Website: www.brentwoodmagazine.com. **Contact:** Dawnya Pring, editor. **100% freelance written.** Bimonthly magazine covering entertainment, business, lifestyles, reviews. "Wanting in-depth interviews with top entertainers, politicians, and similar individuals. Also travel, sports, adventure." Estab. 1995. Circ. 50,000. Pays on publication. Byline given. Editorial lead time 3 months. Submit seasonal material 3 months in advance. Accepts queries by mail, e-mail, phone. Accepts simultaneous submissions. Sample copy for $5. Writer's guidelines available.

   O╌ Break in with "strong editorial pitches on unique personalities, trends, or travel destinations."

Nonfiction Book excerpts, exposé, general interest, historical/nostalgic, humor, interview/profile, new product, opinion, personal experience, photo feature, travel. **Buys 80 mss/year.** Query with published clips. Length: 1,000-2,500 words. **Pays 20¢/word.**

Photos State availability with submission. Reviews contact sheets, negatives, prints. Offers no additional payment for photos accepted with ms. Captions, identification of subjects required.

Columns/Departments Reviews (film/books/theater/museum), 100-500 words; Sports (Southern California angle), 200-600 words. **Buys 20 mss/year.** Query with or without published clips or send complete ms. **Pays 15¢/word.**

Tips "Los Angeles-based writers preferred for most articles."

$ $ $ $ DIABLO MAGAZINE

The Magazine of the East Bay, Diablo Publications, 2520 Camino Diablo, Walnut Creek CA 94597. Fax: (925)943-1045. E-mail: dmail@diablopubs.com. Website: www.diablomag.com. **50% freelance written.** Monthly magazine covering regional travel, food, homestyle, and profiles in Contra Costa and southern Alameda counties and selected areas of Oakland and Berkeley. Estab. 1979. Circ. 45,000. **Pays on acceptance.** Publishes ms an average of 3 months after acceptance. Byline given. Offers 25% kill fee. Buys first rights. Editorial lead time 3 months. Submit seasonal material 5 months in advance. Accepts queries by mail, e-mail, fax. Sample copy and writer's guidelines online.

Nonfiction General interest, interview/profile, new product, photo feature, technical, travel. No restaurant profiles, out of country travel, nonlocal topics. **Buys 60 mss/year.** Query with published clips. Length: 600-3,000 words. **Pays $300-2,000.** Sometimes pays expenses of writers on assignment.

Photos State availability with submission. Buys one-time rights. Negotiates payment individually.

Columns/Departments Education; Parenting; Homestyle; Food; Books; Health; Profiles; Regional Politics. Query with published clips.

Tips "We prefer San Francisco Bay area writers who are familiar with the area."

$ $THE EAST BAY MONTHLY

The Berkeley Monthly, Inc., 1301 59th St., Emeryville CA 94608. (510)658-9811. Fax: (510)658-9902. E-mail: editorial@themonthly.com. **Contact:** Kira Halpern and Kate Rix, co-editors. **95% freelance written.** Monthly tabloid. "We feature distinctive, intelligent articles of interest to *East Bay* readers." Estab. 1970. Circ. 80,000. Pays on publication. Byline given. Buys first, second serial (reprint) rights. Editorial lead time 2+ months. Submit seasonal material 3 months in advance. Accepts queries by mail, e-mail. Accepts simultaneous submissions. Responds in 1 month. Sample copy for $1. Writer's guidelines for #10 SASE or by e-mail.

Nonfiction All articles must have a local angle. Topics include essays (first person), exposés, general interest, humor, interview/profile, personal experience, arts, culture, lifestyles. No fiction or poetry. Query with published clips. Length: 1,500-3,000 words. **Pays $250-700.**

Reprints Send tearsheet and information about when and where the material previously appeared.

Photos State availability with submission. Negotiates payment individually. Identification of subjects required.

Columns/Departments Shopping Around (local retail news), 2,000 words; First Person, 2,000 words. Query with published clips.

$ $FOR SENIORS MAGAZINE

Uptown Marketing Publications, 7309 E. Saddlehorn Way, Orange CA 92869. Fax: (714)744-2883. E-mail: articles@upmarketgroup.com. Website: www.upmarketgroup.com. **Contact:** Joan Yankowitz, editor. Quarterly magazine covering Orange County seniors (health, fitness, home, family, legal, finance, travel, leisure). "*For Seniors Magazine* provides Orange County seniors with timely, in-depth editorial on health, fitness, home, family, careers, legal, finance, travel, leisure topics." Estab. 2004. Circ. 45,000. Pays on publication. Publishes ms an average of 2 months after acceptance. Byline given. Buys first North American serial, electronic rights. Editorial lead time 3 months. Submit seasonal material 3 months in advance. Accepts queries by mail, e-mail, fax. Accepts previously published material. Accepts simultaneous submissions. Responds in 3 months. Sample copy online. Writer's guidelines for #10 SASE or online.

Nonfiction Book excerpts, humor, interview/profile, new product, personal experience, photo feature, travel. **Buys 40 mss/year.** Query with published clips or send complete ms. Length: 1,000-1,200 words. **Pays 10¢/word.**

Photos Reviews contact sheets. Buys one-time rights. Offers no additional payment for photos accepted with ms. Captions, identification of subjects, model releases required.

Columns/Departments Buys 10 mss/year. Query with or without published clips or send complete ms. **Pays 10¢/word.**

Fillers Anecdotes, facts, gags to be illustrated by cartoonist, short humor. **Buys 30/year.** Length: 100-300 words. **Pays 10¢/word.**

$ $FORTY PLUS MAGAZINE

Uptown Marketing Publications, 7309 E. Saddlehorn Way, Orange CA 92869. Fax: (714)744-2883. E-mail: articles@upmarketgroup.com. Website: www.upmarketgroup.com. **Contact:** Joan Yankowitz, editor. **100% freelance written.** Quarterly magazine covering Orange City baby boomers. "*Forty Plus Magazine* provides Orange County California baby boomers with timely, in-depth editorial on health, fitness, home, family, careers, legal, finance, travel, leisure topics." Estab. 2004. Circ. 45,000. Pays on publication. Publishes ms an average of 2 months after acceptance. Byline given. Buys first North American serial, second serial (reprint), electronic rights. Editorial lead time 3 months. Submit seasonal material 3 months in advance. Accepts queries by mail, e-mail, fax. Accepts previously published material. Accepts simultaneous submissions. Responds in 3 months. Sample copy online. Writer's guidelines for #10 SASE or online.

Nonfiction Book excerpts, humor, interview/profile, new product, personal experience, photo feature, travel. **Buys 40 mss/year.** Query with published clips or send complete ms. Length: 1,000-1,200 words. **Pays 10¢/word.**

Photos State availability with submission. Reviews contact sheets. Buys one-time rights. Offers no additional payment for photos accepted with ms. Captions, identification of subjects, model releases required.

Columns/Departments Buys 10 mss/year. Query with or without published clips or send complete ms. **Pays 10¢/word.**

Fillers Anecdotes, facts, gags to be illustrated by cartoonist, short humor. **Buys 30/year.** Length: 100-300 words. **Pays 10¢/word.**

$ $ ORANGE COAST MAGAZINE

The Magazine of Orange County, Orange Coast Kommunications, Inc., 3701 Birch St., Suite 100, Newport Beach CA 92660. (949)862-1133. Fax: (949)862-0133. Website: www.orangecoastmagazine.com. **Contact:** Tina Borgatta, editor. **90% freelance written.** Monthly magazine ''designed to inform and enlighten the educated, upscale residents of Orange County, California; highly graphic and well researched.'' Estab. 1974. Circ. 52,000. Pays on publication. Publishes ms an average of 4 months after acceptance. Byline given. Offers 20% kill fee. Buys first North American serial rights. Editorial lead time 5 months. Submit seasonal material 6 months in advance. Accepts queries by mail. Accepts simultaneous submissions. Responds in 3 months. Sample copy for #10 SASE and 6 first-class stamps. Writer's guidelines for #10 SASE.

    ○┱ Break in with Short Cuts (topical briefs of about 250 words).

Nonfiction Absolutely no phone queries. General interest (with Orange County focus), inspirational, interview/profile (prominent Orange County citizens), personal experience, religious, guides to activities and services. Special issues: Health, Beauty, and Fitness (January); Dining (March); International Travel (April); Home Design (June); Family/Education (August); Arts (September); Local Travel (October). ''We do not accept stories that do not have specific Orange County angles. We want profiles on local people, stories on issues going on in our community, and informational stories using Orange County-based sources. We cannot emphasize the local angle enough.'' **Buys up to 65 mss/year.** Query with published clips. Length: 1,000-2,000 words. **Pays 30¢/word for assigned articles.**

Photos State availability with submission. Buys one-time rights. Negotiates payment individually. Captions, identification of subjects required.

Columns/Departments Short Cuts (stories for the front of the book that focus on Orange County issues, people, and places), 150-250 words. **Buys up to 25 mss/year.** Query with published clips. **Pays 30¢/word.**

Tips ''We're looking for more local personality profiles, analysis of current local issues, and local takes on national issues. Most features are assigned to writers we've worked with before. Don't try to sell us 'generic' journalism. *Orange Coast* prefers articles with specific and unusual angles focused on Orange County. A lot of freelance writers ignore our Orange County focus. We get far too many generalized manuscripts.''

$ $ PALM SPRINGS LIFE

The California Prestige Magazine, Desert Publications, Inc., 303 N. Indian Canyon, Palm Springs CA 92262. (760)325-2333. Fax: (760)325-7008. E-mail: steven@palmspringslife.com. **Contact:** Steven R. Biller, editor. **80% freelance written.** Monthly magazine covering ''affluent Palm Springs-area desert resorts. *Palm Springs Life* celebrates the good life.'' Estab. 1958. Circ. 20,000. Pays on publication. Publishes ms an average of 3 months after acceptance. Byline given. Offers 20% kill fee. Buys one-time rights (negotiable). Submit seasonal material 6 months in advance. Responds in 4-6 weeks to queries. Sample copy for $3.95. Writer's guidelines not available.

    ● Increased focus on desert style, home, fashion, art, culture, personalities, celebrities.

Nonfiction Book excerpts, essays, interview/profile, feature stories, celebrity, fashion, spa, epicurean. Query with published clips. Length: 500-2,500 words. **Pays $100-500.**

Photos State availability with submission. Reviews contact sheets. Buys one-time rights. Pays $75-350/photo. Captions, identification of subjects, model releases required.

Columns/Departments The Good Life (art, fashion, fine dining, philanthropy, entertainment, luxury living, luxury auto, architecture), 250-750 words. **Buys 12 mss/year.** Query with or without published clips. **Pays $200-350.**

$ $ $ SACRAMENTO MAGAZINE

Sacramento Magazines Corp., 706 56th St., Suite 210, Sacramento CA 95819. (916)452-6200. Fax: (916)452-6061. E-mail: krista@sacmag.com. Website: www.sacmag.com. Managing Editor: Darlena Belushin McKay. **Contact:** Krista Minard, editor. **80% freelance written.** Works with a small number of new/unpublished writers each year. Monthly magazine with a strictly local angle on local issues, human interest and consumer items for readers in the middle to high income brackets. Prefers to work with writers local to Sacramento area. Estab. 1975. Circ. 50,000. Pays on publication. Publishes ms an average of 3 months after acceptance. Generally buys shared North American serial rights and electronic rights. Accepts queries by mail. Responds in 3 months. Sample copy for $4.50. Writer's guidelines for #10 SASE.

    ○┱ Break in with submissions to UpFront.

Nonfiction Local issues vital to Sacramento quality of life. ''No e-mail, fax, or phone queries will be answered.''

Buys 5 unsolicited feature mss/year. Query. Length: 1,500-3,000 words, depending on author, subject matter and treatment. **Pays $400 and up.** Sometimes pays expenses of writers on assignment.

Photos Send photos with submission. Buys one-time rights. Payment varies depending on photographer, subject matter and treatment. Captions, identification of subjects, location and date required.

Columns/Departments Business, home and garden, first person essays, regional travel, gourmet, profile, sports, city arts, health, home and garden, profiles of local people (1,000-1,800 words); UpFront (250-300 words). **Pays $600-800.**

$ $SACRAMENTO NEWS & REVIEW

Chico Community Publishing, 1015 20th St., Sacramento CA 95814. (916)498-1234. Fax: (916)498-7920. E-mail: billf@newsreview.com; beccac@newsreview.com. Website: www.newsreview.com. **Contact:** Tom Walsh, editor; Bill Forman, news editor; Becca Costello, arts and lifestyle editor. **25% freelance written.** Magazine "We are an alternative news and entertainment weekly. We maintain a high literary standard for submissions; unique or alternative slant. Publication aimed at a young, intellectual audience; submissions should have an edge and strong voice. We have a decided preference for stories with a strong local slant." Estab. 1989. Circ. 95,000. Pays on publication. Publishes ms an average of 2 months after acceptance. Byline given. Offers 10% kill fee. Buys first, electronic rights. Editorial lead time 2 months. Submit seasonal material 2 months in advance. Accepts queries by mail, e-mail, fax, phone. Accepts simultaneous submissions. Responds in 1 month to queries; 2 months to mss. Sample copy for 50¢.

Nonfiction Essays, exposé, general interest, humor, interview/profile, personal experience. Does not want to see travel, product stories, business profile. **Buys 20-30 mss/year.** Query with published clips. Length: 750-5,000 words. **Pays $40-500.** Sometimes pays expenses of writers on assignment.

Photos State availability with submission. Reviews 8×10 prints. Buys one-time rights. Negotiates payment individually. Identification of subjects required.

Columns/Departments In the Mix (CD/TV/book reviews), 150-750 words. **Buys 10-15 mss/year.** Query with published clips. **Pays $10-200.**

$ $SAN DIEGO MAGAZINE

San Diego Magazine Publishing Co., 1450 Front St., San Diego CA 92101. (619)230-9292. Fax: (619)230-0490. E-mail: tblair@sandiegomag.com. Website: www.sandiegomag.com. **Contact:** Tom Blair, editor-in-chief. **30% freelance written.** Monthly magazine. "We produce informative and entertaining features and investigative reports about politics; community and neighborhood issues, lifestyle, sports, design, dining, arts, and other facets of life in San Diego." Estab. 1948. Circ. 55,000. Pays on publication. Publishes ms an average of 2 months after acceptance. Byline given. Offers 25% kill fee. Buys first North American serial, second serial (reprint) rights. Editorial lead time 2 months. Submit seasonal material 4 months in advance. Accepts simultaneous submissions.

Nonfiction Exposé, general interest, historical/nostalgic, how-to, interview/profile, travel, lifestyle. **Buys 12-24 mss/year.** Query with published clips or send complete ms. Length: 1,000-3,000 words. **Pays $250-750.** Sometimes pays expenses of writers on assignment.

Photos State availability with submission. Buys one-time rights. Offers no additional payment for photos accepted with ms.

$ $ $ $SAN FRANCISCO

Focus on the Bay Area, 243 Vallejo St., San Francisco CA 94111. (415)398-2800. Fax: (415)398-6777. Website: www.sanfran.com. **Contact:** Bruce Kelley, editor-in-chief. **50% freelance written.** Prefers to work with published/established writers. Monthly city/regional magazine. Estab. 1968. Circ. 180,000. Pays on publication. Publishes ms an average of 2 months after acceptance. Byline given. Offers 25% kill fee. Submit seasonal material 5 months in advance. Responds in 2 months. Sample copy for $3.95.

Nonfiction All stories should relate in some way to the San Francisco Bay Area (travel excepted). Exposé, interview/profile, travel, arts, politics, public issues, sports, consumer affairs. Query with published clips. Length: 200-4,000 words. **Pays $100-2,000 and some expenses.**

Ⓝ $ $ $SAN JOSE

The Magazine for Silicon Valley, Renaissance Publications, Inc., 25 Metro Dr., Suite 550, San Jose CA 95110. (408)975-9300. Fax: (408)975-9900. E-mail: gilbert@sanjosemagazine.com. Website: www.sanjosemagazine.com. Managing Editor: Jodi Engle. **Contact:** Gilbert Sangari, publisher/editor. **10% freelance written.** Monthly magazine. "As the lifestyle magazine for those living at the center of the technological revolution, we cover the people and places that make Silicon Valley the place to be for the new millennium. All stories must have a local angle, though they should be of national relevance." Estab. 1997. Circ. 60,000. Pays on publication. Publishes ms an average of 3 months after acceptance. Byline given. Offers 10% kill fee. Buys first North

American serial rights. Pays a flat $25 electronic rights fee. Editorial lead time 18 weeks. Submit seasonal material 6 months in advance. Accepts queries by mail, e-mail, fax. Accepts simultaneous submissions. Responds in 1 month to queries. Sample copy for $5. Writer's guidelines for #10 SASE.

- O— "Get your feet wet by writing smaller pieces (200-500 words). Writers can get into my good graces by agreeing to write some of our unsigned pieces. What impresses the editor the most is meeting the assigned length and meeting deadlines."

Nonfiction General interest, interview/profile, photo feature, travel. "No technical, trade, or articles without a tie-in to Silicon Valley." **Buys 12 mss/year.** Query with published clips. Length: 1,000-2,000 words. **Pays 35¢/word.**

Photos State availability with submission. Offers no additional payment for photos accepted with ms. Captions, identification of subjects, model releases required.

Columns/Departments Fast Forward (a roundup of trends and personalities and news that has Silicon Valley buzzing; topics include health, history, politics, nonprofits, education, Q&As, business, technology, dining, wine and fashion). **Buys 5 mss/year.** Query. **Pays 35¢/word.**

Tips "Study our magazine for style and content. Nothing is as exciting as reading a tightly written query and discovering a new writer."

COLORADO

$ $ $ ASPEN MAGAZINE

Ridge Publications, 720 E. Durant Ave., Suite E8, Aspen CO 81611. (970)920-4040. Fax: (970)920-4044. E-mail: judge@aspenmagazine.com. Website: www.aspenmagazine.com. Editor: Janet C. O'Grady. **Contact:** Liz Judge, managing editor. **30% freelance written.** Bimonthly magazine covering Aspen and the Roaring Fork Valley. "All things Aspen, written in a sophisticated, insider-oriented tone." Estab. 1974. Circ. 20,000. Pays within 3 months of publication. Byline sometimes given. Offers 10% kill fee. Buys first North American serial, electronic rights. Editorial lead time 2 months. Accepts queries by mail, e-mail, fax. Accepts simultaneous submissions. Responds in 2 months to queries; 6 months to mss. Sample copy for 9×12 SAE and 10 first-class stamps. Writer's guidelines for #10 SASE.

- Responds only to submissions including a SASE.

Nonfiction Essays, new product, photo feature, historical, environmental and local issues, architecture and design, sports and outdoors, arts. "We do not publish general interest articles without a strong Aspen hook. We do not publish 'theme' (skiing in Aspen) or anniversary (40th year of Aspen Music Festival) articles, fiction, poetry, or prewritten manuscripts." **Buys 30-60 mss/year.** Query with published clips. Length: 50-4,000 words. **Pays $50-1,000.** Sometimes pays expenses of writers on assignment.

Photos State availability with submission. Reviews contact sheets, negatives, transparencies, prints. Identification of subjects, model releases required.

$ $ STEAMBOAT MAGAZINE

P.O. Box 881659, Steamboat Springs CO 80488. (970)871-9413. Fax: (970)871-1922. E-mail: info@steamboatmagazine.com. Website: www.steamboatmagazine.com. **Contact:** Stacey Kramer, editor. **80% freelance written.** Semiannual magazine "showcasing the history, people, lifestyles, and interests of Northwest Colorado. Our readers are generally well-educated, well-traveled, upscale, active people visiting our region to ski in winter and recreate in summer. They come from all 50 states and many foreign countries. Writing should be fresh, entertaining, and informative." Estab. 1978. Circ. 30,000. Pays 50% on acceptance, 50% on publication. Publishes ms an average of 6 months after acceptance. Byline given. Buys exclusive rights. Submit seasonal material 1 year in advance. Accepts queries by mail, e-mail, fax, phone. Responds in 3 months to queries. Sample copy for $4.95 and SAE with 10 first-class stamps. Writer's guidelines free.

Nonfiction Book excerpts, essays, general interest, historical/nostalgic, humor, interview/profile, photo feature, travel. **Buys 10-15 mss/year.** Query with published clips. Length: 150-1,500 words. **Pays $50-300 for assigned articles.** Sometimes pays expenses of writers on assignment.

Photos "Prefers to review viewing platforms, JPEGs, and dupes. Will request original transparencies when needed." State availability with submission. Buys one-time rights. Pays $50-250/photo. Captions, identification of subjects required.

Tips "Stories must be about Steamboat Springs and the Yampa Valley to be considered. We're looking for new angles on ski/snowboard stories in the winter and activity-related stories all year round. Please query first with ideas to make sure subjects are fresh and appropriate. We try to make subjects and treatments 'timeless' in nature because our magazine is a 'keeper' with a multi-year shelf life."

CONNECTICUT

$ $ $ CONNECTICUT MAGAZINE

Journal Register Co., 35 Nutmeg Dr., Trumbull CT 06611. (203)380-6600. Fax: (203)380-6610. E-mail: dsalm@co nnecticutmag.com. Website: www.connecticutmag.com. Editor: Charles Monagan. **Contact:** Dale Salm, managing editor. **75% freelance written.** Prefers to work with published/established writers who know the state and live/have lived here. Monthly magazine "for an affluent, sophisticated, suburban audience. We want only articles that pertain to living in Connecticut." Estab. 1971. Circ. 93,000. Pays on publication. Publishes ms an average of 4 months after acceptance. Byline given. Offers 20% kill fee. Buys first North American serial rights. Submit seasonal material 4 months in advance. Accepts queries by mail, e-mail, fax. Responds in 6 weeks to queries. Sample copy not available. Writer's guidelines for #10 SASE.

> O➔ Freelancers can best break in with "First" (short, trendy pieces with a strong Connecticut angle); find a story that is offbeat and write it in a lively, interesting manner.

Nonfiction Interested in seeing hard-hitting investigative pieces and strong business pieces (not advertorial). Book excerpts, exposé, general interest, interview/profile, topics of service to Connecticut readers. Special issues: Dining/entertainment, Northeast/travel, home/garden, and Connecticut bride twice/year. Also, business (January) and healthcare once/year. No personal essays. **Buys 50 mss/year.** Query with published clips. Length: 3,000 words maximum. **Pays $600-1,200.** Sometimes pays expenses of writers on assignment.

Photos Send photos with submission. Reviews contact sheets, transparencies. Buys one-time rights. Pays $50 minimum/photo. Identification of subjects, model releases required.

Columns/Departments Business, Health, Politics, Connecticut Calendar, Arts, Dining Out, Gardening, Environment, Education, People, Sports, Media, From the Field (quirky, interesting regional stories with broad appeal). Length: 1,500-2,500 words. **Buys 50 mss/year.** Query with published clips. **Pays $400-700.**

Fillers Short pieces about Connecticut trends, curiosities, interesting short subjects, etc. Length: 150-400 words. **Pays $75-150.**

> ▣ The online magazine carries original content not found in the print edition. Contact: Charles Monagan, online editor.

Tips "Make certain your idea has not been covered to death by the local press and can withstand a time lag of a few months. Again, we don't want something that has already received a lot of press."

Ⓝ $ $ $ $ NORTHEAST MAGAZINE

The Hartford Courant, 285 Broad St., Hartford CT 06115-2510. (860)241-3700. Fax: (860)241-3853. E-mail: northeast@courant.com. Website: www.ctnow.com. Editor: Jennifer Frank. **Contact:** Stephanie Summers or David Funkhouser. **30% freelance written.** Weekly magazine for a Connecticut audience. Estab. 1982. Circ. 281,000. **Pays on acceptance.** Publishes ms an average of 5 months after acceptance. Byline given. Accepts queries by mail. Responds in 3 months to queries. Writer's guidelines available.

Nonfiction "We are primarily interested in hard-hitting nonfiction articles spun off the news and compelling personal stories. We have a strong emphasis on Connecticut subject matter." General interest (has to have a strong Connecticut tie-in), historical/nostalgic, in-depth investigations of stories behind the news (has to have strong Connecticut tie-in), personal essays (humorous or anecdotal). No poetry. **Buys 40-50 mss/year.** Query. Length: 750-4,000 words. **Pays $200-1,500.**

Photos Most are assigned. "Do not send originals." State availability with submission.

Fiction "We run an occasional fiction issue and more frequently excerpts of soon-to-be published books by Connecticut authors or with Connecticut tie-ins." Length: 750-1,500 words.

Tips "Less space available for all types of writing means our standards for acceptance will be much higher. It is to your advantage to read several issues of the magazine before submitting a manuscript or query. Virtually all our pieces are solicited and assigned by us, with a small percentage of what we publish coming in 'over the transom.'"

DELAWARE

$ $ DELAWARE TODAY

3301 Lancaster Pike, Suite 5C, Wilmington DE 19805. (302)656-1809. Fax: (302)656-5843. E-mail: editors@dela waretoday.com. Website: www.delawaretoday.com. **50% freelance written.** Monthly magazine geared toward Delaware people, places and issues. "All stories must have Delaware slant. No pitches such as Delawareans will be interested in a national topic." Estab. 1962. Circ. 25,000. Pays on publication. Publishes ms an average of 4 months after acceptance. Byline given. Offers 50% kill fee. Buys all rights for 1 year. Editorial lead time 3 months. Submit seasonal material 6 months in advance. Responds in 2 months to queries. Sample copy for $2.95.

Nonfiction Historical/nostalgic, interview/profile, photo feature, lifestyles, issues. Special issues: Newcomer's Guide to Delaware. **Buys 40 mss/year.** Query with published clips. Length: 100-3,000 words. **Pays $50-750 for assigned articles.** Sometimes pays expenses of writers on assignment.

Photos State availability with submission. Buys one-time rights. Negotiates payment individually. Identification of subjects required.

Columns/Departments Business; Health; History; People, all 1,500 words. **Buys 24 mss/year.** Query with published clips. **Pays $150-250.**

Fillers Anecdotes, newsbreaks, short humor. **Buys 10/year.** Length: 100-200 words. **Pays $50-75.**

Tips "No story ideas that we would know about, i.e., a profile of the governor. Best bets are profiles of quirky/unique Delawareans that we'd never know about or think of."

DISTRICT OF COLUMBIA

$ $ WASHINGTON CITY PAPER

2390 Champlain St. NW, Washington DC 20009. (202)332-2100. Fax: (202)332-8500. E-mail: kmarsh@washingtoncitypaper.com. Website: www.washingtoncitypaper.com. **Contact:** Kate Marsh. **50% freelance written.** "Relentlessly local alternative weekly in nation's capital covering city and regional politics, media, and arts. No national stories." Estab. 1981. Circ. 93,000. Pays on publication. Publishes ms an average of 6 weeks after acceptance. Byline given. Offers 10% kill fee for assigned stories. Buys first rights. Editorial lead time 7-10 days. Responds in 1 month to queries. Writer's guidelines online.

Nonfiction "Our biggest need for freelancers is in the District Line section of the newspaper: short, well-reported local stories. These range from carefully-drawn profiles to sharp, hooky approaches to reporting on local institutions. We don't want op-ed articles, fiction, poetry, service journalism, or play-by-play accounts of news conferences or events. We also purchase, but more infrequently, longer 'cover-length' stories that fit the criteria stated above. Full guide to freelance submissions can be found on website." **Buys 100 mss/year.** Query by e-mail with published clips or send complete ms. Length: District Line: 800-1,500 words; Covers: 2,500-10,000 words. **Pays 10-40¢/word.** Sometimes pays expenses of writers on assignment.

Photos Make appointment to show portfolio to Pete Morelewicz, art director. Pays minimum of $75.

Columns/Departments Music Writing (eclectic). **Buys 100 mss/year.** Query with published clips or send complete ms. **Pays 10-40¢/word.**

Tips "Think local. Great ideas are a plus. We are willing to work with anyone who has a strong idea, regardless of vita."

$ $ $ THE WASHINGTONIAN

1828 L St. NW, Suite 200, Washington DC 20036. (202)296-3600. E-mail: editorial@washingtonian.com. Website: www.washingtonian.com. **20-25% freelance written.** Monthly magazine. "Writers should keep in mind that we are a general interest city and regional magazine. Nearly all our articles have a hard Washington connection. And, please, no political satire." Estab. 1965. Circ. 160,000. Pays on publication. Publishes ms an average of 3 months after acceptance. Byline given. Buys first North American serial, limited, nonexclusive electronic rights. Editorial lead time 10 weeks. Accepts queries by mail, fax. Writer's guidelines online.

Nonfiction Book excerpts, exposé, general interest, historical/nostalgic (with specific Washington, D.C. focus), interview/profile, personal experience, photo feature, travel. **Buys 15-30 mss/year.** Query with published clips. **Pays 50¢/word.** Sometimes pays expenses of writers on assignment.

Columns/Departments First Person (personal experience that somehow illuminates life in Washington area), 650-700 words. **Buys 9-12 mss/year.** Query. **Pays $325.**

Tips "The types of articles we publish include service pieces; profiles of people; investigative articles; rating pieces; institutional profiles; first-person articles; stories that cut across the grain of conventional thinking; articles that tell the reader how Washington got to be the way it is; light or satirical pieces (send the complete manuscript, not the idea, because in this case execution is everything). Subjects of articles include the federal government, local government, dining out, sports, business, education, medicine, fashion, environment, how to make money, how to spend money, real estate, performing arts, visual arts, travel, health, nightlife, home and garden, self-improvement, places to go, things to do, and more. Again, we are interested in almost anything as long as it relates to the Washington area. We don't like puff pieces or what we call 'isn't-it-interesting' pieces. In general, we try to help our readers understand Washington better, to help our readers live better, and to make Washington a better place to live. Also, remember—a magazine article is different from a newspaper story. Newspaper stories start with the most important facts, are written in short paragraphs with a lot of transitions, and usually can be cut from the bottom up. A magazine article usually is divided into sections that are like 400-word chapters of a very short book. The introductory section is very important—it captures the reader's interest and sets the tone for the article. Scenes or anecdotes often are used to draw the reader into the subject matter. The next section then might foreshadow what the article is about without trying to summarize it—you want to make the reader curious. Each succeeding section develops the subject. Any evaluations or conclusions come in the closing section."

FLORIDA

$ $ $ $ BOCA RATON MAGAZINE

JES Publishing, 6413 Congress Ave., Suite 100, Boca Raton FL 33487. (561)997-8683. Fax: (561)997-8909. Website: www.bocamag.com. **Contact:** Marie Speed, editor-in-chief. **70% freelance written.** Bimonthly lifestyle magazine "devoted to the residents of South Florida, featuring fashion, interior design, food, people, places, and issues that shape the affluent South Florida market." Estab. 1981. Circ. 20,000. **Pays on acceptance.** Publishes ms an average of 3 months after acceptance. Byline given. Buys second serial (reprint) rights. Submit seasonal material 7 months in advance. Accepts simultaneous submissions. Responds in 1 month to queries. Sample copy for $4.95 and 10×13 SAE with 10 first-class stamps. Writer's guidelines for #10 SASE.

Nonfiction General interest, historical/nostalgic, humor, interview/profile, photo feature, travel. Special issues: Interior Design (September-October); Real Estate (March-April); Best of Boca (July-August). Query with published clips or send complete ms. Length: 800-2,500 words. **Pays $350-1,500.**

Reprints Send tearsheet. Payment varies.

Photos Send photos with submission.

Columns/Departments Body & Soul (health, fitness and beauty column, general interest); Hitting Home (family and social interactions); History or Arts (relevant to South Florida), all 1,000 words. Query with published clips or send complete ms. **Pays $350-400.**

Tips "We prefer shorter manuscripts, highly localized articles, and excellent art/photography."

$ $ EMERALD COAST MAGAZINE

Rowland Publishing, Inc., 1932 Miccosukee Rd., Tallahassee FL 32308. E-mail: editorial@rowlandinc.com. Website: www.rowlandinc.com. **Contact:** James Call, editor. **50% freelance written.** Bimonthly lifestyle publication celebrating life on Florida's Emerald Coast. "All content has an Emerald Coast (Northwest Florida) connection. This includes Panama City, Seaside, Sandestin, Destin, Fort Walton Beach, and Pensacola." Estab. 2000. Circ. 18,000. **Pays on acceptance.** Publishes ms an average of 3 months after acceptance. Byline given. Buys first North American serial rights. Editorial lead time 4 months. Submit seasonal material 6 months in advance. Accepts queries by mail, e-mail. Accepts previously published material. Accepts simultaneous submissions. Responds in 3 months. Sample copy for $4. Writer's guidelines by e-mail.

Nonfiction All must have an Emerald Coast slant. Book excerpts, essays, historical/nostalgic, inspirational, interview/profile, new product, personal experience, photo feature. No fiction, poetry, travel or general interest. **Buys 10-15 mss/year.** Query with published clips. Length: 1,800-2,000 words. **Pays $100-250.** Pays in contributor copies as special arrangements through publisher.

Photos Send photos with submission. Reviews prints, GIF/JPEG files. Buys one-time rights. Negotiates payment individually. Captions, identification of subjects, model releases required.

Tips "We're looking for fresh ideas and new slants that are related to Florida's Emerald Coast. Because we work so far in advance, it is difficult to be timely, so be sure to give us ideas that aren't too time specific."

$ $ FLORIDA MONTHLY MAGAZINE

Florida Media, Inc., 801 Douglas Ave., Suite 100, Altamonte Springs FL 32714. (407)816-9596. Fax: (407)816-9373. E-mail: exec-editor@floridamagazine.com. Website: www.floridamagazine.com. Publisher: E. Douglas Cifers. Monthly lifestyle magazine covering Florida travel, food and dining, heritage, homes and gardens, and all aspects of Florida lifestyle. Full calendar of events each month. Estab. 1981. Circ. 225,235. Pays on publication. Publishes ms an average of 5 months after acceptance. Byline given. Buys first rights. Editorial lead time 3 months. Submit seasonal material 6 months in advance. Accepts queries by mail, e-mail, fax. Responds in 2 months to queries. Sample copy for $5. Writer's guidelines for #10 SASE.

- Interested in material on areas outside of the larger cities.
- Break in with stories specific to Florida showcasing the people, places, events, and things that are examples of Florida's rich history and culture.

Nonfiction Historical/nostalgic, interview/profile, travel, general Florida interest, out-of-the-way Florida places, dining, attractions, festivals, shopping, resorts, bed & breakfast reviews, retirement, real estate, business, finance, health, recreation, sports. **Buys 50-60 mss/year.** Query with published clips. Length: 500-2,500 words. **Pays $100-400 for assigned articles; $50-250 for unsolicited articles.**

Photos Send photos with submission. Reviews 3×5 color prints and slides. Offers $6/photo. Captions required.

Columns/Departments Golf; Homes & Gardenings; Heritage (all Florida-related), 750 words. **Buys 24 mss/ year.** Query with published clips. **Pays $75-250.**

$FT. MYERS MAGAZINE

And Pat, LLC, 15880 Summerlin Rd., Suite 189, Fort Myers FL 33908. E-mail: ftmyers@optonline.net. Website: www.ftmyersmagazine.com. Director/Designer: Andrew Elias. **Contact:** Pat Simms-Elias, editorial director. **90% freelance written.** Bimonthly magazine covering regional arts and living. Audience: educated, active, successful and creative residents of Fort Myers and Lee County, Florida, and guests at resorts and hotels in Lee County. Content: arts, entertainment, media, travel, sports, health, home. Estab. 2001. Circ. 20,000. Pays on publication. Publishes ms an average of 3 months after acceptance. Byline given. Offers 50% kill fee. Buys one-time, second serial (reprint) rights. Editorial lead time 3 months. Submit seasonal material 3 months in advance. Accepts queries by e-mail. Accepts simultaneous submissions. Responds in 3 months. Writer's guidelines for #10 SASE or by e-mail.

Nonfiction Essays, general interest, historical/nostalgic, how-to, humor, interview/profile, personal experience, reviews, previews, news, informational. **Buys 60-75 mss/year.** Query with or without published clips or send complete ms. Length: 300-1,500 words. **Pays $40-150.** Will pay in copies or in ad barter at writer's request. Sometimes pays expenses of writers on assignment.

Reprints Accepts previously published submissions.

Photos State availability of or send photos with submission. Reviews 4×5 to 8×10 prints. Buys one-time rights. Negotiates payment individually; generally offers $100/photo or art. Captions, identification of subjects required.

Columns/Departments Media: books, music, video, film, theater, Internet, software (news, previews, reviews, interviews, profiles), 300-1,500 words. Lifestyles: art & design, science & technology, house & garden, health & fitness, sports & recreation, travel & leisure, food & drink (news, interviews, previews, reviews, profiles, advice), 300-1,500 words. **Buys 60 mss/year.** Query with or without published clips or send complete ms. **Pays $40-150.**

$ $ $ GULFSHORE LIFE

9051 N. Tamiami Trail, Suite 202, Naples FL 34108. (239)594-9980. Fax: (239)594-9986. E-mail: hobartr@gulfsh orelifemag.com. Website: www.gulfshorelifemag.com. **Contact:** Hobart Rowland, senior editor. **75% freelance written.** Magazine published 10 times/year for "southwest Florida, the workings of its natural systems, its history, personalities, culture, and lifestyle." Estab. 1970. Circ. 35,000. Pays on publication. Publishes ms an average of 4 months after acceptance. Byline given. Submit seasonal material 8 months in advance. Accepts queries by mail, e-mail, fax. Accepts simultaneous submissions. Sample copy for 9×12 SAE and 10 first-class stamps.

Nonfiction All articles must be related to southwest Florida. Historical/nostalgic, interview/profile, issue/trend. **Buys 100 mss/year.** Query with published clips. Length: 500-3,000 words. **Pays $100-1,000.**

Photos Send photos with submission. Reviews 35mm transparencies, 5×7 prints. Buys one-time rights. Pays $50-100. Identification of subjects, model releases required.

Tips "We buy superbly written stories that illuminate southwest Florida personalities, places, and issues. Surprise us!"

$ $ JACKSONVILLE

White Publishing Co., 534 Lancaster St., Jacksonville FL 32204. (904)358-8330. Fax: (904)358-8668. Website: www.jacksonvillemag.com. **Contact:** Joseph White, editor/publisher. **50% freelance written.** Monthly magazine covering life and business in northeast Florida "for upwardly mobile residents of Jacksonville and the Beaches, Orange Park, St. Augustine, and Amelia Island, Florida." Estab. 1985. Circ. 25,000. Pays on publication. Byline given. Offers 25-33% kill fee to writers on assignment. Buys first North American serial, second serial (reprint) rights. Editorial lead time 3 months. Submit seasonal material 4 months in advance. Responds in 6 weeks to queries; 1 month to mss. Sample copy for $5 (includes postage).

Nonfiction All articles must have relevance to Jacksonville and Florida's First Coast (Duval, Clay, St. John's, Nassau, Baker counties). Book excerpts, exposé, general interest, historical/nostalgic, how-to (service articles), humor, interview/profile, personal experience, photo feature, travel, commentary, local business successes, trends, personalities, community issues, how institutions work. **Buys 50 mss/year.** Query with published clips. Length: 1,200-3,000 words. **Pays $50-500 for feature-length pieces.** Sometimes pays expenses of writers on assignment.

Reprints Send photocopy. Payment varies.

Photos State availability with submission. Reviews contact sheets, transparencies. Buys one-time rights. Negotiates payment individually. Captions, model releases required.

Columns/Departments Business (trends, success stories, personalities); Health (trends, emphasis on people, hopeful outlooks); Money (practical personal financial advice using local people, anecdotes and examples); Real Estate/Home (service, trends, home photo features); Travel (weekends; daytrips; excursions locally and regionally), all 1,000-1,200 words; occasional departments and columns covering local history, sports, family issues, etc. **Buys 40 mss/year. Pays $150-250.**

Tips "We are a writer's magazine and demand writing that tells a story with flair."

$ $TALLAHASSEE MAGAZINE

Rowland Publishing, Inc., 1932 Miccosukee Rd., Tallahassee FL 32308. E-mail: editorial@rowlandinc.com. Website: www.rowlandinc.com. **Contact:** James Call, editor. **50% freelance written.** Bimonthly magazine covering life in Florida's Capital Region. "All content has a Tallahassee, Florida connection." Estab. 1978. Circ. 18,000. **Pays on acceptance.** Publishes ms an average of 2 months after acceptance. Byline given. Buys first North American serial rights. Editorial lead time 4 months. Submit seasonal material 6 months in advance. Accepts queries by mail, e-mail. Accepts simultaneous submissions. Responds in 3 months. Sample copy for $4. Writer's guidelines by e-mail.

Nonfiction All must have a Tallahassee slant. Book excerpts, essays, historical/nostalgic, inspirational, interview/profile, new product, personal experience, photo feature, travel, sports, business, Calendar items. No fiction, poetry, travel or general interest. **Buys 15 mss/year.** Query with published clips. Length: 1,000-2,000 words. **Pays $100-250.**

Photos Send photos with submission. Reviews prints, GIF/JPEG files. Buys one-time rights. Negotiates payment individually. Captions, identification of subjects, model releases required.

Tips "We're looking for fresh ideas and new slants that are related to Florida's Capital Region. Because we work so far in advance, it is difficult to be timely, so be sure to give us ideas that aren't too time specific."

GEORGIA

$ $ $ $ATLANTA MAGAZINE

260 Peachtree St., Suite 300, Atlanta GA 30303. (404)527-5500. Fax: (404)527-5575. Website: www.atlantamaga zine.com. Monthly magazine that explores people, pleasures, useful information, regional happenings, restaurants, shopping, etc., for a general adult audience in Atlanta, including subjects in government, sports, pop culture, urban affairs, arts, and entertainment. "*Atlanta* magazine articulates the special nature of Atlanta and appeals to an audience that wants to understand and celebrate the uniqueness of the region. The magazine's mission is to engage our community through provacative writing, authoritative reporting, and superlative design that illuminates the people, trends, and events that define our city." Circ. 69,000. **Pays on acceptance.** Byline given. Offers 25% kill fee. Buys first North American serial rights. Accepts queries by mail. Responds in 3 months to queries. Sample copy online.

Nonfiction General interest, interview/profile, travel. **Buys 36-40 mss/year.** Query with published clips. Length: 1,500-5,000 words. **Pays $300-2,000.** Pays expenses of writers on assignment.

Columns/Departments Essay, travel. **Length:** 1,000-1,500 words. **Buys 30 mss/year.** Query with published clips. **Pays $500.**

Fiction Novel excerpts. Need short stories for 2 annual reading issues—Winter & Summer. "We prefer all fiction to be by Georgia writers and/or have a Georgia/Southern theme. Length: 1,500-5,000 words.

Fillers Buys 80/year. Length: 75-175 words. **Pays $50-100.**

Tips "Writers must know what makes their piece a story rather than just a subject."

$ $ATLANTA TRIBUNE: THE MAGAZINE

Black Atlanta's Business & Politics, L&L Communications, 875 Old Roswell Rd, Suite C-100, Roswell GA 30076. (770)587-0501. Fax: (770)642-6501. E-mail: frobinson@atlantatribune.com. Website: www.atlantatribune.com. **Contact:** Fred Robinson, editor. **30% freelance written.** Monthly magazine covering African-American business, careers, technology, wealth-building, politics, and education. "The *Atlanta Tribune* is written for Atlanta's black executives, professionals, and entrepreneurs with a primary focus of business, careers, technology, wealth-building, politics, and education. Our publication serves as an advisor that offers helpful information and direction to the black entrepreneur." Estab. 1987. Circ. 30,000. Pays on publication. Byline given. Offers 10% kill fee. Buys electronic, all rights. Editorial lead time 3 months. Submit seasonal material 4 months in advance. Accepts queries by e-mail. Responds in 6 weeks to queries. Sample copy online or mail a request. Writer's guidelines online.

○┐ Break in with "the ability to write feature stories that give insight into Black Atlanta's business community, technology, businesses, and career and wealth-building opportunities. Also, stories with real social, political or economic impact."

Nonfiction "Our special sections include Black History; Real Estate; Scholarship Roundup." Book excerpts, how-to (business, careers, technology), interview/profile, new product, opinion, technical. **Buys 100 mss/ year.** Query with published clips. Length: 1,400-2,500 words. **Pays $250-600.** Sometimes pays expenses of writers on assignment.

Photos State availability with submission. Reviews 2¼×2¼ transparencies. Buys one-time rights. Negotiates payment individually. Identification of subjects, model releases required.

Columns/Departments Business; Careers; Technology; Wealth-Building; Politics and Education; all 400-600 words. **Buys 100 mss/year.** Query with published clips. **Pays $100-200.**

Tips "Send a well-written, convincing query by e-mail that demonstrates that you have thoroughly read previous issues and reviewed our online writer's guidelines."

$ $ GEORGIA BACKROADS

(formerly *North Georgia Journal*), Legacy Communications, Inc., P.O. Box 127, Roswell GA 30077. (770)642-5569. E-mail: info@georgiahistory.ws. Website: www.georgiahistory.ws. **Contact:** Olin Jackson, editor/publisher. **70% freelance written.** Quarterly magazine "for readers interested in travel, history, and lifestyles in Georgia." Estab. 1984. Circ. 18,861. Pays on publication. Publishes ms an average of 5 months after acceptance. Byline given. Offers 25% kill fee. Usually buys all rights (negotiable). Editorial lead time 3 months. Submit seasonal material 6 months in advance. Accepts queries by mail, e-mail, fax. Sample copy for 9×12 SAE and 8 first-class stamps or online. Writer's guidelines for #10 SASE.

Nonfiction Historical/nostalgic, how-to (survival techniques, mountain living, do-it-yourself home construction and repairs, etc.), interview/profile (celebrity), personal experience (anything unique or unusual pertaining to Georgia history), photo feature (any subject of a historic nature which can be photographed in a seasonal context, i.e., old mill with brilliant yellow jonquils in foreground), travel (subjects highlighting travel opportunities in north Georgia). Query with published clips. **Pays $75-350.**

Photos Send photos with submission. Reviews contact sheets, transparencies. Rights negotiable. Negotiates payment individually. Captions, identification of subjects, model releases required.

Fiction Novel excerpts.

Tips "Good photography is crucial to acceptance of all articles. Send written queries, then wait for a response. *No telephone calls, please.* The most useful material involves a first-person experience of an individual who has explored a historic site or scenic locale and interviewed a person or persons who were involved with or have first-hand knowledge of a historic site/event. Interviews and quotations are crucial. Articles should be told in the writer's own words."

$ $ GEORGIA MAGAZINE

Georgia Electric Membership Corp., P.O. Box 1707, Tucker GA 30085. (770)270-6950. E-mail: ann.orowski@georgiaemc.com. Website: www.georgiamagazine.org. **Contact:** Ann Orowski, editor. **50% freelance written.** "We are a monthly magazine for and about Georgians, with a friendly, conversational tone and human interest topics." Estab. 1945. Circ. 460,000. Pays on publication. Publishes ms an average of 4 months after acceptance. Byline given. Buys first North American serial, electronic rights. Editorial lead time 2 months. Submit seasonal material 6 months in advance. Accepts simultaneous submissions. Responds in 1 month (if interested) to queries. Sample copy for $2. Writer's guidelines for #10 SASE.

Nonfiction General interest (Georgia-focused), historical/nostalgic, how-to (in the home and garden), humor, inspirational, interview/profile, photo feature, travel. **Buys 24 mss/year.** Query with published clips. Length: 800-1,000 words; 500 words for smaller features and departments. **Pays $150-500.**

Photos State availability with submission. Reviews contact sheets, transparencies, prints. Buys one-time rights. Negotiates payment individually. Identification of subjects, model releases required.

$ $ KNOW ATLANTA MAGAZINE

New South Publishing, 1303 Hightower Trail, Suite 101, Atlanta GA 30350. (770)650-1102. Fax: (770)650-2848. E-mail: editor1@knowatlanta.com. Website: www.knowatlanta.com. **Contact:** Riley McDermid, editor. **80% freelance written.** Quarterly magazine covering the Atlanta area. "Our articles offer information on Atlanta that would be useful to newcomers—homes, schools, hospitals, fun things to do, anything that makes their move more comfortable." Estab. 1986. Circ. 192,000. Pays on publication. Byline given. Offers 100% kill fee. Buys first North American serial rights. Editorial lead time 2 months. Submit seasonal material 2 months in advance. Accepts queries by mail, e-mail, fax. Accepts previously published material. Sample copy for free.

> ○━ "Know the metro Atlanta area, especially hot trends in real estate. Writers who know about international relocation trends and commercial real estate topics are hot."

Nonfiction General interest, how-to (relocate), interview/profile, personal experience, photo feature. No fiction. **Buys 20 mss/year.** Query with clips. Length: 1,000-2,000 words. **Pays $100-500 for assigned articles; $100-300 for unsolicited articles.** Sometimes pays expenses of writers on assignment.

Reprints Accepts previously published submissions.

Photos Send photos with submission, if available. Reviews contact sheets. Buys one-time rights. Negotiates payment individually. Captions, identification of subjects required.

$ $ POINTS NORTH MAGAZINE

Serving Atlanta's Stylish Northside, All Points Interactive Media Corp., 568 Peachtree Pkwy., Cumming GA 30041-6820. (770)844-0969. Fax: (770)844-0968. E-mail: julie@ptsnorth.com. Website: www.ptsnorth.com. **Contact:** Julie Clark, editor. **85% freelance written.** Monthly magazine covering lifestyle (regional). *"Points North is a first-class lifestyle magazine for affluent residents of suburban communities in north metro Atlanta."* Estab. 2000. Circ. 81,000. Pays on publication. Publishes ms an average of 1 month after acceptance. Byline given. Offers negotiable (for assigned articles only) kill fee. Buys electronic, first serial (in the southeast with a 6-month moratorium) rights. Editorial lead time 3 months. Submit seasonal material 6 months in advance. Accepts queries by mail, e-mail, fax. Accepts previously published material. Responds in 6-8 weeks to queries; 6-8 months to mss. Sample copy for $3.

Nonfiction Managing Editor. General interest (only topics pertaining to Atlanta area), historical/nostalgic, interview/profile, travel. **Buys 50-60 mss/year.** Query with published clips. Length: 1,200-2,500 words. **Pays $250-500.**

Photos "We do not accept photos until the article is accepted. Do not send photos with query." State availability with submission. Reviews slide transparencies, 4×6 prints, GIF/JPEG files. Offers no additional payment for photos accepted with ms. Captions, identification of subjects, model releases required.

Tips "The best way for a freelancer who is interested in being published is to get a sense of the types of articles we're looking for by reading the magazine."

HAWAII

$ $ HONOLULU MAGAZINE

PacificBasin Communications, 1000 Bishop St., Suite 405, Honolulu HI 96813. (808)537-9500. Fax: (808)537-6455. E-mail: johnh@pacificbasin.net. Website: www.honolulumagazine.com. **Contact:** John Heckathorn, editor. Prefers to work with published/established writers. Monthly magazine covering general interest topics relating to Hawaii residents. Estab. 1888. Circ. 30,000. Pays on publication. Byline given. Makes work-for-hire assignments. Accepts queries by mail, e-mail. Writer's guidelines online.

Nonfiction Historical/nostalgic, interview/profile, sports, politics, lifestyle trends, all Hawaii-related. "We write for Hawaii residents, so travel articles about Hawaii are not appropriate." Query with published clips or send complete ms. Length: determined when assignments discussed. **Pays $100-700.** Sometimes pays expenses of writers on assignment.

Photos Jayson Harper, art director. State availability with submission. Pays $50-200. Captions, identification of subjects, model releases required.

Columns/Departments Length determined when assignments discussed. Query with published clips or send complete ms. **Pays $100-300.**

IDAHO

$ $ SUN VALLEY MAGAZINE

Valley Publishing, LLC, 12 E. Bullion, Suite B, Hailey ID 83333. (208)788-0770. Fax: (208)788-3881. E-mail: edit@sunvalleymag.com. Website: www.sunvalleymag.com. **95% freelance written.** Quarterly magazine covering the lifestyle of the Sun Valley area. *Sun Valley Magazine* "presents the lifestyle of the Sun Valley area and the Wood River Valley, including recreation, culture, profiles, history, and the arts." Estab. 1973. Circ. 17,000. Pays on publication. Publishes ms an average of 5 months after acceptance. Byline given. Buys first North American serial, electronic rights. Editorial lead time 1 year. Submit seasonal material 14 months in advance. Accepts queries by mail. Accepts previously published material. Accepts simultaneous submissions. Responds in 5 weeks to queries; 2 months to mss. Sample copy for $4.95 and $3 postage. Writer's guidelines for #10 SASE.

Nonfiction "All articles are focused specifically on Sun Valley, the Wood River Valley, and immediate surrounding areas." Historical/nostalgic, interview/profile, photo feature, travel. Special issues: Sun Valley home design and architecture (Spring); Sun Valley weddings/wedding planner (Summer). Query with published clips. **Pays $40-500.** Sometimes pays expenses of writers on assignment.

Reprints Only occasionally purchases reprints.

Photos State availability with submission. Reviews transparencies. Buys one-time rights and some electronic rights. Offers $60-275/photo. Identification of subjects, model releases required.

Columns/Departments Conservation issues, winter/summer sports, health & wellness, mountain-related activities and subjects, home (interior design), garden. All columns must have a local slant. Query with published clips. **Pays $40-300.**

Tips "Most of our writers are locally based. Also, we rarely take submissions that are not specifically assigned, with the exception of fiction. However, we always appreciate queries."

ILLINOIS

$CHICAGO LIFE

1300 W. Belmont Ave., Suite 225, Chicago IL 60657-3260. (773)880-1360. Publisher: Pam Berns. **Contact:** Jessica Curry, editor. **90% freelance written.** Bimonthly magazine on Chicago life for educated, affluent professionals, 25-60 years old. Estab. 1984. Circ. 50,000. Pays on publication. Byline given. Kill fee varies. Submit seasonal material 8 months in advance. Accepts simultaneous submissions. Responds in 3 months to queries. Sample copy for 9×12 SAE and 7 first-class stamps.

Nonfiction Exposé, environment, health, interior design, politics, local issues, finance. **Buys 50 mss/year.** Send complete ms. Length: 400-2,000 words. Sometimes pays expenses of writers on assignment.

Reprints Send photocopy and information about when and where the material previously appeared.

Photos Send photos with submission. Reviews contact sheets, negatives, transparencies, prints. Buys one-time rights. Offers $15-30/photo.

Columns/Departments Law; Book Reviews; Health; Environment; Home Decorating, 500 words. Send complete ms. **Payment depends on length and topic.**

Fillers Facts. **Pays $15-30.**

Tips "Please send finished work with visuals (photos, if possible). Topics open include environmental concerns, health, interior design, travel. Especially appealing articles include a local angle."

$ $ $ $CHICAGO MAGAZINE

435 N. Michigan Ave., Suite 1100, Chicago IL 60611. E-mail: stritsch@chicagomag.com. Website: www.chicagomag.com. **Contact:** Shane Tritsch, managing editor. **50% freelance written.** Prefers to work with published/established writers. Monthly magazine for an audience which is "95% from Chicago area; 90% college educated; upper income, with overriding interests in the arts, politics, dining, and good life in the city and suburbs. Most are in 25-50 age bracket, well-read, and articulate." Estab. 1968. Circ. 175,000. **Pays on acceptance.** Publishes ms an average of 3 months after acceptance. Buys first rights. Submit seasonal material 4 months in advance. Accepts queries by mail, e-mail. Responds in 1 month to queries. For sample copy, send $3 to Circulation Dept. Writer's guidelines for #10 SASE.

Nonfiction "On themes relating to the quality of life in Chicago: past, present, and future." Writers should have "a general awareness that the readers will be concerned, influential, longtime Chicagoans. We generally publish material too comprehensive for daily newspapers." Exposé, humor, personal experience, think pieces, profiles, spot news, historical articles. **Buys 100 mss/year.** Query; indicate specifics, knowledge of city and market, and demonstrable access to sources. Length: 200-6,000 words. **Pays $100-3,000 and up.** Pays expenses of writers on assignment.

Photos Usually assigned separately, not acquired from writers. Reviews 35mm transparencies, color and b&w glossy prints.

Tips "Submit detailed queries; be business-like and avoid clichéd ideas."

N $ $ $ $CHICAGO READER

Chicago's Free Weekly, Chicago Reader, Inc., 11 E. Illinois St., Chicago IL 60611. (312)828-0350. Fax: (312)828-9926. E-mail: mail@chicagoreader.com. Website: www.chicagoreader.com. Editor: Alison True. **Contact:** Kiki Yablon, managing editor. **50% freelance written.** Weekly alternative tabloid for Chicago. Estab. 1971. Circ. 120,000. Pays on publication. Publishes ms an average of 2 weeks after acceptance. Byline given. Buys one-time rights. Editorial lead time up to 6 months. Accepts queries by mail, e-mail, fax. Accepts simultaneous submissions. Responds if interested to queries. Sample copy for free. Writer's guidelines free or online.

Nonfiction Magazine-style features; also book excerpts, essays, humor, interview/profile, opinion, personal experience, photo feature. **Buys 500 mss/year.** Send complete ms. Length: 500-50,000 words. **Pays $100-3,000.** Sometimes pays expenses of writers on assignment.

Reprints Occasionally accepts previously published submissions.

Columns/Departments Local color, 500-2,500 words; arts and entertainment reviews, up to 1,200 words; calendar items, 400-1,000 words.

Tips "Our greatest need is for full-length magazine-style feature stories on Chicago topics. We're not looking for: hard news (what the mayor said about the schools yesterday); commentary and opinion (what I think about what the mayor said about the schools yesterday); poetry. We are not particularly interested in stories of national (as opposed to local) scope, or in celebrity for celebrity's sake (à la *Rolling Stone, Interview*, etc.). More than half the articles published in the *Reader* each week come from freelancers, and once or twice a month we publish one that's come in 'over the transom'—from a writer we've never heard of and may never hear from again. We think that keeping the *Reader* open to the greatest possible number of contributors makes a fresher, less predictable, more interesting paper. We not only publish unsolicited freelance writing, we depend on it. Our last issue in December is dedicated to original fiction.''

$ $ $ ⊘ CS

Chicago Social, Modern Luxury, Inc., 200 W. Hubbard, Chicago IL 60610. (312)274-2500. E-mail: gbazer@mode rnluxury.com. Website: www.modernluxury.com. **Contact:** Gina Bazer, editor-in-chief. **70% freelance written.** Monthly luxury lifestyle magazine. ''We cover the good things in life—fashion, fine dining, the arts, etc.—from a sophisticated, cosmopolitan, well-to-do perspective.'' Circ. 75,000. Pays 2 months after receipt of invoice. Byline given. Offers kill fee. Buys first rights and all rights. Editorial lead time 6 months. Submit seasonal material 3-6 months in advance. Responds in 1 month to queries. Sample copy for $7.15 for current issue; $8.20 for back issue. Writer's guidelines not available.

Nonfiction General interest, how-to (gardening, culinary, home design), interview/profile, photo feature (occasional), travel. No fiction. *No unsolicited mss.* Query with published clips only. Length: 500-4,500 words. **Pays $50-900.** Pays expenses of writers on assignment.

Photos State availability with submission. Reviews transparencies, prints. Buys one-time rights. ''We pay for film and processing only.''

Columns/Departments Few Minutes With (Q&A), 800 words; City Art; Home Design, both 2,000 words. Query with published clips only. **Pays $150-400.**

Tips ''Send résumé, clips and story ideas. Mention interest and expertise in cover letter. We need writers who are knowledgeable about home design, architecture, art, culinary arts, entertainment, fashion, and retail.''

$ $ NEWCITY

Chicago's News and Arts Weekly, New City Communications, Inc., 770 N. Halsted, Chicago IL 60622. (312)243-8786. Fax: (312)243-8802. E-mail: brian@newcity.com. Website: www.newcitychicago.com. **Contact:** Brian Hieggelke, editor. **50% freelance written.** Weekly magazine. Estab. 1986. Circ. 70,000. Pays 2-4 months after publication. Publishes ms an average of 1 month after acceptance. Byline given. Offers 20% kill fee in certain cases. Buys first rights and non-exclusive electronic rights. Editorial lead time 2 months. Submit seasonal material 2 months in advance. Accepts queries by e-mail. Responds in 1 month to mss. Sample copy for $3. Writer's guidelines online.

Nonfiction Essays, exposé, general interest, interview/profile, personal experience, travel (related to traveling from Chicago and other issues particularly affecting travelers from this area), service. **Buys 100 mss/year.** Query by e-mail only. Length: 100-4,000 words. **Pays $15-450.** Rarely pays expenses of writers on assignment.

Photos State availability with submission. Reviews contact sheets. Buys one-time rights. Captions, identification of subjects, model releases required.

Columns/Departments Lit (literary supplement), 300-2,000 words; Music, Film, Arts (arts criticism), 150-800 words; Chow (food writing), 300-2,000 words. **Buys 50 mss/year.** Query by e-mail. **Pays $15-300.**

Tips ''E-mail a solid, sharply written query that has something to do with what our magazine publishes.''

INDIANA

$ $ EVANSVILLE LIVING

Tucker Publishing Group, 100 NW Second St., Suite 220, Evansville IN 47708. (812)426-2115. Fax: (812)426-2134. E-mail: ktucker@evansvilleliving.com. Website: www.evansvilleliving.com. **Contact:** Kristen Tucker, editor/publisher. **80-100% freelance written.** Bimonthly magazine covering the greater Evansville, Indiana area. ''*Evansville Living* is the only full-color, glossy, 100+ page city magazine for Evansville.'' Estab. 2000. Circ. 50,000. **Pays on acceptance.** Publishes ms an average of 3 months after acceptance. Byline given. Buys all rights. Editorial lead time 6 months. Submit seasonal material 6 months in advance. Accepts queries by mail, e-mail, fax. Accepts previously published material. Sample copy for $5 or online. Writer's guidelines for free or by e-mail.

Nonfiction Essays, general interest, historical/nostalgic, photo feature, travel. **Buys 60-80 mss/year.** Query with published clips. Length: 200-2,000 words. **Pays $100-300.** Sometimes pays expenses of writers on assignment.

Reprints Accepts previously published submissions.

Photos State availability with submission. Reviews contact sheets, negatives, transparencies, prints. Buys all rights. Negotiates payment individually. Captions, identification of subjects required.

Columns/Departments Home Style; Garden Style; Day Tripping; Sporting Life; Local Flavor, all 1,500 words. Query with published clips. **Pays $100-300.**

Ⓝ $ $ $ INDIANAPOLIS MONTHLY

Emmis Publishing Corp., 1 Emmis Plaza, 40 Monument Circle, Suite 100, Indianapolis IN 46204. (317)237-9288. Website: www.indianapolismonthly.com. **30% freelance written.** Prefers to work with published/established writers. "*Indianapolis Monthly* attracts and enlightens its upscale, well-educated readership with bright, lively editorial on subjects ranging from personalities to social issues, fashion to food. Its diverse content and attention to service make it the ultimate source by which the Indianapolis area lives." Estab. 1977. Circ. 45,000. **Pays on acceptance.** Publishes ms an average of 2 months after acceptance. Byline given. Offers negotiable kill fee. Buys first North American serial, one-time rights. Editorial lead time 3 months. Submit seasonal material 3 months in advance. Accepts queries by mail, e-mail. Accepts simultaneous submissions. Responds in 3 weeks to queries. Sample copy for $6.10.

- This magazine is using more first-person essays, but they must have a strong Indianapolis or Indiana tie. It will consider nonfiction book excerpts of material relevant to its readers.

Nonfiction Must have a strong Indianapolis or Indiana angle. Book excerpts (by Indiana authors or with strong Indiana ties), essays, exposé, general interest, interview/profile, photo feature. No poetry, fiction, or domestic humor; no "How Indy Has Changed Since I Left Town," "An Outsider's View of the 500," or generic material with no or little tie to Indianapolis/Indiana. **Buys 35 mss/year.** Query by mail with published clips. Length: 200-3,000 words. **Pays $50-1,000.**

Reprints Send ms with rights for sale noted and information about when and where the material previously appeared. *Accepts reprints only from noncompeting markets.*

Photos State availability with submission. Buys one-time rights. Negotiates payment individually. Captions, identification of subjects, model releases required.

Tips "Our standards are simultaneously broad and narrow: Broad in that we're a general interest magazine spanning a wide spectrum of topics, narrow in that we buy only stories with a heavy emphasis on Indianapolis (and, to a lesser extent, Indiana). Simply inserting an Indy-oriented paragraph into a generic national article won't get it: All stories must pertain primarily to things Hoosier. Once you've cleared that hurdle, however, it's a wide-open field. We've done features on national celebrities—Indianapolis native David Letterman and *Mir* astronaut David Wolf of Indianapolis, to name 2—and we've published 2-paragraph items on such quirky topics as an Indiana gardening supply house that sells insects by mail. Query with clips showing lively writing and solid reporting. No phone queries, please."

KANSAS

☑ $ $ KANSAS!

Kansas Department of Commerce, 1000 SW Jackson St., Suite 100, Topeka KS 66612-1354. (785)296-3479. Fax: (785)296-6988. E-mail: ksmagazine@kansascommerce.com. Website: www.kansmag.com. **90% freelance written.** Quarterly magazine emphasizing Kansas travel attractions and events. Estab. 1945. Circ. 52,000. **Pays on acceptance.** Publishes ms an average of 1 year after acceptance. Byline given. Buys one-time rights. Submit seasonal material 8 months in advance. Accepts queries by mail. Responds in 2 months to queries. Sample copy and writer's guidelines available.

Nonfiction "Material must be Kansas-oriented and have good potential for color photographs. The focus is on travel with articles about places and events that can be enjoyed by the general public. In other words, events must be open to the public, places also. Query letter should clearly outline story. We are especially interested in Kansas freelancers who can supply their own quality photos." General interest, photo feature, travel. Query by mail. Length: 750-1,250 words. **Pays $200-350.** Pays mileage only for writers on assignment.

Photos "We are a full-color photo/manuscript publication." Send photos (original transparencies only) with query. Pays $50-75 (generally included in ms rate) for 35mm or larger format transparencies. Captions required.

Tips "History and nostalgia stories do not fit into our format because they can't be illustrated well with color photos. Submit a query letter describing 1 appropriate idea with outline for possible article and suggestions for photos. Do not send unsolicited manuscripts."

Ⓝ $ $ RELOCATING IN KANSAS CITY

Network Communicatons, Inc., 5301 W. 75th St., Prairie Village KS 66208. (913)648-5757. Fax: (913)648-5783. Editor: Andrea Darr. Annual relocation guides, free for people moving to the area. Estab. 1986. Pays on publication. Byline given. Buys one-time rights. Editorial lead time 4 months. Submit seasonal material 4 months in advance. Accepts queries by mail, fax. Accepts previously published material. Accepts simultaneous submissions. Responds in 1 month. Sample copy for $5.

Nonfiction Historical/nostalgic, travel, local issues. **Buys 8 mss/year.** Query with published clips. Length: 600-1,000 words. **Pays $60-350.**

Reprints Accepts previously published submissions.

Photos Reviews transparencies. Buys one-time rights. Offers no additional payment for photos accepted with ms. Identification of subjects required.

Tips "Really read and understand our audience."

KENTUCKY

$ BACK HOME IN KENTUCKY

Back Home in Kentucky, Inc., P.O. Box 710, Clay City KY 40312-0710. (606)663-1011. Fax: (606)663-1808. E-mail: info@backhomeinky.com. **Contact:** Jerlene Rose, editor/publisher. **50% freelance written.** Bimonthly magazine "covering Kentucky heritage, people, places, events. We reach Kentuckians and 'displaced' Kentuckians living outside the state." Estab. 1977. Circ. 8,000. Pays on publication. Publishes ms an average of 6 months after acceptance. Byline given. Buys first North American serial rights. Submit seasonal material 6 months in advance. Responds in 2 months to queries. Sample copy for $3 and 9×12 SAE with $1.23 postage affixed. Writer's guidelines for #10 SASE.

    O— Interested in profiles of Kentucky people and places, especially historic interest.

Nonfiction Historical/nostalgic (Kentucky-related eras or profiles), photo feature (Kentucky places and events), travel (unusual/little-known Kentucky places), profiles (Kentucky cooks, gardeners, and craftspersons), memories (Kentucky related). No inspirational or religion. **Buys 20-25 mss/year.** Query with or without published clips or send complete ms. Length: 500-2,000 words. **Pays $50-150 for assigned articles; $50-100 for unsolicited articles.** "In addition to normal payment, writers receive 2 copies of issue containing their article."

Photos Looking for color transparencies, slides, or digital (high resolution) for covers (inquire for specific topics). Vertical format. Pays $50-150. Photo credits given. For inside photos, send photos with submission. Reviews transparencies, 4×6 prints. Rights purchased depends on situation. Occasionally offers additional payment for photos accepted with ms. Identification of subjects, model releases required.

Columns/Departments Travel, crafts, profile, and cookbooks (all Kentucky related), 500-750 words. **Buys 10-12 mss/year.** Query with published clips. **Pays $15-40.**

Tips "We work mostly with unpublished or emerging writers who have a feel for Kentucky's people, places, and events. Areas most open are little known places in Kentucky, unusual history, profiles of interesting Kentuckians, and Kentuckians with unusual hobbies or crafts."

$ $ KENTUCKY LIVING

Kentucky Association of Electric Co-Ops, P.O. Box 32170, Louisville KY 40232. (502)451-2430. Fax: (502)459-1611. E-mail: e-mail@kentuckyliving.com. Website: www.kentuckyliving.com. **Contact:** Paul Wesslund, editor. Mostly freelance written. Prefers to work with published/established writers. Monthly feature magazine primarily for Kentucky residents. Estab. 1948. Circ. 470,000. **Pays on acceptance.** Publishes ms an average of 1 year after acceptance. Byline given. Buys first serial rights for Kentucky. Submit seasonal material at least 6 months in advance. Accepts previously published material. Accepts simultaneous submissions. Responds in 1 month to queries. Sample copy for 9×12 SAE and 4 first-class stamps.

Nonfiction Kentucky-related profiles (people, places or events), recreation, travel, leisure, lifestyle articles, book excerpts. **Buys 18-24 mss/year.** Query with or without published clips or send complete ms. **Pays $75-600.** Sometimes pays expenses of writers on assignment.

Photos State availability of or send photos with submission. Reviews color slides and prints. Payment for photos included in payment for ms. Identification of subjects required.

Tips "The quality of writing and reporting (factual, objective, thorough) is considered in setting payment price. We prefer general interest pieces filled with quotes and anecdotes. Avoid boosterism. Well-researched, well-written feature articles are preferred. All articles must have a strong Kentucky connection."

$ $ KENTUCKY MONTHLY

Vested Interest Publications, 213 St. Clair St., Frankfort KY 40601. (502)227-0053. Fax: (502)227-5009. E-mail: membry@kentuckymonthly.com; steve@kentuckymonthly.com. Website: www.kentuckymonthly.com. Publisher: Stephen M. Vest. **Contact:** Michael Embry, editor. **75% freelance written.** Monthly magazine. "We publish stories about Kentucky and by Kentuckians, including those who live elsewhere." Estab. 1998. Circ. 40,000. Pays within 3 months of publication. Publishes ms an average of 3 months after acceptance. Byline given. Buys first North American serial rights. Editorial lead time 3 months. Submit seasonal material 4 months in advance. Accepts queries by mail, e-mail, fax. Accepts simultaneous submissions. Responds in 1 month. Sample copy and writer's guidelines online.

Nonfiction Book excerpts, general interest, historical/nostalgic, how-to, humor, interview/profile, photo feature, religious, travel, all with a Kentucky angle. **Buys 60 mss/year.** Query with or without published clips. Length: 300-2,000 words. **Pays $25-350 for assigned articles; $20-100 for unsolicited articles.**

Photos State availability with submission. Reviews negatives. Buys all rights. Captions required.

Fiction Adventure, historical, mainstream, novel excerpts. **Buys 10 mss/year.** Query with published clips. Length: 1,000-5,000 words. **Pays $50-100.**

Tips "We're looking for more fashion, home, and garden, first-person experience, mystery. Please read the magazine to get the flavor of what we're publishing each month."

LOUISIANA

$ $ SUNDAY ADVOCATE MAGAZINE

P.O. Box 588, Baton Rouge LA 70821-0588. (225)383-1111, ext. 0199. Fax: (225)388-0351. E-mail: glangley@the advocate.com. Website: www.theadvocate.com. **Contact:** Tim Belehrad, news/features editor. **5% freelance written.** "Freelance features are put on our website." Estab. 1925. Pays on publication. Publishes ms an average of 3 months after acceptance. Byline given. Buys one-time rights.

O—π Break in with travel articles.

Nonfiction Well-illustrated, short articles; must have local, area, or Louisiana angle—in that order of preference. **Buys 24 mss/year. Pays $100-200.**

Reprints Send tearsheet or typed ms with rights for sale noted and information about when and where the material previously appeared. Pays $100-200.

Photos Photos purchased with ms. Pays $30/published color photo.

Tips "Style and subject matter vary. Local interest is most important. No more than 4-5 typed, double-spaced pages."

MAINE

$ MAINE MAGAZINE

The Magazine of Maine's Treasures, County Wide Communications, Inc., P.O. Box 497, 26 Main St., Machias ME 04654. (207)753-0919. Website: www.mainemagazine.com. Publisher/Book Review Editor: Bob Berta. **Contact:** Lester J. Reynolds, managing editor. **30% freelance written.** Monthly magazine and website covering Maine and its people. Estab. 1977. Circ. 16,000. Pays on acceptance or publication (negotiable). Byline sometimes given. Offers 100% kill fee. Buys electronic, all rights. Editorial lead time 9 months. Submit seasonal material 9 months in advance. Accepts queries by mail. Accepts simultaneous submissions. Responds in 30 days to queries. Sample copy and writer's guidelines for $4 or online.

Nonfiction "First person not interesting unless you're related to a rich and famous or unique Mainer." Book excerpts, essays, how-to, humor, inspirational, interview/profile, new product, personal experience, photo feature, religious, travel. Query. Length: 1,000-2,000 words. **Pays $25-50.** Sometimes pays expenses of writers on assignment.

Photos Reviews contact sheets, negatives, transparencies. Buys all rights. Offers $15/photo or negotiates payment individually. Captions, identification of subjects required.

Columns/Departments Buys 10 or fewer mss/year. Query. **Pays $10-20.**

Poetry "Many are submitted by readers who love Maine." **Buys 10 or fewer poems/year. Pays $5.**

Tips "We're looking for work that is unique and about Maine—unusual people, places. We always want Stephen King interviews—good luck. We can give you his office address."

MARYLAND

$ $ BALTIMORE MAGAZINE

Inner Harbor E. 1000 Lancaster St., Suite 400, Baltimore MD 21202. (410)752-4200. Fax: (410)625-0280. Website: www.baltimoremagazine.net. **Contact:** Appropriate Editor. **50-60% freelance written.** Monthly magazine. "Pieces must address an educated, active, affluent reader and must have a very strong Baltimore angle." Estab. 1907. Circ. 70,000. Pays within 1 month of publication. Byline given. first rights in all media Submit seasonal material 4 months in advance. Accepts queries by mail, e-mail. Sample copy for $4.45. Writer's guidelines online.

O—π Break in through "Baltimore Inc. and B-Side—these are our shortest, newsiest sections and we depend heavily on tips and reporting from strangers. Please note that we are exclusively local. Submissions without a Baltimore angle may be ignored." Look online for appropriate editor to query via e-mail.

Nonfiction Book excerpts (Baltimore subject or author), essays, exposé, general interest, historical/nostalgic, humor, interview/profile (with a Baltimorean), new product, personal experience, photo feature, travel (local and regional to Maryland only). "Nothing that lacks a strong Baltimore focus or angle." Query by mail with published clips or send complete ms. Length: 1,600-2,500 words. **Pays 30-40¢/word.** Sometimes pays expenses of writers on assignment.

Columns/Departments Hot Shot, Health, Education, Sports, Parenting, Politics. Length: 1,000-2,500 words. Query with published clips.

Tips "Writers who live in the Baltimore area can send résumé and published clips to be considered for first assignment. Must show an understanding of writing that is suitable to an educated magazine reader and show ability to write with authority, describe scenes, help reader experience the subject. Too many writers send us newspaper-style articles. We are seeking: 1) Human interest features—strong, even dramatic profiles of

Baltimoreans of interest to our readers; 2) First-person accounts of experience in Baltimore, or experiences of a Baltimore resident; 3) Consumer—according to our editorial needs, and with Baltimore sources. Writers should read/familiarize themselves with style of *Baltimore Magazine* before submitting.''

CHESAPEAKE LIFE MAGAZINE

Alter Communications, 1040 Park Ave., Suite 200, Baltimore MD 21201. (443)451-6023. Fax: (443)451-6027. E-mail: editor@chesapeakelifemag.com. Website: www.chesapeakelifemag.com. **Contact:** Kessler Burnett, editor. **80% freelance written.** Bimonthly magazine covering restaurant reviews, personalities, home design, travel, regional calendar of events, feature articles, gardening. ''*Chesapeake Life* is a regional magazine covering the Chesapeake areas of Maryland, Virginia, and Southern Delaware.'' Estab. 1995. Circ. 85,000. Pays on publication. Byline given. Buys first North American serial rights. Editorial lead time 2 months. Accepts queries by mail, e-mail, fax, phone.

Nonfiction Book excerpts, general interest, historical/nostalgic, interview/profile, photo feature, travel. Query with published clips. Length: Open.

Photos Send photos with submission. Buys one-time rights. Negotiates payment individually.

MASSACHUSETTS

BOSTON GLOBE MAGAZINE

P.O. Box 58819, Boston MA 02205-5819. (617)929-2000. Website: www.globe.com/globe/magazine. **Contact:** Doug Most, magazine editor. **75% freelance written.** Weekly magazine. Circ. 706,153. Pays on publication. Publishes ms an average of 2 months after acceptance. Buys non exclusive electronic rights. Editorial lead time 2 months. Submit seasonal material 3 months in advance. Sample copy for 9×12 SAE and 2 first-class stamps.

Nonfiction Book excerpts (first serial rights only), interview/profile (not Q&A), narratives, trend pieces, profiles. Especially interested in medicine, science, higher education, sports, and the arts. No travelogs or poetry. **Buys up to 100 mss/year.** Query; SASE must be included with ms or queries for return. Length: 1,000-4,000 words. **Payment negotiable.**

Photos Purchased with accompanying ms or on assignment. Reviews contact sheets. Pays standard rates according to size used. Captions required.

⊘ BOSTON MAGAZINE

300 Massachusetts Ave., Boston MA 02115. (617)262-9700. Fax: (617)267-1774. E-mail: editor@bostonmagazine.com. Website: www.bostonmagazine.com. **Contact:** Jon Marcus, editor. **10% freelance written.** Monthly magazine covering the city of Boston. Estab. 1962. Circ. 125,000. Pays on publication. Publishes ms an average of 3 months after acceptance. Byline given. Offers 20% kill fee. Buys first North American serial rights. Editorial lead time 2 months. Submit seasonal material 4 months in advance. Accepts queries by mail, fax. Responds in 2 weeks to queries.

Nonfiction Book excerpts, exposé, general interest, interview/profile, politics, crime, trends, fashion. **Buys 20 mss/year.** Query. *No unsolicited mss.* Length: 1,200-12,000 words. Pays expenses of writers on assignment.

Photos State availability with submission. Buys one-time rights. Negotiates payment individually.

Columns/Departments Dining, Finance, City Life, Personal Style, Politics, Ivory Tower, Media, Wine, Boston Inc., Books, Theater, Music. Query.

Tips ''Read *Boston*, and pay attention to the types of stories we use. Suggest which column/department your story might best fit, and keep your focus on the city and its environs. We like a strong narrative style with a slightly 'edgy' feel—we rarely do 'remember when' stories. Think *city* magazine.''

Ⓝ $ $ CAPE COD LIFE

including Martha's Vineyard and Nantucket, Cape Cod Life, Inc., 270 Communication Way, Building #6, Hyannis MA 02601. (508)775-9800. Fax: (508)775-9801. Website: www.capecodlife.com. **Contact:** Janice Rohlf, editor-in-chief. **80% freelance written.** Magazine published 7 times/year focusing on ''area lifestyle, history and culture, people and places, business and industry, and issues and answers for year-round and summer residents of Cape Cod, Nantucket, and Martha's Vineyard, as well as nonresidents who spend their leisure time here.'' Circ. 45,000. Pays 1 month after publication. Byline given. Offers 20% kill fee. Buys first North American serial rights, makes work-for-hire assignments. Submit seasonal material 6 months in advance. Accepts queries by mail. Responds in 3 months. Sample copy for $5. Writer's guidelines for #10 SASE.

Nonfiction Book excerpts, general interest, historical/nostalgic, interview/profile, new product, photo feature, travel, gardening, marine, nautical, nature, arts, antiques. **Buys 20 mss/year.** Query with or without published clips. Length: 1,000-3,000 words. **Pays $100-500.**

Photos Photo guidelines for #10 SASE. Buys first rights with right to reprint. Pays $25-225. Captions, identification of subjects required.

Tips "Freelancers submitting quality spec articles with a Cape Cod and Islands angle have a good chance at publication. We like to see a wide selection of writer's clips before giving assignments. We also publish *Cape Cod Home: Living and Gardening on the Cape and Islands* covering architecture, landscape design, and interior design with a Cape and Islands focus."

$ $ PROVINCETOWN ARTS

Provincetown Arts, Inc., 650 Commercial St., P.O. Box 35, Provincetown MA 02657. (508)487-3167. E-mail: cbusa@comcast.net. Website: www.provincetownarts.org. **Contact:** Christopher Busa, editor. **90% freelance written.** Annual magazine covering contemporary art and writing. "*Provincetown Arts* focuses broadly on the artists and writers who inhabit or visit the Lower Cape, and seeks to stimulate creative activity and enhance public awareness of the cultural life of the nation's oldest continuous art colony. Drawing upon a 75-year tradition rich in visual art, literature, and theater, *Provincetown Arts* offers a unique blend of interviews, fiction, visual features, reviews, reporting, and poetry." Estab. 1985. Circ. 8,000. Pays on publication. Publishes ms an average of 4 months after acceptance. Offers 50% kill fee. Buys first, one-time, second serial (reprint) rights. Editorial lead time 6 months. Submit seasonal material 6 months in advance. Accepts simultaneous submissions. Responds in 3 weeks to queries; 2 months to mss. Sample copy for $10. Writer's guidelines for #10 SASE.
Nonfiction Book excerpts, essays, humor, interview/profile. **Buys 40 mss/year.** Send complete ms. Length: 1,500-4,000 words. **Pays $150 minimum for assigned articles; $125 minimum for unsolicited articles.**
Photos Send photos with submission. Reviews 8×10 prints. Buys one-time rights. Offers $20-$100/photo. Identification of subjects required.
Fiction Mainstream, novel excerpts. **Buys 7 mss/year.** Send complete ms. Length: 500-5,000 words. **Pays $75-300.**
Poetry Buys 25 poems/year. Submit maximum 3 poems. **Pays $25-150.**

Ⓝ $ $ WORCESTER MAGAZINE

172 Shrewsbury St., Worcester MA 01604-4636. (508)755-8004. Fax: (508)755-4734. E-mail: mwarshaw@worcestermag.com. Website: www.worcestermag.com. **Contact:** Michael Warshaw, editor. **10% freelance written.** Weekly tabloid emphasizing the central Massachusetts region, especially the city of Worcester. Estab. 1976. Circ. 40,000. Pays on publication. Publishes ms an average of 3 weeks after acceptance. Byline given. Buys all rights. Submit seasonal material 2 months in advance. Accepts queries by mail, e-mail, fax.
● Does not respond to unsolicited material.
○┐ Break in with "back of the book arts and entertainment articles."
Nonfiction "We are interested in any piece with a local angle." Essays, exposé (area government, corporate), general interest, historical/nostalgic, humor, opinion (local), personal experience, photo feature, religious, interview (local). **Buys less than 75 mss/year.** Length: 500-1,500 words. **Pays 10¢/word.**

MICHIGAN

$ $ $ ANN ARBOR OBSERVER

Ann Arbor Observer Co., 201 E. Catherine, Ann Arbor MI 48104. Fax: (734)769-3375. E-mail: hilton@aaobserver.com. Website: www.arborweb.com. **Contact:** John Hilton, editor. **50% freelance written.** Monthly magazine. "We depend heavily on freelancers and we're always glad to talk to new ones. We look for the intelligence and judgment to fully explore complex people and situations, and the ability to convey what makes them interesting." Estab. 1976. Circ. 63,500. Pays on publication. Publishes ms an average of 2 months after acceptance. Byline given. Accepts queries by mail, e-mail, fax, phone. Responds in 3 weeks to queries; several months to mss. Sample copy for 12½×15 SAE with $3 postage. Writer's guidelines for #10 SASE.
Nonfiction Historical, investigative features, profiles, brief vignettes. Must pertain to Ann Arbor. **Buys 75 mss/ year.** Length: 100-5,000 words. **Pays up to $1,000.** Sometimes pays expenses of writers on assignment.
Columns/Departments Up Front (short, interesting tidbits), 150 words. **Pays $75.** Inside Ann Arbor (concise stories), 300-500 words. **Pays $150.** Around Town (unusual, compelling ancedotes), 750-1,500 words. **Pays $150-200.**
Tips "If you have an idea for a story, write a 100-200-word description telling us why the story is interesting. We are open most to intelligent, insightful features of up to 5,000 words about interesting aspects of life in Ann Arbor."

$ $ GRAND RAPIDS MAGAZINE

Gemini Publications, 549 Ottawa Ave. NW, Suite 201, Grand Rapids MI 49503-1444. (616)459-4545. Fax: (616)459-4800. E-mail: cvalade@geminipub.com. Website: www.grmag.com. **Contact:** Carole Valade, editor. "*Grand Rapids* is a general interest life and style magazine designed for those who live in the Grand Rapids metropolitan area or desire to maintain contact with the community." Estab. 1964. Pays on publication. Byline given. Editorial lead time 2 months. Submit seasonal material 2 months in advance. Sample copy for $2 and an SASE with $1.50 postage. Writer's guidelines for #10 SASE.

Nonfiction *"Grand Rapids Magazine* is approximately 60% service articles—dining guide, calendar, travel, personal finance, humor and reader service sections—and 40% topical and issue-oriented editorial that centers on people, politics, problems, and trends in the region. In 2003, the editors added a section called 'Design,' which provides a focus on every aspect of the local design community—from Maya Lin's urban park installation and the new 125-acre sculpture park, to architecture and the world's Big Three office furniture manufacturers headquartered here." Query. **Pays $25-500.**

HOUR DETROIT

Hour Media, LLC, 117 W. Third St., Royal Oak MI 48067. (248)691-1800. Website: www.hourdetroit.com. **50% freelance written.** Monthly magazine. "General interest/lifestyle magazine aimed at a middle- to upper-income readership aged 17-70." Estab. 1996. Circ. 45,000. **Pays on acceptance.** Publishes ms an average of 2 months after acceptance. Byline given. Offers 30% kill fee. Buys first North American serial rights. Editorial lead time 6 weeks. Submit seasonal material 1 year in advance. Accepts queries by mail. Sample copy for $6.

Nonfiction Book excerpts, exposé, general interest, historical/nostalgic, interview/profile, new product, photo feature, technical. **Buys 150 mss/year.** Query with published clips. Length: 300-2,500 words. Sometimes pays expenses of writers on assignment.

Photos State availability with submission.

$ $MICHIGAN HISTORY

Michigan Historical Center, Michigan Dept. of History, Arts & Libraries, 702 W. Kalamazoo, Box 30741, Lansing MI 48909-8241. (800)366-3703. Fax: (517)241-4909. E-mail: editor@michigan.gov. Website: www.michiganhist orymagazine.com. Editor: Roger Rosentreter. **75% freelance written.** Bimonthly magazine covering Michigan history. "We want historical accuracy on Michigan-related content." Estab. 1917. Circ. 30,000. Pays on publication. Publishes ms an average of 16 months after acceptance. Byline given. Buys one-time, electronic rights. Editorial lead time 1 year. Submit seasonal material 1 year in advance. Accepts queries by mail, e-mail, phone. Responds in 3 months to queries; 6 months to mss. Sample copy and writer's guidelines free.

Nonfiction C. Damstra, assistant editor. Book excerpts, general interest, historical/nostalgic, interview/profile, personal experience, photo feature. Nothing already published, fictional. **Buys 20-24 mss/year.** Send complete ms. Length: 1,000-10,000 words. **Pays $100-500.** Sometimes pays expenses of writers on assignment.

Photos C. Schwerin, assistant editor. State availability with submission. Reviews contact sheets, negatives, transparencies, prints, GIF/JPEG files. Buys one-time and electronic use rights. Negotiates payment individually. Identification of subjects, model releases required.

Columns/Departments Remember the Time (personal account of historical event, person, experience), 500-2,000 words. **Buys 5 mss/year.** Send complete ms. **Pays $100-400.**

Tips "Send complete manuscripts, including photocopies of photos to use as illustrations. Be historically accurate, interesting, and informative."

$ $TRAVERSE

Northern Michigan's Magazine, Prism Publications, 148 E. Front St., Traverse City MI 49684. (231)941-8174. Fax: (231)941-8391. Website: www.traversemagazine.com. **20% freelance written.** Monthly magazine covering northern Michigan life. *"Traverse* is a celebration of the life and environment of northern Michigan." Estab. 1981. Circ. 30,000. **Pays on acceptance.** Byline given. Offers 10% kill fee. Buys first North American serial rights. Editorial lead time 1 year. Submit seasonal material 1 year in advance. Accepts queries by mail, fax, phone. Accepts simultaneous submissions. Responds in 2 months to queries. Sample copy for $3. Writer's guidelines for #10 SASE.

Nonfiction Book excerpts, essays, general interest, historical/nostalgic, humor, interview/profile, personal experience, photo feature, travel. No fiction or poetry. **Buys 24 mss/year.** Query with published clips or send complete ms. Length: 1,000-3,200 words. **Pays $150-500.** Sometimes pays expenses of writers on assignment.

Photos State availability with submission. Buys one-time rights. Negotiates payment individually.

Columns/Departments Up in Michigan Reflection (essays about northern Michigan); Reflection on Home (essays about northern homes), both 700 words. **Buys 18 mss/year.** Query with published clips or send complete ms. **Pays $100-200.**

Tips "When shaping an article for us, consider first that it must be strongly rooted in our region. The lack of this foundation element is one of the biggest reasons for our rejecting material. If you send us a piece about peaches, even if it does an admirable job of relaying the history of peaches, their medicinal qualities, their nutritional magnificence, and so on, we are likely to reject if it doesn't include local farms as a reference point. We want sidebars and extended captions designed to bring in a reader not enticed by the main subject. We cover the northern portion of the Lower Peninsula and to a lesser degree the Upper Peninsula. General categories of interest include nature and the environment, regional culture, personalities, the arts (visual, performing, literary), crafts, food & dining, homes, history, and outdoor activities (i.e., fishing, golf, skiing, boating, biking, hiking, birding, gardening). We are keenly interested in environmental and land-use issues but seldom use material dealing with such issues as health care, education, social services, criminal justice, and local politics. We use service pieces and a small number of how-to pieces, mostly focused on small projects for the home or yard. Also, we value research. We need articles built with information. Many of the pieces we reject use writing style to fill in for information voids. Style and voice are strongest when used as vehicles for sound research.''

MINNESOTA

$ $LAKE COUNTRY JOURNAL MAGAZINE

Evergreen Press of Brainerd, 201 W. Laurel St., P.O. Box 465, Brainerd MN 56401. (218)828-6424, ext. 14. Fax: (218)825-7816. E-mail: jodi@lakecountryjournal.com. Website: www.lakecountryjournal.com. **Contact:** Jodi Schwen, editor or Beth Hautala, assistant editor. **90% freelance written.** Bimonthly magazine covering central Minnesota's lake country. ''We target a specific geographical niche in central Minnesota. The writer must be familiar with our area. We promote positive family values, foster a sense of community, increase appreciation for our natural and cultural environments, and provide ideas for enhancing the quality of our lives.'' Estab. 1996. Circ. 14,500. Pays on publication. Publishes ms an average of 6 months after acceptance. Byline given. Offers 25% kill fee. Buys first North American serial, second serial (reprint), electronic rights. Submit seasonal material 1 year in advance. Accepts queries by mail, e-mail. Responds in 2 months to queries; 3 months to mss. Sample copy for $6. Writer's guidelines online.

    O—¬ Break in by ''submitting department length first—they are not scheduled as far in advance as features. Always in need of original fillers.''

Nonfiction Essays, general interest, how-to, humor, interview/profile, personal experience, photo feature. ''No articles that come from writers who are not familiar with our target geographical location.'' **Buys 30 mss/year.** Query with or without published clips. Length: 1,000-1,500 words. **Pays $100-200.** Sometimes pays expenses of writers on assignment.

Reprints Accepts previously published submissions.

Photos State availability with submission. Reviews transparencies. Buys one-time rights. Negotiates payment individually. Identification of subjects, model releases required.

Columns/Departments Profile-People from Lake Country, 800 words; Essay, 800 words; Health (topics pertinent to central Minnesota living), 500 words. **Buys 40 mss/year.** Query with published clips. **Pays $50-75.**

Fiction Adventure, humorous, mainstream, slice-of-life vignettes, literary, also family fiction appropriate to Lake Country and seasonal fiction. **Buys 6 mss/year.** Length:1,500 words. **Pays $100-200.**

Poetry Free verse. ''Never use rhyming verse, avant-garde, experimental, etc.'' **Buys 6 poems/year.** Submit maximum 4 poems. Length: 8-32 lines. **Pays $25.**

Fillers Anecdotes, short humor. **Buys 20/year.** Length: 100-300 words. **Pays $25.**

Tips ''Most of the people who will read your articles live in the north central Minnesota lakes area. All have some significant attachment to the area. We have readers of various ages, backgrounds, and lifestyles. After reading your article, we hope to have a deeper understanding of some aspect of our community, our environment, ourselves, or humanity in general.''

$ $LAKE SUPERIOR MAGAZINE

Lake Superior Port Cities, Inc., P.O. Box 16417, Duluth MN 55816-0417. (218)722-5002. Fax: (218)722-4096. E-mail: edit@lakesuperior.com. Website: www.lakesuperior.com. **Contact:** Konnie LeMay, editor. **40% freelance written.** Works with a small number of new/unpublished writers each year. Please include phone number and address with e-mail queries. Bimonthly magazine covering contemporary and historic people, places and current events around Lake Superior. Estab. 1979. Circ. 20,000. Pays on publication. Publishes ms an average of 10 months after acceptance. Byline given. Buys first North American serial, second serial (reprint) rights. Submit seasonal material 1 year in advance. Accepts queries by mail, e-mail. Responds in 3 months to queries. Sample copy for $3.95 and 5 first-class stamps. Writer's guidelines for #10 SASE.

Nonfiction Book excerpts, general interest, historical/nostalgic, humor, interview/profile (local), personal experience, photo feature (local), travel (local), city profiles, regional business, some investigative. **Buys 15 mss/ year.** Query with published clips. Length: 300-2,200 words. **Pays $60-600.** Sometimes pays expenses of writers on assignment.

Photos ''Quality photography is our hallmark.'' Send photos with submission. Reviews contact sheets, 2×2 and larger transparencies, 4×5 prints. Offers $50/image; $150 for covers. Captions, identification of subjects, model releases required.

Columns/Departments Current events and things to do (for Events Calendar section), less than 300 words; Around The Circle (media reviews, short pieces on Lake Superior, Great Lakes environmental issues, themes, letters and short pieces on events and highlights of the Lake Superior Region); I Remember (nostalgic lake-specific pieces), up to 1,100 words; Life Lines (single personality profile with photography), up to 900 words. Other headings include Destinations, Wild Superior, Lake Superior Living, Heritage, Shipwreck, Chronicle, Lake Superior's Own. **Buys 20 mss/year.** Query with published clips. **Pays $60-90.**

Fiction Ethnic, historic, humorous, mainstream, novel excerpts, slice-of-life vignettes, ghost stories. Must be targeted regionally. "Wants stories that are Lake Superior related." **Buys 2-3 mss/year.** Query with published clips. Length: 300-2,500 words. **Pays $50-125.**

■ The online magazine carries original content not found in the print edition. Contact: Konnie LeMay, online editor.

Tips "Well-researched queries are attended to. We actively seek queries from writers in Lake Superior communities. We prefer manuscripts to queries. Provide enough information on why the subject is important to the region and our readers, or why and how something is unique. We want details. The writer must have a thorough knowledge of the subject and how it relates to our region. We prefer a fresh, unused approach to the subject which provides the reader with an emotional involvement. Almost all of our articles feature quality photography, color or black and white. It is a prerequisite of all nonfiction. All submissions should include a short biography of author/photographer; mug shot sometimes used. Blanket submissions need not apply."

MINNESOTA MONTHLY

600 U.S. Trust Bldg., 730 S. Second Ave., Minneapolis MN 55402. (612)371-5800. Fax: (612)371-5801. E-mail: editor@minnesotamonthly.com. Website: www.mnmo.com. **Contact:** Jeff Johnson, editor. **50% freelance written.** "*Minnesota Monthly* is a regional lifestyle publication written for a sophisticated, well-educated audience living in the Twin Cities area and in greater Minnesota." Estab. 1967. Circ. 80,000. **Pays on acceptance.** Accepts queries by mail, e-mail. Writer's guidelines online.

  ○┓ "The Journey column/department (2,000 words) is probably the best break-in spot for freelancers. Submit, in its entirety, a diary or journal of a trip, event, or experience that changed your life. Past journeys: being an actress on a cruise ship, a parent's death, making a movie."

Nonfiction Regional issues, arts, services, places, people, essays, exposé, general interest, historical/nostalgia, interview/profile, new product, photo feature, travel in Minnesota. "We want exciting, excellent, compelling writing with a strong Minnesota angle." Query with résumé, published clips, and SASE. Length: 1,000-4,000 words. **Payment negotiable.**

Columns/Departments Portrait (photo-driven profile), 360 words; Just Asking (sassy interview with a Minnesota character or celebrity), 900 words; Midwest Traveler, 950-2,000 words; Postcards (chatty notes from Midwest towns), 300 words; Journey (diary/journal of a life-changing experience), 2,000 words. Query with résumé, published clips, and SASE. **Payment negotiable.**

Fiction Fiction in the June issue, and a November fiction contest—The Tamarack Awards.

Tips "Our readers are bright, artsy, and involved in their communities. Writing should reflect that. Stories must all have a strong Minnesota angle. If you can write well, try us! Familiarize yourself with a few recent issues before you query."

$ $ $MPLS. ST. PAUL MAGAZINE

MSP Communications, 220 S. 6th St., Suite 500, Minneapolis MN 55402. (612)339-7571. Fax: (612)339-5806. E-mail: banderson@mspcommunications.com. Website: www.mspmag.com. Editor: Brian Anderson. Managing Editor: Jean Marie Hamilton. Monthly magazine. "*Mpls. St. Paul Magazine* is a city magazine serving upscale readers in the Minneapolis-St. Paul metro area." Circ. 75,000. Pays on publication. Buys all rights. Editorial lead time 3 months. Accepts queries by mail, e-mail, fax. Sample copy for $9.25. Writer's guidelines online.

Nonfiction Book excerpts, essays, exposé, general interest, historical/nostalgic, interview/profile, personal experience, photo feature, travel. **Buys 150 mss/year.** Query with published clips. Length: 500-4,000 words. **Pays 50¢/word for assigned articles.**

MISSISSIPPI

N $ $MISSISSIPPI MAGAZINE

Downhome Publications, 5 Lakeland Circle, Jackson MS 39216. (601)982-8418. Fax: (601)982-8447. **Contact:** Kelli Bozeman, editor. **90% freelance written.** Bimonthly magazine covering Mississippi—the state and its lifestyles. "We are interested in positive stories reflecting Mississippi's rich traditions and heritage, and focusing on the contributions the state and its natives have made to the arts, literature, and culture. In each issue we showcase homes and gardens, lifestyle issues, food, design, art, and more." Estab. 1982. Circ. 39,000. Pays on publication. Publishes ms an average of 6 months after acceptance. Byline given. Offers 50% kill fee. Buys first North American serial rights. Editorial lead time 6 months. Submit seasonal material 1 year in advance. Accepts queries by mail, fax. Responds in 2 months to queries. Writer's guidelines for #10 SASE.

Nonfiction General interest, historical/nostalgic, how-to (home decor), interview/profile, personal experience, travel. "No opinion, political, essay, sports, exposé." **Buys 15 mss/year.** Query. Length: 900-1,500 words. **Pays $150-350.**

Photos Send photos with query. Reviews transparencies, prints, digital images on CD. Buys one-time rights. Negotiates payment individually. Captions, identification of subjects, model releases required.

Columns/Departments Gardening (short informative article on a specific plant or gardening technique), 750-1,000 words; Culture Center (story about an event or person relating to Mississippi's art, music, theatre, or literature), 750-1,000 words; On Being Southern (personal essay about life in Mississippi; only ms submissions accepted), 750 words. **Buys 6 mss/year.** Query. **Pays $150-225.**

MISSOURI

$ $ KANSAS CITY HOMES & GARDENS

Network Communications, Inc., 5301 W. 75th St., Prairie Village KS 66208. (913)648-5757. Fax: (913)648-5783. E-mail: adarr@kc-hg.com. Website: www.kchomesandgardens.com. Publisher: Keith Sauro. Managing Editor: Andrea Darr. Bimonthly magazine. "Since 1986, Kansas City residents (mainly women) have embraced a local publication that speaks to them. Their home, lifestyle and family are featured with emphasis on high-quality, upscale decorating, building and living." Estab. 1986. Circ. 18,000. Pays on publication. Byline given. Buys one-time rights. Editorial lead time 4 months. Submit seasonal material 4 months in advance. Accepts queries by mail, e-mail, fax. Accepts previously published material. Accepts simultaneous submissions. Responds in 1 month. Sample copy for $7.50 or online. Writer's guidelines online.

Nonfiction Travel, home and garden. **Buys 8 mss/year.** Query with published clips. Length: 600-1,000 words. **Pays $100-350.** Sometimes pays expenses of writers on assignment.

Reprints Accepts previously published submissions.

Photos State availability of or send photos with submission. Reviews transparencies. Buys one-time rights. Offers no additional payment for photos accepted with ms. Identification of subjects required.

Columns/Departments Time Away (places to take vacations to), 800 words. Query with published clips. **Pays $100-350.**

Tips "Really read and understand our audience. Who are they and what do they want?"

$ $ MISSOURI LIFE

Missouri Life, Inc., P.O. Box 421, Fayette MO 65248-0421. (660)248-3489. Fax: (660)248-2310. E-mail: info@missourilife.com. Website: www.missourilife.com. Editor-in-Chief: Danita Allen Wood. **Contact:** Martha M. Everett, managing editor. **85% freelance written.** Bimonthly magazine covering the state of Missouri. "*Missouri Life*'s readers are mostly college-educated people with a wide range of travel and lifestyle interests. Our magazine discovers the people, places, and events—both past and present—that make Missouri a great place to live and/or visit." Estab. 1973. Circ. 20,000. Pays on publication. Byline given. Buys all, nonexclusive rights. Editorial lead time 3 months. Submit seasonal material 6 months in advance. Accepts queries by mail, e-mail, fax. Responds in 2 months to queries. Writer's guidelines online.

Nonfiction General interest, historical/nostalgic, travel, all Missouri related. Length: 300-2,000 words. **Pays $50-600; 20¢/word.**

Photos State availability in query; buys all rights nonexclusive. Offers $50-150/photo. Captions, identification of subjects, model releases required.

Columns/Departments All Around Missouri (people and places, past and present, written in an almanac style), 300 words; Missouri Artist (features a Missouri artist), 500 words; Made in Missouri (products and businesses native to Missouri), 500 words; Missouri Memory (a personal memory of Missouri gone by), 500 words.

$ RIVER HILLS TRAVELER

Todd Publishing, Route 4, Box 4396, Piedmont MO 63957. (573)223-7143. Fax: (573)223-2117. E-mail: btodd@riverhillstraveler.com. Website: www.riverhillstraveler.com. **Contact:** Bob Todd, online editor. **50% freelance written.** Monthly tabloid covering "outdoor sports and nature in the southeast quarter of Missouri, the east and central Ozarks. Topics like those in *Field & Stream* and *National Geographic*." Estab. 1973. Circ. 7,500. Pays on publication. Publishes ms an average of 2 months after acceptance. Byline given. Buys one-time rights. Editorial lead time 2 months. Submit seasonal material 1 year in advance. Accepts queries by e-mail. Accepts simultaneous submissions. Responds in 2 months to queries. Sample copy for SAE or online. Writer's guidelines online.

Nonfiction Historical/nostalgic, how-to, humor, opinion, personal experience, photo feature, technical, travel. "No stories about other geographic areas." **Buys 80 mss/year.** Query with writing samples. Length: 1,500 word maximum. **Pays $15-50.** Sometimes pays expenses of writers on assignment.

Reprints Send ms with rights for sale noted and information about when and where the material previously appeared.

Photos Send photos with submission. Reviews JPEG/TIFF files. Buys one-time rights. Negotiates payment individually. Pays $25 for covers.

■ The online magazine carries original content not found in the print edition and includes writer's guidelines. Contact: Bob Todd, online editor.

Tips "We prefer stories that relate an adventure that causes a reader to relive an adventure of his own or consider embarking on a similar adventure. Think of an adventure in camping or cooking, not just fishing and hunting. How-to is great, but not simple instructions. We encourage good first-person reporting. We like to get stories as part of an e-mail, not an attached document."

$ $ SPRINGFIELD! MAGAZINE

Springfield Communications, Inc., P.O. Box 4749, Springfield MO 65808-4749. (417)882-4917. **Contact:** Robert Glazier, editor. **85% freelance written.** Eager to work with a small number of new/unpublished writers each year. "This is an extremely local and provincial monthly magazine. No general interest articles." Estab. 1979. Circ. 10,000. Pays on publication. Publishes ms an average of 3-24 months after acceptance. Byline given. Buys first serial rights. Submit seasonal material 1 year in advance. Responds in 3 months to queries; 6 months to mss. Sample copy for $5.30 and 9½×12½ SAE.

Nonfiction Local interest only; no material that could appeal to other magazines elsewhere. Book excerpts (Springfield authors only), exposé (local topics only), historical/nostalgic (top priority, but must be local history), how-to, humor, interview/profile (needs more on females than males), personal experience, photo feature, travel (1 page/month). **Buys 150 mss/year.** Query with published clips by mail only or send complete ms with SASE. Length: 500-3,000 words. **Pays $35-250 for assigned articles.**

Photos Send photos with query or ms. "Needs more photo features of a nostalgic bent." Reviews contact sheets, 4×6 color, 5×7 b&w glossy prints. Buys one-time rights. Pays $5-$35 for b&w, $10-50 for color. Captions, identification of subjects, model releases required.

Columns/Departments Buys 150 mss/year. Query by mail or send complete ms.

Tips "We prefer writers read 8-10 copies of our magazine prior to submitting any material for our consideration. The magazine's greatest need is for features which comment on these times in Springfield. We are overstocked with nostalgic pieces right now. We also need profiles about young women and men of distinction."

MONTANA

$ $ MONTANA MAGAZINE

Lee Enterprises, P.O. Box 5630, Helena MT 59604-5630. Fax: (406)443-5480. E-mail: editor@montanamagazine. com. Website: www.montanamagazine.com. **Contact:** Beverly R. Magley, editor. **90% freelance written.** Bimonthly magazine. "Strictly Montana-oriented magazine that features community profiles, contemporary issues, wildlife and natural history, travel pieces." Estab. 1970. Circ. 40,000. Publishes ms an average of 1 year after acceptance. Byline given. Buys one-time rights. Submit seasonal material 1 year in advance. Accepts simultaneous submissions. Responds in 6 months to queries. Sample copy for $5 or online. Writer's guidelines online.

● Accepts queries by e-mail. No phone calls.

Nonfiction Query by September for summer material; March for winter material. Essays, general interest, interview/profile, photo feature, travel. Special issues: Special features on summer and winter destination points. No 'me and Joe' hiking and hunting tales; no blood-and-guts hunting stories; no poetry; no fiction; no sentimental essays. **Buys 30 mss/year.** Query with samples and SASE. Length: 300-3,000 words. **Pays 20¢/word.** Sometimes pays expenses of writers on assignment.

Reprints Send photocopy of article with rights for sale noted and information about when and where the material previously appeared. Pays 50% of amount paid for an original article.

Photos Send photos with submission. Reviews contact sheets, 35mm or larger format transparencies, 5×7 prints. Buys one-time rights. Offers additional payment for photos accepted with ms. Captions, identification of subjects, model releases required.

Columns/Departments Memories (reminisces of early-day Montana life), 800-1,000 words; Outdoor Recreation, 1,500-2,000 words; Community Festivals, 500 words, plus b&w or color photo; Montana-Specific Humor, 800-1,000 words. Query with samples and SASE.

Tips "We avoid commonly known topics so Montanans won't ho-hum through more of what they already know. If it's time to revisit a topic, we look for a unique slant."

NEVADA

$ $ NEVADA MAGAZINE

401 N. Carson St., Carson City NV 89701-4291. (775)687-5416. Fax: (775)687-6159. E-mail: editor@nevadamaga zine.com. Website: www.nevadamagazine.com. Editor: David Moore. **Contact:** Joyce Hollister, associate editor. **50% freelance written.** Works with a small number of new/unpublished writers each year. Bimonthly magazine published by the state of Nevada to promote tourism. Estab. 1936. Circ. 80,000. Pays on publication. Publishes ms an average of 8 months after acceptance. Byline given. Buys first North American serial rights. Submit seasonal material 6 months in advance. Accepts queries by mail, e-mail. Responds in 1 month to queries.

○→ Break in with shorter departments, rather than trying to tackle a big feature. Good bets are Dining Out, Recreation, Casinoland, Side Trips, and Roadside Attractions.

Nonfiction "We welcome stories and photos on speculation." Nevada topics only. Historical/nostalgic, humor, interview/profile, personal experience, photo feature, travel, recreational, think pieces. **Buys 40 unsolicited mss/year.** Send complete ms or query. Length: 500-1,800 words. **Pays $50-500.**

Photos Send photo material with accompanying ms. Name, address, and caption should appear on each photo or slide. Also accepts 300 dpi JPEG files. Denise Barr, art director. Buys one-time rights. Pays $20-100 for color transparencies and glossy prints.

Tips "Keep in mind the magazine's purpose is to promote Nevada tourism. Keys to higher payments are quality and editing effort (more than length). Send cover letter; no photocopies. We look for a light, enthusiastic tone of voice without being too cute; articles bolstered by facts and thorough research; and unique angles on Nevada subjects."

NEW HAMPSHIRE

$ $ NEW HAMPSHIRE MAGAZINE

McLean Communications, Inc., 150 Dow St., Manchester NH 03101. (603)624-1442. E-mail: editor@nhmagazin e.com. Website: www.nhmagazine.com. **Contact:** Rick Broussard, editor. **50% freelance written.** Monthly magazine devoted to New Hampshire. "We want stories written for, by, and about the people of New Hampshire with emphasis on qualities that set us apart from other states. We feature lifestyle, adventure, and home-related stories with a unique local angle." Estab. 1986. Circ. 26,000. Pays on publication. Byline given. Offers 25% kill fee. Buys all rights. Editorial lead time 3 months. Submit seasonal material 3 months in advance. Accepts queries by mail, e-mail, fax. Accepts simultaneous submissions. Responds in 2 months to queries; 3 months to mss. Writer's guidelines online. Editorial calendar online.

Nonfiction Essays, general interest, historical/nostalgic, photo feature, business. **Buys 30 mss/year.** Query with published clips. Length: 800-2,000 words. **Pays $50-500.** Sometimes pays expenses of writers on assignment.

Photos State availability with submission. Rights purchased vary. Possible additional payment for photos accepted with ms. Captions, identification of subjects, model releases required.

Fillers Upfront items, sidebars. Length: 200-400 words.

▣ The online magazine carries original content not found in the print edition. Contact: Rick Broussard, online editor.

Tips Network Publications publishes 1 monthly magazine entitled *New Hampshire Magazine* and a "specialty" publication called *Destination New Hampshire*. "In general, our articles deal with the people of New Hampshire—their lifestyles and interests. We also present localized stories about national and international issues, ideas, and trends. We will only use stories that show our readers how these issues have an impact on their daily lives. We cover a wide range of topics, including healthcare, politics, law, real-life dramas, regional history, medical issues, business, careers, environmental issues, the arts, the outdoors, education, food, recreation, etc. Many of our readers are what we call 'The New Traditionalists'—aging Baby Boomers who have embraced solid American values and contemporary New Hampshire lifestyles."

NEW JERSEY

ℕ $ $ $ $ NEW JERSEY MONTHLY

The Magazine of the Garden State, New Jersey Monthly, LLC, 55 Park Place, P.O. Box 920, Morristown NJ 07963-0920. (973)539-8230. Fax: (973)538-2953. E-mail: editor@njmonthly.com. Website: www.njmonthly.c om. **Contact:** Christopher Hann, senior editor. **75-80% freelance written.** Monthly magazine covering "just about anything to do with New Jersey, from news, politics, and sports, to decorating trends and lifestyle issues. Our readership is well-educated, affluent, and on average our readers have lived in New Jersey 20 years or more." Estab. 1976. Circ. 95,000. Pays on completion of fact-checking. Publishes ms an average of 3 months after acceptance. Byline given. Offers 20% kill fee. Buys first North American serial rights. Editorial lead time

3 months. Submit seasonal material 6 months in advance. Accepts queries by mail, e-mail, fax, phone. Accepts simultaneous submissions. Responds in 2 months to queries.

- This magazine continues to look for strong investigative reporters with novelistic style and solid knowledge of New Jersey issues.

Nonfiction Book excerpts, essays, exposé, general interest, historical/nostalgic, humor, interview/profile, personal experience, photo feature, travel (within New Jersey), arts, sports, politics. "No experience pieces from people who used to live in New Jersey or general pieces that have no New Jersey angle." **Buys 90-100 mss/ year.** Query with published magazine clips and SASE. Length: 800-3,000 words. **Pays $750-2,500.** Pays reasonable expenses of writers on assignment with prior approval.

Photos Donna Panagakos, art director. State availability with submission. Reviews transparencies, prints. Buys one-time rights. Payment negotiated. Identification of subjects, model releases required.

Columns/Departments Exit Ramp (back page essay usually originating from personal experience but written in a way that tells a broader story of statewide interest), 1,200 words. **Buys 12 mss/year.** Query with published clips. **Pays $400.**

Fillers Anecdotes (for front-of-book). **Buys 12-15/year.** Length: 200-250 words. **Pays $100.**

Tips "The best approach: Do your homework! Read the past year's issues to get an understanding of our well-written, well-researched articles that tell a tale from a well-established point of view."

$ $NEW JERSEY SAVVY LIVING

CTB, LLC, 30B Vreeland Rd., Florham Park NJ 07932. (973)966-0997. Fax: (973)966-0210. E-mail: njsavvyliving @ctbintl.com. Website: www.njsavvyliving.com. **90% freelance written.** Bimonthly magazine covering New Jersey residents with affluent lifestyles. "*Savvy Living* is a regional magazine for an upscale audience, ages 35-65. We focus on lifestyle topics such as home design, fashion, the arts, travel, personal finance, and health and well being." Estab. 1997. Circ. 50,000. Pays on publication. Publishes ms an average of 3 months after acceptance. Byline given. Offers $50 kill fee. Buys variable rights. Editorial lead time 3 months. Accepts queries by mail. Accepts simultaneous submissions. Sample copy for 9×12 SAE.

Nonfiction Interview/profile (people of national and regional importance), photo feature, travel, home/decorating, finance, health, fashion, beauty. No investigative, fiction, personal experience, and non-New Jersey topics (excluding travel). **Buys 50 mss/year.** Query with published clips. Length: 900-2,000 words. **Pays $250-500.**

Photos State availability with submission. Buys one-time rights. Offers no additional payment for photos accepted with ms. Captions, identification of subjects, model releases required.

Columns/Departments Savvy Shoppers (inside scoop on buying); Dining Out (restaurant review); Home Gourmet (gourmet cooking and entertaining). **Buys 25 mss/year.** Query with published clips. **Pays $300.**

Tips "Offer ideas of interest to a savvy, upscale New Jersey readership. We love articles that utilize local sources and are well focused and keep our readers informed about trends affecting their lives. We work with experienced and stylish writers. Please provide clips."

$ $THE SANDPAPER

Newsmagazine of the Jersey Shore, The SandPaper, Inc., 1816 Long Beach Blvd., Surf City NJ 08008-5461. (609)494-5900. Fax: (609)494-1437. E-mail: letters@thesandpaper.net. **Contact:** Jay Mann, managing editor (jaymann@thesandpaper.net). **10% freelance written.** Weekly tabloid covering subjects of interest to Jersey shore residents and visitors. "*The SandPaper* publishes 2 editions covering many of the Jersey Shore's finest resort communities including Long Beach Island and Ocean City, New Jersey. Each issue includes a mix of news, human interest features, opinion columns, and entertainment/calendar listings." Estab. 1976. Circ. 60,000. Pays on publication. Publishes ms an average of 1 month after acceptance. Byline given. Offers 100% kill fee. Buys first, all rights. Submit seasonal material 3 months in advance. Accepts queries by mail, e-mail, fax, phone. Accepts simultaneous submissions. Responds in 1 month to queries. Sample copy for 9×12 SAE with 8 first-class stamps.

○┐ "The opinion page and columns are most open to freelancers." Send SASE for return of ms.

Nonfiction Must pertain to New Jersey shore locale. Essays, general interest, historical/nostalgic, humor, opinion, arts, entertaining news, reviews; also environmental submissons relating to the ocean, wetlands, and pinelands. **Buys 10 mss/year.** Send complete ms. Length: 200-2,000 words. **Pays $25-200.** Sometimes pays expenses of writers on assignment.

Reprints Send photocopy and information about when and where the material previously appeared. Pays 25-50% of amount paid for an original article.

Photos Send photos with submission. Buys one-time or all rights. Offers $8-25/photo.

Columns/Departments Speakeasy (opinion and slice-of-life, often humorous); Commentary (forum for social science perspectives); both 1,000-1,500 words, preferably with local or Jersey Shore angle. **Buys 50 mss/year.** Send complete ms. **Pays $30.**

Tips "Anything of interest to sun worshippers, beach walkers, nature watchers, and water sports lovers is of potential interest to us. There is an increasing coverage of environmental issues. We are steadily increasing the amount of entertainment-related material in our publication. Articles on history of the shore area are always in demand.''

NEW MEXICO

$ $ NEW MEXICO MAGAZINE

Lew Wallace Bldg., 495 Old Santa Fe Trail, Santa Fe NM 87501. (505)827-7447. E-mail: submissions@nmmagazine.com. Website: www.nmmagazine.com. Editor-in-Chief: Emily Drabanski. Managing Editor: Walter K. Lopez. Associate Editor/Photo Editor: Steve Larese. Editorial Assistant: Carol Kay. **Contact:** Any editor. Monthly magazine emphasizing New Mexico for a college-educated readership with above-average income and interest in the Southwest. Estab. 1923. Circ. 120,000. **Pays on acceptance.** Publishes ms an average of 8 months after acceptance. Buys first North American serial rights. Submit seasonal material 1 year in advance. Accepts queries by mail. Accepts previously published material. Responds in 2 months to queries. Sample copy for $3.95. Writer's guidelines for SASE.

Nonfiction New Mexico subjects of interest to travelers. Historical, cultural, informational articles. ''We are looking for more short, light and bright stories for the Poquito Mas section. Also, we are buying 12 mss per year for our Makin Tracks series.'' Send those submissions to Steve Larese. **Buys 7-10 mss/issue.** General interest, historical/nostalgic, interview/profile, travel. ''No columns, cartoons, poetry or non-New Mexico subjects.'' Query by mail with 3 published writing samples. No phone or fax queries. Length: 250-2,500 words. **Pays 30¢/word.**

Reprints Rarely publishes reprints but sometimes publishes excerpts from novels and nonfiction books.

Photos Purchased as portfolio or on assignment. ''Photographers interested in photo assignments should send tearsheets to photo editor Steve Larese; slides or transparencies with complete caption information are accepted. Photographer's name and telephone number should be affixed to the image mount.'' Buys one-time rights. Captions, model releases required.

Tips ''Your best bet is to write a fun, lively short feature (200-250 words) for our Poquito Mas section that is a superb short manuscript on a little-known person, aspect of history, or place to see in New Mexico. Faulty research will ruin a writer's chances for the future. Good style, good grammar. No generalized odes to the state or the Southwest. No sentimentalized, paternalistic views of Indians or Hispanics. No glib, gimmicky 'travel brochure' writing. No first-person vacation stories. We're always looking for well-researched pieces on unusual aspects of New Mexico and lively writing.''

NEW YORK

$ $ ADIRONDACK LIFE

P.O. Box 410, Jay NY 12941-0410. (518)946-2191. Fax: (518)946-7461. E-mail: aledit@adirondacklife.com. Website: www.adirondacklife.com. **Contact:** Mary Thill and Galen Crane, co-editors. **70% freelance written.** Prefers to work with published/established writers. Magazine published 8 issues/year—including special Annual Outdoor Guide—emphasizing the Adirondack region and the North Country of New York state in articles covering outdoor activities, history, and natural history directly related to the Adirondacks. Estab. 1970. Circ. 50,000. Pays 2-3 months after acceptance. Publishes ms an average of 6 months after acceptance. Byline given. Buys first North American serial, Web rights. Submit seasonal material 1 year in advance. Accepts queries by mail, e-mail. Sample copy for $3 and 9×12 SAE. Writer's guidelines online.

○┬ ''For new writers, the best way to break in to the magazine is through departments.''

Nonfiction ''*Adirondack Life* attempts to capture the unique flavor and ethos of the Adirondack mountains and North Country region through feature articles directly pertaining to the qualities of the area.'' Special issues: Outdoors (May); Single-topic Collector's issue (September). **Buys 20-25 unsolicited mss/year.** Query with published clips. Length: 2,000-4,000 words. **Pays 25¢/word.** Sometimes pays expenses of writers on assignment.

Photos All photos must have been taken in the Adirondacks. Each issue contains a photo feature. Purchased with or without ms on assignment. All photos must be individually identified as to the subject or locale and must bear the photographer's name. Send photos with submission. Reviews color transparencies, b&w prints. Pays $150 for full page, b&w, or color; $400 for cover (color only, vertical in format). Credit line given.

Columns/Departments Special Places (unique spots in the Adirondack Park); Watercraft; Barkeater (personal to political essays); Wilderness (environmental issues); Working (careers in the Adirondacks); Home; Yesteryears; Kitchen; Profile; Historic Preservation; Sporting Scene. Length: 1,200-2,400 words. Query with published clips. **Pays 25¢/word.**

Fiction Considers first-serial novel excerpts in its subject matter and region.

Tips "Do not send a personal essay about your meaningful moment in the mountains. We need factual pieces about regional history, sports, culture, and business. We are looking for clear, concise, well-organized manuscripts that are strictly Adirondack in subject. Check back issues to be sure we haven't already covered your topic. Please do not send unsolicited manuscripts via e-mail. Check out our guidelines online."

$BEYOND THE BADGE

(formerly *Police Officer's Quarterly*), 47-01 Greenpoint Ave., #114, Sunnyside NY 11104-1709. Fax: (718)732-2998. E-mail: editor@beyondthebadgemag.com. Website: www.badgemag.com. **Contact:** Liz Martinez, editor. Quarterly magazine. *Beyond the Badge* is distributed to police officers, peace officers, federal agents, corrections officers, auxiliary police officers, probation and parole officers, civilian employees of law enforcement agencies, etc., in the Long Island, New York area (Nassau and Suffolk Counties), plus NYPD precincts in Eastern Queens, adjacent to Nassau County. Estab. 2001. Buys one-time rights. Accepts queries by e-mail. Accepts previously published material. Accepts simultaneous submissions. Sample copy for $5, plus a 9×12 SASE. Writer's guidelines by e-mail.

Nonfiction "We are seeking stories on travel; law enforcement product/news; books with a LE hook; movies and other entertainment that our readers would enjoy knowing about; worthy LE-related Internet sites; the latest developments in forensics and technology; health articles with a LE spin; investigation techniques; innovative international, national, regional, or local (inside and outside of the New York area) approaches to LE or crime prevention issues; other topics of interest to our reader population. General interest. Special issues: Summer Camps (Summer 2005); Education (Fall 2005); Washington D.C. Travel/Police Week (Winter 2006); Family Vacation Guide (Spring 2006). Please submit supplemental and seasonal topics 5 months in advance. "We see too many pieces that are dry and not enjoyable to read. Even if the topic is serious or scientific, present the material as though you were telling a friend about it." Query. Length: 1,000-1,500 words. **Pays $100.**

Photos Photos are very helpful and much appreciated; however, there is no additional pay for photos. Inclusion of photos does increase chances of publication.

Columns/Departments Book'Em (book reviews/excerpts/author interviews); Internet Guide; Screening Room (movie reviews); Your Finances; Management in Focus; Health Department; Forensics Lab; Technology. Query. **Pays $75.**

Tips "Writers should keep in mind that this is a lifestyle magazine whose readers happen to be cops, not a cop magazine with some lifestyle topics in it."

$ $BUFFALO SPREE MAGAZINE

David Laurence Publications, Inc., 6215 Sheridan Dr., Buffalo NY 14221. (716)634-0820. Fax: (716)810-0075. E-mail: elicata@buffalospree.com. Website: www.buffalospree.com. **Contact:** Elizabeth Licata, editor. **90% freelance written.** City regional magazine published 8 times/year. Estab. 1967. Circ. 25,000. Pays on publication. Publishes ms an average of 1 month after acceptance. Byline given. Buys first North American serial rights. Accepts queries by mail, e-mail, fax. Responds in 6 months to queries. Sample copy for $3.95 and 9×12 SAE with 9 first-class stamps.

Nonfiction "Most articles are assigned, not unsolicited." Interview/profile, travel, issue-oriented features, arts, living, food, regional. Query with résumé and published clips. Length: 1,000-2,000 words. **Pays $125-250.**

Tips "Send a well-written, compelling query or an interesting topic, and great clips. We no longer regularly publish fiction or poetry. Prefers material that is Western New York related."

$ $ $ $CITY LIMITS

New York's Urban Affairs News Magazine, City Limits Community Information Service, 120 Wall St., 20th Floor, New York NY 10005. (212)479-3344. Fax: (212)344-6457. E-mail: citylimits@citylimits.org. Website: www.citylimits.org. **Contact:** Alyssa Katz, editor. **50% freelance written.** Monthly magazine covering urban politics and policy. "*City Limits* is a 29-year-old nonprofit magazine focusing on issues facing New York City and its neighborhoods, particularly low-income communities. The magazine is strongly committed to investigative journalism, in-depth policy analysis, and hard-hitting profiles." Estab. 1976. Circ. 4,000. Pays on publication. Publishes ms an average of 3 months after acceptance. Byline given. Offers 50% kill fee. Buys first North American serial, second serial (reprint) rights. Editorial lead time 2 months. Accepts queries by mail, e-mail, fax. Accepts simultaneous submissions. Sample copy for $2.95. Writer's guidelines free.

Nonfiction Book excerpts, exposé, humor, interview/profile, opinion, photo feature. No essays, polemics. **Buys 25 mss/year.** Query with published clips. Length: 400-3,500 words. **Pays $150-2,000 for assigned articles; $100-800 for unsolicited articles.** Pays expenses of writers on assignment.

Photos State availability with submission. Reviews contact sheets, negatives, transparencies. Offers $50-100/photo.

Columns/Departments Making Change (nonprofit business); Big Idea (policy news); Book Review, all 800 words; Urban Legend (profile); First Hand (Q&A), both 350 words. **Buys 15 mss/year.** Query with published clips.

Tips *"City Limits'* specialty is covering low-income communities. We want to report untold stories about news affecting neighborhoods at the grassroots. We're looking for stories about housing, healthcare, criminal justice, child welfare, education, economic development, welfare reform, politics and government."

$ $ $ HUDSON VALLEY

Today Media, Inc., 22 IBM Rd., Suite 108, Poughkeepsie NY 12601. (845)463-0542. Fax: (845)463-1544. E-mail: rsparling@hvmag.com. Website: www.hudsonvalleymagazine.com. **Contact:** Reed Sparling, editor-in-chief. Monthly magazine for residents of the Hudson Valley. Byline given. Offers 25% kill fee. Buys first North American serial rights. Accepts queries by mail, e-mail. Accepts simultaneous submissions. Responds in 3 months to queries. Sample copy for free. Writer's guidelines for #10 SASE.

Nonfiction Buys 50-80 mss/year. Query with published clips. Length: 200-5,000 words. **Pays $500-800/feature, $50-250/department article, $25-75/short piece.**

IN NEW YORK

Morris Communications, 261 Madison Ave., 9th Floor, New York NY 10016. (212)716-8562. E-mail: trisha.mcma hon@in-newyorkmag.com. Website: www.in-newyorkmag.com. Editor: Trisha S. McMahon. Monthly magazine created exclusively for sophisticated travelers to the New York Metropolitian area and distributed at most hotels, tourist centers, and popular sights. Circ. 125,000. Sample copy for free in upscale hotels at concierge desk.

$ $ $ $ NEW YORK MAGAZINE

Primedia Magazines, 444 Madison Ave., 14th Floor, New York NY 10022. Website: www.newyorkmetro.com. **Contact:** Ben Mathis-Lilley. **25% freelance written.** Weekly magazine focusing on current events in the New York metropolitan area. Circ. 433,813. **Pays on acceptance.** Offers 25% kill fee. Buys electronic, first world serial rights. Submit seasonal material 2 months in advance. Responds in 1 month to queries. Sample copy for $3.50 or on website. Writer's guidelines not available.

Nonfiction New York-related journalism that covers lifestyle, politics and business. Query by mail. **Pays $1/ word.** Pays expenses of writers on assignment.

$ $ SYRACUSE NEW TIMES

A. Zimmer, Ltd., 1415 W. Genesee St., Syracuse NY 13204. Fax: (315)422-1721. E-mail: editorial@syracusenewti mes.com. Website: www.syracusenewtimes.com. **Contact:** Molly English, editor. **50% freelance written.** Weekly tabloid covering news, sports, arts, and entertainment. *"Syracuse New Times* is an alternative weekly that can be topical, provocative, irreverent, and intensely local." Estab. 1969. Circ. 46,000. Pays on publication. Publishes ms an average of 1 month after acceptance. Byline given. Buys one-time rights. Editorial lead time 3 months. Submit seasonal material 3 months in advance. Accepts simultaneous submissions. Responds in 2 weeks to queries; 1 month to mss. Sample copy for 9×12 SAE and 2 first-class stamps. Writer's guidelines for #10 SASE.

Nonfiction Essays, general interest. **Buys 200 mss/year.** Query by mail with published clips. Length: 250-2,500 words. **Pays $25-200.**

Photos State availability of or send photos with submission. Reviews 8×10 prints, color slides. Buys one-time rights. Offers $10-25/photo or negotiates payment individually. Identification of subjects required.

Tips "Move to Syracuse and query with strong idea."

☑ TIME OUT NEW YORK

Time Out New York Partners, LP, 475 10th Ave., 12th Floor, New York NY 10018. (646)432-3000. Fax: (646)432-3160. E-mail: letters@timeoutny.com. Website: www.timeoutny.com. Editor-in-Chief: Joe Angio. **Contact:** Erin Clements, editorial assistant. **20% freelance written.** Weekly magazine covering entertainment in New York City. "Those who want to contribute to *Time Out New York* must be intimate with New York City and its environs." Estab. 1995. Circ. 120,000. Pays on publication. Publishes ms an average of 1 month after acceptance. Byline sometimes given. Offers 25% kill fee. Makes work-for-hire assignments. Accepts queries by mail, fax, phone. Responds in 2 months to queries.

☞ Pitch ideas to the editor of the section to which you would like to contribute (i.e., film, music, dance, etc.). Be sure to include clips or writing samples with your query letter. No unsolicited mss.

Nonfiction Essays, general interest, how-to, humor, interview/profile, new product, travel (primarily within NYC area), reviews of various entertainment topics. No essays, articles about trends, unpegged articles. Query with published clips. Length: 250-1,500 words.

Columns/Departments Around Town (Ethan LaCroix); Art (Andrea Scott); Books & Poetry (Maureen Shelly);

Cabaret (Adam Feldman); Check Out (Marissa Patlingrao Cooley); Clubs (Bruce Tantum); Comedy (Jane Borden); Dance (Gia Kourlas); Eat Out (Maile Carpenter); Film (Darren S'Addario); Gay & Lesbian (Beth Greenfield); Kids (Barbara Aria); Music (Mike Wolf); Radio/TV/Video (Andrew Johnston); Sports (Reed Tucker); Theater (David Cote).

Tips ''We're always looking for quirky, less-known news about what's going on in New York City.''

NORTH CAROLINA

ℕ $ $ CARY MAGAZINE

Western Wake Media, Westview at Weston, 301 Cascade Pointe Lane, #101, Cary NC 27513. (919)674-6020. Fax: (919)674-6027. E-mail: editor@carymagazine.com. Website: www.carymagazine.com. **Contact:** Danielle Caspar. **40% freelance written.** Bimonthly magazine. Lifestyle publication for the affluent communities of Cary, Apex, Morrisville, Holly Springs, Fuquay-Varina and RTP. ''Our editorial objective is to entertain, enlighten and inform our readers with unique and engaging editorial and vivid photography.'' Estab. 2004. Circ. 23,000. Byline given. Buys first North American serial rights. Editorial lead time 2 months. Submit seasonal material 3 months in advance. Accepts queries by mail, e-mail. Responds in 2-4 weeks to queries; 1 month to mss. Sample copy for $4.95. Writer's guidelines free.

Nonfiction Historical/nostalgic (specific to Western Wake County, North Carolina), inspirational, interview/profile (human interest), personal experience. ''Don't submit articles with no local connection.'' **Buys 2 mss/year.** Query with published clips. Sometimes pays expenses of writers on assignment.

Photos Freelancers should state the availability of photos with their submission or send the photos with their submission. Reviews GIF/JPEG files. Buys one-time rights. Negotiates payment individually. Identification of subjects required.

Tips Prefer experienced feature writers with exceptional interviewing skills who can take a fresh perspective on a topic; writes with a unique flare, but clearly with a good hook to engage the reader and evoke emotion; adheres to AP Style and follows basic journalism conventions; and takes deadlines seriously. E-mail inquiries preferred.

$ $ CHARLOTTE MAGAZINE

Abarta Media, 127 W. Worthington Ave., Suite 208, Charlotte NC 28203. (704)335-7181. Fax: (704)335-3739. E-mail: richard.thurmond@charlottemagazine.com. Website: www.charlottemagazine.com. **Contact:** Richard H. Thurmond, editorial director. **75% freelance written.** Monthly magazine covering Charlotte life. ''This magazine tells its readers things they didn't know about Charlotte, in an interesting, entertaining, and sometimes provocative style.'' Circ. 30,000. Pays within 30 days of acceptance. Publishes ms an average of 3 months after acceptance. Byline given. Offers 25% kill fee. Buys first North American serial rights. Editorial lead time 3 months. Submit seasonal material 6 months in advance. Accepts queries by mail, e-mail. Accepts simultaneous submissions. Responds in 6 months to mss. Sample copy for 8½×11 SAE and $2.09.

Nonfiction Book excerpts, exposé, general interest, historical/nostalgic, interview/profile, photo feature, travel. **Buys 90-100 mss/year.** Query with published clips. Length: 200-3,000 words. **Pays 20-40¢/word.** Sometimes pays expenses of writers on assignment.

Photos State availability with submission. Buys one-time rights. Negotiates payment individually. Identification of subjects required.

Columns/Departments Buys 35-50 mss/year. Pays 20-40¢/word.

Tips ''A story for *Charlotte* magazine could only appear in *Charlotte* magazine. That is, the story and its treatment are particularly germane to this area.''

$ $ OUR STATE

Down Home in North Carolina, Mann Media, P.O. Box 4552, Greensboro NC 27404. (336)286-0600. Fax: (336)286-0100. E-mail: editorial@ourstate.com. Website: www.ourstate.com. **95% freelance written.** Monthly magazine covering North Carolina. ''*Our State* is dedicated to providing editorial about the history, destinations, out-of-the-way places, and culture of North Carolina.'' Estab. 1933. Circ. 112,000. Pays on publication. Publishes ms an average of 6-24 months after acceptance. Byline given. Buys first North American serial rights. Editorial lead time 4 months. Submit seasonal material 4 months in advance. Accepts queries by mail, e-mail, fax. Responds in 6 weeks to queries; 2 months to mss. Sample copy for $6. Writer's guidelines for #10 SASE.

Nonfiction Historical/nostalgic, travel, North Carolina culture, folklore. **Buys 250 mss/year.** Send complete ms. Length: 1,200-1,500 words. **Pays $300-500.**

Photos State availability with submission. Reviews 35mm or 4×6 transparencies. Buys one-time rights. Negotiates payment individually. Pays $15-350/photo, depending on size; $125-500 for photos assigned to accompany specific story; $500 maximum for cover photos. Identification of subjects required.

Columns/Departments Tar Heel Memories (remembering something specific about North Carolina), 1,200 words; Tar Heel Profile (profile of interesting North Carolinian), 1,500 words; Tar Heel Literature (review of books by North Carolina writers and about North Carolina), 300 words. **Buys 40 mss/year.** Send complete ms. **Pays $50-300.**

Tips "We are developing a style for travel stories that is distinctly *Our State*. That style starts with outstanding photographs, which not only depict an area, but interpret it and thus become an integral part of the presentation. Our stories need not dwell on listings of what can be seen. Concentrate instead on the experience of being there, whether the destination is a hiking trail, a bed and breakfast, a forest, or an urban area. What thoughts and feelings did the experience evoke? We want to know why you went there, what you experienced, and what impressions you came away with. With at least 1 travel story an issue, we run a short sidebar called, 'If You're Going.' It explains how to get to the destination; rates or admission costs if there are any; a schedule of when the attraction is open or list of relevant dates; and an address and phone number for readers to write or call for more information. This sidebar eliminates the need for general-service information in the story."

NORTH DAKOTA

N $ $ NORTH DAKOTA LIVING MAGAZINE

North Dakota Association of Rural Electric Cooperatives, 3201 Nygren Dr. NW, P.O. Box 727, Mandan ND 58554-0727. (701)663-6501. Fax: (701)663-3745. E-mail: kbrick@ndarec.com. Website: www.ndarec.com. **Contact:** Kent Brick, editor. **20% freelance written.** Monthly magazine covering information of interest to memberships of electric cooperatives and telephone cooperatives. "We publish a general interest magazine for North Dakotans. We treat subjects pertaining to living and working in the northern Great Plains. We provide progress reporting on electric cooperatives and telephone cooperatives." Estab. 1954. Circ. 70,000. **Pays on acceptance.** Publishes ms an average of 6 months after acceptance. Byline given. Buys one-time rights, makes work-for-hire assignments. Editorial lead time 6 months. Submit seasonal material 6 months in advance. Accepts queries by mail, e-mail. Accepts previously published material. Accepts simultaneous submissions. Sample copy and writer's guidelines not available.

Nonfiction General interest, historical/nostalgic, how-to, humor, interview/profile, new product, travel. **Buys 20 mss/year.** Query with published clips. Length: 1,500-2,000 words. **Pays $100-500 minimum for assigned articles; $300-600 for unsolicited articles.** Sometimes pays expenses of writers on assignment.

Photos State availability with submission. Reviews contact sheets. Buys one-time rights. Negotiates payment individually. Identification of subjects required.

Columns/Departments Energy Use and Financial Planning, both 750 words. **Buys 6 mss/year.** Query with published clips. **Pays $100-300.**

Fiction Historical, humorous, slice-of-life vignettes, western. **Buys 1 mss/year.** Query with published clips. Length: 1,000-2,500 words. **Pays $100-400.**

Tips "Deal with what's real: real data, real people, real experiences, real history, etc."

OHIO

$ BEND OF THE RIVER MAGAZINE

P.O. Box 859, Maumee OH 43537. (419)893-0022. **Contact:** R. Lee Raizk, publisher. **98% freelance written.** This magazine reports that it is eager to work with all writers. "We buy material that we like whether it is by an experienced writer or not." Monthly magazine for readers interested in northwestern Ohio history and nostalgia. Estab. 1972. Circ. 7,500. Pays on publication. Publishes ms an average of 6 months after acceptance. Byline given. Buys one-time rights. Submit seasonal material 2 months in advance. Responds in 1 month to queries. Sample copy for $1.25. Writer's guidelines not available.

Nonfiction "We are looking for old snapshots of the Toledo area to accompany articles, personal reflection, etc." Historical/nostalgic. **Buys 75 unsolicited mss/year.** Query with or without published clips or send complete ms. Length: 1,500 words. **Pays $50 and up.**

Tips "Our stockpile is low. Send us anything!"

$ $ $ CINCINNATI MAGAZINE

Emmis Publishing Corp., One Centennial Plaza, 705 Central Ave., Suite 175, Cincinnati OH 45202. (513)421-4300. Fax: (513)562-2746. E-mail: editor@cintimag.emmis.com. **Contact:** Linda Vaccariello, executive editor. Monthly magazine emphasising Cincinnati living. Circ. 30,000. Pays on publication. Byline given. Buys all periodical rights. Sample copy and writer's guidelines free.

Nonfiction Articles on personalities, business, sports, lifestyle relating to Cincinnati and Northern Kentucky. **Buys 12 mss/year.** Query. Length: 2,500-3,500 words. **Pays $500-1,000.**

Columns/Departments Topics are Cincinnati media, arts and entertainment, people, politics, sports, business, regional. Length: 1,000-1,500 words. **Buys 10-15 mss/year.** Query. **Pays $200-400.**

Tips "It's most helpful if you query in writing, with clips. All articles have a local focus. No generics, please. Also: No movie, book, theater reviews, poetry, or fiction. Freelancers may also be interested in our special advertising sections and our bridal publication (2 times/year). For these, query special projects editor Elissa Sonnenberg."

$ $ $ CLEVELAND MAGAZINE

City Magazines, Inc., 1422 Euclid Ave., Suite 730, Cleveland OH 44115. (216)771-2833. Fax: (216)781-6318. E-mail: editorial@clevelandmagazine.com. Website: www.clevelandmagazine.com. **Contact:** Steve Gleydura, editorial director. **60% freelance written.** Mostly by assignment. Monthly magazine with a strong Cleveland/Northeast Ohio angle. Estab. 1972. Circ. 50,000. Pays on publication. Publishes ms an average of 3 months after acceptance. Byline given. Buys first, second serial (reprint), electronic rights. Editorial lead time 6 months. Submit seasonal material 8 months in advance. Accepts queries by mail, e-mail, fax. Accepts simultaneous submissions. Responds in 2 months to queries. Sample copy not available.

Nonfiction General interest, historical/nostalgic, humor, interview/profile, travel, home and garden. Query with published clips. Length: 800-4,000 words. **Pays $250-1,200.**

Columns/Departments My Town (Cleveland first-person stories), 1,100-1,500 words. Query with published clips. **Pays $300.**

$ $ COLUMBUS MONTHLY

P.O. Box 29913, Columbus OH 43229-7513. (614)888-4567. Fax: (614)848-3838. Editor: Lenore E. Brown. **20-40% freelance written.** Prefers to work with published/established writers. Monthly magazine emphasizing subjects specifically related to Columbus and Central Ohio. Circ. 38,000. Pays on publication. Publishes ms an average of 2 months after acceptance. Byline given. Buys all rights. Responds in 1 month to queries. Sample copy for $6.50. Writer's guidelines not available.

Nonfiction "We like query letters that are well written, indicate the author has some familiarity with *Columbus Monthly*, give us enough detail to make a decision, and include at least a basic résumé of the writer." No humor, essays, or first-person material. **Buys 2-3 unsolicited mss/year.** Query. Length: 400-4,500 words. **Pays $50-400.** Sometimes pays expenses of writers on assignment.

Columns/Departments Art, business, food and drink, politics, sports, theatre. Length: 1,000-2,000 words. Query. **Pay varies.**

Tips "It makes sense to start small—something for our City Journal section, perhaps. Stories for that section run between 400-1,000 words."

$ DARKE COUNTY PROFILE

4952 Bishop Rd., Greenville OH 45331. (937)547-0048. E-mail: profile@woh.rr.com. **Contact:** Diana J. Linder, editor. **15% freelance written.** Monthly magazine covering people and places in the Darke County area. Estab. 1994. Circ. 500. Pays on publication. Publishes ms an average of 3-6 months after acceptance. Byline given. Buys one-time rights. Editorial lead time 3 months. Submit seasonal material 3 months in advance. Accepts previously published material. Responds in 3-6 months to mss. Sample copy for $2. Writer's guidelines by e-mail.

Nonfiction General interest, how-to (crafts), humor, inspirational, personal experience, travel. No foul language, graphic violence, or pornography. **Buys 10-12 mss/year.** Send complete ms. Length: 500-1,500 words. **Pays $15-20.** Pays 1-year subscription for work published for the first time in the *Profile*.

Photos Send photos with submission. Buys one-time rights. Pays $3.50/photo. Captions required.

Fiction Adventure, condensed novels, humorous, mainstream, mystery, romance, suspense, western. No violence, foul language, or sexually explicit material. **Buys 12-14 mss/year.** Send complete ms. Length: 500-1,500 words. **Pays $15-20.**

Fillers Anecdotes, facts, short humor. **Buys 6-12/year.** Length: 250-500 words. **Pays $5-10.**

Tips "Write tight and send neatly typed mss with a SASE."

$ $ $ NORTHERN OHIO LIVE

LIVE Publishing Co., 11320 Juniper Rd., Cleveland OH 44106. (216)721-1800. Fax: (216)721-2525. E-mail: ssphar@livepub.com. **Contact:** Sarah R. Sphar, managing editor. **70% freelance written.** Monthly magazine covering Northern Ohio politics, arts, entertainment, education, and dining. "Reader demographic is mid-30s to 50s, though we're working to bring in the late 20s. Our readers are well-educated, many with advanced degrees. They're interested in Northern Ohio's cultural scene and support it." Estab. 1980. Circ. 35,000. Pays on 20th of publication month. Publishes ms an average of 1 month after acceptance. Byline given. Offers 33% kill fee. Buys first North American serial rights. Editorial lead time 3 months. Submit seasonal material 4 months in advance. Responds in 3 weeks to queries; 2 months to mss. Sample copy for $3. Writer's guidelines not available.

Nonfiction All submission/pitches should have a Northern Ohio slant. Essays, exposé, general interest, humor, interview/profile, photo feature, travel. Special issues: Gourmet Guide (restaurants—May). **Buys 100 mss/year.** Query with published clips. Length: 1,000-3,500 words. **Pays $100-1,000.** Sometimes pays expenses of writers on assignment.

Reprints Send photocopy and information about when and where the material previously appeared.

Photos State availability with submission. Reviews contact sheets, 4×5 transparencies, 3×5 prints. Buys one-time rights. Negotiates payment individually. Identification of subjects required.

Columns/Departments News & Reviews (arts previews, personality profiles, general interest), 800-1,800 words. **Pays $200-300.** Time & Place (personal essay), 400-450 words. **Pays $100.** Must be local authors. **Buys 60-70 mss/year.** Query with published clips.

Fiction Novel excerpts.

Tips "Don't send submissions not having anything to do with Northern Ohio. Must have some tie to the Northeast Quadrant of Ohio. We are not interested in stories appearing in every other outlet in town. What is the new angle?"

$ $ $ $ OHIO MAGAZINE

Great Lakes Publishing Co., 1422 Euclid Ave., Suite 730, Cleveland OH 44115. (216)771-2833. E-mail: editorial@ ohiomagazine.com. Website: www.ohiomagazine.com. **Contact:** Richard Osborne, editorial director. **50% freelance written.** Monthly magazine emphasizing Ohio-based travel, news and feature material that highlights what's special and unique about the state. Estab. 1978. Circ. 80,000. Pays on publication. Publishes ms an average of 6 months after acceptance. Byline given. Buys first North American serial, one-time, second serial (reprint), all rights. Buys first serial rights. Submit seasonal material 6 months in advance. Accepts queries by mail, e-mail, fax. Responds in 3 months. Sample copy for $3.95 and 9×12 SAE or online. Writer's guidelines online.

O— Break in by "knowing the magazine—read it thoroughly for several issues. Send clips that show your ability to write on topics we cover. We're looking for thoughtful stories on topics that are more contextual and less shallow. I want queries that show the writer has some passion for the subject."

Nonfiction Length: 1,000-3,000 words. **Pays $300-1,200.** Sometimes pays expenses of writers on assignment.

Reprints Send tearsheet or photocopy and information about when and where the material previously appeared. Pays 50% of amount paid for an original article.

Photos Rob McGarr, art director. Rate negotiable.

Columns/Departments Buys minimum 20 unsolicited mss/year. Pays $50-500.

Tips "Freelancers should send all queries in writing (either by mail or e-mail), not by telephone. Successful queries demonstrate an intimate knowledge of the publication. We are looking to increase our circle of writers who can write about the state in an informative and upbeat style. Strong reporting skills are highly valued."

$ $ OVER THE BACK FENCE

Ohio: Neighbor to Neighbor, Panther Publishing, LLC, P.O. Box 756, Chillicothe OH 45601. (740)772-2165. Fax: (740)773-7626. E-mail: backfenc@bright.net. Website: www.pantherpublishing.com. Sarah Williamson, managing editor. Quarterly magazine. "We are a regional magazine serving 38 counties in Southern Ohio. *Over The Back Fence* has a wholesome, neighborly style. It appeals to readers from young adults to seniors, showcasing art and travel opportunities in the area." Estab. 1994. Circ. 15,000. Pays on publication. Publishes ms an average of 1 year after acceptance. Byline given. Buys one-time North American serial rights, makes work-for-hire assignments. Editorial lead time 1 year. Submit seasonal material 1 year in advance. Accepts queries by mail. Accepts simultaneous submissions. Responds in 3 months to queries. Sample copy for $4 or on website. Writer's guidelines online.

O— Break in with personality profiles (1,000 words), short features, columns (600 words), and features (1,000 words).

Nonfiction General interest, historical/nostalgic, humor, inspirational, interview/profile, personal experience, photo feature, travel. **Buys 9-12 mss/year.** Query with or without published clips or send complete ms. Length: 750-1,000 words. **Pays 10¢/word minimum, negotiable depending on experience.**

Reprints Send photocopy of article or short story and typed ms with rights for sale noted, and information about when and where the material previously appeared. Payment negotiable.

Photos "If sending photos as part of a text/photo package, please request our photo guidelines and submit color transparencies." Reviews color, 35mm or larger transparencies, prints. Buys one-time rights. Pays $25-100/photo. Captions, identification of subjects, model releases required.

Columns/Departments The Arts, 750-1,000 words; History (relevant to a designated county), 750-1,000 words; Inspirational (poetry or short story), 600-850 words; Profiles From Our Past, 300-600 words; Sport & Hobby,

750-1,000 words; Our Neighbors (i.e., people helping others), 750-1,000 words. All must be relevant to Southern Ohio. **Buys 24 mss/year.** Query with or without published clips or send complete ms. **Pays 10¢/word minimum, negotiable depending on experience.**

Fiction Humorous. **Buys 4 mss/year.** Query with published clips. Length: 600-800 words. **Pays 10¢/word minimum, negotiable depending on experience.**

Poetry Wholesome, traditional free verse, light verse, and rhyming. **Buys 4 poems/year.** Submit maximum 4 poems. Length: 4-32 lines. **Pays 10¢/word or $25 minimum.**

Tips "Our approach can be equated to a friendly and informative conversation with a neighbor about interesting people, places, and events in Southern Ohio (counties: Adams, Athens, Brown, Clark, Clermont, Clinton, Coshocton, Fayette, Fairfield, Franklin, Gallia, Greene, Guernsey, Highland, Hocking, Holmes, Jackson, Lawrence, Licking, Madison, Meigs, Miami, Morgan, Muskingum, Noble, Perry, Pickaway, Pike, Ross, Scioto, Vinton, Warren, Washington, and Wayne)."

$ $ THE PLAIN DEALER SUNDAY MAGAZINE

Plain Dealer Publishing Co., Plain Dealer Plaza, 1801 Superior Ave., Cleveland OH 44114. (216)999-4546. Fax: (216)515-2039. E-mail: eburbach@plaind.com. **Contact:** Ellen Stein Burbach, editor. **50% freelance written.** Weekly magazine focusing on Cleveland and Northeastern Ohio. Circ. 450,000. Pays on publication. Publishes ms an average of 2 months after acceptance. Byline given. Buys first, one-time, all Web rights. Submit seasonal material 2 months in advance. Accepts queries by mail, e-mail, fax. Responds in 1 month to queries; 2 months to mss.

- Recommends looking at sample articles online.
- ⚬╾ "Start small, with 'North by Northeast' pieces."

Nonfiction Must include focus on Northeast Ohio people, places, and issues. Book excerpts, essays, exposé, general interest, historical/nostalgic, humor, inspirational, interview/profile, new product, personal experience, photo feature, travel (only personal essays or local ties). **Buys hundreds of shorter pieces and 50-100 feature mss/year.** Query with published clips or send complete ms. Length: 800-4,000 words. **Pays $150-700 for assigned articles.**

Reprints Send ms with rights for sale noted and information about when and where the material previously appeared.

Columns/Departments North by Northeast (short upfront pieces), **pays $25-75**; Essays (personal perspective, memoir OK), **pays $200-250**, 900 words maximum; The Back Burner (food essays with recipe), **pays $200**.

Tips "We're always looking for great stories and superior writers."

OKLAHOMA

$ $ OKLAHOMA TODAY

P.O. Box 1468, Oklahoma City OK 73101. (405)521-2496. Fax: (405)522-4588. E-mail: mccune@oklahomatoday. com. Website: www.oklahomatoday.com. **Contact:** Louisa McCune, editor-in-chief. **80% freelance written.** Works with approximately 25 new/unpublished writers each year. Bimonthly magazine covering people, places, and things Oklahoman. "We are interested in showing off the best Oklahoma has to offer; we're pretty serious about our travel slant but regularly run history, nature, and personality profiles." Estab. 1956. Circ. 45,000. Pays on publication. Publishes ms an average of 6 months after acceptance. Byline given. Buys first worldwide serial rights. Submit seasonal material 1 year in advance. Accepts queries by mail, e-mail. Responds in 4 months to queries. Sample copy for $3.95 and 9×12 SASE or online. Writer's guidelines online.

- ⚬╾ "Start small. Look for possibilities for 'The Range.' Even letters to the editor are good ways to 'get some ink.' "

Nonfiction Book excerpts (on Oklahoma topics), historical/nostalgic (Oklahoma only), interview/profile (Oklahomans only), photo feature (in Oklahoma), travel (in Oklahoma). No phone queries. **Buys 20-40 mss/year.** Query with published clips. Length: 250-3,000 words. **Pays $25-750.**

Photos "We are especially interested in developing contacts with photographers who live in Oklahoma or have shot here. Send samples." Photo guidelines for SASE. Reviews 4×5, 2¼×2¼, and 35mm color transparencies, high-quality transparencies, slides, and b&w prints. Buys one-time rights to use photos for promotional purposes. Pays $50-750 for color. Captions, identification of subjects required.

Fiction Novel excerpts, occasionally short fiction.

Tips "The best way to become a regular contributor to *Oklahoma Today* is to query us with 1 or more story ideas, each developed to give us an idea of your proposed slant. We're looking for lively, concise, well-researched and reported stories, stories that don't need to be heavily edited and are not newspaper style. We have a 3-person full-time editorial staff, and freelancers who can write and have done their homework get called again and again."

OREGON

$ $ OREGON COAST

4969 Highway 101 N. #2, Florence OR 97439. (541)997-8401. Website: www.northwestmagazines.com. **65% freelance written.** Bimonthly magazine covering the Oregon Coast. Estab. 1982. Circ. 50,000. Pays after publication. Publishes ms an average of up to 1 year after acceptance. Byline given. Offers 33% (on assigned stories only, not on stories accepted on spec) kill fee. Buys first North American serial rights. Submit seasonal material 6 months in advance. Accepts queries by mail. Responds in 3 months to queries. Sample copy for $4.50. Writer's guidelines for #10 SASE.

- This company also publishes *Northwest Travel*.
- O→ "Break in with great photos with a story that has a great lead and no problems during fact-checking. We like stories that have a slightly different take on 'same-old' subjects and have good anecdotes and quotes. Stories should have satisfying endings."

Nonfiction "A true regional with general interest, historical/nostalgic, humor, interview/profile, personal experience, photo feature, travel, and nature as pertains to Oregon Coast." **Buys 55 mss/year.** Query with published clips. Length: 500-1,500 words. **Pays $75-250, plus 2-5 contributor copies.**

Reprints Send tearsheet or photocopy and information about when and where the material previously appeared. Pays an average of 60% of the amount paid for an original article.

Photos Photo submissions with no ms or stand alone or cover photos. Send photos with submission. Reviews 35mm or larger transparencies. Buys one-time rights. Captions, identification of subjects, model releases (for cover), photo credits required.

Fillers Newsbreaks (no-fee basis).

Tips "Slant article for readers who do not live at the Oregon Coast. At least 1 historical article is used in each issue. Manuscript/photo packages are preferred over manuscripts with no photos. List photo credits and captions for each historic print or color slide. Check all facts, proper names, and numbers carefully in photo/manuscript packages. Must pertain to Oregon Coast somehow."

PENNSYLVANIA

$ $ BERKS COUNTY LIVING

West Lawn Graphic Communications, P.O. Box 642, Shillington PA 19607. (610)775-0640. Fax: (610)775-7412. E-mail: editor@berkscountyliving.com. Website: www.berkscountyliving.com. **Contact:** Kristin Kramer, editor. **90% freelance written.** Bimonthly magazine covering topics of interest to people living in Berks County, Pennsylvania. Estab. 2000. Circ. 36,000. Pays on publication. Publishes ms an average of 4 months after acceptance. Byline given. Offers 25% kill fee. Buys first North American serial rights. Editorial lead time 3 months. Submit seasonal material 4 months in advance. Accepts queries by mail, e-mail. Accepts previously published material. Accepts simultaneous submissions. Responds in 1 week to queries; 1 month to mss. Sample copy for 9×12 SAE and 2 first-class stamps. Writer's guidelines online.

Nonfiction Articles must be associated with Berks County, Pennsylvania. Exposé, general interest, historical/nostalgic, how-to, humor, inspirational, interview/profile, new product, photo feature, travel, food, health. **Buys 25 mss/year.** Query. Length: 750-2,000 words. **Pays $150-400.** Sometimes pays expenses of writers on assignment.

Reprints Accepts previously published submissions.

Photos State availability with submission. Reviews 35mm or greater transparencies, any size prints. Buys one-time rights. Negotiates payment individually. Captions, identification of subjects, model releases required.

$ $ CENTRAL PA

WITF, Inc., 1982 Locust Lane, Harrisburg PA 17109. (717)221-2800. Fax: (717)221-2630. E-mail: steve_kennedy @centralpa.org. Website: www.centralpa.org. **Contact:** Steve Kennedy, senior editor. **75% freelance written.** Monthly magazine covering life in Central Pennsylvania. Estab. 1982. Circ. 42,000. Pays on publication. Publishes ms an average of 4 months after acceptance. Offers 20% kill fee. Buys first North American serial rights. Editorial lead time 3 months. Submit seasonal material 6 months in advance. Accepts queries by mail, e-mail, fax. Accepts simultaneous submissions. Responds in 6 weeks to queries. Sample copy for $3.50 and SASE. Writer's guidelines online.

- O→ Break in through Central shorts, essay.

Nonfiction Essays, general interest, historical/nostalgic, how-to, humor, interview/profile, opinion, personal experience, photo feature, travel. Special issues: Dining/Food (January). **Buys 50 mss/year.** Query with published clips or send complete ms. Length: 175-1,500 words. **Pays $50-500.** Sometimes pays expenses of writers on assignment.

Photos State availability with submission. Reviews contact sheets, transparencies, prints. Buys one-time rights. Negotiates payment individually. Identification of subjects required.

Columns/Departments Central Shorts (quirky, newsy, regional), 175 words; Thinking Aloud (essay), 1,100 words; Cameo (interview), 1,000 words. **Buys 90 mss/year.** Query with published clips or send complete ms. **Pays $50-100.**

Tips "Wow us with something you wrote, either a clip or a manuscript on spec. If it's off target but shows you can write well and know the region, we'll ask for more. We're looking for creative nonfiction, with an emphasis on conveying valuable information through near literary-quality narrative. Strong central PA interest an absolute must."

$ $PENNSYLVANIA

Pennsylvania Magazine Co., P.O. Box 755, Camp Hill PA 17001-0755. (717)697-4660. E-mail: pamag@aol.com. Website: www.pa-mag.com. Publisher: Albert E. Holliday. **Contact:** Matt Holliday, editor. **90% freelance written.** Bimonthly magazine covering people, places, events, and history in Pennsylvania. Estab. 1981. Circ. 33,000. Pays on acceptance except for articles (by authors unknown to us) sent on speculation. Publishes ms an average of 9 months after acceptance. Byline given. 25% kill fee for assigned articles. Buys first North American serial, one-time rights. Submit seasonal material 9 months in advance. Accepts queries by mail, e-mail. Responds in 4-6 weeks to queries. Sample copy for $2.95. Writer's guidelines for #10 SASE.

O﹁ Break in with "a text/photo package—learn to take photos or hook up with a photographer who will shoot for our rates."

Nonfiction Features include general interest, historical, photo feature, vacations and travel, people/family success stories—all dealing with or related to Pennsylvania. Send photocopies of possible illustrations with query or ms. Include SASE. Nothing on Amish topics, hunting, or skiing. **Buys 75-120 mss/year.** Query. Length: 750-2,500 words. **Pays 10-15¢/word.**

Reprints Send photocopy with rights for sale noted and information about when and where the material previously appeared. Pays 5¢/word.

Photos No original slides or transparencies. Photography Essay (highlights annual photo essay contest entries). Reviews 35mm $2\frac{1}{4} \times 2\frac{1}{4}$ color transparencies, 5×7 to 8×10 color prints. Buys one-time rights. Pays $15-25 for inside photos; $100 for covers. Captions, thumbnail sheet for digital submissions required.

Columns/Departments Round Up (short items about people, unusual events, museums, historical topics/events, family and individually owned consumer-related businesses), 250-1,300 words; Town and Country (items about people or events illustrated with commissioned art), 500 words. Include SASE. Query. **Pays 12-15¢/word.**

Tips "Our publication depends upon freelance work—send queries."

Ⓝ $ $PENNSYLVANIA HERITAGE

Pennsylvania Historical and Museum Commission and the Pennsylvania Heritage Society, Commonwealth Keystone Bldg., Plaza Level, 400 North St., Harrisburg PA 17120-0053. (717)787-7522. Fax: (717)787-8312. E-mail: miomalley@state.pa.us. Website: www.paheritage.org. **Contact:** Michael J. O'Malley III, editor. **90% freelance written.** Prefers to work with published/established writers. Quarterly magazine. "*Pennsylvania Heritage* introduces readers to Pennsylvania's rich culture and historic legacy; educates and sensitizes them to the value of preserving that heritage; and entertains and involves them in such a way as to ensure that Pennsylvania's past has a future. The magazine is intended for intelligent lay readers." Estab. 1974. Circ. 10,000. Pays on publication. Publishes ms an average of 1 year after acceptance. Byline given. Buys all rights. Accepts queries by mail, e-mail. Responds in 10 weeks to queries; 8 months to mss. Sample copy for $5 and 9×12 SAE or online. Writer's guidelines for #10 SASE or online.

● *Pennsylvania Heritage* is now considering freelance submissions that are shorter in length (2,000-3,000 words); pictorial/photographic essays; biographies of famous (and not-so-famous) Pennsylvanians; and interviews with individuals who have helped shape, make, and preserve the Keystone State's history and heritage.

Nonfiction "Our format requires feature-length articles. Manuscripts with illustrations are especially sought for publication. We are now looking for shorter (2,000 words) manuscripts that are heavily illustrated with publication-quality photographs or artwork. We are eager to work with experienced travel writers for destination pieces on historical sites and museums that make up 'The Pennsylvania Trail of History.'" Art, science, biographies, industry, business, politics, transportation, military, historic preservation, archaeology, photography, etc. No articles which do not relate to Pennsylvania history or culture. **Buys 20-24 mss/year.** Prefers to see mss with suggested illustrations. Length: 2,000-3,500 words. **Pays $100-500.**

Photos State availability of or send photos with submission. Buys one-time rights. Pays $25-200 for transparencies; $5-75 for b&w photos. Captions, identification of subjects required.

Tips "We are looking for well-written, interesting material that pertains to any aspect of Pennsylvania history or culture. Potential contributors should realize that, although our articles are popularly styled, they are not light, puffy, or breezy; in fact they demand strident documentation and substantiation (sans footnotes). The most frequent mistake made by writers in completing articles for us is making them either too scholarly or too sentimental or nostalgic. We want material which educates, but also entertains. Authors should make history readable and enjoyable. Our goal is to make the Keystone State's history come to life in a meaningful, memorable way.''

PHILADELPHIA MAGAZINE

1818 Market St., 36th Floor, Philadelphia PA 19103. (215)564-7700. Website: www.phillymag.com. **Contact:** Editor: Larry Platt. Monthly magazine. ''*Philadelphia* is edited for the area's community leaders and their families. It provides in-depth reports on crucial and controversial issues confronting the region—business trends, political analysis, metropolitan planning, sociological trends—plus critical reviews of the cultural, sports and entertainment scene.'' Estab. 1908. Circ. 133,083. **Pays on acceptance.** Accepts queries by mail.

> O–⊓ Break in by sending queries along with clips. ''Remember that we are a general interest magazine that focuses exclusively on topics of interest in the Delaware Valley.''

Nonfiction ''Articles range from law enforcement to fashion, voting trends to travel, transportation to theater, also includes the background studies of the area newsmakers.'' Query with clips and SASE.

Tips ''*Philadelphia Magazine* readers are an affluent, interested and influential group who can afford the best the region has to offer. They're the greater Philadelphia area residents who care about the city and its politics, lifestyles, business and culture.''

$ $ PHILADELPHIA STYLE

Philadelphia's Premier Magazine for Lifestyle & Fashion, Philadelphia Style Magazine, LLC, 141 League St., Philadelphia PA 19147. (215)468-6670. Fax: (215)468-6530. E-mail: pete@phillystylemag.com. Website: www.p hillystylemag.com. Executive Editor: Susan M. Stapleton. **Contact:** Peter Mazzaccaro, articles editor. **90% freelance written.** Bimonthly magazine covering upscale living in the Philadelphia region. Topics include: fashion (men's and women's), home and design, real estate, dining, beauty, travel, arts and entertainment, and more. ''Our magazine is a positive look at the best ways to live in the Philadelphia region. Submitted articles should speak to an upscale, educated audience of professionals that live in the Delaware Valley.'' Estab. 1999. Circ. 45,000. Pays on publication. Publishes ms an average of 3 months after acceptance. Byline given. Offers 25% kill fee. Buys first rights. Editorial lead time 2-4 months. Submit seasonal material 6 months in advance. Accepts queries by mail, e-mail, fax.

> O–⊓ Break in ''with ideas for our real estate section (reviews/stories of area neighborhoods, home and design, architecture, and other new ideas you may have).''

Nonfiction General interest, interview/profile, travel, region-specific articles. ''We are not looking for articles that do not have a regional spin.'' **Buys 100+ mss/year.** Query with published clips or send complete ms. Length: 300-2,500 words. **Pays $50-500.**

Columns/Departments Life in the City (fresh, quirky, regional reporting on books, real estate, art, retail, dining, events, and little-known stories/facts about the region), 100-500 words; Vanguard (people on the forefront of Philadelphia's arts, media, fashion, business, and social scene), 500-700 words; In the Neighborhood (reader-friendly reporting on up-and-coming areas of the region including dining, shopping, attractions, and recreation), 2,000-2,500 words. Query with published clips or send complete ms. **Pays $50-500.**

Tips ''Mail queries with clips or manuscripts. Articles should speak to a stylish, educated audience.''

N $ $ $ $ PITTSBURGH MAGAZINE

WQED Pittsburgh, 4802 Fifth Ave., Pittsburgh PA 15213. (412)622-1360. Website: www.pittsburghmag.com. **Contact:** Stephen Segal, managing editor. **70% freelance written.** Monthly magazine. ''*Pittsburgh* presents issues, analyzes problems, and strives to encourage a better understanding of the community. Our region is Western Pennsylvania, Eastern Ohio, Northern West Virginia, and Western Maryland.'' Estab. 1970. Circ. 75,000. Pays on publication. Publishes ms an average of 2 months after acceptance. Byline given. Offers kill fee. Buys first North American serial, second serial (reprint) rights. Submit seasonal material 6 months in advance. Accepts queries by mail. Responds in 2 months to queries. Sample copy for $2 (old back issues). Writer's guidelines online or via SASE.

> ● The editor reports a need for more hard news and stories targeting readers in their 30s and 40s, especially those with young families. Prefers to work with published/established writers. The monthly magazine is purchased on newsstands and by subscription, and is given to those who contribute $40 or more/year to public TV in western Pennsylvania.

Nonfiction ''Without exception—whether the topic is business, travel, the arts, or lifestyle—each story is clearly oriented to Pittsburghers of today and to the greater Pittsburgh region of today.'' Must have greater Pittsburgh angle. No fax, phone, or e-mail queries. No complete mss. Exposé, lifestyle, sports, informational, service, business, medical, profile. "We have minimal interest in historical articles and we do not publish fiction, poetry, advocacy, or personal reminiscence pieces." Query in writing with outline and clips. Length: 1,200-4,000 words. **Pays $300-1,500+.**

Photos Query. Pays prenegotiated expenses of writer on assignment. Model releases required.

Columns/Departments The Front (short, front-of-the-book items). Length: 300 words maximum. **Pays $50-150.**

Tips "Best bet to break in is through hard news with a region-wide impact or service pieces or profiles with a regional interest. The point is that we want more stories that reflect our region, not just a tiny part. And we *never* consider any story without a strong regional focus. We do not respond to fax and e-mail queries."

$SUSQUEHANNA LIFE

Central Pennsylvania's Lifestyle Magazine, ELS & Associates, 637 Market St., Lewisburg PA 17837. Fax: (570)524-7796. E-mail: info@susquehannalife.com. Website: www.susquehannalife.com. **Contact:** Erica Shames, publisher. **80% freelance written.** Quarterly magazine covering Central Pennsylvania lifestyle. Estab. 1993. Circ. 45,000. Pays on publication. Publishes ms an average of 6-9 months after acceptance. Byline given. Offers 50% kill fee. Not copyrighted. Buys first North American serial, electronic rights. Editorial lead time 3-6 months. Submit seasonal material 4-6 months in advance. Accepts queries by e-mail. Responds in 4-6 weeks to queries; 1-3 months to mss. Sample copy for $4.95 and 5 first-class stamps. Writer's guidelines for #10 SASE.

Nonfiction Book excerpts, general interest, historical/nostalgic, how-to, inspirational, interview/profile, photo feature, travel. Does not want poetry or fiction. **Buys 30-40 mss/year.** Query or send complete ms. Length: 800-1,200 words. **Pays $75-125.** Sometimes pays expenses of writers on assignment.

Photos Send photos with submission. Reviews contact sheets, prints, GIF/JPEG files. Buys one-time rights. Offers $20-25/photo. Captions, identification of subjects, model releases required.

Tips "When you query, do not address letter to 'Dear Sir'—address the letter to the name of the publisher/editor. Demonstrate your ability to write. You need to be familiar with the type of articles we use and the particular flavor of the region."

$ $WESTSYLVANIA

Westsylvania Heritage Corp., P.O. Box 565, 105 Zee Plaza, Hollidaysburg PA 16648-0565. (814)696-9380. Fax: (814)696-9569. E-mail: jschumacher@westsylvania.org. Website: www.westsylvania.com. **Contact:** Jerilynn "Jerry" Schumacher, editor. **50% freelance written.** Quarterly magazine in Western Pennsylvania, plus parts of Ohio, Maryland, West Virginia, Virginia, and Kentucky. "*Westsylvania* magazine celebrates the cultural and natural heritages of south-central and southwestern Pennsylvania. Articles must reflect the writer's keen knowledge of the region. Writers should strive to show what residents are doing to preserve and protect their natural and cultural heritages. This is not a typical history or travel magazine. Stories should show how building on the region's history can make it a great place to live and visit." Estab. 1997. Circ. 10,000-14,000. Pays on publication. Publishes ms an average of 4 months after acceptance. Byline given. Buys first North American serial, web rights. Editorial lead time 6-24 months. Accepts queries by mail, e-mail, fax. Accepts simultaneous submissions. Sample copy sent with request for writer's or photographer's guidelines.

  ➤ Break in with "a well-written query that spotlights stories on what people are doing to preserve their own heritage, such as cleaning up a trout stream, protecting endangered species, finding new uses for historic buildings, or helping others understand the past through art or music. First-person accounts accepted only for assigned columns."

Nonfiction Book excerpts, historical/nostalgic, interview/profile, religious, travel (heritage), business, wildlife, outdoors, photography. *No unsolicited mss.* **Buys 30 mss/year.** Query with published clips. Length: 750-2,200 words. **Pays $75-300 for assigned articles.**

Photos State photo ideas or availability with submission. Use of high-quality digital images a must. Gives assignments to experienced photographers who supply introductory letters, résumés, and samples of past work. Buys one-time rights for magazine and website. Negotiates payments individually. Captions, identification of subjects, model releases required.

Columns/Departments On the Back Porch (introduces readers to a special time or place in Westsylvania), 750 words; Vintage Ventures (stories about businesses 100 or more years old), 750 words. **Buys 8 mss/year.** Query with published clips. **Pays with free subscription or check up to $125, depending.**

Tips Poorly written queries will receive no response. "Look for stories that are uniquely Westsylvania. We will not accept generic articles that do not have a Westsylvania slant."

RHODE ISLAND

$ $ $RHODE ISLAND MONTHLY

The Providence Journal Co., 280 Kinsley Ave., Providence RI 02903. (401)277-8200. Website: www.rimonthly.com. **50% freelance written.** Monthly magazine. "*Rhode Island Monthly* is a general interest consumer magazine with a strict Rhode Island focus.'' Estab. 1988. Circ. 41,000. **Pays on acceptance.** Publishes ms an average of 3 months after acceptance. Byline given. Offers 25% kill fee. Buys all rights for 90 days from date of publication. Editorial lead time 3 months. Submit seasonal material 6 months in advance. Accepts queries by mail, e-mail, fax. Responds in 6 weeks to queries. Writer's guidelines free.

Nonfiction Exposé, general interest, interview/profile, photo feature. **Buys 40 mss/year.** Query with published clips. Length: 1,800-3,000 words. **Pays $600-1,200.** Sometimes pays expenses of writers on assignment.

SOUTH CAROLINA

CHARLESTON MAGAZINE

P.O. Box 1794, Mt. Pleasant SC 29465-1794. (843)971-9811. E-mail: dshankland@charlestonmag.com. Website: charlestonmag.com. **Contact:** Darcy Shankland, editor. **80% freelance written.** Bimonthly magazine covering current issues, events, arts and culture, leisure pursuits, travel, and personalities, as they pertain to the city of Charleston and surrounding areas. ''A Lowcountry institution for more than 30 years, *Charleston Magazine* captures the essence of Charleston and her surrounding areas—her people, arts and architecture, culture and events, and natural beauty.'' Estab. 1972. Circ. 25,000. Pays 1 month after publication. Byline given. Buys one-time rights. Submit seasonal material 4 months in advance. Accepts queries by mail, e-mail, fax. Sample copies may be ordered at cover price from office. Writer's guidelines for #10 SASE.

Nonfiction ''Must pertain to the Charleston area and its present culture.'' General interest, humor, interview/profile, opinion, photo feature, travel, food, architecture, sports, current events/issues, art. ''Not interested in 'Southern nostalgia' articles or gratuitous history pieces.'' **Buys 40 mss/year.** Query with published clips and SASE. Length: 150-1,500 words. **Payment negotiated.** Sometimes pays expenses of writers on assignment.

Reprints Send photocopy and information about when and where the material previously appeared. Payment negotiable.

Photos Send photos with submission. Reviews contact sheets, transparencies, slides. Buys one-time rights. Identification of subjects required.

Columns/Departments Channel Markers (general local interest), 50-400 words; Local Seen (profile of local interest), 500 words; In Good Taste (restaurants and culinary trends in the city), 1,000-1,200 words, plus recipes; Chef at Home (profile of local chefs), 1,200 words, plus recipes; On the Road (travel opportunities near Charleston), 1,000-1,200 words; Southern View (personal experience about Charleston life), 750 words; Doing Business (profiles of exceptional local businesses and entrepreneurs), 1,000-1,200 words; Native Talent (local profiles), 1,000-1,200 words; Top of the Shelf (reviews of books with Southern content or by a Southern author), 750 words.

Tips ''Charleston, although a city with a 300-year history, is a vibrant, modern community with a tremendous dedication to the arts and no shortage of newsworthy subjects. We're looking for the freshest stories about Charleston—and those don't always come from insiders, but also outsiders who are keenly observant.''

$ $ HILTON HEAD MONTHLY

Frey Media, Inc., 2 Park Lane, Hilton Head Island SC 29928. Fax: (843)842-5743. E-mail: bkaufman@freymedia.com; blt1@freymedia.com. Website: www.hiltonheadmonthly.com. **Contact:** Blanche L. Tomaszewski, editor; Barry Kaufman, assistant editor. **75% freelance written.** Monthly magazine covering the business, people, and lifestyle of Hilton Head, South Carolina. ''Our mission is to provide fresh, upbeat reading about the residents, lifestyle and community affairs of Hilton Head Island, an upscale, intensely pro-active resort community on the East Coast. We are not even remotely 'trendy,' but we like to see how national trends/issues play out on a local level. Especially interested in: home design and maintenance, entrepreneurship, health issues, nature, area history, golf/tennis/boating, volunteerism.'' Circ. 28,000. Pays on publication. Publishes ms an average of 6 months after acceptance. Byline given. Offers 50% kill fee. Buys first North American serial rights, makes work-for-hire assignments. Editorial lead time 3 months. Submit seasonal material 4 months in advance. Accepts queries by mail, e-mail, fax. Accepts previously published material. Accepts simultaneous submissions. Responds in 1 week to queries; 4 months to mss. Sample copy for $3.

Nonfiction General interest, historical/nostalgic (history only), how-to (home related), humor, interview/profile (Hilton Head residents only), opinion (general humor or Hilton Head Island community affairs), personal experience, travel. No ''exposé interviews with people who are not Hilton Head residents; profiles of people, events, or businesses in Beaufort, South Carolina; Savannah, Georgia; Charleston; or other surrounding cities, unless it's within a travel piece.'' **Buys 225-250 mss/year.** Query with published clips.

Photos State availability with submission. Reviews contact sheets, prints, slides; any size. Buys one-time rights. Negotiates payment individually.

Columns/Departments News; Business; Lifestyles (hobbies, health, sports, etc.); Home; Around Town (local events, charities and personalities); People (profiles, weddings, etc.). Query with synopsis. **Pays 15¢/word.**

Tips "Give us concise, bullet-style descriptions of what the article covers (in the query letter); choose upbeat, pro-active topics; delight us with your fresh (not trendy) description and word choice."

$SANDLAPPER

The Magazine of South Carolina, The Sandlapper Society, Inc., P.O. Box 1108, Lexington SC 29071-1108. (803)359-9941. Fax: (803)359-0629. E-mail: aida@sandlapper.org. Website: www.sandlapper.org. Editor: Robert P. Wilkins. **Contact:** Aida Rogers, managing editor. **60% freelance written.** Quarterly magazine focusing on the positive aspects of South Carolina. "*Sandlapper* is intended to be read at those times when people want to relax with an attractive, high-quality magazine that entertains and informs them about their state." Estab. 1989. Circ. 18,000 with a readership of 60,000. Pays during the dateline period. Publishes ms an average of 1 year after acceptance. Byline given. Buys first North American serial rights and the right to reprint. Submit seasonal material 6 months in advance. Accepts queries by mail, e-mail, fax. Sample copy online. Writer's guidelines for #10 SASE.

Nonfiction Feature articles and photo essays about South Carolina's interesting people, places, cuisine, things to do. Occasional history articles. Essays, general interest, humor, interview/profile, photo feature. Query with clips and SASE. Length: 500-2,500 words. **Pays $100/published page.** Sometimes pays expenses of writers on assignment.

Photos "*Sandlapper* buys b&w prints, color transparencies, and art. Photographers should submit working cutlines for each photograph. While prints and slides are preferred, we do accept digital images in the following format only: JPEGs at 300 dpi (minimum), at 8½×11. Please provide digital images on CD or IBM-compatible disk, accompanied by a proof or laser print." Pays $25-75/photo, $100/cover or centerspread photo.

The online version contains material not found in the print edition. Contact: Dan Harmon.

Tips "We're not interested in articles about topical issues, politics, crime, or commercial ventures. Avoid first-person nostalgia and remembrances of places that no longer exist. We look for top-quality literature. Humor is encouraged. Good taste is a standard. Unique angles are critical for acceptance. Dare to be bold, but not too bold."

SOUTH DAKOTA

$DAKOTA OUTDOORS

South Dakota, Hipple Publishing Co., P.O. Box 669 333 W. Dakota Ave., Pierre SD 57501-0669. (605)224-7301. Fax: (605)224-9210. E-mail: office@capjournal.com. Editor: Kevin Hipple. **Contact:** Rachel Engbrecht, managing editor. **85% freelance written.** Monthly magazine on Dakota outdoor life, focusing on hunting and fishing. Estab. 1974. Circ. 7,000. Pays on publication. Publishes ms an average of 1-2 months after acceptance. Byline given. Submit seasonal material 3 months in advance. Accepts queries by mail, e-mail. Accepts simultaneous submissions. Responds in 3 months to queries. Sample copy for 9×12 SAE and 3 first-class stamps. Writer's guidelines by e-mail.

Nonfiction "Topics should center on fishing and hunting experiences and advice. Other topics such as boating, camping, hiking, environmental concerns and general nature will be considered as well." General interest, how-to, humor, interview/profile, personal experience, technical (all on outdoor topics-prefer in the Dakotas). **Buys 120 mss/year.** Send complete ms. Length: 500-2,000 words. **Pays $5-50.** Sometimes pays in contributor's copies or other premiums (inquire).

Reprints Send ms with rights for sale noted and information about when and where the material previously appeared. 50% of amount paid for an original article.

Photos Send photos with submission. Reviews 3×5 or 5×7 prints. Buys one-time rights. Offers no additonal payment for photos accepted with ms or negotiates payment individually. Identification of subjects required.

Columns/Departments Kids Korner (outdoors column addressing kids 12-16 years of age). Length: 50-500 words. **Pays $5-15.**

Fiction Adventure, humorous. Does not want stories about vacations or subjects that don't include hunting and fishing. **Buys 15 mss/year.** Send complete ms. Length: 750-1,500 words.

Fillers Anecdotes, facts, gags to be illustrated by cartoonist, newsbreaks, short humor, line drawings of fish and game. **Buys 10/year.**

Tips "Submit samples of manuscript or previous works for consideration; photos or illustrations with manuscript are helpful."

TENNESSEE

$ $MEMPHIS

Contemporary Media, P.O. Box 1738, Memphis TN 38101. (901)521-9000. Fax: (901)521-0129. E-mail: memmag @memphismagazine.com. Website: www.memphismagazine.com. **30% freelance written.** Works with a small number of new/unpublished writers. Monthly magazine covering Memphis and the local region. "Our mission is to provide Memphis with a colorful and informative look at the people, places, lifestyles and businesses that make the Bluff City unique." Estab. 1976. Circ. 24,000. Pays on publication. Publishes ms an average of 2 months after acceptance. Byline given. Offers 25% kill fee. Buys first North American serial rights. Editorial lead time 2 months. Submit seasonal material 3 months in advance. Accepts queries by mail, e-mail, fax. Accepts simultaneous submissions. Responds in 2 months to queries. Sample copy for free or online. Writer's guidelines free.

Nonfiction "Virtually all of our material has strong Memphis area connections." Essays, general interest, historical/nostalgic, interview/profile, photo feature, travel, Interiors/exteriors. Special issues: Restaurant Guide and City Guide. **Buys 20 mss/year.** Query with published clips. Length: 500-3,000 words. **Pays 10-30¢/word.** Sometimes pays expenses of writers on assignment.

Photos State availability with submission. Reviews contact sheets, transparencies. Buys one-time rights.

Columns/Departments IntroSpective (personal experiences/relationships), 1,000-1,500 words; CityScape (local events/issues), 1,500-2,000 words; City Beat (peaople, places and things—some quirky), 200-400 words. **Buys 10 mss/year.** Query. **Pays 10-20¢/word.**

Fiction One story published annually as part of contest. Send complete ms. Length: 1,500-3,000 words.

Tips "Send a query letter with specific ideas that apply to our short columns and departments. Good ideas that apply specifically to these sections will often get published."

TEXAS

Ⓝ $HILL COUNTRY SUN

Sun Country Publications, Inc., P.O. Box 1482, Wimberley TX 78676. (512)847-5162. Fax: (512)847-5162. E-mail: allan@hillcountrysun.com. Website: www.hillcountrysun.com. **Contact:** Allan Kimball, editor. **75% free-lance written.** Monthly tabloid covering traveling in the Central Texas Hill Country. "We publish stories of interesting people, places and events in the Central Texas Hill Country." Estab. 1990. Circ. 30,000. **Pays on acceptance.** Publishes ms an average of 2 months after acceptance. Byline given. Buys one-time rights. Editorial lead time 1 month. Submit seasonal material 2 months in advance. Accepts queries by mail, e-mail. Responds in 1 week to queries; 1 month to mss. Sample copy for free. Writer's guidelines online.

Nonfiction Interview/profile, travel. No first person articles. **Buys 50 mss/year.** Query. Length: 600-800 words. **Pays $50-60.**

Photos State availability of or send photos with submission. Reviews 5×7 prints. Buys one-time rights. No additional payment for photos accepted with ms. Identification of subjects required.

Tips "Writers must be familiar with both the magazine's style and the Texas Hill Country."

$ $ $HOUSTON PRESS

New Times, Inc., 1621 Milam, Suite 100, Houston TX 77002. (713)280-2400. Fax: (713)280-2444. E-mail: melissa .sonzala@houstonpress.com. Website: www.houstonpress.com. Editor: Margaret Downing. Managing Editor: George Flynn. Associate Editor: Cathy Matusow. **Contact:** Melissa Sonzala, editorial assistant. **40% freelance written.** Weekly tabloid covering "news and arts stories of interest to a Houston audience. If the same story could run in Seattle, then it's not for us." Estab. 1989. Pays on publication. Publishes ms an average of 2 weeks after acceptance. Byline given. Buys first North American serial, website rights. Editorial lead time 2 months. Submit seasonal material 3 months in advance. Sample copy for $3.

Nonfiction Exposé, general interest, interview/profile, arts reviews; music. Query with published clips. Length: 300-4,500 words. **Pays $10-1,000.** Sometimes pays expenses of writers on assignment.

Photos State availability with submission. Buys all rights. Negotiates payment individually. Identification of subjects required.

$ $ $PAPERCITY

Dallas Edition, Urban Publishers, 3303 Lee Parkway, #340, Dallas TX 75219. (214)521-3439. Fax: (214)521-3178. E-mail: trish@papercitymag.com. **Contact:** Brooke Hortenstine, Dallas co-editor; Holly Moore, editor-in-chief. **5% freelance written.** Monthly magazine. "*Papercity* covers fashion, food, entertainment, home design and decoratives for urban Dallas, Houston, San Francisco, and Atlanta. Our writing is lively, brash, sexy—it's where to read about the hottest restaurants, great chefs, where to shop, what's cool to buy, where to go and the chicest places to stay—from sexy, small hotels in New York, Los Angeles, London and Morocco, to where to buy the newest trends in Europe. We cover local parties with big photo spreads, and a hip nightlife column." Estab. 1994 (Houston); 1998 (Dallas); 2002 (San Francisco); 2004 (Atlanta). Circ. 85,000 (Dallas). Pays on publication. Publishes ms an average of 1 month after acceptance. Byline given. Offers 10% kill fee. Buys first North American serial rights. Editorial lead time 2 months. Submit seasonal material 4 months in advance. Accepts queries by mail, e-mail, fax. Accepts simultaneous submissions. Responds in 3 weeks to queries; 1

month to mss. Sample copy for 9×12 SAE with $1.50 in first-class stamps. Writer's guidelines for #10 SASE or by e-mail.

Nonfiction General interest, interview/profile, new product, travel, home decor, food. Special issues: Bridal (February); Travel (April); Restaurants (August). No straight profiles on anyone, especially celebrities. **Buys 10-12 mss/year.** Query with published clips. Length: 150-3,000 words. **Pays 35-50¢/word.**

Photos State availability with submission. Reviews contact sheets, transparencies, prints. Buys one-time rights. Negotiates payment individually.

Tips "Read similar publications such as *W, Tattler, Wallpaper, Martha Stewart Living* for new trends, style of writing, hip new restaurants. We try to be very 'of the moment' so give us something in Dallas, Houston, New York, Los Angeles, London, etc., that we haven't heard yet. Chances are if other hip magazines are writing about it so will we."

$ $ $TEXAS HIGHWAYS

The Travel Magazine of Texas, Box 141009, Austin TX 78714-1009. (512)486-5858. Fax: (512)486-5879. E-mail: editors@texashighways.com. Website: www.texashighways.com. **80% freelance written.** Monthly magazine "encourages travel within the state and tells the Texas story to readers around the world." Estab. 1974. Circ. 275,000. **Pays on acceptance.** Publishes ms an average of 1 year after acceptance. Buys first North American serial, electronic rights. Accepts queries by mail. Responds in 2 months to queries. Writer's guidelines online.

Nonfiction "Subjects should focus on things to do or places to see in Texas. Include historical, cultural, and geographical aspects if appropriate. Text should be meticulously researched. Include anecdotes, historical references, quotations and, where relevant, geologic, botanical, and zoological information." Query with description, published clips, additional background materials (charts, maps, etc.) and SASE. Length: 1,200-1,500 words. **Pays 40-50¢/word.**

Tips "We like strong leads that draw in the reader immediately and clear, concise writing. Be specific and avoid superlatives. Avoid overused words. Don't forget the basics—who, what, where, when, why, and how."

TEXAS PARKS & WILDLIFE

3000 South I.H. 35, Suite 120, Austin TX 78704. (512)912-7000. Fax: (512)707-1913. E-mail: michael.berryhill@tpwd.state.tx.us. Website: www.tpwmagazine.com. **Contact:** Robert Macias, editorial director. **80% freelance written.** Monthly magazine featuring articles about Texas hunting, fishing, birding, outdoor recreation, game and nongame wildlife, state parks, environmental issues. All articles must be about Texas. Estab. 1942. Circ. 150,000. **Pays on acceptance.** Publishes ms an average of 6 months after acceptance. Byline given. Kill fee determined by contract, usually $200-250. Buys first rights. Submit seasonal material 6 months in advance. Accepts queries by mail. Responds in 1 month to queries; 3 months to mss. Sample copy and writer's guidelines online.

⌐ *Texas Parks & Wildlife* needs more hunting and fishing material.

Nonfiction General interest (Texas only), how-to (outdoor activities), photo feature, travel (state parks). **Buys 60 mss/year.** Query with published clips. Length: 500-2,500 words.

Photos Send photos to photo editor. Reviews transparencies. Buys one-time rights. Offers $65-350/photo. Captions, identification of subjects required.

Tips "Read outdoor pages of statewide newspapers to keep abreast of news items that can lead to story ideas. Feel free to include more than one story idea in one query letter. All areas are open to freelancers. All articles must have a Texas focus."

Ⓝ $ $WHERE DALLAS MAGAZINE

Morris Communications, 8111 LBJ Freeway, Suite 100, Dallas TX 75251. (214)522-0050. Fax: (214)522-0504. E-mail: fokunbolade@abartapub.com. **Contact:** Funmi Okunbolade, editor. **75% freelance written.** Monthly magazine. "*WHERE Dallas* is part of the *WHERE Magazine International* network, the world's largest publisher of travel magazines. Published in more than 46 cities around the world, travelers trust *WHERE* to guide them to the best in shopping, dining, nightlife, and entertainment." Estab. 1996. Circ. 45,000. Pays on publication. Publishes ms an average of 2 months after acceptance. Byline given. Buys all rights. Editorial lead time 2 months. Submit seasonal material 2 months in advance. Accepts queries by mail, e-mail. Accepts simultaneous submissions. Sample copy for $3.

⌐ Break in with "a solid idea—solid meaning the local Dallas angle is everything. We're looking for advice and tips that would/could only come from those living in the area."

Nonfiction General interest, historical/nostalgic, photo feature, travel, special events. **Buys 20 mss/year.** Query with published clips. Length: 650-1,000 words. **Pays $200-300.** Sometimes pays expenses of writers on assignment.

Photos Send photos with submission. Reviews transparencies. Buys one time rights, all rights on cover photos. Captions, identification of subjects, model releases required.

Columns/Departments Pays $100-450.

Tips "To get our attention, send clips with clever, punchy writing, like you might find in a society or insider column in the newspaper. We're also looking for writers with an expertise in shopping, with knowledge of fashion/art/antiques/collectibles."

VERMONT

$ $VERMONT LIFE MAGAZINE

6 Baldwin St., Montpelier VT 05602-2109. (802)828-3241. Fax: (802)828-3366. E-mail: tom.slayton@state.vt.us. Website: www.vtlife.com. **Contact:** Thomas K. Slayton, editor-in-chief. **90% freelance written.** Prefers to work with published/established writers. Quarterly magazine. "*Vermont Life* is interested in any article, query, story idea, photograph or photo essay that has to do with Vermont. As the state magazine, we are most favorably impressed with pieces that present positive aspects of life within the state's borders." Estab. 1946. Circ. 75,000. Publishes ms an average of 9 months after acceptance. Byline given. Offers kill fee. Buys first North American serial rights. Submit seasonal material 1 year in advance. Accepts queries by mail, e-mail, fax. Responds in 1 month to queries. Writer's guidelines online.

O→ Break in with "short humorous Vermont anecdotes for our 'Postboy' column."

Nonfiction Wants articles on today's Vermont, those which portray a typical or, if possible, unique aspect of the state or its people. Style should be literate, clear, and concise. Subtle humor favored. No "Vermont clichés," and please do not send first-person accounts of your vacation trip to Vermont. **Buys 60 mss/year.** Query. Length: 1,500 words average. **Pays 25¢/word.**

Photos Buys photos with mss; buys seasonal photographs alone. Prefers b&w contact sheets to look at first on assigned material. Color submissions must be 4×5 or 35mm transparencies. Gives assignments but only with experienced photographers. Query in writing. Buys one-time rights. Pays $75-200 for inside color; $500 for cover. Captions, identification of subjects, model releases required.

The online version contains material not found in the print edition. Contact: Andrew Jackson.

Tips "Writers who read our magazine are given more consideration because they understand that we want authentic articles about Vermont. If a writer has a genuine working knowledge of Vermont, his or her work usually shows it. Vermont is changing and there is much concern here about what this state will be like in years ahead. It is a beautiful, environmentally sound place now and the vast majority of residents want to keep it so. Articles reflecting such concerns in an intelligent, authoritative, non-hysterical way will be given very careful consideration. The growth of tourism makes us interested in intelligent articles about specific places in Vermont, their history and attractions to the traveling public."

VIRGINIA

$ $ALBEMARLE

Living in Jefferson's Virginia, Carden Jennings Publishing, 375 Greenbrier Dr., Suite 100, Charlottesville VA 22901. (434)817-2000. Fax: (434)817-2020. Website: www.cjp.com. **80% freelance written.** Bimonthly magazine. "Lifestyle magazine for central Virginia." Estab. 1987. Circ. 10,000. Pays on publication. Publishes ms an average of 4 months after acceptance. Byline given. Offers 30% kill fee. Buys first North American serial rights. Editorial lead time 6 months. Submit seasonal material 6 months in advance. Accepts queries by mail, fax. Accepts simultaneous submissions. Responds in 1 month to queries; 2 months to mss. Sample copy for 10×12 SAE and 5 first-class stamps. Writer's guidelines for #10 SASE.

O→ Break in with "a strong idea backed by good clips to prove abilities. Ideas should be targeted to central Virginia and lifestyle, which can be very broad—a renaissance man or woman approach to living."

Nonfiction Essays, historical/nostalgic, interview/profile, photo feature, travel. "No fiction, poetry or anything without a direct tie to central Virginia." **Buys 30-35 mss/year.** Query with published clips. Length: 900-3,500 words. **Pays $75-225 for assigned articles; $75-175 for unsolicited articles.** Sometimes pays expenses of writers on assignment.

Photos State availability with submission. Reviews transparencies. Buys one-time rights. Negotiates payment individually. Captions, identification of subjects, model releases required.

Columns/Departments Etcetera (personal essay), 900-1,200 words; Flavors of Virginia (food), 900-1,100 words; Leisure (travel, sports), 3,000 words. **Buys 20 mss/year.** Query with published clips. **Pays $75-150.**

Tips "Be familiar with the central Virginia area and lifestyle. We prefer a regional slant, which should include a focus on someone or something located in the region, or a focus on someone or something from the region making an impact in other parts of the world. Quality writing is a must. Story ideas that lend themselves to multiple sources will give you a leg up on the competition."

Ⓝ $ $ HAMPTON ROADS SHIELD

A Magazine for Law Enforcement Officers in Hampton Roads, One Offer Publishing, P.O. Box 99052, Norfold VA 23509-9052. E-mail: hrshieldqueries@aol.com. **Contact:** Cindy Smith. **85% freelance written.** Bimonthly magazine covering all subjects of interest to law enforcement officers in the Hampton Roads, Virginia area. "We cover items of interest that are both job related and non-job related." This magazine is specifically for law enforcement, correctional and security officers working in the Hampton Roads, Virginia area. Estab. 2004. Circ. 5,000. Pays on publication. Publishes ms an average of 3-4 months after acceptance. Byline given. Offers 10% kill fee. Buys first North American serial rights. Editorial lead time 4-6 months. Submit seasonal material 6 months in advance. Accepts queries by mail, e-mail. Responds in 6-8 weeks to queries; 1-2 months to mss. Writer's guidelines by e-mail.

- "This is not a trade magazine, but rather a magazine that strives to bring stories of humor, interest and information to our audience."

Nonfiction Essays, general interest, historical/nostalgic, humor, inspirational, interview/profile, new product, opinion, personal experience, photo feature. Doesn't want anything anti-law enforcement or anything overly dramatic or flowery. **Buys 30/year mss/year.** Query. Length: 300-1,000 words.

Photos State availability with submission. Reviews prints, GIF/JPEG files. Buys one-time rights. Negotiates payment individually. Captions, identification of subjects, model releases required.

Columns/Departments Excuses, Excuses! (stories of humorous excuses offered by criminals), any word length; Shield Gear (highlights law enforcement-related products), 300-500 words; Brother to Brother (written by law enforcement officials), 300-700 words.

Poetry Poems must be related to law enforcement. Avant-garde, free verse, light verse, traditional. **Buys 2-3/year poems/year.** Submit maximum 5 poems. Length: 10-30 lines.

Fillers Anecdotes, facts, short humor. **Buys 50-60/year.** Length: Maximum of 250 words.

Tips Remember the audience and speak to them. "We also welcome ideas for regular departments. New writers are welcome, but please be sure your idea will be of interest to law enforcement officers in Hampton Roads, Virginia. You do not need to be from this area to write effectively for this audience."

$ $ THE ROANOKER

Leisure Publishing Co., 3424 Brambleton Ave., P.O. Box 21535, Roanoke VA 24018-9900. (540)989-6138. Fax: (540)989-7603. E-mail: krheinheimer@leisurepublishing.com. Website: www.theroanoker.com. **Contact:** Kurt Rheinheimer, editor. **75% freelance written.** Works with a small number of new/unpublished writers each year. Magazine published 6 times/year. "*The Roanoker* is a general interest city magazine for the people of Roanoke, Virginia and the surrounding area. Our readers are primarily upper-income, well-educated professionals between the ages of 35 and 60. Coverage ranges from hard news and consumer information to restaurant reviews and local history." Estab. 1974. Circ. 12,000. Pays on publication. Publishes ms an average of 4 months after acceptance. Byline given. Buys all rights, makes work-for-hire assignments. Submit seasonal material 4 months in advance. Accepts queries by mail, e-mail, fax. Responds in 2 months to queries. Sample copy for $2 and 9×12 SAE with 5 first-class stamps or online.

Nonfiction "We're looking for more photo feature stories based in western Virginia. We place special emphasis on investigative and exposé articles." Exposé, historical/nostalgic, how-to (live better in western Virginia), interview/profile (of well-known area personalities), photo feature, travel (Virginia and surrounding states), periodic special sections on fashion, real estate, media, banking, investing. **Buys 30 mss/year.** Query with published clips or send complete ms. Length: 1,400 words maximum. **Pays $35-200.**

Reprints Send tearsheet. Pays 50% of amount paid for an original article.

Photos Send photos with submission. Reviews color transparencies. Rights purchased vary. Pays $5-10 for 5×7 or 8×10 b&w prints; $10-50 for color transparencies. Captions, model releases required.

Columns/Departments Skinny (shorts on people, Roanoke-related books, local issues, events, arts and culture).

Tips "We're looking for more pieces on contemporary history (1930s-70s). It helps if freelancer lives in the area. The most frequent mistake made by writers in completing an article for us is not having enough Roanoke-area focus: use of area experts, sources, slants, etc."

Ⓝ $ $ VIRGINIA LIVING

Cape Fear Publishing, 109 E. Cary St., Richmond VA 23219. (804)343-7539. Fax: (804)649-0306. E-mail: gpollard @capefear.com. Website: www.virginialiving.com. **Contact:** Garland Pollard, editor. **95% freelance written.** Bimonthly magazine covering life and lifestyle in Virginia. "We are a large-format (10×13) glossy magazine covering life in Virginia, from food, architecture, and gardening, to issues, profiles, and travel. Estab. 2002. Circ. 50,000. Pays on publication. Publishes ms an average of 4 months after acceptance. Byline given. Offers 50% kill fee. Not copyrighted. Buys first North American serial rights. Editorial lead time 6 months. Submit seasonal material 6 months in advance. Accepts queries by mail. Accepts simultaneous submissions. Responds in 5 weeks to queries; 1 month to mss. Sample copy for $5.

Nonfiction Book excerpts, essays, exposé, general interest, historical/nostalgic, interview/profile, new product, personal experience, photo feature, travel. No fiction, poetry, previously published articles, and stories with a firm grasp of the obvious. **Buys 180 mss/year.** Query with published clips or send complete ms. Length: 300-3,000 words. **Pays $60-700.** Sometimes pays expenses of writers on assignment.

Photos Tyler Darden, art director. Reviews contact sheets, 6×7 transparencies, 8×10 prints, GIF/JPEG files. Buys one-time rights. Negotiates payment individually. Captions, identification of subjects, model releases required.

Columns/Departments Beauty; Travel; Books; Events; Sports (all with a unique Virginia slant), all 1,000-1,500 words. **Buys 50 mss/year.** Send complete ms. **Pays $120-200.**

Tips "A freelancer would get the best reception if they send clips via mail before they query. I can then sit down with them and read them. In addition, queries should be about fresh subjects in Virginia. Stories about Williamsburg, Chincoteague ponies, Monticello, the Civil War, and other press release-type stories. We prefer to introduce new subjects, faces, and ideas, and get beyond the many clichés of Virginia. Freelancers would also do well to think about what time of the year they are pitching stories for, as well as art possibilities. We are a large-format magazine close to the size of the old-look magazine, so photography is a key component to our stories."

WASHINGTON

$ $ SEATTLE MAGAZINE

Tiger Oak Publications Inc., 1505 Western Ave., Suite 500, Seattle WA 98101. (206)284-1750. Fax: (206)284-2550. E-mail: rachel@seattlemag.com. Website: www.seattlemagazine.com. **Contact:** Rachel Hart, editor. Monthly magazine "serving the Seattle metropolitan area. Articles should be written with our readers in mind. They are interested in social issues, the arts, politics, homes and gardens, travel and maintaining the region's high quality of life." Estab. 1992. Circ. 45,000. Pays on or about 30 days after publication. Publishes ms an average of 3 months after acceptance. Byline given. Offers 25% kill fee. Buys first rights. Editorial lead time 6 months. Submit seasonal material 6 months in advance. Accepts queries by mail, e-mail, fax. Responds in 2 months to queries. Sample copy for #10 SASE. Writer's guidelines online.

○→ Break in by "suggesting short, newsier stories with a strong Seattle focus."

Nonfiction Book excerpts (local), essays, exposé, general interest, humor, interview/profile, photo feature, travel, local/regional interest. No longer accepting queries by mail. Query with published clips. Length: 100-2,000 words. **Pays $50 minimum.**

Photos State availability with submission. Buys one-time rights. Negotiates payment individually.

Columns/Departments Scoop, Urban Safari, Voice, Trips, People, Environment, Hot Button, Fitness, Fashion, Eat and Drink. Query with published clips. **Pays $225-400.**

Tips "The best queries include some idea of a lead and sources of information, plus compelling reasons why the article belongs specifically in *Seattle Magazine*. In addition, queries should demonstrate the writer's familiarity with the magazine. New writers are often assigned front- or back-of-the-book contents, rather than features. However, the editors do not discourage writers from querying for longer articles and are especially interested in receiving trend pieces, in-depth stories with a news hook and cultural criticism with a local angle."

$ $ $ SEATTLE WEEKLY

Village Voice, 1008 Western Ave., Suite 300, Seattle WA 98104. (206)623-0500. Fax: (206)467-4377. Website: seattleweekly.com. **Contact:** Appropriate Editor. **20% freelance written.** Weekly tabloid covering arts, politics, food, business and books with local and regional emphasis. Estab. 1976. Circ. 105,000. Pays on publication. Publishes ms an average of 1 month after acceptance. Byline given. Offers variable kill fee. Buys first North American serial rights. Submit seasonal material 2 months in advance. Responds in 1 month to queries. Sample copy for $3. Writer's guidelines online.

○→ Read online guide for freelancers for specific editors and e-mail addresses.

Nonfiction Book excerpts, exposé, general interest, historical/nostalgic (Northwest), humor, interview/profile, opinion. **Buys 6-8 mss/year.** Query with cover letter, résumé, published clips and SASE. Length: 300-4,000 words. **Pays $50-800.** Sometimes pays expenses of writers on assignment.

Reprints Send tearsheet. Payment varies.

Tips "The *Seattle Weekly* publishes stories on Northwest politics and art, usually written by regional and local writers, for a mostly upscale, urban audience; writing is high-quality magazine style."

WISCONSIN

$ $ $ MILWAUKEE MAGAZINE

417 E. Chicago St., Milwaukee WI 53202. (414)273-1101. Fax: (414)273-0016. E-mail: milmag@qg.com. Website: www.milwaukeemagazine.com. **Contact:** John Fennell, editor. **40% freelance written.** Monthly magazine.

"We publish stories about Milwaukee, of service to Milwaukee-area residents and exploring the area's changing lifestyle, business, arts, politics, and dining." Circ. 40,000. Pays on publication. Publishes ms an average of 2 months after acceptance. Byline given. Offers 20% kill fee. Buys first rights. Submit seasonal material 6 months in advance. Accepts queries by mail, e-mail. Responds in 6 weeks to queries. Sample copy for $4.

Nonfiction Essays, exposé, general interest, historical/nostalgic, interview/profile, photo feature, travel, food and dining, and other services. "No articles without a strong Milwaukee or Wisconsin angle." Length: 2,500-6,000 words for full-length features; 800 words for 2-page "breaker" features (short on copy, long on visuals). **Buys 30-50 mss/year.** Query with published clips. **Pays $400-1,000 for full-length, $150-400 for breaker.** Sometimes pays expenses of writers on assignment.

Columns/Departments Insider (inside information on Milwaukee, exposé, slice-of-life, unconventional angles on current scene), up to 500 words; Mini Reviews for Insider, 125 words. Query with published clips.

Tips "Pitch something for the Insider, or suggest a compelling profile we haven't already done. Submit clips that prove you can do the job. The department most open is Insider. Think short, lively, offbeat, fresh, people-oriented. We are actively seeking freelance writers who can deliver lively, readable copy that helps our readers make the most out of the Milwaukee area. Because we're only human, we'd like writers who can deliver copy on deadline that fits the specifications of our assignment. If you fit this description, we'd love to work with you."

$ $ WISCONSIN TRAILS

P.O. Box 317, Black Earth WI 53515-0317. (608)767-8000. Fax: (608)767-5444. E-mail: lkearney@wistrails.com. Website: www.wistrails.com. **Contact:** Laura Kearney, associate editor. **40% freelance written.** Bimonthly magazine for readers interested in Wisconsin and its contemporary issues, personalities, recreation, history, natural beauty, and arts. Estab. 1960. Circ. 55,000. Pays 1 month from publication. Publishes ms an average of 6 months after acceptance. Byline given. Buys first North American serial, one-time rights. Submit seasonal material 1 year in advance. Accepts queries by mail, e-mail, fax. Responds in 4 months to queries. Sample copy for $4.95. Writer's guidelines for #10 SASE or online.

○┐ "We're looking for active articles about people, places, events, and outdoor adventures in Wisconsin. We want to publish 1 in-depth article of statewide interest or concern/issue, and several short (600-1,500 words) articles about short trips, recreational opportunities, personalities, restaurants, inns, history, and cultural activities. We're looking for more articles about out-of-the-way Wisconsin places that are exceptional in some way and engaging pieces on Wisconsin's little-known and unique aspects."

Nonfiction "Our articles focus on some aspect of Wisconsin life: an interesting town or event, a person or industry, history or the arts, and especially outdoor recreation. We do not use first-person essays or biographies about people who were born in Wisconsin but made their fortunes elsewhere. No fiction. No articles that are too local for our regional audience, or articles about obvious places to visit in Wisconsin. We need more articles about the new and little-known." **Buys 3 unsolicited mss/year.** Query or send outline. Length: 1,000-3,000 words. **Pays 25¢/word for assigned articles.** Sometimes pays expenses of writers on assignment.

Photos Photographs purchased with or without mss, or on assignment. Color photos usually illustrate an activity, event, region, or striking scenery. Prefer photos with people in scenery. Reviews 35mm or larger transparencies. Pays $45-175 for inside color; $250 for covers. Captions, labels with photographer's name required.

Tips "When querying, submit well-thought-out ideas about stories specific to people, places, events, arts, outdoor adventures, etc., in Wisconsin. Include published clips with queries. Do some research—many queries we receive are pitching ideas for stories we recently have published. Know the tone, content, and audience of the magazine. Refer to our writer's guidelines, or request them, if necessary."

WYOMING

$ WYOMING RURAL ELECTRIC NEWS (WREN)

P.O. Box 549, Gillette WY 82717. (307)682-7527. Fax: (307)682-7528. E-mail: wren@coffey.com. **Contact:** Kris Wendtland, editor. **20% freelance written.** Monthly magazine for audience of small town residents, vacation-home owners, farmers, and ranchers. Estab. 1954. Circ. 35,000. Pays on publication. Publishes ms an average of 1 month after acceptance. Byline given. Buys one-time rights. Submit seasonal material 2 months in advance. Accepts queries by mail, e-mail, fax, phone. Responds in 3 months to queries. Sample copy for $2.50 and 9×12 SASE. Writer's guidelines for #10 SASE.

○┐ "You have just learned something. It is so amazing you just have to find out more. You call around. You search on the Web. You go to the library. Everything you learn about it makes you want to know more. In a matter of days, all your friends are aware that you are into something. You don't stop talking about it. You're totally confident that they find it interesting too. Now, write it down and send it to us. We are excited just wondering what you find so amazing! Come on, tell us! Tell us!"

Nonfiction "We print science, ag, how-to, and human interest but not fiction. Topics of interest in general include: hunting, cooking, gardening, commodities, sugar beets, wheat, oil, coal, hard rock mining, beef cattle, electric technologies such as lawn mowers, car heaters, air cleaners and assorted gadgets, surge protectors, pesticators, etc." Wants science articles with question/answer quiz at end—test your knowledge. Buys electrical appliance articles. Articles welcome that put present and/or future in positive light. No nostalgia. No sad stories. **Buys 4-10 mss/year.** Send complete ms. Length: 500-800 words. **Pays up to $140, plus 4 copies.**

Reprints Send tearsheet or photocopy and information about when and where the material previously appeared.

Photos Color only.

Tips "Always looking for fresh, new writers, original perspectives. Submit entire manuscript. Don't submit a regionally set story from some other part of the country. Photos and illustrations (if appropriate) are always welcomed. We don't care if you misspell words. We don't care if your grammar is poor. We want factual articles that are blunt, to the point, accurate."

CANADIAN & INTERNATIONAL

$ $ ABACO LIFE

Caribe Communications, P.O. Box 37487, Raleigh NC 27627. (919)859-6782. Fax: (919)859-6769. E-mail: jimkerr @mindspring.com. Website: www.abacolife.com. Managing Editor: Cathy Kerr. **Contact:** Jim Kerr, editor/ publisher. **50% freelance written.** Quarterly magazine covering Abaco, an island group in the Northeast Bahamas. "*Abaco Life* editorial focuses entirely on activities, history, wildlife, resorts, people and other subjects pertaining to the Abacos. Readers include locals, vacationers, second-home owners, and other visitors whose interests range from real estate and resorts to scuba, sailing, fishing, and beaches. The tone is upbeat, adventurous, humorous. No fluff writing for an audience already familiar with the area." Estab. 1979. Circ. 10,000. Pays on publication. Publishes ms an average of 2 months after acceptance. Byline given. Offers 40% kill fee. Buys one-time rights. Editorial lead time 2 months. Submit seasonal material 4 months in advance. Accepts queries by mail, e-mail. Accepts simultaneous submissions. Responds in 2 weeks to queries; 2 months to mss. Sample copy for $2. Writer's guidelines free.

Nonfiction General interest, historical/nostalgic, how-to, interview/profile, personal experience, photo feature, travel. "No general first-time impressions. Articles must be specific, show knowledge and research of the subject and area—'Abaco's Sponge Industry'; 'Diving Abaco's Wrecks'; 'The Hurricane of '36.'" **Buys 8-10 mss/year.** Query or send complete ms. Length: 400-2,000 words. **Pays $250-600.**

Photos State availability of or send photos with submission. Reviews transparencies, prints. Buys one-time rights. Offers $25-100/photo. Negotiates payment individually. Captions, identification of subjects, model releases required.

> The online magazine carries original content not found in the print edition. Contact: Jim Kerr, online editor.

Tips "Travel writers must look deeper than a usual destination piece, and the only real way to do that is spend time in Abaco. Beyond good writing, which is a must, we like submissions on Microsoft Word, but that's optional. Color slides are also preferred over prints, and good ones go a long way in selling the story. We prefer digital photos saved to a disc at 300 dpi minimum JPEG format. Read the magazine to learn its style."

$ $ $ $ ALBERTAVIEWS

The Magazine About Alberta for Albertans, AlbertaViews, Ltd., Suite 208-320 23rd Ave. SW, Calgary AB T2S 0J2 Canada. (403)243-5334. Fax: (403)243-8599. E-mail: editor@albertaviews.ab.ca. Website: www.albertavie ws.ab.ca. Publisher/Executive Editor: Jackie Flanagan. **Contact:** Erin Waite, editor. **50% freelance written.** Bimonthly magazine covering Alberta culture: politics, economy, social issues, and art. "We are a regional magazine providing thoughtful commentary and background information on issues of concern to Albertans. Most of our writers are Albertans." Estab. 1997. Circ. 30,000. Pays on publication. Publishes ms an average of 3 months after acceptance. Byline given. Offers 50% kill fee. Buys first North American serial, electronic rights. Editorial lead time 4 months. Submit seasonal material 3 months in advance. Accepts queries by e-mail. Responds in 6 weeks to queries; 2 months to mss. Sample copy for free. Writer's guidelines online.

• No phone queries.

Nonfiction Does not want anything not directly related to Alberta. Essays. **Buys 18 mss/year.** Query with published clips. Length: 3,000-5,000 words. **Pays $1,000-1,500 for assigned articles; $350-750 for unsolicited articles.** Sometimes pays expenses of writers on assignment.

Photos State availability with submission. Buys one-time rights, Web rights. Negotiates payment individually.

Fiction Only fiction by Alberta writers. **Buys 6 mss/year.** Send complete ms. Length: 2,500-4,000 words. **Pays $1,000 maximum.**

$ $⬚ THE ATLANTIC CO-OPERATOR

Promoting Community Ownership, Atlantic Co-operative Publishers, 123 Halifax St., Moncton NB E1C 8N5 Canada. Fax: (506)858-6615. E-mail: editor@theatlanticco-operator.coop. Website: www.theatlanticco-operator.coop. **Contact:** Mark Higgins, editor. **95% freelance written.** Bimonthly tabloid covering co-operatives. "We publish articles of interest to the general public, with a special focus on community ownership and community economic development in Atlantic Canada." Estab. 1933. Pays on publication. Publishes ms an average of 2 months after acceptance. Byline given. Editorial lead time 2 months. Submit seasonal material 2 months in advance. Accepts queries by mail, e-mail, fax. Accepts simultaneous submissions. Responds in 3 weeks to queries. Sample copy not available.

Nonfiction Exposé, general interest, historical/nostalgic, interview/profile. No political stories, economical stories, sports. **Buys 90 mss/year.** Query with published clips. Length: 500-2,000 words. **Pays 22¢/word.** Pays expenses of writers on assignment.

Reprints Accepts previously published submissions.

Photos State availability with submission. Reviews prints, GIF/JPEG files. Buys one-time rights. Offers $25/ photo. Identification of subjects required.

Columns/Departments Health and Lifestyle (anything from recipes to travel), 800 words; International Page (co-operatives in developing countries, good ideas from around the world). **Buys 10 mss/year.** Query with published clips. **Pays 15¢/word.**

$ $ $⬚ THE BEAVER

Canada's History Magazine, Canada's National History Society, 478-167 Lombard Ave., Winnipeg MB R3B 0T6 Canada. (204)988-9300. Fax: (204)988-9309. E-mail: articlequeries@historysociety.ca. Website: www.thebeaver.ca. **50% freelance written.** Bimonthly magazine covering Canadian history. Estab. 1920. Circ. 41,000. **Pays on acceptance.** Byline given. Offers $200 kill fee. Buys first North American serial, electronic rights. Editorial lead time 4 months. Submit seasonal material 8 months in advance. Accepts queries by mail. Accepts simultaneous submissions. Responds in 6 weeks to queries; 2 months to mss. Sample copy for 9×12 SAE and 2 first-class stamps. Writer's guidelines online.

⦿ Break in with a "new interpretation based on solid new research; entertaining magazine style."

Nonfiction Photo feature (historical), historical (Canadian focus). Does not want anything unrelated to Canadian history. **Buys 30 mss/year.** Query with published clips. Length: 600-3,500 words. **Pays $400-1,000 for assigned articles; $300-600 for unsolicited articles.** Sometimes pays expenses of writers on assignment.

Photos State availability with submission. Buys one-time rights. Offers no additional payment for photos accepted with ms. Identification of subjects, model releases required.

Columns/Departments Book and other media reviews and Canadian history subjects, 600 words ("These are assigned to freelancers with particular areas of expertise, i.e., women's history, labour history, French regime, etc."). **Buys 15 mss/year. Pays $125.**

Tips "*The Beaver* is directed toward a general audience of educated readers, as well as to historians and scholars. We are in the market for lively, well-written, well-researched, and informative articles about Canadian history that focus on all parts of the country and all areas of human activity. Subject matter covers the whole range of Canadian history, with particular emphasis on social history, politics, exploration, discovery and settlement, aboriginal peoples, business and trade, war, culture and sport. Articles are obtained through direct commission and by submission. Queries should be accompanied by a stamped, self-addressed envelope. *The Beaver* publishes articles of various lengths, including long features (from 1,500-3,500 words) that provide an in-depth look at an event, person or era; short, more narrowly focused features (from 600-1,500 words). Longer articles may be considered if their importance warrants publication. Articles should be written in an expository or interpretive style and present the principal themes of Canadian history in an original, interesting and informative way."

$ $ $⬚ CANADIAN GEOGRAPHIC

39 McArthur Ave., Ottawa ON K1L 8L7 Canada. (613)745-4629. Fax: (613)744-0947. E-mail: editorial@canadiangeographic.ca. Website: www.canadiangeographic.ca. **Contact:** Rick Boychuk, editor. **90% freelance written.** Works with a small number of new/unpublished writers each year. Bimonthly magazine. "*Canadian Geographic*'s colorful portraits of our ever-changing population show readers just how important the relationship between the people and the land really is." Estab. 1930. Circ. 240,000. **Pays on acceptance.** Publishes ms an average of 3 months after acceptance. Buys first Canadian rights. Accepts queries by mail, e-mail, fax. Responds in 1 month to queries. Sample copy for $5.95 (Canadian) and 9×12 SAE or online.

• *Canadian Geographic* reports a need for more articles on earth sciences. Canadian writers only.

Nonfiction Buys authoritative geographical articles, in the broad geographical sense, written for the average person, not for a scientific audience. Predominantly Canadian subjects by Canadian authors. **Buys 30-45 mss/**

year. Query. Length: 1,500-3,000 words. **Pays 80¢/word minimum.** Sometimes pays expenses of writers on assignment.

Photos Pays $75-400 for color photos, depending on published size.

$ $⬚ THE COTTAGE MAGAZINE

Country Living in Western Canada, OP Publishing, Ltd., Box 148, Rockyford AB T0J 2R0 Canada. (604)606-4644. Fax: (604)687-1925. E-mail: editor@cottagemagazine.com. Website: www.cottagemagazine.com. **Contact:** Michael Love, editor. **80% freelance written.** Bimonthly magazine covering do-it-yourself projects, profiles of people and their innovative solutions to building and maintaining their country homes, issues that affect rural individuals and communities, and the R&R aspect of country living. "Our readers want solid, practical information about living in the country—including alternative energy and sustainable living. The also like to have fun in a wide range of recreational pursuits, from canoeing, fishing, and sailing to water skiing, snowmobiling, and entertaining." Estab. 1992. Circ. 10,000. Pays within 1 month of publication. Publishes ms an average of 6 months after acceptance. Byline given. Offers 50% kill fee. Buys first North American serial rights. Accepts queries by e-mail, fax. Accepts simultaneous submissions. Responds in 1 month to queries. Sample copy for $2. Writer's guidelines online.

Nonfiction Buys 18-24 mss/year. Query. Length: Up to 1,500 words. **Pays $200-450 (including visuals).**

Photos Send photos with submission. Reviews with negatives prints, slides. Pays $15-25. Cover submissions also accepted.

Columns/Departments Utilities (solar and/or wind power), 800 words; Weekend Project (a how-to most homeowners can do themselves), 800 words; Government (new regulations, processes, problems), 800 words; Diversions (advisories, ideas, and how-tos about the fun things that people do), 800 words; InRoads (product reviews), 50-600 words; This Land (personal essays or news-based story with a broader context), 800 words; Last Word or Cabin Life (personal essays and experiences), 800 words; Elements (short articles focusing on a single feature of a cottage), 600 words; Alternatives (applied alternative energy), 600 words. Query. **Pays 20¢/published word.**

Fillers Anecdotes, facts, newsbreaks, seasonal tips. **Buys 12/year.** Length: 50-200 words. **Pays 20¢/word.**

Tips "We serve all of Western Canada, so while it's OK to have a main focus on one region, reference should be made to similarities/differences in other provinces. Even technical articles should have some anecdotal content. Some of our best articles come from readers themselves or from writers who can relay that 'personal' feeling. Cottaging is about whimsy and fun as well as maintenance and chores. Images, images, images: We require sharp, quality photos, and the more, the better."

$ $⬚ OUTDOOR CANADA MAGAZINE

340 Ferrier St., Suite 210, Markham ON L3R 2Z5 Canada. (905)475-8440. Fax: (905)475-9246. E-mail: editorial@outdoorcanada.ca. Website: www.outdoorcanada.ca. **Contact:** Patrick Walsh, editor-in-chief. **90% freelance written.** Works with a small number of new/unpublished writers each year. Magazine published 8 times/year emphasizing hunting, fishing, and related pursuits in Canada *only*. Estab. 1972. Circ. 80,000. Pays on publication. Publishes ms an average of 8 months after acceptance. Byline given. Buys first rights. Submit seasonal material 1 year in advance. Accepts queries by mail, e-mail. Responds in 1 month to queries. Writer's guidelines online.

Nonfiction How-to, fishing, hunting, outdoor issues, outdoor destinations in Canada. **Buys 35-40 mss/year.** Query. Length: 2,500 words. **Pays $500 and up for assigned articles.**

Reprints Send information about when and where the article previously appeared. Payment varies.

Photos Emphasize people in the Canadian outdoors. Pays $100-250 for 35mm transparencies and $400/cover. Captions, model releases required.

Fillers Short news pieces. **Buys 30-40/year.** Length: 100-500 words. **Pays $50 and up.**

⬛ The online magazine carries original content not found in the print edition. Contact: Aaron Kylie, online editor.

$ $ $ $⬚ TORONTO LIFE

111 Queen St. E., Suite 320, Toronto ON M5C 1S2 Canada. (416)364-3333. Fax: (416)861-1169. E-mail: editorial@torontolife.com. Website: www.torontolife.com. **Contact:** John Macfarlane, editor. **95% freelance written.** Prefers to work with published/established writers. Monthly magazine emphasizing local issues and social trends, short humor/satire, and service features for upper income, well-educated and, for the most part, young Torontonians. Circ. 92,039. **Pays on acceptance.** Publishes ms an average of 4 months after acceptance. Byline given. Pays 50% kill fee for commissioned articles only. Buys first North American serial rights. Responds in 3 weeks to queries. Sample copy for $4.95 with SAE and IRCs.

Nonfiction Uses most types of articles. **Buys 17 mss/issue.** Query with published clips and SASE. Length: 1,000-6,000 words. **Pays $500-5,000.**

Columns/Departments Query with published clips and SASE. **Pays $2,000.**

Tips "Submissions should have strong Toronto orientation."

$ $ 🌐 THE UKRANIAN OBSERVER

The Willard Group, 4/6 Desiatynna St., 4th Floor, Kiev 01025 Ukraine. (38044) 230 2080. Fax: (38044) 230 2083. E-mail: scott@twg.com.ua. Website: www.ukraine-observer.com. Editor: Glen Willard. **Contact:** Scott Lewis, managing editor. **75% freelance written.** Monthly magazine covering Ukrainian news, culture, travel, and history. "Our English-language content is entirely Ukraine-centered. A writer unfamiliar with the country, its politics, or its culture is unlikely to be successful with us." Estab. 2000. Circ. 15,000. Pays on publication. Publishes ms an average of 2 months after acceptance. Byline given. Offers 50% kill fee. Buys all rights. Editorial lead time 2 months. Submit seasonal material 4 months in advance. Accepts queries by mail, e-mail. Responds in 2 weeks to queries; 1 month to mss. Sample copy free by post to Ukraine addresses only; $3 USD to foreign addresses. Writer's guidelines by e-mail.

Nonfiction General interest (Ukrainian life, history, culture and travel, and significant Ukrainians abroad), historical/nostalgic (Ukrainian history, particular little-known events with significant impact), interview/profile (prominent Ukrainians or foreign expatriates living in Ukraine), photo feature (current or historical photo essays on Ukrainian life, history, culture, and travel), travel (within Ukraine). Does not want poetry, nostalgic family stories, personal experiences or recollections. **Buys 30-40 mss/year.** Query with or without published clips or send complete ms. Length: 800-1,500 words. **Pays $25-250 for assigned articles; $25-50 for unsolicited articles.** Sometimes pays expenses of writers on assignment.

Photos Send photos with submission. Reviews negatives, GIF/JPEG files. Buys one-time rights. Pays $10/photo. Captions, identification of subjects, model releases required.

Fiction All fiction should have a Ukrainian setting and/or theme. Adventure, ethnic, historical, humorous, mainstream, slice-of-life vignettes. Does not want erotica. **Buys 12 mss/year.** Query with or without published clips or send complete ms. Length: 3,500-4,500 words. **Pays $25-150.**

Tips "Obtain, read, and follow our writer's guidelines. We follow Western journalism rules. We are not interested in the writer's opinion—our readers want information to be attributed to experts interviewed for the story. An interesting story that has credible sources and lots of good, direct quotes will be a hit with us. Stories covering political or controversial issues should be balanced and fair."

🔲 UP HERE

Explore Canada's Far North, Up Here Publishing, Ltd., P.O. Box 1350, Yellowknife NT X1A 2N9 Canada. (867)766-6710. Fax: (867)873-2844. E-mail: liz@uphere.ca. Website: www.uphere.ca. **Contact:** Liz Crompton, editor. **50% freelance written.** Magazine published 8 times/year covering general interest about Canada's Far North. "We publish features, columns, and shorts about people, wildlife, native cultures, travel, and adventure in Yukon, Northwest Territories, and Nunavut. Be informative, but entertaining." Estab. 1984. Circ. 30,000. Pays on publication. Byline given. Offers 50% kill fee. Buys first North American serial rights. Editorial lead time 6 months. Accepts queries by mail, e-mail, fax. Sample copy for $3.95 (Canadian) and 9×12 SASE.

　　O┈ Break in with "precise queries with well-developed focuses for the proposed story."

Nonfiction Essays, general interest, how-to, humor, interview/profile, personal experience, photo feature, technical, travel, lifestyle/culture, historical. **Buys 25-30 mss/year.** Query. Length: 1,500-3,000 words. **Fees are negotiable.**

Photos "*Please* do not send unsolicited original photos, slides." Send photos with submission. Reviews transparencies, prints. Buys one-time rights. Captions, identification of subjects required.

Columns/Departments Buys 25-30 mss/year. Query with published clips.

　　🖳 The online magazine carries original content not found in the print edition. Contact: Mifi Purvis, online editor (mifi@uphere.ca).

Tips "We like well-researched, concrete adventure pieces, insights about Northern people and lifestyles, readable natural history. Features are most open to freelancers—travel, adventure, and so on. We don't want a comprehensive 'How I spent my summer vacation' hour-by-hour account. We want stories with angles, articles that look at the North through a different set of glasses. Photos are important; you greatly increase your chances with top-notch images."

$ $ $🔲 VANCOUVER MAGAZINE

Transcontinental Publications, Inc., Suite 500, 2608 Granville St., Vancouver BC V6H 3V3 Canada. E-mail: mail@vancouvermagazine.com. Website: www.vancouvermagazine.com. **Contact:** Matthew Mallon, editor. **70% freelance written.** Monthly magazine covering the city of Vancouver. Estab. 1967. Circ. 65,000. **Pays on acceptance.** Byline given. Offers negotiable kill fee. Buys first North American serial rights. Editorial lead time 2 months. Submit seasonal material 6 months in advance. Accepts queries by mail, e-mail, fax, phone. Accepts simultaneous submissions. Responds in 2 weeks to queries; 1 month to mss. Sample copy for $5. Writer's guidelines for #10 SASE or by e-mail.

Nonfiction "We prefer to work with writers from a conceptual stage and have a 6-week lead time. Most stories are under 1,500 words. Please be aware that we don't publish poetry and rarely publish fiction." Book excerpts, essays, historical/nostalgic, humor, interview/profile, new product, personal experience, photo feature, travel. **Buys 200 mss/year.** Query. Length: 200-3,000 words. **Pays 50¢/word.** Sometimes pays expenses of writers on assignment.

Photos State availability with submission. Reviews contact sheets, negatives, transparencies, prints, GIF/JPEG files. Buys negotiable rights. Negotiates payment individually. Captions, identification of subjects, model releases required.

Columns/Departments Sport; Media; Business; City Issues, all 1,500 words. Query. **Pays 50¢/word.**

Tips "Read back issues of the magazine, or visit our website. Almost all of our stories have a strong Vancouver angle. Submit queries by e-mail. Do not send complete stories."

RELATIONSHIPS

$ $⊘ MARRIAGE PARTNERSHIP

Christianity Today International, 465 Gundersen Dr., Carol Stream IL 60188. Fax: (630)260-0114. E-mail: mp@marriagepartnership.com. Website: www.marriagepartnership.com. **Contact:** Ginger E. Kolbaba, managing editor. **50% freelance written.** Quarterly magazine covering Christian marriages. "Our readers are married Christians. Writers must understand our readers." Estab. 1988. Circ. 55,000. **Pays on acceptance.** Publishes ms an average of 9 months after acceptance. Byline given. Offers 50% kill fee. Buys first North American serial rights. Editorial lead time 6 months. Submit seasonal material 1 year in advance. Accepts queries by mail, e-mail, fax. Responds in 10 weeks to queries; 2 months to mss. Sample copy for $5 or online. Writer's guidelines online.

• *Does not accept unsolicited mss.*

Nonfiction Book excerpts, essays, how-to, humor, inspirational, interview/profile, opinion, personal experience, religious. **Buys 20 mss/year.** Query with or without published clips. Length: 1,000-2,000 words. **Pays 15-30¢/word for assigned articles; 15¢/word for unsolicited articles.**

Columns/Departments Starting Out (opinion by/for newlyweds), 1,000 words; Soul to Soul (inspirational), 1,500 words; Work It Out (problem-solving), 1,000 words; Back from the Brink (marriage in recovery), 1,800 words. **Buys 10 mss/year.** Query with or without published clips. **Pays 15-30¢/word.**

Tips "Think of topics with a fresh slant. Be ever mindful of our readers. Writers who can communicate with freshness, clarity, and insight will receive serious consideration. We are looking for writers who are willing to candidly speak about their own marriages. We strongly urge writers who are interested in contributing to *Marriage Partnership* to read several issues to become thoroughly acquainted with our tone and slant."

RELIGIOUS

ALIVE NOW

1908 Grand Ave., P.O. Box 340004, Nashville TN 37203-0004. E-mail: alivenow@upperroom.org. Website: www.alivenow.org. **Contact:** Melissa Tidwell. Bimonthly thematic magazine for a general Christian audience interested in reflection and meditation. Circ. 70,000. Writer's guidelines online.

Poetry Avant-garde, free verse. Length: 10-45 lines.

$ $ AMERICA

106 W. 56th St., New York NY 10019. (212)581-4640. Fax: (212)399-3596. E-mail: articles@americamagazine.org. Website: www.americamagazine.org. **Contact:** The Rev. Thomas J. Reese, editor. Published weekly for adult, educated, largely Roman Catholic audience. Estab. 1909. **Pays on acceptance.** Byline given. Buys all rights. Responds in 3 weeks to queries. Writer's guidelines online.

Nonfiction "We publish a wide variety of material on religion, politics, economics, ecology, and so forth. We are not a parochial publication, but almost all pieces make some moral or religious point." Articles on theology, spirituality, current political, social issues. "We are not interested in purely informational pieces or personal narratives which are self-contained and have no larger moral interest." Length: 1,500-2,000 words. **Pays $50-300.**

Poetry Only 10-12 poems published a year, thousands turned down. Paul Mariani, poetry editor. **Buys 10-12 poems/year.** Length: 15-30 lines.

ⓃＳＳ ANGELS ON EARTH

Guideposts, 16 E. 34th St., New York NY 10016. (212)251-8100. E-mail: angelsedtr@guideposts.org. **Contact:** Colleen Hughes, editor-in-chief. **90% freelance written.** Bimonthly magazine. "*Angels on Earth* publishes true stories about God's messengers at work in today's world. We are interested in stories of heavenly angels and stories involving humans who have played angelic roles in daily life." Estab. 1995. Circ. 550,000. Pays on publication. Buys all rights. Editorial lead time 6 months. Submit seasonal material 6 months in advance. Accepts queries by mail. Responds in 3 months to queries.

Nonfiction True, inspirational, personal experience (most stories are first-person experiences but can be ghost-written). Nothing that directly preaches, no how-to. **Buys 100 mss/year.** Send complete ms with SASE. Length: 100-2,000 words. **Pays $25-500.**

Photos State availability with submission. Buys one-time rights. Offers no additional payments for photos accepted with ms.

Columns/Departments Meg Belviso, departments editor. Earning Their Wings (unusual stories of good deeds worth imitating); Only Human? (Is the angelic character a human being? The narrator is pleasantly unsure and so is the reader), both 350 words. **Pays $50-100.** Messages (brief, mysterious happenings, or letters describing how a specific article helped you). **Pays $25. Buys 50 mss/year.** Send complete ms with SASE.

ⓃＳ🔲 THE ANNALS OF SAINT ANNE DE BEAUPRÉ

Redemptorist Fathers, P.O. Box 1000, St. Anne De Beaupré QC G0A 3C0 Canada. (418)827-4538. Fax: (418)827-4530. Editor: Father Bernard Mercier, C.Ss.R. **Contact:** Father Roch Achard, C.Ss.R., managing editor. **20% freelance written.** Releases 11 issues/year; July and August are one issue. religious magazine. "Our mission statement includes dedication to Christian family values and devotion to St. Anne." Estab. 1885. Circ. 32,000. **Pays on acceptance.** Buys first North American serial rights. "Please state rights for sale." Editorial lead time 6 months. Submit seasonal material 6 months in advance. Responds in 4-6 weeks to queries. Sample copy and writer's guidelines for $8^{1}/_{2} \times 11$ SAE and IRCs.

● No e-mail or fax queries.

Nonfiction Inspirational, religious. **Buys 40 mss/year.** Send complete ms. Length: 500-1,500 words. **Pays 3-4¢/word, plus 3 copies.**

Fiction Father Roch Achard, C.Ss.R., editor. Religious. No senseless mockery or anti-Christian materials. **Buys 25 mss/year.** Send complete ms. Length: 500-1,500 words. **Pays 3-4¢/word, plus 3 copies.**

Tips "Write something uplifting and/or inspirational. Report-writing is simply not remarkable. We maintain an article bank of unsolicited manuscripts awaiting publication. It may take 3 or more years to see any new article in print."

Ｓ THE ASSOCIATE REFORMED PRESBYTERIAN

Associate Reformed Presbyterian General Synod, 1 Cleveland St., Suite 110, Greenville SC 29601-3696. (864)232-8297, ext. 237. Fax: (864)271-3729. E-mail: arpmaged@arpsynod.org. Website: www.arpsynod.org. **Contact:** Sabrina Cooper, editor. **5% freelance written.** Monthly Christian magazine serving a conservative, evangelical, and Reformed denomination. "As the official publication of our denomination, most articles deal with events/news that occur within the denomination." Estab. 1976. Circ. 5,000. **Pays on acceptance.** Publishes ms an average of 4 months after acceptance. Byline given. Not copyrighted. Buys first, one-time, second serial (reprint) rights. Submit seasonal material 4 months in advance. Accepts queries by mail, fax. Accepts simultaneous submissions. Responds in 1 month to queries. Sample copy for $2. Writer's guidelines for #10 SASE or by e-mail.

Nonfiction Essays, inspirational, personal experience, religious. **Buys 1-5 mss/year.** Query. Length: 400-2,000 words. **Pays $25-75.**

Reprints Send information about when and where the article previously appeared. Pays 100% of amount paid for an original article.

Photos State availability with submission. Buys one-time rights. Offers $25 maximum/photo. Captions, identification of subjects required.

Fiction Ben Johnston, editor. "Currently overstocked." Religious, children's. "Stories should portray Christian values. No retelling of Bible stories or 'talking animal' stories. Stories for youth should deal with resolving real issues for young people." Length: 300-750 words (children); 1,250 maximum (youth). **Pays $50 maximum.**

Tips "Writers should understand that we are denominational, conservative, evangelical, Reformed, and Presbyterian. A writer who appreciates these nuances would stand a much better chance of being published here than one who does not."

ＳＳ BGC WORLD

Magazine of the Baptist General Conference, Baptist General Conference, 2002 S. Arlington Heights Rd., Arlington Heights IL 60005. Fax: (847)228-5376. E-mail: bputman@baptistgeneral.org. Website: www.bgcworld.org.

Contact: Bob Putman, editor. **35% freelance written.** Nonprofit, religious, evangelical Christian magazine published 10 times/year covering the Baptist General Conference. "*BGC-WORLD* is the official magazine of the Baptist General Conference (BGC). Articles related to the BGC, our churches, or by/about BGC people receive preference." Circ. 40,000. Pays on publication. Byline given. Offers 50% kill fee. Buys first rights. Editorial lead time 6 months. Submit seasonal material 6 months in advance. Accepts queries by e-mail. Responds in 1 month to queries; 2 months to mss. Sample copy for #10 SASE. Writer's guidelines, theme list free.

Nonfiction General interest, photo feature, religious, profile, infographics, sidebars related to theme. No sappy religious pieces, articles not intended for our audience. Ask for a sample instead of sending anything first. **Buys 20-30 mss/year.** Query with published clips. Length: 300-1,200 words. **Pays $60-280.** Sometimes pays expenses of writers on assignment.

Photos State availability with submission. Reviews prints, some high-resolution digital. Buys one-time rights. Offers $15-60/photo. Captions, identification of subjects, model releases required.

Columns/Departments Around the BGC (blurbs of news happening in the BGC), 50-150 words. Send complete ms. **Pays $15-20.**

Tips "Please study the magazine and the denomination. We will send sample copies to interested freelancers and give further information about our publication needs upon request. Freelancers who are interested in working on assignment are welcome to express their interest."

N $ BIBLE ADVOCATE

Bible Advocate Press, Church of God (Seventh Day), P.O. Box 33677, Denver CO 80233. (303)452-7973. E-mail: bibleadvocate@cog7.org. Website: www.cog7.org/publications/ba/. **Contact:** Editor. **25% freelance written.** Religious magazine published 10 times/year. "Our purpose is to advocate the Bible and represent the Church of God (Seventh Day) to a Christian audience." Estab. 1863. Circ. 13,500. Pays on publication. Publishes ms an average of 9 months after acceptance. Byline given. Offers 50% kill fee. Buys first, second serial (reprint), electronic rights. Editorial lead time 3 months. Submit seasonal material 6 months in advance. Accepts queries by mail, e-mail. Accepts simultaneous submissions. Responds in 2 months to queries. Sample copy for 9×12 SAE and 3 first-class stamps. Writer's guidelines online.

Nonfiction Inspirational, opinion, personal experience, religious, Biblical studies. No articles on Christmas or Easter. **Buys 20-25 mss/year.** Send complete ms and SASE. Length: 1,500 words. **Pays $25-55.**

Reprints Send ms with rights for sale noted.

Photos Send photos with submission. Reviews prints. Offers payment for photos accepted with ms. Identification of subjects required.

Columns/Departments Viewpoint (opinion), 600-700 words. **Buys 3 mss/year.** Send complete ms and SASE. **No payment for opinion pieces.**

Poetry Free verse, traditional. No avant-garde. **Buys 10-12 poems/year.** Submit maximum 5 poems. Length: 5-20 lines. **Pays $20.**

Fillers Anecdotes, facts. **Buys 5/year.** Length: 50-400 words. **Pays $10-20.**

Tips "Be fresh, not preachy! We're trying to reach a younger audience now, so think how you can cover contemporary and biblical topics with this audience in mind. Articles must be in keeping with the doctrinal understanding of the Church of God (Seventh Day). Therefore, the writer should become familiar with what the Church generally accepts as truth as set forth in its doctrinal beliefs. We reserve the right to edit manuscripts to fit our space requirements, doctrinal stands and church terminology. Significant changes are referred to writers for approval. No fax or handwritten submissions, please."

$ $ CATHOLIC DIGEST

475 Riverside Dr., Suite 248, New York NY 10115. (212)870-2548. Fax: (212)870-2540. E-mail: cdsubmissions@ bayard-inc.com. Website: www.catholicdigest.com. Editor: Joop Koopman. **Contact:** Articles Editor. **15% freelance written.** Monthly magazine. "Publishes features and advice on topics ranging from health, psychology, humor, adventure, and family, to ethics, spirituality, and Catholics, from modern-day heroes to saints through the ages. Helpful and relevant reading culled from secular and religious periodicals." Estab. 1936. Circ. 350,000. Pays on acceptance for articles. Publishes ms an average of 4 months after acceptance. Byline given. Buys first, one-time, second serial (reprint) rights. Editorial lead time 4 months. Submit seasonal material 5 months in advance. Accepts queries by mail, e-mail, fax. Responds in 2 months to mss. Sample copy free.

Nonfiction "Most articles we use are reprinted." Book excerpts, essays, general interest, historical/nostalgic, how-to, humor, inspirational, interview/profile, personal experience, religious, travel. **Buys 60 mss/year.** Send complete ms. Length: 750-2,000 words. **Pays $200-400.**

Reprints Send tearsheet or typed ms with rights for sale noted and information about when and where the material previously appeared. Pays $100.

Photos State availability with submission. Reviews contact sheets, transparencies, prints. Negotiates payment individually. Captions, identification of subjects, model releases required.

Columns/Departments Buys 75 mss/year. Send complete ms. **Pays $4-50.**

Fillers Filler Editor. Open Door (statements of true incidents through which people are brought into the Catholic faith, or recover the Catholic faith they had lost), 200-500 words; also publishes jokes, short anecdotes, and factoids. **Buys 200/year.** Length: 1 line minimum, 500 words maximum. **Pays $2/per published line upon publication.**

Tips "Spiritual, self-help, and all wellness is a good bet for us. We would also like to see material with an innovative approach to daily living, articles that show new ways of looking at old ideas, problems. You've got to dig beneath the surface."

$ $ CATHOLIC FORESTER

Catholic Order of Foresters, 355 Shuman Blvd., P.O. Box 3012, Naperville IL 60566-7012. Fax: (630)983-3384. E-mail: magazine@catholicforester.com. Website: www.catholicforester.com. **Contact:** Mary Ann File, editor. **20% freelance written.** Quarterly magazine for members of the Catholic Order of Foresters, a fraternal insurance benefit society. *Catholic Forester* articles cover varied topics to create a balanced issue for the purpose of informing, educating, and entertaining our readers. Circ. 100,000. **Pays on acceptance.** Buys first North American serial rights. Editorial lead time 6 months. Submit seasonal material 6 months in advance. Responds in 3 months to mss. Sample copy for 9×12 SAE and 4 first-class stamps. Writer's guidelines online.

Nonfiction Inspirational, religious, travel, health, parenting, financial, money management, humor. **Buys 12-16 mss/year.** Send complete ms by mail, fax, or e-mail. Rejected material will not be returned without accompanying SASE. Length: 500-1,500 words. **Pays 30¢/word.**

Photos State availability with submission. Buys one-time rights. Negotiates payment individually.

Fiction Humorous, religious. **Buys 12-16 mss/year.** Length: 500-1,500 words. **Pays 30¢/word.**

Poetry Light verse, traditional. **Buys 3 poems/year.** Length: 15 lines maximum. **Pays 30¢/word.**

Tips "Our audience includes a broad age spectrum, ranging from youth to seniors. Nonfiction topics that appeal to our members include health and wellness, money management and budgeting, parenting and family life, interesting travels, insurance, nostalgia, and humor. A good children's story with a positive lesson or message would rate high on our list."

N $ $ $ CHARISMA & CHRISTIAN LIFE

The Magazine About Spirit-Led Living, Strang Communications Co., 600 Rinehart Rd., Lake Mary FL 32746. (407)333-0600. Fax: (407)333-7133. E-mail: charisma@strang.com. Website: www.charismamag.com. Editor: J. Lee Grady. Managing Editor: Jimmy Stewart. **Contact:** Adrienne Gaines, associate editor. **80% freelance written.** Monthly magazine covering items of interest to the Pentecostal or independent charismatic reader. "More than half of our readers are Christians who belong to Pentecostal or independent charismatic churches, and numerous others participate in the charismatic renewal in mainline denominations." Estab. 1975. Circ. 250,000. Pays on publication. Publishes ms an average of 3 months after acceptance. Byline given. Offers $50 kill fee. Buys all rights. Editorial lead time 4 months. Submit seasonal material 5 months in advance. Accepts queries by mail, e-mail. Sample copy for free. Writer's guidelines by e-mail.

Nonfiction Andy Butcher, senior writer. Book excerpts, exposé, general interest, interview/profile, religious. No fiction, poetry, columns/departments, or sermons. **Buys 40 mss/year.** Query. Length: 2,000-3,000 words. **Pays $1,000 (maximum) for assigned articles.** Pays expenses of writers on assignment.

Photos Rachel Campbell. State availability with submission. Reviews contact sheets, $2^{1}/_{4} \times 2^{1}/_{4}$ transparencies, 3×5 or larger prints, GIF/JPEG files. Buys one-time rights. Negotiates payment individually. Model releases required.

Tips "Be especially on the lookout for news stories, trend articles, or interesting personality profiles that relate specifically to the Christian reader."

$ $ THE CHRISTIAN CENTURY

104 S. Michigan Ave., Suite 700, Chicago IL 60603-5901. (312)263-7510. Fax: (312)263-7540. E-mail: main@christiancentury.org. Website: www.christiancentury.org. **Contact:** David Heim, executive editor. **90% freelance written.** Works with new/unpublished writers. Biweekly magazine for ecumenically-minded, progressive Protestant church people, both clergy and lay. "Authors must have a critical and analytical perspective on the church and be familiar with contemporary theological discussion." Estab. 1884. Circ. 30,000. Pays on publication. Byline given. Buys all rights. Editorial lead time 1 month. Submit seasonal material 4 months in advance. Accepts queries by mail, e-mail. Responds in 1 week to queries; 3 months to mss. Sample copy for $3. Writer's guidelines online.

Nonfiction "We use articles dealing with social problems, ethical dilemmas, political issues, international affairs, and the arts, as well as with theological and ecclesiastical matters. We focus on issues of church and society, and church and culture." Essays, humor, interview/profile, opinion, religious. No inspirational. **Buys 150 mss/**

year. Send complete ms; query appreciated, but not essential. Length: 1,000-3,000 words. **Pays variable amount for assigned articles; $75-150 for unsolicited articles.**

Photos State availability with submission. Reviews any size prints. Buys one-time rights. Offers $25-100/photo.

Fiction Humorous, religious, slice-of-life vignettes. No moralistic, unrealistic fiction. Send complete ms. Length: 1,000-3,000 words. **Pays $75-200.**

Poetry Jill Peláez Baumgaertner, poetry editor. Avant-garde, free verse, haiku, traditional. No sentimental or didactic poetry. **Buys 50 poems/year.** Length: 20 lines. **Pays $50.**

Tips ''We seek manuscripts that articulate the public meaning of faith, bringing the resources of Christian tradition to bear on such topics as poverty, human rights, economic justice, international relations, national priorities, and popular culture. We are equally interested in articles that probe classical theological themes. We welcome articles that find fresh meaning in old traditions and which adapt or apply religious traditions to new circumstances. Authors should assume that readers are familiar with main themes in Christian history and theology; are not threatened by the historical-critical study of the Bible; and are already engaged in relating faith to social and political issues. Many of our readers are ministers or teachers of religion at the college level.''

$ $ CHRISTIAN HOME & SCHOOL

Christian Schools International, 3350 E. Paris Ave. SE, Grand Rapids MI 49512. (616)957-1070, ext. 239. Fax: (616)957-5022. E-mail: rogers@csionline.org. Executive Editor: Gordon L. Bordewyk. **Contact:** Roger Schmurr, senior editor. **30% freelance written.** Works with a small number of new/unpublished writers each year. Bimonthly magazine covering family life and Christian education. ''*Christian Home & School* is designed for parents in the United States and Canada who send their children to Christian schools and are concerned about the challenges facing Christian families today. These readers expect a mature, Biblical perspective in the articles, not just a Bible verse tacked onto the end.'' Estab. 1922. Circ. 67,000. Pays on publication. Publishes ms an average of 4 months after acceptance. Byline given. Buys first North American serial rights. Submit seasonal material 4 months in advance. Accepts queries by mail, e-mail. Responds in 1 month to queries. Sample copy and writer's guidelines for 9 × 12 SAE with 4 first-class stamps. Writer's guidelines only for #10 SASE or online.

> ⊶ Break in by picking a contemporary parenting situation/problem and writing to Christian parents. The editor reports an interest in seeing articles on how to experience and express forgiveness in your home, make summer interesting and fun for your kids, help your child make good choices, and raise kids who are opposites, and promote good educational practices in Christian schools.

Nonfiction ''We publish features on issues that affect the home and school.'' Book excerpts, interview/profile, opinion, personal experience, articles on parenting and school life. **Buys 30 mss/year.** Send complete ms. Length: 1,000-2,000 words. **Pays $175-250.**

Tips ''Features are the area most open to freelancers. We are publishing articles that deal with contemporary issues that affect parents. Use an informal easy-to-read style rather than a philosophical, academic tone. Try to incorporate vivid imagery and concrete, practical examples from real life. We look for manuscripts with a mature Christian perspective.''

Ⓝ $ $ CHRISTIAN LEADER

U.S. Conference of Mennonite Brethren Churches, Box 220, Hillsboro KS 67063. (620)947-5543. Fax: (620)947-3266. E-mail: christianleader@usmb.org. **Contact:** Connie Faber, editor. **10% freelance written.** Monthly magazine covering news and issues related to the Mennonite Brethren denomination. Estab. 1936. Circ. 10,000. Pays on publication. Publishes ms an average of 5 months after acceptance. Byline given. Buys first rights. Editorial lead time 3 months. Submit seasonal material 5 months in advance. Accepts queries by mail, e-mail, fax. Accepts previously published material. Accepts simultaneous submissions. Sample copy for $1.60. Writer's guidelines free.

Nonfiction Book excerpts, essays, how-to, humor, inspirational, religious. **Buys 12 mss/year.** Query or send complete ms. Length: 1,000-2,500 words. **Pays 10¢/word.** Sometimes pays expenses of writers on assignment.

Photos State availability with submission. Buys one-time rights.

Fiction Religious. **Buys 2 mss/year.** Length: 1,000-2,500 words. **Pays 10¢/word.**

Poetry Avant-garde, free verse, haiku, light verse, traditional. Buys 1 poem/year.

Tips ''We ask that writers contact the editor if they are interested in writing an article or have one they've already written. The *Leader* operates on the 'theme' approach, laying out topics we will tackle each month, so we tend to look for articles on those specific topics. However, we have up to 4 issues a year that do not have 'themes'; we publish a variety of articles on different topics in those issues. Most articles published are between 1,200 and 1,700 words; and we operate on a 'first-rights' basis. We also ask writers to submit articles by e-mail via an attachment in Microsoft Word.''

$ $ CHRISTIAN RESEARCH JOURNAL

30162 Tomas, Rancho Santa Margarita CA 92688-2124. (949)858-6100. Fax: (949)858-6111. E-mail: submissions @equip.org. Website: www.equip.org. Managing Editor: Melanie Cogdill. **Contact:** Elliot Miller, editor-in-chief.

75% freelance written. Quarterly magazine. "The *Journal* is an apologetics magazine probing today's religious movements, promoting doctrinal discernment and critical thinking, and providing reasons for Christian faith and ethics." Pays on publication. Publishes ms an average of 3 months after acceptance. Byline sometimes given. Offers 50% kill fee. Buys first rights. Submit seasonal material 4 months in advance. Accepts queries by mail, e-mail, fax. Accepts simultaneous submissions. Responds in 4 months. Sample copy for $6. Writer's guidelines by e-mail at guidelines@equip.org.

Nonfiction Essays, opinion (religious viewpoint), religious, ethics, book reviews, features on cults, witnessing tips. No fiction or general Christian living topics. **Buys 25 mss/year.** Query or send complete ms (if e-mail ms, must mail disk with ms as well). **Pays 16¢/word.**

Columns/Departments Features, 4,500 words; Effective Evangelism, 1,700 words; Viewpoint, 875 words; News Watch, 2,500 words. Query or send complete ms to submissions@equip.org.

Tips "We are most open to features on cults, apologetics, Christian discernment, ethics, book reviews, opinion pieces, and witnessing tips. Be familiar with the *Journal* in order to know what we are looking for."

N $ $ CHRISTIANITY TODAY

465 Gundersen Dr., Carol Stream IL 60188-2498. (630)260-6200. Fax: (630)260-8428. E-mail: cteditor@christianitytoday.com. Website: www.christianitytoday.com. **Contact:** Mark Galli, managing editor. **80% freelance written, but mostly assigned**. Works with a small number of new/unpublished writers each year. Monthly magazine. *Christianity Today* believes that the vitality of the American church depends on its adhering to and applying the Biblical teaching as it meets today's challenges. It attempts to Biblically assess people, events, and ideas that shape evangelical life, thought, and mission. It employs analytical reporting, commentary, doctrinal essays, interviews, cultural reviews, and the occasional realistic narrative." Estab. 1956. Circ. 154,000. Publishes ms an average of 6 months after acceptance. Buys first rights. Submit seasonal material at least 8 months in advance. Accepts queries by mail, e-mail, fax. Responds in 3 months to queries. Sample copy and writer's guidelines for 9 × 12 SAE with 3 first-class stamps.

Nonfiction Buys 6 unsolicited mss/year. Query. Length: 1,200-5,200 words. **Pays 25-35¢/word.** Sometimes pays expenses of writers on assignment.

Reprints Rarely accepts previously published submissions. Pays 25% of amount paid for an original article.

Columns/Departments The CT Review (books, the arts, and popular culture). Length: 700-1,500 words. **Buys 6 mss/year.** Query.

　　The online magazine carries original content not found in the print edition. Contact: Ted Olsen, online editor.

Tips "We are developing more of our own manuscripts and requiring a much more professional quality from others. Queries without a SASE will not be answered and manuscripts not containing a SASE will not be returned."

$ $ CHRYSALIS READER

1745 Gravel Hill Rd., Dillwyn VA 23936. (434)983-3021. E-mail: chrysalis@direcway.com. Website: www.swedenborg.com. Managing Editor: Susanna van Rensselaer. **Contact:** Patti Cramer, editorial associate. **90% freelance written.** Annual literary magazine on spiritually related topics. "It is very important to send for writer's guidelines and sample copies before submitting. Content of fiction, articles, reviews, poetry, etc., should be directly focused on that issue's theme and directed to the educated, intellectually curious reader." Estab. 1985. Circ. 2,000. Pays at page-proof stage. Publishes ms an average of 9 months after acceptance. Byline given. Buys first rights, makes work-for-hire assignments. Accepts queries by mail, e-mail. Responds in 1 month to queries; 4 months to mss. Sample copy for $10 and 8½ × 11 SAE. Writer's guidelines online.

　　● E-mail for themes and guidelines (no mss will be accepted by e-mail).

Nonfiction Relationships (2005), Passages (2006), Discovering Heavenly Realms (2007). Essays, interview/profile. **Buys 20 mss/year.** Query. Length: no longer than 3,000 words. **Pays $50-250 for assigned articles; $50-150 for unsolicited articles.**

Photos Send suggestions for illustrations with submission. Buys original artwork for cover and inside copy; b&w illustrations related to theme; **pays $25-150**. Buys one-time rights. Offers no additional payment for photos accepted with ms. Captions, identification of subjects required.

Fiction Robert Tucker, fiction editor. Short fiction more likely to be published. Adventure, experimental, historical, mainstream, mystery, science fiction, fiction (leading to insight), contemporary, spiritual, sports. No religious works. **Buys 10 mss/year.** Query. Length: no longer than 3,000 words. **Pays $50-150.**

Poetry Rob Lawson, senior editor. Avant-garde, traditional. **Buys 15 poems/year.** Submit maximum 6 poems. **Pays $25, and 5 copies of the issue.**

$ $ CONSCIENCE

The Newsjournal of Catholic Opinion, Catholics for a Free Choice, 1436 U St. NW, Suite 301, Washington DC 20009-3997. (202)986-6093. E-mail: conscience@catholicsforchoice.org. Website: www.catholicsforchoice.org.

Contact: Editor. **60% freelance written.** Sometimes works with new/unpublished writers. Quarterly newsjournal covering reproductive health and rights including, but not limited to, abortion rights in the church, and church-state issues in US and worldwide. "A feminist, pro-choice perspective is a must, and knowledge of Christianity and specifically Catholicism is helpful." Estab. 1980. Circ. 12,000. Pays on publication. Publishes ms an average of 2 months after acceptance. Byline given. Buys first North American serial rights, makes work-for-hire assignments. Accepts queries by mail, e-mail. Responds in 4 months to queries. Sample copy for 9×12 SAE and 4 first-class stamps. Writer's guidelines for #10 SASE.

Nonfiction Especially needs material that recognizes the complexity of reproductive issues and decisions, and offers original, honest insight. "Writers should be aware that we are a nonprofit organization." Book excerpts, interview/profile, opinion, personal experience (a small amount), issue analysis. **Buys 4-8 mss/year.** Query with published clips or send complete ms. Length: 1,500-3,500 words. **Pays $200 negotiable.**

Reprints Send ms with rights for sale noted and information about when and where the material previously appeared. Pays 20-30% of amount paid for an original article.

Photos Prefers b&w prints. State availability with submission. Identification of subjects required.

Columns/Departments Book Reviews, 600-1,200 words. **Buys 4-8 mss/year. Pays $75.**

Tips "Say something new on the issue of abortion, or sexuality, or the role of religion or the Catholic church, or women's status in the church. Thoughtful, well-researched, and well-argued articles needed. The most frequent mistakes made by writers in submitting an article to us are lack of originality and wordiness."

$THE COVENANT COMPANION

Covenant Publications of the Evangelical Covenant Church, 5101 N. Francisco Ave., Chicago IL 60625. E-mail: communication@covchurch.org. Website: www.covchurch.org. **Contact:** Donald L. Meyer, editor or Jane K. Swanson-Nystrom, managing editor. **10-15% freelance written.** "As the official monthly periodical of the Evangelical Covenant Church, we seek to inform the denomination we serve and encourage dialogue on issues within the church and in our society." Circ. 16,000. Publishes ms an average of 2 months after acceptance. Byline given. Submit seasonal material 4 months in advance. Accepts queries by mail, e-mail. Accepts simultaneous submissions. Writer's guidelines online.

Nonfiction Inspirational, religious, contemporary issues. **Buys 40 mss/year.** Send complete ms. Unused mss returned only if accompanied by SASE. Length: 1,200-1,800 words. **Pays $50-100 for assigned articles.**

Reprints Send tearsheet, photocopy or typed ms with rights for sale noted and information about when and where the material previously appeared.

Photos Send photos with submission. Reviews prints. Buys one-time rights. Offers no additional payment for photos accepted with ms. Identification of subjects required.

$ $DECISION

Billy Graham Evangelistic Association, 1 Billy Graham Parkway, Charlotte NC 28201. (704)401-2432. Fax: (704)401-3009. E-mail: submissions@bgea.org. Website: www.decisionmag.org. **Contact:** Bob Paulson, managing editor. **5% freelance written.** Works each year with small number of new/unpublished writers. Magazine published 11 times/year with a mission "to extend the ministry of Billy Graham Evangelistic Association; to communicate the Good News of Jesus Christ in such a way that readers will be drawn to make a commitment to Christ; and to encourage, strengthen and equip Christians in evangelism and discipleship." Estab. 1960. Circ. 800,000. Pays on publication. Publishes ms an average of up to 18 months after acceptance. Byline given. Offers 50% kill fee. Buys first rights. Assigns work-for-hire mss, articles, projects. Editorial lead time 6 months. Submit seasonal material 6 months in advance. Sample copy for 9×12 SAE and 4 first-class stamps. Writer's guidelines online.

    O-π "The best way to break in to our publication is to submit an article that has some connection to the Billy Graham Evangelistic Association or Samaritan's Purse, but also has strong takeaway for the personal lives of the readers." Include telephone number with submission.

Nonfiction Personal experience, testimony. **Buys approximately 8 mss/year.** Send complete ms. Length: 400-1,500 words. **Pays $200-400.** Pays expenses of writers on assignment.

Photos State availability with submission. Reviews prints. Buys one-time rights. Captions, identification of subjects, model releases required.

Columns/Departments Finding Jesus (people who have become Christians through Billy Graham Ministries), 500-600 words. **Buys 11 mss/year.** Send complete ms. **Pays $200.**

Poetry Amanda Knoke, assistant editor. Free verse, light verse, traditional. **Buys 6 poems/year.** Submit maximum 7 poems. Length: 4-16 lines. **Pays $1/word.**

Tips "Articles should have some connection to the ministry of Billy Graham or Franklin Graham. For example, you may have volunteered in one of these ministries or been touched by them. The article does not need to be entirely about that connection, but it should at least mention the connection. Testimonies and personal experience articles should show how God intervened in your life and how you have been transformed by God. SASE required with submissions."

DEVO'ZINE

Just for Teens, 1908 Grand Ave., P.O. Box 340004, Nashville TN 37203-0004. (615)340-7247. Fax: (615)340-1783. E-mail: smiller@upperroom.org. Website: www.devozine.org. Editor: Sandy Miller. Bimonthly magazine for youth ages 12-18. Offers meditations, scripture, prayers, poems, stories, songs, and feature articles to "aid youth in their prayer life, introduce them to spiritual disciplines, help them shape their concept of God, and encourage them in the life of discipleship." Writer's guidelines online.

Nonfiction General interest, inspirational, personal experience, religious, devotional.

Poetry Length: 20 lines.

$ $DISCIPLESHIP JOURNAL

NavPress, a division of The Navigators, P.O. Box 35004, Colorado Springs CO 80935-0004. (719)531-3514. Fax: (719)598-7128. E-mail: sue.kline@navpress.com. Website: www.discipleshipjournal.com. **Contact:** Sue Kline, editor. **90% freelance written.** Works with a small number of new/unpublished writers each year. Bimonthly magazine. "The mission of *Discipleship Journal* is to help believers develop a deeper relationship with Jesus Christ, and to provide practical help in understanding the scriptures and applying them to daily life and ministry. We prefer those who have not written for us before to begin with nontheme articles about almost any aspect of Christian living. We'd like more articles that explain a Bible passage and show how to apply it to everyday life, as well as articles about developing a relationship with Jesus; reaching the world; growing in some aspect of Christian character; or specific issues related to leadership and helping other believers grow." Estab. 1981. Circ. 120,000. **Pays on acceptance.** Publishes ms an average of 8-12 months after acceptance. Byline given. Buys first North American serial, second serial (reprint), electronic rights. Submit seasonal material 6 months in advance. Accepts queries by mail, e-mail, fax. Responds in 6-8 weeks to queries. Sample copy for $2.56 and 9×12 SAE or online. Writer's guidelines online.

    O→ Break in through departments (One to One, DJ Plus) and with nontheme feature articles.

Nonfiction "We'd like to see more articles that encourage involvement in world missions; help readers in personal evangelism, follow-up, and Christian leadership; or show how to develop a real relationship with Jesus." Book excerpts (rarely), how-to (grow in Christian faith and disciplines; help others grow as Christians; serve people in need; understand and apply the Bible), inspirational, interpretation/application of the Bible. No personal testimony; humor; poetry; anything not directly related to Christian life and faith; politically partisan articles. **Buys 80 mss/year.** Query with published clips and SASE only. Length: 500-2,500 words. **Pays 25¢/word for first rights.** Sometimes pays expenses of writers on assignment.

Reprints Send tearsheet and information about when and where the material previously appeared. Pays 5¢/word for reprints.

Tips "Our articles are meaty, not fluffy. Study writer's guidelines and back issues and try to use similar approaches. Don't preach. Polish before submitting. About half of the articles in each issue are related to one theme. We are looking for more practical articles on ministering to others and more articles on growing in Christian character. Be vulnerable. Show the reader that you have wrestled with the subject matter in your own life. Use personal illustrations. We can no longer accept unsolicited manuscripts. Query first."

$ $DISCIPLESWORLD

A Journal of News, Opinion, and Mission for the Christian Church, DisciplesWorld, Inc., P.O. Box 11469, Indianapolis IN 46201-0469. (317)375-8846. Fax: (317)375-8849. E-mail: news@disciplesworld.com. Website: www.disciplesworld.com. **75% freelance written.** Monthly magazine covering faith issues, especially those with a "Disciples slant. We are the journal of the Christian Church (Disciples of Christ) in North America. Our denomination numbers roughly 800,000. Disciples are a mainline Protestant group. Our readers are mostly laity, active in their churches, and interested in issues of faithful living, political and church news, ethics, and contemporary social issues." Estab. 2002. Circ. 14,000. Pays on publication. Publishes ms an average of 6 months after acceptance. Byline given. Buys first North American serial rights. Editorial lead time 3 months. Submit seasonal material 3 months in advance. Accepts queries by mail, e-mail. Accepts simultaneous submissions. Responds in 2 weeks to queries; 2 months to mss. Sample copy for #10 SASE. Writer's guidelines online.

Nonfiction Essays, general interest, inspirational, interview/profile, opinion, personal experience, religious. Does not want preachy or didactic articles. "Our style is conversational rather than academic." **Buys 40 mss/year.** Query with or without published clips or send complete ms. Length: 400-1,500 words. **Pays $100-300 for assigned articles; $25-300 for unsolicited articles.** Sometimes pays expenses of writers on assignment.

Photos Send photos with submission. Buys one-time rights. Negotiates payment individually. Identification of subjects, model releases required.

Columns/Departments Browsing the Bible (short reflections on the applicability of books of the Bible), 400 words; Speak Out (opinion pieces about issues facing the church), 600 words. **Buys 12-15 mss/year.** Send complete ms. **Pays $100.**

Fiction Ethnic, mainstream, novel excerpts, religious, serialized novels, slice-of-life vignettes. "We're a religious publication, so use common sense! Stories do not have to be overtly 'religious,' but they should be uplifting and positive." **Buys 8-10 mss/year.** Send complete ms. Length: 150-1,500 words. **Pays $25-300.**

Poetry Free verse, light verse, traditional. **Buys 6-10 poems/year.** Submit maximum 3 poems. Length: 30 maximum lines.

Fillers Anecdotes, short humor. **Buys 20/year.** Length: 25-400 words. **Pays $0-100.**

Tips "Send a well-written (and well-proofed!) query explaining what you would like to write about and why you are the person to do it. Write about what you're passionate about. We are especially interested in social justice issues, and we like our writers to take a reasoned and well-argued stand."

$ DOVETAIL

A Journal By and For Jewish/Christian Families, Dovetail Institute for Interfaith Family Resources, 775 Simon Greenwell Lane, Boston KY 40107. (502)549-5499. Fax: (502)549-3543. E-mail: di-ifr@bardstown.com. Website: www.dovetailinstitute.org. **Contact:** Debi Tenner, editor, 45 Lilac Lane, Hamden CT 06517. E-mail: debit4rls@a ol.com. **75% freelance written.** Bimonthly newsletter for interfaith families. "All articles must pertain to life in an interfaith (primarily Jewish/Christian) family. We are broadening our scope to include other sorts of interfaith mixes. We accept all kinds of opinions related to this topic." Estab. 1992. Circ. 1,500. Pays on publication. Publishes ms an average of 9 months after acceptance. Byline given. Buys first, one-time, second serial (reprint) rights. Editorial lead time 6 months. Submit seasonal material 6 months in advance. Accepts queries by mail, e-mail, fax, phone. Accepts previously published material. Accepts simultaneous submissions. Responds in 3 months to queries. Sample copy for 9 × 12 SAE and 3 first-class stamps. Writer's guidelines free.

O— Break in with "a fresh approach to standard interfaith marriage situations."

Nonfiction Book reviews, 500 words. **Pays $15, plus 2 copies.** Book excerpts, interview/profile, opinion, personal experience. No fiction. **Buys 5-8 mss/year.** Send complete ms. Length: 800-1,000 words. **Pays $25, plus 2 copies.**

Photos Send photos with submission. Reviews 5 × 7 prints. Buys one-time rights. Offers no additional payment for photos accepted with ms. Identification of subjects, model releases required.

Fillers Anecdotes, short humor. **Buys 1-2/year.** Length: 25-100 words. **Pays $10.**

Tips "Write on concrete, specific topics related to Jewish/Christian or other dual-faith intermarriage: no prose-lytizing, sermonizing, or general religious commentary. Successful freelancers are part of an interfaith family themselves, or have done solid research/interviews with members of interfaith families. We look for honest, reflective personal experience. We're looking for more on alternative or nontraditional families, i.e., interfaith gay/lesbian, single parent raising child in departed partner's faith."

$ $ EFCA TODAY

Evangelical Free Church of America, 418 Fourth St., NE, Charlottesville VA 22902. E-mail: dianemc@journeygro up.com. Website: www.efca.org/today. Associate Editor: Chris Moquist. **Contact:** Diane J. McDougall, editor. **30% freelance written.** Quarterly magazine. "*EFCA Today* informs readers of the vision and activities of the Evangelical Free Church of America. Its readers are EFCA leaders—pastors, elders, deacons, Sunday-school teachers, ministry volunteers." Estab. 1931. Circ. 44,000. **Pays on acceptance.** Publishes ms an average of 3 months after acceptance. Byline given. Offers 50% kill fee. Buys first North American serial, electronic, efca-related church use (if free) rights, makes work-for-hire assignments. Editorial lead time 5 months. Submit seasonal material 6 months in advance. Accepts queries by mail, e-mail. Accepts previously published material and simultaneous submissions. Sample copy for $1 with SAE and 5 first-class stamps. Writer's guidelines free.

Nonfiction Interview/profile, religious. No general-interest "inspirational" articles. Send complete ms. Length: 200-1,100 words. **Pays $75-325 for assigned articles; $46-250 for unsolicited articles.** Sometimes pays expenses of writers on assignment.

Columns/Departments On the Radar (significant trends/news of EFCA), 200-700 words; Breakthrough (innovative outreaches and practices of the EFCA); Impressions (thoughts from EFCA leaders); Among All People (celebration of EFCA diversity); Across the Movement (stories of God at work in the EFCA); all 500-1,000 words. Send complete ms. **Pays $46-250.**

$ $ ENRICHMENT

The General Council of the Assemblies of God, 1445 N. Boonville Ave., Springfield MO 65802. (417)862-2781. Fax: (417)862-0416. E-mail: enrichmentjournal@ag.org. Website: www.enrichmentjournal.ag.org. Executive Editor: Gary Allen. **Contact:** Rick Knoth, managing editor. **15% freelance written.** Quarterly journal covering church leadership and ministry. "*Enrichment* offers enriching and encouraging information to equip and empower spirit-filled leaders." Circ. 33,000. Pays on publication. Publishes ms an average of 1 year after acceptance. Byline given. Buys first rights. Editorial lead time 18 months. Submit seasonal material 18 months in advance. Accepts queries by mail, e-mail, fax, phone. Sample copy for $7. Writer's guidelines free.

Nonfiction Religious. Query with or without published clips or send complete ms. Length: 1,000-3,000 words. **Pays up to 10¢/word.**

$⊡ THE EVANGELICAL BAPTIST

Fellowship of Evangelical Baptist Churches in Canada, 18 Louvigny, Lorraine QC J6Z 1T7 Canada. (450)621-3248. Fax: (450)621-0253. E-mail: eb@fellowship.ca. Website: www.fellowship.ca. **Contact:** Ginette Cotnoir, managing editor. **30% freelance written.** Magazine published 5 times/year covering religious, spiritual, Christian living, denominational, and missionary news. "We exist to enhance the life and ministry of the church leaders of our association of churches—including pastors, elders, deacons, and all the men and women doing the work of the ministry in local churches." Estab. 1953. Circ. 3,000. Pays on publication. Publishes ms an average of 6 months after acceptance. Byline given. Buys one-time, second serial (reprint) rights. Editorial lead time 4 months. Accepts queries by mail, e-mail. Accepts previously published material and simultaneous submissions. Sample copy for 9×12 SAE with $1.50 in Canadian first-class stamps. Writer's guidelines by e-mail.

    O⌐ Break in with items for "Church Life (how-to and how-we articles about church ministries) or columns (Joy in the Journey)."

Nonfiction Religious. No poetry, fiction, puzzles. **Buys 12-15 mss/year.** Send complete ms. Length: 500-2,400 words. **Pays $30-150.**

Photos State availability with submission. Reviews prints. Buys one-time rights. Offers no additional payment for photos accepted with ms. Captions required.

Columns/Departments Church Life (practical articles about various church ministries, i.e., worship, Sunday school, missions, seniors, youth, discipleship); Joy in the Journey (devotional article regarding a lesson learned from God in everyday life), all 600-800 words. **Buys 10 mss/year.** Send complete ms. **Pays $25-50.**

$ EVANGELICAL MISSIONS QUARTERLY

A Professional Journal Serving the Missions Community, Billy Graham Center/Wheaton College, P.O. Box 794, Wheaton IL 60189. (630)752-7158. Fax: (630)752-7155. E-mail: emqjournal@aol.com. Website: www.billygrahamcenter.org/emis. Editor: A. Scott Moreau. **Contact:** Managing Editor. **67% freelance written.** Quarterly magazine covering evangelical missions. "This is a professional journal for evangelical missionaries, agency executives, and church members who support global missions ministries." Estab. 1964. Circ. 7,000. Pays on publication. Publishes ms an average of 18 months after acceptance. Byline given. Offers negotiable kill fee. Buys electronic, all rights. Editorial lead time 1 year. Accepts queries by mail, e-mail, fax, phone. Responds in 2 weeks to queries. Sample copy free. Writer's guidelines online.

Nonfiction Essays, interview/profile, opinion, personal experience, religious. No sermons, poetry, straight news. **Buys 24 mss/year.** Query. Length: 800-3,000 words. **Pays $50-100.**

Photos Send photos with submission. Buys first rights. Offers no additional payment for photos accepted with ms. Identification of subjects required.

Columns/Departments In the Workshop (practical how to's), 800-2,000 words; Perspectives (opinion), 800 words. **Buys 8 mss/year.** Query. **Pays $50-100.**

$ $ EVANGELIZING TODAY'S CHILD

Child Evangelism Fellowship, Inc., Box 348, Warrenton MO 63383-0348. (636)456-4321. Fax: (636)456-4321. E-mail: etceditor@cefonline.com. Website: www.cefonline.com/etcmag. **Contact:** Elsie Lippy, editor. **50% freelance written.** Bimonthly magazine. "Our purpose is to equip Christians to win the world's children to Christ and disciple them. Our readership is Sunday school teachers, Christian education leaders, and children's workers in every phase of Christian ministry to children 4-12 years old." Estab. 1942. Circ. 12,000. Pays within 2 months of acceptance. Publishes ms an average of 6 months after acceptance. Byline given. Offers kill fee if assigned. Buys first North American serial, electronic rights. Submit seasonal material 6 months in advance. Accepts queries by mail, e-mail. Responds in 1 month to queries. Sample copy for $2. Writer's guidelines online.

Nonfiction Unsolicited articles welcomed from writers with Christian education training or current experience in working with children. **Buys 50 mss/year.** Query. Length: 900 words. **Pays 12-15¢/word.**

Reprints Send photocopy and information about when and where the material previously appeared. Pays 35% of amount paid for an original article.

$ $⊡ FAITH TODAY

Seeking to Inform, Equip, and Inspire Christians Across Canada, Evangelical Fellowship of Canada, MIP Box 3745, Markham ON L3R 0Y4 Canada. (905)479-5885. Fax: (905)479-4742. E-mail: fteditor@efc-canada.com. Website: www.faithtoday.ca. Bimonthly magazine. "*FT* is an interdenominational, evangelical magazine that informs Canadian Christians on issues facing church and society, and on events within the church community. It focuses on the communal life of local congregations and corporate faith interacting with society more than on personal spiritual life. Writers should have a thorough understanding of the Canadian evangelical community." Estab. 1983. Circ. 18,000. Pays on publication. Publishes ms an average of 4 months after acceptance. Byline given. Offers 30-50% kill fee. Buys first rights. Editorial lead time 4 months. Accepts queries by mail, e-mail, fax. Responds in 6 weeks to queries. Sample copy for SASE in Canadian postage. Writer's guidelines online.

O→ Break in by "researching the Canadian field and including in your query a list of the Canadian contacts (Christian or not) that you intend to interview."

Nonfiction Book excerpts (Canadian authors only), essays (Canadian authors only), interview/profile (Canadian subjects only), opinion, religious, news feature. **Buys 75 mss/year.** Query. Length: 400-2,000 words. **Pays $100-500 Canadian, more for cover topic material.** Sometimes pays expenses of writers on assignment.

Reprints Send photocopy. Rarely used. Pays 50% of amount paid for an original article.

Photos State availability with submission. Reviews contact sheets. Buys one-time rights. Identifcation of subjects (except for concept/stock photos) required.

Tips "Query should include brief outline and names of the sources you plan to interview in your research. Use Canadian postage on SASE."

$THE FIVE STONES

Newsletter for Small Churches, The American Baptist Churches—USA, 155 Brown St., Providence RI 02906. Phone/Fax: (401)861-9405. E-mail: pappas@tabcom.org. **Contact:** Anthony G. Pappas, editor. **50% freelance written.** Quarterly magazine covering congregational dynamics in smaller churches. "*The Five Stones* is a resource for leaders in smaller congregations. Target audience: pastors, lay leaders, denominational officers." Estab. 1980. Circ. 500. Pays on publication. Publishes ms an average of 1 year after acceptance. Byline given. Not copyrighted. Buys one-time rights. Editorial lead time 6 months. Submit seasonal material 6 months in advance. Accepts queries by mail, e-mail, fax, phone. Accepts previously published material. Accepts simultaneous submissions. Responds in 6 weeks to queries; 6 months to mss. Sample copy and writer's guidelines for #10 SASE.

Nonfiction "Articles must be specific to small church-related issues." Book excerpts, essays, historical/nostalgic, how-to, humor, inspirational, interview/profile, personal experience, religious. **Buys 8-12 mss/year.** Send complete ms. Length: 500-3,000 words. **Pays $10.**

Reprints Accepts previously published submissions.

Photos State availability with submission. Reviews GIF/JPEG files. Buys one-time rights. Offers no additional payment for photos accepted with ms. Identification of subjects required.

Columns/Departments Small Town; Urban; Stewardship; Evangelism; Mission; Church Life; Reources; Humor (all first-person), all 500-2,500 words. **Buys 20 mss/year.** Send complete ms. **Pays $10.**

Fiction Ethnic, historical, humorous, religious, slice-of-life vignettes. **Buys 4 mss/year.** Send complete ms. Length: 300-3,000 words. **Pays $5 (maximum), and 2 contributor's copies.**

Tips "First-person experiences. Focus on current issues of congregational life. Submit stories of positive events or learnings from negative ones."

$FORWARD IN CHRIST

The Word From the WELS, WELS, 2929 N. Mayfair Rd., Milwaukee WI 53222-4398. (414)256-3210. Fax: (414)256-3862. E-mail: fic@sab.wels.net. Website: www.wels.net. **Contact:** Gary P. Baumler, editor. **5% freelance written.** Monthly magazine covering WELS news, topics, issues. The material usually must be written by or about WELS members. Estab. 1913. Circ. 56,000. Pays on publication. Publishes ms an average of 6 months after acceptance. Byline given. Buys one-time rights. Editorial lead time 3 months. Submit seasonal material 4 months in advance. Accepts queries by mail, e-mail, fax. Responds in 2 months to queries. Sample copy and writer's guidelines free.

Nonfiction Personal experience, religious. Query. Length: 550-1,200 words. **Pays $75/page, $125/2 pages.** Sometimes pays expenses of writers on assignment.

Photos State availability with submission. Reviews contact sheets. Buys one-time rights, plus 1 month on Web. Negotiates payment individually. Captions, identification of subjects, model releases required.

Tips "Topics should be of interest to the majority of the members of the synod—the people in the pews. Articles should have a Christian viewpoint, but we don't want sermons. We suggest you carefully read at least 5 or 6 issues with close attention to the length, content, and style of the features."

☑ FOURSQUARE WORLD ADVANCE

International Church of the Foursquare Gospel, 1910 W. Sunset Blvd., Suite 400, Los Angeles CA 90026. E-mail: bshepson@foursquare.org. Website: www.advancemagazine.org. **Contact:** Bill Shepson, editorial director. **90% freelance written.** Quarterly magazine covering devotional/religious material, news, book and product reviews. "The official publication of the International Church of the Foursquare Gospel is distributed without charge to members and friends of the Foursquare Church." Estab. 1917. Circ. 98,000. Pays on publication. Buys all rights. Accepts queries by mail, e-mail. Accepts previously published material. Responds in 2 weeks to queries. Sample copy for free. Writer's guidelines online.

- *Does not accept unsolicited mss.*

$ GOD ALLOWS U-TURNS

The God Allows U-Turns Project, P.O. Box 717, Faribault MN 55021-0717. Fax: (507)334-6464. E-mail: editor@g odallowsuturns.com. Website: www.godallowsuturns.com. **Contact:** Allison Gappa Bottke, editor. **100% freelance written.** Christian inspirational book series. "Each anthology contains approximately 50 dramatically compelling true stories written by contributors from all over the world. Multiple volumes are planned." Pays on publication. Byline given. Accepts previously published material. Accepts simultaneous submissions. Writer's guidelines online.

- Accepts stories by mail and e-mail. Responds *only* when a story is selected for publication. For a list of current *God Allows U-Turns* answered prayer books open to submissions, as well as related opportunities, go to website. Timelines vary, so send stories any time as they may fit another volume. When submitting, indicate which volume it is for.

Nonfiction "Open to well-written personal inspirational pieces showing how faith in God can inspire, encourage, and heal. True stories that must touch our emotions." Essays, historical/nostalgic, humor, inspirational, interview/profile, personal experience, religious. **Buys 100+ mss/year. Pays $50, plus 1 copy of anthology.**

Tips "Read a current volume. See the website for a sample story. Keep it real. Ordinary people doing extraordinary things with God's help. These true stories must touch our emotions. Our contributors are a diverse group with no limits on age or denomination."

$ $ GROUP MAGAZINE

Group Publishing, Inc., P.O. Box 481, Loveland CO 80539. Fax: (970)292-4373. E-mail: greditor@youthministry. com. Website: www.groupmag.com. **Contact:** Kathy Dietrich. **60% freelance written.** Bimonthly magazine covering youth ministry. "Writers must be actively involved in youth ministry. Articles we accept are practical, not theoretical, and focused for local church youth workers." Estab. 1974. Circ. 57,000. **Pays on acceptance.** Publishes ms an average of 6 months after acceptance. Byline given. Offers $20 kill fee. Buys all rights. Submit seasonal material 7 months in advance. Responds in 2 months to queries. Sample copy for $2 and 9×12 SAE. Writer's guidelines online.

Nonfiction How-to (youth ministry issues). No personal testimony, theological or lecture-style articles. **Buys 50-60 mss/year.** Query. Length: 250-2,200 words. **Pays $40-350.** Sometimes pays expenses of writers on assignment.

Tips "Submit a youth ministry idea to one of our mini-article sections—we look for tried-and-true ideas youth ministers have used with kids."

$ $ GUIDEPOSTS MAGAZINE

16 E. 34th St., New York NY 10016-4397. (212)251-8100. Website: www.guideposts.com. **Contact:** James McDermott, articles editor. **40% freelance written.** Works with a small number of new/unpublished writers each year. Monthly magazine. "*Guideposts* is an inspirational monthly magazine for people of all faiths, in which men and women from all walks of life tell in true, first-person narrative how they overcame obstacles, rose above failures, handled sorrow, gained new spiritual insight, and became more effective people through faith in God." Estab. 1945. Pays on publication. Publishes ms an average of several months after acceptance. Offers 20% kill fee on assigned stories, but not to first-time freelancers. Buys all rights. Writer's guidelines online.

- "Many of our stories are ghosted articles, so the writer would not get a byline unless it was his/her own story. Because of the high volume of mail the magazine receives, we regret we *cannot* return manuscripts, and will contact writers only if their material can be used."

Nonfiction Articles and features should be true stories written in simple, anecdotal style with an emphasis on human interest. Short mss of approximately 250-750 words (pays $100-250) considered for such features as "Angels Among Us," "His Mysterious Ways," and general 1-page stories. Address short items to Celeste McCauley. For full-length mss, 750-1,500 words, pays $250-500. All mss should be typed, double-spaced, and accompanied by e-mail address, if possible. Annually awards scholarships to high school juniors and seniors in writing contest. **Buys 40-60 unsolicited mss/year.** Length: 250-1,500 words. **Pays $100-500.** Pays expenses of writers on assignment.

Tips "Study the magazine before you try to write for it. Each story must make a single spiritual point that readers can apply to their own daily lives. And it may be easier to just sit down and write them than to have to go through the process of preparing a query. They should be warm, well written, intelligent, and upbeat. We require personal narratives that are true and have some spiritual aspect, but the religious element can be subtle and should *not* be sermonic. A writer succeeds with us if he or she can write a true article using short-story techniques with scenes, drama, tension, and a resolution of the problem presented.''

$HORIZONS

The Magazine for Presbyterian Women, 100 Witherspoon St., Louisville KY 40202-1396. (502)569-5688. Fax: (502)569-8085. Website: www.pcusa.org/horizons/. Bimonthly Magazine owned and operated by Presbyterian women offering ''information and inspiration for Presbyterian women by addressing current issues facing the church and the world.'' Estab. 1988. Circ. 25,000. Pays on publication. Publishes ms an average of 4 months after acceptance. Buys all rights. Responds in 3 months to mss. Sample copy for $4 and 9×12 SAE. Writer's guidelines for #10 SASE.

● Prefers complete ms over query. Include SASE.

Fiction Send complete ms. Length: 800-1,200 words. **Pays $50/600 words and 2 contributor's copies.**

N $JEWISH FRONTIER

Labor Zionist Alliance, 114 W. 26th St., #1006, New York NY 10001. (212)366-1194. Fax: (212)675-7685. Website: www.laborzionist.org. **Contact:** Jamie Levin, executive editor. **100% freelance written.** Bimonthly intellectual journal covering progressive Jewish issues. ''Reportage, essays, reviews, and occasional fiction and poetry, with a progressive Jewish perspective, and a particular interest in Israeli and Jewish-American affairs.'' Estab. 1934. Circ. 2,600. **Pays on acceptance.** Publishes ms an average of 4 months after acceptance. Byline given. Buys first, second serial (reprint), electronic rights. Editorial lead time 4 months. Submit seasonal material 2 months in advance. Accepts queries by mail, e-mail. Accepts previously published material. Accepts simultaneous submissions. Responds in 1 month to queries; 2 months to mss. Sample copy for 9×12 SAE and 3 first-class stamps or online. Writer's guidelines online.

Nonfiction Must have progressive Jewish focus or will not be considered. Book excerpts, essays, exposé, historical/nostalgic, interview/profile, opinion, personal experience. **Buys 20 mss/year.** Query. Length: 1,000-2,500 words. **Pays 5¢/word.**

Photos State availability with submission. Buys all rights. Offers no additional payment for photos accepted with ms. Captions, identification of subjects required.

Columns/Departments Essays (progressive Jewish opinion), 1,000-2,500 words; Articles (progressive Jewish reportage), 1,000-2,500 words; Reviews, 500-1,000 words. **Buys 12 mss/year.** Query. **Pays 5¢/word.**

Poetry Avant-garde, free verse, haiku, traditional. **Buys 12 poems/year.** Submit 3 poems. Length: 7-25 lines. **Pays 5¢/word.**

Tips ''Send queries with strong ideas first. *Jewish Frontier* particularly appreciates original thinking on its topics related to progressive Jewish matters.''

$ LIFEGLOW

Christian Record Services, P.O. Box 6097, Lincoln NE 68506. Website: www.christianrecord.org. **Contact:** Gaylena Gibson, editor. **95% freelance written.** Large print Christian publication for sight-impaired over age 25 covering health, handicapped people, uplifting articles. Estab. 1984. Circ. 35,000. **Pays on acceptance.** Publishes ms an average of 3 years after acceptance. Byline given. Buys one-time rights. Accepts previously published material. Accepts simultaneous submissions. Responds in 1 year to mss. Sample copy for 7×10 SAE and 5 first-class stamps. Writer's guidelines for #10 SASE.

● Due to a current overabundance of mss, *Lifeglow* will not be accepting mss until 2009.

○→ ''Write for an interdenominational Christian audience.''

Nonfiction Essays, general interest, historical/nostalgic, humor, inspirational, interview/profile, personal experience, travel, adventure, biography, careers, handicapped, health, hobbies, marriage, nature. **Buys 40 mss/year.** Length: 200-1,400 words. **Pays 4-5¢/word, and complimentary copies.**

Photos Send photos with submission. Buys one-time rights. Negotiates payment individually.

Columns/Departments Baffle U! (puzzle), 150 words, **pays $15-25/puzzle;** Vitality Plus (current health topics), length varies, **pays 4¢/word. Buys 10 mss/year.**

Fillers Anecdotes, facts, short humor. **Buys very few/year.** Length: 300 words maximum. **Pays 4¢/word.**

Tips ''Make sure manuscript has a strong ending that ties everything together and doesn't leave us dangling. Pretend someone else wrote it—would it hold your interest? Draw your readers into the story by being specific rather than abstract or general.''

$ $LIGHT AND LIFE MAGAZINE

Free Methodist Church of North America, P.O. Box 535002, Indianapolis IN 46253-5002. (317)244-3660. Fax: (317)248-9055. E-mail: llmauthors@fmcna.org. Website: www.freemethodistchurch.org/magazine. **Contact:** Doug Newton, editor; Cynthia Schnereger, managing editor. Works with a small number of new/unpublished writers each year. Bimonthly magazine for maturing Christians emphasizing a holiness lifestyle, contemporary issues, and a Christ-centered worldview. Includes pull-out discipleship and evangelism tools and encouragement cards, leadership tips and profiles, denominational news. Estab. 1868. Circ. 13,000. **Pays on acceptance.** Byline given. Buys first North American serial rights. Sample copy for $4. Writer's guidelines online.

Nonfiction Query. Length: 500-1,700 words (LifeNotes 1,000 words). **Pays 15¢/word.**

$ $ LIGUORIAN

One Liguori Dr., Liguori MO 63057-9999. (636)464-2500. Fax: (636)464-8449. E-mail: liguorianeditor@liguori.org. Website: www.liguorian.org. Managing Editor: Cheryl Plass. **Contact:** Fr. William J. Parker, CSSR, editor-in-chief. **25% freelance written.** Prefers to work with published/established writers. Magazine published 10 times/year for Catholics. "Our purpose is to lead our readers to a fuller Christian life by helping them better understand the teachings of the gospel and the church and by illustrating how these teachings apply to life and the problems confronting them as members of families, the church, and society." Estab. 1913. Circ. 200,000. **Pays on acceptance.** Offers 50% kill fee. Buys first rights. Submit seasonal material 8 months in advance. Accepts queries by mail, e-mail, fax, phone. Responds in 3 months to mss. Sample copy for 9×12 SAE with 3 first-class stamps or online. Writer's guidelines for #10 SASE and on website.

Nonfiction Pastoral, practical, and personal approach to the problems and challenges of people today. "No travelogue approach or unresearched ventures into controversial areas. Also, no material found in secular publications—fad subjects that already get enough press, pop psychology, negative or put-down articles." **Buys 40-50 unsolicited mss/year.** Length: 400-2,000 words. **Pays 10-15¢/word.** Sometimes pays expenses of writers on assignment.

Photos Photographs on assignment only unless submitted with and specific to article.

Fiction Religious, senior citizen/retirement. Send complete ms. Length: 1,500-2,000 words preferred. **Pays 10-15¢/word and 5 contributor's copies.**

$ THE LIVING CHURCH

Living Church Foundation, 816 E. Juneau Ave., P.O. Box 514036, Milwaukee WI 53203. (414)276-5420. Fax: (414)276-7483. E-mail: tlc@livingchurch.org. Managing Editor: John Schuessler. **Contact:** David Kalvelage, editor. **50% freelance written.** Weekly magazine on the Episcopal Church. News or articles of interest to members of the Episcopal Church. Estab. 1878. Circ. 9,500. Does not pay unless article is requested. Publishes ms an average of 3 months after acceptance. Byline given. Buys one-time rights. Editorial lead time 3 weeks. Submit seasonal material 2 months in advance. Accepts queries by mail, e-mail, fax. Responds in 2 weeks to queries; 1 month to mss. Sample copy for free.

Nonfiction Opinion, personal experience, photo feature, religious. **Buys 10 mss/year.** Send complete ms. Length: 1,000 words. **Pays $25-100.** Sometimes pays expenses of writers on assignment.

Photos Send photos with submission. Reviews any size prints. Buys one-time rights. Offers $15-50/photo.

Columns/Departments Benediction (devotional), 250 words; Viewpoint (opinion), under 1,000 words. Send complete ms. **Pays $50 maximum.**

Poetry Light verse, traditional.

N $ $ THE LOOKOUT

For Today's Growing Christian, Standard Publishing, 8121 Hamilton Ave., Cincinnati OH 45231-9981. (513)931-4050. Fax: (513)931-0950. E-mail: lookout@standardpub.com. Website: www.lookoutmag.com. Administrative Assistant: Sheryl Overstreet. **Contact:** Shawn McMullen, editor. **50% freelance written.** Weekly magazine for Christian adults, with emphasis on spiritual growth, family life, and topical issues. "Our purpose is to provide Christian adults with practical, Biblical teaching and current information that will help them mature as believers." Estab. 1894. Circ. 100,000. **Pays on acceptance.** Publishes ms an average of 1 year after acceptance. Byline given. Offers 33% kill fee. Buys first, one-time rights. Editorial lead time 9 months. Submit seasonal material 1 year in advance. Accepts simultaneous submissions. Responds in 4-6 weeks to queries; 10 weeks to mss. Sample copy for $1. Writer's guidelines by e-mail.

● Audience is mainly conservative Christians. Manuscripts only accepted by mail.

Nonfiction "Writers need to send for current theme list. We also use inspirational short pieces." Inspirational, interview/profile, opinion, personal experience, religious. No fiction or poetry. **Buys 100 mss/year.** Query with or without published clips or send complete ms. Length: Check guidelines. **Pays 5-12¢/word.** Sometimes pays expenses of writers on assignment.

Photos State availability with submission. Buys one-time rights. Offers no additional payment for photos accepted with ms. Identification of subjects required.

Tips "*The Lookout* publishes from a theologically conservative, nondenominational, and noncharismatic perspective. It is a member of the Evangelical Press Association. We have readers in every adult age group, but we aim primarily for those aged 30-55. Most readers are married and have elementary to young adult children, but a large number come from other home situations as well. Our emphasis is on the needs of ordinary Christians who want to grow in their faith, rather than on trained theologians or church leaders. As a Christian general-interest magazine, we cover a wide variety of topics—from individual discipleship to family concerns to social involvement. We value well-informed articles that offer lively and clear writing as well as strong application. We often address tough issues and seek to explore fresh ideas or recent developments affecting today's Christians.''

$THE LUTHERAN DIGEST

The Lutheran Digest, Inc., P.O. Box 4250, Hopkins MN 55343. (952)933-2820. Fax: (952)933-5708. E-mail: tldi@lutherandigest.com. Website: www.lutherandigest.com. **Contact:** David L. Tank, editor. **95% freelance written.** Quarterly magazine covering Christianity from a Lutheran perspective. ''Articles frequently reflect a Lutheran Christian perspective, but are not intended to be sermonettes. Popular stories show how God has intervened in a person's life to help solve a problem.'' Estab. 1953. Circ. 105,000. **Pays on acceptance.** Publishes ms an average of 6 months after acceptance. Byline given. Buys first, second serial (reprint) rights. Editorial lead time 9 months. Submit seasonal material 9 months in advance. Accepts queries by mail. Accepts previously published material. Accepts simultaneous submissions. Responds in 1 month to queries; 4 months to mss. Sample copy for $3.50. Writer's guidelines online.

> O→ Break in with ''reprints from other publications that will fill less than three pages of *TLD*. Articles of 1 or 2 pages are even better. As a digest, we primarily look for previously published articles to reprint, however, we do publish about twenty to thirty percent original material. Articles from new writers are always welcomed and seriously considered.''

Nonfiction General interest, historical/nostalgic, how-to (personal or spiritual growth), humor, inspirational, personal experience, religious, nature, God's unique creatures. Does not want to see ''personal tributes to deceased relatives or friends. They are seldom used unless the subject of the article is well known. We also avoid articles about the moment a person finds Christ as his or her personal savior.'' **Buys 50-60 mss/year.** Send complete ms. Length: 1,500 words. **Pays $35-50.**

Reprints Accepts previously published submissions. ''We prefer this as we are a digest and 70-80% of our articles are reprints.''

Photos ''We seldom print photos from outside sources.'' State availability with submission. Buys one-time rights.

Tips ''An article that tugs on the 'heart strings' just a little and closes leaving the reader with a sense of hope is a writer's best bet to breaking into *The Lutheran Digest*.''

$THE LUTHERAN JOURNAL

Apostolic Publishing Co., Inc., P.O. Box 28158, Oakdale MN 55128. (651)702-0086. Fax: (651)702-0074. Publisher: Vance Lichty. **Contact:** Editorial Assistant. Semiannual Magazine published 2 times/year for Lutheran Church members, middle age and older. ''A family magazine providing wholesome and inspirational reading material for the enjoyment and enrichment of Lutherans.'' Estab. 1938. Circ. 200,000. Pays on publication. Byline given. Buys first, all rights. Accepts simultaneous submissions. Responds in 4 months to queries. Sample copy for 9×12 SAE with 60¢ postage.

Nonfiction Historical/nostalgic, how-to, humor, inspirational, interview/profile, personal experience, religious, interesting or unusual church projects, think articles. **Buys 25-30 mss/year.** Send complete ms. Length: 1,500 words maximum; occasionally 2,000 words. **Pays 1-4¢/word.**

Reprints Send tearsheet, photocopy or typed ms with rights for sale noted and information about when and where the material previously appeared. Pays up to 50% of amount paid for an original article.

Photos Send photocopies of b&w and color photos with accompanying ms. Please do not send original photos.

Fiction Religious, romance, senior citizen/retirement. Must be appropriate for distribution in the churches. Send complete ms. Length: 1,000-1,500 words. **Pays $20-50 and one contributor's copy.**

Poetry Buys 2-3 poems/issue, as space allows. **Pays $10-30.**

Tips ''We strongly prefer a warm, personal style of writing that speaks directly to the reader. In general, writers should seek to convey information rather than express personal opinion, though the writer's own personality should be reflected in the article's style. Send submissions with SASE so we may respond.''

$LUTHERAN PARTNERS

Augsburg Fortress, Publishers, ELCA (DM), 8765 W. Higgins Rd., Chicago IL 60631-4195. (773)380-2884. Fax: (773)380-2829. E-mail: lpartmag@elca.org. Website: www.elca.org/lp. **Contact:** William A. Decker, editor. **40% freelance written.** Bimonthly magazine covering issues of religious leadership. ''Lutheran Partners provides a forum for the discussion of issues surrounding gospel-centered ministry which are vital to scripture, theology, leadership, and mission in congregations and other settings of the church.'' Estab. 1979. Circ. 20,000. Pays on publication. Publishes ms an average of 6 months after acceptance. Byline given. Buys first, one-time, second serial (reprint), electronic rights. Editorial lead time 6 months. Submit seasonal material 6 months in advance. Accepts queries by mail, e-mail, fax, phone. Accepts previously published material. Accepts simultaneous submissions. Responds in 1 month to queries; 6 months to mss. Sample copy for $2. Writer's guidelines online.

- The editor reports an interest in seeing articles on various facets of ministry from the perspectives of ELCA Lutheran ethnic authors (Hispanic, African-American, Asian, Native American, Arab-American), as well as material on youth leadership and ministry, parish education, outreach, and preaching.

O— Break in through "Jottings" (practical how-to articles involving congregational ministry ideas, 500 words maximum)."

Nonfiction Historical/nostalgic, how-to (leadership in faith communities), humor (religious cartoon), inspirational, opinion (religious leadership issues), religious, book reviews (query book review editor). "No exposés, articles primarily promoting products/services, or anti-religion." **Buys 15-20 mss/year.** Query with published clips or send complete ms. Length: 500-1,500 words. **Pays $25-170.** Pays in copies for book reviews.

Photos State availability with submission. Buys one-time rights. Generally offers no additional payment for photos accepted with ms. Captions, identification of subjects required.

Columns/Departments Review Editor. Partners Review (book reviews), 700 words. Query or submit ms. **Pays in copies.**

Fiction Rarely accepts religious fiction. Query.

Poetry Free verse, haiku, light verse, traditional, hymns. **Buys 3-6 poems/year.** Submit maximum 4 poems. **Pays $50-75.**

Fillers Practical ministry (education, music, youth, social service, administration, worship, etc.) in congregation. **Buys 1-3/year.** Length: 500 words. **Pays $25.**

Tips "Know congregational life, especially from the perspective of leadership, including both ordained pastor and lay staff. Think current and future leadership needs. It would be good to be familiar with ELCA rostered pastors, lay ministers, and congregations."

$ $ THE LUTHERAN

Magazine of the Evangelical Lutheran Church in America, 8765 W. Higgins Rd., Chicago IL 60631-4183. (773)380-2540. Fax: (773)380-2751. E-mail: lutheran@lutheran.org. Website: www.thelutheran.org. Managing Editor: Sonia Solomonson. **Contact:** David L. Miller, editor. **15% freelance written.** Monthly magazine for "lay people in church. News and activities of the Evangelical Lutheran Church in America, news of the world of religion, ethical reflections on issues in society, personal Christian experience." Estab. 1988. Circ. 600,000. **Pays on acceptance.** Publishes ms an average of 6 months after acceptance. Byline given. Offers 50% kill fee. Buys first rights. Submit seasonal material 4 months in advance. Accepts queries by mail, e-mail. Responds in 6 weeks to queries. Sample copy free. Writer's guidelines online.

O— Break in by checking out the theme list on the website and querying with ideas related to these themes.

Nonfiction Inspirational, interview/profile, personal experience, photo feature, religious. "No articles unrelated to the world of religion." **Buys 40 mss/year.** Query with published clips. Length: 400-1,400 words. **Pays $75-600.** Pays expenses of writers on assignment.

Photos Send photos with submission. Reviews contact sheets, transparencies, prints. Buys one-time rights. Offers $50-175/photo. Captions, identification of subjects required.

Columns/Departments Lite Side (humor—church, religious), In Focus, Living the Faith, Values & Society, In Our Churches, Our Church at Work, 25-100 words. Send complete ms. **Pays $10.**

Tips "Writers have the best chance selling us feature articles."

$ ⊠ MENNONITE BRETHREN HERALD

3-169 Riverton Ave., Winnipeg MB R2L 2E5 Canada. (888)669-6575. Fax: (204)654-1865. E-mail: mbherald@mb conf.ca. Website: www.mbherald.com. **Contact:** Susan Brandt, editor. **25% freelance written.** Triweekly family publication "read mainly by people of the Mennonite Brethren faith, reaching a wide cross section of professional and occupational groups, including many homemakers. Readership includes people from both urban and rural communities. It is intended to inform members of events in the church and the world, serve personal and corporate spiritual needs, serve as a vehicle of communication within the church, serve conference agencies and reflect the history and theology of the Mennonite Brethren Church." Estab. 1962. Circ. 16,500. Pays on publication. Publishes ms an average of 6 months after acceptance. Byline given. Not copyrighted. Buys one-time rights. Accepts queries by e-mail, fax. Responds in 6 months to queries. Sample copy for $1 and 9×12 SAE with 2 IRCs. Writer's guidelines online.

- "Articles and manuscripts not accepted for publication will be returned if a SASE (Canadian stamps or IRCs) is provided by the writers."

Nonfiction Articles with a Christian family orientation; youth directed, Christian faith and life, and current issues. Wants articles critiquing the values of a secular society, attempting to relate Christian living to the practical situations of daily living; showing how people have related their faith to their vocations. Send complete ms. Length: 250-1,500 words. **Pays $30-40.** Pays expenses of writers on assignment.

Reprints Send tearsheet, photocopy or typed ms with rights for sale noted and information about when and where the material previously appeared. Pays 70% of amount paid for an original article.

Photos Photos purchased with ms.

Columns/Departments Viewpoint (Christian opinion on current topics), 850 words. Crosscurrent (Christian opinion on music, books, art, TV, movies), 350 words.

Poetry Length: 25 lines maximum.

Tips "We like simple style, contemporary language and fresh ideas. Writers should take care to avoid religious cliches."

$ $ MESSAGE MAGAZINE

Review and Herald Publishing Association, 55 West Oak Ridge Dr., Hagerstown MD 21740. (301)393-4099. Fax: (301)393-4103. E-mail: message@rhpa.org. Website: www.messagemagazine.org. **Contact:** Dr. Ron C. Smith, editor. **10-20% freelance written.** Bimonthly magazine. "*Message* is the oldest religious journal addressing ethnic issues in the country. Our audience is predominantly Black and Seventh-day Adventist; however, *Message* is an outreach magazine geared to the unchurched." Estab. 1898. Circ. 110,000. **Pays on acceptance.** Publishes ms an average of 1 year after acceptance. Byline given. first North American serial rights Editorial lead time 6 months. Submit seasonal material 6 months in advance. Responds in 9 months to queries. Sample copy and writer's guidelines by e-mail.

Nonfiction General interest (to a Christian audience), how-to (overcome depression; overcome defeat; get closer to God; learn from failure, etc.), inspirational, interview/profile (profiles of famous African Americans), personal experience (testimonies), religious. **Buys variable number of mss/year.** Send complete ms. Length: 800-1,200 words. **Payment varies.**

Photos State availability with submission. Buys one-time rights. Identification of subjects required.

Columns/Departments Voices in the Wind (community involvement/service/events/health info); Message, Jr. (stories for children with a moral, explain a biblical or moral principle); Recipes (no meat or dairy products—12-15 recipes and an intro); Healthspan (health issues); all 500 words. Send complete ms. for Message, Jr. and Healthspan. Query editor with published clips for Voices in the Wind and Recipes. **Pays $50-300.**

Tips "Please look at the magazine before submitting manuscripts. *Message* publishes a variety of writing styles as long as the writing style is easy to read and flows—please avoid highly technical writing styles."

$ ▧ THE MESSENGER OF THE SACRED HEART

Apostleship of Prayer, 661 Greenwood Ave., Toronto ON M4J 4B3 Canada. (416)466-1195. **Contact:** Rev. F.J. Power, S.J., editor. **20% freelance written.** Monthly magazine for "Canadian and US Catholics interested in developing a life of prayer and spirituality; stresses the great value of our ordinary actions and lives." Estab. 1891. Circ. 11,000. **Pays on acceptance.** Byline given. Buys first North American serial, first rights. Submit seasonal material 5 months in advance. Responds in 1 month to queries. Sample copy for $1 and 7½×10½ SAE. Writer's guidelines for #10 SASE.

Fiction Rev. F.J. Power, S.J. and Alfred DeManche, editors. Religious, stories about people, adventure, heroism, humor, drama. No poetry. **Buys 12 mss/year.** Send complete ms. Length: 750-1,500 words. **Pays 6¢/word, and 3 contributor's copies.**

Tips "Develop a story that sustains interest to the end. Do not preach, but use plot and characters to convey the message or theme. Aim to move the heart as well as the mind. Before sending, cut out unnecessary or unrelated words or sentences. If you can, add a light touch or a sense of humor to the story. Your ending should have impact, leaving a moral or faith message for the reader."

$ THE MIRACULOUS MEDAL

The Central Association of the Miraculous Medal, 475 E. Chelten Ave., Philadelphia PA 19144-5785. (215)848-1010. Website: www.cammonline.org. **Contact:** Rev. James Kiernan, editor. **40% freelance written.** Quarterly magazine. Estab. 1915. **Pays on acceptance.** Publishes ms an average of 2 years after acceptance. Buys first North American serial rights. Accepts queries by mail. Responds in 3 months to queries. Sample copy for 6×9 SAE and 2 first-class stamps. Writer's guidelines free.

Fiction Charles Kelly, general manager. Wants good general fiction—not necessarily religious, but if religion is basic to the story, the writer should be sure of his facts. Only restriction is that subject matter and treatment must not conflict with Catholic teaching and practice. Can use seasonal material, Christmas stories. Religious. Should not be pious or sermon-like. Length: 2,000 words maximum. Occasionally uses short-shorts from 1,000-1,500 words. **Pays 3¢/word minimum.**

Poetry Preferably about the Virgin Mary or at least with a religious slant. Length: 20 lines maximum. **Pays $1/ line minimum.**

N $ THE MONTANA CATHOLIC

Diocese of Helena, P.O. Box 1729, Helena MT 59624. (406)442-5820. Fax: (406)442-5191. E-mail: rstmartin@dio
cesehelena.org. **Contact:** Renee St. Martin Wizeman, editor. **5% freelance written.** Monthly tabloid. "We
publish news and features from a Catholic perspective, particularly as they pertain to the church in western
Montana." Estab. 1932. Circ. 9,200. **Pays on acceptance.** Publishes ms an average of 6 months after acceptance.
Byline given. Offers 25% kill fee. Buys first, one-time, simultaneous rights. Editorial lead time 1 month. Accepts
queries by mail, e-mail. Accepts simultaneous submissions. Responds in 1 month to queries. Writer's guidelines
for #10 SASE.

Nonfiction Special issues: Vocations (January); Lent; Easter; Advent; Christmas. **Buys 5 mss/year.** Send complete ms with SASE for reply and/or return of ms. Length: 400-1,200 words. **Pays 10¢/word for assigned
articles; 5¢/word for unsolicited articles.**

Photos Reviews contact sheets, prints. Buys one-time rights. Offers $5-20/photo. Identification of subjects
required.

Tips "Best bets are seasonal pieces, topics related to our special supplements, and features with a tie-in to
western Montana—always with a Catholic angle. No poetry, please."

$ $ MY DAILY VISITOR

Our Sunday Visitor, Inc., 200 Noll Plaza, Huntington IN 46750. (260)356-8400. Fax: (260)356-8472. E-mail:
mdvisitor@osv.com. Website: www.osv.com. **99% freelance written.** Bimonthly magazine of Scripture meditations based on the day's Catholic Mass readings. Circ. 33,000. **Pays on acceptance.** Publishes ms an average
of 6 months after acceptance. Byline given. Not copyrighted. Buys one-time rights. Accepts queries by mail, e-
mail. Responds in 2 months to queries. Sample copy and writer's guidelines for #10 SAE with 3 first-class
stamps. Sample meditations and guidelines online.

● Each writer does 1 full month of meditations on assignment basis only.

Nonfiction Inspirational, personal experience, religious. **Buys 12 mss/year.** Query with published clips. Length:
130-140 words times the number of days in month. **Pays $500 and 5 free copies for 1 month (28-31) of
meditations.**

Tips "Previous experience in writing Scripture-based Catholic meditations or essays is helpful."

N $ NORTH AMERICAN VOICE OF FATIMA

Barnabite Fathers-North American Province, National Shrine Basilica of Our Lady of Fatima, 1023 Swann Rd.,
P.O. Box 167, Youngstown NY 14174-0167. (716)754-7489. Fax: (716)754-9130. E-mail: voice@fatimashrine.c
om. Website: www.fatimashrine.com. **Contact:** Rev. Peter M. Calabrese, CRSP, editor. **90% freelance written.**
Quarterly magazine covering Catholic spirituality. "The Barnabite Fathers wish to share the joy and challenge
of the Gospel and to foster devotion to Our Lady, Mary, the Mother of the Redeemer and Mother of the Church
who said at Cana: 'Do whatever He tells you.'" Estab. 1961. Circ. 1,200. Pays on publication. Publishes ms an
average of 3 months after acceptance. Byline given. Buys first North American serial, one-time, second serial
(reprint) rights, makes work-for-hire assignments. Editorial lead time 2 months. Submit seasonal material 2
months in advance. Accepts queries by mail, e-mail. Accepts simultaneous submissions. Responds in 3 weeks
to queries. Sample copy for free. Writer's guidelines online.

Nonfiction Inspirational, personal experience, religious. **Buys 32 mss/year.** Send complete ms. Length: 500-
1,250 words. **Pays 5¢/word.**

Photos Send photos with submission. Buys one-time rights. Offers no additional payment for photos accepted
with ms. Identification of subjects required.

Columns/Departments Book Reviews (religious), 500 words or less. Send complete ms. **Pays 5¢/word.**

Poetry Free verse, traditional. **Buys 16-20 poems/year.** Length: 4 lines minimum. **Pays $10-25.**

Tips "We are a Catholic spirituality magazine that publishes articles on faith-based themes—also inspirational
or uplifting stories. While Catholic, we also publish articles by non-Catholic Christians."

$ $ ON MISSION

North American Mission Board, SBC, 4200 North Point Pkwy., Alpharetta GA 30022-4176. E-mail: cpipes@namb
.net. Website: www.onmission.com. **50% freelance written.** Quarterly lifestyle magazine that popularizes
evangelism, church planting and missions. "*On Mission*'s primary purpose is to help readers and churches
become more intentional about personal evangelism, church planting, and missions. *On Mission* equips Christians for leading people to Christ and encourages churches to reach new people through new congregations."
Estab. 1997. Circ. 100,000. **Pays on acceptance.** Publishes ms an average of 6 months after acceptance. Byline
given. Buys first, electronic, first north american rights. Editorial lead time 9 months. Submit seasonal material
9 months in advance. Accepts queries by mail, e-mail. Responds in 6 months. Sample copy and writer's guidelines online.

○┐ Break in with a 600-word how-to article.

Nonfiction How-to, humor, personal experience (stories of sharing your faith in Christ with a non-Christian). **Buys 30 mss/year.** Query with published clips. Length: 350-1,200 words. **Pays 25¢/word, more for cover stories.** Pays expenses of writers on assignment.

Photos Most are shot on assignment. Buys one-time rights. Captions, identification of subjects required.

Columns/Departments Buys 2 mss/year. Query. **Pays 25¢/word.**

Tips ''Readers might be intimidated if those featured appear to be 'super Christians' who seem to live on a higher spiritual plane. Try to introduce subjects as three-dimensional, real people. Include anecdotes or examples of their fears and failures, including ways they overcame obstacles. In other words, take the reader inside the heart of the on mission Christian and reveal the inevitable humanness that makes that person not only believable, but also approachable. We want the reader to feel encouraged to become on mission by identifying with people like them who are featured in the magazine.''

Ⓝ $ $ONE

Catholic Near East Welfare Association, 1011 First Ave., New York NY 10022-4195. (212)826-1480. Fax: (212)826-8979. E-mail: cnewa@cnewa.org. Website: www.cnewa.org. **50% freelance written.** Bimonthly magazine for a Catholic audience with interest in the Near East, particularly its current religious, cultural and political aspects. Estab. 1974. Circ. 100,000. Pays on publication. Publishes ms an average of 6 months after acceptance. Byline given. Buys all rights. Accepts queries by mail, fax. Responds in 2 months to queries. Sample copy and writer's guidelines for 7½×10½ SAE with 2 first-class stamps.

Nonfiction ''Cultural, devotional, political, historical material on the Near East, with an emphasis on the Eastern Christian churches. Style should be simple, factual, concise. Articles must stem from personal acquaintance with subject matter, or thorough up-to-date research.'' Length: 1,200-1,800 words. **Pays 20¢/edited word.**

Photos ''Photographs to accompany manuscript are welcome; they should illustrate the people, places, ceremonies, etc. which are described in the article. We prefer color transparencies but occasionally use b&w.'' Pay varies depending on use—scale from $50-300.

Tips ''We are interested in current events in the Near East as they affect the cultural, political and religious lives of the people.''

$ $OUR SUNDAY VISITOR

Our Sunday Visitor, Inc., 200 Noll Plaza, Huntington IN 46750. (260)356-8400. Fax: (260)356-8472. E-mail: oursunvis@osv.com. Website: www.osv.com. **Contact:** Editor. **10% freelance written.** (Mostly assigned). Weekly tabloid covering world events and culture from a Catholic perspective. Estab. 1912. Circ. 70,000. **Pays on acceptance.** Publishes ms an average of 1 month after acceptance. Byline given. Buys first rights. Accepts queries by mail, e-mail.

Ⓝ $ $OUTREACH MAGAZINE

Outreach, Inc., 2560 Progress St., Vista CA 92081-8422. (760)940-0600. Fax: (760)597-2314. E-mail: lwarren@ou treach.com. Website: www.outreachmagazine.com. Editor: Lynne Marian. **Contact:** Lindy Warren, managing editor. **80% freelance written.** Bimonthly magazine covering outreach. ''*Outreach* is designed to inspire, challenge, and equip churches and church leaders to reach out to their communities with the love of Jesus Christ.'' Circ. 30,000, plus newsstand. Pays on publication. Publishes ms an average of 2 months after acceptance. Byline given. Offers 10% kill fee. Buys first North American serial, electronic rights. Editorial lead time 6 months. Submit seasonal material 6 months in advance. Accepts queries by mail, e-mail, fax. Accepts previously published material. Accepts simultaneous submissions. Responds in 2 months to queries; 8 months to mss. Sample copy and writer's guidelines free.

Nonfiction Book excerpts, how-to, humor, inspirational, interview/profile, personal experience, photo feature, religious. Special issues: Vacation Bible School (January); America's Fastest-Growing Churches (July/August). Does not want fiction, poetry, non-outreach-related articles. **Buys 30 mss/year.** Query with published clips. Length: 1,200-2,000 words. **Pays $375-600 for assigned articles; $375-500 for unsolicited articles.** Sometimes pays expenses of writers on assignment.

Photos Christi Osselaer, lead designer. Send photos with submission. Reviews GIF/JPEG files. Buys all rights. Negotiates payment individually. Identification of subjects required.

Columns/Departments Outreach Pulse (short stories about outreach-oriented churches and ministries), 75-250 words; Questions & Perspectives (a first-person expert perspective on a question related to outreach), 300-400 words; Soulfires (an as-told-to interview with a person about the stories and people that have fueled their passion for outreach), 900 words; From the Front Line (a profile of a church that is using a transferable idea or concept for outreach), 800 words, plus sidebar; Soujourners (short interviews with everyday people about the stories and people that have informed their worldview and faith perspective), 800 words. **Buys 6 mss/year.** Query with published clips. **Pays $100-375.**

Fillers Facts, gags to be illustrated by cartoonist. **Buys 6/year.** Length: 25-100 words. **Pays negotiable fee.**

Tips "Study our writer's guidelines. Send published clips that showcase tight, bright writing as well as your ability to interview, research, and organize numerous sources into an article, and your ability to write a 100-word piece as well as a 1,600-word piece."

$ $⊘ THE PLAIN TRUTH

Christianity Without the Religion, Plain Truth Ministries, 300 W. Green St., Pasadena CA 91129. Fax: (626)304-8172. E-mail: managing.editor@ptm.org. Website: www.ptm.org. **90% freelance written.** Bimonthly magazine. "We seek to reignite the flame of shattered lives by illustrating the joy of a new life in Christ." Estab. 1935. Circ. 70,000. Pays on publication. Publishes ms an average of 8 months after acceptance. Byline given. Offers $50 kill fee. Buys all-language rights for *The Plain Truth* and its affiliated publications. Editorial lead time 6 months. Submit seasonal material 6 months in advance. Accepts queries by mail, e-mail. Accepts simultaneous submissions. Sample copy for 9 × 12 SAE and 5 first-class stamps. Writer's guidelines online.

Nonfiction Inspirational, interview/profile, personal experience, religious. **Buys 48-50 mss/year.** Query with published clips and SASE. *No unsolicited mss.* Length: 750-2,500 words. **Pays 25¢/word.**

Reprints Send tearsheet or photocopy of article or typed ms with rights for sale noted and information about when and where the article previously appeared with SASE for response. Pays 15¢/word.

Photos State availability with submission. Reviews transparencies, prints. Buys one-time rights. Negotiates payment individually. Captions required.

Tips "Material should offer Biblical solutions to real-life problems. Both first-person and third-person illustrations are encouraged. Articles should take a unique twist on a subject. Material must be insightful and practical for the Christain reader. All articles must be well researched and Biblically accurate without becoming overly scholastic. Use convincing arguments to support your Christian platform. Use vivid word pictures, simple and compelling language, and avoid stuffy academic jargon. Captivating anecdotes are vital."

$⊡ PRAIRIE MESSENGER

Catholic Journal, Benedictine Monks of St. Peter's Abbey, P.O. Box 190, Muenster SK S0K 2Y0 Canada. (306)682-1772. Fax: (306)682-5285. E-mail: pm.canadian@stpeters.sk.ca. Website: www.stpeters.sk.ca/prairie_messenger. Managing Editor: Peter Novecosky, OSB. **Contact:** Maureen Weber, associate editor. **10% freelance written.** Weekly Catholic journal with strong emphasis on social justice, Third World, and ecumenism. Estab. 1904. Circ. 7,300. Pays on publication. Publishes ms an average of 4 months after acceptance. Byline given. Not copyrighted. Buys first North American serial, first, one-time, second serial (reprint), simultaneous rights. Submit seasonal material 3 months in advance. Accepts queries by mail, e-mail, fax, phone. Responds in 2 months to queries. Sample copy for 9 × 12 SAE with $1 Canadian postage or IRCs. Writer's guidelines online.

Nonfiction Interview/profile, opinion, religious. "No articles on abortion." **Buys 15 mss/year.** Send complete ms. Length: 250-600 words. **Pays $40-60.** Sometimes pays expenses of writers on assignment.

Photos Send photos with submission. Reviews 3 × 5 prints. Buys all rights. Offers $20/photo. Captions required.

$⊡ PRESBYTERIAN RECORD

50 Wynford Dr., Toronto ON M3C 1J7 Canada. (416)444-1111. Fax: (416)441-2825. E-mail: dharris@presbyterian.ca. Website: www.presbyterian.ca/record. **Contact:** David Harris, editor. **5% freelance written.** Monthly magazine for a church-oriented, family audience. Circ. 41,000. Pays on publication. Publishes ms an average of 4 months after acceptance. Buys first North American serial, one-time, simultaneous rights. Submit seasonal material 3 months in advance. Accepts queries by e-mail. Responds in 2 months on accepted ms. Sample copy for 9 × 12 SAE with $1 Canadian postage or IRCs.

Nonfiction Check a copy of the magazine for style. Inspirational, interview/profile, personal experience, religious. Special issues: Evangelism; Spirituality; Education. No material solely or mainly US in context. No sermons, accounts of ordinations, inductions, baptisms, receptions, church anniversaries, or term papers. **Buys 5-10 unsolicited mss/year.** Query. Length: 700-1,500 words. **Pays $75-150 (Canadian).** Sometimes pays expenses of writers on assignment.

Reprints Send tearsheet, photocopy or typed ms with rights for sale noted and information about when and where the material previously appeared.

Photos When possible, photos should accompany ms; i.e., current events, historical events, and biographies. Pays $50 (Canadian) for glossy photos.

Columns/Departments Items of contemporary and often controversial nature, 700 words; Mission Knocks (new ideas for congregational mission and service), 700 words.

Tips "There is a trend away from maudlin, first-person pieces redolent with tragedy and dripping with simplistic, pietistic conclusions. Writers often leave out those parts which would likely attract readers, such as anecdotes and direct quotes. Using active rather than passive verbs also helps most manuscripts."

$ $PRESBYTERIANS TODAY

Presbyterian Church (U.S.A.), 100 Witherspoon St., Louisville KY 40202-1396. (502)569-5637. Fax: (502)569-8632. E-mail: today@pcusa.org. Website: www.pcusa.org/today. **Contact:** Eva Stimson, editor. **25% freelance written.** Prefers to work with published/established writers. Denominational magazine published 10 times/year covering religion, denominational activities, and public issues for members of the Presbyterian Church (U.S.A.). "The magazine's purpose is to increase understanding and appreciation of what the church and its members are doing to live out their Christian faith." Estab. 1867. Circ. 58,000. **Pays on acceptance.** Publishes ms an average of 6 months after acceptance. Byline given. Offers 50% kill fee. Buys first North American serial rights. Editorial lead time 3 months. Submit seasonal material 3 months in advance. Accepts queries by mail, e-mail, fax, phone. Responds in 2 weeks to queries; 1 month to mss. Sample copy free. Writer's guidelines online.

O⌐ Break in with a "short feature for our Spotlight department (300 words)."

Nonfiction "Most articles have some direct relevance to a Presbyterian audience; however, *Presbyterians Today* also seeks well-informed articles written for a general audience that help readers deal with the stresses of daily living from a Christian perspective." How-to (everyday Christian living), inspirational, Presbyterian programs, issues, people. **Buys 20 mss/year.** Send complete ms. Length: 1,000-1,800 words. **Pays $300 maximum for assigned articles; $75-300 for unsolicited articles.**

Photos State availability with submission. Reviews contact sheets, transparencies, color prints, digital images. Buys one-time rights. Negotiates payment individually. Identification of subjects required.

$ $PRISM MAGAZINE

America's Alternative Evangelical Voice, Evangelicals for Social Action, 10 E. Lancaster Ave., Wynnewood PA 19096. (610)645-9391. Fax: (610)649-8090. E-mail: kristyn@esa-online.org. Website: www.esa-online.org. **Contact:** Kristyn Komarnicki, editor. **50% freelance written.** Bimonthly magazine covering Christianity and social justice. For holistic, Biblical, socially-concerned, progressive Christians. Estab. 1993. Circ. 5,000. Pays on publication. Publishes ms an average of 4-6 months after acceptance. Byline given. Buys first North American serial rights. Editorial lead time 4 months. Submit seasonal material 4 months in advance. Accepts queries by mail, e-mail. Responds in 1 month to queries; 3 months to mss. Sample copy for $3. Writer's guidelines free.

• "We're a nonprofit, some writers are pro bono." Occasionally accepts previously published material.

Nonfiction Book excerpts (to coincide with book release date), essays, interview/profile (ministry). **Buys 10-12 mss/year.** Send complete ms. Length: 500-3,000 words. **Pays $75-300 for assigned articles; $25-200 for unsolicited articles.**

Photos Send photos with submission. Reviews prints, JPEG files. Buys one-time rights. Pays $25/photo published; $150 if photo used on cover.

Tips "We look closely at stories of holistic ministry. It's best to request a sample copy to get to know *Prism*'s focus/style before submitting—we receive so many submissions that are not appropriate."

$PURPOSE

616 Walnut Ave., Scottdale PA 15683-1999. (724)887-8500. Fax: (724)887-3111. E-mail: horsch@mph.org. Website: www.mph.org. **Contact:** James E. Horsch, editor. **95% freelance written.** Weekly magazine "for adults, young and old, general audience with varied interests. My readership is interested in seeing how Christianity works in difficult situations. Magazine focuses on Christian discipleship—how to be a faithful Christian in the midst of everday life situations. Uses personal story form to present models and examples to encourage Christians in living a life of faithful discipleship." Estab. 1968. Circ. 9,000. **Pays on acceptance.** Publishes ms an average of 10 months after acceptance. Buys one-time rights. Submit seasonal material 6 months in advance. Accepts queries by e-mail. Accepts previously published material. Accepts simultaneous submissions. Responds in 3 months to queries. Sample copy and writer's guidelines for 6×9 SAE and $2.

Nonfiction Inspirational stories from a Christian perspective. "I want upbeat stories that deal with issues faced by believers in family, business, politics, religion, gender, and any other areas—and show how the Christian faith resolves them. *Purpose* conveys truth through quality fiction or true life stories. Our magazine accents Christian discipleship. Christianity affects all of life, and we expect our material to demonstrate this. I would like story-type articles about individuals, groups, and organizations who are intelligently and effectively working at such problems as hunger, poverty, international understanding, peace, justice, etc., because of their faith. Essays, fiction, and how-to-do-it pieces must include a lot of anecdotal, life exposure examples." **Buys 130 mss/year.**

Reprints Send tearsheet, photocopy or typed ms with rights for sale noted and information about when and where the material previously appeared.

Photos Photos purchased with ms must be sharp enough for reproduction; requires prints in all cases. Captions required.

Fiction "Produce the story with specificity so that it appears to take place somewhere and with real people."

Historical, humorous, religious. No militaristic/narrow patriotism or racism. Send complete ms. Length: 700 words. **Pays up to 6¢ and 2 contributor's copies.**

Poetry Free verse, light verse, traditional, blank verse. **Buys 130 poems/year.** Length: 12 lines. **Pays $7.50-20/poem depending on length and quality.**

Fillers Anecdotal items up to 400 words. **Pays 5¢/word maximum.**

$ QUEEN OF ALL HEARTS

Montfort Missionaries, 26 S. Saxon Ave., Bay Shore NY 11706-8993. (631)665-0726. Fax: (631)665-4349. E-mail: montfort@optonline.net. Website: www.montfortmissionaries.com. **Contact:** Roger Charest, S.M.M., managing editor. **50% freelance written.** Bimonthly magazine covering "Mary, Mother of Jesus, as seen in the sacred scriptures, tradition, history of the church, the early Christian writers, lives of the saints, poetry, art, music, spiritual writers, apparitions, shrines, ecumenism, etc." Magazine of "stories, articles and features on the Mother of God by explaining the Scriptural basis and traditional teaching of the Catholic Church concerning the Mother of Jesus, her influence in fields of history, literature, art, music, poetry, etc." Estab. 1950. Circ. 2,000. **Pays on acceptance.** Publishes ms an average of 6-12 months after acceptance. Byline given. Not copyrighted. Submit seasonal material 6 months in advance. Accepts queries by mail, e-mail, fax, phone. Responds in 2 months to queries. Sample copy for $2.50 with 9×12 SAE.

Nonfiction Essays, inspirational, interview/profile, personal experience, religious (Marialogical and devotional). **Buys 25 mss/year.** Send complete ms. Length: 750-2,500 words. **Pays $40-60.**

Photos Send photos with submission. Reviews transparencies. Buys one-time rights. Pay varies.

Fiction Roger M. Charest, S.M.M., managing editor. Religious. "No mss not about Our Lady, the Mother of God, the Mother of Jesus." **Buys 6 mss/year.** Send complete ms. Length: 1,500-2,500 words. **Pays $40-60.**

Poetry Joseph Tusiani, poetry editor. Free verse. **Buys approximately 10 poems/year.** Submit maximum 2 poems. **Pays in contributor copies.**

$ $ REFORM JUDAISM

Union for Reform Judaism, 633 Third Ave. 7th Floor, New York NY 10017-6778. (212)650-4240. Fax: (212)650-4249. E-mail: rjmagazine@urj.org. Website: www.urj.org/rjmag/. **Contact:** Joy Weinberg, managing editor. **30% freelance written.** Quarterly magazine of Reform Jewish issues. "*Reform Judaism* is the official voice of the Union for Reform Judaism, linking the institutions and affiliates of Reform Judaism with every Reform Jew. *RJ* covers developments within the movement while interpreting events and Jewish tradition from a reform perspective." Estab. 1972. Circ. 310,000. Pays on publication. Publishes ms an average of 3 months after acceptance. Byline given. Offers kill fee for commissioned articles. Buys first North American serial rights. Submit seasonal material 6 months in advance. Accepts previously published material. Accepts simultaneous submissions. Responds in 2 months. Sample copy for $3.50. Writer's guidelines online.

Nonfiction Book excerpts, exposé, general interest, historical/nostalgic, inspirational, interview/profile, opinion, personal experience, photo feature, travel. **Buys 30 mss/year.** Submit complete ms with SASE. Length: Cover stories: 2,500-3,500 words; major feature: 1,800-2,500 words; secondary feature: 1,200-1,500 words; department (i.e., Travel): 1,200 words; letters: 200 words maximum; opinion: 525 words maximum. **Pays 30¢/word.** Sometimes pays expenses of writers on assignment.

Reprints Send tearsheet, photocopy or typed ms with rights for sale noted and information about when and where the material previously appeared. Usually does not publish reprints.

Photos Send photos with submission. Reviews 8×10 color slides and b&w prints. Buys one-time rights. Pays $25-75. Identification of subjects required.

Fiction Humorous, religious, sophisticated, cutting-edge, superb writing. **Buys 4 mss/year.** Send complete ms. Length: 600-2,500 words. **Pays 30¢/word.**

The online magazine carries original content not found in the print edition and includes writer's guidelines.

Tips "We prefer a stamped postcard including the following information/checklist: __Yes, we are interested in publishing; __No, unfortunately the submission doesn't meet our needs; __Maybe, we'd like to hold on to the article for now. Submissions sent this way will receive a faster response."

$ $ THE REPORTER

Women's American ORT, Inc., 250 Park Ave. S., Suite 600, New York NY 10003. (212)505-7700. Fax: (212)674-3057. E-mail: dasher@waort.org. Website: www.waort.org. **Contact:** Dana Asher, editor. **85% freelance written.** Semiannual nonprofit journal published by Jewish women's organization covering Jewish women celebrities, issues of contemporary Jewish culture, Israel, anti-Semitism, women's rights, Jewish travel, and the international Jewish community. Estab. 1966. Circ. 50,000. **Pays on acceptance.** Publishes ms an average of 1 year after acceptance. Byline given. Buys first North American serial rights. Submit seasonal material 6 months in advance. Accepts queries by mail, e-mail. Responds in 3 months to queries. Sample copy for 9 × 12 SAE and 3 first-class stamps. Writer's guidelines for #10 SASE.

O→ Break in with "a different look at a familiar topic, i.e., 'Jews without God' (Winter 2000). Won't consider handwritten or badly-typed queries. Unpublished writers are welcome. Others, include credits."

Nonfiction Cover feature profiles a dynamic Jewish woman making a difference in Judaism, women's issues, education, entertainment, profiles, business, journalism, arts. Essays, exposé, humor, inspirational, opinion, personal experience, photo feature, religious, travel. Query. Length: 1,800 words maximum. **Pays $200 and up.**

Photos Send photos with submission. Identification of subjects required.

Columns/Departments Education Horizon; Destination (Jewish sites/travel); Inside Out (Advocacy); Women's Business; Art Scene (interviews, books, films); Lasting Impression (uplifting/inspirational).

Fiction Publishes novel excerpts and short stories as part of Lasting Impressions column. Length: 800 words. **Pays $150-300.**

Tips "Send query only by e-mail or postal mail. Show us a fresh look, not a rehash. Particularly interested in stories of interest to younger readers."

$ REVIEW FOR RELIGIOUS

3601 Lindell Blvd., Room 428, St. Louis MO 63108-3393. (314)977-7363. Fax: (314)977-7362. E-mail: review@sl u.edu. Website: www.reviewforreligious.org. **Contact:** David L. Fleming, S.J., editor. **100% freelance written.** Quarterly magazine for Roman Catholic priests, brothers, and sisters. Estab. 1942. Pays on publication. Publishes ms an average of 9 months after acceptance. Byline given. Buys first North American serial rights. Rarely buys second serial (reprint) rights. Accepts queries by mail, fax. Responds in 2 months to queries. Writer's guidelines online.

Nonfiction Spiritual, liturgical, canonical matters only. Not for general audience. Length: 1,500-5,000 words. **Pays $6/page.**

Tips "The writer must know about religious life in the Catholic Church and be familiar with prayer, vows, community life, and ministry."

$ $ ST. ANTHONY MESSENGER

28 W. Liberty St., Cincinnati OH 45202-6498. (513)241-5615. Fax: (513)241-0399. E-mail: stanthony@americanc atholic.org. Website: www.americancatholic.org. **Contact:** Father Pat McCloskey, O.F.M., editor. **55% freelance written.** Monthly general interest magazine for a national readership of Catholic families, most of which have children or grandchildren in grade school, high school, or college. "*St. Anthony Messenger* is a Catholic family magazine which aims to help its readers lead more fully human and Christian lives. We publish articles which report on a changing church and world, opinion pieces written from the perspective of Christian faith and values, personality profiles, and fiction which entertains and informs." Estab. 1893. Circ. 324,000. **Pays on acceptance.** Publishes ms an average of 1 year after acceptance. Byline given. Buys first North American serial, electronic rights. first worldwide serial rights. Submit seasonal material 6 months in advance. Accepts queries by mail, e-mail, fax. Responds in 3 weeks to queries; 2 months to mss. Sample copy for 9 × 12 SAE with 4 first-class stamps. Writer's guidelines online.

Nonfiction How-to (on psychological and spiritual growth, problems of parenting/better parenting, marriage problems/marriage enrichment), humor, inspirational, interview/profile, opinion (limited use; writer must have special qualifications for topic), personal experience (if pertinent to our purpose), photo feature, informational, social issues. **Buys 35-50 mss/year.** Query with published clips. Length: 1,500-2,500 words. **Pays 16¢/word.** Sometimes pays expenses of writers on assignment.

Fiction Mainstream, religious, senior citizen/retirement. "We do not want mawkishly sentimental or preachy fiction. Stories are most often rejected for poor plotting and characterization; bad dialogue—listen to how people talk; inadequate motivation. Many stories say nothing, are 'happenings' rather than stories." No fetal journals, no rewritten Bible stories. **Buys 12 mss/year.** Send complete ms. Length: 2,000-3,000 words. **Pays 16¢/word maximum and 2 contributor's copies; $1 charge for extras.**

Poetry "Our poetry needs are very limited." Submit maximum 4-5 poems. Length: up to 20-25 lines; the shorter, the better. **Pays $2/line; $20 minimum.**

Tips "The freelancer should consider why his or her proposed article would be appropriate for us, rather than for *Redbook* or *Saturday Review*. We treat human problems of all kinds, but from a religious perspective. Articles should reflect Catholic theology, spirituality, and employ a Catholic terminology and vocabulary. We need more articles on prayer, scripture, Catholic worship. Get authoritative information (not merely library research); we want interviews with experts. Write in popular style; use lots of examples, stories, and personal quotes. Word length is an important consideration."

ℕ $ $ $ SCIENCE & SPIRIT

Heldref Publications, 162 Old Colony Ave., 3rd Floor, Quincy MA 02170. Fax: (617)847-5924. E-mail: freelance@science-spirit.org. Website: www.science-spirit.org. Editor: Marc Kaufman. **Contact:** Ami Albernaz, books editor. **75% freelance written.** Bimonthly magazine covering science and religion. *"Science & Spirit* examines the implications of scientific issues for the human condition. We take both science and religion very seriously and look for connections where they enrich each other. We look for solidly reported pieces relayed in a narrative voice." Circ. 7,500. **Pays on acceptance.** Publishes ms an average of 4 months after acceptance. Byline given. Makes work-for-hire assignments. Editorial lead time 4-6 months. Submit seasonal material 6 months in advance. Accepts queries by e-mail. Responds in 1 month to queries. Sample copy online. Writer's guidelines by e-mail.

Nonfiction Essays, interview/profile, religious, science, reported pieces. "No New Age pieces. In general, we look for solidly reported articles." **Buys 40 mss/year.** Query with published clips. Length: 1,200-2,500 words. **Pays 20-75¢/word for assigned articles; 20-50¢/word for unsolicited articles.** Sometimes pays expenses of writers on assignment.

Columns/Departments Interlude, 1,200-1,600 words. "We accept essays on a range of topics for this section. Please refer to the magazine or website for examples." **Buys 6 mss/year.** Query with published clips. **Pays 20-35¢/word.**

Tips "The best way to improve odds of publication is to really familiarize yourself with the magazine. Unless you are a well-established writer, it is probably best to begin with us by writing reported pieces."

$ THE SECRET PLACE

National Ministries, ABC/USA, P.O. Box 851, Valley Forge PA 19482-0851. (610)768-2240. E-mail: thesecretplace@abc-usa.org. **Contact:** Kathleen Hayes, senior editor. **100% freelance written.** Quarterly devotional covering Christian daily devotions. Estab. 1938. Circ. 150,000. **Pays on acceptance.** Byline given. Buys first rights. Editorial lead time 1 year. Submit seasonal material 9 months in advance. For free sample and guidelines, send 6×9 SASE.

Nonfiction Inspirational. **Buys about 400 mss/year.** Send complete ms. Length: 100-200 words. **Pays $15.**

Poetry Avant-garde, free verse, light verse, traditional. **Buys 12-15/year poems/year.** Submit maximum 6 poems. Length: 4-30 lines. **Pays $15.**

Tips Accepts submissions via e-mail.

$ $ SHARING THE VICTORY

Fellowship of Christian Athletes, 8701 Leeds Rd., Kansas City MO 64129. (816)921-0909. Fax: (816)921-8755. E-mail: stv@fca.org. Website: www.fca.org. Editor: Jill Ewert. **50% freelance written.** Prefers to work with published/established writers, but works with a growing number of new/unpublished writers each year. Published 9 times/year. "We seek to serve as a ministry tool of the Fellowship of Christian Athletes by informing, inspiring and involving coaches, athletes and all whom they influence, that they may make an impact for Jesus Christ." Estab. 1959. Circ. 80,000. Pays on publication. Publishes ms an average of 4 months after acceptance. Byline given. Buys first rights. Submit seasonal material 6 months in advance. Responds in 3 months. Sample copy for $1 and 9×12 SAE with 3 first-class stamps. Writer's guidelines online.

Nonfiction Inspirational, interview/profile (with name athletes and coaches solid in their faith), personal experience, photo feature. **Buys 5-20 mss/year.** Query. Length: 500-1,000 words.

Photos State availability with submission. Reviews contact sheets. Buys one-time rights. Pay based on size of photo.

Tips "Profiles and interviews of particular interest to coed athlete, primarily high school and college age. Our graphics and editorial content appeal to youth. The area most open to freelancers is profiles on or interviews with well-known athletes or coaches (male, female, minorities) who have been or are involved in some capacity with FCA."

$ $ SIGNS OF THE TIMES

Pacific Press Publishing Association, P.O. Box 5353, Nampa ID 83653-5353. (208)465-2579. Fax: (208)465-2531. E-mail: mmoore@pacificpress.com. **Contact:** Marvin Moore, editor. **40% freelance written.** Works with a small number of new/unpublished writers each year. Monthly magazine. "We are a monthly Seventh-day Adventist magazine encouraging the general public to practice the principles of the Bible." Estab. 1874. Circ. 170,000. **Pays on acceptance.** Publishes ms an average of 6-18 months after acceptance. Byline given. Offers kill fee. Buys first North American serial, one-time, second serial (reprint) rights. Editorial lead time 1 year. Submit seasonal material 1 year in advance. Responds in 1 month to queries; 2-3 months to mss. Sample copy and writer's guidelines for 9×12 SAE with 3 first-class stamps. Writer's guidelines online.

Nonfiction "We want writers with a desire to share the good news of reconciliation with God. Articles should be people-oriented, well-researched, and should have a sharp focus. Gospel articles deal with salvation and how to experience it. While most of our gospel articles are assigned or picked up from reprints, we do occasionally accept unsolicited manuscripts in this area. Gospel articles should be 1,250 words. Christian lifestyle articles deal with the practical problems of everyday life from a Biblical and Christian perspective. These are typically 1,000-1,200 words. We request that authors include sidebars that give additional information on the topic whenever possible. First-person stories must illuminate a spiritual or moral truth that the individual in the story learned. We especially like stories that hold the reader in suspense or that have an unusual twist at the end. First-person stories are typically 1,000 words long.'' General interest, how-to, humor, inspirational, interview/profile, personal experience, religious. **Buys 75 mss/year.** Query by mail only with or without published clips or send complete ms. Length: 500-1,500 words. **Pays 10-20¢/word.**

Reprints Send tearsheet, photocopy or typed ms with rights for sale noted and information about when and where the material previously appeared. Pays 50% of amount paid for an original article.

Photos Reviews b&w contact sheets, 35mm color transparencies, 5×7 or 8×10 b&w prints. Buys one-time rights. Pays $35-300 for transparencies; $20-50 for prints. Captions, identification of subjects, model releases required.

Fillers ''Short fillers can be inspirational/devotional, Christian lifestyle, stories, comments that illuminate a Biblical text—in short, anything that might fit in a general Christian magazine.'' Length: 500-600 words.

Tips ''The audience for *Signs of the Times* includes both Christians and non-Christians of all ages. However, we recommend that our authors write with the non-Christian in mind, since most Christians can easily relate to articles that are written from a non-Christian perspective, whereas many non-Christians will have no interest in an article that is written from a Christian perspective. While *Signs* is published by Seventh-day Adventists, we mention even our own denominational name in the magazine rather infrequently. The purpose is not to hide who we are but to make the magazine as attractive to non-Christian readers as possible. We are especially interested in articles that respond to the questions of everyday life that people are asking and the problems they are facing. Since these questions and problems nearly always have a spiritual component, articles that provide a Biblical and spiritual response are especially welcome. Any time you can provide us with 1 or more sidebars that add information to the topic of your article, you enhance your chance of getting our attention. Two kinds of sidebars seem to be especially popular with readers: those that give information in lists, with each item in the list consisting of only a few words or at the most a sentence, or those that give technical information or long explanations that in the main article might get the reader too bogged down in detail. Whatever their length, sidebars need to be part of the total word count of the article. We like the articles in *Signs of the Times* to have interest-grabbing introductions. One of the best ways to do this is with anecdotes, particularly those that have a bit of suspense or conflict.''

$SOCIAL JUSTICE REVIEW

3835 Westminster Place, St. Louis MO 63108-3472. (314)371-1653. Fax: (314)371-0889. E-mail: centbur@juno.com. Website: www.socialjusticereview.org. **Contact:** The Rev. John H. Miller, C.S.C., editor. **25% freelance written.** Works with a small number of new/unpublished writers each year. Bimonthly magazine. Estab. 1908. Publishes ms an average of 1 year after acceptance. Not copyrighted, however special articles within the magazine may be copyrighted, or an occasional special issue has been copyrighted due to author's request. Buys first North American serial rights. Accepts queries by mail. Sample copy for 9×12 SAE and 3 first-class stamps.

Nonfiction Scholarly articles on society's economic, religious, social, intellectual, and political problems with the aim of bringing Catholic social thinking to bear upon these problems. Query by mail only with SASE. Length: 2,500-3,000 words. **Pays about 2¢/word.**

Reprints Send ms with rights for sale noted and information about when and where the material previously appeared. Pays about 2¢/word.

Tips ''Write moderate essays completely compatible with papal teaching and readable to the average person.''

Ⓝ $SPIRITUAL LIFE

2131 Lincoln Rd. NE, Washington DC 20002-1199. (202)832-5505. Fax: (202)832-8967. E-mail: edodonnell@aol.com. Website: www.spiritual-life.org. **Contact:** Br. Edward O'Donnell, O.C.D., editor. **80% freelance written.** Prefers to work with published/established writers. Quarterly magazine for ''largely Christian, well-educated, serious readers.'' Circ. 12,000. **Pays on acceptance.** Publishes ms an average of 1 year after acceptance. Buys first North American serial rights. Responds in 2 months to queries. Sample copy and writer's guidelines for 7x10 or larger SAE with 5 first-class stamps.

Nonfiction Serious articles of contemporary spirituality and its pastoral application to everday life. High quality articles about our encounter with God in the present day world. Language of articles should be college level. Technical terminology, if used, should be clearly explained. Material should be presented in a postive manner. Buys inspirational and think pieces. ''Brief autobiographical information (present occupation, past occupations, books and articles published, etc.) should accompany article.'' Sentimental articles or those dealing with specific devotional practices not accepted. No fiction or poetry. **Buys 20 mss/year.** Length: 3,000-5,000 words. **Pays $50 minimum, and 2 contributor's copies.**

$STANDARD

Nazarene International Headquarters, 6401 The Paseo, Kansas City MO 64131. (816)333-7000. Fax: (816)333-4439. E-mail: cyourdon@nazarene.org; evlead@nazarene.org. Website: www.nazarene.org. **Contact:** Dr. Everett Leadingham, editor or Charlie L. Yourdon, managing editor. **100% freelance written.** Works with a small number of new/unpublished writers each year. Weekly inspirational paper with Christian reading for adults. "In *Standard* we want to show Christianity in action, and we prefer to do that through stories that hold the reader's attention." Estab. 1936. Circ. 130,000. **Pays on acceptance.** Publishes ms an average of 14-18 months after acceptance. Byline given. Buys first or reprint rights. Submit seasonal material 6 months in advance. Accepts simultaneous submissions. Writer's guidelines and sample copy for SAE with 2 first-class stamps or by e-mail.
  • Accepts submissions by mail, e-mail. No queries needed.
Fiction Prefers fiction-type stories showing Christianity in action. Send complete ms. Length: 600-1,800 words. **Pays 3½¢/word for first rights; 2¢/word for reprint rights, and contributor's copies.**
Poetry Free verse, haiku, light verse, traditional. **Buys 25 poems/year.** Submit maximum 5 poems. Length: 30 lines. **Pays 25¢/line.**
Tips "Stories should express Christian principles without being preachy. Setting, plot, and characterization must be realistic."

N $THESE DAYS

Presbyterian Publishing Corp., 100 Witherspoon St., Louisville KY 40202-1396. (502)569-5102. Fax: (502)569-5113. E-mail: vpatton@presbypub.com. **Contact:** Vince Patton, editor. **95% freelance written.** Quarterly magazine covering religious devotionals. "*These Days* is published especially for the Cumberland Presbyterian Church, The Presbyterian Church in Canada, The Presbyterian Church (U.S.A.), The United Churches of Canada, and The United Church of Christ as a personal, family, and group devotional guide." Estab. 1970. Circ. 200,000. **Pays on acceptance.** Publishes ms an average of 8 months after acceptance. Byline given. Buys all rights, makes work-for-hire assignments. Editorial lead time 8 months. Submit seasonal material 1 year in advance. Accepts queries by mail, e-mail. Responds in 6 months to queries; 10 months to mss. Sample copy for 6×9 SAE and 3 first-class stamps. Writer's guidelines for #10 SASE.
Nonfiction "Use freelance in all issues. Only devotional material will be accepted. Send for application form and guidelines. Enclose #10 SASE." Publishes very few unsolicited devotionals. **Buys 365 mss/year.** Query with or without published clips. Length: Devotionals, 200 words; These Moments, 475 words; These Times, 750 words. **Pays $14.25 for devotions; $30 for These Moments; $45 for These Times.**
Poetry Buys 2-4 poems/year. Submit maximum 5 poems. Length: 3-20 lines. **Pays $15.**
Tips "The best way to be considered is to send a 1-page query that includes your religious affiliation and your religious, writing-related experience, plus a sample devotion in our format and/or published clips of similar material. Read a current issue devotionally to get a feel for the magazine. We would also like to see more minority and Canadian writers."

$ $TODAY'S CHRISTIAN

Stories of Faith, Hope and God's Love, Christianity Today, 465 Gundersen Dr., Carol Stream IL 60188. (630)260-6200. Fax: (630)260-0114. E-mail: tceditor@todays-christian.com. Website: www.christianitytoday.com/todays christian. Managing Editor: Edward Gilbreath. **Contact:** Cynthia Thomas, editorial coordinator. **25% freelance written.** Bimonthly magazine for adult evangelical Christian audience. Estab. 1963. Circ. 125,000. Pays on acceptance; on publication for humor pieces. Byline given. Editorial lead time 5 months. Submit seasonal material 8 months in advance. Accepts queries by mail. Accepts simultaneous submissions. Responds in 1 month to queries. Sample copy for 5×8 SAE and 4 first-class stamps. Writer's guidelines online.
Nonfiction Book excerpts, general interest, historical/nostalgic, humor, inspirational, interview/profile, personal experience, photo feature, religious. **Buys 100-125 mss/year.** Query with or without published clips or send complete ms. Length: 250-1,500 words. **Pays $125-600 depending on length.** Pays expenses of writers on assignment.
Reprints Send tearsheet, photocopy or typed ms with rights for sale noted and information about when and where the material previously appeared. Pays 35-50% of amount paid for an original article.
Photos Send photos with submission. Reviews transparencies, prints. Buys one-time rights. Negotiates payment individually. Identification of subjects required.
Columns/Departments Humor Us (adult church humor, kids say and do funny things, and humorous wedding tales), 50-200 words. **Pays $35.**
Fillers Anecdotes, short fillers. **Buys 10-20/year.** Length: 100-250 words. **Pays $35.**

Tips "Most of our articles are reprints or staff written. Freelance competition is keen, so tailor submissions to meet our needs by observing the following: *Today's Christian* audience is truly a general interest one, including men and women, urban professionals and rural homemakers, adults of every age and marital status, and Christians of every church affiliation. We seek to publish a magazine that people from the variety of ethnic groups in North America will find interesting and relevant."

N $ TODAY'S PENTECOSTAL EVANGEL

The General Council of the Assemblies of God, 1445 N. Boonville, Springfield MO 65802-1894. (417)862-2781. Fax: (417)862-0416. E-mail: pe@ag.org. Website: www.pe.ag.org. Editor: Hal Donaldson. **5% freelance written.** Works with a small number of new/unpublished writers each year. Weekly magazine emphasizing news of the Assemblies of God for members of the Assemblies and other Pentecostal and charismatic Christians. Estab. 1913. Circ. 215,000. **Pays on acceptance.** Publishes ms an average of 6 months after acceptance. Byline given. Buys first North American serial, second serial (reprint), electronic rights. Submit seasonal material 6 months in advance. Accepts queries by mail, e-mail, fax, phone. Responds in 3 months to queries. Sample copy for $1 or online. Writer's guidelines online.

Nonfiction Inspirational, personal experience, informational (articles on homelife that convey Christian teaching), news, human interest, evangelical, current issues, seasonal. Send complete ms. Length: 500-1,200 words. **Pays up to $150.**

Photos Photos purchased without accompanying ms. Pays $30 for 8×10 b&w glossy prints; $50 for 35mm or larger color transparencies Total purchase price for ms includes payment for photos.

Tips "We publish first-person articles concerning spiritual experiences; that is, answers to prayer for help in a particular situation, of unusual conversions or healings through faith in Christ. All articles submitted to us should be related to religious life. We are Protestant, evangelical, Pentecostal, and any doctrines or practices portrayed should be in harmony with the official position of our denomination (Assemblies of God)."

N $ TOGETHER

Shalom Publishers, 1251 Virginia Ave., Harrisonburg VA 22802. E-mail: tgether@aol.com. Website: www.churchoutreach.com. Managing Editor: Dorothy Hartman. **Contact:** Melodie M. Davis, editor. **90% freelance written.** Quarterly tabloid covering religion and inspiration for a nonchurched audience. "*Together* is directed as an outreach publication to those who are not currently involved in a church; therefore, we need general inspirational articles that tell stories of personal change, especially around faith issues. Also, stories that will assist our readers in dealing with the many stresses and trials of everday life—family, financial, career, community. Estab. 1980. Circ. 50,000. Pays on publication. Publishes ms an average of 6-12 months after acceptance. Byline given. Buys first, electronic rights. Editorial lead time 6-9 months. Submit seasonal material 6 months in advance. Accepts queries by mail, e-mail. Accepts previously published material. Accepts simultaneous submissions. Responds in 2 months to queries; 4 months to mss. Sample copy online. Writer's guidelines free.

> O₋ "We aim for articles that are well written, understandable, challenging (not the same old thing you've read elsewhere); that stimulate readers to dig a little deeper, but not too deep with academic or technical lanugage; that are interesting and fitting for our theological perspective (Christian), but are not preachy or overly patriotic. No mentions of smoking, drinking, cursing, etc."

Nonfiction Essays, general interest, how-to, humor, inspirational, interview/profile, personal experience (testimony), religious. No pet stories. "We have limited room for stories about illness, dying, or grief, but we do use them occasionally. We publish in March, June, September, and December, so holidays that occur in other months are not usually the subject of articles." **Buys 16 mss/year.** Query with or without published clips or send complete ms. Length: 500-1,200 words. **Pays $35-60.**

Photos Dorothy Hartman. State availability with submission. Reviews 4×6 prints, GIF/JPEG files. Buys one-time rights. Offers $15-25/photo. Captions, identification of subjects, model releases required.

Tips "We prefer 'good news' stories that are uplifting and noncontroversial in nature. We can use stories of change and growth in religious journey from a Christian slant, including 'salvation' stories. We generally want articles that tell stories of people solving problems and dealing with personal issues rather than essays or 'preaching.' If you submit electronically, it is very helpful if you put the specific title of the submission in the subject line and include your e-mail address in the body of the e-mail or on your manuscript. Also, always include your address and phone number."

TRICYCLE

The Buddhist Review, The Buddhist Ray, Inc, 92 Vandam St., New York NY 10013. (212)645-1143. Fax: (212)645-1493. E-mail: editorial@tricycle.com. Website: www.tricycle.com. Editor-in-Chief: James Shaheen. **Contact:** Alexandra Kaloyanid, associate editor. **80% freelance written.** Quarterly magazine covering the impact of Buddhism on Western culture. "*Tricycle* readers tend to be well educated and open minded." Estab. 1991. Circ. 60,000. Pays on publication. Byline given. Offers 25% kill fee. Buys one-time rights. Editorial lead time 3 months. Accepts queries by mail, e-mail, fax. Accepts simultaneous submissions. Responds in 3 months. Sample copy for $7.50 or online. Writer's guidelines online.

Nonfiction Book excerpts, essays, general interest, historical/nostalgic, humor, inspirational, interview/profile, personal experience, photo feature, religious, travel. **Buys 4-6 mss/year.** Length: 1,000-5,000 words.

Photos State availability with submission. Reviews contact sheets. Buys one-time rights. Negotiates payment individually. Captions, identification of subjects required.

Columns/Departments Buys 6-8 mss/year. Query.

Poetry *Tricycle* reports that they publish "very little poetry" and do not encourage unsolicited submissions.

Tips "*Tricycle* is a Buddhist magazine, and we can only consider Buddhist-related submissions."

$ $U.S. CATHOLIC

Claretian Publications, 205 W. Monroe St., Chicago IL 60606. (312)236-7782. Fax: (312)236-8207. E-mail: editors @uscatholic.org. Website: www.uscatholic.org. Editor: Fr. John Molyneux, CMF. Managing Editor: Heidi Schlumpf. Executive Editor: Meinrad Scherer-Emunds. **Contact:** Fran Hurst, editorial assistant. **100% freelance written.** Monthly magazine covering Roman Catholic spirituality. "*U.S. Catholic* is dedicated to the belief that it makes a difference whether you're Catholic. We invite and help our readers explore the wisdom of their faith tradition and apply their faith to the challenges of the 21st century." Estab. 1935. Circ. 40,000. **Pays on acceptance.** Publishes ms an average of 2-3 months after acceptance. Byline given. Buys all rights. Editorial lead time 8 months. Submit seasonal material 6 months in advance. Accepts queries by mail, e-mail, fax, phone. Responds in 1 month to queries; 2 months to mss. Sample copy for large SASE. Guidelines by e-mail or on website.

• Please include SASE with written ms.

Nonfiction Essays, inspirational, opinion, personal experience, religious. **Buys 100 mss/year.** Send complete ms. Length: 2,500-3,500 words. **Pays $250-600.** Sometimes pays expenses of writers on assignment.

Photos State availability with submission.

Columns/Departments Pays $250-600.

Fiction Maureen Abood, literary editor. Ethnic, mainstream, religious, slice-of-life vignettes. **Buys 4-6 mss/year.** Send complete ms. Length: 2,500-3,000 words. **Pays $300.**

Poetry Maureen Abood, literary editor. Free verse. "No light verse." **Buys 12 poems/year.** Submit maximum 5 poems. Length: 50 lines. **Pays $75.**

◫ THE UNITED CHURCH OBSERVER

478 Huron St., Toronto ON M5R 2R3 Canada. (416)960-8500. Fax: (416)960-8477. E-mail: mduncan@ucobserve r.org. Website: www.ucobserver.org. **Contact:** Muriel Duncan, editor. **20% freelance written.** Prefers to work with published/established writers. Monthly newsmagazine for people associated with The United Church of Canada. Deals primarily with events, trends, and policies having religious significance. Most coverage is Canadian, but reports on international or world concerns will be considered. Pays on publication. Publishes ms an average of 4 months after acceptance. Byline usually given. Buys first serial rights and occasionally all rights. Accepts queries by mail, e-mail, fax.

Nonfiction Occasional opinion features only. Extended coverage of major issues is usually assigned to known writers. Submissions should be written as news, no more than 1,200 words, accurate, and well-researched. No poetry. Queries preferred. **Rates depend on subject, author, and work involved.** Pays expenses of writers on assignment as negotiated.

Reprints Send tearsheet or photocopy and information about when and where the material previously appeared. Payment negotiated.

Photos Buys color photographs with mss. Send via e-mail. Payment varies.

Tips "The writer has a better chance of breaking in at our publication with short articles; this also allows us to try more freelancers. Include samples of previous news writing with query. Indicate ability and willingness to do research, and to evaluate that research. The most frequent mistakes made by writers in completing an article for us are organizational problems, lack of polished style, short on research, and a lack of inclusive language."

$THE UPPER ROOM

Daily Devotional Guide, P.O. Box 340004, Nashville TN 37203-0004. (615)340-7252. Fax: (615)340-7267. E-mail: theupperroommagazine@upperroom.org. Website: www.upperroom.org. Editor and Publisher: Stephen D. Bryant. **Contact:** Marilyn Beaty, editorial assistant. **95% freelance written.** Eager to work with new/unpublished writers. Bimonthly magazine "offering a daily inspirational message which includes a Bible reading, text, prayer, 'Thought for the Day,' and suggestion for further prayer. Each day's meditation is written by a different person and is usually a personal witness about discovering meaning and power for Christian living through scripture study which illuminates daily life." Circ. 2.2 million (US); 385,000 outside US. Pays on publication. Publishes ms an average of 1 year after acceptance. Byline given. Buys first North American serial, translation rights. Submit seasonal material 14 months in advance. Sample copy and writer's guidelines with a 4×6 SAE and 2 first-class stamps. Guidelines only for #10 SASE or online.

- "Manuscripts are not returned. If writers include a stamped, self-addressed postcard, we will notify them that their writing has reached us. This does not imply acceptance or interest in purchase. Does not respond unless material is accepted for publication."

Nonfiction Inspirational, personal experience, Bible-study insights. Special issues: Lent and Easter; Advent. No poetry, lengthy "spiritual journey" stories. **Buys 365 unsolicited mss/year.** Send complete ms by mail or e-mail. Length: 300 words. **Pays $25/meditation.**

Tips "The best way to break in to our magazine is to send a well-written manuscript that looks at the Christian faith in a fresh way. Standard stories and sermon illustrations are immediately rejected. We very much want to find new writers and welcome good material. We are particularly interested in meditations based on Old Testament characters and stories. Good repeat meditations can lead to work on longer assignments for our other publications, which pay more. A writer who can deal concretely with everyday situations, relate them to the Bible and spiritual truths, and write clear, direct prose should be able to write for *The Upper Room*. We want material that provides for interaction on the part of the reader—meditation suggestions, journaling suggestions, space to reflect and link personal experience with the meditation for the day. Meditations that are personal, authentic, exploratory, and full of sensory detail make good devotional writing."

$ $THE WAR CRY

The Salvation Army, 615 Slaters Lane, Alexandria VA 22314. (703)684-5500. Fax: (703)684-5539. E-mail: war_cry@usn.salvationarmy.org. Website: www.salpubs.com. Managing Editor: Jeff McDonald. **Contact:** Lt. Colonel Marlene Chase, editor-in-chief. **10% freelance written.** Biweekly magazine covering army news and Christian devotional writing. Estab. 1881. Circ. 300,000. **Pays on acceptance.** Publishes ms an average of 2 months-1 year after acceptance. Byline given. Buys first, one-time rights. Editorial lead time 6 weeks. Submit seasonal material 1 year in advance. Accepts previously published material. Accepts simultaneous submissions. Responds in 2 months to mss. Sample copy, theme list, and writer's guidelines free for #10 SASE or online.

- Responds in 4-6 weeks to articles submitted on speculation.
- "A best bet would be a well-written profile of an exemplary Christian or a recounting of a person's experiences that deepened the subject's faith and showed God in action. Most popular profiles are of Salvation Army programs and personnel."

Nonfiction Humor, inspirational, interview/profile, personal experience, religious. No missionary stories, confessions. **Buys 75-100 mss/year.** Send complete ms. **Pays up to 25¢/word.** Sometimes pays expenses of writers on assignment.

Reprints Send ms with rights for sale noted and information about when and where the material previously appeared. Pays 15¢/word.

Photos Buys one-time rights. Offers up to $350/color cover; $200/full page; $75/inside. Identification of subjects required.

Fiction Religious. "No fantasy, science fiction or New Age." **Buys 5-10 mss/year.** Send complete ms. Length: 350-1,500 words.

Poetry Free verse. **Buys 10-20/year poems/year.** Submit maximum 5 poems. Length: 16 lines limit. **Pays $25-100.**

Fillers Anecdotes (inspirational). **Buys 10-20/year.** Length: 200-500 words. **Pays 15-20¢/word.**

Tips "We are soliciting more short fiction, inspirational articles and poetry, interviews with Christian athletes, evangelical leaders and celebrities, and theme-focused articles."

$WESLEYAN LIFE

(formerly *The Wesleyan Advocate*), The Wesleyan Publishing House, P.O. Box 50434, Indianapolis IN 46250-0434. (317)774-7909. Fax: (317)774-7913. E-mail: communications@wesleyan.org. Editor: Dr. Norman G. Wilson. **Contact:** Jerry Brecheisen, managing editor. Quarterly magazine of The Wesleyan Church. Estab. 1842. Circ. 20,000. Pays on publication. Byline given. Buys first rights or simultaneous rights (prefers first rights). Submit seasonal material 6 months in advance. Accepts simultaneous submissions.

Nonfiction Inspirational, religious. No poetry accepted. Send complete ms. Length: 250-400 words. **Pays $25-150.**

$ $THE WITTENBURG DOOR

(formerly *The Door*), P.O. Box 1444, Waco TX 76703-1444. (214)827-2625. Fax: (254)752-4915. E-mail: dooreditor@earthlink.net. Website: www.thedoormagazine.com. **Contact:** Robert Darden, senior editor. **90% freelance written.** Works with a large number of new/unpublished writers each year. Bimonthly magazine. "*The Wittenburg Door* is the world's oldest and largest religious humor and satire magazine." Estab. 1969. Circ. 7,500. Pays on publication. Publishes ms an average of 1 year after acceptance. Buys first rights. Accepts queries by mail. Responds in 3 months to mss. Sample copy for $5.95. Writer's guidelines online.

O— Read several issues of the magazine first! Get the writer's guidelines.

Nonfiction Looking for humorous/satirical articles on church renewal, Christianity and organized religion. Exposé, humor, interview/profile, religious. No book reviews or poetry. **Buys 45-50 mss/year.** Send complete ms. Length: 1,500 words maximum; 750-1,000 preferred. **Pays $50-250.** Sometimes pays expenses of writers on assignment.

Reprints Send ms with rights for sale noted and information about when and where the material previously appeared.

■ The online magazine carries original content not found in the print edition. Contact: Robert Darden.

Tips "We look for someone who is clever, on our wave length, and has some savvy about the evangelical church. We are very picky and highly selective. The writer has a better chance of breaking in with our publication with short articles since we are a bimonthly publication with numerous regular features and the magazine is only 52 pages. The most frequent mistake made by writers is that they do not understand satire. They see we are a humor magazine and consequently come off funny/cute (like *Reader's Digest*) rather than funny/satirical (like *National Lampoon*)."

$WOMAN'S TOUCH

Assemblies of God Women's Ministries Department (GPH), 1445 N. Boonville Ave., Springfield MO 65802-1894. E-mail: womanstouch@ag.org. Website: www.ag.org/womanstouch. Editor: Arlene Allen. **Contact:** Darla Knoth, managing editor. **50% freelance written.** Willing to work with new/unpublished writers. Bimonthly inspirational magazine for women. "Articles and contents of the magazine should be compatible with Christian teachings as well as human interests. The audience is women of all walks of life." Estab. 1977. Circ. 15,000. Pays on publication. Publishes ms an average of 10 months after acceptance. Byline given. Buys first, second, or one-time and electronic rights. Editorial lead time 10 months. Submit seasonal material 10 months in advance. Accepts queries by mail, e-mail, fax. Responds in 3 months to queries. Sample copy for 9½×11 SAE with 3 first-class stamps or online. Writer's guidelines online.

Nonfiction Book excerpts, general interest, inspirational, personal experience, religious, health. No fiction, poetry. **Buys 30 mss/year.** Send complete ms. Length: 200-600 words. **Pays $10-50 for assigned articles; $10-35 for unsolicited articles.**

Reprints Send photocopy and information about when and where the material previously appeared. Pays 50-75% of amount paid for an original article.

Columns/Departments A Final Touch (inspirational/human interest), 400 words; A Better You (health/wellness), 400 words; A Lighter Touch (true, unpublished anecdotes), 100 words.

Tips "Submit manuscripts on current issues of interest to women. Familiarize yourself with *Woman's Touch* by reading 2 issues before submitting an article."

RETIREMENT

$ALIVE!

A Magazine for Vibrant Christians Over 50, Christian Seniors Fellowship, P.O. Box 46464, Cincinnati OH 45246-0464. (513)825-3681. Editor: J. David Lang. **Contact:** A. June Lang, office editor. **60% freelance written.** Quarterly magazine for senior adults 50 and older. "We need timely articles about Christian seniors in vital, productive lifestyles, travel, or ministries." Estab. 1988. Pays on publication. Byline given. Buys first, second serial (reprint) rights. Submit seasonal material 6 months in advance. Responds in 2 months to mss. Sample copy for 9×12 SAE with 3 first-class stamps. Writer's guidelines for #10 SASE.

● Membership $18/year. Organization membership may be deducted from payment at writer's request.

Nonfiction General interest, humor, inspirational, interview/profile, photo feature, religious, travel. **Buys 25-50 mss/year.** Send complete ms and SASE. Length: 600-1,200 words. **Pays $18-75.**

Reprints Send tearsheet, photocopy or typed ms with rights for sale noted and information about when and where the material previously appeared. Pays 60-75% of amount paid for an original article.

Photos State availability with submission. Buys one-time rights. Offers $10-25. Identification of subjects, model releases required.

Columns/Departments Heart Medicine (humorous personal anecdotes; prefer grandparent/granchild stories or anecdotes), 10-100 words. **Buys 50 mss/year.** Send complete ms and SASE. **Pays $5-25.**

Fiction Adventure, humorous, religious, romance, slice-of-life vignettes, motivational, inspirational. **Buys 12 mss/year.** Send complete ms. Length: 600-1,200 words. **Pays $40-60.**

Fillers Anecdotes, facts, short humor. **Buys 15/year.** Length: 50-500 words. **Pays $2-15.**

Tips "Include SASE and information regarding whether manuscript is to be returned or tossed."

$FIFTY SOMETHING MAGAZINE

1168 Beachview Dr., Willoughby OH 44094. (440)951-2468. Fax: (440)951-1015. **Contact:** Linda L. Lindeman DeCarlo, publisher. **80% freelance written.** Quarterly magazine covering nostalgia. "We are focusing on the 50-and-better reader." Estab. 1990. Circ. 10,000. Pays on publication. Publishes ms an average of 6 months after acceptance. Byline given. Offers 5% kill fee. Buys one-time, second serial (reprint), simultaneous rights. Editorial lead time 6 months. Submit seasonal material 6 months in advance. Accepts previously published material. Accepts simultaneous submissions. Responds in 3 months. Sample copy for 9×12 SAE and 4 first-class stamps. Writer's guidelines for #10 SASE.

Nonfiction Book excerpts, essays, exposé, general interest, historical/nostalgic, how-to, humor, inspirational, interview/profile, new product, opinion, personal experience, photo feature, travel. **Buys 20 mss/year.** Length: 500-1,500 words. **Pays $10-100.** Sometimes pays expenses of writers on assignment.

Photos Send photos with submission. Reviews 4×6 prints, GIF/JPEG files. Buys one-time rights. Negotiates payment individually. Captions, identification of subjects, model releases required.

Columns/Departments Health & Fitness (good news/tips), 500 words; Travel (unique trips), 1,000 words; Humor (aging issues), 500 words; Finance (tips), 500 words. **Buys 10 mss/year.** Send complete ms. **Pays $10-100.**

Fiction Adventure, confessions, ethnic, experimental, fantasy, historical, humorous, mainstream, mystery, novel excerpts, romance, slice-of-life vignettes, suspense, western. No erotica or horror. **Buys 10 mss/year.** Send complete ms. Length: 500-1,000 words. **Pays $10-100.**

Poetry Avant-garde, free verse, light verse, traditional. **Buys 10 poems/year.** Submit maximum 5 poems. Length: 10-25 lines.

Fillers Anecdotes, facts, gags to be illustrated by cartoonist, newsbreaks, short humor. **Buys 10/year.** Length: 50-150 words. **Pays $10-100.**

N $MATURE LIVING

A Magazine for Christian Senior Adults, Lifeway Christian Resources, 1 Lifeway Plaza, Nashville TN 37234. E-mail: matureliving@lifeway.com. Website: www.lifeway.com. **Contact:** David Seay, editor-in-chief. **90% freelance written.** Monthly leisure reading magazine for senior adults 55 and older. *"Mature Living* is Christian in content and the material required is what would appeal to 55 and over age group: inspirational, informational, nostalgic, humorous. Our magazine is distributed mainly through churches (especially Southern Baptist churches) that buy the magazine in bulk and distribute it to members in this age group." Estab. 1977. Circ. 320,000. **Pays on acceptance.** Publishes ms an average of 7-8 weeks after acceptance. Byline given. Purchases all rights if writer agrees. Submit seasonal material 1 year in advance. Responds in 3 months to mss. Sample copy for 9×12 SAE with 4 first-class stamps. Writer's guidelines for #10 SASE.

Nonfiction General interest, historical/nostalgic, how-to, humor, inspirational, interview/profile, personal experience, travel, crafts. No pornography, profanity, occult, liquor, dancing, drugs, gambling. **Buys 100 mss/year.** Length: 600-1,200 words. **Pays $75-105.**

Photos State availability with submission. Offers $10-25/photo. Pays on publication.

Columns/Departments Cracker Barrel (brief, humorous, original quips and verses), **pays $15**; Grandparents' Brag Board (something humorous or insightful said or done by your grandchild or great-grandchild), **pays $15**; Inspirational (devotional items), **pays $25**; Food (introduction and 4-6 recipes), **pays $50**; Over the Garden Fence (vegetable or flower gardening), **pays $40**; Crafts (step-by-step procedures), **pays $40**; Game Page (crossword or word-search puzzles and quizzes), **pays $40.**

Fiction Humorous, religious, senior citizen/retirement. No reference to liquor, dancing, drugs, gambling; no pornography, profanity or occult. **Buys 12 mss/year.** Send complete ms. Length: 900-1,200 words preferred. **Pays $75-105 and 3 contributor's copies.**

Poetry Buys 24 poems/year. Submit maximum 5 poems. Length: 12-16 lines. **Pays $25.**

$MATURE YEARS

The United Methodist Publishing House, 201 Eighth Ave. S., Nashville TN 37202-0801. (615)749-6292. Fax: (615)749-6512. E-mail: matureyears@umpublishing.org. **Contact:** Marvin W. Cropsey, editor. **50% freelance written.** Prefers to work with published/established writers. Quarterly magazine "designed to help persons in and nearing the retirement years understand and appropriate the resources of the Christian faith in dealing with specific problems and opportunities related to aging." Estab. 1954. Circ. 55,000. **Pays on acceptance.** Publishes ms an average of 1 year after acceptance. Buys first North American serial rights. Submit seasonal material 14 months in advance. Responds in 2 weeks to queries; 2 months to mss. Sample copy for $5 and 9×12 SAE. Writer's guidelines for #10 SASE or by e-mail.

Nonfiction Especially important are opportunities for older adults to read about service, adventure, fulfillment, and fun. How-to (hobbies), inspirational, religious, travel (special guidelines), older adult health, finance issues.

Buys 75-80 mss/year. Send complete ms; e-mail submissions preferred. Length: 900-2,000 words. **Pays $45-125.** Sometimes pays expenses of writers on assignment.

Reprints Send tearsheet, photocopy or typed ms with rights for sale noted and information about when and where the material previously appeared. Pays at same rate as for previously unpublished material.

Photos Send photos with submission. Typically buys one-time rights. Negotiates pay individually. Captions, model releases required.

Columns/Departments Health Hints (retirement, health), 900-1,500 words; Going Places (travel, pilgrimage), 1,000-1,500 words; Fragments of Life (personal inspiration), 250-600 words; Modern Revelations (religious/inspirational), 900-1,500 words; Money Matters (personal finance), 1,200-1,800 words; Merry-Go-Round (cartoons, jokes, 4-6 line humorous verse); Puzzle Time (religious puzzles, crosswords). **Buys 4 mss/year.** Send complete ms. **Pays $25-45.**

Fiction Marvin Cropsey, editor. Humorous, religious, slice-of-life vignettes, retirement years nostalgia, intergenerational relationships. ''We don't want anything poking fun at old age, saccharine stories, or anything not for older adults. Must show older adults (age 55 plus) in a positive manner.'' **Buys 4 mss/year.** Send complete ms. Length: 1,000-2,000 words. **Pays $60-125.**

Poetry Free verse, haiku, light verse, traditional. **Buys 24 poems/year.** Submit maximum 6 poems. Length: 3-16 lines. **Pays $5-20.**

ROMANCE & CONFESSION

N $ THE BLACK ROMANCE GROUP

Black Confessions, Black Romance, Black Secrets, Bronze Thrills, Jive, Sterling/McFadden Partnership, 333 7th Ave., 11th Floor, New York NY 10001. (212)780-3500. Fax: (212)979-4825. Website: www.sterlingmacfadden.com. **Contact:** Takesha Powell or Lisa Finn, editors. **100% freelance written.** Eager to work with new/unpublished writers. Monthly magazine of romance and love. Circ. 70,000. Pays on publication. Publishes ms an average of 2 months after acceptance. Byline given on special feature articles only but not short stories. Company maintains all property rights of stories. Accepts queries by mail, phone. Responds in 4 months to mss. Sample copy for 9×12 SAE with 5 first-class stamps. Writer's guidelines free.

Nonfiction ''We like our articles to have a down-to-earth flavor. They should be written in the spirit of sisterhood, fun, and creativity. Come up with an original idea our readers may not have thought of but will be dying to try out.'' How-to (relating to romance and love), feature articles on any aspect of relationships. Query with published clips. Length: 4-5 typed pages. **Pays $125.**

Fiction Romance confessional stories told from an African-American female perspective. Stories should include 2 love scenes, alluding to sex. Include spicy, sexual topics of forbidden love, but not graphic detail. Stories must include a conflict between the heroine and her love interest. The age of characters can range from mid-teenage years through late 30s. Make stories exciting, passionate (uninhibited sexual fantasies), and romantic. Send complete ms. Length: 5,000 words. **Pays $100.**

Poetry Accepts poetry, but does not pay.

Tips ''Follow our writer's guidelines and read a few sample copies before submitting your manuscript. Use a romance writer's phrase book as a guide when writing stories, especially love scenes. Submit stories with original, modern conflicts. Incorporate romance and sex in manuscripts uninhibitedly—making the stories an exciting, passionate escape for readers to imagine fulfilling their secret desires.''

$ TRUE CONFESSIONS

Macfadden Women's Group, 333 Seventh Ave., New York NY 10001. (212)979-4898. Fax: (212)979-4825. E-mail: trueconfessionstales@yahoo.com. **Contact:** Pat Byrdsong, editor. **94% freelance written.** Monthly magazine for high school-educated, working class women—teens through maturity. ''*True Confessions* is a women's magazine featuring true-to-life stories about working class women and their families.'' Circ. 200,000. Pays 1 month after publication. Publishes ms an average of 4 months after acceptance. Buys all rights. Submit seasonal material 8 months in advance. Accepts queries by e-mail. Responds in 3 months to queries; 1 year to mss. Sample copy for $4.49.

- Eager to work with new/unpublished writers. Prefers writers to query via e-mail before submitting stories.
- O→ ''If you have a strong story to tell, tell it simply and convincingly. We always have a need for 4,000-word stories with dramatic impact about dramatic events.'' Asian-, Latina-, Native- and African-American stories are encouraged.

Nonfiction Timely, exciting, true, emotional first-person stories on the problems that face today's women. The narrators should be sympathetic, and the situations they find themselves in should be intriguing, yet realistic. Many stories may have a strong romantic interest and a high moral tone; however, personal accounts or ''confessions,'' no matter how controversial the topic, are encouraged and accepted. Careful study of current issue is suggested. Send complete ms. No simultaneous submissions. SASE required. Length: 4,000-7,000 words, and mini stories 1,000-1,500 words. **Pays 3¢/word.**

Columns/Departments Family Zoo (pet feature), 50 words or less, **pays $50 for pet photo and story.** My Moment With God (a short prayer); Incredible But True (an incredible/mystical/spiritual experience); My Man (a man who has been special in your life); Woman to Woman (a point of view about a contemporary subject matter or a woman overcoming odds), all 200-300 words. **Pays $65** for all features; **$75** for My Moment With God. Send complete ms and SASE.

Fiction Pat Byrdsong, editor. Query. Length: 3,000-7,500 words. **Pays 3¢/word or a flat $100 rate for mini-stories and 1 contributor's copy.**

Poetry Poetry should rhyme. Length: 4-20 lines. **Pays $10 minimum.**

Tips "Our magazine is almost 100% freelance. We purchase all stories that appear in our magazine. Read 3-4 issues before sending submissions. Do not talk down to our readers. We prefer manuscripts on disk (saved as RTF file) as well as hard copy."

$TRUE ROMANCE

Dorchester Media, 333 Seventh Ave., New York NY 10001. (212)780-3500. E-mail: nmiller@dorchestermedia.com. Website: www.trueromancemag.com. Associate Editor: Elise Revere. **Contact:** Nell Miller, senior editor. **100% freelance written.** Monthly magazine for women, teens through retired, offering compelling confession stories based on true happenings, with reader identification and strong emotional tone. No third-person material. Estab. 1923. Circ. 225,000. Pays 1 month after publication. Buys all rights. Submit seasonal material 6 months in advance. Accepts queries by mail, e-mail, fax. Responds in 8 months to queries.

Nonfiction Confessions, true love stories, mini-adventures, problems and solutions, dating and marital difficulties. Realistic, yet unique stories dealing with current problems, everyday events; strong emotional appeal; controversial topics of interest to women. **Buys 180 mss/year.** Submit ms. Length: 6,000-9,000 words. **Pays 3¢/word; slightly higher rates for short-shorts.**

Columns/Departments Happily Ever After; Family Recipe; Loving Pets, **all pay $50;** Cupid's Corner, **pays $100;** Passages, **pays 3¢/word.**

Poetry Light romantic poetry. Length: 24 lines maximum. **Pays $10-30.**

Tips "A timely, well-written story that is told by a sympathetic narrator who sees the central problem through to a satisfying resolution is all important to break into *True Romance*. We are always looking for interesting, emotional, identifiable stories."

RURAL

$ $◪ THE COUNTRY CONNECTION

Ontario's Magazine of Choice, Pinecone Publishing, P.O. Box 100, Boulter ON K0L 1G0 Canada. (613)332-3651. E-mail: editor@pinecone.on.ca. Website: www.pinecone.on.ca. **Contact:** Joanne Healy, editor. **100% freelance written.** Magazine published 4 times/year covering nature, environment, history and nostalgia, the arts, and green travel. "*The Country Connection* is a magazine for true nature lovers and the rural adventurer. Building on our commitment to heritage, cultural, artistic, and environmental themes, we continually add new topics to illuminate the country experience of people living within nature. Our goal is to chronicle rural life in its many aspects, giving 'voice' to the countryside." Estab. 1989. Circ. 4,000. Pays on publication. Publishes ms an average of 4 months after acceptance. Byline given. Buys first rights. Editorial lead time 4 months. Accepts queries by mail, e-mail, phone. Sample copy for $5.69. Writer's guidelines online.

Nonfiction General interest, historical/nostalgic, humor, opinion, personal experience, travel, lifestyle, leisure, art and culture, vegan recipes. No hunting, fishing, animal husbandry, or pet articles. **Buys 60 mss/year.** Send complete ms. Length: 500-2,000 words. **Pays 10¢/word.**

Photos Send photos with submission. Reviews transparencies, prints. Buys one-time rights. Offers $10-50/photo. Captions required.

Fiction Adventure, fantasy, historical, humorous, slice-of-life vignettes, country living. **Buys 10 mss/year.** Send complete ms. Length: 500-1,500 words. **Pays 10¢/word.**

🖳 The online magazine carries original content not found in the print edition. Contact: Joanne Healy.

Tips "Canadian content only. Send manuscript with appropriate support material such as photos, illustrations, maps, etc."

$COUNTRY FOLK

Salaki Publishing & Design, HC77, Box 580, Pittsburg MO 65724. (417)993-5944. E-mail: salaki@countryfolkmag.com. Website: www.countryfolkmag.com. **Contact:** Susan Salaki, editor. **100% freelance written.** Bimonthly magazine. "*Country Folk* publishes true stories and history of the Ozarks." Estab. 1994. Circ. 16,700. Pays on publication. Publishes ms an average of 3 months after acceptance. Byline given. Buys first rights. Editorial lead time 2 months. Submit seasonal material 3 months in advance. Accepts queries by mail, e-mail, phone. Responds in 1 month to queries; 2 months to mss. Writer's guidelines online.

- *Country Folk* has increased from quarterly to bimonthly and doubled its circulation.

Nonfiction Historical/nostalgic (true pieces with family names and real places), how-to, humor, inspirational, personal experience, photo feature, true ghost stories of the Ozarks. **Buys 10 mss/year.** Prefers e-mail submissions. Length: 750-1,000 words. **Pays $5-20.** ''Pays writers with contributor copies or other premiums if we must do considerable editing to the work.''

Photos Send photos with submission. Buys one-time rights.

Fiction Historical, humorous, mystery, novel excerpts. **Buys 10 mss/year.** Send complete ms. Length: 750-1,000 words. **Pays $5-50.**

Poetry Haiku, light verse, traditional. **Buys 25 poems/year.** Submit maximum 3 poems. **Pays $1-5.**

Fillers Anecdotes, facts, gags to be illustrated by cartoonist, newsbreaks, short humor. **Buys 25/year. Pays $1-5.**

Tips ''We want material from or about people who were born and raised in the Ozarks. We accept submissions in any form, handwritten or typed. Many of the writers and poets whose work we publish are first-time submissions. Most of the work we publish is written by older men and women who have heard stories from their parents and grandparents about how the Ozark region was settled in the 1800s. Almost any writer who writes from the heart about a true experience from his or her youth will get published. Our staff edits for grammar and spelling errors. All the writer has to be concerned about is conveying the story. We also publish recipes, old photos, and humorous anecdotes. Please visit our website to read material we have published in previous issues and/or to print a copy of our writer's guidelines. We look forward to reading your work.''

$ $FARM & RANCH LIVING

Reiman Media Group, 5925 Country Lane, Greendale WI 53129. (414)423-0100. Fax: (414)423-8463. E-mail: editors@farmandranchliving.com. Website: www.farmandranchliving.com. **Contact:** Nick Pabst, editor. **30% freelance written.** Eager to work with new/unpublished writers. Bimonthly magazine aimed at families that farm or ranch full time. ''F&RL is not a 'how-to' magazine—it focuses on people rather than products and profits.'' Estab. 1978. Circ. 400,000. Pays on publication. Publishes ms an average of 6 months after acceptance. Byline given. Buys first, one-time rights. Submit seasonal material 6 months in advance. Accepts queries by mail, e-mail, fax. Responds in 6 weeks to queries. Sample copy for $2. Writer's guidelines for #10 SASE.

○→ Break in with ''photo-illustrated stories about present-day farmers and ranchers.''

Nonfiction Humor (rural only), inspirational, interview/profile, personal experience (farm/ranch related), photo feature, nostalgia, prettiest place in the country (photo/text tour of ranch or farm). No how-to articles or stories about ''hobby farmers'' (doctors or lawyers with weekend farms); no issue-oriented stories (pollution, animal rights, etc.). **Buys 30 mss/year.** Query with or without published clips or send complete ms. Length: 600-1,200 words. **Pays up to $300 for text/photo package. Payment for Prettiest Place negotiable.**

Reprints Send photocopy with rights for sale noted. Payment negotiable.

Photos Scenic. State availability with submission. Buys one-time rights. Pays $75-200 for 35mm color slides.

Tips ''Our readers enjoy stories and features that are upbeat and positive. A freelancer must see *F&RL* to fully appreciate how different it is from other farm publications—ordering a sample is strongly advised (not available on newsstands). Photo features (about interesting farm or ranch families) and personality profiles are most open to freelancers.''

N $ $HOBBY FARMS

Rural Living for Pleasure and Profit, Bowtie, Inc., P.O. Box 8237, Lexington KY 40533. Fax: (859)260-9814. E-mail: hobbyfarms@bowtieinc.com. Website: www.hobbyfarmsmagazine.com. Associate Editor: Sarah Coleman. **Contact:** Karen Keb Acevedo, editor. **75% freelance written.** Bimonthly magazine covering small farms and rural lifestyle. ''*Hobby Farms* is the magazine for rural enthusiasts. Whether you have a small garden or 100 acres, there is something in *Hobby Farms* to educate, enlighten or inspire you.'' Estab. 2000. Circ. 50,000. Pays on publication. Publishes ms an average of 6 years after acceptance. Byline given. Offers 30% kill fee. Buys first North American serial rights, makes work-for-hire assignments. Editorial lead time 3 months. Submit seasonal material 6 months in advance. Accepts queries by mail, e-mail. Responds in 2 months. Sample copy for 10×12 SAE and 3 first-class stamps. Writer's guidelines free.

- Writing tone should be conversational, but authoritative.

Nonfiction Historical/nostalgic, how-to (farm or livestock management, equipment, etc.), interview/profile, personal experience, technical, breed or crop profiles. **Buys 10 mss/year.** Query with or without published clips or send complete ms. Length: 1,500-2,500 words. Sometimes pays expenses of writers on assignment.

Photos State availability of or send photos with submission. Reviews transparencies, GIF/JPEG files. Buys one-time rights. Negotiates payment individually. Identification of subjects, model releases required.

Tips "Please state your specific experience with any aspect of farming (livestock, gardening, equipment, marketing, etc)."

Ⓝ $MOTHER EARTH NEWS

Ogden Publications, 1503 SW 42nd St., Topeka KS 66609-1265. (785)274-4300. E-mail: letters@motherearthnews.com. Website: www.motherearthnews.com. Managing Editor: Nancy Smith. **Contact:** Cheryl Long, editor. Mostly written by staff and team of established freelancers. Bimonthly magazine emphasizing country living, country skills, natural health and sustainable technologies for both long-time and would-be ruralists. "*Mother Earth News* is dedicated to presenting information that helps readers be more self-sufficient, financially independent, and environmentally aware." Circ. 350,000. Pays on publication. Byline given. Submit seasonal material 5 months in advance. Responds in 6 months to mss. Sample copy for $5. Writer's guidelines for #10 SASE.

Nonfiction How-to, alternative energy systems, organic gardening, home building, home retrofit and maintenance, energy-efficient structures, seasonal cooking, home business. No fiction, please. **Buys 35-50 mss/year.** Query. "Sending us a short, to-the-point paragraph is often enough. If it's a subject we don't need at all, we can answer it immediately. If it tickles our imagination, we'll ask to take a look at the whole piece." Length: 300-3,000 words. **Pays $25-100.**

Columns/Departments Country Lore (down-home solutions to everyday problems); Herbs & Remedies (home healing, natural medicine); Energy & Environment (ways to conserve energy while saving money; also alternative energy).

Tips "Probably the best way to break in is to study our magazine, digest our writer's guidelines, and send us a concise article illustrated with color transparencies that we can't resist. When folks query and we give a go-ahead on speculation, we often offer some suggestions. Failure to follow those suggestions can lose the sale for the author. We want articles that tell what real people are doing to take charge of their own lives. Articles should be well-documented and tightly written treatments of topics we haven't already covered."

$RANGE MAGAZINE

The Cowboy Spirit on American Outback, Purple Coyote, 106 E. Adams, Carson City NV 89706. (775)884-2200. Fax: (775)884-2213. Website: www.rangemagazine.com. Editor: C.J. Hadley. **Contact:** Barbara Wies, associate publisher. **70% freelance written.** Quarterly magazine. "*RANGE* magazine covers ranching and farming as available resources." Estab. 1991. Pays on publication. Publishes ms an average of 6 months after acceptance. Buys first North American serial rights, makes work-for-hire assignments. Accepts queries by mail. Responds in 6-8 weeks to queries; 3-6 months to mss. Sample copy for $2. Writer's guidelines for #10 SASE.

Nonfiction Book excerpts, humor, interview/profile, personal experience, photo feature. No rodeos or anything by a writer not familiar with *Range*. Query. Length: 1,000-1,500 words. **Pays $100.** Sometimes pays expenses of writers on assignment.

Photos C.J. Hadley, editor/publisher. State availability with submission. Reviews 35mm transparencies, 4×6 prints. Buys one-time rights. Negotiates payment individually. Captions, identification of subjects, model releases required.

$RURAL HERITAGE

281 Dean Ridge Lane, Gainesboro TN 38562-5039. (931)268-0655. E-mail: editor@ruralheritage.com. Website: www.ruralheritage.com. Publisher: Allan Damerow. **Contact:** Gail Damerow, editor. **98% freelance written.** Willing to work with a small number of new/unpublished writers. Bimonthly magazine devoted to the training and care of draft animals. Estab. 1976. Circ. 9,500. Pays on publication. Publishes ms an average of 6 months after acceptance. Byline given. Buys first English language rights. Submit seasonal material 6 months in advance. Accepts queries by mail, e-mail. Responds in 3 months to queries. Sample copy for $8. Writer's guidelines online.

Nonfiction How-to (farming with draft animals), interview/profile (people using draft animals), photo feature. No articles on mechanized farming. **Buys 200 mss/year.** Query or send complete ms. Length: 1,200-1,500 words. **Pays 5¢/word.**

Photos Six covers/year, animals in harness $200. Photo guidelines for #10 SASE or on website. Buys one-time rights. Pays $10. Captions, identification of subjects required.

Poetry Traditional. **Pays $5-25.**

Tips "Thoroughly understand our subject: working draft animals in harness. We'd like more pieces on plans and instructions for constructing various horse-drawn implements, and vehicles. Always welcome are: 1) Detailed descriptions and photos of horse-drawn implements; 2) Prices and other details of draft animal and implement auctions and sales."

$ $RURALITE

P.O. Box 558, Forest Grove OR 97116-0558. (503)357-2105. Fax: (503)357-8615. E-mail: ruralite@ruralite.org. Website: www.ruralite.org. **Contact:** Curtis Condon, editor-in-chief. **80% freelance written.** Works with new, unpublished writers. Monthly magazine aimed at members of consumer-owned electric utilities throughout 10 western states, including Alaska. Publishes 48 regional editions. Estab. 1954. Circ. 325,000. **Pays on acceptance.** Byline given. Buys first, sometimes reprint rights. Accepts queries by mail. Responds in 1 month to queries. Sample copy for 10×13 SAE with 4 first-class stamps; guidelines also online. Writer's guidelines online.

Nonfiction Looking for well-written nonfiction, dealing primarily with human interest topics. Must have strong Northwest perspective and be sensitive to Northwest issues and attitudes. Wide range of topics possible, from energy-related subjects to little-known travel destinations to interesting people living in areas served by consumer-owned electric utilities. Family-related issues, Northwest history (no encyclopedia rewrites), people and events, unusual tidbits that tell the Northwest experience are best chances for a sale. **Buys 50-60 mss/year.** Query first; unsolicited mss submitted without request rarely read by editors. Length: 300-2,000 words. **Pays $50-450.**

Reprints Send ms with rights for sale noted and information about when and where the material previously appeared. Pays 50% of amount paid for an original article.

Photos "Illustrated stories are the key to a sale. Stories without art rarely make it. B&W prints, color slides, all formats accepted."

Tips "Study recent issues. Follow directions when given an assignment. Be able to deliver a complete package (story and photos). We're looking for regular contributors to whom we can assign topics from our story list after they've proven their ability to deliver quality mss."

SCIENCE

$ $ $ $ AMERICAN ARCHAEOLOGY

The Archaeological Conservancy, 5301 Central Ave. NE, #902, Albuquerque NM 87108-1517. (505)266-9668. Fax: (505)266-0311. E-mail: tacmag@nm.net. Website: www.americanarchaeology.org. Assistant Editor: Tamara Stewart. **Contact:** Michael Bawaya, editor. **60% freelance written.** Quarterly magazine. "We're a popular archaeology magazine. Our readers are very interested in this science. Our features cover important digs, prominent archaeologists, and most any aspect of the science. We only cover North America." Estab. 1997. Circ. 35,000. **Pays on acceptance.** Publishes ms an average of 3 months after acceptance. Byline given. Offers 20% kill fee. Buys one-time, electronic rights. Editorial lead time 3 months. Accepts queries by mail, e-mail, fax. Responds in 3 weeks to queries; 1 month to mss.

Nonfiction Archaeology. No fiction, poetry, humor. **Buys 15 mss/year.** Query with published clips. Length: 1,500-3,000 words. **Pays $700-1,500.** Pays expenses of writers on assignment.

Photos State availability with submission. Reviews transparencies, prints. Buys one-time rights. Offers $400-600/photo shoot. Negotiates payment individually. Identification of subjects required.

Tips "Read the magazine. Features must have a considerable amount of archaeological detail."

$ $ $ $ ARCHAEOLOGY

Archaeological Institute of America, 36-36 33rd St., Long Island NY 11106. (718)472-3050. Fax: (718)472-3051. E-mail: peter@archaeology.org. Website: www.archaeology.org. **Contact:** Peter A. Young, editor-in-chief. **35% freelance written.** "*Archaeology* combines worldwide archaeological findings with photography, specially rendered maps, drawings, and charts. Articles cover current excavations, recent discoveries, and special studies of ancient cultures. Regular features: newsbriefs, film and book reviews, current museum exhibits. The only magazine of its kind to bring worldwide archaeology to the attention of the general public." Estab. 1948. Circ. 220,000. **Pays on acceptance.** Byline given. Offers 25% kill fee. Buys world rights. Submit seasonal material 6 months in advance. Accepts queries by mail, e-mail, fax. Accepts simultaneous submissions. Sample copy and writer's guidelines free.

Nonfiction Essays, general interest. **Buys 6 mss/year.** Query preferred. Length: 1,000-3,000 words. **Pays $1,500 maximum.** Sometimes pays expenses of writers on assignment.

Photos Send photos with submission. Reviews 4×5 color transparencies, 35mm color slides. Identification of subjects, credits required.

The online magazine carries original content not found in the print edition. Contact: Mark Rose, online editor.

Tips "We reach nonspecialist readers interested in art, science, history, and culture. Our reports, regional commentaries, and feature-length articles introduce readers to recent developments in archaeology worldwide."

$ $ ASTRONOMY

Kalmbach Publishing, 21027 Crossroads Circle, P.O. Box 1612, Waukesha WI 53187-1612. (262)796-8776. Fax: (262)798-6468. E-mail: astro@astronomy.com. Editor: David J. Eicher. Managing Editor: Dick McNally. **50% of articles submitted and written by science writers; includes commissioned and unsolicited.** Monthly magazine covering the science and hobby of astronomy. "Half of our magazine is for hobbyists (who are active observers of the sky); the other half is directed toward armchair astronomers who are intrigued by the science." Estab. 1973. Circ. 150,000. **Pays on acceptance.** Byline given. Buys first North American serial, one-time, all rights. Responds in 1 month to queries; 3 months to mss. Writer's guidelines for #10 SASE or online.

- "We are governed by what is happening in astronomical research and space exploration. It can be up to a year before we publish a manuscript." Query for electronic submissions.

Nonfiction Book excerpts, new product (announcements), photo feature, technical, space, astronomy. **Buys 75 mss/year.** Query. Length: 500-3,000 words. **Pays $100-1,000.**

Photos Send photos with submission. Pays $25/photo. Captions, identification of subjects, model releases required.

Tips "Submitting to *Astronomy* could be tough. (Take a look at how technical astronomy is.) But if someone is a physics teacher or an amateur astronomer, he or she might want to study the magazine for a year to see the sorts of subjects and approaches we use, and then submit a proposal."

N POPULAR SCIENCE

The What's New Magazine, Time4Media, 2 Park Ave., 9th Floor, New York NY 10016. Website: www.popsci.com. **Contact:** Editorial Department. **50% freelance written.** Monthly magazine for the well-educated adult, interested in science, technology, new products. "*Popular Science* is devoted to exploring (and explaining) to a nontechnical, but knowledgeable, readership the technical world around us. We cover all of the sciences, engineering, and technology, and above all, products. We are largely a 'thing'-oriented publication: things that fly or travel down a turnpike, or go on or under the sea, or cut wood, or reproduce music, or build buildings, or make pictures. We are especially focused on the new, the ingenious, and the useful. Contributors should be as alert to the possibility of selling us pictures and short features as they are to major articles. Freelancers should study the magazine to see what we want and avoid irrelevant submissions." Estab. 1872. Circ. 1,450,000. **Pays on acceptance.** Byline given. Offers 25% kill fee. Buys first North American serial, second serial (reprint) rights. Editorial lead time 3 months. Accepts queries by mail, e-mail, fax. Responds in 1 month to queries. Writer's guidelines online.

Nonfiction "We publish stories ranging from hands-on product reviews to investigative feature stories, on everything from black holes to black-budget airplanes." Query.

Tips "Probably the easiest way to break in here is by covering a news story in science and technology that we haven't heard about yet. We need people to be acting as scouts for us out there, and we are willing to give the most leeway on these performances. We are interested in good, sharply focused ideas in all areas we cover. We prefer a vivid, journalistic style of writing, with the writer taking the reader along with him, showing the reader what he saw, through words."

$ $ $ $ SCIENTIFIC AMERICAN

415 Madison Ave., New York NY 10017. (212)754-0550. E-mail: editors@sciam.com. Website: www.sciam.com. Monthly magazine covering developments and topics of interest in the world of science. Query before submitting. "*Scientific American* brings its readers directly to the wellspring of exploration and technological innovation. The magazine specializes in first-hand accounts by the people who actually do the work. Their personal experience provides an authoritative perspective on future growth. Over 100 of our authors have won Nobel Prizes. Complementing those articles are regular departments written by *Scientific American*'s staff of professional journalists, all specialists in their fields. *Scientific American* is the authoritative source of advance information. Authors are the first to report on important breakthroughs, because they're the people who make them. It all goes back to *Scientific American*'s corporate mission: to link those who use knowledge with those who create it." Estab. 1845. Circ. 710,000.

Nonfiction Freelance opportunities mostly in the news scan section; limited opportunity in feature well. **Pays $1/word average.** Pays expenses of writers on assignment.

$ $ SKY & TELESCOPE

The Essential Magazine of Astronomy, Sky Publishing Corp., 49 Bay State Rd., Cambridge MA 02138. (617)864-7360. Fax: (617)576-0336. E-mail: editors@skyandtelescope.com. Website: skyandtelescope.com. Editor: Richard Tresch Fienberg. **Contact:** Bud Sadler, managing editor. **15% freelance written.** Monthly magazine covering astronomy. "*Sky & Telescope* is the magazine of record for astronomy. We cover amateur activities, research news, equipment, book, and software reviews. Our audience is the amateur astronomer who wants to learn more about the night sky." Estab. 1941. Circ. 125,000. Pays on publication. Publishes ms an average of 6 months after acceptance. Byline given. Buys first rights. Editorial lead time 4 months. Submit seasonal material 1 year in advance. Accepts queries by mail, e-mail, fax. Responds in 3 weeks to queries; 1 month to mss. Sample copy for $4.99. Writer's guidelines online.

Nonfiction Essays, historical/nostalgic, how-to, opinion, personal experience, photo feature, technical. No poetry, crosswords, New Age, or alternative cosmologies. **Buys 10 mss/year.** Query. Length: 1,500-2,500 words. **Pays at least 25¢/word.** Sometimes pays expenses of writers on assignment.

Photos Send photos with submission. Reviews contact sheets. Buys one-time rights. Negotiates payment individually. Identification of subjects required.

Columns/Departments Focal Point (opinion), 700 words; Books & Beyond (reviews), 800 words; The Astronomy Scene (profiles), 1,500 words. **Buys 20 mss/year.** Query. **Pays 25¢/word.**

Tips "Good artwork is key. Keep the text lively and provide captions."

$\boxed{\text{N}}$ $ $ $ $∅ STARDATE

University of Texas, 1 University Station, A2100, Austin TX 78712. (512)471-5285. Fax: (512)471-5060. Website: stardate.org. **80% freelance written.** Bimonthly magazine covering astronomy. "*StarDate* is written for people with an interest in astronomy and what they see in the night sky, but no special astronomy training or background." Estab. 1975. Circ. 10,000. **Pays on acceptance.** Publishes ms an average of 4 months after acceptance. Byline given. Offers 25% kill fee. Buys first North American serial, electronic rights. Editorial lead time 6 months. Submit seasonal material 6 months in advance. Accepts queries by mail, e-mail, fax. Responds in 6 weeks to queries. Sample copy and writer's guidelines free.

- *No unsolicited mss.*
- "*StarDate* magazine covers a wide range of topics related to the science of astronomy, space exploration, skylore, and skywatching. Many of our readers rely on the magazine for most of their astronomy information, so articles may cover recent discoveries or serve as a primer on basic astronomy or astrophysics. We also introduce our readers to historical people and events in astronomy and space exploration, as well as look forward to what will make history next year or 50 years from now. *StarDate* topics should appeal to a wide audience, not just professional or amateur astronomers. Topics are not limited to hard-core science. When considering topics, look for undercovered subjects, or give a familiar topic a unique spin. Research findings don't have to make the front page of every newspaper in the country to be interesting. Also, if you'd like to write an historical piece, look for offbeat items and events; we've already covered Copernicus, Kepler, Tycho, Newton and the like pretty well."

Nonfiction General interest, historical/nostalgic, interview/profile, photo feature, technical, travel, research in astronomy. "No first-person; first stargazing experiences; paranormal." **Buys 8 mss/year.** Query with published clips. Length: 1,500-3,000 words. **Pays $500-1,500.** Sometimes pays expenses of writers on assignment.

Photos Send photos with submission. Reviews transparencies, prints. Buys one-time rights. Negotiates payment individually. Identification of subjects required.

Columns/Departments Astro News (short astronomy news item), 250 words. **Buys 6 mss/year.** Query with published clips. **Pays $100-200.**

Tips "Keep up to date with current astronomy news and space missions. No technical jargon."

$ $WEATHERWISE

The Magazine About the Weather, Heldref Publications, 1319 18th St. NW, Washington DC 20036. (202)296-6267. Fax: (202)296-5149. E-mail: ww@heldref.org. Website: www.weatherwise.org. Associate Editor: Amy Souza. **Contact:** Lynn Elsey, managing editor. **75% freelance written.** Bimonthly magazine covering weather and meteorology. "*Weatherwise* is America's only magazine about the weather. Our readers range from professional weathercasters and scientists to basement-bound hobbyists, but all share a common interest in craving information about weather as it relates to the atmospheric sciences, technology, history, culture, society, art, etc." Estab. 1948. Circ. 22,000. Pays on publication. Publishes ms an average of 6 months after acceptance. Byline given. Buys all rights. Editorial lead time 6-9 months. Submit seasonal material 9 months in advance. Accepts queries by mail, e-mail, fax, phone. Responds in 2 months to queries. Sample copy for $4 and 9×12 SAE with 10 first-class stamps. Writer's guidelines online.

- "First, familiarize yourself with the magazine by taking a close look at the most recent issues. (You can also visit our website, which features the full text of many recent articles.) This will give you an idea of the style of writing we prefer in *Weatherwise*. Then, read through our writer's guidelines (available from our office or on our website) which detail the process for submitting a query letter. As for the subject matter, keep your eyes and ears open for the latest research and/or current trends in meteorology and climatology that may be appropriate for the general readership of *Weatherwise*. And always keep in mind weather's awesome power and beauty—its 'fun, fury, and fascination' that so many of our readers enjoy."

Nonfiction Book excerpts, essays, general interest, historical/nostalgic, how-to, interview/profile, new product, opinion, personal experience, photo feature, technical, travel. Special issues: Photo Contest (September/October, deadline June 1). "No blow-by-blow accounts of the biggest storm to ever hit your backyard." **Buys 15-18 mss/year.** Query with published clips. Length: 1,000-2,000 words. **Pays $200-500 for assigned articles; $0-300 for unsolicited articles.**

Photos Reviews contact sheets, negatives, prints, electronic files. Buys one-time rights. Negotiates payment individually. Captions, identification of subjects required.

Columns/Departments Front & Center (news, trends, opinion), 300-400 words; Weather Talk (folklore and humor), 650-1,000 words. **Buys 12-15 mss/year.** Query with published clips. **Pays $0-200.**

Tips "Don't query us wanting to write about broad types like the Greenhouse Effect, the Ozone Hole, El Niño, etc. Although these are valid topics, you can bet you won't be able to cover it all in 2,000 words. With these topics and all others, find the story within the story. And whether you're writing about a historical storm or new technology, be sure to focus on the human element—the struggles, triumphs, and other anecdotes of individuals."

SCIENCE FICTION, FANTASY & HORROR

$ ABSOLUTE MAGNITUDE

Science Fiction Adventures, DNA Publications, P.O. Box 2988, Radford VA 24143-2988. Website: www.dnapubli cations.com/. **Contact:** Warren Lapine, editor-in-chief. Poetry Address: P.O. Box 13511, Roanoke VA 24034-3511. **Contact:** Mike Allen, poetry editor. **95% freelance written.** Quarterly magazine featuring science fiction short stories. "We specialize in action/adventure science fiction with an emphasis on hard science fiction short stories." Estab. 1993. Circ. 8,000. **Pays on acceptance.** Publishes ms an average of 1 year after acceptance. Byline given. Buys first, first english language serial rights. Editorial lead time 6 months. Accepts simultaneous submissions. Responds in 1 month to mss. Sample copy for $6. Writer's guidelines online.

- This editor is still looking for tightly plotted stories that are character driven. He is now purchasing more short stories than before. "Do not query—send complete manuscript."

Fiction Science fiction. No fantasy, horror, funny science fiction. **Buys 40 mss/year.** Send complete ms. Length: 1,000-20,000 words. **Pays 2-6¢/word.**

Poetry Any form. Best chance with light verse. **Buys 4 poems/issue.** Submit maximum 5 poems. Length: up to 25,000 words. **Pays 2-6¢/word.**

Tips "We are very interested in working with new writers, but we are not interested in 'drawer-cleaning' exercises. There is no point in sending less than your best effort if you are interested in a career in writing. We do not use fantasy, horror, satire, or funny science fiction. We're looking for character-driven, action/adventure-based technical science fiction. We want tightly plotted stories with memorable characters. Characters should be the driving force behind the action of the story; they should not be thrown in as an afterthought. We need to see both plot development and character growth. Stories which are resolved without action on the protagonist's part do not work for us; characters should not be spectators in situations completely beyond their control or immune to their influence. Some of our favorite writers are Roger Zelazny, Frank Herbert, Robert Silverberg, and Fred Saberhagen."

$ AMAZING JOURNEYS MAGAZINE

Journey Books Publishing, 3205 Hwy. 431, Spring Hill TN 37174. (615)791-8006. E-mail: journey@journeybooks publishing.com. Website: www.journeybookspublishing.com. Managing Editor: Donnie Clemons. **Contact:** Edward Knight, editor. **80% freelance written.** Quarterly magazine covering science fiction and fantasy. "We are seeking the best in up-and-coming authors who produce great stories that appeal to a wide audience. Each issue will be packed with exciting, fresh material. *Amazing Journeys* will be a fun read, designed to stimulate the senses without offending them. With the introduction of *Amazing Journeys*, we intend to reintroduce the style of writing that made the Golden Age of science fiction 'golden.' If you are tired of 'shock culture' stories or stories written strictly to appeal to a commercial audience, then *Amazing Journeys* is the right magazine for you." Estab. 2003. **Pays on acceptance.** Publishes ms an average of 1-12 months after acceptance. Byline given. Buys first North American serial rights. Editorial lead time 3 months. Accepts queries by mail, e-mail. Responds in 1 week to queries; 2 months to mss. Sample copy for $4.99, plus 1 SAE with 3 First-Class stamps. Writer's guidelines for #10 SASE.

Fiction Fantasy, science fiction. "Absolutely no sexual content will be accepted. Profanity is greatly restricted (none is preferred). **Buys 20-30 mss/year.** Send complete ms. Length: 2,000-10,000 words. **Pays ¼¢/word, $10 minimum.**

Tips "Send us good, clean stories that are fun to read. Do not try to shock us. Entertain us. We are a conservative market. We are new and very small. We are interested in authors who can help us grow. Also, extra comments on how you, as an author, can broaden our subscription base or sell our magazine is greatly appreciated in your cover letter."

$ $ ANALOG SCIENCE FICTION & FACT

Dell Magazine Fiction Group, 475 Park Ave. S., 11th Floor, New York NY 10016. (212)686-7188. Fax: (212)686-7414. E-mail: analog@dellmagazines.com. Website: www.analogsf.com. **Contact:** Dr. Stanley Schmidt, editor.

100% freelance written. Eager to work with new/unpublished writers. Monthly magazine for general future-minded audience. Estab. 1930. Circ. 50,000. **Pays on acceptance.** Publishes ms an average of 10 months after acceptance. Byline given. Not copyrighted. Buys first North American serial, nonexclusive foreign serial rights. Sample copy for $5. Writer's guidelines online.

O— Break in by telling an "unforgettable story in which an original, thought-provoking, plausible idea plays an indispensible role."

Nonfiction Looking for illustrated technical articles dealing with subjects of not only current but future interest, i.e., topics at the present frontiers of research whose likely future developments have implications of wide interest. **Buys 11 mss/year.** Send complete ms. Length: 5,000 words. **Pays 6¢/word.**

Fiction "Basically, we publish science fiction stories. That is, stories in which some aspect of future science or technology is so integral to the plot that, if that aspect were removed, the story would collapse. The science can be physical, sociological, or psychological. The technology can be anything from electronic engineering to biogenetic engineering. But the stories must be strong and realistic, with believable people doing believable things—no matter how fantastic the background might be. No fantasy or stories in which the scientific background is implausible or plays no essential role." **Buys 60-100 unsolicited mss/year.** Send complete ms. Length: 2,000-80,000 words. **Pays 4¢/word for novels; 5-6¢/word for novelettes; 6-8¢/word for shorts under 7,500 words; $450-600 for intermediate lengths.**

Tips "In query give clear indication of central ideas and themes and general nature of story line—and what is distinctive or unusual about it. We have no hard-and-fast editorial guidelines because science fiction is such a broad field that I don't want to inhibit a new writer's thinking by imposing 'Thou Shalt Nots.' Besides, a really good story can make an editor swallow his preconceived taboos. I want the best work I can get, regardless of who wrote it—and I need new writers. So I work closely with new writers who show definite promise, but of course it's impossible to do this with every new writer. No occult or fantasy."

N $AOIFE'S KISS

A Magazine of Speculative Fiction, Sam's Dot Publishing, P.O. Box 782, Cedar Rapids IA 52406. E-mail: aoife@samsdotpublishing.com. Website: www.samsdotpublishing.com/aoife/cover.htm. **Contact:** Tyree Campbell, managing editor. **100% freelance written.** Quarterly magazine publishing science fiction, fantasy, horror, sword & sorcery, and slipstream short stories that are well-plotted and have memorable characters, as well as poetry in these genres that addresses the human condition in space or in magic. Estab. 2002. Circ. 100. Pays on publication. Publishes ms an average of 3-6 months after acceptance. Byline given. Offers 100% kill fee. Buys first North American serial, one-time, second serial (reprint) rights. Editorial lead time 6 months. Submit seasonal material 6 months in advance. Accepts queries by e-mail. Accepts previously published material. Responds in 2 weeks to queries; 2-3 months to mss. Sample copy for $7. Writer's guidelines online.

Nonfiction Interview/profile, book and movie reviews. **Buys 10-18 mss/year.** Send complete ms. Length: 4,000 words. **Pays $5.** Sometimes pays with contributor copies, per request of writer only.

Fiction Fantasy, horror, science fiction, sword & sorcery, slipstream. **Buys 30-40 mss/year.** Send complete ms. Length: 7,500 words. **Pays $5 or ¼¢/word.**

Poetry "We're open to almost anything, but it must be related to the genres we publish." Avant-garde, free verse, light verse, traditional. **Buys 40-50 poems/year.** Submit maximum 5 poems. Length: 200 lines.

Tips "*Aoife's Kiss* loves to publish beginning writers as well as seasoned veterans. Be sure to read and follow the guidelines before submitting your work. Best advice for beginning writers: Send your best effort, not your first draft."

$ARTEMIS MAGAZINE

Science and Fiction for a Space-Faring Age, LRC Publications, Inc., 1380 E. 17th St., Suite 201, Brooklyn NY 11230-6011. E-mail: magazine@lrcpubs.com. Website: www.lrcpublications.com. **Contact:** Ian Randal Strock, editor. **90% freelance written.** Quarterly magazine covering the Artemis Project and manned space flight/colonization in general. "As part of the Artemis Project, we present lunar and space development in a positive light. The magazine is an even mix of science and fiction. We are a proud sponsor of the Artemis Project, which is constructing a commercial, manned moon base. We publish science articles for the intelligent layman, and near-term, near-Earth hard science fiction stories." Estab. 1999. **Pays on acceptance.** Publishes ms an average of 3-12 months after acceptance. Byline given. Buys first world English serial rights. Editorial lead time 3 months. Accepts queries by mail. Responds in 2 months to queries. Sample copy for $5 and a 9×12 SAE with 4 first-class stamps. Writer's guidelines for SASE or on website.

Nonfiction Essays, general interest, how-to (get to, build, or live in a lunar colony), humor, interview/profile, new product, opinion, technical, travel. **Buys 12-16 mss/year.** Query. Length: 5,000 words maximum. **Pays 3-5¢/word.**

Photos State availability of or send photos with submission. Reviews transparencies, prints. Buys one-time rights. Negotiates payment individually. Captions, identification of subjects, model releases required.

Columns/Departments News Notes (news of interest regarding the moon and manned space flight), under 300 words. **Buys 15-20 mss/year.** Send complete ms. **Pays 3-5¢/word.**

Fiction Ian Randal Stock, editor. "We publish near-term, near-Earth, hard science fiction." Adventure, science fiction. No fantasy, inspirational. **Buys 12-16 mss/year.** Send complete ms. Length: 15,000 words maximum (shorter is better). **Pays 3-5¢/word and 3 contributor's copies.**

Fillers Newsbreaks, short humor, cartoons. **Buys 4-12/year.** Length: 100 words maximum. **Pays 3-5¢/word.**

Tips "Know your material, and write me the best possible article/story you can. You want us to read your manuscript, so show us the courtesy of reading our magazine. Also, the Artemis Project website (www.asi.org) may be a good source of inspiration."

$ASIMOV'S SCIENCE FICTION

Dell Magazine Fiction Group, 475 Park Ave. S., 11th Floor, New York NY 10016. (212)686-7188. Fax: (212)686-7414. E-mail: asimovs@dellmagazines.com. Website: www.asimovs.com. **Contact:** Sheila Williams, editor. **98% freelance written.** Works with a small number of new/unpublished writers each year. Magazine published 10 times/year, including 2 double issues. Magazine consists of science fiction and fantasy stories for adults and young adults. Publishes "the best short science fiction available." Estab. 1977. Circ. 50,000. **Pays on acceptance.** Publishes ms an average of 6-12 months after acceptance. Buys first North American serial, nonexclusive foreign serial rights; reprint rights occasionally. Accepts queries by mail. Accepts previously published material. Responds in 2 months to queries; 3 months to mss. Sample copy for $5. Writer's guidelines for #10 SASE or online.

Fiction Science fiction primarily. Some fantasy and humor but no sword and sorcery. No explicit sex or violence that isn't integral to the story. "It is best to read a great deal of material in the genre to avoid the use of some very old ideas." **Buys 10 mss/issue.** Send complete ms and SASE with all submissions. Fantasy, science fiction. No horror or psychic/supernatural. Would like to see more hard science fiction. Length: 750-15,000 words. **Pays 5-8¢/word.**

Poetry Length: 40 lines maximum. **Pays $1/line.**

Tips "In general, we're looking for 'character-oriented' stories, those in which the characters, rather than the science, provide the main focus for the reader's interest. Serious, thoughtful, yet accessible fiction will constitute the majority of our purchases, but there's always room for the humorous as well. Borderline fantasy is fine, but no sword & sorcery, please. A good overview would be to consider that all fiction is written to examine or illuminate some aspect of human existence, but that in science fiction the backdrop you work against is the size of the universe. Please do not send us submissions on disk or via e-mail. We've bought some of our best stories from people who have never sold a story before."

$FLESH AND BLOOD

Tales of Horror & Dark Fantasy, Flesh & Blood Press, 121 Joseph St., Bayville NJ 08721. E-mail: horrorjackf@aol.com. Website: zombie.horrorseek.com/horror/fleshnblood/index2.html. **Contact:** Jack Fisher, editor-in-chief. **99% freelance written.** Quarterly magazine covering horror/dark fantasy. "We publish fiction with heavy emphasis on the supernatural, fantastic, and/or bizarre." Estab. 1997. Circ. 1,000. Pays on publication. Publishes ms an average of 10 months after acceptance. Editorial lead time 1 month. Accepts queries by mail, e-mail. Responds in 2 weeks to queries; 1 month to mss. Sample copy for $6 (check payable to Jack Fisher). Writer's guidelines online.

● The editor reports an interest in seeing powerful vignettes/stories with surrealism-avante-garde(ism) to them and original, unique ghost stories.

Fiction Horror, slice-of-life vignettes, dark fantasy. "Nothing that isn't dark, strange, odd, and/or offbeat." **Buys 32-36 mss/year.** Length: 100-5,000 words. **4-5¢/word.**

Poetry Avant-garde, free verse, horror/dark fantasy surreal, bizarre. "No rhyming poetry." **Buys 24-36 poems/year.** Submit maximum 5 poems. **Pays $10-20.**

Tips "We like subtle horror over gore. Don't let the title of the magazine deceive you; we don't want 'flesh' and 'blood'—we want just the opposite: subtle horror, dark fantasy, stories and poems that are strange, unclassifiable, fantastic, bizzare, quirky, weird, but always dark in theme, style, plot, and tone."

N $LEADING EDGE

Science Fiction and Fantasy, 3146 JKHB, Provo UT 84601. E-mail: tle@byu.edu. Website: tle.byu.edu. Editor: Christopher Kugler. Managing Editor: Jason Wallace. **Contact:** Jillena O'Brien, fiction director. **100% freelance written.** Semiannual magazine covering science fiction and fantasy. "*Leading Edge* is a magazine dedicated to new and upcoming talent in the field of science fiction and fantasy." Estab. 1980. Circ. 400. Pays on publication. Publishes ms an average of 2-4 months after acceptance. Byline given. Buys first North American serial rights. Accepts queries by mail. Sample copy for $4.95. Writer's guidelines online.

Nonfiction Matthew Gibbins, nonfiction director. Science fiction- and fantasy-themed articles. Send complete ms. Length: 1,000-10,000 words. **Pays in contributor copies for nonfiction.**

Fiction Fantasy, science fiction. **Buys 14-16 mss/year.** Send complete ms. Length: Length: 17,000 words maximum. **Pays $10-100.**

Poetry Matthew Gibbins, poetry director. Avant-garde, haiku, light verse, traditional. **Buys 4-6 poems/year.** Submit maximum 10 poems. Length: $10.

$ THE MAGAZINE OF FANTASY & SCIENCE FICTION

Spilogale, Inc., P.O. Box 3447, Hoboken NJ 07030. E-mail: fandsf@aol.com. Website: www.fsfmag.com. **Contact:** Gordon Van Gelder, editor. **100% freelance written.** Monthly magazine covering fantasy fiction and science fiction. *"The Magazine of Fantasy & Science Fiction* publishes various types of science fiction and fantasy short stories and novellas, making up about 80% of each issue. The balance of each issue is devoted to articles about science fiction, a science column, book and film reviews, cartoons, and competitions." Estab. 1949. Circ. 40,000. **Pays on acceptance.** Publishes ms an average of 9-12 months after acceptance. Byline given. Buys first North American serial, foreign serial rights. Submit seasonal material 8 months in advance. Accepts previously published material. Responds in 2 months to queries. Sample copy for $5. Writer's guidelines for SASE, by e-mail or on website.

Fiction Prefers character-oriented stories. "We receive a lot of fantasy fiction, but never enough science fiction." Adventure, fantasy, horror, science fiction. No electronic submissions. **Buys 70-100 mss/year.** Send complete ms. Length: up to 25,000 words. **Pays 5-9¢/word.**

Tips "We need more hard science fiction and humor."

$ ON SPEC

P.O. Box 4727, Station South, Edmonton AB T6E 5G6 Canada. (780)413-0215. Fax: (780)413-1538. E-mail: editor@earthling.net. Website: www.onspec.ca/. **Contact:** Diane L. Walton. **95% freelance written.** Quarterly magazine covering Canadian science fiction, fantasy and horror. "We publish speculative fiction by new and established writers, with a strong preference for Canadian authored works." Estab. 1989. Circ. 2,000. **Pays on acceptance.** Publishes ms an average of 6-18 months after acceptance. Byline given. Buys first North American serial rights. Editorial lead time 6 months. Accepts queries by mail, phone. Accepts simultaneous submissions. Responds in 2 weeks to queries; 2 months after deadline to mss. Sample copy for $7. Writer's guidelines for #10 SASE or on website.

Nonfiction Commissioned only.

Fiction Fantasy, horror, science fiction, magic realism. No media tie-in or shaggy-alien stories. No condensed or excerpted novels, religious/inspirational stories, fairy tales. **Buys 50 mss/year.** Send complete ms. Length: 1,000-6,000 words. **Pays $50-180 for fiction. Short stories (under 1,000 words): $50 plus 1 contributor's copy.**

Poetry "We rarely buy rhyming or religious material." Avant-garde, free verse. **Buys 6 poems/year.** Submit maximum 10 poems. Length: 4-100 lines. **Pays $20.**

Tips "We want to see stories with plausible characters, a well-constructed, consistent, and vividly described setting, a strong plot and believable emotions; characters must show us (not tell us) their emotional responses to each other and to the situation and/or challenge they face. Also, don't send us stories written for television. We don't like media tie-ins, so don't watch TV for inspiration! Read, instead! Absolutely no e-mailed or faxed submissions. Strong preference given to submissions by Canadians."

$ PENNY BLOOD

New York NY 10012. E-mail: editor@pennyblood.com. Website: www.pennyblood.com. Editor: Nick Louras. **70% freelance written.** Semiannual magazine covering horror in entertainment. *"Penny Blood Magazine* is a survey of horror and cult entertainment. We are looking for horror movie retrospectives and interviews with genre personalities." Estab. 2004. Circ. 4,000. **Pays on acceptance.** Byline given. Offers 100% kill fee. Buys first North American serial rights. Accepts queries by e-mail. Responds in 2 weeks to queries; 1 month to mss. Sample copy not available. Writer's guidelines online.

Nonfiction Essays, interview/profile. **Buys 20-30 mss/year.** Send complete ms. **Pays 3¢/word.** Pays in contributor copies for filler material.

Tips "We accept submissions by e-mail only. We are seeking interviews particularly and our highest pay rates go for these."

$ RED SCREAM

Eldritch Press, 166 Kelvin Dr., Buffalo NY 14223. E-mail: dwilliams@redscream.com. Website: www.redscream.com. **Contact:** David R. Williams and R. Moore, editors. **100% freelance written.** Quarterly magazine covering horror. "Looking for dark horror and erotic fiction that isn't just edgy, but is over the edge. Fiction that doesn't just push the envelope, but shreds the envelope and stomps the pieces into the muck. If you've ever written anything you wouldn't dare show your family or friends for fear they would disown you or call for the straightjacket—we want to see it.'' Estab. 2004. **Pays on acceptance.** Publishes ms an average of 3-6 months after acceptance. Byline given. Not copyrighted. Buys one-time, second serial (reprint) rights. Editorial lead time 3-6 months. Accepts queries by e-mail. Responds in 1 week to queries; 1-3 months to mss. Sample copy for $5. Writer's guidelines online.

Fiction Erotica, experimental, horror. Does not want to see knock-offs of your favorite movie. ''Get strangers to read your work. If they drop it and run in fear, we might be interested. If your parents or girlfriend think you're the next Stephen King, good luck and have a happy life, but leave us alone.'' **Buys 50-100 mss/year.** Send complete ms. Length: 2,500-7,000 words. **Pays 5¢/word.**

N $ SCIFAIKUEST

P.O. Box 782, Cedar Rapids IA 52406-0782. E-mail: samsnutmeg@yahoo.com. Website: www.samsdotpublishing.com/scifaikuest/. **Contact:** L.A. Story Houry. **100% freelance written.** Quarterly chapbook-sized magazine. *Scifaikuest* publishes original scifaiku, senryu, tanka, haibun, and other minimalist poetry forms in the genres of science fiction, fantasy, horror, sword & sorcery, and slipstream. It also publishes articles, how-to articles, and reviews of collections, all limited to these poetry forms. Estab. 2003. Circ. 60. Pays on publication. Publishes ms an average of 1-3 months after acceptance. Byline given. Offers 100% kill fee. Buys first North American serial rights. Editorial lead time 2 months. Submit seasonal material 6 months in advance. Accepts queries by e-mail. Responds in 2 weeks to queries; 1-2 months to mss. Sample copy for $7. Writer's guidelines online.

Nonfiction *Scifaikuest* buys/publishes reviews of poetry and poetry collections and how-to articles related to minimalist poetry forms. It also publishes interviews with poets, writers, and teachers, so long as the interviews are related to the magazine's specialty. **Buys 5-8 mss/year.** Send complete ms. Length: 1,000 words. **Pays $4 for unsolicited articles.** Pays in contributer copies at author's request.

Poetry Scifaiku, senryu, tanka, haibun, and other minimalist form. **Buys 80-100 poems/year.** Submit maximum 5 poems.

Tips ''*Scifaikuest* loves to publish beginning writers, as well as seasoned veterans. Be sure to read and follow the guidelines before submitting your work. The best advice for beginning writers is to send your best effort, not your first attempt.''

N $ $ STARLOG MAGAZINE

The Science Fiction Universe, Starlog Group, 475 Park Ave. S., 7th Floor, New York NY 10016-1689. Fax: (212)889-7933. E-mail: allan.dart@starloggroup.com. Website: www.starlog.com. **Contact:** David McDonnell, editor. **90% freelance written.** Monthly magazine covering ''the science fiction/fantasy genre: its films, TV, books, art, and personalities. We often provide writers with a list of additional questions for them to ask interviewees. Manuscripts must be submitted by e-mail. We are somewhat hesitant to work with unpublished writers. We concentrate on interviews with actors, directors, writers, producers, special effects technicians, and others. Be aware that 'science fiction' and 'Trekkie' are seen as derogatory terms by our readers and by us.'' Estab. 1976. Pays on publication. Publishes ms an average of 3 months after acceptance. Byline given. Offers kill fee only to mss. Buys all rights. Accepts queries by mail, e-mail, fax. Responds in 1 month to queries. Sample copy for $7. Writer's guidelines for #10 SASE.

○→ Break in by ''doing something fresh, imaginative, or innovative—or all 3, or by getting an interview we can't get or didn't think of. The writers who sell to us try hard and manage to meet 1 or more challenges. It helps to read the magazine.''

Nonfiction ''We also sometimes cover science fiction/fantasy animation. We prefer article format as opposed to Q&A interviews.'' Book excerpts (having directly to do with science fiction films, TV, or literature), interview/profile (actors, directors, screenwriters—who've done science fiction films—and science fiction novelists), movie/TV set visits. No personal opinion think pieces/essays. No first person. Avoid articles on horror films/creators. Query first with published clips. Length: 500-3,000 words. **Pays $35 (500 words or less); $50-75 (sidebars); $150-300 (1,000-4,000 words).** Pays $50 for each reprint in each foreign edition or such.

Photos ''No separate payment for photos provided by film studios or TV networks.'' State availability with submission. Buys all rights. Photo credit given. Pays $10-25 for color digital images depending on quality. Captions, identification of subjects, credit line required.

Columns/Departments Booklog (book reviews by assignment only). **Buys 150 reviews/year.** Book review, 125 words maximum. No kill fee. Query with published clips. **Pays $15 each.**

■ This online magazine carries original content not found in the print edition. Contact: David McDonnell, online editor.

Tips ''Absolutely no fiction. We do not publish it, and we throw away fiction manuscripts from writers who can't be bothered to include SASE. Nonfiction only please! We are always looking for fresh angles on the various *Star Trek* shows and *Star Wars*. Read the magazine more than once, and don't just rely on this listing. Know something about science fiction films, TV, and literature. Most full-length major assignments go to freelancers with whom we're already dealing. But if we like your clips and ideas, it's possible we'll give you a chance. No phone calls for any reason please—we mean that!''

N $ SURREAL MAGAZINE

Cavern Press, P.O. Box 1424, Salem NH 03079. (603)458-1234. E-mail: submissions@surrealmag.com. Website: www.surrealmag.com. Editors: Mike Miller, Jason D'Aprile. **80% freelance written.** Quarterly magazine covering the horror/thriller genre. ''*Surreal Magazine* publishes original fiction with a horror/thriller theme, and nonfiction articles dealing with the horror industry.'' Estab. 2005. Circ. 1,000 (quarterly). **Pays on acceptance.** Publishes ms an average of 3 months after acceptance. Byline given. Offers 100% kill fee. Buys first, electronic rights, makes work-for-hire assignments. Editorial lead time 2-4 months. Submit seasonal material 6 months in advance. Accepts queries by e-mail. Responds in 3 months to queries. Writer's guidelines online.

Nonfiction Book excerpts, exposé, interview/profile, horror/book/movie/games. Nothing unrelated to the horror industry; no explicit language or scenes. **Buys 20-50 mss/year.** Query with published clips. Length: 500-3,000 words. **Pays $25-150.** Sometimes pays expenses of writers on assignment.

Photos State availability with submission. Negotiates payment individually.

Fiction Horror, surreal fiction. No fantasy, romance, science fiction, or explicit language/scenes. **Buys 100 mss/year.** Send complete ms. Length: 500-9,000 words. **Pays 3-5¢/word.**

Poetry Dark, Poe-like poetry. **Buys up to 20 poems/year.** Length: 500 words maximum.

Fillers Anecdotes, facts, gags to be illustrated by cartoonist, short humor. **Buys 20/year.** Length: 500 words maximum. **Pays $25.**

Tips ''Queries should not be vague and should include samples of your writing. Unpublished writers are welcome and encouraged to query.''

N $ TALES OF THE TALISMAN

Hadrosaur Productions, P.O. Box 2194, Mesilla Park NM 88047-2194. E-mail: hadrosaur@zianet.com. Website: www.zianet.com/hadrosaur. **Contact:** David Lee Summers, editor. **95% freelance written.** Triannual magazine covering science fiction and fantasy. ''*Tales of the Talisman* is a literary science fiction and fantasy magazine published 3 times a year. We publish short stories, poetry, and articles with themes related to science fiction and fantasy. Above all, we are looking for thought-provoking ideas and good writing. Speculative fiction set in the past, present, and future is welcome. Likewise, contemporary or historical fiction is welcome as long as it has a mythic or science fictional element. Our target audience includes adult fans of the science fiction and fantasy genres along with anyone else who enjoys thought-provoking and entertaining writing.'' Estab. 1995. Circ. 150. **Pays on acceptance.** Publishes ms an average of 9 months after acceptance. Byline given. Offers 100% kill fee. Buys one-time rights. Editorial lead time 9-12 months. Submit seasonal material 1 year in advance. Accepts queries by mail, e-mail. Accepts previously published material. Responds in 1 week to queries; 1 month to mss. Sample copy for $6.95. Writer's guidelines online.

Nonfiction Interview/profile, technical, articles on the craft of writing. ''We do not want to see unsolicited articles—please query first if you have an idea that you think would be suitable for *Tales of the Talisman*'s audience. We do not want to see negative or derogatory articles.'' **Buys 1-3 mss/year.** Query. Length: 1,000-3,000 words. **Pays $4-6 for assigned articles.**

Fiction David L. Summers, editor. Erotica, fantasy, horror, science fiction. ''We do not want to see stories with graphic violence. Do not send 'mainstream' fiction with no science fictional or fantastic elements. Do not send stories with copyrighted characters, unless you're the copyright holder.'' **Buys 25-30 mss/year.** Send complete ms. Length: 1,000-6,000 words. **Pays $6-10.**

Poetry Avant-garde, free verse, haiku, light verse, traditional. ''Do not send 'mainstream' poetry with no science fictional or fantastic elements. Do not send poems featuring copyrighted characters, unless you're the copyright holder.'' **Buys 24-30 poems/year.** Submit maximum 5 poems. Length: 3-50 lines.

Tips ''Let your imagination soar to its greatest heights and write down the results. Above all, we are looking for thought-provoking ideas and good writing. Our emphasis is on character-oriented science fiction and fantasy. If we don't believe in the people living the story, we generally won't believe in the story itself. Queries are accepted year-round. Please submit complete manuscripts only during our annual reading periods: May 1-June 15 and November 1-December 15.''

SEX

N $ BLACK MALE FOR MEN

Go West Media Group, LLC, 3230 E. Flamingo Rd., #8-171, Las Vegas NV 89121. (877)446-8682. Fax: (702)974-0585. E-mail: wes@gowestmediagroup.com. Website: www.blackmaleformen.com. **Contact:** Wes Miller, Raul Mangubat. **80% freelance written.** Works with a small number of new/unpublished writers each year. Monthly magazine covering the gay black male lifestyle, gay humor, entertainment, and erotica. Estab. 1998. Circ. 60,000. Pays on publication. Byline given, pseudonym OK. Buys unlimited rights to print (magazine and anthology) and electronic (website) publication. Accepts queries by mail, e-mail, fax. Accepts simultaneous submissions. Responds in 2 months to queries. Sample copy for $7.99. Writer's guidelines online.

> O—π Break in with "a clear, solid story that can be sent on disk, uploaded on the website, or sent via e-mail."

Nonfiction Black entertainment and music/movie interests. **Buys 12-18 mss/year.** Send complete ms. Length: 3,000-3,500 words. **Pays $50-125.**

Photos Send photos with submission. Reviews contact sheets, transparencies, prints. Buys one-time print and electronic (website) posting rights. Offers $25/photo. Captions, identification of subjects, model releases required. Also buys up to 36 illustrations/year to complement erotic fiction (pays $125).

Fiction Gay black male erotica. **Buys up to 36 mss/year.** Send complete ms. Length: 3,000-3,500 words. **Pays $75-125.**

Fillers Short humor. **Buys 12-18/year.** Length: 1,500-2,500 words. **Pays $25-35.**

Tips "Our publications feature male nude photos, plus 2-3 fiction pieces, several articles, cartoons, humorous comments on items from the media, photo features, and entertainment/music information. We present the positive aspects of gay lifestyle, with an emphasis on humor and fitness. Humorous pieces may be erotic in nature. We are open to all submissions that fit our gay male format; the emphasis, however, is on humor and the upbeat. We receive many fiction manuscripts, but not nearly enough unique, innovative, or even experimental material."

Ⓝ $ $ EXOTIC MAGAZINE

X Publishing, 818 SW 3rd Ave., #1324, Portland OR 97204. Fax: (503)241-7239. E-mail: vivacide@hotmail.com. Website: www.xmag.com. Monthly magazine covering adult entertainment, sexuality. "*Exotic* is pro-sex, informative, amusing, mature, intelligent. Our readers rent and/or buy adult videos, visit strip clubs, and are interested in topics related to the adult entertainment industry and sexuality/culture. Don't talk down to them or fire too far over their heads. Many readers are computer literate and well-traveled. We're also interested in insightful fetish material. We are not a 'hard core' publication." Estab. 1993. Circ. 120,000. Pays 30 days after publication. Byline given. Buys first North American serial rights and online rights; may negotiate second serial (reprint) rights. Accepts queries by fax. Accepts simultaneous submissions. Responds in 2 weeks to queries; 2 months to mss. Sample copy for 9×12 SAE and 5 first-class stamps. Writer's guidelines for #10 SASE.

Nonfiction Interested in seeing articles about Viagra, auto racing, gambling, insider porn industry, and real sex worker stories. Exposé, general interest, historical/nostalgic, how-to, humor, interview/profile, travel, news. No "men writing as women, articles about being a horny guy, opinion pieces pretending to be fact pieces." **Buys 36 mss/year.** Send complete ms. Length: 1,000-1,800 words. **Pays 10¢/word up to $150.**

Reprints Send ms with rights for sale noted and information about when and where the material previously appeared. Pays 100% of amount paid for an original article.

Photos Rarely buys photos. Most provided by staff. Reviews prints. Negotiates payment individually. Model releases required.

Fiction "We are currently overwhelmed with fiction submissions. Please only send fiction if it's really amazing." Erotica, slice-of-life vignettes. Send complete ms. Length: 1,000-1,800 words. **Pays 10¢/word up to $150.**

Tips "Read adult publications, spend time in the clubs doing more than just tipping and drinking. Look for new insights in adult topics. For the industry to continue to improve, those who cover it must also be educated consumers and affiliates. Please type, spell-check and be realistic about how much time the editor can take 'fixing' your manuscript."

$ FIRST HAND

Experiences For Loving Men, Firsthand, Ltd., 310 Cedar Lane, Teaneck NJ 07666. (201)836-9177. Fax: (201)836-5055. E-mail: firsthand3@aol.com. Publisher: Sal Nolan. **Contact:** Don Dooley, editor. **75% freelance written.** Eager to work with new/unpublished writers. Monthly magazine published 12 times/year covering homosexual erotica. "Half of the magazine is made up of our readers' own gay sexual experience. Rest is fiction and columns devoted to health, travel, books, etc." Estab. 1980. Circ. 70,000. Pays on publication. Publishes ms an average of 9-18 months after acceptance. Byline given. Buys all rights (exceptions made) and second serial (reprint) rights. Submit seasonal material 10 months in advance. Responds in 2 months to queries; 4 months to mss. Sample copy for $5.99. Writer's guidelines for #10 SASE.

Reprints Send photocopy. Pays 50% of amount paid for original articles.

Fiction "We prefer fiction in the first person which is believable—stories based on the writer's actual experience have the best chance. We're not interested in stories which involve underage characters in sexual situations. Other taboos include bestiality, rape—except in prison stories, as rape is an unavoidable reality in prison—and heavy drug use. Writers with questions about what we can and cannot depict should write for our guidelines, which go into this in more detail. We print mostly self-contained stories; we will look at novel excerpts, but only if they stand on their own." No science fiction or fantasy. Erotica should detail experiences based in reality. Send complete ms. Length: 2,500-3,750 words. **Pays $75.**

Tips "*First Hand* is a very reader-oriented publication for gay men. Half of each issue is made up of letters from our readers describing their personal experiences, fantasies, and feelings. Our readers are from all walks of life, all races and ethnic backgrounds, all classes, all religious and political affiliations, and so on. They are very diverse, and many live in far-flung rural areas or small towns. For some of them, our magazines are the primary source of contact with gay life and in some cases the only support for their gay identity. Our readers are very loyal and save every issue. We return that loyalty by trying to reflect their interests—for instance, by striving to avoid the exclusively big-city bias so common to national gay publications. So bear in mind the diversity of the audience when you write."

N $ ⊕ FOR WOMEN

P.O. Box 381, 4 Selsdon Way, London E14 9GL England. 020 7308 5363. E-mail: elizabeth.coldwell@nasnet.co. uk. Editor: Liz Beresford. Managing Editor: Karen Denman. **Contact:** Elizabeth Coldwell, fiction editor. **50% freelance written.** Magazine published every 6 weeks covering women's sexuality and relationships. Estab. 1992. Circ. 60,000. Pays at the end of the month of publication. Publishes ms an average of 3-4 months after acceptance. Byline given. Buys all rights. Sample copy not available. Writer's guidelines by e-mail.

Fiction "We are allowed to be explicit in the language we use, but the erotic content should be sensual, rather than crude. Stories with a gay/lesbian theme or those which deal with mild bondage/SM are acceptable as long as it is made clear that both partners are willing participants. Some attempt should be made to incorporate a plot. Detailed descriptions of sexual encounters are often very erotic, but our readers also like believable characters and an imaginative setting for the action. We are not allowed to print stories which deal with anything illegal, including underage sex, anal sex (unless those taking part are over 18 and in private—i.e. no threesomes!), incest, beastiality, and anything which features extreme violence or appears to glorify rape or the use of force in a sexual encounter." No stories where a character's motivation is to extract revenge for a previous sexual wrong or in which a character is punished in some way for expressing his/her sexuality. **Buys 18 mss/year.** Send complete ms. Length: 2,000-3,000 words. **Pays £150.**

Tips "Please try to avoid the following plot twists, which we receive more frequently than any other, and which have become increasingly hard to render in an original or surprising way: woman has sexual encounter with a 'stranger' who turns out to be her husband/regular partner; woman has sexual encounter with a 'stranger' who turns out to be a ghost/vampire; or man has sexual encounter with a 'woman' who turns out to be a man. We have also received too many stories set on trains or between characters in cyberspace, so no more of those for the time being, please."

$ $ $ $ HUSTLER

HG Inc., 8484 Wilshire Blvd., Suite 900, Beverly Hills CA 90211. Fax: (323)651-2741. E-mail: features@lfp.com. Website: www.hustler.com. Editor: Bruce David. **Contact:** Carolyn Sinclair, features editor. **60% freelance written.** Magazine published 13 times/year. "*Hustler* is the no-nonsense men's magazine, one that is willing to speak frankly about society's sacred cows and expose its hypocrites. The *Hustler* reader expects honest, unflinching looks at hard topics—sexual, social, political, personality profile, true crime." Estab. 1974. Circ. 750,000. Pays as boards ship to printer. Publishes ms an average of 3 months after acceptance. Byline given. Offers 20% kill fee. Buys all rights. Editorial lead time 4 months. Submit seasonal material 6 months in advance. Accepts queries by mail, e-mail, fax. Responds in 2 weeks to queries; 1 month to mss. Writer's guidelines for #10 SASE.

    O— *Hustler* is most interested in well-researched nonfiction reportage focused on sexual practices and sub-cultures.

Nonfiction Book excerpts, exposé, general interest, how-to, interview/profile, personal experience, trends. **Buys 30 mss/year.** Query. Length: 3,500-4,000 words. **Pays $1,500.** Sometimes pays expenses of writers on assignment.

Columns/Departments Sex play (some aspect of sex that can be encapsulated in a limited space), 2,500 words. **Buys 13 mss/year.** Send complete ms. **Pays $750.**

Fillers Jokes and "Graffilthy," bathroom wall humor. **Pays $50-100.**

Tips "Don't try and mimic the *Hustler* style. If a writer needs to be molded into our voice, we'll do a better job of it than he or she will. Avoid first- and second-person voice. The ideal manuscript is quote-rich, visual, and is narratively driven by events and viewpoints that push one another forward."

N $ IN TOUCH FOR MEN

Go West Media Group, LLC, 3230 E. Flamingo Rd., #8-171, Las Vegas NV 89121. (877)446-8682. Fax: (702)974-0585. E-mail: wes@gowestmediagroup.com. Website: www.intouchformen.com. **Contact:** Wes Miller, Raul

Mangubat. **80% freelance written.** Works with a small number of new/unpublished writers each year. Monthly magazine covering the gay male lifestyle, gay humor, and erotica. Estab. 1973. Circ. 70,000. Pays on publication. Byline given, pseudonym OK. Buys unlimited rights to print (magazine and anthology) and electronic (website) publication. Accepts queries by mail, e-mail, fax. Accepts simultaneous submissions. Responds in 2 months to queries. Sample copy for $7.99. Writer's guidelines online.

O→ Break in with "a clear, solid story that can be sent on disk, uploaded on the website, or sent via e-mail."

Nonfiction Rarely buys nonfiction. Send complete ms. Length: 3,000-3,500 words. **Pays $50-125.**

Photos Send photos with submission. Reviews contact sheets, transparencies, prints. Buys one-time and electronic (website) posting rights. Offers $25/photo. Captions, identification of subjects, model releases. Also buys up to 36 illustrations/year to complement erotic fiction (pays $125).

Fiction Gay male erotica. **Buys up to 36 mss/year.** Send complete ms. Length: 3,000-3,500 words. **Pays $75-125.**

Fillers Short humor. **Buys 12-18/year.** Length: 1,500-2,500 words. **Pays $25-35.**

Tips "Our publications feature male nude photos, plus 2-3 fiction pieces, several articles, cartoons, humorous comments on items from the media, and photo features. We present the positive aspects of gay lifestyle, with an emphasis on humor. Humorous pieces may be erotic in nature. We are open to all submissions that fit our gay male format; the emphasis, however, is on humor and the upbeat. We receive many fiction manuscripts but not nearly enough unique, innovative, or even experimental material."

N $INDULGE FOR MEN

Go West Media Group, LLC, 3230 E. Flamingo Rd., #8-171, Las Vegas NV 89121. (877)446-8682. Fax: (702)974-0585. E-mail: wes@gowestmediagroup.com. Website: www.indulgeformen.com. **Contact:** Wes Miller, Raul Mangubat. **80% freelance written.** Works with a small number of new/unpublished writers each year. Monthly magazine covering the gay male lifestyle, gay humor, fitness, and erotica. Estab. 1985. Circ. 60,000. Pays on publication. Byline given, pseudonym OK. Buys unlimited rights to print (magazine and anthology) and electronic (website) publication. Accepts queries by mail, e-mail, fax. Accepts simultaneous submissions. Responds in 2 months to queries. Sample copy for $7.99. Writer's guidelines online.

O→ Break in with "a clear, solid story that can be sent on disk, uploaded on the website, or sent via e-mail."

Nonfiction Fitness and health interests. **Buys 12-18 mss/year.** Send complete ms. Length: 3,000-3,500 words. **Pays $50-125.**

Photos Send photos with submission. Reviews contact sheets, transparencies, prints. Buys one-time print rights and electronic (website) posting rights. Offers $25/photo. Captions, identification of subjects, model releases. Also buys up to 36 illustrations/year to complement erotic fiction (pays $125).

Fiction Gay male erotica. **Buys up to 36 mss/year.** Send complete ms. Length: 3,000-3,500 words. **Pays $75-125.**

Fillers Short humor. **Buys 12-18/year.** Length: 1,500-2.500 words. **Pays $25-35.**

Tips "Our publications feature male nude photos, plus 2-3 fiction pieces, several articles, cartoons, humorous comments on items from the meda, photo features, fitness training, and wellness information. We present the positive aspects of gay lifestyle, with an emphasis on humor and fitness. Humorous pieces may be erotic in nature. We are open to all submissions that fit our gay male format; the emphasis, however, is on humor and the upbeat. We receive many fiction manuscripts, but not nearly enough unique, innovative, or even experimental material."

$ $ $ $PENTHOUSE

General Media Communications, 11 Penn Plaza, 12th Floor, New York NY 10001. (212)702-6000. Fax: (212)702-6279. E-mail: forum.submission@generalmedia.com. Website: www.penthouse.com. Monthly magazine. "*Penthouse* is for the sophisticated male. Its editorial scope ranges from outspoken contemporary comment to photography essays of beautiful women. *Penthouse* features interviews with personalities, sociological studies, humor, travel, food and wines, and fashion and grooming for men." Estab. 1969. Circ. 640,000. Pays 2 months after acceptance. Byline given. Offers 25% kill fee. Buys all rights. Editorial lead time 3 months. Accepts simultaneous submissions. Writer's guidelines for #10 SASE.

Nonfiction Exposé, general interest (to men), interview/profile. **Buys 50 mss/year.** Query with published clips or send complete ms. Length: 4,000-6,000 words. **Pays $3,000.**

Columns/Departments Buys 25 mss/year. Query with published clips or send complete ms. **Pays $500.**

Tips "Because of our long lead time, writers should think at least 6 months ahead. We take chances. Go against the grain; we like writers who look under rocks and see what hides there."

$ $ PENTHOUSE VARIATIONS

Penthouse Media Group, 2 Penn Plaza, 12th Floor, New York NY 10121. (212)702-6000. E-mail: variations@pent house.com. **Contact:** Barbara Pizio, executive editor. **100% freelance written.** Monthly category-oriented erotica magazine. Estab. 1978. Circ. 100,000. **Pays on acceptance.** Publishes ms an average of 14 months after acceptance. Buys all rights. Editorial lead time 7 months. Submit seasonal material 10 months in advance. Responds in 1 month to queries; 3 months to mss. Writer's guidelines for #10 SASE or by e-mail.

Nonfiction Book excerpts, interview/profile, personal experience. ''No previously published fiction, no humor, no poetry, no children, no one under 21, no relatives, no pets, no coercion.'' **Buys 50 mss/year.** Query by mail only or send complete ms. Do not submit unsolicited mss via e-mail.

Fiction ''*Variations* publishes primarily heterosexual stories in vanilla sex categories as well as various types of S&M and fetishism.'' Erotica. Length: 3,000-3,500 words. **Pays $400 maximum.**

Tips ''Story submissions should be first-person narratives containing at least 2 explicit sex scenes. These sex scenes should be focused within a specific category of sexuality and placed within the context of a realistic plot with well-developed characters.''

$ $ $ $ PLAYBOY MAGAZINE

Playboy Enterprises, Inc., 680 N. Lake Shore Dr., Chicago IL 60611. (212)261-5000. Fax: (212)957-2900. E-mail: articles@playboy.com. Website: www.playboy.com. Monthly magazine. ''As the world's largest general interest lifestyle magazine for men, *Playboy* spans the spectrum of contemporary men's passions. From hard-hitting investigative journalism to light-hearted humor, the latest in fashion and personal technology to the cutting edge of the popular culture, *Playboy* is and always has been guidebook and dream book for generations of American men . . . the definitive source of information and ideas for over 10 million readers each month. In addition, *Playboy*'s 'Interview' and '20 Questions' present profiles of politicians, athletes, and today's hottest personalities.'' Estab. 1953. Circ. 3,200,000. Buys first North American serial rights. Editorial lead time 6 months. Accepts queries by mail. Responds in 2 months to queries. Writer's guidelines for #10 SASE or online.

•*Playboy* does not consider poetry, plays, story outlines or novel-length mss.

Nonfiction ''*Playboy* regularly publishes nonfiction articles on a wide range of topics—sports, politics, music, topical humor, personality profiles, business and finance, science, technology, and other topics that have a bearing on our readers' lifestyles. You can best determine what we're looking for by becoming familiar with the nonfiction we are currently publishing. We frequently reject ideas and articles simply because they are inappropriate to our publication.'' General interest, humor, interview/profile. Mss should be typed, double-spaced and accompanied by a SASE. Writers who submit mss without a SASE will receive neither the ms nor a printed rejection. Submit brief query that outlines idea, explains why it's right for *Playboy*, and ''tells us something about yourself.'' Length: 4,000-5,000 words. **Pays $3,000 minimum.**

Fiction ''*Playboy* is considered one of the top fiction markets in the world. We publish serious contemporary stories, mystery, suspense, humor, science fiction, and sports stories. It pays to take a close look at the magazine before submitting material; we often reject stories of high quality because they are inappropriate to our publication.'' Humorous, mainstream, mystery, science fiction, suspense. Writers should remember that the magazine's appeal is chiefly to a well-informed, young male audience. Fairy tales, extremely experimental fiction and outright pornography all have their place, but it is not in *Playboy*. Handwritten submissions will be returned unread. ''We will not consider stories submitted electronically or by fax.'' Query. Length: 1,000-6,000 words.

Tips ''A bit of advice for writers: Please bear in mind that *Playboy* is not a venue where beginning writers should expect to be published. Nearly all of our writers have long publication histories, working their way up through newspapers and regional publications. Aspiring writers should gain experience and an extensive file of by-lined features before approaching *Playboy*. Please don't call our offices to ask how to submit a story or to explain a story. Don't ask for sample copies, a statement of editorial policy, a reaction to an idea for a story, or a detailed critique. We are unable to provide these, as we receive dozens of submissions daily.''

SPORTS

ARCHERY & BOWHUNTING

$ $ BOW & ARROW HUNTING

Y-Visionary Publishing, LP, 265 S. Anita Dr., Suite 120, Orange CA 92868-3310. (714)939-9991. Fax: (714)939-9909. E-mail: editorial@bowandarrowhunting.com. Website: www.bowandarrowhunting.com. **Contact:** Joe Bell, editor. **70% freelance written.** Magazine published 9 times/year covering bowhunting. ''Dedicated to serve the serious bowhunting enthusiast. Writers must be willing to share their secrets so our readers can become better bowhunters.'' Estab. 1962. Circ. 90,000. Pays on publication. Publishes ms an average of 2 months after acceptance. Byline given. Buys all rights. Submit seasonal material 6 months in advance. Accepts queries by mail. Accepts simultaneous submissions. Responds in 1 month to queries; 6 weeks to mss. Sample copy and writer's guidelines free.

Nonfiction How-to, humor, interview/profile, opinion, personal experience, technical. **Buys 60 mss/year.** Send complete ms. Length: 1,700-3,000 words. **Pays $200-450.**

Photos Send photos with submission. Reviews contact sheets, 35mm and $2\frac{1}{4} \times 2\frac{1}{4}$ transparencies, 5×7 prints. Buys one-time or all rights. Offers no additional payment for photos accepted with ms. Captions required.

Fillers Facts, newsbreaks. **Buys 12/year.** Length: 500 words. **Pays $20-100.**

Tips ''Inform readers how they can become better at the sport, but don't forget to keep it fun! Sidebars are recommended with every submission.''

$ $BOWHUNTER

The Number One Bowhunting Magazine, Primedia Consumer Media & Magazine Group, 6405 Flank Dr., Harrisburg PA 17112. (717)657-9555. Fax: (717)657-9552. E-mail: bowhunter_magazine@primediamags.com. Website: www.bowhunter.com. Founder/Editor Emeritus: M.R. James. **Contact:** Jeff Waring, publisher. **50% freelance written.** Bimonthly magazine covering hunting big and small game with bow and arrow. ''We are a special-interest publication, produced by bowhunters for bowhunters, covering all aspects of the sport. Material included in each issue is designed to entertain and inform readers, making them better bowhunters.'' Estab. 1971. Circ. 158,446. **Pays on acceptance.** Publishes ms an average of 3 months to 2 years after acceptance. Byline given. Buys exclusive first, worldwide publication rights. Submit seasonal material 8 months in advance. Accepts queries by mail, e-mail, fax. Responds in 2 weeks to queries; 1 month to mss. Sample copy for $2 and $8\frac{1}{2} \times 11$ SAE with appropriate postage. Writer's guidelines for #10 SASE or on website.

Nonfiction ''We publish a special 'Big Game' issue each Fall (September) but need all material by mid-March. Another annual publication, Whitetail Bowhunter, is staff written or by assignment only. Our latest special issue is the Gear Specia, which highlights the latest in equipment. We don't want articles that graphically deal with an animal's death. And, please, no articles written from the animal's viewpoint.'' General interest, howto, interview/profile, opinion, personal experience, photo feature. **Buys 60 plus mss/year.** Query. Length: 250-2,000 words. **Pays $500 maximum for assigned articles; $100-400 for unsolicited articles.** Sometimes pays expenses of writers on assignment.

Photos Send photos with submission. Reviews 35mm and $2\frac{1}{4} \times 2\frac{1}{4}$ transparencies, 5×7 and 8×10 prints. Buys one-time rights. Offers $75-250/photo. Captions required.

Fiction Dwight Schuh, editor. Bowhunting, outdoor adventure. Send complete ms. Length: 500-2,000 words. **Pays $100-350.**

Tips ''A writer must know bowhunting and be willing to share that knowledge. Writers should anticipate *all* questions a reader might ask, then answer them in the article itself or in an appropriate sidebar. Articles should be written with the reader foremost in mind; we won't be impressed by writers seeking to prove how good they are—either as writers or bowhunters. We care about the reader and don't need writers with 'I' trouble. Features are a good bet because most of our material comes from freelancers. The best advice is: Be yourself. Tell your story the same as if sharing the experience around a campfire. Don't try to write like you think a writer writes.''

$ $BOWHUNTING WORLD

Ehlert Publishing Group, 6420 Sycamore Lane N., #100, Maple Grove MN 55369. (763)383-4418. Fax: (763)383-4499. E-mail: mstrandlund@ehlertpublishing.com. Website: www.bowhuntingworld.com. **Contact:** Mike Strandlund, editor. **50% freelance written.** Bimonthly magazine with 3 additional issues for bowhunting and archery enthusiasts who participate in the sport year-round. Estab. 1952. Circ. 95,000. **Pays on acceptance.** Publishes ms an average of 5 months after acceptance. Byline given. Buys first, second serial (reprint) rights. Responds in 1 week (e-mail queries) to queries; 6 weeks to mss. Sample copy for $3 and 9×12 SAE with 10 first-class stamps. Writer's guidelines for #10 SASE.

● Accepts queries by mail, but prefers e-mail.

Nonfiction How-to articles with creative slants on knowledgeable selection and use of bowhunting equipment and bowhunting methods. Articles must emphasize knowledgeable use of archery or hunting equipment, and/or specific bowhunting techniques. Contributors must be authorities in the areas of archery and bowhunting. Straight hunting adventure narratives and other types of articles now appear only in special issues. Equipment-oriented articles must demonstrate wise and insightful selection and use of archery equipment and other gear related to the archery sports. Some product-review, field-test, equipment how-to, and technical pieces will be purchased. We are not interested in articles whose equipment focuses on random mentioning of brands. Technique-oriented articles most sought are those that briefly cover fundamentals and delve into leading-edge bowhunting or recreational archery methods. **Buys 60 mss/year.** Query with or without published clips or send complete ms. Length: 1,500-2,500 words. **Pays $350-600.**

Photos ''We are seeking cover photos that depict specific behavioral traits of the more common big game animals (scraping whitetails, bugling elk, etc.) and well-equipped bowhunters in action. Must include return postage.''

Tips ''Writers are strongly advised to adhere to guidelines and become familiar with our format, as our needs are very specific. Writers are urged to query by e-mail. We prefer detailed outlines of 6 or so article ideas/query. Assignments are made for the next 18 months.''

PETERSEN'S BOWHUNTING

Primedia Specialty Group, 6420 Wilshire Blvd., Los Angeles CA 90048. (323)782-2563. Fax: (323)782-2477. Website: www.bowhuntingmag.com. Editor: Jay Michael Strangis. **70% freelance written.** Magazine published 9 times/year covering bowhunting. ''Very equipment oriented. Our readers are 'superenthusiasts,' therefore our writers must have an advanced knowledge of hunting archery.'' Circ. 196,000. **Pays on acceptance.** Byline given. Buys all rights. Editorial lead time 6 months. Submit seasonal material 6 months in advance. Accepts queries by mail. Responds in 1 month to queries. Writer's guidelines free.

Nonfiction Emphasis is on how-to instead of personal. How-to, humor, interview/profile, new product, opinion, personal experience, photo feature. **Buys 50 mss/year.** Query. Length: 2,000 words.

Photos Send photos with submission. Reviews contact sheets, 35mm transparencies, 5×7 prints. Buys one-time rights. Captions, model releases required.

Columns/Departments Query.

Fillers Facts, newsbreaks. **Buys 12/year.** Length: 150-400 words.

BASEBALL

Ⓝ $ FANTASY BASEBALL

Krause Publications, Inc., 700 E. State St., Iola WI 54990-0001. (715)445-2214. Fax: (715)445-4087. E-mail: info@krause.com. Website: www.collect.com. Editor: Greg Ambrosius. Quarterly magazine for fantasy baseball league players. Circ. 130,000. Editorial lead time 6 weeks.

$ JUNIOR BASEBALL

America's Youth Baseball Magazine, 2D Publishing, P.O. Box 9099, Canoga Park CA 91309. (818)710-1234. Fax: (818)710-1877. E-mail: dave@juniorbaseball.com. Website: www.juniorbaseball.com. **Contact:** Dave Destler, editor/publisher. **25% freelance written.** Bimonthly magazine covering youth baseball. ''Focused on youth baseball players ages 7-17 (including high school) and their parents/coaches. Edited to various reading levels, depending upon age/skill level of feature.'' Estab. 1996. Circ. 50,000. Pays on publication. Publishes ms an average of 4 months after acceptance. Byline given. Buys all rights. Editorial lead time 3 months. Submit seasonal material 4 months in advance. Accepts simultaneous submissions. Responds in 2 weeks to queries; 1 month to mss. Sample copy for $5 and online.

Nonfiction How-to (skills, tips, features, how to play better baseball, etc.), interview/profile (with major league players; only on assignment), personal experience (from coaches' or parents' perspective). ''No trite first-person articles about your kid.'' No fiction or poetry. **Buys 8-12 mss/year.** Query. Length: 500-1,000 words. **Pays $50-100.**

Photos Photos can be e-mailed in 300 dpi JPEGs. State availability with submission. Reviews 35mm transparencies, 3×5 prints. Offers $10-100/photo; negotiates payment individually. Captions, identification of subjects required.

Columns/Departments When I Was a Kid (a current Major League Baseball player profile); Parents Feature (topics of interest to parents of youth ball players); all 1,000-1,500 words. In the Spotlight (news, events, new products), 50-100 words; Hot Prospect (written for the 14 and older competitive player. High school baseball is included, and the focus is on improving the finer points of the game to make the high school team, earn a college scholarship, or attract scouts, written to an adult level), 500-1,000 words. **Buys 8-12 mss/year. Pays $50-100.**

Tips ''Must be well-versed in baseball! Having a child who is very involved in the sport, or have extensive hands-on experience in coaching baseball, at the youth, high school or higher level. We can always use accurate, authoritative skills information and good photos to accompany is a big advantage! This magazine is read by experts.''

BICYCLING

$ $ $ ADVENTURE CYCLIST

Adventure Cycling Assn., Box 8308, Missoula MT 59807. (406)721-1776, ext. 222. Fax: (406)721-8754. E-mail: editor@adventurecycling.org. Website: www.adventurecycling.org. **Contact:** Mike Deme, editor. **75% free-**

lance written. Magazine published 9 times/year for Adventure Cycling Association members. Estab. 1975. Circ. 30,000. Pays on publication. Byline given. Buys first rights. Submit seasonal material 9 months in advance. Sample copy and guidelines for 9×12 SAE with 4 first-class stamps.

Nonfiction How-to, humor, interview/profile, photo feature, technical, travel, US or foreign tour accounts; special focus (on tour experience). **Buys 20-25 mss/year.** Query with or without published clips or send complete ms. Length: 800-2,500 words. **Pays $450-1,500.**

Photos Bicycle, scenery, portraits. State availability with submission. Reviews color transparencies. Identification of subjects, model releases required.

Ⓝ BICYCLING

Rodale Press, Inc., 135 N. Sixth St., Emmaus PA 18098. (610)967-8722. Fax: (610)967-8960. Website: www.bicycling.com. **Contact:** William Strickland, executive editor. **50% freelance written.** Magazine published 11 times/year. "*Bicycling* features articles about fitness, training, nutrition, touring, racing, equipment, clothing, maintenance, new technology, industry developments, and other topics of interest to committed bicycle riders. Editorially, we advocate for the sport, industry, and the cycling consumer." Estab. 1961. Circ. 280,000. **Pays on acceptance.** Byline given. Buys all rights. Submit seasonal material 6 months in advance. Accepts previously published material. Responds in 2 months to queries. Sample copy for $3.50. Writer's guidelines for #10 SASE.

> Oₙ "There are 2 great break-in opportunities for writers: 1.) 'Noblest Invention' (750-word column) offers writers a chance to tell us why the bicycle is the greatest bit of machinery ever created. 2.) 'Ask the Wrench' maintenance feature showcases a local bike mechanic's know-how. If you know a great mechanic, this is a chance to get in the magazine."

Nonfiction "We are a cycling lifestyle magazine. We seek readable, clear, well-informed pieces that show how cycling is part of our readers' lives. We sometimes run articles that are inspirational, and inspiration might flavor even our most technical pieces. No fiction or poetry." How-to (on all phases of bicycle touring, repair, maintenance, commuting, new products, clothing, riding technique, nutrition for cyclists, conditioning), photo feature (on cycling events), technical (opinions about technology), travel (bicycling must be central here), fitness. **Buys 10 unsolicited mss/year.** Query. **Payment varies.** Sometimes pays expenses of writers on assignment.

Reprints Send tearsheet or photocopy and information about when and where the material previously appeared.

Photos State availability of or send photos with submission. Pays $15-250/photo. Captions, model releases required.

Tips "Don't send us travel pieces about where you went on summer vacation. Travel/adventure stories have to be about something larger than just visiting someplace on your bike and meeting quirky locals."

$ $ BIKE MAGAZINE

Primedia Enthusiast, P.O. Box 1028, Dana Point CA 92629. (949)496-5922. Fax: (949)496-7849. E-mail: bikemag @primedia.com. Website: www.bikemag.com. **Contact:** Ron Ige, editor. **35% freelance written.** Magazine publishes 8 times/year covering mountain biking. Estab. 1993. Circ. 170,000. Pays on publication. Publishes ms an average of 2 months after acceptance. Byline given. Offers 25% kill fee. Buys first North American serial rights. Editorial lead time 4 months. Submit seasonal material 6 months in advance. Responds in 2 months to queries. Sample copy for $8. Writer's guidelines for #10 SASE.

> Oₙ *Bike* receives many travel-related queries and is seeking more investigative journalism on matters that affect mountain bikers. Writers have a much better chance of publication if they tackle larger issues that affect mountain bikers, such as trail access or sport controversies (i.e., drugs in cycling). If you do submit a travel article, know that a great location is not a story in itself—there must also be a theme. Examine back issues before submitting a travel story; if *Bike* has covered your location before, they won't again (for at least 4-5 years).

Nonfiction Writers should submit queries in March (April 1 deadline) for consideration for the following year's editions. All queries received by April 1 will be considered and editors will contact writers about stories they are interested in. Queries should include word count. Humor, interview/profile, personal experience, photo feature, travel. **Buys 20 mss/year.** Length: 1,000-2,500 words. **Pays 50¢/word.** Sometimes pays expenses of writers on assignment.

Photos David Reddick, photo editor. Send photos with submission. Reviews color transparencies, b&w prints. Buys one-time rights. Negotiates payment individually. Captions, identification of subjects required.

Columns/Departments Splatter (news), 300 words; Urb (details a great ride within 1 hour of a major metropolitan area), 600-700 words. Query year-round for Splatter and Urb. **Buys 20 mss/year. Pays 50¢/word.**

Tips "Remember that we focus on hard core mountain biking, not beginners. We're looking for ideas that deliver the excitement and passion of the sport in ways that aren't common or predictable. Ideas should be vivid, unbiased, irreverent, probing, fun, humorous, funky, quirky, smart, good. Great feature ideas are always welcome, especially features on cultural matters or issues in the sport. However, you're much more likely to get published in *Bike* if you send us great ideas for short articles. In particular we need stories for our Splatter, a front-of-the-book section devoted to news, funny anecdotes, quotes, and odds and ends. These stories range from 50 to 300 words. We also need personality profiles of 600 words or so for our People Who Ride section. Racers are OK but we're more interested in grassroots people with interesting personalities—it doesn't matter if they're Mother Theresas or scumbags, so long as they make mountain biking a little more interesting. Short descriptions of great rides are very welcome for our Urb column; the length should be from 600-700 words.''

$ BIKE MIDWEST

Columbus Sports Publications, 1350 W. Fifth Ave., #30, Columbus OH 43212. (614)486-2202. Fax: (614)486-3650. E-mail: nweis@buckeyesports.com. **Contact:** Nicole Weis, editor. **35% freelance written.** Monthly (April-October) tabloid covering bicycling. ''We like articles to be in a more casual voice so our readers feel more like a friend than just a customer.'' Estab. 1986. Circ. 35,000. Pays on publication. Publishes ms an average of 1 month after acceptance. Byline given. Offers 100% or $75 kill fee. Buys all rights. Editorial lead time 1 month. Submit seasonal material 1 month in advance. Accepts queries by mail, e-mail, fax. Accepts simultaneous submissions. Responds in 2 months. Sample copy and writer's guidelines free.

Nonfiction Essays, general interest, historical/nostalgic, how-to (bicycle mechanics, i.e., how to change a flat tire, etc.), humor, inspirational, interview/profile, new product, opinion, personal experience, technical, travel. Special issues: April and October issues cover travel and tourism by bicycle. Nothing nonbike related. **Buys 14 mss/year.** Send complete ms. Length: 1,000-2,000 words. **Pays $35-75.**

Reprints Accepts previously published submissions.

Photos Send photos with submission. Reviews negatives, $3\frac{1}{2} \times 5$ prints. Buys all rights. Offers $25-50/photo. Captions, identification of subjects, model releases required.

Columns/Departments Metal Cowboy (experiences on a bicycle), 1,800 words; Bicycling News (experiences in bicycling), 1,200 words. **Buys 14 mss/year.** Send complete ms. **Pays $35-75.**

Tips ''Articles must be informative and/or engaging. Our readers like to be entertained. They also look for lots of information when articles are technical (product reviews, etc.)''

$ $ CYCLE CALIFORNIA! MAGAZINE

1702-H Meridian Ave., #289, San Jose CA 95125. (408)924-0270. Fax: (408)292-3005. E-mail: tcorral@cyclecalifornia .com. Website: www.cyclecalifornia.com. **Contact:** Tracy L. Corral, editor/publisher. **75% freelance written.** Magazine published 11 times/year ''covering Northern California bicycling events, races, people. Issues (topics) covered include bicycle commuting, bicycle politics, touring, racing, nostalgia, history, anything at all to do with riding a bike.'' Estab. 1995. Circ. 26,000. Pays on publication. Publishes ms an average of 3 months after acceptance. Byline given. Buys first North American serial rights. Editorial lead time 6 weeks. Submit seasonal material 6 weeks in advance. Accepts queries by mail, e-mail, phone. Accepts simultaneous submissions. Responds in 1 month to queries. Sample copy for 10×13 SAE with 3 first-class stamps. Writer's guidelines for #10 SASE.

Nonfiction Historical/nostalgic, how-to, interview/profile, opinion, personal experience, technical, travel. Special issues: Bicycle Tour & Travel (January/February). No articles about any sport that doesn't relate to bicycling, no product reviews. **Buys 36 mss/year.** Query with or without published clips. Length: 500-1,500 words. **Pays 3-10¢/word.**

Photos Send photos with submission. Reviews 3×5 prints. Buys one-time rights. Negotiates payment individually. Identification of subjects required.

Columns/Departments Buys 2-3 mss/year. Query with published clips. **Pays 3-10¢/word.**

Tips ''E-mail or call editor with good ideas. While we don't exclude writers from other parts of the country, articles really should reflect a Northern California slant, or be of general interest to bicyclists. We prefer stories written by people who like and use their bikes.''

⊘ CYCLE WORLD

Hachette Filipacchi Media U.S., Inc., 1499 Monrovia Ave., Newport Beach CA 92663. (949)720-5300. E-mail: cycleworld@hfmus.com. Website: www.cycleworld.com. Editor-in-Chief: David Edwards. Monthly magazine geared towards motorcycle owners and buyers, accesory buyers, potential buyers and enthusiasts of the overall sport of motorcycling. Circ. 319,489.

• Query before submitting.

Ⓝ ⊘ MOUNTAIN BIKE

Rodale, Inc., 135 N. 6th Street, Emmaus PA 18049-2441. (610)967-8722. Fax: (610)967-8960. Website: www.mo untainbike.com. Editor-in-Chief: Stephen Madden. Magazine published 11 times/year covering every aspect of the bicycle sport including new products and technology, riding techniques, destinations, health and fitness as well as racing and enviromental issues. Circ. 150,328.

- Query before submitting.

N THE RIDE

East Coast Bike Culture, P.O. Box 750064, Arlington MA 02475. (781)641-9515. Fax: (781)641-9527. E-mail: ridezine@ridezine.com. Website: www.ridezine.com. Editor: Richard Fries. **Contact:** Francine Latil, managing editor. **25% freelance written.** Magazine published 8 times/year covering cycling culture in the Northeast. *The Ride* probes and merges the different genres of cyclists that make up East Coast bike culture. "Our readers look to the magazine as their main resource for provocative articles on racing, advocacy, industry, history, travel, and tourism." Estab. 1993. Circ. 10,000. Pays on publication. Publishes ms an average of 2 months after acceptance. Byline given. Buys first rights. Editorial lead time 2-3 months. Submit seasonal material 4 months in advance. Accepts queries by mail, e-mail. Accepts simultaneous submissions. Responds in 1 month to queries; 2 months to mss. Sample copy for $5.

Nonfiction "We seek articles with distinct and intriguing East Coast angles. We look for articles that report on people, places, industries, and things that help shape bike culture in our region." Exposé, interview/profile, travel. "No fiction or poetry, and please don't send a proposal for a bike ride you took in our region unless it is uniquely tied in with the topics we cover." Query with published clips. Length: 500-1,500 words. **Payment varies.**

Photos Deb Fries, production manager. State availability with submission. Reviews GIF/JPEG files.

Columns/Departments Lanterne Rouge (personal experience), 700-1,100 words; Racing (race reporting), 500-700 words; Urban Fringe (urban riding/racing and couriers), 500-700 words; Outta' Here (travel by bike). Query with published clips. **Payment varies.**

Tips "That a bike-related event occurs in our region is a basic foundation for our articles, but we want to show our readers how/why it matters (i.e. politically, historically, recreationally, or culturally)."

BOATING

N BASS & WALLEYE BOATS

The Magazine of Performance Fishing Boats, Poole Publications, Inc., 20700 Belshaw Ave., Carson CA 90746. (310)537-6322. Fax: (310)537-8735. E-mail: info@bassandwalleyeboats.com. Website: www.bassandwalleyeboats.com. Editor: Steve Quinlan. **Contact:** Sylvia Alarid, managing editor. **50% freelance written.** "*Bass & Walleye Boats* is published 9 times/year for the bass and walleye fisherman/boater. Directed to give priority to the boats, the tech, the how-to, the after-market add-ons and the devices that help anglers enjoy their boating experience." Estab. 1994. Circ. 65,000. **Pays on acceptance.** Byline given. Offers 25% kill fee. Buys first North American serial rights. Editorial lead time 2 months. Submit seasonal material 3 months in advance. Accepts queries by mail. Sample copy for $3.95 and 9 × 12 SAE with 7 first-class stamps. Writer's guidelines free.

Nonfiction General interest, how-to, interview/profile, photo feature, technical. No fiction. **Buys about 120 mss/year.** Query. Length: 1,000-3,000 words.

Photos State availability with submission. Reviews transparencies, 35mm slides. Buys one-time rights. Negotiates payment individually. Captions, identification of subjects required.

Tips "Write from and for the bass and walleye boaters' perspective."

N $ $ BOATWORKS

98 N. Washington St., 2nd Floor, Boston MA 02114. (617)720-8600. Fax: (617)723-0912. E-mail: bwmail@boatworksmagazine.com. Website: www.boatworksmagazine.com. Editor: Peter Nielsen. **Contact:** Mark Corke, senior editor. **50% freelance written.** Quarterly DIY magazine for practically-minded boat owners. Explains how boat systems work in easy-to-understand, profusely illustrated features. Each issue has several step-by-step photographic guides to carrying out maintenance and improvement projects. Explains boat design and construction, and all technical aspects of sailing and boating. Readers are encouraged to submit stories based on their own projects and experiences.

Nonfiction Buys 30 mss/year. Length: 250-3,000 words. **Pays $100-750.**

Photos Prefers transparencies, but high resolution digital photos (300 dpi) are also accepted, as are high-quality color prints. Prints should have negatives attached. Pays $25 and up, depending on the size used.

N $ $ $ CANOE & KAYAK MAGAZINE

Canoe America Associates, 10526 NE 68th St., Suite 3, Kirkland WA 98033. (425)827-6363. Website: www.canoekayak.com. Editor: Ross Prather. **Contact:** Robin Stanton, managing editor. **75% freelance written.** Bimonthly magazine. "*Canoe & Kayak Magazine* is North America's No. 1 paddlesports resource. Our readers include flatwater and whitewater canoeists and kayakers of all skill levels. We provide comprehensive information on destinations, technique and equipment. Beyond that, we cover canoe and kayak camping, safety, the environment, and the history of boats and sport." Estab. 1972. Circ. 70,000. Pays on publication. Publishes ms an average of 6 months after acceptance. Byline given. first international rights, which includes electronic and anthology rights Editorial lead time 6 months. Submit seasonal material 8 months in advance. Accepts queries by mail, e-mail. Responds in 2 months to queries. Sample copy and writer's guidelines for 9×12 SAE with 7 first-class stamps.

> O⚊ Break in with good out-of-the-way destination or Put-In (news) pieces with excellent photos. "Take a good look at the types of articles we publish before sending us any sort of query."

Nonfiction Historical/nostalgic, how-to (canoe, kayak camp, load boats, paddle whitewater, etc.), personal experience, photo feature, technical, travel. Special issues: Whitewater Paddling; Beginner's Guide; Kayak Touring; Canoe Journal. "No cartoons, poems, stories in which bad judgement is portrayed or 'Me and Molly' articles." **Buys 25 mss/year.** Query with or without published clips or send complete ms. Length: 400-2,500 words. **Pays $100-800 for assigned articles; $100-500 for unsolicited articles.**

Photos "Some activities we cover are canoeing, kayaking, canoe fishing, camping, canoe sailing or poling, backpacking (when compatible with the main activity) and occasionally inflatable boats. We are not interested in groups of people in rafts, photos showing disregard for the environment or personal safety, gasoline-powered engines unless appropriate to the discussion, or unskilled persons taking extraordinary risks." State availability with submission. Reviews 35mm transparencies, 4×6 prints. Buys one-time rights. Offers $75-500/photo. Captions, identification of subjects, model releases required.

Columns/Departments Put In (environment, conservation, events), 500 words; Destinations (canoe and kayak destinations in US, Canada), 1,500 words; Essays, 750 words. **Buys 40 mss/year.** Send complete ms. **Pays $100-350.**

Fillers Anecdotes, facts, newsbreaks. **Buys 20/year.** Length: 200-500 words. **Pays $25-50.**

Tips "Start with Put-In articles (short featurettes) or short, unique equipment reviews. Or give us the best, most exciting article we've ever seen—with great photos. Read the magazine before submitting."

$ $ $ CHESAPEAKE BAY MAGAZINE

Boating at Its Best, Chesapeake Bay Communications, 1819 Bay Ridge Ave., Annapolis MD 21403. (410)263-2662. Fax: (410)267-6924. E-mail: editor@cbmmag.net. **Contact:** Jane Meneely, managing editor. **60% freelance written.** Monthly magazine covering boating and the Chesapeake Bay. "Our readers are boaters. Our writers should know boats and boating. Read the magazine before submitting." Estab. 1972. Circ. 46,000. Pays within 2 months after acceptance. Publishes ms an average of 1 year after acceptance. Byline given. Buys first North American serial rights. Editorial lead time 1 year. Submit seasonal material 1 year in advance. Accepts queries by mail, e-mail, fax, phone. Accepts simultaneous submissions. Responds in 2 months to queries; 3 months to mss. Sample copy for $5.19 prepaid.

> O⚊ "Read our Channel 9 column and give us some new ideas. These are short news items, profiles, and updates (200-800 words)."

Nonfiction Destinations, boating adventures, how-to, marina reviews, history, nature, environment, lifestyles, personal and institutional profiles, boat-type profiles, boatbuilding, boat restoration, boating anecdotes, boating news. **Buys 30 mss/year.** Query with published clips. Length: 300-3,000 words. **Pays $100-1,000.** Pays expenses of writers on assignment.

Photos Buys one-time rights. Offers $75-250/photo, $400/day rate for assignment photography. Captions, identification of subjects required.

Tips "Send us unedited writing samples (not clips) that show the writer can write, not just string words together. We look for well-organized, lucid, lively, intelligent writing."

$ $ $ $ CRUISING WORLD

The Sailing Co., 5 John Clarke Rd., Newport RI 02840-0992. (401)845-5100. Fax: (401)845-5180. Website: www.cruisingworld.com. Editor: Herb McCormick. Managing Editor: Elaine Lembo. **Contact:** Tim Murphy, executive editor. **60% freelance written.** Monthly magazine covering sailing, cruising/adventuring, do-it-yourself boat improvements. *Cruising World* is a publication by and for sailboat owners who spend time in home waters as well as voyaging the world. Its readership is extremely loyal, savvy, and driven by independent thinking." Estab. 1974. Circ. 155,000. **Pays on acceptance for articles;** on publication for photography. Publishes ms an average of 18 months after acceptance. Byline given. Buys 6-month, all-world, first time rights (amendable). Editorial lead time 3 months. Submit seasonal material 1 year in advance. Accepts queries by mail. Responds in 1 month to queries; 4 months to mss. Sample copy for free. Writer's guidelines online.

Nonfiction Book excerpts, essays, exposé, general interest, historical/nostalgic, how-to, humor, interview/ profile, new product, opinion, personal experience, photo feature, technical, travel. No travel articles that have nothing to do with cruising aboard sailboats from 20-50 feet in length. **Buys dozens of mss/year.** Send complete ms. **Pays $50-1,500 for assigned articles; $50-1,000 for unsolicited articles.** Sometimes pays expenses of writers on assignment.

Photos Send photos with submission. Reviews negatives, transparencies, color slides preferred. Buys one-time rights. Negotiates payment individually. Also buys stand-alone photos. Captions required.

Columns/Departments Shoreline (sailing news, people, and short features; contact Nim Marsh), 500 words maximum; Hands-on Sailor (refit, voyaging, seamanship, how-to; contact Darrell Nicholson), 1,000-1,500 words. **Buys dozens of mss/year.** Query with or without published clips or send complete ms. **Pays $100-700.**

Tips "*Cruising World's* readers know exactly what they want to read, so our best advice to freelancers is to carefully read the magazine and envision which exact section or department would be the appropriate place for proposed submissions."

Ⓝ $ $ GO BOATING MAGAZINE

America's Family Boating Magazine, Duncan McIntosh Co., 17782 Cowan, Suite C, Irvine CA 92614. (949)660-6150. E-mail: editorial@goboatingamerica.com. Website: www.goboatingamerica.com. **Contact:** Mike Telleria, managing editor. **60% freelance written.** Magazine published 8 times/year covering recreational trailer boats. Typical reader "owns a power boat between 14 and 32 feet long and has 3-9 years experience. Boat reports are mostly written by staff while features and most departments are provided by freelancers. We are looking for freelancers who can write well and who have at least a working knowledge of recreational power boating and the industry behind it." Estab. 1997. Circ. 100,000. Pays on publication. Publishes ms an average of 4 months after acceptance. Accepts simultaneous submissions. Responds in 3 months to queries. Sample copy for free. Writer's guidelines for #10 SASE.

Nonfiction General interest, how-to, humor, new product, personal experience, travel. **Buys 20-25 mss/year.** Query. Length: 1,400-1,600 words. **Pays $150-450.** Sometimes pays expenses of writers on assignment.

Photos State availability with submission. Reviews transparencies, prints, digital images. Buys one-time rights. Offers $50-250/photo. Identification of subjects, model releases required.

Fillers Anecdotes, facts, newsbreaks. Length: 250-500 words. **Pays $50-100.**

Tips "We are looking for solid writers who are familiar with power boating and who can educate, entertain, and enlighten our readers with well-written and researched feature stories."

GOOD OLD BOAT

The Sailing Magazine for the Rest of Us, Partnership for Excellence, Inc., 7340 Niagara Lane N., Maple Grove MN 55311. (763)420-8923. Fax: (763)420-8921. E-mail: karen@goodoldboat.com. Website: www.goodoldboat.com. **Contact:** Karen Larson, editor. **90% freelance written.** Bimonthly magazine covering sailing. "*Good Old Boat* magazine focuses on maintaining, upgrading, and loving cruising sailboats that are 10 years old and older. Readers see themselves as part of a community of sailors who share similar maintenance and replacement concerns which are not generally addressed in the other sailing publications. Our readers do much of the writing about projects they have done on their boats and the joy they receive from sailing them." Estab. 1998. Circ. 30,000. Pays 2 months in advance of publication. Publishes ms an average of 12-18 months after acceptance. Buys first North American serial rights. Editorial lead time 4 months. Submit seasonal material 12-15 months in advance. Accepts queries by mail, e-mail, fax. Accepts simultaneous submissions. Responds in 1-2 weeks to queries; 2-6 months to mss. Sample copy for free. Writer's guidelines online.

Nonfiction General interest, historical/nostalgic, how-to, interview/profile, personal experience, photo feature, technical. "Articles which are written by nonsailors serve no purpose for us." **Buys 150 mss/year.** Query or send complete ms. **Payment varies, refer to published rates on website.**

Photos State availability of or send photos with submission. "We do not pay additional fees for photos except when they run as covers, center spread photo features, or are specifically requested to support an article."

Tips "Our shorter pieces are the best way to break into our magazine. We publish many Simple Solutions and Quick & Easy pieces. These are how-to tips that have worked for sailors on their boats. In addition, our readers send lists of projects which they've done on their boats and which they could write for publication. We respond to these queries with a thumbs up or down by project. Articles are submitted on speculation, but they have a better chance of being accepted once we have approved of the suggested topic."

$ $ HEARTLAND BOATING

The Waterways Journal, Inc., 319 N. Fourth St., Suite 650, St. Louis MO 63102. (314)241-4310. Fax: (314)241-4207. E-mail: info@heartlandboating.com. Website: www.heartlandboating.com. **Contact:** Lee Braff, editor. **70% freelance written.** Magazine published 9 times/year covering recreational boating on the inland waterways of mid-America, from the Great Lakes south to the Gulf of Mexico and over to the east. "Our writers must have experience with, and a great interest in, boating, particularly in the area described above. *Heartland Boating's* content is both informative and humorous—describing boating life as the heartland boater knows it. We are boaters and enjoy the outdoor, water-oriented way of life. The content reflects the challenge, joy, and excitement of our way of life afloat. We are devoted to both power and sailboating enthusiasts throughout middle America; houseboats are included. The focus is on the freshwater inland rivers and lakes of the heartland, primarily the waters of the Arkansas, Tennessee, Cumberland, Ohio, Missouri, Illinois, and Mississippi rivers, the Tennessee-Tombigbee Waterway, The Gulf Intracoastal Waterway, and the lakes along these waterways." Estab. 1989. Circ. 12,000. Pays on publication. Byline given. Buys first North American serial, first, electronic rights. Editorial lead time 3 months. Submit seasonal material 6 months in advance. Accepts queries by mail, e-mail, phone. Accepts previously published material. Responds in 2 months to queries. Sample copy for $5. Writer's guidelines by e-mail.

Nonfiction How-to (articles about navigation maintenance, upkeep, or making time spent aboard easier and more comfortable), humor, personal experience, technical, travel (along waterways and on-land stops). Special issues: Annual Boat Show issue in January/February looks at what is coming out on the market for the coming year. **Buys 100 mss/year.** Query with published clips or send complete ms. Length: 850-1,500 words. **Pays $100-250.**

Reprints Send tearsheet, photocopy or typed ms and information about when and where the material previously appeared.

Photos Send photos with submission. Reviews transparencies, prints, digital images. Buys one-time rights. Offers no additional payment for photos accepted with ms.

Columns/Departments Books Aboard (book reviews), Handy Hints (small boat improvement projects), both 850 words. **Buys 18 mss/year.** Query with published clips or send complete ms. **Pays $75-150.**

Tips "We plan the next year's schedule starting in mid-May. So submitting material between May and July will be most helpful for planning, although we accept submissions year-round."

$ $⊘ HOUSEBOAT MAGAZINE

The Family Magazine for the American Houseboater, Harris Publishing, Inc., 360 B St., Idaho Falls ID 83402. Fax: (208)522-5241. E-mail: hbeditor@houseboatmagazine.com. Website: www.houseboatmagazine.com. **Contact:** Brady L. Kay, managing editor. **40% freelance written.** Monthly magazine for houseboaters, who enjoy reading everything that reflects the unique houseboating lifestyle. If it is not a houseboat-specific article, please do not query. Estab. 1990. Circ. 25,000. Pays on publication. Publishes ms an average of 3 months after acceptance. Byline given. Offers 25% kill fee. Buys first North American serial, electronic rights. Editorial lead time 6 months. Submit seasonal material 6 months in advance. Accepts simultaneous submissions. Responds in 1 month to queries; 2 months to mss. Sample copy for $5. Writer's guidelines online.

• *No unsolicited mss.* Accepts queries by mail and fax, but e-mail strongly preferred.

Nonfiction How-to, interview/profile, new product, personal experience, travel. **Buys 36 mss/year.** Query. Length: 1,000-1,200 words. **Pays $150-300.**

Photos Often required as part of submission package. Color prints discouraged. Digital prints are unacceptable. Seldom purchases photos without ms, but occasionally buys cover photos. Reviews transparencies, high-resolution electronic images. Buys one-time rights. Offers no additional payment for photos accepted with ms. Captions, model releases required.

Columns/Departments Pays $100-200.

Tips "As a general rule, how-to articles are always in demand. So are stories on unique houseboats or houseboaters. You are less likely to break in with a travel piece that does not revolve around specific people or groups. Personality profile pieces with excellent supporting photography are your best bet."

$ $ LAKELAND BOATING

The Magazine for Great Lakes Boaters, O'Meara-Brown Publications, Inc., 727 S. Dearborn, Suite 812, Chicago IL 60605. (312)276-0610. Fax: (312)276-0619. E-mail: lb@omeara-brown.com. Website: www.lakelandboating. com. **50% freelance written.** Magazine covering Great Lakes boating. Estab. 1946. Circ. 38,000. Pays on publication. Byline given. Buys first North American serial rights. Accepts queries by e-mail. Responds in 4 months to queries. Sample copy for $5.50 and 9×12 SAE with 6 first-class stamps. Writer's guidelines free.

Nonfiction Book excerpts, historical/nostalgic, how-to, interview/profile, personal experience, photo feature, technical, travel, must relate to boating in Great Lakes. No inspirational, religious, exposé or poetry. **Buys 20-30 mss/year.** Length: 800-3,00 words. **Pays $100-600.**

Photos State availability with submission. Reviews prefers 35mm transparencies. Buys one-time rights. Captions required.

Columns/Departments Bosun's Locker (technical or how-to pieces on boating), 100-1,000 words. **Buys 40 mss/year.** Query. **Pays $30-100.**

$ LIVING ABOARD

Acres, U.S.A., P.O. Box 91299, Austin TX 78709-1299. (512)892-4446. Fax: (512)892-4448. E-mail: editor@living aboard.com. Website: www.livingaboard.com. Managing Editor: Fred Walters. **Contact:** Linda Ridihalgh, edi-

Consumer Magazines

tor. **95% freelance written.** Bimonthly magazine covering living on boats/cruising. Estab. 1973. Circ. 7,500. Pays on publication. Publishes ms an average of 3-6 months after acceptance. Byline given. Buys first North American serial, first, one-time, second serial (reprint) rights. Accepts queries by mail, e-mail, fax. Responds in 1-2 weeks to queries; 1-2 months to mss. Sample copy online. Writer's guidelines free.

Nonfiction How-to (buy, furnish, maintain, provision a boat), interview/profile, personal experience, technical (as relates to boats), travel (on the water), Cooking Aboard with Recipes. Send complete ms. **Pays 5¢/word.**

Photos Pays $5/photo; $50/cover photo.

Columns/Departments Cooking Aboard (how to prepare healthy and nutritious meals in the confines of a galley; how to entertain aboard a boat), 1,000-1,500 words; Environmental Notebook (articles pertaining to clean water, fish, waterfowl, water environment), 750-1,000 words. **Buys 6 mss/year.** Send complete ms. **Pays 5¢/word.**

Tips "Articles should have a positive tone and promote the liveaboard lifestyle."

MOTOR BOATING

Time 4 Media, 18 Marshall St., Suite 114, Norwalk CT 06854-2237. (203)299-5950. Fax: (203)299-5951. Website: www.motorboating.com. Monthly magazine geared toward the owners of power boats 20' to 60'. Devoted to helping its readers make educated decisions about how to buy, equip, maintain, and enjoy their boats. Circ. 155,000. Editorial lead time 6 weeks. Accepts queries by mail. Responds in 6-8 weeks to queries.

Nonfiction "We look for articles on adventure travel by boat; investigative stories on issues important to recreational power boaters; and informative service pieces on boat/engine care and maintenance." Short tips on boat maintenance and repair. Query with published clips. Length: 1,500-2,000 words.

$ NORTHERN BREEZES, SAILING MAGAZINE

Northern Breezes, Inc., 3949 Winnetka Ave. N, Minneapolis MN 55427. E-mail: alan@sailingbreezes.com. Website: www.sailingbreezes.com. **Contact:** Alan Kretzschmar. **70% freelance written.** Magazine published 8 times/year for the Great Lakes and Midwest sailing community. Focusing on regional cruising, racing, and day sailing. Estab. 1989. Circ. 22,300. Pays on publication. Byline given. Buys first North American serial rights. Editorial lead time 1 months. Submit seasonal material 3 months in advance. Accepts queries by mail, e-mail, fax, phone. Accepts previously published material. Responds in 1 month to queries; 2 months to mss. Sample copy for free. Writer's guidelines online.

Nonfiction Book excerpts, how-to (sailing topics), humor, inspirational, interview/profile, new product, personal experience, photo feature, technical, travel. No boating reviews. **Buys 24 mss/year.** Query with published clips. Length: 300-3,500 words.

Reprints Accepts previously published submissions.

Photos Send photos with submission. Reviews negatives, 35mm slides, 3×5 or 4×6 prints. Buys one-time rights. Offers no additional payment for photos accepted with ms. Captions required.

Columns/Departments This Old Boat (sailboat), 500-1,000 words; Surveyor's Notebook, 500-800 words. **Buys 8 mss/year.** Query with published clips. **Pays $50-150.**

Tips "Query with a regional connection already in mind."

$ $ $ $ OFFSHORE

Northeast Boating at Its Best, Offshore Communications, Inc., 500 Victory Rd., Marina Bay, North Quincy MA 02171. (617)221-1400. Fax: (617)847-1871. E-mail: editors@offshoremag.net. Website: www.offshoremag.net. **Contact:** Editorial Department. **80% freelance written.** Monthly magazine covering power and sailboating on the coast from Maine to New Jersey. Estab. 1976. Circ. 35,000. **Pays on acceptance.** Publishes ms an average of 5 months after acceptance. Byline given. Offers 50% kill fee. Buys first North American serial rights. Submit seasonal material 6 months in advance. Accepts queries by mail. Accepts simultaneous submissions. Writer's guidelines for #10 SASE.

Nonfiction Articles on boats, boating, New York, New Jersey, and New England coastal places and people, Northeast coastal history. **Buys 90 mss/year.** Query with or without published clips or send complete ms. Length: 1,200-2,500 words. **Pays $500-1,500 for features, depending on length.**

Photos Reviews 35mm slides and digital images. Buys one-time rights. Pays $150-800. Identification of subjects required.

Tips "Writers must demonstrate a familiarity with boats and with the Northeast coast. Specifically we are looking for articles on boating destinations, boating events (such as races, rendezvous, and boat parades), on-the-water boating adventures, boating culture, maritime museums, maritime history, boating issues (such as safety and the environment), seamanship, fishing, how-to stories, and essays. Note: Since *Offshore* is a regional magazine, all stories must focus on the area from New Jersey to Maine. We are always open to new people, the best of whom may gradually work their way into regular writing assignments. Important to ask for (and follow) our writer's guidelines if you're not familiar with our magazine."

$ $⬚ PACIFIC YACHTING

Western Canada's Premier Boating Magazine, OP Publishing, Ltd., 1080 Howe St., Suite 900, Vancouver BC V6Z 2T1 Canada. (604)606-4644. Fax: (604)687-1925. E-mail: editor@pacificyachting.com. Website: www.pacificyachting.com. **90% freelance written.** Monthly magazine covering all aspects of recreational boating on British Columbia's coast. "The bulk of our writers and photographers not only come from the local boating community, many of them were long-time *PY* readers before coming aboard as a contributor. The *PY* reader buys the magazine to read about new destinations or changes to old haunts on the British Columbia coast and to learn the latest about boats and gear." Circ. 19,000. Pays on publication. Publishes ms an average of 6 months after acceptance. Byline given. Buys first North American serial, simultaneous rights. Editorial lead time 4 months. Submit seasonal material 6 months in advance. Accepts queries by mail, e-mail, fax. Sample copy for $5.95, plus postage charged to credit card. Writer's guidelines free.

Nonfiction Historical/nostalgic (British Columbia coast only), how-to, humor, interview/profile, personal experience, technical (boating related), travel, cruising, and destination on the British Columbia coast. "No articles from writers who are obviously not boaters!" Query. Length: 1,500-2,000 words. **Pays $150-500.** Pays expenses of writers on assignment.

Photos Send photos with submission. Reviews transparencies, 4×6 prints, and slides. Buys one-time rights. Offers no additional payment for photos accepted with ms. Offers $25-300 for photos accepted alone. Identification of subjects required.

Columns/Departments Currents (current events, trade and people news, boat gatherings, and festivities), 50-250 words. Reflections; Cruising, both 800-1,000 words. Query. **Pay varies.**

Tips "Our reader wants you to balance important navigation details with first-person observations, blending the practical with the romantic. Write tight, write short, write with the reader in mind, write to inform, write to entertain. Be specific, accurate, and historic."

$ $ PONTOON & DECK BOAT

Harris Publishing, Inc., 360 B. St., Idaho Falls ID 83402. (208)524-7000. Fax: (208)522-5241. E-mail: brady@pdbmagazine.com. Website: www.pdbmagazine.com. **Contact:** Brady L. Kay, editor. **15% freelance written.** Magazine published 10 times/year. "We are a boating niche publication geared toward the pontoon and deck boating lifestyle and consumer market. Our audience is comprised of people who utilize these boats for varied family activities and fishing. Our magazine is promotional of the PDB industry and its major players. We seek to give the reader a twofold reason to read our publication: to celebrate the lifestyle, and to do it aboard a first-class craft." Estab. 1995. Circ. 84,000. Pays on publication. Byline given. Buys one-time rights. Editorial lead time 2 months. Submit seasonal material 3 months in advance. Accepts simultaneous submissions. Responds in 6 weeks to queries; 3 months to mss. Sample copy and writer's guidelines free.

Nonfiction How-to, personal experience, technical, remodeling, rebuilding. "We are saturated with travel pieces, no general boating, humor, fiction, or poetry." **Buys 15 mss/year.** Query with or without published clips or send complete ms. Length: 600-2,000 words. **Pays $50-300.** Sometimes pays expenses of writers on assignment.

Photos State availability with submission. Reviews transparencies. Rights negotiable. Captions, model releases required.

Columns/Departments No Wake Zone (short, fun quips); Better Boater (how-to). **Buys 6-12 mss/year.** Query with published clips. **Pays $50-150.**

Tips "Be specific to pontoon and deck boats. Any general boating material goes to the slush pile. The more you can tie together the lifestyle, attitudes, and the PDB industry, the more interest we'll take in what you send us."

$ $ $⬚ POWER & MOTORYACHT

Primedia, Inc., 260 Madison Ave., 8th Floor, New York NY 10016. (917)256-2200. Fax: (917)256-2282. E-mail: diane.byrne@primedia.com. Website: www.powerandmotoryacht.com. Editor: Richard Thiel. Managing Editor: Eileen Mansfield. **Contact:** Diane M. Byrne, executive editor. **25% freelance written.** Monthly magazine covering powerboats 24 feet and larger with special emphasis on the 35-foot-plus market. "Readers have an average of 32 years experience boating, and we give them accurate advice on how to choose, operate, and maintain their boats as well as what electronics and gear will help them pursue their favorite pastime. In addition, since powerboating is truly a lifestyle and not just a hobby for them, *Power & Motoryacht* reports on a host of other topics that affect their enjoyment of the water: chartering, sportfishing, and the environment, among others. Articles must therefore be clear, concise, and authoritative; knowledge of the marine industry is mandatory. Include personal experience and information for marine industry experts where appropriate." Estab. 1985. Circ. 157,000. **Pays on acceptance.** Publishes ms an average of 4-6 months after acceptance. Byline given. Offers 33% kill fee. Buys all rights. Editorial lead time 4-6 months. Submit seasonal material 4-6 months in advance. Accepts queries by mail, e-mail, fax. Responds in 1 month to queries. Sample copy for 10×12 SASE. Writer's guidelines for #10 SASE.

Nonfiction How-to, interview/profile, personal experience, photo feature, travel. *No unsolicited mss* or articles about sailboats and/or sailing yachts (including motorsailers). **Buys 20-25 mss/year.** Query with published clips. Length: 800-1,500 words. **Pays $500-1,000 for assigned articles.** Sometimes pays expenses of writers on assignment.

Photos Aimee Colon, art director. State availability with submission. Reviews 8×10 transparencies, GIF/JPEG files (minimum 300 dpi). Buys one-time rights. Offers no additional payment for photos accepted with ms. Captions, identification of subjects required.

Tips "Take a clever or even unique approach to a subject, particularly if the topic is dry/technical. Pitch us on yacht cruises you've taken, particularly if they're in off-the-beaten-path locations."

$ $⬛ POWER BOATING CANADA

1020 Brevik Place, Suites 4 & 5, Mississauga ON L4W 4N7 Canada. (905)624-8218. Fax: (905)624-6764. E-mail: editor@powerboating.com. Website: www.powerboating.com. **70% freelance written.** Bimonthly magazine covering recreational power boating. "*Power Boating Canada* offers boating destinations, how-to features, boat tests (usually staff written), lifestyle pieces—with a Canadian slant—and appeal to recreational power boaters across the country." Estab. 1984. Circ. 42,000. Pays on publication. Publishes ms an average of 3 months after acceptance. Byline given. Buys first North American serial rights. Editorial lead time 2 months. Submit seasonal material 3 months in advance. Accepts previously published material. Responds in 1 month to queries; 2 months to mss. Sample copy for free.

Nonfiction "Any articles related to the sport of power boating, especially boat tests." Historical/nostalgic, how-to, interview/profile, personal experience, travel (boating destinations). No general boating articles or personal anectdotes. **Buys 40-50 mss/year.** Query. Length: 1,200-2,500 words. **Pays $150-300 (Canadian).** Sometimes pays expenses of writers on assignment.

Reprints Send photocopy with rights for sale noted and information about when and where the material previously appeared.

Photos Send photos with submission. Reviews contact sheets, negatives, transparencies, prints. Buys one-time rights. Pay varies; no additional payment for photos accepted with ms. Captions, identification of subjects required.

ℕ $ $ $⊘ POWERBOAT

Nordskog Publishing Inc., 1691 Spinnaker Dr., #206, Ventura CA 93001. (805)639-2222. Fax: (805)639-2220. Website: www.powerboatmag.com. **25% freelance written.** Magazine published 11 times/year covering performance boating. Estab. 1973. Circ. 50,000. Pays on publication. Publishes ms an average of 3 months after acceptance. Byline given. Offers negotiable kill fee. Buys first North American serial, electronic rights. Editorial lead time 3 months. Submit seasonal material 4 months in advance. Accepts queries by mail, e-mail, fax. Sample copy online.

• *No unsolicited mss.*

Nonfiction Features highly focused storied on performance boats and boating. How-to, interview/profile, new product, photo feature. No general interest boating stories. **Buys numerous mss/year.** Query. Length: 300-2,000 words. **Pays $125-1,200.** Sometimes pays expenses of writers on assignment.

Photos State availability with submission. Reviews negatives. Buys one-time rights. Captions required.

$ $ $ SAIL

98 N. Washington St., 2nd Floor, Boston MA 02114. (617)720-8600. Fax: (617)723-0912. E-mail: sailmail@prime diasi.com. Website: www.sailmagazine.com or www.sailbuyersguide.com. Editor: Peter Nielsen. **Contact:** Amy Ullrich, managing editor. **30% freelance written.** Monthly magazine "written and edited for everyone who sails—aboard a coastal or bluewater cruiser, trailerable, one-design or offshore racer, or daysailer. How-to and technical articles concentrate on techniques of sailing and aspects of design and construction, boat systems, and gear; the feature section emphasizes the fun and rewards of sailing in a practical and instructive way." Estab. 1970. Circ. 180,000. **Pays on acceptance.** Publishes ms an average of 1 year after acceptance. Byline given. Buys first North American and other rights. Accepts queries by mail, e-mail, fax. Responds in 3 months to queries. Writer's guidelines for SASE or online (download).

Nonfiction How-to, personal experience, technical, distance cruising, destinations. Special issues: "Cruising, chartering, commissioning, fitting-out, special race (i.e., America's Cup), Top 10 Boats." **Buys 50 mss/year.** Query. Length: 1,500-3,000 words. **Pays $200-800.** Sometimes pays expenses of writers on assignment.

Photos Prefers transparencies. Payment varies, up to $700 if photo used on cover. Captions, identification of subjects, credits required.

Columns/Departments Sailing Memories (short essay); Sailing News (cruising, racing, legal, political, environmental); Under Sail (human interest). Query. **Pays $25-400.**

🖥 The online magazine carries original content not found in the print edition and includes writer's guidelines. Contact: Kimball Livingston, online editor.

Tips "Request an articles' specification sheet. We look for unique ways of viewing sailing. Skim old issues of *Sail* for ideas about the types of articles we publish. Always remember that *Sail* is a sailing magazine. Stay away from gloomy articles detailing all the things that went wrong on your boat. Think constructively and write about how to avoid certain problems. You should focus on a theme or choose some aspect of sailing and discuss a personal attitude or new philosophical approach to the subject. Notice that we have certain issues devoted to special themes—for example, chartering, electronics, commissioning, and the like. Stay away from pieces that chronicle your journey in the day-by-day style of a logbook. These are generally dull and uninteresting. Select specific actions or events (preferably sailing events, not shorebound activities), and build your articles around them. Emphasize the sailing."

$ $ $ SAILING MAGAZINE

125 E. Main St., Port Washington WI 53074-0249. (262)284-3494. Fax: (262)284-7764. E-mail: editorial@sailing magazine.net. Website: www.sailingonline.com. Publisher: William F. Schanen. Managing Editor: Greta Schanen. Monthly magazine for the experienced sailor. Estab. 1966. Circ. 45,000. Pays after publication. Buys one-time rights. Accepts queries by mail, e-mail. Responds in 2 months to queries. Editorial calendar online.

○┅ "Let us get to know your writing with short, newsy, sailing-oriented pieces with good slides for our Splashes section. Query for upcoming theme issues; read the magazine; writing must show the writer loves sailing as much as our readers. We are always looking for fresh stories on new destinations with vibrant writing and top-notch photography. Always looking for short (100-1,500 word) articles or newsy items."

Nonfiction "Experiences of sailing, cruising, and racing or cruising to interesting locations, whether a small lake near you or islands in the Southern Ocean, with first-hand knowledge and tips for our readers. Top-notch photos with maps, charts, cruising information complete the package. No regatta sports unless there is a story involved." Book excerpts, how-to (tech pieces on boats and gear), interview/profile, personal experience, travel (by sail). **Buys 15-20 mss/year.** Length: 750-2,500 words. **Pays $100-800.**

Photos Reviews color transparencies. Pays $50-400. Captions required.

Tips Prefers text in Word on disk for Mac or to e-mail address.

$ $ SAILING WORLD

World Publications, 55 Hammarlund Way, Middletown RI 02842. (401)845-5100. Fax: (401)848-5180. E-mail: editorial@sailingworld.com. Website: www.sailingworld.com. **40% freelance written.** Magazine published 10 times/year covering performance sailing. Estab. 1962. Circ. 60,000. Pays on publication. Publishes ms an average of 4 months after acceptance. Byline given. Buys first North American serial rights and world serial rights. Responds in 1 month to queries. Sample copy for $5.

○┅ Break in with short articles and fillers such as regatta news reports from your own area.

Nonfiction How-to (for racing and performance-oriented sailors), interview/profile, photo feature, Regatta sports and charter. No travelogs. **Buys 5-10 unsolicited mss/year.** Query. Length: 400-1,500 words. **Pays $400 for up to 2,000 words.** Does not pay expenses of writers on assignment unless pre-approved.

Tips "Send query with outline and include your experience. Prospective contributors should study recent issues of the magazine to determine appropriate subject matter. The emphasis here is on performance sailing: keep in mind that the *Sailing World* readership is relatively educated about the sport. Unless you are dealing with a totally new aspect of sailing, you can and should discuss ideas on an advanced technical level. 'Gee-whiz' impressions from beginning sailors are generally not accepted."

$ $ SEA KAYAKER

Sea Kayaker, Inc., P.O. Box 17029, Seattle WA 98127. (206)789-1326. Fax: (206)781-1141. E-mail: editorial@sea kayakermag.com. Website: www.seakayakermag.com. Editor: Christopher Cunningham. **Contact:** Gretchen Bay, executive editor. **95% freelance written.** "*Sea Kayaker* is a bimonthly publication with a worldwide readership that covers all aspects of kayak touring. It is well known as an important source of continuing education by the most experienced paddlers." Estab. 1984. Circ. 30,000. Pays on publication. Publishes ms an average of 6 months after acceptance. Byline given. Offers 10% kill fee. Buys first North American serial rights. Editorial lead time 4 months. Submit seasonal material 4 months in advance. Accepts queries by mail, e-mail, fax, phone. Responds in 2 months to queries. Sample copy for $7.30 (US), samples to other countries extra. Writer's guidelines online.

Nonfiction Essays, historical/nostalgic, how-to (on making equipment), humor, new product, personal experience, technical, travel. Unsolicited gear reviews are not accepted. **Buys 50 mss/year.** Query with or without published clips or send complete ms. Length: 1,500-5,000 words. **Pays 18-20¢/word for assigned articles; 15-17¢/word for unsolicited articles.**

Photos Send photos with submission. Reviews transparencies, prints. Buys one-time rights. Offers $15-400. Captions, identification of subjects required.

Columns/Departments Technique; Equipment; Do-It-Yourself; Food; Safety; Health; Environment; Book Reviews; all 1,000-2,500 words. **Buys 40-45 mss/year.** Query. **Pays 15-20¢/word.**

Tips "We consider unsolicited manuscripts that include a SASE, but we give greater priority to brief descriptions (several paragraphs) of proposed articles accompanied by at least 2 samples—published or unpublished—of your writing. Enclose a statement as to why you're qualified to write the piece and indicate whether photographs or illustrations are available to accompany the piece."

SEA MAGAZINE

America's Western Boating Magazine, Duncan McIntosh Co., 17782 Cowan, Suite A, Irvine CA 92614. (949)660-6150. Fax: (949)660-6172. Website: www.goboatingamerica.com. **Contact:** Holly Simpson, managing editor. Monthly magazine covering West Coast power boating. Estab. 1908. Circ. 50,000. Pays on publication. Publishes ms an average of 3 months after acceptance. Byline given. Buys first North American serial rights. Editorial lead time 3 months. Submit seasonal material 6 months in advance. Accepts simultaneous submissions. Responds in 3 months to queries. Writer's guidelines online.

Nonfiction "'News you can use' is kind of our motto. All articles should aim to help boat owners make the most of their boating experience." How-to, new product, personal experience, technical, travel. **Buys 36 mss/year.** Query with or without published clips or send complete ms. Length: 1,000-1,500 words. **Payment varies.** Sometimes pays expenses of writers on assignment.

Photos State availability with submission. Reviews transparencies. Buys one-time rights. Offers $50-250/photo. Captions, identification of subjects, model releases required.

ℕ $ $ SOUTHERN BOATING MAGAZINE

The South's Largest Boating Magazine, Southern Boating & Yachting, Inc., 330 N. Andrews Ave., Ft. Lauderdale FL 33301. (954)522-5515. Fax: (954)522-2260. E-mail: sboating@southernboating.com. Website: southernboating.com. Editor: Skip Allen. **Contact:** Bill Lindsey, executive editor. **50% freelance written.** Monthly magazine. Upscale yachting magazine focusing on the Southeast US, Bahamas, Caribbean, and Gulf of Mexico. Estab. 1972. Circ. 40,000. Pays on publication. Publishes ms an average of 2 months after acceptance. Byline given. Buys one-time rights. Editorial lead time 6 weeks. Submit seasonal material 2 months in advance. Accepts queries by mail, e-mail, fax, phone. Accepts previously published material. Sample copy for free.

  ○┐ Break in with destination, how-to, and technical articles.

Nonfiction How-to (boat maintenance), travel (boating related, destination pieces). **Buys 100 mss/year.** Query. Length: 1,000 words. **Pays $500 with art.**

Photos State availability of or send photos with submission. Reviews transparencies, prints. Buys one-time rights. Offers $50/photo maximum. Captions, identification of subjects, model releases required.

Columns/Departments Weekend Workshop (how-to/maintenance), 1,000 words; What's New in Electronics (electronics), 1,000 words; Engine Room (new developments), 1,000 words. **Buys 24 mss/year.** Query. **Pays $500.**

ℕ $ $ $ TRAILER BOATS MAGAZINE

Ehlert Publishing Group, Inc., 20700 Belshaw Ave., Carson CA 90746-3510. (310)537-6322. Fax: (310)537-8735. Website: www.trailerboats.com. Editor: Ron Eldridge. **50% freelance written.** Monthly magazine covering legally trailerable power boats and related powerboating activities. Estab. 1971. Circ. 100,000. **Pays on acceptance.** Publishes ms an average of 3 months after acceptance. Byline given. Buys all rights. Editorial lead time 4 months. Submit seasonal material 5 months in advance. Responds in 1 month to queries. Sample copy for 9×12 SAE with 7 first-class stamps.

Nonfiction General interest (trailer boating activities), historical/nostalgic (places, events, boats), how-to (repair boats, installation, etc.), humor (almost any power boating-related subject), interview/profile, personal experience, photo feature, technical, travel (boating travel on water or highways), product evaluations. Special issues: annual New Boat Review. No "How I Spent My Summer Vacation" stories, or stories not directly connected to trailerable boats and related activities. **Buys 70-80 unsolicited mss/year.** Query. Length: 1,000-2,500 words. **Pays $150-1,000.** Sometimes pays expenses of writers on assignment.

Photos Send photos with submission. Reviews transparencies, 2¼×2¼ and 35mm slides, and high-resolution digital images (300 dpi). Buys all rights. Captions, identification of subjects, model releases required.

Columns/Departments Over the Transom (funny or strange boating photos); Watersports (boat-related); Marine Electronics (what and how to use); Boating Basics (elementary boating tips), all 1,000-1,500 words. **Buys 60-70 mss/year.** Query. **Pays $250-500.**

Tips "Query should contain short general outline of the intended material; what kind of photos; how the photos illustrate the piece. Write with authority, covering the subject with quotes from experts. Frequent mistakes are not knowing the subject matter or the audience. The writer may have a better chance of breaking in at our publication with short articles and fillers if they are typically hard-to-find articles. We do most major features in-house, but try how-to stories dealing with smaller boats, installation and towing tips, boat trailer repair. Good color photos will win our hearts every time."

$WATERFRONT NEWS

Ziegler Publishing Co., Inc., 1515 SW 1st Ave., Ft. Lauderdale FL 33315. (954)524-9450. Fax: (954)524-9464. E-mail: editor@waterfront-news.com. Website: www.waterfront-news.com. **Contact:** Jennifer Heit, editor. **20% freelance written.** Monthly tabloid covering marine and boating topics for the Greater Ft. Lauderdale waterfront community. Estab. 1984. Circ. 39,000. Pays on publication. Publishes ms an average of 2 months after acceptance. Byline given. Buys first, second serial (reprint), simultaneous rights in certain circumstances. Submit seasonal material 3 months in advance. Responds in 1 month to queries. Sample copy for 9 × 12 SAE and 4 first-class stamps.

O→ Travel pieces written for recreational boaters are most needed. Include photos, prints or digital.

Nonfiction Interview/profile (of people important in boating, i.e., racers, boat builders, designers, etc. from south Florida), Regional articles on south Florida's waterfront issues; marine communities. Length: 500-1,000 words. **Pays $100-125 for assigned articles.**

Photos Send photos with submission. Reviews JPEG/TIFF files.

Tips "No fiction. Keep it under 1,000 words. Photos or illustrations help. Send for a sample copy of *Waterfront News* so you can acquaint yourself with our publication and our unique audience. Although we're not necessarily looking for technical articles, it helps if the writer has sailing or powerboating experience. Writers should be familiar with the region and be specific when dealing with local topics."

$ $WATERWAY GUIDE

326 First St., Suite 400, Annapolis MD 21403. (443)482-9377. Fax: (443)482-9422. E-mail: greich@waterwayguide.com. Website: www.waterwayguide.com. **Contact:** Gary Reich, editor. **90% freelance written.** Triannual magazine covering intracoastal waterway travel for recreational boats. "Writer must be knowledgeable about navigation and the areas covered by the guide." Estab. 1947. Circ. 30,000. Pays on publication. Publishes ms an average of 3 months after acceptance. Byline given. Buys first North American serial, electronic rights, makes work-for-hire assignments. Editorial lead time 4 months. Submit seasonal material 3 months in advance. Accepts queries by mail, phone. Responds in 6 weeks to queries; 2 months to mss. Sample copy for $39.95 with $3 postage.

Nonfiction Essays, historical/nostalgic, how-to, photo feature, technical, travel. **Buys 6 mss/year.** Query with or without published clips or send complete ms. Length: 250-5,000 words. **Pays $50-500.** Pays in contributor copies or other premiums for helpful tips and useful information.

Photos Send photos with submission. Reviews transparencies, 3 × 5 prints. Buys all rights. Offers $25-50/photo. Captions, identification of subjects required.

Tips "Must have on-the-water experience and be able to provide new and accurate information on geographic areas covered by *Waterway Guide.*"

$✉ WAVELENGTH MAGAZINE

2735 North Rd., Gabriola Island BC V0R 1X7 Canada. (250)247-8858. E-mail: info@wavelengthmagazine.com. Website: www.wavelengthmagazine.com. **Contact:** Alan Wilson, editor. **75% freelance written.** Bimonthly magazine covering sea kayaking. "We promote safe paddling, guide paddlers to useful products and services and explore coastal environmental issues." Estab. 1991. Circ. 60,000 print and electronic readers. Pays on publication. Publishes ms an average of 4 months after acceptance. Byline given. Offers 10% kill fee. Buys first North American serial, electronic rights. Editorial lead time 4 months. Submit seasonal material 4 months in advance. Accepts queries by mail, e-mail, phone. Responds in 2 months to queries. Sample copy and writer's guidelines online.

O→ "Sea kayaking content, even if from a beginner's perspective, is essential. We like a light approach to personal experiences and humor is appreciated. Good detail (with maps and pics) for destinations material. Write to our feature focus."

Nonfiction How-to (paddle, travel), humor, new product, personal experience, technical, travel, trips; advice. **Buys 25 mss/year.** Query. Length: 1,000-1,500 words. **Pays $50-75.**

Photos State availability with submission. Reviews low res JPEGs. Buys first and electronic rights. Offers $25-50/photo. Captions, identification of subjects required.

Tips "You must know paddling—although novice paddlers are welcome. A strong environmental or wilderness appreciation component is advisable. We are willing to help refine work with flexible people. E-mail queries preferred. Check out our Editorial Calendar for our upcoming features."

$ $ WOODENBOAT MAGAZINE

The Magazine for Wooden Boat Owners, Builders, and Designers, WoodenBoat Publications, Inc., P.O. Box 78, Brooklin ME 04616. (207)359-4651. Fax: (207)359-8920. Website: www.woodenboat.com. Editor-in-Chief: Jonathan A. Wilson. Senior Editor: Mike O'Brien. Associate Editor: Tom Jackson. **Contact:** Matthew P. Murphy, editor. **50% freelance written.** Bimonthly magazine for wooden boat owners, builders, and designers. "We are devoted exclusively to the design, building, care, preservation, and use of wooden boats, both commercial and pleasure, old and new, sail and power. We work to convey quality, integrity, and involvement in the creation and care of these craft, to entertain, inform, inspire, and to provide our varied readers with access to individuals who are deeply experienced in the world of wooden boats." Estab. 1974. Circ. 106,000. Pays on publication. Publishes ms an average of 1 year after acceptance. Byline given. Offers variable kill fee. Buys first North American serial rights. Accepts previously published material. Accepts simultaneous submissions. Responds in 2 months. Sample copy for $4.50. Writer's guidelines for #10 SASE.

Nonfiction Technical (repair, restoration, maintenance, use, design, and building wooden boats). No poetry, fiction. **Buys 50 mss/year.** Query with published clips. Length: 1,500-5,000 words. **Pays $300/1,000 words.** Sometimes pays expenses of writers on assignment.

Reprints Send tearsheet or typed ms with rights for sale noted and information about when and where the material previously appeared.

Photos Send photos with submission. Reviews negatives. Buys one-time rights. Pays $15-75 b&w, $25-350 color. Identification of subjects required.

Columns/Departments Currents pays for information on wooden boat-related events, projects, boatshop activities, etc. Uses same columnists for each issue. Length: 250-1,000 words. Send complete information. **Pays $5-50.**

Tips "We appreciate a detailed, articulate query letter, accompanied by photos, that will give us a clear idea of what the author is proposing. We appreciate samples of previously published work. It is important for a prospective author to become familiar with our magazine. Most work is submitted on speculation. The most common failure is not exploring the subject material in enough depth."

GENERAL INTEREST

N $ $ METROSPORTS

New York, MetroSports Publishing, Inc., 259 W. 30th St., 3rd Floor, New York NY 10001. (212)563-7329. Fax: (212)563-7573. E-mail: jshweder@metrosports.com. Website: www.metrosportsny.com. **Contact:** Jeremy Shweder, editor. **50% freelance written.** Monthly magazine covering amateur sports and fitness. "We focus on participatory sports (not team sports) for an active, young audience that likes to exercise." Estab. 1987. Circ. 100,000. Pays on publication. Byline given. Offers 50% kill fee. Buys first, electronic rights. Editorial lead time 3 months. Submit seasonal material 6 months in advance. Accepts queries by mail, e-mail, fax. Accepts previously published material. Accepts simultaneous submissions. Responds in 3-4 weeks to queries; 1-2 months to mss. Sample copy online. Writer's guidelines by e-mail.

Nonfiction Essays, general interest, historical/nostalgic, how-to (train for a triathlon, train for an adventure race, etc.), humor, inspirational, interview/profile, new product, opinion, personal experience, technical, travel. Special issues: Holiday Gift Guide (December). "We don't publish anything related to team sports (basketball, baseball, football, etc.), golf, tennis." **Buys 24 mss/year.** Query with published clips. Length: 800-3,000 words. **Pays $100-300.** Sometimes pays expenses of writers on assignment.

Photos State availability with submission. Reviews slides transparencies, 3 × 5 prints, GIF/JPEG files (300 dpi). Buys one-time rights. Negotiates payment individually. Captions, identification of subjects required.

Columns/Departments Running (training, nutrition, profiles); Cycling (training, nutrition, profiles), both 800 words. **Buys 15 mss/year.** Query with published clips. **Pays $100-250.**

Tips "Read the magazine, know what we cover. E-mail queries or mail with published clips. No phone calls, please."

$ OUTDOORS NW

(formerly *Sports Etc*), 11715 Greenwood Ave. N., Seattle WA 98133. (206)418-0747. Fax: (206)418-0746. E-mail: outdoorsnw@msn.com. Website: www.sportsetc.com. **Contact:** Becky Brun, editor. **80% freelance written.** Monthly magazine covering outdoor recreation in the Pacific Northwest. "Writers must have a solid knowledge of the sport they are writing about. They must be doers." Estab. 1988. Circ. 40,000. Pays on publication. Publishes ms an average of 3 months after acceptance. Byline given. Buys first rights. Editorial lead time 2 months. Submit seasonal material 4 months in advance. Accepts queries by mail, e-mail, fax. Accepts previously published material. Accepts simultaneous submissions. Sample copy and writer's guidelines for $3.

Nonfiction Interview/profile, new product, travel. Query with published clips. Length: 750-1,500 words. **Pays $10-50.** Sometimes pays expenses of writers on assignment.

Photos Send photos with submission. Reviews negatives, transparencies. Buys all rights. Captions, identification of subjects, model releases required.

Columns/Departments Faces, Places, Puruits (750 words). **Buys 10-12 mss/year.** Query with published clips. **Pays $40-50.**

Tips "*Outdoors NW* is written for the serious Pacific Northwest outdoor recreationalist. The magazine's look, style and editorial content actively engage the reader, delivering insightful perspectives on the sports it has come to be known for—alpine skiing, bicycling, adventure racing, triathlon and multi-sport, hiking, in-line skating, kayaking, marathons, mountain climbing, Nordic skiing, running, and snowboarding. *Outdoors NW* magazine wants vivid writing, telling images, and original perspectives to produce its smart, entertaining monthly."

$ $ ROCKY MOUNTAIN SPORTS MAGAZINE

Rocky Mountain Sports, Inc., 2525 15th St., #1A, Denver CO 80211. (303)477-9770. Fax: (303)477-9747. E-mail: rheaton@rockymountainsports.com. Website: www.rockymountainsports.com. Publisher: Mary Thorne. **Contact:** Rebecca Heaton, editor. **50% freelance written.** Monthly magazine covering nonteam-related sports in Colorado. "*Rocky* is a magazine for sports-related lifestyles and activities. Our mission is to reflect and inspire the active lifestyle of Rocky Mountain residents." Estab. 1986. Circ. 80,000. Pays on publication. Publishes ms an average of 2 months after acceptance. Byline given. Buys second serial (reprint) rights. Editorial lead time 3 months. Submit seasonal material 5 months in advance. Accepts queries by mail, e-mail, fax. Accepts previously published material. Responds in 3 weeks to queries; 2 months to mss. Sample copy and writer's guidelines for #10 SASE.

  • The editor says she wants to see mountain outdoor sports writing *only*. No ball sports, hunting, or fishing.

  Oₙ Break in with "Rocky Mountain angle—off-the-beaten-path."

Nonfiction How-to, humor, inspirational, interview/profile, new product, opinion, personal experience, photo feature, travel. Special issues: Skiing & Snowboarding (November); Nordic/Snowshoeing (December); Marathon (January); Running (March); Adventure Travel (April); Triathlon (May); Paddling and Climbing (June); Road Cycling & Camping (July); Mountain Bike & Hiking (August); Women's Sports & Marathon (September); Health Club (October). No articles on football, baseball, basketball, or other sports covered in depth by newspapers. **Buys 24 mss/year.** Query with published clips. Length: 1,500 words maximum. **Pays $150 minimum.**

Reprints Send photocopy and information about when and where the material previously appeared. Pays 20-25% of amount paid for original article.

Photos State availability with submission. Reviews transparencies, prints. Buys one-time rights. Captions, identification of subjects required.

Columns/Departments Starting Lines (short newsy items); Running; Cycling; Climbing; Triathlon; Fitness, Nutrition; Sports Medicine; Off the Beaten Path (sports we don't usually cover). **Buys 20 mss/year.** Query. **Pays $25-300.**

Tips "Have a Colorado angle to the story, a catchy cover letter, good clips, and demonstrate that you've read and understand our magazine and its readers."

$ SILENT SPORTS

Waupaca Publishing Co., P.O. Box 152, Waupaca WI 54981-9990. (715)258-5546. Fax: (715)258-8162. E-mail: info@silentsports.net. Website: www.silentsports.net. **75% freelance written.** Monthly magazine covering running, cycling, cross-country skiing, canoeing, kayaking, snowshoeing, in-line skating, camping, backpacking, and hiking aimed at people in Wisconsin, Minnesota, northern Illinois, and portions of Michigan and Iowa. "Not a coffee table magazine. Our readers are participants from rank amateur weekend athletes to highly competitive racers." Estab. 1984. Circ. 10,000. Pays on publication. Publishes ms an average of 3 months after acceptance. Byline given. Offers 20% kill fee. Buys one-time rights. Submit seasonal material 4 months in advance. Accepts queries by mail, e-mail, fax. Accepts previously published material. Responds in 3 months to queries. Sample copy and writer's guidelines for 10×13 SAE with 7 first-class stamps.

  • The editor needs local angles on in-line skating, recreation bicycling, and snowshoeing.

Nonfiction All stories/articles must focus on the Upper Midwest. General interest, how-to, interview/profile, opinion, technical, travel. **Buys 25 mss/year.** Query. Length: 2,500 words maximum. **Pays $15-100.** Sometimes pays expenses of writers on assignment.

Reprints Send ms with rights for sale noted and information about when and where the material previously appeared. Pays 50% of amount paid for an original article.

Photos State availability with submission. Reviews transparencies. Buys one-time rights. Pays $5-15 for b&w story photos; $50-100 for color covers.

Tips ''Where-to-go and personality profiles are areas most open to freelancers. Writers should keep in mind that this is a regional, Midwest-based publication. We want only stories/articles with a focus on our region.''

$ $ TWIN CITIES SPORTS

Twin Cities Sports Publishing, Inc., 3009 Holmes Ave. S., Minneapolis MN 55408. (612)825-1034. Fax: (612)825-6452. E-mail: kyle@metrosports.com. Website: www.twincitiessports.com. Editor: Jeff Banowetz. **Contact:** Kyle Ryan, managing editor. **75% freelance written.** Monthly magazine covering amateur sports and fitness. ''We focus on participatory sports (not team sports) for an active, young audience that likes to exercise.'' Estab. 1987. Circ. 40,000. Pays on publication. Publishes ms an average of 2 months after acceptance. Byline given. Offers 50% kill fee. Buys first, electronic rights. Editorial lead time 3 months. Submit seasonal material 6 months in advance. Accepts queries by mail, e-mail, fax. Accepts previously published material. Accepts simultaneous submissions. Responds in 3-4 weeks to queries; 1-2 months to mss. Sample copy online. Writer's guidelines by e-mail.

Nonfiction Essays, general interest, historical/nostalgic, how-to (train for a triathlon, set a new 5K PR, train for an adventure race), humor, inspirational, interview/profile, new product, opinion, personal experience, technical, travel. Special issues: Holiday Gift Guide (December). ''We don't publish anything related to team sports (basketball, baseball, football, etc.), golf, tennis. **Buys 24 mss/year.** Query with published clips. Length: 800-3,000 words. **Pays $100-300.** Sometimes pays expenses of writers on assignment.

Photos State availability with submission. Reviews slides transparencies, 3×5 prints, GIF/JPEG files (300 dpi). Buys one-time rights. Negotiates payment individually. Captions, identification of subjects required.

Columns/Departments Running (training, nutrition, profiles), 800 words; Cycling (training, nutrition, profiles), 800 words; Cool Down (first-person essay), 800-1,000 words. **Buys 15 mss/year.** Query with published clips. **Pays $100-250.**

Tips ''Read the magazine, know what we cover. E-mail queries or mail with published clips. No phone calls, please.''

GOLF

N $ $ ARIZONA, THE STATE OF GOLF

Arizona Golf Association, 7226 N. 16th St., Suite 200, Phoenix AZ 85020. (602)944-3035. Fax: (602)944-3228. Website: www.azgolf.org. **50% freelance written.** Quarterly magazine covering golf in Arizona, the official publication of the Arizona Golf Association. Estab. 1999. Circ. 45,000. **Pays on acceptance.** Byline given. Buys all rights. Editorial lead time 6 months. Submit seasonal material 3 months in advance. Accepts queries by mail. Accepts previously published material. Accepts simultaneous submissions. Sample copy and writer's guidelines free.

Nonfiction Book excerpts, essays, historical/nostalgic, how-to (golf), humor, inspirational, interview/profile, new product, opinion, personal experience, photo feature, travel (destinations). **Buys 5-10 mss/year.** Query with or without published clips. Length: 500-2,000 words. **Pays $50-500.** Sometimes pays expenses of writers on assignment.

Reprints Accepts previously published submissions.

Photos State availability with submission. Reviews contact sheets. Rights purchased varies. Negotiates payment individually. Captions, identification of subjects required.

Columns/Departments Short Strokes (golf news and notes), Improving Your Game (golf tips), Out of Bounds (guest editorial, 800 words). Query.

N $ $ $ GOLF CANADA

Official Magazine of the Royal Canadian Golf Association, RCGA/Relevant Communications, Golf House Suite 1, 1333 Dorval Dr., Oakville ON L6M 4X7 Canada. (905)849-9700. Fax: (905)845-7040. E-mail: golfcanada@rcga .org. Website: www.rcga.org. **Contact:** John Tenpenny, editor. **80% freelance written.** Magazine published 5 times/year covering Canadian golf. ''*Golf Canada* is the official magazine of the Royal Canadian Golf Association, published to entertain and enlighten members about RCGA-related activities and to generally support and promote amateur golf in Canada.'' Estab. 1994. Circ. 159,000. **Pays on acceptance.** Byline given. Offers 100% kill fee. Buys first translation, electronic rights. Editorial lead time 3 months. Submit seasonal material 6 months in advance. Accepts queries by mail, e-mail, fax, phone. Accepts previously published material. Sample copy for free.

Nonfiction Historical/nostalgic, interview/profile, new product, opinion, photo feature, travel. No professional golf-related articles. **Buys 42 mss/year.** Query with published clips. Length: 750-3,000 words. **Pays 60¢/word, including electronic rights.** Sometimes pays expenses of writers on assignment.

Photos State availability with submission. Reviews contact sheets, negatives, transparencies, prints. Buys all rights. Negotiates payment individually. Captions required.

Columns/Departments Guest Column (focus on issues surrounding the Canadian golf community), 700 words. Query. **Pays 60¢/word, including electronic rights.**

Tips "Keep story ideas focused on Canadian competitive golf."

⊘ GOLF DIGEST

The Golf Digest Companies, 20 Westport Rd., Box 20, Wilton CT 06897. (203)761-5100. Fax: (203)761-5129. E-mail: editor@golfdigest.com. Website: www.golfdigest.com. Editor: Jerry Tarde. Managing Editor: Roger Schiffman. **Contact:** Craig Bestrom; features editor. Monthly magazine covering the sport of golf. Written for all golf enthusiasts, whether recreational, amateur, or professional player. Estab. 1950. Circ. 1,550,000. Editorial lead time 6 months. Accepts queries by mail. Sample copy for $3.95.

* *No unsolicited materials.*

Nonfiction Query.

GOLF FOR WOMEN

The Golf Digest Companies, P.O. Box 850, Wilton CT 06897. (203)761-5100. E-mail: editors@golfforwomen.com. Website: www.golfdigest.com/gfw. **50% freelance written.** Bimonthly magazine covering golf instruction, travel, lifestyle. "Our magazine is the leading authority on the game for women. We celebrate the traditions and lifestyle of golf, explore issues surrounding the game with incisive features, and we present traditional women's and fashion magazine fare—fashion, beauty, relationship stories—all with a strong golf angle. Travel is also a big component of our coverage. We package everything in a modern, sophisticated way that suits our affluent, educated readers." Circ. 500,000. **Pays on acceptance.** Byline given. Offers variable kill fee (25% standard). Buys all rights, including online. Accepts queries by mail, e-mail, fax.

Nonfiction Book excerpts, essays, general interest, historical/nostalgic, how-to (golf related), humor, inspirational, interview/profile, new product, personal experience, photo feature, travel. **Buys 50 mss/year.** Query. Length: 250-2,500 words. **Payment negotiated.** Sometimes pays expenses of writers on assignment.

Photos State availability with submission. Buys one-time rights and online usage rights. Negotiates payment individually. Model releases required.

Columns/Departments Fitness; Beauty; Get There (travel); Fashion; First Person; Health. **Pays per piece or per word; fees negotiated.**

$ $ GOLF NEWS MAGAZINE

Premier Golf Magazine Since 1984, Golf News Magazine, P.O. Box 1040, Rancho Mirage CA 92270. (760)321-8800. Fax: (760)328-3013. E-mail: golfnews@aol.com. Website: www.golfnewsmag.com. **Contact:** Dan Poppers, editor/publisher. **70% freelance written.** Monthly magazine covering golf. "Our publication specializes in the creative treatment of the sport of golf, offering a variety of themes and slants as related to golf. If it's good writing and relates to golf, we're interested." Estab. 1984. Circ. 14,000. **Pays on acceptance.** Publishes ms an average of 4 months after acceptance. Byline given. Offers negotiable kill fee. Buys first rights, makes work-for-hire assignments. Editorial lead time 2 months. Submit seasonal material 2 months in advance. Accepts queries by mail, e-mail, fax. Accepts previously published material. Accepts simultaneous submissions. Responds in 1 month to queries; 3 months to mss. Sample copy for $2 and 9×12 SAE with 4 first-class stamps.

Nonfiction "We will consider any topic related to golf that is written well with high standards." Book excerpts, essays, exposé, general interest, historical/nostalgic, how-to, humor, inspirational, interview/profile, opinion, personal experience, photo feature, technical, real estate. **Buys 20 mss/year.** Query with published clips. **Pays $75-350.**

Photos State availability with submission. Buys one-time rights. Negotiates payment individually. Identification of subjects required.

Columns/Departments Buys 10 mss/year. Query with published clips.

🖳 The online magazine carries content not found in the print edition.

Tips "Solid, creative, good, professional writing. Stay away from cliches and the hackneyed. Only good writers need apply. We are a national award-winning magazine looking for the most creative writers we can find."

Ⓝ $ $ $ GOLF TIPS

The Game's Most In-Depth Instruction & Equipment Magazine, Werner Publishing Corp., 12121 Wilshire Blvd., Suite 1200, Los Angeles CA 90025. E-mail: editors@golftipsmag.com. Website: www.golftipsmag.com. **95% freelance written.** Magazine published 9 times/year covering golf instruction and equipment. "We provide mostly concise, very clear golf instruction pieces for the serious golfer." Estab. 1986. Pays on publication. Publishes ms an average of 2 months after acceptance. Byline given. Offers 33% kill fee. Buys first, second serial (reprint) rights. Editorial lead time 3 months. Submit seasonal material 4 months in advance. Accepts previously published material. Responds in 1 month to queries. Sample copy free. Writer's guidelines online.

Nonfiction Book excerpts, how-to, interview/profile, new product, photo feature, technical, travel, all golf related. "Generally golf essays rarely make it." **Buys 125 mss/year.** Send complete ms. Length: 250-2,000 words. **Pays $300-1,000 for assigned articles; $300-800 for unsolicited articles.** Occassionally negotiates other forms of payment. Sometimes pays expenses of writers on assignment.

Photos State availability with submission. Reviews 2×2 transparencies. Buys all rights. Negotiates payment individually. Captions, identification of subjects required.

Columns/Departments Stroke Saver (very clear, concise instruction), 350 words; Lesson Library (book excerpts—usually in a series), 1,000 words; Travel Tips (formatted golf travel), 2,500 words. **Buys 40 mss/year.** Query with or without published clips or send complete ms. **Pays $300-850.**

Tips "Contact a respected PGA Professional and find out if they're interested in being published. A good writer can turn an interview into a decent instruction piece."

$ $ THE GOLFER

551 5th Ave., New York NY 10176. (212)867-7070. Fax: (212)867-8550. E-mail: thegolfer@walrus.com. Editor: H.K. Pickens. **Contact:** Colin Sheehan, senior editor. **40% freelance written.** Bimonthly magazine covering golf. "A sophisticated tone for a lifestyle-oriented magazine." Estab. 1994. Circ. 253,000. Pays on publication. Publishes ms an average of 2 months after acceptance. Byline given. Offers negotiable kill fee. Buys all rights. Editorial lead time 2 months. Submit seasonal material 4 months in advance. Accepts queries by mail, e-mail, fax. Accepts previously published material. Accepts simultaneous submissions. Sample copy for free.

Nonfiction Book excerpts, essays, general interest, historical/nostalgic, how-to, humor, inspirational, interview/ profile, new product, opinion, personal experience, photo feature, technical, travel. Send complete ms. Length: 300-2,000 words. **Pays $150-600.**

Reprints Accepts previously published submissions.

Photos Send photos with submission. Reviews any size digital files. Buys one-time rights.

$ $ $ MINNESOTA GOLFER

6550 York Ave. S., Suite 211, Edina MN 55435. (952)927-4643. Fax: (952)927-9642. E-mail: editor@mngolf.org. Website: www.mngolfer.com. **Contact:** W.P. Ryan, editor. **75% freelance written.** Bimonthly magazine covering golf in Minnesota, the official publication of the Minnesota Golf Association. Estab. 1975. Circ. 66,000. Pays on acceptance or publication. Byline given. Buys first rights. Editorial lead time 3 months. Accepts queries by mail, e-mail, fax.

Nonfiction Historical/nostalgic, interview/profile, new product, travel, book reviews, instruction, golf course previews. Query with published clips. Length: 400-2,000 words. **Pays $50-750.** Sometimes pays expenses of writers on assignment.

Photos State availability with submission. Reviews contact sheets, transparencies, digital images. Image rights by assignment. Negotiates payment individually. Captions, identification of subjects required.

Columns/Departments Punch shots (golf news and notes); Q School (news and information targeted to beginners, junior golfers and women); Great Drives (featuring noteworthy golf holes in Minnesota); Instruction.

N $ $ TEXAS GOLFER MAGAZINE

Golfer Magazines, Inc., 4920 Center St., Houston TX 77007. (713)426-0179. Fax: (713)680-0138. **Contact:** Wayne A. Morkovsky, president. **10% freelance written.** Monthly tabloid covering golf in Texas. Estab. 1984. Circ. 50,000. Pays 10 days after publication. Publishes ms an average of 2 months after acceptance. Byline given. Buys first, one-time, second serial (reprint) rights. Editorial lead time 2 months. Submit seasonal material 3 months in advance. Responds in 2 weeks to queries; 1 month to mss. Sample copy for free. Prefers direct phone discussion for writer's guidelines.

● *Texas Golfer Magazine* was created by the merger of two publications: *Gulf Coast Golfer* and *North Texas Golfer*.

Nonfiction Book excerpts, humor, personal experience, all golf-related. Travel pieces accepted about golf outside of Texas. **Buys 20 mss/year.** Query. **Pays 25-40¢/word.**

Photos State availability with submission. Reviews contact sheets, prints. Buys one-time rights. No additional payment for photos accepted with ms, but pays $125 for cover photo. Captions, identification of subjects required.

Tips "Most of our purchases are in the how-to area, so writers must know golf quite well and play the game."

TRAVEL + LEISURE GOLF

(formerly *T&L Golf*), American Express Publishing Corp., 1120 Avenue of the Americas, 11th Floor, New York NY 10036. E-mail: tlgletters@tlgolf.com. Website: www.tlgolf.com. Editor: Yossi Langer. **95% freelance written.** Bimonthly magazine for those who see golf not only as a game but as a lifestyle. Circ. 600,000. **Pays on acceptance.** Buys first time world rights.

Nonfiction Query through website.

Tips "It is rare we will assign a feature article to a writer with whom we have not worked. The best sections to start with are departments in the front of the magazine."

$ $ VIRGINIA GOLFER

TPG Sports, Inc., 600 Founders Bridge Blvd., Midlothian VA 23113. (804)378-2300. Fax: (804)378-2369. Website: www.vsga.org. **Contact:** Andrew Blair, editor. **65% freelance written.** Bimonthly magazine covering golf in Virginia, the official publication of the Virginia Golf Association. Estab. 1983. Circ. 45,000. Pays on publication. Byline given. Buys all rights. Editorial lead time 6 months. Submit seasonal material 3 months in advance. Accepts queries by mail, e-mail. Accepts previously published material. Accepts simultaneous submissions. Sample copy and writer's guidelines free.

Nonfiction Book excerpts, essays, historical/nostalgic, how-to (golf), humor, inspirational, interview/profile, personal experience, photo feature, technical (golf equipment), where to play, golf business. **Buys 30-40 mss/year.** Query with or without published clips or send complete ms. Length: 500-2,500 words. **Pays $50-200.** Sometimes pays expenses of writers on assignment.

Reprints Accepts previously published submissions.

Photos State availability with submission. Reviews contact sheets. Rights purchased varies. Negotiates payment individually. Captions, identification of subjects required.

Columns/Departments Chip ins & Three Putts (news notes), Rules Corner (golf rules explanations and discussion), Pro Tips, Golf Travel (where to play), Golf Business (what's happening?). Query.

GUNS

$ $ THE ACCURATE RIFLE

Precision Shooting, Inc., 222 McKee St., Manchester CT 06040-4800. (860)645-8776. Fax: (860)643-8215. Website: www.theaccuraterifle.com. **Contact:** Dave Brennan, editor. **30-35% freelance written.** Monthly magazine covering "the specialized field of 'extreme rifle accuracy' excluding rifle competition disciplines." Estab. 2000. Circ. 8,000. Pays on publication. Publishes ms an average of 3 months after acceptance. Byline given. Buys first North American serial rights. Editorial lead time 2 months. Submit seasonal material 3 months in advance. Accepts queries by mail, fax. Responds in 2 weeks to queries; 1 month to mss. Sample copy for free. Writer's guidelines not available.

Nonfiction General interest, historical/nostalgic, how-to, humor, interview/profile, personal experience. "Nothing common to newsstand firearms publications. This has a very sophisticated and knowledgable readership." **Buys 36 mss/year.** Query. Length: 1,800-3,000 words. **Pays $200-500.**

Photos Send photos with submission. Reviews 4×6 prints. Buys one-time rights. Offers no additional payment for photos accepted with ms. Captions required.

Tips "Call the editor first and tell him what topic you propose to write about. Could save time and effort."

$ $ GUN DIGEST

DBI Books, Inc., Division of Krause Publications, 700 E. State St., Iola WI 54990. (888)457-2873. Fax: (715)445-4087. **Contact:** Ken Ramage, editor-in-chief. **50% freelance written.** Prefers to work with published/established writers, but works with a small number of new/unpublished writers each year. Annual journal covering guns and shooting. Estab. 1944. **Pays on acceptance.** Publishes ms an average of 20 months after acceptance. Byline given. Buys all rights. Accepts queries by mail. Responds as time allows.

Nonfiction Buys 25 mss/year. Query. Length: 500-5,000 words. **Pays $100-600 for text/art package.**

Photos Prefers 8×10 b&w prints. Slides, transparencies OK. No digital. State availability with submission. Payment for photos included in payment for ms. Captions required.

Tips Award of $1,000 to author of best article (juried) in each issue.

$ $ MUZZLE BLASTS

National Muzzle Loading Rifle Association, P.O. Box 67, Friendship IN 47021. (812)667-5131. Fax: (812)667-5137. E-mail: mblastdop@seidata.com. Website: www.nmlra.org. Editor: Eric A. Bye. **Contact:** Terri Trowbridge, director of publications. **65% freelance written.** Monthly magazine. "Articles must relate to muzzleloading or the muzzleloading era of American history." Estab. 1939. Circ. 20,000. Pays on publication. Publishes ms an average of 6 months after acceptance. Byline given. Offers $50 kill fee. Buys first North American serial, one-time, second serial (reprint) rights. Editorial lead time 4 months. Submit seasonal material 6 months in advance. Responds in 1 month to mss. Sample copy and writer's guidelines free.

Nonfiction Book excerpts, general interest, historical/nostalgic, how-to, humor, interview/profile, new product, personal experience, photo feature, technical, travel. "No subjects that do not pertain to muzzleloading." **Buys 80 mss/year.** Query. Length: 2,500 words. **Pays $150 minimum for assigned articles; $50 minimum for unsolicited articles.**

Photos Send photos with submission. Reviews 5×7 prints. Buys one-time rights. Negotiates payment individually. Captions, model releases required.

Columns/Departments Buys 96 mss/year. Query. **Pays $50-200.**

Fiction Must pertain to muzzleloading. Adventure, historical, humorous. **Buys 6 mss/year.** Query. Length: 2,500 words. **Pays $50-300.**

Fillers Facts. **Pays $50.**

$ $ PRECISION SHOOTING

Precision Shooting, Inc., 222 McKee St., Manchester CT 06040-4800. (860)645-8776. Fax: (860)643-8215. Website: www.precisionshooting.com. **Contact:** Dave Brennan, editor. **30-35% freelance written.** Monthly magazine covering "the specialized field of 'extreme rifle accuracy' including rifle competition disciplines." Estab. 1956. Circ. 17,500. Pays on publication. Publishes ms an average of 3 months after acceptance. Byline given. Buys first North American serial rights. Editorial lead time 2 months. Submit seasonal material 3 months in advance. Accepts queries by mail, fax. Responds in 2 weeks to queries; 1 month to mss. Sample copy for free. Writer's guidelines not available.

Nonfiction General interest, historical/nostalgic, how-to, humor, interview/profile, personal experience. "Nothing common to newsstand firearms publications. This has a very sophisticated and knowledgeable readership." **Buys 36 mss/year.** Query. Length: 1,800-3,000 words. **Pays $200-500.**

Photos Send photos with submission. Reviews 4×6 prints. Buys one-time rights. Offers no additional payment for photos accepted with ms. Captions required.

Tips "Call the editor first and tell him what topic you propose to write about. Could save time and effort."

$ $ SHOTGUN NEWS

Primedia, Box 1790, Peoria IL 61656. (800)521-2885. Fax: (309)679-5476. E-mail: sgnews@primediasi.com. Website: www.shotgunnews.com. **95% freelance written.** Tabloid published every 10 days covering firearms, accessories, ammunition and militaria. "The nation's oldest and largest gun sales publication. Provides up-to-date market information for gun trade and consumers." Estab. 1946. Circ. 100,000. **Pays on acceptance.** Publishes ms an average of 3 months after acceptance. Byline given. Buys first North American serial rights. Editorial lead time 1 month. Submit seasonal material 3 months in advance. Responds in 1 month to queries. Sample copy for free.

Nonfiction Historical/nostalgic, how-to, technical. No political pieces, fiction or poetry. **Buys 50 mss/year.** Query. Length: 1,000-3,000 words. **Pays $200-500 for assigned articles.** Sometimes pays expenses of writers on assignment.

Photos Send photos with submission. Reviews prints. Buys one-time rights. Offers no additional payment for photos accepted with ms. Captions required.

HIKING & BACKPACKING

$ $ $ $ BACKPACKER

Rodale, 33 E. Minor St., Emmaus PA 18098. (610)967-8296. Fax: (610)967-8181. E-mail: pflax@backpacker.com. Website: www.backpacker.com. **Contact:** Peter Flax, deputy editor. **50% freelance written.** Magazine published 9 times/year covering wilderness travel for backpackers. Estab. 1973. Circ. 295,000. **Pays on acceptance.** Byline given. Buys one-time, all rights. Accepts queries by mail, e-mail, fax. Responds in 6 weeks to queries. Writer's guidelines online.

Nonfiction "What we want are features that let us and the readers 'feel' the place, and experience your wonderment, excitement, disappointment, or other emotions encountered 'out there.' If we feel like we've been there after reading your story, you've succeeded." Essays, exposé, historical/nostalgic, how-to, humor, inspirational, interview/profile, new product, personal experience, technical, travel. No step-by-step accounts of what you did on your summer vacation—stories that chronicle every rest stop and gulp of water. Query with published clips. Length: 750-4,000 words. **Pays 60¢-$1/word.**

Photos State availability with submission. Buys one-time rights. Payment varies.

Columns/Departments Signpost, "News From All Over" (adventure, environment, wildlife, trails, techniques, organizations, special interests—well-written, entertaining, short, newsy item), 50-500 words; Getaways (great hiking destinations, primarily North America), includes weekend, 250-500 words, weeklong, 250-1000, multi-destination guides, 500-1500 words, and dayhikes, 50-200 words, plus travel news and other items; Fitness (in-the-field health column), 750-1,200 words; Food (food-related aspects of wilderness: nutrition, cooking techniques, recipes, products and gear), 500-750 words; Know How (ranging from beginner to expert focus, written by people with solid expertise, details ways to improve performance, how-to-do-it instructions, information on equipment manufacturers, and places readers can go), 300-1,000 words; Senses (capturing a moment in backcountry through sight, sound, smell, and other senses, paired with an outstanding photo), 150-200 words. **Buys 50-75 mss/year.**

Tips "Our best advice is to read the publication—most freelancers don't know the magazine at all. The best way to break in is with an article for the Weekend Wilderness, Know How, or Signpost Department."

$ $ $⊘ HOOKED ON THE OUTDOORS

2040 30th St., Suite A, Boulder CO 80301. (303)449-5119. Website: www.ruhooked.com. **60% freelance written.** "*Hooked on the Outdoors* magazine is a bimonthly travel and gear guide for outdoorsy folk of all ages, shapes, sizes, religions, and mantras. No matter the background, all have the North American backyard in common. *Hooked* is the outdoor guide for readers who are multi-sport oriented and, just the same, people new to the outdoors, providing affordable, close to home destinations and gear alternative." Estab. 1998. Circ. 150,000. Pays within 30 days of publication. Publishes ms an average of 4 months after acceptance. Byline given. Offers 15% kill fee. Buys first North American serial, electronic rights. Editorial lead time 3 months. Submit seasonal material 1 year in advance. Accepts queries by mail, e-mail. Accepts simultaneous submissions. Responds in 6 weeks to queries. Sample copy for $5 and SAE with $1.75 postage. Writer's guidelines online.

Nonfiction Book excerpts, essays, exposé, general interest, humor, interview/profile, new product, opinion, personal experience, photo feature, travel. **Buys 4 mss/year.** Query with published clips. Length: 350-2,500 words. **Pays 35-50¢/word.** Sometimes pays expenses of writers on assignment.

Photos State availability with submission. Reviews contact sheets. Buys one-time rights. Offers $25-290. Captions, model releases required.

Columns/Departments **Buys 30 mss/year.** Query with published clips. **Pays 35-50¢/word.**

Tips "Send well thought out, complete queries reflective of research. Writers ought not query on topics already covered."

OUTSIDE

Mariah Media, Inc., Outside Plaza, 400 Market St., Santa Fe NM 87501. Website: www.outsidemag.com. Editor: Hal Espen. **Contact:** Editorial Department. **90% freelance written.** Monthly magazine. "*Outside* is a monthly national magazine for active, educated, upscale adults who love the outdoors and are concerned about its preservation." Estab. 1977. Circ. 550,000. Pays after acceptance. Publishes ms an average of 3 months after acceptance. Byline given. Offers 25% kill fee. Buys first North American serial rights. Submit seasonal material 5 months in advance. Writer's guidelines online. Editorial calendar online.

Nonfiction Book excerpts, essays, general interest, how-to, interview/profile (major figures associated with sports, travel, environment, outdoor), photo feature (outdoor photography), technical (reviews of equipment, how-to), travel (adventure, sports-oriented travel). Do not want to see articles about sports that we don't cover (basketball, tennis, golf, etc.). **Buys 40 mss/year.** Query with published clips. Length: 1,500-5,000 words. Pays expenses of writers on assignment.

Photos "Do not send photos; if we decide to use a story, we may ask to see the writer's photos." Reviews transparencies. Buys one-time rights. Captions, identification of subjects required.

Columns/Departments Dispatches (news, events, short profiles relevant to outdoors), 100-800 words; Destinations (places to explore, news, and tips for adventure travelers), 300-1,000 words; Review (evaluations of products), 200-1,500 words. **Buys 180 mss/year.** Query with published clips.

Tips "Prospective writers should study the magazine before querying. Look at the magazine for our style, subject matter, and standards." The departments are the best areas for freelancers to break in.

HOCKEY

$ $ MINNESOTA HOCKEY JOURNAL

Official Publication of Minnesota Hockey, Inc., % TPG Sports, Inc., 6160 Summit Dr., Suite 375, Minneapolis MN 55430. (763)595-0808. Fax: (763)595-0016. E-mail: greg@tpgsports.com. Website: www.tpgsports.com. Editor: Greg Anzlec. **50% freelance written.** Journal published 4 times/year. Estab. 2000. Circ. 40,000. Pays on publication. Byline given. Buys all rights. Editorial lead time 6 months. Submit seasonal material 4 months in advance. Accepts previously published material. Accepts simultaneous submissions. Sample copy and writer's guidelines free.

Nonfiction Essays, general interest, historical/nostalgic, how-to (play hockey), humor, inspirational, interview/ profile, new product, opinion, personal experience, photo feature, travel, hockey camps, pro hockey, juniors, college, Olympics, youth, etc. **Buys 3-5 mss/year.** Query. Length: 500-1,500 words. **Pays $100-300.**

Reprints Accepts previously published submissions.

Photos State availability with submission. Reviews contact sheets. Rights purchased vary. Negotiates payment individually. Captions, identification of subjects required.

⚛ $ $ $USA HOCKEY MAGAZINE

Official Publication of USA Hockey, TPG Sports, Inc., 6160 Summit Dr., Suite 375, Minneapolis MN 55430. (763)595-0808, ext. 114. Fax: (763)595-0016. E-mail: info@tpgsports.com. Website: www.usahockey.com. Managing Editor: Harry Thompson. **Contact:** Greg Anzelc, publications manager. **60% freelance written.** Magazine published 10 times/year covering amateur hockey in the US. "The world's largest hockey magazine, *USA Hockey Magazine* is the official magazine of USA Hockey, Inc., the national governing body of hockey." Estab. 1980. Circ. 444,000. Pays on acceptance or publication. Byline given. Buys all rights. Editorial lead time 6 months. Submit seasonal material 4 months in advance. Accepts previously published material. Accepts simultaneous submissions. Sample copy and writer's guidelines free.

Nonfiction Essays, general interest, historical/nostalgic, how-to (play hockey), humor, inspirational, interview/profile, new product, opinion, personal experience, photo feature, travel, hockey camps, pro hockey, juniors, college, NCAA hockey championships, Olympics, youth, etc. **Buys 20-30 mss/year.** Query. Length: 500-5,000 words. **Pays $50-750.** Pays expenses of writers on assignment.

Reprints Accepts previously published submissions.

Photos State availability with submission. Reviews contact sheets. Rights purchased varies. Negotiates payment individually. Captions, identification of subjects required.

Columns/Departments Short Cuts (news and notes); Coaches' Corner (teaching tips); USA Hockey; Inline Notebook (news and notes). **Pays $150-250.**

Fiction Adventure, humorous, slice-of-life vignettes. **Buys 10-20 mss/year. Pays $150-1,000.**

Fillers Anecdotes, facts, gags to be illustrated by cartoonist, newsbreaks, short humor. **Buys 20-30/year.** Length: 10-100 words. **Pays $25-250.**

Tips Writers must have a general knowledge and enthusiasm for hockey, including ice, inline, street, and other. The primary audience is youth players in the US.

HORSE RACING

$ $AMERICAN TURF MONTHLY

All Star Sports, Inc., 299 East Shore Rd., Suite 204, Great Neck NY 11023. (516)773-4075. Fax: (516)773-2944. E-mail: editor@americanturf.com. Website: www.americanturf.com. **Contact:** James Corbett, editor-in-chief. **90% freelance written.** Monthly magazine covering Thoroughbred racing, handicapping, and wagering. "Squarely focused on Thoroughbred handicapping and wagering. *ATM* is a magazine for horseplayers, not owners, breeders, or 12-year-old girls enthralled with ponies." Estab. 1946. Circ. 28,000. Pays on publication. Publishes ms an average of 4 months after acceptance. Byline given. Makes work-for-hire assignments. Editorial lead time 2 months. Submit seasonal material 2 months in advance. Accepts queries by mail, e-mail. Responds in 1 month to queries. Sample copy and writer's guidelines free.

Nonfiction Handicapping and wagering features. Special issues: Triple Crown/Kentucky Derby (May); Saratoga/Del Mar (August); Breeder's Cup (November). No historical essays, bilious 'guest editorials,' saccharine poetry, fiction. **Buys 50 mss/year.** Query. Length: 800-2,000 words. **Pays $75-300 for assigned articles; $100-500 for unsolicited articles.**

Photos Send photos with submission. Reviews 3×5 transparencies, prints, 300 dpi TIF images on CD-ROM. Buys one-time rights. Offers $25 interior; $150 for cover. Identification of subjects required.

Fillers Newsbreaks, short humor. **Buys 5/year.** Length: 400 words. **Pays $25.**

▣ The online magazine carries original content not found in the print version.

Tips "Send a good query letter specifically targeted at explaining how this contribution will help our readers to cash a bet at the track!"

HUNTING & FISHING

⚛ $ $ALABAMA GAME & FISH

Game & Fish, P.O. Box 741, Marietta GA 30061. (770)953-9222. Fax: (770)933-9510. E-mail: jimmy.jacobs@primedia.com. Website: www.alabamagameandfish.com. **Contact:** Jimmy Jacobs, editor. See *Game & Fish*.

$ $AMERICAN ANGLER

The Magazine of Fly Fishing & Fly Tying, Abenaki Publishers, Inc., P.O. Box 4100, Bennington VT 05201. E-mail: americanangler@flyfishingmagazines.com. Website: www.flyfishingmagazines.com. **Contact:** Philip Monahan, editor. **95% freelance written.** Bimonthly magazine covering fly fishing. "*American Angler* is dedicated to giving fly fishers practical information they can use—wherever they fish, whatever they fish for." Estab. 1976. Circ. 60,000. Pays on publication. Publishes ms an average of 6 months after acceptance. Byline given. Buys first North American serial, one-time rights. Editorial lead time 3 months. Submit seasonal material

5 months in advance. Accepts queries by mail, fax. Accepts previously published material. Accepts simultaneous submissions. Responds in 6 weeks to queries; 2 months to mss. Sample copy for $6. Writer's guidelines for #10 SASE.

Nonfiction How-to (most important), personal experience, photo feature (seldom), technical. No promotional flack of pay back free trips or freebies, no superficial, broad-brush coverage of subjects. **Buys 45-60 mss/year.** Query with published clips. Length: 800-2,200 words. **Pays $200-400.**

Reprints Send information about when and where the material previously appeared. Pay negotiable.

Photos "Photographs are important. A fly-tying submission should always include samples of flies to send to our staff photographer, even if photos of the flies are included." Send photos with submission. Reviews contact sheets, transparencies. Buys one-time rights. Offers no additional payment for photos accepted with ms. Captions, identification of subjects required.

Columns/Departments One-page shorts (problem solvers), 350-750 words. Query with published clips. **Pays $100-300.**

Tips "If you are new to this editor, please submit complete queries."

$ $ $ AMERICAN HUNTER

11250 Waples Mill Rd., Fairfax VA 22030-9400. (703)267-1335. Fax: (703)267-3971. E-mail: publications@nrahq .org. Website: www.nra.org. **Editor-in-Chief:** J. Scott Olmstead. **Contact:** Frank Minter, executive editor. Monthly magazine for hunters who are members of the National Rifle Association. "*American Hunter* contains articles dealing with various sport hunting and related activities both at home and abroad. With the encouragement of the sport as a prime game management tool, emphasis is on technique, sportsmanship and safety. In each issue hunting equipment and firearms are evaluated, legislative happenings affecting the sport are reported, lore and legend are retold and the business of the Association is recorded in the Official Journal section." Circ. 1,000,000. **Pays on acceptance.** Byline given. Buys first North American serial, second serial (reprint) rights. Accepts queries by mail, e-mail. Responds in 6 months to queries. Writer's guidelines for #10 SASE.

Nonfiction Factual material on all phases of hunting: Expository how-to, where-to, and general interest pieces; humor: personal narratives; and semi-technical articles on firearms, wildlife management or hunting. Features fall into five categories: Deer, upland birds, waterfowl, big game and varmints/small game. Special issues: Pheasants, whitetail tactics, black bear feed areas, mule deer, duck hunters' transport by land and sea, tech topics to be decided; rut strategies, muzzleloader moose and elk, fall turkeys, staying warm, goose talk, long-range muzzleloading. Not interested in material on fishing, camping, or firearms knowledge. Query. Length: 1,800-2,000 words. **Pays up to $800.**

Reprints Send ms with rights for sale noted and information about when and where the material previously appeared.

Photos No additional payment made for photos used with ms; others offered from $75-600.

Columns/Departments Hunting Guns, Hunting Loads and Public Hunting Grounds. Study back issues for appropriate subject matter and style. Length: 1,200-1,500 words. **Pays $300-450.**

Tips "Although unsolicited manuscripts are welcomed, detailed query letters outlining the proposed topic and approach are appreciated and will save both writers and editors a considerable amount of time. If we like your story idea, you will be contacted by mail or phone and given direction on how we'd like the topic covered. NRA Publications accept all manuscripts and photographs for consideration on a specualtion basis only. Story angles should be narrow, but coverage must have depth. How-to articles are popular with readers and might range from methods for hunting to techniques on making gear used on successful hunts. Where-to articles should contain contacts and information needed to arrange a similar hunt. All submissions are judged on three criteria: Story angle (it should be fresh, interesting, and informative); quality of writing (clear and lively—capable of holding the readers' attention throughout); and quality and quantity of accompanying photos (sharpness, reproduceability, and connection to text are most important)."

N $ $ ARKANSAS SPORTSMAN

Game & Fish, P.O. Box 741, Marietta GA 30061. (770)953-9222. Fax: (770)933-9510. E-mail: ronell.smith@prime dia.com. Website: www.arkansassportsmanmag.com. **Contact:** Ronell Smith, editor. See *Game & Fish*.

$ $ BASSMASTER MAGAZINE

B.A.S.S. Publications, 5845 Carmichael Pkwy., Montgomery AL 36117. (334)272-9530. Fax: (334)396-8230. E-mail: editorial@bassmaster.com. Website: www.bassmaster.com. **Contact:** James Hall, editor. **80% freelance written.** Magazine published 11 times/year about largemouth, smallmouth, and spotted bass, offering "how-to" articles for dedicated beginning and advanced bass fishermen, including destinations and new product reviews. Estab. 1968. Circ. 600,000. **Pays on acceptance.** Publishes ms an average of less than 1 year after acceptance. Byline given. Buys electronic rights. Editorial lead time 2 months. Submit seasonal material 6 months in advance. Accepts queries by mail, e-mail. Responds in 2 months to queries. Sample copy for $2. Writer's guidelines for #10 SASE.

> • Needs destination stories (how to fish a certain area) for the Northwest and Northeast.

Nonfiction Historical/nostalgic, how-to (patterns, lures, etc.), interview/profile (of knowledgeable people in the sport), new product (reels, rods, and bass boats), travel (where to go fish for bass), conservation related to bass fishing. "No first-person, personal experience-type articles." **Buys 100 mss/year.** Query. Length: 500-1,500 words. **Pays $100-600.**

Photos Send photos with submission. Reviews transparencies. Buys all rights. Offers no additional payment for photos accepted with ms, but pays $700 for color cover transparencies. Captions, model releases required.

Columns/Departments Short Cast/News/Views/Notes/Briefs (upfront regular feature covering news-related events such as new state bass records, unusual bass fishing happenings, conservation, new products, and editorial viewpoints). Length: 250-400 words. **Pays $100-300.**

Fillers Anecdotes, newsbreaks. **Buys 4-5/year.** Length: 250-500 words. **Pays $50-100.**

Tips "Editorial direction continues in the short, more direct how-to article. Compact, easy-to-read information is our objective. Shorter articles with good graphics, such as how-to diagrams, step-by-step instruction, etc., will enhance a writer's articles submitted to *Bassmaster Magazine*. The most frequent mistakes made by writers in completing an article for us are poor grammar, poor writing, poor organization, and superficial research. Send in detailed queries outlining specific objectives of article, obtain writer's guidelines. Be as concise as possible."

◩ BC OUTDOORS SPORT FISHING AND OUTDOOR ADVENTURE

OP Publishing, 1080 Howe St., Suite 900, Vancouver BC V6Z 2T1 Canada. (604)678-2586. E-mail: bcoutdoors@oppublishing.com. Website: www.bcosportfishing.com. **Contact:** D. Ryan Pohl, editor. **80% freelance written.** Magazine published 6 times/year covering fresh and saltwater fishing, camping, and backroads. Pays on publication. Publishes ms an average of 3 months after acceptance. Byline given. Offers kill fee. Buys first North American serial rights. Writer's guidelines for 8×10 SAE with 7 Canadian first-class stamps.

Nonfiction "We would like to receive how-to, where-to features dealing with fishing in British Columbia." How-to (new or innovative articles on fishing subjects), personal experience (outdoor adventure), outdoor topics specific to British Columbia. Query features in early spring. Length: 1,700-2,000 words.

Photos State availability with submission. Buys one-time rights. Captions, identification of subjects required.

Tips "Wants in-depth information, professional writing only. Emphasis on environmental issues. Those pieces with a conservation component have a better chance of being published. Subject must be specific to British Columbia. We receive many manuscripts written by people who obviously do not know the magazine or market. The writer has a better chance of breaking in with short, lesser-paying articles and fillers, because we have a stable of regular writers who produce most main features."

◩ $ $ THE BIG GAME FISHING JOURNAL

Informational Publications, Inc., 1800 Bay Ave., Point Pleasant NJ 08742. Fax: (732)223-2449. Website: www.bgf-journal.com. **90% freelance written.** Bimonthly magazine covering big game fishing. "We require highly instructional articles prepared by qualified writers/fishermen." Estab. 1994. Circ. 45,000. Pays on publication. Byline given. Offers 50% kill fee. Buys first North American serial rights. Editorial lead time 3 months. Submit seasonal material 3 months in advance. Accepts queries by mail, e-mail. Accepts simultaneous submissions. Responds in 2 weeks to queries; 1 month to mss. Writer's guidelines free.

Nonfiction How-to, interview/profile, technical. **Buys 50-70 mss/year.** Send complete ms. Length: 2,000-3,000 words. **Pays $200-400.** Sometimes pays expenses of writers on assignment.

Photos Send photos with submission. Reviews transparencies. Buys one-time rights. Offers no additional payment for photos accepted with ms. Captions required.

Tips "Our format is considerably different than most publications. We prefer to receive articles from qualified anglers on their expertise—if the author is an accomplished writer, all the better. We require highly-instructional articles that teach both novice and expert readers."

$ $ BUGLE

Rocky Mountain Elk Foundation, P.O. Box 8249, 2291 W. Broadway, Missoula MT 59808. E-mail: bugle@rmef.org. Website: www.elkfoundation.org. Editor: Dan Crockett. **Contact:** Paul Queneau, assistant editor. **50% freelance written.** Bimonthly magazine covering elk conservation and elk hunting. *Bugle* is the membership publication of the Rocky Mountain Elk Foundation, a nonprofit wildlife conservation group. "Our readers are predominantly hunters, many of them conservationists who care deeply about protecting wildlife habitat." Estab. 1984. Circ. 132,000. **Pays on acceptance.** Publishes ms an average of 1-36 months after acceptance. Byline given. Offers variable kill fee. Buys one-time rights. Editorial lead time 6 months. Submit seasonal material 6 months in advance. Accepts queries by mail, e-mail, fax. Accepts previously published material.

Responds in 1 month to queries; 3 months to mss. Sample copy for $5. Writer's guidelines online.

    ○┓ Preparation: "Read as many issues of *Bugle* as possible to know what the Elk Foundation and magazine are about. Queries should include clips of published or unpublished work representative of story being proposed." Unsolicited mss welcome. Electronic submissions preferred.

Nonfiction "We're looking for elk-related science, conservation and natural history articles, interviews/profiles, essays, book excerpts, humor, nostalgia, general interest, western, vignettes, anecdotes, narratives, photo essays." **Buys 30-40 mss/year.** Query with published clips. Length: up to 6,000 words. **Pays 20¢/word.**

Reprints Send ms with rights for sale noted and information about when and where the material previously appeared. Pays 10¢/word.

Columns/Departments Elk-related, 100-3,000 words. Query with published clips. **Pays 20¢/word.**

Fiction Elk-related stories. **Pays 20¢/word.**

Poetry Elk-related.

Tips "We're hungry for situation ethics, thoughts and theories, women in the outdoors, natural history, humor, and straight hunting stories."

🅽 $ $ CALIFORNIA GAME & FISH

Game & Fish, P.O. Box 741, Marietta GA 30061. (770)953-9222. Fax: (770)933-9510. E-mail: burt.carey@primedia.com. Website: www.californiagameandfish.com. **Contact:** Burt Carey, editor. See *Game & Fish*.

🅽 $ $ DEER & DEER HUNTING

Krause Publications, a Division of F+W Publications, Inc., 700 E. State St., Iola WI 54990-0001. E-mail: dan.schmidt@fwpubs.com. Website: www.deeranddeerhunting.com. **Contact:** Daniel E. Schmidt, editor. **95% freelance written.** Magazine published 10 times/year covering white-tailed deer. "Readers include a cross section of the deer hunting population—individuals who hunt with bow, gun, or camera. The editorial content of the magazine focuses on white-tailed deer biology and behavior, management principle and practices, habitat requirements, natural history of deer, hunting techniques, and hunting ethics. We also publish a wide range of 'how-to' articles designed to help hunters locate and get close to deer at all times of the year. The majority of our readership consists of 2-season hunters (bow and gun) and approximately one-third camera hunt." Estab. 1977. Circ. 130,000. **Pays on acceptance.** Publishes ms an average of 18 months after acceptance. Byline given. Buys all rights. Editorial lead time 6 months. Submit seasonal material 12 months in advance. Accepts queries by mail, e-mail. Responds in 1 month to queries; 2 months to mss. Sample copy for 9×12 SASE. Writer's guidelines online.

Nonfiction General interest, historical/nostalgic, how-to, photo feature, technical. No "Joe and me" articles. **Buys 100 mss/year.** Send complete ms. Length: 1,000-1,700 words. **Pays $150-500 for assigned articles; $150-400 for unsolicited articles.** Pays in contributor copies for small articles about hunter-killed deer. Sometimes pays expenses of writers on assignment.

Photos Send photos with submission. Reviews transparencies. Buys one-time rights. Offers $75-250/photo; $600 for cover photos. Captions required.

Columns/Departments Deer Browse (odd occurrences), 500 words. **Buys 10 mss/year.** Query. **Pays $50-300.**

Fiction "Mood" deer hunting pieces. **Buys 9 mss/year.** Send complete ms.

Fillers Facts, newsbreaks. **Buys 40-50/year.** Length: 100-500 words. **Pays $15-150.**

Tips "Feature articles dealing with deer biology or behavior should be documented by scientific research (the author's or that of others) as opposed to a limited number of personal observations."

🅽 $ $ THE DRAKE MAGAZINE

For Those Who Fly-Fish, 34145 PCH #319, Dana Point CA 92629. E-mail: bieline@aol.com. Website: www.drakemag.com. **Contact:** Tom Bie, managing editor. **70% freelance written.** Annual magazine for people who love fishing. Pays 1 month after publication. Publishes ms an average of 1 year after acceptance. Byline given. Buys first North American serial rights. Editorial lead time 1 year. Submit seasonal material 1 year in advance. Accepts queries by mail. Responds in 6 months to mss.

    ○┓ To break in "Tippets is the best bet: Short, 200-600 word essays on any aspect of the fishing world. Rodholders is another good area (profiles of people who fish)."

Nonfiction Book excerpts, essays, general interest, historical/nostalgic, humor, interview/profile, opinion, personal experience, photo feature, travel (fishing related). **Buys 8 mss/year.** Query. Length: 250-3,000 words. **Pays 10-20¢/word** "depending on the amount of work we have to put into the piece."

Photos State availability with submission. Reviews contact sheets, negatives, transparencies. Buys one-time rights. Offers $25-250/photo.

    🖥 The online magazine carries original content not found in the print version. Contact: Tom Bie, online editor.

$ $ $ FIELD & STREAM

2 Park Ave., Time 4 Media, New York NY 10016-5695. (212)779-5000. Fax: (212)779-5114. E-mail: fsletters@time4.com. Website: fieldandstream.com. Editor: Sid Evans. **Contact:** Sid Evans, editor. **50% freelance written.** Monthly magazine. ''Broad-based service magazine for the hunter and fisherman. Editorial content consists of articles of penetrating depth about national hunting, fishing, and related activities. Also humor, personal essays, profiles on outdoor people, conservation, sportsmen's insider secrets, tactics and techniques, and adventures.'' Estab. 1895. Circ. 1,500,000. **Pays on acceptance for most articles.** Byline given. Buys first rights. Accepts queries by mail. Responds in 1 month to queries. Sample copy not available. Writer's guidelines online.

Nonfiction Length: 1,500 words for features. Payment varies depending on the quality of work, importance of the article. **Pays $800-1,000 and more on a sliding scale for major features.** Query by mail.

Photos Send photos with submission. Reviews slides (prefers color). Buys first rights. When purchased separately, pays $450 minimum for color.

□ Online version of magazine carries original content not contained in the print edition. Contact: Elizabeth Burnham.

Tips ''Writers are encouraged to submit queries on article ideas. These should be no more than a paragraph or 2, and should include a summary of the idea, including the angle you will hang the story on, and a sense of what makes this piece different from all others on the same or a similar subject. Many queries are turned down because we have no idea what the writer is getting at. Be sure that your letter is absolutely clear. We've found that if you can't sum up the point of the article in a sentence or 2, the article doesn't have a point. Pieces that depend on writing style, such as humor, mood, and nostalgia or essays often can't be queried and may be submitted in manuscript form. The same is true of short tips. All submissions to *Field & Stream* are on an on-spec basis. Before submitting anything, however, we encourage you to *study*, not simply read, the magazine. Many pieces are rejected because they do not fit the tone or style of the magazine, or fail to match the subject of the article with the overall subject matter of *Field & Stream*. Above all, study the magazine before submitting anything.''

$ FISHING & HUNTING NEWS

Outdoor Empire Publishing, 424 N. 130th St., Seattle WA 98133. (206)624-3845. Fax: (206)695-8512. E-mail: staff@fishingandhuntingnews.com. Website: www.fhnews.com/. **Contact:** John Marsh, managing editor. **95% freelance written.** Bimonthly magazine covering fishing and hunting. ''We focus on upcoming fishing and hunting opportunities in your area—where to go and what to do once you get there.'' Estab. 1954. Circ. 96,000. Pays on publication. Publishes ms an average of 1 month after acceptance. Byline given. Buys first North American serial, second serial (reprint), electronic rights. Editorial lead time 1 month. Submit seasonal material 2 months in advance. Accepts queries by mail, e-mail. Sample copy and writer's guidelines free.

Nonfiction How-to (local fishing and hunting), where-to. **Buys 5,000 mss/year.** Query with published clips. Length: 350-2,000 words. **Pays $25-125 and up.** Seldom pays expenses of writers on assignment.

Photos State availability with submission. Buys all rights. Captions required.

Tips ''*F&H News* is published in 7 local editions across the western US, Great Lakes, and mid-Atlantic states. We look for reports of current fishing and hunting opportunity, plus technique- or strategy-related articles that can be used by anglers and hunters in these areas.''

N $ $ FLORIDA GAME & FISH

Game & Fish, P.O. Box 741, Marietta GA 30061. (770)953-9222. Fax: (770)933-9510. E-mail: jimmy.jacobs@primedia.com. Website: www.floridagameandfish.com. **Contact:** Jimmy Jacobs, editor. See *Game & Fish*.

$ $ FLORIDA SPORTSMAN

Wickstrom Communications Division of Primedia Special Interest Publications, 2700 S. Kanner Hwy., Stuart FL 34994. (772)219-7400. Fax: (772)219-6900. E-mail: editor@floridasportsman.com. Website: www.floridasportsman.com. **Contact:** Jeff Weakley, editor. **30% freelance written.** Monthly magazine covering fishing, boating, and related sports—Florida and Caribbean only. ''*Florida Sportsman* is edited for the boatowner and off-shore, coastal, and fresh water fisherman. It provides a how, when, and where approach in its articles, which also includes occasional camping, diving, and hunting stories—plus ecology; in-depth articles and editorials attempting to protect Florida's wilderness, wetlands, and natural beauty.'' Circ. 115,000. **Pays on acceptance.** Publishes ms an average of 6 months after acceptance. Byline given. Buys nonexclusive additional rights. Submit seasonal material 6 months in advance. Accepts queries by mail. Responds in 2 months to queries; 1 month to mss. Sample copy for free. Writer's guidelines for #10 SASE.

Nonfiction ''We use reader service pieces almost entirely—how-to, where-to, etc. One or 2 environmental pieces/issue as well. Writers must be Florida based, or have lengthy experience in Florida outdoors. All articles must have strong Florida emphasis. We do not want to see general how-to-fish-or-boat pieces which might well appear in a national or wide-regional magazine.'' Essays (environment or nature), how-to (fishing, hunting, boating), humor (outdoors angle), personal experience (in fishing, etc.), technical (boats, tackle, etc., as particularly suitable for Florida specialities). **Buys 40-60 mss/year.** Query. Length: 1,500-2,500 words. **Pays $475.**

Photos Send photos with submission. Reviews 35mm transparencies, 4×5 and larger prints. Buys all rights. Offers no additional payment for photos accepted with ms. Pays up to $750 for cover photos.

Tips "Feature articles are most open to freelancers; however there is little chance of acceptance unless contributor is an accomplished and avid outdoorsman *and* a competent writer-photographer with considerable experience in Florida."

$FLY FISHERMAN MAGAZINE

Primedia Enthusiast Group, 6405 Flank Dr., Harrisburg PA 17112. (717)540-6701. Fax: (717)657-9552. Website: www.flyfisherman.com. Editor: John Randolph. Published 6 times/year covering fly fishing. Written for anglers who fish primarily with a fly rod and for other anglers who would like to learn more about fly fishing. Circ. 122,560. Sample copy not available.

ℕ $ $FLYFISHING & TYING JOURNAL

A Compendium for the Complete Fly Fisher, Frank Amato Publications, P.O. Box 82112, Portland OR 97282. (503)653-8108. Fax: (503)653-2766. E-mail: kim@amatobooks.com. Website: www.amatobooks.com. **Contact:** Kim Koch, editor. **100% freelance written.** Quarterly magazine covering flyfishing and fly tying for both new and veteran anglers. Every issue is seasonally focused: Spring, Summer, Fall, and Winter. Estab. 1980. Circ. 60,000. Pays on publication. Byline given. Buys first rights. Editorial lead time up to 1 year. Submit seasonal material up to 1 year in advance. Accepts queries by mail, e-mail. Responds in 2 months. Writer's guidelines for #10 SASE, Attn: Kim Koch.

Nonfiction How-to. **Buys 55-60 mss/year.** Query. Length: 1,000-2,000 words. **Pays $200-600.**

Photos State availability with submission. Reviews transparencies. Buys one-time rights. Offers no additional payment for photos accepted with ms. Captions, identification of subjects, model releases required.

ℕ $ $FUR-FISH-GAME

2878 E. Main, Columbus OH 43209-9947. **Contact:** Mitch Cox, editor. **65% freelance written.** Monthly magazine for outdoorsmen of all ages who are interested in hunting, fishing, trapping, dogs, camping, conservation, and related topics. Estab. 1900. Circ. 111,000. **Pays on acceptance.** Publishes ms an average of 7 months after acceptance. Byline given. Buys first, all rights. Responds in 2 months to queries. Sample copy for $1 and 9×12 SAE. Writer's guidelines for #10 SASE.

Nonfiction "We are looking for informative, down-to-earth stories about hunting, fishing, trapping, dogs, camping, boating, conservation, and related subjects. Nostalgic articles are also used. Many of our stories are 'how-to' and should appeal to small-town and rural readers who are true outdoorsmen. Some recents articles have told how to train a gun dog, catch big-water catfish, outfit a bowhunter, and trap late-season muskrat. We also use personal experience stories and an occasional profile, such as an article about an old-time trapper. 'Where-to' stories are used occasionally if they have broad appeal." Query. Length: 500-3,000 words. **Pays $50-250 or more for features depending upon quality, photo support, and importance to magazine.**

Photos Send photos with submission. Reviews transparencies, color prints (5×7 or 8×10). Pays $25 for separate freelance photos. Captions, credits required.

Tips "We are always looking for quality how-to articles about fish, game animals, or birds that are popular with everyday outdoorsmen but often overlooked in other publications, such as catfish, bluegill, crappie, squirrel, rabbit, crows, etc. We also use articles on standard seasonal subjects such as deer and pheasant, but like to see a fresh approach or new technique. Instructional trapping articles are useful all year. Articles on gun dogs, ginseng, and do-it-yourself projects are also popular with our readers. An assortment of photos and/or sketches greatly enhances any manuscript, and sidebars, where applicable, can also help. No phone queries, please."

$ $GAME & FISH

2250 Newmarket Pkwy., Suite 110, Marietta GA 30067. (770)953-9222. Fax: (770)933-9510. E-mail: ken.dunwoody@primedia.com. Website: www.gameandfishmag.com. **Contact:** Ken Dunwoody, editorial director. **90% freelance written.** Publishes 30 different monthly outdoor magazines, each one covering the fishing and hunting opportunities in a particular state or region (see individual titles to contact editors). Estab. 1975. Circ. 570,000. Pays 3 months prior to cover date of issue. Publishes ms an average of 7 months after acceptance. Byline given. Offers negotiable kill fee. Buys first North American serial rights. Submit seasonal material 8 months in advance. Accepts queries by mail, e-mail, fax. Responds in 3 months to queries. Sample copy for $3.50 and 9×12 SASE. Writer's guidelines for #10 SASE.

Nonfiction Prefers queries over unsolicited mss. Length: 1,500-2,400 words. **Pays $150-300; additional payment made for electronic rights.**

Photos Reviews transparencies, prints, digital images. Buys one-time rights. Cover photos $250, inside color $75, and b&w $25. Captions, identification of subjects required.

🖳 Online magazine occasionally carries original content not found in the print edition. Contact: Dave Schaefer.

Tips "Our readers are experienced anglers and hunters, and we try to provide them with useful, specific articles about where, when, and how to enjoy the best hunting and fishing in their state or region. We also cover topics concerning game and fish management. Most articles should be tightly focused and aimed at outdoorsmen in 1 particular state. After familiarizing themselves with our magazine(s), writers should query the appropriate state editor (see individual listings) or send to Ken Dunwoody."

N $ $ GEORGIA SPORTSMAN

Game & Fish, P.O. Box 741, Marietta GA 30061. (770)953-9222. Fax: (770)933-9510. E-mail: jimmy.jacobs@primedia.com. Website: www.georgiasportsmanmag.com. **Contact:** Jimmy Jacobs, editor. See *Game & Fish*.

N $ $ GREAT PLAINS GAME & FISH

Game & Fish, P.O. Box 741, Marietta GA 30061. (770)953-9222. Fax: (770)933-9510. E-mail: nick.gilmore@primedia.com. Website: www.greatplainsgameandfish.com. **Contact:** Nick Gilmore, editor. See *Game & Fish*.

N ⊘ GUN WORLD

Y-Visionary Publishing, L.P., 265 Anita Dr., Suite 120, Orange CA 92868-3310. (714)939-9991. Fax: (714)939-9909. E-mail: editorial@gunworld.com. Website: www.gunworld.com. Editor: Jan Libourel. Monthly magazine edited for hunters and target shooters, with frequent articles on new innovations in police and military armament. Circ. 126,402. Editorial lead time 2 months.

● Query before submitting.

GUNS & AMMO

Primedia Enthusiast Group, 6420 Wilshire Blvd., Los Angeles CA 90048. (323)782-2000. Fax: (323)782-2867. E-mail: gunsandammo@primedia.com. Website: www.gunsandammomag.com. Editor: Lee Hoots. Monthly magazine for recreational shooters, hunters, target shooters, plinkers and collectors. Circ. 607,971. Editorial lead time 4 months. Sample copy not available.

N $ $ ILLINOIS GAME & FISH

Game & Fish, P.O. Box 741, Marietta GA 30061. (770)953-9222. Fax: (770)933-9510. E-mail: dennis.schmidt@primedia.com. Website: www.illinoisgameandfish.com. **Contact:** Dennis Schmidt, editor. See *Game & Fish*.

N ⊘ IN-FISHERMAN

Primedia Enthusiast Group, 7819 Highland Scenic Rd., Baxter MN 56425. (218)829-1648. Fax: (218)829-3091. Website: www.in-fisherman.com. Magazine published 8 times/year for freshwaters anglers from beginners to professionals. Circ. 301,258. Editorial lead time 2 months.

● Query before submitting.

N $ $ INDIANA GAME & FISH

Game & Fish, P.O. Box 741, Marietta GA 30061. (770)953-9222. Fax: (770)933-9510. E-mail: ken.freel@primedia.com. Website: www.indianagameandfish.com. **Contact:** Ken Freel, editor. See *Game & Fish*.

N $ $ IOWA GAME & FISH

Game & Fish, P.O. Box 741, Marietta GA 30061. (770)953-9222. Fax: (770)933-9510. E-mail: ronell.smith@primedia.com. Website: www.iowagameandfish.com. **Contact:** Ronell Smith, editor. See *Game & Fish*.

N $ $ KENTUCKY GAME & FISH

Game & Fish, P.O. Box 741, Marietta GA 30061. (770)953-9222. Fax: (770)933-9510. E-mail: ken.freel@primedia.com. Website: www.kentuckygameandfish.com. **Contact:** Ken Freel, editor. See *Game & Fish*.

N $ $ LOUISIANA GAME & FISH

Game & Fish, P.O. Box 741, Marietta GA 30061. (770)953-9222. Fax: (770)933-9510. E-mail: ronell.smith@primedia.com. Website: www.lagameandfish.com. **Contact:** Ronell Smith, editor. See *Game & Fish*.

N $ $ THE MAINE SPORTSMAN

P.O. Box 910, Yarmouth ME 04096. (207)846-9501. Fax: (207)846-1434. E-mail: harry.vanderweide@verizon.net. Website: www.mainesportsman.com. **Contact:** Harry Vanderweide, editor. **80% freelance written.** Monthly tabloid. "Eager to work with new/unpublished writers, but because we run over 30 regular columns, it's hard to get into *The Maine Sportsman* as a beginner." Estab. 1972. Circ. 30,000. Pays during month of publication. Publishes ms an average of 3 months after acceptance. Byline given. Buys first rights. Accepts queries by mail, e-mail. Accepts previously published material. Responds in 2 weeks to queries.

Nonfiction "We publish only articles about Maine hunting and fishing activities. Any well-written, researched, knowledgeable article about that subject area is likely to be accepted by us." **Buys 25-40 mss/year.** Send complete ms via e-mail. Length: 200-2,000 words. **Pays $20-300.** Sometimes pays expenses of writers on assignment.

Reprints Yes, send typed ms via e-mail or query. with rights for sale noted. Pays 100% of amount paid for an original article.

Photos Send color slides, color prints, or JPEGs/TIFFs via e-mail. Pays $5-50 for b&w print.

Tips "We publish numerous special sections each year and are eager to buy Maine-oriented articles on snowmobiling, ice fishing, boating, salt water and deer hunting. Send articles or queries. You can e-mail us at ursushpv@mint.net."

N $ $ MARLIN

The International Sportfishing Magazine, World Publications, Inc., P.O. Box 8500, Winter Park FL 32790. (407)628-4802. Fax: (407)628-7061. E-mail: editor@marlinmag.com. Website: www.marlinmag.com. **Contact:** Dave Ferrell, editor. **90% freelance written.** Magazine published 8 times/year covering the sport of big game fishing (billfish, tuna, dorado, and wahoo). "Our readers are sophisticated, affluent, and serious about their sport—they expect a high-class, well-written magazine that provides information and practical advice." Estab. 1982. Circ. 50,000. **Pays on acceptance.** Publishes ms an average of 3 months after acceptance. Byline given. Buys first North American serial rights. Submit seasonal material 3 months in advance. Accepts previously published material. Sample copy free with SASE. Writer's guidelines online.

Nonfiction General interest, how-to (bait-rigging, tackle maintenance, etc.), new product, personal experience, photo feature, technical, travel. "No freshwater fishing stories. No 'Me & Joe went fishing' stories." **Buys 30-50 mss/year.** Query with published clips. Length: 800-3,000 words. **Pays $250-500.**

Reprints Send photocopy and information about when and where the material previously appeared. Pays 50-75% of amount paid for original article.

Photos State availability with submission. Reviews original slides. Buys one-time rights. Offers $50-300 for inside use, $1,000 for a cover.

Columns/Departments Tournament Reports (reports on winners of major big game fishing tournaments), 200-400 words; Blue Water Currents (news features), 100-400 words. **Buys 25 mss/year.** Query. **Pays $75-250.**

Tips "Tournament reports are a good way to break in to *Marlin*. Make them short but accurate, and provide photos of fishing action or winners' award shots (*not* dead fish hanging up at the docks). We always need how-tos and news items. Our destination pieces (travel stories) emphasize where and when to fish, but also include information on where to stay. For features: Crisp, high-action stories with emphasis on exotic nature, adventure, personality, etc.—nothing flowery or academic. Technical/how-to: concise and informational—specific details. News: Again, concise with good details—watch for legislation affecting big game fishing, outstanding catches, new clubs and organizations, new trends, and conservation issues."

$ MICHIGAN OUT-OF-DOORS

P.O. Box 30235, Lansing MI 48909. (517)371-1041. Fax: (517)371-1505. E-mail: magazine@mucc.org. Website: www.mucc.org. **Contact:** Dennis C. Knickerbocker, editor. **75% freelance written.** Monthly magazine emphasizing Michigan outdoor recreation, especially hunting and fishing, conservation, nature, and environmental affairs. Estab. 1947. Circ. 90,000. **Pays on acceptance.** Publishes ms an average of 6 months after acceptance. Byline given. Buys first North American serial rights. Submit seasonal material 6 months in advance. Accepts queries by mail, phone. Responds in 1 month to queries. Sample copy for $3.50. Writer's guidelines for free or on website.

Break in by "writing interestingly about an *unusual* aspect of Michigan natural resources and/or outdoor recreation.

Nonfiction "Stories must have a Michigan slant unless they treat a subject of universal interest to our readers." Exposé, historical/nostalgic, how-to, interview/profile, opinion, personal experience, photo feature. Special issues: Archery Deer and Small Game Hunting (October); Firearm Deer Hunting (November); Cross-country Skiing and Early-ice Lake Fishing (December or January); Camping/Hiking (May); Family Fishing (June). No humor or poetry. **Buys 96 mss/year.** Send complete ms. Length: 1,000-2,000 words. **Pays $90 minimum for feature stories.**

Photos Buys one-time rights. Offers no additional payment for photos accepted with ms; others $20-175. Captions required.

Tips ''Top priority is placed on true accounts of personal adventures in the out-of-doors—well-written tales of very unusual incidents encountered while hunting, fishing, camping, hiking, etc.''

ℕ $ $ MICHIGAN SPORTSMAN

Game & Fish, P.O. Box 741, Marietta GA 30061. (770)953-9222. Fax: (770)933-9510. E-mail: dennis.schmidt@pri media.com. Website: www.michigansportsmanmag.com. **Contact:** Dennis Schmidt, editor. See *Game & Fish*.

ℕ $ $ MID-ATLANTIC GAME & FISH

Game & Fish, P.O. Box 741, Marietta GA 30061. (770)953-9222. Fax: (770)933-9510. E-mail: ken.freel@primedia. com. Website: www.midatlanticgameandfish.com. **Contact:** Ken Freel, editor. See *Game & Fish*.

$ MIDWEST OUTDOORS

MidWest Outdoors, Ltd., 111 Shore Dr., Burr Ridge IL 60527-5885. (630)887-7722. Fax: (630)887-1958. Website: www.midwestoutdoors.com. **Contact:** Gene Laulunen, editor. **100% freelance written.** Monthly tabloid emphasizing fishing, hunting, camping, and boating. Estab. 1967. Circ. 45,000. Pays on publication. Publishes ms an average of 3 months after acceptance. Byline given. Buys simultaneous rights. Submit seasonal material 2 months in advance. Accepts previously published material. Accepts simultaneous submissions. Responds in 3 weeks to queries. Sample copy for $1 or online. Writer's guidelines for #10 SASE or online.

• Submissions may be e-mailed to info@midwestoutdoors.com (Microsoft Word format preferred).

Nonfiction How-to (fishing, hunting, camping in the Midwest), where-to-go (fishing, hunting, camping within 500 miles of Chicago). ''We do not want to see any articles on 'my first fishing, hunting, or camping experiences,' 'cleaning my tackle box,' 'tackle tune-up,' 'making fishing fun for kids,' or 'catch and release.''' **Buys 1,800 unsolicited mss/year.** Send complete ms. Length: 1,000-1,500 words. **Pays $15-30.**

Reprints Send tearsheet.

Photos Reviews slides and b&w prints. Buys all rights. Offers no additional payment for photos accompanying ms. Captions required.

Columns/Departments Fishing; Hunting. Send complete ms. **Pays $30.**

Tips ''Break in with a great unknown fishing hole or new technique within 500 miles of Chicago. Where, how, when, and why. Know the type of publication you are sending material to.''

ℕ $ $ MINNESOTA SPORTSMAN

Game & Fish, P.O. Box 741, Marietta GA 30061. (770)953-9222. Fax: (770)933-9510. E-mail: dennis.schmidt@pri media.com. Website: www.minnesotasportsmanmag.com. **Contact:** Dennis Schmidt, editor. See *Game & Fish*.

ℕ $ $ MISSISSIPPI GAME & FISH

Game & Fish, P.O. Box 741, Marietta GA 30061. (770)953-9222. Fax: (770)933-9510. E-mail: jimmy.jacobs@prim edia.com. Website: www.mississippigameandfish.com. **Contact:** Jimmy Jacobs, editor. See *Game & Fish*.

ℕ $ $ MISSOURI GAME & FISH

Game & Fish, P.O. Box 741, Marietta GA 30061. (770)953-9222. Fax: (770)933-9510. E-mail: ronell.smith@prime dia.com. Website: www.missourigameandfish.com. **Contact:** Ronell Smith, editor. See *Game & Fish*.

ℕ $ $ MUSKY HUNTER MAGAZINE

P.O. Box 340, St. Germain WI 54558. (715)477-2178. Fax: (715)477-8858. Editor: Jim Saric. **Contact:** Steve Heiting. **90% freelance written.** Bimonthly magazine on musky fishing. ''Serves the vertical market of musky fishing enthusiasts. We're interested in how-to, where-to articles.'' Estab. 1988. Circ. 34,000. Pays on publication. Publishes ms an average of 4 months after acceptance. Byline given. Buys first, one-time rights. Submit seasonal material 4 months in advance. Responds in 2 months to queries. Sample copy for 9×12 SAE with $1.93 postage. Writer's guidelines for #10 SASE.

Nonfiction Historical/nostalgic (related only to musky fishing), how-to (modify lures, boats, and tackle for musky fishing), personal experience (must be musky fishing experience), technical (fishing equipment), travel (to lakes and areas for musky fishing). **Buys 50 mss/year.** Send complete ms. Length: 1,000-2,500 words. **Pays $100-300 for assigned articles; $50-300 for unsolicited articles.** Payment of contributor copies or other premiums negotiable.

Photos Send photos with submission. Reviews 35mm transparencies, 3×5 prints. Buys one-time rights. Offers no additional payment for photos accepted with ms. Identification of subjects required.

ℕ $ $ NEW ENGLAND GAME & FISH

Game & Fish, P.O. Box 741, Marietta GA 30061. (770)953-9222. Fax: (770)933-9510. E-mail: steve.carpenteri@pr imedia.com. Website: www.newenglandgameandfish.com. **Contact:** Steve Carpenteri, editor. See *Game & Fish*.

N $ $ NEW YORK GAME & FISH

Game & Fish, P.O. Box 741, Marietta GA 30061. (770)953-9222. Fax: (770)933-9510. E-mail: steve.carpenteri@primedia.com. Website: www.newyorkgameandfish.com. **Contact:** Steve Carpenteri, editor. See *Game & Fish*.

$ $ NORTH AMERICAN WHITETAIL

The Magazine Devoted to the Serious Trophy Deer Hunter, Game & Fish, 2250 Newmarket Pkwy., Suite 110, Marietta GA 30067. (770)953-9222. Fax: (770)933-9510. Website: northamericanwhitetail.com. **Contact:** Duncan Dobie, editor. **70% freelance written.** Magazine published 8 times/year about hunting trophy-class white-tailed deer in North America, primarily the US. "We provide the serious hunter with highly sophisticated information about trophy-class whitetails and how, when, and where to hunt them. We are not a general hunting magazine or a magazine for the very occasional deer hunter." Estab. 1982. Circ. 130,000. Pays 65 days prior to cover date of issue. Publishes ms an average of 6 months after acceptance. Byline given. Offers negotiable kill fee. Buys first North American serial rights. Submit seasonal material 10 months in advance. Accepts queries by mail, fax, phone. Responds in 3 months to mss. Sample copy for $3.50 and 9×12 SAE with 7 first-class stamps. Writer's guidelines for #10 SASE.

Nonfiction How-to, interview/profile. **Buys 50 mss/year.** Query. Length: 1,000-3,000 words. **Pays $150-400.**

Photos Send photos with submission. Reviews 35mm transparencies, color prints, high quality digital images. Buys one-time rights. Offers no additional payment for photos accepted with ms. Captions, identification of subjects required.

Columns/Departments Trails and Tails (nostalgic, humorous, or other entertaining styles of deer-hunting material, fictional or nonfictional), 1,200 words. **Buys 8 mss/year.** Send complete ms. **Pays $150.**

Tips "Our articles are written by persons who are deer hunters first, writers second. Our hard-core hunting audience can see through material produced by nonhunters or those with only marginal deer-hunting expertise. We have a continual need for expert profiles/interviews. Study the magazine to see what type of hunting expert it takes to qualify for our use, and look at how those articles have been directed by the writers. Good photography of the interviewee and his hunting results must accompany such pieces."

$ $ NORTH CAROLINA GAME & FISH

Game & Fish, P.O. Box 741, Marietta GA 30061. (770)953-9222. Fax: (770)933-9510. E-mail: david.johnson@primedia.com. Website: www.ncgameandfish.com. **Contact:** David Johnson, editor. See *Game & Fish*.

N $ $ OHIO GAME & FISH

Game & Fish, P.O. Box 741, Marietta GA 30061. (770)953-9222. Fax: (770)933-9510. E-mail: steve.carpenteri@primedia.com. Website: www.ohiogameandfish.com. **Contact:** Steve Carpenteri, editor. See *Game & Fish*.

$ $ OKLAHOMA GAME & FISH

Game & Fish, P.O. Box 741, Marietta GA 30061. (770)953-9222. Fax: (770)933-9510. E-mail: nick.gilmore@primedia.com. Website: www.oklahomagameandfish.com. **Contact:** Nick Gilmore, editor. See *Game & Fish*.

$ $ ONTARIO OUT OF DOORS

Roger's Media, 1 Mt. Pleasant Rd., Isabella Tower, Toronto ON M4Y 2Y5 Canada. (416)764-1652. Fax: (416)764-1751. Website: www.ontariooutofdoors.com. Editor: Burt Myers. **Contact:** John Kerr, managing editor. **90% freelance written.** Magazine published 10 times/year covering the outdoors (hunting, fishing, camping). Estab. 1968. Circ. 93,865. **Pays on acceptance.** Publishes ms an average of 6 months after acceptance. Byline given. Buys first, electronic rights. Editorial lead time 6 months. Submit seasonal material 6 months in advance. Accepts queries by mail, e-mail, fax. Responds in 3 months to queries. Sample copy and writer's guidelines free.

Nonfiction Book excerpts, essays, exposé, how-to (fishing and hunting), humor, inspirational, interview/profile, new product, opinion, personal experience, photo feature, technical, travel (where-to), wildlife management; environmental concerns. "No 'Me and Joe' features or articles written from a women's point of view on how to catch a bass." **Buys 100 mss/year.** Length: 500-2,500 words. **Pays $750 maximum for assigned articles; $700 maximum for unsolicited articles.** Sometimes pays expenses of writers on assignment.

Photos Send photos with submission. Reviews transparencies. Buys one time and electronic rights. Pays $450-750 for covers. Captions required.

Columns/Departments Trips & Tips (travel pieces), 50-150 words; Short News, 50-500 words. **Buys 30-40 mss/year.** Query. **Pays $50-250.**

Fiction Humorous, novel excerpts. **Buys 6 mss/year.** Send complete ms. Length: 1,000 words. **Pays $500 maximum.**

Fillers Facts, newsbreaks. **Buys 40/year.** Length: 25-100 words. **Pays $15-50.**

Tips "With the exception of short news stories, it is suggested that writers query prior to submission."

$THE OUTDOORS MAGAZINE

For the Better Hunter, Angler & Trapper, Elk Publishing, Inc., 531 Main St., Colchester VT 05446. (800)499-0447. Fax: (802)879-2015. E-mail: james@elkpublishing.com. Website: www.outdoorsmagazine.net. **Contact:** James Ehlers, publisher. **80% freelance written.** Monthly magazine covering wildlife conservation. "New England hunting, fishing, and trapping magazine covering news, tips, destinations, and good old-fashioned stories." Estab. 1996. Circ. 14,000. Pays on publication. Publishes ms an average of 1 year after acceptance. Byline given. Offers 10% kill fee. Buys first North American serial rights. Editorial lead time 1 year. Submit seasonal material 6 months in advance. Accepts queries by mail. Accepts previously published material. Responds in 1 month to queries; 3 month to mss. Sample copy online or by e-mail. Writer's guidelines free.

Nonfiction Book excerpts, essays, exposé, general interest, historical/nostalgic, how-to, interview/profile, new product, opinion, personal experience, technical. **Buys 200 mss/year.** Query with published clips. Length: 750-2,500 words. **Pays $20-150 for assigned articles.**

Photos State availability with submission. Reviews contact sheets. Buys one-time rights. Pays $15-75/photo. Identification of subjects required.

Columns/Departments Buys 100 mss/year. Query with published clips. **Pays $20-60.**

Fillers Anecdotes, facts.

Tips *"Know* the publication, not just read it, so you understand the audience. Patience and thoroughness will go a long way."

$ $⊘ PENNSYLVANIA ANGLER & BOATER

Pennsylvania Fish & Boat Commission, P.O. Box 67000, Harrisburg PA 17106-7000. (717)705-7844. E-mail: amichaels@state.pa.us. Website: www.fish.state.pa.us. **Contact:** Art Michaels, editor. **40% freelance written.** Bimonthly magazine covering fishing, boating, and related conservation topics in Pennsylvania. Circ. 30,000. Pays 2 months after acceptance. Publishes ms an average of 8 months after acceptance. Byline given. Buys varying rights. Submit seasonal material 8 months in advance. Responds in 1 month to queries; 2 months to mss. Sample copy for 9×12 SAE with 9 first-class stamps. Writer's guidelines for #10 SASE.

• *No unsolicited mss.*

Nonfiction How-to (and where-to), technical. No saltwater or hunting material. **Buys 75 mss/year.** Query. Length: 500-2,500 words. **Pays $25-300.**

Photos Send photos with submission. Reviews 35mm and larger transparencies. Rights purchased vary. Offers no additional payment for photos accompanying mss. Captions, identification of subjects, model releases required.

Ⓝ $ $ PENNSYLVANIA GAME & FISH

Game & Fish, P.O. Box 741, Marietta GA 30061. (770)953-9222. Fax: (770)933-9510. E-mail: steve.carpenteri@primedia.com. Website: www.pagameandfish.com. **Contact:** Steve Carpenteri, editor. See *Game & Fish.*

PETERSEN'S HUNTING

Primedia Enthusiast Group, 6420 Wilshire Blvd., Los Angeles CA 90048. (323)782-2563. Fax: (323)782-2477. Website: www.huntingmag.com. **Contact:** Scott Rupp, editor. **10% freelance written.** Magazine published 10 times/year covering sport hunting. "We are a 'how-to' magazine devoted to all facets of sport hunting, with the intent to make our readers more knowledgeable, more successful and safer hunters." Circ. 350,000. Pays on scheduling. Publishes ms an average of 9 months after acceptance. Byline given. Buys all rights. Writer's guidelines on request.

Nonfiction General interest, how-to (on hunting techniques), travel. **Buys 15 mss/year.** Query. Length: 2,400 words.

Photos Send photos with submission. Reviews 35mm transparencies. Buys one-time rights. Captions, identification of subjects, model releases required.

Ⓝ PETERSEN'S RIFLE SHOOTER

Primedia Enthusiast Group, 6420 Wilshire Blvd., 14th Floor, Los Angeles CA 90048. (323)782-2000. Fax: (323)782-2867. E-mail: rifles@primedia.com. Website: www.rifleshootermag.com. Editor: Jerry Lee. Bimonthly magazine for the dedicated and serious rifle enthusiast. Circ. 150,000. Editorial lead time 4 months.

$ $RACK MAGAZINE

Adventures in Trophy Hunting, Buckmasters, Ltd., P.O. Box 244022, Montgomery AL 36124-4022. (800)240-3337. Fax: (334)215-3535. E-mail: mhandley@buckmasters.com. Website: www.rackmag.com. **Contact:** Mike Handley, editor. **10-15% freelance written.** Hunting magazine published monthly (August-January). "*Rack Magazine* caters to deer hunters and chasers of other big game animals who prefer short stories detailing the harvests of exceptional specimens. There are no how-to, destination, or human interest stories; only pieces describing particular hunts.'' Estab. 1999. Circ. 140,000. Pays on publication. Publishes ms an average of 11 months after acceptance. Byline given. Buys first North American serial, second serial (reprint) rights. Editorial lead time 9 months. Accepts queries by e-mail, phone. Accepts previously published material. Accepts simultaneous submissions. Responds in 1 month to queries. Sample copy for free. Writer's guidelines by e-mail.

Nonfiction Interview/profile, personal experience. *Rack Magazine* does not use how-to, destination, humor, general interest, or hunter profiles. **Buys 35-40 mss/year.** Query. Length: 500-1,500 words. **Pays $250.**

Reprints Accepts previously published submissions.

Photos Send photos with submission. Reviews transparencies. Captions, identification of subjects required.

Tips ''We're only interested in stories about record book animals (those scoring high enough to qualify for BTR, B&C, P&Y, SCI, or Longhunter). Whitetails must be scored by a certified BTR/Buckmasters measurer and their antlers must register at least 160-inches on the BTR system. Deer scoring 190 or better on the B&C or P&Y scales would be candidates, but the hunter would have to have his or her buck scored by a BTR measurer.''

$ $ROCKY MOUNTAIN GAME & FISH

Game & Fish, Box 741, Marietta GA 30061. (770)935-9222. Fax: (770)933-9510. E-mail: burt.carey@primedia.com. Website: www.rmgameandfish.com. **Contact:** Burt Carey, editor. See *Game & Fish*.

$ $SALT WATER SPORTSMAN MAGAZINE

2 Park Ave., New York NY 10016. (212)779-5179. Fax: (212)779-5479. E-mail: editor@saltwatersportsman.com. Website: www.saltwatersportsman.com. **Contact:** David Dibenedetto, editor. **85% freelance written.** Monthly magazine. ''*Salt Water Sportsman* is edited for serious marine sport fishermen whose lifestyle includes the pursuit of game fish in US waters and around the world. It provides information on fishing trends, techniques, and destinations, both local and international. Each issue reviews offshore and inshore fishing boats, high-tech electronics, innovative tackle, engines, and other new products. Coverage also focuses on sound fisheries management and conservation.'' Circ. 170,000. **Pays on acceptance.** Publishes ms an average of 5 months after acceptance. Byline given. Offers kill fee. Buys first North American serial rights. Submit seasonal material 8 months in advance. Accepts queries by mail, e-mail, fax. Accepts previously published material. Responds in 1 month to queries. Sample copy for #10 SASE. Writer's guidelines online.

Nonfiction ''Readers want solid how-to, where-to information written in an enjoyable, easy-to-read style. Personal anecdotes help the reader identify with the writer.'' How-to, personal experience, technical, travel (to fishing areas). **Buys 100 mss/year.** Query. Length: 1,200-2,000 words. **Pays $300-750.**

Reprints Send tearsheet. Pays up to 50% of amount paid for original article.

Photos Reviews color slides. Pays $1,500 minimum for 35mm, $2\frac{1}{4} \times 2\frac{1}{4}$ or 8×10 transparencies for cover. Offers additional payment for photos accepted with ms. Captions required.

Columns/Departments Sportsman's Tips (short, how-to tips and techniques on salt water fishing, emphasis is on building, repairing, or reconditioning specific items or gear). Send complete ms.

Tips ''There are a lot of knowledgeable fishermen/budding writers out there who could be valuable to us with a little coaching. Many don't think they can write a story for us, but they'd be surprised. We work with writers. Shorter articles that get to the point which are accompanied by good, sharp photos are hard for us to turn down. Having to delete unnecessary wordage—conversation, clichés, etc.—that writers feel is mandatory is annoying. Often they don't devote enough attention to specific fishing information.''

$ $SHOTGUN SPORTS MAGAZINE

P.O. Box 6810, Auburn CA 95604. (530)889-2220. Fax: (530)889-9106. E-mail: shotgun@shotgunsportsmagazine.com. **Contact:** Linda Martin, production coordinator. **50% freelance written.** Welcomes new writers. Monthly magazine covering all the shotgun sports and shotgun hunting—sporting clays, trap, skeet, hunting, gunsmithing, shotshell patterning, shotsell reloading, mental training for the shotgun sports, shotgun tests, anything ''shotgun.'' Pays on publication. Publishes ms an average of 1-6 months after acceptance. Buys all rights. Sample copy and writer's guidelines available by contacting Linda Martin, production coordinator.

● Responds within 3 weeks. Subscription: $32.95 (US); $39.95 (Canada); $60 (foreign).

Nonfiction Current needs: ''Anything with a 'shotgun' subject. Tests, think pieces, roundups, historical, interviews, etc. No articles promoting a specific club or sponsored hunting trip, etc.'' Submit complete ms with photos by mail with SASE. Can submit by e-mail. Length: 1,000-5,000 words. **Pays $50-200.**

Photos ''5×7 or 8×10 b&w or 4-color with appropriate captions. On disk or e-mailed at least 5-inches and 300 dpi (contact Graphics Artist for details).'' Reviews transparencies (35 mm or larger), b&w, or 4-color. Send photos with submission.

Tips ''Do not fax manuscript. Send good photos. Take a fresh approach. Create a professional, yet friendly article. Send diagrams, maps, and photos of unique details, if needed. For interviews, more interested in 'words of wisdom' than a list of accomplishments. Reloading articles must include source information and backup data. Check your facts and data! If you can't think of a fresh approach, don't bother. If it's not about shotguns or shotgunners, don't send it. Never say, 'You don't need to check my data; I never make mistakes.'"

N $ $ SOUTH CAROLINA GAME & FISH

Game & Fish, P.O. Box 741, Marietta GA 30061. (770)953-9222. Fax: (770)933-9510. E-mail: david.johnson@pri media.com. Website: www.scgameandfish.com. **Contact:** David Johnson, editor. See *Game & Fish*.

$ $ SPORT FISHING

The Magazine of Saltwater Fishing, 460 N. Orlando Ave., Suite 200, Winter Park FL 32789-7061. (407)571-4576. Fax: (407)571-4577. E-mail: doug.olander@worldpub.net. **Contact:** Doug Olander, editor-in-chief. **50% freelance written.** Magazine covering saltwater sports fishing. Estab. 1986. Circ. 150,000. Pays within 6 weeks of acceptance. Byline given. Offers $100 kill fee. Buys first North American serial, one-time rights. Submit seasonal material 5 months in advance. Accepts queries by mail, e-mail, fax. Responds in 2 weeks to queries. Sample copy for #10 SASE. Writer's guidelines for #10 SASE or by e-mail.

○→ Break in with freelance pieces for the "Tips & Techniques News" and "Fish Tales" departments.

Nonfiction How-to (rigging & techniques tips), technical, conservation, where-to (all on sport fishing). **Buys 32-40 mss/year.** Query. Length: 2,000-3,000 words. **Pays $500 (payment for photos is separate).**

Photos Send photos with submission. Reviews transparencies and returns within 1 week. Buys one-time rights. Pays $75-400 inside; $1,000 cover.

Columns/Departments Fish Tales (humorous sport fishing anecdotes); Rigging (how-to rigging for sport fishing); Technique (how-to technique for sport fishing), 800-1,200 words. **Buys 8-24 mss/year.** Send complete ms. **Pays $250.**

Tips "Don't query unless you are familiar with the magazine; note—*saltwater only*. Find a fresh idea or angle to an old idea. We welcome the chance to work with new/unestablished writers who know their stuff—and how to say it."

N $ $ TENNESSEE SPORTSMAN

Game & Fish, P.O. Box 741, Marietta GA 30061. (770)953-9222. Fax: (770)933-9510. E-mail: david.johnson@pri media.com. Website: www.tennesseesportsmanmag.com. **Contact:** David Johnson, editor. See *Game & Fish*.

N $ $ TEXAS SPORTSMAN

Game & Fish, P.O. Box 741, Marietta GA 30061. (770)953-9222. Fax: (770)933-9510. E-mail: nick.gilmore@prime dia.com. Website: www.texassportsmanmag.com. **Contact:** Nick Gilmore, editor. See *Game & Fish*.

N $ $ TRAPPER & PREDATOR CALLER

Krause Publications, a Division of F+W Publications, Inc., 700 E. State St., Iola WI 54990. (715)445-2214. E-mail: waitp@krause.com. Website: www.trapperpredatorcaller.com. **Contact:** Paul Wait, editor. **95% freelance written.** Tabloid published 10 times/year covering trapping and predator calling, fur trade. "Must have mid-level to advanced knowledge, because *T&PC* is heavily how-to focused." Estab. 1975. Circ. 38,000. Pays on publication. Publishes ms an average of 6 months after acceptance. Byline given. Buys one-time rights. Editorial lead time 1 year. Submit seasonal material 1 year in advance. Accepts queries by e-mail.

Nonfiction How-to, interview/profile, personal experience, travel. **Buys 100 mss/year.** Query with or without published clips or send complete ms. Length: 1,000-2,500 words. **Pays $100-250 for assigned articles; $80-200 for unsolicited articles.**

Photos Send photos with submission. Reviews negatives, prints. Buys one-time rights.

N $ $ TURKEY & TURKEY HUNTING

Krause Publications, a Division of F+W Publications, Inc., 700 E. State St., Iola WI 54990-0001. Website: www.turkeyandturkeyhunting.com. **Contact:** James Schlender, editor. **50% freelance written.** Bimonthly magazine filled with practical and comprehensive information for wild turkey hunters. Estab. 1982. Circ. 40,000. **Pays on acceptance.** Publishes ms an average of 8 months after acceptance. Byline given. Offers 50% kill fee. Buys one-time rights. Editorial lead time 1 year. Submit seasonal material 1 year in advance. Accepts queries by mail. Responds in 1 month to queries; 6 months to mss. Sample copy for $4. Ms and photo guidelines online.

Nonfiction Does not want "Me and Joe went hunting and here's what happened" articles. **Buys 20 mss/year.** Send complete ms. Length: 1,500-2,500 words. **Pays $275-400.**

Photos Send photos with submission. Reviews contact sheets, 2×2 transparencies, any size prints. Buys one-time rights. Offers $75-200/photo. Negotiates payment individually. Identification of subjects required.

Tips "Turkey hunting is a continually growing and changing sport. Search for topics that reflect this trend. Our audience is sophisticated and experienced. We have several contributing editors who write most of our how-to articles, so we buy few articles of this type from freelancers. Well-written mood/essay articles are always welcome for review. If you have not written for *Turkey & Turkey Hunting*, it is best to send a finished manuscript. We do not assign articles based on query letters.''

N $ $ VIRGINIA GAME & FISH

Game & Fish, P.O. Box 741, Marietta GA 30061. (770)953-9222. Fax: (770)933-9510. E-mail: david.johnson@pri media.com. Website: www.virginiagameandfish.com. **Contact:** David Johnson, editor. See *Game & Fish*.

N $ $ WASHINGTON-OREGON GAME & FISH

Game & Fish, P.O. Box 741, Marietta GA 30061. (770)953-9222. Fax: (770)933-9510. E-mail: burt.carey@primedi a.com. Website: www.wogameandfish.com. **Contact:** Burt Carey, editor. See *Game & Fish*.

N $ $ WEST VIRGINIA GAME & FISH

Game & Fish, P.O. Box 741, Marietta GA 30061. (770)953-9222. Fax: (770)933-9510. E-mail: ken.freel@primedia. com. Website: www.wvgameandfish.com. **Contact:** Ken Freel, editor. See *Game & Fish*.

$ $ WESTERN OUTDOORS

185 Avenida La Pata, San Clemente CA 92673. (949)366-0030. Fax: (949)366-0804. E-mail: lew@wonews.com. **Contact:** Lew Carpenter, editor. **60% freelance written.** Magazine emphasizing fishing, boating for California, Oregon, Washington, Baja California, and Alaska. ''We are the West's leading authority on fishing techniques, tackle and destinations, and all reports present the latest and most reliable information.'' Estab. 1961. Circ. 100,000. **Pays on acceptance.** Publishes ms an average of 6 months after acceptance. Buys first North American serial rights. Submit seasonal material 6 months in advance. Accepts queries by mail, e-mail, fax. Responds in 6 weeks to queries. Sample copy for free. Writer's guidelines for #10 SASE.

Nonfiction Where-to (catch more fish, improve equipment, etc.), how-to informational, photo feature. ''We do not accept poetry or fiction.'' **Buys 36-40 assigned mss/year.** Query. Length: 1,500-2,000 words. **Pays $450-600.**

Photos Reviews 35mm slides. Offers no additional payment for photos accepted with ms; pays $350-500 for covers. Captions required.

Tips ''Provide a complete package of photos, map, trip facts and manuscript written according to our news feature format. Excellence of color photo selections make a sale more likely. Include sketches of fishing patterns and techniques to guide our illustrators. Graphics are important. The most frequent mistake made by writers in completing an article for us is that they don't follow our style. Our guidelines are quite clear. One query at a time via mail, e-mail, fax. No phone calls. You can become a regular *Western Outdoors* byliner by submitting professional quality packages of fine writing accompanied by excellent photography. Pros anticipate what is needed, and immediately provide whatever else we request. Furthermore, they meet deadlines!''

WESTERN SPORTSMAN

Suite 900, 1080 Howe St., Vancouver BC V6Z 2T1 Canada. E-mail: editor@westernsportsman.com. **Contact:** David Webb. **90% freelance written.** Bimonthly magazine for anglers, hunters, and others interested in outdoor recreation. ''Note that our main coverage area is British Columbia, Alberta, Saskatchewan, Manitoba, with occasional coverage of the Yukon and Northwest Territories/Nunavut. We occasionally publish adventure destination stories that cover parts of the country as well. Short news items pertaining to all provinces/territories are also accepted. We try to include as much information as possible on all subjects in each edition.'' Estab. 1968. Circ. 35,000. Pays on publication. Byline given. Buys first North American serial rights. Accepts queries by mail, e-mail, fax. Responds in 1 month to queries. Writer's guidelines for free with SAE.

● Familiarize yourself with the magazine before submitting. Queries accepted year-round.

Nonfiction ''It is necessary that all articles can identify with our coverage area. We are interested in manuscripts from writers who have had an interesting fishing or hunting experience. We also publish other informational pieces as long as they relate to our coverage area. We are most interested in articles which tell about the average guy living on beans, piloting his own boat, stalking his game and generally doing his own thing in Western Canada than a story describing a well-to-do outdoorsmen traveling by motorhome, staying at an expensive lodge with guides doing everything for him except catching the fish or shooting the big game animal. The articles submitted to us need to be prepared in a knowledgeable way and include more information than the actual fish catch or animal or bird kill. Discuss the terrain, the people involved on the trip, the water or weather conditions, the costs, the planning that went into the trip, the equipment and other data closely associated with the particular event. We're always looking for new writers.'' **Buys 60 mss/year.** Length: 1,500-2,000 words for features; 600-1,000 words for columns; 150-300 words for news items. **Payment negotiable.**

Photos Photos purchased with ms with no additional payment. Also purchased without ms. Pays up to $250 for front cover.

🅝 $ $ WISCONSIN OUTDOOR JOURNAL

Krause Publications, a Division of F+W Publications, Inc., 700 E. State St., Iola WI 54990-0001. (715)445-2214. E-mail: waitp@krause.com. Website: www.wisoutdoorjournal.com. **Contact:** Paul Wait, editor. **90% freelance written.** Magazine published 8 times/year covering Wisconsin fishing, hunting, and outdoor lifestyles. Estab. 1987. Circ. 25,000. **Pays on acceptance.** Publishes ms an average of 1 year after acceptance. Byline given. Buys one-time rights. Editorial lead time 1 year. Submit seasonal material 1 year in advance. Accepts queries by e-mail.

Nonfiction Book excerpts, exposé, how-to, humor, interview/profile, personal experience, travel (within Wisconsin). **Buys 45-50 mss/year.** Query or send complete ms. **Pays $150-225 for assigned articles; $200 for unsolicited articles.**

Photos Send photos with submission. Reviews negatives, prints. Buys one-time rights. Offers $25-200/photo. Identification of subjects required.

Fiction Adventure, historical, nostalgic. "No eulogies of a good hunting dog." **Buys 10 mss/year.** Send complete ms. Length: 1,500-2,000 words. **Pays $100-250.**

🅝 $ $ WISCONSIN SPORTSMAN

Game & Fish, P.O. Box 741, Marietta GA 30061. (770)953-9222. Fax: (770)933-9510. E-mail: dennis.schmidt@primedia.com. Website: www.wisconsinsportsmanmag.com. **Contact:** Dennis Schmidt, editor. See *Game & Fish*.

MARTIAL ARTS

$ $ BLACK BELT

Black Belt Communications, LLC, 24900 Anza Dr., Unit E, Valencia CA 91355. Fax: (661)257-3028. E-mail: byoung@aimmedia.com. Website: www.blackbeltmag.com. **Contact:** Robert Young, executive editor. **80% freelance written.** Works with a small number of new/unpublished writers each year. Monthly magazine emphasizing martial arts for both experienced practitioner and layman. Estab. 1961. Circ. 100,000. Pays on publication. Publishes ms an average of 1 year after acceptance. Buys all rights. Submit seasonal material 6 months in advance. Accepts queries by mail, e-mail, fax. Accepts simultaneous submissions. Responds in 3 weeks to queries. Writer's guidelines online.

Nonfiction Exposé, how-to, interview/profile, new product, personal experience, technical, travel, Informational; Health/fitness; Training. "We never use personality profiles." **Buys 40-50 mss/year.** Query with outline. Length: 1,200 words minimum. **Pays $100-300.**

Photos Very seldom buys photographs without accompanying ms. Total purchase price for ms includes payment for photos. Captions, model releases required.

🅝 $ $ INSIDE KUNG-FU

The Ultimate In Martial Arts Coverage!, CFW Enterprises, 4201 Vanowen Place, Burbank CA 91505. (818)845-2656. Fax: (818)845-7761. E-mail: davecater@cfwenterprises.com. **Contact:** Dave Cater, editor. **90% freelance written.** Monthly magazine for those with "traditional, modern, athletic, and intellectual tastes. The magazine slants toward little-known martial arts and little-known aspects of established martial arts." Estab. 1973. Circ. 125,000. Pays on publication date on magazine cover. Publishes ms an average of 6 months after acceptance. Byline given. Buys first North American serial rights. Editorial lead time 6 months. Submit seasonal material 6 months in advance. Accepts simultaneous submissions. Responds in 1 month to queries; 2 months to mss. Sample copy for $5.95 and 9×12 SAE with 5 first class stamps. Writer's guidelines for #10 SASE.

Nonfiction "Articles must be technically or historically accurate." *Inside Kung-Fu* is looking for external type articles (fighting, weapons, multiple hackers). Book excerpts, essays, exposé (topics relating to martial arts), general interest, historical/nostalgic, how-to (primarily technical materials), inspirational, interview/profile, new product, personal experience, photo feature, technical, travel, cultural/philosophical. No "sports coverage, first-person articles, or articles which constitute personal aggrandizement." **Buys 120 mss/year.** Query or send complete ms. Length: 1,500-3,000 words (8-10 pages, typewritten and double-spaced). **Pays $125-175.**

Reprints Send tearsheet or typed ms with rights for sale noted and information about when and where the material previously appeared. No payment.

Photos State availability of or send photos with submission. Reviews contact sheets, negatives, 5×7 or 8×10 color prints. Buys all rights. No additional payment for photos. Captions, identification of subjects, model releases required.

Fiction "Fiction must be short (1,000-2,000 words) and relate to the martial arts. We buy very few fiction pieces." Adventure, historical, humorous, mystery, novel excerpts, suspense. **Buys 2-3 mss/year.**

Tips "See what interests the writer. May have a better chance of breaking in at our publication with short articles and fillers since smaller pieces allow us to gauge individual ability, but we're flexible—quality writers get published, period. The most frequent mistakes made by writers in completing an article for us are ignoring photo requirements and model releases (always No. 1—and who knows why? All requirements are spelled out in writer's guidelines).''

$ $ JOURNAL OF ASIAN MARTIAL ARTS

Via Media Publishing Co., 821 W. 24th St., Erie PA 16502-2523. Website: www.goviamedia.com. **Contact:** Michael A. DeMarco, publisher. **90% freelance written.** Quarterly magazine covering ''all historical and cultural aspects related to Asian martial arts, offering a mature, well-rounded view of this uniquely fascinating subject. Although the journal treats the subject with academic accuracy (references at end), writing need not lose the reader!'' Estab. 1991. Pays on publication. Publishes ms an average of 1 year after acceptance. Byline given. Buys first, second serial (reprint) rights. Submit seasonal material 6 months in advance. Responds in 1 month to queries; 2 months to mss. Sample copy for $10. Writer's guidelines for #10 SASE.

Nonfiction ''All articles should be backed with solid, reliable reference material.'' Essays, exposé, historical/nostalgic, how-to (martial art techniques and materials, i.e., weapons), interview/profile, personal experience, photo feature (place or person), religious, technical, travel. ''No articles overburdened with technical/foreign/scholarly vocabulary, or material slanted as indirect advertising or for personal aggrandizement.'' **Buys 30 mss/year.** Query with short background and martial arts experience. Length: 2,000-10,000 words. **Pays $150-500.**

Photos State availability with submission. Reviews contact sheets, negatives, transparencies, prints. Buys one-time and reprint rights. Offers no additional payment for photos accepted with ms. Identification of subjects, model releases required.

Columns/Departments Location (city, area, specific site, Asian or non-Asian, showing value for martial arts, researchers, history); Media Review (film, book, video, museum for aspects of academic and artistic interest).- **Length:** 1,000-2,500 words. **Buys 16 mss/year.** Query. **Pays $50-200.**

Fiction Adventure, historical, humorous, slice-of-life vignettes, translation. No material that does not focus on martial arts culture. **Buys 1 ms/year.** Query. Length: 1,000-10,000 words. **Pays $50-500, or copies.**

Poetry Avant-garde, free verse, haiku, light verse, traditional, translation. ''No poetry that does not focus on martial arts culture.'' **Buys 2 poems/year.** Submit maximum 10 poems. **Pays $10-100, or copies.**

Fillers Anecdotes, facts, gags to be illustrated by cartoonist, newsbreaks, short humor. **Buys 2/year.** Length: 25-500 words. **Pays $1-50, or copies.**

Tips ''Always query before sending a manuscript. We are open to varied types of articles; most however require a strong academic grasp of Asian culture. For those not having this background, we suggest trying a museum review, or interview, where authorities can be questioned, quoted, and provide supportive illustrations. We especially desire articles/reports from Asia, with photo illustrations, particularly of a martial art style, so readers can visually understand the unique attributes of that style, its applications, evolution, etc. 'Location' and media reports are special areas that writers may consider, especially if they live in a location of martial art significance.''

$ KUNG FU TAI CHI

Wisdom for Body and Mind, Pacific Rim Publishing, 40748 Encyclopedia Circle, Fremont CA 94538. (510)656-5100. Fax: (510)656-8844. E-mail: gene@kungfumagazine.com. Website: www.kungfumagazine.com. **Contact:** Gene Ching. **70% freelance written.** Bimonthly magazine covering Chinese martial arts and culture. ''*Kung Fu Tai Chi* covers the full range of Kung Fu culture, including healing, philosophy, meditation, yoga, Fengshui, Buddhism, Taoism, history, and the latest events in art and culture, plus insightful features on the martial arts.'' Circ. 50,000. Pays on publication. Byline given. Buys first North American serial, electronic rights. Editorial lead time 4 months. Submit seasonal material 4 months in advance. Accepts queries by mail, e-mail, fax, phone. Responds in 2 months to queries; 3 months to mss. Sample copy for $3.99 or online. Writer's guidelines online.

Nonfiction General interest, historical/nostalgic, how-to, interview/profile, personal experience, photo feature, religious, technical, travel, cultural perspectives. No poetry or fiction. **Buys 70 mss/year.** Query. Length: 500-2,500 words. **Pays $35-125.**

Photos Send photos with submission. Reviews 5×7 prints, GIF/JPEG files. Buys one-time rights. Offers no additional payment for photos accepted with ms. Captions, identification of subjects required.

Tips ''Check out our website and get an idea of past articles.''

$ $ T'AI CHI

Leading International Magazine of T'ai Chi Ch'uan, Wayfarer Publications, P.O. Box 39938, Los Angeles CA 90039. (323)665-7773. Fax: (323)665-1627. E-mail: taichi@tai-chi.com. Website: www.tai-chi.com/magazine.htm. **Contact:** Marvin Smalheiser, editor. **90% freelance written.** Bimonthly magazine covering T'ai Chi Ch'uan as a martial art and for health and fitness. ''Covers T'ai Chi Ch'uan and other internal martial arts, plus qigong and Chinese health, nutrition, and philosophical disciplines. Readers are practitioners or laymen interested in developing skills and insight for self-defense, health, and self-improvement.'' Estab. 1977. Circ. 50,000. Pays on publication. Publishes ms an average of 6 months after acceptance. Byline given. Buys first North American serial rights. Editorial lead time 3 months. Submit seasonal material 6 months in advance. Accepts queries by mail, e-mail, fax. Responds in 3 weeks to queries; 3 months to mss. Sample copy for $3.95. Writer's guidelines online.

o—r Break in by "understanding the problems our readers have to deal with learning and practicing T'ai Chi, and developing an article that deals with 1 or more of those problems.

Nonfiction Book excerpts, essays, how-to (on T'ai Chi Ch'uan, qigong, and related Chinese disciplines), interview/profile, personal experience. "Do not want articles promoting an individual, system, or school." **Buys 100-120 mss/year.** Query with or without published clips or send complete ms. Length: 1,200-4,500 words. **Pays $75-500.** Sometimes pays expenses of writers on assignment.

Photos Send photos with submission. Reviews color transparencies, color or b&w 4×6 or 5×7 prints. Buys one-time and reprint rights. Offers no additional payment for photos accepted with ms, but overall payment takes into consideration the number and quality of photos. Captions, identification of subjects, model releases required.

Tips "Think and write for practitioners and laymen who want information and insight, and who are trying to work through problems to improve skills and their health. No promotional material."

MISCELLANEOUS

$ACTION PURSUIT GAMES
CFW Enterprises, Inc., P.O. Box 417, Licking MO 65542. E-mail: editor@actionpursuitgames.com. Website: www.actionpursuitgames.com. **Contact:** Daniel Reeves, editor. **60% freelance written.** Monthly magazine covering paintball. Estab. 1987. Circ. 85,000. Pays on publication. Publishes ms an average of 2 months after acceptance. Byline given. Buys electronic rights. print rights Editorial lead time 3 months. Submit seasonal material 6 months in advance. Accepts queries by e-mail. Sample copy for 9×12 SAE and 5 first-class stamps. Writer's guidelines online.

Nonfiction Essays, exposé, general interest, historical/nostalgic, how-to, humor, interview/profile, new product, opinion, personal experience, technical, travel, all paintball-related. No sexually oriented material. **Buys 100+ mss/year.** Length: 500-1,000 words. **Pays $100.** Sometimes pays expenses of writers on assignment.

Photos Send photos with submission. Reviews transparencies, prints. Buys all rights, web and print. Negotiates payment individually. Captions, identification of subjects, model releases required.

Columns/Departments Guest Commentary, 400 words; TNT (tournament news), 500-800 words; Young Guns, 300 words; Scenario Game Reporting, 300-500 words. **Buys 24 mss/year. Pays $100.**

Fiction Adventure, historical, must be paintball related. **Buys 1-2 mss/year.** Send complete ms. Length: 500 words. **Pays $100.**

Poetry Avant-garde, free verse, haiku, light verse, traditional, must be paintball related. **Buys 1-2 poems/year.** Submit maximum 1 poem. Length: 20 lines.

Fillers Anecdotes, gags to be illustrated by cartoonist. **Buys 2-4/year.** Length: 20-50 words. **Pays $25.**

Tips "Good graphic support is critical. Read writer's guidelines at website; read website, www.actionpursuitgames.com, and magazine."

$ $AMERICAN CHEERLEADER
Lifestyle Media, Inc., 110 William St., 23rd Floor, New York NY 10038. (646)459-4800. Fax: (646)459-4900. E-mail: snoone@lifestylemedia.com. Website: www.americancheerleader.com. Managing Editor: Marisa Walker. Senior Editor: Jennifer Smith. **Contact:** Sheila Noone, editorial director. **30% freelance written.** Bimonthly magazine covering high school, college, and competitive cheerleading. "We try to keep a young, informative voice for all articles—'for cheerleaders, by cheerleaders.'" Estab. 1995. Circ. 200,000. Pays on publication. Publishes ms an average of 4 months after acceptance. Byline given. Offers 25% kill fee. Buys all rights. Editorial lead time 3 months. Submit seasonal material 4 months in advance. Accepts queries by mail, e-mail. Responds in 4 weeks to queries; 2 months to mss. Sample copy for $2.95. Writer's guidelines free.

Nonfiction How-to (cheering techniques, routines, pep songs, etc.), interview/profile (celebrities and media personalities who cheered). Special issues: Tryouts (April); Camp Basics (June); College (October); Competition (December). No professional cheerleading stories, i.e., no Dallas Cowboy cheerleaders. **Buys 12-16 mss/year.** Query with published clips. Length: 400-1,500 words. **Pays $100-250 for assigned articles; $100 maximum for unsolicited articles.** Sometimes pays expenses of writers on assignment.

Photos State availability with submission. Reviews transparencies, 5×7 prints. Rights purchased varies. Offers $50/photo. Model releases required.

Columns/Departments Gameday Beauty (skin care, celeb how-tos), 600 words; Health & Fitness (teen athletes), 1,000 words; Profiles (winning squads), 1,000 words. **Buys 12 mss/year.** Query with published clips. **Pays $100-250.**

▣ The online magazine carries original content not found in the print edition.

Tips "We invite proposals from freelance writers who are involved in or have been involved in cheerleading—i.e., coaches, sponsors, or cheerleaders. Our writing style is upbeat and 'sporty' to catch and hold the attention of our teenaged readers. Articles should be broken down into lots of sidebars, bulleted lists, Q&As, etc."

$ $ $ ATV MAGAZINE/ATV SPORT

Ehlert Publishing, 6420 Sycamore Lane, Maple Grove MN 55369. E-mail: crice@ehlertpublishing.com. Website: www.atvnews.com. **Contact:** Chaz Rice, editor. **20% freelance written.** Bimonthly magazine covering all-terrain vehicles. "Devoted to covering all the things ATV owners enjoy, from hunting to racing, farming to trail riding." Pays on magazine shipment to printer. Byline given. Buys all rights. Editorial lead time 6 months. Accepts queries by mail, e-mail, fax. Responds in 3 weeks to queries. Sample copy and writer's guidelines for #10 SASE.

Nonfiction How-to, interview/profile, new product, personal experience, photo feature, technical, travel. **Buys 15-20 mss/year.** Query with published clips. Length: 200-2,000 words. **Pays $100-1,000.** Sometimes pays expenses of writers on assignment.

Photos State availability with submission. Rights purchased vary. Negotiates payment individually. Captions, identification of subjects required.

Tips "Writers must have experience with ATVs, and should own one or have regular access to at least one ATV."

$ ▣ CANADIAN RODEO NEWS

Canadian Rodeo News, Ltd., #223, 2116 27th Ave. NE, Calgary AB T2E 7A6 Canada. (403)250-7292. Fax: (403)250-6926. E-mail: crn@rodeocanada.com. Website: www.rodeocanada.com. **Contact:** Darell Hartlen, editor. **80% freelance written.** Monthly tabloid covering "Canada's professional rodeo (CPRA) personalities and livestock. Read by rodeo participants and fans." Estab. 1964. Circ. 4,000. Pays on publication. Publishes ms an average of 1 month after acceptance. Byline given. Buys first, second serial (reprint) rights. Editorial lead time 1 month. Submit seasonal material 1 month in advance. Accepts queries by mail, e-mail, fax. Accepts simultaneous submissions. Responds in 1 month to queries; 2 months to mss. Sample copy and writer's guidelines free with SASE.

Nonfiction General interest, historical/nostalgic, interview/profile. **Buys 70-80 mss/year.** Query. Length: 400-1,200 words. **Pays $30-60.**

Reprints Send photocopy of article or typed ms with rights for sale noted and information about when and where the material previously appeared. Pays 100% of amount paid for an original article.

Photos Send photos with submission. Reviews digital only. Buys one-time rights. Offers $15-25/cover photo.

Tips "Best to call first with the story idea to inquire if it is suitable for publication. Readers are very knowledgeable of the sport, so writers need to be as well."

$ $ FENCERS QUARTERLY MAGAZINE

848 S. Kimbrough, Springfield MO 65806. (417)866-4370. E-mail: editor@fencersquarterly.com. Editor-in-Chief: Nick Evangelista. **Contact:** Anita Evangelista, managing editor. **60% freelance written.** Quarterly magazine covering fencing, fencers, history of sword/fencing/dueling, modern techniques and systems, controversies, personalities of fencing, personal experience. "This is a publication for all fencers and those interested in fencing; we favor the grassroots level rather than the highly-promoted elite. Readers will have a grasp of terminology of the sword and refined fencing skills—writers must be familiar with fencing and current changes and controversies. We are happy to air any point of view on any fencing subject, but the material must be well-researched and logically presented." Estab. 1996. Circ. 5,000. Pays prior to or at publication. Publishes ms an average of 6 months after acceptance. Byline given. Offers 25% kill fee. Buys first North American serial, second serial (reprint), electronic rights, makes work-for-hire assignments. Editorial lead time 3 months. Submit seasonal material 6 months in advance. Accepts queries by mail, e-mail. Accepts simultaneous submissions. Sample copy and writer's guidelines by request.

● Responds in 1 week or less for e-mail; 1 month for snail mail if SASE; no reply if no SASE and material not usable.

Nonfiction "All article types acceptable—however, we have seldom used fiction or poetry (though will consider if has special relationship to fencing)." How-to should reflect some aspect of fencing or gear. Personal experience welcome. No articles "that lack logical progression of thought, articles that rant, 'my weapon is better than your weapon' emotionalism, puff pieces, or public relations stuff." **Buys 100 mss/year.** Query with or without published clips or send complete ms. Length: 100-4,000 words. **Pays $100-200 (rarely) for assigned articles; $10-60 for unsolicited articles.**

Photos Send photos by mail or as e-mail attachment. Prefers prints, all sizes. Buys all rights. Negotiates payment individually. Captions, identification of subjects, model releases required.

Columns/Departments Cutting-edge news (sword or fencing related), 100 words; Reviews (books/films), 300 words; Fencing Generations (profile), 200-300 words; Tournament Results (veteran events only, please), 200 words. **Buys 40 mss/year.** Send complete ms. **Pays $10-20.**

Fiction Will consider all as long as strong fencing/sword slant is major element. No erotica. Query with or without published clips or send complete ms. Length: 1,500 words maximum. **Pays $25-100.**

Poetry Will consider all which have distinct fencing/sword element as central. No erotica. Submit maximum 10 poems. Length: Up to 100 lines. **Pays $10.**

Fillers Anecdotes, facts, gags to be illustrated by cartoonist, newsbreaks. **Buys 30/year.** Length: 100 words maximum. **Pays $5.**

Tips "We love new writers! Professionally presented work impresses us. We prefer complete submissions, and e-mail or disk (in rich text format) are our favorites. Ask for our writer's guidelines. Always aim your writing to knowledgeable fencers who are fascinated by this subject, take their fencing seriously, and want to know more about its history, current events, and controversies. Action photos should show proper form—no flailing or tangled-up images, please. We want to know what the 'real' fencer is up to these days, not just what the Olympic contenders are doing. If we don't use your piece, we'll tell you why not."

Ⓝ $ $ HER SPORTS

Active Sports Lifestyles, Wet Dog Media, 245 Central Ave., Suite C, St. Petersburg FL 33701. E-mail: editorial@hersports.com. Website: www.hersports.com. **Contact:** Christina Gandolfo, editor-in-chief. **60% freelance written.** Bimonthly magazine covering women's outdoor and individual sports. "*Her Sports* is for active women ages 25-49 who regard sports and being active an important part of their lifestyle. Our readers are beyond 'quick-fix diets' and '5-minute' exercise routines, and are looking for a way to balance being active and healthy with a busy lifestyle. We focus on health, nutrition, sports and sports training, travel, and profiles on everyday athletes and professional athletes with unique and motivational stories." Estab. 2004. Circ. 50,000. Pays on publication. Publishes ms an average of 3 months after acceptance. Byline given. Offers 50% kill fee. Buys all rights. Editorial lead time 3 months. Submit seasonal material 6-8 months in advance. Accepts queries by e-mail. Responds in 2 weeks to queries; 1 month to mss. Sample copy for $4.99 and SASE with 5 first-class stamps. Writer's guidelines online.

Nonfiction Personal experience. "Please do not send articles pertaining to team sports; we cover only outdoor individual sports." **Buys 6 mss/year.** Query with published clips. Length: 800-1,200 words. **Pays $200-300 for assigned articles.**

Photos Kristin Mayer, creative director. State availability with submission. Reviews GIF/JPEG files. Buys one-time rights. Negotiates payment individually. Captions, identification of subjects required.

Columns/Departments Body & Mind (nutrition, mental training, fitness training, body/mind exercise), 1,200 words; Adventure Journal (personal experience with a sport or outdoor adventure), 800-1,200 words; Discoveries (travel articles of interest to active women), 1,500-2,000 words; Weekend Warrior (how-to tips for mastering the sports we cover), 1,000-1,200 words; Her Story (short profile on "everyday athletes" who are an inspiration to others), 650 words. **Buys at least 24 mss/year.** Query. **Pays $250-350.**

Tips "Persistence pays off but burying the editor with multiple submissions will quickly lose you points. If you're asked to check back in 2 months, do so, but if the editor tells you she's on deadline, simply inquire about a better time to get back in touch."

Ⓝ $ $ POINTE MAGAZINE

Ballet At Its Best, Lifestyle Media, Inc., 110 William St., 23rd Floor, New York NY 10038. (646)459-4800. Fax: (646)459-4900. E-mail: pointe@lifestylemedia.com. Website: www.pointemagazine.com. Editor-in-Chief: Virginia Johnson. Managing Editor: Jocelyn Anderson. Bimonthly magazine covering ballet. "*Pointe Magazine* is the only magazine dedicated to ballet. It offers practicalities on ballet careers as well as news and features." Estab. 2000. Circ. 38,000. Pays on publication. Byline given. Buys all rights. Accepts simultaneous submissions. Responds in 1 month. Sample copy for 9×12 SAE and 6 first-class stamps.

Nonfiction Historical/nostalgic, how-to, interview/profile, biography, careers, health, news. **Buys 60 mss/year.** Query with published clips. Length: 400-1,500 words. **Pays $125-400.**

Photos Colin Fowler, photo editor. State availability with submission. Reviews 2¼×2¼ or 35mm transparencies, 8×11 prints. Buys one-time rights. Negotiates payment individually. Captions required.

$ $ POLO PLAYERS' EDITION

Rizzo Management Corp., 3500 Fairlane Farms Rd., Suite 9, Wellington FL 33414. (561)793-9524. Fax: (561)793-9576. E-mail: info@poloplayersedition.com. Website: www.poloplayersedition.com. **Contact:** Gwen Rizzo, editor. Monthly magazine on polo—the sport and lifestyle. "Our readers are affluent, well educated, well read, and highly sophisticated." Circ. 6,150. **Pays on acceptance.** Publishes ms an average of 2 months after acceptance. Kill fee varies. Buys first North American serial rights, makes work-for-hire assignments. Submit seasonal material 3 months in advance. Accepts queries by mail, e-mail, fax. Accepts simultaneous submissions. Responds in 3 months to queries. Writer's guidelines for #10 SAE with 2 stamps.

Nonfiction Historical/nostalgic, interview/profile, personal experience, photo feature, technical, travel. Special issues: Annual Art Issue/Gift Buying Guide; Winter Preview/Florida Supplement. **Buys 20 mss/year.** Query with published clips or send complete ms. Length: 800-3,000 words. **Pays $150-400 for assigned articles; $100-300 for unsolicited articles.** Sometimes pays expenses of writers on assignment.

Reprints Send tearsheet or typed ms with rights for sale noted and information about when and where the material previously appeared. Pays 50% of amount paid for an original article.

Photos State availability of or send photos with submission. Reviews contact sheets, transparencies, prints. Buys one-time rights. Offers $20-150/photo. Captions required.

Columns/Departments Yesteryears (historical pieces), 500 words; Profiles (clubs and players), 800-1,000 words. **Buys 15 mss/year.** Query with published clips. **Pays $100-300.**

Tips "Query us on a personality or club profile or historic piece or, if you know the game, state availability to cover a tournament. Keep in mind that ours is a sophisticated, well-educated audience."

$RUGBY MAGAZINE

Rugby Press, Ltd., 459 Columbus Ave., #1200, New York NY 10024. (212)787-1160. Fax: (212)787-1161. E-mail: rugbymag@aol.com. Website: www.rugbymag.com. **75% freelance written.** Monthly tabloid. "*Rugby Magazine* is the journal of record for the sport of rugby in the US. Our demographics are among the best in the country." Estab. 1975. Circ. 10,000. Pays on publication. Publishes ms an average of 2 months after acceptance. Byline given. Buys all rights. Editorial lead time 1 month. Submit seasonal material 2 months in advance. Accepts queries by mail, e-mail, fax, phone. Accepts simultaneous submissions. Responds in 2 weeks to queries; 1 month to mss. Sample copy for $4. Writer's guidelines free.

Nonfiction Book excerpts, essays, general interest, historical/nostalgic, how-to, humor, interview/profile, new product, opinion, personal experience, photo feature, technical, travel. **Buys 15 mss/year.** Send complete ms. Length: 600-2,000 words. **Pays $50 minimum.** Pays expenses of writers on assignment.

Reprints Send tearsheet or typed ms with rights for sale noted and information about when and where the material previously appeared. Payment varies.

Photos Send photos with submission. Reviews negatives, transparencies, prints. Buys all rights. Offers no additional payment for photos accepted with ms.

Columns/Departments Nutrition (athletic nutrition), 900 words; Referees' Corner, 1,200 words. **Buys 2-3 mss/year.** Query with published clips. **Pays $50 maximum.**

Fiction Condensed novels, humorous, novel excerpts, slice-of-life vignettes. **Buys 1-3 mss/year.** Query with published clips. Length: 1,000-2,500 words. **Pays $100.**

Tips "Give us a call. Send along your stories or photos; we're happy to take a look. Tournament stories are a good way to get yourself published in *Rugby Magazine.*"

Ⓝ ⊘ SKATEBOARDER

Primedia Enthusiast Group, P.O. Box 1028, Dana Point CA 92629. (949)661-5150. E-mail: peech@skateboardermag.com. Website: www.skateboardermag.com. Editor: Brian Peech. Monthly magazine for begining and experienced skateboarders. Circ. 105,000.

● Query before submitting.

$SKYDIVING

1725 N. Lexington Ave., DeLand FL 32724. (386)736-4793. Fax: (386)736-9786. E-mail: editor@skydivingmagazine.com. Website: skydivingmagazine.com. **Contact:** Sue Clifton, editor. **25% freelance written.** Monthly tabloid featuring skydiving for sport parachutists, worldwide dealers and equipment manufacturers. "*Skydiving* is a news magazine. Its purpose is to deliver timely, useful and interesting information about the equipment, techniques, events, people and places of parachuting. Our scope is national. *Skydiving*'s audience spans the entire spectrum of jumpers, from first-jump students to veterans with thousands of skydives. Some readers are riggers with a keen interest in the technical aspects of parachutes, while others are weekend 'fun' jumpers who want information to help them make travel plans and equipment purchases." Circ. 14,200. Pays on publication. Publishes ms an average of 3 months after acceptance. Byline given. Buys one-time rights. Accepts previously published material. Accepts simultaneous submissions. Responds in 1 month to queries. Sample copy for $2. Writer's guidelines online.

Nonfiction Average issue includes 3 feature articles and 3 columns of technical information. "Send us news and information on how-to, where-to, equipment, techniques, events and outstanding personalities who skydive. We want articles written by people who have a solid knowledge of parachuting." No personal experience or human interest articles. Query. Length: 500-1,000 words. **Pays $25-100.** Sometimes pays expenses of writers on assignment.

Photos State availability with submission. Reviews 5×7 and larger b&w glossy prints. Offers no additional payment for photos accepted with ms. Captions required.

Fillers Newsbreaks. Length: 100-200 words. **Pays $25 minimum.**

Tips "The most frequent mistake made by writers in completing articles for us is that the writer isn't knowledgeable about the sport of parachuting. Articles about events are especially time-sensitive so yours must be submitted quickly. We welcome contributions about equipment. Even short, 'quick look' articles about new products are appropriate for *Skydiving*. If you know of a drop zone or other place that jumpers would like to visit, write an article describing its features and tell them why you liked it and what they can expect to find if they visit it. Avoid first-person articles."

✅ TRANSWORLD SKATEBOARDING

Time 4 Media, 353 Airport Rd., Oceanside CA 92054. (760)722-7777. Website: www.skateboarding.com. Monthly magazine for skateboarding enthusiasts. Circ. 243,000. Editorial lead time 3 months.

- Query before submitting.

$ $ WINDY CITY SPORTS

Windy City Publishing, 1450 W. Randolph St., Chicago IL 60607. (312)421-1551. Fax: (312)421-1454. E-mail: jeff@windycitysports.com. Website: www.windycitysports.com. **Contact:** Jeff Banowetz, editorial director. **50% freelance written.** Monthly tabloid. "Writers should have knowledge of the sport they've been hired to cover. In most cases, these are endurance sports, such as running, cycling, triathlon, or adventure racing. Please read the magazine and visit the website to famliarize yourself with our subject matter and our style. Poorly-tailored queries reflect badly on your journalistic skills. If you query us on a golf story, you will not only suffer the shame of rejection, but your name shall be added to our 'clueless freelancer' list, and we will joke about you at the water cooler." Circ. 110,000. Pays on publication. Publishes ms an average of 1 month after acceptance. Byline given. Buys one-time rights. Editorial lead time 2 months. Accepts queries by e-mail. Sample copy and writer's guidelines online.

Nonfiction Essays, general interest, how-to, humor, interview/profile, opinion, personal experience, photo feature, technical. **Buys up to 35 mss/year.** Query with published clips. Length: 700-1,500 words. **Pays $150-300 for assigned articles; $0-300 for unsolicited articles.** Sometimes pays expenses of writers on assignment.

Photos Send photos with submission. Reviews prints. Buys one-time rights. Negotiates payment individually. Captions, identification of subjects required.

Columns/Departments Cool Down (humorous, personal experience), 800-1,000 words; Nutrition (advice and information on diet), 500-800 words; Health/Wellness (advice and information on general health), 500-800 words. Query with published clips. **Pays $50-150.**

Tips "You should try to make it fun. We like to see anecdotes, great quotes and vivid descriptions. Quote Chicago area people as often as possible. If that's not possible, try to stick to the Midwest or people with Chicago connections."

MOTOR SPORTS

✅ AUTOMOBILE MAGAZINE

Primedia Broad Reach Magazines, 120 E. Liberty St., 2nd Floor, Ann Arbor MI 48104. (734)994-3500. Website: www.automobilemag.com. Editor: Jean Jennings. Managing Editor: Amy Skogstrom. Monthly magazine covering automobiles. Edited for the automotive enthusiast interested in the novelty as well as the tradition of all things automotive. Circ. 644,000. Editorial lead time 6 weeks.

- Query before submitting.

🆕 DIRT RIDER

Primedia Enthusiast Group, 6420 Wilshire Blvd., 17th Floor, Los Angeles CA 90048. (323)782-2390. Fax: (323)782-2372. E-mail: drmail@primedia.com. Website: www.dirtrider.com. Editor: Jimmy Lewis. Managing Editor: Terry Masaoka. Monthly magazine devoted to the sport of off-road motorcycle riding that showcases the many ways enthusiast can enjoy dirt bikes. Circ. 201,342. Sample copy not available.

$ THE HOOK MAGAZINE

The Magazine for Antique & Classic Tractor Pullers, Greer Town, Inc., 209 S. Marshall, Box 16, Marshfield MO 65706. (417)468-7000. Fax: (417)859-6075. E-mail: thehook@pcis.net. Website: pcis.net/thehook. **Contact:** Dana Greer Marlin, owner/president. **80% freelance written.** Bimonthly magazine covering tractor pulling. Estab. 1992. Circ. 6,000. Pays on publication. Byline given. Buys one-time, electronic rights. Editorial lead time 6 months. Submit seasonal material 6 months in advance. Accepts queries by mail, e-mail, fax. Accepts previously published material. Accepts simultaneous submissions. Responds in 3 weeks to queries; 2 months to mss.

Sample copy for 8½×11 SAE with 4 first-class stamps or online. Writer's guidelines for #10 SASE.

O→ "Our magazine is easy to break into. Puller profiles are your best bet. Features on individuals and their tractors, how they got into the sport, what they want from competing."

Nonfiction How-to, interview/profile, new product, personal experience, photo feature, technical, event coverage. **Buys 25 mss/year.** Send complete ms. Length: 500-1,500 words. **Pays $70 for technical articles; $35 for others.**

Photos Send photos with submission. Reviews 3×5 prints. Buys one-time and online rights. Negotiates payment individually. Captions, identification of subjects, model releases required.

Fillers Anecdotes, short humor. **Buys 6/year.** Length: 100 words.

Tips "Write 'real'; our readers don't respond well to scholarly tomes. Use your everyday voice in all submissions and your chances will go up radically."

$ $ SAND SPORTS MAGAZINE

Wright Publishing Co., Inc., P.O. Box 2260, Costa Mesa CA 92628. (714)979-2560, ext. 107. Fax: (714)979-3998. Website: www.sandsports.net. **Contact:** Michael Sommer, editor. **20% freelance written.** Bimonthly magazine covering vehicles for off-road and sand dunes. Estab. 1995. Circ. 35,000. Pays on publication. Byline given. Buys first, one-time rights. Editorial lead time 3 months. Submit seasonal material 6 months in advance. Accepts queries by mail. Sample copy and writer's guidelines free.

Nonfiction How-to (technical-mechanical), photo feature, technical. **Buys 20 mss/year.** Query. Length: 1,500 words minimum. **Pays $175/page.** Sometimes pays expenses of writers on assignment.

Photos Send photos with submission. Reviews color slides or high res digital images. Buys one-time rights. Negotiates payment individually. Captions, identification of subjects, model releases required.

$ $ SPEEDWAY ILLUSTRATED

Performance Media, LLC, 107 Elm St., Salisbury MA 01952. (978)465-9099. Fax: (978)465-9033. E-mail: editorial @speedwayillustrated.com. Website: www.speedwayillustrated.com. Executive Editor: Dick Berggren. **Contact:** Rob Sneddon, editor. **40% freelance written.** Monthly magazine covering stock car racing. Estab. 2000. Circ. 130,000. Pays on publication. Byline given. Buys first rights. Editorial lead time 6 weeks. Accepts queries by mail, e-mail, fax. Responds in 2 weeks to queries. Sample copy and writer's guidelines free.

Nonfiction Interview/profile, opinion, personal experience, photo feature, technical. **Buys 30 mss/year.** Query. **Pays variable rate.**

Photos Send photos with submission. Reviews transparencies, digital. Buys all rights. Offers $40-250/photo. Captions, identification of subjects, model releases required.

Tips "We seek short, high-interest value pieces that are accompanied by strong photography, in short—knock our socks off."

OLYMPICS

USA GYMNASTICS

201 S. Capitol Ave., Suite 300, Pan American Plaza, Indianapolis IN 46225. (317)237-5050. Fax: (317)237-5069. E-mail: lpeszek@usa-gymnastics.org. Website: www.usa-gymnastics.org. **Contact:** Luan Peszek, editor. **5% freelance written.** Bimonthly magazine covering gymnastics—national and international competitions. Designed to educate readers on fitness, health, safety, technique, current topics, trends, and personalities related to the gymnastics/fitness field. Readers are gymnasts ages 7-18, parents, and coaches. Estab. 1981. Circ. 95,000. Pays on publication. Publishes ms an average of 4 months after acceptance. Byline given. Buys all rights. Submit seasonal material 4 months in advance. Accepts queries by e-mail, fax. Accepts simultaneous submissions. Responds in 2 months to queries. Sample copy for $5.

Nonfiction General interest, how-to (related to fitness, health, gymnastics), inspirational, interview/profile, opinion (Open Floor section), photo feature. **Buys 3 mss/year.** Query. Length: 1,500 words maximum. **Payment negotiable.**

Reprints Send photocopy.

Photos Send photos with submission. Buys all rights. Offers no additional payment for photos accepted with ms. Identification of subjects required.

Tips "Any articles of interest to gymnasts (men, women, rhythmic gymnastics, trampoline, and tumbling and sports acrobatics), coaches, judges, and parents. This includes nutrition, toning, health, safety, trends, techniques, timing, etc."

RUNNING

Ⓝ $ INSIDE TEXAS RUNNING

14201 Memorial Dr., Suite 204, Houston TX 77079. (281)759-0555. Fax: (281)759-7766. E-mail: lance@running mags.com. Website: www.insidetexasrunning.com. **Contact:** Lance Phegley, editor. **70% freelance written.** Monthly (except June and August) tabloid covering running and running-related events. "Our audience is made up of Texas runners who may also be interested in cross training." Estab. 1977. Circ. 10,000. **Pays on acceptance.** Publishes ms an average of 2 months after acceptance. Byline given. Buys one-time, exclusive Texas rights. Submit seasonal material 2 months in advance. Responds in 1 month to mss. Sample copy for $1.50. Writer's guidelines for #10 SASE.

    Oⲯ "The best way to break in to our publication is to submit brief (2 or 3 paragraphs) fillers for our Texas Roundup section."

Nonfiction Various topics of interest to runners: Profiles of newsworthy Texas runners of all abilities; unusual events; training interviews. Special issues: Shoe Review (March); Fall Race Review (September); Marathon Focus (October); Resource Guide (December). **Buys 20 mss/year.** Send complete ms. Length: 500-1,500 words. **Pays $100 maximum for assigned articles; $50 maximum for unsolicited articles.**

Reprints Send tearsheet, photocopy or typed ms with rights for sale noted and information about when and where the material previously appeared.

Photos Send photos with submission. Buys one-time rights. Offers $25 maximum/photo. Captions required.

    🖵 The online magazine carries original content not found in the print edition.

Tips "Writers should be familiar with the sport and the publication."

$ $ NEW YORK RUNNER

New York Road Runners, 9 E. 89th St., New York NY 10128. (212)423-2260. Fax: (212)423-0879. E-mail: newyorkrun@nyrr.org. Website: www.nyrr.org. **Contact:** Gordon Bakoulis, editor. Quarterly magazine covering running, walking, nutrition, and fitness. Estab. 1958. Circ. 45,000. **Pays on acceptance.** Byline given. Buys first North American serial rights. Submit seasonal material 4 months in advance. Accepts queries by mail, e-mail, fax. Responds in 2 months to queries. Sample copy for $3. Writer's guidelines for #10 SASE.

    • Material should be of interest to members of the New York Road Runners.

Nonfiction Running and marathon articles. Interview/profile (of runners). **Buys 15 mss/year.** Query. Length: 750-1,000 words. **Pays $50-350.**

Columns/Departments Running Briefs (anything noteworthy in the running world), 250-500 words. Query.

Tips "Be knowledgeable about the sport of running."

$ $ $ RUNNER'S WORLD

Rodale, 135 N. 6th St., Emmaus PA 18098. (610)967-5171. Fax: (610)967-8883. E-mail: rwedit@rodale.com. Website: www.runnersworld.com. **Contact:** David Willey, editor-in-chief. **5% freelance written.** Monthly magazine on running, mainly long-distance running. "The magazine for and about distance running, training, health and fitness, nutrition, motivation, injury prevention, race coverage, personalities of the sport." Estab. 1966. Circ. 500,000. Pays on publication. Publishes ms an average of 6 months after acceptance. Byline given. Buys all rights. Submit seasonal material 6 months in advance. Accepts queries by mail. Responds in 2 months to queries. Writer's guidelines online.

    Oⲯ Break in through columns 'Human Race' and 'Finish Line.' Also 'Warmups,' which mixes international running news with human interest stories. If you can send us a unique human interest story from your region, we will give it serious consideration.

Nonfiction How-to (train, prevent injuries), interview/profile, personal experience. No "my first marathon" stories. No poetry. **Buys 5-7 mss/year.** Query. **Pays $1,500-2,000.** Pays expenses of writers on assignment.

Photos State availability with submission. Buys one-time rights. Identification of subjects required.

Columns/Departments Finish Line (back-of-the-magazine essay, personal experience—humor). **Buys 24 mss/year.** Send complete ms. **Pays $300.**

Tips "We are always looking for 'Adventure Runs' from readers—runs in wild, remote, beautiful, and interesting places. These are rarely race stories but more like backtracking/running adventures. Great color slides are crucial, 2,000 words maximum."

$ $ RUNNING TIMES

The Runner's Best Resource, Fitness Publishing, Inc., 213 Danbury Rd., Wilton CT 06897. (203)761-1113. Fax: (203)761-9933. E-mail: editor@runningtimes.com. Website: www.runningtimes.com. Managing Editor: Marc Chalufour. **Contact:** Jonathan Beverly, editor-in-chief. **40% freelance written.** Magazine published 10 times/year covering distance running and racing. "*Running Times* is the national magazine for the experienced running participant and fan. Our audience is knowledgeable about the sport and active in running and racing.

All editorial relates specifically to running: improving performance, enhancing enjoyment, or exploring events, places, and people in the sport.'' Estab. 1977. Circ. 75,000. Pays on publication. Publishes ms an average of 3 months after acceptance. Byline given. Buys first North American serial, second serial (reprint), electronic rights. Editorial lead time 4 months. Submit seasonal material 6 months in advance. Accepts queries by mail, e-mail. Responds in 1 month to queries; 2 months to mss. Sample copy for $5. Writer's guidelines online.

Nonfiction Book excerpts, essays, historical/nostalgic, how-to (training), humor, inspirational, interview/profile, new product, opinion, personal experience (with theme, purpose, evidence of additional research and/or special expertise), photo feature, travel, news, reports. No basic, beginner how-to, generic fitness/nutrition, or generic first-person accounts. **Buys 25 mss/year.** Query. Length: 1,500-3,000 words. **Pays $200-600 for assigned articles; $100-300 for unsolicited articles.** Sometimes pays expenses of writers on assignment.

Photos State availability with submission. Buys one-time rights. Negotiates payment individually. Identification of subjects required.

Columns/Departments Training (short topics related to enhancing performance), 1,000 words; Sports-Med (application of medical knowledge to running), 1,000 words; Nutrition (application of nutritional principles to running performance), 1,000 words. **Buys 10 mss/year.** Query. **Pays $50-200.**

Fiction Any genre, with running-related theme or characters. **Buys 1 ms/year.** Send complete ms. Length: 1,500-3,000 words. **Pays $100-500.**

Tips ''Thoroughly get to know runners and the running culture, both at the participant level and the professional, elite level.''

$ $TRAIL RUNNER

The Magazine of Running Adventure, Big Stone Publishing, 1101 Village Rd. UL-4D, Carbondale CO 81623. (970)704-1442. Fax: (970)963-4965. E-mail: mbenge@bigstonepub.com. Website: www.trailrunnermag.com. **Contact:** Michael Benge, editor. **65% freelance written.** Bimonthly magazine covering all aspects of off-road running. ''The only nationally circulated 4-color glossy magazine dedicated to covering trail running.'' Estab. 1999. Circ. 40,000. Pays on publication. Publishes ms an average of 2 months after acceptance. Byline given. Offers $50 kill fee. Buys first North American serial, electronic rights. Editorial lead time 3 months. Submit seasonal material 5 months in advance. Accepts queries by mail, e-mail. Accepts simultaneous submissions. Responds in 3 weeks to queries; 2 months to mss. Sample copy for $3. Writer's guidelines online.

Nonfiction Essays, exposé, general interest, historical/nostalgic, how-to, humor, inspirational, interview/profile, new product, opinion, personal experience, photo feature, technical, travel, racing. No gear reviews, race results. **Buys 30-40 mss/year.** Query with published clips. Length: 800-2,000 words. **Pays 30-40¢/word.** Sometimes pays expenses of writers on assignment.

Photos Send photos with submission. Reviews 35mm transparencies, prints. Buys one-time rights. Offers $50-250/photo. Identification of subjects, model releases required.

Columns/Departments Monique Cole, senior editor. Training (race training, altitude training, etc.), 800 words; Adventure (off-beat aspects of trail running), 600-800 words; Wanderings (personal essay on any topic related to trail running), 600 words; Urban Escapes (urban trails accessible in and around major US sites), 800 words; Personalities (profile of a trail running personality), 1,000 words. **Buys 5-10 mss/year.** Query with published clips. **Pays 30-40¢/word.**

Fiction Adventure, fantasy, slice-of-life vignettes. **Buys 1-2 mss/year.** Query with published clips. Length: 1,000-1,500 words. **Pays 25-35¢/word.**

Fillers Anecdotes, facts, gags to be illustrated by cartoonist, newsbreaks, short humor. **Buys 50-60/year.** Length: 75-400 words. **Pays 25-35¢/word.**

Tips ''Best way to break in is with interesting and unique trail running news, notes, and nonsense from around the world. Also, check the website for more info.''

$ $TRIATHLETE MAGAZINE

The World's Largest Triathlon Magazine, Triathlon Group of North America, 328 Encinitas Blvd., Suite 100, Encinitas CA 92024. (760)634-4100. Fax: (760)634-4110. E-mail: betsy@triathletemag.com. Website: www.triathletemag.com. **Contact:** Betsy Redfern, managing editor. **50% freelance written.** Monthly magazine. ''In general, articles should appeal to seasoned triathletes, as well as eager newcomers to the sport. Our audience includes everyone from competitive athletes to people considering their first event.'' Estab. 1983. Circ. 50,000. Pays on publication. Byline given. Buys second serial (reprint), all rights. Editorial lead time 3 months. Submit seasonal material 6 months in advance. Accepts queries by mail, e-mail. Accepts simultaneous submissions. Sample copy for $5.

Nonfiction How-to, interview/profile, new product, photo feature, technical. ''No first-person pieces about your experience in triathlon or my-first-triathlon stories.'' **Buys 36 mss/year.** Query with published clips. Length: 1,000-3,000 words. **Pays $200-600.** Sometimes pays expenses of writers on assignment.

Photos State availability with submission. Reviews transparencies. Buys first North American rights. Offers $50-300/photo.

Tips "Writers should know the sport and be familiar with the nuances and history. Training-specific articles that focus on new, but scientifically based, methods are good, as are seasonal training pieces."

SKIING & SNOW SPORTS

$ AMERICAN SNOWMOBILER

The Enthusiast Magazine, Kalmbach Publishing Co., P.O. Box 1612, Waukesha WI 53187. Website: www.amsnow.com. **30% freelance written.** Magazine published 6 times seasonally covering snowmobiling. Estab. 1985. Circ. 90,000. **Pays on acceptance.** Publishes ms an average of 4 months after acceptance. Byline given. Buys all rights. Editorial lead time 4 months. Submit seasonal material 6 months in advance. Accepts queries by mail, e-mail, fax. Responds in 1 month to queries; 2 months to mss. Writer's guidelines for #10 SASE.

> **O—** Break in with "a packet complete with résumé, published clips and photos (or color copies of available photos) and a complete query with a few paragraphs to get me interested and to give an idea of the angle the writer will be taking. When sending an e-mail, do not attach anything."

Nonfiction Seeking race coverage for online version. General interest, historical/nostalgic, how-to, interview/profile, new product, personal experience, photo feature, travel. **Buys 10 mss/year.** Query with published clips. Length: 1,000-2,000 words. **Pay varies for assigned articles; $100 minimum for unsolicited articles.**

Photos State availability with submission. Buys all rights. Offers no additional payment for photos accepted with ms. Captions, identification of subjects, model releases required.

ℕ $ SKATING

United States Figure Skating Association, 20 First St., Colorado Springs CO 80906-3697. (719)635-5200. Fax: (719)635-9548. E-mail: skatingmagazine@usfigureskating.org. **Contact:** Amy G. Partain, editor. Magazine published 10 times/year. "*Skating* magazine is the official publication of US Figure Skating, and thus we cover skating at both the championship and grass roots level." Estab. 1923. Circ. 45,000. Pays on publication. Publishes ms an average of 3 months after acceptance. Byline given. Buys first rights. Accepts queries by mail, e-mail, fax.

> **O—** The best way for a writer to break in is with features on US Figure Skating members (skaters, volunteers, etc.) who have unique or interesting stories to tell. This is a feature that highlights members and their accomplishments, and stories on and off the ice (800-1,500 words).

Nonfiction General interest, historical/nostalgic, how-to, interview/profile (background and interests of skaters, volunteers, or other US Figure Skating members), photo feature, technical and competition reports, figure skating issues and trends, sports medicine. **Buys 10 mss/year.** Query. Length: 500-2,500 words. **Payment varies.**

Photos Photos purchased with or without accompanying ms. Query. Pays $10 for 8×10 or 5×7 b&w glossy prints, and $25 for color prints or transparencies.

Columns/Departments Ice Breaker (news briefs); Foreign Competition Reports; Health and Fitness; In Synch (synchronized skating news); Takeoff (up-and-coming athletes), all 500-2,000 words.

Tips "We want writing by experienced persons knowledgeable in the technical and artistic aspects of figure skating with a new outlook on the development of the sport. Knowledge and background in technical aspects of figure skating is helpful, but not necessary to the quality of writing expected. We would like to see articles and short features on US Figure Skating volunteers, skaters, and other US Figure Skating members who normally wouldn't get recognized, as opposed to features on championship-level athletes, which are usually assigned to regular contributors. Good quality color photos are a must with submissions. Also would be interested in seeing figure skating 'issues and trends' articles, instead of just profiles. No professional skater material. Synchronized skating and adult skating are the 2 fastest growing aspects of the US Figure Skating. We would like to see more stories dealing with these unique athletes."

$ $ $⊘ SKI MAGAZINE

Times Mirror Magazines, 929 Pearl St., Suite 200, Boulder CO 80302. E-mail: editor@skimag.com. Website: www.skimag.com. **Contact:** Kendall Hamilton, editor-in-chief. **60% freelance written.** Magazine published 8 times/year. "*Ski* is a ski-lifestyle publication written and edited for recreational skiers. Its content is intended to help them ski better (technique), buy better (equipment and skiwear), and introduce them to new experiences, people, and adventures." Estab. 1936. Circ. 430,000. **Pays on acceptance.** Publishes ms an average of 3 months after acceptance. Byline given. Offers 15% kill fee. Buys first North American serial rights. Submit seasonal material 8 months in advance. Accepts queries by mail, e-mail. Sample copy for 9×12 SAE and 5 first-class stamps.

• *Does not accept unsolicited mss, and assumes no responsibility for their return.*

Nonfiction Essays, historical/nostalgic, how-to, humor, interview/profile, personal experience. **Buys 5-10 mss/year.** Send complete ms. Length: 1,000-3,500 words. **Pays $500-1,000 for assigned articles; $300-700 for unsolicited articles.** Pays expenses of writers on assignment.

Photos Send photos with submission. Buys one-time rights. Offers $75-300/photo. Captions, identification of subjects, model releases required.

Fillers Facts, short humor. **Buys 10/year.** Length: 60-75 words. **Pays $50-75.**

Tips "Writers must have an extensive familiarity with the sport and know what concerns, interests, and amuses skiers. Start with short pieces ('hometown hills,' 'dining out,' 'sleeping in'). Columns are most open to freelancers."

N $ $ $ $ SKIING

Time 4 Media, Inc., 929 Pearl St., Suite 200, Boulder CO 80302. (303)448-7600. Fax: (303)448-7676. E-mail: editors@skiingmag.com. Website: www.skiingmag.com. Editor-in-Chief: Marc Peruzzi. **Contact:** Evelyn Spence, articles editor. Magazine published 7 times/year for skiers who deeply love winter, who live for travel, adventure, instruction, gear, and news. "*Skiing* is the user's guide to winter adventure. It is equal parts jaw-dropping inspiration and practical information, action and utility, attitude and advice. It relates the lifestyles of dedicated skiers and captures their spirit of daring and exploration. Dramatic photography transports readers to spine-tingling mountains with breathtaking immediacy. Reading *Skiing* is almost as much fun as being there." Estab. 1948. Circ. 400,000. Byline given. Offers 40% kill fee.

Nonfiction Buys 10-15 feature (1,500-2,000 words) and 12-24 short (100-500 words) mss/year. Query. **Pays $1,000-2,500/feature; $100-500/short piece.**

Columns/Departments Buys 2-3 mss/year. Query. **Pays $150-1,000.**

■ The online magazine carries original content not found in the print edition. Contact: Doug Sabonosh, online managing editor.

Tips "Consider less obvious subjects: smaller ski areas, specific local ski cultures, unknown aspects of popular resorts. Be expressive, not merely descriptive. We want readers to feel the adventure in your writing—to tingle with the excitement of skiing steep powder, of meeting intriguing people, of reaching new goals or achieving dramatic new insights. We want readers to have fun, to see the humor in and the lighter side of skiing and their fellow skiers."

N $ $ SNOW GOER

Ehlert Publishing Group, 6420 Sycamore Lane, Maple Grove MN 55369. Fax: (763)383-4499. E-mail: terickson@ehlertpublishing.com. Website: www.snowmobilenews.com. **Contact:** Tim Erickson, editor. **5% freelance written.** Magazine published 7 times/year covering snowmobiling. "*Snow Goer* is a hard-hitting, tell-it-like-it-is magazine designed for the ultra-active snowmobile enthusiast. It is fun, exciting, innovative, and on the cutting edge of technology and trends." Estab. 1967. Circ. 64,000. Pays on publication. Publishes ms an average of 5 months after acceptance. Byline given. Buys first, one-time rights. Editorial lead time 5 months. Submit seasonal material 6 months in advance. Accepts queries by mail, e-mail, fax. Accepts simultaneous submissions. Responds in 3 months to queries. Sample copy for 8×10 SAE and 4 first-class stamps.

Nonfiction General interest, how-to, interview/profile, new product, personal experience, photo feature, technical, travel. **Buys 6 mss/year.** Query. Length: 500-4,000 words. **Pays $50-500.** Sometimes pays expenses of writers on assignment.

Photos State availability with submission. Reviews contact sheets, prints. Buys one-time rights or all rights. Negotiates payment individually. Captions, identification of subjects required.

N $ $ SNOW WEEK

The Snowmobile Racing Authority, Ehlert Publishing Group, 6420 Sycamore Lane N., Maple Grove MN 55369. (763)383-4400. Fax: (763)383-4499. E-mail: terickson@ehlertpublishing.com. Website: www.snowmobilenews.com. Associate Editors: Andy Swanson, Colby Johnson. **Contact:** Tim Erickson, editor. **15% freelance written.** Magazine published 14 times/year covering snowmobile racing. "We cover snowmobile racing from coast to coast for hard core fans. We get in the pits, inside the race trailers and pepper our race coverage with behind the scenes details." Estab. 1973. Circ. 26,000. Pays on publication. Publishes ms an average of 2 months after acceptance. Byline given. Buys first, one-time, simultaneous rights. Editorial lead time 2 weeks. Accepts queries by mail, e-mail, fax, phone. Sample copy for 8×11 SAE and 4 first-class stamps.

Nonfiction Technical, race coverage. **Buys 20 mss/year.** Query. Length: 500-4,000 words. **Pays 50-450.** Sometimes pays expenses of writers on assignment.

Photos State availability with submission. Reviews contact sheets, prints. Buys one-time rights. Offers no additional payment for photos accepted with ms. Captions, identification of subjects required.

Tips "Writers should also be fans of the sport, know how to write and photograph races."

Ⓝ ⊘ SNOWBOARDER

Primedia Enthusiast Group, P.O. Box 1028, Dana Point CA 92629-5028. (949)496-5922. Fax: (949)496-7849. E-mail: pat.bridges@primedia.com. Website: www.snowboardermag.com. Editor: Pat Bridges. Magazine published 8 times/year for snowboard enthusiasts. Circ. 137,800. Editorial lead time 3 months.

• Query before submitting.

$ $ SNOWEST MAGAZINE

Harris Publishing, 360 B St., Idaho Falls ID 83402. (208)524-7000. Fax: (208)522-5241. E-mail: lindstrm@snowest.com. Website: snowest.com. Publisher: Steve Janes. **Contact:** Lane Lindstrom, editor. **10-25% freelance written.** Monthly magazine. "*SnoWest* covers the sport of snowmobiling, products, and personalities in the western states. This includes mountain riding, deep powder, and trail riding, as well as destination pieces, tech tips, and new model reviews." Estab. 1972. Circ. 150,000. Pays on publication. Publishes ms an average of 2 months after acceptance. Byline given. Buys first North American serial rights. Editorial lead time 6 months. Submit seasonal material 3 months in advance. Sample copy and writer's guidelines free.

Nonfiction How-to (fix a snowmobile, make it high performance), new product, technical, travel. **Buys 3-5 mss/year.** Query with published clips. Length: 500-1,500 words. **Pays $150-300.**

Photos Send photos with submission. Buys one-time rights. Negotiates payment individually. Captions, identification of subjects required.

Ⓝ ⊘ TRANSWORLD SNOWBOARDING

Transworld Media, 353 Airport Rd., Oceanside CA 92054. (760)722-7777. Fax: (760)722-0653. Website: www.transworldsnowboarding.com. Editor: Kurt Hoy. Magazine published 8 times/year for the snowboarding enthusiast. Circ. 250,000. Editorial lead time 3 months.

• Query before submitting.

WATER SPORTS

Ⓝ ⊘ BOATING

Hachette Filipacchi Media U.S., Inc., 1633 Broadway, 41st Floor, New York NY 10019. (212)767-6041. Fax: (212)767-4831. Website: www.boatingmag.com. Monthly magazine dedicated to manufactures, distributors and consumers involved in the boating industry. Circ. 201,171. Editorial lead time 3 months.

• Query before submitting.

$ ◩ DIVER

241 E. 1st St., North Vancouver BC V7L 1B4 Canada. (604)948-9337. Fax: (604)948-9985. E-mail: divermag@axion.net. Website: www.divermag.com. Magazine published 8 times/year emphasizing scuba diving, ocean science, and technology for a well-educated, outdoor-oriented readership. Circ. 7,000. Accepts queries by mail, e-mail.

Nonfiction "Well-written and illustrated Canadian and North American regional dive destination articles. Most travel articles are committed up to a year in advance, and there is limited scope for new material." Reading period for unsolicited articles July through August. Length: 500-1,000 words. **Pays $2.50/column inch.**

Photos Reviews 5×7 prints, JPEG/TIFF files (300 dpi), slides, maps, drawings. Captions, identification of subjects required.

Ⓝ $ $ IMMERSED MAGAZINE

The International Technical Diving Magazine, Immersed, LLC, P.O. Box 638, Chester NY 10918. E-mail: jeff@immersed.com. Website: www.immersed.com. **Contact:** Jeff Bonzanic, editor. **60% freelance written.** Quarterly magazine covering scuba diving. "Advances on the frontier of scuba diving are covered in theme-oriented issues that examine archeology, biology, history, gear, and sciences related to diving. We emphasize training, education, and safety." Estab. 1996. Circ. 25,000. Pays on publication. Byline given. Offers kill fee. Buys one-time, electronic rights. Editorial lead time 6 months. Accepts queries by mail, e-mail, fax, phone. Sample copy online. Writer's guidelines for #10 SASE.

    ☞ Break in with "how-to equipment rigging stories or travel stories on unusual but accessible destinations."

Nonfiction Historical/nostalgic, how-to, interview/profile, new product, personal experience, photo feature, technical, travel. No poetry, opinion diatribes, axe-grinding exposés. **Buys 30 mss/year.** Query. Length: 500-2,000 words. **Pays $150-250.** Sometimes pays expenses of writers on assignment.

Photos Send photos with submission. Reviews transparencies, prints. Buys one-time and promotional website rights. Offers no additional payment for photos accepted with ms. Captions required.

Columns/Departments Technically Destined (travel), 1,200 words; Rigging For Success (how-to, few words/

heavily illustrated); Explorer (personality profile), 2,000 words; Tech Spec (product descriptions), 1,000 words; New Products (product press releases), 200 words; Book Review (book review), 800 words. **Buys 12 mss/year.** Query. **Pays $150-250.**

Fillers Newsbreaks. **Pays 35¢/word.**

Tips "Query first with a short, punchy paragraph that describes your story and why it would be of interest to our readers. There's bonus points for citing which feature or department would be most appropriate for your story."

$ $ PADDLER MAGAZINE

World's No. 1 Canoeing, Kayaking and Rafting Magazine, Paddlesport Publishing, P.O. Box 775450, Steamboat Springs CO 80477-5450. (970)879-1450. E-mail: rico@paddlermagazine.com. Website: www.paddlermagazine. com. **70% freelance written.** Bimonthly magazine covering paddle sports. "*Paddler* magazine is written by and for those knowledgeable about river running, flatwater canoeing and sea kayaking. Our core audience is the intermediate to advanced paddler, yet we strive to cover the entire range from beginners to experts. Our editorial coverage is divided between whitewater rafting, whitewater kayaking, canoeing and sea kayaking. We strive for balance between the Eastern and Western US paddling scenes and regularly cover international expeditions. We also try to integrate the Canadian paddling community into each publication." Estab. 1991. Circ. 80,000. Pays on publication. Publishes ms an average of 6 months after acceptance. Byline given. Buys first North American serial, one-time electronic rights rights. Editorial lead time 3 months. Submit seasonal material 6 months in advance. Accepts queries by mail, e-mail. Responds in 6 months to queries. Sample copy for $3 with 8½×11 SASE. Writer's guidelines online.

O— Break in through "The Hotline section at the front of the magazine."

Nonfiction Book excerpts, essays, general interest, historical/nostalgic, how-to, humor, inspirational, interview/ profile, new product, opinion, personal experience, photo feature, technical, travel (must be paddlesport related). **Buys 75 mss/year.** Query. Length: 100-3,000 words. **Pays 10-25¢/word (more for established writers) for assigned articles; 10-20¢/word for unsolicited articles.** Sometimes pays expenses of writers on assignment.

Photos Submissions should include photos or other art. State availability with submission. Reviews contact sheets, negatives, transparencies. Buys one-time rights. Offers $25-200/photo.

Columns/Departments Hotline (timely news and exciting developments relating to the paddling community. Stories should be lively and newsworthy), 150-750 words; Paddle People (unique people involved in the sport and industry leaders), 600-800 words; Destinations (informs paddlers of unique places to paddle—we often follow regional themes and cover all paddling disciplines); submissions should include map and photo, 800 words. Marketplace (gear reviews, gadgets and new products, and is about equipment paddlers use, from boats and paddles to collapsible chairs, bivy sacks and other accessories), 250-800 words. Paddle Tales (short, humorous anecdotes), 75-300 words. Skills (a "How-to" forum for experts to share tricks of the trade, from playboating techniques to cooking in the backcountry), 250-1,000 words. Query. **Pays 20-25¢/word.**

Tips "We prefer queries, but will look at manuscripts on speculation. No phone queries please. Be familiar with the magazine and offer us unique, exciting ideas. Most positive responses to queries are on spec, but we will occasionally make assignments."

N SCUBA DIVING

a Division of F+W Publications, Inc., 6600 Abercorn St., Suite 208, Savannah GA 31405. (912)351-0855. Fax: (912)351-0735. E-mail: edit@scubadiving.com. Website: www.scubadiving.com. **Contact:** Buck Butler, editor (bbutler@scubadiving.com); Keith Phillips, senior editor (kphillips@scubadiving.com); Deborah Kirk, travel editor (dkirk@scubadiving.com). Monthly magazine for scuba divers of all skill levels. Estab. 1992. Circ. 185,000. Buys all rights. Editorial lead time 10 weeks. Accepts queries by mail, e-mail, fax, phone. Sample copy for $3.50. Writer's guidelines by e-mail.

Nonfiction "No first person essays or puff pieces on dive destinations and operators." Query.

Columns/Departments Currents (lively and engaging stories that are heavy on news and/or how-to information), 500 words or less; North American Travel (great diving/scuba adventures that are close to home and can be done in a long weekend), 750 words, including Dive In sidebar. Query.

N $ ⊘ SURFER MAGAZINE

Primedia Enthusiast Group, P.O. Box 1028, Dana Point CA 92629-5028. (949)661-5150. E-mail: chris.mauro@pri media.com. Website: www.surfermag.com. Editor: Chris Mauro. Monthly magazine edited for the avid surfers and those who follow the beach, wave riding scene. Circ. 118,570. Editorial lead time 10 weeks.

● Query before submitting.

N ⊘ SURFING

Primedia Enthusiast Group, 950 Calle Amanecer, Suite C, San Clemente CA 93673. (949)492-7873. E-mail: matt.walker@primedia.com. Website: www.surfingthemag.com. Editor: Evan Slater. **Contact:** Matt Walker, senior editor. Monthly magazine covering surfing. Edited for the active surfing enthusiast who enjoys the beach lifestyle. Estab. 1964. Circ. 108,035. Sample copy for $3.99.

  ● Query before submitting.

$ $ SWIMMING TECHNIQUE

Sports Publications, Inc., P.O. Box 20337, Sedona AZ 86341. (520)284-4005. Fax: (520)284-2477. Website: www.swiminfo.com. **75% freelance written.** Quarterly magazine for professional swim coaches, covering swimming techniques. "Covers all aspects of swimming technique and training." Estab. 1963. Circ. 9,000. Pays on publication. Publishes ms an average of 4 months after acceptance. Byline given. Buys first, all rights. Editorial lead time 4 months. Submit seasonal material 4 months in advance. Accepts queries by mail, e-mail, fax, phone. Accepts previously published material. Responds in 1 month to queries. Sample copy for $5. Writer's guidelines free.

Nonfiction Book excerpts, essays, how-to (swim & technique), interview/profile, opinion, personal experience, technical. **Buys 16-20 mss/year.** Query with published clips. Length: 500-4,000 words. **Pays 12-15¢/word.** Sometimes pays expenses of writers on assignment.

Photos Send photos with submission. Buys all rights. Negotiates payment individually. Captions, identification of subjects required.

$ $ SWIMMING WORLD

Sports Publications, Inc., P.O. Box 20337, Sedona AZ 86341. (520)284-4005. Fax: (520)284-2477. Website: www.swiminfo.com. **50% freelance written.** Monthly magazine. "*Swimming World* is recognized as the authoritative source in the sport of swimming. It publishes articles about all aspects of competitive swimming." Estab. 1959. Circ. 39,700. Pays on publication. Byline given. Kill fee negotiated. Buys all rights. Editorial lead time 2 months. Submit seasonal material 3 months in advance. Accepts queries by mail, e-mail, fax, phone. Accepts simultaneous submissions. Responds in 1 month to queries. Sample copy for $5 and SAE with 4 first-class stamps. Writer's guidelines free.

Nonfiction Book excerpts, essays, exposé, general interest, historical/nostalgic, how-to, humor, inspirational, interview/profile, new product, opinion, personal experience, photo feature, technical, travel. **Buys 30 mss/ year.** Query. Length: 300-3,000 words. **Pays $75-400.** Sometimes pays expenses of writers on assignment.

Photos State availability with submission. Reviews prints. Buys negotiable rights. Negotiates payment individually. Captions, identification of subjects, model releases required.

Columns/Departments Buys 18 mss/year. Query with published clips. **Pays $75-200.**

Ⓝ TRANSWORLD SURF

Transworld Media (a division of Time 4 Media), 353 Airport Rd., Oceanside CA 92054. (760)722-7777. Fax: (760)722-0653. Website: www.transworldsurf.com. Editor-in-Chief: Joel Patterson. Monthly magazine designed to promote the growth of the sport of surfing. Circ. 85,000.

TEEN & YOUNG ADULT

BOP

Laufer Media, 6430 Sunset Blvd., Hollywood CA 90028. (323)462-4267. Fax: (323)462-4341. Editor: Leesa Coble. Monthly magazine. Top teen entertainment magazine covers today's hottest stars. Features, news, gossip, quizzes. Does not want poetry, fiction or real-person stories. Circ. 200,000. Sample copy not available.

$ $ BREAKAWAY MAGAZINE

Focus on the Family, 8605 Explorer Dr., Colorado Springs CO 80920. (719)531-3400. Website: www.breakaway mag.com. Editor: Michael Ross. Associate Editor: Jeremy V. Jones. **Contact:** Carey Posey, editorial assistant. **25% freelance written.** Monthly magazine covering extreme sports, Christian music artists, and new technology relevant to teen boys. "This fast-paced, 4-color publication is designed to creatively teach, entertain, inspire, and challenge the emerging teenager. It also seeks to strengthen a boy's self-esteem, provide role models, guide a healthy awakening to girls, make the Bible relevant, and deepen their love for family, friends, church, and Jesus Christ." Estab. 1990. Circ. 96,000. **Pays on acceptance.** Publishes ms an average of 5-12 months after acceptance. Byline given. Offers $25 kill fee. Buys first North American serial, first, one-time, electronic rights. Editorial lead time 5 months. Submit seasonal material 8 months in advance. Accepts queries by mail. Responds in 2-3 months. Sample copy for $1.50 and 9×12 SASE with 3 first-class stamps. Writer's guidelines for #10 SASE.

Nonfiction Inspirational, interview/profile, personal experience. **Buys up to 6 mss/year.** Send complete ms. Length: 700-2,000 words. **Pays 12-15¢/word.**

Columns/Departments Epic Truth (spiritual/Biblical application devotional for teen guys), 800 words; Weird, Wild, WOW! (technology, culture, science), 200-400 words. **Buys 2-3 mss/year.** Send complete ms. **Pays 12-15¢/word.**

Fiction Adventure, humorous, religious, suspense. "Avoid Christian jargon, clichés, preaching, and other dialogue that isn't realistic or that interrupts the flow of the story." **Buys 3-4 mss/year.** Send complete ms. Length: 600-2,000 words. **Pays 15-20¢/word.**

Tips "Some of our readers get spiritual nurture at home and at church; many don't. To reach both groups, the articles must be written in ways that are compelling, bright, out of the ordinary. Nearly every adult in a boy's life is an authority figure. We would like you, through the magazine, to be seen as a friend! We also want *Breakaway* to be a magazine any pre-Christian teen could pick up and understand without first learning 'Christianese.' Stories should spiritually challenge, yet be spiritually inviting."

N $ $⊘ CAMPUS LIFE

Christianity Today, Inc., 465 Gundersen Dr., Carol Stream IL 60188. (630)260-6200. Fax: (630)480-2004. E-mail: clmag@campuslife.net. Website: www.campuslife.net. **Contact:** Chris Lutes, editor. **35% freelance written.** Bimonthly magazine published 9 times/year for the Christian life as it relates to today's teen. "*Campus Life* is a magazine for high-school and early college-age teenagers. Our editorial slant is not overtly religious. The indirect style is intended to create a safety zone with our readers and to reflect our philosophy that God is interested in all of life. Therefore, we publish 'message stories' side by side with general interest, humor, etc. We are also looking for stories that help high school students consider a Christian college education." Estab. 1942. Circ. 100,000. **Pays on acceptance.** Publishes ms an average of 5 months after acceptance. Byline given. Offers 50% kill fee. Buys first, one-time rights. Editorial lead time 4 months. Responds in 6 weeks to queries. Sample copy for $3 and 9½×11 SAE with 3 first-class stamps. Writer's guidelines online.

● *No unsolicited mss.*

Nonfiction Humor, personal experience, photo feature. **Buys 15-20 mss/year.** Query with published clips. Length: 750-1,500 words. **Pays 15-20¢/word minimum.**

Reprints Send tearsheet, photocopy or typed ms with rights for sale noted and information about when and where the material previously appeared. Pays $50.

Fiction Buys 1-5 mss/year. Query. Length: 1,000-2,000 words. **Pays 15-20¢/word, and 2 contributor's copies.**

Tips "The best way to break in to *Campus Life* is through writing first-person or as-told-to first-person stories. We want stories that capture a teen's everyday 'life lesson' experience. A first-person story must be highly descriptive and incorporate fictional technique. While avoiding simplistic religious answers, the story should demonstrate that Christian values or beliefs brought about a change in the young person's life. But query first with theme information telling the way this story would work for our audience."

$ COLLEGEBOUND TEEN MAGAZINE

The College Bound Network, 1200 South Ave., Suite 202, Staten Island NY 10314. (718)761-4800. Fax: (718)761-3300. E-mail: editorial@collegebound.net. Website: www.collegeboundteen.com. Editor-in-Chief: Gina LaGuardia. **Contact:** Dawn Papandrea, managing editor. **70% freelance written.** Monthly magazine. "*CollegeBound Teen Magazine* is designed to provide high school students with an inside look at all aspects of college life academics and socials. College students from around the country (and those young at heart!) are welcome to serve as correspondents to provide our teen readership with real-life accounts and cutting-edge, expert advice on the college admissions process and beyond." Estab. 1987. Circ. 100,000 (regional issues). Pays 6 weeks upon publication. Publishes ms an average of 3-4 months after acceptance. Byline given. Buys first North American serial, first, electronic rights. Editorial lead time 4 months. Submit seasonal material 4 months in advance. Accepts queries by mail, e-mail. Responds in 6 weeks to queries; 2 months to mss. Sample copy for 9×12 SAE and $3.85 postage. Writer's guidelines online.

Nonfiction How-to (apply for college, prepare for the interview, etc.), unique teen stories related to college admission and college life. No fillers, poetry, or fiction. **Buys 100 mss/year.** Query with published clips. Length: 650-1,500 words. **Pays $50-100, plus 2 issues of magazine.**

Photos Gina LaGuardia, editor-in-chief. State availability with submission. Buys one-time rights. Offers no additional payment for photos accepted with ms. Captions, identification of subjects required.

Columns/Departments Buys 15 mss/year. Query with published clips. **Pays $40-70.**

Tips "We're looking for well-researched, well-reported articles packed with real-life student anecdotes and expert insight on everything from dealing with dorm life, choosing the right college, and joining a fraternity or sorority, to college dating, cool campus happenings, scholarship scoring strategies, and other college issues."

N $ THE CONQUEROR

United Pentecostal Church International, 8855 Dunn Rd., Hazelwood MO 63042-2299. (314)837-7300. Fax: (314)837-4503. E-mail: youth@upci.org. Website: www.upci.org/youth. **Contact:** Shay Mann, editor. **80%**

freelance written. Bimonthly magazine covering Christian youth. "*The Conqueror* addresses the social, intellectual, and spiritual concerns of youth aged 12-21 years from a Christian viewpoint." Estab. 1957. Circ. 6,000. Pays on publication. Publishes ms an average of 4 months after acceptance. Buys one-time rights. Editorial lead time 4 months. Submit seasonal material 4 months in advance. Accepts queries by mail, e-mail, fax. Accepts simultaneous submissions. Responds in 2 months to mss. Sample copy for 9 × 12 SAE with 3 first-class stamps. Writer's guidelines online.

Nonfiction Essays, general interest, historical/nostalgic, inspirational, personal experience, religious. **Buys 18 mss/year.** Send complete ms. Length: 250-1,250 words. **Pays 6¹/₂¢/word.**

Reprints Accepts previously published submissions.

Photos State availability with submission. Offers no additional payment for photos accepted with ms.

Columns/Departments Buys 6-10 mss/year. Send complete ms. **Pays 6¹/₂¢/word.**

Fiction Adventure, ethnic, historical, humorous, mainstream, religious, slice-of-life vignettes. Send complete ms. Length: 250-1,250 words. **Pays 6¹/₂¢/word.**

Poetry Traditional. **Buys 2-4 poems/year.** Submit maximum 5 poems. **Pays $15.**

Fillers Anecdotes, gags to be illustrated by cartoonist, short humor. **Buys 4/year.** Length: 100 words. **Pays $15.**

Tips "Choose subjects relevant to single youth. Most subjects are relevant if properly handled. Today's youth are interested in more than clothes, fashion, careers, and dating. Remember our primary objective: Inspiration— to portray happy, victorious living through faith in God."

$ $ GUIDEPOSTS SWEET 16

(formerly *Guideposts for Teens*), 1050 Broadway, Suite 6, Chesterton IN 46304. (219)929-4429. Fax: (219)926-3839. E-mail: writers@guidepostssweet16mag.com. Website: www.guidepostssweet16mag.com. Editor-in-Chief: Mary Lou Carney. **Contact:** Betsy Kohn, managing editor. **90% freelance written.** Bimonthly magazine serving as an inspiration for teens. "*Sweet 16* is a general interest magazine for teenage girls (ages 11-17). We are an inspirational publication that offers true, first-person stories about real teens. Our watchwords are 'wholesome,' 'current,' 'fun,' and 'inspiring.' We also publish shorter pieces on fashion, beauty, celebrity, boys, embarrassing moments, and advice columns." Estab. 1998. Circ. 195,000. **Pays on acceptance.** Byline sometimes given. Offers 25% kill fee. Buys all rights. Editorial lead time 6 months. Submit seasonal material 6 months in advance. Accepts queries by mail, e-mail. Accepts simultaneous submissions. Responds in 6 weeks. Sample copy for $4.50. Writer's guidelines online.

Nonfiction Nothing written from an adult point of view. How-to, humor, inspirational, interview/profile, personal experience. **Buys 80 mss/year.** Query. Length: 200-1,500 words. **Pays $300-500 for assigned articles; $100-300 for unsolicited articles.** Pays expenses of writers on assignment.

Photos State availability with submission. Buys one-time rights. Negotiates payment individually. Identification of subjects required.

Columns/Departments Quiz (teen-related topics/teen language), 1,000 words; Positive Thinker (first-person stories of teen who've overcome something remarkable and kept a positive outlook), 300-500 words; Mysterious Moments (first-person "strange-but-true" miracle stories), 250 words; The Day I . . . (first-person "the day my life changed" experience stories), 500 words; Too Good to be True (profile of a cute wholesome teen guy who has more than looks/has done something very cool/has overcome something extraordinary), 400 words. **Buys 40 mss/year.** Query with published clips. **Pays $175-400.**

Tips "We are eagerly looking for a number of things: teen profiles, quizzes, DIYs. Most of all, though, we are about true stories in the *Guideposts* tradition. Teens in dangerous, inspiring, miraculous situations. These first-person (ghostwritten) true narratives are the backbone of *Sweet 16*—and what sets us apart from other publications."

$ GUMBO MAGAZINE

The National Magazine Written by Teens for Teens, Strive Media Institute, 1818 N. Dr. Martin Luther King Dr., Milwaukee WI 53212. (414)374-3511. Fax: (414)374-3512. E-mail: info@mygumbo.com. Website: www.mygumbo.com. Editor: Corbin Robinson. **Contact:** Tiffany Wynn, managing editor. **25% freelance written.** Bimonthly magazine covering teen issues (arts, entertainment, social issues, etc.). "All articles must be written by teens (13-19 year-olds) and for teens. Tone is modern, hip, and urban. No adults may write for magazine." Estab. 1998. Circ. 25,000. Pays on publication. Publishes ms an average of 6 months after acceptance. Byline given. Buys one-time rights. Editorial lead time 6 months. Submit seasonal material 6 months in advance. Accepts queries by mail, e-mail, fax. Accepts previously published material. Accepts simultaneous submissions. Responds in 2 weeks to queries; 2 months to mss. Sample copy and writer's guidelines free.

Nonfiction General interest, humor, inspirational, interview/profile, opinion, personal experience, photo feature, technical, book & CD reviews. Does not want unsolicited articles or fiction other than poetry. All news stories require approval from Managing Editor prior to submission. **Buys 50-70 mss/year.** Query. Length: 500-1,000 words. **Pays $25.** Sometimes pays expenses of writers on assignment.

Photos State availability of or send photos with submission. Reviews prints, GIF/JPEG files. Buys one-time rights. Offers no additional payment for photos accepted with ms. Captions, identification of subjects required.

Poetry Any poetry is acceptable provided author is 13-19 years of age. Avant-garde, free verse, haiku, light verse, traditional. Submit maximum 3 poems. Length: 5-50 lines.

Tips "Writers need to apply online or mail in an application from an issue of the magazine."

$ INSIGHT

Because Life Is Full of Decisions, The Review and Herald Publishing Association, 55 W. Oak Ridge Dr., Hagerstown MD 21740. E-mail: insight@rhpa.org. Website: www.insightmagazine.org. **Contact:** Dwain Neilson Esmond, editor. **80% freelance written.** Weekly magazine covering spiritual life of teenagers. "*Insight* publishes true dramatic stories, interviews, and community and mission service features that relate directly to the lives of Christian teenagers, particularly those with a Seventh-day Adventist background." Estab. 1970. Circ. 20,000. Pays on publication. Publishes ms an average of 4 months after acceptance. Byline given. Buys first, second serial (reprint) rights. Editorial lead time 6 months. Submit seasonal material 6 months in advance. Accepts queries by mail, e-mail, fax. Responds in 1 month to mss. Sample copy for $2 and #10 SASE. Writer's guidelines online.

● "'Big Deal' appears in *Insight* often, covering a topic of importance to teens. Each feature contains: An opening story involving real teens (can be written in first-person), "Scripture Picture" (a sidebar that discusses what the Bible says about the topic) and another sidebar (optional) that adds more perspective and help.

Nonfiction How-to (teen relationships and experiences), humor, interview/profile, personal experience, photo feature, religious. **Buys 120 mss/year.** Send complete ms. Length: 500-2,000 words. **Pays $25-150 for assigned articles; $25-125 for unsolicited articles.**

Reprints Send ms with rights for sale noted and information about when and where the material previously appeared. Pays $50.

Photos State availability with submission. Reviews contact sheets, negatives, transparencies, prints. Buys one-time rights. Negotiates payment individually. Model releases required.

Columns/Departments Send complete ms. **Pays $25-125.**

Tips "Skim 2 months of *Insight*. Write about your teen experiences. Use informed, contemporary style and vocabulary. Follow Jesus' life and example."

$ $ LISTEN MAGAZINE

Celebrating Positive Choices, The Health Connection, 55 W. Oak Ridge Dr., Hagerstown MD 21740. (301)393-4010. E-mail: editor@listenmagazine.org. Website: www.listenmagazine.org. **Contact:** Celeste Perrino-Walker, editor. **50% freelance written.** Monthly magazine specializing in tobacco, drug, and alcohol prevention, presenting positive alternatives to various tobacco, drug, and alcohol dependencies. "*Listen* is used in many high school classes and by professionals: medical personnel, counselors, law enforcement officers, educators, youth workers, etc. *Listen* publishes true-to-life stories about giving teens choices about real-life situations and moral issues in a secular way." Circ. 40,000. Publishes ms an average of 6 months after acceptance. Byline given. Pays on acceptance for first rights for use in *Listen*, reprints, and associated material. Accepts queries by mail, e-mail, fax. Accepts previously published material. Accepts simultaneous submissions. Responds in 2 months to queries. Sample copy for $2 and 9×12 SASE. Writer's guidelines for SASE, by e-mail, fax or on website.

○┑ Break in with "by telling me something I don't know. Our topics are fairly limited; make the material fresh."

Nonfiction Seeks articles that deal with causes of drug use such as poor self-concept, family relations, social skills, peer pressure. Especially interested in youth-slanted articles or personality interviews encouraging nonalcoholic and nondrug ways of life and showing positive alternatives. Also interested in good activity articles of interest to teens; an activity that teens would want to do instead of taking abusive substances because they're bored. Teenage point of view is essential. **Pays $250 for Personalities (1,200 words); $125 for hobby/sport/activity (1,000 words); $100 for factuals (1,000 words); $50 for quizzes/shorts (500 words); and 3 contributor's copies (additional copies $2). Buys 30-50 unsolicited mss/year.** Query.

Reprints Send photocopy of article or typed ms with rights for sale noted and information about when and where the material previously appeared. Pays their regular rates.

Photos Color photos preferred, but b&w acceptable. Purchased with accompanying ms. Captions required.

Fiction Seeks narratives which portray teens dealing with youth conflicts, especially those related to the use of or temptation to use harmful substances. For *Listen*, it needs to be more than well-written or entertaining. "Our fiction has to help kids understand the consequences of bad choices, or empower them to make good ones in bad situations. We are also being inundated with drunk-driving accident stories and 'new kid at school' stories. Unless yours is unique, consider another topic." Anti-drug, alcohol, tobacco, positive role models. Query with published clips or send complete ms. **Pays $80 for fiction (500 words); and 3 contributor's copies (additional copies $2).**

Tips "True stories are good, especially if they have a unique angle. Other authoritative articles need a fresh approach. In query, briefly summarize article idea and logic of why you feel it's good. Make sure you've read the magazine to understand our approach. A large percentage of the fiction we receive is about alcohol and tobacco. For a better chance at publication, query us on other topics. Yearly theme lists available upon requst."

$ $LIVE

A Weekly Journal of Practical Christian Living, Gospel Publishing House, 1445 N. Boonville Ave., Springfield MO 65802-1894. (417)862-2781. Fax: (417)862-6059. E-mail: rl-live@gph.org. Website: www.radiantlife.org. **Contact:** Paul W. Smith, senior editor, adult resources. **100% freelance written.** Weekly magazine for weekly distribution covering practical Christian living. "*LIVE* is a take-home paper distributed weekly in young adult and adult Sunday school classes. We seek to encourage Christians in living for God through fiction and true stories which apply Biblical principles to everyday problems." Estab. 1928. Circ. 70,000. **Pays on acceptance.** Publishes ms an average of 18 months after acceptance. Byline given. Buys first, second serial (reprint) rights. Editorial lead time 12 months. Submit seasonal material 18 months in advance. Accepts queries by mail, e-mail, fax. Accepts simultaneous submissions. Responds in 2 weeks to queries; 6 weeks to mss. Sample copy and writer's guidelines for #10 SASE.

    O-π Break in with "true stories that demonstrate how the principles in the Bible work in everyday circumstances as well as crises."

Nonfiction Inspirational, religious. No preachy articles or stories that refer to religious myths (i.e., Santa Claus, Easter Bunny, etc.). **Buys 50-100 mss/year.** Send complete ms. Length: 400-1,200 words. **Pays 7-10¢/word.**

Reprints Send tearsheet, photocopy or typed ms with rights for sale noted and information about when and where the material previously appeared. Pays 7¢/word.

Photos Send photos with submission. Reviews 35mm transparencies and 3×4 prints or larger. Buys one-time rights. Offers $35-60/photo. Identification of subjects required.

Fiction Paul W. Smith, editor. Religious, inspirational, prose poem. No preachy fiction, fiction about Bible characters, or stories that refer to religious myths (i.e., Santa Claus, Easter Bunny, etc.). No science or Bible fiction. No controversial stories about such subjects as feminism, war or capital punishment. **Buys 20-50 mss/year.** Send complete ms. Length: 800-1,200 words. **Pays 7-10¢/word.**

Poetry Free verse, haiku, light verse, traditional. **Buys 15-24 poems/year.** Submit maximum 3 poems. Length: 12-25 lines. **Pays $35-60.**

Fillers Anecdotes, short humor. **Buys 12-36/year.** Length: 300-600 words. **Pays 7-10¢/word.**

Tips "Don't moralize or be preachy. Provide human interest articles with Biblical life application. Stories should consist of action, not just thought-life; interaction, not just insight. Heroes and heroines should rise above failures, take risks for God, prove that scriptural principles meet their needs. Conflict and suspense should increase to a climax! Avoid pious conclusions. Characters should be interesting, believable, and realistic. Avoid stereotypes. Characters should be active, not just pawns to move the plot along. They should confront conflict and change in believable ways. Describe the character's looks and reveal his personality through his actions to such an extent that the reader feels he has met that person. Readers should care about the character enough to finish the story. Feature racial, ethnic, and regional characters in rural and urban settings."

$ $THE NEW ERA

50 E. North Temple, Salt Lake City UT 84150. (801)240-2951. Fax: (801)240-2270. E-mail: cur-editorial-newera dschurch.org. **Contact:** Val Johnson, managing editor. **20% freelance written.** Monthly magazine for young people (ages 12-18) of the Church of Jesus Christ of Latter-day Saints (Mormon), their church leaders and teachers. Estab. 1971. Circ. 230,000. **Pays on acceptance.** Publishes ms an average of 1 year after acceptance. Byline given. Buys all rights. Submit seasonal material 1 year in advance. Accepts queries by mail, e-mail, fax. Responds in 2 months to queries. Sample copy for $1.50 and 9×12 SAE with 2 first-class stamps. Writer's guidelines for SASE.

Nonfiction Material that shows how the Church of Jesus Christ of Latter-day Saints is relevant in the lives of young people today. Must capture the excitement of being a young Latter-day Saint. Special interest in the experiences of young Mormons in other countries. No general library research or formula pieces without the *New Era* slant and feel. How-to, humor, inspirational, interview/profile, personal experience, informational. Query. Length: 150-1,200 words. **Pays 3-12¢/word.** Pays expenses of writers on assignment.

Photos Uses b&w photos and transparencies with manuscripts. Individual photos used for *Photo of the Month*. Payment depends on use, $10-125 per photo.

Columns/Departments What's Up? (news of young Mormons around the world); How I Know; Scripture Lifeline. **Pays 3-12¢/word.**

Poetry Must relate to editorial viewpoint. Free verse, light verse, traditional, blank verse, all other forms. **Pays 25¢/line minimum.**

Tips ''The writer must be able to write from a Mormon point of view. We're especially looking for stories about successful family relationships and personal growth. Well-written, personal experiences are always in demand.''

$ $ $ $ SEVENTEEN

1440 Broadway, 13th Floor, New York NY 10018. (917)934-6500. Fax: (917)934-6574. Website: www.seventeen. com. Features Assistant: Melanie Abrahams. Features Editor: Sarah Nanus. **20% freelance written.** Monthly magazine. ''*Seventeen* is a young woman's first fashion and beauty magazine. Tailored for young women in their teens and early twenties, *Seventeen* covers fashion, beauty, health, fitness, food, college, entertainment, fiction, plus crucial personal and global issues.'' Estab. 1944. Circ. 2,400,000. **Pays on acceptance.** Publishes ms an average of 6 months after acceptance. Byline given. Offers 25% kill fee. Buys one-time rights. Accepts queries by mail. Responds in 3 months to queries. Sample copy not available. Writer's guidelines available online.

- ● ''We no longer accept fiction submissions.''
- ○➔ Break in with the Who Knew section, which contains shorter items, or *Quiz*.

Nonfiction Articles and features of general interest to young women who are concerned with intimate relationships and how to realize their potential in the world; strong emphasis on topicality and service. Send brief outline and query, including typical lead paragraph, summing up basic idea of article, with clips of previously published works. Articles are commissioned after outlines are submitted and approved. Length: 1,200-2,500 words. **Pays $1/word, occasionally more for assigned articles.** Pays expenses of writers on assignment.

Photos Photos usually by assignment only. Elizabeth Kildahl, photo editor.

🖳 The online magazine carries original content not found in the print edition. Contact: Fiona Gibb, editorial director.

Tips ''Writers have to ask themselves whether or not they feel they can find the right tone for a *Seventeen* article—a tone which is empathetic, yet never patronizing; lively, yet not superficial. Not all writers feel comfortable with, understand, or like teenagers. If you don't like them, *Seventeen* is the wrong market for you. An excellent way to break in to the magazine is by contributing ideas for quizzes or the 'My Story' (personal essay) column.''

$ $ SPIRIT

Lectionary-based Weekly for Catholic Teens, Good Ground Press, 1884 Randolph Ave., St. Paul MN 55105-1700. (651)690-7010. Fax: (651)690-7039. E-mail: jmcsj9@aol.com. Publisher: Joan Mitchell, CSJ; Managing Editor: Therese Sherlock, CSJ. **Contact:** Constance Fourre, editor. **50% freelance written.** Weekly newsletter for religious education of Catholic high schoolers. ''We want realistic fiction and nonfiction that raises current ethical and religious questions and that deals with conflicts that teens face in multi-racial contexts. The fact we are a religious publication does *not* mean we want pious, moralistic fiction.'' Estab. 1981. Circ. 26,000. Pays on publication. Publishes ms an average of 6 months after acceptance. Byline given. Buys all rights. Editorial lead time 6 months. Submit seasonal material 6 months in advance. Accepts queries by mail, e-mail, fax. Accepts simultaneous submissions. Responds in 1 month to queries. Sample copy and writer's guidelines free.

Nonfiction ''No Christian confessional, born-again pieces.'' Interview/profile, personal experience, religious, Roman Catholic leaders, human interest features, social justice leaders, projects, humanitarians. **Buys 4 mss/ year.** Query with published clips or send complete ms. Length: 1,000-1,200 words. **Pays $200-225 for assigned articles; $150 for unsolicited articles.**

Photos State availability with submission. Reviews 8×10 prints. Buys one-time rights. Offers $85-125/photo. Identification of subjects required.

Fiction ''We want realistic pieces for and about teens—nonpedantic, nonpious. We need good Christmas stories that show spirit of the season, and stories about teen relationship conflicts (boy/girl, parent/teen).'' Conflict vignettes. **Buys 10 mss/year.** Query with published clips or send complete ms. Length: 1,000-1,200 words. **Pays $150-200.**

Tips ''Writers must be able to write from and for teen point of view rather than adult or moralistic point of view. In nonfiction, interviewed teens must speak for themselves. Query to receive call for stories, spec sheet, sample issues.''

$ $ ⊘ TEEN MAGAZINE

Hearst Magazines, 3000 Ocean Park Blvd., Suite 3048, Santa Monica CA 90405. (310)664-2950. Fax: (310)664-2959. Website: www.teenmag.com. **Contact:** Jane Fort, editor-in-chief (fashion, beauty, TeenPROM); Damon Romine, deputy editor (entertainment, movies, TV, music, books, covers); Heather Hewitt, managing editor (manufacturing, advertising, new products, what's hot). Quarterly magazine for ''a pure Jr. high school female audience. *TEEN* teens are upbeat and want to be informed. Estab. 1957. **Pays on acceptance.** Buys all rights.

• *No unsolicited materials accepted.*

Nonfiction How-to, interview/profile, travel, arts/crafts, fashion, games/puzzles, careers, cooking, health, multicultural, problem-solving, social issues. Does not want to see adult-oriented, adult point of view.'' **Pays $50-500.**

Fiction Does not want to see ''that which does not apply to our market—i.e., science fiction, history, religious, adult-oriented.'' **Pays $100-400.**

TIGER BEAT

Laufer Media, 6430 Sunset Blvd., Suite 700, Hollywood CA 90028. (323)462-4267. Fax: (323)462-4341. Editor: Leesa Coble. Monthly magazine. Leading teen entertainment magazine written for girls. Features news, gossip and features on today's hottest stars. Does not want poetry, fiction, or real-person stories. Circ. 200,000. Editorial lead time 2 months. Sample copy not available.

[N] TWIST

Bauer Publishing, 270 Sylvan Ave., Englewood Cliffs NJ 07632. E-mail: twistmail@twistmagazine.com. Website: www.twistmagazine.com. **5% freelance written.** Monthly entertainment magazine targeting 14- to 19-year-old girls. Estab. 1997. Circ. 700,000. **Pays on acceptance.** Publishes ms an average of 3 months after acceptance. Offers 20% kill fee. Buys first North American serial rights. Editorial lead time 3 months. Submit seasonal material 4 months in advance. Accepts queries by mail. Accepts simultaneous submissions. Responds in 1 month to queries. Writer's guidelines online.

Nonfiction ''No articles written from an adult point of view about teens—i.e., a mother's or teacher's personal account.'' Personal experience (real teens' experiences, preferably in first person). **Payment varies according to assignment.** Pays expenses of writers on assignment.

Photos State availability with submission. Negotiates payment individually. Identification of subjects, model releases required.

Tips ''Tone must be conversational, neither condescending to teens nor trying to be too slangy. If possible, send clips that show an ability to write for the teen market. We are in search of real-life stories, and writers who can find teens with compelling real-life experiences (who are willing to use their full names and photographs in the magazine). Please refer to a current issue to see examples of tone and content. No e-mail queries or submissions, please.''

$ $ [] WHAT'S HERS/WHAT'S HIS MAGAZINES

(formerly *What Magazine*), What! Publishers Inc., 108-93 Lombard Ave., Winnipeg MB R3B 3B1 Canada. (204)985-8160. Fax: (204)957-5638. E-mail: letters@whatshers.com; letters@whatshis.com. **Contact:** Barbara Chabai, *What's HERS* editor; Dan Kenning, *What's HIS* editor. **40% freelance written.** Magazine published 5 times during the school year covering teen issues and pop culture. ''*What's HERS* and *What's HIS* magazines are distributed to high school students across Canada. We produce 2 gender specific magazines that are empowering, interactive and entertaining. We respect the reader—today's teens are smart and creative (and critical).'' Estab. 1987. Circ. 280,000 (180,000 HERS; 100,000 HIS). Pays 1 month after publication. Publishes ms an average of 3 months after acceptance. Byline given. Offers negotiable kill fee. Buys first North American serial rights. Editorial lead time 5 months. Submit seasonal material 5 months in advance. Accepts queries by mail, e-mail, fax. Responds in 2 months to queries; 1 month to mss. Sample copy for 9×12 SAE with Canadian postage. Writer's guidelines for #10 SAE with Canadian postage.

Nonfiction General interest, interview/profile, issue-oriented features. No cliché teen material. **Buys 6-10 mss/ year.** Query with published clips. Length: 500-1,800 words. **Pays $150-400 (Canadian).** Sometimes pays expenses of writers on assignment.

Photos Send photos with submission. Reviews transparencies, 4×6 prints. Negotiates payment individually. Identification of subjects required.

Tips ''We have an immediate need for savvy freelancers to contribute features, short articles, interviews, and reviews that speak to our intelligent teen audience. Looking for fresh talent and new ideas in the areas of entertainment, gaming, pop culture, teen issues, international events as they relate to readers, celebs and 'real people' profiles, lifestyle articles, extreme sports and any other stories of relevance to today's Canadian teen.''

$ WINNER

Saying No To Drugs and Yes To Life, The Health Connection, 55 W. Oak Ridge Dr., Hagerstown MD 21740. (301)393-4082. Fax: (301)393-4055. E-mail: winner@healthconnection.org. Website: www.winnermagazine.org. **Contact:** Anita Jacobs, editor. **30% freelance written.** Monthly magazine covering positive lifestyle choices for students in grades 4-6. ''*Winner* is a teaching tool to help students learn the dangers in abusive substances, such as tobacco, alcohol, and other drugs, as well as at-risk behaviors. It also focuses on everyday problems such as dealing with divorce, sibling rivalry, coping with grief, and healthy diet, to mention just a few.'' Estab.

1956. Circ. 12,000. **Pays on acceptance.** Publishes ms an average of 6-9 months after acceptance. Byline sometimes given. Offers 50% kill fee. Buys first North American serial, first rights. Editorial lead time 5 months. Submit seasonal material 6-8 months in advance. Accepts queries by mail, e-mail, fax, phone. Accepts simultaneous submissions. Responds in 4-6 weeks to queries; 2-3 months to mss. Sample copy for $2 and 9×12 SAE with 2 first-class stamps. Writer's guidelines for SASE, by e-mail, fax or on website.

Nonfiction General interest, humor, drug/alcohol/tobacco activities, personalities, family relationships, friends. No occult, mysteries. "I prefer true-to-life stories." Query or send complete ms. Length: 600-650 words. **Pays $50-80.** Sometimes pays expenses of writers on assignment.

Photos State availability of or send photos with submission. Reviews GIF/JPEG files. Buys one-time rights. Negotiates payment individually. Model releases required.

Columns/Departments Personality (kids making a difference in their community), 600-650 words; Fun & Games (dangers of tobacco, alcohol, and other drugs), 400 words. **Buys 9 mss/year.** Query. **Pays $50-80.**

Fiction True-to-life stories dealing with problems preteens face. No suspense or mystery. **Buys 18 mss/year.** Send complete ms. Length: 600-650 words. **Pays $50-80.**

N $WITH

The Magazine for Radical Christian Youth, Faith and Life Press, 722 Main St., P.O. Box 347, Newton KS 67114-0347. (316)283-5100. Fax: (316)283-0454. E-mail: carold@mennoniteusa.org. Website: www.withonline.org. **Contact:** Carol Duerksen, editor. **60% freelance written.** Magazine published 6 times/year for teenagers. "We are a Christian youth magazine that strives to help youth be radically commited to a personal relationship with Jesus Christ, to peace and justice, and to sharing God's good news through word and action." Estab. 1968. Circ. 3,000. **Pays on acceptance.** Publishes ms an average of 1 year after acceptance. Byline given. Buys one-time rights. Submit seasonal material 6 months in advance. Accepts queries by mail, fax. Accepts previously published material. Accepts simultaneous submissions. Responds in 1 month to queries; 2 months to mss. Sample copy for 9×12 SAE with 4 first-class stamps. Writer's guidelines and theme list for #10 SASE. Additional detailed guidelines for first-person stories, how-to articles, and/or fiction available for #10 SASE.

O→ Break in with "well-written true stories from teen's standpoint."

Nonfiction How-to, humor, personal experience, religious, youth. **Buys 15 mss/year.** Send complete ms. Length: 400-1,800 words. **Pays 5¢/word for simultaneous rights, higher rates for articles written on assignment; 3¢/word for reprint rights and for unsolicited articles.** Sometimes pays expenses of writers on assignment.

Reprints Send ms with rights for sale noted and information about when and where the material previously appeared. Pays 60% of amount paid for an original article.

Photos Send photos with submission. Reviews 8×10 color prints. Buys one-time rights. Offers $10-50/photo. Identification of subjects required.

Fiction Ethnic, humorous, mainstream, religious, youth, parables. **Buys 15 mss/year.** Send complete ms. Length: 500-1,500 words. **Pays 5¢/word for simultaneous rights, higher rates for articles written on assignment; 3¢/word for reprint rights and for unsolicited articles.**

Poetry Avant-garde, free verse, haiku, light verse, traditional. **Buys 10-12 poems/year. Pays $10-25.**

Tips "Most of all, we are looking for true stories, along with some humor, fiction, light verse, and cartoons. Please don't send manuscripts that aren't related to our themes."

$⊘ YOUNG & ALIVE

Christian Record Services, P.O. Box 6097, Lincoln NE 68506. Website: www.christianrecord.org. **Contact:** Gaylena Gibson, editor. **95% freelance written.** Large-print Christian material for sight-impaired people age 12-25 (also in braille), covering health, handicapped people, uplifting articles. "Write for an interdenominational Christian audience—we also like to portray handicapped individuals living normal lives or their positive impact on those around them." Submit seasonal material anytime. Estab. 1976. Circ. 25,000 large print; 3,000 braille. **Pays on acceptance.** Publishes ms an average of 3 years after acceptance. Byline given. Buys one-time rights. Accepts simultaneous submissions. Responds in 1 year to mss. Sample copy for 7×10 SAE with 5 first-class stamps. Writer's guidelines for #10 SASE or included with sample copy.

● Due to the overabundance of mss, *Young & Alive* will not be accepting mss until 2009.

Nonfiction Essays, general interest, historical/nostalgic, humor, inspirational, personal experience, travel, adventure (true), biography, camping, careers, handicapped, health, hobbies, holidays, nature, sports. **Buys 40 mss/year.** Send complete ms. Length: 200-1,400 words. **Pays 4-5¢/word, and complimentary copies.**

Photos Send photos with submission. Reviews 3×5 to 10×12 prints. Buys one-time rights. Negotiates payment individually. Model releases required.

Fillers Anecdotes, facts, short humor. Length: 300 words maximum. **Pays 4¢/word.**

Tips "Make sure article has a strong ending that ties everything together. Pretend someone else wrote it—would it hold your interest? Draw your readers into the story by being specific rather than abstract or general."

$ $ YOUNG SALVATIONIST

The Salvation Army, P.O. Box 269, Alexandria VA 22313-0269. (703)684-5500. Fax: (703)684-5539. E-mail: ys@usn.salvationarmy.org. Website: www.thewarcry.com. **Contact:** Lt. Col. Marlene Chase, editor. **80% freelance written.** Monthly magazine for high school and early college youth. "Only material with Christian perspective with practical real-life application will be considered." Circ. 48,000. **Pays on acceptance.** Publishes ms an average of 6 months after acceptance. Byline given. Buys first North American serial, first, one-time, second serial (reprint) rights. Submit seasonal material 6 months in advance. Responds in 2 months to mss. Sample copy for 9×12 SAE with 3 first-class stamps or on website. Writer's guidelines and theme list for #10 SASE or on website.

- Works with a small number of new/unpublished writers each year. Accepts complete mss by mail and e-mail.

O— "Our greatest need is for nonfiction pieces based in real life rather than theory or theology. Practical living articles are especially needed. We receive many fiction submissions but few good nonfiction."

Nonfiction "Articles should deal with issues of relevance to teens (high school students) today; avoid 'preachiness' or moralizing." How-to, humor, inspirational, interview/profile, personal experience, photo feature, religious. **Buys 60 mss/year.** Send complete ms. Length: 1,000-1,500 words. **Pays 15¢/word for first rights.**

Reprints Send tearsheet, photocopy or typed ms with rights for sale noted and information about when and where the material previously appeared. Pays 10¢/word for reprints.

Fiction Only a small amount is used. Adventure, fantasy, humorous, religious, romance, science fiction, (all from a Christian perspective). **Buys few mss/year.** Length: 500-1,200 words. **Pays 15¢/word.**

Tips "Study magazine, familiarize yourself with the unique 'Salvationist' perspective of *Young Salvationist*; learn a little about the Salvation Army; media, sports, sex, and dating are strongest appeal."

TRAVEL, CAMPING & TRAILER

$ AAA GOING PLACES

Magazine for Today's Traveler, AAA Auto Club South, 1515 N. Westshore Blvd., Tampa FL 33607. (813)289-5923. Fax: (813)288-7935. Editor-In-Chief: Sandy Klim. **50% freelance written.** Bimonthly magazine on auto tips, cruise travel, tours. Estab. 1982. Circ. 2,500,000. Pays on publication. Publishes ms an average of 6 months after acceptance. Byline given. Buys one-time rights. Submit seasonal material 9 months in advance. Accepts simultaneous submissions. Responds in 2 months to mss. Sample copy not available. Writer's guidelines for SAE.

Nonfiction Travel stories feature domestic and international destinations with practical information and where to stay, dine, and shop, as well as personal anecdotes and historical background. Historical/nostalgic, how-to, humor, interview/profile, personal experience, photo feature, travel. **Buys 15 mss/year.** Send complete ms. Length: 500-1,200 words. **Pays $50/printed page.**

Photos State availability with submission. Reviews 2×2 transparencies, 300 dpi digital images. Offers no additional payment for photos accepted with ms. Captions required.

Columns/Departments What's Happening (local attractions in Florida, Georgia, or Tennessee).

Tips "We prefer lively, upbeat stories that appeal to a well-traveled, sophisticated audience, bearing in mind that AAA is a conservative company."

$ $ AAA MIDWEST TRAVELER

AAA Auto Club of Missouri, 12901 N. 40 Dr., St. Louis MO 63141. (314)523-7350 ext. 6301. Fax: (314)523-6982. E-mail: dreinhardt@aaamissouri.com. Website: www.travelermags.com. Editor: Michael J. Right. **Contact:** Deborah Reinhardt, managing editor. **80% freelance written.** Bimonthly magazine covering travel and automotive safety. "We provide members with useful information on travel, auto safety and related topics." Estab. 1901. Circ. 465,000. **Pays on acceptance.** Byline given. Offers $50 kill fee. Not copyrighted. Buys first North American serial, second serial (reprint), electronic rights. Editorial lead time 1 year. Submit seasonal material 6 months in advance. Accepts queries by mail, e-mail, fax. Accepts simultaneous submissions. Responds in 1 month. Sample copy for 10×13 SAE and 4 first-class stamps. Writer's guidelines for #10 SASE.

Nonfiction Travel. No humor, fiction, poetry or cartoons. **Buys 20-30 mss/year.** Query; query with published clips the first time. Length: 800-1,200 words. **Pays $250-350.**

Photos State availability with submission. Reviews transparencies, prints. Buys one-time and electronic rights. Offers no additional payment for photos accepted with ms. Captions required.

Tips "Send queries between December and February, as we plan our calendar for the following year. Request a copy. Serious writers ask for media kit to help them target their piece. Send a SASE or download online. Travel destinations and tips are most open to freelancers; all departments and auto-related news handled by staff. We see too many 'Here's a recount of our family vacation' manuscripts. Go easy on first-person accounts."

$ $ ⚑ ARUBA NIGHTS

Nights Publications, Inc., 1831 Rene Levesque Blvd. W., Montreal QC H3H 1R4 Canada. (514)931-1987. Fax: (514)931-6273. E-mail: editor@nightspublications.com. Website: www.nightspublications.com. **90% freelance written.** Annual magazine covering the Aruban vacation lifestyle experience with an upscale, upbeat touch. Estab. 1988. Circ. 225,000. **Pays on acceptance.** Publishes ms an average of 9 months after acceptance. Byline given for feature articles. Buys North American and Caribbean serial rights. Editorial lead time 1 month. Accepts queries by mail, e-mail, fax. Responds in 2 weeks to queries; 1 month to mss. Writer's guidelines by e-mail.

○→ *Aruba Nights* is looking for more articles on nightlife experiences.

Nonfiction General interest, historical/nostalgic, how-to (relative to Aruba vacationers), humor, inspirational, interview/profile, opinion, personal experience, photo feature, travel, ecotourism, Aruban culture, art, activities, entertainment, topics relative to vacationers in Aruba. "No negative pieces." **Buys 5-10 mss/year.** Send complete ms, include SAE with Canadian postage or IRC. Length: 250-750 words. **Pays $100-250.**

Photos State availability with submission. Reviews transparencies. Buys one-time rights. Pays $50/photo. Captions, identification of subjects, model releases required.

Tips "Be descriptive and entertaining and make sure stories are factually correct. Stories should immerse the reader in a sensory adventure. Focus on specific, individual aspects of the Aruban lifestyle and vacation experience (i.e., art, music, culture, a colorful local character, a personal experience, etc.), rather than generalized overviews. Provide an angle that will be entertaining to vacationers who are already there. E-mail submissions preferred."

$ $ ASU TRAVEL GUIDE

ASU Travel Guide, Inc., 448 Ignacio Blvd. #333, Novato CA 94949. (415)898-9500. Fax: (415)898-9501. E-mail: christopher_gil@asutravelguide.com. Website: www.asutravelguide.com. **Contact:** Christopher Gil, managing editor. **80% freelance written.** Quarterly guidebook covering international travel features and travel discounts for well-traveled airline employees. Estab. 1970. Circ. 36,000. **Pays on acceptance.** Publishes ms an average of 4 months after acceptance. Byline given. Buys first North American serial, first, second serial (reprint) rights. Submit seasonal material 6 months in advance. Accepts previously published material. Accepts simultaneous submissions. Responds in 1 year. Sample copy for 6×9 SAE and 5 first-class stamps. Writer's guidelines for #10 SASE.

Nonfiction International travel articles "similar to those run in consumer magazines. Not interested in amateur efforts from inexperienced travelers or personal experience articles that don't give useful information to other travelers." Destination pieces only; no "Tips on Luggage" articles. Unsolicited mss or queries without SASE will not be acknowledged. No telephone queries. Travel (international). **Buys 12 mss/year.** Length: 1,800 words. **Pays $200.**

Reprints Send tearsheet and information about when and where the material previously appeared. Pays 100% of amount paid for an original article.

Photos "Interested in clear, high-contrast photos." Reviews 5×7 and 8×10 b&w or color prints, JPEGs (300 dpi). Payment for photos is included in article price; photos from tourist offices are acceptable.

Tips "Query with samples of travel writing and a list of places you've recently visited. We appreciate clean and simple style. Keep verbs in the active tense and involve the reader in what you write. Avoid 'cute' writing, coined words, and stale clichés. The most frequent mistakes made by writers in completing an article for us are: 1) Lazy writing—using words to describe a place that could describe any destination such as 'there is so much to do in (fill in destination) that whole guidebooks have been written about it'; 2) Including fare and tour package information—our readers make arrangements through their own airline."

$ ⚑ BONAIRE NIGHTS

Nights Publications, Inc., 1831 René Levesque Blvd. W., Montreal QC H3H 1R4 Canada. (514)931-1987. Fax: (514)931-6273. E-mail: editor@nightspublications.com. **90% freelance written.** Annual magazine covering Bonaire vacation experience. Estab. 1993. Circ. 65,000. Byline given for features. Buys North American and Caribbean serial rights. Editorial lead time 1 month. Accepts queries by mail, e-mail, fax. Responds in 2 weeks to queries; 1 month to mss. Writer's guidelines by e-mail.

Nonfiction General interest, historical/nostalgic, how-to, humor, interview/profile, opinion, personal experience, photo feature, travel, lifestyle, local culture, art, architecture, activities, scuba diving, snorkeling, ecotourism. **Buys 6-9 mss/year.** E-mail submissions preferred. Mailed mss must include an e-mail address for correspondence. Length: 250-750 words. **Pays $100.**

Photos State availability with submission. Pays $50/published photo. Captions, identification of subjects, model releases required.

Tips "Focus on the Bonaire lifestyle, what sets it apart from other islands. We want personal experience on specific attractions and culture, not generalized overviews. Be positive and provide an angle that will appeal to vacationers who are already there. Our style is upbeat, friendly, fluid, and descriptive."

$CAMPING TODAY

Official Publication of the Family Campers & RVers, 126 Hermitage Rd., Butler PA 16001-8509. (724)283-7401. **Contact:** DeWayne Johnston, June Johnston, editors. **30% freelance written.** Monthly official membership publication of the FCRV. *Camping Today* is "the largest nonprofit family camping and RV organization in the United States and Canada. Members are heavily oriented toward RV travel, both weekend and extended vacations. Concentration is on member activities in chapters. Group is also interested in conservation and wildlife. The majority of members are retired." Estab. 1983. Circ. 10,000. Pays on publication. Publishes ms an average of 6 months after acceptance. Byline given. Buys one-time rights. Submit seasonal material 3 months in advance. Accepts simultaneous submissions. Responds in 2 months. Sample copy and guidelines for 4 first-class stamps.

Nonfiction Humor (camping or travel related), interview/profile (interesting campers), new product, technical (RVs related), travel (interesting places to visit by RV, camping). **Buys 10-15 mss/year.** Query by mail only or send complete ms with photos. Length: 750-2,000 words. **Pays $50-150.**

Reprints Send ms with rights for sale noted and information about when and where the material previously appeared. Pays 35-50% of amount paid for original article.

Photos "Need b&w or sharp color prints inside (we can make prints from slides) and vertical transparencies for cover." Send photos with submission. Captions required.

Tips "Freelance material on RV travel, RV maintenance/safety, and items of general camping interest throughout the United States and Canada will receive special attention. Good photos increase your chances."

$ $ $COAST TO COAST MAGAZINE

Affinity Group, Inc., 2575 Vista Del Mar Dr., Ventura CA 93001. (805)667-4100. Fax: (805)667-4217. E-mail: vlaw@affinitygroup.com. Website: www.coastresorts.com. **Contact:** Valerie Law, editorial director. **80% freelance written.** Magazine published 8 times/year for members of Coast to Coast Resorts. "*Coast to Coast* focuses on travel, recreation, and good times, with most stories targeted to recreational vehicle owners." Estab. 1983. Circ. 125,000. **Pays on acceptance.** Publishes ms an average of 4 months after acceptance. Byline given. Offers 33% kill fee. Buys first North American serial rights. Editorial lead time 5 months. Submit seasonal material 5 months in advance. Accepts queries by mail, e-mail, fax. Accepts previously published material. Accepts simultaneous submissions. Responds in 6-8 weeks to queries; 1-2 months to mss. Sample copy for $4 and 9 × 12 SASE. Writer's guidelines for #10 SASE.

Nonfiction Book excerpts, essays, general interest, how-to, interview/profile, new product, personal experience, photo feature, technical, travel. No poetry, cartoons. **Buys 70 mss/year.** Query with published clips or send complete ms. Length: 800-2,500 words. **Pays $75-1,200.**

Reprints Send photocopy and information about when and where the material previously appeared. Pays approximately 50% of amount paid for original article.

Columns/Departments Pays $150-400.

Tips "Send clips or other writing samples with queries, or story ideas will not be considered."

$ $ CURACAO NIGHTS

Nights Publications, Inc., 1831 Rene Levesque Blvd. W., Montreal QC H3H 1R4 Canada. (514)931-1987. Fax: (514)931-6273. E-mail: editor@nightspublications.com. **90% freelance written.** Annual magazine covering the Curacao vacation experience. "We are seeking upbeat, entertaining lifestyle articles; colorful profiles of locals; lively features on culture, activities, nightlife, ecotourism, special events, gambling, how-to features, humor. Our audience is North American vacationers." Estab. 1989. Circ. 155,000. Byline given. Buys North American and Caribbean serial rights. Editorial lead time 1 month. Accepts queries by mail, e-mail, fax. Responds in 2 weeks to queries; 1 month to mss. Writer's guidelines by e-mail.

Nonfiction General interest, historical/nostalgic, how-to (help a vacationer get the most from their vacation), humor, interview/profile, opinion, personal experience, photo feature, travel, ecotourism, lifestyle, local culture, art, activities, nightlife, topics relative to vacationers in Curacao. "No negative pieces, generic copy, or stale rewrites." **Buys 5-10 mss/year.** Query with published clips, include SASE and either Canadian postage or IRC, though e-mail submissions are preferred. Length: 250-750 words. **Pays $100-300.**

Photos State availability with submission. Reviews transparencies. Buys one-time rights. Pays $50/photo. Captions, identification of subjects, model releases required.

Tips "Demonstrate your voice in your query letter. Focus on individual aspects of the island lifestyle and vacation experience (i.e., art, music, culture, a colorful local character, a personal experience, etc.), rather than a generalized overview. Provide an angle that will be entertaining to vacationers who are already on the island. Our style is upbeat, friendly, and fluid."

$ $DURANGO MAGAZINE

For People Who Love Durango, Schultz & Associates, Inc., P.O. Box 3408, Durango CO 81302. (970)385-4030. Fax: (970)385-4436. E-mail: drgomag@animas.net. Website: www.durangomagazine.com. **Contact:** Julianne

W. Schultz, editor/publisher. **75% freelance written.** Semiannual magazine covering travel and tourism, city and regional. "Readers want to know what to see and do in the Durango area. Locals need more in-depth information than visitors, but subjects of interest to both are covered. People profiles, area attractions, history, arts & culture, outdoor pursuits, entertainment are subjects covered." Estab. 1986. Circ. 325,000. Pays on publication. Publishes ms an average of 3 months after acceptance. Byline given. Offers 50% kill fee. Buys first North American serial rights. Editorial lead time 4 months. Submit seasonal material 5 months in advance. Accepts queries by mail, e-mail. Accepts previously published material. Accepts simultaneous submissions. Responds in 6 weeks to queries. Sample copy for $3.95, plus mailing. Writer's guidelines free.

Nonfiction Book excerpts, historical/nostalgic, humor, interview/profile, personal experience, photo feature, travel. Does not want to see anything not assigned. Query with or without published clips. **Pays 30-50¢/word.** Sometimes pays expenses of writers on assignment.

Photos State availability of or send photos with submission. Buys one-time rights. Negotiates payment individually. Identification of subjects required.

$ $ $ $ ENDLESS VACATION MAGAZINE

Endless Vacation, 9998 N. Michigan Rd., Carmel IN 46032-9640. Fax: (317)805-9507. Website: www.evmedia-kit.com.; www.rci.com. **Contact:** Julie Woodard, senior editor. Prefers to work with published/established writers. Bimonthly magazine. "*Endless Vacation* is the vacation-idea magazine edited for people who love to travel. Each issue offers articles for America's dedicated and frequent leisure travelers—time-share owners. Articles and features explore the world through a variety of vacation opportunities and options for travelers who average 4 weeks of leisure travel each year. The goal of the magazine is to provide vibrant, interesting and informative editorial that engages and inspires the reader to travel, focusing more on active, 'do-able' dream vacations rather than aspirational arm-chair travel." Estab. 1974. Circ. 1,541,107. **Pays on acceptance.** Publishes ms an average of 6 months after acceptance. Byline given. Buys first North American serial rights. Accepts queries by mail, e-mail, fax. Accepts simultaneous submissions. Responds in 2 months to queries. Sample copy for $5 and 9×12 SAE with 5 first-class stamps. Writer's guidelines for #10 SASE.

Nonfiction Most articles are from established writers already published in *Endless Vacation. Accepts very few unsolicited pieces.* **Buys 30 feature mss/year.** Query with published clips (no phone calls). Length: 500-1,500 words. **Pays $500-1,500 for feature articles.** Sometimes pays expenses of writers on assignment.

Photos Reviews transparencies, 35mm slides. Buys one-time rights. Pays $300-1,300/photo. Identification of subjects required.

Columns/Departments Weekender (on domestic weekend vacation travel); Healthy Traveler; Cruise Currents; Family Vacationing; Value Travel Destinations, up to 1,200 words. Also Taste (on food-related travel topics) and news items for Ready, Set, Go column on products and the useful and unique in travel, 100-200 words. **Pays $100-900.**

Tips "Study the magazine and the writer's guidelines before you query us. Also check out www.evmediakit.com, which includes a reader profile and the magazine's current editorial calendar. The best way to break in to writing for *Endless Vacation* is through departments (Weekender, for example) and smaller pieces (Ready, Set, Go and Taste). Queries should be well developed."

$ ESCAPEES MAGAZINE

Sharing the RV Lifestyle, Escapees Inc., 100 Rainbow Dr., Livingston TX 77351-9300. (936)327-8873. Fax: (936)327-4388. E-mail: editor@escapees.com. Website: www.escapees.com. Editor: Janice Lasko. **Contact:** Tammy Johnson, departments editor. **90% freelance written.** Bimonthly magazine published for members of Escapees RV Club. "Articles must be RV related. *Escapees Magazine* readers are seeking RVing knowledge beyond what is found in conventional RV magazines." Estab. 1978. Circ. 35,000. Pays on publication. Publishes ms an average of 6 months after acceptance. Byline given. Buys first North American serial, first, one-time, second serial or electronic rights. Editorial lead time 6 months. Submit seasonal material 6 months in advance. Accepts previously published material. Writer's guidelines online.

Nonfiction All articles must be RV related. General interest, historical/nostalgic, how-to, humor, inspirational, interview/profile, new product, personal experience, photo feature, technical, travel, mechanical, finances, working, volunteering, boondocking. Travelogues, consumer advocacy issues, poetry and recipes are not generally published. **Buys 100-125 mss/year.** Send complete ms. Length: 1,400 words maximum. **Pays $150 maximum.**

Reprints Accepts previously published submissions.

Photos Send photos with submission. Reviews contact sheets, transparencies, prints. Buys one-time rights. Negotiates payment individually. Captions required.

Fiction All fiction must be RV related. Adventure, historical, humorous, mainstream, mystery, slice-of-life vignettes, western. **Buys 2-6 mss/year.** Send complete ms. Length: 1,400 words maximum. **Pays $150 maximum.**

Tips "Please do not send queries. Send complete manuscripts."

N ⊘ EXECUTIVE TRAVEL

American Express Publishing, 1120 Avenue of the Americas, New York NY 10036. E-mail: editor@executivetravelmag.com. Website: www.skyguide.net. Editor: Janet Libert. Quarterly magazine for affluent, educated professionals who are constantly on the go. Circ. 130,000.

● Query before submitting.

$ $ FAMILY MOTOR COACHING

Official Publication of the Family Motor Coach Association, 8291 Clough Pike, Cincinnati OH 45244. (513)474-3622. Fax: (513)388-5286. E-mail: magazine@fmca.com. Website: www.fmca.com. Publishing Director: Pamela Wisby Kay. **Contact:** Robbin Gould, editor. **80% freelance written.** "We prefer that writers be experienced RVers." Monthly magazine emphasizing travel by motorhome, motorhome mechanics, maintenance, and other technical information. "*Family Motor Coaching* magazine is edited for the members and prospective members of the Family Motor Coach Association who own or are about to purchase self-contained, motorized recreational vehicles known as motorhomes. Featured are articles on travel and recreation, association news and activities, plus articles on new products and motorhome maintenance and repair. Approximately ⅓ of editorial content is devoted to travel and entertainment, ⅓ to association news, and ⅓ to new products, industry news, and motorhome maintenance." Estab. 1963. Circ. 140,000. **Pays on acceptance.** Publishes ms an average of 8 months after acceptance. Byline given. Buys first North American serial rights. Submit seasonal material 4 months in advance. Accepts queries by mail, e-mail, fax. Responds in 3 months to queries. Sample copy for $3.99; $5 if paying by credit card. Writer's guidelines for #10 SASE.

Nonfiction How-to (do-it-yourself motorhome projects and modifications), humor, interview/profile, new product, technical, motorhome travel (various areas of North America accessible by motorhome), bus conversions, nostalgia. **Buys 90-100 mss/year.** Query with published clips. Length: 1,000-2,000 words. **Pays $100-500, depending on article category.**

Photos State availability with submission. Prefers North American serial rights but will consider one-time rights on photos only. Offers no additional payment for b&w contact sheets, 35mm 2¼×2¼ color transparencies, or high-resolution electronic images (300 dpi and at least 4×5 in size). Captions, model releases, photo credits required.

Tips "The greatest number of contributions we receive are travel; therefore, that area is the most competitive. However, it also represents the easiest way to break in to our publication. Articles should be written for those traveling by self-contained motorhome. The destinations must be accessible to motorhome travelers and any peculiar road conditions should be mentioned."

$ GO MAGAZINE

AAA Carolinas, 6600 AAA Dr., Charlotte NC 28212. (704)569-7733. Fax: (704)569-7815. E-mail: trcrosby@aaaqa.com. Website: www.aaacarolinas.com. **Contact:** Sarah Davis, assistant editor. Bimonthly magazine covering travel, automotive, safety (traffic), and insurance. "Consumer-oriented membership publication providing information on things such as car buying, vacations, travel safety problems, etc." Estab. 1928. Circ. 750,000. Pays on publication. Makes work-for-hire assignments. Editorial lead time 2 months. Accepts queries by mail, fax. Responds in 6 weeks to queries; 3 months to mss. Sample copy for 1 SAE and 4 first-class stamps. Writer's guidelines for #10 SASE.

Nonfiction How-to (fix auto, travel safety, etc.), travel, automotive insurance, traffic safety. **Buys 12-14 mss/year.** Query with published clips. Length: 600-900 words. **Pays $150/published story.**

Photos Send photos with submission. Buys one-time rights. Offers no additional payment for photos accepted with ms.

HIGHWAYS

The Official Publication of the Good Sam Club, Affinity Group, Inc., 2575 Vista Del Mar Dr., Ventura CA 93001. (805)667-4100. Fax: (805)667-4454. E-mail: goodsam@goodsamclub.com. Website: www.goodsamclub.com/highways. **Contact:** Dee Reed, managing editor. **30% freelance written.** Monthly magazine covering recreational vehicle lifestyle. "All of our readers own some type of RV—a motorhome, trailer, pop-up, tent—so our stories need to include places that you can go with large vehicles, and campgrounds in and around the area where they can spend the night." Estab. 1966. Circ. 975,000. **Pays on acceptance.** Publishes ms an average of 6 months after acceptance. Byline given. Offers 50% kill fee. Buys first North American serial, electronic rights. Accepts queries by e-mail. Responds in 2 weeks to queries. Sample copy and writer's guidelines free or online.

Nonfiction How-to (repair/replace something on an RV), humor, technical, travel (all RV related). **Buys 15-20 mss/year.** Query. Length: 800-1,100 words.

Photos Do not send or e-mail unless approved by staff.

Columns/Departments On the Road (issue related); RV Insight (for people new to the RV lifestyle); Action

Line (consumer help); Tech Topics (tech Q&A); Camp Cuisine (cooking in an RV); Product Previews (new products). No plans on adding new columns/departments.

Tips "Know something about RVing. People who drive motorhomes or pull trailers have unique needs that have to be incorporated into our stories. We're looking for well-written, first-person stories that convey the fun of this lifestyle and way to travel."

$ $🌐 INTERNATIONAL LIVING

Agora Ireland, Ltd., 5 Catherine St., Waterford Ireland. (800)643-2479. Fax: 353-51-304-561. E-mail: editor@internationalliving.com. Website: www.internationalliving.com. Managing Editor: Laura Sheridan. **50% freelance written.** Monthly newsletter covering retirement, travel, investment, and real estate overseas. "We do not want descriptions of how beautiful places are. We want specifics, recommendations, contacts, prices, names, addresses, phone numbers, etc. We want offbeat locations and off-the-beaten-track spots." Estab. 1981. Circ. 500,000. Pays on publication. Publishes ms an average of 3 months after acceptance. Byline given. Offers 25-50% kill fee. Buys all rights. Editorial lead time 2 months. Submit seasonal material 3 months in advance. Accepts queries by mail, e-mail, fax. Accepts simultaneous submissions. Responds in 2 months to mss. Sample copy for #10 SASE. Writer's guidelines online.

    🔑 "Break in by writing about something real. If you find it a chore to write the piece you're sending us, then chances are, we don't want it."

Nonfiction How-to (get a job, buy real estate, get cheap airfares overseas, start a business, etc.), interview/profile (entrepreneur abroad), new product (travel), personal experience, travel, shopping, cruises. Special issues: "We produce special issues each year focusing on Asia, Eastern Europe, and Latin America." No descriptive, run-of-the-mill travel articles. **Buys 100 mss/year.** Send complete ms. Length: 500-2,000 words. **Pays $200-500 for assigned articles; $100-400 for unsolicited articles.**

Photos State availability with submission. Reviews contact sheets, negatives, transparencies, prints. Buys all rights. Offers $50/photo. Identification of subjects required.

Fillers Facts. **Buys 20/year.** Length: 50-250 words. **Pays $25-50.**

Tips "Make recommendations in your articles. We want first-hand accounts. Tell us how to do things: how to catch a cab, order a meal, buy a souvenir, buy property, start a business, etc. *International Living*'s philosophy is that the world is full of opportunities to do whatever you want, whenever you want. We will show you how."

$ THE INTERNATIONAL RAILWAY TRAVELER

Hardy Publishing Co., Inc., P.O. Box 3747, San Diego CA 92163. (619)260-1332. Fax: (619)296-4220. E-mail: irteditor@aol.com. Website: www.irtsociety.com. **Contact:** Gena Holle, editor. **100% freelance written.** Monthly newsletter covering rail travel. Estab. 1983. Circ. 3,500. Pays within 1 month of the publication date. Byline given. Offers 25% kill fee. Buys first North American serial, all electronic rights. Editorial lead time 4 months. Submit seasonal material 6 months in advance. Responds in 1 month to queries; 2 months to mss. Sample copy for $6. Writer's guidelines for #10 SASE or via e-mail.

Nonfiction General interest, how-to, interview/profile, new product, opinion, personal experience, travel, book reviews. **Buys 48-60 mss/year.** Query with published clips or send complete ms. Length: 800-1,200 words. **Pays 3¢/word.**

Photos Include SASE for return of photos. Send photos with submission. Reviews contact sheets, negatives, transparencies, 8×10 (preferred) and 5×7 prints, digital photos preferred (minimum 300 dpi). Buys first North American serial rights, all electronic rights. Offers $10 b&w; $20 cover photo. Costs of converting slides and negatives to prints are deducted from payment. Captions, identification of subjects required.

Tips "We want factual articles concerning world rail travel which would not appear in the mass-market travel magazines. *IRT* readers and editors love stories and photos on off-beat train trips as well as more conventional train trips covered in unconventional ways. With *IRT*, the focus is on the train travel experience, not a blow-by-blow description of the view from the train window. Be sure to include details (prices, passes, schedule info, etc.) for readers who might want to take the trip. E-mail queries, submissions encouraged. Digital photo submissions (at least 300 dpi) are encouraged. Please stay within word-count guidelines."

$ $ $ $ ISLANDS

Islands Media Corp., 6267 Carpinteria Ave., Suite 200, Carpinteria CA 93013. (805)745-7100. Fax: (805)745-7102. E-mail: editorial@islands.com. Website: www.islands.com. **Contact:** Lisa Gosselin, editor. **95% freelance written.** Magazine published 8 times/year covering "accessible and once-in-a-lifetime islands from many different perspectives: travel, culture, lifestyle. We ask our authors to give us the essence of the island and do it with literary flair." Estab. 1981. Circ. 220,000. Pays on publication. Publishes ms an average of 8 months after acceptance. Byline given. Offers 25% kill fee. Buys all rights. Accepts queries by mail, e-mail, fax. Responds in 2 months to queries; 6 weeks to mss. Sample copy for $6. Writer's guidelines for #10 SASE or online.

Nonfiction Book excerpts, essays, general interest, interview/profile, photo feature, travel, service shorts, island-related material. **Buys 25 feature mss/year.** Query with published clips or send complete ms. Length: 2,000-4,000 words. **Pays $750-2,500.** Sometimes pays expenses of writers on assignment.

Photos "Fine color photography is a special attraction of *Islands*, and we look for superb composition, technical quality, and editorial applicability." Will not accept or be responsible for unsolicited images or artwork.

Columns/Departments Discovers section (island related news), 200-600 words; On Island (travel experiences, classic island hotels), 700-1,000 words; Adventures (things to do), 800 words. **Buys 50 mss/year.** Query with published clips. **Pays $25-1,000.**

Tips "A freelancer can best break in to our publication with front- or back-of-the-book stories. Stay away from general topics and features."

N $ $ MOTORHOME

TL Enterprises, 2575 Vista Del Mar Dr., Ventura CA 93001. (805)667-4100. Fax: (805)667-4484. Website: www.motorhomemagazine.com. Editorial Director: Barbara Leonard. **Contact:** Bruce Hampson, senior managing editor. **60% freelance written.** Monthly magazine. "*MotorHome* is a magazine for owners and prospective buyers of motorized recreational vehicles who are active outdoorsmen and wide-ranging travelers. We cover all aspects of the RV lifestyle; editorial material is both technical and nontechnical in nature. Regular features include tests and descriptions of various models of motorhomes, travel adventures, and hobbies pursued in such vehicles, objective analysis of equipment and supplies for such vehicles, and do-it-yourself articles. Guides within the magazine provide listings of manufacturers, rentals, and other sources of equipment and accessories of interest to enthusiasts. Articles must have an RV slant and excellent transparencies accompanying text." Estab. 1968. Circ. 150,000. **Pays on acceptance.** Publishes ms an average of within 1 year after acceptance. Byline given. Offers 30% kill fee. Buys first North American serial, electronic rights. Editorial lead time 4 months. Submit seasonal material 6 months in advance. Accepts queries by mail, fax. Responds in 1 month to queries; 2 months to mss. Sample copy for free. Writer's guidelines for #10 SASE.

O➛ Break in with *Crossroads* items.

Nonfiction General interest, historical/nostalgic, how-to, humor, interview/profile, new product, personal experience, photo feature, technical, travel, celebrity profiles, recreation, lifestyle, legislation, all RV related. No diaries of RV trips or negative RV experiences. **Buys 120 mss/year.** Query with or without published clips. Length: 250-2,500 words. **Pays $300-600.**

Photos Digital photography accepted depending upon topic/anticipated use. Send photos with submission. Reviews 35mm slides. Buys one-time rights. Offers no additional payment for art accepted with ms. Pays $500 (minimum) for covers. Captions, identification of subjects, model releases required.

Columns/Departments Crossroads (offbeat briefs of people, places, and events of interest to travelers), 100-200 words; Keepers (tips, resources). Query with or without published clips or send complete ms. **Pays $100.**

▣ The online magazine carries original content not found in the print version. Contact: Barbara Leonard, editorial director.

Tips "If a freelancer has an idea for a good article, it's best to send a query and include possible photo locations to illustrate the article. We prefer to assign articles and work with the author in developing a piece suitable to our audience. We are in a specialized field with very enthusiastic readers who appreciate articles by authors who actually enjoy motorhomes. The following areas are most open: Crossroads—brief descriptions of places to see or special events, with 1 photo/slide, 100-200 words; Travel—places to go with a motorhome, where to stay, what to see and do, etc; and How-to—personal projects on author's motorhomes to make travel easier, unique projects, accessories. Also articles on motorhome-owning celebrities, humorous experiences. Be sure to submit appropriate photography (35mm slides) with at least 1 good motorhome shot to illustrate travel articles. No phone queries, please."

N $ $ NORTHWEST TRAVEL

Northwest Regional Magazines, 4969 Hwy. 101 N., Suite 2, Florence OR 97439. (541)997-8401 or (800)348-8401. Fax: (541)902-0400. Website: www.northwestmagazines.com. **Contact:** Vickie S. Higgins, editor. **60% freelance written.** Bimonthly magazine. "We like energetic writing about popular activities and destinations in the Pacific Northwest. *Northwest Travel* aims to give readers practical ideas on where to go in the region. Magazine covers Oregon, Washington, Idaho, British Columbia, and western Montana; occasionally Alaska." Estab. 1991. Circ. 50,000. Pays after publication. Publishes ms an average of 8 months after acceptance. Buys first North American serial rights. Submit seasonal material 6 months in advance. Accepts queries by mail, e-mail. Responds in 3 months. Sample copy for $4.50. Writer's guidelines online.

O➛ Have good slides to go with a story that is lively with compelling leads, quotes, anecdotes, and no grammar problems.

Nonfiction Book excerpts, general interest, historical/nostalgic, interview/profile (rarely), photo feature, travel (only in Northwest region). "No cliché-ridden pieces on places that everyone covers." **Buys 40 mss/year.**

Query with or without published clips. Submit hard copy of ms, plus copy on disk or via e-mail. Length: 1,250-2,000 words. **Pays $100-750 for feature articles, and 2-5 contributor copies.**

Reprints Send photocopy and information about when and where the material previously appeared. Pays 50% of amount paid for original article.

Photos "Provide credit and model release information on cover photos—will pay extra for those requiring model releases." State availability with submission. Reviews transparencies, prefers dupes. Buys one-time rights. Pays $350 for cover; $100 for Back Page. Captions, identification of subjects required.

Columns/Departments Worth a Stop (brief items describing places "worth a stop"), 300-700 words. **Pays $50-100.** Back Page (photo and text package on a specific activity, season, or festival with some technical photo info), 80 words and 1 slide. **Pays $100. Buys 25-30 mss/year.**

Tips "Write fresh, lively copy (avoid clichés), and cover exciting travel topics in the region that haven't been covered in other magazines. A story with stunning photos will get serious consideration. The department most open to freelancers is the Worth a Stop department. Take us to fascinating places we may not otherwise discover."

$PATHFINDERS

Travel Information for People of Color, 6325 Germantown Ave., Philadelphia PA 19144. (215)438-2140. Fax: (215)438-2144. E-mail: editors@pathfinderstravel.com. Website: www.pathfinderstravel.com. **Contact:** Joseph P. Blake, managing editor. **75% freelance written.** Quarterly magazine covering travel for people of color, primarily African-Americans. "We look for lively, original, well-written stories that provide a good sense of place, with useful information and fresh ideas about travel and the travel industry. Our main audience is African-Americans, though we do look for articles relating to other persons of color: Native Americans, Hispanics and Asians." Estab. 1997. Circ. 100,000. **Pays on acceptance.** Byline given. Buys first North American serial, electronic rights. Accepts queries by mail, e-mail. Responds in 1 month to queries; 2 months to mss. Sample copy at bookstores (Barnes & Noble, Borders, Waldenbooks). Writer's guidelines online.

    O→ Break in through *Looking Back*, 600-word essay on travel from personal experience that provides a historical perspective and US travel with cultural perspective. Also Chef's Table column, featuring information on African American chefs.

Nonfiction Interested in seeing more Native American stories, places that our readers can visit and rodeos (be sure to tie-in African-American cowboys). Essays, historical/nostalgic, how-to, personal experience, photo feature, travel (all vacation travel oriented). "No more pitches on Jamaica. We get these all the time." **Buys 16-20 mss/year.** Send complete ms. Length: 1,200-1,400 words for cover stories; 1,000-1,200 words for features. **Pays $150.**

Photos State availability with submission.

Columns/Departments Chef's Table, Post Cards From Home; Looking Back; City of the Month, 500-600 words. Send complete ms. **Pays $150.**

Tips "We prefer seeing finished articles rather than queries. All articles are submitted on spec. Articles should be saved in either WordPerfect of Microsoft Word, double-spaced and saved as a text-only file. Include a hard copy. E-mail articles are accepted only by request of the editor. No historical articles."

$ $PILOT GETAWAYS MAGAZINE

Airventure Publishing LLC, P.O. Box 550, Glendale CA 91209-0550. (818)241-1890. Fax: (818)241-1895. E-mail: editor@pilotgetaways.com. Website: www.pilotgetaways.com. **Contact:** John Kounis, editor. **90% freelance written.** Quarterly magazine covering aviation travel for private pilots. "*Pilot Getaways* is a travel magazine for private pilots. Our articles cover destinations that are easily accessible by private aircraft, including details such as airport transportation, convenient hotels, and attractions. Other regular features include Fly-in dining, Flying Tips, and Bush Flying." Estab. 1998. Circ. 20,000. Pays on publication. Byline given. Buys first North American serial, electronic rights. Editorial lead time 4 months. Submit seasonal material 9 months in advance. Accepts queries by mail, e-mail, fax, phone. Accepts simultaneous submissions. Responds in 2 weeks to queries; 2 months to mss. Sample copy and writer's guidelines free.

Nonfiction Travel (specifically travel guide articles). "We rarely publish articles about events that have already occurred, such as travel logs about trips the authors have taken or air show reports." **Buys 30 mss/year.** Query. Length: 1,000-3,500 words. **Pays $100-500.**

Reprints Accepts previously published submissions.

Photos State availability with submission. Reviews contact sheets, negatives, 35mm transparencies, prints, GIF/JPEG files. Buys one-time rights. Negotiates payment individually. Captions, identification of subjects required.

Columns/Departments Weekend Getaways (short fly-in getaways), 2,000 words; Fly-in Dining (reviews of airport restaurants), 1,200 words; Flying Tips (tips and pointers on flying technique), 1,000 words; Bush Flying (getaways to unpaved destinations), 1,500 words. **Buys 20 mss/year.** Query. **Pays $100-500.**

Tips *"Pilot Getaways* follows a specific format, which is factual and informative. We rarely publish travel logs that chronicle a particular journey. Rather, we prefer travel guides with phone numbers, addresses, prices, etc., so that our readers can plan their own trips. The exact format is described in our writer's guidelines."

$ $ $ PORTHOLE CRUISE MAGAZINE

The PPI Group, 4517 NW 31st Ave., Ft. Lauderdale FL 33309-3403. (954)377-7777. Fax: (954)377-7000. E-mail: jornstein@ppigroup.com. Website: www.porthole.com. **Contact:** Jodi Ornstein, managing editor; Jeffrey Laign, editorial director. **70% freelance written.** Bimonthly magazine covering the cruise industry. *"Porthole Cruise Magazine* entices its readers to take a cruise vacation by delivering information that is timely, accurate, colorful, and entertaining."* Estab. 1992. Circ. 2,000,000. Pays on publication. Publishes ms an average of 6 months after acceptance. Byline given. Offers 20% kill fee. Buys first North American serial, electronic rights. Editorial lead time 8 months. Submit seasonal material 5 months in advance. Accepts queries by e-mail. Accepts simultaneous submissions.

Nonfiction General interest (cruise related), historical/nostalgic, how-to (pick a cruise, not get seasick, travel tips), humor, interview/profile (crew on board or industry executives), new product, personal experience, photo feature, travel (off-the-beaten-path, adventure, ports, destinations, cruises), onboard fashion, spa articles, duty-free shopping, port shopping, ship reviews. No articles on destinations that can't be reached by ship. **Buys 30 mss/year.** Length: 1,000-1,200 words. **Pays $500-600 for assigned feature articles.**

Photos Linda Douthat, creative director. State availability with submission. Reviews digital images and original transparencies. Buys one-time rights. Rates available upon request to ldorthal@ppigroup.com. Captions, identification of subjects, model releases required.

◫ RV LIFESTYLE MAGAZINE

(formerly *Camping Canada's RV Lifestyle Magazine*), 1020 Brevik Place, Unit 5, Mississauga ON L4W 4N7 Canada. (905)624-8218. Fax: (905)624-6764. E-mail: editor@rvlifemag.com. Website: www.rvlifemag.com. **50% freelance written.** Magazine published 7 times/year (monthly December-May and October). *"RV Lifestyle Magazine* is geared to readers who enjoy travel/camping. Upbeat pieces only. Readers vary from owners of towable trailers or motorhomes to young families and entry-level campers (no tenting)."* Estab. 1971. Circ. 45,000. Pays on publication. Byline given. Buys first North American serial rights. Editorial lead time 2 months. Responds in 1 month to queries; 2 months to mss. Sample copy for free.

Nonfiction How-to, personal experience, technical, travel. No inexperienced, unresearched, or too general pieces. **Buys 30-40 mss/year.** Query. Length: 1,200-2,000 words. **Payment varies.**

Photos Send photos with submission. Reviews low-ISO 35mm slides or JPEG/TIFF files saved at 300 dpi minimum at 5×7. Buys one-time rights. Offers no additional payment for photos accepted with ms.

Tips "Pieces should be slanted toward RV living. All articles must have an RV slant. Canadian content regulations require 95% Canadian writers."

$ $ ◫ ST. MAARTEN NIGHTS

Nights Publications, Inc., 1831 Rene Levesque Blvd. W., Montreal QC H3H 1R4 Canada. (514)931-1987. Fax: (514)931-6273. E-mail: editor@nightspublications.com. Website: www.nightspublications.com. **90% freelance written.** Annual magazine covering the St. Maarten/St. Martin vacation experience seeking "upbeat, entertaining, lifestyle articles. Our audience is the North American vacationer." Estab. 1981. Circ. 225,000. **Pays on acceptance.** Publishes ms an average of 9 months after acceptance. Byline given. Buys North American and Caribbean serial rights. Editorial lead time 1 month. Accepts queries by mail, e-mail, fax. Responds in 2 weeks to queries; 1 month to mss. Writer's guidelines by e-mail.

• E-mail queries preferred. All submissions must include an e-mail address for correspondence.

○┓ "Let the reader experience the story; utilize the senses; be descriptive."

Nonfiction Lifestyle with a lively, upscale touch. Include SASE with Canadian postage or IRC. General interest, historical/nostalgic, how-to (gamble), humor, interview/profile, opinion, personal experience, photo feature, travel, colorful profiles of islanders, sailing, ecological, ecotourism, local culture, art, activities, entertainment, nightlife, special events, topics relative to vacationers in St. Maarten/St. Martin. **Buys 8-10 mss/year.** Query with published clips. Length: 250-750 words. **Pays $100-300.**

Photos State availability with submission. Reviews transparencies. Buys one-time rights. Pays $50/photo. Captions, identification of subjects, model releases required.

Tips "Our style is upbeat, friendly, fluid, and descriptive. Our magazines cater to tourists who are already at the destination, so ensure your story is of interest to this particular audience. We welcome stories that offer fresh angles to familiar tourist-related topics."

$ $ THE SOUTHERN TRAVELER

AAA Auto Club of Missouri, 12901 N. Forty Dr., St. Louis MO 63141. (314)523-7350. Fax: (314)523-6982. Website: www.aaatravelermags.com. Editor: Michael J. Right. **Contact:** Deborah Reinhardt, managing editor.

80% freelance written. Bimonthly magazine. Estab. 1997. Circ. 170,000. **Pays on acceptance.** Byline given. Not copyrighted. Buys first North American serial, second serial (reprint) rights. Accepts simultaneous submissions. Responds in 1 month. Sample copy for 12½×9½ SAE and 3 first-class stamps. Writer's guidelines online.

O→ Query, with best chance for good reception January-March for inclusion in following year's editorial calendar.

Nonfiction "We feature articles on regional and world travel, area history, auto safety, highway and transportation news." **Buys 30 mss/year.** Query. Length: 2,000 words maximum. **Pays $300 maximum.**

Reprints Send ms with rights for sale noted and information about when and where the material previously appeared. Pays $125-200.

Photos State availability with submission. Reviews transparencies. One-time photo reprint rights. Offers no additional payment for photos accepted with ms. Captions required.

Tips "Editorial schedule is set 6-9 months in advance (available online). Some stories available throughout the year, but most are assigned early. Travel destinations and tips are most open to freelancers; auto-related topics handled by staff. Make story bright and quick to read. We see too many 'Here's what I did on my vacation' manuscripts. Go easy on first-person accounts."

$ $ $ $ SPA

Healthy Living, Travel & Renewal, Islands Media, 6267 Carpinteria Ave., Suite 200, Santa Barbara CA 93013. (805)745-7100. Fax: (805)745-7105. Website: www.spamagazine.com. Bimonthly magazine covering health spas: treatments, travel, cuisine, fitness, beauty. "Approachable and accessible, yet authoritative and full of advice, *Spa* is the place to turn for information and tips on nutrition, spa cuisine/recipes, beauty, health, skin care, travel (to spas), fitness, wellness, and renewal. Sometimes humorous and light, sometimes thoughtful and introspective, *Spa* is always helpful, insightful and personal." Byline given. Offers 25% kill fee. Buys first North American serial, all rights. Editorial lead time 3 months. Accepts queries by mail. Sample copy for $6.

Nonfiction Essays, how-to (beauty), humor, personal experience, travel. Does not want "a general article on a spa you have visited." **Buys 30 mss/year.** Query with published clips. Length: 1,500-3,000 words. **Pays $1,125-2,500.** Sometimes pays expenses of writers on assignment.

Columns/Departments Being Well (news and trends on health and healing, wellness and workouts); Spa Talk (new spas, spa programs, treatments); Lotions & Potions (beauty, fragrance); Living Wardrobe (personal style, fashion); Living Well (home, garden, books, music, internet). **Buys 60 mss/year.** Query with published clips. **Pays $100-1,500.**

$ $ 🖳 TIMES OF THE ISLANDS

The International Magazine of the Turks & Caicos Islands, Times Publications, Ltd., P.O. Box 234, Southwind Plaza, Providenciales Turks & Caicos Islands British West Indies. (649)946-4788. Fax: (649)946-4788. E-mail: timespub@tciway.tc. Website: www.timespub.tc. **Contact:** Kathy Borsuk, editor. **60% freelance written.** Quarterly magazine covering the Turks & Caicos Islands. "*Times of the Islands* is used by the public and private sector to inform visitors and potential investors/developers about the Islands. It goes beyond a superficial overview of tourist attractions with in-depth articles about natural history, island heritage, local personalities, new development, offshore finance, sporting activities, visitors' experiences, and Caribbean fiction." Estab. 1988. Circ. 10,000. Pays on publication. Publishes ms an average of 6 months after acceptance. Byline given. Buys second serial (reprint) rights. Publication rights for 6 months with respect to other publications distributed in Caribbean. Editorial lead time 4 months. Submit seasonal material at least 4 months in advance. Accepts queries by mail, fax. Accepts simultaneous submissions. Responds in 6 weeks to queries; 2 months to mss. Sample copy for $6. Writer's guidelines online.

Nonfiction Book excerpts, essays, general interest (Caribbean art, culture, cooking, crafts), historical/nostalgic, humor, interview/profile (locals), personal experience (trips to the Islands), photo feature, technical (island businesses), travel, book reviews, nature, ecology, business (offshore finance), watersports. **Buys 20 mss/year.** Query. Length: 500-3,000 words. **Pays $200-600.**

Reprints Send photocopy and information about when and where the material previously appeared. Payment varies.

Photos Send photos with submission. Reviews slides, prints, digital photos. Pays $15-100/photo. Identification of subjects required.

Columns/Departments On Holiday (unique experiences of visitors to Turks & Caicos), 500-1,500 words. **Buys 4 mss/year.** Query. **Pays $200.**

Fiction Adventure, ethnic, historical, humorous, mystery, novel excerpts. **Buys 2-3 mss/year.** Query. Length: 1,000-3,000 words. **Pays $250-400.**

Tips "Make sure that the query/article specifically relates to the Turks and Caicos Islands. The theme can be general (ecotourism, for instance), but the manuscript should contain specific and current references to the islands. We're a high-quality magazine with a small budget and staff, and are very open-minded to ideas (and manuscripts). Writers who have visited the islands at least once would probably have a better perspective from which to write.''

$ $ TRAILER LIFE

America's No. 1 RV Magazine, Affinity Group, Inc., 2575 Vista Del Mar Dr., Ventura CA 93001. Fax: (805)667-4484. E-mail: info@trailerlife.com. Website: www.trailerlife.com. **40% freelance written.** Monthly magazine. ''*Trailer Life* magazine is written specifically for active people whose overall lifestyle is based on travel and recreation in their RV. Every issue includes product tests, travel articles, and other features—ranging from lifestyle to vehicle maintenance.'' Estab. 1941. Circ. 270,000. **Pays on acceptance.** Publishes ms an average of 6 months after acceptance. Byline given. Offers 30% kill fee for assigned articles that are not acceptable. Buys first North American serial, electronic rights. Editorial lead time 4 months. Submit seasonal material 6 months in advance. Accepts queries by mail. Responds in 2 months. Sample copy for free. Writer's guidelines for #10 SASE.

> **O─** Break in with a ''small piece for the Campground Spotlight or Etc. section; a short article on an interesting RV trip.''

Nonfiction Historical/nostalgic, how-to (technical), humor, new product, opinion, personal experience, travel. No vehicle tests, product evaluations, or road tests; tech material is strictly assigned. No diaries or trip logs, no non-RV trips; nothing without an RV-hook. **Buys 75 mss/year.** Query with or without published clips. Length: 250-2,500 words. **Pays $125-700.** Sometimes pays expenses of writers on assignment.

Photos Send photos with submission. Reviews transparencies, b&w contact sheets. Buys one-time and occasionally electronic rights. Offers no additional payment for photos accepted with ms; does pay for supplemental photos. Identification of subjects, model releases required.

Columns/Departments Campground Spotlight (report with 1 photo of campground recommended for RVers), 250 words; Around the Bend (news, trends of interest to RVers), 100 words; Etcetera (useful tips and information affecting RVers), 240 words. **Buys 70 mss/year.** Query or send complete ms. **Pays $75-250.**

Tips ''Prerequisite: Must have RV focus. Photos must be magazine quality. These are the 2 biggest reasons why manuscripts are rejected. Our readers are travel enthusiasts who own all types of RVs (travel trailers, truck campers, van conversions, motorhomes, tent trailers, fifth-wheels) in which they explore North America and beyond, and embrace the great outdoors in national, state and private parks. They're very active and very adventurous.''

$ TRANSITIONS ABROAD

P.O. Box 745, Bennington VT 05201. Phone/Fax: (802)442-4827. E-mail: editor@transitionsabroad.com. Website: www.transitionsabroad.com. **Contact:** Sherry Schwarz, editor. **80-90% freelance written.** Bimonthly magazine resource for low-budget international travel, often with an educational or volunteer/work component. Focus is on the alternatives to mass tourism. Estab. 1977. Circ. 12,000. Pays on publication. Byline given. Buys first, second serial (reprint) rights. Accepts queries by e-mail. Responds in 1 month. Sample copy for $6.45. Writer's guidelines online.

> **O─** Break in by sending ''a concisely written fact-filled article—or even a letter to Info Exchange—of no more than 1,000 words with up-to-date practical information, based on your own experience, on how readers can combine travel and learning or travel and work.''

Nonfiction Lead articles (up to 1,500 words) provide first-hand practical information on independent travel to featured country or region (see topics schedule). Also, how to find educational and specialty travel opportunities, practical information (evaluation of courses, special interest and study tours, economy travel), travel (new learning and cultural travel ideas). Foreign travel only. Few destination (''tourist'') pieces or first-person narratives. *Transitions Abroad* is a resource magazine for independent, educated, and adventurous travelers, not for armchair travelers or those addicted to packaged tours or cruises. Emphasis on information—which must be usable by readers—and on interaction with people in host country. **Buys 120 unsolicited mss/year.** Prefer e-mail queries that indicate familiarity with the magazine. Query with credentials and SASE. Include author's bio and e-mail with submissions. Length: 500-1,500 words. **Pays $2/column inch.**

Photos Photos increase likelihood of acceptance. Send photos with submission. Buys one-time rights. Pays $10-25 for color prints or color slides (prints preferred), $150 for covers. Captions, identification of subjects required.

Columns/Departments Worldwide Travel Bargains (destinations, activities, and accomodations for budget travelers—featured in every issue); Tour and Program Notes (new courses or travel programs); Travel Resources (new information and ideas for independent travel); Working Traveler (how to find jobs and what to expect); Activity Vacations (travel opportunities that involve action and learning, usually by direct involvement in host culture); Responsible Travel (information on community-organized tours). Length: 1,000 words maximum. **Buys 60 mss/year.** Send complete ms. **Pays $2/column inch.**

Fillers Info Exchange (first-hand information having to do with travel, particularly offbeat educational travel and work or study abroad). **Buys 30/year.** Length: 750 words maximum. **Pays complimentary 1-year subscription.**

📷 The online magazine carries original content not found in the print edition and includes writer's guidelines.

Tips "We like nuts and bolts stuff, practical information, especially on how to work, live, and cut costs abroad. Our readers want usable information on planning a travel itinerary. Be specific: names, addresses, current costs. We are very interested in educational and long-stay travel and study abroad for adults and senior citizens. *Overseas Travel Planner* is published each year in July and provides the best information sources on work, study, and independent travel abroad. Each bimonthly issue contains a worldwide directory of educational and specialty travel programs."

N $ $ TRAVEL AMERICA

The U.S. Vacation Magazine, World Publishing Co., 990 Grove St., Evanston IL 60201-4370. (847)491-6440. **Contact:** Randy Mink, editor. **80% freelance written.** Bimonthly magazine covering US vacation travel. Estab. 1985. Circ. 240,000. Byline given. Buys first North American serial rights. Submit seasonal material 6 months in advance. Accepts queries by mail. Responds in 1 month. Sample copy for $5 and 9×12 SASE with $1.29 postage.

Nonfiction Primarily destination-oriented travel articles and resort/hotel profiles and roundups, but will consider essays, how-to, humor, nostalgia, Americana. "US destination travel features must have personality and strong sense of place, developed through personal experiences, quotes, humor, human interest, local color. We prefer people-oriented writing, not dry guidebook accounts and brochure-style fluff. Always in the market for nationwide roundup stories—past roundups have included US Gambling Meccas and Top 10 Amusement Parks. Also short slices of Americana focusing on nostalgia, collectibles and crafts, ethnic communities and celebrations, special events. It is best to study current contents and query by mail only first." **Buys 60 mss/year.** Length: 1,000 words. **Pays $150-300.**

Reprints Send ms with rights for sale noted. Payment varies.

Photos Top-quality original color slides preferred. Prefers photo feature package (ms, plus slides), but will purchase slides only to support a work-in-progress. Buys one-time rights. Captions required.

Tips "Because we are heavily photo-oriented, superb slides are our foremost concern. The most successful approach is to send 2-3 sheets of slides with the query or complete manuscript. Include a list of other subjects you can provide as a photo feature package."

$ $ $ $ TRAVEL + LEISURE

American Express Publishing Corp., 1120 Ave. of the Americas, New York NY 10036. (212)382-5600. Website: www.travelandleisure.com. Editor-in-Chief: Nancy Novogrod. Managing Editor: Michael S. Cain. **Contact:** Editor. **80% freelance written.** "*Travel + Leisure* is a monthly magazine edited for affluent travelers. It explores the latest resorts, hotels, fashions, foods, and drinks, as well as political, cultural, and economic issues affecting travelers." Circ. 925,000. **Pays on acceptance.** Byline given. Offers 25% kill fee. Buys first world rights, as well as rights to republish in international editions and online. Accepts queries by mail, e-mail. Responds in 6 weeks. Sample copy for $5.50 from (800)888-8728. Writer's guidelines online.

➤ There is no single editorial contact for *Travel + Leisure*. It is best to find the name of the editor of each section, as appropriate for your submission.

Nonfiction Travel. **Buys 40-50 feature (3,000-5,000 words) and 200 short (125-500 words) mss/year.** Query (e-mail preferred). **Pays $4,000-6,000/feature; $100-500/short piece.** Pays expenses of writers on assignment.

Photos Discourages submission of unsolicited transparencies. Buys one-time rights. Payment varies. Captions required.

Columns/Departments Length: 2,500-3,500 words. **Buys 125-150 mss/year. Pays $2,000-3,500.**

Tips "Queries should not be generic, but should specify what is new or previously uncovered in a destination or travel-related subject area."

N $ TRAVEL SMART

Communications House, Inc., P.O. Box 397, Dobbs Ferry NY 10522. E-mail: travelsmartnow@aol.com. Website: www.travelsmartnewsletter.com. **Contact:** Nancy Dunnan, editor. Monthly newsletter covering information on "good-value travel." Estab. 1976. Circ. 20,000. Pays on publication. Buys all rights. Accepts queries by mail, e-mail. Responds in 6 weeks. Sample copy and writer's guidelines for 9×12 SAE with 3 first-class stamps.

Nonfiction "Interested primarily in bargains or little-known deals on transportation, lodging, food, unusual destinations that are really good values. No destination stories on major Caribbean islands, London, New York, no travelogs, 'my vacation,' poetry, fillers. No photos or illustrations other than maps. Just hard facts. We are not part of 'Rosy fingers of dawn . . .' school." Write for guidelines, then query. Query. Length: 100-1,500 words. **Pays $150 maximum.**

Tips "When you travel, check out small hotels offering good prices, good restaurants, and send us brief rundown (with prices, phone numbers, addresses). Information must be current. Include your phone number with submission, because we sometimes make immediate assignments.''

Ⓝ $ $ VOYAGEUR

The Magazine of Carlson Hospitality Worldwide, Pace Communications, 1301 Carolina St., Greensboro NC 27401. (336)378-6065. Fax: (336)378-8272. Editor: Mark Caskie. **Contact:** Sarah Lindsay, senior editor. **90% freelance written.** Quarterly in-room magazine for Radisson hotels and affiliates. ''*Voyageur* is an international magazine published quarterly for Carlson Hospitality Worldwide and distributed in the rooms of Radisson Hotels & Resorts, Park Plaza and Park Inn hotels, and Country Inns & Suites By Carlson throughout North and South America, Europe, Australia, Africa, Asia, and the Middle East. All travel-related stories must be in destinations where Carlson has a presence.'' Estab. 1992. Circ. 160,000. Pays on publication. Publishes ms an average of 2 months after acceptance. Offers 25% kill fee. Buys first North American serial rights. Editorial lead time 4 months. Submit seasonal material 6 months in advance. Accepts queries by mail. Responds in 2 months. Sample copy for $5. Writer's guidelines for #10 SASE.

Oᵣ Break in with a ''well-thought-out, well-written, well-researched query on a city or area the writer lives in or knows well—one where Carlson has a presence (Radisson, Country Inns, or Park).''

Nonfiction The cover story is ''a multi-destination feature with an overall theme, such as romantic weekend getaways. We like these articles to capture the distinctive atmosphere of a destination, while at the same time providing readers with a possible itinerary for a visit. All destinations are locations where Carlson has a major presence. We have a strong preference for writers who live in the city/region covered by the story. Typically, we use 4 different writers for 4 separate destinations in a single issue.'' Length: 425 words, plus sidebar of contact information for travelers. Adventures are first-person articles (with an ''in-the-moment'' feel) that ''focus on active travel opportunities that reflect the unique aspects of a destination. They usually describe adventures that can be accomplished in a weekend or less (i.e., traditional outdoor sports, visits to historic sites, a 1-day cooking class at a local cooking school). Activities must be near destinations with Carlson properties.'' Length: 475 words. Travel. Query with published clips. **Pays $500-525/piece.** Sometimes pays expenses of writers on assignment.

Photos State availability with submission. Reviews contact sheets, transparencies, prints. Buys one-time rights. Negotiates payment individually. Identification of subjects, model releases required.

Columns/Departments A place-specific shopping story with cultural context and upscale attitude, 300 words and 50-word mini-sidebar; Agenda (insights into conducting business and traveling for business internationally), 350 words; Port of Call (an evocative first-person look back at an appealing destination visited by Radisson Seven Seas Cruises), 350 words. **Buys 28-32 mss/year.** Query with published clips. **Pays $375.**

Tips ''We look for authoritative, energetic, and vivid writing to inform and entertain business and leisure travelers, and we are actively seeking writers with an authentic European, Asian, Latin American, African, or Australian perspective. Travel stories should be authoritative yet personal.''

$ WESTERN RV NEWS & RECREATION

P.O. Box 847, Redmond OR 97756. (541)548-2255. Fax: (541)548-2288. E-mail: editor@westernrvnews.com. Website: www.westernrvnews.com. **Contact:** Terie Snyder, editor. **50% freelance written.** Monthly magazine for owners of recreational vehicles and those interested in the RV lifestyle. Estab. 1966. Pays on publication. Publishes ms an average of 6 months after acceptance. Byline given. Buys first, second serial (reprint) rights. Accepts queries by mail, e-mail, fax. Accepts simultaneous submissions. Responds in 2 months. Sample copy for 9×12 SAE and 5 first-class stamps. Writer's guidelines for #10 SASE.

Nonfiction How-to (RV oriented, purchasing considerations, maintenance), humor (RV experiences), new product (with ancillary interest to RV lifestyle), personal experience (varying or unique RV lifestyles), technical (RV systems or hardware), travel. ''No articles without an RV slant.'' **Buys 100 mss/year.** Submit complete ms on paper, disk, or by e-mail. Length: 250-1,400 words. **Pays 8¢/word for first rights.**

Reprints Photocopy of article or typed ms with rights for sale noted and information about when and where the material previously appeared. Pays 5¢/word.

Photos Color slides and prints are accepted with article at a rate of $5/photo used. Digital photos are also accepted through e-mail or on disk (CD, Zip, etc.), but must be at a minimum resolution of 300 dpi at published size (generally, 5×7 inches is adequate). Captions, identification of subjects, model releases required.

Fillers Encourage anecdotes, RV-related tips, and short humor. Length: 50-250 words. **Pays $5-25.**

Tips ''Highlight the RV lifestyle! Western travel articles should include information about the availability of RV sites, dump stations, RV parking, and accessibility. Thorough research and a pleasant, informative writing style are paramount. Technical, how-to, and new product writing is also of great interest. Photos enhance the possibility of article acceptance.''

$ $ WOODALL'S REGIONALS

2575 Vista Del Mar Dr., Ventura CA 93001. Website: www.woodalls.com. Monthly magazine for RV and camping enthusiasts. Woodall's Regionals include *Camper Ways*, *Midwest RV Traveler*, *Northeast Outdoors*, *Florida RV Traveler*, *Southern RV*, *Texas RV*, and *Southwest RV Traveler*. Byline given. Buys first rights. Accepts queries by mail, e-mail. Responds in 1-2 months to queries. Sample copy and writer's guidelines free.

Nonfiction "We need interesting and tightly focused feature stories on RV travel and lifestyle, campground spotlights, and technical articles that speak to both novices and experienced RVers." **Buys 500 mss/year.** Query with published clips. Length: 500-1,700 words. **Pays $180-250/feature; $75-100/department article and short piece.**

WOMEN'S

$ $ $ $ BODY & SOUL

Martha Stewart Living Omnimedia, 42 Pleasant St., Watertown MA 02472. (617)926-0200. Website: www.bodyandsoulmag.com. Editor-in-Chief: Seth Bauer. Managing Editor: Tania Hannan. **Contact:** Editorial Department. **60% freelance written.** Works with a small number of new/unpublished writers each year. Magazine published 8 times/year emphasizing "personal fulfillment and social change. The audience we reach is primarily female, college-educated, 25-55 years of age, concerned about social values, humanitarianism, and balance in personal life." Estab. 1974. Circ. 275,000. Publishes ms an average of 4 months after acceptance. Byline given. Offers 25% kill fee. Buys first North American serial, electronic rights. Editorial lead time 6 months. Submit seasonal material 6 months in advance. Accepts queries by mail. Accepts simultaneous submissions. Responds in 2 months. Sample copy for $5 and 9×12 SAE. Writer's guidelines online.

O⁻ No phone calls. The process of decision making takes time and involves more than one editor. An answer cannot be given over the phone.

Nonfiction Book excerpts, essays, how-to, inspirational, interview/profile, new product, personal experience, travel, spiritual. **Buys 50 mss/year.** Query with published clips. Length: 100-2,500 words. **Pays 75¢-$1/word.** Pays expenses of writers on assignment.

Reprints Send tearsheet or photocopy.

Columns/Departments Health, beauty, fitness, home, healthy eating, personal growth, and spirituality, 600-1,300 words. **Buys 50 mss/year.** Query with published clips. **Pays 75¢-$1/word.**

Tips "Read the magazine and get a sense of the type of writing run in column. In particular, we are looking for new or interesting approaches to subjects such as mind-body fitness, earth-friendly products, Eastern and herbal medicine, self-help, community, healthy eating, etc. No e-mail or phone queries, please. Begin with a query, résumé and published clips—we will contact you for the manuscript. A query is 1 to 2 paragraphs—if you need more space than that to *present* the idea, then you don't have a clear grip on it."

$ $ $ BRIDAL GUIDE

R.F.P., LLC, 3 E. 54th St., 15th Floor, New York NY 10022. (212)838-7733. Fax: (212)308-7165. Website: www.bridalguide.com. **Contact:** Valerie Berrios, assistant editor. **20% freelance written.** Bimonthly magazine covering relationships, sexuality, fitness, wedding planning, psychology, finance, travel. Only works with experienced/published writers. **Pays on acceptance.** Accepts queries by mail. Responds in 3 months. Sample copy for $5 and SAE with 4 first-class stamps. Writer's guidelines available.

Nonfiction "Please do not send queries concerning beauty, fashion, or home design stories since we produce them in-house. We do not accept personal wedding essays, fiction, or poetry. Address travel queries to travel editor." All correspondence accompanied by an SASE will be answered. **Buys 100 mss/year.** Query with published clips from national consumer magazines. Length: 1,000-2,000 words. **Pays 50¢/word.**

Photos Photography and illustration submissions should be sent to the art department.

Tips "We are looking for service-oriented, well-researched pieces that are journalistically written. Writers we work with use at least 3 top expert sources, such as physicians, book authors, and business people in the appropriate field. Our tone is conversational, yet authoritative. Features are also generally filled with real-life anecdotes. We also do features that are completely real-person based—such as roundtables of bridesmaids discussing their experiences, or grooms-to-be talking about their feelings about getting married. In queries, we are looking for a well-thought-out idea, the specific angle of focus the writer intends to take, and the sources he or she intends to use. Queries should be brief and snappy—and titles should be supplied to give the editor an even better idea of the direction in which the writer is going."

Ⓝ $ $ $ $ 🖂 CHATELAINE

One Mount Pleasant Rd., 8th Floor, Toronto ON M4Y 2Y5 Canada. (416)764-1888. Fax: (416)764-2431. Website: www.chatelaine.com. **Contact:** Kim Pittaway, managing editor. Monthly magazine. "*Chatelaine* is edited for

Canadian women ages 25-49, their changing attitudes and lifestyles. Key editorial ingredients include health, finance, social issues and trends, as well as fashion, beauty, food and home decor. Regular departments include Health pages, Entertainment, Humour, How-to." **Pays on acceptance.** Byline given. Offers 25-50% kill fee. Buys first, electronic rights. Accepts queries by mail. Writer's guidelines for #10 SASE with postage.

Nonfiction Seeks "agenda-setting reports on Canadian national issues and trends as well as pieces on health, careers, personal finance and other facts of Canadian life." **Buys 50 mss/year.** Query with published clips and SASE. Length: 1,000-2,500 words. **Pays $1,000-2,500.** Pays expenses of writers on assignment.

Columns/Departments Length: 500-1,000 words. Query with published clips and SASE. **Pays $500-750.**

N $ CINCINNATI WOMAN MAGAZINE

Niche Publishing and Media, LLC, P.O. Box 8170, West Chester OH 45069-8170. Phone/Fax: (513)779-2098. E-mail: cincinnatiwoman@cinci.rr.com. Editor: Cathy Habes. **Contact:** Alicia Wiehe, publisher. **90% freelance written.** Monthly magazine covering women's issues and needs. "Dedicated exclusively to capturing the spirit of Cincinnati-area women, we are committed to providing our readers with information as well as inspiration." Estab. 1998. Circ. 35,000. Pays on publication. Publishes ms an average of 4 months after acceptance. Byline given. Buys one-time rights. Editorial lead time 2 months. Submit seasonal material 3 months in advance. Accepts queries by mail, e-mail. Accepts simultaneous submissions. Responds in 2 weeks to queries. Sample copy for 8×10 SAE and 3 first-class stamps. Writer's guidelines for #10 SASE.

Nonfiction Book excerpts, essays, general interest, how-to, humor, inspirational, interview/profile, new product, opinion, personal experience, photo feature, travel, health/beauty. **Buys 50 mss/year.** Query with published clips or send complete ms. Length: 500-1,000 words. **Pays $80 maximum for assigned articles; $30 maximum for unsolicited articles.**

Reprints Send photocopy of article or typed ms with rights for sale noted and information about when and where the material previously appeared.

Photos State availability with submission. Reviews transparencies, 4×6 prints. Buys one-time rights. Offers no additonal payment for photos accepted with ms. Captions, identification of subjects required.

Columns/Departments Body Shop (health/beauty nuggets); *CWM* Cooks (entertaining and recipes); *CWM* Style (women's fashion); *CWM* Travel, all 700 words. **Buys 30 mss/year.** Query with published clips or send complete ms. **Pays $30.**

Fiction Adventure, confessions, horror, humorous, mainstream, mystery, religious, romance, slice-of-life vignettes. **Buys 20 mss/year.** Query with published clips or send complete ms. Length: 700-1,200 words. **Pays $30.**

Poetry Avant-garde, free verse, light verse, traditional. **Buys 5 poems/year.** Submit maximum 3 poems. Length: 5-60 lines. **Pays $20.**

Fillers Anecdotes, facts, newsbreaks, short humor. **Buys 5/year.** Length: 50-100 words. **Pays $15.**

Tips "We're looking for material on 20-something, dating, fashion, first-time mom experiences, holistic health, cooking, short personal essays."

N $ $ COMPLETE WOMAN

For All The Women You Are, Associated Publications, Inc., 875 N. Michigan Ave., Suite 3434, Chicago IL 60611. (312)266-8680. Editor-in-Chief: Bonnie L. Krueger. **Contact:** Lora Wintz, executive editor. **90% freelance written.** Bimonthly magazine. "Manuscripts should be written for today's busy women in a concise, clear format with useful information. Our readers want to know about the important things: sex, love, relationships, career, and self-discovery. Examples of true-life anecdotes incorporated into articles work well for our readers, who are always interested in how other women are dealing with life's ups and downs." Estab. 1980. Circ. 300,000. Pays 45 days after acceptance. Publishes ms an average of 6 months after acceptance. Byline given. Buys first North American serial, second serial (reprint), simultaneous rights. Editorial lead time 6 months. Submit seasonal material 5 months in advance. Accepts queries by mail. Accepts simultaneous submissions. Responds in 2 months. Sample copy not available. Writer's guidelines for #10 SASE.

O→ "Break in with writing samples that relate to the magazine. Also, the editor reports a need for more relationship stories."

Nonfiction "We want self-help articles written for today's woman. Articles that address dating, romance, sexuality, and relationships are an integral part of our editorial mix, as well as inspirational and motivational pieces." Book excerpts, exposé (of interest to women), general interest, how-to (beauty/diet-related), humor, inspirational, interview/profile (celebrities), new product, personal experience, photo feature, sex, love, relationship advice. **Buys 60-100 mss/year.** Query with published clips or send complete ms. Length: 800-2,000 words. **Pays $160-400.** Sometimes pays expenses of writers on assignment.

Reprints Send tearsheet, photocopy or typed ms with rights for sale noted and information about when and where the material previously appeared.

Photos Photo features with little or no copy should be sent to Mary Munro. Send photos with submission.

Reviews 2.25 or 35mm transparencies, 5×7 prints. Buys one-time rights. Pays $35-100/photo..Captions, identification of subjects, model releases required.

Tips ''Freelance writers should review the publication and writer's guidelines, then submit their articles for review. We're looking for new ways to explore the usual topics, written in a format that will be easy for our readers (ages 24-40+) to understand. We also like sidebar information that readers can review quickly before or after reading the article. Our focus is relationship-driven, with an editorial blend of beauty, health, and career.''

N COUNTRY WOMAN

Reiman Publications, 5400 S. 60th St., Greendale WI 53129. (414)423-0100. E-mail: editors@countrywomanmag azine.com. Website: www.countrywomanmagazine.com. **75-85% freelance written.** Bimonthly magazine. ''*Country Woman* is for contemporary rural women of all ages and backgrounds and from all over the US and Canada. It includes a sampling of the diversity that makes up rural women's lives—love of home, family, farm, ranch, community, hobbies, enduring values, humor, attaining new skills and appreciating present, past and future all within the context of the lifestyle that surrounds country living.'' Estab. 1970. **Pays on acceptance.** Byline given. Buys first North American serial, one-time, second serial (reprint) rights. Submit seasonal material 5 months in advance. Accepts queries by mail. Accepts previously published material. Accepts simultaneous submissions. Responds in 2 months to queries; 3 months to mss. Sample copy for $2 and SASE. Writer's guidelines for #10 SASE.

    O—x Break in with ''fiction, nostalgia, and inspirational pieces. Study the magazine carefully before submitting.''

Nonfiction Articles must be written in a positive, light, and entertaining manner. General interest, historical/nostalgic, how-to (crafts, community projects, decorative, antiquing, etc.), humor, inspirational, interview/profile, personal experience, photo feature (packages profiling interesting country women—all pertaining to rural women's interests). Query. Length: 1,000 words maximum.

Reprints Send ms with rights for sale noted and information about when and where the material previously appeared. Payment varies.

Photos Uses only excellent quality color photos. No b&w. ''We pay for photo/feature packages.'' State availability of or send photos with submission. Reviews 35mm or 2.25 transparencies, excellent quality color prints. Buys one-time rights. Captions, identification of subjects, model releases required.

Columns/Departments Why Farm Wives Age Fast (humor); I Remember When (nostalgia); Country Decorating. Length: 500-1,000 words. **Buys 10-12 mss/year.** Query or send ms.

Fiction Kathleen Anderson, managing editor. Main character must be a country woman. All fiction must have a country setting. Fiction must have a positive, upbeat message. Includes fiction in every issue. Would buy more fiction if stories suitable for our audience were sent our way. ''No contemporary, urban pieces that deal with divorce, drugs, etc.'' Send complete ms. Length: 750-1,000 words.

Poetry Light verse, traditional. ''Poetry must have rhythm and rhyme! It must be country-related, positive, and upbeat. Always looking for seasonal poetry.'' **Buys 6-12 poems/year.** Submit maximum 6 poems. Length: 4-24 lines.

Tips ''We have broadened our focus to include 'country' women—not just women on farms and ranches, but also women who live in a small town or country home and/or simply have an interest in country-oriented topics. This allows freelancers a wider scope in material. Write as clearly and with as much zest and enthusiasm as possible. We love good quotes, supporting materials (names, places, etc.) and strong leads and closings. Readers relate strongly to where they live and the lifestyle they've chosen. They want to be informed and entertained, and that's exactly why they subscribe. Readers are busy—not too busy to read—but when they do sit down, they want good writing, reliable information, and something that feels like a reward. How-to, humor, personal experience and nostalgia are areas most open to freelancers. Profiles, to a certain degree, are also open. Be accurate and fresh in approach.''

N ESSENCE

1500 Broadway, New York NY 10036. (212)642-0600. Fax: (212)921-5173. Website: www.essence.com. Entertainment Editor: Cori Murray. **Contact:** Editorial Department. Monthly magazine. ''*Essence* is the magazine for today's Black women. Edited for career-minded, sophisticated and independent achievers, *Essence*'s editorial is dedicated to helping its readers attain their maximum potential in various lifestyles and roles. The editorial content includes career and educational opportunities; fashion and beauty; investing and money management; health and fitness; parenting; information on home decorating and food; travel; cultural reviews; fiction; and profiles of achievers and celebrities.'' Estab. 1970. Circ. 1,000,000. **Pays on acceptance.** Byline given. Offers 25% kill fee. Makes assignments on a one-time serial rights basis. Editorial lead time 6 months. Submit seasonal material 6 months in advance. Accepts queries by mail, fax. Accepts previously published material. Responds in 2 months. Sample copy for $3.25. Writer's guidelines for #10 SASE.

Nonfiction Book excerpts, novel excerpts. **Buys 200 mss/year.** Query. Length: given upon assignment. **Pays by the word.**

Reprints Send tearsheet and information about when and where the material previously appeared. Pays 50% of the amount paid for the original article.

Photos ''We particularly would like to see photographs for our travel section that feature Black travelers.'' State availability with submission. Pays $200 and up depending on the size of the image. Model releases required.

Tips ''Please note that *Essence* no longer accepts unsolicited mss for fiction or nonfiction, except for the Brothers, Where There's a Will, Making Love Work, Our World, Back Talk and Interiors columns. So please only send query letters for nonfiction story ideas.''

$ $ $ $ FAMILY CIRCLE MAGAZINE

Gruner & Jahr, 375 Lexington Ave., New York NY 10017-5514. (212)499-2000. Fax: (212)499-1987. E-mail: nclark@familycircle.com. Website: www.familycircle.com. Editor-in-Chief: Susan Ungaro. **Contact:** Nancy Clark, deputy editor. **80% freelance written.** Magazine published every 3 weeks. ''We are a national women's service magazine which covers many stages of a woman's life, along with her everyday concerns about social, family, and health issues.'' Estab. 1932. Circ. 4,200,000. Byline given. Offers 20% kill fee. Buys one-time, all rights. Editorial lead time 4 months. Submit seasonal material 4 months in advance. Responds in 2 months. Sample copy not available. Writer's guidelines online.

   O── Break in with ''Women Who Make A Difference.'' Send queries to Nancy Clark, deputy editor.

Nonfiction ''We look for well-written, well-reported stories told through interesting anecdotes and insightful writing. We want well-researched service journalism on all subjects.'' Essays, humor, opinion, personal experience, women's interest subjects such as family and personal relationships, children, physical and mental health, nutrition, and self-improvement. No fiction or poetry. **Buys 200 mss/year.** Query with SASE. Length: 1,000-2,500 words. **Pays $1/word.** Pays expenses of writers on assignment.

Columns/Departments Women Who Make a Difference (profiles of volunteers who have made a significant impact on their community), 1,500 words; Profiles in Courage/Love (dramatic narratives about women and families overcoming adversity), 2,000 words; Full Circle (opinion/point of view on current issue/topic of general interest to our readers), 750 words; Humor, 750 words. **Buys 200 mss/year.** Query with published clips and SASE. **Pays $1/word.**

Tips ''Query letters should be concise and to the point. Also, writers should keep close tabs on *Family Circle* and other women's magazines to avoid submitting recently run subject matter.''

$ $ $ $ 🖳 FLARE MAGAZINE

One Mt. Pleasant Rd., 8th Floor, Toronto ON M4Y 2Y5 Canada. (416)764-2863. Fax: (416)764-2866. E-mail: editors@flare.com. Website: www.flare.com. Monthly magazine for women ages 17-34. Byline given. Offers 50% kill fee. Buys first North American serial, electronic rights. Accepts queries by e-mail. Sample copy for #10 SASE. Writer's guidelines online.

Nonfiction Looking for ''women's fashion, beauty, health, sociological trends, and celebrities.'' **Buys 24 mss/year.** Query. Length: 200-1,200 words. **Pays $1/word.** Pays expenses of writers on assignment.

Tips ''Study our masthead to determine if your topic is handled by regular contributing staff or a staff member.''

Ⓝ $ THE GODLY BUSINESS WOMAN MAGAZINE

All Women are Business Women, The Godly Business Women Magazine Corp., P.O. Box 181004, Casselberry FL 32718-1004. (407)696-2805. Fax: (407)695-8033. E-mail: editor@godlybusinesswoman.com. Website: www. godlybusinesswoman.com. Managing Editor: Tracey Davison. **45% freelance written.** Quarterly magazine covering Christian business women. ''Editorial is focused on issues Christian women face in the workplace. We consider all women as businesswomen (whether at home or in a corporate setting). Articles are hard-hitting and include 'take-away' information for busy women.'' Estab. 1999. **Pays on acceptance.** Publishes ms an average of 6-12 months after acceptance. Byline given. Buys one-time rights. Editorial lead time 4-6 months. Accepts queries by e-mail. Accepts previously published material. Sample copy for free. Writer's guidelines online.

Nonfiction Book excerpts, inspirational, interview/profile, personal experience, business. Query. Length: 400-1,200 words. **Pays $20 minimum for assigned articles.**

$ $ $ $ GOOD HOUSEKEEPING

Hearst Corp., 250 W. 55th St., New York NY 10019. (212)649-2200. Fax: (212)649-2340. Website: www.goodhou sekeeping.com. Editor-in-Chief: Ellen Levine. **Contact:** Judith Coyne, executive editor. Monthly magazine. ''*Good Housekeeping* is edited for the 'New Traditionalist.' Articles which focus on food, fitness, beauty, and child care draw upon the resources of the Good Housekeeping Institute. Editorial includes human interest stories, articles that focus on social issues, money management, health news, travel." Circ. 5,000,000. **Pays on acceptance.** Byline given. Offers 25% kill fee. Buys first North American serial rights. Submit seasonal material 6 months in advance. Responds in 2-3 months. For sample copy, call (800)925-0485. Writer's guidelines for #10 SASE.

Nonfiction Consumer, social issues, dramatic narrative, nutrition, work, relationships, psychology, trends. **Buys 4-6 mss/issue.** Query. Length: 1,500-2,500 words. Pays expenses of writers on assignment.

Photos Photos purchased on assignment mostly. Melissa Paterno, art director. Toni Paciello, photo editor. State availability with submission. Pays $100-350 for b&w; $200-400 for color photos. Model releases required.

Columns/Departments Profiles (inspirational, activist or heroic women), 400-600 words. Query with published clips. **Pays $1/word for items 300-600 words.**

Fiction Laura Mathews, fiction editor. No longer accepts unagented fiction submissions. Because of heavy volume of fiction submissions, *Good Housekeeping* is not accepting unsolicited submissions at this time. Length: 1,500 words (short-shorts); novel according to merit of material; average 5,000 word short stories. **Pays $1,000 minimum.**

Tips "Always send a SASE and clips. We prefer to see a query first. Do not send material on subjects already covered in-house by the Good Housekeeping Institute—these include food, beauty, needlework, and crafts."

$ $ $ $☑ LADIES' HOME JOURNAL

Meredith Corp., 125 Park Ave., 20th Floor, New York NY 10017-5516. (212)557-6600. Fax: (212)455-1313. E-mail: lhj@meredith.com. Website: www.lhj.com. **50% freelance written.** Monthly magazine focusing on issues of concern to women 30-45. They cover a broader range of news and political issues than many women's magazines. *"Ladies' Home Journal* is for active, empowered women who are evolving in new directions. It addresses informational needs with highly focused features and articles on a variety of topics including beauty and fashion, food and nutrition, health and medicine, home decorating and design, parenting and self-help, personalities and current events." Circ. 13,371,000. **Pays on acceptance.** Publishes ms an average of 4-12 months after acceptance. Offers 25% kill fee. Buys first North American serial rights. Rights bought vary with submission. Accepts queries by mail. Accepts simultaneous submissions. Responds in 3 months to queries. Sample copy not available. Writer's guidelines online.

Nonfiction Submissions on the following subjects should be directed to the editor listed for each: investigative reports, news-related features, psychology/relationships/sex; celebrities/entertainment. Query with published clips. Length: 2,000-3,000 words. **Pays $2,000-4,000.** Pays expenses of writers on assignment.

Photos *LHJ* arranges for its own photography almost all the time. State availability with submission. Rights bought vary with submission. Offers variable payment for photos accepted with ms. Captions, identification of subjects, model releases required.

Fiction Only short stories and novels submitted by an agent or publisher will be considered. No poetry of any kind. **Buys 12 mss/year.** Send complete ms. Length: 2,000-2,500.

$ $☑ THE LINK & VISITOR

Baptist Women of Ontario and Quebec, 1-315 Lonsdale Rd., Toronto ON M4V 1X3 Canada. (416)544-8550. E-mail: linkvis@baptistwomen.com. **Contact:** Editor. **50% freelance written.** Magazine published 6 times/ year "designed to help Baptist women grow their world, faith, relationships, creativity, and mission vision (evangelical, egalitarian, Canadian)." Estab. 1878. Circ. 4,000. Pays on publication. Publishes ms an average of 6 months after acceptance. Byline given. Buys one-time, second serial (reprint), simultaneous rights, makes work-for-hire assignments. Editorial lead time 2 months. Submit seasonal material 4 months in advance. Accepts simultaneous submissions. Sample copy for 9×12 SAE with 2 first-class Canadian stamps. Writer's guidelines free.

Nonfiction "Articles must be Biblically literate. No easy answers, American mindset or US focus, retelling of Bible stories, sermons." Inspirational, interview/profile, religious. **Buys 30-35 mss/year.** Send complete ms. Length: 750-2,000 words. **Pays 5-10¢/word (Canadian).** Sometimes pays expenses of writers on assignment.

Photos State availability with submission. Reviews prints. Buys one-time rights. Offers no additional payment for photos accepted with ms. Captions required.

Tips "We cannot use unsolicited manuscripts from non-Canadian writers. When submitting by e-mail, please send stories as messages, not as attachments."

$ LONG ISLAND WOMAN

Maraj, Inc., P.O. Box 176, Malverne NY 11565. E-mail: editor@liwomanonline.com. Website: www.liwomanonline.com. **Contact:** A. Nadboy, managing editor. **40% freelance written.** Monthly magazine covering issues of importance to women—health, family, finance, arts, entertainment, fitness, travel, home. Estab. 2001. Circ. 40,000. Pays within 1 month of publication. Publishes ms an average of 3 months after acceptance. Byline given. Offers 33% kill fee. Buys one-time rights for print and online use. Editorial lead time 3 months. Submit seasonal material 3 months in advance. Accepts queries by mail, e-mail. Accepts previously published material.

Accepts simultaneous submissions. Responds in 2 months to queries; 3 months to mss. Sample copy for $5. Writer's guidelines and editorial calendar online.

● Responds if interested in using reprints that were submitted.

Nonfiction Book excerpts, general interest, how-to, humor, interview/profile, new product, travel, reviews. **Buys 25-30 mss/year.** Query with published clips or send complete ms. Length: 500-1,800 words. **Pays $35-150.**

Reprints Accepts previously published submissions.

Photos State availability of or send photos with submission. Reviews 5×7 prints. Captions, identification of subjects, model releases required.

Columns/Departments Humor; Health Issues; Family Issues; Financial and Business Issues; Book Reviews and Books; Arts and Entertainment; Travel and Leisure; Home and Garden; Fitness.

N MORE MAGAZINE

Meredith Corp., 125 Park Ave., New York NY 10017. Fax: (212)455-1433. Editor-in-Chief: Peggy Northrop. **Contact:** Nanette Varian, features editor. **90% freelance written.** Magazine published 10 times/year covering smart, sophisticated women from 40-60. Estab. 1998. Circ. 1,000,000. **Pays on acceptance.** Publishes ms an average of 3 months after acceptance. Byline given. Offers 25% kill fee. Buys first North American serial, all rights. Editorial lead time 4 months. Submit seasonal material 6 months in advance. Accepts queries by mail, e-mail, fax. Responds in 3 months. Sample copy not available. Writer's guidelines for #10 SASE.

Nonfiction Essays, exposé, general interest, interview/profile, personal experience, travel, crime, food. **Buys 50 mss/year.** Query with published clips. Length: 300-2,500 words. **Pays variable rate depending on writer and/or story length.** Pays expenses of writers on assignment.

Photos State availability with submission. Negotiates payment individually. Captions, identification of subjects, model releases required.

Columns/Departments Buys 20 mss/year. Query with published clips.

$ $ $ $ MS. MAGAZINE

433 S. Beverly Dr., Beverly Hills CA 90212. (310)556-2515. Fax: (310)556-2514. E-mail: info@msmagazine.com. Website: www.msmagazine.com. **Contact:** Manuscripts Editor. **30% freelance written.** Quarterly magazine on women's issues and news. Estab. 1972. Circ. 150,000. Byline given. Offers 30% kill fee. Buys all rights. Responds in 2 months. Sample copy for $9. Writer's guidelines online.

● No unsolicited fiction or poetry.

Nonfiction International and national (US) news, the arts, books, popular culture, feminist theory and scholarship, ecofeminism, women's health, spirituality, political and economic affairs, photo essays. **Buys 4-5 feature (3,500 words) and 4-5 short (500 words) mss/year.** Query with published clips. Length: 300-3,500 words. **Pays $1/word; 50¢/word for news stories.** Pays expenses of writers on assignment.

Reprints Send tearsheet or typed ms with rights for sale noted and information about when and where the material previously appeared. Pays 50% of amount paid for original article.

Photos State availability with submission. Buys one-time rights. Identification of subjects, model releases required.

Columns/Departments Buys 4-5 mss/year. Pays $1/word.

Tips Needs "international and national women's news, investigative reporting, personal narratives, humor, world-class fiction and poetry, and prize-winning journalists and feminist thinkers."

$ $ $ REDBOOK MAGAZINE

Hearst Corp., 224 W. 57th St., 6th Floor, New York NY 10019. Website: www.redbookmag.com. Monthly magazine. "*Redbook* addresses young married women, ages 28-44. Most of our readers are married with children 10 and under; over 60 percent work outside the home. The articles entertain, educate, and inspire our readers to confront challenging issues. Each article must be timely and relevant to *Redbook* readers' lives." Estab. 1903. Circ. 2,300,000. **Pays on acceptance.** Publishes ms an average of 6 months after acceptance. Rights purchased vary with author and material. Responds in 3 months. Sample copy not available. Writer's guidelines online.

○┓ "Please review at least the past 6 issues of *Redbook* to better understand subject matter and treatment."

Nonfiction Subjects of interest: social issues, parenting, sex, marriage, news profiles, true crime, dramatic narratives, health. Query with published clips and SASE. Length: 2,500-3,000 words/articles; 1,000-1,500 words/short articles.

Tips "Most *Redbook* articles require solid research, well-developed anecdotes from on-the-record sources, and fresh, insightful quotes from established experts in a field that pass our 'reality check' test. Articles must apply to women in our demographics."

$ $ TODAY'S CHRISTIAN WOMAN

465 Gundersen Dr., Carol Stream IL 60188-2498. (630)260-6200. Fax: (630)260-0114. E-mail: tcwedit@christiani tytoday.com. Website: www.todayschristianwoman.net. Editor: Jane Johnson Struck. Managing Editor: Cam-

erin Courtney. **Contact:** Lisa Cockrel, associate editor. **50% freelance written.** Bimonthly magazine for Christian women of all ages, single and married, homemakers, and career women. *"Today's Christian Woman* seeks to help women deal with the contemporary issues and hot topics that impact their lives, as well as provide depth, balance, and a Biblical perspective to the relationships they grapple with daily in the following arenas: family, friendship, faith, marriage, single life, self, work, and health." Estab. 1978. Circ. 260,000. **Pays on acceptance.** Publishes ms an average of 6-12 months after acceptance. Byline given. Buys first rights. Submit seasonal material 9 months in advance. Accepts queries by mail, e-mail, fax. Responds in 2 months. Sample copy for $5. Writer's guidelines for #10 SASE or online.

Nonfiction How-to, narrative, inspirational. Practical spiritual living articles, 1,500-1,800 words. Humor (light, first-person pieces that include some spiritual distinctive), 1,000-1,500 words. Issues (third-person, anecdotal articles that report on scope of trends or hot topics, and provide perspective and practical take away on issues, plus sidebars), 1,800 words. Query. *No unsolicited mss.* "The query should include article summary, purpose, reader value, author's qualifications, suggested length, date to send, and SASE for reply." **Pays 20-25¢/word.**

Columns/Departments Readers' Picks (a short review of your current favorite CD or book and why), 200 words; **pays $25.** My Story (first-person, true-life dramatic story of how you solved a problem or overcame a difficult situation), 1,500-1,800 words; **pays $300.** Does not return or acknowledge submissions to these departments.

Tips "Articles should be practical and contain a distinct evangelical Christian perspective. While *TCW* adheres strictly to this underlying perspective in all its editorial content, articles should refrain from using language that assumes a reader's familiarity with Christian or church-oriented terminology. Bible quotes and references should be used selectively. All Bible quotes should be taken from the New International Version if possible. All articles should be highly anecdotal, personal in tone, and universal in appeal."

$ $ ☑ WEDDINGBELLS (CANADA)

WEDDINGBELLS, Inc., 34 King St. E., Suite 1200, Toronto ON M5C 2X8 Canada. E-mail: editorial@weddingbells.com. Website: www.weddingbells.com. **Contact:** Crys Stewart. **10% freelance written.** Semiannual magazine covering bridal, wedding, setting up home. Estab. 1985. Circ. 107,000. Pays on completion of assignment. Publishes ms an average of 6 months after acceptance. Offers 25% kill fee. Buys first North American serial, second serial (reprint), electronic rights. Accepts queries by mail, fax. Responds in 2 months.

Nonfiction Book excerpts, bridal service pieces. **Buys 22 mss/year.** Query with published clips. **Pays variable rates for assigned articles.** Sometimes pays expenses of writers on assignment.

⊘ ☑ WEDDINGBELLS (U.S.)

WEDDINGBELLS, Inc., 34 King St. E., Suite 1200, Toronto ON M5C 2X8 Canada. (416)363-1574. Fax: (416)363-6004. E-mail: editorialdept@weddingbells.com. Website: www.weddingbells.com. Editor: Crys Stewart. **Contact:** Michael Killingsworth, managing editor. **10% freelance written.** Quarterly magazine covering bridal, wedding, setting up home. Estab. 2000. Circ. 350,000. Pays on completion of assignment. Publishes ms an average of 6 months after acceptance. Byline sometimes given. Offers 25% kill fee. Buys first North American serial, second serial (reprint), electronic rights. Accepts queries by mail, fax. Responds in 2 months to queries.

• *Does not accept unsolicited materials.*

Nonfiction Book excerpts, bridal service pieces. **Buys 22 mss/year.** Query with published clips. **Pays variable rates for assigned articles.**

$ $ ⊕ WOMAN'S DAY

54-58 Park St., Sydney NSW 2000 Australia. 9282 8000. Fax: 9267 4360. Weekly magazine "for women of all ages (and the men in their lives enjoy it too)." Buys the first Australian and New Zealand rights. Accepts queries by e-mail, fax.

Fiction Julie Redlich, fiction editor. **Payment is usually $350 (Australian) for under 1,000 words; $450 for stories up to 2,500 words.**

Ⓝ $ $ WOMAN'S LIFE

A Publication of Woman's Life Insurance Society, 1338 Military St., P.O. Box 5020, Port Huron MI 48061-5020. (800)521-9292. Fax: (810)985-6970. E-mail: wkrabach@womanslifeins.com. Website: www.womanslifeins.com. Editor: Janice U. Whipple. **Contact:** Wendy L. Krabach, director of sales and marketing. **30% freelance written.** Quarterly magazine published for a primarily female membership to help them care for themselves and their families. Estab. 1892. Circ. 32,000. Pays on publication. Publishes ms an average of 1 year after acceptance. Byline given. Not copyrighted. Buys one-time, second serial (reprint), simultaneous rights. Submit seasonal material 6 months in advance. Accepts queries by mail, e-mail, fax. Accepts simultaneous submissions. Responds in 1 year. Sample copy for 9×12 SAE and 4 first-class stamps. Writer's guidelines for #10 SASE.

• Works only with published/established writers.

Nonfiction Looking primarily for general interest stories for women aged 25-55 regarding physical, mental, and emotional health and fitness; and financial/fiscal health and fitness. "We would like to see more creative financial pieces that are directed at women.'' **Buys 4-10 mss/year.** Send complete ms. Length: 1,000-2,000 words. **Pays $150-500.**

Reprints Send tearsheet, photocopy or typed ms with rights for sale noted and information about when and where the material previously appeared. Pays 15% of amount paid for an original article.

Photos Only interested in photos included with ms. Identification of subjects, model releases required.

$WOMEN ALIVE

Encouraging Excellence in Holy Living, Women Alive, Inc., P.O. Box 480052, Kansas City MO 64145. Phone/Fax: (913)402-1369. E-mail: ahinthorn@kc.rr.com. Website: www.womenalivemagazine.org. Managing Editor: Jeanette Littleton. **Contact:** Aletha Hinthorn, editor. **50% freelance written.** Bimonthly magazine covering Christian living. ''*Women Alive* encourages and equips women to live holy lives through teaching them to live out Scripture.'' Estab. 1984. Circ. 4,000. Pays on publication. Publishes ms an average of 6 months after acceptance. Byline given. Buys first North American serial, first, one-time, second serial (reprint), simultaneous rights. Editorial lead time 4 months. Submit seasonal material 4 months in advance. Accepts queries by mail, e-mail. Accepts simultaneous submissions. Responds in 6 weeks to mss. Sample copy and writer's guidelines for 9×12 SAE and 3 first-class stamps.

Nonfiction Inspirational, opinion, personal experience, religious. **Buys 30 mss/year.** Send complete ms. Length: 500-1,500 words.

Photos State availability with submission. Offers no additional payment for photos accepted with ms.

Trade Journals

Many writers who pick up *Writer's Market* for the first time do so with the hope of selling an article to one of the popular, high-profile consumer magazines found on newsstands and in bookstores. Many of those writers are surprised to find an entire world of magazine publishing exists outside the realm of commercial magazines—trade journals. Writers who *have* discovered trade journals have found a market that offers the chance to publish regularly in subject areas they find interesting, editors who are typically more accessible than their commercial counterparts, and pay rates that rival those of the big-name magazines. **(Note: All of the magazines listed in the Trade Journals section are paying markets. However, some of the magazines are not identified by payment rates ($ – $ $ $) because the magazines preferred not to disclose specific payment information.)**

Trade journal is the general term for any publication focusing on a particular occupation or industry. Other terms used to describe the different types of trade publications are business, technical, and professional journals. They are read by truck drivers, bricklayers, farmers, fishermen, heart surgeons, and just about everyone else working in a trade or profession. Trade periodicals are sharply angled to the specifics of the professions on which they report. They offer business-related news, features, and service articles that will foster their readers' professional development.

Trade magazine editors tell us their audience is made up of knowledgeable and highly interested readers. Writers for trade magazines have to either possess knowledge about the field in question or be able to report it accurately from interviews with those who do. Writers who have or can develop a good grasp of a specialized body of knowledge will find trade magazine editors are eager to hear from them.

An ideal way to begin your foray into trade journals is to write for those that report on your present profession. Whether you've been teaching dance, farming, or working as a paralegal, begin by familiarizing yourself with the magazines that serve your occupation. After you've read enough issues to have a feel for the kinds of pieces the magazines run, approach the editors with your own article ideas. If you don't have experience in a profession, but can demonstrate an ability to understand (and write about) the intricacies and issues of a particular trade that interests you, editors will still be willing to hear from you.

Information on trade publications listed in the previous edition of *Writer's Market*, but not included in this edition, can be found in the General Index.

ADVERTISING, MARKETING & PR

$ $ BIG IDEA

Detroit's Connection to the Communication Arts, Big Idea, 2145 Crooks Rd., Suite 208, Troy MI 48084. (248)458-5500. Fax: (248)458-7099. E-mail: info@bigideaweb.com. Website: www.bigideaweb.com. **Contact:** Kate Grace, managing editor. **75% freelance written.** Monthly magazine covering creative and communication arts in Southeastern Michigan. "We are a trade magazine specifically for creative professionals in the advertising, marketing and communication arts industry in Southeastern Michigan. Detroit is the third largest advertising market in the U.S. We are the resource for anyone in the agency: film and video, printing, post production, interactive, art and design, illustration, or photography." Estab. 1994. Circ. 10,000. **Pays on acceptance.** Publishes ms an average of 2 months after acceptance. Byline sometimes given. Offers 100% kill fee. Editorial lead time 2 months. Accepts queries by mail, e-mail, fax. Accepts previously published material. Responds in 6 weeks to queries.

Nonfiction Buys 10-12 mss/year. Query with published clips. Length: 1,500-2,500 words. **Pays $100-350 for assigned articles.** Sometimes pays expenses of writers on assignment.

Photos State availability with submission. Reviews GIF/JPEG files. Offers no additional payment for photos accepted with ms. Captions, identification of subjects, model releases required.

$ $ $ BRAND PACKAGING

Stagnito Communications, 155 Pfingsten Rd., Suite 205, Deerfield IL 60015. (847)205-5660. Fax: (847)205-5680. E-mail: jacevedo@stagnito.com. Website: www.brandpackaging.com. Senior Editor: Jim George. **Contact:** Jennifer Acevedo, editor-in-chief. **15% freelance written.** Magazine published 10 times/year covering how packaging can be a marketing tool. "We publish strategies and tactics to make products stand out on the shelf. Our market is brand managers who are marketers but need to know something about packaging." Estab. 1997. Circ. 33,000. **Pays on acceptance.** Publishes ms an average of 2 months after acceptance. Byline given. Makes work-for-hire assignments. Editorial lead time 3 months. Submit seasonal material 3 months in advance. Accepts queries by mail, fax. Sample copy for free.

Nonfiction How-to, interview/profile, new product. **Buys 10 mss/year.** Send complete ms. Length: 600-2,400 words. **Pays 40-50¢/word.**

Photos State availability with submission. Reviews contact sheets, 35mm transparencies, 4×5 prints. Buys one-time rights. Negotiates payment individually. Identification of subjects required.

Columns/Departments Emerging Technology (new packaging technology), 600 words. **Buys 10 mss/year.** Query. **Pays $150-300.**

Tips "Be knowledgeable on marketing techniques and be able to grasp packaging techniques. Be sure you focus on packaging as a marketing tool. Use concrete examples. We are not seeking case histories at this time."

$ DECA DIMENSIONS

1908 Association Dr., Reston VA 20191. (703)860-5000. Fax: (703)860-4013. E-mail: decainc@aol.com. Website: www.deca.org. **30% freelance written.** Quarterly magazine covering marketing, professional development, business, career training during school year (no issues published May-August). "*DECA Dimensions* is the membership magazine for DECA—The Association of Marketing Students—primarily ages 15-19 in all 50 states, the U.S. territories, Germany, and Canada. The magazine is delivered through the classroom. Students are interested in developing professional, leadership, and career skills." Estab. 1947. Circ. 160,000. Pays on publication. Byline given. Buys first, second serial (reprint) rights. Editorial lead time 3 months. Submit seasonal material 4 months in advance. Accepts queries by mail, e-mail, fax, phone. Accepts simultaneous submissions. Sample copy for free.

Nonfiction "Interested in seeing trends/forecast information of interest to audience (How do you forecast? Why? What are the trends for the next 5 years in fashion or retail?)." Essays, general interest, how-to (get jobs, start business, plan for college, etc.), interview/profile (business leads), personal experience (working), leadership development. **Buys 10 mss/year.** Send complete ms. Length: 800-1,000 words. **Pays $125 for assigned articles; $100 for unsolicited articles.**

Reprints Send ms and information about when and where the material previously appeared. Pays 85% of amount paid for an original article.

Columns/Departments Professional Development; Leadership, 350-500 words. **Buys 6 mss/year.** Send complete ms. **Pays $75-100.**

MEDIA INC.

Pacific Northwest Media, Marketing and Creative Services News, P.O. Box 24365, Seattle WA 98124-0365. (206)382-9220. Fax: (206)382-9437. E-mail: editor@media-inc.com. Website: www.media-inc.com. Publisher: James Baker. **30% freelance written.** Bimonthly magazine covering Northwest US media, advertising, marketing, and creative-service industries. Audience is Northwest ad agencies, marketing professionals, media, and creative-service professionals. Estab. 1987. Circ. 10,000. Byline given. Responds in 1 month to queries. Sample copy for 9×12 SAE and 6 first-class stamps.

Tips "It is best if writers live in the Pacific Northwest and can report on local news and events in Media Inc.'s areas of business coverage."

$ $ $ PROMO MAGAZINE

Insights and Ideas for Building Brands, Primedia, 11 Riverbend Dr., Stamford CT 06907. (203)358-4226. Fax: (203)358-9900. E-mail: kjoyce@primediabusiness.com. Website: www.promomagazine.com. **Contact:** Kathleen Joyce, editor. **5% freelance written.** Monthly magazine covering promotion marketing. "*Promo* serves marketers, and stories must be informative, well written, and familiar with the subject matter." Estab. 1987. Circ. 25,000. Pays on publication. Publishes ms an average of 2 months after acceptance. Byline given. Offers 25% kill fee. Buys first North American serial rights. Editorial lead time 3 months. Submit seasonal material 3 months in advance. Responds in 1 month to queries. Sample copy for $5.

Nonfiction Exposé, general interest, how-to (marketing programs), interview/profile, new product (promotion). "No general marketing stories not heavily involved in promotions." Generally does not accept unsolicited mss, query first. **Buys 6-10 mss/year.** Query with published clips. Length: Variable. **Pays $1,000 maximum for assigned articles; $500 maximum for unsolicited articles.** Sometimes pays expenses of writers on assignment. **Photos** State availability with submission. Reviews contact sheets, negatives. Negotiates payment individually. Captions, identification of subjects, model releases required.

Tips "Understand that our stories aim to teach marketing professionals about successful promotion strategies. Case studies or new promos have the best chance."

$ $ SIGN BUILDER ILLUSTRATED

America's How-To Sign Magazine, Simmons-Boardman Publishing Corp., 345 Hudson St., 12th Floor, New York NY 10014. (252)355-5806. Fax: (252)355-5690. E-mail: jwooten@sbpub.com. Website: www.signshop.com. Associate Editor: Chris Ytuarte. **Contact:** Jeff Wooten, editor. **40% freelance written.** Monthly magazine covering sign and graphic industry. "*Sign Builder Illustrated* targets sign professionals where they work: on the shop floor. Our topics cover the broadest spectrum of the sign industry, from design to fabrication, installation, maintenance and repair. Our readers own a similarly wide range of shops, including commercial, vinyl, sign erection and maintenance, electrical and neon, architectural, and awnings." Estab. 1987. Circ. 14,500. **Pays on acceptance.** Publishes ms an average of 3 months after acceptance. Byline given. Offers 10% kill fee. Buys all rights. Editorial lead time 3 months. Submit seasonal material 4 months in advance. Accepts queries by mail, e-mail, fax, phone. Accepts simultaneous submissions. Responds in 1 month to queries. Sample copy and writer's guidelines free.

Nonfiction Historical/nostalgic, how-to, humor, interview/profile, photo feature, technical. **Buys 50-60 mss/ year.** Query. Length: 1,000-1,500 words. **Pays $250-550 for assigned articles.**

Photos Send photos with submission. Reviews 3×5 prints. Buys all rights. Negotiates payment individually. Captions, identification of subjects required.

Tips "Be very knowledgeable about a portion of the sign industry you are covering. We want our readers to come away from each article with at least one good idea, one new technique, or one more 'trick of the trade.' At the same time, we don't want a purely textbook listing of 'do this, do that.' Our readers enjoy *Sign Builder Illustrated* because the publication speaks to them in a clear and lively fashion, from one sign professional to another. We want to engage the reader who has been in the business for some time. While there might be a place for basic instruction in new techniques, our average paid subscriber has been in business over 20 years, employs over seven people, and averages $800,000 in annual sales. These people aren't neophytes content with retread articles they can find anywhere. It's important for our writers to use anecdotes and examples drawn from the daily sign business."

$ $ SIGNCRAFT

The Magazine for Today's Sign Maker, SignCraft Publishing Co., Inc., P.O. Box 60031, Fort Myers FL 33906. (239)939-4644. Fax: (239)939-0607. E-mail: signcraft@signcraft.com. Website: www.signcraft.com. **Contact:** Tom McIltrot, editor. **10% freelance written.** Bimonthly magazine covering the sign industry. "Like any trade magazine, we need material of direct benefit to our readers. We can't afford space for material of marginal interest." Estab. 1980. Circ. 14,000. Pays on publication. Publishes ms an average of 6 months after acceptance. Byline given. Offers negotiable kill fee. Buys first North American serial, all rights. Accepts queries by mail, e-mail, fax. Responds in 1 month to queries. Sample copy and writer's guidelines for $3.

Nonfiction "All articles should be directly related to quality commercial signs. If you are familiar with the sign trade, we'd like to hear from you." Interview/profile. **Buys 10 mss/year.** Query with or without published clips. Length: 500-2,000 words.

$ $ SIGNS OF THE TIMES

The Industry Journal Since 1906, ST Publications, Dept. WM, 407 Gilbert Ave., Cincinnati OH 45202-2285. (513)421-2050. Fax: (513)421-5144. Website: www.signweb.com. **15-30% freelance written.** Monthly magazine covering the sign and outdoor advertising industries. Estab. 1906. Circ. 17,000. Pays on publication. Publishes ms an average of 3 months after acceptance. Byline given. Buys variable rights. Accepts queries by mail, e-mail, fax, phone. Responds in 3 months to queries. Sample copy and writer's guidelines for 9×12 SAE with 10 first-class stamps.

Nonfiction Historical/nostalgic (regarding the sign industry), how-to (carved signs, goldleaf, etc.), interview/profile (focusing on either a signshop or a specific project), photo feature (query first), technical (sign engineering, etc.). Nothing "nonspecific on signs, an example being a photo essay on 'signs I've seen.' We are a trade journal with specific audience interests." **Buys 15-20 mss/year.** Query with published clips. **Pays $150-500.**

Reprints Send tearsheet or typed ms with rights for sale noted and information about when and where the material previously appeared. Payment is negotiated.

Photos "Sign industry-related photos only. We sometimes accept photos with funny twists or misspellings." Send photos with submission.

Fillers Open to queries; request rates.

⬚ The online version contains material not found in the print edition.

Tips "Be thoroughly familiar with the sign industry, especially in the CAS-related area. Have an insider's knowledge plus an insider's contacts."

ART, DESIGN & COLLECTIBLES

$ $ AIRBRUSH ACTION MAGAZINE

Action, Inc., 3209 Atlantic Ave., P.O. Box 438, Allenwood NJ 08720. (732)223-7878. Fax: (732)223-2855. E-mail: editor@airbrushaction.com. Website: www.airbrushaction.com. **80% freelance written.** Bimonthly magazine covering the spectrum of airbrush applications: automotive and custom paint applications, illustration, T-shirt airbrushing, fine art, automotive and sign painting, hobby/craft applications, wall murals, fingernails, temporary tattoos, artist profiles, reviews, and more. Estab. 1985. Circ. 35,000. Pays 1 month after publication. Publishes ms an average of 6 months after acceptance. Byline given. Buys all rights. Editorial lead time 6 months. Submit seasonal material 6 months in advance. Accepts queries by mail, e-mail, fax, phone. Accepts simultaneous submissions.

Nonfiction Current primary focus is on automotive, motorcycle, and helmet kustom kulture arts. How-to, humor, inspirational, interview/profile, new product, personal experience, technical. Nothing unrelated to airbrush. Query with published clips. **Pays 15¢/word.** Sometimes pays expenses of writers on assignment.

Photos Send photos with submission. Digital images preferred. Buys all rights. Negotiates payment individually. Captions, identification of subjects, model releases required.

Columns/Departments Query with published clips.

⬚ The online version contains material not found in the print edition.

Tips "Send bio and writing samples. Send well-written technical information pertaining to airbrush art. We publish a lot of artist profiles—they all sound the same. Looking for new pizzazz!"

$ $ ANTIQUEWEEK

DMG World Media (USA), P.O. Box 90, Knightstown IN 46148-0090. (800)876-5133. Fax: (800)695-8153. E-mail: connie@antiqueweek.com. Website: www.antiqueweek.com. Managing Editor: Connie Swaim. **80% freelance written.** Weekly tabloid covering antiques and collectibles with 2 editions: Eastern and Central, plus monthly *AntiqueWest*. "*AntiqueWeek* has a wide range of readership from dealers and auctioneers to collectors, both advanced and novice. Our readers demand accurate information presented in an entertaining style." Estab. 1968. Circ. 50,000. Pays on publication. Byline given. Offers 10% kill fee or $25. Buys first, second serial (reprint) rights. Submit seasonal material 1 month in advance. Accepts queries by mail, e-mail, fax. Sample copy for free. Writer's guidelines for #10 SASE.

Nonfiction Historical/nostalgic, how-to, interview/profile, opinion, personal experience, antique show and auction reports, feature articles on particular types of antiques and collectibles. **Buys 400-500 mss/year.** Query. Length: 1,000-2,000 words. **Pays $50-250.**

Reprints Send tearsheet or typed ms with rights for sale noted and information about when and where the material previously appeared.

Photos Send photos with submission. Identification of subjects required.

Tips "Writers should know their topics thoroughly. Feature articles must be well researched and clearly written. An interview and profile article with a knowledgeable collector might be the break for a first-time contributor. We seek a balanced mix of information on traditional antiques and 20th century collectibles."

$THE APPRAISERS STANDARD

New England Appraisers Association, 5 Gill Terrace, Ludlow VT 05149-1003. (802)228-7444. Fax: (802)228-7444. E-mail: llt44@ludl.tds.net. Website: www.newenglandappraisers.net. **Contact:** Linda L. Tucker, publisher/editor. **50% freelance written.** Works with a small number of new/unpublished writers each year. Quarterly publication covering the appraisals of antiques, art, collectibles, jewelry, coins, stamps, and real estate. "The writer should be knowledgeable on the subject, and the article should be written with appraisers in mind, with prices quoted for objects, good pictures, and descriptions of articles being written about." Estab. 1980. Circ. 1,300. Pays on publication. Publishes ms an average of 1 year after acceptance. Short bio and byline given. Buys first and simultaneous rights. Submit seasonal material 2 months in advance. Accepts queries by mail, e-mail. Accepts simultaneous submissions. Responds in 1 month to queries; 2 months to mss. Sample copy for 9×12 SAE with 78¢ postage. Writer's guidelines for #10 SASE.

Nonfiction "All geared toward professional appraisers." Interview/profile, personal experience, technical, travel. Query with or without published clips or send complete ms. Length: 700 words. **Pays $50.**

Reprints Send ms with rights for sale noted and information about when and where the material previously appeared.

Photos Send photos with submission. Reviews negatives, prints. Buys one-time rights. Offers no additional payment for photos accepted with ms. Identification of subjects required.

Tips "Interviewing members of the association for articles, reviewing shows, and large auctions are all ways for writers who are not in the field to write articles for us. Articles should be geared to provide information which will help the appraisers with ascertaining value, detecting forgeries or reproductions, or simply providing advice on appraising the articles."

$ $ART CALENDAR MAGAZINE

The Business Magazine for Visual Artists, P.O. Box 2675, Salisbury MD 21802. Fax: (410)749-9626. E-mail: info@artcalendar.com. Website: www.artcalendar.com. **Contact:** Carolyn Proeber, publisher. **100% freelance written.** Monthly magazine. Estab. 1986. Circ. 23,000. Pays on publication. Accepts previously published material. Sample copy for $5. Writer's guidelines online.

- "We welcome nuts-and-bolts, practical articles of interest to serious visual artists, emerging or professional. Examples: marketing how-to's, first-person stories on how an artist has built his career or an aspect of it, interviews with artists (business/career-building emphasis), and pieces on business practices and other topics of use to artists. The tone of our magazine is practical, can-do, and uplifting. Writers may use as many or as few words as necessary to tell the whole story."

Nonfiction Essays (the psychology of creativity), how-to, interview/profile (successful artists with a focus on what made them successful—not necessarily rich and famous artists, but the guy next door who paints all day and makes a decent living doing it), personal experience (artists making a difference—art teachers working with disabled students, bringing a community together, etc.), technical (new equipment, new media, computer software, Internet sites that are way cool that no one has heard of yet), cartoons, art law, including pending legislation that affects artists (copyright law, Internet regulations, etc.). "We like nuts-and-bolts information about making a living as an artist. We do not run reviews or art historical pieces, nor do we like writing characterized by 'critic-speak,' philosophical hyperbole, psychological arrogance, politics, or New Age religion. Also, we do not condone a get-rich-quick attitude." Send complete ms. **Pays $200.** We can make other arrangements in lieu of pay, i.e. a subscription or copies of the magazine in which your article appears.

Reprints Send photocopy or typed ms and information about when and where the material previously appeared. Pays $50.

Photos Reviews b&w glossy or color prints. Pays $25.

Columns/Departments "If an artist or freelancer sends us good articles regularly, and based on results we feel that she is able to produce a column at least 3 times per year, we will invite him to be a contributing writer. If a gifted artist-writer can commit to producing an article on a monthly basis, we will offer him a regular column and the title contributing editor." Send complete ms.

$ $ART MATERIALS RETAILER

Fahy-Williams Publishing, P.O. Box 1080, Geneva NY 14456. (315)789-0458. Fax: (315)789-4263. E-mail: tmanzer@fwpi.com. Website: www.artmaterialsretailer.com. **Contact:** Tina Manzer, editor. **10% freelance written.** Quarterly magazine. Estab. 1998. Pays on publication. Byline given. Buys one-time rights. Editorial lead time 2 months. Submit seasonal material 3 months in advance. Accepts simultaneous submissions. Responds in 3 weeks to queries; 3 months to mss. Sample copy and writer's guidelines free.

Nonfiction Book excerpts, how-to, interview/profile, personal experience. **Buys 2 mss/year.** Send complete ms. Length: 1,500-3,000 words. **Pays $50-250.** Sometimes pays expenses of writers on assignment.

Photos State availability with submission. Reviews transparencies. Buys one-time rights. Offers no additional payment for photos accepted with ms. Identification of subjects required.

Fillers Anecdotes, facts, newsbreaks. **Buys 5/year.** Length: 500-1,500 words. **Pays $50-125.**

Tips "We like to review manuscripts rather than queries. Artwork (photos, drawings, etc.) is a real plus. We enjoy (our readers enjoy) practical, nuts-and-bolts, news-you-can-use articles."

$ARTS MANAGEMENT

110 Riverside Dr., Suite 4E, New York NY 10024. (212)579-2039. **Contact:** A.H. Reiss, editor. **1% freelance written.** Magazine published 5 times/year for cultural institutions. Estab. 1962. Circ. 6,000. Pays on publication. Byline given. Buys all rights. Accepts queries by mail. Responds in 2 months to queries. Writer's guidelines for #10 SASE.

• *Arts Management* is almost completely staff-written and uses very little outside material.

Nonfiction Short articles, 400-900 words, tightly written, expository, explaining how arts administrators solved problems in publicity, fund raising, and general administration; actual case histories emphasizing the how-to. Also short articles on the economics and sociology of the arts and important trends in the nonprofit cultural field. Must be fact filled, well organized, and without rhetoric. No photographs or pictures. **Pays 2-4¢/word.**

$ $INTERIOR BUSINESS MAGAZINE

GIE Media, Inc., 4012 Bridge Ave., Cleveland OH 44113. (800)456-0707. Fax: (216)961-0364. E-mail: acybulski@ gie.net. Website: www.interiorbusinessonline.com. **Contact:** Ali Cybulski, editor. **5-10% freelance written.** Magazine covering interior landscaping. "*Interior Business* addresses the concerns of the professional interior landscape contractor. It's devoted to the business management needs of interior landscape professionals." Estab. 2000. Circ. 6,000. Pays on publication. Publishes ms an average of 3 months after acceptance. Editorial lead time 3 months. Submit seasonal material 5 months in advance. Responds in 1 week to queries.

Nonfiction Interior landscaping. "No articles oriented to the consumer or homeowner." **Buys 2 mss/year.** Length: 1,000-2,500 words. **Pays $250-500.**

Tips "Know the audience. It's the professional business person, not the consumer."

N $ $THE PASTEL JOURNAL

The Magazine for Pastel Artists, F+W Publications, Inc., 4700 E. Galbraith Rd., Cincinnati OH 45236. (513)531-2690. Fax: (513)531-0798. Website: www.pasteljournal.com. Editor: Maureen Bloomfield. Editorial Assistant: Kate Mesch. **Contact:** Loraine Crouch, senior editor. Bimonthly magazine covering pastel artistry. "*The Pastel Journal* is the only national magazine devoted to the medium of pastel. Addressing the working professional as well as passionate amateurs, *The Pastel Journal* offers inspiration and instruction to our educated readers." Estab. 1999. Circ. 17,000. **Pays on acceptance.** Publishes ms an average of 3-6 months after acceptance. Byline given. Offers 25% kill fee. Buys first North American serial rights. Editorial lead time 6 months. Submit seasonal material 6 months in advance. Accepts queries by mail. Accepts simultaneous submissions. Responds in 4-6 weeks to queries. Sample copy and writer's guidelines free.

Nonfiction Book excerpts, how-to, interview/profile, new product. Does not want articles that aren't art-related. Review magazine before submitting. Query with or without published clips or send complete ms. Length: 500-2,500 words. **Pays $150-600.**

Photos State availability of or send photos with submission. Reviews transparencies, prints, GIF/JPEG files. Buys one-time rights. Offers no additional payment for photos accepted with ms. Captions required.

Fillers Anecdotes, facts, newsbreaks. **Pays $25-100.**

$ $ $PRINT

America's Graphic Design Magazine, F+W Publications, 38 E. 29th St., 3rd Floor, New York NY 10016. (212)447-1400. Fax: (212)447-5231. E-mail: info@printmag.com. Website: www.printmag.com. **75% freelance written.** Bimonthly magazine covering graphic design and visual culture. "*PRINT*'s articles, written by design specialists and cultural critics, focus on the social, political, and historical context of graphic design, and on the places where consumer culture and popular culture meet. We aim to produce a general interest magazine for professionals with engagingly written text and lavish illustrations. By covering a broad spectrum of topics, both international and local, we try to demonstrate the significance of design in the world at large." Estab. 1940. Circ. 45,000. **Pays on acceptance.** Publishes ms an average of 3 months after acceptance. Byline given. Offers 25% kill fee. Buys first North American serial rights. Editorial lead time 3 months. Submit seasonal material 3 months in advance. Accepts queries by e-mail. Responds in 2 weeks to queries; 1 month to mss. Sample copy not available.

Nonfiction Essays, interview/profile, opinion. **Buys 35-40 mss/year.** Query with published clips. Length: 1,000-2,500 words. **Pays $1,250.** Sometimes pays expenses of writers on assignment.

Columns/Departments Query with published clips. **Pays $800.**

Tips "Be well versed in issues related to the field of graphic design; don't submit ideas that are too general or geared to nonprofessionals."

$TEXAS ARCHITECT

Texas Society of Architects, 816 Congress Ave., Suite 970, Austin TX 78701. (512)478-7386. Fax: (512)478-0528. E-mail: editor@texasarchitect.org. Website: www.texasarchitect.org. **Contact:** Stephen Sharpe, editor. **30% freelance written.** Mostly written by unpaid members of the professional society. Bimonthly journal covering architecture and architects of Texas. "*Texas Architect* is a highly visually-oriented look at Texas architecture, design, and urban planning. Articles cover varied subtopics within architecture. Readers are mostly architects and related building professionals." Estab. 1951. Circ. 12,000. Pays on publication. Publishes ms an average of 3 months after acceptance. Byline given. Buys one-time, all rights, makes work-for-hire assignments. Submit seasonal material 4 months in advance. Accepts queries by mail, e-mail. Responds in 6 weeks to queries. Writer's guidelines online.

Nonfiction Interview/profile, photo feature, technical, book reviews. Query with published clips. Length: 100-2,000 words. **Pays $50-100 for assigned articles.**

Photos Send photos with submission. Reviews contact sheets, 35mm or 4×5 transparencies, 4×5 prints. Buys one-time rights. Offers no additional payment for photos accepted with ms. Identification of subjects required.

Columns/Departments News (timely reports on architectural issues, projects, and people), 100-500 words. **Buys 10 mss/year.** Query with published clips. **Pays $50-100.**

Ⓝ $ $WATERCOLOR MAGIC

The No. 1 Magazine for Watercolor Artists, F+W Publications, Inc., 4700 E. Galbraith Rd., Cincinnati OH 45236. (513)531-2690. Fax: (513)531-2902. Website: www.watercolormagic.com. Editor: Kelly Kane. Editorial Assistant: Kathe Mesch. **Contact:** Loraine Crouch, senior editor. Bimonthly magazine covering watercolor arts. "*Watercolor Magic* is the definitive source of how-to instruction and creative inspiration for artists working in water-based media." Estab. 1984. Circ. 92,000. **Pays on acceptance.** Publishes ms an average of 3-6 months after acceptance. Byline given. Offers 25% kill fee. Buys first North American serial rights. Editorial lead time 6 months. Submit seasonal material 6 months in advance. Accepts queries by mail. Accepts simultaneous submissions. Responds in 4-6 weeks to queries. Sample copy and writer's guidelines free.

Nonfiction Book excerpts, essays, how-to, inspirational, interview/profile, new product, personal experience. Does not want articles that aren't art-related. Review magazine before submitting. **Buys 36 mss/year.** Query with or without published clips or send complete ms. Length: 350-2,500 words. **Pays $150-600.**

Photos State availability of or send photos with submission. Reviews transparencies, prints, slides, GIF/JPEG files. Buys one-time rights. Captions required.

Fillers Anecdotes. Length: 20-300 words. **Pays $25-100.**

AUTO & TRUCK

$ $AUTOINC.

Automotive Service Association, P.O. Box 929, Bedford TX 76095. (800)272-7467. Fax: (817)685-0225. E-mail: editor@asashop.org. Website: www.autoinc.org. Assistant Editor: Levy Joffrion. **Contact:** Leona Dalavai Scott, editor. **10% freelance written.** Monthly magazine covering independent automotive repair. "The mission of *AutoInc.*, ASA's official publication, is to be the informational authority for ASA and industry members nationwide. Its purpose is to enhance the professionalism of these members through management, technical and legislative articles, researched and written with the highest regard for accuracy, quality, and integrity." Estab. 1952. Circ. 14,000. Pays on publication. Publishes ms an average of 3 months after acceptance. Byline given. Buys all rights. Editorial lead time 2 months. Accepts queries by mail, e-mail, fax. Accepts simultaneous submissions. Responds in 6 weeks to queries; 2 months to mss. Sample copy for $5 or online. Writer's guidelines and editorial calendar online.

Nonfiction How-to (automotive repair), technical. No coverage of staff moves or financial reports. **Buys 6 mss/year.** Query with published clips. Length: 1,200 words. **Pays $250.** Sometimes pays phone expenses of writers on assignment.

Photos State availability of or send photos with submission. Reviews 2×3 transparencies, 3×5 prints, high resolution digital images. Buys one-time and electronic rights. Negotiates payment individually. Captions, identification of subjects, model releases required.

Tips "Learn about the automotive repair industry, specifically the independent shop segment. Understand the high-tech requirements needed to succeed today. We target professional repair shop owners rather than consumers."

$ $BUSINESS FLEET

Bobit Publishing, 3520 Challenger St., Torrance CA 90501-1711. (310)533-2400. E-mail: chris.brown@bobit.com. Website: www.businessfleet.com. **Contact:** Chris Brown, associate editor. **10% freelance written.** Bimonthly magazine covering businesses which operate 10-50 company vehicles. "While it's a trade publication aimed at a business audience, *Business Fleet* has a lively, conversational style. The best way to get a feel for our 'slant' is to read the magazine." Estab. 2000. Circ. 100,000. Pays on publication. Publishes ms an average of 3 months after acceptance. Byline given. Offers 25% kill fee. Buys first, second serial (reprint), electronic rights. Editorial lead time 2 months. Submit seasonal material 2 months in advance. Accepts queries by mail, e-mail, fax. Responds in 3 weeks to queries; 2 months to mss. Sample copy and writer's guidelines free.

Nonfiction How-to, interview/profile, new product, personal experience, photo feature, technical. **Buys 16 mss/year.** Query with published clips. Length: 500-2,000 words. **Pays $100-400.** Pays with contributor copies or other premiums by prior arrangement. Sometimes pays expenses of writers on assignment.

Photos State availability with submission. Reviews 3×5 prints. Buys one-time, reprint, and electronic rights. Negotiates payment individually. Captions required.

Tips "Our mission is to educate our target audience on more economical and efficient ways of operating company vehicles, and to inform the audience of the latest vehicles, products, and services available to small commercial companies. Be knowledgeable about automotive and fleet-oriented subjects."

$ $ FLEET EXECUTIVE

The Magazine of Vehicle Management, The National Association of Fleet Administrators, Inc., 100 Wood Ave. S., Suite 310, Iselin NJ 08830-2716. (732)494-8100. Fax: (732)494-6789. E-mail: publications@nafa.org. Website: www.nafa.org. **Contact:** Carolann McLoughlin, managing editor. **50% freelance written.** Magazine published 8 times/year covering automotive fleet management. "*NAFA Fleet Executive* focuses on car, van, and light-duty truck management in US and Canadian corporations, government agencies, and utilities. Editorial emphasis is on general automotive issues; improving jobs skills, productivity, and professionalism; legislation and regulation; alternative fuels; safety; interviews with prominent industry personalities; technology; association news; public service fleet management; and light-duty truck fleet management." Estab. 1957. Circ. 4,000. Pays on publication. Publishes ms an average of 4 months after acceptance. Buys all rights. Editorial lead time 2 months. Accepts queries by mail, e-mail, fax. Accepts simultaneous submissions. Responds in 1 month to queries. Sample copy online. Writer's guidelines free.

Nonfiction "NAFA hosts its Fleet Management Institute, an educational conference and trade show, which is held in a different city in the US and Canada each year. *Fleet Executive* would consider articles on regional attractions, particularly those that might be of interest to the automotive industry, for use in a conference preview issue of the magazine. The preview issue is published one month prior to the conference. Information about the conference, its host city, and conference dates in a given year may be found on NAFA's website, www.nafa.org, or by calling the association at (732)494-8100." Interview/profile, technical. **Buys 24 mss/year.** Query with published clips. Length: 500-3,000 words. **Pays $500 maximum.**

Photos State availability with submission. Reviews electronic images.

Tips "The sample articles online at www.nafa.org/fleetexecutive should help writers get a feel of the journalistic style we require."

$ $ LIGHT TRUCK & SUV ACCESSORY BUSINESS & PRODUCT NEWS

(formerly *Sport Truck & SUV Accessory Business*), Cygnus Business Media, 1233 Janesville Ave., Fort Atkinson WI 53538. (920)563-6388. Fax: (920)563-1702. E-mail: pat.walker@cygnusb2b.com. Website: www.sportstruck .com. **Contact:** Pat Walker, editor. **25% freelance written.** "*Light Truck & SUV Accessory Business & Product News* is a bimonthly trade magazine designed to provide light truck accessory dealers and installers with advice on improving their retail business practices, plus timely information about industry trends and events. Each issue's editorial package includes a dealer profile, plus features aimed at meeting the distinct needs of store owners, managers and counter sales people. The magazine also provides aftermarket, OEM and trade association news, three separate new product sections, plus an analysis of light truck sales." Estab. 1996. Circ. 15,000. Pays 30 days after publication. Publishes ms an average of 3 months after acceptance. Byline given. Buys first North American serial rights. Editorial lead time 3 months. Submit seasonal material 4 months in advance. Accepts simultaneous submissions. Responds in 1 month to queries. Sample copy and writer's guidelines free.

    O— Break in with "a feature on a top truck or SUV retailer in your area."

Nonfiction General interest, interview/profile, new product, technical, Considers cartoons. No travel, installation how-to's. **Buys 20-30 mss/year.** Query. Length: 1,000-2,000 words. **Pays $300-500.**

Photos Send photos with submission. Reviews transparencies, prints. Buys one-time rights. Negotiates payment individually. Model releases required.

Tips "Send query with or without completed manuscripts. Background/experience and published clips are required."

MOTOR AGE

Advanstar Communications, Inc., 150 Strafford Ave., Suite 210, Wayne PA 19087-3114. (610)687-2587. Fax: (610)687-1419. Website: www.motorage.com. Editor: Bill Cannon. Monthly magazine. Edited as a technical journal for automotive service dealers and technicians in the US. Estab. 1899. Circ. 143,147. Sample copy not available.

OLD CARS WEEKLY

News & Marketplace, Krause Publications, a Division of F+W Publications, Inc., 700 E. State St., Iola WI 54990-0001. (715)445-4612. Fax: (715)445-2214. E-mail: vanbogarta@krause.com; brendan.dooley@krause.com. Website: www.collect.com. **Contact:** Angelo Van Bogart or Brendan Dooley. **50% freelance written.** Weekly tabloid for anyone restoring, selling or driving an old car. Estab. 1971. Circ. 65,000. Pays in the month after publication date. Publishes ms an average of 6 months after acceptance. Byline given. Call circulation department for sample copy. Writer's guidelines for #10 SASE.

Nonfiction How-to, technical, auction prices realized lists. No "Grandpa's Car," "My First Car" or "My Car" themes. **Buys 1,600 mss/year.** Send complete ms. Length: 400-1,600 words. **Payment varies.**

Photos Send photos with submission. Pays $5/photo. Offers no additional payment for photos accepted with ms. Captions, identification of subjects required.

Tips "Ninety percent of our material is done by a small group of regular contributors. Many new writers break in here, but we are usually overstocked with material and never seek nostalgic or historical pieces from new authors. Our big need is for well-written items that fit odd pieces in a tabloid page layout. Budding authors should try some short, catchy items that help us fill odd-ball 'news holes' with interesting writing. Authors with good skills can work up to longer stories. The best queries are 'checklists' where we can quickly mark a 'yes' or 'no' to article ideas."

$ $ $ OVERDRIVE

The Voice of the American Trucker, Randall Publishing Co./Overdrive, Inc., 3200 Rice Mine Rd., Tuscaloosa AL 35406. (205)349-2990. Fax: (205)750-8070. E-mail: mheine@randallpub.com. Website: www.etrucker.net. Editor: Linda Longton. **Contact:** Max Heine, editorial director. **5% freelance written.** Monthly magazine for independent truckers. Estab. 1961. Circ. 100,000. Pays on publication. Publishes ms an average of 2 months after acceptance. Byline given. Offers 10% kill fee. Buys all North American rights, including electronic rights. Responds in 2 months to queries. Sample copy for 9×12 SASE.

Nonfiction All must be related to independent trucker interest. Essays, exposé, how-to (truck maintenance and operation), interview/profile (successful independent truckers), personal experience, photo feature, technical. Query with or without published clips or send complete ms. Length: 500-2,000 words. **Pays $200-1,000 for assigned articles.**

Photos Send photos with submission. Reviews transparencies, prints, slides. Buys all rights. Offers $25-150/photo.

Tips "Talk to independent truckers. Develop a good knowledge of their concerns as small-business owners, truck drivers, and individuals. We prefer articles that quote experts, people in the industry, and truckers, to first-person expositions on a subject. Get straight facts. Look for good material on truck safety, on effects of government regulations, and on rates and business relationships between independent truckers, brokers, carriers, and shippers."

PARTS & PEOPLE

(formerly *Northwest Motor*), Automotive Counseling & Publishing Co., P.O. Box 18731, Denver CO 80218. (303)765-4664. Fax: (303)765-4650. E-mail: kevin@partsandpeople.com. Website: www.partsandpeople.com. **Contact:** Kevin Loewen, managing editor. **5% freelance written.** Five monthly magazines covering the automotive industry. Estab. 1985. Circ. 60,000. Pays on publication. Byline given. Offers 10% kill fee. Buys all rights. Editorial lead time 1 month. Submit seasonal material 2 months in advance. Accepts queries by mail, e-mail. Accepts simultaneous submissions. Sample copy for $2.

Nonfiction How-to, new product, photo feature, technical, business features. **Buys 20 mss/year.** Query. Length: 250-1,200 words. **Payment varies.** Sometimes pays expenses of writers on assignment.

Photos Send photos with submission. Reviews 3×5 prints. Buys all rights. Negotiates payment individually.

Columns/Departments Buys 20 mss/year. Query. **Payment varies.**

Fillers Anecdotes, facts. **Buys 4-9/year.** Length: 15-100 words. **Pays variable amount.**

$ PML

The Market Letter for Porsche Automobiles, PML Consulting, P.O. Box 567, Socorro NM 87801. Fax: (505)838-1222. E-mail: phil@pmletter.com. Website: www.pmletter.com. **Contact:** Phil Van Buskirk, owner. **100% freelance written.** Monthly magazine covering technical tips, personality profiles and race coverage of Porsche automobiles. Estab. 1981. Circ. 1,500. Pays on publication. Publishes ms an average of 2 months after acceptance. Byline given. Buys one-time rights. Editorial lead time 2 months. Submit seasonal material 2 months in advance. Accepts queries by mail, e-mail, fax, phone. Accepts previously published material. Accepts simultaneous submissions. Responds in 2 weeks to queries; 1 month to mss. Sample copy for $5. Writer's guidelines for #10 SASE.

Nonfiction General interest, historical/nostalgic, how-to, humor, interview/profile, new product, personal experience, photo feature, technical, travel, race results. **Buys 30-40 mss/year.** Query with published clips. Length: 500-2,000 words. **Pays $30-50 and up, depending on length and topic.** Sometimes pays expenses of writers on assignment.

Photos Send photos with submission. Reviews 8×10 b&w prints. Buys one-time rights. Negotiates payment individually. Captions, identification of subjects, model releases required.

Fillers Anecdotes, facts, gags to be illustrated by cartoonist, newsbreaks, short humor. **Pays negotiable amount.**

Tips "Check any auto-related magazine for types, styles of articles. We are looking for people doing anything unusual or interesting in the Porsche world. Submit well-prepared, thoroughly-edited articles with photos."

$ ROAD KING MAGAZINE

For the Professional Driver, Parthenon Publishing, 28 White Bridge Rd., Suite 209, Nashville TN 37205. (615)627-2250. Fax: (615)690-3401. E-mail: submissions@roadking.com. Website: www.roadking.com. **80% freelance written.** Bimonthly magazine. "*Road King* is published bimonthly for long-haul truckers. It celebrates the lifestyle and work and profiles interesting and/or successful drivers. It also reports on subjects of interest to our audience, including outdoors, vehicles, music, and trade issues." Estab. 1963. Circ. 229,900. Pays 3 weeks after acceptance. Publishes ms an average of 4 months after acceptance. Byline given. Offers negotiable kill fee. Buys first North American serial, electronic rights. Editorial lead time 4 months. Submit seasonal material 6 months in advance. Accepts queries by mail, e-mail. Responds in 2 months to queries. Sample copy for 9×12 SAE and 5 first-class stamps. Writer's guidelines online.

Nonfiction How-to (trucking-related), interview/profile, new product, photo feature, technical, travel. Special issues: Road Gear (the latest tools, techniques and industry developments to help truckers run a smarter, more efficient trucking business); At Home on the Road ("creature comfort" products, services, and information for the road life, including what's new, useful, interesting, or fun for cyber-trucking drivers). "No fiction, poetry." **Buys 20 mss/year.** Query with published clips. Length: 850-2,000 words. **Payment negotiable.** Sometimes pays expenses of writers on assignment.

Photos State availability with submission. Reviews contact sheets. Buys negotiable rights. Negotiates payment individually. Identification of subjects, model releases required.

Columns/Departments Lead Driver (profile of outstanding trucker), 250-500 words; Roadrunner (new products, services suited to the business of trucking or to truckers' lifestyles), 100-250 words. **Buys 6-10 mss/year.** Query. **Payment negotiable.**

Fillers Anecdotes, facts, gags to be illustrated by cartoonist, short humor. Length: 100-250 words. **Pays $50.**

The online magazine of *Road King* carries original content not found in the print edition.

$ $ RV TRADE DIGEST

Your Source for Management, Marketing and Production Information, Cygnus Business Media, Inc., 1233 Janeville Ave., Fort Atkinson WI 53538. (920)568-8349. Fax: (920)563-1702. E-mail: editor@rvtradedigest.com. Website: www.rvtradedigest.com. **Contact:** Greg Gerber, editor-in-chief. **10% freelance written.** Magazine published 9 times/year. "*RV Trade Digest* seeks to help RV dealers become more profitable and efficient. We don't want fluff and theory. We want tested and proven ideas other dealers can apply to their own businesses. We believe sharing best practices helps everyone in the industry stay strong." Estab. 1980. Circ. 16,000. Pays 1 month after publication. Publishes ms an average of 3 months after acceptance. Byline given. Buys first North American serial rights. Requires exclusive use of all material for 3 months following publication. Editorial lead time 3 months. Submit seasonal material 4 months in advance. Accepts queries by mail, e-mail. Accepts simultaneous submissions. Responds in 2 months to queries. Sample copy and writer's guidelines free.

Nonfiction How-to (install, service parts, accessories), interview/profile (of industry leaders or successful RV dealers), new product (with emphasis on how to best sell and market the product), technical, business subjects, mobile electronics. Does not want articles about RV travel experience. **Buys 1-2 mss/year.** Length: 1,000-2,000 words. **Pays $300-500.** Pays expenses of writers on assignment.

Photos Send photos with submission. Reviews transparencies, prints, GIF/JPEG files. Buys one-time rights. Negotiates payment individually. Model releases required.

Columns/Departments Dealer Pro-File; Profit Central; Modern Manager; Industry Insider.

Tips "Propose an idea that will have broad appeal to the RV industry in that it will be interesting and useful to RV dealers, manufacturers, and suppliers. Queries must include background/experience and published clips."

$ $ TODAY'S TRUCKING

New Communications Group, 451 Attwell Dr., Toronto ON M9W 5C4 Canada. (416)614-2200. Fax: (416)614-8861. E-mail: editors@todaystrucking.com. Website: www.todaystrucking.com. Editor: Peter Carter. **Contact:** Rolf Lockwood. **15% freelance written.** Monthly magazine covering the trucking industry in Canada. "We reach nearly 30,000 fleet owners, managers, owner-operators, shop supervisors, equipment dealers, and parts distributors across Canada. Our magazine has a strong service slant, combining useful how-to journalism with analysis of news, business issues, and heavy-duty equipment trends. Before you sit down to write, please take time to become familiar with *Today's Trucking*. Read a few recent issues.'' Estab. 1987. Circ. 30,000. **Pays on acceptance.** Byline given. Buys first North American serial, second serial (reprint) rights. Editorial lead time 2 months. Submit seasonal material 3 months in advance. Accepts queries by mail, e-mail, fax. Sample copy and writer's guidelines free.

Nonfiction How-to, interview/profile, technical. **Buys 20 mss/year.** Query with published clips. Length: 500-2,000 words. **Pays 40¢/word.** Sometimes pays expenses of writers on assignment.

Photos State availability with submission.

Columns/Departments Pays 40¢/word.

ℕ WARD'S AUTOWORLD

Primedia Business Magazines and Media, 3000 Town Center, Suite 2750, Southfield MI 48075-1245. (248)357-0800. Fax: (248)357-0810. Website: www.wardsauto.com. Editor: Drew Winter. Monthly magazine edited for personnel involved in the original equipment manufacturing industry. Circ. 101,349. Editorial lead time 1 month. Sample copy not available.

ℕ WARD'S DEALER BUSINESS

Primedia Business Magazines and Media, 3000 Town Center, Suite 2750, Southfield MI 48075-1245. (248)357-0800. Fax: (248)357-0810. Website: www.wardsauto.com. Editor: Steve Finlay. Monthly magazine edited for personnel involved in aftermarket sales. Circ. 30,000. Editorial lead time 1 month. Sample copy not available.

$ $⊡ WESTERN CANADA HIGHWAY NEWS

Craig Kelman & Associates, 3C-2020 Portage Ave., Winnipeg MB R3J 0K4 Canada. (204)985-9785. Fax: (204)985-9795. E-mail: terry@kelman.ca. **Contact:** Terry Ross, managing editor. **30% freelance written.** Quarterly magazine covering trucking. ''The official magazine of the Alberta, Saskatchewan, and Manitoba trucking associations.'' Estab. 1995. Circ. 4,500. Pays on publication. Publishes ms an average of 2 months after acceptance. Byline given. Buys one-time rights. Editorial lead time 3 months. Submit seasonal material 3 months in advance. Accepts simultaneous submissions. Responds in 1 month to queries; 1 month to mss. Sample copy for 10×13 SAE with 1 IRC. Writer's guidelines for #10 SASE.

Nonfiction Essays, general interest, how-to (run a trucking business), interview/profile, new product, opinion, personal experience, photo feature, technical, profiles in excellence (bios of trucking or associate firms enjoying success). **Buys 8-10 mss/year.** Query. Length: 500-3,000 words. **Pays 18-25¢/word.** Sometimes pays expenses of writers on assignment.

Photos State availability with submission. Reviews 4×6 prints. Buys one-time rights. Identification of subjects required.

Columns/Departments Safety (new safety innovation/products), 500 words; Trade Talk (new products), 300 words. Query. **Pays 18-25¢/word.**

Tips ''Our publication is fairly time sensitive regarding issues affecting the trucking industry in Western Canada. Current 'hot' topics are international trucking, security, driver fatigue, health and safety, emissions control, and national/international highway systems.''

AVIATION & SPACE

$ $ AIRCRAFT MAINTENANCE TECHNOLOGY

Cygnus Business Media, 1233 Janesville Ave., Fort Atkinson WI 53538. (920)563-6388. Fax: (920)563-1702. E-mail: editor@amtonline.com. Website: www.amtonline.com. Editor: Joe Escobar. **10% freelance written.** Magazine published 10 times/year covering aircraft maintenance. ''*Aircraft Maintenance Technology* provides aircraft maintenance professionals worldwide with a curriculum of technical, professional, and managerial development information that enables them to more efficiently and effectively perform their jobs. Estab. 1989. Circ. 41,500 worldwide. Pays on publication. Publishes ms an average of 2 months after acceptance. Byline given. Buys all rights, makes work-for-hire assignments. Editorial lead time 3 months. Submit seasonal material 6 months in advance. Accepts queries by mail, e-mail, fax. Accepts simultaneous submissions. Responds in 2 weeks to queries; 1 month to mss. Sample copy for free. Writer's guidelines for #10 SASE or by e-mail.

Nonfiction How-to, technical, safety; human factors. Special issues: Aviation career issue (August). No travel/pilot-oriented pieces. **Buys 10-12 mss/year.** Query with published clips. Length: 600-1,500 words, technical articles 2,000 words. **Pays $200.**

Photos State availability with submission. Buys one-time rights. Offers no additional payment for photos accepted with ms. Captions, identification of subjects, model releases required.

Columns/Departments Professionalism, 1,000-1,500 words; Safety Matters, 600-1,000 words; Human Factors, 600-1,000 words. **Buys 10-12 mss/year.** Query with published clips. **Pays $200.**

Tips "This is a technical magazine approved by the FAA and Transport Canada for recurrency training for technicians. Freelancers should have a strong background in aviation, particularly maintenance, to be considered for technical articles. Columns/Departments: Freelancers still should have a strong knowledge of aviation to slant professionalism, safety, and human factors pieces to that audience."

$ $ AIRPORT OPERATIONS

Flight Safety Foundation, Suite 300, 601 Madison St., Alexandria VA 22314-1756. (703)739-6700. Fax: (703)739-6708. E-mail: rozelle@flightsafety.org. Website: www.flightsafety.org. **Contact:** Roger Rozelle, director of publications. **25% freelance written.** Bimonthly newsletter covering safety aspects of airport operations. "*Airport Operations* directs attention to ground operations that involve aircraft and other equipment, airport personnel and services, air traffic control (ATC), and passengers." Estab. 1974. Circ. 2,000. Pays on publication. Publishes ms an average of 3 months after acceptance. Byline given. Buys all rights. Editorial lead time 3 months. Accepts queries by mail, e-mail, fax. Accepts previously published material. Responds in 3 weeks to queries. Sample copy and writer's guidelines online.

Nonfiction Technical. No argumentation, crusading, inspiration, anecdotes, or humor. **Buys 6 mss/year.** Query. Length: 2,500-8,750 words. **Pays $200/printed page, plus 6 copies of publication.**

Photos Send photos with submission. Reviews contact sheets, negatives, 35mm or larger transparencies, 5×7 minimum prints, GIF/JPEG files. Buys all rights. Offers $25/photo. Captions, identification of subjects, model releases required.

Tips "Study the guidelines carefully. Be concerned above all with accuracy, fairness, and objectivity, but if you have information that you believe meets those standards, do not hesitate to query even if you aren't sure of format or style. If you have the content we need, our editorial staff will work with you to put the material into shape."

$ $ AVIATION INTERNATIONAL NEWS

The Convention News Co., 214 Franklin Ave., Midland Park NJ 07432. (201)444-5075. Fax: (201)444-4647. E-mail: rpadfield@ainonline.com. Website: www.ainonline.com. Editor *AIN* Monthly Edition: Nigel Moll. **Contact:** R. Randall Padfield, editor-in-chief. **30-40% freelance written.** Monthly magazine (with onsite issues published at 3 conventions and 2 international air shows each year) covering business and commercial aviation with news features, special reports, aircraft evaluations, and surveys on business aviation worldwide, written for business pilots and industry professionals. "While the heartbeat of *AIN* is driven by the news it carries, the human touch is not neglected. We pride ourselves on our people stories about the industry's 'movers and shakers' and others in aviation who make a difference." Estab. 1972. Circ. 40,000. **Pays on acceptance and upon receipt of writer's invoice.** Publishes ms an average of 2 months after acceptance. Byline given. Offers variable kill fee. Buys first North American serial and second serial (reprint) rights and makes work-for-hire assignments. Editorial lead time 2 months. Submit seasonal material 3 months in advance. Accepts queries by mail, e-mail, fax. Responds in 6 weeks to queries; 2 months to mss. Sample copy for $10. Writer's guidelines for 9×12 SAE with 3 first-class stamps.

- Do not send mss by e-mail unless requested.
- Break in with "local news stories relating to business, commercial and regional airline aviation—think turbine-powered aircraft (no stories about national airlines, military aircraft, recreational aviation or history."

Nonfiction "We hire freelancers to work on our staff at 3 aviation conventions and 2 international airshows each year. Must have strong reporting and writing skills and knowledge of aviation." How-to (aviation), interview/profile, new product, opinion, personal experience, photo feature, technical. No puff pieces. "Our readers expect serious, real news. We don't pull any punches. *AIN* is not a 'good news' publication: It tells the story, both good and bad." **Buys 150-200 mss/year.** Query with published clips. Length: 200-3,000 words. **Pays 30¢/word to first timers, higher rates to proven *AIN* freelancers.** Pays expenses of writers on assignment.

Photos Send photos with submission. Reviews contact sheets, transparencies, prints, TIFF files (300 dpi). Buys one-time rights. Negotiates payment individually. Captions required.

Tips "Our core freelancers are professional pilots with good writing skills, or good journalists and reporters with an interest in aviation (some with pilot licenses) or technical experts in the aviation industry. The ideal *AIN* writer has an intense interest in and strong knowledge of aviation, a talent for writing news stories, and journalistic cussedness. Hit me with a strong news story relating to business aviation that takes me by surprise—something from your local area or area of expertise. Make it readable, fact-filled, and in the inverted-pyramid style. Double-check facts and names. Interview the right people. Send me good, clear photos and illustrations. Send me well-written, logically ordered copy. Do this for me consistently and we may take you along on our staff to one of the conventions in the U.S. or an airshow in Paris, Singapore, London, or Dubai."

$ $AVIATION MAINTENANCE

Access Intelligence, 1201 Seven Locks Rd., Suite 300, Potomac MD 20854. (301)354-1831. Fax: (301)340-8741. E-mail: am@accessintel.com. Website: www.aviationmx.com. Managing Editor: Joy Finnegan. **Contact:** Matt Thurber, editor. **60% freelance written.** Monthly magazine covering aircraft maintenance from small to large aircraft. *Aviation Maintenance* delivers news and information about the aircraft maintenance business for mechanics and management at maintenance shops, airlines, and corporate flight departments. Estab. 1982. Circ. 25,000. **Pays on acceptance.** Publishes ms an average of 2 months after acceptance. Byline given. Kill fee varies. Buys all rights. Editorial lead time 3 months. Submit seasonal material 3 months in advance. Accepts queries by mail, e-mail, fax, phone. Responds in 1 week to queries; 1 month to mss. Sample copy online. Writer's guidelines free.

Nonfiction Exposé, interview/profile, technical. No fiction, technical how-to, or poetry. **Buys 50 mss/year.** Query with or without published clips. Length: 200-500 words. **Pays 35¢/word.** Pays expenses of writers on assignment.

Photos State availability with submission. Buys all rights. Negotiates payment individually. Captions, identification of subjects required.

Columns/Departments Buys 12 mss/year. Query with or without published clips. **Pays $200-250.**

Tips "Writer must be intimately familiar with, or involved in, aviation, either as a pilot or preferably a mechanic or a professional aviation writer. Best place to break in is in the Intelligence News section or with a Postflight profile of an interesting mechanic."

$AVIATION MECHANICS BULLETIN

Flight Safety Foundation, Suite 300, 601 Madison St., Alexandria VA 22314-1756. (703)739-6700. Fax: (703)739-6708. E-mail: rozelle@flightsafety.org. Website: www.flightsafety.org. **Contact:** Roger Rozelle, director of publications. **25% freelance written.** Bimonthly newsletter covering safety aspects of aviation maintenance (airline and corporate). Estab. 1953. Circ. 2,000. Pays on publication. Publishes ms an average of 3 months after acceptance. Byline given. Buys all rights. Editorial lead time 3 months. Accepts queries by mail, e-mail, fax. Accepts previously published material. Responds in 3 weeks to queries. Sample copy and writer's guidelines online.

Nonfiction Technical. No argumentation, crusading, inspiration, anecdotes, or humor. **Buys 6 mss/year.** Query. Length: 2,000-5,500 words. **Pays $100/printed pocket-sized page, plus 6 copies of publication.**

Photos Send photos with submission. Reviews contact sheets, negatives, 35mm or larger transparencies, 5×7 minimum prints, GIF/JPEG files. Buys all rights. Offers $25/photo. Captions, identification of subjects, model releases required.

Tips "Study guidelines carefully. Be concerned above all with accuracy, but if you have information that you believe meets those standards, do not hesitate to query even if you aren't sure of format or style. If you have the content we need, our editorial staff will work with you to put the material into shape."

$ $CABIN CREW SAFETY

Flight Safety Foundation, Suite 300, 601 Madison St., Alexandria VA 22314-1756. (703)739-6700. Fax: (703)739-6708. E-mail: rozelle@flightsafety.org. Website: www.flightsafety.org. **Contact:** Roger Rozelle, director of publications. **25% freelance written.** Bimonthly newsletter covering safety aspects of aircraft cabins (airline and corporate aviation) for cabin crews and passengers. Estab. 1956. Circ. 2,000. Pays on publication. Publishes ms an average of 3 months after acceptance. Byline given. Buys all rights. Editorial lead time 3 months. Accepts queries by mail, e-mail, fax. Accepts previously published material. Responds in 3 weeks to queries. Sample copy and writer's guidelines online.

Nonfiction Technical. No argumentation, crusading, inspiration, anecdotes, or humor. **Buys 6 mss/year.** Query. Length: 2,500-8,750 words. **Pays $200/printed page, plus 6 copies of publication.**

Photos Send photos with submission. Reviews contact sheets, negatives, 35mm or larger transparencies, 5×7 minimum prints, GIF/JPEG files. Buys all rights. Offers $25/photo. Captions, identification of subjects, model releases required.

Tips "Study guidelines carefully. Be concerned above all with accuracy, fairness, and objectivity, but if you have information that you believe meets those standards, do not hesitate to query even if you aren't sure of format or style. If you have the content we need, our editorial staff will work with you to put the material into shape."

$ $FLIGHT SAFETY DIGEST

Flight Safety Foundation, Suite 300, 601 Madison St., Alexandria VA 22314-1756. (703)739-6700. Fax: (703)739-6708. E-mail: rozelle@flightsafety.org. Website: www.flightsafety.org. **Contact:** Roger Rozelle, director of publications. **25% freelance written.** Monthly magazine covering significant issues in airline and corporate aviation safety. "*Flight Safety Digest* offers the page space to explore subjects in greater detail than in other Foundation periodicals." Estab. 1982. Circ. 2,000. Pays on publication. Publishes ms an average of 3 months after acceptance. Byline given. Buys all rights. Editorial lead time 3 months. Accepts queries by mail, e-mail, fax. Accepts previously published material. Responds in 3 weeks to queries. Sample copy and writer's guidelines online.

Nonfiction Technical. No argumentation, crusading, inspiration, anecdotes, or humor. **Buys 6 mss/year.** Query. Length: 4,000-15,000 words. **Pays $200/printed page, plus 6 copies of publication.**

Photos Send photos with submission. Reviews contact sheets, negatives, 35mm or larger transparencies, 5×7 minimum prints, GIF/JPEG files. Buys all rights. Offers $25/photo. Captions, identification of subjects, model releases required.

Tips "Study guidelines carefully. Be concerned above all with accuracy, fairness, and objectivity, but if you have information that you believe meets those standards, do not hesitate to query even if you aren't sure of format or style. If you have the content we need, our editorial staff will work with you to put the material into shape."

$ $GROUND SUPPORT MAGAZINE

Cygnus Business Media, 1233 Janesville Ave., Fort Atkinson WI 53538. (920)563-1622. Fax: (920)563-1699. E-mail: karen.reinhardt@cygnuspub.com. Website: www.groundsupportmagazine.com. **Contact:** Karen Reinhardt, editor. **20% freelance written.** Magazine published 10 times/year. "Our readers are those aviation professionals who are involved in ground support—the equipment manufacturers, the suppliers, the ramp operators, ground handlers, airport and airline managers. We cover issues of interest to this community—deicing, ramp safety, equipment technology, pollution, etc." Estab. 1993. Circ. 15,000. Pays on publication. Publishes ms an average of 2 months after acceptance. Buys all rights. Editorial lead time 2 months. Accepts queries by mail, e-mail, fax. Responds in 3 weeks to queries; 3 months to mss. Sample copy for 9×11 SAE and 5 first-class stamps.

Nonfiction How-to (use or maintain certain equipment), interview/profile, new product, opinion, photo feature, technical aspects of ground support and issues, industry events, meetings, new rules and regulations. **Buys 12-20 mss/year.** Send complete ms. Length: 500-2,000 words. **Pays $100-300.**

Photos Send photos with submission. Reviews 35mm prints, electronic preferred, slides. Buys all rights. Offers additional payment for photos accepted with ms. Identification of subjects required.

Tips "Write about subjects that relate to ground services. Write in clear and simple terms—personal experience is always welcome. If you have an aviation background or ground support experience, let us know."

$ $HELICOPTER SAFETY

Flight Safety Foundation, Suite 300, 601 Madison St., Alexandria VA 22314-1756. (703)739-6700. Fax: (703)739-6708. E-mail: rozelle@flightsafety.org. Website: www.flightsafety.org. **Contact:** Roger Rozelle, director of publications. **50% freelance written.** Bimonthly newsletter covering safety aspects of helicopter operations. "*Helicopter Safety* highlights the broad spectrum of real-world helicopter operations. Topics have ranged from design principles and primary training to helicopter utilization in offshore applications and in emergency medical service (EMS)." Estab. 1956. Circ. 2,000. Pays on publication. Publishes ms an average of 3 months after acceptance. Byline given. Buys all rights. Editorial lead time 3 months. Accepts queries by mail, e-mail, fax. Accepts previously published material. Responds in 3 weeks to queries. Sample copy and writer's guidelines online.

Nonfiction Technical. No argumentation, crusading, inspiration, anecdotes, or humor. **Buys 6 mss/year.** Query. Length: 2,500-8,750 words. **Pays $200/printed page, plus 6 copies of publication.**

Photos Send photos with submission. Reviews contact sheets, negatives, 35mm or larger transparencies, 5×7 minimum prints. Buys all rights. Offers $25/photo. Captions, identification of subjects, model releases required.

Tips "Study guidelines carefully. Be concerned above all with accuracy, fairness, and objectivity, but if you have information that you believe meets those standards, do not hesitate to query even if you aren't sure of format or style. If you have the content we need, our editorial staff will work with you to put the material into shape."

$ $HUMAN FACTORS & AVIATION MEDICINE

Flight Safety Foundation, Suite 300, 601 Madison St., Alexandria VA 22314-1756. (703)739-6700. Fax: (703)739-6708. E-mail: rozelle@flightsafety.org. Website: www.flightsafety.org. **Contact:** Roger Rozelle, director of publications. **50% freelance written.** Bimonthly newsletter covering medical aspects of aviation, primarily for airline and corporate aviation pilots. "*Human Factors & Aviation Medicine* allows specialists, researchers, and physicians to present information critical to the training, performance, and health of aviation professionals." Estab. 1953. Circ. 2,000. Pays on publication. Publishes ms an average of 3 months after acceptance. Byline given. Buys all rights. Editorial lead time 3 months. Accepts queries by mail, e-mail, fax. Accepts previously published material. Responds in 3 weeks to queries. Sample copy and writer's guidelines online.

Nonfiction Technical. No argumentation, crusading, inspiration, anecdotes, or humor. **Buys 6 mss/year.** Query. Length: 2,500-8,750 words. **Pays $200/printed page, plus 6 copies of publication.**

Photos Send photos with submission. Reviews contact sheets, negatives, 35mm or larger transparencies, 5×7 minimum prints, GIF/JPEG files. Buys all rights. Offers $25/photo. Captions, identification of subjects, model releases required.

Tips "Study guidelines carefully. Be concerned above all with accuracy, fairness, and objectivity, but if you have information that you believe meets those standards, do not hesitate to query even if you aren't sure of format or style. If you have the content we need, our editorial staff will work with you to put the material into shape."

$ $ $PROFESSIONAL PILOT

Queensmith Communications, 30 S. Quaker Lane, Suite 300, Alexandria VA 22314. (703)370-0606. Fax: (703)370-7082. E-mail: editor@propilotmag.com. Website: www.propilotmag.com. **Contact:** Phil Rose, managing editor. **75% freelance written.** Monthly magazine covering regional airline, corporate and various other types of professional aviation. "The typical reader has a sophisticated grasp of piloting/aviation knowledge and is interested in articles that help him/her do the job better or more efficiently." Estab. 1967. Circ. 44,000. Pays on publication. Publishes ms an average of 2-3 months after acceptance. Byline given. Kill fee negotiable. Buys all rights. Accepts queries by mail, e-mail, fax, phone.

> O→ "Affiliation with an active flight department, weather activity of Air Traffic Control (ATC) is helpful. Our readers want tool tech stuff from qualified writers with credentials."

Nonfiction "Typical subjects include new aircraft design, new product reviews (especially avionics), pilot techniques, profiles of regional airlines, fixed base operations, profiles of corporate flight departments and technological advances." All issues have a theme such as regional airline operations, maintenance, avionics, helicopters, etc. **Buys 40 mss/year.** Query. Length: 750-2,500 words. **Pays $200-1,000, depending on length. A fee for the article will be established at the time of assignment.** Sometimes pays expenses of writers on assignment.

Photos Send photos with submission. Prefers transparencies or slides. Buys all rights. Additional payment for photos negotiable. Captions, identification of subjects required.

Tips Query first. "Freelancer should be a professional pilot or have background in aviation. Authors should indicate relevant aviation experience and pilot credentials (certificates, ratings and hours). We place a greater emphasis on corporate operations and pilot concerns."

BEAUTY & SALON

$ $BEAUTY STORE BUSINESS

Creative Age Communications, 7628 Densmore Ave., Van Nuys CA 91406-2042. (818)782-7328, ext. 353. Fax: (818)782-7450. E-mail: klissak@creativeage.com. **Contact:** Keith Lissak, executive editor. **50% freelance written.** Monthly magazine covering beauty store business management and news. "The primary readers of the publication are owners, managers, and buyers at open-to-the-public beauty stores, including general-market and multicultural market-oriented ones with or without salon services. Our secondary readers are those at beauty stores only open to salon industry professionals. We also go to beauty distributors." Estab. 1994. Circ. 15,000. **Pays on acceptance.** Publishes ms an average of 3 months after acceptance. Byline given. Offers negotiable kill fee. Buys all rights. Editorial lead time 3 months. Submit seasonal material 4 months in advance. Accepts queries by mail, e-mail, fax. Responds in 1 week to queries. Responds in 2 weeks, if interested, to mss. Sample copy for free.

Nonfiction "If your business-management article will help a specialty retailer, it should be of assistance to our readers. We're also always looking for writers who are fluent in Korean." How-to (business management, merchandising, e-commerce, retailing), interview/profile (industry leaders). **Buys 20-30 mss/year.** Query. Length: 1,800-2,200 words. **Pays $250-525 for assigned articles.** Sometimes pays expenses of writers on assignment.

Photos Do not send computer art electronically. State availability with submission. Reviews transparencies, computer art (artists work on Macs, request 300 dpi, on CD or Zip disk, saved as JPEG, TIFF, or EPS). Buys all rights. Negotiates payment individually. Captions, identification of subjects required.

$ $▧ COSMETICS

Canada's Business Magazine for the Cosmetics, Fragrance, Toiletry, and Personal Care Industry, Rogers, 1 Mt. Pleasant Rd., 7th Floor, Toronto ON M4Y 2Y5 Canada. (416)764-1680. Fax: (416)764-1704. E-mail: dave.lackie@ cosmetics.rogers.com. Website: www.cosmeticsmag.com. **Contact:** Dave Lackie, editor. **10% freelance written.** Bimonthly magazine. "Our main reader segment is the retail trade—department stores, drugstores, salons, estheticians—owners and cosmeticians/beauty advisors; plus manufacturers, distributors, agents, and suppliers to the industry.'' Estab. 1972. Circ. 13,000. **Pays on acceptance.** Publishes ms an average of 3 months after acceptance. Byline given. Offers 50% kill fee. Buys all rights. Editorial lead time 4 months. Submit seasonal material 4 months in advance. Accepts queries by mail. Responds in 1 month to queries. Sample copy for $6 (Canadian) and 8% GST.

Nonfiction General interest, interview/profile, photo feature. **Buys 1 mss/year.** Query. Length: 250-1,200 words. **Pays 25¢/word.** Sometimes pays expenses of writers on assignment.

Photos Send photos with submission. Reviews 2½ up to 8×10 transparencies, 4×6 up to 8×10 prints, 35mm slides, e-mail pictures in 300 dpi JPEG format. Buys all rights. Offers no additional payment for photos accepted with ms. Captions, identification of subjects, model releases required.

📧 The online magazine carries original content not found in the print edition. Contact: Jim Hicks, publisher/online editor.

Tips ''Must have broad knowledge of the Canadian cosmetics, fragrance, and toiletries industry and retail business. 99.9% of freelance articles are assigned by the editor to writers involved with the Canadian cosmetics business.''

$ $DAYSPA

For the Salon of the Future, Creative Age Publications, 7628 Densmore Ave., Van Nuys CA 91406. (818)782-7328. Fax: (818)782-7450. E-mail: dayspa@creativeage.com. Website: www.dayspamagazine.com. Managing Editor: Linda Jacobson-Kossoff. **Contact:** Linda Lewis, executive editor. **50% freelance written.** Monthly magazine covering the business of day spas, skin care salons, wellness centers. ''*Dayspa* includes only well-targeted business articles directed at the owners and managers of high-end, multi-service salons, day spas, resort spas, and destination spas.'' Estab. 1996. Circ. 31,000. **Pays on acceptance.** Publishes ms an average of 4 months after acceptance. Byline given. Buys first, one-time rights. Editorial lead time 4 months. Submit seasonal material 4 months in advance. Accepts queries by mail, e-mail, fax, phone. Responds in 2 months to queries. Sample copy for $5.

Nonfiction Buys 40 mss/year. Query. Length: 1,200-3,000 words. **Pays $150-500.**

Photos Send photos with submission. Buys one-time rights. Negotiates payment individually. Identification of subjects, model releases required.

Columns/Departments Legal Pad (legal issues affecting salons/spas); Money Matters (financial issues), both 1,200-1,500 words. **Buys 20 mss/year.** Query. **Pays $150-300.**

$DERMATOLOGY INSIGHTS

A Patient's Guide to Healthy Skin, Hair, and Nails, American Academy of Dermatology, P.O. Box 4014, Schaumburg IL 60168. Website: www.aad.org. **30% freelance written.** Semiannual magazine covering dermatology. *Dermatology Insights* contains ''educational and informative articles for consumers about dermatological subjects.'' Estab. 2000. **Pays on acceptance.** Publishes ms an average of 4 months after acceptance. Byline given. Buys all rights, makes work-for-hire assignments. Editorial lead time 4 months. Submit seasonal material 4 months in advance. Accepts queries by mail, e-mail. Responds in 3 weeks to queries; 1 month to mss. Sample copy for free. Writer's guidelines not available.

Nonfiction General interest, how-to, interview/profile, new product, personal experience, photo feature, technical. **Buys 10-15 mss/year.** Query. Length: 750 words maximum. **Pays flat rate of $40/hour.** Sometimes pays expenses of writers on assignment.

Photos State availability with submission. Buys all rights. Negotiates payment individually. Identification of subjects required.

Columns/Departments Patient Perspective (patient's first-hand account). **Buys 2-3 mss/year.** Query. **Pays flat rate of $40/hour.**

MASSAGE & BODYWORK

Associated Bodywork & Massage Professionals, 1271 Sugarbush Dr., Evergreen CO 80439-9766. (303)674-8478 or (800)458-2267. Fax: (303)674-0859. E-mail: editor@abmp.com. Website: www.massageandbodywork.com. **Contact:** Leslie A. Young, PhD, editor-in-chief. **85% freelance written.** Bimonthly magazine covering therapeutic massage/bodywork. ''A trade publication for the massage therapist, bodyworker, and skin care professional. An all-inclusive publication encompassing everything from traditional Swedish massage to energy work to other complementary therapies (i.e., homeopathy, herbs, aromatherapy, etc.).'' **Pays on acceptance.** Publishes ms an average of 6 months after acceptance. Buys first North American serial, one-time, electronic rights. Editorial lead time 6 months. Submit seasonal material 6 months in advance. Accepts queries by mail, e-mail, fax, phone. Responds in 1 month to queries; 5 months to mss. Writer's guidelines online.

Nonfiction Essays, exposé, how-to (technique/modality), interview/profile, opinion, personal experience, technical, travel. No fiction. **Buys 60-75 mss/year.** Query with published clips. Length: 1,000-3,000 words.

Reprints Accepts previously published submissions.

Photos State availability with submission. Reviews contact sheets. Buys one-time rights. Negotiates payment individually. Captions, identification of subjects, model releases required.

Columns/Departments Buys 20 mss/year.

Tips "Know your topic. Offer suggestions for art to accompany your submission. *Massage & Bodywork* looks for interesting, tightly focused stories concerning a particular modality or technique of massage, bodywork, somatic and skin care therapies. The editorial staff welcomes the opportunity to review manuscripts which may be relevant to the field of massage, bodywork, and skin care practices, in addition to more general pieces pertaining to complementary and alternative medicine. This would include the widely varying modalities of massage and bodywork (from Swedish massage to Polarity therapy), specific technical or ancillary therapies, including such topics as biomagnetics, aromatherapy, and facial rejuvenation. Reference lists relating to technical articles should include the author, title, publisher, and publication date of works cited. Word count: 1,500-4,000 words; longer articles negotiable."

$ $ MASSAGE MAGAZINE

Exploring Today's Touch Therapies, 1636 W. First Ave., Suite 100, Spokane WA 99204. (800)533-4263. E-mail: karen@massagemag.com. Website: www.massagemag.com. **Contact:** Karen Menehan, editor. **60% freelance written.** Bimonthly magazine covering massage and other touch therapies. Estab. 1985. Circ. 50,000. **Pays on acceptance.** Publishes ms an average of 1 year after acceptance. Byline given. Buys first North American serial rights. Accepts queries by mail, e-mail. Responds in 2 months to queries; 3 months to mss. Sample copy free. Writer's guidelines online.

Nonfiction Book excerpts, essays, general interest, how-to, inspirational, interview/profile, personal experience, photo feature, technical, experiential. Length: 600-2,000 words. **Pays $75-300 for assigned articles.**

Reprints Send tearsheet of article and typed ms with rights for sale noted and information about when and where the material previously appeared. Pays 50-75% of amount paid for an original article.

Photos Send photos with submission via e-mail. Buys one-time rights. Offers $25-100/photo. Identification of subjects, identification of photographer required.

Columns/Departments Profiles; Table Talk (news briefs); Practice Building (business); Technique; Body/Mind. Length: 800-1,200 words. **$75-300 for assigned articles.**

Fillers Facts, newsbreaks. Length: 100-800 words. **Pays $125 maximum.**

Tips "Our readers seek practical information on how to help their clients, improve their techniques, and/or make their businesses more successful, as well as feature articles that place massage therapy in a positive or inspiring light. Since most of our readers are professional therapists, we do not publish articles on topics like 'How Massage Can Help You Relax.' Please study a few back issues so you know what types of topics and tone we're looking for."

$ $ NAILPRO

The Magazine for Nail Professionals, Creative Age Publications, 7628 Densmore Ave., Van Nuys CA 91406. (818)782-7328. Fax: (818)782-7450. E-mail: jmills@creativeage.com. Website: www.nailpro.com. **Contact:** Jodi Mills, executive editor. **75% freelance written.** Monthly magazine written for manicurists and nail technicians working in full-service salons or nails-only salons. It covers technical and business aspects of working in and operating a nail-care service, as well as the nail-care industry in general. Estab. 1989. Circ. 65,000. **Pays on acceptance.** Publishes ms an average of 6 months after acceptance. Byline given. Buys first North American serial rights. Editorial lead time 3 months. Submit seasonal material 3 months in advance. Accepts queries by mail, e-mail, fax. Accepts simultaneous submissions. Responds in 6 weeks to queries. Sample copy for $2 and 8½×11 SASE.

Nonfiction Book excerpts, how-to, humor, inspirational, interview/profile, personal experience, photo feature, technical. No general interest articles or business articles not geared to the nail-care industry. **Buys 50 mss/year.** Query. Length: 1,000-3,000 words. **Pays $150-450.**

Reprints Send ms with rights for sale noted and information about when and where the material previously appeared. Pays 25-50% of amount paid for an original article.

Photos Send photos with submission. Reviews transparencies, prints. Buys one-time rights. Negotiates payment individually. Identification of subjects, model releases required.

Columns/Departments Building Business (articles on marketing nail services/products), 1,200-2,000 words; Shop Talk (aspects of operating a nail salon), 1,200-2,000 words. **Buys 50 mss/year.** Query. **Pays $200-300.**

■ The online magazine carries original content not found in the print edition. Contact: Jodi Mills.

$ $ ☑ NAILS

Bobit Publishing, 3520 Challenger St., Torrance CA 90503. (310)533-2400. Fax: (310)533-2507. E-mail: nailsmag @nailsmag.com. Website: www.nailsmag.com. **Contact:** Cyndy Drummey, editor. **10% freelance written.** Monthly magazine. "*NAILS* seeks to educate its readers on new techniques and products, nail anatomy and health, customer relations, working safely with chemicals, salon sanitation, and the business aspects of running a salon." Estab. 1983. Circ. 55,000. **Pays on acceptance.** Byline given. Buys all rights. Submit seasonal material 4 months in advance. Accepts queries by mail, e-mail, fax. Responds in 3 months to queries. Sample copy and writer's guidelines for #10 SASE.

Nonfiction Historical/nostalgic, how-to, inspirational, interview/profile, personal experience, photo feature, technical. "No articles on one particular product, company profiles or articles slanted toward a particular company or manufacturer." **Buys 20 mss/year.** Query with published clips. Length: 1,200-3,000 words. **Pays $200-500.** Sometimes pays expenses of writers on assignment.

Photos State availability with submission. Reviews contact sheets, transparencies, prints (any standard size acceptable). Buys all rights. Offers $50-200/photo. Captions, identification of subjects, model releases required.

 The online version contains material not found in the print edition. Contact: Hannah Lee.

Tips "Send clips and query; *do not send unsolicited manscripts*. We would like to see ideas for articles on a unique salon or a business article that focuses on a specific aspect or problem encountered when working in a salon. The Modern Nail Salon section, which profiles nail salons and full-service salons, is most open to freelancers. Focus on an innovative business idea or unique point of view. Articles from experts on specific business issues—insurance, handling difficult employees, cultivating clients—are encouraged."

$ $ SKIN INC. MAGAZINE

The Complete Business Guide for Face & Body Care, Allured Publishing Corp., 362 S. Schmale Rd., Carol Stream IL 60188. (630)653-2155. Fax: (630)653-2192. E-mail: taschetta-millane@allured.com. Website: www.skininc.com. Publisher: Marian Raney. **Contact:** Melinda Taschetta-Millane, editor. **30% freelance written.** Magazine published 12 times/year. "Manuscripts considered for publication that contain original and new information in the general fields of skin care and makeup, dermatological and esthetician-assisted surgical techniques. The subject may cover the science of skin, the business of skin care and makeup, and plastic surgeons on healthy (i.e., nondiseased) skin. Subjects may also deal with raw materials, formulations, and regulations concerning claims for products and equipment." Estab. 1988. Circ. 16,000. Pays on publication. Publishes ms an average of 6 months after acceptance. Byline given. Buys all rights. Editorial lead time 6 months. Submit seasonal material 1 year in advance. Accepts queries by mail, e-mail, fax, phone. Responds in 2 weeks to queries; 1 month to mss. Sample copy and writer's guidelines free.

Nonfiction General interest, how-to, interview/profile, personal experience, technical. **Buys 6 mss/year.** Query with published clips. Length: 2,000 words. **Pays $100-300 for assigned articles; $50-200 for unsolicited articles.**

Photos State availability with submission. Reviews 3×5 prints. Buys one-time rights. Offers no additional payment for photos accepted with ms. Captions, identification of subjects, model releases required.

Columns/Departments Finance (tips and solutions for managing money), 2,000-2,500 words; Personnel (managing personnel), 2,000-2,500 words; Marketing (marketing tips for salon owners), 2,000-2,500 words; Retail (retailing products and services in the salon environment), 2,000-2,500 words. Query with published clips. **Pays $50-200.**

Fillers Facts, newsbreaks. **Buys 6/year.** Length: 250-500 words. **Pays $50-100.**

Tips "Have an understanding of the skin care industry."

BEVERAGES & BOTTLING

$ $ BAR & BEVERAGE BUSINESS MAGAZINE

Mercury Publications, Ltd., 1839 Inkster Blvd., Winnipeg MB R2X 1R3 Canada. (204)954-2085. Fax: (204)954-2057. E-mail: editorial@mercury.mb.ca. Website: www.barandbeverage.com. Editor: Kelly Gray. **Contact:** Kristi Balon, editorial production manager. **33% freelance written.** Bimonthly magazine providing information on the latest trends, happenings, buying-selling of beverages and product merchandising. Estab. 1998. Circ. 16,077. Pays 30-45 days from receipt of invoice. Byline given. Offers 33% kill fee. Buys all rights. Submit seasonal material 3 months in advance. Accepts simultaneous submissions. Sample copy and writer's guidelines free or by e-mail.

• Does not accept queries for specific stories. Assigns stories to Canadian writers.

Nonfiction How-to (making a good drink, training staff, etc.), interview/profile. Industry reports, profiles on companies. Query with published clips. Length: 500-9,000 words. **Pays 25-35¢/word.** Sometimes pays expenses of writers on assignment.

Photos State availability with submission. Reviews negatives, transparencies, 3×5 prints, JPEG, EPS or TIFF files. Buys all rights. Negotiates payment individually. Captions required.

Columns/Departments Out There (bar & bev news in various parts of the country), 100-500 words. Query. **Pays $0-100.**

$BEER, WINE & SPIRITS BEVERAGE RETAILER

The Marketing & Merchandising Magazine for Off-Premise Innovators, Oxford Publishing Co., 307 W. Jackson Ave., Oxford MS 38655-2154. (662)236-5510. Fax: (662)236-5541. E-mail: brenda@oxpub.com. Website: www. beverage-retailer.com. **Contact:** Brenda Owen, editor. **2-5% freelance written.** Magazine published 6 times a year covering alcohol beverage retail industry (off-premise). "Our readership of off-premise beverage alcohol retailers (owners and operators of package liquor stores, wine cellars, beer barns, etc.) appreciates our magazine's total focus on helping them increase their revenue and profits. We particulary emphasize stories on retailers' own ideas and efforts to market their products and their stores' images." Estab. 1997. Circ. 20,000. **Pays on acceptance.** Publishes ms an average of 7 months after acceptance. Byline given. Buys first North American serial rights. Editorial lead time 6 months. Submit seasonal material 6 months in advance. Accepts queries by mail. Responds in 2 weeks to queries; 1 month to mss. Sample copy for $5 or online at website.

⊶ Break in with a "successful retailer" profile or product feature that shows your grasp on moneymaking tips, marketing, and merchandising ideas.

Nonfiction General interest, how-to, interview/profile, industry commentary. "No book reviews; no product stories narrowly focused on one manufacturer's product; no general stories on beverage categories (scotch, tequila, etc.) unless trend-oriented." **Buys 4-6 mss/year.** Query with published clips or send complete ms. Length: 350-800 words. **Pays $100 for assigned articles.** Pays phone expenses only of writers on assignment.

Photos State availability of or send photos with submission. Reviews contact sheets, transparencies (all sizes), prints (all sizes). Buys all rights. Offers no additional payment for photos accepted with ms on most features. Negotiates payment individually on cover stories and major features. Captions, identification of subjects, model releases required.

Columns/Departments Successful Retailers (What business practice, unique facility feature, or other quality makes this business so successful?), 350-400 words; Marketing & Merchandising (brief stories of innovative efforts by retailers—displays, tastings and other events, celebrity appearances, special sales, etc.) 50-350 words. Query with published clips or send complete ms. **Pays $25-100.**

Tips "Rely solely on off-premise beverage alcohol retailers (and, in some cases, leading industry experts) as your sources. Make certain every line of your story focuses on telling the reader how to improve his business' revenue and profits. Keep your story short, and include colorful, intelligent, and concise retailer quotes. Include a few relevant and irresistible statistics. We particularly appreciate trend or analysis stories when we get them early enough to publish them in a timely fashion."

$$PATTERSON'S CALIFORNIA BEVERAGE JOURNAL

Interactive Color, Inc., 4910 San Fernando Rd., Glendale CA 91204. (818)291-1125. Fax: (818)547-4607. E-mail: mmay@interactivecolor.com. Website: www.beveragelink.com. **Contact:** Meridith May, associate publisher/senior editor. **25% freelance written.** Monthly magazine covering the alcohol, beverage, and wine industries. "*Patterson's* reports on the latest news in product information, merchandising, company appointments, developments in the wine industry, and consumer trends. Our readers can be informed, up-to-date and confident in their purchasing decisions." Estab. 1962. Circ. 25,000. Byline given. Offers negotiable kill fee. Editorial lead time 1 month. Submit seasonal material 1 month in advance. Accepts queries by mail, e-mail, fax. Sample copy and writer's guidelines free.

Nonfiction Interview/profile, new product, market reports. "No consumer-oriented articles or negative slants on industry as a whole." **Buys 200 mss/year.** Query with published clips. Length: 500-750 words. **Pays $60-200.**

Photos State availability with submission. Reviews transparencies. Buys all rights. Offers no additional payment for photos accepted with ms. Captions, identification of subjects required.

Columns/Departments Query with published clips.

$$$VINEYARD & WINERY MANAGEMENT

P.O. Box 2358, Windsor CA 95492-2358. (707)836-6820. Fax: (707)836-6825. E-mail: gparnell@vwm-online.com. Website: www.vwm-online.com. **Contact:** Graham Parnell, managing editor. **70% freelance written.** Bimonthly magazine of professional importance to grape growers, winemakers, and winery sales and business people. Estab. 1975. Circ. 6,500. Pays on publication. Byline given. Buys first North American serial, simultaneous rights. Accepts queries by e-mail. Responds in 3 weeks to queries; 1 month to mss. Sample copy for free. Writer's guidelines for #10 SASE.

Nonfiction Subjects are technical in nature and explore the various methods people in these career paths use to succeed and the equipment and techniques they use successfully. Business articles and management topics are also featured. The audience is national with western dominance. How-to, interview/profile, new product, technical. **Buys 30 mss/year.** Query. Length: 1,800-5,000 words. **Pays $30-1,000.** Sometimes pays expenses of writers on assignment.

Photos State availability with submission. Reviews contact sheets, negatives, transparencies, digital photos.

Black & white often purchased for $20 each to accompany story material; 35mm and/or 4×5 transparencies for $50 and up; 6/year of vineyard and/or winery scene related to story. Captions, identification of subjects required.

Tips "We're looking for long-term relationships with authors who know the business and write well. Electronic submissions required; query for formats."

$ $ WINES & VINES MAGAZINE

The Authoritative Voice of the Grape and Wine Industry Since 1919, Wine Communications Group, 1800 Lincoln Ave., San Rafael CA 94901. (415)453-9700. Fax: (415)453-2517. E-mail: edit@winesandvines.com. Website: www.winesandvines.com. **50% freelance written.** Monthly magazine covering the international winegrape and winemaking industry. "Since 1919 *Wines & Vines Magazine* has been the authoritative voice of the wine and grape industry—from prohibition to phylloxera, we have covered it all. Our paid circulation reaches all 50 states and many foreign countries. Because we are intended for the trade—including growers, winemakers, winery owners, wholesalers, restauranteurs, and serious amateurs—we accept more technical, informative articles. We do not accept wine reviews, wine country tours, or anything of a wine consumer nature." Estab. 1919. Circ. 5,000. Pays 30 days after acceptance. Publishes ms an average of 3 months after acceptance. Byline given. Buys first, electronic rights. Editorial lead time 2 months. Submit seasonal material 4 months in advance. Accepts queries by e-mail. Responds in 2-3 weeks to queries. Sample copy for $5. Writer's guidelines free.

Nonfiction Interview/profile, new product, technical. No wine reviews, wine country travelogues, 'lifestyle' pieces, or anything aimed at wine consumers. "Our readers are professionals in the field." **Buys 60 mss/year.** Query with published clips. Length: 1,000-2,000 words. **Pays flat fee of $500 for assigned articles.**

Photos Prefers JPEG files (JPEG, 300 dpi minimum). Can use high-quality prints. State availability of or send photos with submission. Does not pay for photos submitted by author, but will give photo credit. Captions, identification of subjects required.

BOOK & BOOKSTORE

$ $ FOREWORD MAGAZINE

ForeWord Magazine, Inc., 129½ E. Front St., Traverse City MI 49684. (231)933-3699. Fax: (231)933-3899. E-mail: alex@forewordmagazine.com. Website: www.forewordmagazine.com. **Contact:** Alex Moore, managing editor. **95% freelance written.** Bimonthly magazine covering independent and university presses for booksellers and librarians with articles, news, book reviews. Estab. 1998. Circ. 8,000. Pays 2 months after publication. Publishes ms an average of 2-3 months after acceptance. Byline given. Buys all rights. Editorial lead time 3-4 months. Submit seasonal material 5 months in advance. Accepts queries by mail, e-mail. Responds in 1 month to queries; 1 month to mss. Sample copy for $10 and 8½×11 SASE with $1.50 postage.

Nonfiction Reviews, 85% nonfiction and 15% fiction/poetry. Query with published clips. Length: 400-1,500 words. **Pays $25-200 for assigned articles.**

Tips "Be knowledgeable about the needs of booksellers and librarians—remember we are an industry trade journal, not a how-to or consumer publication. We review books prior to publication, so book reviews are always assigned—but send us a note telling subjects you wish to review, as well as a résumé."

THE HORN BOOK MAGAZINE

The Horn Book, Inc., 56 Roland St., Suite 200, Boston MA 02129. (617)628-0225. Fax: (617)628-0882. E-mail: magazine@hbook.com. Website: www.hbook.com. **Contact:** Roger Sutton, editor-in-chief. **75% freelance written.** Prefers to work with published/established writers. Bimonthly magazine covering children's literature for librarians, booksellers, professors, teachers and students of children's literature. Estab. 1924. Circ. 16,000. Pays on publication. Publishes ms an average of 4 months after acceptance. Byline given. Submit seasonal material 6 months in advance. Accepts queries by mail, e-mail, fax. Accepts simultaneous submissions. Responds in 3 months to queries. Sample copy and writer's guidelines online.

Nonfiction Interested in seeing strong, authoritative pieces about children's books and contemporary culture. Writers should be familiar with the magazine and its contents. Interview/profile (children's book authors and illustrators), topics of interest to the children's bookworld. **Buys 20 mss/year.** Query or send complete ms. Length: 1,000-2,800 words. **Pays honorarium upon publication.**

Tips "Writers have a better chance of breaking into our publication with a query letter on a specific article they want to write."

BRICK, GLASS & CERAMICS

$ $ GLASS MAGAZINE

For the Architectural Glass Industry, National Glass Association, 8200 Greensboro Dr., Suite 302, McLean VA 22102. (866)342-5642. Fax: (703)442-0630. E-mail: editorialinfo@glass.org. Website: www.glass.org. **Contact:**

Nancy Davis, editor-in-chief. **10% freelance written.** Prefers to work with published/established writers. Monthly magazine covering the architectural glass industry. Circ. 23,291. **Pays on acceptance.** Publishes ms an average of 6 months after acceptance. Byline given. Kill fee varies. Buys first rights. Accepts queries by mail, e-mail, fax. Responds in 2 months to mss. Sample copy for $5 and 9×12 SAE with 10 first-class stamps.

Nonfiction Interview/profile (of various glass businesses; profiles of industry people or glass business owners), new product, technical (about glazing processes). **Buys 5 mss/year.** Query with published clips. Length: 1,000 words minimum. **Pays $150-300 for assigned articles.**

Photos State availability with submission.

Tips *Glass Magazine* is doing more inhouse writing; freelance cut by half. "Do not send in general glass use stories. Research the industry first, then query."

$ STAINED GLASS

Stained Glass Association of America, 10009 E. 62nd St., Raytown MO 64133. (800)438-9581. Fax: (816)737-2801. E-mail: sgaa@kcnet.com. Website: www.stainedglass.org. **70% freelance written.** Quarterly magazine. "Since 1906, *Stained Glass* has been the official voice of the Stained Glass Association of America. As the oldest, most respected stained glass publication in North America, *Stained Glass* preserves the techniques of the past as well as illustrates the trends of the future. This vital information, of significant value to the professional stained glass studio, is also of interest to those for whom stained glass is an avocation or hobby." Estab. 1906. Circ. 8,000. Pays on publication. Publishes ms an average of 1 year after acceptance. Byline given. Buys one-time rights. Editorial lead time 6 months. Submit seasonal material 8 months in advance. Accepts queries by mail, e-mail, fax. Responds in 3 months to queries. Sample copy and writer's guideline free.

Oᴈ Break in with "excellent photography and in-depth stained glass architectural knowledge."

Nonfiction Strong need for technical and how to create architectural type stained glass. Glass etching, use of etched glass in stained glass compositions, framing. How-to, humor, interview/profile, new product, opinion, photo feature, technical. **Buys 9 mss/year.** Query or send complete ms but must include photos or slides—very heavy on photos. **Pays $125/illustrated article; $75/nonillustrated.**

Reprints Accepts previously published submissions from nonstained glass publications only. Send tearsheet of article. Payment negotiable.

Photos Send photos with submission. Reviews 4×5 transparencies, send slides with submission. Buys one-time rights. Pays $75 for non-illustrated. Pays $125, plus 3 copies for line art or photography. Identification of subjects required.

Columns/Departments Teknixs (technical, how-to, stained and glass art), word length varies by subject. **Buys 4 mss/year.** Query or send complete ms, but must be illustrated.

Tips "We need more technical articles. Writers should be extremely well versed in the glass arts. Photographs are extremely important and must be of very high quality. Submissions without photographs or illustrations are seldom considered unless something special and writer states that photos are available. However, prefer to see with submission."

$ $ US GLASS, METAL & GLAZING

Key Communications, Inc., P.O. Box 569, Garrisonville VA 22463. (540)720-5584. Fax: (540)720-5687. E-mail: info@usglassmag.com. Website: www.usglassmag.com. **25% freelance written.** Monthly magazine for companies involved in the flat glass trades. Estab. 1966. Circ. 27,000. Pays on publication. Publishes ms an average of 3 months after acceptance. Byline given. Buys all rights. Editorial lead time 3 months. Submit seasonal material 2 months in advance. Accepts queries by mail, e-mail, fax. Accepts simultaneous submissions. Responds in 1 month to queries; 2 months to mss. Sample copy and writer's guidelines online.

Nonfiction Buys 12 mss/year. Query with published clips. **Pays $300-600 for assigned articles.** Sometimes pays expenses of writers on assignment.

Photos State availability with submission. Reviews contact sheets. Buys first North American rights. Offers no additional payment for photos accepted with ms. Captions, identification of subjects required.

BUILDING INTERIORS

$ $ PWC

Painting & Wallcovering Contractor, Finan Publishing Co., Inc., 107 W. Pacific Ave., St. Louis MO 63119. (314)961-6644. Fax: (314)961-4809. E-mail: jbeckner@finan.com. Website: www.paintstore.com. **Contact:** Jeff Beckner, editor. **90% freelance written.** Bimonthly magazine. "*PWC* provides news you can use: information helpful to the painting and wallcovering contractor in the here and now." Estab. 1928. Circ. 30,000. Pays 1 month after acceptance. Publishes ms an average of 1 month after acceptance. Byline given. Offers variable kill fee. Buys first North American serial rights. Editorial lead time 2 months. Submit seasonal material 2 months in advance. Accepts simultaneous submissions. Responds in 2 weeks to queries. Sample copy for free.

Nonfiction Essays, exposé, how-to (painting and wallcovering), interview/profile, new product, opinion, personal experience. **Buys 40 mss/year.** Query with published clips. Length: 1,500-2,500 words. **Pays $300 minimum.** Pays expenses of writers on assignment.

Reprints Send photocopy and information about when and where the material previously appeared. Negotiates payment.

Photos State availability of or send photos with submission. Reviews contact sheets, negatives, transparencies, digital prints. Buys all rights. Offers no additional payment for photos accepted with ms. Identification of subjects required.

Columns/Departments Anything of interest to the small businessman, 1,250 words. **Buys 2 mss/year.** Query with published clips. **Pays $50-100.**

Tips "We almost always buy on an assignment basis. The way to break in is to send good clips, and I'll try and give you work."

$ $ QUALIFIED REMODELER

The Business Management Tool for Professional Remodelers, Cygnus Business Media, 1233 Janesville Ave., Fort Atkinson WI 53538. E-mail: patrick.otoole@cygnusb2b.com. Website: www.qualifiedremodeler.com. Editor-in-Chief: Patrick O'Toole. **Contact:** Chaya Chang, managing editor. **5% freelance written.** Monthly magazine covering residential remodeling. Estab. 1975. Circ. 83,500. **Pays on acceptance.** Publishes ms an average of 1 month after acceptance. Byline given. Buys all rights. Editorial lead time 3 months. Submit seasonal material 2 months in advance. Accepts queries by mail, e-mail, fax, phone. Sample copy online.

Nonfiction How-to (business management), new product, photo feature, best practices articles, innovative design. **Buys 12 mss/year.** Query with published clips. Length: 1,200-2,500 words. **Pays $300-600 for assigned articles; $200-400 for unsolicited articles.** Sometimes pays expenses of writers on assignment.

Photos Send photos with submission. Reviews negatives, transparencies. Buys one-time rights. Negotiates payment individually.

Columns/Departments Query with published clips. **Pays $400.**

▣ The online version contains material not found in the print edition.

Tips "We focus on business management issues faced by remodeling contractors. For example, sales, marketing, liability, taxes, and just about any matter addressing small business operation."

$ $ $ $ REMODELING

HanleyWood, LLC, One Thomas Circle NW, Suite 600, Washington DC 20005. (202)452-0800. Fax: (202)785-1974. E-mail: chartman@hanleywood.com. Website: www.remodelingmagazine.com. Editor-in-Chief: Sal Alfano. **Contact:** Christine Hartman, managing editor. **10% freelance written.** Monthly magazine covering residential and light commercial remodeling. "We cover the best new ideas in remodeling design, business, construction and products." Estab. 1985. Circ. 80,000. Pays on publication. Publishes ms an average of 3 months after acceptance. Byline given. Offers 5¢/word kill fee. Buys first North American serial rights. Accepts queries by mail, e-mail, fax. Sample copy for free.

Nonfiction Interview/profile, new product, technical, small business trends. **Buys 6 mss/year.** Query with published clips. Length: 250-1,000 words. **Pays $1/word.** Sometimes pays expenses of writers on assignment.

Photos State availability with submission. Reviews 4×5 transparencies, slides, 8×10 prints. Buys one-time rights. Offers $25-125/photo. Captions, identification of subjects, model releases required.

▣ The online magazine carries original content not included in the print edition. Contact: John Butterfield, online editor.

Tips "We specialize in service journalism for remodeling contractors. Knowledge of the industry is essential."

$ $ WALLS & CEILINGS

2401 W. Big Beaver Rd., Suite 700, Troy MI 48084. (248)244-6244. Fax: (248)362-5103. E-mail: morettin@bnpmedia.com. Website: www.wconline.com. **Contact:** Nick Moretti, editor. **20% freelance written.** Monthly magazine for contractors involved in lathing and plastering, drywall, acoustics, fireproofing, curtain walls, and movable partitions, together with manufacturers, dealers, and architects. Estab. 1938. Circ. 30,000. Pays on publication. Publishes ms an average of 6 months after acceptance. Byline given. Buys all rights. Submit seasonal material 4 months in advance. Accepts queries by mail, e-mail, phone. Accepts simultaneous submissions. Responds in 6 months to queries. Sample copy for 9×12 SAE with $2 postage. Writer's guidelines for #10 SASE.

o╼ Break in with technical expertise in drywall, plaster, stucco.

Nonfiction How-to (drywall and plaster construction and business management), technical. **Buys 20 mss/year.** Query or send complete ms. Length: 1,000-1,500 words. **Pays $50-500.** Sometimes pays expenses of writers on assignment.

Reprints Send tearsheet or photocopy with rights for sale noted and information about when and where the material previously appeared. Pays 50% of the amount paid for an original article.

Photos Send photos with submission. Reviews contact sheets, negatives, transparencies, prints. Buys one-time rights. Captions, identification of subjects required.

⬛ The online magazine carries original content not included in the print edition.

BUSINESS MANAGEMENT

$ $ $ $ ACROSS THE BOARD

The Conference Board Magazine, The Conference Board, 845 Third Ave., New York NY 10022. (212)759-0900. Fax: (212)836-3828. Website: www.acrosstheboardmagazine.com. **Contact:** Al Vogl, editor. **60% freelance written.** Bimonthly magazine covering business—focuses on higher management. "*Across the Board* is a non-profit magazine of ideas and opinions for leaders in business, government, and other organizations. The editors present business perspectives on timely issues, including management practices, foreign policy, social issues, and science and technology. *Across the Board* is neither an academic business journal nor a 'popular' manual. That means we aren't interested in highly technical articles about business strategy. It also means we don't publish oversimple 'how-to' articles. We are an idea magazine, but the ideas should have practical overtones. We let *Forbes, Fortune* and *Business Week* do most of the straight reporting, while we do some of the critical thinking; that is, we let writers explore the implications of the news in depth. *Across the Board* tries to provide different angles on important topics, and to bring to its readers' attention issues that they might otherwise not devote much thought to." Circ. 30,000. Pays on publication. Publishes ms an average of 4 months after acceptance. Byline given. Offers 20% kill fee. Buys first rights. Editorial lead time 6 months. Submit seasonal material 6 months in advance. Accepts queries by mail, e-mail, fax. Accepts simultaneous submissions. Responds in 3 weeks to queries. Sample copy for free. Writer's guidelines online.

Nonfiction Book excerpts, essays, humor, opinion, personal experience. No new product information. **Buys 30 mss/year.** Query with published clips or send complete ms. Length: 500-4,000 words. **Pays $50-2,500.** Sometimes pays expenses of writers on assignment.

Photos State availability with submission. Reviews contact sheets. Buys one-time or all rights. Negotiates payment individually. Captions, identification of subjects required.

Tips "We emphasize the human side of organizational life at all levels. We're as concerned with helping managers who are 'lonely at the top' as with motivating workers and enhancing job satisfaction."

$ $ AMERICAN DRYCLEANER/COIN-OP/AMERICAN LAUNDRY NEWS

Crain Communications Inc., 500 N. Dearborn, Suite 1000, Chicago IL 60610. (312)337-7700. **20% freelance written.** Monthly tabloid covering drycleaning, coin laundry, coin car cleaning, institutional laundry. Estab. 1934. Circ. 25,000. Pays on publication. Publishes ms an average of 1 month after acceptance. Byline given. Offers 10% kill fee. Buys first, second serial (reprint), all rights. Editorial lead time 2 months. Submit seasonal material 2 months in advance. Accepts queries by mail, e-mail, fax, phone. Accepts simultaneous submissions. Responds in 1 month to queries; 4 months to mss. Sample copy for 6×9 SAE and 2 first-class stamps.

Nonfiction How-to (general biz, industry-specific), interview/profile, new product, personal experience, technical. No inspirational, consumer-geared. **Buys 12-15 mss/year.** Query. Length: 600-2,000 words. **Pays $50-500 for assigned articles; $25-250 for unsolicited articles.** Sometimes pays expenses of writers on assignment.

Photos State availability with submission. Reviews contact sheets, negatives, 4×5 or slide transparencies, 3×5-5×7 prints. Buys one-time rights. Negotiates payment individually. Identification of subjects required.

Columns/Departments General Business, 1,200 words. **Buys 72 mss/year.** Send complete ms. **Pays $50-150.**

Tips "Each magazine is geared toward small-business owners in these specific industries. Writers will find professional experience in the industry is a plus; general small-business articles are often used, but tailored to each magazine's audience."

Ⓝ $ $ ⬚ ASSOCIATION & MEETING DIRECTOR

Canada's Number One Association Management & Meeting Magazine, August Communications, 225-530 Century St., Winnipeg MB R3H 0Y4 Canada. (888)573-1136. Fax: (866)957-0217. E-mail: r.mcilroy@august.ca. Website: www.associationdirector.ca. **Contact:** Randal McIlroy, editor. **70% freelance written.** Bimonthly magazine covering association management and corporate meeting planners. "*Association & Meeting Director* is direct mailed to Canadian association executives and corporate meeting professionals. It has the aim of exploring both the Canadian corporate and association marketplace." Estab. 2000. Circ. 15,000. Pays 1 month after publication. Publishes ms an average of 2 months after acceptance. Byline given. Buys all rights. Editorial lead time 3 months. Submit seasonal material 3 months in advance. Accepts queries by mail, e-mail, fax. Responds in 1 week to queries. Sample copy and writer's guidelines free.

Nonfiction How-to, inspirational, interview/profile, new product, technical, travel. **Buys 18 mss/year.** Query with published clips. Length: 700-2,000 words. **Pays 20-40¢/word for assigned articles.**

Photos State availability with submission. Reviews GIF/JPEG files. Buys all rights. Negotiates payment individually. Identification of subjects required.

Columns/Departments Buys 12 mss/year. Query with published clips. **Pays 20-40¢/word.**

$ $ $ $ BEDTIMES

The Business Journal for the Sleep Products Industry, International Sleep Products Association, 501 Wythe St., Alexandria VA 22314-1917. (703)683-8371. E-mail: jpalm@sleepproducts.org. Website: www.sleepproducts.org. **Contact:** Julie Palm, editor-in-chief. **20-40% freelance written.** Monthly magazine covering the mattress manufacturing industry. "Our news and features are straightforward—we are not a lobbying vehicle for our association. No special slant." Estab. 1917. Circ. 3,700. **Pays on acceptance.** Publishes ms an average of 4 months after acceptance. Byline given. Buys first North American serial rights. Editorial lead time 2 months. Accepts queries by e-mail, fax. Accepts simultaneous submissions. Responds in 1 month to queries. Sample copy for $4. Writer's guidelines free for #10 SASE or by e-mail.

  O→ Break in with short news stories. "We also use freelancers for monthly features including Newsmakers, company and individual profiles, and other features."

Nonfiction "No pieces that do not relate to business in general or mattress industry in particular." **Buys 15-25 mss/year.** Query with published clips. Length: 500-2,500 words. **Pays 50¢-$1/word for short features; $2,000 for cover story.**

Photos State availability with submission. Buys one-time rights. Negotiates payment individually. Identification of subjects required.

Columns/Departments Millennium Milestones (companies marking anniversaries from 25-150 years), 1,000 words. Query with 3 published clips.

Tips "Cover topics have included annual industry forecast; physical expansion of industry facilities; e-commerce; flammability and home furnishings; the risks and rewards of marketing overseas; the evolving family business; the shifting workplace environment; and what do consumers really want?"

▉ CA MAGAZINE

Canadian Institute of Chartered Accountants, 277 Wellington St. W, Toronto ON M5V 3H2 Canada. (416)977-3222. Fax: (416)204-3409. E-mail: camagazineinfo@cica.ca. Website: www.camagazine.com. **Contact:** Christian Bellavance, editor-in-chief. **30% freelance written.** Magazine published 10 times/year covering accounting. "*CA Magazine* is the leading accounting publication in Canada and the preferred information source for chartered accountants and financial executives. It provides a forum for discussion and debate on professional, financial, and other business issues." Estab. 1911. Circ. 74,834. **Pays on acceptance.** Publishes ms an average of 3 months after acceptance. Byline given. Offers 30% kill fee. Buys all rights. Editorial lead time 4 months. Accepts queries by e-mail. Responds in 1 month to queries. Sample copy and writer's guidelines online.

Nonfiction Book excerpts, financial/accounting business. **Buys 30 mss/year.** Query. Length: 2,500-3,500 words. **Pays honorarium for chartered accountants; freelance rate varies.**

▉ CIO INSIGHT

Ziff-Davis Media, Inc., 28 E. 28th St., New York NY 10016. (212)503-3500. Fax: (212)503-5636. E-mail: editors@cioinsight-ziffdavis.com. Website: www.cioinsight.com. Editor-in-Chief: Ellen Pearlman. Managing Editor: Pat Perkowski. **Contact:** Editorial Assistant. Monthly magazine covering team management, wireless strategies, investment planning and profits, and Web-hosting security issues. "Written for senior-level executives with key interests in strategic information technology, including CIOs, chief technology officers and IS/IT/MIS vice presidents and managers." Accepts queries by e-mail. Accepts previously published material. Writer's guidelines online.

  ● No unsolicited mss.

Nonfiction "We welcome well-thought out story proposals from experienced journalists and experts in technology and business subjects. If you have a compelling and/or original story idea, you may send us your pitch via e-mail. We are particularly interested in case studies, trend and analysis articles, and ideas for whiteboards. Story pitches should be clear about the focus of the proposed article, why the topic is timely, and the key questions to be answered in the article."

$ $ CONTRACT MANAGEMENT

National Contract Management Association, 8260 Greensboro Dr., Suite 200, McLean VA 22102. (571)382-0082. Fax: (703)448-0939. E-mail: miedema@ncmahq.org. Website: www.ncmahq.org. **Contact:** Amy Miedema, director of communications. **10% freelance written.** Monthly magazine covering contract and business management. "Most of the articles published in *Contract Management (CM)* are written by members, although one does not have to be an NCMA member to be published in the magazine. Articles should concern some aspect of the contract management profession, whether at the level of a beginner or that of the advanced practitioner." Estab. 1960. Circ. 23,000. Pays on publication. Publishes ms an average of 3 months after acceptance. Byline given. Buys one-time rights. Editorial lead time 10 weeks. Submit seasonal material 3 months in advance. Accepts queries by mail, e-mail, fax, phone. Accepts previously published material. Accepts simultaneous submissions. Responds in 2 weeks to queries; 1 month to mss. Sample copy and writer's guidelines free.

Nonfiction Essays, general interest, how-to, humor, inspirational, new product, opinion, technical. No company or CEO profiles—please read a copy of publication before submitting. **Buys 6-10 mss/year.** Query with published clips. Length: 2,500-3,000 words. **Pays $300, association members paid in 3 copies.**

Reprints Accepts previously published submissions.

Photos State availability with submission. Buys one-time rights. Offers no additional payment for photos accepted with ms. Captions, identification of subjects required.

Columns/Departments Professional Development (self-improvement in business), 1,000-1,500 words; Back to Basics (basic how-tos and discussions), 1,500-2,000 words. **Buys 2 mss/year.** Query with published clips. **Pays $300.**

Tips "Query and read at least 1 issue. Visit website to better understand our audience."

CONVENTION SOUTH

P.O. Box 2267, Gulf Shores AL 36547. (251)968-5300. Fax: (251)968-4532. E-mail: info@conventionsouth.com. Website: www.conventionsouth.com. Editor: J. Talty O'Connor. **Contact:** Kristen McIntosh, executive editor. **50% freelance written.** Monthly business journal for meeting planners who plan events in the South. Topics relate to the meetings industry—how-to articles, industry news, destination spotlights. Estab. 1983. Circ. 16,000. Pays on publication. Publishes ms an average of 2 months after acceptance. Byline given. Buys first, second serial (reprint) rights. Editorial lead time 3 months. Submit seasonal material 4 months in advance. Accepts queries by mail, e-mail, fax. Accepts simultaneous submissions. Responds in 2 months to queries. Sample copy for free. Writer's guidelines for #10 SASE.

Nonfiction How-to (relative to meeting planning/travel), interview/profile, photo feature, technical, travel. **Buys 50 mss/year.** Query. Length: 750-1,250 words. **Payment negotiable.** Pays in contributor copies or other premiums if arranged in advance. Sometimes pays expenses of writers on assignment.

Reprints Send photocopy and information about when and where the material previously appeared. Payment negotiable.

Photos Send photos with submission. Reviews 5×7 prints. Buys one-time rights. Offers no additional payment for photos accepted with ms. Captions, identification of subjects required.

Columns/Departments How-to (related to meetings), 700 words. **Buys 12 mss/year.** Query with published clips. **Payment negotiable.**

Tips "Know who our audience is and make sure articles are appropriate for them."

$ $EXECUTIVE UPDATE

Greater Washington Society of Association Executives, Reagan Building & International Trade Center, 1300 Pennsylvania Ave. NW, Washington DC 20004. (202)326-9550. Fax: (202)326-0999. E-mail: general@centeronline.org. Website: www.executiveupdate.com. **60% freelance written.** Monthly magazine "exploring a broad range of association management issues and for introducing and discussing management and leadership philosophies. It is written for individuals at all levels of association management, with emphasis on senior staff and CEOs." Estab. 1979. Circ. 14,000. **Pays on acceptance.** Publishes ms an average of 6 months after acceptance. Byline given. Offers 20% kill fee. Buys first rights. Editorial lead time 3 months. Submit seasonal material 6 months in advance. Accepts queries by mail, e-mail, fax, phone. Accepts simultaneous submissions. Responds in 1 month to queries; 2 months to mss. Sample copy free. Writer's guidelines online.

Nonfiction How-to, humor, interview/profile, opinion, personal experience, travel, management and workplace issues. **Buys 24-36 mss/year.** Query with published clips. Length: 1,750-2,250 words. **Pays $500-700.** Pays expenses of writers on assignment.

Columns/Departments Intelligence (new ways to tackle day-to-day issues), 500-700 words; Off the Cuff (guest column for association executives). Query. **Pays $100-200.**

$ $EXPANSION MANAGEMENT MAGAZINE

Growth Strategies for Companies On the Move, Penton Media, Inc., 1300 E. 9th St., Cleveland OH 44114. (216)931-9578. Fax: (216)931-9145. Editor: Bill King. **Contact:** Ken Krizner, managing editor. **50% freelance written.** Monthly magazine covering economic development. Estab. 1986. Circ. 45,000. **Pays on acceptance.** Publishes ms an average of 1 month after acceptance. Byline given. Buys all rights, makes work-for-hire assignments. Editorial lead time 2 months. Sample copy for $7. Writer's guidelines free.

Nonfiction *"Expansion Management* presents articles and industry reports examining relocation trends, strategic planning, work force hiring, economic development agencies, and relocation consultants and state, province, and county reviews and profiles to help readers select future expansions and relocation sites." **Buys 120 mss/ year.** Query with published clips. Length: 800-1,200 words. **Pays $200-400 for assigned articles.** Sometimes pays expenses of writers on assignment.

Photos Send photos with submission. Buys one-time rights. Offers no additional payment for photos accepted with ms. Captions required.

Tips "Send clips first, then call me."

$ $ $EXPO

Atwood Publishing, LLC, 11600 College Blvd., Overland Park KS 66210. (913)469-1185. Fax: (913)469-0806. E-mail: dvasos@expoweb.com. Website: www.expoweb.com. **Contact:** Danica Tormohlen, editor-in-chief. **80% freelance written.** Magazine covering expositions. "*EXPO* is the information and education resource for the exposition industry. It is the only magazine dedicated exclusively to the people with direct responsibility for planning, promoting and operating trade and consumer shows. Our readers are show managers and their staff, association executives, independent show producers and industry suppliers. Every issue of *EXPO* contains in-depth, how-to features and departments that focus on the practical aspects of exposition management, including administration, promotion and operations." Pays on publication. Byline given. Offers 50% kill fee. Buys first North American serial rights. Editorial lead time 3 months. Accepts queries by mail, e-mail, fax. Responds in 3 weeks to queries. Sample copy for free. Writer's guidelines online.

Nonfiction How-to, interview/profile. Query with published clips. Length: 600-2,400 words. **Pays 50¢/word.** Pays expenses of writers on assignment.

Photos State availability with submission.

Columns/Departments Profile (personality profile), 650 words; Exhibitor Matters (exhibitor issues) and EXPO-Tech (technology), both 600-1,300 words. **Buys 10 mss/year.** Query with published clips.

Tips "*EXPO* now offers shorter features and departments, while continuing to offer in-depth reporting. Editorial is more concise, using synopsis, bullets and tidbits whenever possible. Every article needs sidebars, call-outs, graphs, charts, etc., to create entry points for readers. Headlines and leads are more provocative. And writers should elevate the level of shop talk, demonstrating that *EXPO* is the leader in the industry. We plan our editorial calendar about one year in advance, but we are always open to new ideas. Please query before submitting a story to *EXPO*—tell us about your idea and what our readers would learn. Include your qualifications to write about the subject and the sources you plan to contact."

$ $ $FAMILY BUSINESS

The Guide for Family Companies, Family Business Publishing Co., 1845 Walnut St., Philadelphia PA 19103. Fax: (215)405-6078. E-mail: bspector@familybusinessmagazine.com. Website: www.familybusinessmagazine.com. **Contact:** Barbara Spector, editor-in-chief. **25% freelance written.** Quarterly magazine covering family-owned companies. "Written expressly for family company owners and advisors. Focuses on business and human dynamic issues unique to family enterprises. Offers practical guidance and tried-and-true solutions for business stakeholders." Estab. 1989. Circ. 6,000. **Pays on acceptance.** Publishes ms an average of 3-6 months after acceptance. Byline given. Offers 30% kill fee. Buys first, electronic rights. Editorial lead time 4 months. Submit seasonal material 6 months in advance. Accepts queries by e-mail. Writer's guidelines online.

Nonfiction Book excerpts, how-to (family business related only), interview/profile, personal experience. No "articles that aren't specifically related to multi-generational family companies (no general business advice). No success stories—there must be an underlying family or business lesson." **No payment for articles written by** *Family Business* **advisors and other service providers. Buys 8 mss/year.** Query with published clips. Length: 2,000-2,500 words. **Pays $50-1,000 for articles written by freelance reporters.**

Photos State availability with submission. Buys one-time rights. Offers $50-500 maximum/shoot. Captions, identification of subjects, model releases required.

$HOMEBUSINESS JOURNAL

Steffen Publishing Co., 9584 Main St., Holland Patent NY 13354. Fax: (315)865-4000. E-mail: kim@homebusinessjournal.net. Website: www.homebusinessjournal.net. **Contact:** Joanne Steffen, managing editor. **90% freelance written.** Bimonthly magazine covering home businesses. "*HomeBusiness Journal* publishes material pertinent to home-based entrepreneurs." Circ. 25,000. Pays on publication. Publishes ms an average of 3-4 months after acceptance. Byline given. Buys first North American serial, second serial (reprint) rights. Editorial lead time 4-6 months. Submit seasonal material 4 months in advance. Accepts queries by mail, e-mail, fax. Accepts previously published material. Accepts simultaneous submissions. Responds in 1-2 months to queries. Sample copy for 9×12 SAE and 5 first-class stamps. Writer's guidelines online.

Nonfiction Book excerpts, general interest, how-to, humor, interview/profile, tax, marketing, finance as they

Trade Journals

apply to home business issues. No highly technical, "small," or "mid-size" business articles, advertorials. **Buys 50 mss/year.** Query. Length: 700-1,100 words. **Pays $75.**

Photos State availability with submission. Reviews 3×5 prints, GIF/JPEG files. Buys one-time rights. Offers no additional payment for photos accepted with ms. Identification of subjects, model releases required.

Columns/Departments Neighborhood CEO (profiling home-based entrepreneurs), 700 words. **Buys 24 mss/ year.** Query. **Pays $75.**

Tips "Visit our website to view articles previously published, have a good understanding of the issues home-based entrepreneurs face, and work on creative angles for queries."

$ $IN TENTS

The Magazine for the Tent Rental and Fabric Structure Industries, Industrial Fabrics Association International, 1801 County Rd. B W., Roseville MN 55113-4061. (651)225-6970. Fax: (651)225-6966. E-mail: intents@ifai.com. Website: www.ifai.com. **Contact:** Katie Harholdt, editor. **50% freelance written.** Quarterly magazine covering tent-rental and fabric structure industries. Estab. 1994. Circ. 12,000. **Pays on acceptance.** Publishes ms an average of 2 months after acceptance. Byline given. Buys all rights. Editorial lead time 3 months. Accepts queries by mail, e-mail, fax. Sample copy and writer's guidelines free.

    ○━ Break in with familiarity of tent rental, special events, tent manufacturing, and fabric structure industries, or lively, intelligent writing on technical subjects.

Nonfiction How-to, interview/profile, new product, photo feature, technical. **Buys 10-12 mss/year.** Query. Length: 800-2,000 words. **Pays $100-500.** Sometimes pays expenses of writers on assignment.

Photos State availability with submission. Reviews contact sheets, negatives, transparencies, prints, digital images. Buys one-time rights. Negotiates payment individually. Captions, identification of subjects, model releases required.

Tips "We look for lively, intelligent writing that makes technical subjects come alive."

$ $MAINEBIZ

Maine's Business News Source, Mainebiz Publications, Inc., 30 Milk St., 3rd Floor, Portland ME 04101. (207)761-8379. Fax: (207)761-0732. E-mail: mcavallaro@mainebiz.biz. Website: www.mainebiz.biz. **Contact:** Michaela Cavallaro, editor. **25% freelance written.** Biweekly tabloid covering business in Maine. "*Mainebiz* is read by business decision makers across the state. They look to the publication for business news and analysis." Estab. 1994. Circ. 13,000. Pays on publication. Publishes ms an average of 1 month after acceptance. Byline given. Offers 10% kill fee. Buys all rights. Editorial lead time 1 month. Submit seasonal material 2 months in advance. Accepts queries by mail, e-mail. Responds in 3 weeks to queries. Sample copy and writer's guidelines online.

Nonfiction "All pieces are reported and must comply with accepted journalistic standards. We only publish stories about business in Maine." Essays, exposé, interview/profile, business trends. Special issues: See website for editorial calendar. **Buys 50+ mss/year.** Query with published clips. Length: 500-2,500 words. **Pays $50-250.** Pays expenses of writers on assignment.

Photos State availability with submission. Reviews GIF/JPEG files. Buys one-time rights. Negotiates payment individually. Identification of subjects required.

Tips "Stories should be well thought out with specific relevance to Maine. Arts and culture-related queries are welcome, as long as there is a business angle. We appreciate unusual angles on business stories and regularly work with new freelancers. Please, no queries unless you have read the paper."

○ NORTHEAST EXPORT

A Magazine for New England Companies Engaged in International Trade, Commerce Publishing Company, Inc., P.O. Box 254, Northborough MA 01532. (508)351-2925. Fax: (508)351-6905. E-mail: editor@northeast-export.com. Website: www.northeast-export.com. **Contact:** Carlos Cunha, editor. **30% freelance written.** Bimonthly business-to-business magazine. "*Northeast Export* is the only publication directly targeted at New England's international trade community. All stories relate to issues affecting New England companies and feature only New England-based profiles and examples. Estab. 1997. Circ. 13,500. **Pays on acceptance.** Byline given. Offers 10% kill fee. Buys all rights. Editorial lead time 2 months. Accepts queries by mail, e-mail, fax. Sample copy for free.

Nonfiction How-to, interview/profile, travel, industry trends/analysis. **Buys 10-12 mss/year.** Query with published clips and SASE. *No unsolicited mss.* Length: 800-2,000 words. **Payment varies.**

Photos State availability of or send photos with submission. Reviews 2¼ transparencies, 5×7 prints. Buys one-time rights. Negotiates payment individually. Captions, identification of subjects, model releases required.

Tips "We're looking for writers with availability; the ability to write clearly about tough, sometimes very technical subjects; the fortitude to slog through industry jargon to get the story straight; a knowledge of international trade issues and/or New England transportation infrastructure. We're interested in freelancers with business writing and magazine experience, especially those with contacts in the New England manufacturing, finance, and transportation communities."

PROFESSIONAL COLLECTOR

Pohly & Partners, 27 Melcher St., 2nd Floor, Boston MA 02210-1516. (617)451-1700. Fax: (617)338-7767. E-mail: procollector@pohlypartners.com. Website: www.pohlypartners.com. **Contact:** Karen English, editor. **50% freelance written.** Magazine published 3 times/year for Western Union's Financial Services, Inc.'s Quick Collect Service, covering debt collection business/lifestyle issues. "We gear our articles directly to the debt collectors and their managers. Each issue offers features covering the trends and players, the latest technology, and other issues affecting the collections industry. It's all designed to help collectors be more productive and improve their performance." Estab. 1993. Circ. 161,000. Pays on publication. Byline given. Buys first North American serial rights. Editorial lead time 9 months. Submit seasonal material 9 months in advance. Accepts queries by mail, e-mail, fax. Sample copy for free. Writer's guidelines online.

Nonfiction General interest, how-to (tips on good collecting), humor, interview/profile, new product, book reviews. **Buys 10-15 mss/year.** Query with published clips. Length: 400-1,000 words. **Payment negotiable for assigned articles.** Sometimes pays expenses of writers on assignment.

Photos State availability with submission. Reviews contact sheets, 3×5 prints. Buys one-time rights. Negotiates payment individually. Captions, identification of subjects, model releases required.

Columns/Departments Industry Roundup (issues within industry), 500-1,000 words; Tips, 750-1,000 words; Q&A (questions & answers for collectors), 1,500 words. **Buys 15-20 mss/year.** Query with published clips. **Payment negotiable.**

Tips "Writers should be aware that *Professional Collector* is a promotional publication, and that its content must support the overall marketing goals of Western Union. It helps to have extensive insider knowledge about the debt collection industry."

$ $ PROGRESSIVE RENTALS

The Voice of the Rental-Purchase Industry, Association of Progressive Rental Organizations, 1504 Robin Hood Trail, Austin TX 78703. (800)204-2776. Fax: (512)794-0097. E-mail: jsherrier@aprovision.org. Website: www.aprovision.org. **Contact:** Julie Stephen Sherrier, editor. **50% freelance written.** Bimonthly magazine covering the rent-to-own industry. "*Progressive Rentals* is the only publication representing the rent-to-own industry and members of APRO. The magazine covers timely news and features affecting the industry, association activities, and member profiles. Awarded best 4-color magazine by the American Society of Association Executives in 1999." Estab. 1980. Circ. 5,500. **Pays on acceptance.** Publishes ms an average of 2 months after acceptance. Byline given. Offers 25% kill fee. Buys first North American serial rights. Editorial lead time 2 months. Submit seasonal material 4 months in advance. Accepts queries by mail, e-mail, fax, phone. Accepts simultaneous submissions. Responds in 1 month to queries; 2 months to mss. Sample copy for free.

Nonfiction Exposé, general interest, how-to, inspirational, interview/profile, technical, industry features. **Buys 12 mss/year.** Query with published clips. Length: 1,200-2,500 words. **Pays $150-700.** Sometimes pays expenses of writers on assignment.

RENTAL MANAGEMENT

American Rental Association, 1900 19th St., Moline IL 61265. (309)764-2475. Fax: (309)764-1533. E-mail: brian.alm@ararental.org. Website: www.rentalmanagementmag.com. **Contact:** Brian R. Alm, editor. **50% freelance written.** Monthly magazine for the equipment rental industry worldwide (*not* property, real estate, appliances, furniture, or cars), emphasizing management topics in particular but also marketing, merchandising, technology, etc. Estab. 1970. Circ. 18,500. **Pays on acceptance.** Publishes ms an average of 3 months after acceptance. Byline given. Buys first North American serial rights. Editorial lead time 2 months. Submit seasonal material 3 months in advance. Accepts queries by mail, e-mail, fax.

Nonfiction Business management and marketing. **Buys 25-30 mss/year.** Query with published clips. Does not respond to unsolicited work unless being considered for publication. Length: 600-1,500 words. **Payment negotiable.** Sometimes pays expenses of writers on assignment.

Reprints Send tearsheet or typed ms with rights for sale noted and information about when and where the material previously appeared.

Photos State availability with submission. Reviews contact sheets, negatives (35mm or 2¼), transparencies (any size), prints, digital (300 dpi EPS/TIFF/JPEG on e-mail or CD). Buys one-time rights. Negotiates payment individually. Identification of subjects required.

Tips "Show me you can write maturely, cogently, and fluently on management matters of direct and compelling interest to the small-business owner or manager in a larger operation; no sloppiness, no unexamined thoughts, no stiffness or affectation—genuine, direct, and worthwhile English. Knowledge of the equipment rental industry is a distinct plus."

$ $ RETAIL INFO SYSTEMS NEWS

Where Retail Management Shops for Technology, Edgell Communications, 4 Middlebury Blvd., Suite 1, Randolph NJ 07869. (973)252-0100. Fax: (973)252-9020. E-mail: jskorupa@edgellmail.com. Website: www.risnews .com. **Contact:** Joe Skorupa, editor. **65% freelance written.** Monthly magazine. "Readers are functional managers/executives in all types of retail and consumer goods firms. They are making major improvements in company operations and in alliances with customers/suppliers." Estab. 1988. Circ. 20,000. Pays on publication. Publishes ms an average of 2 months after acceptance. Byline sometimes given. Buys first North American serial, second serial (reprint), electronic, all rights. Editorial lead time 3 months. Submit seasonal material 3 months in advance. Accepts queries by mail. Sample copy online.

Nonfiction Essays, exposé, how-to, humor, interview/profile, technical. **Buys 80 mss/year.** Query with published clips. Length: 700-1,900 words. **Pays $600-1,200 for assigned articles.** Sometimes pays in contributor copies as negotiated. Sometimes pays expenses of writers on assignment.

Photos State availability of or send photos with submission. Buys one-time rights plus reprint, if applicable. Negotiates payment individually. Identification of subjects required.

Columns/Departments News/trends (analysis of current events), 150-300 words. **Buys 4 mss/year.** Query with published clips. **Pays $100-300.**

Tips "Case histories about companies achieving substantial results using advanced management practices and/ or advanced technology are best."

ⓝ SMALL TIMES

Big News in Small Tech, Small Times Media, LLC, 755 Phoenix Dr., Ann Arbor MI 48108. (734)994-1106. Fax: (734)994-1554. E-mail: news@smalltimes.com. Website: www.smalltimes.com. Editor: Candace Stuart. Bimonthly magazine. "*Small Times* magazine details technological advances, applications, and investment opportunities to help business leaders stay informed about the rapidly changing business of small tech, from biotech to defense, telecom to transportation." Estab. 2001. Circ. 26,000.

Nonfiction Query.

$ $ SMART BUSINESS

Smart Business Network, Inc., 835 Sharon Dr., Cleveland OH 44145. (440)250-7000. Fax: (440)250-7001. E-mail: dsklein@sbnonline.com. Website: www.sbnonline.com. **Contact:** Dustin S. Klein, executive editor. **5% freelance written.** Monthly business magazine with an audience made up of business owners and top decision makers. "*Smart Business* is one of the fastest growing national chains of regional management journals for corporate executives. Every issue delves into the minds of the most innovative executives in each of our regions to report on how market leaders got to the top and what strategies they use to stay there." Estab. 1989. Pays on publication. Publishes ms an average of 2 months after acceptance. Byline given. Offers 50% kill fee. Buys first North American serial, second serial (reprint), electronic rights. Editorial lead time 3 months. Submit seasonal material 3 months in advance. Accepts queries by mail, e-mail. Responds in 2 weeks to queries; 1 month to mss. Sample copy online. Writer's guidelines by e-mail.

  • Publishes local editions in Philadephia, Cincinnati, Detroit, Los Angeles, Broward/Palm Beach, Cleveland, Akron/Canton, Columbus, Pittsburgh, Atlanta, Chicago, and Indianapolis.

Nonfiction How-to, interview/profile. No breaking news or news features. **Buys 10-12 mss/year.** Query with published clips. Length: 1,150-2,000 words. **Pays $200-500.** Sometimes pays expenses of writers on assignment.

Reprints Accepts previously published submissions.

Photos State availability with submission. Reviews negatives, prints. Buys one-time, reprint, or Web rights. Offers no additional payment for photos accepted with ms. Identification of subjects required.

  The online magazine carries original content not found in the print edition. Contact: Dustin S. Klein, executive editor.

Tips "The best way to submit to *Smart Business* is to read us—either online or in print. Remember, our audience is made up of top level business executives and owners."

$ $ ⊘ SMART BUSINESS

Pittsburgh Edition, SBN, Inc., 11632 Frankstown Rd., #313, Pittsburgh PA 15235. (412)371-0451. Fax: (412)371-0452. E-mail: rmarano@sbnonline.com. Website: www.sbnonline.com. **Contact:** Ray Marano, editor. Monthly magazine. "We provide information and insight designed to help companies grow. Our focus is on local companies with 50 or more employees and their successful business strategies, with the ultimate goal of educating entrepreneurs. Our target audience is business owners and other top executives." Estab. 1994. Circ. 12,000. Editorial lead time 2 months.

Nonfiction How-to, interview/profile, opinion. "No basic profiles about 'interesting' companies or stories about companies with no ties to Pittsburgh."

Reprints Accepts reprints (mainly columns from business professionals).

Photos Reviews high resolution digital images.

Tips "We have articles localized to the Pittsburgh and surrounding areas. We write articles that will help our readers and educate them on a business strategy that another company may be using that can help their companies grow."

$ $ STAMATS MEETINGS MEDIA

550 Montgomery St., #750, San Francisco CA 94111. Fax: (415)788-0301. E-mail: editor@meetingsmedia.com. Website: www.meetingsmedia.com. Destinations Editor: Lori Tenny. **Contact:** Tyler Davidson, editor (columnists, cover stories). **75% freelance written.** Monthly tabloid covering meeting, event, and conference planning. Estab. 1986. Circ. *Meetings East* and *Meetings South* 22,000; *Meetings West* 26,000. Pays 1 month after publication. Publishes ms an average of 1 month after acceptance. Byline given. Buys first North American serial, electronic rights. Editorial lead time 3 months. Submit seasonal material 3 months in advance. Accepts queries by mail, e-mail, fax. Responds in 3 weeks to queries. Sample copy for 9 × 13 SAE and 5 first-class stamps. Editorial calendar online.

    ○┐ Queries and pitches are accepted on columns and cover stories only. All other assignments (Features and Site Inspections) are based exclusively on editorial calendar. Interested writers should send a résumé and 2-3 relevant clips, which must show familiarity with meetings/conventions topics, by e-mail.

Nonfiction How-to, travel (as it pertains to meetings and conventions). "No first-person fluff. We are a business magazine." **Buys 150 mss/year.** Query with published clips. Length: 1,200-2,000 words. **Pays $500 flat rate/ package.**

Photos State availability with submission. Buys one-time rights. Offers no additional payment for photos accepted with ms. Identification of subjects required.

Tips "We're always looking for freelance writers who are local to our destination stories. For Site Inspections, get in touch in late September or early October, when we usually have the following year's editorial calendar available."

$ THE STATE JOURNAL

West V Media Management, LLC, 13 Kanawha Blvd. W., Suite 100, Charleston WV 25302. (304)344-1630. E-mail: info@statejournal.com. Website: www.statejournal.com. **Contact:** Dan Page, editor. **30% freelance written.** "We are a weekly journal dedicated to providing stories of interest to the business community in West Virginia." Estab. 1984. Circ. 10,000. Pays on publication. Publishes ms an average of 3 weeks after acceptance. Byline given. Buys first rights. Submit seasonal material 4 months in advance. Accepts queries by mail, e-mail, fax. Sample copy and writer's guidelines for #10 SASE.

Nonfiction General interest, interview/profile, new product, (all business related). **Buys 400 mss/year.** Query. Length: 250-1,500 words. **Pays $50.** Sometimes pays expenses of writers on assignment.

Photos State availability with submission. Reviews contact sheets. Buys one-time rights. Offers $15/photo. Captions required.

Tips "Localize your work—mention West Virginia specifically in the article; or talk to business people in West Virginia."

$ $ SUSTAINABLE INDUSTRIES JOURNAL NW

Sustainable Industries Media, LLC, 3941 SE Hawthorne Blvd., Portland OR 97214. (503)226-7798. Fax: (503)226-7917. E-mail: brian@celilo.net. Website: www.sijournal.com. Associate Editor: April Streeter. **Contact:** Brian J. Back, editor. **20% freelance written.** Monthly magazine covering environmental innovation in business (Northwest focus). "We seek high quality, balanced reporting aimed at business readers. More compelling writing than is typical in standard trade journals." Estab. 2003. Circ. 2,500. Pays on publication. Publishes ms an average of 1-3 months after acceptance. Byline sometimes given. Not copyrighted. Buys all rights. Editorial lead time 1-2 months. Accepts queries by mail, e-mail, fax. Accepts simultaneous submissions.

Nonfiction General interest, how-to, interview/profile, new product, opinion, news briefs. Issue themes rotate on the following topics: Agriculture & Natural Resources; Green Building; Energy; Government; Manufacturing & Technology; Retail & Service; Transportation & Tourism—though all topics are covered in each issue. No prosaic essays or extra-long pieces. Query with published clips. Length: 500-1,500 words. **Pays $0-500.**

Photos State availability with submission. Reviews prints, GIF/JPEG files. Buys all rights. Offers no additional payment for photos accepted with ms.

Columns/Departments Business trade columns on specific industries, 500-1,000 words. Query.

$ $ ⊕ VENECONOMY/VENECONOMÍA

VenEconomía, Edificio Gran Sabana, Piso 1, Avendia Abraham Lincoln No. 174, Blvd. de Sabana Grande, Caracas Venezuela. (+58)212-761-8121. Fax: (+58)212-762-8160. E-mail: mercadeo@veneconomia.com.

Website: www.veneconomia.com; www.veneconomy.com. **70% freelance written.** Monthly business magazine covering business, political and social issues in Venezuela. "*VenEconomy*'s subscribers are mostly businesspeople, both Venezuelans and foreigners doing business in Venezuela. Some academics and diplomats also read our magazine. The magazine is published monthly both in English and Spanish—freelancers may query us in either language. Our slant is decidedly pro-business, but not dogmatically conservative. Development, human rights, political and environmental issues are covered from a business-friendly angle." Estab. 1983. Pays on publication. Publishes ms an average of 1 month after acceptance. Byline given. Offers 50% kill fee. Makes work-for-hire assignments. Editorial lead time 1-2 months. Submit seasonal material 1 month in advance. Accepts queries by e-mail. Accepts simultaneous submissions. Responds in 2 weeks to queries; 4 months to mss. Sample copy by e-mail.

Nonfiction Francisco Toro, political editor. Essays, exposé, interview/profile, new product, opinion. No first-person stories or travel articles. **Buys 50 mss/year.** Query. Length: 1,100-3,200 words. **Pays 10-15¢/word for assigned articles.** Sometimes pays expenses of writers on assignment.

Tips "A Venezuela tie-in is absolutely indispensable. While most of our readers are businesspeople, *VenEconomy* does not limit itself strictly to business-magazine fare. Our aim is to give our readers a sophisticated understanding of the main issues affecting the country as a whole. Stories about successful Venezuelan companies, or foreign companies doing business successfully with Venezuela are particularly welcome. Stories about the oil-sector, especially as it relates to Venezuela, are useful. Other promising topics for freelancers outside Venezuela include international trade and trade negotiations, US-Venezuela bilateral diplomatic relations, international investors' perceptions of business prospects in Venezuela, and international organizations' assessments of environmental, human rights, or democracy and development issues in Venezuela, etc. Both straight reportage and somewhat more opinionated pieces are acceptable, articles that straddle the borderline between reportage and opinion are best. Before querying, ask yourself: Would this be of interest to me if I was doing business in or with Venezuela?"

$ $ $ WORLD TRADE

"For the Executive with Global Vision", 23421 S. Pointe Dr., Suite 280, Laguna Hills CA 92653. (949)830-1340. Fax: (949)830-1328. E-mail: laras@worldtrademag.com. Website: www.worldtrademag.com. Editorial Director: Neil Shister. **Contact:** Lara Sowinski, associate editor. **50% freelance written.** Monthly magazine covering international business. Estab. 1988. Circ. 75,000. Pays on publication. Publishes ms an average of 1 month after acceptance. Byline given. Buys all rights. Editorial lead time 3 months. Accepts queries by mail, fax.

Nonfiction "See our editorial calendar online." Interview/profile, technical, market reports, finance, logistics. **Buys 40-50 mss/year.** Query with published clips. Length: 450-1,500 words. **Pays 50¢/word.**

Photos State availability with submission. Reviews transparencies, prints. Buys all rights. Negotiates payment individually. Identification of subjects required.

Columns/Departments International Business Services, 800 words; Shipping, Supply Chain Management, Logistics, 800 words; Software & Technology, 800 words; Economic Development (US, International), 800 words. **Buys 40-50 mss/year. Pays 50¢/word.**

Tips "We seek writers with expertise in their subject areas, as well as solid researching and writing skills. We want analysts more than reporters. We don't accept unsolicited manuscripts, and we don't want phone calls. Please read *World Trade* before sending a query."

CHURCH ADMINISTRATION & MINISTRY

THE AFRICAN AMERICAN PULPIT

P.O. Box 15347, Pittsburgh PA 15237. Phone/Fax: (412)364-1688. E-mail: info@theafricanamericanpulpit.com. Website: www.theafricanamericanpulpit.com. Editor: Katara Washington. Publisher: Martha Simmons. **Contact:** Victoria McGoey, project manager. **100% freelance written.** Quarterly magazine covering African American preaching. "*The African American Pulpit* is a quarterly journal that serves as a repository for the very best of African American preaching and provides practical and creative resources for persons in ministry." Estab. 1997. Circ. 3,000. Pays on publication. Publishes ms an average of 6 months after acceptance. Byline always given. Editorial lead time 9 months. Submit seasonal material 1 year in advance. Accepts queries by mail, e-mail, fax, phone. Accepts simultaneous submissions. Writer's guidelines online.

Nonfiction Sermons and articles relating to African American preaching and the African American Church. Book excerpts, essays, how-to (craft a sermon), inspirational, interview/profile, opinion, religious. **Buys 60 mss/year.** Send complete ms. Length: 1,500-3,000 words.

$ CHRISTIAN COMMUNICATOR

9731 N. Fox Glen Dr., #6F, Niles IL 60714-4222. (847)296-3964. Fax: (847)296-0754. E-mail: lin@wordprocomm unications.com. **Contact:** Lin Johnson, managing editor. **90% freelance written.** Monthly magazine covering

Christian writing and speaking. Circ. 4,000. Pays on publication. Publishes ms an average of 6-12 months after acceptance. Byline given. Buys first, second serial (reprint) rights. Editorial lead time 3 months. Submit seasonal material 9 months in advance. Accepts queries by e-mail. Responds in 4-6 weeks to queries; 4-6 weeks to mss. Sample copy for SAE and 5 first-class stamps. Writer's guidelines for SASE or by e-mail.

Nonfiction How-to, interview/profile, opinion, book reviews. **Buys 90 mss/year.** Query or send complete ms only by e-mail. Length: 300-1,000 words. **Pays $10.**

Columns/Departments Speaking, 650-1,000 words. **Buys 11 mss/year.** Query. **Pays $10.**

Poetry Free verse, light verse, traditional. **Buys 11 poems/year.** Submit maximum 3 poems. Contact: Gretchen Sousa, poetry editor (gretloriat@earthlink.net) Length: 4-20 lines. **Pays $5.**

Fillers Anecdotes, short humor. **Buys 10-30/year.** Length: 50-300 words. **Pays cassette tape.**

Tips "We primarily use 'how to' articles and personality features on experienced writers and editors. However, we're willing to look at any other pieces geared to the writing life."

$CHURCH EDUCATOR

Educational Ministries, Inc., 165 Plaza Dr., Prescott AZ 86303. (928)771-8601. Fax: (928)771-8621. E-mail: edmin2@aol.com. **Contact:** Linda Davidson, editor. **95% freelance written.** Monthly magazine covering resources for Christian educators. "*Church Educator* has programming ideas for the Christian educator in the mainline Protestant church. We are *not* on the conservative, fundamental side theologically, so slant articles to the liberal side. Programs should offer lots of questions and not give pat answers." Estab. 1978. Circ. 2,500. Pays 60 days after publication. Publishes ms an average of 2 months after acceptance. Byline given. Buys first rights. Editorial lead time 3 months. Submit seasonal material 7 months in advance. Accepts queries by mail, e-mail, fax, phone. Accepts simultaneous submissions. Responds in 2 weeks to queries; 4 months to mss. Sample copy for 9×12 SAE and 4 first-class stamps. Writer's guidelines free.

Nonfiction How-to, religious. Special issues: How to recruit volunteers; Nurturing faith development of children. No testimonials. **Buys 200 mss/year.** Send complete ms. Length: 500-2,000 words. **Pays 3¢/word.**

Fiction Religious. "No 'How God Saved My Life' or 'How God Answers Prayers.'" **Buys 10 mss/year.** Send complete ms. Length: 500-1,500 words. **Pays 3¢/word.**

Tips "We are always looking for material on the seasons of the church year: Advent, Lent, Pentecost, Epiphany. Write up a program for one of those seasons directed toward children, youth, adults or intergenerational. We added a Worship section, and are looking for material in that area."

N $THE CLERGY JOURNAL

Personal and Professional Development for Pastors and Church Administrators, Logos Productions, Inc., 6160 Carmen Ave. E., Inner Grove Heights MN 55076-4422. E-mail: editorial@logosstaff.com. Website: www.logosproductions.com. Editor: Rebecca Grothe. **Contact:** *The Clergy Journal.* **98% freelance written.** Magazine published 9 times/year covering articles for continuing education and practical help for Christian clergy who are currently serving congregations. "The focus of *The Clergy Journal* is personal and professional development for clergy. Each issue focuses on a current topic related to ministers and the church, and also includes preaching illustrations, sermons, and worship aids based on the Revised Common Lectionary. There is an insert in each issue on financial management topics. Most readers are from mainline Protestant traditions, especially Methodist, Presbyterian, Lutheran, and United Church of Christ." Estab. 1924. Circ. 6,000. Pays on publication. Publishes ms an average of 9 months after acceptance. Byline given. Buys first rights, makes work-for-hire assignments. Editorial lead time 4 months. Submit seasonal material 9 months in advance. Accepts queries by e-mail. Responds in 2 weeks to queries; 2 months to mss. Sample copy for free. Writer's guidelines by e-mail.

Nonfiction "We are seeking articles that address current issues of interest to Christian clergy; emphasis on practical help for parish pastors." Religious. **Buys 90 mss/year.** Query or send complete ms. Length: 1,200-1,500 words. **Pays $125 for assigned articles.**

Tips "Here are my 4 'pet peeves' as an editor: 1. Manuscripts that are over the word count. 2. Manuscripts that do not respect the reader. 3. Manuscripts that are not well organized. 4. Manuscripts that do not have an appropriate 'human touch.'"

$CREATOR MAGAZINE

Bimonthly Magazine of Balanced Music Ministries, P.O. Box 480, Healdsburg CA 95448. (707)837-9071. E-mail: creator@creatormagazine.com. Website: www.creatormagazine.com. **Contact:** Rod Ellis, editor. **35% freelance written.** Bimonthly magazine. "Most readers are church music directors and worship leaders. Content focuses on the spectrum of worship styles from praise and worship to traditional to liturgical. All denominations subscribe. Articles on worship, choir rehearsal, handbells, children's/youth choirs, technique, relationships, etc." Estab. 1978. Circ. 6,000. Pays on publication. Publishes ms an average of 3 months after acceptance. Byline given. Buys first, one-time, second serial (reprint) rights. Occasionally buys no rights. Editorial lead time 3 months. Submit seasonal material 4 months in advance. Accepts queries by mail. Accepts simultaneous submissions. Sample copy for 9×12 SAE and 5 first-class stamps. Writer's guidelines free.

Nonfiction Essays, how-to (be a better church musician, choir director, rehearsal technician, etc.), humor (short personal perspectives), inspirational, interview/profile (call first), new product (call first), opinion, personal experience, photo feature, religious, technical (choral technique). Special issues: July/August is directed toward adult choir members, rather than directors. **Buys 20 mss/year.** Query or send complete ms. Length: 1,000-10,000 words. **Pays $30-75 for assigned articles; $30-60 for unsolicited articles.** Pays expenses of writers on assignment.

Photos State availability of or send photos with submission. Reviews negatives, 8×10 prints. Buys one-time rights. Offers no additional payment for photos accepted with ms. Captions required.

Columns/Departments Hints & Humor (music ministry short ideas, cute anecdotes, ministry experience), 75-250 words; Inspiration (motivational ministry stories), 200-500 words; Children/Youth (articles about specific choirs), 1,000-5,000 words. **Buys 15 mss/year.** Query or send complete ms. **Pays $20-60.**

The online magazine carries original content not found in the print edition.

Tips "Request guidelines and stick to them. If theme is relevant and guidelines are followed, we'll probably publish your article."

$ $GROUP MAGAZINE

Group Publishing, Inc., 1515 Cascade Ave., Loveland CO 80538. (970)669-3836. Fax: (970)292-4360. E-mail: greditor@grouppublishing.com. Website: www.groupmag.com. Editor: Rick Lawrence. **Contact:** Kathy Dieterich, assistant editor. **50% freelance written.** Bimonthly magazine for Christian youth workers. *"Group* is the interdenominational magazine for leaders of Christian youth groups. *Group*'s purpose is to supply ideas, practical help, inspiration, and training for youth leaders." Estab. 1974. Circ. 55,000. **Pays on acceptance.** Byline sometimes given. Buys all rights. Editorial lead time 4 months. Submit seasonal material 5 months in advance. Accepts queries by mail, e-mail, fax. Responds in 6 weeks to queries; 2 months to mss. Sample copy for $2, plus 10×12 SAE and 3 first-class stamps. Writer's guidelines online.

Nonfiction Inspirational, personal experience, religious. No fiction. **Buys 100 mss/year.** Query. Length: 175-2,000 words. **Pays $125-350.** Sometimes pays expenses of writers on assignment.

Columns/Departments Try This One (short ideas for group use), 300 words; Hands-On-Help (tips for youth leaders), 175 words; Strange But True (profiles remarkable youth ministry experience), 500 words. **Pays $40.**

$ $THE JOURNAL OF ADVENTIST EDUCATION

General Conference of SDA, 12501 Old Columbia Pike, Silver Spring MD 20904-6600. (301)680-5075. Fax: (301)622-9627. E-mail: rumbleb@gc.adventist.org. Website: education.gc.adventist.org/jae. **Contact:** Beverly J. Robinson-Rumble, editor. Bimonthly (except skips issue in summer) professional journal covering teachers and administrators in Seventh Day Adventist school systems. Estab. 1939. Circ. 7,500. Pays on publication. Publishes ms an average of 1 year after acceptance. Byline given. Buys first rights. Editorial lead time 1 year. Accepts queries by mail, e-mail, fax, phone. Responds in 6 weeks to queries; 4 months to mss. Sample copy for 10×12 SAE and 5 first-class stamps. Writer's guidelines free.

Nonfiction Theme issues have assigned authors. Book excerpts, essays, how-to (education-related), personal experience, photo feature, religious, education. "No brief first-person stories about Sunday Schools." Query. Length: 1,000-1,500 words. **Pays $25-300.**

Reprints Send tearsheet or photocopy and information about when and where the material previously appeared.

Photos Submit glossy prints, high resolution (300 dpi) scans or digital photos in TIFF/JPEG format. No PowerPoint presentations or photos imbedded in Word documents. State availability of or send photos with submission. Buys one-time rights. Negotiates payment individually. Captions required.

Tips "Articles may deal with educational theory or practice, although the *Journal* seeks to emphasize the practical. Articles dealing with the creative and effective use of methods to enhance teaching skills or learning in the classroom are especially welcome. Whether theoretical or practical, such essays should demonstrate the skillful integration of Seventh-day Adventist faith/values and learning."

$KIDS' MINISTRY IDEAS

Review and Herald Publishing Association, 55 W. Oak Ridge Dr., Hagerstown MD 21740. (301)393-4115. Fax: (301)393-4055. E-mail: kidsmin@rhpa.org. Editor: Ginger Church. **Contact:** Editor. **95% freelance written.** "A quarterly resource for those leading children to Jesus, *Kids' Ministry Ideas* provides affirmation, pertinent and informative articles, program ideas, resource suggestions, and answers to questions from a Seventh-day Adventist Christian perspective." Estab. 1991. Circ. 3,000. **Pays on acceptance.** Publishes ms an average of 3 months after acceptance. Byline given. Buys first North American serial, electronic rights. Editorial lead time 3 months. Submit seasonal material 6 months in advance. Accepts queries by mail, e-mail, fax. Responds in 3 weeks to queries; 3 months to mss. Sample copy and writer's guidelines free.

Nonfiction Inspirational, new product (related to children's ministry), articles fitting the mission of *Kids' Minis-*

try Ideas. **Buys 40-60 mss/year.** Send complete ms. Length: 300-1,000 words. **Pays $30-100 for assigned articles; $30-70 for unsolicited articles.**

Photos State availability with submission. Buys one-time rights. Captions required.

Columns/Departments Buys 20-30 mss/year. Query. **Pays $30-100.**

Tips "Request writer's guidelines and a sample issue."

$ $LEADERSHIP

Real Ministry in a Complex World, Christianity Today International, 465 Gundersen Dr., Carol Stream IL 60188. (630)260-6200. Fax: (630)260-0114. E-mail: ljeditor@leadershipjournal.net. Website: www.leadershipjournal.net. Editor: Marshall Shelley. Managing Editor: Eric Reed. Associate Editor: Skye Jethani. **Contact:** Dawn Zemke, editorial coordinator. **75% freelance written.** Works with a small number of new/unpublished writers each year. Quarterly magazine. Writers must have a "knowledge of and sympathy for the unique expectations placed on pastors and local church leaders. Each article must support points by illustrating from real life experiences in local churches." Estab. 1980. Circ. 65,000. **Pays on acceptance.** Publishes ms an average of 6 months after acceptance. Byline given. Offers 33% kill fee. Buys first, electronic rights. Editorial lead time 6 months. Submit seasonal material 6 months in advance. Accepts queries by mail, e-mail, fax. Responds in 3 weeks to queries; 2 months to mss. Sample copy for $5 or online. Writer's guidelines online.

Nonfiction How-to, humor, interview/profile, personal experience, sermon illustrations. "No articles from writers who have never read our journal." **Buys 60 mss/year.** Query. Length: 300-3,000 words. **Pays $35-400.** Sometimes pays expenses of writers on assignment.

Columns/Departments Eric Reed, managing editor. Toolkit (book/software reviews), 500 words. **Buys 8 mss/year.** Query.

Tips "Every article in *Leadership* must provide practical help for problems that church leaders face. *Leadership* articles are not essays expounding a topic or editorials arguing a position or homilies explaining Biblical principles. They are how-to articles, based on first-person accounts of real-life experiences in ministry. They allow our readers to see 'over the shoulder' of a colleague in ministry who then reflects on those experiences and identifies the lessons learned. As you know, a magazine's slant is a specific personality that readers expect (and it's what they've sent us their subscription money to provide). Our style is that of friendly conversation rather than directive discourse—what I learned about local church ministry rather than what you need to do."

$MOMENTUM

Official Journal of the National Catholic Educational Association, National Catholic Educational Association, 1077 30th St. NW, Suite 100, Washington DC 20007-3852. (202)337-6232. Fax: (202)333-6706. E-mail: momentum@ncea.org. Website: www.ncea.org. **Contact:** Brian E. Gray, editor. **65% freelance written.** Quarterly educational journal covering educational issues in Catholic schools and parishes. "*Momentum* is a membership journal of the National Catholic Educational Association. The audience is educators and administrators in Catholic schools K-12, and parish programs." Estab. 1970. Circ. 28,000. Pays on publication. Publishes ms an average of 3 months after acceptance. Byline given. Buys first rights. Accepts queries by e-mail. Sample copy for $5 SASE and 8 first-class stamps. Writer's guidelines online.

Nonfiction Educational trends, issues, research. No articles unrelated to educational and catechesis issues. **Buys 40-60 mss/year.** Query and send complete ms. Length: 1,500 words. **Pays $75 maximum.**

Photos State availability with submission. Reviews prints. Offers no additional payment for photos accepted with ms. Captions, identification of subjects required.

Columns/Departments From the Field (practical application in classroom); DRE Directions (parish catechesis), both 700 words. **Buys 10 mss/year.** Query and send complete ms. **Pays $50.**

$ $THE PRIEST

Our Sunday Visitor, Inc., 200 Noll Plaza, Huntington IN 46750-4304. (260)356-8400. Fax: (260)356-8472. E-mail: tpriest@osv.com. Website: www.osv.com. Editor: Msgr. Owen F. Campion. **Contact:** Murray Hubley, associate editor. **40% freelance written.** Monthly magazine. "We run articles that will aid priests in their day-to-day ministry. Includes items on spirituality, counseling, administration, theology, personalities, the saints, etc." **Pays on acceptance.** Byline given. Buys first North American serial rights. Editorial lead time 3 months. Submit seasonal material 4 months in advance. Accepts queries by mail, e-mail, fax, phone. Responds in 5 weeks to queries; 3 months to mss. Sample copy and writer's guidelines free.

Nonfiction Essays, historical/nostalgic, humor, inspirational, interview/profile, opinion, personal experience, photo feature, religious. **Buys 96 mss/year.** Send complete ms. Length: 1,500-5,000 words. **Pays $200 minimum for assigned articles; $50 minimum for unsolicited articles.**

Photos Send photos with submission. Reviews transparencies, prints. Buys one-time rights. Negotiates payment individually. Captions, identification of subjects required.

Tips "Please do not stray from the magisterium of the Catholic Church."

$ $REV.

P.O. Box 481, Loveland CO 80539-0481. (970)669-3836. Fax: (970)292-4392. E-mail: lsparks@group.com. Website: www.revmagazine.com. Editor: Lee Sparks. **25% freelance written.** Bimonthly magazine for pastors. "We offer practical solutions to revolutionize and revitalize ministry." Estab. 1997. Circ. 45,000. **Pays on acceptance.** Publishes ms an average of 6 months after acceptance. Byline given. Makes work-for-hire assignments. Editorial lead time 6 months. Submit seasonal material 8 months in advance. Accepts queries by mail, e-mail. Responds in 2 months to queries. Writer's guidelines online.

➲ Break in with short, practical department pieces.

Nonfiction Ministry, leadership, and personal articles with practical application. "No devotions, articles for church members, theological pieces." **Buys 18-24 mss/year.** Query or send complete ms. Length: 1,800-2,000 words. **Pays $300-400.**

Columns/Departments Work (preaching, worship, discipleship, outreach, church business & administration, leadership); Life (personal growth, pastor's family); Culture (trends, facts), all 250-300 words. **Buys 25 mss/year.** Send complete ms. **Pays $35-50.**

Fillers Cartoons. **Buys 3/year. Pays $50.**

Tips "We are looking for creative and practical ideas that pastors and other leaders of churches of all sizes can use."

$TEACHERS INTERACTION

Concordia Publishing House, 3558 S. Jefferson Ave., St. Louis MO 63118-3968. (314)268-1083. Fax: (314)268-1329. E-mail: tom.nummela@cph.org. Editorial Associate: Jean Muser. **Contact:** Tom Nummela, editor. **20% freelance written.** Quarterly magazine of practical, inspirational, theological articles for volunteer Sunday school teachers. Material must be true to the doctrines of the Lutheran Church—Missouri Synod. Estab. 1960. Circ. 12,000. Pays on publication. Publishes ms an average of 1 year after acceptance. Byline given. Buys all rights. Submit seasonal material 1 year in advance. Accepts queries by mail, e-mail, fax. Responds in 3 weeks to mss. Sample copy for $4.99. Writer's guidelines for #10 SASE.

Nonfiction How-to (practical help/ideas used successfully in own classroom), inspirational, personal experience (of Sunday School teachers). No freelance theological articles. **Buys 6 mss/year.** Send complete ms. Length: 1,200 words. **Pays up to $120.**

Fillers *Teachers Interaction* buys short 'Toolbox' items—activities and ideas planned and used successfully in a church school classroom." **Buys 48/year.** Length: 200 words maximum. **Pays $20-40.**

Tips "Practical or 'it happened to me' articles would have the best chance. Also short items—ideas used in classrooms; seasonal and in conjunction with our Sunday school material. Our format emphasizes volunteer Sunday school teachers."

$ $TODAY'S CATHOLIC TEACHER

Peter Li Education Group, 2621 Dryden Rd., Suite 300, Dayton OH 45439. (937)293-1415. Fax: (937)293-1310. E-mail: mnoschang@peterli.com. Website: www.catholicteacher.com. **Contact:** Mary C. Noschang, editor. **60% freelance written.** Magazine published 6 times/year during school year covering Catholic education for grades K-12. "We look for topics of interest and practical help to teachers in Catholic elementary schools in all curriculum areas including religion technology, discipline, motivation." Estab. 1972. Circ. 50,000. Pays on publication. Publishes ms an average of 2 months after acceptance. Byline given. Buys first and all rights and makes work-for-hire assignments. Editorial lead time 3 months. Submit seasonal material 6 months in advance. Accepts queries by mail, e-mail, fax. Accepts simultaneous submissions. Responds in 1 month to queries; 3 months to mss. Sample copy for $3 or on website. Writer's guidelines online.

Nonfiction Interested in articles detailing ways to incorporate Catholic values into academic subjects other than religion class. Essays, how-to, humor, interview/profile, personal experience. "No articles pertaining to public education." **Buys 15 mss/year.** Query or send complete ms. Length: 1,500-3,000 words. **Pays $150-300.** Sometimes pays expenses of writers on assignment.

Photos State availability with submission. Reviews transparencies, prints. Buys one-time rights. Offers $20-50/photo. Captions, identification of subjects, model releases required.

Tips "Although our readership is primarily classroom teachers, *Today's Catholic Teacher* is also read by principals, supervisors, superintendents, boards of education, pastors, and parents. *Today's Catholic Teacher* aims to be for Catholic educators a source of information not available elsewhere. The focus of articles should span the interests of teachers from early childhood through junior high. Articles may be directed to just one age group, yet have wider implications. Preference is given to material directed to teachers in grades 4-8. The desired magazine style is direct, concise, informative, and accurate. Writing should be enjoyable to read, informal rather than scholarly, lively, and free of educational jargon."

$TODAY'S CHRISTIAN PREACHER

Right Ideas, Inc., P.O. Box 100, Morgantown PA 19543. (610)856-6830. Fax: (610)856-6831. E-mail: publications @rightideas.us. Editor: Jerry Thacker. **Contact:** Elaine Williams, assistant editor. **10% freelance written.** Quarterly magazine offering articles for pastors. *"Today's Christian Preacher* is designed to meet the personal needs of the man of God." Estab. 1992. Circ. 25,000. Pays on publication. Publishes ms an average of 1 year after acceptance. Buys simultaneous rights. Editorial lead time 1 year. Submit seasonal material 1 year in advance. Accepts queries by mail, e-mail, fax. Accepts simultaneous submissions. Responds in 1 month to queries; 3 months to mss. Sample copy for 9×12 SAE and 4 first-class stamps. Writer's guidelines for #10 SASE.

    ⊶ Break in with "concise, practical information for the pastor in his personal life, not sermons or church issues."

Nonfiction Inspirational, religious articles to help the man of God in his personal life. **Buys 2 mss/year.** Send complete ms. Length: 800-1,000 words. **Pays $150 for assigned articles.**

Photos Offers no additional payment for photos accepted with ms.

$ $ $WORSHIP LEADER MAGAZINE

26311 Junipero Serra, #130, San Juan Capistrano CA 92675. (949)240-9339. Fax: (949)240-0038. E-mail: editor@ wlmag.com. Website: www.worshipleader.com. **80% freelance written.** Bimonthly magazine covering all aspects of Christian worship. *"Worship Leader Magazine* exists to challenge, serve, equip, and train those involved in leading the 21st century church in worship. The intended readership is the worship team (all those who plan and lead) of the local church." Estab. 1992. Circ. 50,000. Pays on publication. Byline given. Offers 50% kill fee. Buys first North American serial, all rights. Editorial lead time 3 months. Submit seasonal material 6 months in advance. Responds in 6 weeks to queries; 3 months to mss. Sample copy for $5. Writer's guidelines online.

Nonfiction General interest, how-to (related to purpose/audience), inspirational, interview/profile, opinion. **Buys 15-30 mss/year.** Query with published clips. Length: 1,200-2,000 words. **Pays $200-800 for assigned articles; $200-500 for unsolicited articles.** Sometimes pays expenses of writers on assignment.

Photos State availability with submission. Buys one-time rights. Negotiate payment individually. Identification of subjects required.

Tips "Our goal has been and is to provide the tools and information pastors, worship leaders, and ministers of music, youth, and the arts need to facilitate and enhance worship in their churches. In achieving this goal, we strive to maintain high journalistic standards, Biblical soundness, and theological neutrality. Our intent is to present the philosophical, scholarly insight on worship, as well as the day-to-day, 'putting it all together' side of worship, while celebrating our unity and diversity."

$ $YOUR CHURCH

Helping You With the Business of Ministry, Christianity Today, Inc., 465 Gundersen Dr., Carol Stream IL 60188. (630)260-6200. Fax: (630)260-0114. E-mail: yceditor@yourchurch.net. Website: www.yourchurch.net. Managing Editor: Mike Schreiter. **90% freelance written.** Bimonthly magazine covering church administration and products. "Articles pertain to the business aspects of ministry pastors are called upon to perform: administration, purchasing, management, technology, building, etc." Estab. 1955. Circ. 85,000 (controlled). **Pays on acceptance.** Publishes ms an average of 3-4 months after acceptance. Byline given. Buys first, electronic rights. Editorial lead time 6 weeks. Submit seasonal material 5 months in advance. Accepts queries by mail, e-mail, fax. Accepts previously published material. Responds in 1 month to queries; 3 months to mss. Sample copy for 9×12 SAE and 4 first-class stamps. Writer's guidelines free.

Nonfiction How-to, new product, technical. **Buys 50-60 mss/year.** Send complete ms. Length: 1,000-4,000 words. **Pays 15-20¢/word.** Sometimes pays expenses of writers on assignment.

Tips "The editorial is generally geared toward brief and helpful articles dealing with some form of church business. Concise, bulleted points from experts in the field are typical for our articles."

$YOUTH AND CHRISTIAN EDUCATION LEADERSHIP

Pathway Press, 1080 Montgomery Ave., P.O. Box 2250, Cleveland TN 37311. (800)553-8506. Fax: (800)546-7590. E-mail: bill_george@pathwaypress.org. Website: www.pathwaypress.org. **Contact:** Bill George, editor. **25% freelance written.** Quarterly magazine covering Christian education. *"Youth and Christian Education Leadership* is written for teachers, youth pastors, children's pastors, and other local Christian education workers." Estab. 1976. Circ. 12,000. Pays on publication. Publishes ms an average of 6 months after acceptance. Buys first or one-time rights. Editorial lead time 3 months. Submit seasonal material 6 months in advance. Accepts queries by mail, e-mail. Accepts simultaneous submissions. Responds in 3 months to mss. Sample copy for $1 and 9×12 SASE. Writer's guidelines online or by e-mail.

Nonfiction How-to, humor (in-class experience), inspirational, interview/profile, motivational, seasonal short skits. **Buys 16 mss/year.** Send complete ms; include SSN. Send SASE for return of ms. Length: 400-1,200 words. **$25-50.**

Reprints Send typed, double-spaced ms with rights for sale noted and information about when and where the material previously appeared. Pays 80% of amount paid for an original article.

Photos State availability with submission. Reviews contact sheets, transparencies. Buys one-time rights. Negotiates payment individually.

Columns/Departments Sunday School Leadership; Reaching Out (creative evangelism); The Pastor and Christian Education; Preschool; Elementary; Teen; Adult; Drawing Closer; Kids Church, all 500-1,000 words. Send complete ms with SASE. **Pays $25-50.**

Tips "Become familiar with the publication's content and submit appropriate material. We are continually looking for 'fresh ideas' that have proven to be successful."

N $ $ YOUTHWORKER JOURNAL

Salem Publishing, 104 Woodmont Blvd., Nashville TN 37205-9759. E-mail: proposals@youthworker.com. Website: www.youthworker.com. **Contact:** Will Penner, editor. **100% freelance written.** Bimonthly magazine covering professional youth ministry in the church and parachurch. "We exist to help meet the personal and professional needs of career, Christian youth workers in the church and parachurch. Proposals accepted on the posted theme, according to the writer's guidelines on our website. It's not enough to write well—you must know youth ministry." Estab. 1984. Circ. 20,000. Pays on publication. Publishes ms an average of 3 months after acceptance. Byline given. "Articles must be first published with us, and we buy unrestricted use for print and electronic media." Editorial lead time 6 months. Submit seasonal material 6 months in advance. Accepts queries by e-mail. Responds in 6 months to queries. Sample copy for $5. Writer's guidelines online.

Nonfiction Essays, new product (youth ministry books only), personal experience, photo feature, religious. Query. Length: 250-3,000 words. **Pays $50-200.** Pays in contributor copies at the request of the author. Sometimes pays expenses of writers on assignment.

Photos Send photos with submission. Reviews GIF/JPEG files. Negotiates payment individually.

CLOTHING

APPAREL

801 Gervais St., Suite 101, Columbia SC 29201. (803)771-7500. Fax: (803)799-1461. E-mail: kdesmarteau@apparelmag.com. Website: www.apparelmag.com. Editor-in-Chief: Kathleen DesMarteau. **25% freelance written.** Monthly magazine for CEO's and top management in apparel and soft goods businesses including manufacturers and retailers. Circ. 18,000. Pays on receipt of article. Byline given. Buys all rights. Responds in 2 weeks to queries. Sample copy and writer's guidelines free.

Columns/Departments R&D; Winning Strategies; International Watch; Best Practices; Retail Strategies; Production Solutions.

Tips "Articles should be written in a style appealing to busy top managers and should in some way foster thought or new ideas, or present solutions/alternatives to common industry problems/concerns. CEOs are most interested in quick read pieces that are also informative and substantive. Articles should not be based on opinions but should be developed through interviews with industry manufacturers, retailers, or other experts, etc. Sidebars may be included to expand upon certain aspects within the article. If available, illustrations, graphs/charts, or photographs should accompany the article."

$ $ EMB-EMBROIDERY/MONOGRAM BUSINESS

1145 Sanctuary Pkwy., Suite 355, Alpharetta GA 30004. (800)241-9034. Fax: (770)569-5105. E-mail: mallison@embmag.com. Website: www.embmag.com. **Contact:** Melanie Allison, senior editor. **30% freelance written.** Monthly magazine covering computerized embroidery and digitizing design. "Readable, practical business and/or technical articles that show our readers how to succeed in their profession." Estab. 1994. Circ. 26,000. Pays on publication. Publishes ms an average of 3 months after acceptance. Byline given. Buys all rights. Editorial lead time 3 months. Submit seasonal material 6 months in advance. Accepts queries by mail, e-mail. Accepts simultaneous submissions. Sample copy for $10. Writer's guidelines not available.

Nonfiction How-to (embroidery, sales, marketing, design, general business info), interview/profile, new product, photo feature, technical (computerized embroidery). **Buys 4-6 mss/year.** Query. Length: 800-2,000 words. **Pays $200 and up for assigned articles.**

Photos Send photos with submission. Reviews transparencies, prints. Negotiates payment individually.

Tips "Show us you have specified knowledge, experience, or contacts in the embroidery industry or a related field."

$ $ MADE TO MEASURE

Halper Publishing Co., 830 Moseley Rd., Highland Park IL 60035. Fax: (847)780-2902. E-mail: mtm@halper.com. Website: www.madetomeasuremag.com. **Contact:** Rick Levine, editor/publisher. **50% freelance written.**

Semiannual magazine covering uniforms and career apparel. "A semi-annual magazine/buyers' reference containing leading sources of supply, equipment, and services of every description related to the Uniform, Career Apparel, and allied trades, throughout the entire US." Estab. 1930. Circ. 25,000. **Pays on acceptance.** Publishes ms an average of 2 months after acceptance. Byline given. Buys first North American serial rights. Editorial lead time 4 months. Submit seasonal material 4 months in advance. Accepts queries by mail, e-mail. Accepts simultaneous submissions. Responds in 3 weeks to queries. Sample copy online.

Nonfiction "Please only consider sending queries related to companies that wear or make uniforms, career apparel, or identify apparel." Interview/profile, new product, personal experience, photo feature, technical. **Buys 6-8 mss/year.** Query with published clips. Length: 1,000-3,000 words. **Pays $300-500.** Sometimes pays expenses of writers on assignment.

Photos State availability with submission. Reviews contact sheets, any prints. Buys one-time rights. Negotiates payment individually.

Tips "We look for features about large and small companies who wear uniforms (restaurants, hotels, industrial, medical, public safety, etc.)."

$ $ TEXTILE WORLD

Billian Publishing Co., 2100 Powers Ferry Rd., Suite 300, Atlanta GA 30339. (770)955-5656. Fax: (770)952-0669. E-mail: editor@textileindustries.com. Website: www.textileindustries.com. **Contact:** James Borneman, editor-in-chief. **5% freelance written.** Monthly magazine covering "the business of textile, apparel, and fiber industries with considerable technical focus on products and processes. No puff pieces pushing a particular product." Estab. 1868. Pays on publication. Byline given. Buys first North American serial rights.

Nonfiction Technical, business. **Buys 10 mss/year.** Query. Length: 500 words minimum. **Pays $200/published page.**

Photos Send photos with submission. Reviews prints. Buys one-time rights. Offers no additional payment for photos accepted with ms. Captions required.

CONSTRUCTION & CONTRACTING

$ $ ADVANCED MATERIALS & COMPOSITES NEWS PLUS COMPOSITES ENEWS

International Business & Technology Intelligence on High Performance M&P, Composites Worldwide, Inc., 991-C Lomas Santa Fe Dr., MC469, Solana Beach CA 92075-2125. (858)755-1372. E-mail: info@compositesnews.com. Website: www.compositesnews.com. Managing Editor: Susan Loud. **Contact:** Steve Loud, editor. **1% freelance written.** Bimonthly newsletter covering advanced materials and fiber-reinforced polymer composites, plus a weekly electronic version called *Composite eNews*, reaching over 15,000 subscribers and many more pass-along readers. *Advanced Materials & Composites News* "covers markets, applications, materials, processes, and organizations for all sectors of the global hi-tech materials world. Audience is management, academics, researchers, government, suppliers, and fabricators. Focus on news about growth opportunities." Estab. 1978. Circ. 15,000 +. Pays on publication. Publishes ms an average of 1 month after acceptance. Byline sometimes given. Buys all rights. Editorial lead time 2 weeks. Submit seasonal material 1 month in advance. Accepts queries by e-mail. Responds in 1 week to queries; 1 month to mss. Sample copy for #10 SASE.

> O─ "We target, contact, and use freelancers with the most industry knowledge, usually people we know personally from the FRP composites industry."

Nonfiction New product, technical, industry information. **Buys 4-6 mss/year.** Query. Length: 300 words. **Pays $200/final printed page.**

Photos State availability with submission. Reviews 4×5 transparencies, prints, 35mm slides, JPEGs (much preferred). Buys all rights. Offers no additional payment for photos accepted with ms. Captions, identification of subjects, model releases required.

$ $ AUTOMATED BUILDER

CMN Associates, Inc., 1445 Donlon St., Suite 16, Ventura CA 93003. (805)642-9735. Fax: (805)642-8820. E-mail: info@automatedbuilder.com. Website: www.automatedbuilder.com. Editor-in-Chief: Don Carlson. **Contact:** Bob Mendel. **10% freelance written.** Monthly magazine specializing in management for industrialized (manufactured) housing and volume home builders. "Our material is technical in content and concerned with new technologies or improved methods for in-plant building and components related to building. Online content is uploaded from the monthly print material." Estab. 1964. Circ. 25,000. **Pays on acceptance.** Publishes ms an average of 3 months after acceptance. Byline given. Buys first North American serial rights. Editorial lead time 2 months. Submit seasonal material 2 months in advance. Accepts queries by mail, e-mail, fax. Responds in 2 weeks to queries. Sample copy for free.

Nonfiction Case history articles on successful home building companies which may be 1) production (big volume) home builders; 2) mobile home manufacturers; 3) modular home manufacturers; 4) prefabricated (panelized) home manufacturers; 5) house component manufacturers; or 6) special unit (in-plant commercial building) manufacturers. Also uses interviews, photo features, and technical articles. "No architect or plan 'dreams.' Housing projects must be built or under construction." **Buys 6-8 mss/year.** Query. Phone queries OK. Length: 250-500 words. **Pays $300.**

Photos Wants 4×5, 5×7, or 8×10 glossies or disks. State availability with submission. Reviews 35mm or larger (35mm preferred) transparencies. Offers no additional payment for photos accepted with ms. Captions, identification of subjects required.

Tips "Stories often are too long, too loose; we prefer 500-750 words. We prefer a phone query on feature articles. If accepted on query, article usually will not be rejected later."

$ $BUILDERNEWS MAGAZINE

Pacific NW Sales & Marketing, Inc., 500 W. 8th St., Suite 270, Vancouver WA 98660. (360)906-0793. Fax: (360)906-0794. Website: www.buildernewsmag.com. "Articles must address pressing topics for builders in our region with a special emphasis on the business aspects of construction." Estab. 1996. Circ. 35,000. Pays on acceptance of revised ms. Publishes ms an average of 1 month after acceptance. Byline given. Buys first North American serial, electronic rights. Editorial lead time 2 months. Submit seasonal material 3 months in advance. Accepts queries by mail, e-mail, fax. Responds in 1 week to queries; 1 month to mss. Sample copy for free or online. Writer's guidelines free.

Nonfiction How-to, interview/profile, new product, technical. No personal bios unless they teach a valuable lesson to those in the building industry. **Buys 400 mss/year.** Query. Length: 500-2,500 words. **Pays $200-500.** Sometimes pays expenses of writers on assignment.

Photos State availability with submission. Buys first North American serial and electronic rights. Offers no additional payment for photos accepted with ms. Captions, identification of subjects, model releases required.

Columns/Departments Query.

Tips "Writers should have an understanding of the residential building industry and its terminology and be prepared to provide a résumé, writing samples, and story synopsis."

CAM MAGAZINE

Construction Association of Michigan, 43636 S. Woodward Ave., Bloomfield Hills MI 48302. (248)972-1000. Fax: (248)972-1001. Website: www.cam-online.com. **Contact:** Amanda Tackett, editor. **5% freelance written.** Monthly magazine covering all facets of the Michigan construction industry. "*CAM Magazine* is devoted to the growth and progress of individuals and companies serving and servicing the industry. It provides a forum on new construction-related technology, products, and services, plus publishes information on industry personnel changes and advancements." Estab. 1980. Circ. 4,300. Byline given. Buys all rights. Editorial lead time 2 months. Submit seasonal material 3 months in advance. Accepts queries by mail, e-mail, fax, phone. Sample copy and editorial subject calendar with query and SASE.

Nonfiction Michigan construction-related only. Query with published clips. Length: Features: 1,000-2,000 words; will also review short pieces.

Photos Digital format preferred. Send photos with submission. Offers no payment for photos accepted with ms.

Tips "Anyone having current knowledge or expertise on trends and innovations related to commercial construction is welcome to submit articles. Our readers are construction experts."

$ $CONCRETE CONSTRUCTION

Hanley-Wood, LLC., 426 S. Westgate St., Addison IL 60101. (630)543-0870. Fax: (630)543-5399. E-mail: preband @hanley-wood.com. Website: www.worldofconcrete.com. Editor: William Palmer. **Contact:** Pat Reband, managing editor. **20% freelance written.** Monthly magazine for concrete contractors, engineers, architects, specifiers, and others who design and build residential, commercial, industrial, and public works, cast-in-place concrete structures. It also covers job stories and new equipment in the industry. Estab. 1956. Circ. 80,000. **Pays on acceptance.** Publishes ms an average of 4 months after acceptance. Byline given. Editorial lead time 4 months. Submit seasonal material 4 months in advance. Accepts queries by mail, e-mail, fax. Responds in 2 weeks to queries; 1 month to mss. Sample copy and writer's guidelines free.

Nonfiction How-to, new product, personal experience, photo feature, technical, job stories. **Buys 7-10 mss/ year.** Query with published clips. Length: 2,000 words maximum. **Pays $250 or more for assigned articles; $200 minimum for unsolicited articles.** Pays expenses of writers on assignment.

Photos Send photos with submission. Reviews contact sheets, negatives, transparencies, prints. Buys one-time rights. Offers no additional payment for photos accepted with ms. Captions required.

Tips "Have a good understanding of the concrete construction industry. How-to stories accepted only from industry experts. Job stories must cover procedures, materials, and equipment used as well as the project's scope."

$ $ $THE CONCRETE PRODUCER

Hanley-Wood, LLC, 426 S. Westgate St., Addison IL 60101. (630)543-0870. Fax: (630)543-3112. Website: www. worldofconcrete.com. **Contact:** Rick Yelton, editor. **30% freelance written.** Monthly magazine covering concrete production. "Our audience consists of producers who have succeeded in making concrete the preferred building material through management, operating, quality control, use of the latest technology, or use of superior materials." Estab. 1982. Circ. 18,000. **Pays on acceptance.** Publishes ms an average of 2 months after acceptance. Byline given. Editorial lead time 4 months. Accepts queries by mail, e-mail, fax, phone. Responds in 1 week to queries; 2 months to mss. Sample copy for $4. Writer's guidelines free.

Nonfiction How-to (promote concrete), new product, technical. **Buys 10 mss/year.** Send complete ms. Length: 500-2,000 words. **Pays $200-1,000.** Sometimes pays expenses of writers on assignment.

Photos Scan photos at 300 dpi. State availability with submission. Reviews transparencies, prints. Offers no additional payment for photos accepted with ms. Captions, identification of subjects required.

N $ $ FRAME BUILDING NEWS

The Official Publication of the National Frame Builders Association, Krause Publications, a Division of F+W Publications, Inc., 700 E. State St., Iola WI 54990-0001. (715)445-4612, ext. 428. Fax: (715)445-4087. E-mail: tappas@krause.com. Website: www.framebuildingnews.com. Associate Editor: Jim Austin. **Contact:** Scott Tappa, editor. **10% freelance written.** Magazine published 5 times/year covering building. *"Frame Building News* is the official publication of the National Frame Builders Association, which represents contractors who specialize in post-frame building construction." Estab. 1990. Circ. 20,000. Pays on publication. Publishes ms an average of 3 months after acceptance. Byline given. Buys all rights. Editorial lead time 3 months. Submit seasonal material 3 months in advance. Accepts queries by mail. Accepts simultaneous submissions. Sample copy for free.

Nonfiction Book excerpts, historical/nostalgic, how-to, interview/profile, new product, opinion, photo feature, technical. No advertorials. **Buys 15 mss/year.** Query with published clips. Length: 750 words minimum. **Pays $100-500 for assigned articles.**

Photos Send photos with submission. Reviews GIF/JPEG files. Buys all rights. Negotiates payment individually. Captions, identification of subjects required.

Columns/Departments Money Talk (taxes for business); Tech Talk (computers for builders); Tool Talk (tools); Management Insights (business management), all 1,000 words. **Buys 15 mss/year.** Send complete ms. **Pays $0-500.**

Tips "Read our magazine online for a sense of our typical subject matter and audience. Contact by regular mail is best. No advertorials, please."

$HARD HAT NEWS

Lee Publications, Inc., 6113 State Highway 5, Palatine Bridge NY 13428. (518)673-3237. Fax: (518)673-2381. E-mail: hrieser@leepub.com. Website: www.hardhat.com. **Contact:** Holly Rieser. **80% freelance written.** Bi-weekly tabloid covering heavy construction, equipment, road, and bridge work. "Our readers are contractors and heavy construction workers involved in excavation, highways, bridges, utility construction, and underground construction." Estab. 1980. Circ. 58,000. Byline given. Editorial lead time 2 weeks. Submit seasonal material 2 weeks in advance. Accepts queries by mail, e-mail, fax, phone. Sample copy and writer's guidelines free.

O— "We especially need writers with some knowledge of heavy construction, although anyone with good composition and interviewing skills is welcome. Focus on major construction in progress in your area."

Nonfiction Job stories (a brief overall description of the project, the names and addresses of the companies and contractors involved, and a description of the equipment used, including manufacturers' names and model numbers; quotes from the people in charge, as well as photos, are important, as are the names of the dealers providing the equipment). Interview/profile, new product, opinion, photo feature, technical. Send complete ms. Length: 50-800 words. **Pays $2.50/inch.** Sometimes pays expenses of writers on assignment.

Photos Send photos with submission. Reviews prints, slides. Offers $15/photo. Captions, identification of subjects required.

Columns/Departments New Products; Association News; Parts and Repairs; Attachments; Trucks and Trailers; People on the Move.

Tips "Every issue has a focus—see our editorial calender. Special consideration is given to a story that coincides with the focus. A color photo is necessary for the front page. Vertical shots work best. We need more writers in metro NY area. Also, we are expanding our distribution into the Mid-Atlantic states and need writers in Virginia, Tennessee, North Carolina, and South Carolina."

$ $MC MAGAZINE

The Voice of the Manufactured Concrete Products Industry, National Precast Concrete Association, 10333 N. Meridian St., Suite 272, Indianapolis IN 46290. (317)571-9500. Fax: (317)571-0041. E-mail: rhyink@precast.org.

Trade Journals

Website: www.precast.org. **Contact:** Ron Hyink, managing editor. **75% freelance written.** Bimonthly magazine covering manufactured concrete products. *"MC Magazine* is a publication for owners and managers of factory-produced concrete products used in construction. We publish business articles, technical articles, company profiles, safety articles, and project profiles, with the intent of educating our readers in order to increase the quality and use of precast concrete." Estab. 1995. Circ. 8,500. **Pays on acceptance.** Publishes ms an average of 6 months after acceptance. Byline given. Buys first North American serial, second serial (reprint), all rights. Editorial lead time 3 months. Accepts queries by mail, e-mail, fax. Accepts simultaneous submissions. Responds in 1 month to queries; 2 months to mss. Sample copy and writer's guidelines online.

Nonfiction How-to (business), interview/profile, technical (concrete manufacturing). "No humor, essays, fiction, or fillers." **Buys 8-14 mss/year.** Query or send complete ms. Length: 1,500-2,500 words. **Pays $250-750.** Sometimes pays expenses of writers on assignment.

Photos State availability with submission. Buys all rights. Offers no additional payment for photos accepted with ms. Captions required.

Tips "Understand the audience and the purpose of the magazine. Understanding audience interests and needs is important and expressing a willingness to tailor a subject to get the right slant is critical. Our primary freelance needs are about general business or technology topics. Of course, if you are an engineer or a writer specializing in industry, construction, or manufacturing technology, other possibilities may exist. Writing style should be concise, yet lively and entertaining. Avoid clichés. We require a third-person perspective, and encourage a positive tone and active voice. For stylistic matters, follow the *AP Style Book.*"

N $ $ METAL ROOFING MAGAZINE

Krause Publications, a Division of F+W Publications, Inc., 700 E. Iola St., Iola WI 54990-0001. (715)445-4612, ext. 281. Fax: (715)445-4087. E-mail: jim.austin@krause.com. Website: www.metalroofingmag.com. **Contact:** Jim Austin, associate editor. **10% freelance written.** Bimonthly magazine covering roofing. *"Metal Roofing Magazine* offers contractors, designers, suppliers, and others in the construction industry a wealth of information on metal roofing—a growing segment of the roofing trade." Estab. 2000. Circ. 25,000. Pays on publication. Publishes ms an average of 3 months after acceptance. Byline given. Buys all rights. Editorial lead time 3 months. Submit seasonal material 3 months in advance. Accepts queries by mail. Accepts simultaneous submissions. Sample copy for free.

Nonfiction Book excerpts, historical/nostalgic, how-to, interview/profile, new product, opinion, photo feature, technical. No advertorials. **Buys 15 mss/year.** Query with published clips. Length: 750 words minimum. **Pays $100-500 for assigned articles.**

Photos Send photos with submission. Reviews GIF/JPEG files. Buys all rights. Negotiates payment individually. Captions, identification of subjects required.

Columns/Departments Money Talk (taxes for business); Tech Talk (computers for builders); Tool Talk (tools); Management Insights (business management), all 1,000 words. **Buys 15 mss/year.** Send complete ms. **Pays $0-500.**

Tips "Read our magazine online for a sense of our typical subject matter and audience. Contact by regular mail is best. No advertorials, please."

MICHIGAN CONTRACTOR & BUILDER

1917 Savannah Lane, Ypsilanti MI 48198-3674. (734)482-0272. Fax: (734)482-0291. E-mail: akalousdian@reedbusiness.com. **Contact:** Aram Kalousdian. **25% freelance written.** Weekly magazine covering the commercial construction industry in Michigan (no home building). *"Michigan Contractor & Builder's* audience is contractors, equipment suppliers, engineers, and architects. The magazine reports on construction projects in Michigan. It does not cover homebuilding. Stories should focus on news or innovative techniques or materials in construction." Estab. 1907. Circ. 2,256. Pays 1 month after publication. Byline given. Buys all rights. Accepts queries by mail, e-mail, fax, phone. Sample copy for free.

Nonfiction Michigan construction projects. **Buys 52 mss/year.** Query with published clips. Length: 1,000 words with 5-7 photos. **Payment is negotiable.**

Photos Send photos with submission. Reviews high resolution digital photos. Buys all rights. Offers no additional payment for photos accepted with ms. Captions required.

$ $ PENNSYLVANIA BUILDER

Pennsylvania Builders Association, 600 N. 12th St., Lemoyne PA 17043. (717)730-4380. Fax: (717)730-4396. E-mail: pba@pahomes.org. Website: www.pahomes.org. **10% freelance written.** "Quarterly trade publication for builders, remodelers, subcontractors, and other affiliates of the home building industry in Pennsylvania." Estab. 1988. Circ. 12,200. Pays on publication. Publishes ms an average of 1 year after acceptance. Byline given. Buys one-time rights. Editorial lead time 3 months. Submit seasonal material 9 months in advance. Accepts queries by mail, e-mail. Accepts simultaneous submissions. Responds in 2 weeks to queries; 3 months to mss. Sample copy for free. Writer's guidelines by e-mail. Editorial calendar online.

Nonfiction General interest, how-to, new product, technical. No personnel or company profiles. **Buys 1-2 mss/year.** Send complete ms. Length: 800-1,200 words. **Pays $250.** Sometimes pays expenses of writers on assignment.

Reprints Accepts previously published submissions.

Photos Send photos with submission. Reviews negatives, transparencies, prints. Buys one-time rights. Negotiates payment individually. Captions, identification of subjects required.

$ $ PERMANENT BUILDINGS & FOUNDATIONS (PBF)

R.W. Nielsen Co., 764 E. 1950 N., Spanish Fork UT 84660. (801)794-1393. Fax: (801)794-2031. E-mail: rnielsen@ permanentbuildings.com. Website: www.permanentbuildings.com. **Contact:** Roger W. Nielsen, editor. **50% freelance written.** Magazine published 8 times/year. "*PBF* readers are contractors who build residential and light commercial concrete buildings. Editorial focus is on new technologies to build solid, energy efficient structures, insulated concrete walls, waterproofing, underpinning, roofing and the business of contracting and construction." Estab. 1989. Circ. 30,000. Pays on publication. Byline given. Buys first North American serial rights. Editorial lead time 1 month. Submit seasonal material 2 months in advance. Accepts queries by mail, e-mail. Responds immediately to queries; 1 month to mss. Sample copy for 9×12 SASE or online. Writer's guidelines free or online.

Nonfiction How-to (construction methods, management techniques), humor, interview/profile, new product, technical, book reviews, tool reviews. Special issues: Water Proofing and Repair (February); Buyer's Guide (October); Insulated Concrete Forming Report (November); Concrete Homes (January); Commercial Market (July). **Buys 5-10 mss/year.** Query. Length: 500-1,500 words. **Pays 20-40¢/word for assigned articles; $50-500 for unsolicited articles.**

Photos State availability with submission. Reviews contact sheets. Buys North American rights. Offers no additional payment for photos accepted with ms. Captions, identification of subjects required.

Columns/Departments Marketing Tips, 250-500 words; Q&A (solutions to contractor problems), 200-500 words. Query.

$ $ REEVES JOURNAL

Business News Publishing Co., 23241 South Pointe Dr., Suite 280, Laguna Hills CA 92653. (949)830-0881. Fax: (949)859-7845. E-mail: jack@reevesjournal.com. Website: www.reevesjournal.com. **Contact:** Jack Sweet, editor. **25% freelance written.** Monthly magazine covering western building subcontractors—plumbers and HVAC contractors in the 14 western United States. Estab. 1920. Circ. 13,800. Pays on publication. Byline given. Buys first North American serial, electronic rights. Editorial lead time 3 months. Accepts queries by mail, e-mail, fax. Responds in 1 month to queries; 2 months to mss. Sample copy for free. Writer's guidelines for #10 SASE.

> O→ "Knowledge of building construction, water science, engineering is extremely helpful. Even better— former plumbing, HVAC experience, and a great command of the English language. We do not consider generic business articles."

Nonfiction "Only articles applicable to plumbing/HVAC subcontracting trade in the western US." How-to, interview/profile, new product, technical. Query with published clips. Length: 1,500-2,000 words. **Pays $100-350.**

Photos State availability with submission. Buys all rights. Negotiates payment individually. Captions, identification of subjects required.

■ The online magazine carries original content not found in the print edition. Contact: Jack Sweet.

Tips "Know the market. We're not just another builder publication and we do not publish or even consider publishing canned, generic articles, so don't even bother querying us with them. Our target audience is the plumbing, HVAC contractor—new construction, mechanical, and service and repair. We cover the western US (plus Texas)."

Ⓝ $ $ RURAL BUILDER

The Business Management Magazine for Rural Contractors, Krause Publications, a Division of F+W Publications, Inc., 700 E. State St., Iola WI 54990-0001. (715)445-4612, ext. 428. Fax: (715)445-4087. E-mail: tappas@kr ause.com. Website: www.ruralbuilder.com. Associate Editor: Jim Austin. **Contact:** Scott Tappa, editor. **10% freelance written.** Magazine published 7 times/year covering building. "*Rural Builder* serves diversified town and country builders, offering them help managing their businesses through editorial and advertising material about metal, wood, post-frame, and masonry construction." Estab. 1967. Circ. 30,000. Pays on publication. Publishes ms an average of 3 months after acceptance. Byline given. Buys all rights. Editorial lead time 3 months. Submit seasonal material 3 months in advance. Accepts queries by mail. Accepts simultaneous submissions. Sample copy for free.

Nonfiction Book excerpts, historical/nostalgic, how-to, interview/profile, new product, opinion, photo feature, technical. No advertorials. **Buys 15 mss/year.** Query with published clips. Length: 750 words minimum. **Pays $100-500.**

Photos Send photos with submission. Reviews GIF/JPEG files. Buys all rights. Negotiates payment individually. Captions, identification of subjects required.

Columns/Departments Money Talk (taxes for business); Tech Talk (computers for builders); Tool Talk (tools); Management Insights (business management); all 1,000 words. **Buys 15 mss/year.** Send complete ms. **Pays $0-500.**

Tips ''Read our magazine online for a sense of our typical subject matter and audience. Contact by regular mail is best. No advertorials, please.''

$ $ UNDERGROUND CONSTRUCTION

Oildom Publishing Co. of Texas, Inc., P.O. Box 941669, Houston TX 77094-8669. (281)558-6930. Fax: (281)558-7029. E-mail: rcarpenter@oildompublishing.com. Website: www.oildompublishing.com. **Contact:** Robert Carpenter, editor. **35% freelance written.** Monthly magazine covering underground oil and gas pipeline, water and sewer pipeline, cable construction for contractors and owning companies. Circ. 34,500. Publishes ms an average of 6 months after acceptance. Buys first North American serial rights. Accepts queries by mail, e-mail, fax, phone. Responds in 1 month to mss.

Nonfiction How-to, job stories. Query with published clips. Length: 1,000-2,000 words. **Pays $3-500.** Sometimes pays expenses of writers on assignment.

Photos Send photos with submission. Reviews color prints and slides. Buys one-time rights. Captions required.

Tips ''We supply guidelines outlining information we need. The most frequent mistake made by writers in completing articles is unfamiliarity with the field.''

DRUGS, HEALTHCARE & MEDICAL PRODUCTS

$ $ $ VALIDATION TIMES

Bio Research Monitoring Alert, Washington Information Source Co., 208 S. King St., Suite 303, Leesburg VA 20175. (703)779-8777. Fax: (703)779-2508. E-mail: editors@fdainfo.com. Website: www.fdainfo.com. **Contact:** Ken Reid, editor. Monthly Newsletters covering regulation of pharmaceutical and medical devices. ''We write to executives who have to keep up on changing FDA policies and regulations, and on what their competitors are doing at the agency.'' Estab. 1992. Pays on publication. Publishes ms an average of 1 month after acceptance. Byline given. Makes work-for-hire assignments. Editorial lead time 1 month. Submit seasonal material 1 month in advance. Accepts queries by mail. Responds in 1 month to queries. Sample copy and writer's guidelines free.

Nonfiction How-to, technical, regulatory. No lay interest pieces. **Buys 50-100 mss/year.** Query. Length: 600-1,500 words. **Pays $100/half day; $200 full day ''to cover meetings and same rate for writing.''** Sometimes pays expenses of writers on assignment.

Tips ''If you're covering a conference for non-competing publications, call me with a drug or device regulatory angle.''

EDUCATION & COUNSELING

$ ARTS & ACTIVITIES

Publishers' Development Corp., Dept. WM, 12345 World Trade Dr., San Diego CA 92128. (858)605-0242. Fax: (858)605-0247. Website: www.artsandactivities.com. **Contact:** Maryellen Bridge, editor-in-chief. **95% freelance written.** Eager to work with new/unpublished writers. Monthly (except July and August) magazine covering art education at levels from preschool through college for educators and therapists engaged in arts and crafts education and training. Estab. 1932. Circ. 20,000. Pays on publication. Publishes ms an average of 1 year after acceptance. Byline given. Buys first North American serial rights. Submit seasonal material 6 months in advance. Accepts queries by mail. Responds in 3 months to queries. Sample copy for 9 × 12 SAE and 8 first-class stamps. Writer's guidelines online.

○┐ Editors here are seeking more materials for upper elementary and secondary levels on printmaking, ceramics, 3-dimensional design, weaving, fiber arts (stitchery, tie-dye, batik, etc.), crafts, painting, and multicultural art.

Nonfiction Historical/nostalgic (arts, activities, history); how-to (classroom art experiences, artists' techniques); interview/profile (of artists); opinion (on arts activities curriculum, ideas of how to do things better, philosophy

Trade Journals

of art education); personal experience (this ties in with the how-to, we like it to be personal, no recipe style); articles of exceptional art programs. **Buys 80-100 mss/year.** Length: 200-2,000 words. **Pays $35-150.**

Tips "Frequently in unsolicited manuscripts, writers obviously have not studied the magazine to see what style of articles we publish. Send for a sample copy to familiarize yourself with our style and needs. The best way to find out if his/her writing style suits our needs is for the author to submit a manuscript on speculation. We prefer an anecdotal style of writing, so that readers will feel as though they are there in the art room as the lesson/project is taking place. Also, good quality photographs of student artwork are important. We are a visual art magazine!"

$ ⬚ THE ATA MAGAZINE

The Alberta Teachers' Association, 11010 142nd St., Edmonton AB T5N 2R1 Canada. (780)447-9400. Fax: (780)455-6481. E-mail: postmaster@teachers.ab.ca. Website: www.teachers.ab.ca. Quarterly magazine covering education. Estab. 1920. Circ. 39,500. Pays on publication. Publishes ms an average of 4 months after acceptance. Byline given. Buys one-time rights. Editorial lead time 2 months. Submit seasonal material 2 months in advance. Accepts queries by mail, e-mail, fax, phone. Accepts simultaneous submissions. Responds in 2 months to queries. Sample copy free. Writer's guidelines online.

Nonfiction Education-related topics. Query with published clips. Length: 500-1,250 words. **Pays $75 (Canadian).**

Photos Send photos with submission. Reviews 4×6 prints. Negotiates rights. Negotiates payment individually. Captions required.

$ $ EARLYCHILDHOOD NEWS

Excelligence Learning Corp., 2 Lower Ragsdale, Suite 200, Monterey CA 93940. (831)333-2000. Fax: (831)333-5510. E-mail: mshaw@excelligencemail.com. Website: www.earlychildhoodnews.com. **Contact:** Megan Shaw, editor. **80% freelance written.** Bimonthly magazine covering early childhood education. Targets teachers and parents of young children (infants to age 8). Estab. 1988. Circ. 55,000. Pays on publication. Publishes ms an average of 2-3 months after acceptance. Byline given. Buys all rights. Editorial lead time 2-4 months. Submit seasonal material 4 months in advance. Accepts queries by mail, e-mail, fax. Responds in 4-6 weeks to queries; 2-4 months to mss. Sample copy and writer's guidelines free.

Nonfiction Essays, general interest, inspirational, interview/profile, research-based. Special issues: Why Humor is the Best Teacher, Classroom Design (January/February); Promoting Development Through Play (March/April); Sizzling Summer Programs, Summer Reading (May/June); Meeting the Needs of Infants & Toddlers, Safety, Preschool Behavior (August/September); How to Measure Learning, Directors' Choice Awards (October); Crystal Clear Communication with Parents, Music, Teaching Kids with Special Needs (November/December). No personal stories. **Buys 40-50 mss/year.** Query. Length: 500-3,000 words. **Pays $75-300 maximum for assigned articles; $100-300 for unsolicited articles.**

Poetry "Poems should have a teacher-directed audience." Light verse, traditional. No "poetry not related to children, teachers, or early childhood." **Buys 6 poems/year.** Length: 10-60 lines. **Pays $50-250.**

Tips "Knowing about the publication and the types of articles we publish is greatly appreciated. Query letters are preferred over complete manuscripts."

$ $ HISPANIC OUTLOOK IN HIGHER EDUCATION

210 Route 4 E., Suite 310, Paramus NJ 07652. (201)587-8800, ext 100. Fax: (201)587-9105. E-mail: sloutlook@aol.com. Website: www.hispanicoutlook.com. Editor: Adalyn Hixson. **Contact:** Sue Lopez-Isa, managing editor. **50% freelance written.** Biweekly magazine. "We're looking for higher education story articles, with a focus on Hispanics and the advancements made by and for Hispanics in higher education." Circ. 28,000. Pays on publication. Publishes ms an average of 2 months after acceptance. Byline given. Editorial lead time 2 months. Submit seasonal material 3 months in advance. Accepts queries by mail, e-mail, fax. Accepts simultaneous submissions. Sample copy for free.

O⊸ Break with "issues articles such as new laws in higher education."

Nonfiction Historical/nostalgic, interview/profile (of academic or scholar), opinion (on higher education), personal experience, all regarding higher education only. **Buys 20-25 mss/year.** Query with published clips. Length: 1,800-2,200 words. **Pays $500 minimum for assigned articles.** Pays expenses of writers on assignment.

Photos Send photos with submission. Reviews color or b&w prints, digital images must be 300 dpi (call for e-mail photo address). Offers no additional payment for photos accepted with ms.

Tips "Articles explore the Hispanic experience in higher education. Special theme issues address sports, law, health, corporations, heritage, women, and a wide range of similar issues; however, articles need not fall under those umbrellas."

$ $PTO TODAY

The Magazine for Parent Group Leaders, PTO Today, Inc., 200 Stonewall Blvd., Suite 6A, Wrentham MA 02093. (800)644-3561. Fax: (508)384-6108. E-mail: editor@ptotoday.com. Website: www.ptotoday.com. **Contact:** Craig Bystrynski, editor. **65% freelance written.** Magazine published 6 times during the school year covering the work of school parent-teacher groups. "We celebrate the work of school parent volunteers and provide resources to help them do that work more effectively." Estab. 1999. Circ. 80,000. Pays on publication. Publishes ms an average of 2-4 months after acceptance. Byline given. Offers 30% kill fee. Buys first North American serial, electronic, all rights. Editorial lead time 4 months. Submit seasonal material 4 months in advance. Accepts queries by e-mail. Sample copy online. Writer's guidelines by e-mail.

Nonfiction Exposé, general interest, how-to (anything related to PTO/PTA), interview/profile, new product, personal experience. **Buys 40 mss/year.** Query. Length: 600-2,000 words. **Pays 20-40¢/word for assigned articles; $50-500 for unsolicited articles.** Sometimes pays expenses of writers on assignment.

Photos State availability with submission. Buys one-time rights. Negotiates payment individually. Identification of subjects required.

Tips "It's difficult for us to find talented writers with strong experience with parent groups. This experience is a big plus. Also, it helps to review our writer's guidelines before querying."

$RTJ

The Magazine for Catechism Formation, (formerly *Religion Teacher's Journal*), Bayard, Inc., P.O. Box 180, 185 Willow St., Mystic CT 06355. (800)321-0411, ext. 163. Fax: (860)536-5674. E-mail: aberger@twentythirdpublicat ions.com. Website: www.religionteachersjournal.com. **Contact:** Alison J. Berger, editor. **40% freelance written.** Newsletter published 7 times during the school year, with combined November/December and April/May issues, covering topics for catechists and religion teachers with teens and children as students. *RTJ* enriches and empowers catechists and religion teachers in their important ministry of faith formation by providing up-to-date religious knowledge, information, practice, and methods in catechesis." Estab. 1966. Circ. 34,000. **Pays on acceptance.** Publishes ms an average of 3-12 months after acceptance. Byline given. Buys First North American rights. Editorial lead time 5 months. Submit seasonal material 6 months in advance. Accepts queries by mail, e-mail, fax. Accepts simultaneous submissions. Responds in 2-3 weeks to queries; 1 month to mss. Sample copy for 9×12 SAE and 3 first-class stamps. Writer's guidelines free.

Nonfiction How-to (short activities that can be used in religion lessons), personal experience (in teaching religion—a practical approach), religious. Special issues: Sacraments (January); Lent/Reconciliation (February); Prayer/Easter/Baptism (March); Catechist Formation/Summer (April/May); Back to School/Teaching Techniques—as applied to religion sessions (September); Scripture/Saints (October); Advent/Christmas/Thanksgiving (November/December). No fiction. Query or send complete ms. Prefers articles by e-mail. Length: 600-1,300 words. **Pays $50-125 for unsolicited articles.**

$SCHOOLARTS MAGAZINE

50 Portland St., Worcester MA 01608-9959. Fax: (610)683-8229. Website: www.davis-art.com. **Contact:** Editor. **85% freelance written.** Monthly magazine (September-May), serving arts and craft education profession, K-12, higher education, and museum education programs written by and for art teachers. Estab. 1901. Pays on publication. Publishes ms an average of 3 months after acceptance. Buys all rights. Accepts queries by mail, phone. Responds in 3 months to queries. Writer's guidelines online.

O→ Break in with "professional quality photography to illustrate art lessons."

Nonfiction Articles on art and craft activities in schools. Should include description and photos of activity in progress, as well as examples of finished artwork. Query or send complete ms and SASE. Length: 600-1,400 words. **Pays $30-150.**

▣ The online version contains material not found in the print edition.

Tips "We prefer articles on actual art projects or techniques done by students in actual classroom situations. Philosophical and theoretical aspects of art and art education are usually handled by our contributing editors. Our articles are reviewed and accepted on merit and each is tailored to meet our needs. Keep in mind that art teachers want practical tips above all—more hands-on information than academic theory. Write your article with the accompanying photographs in hand." The most frequent mistakes made by writers are "bad visual material (photographs, drawings) submitted with articles, a lack of complete descriptions of art processes, and no rationale behind programs or activities. Familiarity with the field of art education is essential. Review recent issues of *SchoolArts*."

$ $ $TEACHER MAGAZINE

Editorial Projects in Education, 6935 Arlington Rd., Suite 100, Bethesda MD 20814. (310)280-3100. Fax: (301)280-3150. Website: www.teachermagazine.org. Managing Editor: Scott Cech. **Contact:** Rich Shea, executive editor. **40% freelance written.** Magazine published 8 times/year covering the teaching profession. "One of the major thrusts of the current school reform movement is to make teaching a true profession. *Teacher Magazine* plays a central role in that effort. It is a national communications network that provides teachers with the information they need to be better practitioners and effective leaders.'' Estab. 1989. Circ. 120,000. Pays on publication. Publishes ms an average of 1 month after acceptance. Byline given. Offers 25% kill fee. Buys first North American serial, electronic rights. Editorial lead time 3 months. Submit seasonal material 4 months in advance. Accepts queries by mail, fax. Responds in 2 months to queries. Sample copy online. Writer's guidelines free.

Nonfiction Book excerpts, essays, interview/profile, personal experience, photo feature, investigative. No ''how-to'' articles. **Buys 56 mss/year.** Query with published clips. Length: 1,000-5,000 words. **Pays 50¢/word.** Sometimes pays expenses of writers on assignment.

Photos State availability with submission. Reviews contact sheets, transparencies, prints. Buys one-time rights. Negotiates payment individually. Identification of subjects, model releases required.

Columns/Departments Current events, forum. Query with published clips. **Pays 50¢/word.**

Tips ''Sending us a well-researched query letter accompanied by clips that demonstrate you can tell a good story is the best way to break into *Teacher Magazine*. Describe the characters in your proposed article. What scenes do you hope to include in the piece?''

[N] TEACHERS & WRITERS MAGAZINE

Teachers & Writers Collaborative, 5 Union Square W., 7th Floor, New York NY 10003. (212)691-6590. E-mail: editors@twc.org. Website: www.twc.org/pubs. **Contact:** Christina Davis, Christopher Edgar. **95% freelance written.** Bimonthly magazine covering how to teach creative writing (kindergarten through university). Teachers & Writers offers readers a rich array of educational and writerly insights. Estab. 1967. Circ. 5,000. Pays on publication. Publishes ms an average of 4-6 months after acceptance. Byline given. Buys one-time rights. Editorial lead time 4 months. Submit seasonal material 4-6 months in advance. Accepts queries by mail, e-mail, phone. Accepts simultaneous submissions. Responds in 4-8 weeks to queries; 3-6 months to mss. Sample copy for $4. Writer's guidelines by e-mail.

○┐ ''Our readership is composed of savvy and innovative grade-school teachers, MFA students, teaching artists and literary autodidacts who are looking for the latest approaches to teaching poetry, fiction, nonfiction and drama.''

Nonfiction Book excerpts (on creative writing education), essays, interview/profile, opinion, personal experience, creative writing exercises.

$ TEACHERS OF VISION

Christian Educators Association, P.O. Box 41300, Pasadena CA 91114. (626)798-1124. Fax: (626)798-2346. E-mail: judy@ceai.org. Website: www.ceai.org. Editorial Director: Forrest L. Turpen. **Contact:** Judy Turpen, contributing editor. **50% freelance written.** Magazine published 6 times/year for Christian teachers in public education. ''*Teachers of Vision*'s articles inspire, inform, and equip teachers and administrators in the educational arena. Readers look for teacher tips, integrating faith and work, and general interest education articles. Topics include union issues, religious expression and activity in public schools, and legal rights of Christian educators. Our audience is primarily public school educators. Other readers include teachers in private schools, university professors, school administrators, parents, and school board members.'' Estab. 1953. Circ. 10,000. Pays on publication. Publishes ms an average of 6 months after acceptance. Byline given. Buys first North American serial, second serial (reprint) rights. Editorial lead time 4 months. Submit seasonal material 4 months in advance. Accepts queries by mail, e-mail, fax. Accepts simultaneous submissions. Responds in 1 month to queries; 3-4 months to mss. Sample copy for 9×12 SAE and 4 first-class stamps. Writer's guidelines online.

Nonfiction How-to, humor, inspirational, interview/profile, opinion, personal experience, religious. ''Nothing preachy.'' **Buys 15-20 mss/year.** Query or send complete ms if 2,000 words or less. Length: 600-2,500 words. **Pays $30-40.**

Reprints Accepts previously published submissions.

Photos State availability with submission. Buys one-time, web and reprint rights by members for educational purposes. Offers no additional payment for photos accepted with ms.

Columns/Departments Query. **Pays $10-30.**

Fillers Send with SASE—must relate to public education.

Tips ''We are looking for material on living out one's faith in appropriate, legal ways in the public school setting.''

$ $ TEACHING THEATRE

Educational Theatre Association, 2343 Auburn Ave., Cincinnati OH 45219-2819. (513)421-3900. Fax: (513)421-7077. E-mail: jpalmarini@edta.org. Website: www.edta.org. **Contact:** James Palmarini, editor. **65% freelance written.** Quarterly magazine covering education theater K-12, primary emphasis on middle and secondary level education. *"Teaching Theatre* emphasizes the teaching, theory, philosophy issues that are of concern to teachers at the elementary, secondary, and—as they relate to teaching K-12 theater—college levels. We publish work that explains specific approaches to teaching (directing, acting, curriculum development and management, etc.); advocates curriculum reform; or offers theories of theater education." Estab. 1989. Circ. 4,000. **Pays on acceptance.** Publishes ms an average of 3 months after acceptance. Byline given. Buys one-time, electronic rights. Editorial lead time 2 months. Accepts previously published material. Accepts simultaneous submissions. Responds in 1 month to queries; 3 months to mss. Sample copy for $2. Writer's guidelines online.

Nonfiction *"Teaching Theatre*'s audience is well educated, and most have considerable experience in their field. Generalist articles are discouraged; readers already possess basic skills." Book excerpts, essays, how-to, interview/profile, opinion, technical theater. **Buys 20 mss/year.** Query. **Pays $100-400.**

Photos State availability with submission. Reviews contact sheets, 5×7 and 8×10 transparencies, prints, digital images (300 dpi minimum). Offers no additional payment for photos accepted with ms.

Tips Wants articles that address the needs of the busy but experienced high school theater educators. "Fundamental pieces on the value of theater education are not of value to us—our readers already know that."

$ $ $ $TEACHING TOLERANCE

The Southern Poverty Law Center, 400 Washington Ave., Montgomery AL 36104. (334)956-8200. Fax: (334)956-8488. Website: www.teachingtolerance.org. **65% freelance written.** Semiannual magazine. *"Teaching Tolerance* is dedicated to helping K-12 teachers promote tolerance and understanding between widely diverse groups of students. Includes articles, teaching ideas, and reviews of other resources available to educators." Estab. 1991. Circ. 600,000. **Pays on acceptance.** Byline given. Buys all rights. Editorial lead time 6 months. Submit seasonal material 6 months in advance. Accepts queries by mail, fax. Sample copy and writer's guidelines free or online.

Nonfiction Essays, how-to (classroom techniques), personal experience (classroom), photo feature. "No jargon, rhetoric or academic analysis. No theoretical discussions on the pros/cons of multicultural education." **Buys 6-8 mss/year.** Query with published clips. Length: 1,000-3,000 words. **Pays $500-3,000 for assigned articles.** Pays expenses of writers on assignment.

Photos State availability with submission. Reviews contact sheets, transparencies. Buys one-time rights. Captions, identification of subjects required.

Columns/Departments Essays (personal reflection, how-to, school program), 400-800 words; Idea Exchange (special projects, successful anti-bias activities), 250-500 words; Student Writings (short essays dealing with diversity, tolerance, justice), 300-500 words. **Buys 8-12 mss/year.** Query with published clips. **Pays $50-1,000.**

The online magazine carries original content not found in the print edition and includes writer's guidelines. Contact: Brian Willoughby, managing editor.

Tips "We want lively, simple, concise writing. The writing style should be descriptive and reflective, showing the strength of programs dealing successfully with diversity by employing clear descriptions of real scenes and interactions, and by using quotes from teachers and students. We ask that prospective writers study previous issues of the magazine and writer's guidelines before sending a query with ideas. Most open to articles that have a strong classroom focus. We are interested in approaches to teaching tolerance and promoting understanding that really work—approaches we might not have heard of. We want to inform our readers; we also want to inspire and encourage them. We know what's happening nationally; we want to know what's happening in your neighborhood classroom."

$TECH DIRECTIONS

Prakken Publications, Inc., P.O. Box 8623, Ann Arbor MI 48107-8623. (734)975-2800. Fax: (734)975-2787. E-mail: susanne@techdirections.com. Website: www.techdirections.com. **Contact:** Susanne Peckham, managing editor. **100% freelance written.** Eager to work with new/unpublished writers. Monthly (except June and July) magazine covering issues, trends, and activities of interest to science, technical, and technology educators at the elementary through post-secondary school levels. Estab. 1934. Circ. 40,000. Pays on publication. Publishes ms an average of 1 year after acceptance. Byline given. Buys all rights. Responds in 1 month to queries. Sample copy for $5. Writer's guidelines online.

Nonfiction Uses articles pertinent to the various teaching areas in science and technology education (woodwork, electronics, drafting, physics, graphic arts, computer training, etc.). Prefers authors who have direct connection with the field of science and/or technical education. "The outlook should be on innovation in educational programs, processes, or projects that directly apply to the technical education area." Main focus: technical career and education. General interest, how-to, personal experience, technical, think pieces. **Buys 50 unsolicited mss/year.** Length: 2,000-3,000 words. **Pays $50-150.**

Photos Send photos with submission. Reviews color prints. Payment for photos included in payment for ms. Will accept electronic art as well.

Columns/Departments Direct from Washington (education news from Washington DC); Technology Today (new products under development); Technologies Past (profiles the inventors of last century); Mastering Computers, Technology Concepts (project orientation).

Tips "We are most interested in articles written by technology and science educators about their class projects and their ideas about the field. We need more and more technology-related articles, especially written for the community college level."

ELECTRONICS & COMMUNICATION

$ $ THE ACUTA JOURNAL OF TELECOMMUNICATIONS IN HIGHER EDUCATION

ACUTA, 152 W. Zandale Dr., Suite 200, Lexington KY 40503-2486. (859)278-3338. Fax: (859)278-3268. E-mail: pscott@acuta.org. Website: www.acuta.org. **Contact:** Patricia Scott, communications manager. **20% freelance written.** Quarterly professional association journal covering telecommunications in higher education. "Our audience includes, primarily, middle to upper management in the telecommunications department on college/university campuses. They are highly skilled, technology-oriented professionals who provide data, voice, and video communications services for residential and academic purposes." Estab. 1997. Circ. 2,200. Pays on publication. Publishes ms an average of 6 months after acceptance. Byline given. Buys first rights. Editorial lead time 6 months. Accepts queries by mail, e-mail, fax, phone. Responds in 1 month to queries; 2 months to mss. Sample copy for 9×12 SAE and 6 first-class stamps. Writer's guidelines free.

> ⊶ Break in with a campus study or case profile. "Contact me with your idea for a story. Convince me you can handle the level of technical depth required."

Nonfiction "Each issue has a focus. Available with writer's guidelines. We are only interested in articles described in article types." How-to (telecom), technical (telecom), case study, college/university application of technology. **Buys 6-8 mss/year.** Query. Length: 1,200-4,000 words. **Pays 8-10¢/word.** Sometimes pays expenses of writers on assignment.

Photos State availability with submission. Reviews prints. Offers no additional payment for photos accepted with ms. Captions, model releases required.

Tips "Our audience expects every article to be relevant to telecommunications on the college/university campus, whether it is related to technology, facilities, or management. Writers must read back issues to understand this focus and the level of technicality we expect."

AMERICA'S NETWORK

Advanstar Communications, 201 E. Sandpointe Ave., Suite 600, Santa Ana CA 92707. (714)513-8834. Fax: (714)513-8845. E-mail: belliott@advanstar.com. Website: www.americasnetwork.com. Editor-in-Chief: Lester Craf. Managing Editor: Al Senia. **Contact:** Bonnie Elliott. Magazine published 18 times/year. Edited for telecommunications executives and professionals who are responsible for the design, construction, sales, purchase, operations and maintenance of telephone/telecom systems. Circ. 43,533. Editorial lead time 3 months.

$ $ DIGITAL OUTPUT

The Only Magazine Dedicated to Capture, Creation, Output and Finishing, The Doyle Group, 5150 Palm Valley Rd., Suite 103, Ponte Vedra Beach FL 32082. (904)285-6020. Fax: (904)285-9944. E-mail: cmason@digitaloutput. net. Website: www.digitaloutput.net. **Contact:** Cathy Mason, editor-in-chief. **70% freelance written.** Monthly magazine covering electronic prepress, desktop publishing, and digital imaging, with articles ranging from digital capture and design to electronic prepress and digital printing. "*Digital Output* is a national business publication for electronic publishers and digital imagers, providing monthly articles which examine the latest technologies and digital methods and discuss how to profit from them. Our readers include service bureaus, prepress and reprographic houses, designers, commercial printers, wide-format printers, ad agencies, corporate communications, sign shops, and others." Estab. 1994. Circ. 30,000. Pays on publication. Publishes ms an average of 2 months after acceptance. Byline given. Offers 10-20% kill fee. Buys one-time rights including electronic rights for archival posting. Editorial lead time 3 months. Submit seasonal material 3 months in advance. Accepts queries by mail, e-mail. Responds in 3 weeks to queries; 1 month to mss. Sample copy for $4.50 or online.

Nonfiction How-to, interview/profile, technical, case studies. **Buys 36 mss/year.** Query with published clips or hyperlinks to posted clips. Length: 1,500-4,000 words. **Pays $250-600.**

Photos Send photos with submission.

Tips "Our readers are graphic arts professionals. The freelance writers we use are deeply immersed in the technology of commercial printing, desktop publishing, digital imaging, color management, PDF workflow, inkjet printing, and similar topics."

$ $ SQL SERVER MAGAZINE

Penton Media, 221 E. 29th St., Loveland CO 80538. (970)663-4700. E-mail: articles@sqlmag.com. Website: www.sqlmag.com. **35% freelance written.** Monthly magazine covering Microsoft SQL Server. *"SQL Server Magazine* is the only magazine completely devoted to helping developers and DBAs master new and emerging SQL Server technologies and issues. It provides practical advice and lots of code examples for SQL Server developers and administrators, and includes how-to articles, tips, tricks, and programming techniques offered by SQL Server experts." Estab. 1999. Circ. 20,000. Pays on publication. Publishes ms an average of 6 months after acceptance. Byline given. Offers $100 kill fee. Buys all rights. Editorial lead time 4+ months. Accepts queries by mail, e-mail. Responds in 6 weeks to queries; 2-3 months to mss. Sample copy and writer's guidelines online.

Nonfiction How-to, technical, SQL Server administration and programming. Nothing promoting third-party products or companies. **Buys 25-35 mss/year.** Query with or without published clips or send complete ms. Length: 1,800-3,000 words. **Pays $200 for feature articles; $500 for Focus articles.** Pays in contributor copies if the writer requests the substitution.

Columns/Departments R2R Editor. Reader to Reader (helpful SQL Server hints and tips from readers), 200-400 words. **Buys 6-12 mss/year.** Send complete ms. **Pays $50.**

Tips "Read back issues and make sure that your proposed article doesn't overlap previous coverage. When proposing articles, state specifically how your article would contain new information compared to previously published information, and what benefit your information would be to *SQL Server Magazine's* readership."

ENERGY & UTILITIES

$ $ ALTERNATIVE ENERGY RETAILER

Zackin Publications, Inc., P.O. Box 2180, Waterbury CT 06722. (800)325-6745. Fax: (203)755-3480. E-mail: griffin@aer-online.com. Website: www.aer-online.com/aer/. **Contact:** Michael Griffin, editor. **5% freelance written.** Prefers to work with published/established writers. Monthly magazine on selling home hearth products—chiefly solid fuel and gas-burning appliances. "We seek detailed how-to tips for retailers to improve business. Most freelance material purchased is about retailers and how they succeed." Estab. 1980. Circ. 10,000. Pays on publication. Publishes ms an average of 2 months after acceptance. Buys first North American serial rights. Submit seasonal material 4 months in advance. Accepts queries by mail, e-mail, fax, phone. Responds in 2 weeks to queries. Sample copy for 9×12 SAE and 4 first-class stamps. Writer's guidelines online.

O— Submit articles that focus on hearth market trends and successful sales techniques.

Nonfiction How-to (improve retail profits and business know-how), interview/profile (of successful retailers in this field). No "general business articles not adapted to this industry." **Buys 10 mss/year.** Query. Length: 1,000 words. **Pays $200.**

Photos State availability with submission. Reviews color transparencies. Buys one-time rights. Pays $25-125 maximum for 5×7 b&w prints. Identification of subjects required.

Tips "A freelancer can best break into our publication with features about readers (retailers). Stick to details about what has made this person a success."

$ $ ELECTRICAL APPARATUS

The Magazine of Electromechanical & Electronic Application & Maintenance, Barks Publications, Inc., 400 N. Michigan Ave., Chicago IL 60611-4198. (312)321-9440. Fax: (312)321-1288. Senior Editor: Kevin N. Jones. **Contact:** Elsie Dickson, editorial director. Monthly magazine for persons working in electrical and electronic maintenance, chiefly in industrial plants, who install and service electrical motors, transformers, generators, controls, and related equipment. Estab. 1967. Circ. 17,000. Pays on publication. Publishes ms an average of 1 month after acceptance. Byline given. Buys all rights unless other arrangements made. Accepts queries by mail, fax. Responds in 1 week to queries; 2 weeks to mss.

Nonfiction Technical. Length: 1,500-2,500 words. **Pays $250-500 for assigned articles.**

Tips "All feature articles are assigned to staff and contributing editors and correspondents. Professionals interested in appointments as contributing editors and correspondents should submit résumé and article outlines, including illustration suggestions. Writers should be competent with a camera, which should be described in résumé. Technical expertise is absolutely necessary, preferably an E.E. degree, or practical experience. We are also book publishers and some of the material in *EA* is now in book form, bringing the authors royalties. Also publishes an annual directory, subtitled *ElectroMechanical Bench Reference*."

Ⓝ $ $⬚ ELECTRICAL BUSINESS

CLB Media, Inc., 240 Edward St., Aurora ON L4G 3S9 Canada. (905)727-0077. Fax: (905)727-0017. E-mail: acapkun@clbmedia.ca. Website: www.ebmag.com. **Contact:** Anthony Capkun, editor. **35% freelance written.**

Tabloid published 10 times/year covering the Canadian electrical industry. "*Electrical Business* targets electrical contractors and electricians. It provides practical information readers can use right away in their work and for running their business and assets." Estab. 1964. Circ. 18,097. **Pays on acceptance.** Publishes ms an average of 1-2 months after acceptance. Byline given. Offers 50% kill fee. Buys simultaneous rights. Editorial lead time 3 months. Submit seasonal material 6 months in advance. Accepts queries by e-mail, phone. Accepts simultaneous submissions. Responds in 1 month. Sample copy online. Writer's guidelines free.

Nonfiction How-to, technical. Special issues: Summer Blockbuster issue (June/July); Special Homebuilders' issue (November/December). **Buys 15 mss/year.** Query. Length: 800-1,200 words. **Pays 40¢/word.** Sometimes pays expenses of writers on assignment.

Photos State availability with submission. Reviews GIF/JPEG files. Buys simultaneous rights. Negotiates payment individually. Captions, identification of subjects, model releases required.

Columns/Departments Atlantic Focus (stories from Atlantic Canada); Western Focus (stories from Western Canada, including Manitoba); Trucks for the Trade (articles pertaining to the vehicles used by electrical contractors); Tools for the Trade (articles pertaining to tools used by contractors); all 800 words. **Buys 6 mss/year.** Query. **Pays 40¢/word.**

Tips "Call me, and we'll talk about what I need, and how you can provide it. Stories must have Canadian content."

ⓝ $ $⊡ FAR NORTH OIL & GAS

Up Here Publishing, Ltd., #800 4920 52nd St., Yellowknife NT X1A 3T1 Canada. (867)920-4343. Fax: (867)873-2844. E-mail: jake@uphere.ca. Website: www.fnog.ca. Managing Editor: Darren Campbell. **Contact:** Jake Kennedy, editor. **60% freelance written.** Quarterly magazine covering the oil and gas industry in the far North (Alaska, Yukon, NWT, Nunavut). "*Far North Gas & Oil* is the leading authority on the oil and gas industry in the far North of Canada and the US." Estab. 1998. Circ. 10,000. Pays on publication. Publishes ms an average of 3 months after acceptance. Byline given. Offers 50% kill fee. Buys first, electronic rights. Editorial lead time 1 year. Submit seasonal material 6 months in advance. Accepts queries by mail, e-mail, fax. Responds in 2 weeks to queries; 1 month to mss. Sample copy for free.

Nonfiction Essays, general interest, historical/nostalgic, interview/profile, new product, opinion, photo feature, technical. **Buys 10 mss/year.** Query. Length: 1,800-2,500 words. **Pays 30-50¢/word.** Sometimes pays expenses of writers on assignment.

Photos State availability with submission. Reviews contact sheets, negatives, transparencies, prints, GIF/JPEG files. Buys one-time rights. Negotiates payment individually. Captions, identification of subjects required.

Columns/Departments Border Patrol (updates/opinions on Alaska's oil and gas), 1,100 words; Opinion (opinions on oil and gas industry), 1,100 words; Final Say (parting thoughts, back page), 800 words. **Buys 12 mss/year.** Query. **Pays $200-400.**

Tips "Query with story ideas, and be familiar with the magazine. You don't need expertise in the oil/gas industry, but you do need to be a good writer."

$ NATIONAL PETROLEUM NEWS

833 W. Jackson, 7th Floor, Chicago IL 60607. (312)846-4600. Fax: (312)977-1042. Website: www.npn-net.com. **15% freelance written.** Prefers to work with published/established writers. Monthly magazine for decision-makers in the petroleum marketing and convenience store industry. Estab. 1909. Circ. 38,000. Pays on acceptance if done on assignment. Publishes ms an average of 2 months after acceptance. variable rights, depending upon author and material; usually buys all rights. Accepts queries by mail, e-mail, fax. Sample copy not available.

⦿ This magazine is particularly interested in articles on national industry-related material.

Nonfiction Material related directly to developments and issues in the petroleum marketing and convenience store industry and "how-to" and "what-with" case studies. "No unsolicited copy, especially with limited attribution regarding information in story." **Buys 9-10 mss/year.** Length: 2,500 words maximum. **Pays $50-150/printed page.** Sometimes pays expenses of writers on assignment.

Reprints Send typed ms on disk with rights for sale noted and information about when and where the article previously appeared.

Photos Pays $150/printed page. Pays for color and b&w photos.

$ $ PUBLIC POWER

Dept. WM, 2301 M St. NW, Washington DC 20037-1484. (202)467-2948. Fax: (202)467-2910. E-mail: jlabella@appanet.org. Website: www.appanet.org. **Contact:** Jeanne LaBella, editor. **60% freelance written.** Prefers to work with published/established writers. Bimonthly trade journal. Estab. 1942. **Pays on acceptance.** Publishes ms an average of 3 months after acceptance. Byline given. Accepts queries by mail, e-mail, fax. Responds in 6 months to queries. Sample copy and writer's guidelines free.

Nonfiction Features on municipal and other local publicly owned electric utilities. **Pays $600 and up.**

Photos Reviews electronic photos (minimum 300 dpi at reproduction size), transparencies, slides, and prints.

Tips "We look for writers who are familiar with energy policy issues."

$ $ $ TEXAS CO-OP POWER

Texas Electric Cooperatives, Inc., 2550 S. IH-35, Austin TX 78704. (512)454-0311. Website: www.texascooppowe r.com. Editor: Kaye Northcott. Managing Editor: Carol Moczygemba. **50% freelance written.** Monthly magazine covering rural and suburban Texas life, people, and places. "*Texas Co-op Power* provides 1 million households and businesses educational and technical information about electric cooperatives in a high-quality and entertaining format to promote the general welfare of cooperatives, their member-owners, and the areas in which they serve." Estab. 1948. Circ. 1 million. **Pays on acceptance.** Publishes ms an average of 6 months after acceptance. Byline given. Buys first, electronic rights. Editorial lead time 4-5 months. Submit seasonal material 6 months in advance. Accepts queries by mail, e-mail, fax. Accepts simultaneous submissions. Responds in 1 month to queries; 3 months to mss. Sample copy online. Writer's guidelines for #10 SASE.

Nonfiction General interest, historical/nostalgic, interview/profile, photo feature, travel. **Buys 30 mss/year.** Query with published clips. Length: 1,000-2,000 words. **Pays $400-1,000.** Sometimes pays expenses of writers on assignment.

Photos State availability with submission. Reviews transparencies, prints. Buys one-time rights. Negotiates payment individually. Identification of subjects, model releases required.

Tips "We're looking for Texas-related, rural-based articles, often first-person, always lively and interesting."

ENGINEERING & TECHNOLOGY

$ $ $ ⬚ CABLING NETWORKING SYSTEMS

12 Concorde Place, Suite 800, North York ON M3C 4J2 Canada. (416)510-6752. Fax: (416)510-5134. E-mail: pbarker@cnsmagazine.com. Website: www.cablingsystems.com. **Contact:** Paul Barker. **50% freelance written.** Magazine published 8 times/year covering structured cabling/telecommunications industry. "*Cabling Systems* is written for engineers, designers, contractors, and end users who design, specify, purchase, install, test and maintain structured cabling and telecommunications products and systems." Estab. 1998. Circ. 11,000. Pays on publication. Publishes ms an average of 1 month after acceptance. Byline given. Buys all rights. Editorial lead time 3 months. Submit seasonal material 1 month in advance. Accepts queries by mail, e-mail, phone. Accepts simultaneous submissions. Sample copy online. Writer's guidelines free.

Nonfiction Technical (case studies, features). "No reprints or previously written articles. All articles are assigned by editor based on query or need of publication." **Buys 12 mss/year.** Query with published clips. Length: 1,500-2,500 words. **Pays 40-50¢/word.** Sometimes pays expenses of writers on assignment.

Photos State availability with submission. Reviews contact sheets, prints. Negotiates payment individually. Captions, identification of subjects required.

Columns/Departments Focus on Engineering/Design; Focus on Installation; Focus on Maintenance/Testing, all 1,500 words. **Buys 7 mss/year.** Query with published clips. **Pays 40-50¢/word.**

Tips "Visit our website to see back issues, and visit links on our website for background."

$ $ $ ⬚ CANADIAN CONSULTING ENGINEER

Business Information Group, 12 Condorde Place, Suite 800, Toronto ON M3C 4J2 Canada. (416)510-5119. Fax: (416)510-5134. E-mail: bparsons@ccemag.com. Website: www.canadianconsultingengineer.com. **Contact:** Bronwen Parsons, editor. **20% freelance written.** Bimonthly magazine covering consulting engineering in private practice. Estab. 1958. Circ. 8,900. Pays on publication. Publishes ms an average of 4 months after acceptance. Byline given depending on length of story. Offers 50% kill fee. Buys first North American serial rights. Editorial lead time 6 months. Responds in 3 months to mss. Sample copy for free.

● Canadian content only.

Nonfiction Historical/nostalgic, new product, technical, engineering/construction projects, environmental/construction issues. **Buys 8-10 mss/year.** Length: 300-1,500 words. **Pays $200-1,000 (Canadian).** Sometimes pays expenses of writers on assignment.

Photos State availability with submission. Buys one-time rights. Negotiates payment individually.

Columns/Departments Export (selling consulting engineering services abroad); Management (managing consulting engineering businesses); On-Line (trends in CAD systems); Employment, all 800 words. **Buys 4 mss/year.** Query with published clips. **Pays $250-400.**

$ $ $ CAREER RECRUITMENT MEDIA

211 W. Wacker Dr., Suite 900, Chicago IL 60606. (312)525-3100. E-mail: vanderson@alloymarketing.com. Website: www.careermedia.com. **50% freelance written.** "Recruitment publications for college engineering/

computer science/allied health students. Our readers are smart, savvy and hip. The writing must be, too." **Pays on acceptance.** Publishes ms an average of 2 months after acceptance. Byline given. Offers $50 kill fee. Buys all rights. Editorial lead time 2 months. Submit seasonal material 6 months in advance. Accepts queries by mail, e-mail. Accepts simultaneous submissions. Responds in 2 weeks to queries; 3 months to mss. Sample copy and writer's guidelines free.

Nonfiction Book excerpts, exposé, interview/profile, personal experience. Special issues: Minorities; Women. **Buys 40 mss/year.** Send complete ms. Length: 1,500-3,000 words. **Pays $200-800 for assigned articles; $50-300 for unsolicited articles.** Sometimes pays expenses of writers on assignment.

Photos Send photos with submission. Reviews 3×5 prints. Buys one-time rights. Offers no additional payment for photos accepted with ms. Identification of subjects required.

Columns/Departments Industry Focus (analysis of hiring market within particular industry), 1,500 words. **Buys 6 mss/year.** Query. **Pays $200-300.**

Tips "Know the hiring market for entry-level professionals and be able to communicate to college students at their level."

$ $ COMPOSITES FABRICATION MAGAZINE

The Official Publication of the American Composites Manufacturers Association, American Composites Manufacturers Association, 1010 N. Glebe Rd., Suite 450, Arlington VA 22201. (703)525-0511. Fax: (703)525-0743. E-mail: arusnak@acmanet.org. Website: www.cfmagazine.org. **Contact:** Andrew Rusnak, editor. Monthly magazine covering any industry that uses reinforced composites: marine, aerospace, infrastructure, automotive, transportation, corrosion, architecture, tub and shower, sports, and recreation. "Primarily, we publish educational pieces, the how-to of the shop environment. We also publish marketing, business trends, and economic forecasts relevant to the composites industry." Estab. 1979. Circ. 12,000. **Pays on acceptance.** Publishes ms an average of 2-3 months after acceptance. Byline given. Buys all rights. Editorial lead time 2 months. Accepts queries by e-mail. Accepts previously published material. Accepts simultaneous submissions. Responds in 1 week to queries; 1 month to mss. Sample copy for free. Writer's guidelines by e-mail.

Nonfiction How-to (composites manufacturing), new product, technical, marketing, related business trends and forecasts. Special issues: "Each January we publish a World Market Report where we cover all niche markets and all geographic areas relevant to the composites industry. Freelance material will be considered strongly for this issue. No need to query company or personal profiles unless there is an extremely unique or novel angle." **Buys 5-10 mss/year.** Query. Length: 1,500-4,000 words. **Pays 20-40¢/word (negotiable).** Sometimes pays expenses of writers on assignment.

Columns/Departments Query. **Pays $300-350.**

Tips "The best way to break into the magazine is to empathize with the entrepreneurial and technical background of readership, and come up with an exclusive, original, creative story idea. We pride ourselves on not looking or acting like any other trade publication (composites industry or otherwise). Our editor is very open to suggestions, but they must be unique. Don't waste his time with canned articles dressed up to look exclusive. This is the best way to get on the 'immediate rejection list.'"

DESIGN NEWS

Reed Business Information, 275 Washington St., Newton MA 02458. (617)558-4329. Fax: (617)558-4402. E-mail: kfield@reedbusiness.com. Website: www.designnews.com. Editor: Karen Field. Magazine published 18 times/year dedicated to reporting on the latest technology that OEM design engineers can use in their jobs. Circ. 170,000. Editorial lead time 4-6 months. Sample copy not available.

ECN ELECTRONIC COMPONENT NEWS

Reed Business Information, 100 Enterprise Dr., Suite 600, Box 912, Rockaway NJ 07866. (973)292-5100. Fax: (973)292-0783. E-mail: akalnoskas@reedbusiness.com. Website: www.ecnmag.com. Editor: Aimee Kalnoskas. Managing Editor: Jean Miller. Monthly magazine. Provides design engineers and engineering management in electronics OEM with a monthly update on new products and literature. Circ. 131,052. Editorial lead time 2 months. Sample copy not available.

$ $ FLOW CONTROL

The Magazine of Fluid Handling Systems, Witter Publishing Corp., 20 Commerce St., Suite 2013, Flemington NJ 08822. (908)788-0343, ext. 124. Fax: (908)788-3782. E-mail: flowcontrol@witterpublishing.com. Website: www.flowcontrolnetwork.com. Managing Editor: Annu Mangat. **Contact:** Matt Migliore, editor. **90% freelance written.** Monthly magazine covering fluid handling technology. "*Flow Control* is the technology resource for the fluid handling industry's critical disciplines of control, containment, and measurement. *Flow Control* provides solutions for system design, operational and maintenance challenges in all process and OEM applications." Estab. 1995. Circ. 36,000. Pays on publication. Publishes ms an average of 1 month after acceptance. Byline given. Buys all rights. Accepts queries by mail, e-mail, fax, phone. Writer's guidelines online.

Nonfiction How-to (design or maintenance), technical. No glorified product releases. **Buys 18 mss/year.** Query with published clips or send complete ms. Length: 1,000-2,500 words. **Pays $250-350.** Sometimes pays writers with contributor copies or other premiums.

Photos Offers no additional payment for photos accepted with ms. Captions, identification of subjects required.

Columns/Departments Query with published clips or send complete ms. **Pays $250.**

Tips "Anyone involved in flow control technology and/or applications may submit a manuscript for publication. Articles should be informative and analytical, containing sufficient technical data to support statements and material presented. Articles should not promote any individual product, service, or company. Case history features, describing the use of flow control technologies in specific applications, are welcomed."

LASER FOCUS WORLD MAGAZINE

PennWell, 98 Spit Brook Rd., Nashua NH 03062-2801. (603)891-0123. Fax: (603)891-0574. E-mail: carols@penn well.com. Website: www.laserfocusworld.com. Publisher: Christine Shaw. Group Editorial Director: Stephen G. Anderson. **Contact:** Carol Settino, managing editor. **1% freelance written.** Monthly magazine for physicists, scientists, and engineers involved in the research and development, design, manufacturing, and applications of lasers, laser systems, and all other segments of optoelectronic technologies. Estab. 1968. Circ. 66,000. Publishes ms an average of 6 months after acceptance. Byline given unless anonymity requested. Buys all rights. Accepts queries by mail, e-mail, fax, phone. Responds in 1 month to queries. Sample copy for free. Writer's guidelines online.

Nonfiction Lasers, laser systems, fiberoptics, optics, detectors, sensors, imaging, and other optoelectronic materials, components, instrumentation, and systems. "Each article should serve our reader's need by either stimulating ideas, increasing technical competence, or improving design capabilities in the following areas: natural light and radiation sources, artificial light and radiation sources, light modulators, optical materials and components, image detectors, energy detectors, information displays, image processing, information storage and processing, subsystem and system testing, support equipment, and other related areas. No flighty prose, material not written for our readership, or irrelevant material. Query first with a clear statement and outline of why the article would be important to our readers."

Photos Drawings: Rough drawings accepted and finished by staff technical illustrator. Send photos with submission. Reviews 4×5 color transparencies, 8×10 b&w glossies.

Tips "The writer has a better chance of breaking in at our publication with short articles because shorter articles are easier to schedule, but they must address more carefully our requirements for technical coverage. Most of our submitted materials come from technical experts in the areas we cover. The most frequent mistake made by writers in completing articles for us is that the articles are too commercial, i.e., emphasize a given product or technology from one company. Also, articles are not the right technical depth, too thin, or too scientific."

$ $LD+A

(formerly *Lighting Design & Application*), Illuminating Engineering Society of North America, 120 Wall St., 17th Floor, New York NY 10005. (212)248-5000. Fax: (212)248-5017. E-mail: ptarricone@iesna.org. Website: www.iesna.org. **Contact:** Paul Tarricone, editor. **20% freelance written.** Monthly magazine. "*LD+A* is geared to professionals in lighting design and the lighting field in architecture, retail, entertainment, etc. From designers to educators to sales reps, *LD+A* has a very unique, dedicated, and well-educated audience." Estab. 1971. Circ. 10,000. **Pays on acceptance.** Publishes ms an average of 4 months after acceptance. Byline given. Buys first rights. Editorial lead time 4 months. Submit seasonal material 6 months in advance. Accepts queries by mail, e-mail, fax, phone. Accepts simultaneous submissions. Responds in 2 weeks to queries. Sample copy for free.

Nonfiction "Every year we have entertainment, outdoor, retail and arts, and exhibits issues." Historical/nostalgic, how-to, opinion, personal experience, photo feature, technical. "No articles blatantly promoting a product, company, or individual." **Buys 6-10 mss/year.** Query. Length: 1,500-2,200 words. **Pays $300-400 for assigned articles.**

Photos Send photos with submission. Reviews 4×5 transparencies. Offers no additional payment for photos accepted with ms. Captions required.

Columns/Departments Essay by Invitation (industry trends), 1,200 words. Query. **Does not pay for columns.**

Tips "Most of our features detail the ins and outs of a specific lighting project. From Ricky Martin at the Grammys to the Getty Museum, *LD+A* gives its readers an in-depth look at how the designer(s) reached their goals."

$ $ $MINNESOTA TECHNOLOGY

Inside Technology and Manufacturing Business, Minnesota Technology, Inc., 111 Third Ave. S., Minneapolis MN 55401. (612)373-2900. Fax: (612)339-5214. E-mail: editor@mntech.org. Website: mntechnologymag.com.

Contact: Chris Mikko, editor. **75% freelance written.** Magazine published 5 times/year. "*Minnesota Technology* is read 5 times a year by owners and top management of Minnesota's technology and manufacturing companies. The magazine covers technology trends and issues, global trade, management techniques, and finance. We profile new and growing companies, new products, and the innovators and entrepreneurs of Minnesota's technology sector." Estab. 1991. Circ. 20,000. **Pays on acceptance.** Publishes ms an average of 3 months after acceptance. Byline given. Offers 25% kill fee. Buys first North American serial rights. Editorial lead time 2 months. Submit seasonal material 1 year in advance. Accepts queries by mail, e-mail, fax. Responds in 1 month to queries. Sample copy for 9×12 SAE and 5 first-class stamps. Writer's guidelines online.

Nonfiction General interest, how-to, interview/profile. **Buys 45 mss/year.** Query with published clips. Length: 500-2,000 words. **Pays $150-1,000.**

Columns/Departments Feature Well (Q&A format, provocative ideas from busines and industry leaders), 2,000 words; Up Front (mini profiles, anecdotal news items), 250-500 words. **Buys 30 mss/year.** Query with published clips. **Pays $150-300.**

    ■ The online magazine includes writer's guidelines. Contact: Linda Ball, online editor.

Tips "Query with ideas for short profiles of fascinating Minnesota technology people and business written to interest even the most nontechnical person."

$ $ MINORITY ENGINEER

An Equal Opportunity Career Publication for Professional and Graduating Minority Engineers, Equal Opportunity Publications, Inc., 445 Broad Hollow Rd., Suite 425, Melville NY 11747. (631)421-9421. Fax: (516)421-0359. E-mail: jschneider@eop.com. Website: www.eop.com. **Contact:** James Schneider, editor. **60% freelance written.** Prefers to work with published/established writers. Triannual magazine covering career guidance for minority engineering students and minority professional engineers. Estab. 1969. Circ. 15,000. Pays on publication. Publishes ms an average of 6 months after acceptance. Byline given. Buys first rights. Accepts queries by mail, e-mail, fax, phone. Accepts simultaneous submissions. Sample copy and writer's guidelines for 9×12 SAE with 5 first-class stamps.

Nonfiction "We're interested in articles dealing with career guidance and job opportunities for minority engineers." Book excerpts, general interest (on specific minority engineering concerns), how-to (land a job, keep a job, etc.), interview/profile (minority engineer role models), opinion (problems of ethnic minorities), personal experience (student and career experiences), technical (on career fields offering opportunities for minority engineers), articles on job search techniques, role models. No general information. Query. Length: 1,000-2,000 words. **Pays 10¢/word, $15/photo used.** Sometimes pays expenses of writers on assignment.

Reprints Send ms with rights for sale noted and information about when and where the material previously appeared. Pays 100% of amount paid for an original article.

Photos State availability with submission. Reviews transparencies, prints. Buys all rights. Pays $15. Captions required.

Tips "Articles should focus on career guidance, role model and industry prospects for minority engineers. Prefer articles related to careers, not politically or socially sensitive."

$ $ WOMAN ENGINEER

An Equal Opportunity Career Publication for Graduating Women and Experienced Professionals, Equal Opportunity Publications, Inc., 445 Broad Hollow Rd., Suite 425, Melville NY 11747. (631)421-9421. Fax: (631)421-0359. E-mail: jschneider@eop.com. Website: www.eop.com. **Contact:** James Schneider, editorial director. **60% freelance written.** Works with a small number of new/unpublished writers each year. Triannual magazine covering career guidance for women engineering students and professional women engineers. Estab. 1968. Circ. 16,000. Pays on publication. Publishes ms an average of 1 year after acceptance. Byline given. Buys first North American serial rights. Accepts queries by e-mail. Responds in 3 months to queries. Sample copy and writer's guidelines free.

Nonfiction "Interested in articles dealing with career guidance and job opportunities for women engineers. Looking for manuscripts showing how to land an engineering position and advance professionally. We want features on job-search techniques, engineering disciplines offering career opportunities to women; companies with career advancement opportunities for women; problems facing women engineers and how to cope with such problems; and role-model profiles of successful women engineers, especially in major US corporations." Query. Length: 1,000-2,500 words. **Pays 10¢/word.**

Photos Reviews color slides but will accept b&w. Buys all rights. Pays $15. Captions, identification of subjects required.

Tips "We are looking for 800-1,000 word first-person 'As I See It, personal perspectives.'"

Trade Journals

ENTERTAINMENT & THE ARTS

$ $ $ AMERICAN CINEMATOGRAPHER

The International Journal of Film & Digital Production Techniques, American Society of Cinematographers, 1782 N. Orange Dr., Hollywood CA 90028. (323)969-4333. Fax: (323)876-4973. E-mail: stephen@ascmag.com. Website: www.theasc.com. Senior Editor: Rachael Bosley. **Contact:** Stephen Pizzello, executive editor. **90% freelance written.** Monthly magazine covering cinematography (motion picture, TV, music video, commercial). "*American Cinematographer* is a trade publication devoted to the art and craft of cinematography. Our readers are predominantly film-industry professionals." Estab. 1919. Circ. 45,000. Pays on publication. Publishes ms an average of 2-3 months after acceptance. Byline given. Offers 50% kill fee. Buys all rights. Editorial lead time 2 months. Submit seasonal material 3 months in advance. Accepts queries by mail, e-mail, phone. Responds in 2 weeks to queries; 2 months to mss. Sample copy and writer's guidelines free.

Nonfiction Stephen Pizzello, editor. Interview/profile, new product, technical. No reviews, opinion pieces. **Buys 20-25 mss/year.** Query with published clips. Length: 1,500-4,000 words. **Pays $600-1,200.** Pays in contributor copies if the writer is promoting his/her own product or company. Sometimes pays expenses of writers on assignment.

Tips "Familiarity with the technical side of film production and the ability to present that information in an articulate fashion to our audience are crucial."

BACK STAGE

VNU Business Media, 770 Broadway, New York NY 10003. (646)654-5500. Fax: (646)654-5743. E-mail: backstage@backstage.com. Website: www.backstage.com. Editor-in-Chief: Sherry Eaker. Managing Editor: David Sheward. Weekly magazine covering performing arts. "*Back Stage* was created for actors, singers, dancers, and associated performing arts professionals." Circ. 33,000. Accepts queries by mail. Sample copy for $3.25; $2.95 for New York, New Jersey, Connecticut.

$ $ BOXOFFICE MAGAZINE

RLD Publishing Co., 155 S. El Molino Ave., Suite 100, Pasadena CA 91101. (626)396-0250. Fax: (626)396-0248. E-mail: editorial@boxoffice.com. Website: www.boxoffice.com. Editor-in-chief: Kim Williamson. Senior editor: Francesca Dinglasan. Film & Technology editor: Anlee Ellingson. **Contact:** Christine James, managing editor. **15% freelance written.** Magazine about the motion picture industry for executives and managers working in the film business, including movie theater owners and operators, Hollywood studio personnel and leaders in allied industries. Estab. 1920. Circ. 8,000. Pays on publication. Publishes ms an average of 3 months after acceptance. Byline given. Buys all rights, including electronic publishing. Submit seasonal material 5 months in advance. Accepts queries by mail, e-mail, fax. Sample copy for $5 in US; $10 outside US.

> **O—** "*Boxoffice Magazine* is particularly interested in freelance writers who can write business articles on the exhibition industry or technical writers who are familiar with projection/sound equipment and new technologies such as digital cinema."

Nonfiction "We are a business news magazine about the motion picture industry in general and the theater industry in particular, and as such publish stories on business trends, developments, problems, and opportunities facing the industry. Almost any story will be considered, including corporate profiles, but we don't want gossip or celebrity coverage." Book excerpts, essays, interview/profile, new product, personal experience, photo feature, technical, investigative "all regarding movie theatre business." Query with published clips. Length: 800-2,500 words. **Pays 10¢/word.**

Photos State availability with submission. Reviews prints, slides and JPEG files. Pays $10 per published image. Captions required.

■ The online version of this magazine carries original content. Contact: Kim Williamson.

Tips Purchase a sample copy and read it. Then, write a clear, comprehensive outline of the proposed story, and enclose a résumé and published clips to the managing editor.

$ $ CAMPUS ACTIVITIES

Cameo Publishing Group, P.O. Box 509, Prosperity SC 29127. (800)728-2950. Fax: (803)321-2049. E-mail: cameopublishing@mac.com. Website: www.campusactivitiesmagazine.com; www.cameopublishing.com; www.americanentertainmentmagazine.com. Editor: Ian Kirby. Managing Editor: Laura Moore. **Contact:** WC Kirby, publisher. **75% freelance written.** Magazine published 8 times/year covering entertainment on college campuses. *Campus Activities* goes to entertainment buyers on every campus in the US. Features stories on artists (national and regional), speakers, and the programs at individual schools. Estab. 1991. Circ. 9,872. Pays on publication. Publishes ms an average of 2 months after acceptance. Byline given. Offers 15% kill fee if accepted and not run. Buys first, second serial (reprint), electronic rights. Editorial lead time 2 months. Submit seasonal material

2 months in advance. Accepts queries by mail, e-mail, fax. Accepts simultaneous submissions. Responds in 1 month to queries; 2 months to mss. Sample copy for $3.50. Writer's guidelines free.

Nonfiction Interview/profile, photo feature. Accepts no unsolicited articles. **Buys 40 mss/year.** Query. Length: 1,400-3,000 words. **Pays 13¢/word.** Sometimes pays expenses of writers on assignment.

Photos State availability with submission. Reviews contact sheets, negatives, 3×5 transparencies, 8×10 prints, electronic media at 300 dpi or higher. Buys one-time rights. Negotiates payment individually. Identification of subjects required.

Tips "Writers who have ideas, proposals, and special project requests should contact the publisher prior to any commitment to work on such a story. The publisher welcomes innovative and creative ideas for stories and works with writers on such proposals which have significant impact on our readers."

Ⓝ $ $ CREATE MAGAZINE

Fueling the Professional Creative Community, Brahn Communications, Inc., 5762 S. Semoran Blvd., Orlando FL 32822. Fax: (407)207-0405. E-mail: info@createmagazine.com; newscfl@createmagazine.com. Website: www.createmagazine.com. **Contact:** Rebecca Ramsey, assistant editor (localized stories); Katherine Johnson, assistant editor (national sotries). **90% freelance written.** Quarterly magazine covering advertising, design, photography, printing, film & video, audio & music, animation, new media. *Create Magazine* is the largest trade publication serving the creative community. "We are looking for experts in our respective industries who have writing experience. We are constantly looking for local writers in the 20 cities where we are published to get the latest scoop on the local creative community." Estab. 2000. Circ. 100,000. Pays on publication. Publishes ms an average of 4 months after acceptance. Byline given. Buys first North American serial, electronic rights. Editorial lead time 4-12 months. Submit seasonal material 5 months in advance. Accepts queries by e-mail, fax. Accepts simultaneous submissions. Sample copy for $7.95. Writer's guidelines online.

> ○➔ "Feature stories are assigned, not received, but queries are accepted for departments. Writers familiar with the fields covered by our trade publication and the people who serve them are encouraged to inquire."

Nonfiction How-to (use design/photo software), inspirational, new product, photo feature, technical. Does not want downtrodden musings and frustrations of particular industries. How poorly certain products perform and stream of consciousness writings are not accepted. Query with published clips. Length: 500-2,500 words. **Pays minimum $300 for assigned articles.** "Pays in contributor copies or other premiums if the writer is an 'expert' in his/her field and we publish company info and details."

Photos State availability with submission. Reviews GIF/JPEG files. Offers no additional payment for photos accepted with ms. Captions required.

Tips "Have plenty of contacts in these industries: advertising, new media, photography, film & video, design, printing, audio & music. Be located in one of our 20 markets (Central Florida, South Florida, Southern California, Atlanta, Chicago, New York—see website for all 20)."

$ $ DANCE TEACHER

The Practical Magazine of Dance, Lifestyle Media, Inc., 250 W. 57th St., Suite 420, New York NY 10107. (212)265-8890, ext. 20. Fax: (212)265-8908. E-mail: csims@lifestyleventures.com. Website: www.dance-teacher.com. **Contact:** Caitlin Sims, editor. **80% freelance written.** Monthly magazine. "Our readers are professional dance educators, business persons, and related professionals in all forms of dance." Estab. 1979. Circ. 8,000. Pays on publication. Publishes ms an average of 3 months after acceptance. Byline given. Negotiates rights and permission to reprint on request. Submit seasonal material 6 months in advance. Accepts queries by mail, e-mail, fax, phone. Responds in 3 months to mss. Sample copy for 9×12 SAE and 6 first-class stamps. Writer's guidelines online.

Nonfiction How-to (teach, business), interview/profile, new product, personal experience, photo feature. Special issues: Summer Programs (January); Music & More (July); Costumes and Production Preview (November); College/Training Schools (December). No PR or puff pieces. All articles must be well researched. **Buys 50 mss/year.** Query. Length: 700-2,000 words. **Pays $100-300.**

Photos Send photos with submission. Reviews contact sheets, negatives, transparencies, prints. Limited photo budget.

> ▣ The online magazine carries original content. Contact: Caitlin Sims.

Tips "Read several issues—particularly seasonal. Stay within writer's guidelines."

$ $ DRAMATICS MAGAZINE

Educational Theatre Association, 2343 Auburn Ave., Cincinnati OH 45219-2815. (513)421-3900. Fax: (513)421-7077. E-mail: dcorathers@edta.org. Website: www.edta.org. **Contact:** Donald Corathers, editor-in-chief. **70% freelance written.** Monthly magazine for theater arts students, teachers, and others interested in theater arts education. "*Dramatics* is designed to provide serious, committed young theater students and their teachers with the skills and knowledge they need to make better theater; to be a resource that will help high school juniors and seniors make an informed decision about whether to pursue a career in theater, and about how to do so; and to prepare high school students to be knowledgeable, appreciative audience members for the rest of their lives." Estab. 1929. Circ. 37,000. **Pays on acceptance.** Publishes ms an average of 3 months after acceptance. Byline given. Buys first North American serial rights. Submit seasonal material 3 months in advance. Accepts queries by mail, e-mail, fax. Accepts previously published material. Accepts simultaneous submissions. Responds in 3 months to queries Responds in longer than 3 months to unsolicited mss. Sample copy for 9×12 SAE with 5 first-class stamps. Writer's guidelines online.

> 0→ "The best way to break in is to know our audience—drama students, teachers, and others interested in theater—and to write for them."

Nonfiction How-to (technical theater, directing, acting, etc.), humor, inspirational, interview/profile, photo feature, technical. **Buys 30 mss/year.** Send complete ms. Length: 750-3,000 words. **Pays $50-400.** Sometimes pays expenses of writers on assignment.

Reprints Send tearsheet, photocopy or typed ms with rights for sale noted and information about when and where the material previously appeared. Pays up to 75% of amount paid for original.

Photos Query. Purchased with accompanying ms. Reviews transparencies. Total price for ms usually includes payment for photos.

Fiction Drama (one-act and full-length plays). Prefers unpublished scripts that have been produced at least once. "No plays for children, Christmas plays, or plays written with no attention paid to the conventions of theater." **Buys 5-9 mss/year.** Send complete ms. **Pays $100-400.**

Tips "Writers who have some practical experience in theater, especially in technical areas, have a leg-up here, but we'll work with anybody who has a good idea. Some freelancers have become regular contributors, others ignore style suggestions included in our writer's guidelines."

$ $ $ EMMY MAGAZINE

Academy of Television Arts & Sciences, 5220 Lankershim Blvd., North Hollywood CA 91601-3109. (818)754-2800. Fax: (818)761-2827. E-mail: emmymag@emmys.org. Website: www.emmys.tv. **90% freelance written.** Prefers to work with published/established writers. Bimonthly magazine on television for TV professionals. Circ. 14,000. Pays on publication or within 6 months. Publishes ms an average of 4 months after acceptance. Byline given. Offers 25% kill fee. Buys first North American serial rights. Accepts queries by mail, e-mail. Responds in 1 month to queries. Sample copy for 9×12 SAE and 6 first-class stamps. Writer's guidelines online.

Nonfiction Articles on contemporary issues, trends, and VIPs (especially those behind the scenes) in broadcast and cable TV; programming and new technology. "Looking for profiles of fascinating people who work 'below the line' in television. Also, always looking for new writers who understand technology and new media and can write about it in an engaging manner. We require TV industry expertise and clear, lively writing." Query with published clips. Length: 1,500-2,000 words. **Pays $1,000-1,200.**

Columns/Departments Most written by regular contributors, but newcomers can break in with filler items in In the Mix or short profiles in Labors of Love. Length: 250-500 words, depending on department. Query with published clips. **Pays $250-500.**

Tips "Please review recent issues before querying us. Query with published, television-related clips. No fanzine, academic, or nostalgic approaches, please. Demonstrate experience in covering the business of television and your ability to write in a lively and compelling manner about programming trends and new technology. Identify fascinating people behind the scenes, not just in the executive suites but in all ranks of the industry."

$ $ RELEASE PRINT

The Magazine of Film Arts Foundation, Film Arts Foundation, 145 9th St., Suite 101, San Francisco CA 94103. (415)552-8760. Fax: (415)552-0882. E-mail: releaseprint@filmarts.org. Website: www.filmarts.org. Editor: Shari Kizirian. **Contact:** Editor. **80% freelance written.** Bimonthly magazine covering US independent filmmaking. "We have a knowledgeable readership of film and videomakers. They are interested in the financing, production, exhibition, and distribution of independent films and videos. They are interested in practical, technical issues and, to a lesser extent, aesthetic ones." Estab. 1977. Circ. 5,000. Pays on publication. Publishes ms an average of 3 months after acceptance. Byline given. Buys all rights for commissioned works. For works submitted on spec, buys first rights and requests acknowledgement of Release Print in any subsequent publication. Editorial lead time 4 months. Accepts queries by e-mail. Responds in 6 weeks to queries; 2 months to mss. Sample copy for $5 (payable to Film Arts Foundation) and 9×12 SASE with $1.52 postage.

> 0→ Break in with a proposal for an article or interview of an American experimental, documentary or very low budget feature film/video maker with ties to the San Francisco Bay area (or an upcoming screening in this area). Submit at least 4 months prior to publication date.

Nonfiction Interview/profile, technical, book recommendations, case studies. No film criticism or reviews. **Buys 70-72 mss/year.** Query. Length: 500-2,000 words. Sometimes pays expenses of writers on assignment.

Photos Send photos with submission. Reviews prints. Buys one-time rights. Offers no additional payment for photos accepted with ms. Identification of subjects required.
Columns/Departments Query. **Pays 10¢/word.**

$ SCREEN MAGAZINE
Screen Enterprises, Inc., 222 W. Ontario St., Suite 500, Chicago IL 60610. (312)640-0800. Fax: (312)640-1928. E-mail: coverage@screenmag.com. Website: www.screenmag.com. **Contact:** Julie Mynatt, editor. **5% freelance written.** Biweekly Chicago-based trade magazine covering advertising and film production in the Midwest and national markets. "*Screen* is written for Midwest producers (and other creatives involved) of commercials, AV, features, independent corporate and multimedia." Estab. 1979. Circ. 15,000. Pays on publication. Publishes ms an average of a few weeks after acceptance. Byline given. Makes work-for-hire assignments. Accepts queries by e-mail. Responds in 3 weeks to queries. Sample copy online.
Nonfiction Interview/profile, new product, technical. "No general AV; nothing specific to other markets; no no-brainers or opinion." **Buys 26 mss/year.** Query with published clips. Length: 750-1,500 words. **Pays $50.**
Photos Send photos with submission. Reviews prints. Offers no additional payment for photos accepted with ms. Captions required.
Tips "Our readers want to know facts and figures. They want to know the news about a company or an individual. We provide exclusive news of this market, in as much depth as space allows without being boring, with lots of specific information and details. We write knowledgably about the market we serve. We recognize the film/video-making process is a difficult one because it 1) is often technical, 2) has implications not immediately discerned."

$ SOUTHERN THEATRE
Southeastern Theatre Conference, P.O. Box 9868, Greensboro NC 27429-0868. (336)292-6041. E-mail: deanna@setc.org. Website: www.setc.org. **Contact:** Deanna Thompson, editor. **100% freelance written.** Quarterly magazine "covering all aspects of theater in the Southeast, from innovative theater companies, to important trends, to people making a difference in the region. All stories must be written in a popular magazine style but with subject matter appropriate for theater professionals (not the general public). The audience includes members of the Southeastern Theatre Conference, founded in 1949 and the nation's largest regional theater organization. These members include individuals involved in professional, community, college/university, children's, and secondary school theater. The magazine also is purchased by more than 100 libraries." Estab. 1962. Circ. 4,200. Pays on publication. Publishes ms an average of 3 months after acceptance. Byline given. Buys first North American serial, first, one-time, second serial (reprint), electronic rights. Editorial lead time 3 months. Submit seasonal material 6 months in advance. Accepts queries by mail, e-mail. Responds in 3 months to queries; 6 months to mss. Sample copy for $6. Writer's guidelines online.
Nonfiction Looking for stories on design/technology, playwriting, acting, directing, all with a Southeastern connection. General interest (innovative theaters and theater programs, trend stories), interview/profile (people making a difference in Southeastern theater). Special issues: Playwriting (Fall issue, all stories submitted by January 1). No scholarly articles. **Buys 15-20 mss/year.** Query with or without published clips or send complete ms. Length: 1,000-3,000 words. **Pays $50 for feature stories.** Pays in contributor copies for book reviews, sidebars, and other short stories.
Photos State availability of or send photos with submission. Reviews transparencies, prints. Offers no additional payment for photos accepted with ms. Captions, identification of subjects, model releases required.
Columns/Departments Outside the Box (innovative solutions to problems faced by designers and technicians), 800-1,000 words; Words, Words, Words (reviews of books on theater), 400-550 words; Rants & Raves (column where theater professionals can sound off on issues), 400-500 words. Query or send complete ms. **No payment for columns.**
Tips "Look for a theater or theater person in your area that is doing something different or innovative that would be of interest to others in the profession, then write about that theater or person in a compelling way. We also are looking for well-written trend stories (talk to theaters in your area about trends that are affecting them), and we especially like stories that help our readers do their jobs more effectively. Send an e-mail detailing a well-developed story idea, and ask if we're interested."

FARM

AGRICULTURAL EQUIPMENT

$ $ IMPLEMENT & TRACTOR
Agri USA, 2302 W. First St., Cedar Falls IA 50613. (319)277-3599. Fax: (319)277-3783. E-mail: mshepherd@cfu.net. Website: www.implementandtractor.com. **Contact:** Mary Shepherd, editor. **10% freelance written.** Bi-

monthly magazine covering the agricultural equipment industry. "*Implement & Tractor* offers equipment reviews and business news for agricultural equipment dealers, ag equipment manufacturers, distributors, and aftermarket suppliers." Estab. 1895. Circ. 5,000. Pays on publication. Publishes ms an average of 3-4 months after acceptance. Byline given. Buys all rights. Editorial lead time 2 months. Accepts queries by mail, e-mail, fax. Responds in 2 months to queries. Sample copy for $6.

◑⇥ The biggest freelance opportunity is for dealership profiles.

Nonfiction No fiction, cartoons, how-to, general farm machinery articles or farmer profiles articles. Length: 600-1,200 words. **Pays $100-200 (including photos).**

Tips "Know the retail agricultural equipment industry, have an engineer's outlook for analyzing machinery and a writer's skills to communicate that information. Technical background is helpful, as is mechanical aptitude."

CROPS & SOIL MANAGEMENT

$ $ AMERICAN AND WESTERN FRUIT GROWER

(formerly *American Fruit Grower*), Meister Media Worldwide, 37733 Euclid Ave., Willoughby OH 44094. (440)942-2000. E-mail: bdsparks@meistermedia.com. Website: www.fruitgrower.com. **Contact:** Brian Sparks, managing editor. **3% freelance written.** Annual magazine covering commercial fruit growing. "How-to" articles are best. Estab. 1880. Circ. 44,000. Pays on publication. Publishes ms an average of 4 months after acceptance. Byline given. Buys first rights. Editorial lead time 2 months. Submit seasonal material 4 months in advance. Accepts queries by mail, e-mail, fax, phone. Responds in 2 weeks to queries; 2 months to mss. Sample copy and writer's guidelines free.

Nonfiction How-to (better grow fruit crops). **Buys 6-10 mss/year.** Query with published clips or send complete ms. Length: 800-1,200 words. **Pays $200-250.** Sometimes pays expenses of writers on assignment.

Photos Send photos with submission. Reviews prints, slides. Buys one-time rights. Negotiates payment individually.

$ $ COTTON GROWER MAGAZINE

Meister Media Worldwide, 65 Germantown Court, #202, Cordova TN 38018. (901)756-8822. Fax: (901)756-8879. E-mail: frgiles@meistermedia.com. **Contact:** Frank Giles, editor. **5% freelance written.** Monthly magazine covering cotton production, cotton markets and related subjects. Readers are mostly cotton producers who seek information on production practices, equipment and products related to cotton. Estab. 1901. Circ. 43,000. **Pays on acceptance.** Publishes ms an average of 2 months after acceptance. Byline given. Buys first rights. Editorial lead time 2 months. Submit seasonal material 2 months in advance. Accepts queries by mail, e-mail, fax, phone. Accepts simultaneous submissions. Sample copy for free. Writer's guidelines not available.

Nonfiction Interview/profile, new product, photo feature, technical. No fiction or humorous pieces. **Buys 5-10 mss/year.** Query with published clips. Length: 500-800 words. **Pays $200-400.** Sometimes pays expenses of writers on assignment.

Photos State availability with submission. Reviews transparencies. Buys all rights. Offers no additional payment for photos accepted with ms. Captions, identification of subjects required.

$ THE FRUIT GROWERS NEWS

Great American Publishing, P.O. Box 128, Sparta MI 49345. (616)887-9008. Fax: (616)887-2666. E-mail: editor@ fruitgrowersnews.com. Website: www.fruitgrowersnews.com. Publisher: Matt McCallum. **Contact:** Kimberly Warren, editor. **25% freelance written.** Monthly tabloid covering agriculture. "Our objective is to provide commercial fruit growers of all sizes with information to help them succeed." Estab. 1970. Circ. 28,000. Pays on publication. Publishes ms an average of 2 months after acceptance. Makes work-for-hire assignments. Editorial lead time 1 month. Submit seasonal material 1 month in advance. Accepts queries by mail, e-mail, fax. Accepts simultaneous submissions. Responds in 2 weeks to queries; 1 month to mss. Sample copy for free.

Nonfiction General interest, interview/profile, new product. No advertorials, other "puff pieces." **Buys 72 mss/ year.** Query with published clips. Length: 800-1,200 words. **Pays $100-125.** Sometimes pays expenses of writers on assignment.

Photos Send photos with submission. Reviews prints. Buys one-time rights. Offers $15/photo. Captions required.

$ GRAIN JOURNAL

Country Publications, Inc., 3065 Pershing Ct., Decatur IL 62526. (217)877-8660. Fax: (217)877-6647. E-mail: ed@grainnet.com. Website: www.grainnet.com. **Contact:** Ed Zdrojewski, editor. **5% freelance written.** Bimonthly magazine covering grain handling and merchandising. "*Grain Journal* serves the North American grain industry, from the smallest country grain elevators and feed mills to major export terminals." Estab. 1972. Circ. 12,000. Pays on publication. Publishes ms an average of 2 months after acceptance. Byline sometimes given. Buys first rights. Editorial lead time 2 months. Submit seasonal material 2 months in advance. Accepts simultaneous submissions. Sample copy for free.

Nonfiction How-to, interview/profile, new product, technical. Query. Length: 750 words maximum. **Pays $100.**

Photos Send photos with submission. Reviews contact sheets, negatives, transparencies, 3×5 prints. Buys one-time rights. Offers $50-100/photo. Captions, identification of subjects required.

Tips "Call with your idea. We'll let you know if it is suitable for our publication."

$ONION WORLD

Columbia Publishing, P.O. Box 9036, Yakima WA 98909-0036. (509)248-2452, ext. 152. Fax: (509)248-4056. E-mail: brent@freshcut.com. Website: www.onionworld.net. **Contact:** Brent Clement, managing editor. Carrie Kennington, editor. **25% freelance written.** Monthly magazine covering the world of onion production and marketing for onion growers and shippers. Estab. 1985. Circ. 5,500. Pays on publication. Publishes ms an average of 1 month after acceptance. Byline given. Not copyrighted. Buys first North American serial rights. Submit seasonal material 1 month in advance. Accepts queries by mail, e-mail, fax, phone. Accepts simultaneous submissions. Responds in 1 month to queries. Sample copy for 9×12 SAE and 5 first-class stamps.

• Columbia Publishing also produces *Fresh Cut*, *The Tomato Magazine*, *Potato Country*, *RVgolfer*, and *Carrot Country*.

Nonfiction General interest, historical/nostalgic, interview/profile. **Buys 30 mss/year.** Query. Length: 1,200-1,250 words. **Pays $5/column inch for assigned articles.**

Reprints Send photocopy and information about when and where the material previously appeared. Pays 50% of amount paid for an original article.

Photos Send photos with submission. Buys all rights. Offers no additional payment for photos accepted with ms, unless it's a cover shot. Captions, identification of subjects required.

Tips "Writers should be familiar with growing and marketing onions. We use a lot of feature stories on growers, shippers, and others in the onion trade—what they are doing, their problems, solutions, marketing plans, etc."

$THE VEGETABLE GROWERS NEWS

Great American Publishing, P.O. Box 128, Sparta MI 49345. (616)887-9008. Fax: (616)887-2666. E-mail: editor@vegetablegrowersnews.com. Website: www.vegetablegrowersnews.com. Publisher: Matt McCallum. **Contact:** Kimberly Warren, editor. **25% freelance written.** Monthly tabloid covering agriculture. "Our objective is to provide commercial vegetable growers of all sizes with information to help them succeed." Estab. 1970. Circ. 28,000. Pays on publication. Publishes ms an average of 2 months after acceptance. Makes work-for-hire assignments. Editorial lead time 1 month. Submit seasonal material 1 month in advance. Accepts queries by mail, e-mail, fax. Accepts simultaneous submissions. Responds in 2 weeks to queries; 1 month to mss. Sample copy for free.

Nonfiction General interest, interview/profile, new product. No advertorials, other "puff pieces." **Buys 72 mss/year.** Query with published clips. Length: 800-1,200 words. **Pays $100-125.** Sometimes pays expenses of writers on assignment.

Photos Send photos with submission. Reviews prints. Buys one-time rights. Offers $15/photo. Captions required.

DAIRY FARMING

$DAIRY GOAT JOURNAL

Central Countryside Publications, Ltd., W11564 State Hwy. 64, Withee WI 54498. (715)785-7979. Fax: (715)785-7414. Website: www.dairygoatjournal.com. **Contact:** Jennifer Stultz, editor. **45% freelance written.** Monthly journal. "We are looking for clear and accurate articles about dairy goat owners, their herds, cheesemaking, and other ways of marketing products. Some readers own two goats; others own 1,500 and are large commercial operations." Estab. 1917. Circ. 8,000, including copies to more than 70 foreign countries. Pays on publication. Byline given.

Nonfiction Information on personalities and on public issues affecting dairy goats and their owners. How-to articles with plenty of practical information. Health and husbandry articles should be written with appropriate experience or academic credentials. **Buys 100 mss/year.** Query with published clips. Length: 750-2,500 words. **Pays $50-150.** Pays expenses of writers on assignment.

Photos Color or b&w. Vertical cover. Goats and/or people. Pays $100 maximum for covers; $20-70 for inside use or for b&w. Identification of subjects required.

$ $HOARD'S DAIRYMAN

W.D. Hoard and Sons, Co., P.O. Box 801, Fort Atkinson WI 53538. (920)563-5551. Fax: (920)563-7298. E-mail: hoards@hoards.com. Website: www.hoards.com. Tabloid published 20 times/year covering dairy industry.

"We publish semi-technical information published for dairy-farm families and their advisors." Estab. 1885. Circ. 100,000. **Pays on acceptance.** Publishes ms an average of 4 months after acceptance. Byline given. Buys first rights. Editorial lead time 2 months. Submit seasonal material 3 months in advance. Accepts queries by mail, e-mail, fax. Responds in 2 weeks to queries; 1 month to mss. Sample copy for 12×15 SAE and $3. Writer's guidelines for #10 SASE.

Nonfiction How-to, technical. **Buys 60 mss/year.** Query. Length: 800-1,500 words. **Pays $150-350.**

Photos Send photos with submission. Reviews 2×2 transparencies. Offers no additional payment for photos accepted with ms.

$ ☐ WESTERN DAIRY FARMER

Bowes Publishers, Ltd., 4504—61 Ave., Leduc AB T9E 3Z1 Canada. (780)980-7488. Fax: (780)986-6397. E-mail: editor-wdf-caf@webcoleduc.com. Website: www.westerndairyfarmer.com. **Contact:** Diana Macleod, editor. **70% freelance written.** Bimonthly magazine covering the dairy industry. *"Western Dairy Farmer* is a trade publication dealing with issues surrounding the dairy industry. The magazine features innovative articles on animal health, industry changes, new methods of dairying, and personal experiences. Sometimes highlights successful farmers." Estab. 1991. Circ. 6,300. Pays on publication. Publishes ms an average of 4 months after acceptance. Byline given. Buys all rights. Editorial lead time 2 months. Submit seasonal material 2 months in advance. Accepts queries by mail, e-mail, fax. Responds in 2 weeks to queries; 2 months to mss. Sample copy for 9×12 SAE.

Nonfiction "All topics/submissions must be related to the dairy industry." General interest, how-to, interview/ profile, new product, personal experience (only exceptional stories), technical. "Not interested in anything vague, trite, or not dairy related." **Buys 50 mss/year.** Query or send complete ms. Length: 900-1,200 words. **Pays $75-150.**

Photos State availability with submission. Reviews GIF/JPEG files. Buys all rights. Offers no additional payment for photos accepted with ms. Captions, identification of subjects, model releases required.

Tips "Know the industry inside and out. Provide contact names and phone numbers (both for writers and subjects) with submissions. Remember, this is a specialized trade publication, and our readers are well-acquainted with the issues and appreciate new up-to-date information."

$ $ WESTERN DAIRYBUSINESS

Dairy Business Communications, Heritage Complex, Suite 218, 4500 S. Laspina, Tulare CA 93274. (559)687-3160. Fax: (559)687-3166. E-mail: rgoble@dairybusiness.com. Website: www.dairybusiness.com. **Contact:** Ron Goble, editor. **10% freelance written.** Prefers to work with published/established writers. Monthly magazine dealing with large-herd commercial dairy industry. Rarely publishes information about non-Western producers or dairy groups and events. Estab. 1922. Circ. 17,000. Pays on publication. Publishes ms an average of 3 months after acceptance. Byline given. Buys first North American serial rights. Submit seasonal material 3 months in advance. Accepts queries by mail, e-mail. Responds in 1 month to queries. Sample copy for 9×12 SAE and 4 first-class stamps.

Nonfiction Special emphasis on: environmental stewardship, herd management systems, business management, facilities/equipment, forage/cropping. Interview/profile, new product, opinion, industry analysis. "No religion, nostalgia, politics, or 'mom and pop' dairies." Query, or send complete ms. Length: 300-1,500 words. **Pays $25-400 for assigned articles.**

Reprints Seldom accepts previously published submissions. Send information about when and where the article previously appeared. Pays 50% of amount paid for an original article.

Photos Photos are a critical part of story packages. Send photos with submission. Reviews contact sheets, 35mm or 2¼×2¼ transparencies. Buys one-time rights. Pays $25 for b&w; $50-100 for color. Captions, identification of subjects required.

Tips "Know the market and the industry, be well-versed in large-herd dairy management and business."

LIVESTOCK

$ $ ANGUS BEEF BULLETIN

Angus Productions, Inc., 3201 Frederick Ave., St. Joseph MO 64506. (816)383-5270. Fax: (816)233-6575. E-mail: shermel@angusjournal.com. Website: www.angusebeefbulletin.com. **Contact:** Shauna Rose Hermel, editor. **45% freelance written.** Tabloid published 4 times/year covering commercial cattle industry. "The *Bulletin* is mailed free to commercial cattlemen who have purchased an Angus bull and had the registration transferred to them and to others who sign a request card." Estab. 1985. Circ. 67,000. Pays on publication. Publishes ms an average of 3 months after acceptance. Byline given. Buys first, electronic rights. Editorial lead time 3 months. Submit seasonal material 3 months in advance. Accepts queries by mail, e-mail. Accepts simultaneous submissions. Responds in 3 weeks to queries; 3 months to mss. Sample copy for $5. Writer's guidelines for #10 SASE.

Nonfiction How-to (cattle production), interview/profile, technical (cattle production). **Buys 10 mss/year.** Query with published clips. Length: 800-2,500 words. **Pays $50-600.** Pays expenses of writers on assignment. **Photos** Send photos with submission. Reviews 5×7 transparencies, 5×7 glossy prints. Buys all rights. Offers $25/photo. Identification of subjects required.

Tips "Read the publication and have a firm grasp of the commercial cattle industry and how the Angus breed fits in that industry."

$ $ $ ANGUS JOURNAL

Angus Productions Inc., 3201 Frederick Ave., St. Joseph MO 64506-2997. (816)383-5270. Fax: (816)233-6575. E-mail: shermel@angusjournal.com. Website: www.angusjournal.com. **Contact:** Shauna Rose Hermel, editor. **40% freelance written.** Monthly magazine covering Angus cattle. "The *Angus Journal* is the official magazine of the American Angus Association. Its primary function as such is to report to the membership association activities and information pertinent to raising Angus cattle." Estab. 1919. Circ. 17,000. Pays on publication. Publishes ms an average of 3 months after acceptance. Byline given. Buys first, electronic rights. Editorial lead time 2 months. Submit seasonal material 3 months in advance. Accepts queries by mail, e-mail, fax. Accepts simultaneous submissions. Responds in 3 weeks to queries; 2 months to mss. Sample copy for $5. Writer's guidelines for #10 SASE.

Nonfiction How-to (cattle production), interview/profile, technical (related to cattle). **Buys 20-30 mss/year.** Query with published clips. Length: 800-3,500 words. **Pays $50-1,000.** Pays expenses of writers on assignment. **Photos** Send photos with submission. Reviews 5×7 glossy prints. Buys all rights. Offers $25-400/photo. Identification of subjects required.

Tips "Read the magazine and have a firm grasp of the cattle industry."

$ $ THE CATTLEMAN

Texas and Southwestern Cattle Raisers Association, 1301 W. 7th St., Ft. Worth TX 76102-2660. (817)332-7064. Fax: (817)332-5446. E-mail: anita@texascattleraisers.org. Website: www.thecattlemanmagazine.com. Editor: Lionel Chambers. Managing Editor: Ellen Humphries. **Contact:** Anita Braddock, director. **25% freelance written.** Monthly magazine covering the Texas/Oklahoma beef cattle industry. "We specialize in in-depth, management-type articles related to range and pasture, beef cattle production, animal health, nutrition, and marketing. We want 'how-to' articles." Estab. 1914. Circ. 15,400. **Pays on acceptance.** Publishes ms an average of 2 months after acceptance. Byline given. Buys exclusive and one-time rights, plus rights to post on website in month of publication. Editorial lead time 2 months. Submit seasonal material 6 months in advance. Accepts queries by mail, e-mail, fax. Sample copy for free. Writer's guidelines online.

○━ Break in with "clips from other cattle magazines and demonstrated knowledge of our audiences."

Nonfiction How-to, interview/profile, new product, personal experience, technical, ag research. Editorial calendar theme issues include: Horses (January); Range and Pasture (February); Livestock Marketing (July); Hereford and Wildlife (August); Feedlots (September); Bull Buyers (October); Ranch Safety (December). Does not want to see anything not specifically related to beef production in the Southwest. **Buys 20 mss/year.** Query with published clips. Length: 1,500-2,000 words. **Pays $200-350 for assigned articles; $100-350 for unsolicited articles.** Sometimes pays expenses of writers on assignment.

Photos Reviews transparencies, prints, digital files. Buys one-time rights. Offers no additional payment for photos accepted with ms. Identification of subjects required.

Tips "In our most recent readership survey, subscribers said they were most interested in the following topics in this order: range/pasture, property rights, animal health, water, new innovations, and marketing. *The Cattleman* prefers to work on an assignment basis. However, prospective contributors are urged to write the managing editor of the magazine to inquire of interest on a proposed subject. Occasionally, the editor will return a manuscript to a potential contributor for cutting, polishing, checking, rewriting, or condensing. Be able to demonstrate background/knowledge in this field. Include tearsheets from similar magazines."

$ $ FEED LOT MAGAZINE

Feed Lot Magazine, Inc., P.O. Box 850, Dighton KS 67839. (620)397-2838. Fax: (620)397-2839. E-mail: feedlot @st-tel.net. Website: www.feedlotmagazine.com. **Contact:** Robert A. Strong, editor (rstrong@st-tel.net). **40% freelance written.** Bimonthly magazine. "The editorial information content fits a dual role: large feedlots and their related cow/calf operations, and large 500pl cow/calf, 100pl stocker operations. The information covers all phases of production from breeding, genetics, animal health, nutrition, equipment design, research through finishing fat cattle. *Feed Lot* publishes a mix of new information and timely articles which directly affect the cattle industry." Estab. 1993. Circ. 12,000. Pays on publication. Publishes ms an average of 2 months after acceptance. Byline given. Offers 50% kill fee. Buys all rights. Editorial lead time 2 months. Submit seasonal material 6 months in advance. Accepts queries by mail, e-mail, fax. Responds in 1 month to queries. Sample copy and writer's guidelines for $1.50.

Nonfiction Interview/profile, new product (cattle-related), photo feature. Send complete ms. Length: 100-400 words. **Pays 20¢/word.**

Reprints Send tearsheet or typed ms with rights for sale noted and information about when and where the material previously appeared. Pays 50% of amount paid for an original article.

Photos State availability of or send photos with submission. Reviews contact sheets. Buys all rights. Negotiates payment individually. Captions, model releases required.

Tips "Know what you are writing about—have a good knowledge of the subject."

$SHEEP! MAGAZINE

Countryside Publications, Ltd., W11564 State Hwy. 64, Withee WI 54498. (715)785-7979. Fax: (715)785-7414. Website: www.sheepmagazine.com. **Contact:** Nathan Griffin, editor. **35% freelance written.** Prefers to work with published/established writers. Bimonthly magazine. "We're looking for clear, concise, useful information for sheep raisers who have a few sheep to a 1,000 ewe flock." Estab. 1980. Circ. 4,000. Pays on publication. Byline given. Offers $30 kill fee. Buys all rights or makes work-for-hire assignments. Submit seasonal material 3 months in advance.

Nonfiction Information (on personalities and/or political, legal, or environmental issues affecting the sheep industry); health and husbandry articles should be written by someone with extensive experience or appropriate credentials (i.e., a veterinarian or animal scientist); features (on small businesses that promote wool products and stories about local and regional sheep producers' groups and their activities); first-person narratives; book excerpts; how-to (on innovative lamb and wool marketing and promotion techniques, efficient record-keeping systems, or specific aspects of health and husbandry); interview/profile (on experienced sheep producers who detail the economics and management of their operation); new product (of value to sheep producers, should be written by someone who has used them); technical (on genetics health and nutrition). **Buys 80 mss/year.** Query with published clips or send complete ms. Length: 750-2,500 words. **Pays $45-150.**

Photos Color—vertical compositions of sheep and/or people—for cover. Use only b&w inside magazine. Black & white, 35mm photos or other visuals improve chances of a sale. Buys all rights. Identification of subjects required.

Tips "Send us your best ideas and photos! We love good writing!"

MANAGEMENT

$AG JOURNAL

Arkansas Valley Publishing, P.O. Box 500, La Junta CO 81050. (800)748-1997. Fax: (719)384-2867. E-mail: ag-edit@centurytel.net. Website: www.agjournalonline.com. **Contact:** Pat R. Ptolemy, editor. **20% freelance written.** Weekly journal covering agriculture. "The *Ag Journal* covers people, issues and events relevant to ag producers in our seven state region (Colorado, Kansas, Oklahoma, Texas, Wyoming, Nebraska, New Mexico)." Estab. 1949. Circ. 11,000. Pays on publication. Publishes ms an average of 2 weeks after acceptance. Byline given. Buys first, one-time rights, makes work-for-hire assignments. Editorial lead time 1 month. Submit seasonal material 1 month in advance. Accepts queries by e-mail. Accepts previously published material. Responds in 2 weeks to queries. Sample copy and writer's guidelines free.

Nonfiction How-to, interview/profile, new product, opinion, photo feature, technical. Query by e-mail only. **Pays 4¢/word.** Sometimes pays expenses of writers on assignment.

Photos State availability with submission. Buys one-time rights. Offers $8/photo. Captions, identification of subjects required.

$ $NEW HOLLAND NEWS

P.O. Box 1895, New Holland PA 17557-0903. Website: www.newholland.com/na. **Contact:** Gary Martin, editor. **60% freelance written.** Works with a small number of new/unpublished writers each year. Magazine published 8 times/year covering agriculture and non-farm country living; designed to entertain and inform farm families and provide ideas for small acreage outdoor projects. Estab. 1960. **Pays on acceptance.** Publishes ms an average of 10 months after acceptance. Byline given. Offers negotiable kill fee. Buys first North American serial rights. Submit seasonal material 6 months in advance. Accepts queries by mail. Responds in 2 months to queries. Sample copy and writer's guidelines for 9×12 SAE with 2 first-class stamps.

    O➤ Break in with an "agricultural 'economic' success story with all the management details."

Nonfiction "We need strong photo support for articles of 1,200-1,700 words on farm management, farm human interest and rural lifestyles." Inspirational, photo feature. **Buys 40 mss/year.** Query. **Pays $700-900.** Pays expenses of writers on assignment.

Photos Send photos with submission. Reviews color photos in any format. Buys one-time rights. Pays $50-300, $500 for cover shot. Captions, identification of subjects, model releases required.

Tips "The writer must have an emotional understanding of agriculture and the farm family and must demonstrate in the article an understanding of the unique economics that affect farming in North America. We want to know about the exceptional farm managers, those leading the way in agriculture. Use anecdotes freely.''

SMALL FARM TODAY

The How-to Magazine of Alternative and Traditional Crops, Livestock, and Direct Marketing, Missouri Farm Publishing, Inc., Ridge Top Ranch, 3903 W. Ridge Trail Rd., Clark MO 65243-9525. (573)687-3525. Fax: (573)687-3148. E-mail: smallfarm@socket.net. Website: www.smallfarmtoday.com. Editor: Ron Macher. **Contact:** Paul Berg, managing editor. Bimonthly magazine ''for small farmers and small-acreage landowners interested in diversification, direct marketing, alternative crops, horses, draft animals, small livestock, exotic and minor breeds, home-based businesses, gardening, vegetable and small fruit crops.'' Estab. 1984 as *Missouri Farm Magazine.* Circ. 12,000. Pays 60 days after publication. Publishes ms an average of 6 months after acceptance. Byline given. Buys first serial and nonexclusive reprint rights (right to reprint article in an anthology). Submit seasonal material 4 months in advance. Accepts queries by mail, e-mail, fax. Responds in 3 months to queries. Sample copy for $3. Writer's guidelines online.

O-- Break in with a detailed ''how-to'' story with budget information on a specific crop or animal.

Nonfiction Practical and how-to (small farming, gardening, alternative crops/livestock). Special issues: Poultry (January); Wool & Fiber (March); Aquaculture (July); Equipment (November). Query letters recommended. Length: 1,200-2,600 words.

Reprints Send tearsheet, photocopy or typed ms with rights for sale noted and information about when and where the material previously appeared. Pays 57% of amount paid for an original article.

Photos Send photos with submission. Buys one-time and nonexclusive reprint rights (for anthologies). Offers $6 for inside photos and $10 for cover photos. Pays $4 for negatives or slides. Captions required.

Tips ''No poetry or humor. Your topic must apply to the small farm or acreage. It helps to provide more practical and helpful information without the fluff. We need 'how-to' articles (how-to grow, raise, market, build, etc.), as well as articles about small farmers who are experiencing success through diversification, specialty/alternative crops and livestock, and direct marketing.''

MISCELLANEOUS

$ $ BEE CULTURE

P.O. Box 706, Medina OH 44256-0706. Fax: (330)725-5624. E-mail: kim@beeculture.com. Website: www.beeculture.com. **Contact:** (Mr.) Kim Flottum, editor. **50% freelance written.** Monthly magazine for beekeepers and those interested in the natural science of honey bees, with environmentally-oriented articles relating to honey bees or pollination. Estab. 1873. Pays on both publication and acceptance. Publishes ms an average of 4 months after acceptance. Buys first North American serial rights. Accepts queries by mail, e-mail, fax, phone. Responds in 1 month to mss. Sample copy for 9×12 SAE and 5 first-class stamps. Writer's guidelines online.

O-- Break in with marketing strategies, interviews of successful beekeepers or beekeeping science, making management of bees easier or less expensive.

Nonfiction Interested in articles giving new ideas on managing bees. Also looking for articles on honey bee/ environment connections or relationships. Also uses success stories about commercial beekeepers. Interview/ profile, personal experience, photo feature. No ''how I began beekeeping'' articles. No highly advanced, technical, and scientific abstracts, or impractical advice. Length: 2,000 words average. **Pays $100-200.**

Reprints Send photocopy and information about when and where the material previously appeared. Pays 50% of amount paid for an original article, on negotiation.

Photos ''B&W or color prints, 5×7 standard, but 3×5 are OK. 35mm slides, mid-format transparencies are excellent. Electronic images accepted and encouraged.'' Pays $7-10 each, $50 for cover photos.

Tips ''Do an interview story on commercial beekeepers who are cooperative enough to furnish accurate, factual information on their operations. Frequent mistakes made by writers in completing articles are that they are too general in nature and lack management knowledge.''

REGIONAL

$ ⬚ CENTRAL ALBERTA FARMER

Bowes Publishers, Ltd., 4504—61 Ave., Leduc AB T9E 3Z1 Canada. (780)986-2271. Fax: (780)986-6397. E-mail: editor-wdf-caf@webcoleduc.com. Website: www.albertafarmer.com. **Contact:** Diana MacLeod, editor. **10% freelance written.** Monthly tabloid covering farming issues specific to or affecting farmers in central Alberta, Canada. ''*Central Alberta Farmer* is an industry magazine-type product that deals with issues in farming. It also highlights value-added efforts in agriculture and features stories on rural lifestyles.'' Estab. 1993. Circ. 36,000. Pays on publication. Publishes ms an average of 3 months after acceptance. Byline given. Buys all rights.

Editorial lead time 3 months. Submit seasonal material 4 months in advance. Accepts queries by mail, e-mail, fax. Accepts simultaneous submissions. Responds in 2 weeks to queries; 2 months to mss. Sample copy for 9×12 SAE.

Nonfiction "All articles must be related to an aspect of farming in the area *Central Alberta Farmer* covers. Freelance articles must be exceptional. Not many are accepted." General interest, how-to, interview/profile, new product, personal experience, technical. "Not interested in anything trite or trivial." **Buys 5 mss/year.** Query or send complete ms. Length: 1,000-1,500 words. **Pays $20-30.**

Photos State availability with submission. Reviews GIF/JPEG files. Buys all rights. Offers no additional payment for photos accepted with ms. Captions, identification of subjects, model releases required.

Tips "Know the industry well. Provide names and phone numbers with submissions (both yours and the people in the article). This is a difficult publication to break into because most copy is generated in-house. So, your submission must be far above average."

$ $ FLORIDA GROWER

The Voice of Florida Agriculture for More Than 90 Years, Meister Media Worldwide, 1555 Howell Branch Rd., Suite C-204, Winter Park FL 32789. (407)539-6552. Fax: (407)539-6544. E-mail: rcpadrick@meistermedia.com. Website: www.floridagrower.net. **Contact:** Roy Padrick, managing editor. **10% freelance written.** Monthly magazine "edited for the Florida farmer with commercial production interest primarily in citrus, vegetables, and other ag endeavors. Our goal is to provide articles which update and inform on such areas as production, ag financing, farm labor relations, technology, safety, education, and regulation." Estab. 1907. Circ. 12,200. Pays on publication. Byline given. Buys all rights. Editorial lead time 2 months. Submit seasonal material 3 months in advance. Accepts queries by mail, e-mail, fax, phone. Responds in 1 month to queries. Sample copy for 9×12 SAE and 5 first-class stamps. Writer's guidelines free.

Nonfiction Interview/profile, photo feature, technical. Query with published clips. Length: 700-1,000 words. **Pays $150-250.**

Photos Send photos with submission.

$ THE LAND

Minnesota's Favorite Ag Publication, Free Press Co., P.O. Box 3169, Mankato MN 56002-3169. (507)345-4523. E-mail: kschulz@thelandonline.com. Website: www.thelandonline.com. **Contact:** Kevin Schulz, editor. **40% freelance written.** Weekly tabloid covering farming in Minnesota. "Although we're not tightly focused on any one type of farming, our articles must be of interest to farmers. In other words, will your article topic have an impact on people who live and work in rural areas?" Prefers to work with Minnesota writers. Estab. 1976. Circ. 33,000. **Pays on acceptance.** Publishes ms an average of 2 months after acceptance. Byline given. Buys first North American serial rights. Editorial lead time 2 months. Submit seasonal material 2 months in advance. Accepts queries by mail, e-mail. Responds in 3 weeks to queries; 2 months to mss. Sample copy for free. Writer's guidelines for #10 SASE.

Nonfiction General interest (ag), how-to (crop, livestock production, marketing). "Nothing that doesn't pertain to Minnesota agricultural or rural life." **Buys 80 mss/year.** Query. Length: 500-750 words. **Pays $40-70 for assigned articles.**

Photos Send photos with submission. Reviews contact sheets. Buys one-time rights. Negotiates payment individually.

Columns/Departments Query. **Pays $10-50.**

Tips "Be enthused about rural Minnesota life and agriculture and be willing to work with our editors. We try to stress relevance. When sending me a query, convince me the story belongs in a Minnesota farm publication."

$ $ MAINE ORGANIC FARMER & GARDENER

Maine Organic Farmers & Gardeners Association, 662 Slab City Rd., Lincolnville ME 04849. (207)763-3043. E-mail: jenglish@midcoast.com. Website: www.mofga.org. **Contact:** Jean English, editor. **40% freelance written.** Prefers to work with published/established local writers. Quarterly magazine. "*MOF&G* promotes and encourages sustainable agriculture and environmentally sound living. Our primary focus is organic farming, gardening, and forestry, but we also deal with local, national, and international agriculture, food, and environmental issues." Estab. 1976. Circ. 10,000. Pays on publication. Publishes ms an average of 8 months after acceptance. Byline and bio offered. Buys first North American serial, first, one-time, second serial (reprint) rights. Submit seasonal material 1 year in advance. Accepts queries by mail, e-mail. Accepts simultaneous submissions. Responds in 2 months to queries. Sample copy for $2 and SAE with 7 first-class stamps from MOFGA, P.O. Box 170, Unity ME 04988. Writer's guidelines free.

Nonfiction Book reviews; how-to based on personal experience, research reports, interviews; profiles of farmers, gardeners, plants; information on renewable energy, recycling, nutrition, health, nontoxic pest control, organic farm management and marketing. "We use profiles of New England organic farmers and gardeners and news reports (500-1,000 words) dealing with US/international sustainable ag research and development, rural development, recycling projects, environmental and agricultural problems and solutions, organic farms with broad impact, cooperatives and community projects." **Buys 30 mss/year.** Query with published clips or send complete ms. Length: 250-3,000 words. **Pays $25-300.**

Reprints Send ms with rights for sale noted and information about when and where the material previously appeared. Pays 50% of amount paid for an original article.

Photos State availability of b&w photos with query; or send 3×5 b&w photos with ms. Buys one-time rights. Captions, identification of subjects, model releases required.

Tips "We are a nonprofit organization. Our publication's primary mission is to inform and educate, but we also want readers to enjoy the articles."

FINANCE

$ $ $⌘ ADVISOR'S EDGE

Canada's Magazine for the Financial Professional, Rogers Media, Inc., 156 Front St. W., 4th Floor, Toronto ON M5J 2L6 Canada. (416)764-3802. Fax: (416)764-3803. E-mail: deanne.gage@advisor.rogers.com. Website: www.advisorsedge.ca. **Contact:** Deanne Gage, managing editor. Monthly magazine covering the financial industry (financial advisors and investment advisors). "*Advisor's Edge* focuses on sales and marketing opportunities for the financial advisor (how they can build their business and improve relationships with clients." Estab. 1998. Circ. 36,000. Pays on publication. Publishes ms an average of 3 months after acceptance. Byline given. Offers 25% kill fee. Buys one-time, electronic rights. Editorial lead time 3 months. Accepts queries by e-mail. Sample copy online.

Nonfiction "We are looking for articles that help advisors do their jobs better." How-to, interview/profile. No articles that aren't relevant to how a financial advisor does his/her job. **Buys 12 mss/year.** Query with published clips. Length: 1,500-2,000 words. **Pays $900 (Canadian).** Pays in contributor copies only if an industry contributor (i.e., an advisor).

$ $ $ $ BANKING STRATEGIES

Bank Administration Institute (BAI), Chicago IL. E-mail: kcline@bai.org. Website: www.bai.org/bankingstrateg ies. **Contact:** Kenneth Cline, senior editor. **70% freelance written.** Magazine covering banking and financial services. "Magazine covers banking from a strategic and managerial perspective for its senior financial executive audience. Each issue includes in-depth trend articles and interviews with influential executives." Offers variable kill fee. Buys all rights. Accepts queries by e-mail. Responds almost immediately to queries.

Nonfiction How-to (articles that help institutions be more effective and competitive in the marketplace), interview/profile (executive interviews). "No topic queries, we assign stories to freelancers. I'm looking for qualifications as opposed to topic queries. I need experienced writers/reporters." **Buys 30 mss/year.** E-queries preferred. **Pays $1.25/word for assigned articles.**

Tips "Demonstrate ability and financial services expertise. I'm looking for freelancers who can write according to our standards, which are quite high."

$ $ $ COLLECTIONS & CREDIT RISK

The Authority for Commercial and Consumer Professionals, Thomson Media, 300 S. Wacker Dr., Suite 1800, Chicago IL 60606. (858)273-5770. E-mail: cladwig1@san.rr.com. Website: www.creditcollectionsworld.com. **Contact:** Catherine (Kit) Ladwig, editor. **33% freelance written.** Monthly journal covering debt collections and credit risk management. "*Collections & Credit Risk* reports and analyzes events and trends affecting consumer and commercial credit practices and debt collections. The entire credit cycle is covered from setting credit policy and making loan decisions to debt recovery, collections, bankruptcy, and debt sales." Estab. 1996. Circ. 30,000. **Pays on acceptance.** Publishes ms an average of 3 months after acceptance. Byline given. Kill fee determined case by case. Buys all rights. Editorial lead time 3 months. Accepts queries by mail, e-mail, fax. Sample copy free or online.

   Oₙ Break in with "a query with clips of business trend stories using 8-10 sources and demonstrating strong analysis."

Nonfiction Interview/profile, technical, business news and analysis. "No unsolicited submissions accepted—freelancers work on assignment only." **Buys 30-40 mss/year.** Query with published clips. Length: 1,000-2,500 words. **Pays $800-1,000.** Sometimes pays expenses of writers on assignment.

Tips "This is a business news and analysis magazine focused on events and trends affecting the credit-risk management and collections professions. Our editorial approach is modeled after *Business Week, Forbes, Fortune, Wall Street Journal.* No fluff accepted."

$ $ COMMUNITY BANKER

900 19th St. NW, Suite 400, Washington DC 20006. (202)857-3142. E-mail: dcope@acbankers.org. Website: www.americascommunitybankers.com/magazine. **Contact:** Debra Cope, editor. **25% freelance written.** Monthly magazine. *"America's Community Banker* is written for senior managers and executives of community financial institutions. The magazine covers all aspects of financial institution management, with an emphasis on strategic business issues and trends. Recent features have included bank technology, trends in home mortgage finance and alternative bank funding." Circ. 14,000. **Pays on acceptance.** Publishes ms an average of 2 months after acceptance. Byline given. Buys first North American serial rights. Editorial lead time 3 months. Submit seasonal material 6 months in advance. Responds in 1 month to queries. Sample copy and writer's guidelines free.

Nonfiction "Articles must be well-researched and backed up by a variety of sources, preferably senior managers of financial institutions or experts associated with the banking industry." How-to (articles on various aspects of a financial institution's operations). **Buys 6 mss/year.** Query with published clips. Length: 1,000-2,700 words. **Pays 50¢/word.**

Photos Send photos with submission. Reviews contact sheets, negatives, prints. Buys one-time rights. Identification of subjects required.

Columns/Departments Nationwide News (news items on banking and finance), 100-500 words; Technology Report (news on techology for community bankers); and Surveys and Trends (information on the banking business and business in general). **Buys 25 mss/year.** Query with published clips.

Tips "The best way to develop a relationship with *America's Community Banker* is through our 2 departments, Nationwide News and Technology Report. If writers can prove themselves reliable there first, major feature assignments may follow."

$ $ CREDIT UNION MANAGEMENT

Credit Union Executives Society, 5510 Research Park Dr., Madison WI 53711. (608)271-2664. Fax: (608)271-2303. E-mail: editors@cues.org. Website: www.cumanagement.org. **Contact:** Mary Arnold or Theresa Sweeney, editors. **44% freelance written.** Monthly magazine covering credit union, banking trends management, HR, marketing issues. "Our philosophy mirrors the credit union industry of cooperative financial services." Estab. 1978. Circ. 7,413. **Pays on acceptance.** Publishes ms an average of 2 months after acceptance. Editorial lead time 3 months. Submit seasonal material 4 months in advance. Accepts queries by mail, e-mail, fax, phone. Accepts simultaneous submissions. Responds in 2 weeks to queries; 1 month to mss. Sample copy and writer's guidelines free.

Nonfiction Book excerpts, how-to (be a good mentor/leader, recruit, etc.), interview/profile, technical. **Buys 74 mss/year.** Query with published clips. Length: 700-2,400 words. **$250-350 for assigned features.** Pays phone expenses only of writers on assignment.

Columns/Departments Management Network (book/Web reviews, briefs), 300 words; e-marketing, 700 words; Point of Law, 700 words; Best Practices (new technology/operations trends), 700 words. Query with published clips.

Tips "The best way is to e-mail an editor; include résumé, cover letter and clips. Knowledge of financial services is very helpful."

$ $ $ THE FEDERAL CREDIT UNION

National Association of Federal Credit Unions, 3138 N. 10th St., Arlington VA 22201. (703)522-4770. Fax: (703)524-1082. E-mail: tfcu@nafcu.org. Website: www.nafcu.org. Executive Editor: Jay Morris. **Contact:** Robin Johnston, publisher/managing editor. **30% freelance written.** "Looking for writers with financial, banking, or credit union experience, but will work with inexperienced (unpublished) writers based on writing skill. Published bimonthly, *The Federal Credit Union* is the official publication of the National Association of Federal Credit Unions. The magazine is dedicated to providing credit union management, staff, and volunteers with in-depth information (HR, technology, security, board management, etc.) they can use to fulfill their duties and better serve their members. The editorial focus includes coverage of management issues, operations, and technology as well as volunteer-related issues." Estab. 1967. Circ. 8,000. Pays on publication. Publishes ms an average of 3 months after acceptance. Byline given. Buys first North American serial rights, rights to publish and archive online. Submit seasonal material 5 months in advance. Accepts queries by mail, e-mail, fax. Accepts simultaneous submissions. Responds in 2 months to queries. Sample copy for 10×13 SAE and 5 first-class stamps. Writer's guidelines for #10 SASE.

O→ Break in with "pithy, informative, thought-provoking items for our 'Management Insight' section (for free or a small fee of $50-200)."

Nonfiction Humor, inspirational, interview/profile. Query with published clips and SASE. Length: 1,200-2,000 words. **Pays $400-1,000.**

Photos Send photos with submission. Reviews 35mm transparencies, 5×7 prints, high-resolution photos. Buys all rights. Offers no additional payment for photos accepted with ms. Pays $50-500. Identification of subjects, model releases required.

■ The online magazine carries original content not found in the print edition, as well as some print copy. Contact: Robin Johnston.

Tips "We would like more articles on how credit unions are using technology to serve their members and more articles on leading-edge technologies they can use in their operations. If you can write on current trends in technology, human resources, or strategic planning, you stand a better chance of being published than if you wrote on other topics."

$ $ $ $ FINANCIAL PLANNING

Source Media, One State St. Plaza, 26th Floor, New York NY 10001. (212)803-8696. Fax: (212)843-9608. E-mail: jennifer.liptow@thomsonmedia.com. Website: www.financial-planning.com. **Contact:** Jennifer Liptow. **50-60% freelance written.** Monthly magazine covering investment strategies, estate planning, practice management, and other issues facing professional financial planners. Estab. 1971. Circ. 100,000. Pays on publication. Publishes ms an average of 3 months after acceptance. Byline given. Buys all rights. Editorial lead time 3 months. Submit seasonal material 4 months in advance. Accepts queries by e-mail. Responds in 1-2 months to queries. Sample copy for $10. Writer's guidelines free.

Nonfiction Book excerpts, how-to, interview/profile, new product, opinion, technical. No product endorsements. Query (e-mail only). Length: 1,800-2,500 words. **Payment varies—averages $1/word.** Sometimes pays expenses of writers on assignment.

Photos State availability with submission. Reviews contact sheets, any size prints. Offers no additional payment for photos accepted with ms. Identification of subjects required.

Tips "Avoid articles that are too general—ours is a professional readership who require a thoughtful, in-depth analysis of financial issues. A submission that includes charts, graphs, and statistical data is much more likely to pique our interest than overviews of investing."

INVESTMENT NEWS

Crain Communications, 711 Third Ave., 3rd Floor, New York NY 10017. (212)210-0775. E-mail: jpavia@crain.com. Website: www.investmentnews.com. Editor: Jim Pavia. **10% freelance written.** Weekly magazine, newsletter, tabloid covering financial planning and investing. "It covers the business of personal finance to keep its audience of planners, brokers and other tax investment professionals informed of the latest news about their industry." Estab. 1997. Circ. 60,000. Pays on publication. Publishes ms an average of 1 month after acceptance. Byline given. Negotiate kill fee. Buys all rights, makes work-for-hire assignments. Editorial lead time 2 weeks. Submit seasonal material 1 month in advance. Sample copy and writer's guidelines free.

Tips "Come to us with a specific pitch, preferably based on a news tip. We prefer to be contacted by fax or e-mail."

MORTGAGE BANKING

The Magazine of Real Estate Finance, Mortgage Bankers Association, 1919 Pennsylvania Ave., NW, Washington DC 20006. (202)557-2853. Fax: (202)721-0245. E-mail: jhewitt@mortgagebankers.org. Website: www.mortgage bankingmagazine.com. Deputy Editor: Lesley Hall. **Contact:** Janet Hewitt, editor-in-chief. Monthly magazine covering real estate finance. "Timely examinations of major news and trends in the business of mortgage lending for both commercial and residential real estate." Estab. 1939. Circ. 10,000. **Pays on acceptance.** Publishes ms an average of 2 months after acceptance. Byline given. Negotiates kill fee. Buys one-time rights, makes work-for-hire assignments. Editorial lead time 2 months. Submit seasonal material 3 months in advance. Accepts queries by mail, e-mail, fax. Accepts simultaneous submissions. Responds in 1 month to queries; 4 months to mss. Sample copy and writer's guidelines free.

Nonfiction Book excerpts, essays, interview/profile, opinion. Special issues: Commercial Real Estate Special Supplemental Issue (January); Internet Guide Supplemental Issue (September). **Buys 30 mss/year.** Query. Length: 3,000 words. **Writers' fees negotiable.** Sometimes pays expenses of writers on assignment.

Photos State availability with submission. Reviews prints. Buys one-time rights. Negotiates payment individually. Identification of subjects, model releases required.

Columns/Departments Book reviews (current, relevant material), 300 words; executive essay (industry executive's personal views on relevant topic), 750-1,000 words. **Buys 2 mss/year.** Query. **Pay negotiated.**

Tips "Trends in technology, current and upcoming legislation that will affect the mortgage industry are good focus."

$ $ $ $ ON WALL STREET

Source Media, One State St. Plaza, 26th Floor, New York NY 10004. (212)803-8782. E-mail: jennifer.liptow@thomsonmedia.com. Website: www.onwallstreet.com. **Contact:** Jennifer Liptow, group assistant managing editor.

50% freelance written. Monthly magazine for retail stockbrokers. "We help 95,000+ stockbrokers build their business." Estab. 1991. Circ. 95,000. Pays on publication. Publishes ms an average of 1-2 months after acceptance. Byline given. Buys all rights. Editorial lead time 3 months. Submit seasonal material 4 months in advance. Accepts queries by e-mail. Responds in 1-2 months to queries; 2 month to mss. Sample copy for $10.

Nonfiction How-to, interview/profile. "No investment-related articles about hot stocks, nor funds or hot alternative investments." **Buys 30 mss/year.** Query. Length: 1,000-3,000 words. **Pays $1/word.**

Photos State availability with submission. Reviews contact sheets. Buys all rights. Negotiates payment individually. Identification of subjects required.

Tips "Articles should be written for a professional, not consumer, audience."

$ $ SERVICING MANAGEMENT

The Magazine for Loan Servicing Professionals, Zackin Publications, P.O. Box 2180, Waterbury CT 06722. (800)325-6745. Fax: (203)755-3480. E-mail: bates@sm-online.com. Website: www.sm-online.com. **Contact:** Michael Bates, editor. **15% freelance written.** Monthly magazine covering residential mortgage servicing. Estab. 1989. Circ. 20,000. **Pays on acceptance.** Publishes ms an average of 2 months after acceptance. Byline given. Buys all rights. Accepts queries by mail, e-mail, fax. Responds in 2 weeks to queries. Sample copy for free. Writer's guidelines online.

> ⚬⚮ Break in by "submitting a query for Servicing Reports, a monthly department featuring news and information about mortgage servicing and the industry. It should be informative, topical and include comments by industry professionals."

Nonfiction How-to, interview/profile, new product, technical. **Buys 10 mss/year.** Query. Length: 1,500-2,500 words. Will pay industry experts with contributor copies or other premiums rather than a cash payment.

Photos State availability with submission. Reviews contact sheets. Buys all rights. Offers no additional payment for photos accepted with ms. Identification of subjects required.

Columns/Departments Buys 5 mss/year. Query. **Pays $200.**

TRADERS MAGAZINE

Thomson Media Group, 1 State St. Plaza, 17th Floor, New York NY 10001. (212)803-8366. Fax: (212)295-1725. E-mail: john.byrne@thomsonmedia.com. Website: www.tradersmagazine.com. **Contact:** John Aidan Byrne, editor. **35% freelance written.** Monthly magazine plus 2 specials covering equity trading and technology. "Provides comprehensive coverage of how institutional trading is performed on NASDAQ and the New York Stock Exchange." Pays on publication. Publishes ms an average of 2 months after acceptance. Byline given. Buys all rights. Editorial lead time 2 months. Submit seasonal material 3 months in advance. Accepts queries by mail, e-mail, phone. Sample copy free to writers on assignment.

> ⚬⚮ Needs more "buy-side" stories (on mutual fund, pension fund traders, etc.), "sell-side" stories on hot-button topics.

Nonfiction Book excerpts, exposé, general interest, historical/nostalgic, how-to, humor, interview/profile, new product, opinion, personal experience, religious, technical. Special issues: Correspondent clearing (every market) and market making survey of broker dealers. No stories that are related to fixed income and other non-equity topics. **Buys 12-20 mss/year.** Query with published clips or send complete ms. Length: 750-2,800 words.

Columns/Departments Special Features (market regulation and human interest), 1600 words; Trading & Technology, 1,600 words; Washington Watch (market regulation), 750 words. Query with published clips.

Fiction Ethnic, historical, humorous, mystery, science fiction, slice-of-life vignettes. No erotica. **Buys 1 mss/year.** Query with or without published clips or send complete ms. Length: 2,100-2,800 words.

> 🖳 The online magazine carries original content not found in the print edition. "We welcome controversy in both mediums." Contact: Jennifer Speck, online editor.

Tips "Boil it all down and don't bore the hell out of readers. Advice from a distinguished scribe which we pass along. Learn to explain equity market making and institutional trading in a simple, direct manner. Don't waffle. Have a trader explain the business to you if necessary. The *Traders Magazine* is highly regarded among Wall Street insiders, trading honchos, and Washington pundits alike."

FISHING

$ $ PACIFIC FISHING

Northwest Publishing Center, 1710 S. Norman St., Seattle WA 98144. (206)709-1840. Fax: (206)324-8939. E-mail: jholland@pfmag.com. Website: www.pfmag.com. **Contact:** Jon Holland, editor. **75% freelance written.** Works with some new/unpublished writers. Monthly magazine for commercial fishermen and others in the commercial fishing industry throughout Alaska, the west coast, and the Pacific. "*Pacific Fishing* views the fisherman as a small businessman and covers all aspects of the industry, including harvesting, processing, and marketing." Estab. 1979. Circ. 8,000. Pays on publication. Publishes ms an average of 2 months after acceptance. Byline given. Buys first North American serial and unlimited re-use rights. Accepts queries by mail, e-mail, fax, phone. Variable response time to queries. Sample copy and writer's guidelines for 9×12 SAE with 10 first-class stamps.

O┑ Study the magazine before querying.

Nonfiction "Articles must be concerned specifically with commercial fishing. We view fishermen as small business operators and professionals who are innovative and success-oriented. To appeal to this reader, *Pacific Fishing* offers 4 basic features: technical, how-to articles that give fishermen hands-on tips that will make their operation more efficient and profitable; practical, well-researched business articles discussing the dollars and cents of fishing, processing, and marketing; profiles of a fisherman, processor, or company with emphasis on practical business and technical areas; and in-depth analysis of political, social, fisheries management, and resource issues that have a direct bearing on commercial fishermen." **Buys 20 mss/year.** Query noting whether photos are available, and enclose samples of previous work and SASE. Length: Varies, one-paragraph news items to 3,000-word features. **Pays 20¢/word for most assignments.** Sometimes pays expenses of writers on assignment.

Photos "We need good, high-quality photography, especially color, of commercial fishing. We prefer 35mm color slides or JPEG files of at least 300 dpi." Our rates are $200 for cover; $50-100 for inside color; $25-75 for b&w; $10 for table of contents.

Tips "Read the magazine before sending a query. Make your pitch fit the magazine. If you haven't read it, don't waste your time and ours."

FLORISTS, NURSERIES & LANDSCAPERS

$ $ DIGGER

Oregon Association of Nurseries, 29751 SW Town Center Loop W., Wilsonville OR 97070. (503)682-5089. Fax: (503)682-5727. E-mail: csivesind@oan.org. Website: www.oan.org. **Contact:** Cam Sivesind, manager of publications and communications. **50% freelance written.** Monthly magazine covering nursery and greenhouse industry. "Our readers are mainly nursery and greenhouse operators and owners who propagate nursery stock/ crops, so we write with them in mind." Circ. 6,000. Pays on receipt of copy. Publishes ms an average of 2 months after acceptance. Byline given. Offers 100% kill fee. Buys first North American serial rights. Editorial lead time 6 weeks. Submit seasonal material 2 months in advance. Accepts queries by mail, e-mail, fax, phone. Sample copy and writer's guidelines free.

Nonfiction General interest, how-to (propagation techniques, other crop-growing tips), interview/profile, personal experience, technical. Special issues: Farwest Edition (August)—this is a triple-size issue that runs in tandem with our annual trade show (13,500 circulation for this issue). "No articles not related or pertinent to nursery and greenhouse industry." **Buys 20-30 mss/year.** Query. Length: 800-2,000 words. **Pays $125-400 for assigned articles; $100-300 for unsolicited articles.** Sometimes pays expenses of writers on assignment.

Photos State availability with submission. Reviews negatives, 5×7 prints, slides. Buys one-time rights. Offers $25-150/photo. Captions, identification of subjects required.

Tips "Our best freelancers are familiar with or have experience in the horticultural industry. Some 'green' knowledge is a definite advantage."

$ GROWERTALKS

Ball Publishing, 335 N. River St., P.O. Box 9, Batavia IL 60510. (630)208-9080. Fax: (630)208-9350. E-mail: beytes@growertalks.com. Website: www.growertalks.com. **Contact:** Chris Beytes, editor. **50% freelance written.** Monthly magazine. "*GrowerTalks* serves the commercial greenhouse grower. Editorial emphasis is on floricultural crops: bedding plants, potted floral crops, foliage and fresh cut flowers. Our readers are growers, managers, and owners. We're looking for writers who've had experience in the greenhouse industry." Estab. 1937. Circ. 9,500. Pays on publication. Publishes ms an average of 3 months after acceptance. Byline given. Buys first North American serial rights. Editorial lead time 4 months. Submit seasonal material 3 months in advance. Accepts queries by mail, e-mail, fax. Responds in 1 month to queries. Sample copy and writer's guidelines free.

Nonfiction How-to (time- or money-saving projects for professional flower/plant growers), interview/profile (ornamental horticulture growers), personal experience (of a grower), technical (about growing process in greenhouse setting). "No articles that promote only one product." **Buys 36 mss/year.** Query. Length: 1,200-1,600 words. **Pays $125 minimum for assigned articles; $75 minimum for unsolicited articles.**

Photos State availability with submission. Reviews 2½×2½ slides and 3×5 prints. Buys one-time rights. Negotiates payment individually. Captions, identification of subjects, model releases required.

Tips "Discuss magazine with ornamental horticulture growers to find out what topics that have or haven't appeared in the magazine interest them."

$ $ THE GROWING EDGE

New Moon Publishing, Inc., P.O. Box 1027, Corvallis OR 97339. (541)757-8477. Fax: (541)757-0028. Website: www.growingedge.com. **Contact:** Tom Weller, editor. **85% freelance written.** Bimonthly magazine covering indoor and outdoor high-tech gardening techniques and tips. Estab. 1980. Circ. 20,000. Pays on publication. Publishes ms an average of 3 months after acceptance. Byline given. Buys first serial and reprint rights. Submit seasonal material 6 months in advance. Accepts queries by mail, e-mail. Responds in 3 months to queries. Sample copy for $3. Writer's guidelines online.

O— Break in with "a detailed, knowledgeable e-mail story pitch."

Nonfiction How-to, interview/profile, personal experience (must be technical), book reviews, general horticulture and agriculture. Query. Length: 500-3,500 words. **Pays 20¢/word (10¢ for first rights, 5¢ for nonexclusive reprint and nonexclusive electronic rights).**

Reprints Send tearsheet, photocopy or typed ms with rights for sale noted and information about when and where the material previously appeared. Payment negotiable.

Photos Buys first and reprint rights. Pays $25-175. Pays on publication. Credit line given.

Tips Looking for more hydroponics articles and information that will give the reader/gardener/farmer the "growing edge" in high-tech gardening and farming on topics such as high intensity grow lights, water conservation, drip irrigation, advanced organic fertilizers, new seed varieties, and greenhouse cultivation.

$ $ ORNAMENTAL OUTLOOK

Your Connection To The South's Horticulture Industry, Meister Media Worldwide, 1555 Howell Branch Rd., Suite C204, Winter Park FL 32789. (407)539-6552. Fax: (407)539-6544. E-mail: tlcallies@meistermedia.com. Website: www.ornamentaloutlook.com. **Contact:** Tacy Callies, editor. **20% freelance written.** Monthly magazine. *"Ornamental Outlook* is written for commercial growers of ornamental plants in the Southeast US. Our goal is to provide interesting and informative articles on such topics as production, legislation, safety, technology, pest control, water management, and new varieties, as they apply to Southeast growers." Estab. 1991. Circ. 11,000. Pays 30 days after publication. Publishes ms an average of 4 months after acceptance. Byline given. Buys all rights. Editorial lead time 2 months. Submit seasonal material 3 months in advance. Accepts queries by mail, e-mail, fax, phone. Responds in 3 months to queries. Sample copy for 9×12 SAE and 5 first-class stamps. Writer's guidelines free.

Nonfiction Interview/profile, photo feature, technical. "No first-person articles. No word-for-word meeting transcripts or all-quote articles." Query with published clips. Length: 600-1,000 words. **Pays $150-300/article including photos.**

Photos Send photos with submission. Reviews contact sheets, transparencies, prints. Buys one-time rights. Captions, identification of subjects required.

Tips "I am most impressed by written queries that address specific subjects of interest to our audience, which is the Southeast grower of commercial horticulture. Our biggest demand is for features, about 700 words, that follow subjects listed on our editorial calendar (which is sent with guidelines). Please do not send articles of national or consumer interest."

$ $ TREE CARE INDUSTRY MAGAZINE

Tree Care Industry Association, 3 Perimeter Rd. Unit 1, Manchester NH 03103-3341. (800)733-2622 or (603)314-5380. Fax: (603)314-5386. E-mail: staruk@treecareindustry.org. Website: www.treecareindustry.org. Managing Editor: Don Staruk. **50% freelance written.** Monthly magazine covering tree care and landscape maintenance. Estab. 1990. Circ. 28,500. Pays within 1 month of publication. Publishes ms an average of 3 months after acceptance. Byline given. Buys all rights. Editorial lead time 10 weeks. Submit seasonal material 3 months in advance. Accepts queries by mail, e-mail, fax, phone. Responds in 2 weeks to queries; 2 months to mss. Sample copy for 9×12 SAE and 6 first-class stamps. Writer's guidelines free.

Nonfiction Book excerpts, historical/nostalgic, interview/profile, new product, technical. **Buys 60 mss/year.** Query with published clips. Length: 900-3,500 words. **Pays negotiable rate.**

Photos Send photos with submission. Reviews prints. Buys one-time and Web rights. Negotiate payment individually. Captions, identification of subjects required.

Columns/Departments Buys 40 mss/year. Send complete ms. **Pays $100 and up.**

Tips "Preference is given to writers with background and knowledge of the tree care industry; our focus is relatively narrow."

GOVERNMENT & PUBLIC SERVICE

$ CHIEF OF POLICE MAGAZINE

National Association of Chiefs of Police, 3801 Biscayne Blvd., Miami FL 33137. Fax: (321)264-0333. Website: www.aphf.org. **Contact:** Jim Gordon, executive editor. Bimonthly journal for law enforcement commanders (command ranks). Circ. 13,500. **Pays on acceptance.** Publishes ms an average of 6 months after acceptance. Byline given. Buys first rights. Submit seasonal material 6 months in advance. Accepts queries by mail, e-mail, fax. Accepts simultaneous submissions. Responds in 2 weeks to queries. Sample copy for $3 and 9×12 SAE with 5 first-class stamps. Writer's guidelines online.

↳ Break in with "a story concerning command officers or police family survivors."

Nonfiction "We want stories about interesting police cases and stories on any law enforcement subject or program that is positive in nature." General interest, historical/nostalgic, how-to, humor, inspirational, interview/profile, new product, personal experience, photo feature, religious, technical. "No exposé types or anti-police." **Buys 50 mss/year.** Send complete ms. Length: 600-2,500 words. **Pays $25-75 for assigned articles; $25-100 for unsolicited articles.** Sometimes pays expenses of writers on assignment.

Photos Send photos with submission. Reviews 5×6 prints. Buys one-time rights. Pays $5-10 for b&w; $10-25 for color. Captions required.

Columns/Departments New Police (police equipment shown and tests), 200-600 words. **Buys 6 mss/year.** Send complete ms. **Pays $5-25.**

Fillers Anecdotes, short humor, law-oriented cartoons. **Buys 100/year.** Length: 100-1,600 words. **Pays $5-25.**

Tips "Writers need only contact law enforcement officers right in their own areas and we would be delighted. We want to recognize good commanding officers from sergeant and above who are involved with the community. Pictures of the subject or the department are essential and can be snapshots. We are looking for interviews with police chiefs and sheriffs on command level with photos."

$ $ COUNTY

Texas Association of Counties, P.O. Box 2131, Austin TX 78768. (512)478-8753. Fax: (512)477-1324. E-mail: jiml@county.org. Website: www.county.org. **Contact:** Jim Lewis, editor. **15% freelance written.** Bimonthly magazine covering county and state government in Texas. "We provide elected and appointed county officials with insights and information that help them do their jobs and enhances communications among the independent office-holders in the courthouse." Estab. 1988. Circ. 5,500. **Pays on acceptance.** Publishes ms an average of 2 months after acceptance. Byline given. Makes work-for-hire assignments. Editorial lead time 2 months. Submit seasonal material 4 months in advance. Accepts queries by mail, e-mail, phone. Responds in 2 weeks to queries; 1 month to mss. Sample copy and writer's guidelines for 8×10 SAE with 3 first-class stamps.

Nonfiction Historical/nostalgic, photo feature, government innovations. **Buys 5 mss/year.** Query with published clips. Length: 1,000-3,000 words. **Pays $500-700.** Sometimes pays expenses of writers on assignment.

Photos State availability with submission. Buys all rights. Negotiates payment individually. Captions, identification of subjects, model releases required.

Columns/Departments Safety; Human Resources; Risk Management (all directed toward education of Texas county officials), maximum length 1,000 words. **Buys 2 mss/year.** Query with published clips. **Pays $500.**

Tips "Identify innovative practices or developing trends that affect Texas county officials, and have the basic journalism skills to write a multi-sourced, informative feature."

$ $ FIRE CHIEF

Primedia Business, 330 N. Wabash, Suite 2300, Chicago IL 60611. (312)595-1080. Fax: (312)595-0295. E-mail: jwilmoth@primediabusiness.com. Website: www.firechief.com. **Contact:** Janet Wilmoth, editor. **60% freelance written.** Monthly magazine. "*Fire Chief* is the management magazine of the fire service, addressing the administrative, personnel, training, prevention/education, professional development, and operational issues faced by chiefs and other fire officers, whether in paid, volunteer, or combination departments. We're potentially interested in any article that can help them do their jobs better, whether that's as incident commanders, financial managers, supervisors, leaders, trainers, planners, or ambassadors to municipal officials or the public." Estab. 1956. Circ. 53,000. Pays on publication. Publishes ms an average of 6 months after acceptance. Byline given. Kill fee negotiable. Buys first, one-time, second serial (reprint), all rights. Editorial lead time 2 months. Submit seasonal material 4 months in advance. Accepts queries by mail, e-mail, fax. Responds in 1 month to queries; 2 months to mss. Sample copy and writer's guidelines free or online.

Nonfiction "If your department has made some changes in its structure, budget, mission, or organizational culture (or really did reinvent itself in a serious way), an account of that process, including the mistakes made and lessons learned, could be a winner. Similarly, if you've observed certain things that fire departments typically could do a lot better and you think you have the solution, let us know." How-to, technical. **Buys 50-**

60 mss/year. Query with published clips. Length: 1,500-8,000 words. **Pays $50-400.** Sometimes pays expenses of writers on assignment.

Photos State availability with submission. Reviews transparencies, prints. Buys one-time or reprint rights. Captions, identification of subjects required.

Columns/Departments Training Perspectives; EMS Viewpoints; Sound Off; Volunteer Voice; all 1,000-1,800 words.

Tips "Writers who are unfamiliar with the fire service are very unlikely to place anything with us. Many pieces that we reject are either too unfocused or too abstract. We want articles that help keep fire chiefs well informed and effective at their jobs."

$ $ FIRE-RESCUE MAGAZINE

Jems Communications, 525 B St., Suite 1900, San Diego CA 92101. E-mail: frm.editor@jems.com. Website: www.jems.com. **Contact:** Michelle Garrido, editor. **75% freelance written.** Monthly magazine covering technical aspects of being a firefighter/rescuer. Estab. 1988. Circ. 50,000. Pays on publication. Buys first North American serial, one-time rights. Submit seasonal material 6 months in advance. Accepts queries by mail, e-mail. Responds in 3 weeks to queries; 2 months to mss. Sample copy and writer's guidelines for 9×12 SAE with 5 first-class stamps or online.

Nonfiction How-to, new product, photo feature, technical, incident review/report. Special issues: fire suppression, incident command, vehicle extrication, rescue training, mass-casualty incidents, water rescue/major issues facing the fire service. **Buys 15-20 mss/year.** Query with published clips or send complete ms. Length: 1,000-3,000 words. **Pays $125-250.** Sometimes pays expenses of writers on assignment.

Photos Send photos with submission. Reviews contact sheets, negatives, 2×2 and 35mm transparencies, 5×7 prints. Buys one-time rights. Offers $20-200.

Tips "Read our magazine, spend some time with a fire department. We focus on all aspects of fire and rescue. Emphasis on techniques and new technology, with color photos as support."

Ⓝ $ FIREFIGHTERS JOURNAL

Firefighters Journal Corp., 47-01 Greenpoint Ave. #114, Sunnyside NY 11104-1709. Fax: (718)732-2992. E-mail: badgemag@yahoo.com. Managing Editor: Ray Phillips. **Contact:** Liz Martinez, editorial director. **85% freelance written.** Quarterly magazine covering FDNY and general interest for firefighters, EMS and civilian fire employees. "Writers should keep in mind that this is a lifestyle magazine whose readers happen to be firefighters or EMS personnel, not a firefighting magazine with some lifestyle topics in it. Keep the tone friendly and informal, rather than dry and dusty." Estab. 2004. Circ. 15,000. Pays on publication. Publishes ms an average of 3 months after acceptance. Byline given. Buys one-time, second serial (reprint) rights, makes work-for-hire assignments. Editorial lead time 5 months. Submit seasonal material 5 months in advance. Accepts queries by mail, e-mail, fax. Accepts previously published material. Accepts simultaneous submissions. Responds in 2 months to queries; 4 months to mss. Sample copy for $5. Writer's guidelines by e-mail.

Nonfiction Book excerpts, historical/nostalgic, interview/profile, new product, photo feature, technical, travel. "We see too many pieces that are dry and not enjoyable to read. Even if the topic is serious or scientific, present the material as though you were telling a friend about it." Query with or without published clips or send complete ms. Length: 500-2,000 words. **Pays $75-100.**

Photos State availability with submission. Reviews GIF/JPEG files (300 dpi minimum). Buys one-time rights. Offers no additional payment for photos accepted with ms.

Columns/Departments Books (book reviews/excerpts/author interviews); Cyber Station (Internet guide); At the Cineplex (movie reviews); The Arts (museums, etc.); Dining Out (restaurant reviews); Your Health; Finance Department; Leadership (management); Technology; A Look Back (historical). "We are seeking stories on travel; firefighting/EMS product/news; books with a firefighting/EMS hook; movies and other entertainment that our readers would enjoy knowing about; worthy fire-related Internet sites; the latest developments in forensics and technology; health articles with a fire/EMS spin; arson investigation techniques; innovative international, national, regional, or local (inside and outside of the New York area) approaches to firefighting or EMS issues; other topics of interest to our reader population." **Buys 16 mss/year.** Query with or without published clips. **Pays $75-100.** Send complete ms. Length: 500-2,000 words. **Pays $50-100.**

Tips "New writers are welcome. We care about quality writing, not previous experience or a portfolio. Please be patient with us—it may take a long time to respond because we consider each query personally and carefully."

$ $ FIREHOUSE MAGAZINE

Cygnus Business Media, 445 Broad Hollow Rd., Suite 21, Melville NY 11747. (631)845-2700. Fax: (631)845-7109. E-mail: editors@firehouse.com. Website: www.firehouse.com. Editor-in-Chief: Harvey Eisner. **Contact:** Elizabeth Friszell, associate editor. **85% freelance written.** Works with a small number of new/unpublished writers each year. Monthly magazine. "*Firehouse* covers major fires nationwide, controversial issues and trends in the fire service, the latest firefighting equipment and methods of firefighting, historical fires, firefighting history and memorabilia. Fire-related books, fire safety education, hazardous-materials incidents, and the emergency medical services are also covered." Estab. 1976. Circ. 127,000. Pays on publication. Byline given. Accepts queries by mail, e-mail, fax. Sample copy for 9×12 SAE and 8 first-class stamps. Writer's guidelines online.

Nonfiction Book excerpts (of recent books on fire, EMS, and hazardous materials); historical/nostalgic (great fires in history, fire collectibles, the fire service of yesteryear); how-to (fight certain kinds of fires, buy and maintain equipment, run a fire department); technical (on almost any phase of firefighting, techniques, equipment, training, administration); trends in the fire service. No profiles of people or departments that are not unusual or innovative, reports of nonmajor fires, articles not slanted toward firefighters' interests. No poetry. **Buys 100 mss/year.** Query with or without published clips. Length: 500-3,000 words. **Pays $50-400 for assigned articles.**

Photos Send photos with submission. Pays $25-200 for transparencies and color prints. Cannot accept negatives. Captions, identification of subjects required.

Columns/Departments Training (effective methods); Book Reviews; Fire Safety (how departments teach fire safety to the public); Communicating (PR, dispatching); Arson (efforts to combat it). Length: 750-1,000 words. **Buys 50 mss/year.** Query or send complete ms. **Pays $100-300.**

Tips "Have excellent fire service credentials and be able to offer our readers new information. Read the magazine to get a full understanding of the subject matter, the writing style, and the readers before sending a query or manuscript. Send photos with manuscript or indicate sources for photos. Be sure to focus articles on firefighters."

$FOREIGN SERVICE JOURNAL

2101 E. St. NW, Washington DC 20037. (202)338-4045. Fax: (202)338-6820. E-mail: dorman@afsa.org. Website: www.afsa.org. **Contact:** Shawn Dorman. **75% freelance written.** Monthly magazine for foreign service personnel and others interested in foreign affairs and related subjects. Estab. 1924. Pays on publication. Publishes ms an average of 3 months after acceptance. Byline given. Buys first North American serial rights. Accepts queries by mail, e-mail, fax. Responds in 1 month to queries. Sample copy for $3.50 and 10×12 SAE with 6 first-class stamps. Writer's guidelines for #10 SASE.

⚬┐ Break in through "Postcard from Abroad—short items (600 words) on life abroad."

Nonfiction Uses articles on "diplomacy, professional concerns of the State Department and foreign service, diplomatic history and articles on foreign service experiences. Much of our material is contributed by those working in the profession. Informed outside contributions are welcomed, however." Essays, exposé, humor, opinion, personal experience. **Buys 15-20 unsolicited mss/year.** Query. Length: 1,000-3,000 words. **Offers $60 honorarium.**

Tips "We're more likely to want your article if it has something to do with diplomacy or US foreign policy."

Ⓝ $ $HSTODAY

Insight and Analysis for Homeland Security Policymakers, KMD Media LLC, P.O. Box 9789, McLean VA. (703)757-0520. Fax: (866)503-5758. E-mail: editor@hstoday.us. Website: www.hstoday.us. Senior Correspondent: Anthony Kimery. **Contact:** David Silverberg, editor. **100% freelance written.** Monthly magazine covering homeland security and everything related to public safety, security, and emergency management. "This is a magazine designed for government officials with decision and policy-making authority and homeland security responsibilities at the federal, state, and local levels. While written for professionals, we want to be accessible to all readers. Accordingly, we seek good, accurate, comprehensive reporting and analysis that delivers new and useful information to our readers in a lively and engaging style. We encourage articles from everyone in the homeland security community, especially people with firsthand knowledge of HS topics or relevant personal experience." Estab. 2004. Circ. 30,000. Pays on publication. Publishes ms an average of 6 weeks after acceptance. Byline given. Buys first North American serial rights. Editorial lead time 6 weeks. Accepts queries by e-mail. Sample copy for #10 SASE. Writer's guidelines free.

Nonfiction "We are looking for analysis and insight related to homeland security topics. The editor should be contacted by e-mail (editor@hstoday.us) before making any proposal." Opinion (essays from people in the homeland security community; must deal with government policy), reporting/analysis. Special issues: HSToday has 2 ongoing special features: ITToday on cybersecurity, software and computer-related topics; and regional reports. In the regional reports, we report on homeland security measures taken in each of these cities and their surrounding regions along with tips on the procurement practices in each municipality. "No vague, alarmist articles chiefly of interest to general consumer audiences. While being aware of the threat, we concentrate on solutions rather than vulnerability. Our audience of government officials, law enforcement, and first responders is very well aware of homeland security vulnerabilities." Query. Length: Length: 1,500 words. **Pays $500.**

Photos State availability with submission. Reviews JPEG files. Offers no additional payment for photos accepted with ms. Captions required.

Columns/Departments Nebraska Ave. (reporting on developments, events, trends, and people in the Dept. of Homeland Security), 700 words; Milestone 1 (reporting on new technology and research related to homeland security just out of the laboratory and not yet commercialized), 700-900 words; ITToday (every other month—see above—reporting on developments affecting computing, information technology, and the Internet), 700-1,000 words; After Action (analysis and lessons learned from past terrorism-related incidents or events), 1,500 words. **Buys 10-12 mss/year.** Query. **Departments pay $250.**

Tips "Best approach is to query editor by e-mail. Some background in reporting on government, law enforcement, defense, homeland security, and/or government procurement is helpful but not essential. We don't publish corporate bylines, technology White Papers, or one product/one company articles. Our best articles are on government practices, innovative solutions to homeland security challenges, and what homeland security professionals are doing in their jurisdictions. While based in the Washington DC area, we're always looking for articles from towns and cities around the country, and we want to build a network of local and international correspondents. We have a particular need for good reporting on funding, appropriations, and federal grantmaking in homeland security."

$ $ THE JOURNAL OF SAFE MANAGEMENT OF DISRUPTIVE AND ASSAULTIVE BEHAVIOR

Crisis Prevention Institute, Inc., 3315-K N. 124th St., Brookfield WI 53005. Fax: (262)783-5906. E-mail: editor@crisisprevention.com. Website: www.crisisprevention.com. **Contact:** Jerilyn Dufresne, director of communications. **75% freelance written.** Semiannual journal covering safe management of disruptive and assaultive behavior. "Our audience is human service and business professionals concerned about workplace violence issues. *CPI* is the world leader in violence prevention training." Estab. 1980. Circ. 17,000. Pays on publication. Publishes ms an average of 6 months after acceptance. Byline given. Offers 50% kill fee. Buys full publication rights for original work and one-time rights for reprints. Editorial lead time 6 months. Submit seasonal material 3 months in advance. Responds in 1 month to queries. Sample copy and writer's guidelines free.

Nonfiction "Each issue is specifically devoted to one topic. Inquire about topics by e-mail or read journal for editorial calendar." Interview/profile, new product, opinion, personal experience, research. **Buys 5-10 mss/year.** Query. Length: 1,500-3,000 words. **Pays $100-300 for assigned articles; $50-100 for unsolicited articles.**

Tips "For more information on CPI, please refer to our website."

$ $ LAW ENFORCEMENT TECHNOLOGY

Cygnus Business Media, P.O. Box 803, 1233 Janesville Ave., Fort Atkinson WI 53538-0803. (920)563-1726. Fax: (920)563-1702. E-mail: ronnie.garrett@cygnuspub.com. Editor: Ronnie Garrett. **50% freelance written.** Monthly magazine covering police management and technology. Estab. 1974. Circ. 35,000. Pays on publication. Publishes ms an average of 6 months after acceptance. Byline given. Offers 25% kill fee. Buys first North American serial rights. Editorial lead time 6 months. Submit seasonal material 6 months in advance. Responds in 1 month to queries; 2 months to mss. Writer's guidelines for #10 SASE.

Nonfiction Book excerpts, how-to, interview/profile, photo feature, police management and training. **Buys 15 mss/year.** Query. Length: 800-1,800 words. **Pays $75-400 for assigned articles.**

Reprints Send ms with rights for sale noted and information about when and where the material previously appeared. Payment negotiable.

Photos Send photos with submission. Reviews contact sheets, negatives, 5×7 or 8×10 prints. Buys one-time rights. Offers no additional payment for photos accepted with ms. Captions required.

Tips "Writer should have background in police work or currently work for a police agency. Most of our articles are technical or supervisory in nature. Please query first after looking at a sample copy."

$ $ NATIONAL FIRE & RESCUE

SpecComm International, Inc., 5808 Faringdon Place, Suite 200, Raleigh NC 27609. (919)872-5040. Fax: (919)876-6531. E-mail: mike@nfrmag.com. Website: www.nfrmag.com. **Contact:** Mike MacDonald, managing editor. **80% freelance written.** "*National Fire & Rescue* is a bimonthly magazine devoted to informing the nation's fire and rescue services, with special emphasis on fire departments serving communities of less than 100,000. It is the *Popular Science* for fire and rescue with easy-to-understand information on science, technology, and training." Estab. 1980. Circ. 30,000. Pays on publication. Publishes ms an average of 5 months after acceptance. Byline given. Offers 50% kill fee. Buys first North American serial rights. Editorial lead time 2 months. Submit seasonal material 3 months in advance. Accepts simultaneous submissions. Responds in 1 month to queries. Call for writer's guidelines.

Nonfiction Book excerpts, how-to, humor, inspirational, interview/profile, new product, personal experience, photo feature. No pieces marketing specific products or services. **Buys 40 mss/year.** Query with published clips. Length: 600-2,000 words. **Pays $100-350 for assigned articles; $100-200 for unsolicited articles.** Pays expenses of writers on assignment.

Photos State availability with submission. Buys one-time rights. Offers $50-200/photo. Identification of subjects required.

Columns/Departments Leadership (management); Training; Special Operations; all 800 words. **Buys 16 mss/year.** Send complete ms. **Pays $100-200.**

Tips "Discuss your story ideas with the editor."

$ $ $ $ NFPA JOURNAL

National Fire Protection Association, P.O. Box 9101, Quincy MA 02269-9101. (617)984-7567. Fax: (617)984-7090. E-mail: nfpajournal@nfpa.org. Website: www.nfpajournal.org. Publisher: Kathie Robinson. **Contact:** John Nicholson, managing editor. Bimonthly magazine covering fire safety, fire science, fire engineering. "The *NFPA Journal*, the official journal of the NFPA, reaches all of the association's various fire safety professionals. Covering major topics in fire protection and suppression, fire protection advances, and public education." Estab. 1969. Circ. 74,000. **Pays on acceptance.** Byline given. Buys all rights. Accepts queries by e-mail, fax. Writer's guidelines online.

Nonfiction Technical. No fiction, product pieces, or human interest. Query. Length: 2,000-2,500 words. **Negotiates payment individually.**

Tips "Query or call. Be familiar with our publication and audience. We happily send out sample issues and guidelines. We appreciate and value quality writers who can provide well-written material on technical subjects related to fire and life safety."

$ $ 9-1-1 MAGAZINE

Official Publications, Inc., 18201 Weston Place, Tustin CA 92780-2251. (714)544-7776. Fax: (714)838-9233. E-mail: publisher@9-1-1magazine.com. Website: www.9-1-1magazine.com. **Contact:** Randall Larson, editor (editor@9-1-1magazine.com). **85% freelance written.** Trade magazine published 9 times/year for knowledgeable emergency communications professionals and those associated with this respectful profession. "Serving law enforcement, fire, and emergency medical services, with an emphasis on communications, *9-1-1 Magazine* provides valuable information to readers in all aspects of the public safety communications and response community. Each issue contains a blending of product-related, technical, operational, and people-oriented stories, covering the skills, training, and equipment which these professionals have in common." Estab. 1989. Circ. 15,000. Pays on publication. Publishes ms an average of 4-6 months after acceptance. Byline given. Offers 20% kill fee. Buys one-time, second serial (reprint) rights. Accepts queries by mail, e-mail, fax. Responds in 1 month to queries; 1 month to mss. Sample copy for 9 × 12 SAE and 5 first-class stamps. Writer's guidelines online.

Nonfiction New product, photo feature, technical, incident report. **Buys 15-25 mss/year.** Query by e-mail. "We prefer queries, but will look at manuscripts on speculation. Most positive responses to queries are considered on spec, but occasionally we will make assignments." Length: 1,000-2,500 words. **Pays 10¢/word.**

Photos Send photos with submission. Reviews color transparencies, prints, high-resolution digital (300 dpi). Buys one-time rights. Offers $50-100/interior, $300/cover. Captions, identification of subjects required.

The online version of this magazine contains material not found in the print version.

Tips "We are looking for writers knowledgable in this field. As a trade magazine, stories should be geared for professionals in the emergency services and dispatch field, not the lay public. We do not use poetry or fiction. Our primary considerations in selecting material are: quality, appropriateness of material, brevity, knowledge of our readership, accuracy, accompanying photography, originality, wit and humor, a clear direction and vision, and proper use of language."

$ P I MAGAZINE

Journal of Professional Investigators, P I Magazine, Inc., 4400 Route 9 S., Suite 1000, P.O. Box 7198, Freehold NJ 07728-7198. (732)308-3800. Fax: (732)308-3314. E-mail: editor@pimagazine.com. Website: www.pimagazine.com. Publisher/Editor-in-Chief: Jimmie Mesis. **Contact:** Don Johnson, editor. **90% freelance written.** Magazine published 6 times/year. "Audience includes US, Canada, and professional investigators in 20-plus countries, law enforcement, attorneys, process servers, paralegals, and other legal professionals." Estab. 1988. Pays on publication. Accepts queries by mail, e-mail. Sample copy for free. Writer's guidelines online.

● No payment for unsolicited materials.

Nonfiction "Manuscripts must include educational material for professional investigators. Profiles are accepted if they offer information on how other professionals can use the knowledge or expertise utilized by the person profiled. Accounts of real cases are used only as part of an educational piece. Investigators with special expertise should query for educational articles to exceed 1,000 words." **Buys up to 75 mss/year.** Query. Length: 1,000-2,000 words. **Pays $50-150 for articles up to 1,000 words; $10-50 for articles of 500 words or less.**

Photos State availability with submission. May offer additional payment for photos accepted with ms. Identification of subjects, model releases required.

Tips *"P I Magazine* has a new publisher and editor-in-chief, a new editor, and a new focus! Please review the current issue online to understand the magazine before submitting a query. Avoid clichés and television inspired concepts of PIs. Great way to get the editor's attention: There are numerous special sections that need shorts of 500 words or less. $10-50."

$ $ $ PLANNING

American Planning Association, 122 S. Michigan Ave., Suite 1600, Chicago IL 60603. (312)431-9100. Fax: (312)431-9985. E-mail: slewis@planning.org. Website: www.planning.org. **Contact:** Sylvia Lewis, editor. **30% freelance written.** Monthly magazine emphasizing urban planning for adult, college-educated readers who are regional and urban planners in city, state, or federal agencies or in private business, or university faculty or students. Estab. 1972. Circ. 35,000. Pays on publication. Publishes ms an average of 2 months after acceptance. Byline given. Buys all rights. Accepts queries by mail, e-mail, fax. Responds in 5 weeks to queries. Sample copy for 9×12 SAE with 5 first-class stamps. Writer's guidelines online.

Nonfiction "It's best to query with a fairly detailed, 1-page letter or e-mail. We'll consider any article that's well written and relevant to our audience. Articles have a better chance if they are timely and related to planning, and if they appeal to a national audience. All articles should be written in magazine-feature style." Exposé (on government or business, but topics related to planning, housing, land use, zoning); general interest (trend stories on cities, land use, government); how-to (successful government or citizen efforts in planning, innovations, concepts that have been applied); technical (detailed articles on the nitty-gritty of planning, transportation, computer mapping, but no footnotes or mathematical models). Special issues: Transportation Issue; Technology Issue. Also needs news stories up to 500 words. **Buys 44 features and 33 news story mss/year.** Length: 500-3,000 words. **Pays $150-1,500.**

Photos "We prefer authors supply their own photos, but we sometimes take our own or arrange for them in other ways." State availability with submission. Buys one-time rights. Pays $100 minimum for photos used on inside pages and $300 for cover photos. Captions required.

$ $ POLICE AND SECURITY NEWS

DAYS Communications, Inc., 1208 Juniper St., Quakertown PA 18951-1520. (215)538-1240. Fax: (215)538-1208. E-mail: jdevery@policeandsecuritynews.com. **Contact:** James Devery, editor. **40% freelance written.** Bimonthly tabloid on public law enforcement and private security. "Our publication is designed to provide educational and entertaining information directed toward management level. Technical information written for the expert in a manner the nonexpert can understand." Estab. 1984. Circ. 22,000. Pays on publication. Publishes ms an average of 2 months after acceptance. Byline given. Buys first North American serial rights. Accepts queries by mail, e-mail, fax, phone. Accepts simultaneous submissions. Sample copy and writer's guidelines for 9×12 SAE with $2.18 postage.

Nonfiction Al Menear, articles editor. Exposé, historical/nostalgic, how-to, humor, interview/profile, opinion, personal experience, photo feature, technical. **Buys 12 mss/year.** Query. Length: 200-4,000 words. **Pays 10¢/ word. Sometimes pays in trade-out of services.**

Reprints Send tearsheet, photocopy or typed ms with rights for sale noted and information about when and where the material previously appeared.

Photos State availability with submission. Reviews 3×5 prints. Buys one-time rights. Offers $10-50/photo.

Fillers Facts, newsbreaks, short humor. **Buys 6/year.** Length: 200-2,000 words. **Pays 10¢/word.**

$ POLICE TIMES

American Federation of Police & Concerned Citizens, Inc., 6350 Horizon Dr., Titusville FL 32780. (321)264-0911. Fax: (321)264-0033. E-mail: policeinfo@aphf.org. Website: www.aphf.org/pt.html. **Contact:** Jim Gordon, executive editor. **80% freelance written.** Eager to work with new/unpublished writers. Quarterly magazine covering "law enforcement (general topics) for men and women engaged in law enforcement and private security, and citizens who are law and order concerned." Circ. 103,000. **Pays on acceptance.** Publishes ms an average of 6 months after acceptance. Byline given. Buys second serial (reprint) rights. Submit seasonal material 4 months in advance. Accepts queries by mail, fax. Accepts simultaneous submissions. Sample copy for $2.50 and 9×12 SAE with 3 first-class stamps. Writer's guidelines for #10 SASE.

Nonfiction Book excerpts, essays (on police science), exposé (police corruption), general interest, historical/ nostalgic, how-to, humor, interview/profile, new product, personal experience (with police), photo feature, technical (all police related). Special issues: "We produce a special edition on police killed in the line of duty. It is mailed May 15 so copy must arrive 6 months in advance. Photos required." No anti-police materials. **Buys 50 mss/year.** Send complete ms. Length: 200-4,000 words. **Pays $25-100. Payment includes right to publish on organization's website.**

Photos Send photos with submission. Reviews 5×6 prints. Buys all rights. Offers $5-25/photo. Identification of subjects required.

Columns/Departments Legal Cases (lawsuits involving police actions); New Products (new items related to police services); Awards (police heroism acts). Length: 200-1,000. **Buys variable number of mss/year.** Send complete ms. **Pays $25-75.**

Fillers Fillers are usually humorous stories about police officer and citizen situations. Special stories on police cases, public corruptions, etc., are most open to freelancers. No cartoons. Anecdotes, facts, newsbreaks. **Buys 100/year.** Length: 50-100 words. **Pays $5-10.**

TRANSACTION/SOCIETY

35 Berrue Circle, Piscataway NJ 08854. (732)445-2280. Fax: (732)445-3138. E-mail: trans@transactionpub.com. Website: www.transactionpub.com. **Contact:** Irving Louis Horowitz, editor. **10% freelance written.** Prefers to work with published/established writers. Bimonthly magazine for social scientists (policymakers with training in sociology, political issues, and economics). Estab. 1962. Circ. 15,000. Pays on publication. Publishes ms an average of 6 months after acceptance. Byline given. Buys all rights. Responds in 3 months to queries. Sample copy and writer's guidelines for 9×12 SAE with 5 first-class stamps.

Nonfiction "Articles of wide interest in areas of specific interest to the social science community. Must have an awareness of problems and issues in education, population, and urbanization that are not widely reported. Articles on overpopulation, terrorism, international organizations." Book excerpts, essays, interview/profile, photo feature. No general think pieces. Query. **Pays for assigned articles only.**

Photos Pays $200 for photographic essays done on assignment or upon publication.

Tips "Submit an article on a thoroughly unique subject, written with good literary quality. Present new ideas and research findings in a readable and useful manner. A frequent mistake is writing to satisfy a journal, rather than the intrinsic requirements of the story itself. Avoid posturing and editorializing."

GROCERIES & FOOD PRODUCTS

AUTOMATIC MERCHANDISER MAGAZINE

Cygnus Business Media, P.O. Box 803, Fort Atkinson WI 53538. (800)547-7377. Fax: (920)568-2305. E-mail: stacey.meacham@amonline.com. Website: www.amonline.com. Editor: Elliot Maras. **Contact:** Stacey Meacham, managing editor. **30% freelance written.** Monthly magazine covering vending and office coffee. Estab. 1940. Circ. 16,000. **Pays on acceptance.** Byline given. Buys first rights. Editorial lead time 1 month. Accepts queries by mail, e-mail, fax. Accepts simultaneous submissions. Sample copy online.

$ $ $ DISTRIBUTION CHANNELS

AWMA's Magazine for Candy, Tobacco, Grocery, Foodservice and General Merchandise Marketers, American Wholesale Marketers Association, 2750 Prosperity Ave., Suite 530, Fairfax VA 22031. (703)208-3358. Fax: (703)573-5738. E-mail: tracic@awmanet.org. Website: www.awmanet.org. **Contact:** Traci Carneal, editor-in-chief. **70% freelance written.** Magazine published 10 times/year. "We cover trends in candy, tobacco, groceries, beverages, snacks, and other product categories found in convenience stores, grocery stores, and drugstores, plus distribution topics. Contributors should have prior experience writing about the food, retail, and/or distribution industries. Editorial includes a mix of columns, departments, and features (2-6 pages). We also cover AWMA programs." Estab. 1948. Circ. 11,000. **Pays on acceptance.** Publishes ms an average of 2 months after acceptance. Byline given. Editorial lead time 4 months. Accepts queries by mail, e-mail, fax. Writer's guidelines online.

Nonfiction How-to, technical, industry trends; also profiles of distribution firms. No comics, jokes, poems, or other fillers. **Buys 40 mss/year.** Query with published clips. Length: 1,200-3,600 words. **Pays 50¢/word.** Sometimes pays industry members who author articles. Pays expenses of writers on assignment.

Photos Authors must provide artwork (with captions) with articles.

Tips "We're looking for reliable, accurate freelancers with whom we can establish a long-term working relationship. We need writers who understand this industry. We accept very few articles on speculation. Most are assigned. To consider a new writer for an assignment, we must first receive his or her résumé, at least 2 writing samples, and references."

$ $ $ $ FOOD PRODUCT DESIGN MAGAZINE

Weeks Publishing, 3400 Dundee Rd., Suite 100, Northbrook IL 60062. (847)559-0385. Fax: (847)559-0389. E-mail: weeksfpd@aol.com. **Contact:** Lynn Kuntz, editor. **50% freelance written.** Monthly magazine covering food processing industry. "The magazine written for food technologists by food technologists. No foodservice/ restaurant, consumer, or recipe development." Estab. 1991. Circ. 30,000. **Pays on acceptance.** Publishes ms an average of 2 months after acceptance. Byline given. Buys one-time, all rights, makes work-for-hire assignments. Editorial lead time 4 months. Sample copy for 9×12 SAE and 5 first-class stamps.

Nonfiction Technical. **Buys 30 mss/year.** Length: 1,500-7,000 words. **Pays $100-1,500.** Sometimes pays expenses of writers on assignment.

Reprints Accepts previously published submissions depending on where it was published.

Photos State availability with submission. Reviews transparencies, prints. Buys rights depending on photo. Offers no additional payment for photos accepted with ms. Captions required.

Columns/Departments Pays $100-500.

Tips "If you haven't worked in the food industry in research & development, or QA/QC, don't bother to call us. If you can't communicate technical information in a way that is clear, easy-to-understand and well organized, don't bother to call us. While perfect grammar is not expected, good grammar and organization is."

$ $ FOODSERVICE DIRECTOR

VNU Business Media, 770 Broadway, New York NY 10003. (646)654-7403. Fax: (646)654-7410. E-mail: jpond@fsdmag.com. Website: www.fsdmag.com. Editor-In-Chief: James Pond. Feature Editor: Karen Weisberg. News Editor: Jennifer Alexis. **20% freelance written.** Monthly tabloid covering noncommercial foodservice operations for operators of kitchens and dining halls in schools, colleges, hospitals/health care, office and plant cafeterias, military, airline/transportation, correctional institutions. Estab. 1988. Circ. 45,000. Pays on publication. Byline sometimes given. Buys all rights for print and online usage. Submit seasonal material 3 months in advance. Accepts simultaneous submissions. Sample copy for free.

Nonfiction How-to, interview/profile. **Buys 60-70 mss/year.** Query with published clips. Length: 700-900 words. **Pays $250-500.**

Photos Send photos with submission. Reviews transparencies. Buys all rights. Offers no additional payment for photos accepted with ms. Identification of subjects required.

Columns/Departments Equipment (case studies of kitchen/serving equipment in use), 700-900 words; Food (specific category studies per publication calendar), 750-900 words. Query.

$ $ FRESH CUT MAGAZINE

The Magazine for Value-added Produce, Columbia Publishing, 417 N. 20th Ave., Yakima WA 98902. (509)248-2452. Fax: (509)248-4056. E-mail: rick@freshcut.com. **Contact:** Brent Clement, editor. **20% freelance written.** Monthly magazine covering the value-added, pre-cut fruit and vegetable industry. The editor is interested in articles that focus on what different fresh-cut processors are doing. Estab. 1993. Circ. 16,000. Pays on publication. Publishes ms an average of 2 months after acceptance. Byline given. Buys all rights. Editorial lead time 2 months. Submit seasonal material well in advance. Accepts queries by mail, e-mail, fax, phone. Responds in 1 month to queries; 2 months to mss. Sample copy for 9×12 SAE. Writer's guidelines for #10 SASE.

○━ "We want to hear of new products, packaging, food safety programs, how they deal with transportation issues—anything of interest to the industry. We're also interested in the use of pre-cut fruit and vegetable products in retail and foodservice—growth trends and perception by chefs, store managers and others."

Nonfiction Historical/nostalgic, new product, opinion, technical. Special issues: Retail (May); Foodservice (February, July); Packaging Technology (December). **Buys 2-4 mss/year.** Query with published clips. **Pays $5/column inch for assigned articles; $75-125 for unsolicited articles.**

Reprints Send tearsheet with rights for sale noted and information about when and where the material previously appeared. Pays 50% of amount paid for an original article.

Photos Send photos with submission. Reviews transparencies. Buys one-time rights. Offers no additional payment for photos accepted with ms. Identification of subjects required.

Columns/Departments Packaging; Food Safety; Processing/Engineering. **Buys 20 mss/year.** Query. **Pays $125-200.**

Fillers Facts. Length: 300 words maximum. **Pays $25-50.**

$ $ HEALTH PRODUCTS BUSINESS

CYGNUS Business Media, Inc., 1233 Jamesville Ave., Fort Atkinson WI 53538. (920)563-1694. Website: www.healthproductsbusiness.com. **Contact:** Kimber Williams, editor. **40% freelance written.** Monthly magazine covering natural health products. "The business magazine for natural products retailers." Estab. 1954. Circ. 15,000. Pays on publication. Publishes ms an average of 3 months after acceptance. Byline given. Buys first North American serial rights. Editorial lead time 4 months. Submit seasonal material 3 months in advance. Accepts queries by mail, fax. Sample copy for $3.

Nonfiction Query first. **Pays $200-450 for articles on natural health retailing.**

Photos State availability with submission.

▣ The online version of this publication contains material not found in the print edition. Contact: Kimber Williams, editor.

Tips "We are always looking for well-written retail-oriented features, but new writers should always query first to receive information. We prefer writers with industry experience/interest. AP Style, a plus."

$ $ PRODUCE MERCHANDISING

Vance Publishing Corp., 10901 W. 84th Terrace, Lenexa KS 66214. (913)438-8700. Fax: (913)438-0691. E-mail: eashby@producemerchandising.com. Website: www.producemerchandising.com. **Contact:** Elizabeth Ashby, editor. **10% freelance written.** Monthly magazine. "The magazine's editorial purpose is to provide information about promotions, merchandising, and operations in the form of ideas and examples. *Produce Merchandising* is the only monthly journal on the market that is dedicated solely to produce merchandising information for retailers." Circ. 12,000. **Pays on acceptance.** Publishes ms an average of 3 months after acceptance. Byline given. Buys all rights. Editorial lead time 3 months. Accepts queries by mail. Responds in 2 weeks to queries. Sample copy for free.

Nonfiction How-to, interview/profile, new product, photo feature, technical (contact the editor for a specific assignment). **Buys 48 mss/year.** Query with published clips. Length: 1,000-1,500 words. **Pays $200-600.** Pays expenses of writers on assignment.

Photos State availability of or send photos with submission. Reviews color slides and 3×5 or larger prints. Buys all rights. Offers no additional payment for photos accepted with ms. Captions, identification of subjects, model releases required.

Columns/Departments Contact editor for a specific assignment. **Buys 30 mss/year.** Query with published clips. **Pays $200-450.**

Tips "Send in clips and contact the editor with specific story ideas. Story topics are typically outlined up to a year in advance."

$ $ THE PRODUCE NEWS

482 Hudson Terrace, Englewood Cliffs NJ 07632. (201)503-9100. Fax: (201)503-9104. E-mail: groh@theproduce news.com. Website: www.theproducenews.com. Publisher: Gordon M. Hochberg. **Contact:** John Groh, editor. **10% freelance written.** Works with a small number of new/unpublished writers each year. Weekly magazine for commercial growers and shippers, receivers and distributors of fresh fruits and vegetables, including chain store produce buyers and merchandisers. Estab. 1897. Pays on publication. Publishes ms an average of 2 weeks after acceptance. Accepts queries by mail, e-mail, fax. Responds in 1 month to queries. Sample copy and writer's guidelines for 10×13 SAE and 4 first-class stamps.

Nonfiction News stories (about the produce industry). Buys profiles, spot news, coverage of successful business operations and articles on merchandising techniques. Query. **Pays $1/column inch minimum.** Sometimes pays expenses of writers on assignment.

Photos Black and white glossies or color prints. Pays $8-10/photo.

Tips "Stories should be trade oriented, not consumer oriented. As our circulation grows in the next year, we are interested in stories and news articles from all fresh-fruit-growing areas of the country."

$ $ ⬛ WESTERN GROCER MAGAZINE

Mercury Publications Ltd., 1839 Inkster Blvd., Winnipeg MB R2X 1R3 Canada. (204)954-2085. Fax: (204)954-2057. E-mail: mp@mercury.mb.ca. Website: www.mercury.mb.ca/. Editor: Frank Yeo. **Contact:** Carly Peters, editorial production manager. **75% freelance written.** Bimonthly magazine covering the grocery industry. Reports profiles on independent food stores, supermarkets, manufacturers and food processors, brokers, distributors, and wholesalers. Estab. 1916. Circ. 15,500. Pays 30-45 days from receipt of invoice. Byline given. Offers 33% kill fee. Buys all rights. Submit seasonal material 3 months in advance. Sample copy and writer's guidelines free or by e-mail.

• Assigns stories to Canadian writers based on editorial needs of publication.

Nonfiction How-to, interview/profile. Industry reports and profiles on companies. Query with published clips. Length: 500-9,000 words. **Pays 25-35¢/word.** Sometimes pays expenses of writers on assignment.

Photos State availability with submission. Reviews negatives, transparencies, 3×5 prints, JPEG, EPS, or TIF files. Buys all rights. Negotiates payment individually. Captions required.

Tips "E-mail, fax, or mail a query outlining your experience, interest, and pay expectations. Include clippings."

HOME FURNISHINGS & HOUSEHOLD GOODS

FINE FURNISHINGS INTERNATIONAL

FFI, Grace McNamara, Inc., 4215 White Bear Parkway, Suite 100, St. Paul MN 55110. (651)293-1544. Fax: (651)653-4308. E-mail: ffiedit@gracemcnamarainc.com. Website: www.ffimagazine.com. **Contact:** Kate Lundquist, managing editor. Quarterly magazine covering the high-end furniture industry. Estab. 1997. Circ. 25,000.

Pays on publication. Buys all rights. Editorial lead time 3-5 months. Accepts queries by mail, e-mail. Sample copy for $5.

Nonfiction Interior designer profiles, high-end residential furnishings, international trade events, and interior-design associations are all featured in our trade publication.

Tips "Writers must have a knowledge of interior design and furnishings that allows them to speak with authority to our to-the-trade audience of interior designers and architects."

$ $ HOME FURNISHINGS RETAILER

National Home Furnishings Association (NHFA), 3910 Tinsley Dr., High Point NC 27265. (336)801-6156. Fax: (336)801-6102. E-mail: tkemerly@nhfa.org. **Contact:** Trisha Kemerly, editor. **75% freelance written.** Monthly magazine published by NHFA covering the home furnishings industry. "We hope home furnishings retailers view our magazine as a profitability tool. We want each issue to help them make or save money." Estab. 1927. Circ. 15,000. **Pays on acceptance.** Publishes ms an average of 6 weeks after acceptance. Byline given. Buys first North American serial rights. Editorial lead time 3 months. Accepts queries by mail, e-mail. Responds in 1 month to queries. Sample copy available with proper postage. Writer's guidelines for #10 SASE.

> O— Break in by "e-mailing queries that pertain to our market—furniture retailers. We publish articles that give our readers tangible ways to improve their business."

Nonfiction Query with published clips. Length: 3,000-5,000 words (features). **Pays $350-500 for assigned articles.**

Photos State availability with submission. Reviews transparencies. Buys one-time rights. Negotiates payment individually. Identification of subjects required.

Columns/Departments Query with published clips.

Tips "Our readership includes owners of small 'Ma and Pa' furniture stores, executives of medium-sized chains (2-10 stores), and executives of big chains. Articles should be relevant to retailers and provide them with tangible information, ideas, and products to better their business."

HOME LIGHTING & ACCESSORIES

Doctorow Communications, Inc., 1011 Clifton Ave., Clifton NJ 07013. (973)779-1600. Fax: (973)779-3242. E-mail: linda@homelighting.com. Website: www.homelighting.com. **Contact:** Linda Longo, editor. **25% freelance written.** Prefers to work with published/established writers. Monthly magazine for lighting showrooms/department stores. Estab. 1923. Circ. 10,000. Pays on publication. Publishes ms an average of 6 months after acceptance. Buys first rights. Submit seasonal material 6 months in advance. Accepts queries by mail, e-mail. Responds in 2 months to queries. Sample copy for 9×12 SAE and 4 first-class stamps.

Nonfiction Interview/profile (with lighting retailers), personal experience (as a businessperson involved with lighting), technical (concerning lighting or lighting design), profile (of a successful lighting retailer/lamp buyer). Special issues: Outdoor (March); Tribute To Tiffanies (August). **Buys less than 10 mss/year.** Query.

Reprints Send tearsheet and information about when and where the material previously appeared.

Photos State availability with submission. Offers no additional payment for 5×7 or 8×10 b&w glossy prints. Captions required.

Tips "Have a unique perspective on retailing lamps and lighting fixtures. We often use freelancers located in a part of the country where we'd like to profile a specific business or person. Anyone who has published an article dealing with any aspect of home furnishings will have high priority."

WINDOW FASHIONS

Grace McNamara, Inc., 4215 White Bear Pkwy., Suite 100, St. Paul MN 55110. Fax: (651)653-4308. E-mail: wfedit@gracemcnamarainc.com. Website: www.window-fashions.com. **Contact:** Linda Henry, editor-in-chief. **30% freelance written.** Monthly magazine "dedicated to the advancement of the window fashions industry, *Window Fashions* provides comprehensive information on design and business principles, window fashion aesthetics, and product applications. The magazine serves the window-treatment and wall-coverings industry, including designers, retailers, dealers, specialty stores, workrooms, manufacturers, fabricators, and others associated with the field of interior design. Writers should be thoroughly knowledgable on the subject, and submissions need to be comprehensive." Estab. 1981. Circ. 30,000. Pays on publication. Publishes ms an average of 3 months after acceptance. Byline given. Buys all rights. Editorial lead time 3 months. Submit seasonal material 4 months in advance. Accepts queries by mail, e-mail. Accepts simultaneous submissions. Sample copy for $5.

Nonfiction How-to (window fashion installation), interview/profile (of designers), personal experience. "No broad topics not specific to the window fashions industry." **Buys 24 mss/year.** Query or send complete ms. Length: 800-1,000 words.

Tips "The most helpful experience is if a writer has knowledge of interior design or, specifically, window treatments. We already have a pool of generalists, although we welcome clips from writers who would like to be considered for assignments. Our style is professional business writing—no flowery prose. Articles tend to be to the point, as our readers are busy professionals who read for information, not for leisure. Most of all we need creative ideas and approaches to topics in the field of window treatments and interior design. A writer needs to be knowledgeable in the field because our readers would know if information was inaccurate.''

HOSPITALS, NURSING & NURSING HOMES

N $ ALZHEIMER'S CARE GUIDE

Freiberg Press Inc., P.O. Box 612, Cedar Falls IA 50613. (319)553-0642. Fax: (319)553-0644. E-mail: bfreiberg@cfu.net. Website: www.care4elders.com. **Contact:** Bill Freiberg, editor. **25% freelance written.** Bimonthly magazine covering Alzheimer's care. Aimed at caregivers of Alzheimer's patients. Interested in either inspirational first-person type stories or features/articles involving authoritative advice or caregiving tips. Estab. 1992. Circ. 10,000. **Pays on acceptance.** Byline sometimes given. Buys all rights. Accepts queries by e-mail.

Nonfiction Book excerpts, interview/profile, personal experience, technical. **Buys 50 mss/year.** Query. Length: 500-2,000 words. **Pays $15 for unsolicited articles.**

$ $ $ HOSPITALS & HEALTH NETWORKS

Health Forum, 1 N. Franklin, 29th Floor, Chicago IL 60606. (312)422-2100. E-mail: bsantamour@healthforum.com. Website: www.hhnmag.com. **Contact:** Bill Santamour, managing editor. **25% freelance written.** Monthly magazine covering hospitals. ''We are a business publication for hospital and health system executives. We use only writers who are thoroughly familiar with the hospital field. Submit résumé and up to 5 samples of health care-related articles. We assign all articles and do not consider manuscripts.'' Estab. 1926. Circ. 85,000. **Pays on acceptance.** Publishes ms an average of 3 months after acceptance. Byline given. Offers variable kill fee. Buys all rights. Editorial lead time 2-3 months. Accepts queries by e-mail. Responds in 2-4 months to queries.

Nonfiction Interview/profile, technical. Query with published clips. Length: 350-2,000 words. **Pays $300-1,500 for assigned articles.**

Tips ''If you demonstrate via published clips that you are thoroughly familiar with the business issues facing health-care executives, and that you are a polished reporter and writer, we will consider assigning you an article for our InBox section to start out. These are generally 350 words on a specific development of interest to hospitals and health system executives. Persistence does not pay with us. Once you've sent your résumé and clips, we will review them. If we have no assignment at that time, we will keep promising freelance candidates on file for future assignments.''

$ $ ⬚ LONG TERM CARE

The Ontario Long Term Care Association, 345 Renfrew Dr., Suite 102-202, Markham ON L3R 9S9 Canada. (905)470-8995. Fax: (905)470-9595. E-mail: hlrpublishing@bellnet.ca. Website: www.oltca.com. Co-Editor: Tracey Ann Coveart. **Contact:** Heather Lang, editor. Quarterly magazine covering ''professional issues and practical articles of interest to staff working in a long-term care setting (nursing home, retirement home): Information must be applicable to a Canadian setting; focus should be on staff and for resident well being.'' Estab. 1990. Circ. 6,000. Pays on publication. Publishes ms an average of 4 months after acceptance. Byline given. Buys one-time rights. Editorial lead time 3 months. Submit seasonal material 5 months in advance. Responds in 3 months to queries. Sample copy for free. Writer's guidelines online.

Nonfiction General interest, how-to (practical, of use to long term care practitioners), inspirational, interview/profile. No product-oriented articles. Query with published clips. Length: 800-1,500 words. **Pays up to $500 (Canadian).**

Photos Send photos with submission. Reviews contact sheets, 5×5 prints. Buys one-time rights. Offers no additional payment for photos accepted with ms. Captions, model releases required.

Columns/Departments Query with published clips. **Pays up to $500 (Canadian).**

Tips ''Articles must be positive, upbeat, and contain helpful information that staff and managers working in the long term care field can use. Focus should be on staff and resident well being. Articles that highlight new ways of doing things are particularly useful. Please call the editor to discuss ideas. Must be applicable to Canadian settings.''

NURSEWEEK

NurseWeek Publishing, 6860 Santa Teresa Blvd., San Jose CA 95119. (800)859-2091. Fax: (408)249-3756. Website: www.nurseweek.com. *NurseWeek* is an independent biweekly news magazine supported by advertising revenue, sales of continuing education, and trade shows. Its editorial mission is to provide nurses with the latest news, resources, and opportunities to help them succeed in their lives and careers. Five regional editions:

California, Mountain West, South Central, Midwest, and Great Lakes. Assigns articles. **Pays on acceptance.**

◼ NurseWeek.com is updated daily with news content and posts new job listings on a daily basis.

$ $ $ NURSING SPECTRUM

Florida Edition, Nursing Spectrum, 1001 W. Cypress Creek Rd., Suite 330, Ft. Lauderdale FL 33309. (954)776-1455. Fax: (954)776-1456. E-mail: pclass@nursingspectrum.com. Website: www.nursingspectrum.com. **Contact:** Phyllis Class, RN, editorial director. **80% freelance written.** Biweekly magazine covering registered nursing. "We support and recognize registered nurses. All articles must have at least one RN in byline. We prefer articles that feature nurses in our region, but articles of interest to all nurses are welcome, too. We look for substantive, yet readable articles. Our bottom line—timely, relevant, and compelling articles that support nurses and help them excel in their clinical and professional careers." Estab. 1991. Circ. 60,000. Pays on publication. Byline given. Buys all rights. Editorial lead time 3 months. Submit seasonal material 4 months in advance. Accepts queries by mail, e-mail, fax, phone. Responds in 1 month to queries; 4 months to mss. Sample copy for free. Writer's guidelines online.

    ⊶ "Having an original idea is paramount and the first step in writing an article. We are looking for success stories, nurses to be proud of, and progress that is helping patients. If you and your colleagues have dealt with and learned from a thorny issue, tell us how. What is new in your field? Consider your audience: all RNs, well educated, and of various specialties. Will they relate, be inspired, learn something? The best articles are both interesting and informative."

Nonfiction General interest, how-to (career management), humor, interview/profile, personal experience, photo feature. Special issues: Critical Care; Nursing Management. **Buys 125 plus mss/year.** Length: 700-1,200 words. **Pays $50-800 for assigned articles.** Sometimes pays expenses of writers on assignment.

Photos Buys one-time rights. Negotiates payment individually. Captions, identification of subjects, model releases required.

Columns/Departments Humor Infusion (cartoon, amusing anecdotes). **Buys 75 mss/year.** Query with published clips. **Pays $50-120.**

Tips "Write in 'magazine' style—as if talking to another RN. Use to-the-point, active language. Narrow your focus. Topics such as 'The Future of Nursing' or 'Dealing With Change' are too broad and nonspecific. Use informative but catchy titles and subheads (we can help with this). If quoting others, be sure quotes are meaningful and add substance to the piece. To add vitality, you may use statistics and up-to-date references. Try to paint a complete picture, using pros and cons. Be both positive and realistic."

$ $ $ NURSING SPECTRUM

Greater Philadelphia/Tri-State edition, Nursing Spectrum, 2002 Renaissance Blvd., Suite 250, King of Prussia PA 19406. (610)292-8000. Fax: (610)292-0179. Website: www.nursingspectrum.com. **Contact:** Donna Novak, editorial director. **80% freelance written.** Biweekly magazine covering registered nursing. "We support and recognize registered nurses. All articles must have at least one RN in byline. We prefer articles that feature nurses in our region, but articles of interest to all nurses are welcome, too. We look for substantive, yet readable articles. Our bottom line—timely, relevant, and compelling articles that support nurses and help them excel in their clinical and professional careers." Estab. 1992. Circ. 74,000. Byline given. Writer's guidelines online.

    ● See *Nursing Spectrum, Florida Edition* for article needs.

$ $ $ NURSING SPECTRUM

New England edition, Nursing Spectrum, 1050 Waltham St., Suite 330, Lexington MA 02421. (781)863-2300. Fax: (781)863-6277. E-mail: tgaffney@nursingspectrum.com. Website: www.nursingspectrum.com. **Contact:** Theresa Gaffney, RN, editor-in-chief. **80% freelance written.** Biweekly magazine covering registered nursing. "We support and recognize registered nurses. All articles must have at least one RN in byline. We prefer articles that feature nurses in our region, but articles of interest to all nurses are welcome, too. We look for substantive, yet readable articles. Our bottom line—timely, relevant, and compelling articles that support nurses and help them excel in their clinical and professional careers." Estab. 1997. Circ. 66,000. Byline given. Accepts queries by mail, e-mail, fax, phone. Writer's guidelines online.

    ◼ The online version carries original content not found in the print edition. Contact: Judith Mitiguy, vice president of editorial.

$ $ $ NURSING SPECTRUM

Washington, DC/Baltimore edition, Nursing Spectrum, 803 W. Broad St., Suite 500, Falls Church VA 22046. (703)237-6515. Fax: (703)237-6299. Website: www.nursingspectrum.com. **Contact:** Pam Meredith, RN, editor. **80% freelance written.** Biweekly journal covering registered nursing. "We support and recognize registered nurses. All articles must have at least one RN in byline. We prefer articles that feature nurses in our region, but articles of interest to all nurses are welcome, too. We look for substantive, yet readable articles. Our bottom line—timely, relevant, and compelling articles that support nurses and help them excel in their clinical and professional careers.'' Estab. 1990. Circ. 1 million. Writer's guidelines online.

● See *Nursing Spectrum, Florida Edition* for article needs.

$ $ NURSING2005

(formerly *Nursing2004*), Lippincott Williams & Wilkins, 323 Norristown Rd., Suite 200, Ambler PA 19002. (215)646-8700. Fax: (215)367-2155. E-mail: nursing@lww.com. Website: www.nursing2005.com. Editor-in-Chief: Cheryl L. Mee, RN, BC, CMSRN, MSN. Managing Editor: Jane Benner. **Contact:** Patricia Wolf, editorial dept. **100% freelance written.** Monthly magazine ''Written by nurses for nurses; we look for practical advice for the direct caregiver that reflects the author's experience. Any form acceptable, but focus must be nursing.'' Estab. 1971. Circ. over 300,000. Pays on publication. Publishes ms an average of 18 months after acceptance. Byline given. Offers 50% kill fee. Buys all rights. Submit seasonal material 8 months in advance. Responds in 2 weeks to queries; 3 months to mss. Sample copy for $5. Writer's guidelines online.

Nonfiction Book excerpts, exposé, how-to (specifically as applies to nursing field), inspirational, opinion, personal experience, photo feature. No articles from patients' point of view, poetry, etc. **Buys 100 mss/year.** Query. Length: 100 words minimum. **Pays $50-400 for assigned articles.**

Reprints Send photocopy and information about when and where the material previously appeared. Pays 50% of amount paid for an original articles.

Photos State availability with submission. Buys all rights. Offers no additional payment for photos accepted with ms. Model releases required.

Tips ''Basically, *Nursing2005* is a how-to journal, full of hands-on, practical articles. We look for the voice of experience from authors and for articles that help our readers deal with problems they face. We're always interested in taking a look at manuscripts that fall into the following categories: clinical articles, drug articles, charting/documentation, emotional problems, legal problems, ethical dilemnas, difficult or challenging cases.''

HOTELS, MOTELS, CLUBS, RESORTS & RESTAURANTS

$ $ BARTENDER MAGAZINE

Foley Publishing, P.O. Box 158, Liberty Corner NJ 07938. (908)766-6006. Fax: (908)766-6607. E-mail: barmag@aol.com. Website: www.bartender.com. Editor: Jaclyn M. Wilson. **Contact:** Jackie Foley, publisher. **100% freelance written.** Prefers to work with published/established writers; eager to work with new/unpublished writers. Quarterly magazine emphasizing liquor and bartending for bartenders, tavern owners, and owners of restaurants with full-service liquor licenses. Circ. 148,225. Pays on publication. Publishes ms an average of 3 months after acceptance. Byline given. Buys first North American serial, first, one-time, second serial (reprint), simultaneous, all rights. Submit seasonal material 3 months in advance. Accepts simultaneous submissions. Responds in 2 months to mss. Sample copy for 9 × 12 SAE and 4 first-class stamps.

Nonfiction General interest, historical/nostalgic, how-to, humor, interview/profile (with famous bartenders or ex-bartenders), new product, opinion, personal experience, photo feature, travel, nostalgia, unique bars, new techniques, new drinking trends, bar sports, bar magic tricks. Special issues: Annual Calendar and Daily Cocktail Recipe Guide. Send complete ms and SASE. Length: 100-1,000 words.

Reprints Send tearsheet and information about when and where the material previously appeared. Pays 25% of amount paid for an original article.

Photos Send photos with submission. Pays $7.50-50 for 8 × 10 b&w glossy prints; $10-75 for 8 × 10 color glossy prints. Captions, model releases required.

Columns/Departments Bar of the Month; Bartender of the Month; Creative Cocktails; Bar Sports; Quiz; Bar Art; Wine Cellar; Tips from the Top (from prominent figures in the liquor industry); One For the Road (travel); Collectors (bar or liquor-related items); Photo Essays. **Length:** 200-1,000 words. Query by mail only with SASE. **Pays $50-200.**

Fillers Anecdotes, newsbreaks, short humor, clippings, jokes, gags. Length: 25-100 words. **Pays $5-25.**

Tips ''To break in, absolutely make sure that your work will be of interest to all bartenders across the country. Your style of writing should reflect the audience you are addressing. The most frequent mistake made by writers in completing an article for us is using the wrong subject.''

$ $ CHEF

The Food Magazine for Professionals, Talcott Communications Corp., 20 W. Kinzie, 12th Floor, Chicago IL 60610. (312)849-2220. Fax: (312)849-2174. Website: www.chefmagazine.com. **Contact:** Editor. **40% freelance written.** Monthly magazine covering chefs in all food-service segments. ''*Chef* is the one magazine that communicates food production to a commercial, professional audience in a meaningful way.'' Circ. 42,000. **Pays on acceptance.** Byline given. Offers 10% kill fee. Buys first North American serial, second serial (reprint) rights.

Editorial lead time 2 months. Submit seasonal material 4 months in advance. Accepts queries by mail, e-mail, fax. Writer's guidelines free.

Nonfiction Book excerpts, essays, exposé, general interest, historical/nostalgic, how-to (create a dish or perform a technique), inspirational, interview/profile, new product, opinion, personal experience, photo feature, technical. **Buys 30-50 mss/year.** Query. Length: 750-1,500 words. **Pays $250-500.** Sometimes pays expenses of writers on assignment.

Reprints Accepts previously published submissions.

Photos State availability with submission. Reviews transparencies. Buys one-time rights. Negotiates payment individually. Captions, identification of subjects required.

Columns/Departments Flavor (traditional and innovative applications of a particular flavor) 1,000-1,200 words; Dish (professional chef profiles), 1,000-1,200 words; Savor (themed recipes), 1,000-1,500 words. **Buys 12-18 mss/year.** Query. **Pays $250-500.**

Tips "Know food and apply it to the business of chefs. Always query first, after you've read our magazine. Tell us how your idea can be used by our readers to enhance their businesses in some way."

CLUB MANAGEMENT

The Resource for Successful Club Operations, Finan Publishing Co., 107 W. Pacific Ave., St. Louis MO 63119. (314)961-6644. Fax: (314)961-4809. E-mail: tjf4@finan.com. Website: www.club-mgmt.com. **Contact:** Tom Finan, editor. Bimonthly magazine covering club management, private club market, hospitality industry. Estab. 1925. Circ. 16,702. Pays on publication. Publishes ms an average of 2 months after acceptance. Buys first North American serial, electronic rights. Accepts queries by mail, e-mail, fax.

Nonfiction General interest, historical/nostalgic, how-to, interview/profile, personal experience, photo feature, technical, travel. **Buys 100 mss/year.** Query with published clips. Length: 2,000-2,500 words.

Photos State availability with submission.

Columns/Departments Sports (private club sports: golf, tennis, yachting, fitness, etc.).

Tips "We don't accept blind submissions. Please submit a résumé and clips of your work. Send copies, not originals."

$ $ EL RESTAURANTE MEXICANO

P.O. Box 2249, Oak Park IL 60303-2249. (708)445-9454. Fax: (708)445-9477. E-mail: kfurore@restmex.com. **Contact:** Kathleen Furore, editor. Bimonthly magazine covering Mexican restaurants. "*El Restaurante Mexicano* offers features and business-related articles that are geared specifically to owners and operators of Mexican, Tex-Mex, Southwestern, and Latin cuisine restaurants." Estab. 1997. Circ. 27,000. Pays on publication. Publishes ms an average of 3 months after acceptance. Byline given. Buys first North American serial rights. Responds in 2 months to queries. Sample copy for free.

Nonfiction Looking for stories about unique Mexican restaurants and about business issues that affect Mexican restaurant owners. "No specific knowledge of food or restaurants is needed; the key qualification is to be a good reporter who knows how to slant a story toward the Mexican restaurant operator." **Buys 2-4 mss/year.** Query with published clips. Length: 800-1,500 words. **Pays $225.** Pays expenses of writers on assignment.

Tips "Query with a story idea, and tell how it pertains to Mexican restaurants."

$ $ FLORIDA HOTEL & MOTEL JOURNAL

The Official Publication of the Florida Hotel & Motel Association, Accommodations, Inc., P.O. Box 1529, Tallahassee FL 32302-1529. (850)224-2888. Fax: (850)668-2884. E-mail: journal@fhma.net. Website: www.flahotel.c om. **Contact:** Lytha Page Belrose, editor. **10% freelance written.** Prefers to work with published/established writers. Bimonthly magazine acting as a reference tool for managers and owners of Florida's hotels, motels, and resorts. Estab. 1978. Circ. 8,500. Pays on publication. Publishes ms an average of 1-2 months after acceptance. Byline given. Buys first rights. Editorial lead time 1-9 months. Submit seasonal material 4-5 months in advance. Accepts queries by mail. Accepts previously published material. Responds in 2-4 months to queries. Sample copy for free. Writer's guidelines online.

> Preference is given to articles that include references to member properties and general managers affiliated with the Florida Hotel and Motel Association. Since the association acquires new members weekly, queries may be made prior to the scheduling of interviews. This does not preclude the use of materials or ideas based on non-member properties, but member property sources are preferable.

Nonfiction How-to (pertaining to hotel management), interview/profile, new product, personal experience, technical. No travel tips or articles aimed at the traveling public, and no promotion of individual property, destination, product, or service. Query with published clips. Length: 500-1,500 words. **Pays 10¢/published word.** Pays in contributor copies if the article is reprinted with persmission, or the author is a paid representative of a company which is publicized in some manner through the article. Sometimes pays expenses of writers on assignment.

Photos State availability with submission. Buys all rights. Offers no additional payment for photos accepted with ms. Captions, identification of subjects, model releases required.

Columns/Departments Management Monograph, 500-1,000 words (expert information for hotel and motel management); Florida Scene, 500 words (Florida-specific, time-sensitive information for hotel managers or owners); National Scene, 500-1,000 words (USA-specific, time-sensitive information for hotel managers or owners); Fillers and Features, 500-700 words (information specific to editorial focus for the issue). Query. **Pays in contributor copies.**

Fillers Anecdotes, facts, short humor. Length: 50-1,000 words. **Pays in contributor copies.**

Tips "We use press releases provided to this office that fit the profile of our magazine's departments, targeting items of interest to the general managers of Florida's lodging operations. Feature articles are written based on an editorial calendar. We also publish an annual buyer's guide that provides a directory of all FH&MA member companies and allied member companies."

$ $ $ $☑ HOSPITALITY TECHNOLOGY

Edgell Communications, 4 Middlebury Blvd., Randolph NJ 07869. (973)252-0100. Fax: (973)252-9020. E-mail: rpaul@edgellmail.com. Website: www.htmagazine.com. **Contact:** Reid Paul, editor-in-chief. **70% freelance written.** Magazine published 9 times/year. "We cover the technology used in foodservice and lodging. Our readers are the operators, who have significant IT responsibilities." Estab. 1996. Circ. 16,000. **Pays on acceptance.** Publishes ms an average of 1 month after acceptance. Byline given. Buys all rights, makes work-for-hire assignments. Editorial lead time 2 months. Accepts queries by mail, e-mail, fax, phone. Responds in 2 weeks to queries.

Nonfiction How-to, interview/profile, new product, technical. Special issues: "We publish 2 studies each year, the Restaurant Industry Technology Study and the Lodging Industry Technology Study." No unsolicited mss. **Buys 40 mss/year.** Query with published clips. Length: 800-1,200 words. **Pays $1/word.** Sometimes pays expenses of writers on assignment.

$ $▣ HOTELIER

Kostuch Publications, Ltd., 23 Lesmill Rd., Suite 101, Don Mills ON M3B 3P6 Canada. (416)447-0888. Fax: (416)447-5333. E-mail: rcaira@foodservice.ca. Website: www.foodserviceworld.com. Associate Editor: Iris Benaroia. **Contact:** Rosanna Caira, editor. **40% freelance written.** Magazine published 8 times/year covering the Canadian hotel industry. Estab. 1989. Circ. 9,000. Pays on publication. Byline given. Buys first North American serial rights. Editorial lead time 3 months. Submit seasonal material 2 months in advance. Accepts queries by mail, fax. Sample copy and writer's guidelines free.

Nonfiction How-to, new product. No case studies. **Buys 30-50 mss/year.** Query with or without published clips. Length: 700-1,500 words. **Pays 35¢/word (Canadian) for assigned articles.** Sometimes pays expenses of writers on assignment.

Photos Send photos with submission. Offers $30-75/photo.

$ $ INSITE

(formerly *Christian Camp & Conference Journal*), Christian Camp & Conference Association, P.O. Box 62189, Colorado Springs CO 80962-2189. (719)260-9400. Fax: (719)260-6398. E-mail: editor@cciusa.org. Website: www.christiancamping.org. **Contact:** Justin Boles, managing editor; Alison Hayhoe, editor. **75% freelance written.** Prefers to work with published/established writers. Bimonthly magazine emphasizing the broad scope of organized camping with emphasis on Christian camps and conference centers. "All who work in youth camps and adult conferences read our magazine for inspiration and to get practical help in ways to serve in their operations." Estab. 1963. Circ. 9,000. Pays on publication. Publishes ms an average of 4 months after acceptance. Byline given. Buys negotiable rights. Submit seasonal material 6 months in advance. Accepts queries by mail, e-mail. Responds in 1 month to queries. Sample copy for $4.95 plus 9×12 SASE. Writer's guidelines online.

Nonfiction General interest (trends in organized camping in general, Christian camping in particular), how-to (anything involved with organized camping, including motivating staff, programming, record keeping, and camper follow-up), inspirational, interview/profile (with movers and shakers in Christian camping; submit a list of basic questions first). **Buys 15-20 mss/year.** Query required. Length: 500-2,000 words. **Pays 16¢/word.**

Reprints Send photocopy and information about when and where the material previously appeared. Pays 50% of amount paid for an original article.

Photos Price negotiable for 35mm color transparencies and high-quality digital photos.

Tips "The most frequent mistake made by writers is that they send articles unrelated to our readers. Review our publication guidelines first. Interviews are the best bet for freelancers."

$ $ $ PIZZA TODAY

The Monthly Professional Guide to Pizza Profits, Macfadden Protech, LLC, 908 S. 8th St., Suite 200, Louisville KY 40203. (502)736-9500. Fax: (502)736-9502. E-mail: jwhite@pizzatoday.com. Website: www.pizzatoday.com.

Contact: Jeremy White, editor-in-chief. **30% freelance written.** Works with published/established writers; occasionally works with new writers. Monthly magazine for the pizza industry, covering trends, features of successful pizza operators, business and management advice, etc. Estab. 1983. Circ. 40,000. **Pays on acceptance.** Publishes ms an average of 2 months after acceptance. Byline given. Offers 10-30% kill fee. Buys all rights. Submit seasonal material 3 months in advance. Accepts queries by mail, e-mail, fax. Responds in 2 months to queries; 3 weeks to mss. Sample copy for 10×13 SAE and 6 first-class stamps. Writer's guidelines for #10 SASE.

Nonfiction Interview/profile, entrepreneurial slants, pizza production and delivery, employee training, hiring, marketing, and business management. No fillers, humor, or poetry. **Buys 50 mss/year.** Length: 1,000 words. **Pays 50¢/word, occasionally more.** Sometimes pays expenses of writers on assignment.

Photos Reviews contact sheets, negatives, transparencies, color slides, 5×7 prints. Captions required.

Tips "We currently need articles that cover ways pizzeria operators can increase profits through the bar area. We are also seeking more marketing articles. Our readers are not looking for generic advice, however. They need truly unique, applicable marketing advice that can be immediately instituted at acceptable costs."

$ $ ▢ WESTERN HOTELIER MAGAZINE

Mercury Publications, Ltd., 1839 Inkster Blvd., Winnipeg MB R2X 1R3 Canada. (204)954-2085. Fax: (204)954-2057. E-mail: mp@mercury.mb.ca. Website: www.mercury.mb.ca/. Editor: Kelly Gray. **Contact:** Carly Peters, editorial production manager. **33% freelance written.** Quarterly magazine covering the hotel industry. "*Western Hotelier* is dedicated to the accommodation industry in Western Canada and US western border states. *WH* offers the West's best mix of news and feature reports geared to hotel management. Feature reports are written on a sector basis and are created to help generate enhanced profitability and better understanding." Circ. 4,342. Pays 30-45 days from receipt of invoice. Byline given. Offers 33% kill fee. Buys all rights. Submit seasonal material 3 months in advance. Accepts queries by mail, e-mail, fax. Accepts simultaneous submissions. Responds in 2 weeks to queries. Sample copy and writer's guidelines free or by e-mail.

Nonfiction How-to (train staff), interview/profile. Industry reports and profiles on companies. Query with published clips. Length: 500-9,000 words. **Pays 25-35¢/word.** Sometimes pays expenses of writers on assignment.

Photos State availability with submission. Reviews negatives, transparencies, 3×5 prints, JPEG, EPS or TIF files. Buys all rights. Negotiates payment individually. Captions required.

Tips "E-mail, fax, or mail a query outlining your experience, interests and pay expectations. Include clippings."

$ $ ▢ WESTERN RESTAURANT NEWS

Mercury Publications, Ltd., 1839 Inkster Blvd., Winnipeg MB R2X 1R3 Canada. (204)954-2085. Fax: (204)954-2057. E-mail: mp@mercury.mb.ca. Website: www.mercury.mb.ca/. Editor: Kelly Gray. **Contact:** Carly Peters, editorial production manager. **20% freelance written.** Bimonthly magazine covering the restaurant trade. Reports profiles and industry reports on associations, regional business developments, etc. "*Western Restaurant News Magazine* is the authoritative voice of the foodservice industry in Western Canada. Offering a total package to readers, *WRN* delivers concise news articles, new product news, and coverage of the leading trade events in the West, across the country, and around the world." Estab. 1994. Circ. 14,532. Pays 30-45 days from receipt of invoice. Byline given. Offers 33% kill fee. Buys all rights. Submit seasonal material 3 months in advance. Accepts queries by mail, e-mail, fax. Accepts simultaneous submissions. Sample copy and writer's guidelines free or by e-mail.

Nonfiction How-to, interview/profile. Industry reports and profiles on companies. Query with published clips. Length: 500-9,000 words. **Pays 25-35¢/word.** Sometimes pays expenses of writers on assignment.

Photos State availability with submission. Reviews negatives, transparencies, 3×5 prints, JPEG, EPS, or TIFF files. Buys all rights. Negotiates payment individually. Captions required.

Tips "E-mail, fax, or mail a query outlining your experience, interests and pay expectations. Include clippings."

INDUSTRIAL OPERATIONS

$ $ CAST POLYMER CONNECTION

International Cast Polymer Alliance of the American Composites Manufacturers Association, 1010 N. Glebe Rd., Suite 450, Arlington VA 22201-5761. (703)525-0511. Fax: (703)525-0743. E-mail: jgorman@acmanet.org. Website: www.icpa-hq.org. Editor: Andy Rusnak. **Contact:** Jen McCabe Gorman, assistant editor. Bimonthly magazine covering cultured marble and solid surface industries. "Articles should focus on small business owners and manufacturers." Circ. 2,000. Pays on publication. Publishes ms an average of 3 months after acceptance. Byline given. Buys all rights. Accepts queries by mail, e-mail.

Nonfiction "We are interested in how-to articles on technical processes, industry-related manufacturing techniques, and small-business operations.'' Historical/nostalgic, how-to, interview/profile, photo feature, technical. **Buys 3-5 mss/year.** Query. Length: 2,000-5,000 words. **Pays $200-350.** Occasionally arrange ad space to swap for editorial. Sometimes pays expenses of writers on assignment.

$ $▩ COMMERCE & INDUSTRY

Mercury Publications, Ltd., 1839 Inkster Blvd., Winnipeg MB R2X 1R3 Canada. (204)954-2085. Fax: (204)954-2057. E-mail: mp@mercury.mb.ca. Website: www.mercury.mb.ca/. Publisher/Editor: Frank Yeo. **Contact:** Carly Peters, editorial production manager. **75% freelance written.** Bimonthly magazine covering the business and industrial sectors. Industry reports and company profiles provide readers with an in-depth insight into key areas of interest in their profession. Estab. 1947. Circ. 18,876. Pays 30-45 days from receipt of invoice. Byline given. Offers 33% kill fee. Buys all rights. Submit seasonal material 3 months in advance. Accepts queries by mail, e-mail, fax. Accepts simultaneous submissions. Responds in 2 weeks to queries. Sample copy and writer's guidelines free or by e-mail.

Nonfiction How-to, interview/profile. Industry reports and profiles on companies. Query with published clips. Length: 500-9,000 words. **Pays 25-35¢/word.** Sometimes pays expenses of writers on assignment.

Photos State availability with submission. Reviews negatives, transparencies, 3×5 prints, JPEG, EPS or TIF files. Buys all rights. Negotiates payment individually. Captions required.

Tips ''E-mail, fax, or mail a query outlining your experience, interests and pay expectations. Include clippings.''

INDUSTRIAL FABRIC PRODUCTS REVIEW

Industrial Fabrics Association International, 1801 County Rd. B W., Roseville MN 55113-4061. (651)222-2508. Fax: (651)225-6966. E-mail: gdnordstrom@ifai.com. Website: www.ifai.com. **Contact:** Galynn Nordstrom, editorial director. **50% freelance written.** Monthly magazine covering industrial textiles and products made from them for company owners, salespeople, and researchers in a variety of industrial textile areas. Estab. 1915. Circ. 11,000. Pays on publication. Publishes ms an average of 2 months after acceptance. Byline given. Buys all rights. Accepts queries by mail, e-mail, phone. Responds in 1 month to queries. Editorial calendar online.

○━ Break in by ''researching the industry/magazine audience and editorial calendar. We rarely buy material not specifically directed at our markets.''

Nonfiction Technical, marketing, and other topics related to any aspect of industrial fabric industry from fiber to finished fabric product. Special issues: New Products; New Fabrics; Equipment. No historical or apparel-oriented articles. **Buys 50-60 mss/year.** Query with phone number. Length: 1,200-3,000 words.

Tips ''We encourage freelancers to learn our industry and make regular, solicited contributions to the magazine. We do not buy photography.''

$ $ MODERN MATERIALS HANDLING

Reed Business Information, 275 Washington St., Newton MA 02458. (617)558-4374. Fax: (617)558-4327. E-mail: pfcampbell@reedbusiness.com. Website: www.mmh.com. **40% freelance written.** Magazine published 11 times/year covering warehousing, distribution centers, inventory. ''*Warehousing Management* is an 11 times-a-year glossy national magazine read by managers of warehouses and distribution centers. We focus on lively, well-written articles telling our readers how they can achieve maximum facility productivity and efficiency. Heavy management components. We cover technology, too.'' Estab. 1945. Circ. 42,000. Pays on acceptance (allow 4-6 weeks for invoice processing). Publishes ms an average of 1 month after acceptance. Byline given. Editorial lead time 3 months. Accepts queries by mail, e-mail, fax. Sample copy and writer's guidelines free.

Nonfiction Articles must be on-point, how-to pieces for managers. How-to, new product, technical. Special issues: State-of-the-Industry Report, Peak Performer, Salary and Wage survey, Warehouse of the Year. Doesn't want to see anything that doesn't deal with our topic—warehousing. No general-interest profiles or interviews. **Buys 25 mss/year.** Query with published clips. **Pays $300-650.**

Photos State availability with submission. Reviews negatives, transparencies, prints. Buys all rights. Offers no additional payment for photos accepted with ms. Captions, identification of subjects required.

Tips ''Learn a little about warehousing, distributors and write well. We typically don't accept specific article queries, but welcome introductory letters from journalists to whom we can assign articles. But authors are welcome to request an editorial calendar and develop article queries from it.''

$ $ $▩ PEM PLANT ENGINEERING & MAINTENANCE

CLB Media, Inc., 240 Edward St., Aurora ON L4G 3S9 Canada. (905)727-0077. Fax: (905)727-0017. E-mail: rrobertson@clbmedia.ca. Website: www.pem-mag.com. **Contact:** Rob Robertson, editor. **30% freelance written.** Bimonthly magazine looking for ''informative articles on issues that affect plant floor operations and maintenance.'' Circ. 18,500. Pays on publication. Publishes ms an average of 3 months after acceptance. Byline given. Buys one-time rights. Editorial lead time 4 months. Submit seasonal material 4 months in advance.

Accepts simultaneous submissions. Responds in 3 weeks to queries; 1 month to mss. Sample copy and writer's guidelines free. Writer's guidelines online.

Nonfiction How-to (keep production downtime to a minimum, better operate an industrial operation), new product, technical. **Buys 6 mss/year.** Query with published clips. Length: 750-4,000 words. **Pays $500-1,400 (Canadian).** Sometimes pays expenses of writers on assignment.

Photos State availability with submission. Reviews transparencies, prints. Buys one-time rights. Negotiates payment individually. Captions required.

Tips "Information can be found at our website. Call us for sample issues, ideas, etc."

INFORMATION SYSTEMS

AIM E-DOC MAGAZINE

(formerly *E-Doc*), 1100 Wayne Ave., Silver Spring MD 20910. (301)916-7182. E-mail: bduhon@aiim.org. Website: www.aiim.org. **Contact:** Bryant Duhon, editor. **30% freelance written.** Prefers to work with writers with business/high tech experience. Bimonthly magazine on document and information management. "Specifically we feature coverage of the business issues surrounding implementation and use of document and information management technologies." Estab. 1943. Circ. 30,000. Pays on submission. Publishes ms an average of 3 months after acceptance. Byline given. Offers $50 kill fee. Buys first North American serial, second serial (reprint) rights. Accepts queries by mail, e-mail, fax, phone. Accepts simultaneous submissions. Sample copy and writer's guidelines online.

Nonfiction Interview/profile, photo feature, technical. **Buys 10-20 mss/year.** Query. Length: 1,500 words. Sometimes pays expenses of writers on assignment.

Photos State availability with submission. Reviews negatives, 4×5 transparencies. Buys all rights. Offers no additional payment for photos accepted with ms. Captions, identification of subjects required.

Columns/Departments Trends (developments across industry segments); Technology (innovations of specific technology); Management (costs, strategies of managing informaiton); Point/Counterpoint. Length: 500-1,500 words. Query.

Fillers Facts. Length: 150-500 words.

Tips "We would encourage freelancers who have access to our editorial calendar to contact us regarding article ideas, inquiries, etc. Our feature section is the area where the need for quality freelance coverage of our industry is most desirable. The most likely candidate for acceptance is someone who has a proven background in business writing, and/or someone with demonstrated knowledge of high-tech industries as they relate to information management."

$ $ $ CARD TECHNOLOGY

The Magazine of Smart Cards, Networks, and ID Solutions, Thomson Media, 300 S. Wacker Dr., Suite 1800, Chicago IL 60606. (312)983-6152. Fax: (312)913-1369. E-mail: don.davis@thomsonmedia.com. Website: www.cardtechnology.com. Publisher: Andy Rowe. **Contact:** Don Davis, editor/associate publisher. **20% freelance written.** Monthly magazine covering smart cards, biometrics, and related technologies. "*Card Technology* covers all uses of smart cards worldwide, as well as other advanced plastic card technologies. Aimed at senior management, not technical staff. Our readership is global, as is our focus." Estab. 1996. Circ. 22,000. **Pays on acceptance.** Byline given. Offers negotiable kill fee. Buys all rights. Editorial lead time 1 month. Submit seasonal material 2 months in advance. Accepts queries by e-mail. Responds in 1 week to queries; 1 month to mss. Sample copy for free.

Nonfiction Interview/profile, opinion. **Buys 15 mss/year.** Query with published clips. Length: 2,000-4,000 words. **Pays $500-1,500.** Sometimes pays expenses of writers on assignment.

Photos State availability with submission. Reviews contact sheets, negatives, transparencies, prints. Rights negotiable. Negotiates payment individually. Identification of subjects required.

Tips "We are especially interested in finding freelancers outside of North America who have experience writing about technology issues for business publications."

$ $ $ DESKTOP ENGINEERING

Design Solutions from Concept Through Manufacture, Helmers Publishing, P.O. Box 874, Peterborough NH 03458. (603)924-9631. Fax: (603)924-4004. E-mail: de-editors@helmers.com. Website: www.deskeng.com. **Contact:** Jonathan Gourlay, features editor. **90% freelance written.** Monthly magazine covering microcomputer hardware/software for hands-on design and mechanical engineers and engineering management. Estab. 1995. Circ. 62,000. Pays on publication. Publishes ms an average of 4 months after acceptance. Byline given. Buys all rights. Editorial lead time 3 months. Accepts queries by mail, e-mail, fax, phone. Responds in 6 weeks to queries; 6 months to mss. Sample copy free; editorial calendar online. Writer's guidelines by e-mail to jgourlay@helmers.com.

Nonfiction How-to, new product, technical, reviews. "No fluff." **Buys 120 mss/year.** Query. Length: 750-1,500 words. **Pays 60¢/word for assigned articles; negotiable for unsolicited articles.** Sometimes pays expenses of writers on assignment.

Photos Send photos with submission. Negotiates payment individually. Captions required.

Columns/Departments Product Briefs (new products), 50-100 words; Reviews (software, hardware), 500-1,500 words. **Buys 30 mss/year.** Query. **Payment varies.**

■ The online magazine carries original content not found in the print edition. Contact: Jonathan Gourlay.
Tips "Call the editors or e-mail them for submission tips."

$ $ $ GAME DEVELOPER

CMP Media LLC, 600 Harrison St., San Francisco CA 94107. (415)947-6000. Fax: (415)947-6090. E-mail: jmoledina@gdmag.com. Website: www.gdmag.com. **Contact:** Jamil Moledina, managing editor. **90% freelance written.** Monthly magazine covering computer game development. Estab. 1994. Circ. 35,000. Pays on publication. Publishes ms an average of 3-6 months after acceptance. Byline given. Buys first North American serial, first, electronic, all rights. Editorial lead time 3 months. Submit seasonal material 4 months in advance. Accepts queries by e-mail. Sample copy for free. Writer's guidelines online.

Nonfiction How-to, personal experience, technical. **Buys 50 mss/year.** Query. Length: 3,000-5,000 words. **Pays $150/page.**

Photos State availability with submission.

Tips "We're looking for writers who are professional game developers with published game titles. We do not target the hobbyist or amateur market."

$ $ $ $ GOVERNMENT COMPUTER NEWS

Post Newsweek Tech Media, 10 G St., NE, Suite 500, Washington DC 20002. (202)772-2500. Fax: (202)772-2516. E-mail: ttemin@postnewsweektech.com. Website: www.gcn.com. **Contact:** Wyatt Kash, editorial director. Biweekly for government information technology managers. **Pays on acceptance.** Byline given. Offers variable kill fee. Buys all rights. Responds in 1 month to queries. Sample copy for free. Writer's guidelines for #10 SASE.

Nonfiction **Buys 30 mss/year.** Query. Length: 600-750 words. **Pays $800-2,000.** Pays expenses of writers on assignment.

Columns/Departments **Buys 75 mss/year.** Query. **Pays $250-400.**

Fillers **Buys 10/year.** Length: 300-500 words. **Pays $250-450.**

Tips Needs "technical case histories of applications of computers to governmental missions and trends in information technology."

$ $ $ INFORMATION WEEK

600 Community Dr., Manhasset NY 11030. (516)562-5189. Fax: (516)562-5036. E-mail: bevans@cmp.com. Website: www.informationweek.com. Editorial Director: Bob Evans. **20% freelance written.** Weekly magazine for information systems managers. Estab. 1985. Circ. 440,000. **Pays on acceptance.** Publishes ms an average of 1 month after acceptance. Byline given. Offers 25% kill fee. Buys first rights. Non-exclusive serial rights Accepts simultaneous submissions. Responds in 1 month to mss. Sample copy for free. Writer's guidelines for #10 SASE.

Nonfiction Book excerpts, how-to, interview/profile, new product, technical, News analysis, company profiles. **Buys 30 mss/year.** Query with published clips. Length: 1,500-4,000 words. **Pays $1.10/word minimum.** Pays expenses of writers on assignment.

Reprints Considers previously published submissions.

Tips Needs "feature articles on technology trends—all with a business angle. We look at implementations by users, new products, management issues, intranets, the Internet, web, networks, PCs, objects, workstations, sewers, etc. Our competitors are tabloids—we're better written, more selective, and more analytical."

$ $ $ iSERIES NEWS

Penton Technology Media, 221 E. 29th St., Loveland CO 80538. (970)663-4700. Fax: (970)663-3285. E-mail: editors@iseriesnetwork.com; vhamende@penton.com. Website: www.iseriesnetwork.com. **Contact:** Vicki Hamende. **40% freelance written.** Magazine published 14 times/year. "Programming, networking, IS management, technology for users of IBM AS/400 platform." Estab. 1982. Circ. 30,000 (international). Pays on publication. Publishes ms an average of 3 months after acceptance. Byline given. Offers 50% kill fee. Buys first, second serial (reprint), all rights. Editorial lead time 4 months. Submit seasonal material 4 months in advance. Accepts queries by mail, e-mail, fax, phone. Responds in 3 weeks to queries; 5 weeks to mss. Writer's guidelines online.

Nonfiction Book excerpts, opinion, technical. **Buys 70 mss/year.** Query. Length: 1,500-2,500 words. **Pays 17-50¢/word for assigned articles.** Pays in contributor copies upon request of the author. Sometimes pays expenses of writers on assignment.

Reprints Send photocopy. Payment negotiable.

Photos State availability with submission. Offers no additional payment for photos accepted with ms.

Columns/Departments Dialog Box (computer industry opinion), 1,500 words; Load'n'go (complete utility). **Buys 24 mss/year.** Query. **Pays $250-1,000.**

Tips "Be familiar with IBM AS/400 computer platform."

$ JOURNAL OF INFORMATION ETHICS

McFarland & Co., Inc., Publishers, P.O. Box 611, Jefferson NC 28640. (320)255-4822. Fax: (320)255-4778. E-mail: hauptman@stcloudstate.edu. **Contact:** Robert Hauptman, LRTS, editor: 720 Fourth Ave. S., St. Cloud State University, St. Cloud MN 56301. **90% freelance written.** Semiannual scholarly journal. "Addresses ethical issues in all of the information sciences with a deliberately interdisciplinary approach. Topics range from electronic mail monitoring to library acquisition of controversial material. The *Journal*'s aim is to present thoughtful considerations of ethical dilemmas that arise in a rapidly evolving system of information exchange and dissemination." Estab. 1992. Pays on publication. Publishes ms an average of 2 years after acceptance. Byline given. Buys all rights. Submit seasonal material 8 months in advance. Accepts queries by mail, e-mail, fax, phone. Sample copy for $21. Writer's guidelines free.

Nonfiction Essays, opinion, book reviews. **Buys 10 mss/year.** Send complete ms. Length: 500-3,500 words. **Pays $25-50 depending on length.**

Tips "Familiarize yourself with the many areas subsumed under the rubric of information ethics, i.e., privacy, scholarly communication, errors, peer review, confidentiality, e-mail, etc. Present a well-rounded discussion of any fresh, current, or evolving ethical topic within the information sciences or involving real-world information collection/exchange."

N $ $ $ $ TECHNOLOGY REVIEW

MIT, 1 Main St., 7th Floor, Cambridge MA 02142. (617)475-8000. Fax: (617)475-8042. Website: www.technologyreview.com. Editor-in-Chief: Jason Pontin. Magazine published 10 times/year covering information technology, biotech, material science, and nanotechnology. "*Technology Review* promotes the understanding of emerging technologies and their impact." Estab. 1899. Circ. 310,000. **Pays on acceptance.** Byline given. Accepts queries by mail, e-mail.

• Contact specific editor via e-mail using firstname.lastname@technologyreview.com

Nonfiction "We place a high premium on in-depth, original reporting that produces stories rich in description, containing lively quotes from key researchers and industry analysts. Summaries of other companies or labratories doing similar work typically supplement articles. Looking for feature articles." Length: 2,000-4,000 words. **Pays $1-3/word.**

Fillers Short tidbits that relate laboratory prototypes on their way to market in 1-5 years. Length: 150-250 words. **Pays $1-3/word.**

WINDOWS DEVELOPER MAGAZINE

CMP Media LLC, 600 Harrison St., San Francisco CA 94107. (650)513-4307. E-mail: wdeditor@cmp.com. Website: www.wd-mag.com. Editor: John Dorsey. **90% freelance written.** Monthly magazine. "*WD* is written for advanced Windows programmers. Articles are practical, advanced, code-intensive, and not product-specific. We expect our authors to be working Windows programmers." Estab. 1990. Circ. 58,000. **Pays on acceptance.** Publishes ms an average of 6 months after acceptance. Byline given. Offers $150 kill fee. Buys all rights. Editorial lead time 3 months. Accepts simultaneous submissions. Responds in 2 weeks to queries. Sample copy for free. Writer's guidelines online.

Nonfiction Technical. **Buys 70-80 mss/year.** Query. Length: Varies. **Payment varies.**

INSURANCE

$ $ $ $ ADVISOR TODAY

NAIFA, 2901 Telestar Court, Falls Church VA 22042. (703)770-8204. E-mail: amseka@naifa.org. Website: www.advisortoday.com. **Contact:** Ayo Mseka, editor-in-chief. **25% freelance written.** Monthly magazine covering life insurance and financial planning. "Writers must demonstrate an understanding at what insurance agents and financial advisors do to earn business and serve their clients." Estab. 1906. Circ. 110,000. Pays on acceptance or publication (by mutual agreement with editor). Publishes ms an average of 3 months after acceptance.

Makes work-for-hire assignments. Editorial lead time 3 months. Submit seasonal material 6 months in advance. Accepts queries by mail, e-mail, fax, phone. Sample copy for free. Writer's guidelines online.

○→ Break in with queries for "pieces about sales techniques and product disclosure issues."

Nonfiction Insurance. **Buys 8 mss/year.** Query. Length: 1,500-6,000 words. **Pays $800-2,000.**

$ $ GEICO DIRECT

K.L. Publications, 2001 Killebrew Dr., Suite 105, Bloomington MN 55425-1879. (952)854-0155. Fax: (952)854-9440. E-mail: klpub@aol.com. **Contact:** Jan Brenny, editor. **60% freelance written.** Semiannual magazine published for the Government Employees Insurance Company (GEICO) policyholders. Estab. 1988. Circ. 5,000,000. **Pays on acceptance.** Byline given. Accepts queries by mail. Responds in 3 months to queries. Writer's guidelines for #10 SASE.

○→ Break in by "submitting an idea (or editorial approach) for auto/home safety or themed regional travel—one theme with several destinations around the country—that is unique, along with proof of research and writing ability."

Nonfiction Americana, home and auto safety, car care, financial, lifestyle. How-to (auto/home related only), technical (auto), travel. Query with published clips. Length: 1,000-2,200 words. **Pays $300-650.**

Photos Reviews 35mm transparencies, websites. Payment varies.

Columns/Departments Moneywise; Your Car. Length: 500-600 words. Query with published clips. **Pays $175-350.**

Tips "We prefer work from published/established writers, especially those with specialized knowledge of the insurance industry, safety issues, and automotive topics."

JEWELRY

$ $ AJM: THE AUTHORITY ON JEWELRY MANUFACTURING

Manufacturing Jewelers and Suppliers of America, 45 Royal Little Dr., Providence RI 02904. (401)274-3840. Fax: (401)274-0265. E-mail: tinaw@ajm-magazine.com. Website: www.ajm-magazine.com. **Contact:** Tina Wojtkielo, editor. **75% freelance written.** Monthly magazine. "*AJM* is a monthly magazine providing technical, marketing and business information for finished jewelry manufacturers and supporting industries." Estab. 1956. **Pays on acceptance.** Publishes ms an average of 6 months after acceptance. Byline given. Buys all rights for limited period of 18 months. Editorial lead time 1 year. Submit seasonal material 6 months in advance. Accepts queries by mail, e-mail, fax. Responds in 2 months to mss. Sample copy and writer's guidelines free.

Nonfiction All articles should focus on jewelry manufacturing techniques, especially how-to and technical articles. How-to, new product, technical. "No generic articles for a wide variety of industries, articles for hobbyists, or articles written for a consumer audience. Our focus is professional jewelry manufacturers and designers, and articles for *AJM* should be carefully targeted for this audience." **Buys 40 mss/year.** Query. Length: 2,500-3,000 words. **Pays $300-500 for assigned articles.** Sometimes pays expenses of writers on assignment.

Reprints Occasionally accepts previously published submissions. Query.

Photos State availability with submission. Buys one-time rights. Negotiates payment individually. Captions required.

Tips "Because our editorial content is highly focused and specific, we assign most article topics rather than relying on outside queries. We are, as a result, always seeking new writers comfortable with business and technical topics who will work with us long term and whom we can develop into 'experts' in jewelry manufacturing. We invite writers to send an introductory letter and clips highlighting business and technical writing skills if they would like to be considered for a specific assignment."

Ⓝ $ $ ◩ CANADIAN DIAMONDS

Up Here Publishing, Ltd., #800 4920 52nd St., Yellowknife NT X1A 3T1 Canada. (867)920-4343. Fax: (867)873-2844. E-mail: jake@uphere.ca. Website: www.canadiandiamondsmagazine.ca. Managing Editor: Tara Fraser. **Contact:** Jake Kennedy, editor. **60% freelance written.** Quarterly magazine "covering the Canadian diamond industry, from mine to exploration, from the boardroom to the jeweller's display case." Estab. 2000. Circ. 5,000. Pays on publication. Publishes ms an average of 3 months after acceptance. Byline given. Offers 50% kill fee. Buys first rights. Editorial lead time 1 year. Submit seasonal material 6 months in advance. Accepts queries by mail, e-mail, phone. Responds in 1 week to queries; 1 month to mss. Sample copy for free.

Nonfiction Book excerpts, essays, exposé, general interest, historical/nostalgic, how-to, interview/profile, new product, opinion, photo feature, technical, travel. **Buys 10 mss/year.** Query. Length: 1,800-2,500 words. **Pays 30-50¢/word.** Sometimes pays expenses of writers on assignment.

Photos State availability with submission. Reviews contact sheets, negatives, transparencies, prints, GIF/JPEG files. Buys one-time rights. Negotiates payment individually. Captions, identification of subjects required.

Columns/Departments Points (back page, general opinion), 750 words; Retail (retail diamond issues), 1,100 words. **Buys 6 mss/year.** Query. **Pays $200-400.**

$ $ COLORED STONE

Lapidary Journal/Primedia, Inc., 300 Chesterfield Parkway, Suite 100, Malvern PA 19355. (610)232-5700. Fax: (610)232-5756. E-mail: cs.editorial@primedia.com. Website: www.colored-stone.com. **Contact:** Morgan Beard, editor-in-chief. **50% freelance written.** Bimonthly magazine covering the colored gemstone industry. *"Colored Stone* covers all aspects of the colored gemstone (i.e., no diamonds) trade. Our readers are manufacturing jewelers and jewelry designers, gemstone dealers, miners, retail jewelers, and gemologists." Estab. 1987. Circ. 11,000. **Pays on acceptance.** Publishes ms an average of 2 months after acceptance. Byline given. Buys one-time, all rights. Editorial lead time 2 months. Submit seasonal material 4 months in advance. Accepts queries by mail, e-mail, fax. Accepts simultaneous submissions. Responds in 1 month to queries; 2 months to mss. Sample copy free. Writer's guidelines online.

Nonfiction Exposé, interview/profile, new product, technical. "No articles intended for the general public." **Buys 35-45 mss/year.** Query with published clips. Length: 400-2,200 words. **Pays $200-600.**

Photos State availability with submission. Reviews any size transparencies, 4×6 prints and up. Buys one-time rights. Offers $15-50/photo. Captions, identification of subjects, model releases required.

Tips "A background in the industry is helpful but not necessary. Please, no recycled marketing/new technology/ etc. pieces."

$ THE DIAMOND REGISTRY BULLETIN

580 Fifth Ave., #806, New York NY 10036. (212)575-0444. Fax: (212)575-0722. E-mail: diamond58@aol.com. Website: www.diamondregistry.com. **Contact:** Joseph Schlussel, editor-in-chief. **50% freelance written.** Monthly newsletter. Estab. 1969. Pays on publication. Buys all rights. Submit seasonal material 1 month in advance. Accepts queries by mail, e-mail. Accepts simultaneous submissions. Responds in about 3 weeks to mss. Sample copy for $5.

Nonfiction How-to (ways to increase sales in diamonds, improve security, etc.), interview/profile (of interest to diamond dealers or jewelers), prevention advice (on crimes against jewelers). Send complete ms. Length: 50-500 words. **Pays $75-150.**

Tips "We seek ideas to increase sales of diamonds."

$ $ THE ENGRAVERS JOURNAL

P.O. Box 318, Brighton MI 48116. (810)229-5725. Fax: (810)229-8320. E-mail: editor@engraversjournal.com. Website: www.engraversjournal.com. Publisher: Michael J. Davis. **Contact:** Claudia Sinta, managing editor. **70% freelance written.** Monthly magazine covering the recognition and identification industry (engraving, marking devices, awards, jewelry, and signage). "We provide practical information for the education and advancement of our readers, mainly retail business owners." Estab. 1975. **Pays on acceptance.** Publishes ms an average of 1 year after acceptance. Byline given. Buys one-time rights, makes work-for-hire assignments. Accepts queries by mail, e-mail, fax. Responds in 2 weeks to mss. Sample copy and writer's guidelines free.

○→ To break in, submit well-written, fairly in-depth general business articles. Topics and article style should focus on the small retail business owner, and should be helpful and informative.

Nonfiction General interest (industry related), how-to (small business subjects, increase sales, develop new markets, use new sales techniques, etc.), technical. No general overviews of the industry. Length: 1,000-5,000 words. **Pays $200 and up.**

Reprints Send tearsheet, photocopy or typed ms with rights for sale noted and information about when and where the material previously appeared. Pays 50-100% of amout paid for original article.

Photos Send photos with submission. Pays variable rate. Captions, identification of subjects, model releases required.

Tips "Articles should always be down to earth, practical, and thoroughly cover the subject with authority. We do not want the 'textbook' writing approach, vagueness, or theory—our readers look to us for sound practical information. We use an educational slant, publishing both trade-oriented articles and general business topics of interest to a small retail-oriented readership."

$ $ LUSTRE

The Jeweler's Magazine on Design & Style, Cygnus Publishing Co., 19 W. 44th St., Suite 1405, New York NY 10036. (212)921-1091. Fax: (212)921-5539. E-mail: steve.feldman@cygnuspub.com. Website: www.lustremag. com. Editor-in-Chief: Lorraine DePasque. **Contact:** Steve Feldman, publisher. Bimonthly magazine covering fine jewelry and related accessories. *"LUSTRE* is dedicated to helping the retail jeweler stock, merchandise, sell and profit from upscale, high-quality brand name and designer jewelry. Many stories are how-to. We also offer sophisticated graphics to showcase new products.'' Estab. 1997. Circ. 12,200. Pays on publication. Publishes ms an average of 4 months after acceptance. Byline given. Offers 50% kill fee. Buys all rights. Editorial lead time 4 months. Submit seasonal material 4 months in advance. Accepts queries by mail. Responds in 4 weeks to queries. Sample copy for free.

Nonfiction How-to, new product. **Buys 18 mss/year.** Query with published clips. Length: 1,000-2,500 words. **Pays $500.** Sometimes pays expenses of writers on assignment.

Photos State availability with submission. Buys one-time rights, plus usage for 1 year after publication date (but not exclusive usage). Offers no additional payment for photos accepted with ms. Captions, identification of subjects required.

Columns/Departments Celebrity Link (tie in designer jewelry with celebrity), 500 words; Details (news about designer jewelry), 500 words; International Eye, 500 words. **Buys 8 mss/year.** Query. **Pays $500.**

MODERN JEWELER

Cygnus Business Media, 445 Broad Hollow Rd., Melville NY 11747. (631)845-2700. Fax: (631)845-7109. Website: www.modernjeweler.com. Publisher: Tim Murphy. **20% freelance written.** Monthly magazine covering fine jewelry and watches. Estab. 1901. Circ. 33,000. **Pays on acceptance.** Publishes ms an average of 2 months after acceptance. Byline given. Buys all rights. Editorial lead time 2 months. Submit seasonal material 2 months in advance. Accepts queries by mail, fax. Responds in 3 weeks to queries; 3 months to mss. Sample copy for SAE.

Nonfiction Technical.

Photos State availability with submission. Reviews transparencies, prints.

Tips ''Requires knowledge of retail business, experience in dealing with retail and manufacturing executives and analytical writing style. We don't frequently use writers who have no ties to or experience with the jewelry manufacturing industry.''

JOURNALISM & WRITING

$ $ $ $ AMERICAN JOURNALISM REVIEW

1117 Journalism Bldg., University of Maryland, College Park MD 20742. (301)405-8803. Fax: (301)405-8323. E-mail: editor@ajr.umd.edu. Website: www.ajr.org. Editor: Rem Rieder. **Contact:** Lori Robertson, managing editor. **80% freelance written.** Bimonthly magazine covering print, broadcast, and online journalism. ''Mostly journalists subscribe. We cover ethical issues, trends in the industry, coverage that falls short.'' Circ. 25,000. Pays within 1 month after publication. Publishes ms an average of 2 months after acceptance. Byline given. Offers 25% kill fee. Buys first North American serial, electronic rights. Editorial lead time 1 month. Accepts queries by mail, e-mail, fax. Responds in 1 month to queries. Sample copy for $4.95 pre-paid or online. Writer's guidelines online.

Nonfiction Exposé, personal experience, ethical issues. **Buys many mss/year.** Query with published clips or send complete ms. Length: 2,000-4,000 words. **Pays $1,500-2,000.** Pays expenses of writers on assignment.

Fillers Anecdotes, facts, short humor, short pieces. Length: 150-1,000 words. **Pays $100-250.**

Tips ''Write a short story for the front-of-the-book section. We prefer queries to completed articles. Include in a page what you'd like to write about, who you'll interview, why it's important, and why you should write it.''

Ⓝ $ AUTHORSHIP

National Writers Association, 10940 S. Parker Rd., #508, Parker CO 80134. (303)841-0246. E-mail: sandywrter@aol.com. Website: www.nationalwriters.com. Editor: Sandy Whelchel. Quarterly magazine covering writing articles only. ''Association magazine targeted to beginning and professional writers. Covers how-to, humor, marketing issues.'' Disk and e-mail submissions preferred. Estab. 1950s. Circ. 4,000. **Pays on acceptance.** Byline given. Buys first North American serial, second serial (reprint) rights. Editorial lead time 3 months. Submit seasonal material 6 months in advance. Accepts simultaneous submissions. Responds in 2 months to queries. Sample copy for 8½×11 envelope.

Nonfiction Writing only. Poetry (January/February). **Buys 25 mss/year.** Query or send complete ms. Length: 900 words. **Pays $10, or discount on memberships and copies.**

Photos State availability with submission. Reviews 5×7 prints. Buys one-time rights. Offers no additional payment for photos accepted with ms. Identification of subjects, model releases required.

Tips ''Members of National Writers Association are given preference. Writing conference in Denver every June.''

$ BOOK DEALERS WORLD

North American Bookdealers Exchange, P.O. Box 606, Cottage Grove OR 97424. (561)258-2625. Website: www.bookmarketingprofits.com. **Contact:** Al Galasso, editorial director. **50% freelance written.** Quarterly magazine covering writing, self-publishing, and marketing books by mail. Circ. 20,000. Pays on publication. Publishes ms an average of 3 months after acceptance. Byline given. Buys first North American serial, second serial (reprint) rights. Accepts simultaneous submissions. Responds in 1 month to queries. Sample copy for $3.

Nonfiction Book excerpts (writing, mail order, direct mail, publishing), how-to (home business by mail, advertising), interview/profile (of successful self-publishers), positive articles on self-publishing, new writing angles, marketing. **Buys 10 mss/year.** Send complete ms. Length: 1,000-1,500 words. **Pays $25-50.**

Reprints Send ms with rights for sale noted and information about when and where the material previously appeared. Pays 80% of amount paid for an original article.

Columns/Departments Publisher Profile (on successful self-publishers and their marketing strategy). Length: 250-1,000 words. **Buys 20 mss/year.** Send complete ms. **Pays $5-20.**

Fillers Fillers concerning writing, publishing, or books. **Buys 6/year.** Length: 100-250 words. **Pays $3-10.**

Tips "Query first. Get a sample copy of the magazine."

$ BYLINE

P.O. Box 5240, Edmond OK 73083-5240. (405)348-5591. E-mail: mpreston@bylinemag.com. Website: www.bylinemag.com. **Contact:** Marcia Preston, editor/publisher. **80% freelance written.** Eager to work with new/unpublished writers or experienced ones. Magazine published 11 times/year for writers and poets. Estab. 1981. **Pays on acceptance.** Publishes ms an average of 3 months after acceptance. Byline given. Buys first North American serial rights. Editorial lead time 3-4 months. Submit seasonal material 6 months in advance. Accepts queries by mail, e-mail. Accepts simultaneous submissions. Responds in 2 months or less to queries. Sample copy for $5 postpaid. Writer's guidelines online.

- Do not send complete mss by e-mail.

○ "First Sale is probably the easiest way to break in."

Nonfiction "We're always searching for appropriate, well-written features on topics we haven't covered for a couple of years." Needs articles of 1,500-1,800 words connected with writing and selling. No profiles of writers. **Buys approximately 75 mss/year.** Prefers queries; will read complete mss. Send SASE. Length: 1,500-1,800 words. **Pays $75.**

Columns/Departments End Piece (humorous, philosophical, or motivational personal essay related to writing), 700 words, **pays $35**; First Sale (account of a writer's first sale), 250-300 words, **pays $20**; Only When I Laugh (writing-related humor), 50-400 words; **pays $15-25**; Great American Bookstores (unique, independent bookstores), 500-600 words. Send complete ms. **Pays $30-40.**

Fiction Mainstream, genre, literary. No science fiction, erotica, or extreme violence. **Buys 11 mss/year.** Send complete ms. Length: 2,000-4,000 words. **Pays $100.**

Poetry "All poetry should connect in some way with the theme of writing or the creative process." Contact: Sandra Soli, poetry editor. Free verse, haiku, light verse, traditional. **Buys 100 poems/year.** Submit maximum 3 poems. Length: Under 30 lines. **Pays $10, plus free issue.**

Tips "We're open to freelance submissions in all categories. We're always looking for clear, concise feature articles on topics that will help writers write better, market smarter, and be more successful. Strangely, we get many more short stories than we do features, but we buy more features. If you can write a friendly, clear, and helpful feature on some aspect of writing better or selling more work, we'd love to hear from you."

$ CANADIAN WRITER'S JOURNAL

P.O. Box 1178, New Liskeard ON P0J 1P0 Canada. (705)647-5424. Fax: (705)647-8366. E-mail: cwj@cwj.ca. Website: www.cwj.ca. **Contact:** Deborah Ranchuk, editor. **75% freelance written.** Bimonthly magazine for writers. Accepts well-written articles by all writers. Estab. 1984. Circ. 350. Pays on publication. Publishes ms an average of 9 months after acceptance. Byline given. Buys one-time rights. Accepts queries by mail, e-mail, fax, phone. Responds in 2 months to queries. Sample copy for $8, including postage. Writer's guidelines online.

Nonfiction Looking for articles on how to break into niche markets. How-to (articles for writers). **Buys 200 mss/year.** Query optional. **Pays $7.50/published magazine page (approx. 450 words).**

Reprints Send ms with rights for sale noted and information about when and where the material previously appeared.

Fiction Requirements being met by annual contest. Send SASE for rules, or see guidelines on website. "Does not want gratuitous violence, sex subject matter."

Poetry Short poems or extracts used as part of articles on the writing of poetry.

Tips "We prefer short, tightly written, informative how-to articles. US writers note that US postage cannot be used to mail from Canada. Obtain Canadian stamps, use IRCs, or send small amounts in cash."

$ CROSS & QUILL

The Christian Writers Newsletter, Christian Writers Fellowship International, 1624 Jefferson Davis Rd., Clinton SC 29325-6401. (864)697-6035. E-mail: cqarticles@cwfi-online.org. Website: www.cwfi-online.org. **Contact:**

Sandy Brooks, editor/publisher. **75% freelance written.** Bimonthly journal featuring information and encouragement for writers. "We serve Christian writers and others in Christian publishing. We like informational and how-to articles." Estab. 1976. Circ. 1,000. Pays on publication. Publishes ms an average of 6-12 months after acceptance. Byline given. Buys first, second serial (reprint) rights. Editorial lead time 6 months. Submit seasonal material 6 months in advance. Accepts queries by mail, e-mail. Responds in 1 month to queries; 2 months to mss. Sample copy for $2 with 9×11 SAE and 2 first-class stamps. Writer's guidelines online or for SAE.

O➥ Break in by writing "good informational, substantive how-to articles. Right now we're particularly looking for articles on juvenile writing and owning and operating writers groups—successes and learning experiences; also organizing and operating writers workshops and conferences."

Nonfiction How-to, humor, inspirational, interview/profile, new product, technical, devotional. **Buys 25 mss/ year.** Send complete ms. Length: 300-800 words. **Pays $10-25.** Sometimes pays in contributor copies or subscriptions for fillers, poetry.

Photos State availability with submission.

Poetry Free verse, haiku, light verse, traditional. **Buys 6 poems/year.** Submit maximum 3 poems. Length: 12 lines. **Pays $5.**

Tips "Study guidelines and follow them. Acceptances of philosophical, personal reflection, or personal experiences is rare. Paste article submissions into an e-mail form. We do not download submissions as attached files due to the risk of viruses. Double-space between paragraphs. Please use plain text. Do not use boldface or bullets."

$ $ $E CONTENT MAGAZINE

Digital Content Strategies & Resources, Online, Inc., 88 Danbury Rd., Suite 1D, Wilton CT 06897. (203)761-1466. Fax: (203)761-1444. E-mail: michelle.manafy@infotoday.com. Website: www.econtentmag.com. **Contact:** Michelle Manafy, editor. **90% freelance written.** Monthly magazine covering digital content trends, strategies, etc. "*E Content* is a business publication. Readers need to stay on top of industry trends and developments." Estab. 1979. Circ. 12,000. Pays within 1 month of publication. Byline given. Offers 20-50% kill fee. Buys all rights. Editorial lead time 4 months. Accepts queries by e-mail. Responds in 3 weeks to queries; 1 month to mss. Sample copy and writer's guidelines online.

Nonfiction Exposé, how-to, interview/profile, new product, opinion, technical, news features, strategic and solution-oriented features. No academic or straight Q&A. **Buys 48 mss/year.** Query with published clips. Length: 500-700 words. **Pays 40-50¢/word.** Sometimes pays expenses of writers on assignment.

Photos State availability with submission. Buys one-time rights. Negotiates payment individually. Captions required.

Columns/Departments Profiles (short profile of unique company, person or product), 1,200 words; New Features (breaking news of content-related topics), 500 words maximum. **Buys 40 mss/year.** Query with published clips. **Pays 30-40¢/word.**

Tips "Take a look at the website. Most of the time, an e-mail query with specific article ideas works well. A general outline of talking points is good, too. State prior experience."

$ 🔲 FELLOWSCRIPT

InScribe Christian Writers' Fellowship, 333 Hunter's Run, Edmonton AB T6R 2N9 Canada. (780)988-5622. Fax: (780)430-0139. E-mail: submissions@inscribe.org. Website: www.inscribe.org. **Contact:** Elsie Montgomery, editor. **100% freelance written.** Quarterly writers' newsletter featuring Christian writing. "Our readers are Christians with a commitment to writing. Among our readership are best-selling authors and unpublished beginning writers. Submissions to us should include practical information, something the reader can immediately put into practice." Estab. 1983. Circ. 250. Pays on publication. Publishes ms an average of 2-6 months after acceptance. Byline given. Buys one-time, second serial (reprint) rights. Editorial lead time 3 months. Submit seasonal material 4 months in advance. Accepts queries by mail, e-mail, fax, phone. Accepts simultaneous submissions. Responds in 1 month to queries; 2-6 months to mss. Sample copy for $3.50, 9×12 SAE, and 2 first-class stamps (Canadian) or IRCs. Writer's guidelines online.

O➥ "The best bet to break in at *FellowScript* is to write something very specific that will be useful to writers. We receive far too many 'general' submissions which try to cover too much territory in one article. Choose your topic and keep a narrow focus."

Nonfiction All must pertain to writing and the writing life. Essays, exposé, how-to (for writers), inspirational, interview/profile, new product, personal experience, photo feature, religious. Does not want poetry, fiction or think piece, commentary articles. **Buys 30-45 mss/year.** Send complete ms. Length: 400-1,200 words. **Pays 2½¢/word (first rights); 1½¢/word reprints (Canadian funds).**

Photos State availability with submission.

Columns/Departments Book reviews, 150-300 words; Market Updates, 50-300 words. **Buys 1-3 mss/year.** Send complete ms. **Pays 1 copy.**

Fillers Facts, newsbreaks. **Buys 5-10/year.** Length: 25-300 words. **Pays 1 copy.**

Tips "Send your complete manuscript by post or e-mail (pasted into the message, no attachments). E-mail is preferred. Tell us a bit about yourself. Write in a casual, first-person, anecdotal style. Be sure your article is full of practical material, something that can be applied. Most of our accepted freelance submissions fall into the 'how-to' category, and involve tasks, crafts, or procedures common to writers. Please do not swamp us with inspirational articles (i.e., 'How I sold My First Story'), as we receive too many of these already."

$⬛ FREELANCE MARKET NEWS

An Essential Guide for Freelance Writers, The Writers Bureau Ltd., Sevendale House, 7 Dale St., Manchester M1 1JB England. (+44)161 228 2362. Fax: (+44)161 228 3533. E-mail: fmn@writersbureau.com. Website: www.writersbureau.com. **Contact:** Angela Cox, editor. **15% freelance written.** Monthly newsletter covering freelance writing. Estab. 1968. **Pays on acceptance.** Publishes ms an average of 3 months after acceptance. Byline given. Buys all rights. Editorial lead time 3 months. Submit seasonal material 3 months in advance. Accepts queries by mail, e-mail, fax. Accepts previously published material. Accepts simultaneous submissions. Sample copy for #10 SASE. Writer's guidelines for #10 SASE.

Nonfiction How-to (sell your writing/improve your writing). **Buys 12 mss/year.** Length: around 700 words. **Pays £50/1,000 words.**

Columns/Departments New Markets (magazines which have recently been published); Fillers & Letters; Overseas Markets (obviously only English-language publications); Market Notes (established publications accepting articles, fiction, reviews, or poetry). All should be between 40 and 200 words. **Pays £35/1,000 words.**

$ $ FREELANCE WRITER'S REPORT

CNW Publishing, Inc., Main St., P.O. Box A, North Stratford NH 03590-0167. (603)922-8338. E-mail: fwrwm@w riters-editors.com. Website: www.writers-editors.com. **Contact:** Dana K. Cassell, editor. **25% freelance written.** Monthly newsletter. "*FWR* covers the marketing and business/office management aspects of running a freelance writing business. Articles must be of value to the established freelancer; nothing basic." Estab. 1982. Pays on publication. Publishes ms an average of 6 months after acceptance. Byline given. Buys one-time rights. Editorial lead time 2 months. Submit seasonal material 2 months in advance. Accepts queries by mail, e-mail. Accepts simultaneous submissions. Responds in 1 week to queries; 1 month to mss. Sample copy for 6×9 SAE with 2 first-class stamps (for back copy); $4 for current copy. Writer's guidelines online.

O─ Most needed are filler tips of up to 400 words.

Nonfiction Book excerpts, how-to (market, increase income or profits). No articles about the basics of freelancing. **Buys 50 mss/year.** Send complete ms. Length: Up to 900 words. **Pays 10¢/word.**

Reprints Accepts previously published submissions.

⬛ The online magazine carries original content not found in the print edition and includes writer's guidelines.

Tips "Write in a terse, newsletter style."

$ MAINE IN PRINT

Maine Writers & Publishers Alliance, 1326 Washington St., Bath ME 04530. (207)386-1400. Fax: (207)386-1401. E-mail: info@mainewriters.org. Website: www.mainewriters.org. Bimonthly newsletter for writers, editors, teachers, librarians, etc., focusing on Maine literature and the craft of writing. Estab. 1975. Circ. 3,000. Pays on publication. Publishes ms an average of 2 months after acceptance. Byline given. Buys one-time rights. Editorial lead time 2 months. Accepts queries by mail. Accepts simultaneous submissions. Sample copy and writer's guidelines free.

Nonfiction Essays, how-to (writing), interview/profile, technical. No creative writing, fiction, or poetry. **Buys 20 mss/year.** Query with published clips. Length: 400-1,500 words. **Pays $25-50 for assigned articles.**

Reprints Send tearsheet and information about when and where the material previously appeared. Pays $25.

Photos State availability with submission. Offers no additional payment for photos accepted with ms.

Columns/Departments Front-page articles (writing related), 500-1,500 words. **Buys 20 mss/year.** Query. **Pays $25 minimum.**

Tips "Become a member of Maine Writers & Publishers Alliance. Become familiar with Maine literary scene."

$ $ $⬛ MASTHEAD

The Magazine About Magazines, North Island Publishing, 1606 Sedlescomb Dr., Unit 8, Mississauga ON L4X 1M6 Canada. (905)625-7070. Fax: (905)625-4856. Website: www.mastheadonline.com. **40% freelance written.** Journal published 10 times/year covering the Canadian magazine industry. "With its lively mix of in-depth features, news stories, service pieces, surveys, tallies, and spirited commentary, this independent journal provides detailed coverage and analysis of the events, issues, personalities, and technologies shaping Canada's magazine industry." Estab. 1987. Circ. 4,200. Pays on publication. Publishes ms an average of 2 months after acceptance. Byline given. Offers 50% kill fee. Buys first North American serial rights. Editorial lead time 1 month. Accepts queries by mail. Accepts simultaneous submissions. Responds in 2 weeks to queries; 1 month to mss. Sample copy for free. Writer's guidelines free or by e-mail.

Nonfiction "We generally pay $600-850 for a cover story running 2,000-2,500 words, depending on the amount of research, etc., required. For the most part, *Masthead* generates feature ideas in-house and then assigns the stories to regular contributors. When space permits, we sometimes run shorter features or service pieces (1,000-1,500 words) for a flat rate of $350." Book excerpts, essays, exposé, historical/nostalgic, how-to, humor, interview/profile, new product, opinion, personal experience, technical. No articles that have nothing to do with Canadian magazines. Length: 100-3,000 words. **Pays $30-850 (Canadian).** Sometimes pays expenses of writers on assignment.

Photos State availability with submission. Negotiates payment individually. Identification of subjects required.

Columns/Departments Back of the Book, the guest column, pays freelancers a flat rate of $350 and runs approximately 950 words. Back of the book columns examine and/or comment on issues or developments relating to any department: editorial, art, production, circulation, publishing, advertising, etc. **Buys 10 mss/ year.** Query with published clips. **Pays $350 (Canadian).**

Fiction Novel excerpts. No excerpts that have nothing to do with Canadian magazines. Query with published clips.

Tips "Have a solid understanding of the Canadian magazine industry. A good way to introduce yourself is to propose small articles on new magazines."

$ $🌐 MSLEXIA

For Women Who Write, Mslexia Publications Ltd., P.O. Box 656, Newcastle upon Tyne NE99 1PZ United Kingdom. (0044) 191 261 6656. E-mail: postbag@mslexia.demon.co.uk. Website: www.mslexia.co.uk. Editor: Debbie Taylor. **Contact:** Melanie Ashby, deputy editor. **60% freelance written.** Quarterly magazine offering advice and publishing opportunities for women writers, plus poetry and prose submissions on a different theme each issue. "*Mslexia* tells you all you need to know about exploring your creativity and getting into print. No other magazine provides *Mslexia*'s unique mix of advice and inspiration; news, reviews, interviews; competitions, events, grants; all served up with a challenging selection of new poetry and prose. *Mslexia* is read by authors and absolute beginners. A quarterly master class in the business and psychology of writing, it's the essential magazine for women who write." Estab. 1998. Circ. 12,000. Pays on publication. Publishes ms an average of 1 month after acceptance. Byline given. Offers 50% kill fee. Buys one-time rights. Editorial lead time 3 months. Submit seasonal material 3 months in advance. Accepts queries by mail, e-mail, phone. Accepts simultaneous submissions. Responds in 3 months to mss. Sample copy online. Writer's guidelines online or by e-mail.

● This publication does not accept e-mail submissions except from overseas writers.

Nonfiction How-to, interview/profile, opinion, personal experience. No general items about women or academic features. "We are only interested in features (for tertiary-educated readership) about women's writing and literature." **Buys 40 mss/year.** Query with published clips. Length: 500-2,000 words. **Pays $70-400 for assigned articles; $70-300 for unsolicited articles. Pays $40/poem and $20/1,000 words for submissions published in the New Writing section of the magazine.** Sometimes pays expenses of writers on assignment.

Columns/Departments "We are open to suggestions, but would only commission 1 new column/year, probably from a UK-based writer." **Buys 12 mss/year.** Query with published clips.

Fiction Helen Christie, editorial assistant. "See guidelines on our website. Submissions not on one of our current themes will be returned (if submitted with a SASE) or destroyed." **Buys 30 mss/year.** Send complete ms. Length: 50-3,000 words.

Poetry Helen Christie, editorial assistant. Avant-garde, free verse, haiku, traditional. **Buys 40 poems/year.** Submit maximum 4 poems.

Tips "Read the magazine; subscribe if you can afford it. *Mslexia* has a particular style and relationship with its readers which is hard to assess at a quick glance. The majority of our readers live in the UK, so feature pitches should be aware of this. We never commission work without seeing a written sample first. We rarely accept unsolicited manuscripts, but prefer a short letter suggesting a feature, plus a brief bio and writing sample."

$ NEW WRITER'S MAGAZINE

Sarasota Bay Publishing, P.O. Box 5976, Sarasota FL 34277-5976. (941)953-7903. E-mail: newriters@aol.com. **Contact:** George S. Haborak, editor. **95% freelance written.** Bimonthly magazine. "*New Writer's Magazine* believes that *all* writers are *new* writers in that each of us can learn from one another. So, we reach pro and nonpro alike." Estab. 1986. Circ. 5,000. Pays on publication. Byline given. Buys first rights. Accepts queries by mail. Responds in 1 month. Sample copy for $3. Writer's guidelines for #10 SASE.

Nonfiction General interest, how-to (for new writers), humor, interview/profile, opinion, personal experience (with pro writer). **Buys 50 mss/year.** Send complete ms. Length: 700-1,000 words. **Pays $10-50.**

Photos Send photos with submission. Reviews 5×7 prints. Offers no additional payment for photos accepted with ms. Captions required.

Fiction Experimental, historical, humorous, mainstream, slice-of-life vignettes. "Again, we do *not* want anything that does not have a tie-in with the writing life or writers in general." **Buys 2-6 mss/year.** Send complete ms. Length: 700-800 words. **Pays $20-40.**

Poetry Free verse, light verse, traditional. Does not want anything *not* for writers. **Buys 10-20 poems/year.** Submit maximum 3 poems. Length: 8-20 lines. **Pays $5 minimum.**

Fillers For cartoons, writing lifestyle slant. Buys 20-30/year. Pays $10 maximum. Anecdotes, facts, newsbreaks, short humor. **Buys 5-15/year.** Length: 20-100 words. **Pays $5 maximum.**

Tips "Any article with photos has a good chance, especially an up close and personal interview with an established professional writer offering advice, etc. Short profile pieces on new authors also receive attention."

Ⓝ $ $ NOVEL & SHORT STORY WRITER'S MARKET

F+W Publications, Inc., 4700 E. Galbraith Rd., Cincinnati OH 45236. E-mail: lauren.mosko@fwpubs.com. **Contact:** Lauren Mosko, editor. **80% freelance written.** Annual resource book covering the fiction market. "In addition to thousands of listings for places to get fiction published, we feature articles on the craft and business of fiction writing, as well as interviews with successful fiction writers, editors, and agents. Our articles are unique in that they always offer an actionable take-away. In other words, readers must learn something immediately useful about the creation or marketing of fiction." Estab. 1981. **Pays on acceptance.** Byline given. Offers 25% kill fee. Buys exclusive first serial rights; nonexclusive electronic rights for reproduction on website. Accepts queries by mail, e-mail. Responds in 1 week to queries. Sample copy not available.

- Accepts proposals during the summer.
- ⊶ "We're especially in need of writers who can cover the genre markets—romance, horror, science fiction, mystery."

Nonfiction How-to (write, sell and promote fiction; find an agent; etc.), interview/profile, personal experience. **Buys 15 mss/year.** Length: 750-2,500 words. **Pays $200-600.**

Photos Send photos with submission. Reviews prints, GIF/JPEG files (hi-res). Offers no additional payment for photos accepted with ms. Identification of subjects required.

Tips "The best way to break into this book is to review the last few years' editions and look for aspects of the fiction industry that we haven't covered recently. Send me a specific, detailed pitch stating the topic, angle, and 'takeaway' of the piece, what sources you intend to use, and what qualifies you to write this article. Freelancers who have published fiction and/or have contacts in the industry have an advantage."

$ OHIO WRITER

Poets' & Writers' League of Greater Cleveland, 12200 Fairhill Rd., Townhouse #3A, Cleveland OH 44120. (216)421-0403. Fax: (216)421-8874. E-mail: pwlgc@yahoo.com. Website: www.pwlgc.com. **75% freelance written.** Bimonthly magazine covering writing and Ohio writers. Estab. 1987. Pays on publication. Publishes ms an average of 4 months after acceptance. Byline given. Buys one-time, second serial (reprint) rights. Editorial lead time 4 months. Submit seasonal material 4 months in advance. Accepts queries by mail, e-mail, fax, phone. Responds in 6 weeks to mss. Sample copy for $2.50. Writer's guidelines for #10 SASE.

Nonfiction "All articles must be related to the writing life of Ohio writers, or the Ohio publishing scene." Essays, how-to, humor, inspirational, interview/profile, opinion, personal experience. **Buys 24 mss/year.** Send complete ms and SASE. Length: 2,000-2,500 words. **Pays $25 minimum, up to $50 for lead article, other payment under arrangement with writer.**

Reprints Send ms with rights for sale noted and information about when and where the material previously appeared. Pays $10 for reprints.

Columns/Departments Buys 6 mss/year. Send complete ms. **Pays $25-50; $5/book review.**

Tips "We look for articles about writers and writing, with a special emphasis on activities in our state. However, we publish articles by writers throughout the country that offer something helpful about the writing life. Profiles and interviews of writers who live in Ohio are always needed. *Ohio Writer* is read by both beginning and experienced writers and hopes to create a sense of community among writers of different genres, abilities, and backgrounds. We want to hear a personal voice, one that engages the reader. We're looking for intelligent, literate prose that isn't stuffy."

$ $ POETS & WRITERS MAGAZINE

72 Spring St., New York NY 10012. E-mail: editor@pw.org. Website: www.pw.org. **Contact:** The Editors. **100% freelance written.** Bimonthly professional trade journal for poets and fiction writers and creative nonfiction writers. Estab. 1973. Circ. 70,000. Pays on acceptance of finished draft. Publishes ms an average of 4 months after acceptance. Byline given. Offers 20% kill fee. Buys first North American serial rights. Submit seasonal

material 4 months in advance. Accepts queries by mail. Responds in 6 weeks to mss. Sample copy for $4.95 to Sample Copy Dept. Writer's guidelines for #10 SASE.

• No poetry or fiction submissions.

Nonfiction How-to (craft of poetry or fiction writing), interview/profile (with poets or fiction writers). "We do not accept submissions by fax or e-mail." **Buys 35 mss/year.** Query with published clips or send complete ms. Length: 500-2,500 (depending on topic) words.

Photos State availability with submission. Reviews b&w prints. Offers no additional payment for photos accepted with ms.

Columns/Departments Literary and Publishing News, 500-1,000 words; Profiles of Emerging and Established Poets and Fiction Writers, 2,000-3,000 words; Regional Reports (literary activity in US), 1,000-2,000 words. Query with published clips or send complete ms. **Pays $150-300.**

$THE WIN INFORMER

The Professional Association for Christian Writers, Writers Information Network, P.O. Box 11337, Bainbridge Island WA 98110. (206)842-9103. Fax: (206)842-0536. E-mail: writersinfonetwork@juno.com. Website: www.christianwritersinfo.net. **Contact:** Elaine Wright Colvin, editor. **33⅓% freelance written.** Bimonthly magazine for the Professional Association for Christian Writers covering the CBA and religious publishing industry. Estab. 1983. Circ. 1,000. **Pays on acceptance.** Publishes ms an average of 1-4 months after acceptance. Byline given. Buys first North American serial rights. Editorial lead time 2 months. Submit seasonal material 2 months in advance. Accepts queries by e-mail. Responds in 1 month to mss. Sample copy for $10, 9 × 12 SAE with 4 first-class stamps. Writer's guidelines online.

○ₜ Break in by "getting involved in the Christian publishing (CBA) industry; interview CBA published authors, CBA editors, or CBA bookstore managers."

Nonfiction For advanced/professional writers only. How-to (writing), humor, inspirational, interview/profile, new product, opinion, personal experience, religious, technical. No beginners basics material used. Send complete ms. Submit material in the body of e-mail only. Length: 100-1,000 words. **Pays $5-50, sometimes pays other than cash.** Sometimes pays expenses of writers on assignment.

Columns/Departments Industry News; Book Publisher News; Editor/Agent Hot News; News of the Magazines; Awards & Bestsellers; Conference Tips; Conference Schedule; New Book Alert; Bulletin Board; Winmember Websites. Send complete ms in body of e-mail or as an e-mail attachment.

Tips "The *Win Informer* is sometimes referred to as ChristianWritersInfo.net."

$WRITER'S APPRENTICE

For Aspiring, Beginning, and Intermediate Writers, Prairie River Publishing, 607 N. Cleveland St., Merrill WI 54452. Phone/Fax: (715)536-3167. E-mail: tina@writersapprentice.com. Website: www.writersapprentice.com. **Contact:** Tina L. Miller, editor-in-chief. **90% freelance written.** Monthly trade magazine. "*Writer's Apprentice* magazine offers real, practical advice for writers—whether writing for pleasure or publication. Specifics, resources, information, encouragement, and answers to the questions they have." Estab. 2002. Circ. 10,000. Pays on publication. Byline given. Not copyrighted. Buys first rights. Editorial lead time 6-9 months. Submit seasonal material 6-9 months in advance. Accepts queries by mail, e-mail, fax. Responds in 3-4 weeks to queries; 6 months to mss. Sample copy for 9 × 12 SAE and 4 first-class stamps. Writer's guidelines online.

Nonfiction Essays, general interest, how-to, humor, inspirational, interview/profile, personal experience, technical. No fiction, poetry, or stories/articles that do not have a practical, take-away value. Query or send complete ms. Length: 300-900 words. **Pays $15-50.**

Photos State availability with submission. Reviews GIF/JPEG files. Buys one-time rights. Negotiates payment individually. Identification of subjects, model releases required.

Columns/Departments The Writing Life (back page essays), 300-600 words. Send complete ms. **Pays $10-25.**

Tips "Pretend your best friend wants to become a writer. Think of all the questions he/she will have. What can you teach him/her that you already know? How can you share the benefit of your experience? What advice would you give? How would you help him/her get started? Become this imaginary new writer's mentor. Write it down in a concise article on a specific topic, and we're very likely to buy it. But remember: It's got to be real, practical, focused, informative, do-able, and contain resources or a how-to. No 'fluff' stories or stories that are too generic."

$ $ $WRITER'S DIGEST

F + W Publications, Inc., 4700 E. Galbraith Rd., Cincinnati OH 45236. (513)531-2690, ext. 1483. E-mail: wdsubmissions@fwpubs.com. Website: www.writersdigest.com. **Contact:** Submissions Editor. **70% freelance written.** Monthly magazine about writing and publishing. "Our readers write fiction, nonfiction, plays, and scripts. They're interested in improving writing skills and the ability to sell their work and find new outlets for their talents." Estab. 1920. Circ. 150,000. **Pays on acceptance.** Publishes ms an average of 9-12 months after accep-

Trade Journals

tance. Byline given. Offers 25% kill fee. Buys first world serial rights for one-time editorial use, possible electronic posting, and magazine promotional use. Pays 25% reprint fee and 10% for electronic use in fee-charging mediums. Sample copy for $5.25/copy to Lyn Menke, at the address above. "A helpful index of each year's contents is published in the December issue. You also may purchase copies online." Writer's guidelines online.

- *Writer's Digest* prefers e-queries and responds in 2 months to e-queries and mail queries w/SASE. The magazine does not accept or read e-queries with attachments.
- ○→ "Break in through Inkwell and Markets sections of the magazine."

Nonfiction "What we need is the how-to article: How to write compelling leads and conclusions, how to improve your character descriptions, how to become more efficient and productive. We like plenty of examples, anecdotes, and details in our articles. On how-to technique articles, we prefer to work with writers with a proven track record of success. For example, don't pitch us an article on creating effective dialogue if you've never had a work of fiction published. Don't query about setting up a book tour if you've never done one. We like our articles to speak directly to the reader through the use of the first-person voice. We are seldom interested in author interviews, and 'evergreen' topics are not accepted unless they are timely and address industry trends. Don't send articles today that would have fit in *WD* 5 years ago. No articles titled 'So You Want to Be a Writer,' and no first-person pieces without something readers can learn from in the sharing of the story. Avoid the 'and then I wrote' article that is a promotional vehicle for you without tips on how others can put your experience to work." **Buys 75 mss/year.** "We only accept electronic final manuscripts." Length: 800-1,500 words. **Pays 40-50¢/word.**

Tips "Keep an eye on InkWell—an expanded upfront section of the magazine. It's the best place for new writers to try and break in, so read it thoroughly to get a feel for the types of articles we include. Please note that all product reviews and book reviews are handled in house. We welcome short reader tips, but we do not pay for these. This is one section of the magazine where you can benefit from sending the complete written piece as opposed to a query. We accept InkWell submissions via e-mail or mail. Note that our standing columns and departments are not open to freelance submissions. Further, we buy at most 2 interviews/profiles per year; nearly all that we publish are staff written. Candidates for First Impressions interviews (all of which are conducted in-house; candidates must be first-time authors) should send galleys and information about themselves at least 5 months before their book's publication date to Maria Schneider at the address above."

$ $THE WRITER

Kalmbach Publishing Co., 21027 Crossroads Circle, P.O. Box 1612, Waukesha WI 53187-1612. E-mail: queries@writermag.com. Website: www.writermag.com. **Contact:** Elfrieda Abbe, editor. **90% freelance written.** Prefers to buy work of published/established writers. Estab. 1887. **Pays on acceptance.** Buys first North American serial rights. Accepts queries by mail, e-mail. Sample copy for $4.95. Writer's guidelines online.

- No phone queries.

Nonfiction Practical articles for writers on how to write for publication, and how and where to market manuscripts in various fields. Considers all submissions promptly. No assignments. Length: 800-3,000 words. **Pays $50-500.**

Reprints Send tearsheet or photocopy and information about when and where the material previously appeared.

Tips "We are looking for articles with plenty of practical, specific advice, tips, and techniques that aspiring and beginning writers can apply to their own work. New types of publications and our continually updated market listings in all fields will determine changes of focus and fact."

$WRITERS' JOURNAL

The Complete Writer's Magazine, Val-Tech Media, P.O. Box 394, Perham MN 56573-0394. (218)346-7921. Fax: (218)346-7924. E-mail: writersjournal@writersjournal.com. Website: www.writersjournal.com. Managing Editor: John Ogroske. **Contact:** Leon Ogroske, editor (editor@writersjournal.com). **90% freelance written.** Bimonthly trade magazine covering writing. "*Writers' Journal* is read by thousands of aspiring writers whose love of writing has taken them to the next step: writing for money. We are an instructional manual giving writers the tools and information necessary to get their work published. We also print works by authors who have won our writing contests." Estab. 1980. Circ. 26,000. Pays on publication. Publishes ms an average of 10 months after acceptance. Byline given. Buys one-time rights. Editorial lead time 8 months. Submit seasonal material 8 months in advance. Accepts queries by mail, e-mail. Accepts simultaneous submissions. Responds in 6 weeks to queries; 6 months to mss. Sample copy for $5.

Nonfiction Looking for articles on fiction writing (plot development, story composition, character development, etc.) and writing "how-to." Book excerpts, essays, exposé, general interest (to writers), humor, inspirational, interview/profile, new product, opinion, personal experience, photo feature, technical. No erotica. **Buys 45 mss/year.** Send complete ms. Length: 800-2,500 words. **Pays with a 1-year subscription, money depending on article and budget, and in contributor copies or other premiums if author agrees.**

Photos State availability with submission. Reviews contact sheets, prints. Buys one-time rights. Negotiates payment individually. Model releases required.

Columns/Departments For Beginners Only (helpful advice to beginners), 800-2,500 words. **Buys 30 mss/year.** Send complete ms. **Pays $20, money depending on article, and a 1-year subscription.**

Fiction "We only publish winners of our fiction contests—16 contests/year." Length: 2,000 words.

Poetry Esther Leiper-Jefferson, poetry editor. Also publishes winners of the 3 poetry contests. No erotica. **Buys 25 poems/year.** Submit maximum 4 poems. Length: 25 lines. **Pays $5.**

Fillers Anecdotes, facts, short humor, cartoons. **Buys 20/year.** Length: 200 words. **Pays up to $10.**

Tips "Appearance must be professional with no grammatical or spelling errors, submitted on white paper, double spaced with easy-to-read font. We want articles that will help writers improve technique in writing, style, editing, publishing, and story construction. We are interested in how writers use new and fresh angles to break into the writing markets."

$ WRITING THAT WORKS

The Business Communications Report, Communications Concepts, Inc., 7481 Huntsman Blvd., #720, Springfield VA 22153-1648. (703)643-2200. Fax: (703)643-2329. Website: www.apexawards.com. **Contact:** John De Lellis, editor/publisher. Monthly newsletter on business writing and communications. "Our readers are company writers, editors, communicators, and executives. They need specific, practical advice on how to write well as part of their job." Estab. 1983. Pays within 45 days of acceptance. Publishes ms an average of 3 months after acceptance. Byline sometimes given. Buys all rights. Editorial lead time 3 months. Accepts queries by mail, e-mail. Responds in 1 month to queries. Sample copy and writer's guidelines online.

Nonfiction Practical, short, how-to articles and quick tips on business writing techniques geared to company writers, editors, publication staff and communicators. "We're always looking for shorts—how-to tips on business writing." **Buys 120 mss/year.** Accepts electronic final mss. Length: 100-500 words. **Pays $35-150.**

Columns/Departments Writing Techniques (how-to business writing advice); Style Matters (grammar, usage, and editing); Online Publishing (writing, editing, and publishing for the Web); Managing Publications; PR & Marketing (writing).

Fillers Short tips on writing or editing. Mini-reviews of communications websites for business writers, editors, and communicators. Length: 100-150 words. **Pays $35.**

Tips "We do not use material on how to get published or how to conduct a freelancing business. Format your copy to follow *Writing That Works* style. Include postal and e-mail addresses, phone numbers, website URLs, and prices for products/services mentioned in articles."

$ $ $ $ WRITTEN BY

The Magazine of the Writers Guild of America, West, 7000 W. Third St., Los Angeles CA 90048. (323)782-4522. Fax: (323)782-4800. Website: www.wga.org. **40% freelance written.** Magazine published 9 times/year. "*Written By* is the premier magazine written by and for America's screen and TV writers. We focus on the craft of screenwriting and cover all aspects of the entertainment industry from the perspective of the writer. We are read by all screenwriters and most entertainment executives." Estab. 1987. Circ. 12,000. **Pays on acceptance.** Publishes ms an average of 2 months after acceptance. Byline given. Offers 10% kill fee. Buys first North American serial, electronic rights. Editorial lead time 4 months. Submit seasonal material 4 months in advance. Accepts queries by mail, e-mail, fax, phone. Writer's guidelines for #10 SASE.

    ○┐ Break in with "an exclusive profile or Q&A with a major TV or screenwriter."

Nonfiction Book excerpts, essays, historical/nostalgic, humor, interview/profile, opinion, personal experience, photo feature, technical (software). No beginner pieces on "how to break into Hollywood," or "how to write scripts." **Buys 20 mss/year.** Query with published clips. Length: 500-3,500 words. **Pays $500-3,500 for assigned articles.** Sometimes pays expenses of writers on assignment.

Photos State availability with submission. Reviews transparencies. Buys one-time rights. Offers no additional payment for photos accepted with ms. Captions, identification of subjects, model releases required.

Columns/Departments Pays $1,000 maximum.

Tips "We are looking for more theoretical essays on screenwriting past and/or present. Also, the writer must always keep in mind that our audience is made up primarily of working writers who are inside the business; therefore all articles need to have an 'insider' feel and not be written for those who are still trying to break in to Hollywood. We prefer a hard copy of submission or e-mail."

LAW

$ $ $ $ ABA JOURNAL

The Lawyer's Magazine, American Bar Association, 321 N. Clark St., Chicago IL 60610. (312)988-6018. Fax: (312)988-6014. E-mail: releases@abanet.org. Website: www.abajournal.com. Editor: Danial J. Kim. **Contact:**

Debra Cassens Weiss, managing editor. **10% freelance written.** Monthly magazine covering law. "The *ABA Journal* is an independent, thoughtful, and inquiring observer of the law and the legal profession. The magazine is edited for members of the American Bar Association." Circ. 380,000. **Pays on acceptance.** Byline given. Makes work-for-hire assignments. Accepts queries by mail, e-mail. Sample copy for free. Writer's guidelines online.

Nonfiction Legal features. "We don't want anything that does not have a legal theme. No poetry or fiction." **Buys 5 mss/year.** Query with published clips. Length: 500-3,500 words. **Pays $300-2,000 for assigned articles.**

Columns/Departments Buys 25 mss/year. Query with published clips. **Pays $300, regardless of story length.**

$ $ $ BENCH & BAR OF MINNESOTA

Minnesota State Bar Association, 600 Nicollet Ave., Suite 380, Minneapolis MN 55402. (612)333-1183. E-mail: jhaverkamp@mnbar.org. Website: www.mnbar.org. **Contact:** Judson Haverkamp, editor. **5% freelance written.** Magazine published 11 times/year. "Audience is mostly Minnesota lawyers. *Bench & Bar* seeks reportage, analysis, and commentary on trends and issues in the law and the legal profession, especially in Minnesota. Preference to items of practical/human interest to professionals in law." Estab. 1931. Circ. 16,000. **Pays on acceptance.** Publishes ms an average of 3 months after acceptance. Byline given. Buys first North American serial rights, makes work-for-hire assignments. Responds in 1 month to queries. Writer's guidelines online or by mail.

Nonfiction How-to (handle particular types of legal/ethical problems in office management, representation, etc.), humor, interview/profile, technical (legal). "We do not want one-sided opinion pieces or advertorial." **Buys 2-3 mss/year.** Query with or without published clips or send complete ms. Length: 1,500-3,000 words. **Pays $300-800.** Sometimes pays expenses of writers on assignment.

Photos State availability with submission. Reviews 5×7 prints. Buys one-time rights. Pays $25-100 upon publication. Identification of subjects, model releases required.

$ $ $ $ CALIFORNIA LAWYER

Daily Journal Corp., 44 Montgomery St., Suite 250, San Francisco CA 94104. (415)296-2400. Fax: (415)296-2482. E-mail: tema_goodwin@dailyjournal.com. Website: www.dailyjournal.com. **Contact:** Tema Goodwin, managing editor. **30% freelance written.** Monthly magazine of law-related articles and general-interest subjects of appeal to lawyers and judges. "Our primary mission is to cover the news of the world as it affects the law and lawyers, helping our readers better comprehend the issues of the day and to cover changes and trends in the legal profession. Our readers are all California lawyers, plus judges, legislators, and corporate executives. Although we focus on California and the West, we have subscribers in every state. *California Lawyer* is a general interest magazine for people interested in law. Our writers are journalists." Estab. 1981. Circ. 140,000. **Pays on acceptance.** Publishes ms an average of 3 months after acceptance. Byline given. Offers 25% kill fee. Buys first North American serial, electronic rights. Editorial lead time 3 months. Accepts queries by mail, e-mail, fax. Sample copy and writer's guidelines for #10 SASE.

⊶ Break in by "showing us clips—we usually start people on short news stories."

Nonfiction Essays, general interest, interview/profile, news and feature articles on law-related topics. "We are interested in concise, well-written and well-researched articles on issues of current concern, as well as well-told feature narratives with a legal focus. We would like to see a description or outline of your proposed idea, including a list of possible sources." **Buys 12 mss/year.** Query with or without published clips or send complete ms. Length: 500-5,000 words. **Pays $50-2,000.** Pays expenses of writers on assignment.

Photos Jake Flaherty, art director. State availability with submission. Reviews prints. Identification of subjects, model releases required.

Columns/Departments California Esq. (current legal trends), 300 words. **Buys 6 mss/year.** Query with or without published clips. **Pays $50-250.**

$ $ $ $ CORPORATE LEGAL TIMES

656 W. Randolph St., #500-E, Chicago IL 60661. (312)654-3500. E-mail: editorial@cltmag.com. Website: www.corporatelegaltimes.com. **Contact:** Robert Vosper, managing editor. **50% freelance written.** Monthly tabloid. "*Corporate Legal Times* is a monthly national magazine that gives general counsel and inhouse attorneys information on legal and business issues to help them better manage corporate law departments. It routinely addresses changes and trends in law departments, litigation management, legal technology, corporate governance and inhouse careers. Law areas covered monthly include: intellectual property, international, technology, project finance, e-commerce and litigation. All articles need to be geared toward the inhouse attorney's perspective." Estab. 1991. Circ. 45,000. Pays on publication. Publishes ms an average of 3 months after acceptance. Byline given. Buys all rights. Editorial lead time 3 months. Submit seasonal material 3 months in advance. Accepts queries by mail, e-mail. Responds in 3 weeks to queries. Sample copy for $17. Writer's guidelines online.

Nonfiction Interview/profile, news about legal aspects of business issues and events. **Buys 12-25 mss/year.** Query with published clips. Length: 500-3,000 words. **Pays $500-2,000.**

Photos Freelancers should state availability of photos with submission. Reviews color transparencies, b&w prints. Buys all rights. Offers $25-150/photo. Identification of subjects required.

Tips "Our publication targets general counsel and inhouse lawyers. All articles need to speak to them—not to the general attorney population. Query with clips and a list of potential in-house sources."

LAW OFFICE COMPUTING

James Publishing, P.O. Box 25202, Costa Mesa CA 92799. (714)755-5450. Fax: (714)751-5508. E-mail: editorloc @jamespublishing.com. Website: www.lawofficecomputing.com. **Contact:** Amanda Flatten, editor and publisher. **90% freelance written.** Bimonthly magazine covering legal technology industry. "*Law Office Computing* is a magazine written for attorneys and other legal professionals. It covers the legal technology field and features software reviews, profiles of prominent figures in the industry, and 'how-to' type articles." Estab. 1991. Circ. 7,000. Pays on publication. Publishes ms an average of 2 months after acceptance. Byline given. Buys first North American serial rights. Editorial lead time 4 months. Submit seasonal material 4 months in advance. Accepts queries by mail, e-mail, fax. Sample copy for free. Writer's guidelines online.

Nonfiction How-to, interview/profile, new product, technical. **Buys 30 mss/year.** Query. Length: 2,000-3,500 words. **Pays on a case-by-case basis.** Sometimes pays expenses of writers on assignment.

Photos State availability with submission.

Columns/Departments Tech profile (profile firm using technology), 1,200 words; My Solution, 1,200 words; Software reviews: Short reviews (a single product), 600 words; Software Shootouts (2 or 3 products going head-to-head), 1,000-1,500 words; Round-Ups/Buyer's Guides (8-15 products), 300-500 words/product. **Buys 6 mss/ year.** Query. **Pays on a case-by-case basis.**

Tips "If you are a practicing attorney, legal MIS, or computer consultant, try the first-person My Solution column or a short review. If you are a professional freelance writer, technology profiles or a news story regarding legal technology are best, since most of our other copy is written by legal technology professionals."

$LEGAL ASSISTANT TODAY

James Publishing, Inc., P.O. Box 25202, Santa Ana CA 92799. (714)755-5468. Fax: (714)751-5508. E-mail: aflatten@jamespublishing.com. Website: www.legalassistanttoday.com. **Contact:** Amanda Flatten, editor/publisher. Bimonthly magazine "geared toward all legal assistants/paralegals throughout the United States and Canada, regardless of specialty (litigation, corporate, bankruptcy, environmental law, etc.). How-to articles to help paralegals perform their jobs more effectively are most in demand, as are career and salary information, and timely news and trends pieces." Estab. 1983. Circ. 8,000. Pays on publication. Byline given. Buys first North American serial, electronic rights, non-exclusive electronic/Internet right and non-exclusive rights to use the article, author's name, image, and biographical data in advertising and promotion. Editorial lead time 10 weeks. Submit seasonal material 3 months in advance. Accepts queries by mail, e-mail, fax. Accepts simultaneous submissions. Responds in 2 months to mss. Sample copy for free. Writer's guidelines online.

Nonfiction Interview/profile (unique and interesting paralegals in unique and particular work-related situations), news (brief, hard news topics regarding paralegals), features (present information to help paralegals advance their careers). **Pays $25-100.**

Photos Send photos with submission.

Tips "Fax a detailed outline of a 2,500 to 3,000-word feature about something useful to working legal assistants. Writers must understand our audience. There is some opportunity for investigative journalism as well as the usual features, profiles, and news. How-to articles are especially desired. If you are a great writer who can interview effectively, and really dig into the topic to grab readers' attention, we need you."

$ $THE NATIONAL JURIST

Crittenden Magazines, P.O. Box 939039, San Diego CA 92193. (858)503-7562. Fax: (858)503-7588. E-mail: keith@crittendenmagazines.com. **Contact:** Keith Carter, managing editor. **25% freelance written.** Bimonthly magazine covering law students and issues of interest to law students. Estab. 1991. Circ. 100,000. Pays on publication. Buys all rights. Accepts queries by mail, e-mail, fax, phone.

Nonfiction General interest, how-to, humor, interview/profile. **Buys 4 mss/year.** Query. Length: 750-3,000 words. **Pays $100-500 for assigned articles.**

Photos State availability with submission. Reviews contact sheets. Negotiates payment individually.

Columns/Departments Pays $100-500.

$ $THE PENNSYLVANIA LAWYER

Pennsylvania Bar Association, P.O. Box 186, 100 South St., Harrisburg PA 17108-0186. E-mail: editor@pabar.o rg. Executive Editor: Marcy Carey Mallory. Editor: Geoff Yuda. **Contact:** Donald C. Sarvey, editorial director.

25% freelance written. Prefers to work with published/established writers. Bimonthly magazine published as a service to the legal profession and the members of the Pennsylvania Bar Association. Estab. 1979. Circ. 30,000. **Pays on acceptance.** Publishes ms an average of 6 months after acceptance. Byline given. Buys first, one-time rights. Submit seasonal material 6 months in advance. Accepts queries by mail, e-mail. Responds in 2 months. Sample copy for $2. Writer's guidelines for #10 SASE or by e-mail.

Nonfiction All features must relate in some way to Pennsylvania lawyers or the practice of law in Pennsylvania. How-to, interview/profile, law-practice management, technology. **Buys 8-10 mss/year.** Query. Length: 1,200-2,000 words. **Pays $50 for book reviews; $75-400 for assigned articles; $150 for unsolicited articles.** Sometimes pays expenses of writers on assignment.

Photos State availability with submission. Reviews contact sheets. Buys one-time rights. Negotiates payment individually. Identification of subjects required.

STUDENT LAWYER

The Membership Magazine of the American Bar Association's Law Student Division, % ABA Publishing, 321 N. Clark St., Chicago IL 60610. (312)988-6048. Fax: (312)988-6081. E-mail: studentlawyer@abanet.org. Website: www.abanet.org/lsd/studentlawyer. **Contact:** Ira Pilchen, editor. Works with a small number of new writers each year. Monthly magazine (September-May). "*Student Lawyer* is a legal-affairs features magazine that competes for a share of law students' limited spare time, so the articles we publish must be informative, well-researched good reads. We are especially interested in articles that provide students with practical advice for navigating the challenges of law school and developing their careers." Estab. 1972. Circ. 35,000. Byline given. Buys first rights. Editorial lead time 6 months. Accepts queries by mail, e-mail, phone. Writer's guidelines online.

Nonfiction No fiction, please. Query with published clips. Length: 2,000-2,500 words.

Tips "We are not a law review; we are a features magazine with law school (in the broadest sense) as the common denominator. Write clearly and well. Expect to work with editor to polish manuscripts to perfection. We do not make assignments to writers with whose work we are not familiar. If you're interested in writing for us, send a detailed, thought-out query with 3 previously published clips. We are always willing to look at material on spec. Sorry, we don't return manuscripts."

LUMBER

$ $ PALLET ENTERPRISE

Industrial Reporting Inc., 10244 Timber Ridge Dr., Ashland VA 23005. (804)550-0323. Fax: (804)550-2181. E-mail: editor@ireporting.com. Website: www.palletenterprise.com. Assistant Publisher: Chaille Brindley. **Contact:** Tim Cox, editor. **40% freelance written.** Monthly magazine covering lumber and pallet operations. Articles should offer technical, solution-oriented information. Anti-forest articles are not accepted. Articles should focus on machinery and unique ways to improve profitability/make money. Estab. 1981. Circ. 14,500. Pays on publication. Buys first, one-time, electronic rights. Makes work-for-hire assignments. May buy all rights. Rights purchased depends on the writer and the article. Editorial lead time 2 months. Submit seasonal material 2 months in advance. Accepts queries by mail, e-mail, fax, phone. Accepts previously published material. Accepts simultaneous submissions. Sample copy online. Writer's guidelines free.

Nonfiction "We only want articles of interest to pallet manufacturers, pallet recyclers, and lumber companies/sawmills." Interview/profile, new product, opinion, technical, industry news, environmental, forests operation/plant features. No lifestyle, humor, general news, etc. **Buys 20 mss/year.** Query with published clips. Length: 1,000-3,000 words. **Pays $200-400 for assigned articles; $100-400 for unsolicited articles.** Call editor to discuss circumstances under which writers are paid in contributor copies. Sometimes pays expenses of writers on assignment.

Photos State availability with submission. Reviews 3 × 5 prints. Buys one time rights and Web rights. Negotiates payment individually. Captions, identification of subjects required.

Columns/Departments Green Watch (environmental news/opinion affecting US forests), 1,500 words. **Buys 12 mss/year.** Query with published clips. **Pays $200-400.**

Tips "Provide unique environmental or industry-oriented articles. Many of our freelance articles are company features of sawmills, pallet manufacturers, pallet recyclers, and wood waste processors."

$ $ SOUTHERN LUMBERMAN

Hatton-Brown Publishers, P.O. Box 2268, Montgomery AL 36102. (334)834-1170. Fax: (334)834-4525. E-mail: rich@hattonbrown.com. Website: www.southernlumberman.com. **Contact:** Rich Donnell, editor. **20% freelance written.** Works with a small number of new/unpublished writers each year. Monthly journal for the sawmill industry. Estab. 1881. Circ. 15,000. Pays on publication. Publishes ms an average of 3 months after

Trade Journals

acceptance. Byline given. Buys first North American serial rights. Submit seasonal material 6 months in advance. Responds in 1 month to queries; 2 months to mss. Sample copy for $3 and 9 × 12 SAE with 5 first-class stamps. Writer's guidelines for #10 SASE.

Nonfiction How-to (sawmill better), technical, equipment analysis, sawmill features. **Buys 10-15 mss/year.** Query with or without published clips or send complete ms. Length: 500-2,000 words. **Pays $150-350 for assigned articles; $100-250 for unsolicited articles.** Sometimes pays expenses of writers on assignment.

Reprints Send tearsheet or photocopy of article and information about when and where the article previously appeared. Pays 25-50% of amount paid for an original article.

Photos Always looking for news feature types of photos featuring forest products, industry materials, or people. Send photos with submission. Reviews transparencies, 4 × 5 color prints. Pays $10-25/photo. Captions, identification of subjects required.

Tips "Like most, we appreciate a clearly-worded query listing the merits of a suggested story—what it will tell our readers they need/want to know. We want quotes, we want opinions to make others discuss the article. Best hint? Find an interesting sawmill operation owner and start asking questions—what's he doing bigger, better, different. I bet a story idea develops. We need color photos, too. We're interested in new facilities, better marketing, and improved production."

$ $ TIMBERLINE

Timber Industry Newsline/Trading Post, Industrial Reporting, Inc., 10244 Timber Ridge Dr., Ashland VA 23005. (804)550-0323. Fax: (804)550-2181. E-mail: editor@ireporting.com. Website: www.timberlinemag.com. Assistant Publisher: Chaille Brindley. **Contact:** Tim Cox, editor. **50% freelance written.** Monthly tabloid covering the forest products industry. Articles should offer technical, solution-oriented information. Anti-forest products, industry articles are not accepted. Articles should focus on machinery and unique ways to improve profitability and make money. Estab. 1994. Circ. 30,000. Pays on publication. Byline given. Buys first, one-time, electronic rights. Makes work-for-hire assignments. May purchase all rights. Rights purchased depends on the writer and the article. Editorial lead time 2 months. Submit seasonal material 2 months in advance. Accepts queries by mail, e-mail, fax, phone. Accepts previously published material. Accepts simultaneous submissions. Sample copy online. Writer's guidelines free.

Nonfiction "We only want articles of interest to loggers, sawmills, wood treatment facilities, etc. Readers tend to be pro-industry/conservative, and opinion pieces must be written to appeal to them." Historical/nostalgic, interview/profile, new product, opinion, technical, industry news, environmental operation/plant features. No lifestyles, humor, general news, etc. **Buys 25 mss/year.** Query with published clips. Length: 1,000-3,000 words. **Pays $200-400 for assigned articles; $100-400 for unsolicited articles.** Call editor to discuss circumstances under which writers are paid in contributor copies. Sometimes pays expenses of writers on assignment.

Photos State availability with submission. Reviews 3 × 5 prints. Buys one time rights and Web rights. Negotiates payment individually. Captions, identification of subjects required.

Columns/Departments From the Hill (legislative news impacting the forest products industry), 1,800 words; Green Watch (environmental news/opinion affecting US forests), 1,500 words. **Buys 12 mss/year.** Query with published clips. **Pays $200-400.**

Tips "Provide unique environmental or industry-oriented articles. Many of our freelance articles are company features of logging operations or sawmills."

$ $ TIMBERWEST

Timber/West Publications, LLC, P.O. Box 610, Edmonds WA 98020-0160. Fax: (425)771-3623. E-mail: timberwest@forestnet.com. Website: www.forestnet.com. **Contact:** Diane Mettler, managing editor. **75% freelance written.** Monthly magazine covering logging and lumber segment of the forestry industry in the Northwest. "We publish primarily profiles on loggers and their operations—with an emphasis on the machinery—in Washington, Oregon, Idaho, Montana, Northern California, and Alaska. Some timber issues are highly controversial and although we will report on the issues, this is a pro-logging publication. We don't publish articles with a negative slant on the timber industry." Estab. 1975. Circ. 10,000. **Pays on acceptance.** Byline given. Not copyrighted. Buys first North American serial, second serial (reprint) rights. Editorial lead time 3 months. Accepts queries by mail, fax. Responds in 3 weeks to queries. Sample copy for $2. Writer's guidelines for #10 SASE.

Nonfiction Historical/nostalgic, interview/profile, new product. No articles that put the timber industry in a bad light—such as environmental articles against logging. **Buys 50 mss/year.** Query with published clips. Length: 1,100-1,500 words. **Pays $350.** Pays expenses of writers on assignment.

Photos Send photos with submission. Reviews contact sheets, transparencies, prints, GIF/JPEG files. Buys all rights. Offers no additional payment for photos accepted with ms. Captions, identification of subjects required.

Fillers Facts, newsbreaks. **Buys 10/year.** Length: 400-800 words. **Pays $100-250.**

Tips "We are always interested in profiles of loggers and their operations in Alaska, Oregon, Washington, Montana, and Northern California. We also want articles pertaining to current industry topics, such as fire abatement, sustainable forests, or new technology. Read an issue to get a clear idea of the type of material *TimberWest* publishes. The audience is primarily loggers and topics that focus on an 'evolving' timber industry versus a 'dying' industry will find a place in the magazine. When querying, a clear overview of the article will enhance acceptance.''

MACHINERY & METAL

N $ ANVIL MAGAZINE

Voice of the Farrier & Blacksmith, P.O. Box 1810, 2770 Sourdough Flat, Georgetown CA 95634. (530)333-2142. Fax: (530)333-2906. E-mail: anvil@anvilmag.com. Website: www.anvilmag.com. Publisher: Rob Edwards. **Contact:** Mimi Clark, associate editor. **40% freelance written.** Monthly magazine covering ''how-to articles on hoof care and horseshoeing and blacksmithing, tips on running your own farrier or blacksmith business and general articles on those subjects.'' Estab. 1978. Circ. 4,000. Pays on publication. Publishes ms an average of 1 year after acceptance. Byline sometimes given. Buys first North American serial rights. Editorial lead time 3 months. Submit seasonal material 6 months in advance. Accepts queries by mail, e-mail, fax. Accepts simultaneous submissions. Sample copy for $6. Writer's guidelines online.

Nonfiction Material has to be specific to the subjects of horseshoeing, hoof care, farrier interests, blacksmithing interest. General interest, historical/nostalgic, how-to, humor, interview/profile, new product, opinion, photo feature, technical, book reviews of farrier/blacksmithing publications. **Buys 8-10 mss/year.** Send complete ms. Length: 1,200-1,600 words. **Pays $25-200.** Sometimes pays expenses of writers on assignment.

Photos Send photos with submission. Reviews transparencies, prints. Buys one-time rights. Offers $25 additional payment for photos accepted with ms. Negotiates payment individually if photos only, such as for a how-to article. Identification of subjects required.

Poetry Traditional on blacksmithing and farriery subjects only. No cowboy poetry. **Buys 5-6 poems/year.** Submit maximum 1-2 poems. Length: 20-40 lines lines. **Pays $25.**

Tips ''Write clearly and concisely. Our readers are professionals. Stay away from generic topics or general horsemanship. Our most popular features are how-to and interviews. For interviews, don't be bashful—ask the tough questions.''

$ $ $ CUTTING TOOL ENGINEERING

CTE Publications, Inc., 400 Skokie Blvd., Suite 395, Northbrook IL 60062-7903.. (847)498-9100. Fax: (847)559-4444. Website: www.ctemag.com. Publisher: Don Nelson. **Contact:** Alan Richter, editor. **40% freelance written.** Monthly magazine covering industrial metal cutting tools and metal cutting operations. ''*Cutting Tool Engineering* serves owners, managers and engineers who work in manufacturing, specifically manufacturing that involves cutting or grinding metal or other materials. Writing should be geared toward improving manufacturing processes.'' Circ. 36,000. Pays 1 week before publication. Publishes ms an average of 2 months after acceptance. Byline given. Offers 50% kill fee. Buys all rights. Editorial lead time 2 months. Accepts queries by mail, fax. Responds in 2 months to mss. Sample copy and writer's guidelines free.

Nonfiction How-to, opinion, personal experience, technical. ''No fiction or articles that don't relate to manufacturing.'' **Buys 30 mss/year.** Length: 1,500-3,000 words. **Pays $450-1,000.** Pays expenses of writers on assignment.

Photos State availability with submission. Reviews transparencies, prints. Buys all rights. Negotiates payment individually. Captions required.

Tips ''For queries, write 2 clear paragraphs about how the proposed article will play out. Include sources that would be in the article.''

$ $ $ THE FABRICATOR

The Croydon Group, Ltd., 833 Featherstone Rd., Rockford IL 61107. (815)399-8700. Fax: (815)484-7700. E-mail: dand@thefabricator.com. Website: www.thefabricator.com. **Contact:** Dan Davis, executive editor. **15% freelance written.** Monthly magazine covering metal forming and fabricating. Our purpose is to disseminate information about modern metal forming and fabricating techniques, machinery, tooling, and management concepts for the metal fabricator. Estab. 1971. Circ. 58,000. Pays on publication. Byline given. Buys all rights. Editorial lead time 6 months. Accepts queries by mail, e-mail. Responds in 2 weeks to queries; 1 month to mss. Sample copy for free. Writer's guidelines online.

Nonfiction How-to, technical, company profile. Query with published clips. Length: 1,200-2,000 words. **Pays 40-80¢/word.**

Photos Request guidelines for digital images. State availability with submission. Reviews transparencies, prints.

Rights purchased depends on photographer requirements. Negotiates payment individually. Captions, identification of subjects required.

▣ The online magazine carries original content not found in the print edition. Contact: Laurie Harshbarger.

MACHINE DESIGN

Penton Media, Penton Media Bldg., 1300 E. 9th St., Cleveland OH 49114-1503. (216)931-9412. Fax: (216)621-8469. E-mail: mdeditor@penton.com. Website: www.machinedesign.com. Editor: Ronald Khol. **Contact:** Kenneth Korane, managing editor. Semimonthly magazine covering machine design. Covers the design engineering of manufactured products across the entire spectrum of the idustry for people who perform design engineering functions. Circ. 185,163. Editorial lead time 10 weeks. Accepts queries by mail, e-mail. Sample copy not available.

Nonfiction How-to, new product, technical. Query with or without published clips or send complete ms.

Columns/Departments Query with or without published clips or send complete ms.

MANUFACTURING BUSINESS TECHNOLOGY

(formerly *MSI*), Reed Business Information, 2000 Clearwater Dr., Oak Brook IL 60523-8809. (630)288-8756. Fax: (630)288-8105. E-mail: rmichel@reedbusiness.com. Website: www.msimag.com. Editorial Director: Kevin Parker. **Contact:** Roberto Michel, editor. Monthly magazine "about the use of information technology to improve productivity in discrete manufacturing and process industries." Estab. 1984. Circ. 105,000. Pays on publication. Publishes ms an average of 3 months after acceptance. Byline sometimes given. Buys all rights. Editorial lead time 3 months. Submit seasonal material 4 months in advance. Accepts queries by e-mail. Sample copy for free. Writer's guidelines online.

Nonfiction Technical. **Buys 30 mss/year.** Query.

Photos No additional payment for photos. Captions required.

$MATERIAL HANDLING WHOLESALER

Specialty Publications International, Inc., P.O. Box 725, Dubuque IA 52004-0725. (877)638-6190 or (563)557-4495. Fax: (563)557-4499. E-mail: editorial@mhwmag.com. Website: www.mhwmag.com. **Contact:** Cathy Murphy, editor. **100% freelance written.** *MHW* is published monthly for new and used equipment dealers, equipment manufacturers, manufacturer reps, parts suppliers, and service facilities serving the material handling industry. Estab. 1979. Circ. 12,000. Pays on publication. Publishes ms an average of 2 months after acceptance. Byline given. Buys first rights. Editorial lead time 1 month. Submit seasonal material 2 months in advance. Accepts queries by mail, e-mail, fax. Accepts simultaneous submissions. Sample copy for $31 annually (3rd class). Writer's guidelines free.

Nonfiction General interest, how-to, inspirational, new product, opinion, personal experience, photo feature, technical, material handling news.

Photos Send photos with submission. Reviews 3×5 prints. Buys all rights. Offers no additional payment for photos accepted with ms.

Columns/Departments Aftermarket (aftermarket parts and service); Battery Tech (batteries for lifts-MH equipment); Marketing Matters (sales trends in MH industry); Internet at Work (internet trends), all 1,200 words. **Buys 3 mss/year.** Query. **Pays $0-50.**

MODERN MACHINE SHOP

Gardner Publications, Inc., 6915 Valley Ave., Cincinnati OH 45244-3029. (513)527-8800. Fax: (513)527-8801. E-mail: malbert@mmsonline.com. Website: www.mmsonline.com. **Contact:** Mark Albert, editor-in-chief. **5% freelance written.** Monthly magazine. Estab. 1928. Pays 1 month following acceptance. Publishes ms an average of 6 months after acceptance. Byline given. Accepts queries by mail, e-mail, fax, phone. Responds in 1 month to mss. Call for sample copy. Writer's guidelines online.

⊶ Advances in metalworking technology are occurring rapidly. Articles that show how this new technology, as embodied in specific products, is being implemented in shops and plants are sought after. Writers are strongly encouraged to call to discuss an idea.

Nonfiction Uses only articles dealing with all phases of metalworking, manufacturing, and machine shop work, with photos. "Ours is an industrial publication, and contributing authors should have a working knowledge of the metalworking industry. We regularly use contributions from machine shop owners, engineers, other technical experts, and suppliers to the metalworking industry. Almost all of these contributors pursue these projects to promote their own commercial interests." **Buys 5 or fewer unsolicited mss/year.** Query. Length: 1,000-3,500 words. **Pays current market rate.**

▣ The online magazine carries original content not found in the print edition. Contact: A.J. Sweatt (ajsweatt@mmsonline.com).

Tips "Although our focus remains on the basics of metalworking/machining processes, we are giving added coverage to lean manufacturing, business strategies, and marketing as critical factors in competitiveness."

$ $ ORNAMENTAL AND MISCELLANEOUS METAL FABRICATOR

National Ornamental And Miscellaneous Metals Association, 532 Forest Pkwy., Suite A, Forest Park GA 30297. Fax: (404)366-1852. E-mail: rachel@nomma.org. **Contact:** Rachel Bailey, editor. **20% freelance written.** Bimonthly magazine "to inform, educate, and inspire members of the ornamental and miscellaneous metalworking industry." Estab. 1959. Circ. 8,000. Pays on publication. Byline given. Buys one-time rights. Editorial lead time 2 months. Accepts queries by mail, e-mail, fax. Responds by e-mail in 1 month (include e-mail address in query) to queries. Writer's guidelines by e-mail.

Nonfiction Book excerpts, essays, exposé, general interest, historical/nostalgic, how-to, humor, inspirational, interview/profile, new product, opinion, personal experience, photo feature, technical. **Buys 8-12 mss/year.** Query. Length: 1,200-2,000 words. **Pays $375-400.** Pays expenses of writers on assignment.

Reprints Send tearsheet, photocopy or typed ms with rights for sale noted and information about when and where the material previously appeared. Pays 100% of amount paid for an original article.

Photos Artwork and sidebars preferred. State availability with submission. Reviews contact sheets, negatives, transparencies, prints. May offer additional payment for artwork accepted with ms. Model releases required.

Columns/Departments 700-900 words. **Pays $50-100.**

Tips "Please request and review recent issues. Contacting the editor for guidance on article topics is welcome."

$ $ $ PRACTICAL WELDING TODAY

The Croydon Group, Ltd., 833 Featherstone Rd., Rockford IL 61107-6302. (815)399-8700. Fax: (815)381-1370. E-mail: stephaniev@thefabricator.com. Website: www.thefabricator.com. **Contact:** Stephanie Vaughan, associate editor. **15% freelance written.** Bimonthly magazine covering welding. "We generally publish how-to and educational articles that teach people about a process or how to do something better." Estab. 1997. Circ. 40,000. Pays on publication. Byline given. Buys all rights. Editorial lead time 6 months. Accepts queries by mail, e-mail. Responds in 2 weeks to queries; 2 months to mss. Sample copy for free. Writer's guidelines online.

Nonfiction How-to, technical, company profiles. Special issues: Forecast issue on trends in welding (January/February). No promotional, one-sided, persuasive articles or unsolicited case studies. **Buys 5 mss/year.** Query with published clips. Length: 800-1,200 words. **Pays 40-80¢/word.** Sometimes pays expenses of writers on assignment.

Photos State availability with submission. Reviews contact sheets. Rights purchased depends on photographer requirements. Negotiates payment individually. Captions, identification of subjects required.

Tips "Follow our author guidelines and editorial policies to write a how-to piece from which our readers can benefit."

$ $ SPRINGS

The International Magazine of Spring Manufacturers, Spring Manufacturers Institute, 2001 Midwest Rd., Suite 106, Oak Brook IL 60523-1335. (630)495-8588. Fax: (630)495-8595. Website: www.smihq.org. **Contact:** Rita Schauer, editor. **10% freelance written.** Quarterly magazine covering precision mechanical spring manufacture. Articles should be aimed at spring manufacturers. Estab. 1962. Circ. 10,800. Pays on publication. Publishes ms an average of 3-6 months after acceptance. Byline given. Buys first rights. Editorial lead time 4 months. Accepts simultaneous submissions. Sample copy free. Writer's guidelines online.

Nonfiction General interest, how-to, interview/profile, opinion, personal experience, technical. **Buys 4-6 mss/year.** Length: 2,000-10,000 words. **Pays $100-600 for assigned articles; $50-300 for unsolicited articles.**

Photos State availability with submission. Reviews prints, digital photos. Buys one-time rights. Offers no additional payment for photos accepted with ms. Captions required.

Fillers Facts, newsbreaks. **Buys 4/year.** Length: 200-1,000 words. **Pays $25-50.**

Tips "Call the editor. Contact springmakers and spring industry suppliers and ask about what interests them. Include interviews/quotes from people in the spring industry in the article. The editor can supply contacts."

$ $ $ STAMPING JOURNAL

Fabricators & Manufacturers Association (FMA), 833 Featherstone Rd., Rockford IL 61107. (815)399-8700. Fax: (815)381-1370. E-mail: katm@thefabricator.com. Website: www.thefabricator.com. **Contact:** Kathleen McLaughlin, associate editor. **15% freelance written.** Bimonthly magazine covering metal stamping. "We look for how-to and educational articles—nonpromotional." Estab. 1989. Circ. 35,000. Pays on publication. Byline given. Buys all rights. Editorial lead time 6 months. Accepts queries by mail, e-mail, fax, phone. Responds in 2 weeks to queries; 2 months to mss. Sample copy and writer's guidelines free.

Nonfiction How-to, technical, company profile. Special issues: Forecast issue (January). No unsolicited case studies.

Buys 5 mss/year. Query with published clips. Length: 1,000 words. **Pays 40-80¢/word.** Sometimes pays expenses of writers on assignment.

Photos State availability with submission. Reviews contact sheets. Rights purchased depends on photographer requirements. Negotiates payment individually. Captions, identification of subjects required.

🖳 The online magazine contains material not found in the print edition. Contact: Vicki Bell, online editor.

Tips "Articles should be impartial and should not describe the benefits of certain products available from certain companies. They should not be biased toward the author's or against a competitor's products or technologies. The publisher may refuse any article that does not conform to this guideline."

$ $ $TPJ—THE TUBE & PIPE JOURNAL

Fabricators & Manufacturers Association (FMA), 833 Featherstone Rd., Rockford IL 61107. (815)399-8700. Fax: (815)381-1370. Website: www.thefabricator.com. **15% freelance written.** Magazine published 8 times/year covering metal tube and pipe. Educational perspective—emphasis is on "how-to" articles to accomplish a particular task or to improve on a process. New trends and technologies are also important topics. Estab. 1990. Circ. 30,000. Pays on publication. Byline given. Buys all rights. Editorial lead time 6 months. Accepts queries by mail, e-mail. Responds in 2 weeks to queries; 2 months to mss. Sample copy for free. Writer's guidelines online.

Nonfiction Any new or improved tube production or fabrication process—includes manufacturing, bending, and forming tube (metal tube only). How-to, technical. Special issues: Forecast issue (January). No unsolicited case studies. **Buys 5 mss/year.** Query with published clips. Length: 800-1,200 words. **Pays 40-80¢/word.** Sometimes pays expenses of writers on assignment.

Photos State availability with submission. Reviews contact sheets. Rights purchased depends on photographer requirements. Negotiates payment individually. Captions, identification of subjects required.

Tips "Submit a detailed proposal, including an article outline, to the editor."

$ $WIRE ROPE NEWS & SLING TECHNOLOGY

Wire Rope News LLC, P.O. Box 871, Clark NJ 07066. (908)486-3221. Fax: (732)396-4215. E-mail: vsent@aol.com. Website: www.wireropenews.com. **100% freelance written.** Bimonthly magazine "published for manufacturers and distributors of wire rope, chain, cordage, related hardware, and sling fabricators. Content includes technical articles, news and reports describing the manufacturing and use of wire rope and related products in marine, construction, mining, aircraft and offshore drilling operations." Estab. 1979. Circ. 4,300. **Pays on acceptance.** Publishes ms an average of 6 months after acceptance. Byline sometimes given. Buys all rights. Editorial lead time 2 months. Submit seasonal material 2 months in advance. Accepts queries by mail, e-mail, fax. Accepts simultaneous submissions.

Nonfiction General interest, historical/nostalgic, interview/profile, photo feature, technical. **Buys 30 mss/year.** Send complete ms. Length: 2,500-5,000 words. **Pays $300-500.**

Photos Send photos with submission. Reviews contact sheets, 5×7 prints, digital. Buys all rights. Offers no additional payment for photos accepted with ms. Identification of subjects required.

Tips "We are accepting more submissions and queries by e-mail."

MAINTENANCE & SAFETY

Ⓝ $ $AMERICAN WINDOW CLEANER MAGAZINE

Voice of the Professional Window Cleaner, P.O. Box 98, Bedford NY 10506. (914)234-2630. Fax: (914)234-2632. Website: www.awcmag.com. **20% freelance written.** Bimonthly magazine window cleaning. "Articles to help window cleaners become more profitable, safe, professional, and feel good about what they do." Estab. 1986. Circ. 8,000. **Pays on acceptance.** Publishes ms an average of 4-8 months after acceptance. Byline given. Offers 33% kill fee. Buys first rights. Editorial lead time 2 months. Submit seasonal material 3 months in advance. Responds in 2 weeks to queries; 1 month to mss. Sample copy for free. Writer's guidelines online.

Nonfiction How-to, humor, inspirational, interview/profile, personal experience, photo feature, technical. "We do not want PR-driven pieces. We want to educate—not push a particular product." **Buys 20 mss/year.** Query. Length: 500-5,000 words. **Pays $50-250.**

Photos State availability with submission. Reviews contact sheets, transparencies, 4×6 prints. Buys one-time rights. Offers $10 per photo. Captions required.

Columns/Departments Window Cleaning Tips (tricks of the trade); 1,000-2,000 words; Humor-anecdotes-feel good-abouts (window cleaning industry); Computer High-Tech (tips on new technology), all 1,000 words. **Buys 12 mss/year.** Query. **Pays $50-100.**

Tips "*American Window Cleaner Magazine* covers an unusual niche that gets people's curiosity. Articles that are technical in nature and emphasize practical tips or safety, and how to work more efficiently, have the best chances of being published. Articles include: window cleaning unusual buildings, landmarks; working for well-known people/celebrities; window cleaning in resorts/casinos/unusual cities; humor or satire about our industry or the public's perception of it. At some point, we make phone contact and chat to see if our interests are compatible.''

⊡ CANADIAN OCCUPATIONAL SAFETY

CLB Media, Inc., 240 Edward St., Aurora ON L4G 3S9 Canada. (905)727-0077. Fax: (905)727-0017. E-mail: kknudsen@clbmedia.ca. Website: www.cos-mag.com. **Contact:** Kerry Knudsen, editor. **40% freelance written.** Bimonthly magazine. ''We want informative articles dealing with issues that relate to occupational health and safety in Canada.'' Estab. 1989. Circ. 14,000. Pays on publication. Publishes ms an average of 3 months after acceptance. Byline given. Buys one-time rights. Editorial lead time 4 months. Submit seasonal material 4 months in advance. Accepts queries by mail, e-mail, fax, phone. Responds in 3 weeks to queries; 1 month to mss. Sample copy and writer's guidelines free.

Nonfiction How-to, interview/profile. **Buys 30 mss/year.** Query with published clips. Length: 500-2,000 words. **Payment varies.** Sometimes pays expenses of writers on assignment.

Photos State availability with submission. Reviews transparencies. Buys one-time rights. Negotiates payment individually. Captions required.

Tips ''Present us with an idea for an article that will interest workplace health and safety professionals, with cross-Canada appeal.''

$ $ EXECUTIVE HOUSEKEEPING TODAY

The International Executive Housekeepers Association, 1001 Eastwind Dr., Suite 301, Westerville OH 43081. (614)895-7166. Fax: (614)895-1248. E-mail: avance@ieha.org. Website: www.ieha.org. **Contact:** Andi Vance, editor. **50% freelance written.** Monthly magazine for ''nearly 5,000 decision makers responsible for housekeeping management (cleaning, grounds maintenance, laundry, linen, pest control, waste management, regulatory compliance, training) for a variety of institutions: hospitality, healthcare, education, retail, government.'' Estab. 1930. Circ. 5,500. **Pays on acceptance.** Publishes ms an average of 6 months after acceptance. Byline given. Buys first North American serial rights. Editorial lead time 2 months. Submit seasonal material 3 months in advance. Accepts queries by mail, e-mail, fax, phone.

Nonfiction General interest, interview/profile, new product (related to magazine's scope), personal experience (in housekeeping profession), technical. **Buys 30 mss/year.** Query with published clips. Length: 500-1,500 words. **Pays $150-250.**

Photos State availability with submission. Buys one-time rights. Offers no additional payment for photos accepted with ms. Identification of subjects required.

Columns/Departments Federal Report (OSHA/EPA requirements), 1,000 words; Industry News; Management Perspectives (industry specific), 500-1,500 words. Query with published clips. **Pays $150-250.**

Tips ''Have a background in the industry or personal experience with any aspect of it.''

$ $ PEST CONTROL MAGAZINE

7500 Old Oak Blvd., Cleveland OH 44130. (440)243-8100. Fax: (440)891-2675. E-mail: pestcon@advanstar.com. Website: www.pestcontrolmag.com. **Contact:** Frank H. Andorka, Jr., editorial director. Monthly magazine for professional pest management professionals and sanitarians. Estab. 1933. Circ. 20,000. Pays on publication. Licenses rights. Submit seasonal material 3 months in advance. Accepts queries by mail, e-mail, phone. Responds in 1 month to mss. Sample copy not available. Writer's guidelines online.

O─ Break in with ''information directly relating to the field—citing sources that are either industry experts (university or otherwise) or direct quotes from pest/management professionals.''

Nonfiction Prefers contributors with pest control industry background. All articles must have trade or business orientation. How-to, humor, inspirational, interview/profile, new product, personal experience (stories about pest management operations and their problems), case histories, new technological breakthroughs. No general information type of articles desired. **Buys 3 mss/year.** Query. Length: 1,000-1,400 words. **Pays $150-400 minimum.**

Photos Digital photos accepted; please query on specs. State availability with submission. No additional payment for photos used with ms.

Columns/Departments Regular columns use material oriented to this profession, 550 words.

MANAGEMENT & SUPERVISION

$ $ ⊡ CONTACT MANAGEMENT

Canada's Professional Customer Contact Solutions Forum, August Communications, 225-530 Century St., Winnipeg MB R3H 0Y4 Canada. (204)957-0265. Fax: (866)957-0217. E-mail: t.rehberg@august.ca. Website: www.co

ntactmanagement.ca. **Contact:** Trina Rehberg, editor. **90% freelance written.** Quarterly magazine covering Canadian contact centres. *"Contact Management* is the only magazine specifically targeted at Canadian contact centres. Direct mailed to managers, executives, and suppliers, the magazine explores topics important to the successful execution and planning of the day-to-day activities in a modern Canadian contact centre." Estab. 2000. Circ. 5,200. Pays 1 month after publication. Publishes ms an average of 2 months after acceptance. Byline given. Buys all rights. Editorial lead time 3 months. Submit seasonal material 3 months in advance. Accepts queries by mail, e-mail, fax. Responds in 1 week to queries. Sample copy for free.

Nonfiction Exposé, how-to, interview/profile, new product, technical. **Buys 12 mss/year.** Query with published clips. Length: 700-2,250 words. **Pays 15-40¢/word for assigned articles.**

Photos State availability with submission. Reviews GIF/JPEG files. Buys all rights. Negotiates payment individually. Identification of subjects required.

Columns/Departments Buys 6 mss/year. Query with published clips. **Pays 15-40¢/word.**

HR MAGAZINE

On Human Resource Management, Society for Human Resource Management, 1800 Duke St., Alexandria VA 22314-3499. (703)548-3440. E-mail: hrmag@shrm.org. Website: www.shrm.org. **90% freelance written.** Monthly magazine covering human resource management profession with special focus on business news that affects the workplace, including compensation, benefits, recruiting, training and development, outsourcing, management trends, court decisions, legislative actions, and government regulations. Accepts queries and mss via website; responds in 45 days. Estab. 1948. Circ. 190,000. **Pays on acceptance.** Publishes ms an average of 2 months after acceptance. Byline given. Buys all rights. Editorial lead time 4 months. Sample copy for free. Writer's guidelines online.

● Must submit queries via website.

○┰ Break in by having "relevant writing experience and a sharp, narrowly-focused article idea on something new or not well covered elsewhere."

Nonfiction Technical, expert advice and analysis, news features. **Buys 75 mss/year.** Query. Length: 1,800-2,500 words. Pays expenses of writers on assignment.

Photos State availability with submission. Buys one-time rights. Identification of subjects, model releases required.

Tips "Readers are members of the Society for Human Resource Management (SHRM), mostly HR managers with private employers ranging from small to very large in size. Our stories must balance business acumen with a concern for the well-being and productivity of employees."

$ $ $HUMAN RESOURCE EXECUTIVE

LRP Publications Magazine Group, 747 Dresher Rd., Suite 500, Harsham PA 19044. (215)784-0910. Fax: (215)784-0275. E-mail: dshadovitz@lrp.com. Website: www.hrexecutive.com. **Contact:** David Shadovitz, editor. **30% freelance written.** "Monthly magazine serving the information needs of chief human resource professionals/executives in companies, government agencies, and nonprofit institutions with 500 or more employees." Estab. 1987. Circ. 75,000. **Pays on acceptance.** Publishes ms an average of 2 months after acceptance. Byline given. Pays 50% kill fee on assigned stories. Buys all rights. Accepts queries by mail, e-mail, fax. Responds in 1 month to mss. Writer's guidelines online.

Nonfiction Book excerpts, interview/profile. **Buys 16 mss/year.** Query with published clips. Length: 1,800 words. **Pays $200-1,000.** Sometimes pays expenses of writers on assignment.

Photos State availability with submission. Reviews contact sheets. Buys first and repeat rights. Offers no additional payment for photos accepted with ms. Identification of subjects required.

$ $INCENTIVE

VNU Business Publications, 770 Broadway, New York NY 10003. (646)654-7636. Fax: (646)654-7650. E-mail: acohen@incentivemag.com. Website: www.incentivemag.com. **Contact:** Andy Cohen, editor-in-chief. Monthly magazine covering sales promotion and employee motivation: managing and marketing through motivation. Estab. 1905. Circ. 41,000. **Pays on acceptance.** Publishes ms an average of 3 months after acceptance. Byline given. Buys all rights. Accepts queries by mail, e-mail, fax. Responds in 1 month to queries; 2 months to mss. Sample copy for 9×12 SAE.

Nonfiction General interest (motivation, demographics), how-to (types of sales promotion, buying product categories, using destinations), interview/profile (sales promotion executives), travel (incentive-oriented), corporate case studies. **Buys 48 mss/year.** Query with published clips. Length: 1,000-2,000 words. **Pays $250-700 for assigned articles; does not pay for unsolicited articles.** Pays expenses of writers on assignment.

Reprints Send tearsheet and information about when and where the material previously appeared. Pays 50% of the amount paid for an original article.

Photos Send photos with submission. Reviews contact sheets, transparencies. Offers some additional payment for photos accepted with ms. Identification of subjects required.

Tips "Read the publication, then query."

$ $ TODAY'S PLAYGROUND

The National Magazine for Today's Playground Design & Standards, Harris Publishing, 360 B St., Idaho Falls ID 83402. (208)524-7000. Fax: (208)522-5241. E-mail: brady@todaysplayground.com. Website: www.todaysplayground.com. Executive Editor: Steve Smede. **Contact:** Brady L. Kay, editor. **25% freelance written.** Magazine published 10 times/year covering playgrounds and the play equipment market. *"Today's Playground* targets a park and recreation management readership. Articles should focus on the playground market as a whole, including aquatic play and surfacing." Estab. 2000. Circ. 35,000. Pays on publication. Publishes ms an average of 6 months after acceptance. Byline given. Buys first North American serial, electronic rights. Editorial lead time 2 months. Submit seasonal material 1 year in advance. Accepts queries by mail, e-mail. Accepts simultaneous submissions. Responds in 2 weeks to queries; 2 months to mss. Sample copy for $5. Writer's guidelines for #10 SASE.

Nonfiction How-to, interview/profile, new product, opinion, personal experience, photo feature, technical, travel. *"Today's Playground* does not publish any articles that do not directly relate to the playground industry." **Buys 4-6 mss/year.** Query with or without published clips. Length: 800-1,500 words. **Pays $50-300 for assigned articles.** Sometimes pays expenses of writers on assignment.

Photos State availability of or send photos with submission. Reviews 35mm transparencies, GIF/JPEG files. Buys one-time rights. Offers no additional payment for photos accepted with ms. Captions, identification of subjects, model releases required.

Columns/Departments Playground Profile (an article that profiles a unique play area and focuses on community involvement, unique design, or human interest), 800-1,200 words. **Buys 2 mss/year.** Query. **Pays $100-300.**

Tips "We are looking for articles that managers can use as a resource when considering playground construction, management, safety, etc. Writers should find unique angles to playground-related features. We are a trade journal that offers up-to-date industry news and features that promote the playground industry."

MARINE & MARITIME INDUSTRIES

$ $ PROFESSIONAL MARINER

Journal of the Maritime Industry, Navigator Publishing, P.O. Box 569, Portland ME 04112. (207)822-4350. Fax: (207)772-2879. E-mail: editors@professionalmariner.com. Website: www.professionalmariner.com. **Contact:** John Gormley, editor. **75% freelance written.** Bimonthly magazine covering professional seamanship and maritime industry news. Estab. 1993. Circ. 29,000. Pays on publication. Byline given. Buys all rights. Editorial lead time 3 months. Accepts queries by mail, e-mail, fax, phone. Accepts simultaneous submissions.

Nonfiction For professional mariners on vessels and ashore. Seeks submissions on industry news, regulations, towing, piloting, technology, engineering, business, maritime casualties, and feature stories about the maritime industry. Does accept "sea stories" and personal professional experiences as correspondence pieces. **Buys 15 mss/year.** Query. Length: varies; short clips to long profiles/features. **Pays 20¢/word.** Sometimes pays expenses of writers on assignment.

Photos Send photos with submission. Reviews prints, slides. Buys one-time rights. Negotiates payment individually. Captions, identification of subjects required.

Tips "Remember that our audience comprises maritime industry professionals. Stories must be written at a level that will benefit this group."

MEDICAL

$ $ $ AHIP COVERAGE

America's Health Insurance Plans, 601 Pennsylvania Ave., Suite 500, Washington DC 20004. (202)778-8493. Fax: (202)331-7487. E-mail: lakey@ahip.org. Website: www.ahip.org. **Contact:** Larry Akey, editor. **75% freelance written.** Bimonthly magazine. *"AHIP Coverage* is geared toward administrators in America's health insurance companies. Articles should inform and generate interest and discussion about topics on anything from patient care to regulatory issues." Estab. 1990. Circ. 12,000. Pays within 30 days of acceptance of article in final form. Publishes ms an average of 2 months after acceptance. Byline given. Offers 30% kill fee. Buys all rights. Editorial lead time 2 months. Submit seasonal material 4 months in advance. Accepts queries by mail, e-mail, fax. Accepts simultaneous submissions. Sample copy for free.

Nonfiction Book excerpts, how-to (how industry professionals can better operate their health plans), opinion.

"We do not accept stories that promote products." Query with published clips or send complete ms. Length: 1,800-2,500 words. **Pays 65¢/word minimum for assigned articles.** Pays phone expenses of writers on assignment. Buys all rights.

Tips "Look for health plan success stories in your community; we like to include case studies on a variety of topics—including patient care, provider relations, regulatory issues—so that our readers can learn from their colleagues. Our readers are members of our trade association and look for advice and news. Topics relating to the quality of health plans are the ones more frequently assigned to writers, whether a feature or department. We also welcome story ideas. Just send us a letter with the details."

AMERICA'S PHARMACIST

National Community Pharmacists Association, 100 Daingerfield Rd., Suite 205, Alexandria VA 22314. (703)683-8200. Fax: (703)683-3619. E-mail: mike.conlan@ncpanet.org. Website: www.ncpanet.org. **Contact:** Michael F. Conlan, editor. **10% freelance written.** Monthly magazine. "*America's Pharmacist* publishes business and management information and personal profiles of independent community pharmacists, the magazine's principal readers." Estab. 1904. Circ. 25,000. Pays on publication. Publishes ms an average of 3 months after acceptance. Byline given. Buys all rights. Editorial lead time 3 months. Submit seasonal material 3 months in advance. Accepts queries by mail, e-mail, fax. Accepts simultaneous submissions. Responds in 1 week to queries; 2 weeks to mss. Sample copy for free.

Nonfiction Interview/profile, business information. **Buys 3 mss/year.** Query. Length: 1,500-2,500 words.

Photos State availability with submission. Reviews contact sheets. Buys one-time rights. Negotiates payment individually. Captions, identification of subjects, model releases required.

N $ $ $ BIOTECHNOLOGY HEALTHCARE

A Guide for Decision Makers on the Biotechnology Revolution, BioCommunications LLC, 780 Township Line Rd., Yardley PA 19067. (267)685-2782. Fax: (267)685-2966. E-mail: editors@biotechnologyhealthcare.com. Website: www.biotechnologyhealthcare.com. **Contact:** Michael D. Dalzell, editor. **100% freelance written.** Bimonthly magazine. "We are a business magazines (not an academic journal) that covers the economic, regulatory, and health policy aspects of biotech therapies and diagnostics. Our audience includes third-party payers, employer purchasers of healthcare, public healthcare agencies, and healthcare professionals who prescribe biotech therapies. Articles should be written in business magazine-style prose and should be focused on the concerns of these audiences." Estab. 2004. Circ. 35,000. **Pays on acceptance.** Publishes ms an average of 3 months after acceptance. Byline given. Offers $300 kill fee. Buys all rights. Editorial lead time 4 months. Accepts queries by mail, e-mail, fax. Responds in 2 weeks to queries; 1 month to mss. Sample copy online. Writer's guidelines by e-mail.

Nonfiction Book excerpts, essays, how-to (manage the cost of biologics, case studies), interview/profile, opinion, photo feature, technical (about biotech therapies, diagnostics, or devices), regulatory developments, cost analyses studies, coverage of hot-button issues in the field. **Buys 30 mss/year.** Query with published clips. Length: 1,650-3,300 words. **Pays 75-85¢/word; $300-1,870 for unsolicited articles.** Pays expenses of writers on assignment.

Photos Philip Denlinger, design director. State availability with submission. Reviews contact sheets, 4×6 or larger, color only prints, PowerPoint slides, TIF files that are 200 dpi or higher. Buys one-time rights. Negotiates pay individually. Captions, identification of subjects required.

Columns/Departments "Our columns are 'spoken for,' but I am always interested in pitches for new columns from qualified writers." **Buys 24 mss/year.** Query with published clips. **Pays $300 minimum for a full piece; 85¢/word maximum for ms 550 words or more.**

Fillers Gags to be illustrated by cartoonist. **Buys 3 cartoons/year. Pays $300 for cartoons upon publication.**

Tips "Biotechnology represents a new age of medicine, and our readers—who struggle with how to provide healthcare benefits to employees and health insurance enrollees in an affordable way—have a strong interest in learning about how these cutting-edge, but very expensive, treatments will affect how they do their jobs. Keep in mind the interests of the managed care medical or pharmacy director, the employer HR/benefits department, the state Medicaid director, or the clinician who provides biotech therapies to patients. Our audience is highly educated, but not versed in the deep science of biotechnology, so write up to their level but be conversational and stay away from jargon. Please avoid sending consumer-health pitches, as we are not a consumer publication."

$ $ JEMS

The Journal of Emergency Medical Services, Jems Communications, 525 B St., Suite 1900, San Diego CA 92101. (800)266-5367, ext. 6847. E-mail: a.j.heightman@elsevier.com. Website: www.jems.com. **Contact:** A.J. Heightman, editor. **95% freelance written.** Monthly magazine directed to personnel who serve the pre-hospital emergency medicine industry: paramedics, EMTs, emergency physicians and nurses, administrators, EMS consultants, etc. Estab. 1980. Circ. 45,000. Pays on publication. Publishes ms an average of 6 months after acceptance. Byline given. Buys all North American serial rights. Submit seasonal material 6 months in advance. Accepts queries by mail, e-mail, fax. Responds in 2-3 months to queries. Sample copy and writer's guidelines free. Writer's guidelines online.

Nonfiction Essays, exposé, general interest, how-to, humor, interview/profile, new product, opinion, personal experience, photo feature, technical, continuing education. **Buys 50 mss/year.** Query. **Pays $200-400.**

Photos State availability with submission. Reviews 4×6 prints. Buys one-time rights. Offers $25 minimum per photo. Identification of subjects, model releases required.

Columns/Departments Length: 850 words maximum. Query with or without published clips. **Pays $50-250.**

Tips "Please submit a 1-page query letter before you send a manuscript. Your query should answer these questions: 1) What specifically are you going to tell *JEMS* readers? 2) Why do *JEMS* readers need to know this? 3) How will you make your case (i.e., literature review, original research, interviews, personal experience, observation)? Your query should explain your qualifications, as well as include previous writing samples."

$ $ $ MANAGED CARE

780 Township Line Rd., Yardley PA 19067-4200. (267)685-2784. Fax: (267)685-2966. E-mail: editors@managedc aremag.com. Website: www.managedcaremag.com. **Contact:** John Marcille, editor. **50% freelance written.** Monthly magazine. "We emphasize practical, usable information that helps HMO medical directors and pharmacy directors cope with the options, challenges, and hazards in the rapidly changing health care industry. Our regular readers understand that 'health care reform' isn't a piece of legislation; it's an evolutionary process that's already well under way. But we hope to help our readers also keep the faith that led them to medicine in the first place." Estab. 1992. Circ. 44,000. **Pays on acceptance.** Publishes ms an average of 6 weeks after acceptance. Byline given. Offers 20% kill fee. Buys all rights. Editorial lead time 3 months. Submit seasonal material 4 months in advance. Accepts queries by mail, e-mail, fax. Responds in 3 weeks to queries; 2 months to mss. Sample copy for free. Writer's guidelines on request.

Nonfiction "I strongly recommend submissions via e-mail. You'll get a faster response." Book excerpts, general interest (trends in health-care delivery and financing, quality of care, and employee concerns), how-to (deal with requisites of managed care, such as contracts with health plans, affiliation arrangements, accreditation, computer needs, etc.), original research and review articles that examine the relationship between health care delivery and financing. Also considered occasionally are personal experience, opinion, interview/profile, and humor pieces, but these must have a strong managed care angle and draw upon the insights of (if they are not written by) a knowledgeable managed care professional. **Buys 40 mss/year.** Query with published clips. Length: 1,000-3,000 words. **Pays 60¢/word.** Pays expenses of writers on assignment.

Photos State availability with submission. Reviews contact sheets, negatives, transparencies, prints. Buys first-time rights. Negotiates payment individually.

Tips "Know our audience (health plan executives) and their needs. Study our website to see what we cover."

$ $ $ $ MEDICAL ECONOMICS

5 Paragon Dr., Montvale NJ 07645-1742. (201)358-7367. Fax: (201)722-2688. E-mail: jsabatie@advanstar.com. Website: www.memag.com. **Contact:** Jeanne Sabatie, outside copy editor. Semimonthly magazine (24 times/year). "*Medical Economics* is a national business magazine read by M.D.s and D.O.s in office-based practice. Our purpose is to be informative and useful to practicing physicians in the professional and financial management of their practices. We look for contributions from writers who know—or will make the effort to learn—the nonclinical concerns of today's physician. These writers must be able to address those concerns in feature articles that are clearly written and that convey authoritative information and advice. Our articles focus very narrowly on a subject and explore it in depth." Circ. 170,000. **Pays on acceptance.** Offers 25% kill fee. Buys first world publication rights. Accepts queries by mail, e-mail, fax. Sample copy and writer's guidelines online.

Nonfiction Articles about private physicians in innovative, pioneering, and/or controversial situations affecting medical care delivery, patient relations, or malpractice prevention/litigation; personal finance topics. "We do not want overviews or pieces that only skim the surface of a general topic. We address physician readers in a conversational, yet no-nonsense tone, quoting recognized experts on office management, personal finance, patient relations, and medical-legal issues." Query with published clips. Length: 1,000-1,800 words. **Pays $1,200-2,000 for assigned articles.** Pays expenses of writers on assignment.

Photos Will negotiate an additional fee for photos accepted for publication.

Tips "We look for articles about physicians who run high-quality, innovative practices suited to the age of managed care. We also look for how-to service articles—on practice-management and personal-finance topics—which must contain anecdotal examples to support the advice. Read the magazine carefully, noting its style and content. Then send detailed proposals or outlines on subjects that would interest our mainly primary-care physician readers."

MEDICAL IMAGING

6100 Center Dr., Suite 1000, Los Angeles CA 90045. (310)642-4400. Fax: (310)641-0831. E-mail: alucas@medpu
bs.com. Website: www.medicalimagingmag.com. **Contact:** Andi Lucas, editor. **80% freelance written.** Monthly
magazine covering diagnostic imaging equipment. Estab. 1986. Circ. 26,000. Pays on publication. Publishes ms
an average of 2 months after acceptance. Byline given. Buys all rights. Editorial lead time 2 months. Sample
copy on request.

Nonfiction Interview/profile, technical. "No general interest/human interest stories about healthcare. Articles
must deal with our industry, diagnostic imaging." **Buys 6 mss/year.** Query with published clips. Length: 1,500-
2,500 words.

Photos State availability with submission. Reviews negatives. Buys all rights. Offers no additional payment for
photos accepted with ms. Identification of subjects, model releases required.

Tips "Send an e-mail or a letter with an interesting story idea that is applicable to our industry, diagnostic
imaging. Then follow up with a phone call. Areas most open to freelancers are features and technology profiles.
You don't have to be an engineer or radiologist, but you have to know how to talk and listen to them."

$ $ $ $ MODERN PHYSICIAN

Essential Business News for the Executive Physician, Crain Communications, 360 N. Michigan Ave., 5th Floor,
Chicago IL 60601. (312)280-3173. Fax: (312)280-3183. E-mail: dburda@crain.com. Website: www.modernphysi
cian.com. **Contact:** David Burda, editor. **10% freelance written.** Monthly magazine covering business and
management news for doctors. "*Modern Physician* offers timely topical news features with lots of business
information—revenues, earnings, financial data." Estab. 1997. Circ. 32, 552. **Pays on acceptance.** Publishes
ms an average of 2 months after acceptance. Byline given. Buys all rights. Editorial lead time 2 months. Accepts
queries by mail, e-mail. Responds in 6 weeks to queries. Sample copy for free. Writer's guidelines sent after
query.

   O─ Break in with a regional story involving business or physicians.

Nonfiction Length: 750-1,000 words. **Pays 75¢-$1/word.**

   ■ The online magazine carries original content not found in the print edition. Contact: Joseph Conn
     (jconn@crain.com).

Tips "Read the publication, know our audience, and come up with a good story idea that we haven't thought
of yet."

$ $ $ $ THE PHYSICIAN AND SPORTSMEDICINE

McGraw-Hill, 4530 W. 77th St., Minneapolis MN 55435. (952)835-3222. Fax: (952)835-3460. E-mail: jim_wappes
@mcgraw-hill.com. Website: www.physsportsmed.com. **Contact:** Jim Wappes, executive editor. **5% freelance
written.** Monthly magazine covering medical aspects of sports and exercise. Prefers to work with published/
established writers. "We publish articles that are of practical, clinical interest to our physician audience." Estab.
1973. Circ. 115,000. **Pays on acceptance.** Publishes ms an average of 4 months after acceptance. Byline given.
Buys all rights. Responds in 2 months to queries. Sample copy for $10. Writer's guidelines for #10 SASE or on
website.

   ● This publication is relying more heavily on the clinical component of the journal, meaning review articles
     written by physicians who have expertise in a specific specialty.

Nonfiction New developments and issues in sports medicine. Query. Length: 250-2,500 words. **Pays $150-
1,800.**

Photos Mary Schill, photo editor. State availability with submission.

$ $ $ PHYSICIANS' TRAVEL & MEETING GUIDE

Quadrant HealthCom, Inc., 26 Main St., Chatham NJ 07928-2402. (973)701-2716. E-mail: bea.riemschneider@c
meplanner.com. Website: www.cmeplanner.com. **Contact:** Bea Riemschneider, editorial director. **60% freelance written.** Monthly magazine covering travel for physicians and their families. *Physicians' Travel & Meeting
Guide* supplies continuing medical education events listings and extensive travel coverage of international and
national destinations. Circ. 142,541. **Pays on acceptance.** Byline given. Buys first North American serial rights.
Submit seasonal material 4-6 months in advance. Accepts queries by mail, e-mail. Responds in 3 months to
queries.

Nonfiction Photo feature, travel. **Buys 25-35 mss/year.** Query with published clips. Length: 450-3,000 words.
Pays $150-1,000 for assigned articles.

Photos State availability of or send photos with submission. Reviews 35mm, 4×5 transparencies. Buys one-
time rights. Captions, identification of subjects required.

$ $ PODIATRY MANAGEMENT

Kane Communications, Inc., P.O. Box 750129, Forest Hills NY 11375. (718)897-9700. Fax: (718)896-5747. E-
mail: bblock@prodigy.net. Website: www.podiatrym.com. Publisher: Scott C. Borowsky. **Contact:** Barry Block,

editor. Magazine published 9 times/year for practicing podiatrists. "Aims to help the doctor of podiatric medicine to build a bigger, more successful practice, to conserve and invest his money, to keep him posted on the economic, legal, and sociological changes that affect him." Estab. 1982. Circ. 14,500. Pays on publication. Byline given. Buys first North American serial, second serial (reprint) rights. Submit seasonal material 4 months in advance. Accepts queries by e-mail. Accepts simultaneous submissions. Responds in 2 weeks to queries. Sample copy for $3 and 9×12 SAE. Writer's guidelines for #10 SASE.

Nonfiction Book excerpts, general interest (taxes, investments, estate, estate planning, recreation, hobbies), how-to (establish and collect fees, practice management, organize office routines, supervise office assistants, handle patient relations), interview/profile (about interesting or well-known podiatrists), personal experience. "These subjects are the mainstay of the magazine, but offbeat articles and humor are always welcome." **Buys 25 mss/year.** Length: 1,200-3,000 words. **Pays $250-600.**

Reprints Send photocopy. Pays 33% of amount paid for an original article.

Photos State availability with submission. Buys one-time rights. Pays $15 for b&w contact sheet.

Tips "We have been persuading writers to use e-mail for the past few years because of the speed, ease of editing, and general efficiency of the process. The tragic events of 9/11/01 along with the anthrax issue now make the policy mandatory—and the trees will also appreciate it!"

$ $⊘ STRATEGIC HEALTH CARE MARKETING

Health Care Communications, 11 Heritage Lane, P.O. Box 594, Rye NY 10580. (914)967-6741. Fax: (914)967-3054. E-mail: healthcomm@aol.com. Website: www.strategichealthcare.com. **Contact:** Michele von Dambrowski, editor. **90% freelance written.** Monthly newsletter covering health care marketing and management in a wide range of settings, including hospitals, medical group practices, home health services, and managed care organizations. Emphasis is on strategies and techniques employed within the health care field and relevant applications from other service industries. Works with published/established writers only. Estab. 1984. Pays on publication. Publishes ms an average of 2 months after acceptance. Byline given. Offers 25% kill fee. Buys first North American serial rights. Accepts queries by mail, e-mail. Responds in 1 month to queries. Sample copy for 9×12 SAE and 3 first-class stamps. Guidelines sent with sample copy only.

- *Strategic Health Care Marketing* is specifically seeking writers with expertise/contacts in managed care, patient satisfaction, and e-health.

Nonfiction "Preferred format for feature articles is the case history approach to solving marketing problems. Crisp, almost telegraphic style." How-to, interview/profile, new product, technical. **Buys 50 mss/year.** *No unsolicited mss.* Length: 700-3,000 words. **Pays $100-500.** Sometimes pays expenses of writers on assignment with prior authorization.

Photos Photos, unless necessary for subject explanation, are rarely used. State availability with submission. Reviews contact sheets. Buys one-time rights. Offers $10-30/photo. Captions, model releases required.

The online magazine carries original content not found in the print edition. Contact: Mark Gothberg.

Tips "Writers with prior experience on the business beat for newspapers or newsletters will do well. We require a sophisticated, in-depth knowledge of health care and business. This is not a consumer publication—the writer with knowledge of both health care and marketing will excel. Absolutely no unsolicited manuscripts; any received will be returned or discarded unread."

$ $ $ $UNIQUE OPPORTUNITIES

The Physician's Resource, U O, Inc., 214 S. 8th St., Suite 502, Louisville KY 40202. Fax: (502)587-0848. E-mail: bett@uoworks.com. Website: www.uoworks.com. Editor: Mollie Vento Hudson. **Contact:** Bett Coffman, associate editor. **55% freelance written.** Bimonthly magazine covering physician relocation and career development. "Published for physicians interested in a new career opportunity. It offers physicians useful information and first-hand experiences to guide them in making informed decisions concerning their first or next career opportunity. It provides features and regular columns about specific aspects of the search process." Estab. 1991. Circ. 80,000 physicians. Pays 1 month after acceptance. Publishes ms an average of 2 months after acceptance. Byline given. Offers 15% kill fee. Buys first North American serial, electronic rights. Editorial lead time 3 months. Submit seasonal material 6 months in advance. Responds in 2 months to queries. Sample copy for 9×12 SAE and 6 first-class stamps. Writer's guidelines online.

Nonfiction Features: Practice options and information of interest to physicians in career transition. **Buys 14 mss/year.** Query with published clips. Length: 1,500-3,500 words. **Pays $750-2,000.** Sometimes pays expenses of writers on assignment.

Photos State availability with submission. Buys electronic rights. Negotiates payment individually. Identification of subjects, model releases required.

Columns/Departments Remarks (opinion from physicians and industry experts on physician career issues), 900-1,500 words. **No payment.**

Trade Journals

■ The online magazine carries original content not found in the print edition.

Tips "Submit queries via letter or e-mail with ideas for articles that directly pertain to physician career issues, such as specific or unusual practice opportunities, relocation, or practice establishment subjects, etc. Feature articles are most open to freelancers. Physician sources are most important with tips and advice from both the physicians and business experts. Physicians like to know what other physicians think and do, and appreciate suggestions from other business people."

MUSIC

$CLASSICAL SINGER MAGAZINE

Classical Publications, Inc., P.O. Box 1710, Draper UT 84020. (801)254-1025, ext. 13. Fax: (801)254-3139. E-mail: cj@classicalsinger.com. Website: www.classicalsinger.com. **Contact:** Ms. CJ Williamson, editor. Monthly magazine covering classical singers. Estab. 1988. Circ. 7,000. Pays on publication. Publishes ms an average of 3 months after acceptance. Byline given, plus bio and contact info. Buys second serial (reprint), all rights. Editorial lead time 3 months. Submit seasonal material 3 months in advance. Accepts queries by e-mail. Accepts previously published material. Responds in 1 month to queries. Potential writers will be given password to website version of magazine and writer's guidelines online.

    O— E-mail, mail, or fax writing sample. If accepted, editor will give assignment. Most future correspondence is done via e-mail. All mss must be submitted electronically in Word 98 or higher.

Nonfiction Editorial calendar available on request. "The best way to find materials for articles is to look on the General Interest forum on our website and see what singers are interested in." Book excerpts, exposé (carefully done), how-to, humor, interview/profile, new product, personal experience, photo feature, religious, technical, travel, crossword puzzles on opera theme. Does not want reviews unless they are assigned. Query with published clips. Length: 500-3,000 words. **Pays 5¢/word ($50 minimum). Writers also receive 10 copies of the magazine.** Pays telephone expenses of writers with assignments when Xerox copy of bill submitted.

Photos Send photos with submission. Buys all rights. Captions required.

    ■ The online magazine carries original content not found in the print edition. Contact editor by e-mail.

Tips "*Classical Singer Magazine* has a full-color glossy cover and glossy b&w and color pages inside. It ranges in size from 56 pages during the summer to 120 pages in September. Articles need to meet this mission statement: 'Information for a classical singer's career, support for a classical singer's life, and enlightenment for a classical singer's art.'"

CLAVIER MAGAZINE

The Instrumentalist Publishing Co., 200 Northfield Rd., Northfield IL 60093. (847)446-5000. Fax: (847)446-6263. **Contact:** Judy Nelson, editor. **1% freelance written.** Magazine published 10 times/year featuring practical information on teaching subjects that are of value to studio piano teachers and interviews with major artists. Estab. 1937. Circ. 14,000. Pays on publication. Publishes ms an average of 18 months after acceptance. Byline given. Buys all rights. Submit seasonal material 6 months in advance. Accepts queries by mail, fax, phone. Responds in 6 weeks to queries. Sample copy and writer's guidelines free.

Nonfiction "Articles should be of interest and direct practical value to concert pianists, harpsichordists, and organists who are teachers of piano, organ, harpsichord, and electronic keyboards. Topics may include pedagogy, technique, performance, ensemble playing, and accompanying." Historical/nostalgic, how-to, interview/profile, photo feature. Length: 10-12 double-spaced pages. **Pays small honorarium.**

Reprints Occasionally we will reprint a chapter in a book.

Photos Digital artwork should be sent in TIFF, EPS, JPEG files for Photoshop at 300 dpi. Send photos with submission. Reviews negatives, $2^{1}/_{4} \times 2^{1}/_{4}$ transparencies, 3×5 prints. Buys all rights. Offers no additional payment for photos accepted with ms. Identification of subjects required.

$⬚ INTERNATIONAL BLUEGRASS

International Bluegrass Music Association, 2 Music Circle S., Suite 100, Nashville TN 37203. (615)256-3222. Fax: (615)256-0450. E-mail: info@ibma.org. Website: www.ibma.org.; www.discoverbluegrass.com. **Contact:** Nancy Cardwell. **10% freelance written.** Bimonthly newsletter. "We are the business publication for the bluegrass music industry. IBMA believes that our music has growth potential. We are interested in hard news and features concerning how to reach that potential and how to conduct business more effectively." Estab. 1985. Circ. 4,500. Pays on publication. Publishes ms an average of 2 months after acceptance. Byline given. Not copyrighted. Buys one-time rights. Submit seasonal material 4 months in advance. Accepts queries by mail, e-mail, phone. Accepts simultaneous submissions. Responds in 1 month to queries. Sample copy for 6×9 SAE and 2 first-class stamps.

Nonfiction Unsolicited mss are not accepted, but unsolicited news about the industry is accepted. Book excerpts, essays, how-to (conduct business effectively within bluegrass music), new product, opinion. No interview/

profiles/feature stories of performers (rare exceptions) or fans. **Buys 6 mss/year.** Query with or without published clips. Length: 1,000-1,200 words. **Pays up to $150/article for assigned articles.**

Reprints Send photocopy of article and information about when and where the article previously appeared. Does not pay for reprints.

Photos Send photos with submission. Buys one-time rights. Offers no additional payment for photos accepted with ms. Captions, identification of subjects, photographer's name required.

Tips "We're interested in a slant strongly toward the business end of bluegrass music. We're especially looking for material dealing with audience development and how to book bluegrass bands outside of the existing market."

$ $ $MIX MAGAZINE

Primedia Business Magazines, 6400 Hollis St., Suite 12, Emeryville CA 94608. Fax: (510)653-5142. E-mail: gpetersen@primediabusiness.com. Website: www.mixonline.com. Editorial Director: George Petersen. **50% freelance written.** Monthly magazine covering pro audio. "*Mix* is a trade publication geared toward professionals in the music/sound production recording and post-production industries. We include stories about music production, sound for picture, live sound, etc. We prefer in-depth technical pieces that are applications-oriented." Estab. 1977. Circ. 50,000. Pays on publication. Publishes ms an average of 3 months after acceptance. Byline given. Offers 50% kill fee. Buys all rights. Editorial lead time 10 weeks. Submit seasonal material 3 months in advance. Responds in 2 weeks to queries; 1 month to mss. Sample copy for $6. Writer's guidelines free.

Nonfiction How-to, interview/profile, new product, technical, project/studio spotlights. Special issues: Sound for picture supplement (April, September), Design issue. **Buys 60 mss/year.** Query. Length: 500-2,000 words. **Pays $300-800 for assigned articles; $300-400 for unsolicited articles.**

Photos State availability with submission. Reviews 4×5 transparencies, prints. Buys one-time rights. Negotiates payment individually. Captions, identification of subjects required.

MUSIC CONNECTION

The West Coast Music Trade Magazine, Music Connection, Inc., 16130 Ventura Blvd., Suite 540, Encino CA 91436. (818)995-0101. E-mail: markn@musicconnection.com. Website: www.musicconnection.com. **Contact:** Mark Nardone, senior editor. **40% freelance written.** "Biweekly magazine geared toward working musicians and/or other industry professionals, including producers/engineers/studio staff, managers, agents, publicists, music publishers, record company staff, concert promoters/bookers, etc." Estab. 1977. Circ. 75,000. Pays after publication. Publishes ms an average of 2 months after acceptance. Byline given. Kill fee varies. Buys all rights. Editorial lead time 2 months. Submit seasonal material 2 months in advance. Sample copy for $5.

Nonfiction How-to (music industry related), interview/profile, new product, technical. Query with published clips. Length: 1,000-5,000 words. **Payment varies.** Sometimes pays expenses of writers on assignment.

Photos State availability with submission. Reviews transparencies, prints. Buys one-time rights. Negotiates payment individually. Identification of subjects required.

Tips "Articles must be informative music/music industry-related pieces, geared toward a trade-reading audience comprised mainly of musicians. No fluff."

$ $ $OPERA NEWS

Metropolitan Opera Guild, Inc., 70 Lincoln Center Plaza, New York NY 10023-6593. (212)769-7080. Fax: (212)769-8500. Website: www.operanews.com. Editor: F. Paul Driscoll. **Contact:** Kitty March, editor. **75% freelance written.** Monthly magazine for people interested in opera; the opera professional as well as the opera audience. Estab. 1936. Circ. 105,000. Pays on publication. Publishes ms an average of 4 months after acceptance. Byline given. Buys first serial rights only. Editorial lead time 4 months. Sample copy for $5. Writer's guidelines not available.

Oᴍ Break in by "showing incisive knowledge of opera and the opera scene. We look for knowledgeable and informed writers who are capable of discussing opera in detailed musical terms—but in an engaging way."

Nonfiction Most articles are commissioned in advance. Monthly issues feature articles on various aspects of opera worldwide. Emphasis is on high quality writing and an intellectual interest to the opera-oriented public. Historical/nostalgic, interview/profile, informational, think pieces, opera, CD, and DVD reviews. Query. Length: 1,500-2,800 words. **Pays $450-1,200.** Sometimes pays expenses of writers on assignment.

Photos State availability with submission. Buys one-time rights.

Columns/Departments Buys 24 mss/year.

$ $VENUES TODAY

The News Behind the Headlines, 18350 Mount Langley, #200, Fountain Valley CA 92647. Fax: (714)378-5400. E-mail: natasha@venuestoday.com. Website: www.venuestoday.com. Editor: Linda Deckard. **Contact:** Natasha

Emmons, managing editor. **70% freelance written.** Weekly magazine covering the live entertainment industry and the buildings that host shows and sports. "We need writers who can cover an exciting industry from the business side, not the consumer side. The readers are venue managers, concert promoters, those in the concert and sports business, not the audience for concerts and sports. So we need business journalists who can cover the latest news and trends in the market." Estab. 2002. Pays on publication. Publishes ms an average of 1 month after acceptance. Byline given. Buys all rights. Editorial lead time 2 months. Submit seasonal material 2 months in advance. Accepts queries by mail, e-mail, fax. Accepts simultaneous submissions. Responds in 1 week to queries. Sample copy online. Writer's guidelines free.

Nonfiction Interview/profile, photo feature, technical, travel. Does not want customer slant, marketing pieces. Query with published clips. Length: 500-1,500 words. **Pays $100-250.** Pays expenses of writers on assignment.

Photos State availability with submission. Reviews GIF/JPEG files. Buys one-time rights. Negotiates payment individually. Captions, identification of subjects required.

Columns/Departments Venue News (new buildings, trend features, etc.); Bookings (show tours, business side); Marketing (of shows, sports, convention centers); Concessions (food, drink, merchandise). Length: 500-1,200 words. **Buys 250 mss/year.** Query with published clips. **Pays $100-250.**

Fillers Gags to be illustrated by cartoonist. **Buys 6/year. Pays $100-300.**

OFFICE ENVIRONMENT & EQUIPMENT

$ $ OFFICE DEALER

Updating the Office Products Industry, OfficeVision, Inc., 252 N. Main St., Suite 200, Mt. Airy NC 27030. (336)783-0000. Fax: (336)783-0045. E-mail: scullen@os-od.com. Website: www.os-od.com. **Contact:** Scott Cullen, managing editor. **80% freelance written.** Bimonthly magazine covering the office product industry. "*Office Dealer* serves independent resellers of office supplies, furniture, and equipment." Estab. 1987. Circ. 15,300. Pays on publication. Byline given. Buys all rights. Editorial lead time 3 months. Submit seasonal material 5 months in advance. Accepts queries by mail, e-mail, fax. Accepts simultaneous submissions. Responds in 1 month to queries. Sample copy and writer's guidelines free.

Nonfiction Interview/profile, new product, technical. **Buys 10 mss/year.** Length: 700-1,500 words. **Pays $300-500.**

Tips "See editorial calendar posted online. Feature articles are written by our staff or by freelance writers. We may accept corporate 'byline' articles. Queries should be a single page or less and include an SASE for response. Samples of a writer's past work and clips concerning the proposed story are helpful."

$ $ OFFICE SOLUTIONS

The Magazine for Office Professionals, OfficeVision Inc., 252 N. Main St., Suite 200, Mt. Airy NC 27030. (336)783-0000. Fax: (336)783-0045. E-mail: scullen@os-od.com. Website: www.os-od.com. **Contact:** Scott Cullen, managing editor. **80% freelance written.** Bimonthly magazine covering the office personnel and environment. "*Office Solutions* subscribers are responsible for the management of their personnel and office environments." Estab. 1984. Circ. 81,250. Pays on publication. Byline given. Buys all rights. Editorial lead time 3 months. Submit seasonal material 4 months in advance. Accepts queries by mail, e-mail, fax. Accepts simultaneous submissions. Responds in 1 month to queries. Sample copy and writer's guidelines free.

Nonfiction "Our audience is responsible for general management of an office environment and personnel, so articles should be broad in scope and not too technical in nature." Interview/profile, new product, technical, human resources. **Buys 18 mss/year.** Query. Length: 1,500-2,200 words. **Pays $200-450.**

Tips "See editorial calendar posted online. Feature articles are written by our staff or by freelance writers. Queries should be a single page or less and include an SASE for response. Samples of a writer's past work and clips concerning the proposed story are helpful."

PAPER

$ $ THE PAPER STOCK REPORT

News and Trends of the Paper Recycling Markets, McEntee Media Corp., 9815 Hazelwood Ave., Cleveland OH 44149. (440)238-6603. Fax: (440)238-6712. E-mail: psr@recycle.cc. Website: www.recycle.cc. **Contact:** Ken McEntee, editor. Biweekly newsletter covering market trends, news in the paper recycling industry. "Audience is interested in new innovative markets, applications for recovered scrap paper, as well as new laws and regulations impacting recycling." Estab. 1990. Circ. 2,000. Pays on publication. Publishes ms an average of 1 month after acceptance. Byline given. Buys first, all rights. Editorial lead time 2 months. Submit seasonal material 2 months in advance. Accepts queries by mail, e-mail, fax, phone. Accepts simultaneous submissions. Responds in 1 month to queries. Sample copy for #10 SAE with 55¢ postage.

Nonfiction Book excerpts, essays, exposé, general interest, historical/nostalgic, interview/profile, new product, opinion, photo feature, technical, all related to paper recycling. **Buys 0-13 mss/year.** Send complete ms. Length: 250-1,000 words. **Pays $50-250 for assigned articles; $25-250 for unsolicited articles.** Pays expenses of writers on assignment.

Photos State availability with submission. Reviews contact sheets. Negotiates payment individually. Identification of subjects required.

📖 The online magazine carries original content not found in the print edition. Contact: Ken McEntee, online editor.

Tips "Article must be valuable to readers in terms of presenting new market opportunities or cost-saving measures."

📇 PULP & PAPER CANADA

1 Holiday St., #705, East Tower, Pointe-Claire QC H9R 5N3 Canada. (514)630-5955. Fax: (514)630-5980. E-mail: anyao@pulpandpapercanada.com. Publisher: Jim Bussiere. **Contact:** Anya Orzechowska, managing editor. **5% freelance written.** Monthly magazine. Prefers to work with published/established writers. Estab. 1903. Circ. 10,361. Pays on publication. Byline given. Negotiates kill fee. Buys first North American serial rights. Accepts queries by mail, e-mail. Responds in 1 month to queries. Sample copy for free.

○┐ Break in with an article about a Canadian paper mill case study, i.e., problem/solution type or maintenance-related articles.

Nonfiction Articles with photographs or other good quality illustrations will get priority review. How-to (related to processes and procedures in the industry), interview/profile (of Canadian leaders in pulp and paper industry), technical (relevant to modern pulp and/or paper industry). No fillers, short industry news items, or product news items. **Buys 5 mss/year.** Query with published clips or send complete ms. Length: 2,200 words maximum (with photos).

Tips "Any return postage must be in either Canadian stamps or International Reply Coupons only."

$ $ RECYCLED PAPER NEWS

Independent Coverage of Environmental Issues in the Paper Industry, McEntee Media Corp., 9815 Hazelwood Ave., Cleveland OH 44149. (440)238-6603. Fax: (440)238-6712. E-mail: rpn@recycle.cc. Website: www.recycle. cc. **Contact:** Ken McEntee, president. **10% freelance written.** Monthly newsletter. "We are interested in any news impacting the paper recycling industry, as well as other environmental issues in the paper industry, i.e., water/air pollution, chlorine-free paper, forest conservation, etc., with special emphasis on new laws and regulations." Estab. 1990. Pays on publication. Publishes ms an average of 2 months after acceptance. Buys first, all rights. Editorial lead time 1 month. Submit seasonal material 1 month in advance. Accepts queries by mail, e-mail, fax, phone. Accepts simultaneous submissions. Responds in 2 months to queries. Sample copy for 9×12 SAE and 55¢ postage. Writer's guidelines for #10 SASE.

Nonfiction Book excerpts, essays, how-to, interview/profile, new product, opinion, personal experience, photo feature, technical, new business, legislation, regulation, business expansion. **Buys 0-5 mss/year.** Query with published clips. **Pays $10-500.** Pays writers with contributor copies or other premiums by prior agreement.

Reprints Accepts previously published submissions.

Columns/Departments Query with published clips. **Pays $10-500.**

Tips "We appreciate leads on local news regarding recycling or composting, i.e., new facilities or businesses, new laws and regulations, unique programs, situations that impact supply and demand for recyclables, etc. International developments are also of interest."

PETS

$ $ PET AGE

H.H. Backer Associates, Inc., 200 S. Michigan Ave., Suite 840, Chicago IL 60604-2383-2404. (312)663-4040. Fax: (312)663-5676. E-mail: petage@hhbacker.com. Editor-In-Chief/Associate Publisher: Karen Long MacLeod. **Contact:** Cathy Foster, senior editor. **90% freelance written.** Monthly magazine for pet/pet supplies retailers, covering the complete pet industry. Prefers to work with published/established writers. Will consider new writers. Estab. 1971. Circ. 23,022. **Pays on acceptance.** Publishes ms an average of 3 months after acceptance. Byline given. Buys first North American serial, one-time rights. Sample copy and writer's guidelines available.

Nonfiction How-to articles on marketing/merchandising companion animals and supplies; how-to articles on retail store management; industry trends and issues; animal health care and husbandry. No profiles of industry members and/or retail establishments or consumer-oriented pet articles. **Buys 80 mss/year.** Query with published clips. Length: 1,500-2,200 words. **Pays 15¢/word for assigned articles.** Pays documented telephone expenses.

Photos Reviews transparencies, slides, and 5×7 glossy prints. Buys one-time rights. Captions, identification of subjects required.

Tips "This is a business publication for busy people, and must be very informative in easy-to-read, concise style. Articles about animal care or business practices should have the pet-retail angle or cover issues specific to this industry."

$ $☐ PET COMMERCE

August Communications, 225-530 Century St., Winnipeg MB R3H 0Y4 Canada. (888)573-1136. Fax: (866)957-0217. E-mail: s.vivian@august.ca. Website: www.petcommerce.ca. Editorial Director: Adam Peeler. **Contact:** Shelley Vivian, editor. **60% freelance written.** Bimonthly magazine covering pet retail and supply industry. Estab. 1997. Circ. 8,416. Pays 1 month after publication. Byline given. Offers 50% kill fee. Buys all rights. Editorial lead time 3 months. Submit seasonal material 3 months in advance. Accepts queries by mail, e-mail, fax. Responds in 1 week to queries. Sample copy online.

Nonfiction General interest, how-to, interview/profile, new product. Special issues: Annual Pond issue (February/March); Pre-PIJAC Convention issue (June/July); PIJAC Trade Show issue (August/September); Post PIJAC Convention issue (October/November). No consumer-related articles. **Buys 35-40 mss/year.** Query with published clips. Length: 1,200-2,000 words. **Pays 20-30¢/word for assigned articles.**

Photos Send photos with submission. Reviews GIF/JPEG files. Buys all rights. Negotiates payment individually. Captions, identification of subjects, model releases required.

Columns/Departments Fish for Thought (fish-related features); Pet Files (behind-the-scenes look at a pet company or pet profession); Career Chase (profile of a working pet); all 1,500 words. **Buys 12 mss/year.** Query with published clips. **Pays 15-30¢/word.**

PLUMBING, HEATING, AIR CONDITIONING & REFRIGERATION

$ $HVACR NEWS

Trade News International, 4444 Riverside Dr., #202, Burbank CA 91505-4048. Fax: (818)848-1306. E-mail: news@hvacrnews.com. Website: www.hvacrnews.com. **Contact:** Gary McCarty. Monthly tabloid covering heating, ventilation, air conditioning, and refrigeration. "We are a national trade publication writing about news and trends for those in the trade." Estab. 1981. Circ. 50,000. Pays on publication. Byline sometimes given. Buys first North American serial rights. Editorial lead time 2 months. Submit seasonal material 2 months in advance. Accepts queries by mail, e-mail. Responds in 1 month to queries. Sample copy online. Writer's guidelines by e-mail.

Nonfiction General interest, how-to, interview/profile, photo feature, technical. **Buys 25 mss/year.** Query with published clips. Length: 250-1,000 words. **Pays 25¢/word.** Sometimes pays expenses of writers on assignment.

Photos Send photos with submission. Buys one-time rights. Offers $10 minimum. Negotiates payment individually. Identification of subjects required.

Columns/Departments Buys 24 mss/year. **Pays 20¢/word.**

Tips "Writers must be knowledgeable about the HVACR industry."

$ $SNIPS MAGAZINE

BNP Media, 2401 W. Big Beaver Rd., Suite 700, Troy MI 48084. (248)244-6416. Fax: (248)362-0317. E-mail: mcconnellm@bnpmedia.com. Website: www.snipsmag.com. **Contact:** Michael McConnell, editor. **2% freelance written.** Monthly magazine for sheet metal, warm air heating, ventilating, air conditioning, and roofing contractors. Estab. 1932. Publishes ms an average of 3 months after acceptance. Buys all rights. Accepts queries by mail, e-mail, fax, phone. Call for writer's guidelines.

⊶ Break in with a "profile of a local contractor in our industries."

Nonfiction Material should deal with information about contractors who do sheet metal, warm air heating, air conditioning, ventilation, and metal roofing work; also about successful advertising and/or marketing campaigns conducted by these contractors and the results. Length: Under 1,000 words unless on special assignment. **Pays $200-300.**

Photos Negotiable.

PRINTING

$ $IN-PLANT GRAPHICS

North American Publishing Co., 401 N. Broad St., Philadelphia PA 19108. (215)238-5321. Fax: (215)238-5457. E-mail: bobneubauer@napco.com. Website: www.ipgonline.com. **Contact:** Bob Neubauer, editor. **50% freelance**

written. "*In-Plant Graphics* features articles designed to help in-house printing departments increase productivity, save money, and stay competitive. *IPG* features advances in graphic arts technology and shows in-plants how to put this technology to use. Our audience consists of print shop managers working for (nonprint related) corporations (i.e., hospitals, insurance companies, publishers, nonprofits), universities, and government departments. They often oversee graphic design, prepress, printing, bindery, and mailing departments." Estab. 1951. Circ. 24,100. Pays on publication. Publishes ms an average of 3 months after acceptance. Byline given. Buys all rights. Editorial lead time 2 months. Submit seasonal material 3 months in advance. Accepts queries by mail, e-mail, fax. Writer's guidelines online.

Nonfiction "Stories include profiles of successful in-house printing operations (not commercial or quick printers); updates on graphic arts technology (new features, uses); reviews of major graphic arts and printing conferences (seminar and new equipment reviews)." New product (graphic arts), technical (graphic arts/printing/prepress). No articles on desktop publishing software or design software. No Internet publishing articles. **Buys 5 mss/year.** Query with published clips. Length: 800-1,500 words. **Pays $350-500.** Pays writers with contributor copies or other premiums for consultants who agree to write just for exposure.

Photos State availability with submission. Reviews transparencies, prints. Buys one-time rights. Negotiates payment individually. Captions, identification of subjects required.

▣ The online magazine carries original content not found in the print edition. Contact: Bob Neubauer.

Tips "To get published in *IPG*, writers must contact the editor with an idea in the form of a query letter that includes published writing samples. Writers who have covered the graphic arts in the past may be assigned stories for an agreed-upon fee. We don't want stories that tout only one vendor's products and serve as glorified commercials. All profiles must be well balanced, covering a variety of issues. If you can tell us about an in-house printing operation is doing innovative things, we will be interested."

$ $SCREEN PRINTING

407 Gilbert Ave., Cincinnati OH 45202-2285. (513)421-2050. Fax: (513)421-5144. E-mail: tom.frecska@stmediagroup.com. Website: www.screenweb.com. **Contact:** Tom Frecska, editor. **30% freelance written.** Monthly magazine for the screen printing industry, including screen printers (commercial, industrial, and captive shops), suppliers and manufacturers, ad agencies, and allied professions. Works with a small number of new/unpublished writers each year. Estab. 1953. Circ. 17,500. Pays on publication. Publishes ms an average of 3 months after acceptance. Byline given. Buys all rights. Accepts queries by mail, e-mail, fax. Sample copy available. Writer's guidelines for #10 SASE.

Nonfiction "Because the screen printing industry is a specialized but diverse trade, we do not publish general interest articles with no pertinence to our readers. Subject matter is open, but should fall into 1 of 4 categories—technology, management, profile, or news. Features in all categories must identify the relevance of the subject matter to our readership. Technology articles must be informative, thorough, and objective—no promotional or 'advertorial' pieces accepted. Management articles may cover broader business or industry specific issues, but they must address the screen printer's unique needs. Profiles may cover serigraphers, outstanding shops, unique jobs and projects, or industry personalities; they should be in-depth features, not PR puff pieces, that clearly show the human interest or business relevance of the subject. News pieces should be timely (reprints from nonindustry publications will be considered) and must cover an event or topic of industry concern." Unsolicited mss not returned. **Buys 10-15 mss/year.** Query. **Pays $400 minimum for major features.**

Photos Cover photos negotiable; b&w or color. Published material becomes the property of the magazine.

Tips "Be an expert in the screen-printing industry with supreme or special knowledge of a particular screen-printing process, or have special knowledge of a field or issue of particular interest to screen-printers. If the author has a working knowledge of screen printing, assignments are more readily available. General management articles are rarely used."

PROFESSIONAL PHOTOGRAPHY

$ $IMAGING BUSINESS

(formerly *Photographic Processing*), Cygnus Business Media, 3 Huntington Quad., Suite 301N, Melville NY 11747. (631)845-2700. Fax: (631)845-7109. E-mail: bill.schiffner@cygnusb2b.com. Website: www.labsonline.com. Publisher: Arthur Hotz. **Contact:** Bill Schiffner, editor-in-chief. **30% freelance written.** Monthly magazine covering photographic (commercial/minilab) and electronic processing markets. Estab. 1965. Circ. 19,000. Pays on publication. Publishes ms an average of 4 months after acceptance. Byline given. Offers $75 kill fee. Editorial lead time 3 months. Submit seasonal material 3 months in advance. Accepts simultaneous submissions. Sample copy and writer's guidelines free.

Nonfiction How-to, interview/profile, new product, photo processing/digital imaging features. **Buys 20-30 mss/**

year. Query with published clips. Length: 1,500-2,200 words. **Pays $275-350 for assigned articles; $250-275 for unsolicited articles.**

Photos Looking for digitally manipulated covers. Send photos with submission. Reviews 4×5 transparencies, 4×6 prints. Buys one-time rights. Offers no additional payment for photos accepted with ms. Captions required.

Columns/Departments Surviving in 2000 (business articles offering tips to labs on how to make their businesses run better), 1,500-1,800 words; Business Side (getting more productivity out of your lab). **Buys 10 mss/year.** Query with published clips. **Pays $150-250.**

$ $ NEWS PHOTOGRAPHER

National Press Photographers Association, Inc., 6677 Whitemarsh Valley Walk, Austin TX 78746. E-mail: magazine@nppa.org. Website: www.nppa.org. **Contact:** Donald R. Winslow, editor. Published 12 times/year. *"News Photographer* magazine is dedicated to the advancement of still and television news photography. The magazine presents articles, interviews, profiles, history, new products, electronic imaging, and news related to the practice of photojournalism." Estab. 1946. Circ. 11,000. **Pays on acceptance.** Publishes ms an average of 4 months after acceptance. Byline given. Offers 100% kill fee. Buys one-time and archival electronic rights. Editorial lead time 2 months. Submit seasonal material 2 months in advance. Accepts queries by mail, e-mail, fax, phone. Accepts previously published material. Accepts simultaneous submissions. Responds in 1 month to queries. Sample copy for 9×12 SAE and 3 first-class stamps. Writer's guidelines free.

Nonfiction Historical/nostalgic, how-to, interview/profile, new product, opinion, personal experience, photo feature, technical. **Buys 10 mss/year.** Query. Length: 1,500 words. **Pays $300.** Pays expenses of writers on assignment.

Photos State availability with submission. Reviews high resolution, digital images only. Buys one-time rights. Negotiates payment individually. Captions, identification of subjects required.

Columns/Departments Query.

$ $ THE PHOTO REVIEW

140 E. Richardson Ave., Suite 301, Langhorne PA 19047. (215)891-0214. Fax: (215)891-9358. E-mail: info@photoreview.org. Website: www.photoreview.org. **Contact:** Stephen Perloff, editor-in-chief. **50% freelance written.** Quarterly magazine covering art photography and criticism. *"The Photo Review* publishes critical reviews of photography exhibitions and books, critical essays, and interviews. We do not publish how-to or technical articles." Estab. 1976. Circ. 2,000. Pays on publication. Publishes ms an average of 9-12 months after acceptance. Byline given. Buys first rights. Editorial lead time 3 months. Submit seasonal material 6 months in advance. Accepts queries by mail. Accepts simultaneous submissions. Responds in 2 months to queries; 3 months to mss. Sample copy for $7. Writer's guidelines for #10 SASE.

Nonfiction Interview/profile, photography essay, critical review. No how-to articles. **Buys 20 mss/year.** Send complete ms. Length: 2-20 typed pages. **Pays $10-250.**

Reprints Send tearsheet, photocopy or typed ms with rights for sale noted and information about when and where the material previously appeared. Payment varies.

Photos Send photos with submission. Reviews contact sheets, transparencies, prints. Buys all rights. Offers no additional payment for photos accepted with ms. Captions required.

SHUTTERBUG

Primedia, 1419 Chaffee Dr., Suite 1, Titusville FL 32780. Fax: (321)225-3149. E-mail: editorial@shutterbug.com. Website: www.shutterbug.com. Managing Editor: Bonnie Paulk. **Contact:** George Schaub, editor. **90% freelance written.** Monthly covering photography and digial imaging. "Written for the avid amateur, part-time, and full-time professional photographers. Covers equipment techniques, profiles, technology and news in both silver-halide and digital imaging." Estab. 1972. Circ. 90,000. Pays on publication. Byline given. Buys first North American serial, second serial (reprint), electronic rights. Editorial lead time 3 months. Submit seasonal material 6 months in advance. Accepts queries by mail. Responds in 1 month to queries; 1 month to mss. Sample copy not available.

Nonfiction Query with or without published clips. Length: 1,000-2,000 words. **Payment rate depends on published length, including photographs.**

Photos Send photos with submission. Reviews contact sheets, transparencies, CD-ROMs. Offers no additional payment for photos. Captions, model releases required.

REAL ESTATE

$ $ AREA DEVELOPMENT MAGAZINE

Sites and Facility Planning, Halcyon Business Publications, Inc., 400 Post Ave., Westbury NY 11590. (516)338-0900, ext. 211. Fax: (516)338-0100. E-mail: gerri@areadevelopment.com. Website: www.areadevelopment.c

om. **Contact:** Geraldine Gambale, editor. **80% freelance written.** Prefers to work with published/established writers. Bimonthly magazine covering corporate facility planning and site selection for industrial chief executives worldwide. Estab. 1965. Circ. 45,000. Pays on publication. Publishes ms an average of 2 months after acceptance. Byline given. Buys all rights. Accepts queries by mail, e-mail, fax. Responds in 3 months to queries. Sample copy for free. Writer's guidelines for #10 SASE.

Nonfiction Related areas of site selection and facility planning such as taxes, labor, government, energy, architecture, and finance. Historical/nostalgic (if it deals with corporate facility planning), how-to (experiences in site selection and all other aspects of corporate facility planning), interview/profile (corporate executives and industrial developers). **Buys 75 mss/year.** Query. Length: 1,500-2,000 words. **Pays 40¢/word.** Sometimes pays expenses of writers on assignment.

Photos State availability with submission. Reviews JPEGS of at least 300 dpi. Negotiates payment individually. Captions, identification of subjects required.

 ▪ The online version of this publication contains material not found in the print edition. Contact: Chris Chiappinelli, online editor.

$ $▧ CANADIAN PROPERTY MANAGEMENT

Mediaedge Communications Inc., 5255 Yonge St., Suite 1000, Toronto ON M2N 6P4 Canada. (416)512-8186. Fax: (416)512-8344. E-mail: barbc@mediaedge.ca. Website: www.mediaedge.ca. **Contact:** Barb Carss, editor. **10% freelance written.** Magazine published 8 times/year covering Canadian commercial, industrial, institutional (medical and educational), residential properties. *"Canadian Property Management* magazine is a trade journal supplying building owners and property managers with Canadian industry news, case law reviews, technical updates for building operations and events listings. Building and professional profile articles are regular features." Estab. 1985. Circ. 14,500. Pays on publication. Publishes ms an average of 3 months after acceptance. Byline given. Buys all rights. Editorial lead time 2 months. Submit seasonal material 2 months in advance. Accepts queries by mail, e-mail, fax, phone. Accepts simultaneous submissions. Responds in 3 weeks to queries; 2 months to mss. Sample copy for $5, subject to availability. Writer's guidelines free.

Nonfiction Interview/profile, technical. "No promotional articles (i.e., marketing a product or service geared to this industry)!" Query with published clips. Length: 700-1,200 words. **Pays 35¢/word.**

Photos State availability with submission. Reviews transparencies, 3×5 prints, digital (at least 300 dpi). Offers no additional payment for photos accepted with ms. Captions, identification of subjects, model releases required.

Tips "We do not accept promotional articles serving companies or their products. Freelance articles that are strong, information-based pieces that serve the interests and needs of property managers and building owners stand a better chance of being published. Proposals and inquiries with article ideas are appreciated the most. A good understanding of the real estate industry (management structure) is also helpful for the writer."

$ $ $ $COMMERCIAL INVESTMENT REAL ESTATE

CCIM, 430 N. Michigan Ave., Suite 800, Chicago IL 60611-4092. (312)321-4460. Fax: (312)321-4530. E-mail: magazine@ccim.com. Website: www.ciremagazine.com. **Contact:** Jennifer Norbut, editor. **10% freelance written.** Bimonthly magazine. *"CIRE* offers practical articles on current trends and business development ideas for commercial investment real estate practitioners." Estab. 1982. Circ. 17,000. **Pays on acceptance.** Publishes ms an average of 4 months after acceptance. Byline given. Buys all rights. Editorial lead time 4 months. Submit seasonal material 4 months in advance. Accepts queries by mail, e-mail, fax. Responds in 2 weeks to queries; 1 month to mss. Sample copy and writer's guidelines online.

 ○▪ Break in by sending résumé and feature-length clips, "including commercial real estate-related clips if available. We keep writers' materials on file for assigning articles."

Nonfiction How-to, technical, business strategies. **Buys 3-4 mss/year.** Query with published clips. Length: 2,000-3,500 words. **Pays $1,000-1,600.**

Photos May ask writers to have sources. Send images to editors.

Tips "Always query first with a detailed outline and published clips. Authors should have a background in writing on business or real estate subjects."

$ $THE COOPERATOR

The Co-op and Condo Monthly, Yale Robbins, Inc., 31 E. 28th St., 12th Floor, New York NY 10016. (212)683-5700. Fax: (212)545-0764. E-mail: editorial@cooperator.com. Website: www.cooperator.com. **70% freelance written.** Monthly tabloid covering real estate in the New York City metro area. *"The Cooperator* covers condominium and cooperative issues in New York and beyond. It is read by condo unit owners and co-op shareholders, real estate professionals, board members and managing agents, and other service professionals." Estab. 1980. Circ. 40,000. Pays on publication. Publishes ms an average of 3 months after acceptance. Byline given. Buys all rights, makes work-for-hire assignments. Submit seasonal material 3 months in advance. Accepts queries by mail, e-mail, fax. Responds in 1 month to queries. Sample copy and writer's guidelines free.

Nonfiction All articles related to co-op and condo ownership. Interview/profile, new product, personal experience. No submissions without queries. Query with published clips. Length: 1,500-2,000 words. **Pays $300.** Sometimes pays expenses of writers on assignment.

Photos State availability with submission. Reviews contact sheets, negatives, transparencies, prints, digital. Rights purchased vary. Negotiates payment individually. Captions, identification of subjects required.

Columns/Departments Profiles of co-op/condo-related businesses with something unique; Building Finance (investment and financing issues); Buying and Selling (market issues, etc.); Management/Board Relations and Interacting With Professionals (issues dealing with board members and the professionals that help run the building); Interior Design (architectural and interior/exterior design, lobby renovation, etc.); Building Maintenance (issues related to maintaining interior/exterior, facades, lobbies, elevators, etc.); Legal Issues Related to Co-Ops/Condos; Real Estate Trends, all 1,500 words. **Buys 50 mss/year.** Query with published clips. **Pays $300.**

Tips "You must have experience in business, legal, or financial. Must have published clips to send in with résumé and query."

$ $ FLORIDA REALTOR MAGAZINE

Florida Association of Realtors, 7025 Augusta National Dr., Orlando FL 32822-5017. (407)438-1400. Fax: (407)438-1411. E-mail: flrealtor@far.org. Website: floridarealtormagazine.com. Associate Editor: Leslie Stone. **Contact:** Doug Damerst, editor-in-chief. **30% freelance written.** Journal published 11 times/year covering Florida real estate and the profession. "As the official publication of the Florida Association of Realtors, we provide helpful articles for our 120,000 members. We try to stay up on the trends and issues that affect business in Florida's real estate market." Estab. 1925. Circ. 120,000. Pays on publication. Publishes ms an average of 2 months after acceptance. Byline given. Editorial lead time 3 months. Accepts queries by mail, e-mail, fax. Sample copy online.

Nonfiction Book excerpts, how-to, inspirational, interview/profile, new product—all with real estate angle. Florida-specific is good. "No fiction, poetry." **Buys varying number of mss/year.** Query with published clips. Length: 800-1,500 words. **Pays $300-700.** Sometimes pays expenses of writers on assignment.

Photos State availability with submission. Buys one-time rights. Negotiates payment individually. Captions, identification of subjects, model releases required.

Columns/Departments Written in-house: You Inc., 900 words, Technology & You, 1,000 words; Realtor Advantage, 1,000 words. **Buys varying number of mss/year. Payment varies.**

Fillers Short humor. **Buys varying number/year.**

Tips "Build a solid reputation for specializing in real estate writing in state/national publications. Query with specific article ideas."

JOURNAL OF PROPERTY MANAGEMENT

Institute of Real Estate Management, 430 N. Michigan Ave., 7th Floor, Chicago IL 60611. (312)329-6058. Fax: (312)410-7958. E-mail: adruckman@irem.org. Website: www.irem.org. **Contact:** Amanda Druckman, managing editor. **30% freelance written.** Bimonthly magazine covering real estate management. "The *Journal* has a feature/information slant designed to educate readers in the application of new techniques and to keep them abreast of current industry trends." Circ. 20,000. **Pays on acceptance.** Publishes ms an average of 3 months after acceptance. Byline given. Buys all rights. Accepts queries by mail, e-mail, fax. Responds in 6 weeks to queries; 1 month to mss. Sample copy for free. Writer's guidelines online.

Nonfiction Demographic shifts in business employment and buying patterns, marketing. How-to, interview/profile, technical (building systems/computers). "No non-real estate subjects, personality, or company humor." **Buys 8-12 mss/year.** Query with published clips. Length: 750-1,500 words. Sometimes pays expenses of writers on assignment.

Reprints Send tearsheet, photocopy or typed ms. Pays 35% of amount paid for an original article.

Photos State availability with submission. Reviews contact sheets. Buys one-time rights. May offer additional payment for photos accepted with ms. Identification of subjects, model releases required.

Columns/Departments Buys 6-8 mss/year. Query.

$ $ PROPERTIES MAGAZINE

Properties Magazine, Inc., P.O. Box 112127, Cleveland OH 44111. (216)251-0035. Fax: (216)251-0064. E-mail: kkrych@propertiesmag.com. Editor: Kenneth C. Krych. **25% freelance written.** Monthly magazine covering real estate, residential, commerical construction. "*Properties Magazine* is published for executives in the real estate, building, banking, design, architectural, property management, tax, and law community—busy people who need the facts presented in an interesting and informative format." Estab. 1946. Circ. over 10,000. Pays on publication. Publishes ms an average of 2 months after acceptance. Byline given. Buys first rights. Editorial lead time 2 months. Submit seasonal material 2 months in advance. Accepts queries by mail, fax. Responds in 3 weeks to queries. Sample copy for $3.95.

Nonfiction General interest, how-to, humor, new product. Special issues: Environmental issues (September); Security/Fire Protection (October); Tax Issues (November); Computers In Real Estate (December). **Buys 30 mss/year.** Send complete ms. Length: 500-2,000 words. **Pays 50¢/column line.** Sometimes pays expenses of writers on assignment.

Photos Send photos with submission. Reviews prints. Buys one-time rights. Offers no additional payment for photos accepted with ms. Negotiates payment individually. Captions required.

Columns/Departments Buys 25 mss/year. Query or send complete ms. **Pays 50¢/column line.**

$ $⊠ REM

The Real Estate Magazine, House Publications, 115 Thorncliff Park Dr., Toronto ON M4C 3E4 Canada. (416)425-3504. Fax: (416)406-0882. E-mail: jim@remonline.com. Website: www.remonline.com. **Contact:** Jim Adair, editor. **35% freelance written.** Monthly trade journal covering real estate. "*REM* provides Canadian real estate agents and brokers with news and opinions they can't get anywhere else. It is an independent publication and not affiliated with any real estate board, association, or company." Estab. 1989. Circ. 50,000. **Pays on acceptance.** Publishes ms an average of 2 months after acceptance. Offers 25% kill fee. Buys first Canadian serial rights. Editorial lead time 3 months. Submit seasonal material 3 months in advance. Accepts queries by mail, e-mail, fax. Accepts previously published material. Accepts simultaneous submissions. Sample copy for free.

Nonfiction Book excerpts, exposé, inspirational, interview/profile, new product, personal experience. No articles geared to consumers about market conditions or how to choose a realtor. Must have Canadian content. **Buys 60 mss/year.** Query. Length: 500-1,500 words. **Pays $200-400.**

Photos Send photos with submission. Reviews transparencies, prints, GIF/JPEG files. Buys one-time rights. Offers $25/photo. Captions, identification of subjects required.

Tips "Stories must be of interest or practical use for Canadian realtors. Check out our website to see the types of stories we require."

RESOURCES & WASTE REDUCTION

$ $COMPOSTING NEWS

The Latest News in Composting and Scrap Wood Management, McEntee Media Corp., 9815 Hazelwood Ave., Cleveland OH 44149. (440)238-6603. Fax: (440)238-6712. E-mail: cn@recycle.cc. **Contact:** Ken McEntee, editor. **5% freelance written.** Monthly newsletter. "We are interested in any news impacting the composting industry including new laws, regulations, new facilities/programs, end-uses, research, etc." Estab. 1992. Circ. 1,000. Pays on publication. Publishes ms an average of 1 month after acceptance. Buys first, all rights. Editorial lead time 1 month. Submit seasonal material 1 month in advance. Accepts queries by mail, e-mail, fax, phone. Accepts previously published material. Accepts simultaneous submissions. Responds in 2 months to queries. Sample copy for 9×12 SAE and 55¢ postage. Writer's guidelines for #10 SASE.

Nonfiction Book excerpts, essays, general interest, how-to, interview/profile, new product, opinion, personal experience, photo feature, technical, new business, legislation, regulation, business expansion. **Buys 0-5 mss/ year.** Query with published clips. Length: 100-5,000 words. **Pays $10-500.** Pays writers with contributor copies or other premiums by prior agreement.

Columns/Departments Query with published clips. **Pays $10-500.**

◼ The online magazine carries original content not found in the print edition. Contact: Ken McEntee.

Tips "We appreciate leads on local news regarding composting, i.e., new facilities or business, new laws and regulations, unique programs, situations that impact supply and demand for composting. International developments are also of interest."

$ $ $EROSION CONTROL

The Journal for Erosion and Sediment Control Professionals, Forester Communications, Inc., 2946 De La Vina St., Santa Barbara CA 93105. (805)682-1300. Fax: (805)682-0200. E-mail: eceditor@forester.net. Website: www.erosioncontrol.com. **Contact:** Janice Kaspersen, editor. **60% freelance written.** Magazine published 7 times/ year covering all aspects of erosion prevention and sediment control. "*Erosion Control* is a practical, hands-on, 'how-to' professional journal. Our readers are civil engineers, landscape architects, builders, developers, public works officials, road and highway construction officials and engineers, soils specialists, farmers, landscape contractors, and others involved with any activity that disturbs significant areas of surface vegetation." Estab. 1994. Circ. 20,000. Pays 1 month after acceptance. Publishes ms an average of 3 months after acceptance. Byline given. Buys all rights. Editorial lead time 4 months. Submit seasonal material 4 months in advance.

Accepts queries by mail, e-mail, fax, phone. Responds in 3 weeks to queries. Sample copy and writer's guidelines free.

Nonfiction Photo feature, technical. **Buys 15 mss/year.** Query with published clips. Length: 3,000-4,000 words. **Pays $700-850.** Sometimes pays expenses of writers on assignment.

Photos Send photos with submission. Reviews transparencies, prints. Buys all rights. Offers no additional payment for photos accepted with ms. Captions, identification of subjects, model releases required.

Tips "Writers should have a good grasp of technology involved and good writing and communication skills. Most of our freelance articles include extensive interviews with engineers, contractors, developers, or project owners, and we often provide contact names for articles we assign."

$ $ MSW MANAGEMENT

The Journal for Municipal Solid Waste Professionals, Forester Communications, Inc., P.O. Box 3100, Santa Barbara CA 93130. (805)682-1300. Fax: (805)682-0200. E-mail: editor@forester.net. Website: www.mswmanagement.net. **Contact:** John Trotti, editor. **70% freelance written.** Bimonthly magazine. "*MSW Management* is written for public sector solid waste professionals—the people working for the local counties, cities, towns, boroughs, and provinces. They run the landfills, recycling programs, composting, incineration. They are responsible for all aspects of garbage collection and disposal; buying and maintaining the associated equipment; and designing, engineering, and building the waste processing facilities, transfer stations, and landfills." Estab. 1991. Circ. 25,000. Pays on publication. Byline given. Buys all rights. Editorial lead time 4 months. Submit seasonal material 4 months in advance. Accepts queries by mail, e-mail, fax, phone. Accepts simultaneous submissions. Responds in 6 weeks to queries; 2 months to mss. Sample copy and writer's guidelines free. Writer's guidelines online.

Nonfiction Photo feature, technical. "No rudimentary, basic articles written for the average person on the street. Our readers are experienced professionals with years of practical, in-the-field experience. Any material submitted that we judge as too fundamental will be rejected." **Buys 15 mss/year.** Query. Length: 3,000-4,000 words. **Pays $350-750.** Sometimes pays expenses of writers on assignment.

Photos Send photos with submission. Reviews transparencies, prints. Buys all rights. Offers no additional payment for photos accepted with ms. Captions, identification of subjects, model releases required.

Tips "We're a small company, easy to reach. We're open to any and all ideas as to possible editorial topics. We endeavor to provide the reader with usable material, and present it in full color with graphic embellishment whenever possible. Dry, highly technical material is edited to make it more palatable and concise. Most of our feature articles come from freelancers. Interviews and quotes should be from public sector solid waste managers and engineers—not PR people, not manufacturers. Strive to write material that is 'over the heads' of our readers. If anything, attempt to make them 'reach.' Anything submitted that is too basic, elementary, fundamental, rudimentary, etc., cannot be accepted for publication."

$ $ $ STORMWATER

The Journal for Surface Water Quality Professionals, Forester Communications, Inc., 2946 De La Vina St., Santa Barbara CA 93105. (805)682-1300. Fax: (805)682-0200. E-mail: sweditor@forester.net. Website: www.stormh2 o.com. **Contact:** Janice Kaspersen, editor. **10% freelance written.** "*Stormwater* is a practical business journal for professionals involved with surface water quality issues, protection, projects, and programs. Our readers are municipal employees, regulators, engineers, and consultants concerned with stormwater management." Estab. 2000. Circ. 20,000. Publishes ms an average of 3 months after acceptance. Byline given. Editorial lead time 4 months. Submit seasonal material 4 months in advance. Accepts queries by mail, e-mail. Responds in 3 weeks to queries. Writer's guidelines free.

Nonfiction Technical. **Buys 8-10 mss/year.** Query with published clips. Length: 3,000-4,000 words. **Pays $700-850.** Sometimes pays expenses of writers on assignment.

Photos Send photos with submission. Buys all rights. Offers no additional payment for photos accepted with ms. Captions, identification of subjects, model releases required.

Tips "Writers should have a good grasp of the technology and regulations involved in stormwater management and good interviewing skills. Our freelance articles include extensive interviews with engineers, stormwater managers, and project owners, and we often provide contact names for articles we assign. See past editorial content online."

$ $ WATER WELL JOURNAL

National Ground Water Association, 601 Dempsey Rd., Westerville OH 43081. Fax: (614)898-7786. E-mail: tplumley@ngwa.org. Website: www.ngwa.org. **Contact:** Thad Plumley, director of publications. **15% freelance written.** Monthly magazine covering the ground water industry; well drilling. "Each month the *Water Well Journal* covers the topics of drilling, rigs and heavy equipment, pumping systems, water quality, business management, water supply, on-site waste water treatment, and diversification opportunities, including geoexchange installations, environmental remediation, irrigation, dewatering, and foundation installation. It also offers updates on regulatory issues that impact the ground water industry." Estab. 1948. Circ. 26,500. Pays on publication. Publishes ms an average of 3 months after acceptance. Byline given. Buys all rights. Editorial lead time 2 months. Submit seasonal material 3 months in advance. Accepts queries by mail, e-mail, fax, phone. Responds in 2 weeks to queries; 1 month to mss. Writer's guidelines free.

Nonfiction Essays (sometimes), historical/nostalgic (sometimes), how-to (recent examples include how to chlorinate a well; how to buy a used rig; how to do bill collections), interview/profile, new product, personal experience, photo feature, technical, business management. No company profiles or extended product releases. **Buys up to 20 mss/year.** Query with published clips. Length: 1,000-4,000 words. **Pays $100-400.**

Photos State availability with submission. Offers $50-250/photo. Captions, identification of subjects required.

Tips "Some previous experience or knowledge in groundwater/drilling/construction industry helpful. Published clips are a must."

SELLING & MERCHANDISING

$$ BALLOONS AND PARTIES MAGAZINE

Partilife Publications, 65 Sussex St., Hackensack NJ 07601. (201)441-4224. Fax: (201)342-8118. E-mail: mark@balloonsandparties.com. Website: www.balloonsandparties.com. **Contact:** Mark Zettler, publisher. **10% freelance written.** International trade journal for professional party decorators and gift delivery businesses published 5 times/year. Estab. 1986. Circ. 7,000. Pays on publication. Publishes ms an average of 3 months after acceptance. Byline given. Buys all rights. Submit seasonal material 6 months in advance. Accepts queries by mail, e-mail, fax, phone. Responds in 6 weeks to queries. Sample copy for 9×12 SAE.

Nonfiction Essays, how-to, interview/profile, new product, personal experience, photo feature, technical, craft. **Buys 12 mss/year.** Query with or without published clips or send complete ms. Length: 500-1,500 words. **Pays $100-300 for assigned articles; $50-200 for unsolicited articles.** Sometimes pays expenses of writers on assignment.

Reprints Send ms with rights for sale noted and information about when and where the material previously appeared Length: up to 2,500 words. Pays 10¢/word.

Photos Send photos with submission. Reviews 2×2 transparencies, 3×5 prints. Buys all rights. Captions, identification of subjects, model releases required.

Columns/Departments Problem Solver (small business issues); Recipes That Cook (centerpiece ideas with detailed how-to), 400-1,000 words. Send complete ms with photos.

Tips "Show unusual, lavish, and outstanding examples of balloon sculpture, design and decorating, and other craft projects. Offer specific how-to information. Be positive and motivational in style."

$$$$ CONSUMER GOODS TECHNOLOGY

Edgell Communications, 4 Middlebury Blvd., Randolph NJ 07869. (973)252-0100. Fax: (973)252-9020. E-mail: tclark@edgellmail.com. Website: www.consumergoods.com. **Contact:** Tim Clark, managing editor. **40% freelance written.** Monthly tabloid benchmarking business technology performance. Estab. 1987. Circ. 25,000. Pays on publication. Publishes ms an average of 2 months after acceptance. Byline given. Buys first North American serial, second serial (reprint), electronic, all rights. Editorial lead time 3 months. Accepts queries by e-mail. Sample copy online. Writer's guidelines by e-mail.

Nonfiction "We create several supplements annually, often using freelance." Essays, exposé, interview/profile. **Buys 60 mss/year.** Query with published clips. Length: 700-1,900 words. **Pays $600-1,200.** Sometimes pays expenses of writers on assignment.

Photos Buys all rights. Negotiates payment individually. Identification of subjects, model releases required.

Columns/Departments Columns 400-750 words—featured columnists. **Buys 4 mss/year.** Query with published clips. **Pays 75¢-$1/word.**

Tips "All stories in *Consumer Goods Technology* are told through the voice of the consumer goods executive. We only quote VP-level or C-level CG executives. No vendor quotes. We're always on the lookout for freelance talent. We look in particular for writers with an in-depth understanding of the business issues faced by consumer goods firms and the technologies that are used by the industry to address those issues successfully. 'Bits and bytes' tech writing is not sought; our focus is on benchmarketing the business technology performance of CG firms, CG executives, CG vendors, and CG vendor products. Our target reader is tech-savvy, CG C-level decision maker. We write to, and about, our target reader."

$$ CONVENIENCE STORE DECISIONS

Penton Media, Inc., Two Greenwood Square, #410, Bensalem PA 19020. (215)245-4555. Fax: (215)245-4060. E-mail: bdonahue@penton.com. Website: www.c-storedecisions.com. Editorial Director: Jay Gordon. **Contact:** Bill Donahue, editor. **15-20% freelance written.** Monthly magazine covering convenience retail/petroleum marketing. "*CSD* is received by top-level executives in the convenience retail and petroleum marketing industry. Writers should have knowledge of the industry and the subjects it encompasses." Estab. 1990. Circ. 42,000. Pays on publication. Byline given. Buys all rights, makes work-for-hire assignments. Editorial lead time 2-4 months. Submit seasonal material 3 months in advance. Accepts queries by mail, e-mail, fax. Accepts simultaneous submissions. Responds in 3 weeks to queries. Sample copy and writer's guidelines free.

> O→ Break in with a "demonstrated knowledge of finance and business, with special emphasis on retail. Keen powers of observation and attention to detail are also prized."

Nonfiction Interview/profile (retailers), photo feature, technical. No self-serving, vendor-based stories. **Buys 12-15 mss/year.** Query with published clips. Length: 400-2,000 words. **Pays $200-600 for assigned articles.** Sometimes pays expenses of writers on assignment.

Photos State availability with submission. Buys all rights. Negotiates payment individually. Identification of subjects required.

Tips Offer experience. "We get queries from freelancers daily. We are looking for writers with industry experience. We need real-life, retailer-based work. Bring us a story."

$ $ COUNTRY SAMPLER'S COUNTRY BUSINESS

The Magazine for Retailers of Country Gifts and Accessories, Emmis Publishing LP, 707 Kautz Rd., St. Charles IL 60174. (630)377-8000. Fax: (630)377-8194. E-mail: cbiz@sampler.emmis.com. Website: www.country-business.com. **Contact:** Susan Wagner, editor. **50% freelance written.** Magazine published 7 times/year covering independent retail, gift and home decor. *Country Business* is a trade publication for independent retailers of gifts and home accents. Estab. 1993. Circ. 32,000. Pays 1 month after acceptance of final ms. Publishes ms an average of 4-6 months after acceptance. Byline given. Offers $50 kill fee. Buys all rights. Editorial lead time 4-6 months. Submit seasonal material 8-10 months in advance. Accepts queries by mail, e-mail, fax. Accepts previously published material. Accepts simultaneous submissions. Usually responds in 4-6 weeks (only if accepted) to queries. Sample articles are available on website. Writer's guidelines by e-mail.

> O→ Articles cover new products and trends in the gift industry, as well as topics related to running retail and small businesses.

Nonfiction How-to (pertaining to retail), interview/profile, new product, finance, legal, marketing, small business. No fiction, poetry, fillers, photos, artwork, or profiles of businesses, unless queried and first assigned. **Buys 20 mss/year.** Query with published clips or send complete ms. Length: 1,000-2,500 words. **Pays $275-500 for assigned articles; $200-350 for unsolicited articles.** Sometimes pays expenses of writers on assignment.

Columns/Departments Display & Design (store design and product display), 1,500 words; Retailer Profile (profile of retailer—assigned only), 1,800 words; Vendor Profile (profile of manufacturer—assigned only), 1,200 words; Technology (Internet, computer-related articles as applies to small retailers), 1,500 words; Marketing (marketing ideas and advice as applies to small retailers), 1,500 words; Finance (financial tips and advice as applies to small retailers), 1,500 words; Legal (legal tips and advice as applies to small retailers), 1,500 words; Employees (tips and advice on hiring, firing, and working with employees as applies to small retailers), 1,500 words. **Buys 15 mss/year.** Query with published clips or send complete ms. **Pays $250-350.**

$ $ GIFTWARE NEWS

Talcott Corp., 20 W. Kinzie, 12th Floor, Chicago IL 60610. (312)849-2220. Fax: (312)849-2174. **Contact:** John Saxtan, editor-in-chief. **20% freelance written.** Monthly magazine covering gifts, collectibles, and tabletops for giftware retailers. Estab. 1976. Circ. 35,000. Pays on publication. Publishes ms an average of 2 months after acceptance. Byline given. Buys all rights. Submit seasonal material 6 months in advance. Responds in 2 months to mss. Sample copy for $8.

Nonfiction How-to (sell, display), new product. **Buys 20 mss/year.** Query with published clips or send complete ms. Length: 1,500-2,000 words. **Pays $400-500 for assigned articles; $200-300 for unsolicited articles.**

Photos Send photos with submission. Reviews 4×5 transparencies, 5×7 prints, electronic images. Offers no additional payment for photos accepted with ms. Identification of subjects required.

Columns/Departments Buys 10 mss/year. Send complete ms. **Pays $100-250.**

Tips "We are not looking so much for general journalists but rather experts in particular fields who can also write."

$ $ NEW AGE RETAILER

1300 N. State St., #105, Bellingham WA 98225. (800)463-9243. Fax: (360)676-0932. E-mail: ray@newageretailer.com. Website: www.newageretailer.com. **Contact:** Ray Hemachandra, editor-in-chief. **60% freelance written.** Bimonthly magazine for retailers of spiritual and New Age books, music, and giftware. "The goal of the articles in *New Age Retailer* is usefulness—we strive to give store owners and managers practical, in-depth information they can begin using immediately. We have 3 categories of articles: retail business methods that give solid information about the various aspects of running an independent store; inventory articles that discuss a particular New Age subject or trend; and education articles that help storeowners and managers gain knowledge and stay current in New Age subjects." Estab. 1987. Circ. 10,000. Pays on publication. Publishes ms an average of 4 months after acceptance. Byline given. Offers 10% kill fee. Buys first North American serial, second serial (reprint), simultaneous, electronic rights. Editorial lead time 4 months. Submit seasonal material 4 months in advance. Accepts queries by mail, e-mail, fax, phone. Accepts simultaneous submissions. Responds in 1 month to queries; 2 months to mss. Sample copy for $5. Writer's guidelines online.

Nonfiction Book excerpts, how-to, interview/profile, new product, opinion, personal experience, technical, business principles, spiritual. No self-promotion for writer's company or product. Writer must understand independent retailing or New Age subjects. **Buys approximately 25 mss/year.** Query with published clips. Length: 2,500-3,500 words. **Pays $150-350 for assigned articles; $100-300 for unsolicited articles.**

Photos State availability of or send photos with submission. Reviews 2×3 minimum size prints, digital images at 300 dpi. Buys one-time rights. Negotiates payment individually. Captions required.

Tips "Describe your expertise in independent retailing or the New Age market and independent retailing. Have an idea for an article ready to pitch. Promise only what you can deliver."

$ $ NICHE

The Magazine For Craft Gallery Retailers, The Rosen Group, 3000 Chestnut Ave., Suite 304, Baltimore MD 21211. (410)889-3093. Fax: (410)243-7089. E-mail: hoped@rosengrp.com. **Contact:** Hope Daniels, editor-in-chief. **80% freelance written.** Quarterly trade magazine for the progressive craft gallery retailer. Each issue includes retail gallery profiles, store design trends, management techniques, financial information, and merchandising strategies for small business owners, as well as articles about craft artists and craft mediums. Estab. 1988. Circ. 25,000. Pays on publication. Publishes ms an average of 9 months after acceptance. Byline given. Buys first North American serial rights. Editorial lead time 9 months. Submit seasonal material 1 year in advance. Accepts queries by mail, e-mail, fax. Responds in 6-8 weeks to queries; 3 months to mss. Sample copy for $3.

Nonfiction *Niche* is looking for in-depth articles on store security, innovative merchandising/display, design trends, or marketing and promotion. Stories of interest to independent retailers, such as gallery owners, may be submitted. Interview/profile, photo feature, articles targeted to independent retailers and small business owners. **Buys 20-28 mss/year.** Query with published clips. **Pays $300-700.** Sometimes pays expenses of writers on assignment.

Photos Send photos with submission. Reviews transparencies, slides, e-images. Negotiates payment individually. Captions required.

Columns/Departments Retail Details (short items at the front of the book, general retail information); Artist Profiles (biographies of American Craft Artists); Retail Resources (including book/video/seminar reviews and educational opportunities pertaining to retailers). Query with published clips. **Pays $25-100.**

$ O&A MARKETING NEWS

KAL Publications, Inc., 559 S. Harbor Blvd., Suite A, Anaheim CA 92805. (714)563-9300. Fax: (714)563-9310. E-mail: kathy@kalpub.com. Website: www.kalpub.com. **Contact:** Kathy Laderman, editor-in-chief. **3% freelance written.** Bimonthly tabloid. "*O&A Marketing News* is editorially directed to people engaged in the distribution, merchandising, installation, and servicing of gasoline, oil, TBA, quick lube, carwash, convenience store, alternative fuel, and automotive aftermarket products in the 13 Western states." Estab. 1966. Circ. 7,500. Pays on publication. Publishes ms an average of 2 months after acceptance. Byline sometimes given. Buys first, electronic rights. Editorial lead time 1 month. Submit seasonal material 1 month in advance. Accepts queries by mail, e-mail, fax. Accepts simultaneous submissions. Responds in 2 months. Sample copy for 9×13 SAE and 10 first-class stamps. Writer's guidelines not available.

Nonfiction Interview/profile, photo feature, industry news. Nothing that doesn't pertain to the petroleum marketing industry in the 13 Western states. **Buys 35 mss/year.** Send complete ms. Length: 100-500 words. **Pays $1.25/column inch.**

Photos State availability of or send photos with submission. Reviews contact sheets, 4×6 prints. Buys electronic rights. Offers $5/photo. Captions, identification of subjects required.

Columns/Departments Oregon News (petroleum marketing news in state of Oregon). **Buys 7 mss/year.** Send complete ms. **Pays $1.25/column inch.**

Fillers Gags to be illustrated by cartoonist, short humor. **Buys 7/year.** Length: 1-200 words. **Pays per column inch.**

Tips "Seeking Western industry news pertaining to the petroleum marketing industry. It can be something simple—like a new gas station or quick lube opening. News from 'outlying' states such as Montana, Idaho, Wyoming, New Mexico, and Hawaii is always needed—but any timely, topical news-oriented stories will also be considered."

$ $ $ $OPERATIONS & FULFILLMENT

Primedia, Inc., 11 Riverbend Dr. S., P.O. Box 4949, Stamford CT 06907-2524. (203)358-4106. E-mail: barnn@pri mediabusiness.com. Website: www.opsandfulfillment.com. **Contact:** Barbara Arnn, managing editor. **25% freelance written.** Monthly magazine covering catalog/direct mail operations. *"Operations & Fulfillment (O&F)* is a monthly publication that offers practical solutions for catalog online, and direct response operations management. The magazine covers such critical areas as material handling, bar coding, facility planning, transportation, call centers, warehouse management, information systems, online fulfillment and human resources." Estab. 1993. Circ. 17,600. Pays on publication. Publishes ms an average of 2 months after acceptance. Buys first North American serial rights. Editorial lead time 2 months. Accepts queries by mail, e-mail, phone. Responds in 1 week to queries. Sample copy and writer's guidelines free.

Nonfiction Book excerpts, how-to, interview/profile, new product, technical. **Buys 4-6 mss/year.** Query with published clips. Length: 2,500-3,000 words. **Pays $1,000-1,800.**

Photos "In addition to the main article, you must include at least one sidebar of about 400 words that contains a detailed example or case study of how a direct-to-customer catalog company implements or benefits from the process you're writing about; a check list or set of practical guidelines (i.e., "Twelve Ways to Ship Smarter") that describe how to implement what you suggest in the article; supporting materials such as flow charts, graphs, diagrams, illustrations and photographs (these must be clearly labeled and footnoted); and an author biography of no more than 75 words." Send photos with submission. Captions, identification of subjects required.

Tips "Writers need some knowledge of the direct-to-customer industry. They should be able to deal clearly with highly technical material and provide attention to detail and painstaking research."

PARTY & PAPER RETAILER

P.O. Box 128, Sparta MI 49345. (616)887-9008. Fax: (616)887-2666. Website: www.partypaper.com. **90% freelance written.** Monthly magazine covering "every aspect of how to do business better for owners of party and fine stationery shops. Tips and how-tos on display, marketing, success stories, merchandising, operating costs, e-commerce, retail technology, etc." Estab. 1986. Circ. 20,000. Pays on publication. Offers 15% kill fee. Buys first North American serial rights. Editorial lead time 6 months. Submit seasonal material 6 months in advance. Accepts queries by mail, e-mail, fax. Responds in 2 months to queries. Sample copy for $6.

    O━ Especially interested in news items on party retail industry for our Press Pages. Also, new column on Internet retailing ("Cyberlink") which covers all Web-related topics.

Nonfiction Book excerpts, how-to (retailing related), new product. No articles written in first person. **Buys 100 mss/year.** Query with published clips. Length: 800-1,800 words. Pays phone expenses only of writers on assignment.

Reprints Send tearsheet or photocopy of article and information about when and where the article previously appeared.

Photos State availability with submission. Reviews transparencies. Buys one-time rights. Negotiates payment individually. Captions, identification of subjects required.

Columns/Departments Shop Talk (successful party/stationery store profile), 1,800 words; Storekeeping (selling, employees, market, running store), 800 words; Cash Flow (anything finance related), 800 words. **Buys 30 mss/year.** Query with published clips. **Payment varies.**

$ $TRAVEL GOODS SHOWCASE

The source for luggage, business cases, and accessories, Travel Goods Association, 5 Vaughn Dr., Suite 105, Princeton NJ 08540. (609)720-1200. Fax: (609)720-0620. E-mail: john@travel-goods.org. Website: www.travel-goods.org. Editor and Publisher: Michele M. Pittenger. **Contact:** John Misiano, senior editor. **5-10% freelance written.** Magazine published 5 times/year. covering travel goods, accessories, trends, and new products. *"Travel Goods Showcase* contains articles for retailers, dealers, manufacturers, and suppliers about luggage, business cases, personal leather goods, handbags, and accessories. Special articles report on trends in fashion, promotions, selling and marketing techniques, industry statistics, and other educational and promotional improvements and advancements." Estab. 1975. Circ. 11,000. **Pays on acceptance.** Publishes ms an average of 2 months after acceptance. Byline given. Offers $50 kill fee. Editorial lead time 3 months. Submit seasonal material 2 months in advance. Accepts queries by mail, e-mail. Responds in 2 weeks to queries; 1 month to mss. Sample copy and writer's guidelines free.

Nonfiction Interview/profile, new product, technical, travel, retailer profiles with photos. "No manufacturer profiles." **Buys 3 mss/year.** Query with published clips. Length: 1,200-1,600 words. **Pays $200-400.**

$ $ $VERTICAL SYSTEMS RESELLER

The news source for channel management, Edgell Communications, Inc., 4 Middlebury Blvd., Suite 1, Randolph NJ 07869. (973)252-0100. Fax: (973)252-9020. E-mail: dbreeman@edgellmail.com. Website: www.verticalsyste msreseller.com. Publisher: Michael Kachmar. **Contact:** Daniel Breeman, managing editor. **60% freelance writ-**

ten. Monthly journal covering channel strategies that build business. Estab. 1992. Circ. 30,000. **Pays on acceptance.** Publishes ms an average of 2 months after acceptance. Byline given. Editorial lead time 3 months. Accepts queries by mail, e-mail, fax. Accepts simultaneous submissions. Responds in 2 weeks to queries; 2 months to mss. Sample copy online.

Nonfiction Interview/profile, opinion, technical, technology/channel issues. **Buys 36 mss/year.** Query with published clips. Length: 1,000-1,700 words. **Pays $200-800 for assigned articles.** Sometimes pays expenses of writers on assignment.

Photos Send photos with submission. Offers no additional payment for photos accepted with ms. Identification of subjects, model releases required.

SPORT TRADE

$ $ARROWTRADE MAGAZINE

A Magazine for Retailers, Distributors & Manufacturers of Bowhunting Equipment, Arrow Trade Publishing Corp., 3479 409th Ave. NW, Braham MN 55006. (320)396-3473. Fax: (320)396-3206. E-mail: atrade@ecenet.com. **Contact:** Tim Dehn, editor and publisher. **40% freelance written.** Bimonthly magazine covering the archery industry. "Our readers are interested in articles that help them operate their business better. They are primarily owners or managers of sporting goods stores and archery pro shops." Estab. 1996. Circ. 11,000. **Pays on acceptance.** Publishes ms an average of 2 months after acceptance. Byline given. Buys first North American serial rights. Editorial lead time 2 months. Accepts queries by mail, e-mail, fax. Responds in 2 weeks. Sample copy for 9×12 SAE and 10 first-class stamps. Writer's guidelines not available.

> O—¬ *ArrowTrade Magazine* needs queries from veterans interested in writing for our industry audience. Our readers are primarily retailers of bowhunting equipment. "Find an unusual business combination, like someone selling archery plus cowboy boots, motorcycles, taxidermy—and submit it (1,100-1,400 words) for 'Archery Plus.'"

Nonfiction Interview/profile, new product. "Generic business articles won't work for our highly specialized audience." **Buys 24 mss/year.** Query with published clips. Length: 1,800-3,800 words. **Pays $350-550.**

Photos Send photos with submission. Reviews contact sheets, negatives, 35mm transparencies, 4×6 prints, digital photos on CD or ZIP disk. Offers no additional payment for photos accepted with ms. Captions required.

Columns/Departments Dealer Workbench (repair and tuning bows), 1,600 words; Bow Report (tests and evaluations of current models), 2,400 words; Archery Plus (short profiles of retailers who combine archery with other product lines.). **Buys 12 mss/year.** Query with published clips. **Pays $250-375.**

Tips "Our readers are hungry for articles that help them decide what to stock and how to do a better job selling or servicing it. Articles needed typically fall into one of these categories: business profiles on outstanding retailers, manufacturers or distributors; equipment articles that cover categories of gear, citing trends in the market and detailing why products have been designed a certain way and what type of use they're best suited for; basic business articles that help dealers do a better job of promoting their business, managing their inventory, training their staff, etc. Good interviewing skills are a must, as especially in the equipment articles we like to see a minimum of 6 sources."

$ $BOATING INDUSTRY INTERNATIONAL

The Management Magazine for the Recreational Marine Industry, Ehlert Publishing Group, 6420 Sycamore Lane, Suite 100, Maple Grove MN 55369. (763)383-4400. Fax: (763)383-4499. E-mail: lwalz@ehlertpublishing.com. Website: www.boating-industry.com. **Contact:** Liz Walz, senior editor. **10-20% freelance written.** Bimonthly magazine covering recreational marine industry management. "We write for those in the industry—not the consumer. Our subject is the business of boating. All of our articles must be analytical and predictive, telling our readers where the industry is going, rather than where it's been." Estab. 1929. Circ. 23,000. **Pays on acceptance.** Publishes ms an average of 2 months after acceptance. Byline given. Offers 50% kill fee. Buys first, electronic rights. Editorial lead time 2 months. Submit seasonal material 2 months in advance. Accepts queries by mail, e-mail, fax. Responds in 1 month to queries. Sample copy online. Writer's guidelines free.

> O—¬ "We actively solicit items for our electronic news service. See the News Flash section of our website. This is an excellent way to break in, especially for writers based outside the US."

Nonfiction Technical, business. **Buys 30 mss/year.** Query with published clips. Length: 250-2,500 words. **Pays $25-250.** Sometimes pays expenses of writers on assignment.

Photos State availability with submission. Reviews 2×2 transparencies, 4×6 prints. Buys one-time rights. Negotiates payment individually. Captions, identification of subjects required.

$ $FITNESS MANAGEMENT

Issues and Solutions in Fitness Services, Leisure Publications, Inc., 4160 Wilshire Blvd., Los Angeles CA 90010. (323)964-4800. Fax: (323)964-4835. E-mail: edit@fitnessmanagement.com. Website: www.fitnessmanagement.

com. Publisher: Chris Ballard. **Contact:** Ronale Tucker Rhodes, editor. **50% freelance written.** Monthly magazine. ''Readers are owners, managers, and program directors of physical fitness facilities. *FM* helps them run their enterprises safely, efficiently, and profitably. Ethical and professional positions in health, nutrition, sports medicine, management, etc., are consistent with those of established national bodies.'' Estab. 1985. Circ. 26,000. Pays on publication. Publishes ms an average of 5 months after acceptance. Byline given. Offers 50% kill fee. Buys all rights (all articles published in *FM* are also published and archived on its website). Submit seasonal material 6 months in advance. Accepts queries by mail, e-mail, fax. Responds in 3 months to queries. Sample copy for $5. Writer's guidelines for #10 SASE.

Nonfiction How-to (manage fitness center and program), new product (no pay), photo feature (facilities/programs), technical, news of fitness research and major happenings in fitness industry. No exercise instructions or general ideas without examples of fitness businesses that have used them successfully. **Buys 50 mss/year.** Query. Length: 750-2,000 words. **Pays $60-300 for assigned articles.** Pays expenses of writers on assignment.

Photos Send photos with submission. Reviews contact sheets, 2×2 and 4×5 transparencies, prefers glossy prints (5×7 to 8×10). Captions, model releases required.

Tips ''We seek writers who are experts in a business or science field related to the fitness-service industry or who are experienced in the industry. Be current with the state of the art/science in business and fitness and communicate it in human terms (avoid intimidating academic language; tell the story of how this was learned and/or cite examples or quotes of people who have applied the knowledge successfully).''

$ $ GOLF COURSE MANAGEMENT

Golf Course Superintendents Association of America, 1421 Research Park Dr., Lawrence KS 66049. (785)841-2240. Fax: (785)932-3665. E-mail: shollister@gcsaa.org. Website: www.gcsaa.org. **Contact:** Scott Hollister, editor. **85% freelance written.** Monthly magazine covering the golf course superintendent. ''*GCM* helps the golf course superintendent become more efficient in all aspects of their job.'' Estab. 1924. Circ. 40,000. **Pays on acceptance.** Publishes ms an average of 6 months after acceptance. Byline given. Buys first North American serial rights, Web rights, and makes work-for-hire assignments. Editorial lead time 6 months. Submit seasonal material 6 months in advance. Accepts simultaneous submissions. Responds in 3 weeks to queries; 1 month to mss. Sample copy and writer's guidelines free.

Nonfiction How-to, interview/profile. No articles about playing golf. **Buys 40 mss/year.** Query. Length: 1,500-2,500 words. **Pays $300-450 for assigned articles.** Sometimes pays expenses of writers on assignment.

Photos Send photos with submission. Buys all rights. Offers no additional payment for photos accepted with ms. Identification of subjects required.

Tips ''Writers should have prior knowledge of the golf course superintendent profession.''

IDEA FITNESS JOURNAL

IDEA Health & Fitness Association, Inc., 10455 Pacific Center Court, San Diego CA 92121. (858)535-8979. Fax: (858)535-8234. E-mail: websters@ideafit.com. Website: www.ideafit.com. **Contact:** Sandy Todd Webster, editor-in-chief. **70% freelance written.** Magazine published 10 times/year ''for fitness professionals—personal trainers, group fitness instructors, and studio and health club owners—covering topics such as exercise science, nutrition, injury prevention, entrepreneurship in fitness, fitness-oriented research, and program design.'' Estab. 1984. Circ. 20,000. **Pays on acceptance.** Publishes ms an average of 4 months after acceptance. Byline given. Buys all rights. Accepts queries by mail, e-mail, fax. Accepts simultaneous submissions. Responds in 2 months to queries. Sample copy for $5. Writer's guidelines online.

Nonfiction How-to, technical. No general information on fitness; our readers are pros who need detailed information. **Buys 15 mss/year.** Query. Length: 1,000-3,000 words. **Payment varies.**

Photos State availability with submission. Buys all rights. Offers no additional payment for photos with ms. Model releases required.

Columns/Departments Research (detailed, specific info—must be written by expert), 750-1,500 words; Industry News (short reports on research, programs, and conferences), 150-300 words; Fitness Handout (exercise and nutrition info for participants), 750 words. **Buys 80 mss/year.** Query. **Payment varies.**

Tips ''We don't accept fitness information for the consumer audience on topics such as why exercise is good for you. Writers who have specific knowledge of, or experience working in, the fitness industry have an edge.''

$ $ NSGA RETAIL FOCUS

National Sporting Goods Association, 1601 Feehanville Dr., Suite 300, Mt. Prospect IL 60056-6035. (847)296-6742. Fax: (847)391-9827. E-mail: info@nsga.org. Website: www.nsga.org. **Contact:** Larry N. Weindruch, editor/publisher. **20% freelance written.** Works with a small number of new/unpublished writers each year. Bimonthly magazine. ''*NSGA Retail Focus* serves as a bimonthly trade journal for sporting goods retailers who are members of the association.'' Estab. 1948. Circ. 2,000. Pays on publication. Publishes ms an average of 1 month after acceptance. Byline given. Offers kill fee. Buys first, second serial (reprint), electronic rights. Submit seasonal material

6 months in advance. Accepts queries by e-mail. Sample copy for 9×12 SAE and 5 first-class stamps.

Nonfiction Interview/profile, photo feature. "No articles written without sporting goods retail businesspeople in mind as the audience. In other words, no generic articles sent to several industries." **Buys 12 mss/year.** Query with published clips. **Pays $150-300.** Sometimes pays expenses of writers on assignment.

Photos State availability with submission. Reviews high-resolution, digital images. Buys one-time rights. Payment negotiable.

Columns/Departments Personnel Management (succinct tips on hiring, motivating, firing, etc.); Sales Management (in-depth tips to improve sales force performance); Retail Management (detailed explanation of merchandising/inventory control); Store Design; Visual Merchandising, all 1,500 words. **Buys 12 mss/year.** Query. **Pays $150-300.**

$ $ PADDLE DEALER

The Trade Magazine for Paddlesports, Paddlesport Publishing, Inc., P.O. Box 775450, Steamboat Springs CO 80477. (970)879-1450. Fax: (970)870-1404. E-mail: jeff@paddlermagazine.com. Website: www.paddlermagazine.com. Editor: Eugene Buchanan. **Contact:** Jeff Moag, managing editor. **70% freelance written.** Quarterly magazine covering the canoeing, kayaking and rafting industry. Estab. 1993. Circ. 7,500. Pays on publication. Publishes ms an average of 6 months after acceptance. Byline given. Buys first North American serial and one-time electronic rights. Editorial lead time 2 months. Submit seasonal material 6 months in advance. Accepts queries by mail, e-mail, fax. Accepts simultaneous submissions. Responds in 3 months to queries. Sample copy for 8½×11 SAE and $1.78. Writer's guidelines for #10 SASE.

Nonfiction New product, technical, business advice. **Buys 8 mss/year.** Query or send complete ms. Length: 2,300 words. **Pays 15-20¢/word.** Sometimes pays expenses of writers on assignment.

Photos State availability with submission. Reviews transparencies, 5×7 prints. Buys one-time rights.

Columns/Departments Profiles, how-to, great ideas, computer corner. **Buys 12 mss/year.** Query or send complete ms. **Pays 10-20¢/word.**

$ $ POOL & SPA NEWS

Hanley-Wood, LLC, 6222 Wilshire Blvd., Los Angeles CA 90048. (323)801-4972. Fax: (323)801-4986. E-mail: etaylor@hanleywood.com. Website: poolspanews.com. **Contact:** Erika Taylor, editor. **15% freelance written.** Semimonthly magazine covering the swimming pool and spa industry for builders, retail stores, and service firms. Estab. 1960. Circ. 16,300. Pays on publication. Publishes ms an average of 2 months after acceptance. Buys all rights. Accepts queries by mail, e-mail. Responds in 1 month to queries. Sample copy for $5 and 9×12 SAE and 11 first-class stamps.

Nonfiction Interview/profile, technical. Send résumé with published clips. Length: 500-2,000 words. **Pays $150-550.** Pays expenses of writers on assignment.

Reprints Send ms with rights for sale noted and information about when and where the material previously appeared. Payment varies.

Photos Payment varies.

Columns/Departments Payment varies.

▣ The online magazine carries original content not found in the print edition. Contact: Margi Millunzi, online editor.

$ $ REFEREE

Referee Enterprises, Inc., P.O. Box 161, Franksville WI 53126. Fax: (262)632-5460. E-mail: jarehart@referee.com. Website: www.referee.com. Editor: Bill Topp. **Contact:** Jim Arehart, senior managing editor. **75% freelance written.** Monthly magazine covering sports officiating. "*Referee* is a magazine for and read by sports officials of all kinds with a focus on baseball, basketball, football, softball, and soccer officiating." Estab. 1976. Circ. 40,000. **Pays on acceptance.** Publishes ms an average of 6 months after acceptance. Byline given. Kill fee negotiable. Buys all rights. Editorial lead time 6 months. Accepts queries by mail, e-mail, fax. Responds in 2 weeks to queries; 1 month to mss. Sample copy for #10 SASE. Writer's guidelines online.

Nonfiction Book excerpts, essays, historical/nostalgic, how-to (sports officiating related), humor, interview/profile, opinion, photo feature, technical (as it relates to sports officiating). "We don't want to see articles with themes not relating to sport officiating. General sports articles, although of interest to us, will not be published." **Buys 40 mss/year.** Query with published clips. Length: 500-2,500 words. **Pays $100-400.** Sometimes pays expenses of writers on assignment.

Photos State availability with submission. Reviews contact sheets, negatives, transparencies, prints. Purchase of rights negotiable. Offers $35-40 per photo. Identification of subjects required.

Tips "Query first and be persistent. We may not like your idea but that doesn't mean we won't like your next one. Professionalism pays off."

$ $ SKI AREA MANAGEMENT

Beardsley Publications, P.O. Box 644, Woodbury CT 06798. (203)263-0888. Fax: (203)266-0452. E-mail: samedit @saminfo.com. Website: www.saminfo.com. **Contact:** Rick Kahl, editor. **85% freelance written.** Bimonthly magazine covering everything involving the management and development of ski resorts. "We are the publication of record for the North American ski industry. We report on new ideas, developments, marketing, and regulations with regard to ski and snowboard resorts. Everyone from the CEO to the lift operator of winter resorts reads our magazine to stay informed about the people and procedures that make ski areas successful." Estab. 1962. Circ. 4,500. Pays on publication. Byline given. Offers kill fee. Buys all rights. Editorial lead time 2 months. Submit seasonal material 3 months in advance. Accepts queries by mail, e-mail. Responds in 2 weeks to queries. Sample copy for 9×12 SAE with $3 postage or online. Writer's guidelines for #10 SASE.

Nonfiction Historical/nostalgic, how-to, interview/profile, new product, opinion, personal experience, technical. "We don't want anything that does not specifically pertain to resort operations, management, or financing." **Buys 25-40 mss/year.** Query. Length: 500-2,500 words. **Pays $50-400.**

Reprints Accepts previously published submissions.

Photos Send photos with submission. Reviews transparencies, prints. Buys one-time rights or all rights. Offers no additional payment for photos accepted with ms. Identification of subjects required.

Tips "Know what you are writing about. We are read by people dedicated to skiing and snowboarding and to making the resort experience the best possible for their customers. It is a trade publication read by professionals."

$ $ THOROUGHBRED TIMES

Thoroughbred Times Co., Inc., 2008 Mercer Rd., P.O. Box 8237, Lexington KY 40533. (859)260-9800. **Contact:** Mark Simon, editor. **10% freelance written.** Weekly tabloid "written for professionals who breed and/or race thoroughbreds at tracks in the US. Articles must help owners and breeders understand racing to help them realize a profit." Estab. 1985. Circ. 20,000. Pays on publication. Publishes ms an average of 1 month after acceptance. Byline given. Offers 50% kill fee. Buys first publication rights. Submit seasonal material 2 months in advance. Responds in 2 weeks to mss. Sample copy not available.

Nonfiction General interest, historical/nostalgic, interview/profile, technical. **Buys 52 mss/year.** Query. Length: 500-2,500 words. **Pays 10-20¢/word.** Sometimes pays expenses of writers on assignment.

Photos State availability with submission. Reviews prints. Buys one-time rights. Offers $25/photo. Identification of subjects required.

Columns/Departments Vet Topics; Business of Horses; Pedigree Profiles; Bloodstock Topics; Tax Matters; Viewpoints; Guest Commentary.

Tips "We are looking for farm stories and profiles of owners, breeders, jockeys, and trainers."

STONE, QUARRY & MINING

$ $ 🖳 CANADIAN MINING JOURNAL

Business Information Group, 12 Concorde Place, Suite 800, Toronto ON M3C 4J2 Canada. (416)510-6742. Fax: (416)510-5138. E-mail: jwerniuk@canadianminingjournal.com. **Contact:** Jane Werniuk, editor. **5% freelance written.** Magazine covering mining and mineral exploration by Canadian companies. "*Canadian Mining Journal* provides articles and information of practical use to those who work in the technical, administrative, and supervisory aspects of exploration, mining, and processing in the Canadian mineral exploration and mining industry." Estab. 1882. Circ. 10,000. Pays on publication. Publishes ms an average of 3 months after acceptance. Byline given. Buys one-time, electronic rights. Makes work-for-hire assignments. Submit seasonal material 3 months in advance. Accepts queries by mail, e-mail, fax, phone. Responds in 1 week to queries; 1 month to mss.

Nonfiction Opinion, technical, operation descriptions. **Buys 6 mss/year.** Query with published clips. Length: 500-1,400 words. **Pays $100-600.** Pays expenses of writers on assignment.

Photos State availability with submission. Reviews 4×6 prints or high-resolution files. Buys one-time rights. Negotiates payment individually. Captions, identification of subjects, credits required.

Columns/Departments Guest editorial (opinion on controversial subject related to mining industry), 600 words. **Buys 3 mss/year.** Query with published clips. **Pays $150.**

Tips "I need articles about mine sites it would be expensive/difficult for me to reach. I also need to know the writer is competent to understand and describe the technology in an interesting way."

$ CONTEMPORARY STONE & TILE DESIGN

Business News Publishing Co., 210 Route 4 E., Suite 311, Paramus NJ 07652. (201)291-9001. Fax: (201)291-9002. E-mail: jennifer@stoneworld.com. Website: www.stoneworld.com. Publisher: Alex Bachrach. **Contact:** Jennifer Adams, editor. Quarterly magazine covering the full range of stone and tile design and architecture—from classic and historic spaces to current projects. Estab. 1995. Circ. 14,000. Pays on publication. Publishes ms an average of 3 months after acceptance. Byline given. Buys first rights. Submit seasonal material 6 months in advance. Responds in 3 weeks to queries. Sample copy for $10.

Nonfiction Overall features on a certain aspect of stone design/tile work, or specific articles on individual architectural projects. Interview/profile (prominent architect/designer or firm), photo feature, technical, architectural design. **Buys 8 mss/year.** Query with published clips. Length: 1,500-3,000 words. **Pays $6/column inch.** Pays expenses of writers on assignment.

Photos State availability with submission. Reviews transparencies, prints. Buys one-time rights. Pays $10/photo accepted with ms. Captions, identification of subjects required.

Columns/Departments Upcoming Events (for the architecture and design community); Stone Classics (featuring historic architecture); question and answer session with a prominent architect or designer. Length: 1,500-2,000 words. **Pays $6/inch.**

Tips "The visual aspect of the magazine is key, so architectural photography is a must for any story. Cover the entire project, but focus on the stonework or tile work and how it relates to the rest of the space. Architects are very helpful in describing their work and often provide excellent quotes. As a relatively new magazine, we are looking for freelance submissions and are open to new feature topics. This is a narrow subject, however, so it's a good idea to speak with an editor before submitting anything."

$ $PIT & QUARRY

Advantar Communications, 7500 Old Oak Blvd., Cleveland OH 44130. (440)891-2607. Fax: (440)891-2675. E-mail: mkuhar@advanstar.com. Website: www.pitandquarry.com. Managing Editor: Darren Constantino. **Contact:** Mark S. Kuhar, editor. **10-20% freelance written.** Monthly magazine covering nonmetallic minerals, mining, and crushed stone. Audience has "knowledge of construction-related markets, mining, minerals processing, etc." Estab. 1916. Circ. 25,000. **Pays on acceptance.** Publishes ms an average of 6 months after acceptance. Byline given. Buys first North American serial rights. Editorial lead time 6 months. Accepts queries by mail, e-mail, fax, phone. Accepts simultaneous submissions. Responds in 1 month to queries; 4 months to mss. Sample copy for 9×12 SAE and 4 first-class stamps.

Nonfiction How-to, interview/profile, new product, technical. No humor or inspirational articles. **Buys 12-15 mss/year.** Query. Length: 1,000-1,500 words. **Pays $250-700 for assigned articles; $250-500 for unsolicited articles.** Pays writers with contributor copies or other premiums for simple news items, etc. Sometimes pays expenses of writers on assignment.

Photos State availability with submission. Buys one-time rights. Offers no additional payment for photos accepted with ms. Identification of subjects, model releases required.

Columns/Departments Brand New; Techwatch; E-business; Software Corner; Equipment Showcase. Length: 250-750 words. **Buys 5-6 mss/year.** Query. **Pays $250-300.**

The online magazine sometimes carries original content not found in the print edition.

Tips "Be familiar with quarry operations (crushed stone or sand and gravel), as opposed to coal or metallic minerals mining. Know construction markets. We always need equipment-focused features on specific quarry operations."

$STONE WORLD

Business News Publishing Co., 210 Route 4 E., Suite 311, Paramus NJ 07652. (201)291-9001. Fax: (201)291-9002. E-mail: michael@stoneworld.com. Website: www.stoneworld.com. **Contact:** Michael Reis, editor. Monthly magazine on natural building stone for producers and users of granite, marble, limestone, slate, sandstone, onyx and other natural stone products. Estab. 1984. Circ. 21,000. Pays on publication. Publishes ms an average of 4 months after acceptance. Byline given. Buys first North American serial, second serial (reprint) rights. Submit seasonal material 6 months in advance. Responds in 2 months to queries. Sample copy for $10.

Nonfiction How-to (fabricate and/or install natural building stone), interview/profile, photo feature, technical, architectural design, artistic stone uses, statistics, factory profile, equipment profile, trade show review. **Buys 10 mss/year.** Query with or without published clips or send complete ms. Length: 600-3,000 words. **Pays $6/column inch.** Pays expenses of writers on assignment.

Reprints Send photocopy with rights for sale noted and information about when and where the material previously appeared. Pays 50% of amount paid for an original article.

Photos State availability with submission. Reviews transparencies, prints, slides, digital images. Buys one-time rights. Pays $10/photo accepted with ms. Captions, identification of subjects required.

Columns/Departments News (pertaining to stone or design community); New Literature (brochures, catalogs, books, videos, etc., about stone); New Products (stone products); New Equipment (equipment and machinery for working with stone); Calendar (dates and locations of events in stone and design communities). Query or send complete ms. Length 300-600 words. **Pays $6/inch.**

Tips "Articles about architectural stone design accompanied by professional color photographs and quotes from designing firms are often published, especially when one unique aspect of the stone selection or installation is highlighted. We are also interested in articles about new techniques of quarrying and/or fabricating natural building stone.''

TOY, NOVELTY & HOBBY

$ PEN WORLD INTERNATIONAL

World Publications, Inc., 3946 Glade Valley Dr., Kingwood TX 77339-2059. (281)359-4363. Fax: (281)359-5748. E-mail: editor@penworld.com. Website: www.penworld.com. Editor: Marie Picon. Magazine published 7 times/year. Published for the collectors and connoiseurs of contemporary and vintage writing instruments. Circ. 105,994. Sample copy not available.

TRANSPORTATION

BUS CONVERSIONS

The First and Foremost Bus Converters Magazine, MAK Publishing, 7246 Garden Grove Blvd., Westminster CA 92683. (714)799-0062. Fax: (714)799-0042. E-mail: editor@busconversions.com. Website: www.busconversions.com. **Contact:** Tiffany Christian, editor. **95% freelance written.** Monthly magazine covering the bus conversion industry. Estab. 1992. Circ. 10,000. Pays on publication. Buys first North American serial rights. Accepts queries by mail, e-mail.

Nonfiction Each month, *Bus Conversions* publishes a minimum of 2 coach reviews, usually anecdotal stories told by those who have completed their own bus conversion. Publishes some travel/destination stories (all of which are related to bus/RV travel). Looking for articles on engine swaps, exterior painting, and furniture. How-to (articles on the electrical, plumbing, mechanical, decorative, and structural aspects of bus conversions; buses that are converted into RVs).

Photos Include color photos (glossy) with submission. Photos not returned unless SASE is included.

Columns/Departments Industry Update; Products of Interest; Ask the Experts; One For the Road; Road Fix.

Tips ''Most of our writers are our readers. Knowledge of bus conversions and the associated lifestyle is a prerequisite.''

$ $ CLEAR DAY LIMOUSINE DIGEST

Digest Publications, 29 Fostertown Rd., Medford NJ 08055. (609)953-4900. Fax: (609)953-4905. E-mail: info@limodigest.com. Website: www.limodigest.com. **Contact:** Susan Keehn, editor. **25% freelance written.** Monthly magazine covering ground transportation. ''Limousine Digest is 'the voice of the luxury ground transportation industry.' We cover all aspects of ground transportation from vehicles to operators, safety issues, and political involvement.'' Estab. 1990. Circ. 14,000. Pays on publication. Publishes ms an average of 2 months after acceptance. Byline given. Makes work-for-hire assignments. Editorial lead time 1 year. Submit seasonal material 2 months in advance. Accepts queries by mail, e-mail, fax. Accepts simultaneous submissions. Sample copy for free.

Nonfiction Historical/nostalgic, how-to (start a company, market your product), humor, inspirational, interview/profile, new product, personal experience, photo feature, technical, travel, industry news, business. **Buys 7-9 mss/year.** Send complete ms. Length: 700-1,900 words. **Pays 15-25¢/word. Will pay authors in advertising trade-outs.**

Reprints Accepts previously published submissions.

Photos Must include photos to be considered. Send photos with submission. Reviews negatives. Buys all rights. Negotiates payment individually. Captions, identification of subjects, model releases required.

Columns/Departments New Model Showcase (new limousines, sedans, buses), 1,000 words; Player Profile (industry members profiled), 700 words; Hall of Fame (unique vehicles featured), 500-700 words; Association News (association issues), 400 words. **Buys 5 mss/year.** Query. **Pays 15-25¢/word.**

$ $ METRO MAGAZINE

Bobit Publishing Co., 3520 Challenger St., Torrance CA 90503. (310)533-2400. Fax: (310)533-2502. E-mail: joseph.campbell@bobit.com. Website: www.metro-magazine.com. Editor: Steve Hirano. **Contact:** Joseph Campbell, managing editor. **10% freelance written.** Magazine published 10 times/year covering transit bus, passenger rail, and motorcoach operations. ''*Metro Magazine* delivers business, government policy, and technology developments that are *industry specific* to public transportation.'' Estab. 1904. Circ. 20,500. **Pays on acceptance.** Publishes ms an average of 2 months after acceptance. Byline given. Offers 10% kill fee. Buys all rights. Editorial lead time 3 months. Submit seasonal material 3 months in advance. Accepts queries by e-mail. Responds in 2 weeks to queries; 1 month to mss. Sample copy for $8. Writer's guidelines by e-mail.

Nonfiction How-to, interview/profile (of industry figures), new product (related to transit—bus and rail—

private bus), technical. **Buys 6-10 mss/year.** Query. Length: 400-1,500 words. **Pays $80-400.**
Photos State availability with submission. Buys all rights. Negotiates payment individually. Captions, identification of subjects, model releases required.
Columns/Departments Query. **Pays 20¢/word.**

$ $ SCHOOL BUS FLEET

Business Media, 3520 Challenger St., Torrance CA 90503. (310)533-2400. Fax: (310)533-2502. E-mail: sbf@bobit .com. Website: www.schoolbusfleet.com. **Contact:** Steve Hirano, editor. **10% freelance written.** Magazine covering school transportation of K-12 population. "Most of our readers are school bus operators, public and private." Estab. 1965. Circ. 24,000. **Pays on acceptance.** Publishes ms an average of 3 months after acceptance. Byline given. Offers 25% kill fee or $50. Buys first North American serial rights. Editorial lead time 3 months. Submit seasonal material 3 months in advance. Accepts queries by mail, e-mail, fax. Responds in 1 month to queries. Sample copy and writer's guidelines free.
Nonfiction Interview/profile, new product, technical. **Buys 6 mss/year.** Query with published clips. Length: 600-1,800 words. **Pays 20-25¢/word.** Sometimes pays expenses of writers on assignment.
Photos State availability with submission. Reviews transparencies, 4×6 prints, digital photos. Buys one-time rights. Negotiates payment individually. Captions, identification of subjects required.
Columns/Departments Shop Talk (maintenance information for school bus mechanics), 650 words. **Buys 2 mss/year.** Query with published clips. **Pays $100-150.**
Tips "Freelancers should submit ideas about innovations in school bus safety and operations."

TRAVEL

$ $ $ CRUISE INDUSTRY NEWS

Cruise Industry News, 441 Lexington Ave., Suite 1209, New York NY 10017. (212)986-1025. Fax: (212)986-1033. E-mail: oivind@cruiseindustrynews.com. Website: www.cruiseindustrynews.com. **Contact:** Oivind Mathisen, editor. **20% freelance written.** Quarterly magazine covering cruise shipping. "We write about the business of cruise shipping for the industry. That is, cruise lines, shipyards, financial analysts, etc." Estab. 1991. Circ. 10,000. Pays on acceptance or on publication. Publishes ms an average of 4 months after acceptance. Byline given. Offers 25% kill fee. Buys first rights. Editorial lead time 3 months. Accepts queries by mail. Reponse time varies to queries. Sample copy for $15. Writer's guidelines for #10 SASE.
Nonfiction Interview/profile, new product, photo feature, business. No travel stories. **Buys more than 20 mss/ year.** Query with published clips. Length: 500-1,500 words. **Pays $500-1,000 for assigned articles.** Sometimes pays expenses of writers on assignment.
Photos State availability with submission. Buys one-time rights. Pays $25-50/photo.

$ $ LEISURE GROUP TRAVEL

Premier Tourism Marketing, 4901 Forest Ave., Downers Grove IL 60515. (630)964-1431. Fax: (630)852-0414. E-mail: johnk@premiertourismmarketing.com. Website: www.premiertourismmarketing.com. **Contact:** John Kloster, editor-in-chief. **35% freelance written.** Bimonthly magazine covering group travel. We cover destinations and editorial relevant to the group travel market. Estab. 1994. Circ. 15,012. Pays on publication. Byline given. Buys first rights, including online publication rights. Editorial lead time 6 months. Submit seasonal material 6 months in advance. Accepts queries by mail, e-mail. Sample copy online.
Nonfiction Travel. **Buys 75 mss/year.** Query with published clips. Length: 1,200-3,000 words. **Pays $0-1,000.**
Tips "Experience in writing for 50+ travel marketplace a bonus."

$ $ SPECIALTY TRAVEL INDEX

Alpine Hansen, P.O. Box 458, San Anselmo CA 94979. (415)455-1643. Fax: (415)455-1648. E-mail: weinreb@spe cialtytravel.com. Website: www.specialtytravel.com. **90% freelance written.** Semiannual magazine covering adventure and special interest travel. Estab. 1980. Circ. 35,000. Pays on receipt and acceptance of all materials. Byline given. Buys one-time rights. Editorial lead time 3 month. Submit seasonal material 3 months in advance. Accepts queries by mail, e-mail. Writer's guidelines on request.
Nonfiction How-to, personal experience, photo feature, travel. **Buys 15 mss/year.** Query. Length: 1,250 words. **Pays $200 minimum.**
Reprints Send tearsheet. Pays 100% of amount paid for an original article.
Photos State availability with submission. Reviews 35mm transparencies, 5×7 prints. Negotiates payment individually. Captions, identification of subjects required.
Tips "Write about group travel and be both creative and factual. The articles should relate to both the travel agent booking the tour and the client who is traveling."

$ STAR SERVICE

NORTHSTAR Travel Media, 200 Brookstown Ave., Suite 301, Winston-Salem NC 27101. (336)714-3328. Fax: (336)714-3168. E-mail: csheaffer@ntmllc.com. Website: www.starserviceonline.com. **Contact:** Cindy Sheaffer, editor-in-chief. "Eager to work with new/unpublished writers as well as those working from a home base abroad, planning trips that would allow time for hotel reporting, or living in major ports for cruise ships." Worldwide guide to accommodations and cruise ships, sold to travel professionals on subscription basis. Estab. 1960. Pays 1 month after acceptance. Buys all rights. Writer's guidelines and list of available assignments for #10 SASE.

- E-mail queries preferred.
- O─ Break in by "being willing to inspect hotels in remote parts of the world."

Nonfiction Objective, critical evauations of hotels and cruise ships suitable for international travelers, based on personal inspections. Freelance correspondents ordinarily are assigned to update an entire state or country. "Assignment involves on-site inspections of all hotels and cruise ships we review; revising and updating published reports; and reviewing new properties. Qualities needed are thoroughness, precision, perserverance, and keen judgment. Solid research skills and powers of observation are crucial. Travel writing experience is highly desirable. Reviews must be colorful, clear, and documented with hotel's brochure, rate sheet, etc. We accept no advertising or payment for listings, so reviews should dispense praise and criticism where deserved." Query should include details on writer's experience in travel and writing, clips, specific forthcoming travel plans, and how much time would be available for hotel or ship inspections. Sponsored trips are acceptable. **Buys 4,500 mss/year. Pays $30/report used.**

Tips "We may require sample hotel or cruise reports on facilities near freelancer's hometown before giving the first assignment. No byline because of sensitive nature of reviews."

$ $ TRAVEL TIPS

Premier Tourism Marketing, 4901 Forest Ave., Downers Grove IL 60515. (630)964-1431. Fax: (630)852-0414. E-mail: johnk@premiertourismmarketing.com. Website: www.premiertourismmarketing.com. **Contact:** John Kloster, editor-in-chief. **75% freelance written.** Bimonthly magazine covering group travel. "We cover destinations and editorial relevant to the group travel market." Estab. 1994. Circ. 12,500. Pays on publication. Byline given. Buys first, electronic rights. Editorial lead time 6 months. Submit seasonal material 6 months in advance. Accepts queries by mail, e-mail. Sample copy online.

Nonfiction Travel. **Buys 36-50 mss/year.** Query with published clips. Length: 1,200-3,000 words. **Pays $0-500.**

Tips "Experience in writing for 50+ travel marketplace a bonus."

VETERINARY

$ $ VETERINARY ECONOMICS

Business Solutions for Practicing Veterinarians, Advanstar Veterinary Healthcare Communications, 8033 Flint, Lenexa KS 66214. (913)492-4300. Fax: (913)492-4157. E-mail: vmpg@vetmedpub.com. Website: www.vetecon.com. **20% freelance written.** Monthly magazine covering veterinary practice management. "We address the business concerns and management needs of practicing veterinarians." Estab. 1960. Circ. 54,000. Pays on publication. Publishes ms an average of 6 months after acceptance. Byline given. Buys all rights. Editorial lead time 3 months. Submit seasonal material 3 months in advance. Accepts queries by mail, e-mail, fax. Accepts simultaneous submissions. Responds in 3 months to queries. Sample copy for free. Writer's guidelines online.

Nonfiction How-to, interview/profile, personal experience. **Buys 24 mss/year.** Query with or without published clips or send complete ms. Length: 1,000-2,000 words. **Pays $50-400.**

Photos Send photos with submission. Reviews transparencies, prints. Buys one-time rights. Offers no additional payment for photos accepted with ms. Captions, identification of subjects required.

Columns/Departments Practice Tips (easy, unique business tips), 200-300 words. Send complete ms. **Pays $35-40.**

Tips "Among the topics we cover: veterinary hospital design, client relations, contractual and legal matters, investments, day-to-day management, marketing, personal finances, practice finances, personnel, collections, and taxes. We also cover news and issues within the veterinary profession; for example, articles might cover the effectiveness of Yellow Pages advertising, the growing number of women veterinarians, restrictive-covenant cases, and so on. Freelance writers are encouraged to submit proposals or outlines for articles on these topics. Most articles involve interviews with a nationwide sampling of veterinarians; we will provide the names and phone numbers if necessary. We accept only a small number of unsolicited manuscripts each year; however, we do assign many articles to freelance writers. All material submitted by first-time contributors is read on speculation, and the review process usually takes 12-16 weeks. Our style is concise yet conversational, and all manuscripts go through a fairly rigorous editing process. We encourage writers to provide specific examples to illustrate points made throughout their articles."

Contests & Awards

The contests and awards listed in this section are arranged by subject. Nonfiction writers can turn immediately to nonfiction awards listed alphabetically by the name of the contest or award. The same is true for fiction writers, poets, playwrights and screenwriters, journalists, children's writers, and translators. You'll also find general book awards, fellowships offered by arts councils and foundations, and multiple category contests.

New contests and awards are announced in various writer's publications nearly every day. However, many lose their funding or fold—and sponsoring magazines go out of business just as often. We have contacted the organizations whose contests and awards are listed here with the understanding that they are valid through 2005-2006. **Contact names**, **entry fees**, and **deadlines** have been highlighted and set in bold type for your convenience.

To make sure you have all the information you need about a particular contest, always send a SASE to the contact person in the listing before entering a contest. The listings in this section are brief, and many contests have lengthy, specific rules and requirements that we could not include in our limited space. Often a specific entry form must accompany your submission.

When you receive a set of guidelines, you will see that some contests are not applicable to all writers. The writer's age, previous publication, geographic location, and length of the work are common matters of eligibility. Read the requirements carefully to ensure you don't enter a contest for which you are not qualified. You should also be aware that every year, more and more contests, especially those sponsored by "little" literary magazines, are charging entry fees.

Winning a contest or award can launch a successful writing career. Take a professional approach by doing a little extra research. Find out who the previous winner of the award was by investing in a sample copy of the magazine in which the prize-winning article, poem, or short story appeared. Attend the staged reading of an award-winning play. Your extra effort will be to your advantage in competing with writers who choose to submit blindly.

Information on contests and awards listed in the previous edition of *Writer's Market*, but not included in this edition, can be found in the General Index.

GENERAL

ARTSLINK PROJECTS AWARD
CEC Artslink, 435 Hudson St., New York NY 10014. (212)643-1985, ext. 22. Fax: (212)643-1996. E-mail: artslink @cecartslink.org. Website: www.cecartslink.org. **Contact:** Tamalyn Miller, program manager. Offered annually to enable artists of all media to work in Central Europe, Russia, and Eurasia with colleagues there on collaborative projects. Check website for deadline and other information. Prize: Up to $10,000.

N BANTA AWARD
Wisconsin Library Association, % Literary Awards Committee, 5250 E. Terrace Dr., Suite A-1, Madison WI 53718-8345. (608)245-3640. Website: www.wla.lib.wi.us. **Contact:** Chair, Literary Award Committee. Offered annually for books published during the year preceding the award. The Literary Awards Committee reviews all works by Wisconsin authors that are not edited, revised editions, textbooks, or written in foreign languages. Review copies or notification of books, along with verification of the author's ties to Wisconsin, may be submitted to the committee by the publisher or author. Only open to writers born, raised, or currently living in Wisconsin. **Deadline: March of calendar year following publication.** Prize: $500, a trophy given by the Banta Corporation Foundation, and presentation at the Annual Conference of the Wisconsin Library Association between late October and early November.

N ☒ DAFOE BOOK PRIZE
J.W. Dafoe Foundation, 359 University College, University of Manitoba, Winnipeg MB R3T 2M8 Canada. **Contact:** Dr. James Fergusson. The Dafoe Book Prize was ''established to honor John Dafoe, editor of the *Winnipeg Free Press* from 1900 to 1944, and is awarded each year to the book that best contributes to our understanding of Canada and/or its relations abroad by a Canadian or author in residence.'' Books must be previously published January-December of contest year. Co-authored books are eligible, but not edited books consisting of chapters from many different authors. Submit 4 copies of book. **Deadline: December 6.** Prize: $10,000. Judged by board members and academics. Authors must be Canadian citizens or landed immigrants.

THE RALPH WALDO EMERSON AWARD
The Phi Beta Kappa Society, 1606 New Hampshire Ave. NW, Washington DC 20009. (202)265-3808. Fax: (202)986-1601. E-mail: sbeasley@pbk.org. Website: www.pbk.org/scholarships/books. **Contact:** Sandra Beasley. Estab. 1960. ''The Ralph Waldo Emerson Award is offered annually for scholarly studies that contribute significantly to interpretations of the intellectual and cultural condition of humanity. This award may recognize work in the fields of history, philosophy, and religion; these fields are conceived in sufficiently broad terms to permit the inclusion of appropriate work in related fields such as anthropology and the social sciences. Biographies of public figures may be eligible if their critical emphasis is primarily on the intellectual and cultural condition of humanity.'' Work must have appeared in print May 1, 2004-April 30, 2005. Entries must be submitted by the publisher. Entries must be preceded by a letter certifying that the book(s) conforms to all the conditions of eligibility and stating the publication date of each entry. If accepted, 8 copies of each entry are required for the Emerson Award. Ineligible entries will be returned by Phi Beta Kappa. Books will not be entered officially in the competition until all copies and the letter of certification have been received. **Deadline: April 30.** Prize: $2,500. Judged by a rotating panel of distinguished scholars and experts in the field. Open only to original works in English, and authors of US residency and publication.

☒ THE MARIAN ENGEL AWARD
The Writers' Trust of Canada, 90 Richmond St. E., Suite 200, Toronto ON M5C 1P1 Canada. (416)504-8222. Fax: (416)504-9090. E-mail: info@writerstrust.com. Website: www.writerstrust.com. The Engel Award is presented annually at the Great Literary Awards Event, held in Toronto each Spring, to a female Canadian writer for a body of work in hope of continued contribution to the richness of Canadian literature. Prize: $15,000. Open to Canadian residents only.

☒ THE TIMOTHY FINDLEY AWARD
The Writers' Trust of Canada, 90 Richmond St. E., Suite 200, Toronto ON M5C 1P1 Canada. (416)504-8222. Fax: (416)504-9090. E-mail: info@writerstrust.com. Website: www.writerstrust.com. **Contact:** James Davies. The Findley Award is presented annually at The Great Literary Awards Event held in Toronto each spring, to a male Canadian writer for a body of work in hope of continued contribution to the richness of Canadian literature. Prize: $15,000. Open to Canadian residents only.

FOREWORD MAGAZINE BOOK OF THE YEAR AWARDS
ForeWord Magazine, 129½ E. Front St., Traverse City MI 49684. (231)933-3699. Fax: (231)933-3899. Website: www.forewordmagazine.com. Awards offered annually. Eligibility: Books must have a 2004 copyright. **Dead-**

line: **January 15.** Prize: $1,500 cash prize will be awarded to a Best Fiction and Best Nonfiction choice as determined by the editors of *ForeWord Magazine*. Judged by a jury of librarians, booksellers, and reviewers who are selected to judge the categories for entry and select winners and finalists in 47 categories based on editorial excellence and professional production as well as the originality of the narrative and the value the book adds to its genre. Open to any writer.

FRIENDS OF THE DALLAS PUBLIC LIBRARY AWARD

The Texas Institute of Letters, 6335 W. Northwest Hwy., #618, Dallas TX 75225. (214)363-7253. E-mail: franvick @aol.com. Website: www.wtamu.edu/til/awards.htm. **Contact:** Fran Vick, secretary. Offered annually for submissions published January 1-December 31 of previous year to recognize the writer of the book making the most important contribution to knowledge. Writer must have been born in Texas, have lived in the state at least 2 consecutive years at some time, or the subject matter of the book should be associated with the state. See website for guidelines. **Deadline: January 3.** Prize: $1,000.

THE JANE GESKE AWARD

Prairie Schooner, 201 Andrews Hall, P.O. Box 880334, Lincoln NE 68588-0334. (402)472-0911. Fax: (402)472-9771. E-mail: kgrey2@unl.edu. Website: www.unl.edu/schooner/psmain.htm. **Contact:** Hilda Raz. Offered annually for work published in *Prairie Schooner* in the previous year. Prize: $250. Open to any writer.

INDEPENDENT PUBLISHER BOOK AWARDS

Jenkins Group/Independent Publisher Online, 400 W. Front St., #4A, Traverse City MI 49684. (231)933-4954, ext. 1011. Fax: (231)933-0448. E-mail: jimb@bookpublishing.com. Website: www.independentpublisher.com. **Contact:** Jim Barnes. "The Independent Publisher Book Awards were conceived as a broad-based, unaffiliated awards program open to all members of the independent publishing industry. The staff at *Independent Publisher* magazine saw the need to bring increased recognition to the thousands of exemplary independent, university, and self-published titles produced each year. The IPPY Awards reward those who exhibit the courage, innovation, and creativity to bring about change in the world of publishing. Independent spirit and expertise comes from publishers of all areas and budgets, and we judge books with that in mind. For 20 years our mission at *Independent Publisher* has been to recognize and encourage the work of publishers who exhibit the courage and creativity necessary to take chances, break new ground, and bring about changes, not only to the world of publishing, but to our society, our environment, and our collective spirit. Entries will be accepted in 55 categories." **Deadline: April 15.** Guidelines for SASE. **Charges $60 until November 15; $65 until January 15; $70 until April 15.** Prize: $500, and a trophy to 1 book in each of the following categories: Most Original Concept; Best Corporate Branding Book; Best Book Arts Craftsmanship; Most Inspirational to Youth; Best Health Book; Most Likely to Save the Planet; Most Unique Design; Story Teller of the Year; Most Life-Changing; Business Breakthrough of the Year. Judged by a panel of experts representing the fields of design, writing, bookselling, library, and reviewing. Open to any published writer.

🄽 🄲 INSCRIBE FALL CONTEST

InScribe Christian Writers' Fellowship, 333 Hunter's Run, Edmonton AB T6R 2N9 Canada. E-mail: info@inscribe .org. Website: www.inscribe.org. **Contact:** Contest Director. Annual contest for unpublished writing; purpose is to encourage quality writing. Categories usually include devotional, free verse, rhymed verse, short story, and nonfiction. See website for details. **Deadline: Usually the first week in August.** Guidelines for SASE. **Charges $10 (Canadian or US dollars).** Prize: 1st Prize: $50; 2nd and 3rd Prize: Cash or books. InScribe reserves the right to publish winning entries in its newsletter, *FellowScript*. Judged by different judges for each category. Judging is blind. Open to any writer.

KORET JEWISH BOOK AWARDS

Koret Foundation, 33 New Montgomery St., Suite 1090, San Francisco CA 94105-4526. (415)882-7740, ext. 3. Fax: (415)882-7775. E-mail: kjba@koretfoundation.org. Website: www.koretfoundation.org. **Contact:** Steven J. Zipperstein, PhD, director, Koret Institute. Annual awards established "to help readers identify the best Jewish books now available in the English language." Books must be published in English; translations are eligible. Edited volumes and anthologies are not eligible. Books must be submitted by publishers on behalf of authors. There are 5 categories: Biography, Autobiography, Children's Literature and Literary Studies; Fiction; History; Philosophy; Thought. **Deadline: Changes annually; see website for details.** Guidelines for SASE. Prize: $10,000 to the winner in each category.

DOROTHEA LANGE—PAUL TAYLOR PRIZE

Center for Documentary Studies at Duke University, 1317 W. Pettigrew St., Durham NC 27705. (919)660-3663. Fax: (919)681-7600. E-mail: alexad@duke.edu. Website: cds.aas.duke.edu/l-t/. **Contact:** Alexa Dilworth.

Offered annually to "promote the collaboration between a writer and a photographer in the formative or fieldwork stages of a documentary project. Collaborative submissions on any subject are welcome." Guidelines for SASE or on website. **Deadline: January 31. Submissions accepted during January only.** Prize: $10,000.

FENIA AND YAAKOV LEVIANT MEMORIAL PRIZE

Modern Language Association of America, 26 Broadway, 3rd Floor, New York NY 10004-1789. (646)576-5141. Fax: (646)458-0030. E-mail: awards@mla.org. Website: www.mla.org. **Contact:** Coordinator of book prizes. This prize is to honor, in alternating years, an outstanding English translation of a Yiddish literary work or an outstanding scholarly work in any language in the field of Yiddish. Offered every two years. In 2008 it will be awarded to a scholarly work published between 2004 and 2007. In 2006 it will be awarded to a translation published between 2002 and 2005. Open to MLA members and nonmembers. Authors or publishers may submit titles. Guidelines for SASE or by e-mail. **Deadline: May 1.** Prize: $500, and a certificate, to be presented at the Modern Language Association's annual convention in December.

THE GLENNA LUSCHEI PRAIRIE SCHOONER AWARD

Prairie Schooner, 201 Andrews Hall, P.O. Box 880334, Lincoln NE 68588-0334. (402)472-0911. Fax: (402)472-9771. E-mail: kgrey2@unl.edu. Website: www.unl.edu/schooner/psmain.htm. **Contact:** Hilda Raz. Offered annually for work published in *Prairie Schooner* in the previous year. Prize: $1,000. Open to any writer.

◪ THE GRANT MACEWAN YOUNG WRITER'S SCHOLARSHIP

Alberta Community Development, 901 Standard Life Centre, 10405 Jasper Ave., Edmonton AB T5J 4R7 Canada. Website: www.cd.gov.ab.ca. This annual award was created by the government of Alberta to honor the life and contributions of the late Dr. Grant MacEwan. Open to young Alberta writers (16-25) who create a literary work reflecting Alberta and/or Dr. MacEwan's interests. **Deadline: December 31.** Guidelines for SASE. Prize: 4 scholarships of $2,500 each. Judged by a panel of Alberta authors and educators. Only open to residents of Alberta.

MISSISSIPPI REVIEW PRIZE

Mississippi Review, U.S.M. 118 College Dr., #5144, Hattiesburg MS 39406-0011. (601)266-4321. Fax: (601)266-5757. E-mail: rief@mississippireview.com. Website: www.mississippireview.com. **Contact:** Rie Fortenberry, contest director. Offered annually for unpublished fiction and poetry. Guidelines available online or with SASE. **Deadline: October 1. Charges $15 fee.** Prize: $1,000 each for fiction and poetry winners; plus winners are published in the print and online editions of the magazine. Open to all US writers except current or former students and employees of USM.

MLA PRIZE IN UNITED STATES LATINA & LATINO AND CHICANA & CHICANO LITERARY AND CULTURAL STUDIES

Modern Language Association of America, 26 Broadway, 3rd Floor, New York NY 10004-1789. (646)576-5141. Fax: (646)458-0030. E-mail: awards@mla.org. Website: www.mla.org. **Contact:** Coordinator of Book Prizes. Award for an outstanding scholarly study in any language of United States Latina & Latino and Chicana & Chicano literature or culture. *Open to current MLA members only.* Authors or publishers may submit titles. **Deadline: May 1.** Guidelines for SASE. Prize: $1,000, and a certificate to be presented at the Modern Language Association's annual convention in December.

NATIONAL OUTDOOR BOOK AWARDS

Box 8128, Idaho State University, Pocatello ID 83209. (208)282-3912. E-mail: wattron@isu.edu. Website: www.isu.edu/outdoor/books. **Contact:** Ron Watters. Eight categories: History/biography, outdoor literature, instructional texts, outdoor adventure guides, nature guides, childrens' books, design/artistic merit, and nature and the environment. Additionally, a special award, the Outdoor Classic Award, is given annually to books which, over a period of time, have proven to be exceptionally valuable works in the outdoor field. Application forms and eligibilty requirements are available online. **Deadline: September 1. Charges $65 fee.** Prize: Winning books are promoted nationally and are entitled to display the National Outdoor Book Award (NOBA) medallion.

◪ NLAPW BIENNIAL GRANTS FOR MATURE WOMEN

The National League of American Pen Women, 1300 17th St. NW, Washington DC 20036. (202)785-1997. E-mail: nlapw1@juno.com. Website: members.aol.com/penwomen/pen.htm. **Contact:** Elaine Waidelich, national scholarship chair. Offered every 2 years to further the 35+ age woman and her creative purposes in art, music, and letters. Open to US citizens. Award announced by March 1, even-numbered years. **Deadline: October 15, odd-numbered years. Charges $8 fee with entry.** Prize: $1,000 each in art, letters, and music. Sister Marquita Margula, art judge: 1837 Grandview Ave., El Paso TX 79902-5195. Lorna Jean Hagstrom, letters judge: 921 S. Hill Ave., DeLand FL 32724-7015. Louise Canepa, music judge: 666 Wall Rd., Napa CA 94558-9583.

OHIOANA WALTER RUMSEY MARVIN GRANT

Ohioana Library Association, 274 E. First Ave., Suite 300, Columbus OH 43201. (614)466-3831. Fax: (614)728-6974. E-mail: ohioana@sloma.state.oh.us. Website: www.ohioana.org. **Contact:** Linda Hengst. Offered annually to encourage young writers; open to writers under age 30 who have not published a book. Entrants must have been born in Ohio or have lived in Ohio for at least 5 years. Enter 1-6 pieces of prose totaling 10-60 pages (double space, 12 pt. font). **Deadline: January 31.** Prize: $1,000.

PEN CENTER USA LITERARY AWARDS

PEN Center USA, 672 S. Lafayette Park Place, Suite 42, Los Angeles CA 90057. (213)365-8500. Fax: (213)365-9616. E-mail: awards@penusa.org. Website: www.penusa.org. **Contact:** Literary Awards Coordinator. Offered for work published or produced in the previous calendar year. Open to writers living west of the Mississippi River. Award categories: drama, screenplay, teleplay, journalism. Guidelines for SASE or download from website. **Deadline: 4 copies must be received by January 31.** Prize: $1,000.

THE PRAIRIE SCHOONER READERS' CHOICE AWARDS

Prairie Schooner, 201 Andrews Hall, P.O. Box 880334, Lincoln NE 68588-0334. (402)472-0911. Fax: (402)472-9771. E-mail: kgrey2@unl.edu. Website: www.unl.edu/schooner/psmain.htm. **Contact:** Hilda Raz. Annual awards (usually 4-6) for work published in *Prairie Schooner* in the previous year. Prize: $250. Open to any writer.

DAVID RAFFELOCK AWARD FOR PUBLISHING EXCELLENCE

National Writers Association, 10940 S. Parker Rd., #508, Parker CO 80134. (303)841-0246. Fax: (303)841-2607. E-mail: sandywrter@aol.com. Website: www.nationalwriters.com. **Contact:** Sandy Whelchel. Contest is offered annually for books published the previous year. The purpose of this contest is to assist published authors in marketing their works and to reward outstanding published works. **Deadline: May 1.** Guidelines for SASE. **Charges $100 fee.** Prize: Publicity tour, including airfare, valued at $5,000.

ROCKY MOUNTAIN ARTISTS' BOOK COMPETITION

Hemingway Western Studies Center, Boise State University, 1910 University Dr., Boise ID 83725. (208)426-1999. Fax: (208)426-4373. E-mail: ttrusky@boisestate.edu. Website: www.boisestate.edu/hemingway/. **Contact:** Tom Trusky. Offered annually "to publish multiple edition artists' books of special interest to Rocky Mountain readers. Topics must be public issues (race, gender, environment, etc.). Authors may hail from Topeka or Ulan Bator, but their books must initially have regional appeal." Acquires first rights. Open to any writer. **Deadline: September 1-December 1.** Guidelines for SASE. Prize: $500, publication, standard royalties.

WILLIAM SANDERS SCARBOROUGH PRIZE

Modern Language Association of America, 26 Broadway, 3rd Floor, New York NY 10004-1789. (646)576-5141. Fax: (646)458-0030. E-mail: awards@mla.org. Website: www.mla.org. **Contact:** Coordinator of book prizes. Offered annually for work published in the previous year. "Given in honor of a distinguished man of letters and the first African-American member of the Modern Language Association, this prize will be awarded to an outstanding scholarly study of black American literature or culture." Open to MLA members and nonmembers. Authors or publishers may enter titles. Guidelines for SASE or by e-mail. **Deadline: May 1.** Prize: $1,000, and a certificate, to be presented at the Modern Language Association's annual convention in December.

JOANNA CATHERINE SCOTT NOVEL EXCERPT PRIZE

National League of American Pen Women, Nob Hill, San Francisco Bay Area Branch, 1544 Sweetwood Dr., Colma CA 94015. E-mail: pennobhill@aol.com. Website: www.soulmakingcontest.us. **Contact:** Eileen Malone. Send first chapter or the first 20 pages, whichever comes first. Include a 1-page synopsis. Annually. **Deadline: November 30.** Guidelines for SASE. **Charges $5/entry (make checks payable to NLAPW, Nob Hill Branch).** Prize: 1st Place: $100; 2nd Place: $50; 3rd Place: $25. Open to any writer.

BYRON CALDWELL SMITH AWARD

The University of Kentucky, Hall Center for the Humanities, 900 Sunnyside Dr., Lawrence KS 66045-0001. (785)864-4798. Website: www.hallcenter.ku.edu. **Contact:** Victor Baily, director. Offered in odd years. To qualify, applicants must live or be employed in Kansas and have written an outstanding book published within the previous 2 calendar years. Translations are eligible. Guidelines for SASE or on website. **Deadline: March 1.** Prize: $2,000. Guidelines for SASE or on website.

N ☑ TICKLED BY THUNDER ARTICLE CONTEST

Tickled by Thunder fiction magazine, 14076 86A Ave., Surrey BC V3W 0V9 Canada. E-mail: wd@tickledbythunder.com. Website: www.tickledbythunder.com. **Contact:** Larry Lindner. Annual contest to encourage writers of unpublished articles. **Deadline: February 15, May 15, August 15 and October 15.** Guidelines for SASE. Prize: $5 (Canadian), publication and 2 copies of the magazine. Judged by the publisher. Only subscribers may enter this contest.

N FRED WHITEHEAD AWARD

Texas Institute of Letters, 6335 W. Northwest Hwy., #618, Dallas TX 75225. (214)363-7253. E-mail: franvick@aol.com. Website: www.wtamu.edu/til/awards.htm. **Contact:** Fran Vick, secretary. Offered annually for the best design for a trade book. Open to Texas residents or those who have lived in Texas for 2 consecutive years. See website for guidelines. **Deadline: January 3.** Prize: $750.

WORLD FANTASY AWARDS ASSOCIATION

P.O. Box 43, Mukilteo WA 98275-0043. Website: www.worldfantasy.org. **Contact:** Peter Dennis Pautz, president. Estab. 1975. Offered annually for previously published work in several categories, including life achievement, novel, novella, short story, anthology, collection, artist, special award-pro, and special award nonpro. Works are recommended by attendees of current and previous 2 years' conventions, and a panel of judges. **Deadline: July 1.**

NONFICTION

AMWA MEDICAL BOOK AWARDS COMPETITION

American Medical Writers Association, 40 W. Gude Dr., Suite 101, Rockville MD 20850-1192. (301)294-5303. Fax: (301)294-9006. E-mail: bonnie@amwa.org. Website: www.amwa.org. **Contact:** Book Awards Committee. Offered annually to honor the best medical book published in the previous year in each of 3 categories: Books for Physicians, Books for Allied Health Professionals, and Trade Books. **Deadline: March 1. Charges $50 fee.**

RAY ALLEN BILLINGTON PRIZE

Organization of American Historians, 112 N. Bryan Ave., Bloomington IN 47408-4199. (812)855-7311. Fax: (812)855-0696. E-mail: nawards@oah.org. Website: www.oah.org. **Contact:** Award and Prize Committee Coordinator. Offered in even years for the best book in American frontier history, defined broadly so as to include the pioneer periods of all geographical areas and comparison between American frontiers and others. Guidelines available on website. **Deadline: October 1 of even-numbered years.** Prize: $1,000, and a plaque.

⊕ BIOGRAPHERS' CLUB PRIZE

Biographers' Club, The Secretary, 17 Sutherland St., London England SW1V 4JU. (020)7828 1274. Fax: (020)7828 7608. E-mail: lownie@globalnet.co.uk. Website: www.booktrust.org.uk. **Contact:** Andrew Lownie. The annual prize is sponsored by the *Daily Mail*, and all previous winners have gone on to secure publishing contracts—some for 6-figure sums. Entries should consist of a 15-20 page synopsis and 10 pages of a sample chapter for a biography. **Deadline: August 1.** Prize: £1,000. Judged by 3 distinguished biographers. Judges have included Michael Holroyd, Victoria Glendinning, Selina Hastings, Frances Spalding, Lyndall Gordon, Anne de Courcy, Nigel Hamilton, Anthony Sampson, and Mary Lovell. Open to any biographer who has not previously been commissioned or written a book.

BOWLING WRITING COMPETITION

American Bowling Congress Publications, 5301 S. 76th St., Greendale WI 53129-1127. Fax: (414)321-8356. E-mail: abcpr@bowl.com. Website: www.bowl.com. **Contact:** Bill Vint, editor. Estab. 1935. Offered for feature, editorial, and news all relating to the sport of bowling. **Deadline: December 15.** Prize: 1st Place in each division: $300. In addition, News and Editorial: $225, $200, $175, $150, $75, and $50; Feature: $225, $200, $175, $150, $125, $100, $75, and $50; with 5 honorable mention certificates awarded in each category.

✚ JOHN BULLEN PRIZE

Canadian Historical Association, 395 Wellington St., Ottawa ON K1A 0N3 Canada. (613)233-7885. Fax: (613)567-3110. E-mail: cha-shc@archives.ca. Website: www.cha-shc.ca. Offered annually for an outstanding historical dissertation for a doctoral degree at a Canadian university. Open only to Canadian citizens or landed immigrants. **Deadline: November 30.** Guidelines for SASE. Prize: $500.

✚ CANADIAN AUTHORS ASSOCIATION LELA COMMON AWARD FOR CANADIAN HISTORY

Box 419, 320 S. Shores Rd., Campbellford ON K0L 1L0 Canada. (705)653-0323. Fax: (705)653-0593. E-mail: admin@canauthors.org. Website: www.canauthors.org. **Contact:** Alec McEachern. Offered annually for a work of historical nonfiction on a Canadian topic by a Canadian author. Entry form required. Obtain entry form from contact name or download from website. **Deadline: December 15.** Guidelines for SASE. **Charges $35 (Canadian) entry fee.** Prize: $2,500, and a silver medal.

◨ CANADIAN LIBRARY ASSOCIATION STUDENT ARTICLE CONTEST

Canadian Library Association, 328 Frank St., Ottawa ON K2P 0X8 Canada. (613)232-9625, ext. 318. Fax: (613)563-9895. Website: www.cla.ca. **Contact:** Brenda Shields. Offered annually to "unpublished articles discussing, analyzing, or evaluating timely issues in librarianship or information science." Open to all students registered in or recently graduated from a Canadian library school, a library techniques program, or faculty of education library program. Submissions may be in English or French. **Deadline: March 31.** Guidelines for SASE. Prize: 1st Place: $150, publication, and trip to CLA's annual conference; 1st runner-up: $150, and $75 in CLA publications; 3rd runner-up: $100, and $75 in CLA publications.

THE DOROTHY CHURCHILL CAPPON CREATIVE NONFICTION AWARD

New Letters, 5101 Rockhill Rd., Kansas City MO 64110. (816)235-1168. Fax: (816)235-2611. E-mail: newletters@ umkc.edu. Website: www.newsletters.org. **Contact:** Amy Lucas. Contest is offered annually for unpublished work to discover and reward emerging writers and to give experienced writers a place to try new genres. Acquires first North American serial rights. Open to any writer. Guidelines for SASE or online. **Deadline: Third week of May. Charges $15 fee (includes a 1-year subscription to** *New Letters*). Prize: 1st Place: $1,000 and publication in a volume of *New Letters*; 1st runner-up will receive a copy of a recent book of poetry or fiction courtesy of our affiliate BkMk Press. All entries will receive consideration for publication in future editions of *New Letters*.

MORTON N. COHEN AWARD

Modern Language Association of America, 26 Broadway, 3rd Floor, New York NY 10004-1789. (646)576-5141. Fax: (646)458-0030. E-mail: awards@mla.org. Website: www.mla.org. **Contact:** Coordinator of Book Prizes. Estab. 1989. Awarded in odd-numbered years for a distinguished edition of letters. At least 1 volume of the edition must have been published during the previous 2 years. Editors need not be members of the MLA. **Deadline: May 1.** Guidelines for SASE. Prize: $1,000 and a certificate.

CARR P. COLLINS AWARD

The Texas Institute of Letters, 6335 W. Northwest Hwy., #618, Dallas TX 75225. (214)363-7253. E-mail: franvick @aol.com. Website: www.wtamu.edu/til/awards.htm. **Contact:** Fran Vick. Offered annually for work published January 1-December 31 of the previous year to recognize the best nonfiction book by a writer who was born in Texas or who has lived in the state for at least 2 consecutive years at one point, or a writer whose work has some notable connection with Texas. See website for guidelines. **Deadline: January 3.** Prize: $5,000.

AVERY O. CRAVEN AWARD

Organization of American Historians, P.O. Box 5457, Bloomington IN 47408-5457. (812)855-9852. Fax: (812)855-0696. Website: www.oah.org. **Contact:** Award and Prize Committee Coordinator. Offered annually for the most original book on the coming of the Civil War, the Civil War years, or the Era of Reconstruction, with the exception of works of purely military history. Guidelines on website. **Deadline: October 1.** Prize: $500.

CREATIVE NONFICTION PRIZE

(formerly Rosalie Fleming Essay and Creative Nonfiction Prize), National League of American Pen Women, Nob Hill, San Francisco Branch, 1544 Sweetwood Dr., Colma CA 94015. E-mail: pennobhill@aol.com. Website: www.soulmakingcontest.us. **Contact:** Eileen Malone. All prose works must be typed, page numbered, stapled, and double-spaced. Each essay/entry up to 3,000 words. Annually. **Deadline: November 30.** Guidelines for SASE. **Charges $5/entry (make checks payable to NLAPW, Nob Hill Branch).** Prize: 1st Place: $100; 2nd Place: $50; 3rd Place: $25. Open to any writer.

A CUP OF COMFORT

Adams Media Corp./F+W Publications Co., 57 Littlefield St., Avon MA 02322. Fax: (541)427-6790. E-mail: cupofcomfort@adamsmedia.com. Website: www.cupofcomfort.com. "A Cup of Comfort is the best-selling book series featuring inspiring true stories about the relationships and experiences that deeply affect our lives. Stories must be true, written in English, uplifting, and appropriate for a mainstream audience. This prize includes publication in an anthology. Contest is offered 2-4 times/year. Deadline is 6-12 months prior to publication. Guidelines on website, for SASE, or by e-mail. Open to aspiring and published writers. Allow 6-9 months for response. Prize: $500 grand prize; $100 for all other stories published in each book (50-60 stories/anthology). Acquires limited rights for a specified period of time; applies only to those stories selected for publication.

MERLE CURTI AWARD

Organization of American Historians, P.O. Box 5457, 112 N. Bryan Ave., Bloomington IN 47408-5457. (812)855-9852. Fax: (812)855-0696. Website: www.oah.org. **Contact:** Award and Prize Committee Coordinator. Offered annually for books in the fields of American social, intellectual, and/or cultural history. Guidelines available on website. **Deadline: October 1.** Prize: $1,000.

ANNIE DILLARD AWARD IN CREATIVE NONFICTION

Bellingham Review, Mail Stop 9053, Western Washington University, Bellingham WA 98225. (360)650-4863. E-mail: bhreview@cc.wwu.edu. Website: www.wwu.edu/~bhreview. **Contact:** Brenda Miller. Offered annually for unpublished essays on any subject and in any style. Guidelines for SASE or on website. **Deadline: December 1-March 15. Charges $15/1st entry, $10/additional entry.** Prize: 1st Place: $1,000, plus publication and copies. All finalists considered for publication. All entrants receive subscription.

GORDON W. DILLON/RICHARD C. PETERSON MEMORIAL ESSAY PRIZE

American Orchid Society, Inc., 16700 AOS Lane, Delray Beach FL 33446-4351. (561)404-2043. Fax: (561)404-2045. E-mail: jmengel@aos.org. Website: www.aos.org. **Contact:** Jane Mengel. Estab. 1985. "An annual contest open to all writers. The theme is announced each May in *Orchids* magazine. All themes deal with an aspect of orchids, such as repotting, growing, hybridizing, etc. Unpublished submissions only." Themes in past years have included Orchid Culture, Orchids in Nature, and Orchids in Use. Acquires one-time rights. **Deadline: November 30.** Prize: Cash award and certificate. Winning entry usually published in the May issue of *Orchids* magazine.

◼ THE DONNER PRIZE

The Award for Best Book on Canadian Public Policy, The Donner Canadian Foundation, 394A King St. E., Toronto ON M5A 1K9 Canada. (416)368-8253 or (416)368-3763. Fax: (416)363-1448. E-mail: meisnerpublicity@sympatico.ca. Website: www.donnerbookprize.com. **Contact:** Meisner Publicity, prize manager; Sherry Naylor or Susan Meisner. Offered annually for nonfiction published January 1-December 31 that highlights the importance of public policy and to reward excellent work in this field. Entries must be published in either English or French. Open to Canadian citizens. **Deadline: November 30.** Guidelines for SASE. Prize: Winner: $30,000; 5 shortlist authors: $5,000 each.

◼ THE DRAINIE-TAYLOR BIOGRAPHY PRIZE

The Writers' Trust of Canada, 90 Richmond St. E., Suite 200, Toronto ON M5C 1P1 Canada. (416)504-8222. Fax: (416)504-9090. E-mail: info@writerstrust.com. Website: www.writerstrust.com. **Contact:** James Davies. Awarded annually to a Canadian author for a significant work of biography, autobiography, or personal memoir. Award presented at the Great Literary Awards event held in Toronto each spring. Prize: $10,000.

◼ EDUCATOR'S AWARD

The Delta Kappa Gamma Society International, P.O. Box 1589, Austin TX 78767-1589. (512)478-5748. Fax: (512)478-3961. E-mail: jillf@deltakappagamma.org. Website: www.deltakappagamma.org. **Contact:** Jill Foltz, program/membership services administrator. Offered annually for quality research and nonfiction published January-December of previous year. This award recognizes educational research and writings of women authors whose work may influence the direction of thought and action necessary to meet the needs of today's complex society. The book must be written by 1 or 2 women who are citizens of any country in which The Delta Kappa Gamma Society International is organized: Canada, Costa Rica, El Salvador, Finland, Germany, Great Britain, Guatemala, Iceland, Mexico, The Netherlands, Norway, Puerto Rico, Sweden, US. Guidelines (required) for SASE. **Deadline: February 1.** Prize: $1,500.

◼ WALLACE K. FERGUSON PRIZE

Canadian Historical Association, 395 Wellington St., Ottawa ON K1A 0N3 Canada. (613)233-7885. Fax: (613)567-3110. E-mail: cha-shc@archives.ca. Website: www.cha-shc.ca. Offered to a Canadian who has published the outstanding scholarly book in a field of history other than Canadian history. **Deadline: December 2.** Guidelines for SASE. Prize: $1,000. Open to Canadian citizens and landed immigrants only.

GEORGE FREEDLEY MEMORIAL AWARD

Theatre Library Association, Benjamin Rosenthal Library, Queens College, C.U.N.Y., 65-30 Kissena Blvd., Flushing NY 11367. (718)997-3672. Fax: (718)997-3753. E-mail: rlw$lib@qc1.qc.edu. Website: tla.library.unt.edu. **Contact:** Richard Wall, book awards committee chair. Estab. 1968. Offered for a book published in the US within the previous calendar year on a subject related to live theatrical performance (including cabaret, circus, pantomime, puppetry, vaudeville, etc.). Eligible books may include biography, history, theory, criticism, reference, or related fields. **Deadline: February 15 of year following eligibility.** Prize: $500 and certificate to the winner; $200 and certificate for honorable mention.

THE CHRISTIAN GAUSS AWARD

The Phi Beta Kappa Society, 1606 New Hampshire Ave. NW, Washington DC 20009. (202)265-3808. Fax: (202)986-1601. E-mail: sbeasley@pbk.org. Website: www.pbk.org/scholarships/books. **Contact:** Sandra Beasley. The Christian Gauss Award is offered annually for books published May 1-April 30 in the field of literary scholarship or criticism. ''The prize was established in 1950 to honor the late Christian Gauss, the distinguished Princeton University scholar, teacher, and dean, who also served as president of the Phi Beta Kappa Society. To be eligible, a literary biography must have a predominantly critical emphasis.'' Entries must be submitted by the publisher. Entries must be preceded by a letter certifying that the book(s) conform to all conditions of eligibility and stating the publication date of each entry. If accepted, 8 copies of each entry are required for the Gauss Award. Ineligible entries will be returned by Phi Beta Kappa. Books will not be entered officially in the competition until all copies and the letter of certification have been received. **Deadline: April 30.** Prize: $2,500. Judged by a rotating panel of distinguished scholars and experts in the field. Open only to original works in English and authors of US residency and publication.

▧ GOVERNOR GENERAL'S LITERARY AWARD FOR LITERARY NONFICTION

Canada Council for the Arts, 350 Albert St., P.O. Box 1047, Ottawa ON K1P 5V8 Canada. (613)566-4414, ext. 5576. Fax: (613)566-4410. E-mail: joanne.larocque-poirier@canadacouncil.ca. Website: www.canadacouncil .ca/prizes/ggla. **Contact:** Joanne Larocque-Poirier. Offered for work published September 1-September 30. Submissions in English must be published between September 1, 2004 and September 30, 2005; submissions in French between July 1, 2004 and June 30, 2005. Publishers submit titles for consideration. **Deadline: March 15 or August 7, depending on the book's publication date.** Prize: Each laureate receives $15,000; nonwinning finalists receive $1,000.

JAMES T. GRADY—JAMES H. STACK AWARD FOR INTERPRETING CHEMISTRY FOR THE PUBLIC

American Chemical Society, 1155 16th St. NW, Washington DC 20036-4800. (202)872-4408. Fax: (202)776-8211. E-mail: awards@acs.org. Website: www.acs.org/awards/grady-stack.html. **Contact:** Nelufar Mohajeri. Offered annually for previously published work to recognize, encourage, and stimulate outstanding reporting directly to the public, which materially increases the public's knowledge and understanding of chemistry, chemical engineering, and related fields. Guidelines online at website. Rules of eligibility: A nominee must have made noteworthy presentations through a medium of public communication to increase the American public's understanding of chemistry and chemical progress. This information shall have been disseminated through the press, radio, television, films, the lecture platform, books, or pamphlets for the lay public. **Deadline: February 1.** Prize: $3,000, medallion with a presentation box, and certificate, plus travel expenses to the meeting at which the award will be presented.

JOHN GUYON NONFICTION PRIZE

Crab Orchard Review, English Department, Southern Illinois University Carbondale, Carbondale IL 62901-4503. E-mail: jtribble@siu.edu. Website: www.siu.edu/ ~ crborchd. **Contact:** Jon C. Tribble, managing editor. Offered annually for unpublished work. This competition seeks to reward excellence in the writing of creative nonfiction. This is not a prize for academic essays. *Crab Orchard Review* acquires first North American serial rights to submitted works. **Deadline: February 1-April 1.** Guidelines for SASE. **Charges $15/essay (limit of 3 essays of up to 6,500 words each).** Prize: $1,500, and publication. Open to US citizens only.

ALBERT J. HARRIS AWARD

International Reading Association, Division of Research and Policy, 800 Barksdale Rd., Newark DE 19714-8139. (302)731-1600, ext. 423. Fax: (302)731-1057. E-mail: research@reading.org. Website: www.reading.org. **Contact:** Marcella Moore. Offered annually to recognize outstanding published works focused on the identification, prevention, assessment, or instruction of learners experiencing difficulty learning to read. Open to any writer. Copies of the applications and guidelines can be downloaded in PDF format from the International Reading Association's website. **Deadline: September 15.** Prize: Monetary award and recognition at the International Reading Association's annual convention.

ELLIS W. HAWLEY PRIZE

Organization of American Historians, P.O. Box 5457, 112 N. Bryan Ave., Bloomington IN 47408-5457. (812)855-9852. Fax: (812)855-0696. Website: www.oah.org. **Contact:** Award and Prize Committee Coordinator. Offered annually for the best book-length historical study of the political economy, politics, or institutions of the US, in its domestic or international affairs, from the Civil War to the present. Books must be written in English. Guidelines available on website. **Deadline: October 1.** Prize: $500.

THE KIRIYAMA PRIZE

Kiriyama Pacific Rim Institute, 650 Delancey St., Suite 101, San Francisco CA 94107. (415)777-1628. Fax: (415)777-1646. E-mail: admin@kiriyamaprize.org. Website: www.kiriyamaprize.org. **Contact:** Jeannine Stronach, prize manager. Offered for work published from January 1 through December 31 of the current prize year to promote books that will contribute to greater mutual understanding and increased cooperation throughout the Pacific Rim and South Asia. Guidelines and entry form on request, or may be downloaded from the prize website. Books must be submitted for entry by the publisher. Proper entry forms must be submitted. Contact the administrators of the prize for complete rules and entry forms. **Deadline: late Fall each year; specific date TBA.** Prize: $30,000 to be divided equally between the author of 1 fiction and 1 nonfiction book.

KATHERINE SINGER KOVACS PRIZE

Modern Language Association of America, 26 Broadway, 3rd Floor, New York NY 10004-1789. (646)576-5141. Fax: (646)458-0030. E-mail: awards@mla.org. Website: www.mla.org. **Contact:** Coordinator of Book Prizes. Estab. 1990. Offered annually for a book published during the previous year in English in the field of Latin American and Spanish literatures and cultures. Books should be broadly interpretive works that enhance understanding of the interrelations among literature, the other arts, and society. Author need not be a member of the MLA. **Deadline: May 1.** Guidelines for SASE. Prize: $1,000 and a certificate.

🌐 KRASZNA-KRAUSZ PHOTOGRAPHY & MOVING IMAGE BOOK AWARDS

Kraszna-Krausz Foundation, 122 Fawnbrake Ave., London England SE24-0BZ. (+44)20-7738-6701. E-mail: awards@k-k.org.uk. Website: www.k-k.org.uk. **Contact:** Andrea Livingstone. These annual awards recognize outstanding achievements in the publishing and writing of books (published between June and May) on the art, history, practice, and technology of photography and the moving image (film, TV, etc.). All submissions must be made by the publisher of the title. **Deadline: July 1.** Guidelines for SASE. Prize: Main Awards (2): £5,000 UK Sterling; Finalist Awards: up to £1,000 UK Sterling. Judged by an international panel of 3 judges which changes annually. Open to any writer.

LERNER-SCOTT PRIZE

Organization of American Historians, P.O. Box 5457, 112 N. Bryan Ave., Bloomington IN 47408-5457. (812)855-9852. Fax: (812)855-0696. Website: www.oah.org. **Contact:** Award and Prize Committee Coordinator. Offered annually for the best doctoral dissertation in US women's history. Guidelines available at website. **Deadline: October 1 for a dissertation completed in the previous academic year (July 1-June 30).** Prize: $1,000.

JAMES RUSSELL LOWELL PRIZE

Modern Language Association of America, 26 Broadway, 3rd Floor, New York NY 10004-1789. (646)576-5141. Fax: (646)458-0030. E-mail: awards@mla.org. Website: www.mla.org. **Contact:** Coordinator of Book Prizes. Offered annually for literary or linguistic study, or critical edition or biography published in previous year. *Open to MLA members only.* **Deadline: March 1.** Guidelines for SASE. Prize: $1,000 and a certificate.

🍁 SIR JOHN A. MACDONALD PRIZE

Canadian Historical Association, 395 Wellington St., Ottawa ON K1A 0N3 Canada. (613)233-7885. Fax: (613)567-3110. E-mail: cha-shc@archives.ca. Website: www.cha-shc.ca. Offered annually to award a previously published nonfiction work of Canadian history "judged to have made the most significant contribution to an understanding of the Canadian past." Open to Canadian citizens only. **Deadline: December 2.** Guidelines for SASE. Prize: $1,000.

🍁 GRANT MACEWAN AUTHOR'S AWARD

Alberta Community Development, 901 Standard Life Centre, 10405 Jasper Ave., Edmonton AB T5J 4R7 Canada. Website: www.cd.gov.ab.ca. This annual award was created by the government to honor the life and contributions of the late Dr. Grant MacEwan. Books submitted must reflect Alberta and/or Dr. MacEwan's interests and must have been published between January 1 and December 31. **Deadline: December 31.** Guidelines for SASE. Prize: $25,000. Judged by a jury of prominent Alberta authors. Open to residents of Alberta only.

HOWARD R. MARRARO PRIZE

Modern Language Association of America, 26 Broadway, 3rd Floor, New York NY 10004-1789. (646)576-5141. Fax: (646)458-0030. E-mail: awards@mla.org. Website: www.mla.org. **Contact:** Coordinator of Book Prizes. Offered in even-numbered years for a scholarly book or essay on any phase of Italian literature or comparative literature involving Italian, published in previous year. Authors must be members of the MLA. **Deadline: May 1, 2006.** Guidelines for SASE. Prize: $1,000, and a certificate.

ⓝ MID-AMERICAN REVIEW CREATIVE NONFICTION AWARD

Mid-Amerian Review, Department of English, BGSU, Bowling Green OH 43403. (419)372-2725. Fax: (419)372-4642. Website: www.bgsu.edu/midamericanreview. **Contact:** Michael Czyzniejewski. Annual contest for unpublished nonfiction. Essays should be 6,000 words or less. **Deadline: October 1.** Guidelines for SASE. **Charges $10/essay.** Prize: $1,000 to the first-place winner. Judged by a well-published author of creative nonfiction (rotates every year). Acquires first North American Serial Rights.

MID-LIST PRESS FIRST SERIES AWARD FOR CREATIVE NONFICTION

Mid-List Press, 4324 12th Ave. S., Minneapolis MN 55407-3218. Fax: (612)823-8387. E-mail: cihlar@midlist.org. Website: www.midlist.org. **Contact:** James Cihlar, executive director. Open to any writer who has never published a book of creative nonfiction. Submit either a collection of essays or a single book-length work; minimum length 50,000 words. Accepts simultaneous submissions. Guidelines and entry form for SASE or on website. **Deadline: July 1. Charges $30 fee.** Prize: Awards include publication and an advance against royalties.

KENNETH W. MILDENBERGER PRIZE

Modern Language Association of America, 26 Broadway, 3rd Floor, New York NY 10004-1789. (646)576-5141. Fax: (646)458-0030. E-mail: awards@mla.org. Website: www.mla.org. **Contact:** Coordinator of Book Prizes. Offered annually for a publication from the previous year in the field of language culture, literacy, or literature with a strong application to the teaching of languages other than English. Author need not be a member. **Deadline: May 1.** Guidelines for SASE. Prize: $1,000, a certificate, and a year's membership in the MLA.

MLA PRIZE FOR A DISTINGUISHED BIBLIOGRAPHY

Modern Language Association of America, 26 Broadway, 3rd Floor, New York NY 10004-1789. (646)576-5141. Fax: (646)458-0030. E-mail: awards@mla.org. Website: www.mla.org. **Contact:** Coordinator of Book Prizes. Offered in even-numbered years for enumerative and descriptive bibliographies published in monographic, book, or electronic format in the 2 years prior to the competition. Open to any writer or publisher. **Deadline: May 1.** Guidelines for SASE. Prize: $1,000, and a certificate.

MLA PRIZE FOR A DISTINGUISHED SCHOLARLY EDITION

Modern Language Association of America, 26 Broadway, 3rd Floor, New York NY 10004-1789. (646)576-5141. Fax: (646)458-0030. E-mail: awards@mla.org. Website: www.mla.org. **Contact:** Coordinator of Book Prizes. Offered in odd-numbered years. To qualify for the award, an edition should be based on an examination of all available relevant textual sources; the source texts and the edited text's deviations from them should be fully described; the edition should employ editorial principles appropriate to the materials edited, and those principles should be clearly articulated in the volume; the text should be accompanied by appropriate textual and other historical contextual information; the edition should exhibit the highest standards of accuracy in the presentation of its text and apparatus; and the text and apparatus should be presented as accessibly and elegantly as possible. Editor need not be a member of the MLA. **Deadline: May 1.** Guidelines for SASE. Prize: $1,000, and a certificate.

MLA PRIZE FOR A FIRST BOOK

Modern Language Association of America, 26 Broadway, 3rd Floor, New York NY 10004-1789. (646)576-5141. Fax: (646)458-0030. E-mail: awards@mla.org. Website: www.mla.org. **Contact:** Coordinator of Book Prizes. Offered annually for the first book-length scholarly publication by a current member of the association. To qualify, a book must be a literary or linguistic study, a critical edition of an important work, or a critical biography. Studies dealing with literary theory, media, cultural history, and interdisciplinary topics are eligible; books that are primarily translations will not be considered. **Deadline: April 1.** Guidelines for SASE. Prize: $1,000, and a certificate.

MLA PRIZE FOR INDEPENDENT SCHOLARS

Modern Language Association of America, 26 Broadway, 3rd Floor, New York NY 10004-1789. (646)576-5141. Fax: (646)458-0030. E-mail: awards@mla.org. Website: www.mla.org. **Contact:** Coordinator of Book Prizes. Offered annually for a book in the field of English, or another modern language, or literature published in the previous year. Authors who are enrolled in a program leading to an academic degree or who hold tenured or tenure-track positions in higher education are not eligible. Authors need not be members of MLA. Guidelines and application form for SASE. **Deadline: May 1.** Prize: $1,000, a certificate, and a year's membership in the MLA.

ⓝ LINDA JOY MYERS MEMOIR PRIZE

National League of American Pen Women, Nob Hill, San Francisco Branch, 1544 Sweetwood Dr., Colma CA 94015-20029. E-mail: pennobhill@aol.com. Website: www.soulmakingcontest.us. **Contact:** Eileen Malone. One memoir/entry, up to 3,000 words, double spaced. Previously published material is acceptable. Annually. **Deadline: November 30.** Guidelines for SASE. **Charges $5/entry (make checks payable to NLAPW, Nob Hill Branch).** Prize: 1st Place: $100; 2nd Place $50; 3rd Place $45. Open to any writer.

GEORGE JEAN NATHAN AWARD FOR DRAMATIC CRITICISM

Cornell University, Department of English, Goldwin Smith Hall, Ithaca NY 14853. (607)255-6801. Fax: (607)255-6661. Website: www.arts.cornell.edu/english/nathan/index.html. **Contact:** Chair, Department of English. Offered annually to the American "who has written the best piece of drama criticism during the theatrical year (July 1-June 30), whether it is an article, an essay, treatise, or book." Only published work may be submitted; author must be an American citizen. Guidelines for SASE. Prize: $10,000 and a trophy.

NATIONAL WRITERS ASSOCIATION NONFICTION CONTEST

The National Writers Association, 10940 S. Parker Rd., #508, Parker CO 80134. (303)841-0246. Fax: (303)841-2607. E-mail: sandywrter@aol.com. Website: www.nationalwriters.com. **Contact:** Sandy Whelchel, director. Annual contest "to encourage writers in this creative form and to recognize those who excel in nonfiction writing." **Deadline: December 31.** Guidelines for SASE. **Charges $18 fee.** Prize: 1st Place: $200; 2nd Place: $100; 3rd Place: $50.

ⓝ THE FREDERIC W. NESS BOOK AWARD

Association of American Colleges and Universities, 1818 R St. NW, Washington DC 20009. (202)387-3760. Fax: (202)265-9532. E-mail: info@aacu.org. Website: www.aacu.org. **Contact:** Bethany Sutton. Offered annually for work published in the previous year. "Each year the Frederic W. Ness Book Award Committee of the Association of American Colleges and Universities recognizes books which contribute to the understanding and improvement of liberal education." Guidelines for SASE and on website. "Writers may nominate their own work; however, we send letters of invitation to publishers to nominate qualified books." **Deadline: May 1.** Prize: $2,000, and presentation at the association's annual meeting; transportation and 1 night hotel for meeting are also provided.

ⓝ NORTH AMERICAN INDIAN PROSE AWARD

University of Nebraska Press, 233 N. Eighth St., Lincoln NE 68588-0255. Fax: (402)472-0308. E-mail: gdunham1@unl.edu. **Contact:** Gary H. Dunham, editor, Native American studies. Offered for the best new nonfiction work by an American-Indian writer. **Deadline: July 1.** Prize: Publication by the University of Nebraska Press with a $1,000 advance.

OUTSTANDING DISSERTATION OF THE YEAR AWARD

International Reading Association, 800 Barksdale Rd., P.O. Box 8139, Newark DE 19714-8139. (302)731-1600, ext. 423. Fax: (302)731-1057. E-mail: research@reading.org. Website: www.reading.org. **Contact:** Marcella Moore. Offered annually to recognize dissertations in the field of reading and literacy. *Applicants must be members of the International Reading Association.* Copies of the applications and guidelines can be downloaded in PDF format from the International Reading Association's website. **Deadline: October 1.** Prize: $1,000.

FRANK LAWRENCE AND HARRIET CHAPPELL OWSLEY AWARD

Southern Historical Association, Dept. of History, University of Georgia, Athens GA 30602-1602. (706)542-8848. Fax: (706)542-2455. Website: www.uga.edu/~sha. **Contact:** Secretary-Treasurer. Estab. 1934. Managing Editor: John B. Boles. Offered in odd-numbered years for recognition of a distinguished book in Southern history published in even-numbered years. Publishers usually submit the books. **Deadline: March 1.**

LOUIS PELZER MEMORIAL AWARD

Organization of American Historians, *Journal of American History*, 1215 E. Atwater Ave., Bloomington IN 47401. (812)855-9852. Fax: (812)855-0696. Website: www.oah.org. Offered annually for the best essay in American history by a graduate student. The essay may be about any period or topic in the history of the US, and the author must be enrolled in a graduate program at any level, in any field. Length: 7,000 words (including endnotes) maximum. Guidelines available on website. **Deadline: December 1.** Prize: $500 and publication of the essay in the *Journal of American History*.

PEN/MARTHA ALBRAND AWARD FOR FIRST NONFICTION

PEN American Center, 588 Broadway, Suite 303, New York NY 10012. (212)334-1660, ext. 101. Fax: (212)334-2181. E-mail: awards@pen.org. **Contact:** Andrew Proctor. Offered annually for a first published book of general nonfiction distinguished by qualities of literary and stylistic excellence. Eligible books must have been published in the calendar year under consideration. Authors must be American citizens or permanent residents. Although there are no restrictions on the subject matter of titles submitted, nonliterary books will not be considered. Books should be of adult nonfiction for the general or academic reader. Publishers, agents, and authors themselves must submit 3 copies of each eligible title. **Deadline: December 15.** Prize: $1,000.

PEN/MARTHA ALBRAND AWARD FOR THE ART OF THE MEMOIR

PEN American Center, 588 Broadway, Suite 303, New York NY 10012. (212)334-1660, ext. 101. Fax: (212)334-2181. E-mail: awards@pen.org. **Contact:** Andrew Proctor. Offered annually to an American author for his/her memoir published in the current calendar year, distinguished by qualities of literary and stylistic excellence. Send 3 copies of each eligible book. Open to American writers. **Deadline: December 15.** Prize: $1,000.

PEN/JERARD FUND

PEN American Center, 588 Broadway, Suite 303, New York NY 10012. (212)334-1660, ext. 101. Fax: (212)334-2181. E-mail: awards@pen.org. **Contact:** Andrew Proctor. Estab. 1986. Biennial grant offered in odd-numbered years for an American woman writer of nonfiction for a book-length work-in-progress. Minimum requirement for applicants is publication of at least one magazine article in a national publication or in a major literary magazine. **Deadline: January 6.** Prize: $5,500 grant.

THE PHI BETA KAPPA AWARD IN SCIENCE

The Phi Beta Kappa Society, 1606 New Hampshire Ave. NW, Washington DC 20009. (202)265-3808. Fax: (202)986-1601. E-mail: sbeasley@pbk.org. Website: www.pbk.org/scholarships/books. **Contact:** Sandra Beasley. Estab. 1959. ''The Phi Beta Kappa Award in Science is offered annually for outstanding contributions by scientists to the literature of science. The intent of the award is to encourage literate and scholarly interpretations of the physical and biological sciences and mathematics; monographs and compendiums are not eligible. To be eligible, biographies of scientists must have a substantial critical emphasis on their scientific research.'' Entries must have been published May 1-April 30. Entries must be submitted by the publisher. Entries must be preceded by a letter certifying that the book(s) conforms to all the conditions of eligibility and stating the publication date of each entry. If accepted, 6 copies of each entry are required for the Science Award. Ineligible entries will be returned by Phi Beta Kappa. Books will not be entered officially in the competition until all copies and the letter of certification have been received. **Deadline: April 30.** Prize: $2,500. Open only to original works in English and authors of US residency and publication.

PRESERVATION FOUNDATION CONTESTS

The Preservation Foundation, Inc., 2213 Pennington Bend, Nashville TN 37214. E-mail: preserve@storyhouse.org. Website: www.storyhouse.org. **Contact:** Richard Loller. Contest offered annually for unpublished nonfiction. ''Our annual contests are to encourage those with a story to tell to share it with others before it is lost or forgotten. General nonfiction category (1,500-5,000 words)—any appropriate nonfiction topic. Travel nonfiction category (1,500-5,000 words)—must be true story of trip by author or someone known personally by author.'' **First entry in each category is free; $5 fee for each additional entry. Deadline: September 30.** Prize: 1st Prize: $100 in each category. Certificates for finalists. Open to any unpublished writer.

JAMES A. RAWLEY PRIZE

Organization of American Historians, P.O. Box 5457, 112 N. Ryan Ave., Bloomington IN 47408-5457. (812)855-9852. Fax: (812)855-0696. Website: www.oah.org. **Contact:** Award and Prize Committee Coordinator. Offered annually for a book dealing with the history of race relations in the US. Books must have been published in the current calendar year. Before submitting a nomination, a listing of current committee members and details about individual prizes must be obtained from the OAH website. **Deadline: October 1; books to be published after October 1 of the calendar year may be submitted as page proofs.** Prize: $1,000.

☑ EVELYN RICHARDSON NONFICTION AWARD

Writers' Federation of Nova Scotia, 1113 Marginal Rd., Halifax NS B3H 4P7 Canada. (902)423-8116. Fax: (902)422-0881. E-mail: talk@writers.ns.ca. Website: www.writers.ns.ca. **Contact:** Jane Buss, executive director. ''Nova Scotia's highest award for a book of nonfiction written by a Nova Scotian, the Evelyn Richardson Nonfiction Award is presented annually by the Writers' Federation of Nova Scotia. The award is named for Nova Scotia writer Evelyn Richardson, whose book *We Keep a Light* won the Governor General's Literary Award for nonfiction in 1945.'' There is **no entry fee** or form. Full-length books of nonfiction written by Nova Scotians, and published as a whole for the first time in the previous calendar year, are eligible. Publishers: Send 4 copies and a letter attesting to the author's status as a Nova Scotian, and the author's current mailing address and telephone number. **Deadline: First Friday in December.** Prize: $1,000.

▚ ROGERS COMMUNICATION LITERARY NONFICTION CONTEST

(formerly Prism International Prize for Literary Nonfiction), PRISM International, Creative Writing Program, UBC, Buch E462—1866 Main Mall, Vancouver BC V6T 1Z1 Canada. (604)822-2514. Fax: (604)822-3616. E-mail: prism@interchange.ubc.ca. Website: prism.arts.ubc.ca. **Contact:** Zoya Harris, executive editor. Offered annually for published and unpublished writers to promote and reward excellence in literary nonfiction writing. *PRISM* buys first North American serial rights upon publication. ''We also buy limited Web rights for pieces selected for the website.'' Open to anyone except students and faculty of the Creative Writing Program at UBC or people who have taken a creative writing course at UBC in the 2 years prior to contest deadline. All entrants receive a 1-year subscription to *PRISM*. **Deadline: September 30.** Guidelines for SASE. **Charges $25, plus $7 for each additional entry (outside Canada use US funds).** Prize: $500 for the winning entry, plus $20/page for the publication of the winner in *PRISM*'s winter issue.

THE CORNELIUS RYAN AWARD

The Overseas Press Club of America, 40 W. 45th St., New York NY 10036. (212)626-9220. Fax: (212)626-9210. Website: www.opcofamerica.org. **Contact:** Sonya Fry, executive director. Offered annually for excellence in a nonfiction book on international affairs. Generally publishers nominate the work, but writers may also submit in their own name. The work must be published and on the subject of foreign affairs. **Deadline: End of January. Charges $125 fee.** Prize: $1,000 and a certificate.

THEODORE SALOUTOS AWARD

Agricultural History, P.O. Box 5075, Minard Hall, NDSU, Fargo ND 58105-5075. (701)231-5831. Fax: (701)231-5832. E-mail: ndsu.agricultural.history@ndsu.nodak.edu. Website: agriculturalhistory.ndsu.nodak.edu. **Contact:** Claire Strom. Offered annually for best book on US agricultural history broadly interpreted. Open nominations. **Deadline: December 31.** Prize: $500.

ALDO AND JEANNE SCAGLIONE PRIZE FOR COMPARATIVE LITERARY STUDIES

Modern Language Association of America, 26 Broadway, 3rd Floor, New York NY 10004-1789. (646)576-5141. Fax: (646)458-0030. E-mail: awards@mla.org. Website: www.mla.org. **Contact:** Coordinator of Book Prizes. Offered annually for outstanding scholarly work published in the preceding year in the field of comparative literary studies involving at least 2 literatures. *Author must be a member of the MLA.* Works of scholarship, literary history, literary criticism, and literary theory are eligible; books that are primarily translations are not eligible. **Deadline: May 1.** Guidelines for SASE. Prize: $2,000 and a certificate.

ALDO AND JEANNE SCAGLIONE PRIZE FOR FRENCH AND FRANCOPHONE STUDIES

Modern Language Association of America, 26 Broadway, 3rd Floor, New York NY 10004-1789. (646)576-5141. Fax: (646)458-0030. E-mail: awards@mla.org. Website: www.mla.org. **Contact:** Coordinator of Book Prizes. Offered annually for work published in the preceding year that is an outstanding scholarly work in the field of French or francophone linguistic or literary studies. *Author must be a member of the MLA.* Works of scholarship, literary history, literary criticism, and literary theory are eligible; books that are primarily translations are not eligible. **Deadline: May 1.** Guidelines for SASE. Prize: $2,000 and a certificate.

ALDO AND JEANNE SCAGLIONE PRIZE FOR ITALIAN STUDIES

Modern Language Association of America, 26 Broadway, 3rd Floor, New York NY 10004-1789. (646)576-5141. Fax: (646)458-0030. E-mail: awards@mla.org. Website: www.mla.org. **Contact:** Coordinator of Book Prizes. Offered in odd-numbered years for a scholarly book on any phase of Italian literature or culture, or comparative literature involving Italian, including works on literary or cultural theory, science, history, art, music, society, politics, cinema, and linguistics, preferably but not necessarily relating other disciplines to literature. Books must have been published in year prior to competition. *Authors must be members of the MLA.* **Deadline: May 1.** Guidelines for SASE. Prize: $2,000 and a certificate.

ALDO AND JEANNE SCAGLIONE PRIZE FOR STUDIES IN GERMANIC LANGUAGES & LITERATURE

Modern Language Association of America, 26 Broadway, 3rd Floor, New York NY 10004-1789. (646)576-5141. Fax: (646)458-0030. E-mail: awards@mla.org. Website: www.mla.org. **Contact:** Coordinator of Book Prizes. Offered in even-numbered years for outstanding scholarly work appearing in print in the previous 2 years and written by a member of the MLA on the linguistics or literatures of the Germanic languages. Works of literary history, literary criticism, and literary theory are eligible; books that are primarily translations are not eligible. **Deadline: May 1.** Guidelines for SASE. Prize: $2,000 and a certificate.

ALDO AND JEANNE SCAGLIONE PRIZE FOR STUDIES IN SLAVIC LANGUAGES AND LITERATURES

Modern Language Association of America, 26 Broadway, 3rd Floor, New York NY 10004-1789. (646)576-5141. Fax: (646)458-0030. E-mail: awards@mla.org. **Contact:** Coordinator of Book Prizes.

Offered each odd-numbered year for books published in the previous 2 years. Membership in the MLA is not required. Works of literary history, literary criticism, philology, and literary theory are eligible; books that are primarily translations are not eligible. **Deadline: May 1.** Guidelines for SASE. Prize: $2,000 and a certificate.

ALDO AND JEANNE SCAGLIONE PUBLICATION AWARD FOR A MANUSCRIPT IN ITALIAN LITERARY STUDIES

Modern Language Association, 26 Broadway, 3rd Floor, New York NY 10004-1789. (646)576-5141. Fax: (646)458-0030. E-mail: awards@mla.org. Website: www.mla.org. **Contact:** Coordinator of Book Prizes. Awarded annually to an author of a ms dealing with any aspect of the languages and literatures of Italy, including medieval Latin and comparative studies, or intellectual history if main thrust is clearly related to the humanities. Materials from ancient Rome are eligible if related to postclassical developments. Also translations of classical works of prose and poetry produced in Italy prior to 1900 in any language (i.e., neo-Latin, Greek) or in a dialect of Italian (i.e., Neapolitan, Roman, Sicilian). Work can be in English or Italian. *Authors must be members of the MLA* and currently reside in the US or Canada. **Deadline: August 1.** Guidelines for SASE. Prize: $8,000. Subvention to press for publication of manuscript, $2,000 and a certificate to author.

SCIENCE WRITING AWARDS IN PHYSICS AND ASTRONOMY

American Institute of Physics, 1 Physics Ellipse, College Park MD 20740-3843. (301)209-3096. Fax: (301)209-0846. E-mail: llancast@aip.org. Website: www.aip.org/aip/writing. **Contact:** Lalena Lancaster. Offered for published articles, booklets, or books "that improve the general public's appreciation and understanding of physics and astronomy." Four categories: articles or books intended for children, preschool-15 years old; broadcast media for radio or television programming; journalism, written by a professional journalist; and books or articles by a scientist. Guidelines by phone, e-mail, or website. **Deadline: March 1.** Prize: $3,000, an engraved Windsor chair, and a certificate awarded in each category.

MINA P. SHAUGHNESSY PRIZE

Modern Language Association of America, 26 Broadway, 3rd Floor, New York NY 10004-1789. (646)576-5141. Fax: (646)458-0030. E-mail: awards@mla.org. Website: www.mla.org. **Contact:** Coordinator of Book Prizes. Offered annually for a scholarly book in the fields of language, culture, literacy or literature with strong application to the teaching of English published during preceding year. Authors need not be members of the MLA. **Deadline: May 1.** Guidelines for SASE. Prize: $1,000, a certificate, and a 1-year membership in the MLA.

FRANCIS B. SIMKINS AWARD

Southern Historical Association, Dept. of History, University of Georgia, Athens GA 30602-1602. (706)542-8848. Fax: (706)542-2455. Website: www.uga.edu/~sha. **Contact:** John C. Inscoe, secretary-treasurer. Estab. 1934. Managing Editor: John B. Boles. The award is sponsored jointly with Longwood College. Offered in odd-numbered years for recognition of the best first book by an author in the field of Southern history over a 2-year period. **Deadline: March 1.**

CHARLES S. SYDNOR AWARD

Southern Historical Association, Dept. of History, University of Georgia, Athens GA 30602. (706)542-8848. Fax: (706)542-2455. Website: www.uga.edu/~sha. **Contact:** Southern Historical Association. Offered in even-numbered years for recognition of a distinguished book in Southern history published in odd-numbered years. Publishers usually submit books. **Deadline: March 1.**

THE THEATRE LIBRARY ASSOCIATION AWARD

Theatre Library Association, Benjamin Rosenthal Library, Queens College, C.U.N.Y., 65-30 Kissena Blvd., Flushing NY 11367. (718)997-3672. Fax: (718)997-3753. E-mail: rlw$lib@qc1.qc.edu. Website: tla.library.unt.edu. **Contact:** Richard Wall, book awards committee chair. Estab. 1973. Offered for a book published in the US within the previous calendar year on a subject related to recorded or broadcast performance (including motion pictures, television, and radio). Eligible books may include biography, history, theory, criticism, reference, or related fields. **Deadline: February 15 of year following eligibility.** Prize: $500 and certificate to the winner; $200 and certificate for honorable mention.

FREDERICK JACKSON TURNER AWARD

Organization of American Historians, P.O. Box 5457, 112 N. Bryan Ave., Bloomington IN 47408-5457. (812)855-9852. Fax: (812)855-0696. Website: www.oah.org. **Contact:** Award and Prize Committee Coordinator. Offered annually for an author's first book on some significant phase of American history and also to the press that submits and publishes it. The entry must comply with the following rules: 1) The work must be the first book-length study of history published by the author; 2) If the author has a PhD, he/she must have received it no earlier than 7 years prior to submission of the ms for publication; 3) The work must be published in the calendar year before the award is given; 4) The work must deal with some significant phase of American history. Before submitting a nomination, a listing of current committee members and details about individual prizes must be obtained from the OAH website. **Deadline: October 1.** Prize: $1,000.

THE ELIE WIESEL PRIZE IN ETHICS ESSAY CONTEST

The Elie Wiesel Foundation for Humanity, 529 Fifth Ave., Suite 1802, New York NY 10017. (212)490-7777. Fax: (212)490-6006. E-mail: info@eliewieselfoundation.org. Website: www.eliewieselfoundation.org. Estab. 1989. ''This annual competition is intended to challenge undergraduate juniors and seniors in colleges and universities throughout the US to analyze ethical questions and concerns facing them in today's complex society. All students are encouraged to write thought-provoking, personal essays.'' **Deadline: Early December.** Guidelines for SASE. Prize: 1st Prize: $5,000; 2nd Prize: $2,500; 3rd Prize: $1,500; Honorable Mentions (2): $500. Judged by a distinguished panel of readers who evaluate all contest entries. A jury, including Elie Wiesel, chooses the winners.

WRITERS' JOURNAL ANNUAL TRAVEL WRITING CONTEST

Val-Tech Media, P.O. Box 394, Perham MN 56573. (218)346-7921. Fax: (218)346-7924. E-mail: writersjournal@ writersjournal.com. Website: www.writersjournal.com. **Contact:** Leon Ogroske. Offered annually for unpublished work. Buys one-time rights. Open to any writer. 2,000 word maximum. No e-mail submissions accepted. Guidelines for SASE and online. **Deadline: November 30. Charges $5 fee.** Prize: 1st Place: $50; 2nd Place: $25; 3rd Place: $15, plus honorable mentions. Prize-winning stories and selected honorable mentions will be published in *Writer's Journal* magazine.

▩ THE WRITERS' TRUST OF CANADA'S SHAUGHNESSY COHEN PRIZE FOR POLITICAL WRITING

The Writers' Trust of Canada, 90 Richmond St. E., Suite 200, Toronto ON M5C 1P1 Canada. (416)504-8222. Fax: (416)504-9090. E-mail: info@writerstrust.com. Website: www.writerstrust.com. **Contact:** James Davies. Awarded annually for ''a nonfiction book of outstanding literary merit that enlarges our understanding of contemporary Canadian political and social issues.'' Presented at the Politics & the Pen event each spring in Ottawa. Prize: $15,000.

FICTION

AIM MAGAZINE SHORT STORY CONTEST

P.O. Box 1174, Maywood IL 60153-8174. (708)344-4414. E-mail: apiladoone@aol.com. Website: www.aimmaga zine.org. **Contact:** Myron Apilado, editor. Estab. 1974. $100 prize offered to contest winner for best unpublished short story (4,000 words maximum) ''promoting brotherhood among people and cultures.'' **Deadline: August 15.** Open to any writer.

THE ALCHEMIST REVIEW PRIZE FOR SHORT FICTION

(formerly Writer's Repertory Short Fiction Literary Award), English Program, University of Illinois at Springfield, One University Plaza, MS BRK 489, Springfield IL 62703. (217)206-7459. E-mail: writersrepertory@hotmail.com. **Contact:** English GA. ''We are seeking unpublished short fiction (15 pages maximum). The contest is designed to celebrate excellence in short fiction. The contest grew out of a graduate assistant's yearlong project.'' **Deadline: January 31.** Guidelines for SASE. **Charges $5 entry fee.** Prize: 1st Place: $300, publication in *The Alchemist Review* (the student-run literary journal produced by the English Department at the University of Illinois at Springfield), and 2 copies of the journal; 2nd Place: $100 and 1 copy of *The Alchemist Review*; 3rd Place: 1 copy of *The Alchemist Review*. Judged by graduate students in the English Department with a primary focus on creative writing. Open to any writer.

▧ THE SHERWOOD ANDERSON FOUNDATION FICTION AWARD

Sherwood Anderson Foundation, % Michael M. Spear, 216 College Rd., Richmond VA 23229. Annual award for short stories and chapters of novels to encourage and support developing writers. Entrants must have published at least 1 book of fiction or have had several short stories published in major literary and/or commercial publications. Do not send your work by e-mail. Only mss in English will be accepted. **Deadline: April 1. Charges $20 application fee (payable to The Sherwood Anderson Foundation).** Prize: $15,000. Open to any writer.

SHERWOOD ANDERSON SHORT FICTION AWARD

Mid-American Review, Dept. of English, Box WM, Bowling Green State University, Bowling Green OH 43403. (419)372-2725. E-mail: mikeczy@bgnet.bgsu.edu. Website: www.bgsu.edu/midamericanreview. **Contact:** Michael Czyzniejewski, fiction editor. Offered annually for unpublished mss. Contest is open to all writers not associated with a judge or *Mid-American Review*. Guidelines available on website or for SASE. **Deadline: October 1. Charges $10.** Prize: $500, plus publication in the spring issue of *Mid-American Review*. Judged by editors and a well-known writer, i.e. Stuart Dybek or Jean Thompson.

✒ ANNUAL GIVAL PRESS NOVEL CONTEST

Gival Press, LLC, P.O. Box 3812, Arlington VA 22203. (703)351-0079. E-mail: givalpress@yahoo.com. Website: www.givalpress.com. **Contact:** Robert L. Giron. Offered annually for a previously unpublished original—not a translation—novel in English of at least 30,000-100,000 words of literary quality. Guidelines online, via e-mail, or by mail with SASE. **Deadline: May 30. Charges $50 (USD) reading fee.** Prize: $3,000, plus publication of book with a standard contract. Open to any writer.

ANNUAL GIVAL PRESS SHORT STORY CONTEST

Gival Press, LLC, P.O. Box 3812, Arlington VA 22203. (703)351-0079. E-mail: givalpress@yahoo.com. Website: www.givalpress.com. **Contact:** Robert L. Giron. Offered annually for a previously unpublished original—not a translation—short story in English of at least 5,000-15,000 words of literary quality. Guidelines by mail with SASE, by e-mail, or online. **Deadline: August 8. Charges $20 (USD) reading fee.** Prize: $1,000, plus publication on website. Open to any writer.

✒ ANNUAL HIDDEN TALENTS SHORT STORY CONTEST

Tall Tales Press, 20 Tuscany Valley Park NW, Calgary AB T3L 2B6 Canada. (403)874-4293. E-mail: talltalespress @shaw.ca. Website: www.talltalespress.com. **Contact:** Steve Van Bakel. Annual contest to "promote new writers and give them the opportunity to have their work published. There are 2 categories: the adult section and the junior writer for all those under the age of 18." **Deadline: May 31.** Guidelines for SASE. **Charges $10 (Canadian) for adult submissions; $5 (Canadian) for junior writer submissions.** Prize: Adult—1st Place: $500; 2nd Place: $250; 3rd Place: $100; 4th Place: $75; Honorable Mentions: $25. Junior Writers—1st Place: $200; 2nd Place: $100; 3rd Place: $50; 4th Place: $25; Honorable Mentions: $10. "We acquire first-time publishing rights to all stories entered. After that, all rights remain with the author." Judged by 4 published authors and the publisher of Tall Tales Press. Open to any writer.

ANTIETAM REVIEW LITERARY AWARD

Antietam Review, 41 S. Potomac St., Hagerstown MD 21740. (301)791-3132. Fax: (240)420-1754. **Contact:** Mary Jo Vincent, managing editor. "We consider all fiction manuscripts sent to *Antietam Review* Literary Contest as entries for inclusion in each issue. We look for well-crafted, serious literary prose fiction under 5,000 words. Contributors may submit up to three poems. Editors seek well-crafted pieces of no more than 30 lines." Offered annually for unpublished work. Reading period: May 1-September 1. Guidelines for SASE. **Charges $15/story; $15 for 3 poems.** Prize: $150 fiction; $100 poem. Open to any writer.

AUTHORMANIA.COM WRITING CONTEST

AuthorMania.com, 1210 Co. Rd. 707, Buna TX 77612. E-mail: teddybearteam@aol.com. Website: www.author mania.com. **Contact:** Cindy Thomas, contest director. Annual contest for unpublished short stories on any topic (no adult or hate), but no more than 5,000 words. "Enter as many times as you wish, but each entry must be mailed separately, and each must include an entry fee. No handwritten submissions." **Deadline: March 31. Charges $20 entry fee.** Prize: $1,000 and publication on AuthorMania.com. Open to any writer.

✒ THE BALTIMORE REVIEW FICTION CONTEST

The Baltimore Review, P.O. Box 36418, Towson MD 21286. E-mail: susan@susanmuaddidarraj.com. Website: www.baltimorereview.org. **Contact:** Susan Muaddi Darraj. **Deadline: December 1. Charges $15, or $25 for fee and 1-year subscription to** *The Baltimore Review*. Prize: 1st Place: $500 and publication; 2nd Place: $250; 3rd Place: $100. Open to any writer.

BARD FICTION PRIZE

Bard College, P.O. Box 5000, Annandale-on-Hudson NY 12504-5000. (845)758-7087. E-mail: bfp@bard.edu. Website: www.bard.edu/bfp. Estab. 2001. **Deadline: July 15.** Guidelines for SASE. Prize: $30,000 cash award and appointment as writer-in-residence at Bard College for 1 semester. Open to younger American writers.

✒ BEST PRIVATE EYE NOVEL CONTEST

Private Eye Writers of America and St. Martin's Press, 175 Fifth Ave., New York NY 11215. (212)674-5151. Fax: (212)254-4553. **Contact:** Toni Plummer. Offered annually for unpublished, book-length mss in the "private-eye" genre. Open to authors who have not published a mystery novel. **Deadline: July 1.** Guidelines for SASE. Prize: Advance against future royalties of $10,000, and publication by St. Martin's Minotaur.

N BEST SF/F EROTICA CONTEST

Circlet Press, 1770 Massachusetts Ave., #278, Cambridge MA 02140. E-mail: editorial@circlet.com. Website: www.circlet.com. Beginning in 2005, all editorial solicitations will be combined into only 1 anthology. This anthology will be a compilation of erotic stories with a sf/fantasy twist, or sf/fantasy stories with an erotic twist. Prefers stories to be 5,000-7,000 words, but anything up to 15,000 words is eligible. Submit via e-mail, or mail a hard copy. **Deadline: Accepts submissions April 15-August 31 only. Charges $5/entry.** Prize: 1st Place: $500; 2nd Place: $250. Runners-up will be published in the anthology for the regular payments ($50-100, depending on the length). Entrants will receive a $5 coupon good for buying anything in the Circlet catalog. If you still have a story in the slush pile from a previous year, it will automatically be considered for the contest. Open to any writer.

BINGHAMTON UNIVERSITY JOHN GARDNER FICTION BOOK AWARD

(formerly The John Gardner Memorial Prize for Fiction), Binghamton University, Dept. of English, General Literature & Rhetoric, P.O. Box 6000, Binghamton NY 13902-6000. (607)777-2408. Website: english.binghamton .edu/cwpro. **Contact:** Maria Mazziotti Gillan. Contest offered annually for a novel or collection of fiction published in 2004. Submit 3 copies of book. Books entered in competition will be donated to the contemporary literature collection at Binghamtom University Library and to the Broome County Library. **Deadline: March 1.** Prize: $1,000.

BOSTON REVIEW SHORT STORY CONTEST

Boston Review, E53-407 MIT, Cambridge MA 02139. Website: bostonreview.net. Stories should not exceed 4,000 words and must be previously unpublished. **Deadline: October 1. Charges $20 fee (check or money order payable to** *Boston Review*). Prize: $1,000 and publication in a later issue of *Boston Review*.

C CANADIAN AUTHORS ASSOCIATION JUBILEE AWARD FOR SHORT STORIES

P.O. Box 419, 320 S. Shores Rd., Campbellford ON K0L 1L0 Canada. (705)653-0323 or (866)216-6222. Fax: (705)653-0593. E-mail: admin@canauthors.org. Website: www.canauthors.org. **Contact:** Alec McEachern. Offered annually for a collection of short stories by a Canadian author. Entry form required. Obtain entry form from contact name or download from website. **Deadline: December 15.** Guidelines for SASE. **Charges $35 fee (Canadian).** Prize: $2,500 and a silver medal.

C CANADIAN AUTHORS ASSOCIATION MOSAID TECHNOLOGIES INC. AWARD FOR FICTION

Box 419, 320 South Shores Rd., Campbellford ON K0L 1L0 Canada. (705)653-0323 or (866)216-6222. Fax: (705)653-0593. E-mail: admin@canauthors.org. Website: www.canauthors.org. **Contact:** Alec McEachern. Offered annually for a full-length novel by a Canadian citizen or landed immigrant. Entry form required. Obtain entry form from contact name or download from website. **Deadline: December 15.** Guidelines for SASE. **Charges $35 fee (Canadian).** Prize: $2,500 and a silver medal.

CAPE FEAR CRIME FESTIVAL SHORT STORY CONTEST

Atticus, Inc., 3026 Grant Ave., Raleigh NC 27607. Phone/Fax: (919)783-2398. E-mail: nikkirs@nc.rr.com. Website: www.galleone.com/cfcf.htm. **Contact:** Nicole Smith, contest director. "The CFCF Short Story Contest was created in concert with the annual Cape Fear Crime Festival, a mystery writer and reader's conference held in North Carolina. The purpose of the annual story contest is to provide a forum in which to discover, publish, and promote new writers, and to introduce readers to promising authors through the publication of the contest's annual chapbook. Contest organizers are also interested in bridging the imagined gap between genre and nongenre fiction." No specific categories, as long as the story has a strong mystery or crime theme. **Deadline: June 1.** Guidelines for SASE. **Charges $8/entry—unlimited entries.** Prize: 1st Place: $100; 2nd Place: $75; 3rd Place: $50. All winning stories will be published in the story contest chapbook, which is distributed to hundreds of festival attendees. Winning authors will also receive free registration to the Cape Fear Crime Festival, and a free Saturday night dinner featuring a celebrated mystery author. Each winning story is subject to editorial review and will be copyedited for grammatical errors, spelling mistakes, and libelous language. All editorial changes will be shared with the winning authors before the chapbook goes to press. Prize-winning stories may be included in a Cape Fear Crime Anthology to be published at a later date. Judged by a panel of local bookstore employees, editors, and librarians to determine the semifinalists. Semifinalist stories are then passed on to a celebrity judge who determines which stories win 1st, 2nd, and 3rd place. 2004 celebrity judge was author Margaret Maron. Open to any writer.

THE ALEXANDER PATTERSON CAPPON FICTION AWARD

New Letters, 5101 Rockhill Rd., Kansas City MO 64110. (816)235-1168. Fax: (816)235-2611. E-mail: newletters@ umkc.edu. Website: www.newletters.org. **Contact:** Amy Lucas. Offered annually for unpublished work to discover and reward new and upcoming writers. Buys first North American serial rights. Open to any writer. **Deadline: Third week in May.** Guidelines for SASE. **Charges $15 (includes a 1-year subscription to** *New Letters*). Prize: 1st Place: $1,000, and publication in a volume of *New Letters*; 2 runners-up will receive a complimentary copy of a recent book of poetry or fiction from our affiliate BkMk Press. All entries will be given consideration for publication in future issues of *New Letters*.

CAPTIVATING BEGINNINGS SHORT STORY CONTEST

Lynx Eye, 581 Woodland Dr., Los Osos CA 93402. (805)528-8146. E-mail: pamccully@aol.com. **Contact:** Pam McCully, co-editor. Annual award for unpublished stories "with engrossing beginnings, stories that will enthrall and absorb readers." **Deadline: January 31.** Guidelines for SASE. **Charges $5/story.** Prize: $100, plus publication; $10 each for 4 honorable mentions, plus publication. Judged by *Lynx Eye* editors. Open to any writer.

KAY CATTARULLA AWARD FOR BEST SHORT STORY

(formerly Brazos Bookstore Short Story Award), Texas Institute of Letters, 6335 W. Northwest Hwy., #618, Dallas TX 75225. (214)363-7253. E-mail: franvick@aol.com. **Contact:** Fran Vick. Offered annually for work published January 1-December 31 of previous year to recognize the best short story. The story submitted must have appeared in print for the first time to be eligible. Writers must have been born in Texas, must have lived in Texas for at least 2 consecutive years, or the subject matter of the work must be associated with Texas. See website for guidelines. **Deadline: January 3.** Prize: $750.

G.S. SHARAT CHANDRA PRIZE FOR SHORT FICTION

BkMk Press, University of Missouri-Kansas City, 5101 Rockhill Rd., Kansas City MO 64110. (816)235-2558. Fax: (816)235-2611. E-mail: bkmk@umkc.edu. Website: www.umkc.edu/bkmk. **Contact:** Ben Furnish. Offered annually for the best book-length ms collection (unpublished) of short fiction in English by a living author. Translations are not eligible. Initial judging is done by a network of published writers. Final judging is done by a writer of national reputation. Guidelines for SASE, by e-mail, or on website. **Deadline: December 1 (postmarked). Charges $25 fee.** Prize: $1,000, plus book publication by BkMk Press.

CAROLYN A. CLARK FLASH FICTION PRIZE

National League of American Pen Women, Nob Hill, San Francisco Branch, 1544 Sweetwood Dr., Colma CA 94015-2029. E-mail: pennobhill@aol.com. Website: www.soulmakingcontest.us. **Contact:** Eileen Malone. Three flash fiction (short-short) stories per entry, under 500 words. Previously published material is accepted. Annually. **Deadline: November 30.** Guidelines for SASE. **Charges $5/entry (make checks payable to NLAPW, Nob Hill Branch).** Prize: 1st Place: $100; 2nd Place: $50; 3rd Place: $25. Open to any writer.

THE ARTHUR C. CLARKE AWARD

60 Bournemouth Rd., Folkestone Kent CT19 5AZ United Kingdom. E-mail: arthurcclarkeaward@yahoo.co.uk. Website: www.clarkeaward.com. **Contact:** Paul Kincaid. Annual award presented to the best science fiction novel, published between January 1 and December 31 of the year in question, receiving its first British publication during the calendar year. **Deadline: 2nd week in December.** Prize: £2,003 (rising by £1 each year), and an engraved bookend. Judged by representatives of the British Science Fiction Association, the Science Fiction Foundation, and the Science Museum. Open to any writer.

COMMONWEALTH WRITERS PRIZE

The Commonwealth Foundation, % Booktrust, Book House, 45 E. Hill, Wandsworth London SW18 2QZ United Kingdom. Fax: (00 44) 20 8516 2978. E-mail: tarryn@booktrust.org.uk. Website: www.commonwealthwriters.com. **Contact:** Tarryn McKay. The purpose of the annual award is "to encourage and reward the upsurge of new Commonwealth fiction and ensure that works of merit reach a wider audience outside their country of origin. The Commonwealth Foundation established the Commonwealth Writers Prize in 1987. For the purpose of the Prize, the Commonwealth is split into 4 regions—Africa, Caribbean and Canada, Eurasia, and Southeast Asia and South Pacific. Each region has 2 regional winners, 1 for the best book and 1 for the best first book. To be eligible for the best book award, the author must have at least 1 work of adult-aimed fiction previously published between January 1 and December 1. To be eligible for the best first book award, the book must be the author's first work of adult-aimed fiction (including a collection of short stories) to be published." This prize is publisher entry only, except in the case of some African and Asian countries where self-published works may be accepted at the administrator's discretion. Please contact Booktrust on this matter. All entries must be from Commonwealth citizens. All work must be written in English—translations are not eligible. **Deadline: November 15.** Prize: £10,000 to the overall best book; £3,000 to the overall best first book; £1,000 to 8 regional winners, 2 from each of the 4 regions. Judged by 4 panels of judges, 1 for each region. Each region has a chairperson and 2 judges. Once the regional winners are announced, the chairpersons read all 8 books and meet to decide which of the winners will receive the overall awards. This judging is headed by an eminent critic/author.

DAVID DORNSTEIN MEMORIAL CREATIVE WRITING CONTEST FOR YOUNG ADULT WRITERS

The Coalition for the Advancement of Jewish Education, 261 W. 35th St., Floor 12A, New York NY 10001. (212)268-4210. Fax: (212)268-4214. E-mail: cajeny@caje.org. Website: www.caje.org. **Contact:** Operations Manager. Contest offered annually for an unpublished short story based on a Jewish theme or topic. Writer must prove age of 18-35 years old. Submit only 1 story each year. Guidelines on website or available on request from CAJE office. **Deadline: December 31.** Prize: 1st Place: $700; 2nd Place: $200; 3rd Place: $100. Option for publication and distribution to CAJE members.

JACK DYER FICTION PRIZE

Crab Orchard Review, Dept. of English, Southern Illinois University Carbondale, Carbondale IL 62901-4503. E-mail: jtribble@siu.edu. Website: www.siu.edu/~crborchd. **Contact:** Jon C. Tribble, managing editor. Offered annually for unpublished short fiction. *Crab Orchard Review* acquires first North American serial rights to all submitted work. Open to any writer. **Deadline: February 1-April 1.** Guidelines for SASE. **Charges $15/entry (can enter up to 3 stories, each story submitted requires a separate fee and can be up to 6,000 words),** which includes a 1-year subscription to *Crab Orchard Review*. Prize: $1,500, and publication. Open to US citizens only.

N ☑ THE FAR HORIZONS AWARD FOR SHORT FICTION

The Malahat Review, Box 1700 STN CSC, Victoria BC V8W 2Y2 Canada. A short fiction contest for emerging writers who have not yet published their stories in book form. Story not to exceed 3,500 words and not previously published or accepted elsewhere. Anonymous judging; name to appear only on separate page. **Deadline: May 1.** Guidelines for SASE. **Charges $25/story (includes 1-year subscription).** Prize: $500, plus payment for publication at $30/page. Open to any writer.

N ⊕ FIRSTWRITER.COM INTERNATIONAL SHORT STORY CONTEST

firstwriter.com, 24 Gibraltar Ave., Halifax HX1 3UL United Kingdom. Website: www.firstwriter.com. **Contact:** J. Paul Dyson. Accepts short stories up to 3,000 words on any subject and in any style. **Deadline: April 1.** Guidelines for SASE. **Charges $7.50 for 1 short story; $12 for 2; $15 for 3; and $20 for 5.** Prize: Prizes total about $300. Ten special commendations will also be awarded and all the winners will be published in *firstwriter* magazine and recieve a free year's subscription to the site worth $28. All submissions are automatically considered for publication in *firstwriter* magazine and may be published there online. Judged by *firstwriter* magazine editors. Open to any writer.

⊕ FISH INTERNATIONAL SHORT STORY COMPETITION

Fish Publishing, Durrus, Bantry, Co. Cork, Ireland. +353(0)27 55645. E-mail: info@fishpublishing.com. Website: www.fishpublishing.com. **Contact:** Prize Coordinator. Offered annually for unpublished fiction mss (maximum 5,000 words). **Deadline: November 30. Charges $30 USD per story.** Prize: 1st Prize: 10,000 Euro (approximately $13,400 USD); 2nd Prize: 1 week at Anam Cara Writers' Retreat in West Cork and 250 Euro (approximately $150 USD); 3rd Prize: 250 Euro. Twelve runners-up will receive 100 Euro. All 15 winning authors will be published in the annual Fish Short Story Anthology and invited to the launch at the West Cork Literary Festival in June. Winners announced March 17. Judged by a panel of international judges which changes every year. Open to any writer.

FLASH FICTION CONTEST

Lumina, Sarah Lawrence College's Literary Magazine, Slonim House, 1 Mead Way, Bronxville NY 10708-5999. E-mail: lumina@slc.edu. Website: pages.slc.edu/%7lumina. **Contact:** Theresa Douglas. Must be unpublished. **Deadline: January 8. Charges $10 for up to 2 pieces; $5 per additional piece.** Prize: 1st Prize: $500, publication of your work, and 2 copies of the publication; 2nd Prize: $100, publication of your work, and 2 copies of the publication; 3rd Prize: publication of your work, and 2 copies of the publication. Judged by Amy Hempel. Open to US residents only.

H.E. FRANCIS SHORT STORY AWARD

The Ruth Hindman Foundation and the University of Alabama in Huntsville English Department, Huntsville AL 35899. Website: www.uah.edu/colleges/liberal/english/whatnewcontest.html. **Contact:** Patricia Sammon, editor. Offered annually for unpublished work, not to exceed 5,000 words. Acquires first-time publication rights. **Deadline: December 31.** Guidelines for SASE. **Charges $15 reading fee (make check payable to the Ruth**

Hindman Foundation). Prize: $1,000. Judged by a panel of nationally recognized, award-winning authors, directors of creative writing programs, and editors of literary journals.

◪ DANUTA GLEED LITERARY AWARD FOR FIRST BOOK OF SHORT FICTION

The Writers' Union of Canada, 90 Richmond St. E., Suite 200, Toronto ON M5C 1P1 Canada. (416)703-8982, ext. 223. Fax: (416)504-9090. E-mail: projects@writersunion.ca. Website: www.writersunion.ca. **Contact:** Deborah Windsor. Offered annually to Canadian writers for the best first collection of published short stories in the English language. Must have been published in the previous calendar year. Submit 4 copies. **Deadline: January 31.** Guidelines for SASE. Prize: 1st Place: $10,000; $500 to each of 2 runners-up.

GLIMMER TRAIN VERY SHORT FICTION AWARD

Glimmer Train Press, Inc., 1211 NW Glisan St., #207, Portland OR 97209. (503)221-0836. Fax: (503)221-0837. E-mail: eds@glimmertrain.com. Website: www.glimmertrain.com. **Contact:** Linda Swanson-Davies. Offered twice yearly to encourage the art of the very short story. Word count: 2,000 maximum. Open April 1-July 31 (Summer contest) or November 1-January 31 (Winter contest). Follow online submission process on website. Results will be e-mailed to all entrants on November 1 (for Summer contest) and May 1 (for Winter contest). **Charges $10 fee/story.** Winner receives $1,200, publication in *Glimmer Train Stories* (circulation 13,000), and 20 copies of that issue; runners-up receive $500/$300, respectively, and consideration for publication.

GLIMMER TRAIN'S FALL SHORT-STORY AWARD FOR NEW WRITERS

Glimmer Train Press, Inc., 1211 NW Glisan St., Suite 207, Portland OR 97209. (503)221-0836. Fax: (503)221-0837. E-mail: eds@glimmertrain.com. Website: www.glimmertrain.com. **Contact:** Linda Swanson-Davies. Offered for any writer whose fiction hasn't appeared in a nationally-distributed publication with a circulation over 5,000. Word limit: 12,000 words. **Open August 1-September 30.** Follow online submission procedure on website. Notification on January 2. **Charges $12 fee/story.** Prize: Winner receives $1,200, publication in *Glimmer Train Stories*, and 20 copies of that issue; runners-up receive $500/$300, respectively.

GLIMMER TRAIN'S SPRING SHORT-STORY AWARD FOR NEW WRITERS

Glimmer Train Press, Inc., 1211 NW Glisan St., Suite 207, Portland OR 97209. (503)221-0836. Fax: (503)221-0837. E-mail: eds@glimmertrain.com. Website: www.glimmertrain.com. **Contact:** Linda Swanson-Davies. Offered for any writer whose fiction hasn't appeared in a nationally-distributed publication with a circulation over 5,000. Word limit: 12,000 words. Contest open February 1-March 31. Follow online submission procedure on website. Notification on July 1. **Charges $12 fee/story.** Prize: Winner receives $1,200, publication in *Glimmer Train Stories* and 20 copies of that issue; runners-up receive $500/$300, respectively.

GLIMMER TRAIN'S SUMMER FICTION OPEN

Glimmer Train Press, Inc., 1211 NW Glisan St., Suite 207, Portland OR 97209. (503)221-0836. Fax: (503)221-0837. E-mail: eds@glimmertrain.com. Website: www.glimmertrain.com. **Contact:** Linda Swanson-Davies. Offered annually for unpublished stories as "a platform for all themes, all lengths (up to 25,000 words), all writers." Open to any writer. Follow online submission procedure on website. **Deadline: June 30. Charges $15 fee/story.** Prize: 1st Place: $2,000, publication in *Glimmer Train Stories*, and 20 copies of that issue; 2nd Place: $1,000 and possible publication in *Glimmer Train Stories*; 3rd Place: $600 and possible publication in *Glimmer Train Stories*.

GLIMMER TRAIN'S WINTER FICTION OPEN

Glimmer Train, Inc., 1211 NW Glisan St., Suite 207, Portland OR 97209. (503)221-0836. Fax: (503)221-0837. E-mail: eds@glimmertrain.com. Website: www.glimmertrain.com. **Contact:** Linda Swanson-Davies. Offered annually for unpublished work as "a platform for all themes, all lengths (up to 25,000 words), and all writers." Follow online submission procedure on website. **Deadline: January 11. Charges $15/story.** Prize: 1st Place: $2,000, publication in *Glimmer Train Stories*, and 20 copies of that issue; 2nd Place: $1,000 and possible publication in *Glimmer Train Stories*; 3rd Place: $600 and possible publication in *Glimmer Train Stories*. Open to any writer.

⊕ THE PHILLIP GOOD MEMORIAL PRIZE

QWF Magazine, P.O. Box 1768, Rugby CV21 4ZA United Kingdom. 01788 334302. E-mail: jo@qwfmagazine.co.uk. Website: www.qwfmagazine.co.uk. **Contact:** The Competition Secretary. Estab. 1998. Annual international short story competition open to all writers over 18. **Deadline: August 21.** Guidelines for SASE. **Charges £5 for each story up to 5,000 words (checks payable to J.M. Good).** Prize: 1st Prize: £300; 2nd Prize: £150; 3rd Prize: £75. Copyright remains with the author, but permissions will be requested to include the winning entries in *QWF Magazine*.

◪ GOVERNOR GENERAL'S LITERARY AWARD FOR FICTION

Canada Council for the Arts, 350 Albert St., P.O. Box 1047, Ottawa ON K1P 5V8 Canada. (613)566-4414, ext. 5576. Fax: (613)566-4410. E-mail: joanne.larocque-poirier@canadacouncil.ca. Website: www.canadacouncil .ca/prizes/ggla. **Contact:** Joanne Larocque-Poirier. Offered annually for the best English-language and the best French-language work of fiction by a Canadian. Submissions in English must be published between September 1, 2004 and September 30, 2005; submissions in French between July 1, 2004 and June 30, 2005. Publishers submit titles for consideration. **Deadline: March 15 or August 7, depending on the book's publication date.** Prize: Each laureate receives $15,000; nonwinning finalists receive $1,000.

◪ THE RICHARD HALL MEMORIAL GAY MEN'S SHORT FICTION CONTEST

The James White Review, P.O. Box 73910, Washington DC 20056-3910. (202)462-7924. E-mail: merlapatrick@a ol.com. Website: www.lambdalit.org. **Contact:** Jim Marks, executive director. Offered annually for unpublished short stories to recognize emerging gay writers. Subject must be gay men. Open to writers not previously published in a magazine with circulation of 10,000 or over. **Deadline: September 1.** Guidelines for SASE. **Charges $15 fee.** Prize: $1,000 and publication.

TOM HOWARD/JOHN H. REID SHORT STORY CONTEST

John H. Reid, % Winning Writers, 351 Pleasant St., PMB 222, Northampton MA 01060-3961. (866)946-9748. E-mail: adam@winningwriters.com. Website: www.winningwriters.com. **Contact:** John Howard Reid. Estab. 1993. **Deadline: March 31.** Guidelines for SASE. **Charges $10 USD/story/essay/prose work.** Prize: 1st Prize: $1,000; 2nd Prize: $500; 3rd Prize: $250. Highly commended entries share a prize pool of $825. Judged by John Howard Reid. Open to any writer.

L. RON HUBBARD'S WRITERS OF THE FUTURE CONTEST

P.O. Box 1630, Los Angeles CA 90078. (323)466-3310. E-mail: contests@authorservicesinc.com. Website: www. writersofthefuture.com. **Contact:** Contest Administrator. Offered for unpublished work "to find, reward, and publicize new speculative fiction writers so they may more easily attain professional writing careers." Open to new and amateur writers who have not professionally published a novel or short novel, more than 1 novelette, or more than 3 short stories. Eligible entries are short stories or novelettes (under 17,000 words) of science fiction or fantasy. Guidelines for SASE, online, or via e-mail. **Deadline: December 31, March 31, June 30, September 30. No entry fee; entrants retain all rights to their stories; judging by professional writers only.** Prize: Awards quarterly 1st Place: $1,000; 2nd Place: $750; and 3rd Place: $500. Annual Grand Prize: $4,000.

INDIANA REVIEW FICTION CONTEST

Indiana Review, BH 465, Indiana University, Bloomington IN 47405-7103. (812)855-3439. Fax: (812)855-4253. E-mail: inreview@indiana.edu. Website: www.indiana.edu/~inreview. **Contact:** Grady Jaynes, editor. Maximum story length is 15,000 words (no minimum). Offered annually for unpublished work. Guidelines on website and with SASE request. **Deadline: October 15. Charges $15 fee (includes a 1-year subscription).** Prize: $1,000. Judged by guest judges; 2004 prize judged by Chang-rae Lee. Open to any writer.

◪ ◪ INTERNATIONAL 3-DAY NOVEL WRITING CONTEST

P.O. Box 95033, Kingsgate RPO, Vancouver BC V5T 4T8 Canada. E-mail: info@3daynovel.com. Website: www.3 daynovel.com. **Contact:** Melissa Edwards. Estab. 1972. Offered annually for the best novel written in 3 days (Labor Day weekend). To register, send SASE (IRC if from outside Canada) for details, or entry form available from website. **Deadline: Friday before Labor Day weekend. Charges $50 fee (lower group rates available).** Prize: 1st place receives publication; 2nd place receives $500; 3rd place receives library of books. Open to all writers. Writing may take place in any location.

JERRY JAZZ MUSICIAN NEW SHORT FICTION AWARD

Jerry Jazz Musician, 2207 NE Broadway, Portland OR 97232. (503)287-5570. Fax: (801)749-9896. E-mail: jm@jer ryjazzmusician.com. Website: www.jerryjazz.com. **Contact:** Joe Maita. Contest is offered 3 times/year. "We value creative writing and wish to encourage writers of short fiction to pursue their dream of being published. *Jerry Jazz Musician*, an online magazine, would like to provide another step in the career of an aspiring writer. Three times a year, *Jerry Jazz Musician* awards a writer who submits, in our opinion, the best original, previously unpublished work of approximately 3,000-5,000 words. The winner will be announced via a special mailing of our *Jerry Jazz* newsletter. Publishers, artists, musicians, and interested readers are among those who subscribe to the newsletter. Additionally, the work will be published on the home page of *Jerry Jazz Musician* and featured there for at least 4 weeks. The *Jerry Jazz Musician* reader tends to have interests in music, history, literature, art, film, and theater, particularly that of the counter-culture of mid-20th century America. Writing should appeal to a reader with these characteristics." Guidelines available online. **Deadline: September, January, and May.** Prize: $200. Judged by the editors of *Jerry Jazz Musician*. Open to any writer.

JESSE H. JONES AWARD
6335 W. Northwest Hwy., #618, Dallas TX 75225. (214)363-7253. E-mail: franvick@aol.com. Website: www.wt amu.edu/til/awards.htm. **Contact:** Fran Vick. Offered annually for work published January 1-December 31 of year before award is given to recognize the writer of the best book of fiction entered in the competition. Writers must have been born in Texas, have lived in the state for at least 2 consecutive years at some time, or the subject matter of the work should be associated with the state. See website for guidelines. **Deadline: January 7.** Prize: $6,000.

JAMES JONES FIRST NOVEL FELLOWSHIP
Wilkes University, English Department, Kirby Hall, Wilkes-Barre PA 18766. (570)408-4530. Fax: (570)408-7829. E-mail: english@wilkes.edu. Website: www.wilkes.edu/humanities/jones.asp. **Contact:** Debra Archavage, co-ordinator. Offered annually for unpublished novels, novellas, and closely-linked short stories (all works in progress). "The award is intended to honor the spirit of unblinking honesty, determination, and insight into modern culture exemplified by the late James Jones." The competition is open to all American writers who have not previously published novels. **Deadline: March 1. Charges $20 fee.** Prize: $10,000; $250 honorarium (runner-up).

SERENA MCDONALD KENNEDY AWARD
Snake Nation Press, 110 W. Force St., Valdosta GA 31601. (229)244-0752. E-mail: jeana@snakenationpress.org. Website: www.snakenationpress.org. **Contact:** Jean Arambula. Contest for a collection of unpublished short stories by a new or underpublished writer. Entries accepted all year. **Deadline: September 1.** Guidelines for SASE. **Charges $30 reading fee.** Prize: $1,000 and publication. Judged by an independent judge. Open to any writer.

E.M. KOEPPEL SHORT FICTION AWARD
Writecorner Press, Koeppel Contest, P.O. Box 140310, Gainesville FL 32614-0310. Website: writecorner.com. **Contact:** Mary Sue Koeppel and Robert B. Gentry. Estab. 2004. Any number of unpublished stories may be entered by any writer. Send 2 title pages. Put only the title on one title page. List the title and the author's name, address, phone, e-mail, and short bio on the second title page. Guidelines for SASE or online. **Deadline: October 1-April 30. Charges $15/story; $10 for each additional story.** Prize: 1st Place: $1,100; Editor's Choices: $100 scholarship each. Open to any writer.

THE LAWRENCE FOUNDATION AWARD
Prairie Schooner, 201 Andrews Hall, P.O. Box 880334, Lincoln NE 68588-0334. (402)472-0911. Fax: (402)472-9771. E-mail: kgrey2@unl.edu. Website: www.unl.edu/schooner/psmain.htm. **Contact:** Hilda Raz. Offered annually for the best short story published in *Prairie Schooner* in the previous year. Prize: $1,000.

⁇ ⁇ LAWRENCE HOUSE CENTRE FOR THE ARTS SHORT STORY CONTEST
Lawrence House Centre for the Arts, 127 Christina St. S., Sarnia ON N7T 2M8 Canada. (519)337-0507. Fax: (519)337-0482. E-mail: lawrencehouse@bellnet.ca. Website: www.lawrencehouse.ca. **Contact:** Literary Representative on Board of Directors. Annual contest to promote unpublished, short fiction (entries must not exceed 2,500 words). Open to Canadians and landed immigrants. **Deadline: September 1.** Guidelines for SASE. **Charges $20 (Canadian) entry fee.** Prize: 1st Prize: $300; 2nd Prize: $200; 3rd Prize: $100. Judged by college professors of English and/or teachers of creative writing. Acquires first-time rights if local paper, *The Sarnia Observer*, publishes the winning entries.

LITERAL LATTÉ FICTION AWARD
Literal Latté, 200 E. 10th St., Suite 240, New York NY 10003. (212)260-5532. E-mail: litlatte@aol.com. Website: www.literal-latte.com. **Contact:** Edward Estlin, contributing editor. Award "to provide talented writers with 3 essential tools for continued success: money, publication, and recognition. Offered annually for unpublished fiction (maximum 6,000 words). Guidelines for SASE, by e-mail, or on website. Open to any writer. **Deadline: January 15.** Prize: 1st Prize: $1,000 and publication in *Literal Latté*; 2nd Prize: $300; 3rd Prize: $200; up to 7 honorable mentions.

LONG FICTION CONTEST
International, White Eagle Coffee Store Press, P.O. Box 383, Fox River Grove IL 60021. (847)639-9200. E-mail: wecspress@aol.com. Website: members.aol.com/wecspress. **Contact:** Frank E. Smith, publisher. Offered

annually since 1993 for unpublished work to recognize and promote long short stories of 8,000-14,000 words (about 30-50 pages). Sample of previous winner: $5.95, including postage. Open to any writer, no restrictions on materials. **Deadline: December 15.** Guidelines for SASE. **Charges $15 fee; $5 for second story in same envelope.** Prize: (A.E. Coppard Prize) $500, publication, and 25 copies of chapbook.

MALICE DOMESTIC GRANTS FOR UNPUBLISHED WRITERS

Malice Domestic, P.O. Box 31137, Bethesda MD 20284-1137. Website: www.malicedomestic.org. **Contact:** Grants chair. Offered annually for unpublished work in the mystery field. Malice awards 2 grants to unpublished writers in the malice domestic genre at its annual convention in May. The competition is designed to help the next generation of malice authors get their first work published and to foster quality malice literature. Malice Domestic literature is loosely described as mystery stories of the Agatha Christie type—i.e., ''traditional mysteries,'' which usually feature an amateur detective, characters who know each other, and no excessive gore, gratuitous violence, or explicit sex. Writers who have been published previously in the mystery field, including publication of a mystery novel, short story, or nonfiction work, are ineligible to apply. Members of the Malice Domestic Board of Directors and their families are ineligible to apply. Malice encourages applications from minority candidates. Guidelines on website. **Deadline: December 15.** Prize: $1,000.

MAYHAVEN AWARDS FOR FICTION

Mayhaven Publishing, P.O. Box 557, Mahomet IL 61853. (217)586-4493. Fax: (217)586-6330. E-mail: mayhaven publishing@mchsi.com. Website: www.mayhavenpublishing.com. **Contact:** Doris Replogle Wenzel. Estab. 1997. Offered annually for unpublished book-length work ''to provide additional opportunities for authors. We give awards in both adult and children's fiction.'' All entrants will be notified of the contest winners. **Deadline: December 31.** Guidelines for SASE. **Charges $50 fee.** Prize: Publication of work and royalties on sales.

MARY MCCARTHY PRIZE IN SHORT FICTION

Sarabande Books, P.O. Box 4456, Louisville KY 40204. (502)458-4028. Fax: (502)458-4065. E-mail: info@saraba ndebooks.org. Website: www.sarabandebooks.org. **Contact:** Kirby Gann, managing editor. Offered annually to publish an outstanding collection of stories, novellas, or short novel (less than 250 pages). All finalists considered for publication. **Deadline: January 1-February 15.** Guidelines for SASE. **Charges $25 fee.** Prize: $2,000 and publication (standard royalty contract).

MID-LIST PRESS FIRST SERIES AWARD FOR SHORT FICTION

Mid-List Press, 4324 12th Ave. S., Minneapolis MN 55407-3218. Fax: (612)823-8387. E-mail: cihlar@midlist.org. Website: www.midlist.org. **Contact:** James Cihlar, executive director. Open to any writer who has never published a book-length collection of short fiction (short stories, novellas); minimum 50,000 words. Accepts simultaneous submissions. Guidelines and entry form for SASE or on website. **Deadline: July 1. Charges $30 (US) fee.** Prize: Awards include publication and an advance against royalties.

MID-LIST PRESS FIRST SERIES AWARD FOR THE NOVEL

Mid-List Press, 4324 12th Ave. S., Minneapolis MN 55407-3218. (612)822-3733. Fax: (612)823-8387. E-mail: cihlar@midlist.org. Website: www.midlist.org. **Contact:** James Cihlar, executive director. Offered annually for unpublished novels to locate and publish quality mss by first-time writers, particularly those mid-list titles that major publishers may be rejecting. Guidelines for SASE or on website. Open to any writer who has never published a novel. **Deadline: February 1. Charges $30 (US) fee.** Prize: Advance against royalties, plus publication.

MILKWEED NATIONAL FICTION PRIZE

Milkweed Editions, 1011 Washington Ave. S., Suite 300, Minneapolis MN 55415. (612)332-3192. Fax: (612)215-2550. Website: www.milkweed.org. **Contact:** Elisabeth Fitz, first reader. Estab. 1986. Annual award for unpublished works. ''Milkweed is looking for a novel, novella, or a collection of short stories. Manuscripts should be of high literary quality and must be double-spaced and between 150-400 pages in length. Due to new postal regulations, writers who need their work returned must include a check for $5 rather than a SASE book mailer. Manuscripts not accompanied by a check for postage will be recycled.'' Winner will be chosen from the mss Milkweed accepts for publication each year. All mss submitted to Milkweed will automatically be considered for the prize. Submission directly to the contest is no longer necessary. ''Must be written in English. Writers should have previously published a book of fiction or 3 short stories (or novellas) in magazines/journals with national distribution.'' Catalog available on request for $1.50. Guidelines for SASE or online. **Deadline: Open.** Prize: Publication by Milkweed Editions, and a cash advance of $5,000 against royalties agreed upon in the contractual arrangement negotiated at the time of acceptance.

C. WRIGHT MILLS AWARD

The Society for the Study of Social Problems, 901 McClung Tower, University of Tennessee, Knoxville TN 37996-0490. (865)689-1531. Fax: (865)689-1534. E-mail: sssp@utk.edu. Website: www.sssp1.org. **Contact:** Michele Smith Koontz, administrative officer. Offered annually for a book published the previous year that most effectively critically addresses an issue of contemporary public importance; brings to the topic a fresh, imaginative perspective; advances social scientific understanding of the topic; displays a theoretically informed view and empirical orientation; evinces quality in style of writing; and explicitly or implicitly contains implications for courses of action. **Deadline: January 15.** Prize: $500 stipend.

🌐 KATHLEEN MITCHELL AWARD

Cauz Group Pty., Ltd., P.O. Box 777, Randwick NSW 2031 Australia. 61-2-93321559. Fax: 61-2-93321298. E-mail: psalter@cauzgroup.com.au. **Contact:** Petrea Salter. Offered in even years for novels published in the previous 2 years. Author must have been under age 30 when the novel was published. Entrants must be Australian or British born or naturalized Australian citizens, and have resided in Australia for the last year. The award is for a novel of the highest literary merit. **Deadline: March 31.** Guidelines for SASE. Prize: $7,500 (Australian).

NATIONAL WRITERS ASSOCIATION NOVEL WRITING CONTEST

The National Writers Association, 10940 S. Parker Rd. #508, Parker CO 80134. (303)841-0246. Fax: (303)841-2607. **Contact:** Sandy Whelchel, director. Annual contest "to help develop creative skills, to recognize and reward outstanding ability, and to increase the opportunity for the marketing and subsequent publication of novel manuscripts." **Deadline: April 1. Charges $35 fee.** Prize: 1st Place: $500; 2nd Place: $300; 3rd Place: $200.

NATIONAL WRITERS ASSOCIATION SHORT STORY CONTEST

The National Writers Association, 10940 S. Parker Rd. #508, Parker CO 80134. (303)841-0246. Fax: (303)841-2607. **Contact:** Sandy Whelchel, director. Annual contest "to encourage writers in this creative form, and to recognize those who excel in fiction writing." **Deadline: July 1.** Guidelines for SASE. **Charges $15 fee.** Prize: 1st Place: $200; 2nd Place: $100; 3rd Place: $50.

Ⓝ THE NELLIGAN PRIZE FOR SHORT FICTION

Colorado Review/Center for Literary Publishing, Dept. of English, Colorado State University, Ft. Collins CO 80523. (970)491-5449. E-mail: creview@colostate.edu. Website: coloradoreview.colostate.edu. **Contact:** Stephanie G'Schwind, editor. Offered annually to an unpublished short story. **Deadline: March 1. Charges $10.** Prize: $1,000 and publication of story in *Colorado Review*. Open to any writer.

NEW YORK STORIES FICTION PRIZE

New York Stories, English Department, E-103, LaGuardia Community College/CUNY, 31-10 Thomson Ave., Long Island City NY 11101. E-mail: nystories@lagcc.cuny.edu. Website: www.newyorkstories.org. **Contact:** Daniel Lynch, contest director. Offered annually for unpublished work to showcase new, quality short fiction. Stories must not exceed 6,500 words. Open to any writer. **Deadline: September 15.** Guidelines for SASE. **Charges $15 fee (payable to New York Stories).** Prize: 1st Place: $500 and publication; 2nd Place: $250 and consideration for publication.

FRANK O'CONNOR AWARD FOR SHORT FICTION

descant, Texas Christian University's literary journal, TCU Box 297270, Fort Worth TX 76129. (817)257-6537. Fax: (817)257-6239. E-mail: descant@tcu.edu. **Contact:** Dave Kuhne, editor. Offered annually for unpublished short stories. Publication retains copyright but will transfer it to the author upon request. **Deadline: September-April.** Guidelines for SASE. Prize: $500.

THE OHIO STATE UNIVERSITY PRIZE IN SHORT FICTION

The Ohio State University Press and the MFA Program in Creative Writing at The Ohio State University, 1070 Carmack Rd., Columbus OH 43210-1002. (614)292-1462. Fax: (614)292-2065. E-mail: ohiostatepress@osu.edu. Website: ohiostatepress.org. Offered annually to published and unpublished writers. Submissions may include short stories, novellas, or a combination of both. Manuscripts must be 150-300 typed pages; novellas must not exceed 125 pages. No employee or student of The Ohio State University is eligible. **Deadline: January 2006 (postmarked). Charges $20 fee.** Prize: $1,500 and publication under a standard book contract.

ONCEWRITTEN.COM FICTION CONTEST

Oncewritten.com, 1850 N. Whitley Ave., #404, Hollywood CA 90028. E-mail: fictioncontest@oncewritten.com. Website: www.oncewritten.com. The purpose of this biannual contest is to find high quality short fiction to feature on the website and in *Off the Press*, our monthly newsletter, which is distributed specifically to people interested in reading about new authors." **Deadline: April 30 and October 31.** Guidelines for SASE. **Charges $15/story.** Prize: Grand Prize: $1,000; 1st Prize: $100; both include publication on website and in newsletter. Judged by editor and 1 industry professional. Open to any writer.

⊕ ORANGE PRIZE FOR FICTION
Orange PCS, % Booktrust, Book House, 45 E. Hill, Wandsworth, London SW18 2QZ United Kingdom. Fax: (00 44) 20 8516 2978. E-mail: tarryn@booktrust.org.uk. Website: www.orangeprize.co.uk. **Contact:** Becky Shaw. This annual award is for a full-length novel written by a woman which fulfills the criteria of excellence in writing, relevance to people's everyday and imaginative lives, accessibility, and originality. The award is open to any full-length novel written in English between April 1 and the following March 31 by a woman of any nationality. Translations are not eligible, neither are novellas or collections of short stories. Books from all genres are encouraged, but all books must be unified and substantial works written by a single author. All entries must be published in the UK between the publication dates, but may have been previously published outside the UK. Publisher entry only. **Deadline: November 26.** Prize: £30,000 and a statuette known as a "Bessie." Judged by a panel of women.

⊠ OTTAWA PUBLIC LIBRARY ANNUAL SHORT STORY CONTEST
Ottawa Public Library, Community Partnerships and Programming, 101 Centrepointe Dr., Ottawa ON K2G 5K7 Canada. (613)580-2424, ext. 41468. E-mail: esme.bailey@library.ottawa.on.ca. Website: www.library.ottawa.on.ca. **Contact:** Esme Bailey. Offered annually for unpublished short stories (written in French or English) to encourage writing in the community. Open to residents of Ottawa, Ontario, age 18 or older. Call for guidelines, or go online. **Deadline: March 8. Charges $5/story.** Prize: 1st Prize: $500; 2nd Prize: $250; 3rd Prize: $100.

PATERSON FICTION PRIZE
One College Blvd., Paterson NJ 07505-1179. (973)684-6555. Fax: (973)684-5843. E-mail: mgillan@pccc.edu. Website: www.pccc.edu/poetry. **Contact:** Maria Mazziotti Gillan, director. Offered annually for a novel or collection of short fiction published the previous calendar year. **Deadline: April 1.** Guidelines for SASE. Prize: $1,000.

WILLIAM PEDEN PRIZE IN FICTION
The Missouri Review, 1507 Hillcrest Hall, Columbia MO 65211. (573)882-4474. Fax: (573)884-4671. Website: www.missourireview.com. **Contact:** Richard Sowienski, managing editor. Offered annually "for the best story published in the past volume year of the magazine. All stories published in *The Missouri Review* are automatically considered." Prize: $1,000 and a reading/reception.

PEEKS & VALLEYS FLASH FICTION CONTEST
Peeks & Valleys, 702 S. Twyckenham Dr., South Bend IN 46615. E-mail: peeksandvalleys@earthlink.net. Website: www.peeksandvalleys.com. Open to all genres, 750 words or less. **Deadline: July 1. Charges $5/story.** Open to any writer.

PEN/FAULKNER AWARDS FOR FICTION
PEN/Faulkner Foundation, 201 E. Capitol St., Washington DC 20003. (202)675-0345. Fax: (202)608-1719. E-mail: delaney@folger.edu. Website: www.penfaulkner.org. **Contact:** Janice F. Delaney, executive director. Offered annually for best book-length work of fiction by an American citizen published in a calendar year. **Deadline: October 31.** Prize: $15,000 (one winner); $5,000 (4 nominees).

THE KATHERINE ANNE PORTER PRIZE FOR FICTION
Nimrod International Journal, 600 S. College Ave., Tulsa OK 74104. (918)631-3080. Fax: (918)631-3033. E-mail: nimrod@utulsa.edu. Website: www.utulsa.edu/nimrod. **Contact:** Francine Ringold. This annual award was established to discover new, unpublished writers of vigor and talent. **Deadline: April 30.** Guidelines for SASE. **Charges $20 (includes a 1-year subscription to** *Nimrod***).** Prize: 1st Place: $2,000 and publication; 2nd Place: $1,000 and publication. *Nimrod* retains the right to publish any submission. Judged by the *Nimrod* editors (finalists), and a recognized author selects the winners. Open to US residents only.

⊠ PRISM INTERNATIONAL ANNUAL SHORT FICTION CONTEST
Prism International, Creative Writing Program, UBC, Buch E462, 1866 Main Mall, Vancouver BC V6T 1Z1 Canada. (604)822-2514. Fax: (604)822-3616. E-mail: prism@interchange.ubc.ca. Website: prism.arts.ubc.ca. **Contact:** Fiction Contest Manager. Offered annually for unpublished work to award the best in contemporary fiction. Works of translation are eligible. Guidelines for SASE, by e-mail, or on website. Acquires first North

American serial rights upon publication, and limited Web rights for pieces selected for website. Open to any writer except students and faculty in the Creative Writing Department at UBC, or people who have taken a creative writing course at UBC within 2 years of the contest deadline. **Deadline: January 31. Charges $25/ story; $7 each additional story (outside Canada pay US currency); includes subscription.** Prize: 1st Place: $2,000; Runners-up (5): $200 each; winner and runners-up published.

◼ THOMAS H. RADDALL ATLANTIC FICTION PRIZE

Writers' Federation of Nova Scotia, 1113 Marginal Rd., Halifax NS B3H 4P7 Canada. (902)423-8116. Fax: (902)422-0881. E-mail: talk@writers.ns.ca. Website: www.writers.ns.ca. **Contact:** Jane Buss, executive director. ''This award was established by the Writers' Federation of Nova Scotia and the Writers' Development Trust in 1990 to honor the achievement of Thomas H. Raddall, and to recognize the best Atlantic Canadian adult fiction. Thomas Head Raddall is probably best-known for *His Majesty's Yankees* (1942), *The Governor's Lady* (1960), *The Nymph and the Lamp* (1950), and *Halifax, Warden of the North* (1948).'' There is no entry fee or form. Full-length books of fiction written by Atlantic Canadians, and published as a whole for the first time in the previous calendar year, are eligible. Entrants must be native or resident Atlantic Canadians who have either been born in Newfoundland, Prince Edward Island, Nova Scotia, or New Brunswick, and spent a substantial portion of their lives living there, or who have lived in 1 or a combination of these provinces for at least 24 consecutive months prior to entry deadline date. Publishers: Send 4 copies and a letter attesting to the author's status as an Atlantic Canadian, and the author's current mailing address and telephone number. **Deadline: First Friday in December.** Prize: $10,000.

RAMBUNCTIOUS REVIEW FICTION CONTEST

Rambunctious Review, 1221 W. Pratt Blvd., Chicago IL 60626. Annual themed contest for unpublished stories. Acquires one-time publication rights. Open to any writer. **Deadline: December 31.** Guidelines for SASE. **Charges $4/story.** Prize: 1st Prize: $100; 2nd Prize: $75; 3rd Prize: $50; all winning stories will be published in future issues of *Rambunctious Review*. Acquires one-time publication rights.

▦ REAL WRITERS SHORT STORY AWARDS

Real Writers Support & Appraisal Service, P.O. Box 170, Chesterfield S40 1FE United Kingdom. E-mail: info@real-writers.com. Website: www.real-writers.com. **Contact:** Lynne Patrick, coordinator. Annual contest for unpublished short stories to provide an outlet for writers of short fiction and to open up opportunities for development. ''We have a good working relationship with a major publisher.'' **Deadline: November 30.** Guidelines for SASE. **Charges £5 sterling (payable by credit card, so converted to dollars of current exchange rate).** Prize: £2500 sterling and section prizes. Judged by an experienced team of readers who select a shortlist from which prize winners are chosen by a smaller team which includes literary agents and editors, and is led by a senior editor from a major publishing house. ''We buy first British serial rights for publication in an anthology.'' Applies only to prize winners. Open to any writer.

HAROLD U. RIBALOW PRIZE

Hadassah WZOA, 50 W. 58th St., New York NY 10019. (212)451-6289 or (212)451-6293. Fax: (212)451-6257. E-mail: imarks@hadassah.org; atigay@hadassah.org. **Contact:** Ian Marks, coordinator. Editor: Alan Tigay. Offered annually for English-language books of fiction (novel or short stories) on a Jewish theme published the previous year. Books should be submitted by the publisher. Administered annually by *Hadassah Magazine*. **Deadline: March 1.** Prize: $3,000. ''The official announcement of the winner will be made in early fall.''

RIVER CITY WRITING AWARDS IN FICTION

The University of Memphis/Hohenberg Foundation, Dept. of English, Memphis TN 38152. (901)678-4591. E-mail: rivercity@memphis.edu. Website: www.people.memphis.edu/~rivercity. Offered annually for unpublished short stories of 7,500 words maximum. Guidelines for SASE or on website. **Deadline: March 1. Charges $12/story, which is put toward a 1-year subscription for** *River City*. Prize: 1st Place: $1,500; 2nd Place: $350; 3rd Place: $150; and publication for each winner.

◼ THE ROGERS WRITERS' TRUST FICTION PRIZE

The Writers' Trust of Canada, 90 Richmond St. E., Suite 200, Toronto ON M5C 1P1 Canada. (416)504-8222. Fax: (416)504-9090. E-mail: info@writerstrust.com. Website: www.writerstrust.com. **Contact:** James Davies. Awarded annually for a distinguished work of fiction—either a novel or short story collection—published within the previous year. Presented at the Great Literary Awards event held in Toronto each spring. Prize: $15,000. Open to Canadian residents only.

🌐 ROONEY PRIZE FOR IRISH LITERATURE

Strathin, Templecarrig, Delgany, Co. Wicklow, Republic of Ireland. (01) 287 4769. Fax: (01) 287 2595. E-mail: rooneyprize@ireland.com. **Contact:** Thelma Cloake. Estab. 1976. Annual award for a published, Irish writer under the age of 40. Prize: 8,000 Euros. Judged by Michael Allen, Ingrid Craigie, Seamus Hosey, Niall MacMonagle, Deirdre Purcell, and Jim Sherwin (chairman).

🍁 SASKATCHEWAN FICTION AWARD

Saskatchewan Book Awards, Inc., Box 1921, Regina SK S4P 3E1 Canada. (306)569-1585. Fax: (306)569-4187. E-mail: director@bookawards.sk.ca. Website: www.bookawards.sk.ca. **Contact:** Glenda James, executive director. Offered annually for work published September 15-September 14 annually. This award is presented to a Saskatchewan author for the best book of fiction (novel or short fiction), judged on the quality of writing. **Deadline: First deadline: July 31; Final deadline: September 14.** Guidelines for SASE. **Charges $20 (Canadian).** Prize: $2,000.

MARY WOLLSTONECRAFT SHELLEY PRIZE FOR IMAGINATIVE FICTION

(formerly Ursula K. Leguin Prize for Imaginative Fiction), *Rosebud*, P.O. Box 459, Cambridge WI 53523. E-mail: jrodclark@smallbytes.net. Website: www.rsbd.net. **Contact:** J. Roderick Clark, editor. Biennial (odd years) contest for unpublished stories. The next 2 contests close on October 1, 2005 and October 1, 2007. Entries are welcome any time. Acquires first rights. Open to any writer. **Deadline: September 30. Charges $10/story.** Prize: $1,000, plus publication in *Rosebud*.

SIDE SHOW CONTEST

Somersault Press, 404 Vista heights Rd., El Cerrito CA 94530. E-mail: somersaultpress@yahoo.com. Website: www.somersaultpress.com. **Contact:** Shelley Anderson and Jean Schiffman. The anthology is published periodically, so there is no fixed deadline. Check website for deadline. Multiple submissions are encouraged. Guidelines for SASE. **Charges $12.50 for all entries sent in the same envelope, plus a sample copy of** *Side Show*. Prize: 1st Prize: $100; 2nd Prize: $75; 3rd Prize: $50. "We also pay every accepted writer $5 per printed page at the time the book is printed." Judged by the editors. First North American Serial Rights are purchased from accepted writers in exchange for payment of $5 per printed page. Open to any writer.

SHEILA K. SMITH SHORT STORY PRIZE

National League of American Pen Women, Nob Hill, San Francisco Bay Area, 1544 Sweetwood Dr., Colma CA 94015-2029. E-mail: pennobhill@aol.com. Website: www.soulmakingcontest.us. **Contact:** Eileen Malone. One story/entry, up to 5,000 words. All prose works must be typed, page numbered, stapled, and double-spaced. Annually. **Deadline: November 30.** Guidelines for SASE. **Charges $5/entry (make checks payable to NLAPW, Nob Hill Branch).** Prize: 1st Place: $100; 2nd Place: $50; 3rd Place: $25. Open to any writer.

KAY SNOW WRITING AWARDS

Willamette Writers, 9045 SW Barbur Blvd., Suite 5A, Portland OR 97219. (503)452-1592. Fax: (503)452-0372. E-mail: wilwrite@teleport.com. Website: www.willamettewriters.com. **Contact:** Marlene Moore. Contest offered annually to "offer encouragement and recognition to writers with unpublished submissions." Acquires right to publish excerpts from winning pieces 1 time in their newsletter. **Deadline: May 15.** Guidelines for SASE. **Charges $15 fee; no fee for student writers.** Prize: 1st Place: $300; 2nd Place: $150; 3rd Place: $50; excerpts published in Willamette Writers newsletter, and winners acknowledged at banquet during writing conference. Student writers win $50 in categories for grades 1-5, 6-8, and 9-12. $500 Liam Callen Memorial Award goes to best overall entry.

Ⓝ SOUTH CAROLINA FICTION PROJECT

South Carolina Arts Commission, 1800 Gervais St., Columbia SC 29201. (803)734-8696. Fax: (803)734-8526. E-mail: goldstsa@arts.state.sc.us. Website: www.state.sc.us/arts. **Contact:** Sara June Goldstein, contest director. Offered annually for unpublished short stories of 2,500 words or less. *The Post and Courier* newspaper (Charleston, South Carolina) purchases first publication rights. Open to any writer who is a legal resident of South Carolina and 18 years of age or older. Up to 12 stories are selected for publication. **Deadline: January 15.** Guidelines for SASE. Prize: $500.

THE SOUTHERN REVIEW/LOUISIANA STATE UNIVERSITY SHORT FICTION AWARD

Louisiana State University, 43 Allen Hall, Baton Rouge LA 70803. (225)578-5108. Fax: (225)578-5098. E-mail: southernreview@lsu.edu; perreaud@lsu.edu. Offered for first collections of short stories by Americans published in the US during the previous year. Publisher or author may enter by mailing 2 copies of the collection. **Deadline: January 31.**

SPOKANE PRIZE FOR SHORT FICTION

Eastern Washington University Press, 705 W. First Ave., Spokane WA 99201. (800)508-9095. Fax: (509)623-4283. E-mail: ewupress@ewu.edu. Website: ewupress.ewu.edu. **Contact:** Chris Howell. "Annual award to publish the finest work the literary world has to offer." **Deadline: May 1.** Guidelines for SASE. **Charges $25.** Prize: $1,500 and publication. Judged by EWU Press staff. Open to any writer.

THE SUNDAY STAR SHORT STORY CONTEST

The Toronto Star, 1 Yonge St., 5th Floor, Toronto ON M5A 4L1 Canada. Website: www.thestar.com. Annual contest for unpublished work offered "to encourage good, quality short story writing." Must be a Canadian citizen if living outside Canada, or a resident of Canada and at least 16 years or older. Guidelines on website or by calling (416)350-3000, ext. 2747. **Deadline: December 31. Charges $5.** Prize: 1st Place: $5,000, plus tuition fee for the Humber School of Writers Creative Correspondence Program; 2nd Place: $2,000; 3rd Place: $1,000; 7 runners-up receive $200 each. Judged by Ryerson Writing Centre (initial judging). Final judging by panel of writers and editors from *The Star*.

THE PETER TAYLOR PRIZE FOR THE NOVEL

Knoxville Writers' Guild and University of Tennessee Press, P.O. Box 2565, Suite 101, Knoxville TN 37901-2565. Website: www.knoxvillewritersguild.org. **Contact:** Brian Griffin. Offered annually for unpublished work to discover and publish novels of high literary quality. Guidelines for SASE or on website. Open to US residents writing in English. Members of the Knoxville Writers' Guild do the initial screening. A widely published novelist chooses the winner from a pool of finalists. **Deadline: February 1-April 30. Charges $25 fee.** Prize: $1,000 and publication by University of Tennessee Press (a standard royalty contract). Judged by Jill McCorkle (2005).

THOROUGHBRED TIMES FICTION CONTEST

P.O. Box 8237, Lexington KY 40533. (859)260-9800. Fax: (859)260-9812. E-mail: copy@thoroughbredtimes.com. Website: www.thoroughbredtimes.com. **Contact:** Amy Owens. Offered every 2 years for unpublished work to recognize outstanding fiction written about the Thoroughbred racing industry. Maximum length: 5,000 words. *Thoroughbred Times* receives first North American serial rights and reserves the right to publish any and all entries in the magazine. **Deadline: December 31.** Prize: 1st Place: $800 and publication in *Thoroughbred Times*; 2nd Place: $400 and publication; 3rd Place: $250 and publication.

TICKLED BY THUNDER FICTION CONTEST

Tickled by Thunder fiction magazine, 14076 86A Ave., Surrey BC V3W 0V9 Canada. E-mail: wd@tickledbythunder.com. Website: www.tickledbythunder.com. **Contact:** Larry Lindner. Annual contest to encourage unpublished fiction writers. **Deadline: February 15.** Guidelines for SASE. **Charges $10/story (free for subscribers).** Prize: $150, subscription, publication, and 2 copies of the magazine. Judged by the publisher and other various writers he knows who have not entered the contest. Open to any writer.

STEVEN TURNER AWARD FOR BEST FIRST WORK OF FICTION

6335 W. Northwest Hwy., #618, Dallas TX 75225. (214)363-7253. E-mail: franvick@aol.com. Website: wtamu.edu/til/. **Contact:** Fran Vick. Offered annually for work published January 1-December 31 for the best first book of fiction. Writers must have been born in Texas, have lived in the state for at least 2 consecutive years at some time, or the subject matter of the work should be associated with the state. Guidelines on website. **Deadline: January 3.** Prize: $1,000.

WHIM'S PLACE CHANGING OF THE SEASONS FLASH FICTION WRITING CONTEST

WhimsPlace.com, P.O. Box 14931, Lenexa KS 66285. E-mail: contest@whimsplace.com. Website: www.whimsplace.com/contest/contest.asp. **Contact:** Betsy Gallup. Offered quarterly for flash fiction. "We love flash fiction! That's why we're having a contest. We also feel that contests are a great way to boost an ego, enhance a résumé, and to just have some plain old fashion fun with your writing. We expect good writing, however. It must be tightly written, organized, and proofread at least 100 times." Submissions are accepted only through Whim's Place online submission form. Entries over 500 words will automatically be disqualified. **Deadline: March 30; June 30; September 30; December 30. Charges $5.** Prize: 1st Place: $150; 2nd Place: $100; 3rd Place: $50; Honorable Mentions (8): $25. Judged by Whim's Place staff members, and an appointed guest judge each season. The special judge will be a published author or an editor. Open to any writer.

GARY WILSON SHORT FICTION AWARD

descant, Texas Christian University's literary journal, TCU, Box 297270, Fort Worth TX 76129. (817)257-6537. Fax: (817)257-6239. E-mail: descant@tcu.edu. **Contact:** David Kuhne, editor. Offered annually for an outstanding story in an issue. Guidelines for SASE. Prize: $250. Open to any writer.

TOBIAS WOLFF AWARD IN FICTION

Bellingham Review, Mail Stop 9053, Western Washington University, Bellingham WA 98225. (360)650-4863. E-mail: bhreview@cc.wwu.edu. Website: www.wwu.edu/~bhreview/. **Contact:** Brenda Miller. Offered annually for unpublished work. Guidelines for SASE or online. **Deadline: December 1-March 15. Charges $15 entry fee for 1st entry; $10 for each additional entry.** Prize: $1,000, plus publication and subscription. All finalists considered for publication. All entrants receive subscription.

WORDSMITTEN'S TENTEN FICTION COMPETITION

WordSmitten Media, P.O. Box 5067, St. Petersburg FL 33737-5067. E-mail: story@wordsmitten.com. Website: www.wordsmitten.com. **Contact:** J.J. Marino. Contest offered annually for unpublished short stories. Requires exactly 1,010 words. "The word count does not include the story title. Make us laugh or make us weep. Above all, pay rigorous attention to the word count. It's why we call it the TenTen. It's a challenge to be precise, be witty, be short!" For more details, visit the website. Guidelines by e-mail or on website. **Deadline: July 1. Charges $18/entry.** Prize: $1,010 and publication in our print edition, the *WordSmitten Quarterly Journal*, which features distinguished authors (Connie May Fowler, Frank McCourt, Thisbe Nissen, Chris Offutt, ZZ Packer) and new voices. Judged by recognized authors, including Thisbe Nissen (*The Good People of New York* and *Osprey Island*), Michael C. White (*The Garden of Martyrs*), and Peter Meinke, winner of the Flannery O'Connor Short Story Award. Acquires one-time rights for publication, then all rights revert to author.

WORDSMITTEN STORYCOVE FLASH FICTION CONTEST

WordSmitten Media, P.O. Box 5067, St. Petersburg FL 33737-5067. E-mail: story@wordsmitten.com. Website: www.wordsmitten.com. **Contact:** J.J. Marino. Offered annually for unpublished, original fiction with memorable characters and interesting consequences with 500 or fewer words. Submit story embedded in an e-mail (no attachments) with your name at the top of the e-mail. Guidelines for SASE, by e-mail, and on website. **Deadline: May 1. Charges $12/entry.** Prize: $250 and "publication in our print edition, the *WordSmitten Quarterly Journal*, which features new voices and distinguished authors (Connie May Fowler, Frank McCourt, Thisbe Nissen, Christ Offutt, ZZ Packer). Judged by recognized authors, including Thisbe Nissen (*The Good People of New York* and *Osprey Island*), Michael C. White (*The Garden of Martyrs*), and Peter Meinke, winner of The Flannery O'Connor Short Story Award. Acquires one-time rights for publication, then all rights revert to author. Open to any writer.

WRITERS' JOURNAL ANNUAL FICTION CONTEST

Val-Tech Media, P.O. Box 394, Perham MN 56573. (218)346-7921. Fax: (218)346-7924. E-mail: writersjournal@writersjournal.com. Website: www.writersjournal.com. **Contact:** Leon Ogroske (editor@writersjournal.com). Offered annually for previously unpublished fiction. Open to any writer. Guidelines for SASE and online. **Deadline: January 30. Charges $15 reading fee.** Prize: 1st Place: $500; 2nd Place: $200; 3rd Place: $100, plus honorable mentions. Prize-winning stories and selected honorable mentions are published in *Writers' Journal*.

WRITERS' JOURNAL ANNUAL HORROR/GHOST CONTEST

Val-Tech Media, P.O. Box 394, Perham MN 56573. (218)346-7921. Fax: (218)346-7924. E-mail: writersjournal@writersjournal.com. Website: www.writersjournal.com. **Contact:** Leon Ogroske. Offered annually for previously unpublished works. Open to any writer. Guidelines for SASE and online. **Deadline: March 30. Charges $5 fee.** Prize: 1st Place: $50; 2nd Place: $25; 3rd Place: $15, plus honorable mentions. Prize-winning stories and selected honorable mentions are published in *Writers' Journal*.

WRITERS' JOURNAL ANNUAL ROMANCE CONTEST

Val-Tech Media, P.O. Box 394, Perham MN 56573. (218)346-7921. Fax: (218)346-7924. E-mail: writersjournal@writersjournal.com. Website: www.writersjournal.com. **Contact:** Leon Ogroske. Offered annually for previously unpublished works. Open to any writer. Guidelines for SASE and online. **Deadline: July 30. Charges $5 fee.** Prize: 1st Place: $50; 2nd Place: $25; 3rd Place: $15, plus honorable mentions. Prize-winning stories and selected honorable mentions are published in *Writers' Journal*.

WRITERS' JOURNAL ANNUAL SHORT STORY CONTEST

Val-Tech Media, P.O. Box 394, Perham MN 56573. (218)346-7921. Fax: (218)346-7924. E-mail: writersjournal@writersjournal.com. Website: www.writersjournal.com. **Contact:** Leon Ogroske. Offered annually for previously unpublished short stories. Open to any writer. Guidelines for SASE and online. **Deadline: May 30. Charges $7 reading fee.** Prize: 1st Place: $300; 2nd Place: $100; 3rd Place: $50, plus honorable mentions. Prize-winning stories and selected honorable mentions are published in *Writers' Journal*.

ZOETROPE SHORT FICTION CONTEST

Zoetrope: All-Story, 916 Kearny St., San Francisco CA 94133. Fax: (415)989-7910. Website: www.all-story.com. **Contact:** Francis Ford Coppola, publisher. Annual contest for unpublished short stories. Guidelines by SASE or on website. Open to any writer. Please clearly mark envelope "short fiction contest." **Deadline: October 1. Charges $15 fee.** Prize: 1st Place: $1,000, 2nd Place: $500, 3rd Place: $250, plus 10 honorable mentions.

POETRY

ACADEMI CARDIFF INTERNATIONAL POETRY COMPETITION

Academi, P.O. Box 438, Cardiff Wales CF10 5 YA United Kingdom. E-mail: competitions@academi.org. Website: www.academi.org. **Contact:** Peter Finch, contest/award director. "This annual competition is open to everyone—the only criteria being that poems submitted are 50 lines or less, written in English, and previously unpublished. All entries must be accompanied by payment and an entry form, which may be downloaded from the Academi website." **Deadline: January 30.** Guidelines for SASE. **Charges £5/poem.** Prize: 1st Prize: £5,000; 2nd Prize: £700; 3rd Prize: £300; 4th-8th Prize: £200. All cash awards include publication in the *New Welsh Review*, Wales' leading literary journal, and on the Academi website. Judged by Les Murray and Gwyneth Lewis.

ACORN-PLANTOS AWARD FOR PEOPLES POETRY

Acorn-Plantos Award Committee, 36 Sunset Ave., Hamilton ON L8R 1V6 Canada. E-mail: jeffseff@allstream.net. **Contact:** Jeff Seffinga. Annual contest for work that appeared in print between January 1, 2004 and December 31, 2004. "This award is given to the Canadian poet who best (through the publication of a book of poems) exemplifies populist or 'peoples' poetry in the tradition of Milton Acorn, Ted Plantos, et al." Work may be entered by the poet or the publisher; the award goes to the poet. Entrants must submit 5 copies of each title. **Deadline: June 15. Charges $25 (CDN)/title.** Prize: $500 (CDN) and a medal. Judged by a panel of poets in the tradition who are not entered in the current year. Poet must be a citizen of Canada or a landed immigrant. Publisher need not be Canadian.

AKRON POETRY PRIZE

University of Akron Press, 374B Bierce Library, Akron OH 44325-1703. (330)972-5342. Fax: (330)972-6896. E-mail: uapress@uakron.edu. Website: www.uakron.edu/uapress/poetry.html. **Contact:** Elton Glaser, poetry editor. Annual book contest for unpublished poetry. "The Akron Poetry Prize brings to the public writers with original and compelling voices. Books must exhibit 3 essential qualities: mastery of language, maturity of feeling, and complexity of thought." Guidelines available online or for SASE. The final selection will be made by a nationally prominent poet. The University of Akron Press has the right to publish the winning ms, inherent with winning the poetry prize. Open to all poets writing in English. **Deadline: May 15-June 30. Charges $25 fee.** Prize: Winning poet receives $1,000 and publication of book.

ANNUAL GIVAL PRESS OSCAR WILDE AWARD

Gival Press, LLC, P.O. Box 3812, Arlington VA 22203. (703)351-0079. E-mail: givalpress@yahoo.com. Website: www.givalpress.com. **Contact:** Robert L. Giron. Award given to the best previously unpublished original poem—written in English of any length, in any style, typed, double-spaced on 1 side only—which best relates alternative lifestyles, often referred to as gay/lesbian/bisexual/transgendered life, by a poet who is 18 or older. Entrants are asked to submit their poems in the following manner: 1) without any kind of identification, with the exception of titles, and 2) with a separate cover page with the following information: name, address (street, city, and state with zip code), telephone number, e-mail address (if available) and a list of poems by title. Checks drawn on American banks should be made out to Gival Press, LLC. **Deadline: June 27 (postmarked). Charges $5 reading fee (USD).** Prize: $100 (USD), and the poem, along with information about the poet, will be published on the website of Gival Press. Open to any writer.

ANNUAL GIVAL PRESS POETRY CONTEST

Gival Press, LLC, P.O. Box 3812, Arlington VA 22203. (703)351-0079. E-mail: givalpress@yahoo.com. Website: www.givalpress.com. **Contact:** Robert L. Giron. Offered annually for a previously unpublished poetry collection of at least 45 pages, which may include previously published poems. The competition seeks to award well-written, original poetry in English on any topic, in any style. Guidelines for SASE, by e-mail, or on website. Entrants are asked to submit their poems in the following manner: 1) without any kind of identification, with the exception of the titles, and 2) with a separate cover page with the following information: name, address (street, city, state, and zip code), telephone number, e-mail address (if available), and a list of the poems by title. Checks drawn on American banks should be made out to Gival Press, LLC. **Deadline: December 15** (postmarked). **Charges $20 reading fee (USD).** Prize: $1,000, plus publication, standard contract, and 20 author's copies. Open to any writer.

THE ANNUAL PRAIRIE SCHOONER STROUSSE AWARD

Prairie Schooner, 201 Andrews Hall, P.O. Box 880334, Lincoln NE 68588-0334. (402)472-0911. Fax: (402)472-9771. E-mail: kgrey2@unl.edu. Website: www.unl.edu/schooner/psmain.htm. **Contact:** Hilda Raz. Offered annually for the best poem or group of poems published in *Prairie Schooner* in the previous year. Prize: $500.

APR/HONICKMAN FIRST BOOK PRIZE

The American Poetry Review, 117 S. 17th St., Suite 910, Philadelphia PA 19103-5009. (215)496-0439. Fax: (215)569-0808. Website: www.aprweb.org. Offered annually for a poet's first unpublished book-length ms. Judging is by a different distinguished poet each year. Past judges include Gerald Stern, Louise Gluck, Robert Creeley, Adrienne Rich, Derek Walcott, and Jorie Graham. Open to US citizens. **Deadline: October 31.** Guidelines for SASE. **Charges $25 fee.** Prize: Publication by *APR* (distrubution by Copper Canyon Press through Consortium), $3,000 cash prize, plus $1,000 to support a book tour.

⊠ ATLANTIC POETRY PRIZE

Writers' Federation of Nova Scotia, 1113 Marginal Rd., Halifax NS B3H 4P7 Canada. (902)423-8116. Fax: (902)422-0881. E-mail: talk@writers.ns.ca. Website: www.writers.ns.ca. **Contact:** Jane Buss, executive director. Full-length books of adult poetry written by Atlantic Canadians, and published as a whole for the first time in the previous calendar year, are eligible. Entrants must be native or resident Atlantic Canadians who have either been born in Newfoundland, Prince Edward Island, Nova Scotia, or New Brunswick, and spent a susbstantial portion of their lives living there, or who have lived in one or a combination of these provinces for at least 24 consecutive months prior to entry deadline date. Publishers: Send 4 copies and a letter attesting to the author's status as an Atlantic Canadian and the author's current mailing address and telephone number. **Deadline: First Friday in December.** Prize: $1,000.

Ⓝ THE BALTIMORE REVIEW POETRY CONTEST

The Baltimore Review, P.O. Box 36418, Towson MD 21286. E-mail: susan@susanmuaddidarraj.com. Website: www.baltimorereview.org. **Contact:** Susan Muaddi Darraj. **Deadline: July 1. Charges $12, or $20 for fee and 1-year subscription to** *The Baltimore Review*. Prize: 1st Place: $300 and publication; 2nd Place: $150; 3rd Place: $50. Open to any writer.

THE BASKERVILLE PUBLISHERS POETRY AWARD & THE BETSY COLQUITT POETRY AWARD

descant, Texas Christian University's literary journal, TCU, Box 297270, Fort Worth TX 76129. (817)257-6537. Fax: (817)257-6239. E-mail: descant@tcu.edu. **Contact:** Dave Kuhne, editor. Annual award for an outstanding poem published in an issue of *descant*. **Deadline: September-April.** Guidelines for SASE. Prize: $250 for Baskerville Award; $500 for Betsy Colquitt Award. Publication retains copyright, but will transfer it to the author upon request. Open to any writer.

THE BINGHAMTON UNIVERSITY MILT KESSLER POETRY BOOK AWARD

Binghamton University Creative Writing Program, Dept. of English, General Literature & Rhetoric, P.O. Box 6000, Binghamton NY 13902-6000. (607)777-2713. E-mail: cwpro@binghamton.edu. Website: english.binghamton.edu/cwpro/bookawards/bookawards.htm. **Contact:** Maria Mazziotti Gillan, creative writing program director. Estab. 2001. Offered annually for previously published work. Book must be published, be 48 pages or more with a press run of 500 copies or more. Each book submitted must be accompanied by an application form. Publisher may submit more than 1 book for prize consideration. Send 3 copies of each book. Guidelines available online or for SASE. **Deadline: March 1.** Prize: $1,000. Judged by professional poet not on Binghamton University faculty. Open to any writer over the age of 40.

BLUE LYNX PRIZE FOR POETRY

(formerly Spokane Prize for Poetry) Eastern Washington University Press, 705 W. First Ave., Spokane WA 99201. (800)508-9095. Fax: (509)623-4283. E-mail: ewupress@ewu.edu. Website: www.ewupress.ewu.edu. **Contact:** Chris Howell. "Annual award to publish the finest work the literary world has to offer." **Deadline: May 1.** Guidelines for SASE. **Charges $25.** Prize: $1,500 and publication. Judged by anonymous judges. Open to any writer.

BLUE MOUNTAIN ARTS/SPS STUDIOS POETRY CARD CONTEST

P.O. Box 1007, Boulder CO 80306. (303)449-0536. Fax: (303)447-0939. E-mail: poetrycontest@sps.com. Website: www.sps.com. "We're looking for original poetry, which can be rhyming or nonrhyming, although we find nonrhyming poetry reads better. Poems may also be considered for possible publication on greeting cards or in book anthologies." Contest is offered biannually. Guidelines online. **Deadline: December 31 and June 30.** Prize: 1st Prize: $300; 2nd Prize: $150; 3rd Prize: $50. Judged by Blue Mountain Arts editorial staff. Open to any writer.

THE BORDIGHERA ITALIAN-AMERICAN POETRY PRIZE

Sonia Raziss-Giop Foundation, 57 Montague St., #8G, Brooklyn NY 11201-3356. E-mail: daniela@garden.net. Website: www.italianamericanwriters.com. **Contact:** Alfredo de Palchi. Offered annually "to find the best un-published manuscripts of poetry in English, by an American of Italian descent, to be translated into quality Italian and published bilingually." No Italian-American themes required, just excellent poetry. **Deadline: May 31.** Guidelines for SASE. Prize: $2,000 and bilingual book publication to be divided between poet and consigned translator. Judged by Daniela Gioseffi, distinguished poet.

BOSTON REVIEW POETRY CONTEST

Boston Review, E-53-407 MIT, Cambridge MA 02139. Website: bostonreview.net. Submit up to 5 unpublished poems, no more than 10 pages total. **Deadline: June 1. Charges $15 fee (check or money order payable to** *Boston Review*). Prize: $1,000 and publication in the October/November issue of *Boston Review.*

BARBARA BRADLEY PRIZE

New England Poetry Club, 16 Cornell St., Arlington MA 02476. E-mail: contests@nepoetryclub.org. Website: www.nepoetryclub.org/contests.htm. **Contact:** Elizabeth Crowell. Offered annually for a poem under 20 lines, written by a woman. **Deadline: June 30.** Guidelines for SASE. **Charges $10 for 3 poems.** Prize: $200.

BRITTINGHAM PRIZE IN POETRY/FELIX POLLAK PRIZE IN POETRY

University of Wisconsin Press, Dept. of English, 600 N. Park St., University of Wisconsin, Madison WI 53706. Website: www.wisc.edu/wisconsinpress/poetryguide.html. **Contact:** Ronald Wallace, contest director. Estab. 1985. Offered for unpublished book-length mss of original poetry. Submissions must be received by the press during the month of September, accompanied by a SASE for contest results. Does not return mss. One entry fee covers both prizes. Guidelines for SASE or online. **Charges $25 fee (payable to University of Wisconsin Press).** Prize: $1,000 and publication of the 2 winning mss.

THE DOROTHY BRUNSMAN POETRY PRIZE

Bear Star Press, 185 Hollow Oak Dr., Cohasset CA 95973. (530)891-0360. E-mail: bspencer@bearstarpress.com. Website: www.bearstarpress.com. **Contact:** Beth Spencer. Offered annually to support the publication of 1 volume of poetry. Guidelines on website. Open to poets living in the Western States (those in Mountain or Pacific time zones, plus Alaska and Hawaii). **Deadline: November 30. Charges $20 fee.** Prize: $1,000 and publication.

▧ CAA JACK CHALMERS POETRY AWARD

Box 419, 320 S. Shores Rd., Campbellford ON K0L 1L0 Canada. (705)653-0323 or (866)216-6222. Fax: (705)653-0593. E-mail: admin@canauthors.org. Website: www.canauthors.org. **Contact:** Alec McEachern. Offered annually for a volume of poetry by a Canadian citizen. Entry form required. Obtain form from contact name or download from website. **Deadline: December 15.** Guidelines for SASE. **Charges $35 fee (Canadian).** Prize: $1,000 and a silver medal.

CAMPBELL CORNER POETRY CONTEST, LANGUAGE EXCHANGE

Graduate Studies/Sarah Lawrence College, One Meadway, Bronxville NY 10708. (914)395-2371. Fax: (914)395-2664. **Contact:** Dean of Graduate Studies. **Deadline: March 15.** Guidelines for SASE. **Charges $25.** Prize: $3,000. The work will also be published on Campbell Corner's Language Exchange. Judged by Phillis Levin. Open to any writer.

HAYDEN CARRUTH AWARD

Copper Canyon Press, P.O. Box 271, Port Townsend WA 98368. (360)385-4925. Fax: (360)385-4985. E-mail: poetry@coppercanyonpress.org. Website: www.coppercanyonpress.org. **Contact:** Office Manager. Offered annually for unpublished work. Contest is for new and emerging poets who have published no more than 2 full-length books of poetry. Chapbooks of 32 pages or less are not considered to be full length, and books published in other genres do not count toward the 2-book limit. **Deadline: November 1-30 (reading period).** Guidelines for SASE. **Charges $25 fee.** Prize: $1,000 advance and book publication by Copper Canyon Press.

THE CENTER FOR BOOK ARTS POETRY CHAPBOOK COMPETITION

The Center for Book Arts, 28 W. 27th St., 3rd Floor, New York NY 10001. (212)481-0295. Fax: (212)481-9853. E-mail: info@centerforbookarts.org. Website: www.centerforbookarts.org. **Contact:** Sarah Nicholls. Offered annually for unpublished collections of poetry. Individual poems may have been previously published. Collection must not exceed 500 lines or 24 pages. **Deadline: December 1 (postmarked).** Guidelines for SASE. **Charges $20 fee.** Prize: $500 award, $500 honorarium for a reading, publication, and 10 copies of chapbook. Judged by Sharon Dolin and Jean Valentine (2005 judges). Open to any writer.

JOHN CIARDI PRIZE FOR POETRY
BkMk Press, University of Missouri-Kansas City, 5101 Rockhill Rd., Kansas City MO 64110. (816)235-2558. Fax: (816)235-2611. E-mail: bkmk@umkc.edu. Website: www.umkc.edu/bkmk. **Contact:** Ben Furnish. Offered annually for the best book-length collection (unpublished) of poetry in English by a living author. Translations are not eligible. Initial judging is done by a network of published writers. Final judging is done by a writer of national reputation. Guidelines for SASE, by e-mail, or on website. **Deadline: December 1 (postmarked). Charges $25 fee.** Prize: $1,000, plus book publication by BkMk Press.

THE COLORADO PRIZE FOR POETRY
Colorado Review/Center for Literary Publishing, Dept. of English, Colorado State University, Ft. Collins CO 80523. (970)491-5449. E-mail: creview@colostate.edu. Website: coloradoreview.colostate.edu. **Contact:** Stephanie G'Schwind, editor. Offered annually to an unpublished collection of poetry. Guidelines for SASE or online. **Deadline: January 15. Charges $25 fee, includes subscription to** *Colorado Review*. Prize: $1,500 and publication of book.

CONTEMPORARY POETRY SERIES
University of Georgia Press, 330 Research Dr., Suite B100, Athens GA 30602-4901. (706)369-6135. Fax: (706)369-6131. Website: www.ugapress.org. Offered 2 times/year. Two awards: 1 for poets who have not had a full-length book of poems published **(deadline in September)**, and 1 for poets with at least 1 full-length publication **(deadline in January)**. Guidelines for SASE. **Charges $20 fee.**

CRAB ORCHARD OPEN COMPETITION SERIES IN POETRY
Crab Orchard Review and Southern Illinois University Press, Dept. of English, Carbondale IL 62901-4503. Website: www.siu.edu/ ~ crborchd. **Contact:** Jon C. Tribble, series editor. Offered annually for collections of unpublished poetry. Visit website for current deadlines. Guidelines for SASE. **Charges $25 fee.** Prize: 1st Place: $3,500 and publication; 2nd Place: $1,500 and publication. Open to US citizens and permanent residents.

ALICE FAY DI CASTAGNOLA AWARD
Poetry Society of America, 15 Gramercy Park S., New York NY 10003. (212)254-9628. Fax: (212)673-2352. Website: www.poetrysociety.org. **Contact:** Programs Associate. Offered annually for a manuscript-in-progress of poetry or verse-drama. Guidelines for SASE or on website. Award open only to PSA members. It is strongly encouraged that applicants read the complete contest guidelines on the PSA website before submitting. **Deadline: October 1-December 22.** Prize: $1,000. Members only.

MILTON DORFMAN POETRY PRIZE
Rome Art & Community Center, 308 W. Bloomfield St., Rome NY 13440. (315)336-1040. Fax: (315)336-1090. Website: www.romeart.org. Estab. 1990. "The purpose of the Milton Dorfman Poetry Prize is to offer poets an outlet for their craft. All submissions must be previously unpublished." **Deadline: April 30.** Guidelines for SASE. **Charges $15 fee/poem.** Prize: 1st Place: $500; 2nd Place: $250; 3rd Place: $150. Judged by a professional, published poet. Awards ceremony and poetry reading in June.

T.S. ELIOT PRIZE FOR POETRY
Truman State University Press, 100 E. Normal St., Kirksville MO 63501-4221. (660)785-7336. Fax: (660)785-4480. E-mail: tsup@truman.edu. Website: tsup.truman.edu. **Contact:** Nancy Rediger. Annual competition for unpublished poetry collection. Guidelines for SASE, on website, or by e-mail. **Deadline: October 31 (postmarked). Charges $25 fee.** Prize: $2,000 and publication.

ROBERT G. ENGLISH/POETRY IN PRINT
P.O. Box 30981, Albuquerque NM 87190-0981. (505)888-3937. Fax: (505)888-3937. Website: www.poets.com/RobertEnglish.html. **Contact:** Robert G. English, owner. Offered annually "to help a poetry writer accomplish their own personal endeavors. Hopefully the prize amount of the Poetry in Print award will grow to a higher significance. The contest is open to any writer of any age. Hopefully to prepare writers other than just journalists with a stronger desire to always tell the truth." No limit to number of entries; 60-line limit/poem. "Please enclose SASE." **Deadline: August 1. Charges $10/poem.** Prize: $1,000.

JANICE FARRELL POETRY PRIZE

National League of American Pen Women, Nob Hill, San Francisco Branch, 1544 Sweetwood Dr., Colma CA 94015-2029. E-mail: pennobhill@aol.com. Website: www.soulmakingcontest.us. **Contact:** Eileen Malone. Poetry may be double- or single-spaced. One-page poems only, and only 1 poem/page. All poems must be titled. Three poems/entry. Annually. **Deadline: November 30.** Guidelines for SASE. **Charges $5/entry (make checks payable to NLAPW, Nob Hill Branch).** Prize: 1st Place: $100; 2nd Place: $50; 3rd Place: $25. Judged by a local San Francisco successfully published poet. Open to any writer.

FIELD POETRY PRIZE

Oberlin College Press/FIELD, 50 N. Professor St., Oberlin OH 44074-1091. (440)775-8408. Fax: (440)775-8124. E-mail: oc.press@oberlin.edu. Website: www.oberlin.edu/ocpress. **Contact:** Linda Slocum, managing editor. Offered annually for unpublished work. "The FIELD Poetry Prize contest seeks to encourage the finest in contemporary poetry writing." Open to any writer. **Deadline: Submit in May only.** Guidelines for SASE. **Charges $22 fee, which includes a 1-year subscription to** *FIELD*. Prize: $1,000, and book published in Oberlin College Press's FIELD Poetry Series.

Ⓝ 🌐 FIRSTWRITER.COM INTERNATIONAL POETRY COMPETITION

firstwriter.com, 24 Gibraltar Ave., Halifax HX1 3UL United Kingdom. Website: www.firstwriter.com. **Contact:** J. Paul Dyson. Accepts original poetry up to 30 lines on any subject and in any style. **Deadline: October 1.** Guidelines for SASE. **Charges $4.50/poem; 3 poems for $11.25; 5 poems for $15; and 10 poems for $22.50.** Prize: Over $700, with $150 for the best runners-up from the US and the United Kingdom. Ten special commendations will also be awarded and all the winners will be published in *firstwriter* magazine and receive a free year's subscription worth $28. Judged by *firstwriter* magazine editors. Open to any writer.

FIVE POINTS JAMES DICKEY PRIZE FOR POETRY

Five Points, Georgia State University, P.O. Box 3999, Atlanta GA 30302-3999. (404)651-0071. Fax: (404)651-3167. E-mail: msexton@gsu.edu. Website: www.webdelsol.com/Five_Points. **Contact:** Megan Sexton. Offered annually for unpublished poetry. Send 3 unpublished poems, no longer than 50 lines each, name and addresses on each poem, SASE for receipt and notification of winner. Winner announced in Spring issue. **Deadline: November 30.** Guidelines for SASE. **Charges $20 fee (includes 1-year subscription).** Prize: $1,000, plus publication.

FOLEY POETRY CONTEST

America Press, 106 W. 56th St., New York NY 10019. (212)581-4640. Fax: (212)399-3596. Website: www.americamagazine.org. **Contact:** Paul Mariani, poetry editor. Estab. 1909. Offered annually for unpublished works between January and April. **Deadline: January 1-April 16.** Guidelines for SASE. Prize: $1,000, usually awarded in June. Open to any writer.

THE 49th PARALLEL POETRY AWARD

Bellingham Review, Mail Stop 9053, Western Washington University, Bellingham WA 98225. (360)650-4863. E-mail: bhreview@cc.wwu.edu. Website: www.wwu.edu/~bhreview/. **Contact:** Brenda Miller. Estab. 1977. Offered annually for unpublished poetry. Guidelines available on website or for SASE. **Deadline: December 1-March 15. Charges $15 for first entry (up to 3 poems), $10 each additional entry (including each additional poem).** Prize: 1st Place: $1,000 and publication. All finalists considered for publication; all entrants receive subscription.

FOUR WAY BOOKS POETRY PRIZES

Four Way Books, P.O. Box 535, Village Station, New York NY 10014. (212)334-5430. Fax: (212)334-5435. E-mail: four_way_editors@yahoo.com. Website: www.fourwaybooks.com. **Contact:** C. Lowen, contest coordinator. Four Way Books runs different prizes annually. For guidelines send a SASE or download from website. **Deadline: March 31.** Prize: Cash honorarium and book publication.

ALLEN GINSBERG POETRY AWARDS

The Poetry Center at Passaic County Community College, One College Blvd., Paterson NJ 07505-1179. (973)684-6555. Fax: (973)684-5843. E-mail: mgillan@pccc.edu. Website: www.pccc.edu/poetry. **Contact:** Maria Mazziotti Gillan, executive director. Offered annually for unpublished poetry "to honor Allen Ginsberg's contribution to American literature." The college retains first publication rights. Open to any writer. **Deadline: April 1.** Guidelines for SASE. **Charges $13, which covers the cost of a subscription to** *The Paterson Literary Review*. Prize: $1,000.

🔷 GOVERNOR GENERAL'S LITERARY AWARD FOR POETRY

Canada Council for the Arts, 350 Albert St., P.O. Box 1047, Ottawa ON K1P 5V8 Canada. (613)566-4414, ext. 5576. Fax: (613)566-4410. E-mail: joanne.larocque-poirier@canadacouncil.ca. Website: www.canadacouncil

.ca/prizes/ggla. **Contact:** Joanne Larocque-Poirier. Offered for the best English-language and the best French-language work of poetry by a Canadian. Submissions in English must be published between September 1, 2004 and September 30, 2005; submissions in French between July 1, 2004 and June 30, 2005. Publishers submit titles for consideration. **Deadline: March 15 or August 7, depending on the book's publication date.** Prize: Each laureate receives $15,000; nonwinning finalists receive $1,000.

GREEN ROSE PRIZE IN POETRY

New Issues Poetry & Prose, Dept. of English, Western Michigan University, 1903 W. Michigan Ave., Kalamazoo MI 49008-5331. (269)387-8185. Fax: (269)387-2562. E-mail: herbert.scott@wmich.edu. Website: www.wmich.edu/newissues. **Contact:** Herbert Scott, editor. Offered annually for unpublished poetry. The university will publish a book of poems by a poet writing in English who has published 1 or more full-length books of poetry. Guidelines for SASE or on website. *New Issues Poetry & Prose* obtains rights for first publication. Book is copyrighted in author's name. **Deadline: May 1-September 30. Charges $20 fee.** Prize: $2,000 and publication of book. Author also receives 10% of the printed edition.

☒ THE GRIFFIN POETRY PRIZE

The Griffin Trust for Excellence in Poetry, 6610 Edwards Blvd., Mississauga ON L5T 2V6 Canada. (905)565-5993. E-mail: info@griffinpoetryprize.com. Website: www.griffinpoetryprize.com. **Contact:** Ruth Smith. Offered annually for work published between January 1 and December 31. **Deadline: December 31.** Prize: Two $40,000 (Canadian) prizes. One prize will go to a living Canadian poet or translator, the other to a living poet or translator from any country, which may include Canada. Judged by a panel of qualified English-speaking judges of stature. Judges are chosen by the Trustees of The Griffin Trust For Excellence in Poetry. Open to any writer.

GROLIER POETRY PRIZE

Grolier Poetry Book Shop, Inc., and Ellen LaForge Memorial Poetry Foundation, Inc., 6 Plympton St., Cambridge MA 02138. (617)253-4452. E-mail: cbjknox@aol.com. **Contact:** Caroline Knox. Estab. 1973. When e-mailing, please put "Grolier Poetry Prize" in subject line. The prize is intended to encourage and introduce developing poets and is open to all poets who have not published a previous volume (chapbook, small press, trade, or vanity) of poetry. Submissions (in duplicate) should include no more than 5 poems (none simultaneously submitted or previously published), running 10 double-spaced pages or 5 single-spaced pages. Separate cover sheet should include poet's address and telephone number, e-mail address, titles of poems, and brief biography. Enclose a self-addressed, stamped postcard for notification of receipt. The author's name and other identifying information should not appear on the same pages as the poems. Entries must be submitted in duplicate. Mss will not be returned. Annually. **Deadline: May 1 (after May 1st, use the book shop address). Charges $7 fee.**

VIOLET REED HAAS POETRY CONTEST

Snake Nation Press, 110 W. Force St., Valdosta GA 31601. (229)244-0752. E-mail: jeana@snakenationpress.org. Website: www.snakenationpress.org. **Contact:** Jean Arambula. Offered annually for poetry mss of 50-75 pages. **Deadline: June 15. Charges $20 reading fee.** Prize: $500 and publication. Judged by an independent judge.

KATHRYN HANDLEY PROSE-POEM PRIZE

National League of American Pen Women, Nob Hill, San Francisco Branch, 1544 Sweetwood Dr., Colma CA 94015-2029. E-mail: pennobhill@aol.com. Website: www.soulmakingcontest.us. **Contact:** Eileen Malone. Poetry may be double- or single-spaced. One-page poems only, and only 1 poem/page. Three poems/entry. Annually. **Deadline: November 30.** Guidelines for SASE. **Charges $5/entry (make checks payable to NLAPW, Nob Hill Branch).** Prize: 1st Place: $100; 2nd Place: $50; 3rd Place: $25. Open to any writer.

IRA LEE BENNETT HOPKINS PROMISING POET AWARD

International Reading Association, P.O. Box 8139, Newark DE 19714-8139. (302)731-1600. Fax: (302)731-1057. E-mail: exec@reading.org. Website: www.reading.org. Offered every 3 years to a promising new poet of children's poetry (for children and young adults up to grade 12) who has published no more than 2 books of children's poetry. Download application from website. **Deadline: December 1.** Guidelines for SASE. Prize: $500.

FIRMAN HOUGHTON PRIZE

New England Poetry Club, 16 Cornell St., Arlington MA 02476. E-mail: contests@nepoetryclug.org. Website: www.nepoetryclub.org/contests.htm. **Contact:** Elizabeth Crowell. Offered annually for a lyric poem in English. **Deadline: June 30.** Guidelines for SASE. **Charges $10 for 3 poems.** Prize: $250.

INDIANA REVIEW POETRY PRIZE

Indiana Review, BH 465, Indiana University, Bloomington IN 47405-7103. (812)855-3439. Fax: (812)855-4253. E-mail: inreview@indiana.edu. Website: www.indiana.edu/~inreview. **Contact:** Grady Jaynes, editor. Offered annually for unpublished work. Judged by guest judges; 2005 prize judged by Marilyn Hacker. Open to any writer. Send no more than 4 poems, 15-page maximum combined (no minimum). Guidelines on website and with SASE request. **Deadline: March 31. Charges $15 fee (includes a 1-year subscription).** Prize: $1,000.

Ⓝ INTERNATIONAL HAIKU CONTEST

National League of American PenWomen, Palomar Branch, 12063 Lomica Dr., San Diego CA 92128. E-mail: wordhog1@juno.com. **Contact:** Faith Frances Berlin. "Our judges are always poets of haiku who have many awards and knowledge in the field. This year our judge is Yvonne M. Hardenbrook—a published haiku author and prize-winning poet." **Deadline: March 1.** Guidelines for SASE. **Charges $5 for 2 haiku poems.** Prize: 1st Prize: $100; 2nd prize: $50; 3rd prize: $25; plus honorable mentions. Winning poems will be published in a chapbook. Purpose is to raise money and provide a scholarship for a deserving student entering college. Open to any writer.

IOWA POETRY PRIZES

University of Iowa Press, 100 Kuhl House, Iowa City IA 52242. (319)335-2000. Fax: (319)335-2055. E-mail: uipress@uiowa.edu. Website: www.uiowapress.org. Offered annually to encourage poets and their work. Submit mss by April 30; put name on title page only. Open to writers of English (US citizens or not). Manuscripts will not be returned. Previous winners are not eligible. **Deadline: April. Charges $20 fee.**

RANDALL JARRELL/HARPERPRINTS POETRY CHAPBOOK COMPETITION

North Carolina Writers' Network, 3501 Highway 54 W., Studio C, Chapel Hill NC 27516. E-mail: mail@ncwriters .org. Website: www.ncwriters.org. **Contact:** Beth Stone. Offered annually for unpublished work "to honor Randall Jarrell and his life at UNC-Greensboro by recognizing the best poetry submitted." Competition is open to North Carolina residents who have not published a full-length collection of poems. **Deadline: January 31. Charges $10 (NCWN members); $15 (nonmembers) entry fee.** Prize: $200, chapbook publication, and a reading and reception.

KALLIOPE'S ANNUAL SUE SANIEL ELKIND POETRY CONTEST

Kalliope, 11901 Beach Blvd., Jacksonville FL 32246. (904)646-2081. Website: www.fccj.org/kalliope. **Contact:** Mary Sue Koeppel, editor. Offered annually for unpublished work. "Poetry may be in any style and on any subject. Maximum poem length is 50 lines. Only unpublished poems are eligible." No limit on number of poems entered by any 1 poet. The winning poem is published, as are the finalists' poems. Copyright then returns to the authors. Guidelines for SASE and on website. **Deadline: November 1. Charges $4/poem; $10 for 3 poems.** Prize: $1,000 and publication of poem in *Kalliope*.

THE WELDON KEES AWARD

(formerly the Backwaters Prize), The Backwaters Press, 3502 N. 52nd St., Omaha NE 68104-3506. (402)451-4052. E-mail: gkosm62735@aol.com. Website: www.thebackwaterspress.homestead.com. **Contact:** Greg Kosmicki. Contest for a chapbook of poetry. Submit 20-30 pages of original poetry by a single poet. This does not include title and contents pages. No style/content restrictions. Send SASE for ms return. **Deadline: December 31 (postmarked). Charges $20 fee for each ms entered.** Prize: Three winners are chosen annually. Each is given $125 in cash and 10% of the press run (30 chapbooks). Judged by editors of the press.

BARBARA MANDIGO KELLY PEACE POETRY AWARDS

Nuclear Age Peace Foundation, PMB 121, 1187 Coast Village Rd., Suite 1, Santa Barbara CA 93108-2794. (805)965-3443. Fax: (805)568-0466. E-mail: communications@napf.org. Website: www.wagingpeace.org. **Contact:** Carah Ong. "The Barbara Mandigo Kelly Peace Poetry Contest was created to encourage poets to explore and illuminate positive visions of peace and the human spirit. The contest honors the late Barbara Kelly, a Santa Barbara poet and longtime supporter of peace issues. Awards are given in 3 categories: adult (over 18 years), youth between 12 and 18 years, and youth under 12." Contest is offered annually. All submitted poems should be unpublished. **Deadline: July 1 (postmarked).** Guidelines for SASE. **Charges $15 for up to 3 poems; no fee for youth entries.** Prize: Adult: $1,000; Youth (13-18): $200; Youth (12 and under): $200. Honorable Mentions may also be awarded. Judged by a committee of poets selected by the Nuclear Age Peace Foundation. The foundation reserves the right to publish and distribute the award-winning poems, including honorable mentions. Open to any writer.

HELEN AND LAURA KROUT MEMORIAL OHIOANA POETRY AWARD

Ohioana Library Association, 274 E. First Ave., Columbus OH 45201. (614)466-3831. Fax: (614)728-6974. E-mail: ohioana@sloma.state.oh.us. Website: www.ohioana.org. **Contact:** Linda R. Hengst. Offered annually ''to an individual whose body of published work has made, and continues to make, a significant contribution to poetry, and through whose work interest in poetry has been developed.'' Recipient must have been born in Ohio or lived in Ohio at least 5 years. **Deadline: December 31.** Guidelines for SASE. Prize: $1,000.

▧ GERALD LAMPERT MEMORIAL AWARD

The League of Canadian Poets, 920 Yonge St., Suite 608, Toronto ON M4W 3C7 Canada. (416)504-1657. Fax: (416)504-0096. E-mail: promotion@poets.ca. Website: www.poets.ca. Offered annually for a first book of poetry by a Canadian poet published in the preceding year. Guidelines for SASE and on website. **Deadline: November 1. Charges $15 fee.** Prize: $1,000. Open to Canadian citizens and landed immigrants only.

THE LEDGE ANNUAL POETRY CHAPBOOK CONTEST

The Ledge Magazine, 40 Maple Ave., Bellport NY 11713. **Contact:** Timothy Monaghan. Offered annually to publish an outstanding collection of poems. Open to any writer. **Deadline: October 31.** Guidelines for SASE. **Charges $15 fee.** Prize: $1,000, publication of chapbook, and 50 copies; all entrants receive a copy of winning chapbook.

THE LEDGE POETRY AWARDS

The Ledge Magazine, 40 Maple Ave., Bellport NY 11713. **Contact:** Timothy Monaghan. Offered annually for unpublished poems of exceptional quality and significance. All poems considered for publication in the magazine. Open to any writer. **Deadline: April 30.** Guidelines for SASE. **Charges $10 for 3 poems; $3/additional poem ($17 subscription gains free entry for the first 3 poems).** Prize: 1st Place: $1,000 and publication in *The Ledge Magazine*; 2nd Place: $250 and publication; 3rd Place: $100 and publication.

LENA-MILES WEVER TODD POETRY SERIES

Pleiades Press & Winthrop University, Dept. of English, Central Missouri State University, Warrensburg MO 64093. (660)543-8106. Fax: (660)543-8544. E-mail: kdp8106@cmsu2.cmsu.edu. Website: www.cmsu.edu/engl phil/pleiades. **Contact:** Kevin Prufer. Offered annually for an unpublished book of poetry by an American or Canadian poet. Guidelines for SASE or by e-mail. The winning book is copyrighted by the author and Pleiades Press. **Deadline: Generally September 30; e-mail for firm deadline. Charges $15, which includes a copy of the winning book.** Prize: $1,000 and publication of winning book in paperback edition. Distribution through Louisiana State University Press. Open to any writer living in the US or Canada.

LEVIS READING PRIZE

Virginia Commonwealth University, Dept. of English, P.O. Box 842005, Richmond VA 23284-2005. (804)828-1329. Fax: (804)828-8684. E-mail: eng_grad@vcu.edu. Website: www.has.vcu.edu/eng/resources/levis_prize. htm. **Contact:** Jeff Lodge. Offered annually for books of poetry published in the previous year to encourage poets early in their careers. The entry must be the writer's first or second published book of poetry. Previously published books in other genres, or previously published chapbooks, do not count as books for this purpose. **Deadline: January 15.** Guidelines for SASE. Prize: $1,000 honorarium and an expense-paid trip to Richmond to present a public reading.

FRANCES LOCKE MEMORIAL POETRY AWARD

The Bitter Oleander Press, 4983 Tall Oaks Dr., Fayetteville NY 13066-9776. (315)637-3047. Fax: (315)637-5056. E-mail: info@bitteroleander.com. Website: www.bitteroleander.com. **Contact:** Paul B. Roth. Offered annually for unpublished, imaginative poetry. Open to any writer. **Deadline: June 15.** Guidelines for SASE. **Charges $10/5 poems; $2/each additional poem.** Prize: $1,000 and 5 copies of the issue.

LOUISIANA LITERATURE PRIZE FOR POETRY

Louisiana Literature, SLU—Box 792, Southeastern Louisiana University, Hammond LA 70402. (504)549-5022. Fax: (504)549-5021. E-mail: lalit@selu.edu. Website: www.selu.edu/orgs/lalit/. **Contact:** Jack Bedell, contest director. Estab. 1984. Offered annually for unpublished poetry. All entries considered for publication. **Deadline: April 1.** Guidelines for SASE. **Charges $12 fee.** Prize: $400.

LOUISE LOUIS/EMILY F. BOURNE STUDENT POETRY AWARD

Poetry Society of America, 15 Gramercy Park S., New York NY 10003. (212)254-9628. Fax: (212)673-2352. Website: www.poetrysociety.org. **Contact:** Programs Associate. Offered annually for unpublished work to promote excellence in student poetry. Open to American high school or preparatory school students (grades 9-12).

Guidelines for SASE and on website. Judged by prominent American poets. It is strongly encouraged that applicants read the complete contest guidelines before submitting. **Deadline: October 1-December 22. Charges $5 for a student submitting a single entry; $20 for a high school submitting unlimited number of its students' poems.** Prize: $250.

PAT LOWTHER MEMORIAL AWARD

920 Yonge St., Suite 608, Toronto ON M4W 3C7 Canada. (416)504-1657. Fax: (416)504-0096. E-mail: promotion @poets.ca. Website: www.poets.ca. Estab. 1966. Offered annually to promote new Canadian poetry/poets and also to recognize exceptional work in each category. Submissions to be published in the preceding year. Enquiries from publishers welcome. Open to Canadians living at home and abroad. The candidate must be a Canadian citizen or landed imigrant, though the publisher need not be Canadian. Call, write, fax, or e-mail for rules. **Deadline: November 1. Charges $15 fee/title.** Prize: $1,000.

THE MACGUFFIN NATIONAL POET HUNT

The MacGuffin, 18600 Haggerty, Livonia MI 48152. E-mail: macguffin@schoolcraft.edu. Website: www.macguff in.org. **Contact:** Managing Editor. "The purpose of the National Poet Hunt contest is to judge each piece blindly in its own right. It is not judged against another poet, only on the merits of the piece of itself. By sponsoring this contest, we've been able to publish new poets and give confidence to those who've entered by assuring those writers that the pieces would be judged on their own merits and that that work would be read by a renowned published poet." Offered annually for unpublished work. **Deadline: April 1, 2005-June 3, 2005 (postmarked).** Guidelines for SASE. **Charges $15 for a 5-poem entry.** Prize: 1st Prize: $500; 2nd Prize: $250; 3rd Prize: $100, and up to 3 Honorable Mentions. All winning poems published in the fall issue of *The MacGuffin*. Judged by Conrad Hilberry in 2005. Past judges include Molly Peacock, Gary Gildner, Richard Tillinghast, and Bob Hicok. Acquires first rights (if piece is published). Once published, all rights revert to the author. Open to any writer.

NAOMI LONG MADGETT POETRY AWARD

Lotus Press, Inc., P.O. Box 21607, Detroit MI 48221. E-mail: lotuspress@aol.com. Website: www.lotuspress.org. **Contact:** Constance Withers. Offered annually to recognize an unpublished poetry ms. Guidelines for SASE, by e-mail, or on website. **Deadline: January 2-March 25.** Prize: $500 and publication by Lotus Press.

THE MALAHAT REVIEW LONG POEM PRIZE

The Malahat Review, Box 1700 STN CSC, Victoria BC V8W 2Y2 Canada. E-mail: malahat@uvic.ca (queries only). Website: malahatreview.ca. **Contact:** Editor. Offered in alternate years with the Novella Contest. Open to unpublished long poems. Preliminary reading by editorial board; final judging by the editor and 2 recognized poets. Obtains first world rights. After publication rights revert to the author. Open to any writer. **Deadline: March 1.** Guidelines for SASE. **Charges $35 fee (includes a 1-year subscription to the *Malahat*, published quarterly).** Prize: 2 prizes of $400, plus payment for publication ($30/page), and additional 1-year subscription.

MORTON MARR POETRY PRIZE

Southwest Review, P.O. Box 750374, Dallas TX 75275-0374. (214)768-1037. Fax: (214)768-1408. E-mail: swr@m ail.smu.edu. Website: www.southwestreview.org. **Contact:** Willard Spiegelman. Annual award given to a poem by a writer who has not yet published a first book. Contestants may submit no more than 6 poems in a "traditional" form (i.e., sonnet, sestina, villanelle, rhymed stanzas, blank verse, etc.). A cover letter with name, address, and other relevant information may accompany the poems which must be printed without any identifying information. Guidelines for SASE or online. **Deadline: November 30. Charges $5/poem.** Prize: $1,000 first prize; $500 second prize; and publication in *The Southwest Review*. Open to any writer who has not yet published a first book.

MID-LIST PRESS FIRST SERIES AWARD FOR POETRY

Mid-List Press, 4324 12th Ave. S., Minneapolis MN 55407-3218. Fax: (612)823-8387. E-mail: cihlar@midlist.org. Website: www.midlist.org. **Contact:** James Cihlar, executive director. Estab. 1990. Offered annually for unpublished book of poetry to encourage new poets. Guidelines for SASE or on website. Contest is open to any writer who has never published a book of poetry. "We do not consider a chapbook to be a book of poetry." **Deadline: February 1. Charges $30 (US) fee.** Prize: Publication and an advance against royalties.

MISSISSIPPI VALLEY NON-PROFIT POETRY CONTEST

Midwest Writing Center, P.O. Box 3188, Rock Island IL 61204-3188. (563)359-1057. **Contact:** Max Molleston, chairman. Estab. 1972. Offered annually for unpublished poetry: adult general, student division, Mississippi

Valley, senior citizen, religious, rhyming, jazz, humorous, haiku, history, and ethnic. Up to 5 poems may be submitted. **Deadline: April 1. Charges $8 fee; $5 for students.** Prize: Cash prizes total $1,200.

FREDERICK MORGAN POETRY PRIZE

(formerly Nicholas Roerich Poetry Prize), Story Line Press, Three Oaks Farm, P.O. Box 1240, Ashland OR 97520-0055. (541)482-9363. E-mail: mail@storylinepress.com. Website: www.storylinepress.com. **Contact:** Morgan Prize Coordinator. Estab. 1988. Offered annually for full-length book of poetry. Any writer who has not previously published a full-length collection of poetry (48 pages or more) in English is eligible to apply. Guidelines for SASE or on website. **Deadline: May 1-October 31. Charges $25 fee.** Prize: $1,000 and publication.

MORSE POETRY PRIZE

Northeastern University English Department, 406 Holmes Hall, Boston MA 02115. (617)437-2512. E-mail: g.rotella@neu.edu. Website: www.casdn.neu.edu/~english. **Contact:** Guy Rotella. Offered annually for previously published poetry book-length mss of first or second books. **Deadline: September 15. Charges $15 fee.** Prize: $1,000 and publication by NU/UPNE.

KATHRYN A. MORTON PRIZE IN POETRY

Sarabande Books, P.O. Box 4456, Louisville KY 40204. (502)458-4028. Fax: (502)458-4065. E-mail: info@sarabandebooks.org. Website: www.sarabandebooks.org. **Contact:** Kristina McGrath, associate editor. Offered annually to publish an outstanding collection of poetry. All finalists considered for publication. **Deadline: January 1-February 15.** Guidelines for SASE. **Charges $20 fee.** Prize: $2,000 and publication with standard royalty contract.

SHEILA MOTTON AWARD

New England Poetry Club, 16 Cornell St., Apt. 2, Arlington MA 02476-7710. **Contact:** Elizabeth Crowell. For a poetry book published in the last 2 years. Send 2 copies of the book and **$10 entry fee.** Prize: $500.

ERIKA MUMFORD PRIZE

New England Poetry Club, 16 Cornell St., Apt. 2, Arlington MA 02476-7710. **Contact:** Elizabeth Crowell. Offered annually for a poem in any form about foreign culture or travel. **Deadline: June 30.** Guidelines for SASE. **Charges $10 for up to 3 entries in NEPC contests.** Prize: $250.

NATIONAL FEDERATION OF STATE POETRY SOCIETIES ANNUAL POETRY CONTEST

National Federation of State Poetry Societies, 30 W. Lester Ave., D 27, Salt Lake City UT 84107. E-mail: theda_bassett2002@yahoo.com. Website: www.nfsps.org/poetry_contests. **Contact:** Theda Bassett. Estab. 1959. Contest for previously unpublished poetry. Fifty categories. Flier lists them all. Guidelines for SASE. Must have guidelines to enter. **Deadline: March 15.** Prize: All awards are announced in June. Top awards only (not honorable mentions) published the following June.

NATIONAL WRITERS ASSOCIATION POETRY CONTEST

The National Writers Association, 10940 S. Parker Rd. #508, Parker CO 80134. (303)841-0246. Fax: (303)841-2607. **Contact:** Sandy Whelchel, director. Annual contest "to encourage the writing of poetry, an important form of individual expression but with a limited commercial market." Guidelines for SASE. **Charges $10 fee.** Prize: 1st Place: $100; 2nd Place: $50; 3rd Place: $25.

HOWARD NEMEROV SONNET AWARD

The Formalist, 320 Hunter Dr., Evansville IN 47711. Website: www2.evansville.edu/theformalist. **Contact:** Mona Baer. Offered annually for an unpublished sonnet to encourage poetic craftsmanship and to honor the memory of the late Howard Nemerov, third US Poet Laureate. Acquires first North American serial rights for those sonnets chosen for publication. Upon publication all rights revert to the author. Open to the international community of writers. Guidelines are on the website. **Deadline: November 15. Charges $3 entry fee/sonnet.** Prize: $1,000 and publication in *The Evansville Review*.

THE PABLO NERUDA PRIZE FOR POETRY

Nimrod International Journal, 600 S. College Ave., Tulsa OK 74104. (918)631-3080. Fax: (918)631-3033. E-mail: nimrod@utulsa.edu. Website: www.utulsa.edu/nimrod. **Contact:** Francine Ringold. Annual award to discover new writers of vigor and talent. **Deadline: April 30.** Guidelines for SASE. **Charges $20 (includes a 1-year subscription to** *Nimrod***).** Prize: 1st Place: $2,000 and publication; 2nd Place: $1,000 and publication. *Nimrod* retains the right to publish any submission. Judged by the *Nimrod* editors (finalists). A recognized author selects the winners. Open to US residents only.

NEW ISSUES FIRST BOOK OF POETRY PRIZE

New Issues Poetry & Prose, Dept. of English, Western Michigan University, 1903 W. Michigan Ave., Kalamazoo MI 49008-5331. (269)387-8185. Fax: (269)387-2562. E-mail: herbert.scott@wmich.edu. Website: www.wmich.edu/newissues. **Contact:** Herbert Scott, editor. Offered annually for publication of a first book of poems by a poet writing in English who has not previously published a full-length collection of poems in an edition of 500 or more copies. *New Issues Poetry & Prose* obtains rights for first publication. Book is copyrighted in author's name. Guidelines for SASE or on website. **Deadline: November 30. Charges $15.** Prize: $2,000 and publication of book. Author also receives 10% of the printed edition.

NEW RIVER POETS QUARTERLY POETRY AWARDS

New River Poets, a chapter of Florida State Poets Association, Inc., 5545 Meadowbrook St., Zephyrhills FL 33541-2715. **Contact:** June Owens, awards coordinator. Offered quarterly (February, May, August, and November) for previously published and unpublished work to acknowledge and reward outstanding poetic efforts. Previous winners have been Donna Jean Tennis, Gwendolyn Carr, and Theda Bassett. **Deadline: February 15, May 15, August 15, and November 15.** Guidelines for SASE. **Charges $5 fee for 1-4 poems; $1 for each additional poem (no limit).** Prize: Awarded each quarter. 1st Prize: $65; 2nd Prize: $45; 3rd Prize: $35; plus 5 honorable mentions at $5 each. Judged by the winning authors in each quarterly competition who judge the first-place unscreened entries in a subsequent competition. Open to any writer.

NO LOVE LOST

Hidden Brook Press, 109 Bayshore Rd., RR#4, Brighton ON K0K 1H0 Canada. (613)475-2368. Fax: (801)751-1837. E-mail: writers@hiddenbrookpress.com. Website: www.hiddenbrookpress.com. No Love Lost is an annual international poetry anthology contest. "Love, hate, lust, desire, passion, jealousy, and ambivalence. Including brotherly, sisterly, parental love, love of country, city." Send 3 poems with SASE. Electronic and hard copy submissions required. Previously published and simultaneous submissions are welcome. **Deadline: November 30. Charges $15 for 3 poems (includes purchase of book).** Prize: 1st Prize: $100; 2nd Prize: $75; 3rd Prize: $50; 4th Prize: $40; 5th Prize: $30; 6th Prize: $25; 7th Prize: $20; 8th Prize: $15; 9th-10th Prize: $10, plus up to 12 Honorable Mentions. Up to 300 poems published. Authors retain copyright. Open to any writer.

THE OHIO STATE UNIVERSITY PRESS/*THE JOURNAL* AWARD IN POETRY

The Ohio State University Press and *The Journal*, 1070 Carmack, Columbus OH 43210. (614)292-6930. Fax: (614)292-2065. E-mail: ohiostatepress@osu.edu. Website: www.ohiostatepress.org. **Contact:** David Citino, poetry editor. Offered annually for unpublished work, minimum of 48 pages of original poetry. **Deadline: Entries accepted September 1-30. Charges $25 fee.** Prize: $3,000 and publication.

ONCEWRITTEN.COM POETRY CONTEST

Oncewritten.com, 1850 N. Whitley Ave., #404, Hollywood CA 90028. E-mail: poetrycontest@oncewritten.com. Website: www.oncewritten.com. The purpose of this biannual contest is "to find high quality, previously unpublished poetry to feature on the website and in *Off the Press*, our monthly newsletter, which is distributed specifically for people interested in reading about new authors." **Deadline: February 28 and August 31.** Guidelines for SASE. **Charges $10.** Prize: Grand Prize: $500; 1st Prize: $100; both include publication on website and in newsletter. Judged by editor and 1 industry professional. Open to any writer.

THE OPEN WINDOW

Hidden Brook Press, 109 Bayshore Rd., RR#4, Brighton ON K0K 1H0 Canada. (613)475-2368. Fax: (801)751-1837. E-mail: writers@hiddenbrookpress.com. Website: www.hiddenbrookpress.com. An annual poetry anthology contest. "A wide open window theme including family, nature, death, rhyming, city, country, war and peace, social—long, short haiku, or any other genre." Send sets of 3 poems with short bio (35-40 words) and a SASE. Electronic and hard copy submissions required. Previously published and simultaneous submissions are welcome. **Deadline: November 30. Charges $15 for 3 poems.** Prize: 1st Prize: $100; 2nd Prize: $75; 3rd Prize: $50; 4th Prize: $40; 5th Prize: $30; 6th Prize: $25; 7th Prize: $20; 8th Prize: $15; 9th-10th Prize: $10, plus up to 12 honorable mentions. All winners, honorable mentions, and runners up receive 1 copy of the book for each published poem. Authors retain copyright. Open to any writer.

NATALIE ORNISH POETRY AWARD

The Texas Institute of Letters, 6335 W. Northwest Hwy., #618, Dallas TX 75225. (214)363-7253. E-mail: franvick@aol.com. Website: www.wtamu.edu/til/awards. **Contact:** Fran Vick, secretary. Offered annually for the best book of poems published January 1-December 31 of previous year. Poet must have been born in Texas, have lived in the state at some time for at least 2 consecutive years, or the subject matter must be associated with the state. See website for guidelines. **Deadline: January 3.** Prize: $1,000.

THE PATERSON POETRY PRIZE

The Poetry Center at Passaic County Community College, One College Blvd., Paterson NJ 07505-6555. (973)684-6555. Fax: (973)684-5843. E-mail: mgillan@pccc.cc.nj.us. Website: www.pccc.edu/poetry. **Contact:** Maria Mazziotti Gillan, director. Offered annually for a book of poetry published in the previous year. **Deadline: February 1.** Guidelines for SASE. Prize: $1,000.

N PAUMANOK POETRY AWARD

English Department, Knapp Hall, Farmingdale State University of New York, 2350 Broadhollow Rd., Route 110, Farmingdale NY 11735. Fax: (631)420-2051. E-mail: brownml@farmingdale.edu. Website: www.farmingdale. edu/campuspages/artsscience/englishhumanities/paward.html. **Contact:** Margery L. Brown, director, Visiting Writers Program. Offered annually for published or unpublished poems. Send cover letter, 1-paragraph bio, 3-5 poems (name and address on each poem). Include SASE for notification of winners. (Send photocopies only; mss will *not* be returned.) **Deadline: September 15. Charges $25 fee, payable to Farmingdale State University VWP.** Prize: 1st Place: $1,000, plus expenses for a reading in 2005-2006 series; Runners-up (2): $500, plus expenses for a reading in series.

PEARL POETRY PRIZE

Pearl Editions, 3030 E. Second St., Long Beach CA 90803. (562)434-4523. Fax: (562)434-4523. E-mail: pearlmag @aol.com. Website: www.pearlmag.com. **Contact:** Marilyn Johnson, editor/publisher. Offered annually "to provide poets with further opportunity to publish their poetry in book-form and find a larger audience for their work." Manuscripts must be original works written in English. Guidelines for SASE or on website. **Deadline: July 15. Charges $20.** Prize: $1,000 and publication by Pearl Editions. Open to all writers. Manuscripts must be original work (no translations) and in English.

PEN/JOYCE OSTERWEIL AWARD FOR POETRY

PEN American Center, 588 Broadway, Suite 303, New York NY 10012. (212)334-1660, ext. 101. E-mail: awards@ pen.org. Website: www.pen.org. **Contact:** Andrew Proctor, coordinator. *Candidates may only be nominated by members of PEN.* This award "recognizes the high literary character of the published work to date of a new and emerging American poet of any age, and the promise of further literary achievement." Nominated writer may not have published more than 1 book of poetry. Offered every 2 years (odd years). **Deadline: January 7.** Prize: $5,000. Judged by a panel of 3 judges selected by the PEN Awards Committee.

PEN/VOELCKER AWARD FOR POETRY

PEN American Center, 588 Broadway, Suite 303, New York NY 10012. (212)334-1600, ext. 101. E-mail: awards@ pen.org. Website: www.pen.org. **Contact:** Literary awards manager. *Candidates may only be nominated by members of PEN.* Award given to an American poet "whose distinguished and growing body of work to date represents a notable and accomplished presence in American literature." Offered even numbered years. **Deadline: January 1 (nominations).** Prize: $5,000 stipend. Judged by a panel of 3-5 poets or other writers.

N PERUGIA PRESS INTRO AWARD

Perugia Press, P.O. Box 60364, Florence MA 01062. E-mail: info@perugiapress.com. Website: www.perugiapres s.com. **Contact:** Susan Kan. Contest for a first or second book by a woman. Some poems in the submission can be previously published, but the ms as a whole must be unpublished. **Deadline: November 15.** Guidelines for SASE. **Charges $20.** Prize: $1,000 and publication. Judged by a panel of judges made up of previous winners of the Perugia Press Intro Award, plus other poets, teachers, scholars, booksellers, and poetry lovers. The contest is open to women poets who are US residents and who have not published more than one book.

PHILBRICK POETRY AWARD

Providence Athenaeum, 251 Benefit St., Providence RI 02903. (401)421-6970. Fax: (401)421-2860. E-mail: smark ley@providenceathenaeum.org. Website: www.providenceathenaeum.org. **Contact:** Sandy Markley. Offered annually for New England poets who have not yet published a book. Previous publication of individual poems in journals or anthologies is allowed. Judged by nationally-known poets. Guidelines for SASE or on website. **Deadline: June 15-October 15. Charges $8 fee (includes copy of previously published chapbook).** Prize: $500, publication of winning ms as a chapbook, and a public reading at Providence Athenaeum with the final judge/award presenter.

POET'S CORNER AWARD

Broken Jaw Press and BS Poetry Society, Box 596 Stn. A, Fredericton NB E3B 5A6 Canada. (506)454-5127. Fax: (506)454-5127. E-mail: jblades@brokenjaw.com. Website: www.brokenjaw.com. Offered annually to recognize the best book-length ms by a Canadian poet. Guidelines for SASE or on website at www.brokenjaw.com/

poetscorner.htm. **Deadline: December 31. Charges $20 fee (which includes copy of winning book upon publication).** Prize: $500, plus trade publication of poetry ms.

POETIC LICENCE CONTEST FOR CANADIAN YOUTH

League of Canadian Poets, 920 Yonge St., Suite 608, Toronto ON M4W 3C7 Canada. (416)504-1657. Fax: (416)504-0096. E-mail: contest@poets.ca. Website: www.poets.ca; www.youngpoets.ca. Offered annually for unpublished work to seek and encourage new poetic talent in 2 categories: grades 7-9 and 10-12. Entry is by e-mail only. Open to Canadian citizens and landed immigrants only. Guidelines for SASE or on website. See website for more information about the contest. **Deadline: December 1.** Prize: 1st Place: $150; 2nd Place: $100; 3rd Place: $50.

THE POETRY CENTER BOOK AWARD

The Poetry Center, San Francisco State University, 1600 Holloway Ave., San Francisco CA 94132-9901. (415)338-2227. Fax: (415)338-0966. E-mail: poetry@sfsu.edu. Website: www.sfsu.edu/~poetry. Estab. 1980. Offered annually for books of poetry and chapbooks, published in year of the prize. "Prize given for an extraordinary book of American poetry written in English." Please include a cover letter noting author name, book title(s), name of person issuing check, and check number. Will not consider anthologies or translations. **Deadline: January 31 for books published and copywrited in the previous year. Charges $10 reading fee/entry.** Prize: $500 and an invitation to read in the Poetry Center Reading Series.

POETRY IN PRINT POETRY CONTEST

Poetry in Print, P.O. Box 30981, Albuquerque NM 87190-0981. (505)888-3937. Fax: (505)888-3937. **Contact:** Robert G. English. No limit to the number of entries; 60 lines of poetry accepted. **Deadline: August 1. Charges $10.** Prize: $1,000. Open to any writer.

RAMBUNCTIOUS REVIEW POETRY CONTEST

Rambunctious Review, 1221 W. Pratt Blvd., Chicago IL 60626. Annual themed contest for unpublished poems. Acquires one-time publication rights. Open to any writer. **Deadline: December 31.** Guidelines for SASE. **Charges $3/poem.** Prize: 1st Prize: $100; 2nd Prize: $75; 3rd Prize: $50; all winning entries will be published in future issues of *Rambunctious Review*.

RIVER CITY WRITING AWARDS IN POETRY

The University of Memphis/Hohenberg Foundation, Dept. of English, Memphis TN 38152. (901)678-4591. E-mail: rivercity@memphis.edu. Website: www.people.memphis.edu/~rivercity. Offered annually for unpublished poems of 2 pages maximum. Guidelines for SASE or on website. **Deadline: March 1. Charges $12 fee for up to 3 poems.** Prize: 1st Place: $1,000; 2nd and 3rd Place: Publication and a 1-year subscription. Open to any writer.

RIVER STYX INTERNATIONAL POETRY CONTEST

River Styx Magazine, 634 N. Grand Blvd., 12th Floor, St. Louis MO 63103. (314)533-4541. Fax: (314)533-3345. Website: www.riverstyx.org. **Contact:** Richard Newman, editor. Offered annually for unpublished poetry. Poets may send up to 3 poems, not more than 14 pages. **Deadline: May 31.** Guidelines for SASE. **Charges $20 reading fee (which includes a 1-year subscription).** Prize: $1,000 and publication in August issue. Judged by Rodney Jones in 2005. Past judges include Miller Williams, Billy Collins, Marylin Hacker, Mark Doty, Molly Peacock, and Philip Levine. Open to any writer.

THE RUNES AWARD

RUNES, A Review of Poetry/Arctos Press, P.O. Box 401, Sausalito CA 94966. Fax: (415)331-3092. E-mail: runesrev @aol.com. Website: members.aol.com/runes. **Contact:** CB Follett or Susan Terris. Offered annually for unpublished poems. Prefer poems less than 100 lines. Theme for Runes 2006 is Hearth; 2007 is Connection. Guidelines online. **Deadline: May 31 postmark (regular and contest submissions accepted in April and May only). Charges $15 for 3 poems (includes a 1-year subscription to *RUNES, A Review of Poetry*);** additional poems $3 each. Prize: $1,000, plus publication in *RUNES, A Review of Poetry*. Judged by Mark Doty (2006 competition). There is no charge for regular submissions, same themes, with equal chance at publication. Acquires one-time publication rights. Open to any writer.

BENJAMIN SALTMAN POETRY AWARD

Red Hen Press, P.O. Box 3537, Granada Hills CA 91394. (818)831-0649. Fax: (818)831-6659. E-mail: editors@red hen.org. Website: www.redhen.org. **Contact:** Kate Gale. Offered annually for unpublished work "to publish a

Contests & Awards

winning book of poetry.'' Open to any writer. **Deadline: October 31.** Guidelines for SASE. **Charges $20 fee.** Prize: $1,000 and publication.

⚄ SASKATCHEWAN POETRY AWARD

Saskatchewan Book Awards, Inc., Box 1921, Regina SK S4P 3E1 Canada. (306)569-1585. Fax: (306)569-4187. E-mail: director@bookawards.sk.ca. Website: www.bookawards.sk.ca. **Contact:** Glenda James, executive director. Offered annually for work published September 15-September 14 annually. This award is presented to a Saskatchewan author for the best book of poetry, judged on the quality of writing. **Deadline: First deadline: July 31; Final deadline: September 14.** Guidelines for SASE. **Charges $20 (Canadian).** Prize: $2,000.

THE HELEN SCHAIBLE INTERNATIONAL SHAKESPEAREAN/PETRARCHAN SONNET CONTEST

Poets' Club of Chicago, 1212 S. Michigan Ave., #2702, Chicago IL 60605. **Contact:** Tom Roby, chair. Offered annually for original and unpublished Shakespearean or Petrarchan sonnets. One entry/author. Submit 2 copies, typed and double-spaced; 1 with name and address, 1 without. All rules printed here. Send SASE for winners list. **Deadline: September 1.** Prize: 1st Place: $50; 2nd Place: $35; 3rd Place: $15; 3 Honorable Mentions; 3 special recognitions.

⚄ SEEDS

Hidden Brook Press, 109 Bayshore Rd., RR#4, Brighton ON K0K 1H0 Canada. (613)475-2368. Fax: (801)751-1837. E-mail: writers@hiddenbrookpress.com. Website: www.hiddenbrookpress.com. ''The *SEEDS* International Poetry Chapbook Anthology Contest is interested in all types and styles of poetry. See the *SEEDS* website for examples of the type of poetry we have published in the past.'' Previously published and multiple submissions are welcome. **Deadline: October 1. Charges $15 for 3 poems.** Prize: 1st Prize: $100; 2nd Prize: $75; 3rd Prize: $50; 4th Prize: $40; 5th Prize: $30; 6th Prize: $25; 7th Prize: $20; 8th Prize: $15; 9th-10th Prize: $10, plus 15-25 Honorable Mentions. Winning poems published in the *SEEDS International Poetry Chapbook Anthology.* All winning and honorable mention submissions receive 1 copy of the book for each published poem. Authors retain copyright. Open to any writer.

SLAPERING HOL PRESS CHAPBOOK COMPETITION

The Hudson Valley Writers' Center, 300 Riverside Dr., Sleepy Hollow NY 10591. (914)332-5953. Fax: (914)332-4825. E-mail: info@writerscenter.org. Website: www.writerscenter.org. **Contact:** Margo Stever, editor. The annual competition is open to poets who have not published a book or chapbook, though individual poems may have already appeared. Limit: 16-20 pages. The press was created in 1990 to provide publishing opportunities for emerging poets. **Deadline: May 15.** Guidelines for SASE. **Charges $15 fee.** Prize: $1,000, publication of chapbook, 10 copies of chapbook, and a reading at The Hudson Valley Writers' Center.

SLIPSTREAM ANNUAL POETRY CHAPBOOK COMPETITION

Slipstream, Box 2071, Niagara Falls NY 14301. (716)282-2616 (after 5 p.m. EST). E-mail: editors@slipstreampress.org. Website: www.slipstreampress.org. **Contact:** Dan Sicoli, co-editor. Offered annually to help promote a poet whose work is often overlooked or ignored. Open to any writer. **Deadline: December 1.** Guidelines for SASE. **Charges $15.** Prize: $1,000 and 50 copies of published chapbook.

Ⓝ THE SOW'S EAR CHAPBOOK PRIZE

The Sow's Ear Poetry Review, 355 Mount Lebanon Rd., Donalds SC 29638-9115. (864)379-8061. E-mail: errol@kitenet.net. **Contact:** Errol Hess, managing editor. Estab. 1988. Offered for poetry mss of 22-26 pages. Guidelines for SASE or by e-mail. **Deadline: Submit March-April. Charges $15 fee.** Prize: $1,000, 25 copies, and distribution to subscribers.

THE SOW'S EAR POETRY PRIZE

The Sow's Ear Poetry Review, 355 Mount Lebanon Rd., Donalds SC 29638-9115. (864)379-8061. E-mail: errol@kitenet.net. **Contact:** Errol Hess, managing editor. Estab. 1988. Offered for previously unpublished poetry. Guidelines for SASE or by e-mail. All submissions considered for publication. **Deadline: Submit September-October. Charges $3 fee/poem.** Prize: $1,000, publication, plus option of publication for 20-25 finalists.

SPOON RIVER POETRY REVIEW EDITORS' PRIZE

Spoon River Poetry Review, Campus Box 4241, English Department, Illinois State University, Normal IL 61790-4241. (309)438-7906. Website: www.litline.org/spoon. **Contact:** Lucia Cordell Getsi, editor. Offered annually for unpublished poetry ''to identify and reward excellence.'' Guidelines on website. Open to all writers. **Deadline: April 15. Charges $16 (entitles entrant to a 1-year subscription valued at $15).** Prize: 1st Place: $1,000; Runners-Up (2): $100 each; publication of 1st Place, runners-up, and selected honorable mentions.

N ANN STANFORD POETRY PRIZE

The Southern California Anthology, % Master of Professional Writing Program, WPH 404, U.S.C., Los Angeles CA 90089-4034. (213)740-3252. Website: www.usc.edu/dept/LAS/mpw. **Contact:** James Ragan, contest director. Estab. 1988. Offered annually for previously unpublished poetry to honor excellence in poetry in memory of poet and teacher Ann Stanford. Submit cover sheet with name, address, phone number, and titles of the 5 poems entered. **Deadline: April 15.** Guidelines for SASE. **Charges $10 fee.** Prize: 1st Place: $1,000; 2nd Place: $200; 3rd Place: $100. Winning poems are published in *The Southern California Anthology*, and all entrants receive a free issue.

THE EDWARD STANLEY AWARD

Prairie Schooner, 201 Andrews Hall, P.O. Box 880334, Lincoln NE 68588-0334. (402)472-0911. Fax: (402)472-9771. E-mail: kgrey2@unl.edu. Website: www.unl.edu/schooner/psmain.htm. **Contact:** Hilda Raz. Offered annually for poetry published in *Prairie Schooner* in the previous year. Prize: $1,000.

THE ELIZABETH MATCHETT STOVER MEMORIAL AWARD

Southwest Review, P.O. Box 750374, Dallas TX 75275-0374. (214)768-1037. Fax: (214)768-1408. E-mail: swr@mail.smu.edu. Website: www.southwestreview.org. **Contact:** Jennifer Cranfill and Willard Spiegelman. Offered annually for unpublished poems or group of poems. Please note that mss are submitted for publication, not for the prizes themselves. Guidelines for SASE and on website. Prize: $250. Judged by Jennifer Cranfill, managing editor, and Willard Spiegelman, editor-in-chief. Open to any writer.

HOLLIS SUMMERS POETRY PRIZE

Ohio University Press, Scott Quadrangle, Athens OH 45701. (740)593-1155. Fax: (740)593-4536. Website: www.ohio.edu/oupress. **Contact:** David Sanders. Offered annually for unpublished poetry books. Books will be eligible if individual poems or sections have been published previously. Open to any writer. Guielines for SASE or on website. **Deadline: October 31. Charges $15.** Prize: $1,000 and publication of the ms in book form.

MAY SWENSON POETRY AWARD

Utah State University Press, 7800 Old Main Hill, Logan UT 84322-7800. (435)797-1362. Fax: (435)797-0313. E-mail: michael.spooner@usu.edu. Website: www.usu.edu/usupress. **Contact:** Michael Spooner. Offered annually in honor of May Swenson, one of America's major poets. Contest for unpublished mss in English, 50-100 pages; not only a "first book" competition. Entries are screened by 6 professional writers and teachers. The finalists are judged by a nationally known poet. Former judges include: Alicia Ostriker, Mark Doty, John Hollander, and Mary Oliver. Open to any writer. **Deadline: September 30.** Guidelines for SASE. **Charges $25 fee.** Prize: $1,000, publication of ms, and royalties.

N ⚡ TICKLED BY THUNDER POETRY CONTEST

Tickled by Thunder fiction magazine, 14076 86A Ave., Surrey BC V3W 0V9 Canada. E-mail: wd@tickledbythunder.com. Website: www.tickledbythunder.com. **Contact:** Larry Lindner. Annual contest to encourage unpublished poets. **Deadline: February 15, May 15, August 15 and October 15.** Guidelines for SASE. Prize: $75 (Canada), subscription, publication, and 2 copies of the magazine. Judged by the publisher and others he knows who have not entered the contest. Open to any writer.

TRANSCONTINENTAL POETRY AWARD

Pavement Saw Press, P.O. Box 6291, Columbus OH 43206. (614)445-0534. E-mail: info@pavementsaw.org. Website: pavementsaw.org. **Contact:** David Baratier, editor. Offered annually for a first book of poetry. Judged by Editor David Baratier and a guest judge. Guidelines on website. **Deadline: August 15. Charges $18 fee.** Prize: $1,500, 30 copies for judge's choice, standard royalty contract for editor's choice. All writers receive one free book for entering. Open to any writer.

KATE TUFTS DISCOVERY AWARD

Claremont Graduate University, 160 E. 10th St., Harper East B7, Claremont CA 91711-6165. (909)621-8974. Fax: (909)607-8438. Website: www.cgu.edu/tufts. **Contact:** Betty Terrell, administrative director. Estab. 1993. Offered annually for a first book by a poet of genuine promise. Entries must be a published book completed September 15, 2004-September 15, 2005. Guidelines for SASE or on website. **Deadline: September 15.** Prize: $10,000. Open to US residents and legal aliens.

KINGSLEY TUFTS POETRY AWARD

Claremont Graduate University, 160 E. 10th St., Harper East B7, Claremont CA 91711-6165. (909)621-8974. Fax: (909)607-8438. Website: www.cgu.edu/tufts. **Contact:** Betty Terrell, administrative director. Estab. 1992.

Offered annually "for a work by a poet, one who is past the very beginning but who has not yet reached the acknowledged pinnacle of his or her career." Guidelines for SASE or on website. **Deadline: September 15.** Prize: $100,000.

N ⬚ UTMOST CHRISTIAN POETRY CONTEST

Utmost Christian Writers Foundation, 121 Morin Maze, Edmonton AB T6K 1V1 Canada. E-mail: nnharms@telus planet.net. Website: www.utmostchristianwriters.com. **Contact:** Nathan Harms. The purpose of this annual contest is "to promote excellence in poetry by poets of Christian faith. All entries are eligible for most of the cash awards, but special categories (each with a $100 prize) have been created for: Best Poem by a US Citizen; Best Poem by a Canadian Citizen; Best Formal Poem (specific form); Best Poem by a Young Poet (under 21)." All entries must be unpublished. **Deadline: February 28.** Guidelines for SASE. **Charges $15/poem (maximum 7 poems).** Prize: Almost all prizes are in cash. In 2005, over $2,700 in cash awards with a top prize of $1,000. Rights are acquired to post winning entries on the organization's website. Judged by a committee of the Directors of Utmost Christian Writers Foundation (who work under the direction of Barbara Mitchell, chief judge). Open to any writer.

DANIEL VAROUJAN AWARD

New England Poetry Club, 16 Cornell St., #2, Arlington MA 02476-7710. **Contact:** Elizabeth Crowell. Offered annually for "an unpublished poem worthy of Daniel Varoujan, a poet killed by the Turks at the onset of the first genocide of the 20th century which decimated three-fourths of the Armenian population." Send poems in duplicate, with name and address of poet on one copy only. **Deadline: June 30.** Guidelines for SASE. **Charges $10 for 3 entries in NEPC contests paying $3,000 in prizes. Make check out to New England Poetry Club.** Prize: $1,000. Open to any writer.

CHAD WALSH POETRY PRIZE

Beloit Poetry Journal, P.O. Box 151, Farmington ME 04938. (207)778-0020. Website: www.bpj.org. **Contact:** Lee Sharkey and John Rosenwald, editors. Offered annually to honor the memory of poet Chad Walsh, a founder of the *Beloit Poetry Journal*. The editors select a strong poem or group of poems from the poems published in the journal that year. Prize: $3,000.

WAR POETRY CONTEST

Winning Writers, 351 Pleasant St., PMB 222, Northhampton MA 01060-3961. (866)946-9748. Fax: (413)280-0539. E-mail: warcontest@winningwriters.com. Website: www.winningwriters.com/annualcontest.htm. **Contact:** Adam Cohen. "This annual contest seeks outstanding, unpublished poetry on the theme of war. Up to 3 poems can be submitted, with a maximum total of 500 lines. English language. No translations, please. Submit online or by mail." **Deadline: November 15-May 31.** Guidelines for SASE. **Charges $12.** Prize: 1st Prize: $1,500 and publication on WinningWriters.com; 2nd Prize: $500 and publication; 3rd Prize: $250 and publication; Honorable Mentions (10): $75. Judged by award-winning poet Jendi Reiter. Acquires nonexclusive right to publish submissions on WinningWriters.com, in e-mail newsletter, and in press releases. Open to any writer.

THE WASHINGTON PRIZE

The Word Works, Inc., P.O. Box 42164, Washington DC 20015. E-mail: editor@wordworksdc.com. Website: www.wordworksdc.com. **Contact:** Miles David Moore. Offered annually "for the best full-length poetry manuscript (48-64 pp.) submitted to The Word Works each year. The Washington Prize contest is the only forum in which we consider unsolicited manuscripts." Acquires first publication rights. Open to any American writer. **Deadline: January 15-March 1.** Guidelines for SASE. **Charges $20 fee.** Prize: $1,500 and book publication; all entrants receive a copy of the winning book.

WERGLE FLOMP POETRY CONTEST

Winning Writers, 351 Pleasant St., PMB 222, Northampton MA 01060-3961. (866)946-9748. Fax: (413)280-0539. E-mail: flompcontest@winningwriters.com. Website: www.winningwriters.com. **Contact:** Adam Cohen. "This annual contest seeks the best parody poem that has been sent to a 'vanity poetry contest' as a joke. Vanity contests are characterized by low standards. Their main purpose is to entice poets to buy expensive products like anthologies, chapbooks, CDs, plaques, and silver bowls. Vanity contests will often praise remarkably bad poems in their effort to sell as much stuff to as many people as possible. The Wergle Flomp Prize will be awarded for the best bad poem. One poem of any length should be submitted, along with the name of the vanity contest that was spoofed. The poem should be in English. Inspired gibberish is also accepted. Submit online at WinningWriters.com. See website for guidelines and examples." **Deadline: August 15-April 1.** Prize: 1st Prize: $1,190; 2nd Prize: $169; 3rd prize: $60. Honorable Mentions get $38 each. All prize winners receive online publication at WinningWriters.com. Non-US winners will be paid in US currency (or PayPal) if a check is inconvenient. Judged by Jendi Reiter in 2004. Acquires nonexclusive right to publish submissions on Winning-Writers.com, in e-mail newsletter, and in press releases. Open to any writer.

WHITE PINE PRESS POETRY PRIZE

White Pine Press, P.O. Box 236, Buffalo NY 14201. E-mail: wpine@whitepine.org. Website: www.whitepine.org. **Contact:** Elaine LaMattina, managing editor. Offered annually for previously published or unpublished poets. Manuscript: Up to 80 pages of original work; translations are not eligible. Poems may have appeared in magazines or limited-edition chapbooks. Open to any US citizen. **Deadline: November 30 (postmarked). Charges $20 fee.** Prize: $1,000 and publication. Judged by a poet of national reputation. All entries are screened by the editorial staff of White Pine Press.

STAN AND TOM WICK POETRY PRIZE

Wick Poetry Center, 301 Satterfield Hall, Kent State University, P.O. Box 5190, Kent OH 44242-0001. (330)672-2067. Fax: (330)672-3152. E-mail: wickpoet@kent.edu. Website: dept.kent.edu/wick. **Contact:** Maggie Anderson, director. Open to anyone writing in English who has not previously published a full-length book of poems (a volume of 48 pages or more published in an edition of 500 or more copies). Send SASE or visit the website for guidelines. **Deadline: May 1. Charges $20 fee.** Prize: $2,000 and publication by the Kent State University Press.

THE RICHARD WILBUR AWARD

The University of Evansville Press, University of Evansville, Evansville IN 47722. **Contact:** The Editors. Offered in even-numbered years for an unpublished poetry collection. Guidelines for SASE and online at english.evansville.edu/english/WilburAwardGuidelines.htm. **Deadline: December 1, 2006. Charges $25 fee.** Prize: $1,000 and publication by the University of Evansville Press.

WILLIAM CARLOS WILLIAMS AWARD

Poetry Society of America, 15 Gramercy Park S., New York NY 10003. (212)254-9628. Fax: (212)673-2352. Website: www.poetrysociety.org. **Contact:** Programs Associate. Offered annually for a book of poetry published by a small press, nonprofit, or university press. Winning books are distributed to PSA Lyric Circle members while supplies last. Books must be submitted directly by publishers. Entry forms are required. It is strongly encouraged that applicants read the complete contest guidelines on the PSA website before submitting. **Deadline: October 1-December 21. Charges $22 fee.** Prize: $500-1,000.

JAMES WRIGHT POETRY AWARD

Mid-American Review, Dept. of English, Bowling Green State University, Bowling Green OH 43403. (419)372-2725. Fax: (419)372-6805. Website: www.bgsu.edu/midamericanreview. **Contact:** Karen Craig. Offered annually for unpublished poetry. Open to all writers not associated with *Mid-American Review* or judge. **Deadline: October 1.** Guidelines for SASE. **Charges $10.** Prize: $1,000 and publication in Spring issue of *Mid-American Review*. Judged by editors and a well known writer, i.e., Kathy Fagan, Bob Hicok, Michelle Boisseau.

WRITERS' JOURNAL POETRY CONTEST

Val-Tech Media, P.O. Box 394, Perham MN 56573. (218)346-7921. Fax: (218)346-7924. E-mail: writersjournal@writersjournal.com. Website: www.writersjournal.com. **Contact:** Esther M. Leiper. Offered for previously unpublished poetry. Guidelines for SASE or online. **Deadline: April 30, August 30, December 30. Charges $3 for each poem entered.** Prize: 1st Place: $50; 2nd Place: $25; 3rd Place: $15. 1st, 2nd, and 3rd place winners, and selected honorable mention winners will be published in *Writers' Journal* magazine.

PLAYWRITING & SCRIPTWRITING

▣ ALBERTA PLAYWRITING COMPETITION

Alberta Playwrights' Network, 2633 Hochwald Ave. SW, Calgary AB T3E 7K2 Canada. (403)269-8564; (800)268-8564. Fax: (403)265-6773. E-mail: apn@nucleus.com. Website: www.nucleus.com/ ~ apn. Offered annually for unproduced plays with full-length and Discovery categories. Discovery is open only to previously unproduced playwrights. Open only to residents of Alberta. **Deadline: January 15. Charges $40 fee (Canadian).** Prize: Full length: $3,500 (Canadian); Discovery: $1,500 (Canadian); plus written critique, workshop of winning play, and reading of winning plays at a Showcase Conference.

ANNUAL INTERNATIONAL ONE-PAGE PLAY COMPETITION

Lamia Ink!, P.O. Box 202, Prince Street Station, New York NY 10012. Website: www.lamiaink.org. **Contact:** Cortland Jessup, founder/artistic director. Offered annually for previously published or unpublished 1-page plays. Acquires "the rights to publish in our magazine and to be read or performed at the prize awarding festival." Playwright retains copyright. There are 3 rounds of judging with invited judges that change from year to year. There are up to 12 judges for finalists round. **Deadline: March 15. Charges $2/play; $5/3 plays (maximum).** Prize: $200, staged reading, and publication of 12 finalists. Open to any writer.

N APPALACHIAN FESTIVAL OF PLAYS & PLAYWRIGHTS
Barter Theatre, Box 867, Abingdon VA 24212-0867. (276)619-3314. Fax: (276)619-3335. E-mail: apfestival@bart ertheatre.com. Website: www.bartertheatre.com. **Contact:** Derek Davidson. "With the annual Appalachian Festival of New Plays & Playwrights, Barter Theatre wishes to celebrate new, previously unpublished/unproduced plays by playwrights from the Appalachian region. (If the playwrights are not from Appalachia, the plays themselves must be about the region.)" **Deadline: April 23.** Guidelines for SASE. Prize: $250, a staged reading performed at Barter's Stage II theater, and some transportation compensation and housing during the time of the festival. There may be an additional award for the best staged readings. Judged by the Barter Theatre's artistic director and associate director.

AUSTIN HEART OF FILM FESTIVAL FEATURE LENGTH SCREENPLAY COMPETITION
1604 Nueces, Austin TX 78701. (512)478-4795. Fax: (512)478-6205. E-mail: info@austinfilmfestival.com. Website: www.austinfilmfestival.com. Offered annually for unpublished screenplays. The Austin Film Festival is looking for quality screenplays which will be read by industry professionals. Two competitions: Adult/Family Category and Comedy Category. Guidelines for SASE or call (800)310-3378. The writer must hold the rights when submitted; it must be original work. The screenplay must be between 90 and 130 pages. It must be in standard screenplay format (industry standard). **Deadline: May 16. Charges $40 entry fee.** Prize: $5,000 in each category.

BAKER'S PLAYS HIGH SCHOOL PLAYWRITING CONTEST
Baker's Plays, P.O. Box 699222, Quincy MA 02269-9222. (617)745-0805. Fax: (617)745-9891. Website: www.ba kersplays.com. **Contact:** Deirdre Shaw, managing editor. Offered annually for unpublished work by high school-age students. Plays can be about any subject, so long as the play can be reasonably produced on the high school stage. Plays may be of any length. Submissions must be accompanied by the signature of the sponsoring high school drama or English teacher, and it is recommended that the play receive a production or a public reading prior to the submission. Multiple submissions and co-authored scripts are welcome. Teachers may not submit a student's work. The ms must be firmly bound, typed, and come with a SASE that includes enough postage to cover the return of the ms. Plays that do not come with a SASE will not be returned. Do not send originals; copies only. **Deadline: January 31.** Guidelines for SASE. Prize: 1st Place: $500 and publication by Baker's Plays; 2nd Place: $250; 3rd Place: $100.

BAY AREA PLAYWRIGHTS FESTIVAL
Produced by Playwrights Foundation, 131 10th St., 3rd Floor, San Francisco CA 94103. (415)626-0453, ext. 106. E-mail: literary@playwrightsfoundation.org. Website: www.playwrightsfoundation.org. **Contact:** Amy Mueller, artistic director; Duca Knezevic, director of literary services. Offered annually for unpublished plays by established and emerging theater writers to support and encourage development of a new work. Unproduced full-length play only. **Deadline: January 15 (postmarked).** Prize: Small stipend and in-depth development process with dramaturg and director, and a professionally staged reading in San Francisco. Open to any writer.

N THE BEVERLY HILLS THEATRE GUILD-JULIE HARRIS PLAYWRIGHT AWARD COMPETITION
P.O. Box 39729, Los Angeles CA 90039-0729. **Contact:** Dick Dotterer. Estab. 1978. "The contest is a national event open to aspiring, emerging, and established playwrights in the United States. Playwrights must be US citizens or legal residents. They may submit 1 unproduced playscript to the competition, accompanied by a signed application form. No one-acts, musicals, or children's plays are eligible." **Deadline: August 1-November 1 (postmark accepted).** Prize: 1st Prize: $3,500; 2nd Prize: $2,500; 3rd Prize: $1,500.

N BIENNIAL PROMISING PLAYWRIGHT CONTEST
Colonial Players, Inc., Box 2167, Annapolis MD 21404. (410)268-7373. **Contact:** Vice President. Offered every 2 years for unpublished full-length plays and adaptations. Open to any aspiring playwright residing in West Virginia, Washington DC, or any of the states descendant from the original 13 colonies (Connecticut, Delaware, Georgia, Maryland, Massachusetts, New Hampshire, New Jersey, New York, North Carolina, Pennsylvania, Rhode Island, South Carolina, and Virginia). Next contest runs September 1-December 1. Send SASE for guidelines, or visit www.cplayers.com. Prize: $1,000 cash award, weekend workshop with playwright participation, and rehearsed reading.

BIG BREAK INTERNATIONAL SCREENWRITING COMPETITION
Final Draft, Inc., 26707 W. Aguora Rd., Suite 205, Calabasas CA 91302. (800)231-4055. Fax: (818)995-4422. E-mail: bigbreak@finaldraft.com. Website: www.bigbreakcontest.com. **Contact:** Liz Alani, contest director. Estab. 2000. Annual global screenwriting competition designed to promote emerging creative talent. Guidelines online or for SASE. **Deadline: Febraury 15-June 15. Charges $40-60, depending on entry date.** Prize: Grand-prize winner is awarded $10,000, meetings with industry professionals and additional prizes worth over $5,000. Past winning scripts have been produced or optioned. The top 10 finalists will receive a copy of Final Draft scriptwriting software, Microsoft software, a screenwriting course from Gothan Writers' Workshop, a 1-year subscription to *Fade In* and *Scr(i)pt* magazines, and a $50 gift certificate from The Writers Store. Judged by industry professionals. Open to any writer.

BUNTVILLE CREW'S AWARD BLUE
Buntville Crew, 118 N. Railroad Ave., Buckley IL 60918-0445. E-mail: buntville@yahoo.fr. **Contact:** Steven Packard, artistic director. Presented annually for the best unpublished/unproduced play script under 15 pages, written by a student enrolled in any Illinois high school. Submit 1 copy of the script in standard play format, a brief biography, and a SASE (scripts will not be returned). Include name, address, telephone number, age, and name of school. **Deadline: May 31.** Guidelines for SASE. Prize: Cash prize and possible productions in Buckley and/or New York City. Judged by panel selected by the theater.

BUNTVILLE CREW'S PRIX HORS PAIR
Buntville Crew, 118 N. Railroad Ave., Buckley IL 60918-0445. E-mail: buntville@yahoo.fr. **Contact:** Steven Packard, artistic director. Annual award for unpublished/unproduced play script under 15 pages. Plays may be in English, French, German, or Spanish (no translations, no adaptations). Submit 1 copy of the script in standard play format, a résumé, and a SASE (scripts will not be returned). Include name, address, and telephone number. **Deadline: May 31.** Guidelines for SASE. **Charges $8.** Prize: $200 and possible production in Buckley and/or New York City. Judged by panel selected by the theater. Open to any writer.

CAA CAROL BOLT AWARD FOR DRAMA
Canadian Authors Association with the support of the Playwrights Guild of Canada and Playwrights Canada Press, 320 S. Shores Rd., P.O. Box 419, Campbellford ON K0L 1L0 Canada. (705)653-0323 or (866)216-6222. Fax: (705)653-0593. E-mail: admin@canauthors.org. Website: www.canauthors.org. **Contact:** Alec McEachern. Annual contest for the best English-language play for adults by an author who is Canadian or a landed immigrant. Submissions should be previously published or performed in the year prior to the giving of the award. **Deadline: December 15, except for plays published or performed in December, in which case the deadline is January 15.** Guidelines for SASE. **Charges $35 (Canadian funds) fee.** Prize: $1,000, and a silver medal. Judged by a trustee for the award (appointed by the CAA). The trustee appoints up to 3 judges. The identities of the trustee and judges are confidential. Short lists are not made public. Decisions of the trustee and judges are final, and they may choose not to award a prize.

CALIFORNIA YOUNG PLAYWRIGHTS CONTEST
Playwrights Project, 450 B St., Suite 1020, San Diego CA 92101-8093. (619)239-8222. Fax: (619)239-8225. E-mail: write@playwrightsproject.com. Website: www.playwrightsproject.com. **Contact:** Cecelia Kouma, managing director. Offered annually for previously unpublished plays by young writers to stimulate young people to create dramatic works, and to nurture promising writers. Scripts must be a minimum of 10 standard typewritten pages; send 2 copies. Scripts will *not* be returned. All entrants receive detailed evaluation letter. Writers must be California residents under age 19 as of the deadline date. Guidelines on website. **Deadline: June 1.** Prize: Professional production of 3-5 winning plays at the Old Globe in San Diego, plus royalty.

COE COLLEGE PLAYWRITING FESTIVAL
Coe College, 1220 First Ave. NE, Cedar Rapids IA 52402-5092. (319)399-8624. Fax: (319)399-8557. E-mail: swolvert@coe.edu. Website: www.public.coe.edu/departments/theatre/. **Contact:** Susan Wolverton. Estab. 1993. Offered biennially for unpublished work to provide a venue for new works for the stage. "There is usually a theme for the festival. We are interested in full-length productions, not one-acts or musicals. There are no specific criteria although a current résumé and synopsis is requested." Open to any writer. **Deadline: November 1. Notification: January 15.** Guidelines for SASE. Prize: $325, plus 1-week residency as guest artist with airfare, room and board provided.

DAYTON PLAYHOUSE FUTUREFEST
The Dayton Playhouse, 1301 E. Siebenthaler Ave., Dayton OH 45414-5357. (937)333-7469. Website: www.daytonplayhouse.com. **Contact:** Dave Seyer, executive director. "Three plays selected for full productions, 3 for readings at July FutureFest weekend. The 6 authors will be given travel and lodging to attend the festival."

Professionally adjudicated. Guidelines for SASE or online. **Deadline: October 30.** Prize: $1,000; $100 to the other 5 playwrights.

DRURY UNIVERSITY ONE-ACT PLAY CONTEST

Drury University, 900 N. Benton Ave., Springfield MO 65802-3344. E-mail: msokol@drury.edu. **Contact:** Mick Sokol. Offered in even-numbered years for unpublished and professionally unproduced plays. One play/playwright. Guidelines for SASE or by e-mail. **Deadline: December 1.**

DUBUQUE FINE ARTS PLAYERS ANNUAL ONE-ACT PLAY CONTEST

Dubuque Fine Arts Players, 1686 Lawndale, Dubuque IA 52001. E-mail: gary.arms@clarke.edu. **Contact:** Gary Arms. "We select 3 one-act plays each year. We award cash prizes of up to $600 for a winning entry. We produce the winning plays in August." Offered annually for unpublished work. Guidelines and application form for SASE. **Deadline: January 31. Charges $10.** Prize: 1st Prize: $600; 2nd Prize: $300; 3rd Prize: $200. Judged by 3 groups who read all the plays; each play is read at least twice. Plays that score high enough enter the second round. The top 10 plays are read by a panel consisting of 3 directors and 2 other final judges. Open to any writer.

EMERGING PLAYWRIGHT'S AWARD

Urban Stages, 17 E. 47th St., New York NY 10017-1920. (212)421-1380. Fax: (212)421-1387. E-mail: tlreilly@urbanstages.org. Website: www.urbanstages.org. **Contact:** T.L. Reilly, producing director. Estab. 1986. Submissions required to be unproduced in New York City. Send script, letter of introduction, production history, author's name, résumé, and SASE. Submissions accepted year-round. Plays selected in August and January for award consideration. One submission/person. **Deadline: Ongoing. Charges $5.** Prize: $1,000 (in lieu of royalties), and a staged production of winning play in New York City. Open to US residents only.

ESSENTIAL THEATRE PLAYWRITING AWARD

The Essential Theatre, P.O. Box 8172, Atlanta GA 30306. (404)212-0815. E-mail: pmhardy@aol.com. Website: www.essentialtheatre.com. **Contact:** Peter Hardy. Offered annually for unproduced, full-length plays by Georgia writers. No limitations as to style or subject matter. **Deadline: January 13.** Prize: $400 and full production.

SHUBERT FENDRICH MEMORIAL PLAYWRITING CONTEST

Pioneer Drama Service, Inc., P.O. Box 4267, Englewood CO 80155. (303)779-4035. Fax: (303)779-4315. E-mail: playwrights@pioneerdrama.com. Website: www.pioneerdrama.com. **Contact:** Lori Conary, assistant editor. Offered annually for unpublished, but previously produced, submissions to encourage the development of quality theatrical material for educational and community theater. Rights acquired only if published. Authors already published by Pioneer Drama are not eligible. **Deadline: March 1 (postmarked).** Guidelines for SASE. Prize: $1,000 royalty advance and publication.

FULL-LENGTH PLAY COMPETITION

West Coast Ensemble, P.O. Box 38728, Los Angeles CA 90038. (323)876-9337. Fax: (323)876-8916. Website: www.wcensemble.org. **Contact:** Les Hanson, artistic director. Offered annually "to nurture, support, and encourage" unpublished playwrights. Permission to present the play is granted if work is selected as finalist. **Deadline: December 31.** Guidelines for SASE. Prize: $500 and presentation of play.

JOHN GASSNER MEMORIAL PLAYWRITING COMPETITION

New England Theatre Conference, PMB 502, 198 Tremont St., Boston MA 02116. E-mail: mail@netconline.org. Website: www.netconline.org. Offered annually to unpublished full-length plays and scripts. Open to New England residents and NETC members. Playwrights living outside New England may participate by joining NETC. **Deadline: April 15.** Guidelines for SASE. **Charges $10 fee.** Prize: 1st Place: $1,000; 2nd Place: $500.

◪ GOVERNOR GENERAL'S LITERARY AWARD FOR DRAMA

Canada Council for the Arts, 350 Albert St., P.O. Box 1047, Ottawa ON K1P 5V8 Canada. (613)566-4414, ext. 5576. Fax: (613)566-4410. E-mail: joanne.larocque-poirier@canadacouncil.ca. Website: www.canadacouncil.ca/prizes/ggla. **Contact:** Joanne Larocque-Poirier. Offered for the best English-language and the best French-language work of drama by a Canadian. Submissions in English must be published between September 1, 2004 and September 30, 2005; submissions in French between July 1, 2004 and June 30, 2005. Publishers submit titles for consideration. **Deadline: March 15 or August 7, 2005, depending on the book's publication date.** Prize: Each laureate receives $15,000; nonwinning finalists receive $1,000.

AURAND HARRIS MEMORIAL PLAYWRITING AWARD

The New England Theatre Conference, Inc., PMB 502, 198 Tremont St., Boston MA 02116-4750. (617)851-8535. E-mail: mail@netconline.org. Website: www.netconline.org. Offered annually for an unpublished full-length play for young audiences. Guidelines for SASE. "No phone calls, please." Open to New England residents and/ or members of the New England Theatre Conference. **Deadline: May 1.** Guidelines for SASE. **Charges $20 fee.** Prize: 1st Place: $1,000; 2nd Place: $500. Open to any writer.

HENRICO THEATRE COMPANY ONE-ACT PLAYWRITING COMPETITION

Henrico Recreation & Parks, P.O. Box 27032, Richmond VA 23273. (804)501-5138. Fax: (804)501-5284. E-mail: per22@co.henrico.va.us. Website: www.co.henrico.va.us/rec. **Contact:** Amy A. Perdue. Offered annually for previously unpublished or unproduced plays or musicals to produce new dramatic works in one-act form. "Scripts with small casts and simpler sets given preference. Controversial themes and excessive language should be avoided." **Deadline: July 1.** Guidelines for SASE. Prize: $300; Runner-Up: $200. Winning entries may be produced; videotape sent to author.

JEWEL BOX THEATRE PLAYWRIGHTING COMPETITION

Jewel Box Theatre, 3700 N. Walker, Oklahoma City OK 73118-7099. (405)521-1786. **Contact:** Charles Tweed, production director. Estab. 1982. Offered annually for full-length plays. Send SASE in October for guidelines. **Deadline: January 15.** Prize: $500.

MARC A. KLEIN PLAYWRITING AWARD FOR STUDENTS

Dept. of Theater and Dance, Case Western Reserve University, 10900 Euclid Ave., Cleveland OH 44106-7077. (216)368-4868. Fax: (216)368-5184. E-mail: ksg@case.edu. Website: www.cwru.edu/artsci/thtr. **Contact:** Ron Wilson, reading committee chair. Estab. 1975. Offered annually for an unpublished, professionally unproduced full-length play, by a student at an American college or university. **Deadline: December 1.** Prize: $1,000, which includes $500 to cover residency expenses, and production.

KUMU KAHUA/UHM THEATRE DEPARTMENT PLAYWRITING CONTEST

Kumu Kahua Theatre, Inc./University of Hawaii at Manoa, Dept. of Theatre and Dance, 46 Merchant St., Honolulu HI 96813. (808)536-4222. Fax: (808)536-4226. E-mail: kkt@pixi.com. Website: www.kumukahua.c om. **Contact:** Harry Wong III, artistic director. Offered annually for unpublished work to honor full-length and short plays. Guidelines available every September. First 2 categories open to residents and nonresidents. For Hawaii Prize, plays must be set in Hawaii or deal with some aspect of the Hawaiian experience. For Pacific Rim prize, plays must deal with the Pacific Islands, Pacific Rim, or Pacific/Asian-American experience—short plays only considered in 3rd category. **Deadline: January 2.** Prize: $500 (Hawaii Prize); $400 (Pacific Rim); $200 (Resident).

LOVE CREEK ANNUAL SHORT PLAY FESTIVAL

Love Creek Productions, % Granville, 162 Nesbit St., Weehawken NJ 07086-6817. E-mail: creekread@aol.com. **Contact:** Cynthia Granville-Callahan, festival manager. Estab. 1985. *E-mail address is for information only.* Annual festival for unpublished plays, unproduced in New York in the previous year. An author may submit no more than 2 English language scripts per submission packet, each not to exceed 40 minutes in length, except for monologues or any 1-person plays, which should be 2-20 minutes in length. "We established the festival as a playwriting competition in which scripts are judged on their merits in performance." All entries must specify "festival" on envelope and must include letter giving permission to produce script, if chosen, and stating whether equity showcase is acceptable. "We are giving strong preference to scripts featuring females in major roles in casts which are predominantly female." **Deadline: Ongoing.** Guidelines for SASE. Prize: Cash prize awarded to overall winner.

MAXIM MAZUMDAR NEW PLAY COMPETITION

Alleyway Theatre, One Curtain Up Alley, Buffalo NY 14202-1911. (716)852-2600. Fax: (716)852-2266. E-mail: email@alleyway.com. Website: alleyway.com. **Contact:** Literary Manager. Estab. 1990. Annual competition. Full Length: Not less than 90 minutes, no more than 10 performers. One-Act: Less than 20 minutes, no more than 6 performers. Children's plays. Musicals must be accompanied by audio tape. Finalists announced October 1. "Playwrights may submit work directly. There is no entry form. Annual playwright's **fee $5**; may submit 1 in each category, but pay only 1 fee. Please specify if submission is to be included in competition. Alleyway Theatre must receive first production credit in subsequent printings and productions." **Deadline: July 1.** Prize: Full length: $400, production, and royalties; One-act: $100, production, and royalties.

McKNIGHT ADVANCEMENT GRANT

The Playwrights' Center, 2301 Franklin Ave. E., Minneapolis MN 55406-1099. (612)332-7481, ext. 10. Fax: (612)332-6037. E-mail: info@pwcenter.org. Website: www.pwcenter.org. **Contact:** Kristen Gandrow, director of new play development. Offered annually for either published or unpublished playwrights to recognize those whose work demonstrates exceptional artistic merit and potential and whose primary residence is in the state of Minnesota. The grants are intended to significantly advance recipients' art and careers, and can be used to support a wide variety of expenses. Applications available December 1. Guidelines for SASE. Additional funds of up to $2,000 are available for workshops and readings. The Playwrights' Center evaluates each application and forwards finalists to a panel of 3 judges from the national theater community. Applicant must have been a citizen or permanent resident of the US and a legal resident of the state of Minnesota since July 1, 2004. (Residency must be maintained during fellowship year.) Applicant must have had a minimum of 1 work fully produced by a professional theater at the time of application. **Deadline: February 4.** Prize: $25,000 which can be used to support a wide variety of expenses, including writing time, artistic costs of residency at a theater or arts organization, travel and study, production, or presentation.

McLAREN MEMORIAL COMEDY PLAY WRITING COMPETITION

Midland Community Theatre, 2000 W. Wadley, Midland TX 79705. (432)682-2544. Fax: (432)682-6136. Website: www.mctmidland.org. **Contact:** Alathea Blischke, McLaren co-chair. Estab. 1990. Offered annually in 2 divisions: one-act and full-length. All entries must be comedies for adults, teens, or children; musical comedies accepted. Work must have never been professionally produced or published. See website for competition guidelines and required entry form. **Charges $15 fee/script.** Prize: $400 for winning full-length play; $200 for winning one-act play; staged readings for finalists in each category.

MOVING ARTS PREMIERE ONE-ACT COMPETITION

Moving Arts, 514 S. Spring St., Los Angeles CA 90013-2304. (213)622-8906. Fax: (213)622-8946. E-mail: treynichols@movingarts.org. Website: www.movingarts.org. **Contact:** Trey Nichols, literary director. Offered annually for unproduced one-act plays in the Los Angeles area and "is designed to foster the continued development of one-act plays." All playwrights are eligible except Moving Arts resident artists. Guidelines for SASE or by e-mail. **Deadline: February 1 (postmarked). Charges $10 fee/script.** Prize: 1st Place: $200, plus a full production with a 4-8 week run; 2nd and 3rd Place: Program mention and possible production.

MUSICAL STAIRS

West Coast Ensemble, P.O. Box 38728, Los Angeles CA 90038. (323)876-9337. Fax: (323)876-8916. **Contact:** Les Hanson. Offered annually for unpublished writers "to nurture, support, and encourage musical creators." Permission to present the musical is granted if work is selected as finalist. **Deadline: June 30.** Prize: $500 and presentation of musical.

NATIONAL AUDIO DRAMA SCRIPT COMPETITION

National Audio Theatre Festivals, 115 Dikeman St., Hempstead NY 11150. (516)483-8321. Fax: (516)538-7583. Website: www.natf.org. **Contact:** Sue Zizza. Offered annually for unpublished radio scripts. "NATF is particularly interested in stories that deserve to be told because they enlighten, intrigue, or simply make us laugh out loud. Contemporary scripts with strong female roles, multi-cultural casting, and diverse viewpoints will be favorably received." Preferred length is 25 minutes. Guidelines on website. Open to any writer. NATF will have the right to produce the scripts for the NATF Live Performance Workshop; however, NATF makes no commitment to produce any script. The authors will retain all other rights to their work. **Deadline: November 15. Charges $25 fee (US currency only).** Prize: $800 split between 2-4 authors, and free workshop production participation.

⚄ NATIONAL CANADIAN ONE-ACT PLAYWRITING COMPETITION

Ottawa Little Theatre, 400 King Edward Ave., Ottawa ON K1N 7M7 Canada. (613)233-8948. Fax: (613)233-8027. E-mail: olt@on-aibn.com. Website: www.o-l-t.com. **Contact:** Elizabeth Holden, office administrator. Estab. 1913. Purpose is "to encourage literary and dramatic talent in Canada." Guidelines for #10 SASE with Canadian postage or #10 SAE with 1 IRC. **Deadline: August 31.** Prize: 1st Place: $1,000; 2nd Place: $700; 3rd Place: $500.

NATIONAL CHILDREN'S THEATRE FESTIVAL

Actors' Playhouse at the Miracle Theatre, 280 Miracle Mile, Coral Gables FL 33134. (305)444-9293. Fax: (305)444-4181. E-mail: maulding@actorsplayhouse.org. Website: www.actorsplayhouse.org. **Contact:** Earl Maulding. Offered annually for unpublished musicals for young audiences. Target age is 3-12. Script length should be 45-60 minutes. Maximum of 8 actors to play any number of roles. Prefer settings which lend themselves to simplified scenery. Bilingual (English/Spanish) scripts are welcomed. Call or visit website for guidelines. Open to any writer. **Deadline: June 1. Charges $10 fee.** Prize: 1st Place: $500 and full production.

NATIONAL LATINO PLAYWRIGHTS AWARD

Arizona Theatre Co., 40 E. 14th St., Tucson AZ 85701. (520)884-8210, ext. 5510. Fax: (520)628-9129. E-mail: eromero@arizonatheatre.org. Website: www.arizonatheatre.org. **Contact:** Elaine Romero, playwright-in-residence. Offered annually for unproduced, unpublished plays over 50 pages in length. "The plays may be in English, bilingual, or in Spanish (with English translation). The award recognizes exceptional full-length plays by Latino playwrights on any subject." Open to Latino playwrights currently residing in the US, its territories, and/or Mexico. Guidelines via e-mail or for SASE. **Deadline: December 30.** Prize: $1,000.

NATIONAL ONE-ACT PLAYWRITING COMPETITION

Little Theatre of Alexandria, 600 Wolfe St., Alexandria VA 22314. Website: www.thelittletheatre.com/oneact. Estab. 1978. Offered annually to encourage original writing for theater. Submissions must be original, unpublished, unproduced, one-act stage plays. "We try to produce top 2 or 3 winners." Guidelines for SASE or on website. **Deadline: Submit scripts January 1-October 31. Charges $20/play; 2-play limit.** Prize: 1st Place: $350; 2nd Place: $250; 3rd Place: $150.

NATIONAL PLAYWRITING COMPETITION

Young Playwrights, Inc., 306 W. 38th St., Suite 300, New York NY 10018. (212)594-5440. Fax: (212)594-5441. E-mail: writeaplay@aol.com. Website: youngplaywrights.org. **Contact:** Literary Department. Offered annually for stage plays of any length (no musicals, screenplays, or adaptations). Writers ages 18 or younger (as of deadline) are invited to send scripts. **Deadline: December 1.** Prize: Invitation to week-long writers' conference in New York City (all expenses paid) and off-Broadway presentation.

NEW AMERICAN COMEDY WORKSHOP

Ukiah Players Theatre, 1041 Low Gap Rd., Ukiah CA 95482. (707)462-1210. Fax: (707)462-1790. E-mail: players @pacific.net. Website: ukiahplayerstheatre.org. **Contact:** Kate Magruder, executive director. Offered every 2 years to playwrights seeking to develop their unproduced, full-length comedies into funnier, stronger scripts. Two scripts will be chosen for staged readings; 1 of these may be chosen for full production. Guidelines for SASE or online. **Deadline: November 30 of odd-numbered years.** Prize: Playwrights chosen for readings will receive a $25 royalty/performance. The playwright chosen for full production will receive a $50 royalty/performance, travel (up to $500) to Ukiah for development workshop/rehearsal, lodging, and per diem.

OGLEBAY INSTITUTE TOWNGATE THEATRE PLAYWRITING CONTEST

Oglebay Institute, Stifel Fine Arts Center, 1330 National Rd., Wheeling WV 26003. (304)242-7700. Fax: (304)242-7747. Website: www.oionline.com. **Contact:** Kate H. Crosbie, director of performing arts. Estab. 1976. Offered annually for unpublished works. "All full-length nonmusical plays that have never been professionally produced or published are eligible." Open to any writer. **Deadline: January 1; winner announced May 31.** Guidelines for SASE. Prize: Run of play and cash award.

ⓝ ONE-ACT PLAY CONTEST

Tennessee Williams/New Orleans Literary Festival, 938 Lafayette St., Suite 328, New Orleans LA 70113. (504)581-1144. E-mail: info@tennesseewilliams.net. Website: www.tennesseewilliams.net. **Contact:** Paul J. Willis. Annual contest for an unpublished play. **Deadline: December 1. Charges $15.** Prize: $1,000 and a staged reading at the festival. The play will also be fully produced at the following year's festival. The Tennessee Williams/New Orleans Literary Festival reserves the right to publish. Judged by an anonymous expert panel. Open to any writer.

MILDRED & ALBERT PANOWSKI PLAYWRITING AWARD

Forest Roberts Theatre, Northern Michigan University, Marquette MI 49855-5364. (906)227-2559. Fax: (906)227-2567. Website: www.nmu.edu/theatre. **Contact:** David Hansen, award coordinator. Estab. 1977. Offered annually for unpublished, unproduced, full-length plays. Guidelines and application for SASE. **Deadline: August 15-November 15 (due at office on the 15th).** Prize: $2,000, a fully-mounted production, and transportation to Marquette to serve as Artist-in-Residence the week of the show.

PERISHABLE THEATRE'S WOMEN'S PLAYWRITING FESTIVAL

P.O. Box 23132, Providence RI 02903. (401)331-2695. Fax: (401)331-7811. E-mail: wpf@perishable.org. Website: www.perishable.org. **Contact:** Rebecca Wolff, festival coordinator. Offered annually for unproduced, one-act plays (up to 30 minutes in length when fully produced) to encourage women playwrights. **Deadline: October 15 (postmarked).** Guidelines for SASE. **Charges $5 fee/playwright (limit 2 plays/playwright).** Prize: $500 and travel to Providence. Judged by a reading committee, the festival director, and the artistic director of the theater. Open to women playwrights exclusively.

PETERSON EMERGING PLAYWRIGHT COMPETITION

Catawba College Theatre Arts Department, 2300 W. Innes St., Salisbury NC 28144. (704)637-4440. Fax: (704)637-4207. E-mail: lfkesler@catawba.edu. Website: www.catawba.edu. **Contact:** Linda Kesler, theatre arts department staff. Offered annually for full-length unpublished work "to assist emerging playwrights in the development of new scripts, hopefully leading to professional production. Competition is open to all subject matter except children's plays. Musicals are accepted. Playwrights may submit more than 1 entry." Guidelines for SASE or by e-mail. **Deadline: December 1 (postmarked).** Prize: Production of the winning play at Catawba College, $2,000 cash award, transportation to and from Catawba College for workshop and performance, lodging and food while in residence, and professional response to the performance of the play. Open to any writer.

ROBERT J. PICKERING AWARD FOR PLAYWRIGHTING EXCELLENCE

Coldwater Community Theater, % 89 Division, Coldwater MI 49036. (517)279-7963. Fax: (517)279-8095. **Contact:** J. Richard Colbeck, committee chairperson. Estab. 1982. Previously unproduced monetarily. "To encourage playwrights to submit their work, to present a previously unproduced play in full production." Submit script with SASE. "We reserve the right to produce winning script." **Deadline: December 31.** Guidelines for SASE. Prize: 1st Place: $300; 2nd Place: $100; 3rd Place: $50.

PLAYHOUSE ON THE SQUARE NEW PLAY COMPETITION

Playhouse on the Square, 51 S. Cooper, Memphis TN 38104. **Contact:** Jackie Nichols. Submissions required to be unproduced. **Deadline: April 1.** Guidelines for SASE. Prize: $500 and production.

Ⓝ PLAYS FOR THE 21ST CENTURY

Playwrights Theater, 6732 Orangewood Dr., Dallas TX 75248-5024. E-mail: info@playwrightstheater.org. Website: www.playwrightstheater.org. **Contact:** Jack Marshall. Annual contest for unpublished or professionally unproduced plays (at time of submission). **Deadline: February 28. Charges $20.** Prize: $1,500 first prize; $500 each for second and third prizes. First prize receives a rehearsed reading. The judges decide on readings for second and third prizes. "Winners and their bios and contact info are posted on our website with a 15-page sample of the play (with playwright's permission)." All rights remain with the author. Judged by an outside panel of 3 theater professionals. The judges are different each year. Open to any writer.

PLAYWRIGHT DISCOVERY AWARD

VSA Arts, 1300 Connecticut Ave. NW, Suite 700, Washington DC 20036. (202)628-2800. Fax: (202)737-0725. E-mail: info@vsarts.org. Website: www.vsarts.org. **Contact:** Director, Performing Arts. Invites students with and without disabilities (grades 6-12) to submit a one-act play that explores the theme of disability. Recipients of the award will receive a scholarship and the opportunity to have their play produced at the John F. Kennedy Center for the Performing Arts in Washington, DC. **Deadline: April 15.**

PLAYWRIGHTS/SCREENWRITERS FELLOWSHIPS

NC Arts Council, Dept. of Cultural Resources, Raleigh NC 27699-4632. (919)715-1519. Fax: (919)733-4834. E-mail: debbie.mcgill@ncmail.net. Website: www.ncarts.org. **Contact:** Deborah McGill, literature director. Offered every even year for a play to support the development and creation of new work. See website for guidelines and other elegibility requirements. **Deadline: November 1.** Prize: $8,000 grant. Judged by a panel of film and theater professionals (playwrights, screenwriters, directors, producers, etc.). Artists must be current North Carolina residents who have lived in the state for at least 1 year as of the application deadline. Grant recipients must maintain their North Carolina status during the grant year and may not pursue academic or professional degrees during that period.

PRINCESS GRACE AWARDS PLAYWRIGHT FELLOWSHIP

Princess Grace Foundation—USA, 150 E. 58th St., 25th Floor, New York NY 10155. (212)317-1470. Fax: (212)317-1473. E-mail: pgfusa@pgfusa.com. Website: www.pgfusa.com. **Contact:** Christine Giancatarino, grants coordinator. Offered annually for unpublished, unproduced submissions to support playwright-through-residency program with New Dramatists, Inc., located in New York City. Entrants must be US citizens or have permanent US status. Guidelines for SASE or on website. **Deadline: March 31.** Prize: $7,500, plus residency with New Dramatists, Inc., in New York City, and representation/publication by Samuel French, Inc.

RICHARD RODGERS AWARDS IN MUSICAL THEATER

American Academy of Arts and Letters, 633 W. 155th St., New York NY 10032-7599. (212)368-5900. Fax: (212)491-4615. **Contact:** Lydia Kaim. Estab. 1978. The Richard Rodgers Awards subsidize full productions, studio productions, and staged readings by nonprofit theaters in New York City of works by composers and writers who are not already established in the field of musical theater. Authors must be citizens or permanent residents of the US. Guidelines and application for SASE. **Deadline: November 1.**

⑤ MORTON R. SARETT NATIONAL PLAYWRITING COMPETITION

UNLV Fine Arts College/Theatre Dept., 4505 Maryland Pkwy., Las Vegas NV 89154-5036. (702)895-3666. Fax: (702)895-0833. E-mail: stacey.jansen@ccmail.nevada.edu. Website: www.theatre.unlv.edu. **Contact:** Dr. Jeffrey Koep, Dean of the College of Fine Arts at UNLV. Original, innovative, full-length plays on any subject in English (or musicals meeting the same standards) which have not been previously produced, adapted, or published may be entered in this competition. Contest occurs every 2 years. **Deadline: February 1.** Guidelines for SASE. Prize: $3,000, plus travel and housing to attend rehearsals and the opening performance. The play will be produced by the Department of Theatre at UNLV. Open to any writer.

SCRIPTAPALOOZA SCREENWRITING COMPETITION

Supported by Writers Guild of America and sponsored by Write Brothers, Inc., 7775 Sunset Blvd., PMB #200, Hollywood CA 90046. (323)654-5809. E-mail: info@scriptapalooza.com. Website: www.scriptapalooza.com. Annual contest open to unpublished scripts from any genre. Open to any writer, 18 or older. Submit 1 copy of a 90-130-page screenplay. Body pages must be numbered, and scripts must be in industry-standard format. All entered scripts will be read and judged by over 50 production companies. **Deadline: Early Deadline: January 5; Deadline: March 7; Late Deadline: April 15.** Guidelines for SASE. **Charges Early Deadline Fee: $40; Fee: $45; Late Deadline Fee: $50.** Prize: 1st Place: $10,000 and software package from Write Brothers, Inc; 2nd Place, 3rd Place, and 10 Runners-Up: Software package from Write Brothers, Inc. The top 13 scripts will be considered by over 50 production companies.

SIENA COLLEGE INTERNATIONAL PLAYWRIGHTS COMPETITION

Siena College Theatre Program, 515 Loudon Rd., Loudonville NY 12211-1462. (518)783-2381. Fax: (518)783-2381. E-mail: maciag@siena.edu. Website: www.siena.edu/theatre. **Contact:** Gary Maciag, director. Offered every 2 years for unpublished plays ''to allow students to explore production collaboration with the playwright. In addition, it provides the playwright an important development opportunity. Plays should be previously unproduced, unpublished, full-length, nonmusicals, and free of copyright and royalty restrictions. Plays should require unit set, or minimal changes, and be suitable for a college-age cast of 3-10. There is a required 4-6 week residency.'' Guidelines for SASE. Guidelines are available after November 1 in odd-numbered years. Winning playwright must agree that the Siena production will be the world premiere of the play. **Deadline: February 1-June 30 in even-numbered years.** Prize: $2,000 honorarium, up to $2,000 to cover expenses for required residency, and full production of winning script.

DOROTHY SILVER PLAYWRITING COMPETITION

The Jewish Community Center of Cleveland, 26001 S. Woodland, Beachwood OH 44122. (216)831-0700. Fax: (216)831-7796. E-mail: dbobrow@clevejcc.org. Website: www.clevejcc.org. **Contact:** Deborah Bobrow, competition coordinator. Estab. 1948. All entries must be original works, not previously produced, suitable for a full-length presentation, and directly concerned with the Jewish experience. **Deadline: May 1.** Prize: Cash award, plus staged reading.

⑤ SOUTHEASTERN THEATRE CONFERENCE NEW PLAY PROJECT

P.O. Box 9868, Greensboro NC 27429. (336)272-3645. Fax: (336)272-8810. E-mail: setc@setc.org. Website: www.setc.org. **Contact:** Kenn Stilson. Offered annually for the discovery, development, and publicizing of worthy new unproduced plays and playwrights. Eligibility limited to members of 10-state SETC Region: Alabama, Florida, Georgia, Kentucky, Mississippi, North Carolina, South Carolina, Tennessee, Virginia, or West Virginia. Submissions accepted on disk only, in Microsoft Word format only. Check the SETC website for full submission details. No musicals or children's plays. **Deadline: March 1-June 1.** Guidelines for SASE. Prize: $1,000, staged reading at SETC Convention, and expenses paid trip to convention.

⑤ SOUTHERN APPALACHIAN PLAYWRIGHTS CONFERENCE

Southern Appalachian Repertory Theatre, P.O. Box 1720, Mars Hill NC 28754. (828)689-1384. Fax: (828)689-1272. E-mail: SART@mhc.edu. Website: www.sarttheatre.com. **Contact:** Andrew Reed, managing director. Offered annually for unpublished, unproduced, full-length plays to promote the development of new plays. All plays are considered for later production with honorarium provided for the winning playwright. **Deadline: October 31 (postmarked).** Guidelines for SASE. Prize: 4-5 playwrights are invited for staged readings in May, room and board provided.

SOUTHERN PLAYWRIGHTS COMPETITION

Jacksonville State University, 700 Pelham Rd. N., Jacksonville AL 36265-1602. (256)782-5414. Fax: (256)782-5441. E-mail: swhitton@jsucc.jsu.edu. Website: www.jsu.edu/depart/english/southpla.htm. **Contact:** Steven J. Whitton. Estab. 1988. Offered annually to identify and encourage the best of Southern playwriting. Playwrights must be a native or resident of Alabama, Arkansas, Florida, Georgia, Kentucky, Louisiana, Missouri, North Carolina, South Carolina, Tennessee, Texas, Virginia, or West Virginia. **Deadline: February 15.** Guidelines for SASE. Prize: $1,000 and production of the play.

STANLEY DRAMA AWARD

Dept. of Theatre Wagner College, One Campus Rd., Staten Island NY 10301. (718)390-3157. Fax: (718)390-3323. **Contact:** Dr. Felicia J. Ruff, director. Offered for original full-length stage plays, musicals, or one-act play sequences that have not been professionally produced or received trade book publication. **Deadline: October 1.** Guidelines for SASE. **Charges $10 submission fee.** Prize: $2,000.

TELEPLAY COMPETITION

(formerly Prime Time Television Competition), Austin Film Festival, 1604 Nueces, Austin TX 78701. (512)478-4795. Fax: (512)478-6205. E-mail: info@austinfilmfestival.con. Website: www.austinfilmfestival.com. Offered annually for unpublished work to discover talented television writers, and introduce their work to production companies. Categories: drama and sitcom (must be based on current television program). Contest open to writers who do not earn a living writing for television or film. **Deadline: June 1.** Guidelines for SASE. **Charges $30.** Prize: $1,000 in each category.

✂ THEATRE BC'S ANNUAL CANADIAN NATIONAL PLAYWRITING COMPETITION

Theatre BC, P.O. Box 2031, Nanaimo BC V9R 6X6 Canada. (250)714-0203. Fax: (250)714-0213. E-mail: pwc@the atrebc.org. Website: www.theatrebc.org. **Contact:** Robb Mowbray, executive director. Offered annually to unpublished plays "to promote the development and production of previously unproduced new plays (no musicals) at all levels of theater. Categories: Full Length (75 minutes or longer); One-Act (less than 75 minutes); and an open Special Merit (juror's discretion). Guidelines for SASE or on website. Winners are also invited to New Play Festival: Up to 16 hours with a professional dramaturg, registrant actors, and a public reading in Kamloops (every Spring). Production and publishing rights remain with the playwright. Open to Canadian residents. All submissions are made under pseudonyms. E-mail inquiries welcome. **Deadline: Fourth Monday in July. Charges $35/entry; optional $25 for written critique.** Prize: Full Length: $1,000; One-Act: $750; Special Merit: $500.

THEATRE CONSPIRACY ANNUAL NEW PLAY CONTEST

Theatre Conspiracy, 10091 McGregor Blvd., Ft. Myers FL 33919. (239)936-3239. Fax: (239)936-0510. E-mail: info@theatreconspiracy.org. **Contact:** Bill Taylor, award director. Offered annually for unproduced full-length plays with 8 or less characters and simple to moderate production demands. One entry per year. Send SASE for reply. **Deadline: March 30. Charges $5 fee.** Prize: $700 and full production. Open to any writer.

✂ THEATREPEI NEW VOICES PLAYWRITING COMPETITION

P.O. Box 1573, Charlottetown PE C1A 7N3 Canada. (902)894-3558. Fax: (902)368-7180. E-mail: theatre@isn.n et. **Contact:** Dawn Binkley, general manager. Offered annually. Open to individuals who have been residents of Prince Edward Island for 6 months preceding the deadline for entries. **Deadline: February 14.** Guidelines for SASE. **Charges $5 fee.** Prize: Monetary.

TRUSTUS PLAYWRIGHTS' FESTIVAL

Trustus Theatre, Box 11721, Columbia SC 29211-1721. (803)254-9732. Fax: (803)771-9153. E-mail: trustus@trus tus.org. Website: www.trustus.org. **Contact:** Jon Tuttle, literary manager. Offered annually for professionally unproduced full-length plays; cast limit of 8; prefer challenging, innovative dramas and comedies; no musicals, plays for young audiences, or "hillbilly" southern shows. Send SASE for guidelines and application. **Deadline: December 1, 2005-February 28, 2006.** Prize: Public staged reading and $250, followed after a 1-year development period by full production, $500, plus travel/accommodations to attend opening.

UNICORN THEATRE NEW PLAY DEVELOPMENT

Unicorn Theatre, 3828 Main St., Kansas City MO 64111. (816)531-7529, ext. 15. Fax: (816)531-0421. Website: www.unicorntheatre.org. **Contact:** Herman Wilson, literary assistant. Offered annually to encourage and assist the development of an unpublished and unproduced play. Acquires 2% subsidiary rights of future productions for a 5-year period. **Deadline: Ongoing.** Guidelines for SASE. Prize: $1,000 royalty and production.

VERMONT PLAYWRIGHT'S AWARD

The Valley Players, P.O. Box 441, Waitsfield VT 05673. (802)496-3751. E-mail: valleyplayers@madriver.com. Website: www.valleyplayers.com. **Contact:** Jennifer Howard, chair. Offered annually for unpublished, nonmusical, full-length plays suitable for production by a community theater group to encourage development of playwrights in Vermont, New Hampshire, and Maine. **Deadline: February 1.** Prize: $1,000.

◪ THE HERMAN VOADEN NATIONAL PLAYWRITING COMPETITION

Drama Department, Queen's University, Kingston ON K7L 3N6 Canada. (613)533-2104. E-mail: hannaca@post. queensu.ca. Website: www.queensu.ca/drama. **Contact:** Carol Anne Hanna. Offered every 2 years for unpublished plays to discover and develop new Canadian plays. See website for deadlines, guidelines. Open to Canadian citizens or landed immigrants. **Charges $30 entry fee.** Prize: $3,000, $2,000, and 8 honorable mentions. 1st- and 2nd-prize winners are offered a 1-week workshop and public reading by professional director and cast. The 2 authors will be playwrights-in-residence for the rehearsal and reading period.

VSA ARTS PLAYWRIGHT DISCOVERY AWARD

VSA Arts, 1300 Connecticut Ave. NW, Suite 700, Washington DC 20036. (202)628-2800. Fax: (202)737-0725. Website: www.vsarts.org. **Contact:** Performing Arts Coordinator. The VSA Arts Playwright Discovery Award challenges students grades 6-12 of all abilities to express their views about disability by writing a one-act play. Two plays will be produced at The Kennedy Center in Washington, DC. The Playwright Discovery Teacher Award honors teachers who bring disability awareness to the classroom through the art of playwriting. Recipient receives funds for playwriting resources, a scholarship, a trip to Washington, DC, and national recognition. **Deadline: April 15.**

WEST COAST ENSEMBLE FULL-PLAY COMPETITION

West Coast Ensemble, P.O. Box 38728, Los Angeles CA 90038. (323)876-9337. Fax: (323)876-8916. **Contact:** Les Hanson, artistic director. Estab. 1982. Offered annually for unpublished plays in Southern California. No musicals or children's plays for full-play competition. No restrictions on subject matter. **Deadline: December 31.**

JACKIE WHITE MEMORIAL NATIONAL CHILDREN'S PLAYWRITING CONTEST

Columbia Entertainment Co., 309 Parkade, Columbia MO 65202. (573)874-5628. **Contact:** Betsy Phillips, director. Offered annually for unpublished plays. ''Searching for good scripts—either adaptations or plays with original story lines—suitable for audiences of all ages.'' Script must include at least 7 well-developed roles. **Deadline: June 1.** Guidelines for SASE. **Charges $10 fee.** Prize: $500. Company reserves the right to grant prize money without production. All entrants receive written evaluation.

WRITE A PLAY! NYC

Young Playwrights, Inc., 306 W. 38th St., Suite 300, New York NY 10018. (212)594-5440. Fax: (212)594-5441. E-mail: writeaplay@aol.com. Website: youngplaywrights.org. **Contact:** Literary Department. Offered annually for plays by NYC elementary, middle, and high school students only. **Deadline: April 1.** Prize: Varies.

YEAR END SERIES (YES) NEW PLAY FESTIVAL

Dept. of Theatre, Nunn Dr., Northern Kentucky University, Highland Heights KY 41099-1007. (859)572-6362. Fax: (859)572-6057. E-mail: forman@nku.edu. **Contact:** Sandra Forman, project director. Receives submissions from May 1-October 31 in even-numbered years for the festivals which occur in April of odd-numbered years. Open to all writers. **Deadline: October 31.** Guidelines for SASE. Prize: $500 and an expense-paid visit to Northern Kentucky University to see the play produced.

ANNA ZORNIO MEMORIAL CHILDREN'S THEATRE PLAYWRITING COMPETITION

University of New Hampshire, Dept. of Theatre and Dance, PCAC, 30 College Rd., Durham NH 03824-3538. (603)862-2919. Fax: (603)862-0298. E-mail: mike.wood@unh.edu. Website: www.unh.edu/theatre-dance/zorn io.html. **Contact:** Michael Wood. Offered every 4 years for unpublished well-written plays or musicals appropriate for young audiences with a maximum length of 60 minutes. May submit more than 1 play, but not more than 3. All plays must be appropriate for children within the K-12 grades. Guidelines and entry forms available as downloads on the website. **Deadline: March 3, 2008.** Prize: $1,000, and play produced and underwritten as part of the season by the UNH Department of Theatre and Dance. Winner will be notified in November 2008. Open to all playwrights in US and Canada. All ages are invited to participate.

Contests & Awards

JOURNALISM

THE AMERICAN LEGION FOURTH ESTATE AWARD

The American Legion, 700 N. Pennsylvania, Indianapolis IN 46206. (317)630-1253. Fax: (317)630-1368. E-mail: pr@legion.org. Website: www.legion.org. Offered annually for journalistic works published the previous calendar year. "Subject matter must deal with a topic or issue of national interest or concern. Entry must include cover letter explaining entry, and any documention or evidence of the entry's impact on the community, state, or nation. No printed entry form." Guidelines for SASE or on website. **Deadline: January 31.** Prize: $2,000 stipend to defray expenses of recipient accepting the award at The American Legion National Convention in August.

AMY WRITING AWARDS

The Amy Foundation, P.O. Box 16091, Lansing MI 48901. (517)323-6233. Fax: (517)323-7293. E-mail: amyfoundtn@aol.com. Website: www.amyfound.org. **Contact:** James Russell, president. Estab. 1985. Offered annually for nonfiction articles containing scripture published in the previous calendar year in the secular media. **Deadline: January 31.** Prize: 1st Prize: $10,000; 2nd Prize: $5,000; 3rd Prize: $4,000; 4th Prize: $3,000; 5th Prize: $2,000; and 10 prizes of $1,000.

⬛ AVENTIS PASTEUR MEDAL FOR EXCELLENCE IN HEALTH RESEARCH JOURNALISM

Canadians for Health Research, P.O. Box 126, Westmount QC H3Z 2T1 Canada. (514)398-7478. Fax: (514)398-8361. E-mail: info@chrcrm.org. Website: www.chrcrm.org. **Contact:** Linda Bazinet. Offered annually for work published the previous calendar year in Canadian newspapers or magazines. Applicants must have demonstrated an interest and effort in reporting health research issues within Canada. Guidelines available from CHR or on website. **Deadline: February.** Prize: $2,500 and a medal.

ERIK BARNOUW AWARD

Organization of American Historians, P.O. Box 5457, 112 N. Bryan Ave., Bloomington IN 47408-5457. (812)855-9852. Fax: (812)855-0696. Website: www.oah.org. **Contact:** Award & Prize Committee Coordinator. One or 2 awards are given annually in recognition of outstanding reporting or programming on network or cable television, or in documentary film, concerned with American history, the study of American history, and/or the promotion of history. Entries must have been released the year of the contest. Guidelines available on website. **Deadline: December 1.** Prize: $1,000.

THE WHITMAN BASSOW AWARD

Overseas Press Club of America, 40 W. 45th St., New York NY 10036. (212)626-9220. Fax: (212)626-9210. Website: www.opcofamerica.org. **Contact:** Sonya Fry, executive director. Offered annually for best reporting in any medium on international environmental issues. Work must be published by US-based publications or broadcast. **Deadline: End of January. Charges $125 fee.** Prize: $1,000 and a certificate.

MIKE BERGER AWARD

Columbia University Graduate School of Journalism, 2950 Broadway, MC 3800, New York NY 10027-7004. (212)854-6468. Fax: (212)854-3800. E-mail: lsr21@columbia.edu. Website: www.jrn.columbia.edu. **Contact:** Lisa Redd, program coordinator. Offered annually honoring in-depth and enterprising reporting on individuals in the tradition of the late Meyer "Mike" Berger. All newspaper reporters whose beat is the Metropolitan New York region (New York state, New Jersey and Connecticut) are eligible—whether they report for dailies, weeklies or monthlies. "We welcome and encourage members of the English-language ethnic press to submit nominations." **Deadline: March 1.** Prize: Cash.

🅽 THE WORTH BINGHAM PRIZE

The Worth Bingham Memorial Fund, 1616 H St. NW, 3rd Floor, Washington DC 20006. (202)737-3700. Fax: (202)737-0530. E-mail: stalalay@icfj.org. Website: www.worthbinghamprize.org. **Contact:** Susan Talaly, project director. Offered annually to articles published during the year of the award. "The prize honors newspaper or magazine investigative reporting of stories of national significance where the public interest is being ill-served. Entries may include a single story, a related series of stories, or up to 3 unrelated stories. Please contact us for guidelines and entry form, or check our website." **Deadline: January 3.** Prize: $10,000.

HEYWOOD BROUN AWARD

The Newspaper Guild-CWA, 501 Third St. NW, Washington DC 20001-2797. (202)434-7173. Fax: (202)434-1472. E-mail: azipser@cwa-union.org. Website: www.newsguild.org. **Contact:** Andy Zipser. Offered annually for works published the previous year. "This annual competition is intended to encourage and recognize individual journalistic achievement by members of the working media, particularly if it helps right a wrong or correct an injustice. First consideration will be given to entries on behalf of individuals or teams of no more than 2." Guidelines for SASE or online. **Deadline: Last Friday in January.** Prize: $5,000 and a plaque.

CONSUMER JOURNALISM AWARD

National Press Club, General Manager's Office, National Press Bldg., 529 14th St. NW, Washington DC 20045. (202)662-8744. Fax: (202)662-7512. E-mail: jbooze@npcpress.org. Website: npc.press.org. **Contact:** Joann Booze. Offered annually to recognize excellence in reporting on consumer topics in the following categories: newspapers, periodicals, television, and radio. Entries must have been published/broadcast in the previous calendar year. Include a letter detailing how the piece or series resulted in action by consumers, the government, the community, or an individual. Guidelines on website. **Deadline:** April 1. Prize: $500 for each category.

Ⓝ O. HENRY AWARD

The Texas Institute of Letters, 6335 W. Northwest Hwy., #618, Dallas TX 75225. (214)363-7253. E-mail: franvick @aol.com. Website: www.wtamu.edu/til/awards.htm. **Contact:** Fran Vick, secretary. Offered annually for work published January 1-December 31 of previous year to recognize the best-written work of journalism appearing in a magazine or weekly newspaper. Judged by a panel chosen by the TIL Council. Writer must have been born in Texas, have lived in Texas for at least 2 consecutive years at some time, or the subject matter of the work should be associated with Texas. See website for guidelines. **Deadline: January 3.** Prize: $1,000.

SANDY HUME MEMORIAL AWARD FOR EXCELLENCE IN POLITICAL JOURNALISM

National Press Club, General Manager's Office, National Press Bldg., 529 14th St. NW, Washington DC 20045. (202)662-8744. Fax: (202)662-7512. E-mail: jbooze@npcpress.org. Website: npc.press.org. **Contact:** Joann Booze. Offered annually for work published in the previous calendar year. "This award honors excellence and objectivity in political coverage. This prize can be awarded for a single story of great distinction or for continuing coverage of 1 political topic. Categories: print, online. Guidelines on website. Open to professional journalists 34 years or younger. **Deadline:** April 1. Prize: $1,000.

ICIJ AWARD FOR OUTSTANDING INTERNATIONAL INVESTIGATIVE REPORTING

International Consortium of Investigative Journalists, A Project of the Center for Public Integrity, 910 17th St. NW, 7th Floor, Washington DC 20006. (202)466-1300. Fax: (202)466-1101. E-mail: info@icij.org. Website: www.icij.org. **Contact:** Andre Verloy. Offered annually for works produced in print, broadcast, and online media between June 1, 2004, and June 1, 2005. Work requires the use of sources in 2 or more countries. Guidelines and application form are on the website. **Deadline: July 15.** Prize: 1st Place: $20,000; up to 5 finalist awards of $1,000 each.

THE IOWA AWARD/THE TIM McGINNIS AWARD

The Iowa Review, 308 EPB, University of Iowa, Iowa City IA 52242. (319)335-0462. E-mail: iowa-review@uiowa. edu. Website: www.uiowa.edu/~ iareview. **Contact:** David Hamilton. "Offered annually for work already published in our magazine, usually within the previous year. The Iowa Award is a judge's choice of the best work of the year. The McGinnis Award is the editors' choice of a work from whatever we publish during the year before that usually expresses an off-beat and (we hope) sophisticated sense of humor. The Iowa Awards result from an annual contest, the submissions for which arrive in January. We send finalists in fiction, poetry, and nonfiction to outside judges to name the winners and publish each winner and several runners-up in our December issue. Please see our online guidelines for current information." Prize: $1,000 for each Iowa Award; $500 for McGinnis Award.

ANSON JONES, M.D. AWARD

Texas Medical Association, 401 W. 15th St., Austin TX 78701-1680. (512)370-1381. Fax: (512)370-1629. E-mail: brent.annear@texmed.org. Website: www.texmed.org. **Contact:** Brent Annear, media relations manager. Offered annually "to the media of Texas for excellence in communicating health information to the public." Open only to Texas general interest media or writers published in Texas. Guidelines posted online. **Deadline: January 15.** Prize: $1,000 for winners in each of the categories.

LIVINGSTON AWARDS FOR YOUNG JOURNALISTS

Mollie Parnis Livingston Foundation, Wallace House, 620 Oxford, Ann Arbor MI 48104. (734)998-7575. Fax: (734)998-7979. E-mail: livingstonawards@umich.edu. Website: www.livawards.org. **Contact:** Charles Eisendrath. Offered annually for journalism published January 1-December 31 the previous year to recognize and further develop the abilities of young journalists. Includes print, online, and broadcast. Guidelines on website. **Deadline: February 1.** Prize: $10,000 each for local reporting, national reporting, and international reporting.

Judges include Charles Gibson, Ellen Goodman, and Tom Brokaw. Open to journalists who are 34 years or younger as of December 31 of previous year and whose work appears in US-controlled print or broadcast media.

FRANK LUTHER MOTT-KAPPA TAU ALPHA RESEARCH AWARD IN JOURNALISM

University of Missouri School of Journalism, 76 Gannett Hall, Columbia MO 65211-1200. (573)882-7685. E-mail: umcjourkta@missouri.edu. Website: www.missouri.edu/~ktahq. **Contact:** Dr. Keith Sanders, executive director, Kappa Tau Alpha. Offered annually for best researched book in mass communication. Submit 6 copies; no forms required. **Deadline: December 9.** Prize: $1,000.

ONLINE JOURNALISM AWARD

National Press Club, General Manager's Office, National Press Bldg., 529 14th St. NW, Washington DC 20045. (202)662-8744. Fax: (202)662-7512. E-mail: jbooze@npcpress.org. Website: npc.press.org. **Contact:** Joanne Booze. Offered annually to recognize the most significant contributions to journalism by the online media in 2 categories: Best Journalism Site (this award honors the best journalistic use of the online medium); and Distinguished Online Contribution (this award goes to the best individual contribution to public service using online technology). Guidelines on website. **Deadline:** April 1. Prize: $1,000 in each category.

ALICIA PATTERSON JOURNALISM FELLOWSHIP

Alicia Patterson Foundation, 1730 Pennsylvania Ave. NW, Suite 850, Washington DC 20006. (202)393-5995. Fax: (301)951-8512. E-mail: info@aliciapatterson.org. Website: www.aliciapatterson.org. **Contact:** Margaret Engel. Offered annually for previously published submissions to give 8-10 full-time print journalists or photojournalists 6 months or one year of in-depth research and reporting. Applicants must have 5 years of professional print journalism experience and be US citizens. Fellows write 4 magazine-length pieces for the *Alicia Patterson Reporter*, a quarterly magazine, during their fellowship year. Fellows must take 6-12 months' leave from their jobs, but may do other freelance articles during the year. Write, call, fax, or check website for applications. **Deadline: October 1.** Prize: $35,000 stipend for calendar year; $17,500 for 6 months.

JOSEPH D. RYLE AWARD FOR EXCELLENCE IN WRITING ON THE PROBLEMS OF GERIATRICS

National Press Club, General Manager's Office, National Press Bldg., Washington DC 20045. (202)662-8744. Fax: (202)662-7512. Website: npc.press.org. **Contact:** Joann Booze. Offered annually for work published in the previous year. This award emphasizes excellence and objectivity in coverage of the problems faced by the elderly. Guidelines on website. Open to professional print journalists. **Deadline:** April 1. Prize: $2,000.

SOVEREIGN AWARD

The Jockey Club of Canada, P.O. Box 66, Station B, Etobiwke ON M9W 5K9 Canada. (416)675-7756. Fax: (416)675-6378. E-mail: jockeyclub@bellnet.ca. Website: www.jockeyclubcanada.ca. **Contact:** Bridget Bimm, executive director. Estab. 1973. Offered annually to recognize outstanding achievement in the area of Canadian thoroughbred racing journalism published November 1-October 31 of the previous year. Categories: Outstanding Newspaper Article, Outstanding Feature Story, Outstanding Photograph, Outstanding Film/Video/Broadcast. Submissions for these media awards must be of Canadian Thoroughbred racing or breeding content. Submissions must have appeared in a media outlet recognized by The Jockey Club of Canada. Submissions must be received in The Jockey Club of Canada no later than 5 p.m. (EDT) on October 31 in the year in which the awards are presented. There is no nominating process other than the writer submitting no more than 1 entry/category. A copy of the newspaper article or magazine story must be provided along with a 3.25" disk containing the story in an ASCII style format. Submissions to the photograph category should include a newspaper cut of the photo and 10 8×11 photos. Submission to the Outstanding Film/Video/Broadcast category should be made by sending a letter detailing what the video is about, the names of the editor, producer, etc., and a VHS or Beta tape of the program, including the date the show aired and where it aired. **Deadline: October 31.**

STANLEY WALKER JOURNALISM AWARD

The Texas Institute of Letters, 6335 W. Northwest Hwy., #618, Dallas TX 75225. (214)363-7253. E-mail: franvick @aol.com. Website: www.wtamu.edu/til/awards.htm. **Contact:** Fran Vick, secretary. Offered annually for work published January 1-December 31 of previous year to recognize the best writing appearing in a daily newspaper. Writer must have been born in Texas, have lived in the state for 2 consecutive years at some time, or the subject matter of the article must be associated with the state. See website for guidelines. **Deadline: January 3.** Prize: $1,000.

WASHINGTON CORRESPONDENCE AWARD

National Press Club, General Manager's Office, National Press Bldg., 529 14th St. NW, Washington DC 20045. (202)662-8744. Fax: (202)662-7512. E-mail: jbooze@npcpress.org. Website: npc.press.org. **Contact:** Joann

Booze. Offered annually to honor the work of reporters who cover Washington for the benefit of the hometown audience. ''This award is for a single report or series on one topic, not for national reporting, nor for a body of work. Entrants must demonstrate a clear knowledge of how Washington works and what it means to the folks back home.'' Categories: print, online. Guidelines on webiste. **Deadline:** April 1. Prize: $1,000.

WRITING FOR CHILDREN & YOUNG ADULTS

ℕ ⊕ ACADEMY OF CHILDREN'S WRITERS' WRITING FOR CHILDREN COMPETITION

Academy of Children's Writers, P.O. Box 95, Huntington Cambridgeshire PE28 5RL England. 01487 832752. Fax: 01487 832752. E-mail: per_ardua@lycos.co.uk. **Contact:** Roger Dewar, contest director. Annual contest for the best unpublished short story writer for children. **Deadline: March 31.** Guidelines for SASE. **Charges $5 (US); £2 (UK).** Prize: 1st Prize: £1,000; 2nd Prize: £300; 3rd Prize: £100. Judged by a panel appointed by the Academy of Children's Writers. Open to any writer.

✠ ASTED/GRAND PRIX DE LITTERATURE JEUNESSE DU QUEBEC-ALVINE-BELISLE

Association pour l'avancement des sciences et des techniques de la documentation, 3414 Avenue du Parc, Bureau 202, Montreal QC H2X 2H5 Canada. (514)281-5012. Fax: (514)281-8219. E-mail: info@asted.org. Website: www.asted.org. **Contact:** Marie-Hélène Parent, president. ''Prize granted for the best work in youth literature edited in French in the Quebec Province. Authors and editors can participate in the contest.'' Offered annually for books published during the preceding year. **Deadline: June 1.** Prize: $1,000.

✠ THE GEOFFREY BILSON AWARD FOR HISTORICAL FICTION FOR YOUNG PEOPLE

The Canadian Children's Book Centre, 40 Orchard View Blvd., Suite 101, Toronto ON M4R 1B9 Canada. (416)975-0010. Fax: (416)975-8970. E-mail: brenda@bookcentre.ca. Website: www.bookcentre.ca. **Contact:** Brenda Halliday, librarian. Created in Geoffrey Bilson's memory in 1988. Offered annually for a previously published ''outstanding work of historical fiction for young people by a Canadian author.'' Open to Canadian citizens and residents of Canada for at least 2 years. **Deadline: January 15.** Prize: $1,000. Judged by a jury selected by the Canadian Children's Book Centre.

IRMA S. AND JAMES H. BLACK AWARD

Bank Street College of Education, 610 W. 112th St., New York NY 10025. (212)875-4450. Fax: (212)875-4558. E-mail: lindag@bankstreet.edu. Website: streetcat.bnkst.edu/html/isb.html. **Contact:** Linda Greengrass, director. Estab. 1972. Offered annually in May for excellence of both text and illustrations in a book for young children. Entries must have been published during the previous calendar year. **Deadline: December 15 of the year the book is published.**

⊕ BOOKTRUST EARLY YEARS AWARDS

(formerly Bookstart Baby Book Award), % Booktrust, Book House, 45 E. Hill, Wandsworth, London SW18 2QZ United Kingdom. Fax: (00 44) 20 8516 2978. E-mail: tarryn@booktrust.org.uk. Website: www.booktrusted.com. **Contact:** Tarryn McKay. The Booktrust Early Years Awards were initially established in 1999 and are awarded annually. The awards are given to the best books, published between September 1 and the following August 31, in the opinion of the judges in each category. The categories are: Baby Book Award, Pre-School Award, and Best New Illustrator Award. Authors and illustrators must be of British nationality, or other nationals who have been residents in the British Isles for at least 10 years. Books can be any format. **Deadline: June.** Prize: £2,000 and a crystal award to each winner. In addition, the publisher receives a crystal award naming them as ''The Booktrust Early Years Awards Publisher of the Year.''

BOSTON GLOBE-HORN BOOK AWARDS

The Boston Globe, Horn Book, Inc., 56 Roland St., Suite 200, Boston MA 02129. (617)628-0225. Website: www.hbook.com. **Contact:** Marika Hoe. Offered annually for excellence in literature for children and young adults (published June 1, 2004-May 31, 2005). Categories: picture book, fiction and poetry, nonfiction. Judges may also name several honor books in each category. Books must be published in the US. Guidelines for SASE or online. **Deadline: May 6.** Prize: Winners receive $500 and an engraved silver bowl; honor book recipients receive an engraved silver plate. Judged by a panel of 3 judges selected each year.

ℕ SANDRA CARON YOUNG ADULT POETRY PRIZE

National League of American Pen Women, Nob Hill, San Francisco Branch, 1544 Sweetwood Dr., Colma CA 94015-2029. E-mail: pennobhill@aol.com. Website: www.soulmakingcontest.us. **Contact:** Eileen Malone. Three poems/entry; one poem/page; one-page poems only from someone in grades 9-12. Annually. **Deadline: Novem-**

Contests & Awards *(side tab)*

ber 30. Guidelines for SASE. **Charges $5/entry (make checks payable to NLAPW, Nob Hill Branch).** Prize: 1st Place: $100; 2nd Place: $50; 3rd Place: $25. Open to any writer.

CHILDREN'S WRITERS FICTION CONTEST

Stepping Stones, P.O. Box 601721, N. Miami Beach FL 33160-1721. (305)944-6491. E-mail: verwil@alumni.pace. edu. **Contact:** V.R. Williams, director. Offered annually for unpublished fiction. **Deadline: July 31.** Guidelines for SASE. **Charges $10.** Prize: $260, and/or publication in *Hodge Podge*. Judged by Williams, Walters & Associates. "Entries are judged for clarity, grammar, punctuation, imagery, content, and suitability for children." Open to any writer.

DELACORTE YEARLING CONTEST FOR A FIRST MIDDLE-GRADE NOVEL

(formerly the Marguerite De Angeli Prize). Delacorte Press Books for Young Readers, Random House, Inc., 1745 Broadway, New York NY 10019. (212)782-9000. Fax: (212)782-9452. Website: www.randomhouse.com/ kids. Estab. 1992. Offered annually for an unpublished fiction ms suitable for readers 8-12 years of age, set in North America, either contemporary or historical. Guidelines on website. **Deadline: April 1-June 30.** Prize: $1,500 in cash, publication, and $7,500 advance against royalties. World rights acquired.

◪ THE NORMA FLECK AWARD FOR CANADIAN CHILDREN'S NONFICTION

The Canadian Children's Book Centre, 40 Orchard View Blvd., Suite 101, Toronto ON M4R 1B9 Canada. (416)975-0010. Fax: (416)975-8970. E-mail: info@bookcentre.ca. Website: www.bookcentre.ca. **Contact:** Shannon Howe, program coordinator. The Norma Fleck Award was established by the Fleck Family Foundation in May 1999 to honor the life of Norma Marie Fleck, and to recognize exceptional Canadian nonfiction books for young people. Publishers are welcome to nominate books using the online form. Offered annually for books published between May 1, 2005, and April 30, 2006. Open to Canadian citizens or landed immigrants. The jury will always include at least 3 of the following: a teacher, a librarian, a bookseller, and a reviewer. A juror will have a deep understanding of, and some involvement with, Canadian children's books. The Canadian Children's Book Centre will select the jury members. **Deadline: March 31 (annually).** Prize: $10,000 goes to the author (unless 40% or more of the text area is composed of original illustrations, in which case the award will be divided equally between the author and the artist).

FRIENDS OF THE AUSTIN PUBLIC LIBRARY AWARD FOR BEST CHILDREN'S AND BEST YOUNG ADULT'S BOOK

6335 W. Northwest Hwy, #618, Dallas TX 75225. (214)363-7253. E-mail: franvick@aol.com. Website: www.wtamu. edu/til/awards.htm. **Contact:** Fran Vick. Offered annually for work published January 1-December 31 of previous year to recognize the best book for children and young people. Writer must have been born in Texas or have lived in the state for at least 2 consecutive years at one time, or the subject matter must be associated with the state. See website for judges and further information. **Deadline: January 3.** Prize: $500 for each award winner.

GOLDEN KITE AWARDS

Society of Children's Book Writers and Illustrators (SCBWI), 8271 Beverly Blvd., Los Angeles CA 90048. (323)782-1010. E-mail: scbwi@scbwi.org. Website: www.scbwi.org. **Contact:** Rebekah Merroll, coordinator. Estab. 1973. Offered annually for children's fiction, nonfiction, and picture illustration books by SCBWI members published in the calendar year. **Deadline: December 15.**

◪ GOVERNOR GENERAL'S LITERARY AWARD FOR CHILDREN'S LITERATURE

Canada Council for the Arts, 350 Albert St., P.O. Box 1047, Ottawa ON K1P 5V8 Canada. (613)566-4414, ext. 5576. Fax: (613)566-4410. E-mail: joanne.larocque-poirier@canadacouncil.ca. Website: www.canadacouncil .ca/prizes/ggla. **Contact:** Joanne Larocque-Poirier. Offered for the best English-language and the best French-language works of children's literature by a Canadian in 2 categories: text and illustration. Submissions in English must be published between September 1, 2004 and September 30, 2005; submissions in French between July 1, 2004 and June 30, 2005. Publishers submit titles for consideration. **Deadline: April 15 or August 7, 2005, depending on the book's publication date.** Prize: Each laureate receives $15,000 and nonwinning finalists receive $1,000.

◪ THE MARILYN HALL AWARDS FOR YOUTH THEATRE

Beverly Hills Theatre Guild, P.O. Box 39729, Los Angeles CA 90039-0729. **Contact:** Dick Dotterer. Estab. 1998. Contest is held annually. Playwrights must be US citizens or legal residents. They may submit up to 2 playscripts to the competition. One production allowed to still be eligible. Guidelines and submission forms available after November each year. **Deadline: January 15-last day in February each year (postmark accepted).** Prize: 1st Place: $500; 2nd Place: $300; 3rd Place: $200.

HIGHLIGHTS FOR CHILDREN FICTION CONTEST

Highlights for Children, 803 Church St., Honesdale PA 18431-1824. (570)253-1080. Website: www.highlights.com. **Contact:** Marileta Robinson, senior editor. Offered for stories for children ages 2-12; category varies each year. Stories should be previously unpublished and limited to 800 words for older readers, 500 words for younger readers. No crime or violence, please. Specify that ms is a contest entry. See website for current theme and guidelines. **Deadline: January 1-February 28 (postmarked).** Guidelines for SASE. Prize: $1,000 to 3 winners, and publication of stories in *Highlights*. All other submissions will be considered for purchase by *Highlights for Children*. Open to anyone 16 years of age or older.

☒ THE VICKY METCALF AWARD FOR CHILDREN'S LITERATURE

The Writers' Trust of Canada, 90 Richmond St. E., Suite 200, Toronto ON M5C 1P1 Canada. (416)504-8222. Fax: (416)504-9090. E-mail: info@writerstrust.com. Website: www.writerstrust.com. **Contact:** James Davies. The Metcalf Award is presented each spring to a Canadian writer for a body of work in children's literature at The Great Literary Awards event in Toronto. Prize: $15,000. Open to Canadian residents only.

MILKWEED PRIZE FOR CHILDREN'S LITERATURE

Milkweed Editions, 1011 Washington Ave. S., Suite 300, Minneapolis MN 55415. (612)332-3192. Fax: (612)215-2550. Website: www.milkweed.org. **Contact:** Elisabeth Fitz, first reader. Estab. 1993. Annual prize for unpublished works. "Milkweed is looking for a novel intended for readers aged 8-13. Manuscripts should be of high literary quality and must be double-spaced, 90-200 pages in length. The Milkweed Prize for Children's Literature will be awarded to the best manuscript for children ages 8-13 that Milkweed accepts for publication during each calendar year by a writer not previously published by Milkweed Editions." All mss submitted to Milkweed will automatically be considered for the prize. Submission directly to the contest is not necessary. Must review guidelines, available at website or for SASE. Catalog for $1.50 postage. Prize: $5,000 advance on royalties agreed upon at the time of acceptance.

▦ NESTLÉ CHILDREN'S BOOK PRIZE

% Booktrust, Book House, 45 E. Hill, Wandsworth London SW18 2QZ United Kingdom. Fax: (00 44) 20 8516 2978. E-mail: hannah@booktrust.org.uk. Website: www.booktrusted.com. **Contact:** Hannah Rutland. "The Nestlé Children's Book Prize was established in 1985 to encourage high standards and stimulate interest in children's books. The prize is split into 3 age categories: 5 and under, 6-8, 9-11, plus the 4Children Special Award. The books are judged by our adult panel, who shortlist 3 outstanding books in each category, and the final decision of who gets Gold, Silver, Bronze, and the 4Children Special Award is left to our young judges. The young judges are chosen from classes of school children who complete a task for their age category; the best 50 from each category go on to judge the 3 books in their age category. The 4Children clubs judge the 6-8 books. From the 200 classes who judge the books, 1 class from each category is invited to present the award at the ceremony in London. The children are chosen from projects they submit with their votes." Open to works of fiction or poetry for children written in English by a citizen of the UK, or an author residing in the UK. All work must be submitted by a UK publisher. **Deadline: July.** Prize: Gold Award winners in each age category: £2,500; Silver Award winners in each age category: £1,500; Bronze Award winners in each age category: £500; certificate for the 4Children Special Award winner.

PATERSON PRIZE FOR BOOKS FOR YOUNG PEOPLE

The Poetry Center at Passaic County Community College, One College Blvd., Paterson NJ 07505-1179. (973)684-6555. Fax: (973)684-5843. E-mail: mgillan@pccc.edu. Website: www.pccc.edu/poetry. **Contact:** Maria Mazziotti Gillan, director. Offered annually for books published the previous calendar year. Three categories: pre-kindergarten-grade 3; grades 4-6; and grades 7-12. Open to any writer. **Deadline: April 1.** Guidelines for SASE. Prize: $500 in each category.

PEN/PHYLLIS NAYLOR WORKING WRITER FELLOWSHIP

PEN American Center, 588 Broadway, Suite 303, New York NY 10012. (212)334-1660, ext. 101. Fax: (212)334-2181. E-mail: awards@pen.org. **Contact:** Andrew Proctor. Offered annually to a "writer of children's or young-adult fiction in financial need, who has published 2-5 books in the past 10 years, which may have been well reviewed and warmly received by literary critics, but which have not generated sufficient income to support the author." Writers must be nominated by an editor or fellow writer. **Deadline: January 7.** Prize: $5,000.

☒ PRIX ALVINE-BELISLE

Association pour L'avancement des sciences et des techniques de la documentation, ASTED, Inc., 3414 av. Parc #202, Montreal QC H2X 2H5 Canada. (514)281-5012. Fax: (514)281-8219. E-mail: info@asted.org. Website: www.asted.org. **Contact:** Louis Cabral, executive director. Offered annually for work published the year before the award to promote authors of French youth literature in Canada. **Deadline: April 1.** Prize: $1,000.

SASKATCHEWAN CHILDREN'S LITERATURE AWARD

Saskatchewan Book Awards, Inc., Box 1921, Regina SK S4P 3E1 Canada. (306)569-1585. Fax: (306)569-4187. E-mail: director@bookawards.sk.ca. Website: www.bookawards.sk.ca. **Contact:** Glenda James, executive director. Offered annually for work published September 15-September 14. This award is presented to a Saskatchewan author for the best book of children's or young adult's literature, judged on the quality of writing. **Deadline: First Deadline: July 31; Final Deadline: September 14.** Guidelines for SASE. **Charges $20 (Canadian).** Prize: $2,000.

SYDNEY TAYLOR BOOK AWARD

Association of Jewish Libraries, % NFJC, 330 7th Ave., 21st Floor, New York NY 10001. (212)725-5359. E-mail: heidi@cbiboca.org or ajllibs@osu.edu. Website: www.jewishlibraries.org. **Contact:** Heidi Estrin, chair. Offered annually for work published in the year of the award. "Given to distinguished contributions to Jewish literature for children. One award for older readers, one for younger." Publishers submit books. **Deadline: December 31.** Guidelines for SASE. Prize: Certificate, cash award, and gold seal for cover of winning book.

TEDDY AWARD FOR BEST CHILDREN'S BOOK

Writers' League of Texas, 1501 W. Fifth St., Suite E-2, Austin TX 78703. (512)499-8914. Fax: (512)499-0441. E-mail: wlt@writersleague.org. Website: www.writersleague.org. **Contact:** Helen Ginger, director. Offered annually for work published June 1-May 31. Honors 2 outstanding books for children published by members of the Writers' League of Texas. Writer's League of Texas dues may accompany entry fee. **Deadline: May 31.** Guidelines for SASE. **Charges $25 fee.** Prize: Two prizes of $1,000, and teddy bears.

TORONTO MUNICIPAL CHAPTER IODE BOOK AWARD

Toronto Municipal Chapter IODE, 40 St. Clair Ave. E., Suite 205, Toronto ON M4T 1M9 Canada. (416)925-5078. Fax: (416)925-5127. **Contact:** Theo Heras (Lillian Smith Library, 239 College St., Toronto). Offered annually for childrens' books published by a Canadian publisher. Author and illustrator must be Canadian citizens residing in or around Toronto. **Deadline: Late November.** Prize: $1,000.

RITA WILLIAMS YOUNG ADULT PROSE PRIZE

National League of American Pen Women, Nob Hill, San Francisco Branch, 1544 Sweetwood Dr., Colma CA 94015-2029. E-mail: pennobhill@aol.com. Website: www.soulmakingcontest.us. **Contact:** Eileen Malone. Up to 3,000 words in story, essay, journal entry, creative nonfiction, or memoir by someone in grades 9-12. Annually. **Deadline: November 30.** Guidelines for SASE. **Charges $5/entry (make checks payable to NLAPW, Nob Hill Branch).** Prize: 1st Place: $100; 2nd Place: $50; 3rd Place: $25. Open to any writer.

PAUL A. WITTY SHORT STORY AWARD

Executive Office, International Reading Association, P.O. Box 8139, Newark DE 19714-8139. (302)731-1600, ext. 221. Fax: (302)731-1057. E-mail: exec@reading.org. Website: www.reading.org. Offered to reward author of an original short story published in a children's periodical during 2005 which serves as a literary standard that encourages young readers to read periodicals. Write for guidelines or download from website. **Deadline: December 1.** Prize: $1,000.

ALICE WOOD MEMORIAL OHIOANA AWARD FOR CHILDREN'S LITERATURE

Ohioana Library Association, 274 E. First Ave., Suite 300, Columbus OH 43201. (614)466-3831. Fax: (614)728-6974. E-mail: ohioana@sloma.state.oh.us. Website: www.ohioana.org. **Contact:** Linda R. Hengst. Offered to an author whose body of work has made, and continues to make, a significant contribution to literature for children or young adults and through their work as a writer, teacher, administrator, and community member, interest in children's literature has been encouraged and children have become involved with reading. Nomination forms for SASE. Recipient must have been born in Ohio or lived in Ohio at least 5 years. **Deadline: December 31.** Prize: $1,000.

WRITING FOR CHILDREN COMPETITION

(formerly The Writer's Union of Canada Writing for Children Competition), The Writers' Union of Canada, 90 Richmond St. E., Suite 200, Toronto ON M5C 1P1 Canada. (416)703-8982, ext. 223. Fax: (416)504-9090. E-mail: projects@writersunion.ca. Website: www.writersunion.ca. **Contact:** Projects Coordinator. Offered annually "to discover developing Canadian writers of unpublished children's/young adult fiction or nonfiction." Open to Canadian citizens or landed immigrants who have not been published in book format, and who do not currently have a contract with a publisher. **Deadline: April 24. Charges $15 entry fee.** Prize: $1,500; the winner and 11 finalists' pieces will be submitted to 3 Canadian publishers of children's books.

TRANSLATION

N ALTA NATIONAL TRANSLATION AWARD

American Literary Translators Association, UTD, Box 830688-JO51, Richardson TX 75083-0688. (972)883-2093. Fax: (972)883-6303. E-mail: derouen@utdallas.edu. Website: www.literarytranslators.org. **Contact:** Rich De-Rouen. Each year, ALTA invites publishers to nominate book-length translation, published in the preceding calendar year, for this award. Translation must be by a US or Canadian publisher and the submission must be a book-length work in English of fiction, poetry, drama, or creative nonfiction (literary criticism and philosophy are not eligible). For nominated books selected as finalists, publishers will be asked to provide an original-language version of the text. Send a letter of nomination and 4 copies of each nominated book. **Deadline: March 31.** Guidelines for SASE. Prize: $1,500; winner announced and featured at annual ALTA conference in the fall; press release distributed to major publications. Judged by panel of translators. Open to any writer.

ASF TRANSLATION PRIZE

The American-Scandinavian Foundation, 58 Park Ave., New York NY 10016-3007. (212)879-9779. Fax: (212)686-2115. E-mail: ahenkin@amscan.org. Website: www.amscan.org. **Contact:** Andrey Henkin. Offered annually to a translation of Scandinavian literature into English of a Nordic author born within the last 200 years. "The prize is for an outstanding English translation of poetry, fiction, drama, or literary prose originally written in Danish, Finnish, Icelandic, Norwegian, or Swedish that has not been previously published in the English language." **Deadline: June 1.** Guidelines for SASE. Prize: $2,000, publication of an excerpt in an issue of *Scandinavian Review*, and a commemorative bronze medallion. Runner-up receives the Leif and Inger Sjöberg Prize of $1,000, publication of an excerpt in an issue of *Scandinavian Review*, and a commemorative bronze medallion.

N DIANA DER-HOVANESSIAN TRANSLATION PRIZE

New England Poetry Club, 16 Cornell St.#2, Arlington MA 02476. **Contact:** Elizabeth Crowell. Annual contest for a poem translated into English. **Deadline: June 30.** Guidelines for SASE. **Charges $10 for 3 poems.** Prize: $200. Open to any writer.

SOEURETTE DIEHL FRASER TRANSLATION AWARD

6335 W. Northwest Hwy., #618, Dallas TX 75225. (214)528-2655. E-mail: franvick@aol.com. **Contact:** Fran Vick. Offered every 2 years to recognize the best translation of a literary book into English. Translator must have been born in Texas or have lived in the state for at least 2 consecutive years at some time. **Deadline: January 3.** Guidelines for SASE. Prize: $1,000.

GERMAN PRIZE FOR LITERARY TRANSLATION

American Translators Association, 225 Reinekers Lane, Suite 590, Alexandria VA 22314. (703)683-6100, ext. 3006. Fax: (703)683-6122. E-mail: ata@atanet.org. Website: www.atanet.org. **Contact:** Walter W. Bacak. Offered in odd-numbered years for a previously published book translated from German to English. In even-numbered years, the Lewis Galentiere Prize is awarded for translations other than German to English. **Deadline: May 15.** Prize: $1,000, a certificate of recognition, and up to $500 toward expenses for attending the ATA Annual Conference.

GOVERNOR GENERAL'S LITERARY AWARD FOR TRANSLATION

Canada Council for the Arts, 350 Albert St., P.O. Box 1047, Ottawa ON K1P 5V8 Canada. (613)566-4414, ext. 5576. Fax: (613)566-4410. E-mail: joanne.larocque-poirier@canadacouncil.ca. Website: www.canadacouncil .ca/prizes/ggla. **Contact:** Joanne Larocque-Poirier. Offered for the best English-language and the best French-language work of translation by a Canadian. Submissions in English must be published between September 1, 2004 and September 30, 2005; submissions in French between July 1 and June 30. Publishers submit titles for consideration. **Deadline: March 15 or August 7, 2005, depending on the book's publication date.** Prize: Each laureate receives $15,000; nonwinning finalists receive $1,000.

THE HAROLD MORTON LANDON TRANSLATION AWARD

The Academy of American Poets, 584 Broadway, Suite 604, New York NY 10012-3210. (212)274-0343. Fax: (212)274-9427. E-mail: rmurphy@poets.org. Website: www.poets.org. **Contact:** Ryan Murphy, awards coordinator. Offered annually to recognize a published translation of poetry from any language into English. Open to living US citizens. Anthologies by a number of translators are ineligible. **Deadline: December 31.** Guidelines for SASE. Prize: $1,000.

🌐 THE MARSH AWARD FOR CHILDREN'S LITERATURE IN TRANSLATION

The Marsh Christian Trust/Administered by NCRCL, Roehampton University, Froebel College, Roehampton Lane, London England SW15 5PJ. 020 8392 3014. Fax: 020 3892 3819. **Contact:** Dr. Gillian Lathey. Offered every 2 years to raise awareness in the UK of the quality of children's books written in other languages and of the work of their translators. Entries must be submitted by British publishing companies and published between June 30, 2004 and June 30, 2006. No translations first published in the US or Australia are eligible for this award. **Deadline: June 30, 2006.** Guidelines for SASE. Prize: £1,000. Judged by critics and translators of children's books.

PEN AWARD FOR POETRY IN TRANSLATION

PEN American Center, 588 Broadway, Suite 303, New York NY 10012. (212)334-1660, ext. 101. E-mail: awards@pen.org. Website: www.pen.org. **Contact:** Literary awards manager. This award "recognizes book-length translations of poetry from any language into English, published during the current calendar year. All books must have been published in the US. Translators may be of any nationality. US residency/citizenship not required." **Deadline: December (inquire for exact date).** Prize: $3,000. Judged by a single translator of poetry appointed by the PEN Translation Committee.

PEN/BOOK-OF-THE-MONTH CLUB TRANSLATION PRIZE

PEN American Center, 588 Broadway, Suite 303, New York NY 10012. (212)334-1660, ext. 101. Fax: (212)334-2181. E-mail: awards@pen.org. **Contact:** Literary Awards Manager. Offered for a literary book-length translation into English published in the calendar year. No technical, scientific, or reference books. Publishers, agents, or translators may submit 3 copies of each eligible title. All eligible titles must have been published in the US. **Deadline: December 15.** Prize: $3,000.

THE RAIZISS/DE PALCHI TRANSLATION FELLOWSHIP

The Academy of American Poets, 588 Broadway, Suite 604, New York NY 10012-3210. (212)274-0343. Fax: (212)274-9427. E-mail: rmurphy@poets.org. Website: www.poets.org. **Contact:** Awards Director. Offered in alternate years to recognize outstanding unpublished translations of modern Italian poetry into English. Applicants must verify permission to translate the poems or that the poems are in the public domain. Open to any US citizen. **Deadline: September 1-November 1.** Guidelines for SASE. Prize: $20,000 and a 6-week residency at the American Academy in Rome.

LOIS ROTH AWARD FOR A TRANSLATION OF A LITERARY WORK

Modern Language Association, 26 Broadway, 3rd Floor, New York NY 10004-1789. (646)576-5141. Fax: (646)458-0030. E-mail: awards@mla.org. Website: www.mla.org. **Contact:** Coordinator of Book Prizes. Offered every 2 years (odd years) for an outstanding translation into English of a book-length literary work published the previous year. Translators need not be members of the MLA. **Deadline: April 1.** Guidelines for SASE. Prize: $1,000 and a certificate.

ALDO AND JEANNE SCAGLIONE PRIZE FOR A TRANSLATION OF A LITERARY WORK

Modern Language Association, 26 Broadway, 3rd Floor, New York NY 10004-1789. (646)576-5141. Fax: (646)458-0030. E-mail: awards@mla.org. Website: www.mla.org. **Contact:** Coordinator of Book Prizes. Offered in even-numbered years for the translation of a book-length literary work appearing in print during the previous year. Translators need not be members of the MLA. **Deadline: April 1.** Guidelines for SASE. Prize: $2,000 and a certificate.

ALDO AND JEANNE SCAGLIONE PRIZE FOR A TRANSLATION OF A SCHOLARLY STUDY OF LITERATURE

Modern Language Association of America, 26 Broadway, 3rd Floor, New York NY 10004-1789. (646)576-5141. Fax: (646)458-0030. E-mail: awards@mla.org. Website: www.mla.org. **Contact:** Coordinator of Book Prizes. Offered in odd-numbered years "for an outstanding translation into English of a book-length work of literary history, literary criticism, philology, or literary theory published during the previous biennium." Translators need not be members of the MLA. **Deadline: May 1.** Guidelines for SASE. Prize: $2,000 and a certificate.

MULTIPLE WRITING AREAS

N ALLIGATOR JUNIPER AWARD

Alligator Juniper/Prescott College, 220 Grove Ave., Prescott AZ 86301. (928)350-2012. E-mail: aj@prescott.edu. Website: www.prescott.edu/highlights/alligator_juniper. **Contact:** Miles Waggener, managing editor. Offered annually for unpublished work. Guidelines on website. All contest entrants receive a copy of the next issue of *Alligator Juniper*, a $7.50 value. **Deadline: October 1. Charges $10 (includes the winning issue).** Prize: $500, plus publication. Judged by the staff and occasional guest judges. Acquires first North American rights. Open to any writer.

AMERICAN LITERARY REVIEW CONTEST

American Literary Review, P.O. Box 311307, University of North Texas, Denton TX 76203-1307. (940)565-2755. E-mail: americanliteraryreview@yahoo.com. Website: www.engl.unt.edu/alr. **Contact:** Managing Editor. Offered annually for unpublished work. This contest alternates annually between poetry and fiction. Open to any writer. Guidelines for SASE or online. **Deadline: Varies each year. Charges $10 entry fee.** Prize: $1,000 and publication.

AMERICAN MARKETS NEWSLETTER COMPETITION

American Markets Newsletter, 1974 46th Ave., San Francisco CA 94116. E-mail: sheila.oconnor@juno.com. **Contact:** Sheila O'Connor. "Accepts fiction and nonfiction up to 2,000 words. Entries are eligible for cash prizes and all entries are eligible for worldwide syndication whether they win or not. Here's how it works: Send us your double-spaced manuscripts with your story/article title, byline, word count, and address on the first page above your article/story's first paragraph (no need for separate cover page). There is no limit to the number of entries you may send." **Deadline: December 31.** Guidelines for SASE. **Charges $10 for 1 entry; $15 for 2 entries; $20 for 3 entries; $25 for 4-5 entries.** Prize: 1st Place: $300; 2nd Place: $100; 3rd Place: $50. Judged by a panel of independent judges. Open to any writer.

ARIZONA AUTHORS' ASSOCIATION ANNUAL NATIONAL LITERARY CONTEST AND BOOK AWARDS

Arizona Authors' Association, P.O. Box 87857, Phoenix AZ 85080-7857. (602)769-2066. Fax: (623)780-0468. E-mail: info@azauthors.com. Website: www.azauthors.com. **Contact:** Toby Heathcotte, contest coordinator. Offered annually for previously unpublished poetry, short stories, essays, and articles. New awards for published books in fiction, anthology, nonfiction, and children's. Winners announced at an award banquet in Phoenix in November, and short pieces and excerpts published in *Arizona Literary Magazine*. **Deadline: July 1. Charges $10 fee for poetry; $15 for short stories and essays; $30 for published books.** Prize: $100 and publication.

ARTS & LETTERS PRIZES

Arts & Letters Journal of Contemporary Culture, Campus Box 89, GC&SU, Milledgeville GA 31061. (478)445-1289. E-mail: al@gcsu.edu. Website: al.gcsu.edu. **Contact:** The Editors. Offered annually for unpublished work. **Deadline: April 1 (postmarked). Charges $15/entry (payable to GC&SU), which includes a 1-year subscription to the journal.** Prize: $1,000 for winners in fiction, poetry, and drama (one-act play). Fiction and poetry winners will attend a weekend program in October, and the drama winner will attend a Spring festival that includes a production of the prize-winning play. Judged by editors (initial screening); 2005 final judges: Julianna Baggott (fiction), Christian Wiman (poetry), Naomi Wallace (drama). Open to any writer.

N ⚫ THE ASSOCIATION OF ITALIAN-CANADIAN WRITERS LITERARY CONTEST

AICW, % Delia De Santis, 2961 Delia Crescent, Bright's Grove ON N0N 1C0 Canada. (519)869-6852. E-mail: delidesantis@yahoo.com. Website: www.aiwa.ca. **Contact:** Venera Fazio. Contest held during even-numbered years for unpublished writers in 3 categories: short fiction (up to 2,500 words); poetry (up to 3 poems, each no longer than 40 lines); and nonficiton (memoir or personal essay up to 2,500 words). Entries may be in French, English or Italian. **Deadline: March 1. Charges $10 for AICW members; $20 for nonmembers.** Prize: $200 and 1 honorary mention for each of the 3 categories. Judged by accomplished writers of Italian origin fluent in French, Italian, and English. Open to all writers in Canada and the US. Not specific to Italian Canadians or Italian Americans.

N AWP AWARD SERIES

Association of Writers & Writing Programs, Carty House, Mail Stop 1E3, George Mason University, Fairfax VA 22030. (703)993-4301. Fax: (703)993-4302. E-mail: awp@awpwriter.org. Website: awpwriter.org. **Contact:** Supriya Bhatnagar. Offered annually to foster new literary talent. Categories: poetry (Donald Hall Poetry Prize), short fiction (Grace Paley Prize in Short Fiction), novel, and creative nonfiction. Guidelines for SASE and on website. Open to any writer. **Deadline: January 1-February 28 (postmarked). Charges $20 for nonmembers; $10 for members.** Prize: Cash honorarium ($4,000 for Donald Hall Prize for Poetry and Grace Paley Prize in Short Fiction, and $2,000 each for novel and creative nonfiction), and publication by a participating press.

N AWP INTRO JOURNALS PROJECT

The Association of Writers & Writing Programs, Dept. of English, Bluffton University, 1 University Dr., Bluffton OH 45817-2104. E-mail: awp@awpwriter.org. Website: www.awpwriter.org. **Contact:** Jeff Gundy. "This is a prize for students in AWP member-university creative writing programs only. Authors are nominated by the head of the Creative Writing Department. Each school may nominate no more than 1 work of nonfiction, 1 work of short fiction, and 3 poems." **Deadline: December 1.** Guidelines for SASE. Prize: $100, plus publication in participating journal. Judged by AWP. Open to students in AWP member-university creative writing programs only.

BAKELESS LITERARY PUBLICATION PRIZES

Bread Loaf Writers' Conference, Middlebury College, Middleburg VT 05753. (802)443-2018. Fax: (802)443-2087. E-mail: bakeless@middlebury.edu. Website: www.bakelessprize.org. **Contact:** Ian Pounds, contest director. Offered annually for unpublished authors of poetry, fiction, and creative nonfiction. Open to all writers who have not yet published a book in English in their entry's genre. **Deadline: October 1-November 15.** Guidelines for SASE. **Charges $10 fee.** Prize: Publication of book-length ms by Houghton Mifflin, and a fellowship to attend the Bread Loaf Writers' Conference.

EMILY CLARK BALCH AWARD

Virginia Quarterly Review, 1 West Range, P.O. Box 400223, Charlottesville VA 22904-4233. (434)924-3124. Fax: (434)924-1397. Website: www.virginia.edu/vqr. **Contact:** Ted Genoways, editor. Annual award for the best short story/poetry accepted and published by the *Virginia Quarterly Review* during a calendar year. No deadline. Prize: $1,000.

THE BOSTON AUTHORS CLUB BOOK AWARDS

The Boston Authors Club, 121 Follen Rd., Lexington MA 02421. E-mail: bostonauthors@aol.com. Website: www.bostonauthorsclub.org. **Contact:** Andrew McAleer, president. Julia Ward Howe Prize offered annually for books published the previous year. Two awards are given, 1 for trade books of fiction, nonfiction, or poetry, and the second for children's books. Authors must live or have lived within 100 miles of Boston. **Deadline: January 2.** Prize: Certificate and honorarioum of $500 in each category.

THE BRIAR CLIFF POETRY, FICTION AND CREATIVE NONFICTION COMPETITION

The Briar Cliff Review, Briar Cliff University, 3303 Rebecca St., Sioux City IA 51104-0100. (712)279-5321. Fax: (712)279-5410. E-mail: curranst@briarcliff.edu. Website: www.briarcliff.edu/bcreview. **Contact:** Tricia Currans-Sheehan, editor. Offered annually for unpublished poetry, fiction and essay. **Deadline: August 1-November 1. No mss returned.** Guidelines for SASE. **Charges $15.** Prize: $500 and publication in Spring issue. Judged by editors. "We guarantee a considerate reading." Open to any writer.

N THE BRIDGE FUND FELLOWSHIP FOR THE CREATION OF ORIGINAL MATERIALS FOR THE TEACHING OF ARKANSAS HISTORY

The Writers' Colony at Dairy Hollow, 515 Spring St., Eureka Springs AR 72632. (479)253-7444. Fax: (479)253-9859. E-mail: director@writerscolony.org. Website: www.writerscolony.org. **Contact:** Sandy Wright, director. Annually. **Deadline: November 15.** Guidelines for SASE. **Charges $35.** Prize: 1-month residency, all-expense paid fellowship at the Writers' Colony at Dairy Hollow, Eureka Springs, Arkansas—plus a $1,500 stipend. Transportation to and from the colony is not included. Judged by literary professionals. Open to any writer.

ARCH & BRUCE BROWN FOUNDATION

The Arch & Bruce Brown Foundation, PMB 503, 31855 Date Palm Dr., Suite 3, Cathedral City CA 92234. E-mail: archwrite@aol.com. Website: www.aabbfoundation.org. **Contact:** Arch Brown, president. Annual contest for unpublished, "gay-positive works based on history." Type of contest changes each year: playwriting (2005); full-length fiction (2006); short fiction (2007). **Deadline: November 30.** Guidelines for SASE. Prize: $1,000 (not limited to a single winner). Open to any writer.

BURNABY WRITERS' SOCIETY CONTEST

E-mail: info@bws.bc.ca. Website: www.bws.bc.ca. **Contact:** Eileen Kernaghan. Offered annually for unpublished work. Open to all residents of British Columbia. Categories vary from year to year. Send SASE for current rules. Purpose is to encourage talented writers in all genres. **Deadline: May 31.** Guidelines for SASE. **Charges $5 fee.** Prize: 1st Place: $200; 2nd Place: $100; 3rd Place: $50; and public reading.

BYLINE MAGAZINE AWARDS

P.O. Box 5240, Edmond OK 73083-5240. (405)348-5591. E-mail: mpreston@bylinemag.com. Website: www.byli nemag.com. **Contact:** Marcia Preston, award director. Contest includes several monthly contests, open to any-one, in various categories that include fiction, nonfiction, poetry, and children's literature; an annual poetry chapbook award which is open to any poet; and an annual *ByLine* Short Fiction and Poetry Award open only to our subscribers. For chapbook award and subscriber awards, publication constitutes part of the prize, and winners grant first North American rights to *ByLine*. **Deadline: Varies. Charges $3-5 for monthly contests; $15 for chapbook contest.** Prize: **Monthly contests:** Cash and listing in magazine; **Chapbook Award:** Publication of chapbook, 50 copies, and $200; *ByLine* **Short Fiction and Poetry Award:** $250 in each category, plus publication in the magazine.

◆ CANADIAN AUTHORS ASSOCIATION AWARDS PROGRAM

P.O. Box 419, Campbellford ON K0L 1L0 Canada. (705)653-0323 or (866)216-6222. Fax: (705)653-0593. E-mail: admin@canauthors.org. Website: www.canauthors.org. **Contact:** Alec McEachern. Offered annually for short stories, fiction, poetry, history, and drama. Entrants must be Canadians by birth, naturalized Canadians, or landed immigrants. Entry form required for all awards. Obtain entry form from contact name or download from website. **Deadline: December 15.** Guidelines for SASE. **Charges $35 (Canadian) fee/title entered.** Prize: $2,500 and a silver medal.

Ⓝ ◆ CANADIAN HISTORICAL ASSOCIATION AWARDS

Canadian Historical Association, 395 Wellington, Ottawa ON K1A 0N3 Canada. (613)233-7885. Fax: (613)567-3110. E-mail: cha-shc@archives.ca. Website: www.cha-shc.ca. **Contact:** Joanne Mineault. Offered annually. Categories: Regional history, Canadian history, history (not Canadian), women's history (published articles, English or French), doctoral dissertations. Open to Canadian writers. **Deadline: Varies.** Guidelines for SASE. Prize: Varies.

Ⓝ ◆ CBC LITERARY AWARDS/PRIX LITTÉRAIRES RADIO-CANADA

CBC Radio/Radio Canada, Canada Council for the Arts, *enRoute* magazine, P.O. Box 6000, Montreal QC H3C 3A8 Canada. (877)888-6788. E-mail: literary_awards@cbc.ca. Website: www.cbc.ca/literaryawards. **Contact:** Carolyn Warren, executive producer. The CBC Literary Awards Competition is the only literary competition that celebrates original, unpublished works in Canada's 2 official languages. There are 3 categories: short story, poetry, and travel writing. Submissions to the short story and travel category must be 2,000-2,500 words; poetry submissions must be 1,500-2,500 words. Poetry submissions can take the form of a long narrative poem, a sequence of connected poems, or a group of unconnected poems. **Deadline: November.** Guidelines for SASE. **Charges $20 CDN.** Prize: There is a first prize of $6,000 and second prize of $4,000 for each category, in both English and French, courtesy of the Canada Council for the Arts. In addition, winning entries are published in Air Canada's *enRoute* magazine and broadcast on CBC radio. First publication rights are granted by winners to *enRoute* magazine and broadcast rights are given to CBC radio. Submissions are judged blind by a jury of qualified writers and editors from around the country. Each category has 3 jurors. Canadian citizens, living in Canada or abroad, and permanent residents of Canada are eligible to enter.

CHAUTAUQUA LITERARY JOURNAL ANNUAL CONTESTS

Chautauqua Literary Journal, a publication of the Writers' Center at Chautauqua, Inc., P.O. Box 2039, York Beach ME 03910. E-mail: cljeditor@aol.com (for contest entries only). **Contact:** Richard Foerster, editor. Offered annually for unpublished work to award literary excellence in the categories of poetry and prose (short stories and/or creative nonfiction). Guidelines for SASE or by e-mail. **Deadline: September 30 (postmarked). Charges $15/entry.** Prize: $1,500 in each of the 2 categories of poetry and prose, plus publication in *Chautauqua Literary Journal*. Judged by the editor and editorial advisory staff of the *Chautauqua Literary Journal*. Acquires first rights and one-time nonexclusive reprint rights. Open to any writer.

CHICANO/LATINO LITERARY CONTEST

Dept. of Spanish and Portuguese, University of California-Irvine, Irvine CA 92697. (949)824-5443. Fax: (949)824-2803. E-mail: cllp@uci.edu. Website: www.hnet.uci.edu/spanishandportuguese/contest.html. **Contact:** David Rink. Estab. 1974. Offered annually ''to promote the dissemination of unpublished Chicano/Latino literature in Spanish or English, and to encourage its development. The call for entries will be genre specific, rotating through 4 categories: poetry (2005), drama (2006), novel, and short story.'' The contest is open to all citizens or permanent residents of the US. **Deadline: June 1.** Guidelines for SASE. Prize: 1st Place: $1,000, publication, and transportation to receive the award; 2nd Place: $500; 3rd Place: $250.

⛰ THE CITY OF VANCOUVER BOOK AWARD

Office of Cultural Affairs, 453 W. 12th Ave., Vancouver BC V5Y 1V4 Canada. (604)871-6434. Fax: (604)871-6005. E-mail: marnie.rice@vancouver.ca. Website: www.vancouver.ca/culture. Offered annually for books published in the previous year which exhibit excellence in the categories of content, illustration, design, and format. The book must contribute significantly to the appreciation and understanding of the city of Vancouver and heighten awareness of 1 or more of the following: Vancouver's history, the city's unique character, or achievements of the city's residents. The book may be fiction, nonfiction, poetry, or drama written for adults or children, and may deal with any aspects of the city—history, geography, current affairs, or the arts. Guidelines on website. Prize: $2,000.

CLEVERKITTY CATERWAULING CONTEST

Cleverkitty.com, 6764 Sugar Hill Dr., Nashville TN 37211. (615)941-5090. E-mail: caterwauling05@cleverkitty.com. Website: www.cleverkitty.com/caterwauling.htm. **Contact:** Kim Cady, contest director. "Our website celebrates all things feline. Our annual contest is for writers of all kinds of short literature, fiction, or nonfiction (stories concerning real-life experiences are accepted as essays) relating to "The Cat." There are no separate categories at this time. The pieces will be judged for impact and overall excellence." **Deadline: February 1-October 1.** Prize: 1st Place: $100; 2nd Place: $50; 3rd Place: $20. In addition, the first-place winner will receive a membership in the "Best Friends Animal Society" (one of the premier animal welfare organizations in the US). Open to all writers.

CNW/FFWA ANNUAL FLORIDA STATE WRITING COMPETITION

Florida Freelance Writers Association, P.O. Box A, North Stratford NH 03590-0167. E-mail: contest@writers-editors.com. Website: www.writers-editors.com. **Contact:** Dana K. Cassell, executive director. Annual award "to recognize publishable talent." Divisions & Categories: Nonfiction (previously published article/essay/column/nonfiction book chapter; unpublished or self-published article/essay/column/nonfiction book chapter); Fiction (unpublished or self-published short story or novel chapter); Children's Literature (unpublished or self-published short story/nonfiction article/book chapter/poem); Poetry (unpublished or self-published free verse/traditional). **Deadline: March 15.** Guidelines for SASE. **Charges $5 (active or new CNW/FFWA members) or $10 (nonmembers) for each fiction/nonfiction entry under 3,000 words; $10 (members) or $20 (nonmembers) for each entry of 3,000 words or longer; and $3 (members) or $5 (nonmembers) for each poem.** Prize: 1st Place: $100; 2nd Place: $75; 3rd Place: $50. All winners and Honorable Mentions will receive certificates as warranted. Judged by editors, librarians, and writers. Open to any writer.

Ⓝ COMMONWEALTH CLUB OF CALIFORNIA BOOK AWARDS

595 Market St., San Francisco CA 94105. (415)597-4846. Fax: (415)597-6729. E-mail: bookawards@commonwealthclub.org. Website: www.commonwealthclub.org/baguidelines. **Contact:** Barbara Lane, book awards director. Estab. 1931. Offered annually for published submissions appearing in print January 1-December 31 of the previous year. "Purpose of award is the encouragement and production of literature in California. Categories include: fiction, nonfiction, poetry, first work of fiction, juvenile up to 10 years old, juvenile 11-16, works in translation, notable contribution to publishing and Californiana." Can be nominated by publisher as well. Open to California residents (or residents at time of publication). Annually. **Deadline: December 31.** Guidelines for SASE. Prize: Medals and cash prizes to be awarded at publicized event.

Ⓝ CORDON D'OR GOLD RIBBON AWARDS

Cordon d'Or Gold Ribbon Inc., P.O. Box 40660, St. Petersburg FL 33743-0660. (727)347-2437. E-mail: cordonor@aol.com. Website: www.cordonorcuisine.com; www.goldribboncookery.com. **Contact:** Noreen Kinney. Contest promotes recognition of food authors, writers, culinary magazines, food stylists and food photographers and other professionals in the culinary field. Full details on all categories can be found on the website. Annually. **Deadline: May 30.** Prize: Cordon d'Or Gold Ribbon Crystal Globe Trophies (with stands) will be presented to winners in each category. An outstanding winner chosen by the judges from among all entries will also win a cash award of $1,000. Judged by professionals in the fields covered in the awards program. Open to any writer. The only criteria is that all entries must be in the English language.

VIOLET CROWN BOOK AWARDS

Writers' League of Texas, 1501 W. Fifth St., Suite E-2, Austin TX 78703. (512)499-8914. Fax: (512)499-0441. E-mail: wlt@writersleague.org. Website: www.writersleague.org. **Contact:** Helen Ginger, director. Offered annually for work published June 1-May 31. Honors 3 outstanding books published in fiction, nonfiction, and literary categories by Writers' League of Texas members. Membership dues may accompany entry fee. **Deadline: May 31.** Guidelines for SASE. **Charges $25 fee.** Prize: Three $1,000 prizes and trophies.

THE CRUCIBLE POETRY AND FICTION COMPETITION

Crucible, Barton College, College Station, Wilson NC 27893. (252)399-6344. E-mail: tgrimes@barton.edu. **Contact:** Terrence L. Grimes, editor. Offered annually for unpublished mss. **Deadline: Late April.** Guidelines for SASE. Prize: 1st Prize: $150; 2nd Prize: $100; publication in *Crucible*. Judged by in-house editorial board. Open to any writer.

CWW ANNUAL AWARDS COMPETITION

Council for Wisconsin Writers, E-mail: mbowen@foleylaw.com. Website: www.wisconsinwriters.org/index.h tm. Offered annually for work published by Wisconsin writers the previous calendar year. Thirteen awards: major/life achievement; short fiction; scholarly book; short nonfiction; nonfiction book; juvenile fiction book; children's picture book; poetry book; fiction book; outdoor writing; juvenile nonfiction book; drama (produced); outstanding service to Wisconsin writers. Open to Wiscconsin residents. Guidelines on website. **Deadline: January 31. Charges $25 fee for nonmembers; $10 for members.** Prize: $100-1,500 and a certificate.

DANA AWARDS IN PORTFOLIO, THE NOVEL, SHORT FICTION AND POETRY

200 Fosseway Dr., Greensboro NC 27445. (336)644-8028. E-mail: danaawards@pipeline.com. Website: www.da naawards.com. **Contact:** Mary Elizabeth Parker, chair. Four awards offered annually for unpublished work written in English. Purpose is monetary award for work that has not been previously published or received monetary award, but will accept work published simply for friends and family. Works previously published online are not eligible. No work accepted by or for persons under 16 for any of the 4 awards. Awards: **Portfolio:** For any combination of 3 mss in novel, short fiction or poetry. For this 3-mss award (as for the single mss award), each novel mss must be the first 50 pp only; each short fiction mss must be 1 short story only; and each poetry mss must be 5 poems only. **Novel:** For the first 50 pages of a novel completed or in progress. **Fiction:** Short fiction (no memoirs) up to 10,000 words. **Poetry:** For best group of 5 poems based on excellence of all 5 (no light verse, no single poem over 100 lines). See website for full guidelines on varied fees for portfolio award. **Deadline: October 31 (postmarked).** Prize: $3,000 for portfolio award; $1,000 each for other categories.

ℕ E.F.S. ANNUAL WRITING COMPETITION

E.F.S. Online Publishing, 2844 Eighth Ave., Suite 6E, New York NY 10039-2171. (212)283-8899. Website: www.efs-enterprises.com. **Contact:** Rita Baxter. Offered annually for unpublished work in the following categories: fiction, nonfiction, poetry, scripts. **Deadline: April 30.** Guidelines for SASE. **Charges $25/ms.** First-prize winners get $50 cash prize or special publishing contract option. E.F.S. reserves the right to extend special contract options to any first-, second- and third-place winners it desires based on the quality, marketability and salability of those manuscripts/entries. Should E.F.S. extend a special publishing contract option to any first-prize winners, the first-prize winner would have the option of choosing the $50 cash award or the publishing contract option. Open to any writer.

ℕ E.F.S. RELIGIOUS FICTION & NONFICTION WRITING COMPETITION

E.F.S. Online Publishing, 2844 Eighth Ave., Suite 6E, New York NY 10039-2171. (212)283-8899. Website: www.efs-enterprises.com. **Contact:** Rita Baxter. Offered annually for unublished work in the following categories: inspirational/religious fiction, inspirational/religious nonfiction. **Deadline: August 31.** Guidelines for SASE. **Charges $25/ms.** Prize: Publishing contract for grand-prize winner. First-prize winner gets $50 cash prize or special publishing contract option. E.F.S reserves the right to extend special publishing options to any first-, second- or third-place winners it desires based on the quality, marketability and salability of those manuscripts/entries. Should E.F.S. extend a special publishing contract to any first-prize winners, the first-prize winners would have the option of choosing the $50 cash award or the publishing contract option. Open to any writer.

EATON LITERARY AGENCY'S ANNUAL AWARDS PROGRAM

Eaton Literary Agency, P.O. Box 49795, Sarasota FL 34230. (941)366-6589. Fax: (941)365-4679. E-mail: eatonlit @aol.com. **Contact:** Richard Lawrence, vice president. Offered annually for unpublished mss. **Deadline: March 31 (mss under 10,000 words); August 31 (mss over 10,000 words).** Guidelines for SASE. Prize: $2,500 (over 10,000 words); $500 (under 10,000 words). Judged by an independent agency in conjunction with some members of Eaton's staff. Open to any writer.

THE VIRGINIA FAULKNER AWARD FOR EXCELLENCE IN WRITING

Prairie Schooner, 201 Andrews Hall, P.O. Box 880334, Lincoln NE 68588-0334. (402)472-0911. Fax: (402)472-9771. E-mail: kgrey2@unl.edu. Website: www.unl.edu/schooner/psmain.htm. **Contact:** Hilda Raz. Offered annually for work published in *Prairie Schooner* in the previous year. Prize: $1,000.

⬛ 📧 FREEFALL SHORT FICTION AND POETRY CONTEST

The Alexandra Writers' Centre Society, 922 9th Ave. SE, Calgary AB T2G 0S4 Canada. (403)264-4730. E-mail: awcs@telusplanet.net. Website: www.alexandrawriters.org. Offered annually for unpublished work in the categories of poetry (5 poems/entry) and fiction (3,000 words or less). The purpose of the award in both categories is to recognize writers and offer publication credits in a literary magazine format. **Deadline: October 1.** Guidelines for SASE. **Charges $20 entry fee.** Prize: 1st Prize: $200 (Canadian); 2nd Prize: $100 (Canadian). Both prizes include publication in the spring edition of *FreeFall Magazine*. Winners will also be invited to read at the launch of that issue if such a launch takes place. Honorable mentions in each category will be published and may be asked to read. Travel expenses not included. Judged by current *FreeFall* editors (who are also published authors in Canada). Acquires first Canadian serial rights (ownership reverts to author after one-time publication). Open to any writer.

⬛ GIGGLEWORKS WRITING COMPETITION

GiggleWorks, 32825 43rd Place SW, Federal Way WA 98023. (253)874-4101. E-mail: giggleworks@aol.com. Website: www.giggleworks.net. **Contact:** Scott M. Sparling. Contest for unpublished authors occurring in July and January. **Deadline: June 30 for July competition; December 31 for January competition.** Guidelines for SASE. **Charges $1.** Prize: $50 reward and possible publication on GiggleWorks.net. Aside from publishing the winning stories on the website, the author retains all rights. Judged by entertainment staff. Open to any writer. Entries must be in English.

⬛ THE GREENSBORO REVIEW LITERARY AWARD IN FICTION AND POETRY

The Greensboro Review, English Department, 134 McIver Bldg., P.O. Box 26170, Greensboro NC 27402-6170. (336)334-5459. E-mail: jlclark@uncg.edu. Website: www.greens024review.com. **Contact:** Jim Clark, editor. Offered annually for fiction (7,500 word limit) and poetry recognizing the best work published in the spring issue of *The Greensboro Review*. Sample issue for $5. **Deadline: September 15.** Guidelines for SASE. Prize: $500 each for best short story and poem. Rights revert to author upon publication. Open to any writer.

GULF COAST POETRY & SHORT FICTION PRIZE

Gulf Coast, English Department, University of Houston, Houston TX 77204-3013. (713)743-3223. Website: www. gulfcoast.uh.edu. Offered annually for poetry, short stories, and creative nonficiton. **Deadline: March 31. Charges $15 fee, which includes subscription.** Prize: $1,000 (poetry and fiction); $500 (nonfiction); publication of winners in *Gulf Coast*. Open to any writer.

⬛ THE JULIA WARD HOWE/BOSTON AUTHORS AWARD

The Boston Authors Club, 79 Moore Rd., Wayland MA 01778. (781)259-7966. E-mail: bostonauthors@aol.com. Website: www.bostonauthorsclub.org. **Contact:** Patty Wolcott. This annual award honors Julia Ward Howe and her literary friends who founded the Boston Authors Club in 1900 to "further the literary purposes and promote social intercourse among authors." It also honors the membership over 103 years, consisting of governors and senators, librarians and philosophers, composers and playwrights, poets, and other luminaries. There are 2 categories: adult books and books for young readers (beginning with chapter books through young adult books). Illustrated books and works of fiction, nonfiction, memoir, poetry, and biography are eligible. Authors must live or have lived (college counts) within a 100-mile radius of Boston. Children's picture books and self-published books are not eligible. **Deadline: January 1.** Prize: $500 in each category.

INDIANA REVIEW ½ K (SHORT-SHORT/PROSE-POEM) PRIZE

Indiana Review, BH 465, Indiana University, Bloomington IN 47405-7103. (812)855-3439. Fax: (812)855-4253. E-mail: inreview@indiana.edu. Website: www.indiana.edu/~inreview. **Contact:** Grady Jaynes. Maximum story/poem length is 500 words. Offered annually for unpublished work. **Deadline: Early June.** Guidelines for SASE. **Charges $15 fee for no more than 3 pieces (includes a 1-year subscription).** Prize: $1,000. Judged by guest judges; Juliana Baggott was 2004 judge. Open to any writer.

⬛ INSIGHT WRITING CONTEST

Insight Magazine, 55 W. Oak Ridge Dr., Hagerstown MD 21740. Fax: (301)393-4055. E-mail: insight@rhpa.org. Website: www.insightmagazine.org. **Contact:** Dwain Esmond, editor. Annual contest for unpublished writers in the categories of student short story, general short story, and student poetry. **Deadline: June 1.** Guidelines for SASE. Prize: **Student Short Story** and **General Short Story**: 1st Prize: $250; 2nd Prize: $200; 3rd Prize: $150. **Student Poetry**: 1st Prize: $100; 2nd Prize: $75; 3rd Prize: $50. Judged by editors. General category is open to all writers; student categories must be age 22 and younger.

IOWA AWARD IN POETRY, FICTION, & ESSAY

The Iowa Review, 308 EPB, The University of Iowa, Iowa City IA 52242. (319)335-0462. Fax: (319)335-2535. E-mail: iowa-review@uiowa.edu. Website: www.uiowa.edu/~iareview. **Deadline: February 1. Charges $15 entry fee.** Prize: $1,000 and publication.

LABYRINTH SOCIETY WRITING CONTEST

The Labyrinth Society, P.O. Box 736, Trumansburg NY 14886-0736. Website: www.labyrinthsociety.org. **Contact:** David Gallagher. Estab. 2004. The Labyrinth Society is looking for short stories, essays, and poems that reflect the many experiences available through the labyrinth. "We want to see your best writing. Stories will be judged on creativity, content, general appeal, and the extent to which the labyrinth is highlighted." Entry forms are available online or by sending a request and SASE to The Labyrinth Society. **Deadline: June 15 (postmarked). Charges $10 (send checks only).** Prize: Grand Prize: free registration for The Labyrinth Society's Annual Gathering/Conference ($500+ value), or $150 if unable to attend; 1st Prize: $75; 2nd Prize: $50; 3rd Prize: $25 in each of the 3 categories. Open to any writer.

LET'S WRITE LITERARY CONTEST

The Gulf Coast Writers Association, P.O. Box 6445, Gulfport MS 39506. E-mail: gcwriters@aol.com. Website: www.gcwriters.org. **Contact:** Victoria Olsen. **Deadline: April 15.** Guidelines for SASE. **Charges $10 for each fiction or nonfiction entry and $5/additional entry (adults); $1 for entry in each category (children).** Prize: **Adult** 1st Prize: $75; 2nd Prize: $50; 3rd Prize: $25. **Young Writer** 1st Prize: $25; 2nd Prize: $15; 3rd Prize: $10. Judged by 5 professional writers. Open to any writer.

LARRY LEVIS EDITORS' PRIZE IN POETRY/THE MISSOURI REVIEW EDITORS' PRIZE IN FICTION & ESSAY

The Missouri Review, 1507 Hillcrest Hall, Columbia MO 65211. (573)882-4474. Fax: (573)884-4671. Website: www.missourireview.com. **Contact:** Richard Sowienski. Offered annually for unpublished work in 3 categories: fiction, essay, and poetry. Guidelines for SASE after June. **Deadline: October 15. Charges $15 fee (includes a 1-year subscription).** Prize: $2,000 in each genre, plus publication; 3 finalists in each category receive a minimum of $100.

THE HUGH J. LUKE AWARD

Prairie Schooner, 201 Andrews Hall, P.O. Box 880334, Lincoln NE 68588-0334. (402)472-0911. Fax: (402)472-9771. E-mail: kgrey2@unl.edu. Website: www.unl.edu/schooner/psmain.htm. **Contact:** Hilda Raz. Offered annually for work published in *Prairie Schooner* in the previous year. Prize: $250.

BRENDA MACDONALD RICHES FIRST BOOK AWARD

Saskatchewan Book Awards, Inc., 120-2505 11th Ave., Regina SK S4P 0K6 Canada. (306)569-1585. Fax: (306)569-4187. E-mail: director@bookawards.sk.ca. Website: www.bookawards.sk.ca. **Contact:** Glenda James, executive director. Offered annually for work published September 15 of year past to September 14 of current year. This award is presented to a Saskatchewan author for the best first book, judged on the quality of writing. Books from the following categories will be considered: children's; drama; fiction (short fiction by a single author, novellas, novels); nonfiction (all categories of nonfiction writing except cookbooks, directories, how-to books, or bibliographies of minimal critical content); poetry. **Deadline: First deadline: July 31; Final deadline: September 14.** Guidelines for SASE. **Charges $20 (Canadian).** Prize: $2,000.

MANITOBA WRITING AND PUBLISHING AWARDS

% Manitoba Writers' Guild, 206-100 Arthur St., Winnipeg MB R3B 1H3 Canada. (204)942-6134 or (888)637-5802. Fax: (204)942-5754. E-mail: info@mbwriter.mb.ca. Website: www.mbwriter.mb.ca. **Contact:** Robyn Maharaj or Jamis Paulson. Offered annually: The McNally Robinson Book of Year Award (adult); The McNally Robinson Book for Young People Awards (8 and under and 9 and older); The John Hirsch Award for Most Promising Manitoba Writer; The Mary Scorer Award for Best Book by a Manitoba Publisher; The Carol Shields Winnipeg Book Award; The Eileen McTavish Sykes Award for Best First Book; The Margaret Laurence Award for Fiction; The Alexander Kennedy Isbister Award for Non-Fiction; The Manuela Dias Book Design of the Year Award; The Best Illustrated Book of the Year Award; and the biennial Le Prix Littéraire Rue-Deschambault. Guidelines and submission forms available on website at www.mbwriter.mb.ca/mwapa.html. Open to Manitoba writers only. **Deadline: December 1 (books published December 1-31 will be accepted until mid-January).** Prize: Several prizes up to $5,000 (Canadian).

MASTERS LITERARY AWARDS

Titan Press, P.O. Box 17897, Encino CA 91416-7897. **Contact:** Contest Coordinator. Offered annually and quarterly for work published within 2 years (preferred) and unpublished work (accepted). Fiction, 15-page maximum; poetry, 5 pages or 150-lines maximum; and nonfiction, 10 pages maximum. "A selection of winning entries may appear in our national literary publication." Winners may also appear on the Internet. Titan Press retains one-time publishing rights to selected winners. **Deadline: Ongoing (nominations made March 15, June 15, September 15, December 15).** Guidelines for SASE. **Charges $15.** Prize: $1,000, and possible publication in the *Titan Press* internet journal.

THE MCGINNIS-RITCHIE MEMORIAL AWARD

Southwest Review, P.O. Box 750374, Dallas TX 75275-0374. (214)768-1037. Fax: (214)768-1408. E-mail: swr@mail.smu.edu. Website: www.southwestreview.org. **Contact:** Jennifer Cranfill and Willard Spiegelman. The McGinnis-Ritchie Memorial Award is given annually to the best works of fiction and nonfiction that appeared in the magazine in the previous year. Manuscripts are submitted for publication, not for the prizes themselves. Guidelines for SASE or on website. Prize: Two cash prizes of $500 each. Judged by Jennifer Cranfill, managing editor, and Willard Spiegelman, editor-in-chief. Open to any writer.

ⓃMIDLAND AUTHORS AWARD

Society of Midland Authors, P.O. Box 10419, Chicago IL 60610-0419. E-mail: writercc@aol.com. Website: www.midlandauthors.com. **Contact:** Carol Jean Carlson. Offered annually for published fiction, nonfiction, poetry, biography, children's fiction, and children's nonfiction. Authors must reside in the states of Illinois, Indiana, Iowa, Kansas, Michigan, Minnesota, Missouri, Nebraska, North Dakota, South Dakota, Wisconsin, or Ohio. Guidelines and submission at website. **Deadline: March 1.** Prize: Monetary award given to winner in each category.

NEW ENGLAND WRITERS FREE VERSE AND FICTION CONTESTS

New England Writers, P.O. Box 5, Windsor VT 05089-0005. (802)674-2315. E-mail: newvtpoet@aol.com. Website: www.newenglandwriters.org. **Contact:** Dr. Frank and Susan Anthony. Poetry line limit: 30 lines. Fiction word limit: 1,000 words. Guidelines for SASE or online. **Deadline: Postmarked June 15. Charges $5 for 3 poems or 1 fiction (multiple entries welcome).** Prize: The winning poems and fiction are published in *The Anthology of New England Writers*. The free verse contest has Robert Penn Warren Awards of $300, $200, and $100, with 10 Honorable Mentions of $20. The short fiction contest has 1 Marjory Bartlett Sanger Award of $300, with 5 Honorable Mentions of $30. Judged by published, working university professors of the genre. Open to any writer, not just New England.

NEW LETTERS LITERARY AWARDS

New Letters, University House, 5101 Rockhill Rd., Kansas City MO 64110-2499. (816)235-1168. Fax: (816)235-2611. E-mail: newletters@umkc.edu. Website: www.newletters.org. **Contact:** Amy Lucas. Award has 3 categories (fiction, poetry, and creative nonfiction) with 1 winner in each. Offered annually for previously unpublished work. Guidelines for SASE or online. **Deadline: May 18. Charges $15 fee (includes a 1-year subscription to** *New Letters* **magazine).** Prize: 1st Place: $1,000, plus publication; First Runners-Up: A copy of a recent book of poetry or fiction courtesy of our affiliate BkMk Press. Preliminary judges are regional writers of prominence and experience. All judging is done anonymously. Winners picked by a final judge of national repute. Previous judges include Maxine Kumin, Albert Goldbarth, Charles Simic, Janet Burroway. Acquires first North American serial rights. Open to any writer.

NEW WRITERS AWARDS

Great Lakes Colleges Association New Writers Awards, The Philadelphia Center, North American Building, 121 S. Broad St., 7th Floor, Philadelphia PA 19107. (215)735-7300. Fax: (215)735-7373. E-mail: clark@philactr.edu. **Contact:** Dr. Mark A. Clark, award director. Offered annually to the best first book of poetry and the best first book of fiction among those submitted by publishers. An honorarium of at least $300 will be guaranteed the author by each of the colleges visited. Open to any first book of poetry or fiction submitted by a publisher. **Deadline: February 28.** Guidelines for SASE. Prize: Winning authors tour the GLCA colleges, where they will participate in whatever activities they and the college deem appropriate.

🌐 THE NOMA AWARD FOR PUBLISHING IN AFRICA

Kodansha Ltd., Japan, P.O. Box 128, Witney Oxon OX8 5XU United Kingdom. (+44) (0)1993-775235. Fax: (+44) (0)1993-709265. E-mail: maryljay@aol.com. Website: www.nomaaward.org. **Contact:** Mary Jay, secretary to the Noma Award Managing Committee. "The Noma Award is open to African writers and scholars whose work is published in Africa. The spirit within which the annual award is given is to encourage and reward genuinely autonomous African publishers, and African writers. The award is given for an outstanding new book in any of these 3 categories: scholarly or academic; books for children; and literature and creative writing (including fiction, drama, poetry, and essays on African literature)." Entries must be submitted by publishers in Africa, who are limited to 3 entries (in any combination of the eligible categories). The award is open to any author who is indigenous to Africa (a national, irrespective of place of domicile). Guidelines at website or from Secretariat. **Deadline: February 28.** Prize: $10,000 (US). Judged by an impartial committee chaired by Mr. Walter Bgoya, comprising African scholars, book experts, and representatives of the international book community. This Managing Committee is the jury. The jury is assisted by independent opinion and assessment from a large and distinguished pool of subject specialists from throughout the world, including many in Africa.

OREGON BOOK AWARDS

Literary Arts, 224 NW 13th Ave., Suite 306, Portland OR 97209. (503)227-2583. E-mail: la@literary-arts.org. Website: www.literary-arts.org. **Contact:** Kristy Athens, program coordinator. The annual Oregon Book Awards celebrate Oregon authors in the areas of poetry, fiction, nonfiction, drama, and young readers' literature published April 1-March 31. Send SASE or go online for guidelines. **Deadline: last Friday in May.** Prize: Finalists are invited on a statewide reading tour and are promoted in bookstores and libraries across the state. Winners receive a cash prize. Judged by out-of-state judges who are selected for their expertise in a genre. Past judges include Dorothy Allison, Chris Offutt, and Maxine Kumin. Open to Oregon residents only.

PEACE WRITING INTERNATIONAL WRITING AWARDS

Peace and Justice Studies Association and Omni: Center for Peace, Justice & Ecology, 2582 Jimmie, Fayetteville AR 72703-3420. (479)442-4600. E-mail: jbennet@uark.edu. Website: www.omnicenter.org. **Contact:** Dick Bennett. Offered annually for unpublished books. "PeaceWriting encourages writing about war and international nonviolent peacemaking and peacemakers. PeaceWriting seeks book manuscripts about the causes, consequences, and solutions to violence and war, and about the ideas and practices of nonviolent peacemaking and the lives of nonviolent peacemakers." Three categories: Nonfiction Prose (history, political science, memoirs); Imaginative Literature (novels, plays, collections of short stories, collections of poetry, collections of short plays); and Works for Young People. Open to any writer. Enclose SASE for ms return. **Deadline: December 1.** Prize: $500 in each category.

PEN CENTER USA ANNUAL LITERARY AWARDS

PEN Center USA, 672 S. Lafayette Park Place, Suite 42, Los Angeles CA 90057. (213)365-8500. Fax: (213)365-9616. E-mail: awards@penusa.org. Website: www.penusa.org. **Contact:** Literary Awards Coordinator. Offered annually for fiction, nonfiction, poetry, children's literature, or translation published January 1-December 31 of the current year. Open to authors west of the Mississippi River. Guidelines for SASE or online. **Deadline: December 16. Charges $35 fee.** Prize: $1,000.

PNWA LITERARY CONTEST

Pacific Northwest Writers Association, P.O. Box 2016, Edmonds WA 98020-9516. (425)673-2665. Fax: (425)771-9588. E-mail: staff@pnwa.org. Website: www.pnwa.org. **Contact:** Dana Murphy-Love. Annual contest for unpublished mss that awards prize money in 10 categories. Categories include: Stella Cameron Romance Genre; Screenwriting; Poetry; Adult Genre Novel; Jean Auel Adult Mainstream Novel; Adult Short Story; Juvenile/Young Adult Novel; Juvenile Short Story or Picture Book; Nonfiction Book/Memoir; Adult Article/Essay/Short Memoir. Each entry receives 2 critiques. **Deadline: February.** Guidelines for SASE. **Charges $35/entry (members); $45/entry (nonmembers).** Prize: 1st Place: $600; 2nd Place: $300; 3rd Place: $150—each place is awarded in all 10 categories. Judged by industry experts. Open to any writer.

⊡ POSTCARD STORY COMPETITION

The Writers' Union of Canada, 90 Richmond St. E., Suite 200, Toronto ON M5C 1P1 Canada. (416)703-8982, ext. 223. Fax: (416)504-9090. E-mail: projects@writersunion.ca. Website: www.writersunion.ca. **Contact:** Project Coordinator. Offered annually for original and unpublished fiction, nonfiction, prose, verse, dialogue, etc., with a maximum length of 250 words. Open to Canadian citizens or landed immigrants only. **Deadline: February 14.** Guidelines for SASE. **Charges $5 entry fee.** Prize: $500.

THE PRESIDIO LA BAHIA AWARD

Sons of the Republic of Texas, 1717 Eighth St., Bay City TX 77414-5033. (979)245-6644. Fax: (979)244-3819. E-mail: srttexas@srttexas.org. Website: www.srttexas.org. **Contact:** Scott Dunbar, chairman. Offered annually "to promote suitable preservation of relics, appropriate dissemination of data, and research into our Texas heritage, with particular attention to the Spanish Colonial period." **Deadline: September 30.** Guidelines for SASE. Prize: $2,000 total; 1st Place: Minimum of $1,200, 2nd and 3rd prizes at the discretion of the judges. Judged by members of the Sons of the Republic of Texas on the Presidio La Bahia Award Committee. Open to any writer.

🔲 QWF LITERARY AWARDS

Quebec Writers' Federation, 1200 Atwater Ave., Montreal QC H3Z 1X4 Canada. (514)933-0878. E-mail: admin@ qwf.org. Website: www.qwf.org. Offered annually for a book published October 1-September 30 to honor excellence in English-language writing in Quebec. Categories: fiction, nonfiction, poetry, first book, and translation. Author must have resided in Quebec for 3 of the past 5 years. **Deadline: May 31 for books; August 15 for books and finished proofs.** Guidelines for SASE. **Charges $10/entry.** Prize: $2,000 in each category.

🔲 REGINA BOOK AWARD

Saskatchewan Book Awards, Inc., 120-2505 11th Ave., Regina SK S4P 0K6 Canada. (306)569-1585. Fax: (306)569-4187. E-mail: director@bookawards.sk.ca. Website: www.bookawards.sk.ca. **Contact:** Glenda James, executive director. Offered annually for work published September 15 of year past to September 14 of current year. In recognition of the vitality of the literary community in Regina, this award is presented to a Regina author for the best book, judged on the quality of writing. Books from the following categories will be considered: children's; drama; fiction (short fiction by a single author, novellas, novels); nonfiction (all categories of nonfiction writing except cookbooks, directories, how-to books, or bibliographies of minimal critical content); poetry. **Deadline: First deadline: July 31; Final deadline: September 14.** Guidelines for SASE. **Charges $20 (Canadian).** Prize: $2,000.

🌐 JOHN LLEWELLYN RHYS PRIZE

(formerly The Mail on Sunday/John Llewellyn Rhys Prize), Booktrust Book House 45 E. Hill, Wandsworth London SW18 2QZ United Kingdom. Fax: (00 44) 20 8516 2978. E-mail: tarryn@booktrust.org.uk. Website: www.booktrust.org.uk. **Contact:** Tarryn McKay. "The prize was founded in 1942 by Jane Oliver, the widow of John Llewellyn Rhys, a young writer killed in action in World War II. This is one of Britain's oldest and most prestigious literary awards, with an unequalled reputation of singling out the fine young writers—poets, novelists, biographers, and travel writers—early in their careers." Entries can be any work of literature written by a British or Commonwealth writer aged 35 or under at the time of publication. Books must be written in English, published between January 1 and December 31 the year of the prize. Translations are not eligible. **Deadline: August.** Prize: £5,000 to the winner and £500 to shortlisted authors.

SUMMERFIELD G. ROBERTS AWARD

Sons of the Republic of Texas, 1717 Eighth St., Bay City TX 77414-5033. (979)245-6644. Fax: (979)244-3819. E-mail: srttexas@srttexas.org. Website: www.srttexas.org. **Contact:** J. Richard Reese, chairman. Offered annually for submissions published during the previous calendar year "to encourage literary effort and research about historical events and personalities during the days of the Republic of Texas, 1836-1846, and to stimulate interest in the period." **Deadline: January 15.** Guidelines for SASE. Prize: $2,500. Judged by the last 3 winners of the contest. Open to any writer.

Ⓝ 🌐 THE ROSS FORTUNE WRITE COLOR AWARDS

Ross Fortune's Syndicate, Design Head Cottage, New No. 66, Old No. 30 B. S. Boag Rd., T. Nagar, Chennai-Madras, Tamil Nadu 600017 India. (044)52071020. E-mail: tiffinbox@rossfortune.com. Website: www.rossfortune.com. **Contact:** Tariq Hyder, editorial director. Annual contest to discover and promote talented, unpublished writers in all genres including fiction, nonfiction, and photography. All entries must be original and not submitted elsewhere. Usually no rights are acquired, but rules vary from year to year. Participating sponsors might acquire all rights. Open to writers worldwide under the age of 50. **Deadline: September 30.** Prize: Award varies each year from a minimum of $100 (USD) to a maximum of $500 (USD). Winning works are published in a sponsoring magazine or newspaper. Internships are awarded to young finalists. All participants receive certificates suitable for framing. Judged by a panel of respected journalists and established writers.

Ⓝ SANTA FE WRITERS PROJECT LITERARY AWARDS PROGRAM

Santa Fe Writers Project, P.O. Box 170, 3509 Connecticut Ave. NW, Washington DC 20008-2470. E-mail: info@sfwp.com. Website: www.sfwp.com. **Contact:** Andrew Gifford. Annual contest seeking fiction and nonfiction of any genre. The Literary Awards Program was founded by a group of authors to offer recognition for excellence in writing in a time of declining support for writers and the craft of literature. Past judges have included Richard Currey, Jayne Anne Phillips, and Chris Offutt. **Deadline: December 30.** The program selects a new judge each year and caters to his/her schedule. The deadline is always either July 15 or December 30. Guidelines for SASE. **Charges $30; $25 for students.** Prize: $6,000 and publication. Open to all writers over the age of 18.

🔲 SASKATCHEWAN BOOK OF THE YEAR AWARD

Saskatchewan Book Awards, Inc., Box 1921, Regina SK S4P 3E1 Canada. (306)569-1585. Fax: (306)569-4187. E-mail: director@bookawards.sk.ca. Website: www.bookawards.sk.ca. **Contact:** Glenda James, executive di-

Contests & Awards

rector. Offered annually for work published September 15-September 14 annually. This award is presented to a Saskatchewan author for the best book, judged on the quality of writing. Books from the following categories will be considered: children's; drama; fiction (short fiction by a single author, novellas, novels); nonfiction (all categories of nonfiction writing except cookbooks, directories, how-to books, or bibliographies of minimal critical content); poetry. Visit website for more details. **Deadline: First deadline: July 31; Final deadline: September 14.** Guidelines for SASE. **Charges $20 (Canadian).** Prize: $2,000.

☒ SASKATOON BOOK AWARD

Saskatchewan Book Awards, Inc., Box 1921, Regina SK S4P 3E1 Canada. (306)569-1585. Fax: (306)569-4187. E-mail: director@bookawards.sk.ca. Website: www.bookawards.sk.ca. **Contact:** Glenda James, executive director. Offered annually for work published September 15-September 14. In recognition of the vitality of the literary community in Saskatoon, this award is presented to a Saskatoon author for the best book, judged on the quality of writing. Books from the following categories will be considered: children's; drama; fiction (short fiction by a single author, novellas, novels); nonfiction (all categories of nonfiction writing except cookbooks, directories, how-to books, or bibliographies of minimal critical content); poetry. **Deadline: First deadline: July 31; Final deadline: September 14.** Guidelines for SASE. **Charges $20 (Canadian).** Prize: $2,000.

☒ MARGARET & JOHN SAVAGE FIRST BOOK AWARD

(formerly Cunard First Book Award), Writers' Federation of Nova Scotia, 1113 Marginal Rd., Halifax NS B3H 4P7 Canada. (902)423-8116. Fax: (902)422-0881. E-mail: talk@writers.ns.ca. Website: www.writers.ns.ca. **Contact:** Jane Buss, executive director. This award was established by the Atlantic Book Week Steering Committee to honor the first published book by an Atlantic-Canadian author. Full-length books of fiction, nonfiction, or poetry written by Atlantic Canadians, and published as a whole for the first time in the previous calendar year, are eligible. Entrants must be native or resident Atlantic Canadians who have either been born in Newfoundland, Prince Edward Island, Nova Scotia, or New Brunswick, and spent a susbstantial portion of their lives living there, or who have lived in 1 or a combination of these provinces for at least 24 consecutive months prior to entry deadline date. Publishers: Send 4 copies and a letter attesting to the author's status as an Atlantic Canadian and the author's current mailing address and telephone number. **Deadline: First Friday in December.** Prize: $500.

THE MONA SCHREIBER PRIZE FOR HUMOROUS FICTION & NONFICTION

11362 Homedale St., Los Angeles CA 90049. (310)471-3280. E-mail: brashcyber@pcmagic.net. Website: www.brashcyber.com. **Contact:** Brad Schreiber. **Deadline: December 1. Charges $5 fee/entry (payable to Mona Schreiber Prize).** Prize: 1st Place: $500; 2nd Place: $250; 3rd Place: $100. All winners receive a copy of *What Are You Laughing At?: How to Write Funny Screenplays, Stories and More*, by Brad Schreiber. Judged by Brad Schreiber, author, journalist, consultant, and instructor at UCLA Extension Writers' Program. Open to any writer.

☒ SHORT GRAIN WRITING CONTEST

Grain Magazine, Box 67, Saskatoon SK S7K 3K1 Canada. (306)244-2828. Fax: (306)244-0255. E-mail: grainmag @sasktel.net. Website: www.grainmagazine.ca. **Contact:** Bobbi Clackson-Walker. Offered annually for unpublished dramatic monologues, postcard stories (narrative fiction) and prose (lyric) poetry, and nonfiction creative prose. Maximum length for short entries, 500 words. Entry guidelines online. All entrants receive a 1-year subscription to *Grain Magazine*. *Grain* purchases first Canadian serial rights only; copyright remains with the author. Open to any writer. No fax or e-mail submissions. **Deadline: January 31. Charges $28 fee for 2 entries; $8 for 3 additional entries; US and international entries $28, plus $6 postage in US funds (non-Canadian).** Prize: $6,000; four prizes of $500 in each category.

☒ SHORT PROSE COMPETITION FOR DEVELOPING WRITERS

The Writers' Union of Canada, 90 Richmond St. E., Suite 200, Toronto ON M5C 1P1 Canada. (416)703-8982, ext. 223. Fax: (416)504-9090. E-mail: projects@writersunion.ca. Website: www.writersunion.ca. **Contact:** Project Coordinator. Offered annually "to discover developing Canadian writers of unpublished prose fiction and nonfiction." Length: 2,500 words maximum. Open to Canadian citizens or landed immigrants who have not been published in book format, and who do not currently have a contract with a publisher. **Deadline: November 3.** Guidelines for SASE. **Charges $25 entry fee.** Prize: $2,500 and possible publication in a literary journal.

THE BERNICE SLOTE AWARD

Prairie Schooner, 201 Andrews Hall, PO Box 880334, Lincoln NE 68588-0334. (402)472-0911. Fax: (402)472-9771. E-mail: kgrey2@unl.edu. Website: www.unl.edu/schooner/psmain.htm. **Contact:** Hilda Raz. Offered annually for the best work by a beginning writer published in *Prairie Schooner* in the previous year. Prize: $500.

[N] SOUTHWEST WRITERS CONTEST

SWW, 3721 Morris St. NE, Suite A, Albuquerque NM 87111-3611. (505)265-9485. Fax: (505)265-9483. E-mail: swriters@aol.com. Website: www.southwestwriters.org. **Contact:** David J. Corwell, contest chair; Joanne Marsh, contest co-chair. **Deadline: May 1. Charges $18/poetry entry (members); $28/poetry entry (nonmembers); $29 for all other entries (members); $44 for all other entries (nonmembers).** Prize: First-, second-, and third-place winners in each category receive cash prizes of $150, $100, and $50 respectively, as well as a certificate of achievement. First-place winners also compete for the $1,000 Storyteller Award. Finalists in all categories are notified by mail and are listed on the SWW website. Winners will be honored at a contest awards banquet. Writer maintains all rights to the work. Judged by editors and literary agents who review all entries and critique the top 3 entries in each category. All entries receive a written critique by a qualified consultant (usually—but not always—a published author). Judges are chosen by the contest chairs. Open to any writer.

WALLACE STEGNER FELLOWSHIPS

Creative Writing Program, Stanford University, Dept. of English, Stanford CA 94305-2087. (650)723-2637. Fax: (650)723-3679. E-mail: vfhess@stanford.edu. Website: www.stanford.edu/dept/english/cw/. **Contact:** Virginia Hess, program administrator. Offered annually for a 2-year residency at Stanford for emerging writers to attend the Stegner workshop to practice and perfect their craft under the guidance of the creative writing faculty. Guidelines available online. **Deadline: December 1 (postmarked). Charges $50 fee.** Prize: Living stipend (currently $22,000/year) and required workshop tuition of $6,500/year.

[N] TALL GRASS WRITERS GUILD LITERARY ANTHOLOGY/CONTEST

Outrider Press, 937 Patricia, Crete IL 60417. (708)672-6630. Fax: (708)672-5820. E-mail: outriderpr@aol.com. Website: www.outriderpr.com. **Contact:** Whitney Scott, senior editor. Competition to collect diverse writings by authors of all ages and backgrounds on the theme of "vacations"—spiritual as well as physical. Word length: 2,500 words or less. Previously published and unpublished submissions accepted. Maximum 2 prose, 8 poetry entries per person. Send SASE. **Deadline: February 28.** Guidelines for SASE. **Charges $16; $12 for members. Make check payable to Tallgrass Writers Guild.** Prize: Publication in anthology, free copy to all published authors, $1,000 in cash prizes. Open to any writer.

TENNESSEE WRITERS ALLIANCE LITERARY COMPETITION

Tennessee Writers Alliance, P.O. Box 120396, Nashville TN 37212. Website: www.tn-writers.org. **Contact:** Jane Hicks, competition director. Offered annually for unpublished short fiction and poetry. Membership open to all, regardless of residence, for $25/year; $15/year for students. "For more information and guidelines visit our website or send a SASE." **Deadline: July 1. Charges $10 fee for members; $15 fee for nonmembers.** Prize: 1st Place: $500; 2nd Place: $250; 3rd Place: $100.

[C] TORONTO BOOK AWARDS

City of Toronto % Toronto Protocol, 100 Queen St. W., 10th Floor, West Tower, City Hall, Toronto ON M5H 2N2 Canada. (416)392-8191. Fax: (416)392-1247. E-mail: bkurmey@toronto.ca. Website: www.toronto.ca/book_awards. **Contact:** Bev Kurmey, protocol officer. Offered annually for previously published fiction, nonfiction, or juvenile books that are "evocative of Toronto." Previously published entries must have appeared in print between January 1 and December 31 the year prior to the contest year. **Deadline: February 28.** Guidelines for SASE. Prize: Awards total $15,000; $1,000 goes to shortlist finalists (usually 4-6) and the remainder goes to the winner. Judged by independent judging committee of 5 people chosen through an application and selection process.

WESTMORELAND POETRY & SHORT STORY CONTEST

Westmoreland Arts & Heritage Festival, 252 Twin Lakes Rd., Latrobe PA 15650-9415. (724)834-7474. Fax: (724)850-7474. E-mail: info@artsandheritage.com. **Contact:** Donnie A. Gutherie. Offered annually for unpublished work. Writers are encouraged to submit short stories from all genres. The purpose of the contest is to provide writers varied competition in 2 categories: short story and poetry. Entries must be 4,000 words or less. No erotica or pornography. **Deadline: March.** Guidelines for SASE. **Charges $10 fee/story; $10 fee/2 poems.** Prize: Up to $200 in prizes.

WILLA LITERARY AWARD

Women Writing the West, 10 N. Johanna Dr., Centerville OH 45459. Phone/Fax: (937)434-5979. E-mail: srick18153@aol.com. Website: www.womenwritingthewest.org. **Contact:** Sarah Rickman, contest director. "The WILLA Literary Award honors the best in literature featuring women's stories set in the West published each year. Women Writing the West (WWW), a nonprofit association of writers and other professionals writing and promoting the Women's West, underwrites and presents the nationally recognized award annually (for work published between January 1 and December 31). The award is named in honor of Pulitzer Prize winner Willa Cather, one of the country's foremost novelists. The award is given in 7 categories: historical fiction, contemporary fiction, original softcover, nonfiction, memoir/essay nonfiction, poetry, and children's/young adult fiction/nonfiction.'' **Deadline: February 1, 2006.** Guidelines for SASE. **Charges $50 entry fee.** Prize: Each winner receives $100 and a trophy. Each finalist receives a plaque. Award announcement is in early August, and awards are presented to the winners and finalists at the annual WWW Fall Conference. Judged by professional librarians not affiliated with WWW. Open to any writer.

WOMEN IN THE ARTS ANNUAL FICTION CONTEST

Women in the Arts, P.O. Box 2907, Decatur IL 62524. (217)872-0811. **Contact:** Vice President. Annual competition for essays, fiction, fiction for children, plays, rhymed poetry, and unrhymed poetry. **Deadline: November 1.** Guidelines for SASE. **Charges $2/submission.** Prize: 1st Prize: $50; 2nd Prize: $35; 3rd Prize: $15. Judged by professional writers. Open to any writer.

N WOMEN'S EMPOWERMENT AWARDS WRITING COMPETITION

E.F.S Online Publishing, 2844 Eighth Ave., Suite 6E, New York NY 10039-2171. (212)283-8899. Website: www.efs-enterprises.com. **Contact:** Rita Baxter. Offered annually, for unpublished work, to both empower women and to provide writers the opportunity to publish their work in the following categories: fiction, playwriting, and nonfiction. **Deadline: November 30.** Guidelines for SASE. **Charges $25/ms.** Prize: Publishing contract for the grand-prize winner. First-prize winners get $50 cash or special publishing contract option. E.F.S. reserves the right to extend special contract options to any first-, second, or third-place winners it desires based on the quality, marketability, and salability of those manuscripts/entries. Should E.F.S. extend a special publishing contract option to any first-prize winners, the first-prize winners would have the option of choosing the $50 cash award or the publishing contract option. Open to any writer.

JOHN WOOD COMMUNITY COLLEGE ADULT CREATIVE WRITING CONTEST

1301 S. 48th St., Quincy IL 62305. Website: www.jwcc.edu. **Contact:** Sherry L. Sparks, contest coordinator. Categories include serious poetry, light poetry, nonfiction, fiction. ''No identification should appear on manuscripts, but send a separate 3×5 card for each entry with name, address, phone number, e-mail address, word count, title of work, and category in which each work should be entered.'' Only for previously unpublished work: serious or light poetry (2 page/poem maximum), fiction (2,000 words maximum), nonfiction (2,000 words maximum). Guidelines for SASE or online. Period of Contest: January 1-April 1. Contest in conjunction with Mid Mississippi Review Writer's Conference. **Charges $5/poem; $7/fiction or nonfiction.** Prize: Cash prizes dictated by the number of entries received.

WORLD'S BEST SHORT SHORT STORY FICTION CONTEST & SOUTHEAST REVIEW POETRY CONTEST

English Department, Writing Program, Florida State University, Tallahassee FL 32306. (850)644-2773. E-mail: southeastreview@english.fsu.edu. Website: www.english.fsu.edu/southeastreview. **Contact:** James Kimbrell, editor, *The Southeast Review.* Estab. 1979. Annual award for unpublished short short stories (no more than 500 words). **Deadline: February 15. Charges $10 fee for up to 3 stories or poems.** Prize: $500 and publication in The *Southeast Review.* Nine finalists in each genre will also be published. Robert Olen Butler judges the World's Best Short Short Story Fiction Contest; Charles Wright judges the Southeast Review Poetry Contest.

THE WORD GUILD CANADIAN WRITING AWARDS

The Word Guild, Box 487, Markham ON L3P 3R1 Canada. E-mail: info@thewordguild.com. Website: www.theword guild.com. This contest is offered ''to encourage first-time Canadian authors to write fiction and nonfiction books expressing Christian faith in a clear, original, and inspiring way.'' The Castle Quay Books Canada and Essence Publishing Award is open to Canadian citizens only and someone who has never had a book published. The God Uses Ink Awards is for a theme-based article, short story, book, or script submitted by an unpublished author. The Word Guild Canadian Christian Writing Awards for work published in the previous year include: Nonfiction Books (life stories, personal growth, relationships, culture, leadership and philosophy, and special—books of poetry, anthology, etc.); Novels (literary/mainstream); Children & Young Adult Books (novels and nonfiction); Self-Published Books; Articles (news, feature, column/editorial/opinion, personal experience, devotional/inspirational, humor); Letter to the Editor; Short Story (fiction); Children & Young Adult (articles and short stories); Poetry (rhymed or free verse; maximum of 40 lines). **Deadline: January for published work; February for unpublished work. Charges $50 (Canadian)/$30 (US) for published books; $20 (Canadian)/$15 (US) for short items.** Prize: Book Awards: $200; Short Items: $100; Castle Quay Books Award: Ms will be published; God Uses ink Award: Registration at the God Uses Ink conference, plus runners-up awards. Judged by writers, editors, etc.

WRITERS NOTES BOOK AWARDS

Writers Notes Magazine, P.O. Box 11, Titusville NJ 08560. Fax: (609)818-1913. E-mail: info@hopepubs.com. Website: www.writersnotes.com. **Contact:** Christopher Klim, senior editor. Annual contest for previously published writing. Recognizes excellence in independent publishing in many unique categories: Art (titles capture the experience, execution, or demonstration of the arts); General Fiction (nongenre-specific fiction); Commercial Fiction (genre-specific fiction); Children (titles for young children); Young Adult (titles aimed at the juvenile and teen markets); Culture (titles demonstrating the human or world experience); Business (titles with application to today's business environment and emerging trends); Reference (titles from traditional and emerging reference areas); Home (titles with practical applications to home or home-related issues); Health/Self-Help (titles promoting the evaluation of mind and/or body); Legacy (titles over 2 years of age that hold particular relevance to any subject matter or form); E-book (all e-book titles in PC format). **Deadline: January 15.** Guidelines for SASE. **Charges $40.** Prize: $100, and international coverage in *Writers Notes Magazine*. Judged by authors, editors, agents, publishers, book producers, artists, experienced category readers, and health and business professionals. Open to any writer.

WRITERS NOTES WRITING AWARDS

Writers Notes Magazine, P.O. Box 11, Titusville NJ 08560. Fax: (609)818-1913. E-mail: info@hopepubs.com. Website: www.writersnotes.com. **Contact:** Christopher Klim, senior editor. Annual contests for unpublished fiction and nonfiction (5,000 words or less). Purchases first publication and one-time anthology rights for winning entries. **Deadline: July 31.** Guidelines for SASE. **Charges $15.** Prize: For both categories—Winner: $150; 1st Runners-up: $50; Honorable Mention: Publication contract. All winners will be published in fall issue or offered a writing contract for future issue. Judged by authors, editors, journalists, agents, and experienced category readers. Open to any writer.

ARTS COUNCILS & FOUNDATIONS

ALABAMA STATE COUNCIL ON THE ARTS FELLOWSHIP-LITERATURE

Alabama State Council on the Arts, 201 Monroe St., Montgomery AL 36130-1800. (334)242-4076, ext. 224. Fax: (334)240-3269. E-mail: randy@arts.state.al.us. Website: www.arts.state.al.us. **Contact:** Randy Shoults. Literature fellowship offered every year (for previously published or unpublished work) to set aside time to create and to improve skills. Two-year Alabama residency required. Guidelines available. **Deadline: March 1.** Prize: $10,000 or $5,000.

ALASKA STATE COUNCIL ON THE ARTS CAREER OPPORTUNITY GRANT AWARD

Alaska State Council on the Arts, 411 W. 4th Ave., Suite 1E, Anchorage AK 99501-2343. (907)269-6610. Fax: (907)269-6601. E-mail: aksca_info@eed.state.ak.us. Website: www.eed.state.ak.us/aksca. **Contact:** Charlotte Fox, executive director. Grants help artists take advantage of impending, concrete opportunities that will significantly advance their work or careers. **Deadline: Applications must be received by the first of the month preceding the month of the proposed activity.** Prize: Up to $1,000. Open to residents of Alaska only.

ARROWHEAD REGIONAL ARTS COUNCIL INDIVIDUAL ARTIST CAREER DEVELOPMENT GRANT

Arrowhead Regional Arts Council, 1301 Rice Lake Rd., Suite 111, Duluth MN 55811. (218)722-0952 or (800)569-8134. Fax: (218)722-4459. E-mail: aracouncil@aol.com. Website: www.aracouncil.org. **Contact:** Robert DeArmond, executive director. For writers residing in the 7 counties of Northeastern Minnesota. **Deadline: November 24 and April 29.** Guidelines for SASE. Prize: Up to $1,000. Judged by ARAC Board. Applicants must live in the 7-county region of Northeastern Minnesota.

ARTIST TRUST/WASHINGTON STATE ARTS COMMISSION FELLOWSHIP AWARDS

Artist Trust, 1835 12th Ave., Seattle WA 98122-2437. (206)467-8734. E-mail: info@artisttrust.org. Website: www.artisttrust.org. **Contact:** Fionn Meade, director of grant programs. "The fellowship is a merit-based award of $6,000 to practicing professional Washington State artists of exceptional talent and demonstrated ability." Literature fellowships are offered every other year, and approximately six $6,000 literature fellowships are awarded. The award is made on the basis of work of the past 5 years. Applicants must be individual artists; Washington State residents; not matriculated students; and generative artists. Offered every 2 years in odd years. Guidelines and application online or for SASE. **Deadline: June.** Prize: $6,000. Judged by a selection panel of artists and/or arts professionals in the field chosen by the Artist Trust staff.

[N] ARTS RECOGNITION AND TALENT SEARCH

National Foundation for Advancement in the Arts, 444 Brickell Ave., Suite P-14, Miami FL 33131. (305)377-1140 or (800)970-ARTS. Fax: (305)377-1149. E-mail: info@nfaa.org. Website: www.artsawards.org. **Contact:**

Vivian Orndorff, programs manager. Estab. 1981. For high school seniors in dance, music, jazz, photography, theater, film & video, visual art, voice, and writing. Applications available on website or by phone request. **Deadline: Early: June 1 ($30 fee); Regular: October 1 ($40 fee).** Prize: Individual awards range from $100-10,000 in an awards package totalling $900,000—$3 million in scholarship opportunities and the chance to be named Presidential Scholars in the Arts.

N GEORGE BENNETT FELLOWSHIP

Phillips Exeter Academy, 20 Main St., Exeter NH 03833-2460. Website: www.exeter.edu. **Contact:** Charles Pratt, coordinator, selection committee. Estab. 1968. Annual award for a fellow "to provide time and freedom from material considerations to a person seriously contemplating or pursuing a career as a writer. Applicants should have a manuscript in progress which they intend to complete during the fellowship period." Duties: To be in residency for the academic year; to make oneself available informally to students interested in writing. Guidelines for SASE or on website. The committee favors writers who have not yet published a book with a major publisher. Residence at the academy during the fellowship period required. **Deadline: December 1.** Prize: $10,000 stipend, room and board.

BUSH ARTIST FELLOWS PROGRAM

The Bush Foundation, 332 Minnesota St., Suite E-900, St. Paul MN 55101. (651)227-0891. Fax: (651)297-6485. Website: www.bushfoundation.org. **Contact:** Kathi Polley, program assistant. Estab. 1976. Award for US citizens or permanent residents of Minnesota, North Dakota, South Dakota, and western Wisconsin. Applicants must be 25 years or older (students are not eligible) and want "to buy 12-24 months of time for the applicant to further his/her own work." All application categories rotate on a 2-year cycle. Publishing, performance, and/or option requirements for eligibility. Applications available August 2006. **Deadline: October.** Prize: Up to 15 fellowships/year, $44,000 each.

ChLA RESEARCH GRANTS

Children's Literature Association, P.O. Box 138, Battle Creek MI 49016-0138. (269)965-8180. Fax: (269)965-8180. E-mail: kkiessling@childlitassn.org. Website: www.childlitassn.org. **Contact:** ChLA Grants Chair. Offered annually. "The grants are awarded for proposals dealing with criticism or original scholarship with the expectation that the undertaking will lead to publication and make a significant contribution to the field of children's literature in the area of scholarship or criticism." Funds are not intended for work leading to the completion of a professional degree. Guidelines available online or send SASE to ChLA office for a print copy. **Deadline: February 1.** Prize: $500-1,000.

CONNECTICUT COMMISSION ON CULTURE & TOURISM ARTIST FELLOWSHIPS

One Financial Plaza, Hartford CT 06103-2601. (860)256-2800. Fax: (860)256-2811. E-mail: artsinfo@ctarts.org. Website: www.ctarts.org/artfellow.htm. **Contact:** Linda Dente, program manager. **Deadline: September 2006.** Prize: $5,000 and $2,500. Judged by peer professionals (writers, editors). Open to Connecticut residents only.

N CREATIVE & PERFORMING ARTISTS & WRITERS FELLOWSHIP

American Antiquarian Society, 185 Salisbury St., Worcester MA 01609. (508)471-2131. Fax: (508)754-9069. E-mail: jmoran@mwa.org. Website: www.americanantiquarian.org. **Contact:** James David Moran. Annual contest for published writers and performers to conduct research in pre-20th century history. **Deadline: October 5.** Prize: $1,200 monthly stipend, plus travel expenses of up to $400. Judged by AAS staff and outside reviewers. Open to any writer.

N ⊕ CREATIVE SCOTLAND AWARD

Scottish Arts Council, 12 Manor Place, Edinburgh Scotland EH3 7DD. (0845) 603 6000. Fax: (0131) 225 9833. E-mail: help.desk@scottisharts.org.uk. Website: www.scottisharts.org.uk. Up to 10 awards annually of £30,000 each to support Scotland's leading artists. The awards provide a unique opportunity for artists to refresh their skills, to experiment, and to create innovative and inspiring work. Guidelines and applications forms are available starting Summer 2005. Guidelines for SASE.

DELAWARE DIVISION OF THE ARTS

820 N. French St., Wilmington DE 19801. (302)577-8284. Fax: (302)577-6561. E-mail: kristin.pleasanton@state.de.us. Website: www.artsdel.org. **Contact:** Kristin Pleasanton, coordinator. Award offered annually "to help further careers of Delaware's emerging and established professional artists." **Deadline: August 1.** Guidelines for SASE. Prize: $10,000 for masters; $5,000 for established professionals; $2,000 for emerging professionals. Judged by out-of-state professionals in each division. Open to Delaware residents only.

DOBIE/PAISANO FELLOWSHIPS

J. Frank Dobie House, 702 E. Dean Keeton St., Austin TX 78705. Fax: (512)471-9997. E-mail: aslate@mail.utexas .edu. Website: www.utexas.edu/ogs/Paisano. **Contact:** Audrey Slate. The Dobie-Paisano Fellowships provide an opportunity for creative writers to live for an extended period of time at a place of literary association. At the time of the application, 1 of the following requirements must be met: 1) be a native Texan; 2) have lived in Texas at some time for at least 3 years; 3) have published writing that has a Texas subject. Criteria for making the awards include quality of work, character of proposed project, and suitability of the applicant for life at Paisano. Applicants must submit examples of their work in triplicate. Guidelines for SASE or online. Annually. **Deadline: January 28. Charges $10 fee.** Prize: 2 fellowships of $2,000/month for 6 months, and 6 months in residence at the late J. Frank Dobie's ranch near Austin, Texas—the first beginning September 1 and the second March 1. The fellowships are known as the Ralph A. Johnston Memorial Fellowship and the Jesse H. Jones Writing Fellowship. Winners are announced in early May. Three copies of the application must be submitted with the rest of the entry and mailed in 1 package. Entries must be submitted on the form.

N GAP (GRANTS FOR ARTIST PROJECTS) PROGRAM

Artist Trust, 1835 12th Ave., Seattle WA 98122. (206)467-8734. Fax: (206)467-9633. E-mail: info@artisttrust.org. Website: www.artisttrust.org. **Contact:** Director of Grant Programs. "The GAP is awarded annually to approximately 50 artists, including writers. The award is meant to help finance a specific project, which can be in very early stages or near completion. Full-time students are not eligible. Open to Washington state residents only. **Deadline: The last Friday of February.** Guidelines for SASE. Prize: Up to $1,400 for artist-generated projects.

HAWAI'I AWARD FOR LITERATURE

Hawai'i State Foundation on Culture and the Arts, 250 S. Hotel St., 2nd Floor, Honolulu HI 96813. (808)586-0769. Fax: (808)586-0308. E-mail: sfca@sfca.state.hi.us. Website: www.state.hi.us/sfca. **Contact:** Hawai'i Literary Arts Council: Box 11213, Honolulu HI 96828-0213. (808)956-7357. Fax: (808)956-6345. E-mail: iwasa@hawaii.edu. "The annual award honors the lifetime achievement of a writer whose work is important to Hawai'i and/or Hawai'i's people." Nominations are a public process; inquiries should be directed to the Hawai'i Literary Arts Council at address listed. "Cumulative work is considered. Self nominations are allowed, but not usual. Fiction, poetry, drama, certain types of nonfiction, screenwriting, and song lyrics are considered. The award is not intended to recognize conventional academic writing and reportage, nor is it intended to recognize more commercial types of writing, i.e., advertising copy, tourist guides, and how-to manuals." **Deadline: November.** Prize: Governor's reception and cash award.

ALFRED HODDER FELLOWSHIP

The Council of the Humanities, Joseph Henry House, Princeton University, Princeton NJ 08544. E-mail: humcou nc@princeton.edu. Website: www.princeton.edu/~humcounc/. The Hodder Fellowship is awarded to exceptional humanists at the early stages of their careers, typically after they have published one book and are working on a second. Preference is given to individuals outside academia. Hodder Fellows spend an academic year in residence in Princeton, pursuing independent projects. Candidates are invited to submit a résumé, a sample of previous work (10-page maximum, not returnable), a project proposal of 2-3 pages, and SASE for acknowledgement. Letters of recommendation are not required. **Deadline: November 1 (postmarked).** Prize: $55,000 stipend.

ILLINOIS ART COUNCIL ARTISTS FELLOWSHIP PROGRAM IN POETRY & PROSE

Illinois Art Council, 100 W. Randolph, Suite 10-500, Chicago IL 60601. (312)814-6740. Fax: (312)814-1471. E-mail: info@arts.state.il.us. Website: www.state.il.us/agency/iac. **Contact:** Director of Literature. Offered biannually for Illinois writers of exceptional talent to enable them to pursue their artistic goals. Applicant must have been a resident of Illinois for at least 1 year prior to the deadline. Guidlines for SASE. **Deadline: September 1, 2005 (prose).** Prize: Nonmatching award of $7,000; finalist award of $700.

CHRISTOPHER ISHERWOOD FELLOWSHIPS

Christopher Isherwood Foundation, PMB 139, 1223 Wilshire Blvd., Santa Monica CA 90403-5040. E-mail: james @isherwoodfoundation.org. Website: www.isherwoodfoundation.org. **Contact:** James P. White, executive director. Several awards are given annually to selected novelists who have published a novel. **Deadline: September 1-October 1 (send to the address posted on the website).** Prize: Fellowship consists of $3,000. Judged by advisory board.

N KORET JEWISH STUDIES PUBLICATIONS PROGRAM

Koret Foundation, 33 New Montgomery St., Suite 1090, San Francisco CA 94105-4526. (415)882-7740. Fax: (415)882-7775. E-mail: jspp@koretfoundation.org. Website: www.koretfoundation.org. **Contact:** Call Koret

Foundation and ask for JSPP Program Officer. "In 1998, the Koret Foundation launched the Jewish Studies Publications Program (JSPP) to provide publication subsidies to first-time authors of original scholarly monographs in the field of Jewish studies. The program was designed to help unpublished scholars bring their work to light. As of August 2004, these grants have assisted in the publication of 65 books. Koret is the only Jewish foundation that has such a program, and the response of publishers and authors has been very positive. The subsidy grants are payable only to nonprofit institutions, organizations, and publishers. The grant funds are to support costs that an interested publisher may not otherwise be able to meet." Equal consideration will be given to applicants whose mss have not yet been accepted by a publisher. **Deadline: Posted on the foundation's website in November.** Guidelines for SASE. Prize: Grants ranging from $3,000-4,000.

KORET YOUNG WRITER ON JEWISH THEMES AWARD

Koret Foundation, 33 New Montgomery St., Suite 1090, San Francisco CA 94105-4526. (415)882-7740, ext. 3. Fax: (415)882-7775. E-mail: kywa@koretfoundation.org. Website: www.koretfoundation.org. **Contact:** Steven J. Zipperstein, PhD, director, Koret Institute. Annual award for "1 writer whose work contains Jewish themes. The residency allows time for writing, participating in and/or leading workshops within the Bay area, and the option of designing and teaching a course at Stanford University." Applicants must be 40 years of age or younger and have published no more than 1 book at the time of application. Scholarly work will not be considered. This award is for fiction, nonfiction, or poetry. **Deadline: November 15.** Prize: $25,000, plus 3-month residency at Stanford University. Judged by a distinguished panel of judges who remain anonymous.

LITERARY GIFT OF FREEDOM

A Room of Her Own Foundation, P.O. Box 778, Placitas NM 87043. E-mail: info@aroomofherownfoundation.org. Website: www.aroomofherownfoundation.org. **Contact:** Darlene Chandler Bassett. Award offered every other year to provide very practical help—both materially and in professional guidance and moral support—to women who need assistance in making their creative contribution to the world. Guidelines available on website. **Deadline: February 1, 2007 (for fiction writers). Charges $25.** Prize: Up to $50,000 over 2 years, also a mentor for advice and dialogue, and access to the Advisory Council for professional and business consultation. Judged by members of AROHO's Board of Directors, Advisory Council, and volunteers from a wide variety of backgrounds. Open to any female resident citizen of the US.

MASSACHUSETTS CULTURAL COUNCIL ARTISTS GRANTS PROGRAM

Massachusetts Cultural Council, 10 St. James Ave., Boston MA 02116-3803. (617)727-3668. Fax: (617)727-0044. E-mail: mcc@art.state.ma.us. Website: www.massculturalcouncil.org. Awards in poetry, fiction, creative nonfiction, and playwriting/new theater works (among other discipline categories) are $5,000 each in recognition of exceptional original work. Criteria: Artistic excellence and creative ability, based on work submitted for review. Judged by independent peer panels composed of artists and art professionals. Must be 18 years or older and a legal residents of Massachusetts for the last 2 years and at time of award. This excludes students in directly-related degree programs and grant recipients within the last 3 years.

JENNY McKEAN/MOORE VISITING WRITER

English Department, George Washington University, Washington DC 20052. (202)994-6180. Fax: (202)994-7915. E-mail: dmca@gwu.edu. Website: www.gwu.edu/~english. **Contact:** David McAleavey. Offered annually to provide 1-year visiting writers to teach 1 George Washington course and 1 free community workshop each semester. Guidelines for SASE or on website. This contest seeks someone specializing in a different genre each year. **Deadline: November 15.** Prize: Annual stipend of approximately $50,000, plus reduced-rent townhouse (not guaranteed).

N MINNESOTA STATE ARTS BOARD INITIATIVE GRANT

Minnesota State Arts Board, Park Square Court, 400 Sibley St., Suite 200, St. Paul MN 55101-1928. (651)215-1600 or (800)866-2787. Fax: (651)215-1602. E-mail: amy.frimpong@arts.state.mn.us. Website: www.arts.state.mn.us. **Contact:** Amy Frimpong. Purpose is to support and assist artists at various stages in their careers. It encourages artistic development, nurtures artistic creativity, and recognizes the contributions of individual artists to make the creative environment of the state of Minnesota. Literary categories include prose, poetry, playwriting, and screenwriting. Open to Minnesota residents. Prize: Bi-annual grants of $2,000-6,000.

MONEY FOR WOMEN

Barbara Deming Memorial Fund, Inc., P.O. Box 630125, The Bronx NY 10463. **Contact:** Susan Pliner. "Small grants to individual feminists in fiction, nonfiction, and poetry, whose work addresses women's concerns and/or speaks for peace and justice from a feminist perspective." Guidelines and required entry forms for SASE. "The fund does not give educational assistance, monies for personal study or loans, monies for dissertation, research projects, or self-publication, grants for group projects, business ventures, or emergency funds for hardships.'' Open to citizens of the US or Canada. The fund also offers 2 awards, the Gertrude Stein Award for outstanding works by a lesbian and the Fannie Lou Hamer Award for work which combats racism and celebrates women of color. No special application necessary for these 2 awards. Recipients will be chosen from all the proposals. **Deadline: December 31 (fiction) and June 30 (nonfiction and poetry).** Prize: Grants up to $1,500.

NEBRASKA ARTS COUNCIL INDIVIDUAL ARTISTS FELLOWSHIPS

Nebraska Arts Council, 3838 Davenport St., Omaha NE 68131-2329. (402)595-2122. Fax: (402)595-2334. E-mail: ltubach@nebraskaartscouncil.org. Website: www.nebraskaartscouncil.org. **Contact:** Lisa Tubach. Estab. 1991. Offered every 3 years (literature alternates with other disciplines) to recognize exemplary achievements by originating artists in their fields of endeavor and support the contributions made by Nebraska artists to the quality of life in this state. "Generally, distinguished achievement awards are $5,000 and merit awards are $1,000-2,000. Funds available are announced in September prior to the deadline.'' Must be a resident of Nebraska for at least 2 years prior to submission date; 18 years of age; not enrolled in an undergraduate, graduate, or certificate-granting program in English, creative writing, literature, or related field. **Deadline: November 15, 2005.** Prize: $5,000; merit awards are $1,000-2,000.

NEW JERSEY STATE COUNCIL ON THE ARTS FELLOWSHIP PROGRAM

New Jersey State Council on the Arts, 225 W. State St., P.O. Box 306, Trenton NJ 08625. (609)292-6130. Fax: (609)989-1440. E-mail: njsca@njartscouncil.org. Website: www.njartscouncil.org. **Contact:** Don Ehman, program associate. Offered every other year. Writers may apply in either poetry, playwriting, or prose. Fellowship awards are intended to provide support for the artist during the year to enable him/her to continue producing new work. Send for guidelines and application, or visit website. Must be New Jersey residents; may *not* be undergraduate or graduate matriculating students. **Deadline: July 15.** Prize: $7,000-12,000.

NORTH CAROLINA ARTS COUNCIL REGIONAL ARTIST PROJECT GRANTS

North Carolina Arts Council, Dept. of Cultural Resources, Raleigh NC 27699-4634. (919)715-1519. Fax: (919)733-4834. E-mail: debbie.mcgill@ncmail.net. Website: www.ncarts.org. **Contact:** Debbie McGill, literature director, or see the website for contact information for the local arts councils that distribute these grants. **Deadline: Varies; generally late summer/early fall.** Prize: $500-3,000 awarded to writers to pursue projects that further their artistic development. Open to any writer living in North Carolina.

NORTH CAROLINA WRITERS' FELLOWSHIPS

North Carolina Arts Council, Dept. of Cultural Resources, Raleigh NC 27699-4632. (919)715-1519. Fax: (919)733-4834. E-mail: debbie.mcgill@ncmail.net. Website: www.ncarts.org. **Contact:** Deborah McGill, literature director. Offered every even year to support writers of fiction, poetry, literary nonfiction, literary translation, and spoken word. See website for guidelines and other eligibility requirements. **Deadline: November 1, 2006.** Prize: $8,000 grant. Judged by a panel of literary professionals (writers, editors). Writers must be current residents of North Carolina for at least 1 year and may not pursue academic or professional degrees while receiving grant.

NORTHWOOD UNIVERSITY'S CREATIVITY FELLOWSHIP

Northwood University, Alden B. Dow Creativity Center, 4000 Whiting Dr., Midland MI 48640-2398. (989)837-4478. Fax: (989)837-4468. E-mail: creativity@northwood.edu. Website: www.northwood.edu/abd. **Contact:** Award Director. Estab. 1979. Ten-week summer residency for individuals in any field who wish to pursue new and creative ideas that have potential impact in their fields. No accommodations for family/pets. Write for guidelines or check website. Authors must be US citizens. **Deadline: December 31 (postmarked).**

OREGON LITERARY FELLOWSHIPS

Literary Arts, Inc., 224 NW 13th Ave., Suite 306, Portland OR 97209. (503)227-2583. E-mail: la@literary-arts.org. Website: www.literary-arts.org. **Contact:** Kristy Athens, program coordinator. The annual Oregon Literary Fellowships support Oregon writers with a monetary award. Guidelines for SASE or online. **Deadline: last Friday in June.** Prize: $500-3,000. Fellows are also offered residencies at Caldera, a writers' retreat in Central Oregon. Judged by out-of-state judges who are selected for their expertise in a genre. Open to Oregon residents only.

⊕ THE CHARLES PICK FELLOWSHIP

School of Literature and Creative Writing, University of East Anglia, Norwich NR4 7TJ United Kingdom. Website: www.uea.ac.uk/eas/fellowships/pick.shtml. "The fellowship is dedicated to the memory of the distinguished publisher and literary agent, Charles Pick. Applicants must be writers of fictional or nonfictional prose (no more than 2,500 words) in English who have not yet published a book.'' All applicants must provide reference from an editor, agent, or accredited teacher of creative writing. **Deadline: January 31.** Guidelines for SASE. Prize: £10,000. Judged by a distinguished panel of writers. Open to any writer.

⊠ REQUEST FOR PROPOSAL

Rhode Island State Council on the Arts, One Capitol Hill, 3rd Floor, Providence RI 02908. (401)222-3880. Fax: (401)222-3018. E-mail: cristina@arts.ri.gov. Website: www.arts.ri.gov. **Contact:** Cristina DiChiera, director of individual artist & public art programs. "Request for Proposal grants enable an artist to create new work and/or complete works-in-progress by providing direct financial assistance. By encouraging significant development in the work of an individual artist, these grants recognize the central contribution artists make to the creative environment of Rhode Island." Guidelines online. Open to Rhode Island residents age 18 or older; students not eligible. **Deadline: October 1 and April 1.** Prize: Nonmatching grants typically under $5,000.

THE SOCIETY FOR THE SCIENTIFIC STUDY OF SEXUALITY STUDENT RESEARCH GRANT

The Society for the Scientific Study of Sexuality, P.O. Box 416, Allentown PA 18105-0416. (610)530-2483. Fax: (610)530-2485. E-mail: thesociety@inetmail.att.net. Website: www.sexscience.org. **Contact:** Ilsa Lottes. Offered twice a year for unpublished works. "The student research grant award is granted twice yearly to help support graduate student research on a variety of sexually related topics." Guidelines and entry forms for SASE. Open to SSSS students pursuing graduate study. **Deadline: February 1 and September 1.** Prize: $1,000.

⊠ TENNESSEE ARTS COMMISSION LITERARY FELLOWSHIP

Tennessee Arts Commission, 401 Charlotte Ave., Nashville TN 37243-0780. (615)532-5934. Website: www.arts.state.tn.us. **Contact:** Kim Leavitt, director of literary programs. Awarded annually in recognition of professional Tennessee artists, i.e., individuals who have received financial compensation for their work as professional writers. Applicants must have a publication history other than vanity press. Two fellowships awarded annually to outstanding literary artists who live and work in Tennessee. Categories are in prose and poetry. **Deadline: January 17.** Guidelines for SASE. Prize: $5,000. Judged by an out-of-state adjudicator.

UCROSS FOUNDATION RESIDENCY

30 Big Red Lane, Clearmont WY 82835. (307)737-2291. Fax: (307)737-2322. E-mail: info@ucross.org. Website: www.ucrossfoundation.org. Eight concurrent positions open for artists-in-residence in various disciplines (includes writers, visual artists, music, humanities, natural sciences) extending from 2 weeks to 2 months. No charge for room, board, or studio space. **Deadline: March 1 and October 1. Charges $20 application fee.**

VERMONT ARTS COUNCIL

136 State St., Drawer 33, Montpelier VT 05633-6001. (802)828-3291. Fax: (802)828-3363. E-mail: mbailey@vermontartscouncil.org. Website: www.vermontartscouncil.org. **Contact:** Michele Bailey. Offered twice a year for previously published or unpublished works. Opportunity Grants are for specific projects of writers (poetry, playwriters, fiction, nonfiction) as well as not-for-profit presses. Also available are Artist Development funds to provide technical assistance for Vermont writers. Write or call for entry information. Open to Vermont residents only. Prize: $250-5,000.

WISCONSIN ARTS BOARD ARTIST FELLOWSHIP AWARDS

Wisconsin Arts Board, 101 E. Wilson St., 1st Floor, Madison WI 53702. (608)266-0190. Fax: (608)267-0380. E-mail: artsboard@arts.state.wi.us. Website: www.arts.state.wi.us. **Contact:** Mark Fraire, grant programs and services specialist. Offered every 2 years (even years), rewarding outstanding, professionally active Wisconsin artists by supporting their continued development, enabling them to create new work, complete work in progress, or pursue activities which contribute to their artistic growth. If the deadline falls on a weekend, the deadline is extended to the following Monday. Application is found on the Wisconsin Arts Board website. The Arts Board requires permission to use the work sample, or a portion thereof, for publicity or educational purposes. Contest open to professionally active artists who have resided in Wisconsin 1 year prior to application. Artists who are full-time students pursuing a degree in the fine arts at the time of application are not eligible. **Deadline: September 13, 2006.** Prize: $8,000 fellowship awarded to 7 Wisconsin writers.

⊕ DAVID T.K. WONG FELLOWSHIP

School of Literature and Creative Writing, University of East Anglia, Norwich NR4 7TJ United Kingdom. Website: www.uea.ac.uk/eas/fellowships/wong/wong.shtml. Offered annually for mss of no more than 2,500 words (in English). The purpose of the award is to promote "excellence in the writing of literature." The fellowship is awarded to a writer planning to produce a work of prose fiction in English which deals seriously with some aspect of life in the Far East. **Deadline: October 31.** Guidelines for SASE. **Charges £10.** Prize: £25,000. Judged by a distinguished international panel. Open to any writer.

N ⊕ WRITER'S & NEW WRITER'S BURSARIES

Scottish Arts Council, 12 Manor Place, Edinburgh EH3 7DD Scotland. 0845 603 6000. Fax: 0131 225 9833. E-mail: help.desk@scottisharts.org.uk. Website: www.scottisharts.org.uk. Support is available to assist playwrights and published writers of literary work that are based in Scotland and need finance for a period of concentrated work on their next book or play. The bursary may be used for a quiet period of writing at home or elsewhere, or it may be used for necessary travel and research. Priority will be given to writers of fiction and poetry, including writers for children, but applications from nonfiction writers whose work is of a literary nature will also be considered. Applications from writers/illustrators are also welcome. For playwrights, the bursary is to assist with the creation of new scripts rather than the revision or rewriting of existing ones. "We also support new writers and plawrights with little or no previous publication or production track record (based in Scotland) who need finance for a period of concentrated work on their writing." Guidelines for SASE.

WRITERS' RESIDENCIES—HEADLANDS CENTER FOR THE ARTS

NC Arts Council, Dept. of Cultural Resources, Raleigh NC 27699-4634. (919)715-1519. Fax: (919)733-4834. E-mail: debbie.mcgill@ncmail.net. Website: www.ncarts.org. **Contact:** Deborah McGill, literature director. **Deadline: June 4.** Guidelines for SASE. Prize: Room, board, round-trip travel, and a $500 monthly stipend for 2-month residency. Judged by a panel assembled by Headlands. In addition, a member of the Headlands staff comes to North Carolina to interview a short list of finalists in order to narrow that list down to 1 grant recipient. Applicants must be residents of North Carolina and have lived in the state at least 1 year prior to the application deadline. NCAC grant recipients must maintain their North Carolina residency status during the grant year and may not pursue academic or professional degrees during that period. See website for other eligibility requirements.

Glossary

Advance. A sum of money a publisher pays a writer prior to the publication of a book. It is usually paid in installments, such as one-half on signing the contract and one-half on delivery of a complete and satisfactory manuscript.

Agent. A liaison between a writer and editor or publisher. An agent shops a manuscript around, receiving a commission when the manuscript is accepted. Agents usually take a 10-15% fee from the advance and royalties.

Assignment. Editor asks a writer to produce a specific article for an agreed-upon fee.

Auction. Publishers sometimes bid for the acquisition of a book manuscript that has excellent sales prospects. The bids are for the amount of the author's advance, advertising and promotional expenses, royalty percentage, etc. Auctions are conducted by agents.

Avant-garde. Writing that is innovative in form, style, or subject; often considered difficult and challenging.

Backlist. A publisher's list of books that were not published during the current season, but that are still in print.

Bimonthly. Every two months.

Bio. A sentence or brief paragraph about the writer; can include education and work experience.

Biweekly. Every two weeks.

Boilerplate. A standardized publishing contract.

Byline. Name of the author appearing with the published piece.

Category fiction. A term used to include all types of fiction.

Chapbook. A small booklet—usually paperback—of poetry, ballads, or tales.

Circulation. The number of subscribers to a magazine.

Clips. Samples, usually from newspapers or magazines, of your published work.

Coffee-table book. A heavily illustrated oversized book.

Commercial novels. Novels designed to appeal to a broad audience. These are often broken down into categories such as western, mystery, and romance. See *genre*.

Contributor's copies. Copies of the issues of magazines sent to the author in which the author's work appears.

Copyediting. Editing a manuscript for grammar, punctuation, printing style, and factual accuracy.

Copyright. A means to protect an author's work.

Cover letter. A brief letter that accompanies the manuscript being sent to an agent or editor.

Creative nonfiction. Nonfictional writing that uses an innovative approach to the subject and creative language.

CV. Curriculum vita. A brief listing of qualifications and career accomplishments.

Electronic submission. A submission made by modem or on computer disk.

Erotica. Fiction or art that is sexually oriented.

Fair use. A provision of the copyright law that says short passages from copyrighted material may be used without infringing on the owner's rights.

Feature. An article giving the reader information of human interest rather than news.

Filler. A short item used by an editor to "fill" out a newspaper column or magazine page. It could be a joke, an anecdote, etc.

Frontlist. A publisher's list of books that are new to the current season.

Galleys. The first typeset version of a manuscript that has not yet been divided into pages.

Genre. Refers either to a general classification of writing, such as the novel or the poem, or to the categories within those classifications, such as the problem novel or the sonnet.

Ghostwriter. A writer who puts into literary form an article, speech, story, or book based on another person's ideas or knowledge.

Graphic novel. An adaptation of a novel in graphic form, long comic strip, or heavily illustrated story; of 40 pages or more; produced in paperback form.

Honorarium. Token payment—small amount of money, or a byline and copies of the publication.

How-to. Books and magazine articles offering a combination of information and advice in describing how something can be accomplished.

Imprint. Name applied to a publisher's specific line of books.

Kill fee. Fee for a complete article that was assigned and then cancelled.

Lead time. The time between the acquisition of a manuscript by an editor and its actual publication.

Literary fiction. The general category of serious, nonformulaic, intelligent fiction.

Mainstream fiction. Fiction that transcends popular novel categories such as mystery, romance, and science fiction.

Mass market. Nonspecialized books of wide appeal directed toward a large audience.

Memoir. A narrative recounting a writer's (or fictional narrator's) personal or family history.

Midlist. Those titles on a publisher's list that are not expected to be big sellers, but are expected to have limited sales.

Model release. A paper signed by the subject of a photograph giving the photographer permission to use the photograph.

Multiple submissions. Sending more than one idea at the same time.

Narrative nonfiction. A narrative presentation of actual events.

Net royalty. A royalty payment based on the amount of money a book publisher receives on the sale of a book after booksellers' discounts, special sales discounts, and returns.

Novella. A short novel, or a long short story; approximately 7,000-15,000 words.

On spec. An editor expresses an interest in a proposed article idea and agrees to consider the finished piece for publication "on speculation." The editor is under no obligation to buy the finished manuscript.

Payment on acceptance. The editor sends you a check for your article, story, or poem as soon as he decides to publish it.

Payment on publication. The editor doesn't send you a check for your material until it is published.

Pen name. The use of a name other than your legal name on articles, stories, or books when you wish to remain anonymous. Also called a pseudonym.

Photo feature. Feature in which the emphasis is on the photographs rather than on accompanying written material.

Proofreading. Close reading and correction of a manuscript's typographical errors.

Proposal. A summary of a proposed book submitted to a publisher, particularly used for nonfiction manuscripts. A proposal often contains an individualized cover letter, one-page overview of the book, marketing information, competitive books, author information, chapter-by-chapter outline, and two to three sample chapters.

Query. A letter that sells an idea to an editor or agent. Usually a query is brief (no more than one page) and uses attention-getting prose.

Remainders. Copies of a book that are slow to sell and can be purchased from the publisher at a reduced price.

Reporting time. The time it takes for an editor to report to the author on his/her query or manuscript.

Royalties, standard hardcover book. 10 percent of the retail price on the first 5,000 copies sold; 12½ percent on the next 5,000; 15 percent thereafter.

Royalties, standard mass paperback book. 4-8 percent of the retail price on the first 150,000 copies sold.

Royalties, standard trade paperback book. No less than 6 percent of list price on the first 20,000 copies; 7½ percent thereafter.

Self-publishing. In this arrangement, the author keeps all income derived from the book, but he pays for its manufacturing, production, and marketing.

Semimonthly. Twice per month.

Semiweekly. Twice per week.

Serial. Published periodically, such as a newspaper or magazine.

Serial fiction. Fiction published in a magazine in installments, often broken off at a suspenseful spot.

Short-short. A complete short story of 250-1,500 words.

Sidebar. A feature presented as a companion to a straight news report (or main magazine article) giving sidelights on human-interest aspects or sometimes elucidating just one aspect of the story.

Simultaneous submissions. Sending the same article, story, or poem to several publishers at the same time. Some publishers refuse to consider such submissions.

Slant. The approach or style of a story or article that will appeal to readers of a specific magazine.

Slice-of-life vignette. A short fiction piece intended to realistically depict an interesting moment of everyday living.

Slush pile. The stack of unsolicited or misdirected manuscripts received by an editor or book publisher.

Subsidy publisher. A book publisher who charges the author for the cost to typeset and print his book, the jacket, etc., as opposed to a royalty publisher who pays the author.

Synopsis. A brief summary of a story, novel, or play. As part of a book proposal, it is a comprehensive summary condensed in a page or page and a half, single-spaced.

Tabloid. Newspaper format publication on about half the size of the regular newspaper page.

Tearsheet. Page from a magazine or newspaper containing your printed story, article, poem, or ad.

TOC. Table of Contents.

Unsolicited manuscript. A story, article, poem, or book that an editor did not specifically ask to see.

YA. Young adult books.

Book Publishers Subject Index

This index will help you find publishers that consider books on specific subjects. Remember that a publisher may be listed here only under a general subject category such as Art and Architecture, while the company publishes *only* art history or how-to books. Be sure to consult each company's individual listing, its book catalog, and several of its books before you send your query or proposal.

FICTION

Adventure

Experimental

Fantasy

Subject Index

Horror

Humor

Juvenile

Literary

Mainstream/Contemporary

Military/War

Occult

Picture Books

Plays

Poetry (Including Chapbooks)

Subject Index

Short Story Collections

Western

Young Adult

NONFICTION

Agriculture/Horticulture

Americana

Animals

Subject Index

Anthropology/Archeology

Art/Architecture

Biography

Business/Economics

Child Guidance/Parenting

Children's/Juvenile

Coffee Table Book

Computers/Electronic

Contemporary Culture

Cookbook

Cooking/Foods/Nutrition

Creative Nonfiction

Education

Ethnic

Fashion/Beauty

Film/Cinema/Stage

Gardening

Gay/Lesbian

History

Subject Index

Subject Index

Hobby

How-To

Subject Index

Language/Literature

Memoirs

Military/War

Multimedia

Music/Dance

Nature/Environment

New Age

Philosophy

Recreation

Reference

Subject Index

Regional

Religion

Science

Self-Help

Sex

Sociology

Software

Technical

Textbook

Translation

Travel

True Crime

Women's Issues/Studies

World Affairs

General Index

This index lists every market appearing in the book; use it to find specific companies you wish to approach. Markets that appeared in the 2005 edition of *Writer's Market*, but are not included in this edition are identified by a code explaining why the market was omitted: (**ED**)—Editorial Decision, (**GLA**)—Included in *Guide to Literary Agents*, (**NS**)—Not Accepting Submissions, (**NR**)—No or Late Response to Listing Request, (**OB**)—Out of Business, (**RR**)—Removed by Market's Request, (**UC**)—Unable to Contact, (**RP**)—Business Restructured or Purchased, (**NP**)—No Longer Pays or Pays in Copies Only, (**SR**)—Subsidy/Royalty Publisher, (**UF**)—Uncertain Future, (**Web**)—a listing that appears on our website at www.WritersMarket.com.

Writer's Digest

WRITE BETTER
GET PUBLISHED

DISCOVER A WORLD OF WRITING SUCCESS!

Are you ready to be praised, published, and paid for your writing? It's time to invest in your future with *Writer's Digest!* Beginners and experienced writers alike have been relying on *Writer's Digest*, the world's leading magazine for writers, for more than 80 years — and it keeps getting better!
Each issue is brimming with:

- Technique articles geared toward specific genres, including fiction, nonfiction, business writing and more
- Business information specifically for writers, such as organizational advice, tax tips, and setting fees
- Tips and tricks for rekindling your creative fire
- The latest and greatest markets for print, online and e-publishing
- And much more!

That's a lot to look forward to every month. Let *Writer's Digest* put you on the road to writing success!

Get 2 FREE ISSUES of Writer's Digest!

NO RISK!
Send No Money Now!

☐ **Yes!** Please rush me my 2 FREE issues of *Writer's Digest* — the world's leading magazine for writers. If I like what I read, I'll get a full year's subscription (12 issues, including the 2 free issues) for only $19.96. That's 72% off the newsstand rate! If I'm not completely satisfied, I'll write "cancel" on your invoice, return it and owe nothing. The 2 FREE issues are mine to keep, no matter what!

Name _____

Address_____

City _____

State_____ZIP _____

E-mail _____

☐ You may contact me about my subscription via e-mail.
(We won't use your address for any other purpose.)

Subscribers in Canada will be charged an additional US$10 (includes GST/HST) and invoiced. Outside the U.S. and Canada, add US$10 and remit payment in U.S. funds with this order. Annual newsstand rate: $71.88. Please allow 4-6 weeks for first-issue delivery.

Writer's Digest

www.writersdigest.com

J5FWMK

Get 2 FREE
TRIAL ISSUES of
Writer's Digest
WRITE BETTER
GET PUBLISHED

Packed with creative inspiration, advice, and tips to guide you on the road to success, *Writer's Digest* offers everything you need to take your writing to the next level! You'll discover how to:

- Create dynamic characters and page-turning plots
- Submit query letters that publishers won't be able to refuse
- Find the right agent or editor
- Make it out of the slush-pile and into the hands of publishers
- Write award-winning contest entries
- And more!

See for yourself — order your 2 FREE trial issues today!